CONTEMPORARY NOVELISTS

Contemporary Writers of the English Language

Contemporary Poets
Contemporary Novelists
(including short story writers)
Contemporary Dramatists
Contemporary Literary Critics

CONTEMPORARY NOVELISTS

THIRD EDITION

PREFACE TO THE FIRST EDITION

WALTER ALLEN

PREFACE TO THE THIRD EDITION

JEROME KLINKOWITZ

EDITOR

JAMES VINSON

ASSOCIATE EDITOR

D.L. KIRKPATRICK

ST. MARTIN'S PRESS

NEW YORK

ST. MARTIN'S PRESS, INC.
175 Fifth Avenue,
New York, N.Y. 10010

ISBN 0-312-16766-0

LC 75-189694

First edition published 1972; second
edition published 1976.

CONTENTS

PREFACE

to the first edition

The novel, we have been told many times in recent years, is dying: the news, as the appearance of this book shows, doesn't seem to have reached novelists themselves. But I don't recall that the assertion was made until about 1945, and perhaps it ought to be examined. We might at least discover why it is made. Ironically, it seems to have been first propounded at just about the time when the study of novels as a serious form of writing was being taken up in the universities. Today, one sometimes has the impression that little else but novels are studied there. The only ones I remember meeting in prescribed courses when I was an undergraduate studying English at the beginning of the Thirties were Jane Austen's—and, of all things, *The Castle of Otranto*, which must have had something to do with something else. I suppose one might cynically say that the very fact that novels are studied so seriously now in the universities is a sign that the form is dying.

If this were so, there would be nothing intrinsically remarkable about it. Literary forms, or significant variations of them, have disappeared before. For the best part of half a century the verse play was the great glory of English literature. Its death was certainly protracted, but for a hundred years it got steadily weaker until it ended not with a bang but a whimper in the closet poetic drama of the Romantics and the Victorians; and attempts to resurrect it in our time have not been conspicuously successful. Literary forms die or dwindle in importance as a result, I think we can say, of technological changes or of changes in men's interests. The novel itself had its origin in both kinds of change.

One thing it seems to me can be said with some certainty: the novel no longer has the central place in current literature and culture that it had in the nineteenth century. Having made the generalisation with some certainty, I find myself drawing back from it. On second thoughts, I suspect that Tennyson and Ruskin, for instance, were regarded with greater awe, as poets and prophets, than Dickens or George Eliot, who, as novelists, were merely entertainers. But *we* see the novel as central to nineteenth-century literature—it may be for reasons that are much the same as those that lead some people to think the novel is dying.

For one thing, as entertainers the Victorian novelists had virtually no competitors except one another. There were no films, no television, no radio. Dickens, indeed, was almost a Hollywood in himself. If you wanted to be beguiled, taken out of yourself, where could you turn but to the novel? And in the novel, in Dickens, Thackeray, George Eliot, Trollope, you could find a synoptic view of society; English life, depicted on a large enough scale, with enough contrast between social classes to suggest the whole of English life, was spread out in front of you. And there was something else, which is indicated by the historian G.M. Young. Writing on the Victorian age, Young has said: "It was part of the felicity of the fifties to possess a literature which was at once topical, contemporary, and classic; to meet the Immortals in the street and to read them with added zest for the encounter." Among these Immortals, even as young men, were Dickens and Thackeray. But the main emphasis, in my view, has to go on the word "classic"; the role was forced upon the great novelists almost by the situation of the times, which enabled them to identify themselves with their public, to speak for it, to an extent that is impossible for a novelist today. They shared the assumptions about the age common to the age, and when they criticised them they did so in much the same way as their readers were doing. In other words, they were the spokesmen of their age, or at least of the most important section of their public, the middle class. But this was not a serious limitation on them, for middle-class values were dominant. The society they wrote for was more homogeneous than ours. Middle-class culture, perhaps even upper middle-class culture was supreme, and seriously to read was to become part of that culture. The notion of cultural splits, the division into highbrow, middle-brow, low-brow, did not exist. And the novelists' identification with their society and their public gave them an authority denied, I suspect, to novelists of our time. Not that the synoptic novelist is unknown today. One thinks of C.P. Snow, whose *Strangers and Brothers* sequence takes in large and diverse areas of experience embracing a whole range of social class from lower-middle to aristocracy. I suspect that Snow's ideal of the novel is the Victorian at the height of its power. But there is a difference, and I think it is fundamental. Snow presents his synoptic, panoramic view of our society through the experiences of his narrator Lewis Eliot, whose life and career bear distinct resemblances to Snow's own. He is pretty obviously a persona for his creator. What Snow gives us, in other words, is one man's view of society. But when Thackeray, Trollope and George Eliot drop into the first person singular we read and accept, I believe, their "I" as "we". We assume an identification with their readers, and for all his idiosyncrasy, we do this with Dickens too. The novelists are not speaking for themselves, but for the consensus of opinion of their age. This is one of the factors that gives their novels a universal quality.

It was such novelists as these that Lionel Trilling had in mind when he wrote his famous passage in *The Liberal Imagination*:

> For our time the most effective agent of the moral imagination has been the novel of the last two hundred years. It was never, either aesthetically or morally, a perfect form and its faults and failures can be quickly enumerated. But its greatness and its practical usefulness lie in its unremitting work of involving the reader himself in the moral life, inviting him to put his own motives under examination, suggesting that reality is not as his conventional education has led him to see it. It taught us, as no other genre ever did, the extent of human variety and the value of this variety. It was the literary form to which the emotions of understanding and forgiveness were indigenous, as if by the definition of the form itself.

For me, these words of Trilling's constitute the great main justification of the novel. I know, though I had not realized until I read Trilling, that this is where my first interest in the novel began, both as reader and as someone who aspired to be a novelist himself. It is not, of course, the end of my interest in the novel. In our time, however, I feel it is increasingly difficult for the novelist to fulfil Trilling's expectations. Why this is so is indicated by Kingsley Amis's hero in *I Like It Here*, as he contemplates the memorial to Henry Fielding in Lisbon:

> Perhaps it was worth dying in your forties if two hundred years later you were the only non-contemporary novelist who could be read with unaffected and whole-hearted interest, the only one who never had to be apologized for or excused on the grounds of changing taste. And how enviable to live in the world of his novels, where duty was plain, evil arose from malevolence and a starving wayfarer could be invited indoors without hesitation and without fear. Did that make it a simplified world? Perhaps, but that hardly mattered beside the existence of a moral seriousness without the aid of evangelical puffing and blowing.

Well, today duty is not plain, and we can no longer confidently say that evil arises from malevolence. Our faith in our moral judgments has been sapped, principally I suppose by the findings of Freud and his followers. But we also live in a world that presses on us in all its intensity of evil so remorselessly as to seem unassimilable in the novel. The paradigm of the evil is the concentration camps of Nazi Germany; but the evil—at the moment of writing in Vietnam, in Ulster, in East Bengal, and God knows where it will be next year—leaps at us nightly from the television screen. It was something the great Victorians didn't have to take into account, or there was less of it to take into account. Equally, it is something we and our contemporaries must. The difficulty of doing so, perhaps indeed the impossibility, has been stated by George Steiner in *Language and Silence*. That even sixty-five years ago the difficulty could be overcome was shown by Conrad in what now seems his prophetic novel *Nostromo*; and we can see it can be handled in our time from Golding's *Lord of the Flies*, from Graham Greene throughout his career and from Saul Bellow's *Mr. Sammler's Planet*. But novels of this order seem almost special cases.

I am putting forward a number of things that differentiate the contemporary novel from the classic novel, by which in the end rightly or wrongly we tend to judge contemporary work. Briefly, the novel is no longer the main medium of entertainment and instruction. The film tells a story at least as well; and a good part of what, even as late as Lawrence, was taken for granted as belonging to the content of the novel, what may be called the journalistic or documentary and argumentative content, has been taken over by television and the non-fiction book. Best-sellers are no longer, as they were fifty years ago, generally novels. The books that are most widely read and argued about are works of non-fiction, works of reportage, scientific theory and speculation, and controversy. The discussion of current ideas and affairs, the exposures of current abuses, these are now presented to us on television. This is a consequence of technological development, and perhaps nothing can be done about it. But the result is a loss to the novel—and also, I think, to the quality of our response to what is happening everywhere in the world. The world, simply, is too much with us, and too immediately so: we lack the filter of fiction and must suffer instead the immediate brutal impact upon us of events and new ideas. In the past, the writing of a novel was a comparatively leisurely affair. It may still be so. To write a novel takes anything from one year to ten: but now, by the time it is published, and irrespective of the length of time in its writing, it may seem to refer to a world that is irredeemably past.

One consequence of this speeding up of life and the decay between the event and the novelist's assimilation of and reaction towards it is, it seems to me, a distrust of fiction, which is seen almost as a luxury. There is perhaps some evidence of this in the large number of *romans fleuves* which has been so striking a feature of the British novel since the war, sequences like those of Snow, Waugh, Powell, Doris Lessing, Durrell and Olivia Manning. Vastly different from one another though these works are, they have one thing in common: the narrator of each one of them seems to be uncommonly close to his creator, so that there appears in these sequences to be a narration of events akin to those the novelist has himself experienced. It is a short step beyond this to something that, though in many ways comparable to the novel, is not the novel. I am thinking of what has been called the "non-fiction novel," notably Truman Capote's *In Cold Blood* and Norman Mailer's *The Armies of the Night*, a work of reporting of personal experience that only a novelist of great brilliance could have written.

But there is another kind of book, which does not profess in any way to relate to the novel, that all the same seems to cater to the interests of readers who half a century ago would have been reading novels or would have had a comparable experience from reading novels. The books I have in mind are a disparate lot; it includes books like Kate Millet's and Germaine Greer's on Woman's Lib., White's *The Organization Man*, Watson's *The Double Helix*, anthropological and sociological works based on taped interviews, Desmond Morris's *The Naked Ape*, the books of Bruno Bettelheim and the psychological writings of R.D. Laing. All in one way or another are about people. And there are two points here. They are in some sense specialised works the contents of which novelists themselves will generally have no more first-hand knowledge of than the non-specialist reading public. And they also appear to be based on recorded fact or what looks like it. They appeal, in other words, to a curiosity that in the past the novelist could satisfy but that now he cannot.

These books may be seen as case-histories. They are of the stuff of fiction but *true*; and it may be that we are in a period when readers prefer to read what they think is history rather than the imaginative re-creation of history that is the novel.

It could also be that this interest in history and in what seems to be the scientifically provable is being counterbalanced by an interest in a fiction of what might be called an extreme kind, one that goes beyond the novel and is akin to the romance that we all thought the novel had displaced two and a half centuries ago. It seems significant that for the past four or five years the works of fiction most eagerly devoured by university students in the United States, and I suspect in Britain too, have been the fantasies of Tolkien and the works of Hermann Hesse, works of fiction that lie outside the novel as I conceive it.

What that is will be apparent. For me, though I recognise variants such as the novels of Melville, the novel is a broadly realistic representation of man's life in society which is also a criticism of life and of society. This, as I see it, makes up the mainstream of the English novel from Fielding to Joyce and Lawrence. All the evidence—and it comes from novels themselves—suggests that during the past two or three decades the contemporary novelist has been forced by pressures of circumstances—technological change, change in men's attitudes towards themselves and towards the universe, the simple facts of history in our time, and the sheer increase of knowledge in many fields from which as a non-specialist he is barred—to yield much of his former territory to other literary forms and media. Despite himself, he has become more subjective, much less sure of himself. He has lost much of the authority his forbears could take for granted. It seems less possible for the novelist to put forward the mimic world he has invented as a convincing paradigm of the world in which he and his readers live.

There is, I am well aware, a factor that so far I have ignored. Invoking the past, I have referred to the very great novelists of the language. We in this second half of the twentieth century follow in the wake of very great novelists. The years from roughly 1900 to 1940 form one of the peak periods in our literature, in poetry and the novel alike. The great names are obvious enough: in the novel, Conrad, Joyce, Lawrence, Virginia Woolf; Dreiser, Fitzgerald, Hemingway perhaps, Faulkner; and a host of smaller but very significant figures flank them. What impresses us in them today is the scope of their ambitions and their success in realising them. If we have no one to set against them, the same seems to me to be true of the novel throughout the world. But history shows that similar situations have existed before, that an age of intense flowering is often followed by one comparatively barren or in which the growths are smaller. The emergence of a new novelist of the calibre of Conrad or Faulkner could change the literary scene as an earthquake changes a landscape and make nonsense of all my generalisations. Figures of Conrad's and Faulkner's stature can't be produced to order—and it may be worth pointing out that the true greatness of some of the novelists of our century, Conrad among them, was not seen until after their deaths and that their influence, which we now take for granted, was posthumous.

Meanwhile, until that monster the new great novelist arrives, we must put up with what we have. If that sounds churlish, it is not meant to be. Our contemporary novelists are ours, they belong to us, the problems that face them face us their readers too. Their fragmentation reflects ours. But much more can be said than that. If I do not believe that we live in one of the peak periods of the novel, I do emphatically believe that we live in a time distinguished by a bigger concentration of talented men and women only less than the great than has ever been seen before in the history of the novel in English. I have spent almost all my life reading novels (and trying to write them) and I could write down the names of I suspect two score and probably more from Britain and America who have given me pleasure, aesthetic or intellectual, of a keenness that makes it almost impossible for me to think they won't be read at least with interest a century hence. The temptation is to write the names down, but it must be resisted.

No, the novel is not dead or dying, even though its stature may be smaller than a century ago—and that, as I have suggested, the arrival of my monster may change. And there is another reason, besides the prodigality of talent on all sides, which shows no sign of drying up, for believing the novel is not dying. This is the sudden and unexpected appearance of the novel within the past three decades or so in the new countries where English is spoken, the Caribbean islands, India, the countries of Africa. For a congenital reader and student of the novel it has been a moving experience to watch these new literatures come into existence during one's reading lifetime, for they are surely signs of life, not of death. The task of these men and women making these new literatures is, no doubt, different from that of contemporary English and American white novelists, for it is to forge, in Joyce's words, the uncreated conscience of their race. But their novels testify to the variety and diversity of human experience and to the human need to set it down and rejoice in it. It is in the consciousness precisely of that variety and diversity that the novel had its origins; and so long as it remains, so long as men are curious about their fellows and themselves, it seems to me unlikely the novel will die.

—WALTER ALLEN

PREFACE

to the Third Edition

Fiction constitutes a way of looking at the world. What a rich and potentially troublesome definition that is! One cannot imagine a novelist from Cervantes to Beckett (himself the last Quixote) who would disagree, yet its very philosophy of form makes fiction the most volatile and controversial literary genre we are likely to encounter.

For example: when we read *Bleak House* or *Great Expectations* we are getting more than just a picture of 19th-century England, rich with documentary material complementary to our social and political histories of the time. In a Dickens novel we are privileged to the author's *way of seeing* the England (and its people) of his day. That view was certainly different from Samuel Butler's or either of the Brontës'. Standing behind the contents of their novels are entire philosophies social, moral, and aesthetic—which determine each author's sense of what should be recorded, and how.

When the world changes, controversies of form are even more pronounced. "In or about December, 1910", Virginia Woolf once remarked, "human character changed." She was referring to the first London exhibition of post-impressionist paintings, in themselves a radical statement on the act of seeing. But those works were part of an emerging world view which influenced her own way of writing novels and the entire culture's manner of judging itself. Painting still remains painting, even though its physical form—from impressionism through cubism and surrealism to abstract expressionism and beyond—changes so radically. It must be the world, then, and our way of seeing it that are transformed. And even more immediately than painting, the novel is there to respond to and express this violent alteration.

To survey the status of the novel in English these days is to describe a battle of the books, both critical and creative, such as has not existed in Anglo-American letters for nearly a century. That long-distant conflict was the H.G. Wells-Henry James debate over the future course of fiction: Was the novel to enter the 20th century as a documentary record of social action, the "novel of saturation" which by its refusal to tamper with reality placed highest value in the writer's ability to perceive and report, or would modern times begin with the Jamesian "novel of selection," picking and choosing among the materials of life to present not the world itself but rather an illusory representation of it?

Both novels, of course, continued to be written. Novelists of saturation (Arnold Bennett, Theodore Dreiser, John Steinbeck) satisfied a wide range of interests from popular entertainment to social advocacy, while the selectivists (Joseph Conrad, Virginia Woolf, F. Scott Fitzgerald) pursued a more formally modernist fiction which helped prepare an aesthetic for such newly invented media as film and an ethic open to the discoveries of psychology and psychoanalysis.

But by midcentury a curious discomfort with the world itself became evident among novelists and critics alike. Reviewing the absurdly ridiculous events of the American 1950's, Philip Roth complained ("Writing American Fiction," in *Reading Myself and Others*, 1975):

> The American writer in the middle of the 20th century has his hands full in trying to understand, and then describe, and then make *credible* much of the American reality. It stupefies, it sickens, it infuriates, and finally it is even a kind of embarrassment to one's meager imagination. The actuality is continually outdoing our talents and the culture tosses up figures almost daily that are the envy of any novelist.

Critics were quick to agree, proclaiming "the death of the novel" on the evidence of form as well as of content, for philosophy and social history had discredited the world view upon which conventions of fiction had been based, as Ronald Sukenick explained in his own short story "The Death of the Novel":

> Realistic fiction presupposed chronological time as the medium of plotted narrative, an irreducible individual psyche as the subject of its characterization, and, above all, the ultimate, concrete reality of things as the object and rationale of its description. In the world of post-realism, however, all of these absolutes have become absolutely problematic.
>
> The contemporary writer—the writer who is acutely in touch with the life of which he is a part—is forced to start from scratch: Reality doesn't exist, time doesn't exist, personality doesn't exist. God was the omniscient author, but he died; now no one knows the plot, and since our reality lacks the sanction of a creator, there's no guarantee as to the authenticity of the received version. Time is reduced to presence, the content of a series of discontinuous moments. Time is no longer purposive, and so there is no destiny, only chance. Reality is, simply, our experience, and objectivity is, of course, an illusion. Personality, after having passed through a phase of awkward self-

consciousness, has become, quite minimally, a mere locus for our experience. In view of these annihilations, it should be no surprise that literature, also, does not exist—how could it? There is only reading and writing, which are things we do, like eating and making love, to pass the time, ways of maintaining a considered boredom in the face of the abyss.

Again, conventionally realistic novels continued to be written—in America by the commercial entertainers but also by such craftsmen and women as John Updike, Saul Bellow, and Joan Didion, and in Britain by Kingsley Amis, Margaret Drabble, and many others. But never again could realism proceed with such confidence and naivety, for in the face of the disruptions just described even simple characterization and linear plotting became necessarily experimental techniques.

The 1960's and 1970's in particular witnessed a sometimes bitter debate over fiction's new aesthetic. Was it to be a vehicle for commentary on man's existence, or simply an artifact of his own making and nothing more? Whether the novel was "about" reality or "about" itself (and hence an addition to experience rather than a report of it) set the terms for a squabble both trans-Atlantic and domestic. "It seems a country-headed thing to say," the novelist William H. Gass admits ("The Medium of Fiction," in *Fiction and the Figures of Life*, 1970), "that literature is language, that stories and the places and the people in them are merely made of words as chairs are made of smoothed sticks and sometimes of cloth and metal tubes.... It seems incredible," he readily agrees, "the ease with which we sink through books quite out of sight, pass clamorous pages into soundless dreams." His own style of metafiction—works whose subject is its own making, its product nothing but its own process—is indeed disruptively revolutionary, especially startling not just for what it does in itself but for what it discredits in the conventional novel. "That novels should be made of words, and merely words, is shocking, really," he concludes. "It's as if you had discovered that your wife were made of rubber: the bliss of all those years, the fears...from sponge."

Opposed to Gass (and to the French theoreticians of literary language—Barthes, Derrida, and Kristeva—who support him) are the moral fictionist John Gardner and the truth-centered critic Gerald Graff. Does literature have a duty beyond its own self-apparency of form? Most certainly, Gardner replies (in *On Moral Fiction*, 1978), citing Tolstoy: God instructs, heroes enact, and writers record. Is writing simply a commentary on other writing, as philosophers from Hegel onward would suggest? Not at all, Graff insists (in *Literature Against Itself*, 1978): "Most theories of the nature of literature are more or less concealed theories of the nature of man and of the good society. In this sense, literary thinking is inseparable from moral and social thinking." The rub is, Graff dismisses entirely the post-modern theory of Derrida, Gass & Co. Fiction still makes truth-claims, he believes, and those claims are just as creditable as the bottom line statements from a bank.

This battle of the books now raging in America bears close resemblance to the stand-off many critics have claimed exists between the contemporary British and American novels. Comparing their states of criticism (and behind them the style of fiction each advocates), Ihab Hassan (in *Georgia Review*, Fall, 1980) sees the best elements in America reflecting the French philosophy of deconstruction (truth in textuality alone) while "England offers nothing bracing in criticism now." Meanwhile in a British symposium for *The New Review* on "The State of Fiction" (Summer 1978) John Braine is asked How Are Things Going? and What's New? and glowers in reply, "A bad time," acknowledging little from the UK and "From the USA, nothing at all, now that John O'Hara's dead." What Malcolm Bradbury calls "a depressing and outdated folklore" informs both views: that since the start of the 19th century American fiction has been vitalized by a searchingly romantic disposition, while the British novel rests smugly within the confidence of Lockean empiricism and the comforts of a hearty life sustained by beef and ale. Is Hassan aware of John Fowles, Lawrence Durrell, and the later works of Doris Lessing? Of course, just as Braine must know of William H. Gass, Ronald Sukenick, Donald Barthelme, and the fuss they have caused at home among supporters and detractors alike. But each chooses to discount such work as either unrepresentative or unworthy of notice, so that the old distinctions might live one more day.

Indeed, the characteristics of British, American, and Commonwealth fiction in the 1980's suggests that novelists are eager to grow beyond such narrowly national groupings and confront the aesthetic issues of their times—and also to acknowledge that simply performing in character and writing what might be expected of them is no longer a satisfactory or rewarding approach to fiction. In Britain romancers such as John Fowles and Lawrence Durrell are eclipsing D.H. Lawrence's belief that Americans have prior claim to license of imagination. As Chris Bigsby explains (*Granta*, Fall 1980), Fowles is still a storyteller who uses most devices of conventional narration, drawing upon all the traditional strengths of the English novel; yet he also appreciates that "the process of invention is itself the source of values. But it is also the origin of coercion," and so involves himself in the metafictional drama described by William H. Gass. In Canada, Margaret Atwood has crafted a series of novels at once womanly and universal, transcending the narrow issues of sexual politics in order to shape a fictive world responsive to the genuinely new lives being led in this era. In America, the moral fiction debate has continued, and the controversy has lent its themes and structures to novels themselves, such as Clarence Major's *Emergency Exit* (which deconstructs a simple narrative into its semiological and linguistic components) and John Gardner's *October Light*, a self-proclaimed moral fiction which contains within itself a parodistic experimental novel.

A common complaint against postwar British fiction is that it was shaped by its contents—an argument summarized in the title of Rubin Rabinovitz's study *The Reaction Against Experiment in the English Novel 1950-1960*, in which "experiment" implies the determinacy of aesthetic form. The newer work of Angus Wilson, Doris Lessing, and many others (as we shall see) in fact turns this assertion on its head: novels such as *No Laughing Matter* and *The Golden*

Notebook adopt new forms which twist content beyond the old habitual patterns of understanding—an exercise in which John Fowles also takes delight. The irony is that so many recent American novelists have distinguished themselves by seeking the very informing-sort of content previously reserved for their British colleagues. Sometimes the same historical event must do double duty, as the execution of accused atom-spies Julius and Ethel Rosenberg serves for E.L. Doctorow's *The Book of Daniel* (where the names are changed but events remain closely factual) and Robert Coover's masterful *The Public Burning* (where the names stay the same but events are subjected to unrestrained fancy). Ishmael Reed turns to black folklore and the mythology of popular culture for his novels *Flight to Canada* and *The Last Days of Louisiana Red*, and in *Mumbo Jumbo* constructs a virtual epic from historical sources dating from the present back to ancient Egypt—all as a way of putting contemporary life in sharper focus and revealing the aesthetic structures of existence. Norman Mailer's *The Executioner's Song* and Doctorow's *Ragtime* mark the extremes of this para-historical approach: the absolute weight of experience forming its own phenomenological poetry, or the delicate dance of several wispy historical threads to create both the spirit of an era and the joy of textual play. At its best, in the hands of Guy Davenport, history yields itself to collage: Kafka at an airshow in Brescia brushing shoulders with Ludwig Wittgenstein (*Tatlin!*), Lenin photographed in a Zurich cafe, self-consciously and properly posed, while undetected (at the time) in the background may be seen James and Nora Joyce haggling with a taxi driver (*Da Vinci's Bicycle*). Rather than being shaped by such contents, recent American fiction of this style uses form itself to reshape history, believing that in any contest between the ethics and aesthetic of truth, the latter must always win.

The alleged conservatism of British fiction against which so many critics, both English and American, have complained, was actually a short-lived and readily explainable phenomenon. Joyce, Woolf, and Lawrence had, of course, helped create the modern novel. Solidly grounded in psychology and myth, its formal experimentalism was scarcely a cause for complaint, for all bases, moral and aesthetic, were covered. In the postwar years, however, a younger generation of university men and women reacted against what they considered the romantic excesses of writers such as Dylan Thomas and Henry Treece, taking counsel from critics F.R. Leavis and William Empson that the goals of literature should be a "marked moral intensity" distinguished by rationalism, realism, empiricism, and above all clarity of expression. Loosely called "The Movement" and more famous for its poetry, it nevertheless included novelists so disposed as Kingsley Amis, Philip Larkin, and John Wain, who believed fiction was not so much a textual display as an instrument of persuasion, what Jonathan Raban called "the nicest and kindest form of paternal dictatorship" (*The Society of the Poem*, 1971) and which Blake Morrison sums up as "a strong determinism to inform, instruct, even manipulate" (*The Movement*, 1980). Behind it all was a new attitude expressed by a new style of hero, the central character of such books as Amis's *Lucky Jim* and Wain's *Hurry on Down*, as described by Walter Allen (*New Statesman*, 30 January 1954):

> A new hero has risen among us. Is he the intellectual tough, or the tough intellectual? He is consciously, even conscientiously, graceless. His face, when not dead-pan, is set in a snarl of exasperation. He has one skin too few, but his is not the sensitiveness of the young man in earlier twentieth-century fiction: it is the phoney to which his nerve-ends are tremblingly exposed, and at the least suspicion of the phoney he goes tough. He is at odds with his conventional university education, though he comes generally from a famous university: he has seen through the academic racket as he sees through all the others.... The Services, certainly, helped to make him; but George Orwell, Dr Leavis and the Logical Positivists—all contributed to his genesis.

It is in reaction to this very coercion and manipulation that the most recent British fiction has defined itself. A conservative attitude is itself coercive, rejecting new ideas as smugly as Dr. Johnson kicking Bishop Berkeley's stone. The novels of Doris Lessing challenge this position. Raised in Southern Rhodesia, she seems to have adopted this colonial displacement for her own posture as a novelist. As Lorna Sage explains (*Granta*, Fall 1980), "Deliberately, traumatically (and now it at last seems serenely) she has mislaid her sense of humor, her sense of proportion, her 'English' personality. The science fiction and fantasy she's writing in her new 'Canopus in Argos' sequence reveals a fragmented cosmos seen by a composite, coolly impersonal eye." Traditional values no longer boast a unifying effect—indeed, the center has not held—but for British fiction this readjustment to the world has proved a godsend. The novels of Angus Wilson, for example, become more lively year by year as they turn to parody and pastiche (rather than social reportage) for their structure. In Malcolm Bradbury's work, the comedy is so hilariously extreme that no predictable form can hold it. The emerging nation of womanhood, as Lorna Sage calls it, provides genuinely new material for the works of Angela Carter, Beryl Bainbridge, and Caroline Blackwood in Britain and Margaret Atwood in Canada—materials of a reality previous generations might not have known existed. In Australia Patrick White abandons conventional wisdom and familiar views to present a totally unstereotyped view of his world. And at the far side of such ethical and aesthetic ponderings, John Fowles writes novels which examine their own structures, particularly those which determine reality, even as their stories continue on. In a fully legitimate manner, British novelists are having it both ways, celebrating what Alan Kennedy calls (in *The Protean Self*, 1974) "the dramatic actions" of a "Protean self" which "testify to a reality underlying, but they do not by any means give the whole of that reality."

Where lies fiction's reality: in its contents or in its form? This has been the central question for debate in our times. If fiction is indeed a way of looking at the world, it lies in each, and the Protean selves of John Fowles's characters and the reinventive and imaginatively transforming heroes of such American novelists as Kurt Vonnegut (*Slaughterhouse Five*) and Jerzy Kosinski (*The Painted Bird*) are the truest fictions of our age. Virginia Woolf's world changed in 1910, as signalled by the post-impressionist painters. If we are to believe the reactions of our finest novelists today, their world changed with the abstract expressionists, who taught that the painter's canvas is not so much a surface upon which to represent but rather an arena within which to act. The contemporary novelist's page shows evidence of this same ethic: what we read is not so much a report of experience as a sample of experience itself, yet in this very activity still reflective of the moral spirit. The last Quixote, as Robert Coover calls him, is still among us, counselling that despite all obstacles we must continue, that even as we say "I can't go on" we *have* gone on to make another statement. Samuel Beckett offers a way of going on without making an affirmation of anything but that creative, continuing act—an act, of course, which speaks volumes and offers hope beyond rational belief.

—JEROME KLINKOWITZ

EDITOR'S NOTE

The selection of writers included in this book is based upon the recommendations of the advisers listed on page xvii.

The entry for each writer consists of a biography, a full bibliography, a comment by the writer on his fiction if he chose to make one (more than half of the writers did make a statement), and a signed critical essay on his fiction.

All uncollected short stories published since the entrant's last collection, plus others the entrant himself has mentioned, have been listed. As a rule, all books written about the entrant are listed in the Critical Studies section; reviews and essays listed have been recommended by the entrant. British and United States editions of all books have been listed; other editions are listed only if they are the first editions.

An appendix of entries has been included for some nine novelists who have died since the 1950's but whose reputations are essentially contemporary.

We would like to thank the entrants and contributors for their patience and cooperation in helping us compile this book.

ADVISERS

Walter Allen
Bernard Bergonzi
Earle Birney
Elmer Borklund
Anthony Burgess
D.D.C. Chambers
Margaret Drabble
Leslie Fiedler
Roy Fuller
Albert Guerard
James B. Hall
John Hawkes
Susan Hill
A. Norman Jeffares
James Korges
John Lehmann
Harry Levin
Harry T. Moore
J.E. Morpurgo
Stephen Murray-Smith
Desmond Pacey
Hal Porter
Anthony Powell
Arthur Ravenscroft
John M. Reilly
Kenneth Rexroth
H. Winston Rhodes
Alan Ross
Barney Rosset
Mark Schorer
Tony Tanner
George Woodcock

CONTRIBUTORS

Walter Allen
Richard Andersen
Alvin Aubert
Jane S. Bakerman
John Barnes
Sally H. Bennett
Alice Bensen
Bernard Bergonzi
Chaim Bermant
Marshall A. Best
William Bittner
William Borden
Elmer Borklund
Frederick Bowers
Anthony Boxill
Malcolm Bradbury
M.E. Bradford
Laurence Brander
Lloyd W. Brown
Dalma H. Brunauer
Herbert C. Burke
Mary Cadogan
Donald Cameron
Frank Campenni
Frederic I. Carpenter
Hayden Carruth
D.D.C. Chambers
Gerda Charles
Ann Charters
Paul Seiko Chihara
Laurie Clancy
Anderson Clark
Gloria Cohen
Ruby Cohn
John Colmer
Mary Conroy
Judy Cooke
R.A. Copland
John Cotton
Hallvard Dahlie
Barrie Davies
Jeanne Desy
Margaret Dick
R.H.W. Dillard
Dale K. Doepke
Paul A. Doyle
Deborah Duckworth
Chester E. Eisinger
Brian Elliott
James A. Emanuel
Richard J. Fein
Brenda R. Ferguson
Paul F. Field
John Figueroa
Barbara Foley
Irving F. Foote
Roberta J. Forsberg
Ruel E. Foster
Warren French
Alan Warren Friedman
Melvin J. Friedman
Lucy Frost
John Fuegi
David Galloway
Norman T. Gates
R.G. Geering
David J. Geherin
James Gindin
Lois Gordon
William Goyen

Robert Greacen
Richard Greenleaf
George Grella
Albert Guerard
Prabhu S. Guptara
Emily Hahn
James B. Hall
John Hall
Cherry Hankin
Maurice Harmon
S.C. Harrex
Carl Harrison-Ford
James A. Hart
Ihab Hassan
David M. Heaton
Leo J. Hertzel
James Hill
Jacqueline Hoefer
Jan Hokenson
Craig Hudziak
Barbara Hults
Van Ikin
Blyden Jackson
Louis James
A. Norman Jeffares
Annibel Jenkins
Margaret Keith
Burton Kendle
Brian Kiernan
H.M. Klein
Marcus Klein
Jerome Klinkowitz
James Korges
Martin L. Kornbluth
Richard Kostelanetz
Leonie Kramer
Ursula Laredo
Margaret Laurence
Chet Leach
Thomas LeClair
Anastasia Leech
Margaret Lewis
Peter Lewis
Stanley W. Lindberg
Bernth Lindfors
Jack Lindsay
John Lucas
Robert E. Lynch
David Madden
Hena Maes-Jelinek
Irving Malin
Paul Marx
Ann Massa
Roland Mathias
Brian E. Matthews
Frank D. McConnell
John McCormick
Frederick P.W. McDowell
Margaret B. McDowell
George McElroy
John Mepham
Patricia Merivale
Naomi Mitchison
John Montague
Gerald Moore
Harry T. Moore
J.E. Morpurgo
Robert K. Morris
Kay J. Mussell
Shyamala A. Narayan
Tom Nelson
Bruce Nesbitt
W.H. New
Leslie Norris
Robert Nye
John P. O'Neill
John Ormond
Bridget O'Toole
Desmond Pacey
Malcolm Page
Joseph Parisi
William Peden
Marian Pehowski
Barbara M. Perkins
George Perkins
Frank T. Phipps
Isabel Quigly
Arthur Ravenscroft
Ian Reid
J.C. Reid
John M. Reilly
Kenneth Rexroth
H. Winston Rhodes
Lawrence Ries
Judith Rodriguez
Trevor Royle
Louis D. Rubin, Jr.
Jack Salzman
Clarence Sandelin
David Sanders
Stewart F. Sanderson
William J. Schafer
Alexander Scott
Ian Scott-Kilvert
Cynthia Secor
Kathryn L. Seidel
T.A. Shippey
Alan R. Shucard
Ben Siegel
Fred Silva
Angela Smith
Curtis C. Smith
Radcliffe Squires
Derek Stanford
Donald E. Stanford
Jane W. Stedman
George Stephenson
Carol Simpson Stern
James R. Stevens
Joan Stevens
Edward Stokes
W.J. Stuckey
Roy Thomas
Derick S. Thomson
Shirley Toulson
William Trevor
Roland Turner
Ivan Van-Sertima
James Vinson
Thomas A. Vogler
Keith Walker
William Walsh
Val Warner
Harold H. Watts
Christof Wegelin
John A. Weigel
Dennis M. Welch
Robert L. Welker
Perry D. Westbrook
Peter R. Weston
Margaret Willy
George Woodcock

CONTEMPORARY NOVELISTS

Ahmad Abbas
Walter Abish
Paul Ableman
Peter Abrahams
Dannie Abse
Chinua Achebe
Brian Aldiss
James Aldridge
Ahmed Ali
Walter Allen
T.M. Aluko
A. Alvarez
Elechi Amadi
Eric Ambler
Kingsley Amis
Martin Amis
Mulk Raj Anand
Michael Anthony
Ayi Kwei Armah
Harriette Arnow
Sylvia Ashton-Warner
Isaac Asimov
Thea Astley
Margaret Atwood
Louis Auchincloss

Paul Bailey
Beryl Bainbridge
Elliott Baker
James Baldwin
David Ballantyne
J.G. Ballard
Amiri Baraka
A.L. Barker
Djuna Barnes
Clive Barry
Stan Barstow
John Barth
Donald Barthelme
Jonathan Baumbach
Nina Bawden
David Beaty
Stephen Becker
Samuel Beckett
Barry Beckham
Sybille Bedford
Saul Bellow
David Benedictus
John Berger
Thomas Berger
Chaim Bermant
Bhabani Bhattacharya
Earle Birney
Caroline Blackwood
Burt Blechman
Fred Bodsworth
Vance Bourjaily
John Bowen
Paul Bowles
Kay Boyle
Malcolm Bradbury
Ray Bradbury
Melvyn Bragg
John Braine
Shasti Brata
Errol Brathwaite
Richard Brautigan
Christine Brooke-Rose
Brigid Brophy
Chandler Brossard
George Mackay Brown
Bryher
George Buchanan
Ernest Buckler
Frederick Buechner
Anthony Burgess
Alan Burns
William S. Burroughs
Janet Burroway
Frederick Busch
A.S. Byatt

Arthur Calder-Marshall
Erskine Caldwell
Hortense Calisher
Morley Callaghan
Philip Callow
W.H. Canaway
Robert Cantwell
Truman Capote
Angela Carter
R.V. Cassill
David Caute
Sid Chaplin
Gerda Charles
Jerome Charyn
John Cheever
Eleanor Clark
Arthur C. Clarke
Austin C. Clarke
Jon Cleary
Leonard Cohen
Matt Cohen
Barry Cole
Cyrus Colter
Alex Comfort
Richard Condon
Evan S. Connell, Jr.
Jack Conroy
Lettice Cooper
William Cooper
Robert Coover
Jack Cope
Peter Cowan
Harry Crews
Michael Crichton
Ian Cross

Roald Dahl
O.R. Dathorne
Guy Davenport
Robertson Davies
Dan Davin
Jennifer Dawson
Len Deighton
Samuel R. Delany
Don DeLillo

Nigel Dennis
Anita Desai
G.V. Desani
Peter De Vries
Philip K. Dick
Monica Dickens
Joan Didion
E.L. Doctorow
J.P. Donleavy
Margaret Drabble
C.J. Driver
Allen Drury
Maureen Duffy
Daphne du Maurier
Elaine Dundy
Nell Dunn
Lawrence Durrell
Geoffrey Dutton

William Eastlake
Cyprian Ekwensi
Stanley Elkin
Ralph Ellison
David Ely
Marian Engel
Isobel English
Peter Everett

Howard Fast
Irvin Faust
Raymond Federman
Elaine Feinstein
Leslie Fiedler
Gabriel Fielding
Eva Figes
Roderick Finlayson
Penelope Fitzgerald
Thomas Flanagan
Shelby Foote
Jesse Hill Ford
Frederick Forsyth
David Foster
John Fowles
Janet Frame
Dick Francis
Michael Frayn
Nicolas Freeling
Gillian Freeman
Bruce Jay Friedman
Daniel Fuchs
Roy Fuller

William Gaddis
Ernest J. Gaines
Mavis Gallant
John Gardner
George Garrett
William H. Gass
Maurice Gee
Martha Gellhorn
Zulfikar Ghose
Stella Gibbons
Brendan Gill
Penelope Gilliatt
Brian Glanville
Julian Gloag
Rumer Godden
Dave Godfrey
Gail Godwin
Herbert Gold
William Golding
William Goldman
Nadine Gordimer
Giles Gordon
Robert Gover
William Goyen
Winston Graham
Shirley Ann Grau
Robert Graves
Simon Gray
Graham Greene
Alfred Grossman
Albert Guerard
A.B. Guthrie, Jr.

William Haggard
Arthur Hailey
Nancy Hale
James B. Hall
Clifford Hanley
Gerald Hanley
James Hanley
Elizabeth Hardwick
Mark Harris
Wilson Harris
Elizabeth Harrower
John Hawkes
Shirley Hazzard
Bessie Head
John Hearne
Roy A.K. Heath
Robert A. Heinlein
Joseph Heller
Xavier Herbert
James Leo Herlihy
John Hersey
Granville Hicks
Aidan Higgins
George V. Higgins
Patricia Highsmith
Carol Hill
Susan Hill
Noel Hilliard
Chester Himes
Thomas Hinde
Edward Hoagland
Laura Z. Hobson
John Clellon Holmes
Hugh Hood
Paul Horgan
Geoffrey Household
Elizabeth Jane Howard
William Bradford Huie
William Humphrey
Emyr Humphreys
Evan Hunter
Kristin Hunter
Maude Hutchins

Witi Ihimaera
Hammond Innes
David Ireland
John Irving
Christopher Isherwood
Charles Israel

Dan Jacobson

C.L.R. James
Storm Jameson
Robin Jenkins
Ruth Prawer Jhabvala
Josephine Johnson
Pamela Hansford Johnson
Glyn Jones
Gwyn Jones
Madison Jones
Marion Jones
Mervyn Jones
Erica Jong
M.K. Joseph
Gabriel Josipovici

David Karp
William Melvin Kelley
Thomas Keneally
Ken Kesey
Ismith Khan
Benedict Kiely
John Oliver Killens
Richard E. Kim
Francis King
Fletcher Knebel
John Knowles
C.J. Koch
Arthur Koestler
Bernard Kops
Jerzy Kosinski
Uys Krige
Robert Kroetsch

Alex La Guma
George Lamming
Margaret Laurence
Mary Lavin
John le Carré
John A. Lee
Ursula K. Le Guin
Rosamond Lehmann
Fritz Leiber
Alan Lelchuk
Doris Lessing
Ira Levin
Meyer Levin
Norman Levine
Janet Lewis
Jack Lindsay
Emanuel Litvinoff
David Lodge
Anita Loos
Earl Lovelace
Robert Lowry
Jack Ludwig
Alison Lurie
Andrew Lytle
David Lytton

Robie Macauley
Ross Macdonald
Hugh MacLennan
David Madden
Norman Mailer
Clarence Major
Bernard Malamud
Manohar Malgonkar
David Malouf
Albert Maltz
Frederick Manfred
Jerre Mangione
Wolf Mankowitz
Leonard Mann
Ethel Mannin
Kamala Markandaya
Wallace Markfield
Ngaio Marsh
Bruce Marshall
Paule Marshall
John Masters
Peter Mathers
Jack Matthews
Peter Matthiessen
Elizabeth Mavor
William Maxwell
Julian Mayfield
Mary McCarthy
Joseph McElroy
Ian McEwan
John McGahern
Thomas McGuane
Tom McHale
Larry McMurtry
James McNeish
James A. McPherson
Aubrey Menen
Leonard Michaels
James A. Michener
O.E. Middleton
Stanley Middleton
Margaret Millar
Mark Mirsky
Adrian Mitchell
Joseph Mitchell
Julian Mitchell
W.O. Mitchell
Naomi Mitchison
N. Scott Momaday
Brian Moore
Frank Moorhouse
Wright Morris
Toni Morrison
Penelope Mortimer
Nicholas Mosley
Ezekiel Mphahlele
John Munonye
Alice Munro
Iris Murdoch

Shiva Naipaul
V.S. Naipaul
R.K. Narayan
Robert Nathan
Bill Naughton
Howard Nemerov
Jay Neugeboren
P.H. Newby
Edward Newhouse
C.J. Newman
Charles Newman
Ngugi wa Thiong'o
Abioseh Nicol
Christopher Nicole
Robert Nye

Barry Oakley
Joyce Carol Oates
Edna O'Brien

Julia O'Faolain
Sean O'Faolain
Liam O'Flaherty
Tillie Olsen
Guy Owen
Cynthia Ozick

Grace Paley
Alan Paton
Orlando Patterson
Bill Pearson
Walker Percy
Kathrin Perutz
Jerzy Peterkiewicz
Harry Mark Petrakis
Ann Petry
Gilbert Phelps
Marge Piercy
David Plante
Frederik Pohl
Hal Porter
Anthony Powell
J.F. Powers
Reynolds Price
J.B. Priestley
V.S. Pritchett
Frederic Prokosch
James Purdy
Mario Puzo
Thomas Pynchon

Thomas Head Raddall
Ayn Rand
Raja Rao
Frederic Raphael
Simon Raven
Piers Paul Read
John Rechy
Ishmael Reed
Vic Reid
Lynne Reid Banks
Mary Renault
Mordecai Richler
Tom Robbins
Daphne Rooke
Sinclair Ross
Leo Rosten
Henry Roth
Philip Roth
Bernice Rubens
Michael Rumaker

Nayantara Sahgal
Garth St. Omer
J.D. Salinger
Andrew Salkey
Frank Sargeson
May Sarton
Budd Schulberg
Hubert Selby, Jr.
Samuel Selvon
Maurice Shadbolt
Margery Sharp
Irwin Shaw
Wilfrid Sheed
Clancy Sigal
Alan Sillitoe
Andrew Sinclair
Jo Sinclair
Isaac Bashevis Singer
Khushwant Singh
Emma Smith
Iain Crichton Smith
Susan Sontag
Gilbert Sorrentino
Terry Southern
Muriel Spark
Colin Spencer
Elizabeth Spencer
Christina Stead
Wallace Stegner
Daniel Stern
James Stern
Richard G. Stern
J.I.M. Stewart
Monica Stirling
Dal Stivens
Irving Stone
Anthony Storey
David Storey
Randolph Stow
Francis Stuart
Jessie Stuart
William Styron
Ronald Sukenick
Hollis Summers
Glendon Swarthout
Frank Swinnerton
Julian Symons
Scott Symons

Robert Taylor
Emma Tennant
Kylie Tennant
Paul Theroux
Audrey Thomas
Gillian Tindall
Peter Tinniswood
Honor Tracy
William Trevor
Rachel Trickett
Alexander Trocchi
Niccolò Tucci
Frank Tuohy
George Turner
Amos Tutuola
Anne Tyler

John Updike
Edward Upward
Leon Uris
Fred Urquhart

Laurens van der Post
Gore Vidal
Kurt Vonnegut, Jr.

David Wagoner
John Wain
Margaret Walker
Rex Warner
Robert Penn Warren
Judah Waten
Keith Waterhouse
David Watmough
Alec Waugh

Auberon Waugh
Jerome Weidman
Fay Weldon
Eudora Welty
Albert Wendt
Glenway Wescott
Anthony West
Anthony C. West
Jessamyn West
Morris West
Paul West
Rebecca West
Jon Manchip White
Patrick White
Rudy Wiebe
John Williams
John A. Williams
Raymond Williams
Tennessee Williams
Wirt Williams
Calder Willingham
Angus Wilson
Colin Wilson
Sloan Wilson
Donald Windham
Adele Wiseman
Larry Woiwode
Bernard Wolfe
Douglas Woolf
Herman Wouk
Charles Wright

James Yaffe
Richard Yates
Frank Yerby
Jose Yglesias
Al Young
Marguerite Young
Sol Yurick

APPENDIX

Walter Van Tilburg Clark
J.G. Farrell
Shirley Jackson
James Jones
Jack Kerouac
Olivia Manning
Carson McCullers
Flannery O'Connor
Paul Scott

ABBAS, (Khwaja) Ahmad. Indian. Born in Panipat, 7 June 1914. Educated at Hali Muslim High School; Aligarh Muslim University, B.A. 1933, LL.B. 1935. Married Mujtabai Khatoon in 1942 (died, 1958); one daughter. Reporter and Sub-Editor, 1936-39, and Editor, Sunday Edition, and Columnist, 1939-47, Bombay *Chronicle*. Since 1947, Contributing Columnist, *Blitz* magazine, Bombay. Since 1951, Proprietor, Naya Sansar film production Company, Bombay. Leader, Indian Film Delegation, U.S.S.R., 1954. Recipient: *Hindustan Times* prize, 1950; President of India's Gold Medal, for film, 1964; Padma Shree, 1969; Haryana State Robe of Honour, 1969. Address: Philomena Lodge, Church Road, Juhu, Bombay-54, India.

PUBLICATIONS

Novels

Tomorrow Is Ours! Bombay, Popular Book Depot, 1943; as *Divided Heart*, New Delhi, Paradise, 1968.
Defeat for Death: A Story Without Names. Baroda, Padmaja, 1944.
Not All Lies! Privately printed, 1949.
Blood and Stones. Bombay, Hind Kitabs, 1947.
Inqilab. Bombay, Jaico, 1955.
When Night Falls. Delhi, Hind, 1968.
Mera Naam, Joker. Delhi, Hind, 1970.
Maria. Delhi, Hind, 1972.
Boy Meets Girl. New Delhi, Sterling, 1973.
Bobby. New Delhi, Sterling, 1973.
Distant Dream. New Delhi, Sterling, 1975.

Short Stories

Rice and Other Stories. Bombay, Kutub, 1947.
Cages of Freedom and Other Stories. Bombay, Hind Kitabs, 1952.
One Thousand Nights on a Bed of Stones and Other Stories. Bombay, Jaico, 1957.
The Black Sun and Other Stories. Bombay, Jaico, 1963.
The Most Beautiful Woman in the World. New Delhi, Paradise, 1968.
The Walls of Glass. New Delhi, Himalaya, 1977.

Plays

Zubeida (produced Bombay, 1944).
Invitation to Immortality. Bombay, Padma, 1944.
Lal Gulab Ki Wapsi (produced Bombay, 1964).

Screenplays: *Naya Sansar*, 1941; *Dr. Kotnis*, 1945; *Dharti Ke Lal*, 1946; *Awara*, 1951; *Anhonee*, 1951; *Rahi*, 1952; *Munna*, 1954; *Shri 420*, 1955; *Pardesi*, 1957; *Chardil Char Rahen*, 1959; *Shehar Aur Sapna*, 1963; *Hamara Gaar*, 1964; *Aasman Bahal*, 1966; *Bambai Raat Ki Bahon Mein*, 1968; *Saat Hindustani*, 1969; *Mera Naam Joker*, 1970; *Do Boond Pani*, 1971; *Bobby*, 1973; *Achanak*, 1973; *Faaslah*, 1974.

Other

Outside India: The Adventures of a Roving Reporter. Delhi, Hali, 1938.
Let India Fight for Freedom. Bombay, Sound Magazine, 1943.
An Indian Looks at America. Bombay, Thacker, 1943.
And One Did Not Come Back: The Story of the Congress Medical Mission to China. Bombay, Sound Magazine, 1944.
Report to Gandhiji, with N.G. Yog. Bombay, Hind Kitabs, 1944.
I Write as I Feel (selections from Bombay *Chronicle*). Bombay, Hind Kitabs, 1948.
Kashmir Fights for Freedom. Bombay, Kutub, 1948.
China Can Make It. Bombay, Bhatt, 1952.
In the Image of Mao Tse-tung. Bombay, Peoples Publishing House, 1953.
Face to Face with Khrushchov. Delhi, Rajpal, 1960.
Till We Reach the Stars: The Story of Yuri Gagarin. London, Asia Publishing House, 1961; New York, Asia Publishing House, 1962.
Indira Gandhi: Return of the Red Rose. Bombay, Popular Prakashan, 1966.
That Woman: Her Seven Years in Power. New Delhi, Indian Book Company, 1973.
Face to Face with Indira Gandhi, with R.K. Karanjia. New Delhi, Chetana, 1974.
Jawaharlal Nehru: Portrait of an Integrated Indian. New Delhi, National Council of Educational Research and Training, 1974.
I Am Not an Island: An Experiment in Autobiography. New Delhi, Vikas, and Columbia, Missouri, South Asia Books, 1977.
The Mad, Mad, Mad World of Indian Films. Delhi, Hind, 1977.
20th March 1977: A Day Like Any Other. New Delhi, Vikas, 1978.
Janata in a Jam? Bombay, Jaico, 1978.
The Naxalites. Delhi, Lok, 1979.

Translator, *I Cannot Die*, by Krishnan Chandar. Poona, Kutub, 1943 (?).
Translator, *Shadows Speak*, by A.H. Sahir Ludhianvi. Bombay, P.P.H. Bookstall, 1958.

Ahmad Abbas comments:

Highbrow literary critics in India have sometimes sneeringly labelled my novels and short stories as "mere journalese." The fact that most of them are inspired by aspects of the contemporary historical reality, as sometimes chronicled in the press, is sufficient to put them beyond the pale of literary creation. I have no quarrel with the critics. Maybe I am an unredeemed journalist and reporter, masquerading as a writer of fiction. But I have always believed that while the inner life of man undoubtedly is, and should be, the primary concern of literature, this inner personal life impinges upon the life of the community—and of humanity—at every critical turning point of human experience. "No man is an island..." said John Donne, and one may add that even if he was, no island is free from the inroads of the sea, as no man is free from the impact of social forces and the life around him.

This inter-action of the individual and society, both in its psychological and social complexity, is of particular interest to me as a writer. It has inspired, provoked, or coloured most of what I have written.

Mirrored in my works are many fragments of our recent history—the war, the religious riots and the killings, the partition, the post-freedom years of disillusionment, of the new hopes engendered, and problems raised, by the industrialization and mechanization of agriculture. But I do hope I have also revealed glimpses of the "inner life" of my contemporaries, the people of a new India, in their moments of tenderness and passion, of frustration and exultation, as they evolve from the passive (but by no means ignoble) fatalism, so characteristic of the Indian peasant rooted in tradition, towards the hopeful dynamism, the remarkable adaptability and the willingness to change, which, paradoxically enough, is also an Indian characteristic.

If there is one thing that I have tried consistently to do in my novels and stories, it is to give the readers a little peep into the hearts and minds, the inner life, of my contemporaries and fellow Indians, to show that their life is being influenced and changed and re-shaped by the historical and social forces that are greater than us and our "destiny."

* * *

Ahmad Abbas's affinities with the "social conscience" and "national brotherhood" schools of Indian fiction are symbolised by the fact that Mulk Raj Anand wrote an epistolary introduction to *Rice and Other Stories* and that Abbas dedicated *Cages of Freedom* to Anand. Abbas's literary interest in the relationship between the individual and society was probably stimulated by Anand's early novels about the social tragedy of India's untouchable, coolie, and peasant poor, who were economically exploited and politically oppressed, victims jointly of British imperialism and Indian vested interests. Abbas in turn has depicted social tragedy, and as such his fiction is conceived as a contribution to Indian humanism. He is essentially a "progressive," "purposeful" writer and sometime propagandist, as he whimsically acknowledges in *Not All Lies!* Although Abbas's literary achievement is only modest and minor, he has centered his attention on important Indian themes.

Mulk Raj Anand has defined the most fundamental of these themes as follows: "the emergence of man from the restraints, inhibitions, codes, conventions and violences of the old society to the status of an individual integrated in a new community of like individuals, so that the development and the expression of human personality should become possible" (*Rice and Other Stories*, p. 9). This "Tradition v. Modernity" crisis is at the centre of Abbas's fiction, particularly his Independence Struggle novels. *Tomorrow Is Ours!* resounds with dated applause for resurgent India's fight for freedom: for "genuine modernism" emerging out of the "ruins of feudalism" and the "tinsel and trash discarded by the West." *Inqilab* (the title is derived from the patriotic battle-cry "Inqilab Zindabad" or Long Live Revolution) competently communicated a sense of what it was like to be committed to the Independence movement during the 1920's and 1930's. *Maria* recalls the endurance and heroism of Goa's struggle against Portuguese colonialism. The Goan heroine is an allegorical soul of India; on her death-bed in 1970, she is destined to re-unite her former Indian comrades who, after their Goan adventure, reverted back into the hostile separatism of communal names and languages and denied their proven common humanity.

In *Inqilab* Abbas explores two themes which are prominent in his writings: the quest for personal identity, and the need for intercommunal brotherhood. Thus Anwar (the dramatic hero of the novel as distinct from Gandhi and Nehru who are its polemical heroes) is Muslim in upbringing but Hindu by birth. The revelation of Anwar's origins results in a traumatic drama of identity, but his discovery of self is also a discovery of India and he is finally integrated into "a strange symbol of unity." Anwar's evolving consciousness and political activities provide a sound basis for Abbas's major comment, which acknowledges the tragedy of sectarian hatred and confusion of aims within the revolutionary movement, but concludes that unity and love can ultimately prevail over division and hate.

That moral integrity is the central value in Abbas's world-view is further exemplified in *When Night Falls* and *Mera Naam, Joker*. However, despite the pertinence of the integrity versus corruption theme in *When Night Falls* (a reporter fights for the poor against a diabolical millionaire and refuses to be bought off), the human significance of this theme and of the social evils exposed is vitiated by Abbas's gaudy melodrama, crude characterisation, and naive style. This novel reveals Abbas endeavoring to reach a potential cinema audience which relishes gauche sensationalism. *Mera Naam, Joker*, by contrast, reveals something of the "inner life" of Indian sensibility. The conceit of the joker's dual personality—the mask of pleasure hiding the man of pain—provides scope for Indian-style expression of emotion which westerners usually dismiss as sentimental. The sad story of the joker's failure to win the women he loves is presented in terms of Indian existentialism; the joker's destiny is divinely inspired, life is "a huge joke" in the cosmos of the absurd.

Abbas's main limitations as a writer—unsubtlety of form and meaning, transparent contrivances, melodrama, sensationalism—weaken the humane effects he is constantly striving for. Nevertheless, his work often reflects genuinely Indian dispositions of the folk spirit (see his more lyrical short stories), and in *Inqilab* he successfully conveys a reportorial sense of "the contemporary historical reality."

—S.C. Harrex

ABISH, Walter. American. Born in Vienna, Austria, 24 December 1931; became American citizen in 1960. Married to the sculptor Cecile Abish. Adjunct Professor, Empire State College, New York, 1973-75; Writer-in-Residence, Wheaton College, Norton, Massachusetts, 1976; Visiting Butler Professor, State University of New York, Buffalo, 1977. Since 1979, Lecturer in English and Comparative Literature, Columbia University, New York. Recipient: New Jersey Council on the Arts Fellowship, 1972; Rose Isabel Williams Foundation grant, 1974; Ingram Merrill Foundation grant, 1977; National Endowment for the Arts Fellowship, 1980; P.E.N.-Faulkner Award, 1981. Address: P.O. Box 485, Cooper Station, New York, New York 10276, U.S.A.

PUBLICATIONS

Novels

Alphabetical Africa. New York, New Directions, 1974.
How German Is It. New York, New Directions, 1980.

Short Stories

Minds Meet. New York, New Directions, 1975.
In the Future Perfect. New York, New Directions, 1977.

Uncollected Short Stories

"Inside Out," in *Personal Injury Magazine 4* (New York), 1978.
"Happiness," in *Parenthèse* (Brewster, New York), 1979.
"Ninety-Nine: The New Meaning," in *Renegade 1* (New York), 1979.
"Auctioning Australia," in *Text-Sound Texts*, edited by Richard Kostelanetz. New York, Morrow, 1980.
"Alphabet of Revelations," in *New Directions in Prose and Poetry 41.* New York, New Directions, 1980.
"The Idea of Switzerland," in *Partisan Review* (New Brunswick, New Jersey), 1980.

Verse

Duel Site. New York, Tibor de Nagy, 1970.

*

Critical Studies: "Through a Continent Darkly," in *Picked-Up Pieces* by John Updike, New York, Knopf, 1975, London, Deutsch, 1976; interview with Jerome Klinkowitz, in *Fiction International* (Canton, New York), Fall 1975, and *The Life of Fiction* by Klinkowitz, Urbana, University of Illinois Press, 1977; "Restrictive Fiction" by Kenneth Baker, in *New Directions in Prose and Poetry 35*, edited by James Laughlin, New York, New Directions, 1977; "Present Imperfect" by Tony Tanner, in *Granta* (Cambridge), 1979; "On the Guideless Guidebooks of Postmodernism" by Charles Caramello, in *Sun and Moon* (College Park, Maryland), Summer 1980; "The Writer-to-Be: An Impression of Living" by Abish, and "The Puzzle of Walter Abish" by Alain Arias-Misson, in *Sub-Stance 27* (Madison, Wisconsin), Winter 1980.

Walter Abish comments:

I spent my childhood in China, seeing an incredibly corrupt society slowly disintegrate. It was as if all the life processes were accentuated and crowded into the period of time I lived in Shanghai.

I have always thought that all the life networks that enable us to proceed wherever we are going, or prevent us from doing so, are predicated on a system called language. This awareness undoubtedly influenced my approach to writing.

* * *

Walter Abish—born in Vienna, raised in China, settled in Israel, and trained as a city planner, the occupation which first brought him to America and a job in New York City—began publishing fiction in 1970. His major work has appeared in the semi-annual anthologies produced by New Directions, the publisher who has also issued his two collections of short fiction and two novels. A master of the stiff-upper-lip, self-consciously presentational prose style made famous by Donald Barthelme, Abish has devised his own techniques by which the language of his stories explores itself in search of the ironies of human communication and behaviour.

His first novel, *Alphabetical Africa*, is a tour de force demonstration of how words can refer to their own artificiality at the same time they operate as linguistic signifiers. The first chapter is titled "A," and every word therein begins with that letter ("Ages ago, Alex, Allen and Alva arrived at Antibes, and Alva allowing all, allowing anyone, against Alex's admonition, against Allen's angry assertion: another African amusement," etc.). The second chapter, "B," adds words beginning with the letter *B*, and so forth until the book expands to its full linguistic possibilities. Such a self-apparent structure makes the reader painfully aware of the words themselves, and of how an artificial discipline of language determines just what reality may transpire. For example, a character named Herman can't appear until chapter "H"; the first person narrator must keep his comments to himself until chapter "I"; and the characters cannot travel to Jedda until chapter "J." By chapter "Z" the full exercise of language may have lulled the reader into complacency. But the book is only half done, for the 27th chapter is titled "Z" once more, followed by "Y," "X," and so forth back through the now-contracting alphabet. Familiar persons, places, and things are lost at each receding chapter as the book's mimetic action literally effaces itself in one's hands, until at the end one is left with the solemn toiling at the minimally expressive letter *A*. Like breathing in and then breathing out, the reader has experienced the expansion and contraction, the life and death of a work of fiction. At no point can one suspend disbelief and sink into the pantomine of suspended disbelief, for at all times attention is riveted to the self-conscious making and unmaking of the physical book.

Minds Meet collects 12 of Abish's short fictions from the early 1970's. The title piece is based upon improvisations with the theme of human communication: "Taken Aback by the Message," "The Abandoned Message," "Abased by the Message," and so forth. Another story, "This Is Not a Film. This Is a Precise Act of Disbelief," employs the semiology of contemporary American culture, whereby the needs of people are served by an assortment of surface details ("pure signifiers" as the structuralists would say). Abish's most characteristic style in these shorter pieces is to write sentences composed of radically different thoughts which collide at the caesura; readers are thus aware of content and linguistic form at the same time, and especially how syntax presupposes judgment—an irony Abish enjoys exploiting with his humor of sexual innuendo. By these collisions, the story moves forward; its real subject is nothing other than itself.

The stories of *In the Future Perfect* are distinguished by their mechanical structures which call attention to their component words. "Ardor/Awe/Atrocity" consists of block paragraphs headed by three superscripted words, their presence in the following sections numbered in alphabetical order. One is thus aware of the 78 key words which will be featured long before they pop up in the narrative; when they do, the reader should be more inclined to treat them as signifiers—as creatures of the writer's invention—than as signified in the outside world of associations. "In So Many Words" assembles the words of each paragraph in alphabetical order before those same terms are repeated in syntactic sense, making attention to the writer's artifice (and the words themselves) more pronounced. Even the apparently conventional stories in this volume, by virtue of their circular technique, return to key elements ("perfection," "repetition") which the author selects at the start of each section.

How German Is It, Abish's second novel, is disarmingly conventional. But only on the surface is it a simple story of a writer's return to "the new Germany." A story from *In the Future Perfect*, "The English Garden," is actually its prolegomena, and the epigraph from John Ashbery indicates Abish's deeper interests in the linguistically contrived nature of human behaviour: "Remnants of the old atrocity subsist, but they are converted into ingenious shifts in scenery, a sort of 'English Garden' effect, to give the required air of naturalness, pathos and hope."

—Jerome Klinkowitz

ABLEMAN, Paul. British. Born in Leeds, Yorkshire, 13 June 1927; brought up in New York. Attended King's College, University of London. Military service: 3 years. Married; one son. Agent: Jonathan Clowes Ltd., 19 Jeffrey's Place, London NW1 9PP. Address: Flat 36, Duncan House, Fellows Road, London N.W.3, England.

PUBLICATIONS

Novels

I Hear Voices. Paris, Olympia Press, 1957; London, New English Library, 1966.
As Near as I Can Get. London, Spearman, 1962.
Vac. London, Gollancz, 1968.
The Twilight of the Vilp. London, Gollancz, 1969.
Tornado Pratt. London, Gollancz, 1977.
Shoestring (novelization of TV play). London, BBC Publications, 1979.
Porridge (novelization of screenplay). London, Pan, 1979.
Shoestring's Finest Hour. London, BBC Publications, 1980.

Uncollected Short Stories

"The Bay Area," in *Transatlantic Review 26* (London), Autumn 1967.
"Sir Jacob's Ordeal," in *Men Only* (London), November 1971.

Plays

Even His Enemy, with Gertrude Macauley (as *Letters to a Lady*, produced London, 1951). London, French, 1948.
Help! (revue; produced London, 1963).
One Hand Clapping (revue; produced Edinburgh, 1964).
Dialogues (produced London, 1965).
Green Julia (produced Edinburgh and London, 1965; Washington, D.C., 1968; New York, 1972). London, Methuen, and New York, Grove Press, 1966.
Tests (playlets). London, Methuen, 1966.
Emily and Heathcliff (produced London, 1967).
Blue Comedy: Madly in Love, Hank's Night (produced London, 1968). London, Methuen, 1968; *Madly in Love* published in *Modern Short Comedies from Broadway and London*, edited by Stanley Richards, New York, Random House, 1969.
The Black General, adaptation of *Othello* (produced London, 1969).
And Hum Our Sword (produced London, 1973).
Little Hopping Robin (produced London, 1973).
The Visitor (produced London, 1974).
Windsor All-Sorts (produced London, 1977).

Radio Play: *The Infant*, 1974.

Television Plays: *Barlowe of the Car Park*, 1961; *That Woman Is Wrecking Our Marriage*, 1969; *Visits from a Stranger*, 1970; *The Catch in a Cold*, 1970.

Verse

Bits: Some Prose Poems. London, Latimer Press, 1969.

Other

The Mouth and Oral Sex. London, Running Man Press, 1969; as *The Mouth*, London, Sphere, 1972; as *The Sensuous Mouth*, New York, Ace, 1972.

Translator, with Veronica Hull, *Egypt*, by Simone Lacourture. London, Vista, 1963.

* * *

Paul Ableman is a comedian whose favourite joke is the reader. His gadfly gifts first came to light in a strange novel, *I Hear Voices*, published by the Olympia Press in 1957. This book is recounted by an imaginary schizophrene, and Philip Toynbee has described it as presenting "a marvellous entanglement of different levels of reality." The hero is confined to his room, where he lies in bed, eats his meals, receives the occasional visitor. But by means of his madness, as Toynbee points out, he becomes a traveller in time and space, well-equipped to encounter "a wonderful series of dream-like adventures." Ableman has also written several plays (including *Green Julia* which had a certain critical success), and he is responsible for a volume of amusing if somewhat hermetic neo-Dadaist dialogues, *Tests*.

As Near As I Can Get confirmed his special, effervescent, slightly secret talent, but not until *Vac* did he go some way towards pleasing a wider public. The title of his novel is exact, fusing the idea of holiday or vacation with that of vacuum. The narrator, Billy Soodernim, exists somewhere between the two. For 12 years he has been married to Lucy, warm, sad, accommodating, vulnerable Lucy; he loves Lucy and has looked after her pretty well, but he never began to promise to be faithful to her, and his flexible notions of the concept of marriage have now become too much for her. Lucy has taken up with a 19-year-old hashish-smoking Turk, Kemal. The two of them visit Billy when he is in the hospital for a hernia operation, but even this act of bizarre emotional generosity cannot divert the marriage from the rocks. When the book opens Billy and Lucy are breaking up. For the rest of the time Billy breaks down. There is a lifelikeness and immediacy to Ableman's "scene," with its parties and car-rides and endless bickerings against the flames of the sex war. But there is also a certain whimsical self-indulgence in his refusal to give imaginative "distance" to his central character. The joke of Billy's name is not a particularly good joke. By the last pixillated page it has been made to seem to be at the reader's expense. As a piece of improvisation, though, *Vac* has the virtues of its own recklessness. The prose is highly alert, and often funny, especially about sex, a remark which applies with equal truth to *The Twilight of the Vilp*, though the filament-thin slightness of this leaves one in doubt as to whether the author is seriously joking or jokingly serious. Perhaps, in a word, and Joyce's at that, he is *jocoserious*?

Bits is a book of experimental prose pieces, all short. In a note, Ableman declares that each "bit" is built round a simple poetic idea, but that this idea has not been explored or embodied in poetic form firstly because he does not think he can write "true" poetry, and secondly because it seems to him that as regards form "the way ahead for literature is a fusion of the chief virtues of prose (breadth, sustained objectivity, naturalness of tone) with those of poetry (syntactical freedom, exactness of expression)." The result is diverting, if rather too determinedly trivial. In a piece such as "A Man Suddenly Remembering" the process of thinking, the movement of the mind, is aptly caught in the quick uncertain sentence constructions, and in "Lichen" and "Strangers" and "The Ghosts of the Mind" something rarer—a moment seized and turned inside-out for its meaning, as in one of Rimbaud's *Illuminations*, or a Sarraute *tropisme*.

—Robert Nye

ABRAHAMS, Peter (Henry). South African. Born in Vrededorp, near Johannesburg, in 1919. Educated at Church of England mission schools and colleges. Married Daphne Elizabeth Miller; three children. Merchant seaman, 1939-41; then lived in England: regular contributor to *The Observer*, London, and the *Herald Tribune*, New York and Paris, 1952-64; Editor, *West Indian Economist*, and Controller, *West Indian News*, Jamaica, 1955-64. Address: Red Hills, St. Andrews, Jamaica.

Publications

Novels

Song of the City. London, Crisp, 1945.
Mine Boy. London, Crisp, 1946; New York, Knopf, 1955.
The Path of Thunder. New York, Harper, 1948; London, Faber, 1952.
Wild Conquest. New York, Harper, 1950; London, Faber, 1951.
A Wreath for Udomo. New York, Knopf, and London, Faber, 1956.
A Night of Their Own. New York, Knopf, and London, Faber, 1965.
This Island Now. London, Faber, 1966; New York, Knopf, 1967.

Short Stories

Dark Testament. London, Allen and Unwin, 1942.

Verse

A Blackman Speaks of Freedom! Poems. Durban, Universal Printing Works, 1938 (?).
Here, Friend. Privately printed, n.d.

Other

Return to Goli (reportage). London, Faber, 1953.
Tell Freedom: Memories of Africa. London, Faber, and New York, Knopf, 1954.
Jamaica: An Island Mosaic. London, Her Majesty's Stationery Office, 1957.
The World of Mankind, with others. New York, Golden Press, 1962.

*

Critical Studies: *Peter Abrahams* by Michael Wade, London, Evans, 1972; *The Writing of Peter Abrahams* by Kolawole Ogungbesan, London, Hodder and Stoughton, 1979.

* * *

Peter Abrahams left South Africa in 1939, when he was only 20 years old, but the racial and political problems of that troubled land have continued to dominate his imagination. All but one of his seven novels have been set entirely or in part in South Africa, and the one exception, *This Island Now*, deals with race and politics in another potentially explosive plural society, an island in the Caribbean with a poverty-stricken black majority and an affluent white minority. Abrahams has also written two autobiographical books, *Tell Freedom* and *Return to Goli*, both of which focus on his experiences as a mulatto in South Africa.

Abrahams's early novels were influenced by Marxist ideas so they tend to be concerned more with race and economics than with politics. *Song of the City* and *Mine Boy* tell of the consequences of urbanization and industrialization on the lives of young black workers who move from the country to the city. *Song of the City* takes place at the time of the second world war, *Mine Boy* against the backdrop of booming gold mines in Johannesburg. In both novels nonwhites are mistreated and oppressed by whites.

In his next novel, *The Path of Thunder*, Abrahams turned to the theme of interracial love, exploring its impact on a young Coloured schoolteacher and an Afrikaner girl whose passionate affair ultimately ends in tragedy when the Afrikaner community discovers they are lovers. Two years later Abrahams moved in yet another direction, this time reconstructing the era of the Afrikaner migration or "Great Trek" in *Wild Conquest*, an historical novel in which he made an effort to be fair to all the major ethnic groups in South Africa—Bantu, Boer and Briton.

After these early works, all of which were written in the 1940's, Abrahams's fiction became more political. *A Wreath for Udomo*, published just before Ghana attained its independence, was an attempt to predict what might happen when independent black African nations were confronted with the choice between the financial advantages of collaborating with the white regimes in southern Africa and the moral imperative of opposing them by actively supporting black liberation movements. *A Night of Their Own* carried the revolutionary theme further by detailing the adventures of an African underground agent involved in smuggling funds to an Indian resistance organization in South Africa. And *This Island Now* told of racial tensions and internal power struggles in a small, black-ruled Caribbean island-state. In each successive novel Abrahams moved further and further away from a depiction of South African social realities to the construction of hypothetical situations which afforded greater creative elbow room. Even *A Night of Their Own*, though set in South Africa, had elements of fantasy and wishful thinking in it. Abrahams's increased dependence on his imagination in these later novels may reflect how far out of touch he is with contemporary conditions in his native land.

Abrahams has always written in a simple, direct prose style which wavers between superior reportage and maudlin romanticizing. He is at his best when transcribing newsworthy events which have a basis in fact; his autobiographical and travel writings, for instance, are superb. But he has a regrettable tendency to sentimentalize personal relationships between men and women, especially if they are of different races, as they so often are in his novels. His accounts of miscegenated love are nearly always literary disasters because they are bathed in lachrymose artificiality.

Yet when he writes of exciting happenings such as spontaneous labor strikes, bloody frontier battles, underground resistance campaigns, or the highly-charged political debates at a Pan-African congress, Abrahams can carry the reader along swiftly and persuasively, building up a spell-binding momentum which is broken only when he suddenly veers from the external world of his characters into the internal world of their thoughts and dreams. Abrahams has not yet learned to write a decent interior monologue, and his novels would be more aesthetically satisfying if his heroes and heroines were less inclined to moments of moody introspection. His surface sketches are much more convincing than his psychological probings.

Because Abrahams was one of the first African writers to achieve international recognition, his works received a good deal of patronizing attention at first. European and American critics were all too eager to embrace him as a literary phenomenon—a nonwhite South African who could not only write but could actually write fairly well!—so they wrote glowing reviews of his early novels, emphasizing their strong points and ignoring obvious flaws. Today, in the midst of an African literary awakening, Abrahams tends to be regarded with less enthusiasm, for his novels are recognized as far less interesting and accomplished than those produced in West Africa by such talented artists as Chinua Achebe, Wole Soyinka, and Ayi Kwei Armah. Abrahams has certainly carved a niche for himself in African literary history, but it is a small niche somewhere at the base of the monument, passionately but clumsily hewn.

—Bernth Lindfors

ABSE, Dannie. Welsh. Born in Cardiff, Glamorgan, 22 September 1923. Educated at St. Illtyd's College, Cardiff; University of South Wales and Monmouthshire, Cardiff; King's College, London; Westminster Hospital, London; qualified as physician 1950, M.R.C.S., L.R.C.P. Served in the Royal Air Force, 1951-54: Squadron Leader. Married Joan Mercer in 1951; one son and two daughters. Since 1954, Specialist in charge of the chest clinic, Central London Medical Establishment. Senior Fellow in Humanities, Princeton University, New Jersey, 1973-74. Since 1978, President, Poetry Society. Recipient: Foyle Award, 1960; Welsh Arts Council award, for verse, 1971. Agent: Anthony Shiel Associates Ltd., 2-3 Morwell Street, London WC1B 3AR. Address: 85 Hodford Road, London N.W.11, England.

PUBLICATIONS

Novels

Ash on a Young Man's Sleeve. London, Hutchinson, 1954; New York, Criterion, 1955.
Some Corner of an English Field. London, Hutchinson, 1956; New York, Criterion, 1957.
O. Jones, O. Jones. London, Hutchinson, 1970.

Uncollected Short Stories

"Tobacconist," in *Commentary* (New York), March 1957.
"Metamorphosis of Reg," in *Twentieth Century* (London), no. 1034, 1967.
"My Father's Red Indian," in *New Stories 2*, edited by Derwent May and Alexis Lykiard. London, Arts Council, 1977.
"Sorry, Miss Crouch," in *The Punch Book of Short Stories.* London, Robson, 1979.

Plays

Fire in Heaven (produced London, 1948). London, Hutchinson, 1956; revised version, as *Is the House Shut?* (produced London, 1964); revised version, as *In the Cage*, in *Three Questor Plays*, 1967.
Hands Around the Wall (produced London, 1950).
House of Cowards (produced London, 1960). Included in *Three Questor Plays*, 1967; in *Twelve Great Plays*, edited by Leonard F. Dean, New York, Harcourt Brace, 1970.
The Eccentric (produced London, 1961). London, Evans, 1961.
Gone (produced London, 1962). Included in *Three Questor Plays*, 1967.
The Joker (produced London, 1962).
Three Questor Plays (includes *House of Cowards, Gone, In the Cage*). Lowestoft, Suffolk, Scorpion Press, 1967.
The Dogs of Pavlov (produced London, 1969; New York, 1974). London, Vallentine Mitchell, 1973.
The Courting of Essie Glass (broadcast, 1975). Published in *The Jewish Quarterly* (London), 1972.

Funland (produced London, 1975).
Pythagoras (produced Birmingham, 1976; London, 1980). London, Hutchinson, 1979.
Gone in January (produced London, 1978).

Radio Plays: *Conform or Die*, 1957; *No Telegrams, No Thunder*, 1962; *You Can't Say Hello to Anybody*, 1964; *A Small Explosion*, 1964; *The Courting of Essie Glass*, 1975.

Verse

After Every Green Thing. London, Hutchinson, 1949.
Walking under Water. London, Hutchinson, 1952.
Tenants of the House. London, Hutchinson, 1957; New York, Criterion, 1958.
Poems, Golders Green. London, Hutchinson, 1962.
Dannie Abse: A Selection. London, Studio Vista, 1963.
A Small Desperation. London, Hutchinson, 1968.
Demo. Frensham, Surrey, Sceptre Press, 1969.
Selected Poems. London, Hutchinson, and New York, Oxford University Press, 1970.
Funland: A Poem in Nine Parts. Portland, Oregon, Portland University Press, 1971.
Corgi Modern Poets in Focus 4, with others, edited by Jeremy Robson. London, Corgi, 1972.
Funland and Other Poems. London, Hutchinson, and New York, Oxford University Press, 1973.
Lunchtime. London, Poem-of-the-Month Club, 1974.
Penguin Modern Poets 26, with D.J. Enright and Michael Longley. London, Penguin, 1975.
Collected Poems 1948-1976. London, Hutchinson, and Pittsburgh, University of Pittsburgh Press, 1977.
Way Out in the Centre. London, Hutchinson, 1981.

Recording: *Poets of Wales*, Argo, 1972.

Other

Medicine on Trial. London, Aldus, 1968; New York, Crown, 1969.
A Poet in the Family (autobiography). London, Hutchinson, 1974.
Miscellany One. Bridgend, Poetry Wales Press, 1981.

Editor, with Howard Sergeant, *Mavericks*. London, Editions Poetry and Poverty, 1957.
Editor, *European Verse*. London, Studio Vista, 1964.
Editor, *Corgi Modern Poets in Focus 1, 3, 5*. London, Corgi, 1971-73.
Editor, *Thirteen Poets*. London, Poetry Book Society, 1973.
Editor, *Poetry Dimension 2-5: The Best of the Poetry Year*. London, Robson, 1974-78; New York, St. Martin's Press, 1976-79; *The Best of the Poetry Year 6-7*, Robson, and Totowa, New Jersey, Rowman and Littlefield, 1979-80.

* * *

Dannie Abse has spoken of clarifying "dangers in the dark" by writing "tiny flashes in the night." Brief and controlled, his novels illuminate deadly pitfalls. But they also put in relief moments of humane concern, projecting these against a darkness at once social and metaphysical.

Abse's skill at threading his narratives on counterpointed leitmotifs makes his novels as "poetic" as they are socially realistic. The leitmotifs are taken from history, literature, even football, but especially from medicine. The symbolic transformation of detail, however, derives from Abse's anxious yet humorous ambivalence toward the antithetical claims of nihilism and social conscience. (In this respect, he has much in common with another physician-novelist, the psychoanalyst Allen Wheelis.) It is always with some image of the dissecting room in mind that Abse's protagonists hunt a tenuous ethical position. Like a war zone, that horrendous place simultaneously negates and compels the search.

Ash on a Young Man's Sleeve is an evocation of adolescence, particularly the amusing side of that period. Set in Cardiff between 1930 and 1940, the story delineates, over against the rise of Fascism, the emergence from boyhood of a Welsh Jew. At first remote, the brutality of Nazism descends in bombs upon the young man's very neighborhood, killing his best friend and eradicating in a split second a precious relationship they had worked out through periods of rivalry and almost laughable bigotry. The "ash" of the title signifies the early encroachment of death into youthful life. The title itself modifies Eliot's lines from "Little Gidding":

> Ash on an old man's sleeve
> Is all the ash burnt roses leave.
> Dust in the air suspended
> Marks the place where a story ended.

which serve as an epigraph to the novel and contrast throughout with a refrain from Hopkins: "Glory be to God for dappled things." The work concludes with an exquisite passage on the falling of leaves and the end of innocence which seems to connect the novel attitudinally to Hopkins's poem "Spring and Fall."

Some Corner of an English Field is set in a post-World War Two R.A.F. station in England and devastates the military by likening it to a new shallowness of spirit. Drinking himself into courage, the central figure, Dr. Henderson, tells his officer colleagues in a farewell speech: "The symbols of our sick internal reality...are here externalized in the airship hangars, in the sound of marching feet, in the shocking uniformity of opinion." The symbolic beating scene which ensues brings the insight to a grim fruition. Henderson is placed, however, between this violent dullness and the temptation of following four drifters in their suicidal meanderings. Of this dilemma, so germane to Abse's work, the narrator says almost imploringly: "Somewhere there was a way between utter acceptance and complete, destructive rebellion."

In the vein of Amis's *Lucky Jim*, *O. Jones, O. Jones* is Abse's most thoroughly comic novel. The "O" stands for Ozymandias, a cognomen the hero grandly hands himself to make up for his own dull "Herbert." As a medical student "Ozy" deals with one devastating event after another. He comes haltingly to something near Shelley's view of Ozymandias. Because, ironically, his character is his fate and life is fortuitous, Ozy's receptivity to experience cancels out his spurious motivation and he seems at last a serious candidate for good works, for labor no longer glimpsed through an adolescent haze.

—David M. Heaton

ACHEBE, Chinua. Nigerian. Born Albert Chinualumogu in Ogidi, 16 November 1930. Educated at Government College, Umuahia, 1944-47; University College, Ibadan, 1948-53, B.A. (London) 1953. Married Christie Okoli in 1961; two sons and two daughters. Talks Producer, Lagos, 1954-57, Controller, Enugu, 1958-61, and Director, Lagos, 1961-66, Nigerian Broadcasting Corporation. Chairman, Citadel Books Ltd., Enugu, 1967. Senior Research Fellow, 1967-73, and since 1973, Professor of English, University of Nigeria, Nsukka. Visiting Professor, University of Massachusetts, Amherst, 1972-75, and University of Connecticut, Storrs, 1975-76. Since 1962, Founding Editor, Heinemann African Writers series, and since 1970, Director, Heinemann Educational Books (Nigeria) Ltd., and Nwankwo-Ifejika Ltd., later Nwamife, publishers, Enugu. Since 1971, Editor, *Okike*, an African journal of new writing. Member, University of Lagos Council, 1966; Chairman, Society of Nigerian Authors, 1966. Recipient: Margaret Wrong Memorial Prize, 1959; Nigerian National Trophy, 1960; Rockefeller Fellowship, 1960; Unesco Fellowship, 1963; Jock Campbell Award (*New Statesman*), 1965; Commonwealth Poetry Prize, 1973; Neil Gunn International Fellowship, 1974; Nigerian National Merit Medal, 1979. D.Litt.: Dartmouth College, Hanover, New Hampshire, 1972; University of Southampton, 1975; University of Ife, 1978; D. Univ.: University of Stirling, 1975; LL.D.: University of Prince Edward Island, Charlottetown, 1976; D.H.L.: University of Massachusetts, 1977. Honorary Fellow, Modern Language Association of America, 1974; Member, Order of the Federal Republic of Nigeria, 1979. Address: University of Nigeria, Nsukka, Nigeria.

PUBLICATIONS

Novels

Things Fall Apart. London, Heinemann, 1958; New York, McDowell Obolensky, 1959.
No Longer at Ease. London, Heinemann, 1960; New York, Obolensky, 1961.
Arrow of God. London, Heinemann, 1964; New York, Day, 1967.
A Man of the People. London, Heinemann, and New York, Day, 1966.

Short Stories

The Sacrificial Egg and Other Stories. Onitsha, Etudo, 1962.
Girls at War. London, Heinemann, and New York, Doubleday, 1972.

Verse

Beware, Soul-Brother and Other Poems. Enugu, Nwankwo-Ifejika, 1971; revised edition, Enugu, Nwamife, and London, Heinemann, 1972.
Christmas in Biafra and Other Poems. New York, Doubleday, 1973.

Other

Chike and the River (juvenile). London and New York, Cambridge University Press, 1966.
How the Leopard Got His Claws (juvenile). Enugu, Nwamife, 1972; New York, Third Press, 1973.
African Aesthetics. Enugu, Nwamife, 1973.
Morning Yet on Creation Day: Essays. London, Heinemann, and New York, Doubleday, 1975.
In Person: Achebe, Awoonor, and Soyinka at the University of Washington. Seattle, University of Washington African Studies Program, 1975.
The Flute (juvenile). Enugu, Fourth Dimension, 1977.
The Drum (juvenile). Enugu, Fourth Dimension, 1977.

Editor, *The Insider: Stories of War and Peace from Nigeria*. Enugu, Nwanko-Ifejika, and Chatham, New Jersey, Chatham Booksellers, 1971.
Co-Editor, *Don't Let Him Die*. Enugu, Fourth Dimension, 1978.

*

Bibliography: in *Africana Library Journal* (New York), Spring 1970.

Critical Studies: *The Novels of Chinua Achebe* by G.D. Killam, London, Heinemann, and New York, Africana, 1969, revised edition, Heinemann, 1977; *Chinua Achebe* by Arthur Ravenscroft, London, Longman, 1969, revised edition, 1977; *Chinua Achebe* by David Carroll, New York, Twayne, 1970, revised edition, London, Macmillan, 1980; *Critical Perspectives on Chinua Achebe* edited by Bernth Lindfors and C.L. Innes, London, Heinemann, and Washington, D.C., Three Continents, 1978; *Achebe's World: The Historical and Cultural Context of Chinua Achebe's Novels* by Robert M. Wren, Washington, D.C., Three Continents, 1980.

Chinua Achebe comments:

I am a political writer. My politics is concerned with universal human communication across racial and cultural boundaries as a means of fostering respect for all people. Such respect can issue only from understanding. So my primary concern is with clearing the channels of communication in my own neighbourhood by hacking away at the thickets that choke them.

Africa's meeting with Europe must be accounted a terrible disaster in this matter of human understanding and respect. The nature of the meeting precluded any warmth of friendship. First Europe was an enslaver; then a colonizer. In either role she had no need and made little effort to understand or appreciate Africa; indeed she easily convinced herself that there was nothing there to justify the effort. Today our world is still bedevilled by the consequences of that cataclysmic encounter.

I was born into the colonial era, grew up in the heady years of nationalist protest and witnessed Africa's resumption of independence. (It was not, however, the same Africa which originally lost her freedom that now regained it, but a different Africa created in the image of Europe—but that's another story.) So I have seen in my not very long lifetime three major eras in precipitate succession, leaving us somewhat dazed. My response as a writer has been to try to keep pace with these torrential changes. First I had to tell Europe that the arrogance on which she sought to excuse her pillage of Africa, i.e., that Africa was the Primordial Void, was sheer humbug; that Africa had a history, a religion, a civilization. We reconstructed this history and civilization and displayed it to challenge the stereotype and the cliché. Actually it was not to Europe alone I spoke. I spoke also to that part of ourselves that had come to accept Europe's opinion of us. And I was not alone nor even the first.

But the gauntlet had barely left our hands when a new historic phase broke on us. Europe conceded independence to us and we promptly began to misuse it, or rather those leaders to whom we entrusted the wielding of our new power and opportunity. So we got mad at them and came out brandishing novels of disenchantment. Actually we had all been duped. No independence was given—it is never given but taken, anyway. Europe had only made a tactical withdrawal on the political front and while we sang our anthem and unfurled our flag she was securing her iron grip behind us in the economic field. And our leaders in whose faces we hurled our disenchantment neither saw nor heard because they were not leaders at all but marionettes.

So the problem remains for Africa, for black people, for all deprived peoples and for the world. And so for the writer, for he is like the puppy in our proverb: that stagnant water in the potsherd is for none other but him. As long as one people sit on another and are deaf to their cry, so long will understanding and peace elude all of us.

* * *

For technical inventiveness both in language and novelistic technique, for profound insight into tragic human experience, for satirical sophistication, and for sustained creative energy, Chinua Achebe must still be regarded as the Anglophone African novelist of most considerable stature. The success of his first novel, *Things Fall Apart*, has led to some underestimation of the books that followed. Because Obi in *No Longer at Ease* is a grandson of Okonkwo in the first novel, the second has been regarded as not only a sequel but an attempt at essentially the same kind of tragic novel, and there has been disappointment that expectations aroused by *Things Fall Apart* are not fulfilled in *No Longer at Ease*. Because *Arrow of God* deals with the same sort of traditional Igbo society as forms the setting of *Things Fall Apart*, it has been seen as a less concise exercise over the same ground. Because there is a surface opposition between the young Odili and the corrupt political boss, Chief Nanga, in *A Man of the People*, much of the subtle satire and moral judgement in this novel has been missed.

Things Fall Apart is rightly praised as a taut, economically written novel that examines the period of the first Igbo contact with white missionaries and colonial officials in terms that are reminiscent of Greek tragedy. The rise of the self-made man, Okonkwo, in such a society, and his ignominious end are often regarded as the peculiar strength of the novel. Yet what happens to Okonkwo is the result of neither blind fate nor inevitable psychological bias. Okonkwo's very warrior-strength comes from his conscious will; he pursues a particular course from deliberate choice, and suppresses all his humaner tendencies so that his natural affections become warped. Other alternatives are open to him, and taken by others equally valiant. His career parallels and illumines the tragedy that overcomes his people; Igbo society is too inflexible to cope with the imperial power. Although Achebe presents traditional African society and his hero Okonkwo with great sympathy, he retains an admirable artistic objectivity about them. He does not allow his desire to show that the pre-colonial African past had a highly developed culture to obscure its weaknesses—precisely those that enabled the missionaries to get a toehold among the Igbos. The point of view is sympathetic, yet delicately balanced, and complex in the means by which it is conveyed. For instance, the most marked linguistic characteristic is Achebe's use of literal English translations of Igbo proverbs. This device not only makes for surface authenticity, but is a means of indicating how Igbo society is simultaneously strengthened and severely limited by its traditional wisdom inherited through gnomic folk sayings. In an oral culture, the spoken word is extraordinarily utilitarian, but also a form of continuing ritual. While the tragedy is the destruction of an admirable, self-contained society by an intrusive culture, the victim is also seen to have serious inadequacies. Achebe's story is not a lament for the past but an analysis of a process of historical change. The blindnesses of those involved on both sides are revealed with a detachment on the novelist's part that is intimately related to his satirical methods in *No Longer at Ease* and *A Man of the People*.

Although *Arrow of God* provides an even richer evocation of traditional culture than *Things Fall Apart* does, it is more than a similar novel on a grander scale. The organic daily life of the Umuaro clan is drawn in great detail, but not simply to anatomize traditional culture. It is necessary for realizing fully the part of the priest Ezeulu in that society, for Ezeulu is the most complex and ambitious study in characterization that Achebe has yet produced, and his tragedy grows out of the conflict within him between the demands of his semi-divine office as priest of the clan's protective deity and his very human desire for personal power. The theme is a man's attitude to the power he already wields, what he does with that power, and the effects of his misuse of it upon himself and his people. In *Arrow of God*, too, Achebe uses Igbo proverbs, but now not merely to suggest the ordinary rituals of traditional life, but also as means of conveying the twilit area between a man's terrestrial life and his function as a semi-spirit mediating on his people's behalf with a deity. It is here that Ezeulu loses his way. Achebe directs the intricate drama with great sympathy and human understanding yet maintains an extraordinary detachment, best illustrated by the sardonic last paragraph of the novel, which casts doubt on the people's over-simple interpretation of Ezeulu's downfall.

In *No Longer at Ease* the characteristics of pre-colonial Igbo culture have become hollow mockeries, just as Obi's youthful idealism is seen to be without foundation before the harsh realities of corruption in modern Lagos. What is satirically laid bare is the chaotic, rootless bewilderment of West African city life, again fully reflected in the character's speech, as they switch from Igbo to pidgin or to English, according to their relationships with other people. The general crisis of culture is particularized—and humanized—in Obi's career, but Achebe's satire underlines the absence of any larger mode for personal integrity to work within.

In *A Man of the People* Achebe attacks political corruption and thuggery, not by conventional means, but by using Odili as an anti-hero who lucidly analyses the evils around him, while taking a share in them himself. The only clue to Odili's real fictional function lies in the false, pseudo-sophisticated speech that Achebe places in his mouth. The novel is a brilliant creation, a superb satirical farce.

Thus far Achebe's experience of the Nigerian Civil War (1967-70), in which he worked for the Biafran government, has been expressed in two compassionate stories in *Girls at War* and some very fine, somber, caustic poems about the dark side of human behaviour in war in *Beware, Soul Brother*.

Perhaps Achebe's greatest strength as a novelist is the steady refinement of his control over language as a means of conveying rather than stating moral insights.

—Arthur Ravenscroft

ALDISS, Brian (Wilson). British. Born in East Dereham, Norfolk, 18 August 1925. Educated at Framlingham College, Suffolk, 1936-39; West Buckland School, 1939-42. Served in the Royal Signals in the Far East, 1943-47. Married Margaret Manson in 1965 (second marriage); four children, two from previous marriage. Bookseller, Oxford, 1947-56; Literary Editor, *Oxford Mail*, 1958-69; Science-Fiction Editor, Penguin Books, London, 1961-64; Art Correspondent, *Guardian*, London. President, British Science Fiction Association, 1960-65; Co-Founder, 1972, and Chairman, 1976-78, John W. Campbell Memorial Award; Co-President, Eurocon Committee, 1975-79; Chairman, Society of Authors, London, 1978-79; Member, Arts Council Literature Panel, 1978-80. Since 1975, Vice-President, Stapledon Society; since 1977, Founding Trustee, World Science Fiction, Dublin. Recipient: World Science Fiction Convention citation, 1959; Hugo Award, 1962; Nebula Award, 1965; Ditmar Award (Australia), 1970; British Science Fiction Association Award, 1972, and Special Award, 1974; Eurocon Award, 1976; James Blish Award, for non-fiction, 1977; Cometa d'Argento (Italy), 1977; Prix Jules Verne, 1977; Pilgrim Award, 1978. Guest of Honour, World Science Fiction Convention, London, 1965, 1979. Agent: A.P. Watt Ltd., 26-28 Bedford Row, London WC1R 4HL. Address: Orchard House, Begbroke, Oxfordshire OX5 1RT, England.

PUBLICATIONS

Novels

The Brightfount Diaries. London, Faber, 1955.

Non-Stop. London, Faber, 1958; as *Starship*, New York, Criterion, 1959.

Vanguard from Alpha. New York, Ace, 1959; as *Equator*, London, Digit, 1961.

Bow Down to Nul. New York, Ace, 1960; as *The Interpreter*, London, Digit, 1961.

The Male Response. New York, Galaxy, 1961; London, Dobson, 1963.

The Primal Urge. New York, Ballantine, 1961; London, Sphere, 1967.

Hothouse. London, Faber, 1962; Boston, Gregg Press, 1976; abridged edition, as *The Long Afternoon of Earth*, New York, New American Library, 1962.

The Dark Light-Years. London, Faber, and New York, New American Library, 1964.

Greybeard. London, Faber, and New York, Harcourt Brace, 1964.

Earthworks. London, Faber, 1965; New York, Doubleday, 1966.

An Age. London, Faber, 1967; as *Cryptozoic!*, New York, Doubleday, 1968.

Report on Probability A. London, Faber, 1968; New York, Doubleday, 1969.
Barefoot in the Head. London, Faber, 1969; New York, Doubleday, 1970.
The Hand-Reared Boy. London, Weidenfeld and Nicolson, and New York, McCall, 1970.
A Soldier Erect; or, Further Adventures of the Hand-Reared Boy. London, Weidenfeld and Nicolson, and New York, Coward McCann, 1971.
Frankenstein Unbound. London, Cape, 1973; New York, Random House, 1974.
The Eighty-Minute Hour. London, Cape, and New York, Doubleday, 1974.
The Malacia Tapestry. London, Cape, 1976; New York, Harper, 1977.
Brothers of the Head. London, Pierrot, 1977; New York, Two Continents, 1978.
Enemies of the System. London, Cape, and New York, Harper, 1978.
A Rude Awakening. London, Weidenfeld and Nicolson, 1978; New York, Random House, 1979.
Brothers of the Head, and Where the Lines Converge. London, Panther, 1979.
Life in the West. London, Weidenfeld and Nicolson, 1980.
Moreau's Other Island. London, Cape, 1980; as *An Island Called Moreau*, New York, Simon and Schuster, 1981.

Short Stories

Space, Time, and Nathaniel: Presciences. London, Faber, 1957; abridged edition, as *No Time Like Tomorrow*, New York, New American Library, 1959.
The Canopy of Time. London, Faber, 1959; revised edition, as *Galaxies Like Grains of Sand*, New York, New American Library, 1960.
The Airs of Earth. London, Faber, 1963.
Starswarm. New York, New American Library, 1964; London, Panther, 1979.
Best Science Fiction Stories of Brian Aldiss. London, Faber, 1965; as *Who Can Replace a Man?*, New York, Harcourt Brace, 1966; revised edition, Faber, 1971.
The Saliva Tree and Other Strange Growths. London, Faber, 1966; Boston, Gregg Press, 1981.
Intangibles Inc. and Other Stories. London, Faber, 1969.
Neanderthal Planet. New York, Avon, 1970.
The Moment of Eclipse. London, Faber, 1970; New York, Doubleday, 1972.
The Book of Brian Aldiss. New York, DAW, 1972; as *Comic Inferno*, London, New English Library, 1973.
Excommunication. London, Post Card Partnership, 1975.
Last Orders and Other Stories. London, Cape, 1977.
New Arrivals, Old Encounters. London, Cape, 1979; New York, Harper, 1980.

Play

Distant Encounters, adaptation of his own stories (produced London, 1978).

Verse

Pile: Petals from St. Klaed's Computer. London, Cape, and New York, Holt Rinehart, 1979.

Other

Cities and Stones: A Traveller's Jugoslavia. London, Faber, 1966.
The Shape of Further Things: Speculations on Change. London, Faber, 1970; New York, Doubleday, 1971.
Billion Year Spree: A History of Science Fiction. London, Weidenfeld and Nicolson, and New York, Doubleday, 1973.
Science Fiction Art, illustrated by Chris Foss. New York, Bounty, 1975; London, Hart Davis, 1976.
Science Fiction as Science Fiction. Frome, Somerset, Bran's Head, 1978.
This World and Nearer Ones: Essays Exploring the Familiar. London, Weidenfeld and Nicolson, 1979.

Editor, *Penguin Science Fiction.* London, Penguin, 1961; *More Penguin Science Fiction*, 1963; *Yet More Penguin Science Fiction*, 1964; 3 vols. collected as *The Penguin Science Fiction Omnibus*, 1973.
Editor, *Best Fantasy Stories.* London, Faber, 1962.
Editor, *Last and First Men*, by Olaf Stapledon. London, Penguin, 1963.
Editor, *Introducing SF.* London, Faber, 1964.
Editor, with Harry Harrison, *Nebula Award Stories 2.* New York, Doubleday, 1967; as *Nebula Award Stories 1967*, London, Gollancz, 1967.
Editor, *Farewell, Fantastic Venus.* London, Macdonald, 1968; abridged edition, as *All about Venus*, New York, Dell, 1968.
Editor, with Harry Harrison, *Best SF 1967* [to *1975*]. New York, Putnam, 7 vols., and Indianapolis, Bobbs Merrill, 2 vols., 1968-75; as *The Year's Best Science Fiction 1-9*, London, Sphere, 9 vols., 1968-76.
Editor, with Harry Harrison, *The Astounding-Analog Reader.* New York, Doubleday, 1972; London, Sphere, 2 vols., 1973.
Editor, *Space Opera.* London, Weidenfeld and Nicolson, 1974; New York, Doubleday, 1975.
Editor, *Space Odysseys.* London, Futura, 1974; New York, Doubleday, 1976.
Editor, with Harry Harrison, *SF Horizons.* New York, Arno Press, 1975.
Editor, with Harry Harrison, *Hell's Cartographers: Some Personal Histories of Science Fiction Writers.* London, Weidenfeld and Nicolson, and New York, Harper, 1975.
Editor, with Harry Harrison, *Decade: The 1940's, The 1950's, The 1960's.* London, Macmillan, 3 vols., 1975-77; *The 1940's* and *The 1950's*, New York, St. Martin's Press, 2 vols., 1978.
Editor, *Evil Earths.* London, Weidenfeld and Nicolson, 1975; New York, Avon, 1979.
Editor, *Galactic Empires.* London, Weidenfeld and Nicolson, 2 vols., 1976; New York, St. Martin's Press, 2 vols., 1977.
Editor, *Perilous Planets.* London, Weidenfeld and Nicolson, 1978; New York, Avon, 1980.

*

Bibliography: *Item Eighty-Three: Brian Aldiss: A Bibliography 1954-1972* by Margaret Aldiss, Oxford, Bocardo Press, 1972.

Manuscript Collection: Bodleian Library, Oxford University.

Critical Studies: "Generic Discontinuities in SF: Brian Aldiss' *Starship*" by Fredric Jameson, in *Science-Fiction Studies* (Terre Haute, Indiana), i, 2, 1973; *Aldiss Unbound: The Science Fiction of Brian W. Aldiss* by Richard Mathews, San Bernardino, California, Borgo Press, 1977.

Brian Aldiss comments:

(1972) Time is the spectre haunting the stage of most of my books: Time in its own right and in one of its nastier disguises, as Change. The characters cope with this as best they can. Sometimes, Time has only a walk-on role, as in *Barefoot in the Head*; sometimes, it even consents to play the fool, as in my current series of sexual-social novels, of which the first two volumes are *The Hand-Reared Boy* and *A Soldier Erect*.

By nature I'm an obsessive writer. Whatever I am writing at present pleases me most, or else I give it up. My science fiction represents a spectrum moving from extreme science-fiction situations in the early novels towards situations merely coloured by the presence of the future; by the time I reached *Report on Probability*

A and *Barefoot*, I was writing a fiction that bears only slight resemblance to traditional SF. The Hand-Reared series (which may run to six or more novels) is a logical extension of this process; here the gaze is directed towards the past, but emphasis is still on Change—change, in this case, as it relates to one man's life. The emphasis in this series is on comedy, with sorrow as a light zither accompaniment; in my science fiction, the arrangement has generally been the other way round.

At present, I am working on a history of science fiction, *The Billion Year Spree*, together with the critic Philip Strick. Perhaps this means (though I hope it doesn't) that the science fiction novel and I are parting company. But I shall continue to write short stories with a futurist-surrealist bent, which may still be considered as my natural medium.

* * *

The great contribution Brian Aldiss has made to the art of science fiction is to help to raise it to the point where it is now accepted, by all but the chronically bigoted, as a literary form worthy of serious consideration. I suspect that this has much to do with the fact that Aldiss has always looked upon himself primarily as a novelist rather than as a writer of SF, and he has written several novels other than those on science-fiction themes.

His first full length science-fiction novel was *Non-Stop* which was based on the almost classic SF theme of a giant space-ship adrift in space. As a piece of story telling it is first class, and it displays all the excellences that are to be found in his later work: the ability to establish by carefully selected detail a convincing atmosphere of place and time, and a logical development of situations so that even the most outlandish become acceptable to the reader. In *Hothouse*, for example, Aldiss creates a world dominated by vegetation where we can sense the continual and overwhelming growth, even breathe the vegetable air, and in *Greybeard* the experience of being in post-atomic Oxford is remarkably vivid. But in *Non-Stop*, while the exploration of the ship (once built by giants) by Roy Complain and his companions has parallels with the sense of awe and wonder experienced by the Old English poets when they encountered the ruins of Roman cities, the space ship becomes a microcosm of Earth which, too, can be seen as a giant ship itself endlessly adrift in space, and the exploration develops into a search for destination and purpose.

A quality which informs Brian Aldiss's work, and which should not be overlooked, is his sense of humour. In *Non-Stop* one aspect of this can be seen in his pursuit of the idea that in the future psychology will develop its own theology and superstitions and replace our present religions. It is a plausible thesis and at the same time an amusing one, and often Aldiss's humour helps to save his SF novels from the over-seriousness that has engulfed other practitioners in this genre. It has been responsible too for the excellent humorous novels. The logical consequences of the invention and universal use of an "Emotional Register" are used in *The Primal Urge* to create a fantastic and hilarious story.

In recent years Brian Aldiss has striven to extend the boundaries of his art. In *Report on Probability A* he attempted the first SF anti-novel, a study in relative phenomena which proved a tour de force, and in *Barefoot in the Head* he produced another "first" where groups of poems and "pop-songs" reflect and comment on the preceding prose chapters. In a Europe reeling psychodelically from an attack by an Arab state with Psycho-Chemical Aerosol Bombs, Chateris, the hero of *Barefoot in the Head*, gradually absorbs the acid-head poison in the atmosphere to find himself a new Messiah. As social and thought patterns disintegrate so does the language, and Aldiss develops a stunning-punning prose reminiscent of the verbal pyrotechnics of Joyce's *Finnegans Wake*. At the same time he creates a nightmare world reflecting trends observable in the situation already with us.

Though not strictly within a discussion of Brian Aldiss's novels, we should not overlook his collections of short stories, *Space, Time, and Nathaniel* and *The Canopy of Time*, of which he is justly proud. A recent enterprise, planned as a group of novels, constitutes a fictional autobiography covering the years from the 1930's to the 1960's, where through the sexual and spiritual development of Horatio Stubbs are examined certain aspects of the poverty of English middle-class life. The first, *The Hand-Reared Boy*, begins with Horatio as a boy, his masturbatory fantasies and his first sexual encounters. The direct and extremely realistic style of the first part of this novel might not be to everyone's taste, but it flowers into a most beautifully controlled story of Horatio's first and hopeless love for an older woman. In the second novel, *A Soldier Erect*, we find Horatio still hard at it in the army and serving in India and Burma where his sexual and social education is broadened. The coarse brutality of wartime soldiering in the Far East is accurately and as brutally portrayed, but redeemed by humour and set in contrast with Horatio's growing awareness of values beyond the more immediately erotic, a theme continued and brought to conclusion in the third novel in the series, *A Rude Awakening*, where Horatio encounters the Dutch, Indian, Japanese, Chinese, and Indonesian forces in Sumatra and finds himself with two girls.

On the SF side, Aldiss's *Frankenstein Unbound* breaks new ground again. As a result of the indiscriminate use of nuclear weapons within the ambits of the Earth-Lunar system the infrastructure of space is seriously damaged to the point where time and space go "on the brink." The consequent "time shifts" find Joe Boderland suddenly transported to Switzerland in the year 1816 where he encounters not only Mary Shelley, the creator of Frankenstein, but Frankenstein himself in a world where reality itself is equally unstable and the dividing line between the real and the imagined world has become confused. In this situation Boderland finds himself unsure of his own role, and it is the discovery and fulfilment of his mission which constitutes the central theme of the narrative. It is a measure of Aldiss's powers as a novelist that he persuades the reader of the *reality* of this fantastic situation. The theme, I suspect, was suggested by his researches into the origins of science fiction which he undertook to produce his history of the genre, *Billion Year Spree*, and in which he makes a powerful case for Mary Shelley's *Frankenstein* as the first true SF novel.

More recent novels increase one's admiration for Brian Aldiss's versatility and unflagging powers of invention. *Brothers of the Head*, the story of Siamese twin boys with a third dominant head which becomes increasingly demanding, is a brilliant if disturbing excursion into the macabre, while *The Malacia Tapestry* almost defies definition. Set in an age old city state, riddled with rival philosophies, under the spell of magicians, and where change is forbidden, it presents the reader with a panorama of dukes, wealthy merchants, thespians, courtesans, spongers, and soldiers. What we are never sure of is whereabouts in the time scale we are. Is it a medieval town? Then just a glimpse of something tells us no. An alternative world? But never explicitly so. The way in which Aldiss makes this totally imaginary world a reality is remarkable, a superb example of how to induce the suspension of disbelief. At the same time a stream of traditional SF stories continues with novels like *Enemies of the System*. An essay on Brian Aldiss is always an interim report.

—John Cotton

ALDRIDGE, (Harold Edward) James. Australian. Born in White Hills, Victoria, 10 July 1918. Educated at Swan Hill High School; London School of Economics. Married Dina Mitchnik in 1942; two sons. Writer, Melbourne *Herald* and *Sun*, 1937-38, and London *Daily Sketch* and *Sunday Dispatch*, 1939; European and Middle East War Correspondent for the Australian Newspaper Service and the North American Newspaper Alliance, 1939-44; Teheran Correspondent, for *Time* and *Life*, 1944. Recipient: Rhys

Memorial Prize, 1945; World Peace Council Gold Medal; International Organization of Journalists prize, 1967; Lenin Memorial Peace Prize, 1972. Address: 21 Kersley Street, London S.W.11, England.

PUBLICATIONS

Novels

Signed with Their Honour. London, Joseph, and Boston, Little Brown, 1942.
The Sea Eagle. London, Joseph, and Boston, Little Brown, 1944.
Of Many Men. London, Joseph, and Boston, Little Brown, 1946.
The Diplomat. London, Lane, 1949; Boston, Little Brown, 1950.
The Hunter. London, Lane, 1950; Boston, Little Brown, 1951.
Heroes of the Empty View. London, Lane, and New York, Knopf, 1954.
I Wish He Would Not Die. London, Bodley Head, 1957; New York, Doubleday, 1958.
The Last Exile. London, Hamish Hamilton, and New York, Doubleday, 1961.
A Captive in the Land. London, Hamish Hamilton, 1962; New York, Doubleday, 1963.
The Statesman's Game. London, Hamish Hamilton, and New York, Doubleday, 1966.
My Brother Tom. London, Hamish Hamilton, 1966; as *My Brother Tom: A Love Story*, Boston, Little Brown, 1967.
A Sporting Proposition. London, Joseph, and Boston, Little Brown, 1973; as *Ride a Wild Pony*, London, Penguin, 1976.
Mockery in Arms. London, Joseph, 1974; Boston, Little Brown, 1975.
The Untouchable Juli. London, Joseph, 1975; Boston, Little Brown, 1976.
One Last Glimpse. London, Joseph, and Boston, Little Brown, 1977.
Goodbye Un-America. London, Joseph, and Boston, Little Brown, 1979.

Short Stories

Gold and Sand. London, Bodley Head, 1960.

Uncollected Short Stories

"Braver Time," in *Redbook* (Dayton, Ohio), May 1967.
"The Unfinished Soldiers," in *Winter's Tales 15*, edited by A.D. Maclean. London, Macmillan, 1969; New York, St. Martin's Press, 1970.
"The Black Ghost of St. Helen," in *After Midnight Ghost Book*, edited by James Hale. London, Hutchinson, 1980.

Plays

The 49th State (produced London, 1947).

Television Plays: scripts for *Robin Hood* series.

Other

Undersea Hunting for Inexperienced Englishmen. London, Allen and Unwin, 1955.
The Flying 19 (juvenile). London, Hamish Hamilton, 1966.
Living Egypt, photographs by Paul Strand. London, MacGibbon and Kee, and New York, Horizon Press, 1969.
Cairo: Biography of a City. Boston, Little Brown, 1969; London, Macmillan, 1970.
The Marvelous Mongolian (juvenile). Boston, Little Brown, and London, Macmillan, 1974.

* * *

James Aldridge left Australia when quite a young man as a war-correspondent; and this fact has largely determined the material and the angle of approach in his work. He went through the Greek campaign and wrote two books based directly on his experiences in it. Here his method was strongly affected by Hemingway; but the books were saved from being mere imitations by the genuine freshness and truth of his presentation. He was learning how to build a narrative full of stirring events and based on historical developments which he knew at first-hand, and at the same time to link the story with the personal problems and struggles of his protagonists. With his next book, a collection of stories, came a break from the Hemingway influence. What he had gained from his apprenticeship was now integrated in his own method and outlook. The tales showed how well he was able to grasp situations with very diverse settings and convincingly to define aspects of national character in a compact form. Still drawing on his wartime experiences as a correspondent, he wrote *The Diplomat*, an ambitious large-scale work, dealing with both the Soviet Union and the region of the Kurds in northern Mesopotamia. With much skill he explored the devious world of diplomacy in the postwar world, making the issues concrete by their basis in the difficult national question of the Kurds. Aldridge emerged as an important political novelist. He showed himself able to handle complicated political themes without losing touch with the essential human issues. The political aspects were removed from triviality or narrowness by being linked with the painful struggles of the protagonist to understand the world in which he found himself an actor. Thus what gave artistic validity to the work, beyond any particular conclusions reached in the search for truth, was the definition of that search itself.

In *The Hunter* Aldridge next refreshed himself by dropping all large themes and turning to Canada in a work more concerned with immediacies of experience; his theme was the world of the hunter, a direct relationship to nature; and he showed he could conjure up a dimension of sheer physical living. But it was perhaps significant that when he turned from the theme of contemporary history and politics, it was to the sphere of nature he looked, not to everyday life in some specific society. For good and bad his uprooting through the war had made him into a novelist of the large national conflicts of our age. His material has thus been born of his journalism, but in transforming it into fiction he has overcome the journalistic limitations and been able to penetrate to deep human issues. He sees the problem in terms of real people and has never been guilty of inventing puppets to represent national or political positions.

He now turned again to the Near East, in *Heroes of the Empty View*, *I Wish He Would Not Die*, and *The Last Exile*, not dealing with such a remote issue as that of the Kurds, but taking up the problems of the Arab world, with special reference to Egypt. He has been helped by having many direct connections and sources of information; but despite his sympathy for the Arabs he has not oversimplified issues or made his works into tracts for a particular point of view. The stories clarify things and deepen one's understanding of the human beings entangled in vast conflicts. In his latest works he has again taken up the question of the Soviet Union but with less force and artistic success than in *The Diplomat* or the books on the Near East. It would be hard to point to any contemporary novelist who has dealt more directly with postwar political problems on the international plane with such success, uniting a warm sympathy for the persons he writes about, with, in the last resort, a true artistic detachment.

—Jack Lindsay

ALI, Ahmed. Pakistani. Born in Delhi, India, 1 July 1910. Educated at Aligarh University; Lucknow University, B.A. 1931, M.A.

1932. Married Bilquees Jehan in 1950; four children. Lecturer, Lucknow University, 1932-33, 1936-41; Professor, Agra College, 1933-34; Lecturer, Allahabad University, 1934-36; Professor, Presidency College, Calcutta, 1945-47; British Council Visiting Professor, National Central University, Nanking, 1946-48; Visiting Professor, Michigan State University, East Lansing, 1975; Fulbright-Hays Professor, Western Kentucky University, Bowling Green, and Southern Illinois University, Carbondale, 1978-79. Representative and Director, BBC, New Delhi, 1941-44. Director of Foreign Publicity, Pakistan Government, Karachi, 1948-49; Counsellor and Chargé d'Affaires, Pakistan Foreign Service, in Karachi, Peking, and Rabat, 1950-60. Since 1970, Managing Director of Lomen Fabrics Ltd., Karachi. Editor, *Indian Writing*, London, 1939-41; *Tomorrow*, Bombay, 1941-42; *PEN Miscellany*, Karachi, 1948-50. Proprietor, Akrash Press, Delhi, 1940-47, and in Karachi since 1963. Founding Fellow, Pakistan Academy of Letters. Address: 21-A Faran, Hyder Ali Road, Karachi 5, Pakistan.

PUBLICATIONS

Novels

Twilight in Delhi. London, Hogarth Press, 1940; New York and London, Oxford University Press, 1967.
Ocean of Night. London, Peter Owen, 1964.

Short Stories (in Urdu)

Angaray. Privately printed, 1932.
Sholay. Lahore, Maktaba Urdu, 1934.
Hamari Gali. Delhi, Akrash Press, 1940.
Qaidkhana. Delhi, Akrash Press, 1942.
Maut Se Pahlay. Delhi, Akrash Press, 1945.
Prima della Morte (bilingual edition). Milan, Vito Salierno, 1967.

Uncollected Short Stories

"When the Funeral Was Crossing the Bridge," in *Lucknow University Journal*, 1929.
"A Stormy Night of Rains," in *Humayun* (Lahore), January 1931.
"Our Lane," in *New Writing* (London), 1936.
"Before Death," in *New Directions 15*. New York, New Directions, 1955.
"The Castle," in *Eastern Horizon* (Hong Kong), October 1965.
"A Feudal House," in *Eastern Horizon* (Hong Kong), November 1966.

Plays

The Land of Twilight (produced Lucknow, 1931). Lucknow, Sreshta, 1937.
Break the Chains (produced Lucknow, 1932).

Verse

Purple Gold Mountain: Poems from China. London, Keepsake Press, 1960.

Other

Mr. Eliot's Penny-World of Dreams. Lucknow, Lucknow University, 1941.
Muslim China. Karachi, Institute of International Affairs, 1949.
Problem of Style and Technique in Ghalib. Karachi, American Centre, 1969.

Editor and Translator, *The Flaming Earth: Poems from Indonesia*. Karachi, Friends of the Indonesian Republic, 1949.
Editor and Translator, *The Bulbul and the Rose: An Anthology of Urdu Poetry*. Karachi, Jamia, 1962.
Editor and Translator, *Ghalib: Selected Poems*. Rome, Ismeo, 1969.
Editor and Translator, *The Golden Tradition: An Anthology of Urdu Poetry in English*. New York, Columbia University Press, 1973.

Translator, *The Falcon and the Hunted Bird* (Urdu verse). Karachi, Kitab, 1950.

*

Critical Studies: "The Novels of Ahmed Ali" by Laurence Brander, in *Journal of Commonwealth Literature* (Leeds, Yorkshire), July 1967; "Ahmed Ali and *Twilight in Delhi*" by David D. Anderson, in *Mahfil* (East Lansing, Michigan), Spring-Summer 1971; "*Twilight in Delhi*: A Study in Lyricism" by Anita S. Kumar, in *Indian Literature* (New Delhi), March-April 1976.

Ahmed Ali comments:

(1972) Starting with poetry and belles lettres as a young student of 16, the writer moved on at 19 to Credo of tragic unbelief in a sad unreal world in short stories like "When the Funeral Was Crossing the Bridge," side by side with poems filled with the anguish of adolescence. Simultaneously he was discovering the realities of life and the degrading state of the nation, the social milieu in India of the Simon Commission and the Non-Cooperation Movement of the late 1920's and early 1930's, which finds its first affirmative expression in the short story "A Stormy Night of Rains." This set him on a career of writing fiction, and led him to found, in association with two friends, the Progressive Writers Movement of India in 1932, and the publication the same year of the now historic and then shocking and banned book of short stories in Urdu—*Angaray* (Burning Coals). Four volumes of short stories followed at irregular intervals, and the publication of the short story "Our Lane," a story giving a cross-section of life in a lane in Delhi, his home town, in which the lane itself becomes a living character with its landmarks of shops and trees and cats and people, and all that happens to them therein. Anyone wanting to understand the writer must read this as the most significant introduction to his work and themes and technique, although from the last point of view his story "Before Death" is equally revealing.

His now most highly considered novel, *Twilight in Delhi*, depicts the life of two generations during the first two decades of this century, going back to 1857 and ending with the start of the National Movement in 1921. On the ideological plane the novel presents the decline of feudalism and, as he wrote in the introduction to the 1966 edition of the novel,

> decay of a whole culture, a particular mode of thought and living, now dead and gone already right before our eyes. Seldom is one allowed to see a pageant of History whirl past and partake in it too. Already, since its publication, the Delhi of the novel has changed beyond recognition. For its culture had been nourished and born within the city walls which lie demolished today; and the distinction between the language of the city and the outside world has disappeared in the rattle of many tongues, even as the homogeneity of its life has been engulfed by the tide of democracy. The British had only built a new Delhi outside the city walls. The present rulers have removed the last relic on which the old culture could have taken a stand within the moat-encircled ground. Thus, the prophecy of the book has come true: Seven Delhis had fallen, and the eighth has gone the way of its predecessors yet to be built and demolished again.

Ocean of Night, the writer's second novel, deals with the life between the Wars and its complex problems, symbolically set against the background of Lucknow, artificial and fleshly, decaying before it was ripe; clash between the feudal and the modern spirit with resultant decay and defeatist violence. The feeling heart, which was still alive in the world of *Twilight in Delhi*, here displays one half of it as atrophied and dead, the other half searching for it and failing in the utter confusion of not knowing what it wants or is looking for. As Laurence Brander has concluded in his essay on the writer:

> It could be a sermon to all Muslims on the besetting sin of pride, while for the rest of us it is an expression of the sense and accord we experience when we stand in the Mosques and tombs of Islam. In the outer world, the Muslim search is for the Friend and for the mystical experience of reconciliation with life.

In the third novel of the trilogy the writer had planned at the inception of the first—*Of Rats and Diplomats*, still unpublished, alas—the story of man is taken up after the Second World War and the consequent loss of values, the mess that man has made of life. The mind has developed, but the heart has died in the madness of power and greed for self. Only a faint, far echo is heard, and even that in memory of something undefined in a world from which the big idea has fled.

* * *

The Muslim civilization of India is centred in Delhi and Agra and Lucknow. Delhi and Agra provide the great monuments. Delhi and Lucknow provide the language and the poetry. In its decline the poetry is drenched in remembrance of things past and this agony before the British went was mingled with prophecy of their going and hope that the ancient Moghul splendour would be revived. In the event, the memories have become shadows of shades and the exquisitely civilized Muslims from the great Moghul cities live in exile in Pakistan.

The two novels of Ahmed Ali are the finest celebration we have in novel form of the nostalgia for former glories and that accompanying Muslim belief in the vanity of earthly life. They are expressions of the pain of our human condition and of the agonized sense of the transitory nature of its happiness. They celebrate aspects of Muslim life in two of the great centres of Muslim culture. The Delhi novel came first. In time, it is set in the early decades of the century. From the old house in a by-lane of Old Delhi we go out to see the Great Durbar held by the King-Emperor in 1911, we see Delhi's reactions during the 1914 War, we glimpse the horror of the influenza epidemic in 1919 which decimated the population and we hear of the political unrest which swept across Northern India in 1920. But these things are on the fringe. At the centre is an old Muslim feudal family, generation following generation in gentle, dignified decay. The essential atmosphere of the novel is of the emptiness of the days as life passes by: the want of meaning. It is a special aspect of the despair which saturated the Gangetic Plain—the earth and air stale with the pain of existence, every atom of dust anguished and exhausted after being so many times vegetable, animal and human.

The story outline is simple and sad. Not tragic; it does not attempt that dimension. Two young people fall in love and for a time their union is thwarted—the girl is of a mere Moghul family, Asian from beyond the Himalayas, while the boy is Arabic, straight from the great families. The difficulties are overcome but eventually his love falters and he is unfaithful. The girl pines but before she dies their love is renewed. The value of the novel is in what is embroidered round this simple tale. The father's delight in the great Delhi pastime of pigeon flying, life in the zenana, the ceremonies at the wedding and the descriptions of all the people in the lanes who must play their part. It is a picture of energetic life and brilliant colour, the energy and colour which make life tolerable with its aching background of despair. Then later, the blows of fate, inevitable and cruel. On one side, the Muslim exuberance; on the other, the acceptance of fate: "Who can meddle in the affairs of God?" *Twilight in Delhi* is the most imaginative picture we have of the old Muslim life in Delhi which disappeared when the British went away; it is a fragment of Muslim history written with the pride of deep affection.

The second novel, *Ocean of Night*, was drafted soon afterwards though put aside and published much later. Instead of the colourful vigour of the first novel we have the mood appropriate to Lucknow, where the story is set. Again we have the Muslim celebration, but this time of the Muslim ideas of love and peace and friendship. The action is sordid, taking place in the house of a dissolute Nawab and the house of his mistress, an accomplished dancing girl. Lucknow is famous as a training ground of courtesans and we see the dancing master and the pimps, and the protector being bled of all his possessions. Sordid, the balancing excess to the expression of another excess, the intensity of mystical Islamic thinking. This more interesting theme is presented as the private search of a Muslim intellectual, a lawyer, for the traditional spiritual fulfillment of Islam. The intensity of this emotion is intellectual, a vivid glimpse of the mystical core of Islam. Religions normally reflect man's search for peace and harmony and in his search this Muslim lawyer had a vision in which the inhabitants of his dream tell him that peace is both love and glory, that friendship and love are what matter and the Muslim must subdue his natural pride for he will experience them only in humility. (Ali develops this theme in his fascinating anthology of Urdu poetry, *The Golden Tradition*.) So are we reconciled with God and man. In these two novels a distinguished Urdu poet offers imaginative glimpses of the grace and glory of Islam as it flourished once on the Gangetic Plain.

—Laurence Brander

ALLEN, Walter (Ernest). British. Born in Birmingham, 23 February 1911. Educated at King Edward's Grammar School, Birmingham; Birmingham University, B.A. (honours) in English 1932. Married Peggy Yorke Joy in 1944; two sons and two daughters. Assistant Master, King Edward's Grammar School, Birmingham, 1934; Visiting Lecturer in English, University of Iowa, Iowa City, 1935; Features Editor, Cater's News Service, Birmingham, 1935-37; Assistant Technical Officer, Wrought Light Alloys Development Association, Birmingham, 1943-45; Margaret Pilcher Visiting Professor of English, Coe College, Cedar Rapids, Iowa, 1955-56; Assistant Literary Editor, 1959-60, and Literary Editor, 1960-61, *New Statesman*, London; Visiting Professor of English, Vassar College, Poughkeepsie, New York, 1963-64, University of Kansas, Lawrence, 1967, and University of Washington, Seattle, 1967; Professor and Chairman of English Studies, New University of Ulster, Coleraine, 1967-73; Berg Professor of English, New York University, 1970-71; Visiting Professor, Dalhousie University, Halifax, Nova Scotia, 1973-74; Miles Professor of English, Virginia Polytechnic Institute and State University, Blacksburg, 1974-75. Fellow, Royal Society of Literature, 1960. Address: 6 Canonbury Square, London N1 2AU, England.

PUBLICATIONS

Novels

Innocence Is Drowned. London, Joseph, 1938.
Blind Man's Ditch. London, Joseph, 1939.
Living Space. London, Joseph, 1940.
Rogue Elephant. London, Joseph, and New York, Morrow, 1946.
Dead Man over All. London, Joseph, 1950; as *Square Peg*, New York, Morrow, 1951.
All in a Lifetime. London, Joseph, 1959; as *Threescore and Ten*, New York, Morrow, 1959.

Uncollected Short Stories

"At Aunt Sarah's," in *New Writing* (London), Spring 1938.
"You Hit Me," in *New Writing* (London), Christmas 1939.
"Hotel Hudson-Potomac," in *English Story*, edited by Woodrow and Susan Wyatt. London, Collins, 1941.

Other

The Black Country (topography). London, Elek, 1946.
The Festive Baked-Potato Cart and Other Stories (juvenile). London, Muller, 1948.
Arnold Bennett. London, Home and Van Thal, 1948; Denver, Swallow, 1949.
Reading a Novel. London, Phoenix House, and Denver, Swallow, 1949; revised edition, Phoenix House, 1956, 1963.
Joyce Cary. London, Longman, 1953; revised edition, 1963, 1971.
The English Novel: A Short Critical History. London, Phoenix House, 1954; New York, Dutton, 1955.
Six Great Novelists: Defoe, Fielding, Scott, Dickens, Stevenson, Conrad. London, Hamish Hamilton, 1955; Folcroft, Pennsylvania, Folcroft Editions, 1969.
The Novel Today. London, Longman, 1955; revised edition, 1960; Folcroft, Pennsylvania, Folcroft Editions, 1969.
George Eliot. New York, Macmillan, 1964; London, Weidenfeld and Nicolson, 1965.
Tradition and Dream: The English and American Novel from the Twenties to Our Time. London, Phoenix House, 1964; as *The Modern Novel in Britain and the United States*, New York, Dutton, 1964.
The British Isles in Colour. London, Batsford, and New York, Viking Press, 1965.
The Urgent West: An Introduction to the Idea of the United States. London, Baker, 1969; as *The Urgent West: The American Dream and Modern Man*, New York, Dutton, 1969.
Some Aspects of the American Short Story (lecture). London, Oxford University Press, 1973.
The Short Story in English. London and New York, Oxford University Press, 1980.

Editor, *Writers on Writing*. London, Phoenix House, 1948; as *The Writer on His Art*, New York, McGraw Hill, 1949.
Editor, *Transatlantic Crossing: American Visitors to Britain and British Visitors to America in the Nineteenth Century*. London, Heinemann, and New York, Morrow, 1971.
Editor, *The Roaring Queen*, by Wyndham Lewis. London, Secker and Warburg, and New York, Liveright, 1973.

*

Walter Allen comments:

My first three novels seem now to have been the outcome of a single impulse, or rather a twin impulse. One side of it was to set down the nature of working-class life as I saw it all about me in the Midland city of Birmingham in a time of industrial depression, the rise of fascism and the threat of war. To this extent, these three novels are very much of the late 1930's. The other side of the impulse was formal: I was concerned with economy, with limits, with unity, almost indeed the Unities, believing that the most intense writing came from a narrow but powerful focus. I found myself unable to write fiction during the war and turned to the writing of criticism, and my first postwar novel, *Rogue Elephant*, turned out to be very different from my earlier work, though it had formal elements in common. I set out to write a work almost of classical comedy. At this time and for a long time to come I was caught up with the novel, as reviewer, publisher's reader and as a historian of the form, to the almost total exclusion of other interests, and this, I am sure, had its consequences. One was that I came increasingly to value what might be called the historical aspects of the novel. I was conscious, writing *Dead Man over All*, that I was attempting a number of disparate things. I wanted to show the influence on individuals of history, heredity, family tradition and so on; to say something about what seemed to me the changing nature of industrialism; to describe life in a factory geared to production for war during war (and that itself would be a contribution of a sort to the history of industry and the recent war); and also to depict a man in what I called an impossible position, impossible because willed for him, as it were, by others, by tradition. All the same, in that novel, I largely retained the narrative pattern of my earlier books. I broke away from it in *All in a Lifetime*. Writing that novel, I was conscious that I was trying to do several things simultaneously: to trace the rise of the British Labour Party through a working man in some sort representative, to adumbrate the growth of a city through half a century, to show the rise to political and cultural awareness of the working class. There was also a personal factor that was probably fundamental to these: I wanted to celebrate my father, who became the model in the novel of my "in some sort representative" working man. But I had to satisfy myself that he might have written what I have him write in the novel—it is in fact the novel—and this dictated the narrative technique of the long letter/Defoe-esque pseudo-autobiographical novel. This emerged only after many false starts.

I don't think my novels have appeared to be particularly playful works; but in the writing of them it is the element of play that I have found most pleasurable, the making of a mimic world through the arrangement, both studied and "accidental," of one's characters. I wouldn't, though, have found much point in the play if it hadn't resulted from time to time in what seemed an acceptable paradigm of the real world.

* * *

The title of Walter Allen's novel *Innocence Is Drowned* comes from Yeats's well-known lines beginning: "Things fall apart; the centre cannot hold/The blood-dimmed tide is loosed, and everywhere/The ceremony of innocence is drowned." Allen had in mind not only the approach of the Second World War but also the manner in which his characters came to recognise not only the cruelty and indifference of others but also the cruelty and indifference in themselves. The novel can be seen as their attempt to come to terms with reality.

Innocence Is Drowned, Allen's first novel, has presumably his home-town of Birmingham for its setting, although no name is given to the place in the book. He introduces us to a working-class family. It is one in which the father, Dick Gardiner, is conscientious, hard-working, politically committed: a man who made the mistake of setting up as a master toolmaker instead of remaining a secure employee. The novel—like *Dead Man over All* and *Living Space*—covers only a few days in time: Tuesday, Wednesday and Thursday.

The narrative is largely conveyed through the minds of Mr. Gardiner, his wife and three sons, Ralph, Eric, and Sydney. One forms a vivid picture of each character and a clear impression of his (or her) relationships both within and outside the family. The actual events are trivial enough—for instance, the detention at school of the youngest boy causes quite a bit of fuss in the family circle—but they are skillfully built up into a convincing re-creation of pre-War life in the Midlands.

Innocence Is Drowned marked the emergence of a writer who has made more impact, perhaps, as a literary critic (he has a specialised knowledge of the English novel from its beginnings to the present day) than as a novelist. It shows, too, how Allen, while not standing aside from the Left-wing current of his time, knew from the start that propaganda and art are ill-sorted bedfellows.

Rogue Elephant represents a considerable advance on the earlier novels. The style is more supple and fluent, and contains less pedestrian descriptive writing. Allen, like all true artists, obviously learned from his first experiments in his craft as well as from the twentieth-century masters about whom he has written so perceptively.

The central character of *Rogue Elephant* is called Henry Ashley, a fat, clever but unintegrated young man who ambles through the novel, a schemer with a soft core in his personality. This is how he looks at himself: "Mr. Henry Ashley...saw himself as the enemy, as miching mallecho which means mischief, as the test-tube of cholera bacillus that is broken into the water supply." For a while Ashley wreaks havoc among two girls (they are cousins) in an upper-class household in Devonshire. Ashley lives for and through his writing. A rising young novelist and critic, he copes with life through ideas and word-spinning. He keeps reality at arm's length. Henry Ashley comes across as a real person, not just as a target for satirical rifle-practice.

Allen's most solid achievement in the novel is undisputably *All in a Lifetime*. It came out, in 1959, at a time when regionalism was beginning to be a potent force in post-War English fiction. That same year saw the publication, for instance, of Keith Waterhouse's *Billy Liar* and Alan Sillitoe's *The Loneliness of the Long-Distance Runner*. Brash, ill-mannered young working-class heroes (or, rather, anti-heroes) without religious, political or moral conviction became fashionable. Allen, an older man than writers such as John Braine, Stan Barstow and the others, stood foursquare against the new gospel of revolt for its own sake.

Billy Ashted, the narrator of *All in a Lifetime*, is in his middle seventies. He looks back calmly on his life and the changes he has lived through. He is portrayed as a man with a strong political faith—a kind of substitute, it may be, for religion—a man who tended to look outward rather than into his own ego. Allen accurately analyses the place held by religion in the Black Country when Billy Ashted was young: the Nonconformist chapel where the preacher was a "great populariser" who "talked of new ideas and movements of ideas in such a way that your curiosity was stimulated to find out about them at first hand." Opposed to the plain services and Christian Socialism of the chapel, there is the High Anglicanism that repels Billy Ashted because it smacks of Popery and aristocracy.

In a comment on the novel Allen says that Billy Ashted is based on his father who, like Ashted, was "a working silversmith in Birmingham all his life and never earning at any time more than £5 a week from his craft." Nevertheless, Allen's father "had a very considerable learning in philosophy and, in the opinion of people much better qualified than me to judge, had genuine ability as a philosopher." Billy Ashted's brief migration to the U.S. was paralleled by Allen's own father's experience in that country. The author tells us that his father had lived in Philadelphia whereas Billy Ashted goes to New York for the good reason that the novelist is more familiar with the topography of New York.

Allen has two aims in writing the novel: first, he wanted to write a chronicle novel in which social change would be explored and the rise of the Labour Party outlined; and second, he wished to write about an old man and so project himself "imaginatively into the experience of old age as it faces death." Already he had, in *Rogue Elephant* and *Dead Man over All*, drawn the portraits of very old men: but they were minor characters and he was determined to essay a major portrait. This he had done with great success, taking care to balance the essentially contemplative Billy Ashted with the more active and politically committed George Thompson.

The novel consists of a "letter" Billy Ashted writes to his sister at a time of family crisis: the ostensible reason for it is to discover how to cope with the present difficulty. He feels this can be achieved by dredging incidents and people from his long life. Thus past and present are intermingled, and the novel takes on a reality and naturalness it might lack had it been written in the third person.

All in a Lifetime did not create much of a stir in the literary world when it appeared. Unlike other novels of the time with a strong regional flavour it has not been filmed or adapted for television. What it lacks in newsworthiness it makes up in sincerity and warmth and, not least, in sheer skill. It will probably be more durable than those novels that have a hard, glittering shell but are soft and cold at the center.

—Robert Greacen

ALUKO, T(imothy) M(ofolorunso). Nigerian. Born in Ilesha, 14 June 1918. Educated at Ilesha primary school; Yaba Higher College; Government College, Ibadan, 1933-38; University of London, 1946-50, B.Sc. in Engineering and Diploma in Town Planning 1950; University of Newcastle upon Tyne (UNESCO Fellow), 1968-69, M.Sc. in Engineering 1969. Married Janet Adebisi Fajemisin in 1950; six children. Engineer, Public Works Department, Lagos, 1943-46; Executive Engineer, Public Works Department, Ibadan and Lagos, 1950-56; Town Engineer, Lagos Town Council, 1956-60; Director and Permanent Secretary, Ministry of Works and Transport, Western Nigeria, 1960-66; Senior Lecturer, University of Ibadan, 1966. Since 1966, Senior Research Fellow in Municipal Engineering at the University of Lagos. Fellow, Institution of Civil Engineers, Institution of Municipal Engineers, and Nigerian Society of Engineers. O.B.E. (Officer, Order of the British Empire), 1963; O.O.N. (Officer, Order of the Niger), 1964. Address: Faculty of Engineering, University of Lagos, Lagos, Nigeria.

PUBLICATIONS

Novels

One Man, One Wife. Lagos, Nigerian Printing and Publishing Company, 1959; London, Heinemann, 1967; New York, Humanities Press, 1968.
One Man, One Matchet. London, Heinemann, 1964; Mystic, Connecticut, Verrey, 1965.
Kinsman and Foreman. London, Heinemann, 1966; New York, Humanities Press, 1967.
Chief the Honourable Minister. London, Heinemann, 1970.
His Worshipful Majesty. London, Heinemann, 1973.

Uncollected Short Story

"The New Engineer," in *African New Writing*. London, Lutterworth Press, 1947.

*

Critical Study: *Long Drums and Cannons* by Margaret Laurence, London, Macmillan, 1968.

* * *

T.M. Aluko's *One Man, One Wife* was the first African novel in English to be published in Nigeria, and in following it up with four more books Aluko became one of the more productive African novelists. Aluko is, however, a much under-rated writer whose very intelligent comic sense has been out of tune with the seriousmindedness of West African fiction generally and has thus caused his work to be overlooked or summarily dismissed. In his first three novels he applies a wry, comic detachment to the stresses between modern and traditional life among the Yoruba people.

Most reviewers and commentators have seen this detachment as a complete lack of commitment in social problems, about which they believe all African writers should be committed, and one suspects that they have sometimes mistaken for Aluko's own the clichés, grandiloquences, and superficial attitudes which, with considerable linguistic sophistication, he mocks by embedding them even in authorial narration; for instance, this bemused reflection upon the Christian catechist Royasin's message on Christmas Day: "How could this same Baby have founded a religion nearly two thousand years old? And how could this same mysterious Baby rule all the world? The invitation to all the faithful to come to Bethlehem, the geographical location of which even the great Royasin could not tell..." (*One Man, One Wife*). In this novel Aluko captures the very accents of various levels of English used in Yorubaland, as he satirizes with amused impartiality the foibles of both Christians and polygamists, of both followers of the new faith who retain a toehold in the old, like Elder Joshua, and the blindly committed converts, like Bible Jeremiah. The comedy is largely verbal and cerebral, the mode dead-pan, like that of the silent-film comedian, Buster Keaton, but it is never malicious, and even as satire it finds cause for celebration in the rich absurdities of human behaviour.

One Man, One Matchet plays upon the differences between the unprincipled, rabble-rousing Benjamin Benjamin, who is no more than a spiv with the gift of the gab, and the newly appointed Nigerian-born administrators trying to do an honest job but suspected by the traditionalists because of their command of "the White Man's language." The purpose is not anti-Nationalist but exposure of the spurious and the absurd wearing Nationalist garb. *Kinsman and Foreman* explores the trials and embarrassments of an overseas-trained Nigerian engineer who is employed by the Public Works Department in his home town and finds that his relations expect him to use his official position for their private benefit. It is a book that bubbles with cross-cultural misunderstandings.

Perhaps as a result of meagre critical attention, Aluko tries to swim in the mainstream of Nigerian writing with *Chief the Honourable Minister*, a novel which, somewhat in the manner of Achebe's *A Man of the People*, deals with post-Independence political developments in Nigeria. This more "serious" venture confirms that Aluko's real gift is a judicious response to the comic, though the presentation of the idealistic Alade Moses's transformation into a corrupt politician is very skillfully done; Moses is for ever putting off as untimely the decision to resign on principle as a Minister in the government, and always succeeds in finding good principles to justify his continuing in office.

With some success *His Worshipful Majesty* treats tragically the inability of an *oba* or traditional king to make the transition from autocratic rule to mere Chairmanship of a Local Government Council hemmed in by bureaucratic regulations. In the details of the story, however, there is a muted return to Aluko's earlier comic manner, and he does achieve an uneasy poise in modulating the comic with the tragic within the same novel.

—Arthur Ravenscroft

ALVAREZ, A(lfred). British. Born in London, 5 August 1929. Educated at Oundle School, Northamptonshire; Corpus Christi College, Oxford (Senior Research Scholar, 1952-53, 1954-55), B.A. 1952, M.A. 1956; Princeton University, New Jersey (Procter Visiting Fellow, 1953-54). Married 1) Ursula Barr in 1956 (marriage dissolved, 1961), one son; 2) Anne Adams, 1966, one son and one daughter. Gauss Lecturer, Princeton University, 1957-58; Visiting Professor, Brandeis University, Waltham, Massachusetts, 1960, and State University of New York, Buffalo, 1966. Advisory Poetry Editor, *The Observer*, London, 1956-66; Editor, *Journal of Education*, 1957; Drama Critic, *New Statesman*, London, 1958-60. Since 1965, Advisory Editor, Penguin Modern European Poets in Translation. Recipient: Rockefeller Fellowship, 1955; D.H. Lawrence Fellowship, 1958; Vachel Lindsay Prize (*Poetry*, Chicago), 1961. Address: c/o The Observer, 8 St. Andrew's Hill, London EC4V 5JA, England.

PUBLICATIONS

Novels

Hers. London, Weidenfeld and Nicolson, 1974; New York, Random House, 1975.
Hunt. London, Macmillan, 1978; New York, Simon and Schuster, 1979.

Uncollected Short Stories

"The Smile," in *Cosmopolitan* (New York), December, 1970.
"Laughter," in *Winter's Tales 17*, edited by Caroline Hobhouse. London, Macmillan, 1971; New York, St. Martin's Press, 1972.
"Summertime," in *Daily Telegraph Magazine* (London), 16 July 1971.
"Night Out," in *New Yorker*, 4 September 1971.
"Veterans," in *The Times Saturday Review* (London), 24 January 1976.

Play

Screenplay: *The Anarchist*, 1969.

Verse

(Poems). Oxford, Fantasy Press, 1952.
The End of It. Privately printed, 1958.
Twelve Poems. London, The Review, 1968.
Lost. London, Turret, 1968.
Penguin Modern Poets 18, with Roy Fuller and Anthony Thwaite. London, Penguin, 1970.
Apparition. Brisbane, University of Queensland Press, 1971.
The Legacy. London, Poem-of-the-Month Club, 1972.
Autumn to Autumn and Selected Poems 1953-1976. London, Macmillan, 1978.

Other

The Shaping Spirit: Studies in Modern English and American Poets. London, Chatto and Windus, 1958; as *Stewards of Excellence: Studies in Modern English and American Poets*, New York, Scribner, 1958.
The School of Donne. London, Chatto and Windus, 1961; New York, Pantheon, 1962.
Under Pressure: The Artist and Society: Eastern Europe and the U.S.A. London, Penguin, 1965.
Beyond All This Fiddle: Essays 1955-1967. London, Allen Lane, 1968; New York, Random House, 1969.
The Savage God: A Study of Suicide. London, Weidenfeld and Nicolson, 1971; New York, Random House, 1972.
Beckett. London, Fontana, and New York, Viking Press, 1973.

Editor, *The New Poetry: An Anthology*. London, Penguin, 1962; revised edition, 1966.

* * *

A. Alvarez's reputation rests primarily upon his criticism. *The Savage God*, with its perceptive essay on Plath, and *Beyond All This Fiddle* express Alvarez's temper, the breadth of his literary interests, and the subtlety of his mind. His poetry and his novels suffer from some of the faults typical of a literary-critic-turned-creative writer: his style is derivative, and a little too self-conscious; he lacks the freedom of invention characteristic of the best writers. Nonetheless, he writes well and is always eminently readable. His poetry suffers from its compression and adherence to formal conventions. His novels at times create a scene or person with life-like vividness, but generally his characters are thin and the plot is slight.

His first novel, *Hers*, is voguish in its subject. It is the story of a middle-aged woman's affair with one of her husband's students, a man some 12 years her junior. Julie, the wife of German extraction with a painful past, is married to the stereotypical university professor of letters, an older man who married her to capture the youth he neglected for his books. Alvarez's caricature of academia is not as rich as Kingsley Amis's in *Lucky Jim*, nor does he have the flair that Iris Murdoch and Joyce Carol Oates have for this subject, but his portrait of Charles, the Professor, is often entertaining. Charles, with his unspeakable air of self-assurance, with his inability to register any emotion without filtering it through the language of literary characters—when he discovers his wife has cuckolded him, he mutters Othello's words—is a perfectly realized representative of a "preordained academic." At one point, he lectures his student, who is his wife's lover, talking to him on morality and literature, quoting his lecture notes, calling upon Arnold and Tolstoy, Wellek and Warren, Eliot and Hume rather than simply confronting him directly with his anger. Julie is a complicated person. Blond, youthful in appearance, fragile and Germanic, she is the mother of two children and a woman who took an older husband to forget the abuse heaped on her by the Russians and the murder of her father by the Nazis. Julie provides Sam every pleasure but the pleasure of being inside her, fearing that the final act will somehow mark her as an infidel. Once she becomes Sam's mistress in every sense, she is driven back into her past. Returning to a sanitorium in Germany, she comes to terms with herself in a fairly predictable way. Probably the best scenes in the novels are those when Charles behaves paranoically, venting his hostility upon all the young, and making himself the prey of a motorcycle gang, and when he violently retakes possession of his wife, making her share in the complicity of their mutual violence.

Hunt is a thriller, written in a manner very like Arthur La Bern's *Goodbye Piccadilly, Farewell Leicester Square*. The drab life of Conrad Jessup, a man dulled by his marriage and tedious job, is depicted with a naturalism typical of Greene at his best. Jessup's quest for excitement and a moment that will give value to his life takes him to the gambling tables and then out into the park, late in the night, where he discovers the body of a woman who has been assaulted. His discovery leads to his arrest on suspicion of murder. Once released, he cannot resist finding the woman and he becomes caught up in her web of international espionage. The plot is slow, and rather obvious. The best moments in the novel are the scenes at the poker table where Conrad's compulsive gambling is so convincingly portrayed that the reader vicariously experiences his excitement and disillusion. The world of pubs, gambling clubs, and boutiques is presented with a good sense of detail. But the story itself has been told before.

It is too early to judge Alvarez as a novelist. He is clever and has a good sense of the modern. His next novel may well surprise us.

—Carol Simpson Stern

AMADI, Elechi. Nigerian. Born in Aluu, 12 May 1934. Educated at University College, Ibadan, 1955-59, B.Sc. in mathematics and physics 1959. Served in the Nigerian Federal Army, 1963-66, 1968-69. Married Dorah Ohale in 1957; eight children. Government survey assistant, Calabar, 1953-55, and surveyor, Enugu, 1959-60; science teacher in mission schools, Oba and Ahoada, 1960-63; Principal, Asa Grammar School, 1967. Administrative Officer, 1970-74, and since 1975, Permanent Secretary, Government of Rivers State, Port Harcourt. Recipient: International Writers Program grant, University of Iowa, 1973. Address: 2 Shitu Alao Street, Box 331, Port Harcourt, Nigeria.

PUBLICATIONS

Novels

The Concubine. London, Heinemann, 1966.
The Great Ponds. London, Heinemann, 1969; New York, Day, 1973.
The Slave. London, Heinemann, 1978.

Plays

Isiburu (in verse; produced Port Harcourt, Nigeria, 1969). London, Heinemann, 1973.
Peppersoup (produced Port Harcourt, Nigeria, 1977). Included in *Peppersoup, and The Road to Ibadan*, 1977.
The Road to Ibadan (produced Port Harcourt, Nigeria, 1977). Included in *Peppersoup, and The Road to Ibadan*, 1977.
Peppersoup, and The Road to Ibadan. Ibadan, Onibonoje Press, 1977.
Dancer of Johannesburg (produced Port Harcourt, Nigeria, 1979). Ibadan, Onibonoje Press, 1979.

Other

Sunset in Biafra: A Civil War Diary. London, Heinemann, 1973.

Translator, with Obiajunwo Wali and Greensille Enyinda, *Okwukwo Eri* (hymnbook). Port Harcourt, Nigeria, CSS Printers, 1969.
Translator, *Okupkpe* (prayerbook). Port Harcourt, Nigeria, CSS Printers, 1969.

Elechi Amadi comments:

I like to think of myself as a painter or composer using words in the place of pictures and musical symbols. I consider commitment in fiction a prostitution of literature. The novelist should depict life as he sees it without consciously attempting to persuade the reader to take a particular viewpoint. Propaganda should be left to journalists.

In my ideal novel the reader should feel a sense of aesthetic satisfaction that he cannot quite explain—the same feeling he gets when he listens to a beautiful symphony. For those readers who insist on being taught, there are always things to learn from a faithful portrayal of life in a well-written novel.

* * *

From his first appearance as a novelist, with *The Concubine* in 1966, Elechi Amadi established himself as a unique figure in African fiction. He was not alone in attempting to convey the day-to-day texture of traditional, pre-colonial life in an African village (Chinua Achebe's *Things Fall Apart* had already done this, at least in its earlier pages), but he distinguished himself by not offering any explicit contrasts between that traditional world and the one that replaced it. Whereas *Things Fall Apart* and many other African novels are concerned, in part at least, with the coming of the white man and the effect of that coming, Amadi's novels have never adverted to alien influences at all. The action of any of his three novels could have taken place either five years or a century before the colonial intrusion upon the area; the dilemmas which confront and finally destroy his heroes or heroines derive entirely from the beliefs, practices, and events of their indigenous culture.

The Concubine was followed by *The Great Ponds* and *The Slave*. Although not thematically related, all three novels take place in what is recognizably the same Ikweore environment. The action of all three appears to turn upon the working out of a fate which falls upon the characters from without, but which it would be meaningless, in this traditional and god-fearing environment, to call unjust. Iheoma, heroine of *The Concubine*, is powerless to avert her spiritual marriage to the sea-king which prevents her having any successful human relationship. Her attraction thus becomes a fatal one, resulting in the deaths of all those who seek to free her from her condition. Likewise, the hero of *The Slave* leaves the shrine of Amadioha to which his late father was bound as an *osu* (cult-slave) and appears to have right on his side in arguing for his emancipation, since he was not actually conceived there. Nevertheless, his brief career in freedom has an obstinately circular form curving through initial success to a series of disasters which brings him, friendless and alone, back to the shrine he had so hopefully deserted.

Amadi maintains a nicely judged ambiguity about the meaning of these events, which must depend entirely upon the reader himself. The society of which he writes would have rejected, perhaps still rejects, any clear distinction between the natural and spiritual orders of existence. These interpenetrate to such an extent that man cannot demand the mastery of his fate through will alone. The highest he can aspire to is to know his fate and tune his soul to its acceptance. Tragedy springs as much from failure to do this, as from the nature of that fate itself.

—Gerald Moore

AMBLER, Eric. British. Born in London, 28 June 1909. Educated at Colfe's Grammar School, London; London University, 1925-28. Served in the Royal Artillery, 1940-46; Assistant Director of Army Kinematography, 1944-46: Bronze Star (USA). Married 1) Louise Crombie in 1939; 2) the writer Joan Harrison in 1958. Engineering apprentice, 1928; advertising copywriter, 1929-37; director of an advertising agency, 1937-38. Recipient: Crime Writers Association Award, 1959, 1962, 1967, 1972; Mystery Writers of America Edgar Allan Poe Award, 1964, and Grand Master Award, 1975; Svenska Deckarakademins Grand Master, 1975. O.B.E. (Officer, Order of the British Empire), 1981. Agent: Linder A G, Jupiterstrasse 1, Postfach CH-8032 Zurich, Switzerland. Address: Avenue Eugène Rambert 20, 1815 Clarens, Switzerland.

PUBLICATIONS

Novels

The Dark Frontier. London, Hodder and Stoughton, 1936.
Uncommon Danger. London, Hodder and Stoughton, 1937; as *Background to Danger*, New York, Knopf, 1937.
Epitaph for a Spy. London, Hodder and Stoughton, 1938; New York, Knopf, 1952.
Cause for Alarm. London, Hodder and Stoughton, 1938; New York, Knopf, 1939.
The Mask of Dimitrios. London, Hodder and Stoughton, 1939; as *A Coffin for Dimitrios*, New York, Knopf, 1939.
Journey into Fear. London, Hodder and Stoughton, and New York, Knopf, 1940.
Skytip (as Eliot Reed, with Charles Rodda). New York, Doubleday, 1950; London, Hodder and Stoughton, 1951.
Judgment on Deltchev. London, Hodder and Stoughton, and New York, Knopf, 1951.
Tender to Danger (as Eliot Reed, with Charles Rodda). New York, Doubleday, 1951; as *Tender to Moonlight*, London, Hodder and Stoughton, 1952.
The Maras Affair (as Eliot Reed, with Charles Rodda). London, Collins, and New York, Doubleday, 1953.
The Schirmer Inheritance. London, Heinemann, and New York, Knopf, 1953.
Charter to Danger (as Eliot Reed, with Charles Rodda). London, Collins, 1954.
The Night-Comers. London, Heinemann, 1956; as *State of Siege*, New York, Knopf, 1956.
Passport to Panic (as Eliot Reed, with Charles Rodda). London, Collins, 1958.
Passage of Arms. London, Heinemann, 1959; New York, Knopf, 1960.
The Light of Day. London, Heinemann, 1962; New York, Knopf, 1963; as *Topkapi*, New York, Bantam, 1964.
A Kind of Anger. London, Bodley Head, and New York, Atheneum, 1964.
Dirty Story. London, Bodley Head, and New York, Atheneum, 1967.
The Intercom Conspiracy. New York, Atheneum, 1969; London, Weidenfeld and Nicolson, 1970.
The Levanter. London, Weidenfeld and Nicolson, and New York, Atheneum, 1972.
Doctor Frigo. London, Weidenfeld and Nicolson, and New York, Atheneum, 1974.
Send No More Roses. London, Weidenfeld and Nicolson, 1977; as *The Siege of the Villa Lipp*, New York, Random House, 1977.
The Care of Time. London, Weidenfeld and Nicolson, and New York, Farrar Straus, 1981.

Uncollected Short Stories

"The Army of the Shadows," in *The Queen's Book of the Red Cross*. London, Hodder and Stoughton, 1939.
"The Intrusions of Dr. Czissar" ("A Bird in the Tree," "The Case of the Emerald Sky," "Case of the Gentleman Poet," "Case of the Landlady's Brother," "Case of the Overheated Flat," "The Case of the Pinchbeck Locket"), in *The Sketch* (London), 1940.
"The Blood Bargain," in *Winter's Crimes 2*, edited by George Hardinge. London, Macmillan, 1970.

Plays

Screenplays: *The Way Ahead*, with Peter Ustinov, 1944; *United States*, 1945; *The October Man*, 1947; *The Passionate Friends (One Woman's Story)*, with David Lean and Stanley Haynes, 1949; *Highly Dangerous*, 1950; *The Clouded Yellow*, 1950; *The Magic Box*, 1951; *Gigolo and Gigolette*, in *Encore*, 1951; *The Card (The Promoter)*, 1952; *Rough Shoot (Shoot First)*, 1953; *The Cruel Sea*, 1953; *Lease of Life*, 1954; *The Purple Plain*, 1954; *Yangtse Incident (Battle Hell)*, 1957; *A Night to Remember*, 1958; *The Wreck of the Mary Deare*, 1960; *Mutiny on the Bounty* (uncredited), with others, 1962; *Love Hate Love*, 1970.

Other

The Ability to Kill and Other Pieces. London, Bodley Head, 1963.

Editor, *To Catch a Spy: An Anthology of Favourite Spy Stories*. London, Bodley Head, 1964; New York, Atheneum, 1965.

*

Bibliography: in *Uber Eric Ambler* edited by Gerd Haffmans, Zurich, Diogenes Verlag, 1979.

Manuscript Collection: Mugar Memorial Library, Boston University.

Critical Studies: "Eric Ambler Issue" of *Hollins Critic* (Hollins College, Virginia), February 1971.

Eric Ambler comments:

I have found that every statement I have ever tried to make on the subject of my work later seems either pretentious or meaningless. Besides, I am an unreliable witness. When *Uber Eric Ambler* was published on my 70th birthday I gave a number of interviews to European journalists. One of them pointed out that I had answered a standard question (where do you get your ideas?) in two entirely different ways. Which answer was the right one? I explained that I always tried to avoid giving an interviewer the same answer as I had given his colleague so that each had something exclusive. He was deeply shocked. Did I not distinguish between truth and falsehood? I could have said, "Not when answering dull or unanswerable questions." Instead, I mumbled something about only trying to be helpful. It failed to satisfy him. I stood convicted of frivolity.

* * *

In Graham Greene's view Eric Ambler is Britain's best thriller writer and there are many reasons for supporting this judgment. The most important is Ambler's capacity for telling a story. He wastes no words; his narrative is economical yet evocative; his grasp of detail matches his control of suspense.

His ability to vary the tempo of a story is subtle. He is a master of reconstruction without boredom. This technique is one of the reasons for the success of an early book, *The Mask of Dimitrios*, where his character Latimer, a detective story writer, becomes obsessed with the mysterious life of a man called Dimitrios whose supposed body he sees in a Turkish morgue. He decides to find out something of the man's odd past, and discovers more and more of his intrigues in many countries, his altering identity, his capacity for murder, pimping, political assassination, drug trafficking, and double crossing. Latimer's own search unfolds slowly, then follows his unwilling cooperation with a former associate and victim of Dimitrios. Gradually the narration speeds up until Latimer is confronted by the fact that Dimitrios is alive, and not only alive but deadly dangerous. The reader is involved in Latimer's searching, in the gradual building up of a biography, in the factual details which reveal the ruthless cleverness of this professional crook. The narration gives us a clear picture of Latimer's thoughts and shows him building up theories about Dimitrios as his knowledge of the man's past increases. Not only does the tension of a search which is progressing steadily despite the inevitable setbacks keep the reader's attention clearly focussed on the details of the story, but the relationship between Latimer and the mysterious Mr. Peters also heightens the intensity.

In *The Mask of Dimitrios* no sympathy is evoked for the successful, ruthless criminal, nor indeed for Mr. Peters, the unsuccessful one. There is some alteration of viewpoint in some of Ambler's later novels. For instance, in *Dirty Story*, the main character, Arthur Simpson (he first appeared in *The Light of Day*), is described in an Interpol dossier as interpreter, chauffeur, waiter, pornographer, and guide. He is also a pimp, and the story begins with his urgent need for a passport. His stormy interview with Her Majesty's Vice-Consul in Athens leaves us no possibility for illusions about the man whose life, according to the Vice-Consul, is nothing but a long dirty story. Driven by lack of money (with which to buy a Panlibhoncan passport) into acting as a casting director of blue films, he eventually becomes a mercenary in Central Africa. He does not cover himself with credit but eventually escapes to Tangier. One of Ambler's particular skills is a capacity to create modern rogue literature. Morally we despise his character, but such is the power of the tense narration that we follow his adventures with an interest which verges between sympathy, as things go hopelessly wrong, and a wry sense of the sheer comedy latent in Arthur Simpson's incongruous, unscrupulous, and ridiculous nature.

The whole unscrupulous world of espionage occupies some of Ambler's attention. In *The Intercom Conspiracy* the protagonist is Theodore Carter, editor of *Intercom*, a journal owned by a retired, somewhat crackpot American general of anti-Communist views. When the general dies the journal is bought by a mysterious Arnold Bloch, who supplies material for the journal which offends west and east alike. Various intelligence agencies become interested in Carter's sources, and eventually, after being, in the space of a few hours, snatched, interrogated under duress, roughed up, threatened, burgled, and gassed, he runs. We know that two clever and unscrupulous colonels have got disgruntled with their role in their respective intelligence services; their plot to play off the major powers and cash in on the situation involves Carter as cats-paw—and, of course, Latimer, Ambler's author character, created much earlier, who is busily writing up the story. The inclusion of Latimer, and his disappearance at the beginning of the book, allows Ambler to tell the story at different levels and from different viewpoints. As usual the tension heightens, the pace speeds up, as the reader becomes sufficiently *au fait* with the complex linkage of events. The story is realistic; its portrayal of the cynicism, indeed the theatrically self-conscious seediness and secrecy of the world of military and political intelligence, is convincing in its detail. Ambler's characters have sufficient depth and individuality to match this superb handling of plot. Carter, the journalist, is given to drink; his marriage has broken up earlier; and he is "a man of undoubted ability who takes pleasure in misusing it." Again, the central character is no orthodox hero, and must be taken with blemishes and all: and the two colonels realise he will have dangerous moments. This is a calculated risk and he must take his chance. And take it he does in the respectable surroundings of Geneva.

Ambler has two kinds of story, the simple and the complex. In *The Night-Comers* he unfolds a simple story of an English consulting engineer who is unwillingly involved in a military coup d'état in an island near Indonesia. He is on his way home, staying for a few days in a friend's flat on the top of the local radio station when the revolution begins. His situation is complicated, indeed endangered by the presence of an Eurasian girl with whom he is having a brief affair when the rebels make this their headquarters. The government forces close in on the radio station, and the novel describes the fighting with skilled economy. Tension is built up, the waiting alternates with hope and despair. Again Ambler's realism keeps the story convincing. At one period, when the Englishman realises that one of the insurgent's leaders is a government agent and that his own life and the girl's are in danger, he is compelled to repair a generator so that the rebel general can broadcast his programme to the outside world. This sudden involvement with the mechanical problems of drying out a generator, damaged by water seeping into the power house after a bomb blast, gives the story an authenticity which is compelling. It adds an extra dimension to the simple narrative by, as it were, describing one aspect of the situation of the insurgents in some depth. The effect of the rising on the hapless spectators, the Englishman and the Eurasian girl, gives the story the necessary counterpointing, and again is used to involve the reader's sympathy, to sharpen and hold his attention.

For Ambler's ability to juggle with a complex plot there is *A Kind of Anger* where a newspaperman becomes involved in the search for a missing girl, the mistress of a murdered Iraqi colonel, a Kurdish conspirator. Here there are rival buyers for the colonel's papers, which the girl possesses, and which the newspaperman, lonely, neurotic, suicidal, eventually helps her to sell. Here the mixture of cross purposes is skillfully woven into the tapestry of the story. This is ingeniously done, and the suspense mounts steadily as the various motives are brought together. While Ambler's plots require sex and violence there is no excess of them, and when they do arise there is a touch of inevitability about them which adds to the conviction his narration has already established in the reader's mind. He is indeed a skilled, professional writer of the highest order.

—A. Norman Jeffares

AMIS, Kingsley (William). British. Born in London, 16 April 1922. Educated at City of London School; St. John's College, Oxford, M.A. Served in the Royal Corps of Signals, 1942-45. Married 1) Hilary Ann Bardwell in 1948 (marriage dissolved, 1965), two sons, including Martin Amis, *q.v.*, and one daughter; 2) Elizabeth Jane Howard, *q.v.*, in 1965. Lecturer in English, University College, Swansea, Wales, 1949-61; Fellow in English, Peterhouse, Cambridge, 1961-63. Visiting Fellow in Creative Writing, Princeton University, New Jersey, 1958-59; Visiting Professor, Vanderbilt University, Nashville, Tennessee, 1967. Recipient: Maugham Award, 1955; *Yorkshire Post* award, 1974; Campbell Memorial Award, 1977. Honorary Fellow, St. John's College, 1976. C.B.E. (Commander, Order of the British Empire), 1981. Agent: Jonathan Clowes Ltd., 19 Jeffrey's Place, London NW1 9PP, England.

PUBLICATIONS

Novels

Lucky Jim. London, Gollancz, and New York, Doubleday, 1954.
That Uncertain Feeling. London, Gollancz, 1955; New York, Harcourt Brace, 1956.
I Like It Here. London, Gollancz, and New York, Harcourt Brace, 1958.
Take a Girl Like You. London, Gollancz, 1960; New York, Harcourt Brace, 1961.
One Fat Englishman. London, Gollancz, 1963; New York, Harcourt Brace, 1964.
The Egyptologists, with Robert Conquest. London, Cape, 1965; New York, Random House, 1966.
The Anti-Death League. London, Gollancz, and New York, Harcourt Brace, 1966.
Colonel Sun: A James Bond Adventure (as Robert Markham). London, Cape, and New York, Harper, 1968.
I Want It Now. London, Cape, 1968; New York, Harcourt Brace, 1969.
The Green Man. London, Cape, 1969; New York, Harcourt Brace, 1970.
Girl, 20. London, Cape, 1971.
The Riverside Villas Murder. London, Cape, and New York, Harcourt Brace, 1973.
Ending Up. London, Cape, and New York, Harcourt Brace, 1974.
The Alteration. London, Cape, 1976; New York, Viking Press, 1977.
Jake's Thing. London, Hutchinson, 1978; New York, Viking Press, 1979.
Russian Hide-and-Seek. London, Hutchinson, 1980.

Short Stories

My Enemy's Enemy. London, Gollancz, 1962; New York, Harcourt Brace, 1963.
Penguin Modern Stories 11, with others. London, Penguin, 1972.
Dear Illusion. London, Covent Garden Press, 1972.
The Darkwater Hall Mystery. Edinburgh, Tragara Press, 1978.
Collected Short Stories. London, Hutchinson, 1980.

Plays

Radio Plays: *Something Strange*, 1962; *The Riverside Villas Murder*, from his own novel, 1976.

Television Plays: *A Question about Hell*, 1964; *The Importance of Being Harry*, 1971; *Dr. Watson and the Darkwater Hall Mystery*, 1974; *See What You've Done* (*Softly, Softly* series), 1974; *We Are All Guilty* (*Against the Crowd* series), 1975; *Break In*, 1975.

Verse

Bright November. London, Fortune Press, 1947.
A Frame of Mind. Reading, Berkshire, University of Reading School of Art, 1953.
(Poems). Oxford, Fantasy Press, 1954.
A Case of Samples: Poems 1946-1956. London, Gollancz, 1956; New York, Harcourt Brace, 1957.
The Evans Country. Oxford, Fantasy Press, 1962.
Penguin Modern Poets 2, with Dom Moraes and Peter Porter. London, Penguin, 1962.
A Look round the Estate: Poems 1957-1967. London, Cape, 1967; New York, Harcourt Brace, 1968.
Wasted, Kipling at Bateman's. London, Poem-of-the-Month Club, 1973.
Collected Poems 1944-1979. London, Hutchinson, 1979; New York, Viking Press, 1980.

Recordings: *Kingsley Amis Reading His Own Poems*, Listen, 1962; *Poems*, with Thomas Blackburn, Jupiter, 1962.

Other

Socialism and the Intellectuals. London, Fabian Society, 1957.
New Maps of Hell: A Survey of Science Fiction. New York, Harcourt Brace, 1960; London, Gollancz, 1961.
The James Bond Dossier. London, Cape, and New York, New American Library, 1965.
Lucky Jim's Politics. London, Conservative Political Centre, 1968.
What Became of Jane Austen? and Other Questions. London, Cape, 1970; New York, Harcourt Brace, 1971.
On Drink. London, Cape, 1972; New York, Harcourt Brace, 1973.
Kipling and His World. London, Thames and Hudson, 1975; New York, Scribner, 1976.
An Arts Policy? London, Centre for Policy Studies, 1979.

Editor, with James Michie, *Oxford Poetry 1949.* Oxford, Blackwell, 1949.
Editor, with Robert Conquest, *Spectrum [1-5]: A Science Fiction Anthology.* London, Gollancz, 5 vols., 1961-65; New York, Harcourt Brace, 5 vols., 1962-67.
Editor, *Selected Short Stories of G.K. Chesterton.* London, Faber, 1972.
Editor, *Tennyson.* London, Penguin, 1973.
Editor, *Harold's Years: Impressions from the New Statesman and The Spectator.* London, Quartet, 1977.
Editor, *The New Oxford Book of Light Verse.* London and New York, Oxford University Press, 1978.
Editor, *The Faber Popular Reciter.* London, Faber, 1978.

*

Bibliography: *Kingsley Amis: A Checklist* by Jack Benoit Gohn, Kent, Ohio, Kent State University Press, 1976; *Kingsley Amis: A Reference Guide* by Dale Salwak, Boston, Hall, 1978.

Manuscript Collection (verse): State University of New York, Buffalo.

Kingsley Amis comments:

(1972) Anything a novelist (or any other artist) says about his own work should be regarded with suspicion. It will depend, at least partly, on his mood, the reception of his latest book, whether the one he is working on at the moment is coming well or badly (actually my own always come well, i.e. slowly but—so far—surely). And a novelist is far from being his own best critic, if only because, as Christopher Isherwood once remarked (in effect), no writer is aware of more than about two-thirds of what he is actually doing and saying. Nor should he be.

Well, anyhow: what I think I am doing is writing novels within the main English-language tradition. That is, trying to tell interesting, believable stories about understandable characters in a reasonably straightforward style: no tricks, no experimental foolery. As the tradition indicates, my subject is the relations between people, and I aim at the traditional wide range of effects: humour, pathos, irony, suspense, description, action, introspection. If I had to find a label for my novels, I should call them serio-comedies, though I like to venture now and again into a kind of genre fiction that has always interested me, and have written a straight espionage thriller, a mainstream novel with espionage and science-fiction elements, and a mainstream novel with a large ghost-story interest. One day I may tackle a straight science-fiction novel and a straight detective story.

What I do not think I am doing, despite what some critics have said, is making any kind of statement about "society." As a private citizen I am deeply interested in politics; as a novelist I merely use political material along with domestic, personal, sexual, farcical, social, and other material. The novelist must always try to get the reader to believe that his story and characters are very probable. To do this he must get his background right, or right as he sees it, which means he must try to describe his times; but this is not his prime object. That object is to portray human nature as it has always been, the permanent human passions of love, sorrow, ambition, fear, anger, frustration, joy, and the rest. No "commitment" for me, except to literature.

* * *

Kingsley Amis's principal distinction, in all his novels and other writings, is the sharp comic texture of his prose. Full of mimicry, elaborate satire of ordinary experience (like the bad taste of food or the pains of waking up with a hangover), stock characters tagged by occupation (dentists' mistresses abound in the early fiction), pseudo-logical analyses of experience, satire of contemporary fads and social attitudes, Amis's prose is generally funny. At times, in some of his later works, like *The Anti-Death League* or *Girl, 20*, the prose is flatter and less referential, the list of grievances less ebullient, but farcical events and sharply observed improbabilities keep the tone and texture comic. And some of the later work, like *Jake's Thing*, displays a biting wit directed against contemporary sex therapy and other fashionable distortions of relationships between the sexes. In some of the later fiction, what was, in Amis, an initial attitude of iconoclasm, mocking pretensions to culture or tourist-like enthusiasms for foreign lands or attempts by characters to transcend themselves, has come to sound like a perverse grumble. Particularly in novels like *One Fat Englishman* or *Girl, 20*, or the more recent *Ending Up*, the spirited and farcical antics of the protagonists, originally, as in *Lucky Jim*, self-protective, turn into a series of aggressive and hostile tricks. Amis sometimes shades the line between the persona of the plain Englishman, fooled by neither the old-fashioned nonsense of faith in official or religious verities nor the contemporary nonsense of various rebellious or international fads, and the persona of the curmudgeon.

Amis is a careful craftsman in a wide variety of literary forms. He has always demonstrated a strong interest in science fiction and the novel of espionage. Within the last decade or so, he has written a ghost story (*The Green Man*), a who-done-it (*The Riverside Villas Murder*), and a novel dependent on the imaginative historical assumption, detailed in terms of 1976, that Martin Luther became Pope instead of founding a new religion (*The Alteration*). The novels set in the more familiar contemporary world are also constructed with careful control. Frequently, thematic strands, embodied in different satirically symbolic characters, are gradually drawn together toward a climactic scene that involves almost everyone in the novel. These culminating scenes, like the drunken lecture in *Lucky Jim* or the party in *Take a Girl Like You* or the therapy workshop week-end in *Jake's Thing*, often take place in public, emphasizing the resolutions of the novel in terms that are publicly and socially visible. For Amis, the novel is a rational construction, and he has frequently demonstrated his respect for the traditional novels of the 18th century, both explicitly, as in the great admiration for Fielding shown in *I Like It Here*, and implicitly, as in all the parallels followed by an ironically reversed conclusion between Richardson's *Pamela* and Amis's *Take a Girl Like You*. Amis's rational constructions lampoon deviation, excessive complexity, or eccentricity, and they resolve mystery, either directly in a novel like *The Riverside Villas Murder* or metaphorically, in social and psychological terms, in a novel like *That Uncertain Feeling*. Amis's fictional structures are never open-ended, finally containing little of the thematic corollaries of the open-ended, of introspection, self-doubt, emotional turbulence, indecision, or romanticism.

In spite of all the journalistic declarations in the late 1950's about "Angry Young Men," a rebellion he supposedly led, Amis has never been or claimed to be an iconoclast about society. Rather, the novels, even, by implication, those transformed in setting like *The Alteration*, demonstrate an acceptance, no matter how ironic or grudging, of the social status quo. Frequently, as in *One Fat Englishman* and *I Want It Now*, Amis begins by satirizing a character who pretends to be iconoclastic by showing that the iconoclasm is merely modish opportunism. As the novel develops, in a characteristic switch, Amis shows that the opportunism is very much like everyone else's, is in fact slightly less selfish and self-deluding than that of others. The energetic iconoclast generally learns to adjust in contemporary society, earns the rewards of jobs and good women by sensibly squelching deviation or insistence on self and following the axioms audible around him. Often, as in *Lucky Jim*, *Take a Girl Like You*, and *I Want It Now*, the central character is helped materially by an aristocrat, a symbolic representative of the pinnacle of society who leans down, like a fairy god-father, to reward the deserving. Committed social rebels, those who would transform society in terms of a new or resurrected vision, are either peripheral fools or non-existent in Amis's fiction.

Amis's attitude toward the social adjustment he endorses has altered in the course of his fictional career. Initially, in *Lucky Jim* and *That Uncertain Feeling*, the value of adjustment was debatable, although the process inevitable for a talented young man. *That Uncertain Feeling*, Amis's least certain, least consoling novel, and the one that seems to catch contemporary social references most strikingly, even develops sympathy for the man who is unable to adjust and must retreat to the provincial society he came from. Later, in *I Like It Here* and *Take a Girl Like You*, questions about the value of adjustment become more a matter of superficial comedy and the worth of adjustment, like that of learning to order a meal, drive a car, or lose virginity, is taken for granted. In *I Want It Now* adjustment becomes a positive virtue contrasted to the selfish deviation of eccentrics who are eventually exposed; in *Girl, 20*, the most curmudgeonly novel, the eccentrics can despoil and destroy contemporary London and can only be countered by a rigid adherence to a non-permissive social code. In more recent fiction, like *Jake's Thing*, adjustment is somewhat gentler, the 60-year-old protagonist's recognition that, although the social forms of sex therapy and the new female consciousness are ludicrous (including the theory that Hamlet was really a woman in disguise), he has learned to modify somewhat and accept the uncomfortable consequences of the male chauvinism by which he has lived. All the emphasis on the rightness of adjustment or accommodation in Amis's fiction is, however, always stated negatively, casually. At the end of *Lucky Jim* Jim Dixon, less arid and phony as a teacher than are the other academics, is rewarded because "It's not that you've got the qualifications.... You haven't got the disqualifications, though, and that's much rarer"; similarly, at the end of *I Want It Now* the hero and heroine are together acknowledging that, although bad, they are not quite as bad as others and they can help "each other not to be as bad as we would be on our own"; Jake, at the end of *Jake's Thing*, learns that the "loss of libido" that propelled his excursion into the ludicrous new psychological world to which he partially adjusted may have been physical in origin after all. In other words, Amis characteristically wraps his resolving accommodations in layers of irony.

Amis's forms, his attitudes, and his ironic resolutions work against any sympathetic presentation of depth or intensity in human emotions. For example, in many of the novels, especially the early ones, sexual encounters are almost always material for comedy. Potentially emotional love-making is interrupted by mosquitoes or wasps or a pseudo-logical analysis of how to defend different parts of the anatomy or a manual of sexual technique to demonstrate the protagonist's social skills. Often, the actual scene generating emotion is omitted or severely compressed; at other times, it is subservient to another irony, as in *The Green Man*, in which the protagonist has wanted most to be in bed with his wife and his mistress simultaneously and meticulously arranges it only to find that the two women shut him out entirely. A similar irony resolves the plot of *The Alteration*, in which the imaginary contemporary theocratic world (a world brilliantly depicted in sharply semi-anachronistic prose) propounds the central question of castrating an exceptionally talented young church singer. Just as the talented boy is about to escape, a sudden illness makes castration medically necessary. When, as in *I Want It Now* and *The Anti-Death League*, Amis tries to depict sexuality or love directly, the comedy disappears, the prose becomes flat and banal, and the scene is sentimental. Only occasionally does the implicit Puritanism surface from underneath the irony. In *The Riverside Villas Murder*, in which the resolution is ratiocinatively clever and all the ends neatly tied but the motivation sketchy and unconvincing, the murderer is the woman who sexually initiated the young narrator in a long and conventionally steamy scene. Here, uncharacteristically, the introduction of Eve, the sensual woman who imposes evil on the innocent boy, overwhelms the design of the novel.

Although less sparkling and skillfully comic than many of his novels, *The Anti-Death League* (in which L.S. Caton, the rather slimy editor and lecturer who writes in green ink and appears in almost all the earlier novels, is finally killed off) is one of Amis's most interesting and illustrative. A group of characters at and near a military base recognize the prospect of death and confront the issues of survival in their political, occupational, personal, and psychological ramifications. But the lovers, facing the possible death of one, are simply silent, as if all talk, all human articulation, is futile or pretentiously silly. The other characters spin off into farce or tricks or deliberate evasion in order to survive. Similarly, in *Ending Up*, in which five old people share Tupenny-Hapenny cottage, Bernard, the most intelligent of them, learns that he has only a few months to live. He indulges in a series of malicious tricks on the others, expresses his defiance of death in hostility (as if a "better" death would necessarily be a mawkish one), and begins a chain of events that kills all five. The comic belligerent pose is that of the author as well as that of the character, as if potential humanity and sensitivity are hiding behind the masks, the tricks, all the paraphernalia of Amis's comic survival kit (one that includes the capacity for self-satire as well), and the professional sharpness and skill. When the pose slips or is discarded, the books are suddenly silent, as if nothing else is there and we can infer sensitivity only from its negation. For the most part, Amis's characteristic virtue, as well as his characteristic limitation, is his sense of distance, his capacity for seeing clearly a great deal of what is ludicrous and pretentious even at the price of omitting what is most profoundly or intensely human.

—James Gindin

AMIS, Martin. British. Born in Oxford, 25 August 1949; son of Kingsley Amis, *q.v.* Educated at Exeter College, Oxford, B.A. (honours) 1971. Editorial assistant, *Times Literary Supplement*, London, 1972-75; Assistant Literary Editor, 1975-77, and Literary Editor, 1977-79, *New Statesman*, London. Recipient: Maugham Award, 1974. Agent: Pat Kavanagh, A.D. Peters Ltd., 10 Buckingham Street, London WC2N 6BU. Address: Flat 3, 14 Kensington Gardens Square, London W.2, England.

PUBLICATIONS

Novels

The Rachel Papers. London, Cape, 1973; New York, Knopf, 1974.
Dead Babies. London, Cape, 1975; New York, Knopf, 1976; as *Dark Secrets*, London, Triad, 1977.
Success. London, Cape, 1978.
Other People: A Mystery Story. London, Cape, and New York, Viking Press, 1981.

Uncollected Short Stories

"Denton's Death," in *Encounter* (London), October 1976.
"Heavy Water," in *New Statesman* (London), December 1978.
"Vernon," in *Penthouse* (London), December 1980.

Play

Screenplay: *Saturn 3*, 1980.

*

Theatrical Activities:

Actor: **Film**—*A High Wind in Jamaica*, 1965.

* * *

Martin Amis has been celebrated as the foremost novelist of his generation; his success has been so rapid—four books in nine years—that it is sometimes hard to see how good he really is. His theme of rotten sweetness is rooted in the decaying idealism of his time but he takes it far beyond the merely topical. He writes taut, satiric prose; he can sketch a scene and sum up a character with economy and style; his sombre observations on cruelty are balanced by an underlying optimism, a bubbling well of comic energy. As a moralist, he is on God's side, and probably knows it.

The Rachel Papers introduced his self-seeking, self-doubting protagonist; clever, young, ambitious, Charles is the essential survivor. He cuts a swathe through the chaos around him and ends up with the prizes, in this case, a place at Oxford and the right girl. Inevitably, his progress was compared to that of a 1950's picaresque hero, Lucky Jim. Jim was always on the way up, true, but by virtue of his own innocence; he could never have been labelled "whiz kid."

Quentin, the central character in *Dead Babies*, is like a rocket fuelled by fashion, the darling of gossip columnists, blonde-haired, green-eyed, literary show biz. This novel shows the full range of Amis's talent; like Burroughs's *Naked Lunch*, the title is meant to shock and the text is thoroughly shocking. It describes a country house party at Appleseed Rectory, home of Quentin and the aristocratic Celia, refuge to a group of English eccentrics, the neurotic Giles, the dwarfish Keith, the simple stud Andy Adorno. A hell hole of degradation and deceit, in fact. Left to themselves, the gilded English might have kept within the sentimentalities of flower power; enter an American trio, Skip, Roseanne, and their spokesman, Dr. Marvell Buzhardt, chemist and philosopher: "We've agreed that life is a rat's ass and it's no fun being yourself at the time.... Fuck all this dead babies about love, understanding, compassion...we have drugs to make you euphoric, sad, horny, violent, lucid, tender." Thus begins the lost weekend of the 1970's, an unremittingly asexual orgy in which the characters destroy themselves. A psychopath is on the loose, an outsider who breaks in, wreaks havoc, and signs himself "Johnny." When his identity is revealed the reader recognises that, on one level, it has been known all along. The narrative is so savage that one had hoped, against all the odds, for a last minute reprieve, a glimpse of the heroic.

After this triumph, black and dazzling, *Success* seemed unresolved, incomplete. It is a study of the relationship between two foster-brothers, Terence and Gregory, neither very likeable and at times indistinguishable. A deeply melancholy book, it ends on one of the author's best lines: "The wind will never cease to craze the frightening leaves."

The cast list preceding *Dead Babies* described Johnny as "a practical joker." He may be the author of *Other People*, a self-styled mystery story in which nothing else is clear, not even the divisions between life and death. Mary Lamb, the central character, exists on a metaphysical seesaw, the focus of both good and evil. We meet her in hospital, dazed, amnesiac, the victim of "special damage"; she wanders out into the city, is rescued, raped, hunted down, and seduced by a sinister saviour, Prince. Is he the devil, the prince of darkness? Does he take her to be murdered? Or is she dead anyway, in hell right from the start of the story? The book invites, but defies, interpretation. Mary seems unavoidably guilty, inextricably bound up with suffering. Like the figure in a Francis Bacon painting, she compels our sympathy and puzzles our understanding. It is a compelling piece of writing.

—Judy Cooke

ANAND, Mulk Raj. Indian. Born in Peshawar, 12 December 1905. Educated at Khalsa College, Amritsar; Punjab University, 1921-24, B.A. (honours) 1924; University College, University of London, 1926-29, Ph.D.; Cambridge University, 1929-30; League of Nations School of Intellectual Cooperation, Geneva, 1930-32. Married 1) the actress Kathleen Van Gelder in 1939 (divorced, 1948); 2) the dancer Shirin Vajifdar in 1950, one daughter. Lecturer, School of Intellectual Cooperation, Summer 1930, and Workers Educational Association, London, intermittently 1932-45; has also taught at the universities of Punjab, of Banares, Varanasai, and of Rajasthan, Jaipur, 1948-66: Tagore Professor of Literature and Fine Art, University of Punjab, 1963-66; Visiting Professor, Institute of Advanced Studies, Simla, 1967-68. Fine Art Chairman, Lalit Kala Akademi (National Academy of Art), New Delhi, 1965-70. Since 1946, Editor of *Marg* magazine, Bombay, and Director, Kutub Publishers, Bombay. Since 1970, President of the Lokayata Trust, for creating a community and cultural centre in Hauz Khas village, New Delhi. Recipient: Leverhulme Fellowship, 1940-42; World Peace Council prize, 1952; Padma Bhushan, India, 1968; Sahitya Academy award, 1974. Member, Indian Academy of Letters. Address: 25 Cuffe Parade, Bombay 5, India.

PUBLICATIONS

Novels

Untouchable. London, Wishart, 1935; revised edition, London, Bodley Head, 1970.
The Coolie. London, Lawrence and Wishart, 1936; as *Coolie*, London, Penguin, 1945; New York, Liberty Press, 1952; revised edition, London, Bodley Head, 1972.
Two Leaves and a Bud. London, Lawrence and Wishart, 1937; New York, Liberty Press, 1954.
The Village. London, Cape, 1939.
Lament on the Death of a Master of Arts. Lucknow, Naya Sansar, 1939.
Across the Black Waters. London, Cape, 1940.
The Sword and the Sickle. London, Cape, 1942.
The Big Heart. London, Hutchinson, 1945.
Seven Summers: The Story of an Indian Childhood. London, Hutchinson, 1951.
Private Life of an Indian Prince. London, Hutchinson, 1953; revised edition, London, Bodley Head, 1970.
The Old Woman and the Cow. Bombay, Kutub, 1960; as *Gauri*, New Delhi, Orient, 1976.
The Road. Bombay, Kutub, 1961.
Death of a Hero. Bombay, Kutub, 1963.
Morning Face. Bombay, Kutub, 1968.
Confession of a Lover. New Delhi, Arnold-Heinemann India, 1976.

Short Stories

The Lost Child and Other Stories. London, J.A. Allen, 1934.
The Barber's Trade Union and Other Stories. London, Cape, 1944.
The Tractor and the Corn Goddess and Other Stories. Bombay, Thacker, 1947.
Reflections on the Golden Bed. Bombay, Current Book House, 1947.
The Power of Darkness. Bombay, Jaico, 1958.
Lajwanti and Other Stories. Bombay, Jaico, 1966.
Between Tears and Laughter. New Delhi, Sterling, 1973.
Selected Short Stories of Mulk Raj Anand, edited by M.K. Naik. New Delhi, Arnold-Heinemann India, 1977.

Play

India Speaks (produced London, 1943).

Other

Persian Painting. London, Faber, 1930.
Curries and Other Indian Dishes. London, Harmsworth, 1932.
The Golden Breath: Studies in Five Poets of the New India. London, Murray, and New York, Dutton, 1933.
The Hindu View of Art. Bombay, Asia Publishing House, and London, Allen and Unwin, 1933; revised edition, Asia Publishing House, 1957.
Letters on India. London, Routledge, 1942.
Apology for Heroism: An Essay in Search of Faith. London, Drummond, 1946.
Homage to Tagore. Lahore, Sangam, 1946.
Indian Fairy Tales: Retold (juvenile). Bombay, Kutub, 1946.
On Education. Bombay, Hind Kitabs, 1947.
The Bride's Book of Beauty, with Krishna Hutheesing. Bombay, Kutub, 1947.
The Story of India (juvenile). Bombay, Kutub, 1948.
The King-Emperor's English; or, The Role of the English Language in the Free India. Bombay, Hind Kitabs, 1948.
Lines Written to an Indian Air: Essays. Bombay, Nalanda, 1949.
The Indian Theatre. London, Dobson, 1950; New York, Roy, 1951.
The Story of Man (juvenile). New Delhi, Sikh Publishing House, 1952.
The Dancing Foot. Delhi, Ministry of Information, 1957.
Kama Kala: Some Notes on the Philosophical Basis of Hindu Erotic Sculpture. London, Skilton, 1958; New York, Lyle Stuart, 1962.
India in Colour. Bombay, Taraporevala, London, Thames and Hudson, and New York, McGraw Hill, 1959.
Homage to Khajuraho, with Stella Kramrisch. Bombay, Marg, 1960.
More Indian Fairy Tales (juvenile). Bombay, Kutub, 1961.
Is There a Contemporary Indian Civilisation? Bombay, Asia Publishing House, 1963.
The Story of Chacha Nehru (juvenile). Delhi, Rajpal, 1965.
Bombay. Bombay, Marg, 1965(?).
The Third Eye: A Lecture on the Appreciation of Art. Patiala, University of Punjab, 1966.
Design for Living. Bombay, Marg, 1967.
The Humanism of M.K. Gandhi: Three Lectures. Ghandigahr, University of Panjab, 1967(?).
Konorak, with others. Bombay, Marg, 1968.
The Volcano: Some Comments on the Development of Rabindranath Tagore's Aesthetic Theories. Baroda, Maharaja Sayajirao University, 1968.
Ajunta, photographs by R.R. Bhurdwaj. Bombay, Marg-McGraw Hill, 1971.
Roots and Flowers: Two Lectures on the Metamorphosis of Technique and Content in the Indian English Novel. Dharwar, Karnatak University, 1972.
Author to Critic: The Letters of Mulk Raj Anand, edited by Saros Cowasjee. Calcutta, Writers Workshop, 1973.
Album of Indian Paintings. New Delhi, National Book Trust, 1973.
Folk Tales of Punjab. New Delhi, Sterling, 1974.
Lepakshi. Bombay, Marg, 1977(?).
Seven Little-Known Birds of the Inner Eye. Rutland, Vermont, Tuttle, 1978.

Editor, *Marx and Engels on India.* Allahabad, Socialist Book Club, 1933.
Editor, with Iqbal Singh, *Indian Short Stories.* London, New India, 1947.
Editor, *Introduction to Indian Art*, by A.K. Coomaraswamy. Madras, Theosophical Publishing House, and Wheaton, Illinois, Theosophical Press, 1956.
Editor, *Experiments: Contemporary Indian Short Stories.* Agra, Kranchalson, 1968.
Editor, *Annals of Childhood.* Agra, Kranchalson, 1968.

Editor, *Contemporary World Sculpture*. Bombay, Marg, 1968.
Editor, *Grassroots*. Agra, Kranchalson, 1968(?).
Editor, *Homage to Jaipur*. Bombay, Marg, 1977.
Editor, *Homage to Amritsar*. Bombay, Marg, 1977.

*

Critical Studies: *Mulk Raj Anand: A Critical Essay* by Jack Lindsay, Bombay, Hind Kitabs, 1948, revised edition, as *The Elephant and the Lotus*, Bombay, Kutub, 1954; "Mulk Raj Anand Issue" of *Contemporary Indian Literature* (New Delhi), 1965; *An Ideal of Man in Anand's Novels* by D. Riemenschneider, Bombay, Kutub, 1969; *Mulk Raj Anand: The Man and the Novelist* by Margaret Berry, Amsterdam, Orienta Press, 1971; *Mulk Raj Anand* by K.N. Sinha, New York, Twayne, 1972; *Mulk Raj Anand* by M.K. Naik, New Delhi and London, Arnold-Heinemann India, and New York, Humanities Press, 1973; *Anand: A Study of His Fiction in Humanist Perspective* by G.S. Gupta, Bareilly, Prakash, 1974; *So Many Freedoms: A Study of the Major Fiction of Mulk Raj Anand* by Saros Cowasjee, Delhi and London, Oxford University Press, 1978.

Mulk Raj Anand comments:

I began to write early—a kind of free verse in the Punjabi and Urdu languages, from the compulsion of the shock of the death of my cousin when she was nine years old. I wrote a letter to God telling him He didn't exist. Later, going through the dark night of another bereavement, when my aunt committed suicide because she was excommunicated for interdining with a Muslim woman, I wrote prose. Again, when I fell in love with a young Muslim girl, who was married off by arrangement, I wrote calf love verse. The poet-philosopher, Muhammad Iqbal, introduced me to the problems of the individual through his long poem "Secrets of the Self." Through him, I also read Nietzsche to confirm my rejection of God. After a short term in jail, my father, who was pro-British, punished my mother for my affiliations with the Gandhi Movement. I went to Europe and studied various philosophical systems and found that these comprehensive philosophies did not answer life's problems. I was beaten up for not blacklegging against workers in 1926, in the coal-miner's strike. I joined a Marxist worker's study circle with Trade Unionist Alan Hutt, and met Palme-Dutt, John Strachey, T.S. Eliot, Herbert Read, Bonamy Dobrée, Harold Laski, Leonard Woolf. During that time I fell in love with a young Welsh girl painter, Irene, whose father was a biologist. For her I wrote a long confession about the break-up of my family, the British impact, and my later life. Nobody would publish the 2,000 word narrative. So I began to rewrite portions, as allegories, short stories, and novels. On a tour with Irene, in Paris, Rome, Vienna, Berlin, Brussels, I discovered Rimbaud, Dante, and Joyce. My first attempt at a novel was revised in Gandhi's Sabarmati Ashram in Ahmedabad, but was turned down by 19 publishers in London. The 20th offered to publish it if E.M. Forster wrote a Preface. This the author of *A Passage to India* did.

Since the publication of this first novel, I have written continuously on the human situation in the lives of people of the lower caste, peasants, lumpen, and other eccentrics, thrown up during the transition from the ancient orthodox Indian society to the self-conscious modernist secular democracy.

I believe that creating literature is the true medium of humanism as against systematic philosophies, because the wisdom of the heart encourages insights in all kinds of human beings who grow to self-consciousness through the conflicts of desire, will, and mood. I am inclined to think that the highest aim of poetry and art is to integrate the individual into inner growth and outer adjustment. The broken bundle of mirrors of the human personality in our time can only become the enchanted mirror if the sensibility is touched in its utmost pain and sheer pleasure and tenderest moments. No rounded answers are possible. Only hunches, insights, and inspirations and the *karuna* that may come from understanding.

The novelist's task is that of an all-comprehending "God," who understands every part of his creation, through pity, compassion, or sympathy—which is the only kind of catharsis possible in art. The word is itself action of the still centre. The struggle to relate the word and the deed in the life of man is part of the process of culture, through which illumination comes to human beings. The world of art is a communication from one individual to another, or to the group through the need to connect. This may ultimately yield the slogan "love one another," if mankind is to survive (against its own inheritance of fear, hatred, and contempt, now intensified through money-power, or privileges, and large-scale violence) into the 21st century, in any human form.

* * *

Mulk Raj Anand's first five novels, including some of his best work, appeared in the 1930's. He was one of three writers (R.K. Narayan and Raja Rao were the others) who defined the area in which the Indian novel was to operate. They established its assumptions, sketched its main themes, drew the first models of its characters, and elaborated its peculiar logic. Each of them used an easy, natural idiom which was unaffected by the opacity of a British inheritance. Their language has been freed of the foggy taste of Britain and transferred to a wholly new setting of brutal heat and brilliant light.

Anand is passionately concerned with the villages, with the ferocious poverty and the cruelties of caste, with orphans, untouchables, and urban labourers. He writes in an angry reformist way, like a less humorous Dickens and a more emotional Wells, of the personal sufferings induced by economics—really economics, one feels, even when he is writing of caste. His sharpest, best organised novel is *Untouchable*, which was very highly thought of by E.M. Forster. It is an interesting combination of hard material, narrow specific theme, and throbbing Shelleyan manner. The action, occupying a single day, is precipitated by a great "catastrophe," an accidental "touching" in the morning. Everything that follows is affected by it, even the innocent and vividly realised hockey match. Of the three solutions hinted at to the problem of the untouchable—Christ, Gandhi, and Main Drainage—it is the last which is most favoured by Anand. He is a committed artist, and what he is committed to is indicated by Bashir's mockery in *Untouchable*: "greater efficiency, better salesmanship, more mass-production, standardisation, dictatorship of the sweepers, Marxian Materialism and all that." "Yes, yes," is the reply, "all that, but no catch-words and cheap phrases, the changes will be organic and not mechanical."

Anand's semi-Marxist categories, his furious, and one must say well-grounded indignation, and his habit of undue explicitness, together with a deficiency in self-criticism make him a writer whose work has to be severely sieved. Like many writers impelled by social motives, however worthy, whose attitude to life is too patently dominated by theory, he has a habit of preaching at the reader. But when his imagination burns, and the dross of propaganda is consumed, as in *Untouchable*, *Coolie*, and *The Big Heart*, there is no doubt that he is a novelist of considerable power.

Even politics, that is, even politics as cerebral and doctrinal as this, can be humanised by the ingathering and melting capacity of the Indian mind. It is a quality working right through *Coolie* where Anand showed himself one of the first Indian writers to look on the savagely neglected and maltreated poor with an angry lack of resignation. The novel combines an acrid indignation at the condition of the poor together with a Dickensian vivacity in physical registration *and* a delicate sense of the psychology of Munoo, the waif-hero, in particular of the rhythms of his growth from boy to adolescent. Munoo's victim-role brings home to one the passive quality of the Asiatic poor in what Anand shows to be a markedly static and hierarchical society, just as the immense tracts, from Simla to Bombay, covered in the boy's forced journeys convey in a way new to Indian fiction that continental vastness and variety of India.

Anand belongs to the tradition of the 19th-century writer—not necessarily just the British tradition for one is aware of a distinctly European set of influences operating on him, particularly French and Russian influences—in his approach to the novel, in his techniques, his weaving together of theme and event, in his sensibility, and in his hope for what the novel may publicly achieve. He is particularly of this tradition in point of his fluency. Creation appears to be no agonising struggle for him, communication something he engages in with an unstrained and vivid enthusiasm, and something of the facility of a Russian writer. He is 19th-century, too, in his conception of the novel, seeing it as an organisation strongly based on a double foundation of character and circumstance: character which has to be clearly defined and then developed, largely through the causality of the other constitutive force, social circumstances and influences, usually of a harshly oppressive sort. He has, too, a natural disposition towards the picaresque. The trilogy *The Village*, *Across the Black Waters*, and *The Sword and the Sickle* takes the peasant boy Lal Singh, from his North Indian village and a life stifled by suffocating layers of custom and religion, into the ferocity of the 1914-18 war and the crass commercialism of Europe, and then back again to India to a new political stance towards life.

The defect which constricts his real creative capacity is the habit of allowing his moral and social purposes to become separate from the particular actuality of the fiction, so that they frequently lead a collateral rather than a unified existence. This is accompanied by a certain passivity on the part of the characters, apt no doubt when they are the victim of circumstances, which they so frequently are, but out of place in those parts of his work where the individual should be more energetically active in the working out of his own nature. The theme of *The Big Heart*, this very Dickensian novel, is stated in a single sentence: "In the centre of Amritsar is Kucha Billimaran, a colony of traditional coppersmiths called thathiars, now uprooted and on the brink of starvation due to the advent of the factory and the consequent loss of their traditional occupation." The contrast of the two worlds is vividly delineated and the theme is a splendid vehicle for Anand's largeness and generosity. It is less impressive in the characterisation of the hero, Ananta, who suffers again from a certain limpness in action. He feels the attractions of the two kinds of life. He is fulfilled in the craft of smoothing the intractable metal, but he is also anguished by the poverty of the half-starved coppersmiths. He combines in his reactions something of the feeling of William Morris and of an angry Trade Union leader. Moreover, there is as much moral prejudice against him from the poor, whom the boy is trying to help, because he is living with a widow, as political opposition from the tyrannical capitalists. In a sense Ananta manifests the kind of inward friction which frays Anand himself as an artist, and which he has managed to assuage only in a handful of his books.

As a writer, Mulk Raj Anand lacks the concrete sagacity, the *finesse*, the "appetite for the illustrational"—to use Henry James's phrase—which marks everything that R.K. Narayan writes; nor does he have that sense of the metaphysical nature of man we find in the other distinguished novelist, Raja Rao. But he has a stricken and genuine feeling for the deprived, a grasp of the social structure of his society and an extraordinary fluency of communication. This fluency of communication has something Russian in it, and Russian too (but in an infinitely more attractive sense than the earlier Marxist-dominated way) are two later works, *Morning Face* and *Private Life of an Indian Prince* (revised, 1970). These two books which are, it appears from Saros Cowasjee's introduction, highly autobiographical, summon up the great name of Dostoevsky in their pouring out of an intensely realised personal grief. They show in addition how the mind which created *Coolie* came to be formed, how the boy Krishna, once folded lovingly into the family, becomes coldly detached and alone. The rhythm of this desperate progress is defined with an unusual purity and precision, and so with the same mastery is the collapse of the prince's mind in *Private Life of an Indian Prince*. In both these works, free as they are from undue political scaffolding, there is an extraordinary combination of psychological perception and human agony.

—William Walsh

ANTHONY, Michael. Trinidadian. Born in Mayaro, 10 February 1932. Educated at Mayaro Roman Catholic School; Junior Technical College, San Fernando, Trinidad. Married Yvette Francesca in 1958; four children. Lived in England, 1954-68: Journalist, Reuters News Agency, London, 1964-68. Lived in Brazil, 1968-70. Returned to Trinidad, 1970. Since 1970, Assistant Editor, Texaco Trinidad, Pointe-à-Pierre. Address: c/o Publications Department, Texaco Trinidad, Pointe-à-Pierre, Trinidad.

PUBLICATIONS

Novels

The Games Were Coming. London, Deutsch, 1963; Boston, Houghton Mifflin, 1968.
The Year in San Fernando. London, Deutsch, 1965.
Green Days by the River. Boston, Houghton Mifflin, and London, Deutsch, 1967.
Streets of Conflict. London, Deutsch, 1976.
All That Glitters. London, Deutsch, 1981.

Short Stories

Sandra Street and Other Stories. London, Heinemann, 1973.
Cricket in the Road. London, Deutsch, 1973.
Folk Tales and Fantasies. Port-of-Spain, Trinidad, Columbus, 1976.

Other

Glimpses of Trinidad and Tobago, with a Glance at the West Indies. Port-of-Spain, Trinidad, Columbus, 1974.
Profile Trinidad: A Historical Survey from the Discovery to 1900. London, Macmillan, 1975.

Editor, with Andrew Carr, *David Frost Introduces Trinidad and Tobago*. London, Deutsch, 1975.

*

Critical Studies: in *London Magazine*, April 1967; "Novels of Childhood" in *The West Indian Novel and Its Background* by Kenneth Ramchand, London, Faber, 1970.

Michael Anthony comments:

I see myself principally as a story-teller. In other words, I am not aware that I have any message. I think both the past life and the fascination of landscape play a most important part in my work.

My infancy has been very important in my literary development and so far almost everything I have written—certainly my novels—are very autobiographical.

It is strange that I have never had the desire to write about England, although I spent fourteen years there. To some people, judging from my writing alone, I have never been out of Trinidad. And this is true in some sort of way.

I feel a certain deep attachment to Trinidad and I want to write about it in such a way that I will give a faithful picture of life here. But when I am writing a story I am not aware that I want to do anything else but tell the story.

* * *

The appearance of Michael Anthony's first novel, *The Games Were Coming*, added a distinctive voice to West Indian fiction. Not only did Anthony, already living in London for nine years, entirely avoid the *Angst* of exile and of intellectual or class alienation which had become so common in that fiction, but he achieved the most difficult of all prose qualities: an impression of lyrical simplicity, freshness and ease. Unlike many of the exile writers of his generation, Anthony was able to avoid a tone of recollection (a tone through which some quality of present separation or anguish is audible); he seemed able to inhabit the mounting excitement of the boy Dolphus in this first novel as completely as he later inhabited the pain and confusion of his other boy-hero, Francis, in *The Year in San Fernando*.

The art which makes possible the limpid flow of his style is evident also in the cunning with which he weaves together the various tensions which culminate in the cycle-race at the end of the first novel, or in the death of Mrs. Chandles at the end of the second. While Leon, the young cycling champion, is training with ever-mounting intensity for his big race, his sweetheart Sylvia is moving through parallel tensions of her own. Her frustration at Leon's long-sustained refusal to make love to her gradually turns to feverish anticipation at the approach of a new lover, then to dread as she learns of her pregnancy by him, and finally to a convergent excitement as she persuades the unwitting Leon, on the eve of the race, to marry her if he wins. Thus the race is finally more decisive for her than for him.

The twelve-year-old Francis, who is suddenly switched from the rural calm of Mayaro to the big town of San Fernando, where he stays for a year as a sort of schoolboy-servant in the Chandles household, is not living with a familiar but heightened excitement like Leon's young brother Dolphus; he lives instead with a new insecurity and uncertainty about adult motives, actions and relationships, far away from his family and the scenes of his boyhood. Only as a suddenly pathetic Mrs. Chandles approaches death and her two violently conflicting sons converge on the death-bed does Francis begin to feel that he has absorbed what he can of this disturbing adult world. He has aged much more than a year as he prepares to return to Mayaro.

Green Days by the River offers a slightly older but sadly confused hero, excitedly exploring the experience of loving two different girls at once. Here, for the first time, Anthony introduces some of the racial complexities of Trinidad, for one of the girls is half-Indian, and her father has all the traditional Indian instinct to protect his daughter's virginity right up to the altar. Far away in Port of Spain the boy's own father is dying, while he himself drifts away from the Indian girl he has given every appearance of courting. Her father brutally recalls him to his responsibilities by setting four fierce dogs on him, but this scene is hard to accept in the spirit intended by the author, for it might as easily have resulted in the boy's death as in his marriage.

The publication of his collected short stories, *Cricket in the Road*, did not really signal any new development in his art, since they are mostly early work, written before his novels. They display many of the same qualities of spontaneity and descriptive power. Especially notable are the Indian traders of "The Enchanted Alley" and the Chinese couple of "Many Things," who are created with all the unself-conscious receptiveness of a child exploring his world and its strange inhabitants. Mayaro is again beautifully recreated in "The Valley of Cocoa," though there is an unsuccessful excursion into whimsy in the story "Peeta of the Deep Sea." This failure bears out Anthony's own remarks in the Introduction, which show an understanding of his particular strength: "It seemed to me that a work of fiction based on fact was more meaningful than one that stemmed totally from the imagination."

With these novels and stories, Anthony seems to have exhausted his capacity to re-create with such totality and freshness the Trinidad of his youth. He will need now to become a new kind of novelist. Speaking in 1968 at Canterbury, he said: "I have really reached the crossroads in my career. If I am to go on writing I feel I must return to the scene of my material." But the Trinidad to which he has now returned is a more bitter, tense and divided island than the one he remembered in these novels.

—Gerald Moore

ARMAH, Ayi Kwei. Ghanaian. Born in Takoradi in 1938. Educated at Achimota College, Accra; Groton School, Connecticut; Harvard University, Cambridge, Massachusetts, A.B. in social studies; Columbia University, New York. Translator, *Révolution Africaine* magazine, Algiers; scriptwriter for Ghana Television; English teacher, Navrongo School, Ghana, 1966; Editor, *Jeune Afrique* magazine, Paris, 1967-68; teacher at Teacher's College, Dar es Salaam, universities of Massachusetts, Amherst, and Lesotho, and currently at the University of Wisconsin, Madison. Address: Department of English, University of Wisconsin, Madison, Wisconsin 53706, U.S.A.

PUBLICATIONS

Novels

The Beautyful Ones Are Not Yet Born. Boston, Houghton Mifflin, 1968; London, Heinemann, 1969.
Fragments. Boston, Houghton Mifflin, 1970; London, Heinemann, 1975.
Why Are We So Blest? New York, Doubleday, 1972; London, Heinemann, 1975.
Two Thousand Seasons. Nairobi, East African Publishing House, 1973; London, Heinemann, 1979; Chicago, Third World Press, 1980.
The Healers. Nairobi, East African Publishing House, 1978; London, Heinemann, 1979.

Uncollected Short Stories

"A Short Story," in *New African* (London), December 1965.
"Yaw Manu's Charm," in *Atlantic* (Boston), May 1968.
"The Offal Kind," in *Harper's* (New York), January 1969.

*

Critical Study: *The Novels of Ayi Kwei Armah* by Robert Fraser, London, Heinemann, 1979.

* * *

Ayi Kwei Armah's masterly control over language forces his reader to suspend his disbelief, however reluctant he may be to do so. The comic or horrific distortion of what is nearly recognisable reality in the first three novels has extraordinary imaginative power.

The title of the first novel refers to an inscription which the central character, known only as "the man," sees on a bus. By implication it refers back to the Teacher's story of Plato's cave, where the one man who escapes from the cave and returns to tell his fellow sufferers of the beautiful world outside is thought to be mad by those in the "reassuring chains." The man is anonymous because he is regarded as mad in his society, modern Accra. His family suffers from his refusal to take bribes in his position as a railway clerk, and his honesty is incomprehensible to "the loved ones." His former friend, Koomson, has become a Minister through corruption, and, though the regime of which he is a part falls, an equally corrupt one takes its place. The fusion of styles in *The Beautyful Ones* can be seen in the first few pages, which give a realistic account of a bus journey but also introduce the controlling symbol in the novel, that of money as decay, or excrement. The bus conductor smells a cedi note and finds it has "a very old smell, very strong, and so very rotten that the stench itself of it came with a curious, satisfying pleasure." This anticipates the comic and horrible way in which Koomson has to escape the new regime, by wriggling through a latrine. The depravity of the society is suggested by the manner in which a young man confesses he has made money in a lottery "in the embarrassed way of a young girl confessing love"; if he escaped from his society the man would only mirror his broken pencil sharpener, whose handle "sped round and round with the futile freedom of a thing connected to nothing else."

Armah's ability to invest apparently insignificant objects or scenes with meaning is clear in *Fragments*. Early in the novel there is a detailed account of the destruction of a mad dog by a man with a gross sexual deformity, while the little boy who loves the dog looks on helplessly. It is so vivid that it prepares the reader for the destruction of the central character, Baako, who returns to Ghana from New York wanting to write film scripts because "Film gets to everyone." He finds that his society wants material evidence of his "been-to" status. The new element in this novel is represented by Naana, Baako's blind grandmother, who is the voice of the traditional culture. Traditional ceremonies, such as Baako's baby nephew's outdooring, have lost their spiritual significance and become an opportunity for ostentation and avarice; the plot suggests that Naana's fears for the baby as the victim of this irreligious display are justified, for he dies in the course of it. The fragments of the title seem to be the members of the new society, placed within the opening and closing sections of the novel which express Naana's sense of meaningful community. The only other hopeful element is the growing love between Baako and the sensitive Puerto Rican, Juana.

Why Are We So Blest? is a more fragmented novel than *Fragments*, jumping between three narrators with no obvious narrative line, though we eventually discover that Solo, a failed revolutionary, is using the notebooks of Aimée, a white American, and Modin, a Ghanaian, intercut with his own text. The savage irony of the title is sustained throughout the novel, which lacks the cynical comedy of the two previous works and is much more overt in its distortion of reality. All the white women in the novel prey on the black men: Modin, a student who drops out of Harvard to go to Laccryville in North Africa as a would-be revolutionary, is used primarily by Aimée, who epitomises the sexual sickness of all the white women. She is frigid when she meets Modin, and uses him as an object to stimulate her sexual fantasies of intercourse with a black servant. Modin's attempt to liberate her into a fuller sensitivity destroys him. The horrific scene, in which Aimée is raped and Modin castrated by white men, fully enacts Aimée's fantasy. She is sexually aroused and kisses Modin's bleeding penis, asking him to say that he loves her. Solo sees Modin as an African who does not know "how deep the destruction has eaten into himself, hoping to achieve a healing juncture with his destroyed people."

Armah's most recent novels are historical. *Two Thousand Seasons* is written in a new style, in its repetitiveness and long leisurely sentences suggesting that it is folk myth: "With what shall the utterers' tongue stricken with goodness, riven silent with the quiet force of beauty, with which mention shall the tongue of the utterers begin a song of praise whose perfect singers have yet to come?" Its narrator is not identified, though he participates in the action. The violation of his people's way of life by Arab and then European invaders is depicted powerfully but the ideal of "the way, our way" remains nebulous. *The Healers* is stylistically much more vigorous, and is set at a precise time in the past, during the Second Asante War. The idea of "inspiration" is gradually defined in the course of the novel as being a healing and creative force which can only work slowly, and Armah perhaps sees himself as one of those prophesied by Damfo in the novel, "healers wherever our people are scattered, able to bring us together again."

—Angela Smith

ARNOW, Harriette (Louisa, née Simpson). American. Born in Wayne County, Kentucky, 7 July 1908. Educated at St. Helen's Academy; Stanton Academy; Burnside High School, graduated 1924; Berea College, Kentucky, 1924-26; University of Louisville, B.A. 1931. Married Harold A. Arnow in 1939; one daughter and one son. Teacher in Pulaski County, Kentucky, 1926-28, 1931-34, and Louisville, 1934; waitress, Cincinnati, 1934-39. Recipient: Berea College Centennial Award, 1955; Friends of American Writers Award, 1955. D.Litt.: Albion College, Michigan; Transylvania University, Lexington, Kentucky. Address: c/o Alfred A. Knopf Inc., 201 East 50th Street, New York, New York 10022, U.S.A.

PUBLICATIONS

Novels

Mountain Path. New York, Covici Friede, 1936.
Hunter's Horn. New York, Macmillan, 1949; London, Collins, 1950.
The Dollmaker. New York, Macmillan, 1954; London, Heinemann, 1955.
The Weedkiller's Daughter. New York, Knopf, 1970.
The Kentucky Trace: A Novel of the American Revolution. New York, Knopf, 1974.

Uncollected Short Stories

"Marigolds and Mules," in *Kosmos* (Philadelphia), August-September 1934.
"A Mess of Pork," in *The New Talent* (New York), October-December 1935.
"Washerwoman's Day," in *Anthology of Stories from the Southern Review*, edited by Cleanth Brooks and Robert Penn Warren. Baton Rouge, Louisiana State University Press, 1953.
"Fra Lippi and Me," in *Georgia Review* (Athens), Winter 1979.

Other

Seedtime on the Cumberland. New York, Macmillan, 1960.
Flowering of the Cumberland. New York, Macmillan, 1963.
Some Musings on the Nature of History (lecture). Ann Arbor, Historical Society of Michigan, 1968.
Old Burnside. Lexington, University Press of Kentucky, 1978.

*

Manuscript Collection: Margaret I. King Library, University of Kentucky, Lexington.

Critical Studies: by Joyce Carol Oates, in *Rediscoveries* edited by David Madden, New York, Crown, 1971; *Harriette Arnow* by Wilton Eckley, New York, Twayne, 1974.

Harriette Arnow comments:

Judging from critical studies, reviews, and letters the main features of my novels are the characters, sometimes praised, but often damned. Perhaps the most notable characters are in *Hunter's Horn* and *The Dollmaker*; at least more has been written of them, particularly of Gertie Nevels in *The Dollmaker*, the story of a rural family's migration to an industrial city during World War II. Most of the characters in *The Weedkiller's Daughter*, set in modern suburbia, were damned. The main character in *The Kentucky Trace*, an historical novel, did somewhat better.

* * *

Harriette Arnow's reputation as an artist rests on three significant volumes: two—*Seedtime on the Cumberland* and *Flowering of the Cumberland*—are cultural histories; one—*The Dollmaker*—is a novel. The histories are remarkable for the brilliant, often lyrical, narrative techniques and for the accuracy and wealth of detail relating the every-day domestic life of the early settlers of the Cumberland. The same attention to life-as-lived detail and to strong prose distinguishes *The Dollmaker*, which Joyce Carol Oates called "a legitimate tragedy, our most unpretentious American masterpiece."

Discounting possible overstatement, most critics would agree with Oates: *The Dollmaker* is a masterpiece, one which does with the folk of Appalachia what Steinbeck's *The Grapes of Wrath* does with the Okies, one which gives the plight of a displaced family heroic stature and epic sweep. Following the archetype of flight from the ruined Eden to the new promised land, the novel dramatizes with authentic precision the collision of two cultures. The mountain family's agrarian values of independence, self-sufficiency, love of the land, and aesthetic based on closeness to the beauty and harshness of nature are epitomized in the mother, Gertie, who with the soul of an artist is a marvel of physical and spiritual strength, ingenuity, and endurance. Rather than the dust bowl and rapacity of landholders, the calamity that springs the exodus from her Eden is World War II which took the men from the mountains and lured them to death in combat or to death-in-life in industrial Detroit. Seduced in part by her own traditions of family loyalty, the mother follows her man's dream of better life in progressive Detroit which promised affluence, untold luxuries, and marvelous conveniences. The incipient callousness and bigotry of Gertie's mountain society also follow to Detroit where they are mass-produced and manufactured on a scale of overwhelming vulgarity. With a fate as persistent, inevitable, finely wrought, and devastating as pursued Jude the Obscure, the horrors of industrialized society are exposed: the family disintegrates and sinks to the lowest levels of violence and misery. Even the artistic soul of Gertie is sacrificed to mass production, standardization, mechanization, and crass commercialism.

Overlaid on the superb rendering of the minutiae of life in Appalachia and Detroit are the same mythic and epic elements as Steinbeck's novel. Ultimately the novel becomes a search for Christ in the world, a Christ freed from the dogma and bigotry of established institutions. Certainly as successful in this attempt as Steinbeck, Arnow shows that beneath the selfishness and ignorance, beneath the degrading impersonalization of modernism, the suppressed folk have a genuine human care for each other that binds them together and gives them the strength to endure their crucifixions. *En masse* they can endure and perhaps overcome the enemy: organized religion, industrialism, false aristocracy, mass media, standardization, public education—anything that depersonalizes and dehumanizes. Salvation seems to be in the mass rather than in the individuals. Thus, finally, Arnow turns from agrarian novelist to proletariat novelist. This paradox or ambiguity is seen in the ending of *The Dollmaker*. Throughout the trials that Gertie endures, the chief sustainer and symbol of her dream of spirituality and human truth has been a block of wood which she has carved, but which she has not finished, awaiting the revelation that will give the figure a face. The figure is amorphous, even to Gertie, and is sometimes a man, sometimes a woman, sometimes a Judas, sometimes a virgin, but ultimately it is to be Christ. In the final pages of the novel, in a pointed counterpart of a religious procession of a holy image, the block of wood is hauled to the saw mill in the midst of crowds of on-lookers. It is cut into blocks to make mass-produced dolls for commercial sale. Her vision is thus sacrificed to the cheap vulgarity and needs of a materialistic and meaningless existence. However, at the last Gertie sees that unseen face of Christ could have been the face of her neighbors—"millions and millions of faces fine enough for him." Christ is to be found in the mass, in the millions of those who are the folk, to which the individual vision must be relinquished.

Arnow's earlier novels, *Mountain Path* and *Hunter's Horn*, are less ambitious and *au courant* with the times, but they are indicative of her skill in depicting mountain scenes and characters. They also show her lesser skill at realistic plotting, especially *Mountain Path*, which indulges in plot clichés and situations common to stereotyped hillbilly life. *The Weedkiller's Daughter* and *The Kentucky Trace* are barely satisfactory for serious reading. *The Weedkiller's Daughter* sets a group of nature-loving, arrogantly deceitful, pseudo-sophisticated, precocious teenagers against a plastic society of stupid and vulgar newly-rich parents. The plot is negligible and a contrivance merely to hold together a narrative designed to deliver every stance posed by the 1960's liberal. *The Kentucky Trace* returns to some of the materials of Arnow's earlier work, but the narrative is a creaking vehicle to utilize her detailed knowledge of the pioneer ways and means of the mountain settlers.

—Robert L. Welker

ASHTON-WARNER, Sylvia (Constance). New Zealander. Born in Stratford, 17 December 1908. Educated at small country schools, including Te Whiti; Wairarapa College, Masterton; Teachers College, Auckland, 1928-29. Married to Keith Dawson Henderson. Taught with her husband at several country schools in New Zealand. Professor of Education, Aspen Community School Teaching Center, Colorado, until 1972. Address: Whenua, 5-9 Levers Road, Otumoetai, Tuaranga, New Zealand.

PUBLICATIONS

Novels

Spinster. London, Secker and Warburg, 1958; New York, Simon and Schuster, 1959.
Incense to Idols. London, Secker and Warburg, and New York, Simon and Schuster, 1960.
Bell Call. New York, Simon and Schuster, 1965; London, Hale, 1971.
Greenstone. New York, Simon and Schuster, 1966; London, Secker and Warburg, 1967.
Three. New York, Knopf, 1970; London, Hale, 1971.

Uncollected Short Stories

"No Longer Blinded by Our Eyes" (as Sylvia Henderson), in *New Zealand Listener* (Wellington), 8 October 1948.
"The Least Thing" (as Sylvia), in *Here and Now* (Auckland), April 1956.
"Floor" (as Sylvia), in *Here and Now* (Auckland), June 1956.
"That Boy Again," in *New Zealand Monthly Review* (Christchurch), March 1961.
"Patricia," in *New Zealand Monthly Review* (Christchurch), May 1962.
"Toll Call," in *New World Writing 20*. Philadelphia, Lippincott, 1962.

Other

Teacher. London, Secker and Warburg, and New York, Simon and Schuster, 1963.
Myself. New York, Simon and Schuster, 1967; London, Secker and Warburg, 1968.
Spearpoint: "Teacher" in America. New York, Knopf, 1972; as *"Teacher" in America*, London, Cassell, 1974.
I Passed This Way. New York, Knopf, 1979; London, Virago, 1980.

* * *

Sylvia Ashton Warner's novels have the great merit of being unpredictable. She burst upon the rather conventional literary scene in New Zealand in 1958 with a work, *Spinster*, that was less a novel than an educational thriller, rich with identifiable persons and places, pulsing with anti-Establishment exasperations, and flaring with emotional highlights. It erupted into the artistic scene as well as the educational one, for its exhibition of the tormented inner life of the teacher-narrator, Anna Vorontosov, was more riotously outspoken than local readers expected.

In all her educational work, Ashton-Warner has one dominant message, that the most vital of human concerns is communication between "Thee" and "Me," whether verbal or physical, intellectual or emotional, loving or destructive. Response, and response alone, confers life. In *Spinster* the novelist portrays the lonely woman whose deprivation of the "Thee and Me" relationship has sharpened her perception of its value. Anna Vorontosov, gifted at art, music, and self-dramatisation, lives through a school year with the reader beside her as absorbed eavesdropper. The tumbling chaos of her inner and outer lives has imposed upon it a framework of the four seasons, threaded through with lines from the poems of Gerard Manley Hopkins (especially "The Caged Skylark," "To Seem the Stranger," "Thou Art Indeed Just Lord," and "To R.B."). Faced with her prefabricated infant room exploding with brown and white children, this teacher tries to find ways of releasing the currents locked within these little beings. The frozen puritan *pakeha* Dennis must thaw; the irrepressible Maori Seven must be drawn into creating instead of destroying; Hinewaka, of the injured feet, must be healed of her hospital terrors; and anxious little Riti, whose hair is full of "those things," must in spite of them be allowed to cuddle close, because physical contact is the only way to make connection.

Anna Vorontosov's personal life is less credible than her professional one. Elements which recur in later novels—the musical and horticultural fantasies, the suiciding lover, the anguish of soul—these flare and collide in *Spinster*, threatening to overbalance the novel into hysteria. Yet there is more substance in it than in most novels, substance so rich and so original that the terms "good" or "bad" hardly seem relevant.

In *Incense to Idols*, however, hysteria has the upper hand. Germaine, the improbable Paris pianist who has come to rest in a small New Zealand town, maintains an exotic narrative flow swirling over sex, religion, alcohol, poetry, and prophecy, with neither pattern nor real significance emerging.

Bell Call, published in New York in 1965 but not in New Zealand until 1971, is an attempt to ignore the school bell altogether. This novel, like *Incense to Idols*, has a bizarre narrative mode, shared as it is between a ghost watching earthly events from some undefined stance, and the ghost's living husband, Daniel Francis, ex-schoolmaster and writer. Tarl Prackett, mother of four, believes that teaching is a sinful intrusion upon a child's free growth. Until a child asks for it, education should not be imposed. These beliefs bring her of course into open conflict with the New Zealand law. She therefore spends the book seeking for the "primitive simplicity" of some retreat where her children can "merge with nature." Playing opposite to Tarl is Angela, Daniel's daughter, with her tidy house and disciplined offspring. The tale is told in strained, posturing, deliberately fanciful language, its basic mystique is that of its quotation from Whitman: "For I confront peace, security, and all the settled laws, to unsettle them.../I heed not, and have never heeded, either experience, cautions, majorities, nor ridicule...."

Greenstone unfortunately is as touristic as its title suggests. It is set on the Wanganui River, where the author taught during the years she describes in *Myself*. Her material, however, seems to be not so much derived from this reality as salvaged from some course of reading in early New Zealand potboilers, with their garbled Maori myths, remittance men figures, halfcaste princesses, and other standard items of popular colonial romance. Ashton-Warner's thesis, the need for racial harmony and integration, does of course need recurring emphasis, but its cause is hardly likely to be advanced by such luxuriant sentimentality.

In 1967 came *Myself*, which purports to be the diary of the author's life from 1941 to 1945 at Pipiriki School on the Wanganui River. Whether *Myself* is an accurate daily record, or a pepped up selection of one, or a fictitious reconstruction—the same problem arises with the diary section of *Teacher*—the effect is certainly creative rather than documentary. Ashton-Warner pictures a woman torn between the different roles of "the wife, the mother, the lover, the teacher, and the violent artist." Her husband, Keith Dawson Henderson, appears in person and by name, a loyal and father-like figure who stands by to offer stability and refuge. The turbulent fluctuations of the author's feelings in these diverse roles are conveyed in a straightforward and therefore more effective prose than she uses elsewhere. However erratic and embarrassing may be the personal revelations of her work and the exotic pranks of her prose, Sylvia Ashton-Warner's writing carries at its heart a core of passionate human concern. It is this which gives her a claim to serious attention.

—Joan Stevens

ASIMOV, Isaac. American. Born in Petrovichi, U.S.S.R., 2 January 1920; emigrated to the United States in 1923; naturalized, 1928. Educated at Columbia University, New York, B.S. 1939, M.A. 1941, Ph.D. 1948. Served in the United States Army, 1945-46. Married 1) Gertrude Blugerman in 1942 (divorced), one son and one daughter; 2) Janet Opal Jeppson in 1973. Instructor in Biochemistry, 1949-51, Assistant Professor, 1951-55, Associate Professor, 1955-79, and since 1979 Professor, Boston University School of Medicine. Recipient: Edison Foundation National Mass Media Award, 1958; Blakeslee Award, for non-fiction, 1960; World Science Fiction Convention Citation, 1963; Hugo Award, 1963, 1966, 1973, 1977; American Chemical Society James T. Grady Award, 1965; American Association for the Advancement of Science-Westinghouse Writing Award, 1967; Nebula Award, 1972, 1976. Address: 10 West 66th Street, Apartment 33-A, New York, New York 10023, U.S.A.

PUBLICATIONS

Novels

Triangle. New York, Doubleday, 1961; as *A Second Isaac Asimov Omnibus*, London, Sidgwick and Jackson, 1969.
- *Pebble in the Sky*. New York, Doubleday, 1950; London, Corgi, 1958.
- *The Stars, Like Dust*. New York, Doubleday, 1951; London, Panther, 1958; as *The Rebellious Stars*, New York, Ace, 1954.
- *The Currents of Space*. New York, Doubleday, 1952; London, Boardman, 1955.

Foundation Trilogy. New York, Doubleday, 1963(?); as *An Isaac Asimov Omnibus*, London, Sidgwick and Jackson, 1966.
- *Foundation*. New York, Gnome Press, 1952; London, Weidenfeld and Nicolson, 1953; abridged edition, as *The Thousand-Year Plan*, New York, Ace, 1956.
- *Foundation and Empire*. New York, Gnome Press, 1952; London, Panther, 1962; as *The Man Who Upset the Universe*, New York, Ace, 1955.
- *Second Foundation*. New York, Gnome Press, 1953.

The Caves of Steel. New York, Doubleday, and London, Boardman, 1954.

The End of Eternity. New York, Doubleday, 1955; London, Panther, 1958.

The Naked Sun. New York, Doubleday, 1957; London, Joseph, 1958.

The Death Dealers. New York, Avon, 1958; as *A Whiff of Death*, New York, Walker, and London, Gollancz, 1968.

Fantastic Voyage (novelization of screenplay). Boston, Houghton Mifflin, and London, Dobson, 1966.

The Gods Themselves. New York, Doubleday, and London, Gollancz, 1972.

Murder at the ABA. New York, Doubleday, 1976; as *Authorized Murder*, London, Gollancz, 1976.

The Collected Fiction: The Far Ends of Time and Earth, Prisoners of the Stars. New York, Doubleday, 2 vols., 1979.

Short Stories

I, Robot. New York, Gnome Press, 1950; London, Grayson, 1952.
The Martian Way and Other Stories. New York, Doubleday, 1955; London, Dobson, 1964.
Earth Is Room Enough. New York, Doubleday, 1957; London, Panther, 1960.
Nine Tomorrows: Tales of the Near Future. New York, Doubleday, 1959; London, Dobson, 1963.
The Rest of the Robots. New York, Doubleday, 1964; London, Dobson, 1967.
Through a Glass, Clearly. London, New English Library, 1967.
Asimov's Mysteries. New York, Doubleday, and London, Rapp and Whiting, 1968.
Nightfall and Other Stories. New York, Doubleday, 1969; London, Rapp and Whiting, 1970.
The Early Asimov; or, Eleven Years of Trying. New York, Doubleday, 1972; London, Gollancz, 1973.
The Best of Isaac Asimov (1939-1972). London, Sidgwick and Jackson, 1973; New York, Doubleday, 1974.
Have You Seen These? Cambridge, Massachusetts, NESFA Press, 1974.
Tales of the Black Widowers. New York, Doubleday, 1974; London, Gollancz, 1975.
Buy Jupiter and Other Stories. New York, Doubleday, 1975; London, Gollancz, 1976.
The Dream, Benjamin's Dream, Benjamin's Bicentennial Blast. Privately printed, 1976.
The Bicentennial Man and Other Stories. New York, Doubleday, and London, Gollancz, 1976.
More Tales of the Black Widowers. New York, Doubleday, 1976; London, Gollancz, 1977.
Good Taste. Topeka, Kansas, Apocalypse Press, 1976.
Casebook of the Black Widowers. New York, Doubleday, and London, Gollancz, 1980.

Verse

Lecherous Limericks. New York, Walker, 1975; London, Corgi, 1977.
More Lecherous Limericks. New York, Walker, 1976.
Still More Lecherous Limericks. New York, Walker, 1977.
Asimov's Sherlockian Limericks. Yonkers, New York, Mysterious Press, 1978.
Limericks: Too Gross, with John Ciardi. New York, Norton, 1978.

Other

Biochemistry and Human Metabolism, with Burnham Walker and William C. Boyd. Baltimore, Williams and Wilkins, 1952; revised edition, 1954, 1957; London, Ballière Tindall and Cox, 1955.
David Starr, Space Ranger (juvenile; as Paul French). New York, Doubleday, 1952; Kingswood, Surrey, World's Work, 1953.
Lucky Starr and the Pirates of the Asteroids (juvenile; as Paul French). New York, Doubleday, 1953; Kingswood, Surrey, World's Work, 1954.
The Chemicals of Life: Enzymes, Vitamins, Hormones. New York, Abelard Schuman, 1954; London,Bell, 1956.
Lucky Starr and the Oceans of Venus (juvenile; as Paul French). New York, Doubleday, 1954; as *The Oceans of Venus,* as Isaac Asimov, London, New English Library, 1973.
Races and Peoples, with William C. Boyd. New York, Abelard Schuman, 1955; London, Abelard Schuman, 1958.
Lucky Starr and the Big Sun of Mercury (juvenile; as Paul French). New York, Doubleday, 1956; as *The Big Sun of Mercury,* as Isaac Asimov, London, New English Library, 1974.
Chemistry and Human Health, with Burnham Walker and M.K. Nicholas. New York, McGraw Hill, 1956.
Inside the Atom. New York and London, Abelard Schuman, 1956; revised edition, 1958, 1961, 1966, 1974.
Lucky Starr and the Moons of Jupiter (juvenile; as Paul French). New York, Doubleday, 1957; as *The Moons of Jupiter,* as Isaac Asimov, London, New English Library, 1974.
Building Blocks of the Universe. New York, Abelard Schuman, 1957; London, Abelard Schuman, 1958; revised edition, 1961, 1974.
Only a Trillion. New York and London, Abelard Schuman, 1957; as *Marvels of Science,* New York, Collier, 1962.
Lucky Starr and the Rings of Saturn (juvenile; as Paul French). New York, Doubleday, 1958; as *The Rings of Saturn,* as Isaac Asimov, London, New English Library, 1974.
The World of Carbon. New York and London, Abelard Schuman, 1958; revised edition, New York, Collier, 1962.
The World of Nitrogen. New York and London, Abelard Schuman, 1958; revised edition, New York, Collier, 1962.
The Clock We Live On. New York and London, Abelard Schuman, 1959; revised edition, New York, Collier, 1962; Abelard Schuman, 1965.
The Living River. New York and London, Abelard Schuman, 1959; revised edition, as *The Bloodstream: River of Life,* New York, Collier, 1961.
Realm of Numbers. Boston, Houghton Mifflin, 1959; London, Gollancz, 1963.
Words of Science and the History Behind Them. Boston, Houghton Mifflin, 1959; London, Harrap, 1974.
Breakthroughs in Science (juvenile). Boston, Houghton Mifflin, 1960.
The Intelligent Man's Guide to Science. New York, Basic, 2 vols., 1960; revised edition, as *The New Intelligent Man's Guide to Science,* 1 vol., 1965; London, Nelson, 1967; as *Asimov's Guide to Science,* Basic, 1972; London, Penguin, 1975.
The Kingdom of the Sun. New York and London, Abelard Schuman, 1960; revised edition, New York, Collier, 1962; Abelard Schuman, 1963.
Realm of Measure. Boston, Houghton Mifflin, 1960.
Satellites in Outer Space (juvenile). New York, Random House, 1960; revised edition, 1964, 1973.
The Double Planet. New York, Abelard Schuman, 1960; London, Abelard Schuman, 1962; revised edition, 1966.
The Wellsprings of Life. New York and London, Abelard Schuman, 1960.
Realm of Algebra. Boston, Houghton Mifflin, 1961; London, Gollancz, 1964.
Words from the Myths. Boston, Houghton Mifflin, 1961; London, Faber, 1963.
Fact and Fancy. New York, Doubleday, 1962.
Life and Energy. New York, Doubleday, 1962; London, Dobson, 1963.
The Search for the Elements. New York, Basic, 1962.
Words in Genesis. Boston, Houghton Mifflin, 1962.
Words on the Map. Boston, Houghton Mifflin, 1962.
View from a Height. New York, Doubleday, 1963; London, Dobson, 1964.
The Genetic Code. New York, Orion Press, 1963; London, Murray, 1964.
The Human Body: Its Structure and Operation. Boston, Houghton Mifflin, 1963; London, Nelson, 1965.
The Kite That Won the Revolution. Boston, Houghton Mifflin, 1963.
Words from the Exodus. Boston, Houghton Mifflin, 1963.
Adding a Dimension: 17 Essays on the History of Science. New York, Doubleday, 1964; London, Dobson, 1966.
The Human Brain: Its Capacities and Functions. Boston, Houghton Mifflin, 1964; London, Nelson, 1965.

Quick and Easy Math. Boston, Houghton Mifflin, 1964; London, Whiting and Wheaton, 1967.
A Short History of Biology. Garden City, New York, Natural History Press, 1964; London, Nelson, 1965.
Planets for Man, with Stephen H. Dole. New York, Random House, 1964.
Asimov's Biographical Encyclopedia of Science and Technology. New York, Doubleday, 1964; London, Allen and Unwin, 1966; revised edition, Doubleday, 1972; London, Pan, 1975.
An Easy Introduction to the Slide Rule. Boston, Houghton Mifflin, 1965; London, Whiting and Wheaton, 1967.
The Greeks: A Great Adventure. Boston, Houghton Mifflin, 1965.
Of Time and Space and Other Things. New York, Doubleday, 1965; London, Dobson, 1967.
A Short History of Chemistry. New York, Doubleday, 1965; London, Heinemann, 1972.
The Neutrino: Ghost Particle of the Atom. New York, Doubleday, and London, Dobson, 1966.
The Genetic Effects of Radiation, with Theodosius Dobzhansky. Washington, D.C., Atomic Energy Commission, 1966.
The Noble Gases. New York, Basic, 1966.
The Roman Republic. Boston, Houghton Mifflin, 1966.
From Earth to Heaven. New York, Doubleday, 1966.
Understanding Physics. New York, Walker, 3 vols., 1966; London, Allen and Unwin, 3 vols., 1967.
The Universe: From Flat Earth to Quasar. New York, Walker, 1966; London, Penguin, 1967; revised edition, Walker, 1971; revised edition, as *The Universe: From Flat Earth to Black Holes—and Beyond*, Walker, 1980.
The Roman Empire. Boston, Houghton Mifflin, 1967.
The Moon (juvenile). Chicago, Follett, 1967; London, University of London Press, 1969.
Is Anyone There? (essays). New York, Doubleday, 1967; London, Rapp and Whiting, 1968.
To The Ends of the Universe. New York, Walker, 1967; revised edition, 1976.
The Egyptians. Boston, Houghton Mifflin, 1967.
Mars (juvenile). Chicago, Follett, 1967; London, University of London Press, 1971.
From Earth to Heaven: 17 Essays on Science. New York, Doubleday, 1967; London, Dobson, 1968.
Environments Out There. New York, Abelard Schuman, 1967; London, Abelard Schuman, 1968.
Science, Numbers, and I: Essays on Science. New York, Doubleday, 1968; London, Rapp and Whiting, 1969.
The Near East: 10,000 Years of History. Boston, Houghton Mifflin, 1968.
Asimov's Guide to the Bible: The Old Testament, The New Testament. New York, Doubleday, 2 vols., 1968-69.
The Dark Ages. Boston, Houghton Mifflin, 1968.
Galaxies (juvenile). Chicago, Follett, 1968; London, University of London Press, 1971.
Stars (juvenile). Chicago, Follett, 1968.
Words from History. Boston, Houghton Mifflin, 1968.
Photosynthesis. New York, Basic, 1968; London, Allen and Unwin, 1970.
The Shaping of England. Boston, Houghton Mifflin, 1969.
Twentieth Century Discovery (juvenile). New York, Doubleday, and London, Macdonald, 1969.
Opus 100 (selection). Boston, Houghton Mifflin, 1969.
ABC's of Space (juvenile). New York, Walker, 1969.
Great Ideas of Science (juvenile). Boston, Houghton Mifflin, 1969.
To the Solar System and Back. New York, Doubleday, 1970.
Asimov's Guide to Shakespeare: The Greek, Roman, and Italian Plays; The English Plays. New York, Doubleday, 2 vols., 1970.
Constantinople. Boston, Houghton Mifflin, 1970.
The ABC's of the Ocean (juvenile). New York, Walker, 1970.
Light (juvenile). Chicago, Follett, 1970.
Best New Thing (juvenile). Cleveland, World, 1971.
The Stars in Their Courses. New York, Doubleday, 1971; London, White Lion, 1974.
What Makes the Sun Shine. Boston, Little Brown, 1971.
The Isaac Asimov Treasury of Humor. Boston, Houghton Mifflin, 1971; London, Vallentine Mitchell, 1972.
The Sensuous Dirty Old Man (as Dr. A.). New York, Walker, 1971.
The Land of Canaan. Boston, Houghton Mifflin, 1971.
ABC's of Earth (juvenile). New York, Walker, 1971.
The Space Dictionary. New York, Starline, 1971.
More Words of Science. Boston, Houghton Mifflin, 1972.
Electricity and Man. Washington, D.C., Atomic Energy Commission, 1972.
The Shaping of France. Boston, Houghton Mifflin, 1972.
Asimov's Annotated "Don Juan." New York, Doubleday, 1972.
ABC's of Ecology (juvenile). New York, Walker, 1972.
The Story of Ruth. New York, Doubleday, 1972.
Worlds Within Worlds. Washington, D.C., Atomic Energy Commission, 1972.
The Left Hand of the Electron (essays). New York, Doubleday, 1972; London, White Lion, 1975.
Ginn Science Program. Boston, Ginn, 5 vols., 1972-73.
How Did We Find Out about Dinosaurs [The Earth Is Round, Electricity, Vitamins, Germs, Comets, Energy, Atoms, Nuclear Power, Numbers, Outer Space, Earthquakes, Black Holes, Our Human Roots, Antarctica, Coal, Oil] (juvenile). New York, Walker, 17 vols., 1973-79; 6 vols. published London, White Lion, 1975-76; 1 vol. published London, Pan, 1980.
The Tragedy of the Moon (essays). New York, Doubleday, 1973; London, Abelard Schuman, 1974.
Comets and Meteors (juvenile). Chicago, Follett, 1973.
The Sun (juvenile). Chicago, Follett, 1973.
The Shaping of North America from the Earliest Times to 1763. Boston, Houghton Mifflin, 1973; London, Dobson, 1975.
Please Explain (juvenile). Boston, Houghton Mifflin, 1973; London, Abelard Schuman, 1975.
Physical Science Today. Del Mar, California, CRM, 1973.
Jupiter, The Largest Planet (juvenile). New York, Lothrop, 1973; revised edition, 1976.
Today, Tomorrow, and.... New York, Doubleday, 1973; London, Abelard Schuman, 1974; as *Towards Tomorrow*, London, Hodder and Stoughton, 1977.
The Birth of the United States 1763-1816. Boston, Houghton Mifflin, 1974.
Earth: Our Crowded Spaceship. New York, Day, and London, Abelard Schuman, 1974.
Asimov on Chemistry. New York, Doubleday, 1974; London, Macdonald and Jane's, 1975.
Asimov on Astronomy. New York, Doubleday, and London, Macdonald, 1974.
Asimov's Annotated "Paradise Lost." New York, Doubleday, 1974.
Our World in Space. Greenwich, Connecticut, New York Graphic Society, and Cambridge, Patrick Stephens, 1974.
The Solar System (juvenile). Chicago, Follett, 1975.
Birth and Death of the Universe. New York, Walker, 1975.
Of Matters Great and Small. New York, Doubleday, 1975.
Our Federal Union: The United States from 1816 to 1865. Boston, Houghton Mifflin, and London, Dobson, 1975.
The Ends of the Earth: The Polar Regions of the World. New York, Weybright and Talley, 1975.
Eyes on the Universe: A History of the Telescope. Boston, Houghton Mifflin, 1975; London, Deutsch, 1976.
Science Past — Science Future. New York, Doubleday, 1975.
The Heavenly Host (juvenile). New York, Walker, 1975; London, Penguin, 1978.
Alpha Centauri, The Nearest Star (juvenile). New York, Lothrop, 1976.
I, Rabbi (juvenile). New York, Walker, 1976.
Asimov on Physics. New York, Doubleday, 1976.

The Planet That Wasn't. New York, Doubleday, 1976; London, Sphere, 1977.
The Collapsing Universe: The Story of Black Holes. New York, Walker, and London, Hutchinson, 1977.
Asimov on Numbers. New York, Doubleday, 1977.
The Beginning and the End. New York, Doubleday, 1977.
Familiar Poems Annotated. New York, Doubleday, 1977.
The Golden Door: The United States from 1865 to 1918. Boston, Houghton Mifflin, and London, Dobson, 1977.
The Key Word and Other Mysteries (juvenile). New York, Walker, 1977.
Mars, The Red Planet (juvenile). New York, Lothrop, 1977.
Life and Time. New York, Doubleday, 1978.
Quasar, Quasar, Burning Bright. New York, Doubleday, 1978.
Animals of the Bible (juvenile). New York, Doubleday, 1978.
Isaac Asimov's Book of Facts. New York, Grosset and Dunlap, 1979; London, Hodder and Stoughton, 1980.
Extraterrestrial Civilizations. New York, Crown, 1979; London, Robson, 1980.
A Choice of Catastrophes. New York, Simon and Schuster, 1979; London, Hutchinson, 1980.
Saturn and Beyond. New York, Lothrop, 1979.
Opus 200 (selection). Boston, Houghton Mifflin, 1979.
In Memory Yet Green: The Autobiography of Isaac Asimov 1920-1954. New York, Doubleday, 1979.
The Road to Infinity. New York, Doubleday, 1979.
Opus (includes *Opus 100* and *Opus 200*). London, Deutsch, 1980.
In Joy Still Felt: The Autobiography of Isaac Asimov 1954-1978. New York, Doubleday, 1980.
The Annotated Gulliver's Travels. New York, Potter, 1980.
In the Beginning: Science Faces God in the Book of Genesis. New York, Crown, 1981.
Asimov on Science Fiction. New York, Doubleday, 1981.
Venus, Near Neighbor of the Sun (juvenile). New York, Lothrop, 1981.

Editor, *The Hugo Winners 1-3.* New York, Doubleday, 3 vols., 1962-77; *1* and *3*, London, Dobson, 2 vols., 1963-77; *2*, London, Sphere, 1973.
Editor, with Groff Conklin, *Fifty Short Science Fiction Tales.* New York, Macmillan, 1963.
Editor, *Tomorrow's Children: 18 Tales of Fantasy and Science Fiction.* New York, Doubleday, 1966; London, Futura, 1974.
Editor, *Where Do We Go from Here?* New York, Doubleday, 1971; London, Joseph, 1973.
Editor, *Nebula Award Stories 8.* New York, Harper, and London, Gollancz, 1973.
Editor, *Before the Golden Age: A Science Fiction Anthology of the 1930's.* New York, Doubleday, and London, Robson, 1974.
Editor, with Martin H. Greenberg and Joseph D. Olander, *100 Great Science Fiction Short-Short Stories.* New York, Doubleday, and London, Robson, 1978.
Editor, with Martin H. Greenberg and Charles G. Waugh, *The Science Fictional Solar System.* New York, Harper, 1979; London, Sidgwick and Jackson, 1980.
Editor, with Martin H. Greenberg and Charles G. Waugh, *The Thirteen Crimes of Science Fiction.* New York, Doubleday, 1979.
Editor, with Martin H. Greenberg, *The Great SF Stories 1-4.* New York, DAW, 4 vols., 1979-80.
Editor, with Martin H. Greenberg and Joseph D. Olander, *Microcosmic Tales: 100 Wondrous Science Fiction Short-Short Stories.* New York, Taplinger, 1980.
Editor, with Martin H. Greenberg and Joseph D. Olander, *Space Mail.* New York, Fawcett, 1980.
Editor, with Martin H. Greenberg and Joseph D. Olander, *The Future in Question.* New York, Fawcett, 1980.
Editor, with Alice Laurance, *Who Done It?* Boston, Houghton Mifflin, 1980.
Editor, with Martin H. Greenberg and Charles G. Waugh, *The Seven Deadly Sins of Science Fiction.* New York, Fawcett, 1980.
Editor, with Martin H. Greenberg and Joseph D. Olander, *Miniature Mysteries: 100 Malicious Little Mystery Stories.* New York, Taplinger, 1981.
Editor, with J.O. Jeppson, *Laughing Space.* Boston, Houghton Mifflin, 1981.

*

Bibliography: *Isaac Asimov: A Checklist of Works Published in the United States March 1939-May 1972* by Marjorie M. Miller, Kent, Ohio, Kent State University Press, 1972; in *In Joy Still Felt*, 1980.

Manuscript Collection: Mugar Memorial Library, Boston University.

Critical Studies: *Asimov Analyzed* by Neil Goble, Baltimore, Mirage Press, 1972; *The Science Fiction of Isaac Asimov* by Joseph F. Patrouch, Jr., New York, Doubleday, 1974, London, Panther, 1976; *Isaac Asimov* edited by Joseph D. Olander and Martin H. Greenberg, New York, Taplinger, and Edinburgh, Harris, 1977; *Asimov: The Foundations of His Science Fiction* by George Edgar Slusser, San Bernardino, California, Borgo Press, 1980.

Isaac Asimov comments:

If there is any category of human being for whom his work ought to speak for itself, it is the writer. If people *insist* on hearing from me, there are my books *Opus 100*, *Opus 200*, *The Early Asimov*, *Before the Golden Age*, *In Memory Yet Green*, and *In Joy Still Felt*, in which I tell people far more about me than they probably want to know.

* * *

It's common to find scientists who write science fiction part-time, but Isaac Asimov is quite the opposite—a writer first and foremost who occasionally dons the garb of a research biochemist. Asimov gained his credentials at Boston University some ten years after making his first sale to a science fiction magazine in 1939. For a time he managed the two careers, but as his output grew it became clear that something had to go and in the end he chose to concentrate upon writing. Not upon science fiction, unfortunately, of which he has written very little since about 1958. While his SF novels have sold in the millions of copies, with one exception they were originally published some 25-30 years ago. Of Asimov's titles to date, in fact, the vast majority are textbooks or popular science, and he has acquired a simultaneous reputation as one of the world's leading science writers, matched only by Arthur C. Clarke from within the science-fiction field.

At the age of 19 Asimov sold a story to *Amazing Stories*, but his real development as a writer took place in the pages of *Astounding* under the wing of the editor John W. Campbell, who was just beginning his marathon 33-year tenure of office. Asimov frankly acknowledges his debt to Campbell, and nowhere is this more apparent than in "Nightfall," the story that can be said to have "made" his name in science-fiction circles. To this day some readers claim this is Asimov's best story, doubtless to the author's great irritation. Its impact in 1941 was considerable, but the basic idea—what if the stars should appear just one night in a thousand years—was pointed out by Campbell. So were the celebrated "Three Laws of Robotics," around which Asimov subsequently wove some two dozen ingenious tales. A selection of these stories appeared in *I, Robot*, in 1950, and not only have they become immensely popular but the "Laws" have come to be tacitly used by an ever-growing body of later science-fiction writers. If robots should ever actually be built it is accepted that they will conform to the assumptions laid down by the 21-year old author in 1941.

Shortly after the publication of "Nightfall" Asimov commenced his most ambitious work, based originally upon a reading of

Decline and Fall of the Roman Empire. He extrapolated this into the collapse and re-birth of a future Galactic civilisation, and gradually assembled the Foundation saga from 1942-49. This was to appear as a hard-cover trilogy during the early 1950's. Both series were noted for their breadth of imagination and intricacy of plotting; now Asimov was to develop a greater degree of characterisation and human warmth in his work. The first result was *Pebble in the Sky*, an excellent novel set within the same general background as the Foundation epic although not part of the series. *The Currents of Space* was written along similar lines.

Then in 1953 Asimov produced what must be regarded in many ways as his best novel. *The Caves of Steel* is in a class by itself, successfully combining the best features of the "robotics" stories (the co-protagonist is a robot) with the social engineering of the Empire novels. It is simultaneously a view of the over-populated "hive" cities of the future, an arresting story of people coming to terms with the steel caves in which they must live, and a stimulating detective mystery, one of the few to be set within a science-fiction framework. Asimov later attempted a sequel, *The Naked Sun*, which was reasonably well received although it lacked much of the depth of vision of its predecessor. He has since resisted all entreatments to write a third novel in the series, although leaving a clear hint that one was originally intended.

During the 1960's he wrote only the occasional short science-fiction/detective story, collecting these under the title *Asimov's Mysteries*. Then in 1971/2 he did the unexpected and produced an entirely new novel, *The Gods Themselves*, which promptly won both Hugo and Nebula Awards for that year. Interesting as it was, many suspect the awards were given in appreciation of Asimov's record, rather than through the virtues of the novel alone. Certainly it is no more representative of his major achievements than was the book *Fantastic Voyage* in 1966, a novel taken from the script of the film of the same name.

But whatever Asimov writes, he writes well, be it a book about prime numbers, the Bible, or of science fiction. He has above all the ability to *communicate*, which will ensure that all of his works will have a lasting appeal.

—Peter R. Weston

ASTLEY, Thea (Beatrice May). Australian. Born in Brisbane, Queensland, 25 August 1925. Educated at the University of Queensland, Brisbane, 1943-47, B.A. 1947. Married Edmund John Gregson in 1948; one child. Taught English in Queensland, 1944-48, and in New South Wales, 1948-67. Since 1968, Senior Tutor, then Fellow, in English, Macquarie University, Sydney. Recipient: Commonwealth Literary Fund Fellowship, 1961, 1964; Miles Franklin Award, 1962, 1965, 1973; Moomba Award, 1965; *The Age* award, 1975. Address: Department of English, Macquarie University, North Ryde, Sydney, New South Wales 2113, Australia.

PUBLICATIONS

Novels

Girl with a Monkey. Sydney, Angus and Robertson, 1958.
A Descant for Gossips. Sydney and London, Angus and Robertson, 1960.
The Well-Dressed Explorer. Sydney and London, Angus and Robertson, 1962.
The Slow Natives. Sydney, Angus and Robertson, 1965; London, Angus and Robertson, 1966; New York, Evans, 1967.
A Boat Load of Home Folk. Sydney and London, Angus and Robertson, 1968.
The Acolyte. Sydney and London, Angus and Robertson, 1972.
A Kindness Cup. Melbourne, Nelson, 1974.
Hunting the Wild Pineapple. Melbourne, Nelson, 1979.

Uncollected Short Stories

"Cubby," in *Coast to Coast*. Sydney, Angus and Robertson, 1961.
"The Scenery Never Changes," in *Coast to Coast*. Sydney, Angus and Robertson, 1963.
"Journey to Olympus," in *Coast to Coast*. Sydney, Angus and Robertson, 1965.
"Seeing Mrs. Landers," in *Festival and Other Stories*, edited by Brian Buckley and Jim Hamilton. Melbourne, Wren, 1974; Newton Abbot, Devon, David and Charles, 1975.

Other

Editor, *Coast to Coast, 1969-1970*. Sydney, Angus and Robertson, 1971.

*

Critical Study: "The Idiot Question" by the author, in *Southerly 1* (Sydney), 1970.

Thea Astley comments:

(1972) My main interest (and has been through my five published and current unpublished novels) is the misfit. Not the spectacular outsider, but the seedy little non-grandiose non-fitter who lives in his own mini-hell. Years ago I was impressed at eighteen or so by *Diary of a Nobody*, delighted by the quality Grossmith gave to the non-achiever and the sympathy which he dealt out. My five published novels have always been, despite the failure of reviewers to see it, a plea for charity—in the Pauline sense, of course—to be accorded to those not ruthless enough or grand enough to be gigantic tragic figures, but which, in their own way, record the same *via crucis*.

* * *

Towards the end of Thea Astley's fifth novel (*A Boat Load of Home Folk*) a hurricane descends upon Port Lena and rages violently while the problems and personal crises of the various characters draw towards some sort of resolution. The hurricane as a destructive natural phenomenon is slightly unusual in the imaginative world of Thea Astley, but, as a symbol, it is not at all unfamiliar. For her characters seem to move perpetually in the artificially calm eye of the universe's innate anarchy: a symbolic storm encloses, yet also by its very existence and threatening nature, divides them. Moving in this constantly endangered pseudo-equilibrium, they brush often the edges of disaster, succumb to it occasionally, make what order they can with the opportunities that offer.

The impending, eager-to-consume anarchy of Astley's world is manifested variously: it can materialise as the chaos of the emotional life, that destroys identity, reduces "to a spineless receptivity" (*Girl with a Monkey*); it may take the form of spiritual annihilation by human viciousness exquisitely applied and cravenly veiled (*A Descant for Gossips*); or act through the confusing yet endlessly fascinating impulses of the uncomprehended self (*The Well-Dressed Explorer*); or emerge as that fatal disjunction from an intolerable world, experienced by those who, like "the wandering islands" of A.D. Hope's poem, ply "the long isolation of the heart" (*The Slow Natives*). Anarchy of a kind crowds in upon Astley's characters and they have few resources with which to resist it.

Because the action is caught, as it were, in the eye of the symbolic storm, her novels, especially the earlier ones, seem at times highly, even excessively, deliberated: characters move in a real enough world, yet often with fleetingly dream-like deliberateness, islands of intense self-consciousness seeking, in assertive almost desperate avowals of identity, bastions against encroaching chaos. Thus Elsie, in *Girl with a Monkey*, is "caught static in a complete island of twenty-four hours"—a metaphor which continually reinforces a sense of extreme deliberation in action and thought. When she hears, at Mass "as through walls of water," it is an apt and summary image for the action of the whole book; similarly, Mrs. Crozier is pictured as moving "Almost epileptically...pruning as she went the ambient roses...." In *A Descant for Gossips* the tragic relationship between Helen, Moller, and Vinny is captured, with momentary statuesqueness at its very inception, as "a dangerous montage," while at the end of the book, Vinny, coming to her crucial decision, is described as seeing everything with "an amazing clarity...the grass stood in millions of separate blades, green and sharp...." This has that quality of the dream that is not blurred and vague but horrifically more real than real. Again, George Brewster, hero of *The Well-Dressed Explorer*, builds his life on fantasy views of himself and dies in a "dream-streaked sleep" in which that life is paraded, insanely truncated, yet paradoxically illuminating and immensely moving. A similar quality is discoverable, though it is admittedly less obvious amidst a growing complexity, in the remaining two books.

This deliberation, even if it is occasionally overdone, is no mere quirk of "style"; it is a quality, a condition, in the characters' lives and an element in the Astley universe. And it is necessary, indeed indispensable, if the people are to affirm identity and a concept of order in the face of a chaos of evil, sordidness, deadly triviality, and cavernous loneliness.

It is difficult to determine what real weapons her characters have in this essentially rearguard action against a universe morally and spiritually anarchic. Perhaps love, but that is plagued by infidelity, impediment, or possessiveness; perhaps the child's innocence, but in this world, that innocence, followed out, brings Vinny Lalor and Keith Leverson to tragedy or near tragedy; perhaps religion. Thea Astley is certainly preoccupied with Catholic experience and upbringing, with Catholicism as an influence on personality and intellect and with the guilt and neurosis traditionally associated with Catholic sexual morality. But religion is not much comfort in the eye of the storm: it is at best irrelevant, at worst grotesque. Indeed grotesquerie and corruption become inseparable from Catholicism in Astley's vision, even if she suggests, in a way reminiscent of Greene, a road to sanctity through intimate knowledge of sin. A deeply personal conflict between religious commitment and revulsion against unhealthy inhibition and veiled corruption seems to be involved. It may be that in *A Boat Load of Home Folk*, where almost excessive sordidness and grotesqueness seem to suggest something like purgation, this conflict has reached a resolution.

Following that novel, Astley published *The Acolyte*—a brilliant, complex portrayal of the egocentric artist who enslaves and preys upon everyone around him, the more exquisitely and ruthlessly because he is blind. Like Brewster, but with much greater sophistication and intent, he creates chaos everywhere. *The Acolyte*, together with *A Kindness Cup*—a tense, remorseless study of fear and guilt which won for her the Australian Book of the Year Award in 1975—is the peak of Astley's achievement so far in the novel form. Most recently she has turned to short stories. Her linked collection *Hunting the Wild Pineapple* is witty, engaging, and relaxed, the characteristically dense, sometimes staccato style never slipping into tortuousness. The wounded and the misfits are all there; life is as uncontrollable as always. But the occasional straining for effect and the self-consciously literary moments of earlier books are gone long since. There are a mellowness and a confidence about the narrative in *Hunting the Wild Pineapple*—a now middle-aged, quizzical Keith Leverson of *The Slow Natives* is the narrator—which are the marks of a fine writer at the height of her powers.

—Brian E. Matthews

ATWOOD, Margaret (Eleanor). Canadian. Born in Ottawa, Ontario, 18 November 1939. Educated at Victoria College, University of Toronto, B.A. 1961; Radcliffe College, Cambridge, Massachusetts, A.M. 1962; Harvard University, Cambridge, Massachusetts. Lecturer in English, University of British Columbia, Vancouver, 1964-65; Instructor in English, Sir George Williams University, Montreal, 1967-68; Writer-in-Residence, University of Toronto, 1972-73. Recipient: E.J. Pratt Medal, 1961; President's Medal, University of Western Ontario, 1965; Governor-General's Award, 1966; Centennial Commission prize, 1967; Union League Civic and Arts Foundation Prize, 1969, and Bess Hokin Prize, 1974 (*Poetry*, Chicago); St. Lawrence Award, 1977; Molson Award, 1981. D.Litt.: Trent University, Peterborough, Ontario, 1973; LL.D.: Queen's University, Montreal, 1974. Lives in Ontario. Address: c/o Phoebe Larmore, 2814 Third Street, Santa Monica, California 90405, U.S.A.

PUBLICATIONS

Novels

The Edible Woman. Toronto, McClelland and Stewart, London, Deutsch, and Boston, Little Brown, 1969.
Surfacing. Toronto, McClelland and Stewart, 1972; London, Deutsch, and New York, Simon and Schuster, 1973.
Lady Oracle. Toronto, McClelland and Stewart, and New York, Simon and Schuster, 1976; London, Deutsch, 1977.
Life Before Man. New York, Simon and Schuster, and London, Cape, 1980.
Bodily Harm. Toronto, McClelland and Stewart, 1981.

Short Stories

Dancing Girls and Other Stories. Toronto, McClelland and Stewart, 1977.

Uncollected Short Story

"Betty," in *Chatelaine* (Toronto), February 1978.

Plays

Television Plays: *The Servant Girl*, 1974; *Snowbird*, 1981.

Verse

Double Persephone. Toronto, Hawkshead Press, 1961.
The Circle Game. Bloomfield Hills, Michigan, Cranbrook Academy of Art, 1964; revised edition, Toronto, Contact Press, 1966.
Talismans for Children. Bloomfield Hills, Michigan, Cranbrook Academy of Art, 1965.
Kaleidoscopes: Baroque. Bloomfield Hills, Michigan, Cranbrook Academy of Art, 1965.
Speeches for Doctor Frankenstein. Bloomfield Hills, Michigan, Cranbrook Academy of Art, 1966.
The Animals in That Country. Toronto, Oxford University Press, 1968; Boston, Little Brown, 1969.
Five Modern Canadian Poets, with others, edited by Eli Mandel. Toronto, Holt Rinehart, 1970.
The Journals of Susanna Moodie. Toronto, Oxford University Press, 1970.
Procedures for Underground. Toronto, Oxford University Press, and Boston, Little Brown, 1970.
Power Politics. Toronto, Anansi, 1972; New York, Harper, 1973.
You Are Happy. Toronto, Oxford University Press, and New York, Harper, 1974.
Selected Poems. Toronto, Oxford University Press, 1976; New York, Simon and Schuster, 1978.

Two-Headed Poems. Toronto, Oxford University Press, 1978; New York, Simon and Schuster, 1981.
True Stories. Toronto, Oxford University Press, 1981.

Recording: *The Poetry and Voice of Margaret Atwood*, Caedmon, 1977.

Other

Survival: A Thematic Guide to Canadian Literature. Toronto, Anansi, 1972.
Up in the Tree (juvenile). Toronto, McClelland and Stewart, 1978.
Anna's Pet (juvenile), with Joyce Bankhouse. Toronto, Loines, 1980.

*

Bibliography: "Margaret Atwood: An Annotated Bibliography (Prose)" by Alan J. Horne, in *The Annotated Bibliography of Canada's Major Authors 1*, edited by Robert Lecker and Jack David, Downsview, Ontario, ECW Press, 1979.

Manuscript Collection: Fisher Library, University of Toronto.

Critical Studies: *Margaret Atwood: A Symposium* edited by Linda Sandler, Victoria, British Columbia, University of Victoria, 1977; *A Violent Duality* by Sherril Grace, Montreal, Vehicule Press, 1979.

* * *

Margaret Atwood is one of Canada's most versatile writers, a fine poet with several collections to her credit, a critic whose *Survival* remains a significant study of writing in Canada, and the author of four novels, *The Edible Woman*, *Surfacing*, *Lady Oracle*, and *Life Before Man*.

The capillary links between Margaret Atwood's poetry, fiction, and criticism are many and clear. Indeed the relationship between her first novel, *The Edible Woman*, and her poems of the same period is so close that perhaps the best way of saying what the novel is about is to quote a verse from her early collection *The Circle Game*:

These days we keep
our weary distances
sparring in the vacant spaces
of peeling rooms
and rented minutes, climbing
all the expected stairs, our voices
abraded with fatigue
our bodies weary.

The Edible Woman too is about distances and defences between human beings, necessary because human beings are predators. *The Edible Woman* is a novel about emotional cannibalism, and its title names the central image. The edible woman is a cake shaped like a woman and iced for verisimilitude, which the heroine—Marian McAlpin—eats at the key point of the novel, when she is released from the doggedly normal life she has been following. Having trapped a highly normal young man into a proposal of marriage, Marian feels herself a victim of his emotional anthropophagy. Victor and victim are one. Marian's recognition of her situation takes the form of a symbolic neurosis. First her tongue closes against meat as she associates it with the living animal, then against vegetables whose agonies she imagines; finally, having tried to escape her marriage and found that escape only makes one another kind of victim, she bakes the edible woman, offers it to her shocked fiancé, and then eats it herself. In consuming the artificial "normal" being she tried to become, she is made whole.

If one associates *The Edible Woman* with Atwood's early poetry, one associates *Surfacing* with the similarly titled critical work, *Survival*, which explores the theme of the victim and his evasion of destruction in Canadian literature. But *Surfacing* resembles *The Edible Woman* in being an account of a *rite de passage*; it is a novel of self-realization, hence of life-realization, but it also contains a strong element of self-mockery. Hearing of her father's disappearance from his cabin on a northern lake, the narrator goes there with three companions, all fake *emancipés*. It is a journey into her past but also, though she does not realize it at first, into her true self. She is significantly nameless, though she names her three companions, who refer to her only as "you." "I" is in the state of inner apathy Marian reaches in *The Edible Woman*; Marian cannot assimilate food, "I" cannot absorb or generate human feeling. She describes herself as just a head, untouched and untouching. Yet, through events that explode out of her return to childhood's scenes, she recovers herself as a whole being. It is a process of surfacing, but only after submersion. The metaphors of drowning recur. Her brother almost drowned as a child; her father, she finally discovers, actually drowned searching for Indian paintings on a rock wall falling sheer to the lake; her own crisis is precipitated when, diving to locate the paintings, she sees her father's floating corpse, weighed down by his camera. Her surfacing becomes almost literally a rising from death into life.

By this time other realizations have surfaced, and "I" must shed all she has acquired, must unlearn adulthood, return through childhood and beyond humanity, become like the victim animals, as she is in the crucial chapter when, fleeing from her companions and living like a beast, she survives until the panic delirium passes away. Then she returns to a consciousness beyond the animistic world of beasts and children. The gods have departed; she is alone. "The lake is quiet, the trees surround me, asking and giving nothing." One senses, as the novel ends, that benign indifference of the universe of which Camus spoke.

In many ways *Lady Oracle* resembles its predecessors. Joan Foster, alias Louisa K. Delacourt, is obsessed with food and morbidly dominated by her parents, like the heroine of the earlier novels. Furthermore, her life exemplifies the abrasive nature of sexual relations, and during the whole present of the novel Joan is in flight from marriage, hiding in a sordid Italian coast resort town, pretending to be dead. Where *Lady Oracle* does differ from the earlier novels is in the sureness of its comedy and the accurate intensity of its satirical representation of Canadian bourgeois life—in its philistine and also its bohemian aspects. An obsessive eater who slims to win an inheritance that will liberate her, Joan has her fat and thin personalities. Out of them emerge the sensational romantic novelist, Louisa K. Delacourt, and Joan Foster the psychic poet, in which role she becomes involved with the strange vagaries of the Canadian literary world. Perhaps most impressive about *Lady Oracle* is the way Atwood has reused old themes and devices, the divided personality, the resentment of child against parent, the fatal abrasiveness of long relationships between man and woman, leading to physical escape from an intolerable situation, and has raised them to a higher level through a remarkable adeptness in the devices of comedy which her early writings had led one to expect. True, a wry ironic wit often surfaces in the earlier poetry and a good deal of sardonic fun is poked at institutions and human types in *The Edible Woman* and *Surfacing*; in both novels grotesque and fanciful situations are used to enhance the absurdity of the central predicament. But it is the sustained and uninhibited comic tone that secures Atwood's fictional achievement in *Lady Oracle* from any doubt that she can sustain her role as a novelist and avoid being caught in a groove of merely poetic fiction.

Atwood's most recent novel, *Life Before Man*, a muted narrative of emotional conflicts among employees of the Royal Ontario Museum, seems a marking of time. It has all the virtues Wilde once attributed to James—"his neat literary style, his felicitous phrases, his swift and caustic satire"—but it disturbingly tends to negate the presupposition on which the novel has been traditionally based, that the lives of men and woman necessarily have a value worth cherishing. All such assumptions are thrown in doubt in a book that rejects the illusions of hope with as much quiet rigour as Camus. I suspect *Life Before Man* does not reject compassion. But Atwood is strangely reticent about declaring it.

—George Woodcock

AUCHINCLOSS, Louis (Stanton). American. Born in Lawrence, New York, 17 September 1917. Educated at Groton School, Connecticut, graduated 1935; Yale University, New Haven, Connecticut, 1935-38; University of Virginia Law School, Charlottesville, LL.B. 1941; admitted to the New York Bar, 1941. Served in the United States Naval Reserve, 1941-45: Lieutenant. Married Adèle Lawrence in 1957; three sons. Associate Lawyer, Sullivan and Cromwell, New York, 1941-51. Associate, 1954-58, and since 1958 Partner, Hawkins Delafield and Wood, New York. Since 1966, President of the Museum of the City of New York. Trustee, Josiah Macy Jr. Foundation, New York; Member of the Executive Committee, Association of the Bar of New York City. D.Litt.: New York University, 1974; Pace College, New York, 1979. Member, American Academy. Address: 1111 Park Avenue, New York, New York 10028, U.S.A.

PUBLICATIONS

Novels

The Indifferent Children (as Andrew Lee). New York, Prentice Hall, 1947.
Sybil. Boston, Houghton Mifflin, 1951; London, Gollancz, 1952.
A Law for the Lion. Boston, Houghton Mifflin, and London, Gollancz, 1953.
The Great World and Timothy Colt. Boston, Houghton Mifflin, 1956; London, Gollancz, 1957.
Venus in Sparta. Boston, Houghton Mifflin, and London, Gollancz, 1958.
Pursuit of the Prodigal. Boston, Houghton Mifflin, 1959; London, Gollancz, 1960.
The House of Five Talents. Boston, Houghton Mifflin, 1960; London, Gollancz, 1961.
Portrait in Brownstone. Boston, Houghton Mifflin, and London, Gollancz, 1962.
The Rector of Justin. Boston, Houghton Mifflin, 1964; London, Gollancz, 1965.
The Embezzler. Boston, Houghton Mifflin, and London, Gollancz, 1966.
A World of Profit. Boston, Houghton Mifflin, 1968; London, Gollancz, 1969.
I Come as a Thief. Boston, Houghton Mifflin, 1972; London, Weidenfeld and Nicolson, 1973.
The Partners. Boston, Houghton Mifflin, and London, Weidenfeld and Nicolson, 1974.
The Winthrop Covenant. Boston, Houghton Mifflin, and London, Weidenfeld and Nicolson, 1976.
The Dark Lady. Boston, Houghton Mifflin, and London, Weidenfeld and Nicolson, 1977.
The Country Cousin. Boston, Houghton Mifflin, and London, Weidenfeld and Nicolson, 1978.
The House of the Prophet. Boston, Houghton Mifflin, and London, Weidenfeld and Nicolson, 1980.
The Cat and the King. Boston, Houghton Mifflin, 1981.

Short Stories

The Injustice Collectors. Boston, Houghton Mifflin, 1950; London, Gollancz, 1951.
The Romantic Egoists: A Reflection in Eight Minutes. Boston, Houghton Mifflin, and London, Gollancz, 1954.
Powers of Attorney. Boston, Houghton Mifflin, and London, Gollancz, 1963.
Tales of Manhattan. Boston, Houghton Mifflin, and London, Gollancz, 1967.
Second Chance. Boston, Houghton Mifflin, 1970; London, Gollancz, 1971.

Uncollected Short Stories

"The Adventures of Johnny Flashback," in *Saturday Review* (New York), 22 October 1955.
"The Trial of Mr. M.," in *Harper's* (New York), October 1956.
"Ghost of Hamlet's Ghost," in *Harper's Bazaar* (New York), June 1971.
"Cup of Coffee," in *Ladies' Home Journal* (Des Moines, Iowa), July 1973.
"Stories of Death and Society," in *New York Magazine*, 23 July 1973.
"The Seagull," in *Atlantic* (Boston), May 1979.

Play

The Club Bedroom (produced New York, 1967).

Other

Edith Wharton. Minneapolis, University of Minnesota Press, 1961.
Reflections of a Jacobite. Boston, Houghton Mifflin, 1961; London, Gollancz, 1962.
Ellen Glasgow. Minneapolis, University of Minnesota Press, 1964.
Pioneers and Caretakers: A Study of 9 American Women Novelists. Minneapolis, University of Minnesota Press, 1965; London, Oxford University Press, 1966.
Motiveless Malignity (on Shakespeare). Boston, Houghton Mifflin, 1969; London, Gollancz, 1970.
Henry Adams. Minneapolis, University of Minnesota Press, 1971.
Edith Wharton: A Woman in Her Time. New York, Viking Press, 1971; London, Joseph, 1972.
Richelieu. New York, Viking Press, 1972; London, Joseph, 1973.
A Writer's Capital (autobiography). Minneapolis, University of Minnesota Press, 1974.
Reading Henry James. Minneapolis, University of Minnesota Press, 1975.
Persons of Consequence: Queen Victoria and Her Circle. New York, Random House, and London, Weidenfeld and Nicolson, 1979.
Life, Law, and Letters: Essays and Sketches. Boston, Houghton Mifflin, 1979; London, Weidenfeld and Nicolson, 1980.

Editor, *An Edith Wharton Reader.* New York, Scribner, 1965.
Editor, *The Warden, and Barchester Towers,* by Trollope. Boston, Houghton Mifflin, 1966.
Editor, *Fables of Wit and Elegance.* New York, Scribner, 1975.

*

Bibliography: *Louis Auchincloss and His Critics: A Bibliographical Record* by Jackson R. Bryer, Boston, Hall, 1977.

Manuscript Collection: Yale University, New Haven, Connecticut.

Louis Auchincloss comments:

(1972) I do not think in general that authors are very illuminating on their own work, but in view of the harshness of recent (1970) reviewers, I should like to quote from a letter of Edith Wharton in my collection. It was written when she was 63, ten years older than I now am, but the mood is relevant. She is speaking of critics who have disliked her last novel: "You will wonder that the priestess of the life of reason should take such things to heart, and I wonder too. I never have minded before, but as my work reaches its close, I feel so sure that it is either nothing or far more than they know. And I wonder, a little desolately, which." Mrs. Wharton's work was far from its close, and I hope mine may be!

* * *

Louis Auchincloss is among the few dedicated novelists of manners at work in contemporary America. He is a successor to Edith Wharton as a chronicler of the New York aristocracy. In this role he necessarily imbues his novels with an elegiac tone as he observes the passing beauties of the city and the fading power of the white Anglo-Saxon Protestants of old family and old money who can no longer sustain their position of dominance in the society or their aristocratic ideals. His principal subject is thus the manners and morals, the money and marriages, the families and houses, the schools and games, the language and arts of the New York aristocracy as he traces its rise, observes its present crisis, and meditates its possible fall and disappearance. The point of vantage from which he often observes the aristocracy is that of the lawyer who serves and frequently belongs to this class.

The idea of good family stands in an uneasy relation to money in Auchincloss's fiction. Auchincloss dramatizes the dilemma of the American aristocracy by showing that it is necessary to possess money to belong to this class but fatal to one's standing within the class to pursue money. People who have connections with those who are still in trade cannot themselves fully qualify as gentlemen, as the opportunistic Mr. Dale in *The Great World and Timothy Colt* shows. On the other hand, Auchincloss is clearly critical of those aristocrats like Bertie Millinder or Percy Prime who do nothing constructive and are engaged simply in the spending of money. Auchincloss recognizes that the family is the most important of aristocratic institutions and that its place in its class is guaranteed by the conservation of its resources. This task of preserving the family wealth falls to the lawyers, and his fiction is rich in the complexities, both moral and financial, of fiduciary responsibility; *Venus in Sparta* is a novel in point. The paradox that Auchincloss reveals but does not seem sufficiently to exploit is that the conservative impulse of the aristocracy, which emphasizes the past, is concerned ultimately with posterity, which of course emphasizes the future.

Auchincloss does, however, fully exploit the conflict between the marriage arranged for the good of the family, often by strong women, and romantic or sexual impulses that are destructive of purely social goals, as *Portrait in Brownstone* illustrates. Sex and love are enemies to the organicism of conservative societies, in which the will of the individual is vested in the whole. Auchincloss observes the workings of this organic notion in the structure of family and marriage as well as in institutions like the school and the club where a consensus judgment about value and behaviour is formulated and handed down. Such institutions preserve a way of life and protect those who live by it from those on the outside who do not. *The Rector of Justin* is the most obvious of Auchincloss's novels to deal with an institution, or with a man as an institution, that performs this function.

Auchincloss's fiction does more than present us with a mere record of the institutions that support the American aristocracy. The dramatic interest in his novels and whatever larger importance may be accorded them lies in his recognition that the entire class is in jeopardy and that individual aristocrats are often failures. The closed, unitary life of the aristocracy is sometimes threatened by outsiders—Jews, for example, as in *The Dark Lady* and *The House of the Prophet*—who must be repelled or at worst absorbed. Sometimes Auchincloss sees problems arising within the context of aristocracy itself, as when individual will or desire comes in conflict with the organicism; perhaps Reese Parmalee, in *Pursuit of the Prodigal*, makes the most significant rebellion of all Auchincloss's characters, but he is rejecting a decadent aristocracy and not aristocracy itself. Auchincloss is severely critical of the idea of the gentleman when it is corrupted by allegiance to superficial qualities, like Guy Prime's capacity to hold his liquor or to behave with virile cordiality in *The Embezzler*. But the real failures are those aristocrats who suffer, as so many of Auchincloss's male characters do, from a sense of inadequacy and insecurity that leads them to self-destructiveness. They are not strong and tough-fibred, as so many of the women are; they seem too fastidious and over-civilized, and they are failing the idea of society and their class. In this way, and in others, Auchincloss regretfully chronicles the passing of the aristocracy, which cannot sustain its own ideals in the contemporary world: *A World of Profit* is the most explicit recognition of this failure.

Auchincloss has made his record of the New York aristocracy in a style which is clear and simple, occasionally elegant and brilliant, and sometimes self-consciously allusive. He has a gift for comedy of manners, which he has not sufficiently cultivated, and a fine model in Oscar Wilde. Other influences upon him include Edith Wharton, in ways already mentioned; Henry James, from whom he learned the manipulation of point of view and the faculty of endowing things, art objects for example, with meaning; and St. Simon, a memorialist who did for the French court what Auchincloss wishes to do for Knickerbocker New York. Yet among his faults as a novelist, especially evident because of the particular genre he has chosen, is a failure to give the reader a richness of detail; he does well with home furnishings but is far less successful with the details of institutions. Furthermore, he sometimes loses control of his novels and permits action to overwhelm theme. The most serious criticism to be made of his work is that while he does indeed pose moral dilemmas for his characters, he too easily resolves their problems for them. He does not sufficiently convey a sense of the bitter cost of honesty or courage or moral superiority, a continuing difficulty for him, as *The Country Cousin* demonstrates. He has given us, on balance, a full enough record of upper-class life in New York, but he has fallen short of the most penetrating and meaningful kinds of social insight that the best of the novelists of manners offer.

—Chester E. Eisinger

BAILEY, Paul. British. Born in Battersea, London, 16 February 1937. Educated at the Sir Walter St. John's School, London, 1948-53; Central School of Speech and Drama, London, 1953-56. Actor, 1956-63. Currently, Publisher's Reader for Jonathan Cape Ltd., London. Recipient: Maugham Award, 1968; Arts Council Award, 1968; Authors' Club Award, 1970; E.M. Forster Award (USA), 1974; Bicentennial Arts Fellowship, 1976. Address: 79 Davisville Road, London W. 12, England.

PUBLICATIONS

Novels

At the Jerusalem. London, Cape, and New York, Atheneum, 1967.
Trespasses. London, Cape, 1970; New York, Harper, 1971.
A Distant Likeness. London, Cape, 1973.
Peter Smart's Confessions. London, Cape, 1977.
Old Soldiers. London, Cape, 1980.

Plays

A Worthy Guest (produced Newcastle upon Tyne, 1973; London, 1974).
Alice (produced Newcastle upon Tyne, 1975).
Crime and Punishment, adaptation of a novel by Dostoevsky (produced Manchester, 1978).

Radio Play: *At Cousin Harry's*, 1964.

Television Play: *We Think the World of You*, with Tristram Powell, 1980.

*

Critical Studies: review by Irving Wardle, in *The Observer* (London), 28 May 1967; Alan Ross, in *London Magazine*, October 1967; Maggie Ross in *The Listener* (London), 30 April 1970.

Paul Bailey comments:

I write novels for many reasons, some of which I have probably never consciously thought of. I don't like absolute moral judgments, the "placing" of people into types—I'm both delighted and appalled by the mysteriousness of my fellow creatures. I enjoy "being" other people when I write, and the novels I admire most respect the uniqueness of other human beings. I like to think I show my characters respect and that I don't sit in judgment on them. This is what, in my small way, I am striving for—to capture, in a shaped and controlled form, something of the mystery of life. I am writing, too, to expand and stimulate my own mind. I hope I will have the courage to be more ambitious, bolder and braver in my search for the ultimately unknowable, with each book I write.

* * *

Paul Bailey's first novel, *At the Jerusalem*, has been rightly acknowledged as one of the outstanding literary debuts of the 1960's in England, and among the reasons why it attracted attention when it appeared was that it departed so markedly from our usual expectations of first novels—autobiographies in thin disguise. What came as a surprise was to find a first novel by a young man in his twenties about old age and its attendant tribulations. Yet Bailey's achievement did not, of course, lie in merely writing about the elderly and their problems, but in doing so with such sympathetic understanding and sensitivity while maintaining sufficient detachment and objectivity to avoid any trace of sentimentality. There is no falsification, no whimsy, none of that awkwardness and emotional uncertainty that tend to afflict writers when dealing with the old. Bailey's depiction of an old people's home, the Jerusalem of the title, and especially of the central character, Mrs. Gadny, whose fairly rapid decline after entering the home is charted, carries complete conviction. Quiet and unpretentious as *At the Jerusalem* is, it is also an extraordinary feat of the imagination.

In retrospect, we can now see that *At the Jerusalem* introduced many of the themes and preoccupations which have come to be integral components of the Bailey world: isolation, suffering, death, suicide, old age, the pain of loss, psychological collapse, role-playing in an attempt to bear or ward off reality. If *At the Jerusalem* is mainly a study of disintegration—Mrs. Gadny's fate is to be taken to a mental hospital—Bailey's second novel, *Trespasses*, partly set in a mental hospital, is about an attempt at reintegration after personal breakdown and fragmentation. Surprisingly for a Bailey novel, *Trespasses* ends on a note of muted optimism, but much of the book is pervaded by anguish, leading to suicide in the case of one character and mental collapse in the case of another. Technically, *Trespasses* is a much more adventurous work than the fairly orthodox and straightforward *At the Jerusalem*. Some sections of the novel are collages of short, fragmented monologues, appropriate enough for the subject but demanding considerable concentration and imaginative involvement on the part of the reader, who has to construct the total picture from the pieces like a jig-saw puzzle. This intricate cross-cutting between different minds is a most economical way of revealing characters and events; narrated in a conventional way, the novel would be very much longer and far less intense than it is, and the technique justifies itself as the pieces finally cohere into a highly organized pattern.

Bailey's pursuit of poetic concentration, a concomitant of his increasing technical sophistication and artistic discipline, is taken a stage further in his third novel, *A Distant Likeness*. Like *Trespasses*, the novel is fragmented and elliptical so that the reader again has to work hard to piece the information together. Bailey is almost as sparing of words as Webern was of musical notes. The book, about a policeman in charge of a murder investigation, is another study in disintegration, resulting in this case from the policeman's inner contradictions. Many critics have felt the "distant likeness" to be between the policeman and the murderer, but the sentence from Simone Weil's *Notebooks* that provides the novel with its title, "Privation is a distant likeness of death," is perhaps the key to the interpretation of this complex book. Bailey's subject is privation, and it appears in various forms. *A Distant Likeness* has been compared to *Crime and Punishment*, but Bailey's novel is not so much like Dostoevsky as a distillation of a super-refined Dostoevskian essence. The extreme compression can be likened to T.S. Eliot's miniaturization of epic form in *The Waste Land*, a parallel that suggests itself because of similarities between the imagery of the two works.

After the minimalist austerity and purity, as well as human bleakness, of *A Distant Likeness*, Bailey altered course somewhat, producing a much more relaxed novel in a comic, even picaresque, vein, *Peter Smart's Confessions*. Here the Dickensian side of his talent, evident but not prominent in his earlier books, is given freer rein, although he maintains his usual technical and stylistic control, never wasting words. *Peter Smart's Confessions* is a kind of *bildungsroman*, dealing with the development of a sensitive and artistic boy surrounded by philistinism and other forms of paralysing opposition. Yet much of the interest lies in the gallery of eccentrics and extraordinary characters with whom Peter comes into contact rather than in Peter himself. The later stages of the novel are more desultory and less subtle than the brilliant first half, but the novel as a whole opened up new possibilities for Bailey.

His most recent novel, *Old Soldiers*, is his most completely satisfying since *At the Jerusalem*, and is also about old age, the two main characters being men in their seventies with unforgettable memories of the First World War—hence the title. Technically, the novel is not as "difficult" as *Trespasses* or *A Distant Likeness*, but it resembles them in its brevity, imagistic density, and dependence on suggestion rather than statement. As usual, much is left unsaid. Bailey's treatment of the two very different men, who are nevertheless drawn together after their paths cross, again reveals one of his central concerns as a novelist to be the essential isolation of human beings, the way in which everyone lives and dies alone. He exposes the vulnerable core at the heart of all individuals, the strategies by which people try to disguise their vulnerability and protect themselves from the daily assault of reality, including the inevitability of death. This marks him as a descendant of Conrad, a novelist he greatly admires. Yet if Bailey peels away the deceptions and self-deceptions, the masks and pretences, by which his characters live, he does so with enormous sympathy for their predicament. Bailey respects the uniqueness of individuals, and possesses the true novelist's fascination with people of every description. His novels succeed in widening our sympathy, extending our imagination, and expanding our consciousness.

—Peter Lewis

BAINBRIDGE, Beryl (Margaret). British. Born in Liverpool, Lancashire, 21 November 1934. Educated at Merchant Taylors' School, London; ballet school in Tring, Hertfordshire. Married Austin Davies in 1955 (divorced, 1959); one son and two daughters. Actress with repertory theatres in Liverpool, Windsor, Salisbury, Wiltshire, London, and Dundee, Scotland, 1949-60; worked as a cellar woman in a bottle factory, London, 1970; Clerk, Gerald Duckworth Ltd., publishers, London, 1971-73. Recipient: *Guardian* Prize, 1974; Whitbread Literary Award, 1977. Fellow, Royal Society of Literature, 1978. Address: 42 Albert Street, London NW1 7NU, England.

PUBLICATIONS

Novels

A Weekend with Claude. London, Hutchinson, 1967.
Another Part of the Wood. London, Hutchinson, 1968; revised edition, London, Duckworth, 1979; New York, Braziller, 1980.
Harriet Said. London, Duckworth, 1972; New York, Braziller, 1973.
The Dressmaker. London, Duckworth, 1973; as *The Secret Glass*, New York, Braziller, 1974.
The Bottle Factory Outing. London, Duckworth, 1974; New York, Braziller, 1975.
Sweet William. London, Duckworth, 1975; New York, Braziller, 1976.
A Quiet Life. London, Duckworth, 1976; New York, Braziller, 1977.
Injury Time. London, Duckworth, 1977; New York, Braziller, 1978.
Young Adolf. London, Duckworth, 1978; New York, Braziller, 1979.
Winter Garden. London, Duckworth, 1980; New York, Braziller, 1981.

Uncollected Short Stories

"Eric on the Agenda," in *Bananas*, edited by Emma Tennant. London, Quartet-Blond and Briggs, 1977.
"Beggars Would Ride," in *Winter's Tales 26*, edited by A.D. Maclean. London, Macmillan, 1980; New York, St. Martin's Press, 1981.

Plays

Screenplay: *Sweet William*, 1980.

Radio Play: *Clap Hands, Here Comes Charlie*, 1981.

Television Plays: *Tiptoe Through the Tulips*, 1976; *Blue Skies from Now On*, 1977; *The Warrior's Return* (*The Velvet Glove* series), 1977; *Words Fail Me*, 1979; *The Journal of Bridget Hitler*, with Philip Saville, 1981; *Somewhere More Central*, 1981.

Other

Editor, *New Stories 6.* London, Hutchinson, 1981.

*

Beryl Bainbridge comments:

(1976) As a novelist I am committing to paper, for my own satisfaction, episodes that I have lived through. If I had had a camera forever ready with a film I might not have needed to write. I am not very good at fiction...it is always me and the experiences I have had. In my last three novels I have used the device of accidental death because I feel that a book has to have a strong narrative line. One's own life, whilst being lived, seems to have no obvious plot and is therefore without tension.

I think writing is a very indulgent pastime and I would probably do it even if nobody ever read anything.

I write about the sort of childhood I had, my parents, the landscape I grew up in: my writing is an attempt to record the past. I am of the firm belief that everybody could write books and I never understand why they don't. After all, everyone speaks. Once the grammar has been learnt it is simply talking on paper and in time learning what not to say.

* * *

With the exception of *Sweet William*, each of Beryl Bainbridge's novels is centered on a death or an act of violence. Her novels are also overshadowed by generalized violence, usually the Second World War. *The Dressmaker* evokes the Liverpudlian home front during the war, while *A Quiet Life* is set in the immediate postwar period, with German prisoners-of-war waiting to be repatriated, and *Harriet Said* slightly later, amid vivid memories of Italian prisoners-of-war. In *A Weekend with Claude*, the old Jewess may not forget the concentration camps, which in a sinisterly different way obsess the "Commandant" of the camping site in the earlier version of *Another Part of the Wood.* Since *Young Adolf* takes off from the possibility that Hitler may have lived in Liverpool in 1909, the book's very conception foreshadows the Holocaust and the war. *Injury Time* draws on a background of terrorism and armed crime in contemporary London, while another London novel, *The Bottle Factory Outing*, relies for its effect on the build-up of a violently foreboding atmosphere in and around the bottle factory, without any historical cause. Beryl Bainbridge's novels in fact work largely by such build-up of violent atmosphere, drawn from both external circumstances and the characters themselves; this typically erupts in a death, albeit apparently accidental, in the characters' immediate circle.

In *A Weekend with Claude* the central act of violence is a shooting, innocuous in its effect whatever its intention. Like her second novel, *Another Part of the Wood*, which Bainbridge later rewrote, it lacks the taut spareness which distinguishes her work from *Harriet Said* on.

The questions of responsibility which her novels often beg so stylishly are twofold in *Harriet Said*; not only is the killing accidental, but it's done by a 13-year-old. On one level, the book is an amusing portrayal by a girl of her friend's sexuality and unnatural "wisdom": "We both tried very hard to give our parents love, and security, but they were too demanding." In *The Dressmaker* a young girl's pathetic first love for an American G.I. unfolds towards death against the stark symbolism of the work of the dressmaker, who "dreamed she was following mother down a country garden, severing with sharp scissors the heads of roses." Through the more flamboyant black comedy of *The Bottle Factory Outing* flickers the rare lyricism that as elsewhere in Bainbridge's work is a measure of her Joycean acceptance of her characters. This lyrical quality derives from the setting; the garden in *A Weekend with Claude* has become Windsor Great Park in the later novel. But the death precludes total acceptance.

In *Sweet William*, a girl bedsitting in London falls disastrously in love with the Don Juan of the title, a philandering playwright who moves nonchalantly among the human wreckage he creates. Outstanding here is the portrait of the girl's mother; it was in reaction against her vicious pettiness that the daughter was vulnerable to William. *A Quiet Life* takes an archetypal nuclear family to focus devastatingly again on what children become in reaction to their parents and, as it's hinted, in turn cause any children they have to react against. Bainbridge begins several novels with a Chapter 0, implying what is to come, and here she both begins and ends with this device, as brother and sister encounter each other 15 years later.

Injury Time describes the unorthodox dinner-party of a middle-aged quartet, accidentally taken as hostages in a siege, to the especial embarrassment of a married man dining *chez* his mistress. Beneath the black comedy, and as moulded by formative early experiences, the meaner and more generous impulses of the two main characters come through, in all their ambivalence.

Young Adolf is Bainbridge's most ambitious book, with the tension deriving from our knowledge of what is to come, historically. Against this appalling factual scenario, details like the brown shirt made for the penniless Adolf by his sister-in-law—so that "he needn't sit wrapped in a blanket while his other one was in the wash"—are the blackest black comedy imaginable, though some readers may feel the subject ultimately precludes any such treatment.

In the revised version of *Another Part of the Wood* a death occurs through negligence, and here the responsibility is sharply brought home. Perhaps some of the other accidental deaths in Beryl Bainbridge's brilliant novels may be mistaken, as by sensationalizing they distract attention from the composite picture of egotisms that the black comedy of her various ambiences pillories so unnervingly.

—Val Warner

BAKER, Elliott. American. Born in Buffalo, New York, 15 December 1911. Educated at Indiana University, Bloomington, B.S. 1944. Served in the United States Army. Recipient: Putnam Award, 1964. Address: c/o Morton L. Leavy, 437 Madison Avenue, New York, New York 10022, U.S.A.

PUBLICATIONS

Novels

A Fine Madness. New York, Putnam, and London, Joseph, 1964.
The Penny Wars. New York, Putnam, 1968; London, Joseph, 1969.
Pocock and Pitt. New York, Putnam, 1971; London, Joseph, 1972.
Klynt's Law. New York, Harcourt Brace, and London, Joseph, 1976.
And We Were Young. New York, Times, 1979; London, Joseph, 1980.

Short Stories

Unrequited Loves. New York, Putnam, and London, Joseph, 1974.

Plays

The Delinquent, *The Hipster*, and *The Square* (broadcast, 1959). Published in *The Delinquent, The Hipster, The Square, and the Sandpile Series*, edited by Alva I. Cox, Jr. St. Louis, Bethany Press, 1962.
The Penny Wars (produced New York, 1969).

Screenplays: *A Fine Madness*, 1966; *Luv*, 1967; *Viva Max*, 1970.

Radio Plays: *The Delinquent*, *The Hipster*, and *The Square*, 1959.

*

Manuscript Collection: Indiana University, Bloomington.

* * *

Elliott Baker's first novels, *A Fine Madness* and *The Penny Wars*, demonstrate a diversity of ideas and themes but focus on moral and psychological growth and the life of the imagination. They are comic views of modern America informed by an underlying sense of tragedy or tragic potential. Baker's later works continue to present this tension.

A Fine Madness depicts the triumph of an artist, a kind of American Gulley Jimson, over the forces of conformity and death-in-life. Samson Shillitoe, a working-class hero, a Blakean poet driven by powerful artistic and sexual urges, is pursued and seized by a group of psychiatric experimenters. He is analyzed, institutionalized, and lobotomized but emerges whole, sane, and uncastrated, his creative (and procreative) energies intact. Baker uses his inside knowledge of modern psychotherapy to show the artist at war with a mechanical world and the mechanized minds of clinical psychology. Shillitoe is obsessed by imagination, driven by forces beyond his control. He is amoral, anti-social, unconcerned with "adjustment" or mental health. The psychologists view him only as a specimen, a sample of neurosis or psychosis. Shillitoe's view triumphs: he conceives and produces an epic-sized poem and his common-law wife conceives his child. Life and creation vanquish death and destruction.

In *The Penny Wars* Baker creates a nostalgic vision of adolescence on the eve of World War II. Tyler Bishop, another rebel, grows up in 1939 in squalor and confusion of values. An unreconstructed liberal, Tyler worries about the Nazis while America's smugness and isolationism seem invincible, worries about his budding sexuality, worries about the world he will inherit. Himself a WASP, he stands up for Jews and Negroes, fights bigotry and ignorance—and loses. Through a series of social confrontations, Tyler begins to find his way toward a self-sufficient individualism.

Unrequited Loves, a set of related novellas, documents the youth (1939-45) of a persona named "Elliott Baker," especially initiations into love and sex. Each story is a comic odyssey wherein the young man discovers the battles and truces in the war between men and women. It is Baker's most genial and optimistic book, focusing the nostalgia of *The Penny Wars* on our national pastimes—love, war, baseball, growing up.

Pocock and Pitt is a satirical exploration of identity and childhood in the modern world. Wendell Pocock, American middle-class victim of repeated heart attacks, becomes Winston Pitt, British worker in an organ bank. A pawn in an international espionage duel, he discovers genuine love and redemption after exhausting the cold consolations of history and philosophy. The novel develops the slapstick meditations of *A Fine Madness* and widens Baker's scope to the state of the whole modern world.

Klynt's Law is a *tour de force* in combining genres—a satirical "college novel," a thriller of Las Vegas criminal shenanigans, a study of parapsychology and gambling compulsions. In it, Tobias Klynt (a.k.a. Kleinmann), an archetypal *klutz*, breaks with his shrewish wife, his university career, and the straight world to put the para-normal talents of four students to work on roulette wheels. They have evolved the perfect "system" to beat Las Vegas but fail to understand that gambling is not for winners. The irony is alternately black and farcical, and, as in all good gambling stories, winners are losers.

The same is true in *And We Were Young*, which traces four ex-rifle-squad members in the red-scare years after World War II. A tangle of coincidences—or synchronistic ironies—brings them together in New York City, where each betrays his youthful desires and beliefs in the enveloping glaciers of the Cold War. The book extends Baker's picture of the generation that grew up with World War II, begun in *The Penny Wars* and *Unrequited Loves*, and develops his vision of our society as it changed radically in a new internationalist world.

—William J. Schafer

BALDWIN, James (Arthur). American. Born in New York City, 2 August 1924. Educated at Public School 139, Harlem, New York, and DeWitt Clinton High School, Bronx, New York. Lived in Europe, mainly in Paris, 1948-56. Member, Actors Studio, New York; National Advisory Board of CORE (Congress on Racial Equality); and National Committee for a Sane Nuclear Policy. Recipient: Saxton Fellowship, 1945; Rosenwald Fellowship, 1948; Guggenheim Fellowship, 1954; American Academy award, 1956; Ford Fellowship, 1958; National Conference of Christians and Jews Brotherhood Award, 1962; George Polk Award, 1963; Foreign Drama Critics Award, 1964; Martin Luther King, Jr., Award, City University of New York, 1978. D.Litt.: University of British Columbia, Vancouver, 1963. Member, American Academy, 1964. Lives in New York City. Agent: Tria G.B. French, 118 Rue la Boétie, Paris 75008, France. Address: c/o Dial Press, 1 Dag Hammarskjold Plaza, New York, New York 10017, U.S.A.

PUBLICATIONS

Novels

Go Tell It on the Mountain. New York, Knopf, 1953; London, Joseph, 1954.
Giovanni's Room. New York, Dial Press, 1956; London, Joseph, 1957.
Another Country. New York, Dial Press, 1962; London, Joseph, 1963.
Tell Me How Long the Train's Been Gone. New York, Dial Press, and London, Joseph, 1968.
If Beale Street Could Talk. New York, Dial Press, and London, Joseph, 1974.
Just above My Head. New York, Dial Press, and London, Joseph, 1979.

Short Stories

Going to Meet the Man. New York, Dial Press, and London, Joseph, 1965.

Uncollected Short Stories

"Any Day Now," in *Partisan Review* (New Brunswick, New Jersey), Spring 1960.
"Exodus," in *American Negro Short Stories*, edited by John Henrik Clarke. New York, Hill and Wang, 1966.
"Equal in Parts," in *Travelers.* New York, Macmillan, 1972.

Plays

The Amen Corner (produced Washington, D.C., 1955; New York, Edinburgh, and London, 1965). New York, Dial Press, 1968.
Blues for Mr. Charlie (produced New York, 1964; London, 1965). New York, Dial Press, 1964; London, Joseph, 1965.
One Day, When I Was Lost: A Scenario Based on "The Autobiography of Malcolm X." London, Joseph, 1972; New York, Dial Press, 1973.
A Deed from the King of Spain (produced New York, 1974).

Screenplay: *The Inheritance*, 1973.

Other

Notes of a Native Son. Boston, Beacon Press, 1955; London, Joseph, 1964.
Nobody Knows My Name: More Notes of a Native Son. New York, Dial Press, 1961; London, Joseph, 1964.
The Fire Next Time. New York, Dial Press, and London, Joseph, 1963.
Nothing Personal, photographs by Richard Avedon. New York, Atheneum, and London, Penguin, 1964.
A Rap on Race, with Margaret Mead. Philadelphia, Lippincott, and London, Joseph, 1971.
No Name in the Street. New York, Dial Press, and London, Joseph, 1972.
A Dialogue: James Baldwin and Nikki Giovanni. Philadelphia, Lippincott, 1973; London, Joseph, 1975.
Little Man, Little Man (juvenile). London, Joseph, 1976; New York, Dial Press, 1977.
The Devil Finds Work: An Essay. New York, Dial Press, and London, Joseph, 1976.

*

Bibliography: "James Baldwin: A Checklist, 1947-1962" by Kathleen A. Kindt, and "James Baldwin: A Bibliography, 1947-1962" by Russell G. Fischer, both in *Bulletin of Bibliography* (Boston), January-April 1965; *James Baldwin: A Reference Guide* by Fred L. and Nancy Standley, Boston, Hall, 1979.

Critical Studies: *The Furious Passage of James Baldwin* by Fern Eckman, New York, Evans, 1966, London, Joseph, 1968; *James Baldwin: A Critical Study* by Stanley Macebuh, New York, Third Press, 1973, London, Joseph, 1975; *James Baldwin: A Collection of Critical Essays* edited by Keneth Kinnamon, Englewood Cliffs, New Jersey, Prentice Hall, 1974; *James Baldwin: A Critical Evaluation* edited by Therman B. O'Daniel, Washington, D.C., Howard University Press, 1975; *James Baldwin* by Louis H. Pratt, Boston, Twayne, 1978; *James Baldwin* by Carolyn W. Sylvander, New York, Ungar, 1981.

Theatrical Activities:

Director: **Film** — *The Inheritance*, 1973.

James Baldwin comments:

I have always found it difficult to speak of my own work. I am not altogether certain that I can identify my "subjects" and "themes." The life that I was born into, or the life that I have lived—which are not, necessarily, the same—certainly account, to some degree, for the structure of my mind. I have made a certain conscious effort to avoid sentimentality. I am still making that effort.

* * *

James Baldwin, the most eloquently intense and morally insistent essayist in midcentury America has published six novels and a book of short stories. Some of his fiction, like some of his drama, has stimulated controversy; but there is general agreement that he has done masterful work in both the novel and the short story forms.

Go Tell It on the Mountain, Baldwin's first and best novel, centered upon the religious conversion of John Grimes the night of his 14th birthday, is divided into three parts. Part I, "The Seventh Day," introduces the Grimes family in Harlem in March 1935. John feels locked in by the repressive, doom-ridden preachments of his father Gabriel, head deacon of the store-front Temple of the Fire Baptized, and is guiltily aware of sex. He hates his father reciprocally, sometimes hates his mother, and will soon hate all white people—whom his father despises—"if God did not change his heart."

Part II, "The Prayers of the Saints," which comprises in flashbacks well over half the novel, provides background for the family dilemma of John. His 60-year-old Aunt Florence, driven by her fear of death from cancer, recalls in her prayer the following: the slavery-time memories of her and Gabriel's mother, who envisioned a dominant masculine role in Black family life; Florence's departure from the South in 1900 after her white employer "proposed that she become his concubine"; and the marital love between her and caramel-colored Frank—ended after ten years by her disdain for his "common nigger" friends and by her jars of skin-whitener (despite Frank's reminder that "black's a mighty pretty color"). Florence ends her prayer bitterly asking why God "preferred her mother and her brother, the old, black woman, and the low, black man, while she, who had sought only to walk upright, was come to die, alone and in poverty, in a dirty, furnished room?"

Gabriel, in the long section on his prayer, relives highlights of his 21st through 40th years, mainly his affair with Esther and the birth and death at 18 of their son Royal. This affair, preceded by wild young Gabriel's marriage of repentance to bony, "sexless" Deborah, humanizes him as trapped in contradictory pietistic and lustful urges so delicately balanced within him as to demand rigid, defensive behavior. Significant are young Gabriel's criticism of "big, comfortable, ordained" ministers at the Twenty-Four Elders Revival Meeting; the intimation of the perfect coincidence of death and life at the burial of Esther and later at the news of her son Royal's death; and John's sense of the artistic value of hatred: "He did not *want* to love his father; he wanted to hate him, to cherish that hatred, and give his hatred words one day." Stylistically notable are the poetic prose description of Gabriel's autumn flight after deserting Esther, and the use of sound, silence, and group movement to signal flashbacks.

Elizabeth, in her section, recalls what love has meant to her. Deprived of her sick mother's questionable love by death, and of her disreputable father's evident love by her aunt's prudishness, Elizabeth finds idyllic love when she and Richard go to New York. But Richard commits suicide after humiliation and beating by police. After the birth of their illegitimate son John, she finds redemption in marriage to Gabriel (Deborah having died), who promises to love her son. In this section about love, the antithesis has its role: Richard's quest for knowledge is energized by hatred of whites; and Elizabeth, after Richard's death, "hated it all—the white city, the white world."

Part III, "The Threshing-Floor," engrossingly describes John's conversion on the floor before the altar, the tortured probings and exhilarations of his mind sharpened by guilt and expanded by hope for salvation. At dawn, the smiling boy, facing an unsmiling father, is confident of his future.

Plainly autobiographical, this novel about a boy's anguished choice between church and jail metaphorically opposes the demands of those institutions as the forces that have long constricted but spiritualized Black people. The "saints" of the store-front church are all martyrs, Florence having been undone by normal ambition, Gabriel by duties too spiritual for his normal flesh, and Elizabeth by love. Jailed within body, family, church, and country, they vacillate between varieties of surrender and feel no sinless ecstasy or power other than singing the mysteries of God. The Biblical enchantment of Baldwin's prose rhythm elevates even his scenes of animal love, and the speech of his characters is vividly true to their heritage.

In *Giovanni's Room*, Baldwin's major fictional deviation from the racial theme, he melodramatically but profoundly explores love as illuminated and defined by homosexuality. The action, set in Paris and recalled by David on the eve of homosexual Giovanni's execution for murdering his exploiter Guillaume, concerns David's love and responsibility for Giovanni, whom he deserts to return to his fiancée Hella. Giovanni's indictment of David is central: "You are not leaving me for a *woman*. If you were really in love with this little girl, you would not have had to be so cruel to me" and "You want to *kill* [me] in the name of all your lying little moralities." Baldwin emphasizes that love inspires magnanimity and charity and that morality begins in honesty about oneself.

Another Country is Baldwin's major attempt to dramatize the racist destruction of interracial affections. In Book I, Rufus Scott, the jazz musician who turns his drums and his Southern white girl friend into objects for the dazzling release of his frustrations over racism, dives suicidally off the George Washington Bridge. His white friends, who failed to imagine his despair, live under its shadow as victims of a loveless, divisive New York. His sister Ida uses Vivaldo Moore's love to hasten her vengeance upon the white world. Vivaldo, loving her partly to shorten the distance that his whiteness maintains, pays in pain the dues that Cass Silenski offers less riskily. In Books II and III, Eric Jones, a young Southern actor who in France discovers his reality homosexually with Yves, moves therapeutically among other characters, teaching as existential man sexual liberation from the chaos of life, love, racism, and death. *Another Country*, although weakened by talkiness, occasionally inconsistent diction, and a questionable ending, is morally keyed to a remark by the preacher at Rufus's funeral: "Try to understand....we got to try to be better than the world."

Tell Me How Long the Train's Been Gone follows Leo Proudhammer from the age of ten in Harlem through his years as a famous actor. More to be noted than the typical inclusion of heterosexual, homosexual, and interracial lovemaking are young Leo's despairing father and idolized brother Caleb. Too much black rum and servility before white men destroy Leo's respect for the former; then police and prison guard brutality, followed by conversion to the ministry during his service in World War II, saps the once admirable militance in Caleb. Leo's affections turn to Christopher, who enters his life as his body-guard and who closes the novel telling him "I think you got to agree that we [Black people] need us some guns." Although Leo, like Christopher, considers religion useless in the racial struggle, he demurs at the thought of violence. This novel is occasionally powerful—in the summer workshop and police station scenes, for example—but it is Baldwin's least impressive long work.

Of the eight stories in *Going to Meet the Man*, the first three focus upon father-son relationships: "The Rockpile" and "The Outing" (both using characters and situations seen in his first novel) and "The Man Child." Three others show people trying to accept their Blackness: "Previous Condition," "Come Out the Wilderness," and the excellent "This Morning, This Evening, So Soon." The other two are also exceptional: "Sonny's Blues," the best story, and "Going to Meet the Man." The former brilliantly probes the failure of sympathy between two brothers, one an addict, and the latter traces the growth of psychopathic race hatred in an impotent deputy sheriff.

In *If Beale Street Could Talk* there is neither love nor mercy in the Black church, neither truth nor justice in American law, and neither hope nor sanctuary in anything but familial and personal love. Probing the racist-fomented dilemmas of his young Harlem narrator, Tish Rivers, and her falsely jailed fiancé, Fonny Hunt, Baldwin transcends his earlier renderings of Black men: the lovers' fathers here, like Fonny, are strong men precisely because they accept as a masculine challenge their Black ancestry and the needs of their children. Tish's narrative style does not fully demand Baldwin's sophisticated powers (although his love scenes and proverbial wisdom are memorable); but his new cynicism and deepened affinities foretell added significance in his future themes.

Baldwin's fiction, even when it falters, aims high, grappling with problems by which people measure themselves as humans and lovers. Unsparing but hopeful in its societal and racial criticism, urging self-acceptance and love in personal relations, his novels and stories pain and elevate the consciousness of his vast audience.

—James A. Emanuel

BALLANTYNE, David (Watt). New Zealander. Born in Auckland, 14 June 1924. Educated at Gisborne High School. Served in the New Zealand Army, 1942-43. Married Vivienne Heise in 1949; one child. Journalist, *Auckland Star*, 1943-47, *Southern Cross*, Wellington, 1947-48, *Auckland Star*, 1949-54, and *Evening News*, London, 1955-63; Editor, *Finding Out*, London, 1964; Journalist, *Evening Standard*, London, 1965. Feature Writer, 1966-77, and since 1977, Literary Editor, *Auckland Star*. Since 1977, Member of the Literary Fund Advisory Committee. Recipient: Hubert Church

Memorial Award, 1949; A.T.V. prize, for television play, 1961; New Zealand Scholarship in Letters, 1968. Address: Auckland Star, P.O. Box 3697, Auckland, New Zealand.

PUBLICATIONS

Novels

The Cunninghams. New York, Vanguard Press, 1948; London, Hale, 1963.
The Last Pioneer. Christchurch, Whitcombe and Tombs, and London, Hale, 1963.
A Friend of the Family. Christchurch, Whitcombe and Tombs, and London, Hale, 1966.
Sydney Bridge Upside Down. Christchurch, Whitcombe and Tombs, and London, Hale, 1968.
The Talkback Man. Palmerston North, Dunmore Press, and London, Hale, 1978.
The Penfriend. Palmerston North, Dunmore Press, and London, Hale, 1980.

Short Stories

And the Glory. Christchurch, Whitcombe and Tombs, and London, Hale, 1963.

Uncollected Short Stories

"Only a Kid of Course," in *New Zealand Weekly News* (Auckland), 21 January 1942.
"A Child's Day," in *New Zealand New Writing 2* (Wellington), October 1943.
"A Couple of Hacks," in *Arena* (Wellington), 1962.

Plays

Television Plays: *Passing Through*, 1963 (UK); *The Night of the Leopard*, 1963 (UK); *Twice upon a Time*, 1965 (UK); *Frances Hodgkins* (documentary), 1969; *Arthur K. Frupp*, 1970; *A Last Look*, 1971.

Other

Editor, *Around the World: Looking at Other Lands* (juvenile). London, Purnell, 1964; Boston, Ginn, 1966.

*

Critical Studies: *New Zealand Literature* by E.H. McCormick, London, Oxford University Press, 1959; *Islands of Innocence* by M.H. Holcroft, Wellington, Reed, 1964; *New Zealand Fiction since 1945* by H. Winston Rhodes, Wellington, McIndoe, 1968; "Whimsical Losers" by C.K. Stead, in *Landfall 132* (Christchurch), December 1979.

David Ballantyne comments:

(1972) I took my earliest themes from what I knew of the ways of life of my fellow countrymen. I wanted to write truthfully about their attitudes and their behaviour. I thought of myself as a realist, in the tradition of writers like Zola, Dreiser, Joyce, Hemingway, and Farrell. I drew upon my own experiences for my fiction, but tried for a detachment that would allow me to see the humour and warmth in life as well as the anxiety and pain. I thought a lean writing style, free of pretty phrases and philosophical flourishes, best suited to what I had to say. This was my approach in my first novel, *The Cunninghams*, and in my short stories. In a later novel, *A Friend of the Family*, written after I had lived in London several years, I used satire to suggest how I viewed certain aspects of contemporary life. And in another novel, *Sydney Bridge Upside Down*, I found parody a useful device. Mainly, though, I have told stories. Some more eventful than others.

* * *

All David Ballantyne's work could well be subtitled, "Scenes from Provincial Life." He began in the 1940's as a writer of short stories, notably "And the Glory," which appeared in *Landfall* in 1948 and gave the title to a collected volume in 1963. In this story, Larry, a lowgrade shop hand reprimanded by the boss, goes home to the suburbs to take out his temper there. He doesn't understand his own state of mind. Though he has "a comfortable job, a wife, a son, the prospect of a State house, good health," he still asks in puzzlement "what more did anybody want?" The answer that Ballantyne intends is, it seems, "the power and the glory." But Larry's ensuing verbal battle with the Electric Power Board (was the pun necessary?) over an unpaid bill provides him with only a shabby "glory." Like most of Ballantyne's shorter fiction, this story is economical and swift. Two other elements in it are also, however, constant in his later work: the mediocre, lower middle class "ordinary joker" as subject, and the under-played, undramatic, would-be-realistic lingo of the presentation.

Ballantyne's first novel, *The Cunninghams*, which also appeared in 1948, is set in New Zealand's depression decade, the 1930's; at full novel length, Ballantyne's grey preoccupation with social realism needs a lift of style or symbol to give some strength of dramatic impact. *The Cunninghams* has only a painstaking documentary accuracy. The people of this novel—Gilbert the ex-soldier father, Helen the overdriven wife, Gilbert the sensitive, inhibited and hopeless son—are recognisable enough, and so is the New Zealand small town setting. But these dreary empty lives repel the reader by that very boredom which is meant to evoke his pity. This is, of course, the difficulty inherent in all fiction of social analysis—how to create interest out of uninteresting lives.

Ballantyne made another attempt at picturing the stagnation of "provincial life" in his next novel, *The Last Pioneer*. To the small town of Mahuta come Mr. Wyatt and his son, in search of the pioneer dream. The minutiae of life are given with scrupulous fidelity. Booze in the kitchen or the pub, drama at the local movies ("the flagons and the flicks," as it might be put) represent the range of Mahuta's non-utilitarian activities, plus of course a little fun with sex. As a "decent joker" Wyatt should have been accepted, for the term is "the New Zealander's highest tribute" as someone remarks. "I mean, a decent joker is an ordinary joker, and *that's* what we want. But you'll have to remember to stay ordinary." Still giving the author's view, the speaker goes on to analyse: "We treasure our smallness down here, you know...the State will do *everything* for you if you let it...you can be as mediocre as the next person, mediocre and safe."

The pioneer, individual and striving, is therefore "out of fashion," and Wyatt's country paradise in its own way rejects him. But as before, no insights transcend for us the banal boredom of the surface so minutely delineated. Ballantyne adds up nothing; the arithmetic of generalised perception is left entirely to the reader, and with neither "power" nor "glory" offered to him, he finds the going dreary.

A Friend of the Family is a livelier book, verging on farce, about a phoney business tycoon and his associates, all in perpetual and pointless motion. The characterisation is shallow and the action slapstick. At the end, the "ordinary joker" who tells the tale gets some of the satisfactions of power from the bizarre revenges which he takes upon his employers, but we hardly know or like the fellow well enough to get much kick out of this.

Sydney Bridge Upside Down (an irrelevant catchpenny title) returns to provincial life. Calliope Bay has a store, a school, a wharf, a river, a railway line, the ruins of the abandoned freezing works, and five houses. The adolescent Harry uses the trailing boyish lingo of the half-educated to tell the story of what he saw and did when his little tart of a cousin, Caroline, came for a country holiday. Neither the manner nor the material is new, and it cannot be said that

Ballantyne has anything to add to his previous emphasis on the undistinguished, the unpleasant, and the squalid in sub-standard lives. His shock tactics make the book saleable enough, but no significant pattern emerges from the mosaic of surface trivialities.

Ballantyne has, however, developed an assured and skilful craftsmanship, which should stand him in good stead when he makes his next move.

—Joan Stevens

BALLARD, J(ames) G(raham). British. Born in Shanghai, China, 15 November 1930. Educated at Leys School, Cambridge; King's College, Cambridge. Served in the Royal Air Force. Married Helen Mary Matthews in 1953 (died, 1964); three children. Agent: John Wolfers, 3 Regent Square, London WC1H 8HZ. Address: 36 Charlton Road, Shepperton, Middlesex, England.

PUBLICATIONS

Novels

The Wind from Nowhere. New York, Berkley, 1962; London, Penguin, 1967.
The Drowned World. New York, Berkley, 1962; London, Gollancz, 1963.
The Burning World. New York, Berkley, 1964; revised edition, as *The Drought*, London, Cape, 1965.
The Crystal World. London, Cape, and New York, Farrar Straus, 1966.
Crash! London, Cape, and New York, Farrar Straus, 1973.
Concrete Island. London, Cape, and New York, Farrar Straus, 1974.
High-Rise. London, Cape, 1975; New York, Holt Rinehart, 1977.
The Unlimited Dream Company. London, Cape, and New York, Holt Rinehart, 1979.
Hello America. London, Cape, 1981.

Short Stories

The Voices of Time and Other Stories. New York, Berkley, 1962.
Billennium and Other Stories. New York, Berkley, 1962.
The Four-Dimensional Nightmare. London, Gollancz, 1963.
Passport to Eternity and Other Stories. New York, Berkley, 1963.
The Terminal Beach. London, Gollancz, 1964; abridged edition, New York, Berkley, 1964.
The Impossible Man and Other Stories. New York, Berkley, 1966.
The Disaster Area. London, Cape, 1967.
The Day of Forever. London, Panther, 1967.
The Overloaded Man. London, Panther, 1967.
The Atrocity Exhibition. London, Cape, 1970; as *Love and Napalm: Export USA*, New York, Grove Press, 1972.
Chronopolis and Other Stories. New York, Putnam, 1971.
Vermilion Sands. New York, Berkley, 1971; London, Cape, 1973.
Low-Flying Aircraft and Other Stories. London, Cape, 1976.
The Best Short Stories of J.G. Ballard. New York, Holt Rinehart, 1978.

Play

The Assassination Weapon (produced London, 1969).

*

Bibliography: in *J.G. Ballard: The First Twenty Years* edited by James Goddard and David Pringle, Hayes, Middlesex, Bran's Head, 1976.

J.G. Ballard comments:

I believe that science fiction is the authentic literature of the 20th century, the only fiction to respond imaginatively to the transforming nature of science and technology. I believe that the true domain of science fiction is that zone I have termed inner space, rather than outer space, and that the present, rather than the future, is now the period of greatest moral urgency for the writer. In my own fiction I have tried to achieve these aims.

* * *

J.G. Ballard's novels and short stories go well beyond the limits that the term "science-fiction" suggests. They reveal a powerful and sensuous imagination which reinforces a serious and universal concern with human despair in the universe of Nature. In its cosmic scale, Ballard's writing makes the reader uncomfortably aware of the slender filament by which man and all his works depend from the general scheme of things. In this respect, it has a distinctly 17th-century flavour—of the preoccupation with death we see in Browne, Burton, and Donne—which is expressed by Ransome in *The Drought*: "I've always thought of life as a kind of disaster area." The dominant images which linger with the reader are of disease limiting human aspirations and achievements, leprous beauty, deformed genius, and cities of Hell presented as sharply as their visual parallels in Delvaux, Dali, and Ernst.

Thematically, Ballard's novels are concerned with the delicate natural equipoise upon which our existence depends, the ease with which the balance may be upset and the consequences of the resulting imbalance. In *The Wind from Nowhere* a global wind turns the world into a dry, howling desert in which human relationships are torn apart and dried of feeling; in *The Drowned World* the earth's protective ionosphere is penetrated as a result of solar storms and the world turned into a vast equatorial swamp in which man returns to the autistic world of the womb. In both these novels the natural balance which we take for granted has been drastically upset by chance, with disastrous consequences for mankind; *The Drought* turns the screw by having mankind the instrument of his own disaster by polluting the oceans to such an extent that they are suffocated by a thin film of non-degradable substance which prevents the formation of clouds; once again, Ballard closely examines the destructive effect of such a disaster on human personality and relationships.

None of these novels, however, should be thought of as mere environmentalist propaganda; they go well beyond such a literal stage to a wider concern about man's desperate place in the universe. That Ballard's preoccupation is with the grander scheme is shown in *The Crystal World* which provides both explanation and solution to the problem of maintaining equipoise. Into a world of physical and social disease comes "time with the Midas touch" which petrifies and purifies what it meets. As in *The Wind from Nowhere* and *The Drowned World* random chance introduces the change, but this time the effect shows the way to solution. The crystallization effect results from the repeated collisions of anti-particles with particles, each of which subtracts "from the universe another quantum of its total share of time." The ultimate consequence is foreseen as a single atom producing "an infinite number of duplicates of itself" and so filling "the entire universe from which simultaneously all time has expired." So Ballard's explanation for natural disaster is the impossibility of maintaining balance in a cosmos where time, and therefore movement, is dominant; his solution (and this novel is compellingly hopeful) is that life can only be found in an ultimate, total stillness out of time.

What is very striking about Ballard's work is the degree to which it explores those particular zones of the wasteland whose approach routes were mapped by T.S. Eliot. The first three novels probe areas which directly relate to particular preoccupations in the Prufrock poems and *The Waste Land*, while *The Crystal World* has the same concern as the *Four Quartets* in its search for "the still point of a turning world." Such a comparison, made in terms of image and thematic concerns, might be expected to diminish Ballard, but it doesn't; nor should one conclude that Ballard's energy is dependent on Eliot; it is rather that both derive their strength from their underlying concern about man in his universe.

—Frederick Bowers

BARAKA, Amiri. American. Born Everett LeRoi Jones in Newark, New Jersey, 7 October 1934. Educated at the Central Avenue School, and Barringer High School, Newark; Howard University, Washington, D.C. Served in the United States Air Force, 1954-56. Married 1) Hettie Cohen in 1958 (divorced, 1965), two daughters; 2) Sylvia Robinson in 1966, five children, two step-daughters, and one other daughter. Taught at the New School for Social Research, New York, 1961-64, and Summers 1977-79; State University of New York, Buffalo, Summer 1964; Columbia University, New York, 1964 and Spring 1980; Visiting Professor, San Francisco State College, 1966-67, Yale University, New Haven, Connecticut, 1977-78, and George Washington University, Washington, D.C., 1978-79. Since 1980, Assistant Professor of African Studies, State University of New York, Stony Brook. Founder, *Yugen* magazine and Totem Press, New York, 1958; Editor, with Diane di Prima, *Floating Bear* magazine, New York, 1961-63; Founding Director, Black Arts Repertory Theatre, Harlem, New York, 1964-66. Since 1966, Founding Director, Spirit House, Newark. Involved in Newark politics: Member of the United Brothers, 1967, and Committee for Unified Newark, 1969-75; Chairman, Congress of Afrikan People, 1972-75. Recipient: Whitney Fellowship, 1961; Obie Award, for drama, 1964; Guggenheim Fellowship, 1965; Dakar Festival Prize, 1966; National Endowment for the Arts grant, 1966. D.H.L.: Malcolm X University, Chicago, 1972. Member, Black Academy of Arts and Letters. Address: 808 South 10th Street, Newark, New Jersey 07108, U.S.A.

PUBLICATIONS

Novel

The System of Dante's Hell. New York, Grove Press, 1965; London, MacGibbon and Kee, 1966.

Short Stories

Tales. New York, Grove Press, 1967; London, MacGibbon and Kee, 1969.

Plays

A Good Girl Is Hard to Find (produced Montclair, New Jersey, 1958).
Dante (produced New York, 1961; as *The 8th Ditch*, produced New York, 1964). Included in *The System of Dante's Hell*, 1965.
The Toilet (produced New York, 1962). Included in *The Baptism, and The Toilet*, 1967.
Dutchman (produced New York, 1964; London, 1967). Included in *Dutchman, and The Slave*, 1964.
The Slave (produced New York, 1964; London, 1972). Included in *Dutchman, and The Slave*, 1964.
Dutchman, and The Slave. New York, Morrow, 1964; London, Faber, 1965.
The Baptism (produced New York, 1964; London, 1971). Included in *The Baptism, and The Toilet*, 1967.
Jello (produced New York, 1965). Chicago, Third World Press, 1970.
Experimental Death Unit No. 1 (also director: produced New York, 1965). Included in *Four Black Revolutionary Plays*, 1969.
A Black Mass (also director: produced Newark, 1966). Included in *Four Black Revolutionary Plays*, 1969.
The Baptism, and The Toilet. New York, Grove Press, 1967.
Arm Yrself or Harm Yrself (produced Newark, 1967). Newark, Jihad, 1967.
Slave Ship: A Historical Pageant (produced Newark, 1967; New York, 1969). Newark, Jihad, 1967.
Madheart (also director: produced San Francisco, 1967). Included in *Four Black Revolutionary Plays*, 1969.
Great Goodness of Life (*A Coon Show*) (also director: produced Newark, 1967; New York, 1969). Included in *Four Black Revolutionary Plays*, 1969.
Home on the Range (produced Newark and New York, 1968). Published in *Drama Review* (New York), Summer 1968.
Police, in *Drama Review* (New York), Summer 1968.
The Death of Malcolm X, in *New Plays from the Black Theatre*, edited by Ed Bullins. New York, Bantam, 1969.
Four Black Revolutionary Plays (includes *Experimental Death Unit No. 1, A Black Mass, Great Goodness of Life* (*A Coon Show*), *Madheart*). Indianapolis, Bobbs Merrill, 1969; London, Calder and Boyars, 1971.
Junkies Are Full of (*SHHH...*), *and Bloodrites* (produced Newark, 1970). Published in *Black Drama Anthology*, edited by Woodie King and Ron Milner, New York, New American Library, 1971.
BA-RA-KA, in *Spontaneous Combustion: Eight New American Plays*, edited by Rochelle Owens. New York, Winter House, 1972.
Columbia the Gem of the Ocean (produced Washington, D.C., 1973).
A Recent Killing (produced New York, 1973).
Sidnee Poet Heroical (also director: produced New York, 1975).
S-1 (also director: produced New York, 1976). Included in *The Motion of History and Other Plays*, 1978.
The Motion of History (also director: produced New York, 1977). Included in *The Motion of History and Other Plays*, 1978.
The Motion of History and Other Plays (includes *S-1* and *Slave Ship*). New York, Morrow, 1978.
What Was the Relationship of the Lone Ranger to the Means of Production? (produced New York, 1979).

Screenplays: *Dutchman*, 1967; *A Fable*, 1971.

Verse

Spring and Soforth. New Haven, Connecticut, Penny Poems, 1960.
Preface to a Twenty Volume Suicide Note. New York, Totem-Corinth, 1961.
The Dead Lecturer. New York, Grove Press, 1964.
Black Art. Newark, Jihad, 1966.
A Poem for Black Hearts. Detroit, Broadside Press, 1967.
Black Magic: Poetry 1961-1967. Indianapolis, Bobbs Merrill, and London, MacGibbon and Kee, 1969.
It's Nation Time. Chicago, Third World Press, 1970.
In Our Terribleness: Some Elements and Meaning in Black Style, with Fundi (Billy Abernathy). Indianapolis, Bobbs Merrill, 1970.
Spirit Reach. Newark, Jihad, 1972.
Afrikan Revolution. Newark, Jihad, 1973.
Hard Facts. Newark, Peoples War, 1976.
Selected Poetry. New York, Morrow, 1979.
AM/TRAK. New York, Phoenix Bookshop, 1979.

Other

Cuba Libre. New York, Fair Play for Cuba Committee, 1961.
Blues People: Negro Music in White America. New York, Morrow, 1963; London, MacGibbon and Kee, 1965.
Home: Social Essays. New York, Morrow, 1966; London, MacGibbon and Kee, 1968.
Black Music. New York, Morrow, 1968.
Trippin': A Need for Change, with Larry Neal and A.B. Spellman. Newark, Cricket, 1969(?).
A Black Value System. Newark, Jihad, 1970.
Raise Race Rays Raze: Essays since 1965. New York, Random House, 1971.
Strategy and Tactics of a Pan African Nationalist Party. Newark, National Involvement, 1971.
Beginning of National Movement. Newark, Jihad, 1972.
The New Nationalism. Chicago, Third World Press, 1972.
National Liberation and Politics. Newark, Congress of African People, 1974.
The Creation of the New Ark. Washington, D.C., Howard University Press, 1975.
Selected Plays and Prose. New York, Morrow, 1979.
Spring Song. Privately printed, 1979.

Editor, *Four Young Lady Poets.* New York, Totem-Corinth, 1962.
Editor, *The Moderns: New Fiction in America.* New York, Corinth, 1963; London, MacGibbon and Kee, 1965.
Editor, with Larry Neal, *Black Fire: An Anthology of Afro-American Writing.* New York, Morrow, 1968.
Editor, *African Congress: A Documentary of the First Modern Pan-African Congress.* New York, Morow, 1972.
Editor, with Diane di Prima, *The Floating Bear: A Newsletter, Numbers 1-37.* La Jolla, California, Laurence McGilvery, 1974.

*

Bibliography: *LeRoi Jones (Imamu Amiri Baraka): A Checklist of Works by and about Him* by Letitia Dace, London, Nether Press, 1971.

Critical Studies: *From LeRoi Jones to Amiri Baraka: The Literary Works* by Theodore Hudson, Durham, North Carolina, Duke University Press, 1973; *Baraka: The Renegade and the Mask* by Kimberly W. Benston, New Haven, Connecticut, Yale University Press, 1976, and *Imamu Amiri Baraka (LeRoi Jones): A Collection of Critical Essays* edited by Benston, Englewood Cliffs, New Jersey, Prentice Hall, 1978; *Amiri Baraka/LeRoi Jones: The Quest for a "Populist Modernism"* by Werner Sollors, New York, Columbia University Press, 1978; *Amiri Baraka* by Lloyd W. Brown, Boston, Twayne, 1980.

Theatrical Activities:

Director: several of his own plays.

* * *

Amiri Baraka (LeRoi Jones), in fictionally expressing his leadership in the 1960's as wayward literary artist in Greenwich Village, as inspirer of authentic Black theatrical work in Harlem and New Jersey, and as promoter of Black cultural nationalism and political activism from his base in "New Ark," published a novel and a collection of short stories.

In his semiautobiographical novel, *The System of Dante's Hell*, Baraka is much less concerned with the elaborately symbolic structure of Dante's poem (to which he refers six or seven times) than with its literal subject, "the state of souls after death." But death-in-life is Baraka's subject. Like Dante, he explores the soul moving through states of perception; but he envisions no Beatrice, no Empyrean, no final, unified illumination making the Newark ghetto anything more than "Hell in the head," where God "is simply a white man" and where most Black people die "in a bathroom of old age and segregation." Baraka's plan, which his final chapter calls movement "from sound and image ('association complexes') into fast narrative," takes form initially as the young narrator's fragmented, introspective memories and revaluations. Sometimes cryptic or almost perversely obscure, they are usually patterned around what he laments as "the breakup of my sensibility," as "indelicate furtive lust" that left him either victim or debaser, and as the peculiar doom of the artist ("I kill everything....I am left only with my small words"). After a series of impregnated girlfriends, "cold sin in the cities" with homosexuals, and an alienating education during which "Eliot, Pound, Cummings, Apollinaire were living across from Kresges," the narrator remains emotionally the boy who would sit silently in his dark closet wearing green glasses, others' beauty and purity reduced to "sad tinny lies" except for his name that "a black catholic girl had written...on a trash can. I love you I love you I love you."

"The Eighth Ditch" (a one-act drama of unrestrained homosexuality) and three short stories resuming the experiences of the narrator—all four previously published—make up the second half of the novel. "The Christians," hinting at satire against technology, culminates in a gang fight at a basement party. The anti-middle class sentiment in "The Rape" gives way to surrealistic excess and almost manic tensions during a wild car ride taken by six young men and a syphilitic whore. The best story, "The Heretics," about two light-skinned Air Force men dissipating in Shreveport, Louisiana, fixes the theme of sexual perversion more intimately in the narrator Roi's guilt complex. In fact, the essential cultural and sexual impasse haunting the protagonist of the novel despite his intellectual and athletic prowess is expressed thus:

> Can you read? Who is T.S. Eliot? So what? A cross. You've got to like girls. Weirdo. Break, Roi, break. Now come back, do it again. Get down, hard. Come up. Keep your legs high, crouch hard when you get the ball.... Talk to me. Goddamnit. Say something. You never talk, just sit there, impossible to love.... Move. Frightened bastard.

Noteworthy in "The Heretics," besides the narrator's pitiful lovemaking with Peaches, are Baraka's new departures in racial themes. For example, a long strip of segregating, white tape sticking to the floor, bar, and counter in the Cotton Club separates interracial "old friends, touching each other, and screaming with laughter." Black people's sensuous dancing, "a rite no one knew, or had use for outside their secret lives," is explained in terms of both "separate flesh" and closed history. And near the end, Roi finds brief but satisfying racial identification and acceptance among Black people as "Peaches' man." His new, real world of "soft black harmonies and color" is given historical dimension by Baraka's advice in the final chapter: that Black people "bring back on ourselves, the absolute pain our people must have felt when they came onto this shore," to recover both selfhood and history.

Filled with private references (the chapter "Thieves" entirely so), thematically intense obscenities, and terse prose-poetry nerved with original metaphor, the novel is Baraka's revolt against a ghetto-minded society that, in toughly preserving its own hell, kept him unaware "of what death and lust [he] fondled and thot to make beautiful."

Tales, including some autobiographical matter in each selection, consists of seven short stories and nine reflective, partly narrative pieces. Most of the latter are variously allegorical ("The Largest Ocean in the World"), anecdotal ("Uncle Tom's Cabin: Alternative Ending"), personal (the tender "New Spirit"), and prophetic of the new Black Consciousness (five near the end of the book, starting with revolutionary idealism in "New-Sense" and ending with "Answers in Progress," in which victorious Black revolutionaries see spaceships land among them, disgorging "them thin cats hopping around us," the blue invaders observing the rounding up of "blanks"—white people—and "gettin cooled out on carrots," their own superdrug.

Of the bona fide short stories, four are important in themselves or as documentation of Baraka's evolving ideas. In "The Alternative" an eccentric fumbler for knowledge sees his university buddies as professionals-to-be who will betray the "flame in the valley" of their Black heritage and, instead, "erect a new world, of lies and stocking caps." In "The Death of Horatio Alger" the skinny narrator suffers a double loss: his call for help, shouted to his best friend in front of jeering companions, somehow emerges as an insulting scream of hatred; and by his shameful failure in the resulting fist fight he incurs the lasting scorn of his parents. "Heroes Are Gang Leaders," in showing the author-narrator reluctant to speak up for his hospital ward-mate being brutalized in police action usable in his own fiction, exemplifies "the airless social compromise that keeps us alive past any use of ourselves." The superior "The Screamers," vividly sensory and tense with the exaltations of intimate dancing and "honking" saxophones, is a steadily impassioned expression of unique Black experience. The saxophonists and the Black audience that follows them dancing into the street to block Newark traffic are perfectly described. The former are "ethnic historians, actors, priests of the unconscious" who give elegant form to their race's "hatred and frustration, secrecy and despair." Of the latter, Baraka says tellingly: "We screamed and screamed at the clear image of ourselves as we should always be. Ecstatic, completed, involved in a secret communal expression."

In his best fiction, LeRoi Jones/Amiri Baraka has been both saxophonist and dancer, blowing "enraged sociologies," his racial memory "ground...past passion or moved so fast it blurred intelligence."

—James A. Emanuel

BARKER, A(udrey) L(ilian). British. Born in Kent, 13 April 1918. Educated at schools in Beckenham, Kent, and Wallington, Surrey. Recipient: Atlantic Award, 1946; Maugham Award, 1947; Cheltenham Festival Award, 1962; Arts Council Award, 1970. Fellow, Royal Society of Literature, 1970. Address: 103 Harrow Road, Carshalton, Surrey SM5 3QF, England.

PUBLICATIONS

Novels

Apology for a Hero. London, Hogarth Press, and New York, Scribner, 1950.
A Case Examined. London, Hogarth Press, 1965.
The Middling: Chapters in the Life of Ellie Toms. London, Hogarth Press, 1967.
John Brown's Body. London, Hogarth Press, 1969.
A Source of Embarrassment. London, Hogarth Press, 1974.
A Heavy Feather. London, Hogarth Press, 1978; New York, Braziller, 1979.

Short Stories

Innocents: Variations on a Theme. London, Hogarth Press, 1947; New York, Scribner, 1948.
Novelette with Other Stories. London, Hogarth Press, and New York, Scribner, 1951.
The Joy-Ride and After. London, Hogarth Press, 1963; New York, Scribner, 1964.
Lost upon the Roundabouts. London, Hogarth Press, 1964.
Penguin Modern Stories 8, with others. London, Penguin, 1971.
Femina Real. London, Hogarth Press, 1971.
Life Stories. London, Chatto and Windus, 1981.

Play

Television Play: *Pringle*, 1958.

* * *

The theme of A.L. Barker's work is the ambivalence of love and the dangers of egoism. She examines those relationships which exist between victor and victim, he who eats and he who is eaten. This material is handled lightly and skillfully; she has the satirist's ability to select detail, placing her characters socially as well as psychologically. Her territory covers childhood, the worlds of the outcast and the ill and the impoverished lives of the lonely. She is close to the English tradition of the comic novel and like Angus Wilson, a major writer in this genre, she often indulges in caricature.

Many of her short stories reveal a fondness for the macabre, introducing elements of horror into seeming calm. Her first collection, *Innocents*, begins with a study of a boy testing his courage in swimming; he becomes involved in a scene of adult violence that is far more dangerous to him than the tree-roots in his river. Innocence in these stories is seen as inexperience, as the blinkered vision of the mad and as the selfishness of the egoist. *Lost upon the Roundabouts* is a further exploration of these ideas and contains two very fine short stories, "Miss Eagle" and "Someone at the Door."

The central characters in Barker's novels are parasites, dependent on other people for a sense of their own identity. For Ellie in *The Middling* love means "turning another person into a colony of myself." Charles Candy, the central character of *Apology for a Hero*, loves his wife Wynne "because she could give him himself." After Wynne's death he acquires a housekeeper and finds that "when he was with her he felt located." He meets death on a reckless voyage, persuaded that sea-trading will, at last, show him the real Mr. Candy.

The egoist in *A Case Examined* is Rose Antrobus, the chairman of a charity committee with the power to allocate money either to a destitute family or to the church hassock fund. Rose has always insulated herself against suffering. She remembers a childhood friend, Solange, whom she credits with the understanding of despair: Solange provokes violence, she feels, by her own wickedness. This fantasy is shattered by a visit to Paris and a meeting with the real Solange, whose account of Nazi persecution shakes Rose into compassion. A bridge has been made between the worlds of the two women, between the petty and the tragic, and the committee decision is altered accordingly.

Barker's latest collection of stories, *Femina Real*, is an entertaining set of portraits, nine studies of the female character. In many of the situations an apparent vulnerability hides an underlying strength. A frail woman dominates those around her; adolescence vanquishes middle-age; a ten-year-old cripple turns the tables on the man holding her prisoner. As always, Barker's clear prose style matches the accuracy of her observations. Hers is a talent to be treasured.

—Judy Cooke

BARNES, Djuna (Chappell). American. Born in Cornwall-on-Hudson, New York, 12 June 1892. Privately educated; studied art at the Pratt Institute, Brooklyn, New York, and the Art Students' League, New York. Journalist and illustrator, 1913-31; also an artist: exhibited at Art of This Century Gallery, New York, 1946.

Since 1961, Trustee, New York Committee, Dag Hammarskjöld Foundation. Recipient: Merrill and Rothko grants. Member, American Academy. Address: 5 Patchin Place, New York, New York 10011, U.S.A.

PUBLICATIONS

Novels

Ryder. New York, Liveright, 1928.
Nightwood. London, Faber, 1936; New York, Harcourt Brace, 1937.

Short Stories

A Book (includes verse and plays). New York, Boni and Liveright, 1923; augmented edition, as *A Night among the Horses*, New York, Liveright, 1929; shortened version, stories only, as *Spillway*, London, Faber, 1962; New York, Harper, 1972.
Vagaries Malicieux: Two Stories. New York, Hallman, 1974.

Plays

Three from the Earth (produced New York, 1919). Included in *A Book*, 1923.
Kurzy of the Sea (produced New York, 1919).
An Irish Triangle (produced New York, 1919). Published in *Playboy* (New York), 1921.
To the Dogs, in *A Book*, 1923.
The Dove (produced New York, 1926). Included in *A Book*, 1923.
She Tells Her Daughter, in *Smart Set* (New York), November 1923.
The Antiphon (produced Stockholm, 1961). London, Faber, and New York, Farrar Straus, 1958.

Verse

The Book of Repulsive Women: Eight Rhythms and Five Drawings. New York, Bruno Chap Books, 1915.

Other

Ladies Almanack: Showing Their Signs and Their Tides; Their Moon and Their Changes; The Seasons as It Is with Them; Their Eclipses and Equinoxes; As Well as a Full Record of Diurnal and Nocturnal Distempers Written and Illustrated by a Lady of Fashion. Privately printed, 1928; New York, Harper, 1972.
Selected Works. New York, Farrar Straus, 1962; London, Faber, 1980.
Greenwich Village as It Is. New York, Phoenix Bookshop, 1978.

*

Bibliography: *Djuna Barnes: A Bibliography* by Douglas Messerli, New York, Lewis, 1975.

Manuscript Collection: University of Maryland, College Park.

Critical Studies: *Djuna Barnes* by James B. Scott, Boston, Twayne, 1976; *The Art of Djuna Barnes: Duality and Damnation* by Louis F. Kannenstine, New York, New York University Press, 1977.

Theatrical Activities:

Actress: **Plays**—in *Power of Darkness* by Tolstoy, New York, 1920; in *The Tidings Brought to Mary* by Paul Claudel, New York, 1922.

* * *

Djuna Barnes was born in 1892, which makes her from five to twelve years younger than the generation of classic American modernists—Wallace Stevens, William Carlos Williams, Ezra Pound, T.S. Eliot, and the rest. Only Ezra Pound was earlier on the scene. Not only was she precocious and supporting herself as a journalist and illustrator before the First War but she was, as a younger girl, a member of the international bohemia of the first quarter of the century, rather than a member of any specific literary set, a very different thing. She was trained as an artist and was considered equally an artist and writer until *Nightwood* established her literary reputation, when she was past forty. These details are important; they account for a remarkable independence as well as for her special sensibility and for her subject matter. This independence was certainly reinforced by her person and personality. She was an exceptionally beautiful woman, unusually intelligent, a great conversationalist, with a drastic, ironic wit, and finally she was the very archetype of the liberated woman. Also, in the days when most American writers read little except their contemporaries, she was deeply and enthusiastically self-educated in classic English literature and in French modernism. Long before such writing became fashionable, she was developing a style compounded of the more complex Elizabethan prose writers and the most alienated French poets of the early twentieth century. Although she is usually grouped with the classic modernists of between-the-wars, she is really one of the most perfected writers to come out of the totally subversive bohemia of the turn of the century and belongs with Tristan Corbière and Alfred Jarry rather than with Wallace Stevens or even Eliot—who may have assimilated the anti-Symbolists but who certainly did not share their life attitudes.

The comparisons that spring most readily to mind are Kafka and Céline. From her first stories, Djuna Barnes's subjects are the possessed, the haunted, ghosts, and automata wandering in nightmares come true. The action almost always takes place beyond the end of night. So the resemblance is not, as one might think, to Dostoevsky, whose people are deranged but real Russians, but to the best horror or science fiction. Her people seem to have a different blood chemistry, ammonia, perhaps, instead of water. They inhabit a bohemia of their own, alienated from the dominant society, but not the comforting community of Greenwich Village or the Café du Dome, but a world of the self-alienated. "I am another," said Rimbaud. The personalities have all split and have begun to disintegrate. Even *Ryder*, a big, eventful novel of domesticity, a satire on masculinity written in a style which owes much to the obstreperous, controversial pamphlets of the Elizabethan Thomas Nashe, is, for all its bawdry and babies, saturated with black humor. When she was writing it she used to say, "I am writing the female *Tom Jones*," but the book would certainly have frightened Henry Fielding, that eminently sane and wholesome man.

In the second novel, *Nightwood*, we are in the limbo of the undamned. The characters are all self-condemned to unreality. They seek reality, not in salvation, which they are incapable of even knowing, but in damnation—which is closed to them—and so they find only an immense frivolity. No exit.

Nightwood achieves more perfectly than any other of her fictions that haunted, obsessed quality, that atmosphere of inescapable nightmare which is her special *métier*. Its influence has been very great. Nathanael West's *Miss Lonelyhearts* and *The Day of the Locust*, Nelson Algren's *A Walk on the Wild Side*, and the work of Edward Dahlberg are only a few of its many descendants. Henry Miller's *Tropic of Cancer, Tropic of Capricorn*, and especially *Black Spring* owe much to the precedent of Djuna Barnes, but Henry Miller is far too normal and conventional a man to realize her special horrors. Djuna Barnes is very far indeed from being a naive writer. Similarly she has been a great influence on Anaïs Nin, in whose novels a character "Djuna" occurs again and again. Here the influence is essentially that of personal admiration. Djuna Barnes is an exemplar for Anaïs Nin. One feels she may have modeled her life rather than her fiction on her—a woman of powerful will, immense talent, independence, sexually free, and very beautiful. In other words Djuna Barnes is at least as influential as a legend as she is as a writer.

T.S. Eliot in introducing *Nightwood* said that it would "appeal primarily to readers of poetry" because it was written with such an acute feeling for language that only people trained on poetry could fully appreciate it. It is true that all of Djuna Barnes's prose stands out from that of her contemporaries, distinguished by her physiological sense of rhythm and a wit that constantly plays with the reverberating meanings and sounds of words. It may be a conscious style, deliberately and painfully worked out—so was Flaubert's, but like Flaubert's it gives little evidence of labor. It seems to flow spontaneously, one just word after another, with a music that comes from the sinews of a uniquely integrated human being. At the same time it is distinguished by its elegance. It is as though she had never read anything but the greatest literature and was saturated with it. Her verse play, *The Antiphon*, is a perfect transmutation of the style, the subject, the very personal being, of the nightmare world of the tragedies of John Webster and Cyril Tourneur into completely modern terms. The speeches echo *The Duchess of Malfi* but echo it in the mid-twentieth century with its own language and its own nightmares.

Djuna Barnes may be considered as a late born voice of the *fin de siècle* literary decadence but she is an early born prophet of the black comedy, theatre of cruelty, and literature of total alienation of the later years of the century, the period of decadence and disintegration of western civilization itself, the time of permanent apocalypse. Hers is a moral esthetic, the esthetic of a "theology of crisis"; "*'We have fashioned ourselves against the Day of Judgment.' This remark was made by Dr. Katrina Silverstaff at the oddest moments, seeming without relevance to anything at all, as one might sigh 'Be still.'* " So begins a story "The Doctors."

—Kenneth Rexroth

BARRY, Clive. Australian. Born in Sydney, New South Wales, in 1922. Served in World War II; prisoner of war. District Education Officer in East Africa since the mid-1950's. Since 1961, United Nations Representative in the Congo. Address: c/o Faber and Faber Ltd., 3 Queen Square, London WC1N 3AU, England.

PUBLICATIONS

Novels

The Spear Grinner. London, Faber, 1963.
Crumb Borne. London, Faber, 1965.
Fly Jamskoni. London, Faber, 1969.

* * *

Clive Barry's first and third novels are comedies animated by the adventures of the same hero; they are, however, unequal achievements. In *The Spear Grinner* Hector Reed, a gruff though well-intentioned Australian, comes as an Administrative Officer to the small imaginary state of Jamskoni in East Africa. His duties are ill-defined but in his one week stay he manages to kill an elephant and just escapes being killed by another; he prevents a whole cargo of hemp from being smuggled to Yemen, takes part in a ludicrous election campaign and avoids being knived by gangsters by blowing up part of his own house. The only real authority in Jamskoni seems to be exercised by the District Commissioner's office boy, an ex-public-school native called the Ostrich after the emblem of his political campaign for the coming elections. He is a pleasant rogue, the "spear grinner" of the title, who in defiance of the proverb "Only a fool laughs at the spear" cultivates a savage grin and thrives on everyone else's inefficiency. The story is told with brilliant gusto. Barry's dry humour, his elliptical style and the detachment with which he frames the most absurd situations, are well suited to his rendering of the anarchy and inverted sense of values that prevail in Jamskoni. Sheer farce alternates with more subtly satirical scenes. In the end, however, the tragic reverse of amusing chaos, which has been played down through most of the novel, is allowed to emerge: Reed's beautiful housekeeper is found killed and horribly mutilated by the gangsters. There is a suggestion throughout the novel that Reed needs Africa as much as Africa needs him. Yet as an uncommitted witness of other people's predicament, it is without remorse that he flies back to the security of a modern suburbia.

In *Fly Jamskoni* Hector Reed comes back to the small newly-independent state as a United Nations Officer. The Ostrich is Minister of Aviation and apparently still runs the show by himself, though he spends most of his time piloting the country's one biplane. Gangsterism has been eradicated by making the head gangster superintendent of police. The one remaining problem for Reed is to stop the camel-herders from smuggling hemp. As his job depends on the continuance of the trade, he befriends the herders and even helps them to smuggle their hemp by aircraft rather than on camels. He has at last learned from the Ostrich the art of compromise. Unlike *The Spear Grinner*, Barry's third novel is hardly more than a succession of loosely connected farcical incidents. His style has lost nothing of its vividness, and he still relies on the paradoxical to raise an occasional laugh. But it is often hard to make head or tail of what is happening, and the reader is more confused than Reed himself about what the latter is doing in Jamskoni.

Crumb Borne portrays an altogether different world: the hopeless society created by a hundred starving prisoners-of-war on a freezing plateau in the middle of nowhere. Their microcosm reproduces the hierarchical functions of the ordinary world even to the need for a scapegoat. The outsider is Frugal, whose quiet self-sufficiency and capacity to survive through strict self-discipline are interpreted by his fellow-prisoners as a threat to their own survival. Actually, Frugal alone remains human while the others' meanness increases with their physical degradation. The cold, matter-of-fact precision with which Barry describes the isolated camp and the prisoners' permanent near-hysteria further enhances the depressing character of the underworld he creates.

—Hena Maes-Jelinek

BARSTOW, Stan(ley). British. Born in Horbury, Yorkshire, 28 June 1928. Educated at Ossett Grammar School. Married Constance Mary Kershaw in 1951; two children. Draftsman and Sales Executive in the engineering industry, 1945-62. Recipient: Writers Guild Award, 1974. Address: Goring House, Goring Park Avenue, Ossett, West Yorkshire WF5 OHX, England.

PUBLICATIONS

Novels

A Kind of Loving. London, Joseph, 1960; New York, Doubleday, 1961.
Ask Me Tomorrow. London, Joseph, 1962.
Joby. London, Joseph, 1964.
The Watchers on the Shore. London, Joseph, 1966; New York, Doubleday, 1967.
A Raging Calm. London, Joseph, 1968; as *The Hidden Part*, New York, Coward McCann, 1969.
The Right True End. London, Joseph, 1976.
A Brother's Tale. London, Joseph, 1980.

Short Stories

The Desperadoes. London, Joseph, 1961.
The Human Element and Other Stories, edited by Marilyn Davies. London, Longman, 1969.
A Season with Eros. London, Joseph, 1971.
A Casual Acquaintance and Other Stories, edited by Marilyn Davies. London, Longman, 1976.

Plays

Ask Me Tomorrow, with Alfred Bradley, adaptation of the novel by Barstow (produced Sheffield, 1964). London, French, 1966.
A Kind of Loving, with Alfred Bradley, adaptation of the novel by Barstow (produced Sheffield, 1965). London, Blackie, 1970.
An Enemy of the People, adaptation of a play by Ibsen (produced Harrogate, Yorkshire, 1969). London, Calder, 1977.
Listen for the Trains, Love, music by Alex Glasgow (produced Sheffield, 1970).
Stringer's Last Stand, with Alfred Bradley (produced York, 1971). London, French, 1972.
We Could Always Fit a Sidecar (broadcast, 1974). Published in *Out of the Air: Five Plays for Radio*, edited by Alfred Bradley, London, Longman, 1978.
Joby, adaptation of his own novel (televised, 1975). London, Blackie, 1977.

Radio Plays: *The Desperadoes*, from his own story, 1965; *We Could Always Fit a Sidecar*, 1974; *The Watchers on the Shore*, from his own novel, 1978; *The Right True End*, from his own novel, 1978.

Television Plays: *The Human Element*, 1964; *The Pity of It All*, 1965; *A World Inside* (documentary), with John Gibson, 1966; *A Family at War* (1 episode), 1970; *Mind You, I Live Here* (documentary), with John Gibson, 1971; *A Raging Calm*, from his own novel, 1974; *South Riding*, from the novel by Winifred Holtby, 1974; *Joby*, 1975; *The Cost of Loving*, 1977; *The Assailants*, 1977; *The Years Between*, 1977; *Travellers*, 1978; *Bright Day*, from the novel by J.B. Priestley, 1980; *A Kind of Loving*, from his own novels, 1981.

Other

Editor, *Through the Green Woods: An Anthology of Contemporary Writing about Youth and Children.* Leeds, Arnold, 1968.

Stan Barstow comments:

Came to prominence about the same time as several other novelists from North of England working-class backgrounds, viz. John Braine, Alan Sillitoe, David Storey, Keith Waterhouse, and saw with satisfaction, and occasional irritation, the gains made in the opening up of the regions and the "elevation" of the people into fit subjects for fictional portrayal absorbed into the popular cultures of the cinema and TV drama series and comedy shows. Still, living in the provinces and using mainly regional settings, consider myself non-metropolitan oriented. The publication of some of my work in the U.S. and its translation into several European languages reassures me that I have not resisted the neurotic trendiness of much metropolitan culture for the sake of mere provincial narrowness; and the knowledge that some of the finest novels in the language are "regional" leads me to the belief that to hoe one's own row diligently, thus seeking out the universal in the particular, brings more worthwhile satisfactions than the frantic pursuit of a largely phoney jet-age internationalism.

* * *

Stan Barstow belongs centrally to that group of northern novelists—Kirkup, Braine, Sillitoe, Waterhouse, Middleton, Storey—who grew to literary prominence in the 1950's and 1960's by their realistic portrayal of working class life. In this common bond they are literary descendants of Gissing, Wells, and Lawrence, but they each demonstrate particular preoccupations which distinguish them from their predecessors and each from the others; Braine and Sillitoe for example are very much concerned with class divisiveness, whereas Kirkup and Waterhouse explore much more closely the fabric and feel of working class life.

Barstow's novels take social class and the industrial environment much more for granted; this is not to say that such matters are only sketched in, for they are solidly presented, but the overriding preoccupation is with the development of human wisdom and love in an environment which is indifferent or hostile. The three major novels each present a central character making a marked shift in worldview, from self-interest to an awareness of others. More particularly, they present the conflict between an environment which is materially and spiritually narrow and the growth of love, which prevails at last, not to reach sublime heights but to manage a modicum of human happiness. Vic Brown's relationship with Ingrid (*A Kind of Loving*) descends from youthful romance to cynical despair as a result of the harm Ingrid's mother has done to their marriage through her shallow notions of morality and her semi-detached snobbery; only with a struggle does he eventually manage to rebuild their marriage and turn his back on both ecstasy and despair. At the end of the novel Vic accepts life as it is: "And if you say what is life about I'll say it's about life, and that's all. And it's enough because there's plenty of good things in life as well as bad."

The presentation of a workaday human love not only as the best that one can hope for but also as an essential condition of life is repeated in *Joby* and *A Raging Calm*. Young Joby's summer of decline into petty theft and tacky child sex mirrors his father's own drift into a clumsy affair with Joby's rather retarded but nubile cousin Mona; both Joby and his father reach a point where disintegration of the family seems inevitable, but Joby manages to see beyond his own troubles to his father's: "He saw for the first time as a person carrying about with him a world of his own...," and he brings his father back into the family. Similarly, Tom Simkins reintegrates the loose ends of his life by taking Norma and her children under his roof.

Barstow sets his theme against the unsympathetic background of Cressley, a West Riding industrial town of terraced houses, ugly factories, garish cinemas and grubby parks. The meanness of the town is shown to breed both narrow morality and generous love; it is up to the individual to choose one or the other, but Barstow points to his choice: Joby persuades his father, "Oh, come on home with me, Dad. It'll be all right. Me mam's waiting for you. You don't care about me Aunt Daisy and them, do you? They don't matter to us, do they?"

Although Barstow makes no technical innovations (he sticks to traditional narrative forms—first person in *A Kind of Loving*, omniscient linked plots in *A Raging Calm* and third person point of view in *Joby*) his novels rise above the ephemeral in their concrete presentation of human character, their solid settings, their natural dialogue and, above all, their forceful and moving expression of what it is to be human.

—Frederick Bowers

BARTH, John (Simmons). American. Born in Cambridge, Maryland, 27 May 1930. Educated at the Juilliard School of Music, New York; Johns Hopkins University, Baltimore, A.B. 1951, M.A. 1952. Married 1) Anne Strickland in 1951, one daughter and two sons; 2) Shelley Rosenberg in 1970. Junior Instructor in English, Johns Hopkins University, 1951-53; Instructor to Associate Professor of English, Pennsylvania State University, University Park, 1953-65; Professor of English, State University of New York, Buffalo, 1965-73. Since 1973, Centennial Professor of English and Creative Writing, Johns Hopkins University. Recipient: Brandeis University Creative Arts Award, 1965; Rockefeller grant, 1965; American Academy grant, 1966; National Book Award, 1973. Litt.D.: University of Maryland, College Park, 1969. Address: c/o Writing Seminars, Johns Hopkins University, Baltimore, Maryland 21218, U.S.A.

PUBLICATIONS

Novels

The Floating Opera. New York, Appleton Century Crofts, 1956; revised edition, New York, Doubleday, 1967; Secker and Warburg, 1968.
The End of the Road. New York, Doubleday, 1958; London, Secker and Warburg, 1962; revised edition, Doubleday, 1967.
The Sot-Weed Factor. New York, Doubleday, 1960; London, Secker and Warburg, 1961; revised edition, Doubleday, 1967.
Giles Goat-Boy; or, The Revised New Syllabus. New York, Doubleday, 1966; London, Secker and Warburg, 1967.
Letters. New York, Putnam, 1979; London, Secker and Warburg, 1980.

Short Stories

Lost in the Funhouse: Fiction for Print, Tape, Live Voice. New York, Doubleday, 1968; London, Secker and Warburg, 1969.
Chimera. New York, Random House, 1972; London, Deutsch, 1974.

Play

The Tragedy of Taliped Decanus, adaptation of his novel *Giles Goat-Boy* (produced New York, 1977).

*

Bibliography: *John Barth: A Descriptive Primary and Annotated Secondary Bibliography* by Joseph Weixlmann, New York, Garland, 1975; *John Barth: An Annotated Bibliography* by Richard A Vine, Metuchen, New Jersey, Scarecrow Press, 1977; *John Barth, Jerzy Kosinski, and Thomas Pynchon: A Reference Guide* by Thomas P. Walsh and Cameron Northouse, Boston, Hall, 1977.

Manuscript Collection: Library of Congress, Washington, D.C.

Critical Studies: *John Barth* by Gerhard Joseph, Minneapolis, University of Minnesota Press, 1970; *John Barth: The Comic Sublimity of Paradox* by Jac Tharpe, Carbondale, Southern Illinois University Press, 1974; *John Barth: An Introduction* by David Morrell, University Park, Pennsylvania State University Press, 1976.

* * *

The heroes of *The Floating Opera*, *The End of the Road*, and *The Sot-Weed Factor*—if "heroes" is the right word—all suffer from "cosmopsis," John Barth's term for the existential fever contracted by a good many writers, or at least their characters, during the 1950's. Barth makes no attempt to hide his debts here: "cosmopsis" or the "cosmic view" is the first stage of existential awareness, the paralyzing realization that, contrary to Christian and other transcendental accounts of the world and man's destiny, life is a purely contingent affair. Being simply *is*; there are no reasons for things to be or to be as they are, no absolute values or sanctions. *The Floating Opera* describes the education in these matters of Todd Andrews, a man painfully aware of his own fragile mortality. Towards the end of the novel he is able to conclude that, first of all, nothing has intrinsic value; secondly, that the values we do attribute to things are ultimately irrational, arbitrary and hence purely "relative"; and finally that there are no right reasons for action of any sort, or indeed for the act of living itself. Thus he plans his suicide ("There is but one truly serious philosophical problem," Camus announces at the start of *The Rebel*, " and that is suicide"); but for purely accidental reasons, the attempt fails. This failure and a sudden flicker of responsibility for the child who may be his illegitimate daughter push Andrews to a further conclusion: he goes on living, not because there is a good intrinsic reason for doing so, but simply because by the same token there is no good reason *not* to go on living. As Barth commented later, he deliberately had Andrews "end up with that brave ethical subjectivism in order that Horner might undo that position in #2 and carry all non-mystical value-thinking to the end of the road." Jacob Horner, the central figure in Barth's second novel, *The End of the Road*, is immobilized by his awareness that there is no justification for any action ("I simply ran out of motives, as a car runs out of gas"). "Human existence," explains his mysterious, self-appointed therapist, "precedes human essence...and a man is free not only to choose his own essence but to change it at will." He advises Horner to live a deliberately chosen role (as a grammar teacher at a small college) and remain true to it, since "a man's integrity consists in being faithful to the script he's written for himself." In Barth's terms Horner is engaging in a course of arbitrary "non-mythic value-thinking"; but in so doing, he becomes disastrously involved with a fellow teacher and his wife, for whose death he is partly responsible. "We've come too far," he says at the end of the novel: "Who can live in such a world?" Barth has called *The Floating Opera* a "nihilistic comedy" ("existential comedy" might be a better tag here, since it might be argued that real nihilists don't write books in the first place) and *The End of the Road* a "nihilistic tragedy." If this is so, it is simply by an act of authorial will. There is no inherent reason why one novel should be comic, the other tragic; both embody the same "system" and cancel each other out, or rather lead to an ethical impasse. In his thoughtful study of Barth's first four novels, Jac Tharpe observes that "whether Barth urges to activity is debatable." And yet he is also forced to add, with some understandable uneasiness, that "Barth is obviously a decent man who, despite his skepticism, cynicism, or severe artistic detachment, has no wish to send out the message that anything goes."

Set during the late 17th century, *The Sot-Weed Factor* seems at first glance utterly unlike Barth's first two novels—a massive parody of the picaresque novel-with-a-moral, complete with endless complications ("I wanted to see if I couldn't make a plot fancier than *Tom Jones*," Barth comments, and he wins, hands down). But the issues here are the same as before. The innocent young hero, Ebenezer Cooke, suffers from a benign form of cosmopsis: he is "dazzled by the beauty of the possible" and "throws up his hands at choice." His mentor, Henry Burlingame, enlightens him, maintaining that men are "by mindless lust engendered, and by mindless wrench expelled, from the Eden of the womb to the motley, mindless world." We are "Chance's fool, the toy of aimless Nature—a Mayfly flitting down the winds of Chaos." But to brood on the absurdity of existence in this way, Burlingame warns, is to court destruction: "One must needs make and seize his soul, and then cleave to't fast, or go babbling in the corner; one must choose his gods and devils on the run, quill his own name up on the universe, and declare, 'Tis I, and the world stands such-a-way!' One must *assert, assert, assert*, or go screaming mad. What other course remains?" "Assertion" here refers, once again, to the act of existential choice, and Cooke does pursue his chosen destiny to become poet laureate of the brave new Maryland territory and claim his father's estate there. Eventually he does so, after interminable adventures and setbacks, during which he quite properly loses his innocence. Thus Cooke learns the real nature of the world and ends his days mocking what he once hoped to praise, weary, but faithfully supporting the dying, pox-ridden prostitute—Barth's reminder of the inevitable corruption of the flesh—to whom he lost his innocence.

Giles, of *Giles Goat-Boy*, is a hero in a quite special sense. Barth tells us that he was fascinated by the archetype of the mythic hero described by Lord Raglan, Otto Rank, and especially Joseph

Campbell, whose Jungian account of the basic "monomyth" (in *The Hero with a Thousand Faces*) is important for understanding the novel. The hero, Campbell writes, is the exceptional man who "ventures forth from the world of common day into a region of supernatural wonder: fabulous forces are there encountered and a decisive victory is won: the hero comes back from his mysterious adventures with the power to bestow boons on his fellow men." But the ascendancy of the hero does not last. He is rejected and dies mysteriously; his "boons" are forgotten or imperfectly understood by a few followers. Barth places his dramatization of this archetypal pattern in the context of a hypertrophic allegory in which the world is represented by the "University," Russia and America by the "East Campus" and "West Campus," and the life-force itself (which is also potentially self-destructive) by the central power source, the computer WESCAC. Giles's mission is to de-program that part of the computer which might lead to all-out atomic war and to become the "Grand Tutor" who understands the true meaning of "Pass" and "Fail." He accomplishes his task and in the belly of the computer has his mystical revelation of the oneness of all being ("There was no East, no West, but an entire seamless campus"). Nevertheless, Giles is soon rejected and like the archetypal hero dies alone and misunderstood. On another occasion Barth remarked, "What does Giles learn in his quest? That the tragedy is you can't transmit wisdom and insight."

Barth's first four novels are clearly "modern" novels—modern, that is, in their preoccupation with new intellectual frameworks and their exploitation of myth and parody, two of the great resources of the great experimental writers of the first half of this century. But in his recent work he moves directly into that ill-defined area known at the moment as the "post-modern." The word has been abused, but it does have some genuine value in calling attention to an altered relationship between artist, work, and audience. In post-modern fiction (what Barth calls the "literature of exhaustion") the artist no longer tries to provide a convincing illusion of reality. He forces his audience to realize that what they are experiencing is an artifice and involves them in the very process of artistic making. There are several reasons for this break with tradition, two of which are relevant for grasping what Barth is now attempting to do. "Contemporary writers," he has said, "can't go on doing what's been done, and done better. I revere Flaubert and Tolstoy, Hemingway and Faulkner; but they're finished as objects of interest to the writer. My God, we're living in the last third of the twentieth century." But even more important for Barth is the fact that the new fiction allows us to see a new connection between art and life. Such fiction, Barth explains, may be defined as

> a kind of true representation of the distortion we all make in life. In other words, it's a representation of a distortion; not a representation of life itself, but a representation of a representation of life. If you acknowledge that premise to begin with, there's no reason why you can't do all sorts of things that could otherwise be objected to.... Art *is* artifice after all.

But perhaps this is simply a new version of realism: with many others these days Barth seems to be saying that all knowledge is fictive, that living itself is a process of creating inevitably distorted versions of reality. Post-modern art intensifies our awareness of how we necessarily live.

Barth's inordinately complex recent work needs and no doubt will receive careful critical scrutiny. But very briefly, *Letters*, which is probably the most demanding novel in English (assuming *Finnegans Wake* is not "in English"), consists of a series of gradually interlocking letters sent to Barth by a set of characters mostly drawn from his earlier fiction. Todd Andrews, at the end, seems about to take his life, this time successfully; Horner is ruined once more; Ambrose (Barth's alter-ego artist-figure) is probably not the father of the child he has tried so hard to produce (children, like works of art, are protests against mortality) and seems to be drawn to the great explosion which probably will occur after the end of the novel. All of the characters fail in their "assertions," but Barth has made us care about some of his drolls and dreamers in a way we have not cared about the types and caricatures who inhabit his earlier fiction. This sympathy—ultimately frustrated or pointless since the characters merely "imagine" they are real—may be another way of reminding us painfully of our own condition: we too imagine we are "real" and go on projecting our claims against the background of an unyielding universe. Like works of art, we are fictive, lost in a very unfunny funhouse. Ambrose has the last word: "He wishes he had never entered the funhouse. But he has. Then he wishes he were dead. But he's not. Therefore he will construct funhouses for others and be their secret operator—though he would rather be among the lovers for whom the funhouses are designed."

—Elmer Borklund

BARTHELME, Donald. American. Born in Philadelphia, Pennsylvania, 7 April 1931. Educated at the University of Houston. Served in the United States Army, 1953-55. Married to Birgit Barthelme; one daughter. Reporter, Houston *Post*, 1951, 1955-56; worked on public relations and news service staff, and founding editor of the university literary magazine *Forum*, University of Houston, 1956-59; Director, Contemporary Arts Museum, Houston, 1961-62; Managing Editor, *Location* magazine, New York, 1962-64. Visiting Professor, State University of New York, Buffalo, 1972, and Boston University, 1973. Since 1974, Visiting Professor, City College, New York. Recipient: Guggenheim Fellowship, 1966; National Book Award, 1972; American Academy Morton Dauwen Zabel Award, 1972. Member, American Academy. Lives in New York City. Address: c/o The New Yorker, 25 West 43rd Street, New York, New York 10036, U.S.A.

PUBLICATIONS

Novels

Snow White. New York, Atheneum, 1967; London, Cape, 1968.
The Dead Father. New York, Farrar Straus, 1975; London, Routledge, 1977.

Short Stories

Come Back, Dr. Caligari. Boston, Little Brown, 1964; London, Eyre and Spottiswoode, 1966.
Unspeakable Practices, Unnatural Acts. New York, Farrar Straus, 1968; London, Cape, 1969.
City Life. New York, Farrar Straus, 1970; London, Cape, 1971.
Sadness. New York, Farrar Straus, 1972; London, Cape, 1973.
Guilty Pleasures. New York, Farrar Straus, 1974.
Amateurs. New York, Farrar Straus, 1976; London, Routledge, 1977.
Great Days. New York, Farrar Straus, and London, Routledge, 1979.

Uncollected Short Stories

"Man's Face," in *New Yorker*, 30 May 1964.
"Then," in *Mother 3* (Northfield, Minnesota), November-December 1964.
"Philadelphia," in *New Yorker*, 30 November 1968.
"Newsletter," in *New Yorker*, 11 July 1970.
"Adventure," in *Harper's Bazaar* (New York), December 1970.
"Alexandra and Henrietta," in *New American Review 12*, edited by Theodore Solotaroff. New York, Simon and Schuster, 1971.
"The Story Thus Far:," in *New Yorker*, 1 May 1971.

"Natural History," in *Harper's* (New York), August 1971.
"The Mothball Fleet," in *New Yorker*, 11 September 1971.
"Three," in *Fiction 1*, 1972.
"Edwards, Amelia," in *New Yorker*, 9 September 1972.
"Wrack," in *New Yorker*, 21 October 1972.
"Over the Sea of Hesitation," in *New Yorker*, 11 November 1972.
"A Man," in *New Yorker*, 30 December 1972.
"The Inauguration," in *Harper's* (New York), January 1973.
"The Bill," in *Viva* (New York), November 1973.
"The Bed," in *Viva* (New York), March 1974.
"The Dassaud Prize," in *New Yorker*, 12 January 1976.
"Monumental Folly," in *Atlantic* (Boston), February 1976.
"The Short Story Contest," in *New York Times Magazine*, 1 February 1976.
"Manfred," with Karen Snow, in *New York Times Magazine*, 18 April 1976.
"The Great Debate," in *New Yorker*, 3 May 1976.
"Presents," in *Penthouse* (New York), December 1977.
"How I Write My Songs, by Bill B. White," in *New Yorker*, 27 November 1978.
"Captain Blood," in *New Yorker*, 1 January 1979.
"Aria," in *New Yorker*, 12 March 1979.
"The Willie and Wade Park," in *Harper's* (New York), June 1979.
"Grandmother," in *New Yorker*, 3 September 1979.
"Heroes," in *New Yorker*, 5 May 1980.
"Bishop," in *New Yorker*, 4 August 1980.

Other

The Slightly Irregular Fire Engine; or, The Thithering Dithering Djinn (juvenile). New York, Farrar Straus, 1971.

*

Bibliography: *Donald Barthelme: A Comprehensive Bibliography and Annotated Secondary Checklist* by Jerome Klinkowitz, Asa Pieratt, and Robert Murray Davis, Hamden, Connecticut, Shoe String Press, 1977.

Critical Study: *Donald Barthelme* by Lois Gordon, Boston, Twayne, 1981.

* * *

Since the mid-1960's, a new literary movement has appeared on both sides of the Atlantic. Given a variety of labels—including post-modernism, surfiction, metafiction, superFiction, parafiction—this avant-garde rejects all the traditions of the conventional novel form and takes as its subject the very act of writing fiction and the difficulties of using language to reflect a reality that in itself may be unknowable. In America the movement includes Donald Barthelme, William Gass, Robert Coover, Ronald Sukenick, Raymond Federman, Ishmael Reed, Steve Katz, John Hawkes, and Gilbert Sorrentino, and the earlier-known and earlier-established John Barth and Vladimir Nabokov. Abroad it includes Cortázar, Calvino, Pinget, Simon, Sollers, Richardou and Le Clézio, with Beckett and Borges its earliest practitioners. Donald Barthelme is one of the most interesting of these writers; he has frequently been called the most brilliant writer in America.

Like the other writers of this "movement," Barthelme rejects the conventional mimetic form—traditional, linear plot and characterization, the unities of time and space, and the assumption that the novel can reflect and comment upon reality. Numerous themes recur through his work, which has often (at least up through *The Dead Father*) been described as verbal collage: the hyper-educated society, brainwashed by packaged slogans and media-marketed expertise ("The Viennese Opera Ball"), the political and social pathology of American life ("The President"), the inhuman and grotesque mentality of its warmongers ("Report"); Barthelme also writes about more personal matters, like the endless war between the sexes ("Indian Uprising"), the father-son relationship ("See the Moon?"), and aging ("The New Jazz"). Throughout, his most persistent theme is the difficulty of using language in both a personal and creative way—not only as an artistic vehicle but also as a satisfactory way of connecting with the world and the human community ("The Balloon"). Some of his best stories treat how "signs sometimes lie" ("Me and Miss Mandible"), how one's experience is always private, and one's efforts to *translate* it into *words* is always inadequate ("Shower of Gold," "Marie, Marie, Hold On Tight," "Robert Kennedy Saved from Drowning").

In his earliest volumes Barthelme was especially concerned with social issues—the contemporary, brainwashed society, bent on mouthing technology and texts, a world totally indifferent to "meaning" and feeling (*Come Back, Dr. Caligari, Unspeakable Practices, Unnatural Acts*). In *City Life* and *Sadness*, while these concerns persist, Barthelme turns to irony as a defense against the spiritually sordid world. What he discovers, however, is that irony permits only a pyrrhic victory. One wants, in fact, not a denial of reality (or annihilation of it through irony) but instead a reconciliation with the world. These two volumes, and stories like "At the Tolstoy Museum," "The Glass Mountain," "Kierkegaard Unfair to Schlegel," "The Temptation of St. Anthony," and "Daumier," are among his finest works.

Guilty Pleasures, which the dust-jacket calls "non-fiction," is Barthelme's funniest book and a good introduction to his variety of parodic forms. It is a wild excursion through the corroded soul of contemporary America. In *Amateurs* Barthelme introduces a new fable form, and in *Great Days* he turns to an entirely new dialogue form to explore larger and more basic issues like time and mortality. He creates more human figures with whom one feels a certain personal kinship. These are not the earlier exaggerated comic creations of *Come Back, Dr. Caligari* or *Unspeakable Practices, Unnatural Acts*.

Barthelme has written two brilliant novels, and one feels impertinent generalizing about them. In portraying Snow White in the modern world, Barthelme underscores the dilemma of one's imprisonment in words, roles, or in a sense "scripts"—i.e., being born as Snow White. In his greatest work, *The Dead Father*, he focuses on one's compulsion both toward and away from "authority" (the dead father), and he projects on to his central figure any number of literary, mythic, historical, political, and linguistic meanings. The book has an encyclopedic scope, and it incorporates a variety of techniques from art, music, and film.

Throughout, one is overwhelmed by Barthelme's inventive use of language. As though to offer an alternative to our immersion in fixed roles and clichés, and our inevitable imprisonment in the fixed structures of language, he subjects the written and spoken forms of language to endless parody and experimentation. Through his extraordinary verbal arrangements he evokes a universe—unborn until then—in his reader's consciousness. He creates (up through *The Dead Father*) a unique form of comedy, with language an emblem of man's relationship to the universe.

In the more recent work, Barthelme writes in a more poetic style. One associates the brilliant verbal collage with the earlier and main body of his work, and the more ineffable and polyphonic techniques of poetry and musical composition with the more recent work. Throughout, he illustrates how words, with all the difficulties (and one's inevitable "failure") in using them, are our only link with the universe, all one has as a barter against annihilation. In "Nothing: A Preliminary Account" he illustrates his central thesis that one must never capitulate to nothingness. He punctuates an unending list of negatives with the phrase "Hurry on" as he embraces life: "How joyous the notion that, try as we may, we cannot do other than fail and fail absolutely and that the task will remain always before us, like a meaning for our lives. Hurry. Quickly. Nothing is not a nail."

—Lois Gordon

BAUMBACH, Jonathan. American. Born in New York City, 5 July 1933. Educated at Brooklyn College, New York, 1951-55, A.B. 1955; Columbia University, New York, 1955-56, M.F.A. 1956; Stanford University, California, 1958-61, Ph.D. 1961. Served in the United States Army, 1956-58. Married 1) Elinor Berkman in 1956 (divorced, 1967), one son and one daughter; 2) Georgia A. Brown in 1968, two sons. Instructor, Stanford University, 1958-60; Instructor, 1961-62, and Assistant Professor, 1962-64, Ohio State University, Columbus; Assistant Professor, New York University, 1964-66. Associate Professor, 1966-70, 1971-72, and since 1972, Professor of English, Brooklyn College, City University of New York. Visiting Professor, Tufts University, Medford, Massachusetts, 1970-71, and University of Washington, Seattle, 1978-79. Since 1974, film critic, *Partisan Review*, New Brunswick, New Jersey. Recipient: *New Republic* award, 1958; Yaddo grant, 1963, 1964, 1965; National Endowment for the Arts Fellowship, 1967; Guggenheim Fellowship, 1978. Agent: Gloria Loomis, A. Watkins, 77 Park Avenue, New York, New York 10016. Address: 42 Montgomery Place, Brooklyn, New York 11215, U.S.A.

PUBLICATIONS

Novels

A Man to Conjure With. New York, Random House, 1965; London, Gollancz, 1966.
What Comes Next. New York, Harper, 1968.
Reruns. New York, Fiction Collective, 1974.
Babble. New York, Fiction Collective, 1976.
Chez Charlotte and Emily. New York, Fiction Collective, 1979.

Short Stories

The Return of Service. Urbana, University of Illinois Press, 1979.

Uncollected Short Stories

"Passion?," in *Prize Stories 1979: The O. Henry Awards*, edited by William Abrahams. New York, Doubleday, 1979.
"A West Coast Story," in *New York Arts Journal*, Spring 1980.
"Errant Melancholy," in *Canto* (Andover, Massachusetts), Winter 1980.
"Familiar Games," in *Antaeus* (New York), Fall 1981.

Play

The One-Eyed Man Is King (produced New York, 1956).

Other

The Landscape of Nightmare: Studies in the Contemporary American Novel. New York, New York University Press, 1965; London, Owen, 1966.

Editor, with Arthur Edelstein, *Moderns and Contemporaries: Nine Masters of the Short Story.* New York, Random House, 1968; revised edition, 1977.
Editor, *Writers as Teachers/Teachers as Writers.* New York, Holt Rinehart, 1970.
Editor, *Statements: New Fiction from the Fiction Collective.* New York, Braziller, 1975.
Editor, with Peter Spielberg, *Statements 2: New Fiction.* New York, Fiction Collective, 1977.

*

Critical Study: *The Life of Fiction* by Jerome Klinkowitz, Urbana, University of Illinois Press, 1977.

Jonathan Baumbach comments:

Novels are an attempt to make sense out of experience and to make experience out of sense, to eschew the illusion of verisimilitude, to give form to what never existed, not to imitate life but to re-invent it out of language, to imagine the processes of the imagination, to imagine the imagining of the processes of the imagination, involved with cinema, dream, and memory, and the underground landscape of their conjunction.

No theory informs the work. It is what it comes to. My fiction is the illusion of itself.

* * *

A helpful preface to Jonathan Baumbach's six books of fiction is his critical study, *The Landscape of Nightmare: Studies in the Contemporary American Novel.* Baumbach is representative of a new style of novelist (which includes Ronald Sukenick, Jerzy Kosinski, and William H. Gass), having earned a graduate degree before writing fiction himself. Baumbach's thesis, that "To live in this world, to live consciously in this world in which madness daily passes for sanity is a kind of madness in itself," describes a problem for literary art against which he poses his own fiction as solution. "Unable to believe in the surface (the *Life* magazine reality) of our world," he argues, "the best of the post-Second-World-War novelists have taken as their terrain the landscape of the psyche." Yet for that "landscape of nightmare" writers such as Bernard Malamud and William Styron were still using techniques more appropriate to social realism. In his own work Baumbach has striven to find a new style suitable for the innovative fiction he writes. As he emphasized to an interviewer in 1973, "I'm not just using the dream in the traditional sense, in the psychological sense where it's an almost compacted parable, with special symbols. I'm just trying to find another way of getting at reality. I mean, my sense is that the conventional novel, for me, anyway, is on its way to a dead end. And I'm trying to get at the way things are in a way that no one has ever seen them before."

Baumbach's first novel, *A Man to Conjure With*, synthesizes various trends outlined in his critical study. Much like William Styron's *Lie Down in Darkness*, Baumbach's work has a protagonist who moves simultaneously backward and forward in time, carefully orchestrating revelations of plot and character so that the present is gradually understood in a plausible and convincing way. As a result, the narrative is assembled as a psychological collage; only in the protagonist's final act do all the elements become clear. Baumbach's technical achievement has been to find a structural form which reflects this psychological state: a thoroughly spatial novel.

What Comes Next is a more tightly written exploration of this same structural theme. Again the situation is psychological: a young college student, beset by sexual and parental problems, is "flipping out," and Baumbach's novel expresses this confusion by its very form. Violence erupts on every page, though primarily as mental device, since it is usually sparked by newspaper headlines and fantasized incidents. The book organizes itself as a literal landscape of nightmare, as all reference points for the character's reality are located within his own disjointed perceptions. As far as temporal narrative, "what comes next" is created from the workings of his mind.

Baumbach's subsequent work has been even more strongly experimental. His third novel, *Reruns*, abandons plot and character entirely in favor of dream-like images from movies rerun page by page. *Babble*, a novel made up of several "baby stories" written through the mid-1970's, is more playful but no less daring in its technical achievement. In order to explore the workings of narrative, Baumbach records the stories his infant son allegedly tells him ("His second story is less fresh than the first, though of greater technical sophistication"; "The robot is after him again, this time disguised as a soda vending machine. 'You can't have any Coke,' the robot says, 'until you wash your face'"). Once more Baumbach has become the critic in order to fashion a new mode for fiction.

Throughout the 1970's Baumbach continued to experiment with

various structures for fiction, including the sub-genre parodies, movie mythologies, and dreamlike obsessions featured throughout his story collection *The Return of Service*. But it is his fifth novel, *Chez Charlotte and Emily*, which displays his greatest facility as a writer. Ostensibly the device by which a bored husband and wife communicate with each other (by proposing a narrative and then critiquing it), the novel is actually an excuse (à la *The Canterbury Tales*) for the telling of stories. Freed from the necessity of plausible context, Baumbach is able to spin out fantasies of shipwreck, sexual adventure, intrigue, and the complexity of human relationships—all as pure writing, justified by the arrangement of the couple's critical debate. Soon the two contexts, critical and fictional, merge—as they must, Baumbach would argue, for it is through works of the imagination that we preserve our consciousness of the world.

—Jerome Klinkowitz

BAWDEN, Nina (née Mabey). British. Born in London, 19 January 1925. Educated at Ilford County High School; Somerville College, Oxford, B.A. 1946, M.A. 1951; Salzburg Seminar in American Studies, 1960. Married 1) H.W. Bawden in 1946, two sons; 2) A.S. Kark in 1954, one son. Assistant, Town and Country Planning Association, 1946-47. Since 1969, Justice of the Peace for Surrey. Regular reviewer, *Daily Telegraph*, London. Member, P.E.N. Executive Committee, 1968-71. Recipient: *Guardian* Award, for children's book, 1976; *Yorkshire Post* Award, 1976. Fellow, Royal Society of Literature, 1970. Address: 22 Noel Road, London N1 8HA, England.

PUBLICATIONS

Novels

Who Calls the Tune. London, Collins, 1953; as *Eyes of Green*, New York, Morrow, 1953.
The Odd Flamingo. London, Collins, 1954.
Change Here for Babylon. London, Collins, 1955.
The Solitary Child. London, Collins, 1956; New York, Lancer, 1966.
Devil by the Sea. London, Collins, 1957; Philadelphia, Lippincott, 1959.
Just Like a Lady. London, Longman, 1960; as *Glass Slippers Always Pinch*, Philadelphia, Lippincott, 1960.
In Honour Bound. London, Longman, 1961.
Tortoise by Candlelight. London, Longman, and New York, Harper, 1963.
Under the Skin. London, Longman, and New York, Harper, 1964.
A Little Love, A Little Learning. London, Longman, 1965; New York, Harper, 1966.
A Woman of My Age. London, Longman, and New York, Harper, 1967.
The Grain of Truth. London, Longman, and New York, Harper, 1968.
The Birds on the Trees. London, Longman, 1970; New York, Harper, 1971.
Anna Apparent. London, Longman, and New York, Harper, 1972.
George Beneath a Paper Moon. London, Allen Lane, and New York, Harper, 1974.
Afternoon of a Good Woman. London, Macmillan, 1976; New York, Harper, 1977.
Familiar Passions. London, Macmillan, and New York, Morrow, 1979.
Walking Naked. London, Macmillan, 1981.

Other (fiction for children)

The Secret Passage. London, Gollancz, 1963; as *The House of Secrets*, Philadelphia, Lippincott, 1964.
On the Run. London, Gollancz, 1964; as *Three on the Run*, Philadelphia, Lippincott, 1965.
The White Horse Gang. London, Gollancz, and Philadelphia, Lippincott, 1966.
The Witch's Daughter. London, Gollancz, and Philadelphia, Lippincott, 1966.
A Handful of Thieves. London, Gollancz, and Philadelphia, Lippincott, 1967.
The Runaway Summer. London, Gollancz, and Philadelphia, Lippincott, 1969.
Squib. London, Gollancz, and Philadelphia, Lippincott, 1971.
Carrie's War. London, Gollancz, and Philadelphia, Lippincott, 1973.
The Peppermint Pig. London, Gollancz, and Philadelphia, Lippincott, 1975.
Rebel on a Rock. London, Gollancz, and Philadelphia, Lippincott, 1978.
The Robbers. London, Gollancz, and New York, Lothrop, 1979.
William Tell. London, Cape, and New York, Lothrop, 1981.

*

Nina Bawden comments:

I find it difficult to comment on my adult novels. I suppose one could say that the later books, from *Just Like a Lady* onwards, are social comedies with modern themes and settings; the characters moral beings, hopefully engaged in living. People try so hard and fail so often, sometimes sadly, sometimes comically; I try to show how and why and to be accurate about relationships and motives. I have been called a "cryptomoralist with a mischievous sense of humour," and I like this description: it is certainly part of what I aim to be.

This quotation, from the *Christian Science Monitor*, though not the most flattering, might be useful:

> Nina Bawden is a writer of unusual precision who can depict human foibles with an almost embarrassing accuracy. Yet for all that she centres dead on target, there is always a note of compassion in her stories. The light thrown on her characters, clear though it is, is no harsh spotlight. It is a more diffuse beam that allows one to peer into the shadows and see causes even while it focuses on effects.

* * *

In her abundant energy and in her occasional recourse to melodrama, Nina Bawden may remind one of her contemporary, Iris Murdoch. Such a comparison is misleading, however, for it is soon apparent that the two women move in opposite directions. Bawden's literary debts are not, like Murdoch's, to continental phenomenology, but to English sources, specifically to Jane Austen and Charles Dickens. Austen and Dickens make an odd mix, but not so odd when it becomes clear that Austen preponderates.

From *Just Like a Lady*, the first of Bawden's novels that is not frankly a thriller, to her most recent, the essential scene is domestic, suburban, and enclosed, even when the ostensible setting, as in *A Woman of My Age*, is Morocco. The style is efficient, witty, and often satirical in the Austen manner. And like Austen's Bawden's best novels, *Just Like a Lady*, *A Woman of My Age*, and *The Birds on the Trees*, are about the central characters' efforts to achieve honesty to self, to separate the genuine from the hypocritical or convenient motive, even at the risk, always resisted, of upsetting the social balance. The catch is that modern society does not provide the elaborate mechanism of manners available to Jane Austen; therefore the parallel can only be schematic.

Bawden is Dickensian in the theme of *Just Like a Lady*, frequently in her conception of minor characters, and at those frequent points in her narratives where manners must give over to melodramas, where manners are either no longer viable or no longer exist. Lucy, of *Just Like a Lady*, has great expectation: an orphan, she is brought up in confining suburban near-squalor by relatives. She refuses conformity for Oxford, a naive marriage to a pompous fool, an affair with a lukewarm lover, and reconciliation of a sort with her foolish husband. Banal in outline, the novel is anything but banal in execution. This English adventure in *bovarysme* carries freshness, conviction, and the power of psychological truth.

The milieu of the later novels is suburban, middle class, and superficially safe. It is not safe in fact, however. At the bottom of the garden lives abject poverty in an abandoned bus, its hair infested by horrors and disease in its body. The bus people, or the people of the gravel pit, in *Tortoise by Candlelight*, live by their wits, outside the law. They threaten the good middle-class children. The criminal poor are chaos and excitement, qualities on which the children thrive and from which they may perish. As in Dickens, the past, too, often comes to upset the present: Bawden's closets have Dickensian rather than phenomenological skeletons in them.

If Bawden is sometimes tedious, it is because of the numerous children, who narrate events, as in *A Little Love, A Little Learning*, or whose coy habits are dwelt on at length, as in *Tortoise by Candlelight*. Or in the many eccentrics whose foibles are merely exhibited, to the detriment of the usually spare narrative. Any tediousness is forgotten, however, in one's realization that with each succeeding novel, a perceptible advance has occurred. The authority of craft and the authority of perception promise further advances. In the meantime, the satiric eye and the admirable energy abound, most welcome in a dry time.

—John McCormick

BEATY, (Arthur) David. British. Born in Hatton, Ceylon, 28 March 1919. Educated at Kingswood School, Bath, Somerset; Merton College, Oxford, 1938-40, M.A. in history 1940; University College, London, 1964-67, 1974-77, M. Phil. in psychology 1977. Served as a Squadron Leader in the Royal Air Force, in the United Kingdom and the Middle East, 1940-46: Distinguished Flying Cross and Bar. Married Betty Smith in 1948; three children. Senior Captain, BOAC (British Overseas Airways Corporation), 1946-53. Instructor, College of Air Training, Hamble, Hampshire, 1963. Principal, Administrative Civil Service, 1966-70; Administrative Secretary, Centre for Educational Development Overseas, London, 1970-72; Principal, Overseas Development Administration, London, 1972-74. Companion, Royal Aeronautical Society. Address: Woodside, Hever, Edenbridge, Kent, England.

PUBLICATIONS

Novels

The Take Off. London, Werner Laurie, 1948; as *The Donnington Legend*, New York, Morrow, 1949.
The Heart of the Storm. London, Secker and Warburg, 1954; as *The Four Winds*, New York, Morrow, 1955.
The Proving Flight. London, Secker and Warburg, 1956; New York, Morrow, 1957.
Cone of Silence. London, Secker and Warburg, and New York, Morrow, 1959.
Call Me Captain (as Paul Stanton). London, Joseph, 1959; New York, Mill, 1960.
Village of Stars (as Paul Stanton). London, Joseph, and New York, Mill, 1960.
The Wind Off the Sea. London, Secker and Warburg, and New York, Morrow, 1962.
The Siren Song. London, Secker and Warburg, and New York, Morrow, 1964.
The Gun Garden (as Paul Stanton). London, Joseph, and New York, Mill, 1965.
Sword of Honour. London, Secker and Warburg, 1965; New York, Morrow, 1966.
The Temple Tree. London, Secker and Warburg, and Boston, Houghton Mifflin, 1971.
Electric Train. London, Secker and Warburg, 1975.
Excellency. London, Secker and Warburg, 1977; New York, Morrow, 1978.
The White Sea-Bird. London, Secker and Warburg, 1979; New York, Morrow, 1980.

Uncollected Short Story

"Kid's Stuff," in *Pick of Today's Short Stories*, edited by John Pudney. London, Putnam, 1954.

Other

Milk and Honey: Travails with a Donkey (as Paul Stanton). London, Joseph, 1964; New York, Mill, 1965.
The Human Factor in Aircraft Accidents. London, Secker and Warburg, 1969; New York, Stein and Day, 1970.
The Water Jump: The Story of Transatlantic Flight. London, Secker and Warburg, and New York, Harper, 1976.
The Complete Skytraveller. London, Methuen, 1979.

*

Critical Studies: *The World of David Beaty*, New York, Twayne, 1971, and *Antoine de Saint-Exupéry and David Beaty: Poets of a New Dimension*, Boston, Hall, 1974, both by Roberta J. Forsberg.

David Beaty comments:

(1972) In my view, the main purpose of a novel is to search out and exhibit truth, illuminating at the same time human behaviour. This should be executed in a way that is both informative and interesting. The reader must be absorbed by what he reads in order to turn the page. The motivation behind the characters' actions, the interacting of their personalities within the plot are most important. I am interested in "why," not simply in the events themselves. My novels are built up on a plan, almost a blueprint. "Belief" is all important, and the sustaining of belief is one of the most difficult things to do. Without belief, the novel is nothing—though belief is of course still possible within fantasy and fairy stories. I see the plot as a symphony composed of incidents, complete in themselves, all with their own note and colour. An incident is "wrong" when it is out of tune or clashes with the colour of its neighbour. Every novel is an attempt to capture time, to weave something solid out of air. The author knows it is an impossible task—that is why he keeps on trying.

(1981) As far as I know, I am the only professional novelist who is qualified in psychology. My characters follow very closely present-day thinking in psychology and human behaviour.

* * *

David Beaty, like Saint-Exupéry, makes his fiction out of the world of commercial aviation. And like his predecessor, his poetic insight enables him to add the symbolic dimension to the realism of his characterization and action. That realism centres on the contemporary dilemma, the human being trapped more and more by his own technology. The novelist particularizes this theme in *The Siren Song* by putting a question, "What is going to happen now that a machine can land an aeroplane a thousand times more safely than a human operator?"

The Beaty concern with man vs. machine has qualities which differentiate his work from that of other writers who discuss the same problem. As reference to the biography will indicate, he is a professional with a distinguished career as a pilot. In addition, he is an expert in certain areas of flying. His most recent research was published in 1969 in *The Human Factor in Aircraft Accidents*. This study of the psychological factors affecting pilot performance was so highly regarded by an international airline that the management wished to serialize it in their house organ. The importance of his past work is that it has an essential bearing on his art, on its emotional depth. In short Beaty draws upon his experience for more than a life-like milieu and professionally performing men and women.

Many facets of his work reveal the ties between his technology and his poetic fiction, but only two of these can be indicated in a short summary essay. The first aspect one can only call fundamental love of the instrument. Like the ship of the sea, the airship is regarded as a living creature. "As always on a runway, he had a sense of having no right to be there; as though this was the property of the machines that came tearing down it, to lift themselves up just before where he was now standing, and launch themselves into their own element." Obviously David Beaty does not belong to the back-to-nature school of critics, those who would denounce what they see as dirty, ugly, caricatures of birds. To airmen like him they are the vital tools for casting off earth's fetters, for seeing a new beauty, and for finding peace of mind and soul. Man and machine, "each dead without the other," must make their lives together, struggle with the elements together. Often the novelist sees the survival of each as equally important.

But man can use this instrument for bringing about his own damnation, even as the path to hell goes down from the gate to paradise. Thus, in the Beaty world of multiple images, the man-machine twinning becomes a warning symbol of ultimate destruction, as well as a sign of the way to a better world on the humanistic level and of joy on the transcendental level. In *The Wind Off the Sea* Gavin Gallagher, the Commander of a nuclear rocket base, has gloried in his god-sized power. "Marching along like this he had a sudden feeling of wisdom and elevation.... He was a giant. God. And he looked on it, and it was Good.... He said...let there be Life. And there was Life.... Let there be Death.... And there was Death. At the turn of a switch.... Quick as God." But a combination of factors culminating in the chilling experience of thinking that he has, through his right-left confusion, accidentally released the rocket, brings him to conversion:

> He walked away down the gravel path, out of the rocket site. Overhead the thin cloud cleared, and the sky was luminous with light....He had the distinct impression that he had been suffocating in a million fragmented thoughts, the metabolism of a life-time's mental processes, a dark pit, a deep sea. And that suddenly he had swum upwards towards a chink of light....He leaned against what had once been a blast wall to protect aircraft. He seemed to see every blade of grass, every branch of every tree, every patch of field and hedge and roadway, every iridescent particle of moonlight in some warm and loving radiance.

Beaty continues to write in two fields, fictional and technical. On the technical side, *The Water Jump* discusses the conquering of the North Atlantic route, and *The Complete Skytraveller* answers in detail the questions asked by the passenger. In fiction, his latest novels, *Excellency*, on a newly formed independent African government, and *The White Sea-Bird*, a moving depiction of sacrifice in World War II, unite his interests, for here he is concerned, as always, to show the human problems connected with the new technological environment man is creating.

—Roberta J. Forsberg

BECKER, Stephen (David). American. Born in Mount Vernon, New York, 31 March 1927. Educated at Harvard University, Cambridge, Massachusetts, 1943-47, B.A. 1947; Yenching University, Peking, 1947-48. Served in the United States Marine Corps, 1945. Married Mary Elizabeth Freeburg in 1947; three children. Instructor, Tsing Hua University, Peking, 1947-48; Teaching Fellow, Brandeis University, Waltham, Massachusetts, 1951-52; Lecturer, University of Alaska, 1967, Bennington College, Vermont, 1971, 1977, 1978, and University of Iowa, Iowa City, 1974. Editor, Western Printing Company, New York, 1955-56. Recipient: Paul Harris Fellowship, 1947; Guggenheim Fellowship, 1954. Address: West End, Tortola, British Virgin Islands.

PUBLICATIONS

Novels

The Season of the Stranger. New York, Harper, and London, Hamish Hamilton, 1951.
Shanghai Incident (as Steve Dodge). New York, Fawcett, 1955.
Juice. New York, Simon and Schuster, 1958; London, Muller, 1959.
A Covenant with Death. New York, Atheneum, and London, Hamish Hamilton, 1965.
The Outcasts. New York, Atheneum, and London, Hamish Hamilton, 1967.
When the War Is Over. New York, Random House, 1969; London, Hamish Hamilton, 1970.
Dog Tags. New York, Random House, 1973; London, Barrie and Jenkins, 1974.
The Chinese Bandit. New York, Random House, 1975; London, Chatto and Windus, 1976.
The Last Mandarin. New York, Random House, and London, Chatto and Windus, 1979.

Uncollected Short Stories

"To Know the Country," in *Harper's* (New York), August 1951.
"The Town Mouse," in *The Best American Short Stories 1953*, edited by Martha Foley. Boston, Houghton Mifflin, 1953.
"A Baptism of Some Importance," in *Story.* New York, McKay, 1953.
"Monsieur Malfait," in *Harper's* (New York), June 1953.
"The New Encyclopaedist," in *The Year's Best SF 10*, edited by Judith Merril. New York, Delacorte Press, 1965.

Other

Comic Art in America: A Social History of the Funnies, the Political Cartoons, Magazine Humor, Sporting Cartoons, and Animated Cartoons. New York, Simon and Schuster, 1959.
Marshall Field III: A Biography. New York, Simon and Schuster, 1964.

Translator, *The Colors of the Day*, by Romain Gary. New York, Simon and Schuster, and London, Joseph, 1953.
Translator, *Mountains in the Desert*, by Louis Carl and Joseph Petit. New York, Doubleday, 1954; as *Tefedest*, London, Allen and Unwin, 1954.
Translator, *The Sacred Forest*, by Pierre-Dominique Gaisseau. New York, Knopf, 1954.
Translator, *Faraway*, by André Dhotel. New York, Simon and Schuster, 1957.
Translator, *Someone Will Die Tonight in the Caribbean*, by René Puissesseau. New York, Knopf, 1958; London, W.H. Allen, 1959.
Translator, *The Last of the Just*, by André Schwarz-Bart. New York, Atheneum, and London, Secker and Warburg, 1961.
Translator, *The Town Beyond the Wall*, by Elie Wiesel. New York, Atheneum, 1964; London, Robson, 1975.

Translator, *The Conquerors*, by André Malraux. New York, Holt Rinehart, 1976.
Translator, *Diary of My Travels in America*, by Louis-Philippe. New York, Delacorte Press, 1977.
Translator, *Ana No*, by Agustin Gomez-Arcos. London, Secker and Warburg, 1980.

* * *

Equally distinguished as a translator, a biographer, a commentator on the popular arts, and a novelist, Stephen Becker brings to his fiction a breadth of experience with world culture and human behavior which yields moral complexity and psychological verity in his work. Two major themes intertwine through his novels—the problems of justice and the necessity for self-knowledge and self-fulfillment.

Beginning most clearly with *Juice*, Becker concentrates on the moral and social complexities of law and justice, continuing this theme in *A Covenant with Death* and *When the War Is Over*. The problem Becker's protagonists face is to distinguish between the arbitrary and mechanical justice of the law and true human justice. The rigidity and absoluteness of law collide with human values—especially the need for expiation, mercy and compassion. The characters' dilemma is to choose between true justice and simple retribution and to use the mechanism of blind justice to solve difficult moral problems. Against this theme is developed another—an existential concept of the self, men struggling with themselves, with nature and with circumstances to become fully alive and functioning beings. This theme is isolated most clearly in *The Outcasts*, which describes a group of engineers building a bridge deep in a primeval jungle. There they must overcome the indifferent force of nature, their own weaknesses, their fears and prejudices.

In *Juice* the theme of human and mechanical justice arises when the central character, Joseph Harrison, kills a pedestrian in an auto accident. His friends and employer try to use the law and the power of money and position ("juice") to whitewash the occurrence, while Harrison demands an absolute judgment to redeem his error. The tensions between views of law and truth reshape Harrison's whole existence. In *A Covenant with Death* a young judge is confronted with a difficult decision in a murder case; through detective work, insights into motivation and a complete understanding of the limits of the law, Judge Lewis is able to render a humane verdict and still satisfy the meaning of law. The forces of procrustean and draconian legalism are averted through the judge's efforts, through an intense moral revaluation which ultimately changes the judge's own life. In this novel, humanity triumphs through the action of the law.

The tragedy of the law is exposed in *When the War Is Over*, Becker's most satisfying novel. It is the story of the last victim of the Civil War, a boy executed as a Confederate guerilla long after hostilities had ceased. The moral struggle is embodied in Lt. Marius Catto, a young career officer caught between a genuine love of peace and justice and a natural inclination toward the arts of war. He works to prevent General Hooker from wreaking vengeance through law on the boy but fails and is left scarred and embittered by disillusionment. The novel, based on historical fact, is a brilliant reconstruction of the time and place and an intense scrutiny of moral and social values. It convincingly examines the mechanism of military order, social justice and our conflicting views of violence and law. The story uncovers basic contradictions in our organization of legal murder.

Dog Tags is another densely detailed chronicle of man at war and his ability to survive it humanly and intelligently. It focuses on Benjamin Beer, a Jew wounded in World War II and later interned in North Korea. His response to war is to become a skilled and humane doctor, as if in expiation for the universal crime of war. His life is a moral struggle for self-knowledge and understanding of man's limitless potentials: "You're worried about good and bad," he says, "well, I'm worried about good and evil." In his quest, Benjamin learns his own abilities and limitations and achieves peace and grace within himself.

Becker's examination of society's structure and limitations and his portrayal of men seeking "grace under pressure" is a significant contribution to contemporary fiction. The existential premises of the works—individuals finding meaning inside the arbitrary bounds of social order—reflect our acceptance of the civilization we have built.

—William J. Schafer

BECKETT, Samuel (Barclay). Irish. Born near Dublin, 13 April 1906. Educated at Portora Royal School, County Fermanagh; Trinity College, Dublin, B.A. in French and Italian 1927, M.A. 1931. Worked at the Irish Red Cross Hospital, St. Lô, France, 1945. Married Suzanne Dechevaux-Dumesnil in 1948. French teacher, Campbell College, Belfast, 1928; Lecturer in English, Ecole Normale Supérieure, Paris, 1928-30; Lecturer in French, Trinity College, Dublin, 1930-31. Closely associated with James Joyce in Paris in the late 1920's and the 1930's. Settled in Paris in 1938, and has written chiefly in French since 1945; translates his own work into English. Recipient: *Evening Standard* award, for drama, 1955; Obie Award, for drama, 1958, 1960, 1962, 1964; Italia Prize, 1959; International Publishers Prize, 1961; Prix Filmcritice, 1965; Tours Film Prize, 1966; Nobel Prize for Literature, 1969. D.Litt: Dublin University, 1959. Address: c/o Editions de Minuit, 7 rue Bernard-Palissy, Paris 6, France.

PUBLICATIONS

Novels

Murphy. London, Routledge, 1938; New York, Grove Press, 1957.
Molloy. Paris, Editions de Minuit, 1951; translated by the author and Patrick Bowles, Paris, Olympia Press, and New York, Grove Press, 1955; London, Calder, 1959.
Malone meurt. Paris, Editions de Minuit, 1951; translated by the author as *Malone Dies*, New York, Grove Press, 1956; London, Calder, 1958.
L'Innommable. Paris, Editions de Minuit, 1953; translated by the author as *The Unnamable*, New York, Grove Press, 1958; London, Calder, 1959.
Watt (written in English). Paris, Olympia Press, 1953; New York, Grove Press, 1959; London, Calder, 1963.
Comment C'Est. Paris, Editions de Minuit, 1961; translated by the author as *How It Is*, New York, Grove Press, and London, Calder, 1964.
Mercier et Camier. Paris, Editions de Minuit, 1970; translated by the author as *Mercier and Camier*, London, Calder and Boyars, 1974; New York, Grove Press, 1975.
Company. London, Calder, and New York, Grove Press, 1980.

Short Stories and Texts

More Pricks Than Kicks. London, Chatto and Windus, 1934; New York, Grove Press, 1970.
Nouvelles et Textes pour Rien. Paris, Editions de Minuit, 1955; translated by the author and Richard Seaver as *Stories and Texts for Nothing*, New York, Grove Press, 1967; in *No's Knife: Selected Shorter Prose, 1945-1966*, 1967.
From an Abandoned Work. London, Faber, 1958.
Imagination morte imaginez. Paris, Editions de Minuit, 1965; translated by the author as *Imagination Dead Imagine*, London, Calder and Boyars, 1965.

Assez. Paris, Editions de Minuit, 1966; translated by the author as *Enough*, in No's Knife, 1967.
Bing. Paris, Editions de Minuit, 1966; translated by the author as *Ping*, in *No's Knife*, 1967.
Têtes-Mortes (includes *D'Un Ouvrage Abandonné, Assez, Bing, Imagination morte imaginez*). Paris, Editions de Minuit, 1967; translated by the author, in *No's Knife*, 1967.
No's Knife: Selected Shorter Prose, 1945-1966 (includes *Stories and Texts for Nothing, From an Abandoned Work, Imagination Dead Imagine, Enough, Ping*). London, Calder and Boyars, 1967.
L'Issue. Paris, Georges Visat, 1968.
Sans. Paris, Editions de Minuit, 1969; translated by the author as *Lessness*, London, Calder and Boyars, 1971.
Séjour. Paris, Georges Richar, 1970.
Premier Amour. Paris, Editions de Minuit, 1970; translated by the author as *First Love*, London, Calder and Boyars, 1973.
Le Dépeupleur. Paris, Editions de Minuit, 1971; translated by the author as *The Lost Ones*, London, Calder and Boyars, 1972.
The North. London, Enitharmon Press, 1972.
First Love and Other Shorts. New York, Grove Press, 1974.
Fizzles. New York, Grove Press, 1976.
For to End Yet Again and Other Fizzles. London, Calder, 1976.
All Strange Away. New York, Gotham Book Mart, 1976; London, Calder, 1979.
Four Novellas (*The Expelled, The Calmative, The End, First Love*). London, Calder, 1977; as *The Expelled and Other Novellas*, London, Penguin, 1980.
Six Residua. London, Calder, 1978.
Mal vu mal dit. Paris, Editions de Minuit, 1981.

Plays

Le Kid, with Georges Pelorson (produced Dublin, 1931).
En Attendant Godot (produced Paris, 1953). Paris, Editions de Minuit, 1952; translated by the author as *Waiting for Godot: Tragicomedy* (produced London, 1955; Miami and New York, 1956), New York, Grove Press, 1954; London, Faber, 1956.
Fin de Partie: Suivi de Acte sans Paroles (produced London, 1957). Paris, Editions de Minuit, 1957; translated by the author as *Endgame: A Play in One Act; Followed by Act Without Words: A Mime for One Player* (*Endgame*, produced New York and London, 1958; *Act Without Words*, produced New York, 1960), New York, Grove Press, and London, Faber, 1958.
All That Fall (broadcast, 1957). New York, Grove Press, 1957; as *All That Fall: A Play for Radio*, London, Faber, 1957.
Krapp's Last Tape (produced London, 1958; New York, 1960). Included in *Krapp's Last Tape and Embers*, 1959; in *Krapp's Last Tape and Other Dramatic Pieces*, 1960.
Embers (broadcast, 1959). Included in *Krapp's Last Tape and Embers*, 1959; in *Krapp's Last Tape and Other Dramatic Pieces*, 1960.
Krapp's Last Tape and Embers. London, Faber, 1959.
Act Without Words II (produced New York, 1959; London, 1960). Included in *Krapp's Last Tape and Other Dramatic Pieces*, 1960; in *Eh Joe and Other Writings*, 1967.
Krapp's Last Tape and Other Dramatic Pieces (includes *All That Fall, Embers, Act Without Words I* and *II*). New York, Grove Press, 1960.
Happy Days (produced New York, 1961; London, 1962). New York, Grove Press, 1961; London, Faber, 1962; bilingual edition, edited by James Knowlson, Faber, 1978.
Words and Music (broadcast, 1962). Included in *Play and Two Short Pieces for Radio*, 1964; in *Cascando and Other Short Dramatic Pieces*, 1968.
Cascando (broadcast, in French, 1963). Paris, Editions de Minuit, 1963; translated by the author as *Cascando: A Radio Piece for Music and Voice* (broadcast, 1964; in *Beckett 3*, produced London, 1970; produced New York, 1976), included in *Play and Two Short Pieces for Radio*, 1964; in *Cascando and Other Short Dramatic Pieces*, 1968.
Play (produced Ulm-Donau, 1963; New York and London, 1964). Included in *Play and Two Short Pieces for Radio*, 1964; in *Cascando and Other Short Dramatic Pieces*, 1968.
Play and Two Short Pieces for Radio (includes *Words and Music* and *Cascando*). London, Faber, 1964.
Eh Joe (televised, 1966; produced New York, 1978). Included in *Eh Joe and Other Writings*, 1967; in *Cascando and Other Short Dramatic Pieces*, 1968.
Come and Go: Dramaticule (produced Paris, 1966; Dublin, 1968; London, 1970; New York, 1974). London, Calder and Boyars, 1967; in *Cascando and Other Short Dramatic Pieces*, 1968.
Eh Joe and Other Writings (includes *Act Without Words II* and *Film*). London, Faber, 1967.
Cascando and Other Short Dramatic Pieces (includes *Words and Music, Eh Joe, Play, Come and Go, Film*). New York, Grove Press, 1968.
Film. New York, Grove Press, 1969; London, Faber, 1971.
Breath (produced Oxford, 1970). Included in *Breath and Other Shorts*, 1971.
Breath and Other Shorts (includes *Come and Go, Act Without Words I* and *II*, and the prose piece *From an Abandoned Work*). London, Faber, 1971.
Not I (produced New York, 1972; London, 1973). London, Faber, 1973; in *First Love and Other Shorts*, 1974.
Tryst (televised, 1976). Included in *Ends and Odds*, 1976.
That Time (produced London and Washington, D.C., 1976; New York, 1977). London, Faber, 1976; in *Ends and Odds*, 1976.
Footfalls (also director: produced London, 1976; Washington, D.C., 1976; New York, 1977). London, Faber, 1976; in *Ends and Odds*, 1976.
Ends and Odds: Dramatic Pieces (includes *That Time, Footfalls, Tryst, Not I*). New York, Grove Press, 1976; as *Ends and Odds: Plays and Sketches* (includes *Not I, That Time, Footfalls, Ghost Trio, ...But the Clouds..., Theatre I* and *II, Radio I* and *II*), London, Faber, 1977.
Rough for Radio (broadcast, 1976). As *Radio II*, included in *Ends and Odds*, 1977.
Shades (televised, 1977). Included in *Ends and Odds*, 1977.
Rockaby (produced Buffalo, New York, and New York City, 1981). Included in *Rockaby and Other Works*, 1981.
Rockaby and Other Works. New York, Grove Press, 1981.

Screenplay: *Film*, 1965.

Radio Plays: *All That Fall*, 1957; *Embers*, 1959; *Words and Music*, 1962; *Cascando*, 1963; *Rough for Radio*, 1976.

Television Plays: *Eh Joe*, 1966; *Tryst*, 1976; *Shades* (*Ghost Trio, Not I*, and *...But the Clouds...*), 1977.

Verse

Whoroscope. Paris, Hours Press, 1930.
Echo's Bones and Other Precipitates. Paris, Europa Press, 1935.
Gedichte (collected poems in English and French, with German translations). Wiesbaden, Limes Verlag, 1959.
Poems in English. London, Calder, 1961; New York, Grove Press, 1963.
Collected Poems in English and French. London, Calder, and New York, Grove Press, 1977.

Other

"Dante...Bruno. Vico..Joyce," in *Our Exagmination round His Factification for Incamination of Work in Progress.* Paris, Shakespeare and Company, 1929; London, Faber, 1936; New York, New Dimensions, 1939.
Proust. London, Chatto and Windus, 1931; New York, Grove Press, 1957; with *Three Dialogues with Georges Duthuit*, London, Calder, 1965.

Bram von Welde, with others. Paris, Georges Fall, 1958; translated by the author and Olive Classe, New York, Grove Press, 1960.
A Samuel Beckett Reader. London, Calder and Boyars, 1967.
I Can't Go On: A Selection from the Work of Samuel Beckett, edited by Richard Seaver. New York, Grove Press, 1976.

Translator, *Anthology of Mexican Poetry*, edited by Octavio Paz. Bloomington, Indiana University Press, 1958; London, Thames and Hudson, 1959.
Translator, *The Old Tune*, by Robert Pinget. Paris, Editions de Minuit, 1960; in *Three Plays*, by Robert Pinget, New York, Hill and Wang, 1966; in *Plays*, London, Calder and Boyars, 1966.
Translator, *Zone*, by Guillaume Apollinaire. Dublin and London, Dolmen Press-Calder and Boyars, 1960.
Translator, *Drunken Boat*, by Arthur Rimbaud, edited by James Knowlson and Felix Leakey. Reading, Whiteknights Press, 1977.

*

Bibliography: *Samuel Beckett: His Work and His Critics: An Essay in Bibliography* by Raymond Federman and John Fletcher, Berkeley, University of California Press, 1970 (through 1966).

Manuscript Collections: University of Texas, Austin; Ohio State University, Columbus; Washington University, St. Louis, Missouri; Dartmouth College, Hanover, New Hampshire; Reading University, England.

Critical Studies (selection): *Samuel Beckett: A Critical Study*, New York, Grove Press, and London, Calder, 1962, revised edition, Berkeley, University of California Press, 1968, and *A Reader's Guide to Samuel Beckett*, New York, Farrar Straus, and London, Thames and Hudson, 1973, both by Hugh Kenner; *Samuel Beckett: The Comic Gamut*, New Brunswick, New Jersey, Rutgers University Press, 1962, and *Back to Beckett*, Princeton, New Jersey, Princeton University Press, 1974, both by Ruby Cohn; *Samuel Beckett* by William York Tindall, New York, Columbia University Press, 1964; *Samuel Beckett* by Richard N. Coe, New York, Grove Press, 1964; *The Novels of Samuel Beckett* by John Fletcher, London, Chatto and Windus, and New York, Barnes and Noble, 1964; *Samuel Beckett: A Collection of Critical Essays* edited by Martin Esslin, Englewood Cliffs, New Jersey, Prentice Hall, 1965; *Journey to Chaos: Samuel Beckett's Early Fiction* by Raymond Federman, Berkeley, University of California Press, 1965, and *Samuel Beckett: The Critical Heritage* edited by Federman and Lawrence Graver, London, Routledge, 1979; *Beckett at 60: A Festschrift* edited by John Calder, London, Calder and Boyars, 1967; *Samuel Beckett* by Ronald Hayman, London, Heinemann, 1968, New York, Ungar, 1974; *Samuel Beckett Now: Critical Approaches to His Novels, Poetry, and Plays* edited by Melvin J. Friedman, Chicago, University of Chicago Press, 1970; *Samuel Beckett: A Study of His Novels* by Eugene Webb, Seattle, University of Washington Press, 1970; *The Fiction of Samuel Beckett: Form and Effect* by H. Porter Abbott, Berkeley, University of California Press, 1973; *Beckett/Beckett* by Vivian Mercier, New York, Oxford University Press, 1977, London, Oxford University Press, 1979; *Samuel Beckett: A Biography* by Dierdre Bair, New York, Harcourt Brace, and London, Cape, 1978; *Beckett and the Voice of Species: A Study of His Prose Fiction* by Eric P. Levy, New York, Barnes and Noble, 1980; *Frescoes of the Skull: The Later Prose and Drama of Samuel Beckett* by James Knowlson and John Pilling, New York, Grove Press, 1980.

Theatrical Activities:

Director: **Plays**—*Come and Go*, Paris, 1966; *Endgame*, Berlin, 1967; *Krapp's Last Tape*, Berlin, 1969; *Krapp's Last Tape* and *Act Without Words*, Paris, 1970; *Krapp's Last Tape* and *Endgame*, London, 1971; *Happy Days*, Berlin, 1971, London, 1979; *Waiting for Godot*, Berlin, 1975, New York, 1977; *Krapp's Last Tape* and *Not I*, Paris, 1975; *Footfalls*, London, 1976; *Krapp's Last Tape*, Berlin, 1977, and London, 1978. **Television**—*Eh Joe*, 1966 (Germany).

* * *

Poet, playwright, and occasional critic, Samuel Beckett considers his most valid work to be the fiction which has changed radically from the modish English written in his twenties, to the dense French written in his seventies.

Beckett's first published short story, "Assumption," appeared in the June 1929 issue of *transition*, along with his essay on Joyce's *Work in Progress*. Beckett then began his own Work in Progress, a novel entitled *Dream of Fair to Middling Women*. After 214 pages, he abandoned it, although he published two excerpts in 1932. More importantly, he salvaged the novel's protagonist, Belacqua Shuah, for a series of short stories, *More Pricks Than Kicks*. The exotic name of the Dublin-based hero is borrowed from Canto IV of Dante's *Purgatorio*, where he sits in fetal position "more indolent than if sloth were his sister." Like his namesake, Beckett's Belacqua inclines to indolence, but circumstances and fair to middling women conspire against him, so that he leads an active short life. Thrice married, Beckett's Belacqua dies in surgery and is replaced by his best friend in the arms of his widow. The book closes in a cemetery, where the ground keeper forgets about Belacqua's remains. "So it goes in the world." For the way of the world is not a way of lingering compassion.

After the 1934 publication of these ten stories that constitute a picaresque novel, Beckett began the novel *Murphy*, more traditionally plotted. In name and spirit, Belacqua was a foreigner in his native Dublin; Murphy the Irishman is a foreigner in London, where Beckett was living when he wrote the novel. Like Belacqua, Murphy cherishes indolence, and like Beckett's Belacqua, Murphy finds that Woman is the main obstacle to the indolent life of the mind. Belacqua's several women crystallize into Murphy's Celia Kelly, a kind-hearted whore about whom the hero's mind and body are in conflict. Despite reluctance on the part of the former, she prevails upon the latter to seek employment so that she need not continue hers. At his place of employment, the Magdalen Mental Mercyseat, Murphy renounces the outside world, including Celia. While this ironic reversal is taking place, a virtual posse has set out in search of Murphy—from Cork through Dublin to London, where they converge upon a Murphyless Celia. Murphy, having retired to a garret, is burned to death in an explosion. Murphy's various hunters find only his charred remains, and they go on with their separate lives. For the way of the world is not a way of lingering compassion.

Murphy was not published until 1938, after Beckett had moved to Paris, where he still lives. His first French fiction was the translation of *Murphy* into French, undertaken with Alfred Péron and completed before the outbreak of World War II. After fleeing from the Nazis to Free France, while working as an agricultural laborer Beckett completed *Watt*. The naive titular hero expects language to explain phenomena. Using his senses, "his most noble faculties," and his mind, "whatever that may be," Watt seeks to make sense of thing, event, and person at Mr. Knott's establishment, where he undertakes service. But reason and senses are incommensurate with Mr. Knott, and Watt leaves Mr. Knott's house. At a later date, Watt moves and speaks in inversions; he lives in a mansion where he meets Sam who lives in his own mansion, and it is Sam who purports to be the recorder of Watt's adventures as narrated by their hero. It is presumably Sam who divides the novel into four numbered parts and an Addendum. Part 2 is the core of Watt's tragedy—his inability to come to terms with the phenomena of Mr. Knott's establishment. Part 2 of *Watt* also contains the precursor of Beckett's French fiction—his predecessor's alogical, first-person narration.

Although Beckett had written poems in French and translated *Murphy* into French, it was not until his return to Paris after World War II that he adopted French as his major writing language. The bulk of Beckett's fiction should be classified as *French* fiction. With an occasional collaborator, however, he has translated his French fiction into English, whose literature he thereby enriches.

After four long stories (*La Fin, L'Expulsé, Premier amour*, and *Le Calmant*) and a novel (*Mercier et Camier*), Beckett embarked on the trilogy, often considered his major work. *Molloy, Malone Dies*, and *The Unnamable*, published separately, are not a trilogy in the usual sense of developing a plot through time. Rather, they progressively concentrate events and characters through heightened intensity of the first-person narrations. *Molloy* is divided into two parts. In the first a grotesque old cripple, hat fastened to his buttonhole by a lace, having arrived mysteriously in his mother's room, writes a disconnected tale of his disconnected voyage toward his mother. In the second part Jacques Moran, a middle-aged Catholic father of an only namesake son, having returned from a mission to seek Molloy, writes a report for his employer Youdi. In *Malone Dies* the paralytic hero, confined to his bed, tries to order the time of his dying by writing an inventory of his possessions, a description of his present state, and stories. The titular speaker-protagonist of *The Unnamable* seeks to penetrate behind fictional and linguistic formulae to himself. His utterances, stripped of Moran's determination, Molloy's passion, and Malone's purpose, attain an incantatory anguish of meaning made music.

After the trilogy, genre designations are difficult for Beckett's non-dramatic work, and plots crumble before any effort at summary. His *Texts for Nothing*, spare of event, might be called prose poems or thematic monologues; Beckett calls them "texts." *How It Is*, whose three parts might be called a novel, traces the itineraries of characters who meet and part, naked in the mud. The grammatical first person dissolves into unpunctuated phrases in irregular verses which, repeated and permuted, carry the burden of a narration climaxed by the tender yet terrifying encounter of Pim and Bom. *How It Is* is the verbal distillation of anguished reaching for a self, and it is Beckett's last fictional expression of pain.

After *How It Is*, Beckett's mainly French fiction is more frankly fiction as it recedes further and further from referential reality, the quasi-mathematical *Residua* leading to *The Lost Ones. How It Is* reached for an infinite series of Pims and Boms, but the protagonist of *The Lost Ones* is a tiny town—two hundred five inhabitants of a desiccated cylinder. These inferno-dwellers manoeuvre fifteen ladders in their vain search for an exit from the cylinder. Searchers, climbers, and vanquished form a perpetual motion machine that (distortedly?) mirrors human societies. Beckett depersonalizes narration, only to create another analogue of suffering.

Company is Beckett's first extended English fiction since *Watt*—after 35 years—and it is marked by lyrical cadences of rich language for dim scenes. "You," a man on his back in the dark, has for "company" a voice—the voice that resonates as early as *Watt*, and that attains full diapason in the post-*Godot* fiction. Further even than *How It Is* from specific setting, *Company* coalesces drama and fiction; *Company* is a dialogue between an inert "you" and an observing "he." *Company* blends autobiographical traces with phrases, themes, incidents of earlier Beckett works—the whole company. *Company* is its own salute to man's capacity for conceiving company.

As though to disdain that capacity, Beckett retreated to French for *Mal vu mal dit*. A Venus-haunted, white-haired woman in black is intermittently perceived in her own perceptions. Alerting the reader by calls of "Attention," the narrative imagination endows her with a dozen disciples, a suffering lamb, and shards of biblical landscapes. No longer goal-oriented as in *How It Is* and *The Lost Ones*, this latest Beckett fiction fragments the myths of our culture. No longer seeking Being beneath the superficies of our civilization, Beckett continues to write, more candidly imagining. "Ill seen, ill said" though his fiction may be, it has been a lodestar of two literatures—English and French.

—Ruby Cohn

BECKHAM, Barry (Earl). American. Born in Philadelphia, Pennsylvania, 19 March 1944. Educated at Brown University, Providence, Rhode Island, 1962-66, A.B. 1966. Married 1) Betty Louise Hope in 1966 (divorced, 1977), one son and one daughter; 2) Geraldine Lynne Palmer in 1979. Public Relations Consultant, 1966-67, and Urban Affairs Associate, 1969-70, Chase Manhattan Bank, New York; Public Relations Consultant, YMCA National Council, New York, 1967-68, and Western Electric Company, New York, 1968-69. Since 1970, Lecturer, then Associate Professor and Director of Graduate Program in Creative Writing, Brown University. Agent: Mel Berger, William Morris Agency, 1350 Avenue of the Americas, New York, New York 10019. Address: 236 Camp Street, Providence, Rhode Island 02906, U.S.A.

PUBLICATIONS

Novels

My Main Mother. New York, Walker, 1969; London, Wingate, 1970; as *Blues in the Night*, London, Tandem, 1974.
Runner Mack. New York, Morrow, 1972.

*

Manuscript Collection: Mugar Memorial Library, Boston University.

Critical Studies: reviews by Peter Rowley, 30 November 1969, and Mel Watkins, 17 September 1972, both in *New York Times Book Review*; interview with Sanford Pinsker, in *Black Images 3* (Toronto), Autumn 1974.

* * *

By and large, Barry Beckham's reputation rests modestly on two small novels published within the three-year period of 1969-72. Both are flawed and somewhat derivative, yet Beckham's talents suggest promising developments in fiction about black experience in America, a field which he thinks "has been inadequately treated for the most part." In both novels, Beckham moves decisively away from the ghetto novel of social protest and literary naturalism to the psychological effects of neglect and exploitation, portrayed in a blend of verbal impressionism and surrealism.

In *My Main Mother* Mitchell Mibbs tells his own story of how he came to murder his beautiful mother, Pearl, in their home in Chatsworth, Maine, where Mitch's grandparents were born. In this tragicomic "confession of the soul," or "proclamation of my own emancipation," Mitchell plans an imaginary press release, a self-mocking and ironic outline-summary of Beckham's first novel: "A young black genius, sitting comfortably in an abandoned auto on the outskirts of town, announced today that he has killed his mother for the best of all concerned. His testimony is a novel, profound manuscript of some eighty thousand words, listing various and sundry acts alleged to have prompted the macabre slaying. The acts have been arranged in narrative form, and the manuscript has been cited by leading authorities as extremely accomplished."

Perhaps the cruelest of mother Pearl's "various and sundry acts" is the exploitation and betrayal of old Mervin Pip, an honest, kindly uncle who serves Mitch *in loco parentis* and is his one true friend. The title is therefore a triple play on the shaping environment: "main" refers to the geographical location, to Uncle Melvin and to Pearl, all of whom have made Mitchell what he is. Throughout, racial themes are both present and understated, while authentic portrayal of main characters, skillful use of point-of-view, and vivid imagery earn our attention. The title phrase is, of course, "black," and so are the idiom, characterizations, and occurrences of the novel without the stridency of naturalism or the "race novel." Present, nevertheless, are the props and concerns found in *Native Son* and *Black Boy*, the ur-works of modern black literary art: besides the title similarities, combined in this one work are Wright's dual depictions of the fatherless boy who murders a beautiful woman, the suppression of aspiration in a bright black boy, the hypocrisy of liberal or well-meaning whites, and the sense of entrapment, betrayal, and waste of youth.

Runner Mack is indebted to that other seminal and symbolic black novel, *Invisible Man*, by Ralph Ellison. Beckham's Henry Adams, not a New England patrician but a poor Mississippi baseball player, comes to New York ostensibly for a baseball try-out ("this is the national past-time, they've got to be fair with me"), and then remains to be educated in the true national sport of "keeping this nigger running." Cheated by a midget manager of his fair chance in athletics (a prime source of upward mobility for American blacks), Henry tries the subtler game of American business, where he is given token opportunity in a dead-end job. In dreamlike sequences, he is hit by a Mack truck (before encountering "Runner Mack," the title character); a heedless Spanish building "super" steals his pajamas; Henry's wife is raped in his presence; a crippled corporation president delivers an inaudible Christmas speech; and a summons arrives requiring Henry to leave at once "to fight for my country." Like Ellison, Barry Beckham casts his young innocent in a picaresque narrative reprise of black-American history, with emphasis on the absurdity of American rituals and the indecencies of American institutions.

Thus, the stage is set for the novel's second half, Henry's army adventures, in a twin parody of war and revolution. Institutionalized racism is patriotically turned against "slopes" and "gooks" instead of blacks, so that even Henry may become both a racist and a good American. The Vietnam war is mysteriously transposed to the white Alaskan wilderness and since no "slopes" are ever found, the men slay seals and herds of Caribou, the ecological equivalent of defoliation. The young soldiers are terrified by the Pentagon mentality of Captain Nevins and the fierce, foul intensity of his need to kill. Then Henry encounters Runnington Mack, a cynical, honest black hipster, who becomes his mentor in a revolutionary plot to bomb the White House. "Runner" Mack, loose as a halfback and solid as a truck, stands in obvious contrast to the hysterical, murderous Captain Nevins, to the deformed baseball manager and corporation president and to the other obsessive, obscene whites whom Henry has had to follow. Swiftly, he learns from Mack of the hypocrisy of American leadership, the futility of reform in a death-directed culture, and the need for violent revolution. Henry Adams' "education" is poignantly completed when Runner Mack's thought-out plan fails abysmally because no one cares and Mack commits suicide in despair.

Although his main characters are believable in both novels, Beckham's characterizations sometimes divide humanity into wholly good or wholly despicable specimens, and nearly all white characters are negatively drawn. Despite this side-choosing, he elicits our sympathy for his good guys, such as Mitch, Henry, and Runner, and hostility toward Mitch's mother, her husband Julius, and assorted villains. His success at evoking reader empathy is largely attributable to Beckham's small-scale scenic method, whereby we see and feel the misery of a rustic old man lost in Harlem, the loneliness of a boy in a rusty, abandoned car in the woods, the isolation of a housewife deafened by television, the panic of a man running to a job interview. These and other carved images become slide-projections or backdrops in the larger enactments of black absurd theatre.

—Frank Campenni

BEDFORD, Sybille. British. Born in Charlottenburg, Germany, 16 March 1911. Educated privately. Married Walter Bedford in 1935. Has worked as a Law Reporter: covered the Auschwitz Trial at Frankfurt for the *Observer*, London, and the *Saturday Evening Post*, New York, 1963-65, and the trial of Jack Ruby at Dallas for *Life*, New York, 1964. Vice-President, P.E.N., 1980. Fellow, Royal Society of Literature, 1964. O.B.E. (Officer, Order of the British Empire), 1981. Address: c/o Coutts Bank, 1 Old Park Lane, London W1Y 4BS, England.

PUBLICATIONS

Novels

A Legacy. London, Weidenfeld and Nicolson, 1956; New York, Simon and Schuster, 1957.

A Favourite of the Gods. London, Collins, and New York, Simon and Schuster, 1963.

A Compass Error. London, Collins, 1968; New York, Knopf, 1969.

Uncollected Short Story

"Compassionata at Hyde Park Corner," in *23 Modern Stories.* New York, Knopf, 1963.

Other

The Sudden View: A Mexican Journey. London, Gollancz, and New York, Harper, 1953; revised edition, New York, Atheneum, 1963; as *A Visit to Don Otavio: A Traveller's Tale from Mexico*, London, Collins, 1960.

The Best We Can Do: An Account of the Trial of John Bodkin Adams. London, Collins, 1958; as *The Trial of Dr. Adams*, New York, Simon and Schuster, 1959.

The Faces of Justice: A Traveller's Report. London, Collins, and New York, Simon and Schuster, 1961.

Aldous Huxley: A Biography. London, Chatto and Windus-Collins, 2 vols., 1973-74; New York, Knopf, 1 vol., 1974.

*

Critical Studies: by Evelyn Waugh, in *The Spectator* (London), 13 April 1956; V.S. Pritchett, in *New Statesman* (London), 11 January 1963; P.N. Furbank, in *Encounter* (London), April 1964; Bernard Levin, in London *Daily Mail*, 12 September 1966; Constantine FitzGibbon, in *Irish Times* (Dublin), 19 October 1968.

* * *

A first glance at Sybille Bedford's fiction suggests the genre of social history, perhaps the subordinate form of the family novel. Yet, although the accoutrements of history and generation are present, strongest in the first novel and diminishing in the next two, the actual core of interest resides in the individual character as such and the validity of his action.

The first novel, *A Legacy*, might have commented on the unification of Germany through a parallelling of the events of the Felden Scandal or the marriages that occupy much of the action. The novel might also have commented on the degeneration of the twin dynamos of the early modern age, Voltaire and Rousseau, through the description of the two major families of the book: the Merzes, "wealthy" Berlin Jews whose retiring and bourgeois interests belie their originating ancestor's intellectual passions; and the von Feldens, petty South German barons who are vaguely agrarian and on occasion Catholic. However, the ties are too tenuous and the long build-up accorded the families only serves as an interesting forepiece to the corrupt morality and inadequate vitality that are revealed in the marriages of Julius von Felden to Melanie Merz and later to Caroline Trafford, the generous-spirited English woman who suddenly appears more than half way through the novel and serves as the reader's sounding board.

The second novel, *A Favourite of the Gods*, running from the turn of the century into the period between the World Wars in Italy and England, draws less extensively on social and historical matters, although the characters reflect regional stereotypes and there is some mention made of the First World War and of the opposition to Mussolini. Principally, however, the novel contrasts Anna, a sexually ingenuous and probably repressed blue-stocking from New England, who marries a Roman prince, with Constanza, her sexually free, liberal-minded, but intellectually poorly-developed daughter.

The third novel, *A Compass Error*, which takes place in Southern France, is the least socio-historical, having only peripheral mention of anti-fascism and the Second World War. An enlargement of an incident in *A Favourite of the Gods*, it details a hybristic error made by Flavia, the daughter of Constanza, and her short-lived English husband. Within the frame of a backward look the middle-aged Flavia recounts her young belief that she could chart out her life, and her subsequent manipulation by the wife of her mother's lover that changed her own as well as her mother's life.

The socio-historical settings of the novels, although never essential to the action, are often fascinating in themselves. Further, they suggest, as a consideration of the characters will show, the possible mastership of Henry James. Besides the indirection of comment, that sometimes maddening characteristic of James, each of the characters who pair off in the novels' action derives from a different country, again typical. In addition each pair exhibits the contrast between fresh, energetic innocence and degenerate, if attractive, worldliness leading to moral insight that James modulated from *The American* to *The Golden Bowl*. Yet, if the characterization is Jamesian, the shifting point of view of the narrator is not. Nor is the large structure of the novels, as evidenced by the overweighted early part of *A Legacy* and the background that Flavia relates in *A Compass Error*, at the end of which her fictional auditor is quite understandably asleep.

Although top literary honors cannot be accorded Sybille Bedford's fiction, we can recognize her civilized and informed attitude and the skillfully drawn characters, the delightful evocation of place and time, and the witty well-rendered scenes that have won her contemporary acclaim.

—John P. O'Neill

BELLOW, Saul. American. Born in Lachine, Quebec, Canada, 10 June 1915; grew up in Montreal; moved with his family to Chicago, 1924. Educated at the University of Chicago, 1933-35; Northwestern University, Evanston, Illinois, 1935-37, B.S. (honors) in sociology and anthropology 1937; did graduate work in anthropology at the University of Wisconsin, Madison, 1937. Served in the United States Merchant Marine, 1944-45. Married 1) Anita Goshkin in 1937 (divorced), one son; 2) Alexandra Tschacbasov in 1956 (divorced), one son; 3) Susan Glassman in 1961, one son. Teacher, Pestalozzi-Froebel Teachers College, Chicago, 1938-42; Member of the Editorial Department, "Great Books" Project, *Encyclopaedia Britannica*, Chicago, 1943-46; Instructor, 1946, and Assistant Professor of English, 1948-49, University of Minnesota, Minneapolis; Visiting Lecturer, New York University, 1950-52; Creative Writing Fellow, Princeton University, New Jersey, 1952-53; Member of the English faculty, Bard College, Annandale-on-Hudson, New York, 1953-54; Associate Professor of English, University of Minnesota, 1954-59; Visiting Professor of English, University of Puerto Rico, Rio Piedras, 1961. Since 1962, Professor, Committee on Social Thought, University of Chicago. Co-Editor, *The Noble Savage*, New York, then Cleveland, 1960-62. Fellow, Academy for Policy Study, 1966; Fellow, Branford College, Yale University, New Haven, Connecticut. Recipient: Guggenheim Fellowship, 1948, 1955; American Academy grant, 1952, and Gold Medal, 1977; National Book Award, 1954, 1965, 1971; Ford grant, 1959, 1960; Friends of Literature Award, 1960; James L. Dow Award, 1964; Prix International de Littérature, 1965; Jewish Heritage Award, 1968; Nobel Prize for Literature, 1976; Pulitzer Prize, 1976; Neil Gunn International Fellowship, 1977; Brandeis University Creative Arts Award, 1978. D.Litt.: Northwestern University, 1962; Bard College, 1963. Member, American Academy. Agent: Harriet Wasserman, Russell and Volkening Inc., 551 Fifth Avenue, New York, New York 10017. Address: Committee on Social Thought, University of Chicago, 1126 East 59th Street, Chicago, Illinois 60637, U.S.A.

PUBLICATIONS

Novels

Dangling Man. New York, Vanguard Press, 1944; London, Lehmann, 1946.
The Victim New York, Vanguard Press, 1947; London, Lehmann, 1948.
The Adventures of Augie March. New York, Viking Press, 1953; London, Weidenfeld and Nicolson, 1954.
Henderson the Rain King. New York, Viking Press, and London, Weidenfeld and Nicolson, 1959.
Herzog. New York, Viking Press, 1964; London, Weidenfeld and Nicolson, 1965.
Mr. Sammler's Planet. New York, Viking Press, and London, Weidenfeld and Nicolson, 1970.
Humboldt's Gift. New York, Viking Press, and London, Alison Press-Secker and Warburg, 1975.
The Dean's December. New York, Harper, 1981.

Short Stories

Seize the Day, with Three Short Stories and a One-Act Play (includes *The Wrecker*). New York, Viking Press, 1956; London, Weidenfeld and Nicolson, 1957.
Mosby's Memoirs and Other Stories. New York, Viking Press, 1968; London, Weidenfeld and Nicolson, 1969.

Uncollected Short Stories

"Burdens of a Lone Survivor," in *Esquire* (New York), December 1974.
"A Silver Dish," in *The Best American Short Stories 1979*, edited by Joyce Carol Oates and Shannon Ravenel. Boston, Houghton Mifflin, 1979.

Plays

The Wrecker (televised, 1964). Included in *Seize the Day*, 1956.
Scenes from Humanitas: A Farce, in *Partisan Review* (New Brunswick, New Jersey), Summer 1962.
The Last Analysis (produced New York, 1964; Derby, 1967). New York, Viking Press, 1965; London, Weidenfeld and Nicolson, 1966.
Under the Weather (includes *Out from Under, A Wen,* and *Orange Soufflé*) (produced Glasgow and New York, 1966; as *The Bellow Plays*, produced London, 1966). *A Wen* published in *Esquire* (New York), January 1965; in *Traverse Plays*, London, Penguin, 1967; *Orange Soufflé* published in *Esquire* (New York), October 1965; in *Traverse Plays*, London, Penguin, 1967.

Other

Dessins, by Jesse Reichek; text by Saul Bellow and Christian Zervos. Paris, Editions Cahiers d'Art, 1960.
Recent American Fiction: A Lecture. Washington, D.C., Library of Congress, 1963.

Like You're Nobody: The Letters of Louis Gallo to Saul Bellow, 1961-62, Plus Oedipus-Schmoedipus, The Story That Started It All. New York, Dimensions Press, 1966.
The Future of the Moon. New York, Viking Press, 1970.
The Portable Saul Bellow, edited by Gabriel Josipovici. New York, Viking Press, 1974; London, Penguin, 1977.
Technology and the Frontiers of Knowledge (lectures), with others. New York, Doubleday, 1975.
To Jerusalem and Back: A Personal Account. New York, Viking Press, and London, Secker and Warburg, 1976.
Nobel Lecture. Stockholm, United States Information Service, 1977.

Editor, *Great Jewish Short Stories.* New York, Dell, 1963; London, Vallentine Mitchell, 1971.

*

Bibliography: *Saul Bellow: A Comprehensive Bibliography* by B.A. Sokoloff and Mark E. Posner, Norwood, Pennsylvania, Norwood Editions, 1973; *Saul Bellow, His Works and His Critics: An Annotated International Bibliography* by Marianne Nault, New York, Garland, 1977.

Critical Studies: *Saul Bellow* by Tony Tanner, Edinburgh, Oliver and Boyd, 1965, New York, Barnes and Noble, 1967; *Saul Bellow* by Earl Rovit, Minneapolis, University of Minnesota Press, 1967, and *Saul Bellow: A Collection of Critical Essays* edited by Rovit, Englewood Cliffs, New Jersey, Prentice Hall, 1975; *Saul Bellow: A Critical Essay* by Robert Detweiler, Grand Rapids, Michigan, Eerdmans, 1967; *The Novels of Saul Bellow* by Keith Michael Opdahl, University Park, Pennsylvania State University Press, 1967; *Saul Bellow and the Critics* edited by Irving Malin, New York, New York University Press, and London, University of London Press, 1967, and *Saul Bellow's Fiction* by Malin, Carbondale, Southern Illinois University Press, 1969; *Saul Bellow: In Defense of Man* by John Jacob Clayton, Bloomington, Indiana University Press, 1968; *Saul Bellow* by Robert R. Dutton, New York, Twayne, 1971; *Saul Bellow's Enigmatic Laughter* by Sarah Blacher Cohen, Urbana, University of Illinois Press, 1974; *Whence the Power? The Artistry and Humanity of Saul Bellow* by M. Gilbert Porter, Columbia, University of Missouri Press, 1974; *Saul Bellow: The Problem of Affirmation* by Chirantan Kulshrestha, New Delhi and London, Arnold-Heinemann India, 1978, New York, Humanities Press, 1979; *Critical Essays on Saul Bellow* edited by Stanley Trachtenberg, Boston, Hall, 1979.

* * *

Saul Bellow is the most distinguished novelist of the post-war period in America. He is the most intellectual of American novelists, but one who, paradoxically, relies finally upon imagination and feeling; in his last novel at this writing, *Humboldt's Gift*, he moves more surely than ever before toward intuition and mysticism, toward a non-rational epistemology. He may be the staunchest defender of the idea of the self in American fiction, but he frequently recognizes claims of brotherhood and love that limit the egoistic pursuit of the self. His fiction rests upon a conception of becoming or possibility, yet he recognizes the human initiative in creating and pursuing process is limited by powerful determinants beyond human control. Bellow is an optimist, despite the prevailing climate of pessimism and despair. His novels are built on these dichotomies and paradoxes and written in a language that is almost always vibrant and resourceful.

The evolution of Bellow's style is a key to the understanding of his fiction. He began, in *Dangling Man* and *The Victim*, with a tight conception of both language and structure, using Flaubert as his model. Both books are disciplined and spare; Bellow has said that he strove for a kind of correctness that would be acceptable to the Anglo-Saxon Protestant world that seemed to dominate American literature. But by the time he came to write *The Adventures of Augie March*, he had discovered rhetoric, he had gained confidence as a writer and as an American, and he had recognized the weakening of the WASP hold on literature in the United States. The result is that the language of this novel streams out of Bellow in a fine, free flow; it is as larky as its protagonist and as various as the many levels of its discourse demand, ranging in its versatility from the talk of Jewish immigrants to the intercourse of University of Chicago intellectuals. As the language expanded, so did the book, and *Augie* is a sprawling, picaresque work in contrast to the carefully contained earlier novels. Succeeding novels show a curbing of rhetorical extravagance, but *Augie* established the essential mode of expression for the fiction Bellow has done since.

Bellow's taste for a vital and even eccentric language is related, first, to his conviction that words are a form of power, and second, to his hope that character can be preserved in contemporary fiction. With respect to the latter, he has made a considerable contribution by assembling in his novels a gallery of ill assorted oddballs, misfits, geniuses, and cranks, like Einhorn in *Augie*, or confidence men, like Dr. Tamkin in *Seize the Day*. Bellow commands Dickensian comic energies in the depiction of character, but he can also give us characters of size, power, subtlety, and cunning like Julius in *Humboldt's Gift*, who has the presence and imperious will of a Medici prince. The idea of character, furthermore, is associated with the survival of the self. Nothing is more important in Bellow's fiction, and Augie March, Henderson, and Tommy Wilhelm, among his protagonists, are all committed to the quest for identity and the salvation of the self. Bellow knows that, beginning in the 19th century, many forces, from Darwinism and Marxism to the Nazis and the logical positivists of the 20th century, have conspired to eliminate the self, and that writers like Joyce and Beckett have joined in this campaign. He believes, as he has said repeatedly in his fiction, that the main business of a man's life is to carry the burden of his personality or "to be the carrier of a load which was his own self," as he puts it in *Seize the Day*. By realizing the self, one asserts his humanity, that is, lays a claim to sharing in human suffering and joy, in the human destiny.

Realization of the self means surrender of the self. Bellow has always recognized this paradox, which he dramatizes nowhere more effectively than in *Henderson the Rain King*. Henderson begins as a man overwhelmed by the demands of his own ego. Neighbors, wives, children—nothing and nobody is permitted to stand in the way of his self gratification as he listens to an inner voice intoning, "I want! I want!" At the end of the book, his African experience has taught him that what men need is a right relation with the world of nature and with humanity as a whole. The guardianship he assumes of the lion cub and the little boy is an expression of love in both realms of being that signifies Henderson's surrender of the ego in order to realize the self through immersion in the order of nature and in the community of man. Similarly, Tommy Wilhelm in *Seize the Day* finds the consummation of his heart's need in the abandonment of self concern and the substitution of a generalized love for mankind.

Mr. Sammler's Planet, however, a novel of the 1970's, is far more critical of the idea of the self than any previous work. It is a book that documents Bellow's conviction that the conception of individualism or the self that we took first from Christianity and then from the Enlightenment has degenerated, in our time, into self-indulgence and license. But even in the face of this bitter revision of the optimistic history of the West, Bellow is unwilling to abandon in this novel the possibility that good may be found in human beings, and he persists in showing the need to pursue definition in one's life.

This hedged optimism in the face of his own pessimistic conclusions about the nature and fate of man is one of the most difficult situations that Bellow must confront in his fiction. Like Charlie Citrine in *Humboldt*, Bellow wonders whether Americans have a theory of evil and speculates that the American experience is "uncorrected by the main history of human suffering." The evidence tells him that man is depraved. Observation shows that men tend to behave, in crisis, like rats in a sack, as H.G. Wells said. Reason crowds him to an acceptance of absurdity as the prime condition of man and the world. But Bellow simply refuses to credit what observation, reason, and ideas thrust before him. He knows that man is less than what the Golden Age promised us, but he refuses to believe that man is nothing. He is something, Bellow says, and saying it he performs an act of faith. He rests his conviction on his feelings, and like the Transcendentalists upon whom he calls so often in his fiction, he resorts to his intuition. *Herzog* is a clear-cut illustration of Bellow's rejection of pessimistic philosophies. Everyone believes that man is a sick animal, says the protagonist of this novel, but he himself refuses to acquiesce in this judgment or to accept such dark interpretations of human experience as are contained in Kierkegaardian despair and absurdity, Spengler's decline of the West, or Eliot's wasteland complex. Herzog is himself a victim in modern America, but he simply refuses to accept his fate. He refuses to accept the empirical evidence. Persisting in his quest for love, he comes at the end to a restoration of sanity and hope for the future.

As Bellow accepts the epistemological implications of feeling, he also accepts or indeed advocates openness to feeling as sentiment. *Dangling Man* contained a rejection of the stiff-lipped Hemingway code which demands the suppression of emotion, and in all subsequent work he tended to expand the role given to emotion. He believes in the power of feeling and thinks that the novel must show a sympathetic devotion to the life of someone else, that the reader, in other words, must be asked to respond with sympathetic devotion to the life of the characters. In this way, Bellow works toward human connection between author and reader, between reader and characters; these are the connections that will lead to understanding. This emphasis upon emotion in Bellow is to be traced, in part, to the influence of Wilhelm Reich, who related the liberation of the emotions to the struggle for life fulfillment, and in part to the influence of Hasidism, the Jewish creed in which the central proposition is that life is holy joy.

The emphasis upon the self, optimism, and feeling must be understood in relation to Bellow's attitude toward death. He believes that one cannot understand life until one comes to terms with death. He treats the theme everywhere in his fiction, but it is enough here to remark it in four of his books. In *Seize the Day*, Tommy Wilhelm is able to come fully into possession of life, to seize the day, only after he confronts death itself and undergoes a symbolic drowning. Death brings him to the recognition of the heart's ultimate need, which is love. Bellow is equally concerned with death in *Henderson the Rain King* but less successful with it. Henderson insists that we hate and fear death, but that there is nothing like it. He means that we all know we must face it and that we learn from facing it, as he learned from facing the lion, the meaning of life. In *Humboldt*, Citrine says repeatedly that Whitman was right: the important question is the death question. One of the major attractions of Rudolf Steiner's anthroposophy for Citrine is that in death the soul will liberate itself from the body. *Mr. Sammler's Planet* is Bellow's most extensive treatment of death. It is an elegiac meditation, first, on the approaching death of Western culture, brought on by a new barbarism represented by those who surrendered traditional concepts of value. And it is, further, the story of a man who has come back from the dead, as it were, whose authority as a spokesman rests upon his knowledge of death: he had dug what was supposed to be his own grave but had, by chance, crawled out of it; he had seen the Arab dead rotting at Gaza; he had himself killed a man. Throughout the novel he watches his friend and benefactor die. To have known death is to know the meaning of life and to know what it means to be a human being.

Bellow's achievement is to have imposed upon the contending forces in his fiction—life and death, optimism and despair, reason and feeling, self and brotherhood—an idea of order. Bellow has always known that the novelist begins at a great depth of distraction and disorder. Out of the chaos of experience and the tensions of conflicting claims, he has sought to create a coherent and compelling vision of experience. But it has been a tentative endeavor marked by a sad, sane, comic skepticism about the power of the artist or intellectual to affect the world in any way. Near the end of *Humboldt* Citrine says an extraordinary poetry is buried in America, "but none of the conventional means known to culture can even begin to extract it.... The agony is too deep, the disorder too big for art enterprises to be undertaken in the old way." The implication is not that we must, in despair, fall into silence, but that we must find another way to express delight and reveal beauty, to listen "in secret to the sound of truth that God puts into us," and achieve in the midst of disorder a framework of order willed by the artist.

—Chester E. Eisinger

BENEDICTUS, David. British. Born in London, 16 September 1938. Educated at Eton College; Balliol College, Oxford, B.A. 1959; University of Iowa, Iowa City. Married in 1971. Assistant Trainee, BBC Radio, London, 1963-64; Drama Director, 1964-65, and Story Editor, "Wednesday Play," 1967, for BBC Television; Trainee Director, Thames Television, Bristol, 1969-70; Assistant Director, Royal Shakespeare Company, London, 1970-71; Writer-in-Residence, Central Library, Sutton, Surrey, 1976, and Kibbutz Gezer, Israel, 1980. Address: 20 Alexandra Road, East Twickenham, Middlesex, England.

PUBLICATIONS

Novels

The Fourth of June. London, Blond, and New York, Dutton, 1962.
You're a Big Boy Now. London, Blond, 1963; New York, Dutton, 1964.
This Animal Is Mischievous. London, Blond, 1965; New York, New American Library, 1966.
Hump; or, Bone by Bone, Alive. London, Blond, 1967.
The Guru and the Golf Club. London, Blond, 1969.
A World of Windows. London, Weidenfeld and Nicolson, 1971.
The Rabbi's Wife. London, Blond and Briggs, and New York, Evans, 1976.
A Twentieth-Century Man. London, Blond and Briggs, 1978.

Uncollected Short Stories

"Mother Love," in *Seventeen* (Radnor, Pennsylvania), September 1963.
"E-Type Charlie," in *Seventeen* (Radnor, Pennsylvania), September 1964.
"The Unworthiness of Caspar," in *Queen* (London), 1 September 1965.
"Eat Me!," in *Status* (New York), November 1968.
"Nose-Job," in *Pointer* (London), 1970.
"Dreamboat," in *Penthouse* (London), 1971.
"The Torture Chambers of the Mind," in *Men Only* (London), 1974.

Plays

The Fourth of June, adaptation of his own novel (produced London, 1964).
Angels (Over Your Grave) and Geese (Over Mine) (produced Edinburgh, 1967).
Dromedary, adaptation of his own novel *Hump* (produced Newcastle upon Tyne, 1969).
The Happy Hypocrite, music by Tony Russell, adaptation of the work by Max Beerbohm (produced Bristol, 1969).
What a Way to Run a Revolution!, music by Guy Wolfenden (produced London, 1971).

Betjemania (also director: produced Richmond, Surrey, 1978).

Radio Play: *Fortune and the Fishmonger*, 1981.

Other

Junk: How and Where to Buy Beautiful Things for Next to Nothing. London, Macmillan, 1976.
The Antique Collector's Guide. London, Macmillan, 1980; New York, Atheneum, 1981.

*

Theatrical Activities:

Director: **Play**—*Betjemania*, Richmond, Surrey, 1978.

David Benedictus comments:

Given peace of mind, financial independence, and a modicum of luck, I may produce a novel to be proud of one day. But then, who wouldn't? In the meantime, I continue to rehearse in public.

* * *

The range of David Benedictus's novels is very broad. Beginning as a penetrating social satirist in his first works—*The Fourth of June, You're a Big Boy Now, This Animal Is Mischievous*—he has become increasingly serious and experimental over the past decade. Throughout his fiction, Benedictus is concerned with British society's most rigid conventions of sexual and political behavior and with the many kinds of victims caused by the abrasions of caste and class. His caustic ironic vision is perhaps closer to that of Nathanael West than that of Evelyn Waugh, to whom he has been compared.

Benedictus poses the stock characters of social comedy—bishops, clubmen, schoolmasters—against individuals often maimed, deranged, or outcast by society. A Kafkaesque quality of irony emerges in the novels. *Hump* is a dystopian fantasy about a humpback who loves his deformity in a world of increasing uniformity. *A World of Windows* is a dialectical drama between a voyeur and his wife, exploring the reciprocal madness of observed and observer. *The Guru and the Golf Club* poses a caricature of Eastern mysticism against a parallel caricature of British middle-class pretensions and aspirations.

The most recent novels, *The Rabbi's Wife* and *A Twentieth-Century Man*, are mordant and tragic investigations of our times through the refracting prism of Jewish experience. Each contrasts norms of British behavior with the catastrophes of the Holocaust and contemporary terrorism against Jews. In *The Rabbi's Wife* Palestinian terrorists separate a young mod rabbi and his wife, murdering children in a synagogue on the Day of Atonement. The terrorists, modern British Jews, and the indifferent mass of the population are detailed against the horrifying events of political diabolism. *A Twentieth-Century Man* establishes the same mordant ironies by juxtaposing scenes from the marriage of a Tory M.P. and his Dutch wife, whom he rescued from Bergen-Belsen in 1945. Bitter, disturbing comparisons arise between the destruction of the human spirit in the death camps and in contemporary urban civilization.

Benedictus's *forte* in his fiction is the creation of vivid, complex characters that represent basic assumptions of our culture. His satire is Swiftian in intensity and in its distorted images of sexuality, violence, and brutality. Moving from the sublimated prison system of the quintessential British public school (Eton) to the torments of urban life, the death camps, and warfare by terrorism, Benedictus has compiled a sardonic catalogue of our century's ills. The collision between dead tradition and the anarchy of the present instant is Benedictus's entree into his characters.

These novels also demonstrate a measure of compassion for individuals trapped by the failures of our culture. Even when afflicted by bizarre sexual compulsions, failures of will and nerve, or base selfishness, many of his characters rise to small moments of love and heroism. If Benedictus's satire does not exempt many from its ironies, it also allows room for individuals' virtues. The survivors of our varied holocausts still struggle to live and love one another.

—William J. Schafer

BERGER, John (Peter). British. Born in Stoke Newington, London, 5 November 1926. Attended the Central School of Art and the Chelsea School of Art, London. Served in the Oxford and Buckinghamshire Infantry, 1944-46. Has three children. Recipient: Booker Prize, 1972; *Guardian* Prize, 1972; Black Memorial Prize, 1973; New York Critics Prize, for screenplay, 1976; George Orwell Memorial Prize, 1977. Address: c/o Weidenfeld and Nicolson, 11 St. John's Hill, London S.W. 11, England.

PUBLICATIONS

Novels

A Painter of Our Time. London, Secker and Warburg, 1958; New York, Simon and Schuster, 1959.
The Foot of Clive. London, Methuen, 1962.
Corker's Freedom. London, Methuen, 1964.
G. London, Weidenfeld and Nicolson, and New York, Viking Press, 1972.

Short Stories

Pig Earth. London, Writers and Readers Cooperative, 1979; New York, Pantheon, 1980.

Plays

Screenplays, with Alain Tanner: *The Salamander*, 1971; *The Middle of the World*, 1974; *Jonah Who Will Be 25 in the Year 2000*, 1976.

Other

Marcel Frishman, with George Besson. Oxford, Cassirer, 1958.
Permanent Red: Essays in Seeing. London, Methuen, 1960; as *Towards Reality*, New York, Knopf, 1962.
The Success and Failure of Picasso. London, Penguin, 1965; New York, Pantheon, 1980.
A Fortunate Man: The Story of a Country Doctor, photographs by Jean Mohr. London, Allen Lane, and New York, Holt Rinehart, 1967.
Art and Revolution: Ernst Neizvestny and the Role of the Artist in the U.S.S.R. London, Weidenfeld and Nicolson, and New York, Pantheon, 1969.
The Moment of Cubism and Other Essays. London, Weidenfeld and Nicolson, and New York, Pantheon, 1969.
The Look of Things, edited by Nikos Stangos. London, Penguin, 1972; New York, Viking Press, 1974.
Ways of Seeing, with others. London, BBC-Penguin, 1972; New York, Viking Press, 1973.
A Seventh Man: Migrant Workers in Europe, photographs by Jean Mohr. London, Penguin, and New York, Viking Press, 1975.
About Looking. London, Writers and Readers Cooperative, and New York, Pantheon, 1980.

Translator, with Anya Bostock, *Poems on the Theatre*, by Bertolt Brecht. London, Scorpion Press, 1961; as *The Great Art of Living Together: Poems on the Theatre*, Bingley, Yorkshire, Granville Press, 1972.
Translator, with Anya Bostock, *Helene Weigel, Actress*, by Bertolt Brecht. Leipzig, Veb Edition, 1961.
Translator, with Anya Bostock, *Return to My Native Land*, by Aimé Césaire. London, Penguin, 1969.

* * *

John Berger does not like one to divide his work up into categories; but if one is to consider the three novels published between 1959 and 1964 in isolation from his other published work then what immediately stands out is that he is a very skilful entertainer as well as a Marxist and a painter. Those two last attributes do, however, have a strong, if indirect, bearing on the novels. Berger is far too much of an artist to mix fiction and polemic, but he is concerned with how his characters behave in a social setting, whether the society is confined to the men's ward of a general hospital, as in *The Foot of Clive*, or a sleazy employment agency in Clapham (*Corker's Freedom*). It is how these microcosms of civilisation affect and shape his characters that matters. For although individuals may have strong ideas about how they intend to fashion their lives, the entrenched structures of society, which somehow always seem to be in a league with their own habitual weaknesses, always prove too much for them.

As a painter, Berger brings to his novels a sensual awareness that is not entirely visual. Reviewing *The Foot of Clive* for *The Observer*, Francis Wyndham wrote, "He can make us smell the ward (lemons and sour milk), taste the tea, hear the Light Programme through the earphones, see the sick men's bodies, above all feel the texture of the sheets, pyjamas, human skin." He also has an artist's awareness of structures and of the various complimentary levels on which all facets of life operate. For instance in the act of speaking, we have at one level the words that actually emerge, but behind these in the speaker's mind are the words he would like to say, his feelings, his fantasies, and his instinctively accurate, and usually highly disturbing, knowledge about the existential facts of the immediate situation. All these levels come clear in the illustrated lecture on Vienna which Corker, the seedy, aged bachelor from Clapham, gives to a Church social gathering.

To both these attributes must be added Berger's skill as an entertainer. He can hold his audience's attention by his dexterity in dealing with his subject matter, and with the wit with which he brings to light the absurd juxtapositions of the human situation.

All these qualities are deepened and extended in his most recent novel, *G.* This work is written more in the form of a film script than an orthodox work of fiction, each paragraph (and some of them only contain one short sentence) being sharp and complete in itself, and often setting a precise visual scene. G is the illegitimate son of a wealthy Italian merchant and rather advanced American girl who later develops Fabian leanings. He was born four years after Garibaldi's death, and the initial by which his author calls him refers equally to that, and to his father's name Giovanni. He was killed in Trieste on the day that Austria declared war on Italy on account of that city. Although G is intrinsically bound up with the historical events of his time, he is almost a-political himself. In this chronicle, Berger has set himself the vast task that Tolstoy undertook: that of depicting how each one of us is history in that we are both monumentally shaped by events and, in small measure, by the mere act of inhabiting our skins, influence their course.

—Shirley Toulson

BERGER, Thomas (Louis). American. Born in Cincinnati, Ohio, 20 July 1924. Educated at the University of Cincinnati, B.A. 1948; Columbia University, New York, 1950-51. Served in the United States Army, 1943-46. Married Jeanne Redpath in 1950. Librarian, Rand School of Social Science, New York, 1948-51; Staff Member, *New York Times Index*, 1951-52; Associate Editor, *Popular Science Monthly*, New York, 1952-54. Recipient: Dial Fellowship, 1962; Western Heritage Award, 1965; Rosenthal Award, 1965. Address: c/o Harold Matson Company, 22 East 40th Street, New York, New York 10016, U.S.A.

PUBLICATIONS

Novels

Crazy in Berlin. New York, Scribner, 1958.
Reinhart in Love. New York, Scribner, 1962; London, Eyre and Spottiswoode, 1963.
Little Big Man. New York, Dial Press, 1964; London, Eyre and Spottiswoode, 1965.
Killing Time. New York, Dial Press, 1967; London, Eyre and Spottiswoode, 1968.
Vital Parts. New York, Baron, 1970; London, Eyre and Spottiswoode, 1971.
Regiment of Women. New York, Simon and Schuster, 1973; London, Eyre Methuen, 1974.
Sneaky People. New York, Simon and Schuster, 1975; London, Methuen, 1980.
Who Is Teddy Villanova? New York, Delacorte Press, and London, Eyre Methuen, 1977.
Arthur Rex: A Legendary Novel. New York, Delacorte Press, 1978; London, Methuen, 1979.
Neighbors. New York, Delacorte Press, 1980.

Uncollected Short Stories

"Professor Hyde," in *Playboy* (Chicago), December 1961.
"A Monkey of His Own," in *Saturday Evening Post* (Philadelphia), 22 May 1965.
"Fatuous Fables," in *Penthouse* (London), March 1973.
"Envy," in *Oui* (Chicago), April 1975.
"The Achievement of Dr. Poon," in *American Review 25*, edited by Theodore Solotaroff. New York, Bantam, 1976.

Play

Other People (produced Berkshire Theatre Festival, Massachusetts, 1970).

*

Manuscript Collection: Boston University Library.

Critical Studies: "Bitter Comedy" by Richard Schickel, in *Commentary* (New York), July 1970; "Thomas Berger's *Little Big Man* as History" by Leo Oliva, in *Western American Literature* (Fort Collins, Colorado), viii, 1-2, 1973; "Thomas Berger's Elan" by Douglas Hughes, in *Confrontation* (New York), Spring-Summer 1976; "The Radical Americanist" by Brooks Landon, and "The Second Decade of *Little Big Man*" by Frederick Turner, both in *The Nation* (New York), 20 August 1977; "Berger and Barth: The Comedy of Decomposition" by Stanley Trachtenberg, in *Comic Relief*, edited by Sarah B. Cohen, Urbana, University of Illinois Press, 1978.

Thomas Berger comments:
I write to amuse and conceal myself.

* * *

Thomas Berger's novels exhibit an extraordinary comic sensibility, a satiric talent for wild caricature, and a concern for the quality of middle-class life in middle America. His novels chronicle the decline and fall of the Common Man in 20th-century America and meticulously detail the absurdities of our civilization. Berger is one of the subtlest and most accurate parodists writing today, with a flawless sense of style and proportion that is charged with comic vitality.

His Reinhart saga (*Crazy in Berlin*, *Reinhart in Love*, and *Vital Parts*) follows Carlo Reinhart from adolescence to middle age, detailing his career as a soldier in occupied Germany, a GI-Bill student and a failed wage-slave and decrepit father in the bewildering America of 1970. Reinhart epitomizes the failure of good intentions. A believer in the American Dream as purveyed in magazines, high-school classrooms, and advertisements, Carlo is a constant victim of deceit and fraud. Like the Good Soldier Schweik, Carlo takes the world at face value and assumes that appearance is reality; unlike Schweik, Carlo is guileless and incapable of hypocrisy, so he is perpetually victimized and disillusioned. The comedy arises in the gulf between Carlo's expectations and his experience.

In *Crazy in Berlin* Carlo is swept up in conspiracy, involved with spies and criminals dividing the spoils of the fallen Nazi state. A good-natured slob and summer soldier, Carlo survives, but he is driven to murder and madness, shattered not by war but by the lunacy of peace. The novel exudes the bitter ironies of sophisticated slap-stick comedy, similar to Preston Sturges's films. Carlo, a bewildered, optimistic average man, is driven mad by the Hobbesian nightmare of Occupied Germany.

The second novel, *Reinhart in Love*, continues the mock-heroic saga. Carlo returns to the purported normality of peacetime America to continue college on the GI Bill. Again he is duped, exploited, and betrayed as Orlando himself, charged with cosmic love: "*Reinhart was in love with everything.*" But as his boss tells him, the world is still a Hobbesian jungle, with every man's hand raised against his fellows: "life, real life, is exactly like the fighting, except in the latter you use guns and therefore don't destroy as many people." The novel ends with Carlo married by deception to a shrew, failed even at suicide and bereft of ideals and ambitions, ready to move upward and onward.

The latest installment in Reinhart's tale is *Vital Parts*, which moves ahead 20 years. He is still married to his shrew and father to a fat, mooning daughter and a vicious ne'er-do-well son. He has failed at every capitalistic venture, lost his hair and youth, gained debts and a paunch. Again in suicidal despair, he becomes involved in a bizarre cryogenics scheme—to immortality via technology. He becomes the guinea pig in a scheme to freeze and revive a human being. Carlo feels he has little to choose between an absurd life, an absurd death, and a remote hope of immortality.

In *Little Big Man* Berger also uses mock-heroic satire, here on the elaborate mythology of the Old West. A tale of cowboys and Indians told from *both* views, the novel describes the only white survivor of the Battle of the Little Big Horn—111-year-old Jack Crabb, victim of Indian attacks, Indian, Indian-fighter, gunfighter, gambler, con man, etc. The novel follows the "half-man, half-alligator" tradition of frontier humor, bursting with gigantic hyperbole. It is also a detailed, convincing picture of prairie life, both with the Cheyenne (the "Human Beings") and with the white settlers. The violence, squalor, and monotomy of life in raw nature are as intensely realized as the farce. Jack Crabb is a frontier Carlo Reinhart, with the same insecurities, the same propensities for confusion and cowardice, the same common humanity.

Arthur Rex may be the finest redaction of the legend since Malory. It is a labor of love for pure story and style in which Berger's brilliant prose is honed like Excalibur itself. A straightforward rendering of the Arthurian material, the novel is a tribute to romance, adventure, and storytelling as the roots of our literature. Berger makes the characters come sharply alive in vigorous, dramatic scenes and retains the mixture of exuberance and nostalgia which defines the ancient cycle.

A theme inherent in Berger's work is that of metamorphosis—transformation, counterfeiting, deception, the shiftiness of reality. In *Who Is Teddy Villanova?* and *Neighbors* this theme dominates. The detective story, from Poe through Dostoevsky, Raymond Chandler, and Dashiell Hammett, provides a parodic skeleton for *Who Is Teddy Villanova?* in which a hapless semi-pro detective named Russel Wren is hurled through a maze of fraud. The parody is bright, literary, and subtly styled. In *Neighbors* the same mode is applied to suburban realities. Earl Keese, prone to hallucinations, is subjected to a series of emotional and mental assaults by a man and woman who move in next door. The story turns on paradoxes and illusions, an increasingly grotesque feeling that things are never what they seem. In Berger's view, our culture has crashed through the looking glass, where absurdity rules all and everything turns by subtle and malicious irony into its opposite.

—William J. Schafer

BERMANT, Chaim (Icyk). British. Born in Breslev, Poland, 26 February 1929. Educated at Queens Park School, Glasgow, 1938-48; Glasgow Rabbinical College, 1949-51; Glasgow University, 1952-55, 1959-61, M.A., M. Litt.; London School of Economics, 1955-57, M. Sc. Married Judith Weil in 1962; four children. Schoolmaster, in London and the home counties, 1955-61; script writer, Scottish Television, Glasgow, 1958-59, and Granada Television, London 1959-60; Features Editor, *Jewish Chronicle*, London, 1964-66. Recipient: Wingate Award (*Jewish Chronicle*), for non-fiction, 1977. Agent: A.P. Watt Ltd., 26-28 Bedford Row, London WC1R 4HL. Address: 18 Hill Rise, London NW11 6NA, England.

PUBLICATIONS

Novels

Jericho Sleep Alone. London, Chapman and Hall, 1964.
Berl Make Tea. London, Chapman and Hall, 1965.
Ben Preserve Us. London, Chapman and Hall, 1965; New York, Holt Rinehart, 1966.
Jericho Sleep Alone and Berl Make Tea. New York, Holt Rinehart, 1966.
Diary of an Old Man. London, Chapman and Hall, 1966; New York, Holt Rinehart, 1967.
Swinging in the Rain. London, Hodder and Stoughton, 1967.
Here Endeth the Lesson. London, Eyre and Spottiswoode, 1969.
Now Dowager. London, Eyre and Spottiswoode, 1971.
Roses Are Blooming in Picardy. London, Eyre Methuen, 1972.
The Last Supper. London, Eyre Methuen, and New York, St. Martin's Press, 1973.
The Second Mrs. Whitberg. London, Allen and Unwin, and New York, St. Martin's Press, 1976.
The Squire of Bor Shachor. London, Allen and Unwin, and New York, St. Martin's Press, 1977.
Now Newman Was Old. London, Allen and Unwin, and New York, St. Martin's Press, 1978.
The Patriarch. New York, St. Martin's Press, 1981.

Play

Television Play: *Pews*, 1980.

Other

Israel. London, Thames and Hudson, and New York, Walker, 1967.
Troubled Eden: An Anatomy of British Jewry. London, Vallentine Mitchell, 1969; New York, Basic Books, 1970.

The Cousinhood: The Anglo-Jewish Gentry. London, Eyre and Spottiswoode, 1971; New York, Macmillan, 1972.
The Walled Garden: The Saga of Jewish Family Life and Tradition. London, Weidenfeld and Nicolson, 1974; New York, Macmillan, 1975.
Point of Arrival: A Study of London's East End. London, Eyre Methuen, 1975; as *London's East End: Point of Arrival*, New York, Macmillan, 1976.
Coming Home. London, Allen and Unwin, 1976.
The Jews. London, Weidenfeld and Nicolson, and New York, Times, 1977.
Ebla: An Archaeological Enigma, with Michael Weitzman. London, Weidenfeld and Nicolson, and New York, Times, 1979.
Belshazzar: A Cat's Story for Humans. London, Allen and Unwin, 1979.

Editor, with Murray Mindlin, *Explorations: An Annual on Jewish Themes*. London, Barrie and Rockliff, 1967; Chicago, Quadrangle, 1968.

*

Manuscript Collection: Mugar Memorial Library, Boston University.

Chaim Bermant comments:

My characters are mainly Jewish, hapless but not helpless, beset by many small calamities which somehow never amount to an irreversible disaster and which certainly do not diminish their hope that even if the worst is not over the best is yet to come. The treatment is humorous, but the intention is serious.

* * *

Of Chaim Bermant's novels the one word consistently used by every reviewer is "funny." And so they are, with a crisp, snip-snap style based largely on word play and repetition, the one-line sentences tripping down the page in a way which makes the easiest of easy reading. Yet, although this accolade is almost the greatest a writer can receive today, one must look for other criteria when attempting judgment. However jokey and ephemeral the fashion of our time, the novel is still a serious art form and its most important task is still the creation of character.

By this standard, Bermant's first novel, *Jericho Sleep Alone*, is genuinely alive and kicking. Its hero is a young Jewish boy living with his Orthodox family and friends in Glasgow. So far, so autobiographical. His growing up, his uncertainty about himself, his bewilderment as to what makes personality, what qualities bring success, his infatuation with (inevitably) the "most popular girl" in his group (the best and most believable female character in the whole of his work)—all this is conveyed in a brisk, lively style. It is a most agreeable book, not sweet, not sour, but tart and fresh and truthful.

With *Berl Make Tea*, that well-known hazard, the second novel, the author, it must be said, doesn't quite make it. Berl is a squat philosophical little Jew, the eternal rubberball, taking all misfortunes and bouncing back every time. He (thankfully) loses his wife, loses his job, drifts from place to place encountering odd people and odd goings on. The characters are—as so often in this writer's work—line drawings rather than people; escapees from a sort of 19th-century, Yiddish, comic strip.

It is perhaps a pity that it was this book rather than *Jericho* which set the pattern for many of Bermant's subsequent novels (mostly written in the first person). *Ben Preserve Us*: the central character a young Rabbi in a Scottish town, eligible and, it is discovered, very rich but also Jewish-mother-ridden. *Swinging in the Rain*: central figure a rich chocolate manufacturer with business worries, a flighty daughter and an oafish son, and so on. (This author, apart from his archetypal Jewish parents, appears to be equally fascinated by the very rich and the oafs. They appear in practically every one of his novels.)

Of the six or seven books of the "middle period" perhaps *Now Dowager*, though written in exactly the same style and tone as the rest is probably the most enjoyable. The "I" character this time is a very rich, old Jewish widow trying to convert a non-Jewish girl to the faith. It is as wildly unbelievable as all his other books but is somehow more attractive and exhibits his abilities at their sparkling best. These abilities are a gift for endless but sometimes very amusing dialogue which, like slated biscuits or crisp celery, one can go on eating—or reading—forever; a real talent for economical, physical description; and powers of invention, shallow perhaps, but so quick and skilful and lively that the critical faculty invariably takes a holiday whilst actually reading. There is also very often a genuine touch of pathos. It is this last which gives the impression that if Bermant, instead of producing books which can be read in an hour and forgotten in twenty minutes (a fair example of Bermant's style of comment) were to forget what appears to have been an over-exposure to P.G. Wodehouse in his youth (since he has neither the ultimate flair nor the meticulous sense of structure which underlies the great, classic comedy writers) he would be not only a much better novelist but also a true humorist rather than a jokester.

This impression is reinforced by the two "sports" among his books. About midway in his career Bermant published a very slender book, hardly a novel, more a *conte*, entitled *Diary of an Old Man*. It is a simple account of one freezing, wintry month in the life of an old man living in one room. Yet, perhaps because of its very brevity, the author was able to give his tale the concentrated care really good fiction demands and the result was an imperfect but very moving little gem; imperfect because too often this author has a slapdash approach which leaves loose, contradictory bits of character and a handful of short ends lying around every novel.

The other exception in his canon is *The Last Supper*; an ambitious attempt to break out of the snap, crackle and pop formula of all his other fiction. It is the story of the week's mourning which Jewish families observe when a close member—in this case the mother—dies. Again the milieu is that of a very rich, Anglo-Jewish, aristocratic family but this time the author has made a genuine try at distinguishing between his characters; brothers and sisters, aunts and uncles, in-laws.... During the week revelations are made, old scandals revived, sub-plots inserted. The book is a failure but the attempt is an honourable one; the characters emerging half-hewn as it were from the stone. Next time it may be that the people will emerge complete, free-standing and believable, even with the jokes.

It is only fair to add that though up till now Bermant cannot be claimed as a novelist really to be reckoned with, he is an admirable and often brilliant journalist and also a respectable hard-backed sociologist, specialising in aspects of Anglo-Jewish life. Both *Troubled Eden* and *The Cousinhood*, a study of the rich, interweaved families of Jewish aristocracy in England have been much praised—as have two other recent books, *Point of Arrival*, a history of the East End of London, and *The Walled Garden*, a study of Jewish family groupings and traditions. He does this kind of thing so much better than the novel, it is easy to see where his true metier lies.

—Gerda Charles

BHATTACHARYA, Bhabani. Indian. Born in Bhagalpur, Bihar, 10 November 1906. Educated at Patna University, B.A. (honours) in English 1927; University of London, 1929-34, B.A. (honours) in history 1931, Ph.D. 1934. Married Salila Mukerji in 1935; three children. Press Attaché, Embassy of India, Washington, D.C., 1949-50; Assistant Editor, *Illustrated Weekly of India*, Bombay, 1950-52; Secretary, Tagore Commemorative Society, New Delhi, 1959-60; Consultant, Ministry of Education, New Delhi,

1961-67; Senior Specialist, East-West Center, Honolulu, 1969-70. Since 1970, Visiting Professor, University of Hawaii, Honolulu, University of Washington, Seattle, and other universities. Lectured as a guest of the government in New Zealand, 1962, Australia, 1962, and West Germany, 1963. Recipient: Universities of New Zealand Prestige Award, 1962; Asia Foundation grant, 1966; Indian National Academy of Letters Award, 1967; Ford grant, 1968, 1969; American Institute of Indian Studies-Indian Council for Cultural Relations grant, 1980. Member of the Advisory Board, Indian National Academy of Letters. Address: 460 Larkspur, Ann Arbor, Michigan 48105, U.S.A.

PUBLICATIONS

Novels

So Many Hungers! Bombay, Hind Kitabs, and London, Gollancz, 1947.
Music for Mohini. New York, Crown, 1952; London, Angus and Robertson, 1959.
He Who Rides a Tiger. New York, Crown, 1954; London, Angus and Robertson, 1960.
A Goddess Named Gold. New York, Crown, 1960.
Shadow from Ladakh. New York, Crown, 1966; London, W.H. Allen, 1967.
A Dream in Hawaii. New Delhi, Macmillan, 1979.

Short Stories

Steel Hawk and Other Stories. New Delhi, Hind, and Thompson, Connecticut, InterCulture, 1968.

Uncollected Short Story

"My Brave Great-Uncle," in *Hemisphere* (Sydney), February 1969.

Other

Some Memorable Yesterdays. Patna, Pustak Bhandar, 1941; revised edition, as *Indian Cavalcade*, Bombay, Nalanda, 1948; as *Glimpses of Indian History*, New Delhi, Sterling, 1976.
Gandhi the Writer: The Image as It Grew. New Delhi, National Book Trust, 1969; revised edition, as *Mahatma Gandhi*, New Delhi, Arnold-Heinemann, 1977.
Education for India: A Collection of Papers, edited by M.K. Banerjee. Calcutta, Banerjee, 1976.
Some Political Currents in Bengal: A 19th Century Perspective. New Delhi, Vikas, 1980.

Editor, *Contemporary Indian Short Stories*, series 2. New Delhi, Sahitya Akademi, 1967.

Translator, *The Golden Boat*, by Tagore. London, Allen and Unwin, 1932; New York, Macmillan, 1933.
Translator, *Towards Universal Man*, by Tagore. Bombay, London, and New York, Asia Publishing House, 1961.

*

Manuscript Collection: Boston University.

Critical Study: *Bhabani Bhattacharya* by Dorothy Shimer, New York, Twayne, 1975.

Bhabani Bhattacharya comments:

How did I happen to become a novelist? When I was a student in London in the 1930's, I started writing a novel. Halfway through, I thought it was no good and I was not destined to be a creative writer—I was not a student of Literature anyway. I tore up the manuscript. However, I wrote some short sketches for *The Spectator*. I translated Tagore. Back in India, I found other preoccupations. Early in the 1940's I tried to do a novel again. When half-written, it found its way into a heap of unwanted papers.

Then the great famine swept down upon Bengal. The emotional stirrings I felt (more than two million men, women and children died of slow starvation amid a man-made scarcity) were a sheer compulsion to creativity. The result was the novel *So Many Hungers!* (The story was concerned with all the intensified hungers of the historic years 1942-43—not food alone: the money hunger, the sex hunger, the hunger to achieve India's political freedom.) Again I tucked the manuscript away. But my wife Salila forced me to have faith in my work. Acceptance by a publisher, and success, were quick.

I have no big literary output, as you see. I have not believed in writing for the sake of writing. I seldom planned a story structure. Each story grew in my subconscious mind, as it were. When it had grown enough, I had to give it a physical form. The characters, even when I had decided how they were going to behave, moved by their own volition often defeating my purpose.

Finally, why did I choose English as my medium of expression? I have loved writing in English. The creative writer must have full freedom to use the language of his choice. If he decides on a foreign tongue, he will have to cross immense technical hurdles, but that is *his* headache. I have enjoyed the challenge of this literary problem—expressing Indian life in the idiom of an alien tongue.

* * *

Bhabani Bhattacharya has stated that he regards art as a criticism of life which reviews current values, and that he conceives the novel as an "idiom of compassion" which is designed to have a curative social effect. His own novels conscientiously reflect these views. Their subject-matter and themes derive from modern Indian history and the problems of contemporary Indian society, and they embody programmes of reform as well as stinging social criticism. This approach, initiated in modern Indian fiction in English by the early novels and short stories of Mulk Raj Anand (from 1935-47), is a feature of the majority of Indian post-Independence novels. Bhattacharya's contributions to the contemporary Indian novel demonstrates that, for literate Indians, fiction is a good medium in which to examine such problems as caste, poverty, ignorance, political injustice, communal intolerance and economic inequality. Many Indian novelists, including Bhattacharya, have revealed how these and many other aspects of Indian life relate to the course of modern Indian history, particularly the Independence struggle, Partition, and "free" India's attempt to create a new social order.

Like many other Indians, Bhattacharya celebrated Independence with the publication of a first novel: *So Many Hungers!* This novel is a harrowing account of famine in Bengal (unfortunately ever-relevant) and a passionate indictment of the human culpability involved, particularly of the grasping parasites (mostly upper-class) who exploit the famine to make black-market fortunes. The story is told from the point of view of the starving peasants who migrated to Calcutta where they died in the streets, and is calculated to shock the reader's sense of humanity in scenes such as that which describes a jackal perched on the thigh of a pregnant woman, tearing at her swollen belly while her screams slash the air.

Bhattacharya's second novel, *Music for Mohini*, is the story of an arranged marriage and the adjustment which the modern city girl, Mohini, has to make to fit into the traditional patterns of life in her husband Jayadev's "Big House," presided over by his aristocratic iron-willed mother. The main theme of the novel is the idea of "synthesis," "a profound union of today with yesterday," whereby the conflict between tradition and modernity will be resolved. Synthesis is achieved in practice as well as theory: finally Mohini and her mother-in-law are agreeably reconciled and Jayadev is transformed, through conjugal and moral stimuli, from ascetic intellectual into village reformer. *Shadow from Ladakh*, set against the background of the Indo-Chinese border conflict following China's annexation of Tibet, is also a variation on the theme of synthesis. Through the relationships of the main characters Bhattacharya advocates for present-day India a cultural fusion based on a love-match between Gandhian idealism and a progressive people's technology.

He Who Rides a Tiger and *A Goddess Named Gold* are social fables and as such are Bhattacharya's most formally sophisticated works. The former is the story of an untouchable who successfully poses as a Brahmin holy man; the plot of the latter is a variation of fairytale in which the heroine and her fellow villagers believe that her amulet has the magical power to transform copper into gold whenever she performs a true act of kindness. In *He Who Rides a Tiger* the social theme is developed in terms of irony in order to dramatise the iniquities and hypocrisies of the caste system, while in *A Goddess Named Gold* the moral supremacy of communal unity over landlord selfishness is proposed as a model for independent India.

Although Bhattacharya has a tendency to load his novels with mechanical sociology, over-simplified philosophies, and naively symbolic relationships (as in *Shadow from Ladakh*), these defects are compensated for by the sincerity of his compassion and the relevance of his vision.

—S.C. Harrex

BIRNEY, Earle. Canadian. Born in Calgary, Alberta, 13 May 1904. Educated at the University of British Columbia, Vancouver, B.A. 1926; University of Toronto, M.A. 1927, Ph.D. 1936; University of California, Berkeley, 1927-30; Queen Mary College, London, 1934-35. Served in the Canadian Army, in the reserves 1940-41, and on active duty 1942-45: Major-in-Charge, Personnel Selection, Belgium and Holland, 1944-45. Married Esther Bull in 1940; one child. Instructor in English, University of Utah, Salt Lake City, 1930-34; Lecturer, later Assistant Professor of English, University of Toronto, 1936-42; Supervisor, European Foreign Language Broadcasts, Radio Canada, Montreal, 1945-46; Professor of Medieval English Literature, 1946-63, and Professor and Chairman of the Department of Creative Writing, 1963-65, University of British Columbia; Writer-in-Residence, University of Toronto, 1965-67, and University of Waterloo, Ontario, 1967-68; Regents Professor in Creative Writing, University of California, Irvine, 1968; Writer-in-Residence, University of Western Ontario, London, 1981-82. Since 1968, free-lance writer and lecturer. Literary Editor, *Canadian Forum*, Toronto, 1936-40; Editor, *Canadian Poetry Magazine*, Edmonton, 1946-48; Editor, *Prism International*, Vancouver, 1964-65; Advisory Editor, *New: American and Canadian Poetry*, Trumansburg, New York, 1966-70. Recipient: Governor-General's Award, for verse, 1943, 1946; Stephen Leacock Medal, 1950; Borestone Mountain Poetry Award, 1951; Canadian Government Overseas Fellowship, 1953, Service Medal, 1970; Lorne Pierce Medal, 1953; President's Medal, University of Western Ontario, 1954; Nuffield Fellowship, 1958; Canada Council Senior Arts Fellowship, 1962, 1974, Medal, 1968, Special Fellowship, 1968, 1978, and Travel Award, 1971, 1974. LL.D.: University of Alberta, Calgary, 1965; D.Litt.: McGill University, Montreal, 1980. Fellow, Royal Society of Canada, 1954. Address: c/o McClelland and Stewart, 25 Hollinger Road, Toronto, Ontario M4B 3G2, Canada.

PUBLICATIONS

Novels

Turvey: A Military Picaresque. Toronto, McClelland and Stewart, 1949; London and New York, Abelard Schuman, 1959; as *The Kootenay Highlander*, London, Four Square, 1960

Down the Long Table. Toronto, McClelland and Stewart, 1955; London, Abelard Schuman, 1959.

Short Stories

Big Bird in the Bush. Oakville, Ontario, Mosaic Press, 1978.

Play

The Damnation of Vancouver: A Comedy in Seven Episodes (broadcast, 1952). Included in *Trial of a City*, 1952; revised version (produced Seattle, 1957; Vancouver, 1978), in *Selected Poems*, 1966.

Radio Play: *The Damnation of Vancouver*, 1952.

Verse

David and Other Poems. Toronto, Ryerson Press, 1942.
Now Is Time. Toronto, Ryerson Press, 1945.
Strait of Anian: Selected Poems. Toronto, Ryerson Press, 1948.
Trial of a City and Other Verse. Toronto, Ryerson Press, 1952.
Ice Cod Bell or Stone. Toronto, McClelland and Stewart, 1962.
Near False Creek Mouth. Toronto, McClelland and Stewart, 1964.
Selected Poems 1940-1966. Toronto, McClelland and Stewart, 1966.
Memory No Servant. Trumansburg, New York, New Books, 1968.
The Poems of Earle Birney. Toronto, McClelland and Stewart, 1969.
Pnomes, Jukollages and Other Stunzas. Toronto, Gronk Press, 1969.
Rag and Bone Shop. Toronto, McClelland and Stewart, 1971.
Four Parts Sand: Concrete Poems, with others. Ottawa, Oberon Press, 1972.
The Bear on the Delhi Road. London, Chatto and Windus, 1973.
What's So Big about Green? Toronto, McClelland and Stewart, 1973.
Collected Poems. Toronto, McClelland and Stewart, 2 vols., 1975.
The Rugging and the Moving Times: Poems New and Uncollected 1976. Coatsworth, Ontario, Black Moss Press, 1976.
Alphabeings and Other Seasyours. London, Ontario, Pikadilly Press, 1976.
Ghost in the Wheels: Selected Poems 1920-1976. Toronto, McClelland and Stewart, 1977; London, Canadabooks, 1978.
Fall by Fury. Toronto, McClelland and Stewart, 1978.
The Mammoth Corridors. Okemos, Michigan, Stone Press, 1980.

Recordings: *David*, 1964; *Earle Birney Reads His Poems*, Barnet, 1970; *Birney*, Ontario Institute for Studies in Education, 1971.

Other

The Creative Writer. Toronto, CBC, 1966.
The Cow Jumped over the Moon: The Writing and Reading of Poetry. Toronto, Holt Rinehart, 1972.
Spreading Time: Remarks on Canadian Writing and Writers, Book I: 1904-49. Montreal, Vehicule Press, 1980.

Editor, *Twentieth Century Canadian Poetry*. Toronto, Ryerson Press, 1953.
Editor, *Record of Service in the Second World War*. Vancouver, University of British Columbia, 1955.
Editor, with others, *New Voices*. Vancouver, Dent, 1956.
Editor, with Margerie Lowry, *Selected Poems of Malcolm Lowry*. San Francisco, City Lights, 1962.
Editor, with Margerie Lowry, *Lunar Caustic*, by Malcolm Lowry. New York, Grossman, 1963; London, Cape, 1968.

*

Bibliography: by Peter C. Noel-Bentley and Earle Birney in *Essays in Canadian Writing* (Toronto), 1980.

Manuscript Collection: Fisher Library, University of Toronto.

Critical Studies: review of *Turvey* by Malcolm Lowry, in *Thunderbird* (Vancouver), December 1949; "Earle Birney and the Compound Ghost" by Paul West, in *Canadian Literature* (Vancouver), 1962; introduction by George Woodcock to *Turvey*, Toronto, McClelland and Stewart, 1963; *Earle Birney* by Frank Davey, Toronto, Copp Clark, 1971; *Earle Birney* by Richard Robillard, Toronto, McClelland and Stewart, 1971; *Earle Birney* edited by Bruce Nesbitt, Toronto, McGraw Hill Ryerson, 1974; *Earle Birney* by Peter Aichinger, Boston, Twayne, 1979; "Earle Birney Issue" of *Essays on Canadian Writing* (Toronto), Spring 1981.

Earle Birney comments:

My short stories have been extensions of my work as a poet. More relaxed in style than my best-known poem *David*, they are nevertheless equally symbolic in technique, and unified around a two-person relationship and a definite action.

My novels, on the other hand, are attempts to contain within one fairly complex form a multitude of experiences none of which seemed to me naturally separable, and much more likely to be effective if handled together. They are to some extent "documentary," aiming at accuracy in dialogue and in reference to the historic frame; but their over-all preoccupations have been with the mores and philosophy of North American society.

Turvey, my first novel, was written out of things that happened to me, or stories told to me, during the Second World War. For the last three years of it my job was interviewing soldiers: in Canada, volunteers, draftees, deserters, or men in sick bays or cells; in England, officer candidates, paratroopers, commandos, psychotics in hospital or psychopaths in detention; in Belgium and Holland, officers and soldiers in every arm and service of an Army, wanting to get into action or out of it, to change their job or their wife, to see a psychiatrist or just to make it back home. This kind of job taught me a lot about the bureaucratic complexity of a modern Army, its capacity for muddle and waste, especially of its human material. The job taught me also something about soldiers in general and the young Canadian one in particular. I came out of the army determined to write a novel whose central character would be a soldier both absurd and eccentric (like me) and wild, funny, naive, and long-suffering (like the average Canadian soldier—and perhaps civilian). *Turvey* is my attempt. His only literary cousin, of whom I was conscious, was the Good Soldier Schweik, Hasek's dumb wily Czech private caught in the Austro-Hungarian army of World War One.

My second novel, *Down the Long Table*, is laid in the Depressed Thirties, its scene shifting from Salt Lake City to Toronto to Vancouver. Like *Turvey* it is somewhat picaresque in form but the tone is more serious and the theme more involved in confrontations of ideas. It is not an autobiographical novel, but many of the characters are based on my acquaintance with young American and Canadian radicals of the Thirties, leaders of mine strikes, organizers of the unemployed, Trotskyist theoreticians, Stalinist bureaucrats, and some plain workers and workless of forty years ago, who were honest and brave and helpless and doomed.

* * *

Earle Birney is best known as one of Canada's finest contemporary poets, and, especially outside Canada, his reputation in this role has tended to obscure his achievements in fiction. He is the author of two novels, *Turvey* and *Down the Long Table*. Both of them, if not autobiographical, deal with times and settings in which the author was deeply and passionately involved: the Canadian army in the Second World War in the case of *Turvey*, and the social despair and political idealism of the Thirties in the case of *Down the Long Table*. Both novels share with Birney's poetry an inclination towards social satire and a preoccupation with colloquial speech patterns; *Down the Long Table* also shares with Birney's later verse an experimental use of the verbal detritus of political propaganda and the mass media in general.

Turvey is described accurately by its author as "a military picaresque." It narrates the adventures of a simple, rustic-minded Canadian, Turvey, who is anxious to serve his country in his local regiment, but becomes involved in a bureaucratic hurdle race which leads him into a series of comic predicaments, out of which in the end he emerges—never having seen a German soldier—to hail with joy his return to civilian life. Inevitably, *Turvey* calls to mind *The Good Soldier Schweik*, but there is a slyness in Schweik which Turvey does not possess. Where from the beginning Schweik seems to use the pretense of stupidity as a subversive weapon, Turvey is throughout the naive enthusiast, and it is the army that condemns itself by its bureaucratic unintelligence. The fighting war is always distant; the real war that Birney invites us to follow is the burlesque combat between a mindless collective machine and Turvey's irrepressible individuality. That Turvey emerges undefeated makes this a statement of faith in the victory of man over the inhumanity of mass organization.

Down the Long Table is a novel of memory, projected from the silent Fifties into the troubled Thirties. The basic structure is Proustian; Professor Gordon Saunders, a Canadian teaching in the United States, is brought before a committee investigating Communist affiliations. Before him at the long table he sees a face from the past, that of an ex-Communist turned informer, and this provokes the chain of memories which forms the substance of the book. Gordon remembers the fatal interconnection between personal relationships and political actions, weaving into a rope that shifts his sentimental idealism into militancy, takes him in and rapidly out of the Communist party, and culminates in a brief, violent, and disillusioning period as the would-be organizer of a Trotskyist movement among the unemployed and skidroad derelicts of Vancouver.

The greatest merit of *Down the Long Table* is the vividness with which the spirit and even the physical feel of the Thirties are recreated. It is when one considers the book as more than an evocative document that its defects become evident. There is an unassimilable implausibility about Professor Saunders sitting at the long table and, in that instant of time which is undoubtedly all the inquisiting senators would allow him, plunging into almost three hundred pages of chronologically sequential recollection, interrupted, not by the impinging voices of the present, but by the chapter-dividing extracts from contemporary newspapers, which enhance the documentary verisimilitude, but which in fictional terms are out of pitch with the essentially romantic tone of the rest of the novel, with its dark but poetic vision of what happens to ideals when they must find expression through human beings twisted and battered by existence. *Turvey* has a wholly convincing comic unity; *Down the Long Table* is divided by the conflict between the historical impulse to reconstruct authentically time past, and the fictional impulse to establish a self-confident imaginary world.

—George Woodcock

BLACKWOOD, Caroline. British. Born in Ireland, in July 1931. Married the poet Robert Lowell in 1972 (died, 1977); one son. Recipient: Higham Award, 1976. Address: c/o Duckworth and Company Ltd., 43 Gloucester Crescent, London NW1 7DY, England.

PUBLICATIONS

Novels

The Stepdaughter. London, Duckworth, 1976; New York, Scribner, 1977.
Great Granny Webster. London, Duckworth, and New York, Scribner, 1977.
The Fate of Mary Rose. London, Cape, and New York, Summit, 1981.

Short Stories

For All That I Found There (includes essays) London, Duckworth, 1973; New York, Braziller, 1974.

Other

Darling, You Shouldn't Have Gone to So Much Trouble (cookbook), with Anna Haycraft. London, Cape, 1980.

* * *

Though Caroline Blackwood's books are quite different in form, the purpose of the form is the same in each case—to enable the author to be as direct as possible. Her unflinching, confrontational style is part of the honesty which often leads her to take as subject the uglier aspects of human relationships, while leaving open as many of the possibilities as one human being's perception can apprehend.

Her first book, *For All That I Found There*, has a threefold division into "Fiction," short stories set in the USA, England, and Ireland, "Fact," reportage on Women's Theatre, a Harlem Free School, Beatniks, and a hospital Burns Unit, and "Ulster," which deals mostly with what seems to be autobiographical material. The rationale for the final section's form is given by the central character in the short story "The Interview," a famous painter's widow, who criticizes a film about her husband as "a little too factual.... One should only ever be linked to the past through one's memory. Luckily memory is the most miserable, and unreliable, old muscle." It's perhaps the same rationale that underlies the "novel" form of *Great Granny Webster*, with its unnamed narrator and possibly autobiographical material.

Highlighting relationships in contemporary, materialistic society, the short stories are hard-hitting. Blackwood needs a longer text for her main strength, the probing of motivation, though, as her novels are very short, clearly she doesn't need the length traditionally associated with the novel of motivation, as written by James, Proust, Anthony Powell.

The Stepdaughter is told entirely in the form of letters to an imaginary friend from a woman who rarely leaves her claustrophobic Manhattan penthouse flat. She is, understandably,obsessed by the repulsive stepdaughter whom her ex-husband has foisted on her. The letters consist mainly of the woman's analysis of the motivation of herself, her stepdaughter, and her ex-husband. The technique throws the focus of interest onto the woman, as we learn about her between the lines. This technique also allows Blackwood to manipulate dextrously the reader's sympathy as we respond to the woman's changing moods. Supremely, the author is able to shift the novel and our sympathies in a quite new direction mid-way, in the course of a few pages.

Great Granny Webster is, apparently, a loosely linked account of the selfish woman of the title, who by force of sheer longevity "had managed to be both the start of a line and the end of a line," and of the main characters in this line—the narrator's grandmother, once mistress of the decaying ancestral home in Ulster, but long in a mental hospital, her flighty Aunt Lavinia, and her father, who died when she was nine. But the new facts and attendant possibilities mean things may not be quite as they seem. Given her "near-religious belief that it was wicked to inflict one's personal despair on others...Aunt Lavinia in some ways had been just as stoical" as her grandmother. Further, much of the real narrative line in the book hinges on the narrator's curiosity as to why her party-going father chose to spend part of his wartime leaves visiting Great Granny Webster; the blurred figure of the narrator's father is at the heart of the novel, doubly lost to her because he died before "the beginning of my memory's photography."

The description of Great Granny Webster's funeral which ends the book is the *pièce de résistance* of Blackwood's characteristic black comedy, as she describes the old lady's bizarrely snowy ashes, "almost exactly like castor sugar that was being poured into a bowl as an ingredient for a wedding cake." But this scene is far more than a gem itself, with the actualizing here of the imagery of black and white which runs all through a book, one of whose purposes is to blur certainties and whose first word is the "I" of the narrator and last word the "eye" of one of the narrated.

For all the amazing compression and the wit of Caroline Blackwood's work, a curious feature of her prose style is its wordiness, though this rather adds authenticity to the voice of her first-person narrators. If it *were* possible for her to pare down her sentences, and also to increase the breadth of her work—its psychological depth is unrivalled—she might write something even more powerful. Yet her very slightly verbose vignettes are unique as chips off a block of totally uncompromising honesty.

—Val Warner

BLECHMAN, Burt. American. Born in Brooklyn, New York, 2 March 1927. Educated at the University of Vermont, Burlington, B.A. 1949 (Phi Beta Kappa). Since 1973, Instructor, New York University Medical School. Recipient: Ingram Merrill Foundation Award, 1965. Address: 200 Waverly Place, New York, New York, 10014, U.S.A.

PUBLICATIONS

Novels

How Much? New York, Obolensky, 1961; London, Eyre and Spottiswoode, 1963.
The War of Camp Omongo. New York, Random House, 1963.
Stations. New York, Random House, 1963; London, Peter Owen, 1966.
The Octopus Papers. New York, Horizon Press, 1965; London, Peter Owen, 1966.
Maybe. Englewood Cliffs, New Jersey, Prentice Hall, and London, Peter Owen, 1967.

*

Critical Studies: article by Alfred Kazin in *The Great Ideas Today*, Chicago, Encyclopaedia Britannica, 1962; essay by Jacques Cabau in *L'Express* (Paris), December 1965; *The Jewish Writer in America* by Allen Guttman, New York, Oxford University Press, 1971.

Burt Blechman comments:

My characters don't reflect, they act. As in tabloids. My work is straight reportage; headlines are enough; brevity, a necessity.

* * *

"For Armageddon is frightening only to those who fear progress." (*Maybe*)

Though his first books, *How Much?* and *The War of Camp Omongo*, treated the same self-searching adolescents, ineffectual fathers, domineering mothers, and crass value systems as the work of other young Jewish novelists of the period, Burt Blechman focused on the total social picture rather than on a young male protagonist and created mothers whose comic vulgarity paradoxically earns them the compassion with which Blechman views all his characters (Mrs. Halpern's obsessive search for candlesticks in *How Much?* and boast of "Creative Shopping" during her brief appearance in *Omongo*, and Mrs. Levine's matching her quarter-carat ring against the three and two-and-one-half carat competition of the wealthier *Omongo* mothers). Just as these characters flesh out their caricature outlines, Blechman's entire fictional world transcends, without denying, the episodic structure and rapid pacing of the comic strip. *Stations*, which dramatizes the surrealistic world of a Catholic homosexual, was even stronger proof of Blechman's individuality, as were *The Octopus Papers* and *Maybe*, though all three books have stylistic and thematic parallels with his earlier novels.

Dramatizing their compulsions, Blechman's characters frantically fear and court the destruction that threatens either as individual confinement to perpetually shrinking spaces or as universal annihilation. "Little Normy Greenberg, the lousiest kid in the whole camp, paddling for all he was worth..." in a desperate attempt to triumph by the camp code he has always despised, achieves the goal he unconsciously sought: "The water was up to his ankles. Faster. Faster. His arms digging, digging, digging. A spade. A shovel. A grave" (*The War of Camp Omongo*). And the atmosphere of the novel tends to reinforce the belief of Eagle, the Indian caretaker, that his fellow Omongos are plotting the total slaughter of the white men who have usurped their land and who encourage catastrophe by the ritual war games they enact at the boys' camp.

In *How Much?* Jenny Stern's desire for independence in the home of her daughter and son-in-law, the Halperns, predictably traps her in a converted closet: "A drape, so Mama will think there's a window. We can even put a light behind so when she pulls the drape, open sesame, a little electric sun." Next Jenny inhabits the morgue, the cheapest room in Dr. Zatz's nursing home, where she must play dead during an inspector's visit. As the Halperns continually cry the title question in the face of bankruptcy, war, failure, and unresponsive auctioneers, "How much, dear God, how much does it cost to be happy?" they hasten the fate they profess to fear.

Myra Russell of *Maybe*, compulsively wasting money and time ("Maybe the biggest problem in life is how to spend it") while she calculates her shrinking future by her dwindling investments ironically resists her son's advice to move into a maisonette that has both a kitchenette and bathroomette, but is too small for a bedroomette. As the enemy's Tyranny Tests, countered by America's Freedom Tests, threaten to explode Myra's world, the newspapers stress the plight of the trapped Cave Girl. The two alternatives converge.

901, the homosexual voyeur of *Stations*, is driven by a conviction of the impending doom embodied in the vice-detective, Dom, to travel the Via Dolorosa of his confining subway "chapels" for what he believes to be the last time. His menacing universe, peopled by Madonna and Mother Superior, and filled with altars and confessionals, depends on a parody of Catholicism that combines elements of Genet with the science fiction-*cum*-paranoia of William Burroughs. Blechman employs a more general biblical parody in *How Much?*, *Maybe*, and in items like Steiner's commandments in *Omongo*: "Thou shalt have no other loyalties before me for I am the Lord Steiner who hath led thee from bondage in the land of thy parents...." Though often brash and crude, Blechman's parody manages to ridicule both modern perversions of religious creeds and the original creeds themselves. Simultaneously, the parody laments a lost pattern of meaning that prevented or at least explained the chaos that perpetually waits to undo the universe. 901's abortive aspirations toward various careers parallel young Bernard Halpern's strivings in *How Much?* (Since Bernard appears in *The Octopus Papers* as B. Halpern, photographer, and in *Maybe* as B. Halpern, caricaturist, he apparently made a choice of a sort. His role as young Fat Stuff Halpern in *Omongo* reinforces the shared world view and tone of the books.)

The Octopus Papers, a collage of documents "selected, adapted, compiled, and annotated by Burt Blechman," is a literary hoax in the manner of *Gulliver's Travels* or *The Dunciad*, though the "Author's Apology" claims to be aping the style of Restoration Comedy. The book traces the history of Arsyn, an organization committed to the synthesis and marketing of the arts. Blechman has more tellingly satirized this tendency in *Omongo*, when a businessman attributed the widespread popularity of Van Gogh's "Sunflowers," in copies with simulated brushstrokes (cf. the "little electric sun" of Jenny's closet), to the artist's brilliant advertising ploy of self-mutilation. Moreover, the shadowy characterizations, thin texture, and surprisingly slow pace of *Octopus* make obtrusive Blechman's perpetual punning, as in the name of the trend-setting Newvoes, while this device seems venial amid the gusto and speed of the other books.

Pathetic little Norman Greenberg (*Omongo*), whose often hilarious obscenity helps define his loveless misery, epitomizes the combination of comic horror and pathos that is Blechman's major achievement. Similarly the humor in Jenny Stern's struggle against the senile amorousness of Mr. Lazar at the nursing home balances the compassionate responses she and her fellow inmates give to the news of their nurse's pregnancy, while they continue their litany of familiar complaints about their own children. What insures Blechman's status as a comic novelist, despite his often horrifying subject-matter, is his complex parody, his word play that exposes an undercutting level of wit, his stylized handling of realistic dialogue, and ultimately, in Rabbi Yeslin's lament for his failure as a marriage broker, a prose that mocks an absurdity otherwise too painful to endure: "Nowadays, men wanted a special type, the kind you found late at night, alone in a delicatessen, waiting" (*The War of Camp Omongo*).

—Burton Kendle

BODSWORTH, (Charles) Fred(erick). Canadian. Born in Port Burwell, Ontario, 11 October 1918. Educated at Port Burwell public and high schools. Married Margaret Neville Banner in 1944; three children. Reporter, *Times-Journal*, St. Thomas, Ontario, 1940-43; Reporter and Editor, *Daily Star* and *Weekly Star*, Toronto, 1943-46; Staff Writer and Editor, *Maclean's Magazine*, Toronto, 1947-55. Since 1955, free-lance writer. Director, and a Past President (1965-67), Federation of Ontario Naturalists: Leader of worldwide ornithological tours. Recipient: Doubleday Canadian Prize Novel Award, 1967. Address: 294 Beech Avenue, Toronto, Ontario M4E 3J2, Canada.

PUBLICATIONS

Novels

The Last of the Curlews. Toronto and New York, Dodd Mead, 1955; London, Museum Press, 1956.
The Strange One. Toronto and New York, Dodd Mead, 1959; London, Longman, 1960.
The Atonement of Ashley Morden. Toronto and New York, Dodd Mead, 1964; as *Ashley Morden*, London, Longman, 1965.
The Sparrow's Fall. New York, Doubleday, and London, Longman, 1967.

Other

The People's Health: Canada and WHO, with Brock Chisholm. Toronto, Canadian Association for Adult Education, 1949.
The Pacific Coast. Toronto, Natural Science of Canada, 1970.
Wilderness Canada, with others. Toronto, Clarke Irwin, 1970.

*

Critical Studies: Introduction by James Stevens to *The Last of the Curlews*, Toronto, McClelland and Stewart, 1963; by Norah Story in *Oxford Companion to Canadian Literature*, Toronto, Oxford University Press, 1967.

Fred Bodsworth comments:

The major part of my work has been novels linking human and animal characters in a fiction format with strong natural history content and wilderness backgrounds. The nature storyteller who uses birds or mammals in fictional situations treads a narrow path if he wishes to be scientifically authentic and portray them as they really are. On the one hand, he has to personalize his animal as well as his human characters or he simply has no dramatic base for his story. Yet if the personalizing of animal characters goes too far and begins turning them into furry or feathered people—the nature writer's sin of anthropomorphism—the result is maudlin nonsense that is neither credible fable nor fiction. I enjoy the challenge of presenting wildlife characters as modern animal behaviour studies are showing them to be—creatures dominated by instinct, but not enslaved by it, beings with intelligence very much subhuman in some areas yet fascinatingly superhuman in others. Out of this blending of human and animal stories comes the theme that I hope is inherent in all my books: that man is an inescapable part of all nature, that its welfare is his welfare, that to survive he cannot continue acting and regarding himself as a spectator looking on from somewhere else.

* * *

Fred Bodsworth, writing in imaginative, uncomplicated prose, has used the Canadian Shield of pine-tree laden granite for the setting in his novels. He calls it "a benign land sometimes amiable, even indulgent, but at other times a land of perverse hostility." These sparsely, Indian-populated lands provide a unique characteristic which distinguishes Canada from its gargantuan neighbor to the south. Bodsworth is then readily identifiable as a Canadian novelist.

The strength of his writing is the skillful portrayal of characters who are dependent upon the milieu and the forces within it. He is able to make his birds and humans unpredictable because of unforeseen but crucial subtleties in the environmental settings. Bodsworth's naturalist and ornithological knowledge fosters such keen insight. Atook, a native hunter in *The Sparrow's Fall*, seems doomed because Christian myth interferes with his hunting prowess. But the will to survive, which resides in all his characters, eventually causes Atook to cast aside his alien beliefs and adjust to his natural surroundings.

The Last of the Curlews is his most stimulating and moving novel. Bodsworth reveals the brutal and senseless slaughter of a bird that has not developed a fear of the earth's most irrational creature, man. In sensitive prose, the tiny bird becomes personalized but not human; thus he avoids sham. The theme of this novel has increased in importance since its writing because of the growing awareness of our threatened environment.

While Bodsworth commits the occasional transgression by allowing his creatures to reason, it does not seriously detract from his animal characters.

In *The Strange One*, he adroitly interweaves the mating of an alien Hebridean Barra goose with a native Canada goose and the love of a young biologist for a Cree maiden, who has been socialized in the whiteman's world. Indian-white miscegenation is as old as Canada itself and this theme intertwined with the geese is unusual in Canadian literature. Bodsworth is the first to write about it. The parallel between man and bird in this novel clearly reveals the interrelationship of man with animal when Rory, the scientist, follows what appear to be almost instinctual feelings, disregards social convention and returns to the beautiful Cree, Kanina.

The Strange One and *The Atonement of Ashley Morden* involve what may be melodramatic relationships between men and birds, but the two themes are drawn together skillfully, and are quite effectively written. An underlying theme in both these novels, as well as the others, is the complicated, often contradictory behaviour of men contrasted with the logical, conditioned instincts of animals and birds.

In the context of Canadian literature, Bodsworth is one of the leading traditional novelists.

—James R. Stevens

BOURJAILY, Vance (Nye). American. Born in Cleveland, Ohio, 17 September 1922. Educated at Bowdoin College, Brunswick, Maine, B.A. 1947. Served in the American Field Service, 1942-44, and in the United States Army, 1944-46. Married Bettina Yensen in 1946; two children. Taught at the Writers Workshop, 1957-58, Associate Professor, 1960-64, 1966-67, 1971-72, University of Iowa, Iowa City. Served on the United States Department of State Mission to South America, 1959. Distinguished Visiting Professor, Oregon State University, Corvallis, Summer 1968. Agent: Russell and Volkening, 551 Fifth Avenue, New York, New York 10017. Address: Route 3, Box 194, Iowa City, Iowa 52240, U.S.A.

PUBLICATIONS

Novels

The End of My Life. New York, Scribner, 1947; London, W.H. Allen, 1963.
The Hound of Earth. New York, Scribner, 1955; London, Secker and Warburg, 1956.
The Violated. New York, Dial Press, 1958; London, W.H. Allen, 1962.
Confessions of a Spent Youth. New York, Dial Press, 1960; London, W.H. Allen, 1961.
The Man Who Knew Kennedy. New York, Dial Press, and London, W.H. Allen, 1967.
Brill among the Ruins. New York, Dial Press, 1970; London, W.H. Allen, 1971.
Now Playing in Canterbury. New York, Dial Press, 1976.
A Game Men Play. New York, Dial Press, 1980.

Uncollected Short Stories

"The Poozle Dreamers," in *Dial* (New York), Fall 1959.
"Fractional Man," in *New Yorker*, 6 August 1960.
"Goose Pits," in *New Yorker*, 25 November 1961.
"Varieties of Religious Experience," in *The Esquire Reader*, edited by Arnold Gingrich and others. New York, Dial Press, 1967.
"A Lover's Mask," in *Saturday Evening Post* (Philadelphia), 6 May 1967.

Play

$4000: An Opera in Five Scenes, in *North American Review* (Mount Vernon, Iowa), Winter 1969.

Other

The Girl in the Abstract Bed (text for cartoons). New York, Tiber Press, 1954.
The Unnatural Enemy (on hunting). New York, Dial Press, 1963.
Country Matters: Collected Reports from the Fields and Streams of Iowa and Other Places. New York, Dial Press, 1973.

Editor, *Discovery 1-6.* New York, Pocket Books, 1953-55.

*

Manuscript Collection: Bowdoin College Library, Brunswick, Maine.

Critical Studies: by the author in *Afterwords*, edited by Thomas McCormack, New York, Harper, 1969; *The Shaken Realist* by John M. Muste, Baton Rouge, Louisana State University Press, 1970.

* * *

Vance Bourjaily's first three novels trace the effects of World War II on his generation of Americans, people who were undergraduates at the time of Munich and Benny Goodman's rendition of "I Got It Bad and That Ain't Good." In the looser structure of *Confessions of a Spent Youth* the war becomes one of several stages in the narrator's growing up, and Bourjaily attempts moods and situation, humor and introspection that had not entered his more rigid earlier work. The novels that have followed this pivotal book have displayed a remarkable variety of subject and technique without gaining for Bourjaily the popularity or critical recognition that many have thought his due over the past 30 years.

The End of My Life recalls the World War I novels centered in the ambulance service, and it suffers from the comparisons. Skinner Galt, Bourjaily's hero, is a young man who believes only in a few friends; any larger society or idea more complex than those friendships is meaningless to him. His accounting for that emptiness makes him sift through his limited reading and experience to understand why he has "no principles, no truths, no ethics, no standards." He is, predictably, surer in suggesting why his war was an intensification of attitudes from the preceding one than he is in guessing why it is itself unprecedented. For all of this, however, Skinner has some of the appeal of Fitzgerald's Amory Blaine struggling to know himself in the midst of his general ignorance, and when the friendship theme is pursued in action rather than in Skinner's disquisitions the book comes to life. *The Hound of Earth* is a parable of American responsibility for nuclear power. It describes the last days of the seven-year flight of an atomic scientist, who has left his family and profession because these ties constantly remind him of the thousands of people he has helped to kill. He adopts a life of bare subsistence only to be run down by his "hound of earth," a persistent humanitarian impulse that results in helpless acts of kindness toward everyone he meets. *The Violated*, a far more ambitious work, shows how four characters invariably violate those whom they would love, and are, in turn, violated by the emptiness of their rapacious lives. The child of one of them (or perhaps of two of them) plays the lead and directs several other children in her own production of *Hamlet* before the parents, who sit as Gertrudes and Claudiuses, stupefied or wary until the moment when, "frighted with false fire," one Claudius rises to end the show. Bourjaily's most sustained and complicated plot thus ends with his first striking outburst of fictional invention.

Confessions of a Spent Youth is a re-telling of *The End of My Life* that relieves the narrator, Quincy Quince, of the burden of philosophical exposition and allows him to reminisce in the manner of his near-namesake about various events in his young life: his friendships, his drinking and brushes with drugs, his loves, and his war service. The autobiographical element in this work, admitted by Bourjaily, is clearest in Quincy's statement that "to recall is a pleasure, " for these stories show the writer let loose with possibilities of fiction he had begun to tap with the children's play in *The Violated*. His earlier writing seems narrow and solemn along Quincy's adventures, his detailed observation of ordinary existence, and the pathos of meeting a girl "so beautiful you wanted to believe your eyes."

In *The Man Who Knew Kennedy* Bourjaily examines the crises that overtake two friends in the months following the president's assassination. The connection between history and private lives is not quite clear enough. Kennedy, according to Bourjaily's narrator, was killed by the psychotic force of someone writhing out of an abyss of frustration. A generation's illusions of invulnerability were smashed in an instant. The gifted, graceful victim of this novel is, on the other hand, destroyed by his inexplicable ties to a woman as depraved as she is helpless. This man had traded on his talent instead of developing it, while the surviving friend realizes that he is the stronger of the two for such reasons as having been "in a solid business of making necessary items out of wood—not fiberglass." *Brill among the Ruins* is Bourjaily's richest novel, and Brill, a middle-aged lawyer from Southern Illinois, is his most fully realized character. He stands among two kinds of ruins, the hard bargain of his small-town life and then the archeological sites of Oaxaca, and develops an understanding of himself that finally arrests his flight from responsibility. The accounts of digging are superb, inferior only to the hunting scene when Brill is "sculling" for ducks alone on the Mississippi before dawn. Among the ruins, he confirms his own integrity.

Now Playing in Canterbury follows Chaucer to the extent of having several characters tell tales within the framework of something that corresponds to a pilgrimage. Their journey is the progress through planning and rehearsal to the performance of an opera commissioned for the opening of a university theater. It is a curious, exciting, but diffuse mixture of extravagant tales and breathless frame narrative. In the troubled early 1970's, Bourjaily implies, only artistic collaboration could draw such people together. Only their talents could withstand the blows of circumstance on their characters. Like most of his work (including the ironically titled *End of My Life*), *Now Playing in Canterbury* seems more a point of departure than either his great book or his summing up.

—David Sanders

BOWEN, John (Griffith). British. Born in Calcutta, India, 5 November 1924. Educated at Queen Elizabeth's Grammar School, Crediton, Devon; Pembroke College, Oxford (Editor, *Isis*), 1948-51; St. Antony's College, Oxford (Frere Exhibitioner in Indian Studies), 1951-53, M.A., 1953; Ohio State University, Columbus, 1952-53. Served in the Mahratha Light Infantry, 1943-47: Captain. Assistant Editor, *The Sketch* magazine, London, 1953-56; Copywriter, J. Walter Thompson Company, London, 1956-58; Head of the Copy Department, S.T. Garland Advertising, London, 1958-60; Script Consultant, Associated Television, London, 1960-67; Producer of Plays, Thames Television, London, 1978-79. Address: Old Lodge Farm, Sugarswell Lane, Edgehill, Banbury, Oxfordshire OX15 6HP, England.

PUBLICATIONS

Novels

The Truth Will Not Help Us: Embroidery on an Historical Theme. London, Chatto and Windus, 1956.
After the Rain. London, Faber, 1958; New York, Ballantine, 1959; revised edition, Faber, 1972.

The Centre of the Green. London, Faber, 1959; New York, McDowell Obolensky, 1960.
Storyboard. London, Faber, 1960.
The Birdcage. London, Faber, and New York, Harper, 1962.
A World Elsewhere. London, Faber, 1965; New York, Coward McCann, 1967.

Uncollected Short Stories

"Another Death in Venice," in *London Magazine*, June 1964.
"The Wardrobe Mistress," in *London Magazine*, January 1971.

Plays

The Essay Prize, with A Holiday Abroad and The Candidate: Plays for Television. London, Faber, 1962.
I Love You, Mrs. Patterson (produced Cambridge and London, 1964). London, Evans, 1964.
The Corsican Brothers, based on the play by Dion Boucicault (televised, 1965; revised version, produced London, 1970). London, Methuen, 1970.
After the Rain, adaptation of his own novel (produced London, 1966; New York, 1967). London, Faber, 1967; New York, Random House, 1968; revised version, Faber, 1972.
The Fall and Redemption of Man (as *Fall and Redemption*, produced London, 1967; as *The Fall and Redemption of Man*, produced New York, 1974). London, Faber, 1968.
Silver Wedding (televised, 1967; revised version, produced, in *We Who Are about to...*, later called *Mixed Doubles*, London, 1969). London, Methuen, 1970.
Little Boxes (includes *The Coffee Lace* and *Trevor*) (produced London, 1968; New York, 1969). London, Methuen, 1968; New York, French, 1970.
The Disorderly Women, adaptation of *The Bacchae* by Euripides (produced Manchester, 1969; London, 1970). London, Methuen, 1969.
The Waiting Room (produced London, 1970). London, French, 1970; New York, French, 1971.
Robin Redbreast (televised, 1970; produced Guildford, Surrey, 1974). Published in *The Television Dramatist*, edited by Robert Muller, London, Elek, 1973.
Diversions (produced London, 1973).
Young Guy Seeks Part-Time Work (televised, 1973; produced London, 1978).
Roger, in *Mixed Blessings* (produced Horsham, Sussex, 1973). Published in *London Magazine*, 1976.
Florence Nightingale (as *Miss Nightingale*, televised, 1974; revised version, as *Florence Nightingale*, produced Canterbury, 1975). London, French, 1976.
Heil Caesar!, adaptation of *Julius Caesar* by Shakespeare (televised, 1974). London, BBC Publications, 1974; revised version (produced Birmingham, 1974), London, French, 1975.
Which Way Are You Facing? (produced Bristol, 1976).
Singles (produced London, 1977).
Bondage (produced London, 1978).
The Inconstant Couple, adaptation of a play by Marivaux (produced Chichester, 1978).

Radio Plays: *Digby* (as Justin Blake, with Jeremy Bullmore), 1959; *Varieties of Love* (revised version of television play *The First Thing You Think Of*), 1968.

Television Plays: created the *Garry Halliday* series; episodes in *Front Page Story, The Power Game, The Guardians* (7 episodes), *Wylde Alliance*, and *The Villains* series; *A Holiday Abroad*, 1960; *The Essay Prize*, 1960; *The Jackpot Question*, 1961; *The Candidate*, 1961; *Nuncle*, from the story by John Wain, 1962; *The Truth about Alan*, 1963; *A Case of Character*, 1964; *Mr. Fowlds*, 1965; *The Corsican Brothers*, 1965; *Finders Keepers*, 1967; *The Whole Truth*, 1967; *A Most Unfortunate Accident*, 1968; *Flotsam and Jetsam*, 1970; *Robin Redbreast*, 1970; *A Woman Sobbing*, 1972; *The Emergency Channel*, 1973; *Young Guy Seeks Part-Time Work*, 1973; *Miss Nightingale*, 1974; *Heil Caesar!*, 1974; *The Treasure of Abbot Thomas*, 1974; *The Snow Queen*, 1974; *A Juicy Case*, 1975; *Brief Encounter*, from the film by Noël Coward, 1976; *A Photograph*, 1977; *Rachel in Danger*, 1978; *A Dog's Ransom*, from the novel by Patricia Highsmith, 1978; *Games*, 1978; *The Ice House*, 1978; *The Letter of the Law*, 1979; *Dying Day*, 1980; *The Specialist*, 1980; *Dark Secret*, 1981.

Other (juvenile)

Pegasus. London, Faber, 1957; New York, A.S. Barnes, 1960.
The Mermaid and the Boy. London, Faber, 1958; New York, A.S. Barnes, 1960.
Garry Halliday and the Disappearing Diamonds [*Ray of Death*; *Kidnapped Five*; *Sands of Time*; *Flying Foxes*] (as Justin Blake, with Jeremy Bullmore). London, Faber, 5 vols., 1960-64.

*

Manuscript Collections: Mugar Memorial Library, Boston University; (television works) Temple University Library, Philadelphia.

Critical Studies: *Postwar British Fiction*, Berkeley, University of California Press, 1962, and "The Fable Breaks Down," in *Wisconsin Studies in Contemporary Literature* (Madison), viii, 7, 1967, both by James Gindin; "Bowen on the Little Box" by Hugh Hebert, in *The Guardian* (London), 6 August 1971.

Theatrical Activities:

Director: **Plays**—at the London Academy of Music and Dramatic Art since 1967; *The Disorderly Women*, Manchester, 1969, London, 1970; *Fall and Redemption*, Pitlochry, Scotland, 1969; *The Waiting Room*, London, 1970.

Actor: **Plays**—in repertory in North Wales, Summers 1950-51; Palace Theatre, Watford, Hertfordshire, 1965.

John Bowen comments:

I have always been interested in problems of form. Thus, in my first novel, *The Truth Will Not Help Us*, I wanted to try to tell a story of an historical occurrence of 1705 in Britain in terms of the political atmosphere and activities of the U.S.A. in 1953; in both those years political witch-hunting caused injustice and harm to innocent persons. My second novel, *After the Rain*, began as an attempt to do for science fiction what Michael Innes had done for the detective story: I failed in this attempt because I soon became more interested in the ideas with which I was dealing than in the form, and anyway made many scientific errors. My third novel was straightforwardly naturalistic, but in my fourth, *Storyboard*, I used an advertising agency as a symbol of a statement about public and private life, just as Zola used a department store in *Au Bonheur des Dames*. In my fifth novel, *The Birdcage*, I attempted to use a 19th-century manner—the objective detachment of Trollope, who presents his characters at some distance, displays and comments on them. In my sixth novel, *A World Elsewhere*, the hero, himself a wounded and needed politician, is writing a fiction about Philoctetes, the wounded archer, and until he has found his own reasons for returning to political life in London, cannot conclude his fiction, because he does not see why Philoctetes should allow himself to accompany Odysseus to Troy. The same interest in different problems of form can be seen in my plays—the first Ibsenesque, the second borrowing from Brecht, Pirandello, and the Chinese theatre, the third a pair of linked one-acters, designed as two halves of the same coin, the fourth an attempt to rework the myth of *The Bacchae* as Sartre, Giraudoux, and Anouilh had used Greek myths, and to blend verse and prose, knockabout comedy, high tragedy, and Shavian argument. My full-length play *The Corsican Brothers* (an expansion of my earlier television play) has songs set within the play to music pirated from 19th-century composers, and I tried to make, from the melodramatic fantasies of Dumas and Dion Boucicault, a kind of Stendhalian statement about a society based on ideas of honour. In two of my television plays, *Miss Nightingale* and *The Emergency Channel*, I experimented with a narrative method that was associative, not lineal.

In this commentary, I am more confident in writing of form than of theme. One's themes are for the critics to set out neatly on a board: one is not always so clearly conscious of them oneself. There is a concern with archetypical patterns of behaviour (therefore with myth). There is a constant war between reasonable man and instinctive man. There is the pessimistic discovery that Bloomsbury values don't work, but that there seem to be no others worth holding. There is a statement of the need for Ibsen's "Life Lie" even when one knows it to be a lie, and Forster's "Only connect" becomes "Only accept" in my work.

I believe that novels and plays should tell a story, that the story is the mechanism by which one communicates one's view of life, and that no symbolism is worth anything unless it also works as an element in the story, since the final symbol is the story itself.

Inasmuch as the influences on one's style are usually those writers whom one has discovered in one's adolescence and early twenties, I might be said to have been influenced as a novelist by Dickens, Trollope, E.M. Forster, Virginia Woolf, E. Nesbit, P.G. Wodehouse, and Evelyn Waugh—perhaps a little also by Hemingway and Faulkner. As a playwright, I have been influenced by Ibsen, Tchekov, Shaw, Pirandello, Anouilh, Giraudoux, and Noël Coward. Most of these names, I am sure, would be on any lists made by most of my contemporaries.

* * *

John Bowen has always been an intelligent and didactic novelist. His first novel, *The Truth Will Not Help Us*, uses a story of English seamen charged with piracy in a Scottish port in 1705 as a metaphor for the political evil of assuming guilt by rumor or association. *A World Elsewhere*, his latest novel, uses the myth of Philoctetes as a parallel to complicated speculation about hypocrisy and engagement in contemporary political life. *The Birdcage* contains a long essay giving an account of the history and development of commercial television; and a defense of advertising as not necessarily more corrupt than any other institution in urban, capitalistic society introduces *Storyboard*. Although Bowen's fictional lessons are invariably complex and thoughtful, the author's presence is always visible arranging, blocking out, and connecting the material. Myth is made pointedly and explicitly relevant; symbols, like the lovebirds in *The Birdcage* or the breaking of a bronze chrysanthemum at a funeral in *The Centre of the Green*, sometimes seem attached heavy-handedly and literally. Bowen always acknowledges his own presence in his fiction, especially in his two most recent novels in which the author addresses the reader directly and becomes playful and intelligently skeptical about the complexities that prevent him from making any easy disposition of the characters and issues he has developed. The author is conspicuously articulate and instructive, but he does not attempt to play God; in fact, the danger of human substitutions for a non-existent or unknowable deity comprises part of the message of *After the Rain* and the skepticism underlying *The Birdcage* and *A World Elsewhere*.

All of Bowen's novels contain sharply memorable and effective scenes: the retired colonel expressing his style and his strength through his garden in *The Centre of the Green*, the nocturnal trip around Soho in which a character is beaten in *The Birdcage*, the picnic on a Greek island in *A World Elsewhere*. Often the best scenes involve a witty and comic treatment of dramatic conflict between two characters involved in close relationship, like the familial and sexual relationships in *The Centre of the Green* and *Storyboard* or the brilliantly handled quarrel between two contemporary London lovers who have lived together too long that takes place in the Piazza San Marco in *The Birdcage*. Bowen's comedy, however, no matter how strident initially, invariably turns into sympathy for his characters, a recognition that they are unable to be more human or more dignified than they are and that no man manages more. This characteristic switch from satire to sympathy is emblematic of most of Bowen's fiction which works on reversals, on dramatically presented and thematically central violations of expected conclusions. The simple, muscle-flexing athlete, not the expected sensitive intellectual, finally defies and defeats the tyrant who would make himself God in *After the Rain*. Humanity and integrity appear in just those places most easily and generally thought the most corrupt in modern society in *Storyboard*. The family in which all members seem, superficially, most selfish and isolated can understand and respect each other in *The Centre of the Green*. This engagingly perverse positivism is often applied to social or political clichés, as in the forceful and complicated treatment of E.M. Forster's "Only connect" in *The Birdcage* or the ramifications on "politics is the art of the possible" developed in *A World Elsewhere*. Such clichés, in Bowen's fictional world, never honestly express the concerns or dilemmas of the characters who use them so glibly, although they may yet be partially true in ways the characters never intend and can seldom comprehend. People, in Bowen's novels, generally haven't a very good idea of what they're about, although this is no reason to deny their humanity or their capacity to invoke sympathy.

Bowen has not published a novel since 1965, but has written several plays for the stage and television. Some of the plays, like *The Disorderly Women* and *The Corsican Brothers*, are, beneath the comedy, darker and more tragic versions of experience than are the novels. Yet drama seems, structurally, the appropriate vehicle for the qualities apparent in Bowen's fiction. Drama compresses the use of myth and symbol, the skill at scenes of dramatic confrontation, and the striking reversals of expectation which underline the humane and intelligent lessons.

—James Gindin

BOWLES, Paul (Frederic). American. Born in New York City, 30 December 1910. Educated at the University of Virginia, Charlottesville, 1928-29; studied music with Aaron Copland in New York and Berlin, 1930-32, and with Virgil Thomson in Paris, 1933-34. Married the writer Jane Sydney Auer (i.e., Jane Bowles) in 1938 (died, 1973). Music Critic, *New York Herald Tribune*, 1942-46; also composer. Recipient: Guggenheim Fellowship, 1941; American Academy award, 1950; Rockefeller grant, 1959; Translation Center grant, 1975; National Endowment for the Arts grant, 1977. Since 1947 has lived in Tangier. Agent: William Morris Agency, 1350 Avenue of the Americas, New York, New York 10019, U.S.A. Address: 2117 Tanger Socco, Tangier, Morocco.

PUBLICATIONS

Novels

The Sheltering Sky. London, Lehmann, and New York, New Directions, 1949.
Let It Come Down. London, Lehmann, and New York, Random House, 1952.
The Spider's House. New York, Random House, 1955; London, Macdonald, 1957.
Up above the World. New York, Simon and Schuster, 1966; London, Owen, 1967.

Short Stories

The Delicate Prey and Other Stories. New York, Random House, 1950.
A Little Stone: Stories. London, Lehmann, 1950.
The Hours after Noon. London, Heinemann, 1959.

A Hundred Camels in the Courtyard. San Francisco, City Lights, 1962.
The Time of Friendship. New York, Holt Rinehart, 1967.
Pages from Cold Point and Other Stories. London, Owen, 1968.
Three Tales. New York, Hallman, 1975.
Things Gone and Things Still Here. Santa Barbara, California, Black Sparrow Press, 1977.
Collected Stories 1939-1976. Santa Barbara, California, Black Sparrow Press, 1979.

Uncollected Short Stories

"The Eye," in *Missouri Review* (Columbia), 1978.
"Midnight Mass," "Here to Learn," "The Dismissal," "Madame and Ahmed," and "Kitty," in *Antaeus* (New York), 1979-80.
"The Husband," in *Michigan Quarterly Review* (Ann Arbor), 1980.
"At the Krungthep Plaza," in *Ontario Review* (Windsor), 1980.

Verse

Scenes. Los Angeles, Black Sparrow Press, 1968.
The Thicket of Spring: Poems 1926-1969. Los Angeles, Black Sparrow Press, 1972.
Next to Nothing. Kathmandu, Starstreams, 1976.

Other

Yallah (travel). Zurich, Manesse, 1956; New York, McDowell Obolensky, 1957.
Their Heads Are Green (travel). London, Owen, 1963; as *Their Heads Are Green and Their Hands Are Blue*, New York, Random House, 1963.
Without Stopping: An Autobiography. London, Owen, and New York, Putnam, 1972.

Translator, *No Exit*, by Jean-Paul Sartre. New York, French, 1946.
Translator, *Lost Trail of the Sahara*, by Roger Frison-Roche. London, Hale, 1956; Englewood Cliffs, New Jersey, Prentice Hall, 1962.
Translator, *A Life Full of Holes*, by Driss ben Hamed Charhadi. New York, Grove Press, 1964; London, Weidenfeld and Nicolson, 1965.
Translator, *Love with a Few Hairs*, by Mohammed Mrabet. London, Owen, 1967; New York, Braziller, 1968.
Translator, *The Lemon*, by Mohammed Mrabet. London, Owen, 1969; New York, McGraw Hill, 1972.
Translator, *Mhashish*, by Mohammed Mrabet. San Francisco, City Lights, 1969.
Translator, *The Boy Who Set the Fire and Other Stories.* Los Angeles, Black Sparrow Press, 1974.
Translator, *For Bread Alone*, by Mohamed Choukri. London, Owen, 1974.
Translator, *Jean Genet in Tangier*, by Mohamed Choukri. New York, Ecco Press, 1974.
Translator, *The Oblivion Seekers*, by Isabelle Eberhardt. San Francisco, City Lights, 1975.
Translator, *Hadidan Aharam*, by Mohammed Mrabet. Los Angeles, Black Sparrow Press, 1975.
Translator, *Harmless Poisons, Blameless Sins*, by Mohammed Mrabet. Santa Barbara, California, Black Sparrow Press, 1976.
Translator, *Look and Move On*, by Mohammed Mrabet. Santa Barbara, California, Black Sparrow Press, 1976.
Translator, *The Big Mirror*, by Mohammed Mrabet. Santa Barbara, California, Black Sparrow Press, 1977.
Translator, *Five Eyes: Short Stories by Five Moroccans.* Santa Barbara, California, Black Sparrow Press, 1979.
Translator, *Tennessee Williams in Tangier*, by Mohamed Choukri. Santa Barbara, California, Cadmus Editions, 1979.
Translator, *The Beach Café, and The Voice*, by Mohammed Mrabet. Santa Barbara, California, Black Sparrow Press, 1980.

Published Music: *Tornado Blues* (chorus); *Music for a Farce* (chamber music); *Piana Sonatina*; *Huapango 1* and *2*; *Six Preludes for Piano*; *El Indio*; *El Bejuco*; *Sayula*; *La Cuelga*; *Sonata for Two Pianos*; *Night Waltz* (two pianos); *Songs: Heavenly Grass*; *Sugar in the Cane*; *Cabin*; *Lonesome Man*; *Letter to Freddy*; *The Years*; *Of All the Things I Love*; *A Little Closer, Please*; *David*; *In the Woods*; *Song of an Old Woman*; *Night Without Sleep*; *Two Skies*; *Que te falta?*; *Ya Llego*; *Once a Lady Was Here*; *Bluebell Mountain*; *Three*; *On a Quiet Conscience*; *El Carbonero*; *Baby, Baby.*

Operas: *Denmark Vesey*, 1937; *The Wind Remains*, 1941.

Ballets: *Yankee Clipper*, 1937; *Pastorella*, 1941; *Sentimental Colloquy*, 1944; *Blue Roses*, 1957.

Incidental Music, for plays: *Horse Eats Hat*, 1936; *Dr. Faustus*, 1937; *My Heart's in the Highlands*, 1939; *Love's Old Sweet Song*, 1940; *Twelfth Night*, 1940; *Liberty Jones*, 1941; *Watch on the Rhine*, 1941; *South Pacific*, 1943; *Jacobowsky and the Colonel*, 1944; *The Glass Menagerie*, 1945; *Twilight Bar*, 1946; *On Whitman Avenue*, 1946; *The Dancer*, 1946; *Cyrano de Bergerac*, 1946; *Land's End*, 1946; *Summer and Smoke*, 1948; *In the Summer House*, 1953; *Edwin Booth*, 1958; *Sweet Bird of Youth*, 1959; *The Milk Train Doesn't Stop Here Anymore*, 1963; for films: *Roots in the Soil*, 1940; *Congo*, 1944.

Recordings: *The Wind Remains*, M.G.M.; *Café Sin Nombre*, New Music; *Sonata for Two Pianos*, Concert Hall; *Night Waltz*, Columbia; *Scènes d'Anabase*, Columbia; *Music for a Farce*, Columbia; *Song for My Sister*, Disc; *They Cannot Stop Death*, Disc; *Night Without Sleep*, Disc; *Sailor's Song*; Disc; *Rain Rots the Wood*, Disc; *Sonata for Flute and Piano*, Art of This Century; *Six Preludes*, Golden Crest; *Huapango 1* and *2*, New Music; *A Picnic Cantata*, Columbia; *El Bejuco* and *El Indio*, Art of This Century; *Blue Mountain Ballads*, Music Library; *Concerto for Two Pianos, Winds and Percussion*, Columbia; *Once a Lady Was Here, Song of an Old Person*, New World.

*

Manuscript Collection: Humanities Research Center, University of Texas, Austin.

Critical Studies: "Paul Bowles and the Natural Man" by Oliver Evans, in *Recent American Fiction*, Boston, Houghton Mifflin, 1963; *Paul Bowles: The Illumination of North Africa* by Lawrence D. Stewart, Carbondale, Southern Illinois University Press, 1974; *Paul Bowles: Staticity and Terror* by Eric Mottram, London, Aloes, 1976; *The Fiction of Paul Bowles: The Soul Is the Weariest Part of the Body* by Hans Bertens, Atlantic Highlands, New Jersey, Humanities Press, 1979.

Paul Bowles comments:

All I can find of interest to say about my work is to mention the key role in the process of writing played by my subconscious. It knows far better than I what should be written and how it should sound in words.

* * *

Since the publication of his first novel, *The Sheltering Sky*, Paul Bowles has provoked sharply partisan feelings in his readers. To some he is a major prophet for our times; to others his work rather luridly exploits the fashionable themes of nihilism, violence, and despair. Few, however, are able to deny the insistent power of his prose—its urgency, clarity, and lyric compactness. Bowles's subtly acute sense of language no doubt owes a major debt to his training as a musician, his work as a translator, and his life-long interest in poetry. The intricate web of language in which his novels are contained often seems the only protection against the horror and despair which threaten to overwhelm his characters.

The Sheltering Sky sounded the major theme with which Bowles was to be concerned in all his work: the elemental clash between the primitive and the civilized. Bowles's central characters, Kit and Port Moresby, arrive in North Africa without any clear past, and make their way through a series of grotesque adventures. They are spiritual somnambulists, exiles, ambassadors from the wasteland of the modern world, and their veneer of civilization is slowly stripped away as they confront the primitive realities of the barren Sahara. *The Sheltering Sky* owes a debt, in its precise rendering of the violence and poverty of the Arab world, to the naturalist tradition, but beneath the novel's precisely rendered surface are undercurrents of symbol and insinuation which continually extend the meaning of the work. Like Edgar Allan Poe, the American writer whom he most admires, Bowles is primarily interested in probing the human soul, and to do so he must first strip it naked. That process most often reveals a spiritual emptiness, a sense of the void which links him to European existentialist writers like Sartre, whose *No Exit* Bowles translated in 1946. As Bowles remarks of one of his own characters, "in order to deal with relative values, he had long since come to deny all purpose to the phenomenon of existence—it was more expedient and more comforting."

Some reviewers felt that *The Sheltering Sky* was merely a retelling of the story of spiritually bankrupt expatriates that Hemingway had recorded in *The Sun Also Rises*. In his second novel, *Let It Come Down*, Bowles made it clear that his interest in *nada* went far beyond Hemingway's essentially romantic attitude toward the dispossessed. The atmosphere of this work is even more stark, malevolent, and absurd than that of the first novel. A sober, sheltered clerk in a New York bank gives up his position in order to work in a friend's travel agency in Tangier; there he discovers the business to be a front for currency black-marketeering, and following that revelation he himself becomes involved in smuggling, narcotics traffic, sexual perversion, espionage, and murder, ultimately absconding with an Arab companion and a bundle of stolen currency. Despite the obvious sensationalism of plot, Bowles is again concerned with the psychic disintegration and moral decay which overtake so-called civilized man when he confronts the primitive; the theme pervades his major writing as it does that of Joseph Conrad.

The hero (or anti-hero) of *Let It Come Down* seeks some place in the world to cancel out his meaningless existence, to find self by losing it; rejecting all conventional ideas of order, he acts in a chaotic way that creates and invites violence. Violence also overtakes and destroys the central characters of *Up above the World* who celebrate their second wedding anniversary with a trip to an obscure plantation republic. As they wander through wild landscapes, their adventures become increasingly feverish, compulsive, and agonized until hallucination and death overtake them.

The world of Paul Bowles's fiction is morally uninhabitable; it closes down on his characters like a hypnotic spell, as it closes down on the reader willing to grant the author's *donnée*: that there is within each of us the capacity for violence, irrational behavior, and madness, and that modern culture proves increasingly ineffective in giving check to those abysses. Nonetheless, Bowles's most memorable characters struggle for some kind of definition and often gamble for meaning with their very souls. Such concerns are equally present in Bowles's poetry, his travel books, and such edited "translations" as *Love with a Few Hairs*, the autobiography of the young Moroccan, Mohammed Mrabet. Many readers will find his vision discomforting, but it has significant parallels in the work of Sartre and Genet, Camus's *L'Etranger*, and the later work of Norman Mailer. Few modern writers have explored so memorably the contrasts between naivety and guile, Puritan restraint and pagan indulgence, Western sophistication and ancient superstition.

Nonetheless, it is difficult to escape the sense that Bowles's agonized vision, his extraordinary range of talent and his richly international experience have never coalesced to produce the single great work on which a major reputation might be established. The hypnotic atmosphere of *The Sheltering Sky* has been equalled in later work, but never surpassed, and while *The Spider's House* and *Up above the World* demonstrate a refinement of narrative power, they seem finally like somewhat redundant variations on long-established gothic themes.

—David Galloway

BOYLE, Kay. American. Born in St. Paul, Minnesota, 19 February 1902. Educated at the Cincinnati Conservatory of Music; Ohio Mechanics Institute, 1917-19. Married 1) Richard Brault in 1921 (divorced); 2) Laurence Vail in 1931 (divorced); 3) Baron Joseph von Franckenstein in 1943 (died, 1963); five daughters and one son. Lived in Europe for 30 years. Foreign Correspondent, *The New Yorker* magazine, 1946-53. Since 1963, Professor of English, San Francisco State College. Lecturer, New School for Social Research, New York, 1962; Fellow, Wesleyan University, Middletown, Connecticut, 1963; Director, New York Writers Conference, Wagner College, New York, 1964; Fellow, Radcliffe Institute for Independent Study, Cambridge, Massachusetts, 1964-65; Writer-in-Residence, University of Massachusetts, Amherst, 1967, and Hollins College, Virginia, 1970-71. Recipient: Guggenheim Fellowship, 1934, 1961; O. Henry Award, for short story, 1935, 1941. D.Litt.: Columbia College, Chicago, 1971; D.H.L.: Skidmore College, Saratoga Springs, New York, 1977. Member, American Academy, 1979. Address: c/o A. Watkins Inc., 77 Park Avenue, New York, New York 10016, U.S.A.

PUBLICATIONS

Novels

Plagued by the Nightingale. New York, Cape and Smith, and London, Cape, 1931.
Year Before Last. New York, Smith, and London, Faber, 1932.
Gentlemen, I Address You Privately. New York, Smith, 1933; London, Faber, 1934.
My Next Bride. New York, Harcourt Brace, 1934; London, Faber, 1935.
Death of a Man. New York, Harcourt Brace, and London, Faber, 1936.
Monday Night. New York, Harcourt Brace, and London, Faber, 1938.
Primer for Combat. New York, Simon and Schuster, 1942; London, Faber, 1943.
Avalanche. New York, Simon and Schuster, and London, Faber, 1944.
A Frenchman Must Die. New York, Simon and Schuster, and London, Faber, 1946.
1939. New York, Simon and Schuster, and London, Faber, 1948.
His Human Majesty. New York, McGraw Hill, 1949; London, Faber, 1950.
The Seagull on the Step. New York, Knopf, and London, Faber, 1955.
Generation Without Farewell. New York, Knopf, 1960.
The Underground Woman. New York, Doubleday, 1975.

Short Stories

Short Stories. Paris, Black Sun Press, 1929.
Wedding Day and Other Stories. New York, Cape and Smith, 1930; London, Pharos, 1932.
The First Lover and Other Stories. New York, Smith and Haas, 1933; London, Faber, 1937.

The White Horses of Vienna and Other Stories. New York, Harcourt Brace, 1936; London, Faber, 1937.
The Crazy Hunter: Three Short Novels. New York, Harcourt Brace, 1940; as *The Crazy Hunter and Other Stories*, London, Faber, 1940.
Thirty Stories. New York, Simon and Schuster, 1946; London, Faber, 1948.
The Smoking Mountain: Stories of Post War Germany. New York, McGraw Hill, 1951; London, Faber, 1952.
Three Short Novels. Boston, Beacon Press, 1958.
Nothing Ever Breaks Except the Heart. New York, Doubleday, 1966.
Fifty Stories. New York, Doubleday, 1980.

Verse

A Statement. New York, Modern Editions Press, 1932.
A Glad Day. New York, New Directions, 1938.
American Citizen: Naturalized in Leadville, Colorado. New York, Simon and Schuster, 1944.
Collected Poems. New York, Knopf, 1962.
Testament for My Students and Other Poems. New York, Doubleday, 1970.

Other

The Youngest Camel (juvenile). Boston, Little Brown, and London, Faber, 1939; revised edition, New York, Harper, 1959; Faber, 1960.
Breaking the Silence: Why a Mother Tells Her Son about the Nazi Era. New York, Institute of Human Relations Press-American Jewish Committee, 1962.
Pinky, The Cat Who Liked to Sleep (juvenile). New York, Crowell Collier, 1966.
Pinky in Persia (juvenile). New York, Crowell Collier, 1968.
Being Geniuses Together 1920-1930, with Robert McAlmon. New York, Doubleday, 1968; London, Joseph, 1970.
The Long Walk at San Francisco State and Other Essays. New York, Grove Press, 1970.
Four Visions of America, with others. Santa Barbara, California, Capra Press, 1977.

Editor, with Laurence Vail and Nina Conarain, *365 Days.* New York, Harcourt Brace, and London, Cape, 1936.
Editor, *The Autobiography of Emanuel Carnevali.* New York, Horizon Press, 1967.
Editor, with Justine Van Gundy, *Enough of Dying! An Anthology of Peace Writings.* New York, Dell, 1972.

Translator, *Don Juan*, by Joseph Delteil. New York, Cape and Smith, 1931.
Translator, *Mr. Knife, Miss Fork*, by R. Crevel. Paris, Black Sun Press, 1931.
Translator, *The Devil in the Flesh*, by Raymond Radiguet. New York, Smith, 1932; London, Grey Walls Press, 1949.

Ghost-writer for the books *Relations and Complications: Being the Recollections of H.H. the Dayang Muda of Sarawak*, by Gladys Palmer Brooke, London, Lane, 1929, and *Yellow Dusk*, by Bettina Bedwell, London, Hurst and Blackett, 1937.

*

Manuscript Collection: Morris Library, Southern Illinois University, Carbondale.

* * *

What I remember most in my reading of Kay Boyle are specific scenes—the sight of the sea tide building and crashing through the mouth of a river; a young man, sick with tuberculosis, leaning over a basin to vomit blood; a bus-driver arguing recklessly with his passengers while the bus careens along a cliff road; a run-over dog pulling itself forward, as its spilled-out entrails drag and turn white in the dust; Americans and Germans waiting over real fox holes in a German forest, ready to club the young foxes as they come out, and underground, moving through the tunnels, now near, now distant, the sound of the yelping pack and pursuing dog.

Boyle's concern here is to heighten our responses to these events. She asks us not only to respond to the vivid and extreme sensations which they present, but to see them in sharp moral and aesthetic terms, as beautiful or dangerous or agonizingly brutal.

It is this intense kind of involvement that Boyle asks from us generally. She offers very little neutral ground on which we may look at these scenes on our own. The youthful idealists, who play a major role in her novels, will give us, I think, the right emotional cues for appreciating her work. Inexperienced in the ways of the world, their feelings are open and unmitigated; they do not quite believe in evil and yet they are deeply troubled by pain and injustice. Bridget, Victoria John, Mary Farrant, Milly Roberts—young Americans whose destinies are connected with Europe—are such figures. If the fictional situation would seem to echo James, there are major differences in its development, for Kay Boyle's morality is active rather than introspective.

Indeed, whether her heroes be young Americans in Europe or former German soldiers, they express themselves in concrete acts—Mary Farrant makes her way up a rocky cliff to save the dwarf Marrakech; a middle-aged dandy, terrified of horses, enters the stall of a blind horse, and, for his daughter's sake, stays there while it kicks and rears in fright; Jaeger, a German journalist and ex-P.O.W. from the Afrika Corps, crawls over a heap of sliding rubble to give a cigarette to a power shovel driver trapped inside his cab.

What her heroes have in common is the courage to act—it is the only thing people ever remember, one character says. But action is, of course, no guarantee of success. Involved in every human venture, it would seem, are elements that bring about its destruction. Those elements may be physical in nature—not malevolent but merely indifferent—stupid accident, or man's incapacity to make a social world that is supportive and helpful.

Thus, in *Plagued by the Nightingale*, the closely bound world of a French family becomes so destructive that three daughters and a son wait desperately for an escape. Only Charlotte, the fourth daughter, loves her richly domestic life and her place within the family; and only Charlotte is deprived of it by death. In *Year Before Last* Martin, a young poet, dying of tuberculosis, and Eve, his aunt, are bound together by their dedication to art. Yet the emotion that shapes their lives is Eve's cruel jealousy of Hanah, whom Martin loves and who would shield him from the agonies of poverty and illness. In *My Next Bride* the artist, Sorrel, uses the common funds of the art colony to buy a magnificent and expensive automobile. In this shallow attempt to escape poverty and ugliness, he betrays the destitute craftsmen who work for him, as well as the artistic creed he has professed to live by.

Boyle's novels have, I think, a potentially tragic feeling. The qualities she projects in her strongest characters—courage to act as a counter to failure, energy rather than hopeless despair—offer this possibility. Very often, it seems wasted, for although Boyle insists upon courageous action, the possible choices she sees in such action are limited. Also, perhaps equally harmful, these choices do not necessarily grow out of the fictional situation; they seem fixed from the beginning. It is for this reason, perhaps, that her characters sometimes take unreal positions—in *Avalanche* the mountain men are total in their dedication to a good cause, the German agent, total in his dedication to a bad one; in *The Seagull on the Step* the doctor commits melodramatic villainies, the teacher-reformer, heroic deeds; in *Generation Without Farewell* the American colonel is brutal and gross, his wife and daughter are gentle and sensitive. Such extreme divisions in realistic novels are unconvincing. In relation to this kind of fictional situation, we are no longer active readers but spectators, waiting for the author to tell us what is right, what is sad and pitiable, what is mean.

There is a problem also, I think, in Boyle's wish to discover in technology and social reform, the elements of high moral adventure. In *Generation Without Farewell*, for example, Jaeger, the German journalist, and his fellow-townsmen drive through the night to pick up an iron lung for Christoph Horn, dying of bulbar polio, and arrive back in time to save Horn's life, if only for a few days. Later, after Horn's death, the director of America House, Honerkamp, erects a huge thermometer in the town square to register donations for an iron lung that, hopefully, the town will now buy for itself. In both instances, we are expected to share the emotions of the major figures, of Jaegar, who sees the journey as "keeping death at bay," and of Honerkamp, who believes that the Germans will learn something about democracy from this community chest effort.

The focus here is on technical solutions—the iron lung for saving a life; the thermometer, for registering a common social effort. Both are stock images that offer very little opportunity for a fresh response. More important, perhaps, they are mechanical and static. Our involvement with them is necessarily limited, for they have no power to draw us into a situation in which our feelings may be deepened and extended. The best we can offer is a set response.

Yet, I am sure that Boyle would never exclude these social possibilities, whatever the literary risks. In an early poem, she uses the phrase "tough taste." It is a good phrase, I think, to describe her conception of what she is doing.

What gives her work strength are not these special interests, but her understanding that our human connections lie finally in our limitations, most of all in our common mortality. From the beginning, she has had this kind of knowledge.

At moments we see it expressed with startling clarity. In her first novel, Charlotte's family is hastily called to her bedside. Those who have waited through the day—Charlotte's young children, her sisters—make their way through the dark, wet fall night, to Charlotte's house, up the great stairs and to her room. There, they wait in silence until the door is opened, and the children walk "calmly into the roar of Charlotte's death." In her recent novel of post-war Germany, a power shovel in downtown Frankfurt accidentally unearths an underground air raid shelter and releases a single survivor, entombed there since the war. As the mad, tattered figure runs wildly across the upturned ground, bewildered by his resurrection, any ideals we may hold about nationality, military success, moral justification, diminish into nothingness. Only a sense of our common inhumanity persists.

In the short stories also, Kay Boyle shows us the complicated devastation that human beings can work on one another and on themselves. Among the best are the stories of postwar Germany in *The Smoking Mountain*. The scale is modest—an American army wife shops in a PX supermarket, three boys search out a center for lost children, a group of local actors put on a play at a Weinstube—the right dimension to make us understand such a catastrophe as an individual, day-to-day experience. Likewise, in the brilliant reportorial piece that opens the collection, on the murder trial of a minor Gestapo official, Heinrich Baab, nothing is obscured by the blare of historical significance. Baab, accused of 57 murders, was, as Boyle says, a "small criminal." For those who sometimes have doubts about the relationship between art and the direct observation of experience, these stories should give a clear answer.

—Jacqueline Hoefer

BRADBURY, Malcolm (Stanley). British. Born in Sheffield, Yorkshire, 7 September 1932. Educated at West Bridgford Grammar School; University College of Leicester, B.A. in English 1953; Queen Mary College, London, M.A. in English 1955; Indiana University, Bloomington, 1955-56; University of Manchester, 1956-58, Ph.D. in American Studies, 1963. Married Elizabeth Salt in 1959; two sons. Staff Tutor in Literature, Extra-Mural Department, University of Hull, Yorkshire, 1959-61; Lecturer in English, University of Birmingham, 1961-65. Lecturer in English, 1965-67, Senior Lecturer, 1967-69, Reader, 1969-70, and since 1970, Professor of American Studies, University of East Anglia, Norwich. Visiting Fellow, All Souls College, Oxford, 1969; Visiting Professor, University of Zurich, 1972. Member of the Committee, British Association for American Studies. Recipient: British Association for American Studies Fellowship, 1958; American Council of Learned Societies Fellowship, 1965; Heinemann Award, 1976. Fellow, Royal Society of Literature. Address: School of English and American Studies, University of East Anglia, Norwich NR4 7TJ, England.

PUBLICATIONS

Novels

Eating People Is Wrong. London, Secker and Warburg, 1959; New York, Knopf, 1960.
Stepping Westward. London, Secker and Warburg, 1965; Boston, Houghton Mifflin, 1966.
The History Man. London, Secker and Warburg, 1975; Boston, Houghton Mifflin, 1976.

Short Stories

Who Do You Think You Are? Stories and Parodies. London, Secker and Warburg, 1976.

Plays

Between These Four Walls, with David Lodge and James Duckett (produced Birmingham, 1963).
Slap in the Middle, with others (produced Birmingham, 1965).

Radio Plays: *This Sporting Life*, with Elizabeth Bradbury, from the novel by David Storey, 1974; *Patterson*, with Christopher Bigsby, 1981.

Television Plays: *The After Dinner Game*, with Christopher Bigsby, 1975; *The Enigma*, from the story by John Fowles, 1980; *Standing In for Henry*, 1980.

Verse

Two Poets, with Allan Rodway. Nottingham, Byron Press, 1966.

Other

Phogey! How to Have Class in a Classless Society. London, Parrish, 1960.
All Dressed Up and Nowhere to Go: The Poor Man's Guide to the Affluent Society. London, Parrish, 1962.
Evelyn Waugh. Edinburgh, Oliver and Boyd, 1964.
What Is a Novel? London, Arnold, 1969.
The Social Context of Modern English Literature. Oxford, Blackwell, and New York, Schocken, 1971.
Possibilities: Essays on the State of the Novel. London, Oxford University Press, 1973.

Editor, *Forster: A Collection of Critical Essays.* Englewood Cliffs, New Jersey, Prentice Hall, 1966.
Editor, *Pudd'nhead Wilson, and Those Extraordinary Twins*, by Mark Twain. London, Penguin, 1969.
Editor, *E.M. Forster: A Passage to India: A Casebook.* London, Macmillan, 1970.
Editor, with David Palmer, *Contemporary Criticism.* London, Arnold, 1970; New York, St. Martin's Press, 1971.

Editor, with Eric Mottram, *U.S.A.*, in *The Penguin Companion to Literature 3.* London, Allen Lane-Penguin Press, and New York, McGraw Hill, 1971.

Editor, with David Palmer, *The American Novel and the Nineteen Twenties.* London, Arnold, 1971.

Editor, with James McFarlane, *Modernism 1890-1930.* London, Penguin, 1976.

Editor, *The Novel Today: Contemporary Writers on Modern Fiction.* Manchester, Manchester University Press, and Totowa, New Jersey, Rowman and Littlefield, 1977.

Editor, with David Palmer, *The Contemporary English Novel.* London, Arnold, 1979; New York, Holmes and Meier, 1980.

Editor, with Howard Temperley, *An Introduction to American Studies.* London, Longman, 1981.

*

Manuscript Collection: Nottingham Public Library.

Malcolm Bradbury comments:

(1972) Both of my novels (and the third one I am now writing) are set in universities; the first in a "redbrick," the second, in part, on an American campus, and the third in a new university. Such criticism as has discussed my work seems to have treated it as a species of the campus novel; I am uneasy with the designation. The settings are relatively incidental (any intellectual milieu might do as well), and my main concern has been, within a more or less comic framework, to explore problems and dilemmas of liberalism and issues of moral responsibility. My main characters are typically confused but concerned moral agents; their liberalism is less a political than a moral perspective; their aim is decency and goodwill, and the comedy and indeed the potential tragedy or at least pathos arises when the world, in its contingency, refuses to let them, or blurs the moral perspectives they fell they possess.

I regard comedy as a main means of fulfilling my purposes because it seems to me the best way of distilling my sense not only of the moral difficulties and insufficiencies of men, but also of the difficult pressures of the claims of modern history on those who live through it; it allows me a certain modified realism and tolerance, and a dialectical range within myself. Perhaps another way of saying that is to remark that comedy allows me the chance to demonstrate the ironical situation of values which concern me, allows me in a time when the language of value has little force in modern fiction to explore them at all.

Critics today—I say this as one myself—have a strong tendency to prescribe the limits of reality, to say how little there is of it with which the novelist may deal, to lay their stress on the game—like elements of the fictive act; that, as critics, is one of *their* essential modern fictions, and I can see how they come to it while not necessarily finding myself amidst such problems when I set out to write a novel.

The fact remains that my earlier novels do owe a considerable amount to a liberal climate which is now threatened and could perhaps be dying; and though in the two published novels these strains on liberalism were part of my theme I find myself, in my new book, putting it under much more onerous threats. To this extent I do see my kind of writing as under an historical pressure. *Eating People Is Wrong*, which was largely written when I was an undergraduate, and then revised much later, in part sees the world of the academy and the intellect from outside; but it respects it and grants it goodwill, rather than condemning it as many students now do. *Stepping Westward* likewise tries to see that we can be misused by the historicist, political mind whether it be radical or reactionary. If both books end by linking the desire to mediate with inertia or a failure of will, this is not to condemn the centre of tolerance that I try to create in them both, even if that tolerance itself has comic dimensions. As for what I am now doing, I find myself increasingly obsessed with formal problems and, linked with that, a far greater ironic distance from my characters and any worlds I can give them to inhabit.

* * *

Ever since the 1959 publication of his first novel, *Eating People Is Wrong*, Malcolm Bradbury has been regarded as an extremely funny satirist, lampooning topical phenomena and issues with brilliant wit. He excels in satirical set pieces: the cautiously wild and slapstick university party that mixes faculty and students in *Eating People Is Wrong*; the American faculty committee meeting to choose a writer-in-residence that begins *Stepping Westward* and is ironically contrasted with a similar meeting, a year later, at the end; the department meeting that combines haggling over procedure, trivia, several forms of self-seeking, and genuine academic concerns in *The History Man*; the adult education class that was apparently cut from *Eating People Is Wrong* and, in revised form, printed in the collection of *Who Do You Think You Are?* All these pieces bring people, representing various points of view on some current question of politics or communal definition, into sharp, comically outrageous conflict. And Bradbury is particularly skillful in handling the large party, like the "with-it," consciously "existential" party, a license for free self-definition, arranged by the "new" university sociologist, Howard Kirk, in *The History Man*. In such pieces, Bradbury exploits his talent for mimicry, not only a mimicry of current attitudes but also one of frequent literary themes and other writers. A long section of *Who Do You Think You Are?*, for example, contains parodies of other contemporary writers, astringent treatments of Snow, Amis, Iris Murdoch, John Braine, Sillitoe, and others, along with less biting and salient echoes of Angus Wilson and Lawrence Durrell. The use of Amis (with whose early work Bradbury's has often been compared) is particularly resonant. Like Amis, Bradbury sometimes includes characters from one fiction in another, like the free-loving psychologist, Flora Beniform, who is both Howard Kirk's uncommitted mistress in *The History Man* and a central character on the television panel concerning modern sexual mores satirized in the story "Who Do You Think You Are?" As an in-joke, Bradbury even appropriates the Amis character who doesn't appear, the fraudulent L.S. Caton used in a number of novels until Amis finally killed him off in *The Anti-Death League*. Bradbury makes him a professor, scheduled to visit Benedict Arnold University in the U.S. to give a lecture on the "angry young men," who never arrives. In spite of all the critical comparisons and interlocking references, Bradbury's satire is different from Amis's, Bradbury always more concerned with issues and ideas, less implicitly committed to pragmatic success in the world or to mocking various forms of contemporary incompetence.

Much of Bradbury's fiction takes place within a university setting: the provincial red-brick during the 1950's in *Eating People Is Wrong*, the American university in the flat wilderness of the Plains states in *Stepping Westward*, the new south coast university in 1972 in *The History Man*. Yet, as Bradbury himself has rightly insisted, the applications of his fiction extend far beyond the university setting, just as the implications of his moral treatments of contemporary experience are far from slapstick comedy. In *Stepping Westward* the Englishman, James Walker, who becomes writer-in-residence at the "moral supermarket" of the American university, begins with his own "decent modest radicalism" and tries to extend himself in America, to assimilate more of the modern world, looking for "sense and design." The plot depends on Walker's public refusal to sign an American loyalty oath, part of his English "faith in unbelief," and, as a result, the America he finds is one of "violence and meaninglessness and anarchy." In *The History Man* Howard Kirk, seen far less sympathetically than James Walker is, seeks "liberation" and "emancipation" in the new university for himself and others, ignoring or condescending to his old friend, Beamish, a rather bumbling locus of value in the novel, who claims "there is an inheritance of worthwhile life in this country." In this novel, written entirely in the rush of the present tense, Kirk chooses instead to redevelop the town, to lie, to manipulate others in the name of "now" and the "new," and to ignore the voice of a young English teacher who sees her function as simply reading and talking about books. In both novels Bradbury's moral focus is clear and searching, although it sometimes seems slightly provincial, and he always attacks the self-seeking, the self-deceptive, and the meretricious, like a career academic named Froelich who becomes chairman in

Stepping Westward and Kirk himself in *The History Man*. Yet some of Bradbury's work has more complexity than outlining the moral framework might suggest. Sometimes, as in *The History Man*, which ends with Kirk's wife deliberately pushing her arm through the window, an act of self-destruction like that more ambivalently performed by Beamish at an earlier party, or in a short story entitled "A Very Hospitable Person," the satire seems brittle, almost cruel, in denying the central figures any humanity or self-doubt. At other times, as in an excellent story called "A Breakdown," about a student having a futile affair with a married man in Chesterfield who runs off to Spain to punish herself, or as in *Stepping Westward*, where James Walker recognizes that America has defeated him, that, in spite of all his morality, he could not really handle his own freedom to define himself, Bradbury's perspective is more humane and sympathetic without diluting the moral concern.

—James Gindin

BRADBURY, Ray(mond Douglas). American. Born in Waukegan, Illinois, 22 August 1920. Educated at Los Angeles High School. Married Marguerite Susan McClure in 1947; four daughters. Since 1943, full-time writer. President, Science-Fantasy Writers of America, 1951-53. Member of the Board of Directors, Screen Writers Guild of America, 1957-61. Recipient: O. Henry Prize, 1947, 1948; Benjamin Franklin Award, 1954; American Academy award, 1954; Boys' Clubs of America Junior Book Award, 1956; Golden Eagle Award, for screenplay, 1957; Ann Radcliffe Award, 1965, 1971; Aviation and Space Writers Award, for television documentary, 1979; Gandalf Award, 1980. D.Litt.: Whittier College, California, 1979. Agent: Don Congdon, Harold Matson Company, 22 East 40th Street, New York, New York 10016. Address: 10265 Cheviot Drive, Los Angeles, California 90064, U.S.A.

PUBLICATIONS

Novels

Fahrenheit 451. New York, Ballantine, 1953; London, Hart Davis, 1954.
Something Wicked This Way Comes. New York, Simon and Schuster, 1962; London, Hart Davis, 1963.

Short Stories

Dark Carnival. Sauk City, Wisconsin, Arkham House, 1947; London, Hamish Hamilton, 1948.
The Martian Chronicles. New York, Doubleday, 1950; as *The Silver Locusts*, London, Hart Davis, 1951.
The Illustrated Man. New York, Doubleday, 1951; London, Hart Davis, 1952.
The Golden Apples of the Sun. New York, Doubleday, and London, Hart Davis, 1953.
The October Country. New York, Ballantine, 1955; London, Hart Davis, 1956.
Dandelion Wine. New York, Doubleday, and London, Hart Davis, 1957.
A Medicine for Melancholy. New York, Doubleday, 1959; as *The Day It Rained Forever*, London, Hart Davis, 1959.
The Small Assassin. London, Ace, 1962; New York, New American Library, 1973.
The Machineries of Joy. New York, Simon and Schuster, and London, Hart Davis, 1964.
The Vintage Bradbury. New York, Random House, 1965.
The Autumn People. New York, Ballantine, 1965.
Tomorrow Midnight. New York, Ballantine, 1966.
Twice Twenty-Two (selection). New York, Doubleday, 1966.
I Sing the Body Electric! New York, Knopf, 1969; London, Hart Davis, 1970.
Bloch and Bradbury, with Robert Bloch. New York, Belmont, 1969; as *Fever Dreams and Other Fantasies*, London, Sphere, 1970.
(*Selected Stories*), edited by Anthony Adams. London, Harrap, 1975.
Long after Midnight. New York, Knopf, 1976; London, Hart Davis MacGibbon, 1977.
The Stories of Ray Bradbury. New York, Knopf, 1980.
The Last Circus, and The Electrocution. Northridge, California, Lord John Press, 1980.

Uncollected Short Stories

"The Fruit at the Bottom of the Bowl," in *Ellery Queen's Mystery Magazine* (New York), January 1953.
"And So Died Riabouchinska," in *The Saint* (New York), June-July 1953.
"The Whole Town's Sleeping," in *Ellery Queen's Mystery Magazine* (New York), June 1954.
"At Midnight, In the Month of June," in *Ellery Queen's Mystery Magazine* (New York), June 1954.
"Shopping for Death," in *The Saint* (New York), February 1955.
"The Screaming Woman," in *The Saint* (New York), September 1955.
"The Town Where No One Got Off," in *Ellery Queen's Mystery Magazine* (New York), October 1958.

Plays

The Meadow, in *Best One-Act Plays of 1947-48*. New York, Dodd Mead, 1948.
The Anthem Sprinters and Other Antics (produced Los Angeles, 1968). New York, Dial Press, 1963.
The World of Ray Bradbury (produced Los Angeles, 1964; New York, 1965).
The Wonderful Ice-Cream Suit (produced Los Angeles, 1965). Included in *The Wonderful Ice-Cream Suit and Other Plays*, 1972.
The Day It Rained Forever. New York, French, 1966.
The Pedestrian. New York, French, 1966.
Christus Apollo, music by Jerry Goldsmith (produced Los Angeles, 1969).
The Wonderful Ice-Cream Suit and Other Plays (includes *The Veldt* and *To the Chicago Abyss*). New York, Bantam, 1972; London, Hart Davis, 1973.
The Veldt, adaptation of his own story (produced London, 1980). Included in *The Wonderful Ice-Cream Suit and Other Plays*, 1972.
Leviathan 99 (produced Los Angeles, 1972).
Pillar of Fire and Other Plays for Today, Tomorrow, and Beyond Tomorrow (includes *Kaleidoscope* and *The Foghorn*). London, Bantam, 1975.
The Foghorn (produced New York, 1977). Included in *Pillar of Fire and Other Plays*, 1975.
That Ghost, That Bride of Time: Excerpts from a Play-in-Progress. Privately printed, 1976.
The Martian Chronicles, adaptation of his own stories (produced Los Angeles, 1977).
Farenheit 451, adaptation of his own novel (produced Los Angeles, 1979).
Dandelion Wine, adaptation of his own story (produced Los Angeles, 1980).

Screenplays: *It Came from Outer Space*, with David Schwartz, 1952; *Moby-Dick*, with John Huston, 1956; *Icarus Montgolfier Wright*, 1961; *The Picasso Summer*, 1967.

Television Plays: *The Jail*, 1962; *The Life Work of Juan Diaz*, 1963.

Verse

Old Ahab's Friend, and Friend to Noah, Speaks His Piece: A Celebration. Privately printed, 1971.
When Elephants Last in the Dooryard Bloomed: Celebrations for Almost Any Day of the Year. New York, Knopf, 1973; London, Hart Davis MacGibbon, 1975.
That Son of Richard III: A Birth Announcement. Privately printed, 1974.
Where Robot Mice and Robot Men Run round in Robot Towns: New Poems, Both Light and Dark. New York, Knopf, 1977; London, Hart Davis MacGibbon, 1979.
Twin Hieroglyphs That Swim the River Dust. Northridge, California, Lord John Press, 1978.
The Bike Repairman. Northridge, California, Lord John Press, 1978.
The Author Considers His Resources. Northridge, California, Lord John Press, 1979.
The Aqueduct. Glendale, California, Squires Press, 1979.
The Attic Where the Meadow Greens. Northridge, California, Lord John Press, 1980.
The Haunted Computer and the Android Pope. New York, Knopf, 1981.

Other

Switch on the Night (juvenile). New York, Pantheon, and London, Hart Davis, 1955.
R Is for Rocket (juvenile). New York, Doubleday, 1962; London, Hart Davis, 1968.
S Is for Space (juvenile). New York, Doubleday, 1966; London, Hart Davis, 1968.
Teacher's Guide: Science Fiction, with Lewy Olfson. New York, Bantam, 1968.
The Halloween Tree (juvenile). New York, Knopf, 1972; London, Hart Davis MacGibbon, 1973.
Mars and the Mind of Man. New York, Harper, 1973.
Zen and the Art of Writing, and The Joy of Writing. Santa Barbara, California, Capra Press, 1973.
The Mummies of Guanajuato, photographs by Archie Lieberman. New York, Abrams, 1978.
Beyond 1984: Remembrance of Things Future. New York, Targ Editions, 1979.
The Ghosts of Forever, illustrated by Aldo Sessa. New York, Rizzoli, 1981.

Editor, *Timeless Stories for Today and Tomorrow.* New York, Bantam, 1952.
Editor, *The Circus of Dr. Lao and Other Improbable Stories.* New York, Bantam, 1956.

*

Critical Studies: interview in *Show* (New York), December 1964; introduction by Gilbert Highet to *The Vintage Bradbury*, 1965; "The Revival of Fantasy" by Russell Kirk, in *Triumph* (Washington, D.C.), May 1968; "Ray Bradbury's *Dandelion Wine*: Themes, Sources, and Style" by Marvin E. Mengeling, in *English Journal* (Champaign, Illinois), October 1971; *The Ray Bradbury Companion* (includes bibliography) by William F. Nolan, Detroit, Gale, 1975; *The Drama of Ray Bradbury* by Benjamin P. Indick, Baltimore, T-K Graphics, 1977; *The Bradbury Chronicles* by George Edgar Slusser, San Bernardino, California, Borgo Press, 1977; *Ray Bradbury* edited by Joseph D. Olander and Martin H. Greenberg, New York, Taplinger, 1979; *Ray Bradbury* by Wayne L. Johnson, New York, Ungar, 1980.

Ray Bradbury comments:

I am not so much a science-fiction writer as I am a magician, an illusionist. From my beginnings as a boy conjurer I grew up frightening myself so as to frighten others so as to cure the midnight in our souls. I have grown into a writer of the History of Ideas, I guess you might say. Any idea, no matter how large or small, that is busy growing itself alive, starting from nowhere and at last dominating a town, a culture, or a world, is of interest. Man the problem solver is the writer of my tales. Science fiction becoming science fact. The machineries of our world putting away and keeping our facts for us so they can be used and learned from. Machines as humanist teachers. Ideas of men built into those machines in order to help us survive and survive well. That's my broad and fascinating field, in which I will wander for a lifetime, writing past science fictions one day, future ones another. And all of it a wonder and a lark and a great love. I can't imagine writing any other way.

* * *

Although he has written the novels *Something Wicked This Way Comes* and *Fahrenheit 451*, Ray Bradbury is primarily a writer of short stories. Ever the storyteller, Bradbury aims in each story at producing the horror, the surprise, or the single dominant effect of Poe, one of his principal mentors. Nonetheless, his short story collections—notably *The Martian Chronicles* and *Dandelion Wine*—have an overall meaning which exceeds the meaning of the parts. Although he often seems to write about disparate bits of experience, Bradbury does have an identifiable view of life.

"Here There Be Tygers" (*R Is for Rocket*) contains several of the elements of that view. Astronauts land on a previously unknown planet. One of them fears that there are dangers ("tygers") on the planet, and he wishes to kill whatever is alive and to exploit the remaining dead matter. He fulfills his own prophecy: the planet kills him. There *are* tygers on this pastoral world, but the other astronauts are drawn to them. The planet is not dead but alive, and when the astronauts dare to dream their favourite forbidden dreams into it, they awake to find them true. Bradbury follows Wordsworth, Coleridge, and Keats in believing that the childlike imagination can create a wonderful but also terrifying, and temporary, pleasure dome. All but one of the astronauts leave the strange Eden.

In *The Martian Chronicles*, the Eden is Mars. The ancient, delicate Martian civilization is destroyed by crass, polluting, materialistic American invaders. Bradbury the dystopian never entirely shuts out Bradbury the believer in fresh starts, however. "The Million Year Panic" concerns a family which escapes from nuclear war on Earth and uses the psychic energy or imaginative force of the dead Martians to make themselves into "Martians," capable of starting a new and more humane civilization.

The Illustrated Man and *Fahrenheit 451* continue the theme of the imagination threatened but ultimately triumphant. In "The Exiles" Poe, Bierce, and other writers of the fantastic and the macabre perish with their creations on Mars. Fahrenheit 451 is the temperature which the firemen of the future generate to burn all books. Both works point ways out, however. In *Fahrenheit 451* a rebel band memorizes books. "The Rocket, " last story in *The Illustrated Man*, concerns a junkman who makes a rocket ship out of tin cans, which creates for his children the illusion of going to Mars.

Thus Bradbury believes that the imagination may operate in humble and private places as well as in space, and that it is as important to make familiar things new as to make the new things of the space age familiar. *Dandelion Wine* grafts suggestions of horror and science-fiction machines onto "Green Town," Illinois (presumably a version of the Waukegan, Illinois, of Bradbury's childhood). A man who can remember the Civil War past becomes a "time machine" to the boys who listen to his stories. Electric cars, lawnmowers, and trolleys become as mysterious as spaceships. Each day of the summer of 1928 a flask of dandelion wine—a noble thing made from a common plant—is put away for winter use. Bradbury's short stories are flasks of this wine: each day, or each story, is a little different and must be tasted separately. No single flask of wine contains all the wonders and terrors of our kaleidoscopic world.

The stories of *A Medicine for Melancholy* and *The Machineries of Joy* use terror and delight to purge the reader of melancholy. In "The Day It Rained Forever" 71-year-old Miss Hillgood, who has let her life pass by while she attended only to music, arrives at Joe Terle's Desert Hotel, where for years past there has been rain only one day of the year. When she begins to play, her music suddenly ceases to be sterile, and it magically causes a permanent end of the drought. To Bradbury, the unexpected can always happen. Life can always take a new turn precisely when and where you think of giving it up.

Both *The Machineries of Joy* and *I Sing the Body Electric!* contain Mars stories and others in the familiar Bradbury manner. But (particularly in the latter book) Bradbury experiments with replacing fantasy and plot twists with atmosphere, interior emotion, and character development. Too often the resulting stories lack the motivation and the logic which the fantastic never required. But Bradbury is a flexible and resourceful writer, and he may yet make successful use of the techniques of mainstream fiction.

Perhaps Bradbury's greatest value is as a social critic and a commentator on technology. Perceiving the madness of expansionist technology, Bradbury no longer shares the teenage boy's worship of the astronaut corps in "R Is for Rocket." But his Martians have a more advanced technology than Earth's, in many respects—their cities last, and Earthmen's do not. "Space travel has made children of us all," says the philosopher on the verso of *The Martian Chronicles*. The American astronauts are childish idiots, but space travel also makes possible the childlike wonder of the million-year picnic. In "The End of the Beginning" (*A Medicine for Melancholy*) a man pauses from mowing his lawn to watch his son rocket into the twilight air to make the first space station. Bradbury suggests the unity of all technology: Ezkiel's wheel in the middle of the air, the wheeling space station and lawnmower, and the wheels in the man's watch. Moreover, life and technology are interrelated. The amoeba's climb from water to land prepared for man's climb from Earth. It is now a new age, but the man finishes mowing the lawn after watching the rocket launching. Bradbury is not against technology. He simply believes that man must look around and back at the same time he looks forward.

In the 1960's and 1970's Bradbury's career has taken an entirely new turn. Few of his recent stories are science fiction or fantasy. Instead, Bradbury now concentrates solely on what was always present in his writing, his compassion for likeable but inadequate people struggling against the tragic ironies of life, and often being successful in ways they did not expect. "The Parrot Who Met Pappa" is about the theft of a parrot who knew Hemingway by a writer, Hemingway's contemporary, whose life is still filled with jealousy of the great man. In "The Utterly Perfect Murder" Douglas returns to Green Town, Bradbury's fabled childhood world, to kill someone he hated as a child. But when Douglas finds this changed and almost pitiful person, his murderous feelings melt. "Have I Got a Chocolate Bar for You!" is the tale of a Catholic priest who saves an Irish Jew from the sin of chocolate addiction.

As we can tell from his essay "Zen and the Art of Writing," Bradbury is an ambitious writer with a theory behind what he is doing. He is trying to convey the zest that life can have in a less-than-ideal universe. Bradbury's early science fiction now seems dated, and the emotion in his more recent fiction is at times overdone. But Bradbury's compassion for his characters and for his readers deserves respect.

—Curtis C. Smith

BRAGG, Melvyn. British. Born in Cumberland, 6 October 1939. Educated at Nelson Thomlinson Grammar School, Wigton, Cumberland, 1950-59; Wadham College, Oxford, M.A. (honours) in modern history 1961. Married 1) Lise Roche (died, 1971), one daughter; 2) Catherine Mary Haste in 1973, one daughter and one son. Producer, BBC Television, London, from 1961: Presenter, *Second House*, 1973-77, and *Read All about It*, 1976-77. Since 1977, Producer, *South Bank Show*, London Weekend Television. Since 1969, Member, and Chairman, 1977-80, Arts Council Literature Panel. Recipient: Writers Guild Award, for screenplay, 1966; Rhys Memorial Prize, 1968; Northern Arts Association Prose Award, 1970; Silver Pen Award, 1970. Fellow, Royal Society of Literature, 1970. Address: 12 Hampstead Hill Gardens, London N.W. 3, England.

PUBLICATIONS

Novels

For Want of a Nail. London, Secker and Warburg, and New York, Knopf, 1965.
The Second Inheritance. London, Secker and Warburg, 1966; New York, Knopf, 1967.
Without a City Wall. London, Secker and Warburg, 1968; New York, Knopf, 1969.
The Hired Man. London, Secker and Warburg, 1969; New York, Knopf, 1970.
A Place in England. London, Secker and Warburg, 1970; New York, Knopf, 1971.
The Nerve. London, Secker and Warburg, 1971.
The Hunt. London, Secker and Warburg, 1972.
Josh Lawton. London, Secker and Warburg, and New York, Knopf, 1972.
The Silken Net. London, Secker and Warburg, and New York, Knopf, 1974.
Autumn Manoeuvres. London, Secker and Warburg, 1976.
Kingdom Come. London, Secker and Warburg, 1980.

Short Story

A Christmas Child. London, Secker and Warburg, 1976.

Uncollected Short Story

"The Initiation," in *Winter's Tales 18*, edited by A.D. Maclean. London, Macmillan, and New York, St. Martin's Press, 1972.

Plays

Mardi Gras, music by Alan Blaikley and Ken Howard (produced London, 1976).

Screenplays: *Play Dirty*, with Lotte Colin, 1968; *Isadora*, with Clive Exton and Margaret Drabble, 1969; *The Music Lovers*, 1970; *Jesus Christ Superstar*, with Norman Jewison, 1973.

Radio Play: *Robin Hood*, 1971.

Television Plays: *Charity Begins at Home*, 1970; *Zinotchka*, 1972; *Orion*, music by Ken Howard and Alan Blaikley, 1977; *Clouds of Glory*, with Ken Russell, 1978.

Other

Speak for England: An Essay on England 1900-1975. London, Secker and Warburg, 1976; as *Speak for England: An Oral History of England 1900-1975*, New York, Knopf, 1977.

Editor, *My Favourite Stories of Lakeland.* Guildford, Surrey, Lutterworth Press, 1981.

*

Critical Studies: by Rodney Pybus, in *Stand* (Newcastle upon Tyne), Summer 1970; by Kenneth John Achuty, in *Kenyon Review 127* (Gambier, Ohio), 1971.

Melvyn Bragg comments:

(1972) The ways in which I came to write are sketched in the last chapters of *A Place in England:* they are made the notions of a fictional self—Douglas Tallentire.

Present ideas on fiction are represented in the novel *The Nerve* and in an essay "Class and the Novel" in *Times Literary Supplement* (London), 15 October 1971.

* * *

Melvyn Bragg began with two good novels about wasted human potential, *For Want of a Nail* and *The Second Inheritance*. But it was *Without a City Wall* which secured for him a deserved reputation as one of the best contemporary novelists. Theme and structure reinforce each other as Bragg traces, first, the awakening of passion in Richard Godwin, a self-imposed exile from the chaos of London, for Janice Beattie, a Cumberland girl of unusual intelligence and powerful ambition; and then, the challenges that the life of consummated passion entails for both of them. The drama develops principally from Janice whose ambition and fastidiousness prove stronger than sexual passion or her sense of responsibility to others. Her passion for Richard contracts, while his for her continues to expand. Richard is driven to the brink of self-destruction but recoils in time to force Janice to some kind of modus vivendi between the claims of his passion and the claims of her individuality. Bragg's more recent novel, *The Silken Net*, also develops the theme of sexual struggle. This book focuses on a restless intellectual, Rosemary Lewis, whose energy alienates her from life in the Cumberland village of Thurston. Her vigor is admirable but her egoism is destructive as she attempts to breed in her husband the same intensities that motivate her. The resulting conflict registers with less authority, however, than that developed in *Without a City Wall*.

The alternation of intensity and apathy in the passional life is again one subject explored in *The Hired Man*. Covering the years 1898 to 1920 in the life of John and Emily Tallentire, the novel articulates the nuances of their emotions. Communication between a man and a woman becomes a function of the body; and estrangement develops when perfect physical accord is broken. After Emily's death at forty John is where he was at the beginning, a man for casual hire on the great farms but now with all zest gone. Bragg's artistry is at its best in his honest portrayal of the hard lives of agricultural laborers in the early 20th century. *A Place in England* has for protagonist Joseph Tallentire, John's son. Bragg is less close to Joseph than to John; in fact, the most memorable pages of the novel feature the now patriarchal John. After much struggle Joseph is able to "be his own man" as owner of a public house; but his success is undercut by the disintegration of his marriage, a loss to him for which he cannot account.

Kingdom Come reveals much of the power found in *The Hired Man* and has much interest for the modern reader, as Bragg presents the contemporary generation of the Tallentire men. Lester, a con man and cousin, and Douglas, the son of Joseph and a writer of talent, lack the purposiveness and inner strength of their ancestors, though Harry, the adopted son who stays in Thurston, retains these qualities in large part. Douglas is the sympathetically presented protagonist who can neither be satisfied with the stern ancestral morality nor get clear of the claims of responsibility which derive from it. His divided nature defeats him because it leads him to betray the woman he loves and whose real worth he realizes too late.

In two other recent novels Bragg has again had recourse to Cumberland and its people. In *Josh Lawton*, a moving parable, Lawton has overtones of a Biblical patriarch and suffers the predictable fate of those who are too good for this world. In *Autumn Manoeuvres* Bragg traces the destructive and self-destructive career of Gareth Johnson. His violent loathing of his stepfather and his own violent self-loathing are linked to the violence of his begetting (his mother had been gang raped in World War I). Is he the victim of fatality or is he his own victim—more the second than the first, Bragg implies.

London figures more than Cumberland in *The Nerve* in which Bragg traces, in a first-person narrative, the stages in the mental breakdown of his protagonist, Ted. Power accrues when Ted, the narrator, actualizes some of his experience of physical and mental pain, but the breakdown which is a "breakthrough" is not precisely characterized.

The immediacy of Bragg's Cumberland milieu is, at least superficially, the quality that impresses most in his fiction. As in Thomas Hardy and D.H. Lawrence, milieu is integrally fused with the fortunes and development of the characters. Like Hardy he has in unusual degree insight into human beings who confront the elemental realities of nature, and like Hardy's his people encounter problems difficult to resolve when they lose rapport with nature. Bragg's eye for detail, his compelling sense of drama, his penetration into the emotional and psychic life of his characters, his sense of the moral verities, and his supple and luminous prose have all contributed to his standing as a distinguished novelist.

—Frederick P.W. McDowell

BRAINE, John (Gerard). British. Born in Bradford, Yorkshire, 13 April 1922. Educated at St. Bede's Grammar School, Bradford; Leeds School of Librarianship, A.L.A. 1949. Served as a telegraphist in the Royal Navy, 1942-43. Married Helen Patricia Wood in 1955; one son and three daughters. Assistant Librarian, 1940-49, and Chief Assistant Librarian, 1949-51, Bingley Public Library, Yorkshire; Branch Librarian, Northumberland County Library, 1954-56, and West Riding County Library, Darton, Yorkshire, 1956-57. Writer-in-Residence, Purdue University, Lafayette, Indiana, Fall 1978. Member, BBC North Regional Advisory Council, 1960-64. Address: Pentons, Onslow Crescent, Woking, Surrey, England.

PUBLICATIONS

Novels

Room at the Top. London, Eyre and Spottiswoode, and Boston, Houghton Mifflin, 1957.

The Vodi. London, Eyre and Spottiswoode, 1959; revised edition, London, Eyre Methuen, 1978; as *From the Hand of the Hunter*, Boston, Houghton Mifflin, 1960.

Life at the Top. London, Eyre and Spottiswoode, and Boston, Houghton Mifflin, 1962.

The Jealous God. London, Eyre and Spottiswoode, 1964; Boston, Houghton Mifflin, 1965.

The Crying Game. London, Eyre and Spottiswoode, and Boston, Houghton Mifflin, 1968.

Stay with Me till Morning. London, Eyre and Spottiswoode, 1970; as *The View from Tower Hill*, New York, Coward McCann, 1971.

The Queen of a Distant Country. London, Methuen, 1972; New York, Coward McCann, 1973.

The Pious Agent. London, Eyre Methuen, 1975; New York, Atheneum, 1976.

Waiting for Sheila. London, Eyre Methuen, 1976.

The Only Game in Town. London, Eyre Methuen, 1976.

Finger of Fire. London, Eyre Methuen, 1977.

One Last Love. London, Eyre Methuen, 1981.

Plays

The Desert in the Mirror (produced Bingley, Yorkshire, 1951).

Television Plays: *Man at the Top* series, 1970, 1972; *Waiting for Sheila*, from his own novel, 1977; *Queen of a Distant Country*, from his own novel, 1978; *Stay with Me till Morning*, from his own novel, 1980.

Other

Writing a Novel (textbook). London, Eyre Methuen, and New York, McGraw Hill, 1975.
J.B. Priestley. London, Weidenfeld and Nicolson, 1978; New York, Barnes and Noble, 1979.

*

Bibliography: *John Braine and John Wain: A Reference Guide* by Dale Salwak, Boston, Hall, 1980.

Manuscript Collection: Central Public Library, Bradford, Yorkshire.

Critical Study: *John Braine* by James W. Lee, New York, Twayne, 1968.

John Braine comments:

What I care about the most is telling the truth about human beings and the world they live in. I'm not interested in making moral judgements as a novelist. I'm not interested in making any sort of propaganda. I do have very strong political beliefs and in a sense can't separate them from my religious beliefs. I'll put it this way: I believe in parliamentary democracy, majority rule, the rule of law, and a fixed morality. I would rather die than live under a government which denied me the freedom to write exactly as I want to. It isn't for me to say whether I write well or badly. But this at least I can say: I have never thought of being anything else but a writer and will never be anything else but a writer. And every word I write is a celebration of my love for the created world and everyone and everything within it.

* * *

John Braine burst upon the literary scene in 1957 with *Room at the Top*, an instantaneous success which enrolled him among "the angry young men," writers who protested the discriminations imposed upon those who came from the working class or the lower middle class. Joe Lampton derives from the wrong class for worldly success to come easily to him. He is cynical of the establishment but determined to exploit it. At this time he does not realize that he may be absorbed by the class whose wealth he intends to share. Against his will he falls in love with Alice Aisgill, an unhappily married middle-aged woman. Out of opportunism he gives her up but feels guilt for her violent death. He marries Susan Brown, his fairy princess, with painful lack of enthusiasm. Braine implies that any society which demands the sacrifice of integrity as the price of "success" is corrupt.

Life at the Top, a sequel, is equally fine. Joe Lampton has by now joined the establishment and become a minor administrator in his father-in-law's firm. He finds that life at the top is empty and that affluence entails severe liabilities. Joe, the rebel against the drabness of Dufton (his native town), now realizes that life at the top can be just as drab, certainly more corrupt, than life in Dufton. Joe reaches beyond torment and materialist values to spiritual triumph when he accepts the child with love whom he discovers is not his own.

The Jealous God is a religious novel which traces the ramifications of Catholicism upon the personal life. Vincent Dungarvan has for long been poised between life as priest and life in the world. His possessive mother is more anxious than Vincent for him to become a priest. In the upshot the church and Mrs. Dungarvan win out over Vincent's desire to marry a divorcee whose husband had been homosexual. Braine depicts with urgency and strength the conflicts inherent in Vincent, the sensual man of deep religious commitment. And life in the provincial town is rendered with knowledge, finesse, and sympathy. *The Vodi* is Braine's least significant novel and chronicles the successful revolt of Dick Corvy against malign supernatural presences (the Vodi).

The Crying Game is a kind of "morality," depicting Frank Batcombe's oscillating attitudes toward the glamor and easy rewards of London, the intense yet transitory quality of its pleasures. The conflicts do not register clearly because Braine fails to keep his characters at a sufficient ironic distance for him to judge them adequately and the values they embody. Like Milton, Braine at times seems to be of the devil's party, represented in the book by Adam Keelby and his sleazy values. Braine, however, seems to be as fascinated by the great world of finance and intrigue as he is critical of it. Frank, a journalist, sees in time the corruption which is about to engulf him as a result of Adam's influence. He turns to his "good angel," Theresa, whom he had thought earlier of being the right girl met at the wrong time. *The Crying Game* does capture the texture of decadent urban life, the corruptness of its luxury, the opportunism inherent in its human relationships, especially in the realm of sex.

In *Stay with Me till Morning* Braine analyzes marital discord for the first time since *Life at the Top*. The protagonists, Robin and Clive Lendrick, have everything: a fine home in a Yorkshire town, economic security, healthy children, mutual affection and understanding. Yet after 20 years together they feel that something has gone from their relationship if ever it were there. Infidelity, Braine seems to imply, is preferable to spiritual lassitude. The difficulties inherent in marriage, and its general inflexibility, are principal themes in this disquieting dissection of modern mores. More constricted in its reach and less impressive generally is *Waiting for Sheila* which is a painful and hardly significant first-person analysis by its lower class protagonist of his sexual difficulties, largely the result of his ignorance and of his lack of imagination.

In *The Queen of a Distant Country* a successful novelist from the provinces, Tom Matfield, becomes aware, finally, that a demanding professional career need not exclude a meaningful personal life. He also faces honestly his indebtedness to Miranda, once among the most acclaimed of writers.

More recently Braine has ventured into the spy novel, with considerable flair and structural expertise. *The Pious Agent* is an intense, disturbing, and sinister book, in which Braine presents the insistent claims made by governmental departments upon the efficient agents which they must use. Whether such departments are justified in exploiting these men for the common political good is one question explored in the book. The agent, Colonel Xavier Flynn, is torn between conflicting impulses: religion, patriotism, moral decency, sexual ardor, desire for serene domesticity, contempt for and fascination with international power politics, compulsion to wield power, and violence. *Finger of Fire* recounts Flynn's confrontations with FIST, an organization dedicated to the penetration of British politics and to the violent overthrow of British democratic government.

Braine has emerged as a writer alternately fascinated and repelled by the present-day upper middle class, especially that segment of it which enjoys prosperity but lacks spiritual stamina. He is a master at analyzing the antagonisms of people thrown together in close association in marriage, friendship, government, and professional life. Some of his characters, satirically treated, never attain awareness: for them sex has none but a perfunctory significance. Others do attain enlightenment, but with much pain, sometimes even with regret. The acknowledgement of the claims of other people upon them coincides with an acknowledgment of their own personal deficiencies. The unregenerate are those whose egotism is impervious to the influence of others. As a creator of characters who embody the tensions existing between themselves and others and between themselves and social institutions and conventions, he achieves his greatest distinction.

—Frederick P.W. McDowell

BRATA, Sasthi (Sasthibrata Chakravarti). British. Born in Calcutta, India, 16 July 1939. Educated at Calcutta Boys School; Presidency College, Calcutta University, B.S. (honours) in physics. Married Pamela Joyce Radcliffe (divorced). Has worked in Europe and New York as lavatory assistant, kitchen porter, barman, air conditioning engineer, and postman. London columnist, *Statesman*, 1977-80. Recipient: Arts Council grant, 1979. Agent: Jonathan Clowes Ltd., 19 Jeffrey's Place, London NW1 9PP; or, Bertha Klausner, 71 Park Avenue, New York, New York 10017, U.S.A. Address: 33 Savernake Road, London N.W. 3, England.

PUBLICATIONS

Novels

Confessions of an Indian Woman Eater. London, Hutchinson, 1971; as *Confessions of an Indian Lover*, New Delhi, Sterling, 1973.
She and He. Delhi, Orient, 1973.
The Sensuous Guru: The Making of a Mystic President. New Delhi, Sterling, 1980.

Short Stories

Encounter. New Delhi, Orient, 1978.

Verse

Eleven Poems. New Delhi, Blue Moon, 1960.

Other

My God Died Young (autobiography). London, Hutchinson, and New York, Harper, 1968.
A Search for Home (autobiography). New Delhi, Orient, 1975.
Astride Two Worlds: Traitor to India. New Delhi, B.I. Publications, 1976; as *Traitor to India: A Search for Home*, London, Elek, 1976.

Sasthi Brata comments:

My first published book, *My God Died Young*, was a self-professed autobiography, written at the age of 28, before I had made any kind of a name for myself as a writer, or anything else. This led a good few publishers, readers, and finally critics to utter the exasperated cry: "What makes you think that the story of your life (woefully unlived-in up to that time) deserves to be told? Or that people will want to read it?" The answer to these questions was within the book itself, of course. But in a sense *all* of my writing, fiction, non-fiction, and journalism, has been an attempt to refute the assumptions lurking behind those superficially plausible and innocent-sounding queries. For they presume that only the heroic and the grand deserve artistic exploration and autobiographical treatment. While I believe, very firmly, that everyone, but everyone has *a* story to tell. The difference between the true artist and the pub bore is that the writer has a sure grasp over the instruments of his trade—words, sentences, paragraphs, syntax, metaphor, melody—and is then able to select, assemble, and present a somewhat more ordered and appetising version of the world than the chaotic, often repetitive jumble of experiences from external reality which make up his raw material.

All my fiction has been supremely autobiographical. Even in those books which are listed as non-fiction on library shelves, I have used fictional devices, and equally freely introduced reportage techniques in books which profess to be novels. I should warn the prospective reader however not to deduce from this that every hero in every one of my novels is an exactly congruent picture of the man I am. In a review of the late Yukio Mishima's novels I wrote: "The obsessionally autobiographical writer may be an invisible man." For while he may not be telling lies, he is not necessarily telling the *truth* either, at least not of the kind the law courts would accept. Since he is an artist, he *has* used his imagination, but he has not necessarily let you into the secret of where the fictive imagination begins or where empirically verifiable reality ends.

There was a time when I used to be irked by attacks on the high sexual content in my writing. I am no longer. Few addicts of hardcore porn would find any of my books satisfactory. Prurient sensibilities, with a cavalier indifference to style and linguistic resonances, might equally be put off by their subject matter. Apologies to neither group.

I would call myself a "radical traditionalist" as a novelist, if only because to be a successful "experimental" writer, in the sense that Joyce and Borges are, requires poetic sensibility I do not possess. It is easy to descend into the wholly bogus or deliberately pedantic in trying to achieve effects about which one is not totally sure. There are no rules in the use of language of course, but I would rather stick within certain wide but strictly defined limits, than stray into those unexplored territories where the arcane, obscure, or simply fraudulent vendors ply their wares. I believe that all my books can be read simply as good tales.

* * *

Most of Sasthi Brata's books are written in the first person, and all his heroes seem to be modelled after the novelist himself. The hero is always a Bengali Brahmin, from a well-to-do family, who lives in Calcutta and studies physics at college. He leaves home in protest after the girl of his choice is married off to someone whom her parents have chosen. He drifts into a number of jobs, including journalism, and finally establishes himself comfortably in Hampstead. His chief hobby is haunting pubs. The narrator of his first novel, *Confessions of an Indian Woman Eater*, differs only in name from the narrator of the autobiographies *My God Died Young* and *Astride Two Worlds*. The physical characteristics remain the same, even if the hero is Zamir Ishmael of *She and He*: he is dark, of medium height, with dark eyes and an attractive smile; his success with women is unlimited. Sasthi Brata's books are quite readable; his style is racy and adequate for his purpose, which is generally limited to describing the exploits of his hero in bed. The exception is *Astride Two Worlds*, the second part of his autobiography, which touches upon many serious topics like racial discrimination in Britain, the involvement of the Indian government in the guerilla activities of the Mukti Bahini in Bangledesh in 1971, and the growing disillusionment of the young with established politicians in India. A couple of chapters, written in the third person, serve to give a proper perspective to this autobiography.

Sasthi Brata's bestselling novel, *Confessions of an Indian Woman Eater*, begins where his first book, *My God Died Young*, an autobiography left off: Amit Ray, like Sasthi Brata, runs away from his Calcutta home. Amit recounts his varied sexual experiences in a number of capitals—New Delhi, Rome, London, Paris, Copenhagen. He finally ends up in Hampstead with a steady job, and becomes a successful writer. For a certain readership the chief attraction of the book would lie in the step-by-step accounts of copulation, found almost every ten pages. The next novel, *She and He*, has a hero born of an Arab father and a French mother; he is at home in England and lands a good job because he can speak the language with the proper accent. He always talks about writing the "Great English Novel," but does nothing about it until one of his ex-girl friends sends him an unfinished novel, having written her side of the story, with blank pages for the hero to fill in. The first person account of Zamir alternating with the third person narrative of Sally is an interesting stylistic innovation, but the hero's mindless drifting from bed to bed is ultimately boring.

The Sensuous Guru: The Making of a Mystic President, perhaps the most imaginative of Sasthi Brata's works, recounts the rise of Ram Chukker (short for Ram Chakravarti, just as Sasthi Barata is the shortened form of Sasthibrata Chakravarti). Chukker initially sets himself up as a Guru in New York, and makes a good living. He writes a short autobiographical novel, *The Making of a Guru*, which outdoes the worst that America can produce in pornography. Through high-pressure promotion with the help of an influential literary agent Chukker wins the Pulitzer Prize, is nominated for the Nobel Prize, manages one for Peace, and is ultimately elected President of the United States of America.

Sasthi Brata has also published a collection of stories; most of them are like his novels (some have appeared, with modifications, as chapters in his novels). One very good story is "Smiles among the Bric-a-Brac," about a young Oxford graduate from a rich English family, comfortably settling down to the girl and the job his parents have chosen for him, though he earlier loves the beautiful Nina Fernandez, of mixed parentage. The first person account, with the hero justifying the way he drops Nina, is a beautiful psychological study of the hero's lack of principles. It is significant that Robert Lomax, from an old English family, is very different from the usual Bengali hero. One feels that Sasthi Brata could write better fiction, especially if he got rid of his autobiographical obsession .

—Shyamala A. Narayan

BRATHWAITE, Errol (Freeman). New Zealander. Born in Clive, Hawkes Bay, 3 April 1924. Educated at Waipukurau District High School, 1929-37; Timaru Boys' High School, 1938-39. Served in the New Zealand Army in the City of Wellington's Own, 1942-43; Royal New Zealand Air Force, 1943-45, 1947-55; Royal New Zealand Signals, 1955-58. Married Alison Irene Whyte in 1948; two children. Cadet, New Zealand Railways, 1940-42, 1945; Farm Trainee, Rehabilitation Department, King Country, 1946; Copywriter, New Zealand Broadcasting Corporation, Christchurch, 1959-62, and Dobbs-Wiggins-McCann-Erickson, Christchurch, 1962-66. Since 1969, Copywriter, and Manager, 1971-73, Carlton Carruthers du Chateau, Christchurch. Recipient: Otago *Daily Times* Centennial Novel Prize, 1961; New Zealand Literary Fund Award, 1962. Address: 12 Fulton Avenue, Fendalton, Christchurch 1, New Zealand.

PUBLICATIONS

Novels

Fear in the Night. Christchurch, Caxton Press, 1959.
An Affair of Men. Auckland and London, Collins, 1961; New York, St. Martin's Press, 1964.
Long Way Home. Christchurch, Caxton Press, 1964.
The Flying Fish. Auckland and London, Collins, 1964; San Francisco, Tri-Ocean, 1969.
The Needle's Eye. Auckland and London, Collins, 1965; San Francisco, Tri-Ocean, 1969.
The Evil Day. Auckland and London, Collins, 1967; San Francisco, Tri-Ocean, 1969.
The Flame Box. Auckland, Collins, 1978.

Uncollected Short Story

"Williams and Christmas," in *New Zealand Weekly* (Auckland), 1968.

Plays

Radio Plays: *An Affair of Men*, 1962; *Long Way Home*, 1966; *The Needle's Eye*, 1969; *Marnot*, 1978; *Marnot and the Power Game*, 1979; *The Rehabilitation of Captain Marnot*, 1979; *Shape Up or Ship Out*, 1979; *Holes in the Air*, 1980.

Other

The Companion Guide to the North [South] Island of New Zealand. Auckland and London, Collins, 2 vols., 1970-72.
New Zealand and Its People. Wellington, New Zealand Government Printer, 1974.
The Beauty of New Zealand. Auckland, Golden Press, 1974.
Historic New Zealand. Christchurch, Kowhai, 1980.
New Zealand. Christchurch, Kowhai, 1980.

*

Errol Brathwaite comments:

It is difficult for me to comment on my own novels, since I never write with any other end in view than to tell a good story and, that being so, any situations around which I build up my story must be rich in dramatic possibilities.

I regard life as a constant battle between good and evil, albeit a highly complex warfare, since both sides in any given encounter have within them leanings towards both good and evil. I strive to make my characters positive, though not necessarily strong—never clean-cut good or evil, though tending infinitely more strongly in one direction (usually towards good) than the other. I acknowledge the complexity of the battle by giving my creations multifaceted characters; and while I comment on life, I try to allow the commentary to grow as a by-product of observations and reportage. I do not deliberately attack attitudes or situations, but merely use them. To do otherwise would be to obtrude, to force myself and my opinions on the reader.

If I want a particular character to be a hero, I make him progress towards an obviously desirable goal somewhat in spite of himself, sometimes fortuitously and always with much stumbling and a modicum of obtuseness. I try to let the reader see the desirable objective, as it were from a height, observing the hero's ground-level side-tracking and stumbling progress. I do this in an attempt to involve the reader, which I regard as being a first principle of good entertainment.

I suppose that this is why war has so often been, if not the subject, then the setting of my novels. It is a pattern, in bold relief, of life itself. It is full of dramatic possibilities. It can face ordinary good/evil man with a rapid series of searing moral and other dilemmas.

I don't expect that I shall always write about war, but I regard conflict as being one of the two major dramatic themes, the other being the "Robinson Crusoe" situation, wherein man overcomes circumstances and bends it to his will.

What else is there to say? I believe that life itself is seldom tidy, and that its conclusion inevitably leaves a number of more or less untidy loose ends flapping around. I realise that in a novel there must be a rather greater degree of contrivance than in life, but I don't care to make my novels too unlifelike.

I suppose, to sum it all up, that I regard myself as an entertainer; a teller, as Kai Lung used to say, of imagined tales. I have, therefore, one source of material, which is human behaviour, and three forms of presentation, which are drama, romance and comedy. Drama and comedy call for high, bold colouring techniques—the dash and splash of bright oils. Romance calls for water-colour treatment, and I don't think that my brushwork is subtle enough. Therefore, I suppose that the highly dramatic will continue to be my chosen form, and that if there is any change, it will be to comedy.

* * *

In Errol Brathwaite's novels, the basic formula is that of men in a dangerous war-situation, submitted to physical and mental stress, which strips them down to basic responses and confronts them with moral dilemmas. His work represents an endeavour to add to the war-novel an extra dimension of moral significance and to highlight the complexity of circumstances which are usually treated in terms of mere physical endurance. His strength lies in his keen historical sense, his ability to tell exciting stories, his understanding of the psychology of fighting men (women make very rare appearances in his fiction) and his clean-cut, unfussy style. His weaknesses are seen in his tendency to view his characters at times as human beings, at others as representing abstract qualities, and his slightly mechanical organisation of moments of tension. But he is one of the most readable of New Zealand novelists and at the same time sets his sights high.

His first two novels were *Fear in the Night* and *Long Way Home*. (Despite the publication date of *An Affair of Men*, 1961, it was written after *Long Way Home*.) Both come from the author's own aviation experience. In *Fear in the Night*, the crew of a bomber forced down in Japanese territory are under pressure to repair the plane before they are captured. Brathwaite's technical knowledge and his eye for detail combine with his skill in exploring the minds of his characters under the strain to create a convincing situation remarkable for its concentration of effect. *Long Way Home*, which deals with a search and rescue operation in New Zealand's Southern Alps, is similarly organised.

There is a real advance in *An Affair of Men*. This time the suspense story does not so much include the moral attitudes as dramatise them. Allied airmen who have crashed on the Pacific island Bougainville are pursued by the Japanese under Captain Itoh. His search is frustrated by a Christian-educated headman, Sedu, who insists on remaining neutral. The clash of wills and ideologies is handled with continual invention and boldness and is resolved in terms of the psychology and background of the antagonists. The drama reflects modern man's dilemma in his choice between two different sets of values, between peace and violence.

Brathwaite's trilogy, *The Flying Fish*, *The Needle's Eye*, and *The Evil Day*, follows the experiences of the fictional Major Williams in the Maori Wars of the 1860's and is the most ambitious treatment of this subject so far written. Again, it is not only the details of strategy and battles which engage Brathwaite and the various kinds of military sensibility which he analyses, although these are treated with careful attention to historical fact, but the personal and moral problems posed by war itself. A further theme is the development of mutual understanding, paradoxically, between Maori and European through the wars and the question of where the real blame for the conflict lay. The characterisation is firm and varied and Major Williams is one of the most completely realised characters in New Zealand fiction.

—J.C. Reid

BRAUTIGAN, Richard. American. Born in Tacoma, Washington, 30 January 1933. Recipient: National Endowment for the Arts grant, 1968. Address: c/o Helen Brann, 14 Sutton Place South, New York, New York 10022, U.S.A.

PUBLICATIONS

Novels

In Watermelon Sugar. San Francisco, Four Seasons, 1964; London, Cape, 1970.
A Confederate General from Big Sur. New York, Grove Press, 1965; London, Cape, 1971.
Trout Fishing in America. San Francisco, Four Seasons, 1967; London, Cape, 1970.
The Abortion: An Historical Romance 1966. New York, Simon and Schuster, 1971; London, Cape, 1973.
The Hawkline Monster: A Gothic Western. New York, Simon and Schuster, 1974; London, Cape, 1975.
Willard and His Bowling Trophy: A Perverse Mystery. New York, Simon and Schuster, 1975; London, Cape, 1976.
Sombrero Fallout: A Japanese Novel. New York, Simon and Schuster, 1976; London, Cape, 1977.
Dreaming of Babylon: A Private Eye Novel 1942. New York, Delacorte Press, 1977; London, Cape, 1978.
The Tokyo-Montana Express. New York, Delacorte Press, 1980; London, Cape, 1981.

Short Stories

Revenge of the Lawn: Stories 1962-1970. New York, Simon and Schuster, 1971; London, Cape, 1972.

Uncollected Short Stories

"Football," in *Tri-Quarterly* (Evanston, Illinois), Winter 1976.
"Great Golden Telescope," in *Redbook* (Des Moines, Iowa), August 1979.

Verse

The Return of the Rivers. San Francisco, Inferno Press, 1957.
The Galilee Hitch-Hiker. San Francisco, White Rabbit Press, 1958.
Lay the Marble Tea: Twenty-Four Poems. San Francisco, Carp Press, 1959.
The Octopus Frontier. San Francisco, Carp Press, 1960.
All Watched Over by Machines of Loving Grace. San Francisco, Communication, 1967.
Please Plant This Book. San Francisco, MacKintosh, 1968.
The Pill Versus the Springhill Mine Disaster (Poems 1957-1968). San Francisco, Four Seasons, 1968; London, Cape, 1970.
The San Francisco Weather Report. Goleta, California, Unicorn, 1969.
Rommel Drives On Deep into Egypt. New York, Delacorte Press, 1970.
Loading Mercury with a Pitchfork. New York, Simon and Schuster, 1975.
June 30th, June 30th. New York, Delacorte Press, 1978.

*

Critical Studies: *Richard Brautigan* by Terence Malley, New York, Warner, 1972.

* * *

In the first section of *Trout Fishing in America* Richard Brautigan asks: "Was it Kafka who learned about America by reading the autobiography of Benjamin Franklin...Kafka who said, 'I like the Americans because they are healthy and optimistic.' " This is as good a center as any for a brief look at his work. Brautigan has found a way for Americans who don't much like themselves as Americans to fall in love with an old American Adam reborn once more. He draws on those qualities which are likeable to a Kafka, because so exotic and remote: innocence and good intentions, naive optimism combined with a practical cunning. The narrator-hero of *The Abortion* says, when forced to leave his library at the end of the book: "Vida was right when she said that I would be a hero in Berkeley." The hero in this case, as always with Brautigan, is not a person or character—he is an attitude, a point of view. He embodies good humor, is unaware of or mystified by evil, and survives catastrophes without even knowing they are there. Brautigan's narrator-heroes are hang-loose and loveable Captain Delanos, with the evil in their worlds pushed even further under the carpet. But for the reader, excluded evil becomes even more conspicious and significant by its absence, like the plot in a plotless novel. Brautigan's version of the "American Dream" leaves out precisely those things writers like Mailer insist on as the basic substance of the dream.

The nameless innocent narrator of *In Watermelon Sugar* is a good example of these Brautigan qualities. He tells us early on that he has a "gentle life," a "comfortable" life, a life "carefully constructed from watermelon sugar and then travelled to the length of our dreams...." The book, too, is made from "watermelon sugar," and things gone into it are travelled in watermelon sugar." What "watermelon sugar" is, then, is indefinable even on the allegorical level. It is like "Trout Fishing in America," a phrase which can be anything from a person to the name of a book. It is a combination of language and attitude, a sense of form and response which is at once amorphous and particulate, innocent and cunning. When the narrator stops sleeping with Margaret and starts sleeping with Pauline, Margaret eventually hangs herself. Before that, Pauline asks the narrator how Margaret feels, saying that she seems terribly upset. "I don't know how she feels," is his response. The narrator-hero learned this response early, having watched some "tigers" kill and eat his parents when he was nine. After their meal, the tigers comment enthusiastically on how nice the day is, then they apologize: "Please try to understand. We tigers are not evil. This is just a thing we have to do." The narrator says, "All right...thanks for helping me with my arithmetic," and the tigers answer: "Think nothing of it." It is precisely this lack of thought, introduced here in a typical Brautigan *double-entendre*, that means any day, even when one's parents have been eaten, can be a "nice day." At the very end, after Margaret hangs herself from the apple tree, there is a traditional way of doing things. No empathy with the motives that might drive the inBOIL gang to cut themselves up ("It's a mystery to us") or drive Margaret to hang herself ("I don't know why") can distract the narrator from the contents of the potato salad, which had a lot of carrots in it.

The more one reads this book, the more uneasy one feels. Perhaps the "point" is as profound as that at the end of *The Brothers Karamazov*. We can't understand the problem of death and evil; so mourn and suffer, but eat pancakes and be happy. Yet here is a book, not really a novel, that does away with the dialectic of mourning and rejoicing altogether. "We take the juice from the watermelons and cook it down until there's nothing left but sugar, and then we work it into the shape of this thing that we have: our lives." This sugary shape, and the virtuoso power of metamorphosis (the sentence is about it and illustrative of it at the same time) are the essence of Brautigan's art. More process than substance, more wit than wisdom—except that he just might be right, after all. One is left with the same ambivalence of attraction and repulsion felt towards the "So it goes" refrain of Vonnegut's *Slaughterhouse Five*; and with the feeling that any response to so understated a form of art risks overstatement.

—Thomas A. Vogler

BROOKE-ROSE, Christine. British. Born in Geneva, Switzerland. Educated at Somerville College, Oxford, 1946-49, B.A., M.A.; University College, London, 1950-54, B.A., Ph.D. Married Jerzy Peterkiewicz, *q.v.*, in 1948 (divorced, 1975). Worked as a free-lance literary journalist, London, 1956-68. Maitre de Conférences, 1969-75, and since 1975, Professeur, University of Paris, Vincennes. Recipient: Society of Authors Travelling Prize, 1965; Black Memorial Prize, 1967; Arts Council Translation Prize, 1969. Address: c/o Hamish Hamilton Ltd., 57-59 Long Acre, London WC2E 9JZ, England.

PUBLICATIONS

Novels

The Languages of Love. London, Secker and Warburg, 1957.
The Sycamore Tree. London, Secker and Warburg, 1958; New York, Norton, 1959.
The Dear Deceit. London, Secker and Warburg, 1960; New York, Doubleday, 1961.
The Middlemen: A Satire. London, Secker and Warburg, 1961.
Out. London, Joseph, 1964.
Such. London, Joseph, 1966.
Between. London, Joseph, 1968.
Thru. London, Hamish Hamilton, 1975.

Short Stories

Go When You See the Green Man Walking. London, Joseph, 1970.

Verse

Gold. Aldington, Kent, Hand and Flower Press, 1955.

Other

A Grammar of Metaphor. London, Secker and Warburg, 1958.
A ZBC of Ezra Pound. London, Faber, 1971; Berkeley, University of California Press, 1976.
A Structural Analysis of Pound's Usura Canto: Jakobson's Method Extended and Applied to Free Verse. The Hague, Mouton, 1976.

Translator, *Children of Chaos*, by Juan Goytisolo. London, MacGibbon and Kee, 1958.
Translator, *Fertility and Survival: Population Problems from Malthus to Mao Tse Tung*, by Alfred Sauvy. New York, Criterion, 1960; London, Chatto and Windus, 1961.
Translator, *In the Labyrinth*, by Alain Robbe-Grillet. London, Calder and Boyars, 1968.

* * *

Christine Brooke-Rose is a European intellectual whose supranational, multi-disciplinary belles lettres might serve as a model for New Renaissance women. Brought up in Geneva and Brussels, she was educated at Oxford, served as a tough practitioner of Fleet Street literary journalism, and subsequently wound up teaching Romance studies at the French government's show-piece university of Vincennes. She started her literary career as a poet, found her verse poor and became adept at turning a brittle, satirical novel, which in turn she found unsatisfactory and abandoned in favour of the analogical novaglot essays of *Out, Such, Between* and *Go When You See the Green Man Walking* (collected stories of the previous eight years).

States of mind and body, the areas between life and death, and the nature of words and the meanings with which man invests them are her concerns. They are not chance preoccupations. At a time when she was still a poet and an academic, her husband became ill and almost died. Her reaction to the state of mind induced by strain was to leave off working on a critical work (*A Grammar of Metaphor*) and for the first time to write a novel. The exercise (*The Languages of Love*—a soufflé based on the goings-on of university philologists) performed the function of therapy and also pointed Brooke-Rose in the direction of her proper literary concern. A few years later, in 1962, she herself fell ill, and was convinced that she would die. She wrote one sentence a day before falling exhausted on her pillows. During the illness her consciousness seemed to function at a different level. She has described the experience as "a sense of being in touch with something else—death perhaps." As a result of this changed awareness, she was able to realise a new kind of sensibility, which, from that time onwards, she has attempted to explore in her fiction.

Her early novels (*The Languages of Love, The Sycamore Tree, The Dear Deceit*, and *The Middlemen*) are works whose value she now denies. They were competent enough vignettes of the witty, intelligent circles in which one might expect to discover Iris Murdoch, and their end result was not far removed from the sum of the parts of Murdoch's own elegant conundrums. One could not help feeling that the authoress was an awfully clever gel, insofar as she could manipulate quite adequately the basic framework of the nineteenth-century novel of manners. Only in *The Dear Deceit* did Brooke-Rose display a certain restlessness over the form of her material—she started her story at the end and wrote on to its beginning.

Out was the first work of her convert period; it is itself the story of a world which has come close to death, and survives in an utterly changed form. Set in some unspecified Afro-Eurasia, in some future time following a catastrophe which is always referred to, euphemistically, as "the displacement," *Out* treats with a society in which colour prejudice has a logical basis. Any colour—black, brown or yellow—is equated with health, and consequently with power and privilege. The whites, who after "the displacement" turn out to be prone to a widespread and fatal blood disease, are treated with the contempt and indifference which, in terms of an objective Darwinian calculation, they merit. But it is more than a story of Black Power through superior anti-radiation pigmentation. The book is pervaded with a sense of anarchy at the door, and its black notables and sick white trash are together attempting to arrive at some technique for coping with disorder, sickness, and more generally, a changed order of things. The book begins with an observation of two flies copulating, and ends with a burst of fire and the conclusion: "We are merely marking time and time is nothing, nothing. A moment of agony, of burning flesh, an aspect of the human element disintegrating to ash, and you are dead. But that's another story."

The stylistic devices with which Brooke-Rose coped with the socio-sci fi of *Out* are characteristic of all her later works. In place of a story she substitutes an apparently formless consideration of states of mind, in which the repetition and reorganization of thoughts occur randomly, as they will in ordinary human consciousness. The language of this statement and restatement is often so determinedly scientific as to fly above the understanding of a lay reader. In *Out* it is the language of bio-chemistry and molecular physics:

> The left foot in its dirty canvas shoe is wholly contained in a benzene ring, the other, a little less dirty, has its big toe on the top dividing line like a carbon atom. If there were a single carbon atom at every angle the result would be graphite ...with the appropriate enzyme, represented perhaps by the left heel in a ribose molecule to the South East and the whole series linked by two energy-rich phosphate bonds, the energy can be quantitively transferred from one molecule to another so that the backward and forward reactions are thermodynamically equivalent....

Such is also a science fiction experiment, and again it deals with death, closely escaped. In this case a man dies at the radio telescope, and in the three minutes time span which the book covers various aspects of his lost psyche are examined before he returns to life like Lazarus or the fortunate subject of a heart masseur. He sees people as a radio telescope sees stars; some are already degenerate matter, others are forming new stars. The metaphor is astro-physical; the vocabulary likewise—even in a mock sentimental duologue between our hero and his woman:

> —Larry, everyone deserves the attention of definiteness.
>
> —Even if they prefer uncertain principles?
>
> —They only pretend to prefer it. They have to. You used to say that. Someone would come along and find a unified theory that would do away with indeterminate interpretations, you'd say, and revert to causality. I thought perhaps you might.
>
> —I thought so too. In psychic terms at least. But I didn't. In the meantime we do the best we can, some of us preferring to pretend causality exists, and others, others preferring to prefer its absence. But you can never know with absolute certainty that what looks like the same particle, with the same identity...
>
> —Yes but for practical purposes you have to, Larry, in the chemistry of people. Otherwise how can you live?
>
> —You can't. Not really. You pretend to. To save appearances.
>
> —Larry, you can't honestly believe that.

Between substitutes for a confusion of astro-physical concepts a tumult of semantic hypotheses. Its protagonist is a simultaneous interpreter from French to German, whose thought processes are affected by three languages and three sensibilities while she receives and transmits, often without understanding, the ideas of conference delegates. Brooke-Rose's characteristic telescoping of time and place are further complicated by a kaleidoscopic narrative which may, during the course of a paragraph, arrange consecutive liaisons of Greek, Latin, German, Czech, Spanish and James Joycese. The link might be an international Nabokovian pun, or simply a leap of the imagination. The confusion is intended; that is what words are for:

> The visitor's attention turns immediately to higher things as the seven-terraced Tower of Babel on the seventh hauteur du ciel way up above the smattering of the mouthpiece in ces capitales que je connais, que je hais, ah, pardonnez-moi cette vilaine jalousie. Je n'ai jamais aime comme ca between the zest of youth and the wisdom of old age through an indefinitely long period called the middle ages...

—John Hall

BROPHY, Brigid (Antonia). British. Born in London, 12 June 1929. Educated at St. Paul's Girls' School; St. Hugh's College, Oxford (Jubilee Scholar), 1947-48. Married Michael Levey in 1954; one daughter. Co-Founder, Writers Action Group, 1972; Executive Councillor, Writers Guild of Great Britain, 1975-78. Since 1974, Vice-President, Anti-Vivisection Society of Great Britain; since 1976, Vice-Chairman, British Copyright Council. Recipient: Cheltenham Festival prize, 1954; *London Magazine* prize, 1962. Fellow, Royal Society of Literature, 1973. Address: Flat 3, 185 Old Brompton Road, London S.W.5, England.

PUBLICATIONS

Novels

Hackenfeller's Ape. London, Hart Davis, 1953; New York, Random House, 1954.

The King of a Rainy Country. London, Secker and Warburg, 1956; New York, Knopf, 1957.

Flesh. London, Secker and Warburg, 1962; Cleveland, World, 1963.

The Finishing Touch. London, Secker and Warburg, 1963.

The Snow Ball. London, Secker and Warburg, 1964.

The Snow Ball, with The Finishing Touch. Cleveland, World, 1964.

In Transit. London, Macdonald, 1969; New York, Putnam, 1970.

The Adventures of God in His Search for the Black Girl: A Novel and Some Fables. London, Macmillan, 1973; Boston, Little Brown, 1974.

Palace Without Chairs: A Baroque Novel. London, Hamish Hamilton, and New York, Atheneum, 1978.

Short Stories

The Crown Princess and Other Stories. London, Collins, and New York, Viking Press, 1953.

Uncollected Short Story

"Pilgrimage," in *Winter's Tales 3.* London, Macmillan, and New York, St. Martin's Press, 1957.

Plays

The Waste-Disposal Unit (broadcast, 1964). Published in *London Magazine*, April 1964; in *Best Short Plays of the World Theatre 1958-67*, New York, Crown, 1968.
The Burglar (produced London, 1967). London, Cape, and New York, Holt Rinehart, 1968.

Radio Play: *The Waste-Disposal Unit*, 1964.

Other

Black Ship to Hell. London, Secker and Warburg, and New York, Harcourt Brace, 1962.
Mozart the Dramatist: A New View of Mozart, His Operas, and His Age. London, Faber, and New York, Harcourt Brace, 1964.
Don't Never Forget: Collected Views and Reviews. London, Cape, 1966; New York, Holt Rinehart, 1967.
Religious Education in State Schools. London, Fabian Society, 1967.
Fifty Works of English and American Literature We Could Do Without, with Michael Levey and Charles Osborne. London, Rapp and Carroll, 1967; New York, Stein and Day, 1968.
Black and White: A Portrait of Aubrey Beardsley. London, Cape, 1968; New York, Stein and Day, 1969.
The Longford Threat to Freedom. London, National Secular Society, 1972.
Prancing Novelist: A Defence of Fiction in the Form of a Critical Biography in Praise of Ronald Firbank. London, Macmillan, and New York, Barnes and Noble, 1973.
Beardsley and His World. London, Thames and Hudson, and New York, Crown, 1976.
Pussy Owl (juvenile). London, BBC Publications, 1976.

*

Manuscript Collection: Lilly Library, University of Indiana, Bloomington.

* * *

In the agreeably self-dramatizing preface to her play *The Burglar*, Brigid Brophy provides a definitive statement of her aims and methods as a critic and novelist. Like Shaw (whom she sees, along with Freud, as one of the "two mainstays of the twentieth century"), Brophy is an evolutionary vitalist, essentially optimistic despite a sharp eye for human failings and hypocrisies. And like Shaw she assumes the existence of a driving Life Force which strives to express itself in ever more competent and complex forms.

Art itself is a "function of the life instinct," which by its potent illusions brings us "into accord with reality" (unlike religion, which makes the mistake of taking its illusions as literal truths). The human race is a species "uniquely capable of imagination, rationality and moral choice," and therein lies man's justification and perilous responsibility. For Brophy, like Shaw once more, knows full well that our powers may be misused, that the human race is frighteningly capable of undoing what the Life Force has accomplished thus far. From Freud Miss Brophy takes over the conception of life as a dynamic struggle between Eros, the binding and civilizing force, and Thanatos, the death instinct which seeks to destroy the work of Eros. Thus *Black Ship to Hell* has as its theme "man as a destructive and, more particularly, a self-destructive animal" and is in effect an encyclopedic investigation of the interrelationships of the two opposing principles in war, politics, art and religion. Brophy sees her work, finally, in the life-affirming tradition of Shaw and Freud: "I too am aiming to reform civilization." The necessary balance between Eros and Thanatos, the integration of work, love, and responsibility, gives Brophy the theme of her fiction: in the long run there may be reason to hope for civilization, but in the short run of individual lives there are failures as well as successes, an infinite fund of dramatic possibilities to be exploited.

Brophy's didacticism is apparent at once in her first collection of short stories, *The Crown Princess*, many of which are no more than fictionalized statements of a thesis or problem. But there is one story here, "Fordie," which unmistakably reveals a writer of remarkable power and intelligence. An intricate fable about the differences between the true creator and the self-seeking failure, "Fordie" belongs in the company of Henry James's great series of artist-parables. *Hackenfeller's Ape*, Brophy's first novel, is a disappointingly thin version of one of her persistent concerns, the treatment of animals "whom we have no right to maim, torture or kill." Embedded here, however, is a dialogue between opposing forces which illustrates clearly the truth of Brophy's statement that all of her works are "baroque," that is, they all "proceed by contraposition; and in a reductive analysis the elements contraposited are always Eros and Thanatos." *The King of a Rainy Country*, a much more engaging novel, dramatizes the disordered forms Eros may assume in individual lives—in regressive, homo-erotic relationships and more specifically in doomed, infantile quests for the "perfect moment." In this comic anti-romance the heroine learns at some painful cost that the static ideal is impossible: "you give from one person and take from another—give and take vitality, I mean. Nobody is a reservoir. It's just an exchange. It goes round in an endless cycle." *Flesh* continues to explore this vital give and take, dramatizing with splendid economy and wit the way in which love reclaims a diffident young man. Brophy avoids sentimentality, however, by indicating that in this particular relationship the cost of investigation has been high; the young man brought to life by Eros is now an object of both horror and desire for his wife; pain becomes a sinister bond in "a hostile and perhaps perverted situation."

The baroque method of construction is increasingly important in Brophy's later work, "deploying masses in such a way that each, as well as performing its own function, constitutes a funnel down which one gets a sharply unexpected view—ironic, tragic or comic." *The Snow Ball* is architectural with a vengeance: its complexity, Brophy boasts, "defies even my own intellectual analysis." But unfortunately the opposite is true: in this brittle, pretentious reworking of the Don Juan-Donna Anna theme (to which Brophy is addicted, seeing in the myth a paradigm of the human sexual emotions), only the contrived and quite obvious design engages the reader's attention. Man is not only *homo faber* and *homo artifax* for Brophy, but *homo Fabergé* as well, and hence her fascination with Beardsley, Firbank, and other aesthetes and dandies. *The Finishing Touch*, besides providing another example of Eros distorted, is an homage to Ronald Firbank, an imitative recreation of the very highest order.

In Transit is a radical departure from the quasi-naturalistic style of the earlier books. In "Fordie" the narrator had reflected that "perhaps the personality surrenders some of its philosophic right to be called a personality when the babbling to oneself, which is the mark of human identity, is halted. I would write a book on the subject, if anyone would attend to it." *In Transit* is that book, and a good deal more, anatomizing the layers of individual personality in a wild, punning Joycean flow of rhetoric which defies coherent description. The hero-heroine (we are hurled into a vortex where sexual differences are superficial) is "in transit," literally waiting to board a plane, but psychically in transit as well, pulled and pushed by a host of new energies. The secondary or simultaneous protagonist of *In Transit* is language itself, which is extended, inverted, parodied, and finally blown to bits by the onslaught of modern life. "I am," the psyche insists, but "communication is broken." In a sleight-of-hand finale, however, which is typical of Brophy's invincible optimism, the psyche is reintegrated "for Love of You"—the "You" being (apparently) the expectant interlocutor our consciousness by necessity posits and the eternal "you" of the audience, waiting for the voice of the artist to bring it back into accord with even the most disruptive modern reality.

The sub-title of *The Adventures of God in His Search for the Black Girl* is misleading. The first section of the book is made up of short fables, very much in the style of *The Crown Princess* and making many of the same points. The long title piece, however, is not really a novel at all, but a kind of philosophic dialogue in the manner of Lucian and Shaw. The chief character, God, is anxious to establish once and for all his "fictitious" nature as a being wholly created by man. The problems arise, he argues, when men take this fiction—or any of their other guiding fictions—as literal, historic truth. The issue here is a familiar one these days: all human beliefs and ideals are, like works of art, purely imaginative constructs. Some are benign, some are not. The implied goal, then, is to construct fictions which will be recognized as such and will still have the power to work for the benefit of mankind. The "Godifesto" is released in a dove-like shower over Rome, but in a wry epilogue Brophy seems to be suggesting that those receiving it will fail to understand what is at stake.

Palace Without Chairs is a novel of sorts, an extended if not entirely clear political allegory. The King and Queen of Evarchia and four of their five children kill themselves or disappear in a series of ludicrous accidents, and a military dictatorship promptly takes over; but the last of the royal children, Heather, a "pachydermous" lesbian, manages to reach London, where our final glimpse of her is an ambiguous one. Drunk in a small hotel bar and happily pursuing another ample lady, she still seems to her former governess (who may not be a reliable witness) to offer "some just cause for hope.... The very elements in her personality that most people condemned were...the sources of a vitality that should surmount both guilt and nostalgia." *Palace Without Chairs* is amusing enough at times but takes few risks and as a result is considerably less impressive than *In Transit*.

—Elmer Borklund

BROSSARD, Chandler. American. Born in Idaho Falls, Idaho, 18 July 1922. Self-educated; left school at 11. Married in 1948; two children. Reporter, *Washington Post*, 1940-42; Writer, *New Yorker*, 1942-43; Senior Editor, *Time* magazine, New York, 1944; Executive Editor, *American Mercury*, New York, 1950-51; Senior Editor, *Look* magazine, New York, 1956-67. Associate Professor, Old Westbury College, Oyster Bay, Long Island, New York, 1968-70; has also taught at the University of Birmingham, England, 1970, Fairleigh Dickinson University, Rutherford, New Jersey, New School for Social Research, New York, and in Paris, 1975-76. Recipient: National Endowment for the Arts grant, 1977. Address: 2350 Woolsey Street, Berkeley, California 94705, U.S.A.

PUBLICATIONS

Novels

Who Walk in Darkness. New York, New Directions, and London, Lehmann, 1952.
The Bold Saboteurs. New York, Farrar Straus, 1953; London, Sphere, 1971.
The Wrong Turn (as Daniel Harper). New York, Avon, 1954.
All Passion Spent. New York, Popular Library, 1954; London, Sphere, 1971; as *Episode with Erika*, New York, Belmont, 1963.
The Double View. New York, Dial Press, 1960; London, Sphere, 1971.
The Girls in Reno. New York, New American Library, 1961; London, New English Library, 1962.
Love Me, Love Me. New York, Fawcett, 1966; as *A Man for All Women*, London, Sphere, 1971.
Wake Up. We're Almost There. New York, Baron, 1971.
Did Christ Make Love? Indianapolis, Bobbs Merrill, 1973.

Short Stories

Raging Joys: Sublime Variations. Wheaton, Maryland, Cherry Valley Editions, 1981.

Plays

Harry the Magician (produced St. Louis, 1961).
Some Dreams Aren't Real (produced St. Louis, 1962).
The Man with Ideas (produced St. Louis, 1962).

Other

The Insane World of Adolf Hitler. New York, Fawcett, 1967.
The Spanish Scene. New York, Viking Press, 1968.

Editor, *The Scene Before You: A New Approach to American Culture.* New York, Rinehart, 1955.
Editor, *The First Time.* New York, Almat, 1957; London, Panther, 1962.

*

Manuscript Collection: George Arents Collection, Syracuse University, New York.

Critical Studies: *The Beat Generation and the Angry Young Men*, edited by Max Gartenberg and Gene Feldman, New York, Citadel Press, 1958; *The Beats*, edited by Seymour Krim, New York, Fawcett, 1960.

Chandler Brossard comments:

(1972) I guess my fiction is concerned with those experiences which society forbids or which one lies to oneself about. One might say the reality of the spiritual-cultural underground. This is sometimes expressed in what I could call hallucinatory fiction, which fiction began in my own case with my second novel, *The Bold Saboteurs.* I might add that I am apparently concerned with the demonism of contemporary society: those drives, those reifications that our society creates, clings to and is being destroyed by. Most lately, in my last work of fiction, *Wake Up. We're Almost There*, I see that I have gone into the labyrinths of linguistics, so to speak. Specifically, I think I could make a case for language as Fiction, since all western fiction has been projected by way of a particular language or style structure (as exemplified by, say, Hemingway on one hand, and Henry James on another). My own language fiction attempts to bring out the hidden meanings—phonemes?—which give the manifest language its base of meaning, and give these hidden deep meanings their full manifest play. Plus one other thing: identity. I am challenging, in my fiction, the concept of identity in western society as represented in its fiction. What I'm saying is that I don't really believe in the validity of individual identity. I think we are all flowing in and out of each other at all times. Identity is simply a kind of negotiation individuals make with other individuals to give each other the illusion of separate independence.

*   *   *

Chandler Brossard is two different men, one a serious novelist of some talent and the other a hack journalist. If he could keep the two identities separate he would have fewer problems as an artist, but it is his fate to be unable to separate them, or even to tell which is which. Thus his novels are published usually under his own name, but at least once under a pseudonym (*The Wrong Turn*, by "Daniel Harper"), sometimes in quality hard cover editions (*Who Walk in Darkness*, New Directions) and sometimes in cheap paperbacks (*All Passion Spent*, reprinted as *Episode with Erika*). All contain passages of good writing and passages of sloppy prose and characterization, with the proportions varying considerably from novel to novel.

Similarly, the theme of duality is common within the works. In *The Double View* a man who has been insane makes love to the wife of his best friend, who is now confined to an asylum. In *All Passion Spent* the narrator leaves the prim academic wife in order to share the bed of a girl whom he later discovers to be not only promiscuously heterosexual but bisexual as well. Psychiatrists appear frequently and are given to sexual exploitation of the female patients whose tangled lives they boast of straightening.

Brossard's recent novel, *Wake Up. We're Almost There*, exhibits these qualities at their worst. Hailed as "Chandler Brossard's masterpiece" on the dust jacket, it runs to a quarter of a million words, and yet, judged by any standard other than weight, *Wake Up* is a dismal failure. It ranges widely—New York to London to Rome to Vietnam to Paris—with the disintegration of Western civilization as its theme. Scenes of photographic accuracy merge with scenes of murky surrealism. The narrative center slips easily from mind to mind and from country to country, but all characters talk the same and all minds operate the same, with sex always as primal and final motivation (taken as an anthology of graphic sexuality the work would be impressive if only all the orgies contained in it were not so similar—except for incidental details of country, race, and physical combinations).

Some of his earlier books are much better. *Who Walk in Darkness* deals with the lower depths of Bohemian life in New York. *The Bold Saboteurs*, hardly a novel at all in any traditional sense, is nevertheless a memorable evocation of a childhood spent in delinquency. It deserves a wider readership than it has thus far obtained. The boy narrator, his brother, and at least one of his companions come sharply to life. Erika, too (from *All Passion Spent*), is disturbingly memorable. Generally in these earlier works the proportion of good prose, accurately captured dialogue, believable characterization, striking description, and meaningful plotting is much higher than it is in later works. Some of these qualities continue to exist in *The Double View*, but that book reads more like the scenario for a novel than a completely realized work—there is little internal evidence to suggest that Brossard spent much time with it. *Wake Up* is certainly the result of time and somewhere within its bulk there may be a novel, but Brossard has not discovered it for us. If we are to give him his due as a writer of fiction we must begin with his earliest works and not be put off by his latest.

—George Perkins

BROWN, George Mackay. British. Born in Stromness, Orkney, Scotland, 17 October 1921. Educated at Stromness Academy; Newbattle Abbey College; Edinburgh University, M.A. 1960. Recipient: Arts Council Award, 1966; Society of Authors Travel Award, 1968; Scottish Arts Council Literature Prize, 1969; Katherine Mansfield Menton Short Story Prize, 1971. M.A.: Open University, 1976; LL.D.: University of Dundee, 1977. Fellow, Royal Society of Literature, 1977. O.B.E. (Officer, Order of the British Empire), 1974. Address: 3 Mayburn Court, Stromness, Orkney KW16 3DH, Scotland.

PUBLICATIONS

Novels

Greenvoe. London, Hogarth Press, and New York, Harcourt Brace, 1972.
Magnus. London, Hogarth Press, 1973.

Short Stories

A Calendar of Love. London, Hogarth Press, 1967; New York, Harcourt Brace, 1968.
A Time to Keep. London, Hogarth Press, 1969; New York, Harcourt Brace, 1970.
Hawkfall and Other Stories. London, Hogarth Press, 1974.
The Sun's Net and Other Stories. London, Hogarth Press, 1976.
Witch and Other Stories. London, Longman, 1977.

Plays

Witch (produced Edinburgh, 1969). Included in *A Calendar of Love*, 1967.
A Spell for Green Corn (broadcast, 1967; produced Edinburgh, 1970). London, Hogarth Press, 1970.
Loom of Light (produced Kirkwall, 1972).
The Storm Watchers (produced Edinburgh, 1976).
The Martyrdom of St. Magnus, music by Peter Maxwell Davies, adaptation of the novel *Magnus* by Brown (produced Kirkwall and London, 1977; Santa Fe, 1979). London, Boosey and Hawkes, 1977.
The Two Fiddlers, music by Peter Maxwell Davies, adaptation of the story by Brown (produced London, 1978). London, Boosey and Hawkes, 1978.

Radio Play: *A Spell for Green Corn*, 1967.

Television Plays: Three stories from *A Time to Keep*, 1969; *Orkney*, 1971; *Miss Barraclough*, 1977; *Four Orkney Plays for Schools*, 1978.

Verse

The Storm. Kirkwall, Orkney Herald Press, 1954.
Loaves and Fishes. London, Hogarth Press, 1959.
The Year of the Whale. London, Hogarth Press, 1965.
The Five Voyages of Arnor. Falkland, Fife, K.D. Duval, 1966.
Twelve Poems. Belfast, Festival, 1968.
Fishermen with Ploughs: A Poem Cycle. London, Hogarth Press, 1971.
Poems New and Selected. London, Hogarth Press, 1971; New York, Harcourt Brace, 1973.
Lifeboat and Other Poems. Credition, Devon, Gilbertson, 1971.
Penguin Modern Poets 21, with Iain Crichton Smith and Norman MacCaig. London, Penguin, 1972.
Winterfold. London, Hogarth Press, 1976.
Selected Poems. London, Hogarth Press, 1977.

Other

An Orkney Tapestry. London, Gollancz, 1969.
The Two Fiddlers (juvenile). London, Chatto and Windus, 1974.
Letters from Hamnavoe (essays). Edinburgh, Wright, 1975.
Edwin Muir: A Brief Memoir. West Linton, Peeblesshire, Castlelaw Press, 1975.
Pictures in the Cave (juvenile). London, Chatto and Windus, 1977.
Under Brinkie's Brae. Edinburgh, Wright, 1979.
Six Lives of Fankle the Cat (juvenile). London, Chatto and Windus, 1980.
Portrait of Orkney. London, Hogarth Press, 1981.

*

Manuscript Collections: Scottish National Library, Edinburgh; Edinburgh University.

Critical Study: *George Mackay Brown* by Alan Bold, Edinburgh, Oliver and Boyd, 1978.

George Mackay Brown comments:

(1972) I find it very difficult to comment on my own work, except in some imaginary context. I have recently finished a short story called "Seal Skin" about a musician. He reads, in Dublin, an old Celtic manuscript, about "the intricate web of creation" that men are mindlessly exploiting and tearing; and he is much moved by it. The last paragraphs are as follows:

> He [Magnus Olafson the musician] thought of the men who have thrown off all restraint and were beginning now to raven in the most secret and delicate and precious places of nature. They were the new priesthood; the world went down on its knees before every tawdry miracle—the phonograph, the motor car, the machine-gun, the wireless—that they held up in triumph. And the spoliation had hardly begun.
>
> Was this then the task of the artist: to keep in repair the sacred web of creation—that cosmic harmony of God and beast and man and star and plant—in the name of humanity, against those who in the name of humanity are mindlessly and systematically destroying it?
>
> If so, what had been taken from him was a necessary sacrifice.

* * *

The ancient undulating landscape of the Orkney islands forms more than a backcloth to the work of George Mackay Brown: it provides motif after motif for his novels and short stories, informing them with a sense of grandeur and venerable antiquity. A favourite description is "very ancient," and this phrase recurs again and again to build up a sense of timelessness where chronology becomes unimportant. In his novel *Greenvoe* Brown views time as "not a conflagration; it is a slow grave sequence of grassblade, fish, apple, star, snowflake," and the natural symbolism is continued in the inevitable demise of the community of Greenvoe and the promise of its resurrection: "The sun rose. The stars were warm. They broke the bread." Although there is death in the novel, the death of a human community, Brown uses the potent concept of renewal through the planting of seed both as a reminder of the island's heritage and as a reiteration of the doctrine of salvation through resurrection. Skarf, the Marxist fisherman, imagines the founding of the Orkney islands with strange visitors from the Mediterranean and Scandinavia bringing with them jars of seed to ensure their survival in a new life.

The descendents of those early invaders are the crofters and fishermen of Orkney who are the life-blood of Brown's fiction. It is they who are the integral part of the circle of life and death and it is they who move inexorably in its rhythm of seedtime, birth, harvest, and death. Their participation and their knowledge of the historical inter-twining of their present with their ancestors' past give a dignity to their lives and also prevents Brown's interest in them from sliding into sentimentality or nostalgia for the irretrievable past.

The theme of renewal is continued in *Hawkfall*, a collection of five related pieces which contemplate the survival of human characteristics in an Orkney family from the Bronze Age to the present day. Through the long sweep of history Brown traces both the story of his islands and the personal relationships that exist between succeeding generations of its people. The stories in *Hawkfall* are in the minor key, sombre and suffused with the ancient heritage of Orkney, and it is fitting that the collection should end with "The Interrogator," a story that examines not the finality and pain of death but its impossible mystery. That same sense of the mystery of creation is present in *The Sun's Net*, a collection of stories imbued with Brown's religious belief that each birth is the re-enactment of the nativity; in "A Winter Tale" the ancient ritual of the sun king and the corn queen is contrasted with the simple birth of a child in mid-winter at a deserted croft. Children grow up to renew the community and in any season are blessed, but this child born at Christmas is seen by all, except the minister who has become blind to miracles, as a promise of the island's salvation.

Brown's fascination with the Christian theme of redemption finds its most vigorous form in his second novel, *Magnus*, which tells the story of the 12th-century Earl of Orkney who was later sanctified for his martyrdom at the hands of his cousin Haakon. The terrible contemplation of Magnus's torment lies at the heart of this deeply religious work, a novel so dense and committed to its central theme that it lacks the simple narrative structure of the best short stories.

Orkney, its history and traditions, the people who have contributed to its story and to its regeneration over succeeding generations: these are the central strands with which Brown has woven a seamless literature, deceptively simple yet universal in its appeal.

—Trevor Royle

BRYHER. British. Born Annie Winifred Ellerman in Margate, Kent, 1894. Educated privately and at Queenwood School, Eastbourne, Sussex. Married 1) the writer Robert McAlmon in 1921 (marriage dissolved, 1926); 2) Kenneth Macpherson in 1927 (marriage dissolved, 1947). Editor, with Kenneth Macpherson, *Close Up* magazine, Territet, Switzerland, and London, 1927-30. Address: Kenwin, Burier, Vaud, Switzerland.

Publications

Novels

Development. London, Constable, and New York, Macmillan, 1920.

Two Selves. Paris, Contact, 1923(?); New York, Chaucer Head, 1927(?).

Civilians. Territet, Switzerland, Pool, 1927; London, Pool, 1930.

The Light-Hearted Student, with Trude Weiss. Dijon, Pool, 1930.

The Fourteenth of October. New York, Pantheon, 1952; London, Collins, 1954.

The Player's Boy. New York, Pantheon, 1953; London, Collins, 1957.

Roman Wall. New York, Pantheon, 1954; London, Collins, 1955.

Beowulf. New York, Pantheon, 1956.

Gate to the Sea. New York, Pantheon, 1958; London, Collins, 1959.

Ruan. New York, Pantheon, 1960; London, Collins, 1961.

The Coin of Carthage. New York, Harcourt Brace, 1963; London, Collins, 1964.

Visa for Avalon. New York, Harcourt Brace, 1965.

This January Tale. New York, Harcourt Brace, 1966; London, Secker and Warburg, 1968.

The Colors of Vaud. New York, Harcourt Brace, 1969.

Uncollected Short Stories

"Chance Encounter," in *Little Review* (Chicago), Autumn 1924-Winter 1925.

"Manchester," in *Life and Letters* (London), December 1935, Spring 1936, and Summer 1936.

Verse

Region of Lutany (as A.W. Ellerman). London, Chapman and Hall, 1914.

Arrow Music, with others. London, Bumpus, 1924.

Other

Amy Lowell: A Critical Appreciation. London, Eyre and Spottiswoode, 1918.
A Picture Geography for Little Children: Asia. London, Cape, 1925.
West (on the USA). London, Cape, 1925.
Film Problems of Soviet Russia. Territet, Switzerland, Pool, 1929.
Cinema Survey, with Robert Herring and Dallas Bower. London, Brendin, 1937.
The Heart to Artemis: A Writer's Memoirs. New York, Harcourt Brace, 1962; London, Collins, 1963.
The Days of Mars: A Memoir 1940-1946. New York, Harcourt Brace, and London, Calder and Boyars, 1972.

Translator, *The Lament for Adonis*, by Bion. London, Humphreys, 1918.

* * *

Anyone interested in the novels of Bryher should read her remarkable autobiography, *The Heart to Artemis*, for in it lies the key to them. There she describes a childhood in which the seeds of all her later interests and achievements were sown. Travel with intelligent parents proved marvellously fruitful, the child gathering her sense of time and place and history through leisurely wanderings around the Mediterranean and the Middle East, acquiring the rudiments, at least, of the extraordinary power that came later to project herself into other worlds, to live in other ages. "Fate was kind and I did few formal lessons in my childhood," she writes, "with the result that my mind developed freely and was ravenous for knowledge.... I was reading history from books written not for children but for scholars by the time I was ten, I could chatter in Arabic, I knew some hieroglyphics. More important perhaps than knowledge, I had been near to poverty, fire and death." The heroes of these stimulating early years were Shakespeare, Homer and *The Swiss Family Robinson*; and G.A. Henty, the writer of boys' books, of whom she says: "He taught me history." Other influences were Colette and Dorothy Richardson, and the autobiography is dedicated "to the memory of my master, Stéphane Mallarmé."

These varied influences converged in a woman of remarkable mental powers; and at the same time of an almost mystical power to absorb the alien and the past, to assimilate other cultures than her own. Her novels are set in the past, generally the distant past, and nearly always at a time of dissolution and transition, when old worlds are crumbling and new ones have yet to emerge from the violence. Fear lies at their centre, a sense of doom and yet of defiance; and at the same time, with hindsight which enriches the whole, we know that out of the ruins other worlds were to grow, that the misery and despair would break down into a compost to nourish other civilisations. This empathy that enables her to live through the past rather than merely to recreate it is found in the best of modern historical novelists, whether they write for adults or the young (the distinction has little meaning, today, at a high level of writing): Marguerite Yourcenar, Henry Treece, Rosemary Sutcliff. In Bryher the sense of other worlds is so strong that one is oneself swept into them, as if through poetry. Edith Sitwell, in an introduction to *The Fourteenth of October*, a story about the Danes invading Yorkshire seen from the point of view of the doomed Saxons, wrote: "the prose rhythms are of great beauty...these rhythms vary, they fluctuate, grow hard and terrible as in the battle scenes, or are exquisite and tender."

What is astonishing is Bryher's range, as well as depth, of historical knowledge and feeling. *Roman Wall* is set in a Roman outpost in what is now Switzerland, when German tribes are massing on the far bank of the Rhine, threatening to pour in. *Ruan* is set in 6th-century Britain, in the Celtic parts—Cornwall and the Scillys, Wales and Ireland—a generation after the death of Arthur. *The Coin of Carthage*, which was distantly inspired by G.A. Henty's *The Young Carthaginian*, is about Greek traders in a Greek settlement on the Italian coast, at the time of Hannibal. *Gate to the Sea* is set in the 4th century BC, when Poseidonia had been conquered by the Lucanians after the death of Alexander. And the same sense of doom (in this case of doom accomplished) hangs over *This January Tale*, which is about England after the Conquest, when, Bryher writes, "Art and learning virtually disappeared. A magnificent language was destroyed." Then, characteristically, she links the ages, making a valid modern parallel: "1940 almost followed the pattern of 1066."

The atmospheric intensity of Bryher's novels makes them stay in the mind, become part of one's own experience.

—Isabel Quigly

BUCHANAN, George (Henry Perrott). British. Born in Kilwaughter, County Antrim, Northern Ireland, 9 January 1904. Educated at Campbell College and Queen's University, Belfast. Served in the Royal Air Force Coastal Command, 1940-45. Married 1) Mary Corn in 1938 (marriage dissolved, 1945); 2) Noel Ritter in 1949 (died, 1951); 3) Janet Margesson in 1952 (died, 1968), two daughters; 4) Sandra McCloy in 1974. Reviewer for the *Times Literary Supplement*, London, 1928-40; on the editorial staff, *The Times*, London, 1930-35; Columnist and Drama Critic, *News Chronicle*, London, 1935-38. Chairman, Town and Country Development Committee, Northern Ireland, 1949-53. Since 1954, Member of the Executive Council of the European Society of Culture, Venice. Address: 27 Ashley Gardens, London S.W.1, England.

PUBLICATIONS

Novels

A London Story. London, Constable, 1935; New York, Dutton, 1936.
Rose Forbes: The Biography of an Unknown Woman (part 1). London, Constable, 1937.
Entanglement. London, Constable, 1938; New York, Appleton Century, 1939.
The Soldier and the Girl. London, Heinemann, 1940.
Rose Forbes (parts 1 and 2). London, Faber, 1950.
A Place to Live. London, Faber, 1952.
Naked Reason. New York, Holt Rinehart, 1971.

Plays

Dance Night (produced London, 1934). London, French, 1935.
A Trip to the Castle (produced London, 1960).
Tresper Revolution (produced London, 1961).
War Song (produced London, 1965).

Verse

Bodily Responses. London, Gaberbocchus, 1958.
Conversation with Strangers. London, Gaberbocchus, 1961.
Annotations. Oxford, Carcanet Press, 1970.
Minute-Book of a City. Oxford, Carcanet Press, 1972.
Inside Traffic. Manchester, Carcanet Press, 1976.
Possible Being. Manchester, Carcanet Press, 1980.

Other

Passage Through the Present: Chiefly Notes from a Journal. London, Constable, 1932; New York, Dutton, 1933.
Words for Tonight: A Notebook. London, Constable, 1936.
Serious Pleasures: The Intelligent Person's Guide to London. London, London Transport, 1938.
Green Seacoast (autobiography). London, Gaberbocchus, 1959; New York, Red Dust, 1968.
Morning Papers (autobiography). London, Gaberbocchus, 1965.
The Politics of Culture. London, Menard Press, 1977.

*

Critical Studies: "George Buchanan Special Supplement" of *Honest Ulsterman 59* (Belfast), 1978.

George Buchanan comments:

A novel is a poetic work. The French emphasis on *écriture*, the Russian Formalists' on "poetic speech," are converging points of view. Novels must have the same sudden careless quality as poems.

I prefer work that is artificial, am against autobiographical novels. (Better to face the truth in an undisguised autobiography, and try to turn the past into knowledge.) A novel should *au fond* be erotic. Otherwise it is on the side of death. Note the quantity of death novels, openly popularising the idea of murder.

The novel is an event in consciousness. Our aim isn't to copy actuality, but to modify and recreate our sense of it. The novelist is inviting the reader to watch a performance in his own brain. The people of the novel are in me and I am in them, from the beginning. I am making, rather than knowing. Much of the making is outside my understanding. I seek to create groups in an imaginary version of society, but a society which is accepted as being in history. These would include neo-persons, individuated constructs of the author. By thinking in a situation, each would be propelled to new positions. Story would thus emerge, not be imposed beforehand. It would also tend to be non-scenic. The characters will theorise, not dramatise, themselves. We don't necessarily grasp life in terms of scenes, as in film and theatre. It is this style of dealing with the drift of persons that is left to the novel. Narrative will be more critical than descriptive. The author will write, as Victor Shklovsky said, with *sang froid*. Detachment, not identification, is the first sign of seriousness.

Allow me to retain my own services as narrator. I rarely employ the technique of impersonating one of the characters. If it is feared that by telling the story myself, I destroy the illusion, I ask, "The illusion of what?" I don't wish the reader to feel that he is watching a piece of actuality. He is reading a book which sets out to give an impression of an imaginary event. But sometimes another voice does begin to be heard behind the author's. The work that I do is not only inside me but also apart from me, so that I address myself to it as an attentive associate, and I must be attentive. For a voice seems always about to speak to me out of the words that I myself write. I must be ready to hear.

It may be that our civilization will depend on the success with which we can make a secondary life, surrounded by imaginary elements. The novel has an important role in this. There may be some value in the notion of treating fiction as an account of the socially possible—not going the length of science fiction but offering limited deviations from familiar functioning. "A large measure of the reader's pleasure comes from participation in an empirical venture. Novels are risks" (Herbert Gold). Perhaps novels will be creating persons on their journey into half-known, half-guessed, half-anticipated areas.

* * *

Genre is less important in George Buchanan's work than in most writers who use diverse forms, as all his work is structured as *textes*. His non-fiction *Passage Through the Present* and *Words for Tonight* include aphorisms, poems, and short stories; the quality of these last makes it a matter of regret that Buchanan has not used this form more often. His poetic perception informs his novels too; as he has written, "By poet I do not mean always a writer in verse; I mean a person whose basic outlook can be described best perhaps in the words 'poetic realism.' Call him the artist-journalist, if you would prefer it."

Buchanan's first novel, *A London Story*, satirizes advertising in a big store, Drancer's. Nicholas, the brother of its successful Publicity Manager, is unfairly dismissed; a casualty of capitalism, he believes that "years later, the personal economic taboo will be regarded as the degrading mark of the early twentieth century." He decides that "the secret of non-specialization is the ability to doubt," doubt being "the great human attainment." One ironic thread is that Nicholas himself was rescued from despair by his wife, Phillida, who scarcely grasps his nebulous theories. This novel's sunlit public park scenes are the first in a series reflecting Buchanan's observation in his autobiography that "the sight of any collective enjoyment is recuperative."

Buchanan aspired to a journalism which "can produce its own kind of literature"; in his longest novel, *Entanglement*, he attempted in a similar way to write a kind of contemporary historical novel. He was careful to avoid characters which "may be too full of a sense of direction to belong credibly to our world of flickering whims." Forty-odd characters from different classes are observed through the menacing year March 1937 to March 1938. Some have no understanding, and none has a monopoly of insight, though the young Kevin Rede comes closest with his emphasis on "the eternal moment." The author refuses to impose a "plot." He subverts the traditional "omnibus" novel in the final chapter, after "a year has passed"; instead of giving the conventional potted biographies of his characters' subsequent lives, he merely remarks that they have all "changed bit by bit."

In *The Soldier and the Girl* the central tension is personal, the course of an Irish girl's marriage to a London painter. The passages of verse linking the parts attempt to give the author-narrator another dimension, while contributing to the book's light-hearted tone. The *tour de force* is a Saturday beach scene, where almost an entire office staff appear by chance. Yet, as in *Entanglement*, undertones of war bring out the relation of death and the moment, for "without the skeleton at the feast, it is questionable whether the feast tastes good."

With *A Place to Live*, set in Ireland, Buchanan returned to the inter-relation of public and private themes. The hotel manager Sinton Kells is urged by a journalist friend to participate in public life; eventually he does so, founding a new party, only to withdraw at the height of his "success." The not untroubled but predominately sunlit domesticity of the closing chapters, as at the end of *Rose Forbes* (1950), is finely evoked.

In all his work, Buchanan examines the position of women. In Part I of *Rose Forbes*, originally published as a complete novel (1937), he gave an effectively dispassionate account of an "ordinary"—if unusually resilient—woman: "Her true biography might be a story of herself drying her face every morning and looking above the towel at a corner of sky." As in all Buchanan's books, the ending was ambivalent, with Rose apparently about to decide against returning to her husband. Part II is different in tone, informed by Rose's gradual realization of "sensual virtue, this value system in the flesh."

Fuller implications of this wider ethical freedom are explored in *Naked Reason*, where Ellie speculates on the use of the sexual act "for the purpose of engendering friendships" instead of family textures. Reflecting on her experiments in this respect, she stresses her "non-advocacy": "I am not advocating anything.... Varying attitudes are a principal charm of the intimate life."

Written after a gap of 19 years, *Naked Reason* gives the stylistic pleasure of Buchanan's other work. The terse sentences are often arranged in short paragraphs that could be canticles from a prose poem. His novels all have an element of fable—open-ended fable. *Naked Reason* gives another slant to George Buchanan's lifelong exploration of the sexual and economic nexus, in the light of habitual human irresolution.

—Val Warner

BUCKLER, Ernest (Redmond). Canadian. Born in Dalhousie West, Nova Scotia, 19 July 1908. Educated at Dalhousie University, Halifax, Nova Scotia, B.A. 1929; University of Toronto, M.A. in philosophy 1930. Actuarial employee, Manufacturers Life Insurance Company, Toronto, 1930-35. Sometime farmer, and free-lance writer, since 1936. Columnist, *Saturday Night*, Toronto, 1947-48; Book Reviewer, *New York Times* and *Los Angeles Times*, 1962-66. Recipient: *Maclean's* magazine prize, 1948; President's Medal, University of Western Ontario, 1957, 1958; Canada Council Fellowship, 1960, 1963, 1966; Leacock Medal, 1978. D.Litt.: University of New Brunswick, Fredericton, 1969; LL.D.: Dalhousie University, 1971. Agent: Curtis Brown Ltd., 575 Madison Avenue, New York, New York 10022, U.S.A. Address: R.R. 2, Bridgetown, Nova Scotia BOS 1CO, Canada.

PUBLICATIONS

Novels

The Mountain and the Valley. New York, Holt, 1952.
The Cruelest Month. Toronto, McClelland and Stewart, 1963.

Short Stories

The Rebellion of Young David and Other Stories, edited by Robert D. Chambers. Toronto, McClelland and Stewart, 1975.

Other

Ox Bells and Fireflies: A Memoir. Toronto, McClelland and Stewart, and New York, Knopf, 1968.
Nova Scotia: Window on the Sea, photographs by Hans Weber. Toronto, McClelland and Stewart, and New York, Potter, 1973.
Whirligig: Selected Prose and Verse. Toronto, McClelland and Stewart, 1977.

*

Manuscript Collection: University of Toronto Library.

Critical Studies: *Ernest Buckler* edited by Gregory M. Cook, Toronto, McGraw Hill Ryerson, 1972; *Ernest Buckler* by Alan Young, Toronto, McClelland and Stewart, 1976.

Ernest Buckler comments:

It is extremely difficult to list the various "themes" of my work—but by far the most recurrent is an attempt to render the texture of life in the Nova Scotian country in all its complexity. Such life, often thought to be crude and simple, is nothing of the kind. It is a microcosm in which every facet of whatever macrocosm one can think of (particularly in cases of the spirit) is illustrated and parabled.

* * *

Though he has written several books and innumerable essays, stories, radio plays, and other works, Ernest Buckler's reputation rests especially on one book: his first novel, *The Mountain and the Valley*.

Set in the time-eroded farmland of Nova Scotia's Annapolis Valley, *The Mountain and the Valley* is one of the most rich, densely textured and complex of Canadian novels—too much so at times, indeed, shading away into occasional over-elaboration and obscurity. As Claude Bissell has said, it is "a novel written in praise of the family," and it traces the development of David Canaan, an unusually sensitive and intelligent boy who loves language and appears something of an artist *manqué*. The promise David shows, the attentiveness with which he notices every nuance of mood and shift in interaction, the capacity he reveals to describe these subtleties—none of these qualities receives full play in the country village to which something in him remains deeply committed. David's health, never robust, is seriously weakened by a fall from a barn loft, and when he dies at thirty, he has been for some time a slightly eccentric bachelor living in the family home with only his grandmother.

But to focus on plot in *The Mountain and the Valley* is to miss the point, for the novel's life is in its characters and its language. Buckler has done graduate study in philosophy, and the reflectiveness, the psychological sophistication, and the intricate symbolic construction of his work leave an impression which has less to do with art narrowly conceived than with wisdom. The book seems slow—until one realizes that the pace is that of country living, allowing time for observation, contemplation, attention to the phenomenon of nature and of man meshed with nature. Despite some obvious weaknesses which spring in part from the nature of Buckler's enterprise, *The Mountain and the Valley* is one of the most rewarding and expressive works of the Canadian imagination.

The Cruelest Month was pummelled by the reviewers, as the successor to a brilliant first novel normally is, and it has rarely been read with the kind of care it warrants. To Paul Creed's guest-house in Nova Scotia comes a disparate group, including a novelist, an aged professor of archaeology and his spinster daughter, a well-to-do couple from Greenwich, Connecticut, and a withdrawn former medical student. Each one—Paul included—faces a personal crisis of some sort. The interplay among these private anguishes forms the action of the novel, which concludes as all but Paul and his housekeeper, Letty, drive away through a roaring forest fire.

The Cruelest Month has Buckler's usual faults. A compulsion to find an exact verbal equivalent for every shade of experience produces over-writing; some passages are merely coy. But if the reviewers were right to find Buckler's second novel less impressive than his first, they were wrong to dismiss it as briskly as many did. Like all Buckler's work, it is shrewd and craftsmanlike; and Buckler at his worst is more serious and more honest than most Canadian novelists at their best.

With *Ox Bells and Fireflies* Buckler abandoned the novel form almost entirely. He calls the book "a fictive memoir": an accurate phrase for an attempt to capture the nimbus of life in his native village fifty years ago. Though it lacks the thrust and intensity of a novel, *Ox Bells and Fireflies* is a beautiful book, with passages which read like verse, bits of folk wisdom imbedded in it like raisins in cake, country words and phrases polished and set like gems, and a haunting feeling for the evanescent terror and magnificence of life which has always spoken to Buckler with a unique intensity in the country.

Ox Bells and Fireflies presents itself as the distillation of a sensitive man's love for common experience. Though no one but Buckler could have written it, it is curiously impersonal, almost the voice of the land and its rooted people themselves. Buckler maintains that the universal inheres in the local, that his own village contains all man's tragedy and joy. His own work is powerful evidence for that theory.

—Donald Cameron

BUECHNER, (Carl) Frederick. American. Born in New York City, 11 July 1926. Educated at Princeton University, New Jersey, A.B. 1947; Union Theological Seminary, New York, B.D. 1958; ordained a Minister of the United Presbyterian Church, 1958. Served in the United States Army, 1944-46. Married Judith Friedrike Merck in 1956; three children. English Master, Lawrenceville School, New Jersey, 1948-53; Instructor in Creative Writing, New York University, summers 1953-54; Head of the Employment Clinic, East Harlem Protestant Parish, New York, 1954-58; Chairman of the Religion Department, 1958-67, and School Minister, 1960-67, Phillips Exeter Academy, New Hampshire. William Belden Noble Lecturer, Harvard University, Cambridge, Massachusetts, 1969; Lyman Beecher Lecturer, Yale Divinity School, New Haven, Connecticut, 1976; Harris Lecturer, Bangor Seminary, Maine, 1979. Recipient: O. Henry Prize, 1955; Rosenthal Award, 1959. Address: Pawlet, Vermont 05761, U.S.A.

PUBLICATIONS

Novels

A Long Day's Dying. New York, Knopf, 1950; London, Chatto and Windus, 1951.
The Seasons' Difference. New York, Knopf, and London, Chatto and Windus, 1952.
The Return of Ansel Gibbs. New York, Knopf, and London, Chatto and Windus, 1958.
The Final Beast. New York, Atheneum, and London, Chatto and Windus, 1965.
The Entrance to Porlock. New York, Atheneum, and London, Chatto and Windus, 1970.
The Book of Bebb. New York, Atheneum, 1979.
  Lion Country. New York, Atheneum, and London, Chatto and Windus, 1971.
  Open Heart. New York, Atheneum, and London, Chatto and Windus, 1972.
  Love Feast. New York, Atheneum, 1974; London, Chatto and Windus, 1975.
  Treasure Hunt. New York, Atheneum, 1977; London, Chatto and Windus, 1978.
Godric. New York, Atheneum, 1980; London, Chatto and Windus, 1981.

Uncollected Short Story

"The Tiger," in *Prize Stories 1955: The O. Henry Awards*, edited by Paul Engle and Hansford Martin. New York, Doubleday, 1955.

Other

The Magnificent Defeats (meditations). New York, Seabury Press, 1966; London, Chatto and Windus, 1967.
The Hungering Dark (meditations). New York, Seabury Press, 1969.
The Alphabet of Grace (autobiography). New York, Seabury Press, 1970.
Wishful Thinking: A Theological ABC. New York, Harper, and London, Collins, 1973.
The Faces of Jesus, photographs by Lee Boltin. Croton-on-Hudson, New York, Riverwood, 1974.
Telling the Truth: The Gospel as Tragedy, Comedy, and Fairy Tale. New York, Harper, 1977.
Peculiar Treasures: A Biblical Who's Who. New York, Harper, 1979.

*

Manuscript Collection: Princeton University, New Jersey.

Frederick Buechner comments:

When I started out writing novels, my greatest difficulty was always in finding a plot. Since then I have come to believe that there is only one plot. It has to do with the way life or reality or God—the name is perhaps not so important—seeks to turn us into human beings, to make us whole, to make us Christs, to "save" us—again, call it what you will. In my fiction and non-fiction alike, this is what everything I have written is about.

* * *

The novels of Frederick Buechner represent a movement from a consideration of psychological textures to an assessment of the religious values that are expressed by those textures. The fact that Buechner is an ordained Presbyterian clergyman may not strike the reader of the earlier novels—*A Long Day's Dying*, *The Seasons' Difference*, and *The Return of Ansel Gibbs*—as particularly relevant to the interpretation of those novels. His early novels, indeed, may impress the casual reader as works that are in the tradition of Henry James, concerned as they are with the rather delicate and tenuously resolved relations among cultivated and privileged Americans. The characters in these novels are preoccupied with resolutions of their difficulties, but these resolutions go no farther than clarification of their identities in relation to each other. This clarification is conveyed in a style that was regarded, at the time of the novels' appearance, as oblique and over-worked. The actual course of event in the early novels issues, as indicated, in changes of orientation that can be spoken of as a clearing out of the psychological undergrowth that impedes the discovery of purpose and self-knowledge on the part of the chief characters. The course of the narratives is marked by a taste for ironic comedy—a comedy that records the experience of living in a world that, unlike the world of some older comedy, is bare of generally shared values. The values that are to be detached are values for a particular person and do not have much wider relevance.

It is in later novels—*The Final Beast*, *The Entrance to Porlock*, and *Lion Country*—that one can see Buechner moving, in an ironic and quite self-protective way, toward concerns that his ordination as a clergyman would suggest. He moves from concern with particular persons in special situations toward more inclusive concerns which announce that lives of individual characters are oblique annunciations of the general constraint and opportunity which all human beings can, if they are responsive, encounter. The psyche is also a soul—a focus of energy that achieves fulfillment by coming into relation with patterns that religion and mythology testify to. The style of the later work becomes simpler, and Buechner delights in reporting farcical aspects of American experience that found little place in his earlier work. And these farcical elements are organized by invocation of narrative patterns that are widely known. The narrative pattern that underpins *The Entrance to Porlock* is drawn from that item of popular culture, *The Wizard of Oz*; the motley company of this novel repeats and varies the quest that took Dorothy Gale and her companions along the Road of Yellow Bricks.

In *Lion Country* and the three novels that succeed it—*Open Heart*, *Love Feast*, and *Treasure Hunt*—the grotesque menagerie of characters has experiences that are organized by nothing less than the traditional patterns of the Christian religion itself. (The four novels are published together under the title of *The Book of Bebb*.) In this series, the Christian religion undergoes parody that on the surface is blasphemous, is offered variation that is ironical rather than confirming, and yet—in the long run—achieves the only kind of validation that is possible at the present time. At the very least the series is a successful counter-weight to novels that confirm conventional piety by exercises in conventional piety. Yet beneath the adultery, farce, and sheer violence of the Bebb series is a set of insights that are very close to the assertions of conventional Christianity. The conventionality—and the sincerity—of Buechner's views can be sampled in the theological ABC contained in *Wishful Thinking* and other meditations.

In summary Buechner can be seen as a novelist who at first was challenged by the sheer complexity of human behavior and who later finds that complexity partially comprehensible when linked with popular myth-work like the Oz books and, finally, with the self-mastery and self-discovery offered by the Christian religion.

—Harold H. Watts

BURGESS, Anthony. Pseudonym for John Anthony Burgess Wilson. British. Born in Manchester, Lancashire, 25 February 1917. Educated at Xaverian College, Manchester; Manchester University, B.A. in English 1940. Served in the British Army Education Corps, 1940-46: Sergeant-Major. Married 1) Llewela Isherwood Jones in 1942 (died, 1968); 2) Liliana Macellari in 1968, one son. Lecturer, Extra-Mural Department, Birmingham University, 1946-48; Education Officer and Lecturer, Central Advisory Council for Adult Education in the Forces, 1946-48; Lecturer, Ministry of Education, 1948-50; English Master, Banbury Grammar School, Oxfordshire, 1950-54; Colonial Service Education Officer, Malaya and Brunei, 1954-59. Writer-in-Residence, University of North Carolina, Chapel Hill, 1969-70; Professor, Columbia University, New York, 1970-71; Visiting Fellow, Princeton University, New Jersey, 1970-71; Distinguished Professor, City University of New York, 1972-73. Since 1972, Literary Adviser, Guthrie Theatre, Minneapolis. Also composer. Fellow, Royal Society of Literature, 1969. Address: 44 Rue Grimaldi, Monaco.

PUBLICATIONS

Novels

Time for a Tiger. London, Heinemann, 1956.
The Enemy in the Blanket. London, Heinemann, 1958.
Beds in the East. London, Heinemann, 1959.
The Right to an Answer. London, Heinemann, 1960; New York, Norton, 1961.
The Doctor Is Sick. London, Heinemann, 1960; New York, Norton, 1966.
The Worm and the Ring. London, Heinemann, 1961; revised edition, 1970.
Devil of a State. London, Heinemann, 1961; New York, Norton, 1970.
One Hand Clapping (as Joseph Kell). London, Davies, 1961; as Anthony Burgess, New York, Knopf, 1972.
A Clockwork Orange. London, Heinemann, 1962; New York, Norton, 1963.
The Wanting Seed. London, Heinemann, 1962; New York, Norton, 1963.
Honey for the Bears. London, Heinemann, 1963; New York, Norton, 1964.
Inside Mr. Enderby (as Joseph Kell). London, Heinemann, 1963.
The Eve of Saint Venus. London, Sidgwick and Jackson, 1964; New York, Norton, 1970.
Nothing Like the Sun: A Story of Shakespeare's Love-Life. London, Heinemann, and New York, Norton, 1964.
The Malayan Trilogy (includes *Time for a Tiger*, *The Enemy in the Blanket*, *Beds in the East*). London, Pan, 1964; as *The Long Day Wanes*, New York, Norton, 1965.
A Vision of Battlements. London, Sidgwick and Jackson, 1965; New York, Norton, 1966.
Tremor of Intent. London, Heinemann, and New York, Norton, 1966.
Enderby Outside. London, Heinemann, 1968.
Enderby (includes *Inside Mr. Enderby* and *Enderby Outside*). New York, Norton, 1968.
MF. London, Cape, and New York, Knopf, 1971.
Napoleon Symphony. London, Cape, and New York, Knopf, 1974.
The Clockwork Testament; or, Enderby's End. London, Hart Davis MacGibbon, 1974; New York, Knopf, 1975.
Beard's Roman Women. New York, McGraw Hill, 1976; London, Heinemann, 1977.
Abba Abba. London, Faber, 1977; Boston, Little Brown, 1978.
1985. London, Hutchinson, and Boston, Little Brown, 1978.
Man of Nazareth. New York, McGraw Hill, 1979; London, Magnum, 1980.
Earthly Powers. London, Hutchinson, and New York, Simon and Schuster, 1980.

Short Story

Will and Testament: A Fragment of Biography. Verona, Plain Wrapper Press, 1977.

Uncollected Short Stories

"From 'It Is the Miller's Daughter,' " in *Transatlantic Review* (London), Spring 1967.
"Somebody's Got to Pay the Rent," in *Partisan Review* (New Brunswick, New Jersey), Winter 1968.
"An American Organ," in *Splinters*, edited by Alex Hamilton. New York, Walker, 1969.
"A Benignant Growth," in *Transatlantic Review* (London), Summer 1969.
"I Wish My Wife Was Dead," in *Transatlantic Review* (London), Winter 1969-70.
"The Muse," in *Best SF 1969*, edited by Brian Aldiss and Harry Harrison. New York, Putnam, and London, Sphere, 1970.

Plays

Cyrano, music by Michael J. Lewis, lyrics by Burgess, adaptation of the play by Rostand (produced Minneapolis, 1971; New York, 1973). New York, Knopf, 1971.
Oedipus the King, adaptation of a play by Sophocles (produced Minneapolis, 1972; Southampton, Hampshire, 1979). Minneapolis, University of Minnesota Press, 1972; London, Oxford University Press, 1973.

Television Plays: *Moses the Law-Giver*, 1975; *Jesus of Nazareth*, with Suso d'Amico and Franco Zeffirelli, 1979; *A Kind of Failure* (documentary; *Writers and Places* series), 1981.

Verse

Moses: A Narrative. London, Dempsey and Squires, and New York, Stonehill, 1976.
A Christmas Recipe. Verona, Plain Wrapper Press, 1977.

Other

English Literature: A Survey for Students (as John Burgess Wilson). London, Longman, 1958.
The Novel Today. London, Longman, 1963; Folcroft, Pennsylvania, Folcroft Editions, 1971.
Language Made Plain. London, English Universities Press, 1964; New York, Crowell, 1965; revised edition, London, Fontana, 1975.
Here Comes Everybody: An Introduction to James Joyce for the Ordinary Reader. London, Faber, 1965; as *Re Joyce*, New York, Norton, 1965.
The Novel Now: A Student's Guide to Contemporary Fiction. London, Faber, and New York, Norton, 1967; revised edition, Faber, 1971.

Urgent Copy: Literary Studies. London, Cape, 1968; New York, Norton, 1969.
Shakespeare. London, Cape, and New York, Knopf, 1970.
Joysprick: An Introduction to the Language of James Joyce. London, Deutsch, 1973; New York, Harcourt Brace, 1975.
Obscenity and the Arts (lecture). Valletta, Malta Library Association, 1973.
A Long Trip to Teatime (juvenile). London, Dempsey and Squires, 1976; New York, Stonehill, 1978.
New York, with the editors of Time-Life books. New York, Time, 1976.
Ernest Hemingway and His World. London, Thames and Hudson, and New York, Scribner, 1978.
The Land Where Ice Cream Grows (juvenile). Tonbridge, Kent, Benn, and New York, Doubleday, 1979.

Editor, *Coaching Days of England.* London, Elek, 1966.
Editor, *A Journal of the Plague Year*, by Daniel Defoe. London, Penguin, 1966.
Editor, *A Shorter Finnegans Wake*, by James Joyce. London, Faber, 1966; New York, Viking Press, 1967.
Editor, with Francis Haskell, *The Age of the Grand Tour.* London, Elek, and New York, Crown, 1967.
Editor, *Malaysian Stories*, by W. Somerset Maugham. Singapore, Heinemann, 1969.

Translator, with Llewela Burgess, *The New Aristocrats*, by Michel de Saint-Pierre. London, Gollancz, 1962.
Translator, with Llewela Burgess, *The Olive Trees of Justice*, by Jean Pelegri. London, Sidgwick and Jackson, 1962.
Translator, *The Man Who Robbed Poor Boxes*, by Jean Servin. London, Gollancz, 1965.

*

Bibliography: *Anthony Burgess: An Enumerative Bibliography* by Paul Boytinck, Norwood, Pennsylvania, Norwood Editions, 1974; *Anthony Burgess: A Bibliography* by Jeutonne Brewer, Metuchen, New Jersey, Scarecrow Press, 1980.

Manuscript Collection: Mills Memorial Library, Hamilton, Ontario.

Critical Studies: in *The Red Hot Vacuum* by Theodore Solotaroff, New York, Atheneum, 1970; *Shakespeare's Lives* by Samuel Schoenbaum, Oxford, Clarendon Press, 1970; *Anthony Burgess* by Carol M. Dix, London, Longman, 1971; *The Consolations of Ambiguity: An Essay on the Novels of Anthony Burgess* by Robert K. Morris, Columbia, University of Missouri Press, 1971; *Anthony Burgess* by A.A. DeVitis, New York, Twayne, 1972; *The Clockwork Universe of Anthony Burgess* by Richard Mathews, San Bernardino, California, Borgo Press, 1978; *Anthony Burgess: The Artist as Novelist* by Geoffrey Aggeler, University, University of Alabama Press, 1979.

Anthony Burgess comments:

I hesitate to say much about my own work, which I can lay less claim to understanding than a really perceptive professional critic. I was shocked to be told that the name of the hero of *A Vision of Battlements* (R. Ennis) spells sinner backwards—a fact it took me fifteen years to realise. Since then, I have become so used to my unconscious mind dictating not only the themes of my novels but also the names and symbols that I regard myself as a mere hen, non-ovivorous. But the novels are probably all about the same thing—man as a sinner, but not sufficiently a sinner to deserve the calamities that are heaped upon him. I suppose I try to make comic novels about man's tragic lot.

* * *

Anthony Burgess's first novel, *A Vision of Battlements*, was written in 1949 but remained unpublished until 1965. As a young man he had been interested in composing music rather than writing books, but he produced *A Vision of Battlements* as an attempt to exorcise the oppressive memory of his war service in Gibraltar. It makes a good starting point for the discussion of his work, as it already displays, if in an undeveloped form, many of the characteristics of his later novels. Its hero, Richard Ennis, a sergeant in an education branch of the British Army in Gibraltar, is a victim of his environment—in this case the military hierarchy—but although he suffers many defeats he fights back resiliently, and wins the occasional tactical victory. He is a lapsed Catholic and the burden of his religious upbringing weighs heavily upon him. Ennis has fairly strong libidinous urges but he is also fastidious in his attitudes to sex, being as much repelled by the flesh as drawn to it; he is at home in squalid surroundings, while aspiring to a materially comfortable life. Life presents itself to him as a rapid alternation of comic and melodramatic incidents. Basically *A Vision of Battlements* is a semipicaresque novel that draws heavily on Burgess's memories of wartime Gibraltar. Yet is is characteristic that he complicated his story by underpinning it with the plot of the *Aeneid* ("Ennis" = Aeneas) in a manner directly imitative of Joyce's use of the *Odyssey* in *Ulysses.* The influence of Joyce is pervasive, too, in Burgess's endless fascination with language and his love of verbal games, an influence reinforced in his later fiction by that of Nabokov. The other dominant influence is that master of cruel comedy, Evelyn Waugh, particularly his early work.

It was to be several more years before Burgess emerged as a novelist. In the 1950's he published his *Malayan Trilogy* which drew on his experiences as a Colonial Civil Servant in Malaya during the final phase of British rule. Here, too, one finds a sad, comic, victimised hero, and a highly episodic story line. The essential nature of Burgess's fiction has not changed since then, though his particular effects have become increasingly sophisticated. He can reasonably be described as a writer of black comedy, who is preoccupied with certain quasi-religious themes. Burgess himself is what he has called a "renegade Catholic," who comes from an old Lancashire Catholic family and attended a Catholic school in Manchester; in the opening of *Tremor of Intent* he describes the terrifyingly repressive atmosphere of such a school, in what reads like an autobiographical account, and which is reminiscent of Joyce's *Portrait of the Artist.* He has remarked that "The God my religious upbringing forced upon me was a God wholly dedicated to doing me harm.... A big vindicitive invisibility." If he has abandoned the practice of Catholicism, Burgess has certainly not turned to the agnostic liberal humanism professed by most English-speaking intellectuals. He remains preoccupied in a Jansenist way by the separation between Nature and Grace, and is deeply suspicious of progressive social ideals and movements. This Augustinian pessimism, which is more convinced of the depravity of man than of the likelihood of transcendent goodness, has antecedents in Baudelaire and Graham Greene and T.S. Eliot, and it pervades Burgess's finest novel, *A Clockwork Orange.*

This novel is an anti-utopian fable about the near future, when teenage gangs habitually terrorize the inhabitants of a shabby metropolis. The story is told in the first person by a young criminal, Alex, in a superb piece of impersonatory writing by Burgess. Alex may be morally vicious but he is mentally alert, and through his flow of complicated slang (much of it of Russian origin) one distinguishes a coherent though desperate view of life. Alex is cruel and ruthless, though usually cheerful, given to beating up older citizens and raping girls and destroying books. And if he acts in this way it is not because he has had an unhappy childhood or lives in an underprivileged community, as liberal-minded psychologists might say, but because he has deliberately chosen evil, as an assertion of spiritual freedom in a world of sub-human conformists. Like all Burgess's novels, *A Clockwork Orange* has a largely episodic plot, but it rises to a powerful climax when Alex is subject by the state to a form of psychological conditioning that removes his capacity to engage in criminal acts. Here Burgess touches on a question of great philosophical importance: in what sense is a man who has been *forced* to be good better than a man who deliberately asserts his humanity by choosing evil? *A Clockwork Orange* works brilliantly as a metaphysical thriller. It has thematic affinities with another accomplished novel, *The Right to an Answer*, which Burgess has described as "a study of provincial England, as seen by a man on leave from the East, with special emphasis on the decay of traditional values in an affluent society." It is one of Burgess's funniest books, but it is pervaded by a profound distaste for the contemporary English scene, where the comic elements are held in tension with a sense that England is a flat and dismal place of petty lusts and feeble adulteries, drawing all its values from the mass media. In *The Wanting Seed* Burgess draws another pessimistic vision of the future, this time of a society grappling with overpopulation, where history moves cyclically, a severe Augustinian ideology persisting for a while, then giving place to a relaxed Pelagian one, and so on indefinitely. These three novels of the early 1960's are full of wit and inventiveness, and are convincing as novels of ideas.

Burgess's later novels are numerous, for he is an extraordinarily prolific writer. They develop the characteristics of his early fiction, notably the combination of verbal brilliance and loose, episodic structure. Although Burgess is sympathetic to experimental fiction, his own work is basically conventional, despite his taste for Joycean manipulations of language. He has become increasingly more ingenious and has turned to a variety of themes or models. *Nothing Like the Sun* is a novel about Shakespeare, who is treated in a very unromantic way, and where Burgess uses Elizabethan language with great finesse. *Tremor of Intent* is an attempt to use the conventions of the sensational spy-story to write a serious novel, though it is little more than a series of bravura episodes. In *Inside Mr. Enderby* and its sequel *Enderby Outside* Burgess returns to familiar Joycean ground; its hero, the middle-aged poet, F.X. Enderby, can only compose in the lavatory. He is a lapsed Catholic, who associates the Catholic religion with his frightful stepmother who has frightened him off women for life. Enderby prefers solitary sex, but in the later part of the story he marries, against his will, and gets involved in a series of fast-moving if incredible adventures. Here, as elsewhere in his fiction, Burgess has devised a convincing and interesting character, but can do nothing with him except thrust him into a rapid episodic narrative. Almost all of Burgess's novels reflect this basic weakness in maintaining and developing a large-scale structure. In his recent novels Burgess has appeared to make a virtue of this limitation, deliberately using external devices as a way of ensuring a sustained fictional structure. Thus, *MF* draws heavily on the anthropology of Lévi-Strauss, mixing riddles and incest myths and identical twins and bird symbolism, with a dazzling range of puns and word-play, spanning many languages. And in *Napoleon Symphony* Burgess brings together his musical and literary interests in a formidably intricate novel about Napoleon whose form closely imitates Beethoven's "Eroica" symphony. Such works show Burgess's ceaseless ingenuity and inventiveness; but they provide few of the ordinary satisfactions of fiction. Burgess remains a uniquely clever and energetic novelist, but his recent development is not encouraging.

—Bernard Bergonzi

BURNS, Alan. British. Born in London, 29 December 1929. Educated at the Merchant Taylors' School, London; Middle Temple, London: called to the Bar, 1956. Served in the Royal Army Education Corps, 1949-51. Married Carol Lynn in 1954; two children. Practised as Barrister, London, 1956-59; Research Assistant, London School of Economics, 1959; Assistant Legal Manager, Beaverbrook Newspapers, London, 1959-62; Lecturer, National County Libraries Summer School, 1970; First Holder, Henfield Fellowship, University of East Anglia, Norwich, 1971; Senior Tutor in Creative Writing, Western Australian Institute of Technology, South Bentley, 1975; Arts Council Writing Fellow, City Literary Institute, London, 1976. Since 1977, Associate Professor of English, University of Minnesota, Minneapolis. Recipient: Arts Council grant, 1967, 1969, and bursary, 1969, 1973; C. Day Lewis Fellowship, 1973. Address: Department of English, University of Minnesota, Minneapolis, Minnesota 55414, U.S.A.

PUBLICATIONS

Novels

Buster, in *New Writers One*. London, Calder, 1961; as *Buster*, New York, Red Dust, 1972.
Europe after the Rain. London, Calder, 1965; New York, Day, 1970.
Celebrations. London, Calder and Boyars, 1967.
Babel. London, Calder and Boyars, 1969; New York, Day, 1970.
Dreamerika! A Surrealist Fantasy. London, Calder and Boyars, 1972.
The Angry Brigade: A Documentary Novel. London, Allison and Busby, 1973.
The Day Daddy Died. London, Allison and Busby, and New York, Shocken, 1981.

Uncollected Short Story

"Wonderland," in *Beyond the Words*. London, Hutchinson, 1975.

Play

Palach (produced London, 1970). London, Penguin, 1974.

Other

To Deprave and Corrupt: Technical Reports of the United States Commission on Obscenity and Pornography. London, Davis Poynter, 1972.
The Imagination on Trial: Conversations with British and American Writers, with Charles Sugnet. London, Allison and Busby, 1980; New York, Shocken, 1981.

*

Critical Studies: two articles by Robert Nye in *The Scotsman* (Edinburgh), 17 April 1965, and 7 October 1967; a profile in *The Guardian* (London), 30 April 1970; an interview in the *Times Educational Supplement* (London), 18 September 1970.

* * *

Alan Burns's novels deserve the attention of serious readers. The first, *Europe after the Rain*, taking its title from a painting by Max Ernst, established him as a kind of infra-realist. Set in the unspecified future, in a Europe devastated by internecine strife within "the party," it deals with ruined figures in a ruined landscape, purposelessly dedicated to "the work" which is the only thing the party will reward with the food necessary to keep alive. The unnamed narrator alone possesses any genuine purpose. His quest to find and take care of the daughter of the Trotskyite leader of the rebel forces is inspired by something like love, doubtfully implicit in his actions, later developed into a statement of hope which comes as the one redeeming human fact in a world blasted beyond the usual trappings of humanity, but arrived at only after much violence: a woman is flogged, a dog stabbed and its legs dislocated, people fight over corpses for the gold fillings in the teeth, a leg is wrenched off a corpse and eaten by a woman, other women pursue and stone and half-crucify and eventually beat to death the commander of the forces who are in power at the book's beginning. To this nightmarish action Burns applies a style which may be described as burnt-out. His sentences are mostly short, or built up of short phrases resting on commas where one might have expected full-stops, the total effect being slipped, stripped, and abrupt.

Celebrations is similarly uncompromising, with six characters and seven funerals. Williams, boss of a factory, has two sons, Michael and Phillip, whom he dominates. A hero to himself, Williams is a most uncertain personality, inconstant in his psychological attributes, extravagant in behaviour which is nevertheless always reported in the same flat and colourless prose. Phillip's death, following an accident which necessitates the amputation of his leg, leaves an even sharper taste of doubt in the reader's mind—for while it throws his father and his brother into grim rivalry for the attention of his widow, Jacqueline, these affairs are chronicled with such irony that they hardly seem to occur. All the time, it appears, we are meant to be reminded of Kierkegaard's dictum, "The thought of death condenses and intensifies life," as Burns piles violence on violence, and funeral on funeral, abbreviating whole lives to a tapestry of gesture.

With *Babel* Burns seems to have reached a dead end, though it confirms him in his role as infra-realist, anti-poet, steely perceiver of disconnections, writing as though he looks down on the rest of us from a private spaceship in unwilling orbit. Here he has assembled an ice-cold report on a world in chaos, stitching together clichés from the newspapers, fragments of misunderstood conversation, a babble of jokes and warnings. The cunningly fragmented styles owe too much to Burroughs and Ballard, and the comedy cannot quite conceal something merely self-disgusted in such furious insistence on unmeaning.

—Robert Nye

BURROUGHS, William S(eward). American. Born in St. Louis, Missouri, 5 February 1914. Educated at John Burroughs and Taylor schools, St. Louis; Los Alamos Ranch School, New Mexico; Harvard University, Cambridge, Massachusetts, A.B. in anthropology 1936; studied medicine at the University of Vienna; Mexico City College, 1948-50. Served in the United States Army, 1942. Married Jean Vollmer in 1945 (died); one son. Has worked as a journalist, private detective, and bartender; now a full-time writer. Heroin addict, 1944-57. Recipient: American Academy award, 1975. Lived for many years in Tangier; now lives in New York City. Agent: Peter Matson, Literistic Ltd., 32 West 40th Street, New York, New York 10018, U.S.A.

PUBLICATIONS

Novels

Junkie: Confessions of an Unredeemed Drug Addict (as William Lee). New York, Ace, 1953; London, Digit, 1957.
The Naked Lunch. Paris, Olympia Press, 1959; London, Calder, 1964; as *Naked Lunch*, New York, Grove Press, 1962.
The Soft Machine. Paris, Olympia Press, 1961; New York, Grove Press, 1966; London, Calder and Boyars, 1968.
The Ticket That Exploded. Paris, Olympia Press, 1962; revised edition, New York, Grove Press, 1967; London, Calder and Boyars, 1968.
Dead Fingers Talk. London,Calder, 1963.
Nova Express. New York, Grove Press, 1964; London, Cape, 1966.
The Wild Boys: A Book of the Dead. New York, Grove Press, 1971; London, Calder and Boyars, 1972; revised edition, London, Calder, 1979.
Exterminator! New York, Viking Press, 1973; London, Calder and Boyars, 1974.
Short Novels. London, Calder, 1978.
Blade Runner: A Movie. Berkeley, California, Blue Wind Press, 1979.
Port of Saints. Berkeley, California, Blue Wind Press, 1980.
Cities of the Red Night: A Boy's Book. London, Calder, and New York, Holt Rinehart, 1981.

Play

The Last Words of Dutch Schultz. London, Cape Goliard Press, 1970; New York, Viking Press, 1975.

Other

The Exterminator, with Brion Gysin. San Francisco, Auerhahn Press, 1960.
Minutes to Go, with others. Paris, Two Cities, 1960; San Francisco, Beach, 1968.
The Yage Letters, with Allen Ginsberg. San Francisco, City Lights, 1963.
Roosevelt after Inauguration. New York, Fuck You Press, 1964.
Valentine Day's Reading. New York, American Theatre for Poets, 1965.
Time. New York, "C" Press, 1965.
Health Bulletin: APO-33: A Metabolic Regulator. New York, Fuck You Press, 1965; revised edition, as *APO—33 Bulletin*, San Francisco, Beach, 1966.
So Who Owns Death TV?, with Claude Pelieu and Carl Weissner. San Francisco, Beach, 1967.
The Dead Star. San Francisco, Nova Broadcast Press, 1969.
Ali's Smile. Brighton, Unicorn, 1969.
Entretiens avec William Burroughs, by Daniel Odier. Paris, Belfond, 1969; translated as *The Job: Interviews with William S. Burroughs* (includes *Electronic Revolution*), New York, Grove Press, and London, Cape, 1970.
The Braille Film. San Francisco, Nova Broadcast Press, 1970.
Brion Gysin Let the Mice In, with Brion Gysin and Ian Somerville, edited by Jan Herman. West Glover, Vermont, Something Else Press, 1973.
Mayfair Academy Series More or Less. Brighton, Urgency Press Rip-Off, 1973.
White Subway, edited by James Pennington. London, Aloes, 1974.
The Book of Breeething. Ingatestone, Essex, OU Press, 1974; Berkeley, California, Blue Wind Press, 1975; revised edition, Blue Wind Press, 1980.
Snack: Two Tape Transcripts, with Eric Mottram. London, Aloes, 1975.
Sidetripping, with Charles Gatewood. New York, Strawberry Hill, 1975.
Ah Pook Is Here and Other Texts: The Book of Breeething, Electronic Revolution. London, Calder, 1979.

*

Bibliography: *William S. Burroughs: An Annotated Bibliography of His Words and Criticism* by Michael B. Goodman, New York, Garland, 1975; *William S. Burroughs: A Bibliography 1953-73* by Joe Maynard and Barry Miles, Charlottesville, University Press of Virginia, 1978.

Critical Study: *William Burroughs: The Algebra of Need* by Eric Mottram, New York Intrepid Press, 1971; London, Calder and Boyars, 1977.

* * *

Critical opinion regarding the work of William S. Burroughs takes an unusually wide range, from the encomiums of Norman

Mailer ("I think William Burroughs is the only American novelist living today who may conceivably be possessed by genius") and Jack Kerouac ("Burroughs is the greatest satirical writer since Jonathan Swift") to the objections of the English critic David Lodge: "Burrough has, principally, two claims on the attention of serious readers: as a moralist, and as an innovator. On both counts, it seems to me, he cannot be considered as more than a minor, eccentric figure. Undoubtedly he has a certain literary talent, particularly for comedy and the grotesque, but in both precept and practice he is deeply confused and ultimately unsatisfying." Burroughs himself has not much assisted appreciation of his work by an interview which he gave *The Paris Review* (Fall 1965) in which he declared his opposition to "the Aristotelian construct" as one of "the great shackles of Western civilisation," nor by the book-length dialogue with Daniel Odier which was published as *The Job*, where he seems determined to talk in headlines, every breath a banner, every sentence a proclamation.

Burroughs's first book, *Junkie*, is a straightforward account of his addiction to morphine. He has allowed this text to be reprinted under his own name but he does not think highly of it. Some readers, however, regard its brutal account of a man's reduction of himself to so many dope-sick cells as an achievement, a solid piece of reporting. Psychologically it is also of interest in that it contains a measure of reasonably sustained self-analysis, from which it emerges that the designation "Dope fiend" gave Burroughs a similar sense of identity to that which Genet found in being branded "Thief," and that once addicted to narcotics the author's principal pleasure lay in the monotony of relief. The book's austere equation of habit and necessity, and its unromantic description of the greyness of the addict's world commands sympathy: "The kick of junk is that you have to have it. Junkies run on junk-time and junk-metabolism. They are subject to junk-climate. They are warmed and chilled by junk. The kick of junk is living under junk conditions." Written in depressed, unpretentious, staccato prose, *Junkie* reads like a report to society from the morgue.

The Naked Lunch also begins as a first-person narrative by a drug addict, but this mode soon breaks down as Burroughs separates himself from the confines of linear discourse and moves in the direction of creating what he has called an "image-track"—that is, a sort of hallucinatory continuum where the viewpoint is in a state of *articulo mortis*. Such coherence as the text possesses is achieved through a repetition of certain phrases and certain kinds of imagery, mostly of a sensationally homosexual nature. There are passages where the narrative dislocations seem justified by the power of the satirical effect resulting, but the book's melodramatic excesses outweigh these. Mary McCarthy suggested that the latter might be derived from "withdrawal" symptoms, and *The Naked Lunch* thus considered as the nightmare of a morphine addict cut off from his drug. Such a reading has something to commend it, but if the book is then compared with another modern novel in which an attempt is made to construct a work of art upon the inferno of addiction—Malcolm Lowry's *Under the Volcano* (1947), in which the drug is alcohol—the clinically limited nature of Burroughs's achievement becomes apparent.

By the time of his next experiments in the novel form—*The Soft Machine* and *The Ticket That Exploded*—Burroughs had learned from a fellow American expatriate, Brion Gysin, a technique which led to what they termed "cut-ups." To make a cut-up demanded a minimum of creative or critical endeavour. One simply took a page with words on it, cut or tore it up, and stuck it together again, preferably with bits from other pages that might be expected to provide baffling or amusing semantic juxtapositions. Gysin himself had already achieved Solomon plus Shakespeare plus Eliot plus St. John Perse plus Aldous Huxley plus Grundig—by jumbling up choice extracts from their works on a tape-recorder and publishing the results as a poem called *The Song of Songs*. Burroughs favoured the more popular parts of James Joyce (the end of "The Dead," for instance), such Shakespeare passages as one might find in an anthology (Prospero on this insubstantial pageant, etc.), a gross of images from Rimbaud, a little Kafka, Conrad, Richard Hughes, Graham Greene, and a good deal of science fiction by less literary writers. Desiring originality, he also developed a novel-making process of his own, which he called "fold-in," involving cross-column reading and random word-play. Since it has been claimed that cut-ups were "invented" in 1881, it seems as well to point out that they are essentially just an extension of the cento technique and therefore at least as old as Ausonius or that life of Christ written by the Empress Eudoxia in lines taken from Homer. There is even a precedent for their name in the work of a 6th-century grammarian, Vergilius Maro, who wrote a series of 15 epitomae on the more unusual literary experiments of his contemporaries. Number 13 is devoted to "Ars Scissendi"—the Art of Cutting Up—and is in all important respects a fair description of what Burroughs does today. According to Vergilius Maro, the ultimate here was achieved by one Galbungus, who chopped up a sentence until it began: PPPP. PPP.RRR.RRR.LM.SSS.

There is nothing quite as impenetrable as this in *Nova Express*, but as a folded-in "composite of many writers living and dead" it remains Burroughs's most opaque and difficult text, a series of syntactic manipulations that only infrequently add up to anything as social as a sentence. Of this author's work in general it may be said that he has a savage sense of comedy, and a cleverly educated ear for the casual but haunting phrase ("So pack your ermines, Mary"). There is also a certain compulsive private rhythm in his writing—see the way he keeps returning to the fragments about Lykin, and the Old Doctor you can't call twice, as well as Mary and her ermines, not just in *Nova Express* but in *The Ticket That Exploded* and *Dead Fingers Talk* as well.

—Robert Nye

BURROWAY, Janet (Gay). American. Born in Tucson, Arizona, 21 September 1936. Educated at the University of Arizona, Tucson, 1954-55; Barnard College, New York, B.A. 1958; Cambridge University, B.A. 1960, M.A. 1965; Yale School of Drama, New Haven, Connecticut, 1960-61. Married 1) Walter Eysselinck in 1961 (divorced, 1973); two children; 2) William Dean Humphries in 1978. Supply teacher and music director, Binghamton public schools, New York, 1961-63; Lecturer in American Studies, University of Sussex, Brighton, 1965-72; Assistant to the Writing Program, University of Illinois, Urbana, 1972. Associate Professor, 1972-77, and since 1977, Professor of English, Florida State University, Tallahassee. Visiting Lecturer, Writers Workshop, University of Iowa, Iowa City, 1980. Recipient: Amoco Award, for teaching, 1974; National Endowment for the Arts grant, 1976. Agent: Jed Mattes, International Creative Management Inc., 1301 Avenue of the Americas, New York, New York 10019. Address: 240 De Soto Street, Tallahassee, Florida 32303, U.S.A.

PUBLICATIONS

Novels

Descend Again. London, Faber, 1960.
The Dancer from the Dance. London, Faber, 1965; Boston, Little Brown, 1968.
Eyes. London, Faber, and Boston, Little Brown, 1966.
The Buzzards. Boston, Little Brown, 1969; London, Faber, 1970.
Raw Silk. Boston, Little Brown, and London, Gollancz, 1977.

Plays

The Fantasy Level (produced Brighton, Sussex, 1968).

The Beauty Operators (produced Brighton, Sussex, 1968).
Poenulus; or, The Little Carthaginian, adaptation of a play by Plautus, in *Five Roman Comedies*, edited by Palmer Boive. New York, Dutton, 1970.

Television Play: *Hoddinott Veiling*, 1970.

Verse

But to the Season. Weston super Mare, Somerset, Universities' Poetry, 1961.
Material Goods. Tallahasee, University Presses of Florida, 1981.

Other

The Truck on the Track (juvenile). London, Cape, 1970; Indianapolis, Bobbs Merrill, 1971.
The Giant Ham Sandwich (verse only; juvenile), with John Vernon Lord. London, Cape, 1972; Boston, Houghton Mifflin, 1973.

*

Manuscript Collection: Florida State University, Tallahassee.

* * *

Janet Burroway depicts contemporary social issues through multiple points-of-view to convey strong, and sometimes nebulous, moral messages. Complicated relationships are neatly interconnected within sharply defined domestic and urban settings, as contrasting characters try to work out crises of conscience. The author's penchant for epigrams and symbols further unifies her narratives, but at the cost of excessive, self-conscious rhetoric. Likewise, while her abrupt and usually ambiguous endings avoid blatant didacticism, they also seriously mar the proportions of her careful structures. Stories do not seem to conclude so much as merely come to a halt. She also favors theatrical surprises which do not proceed necessarily from exigencies of plot but facilely exploit the sensational. These linguistic artifices and narrative ploys intrude more than they enlighten, weakening her otherwise admirable craftsmanship. Burroway's novels are well-paced, however, and she further enhances their popular appeal by providing plenty of practical information.

Eyes views the problems of race prejudice and of ethics in medicine and journalism through the individual perspectives of the four principal characters. Set in the South, the novel examines one day in the life of Dr. Rugg, an eye surgeon; his wife Maeve, who is pregnant at 40; their somewhat estranged son Hilary, a liberal reporter on a conservative paper; and Hilary's fiancée Jadeen, a junior high school teacher. Skillfully Burroway evokes the Southern atmosphere and delineates the elaborate rituals of black-white relations as enacted by her sensitive protagonists. As a newly liberal and insecure daughter of an old Southern family, Jadeen's dilemma becomes acute: to refuse to teach an outrageously biased textbook and thus lose her job and alienate her genteel but bigotted mother, or to cave in and betray her recent convictions and lose her fiancé. Dr. Rugg, awkward in his charity and family relations and preoccupied in his profession, unwittingly destroys his career by casually mentioning his war-time experiments. Hilary, frustrated in his job and resentful of his famous father, carelessly misses the major scandal his father's seemingly innocuous lecture turns out to be—ironically, sent out on the national wires by Dodds, Rugg's soon-to-be-blind patient—which costs him and his mentor their positions. No totally satisfactory solution to these complications is possible. But Rugg heroically refuses to recant to save face for the State Department, and he serenely awaits his final heart-attack. Hilary, given a last chance, refuses to compromise his principles, or betray his father. Jadeen, however, is not strong enough for the sacrifice and buckles under to the "system"; she resigns herself (somewhat illogically) to being a subservient, dull teacher, without Hilary. Only Maeve, always understanding if inarticulate, and calm, maintains stability amid the domestic chaos. At the end, Jadeen points a moral of sorts: "Thoughts are complex. Actions are not. That is the subject of tragedy." Burroway's vignettes are telling, especially when she describes racial tension in a black bar or the techniques of surgery, reporting, teaching. But that's the rub: she prefers to tell more than to show. Dialogue is often wooden, and despite the neat plotting, the separate thematic strands don't quite mesh. The melodrama ends slightly out of focus.

The Dancer from the Dance is an ambitious and often subtle attempt at a novel of manners, in which the young, strangely innocent yet wise Prytania naively brings about the destruction and near-collapse of the older and more sophisticated people irresistibly drawn to her. 60-year-old Powers, the sensitive but detached narrator, gives the hapless girl a job in his UNICEF office in Paris and entrée into his elegant world. Soon Prytania holds all in thrall. Stoddard, a young and unimaginative medical student, she leads on but finally cannot marry. Old Riebenstahl, a primitive sculptor and curious sage, finally commits suicide, because he has acted as go-between for her illicit affair with the talented mime Jean-Claude. Even the worldly wise Mme. de Verbois, with whom she stays, and finally Powers himself are cruelly touched by her strange power. The nuances of social behavior, the curious transformations of character, and the complex emotional entanglements are deftly portrayed in several delicately drawn scenes. Yet, for all that, Prytania remains a shadowy figure, and the narrative barely escapes incredibility. Further, although the pages are cluttered with more witticisms and aphorisms than a Restoration comedy, the general tone is more that of a middling French film about yet another blighted romance. The several ironies and crises come off as contrived and formulaic, and ultimately the novel sadly disappoints: such an anticlimax after so much art.

In *The Buzzards* Burroway turns to the political realm, employing, yet again, several narrators. But as we follow the campaign trail of Alex, the conservative but likeable Senator from Arizona, the multiple perspectives—interior monologues, set speeches, newspaper articles, letters—soon become redundant and tedious. Especially so are the fatuous epigrams which clog the journal of the sententious and most implausible manager, Galcher (he calls them Axioms of God; e.g., "We are not subtle enough to contrive a machine in which disintegration contributes to maintenance and manufacture"). Alex's cold, brittle, and marvelously inept wife, his disaffected son, and neurotic daughter Eleanor (whose near-suicide and Mexican abortion pose serious threats to his chances), like the "allegorical" Galcher, are definite liabilities—not only for Alex but for the reader, who has little reason to be interested in them, let alone to like them. Younger daughter Evie, a vivacious, all-American, plastic pom-pom girl, is equally off-putting, though depicted as an asset in Alex's uphill struggle for re-election. Nonetheless, Burroway still has incisive power to reveal the moral ambiguities, contradictions, and rationalizations of her characters, especially the women. But beyond showing the hectic pace and many stratagems of modern politicking, the novel's rationale is not quite clear. And when Evie is precipitously assassinated in the last few pages, the event seems not tragic but merely expedient in terminating a journey that has no real destination. That a writer of Janet Burroway's obvious talents in use of detail and perspective should ultimately be defeated by a lack of control or malfunction of these very elements is an unfortunate irony of her otherwise impressive work.

—Joseph Parisi

BUSCH, Frederick. American. Born in Brooklyn, New York, 1 August 1941. Educated at Muhlenberg College, Allentown, Pennsylvania, 1958-62, A.B. 1962; Columbia University, New York (Woodrow Wilson Fellow, 1962), 1962-63, M.A. 1967. Married Judith Burroughs in 1963; two sons. Writer and Editor, North American Précis Syndicate, New York, 1964-65, and *School Management* magazine, Greenwich, Connecticut, 1965-66. Instructor, 1966-67, Assistant Professor, 1968-72, Associate Professor, 1973-76, and since 1976, Professor of English, Colgate University, Hamilton, New York. Recipient: National Endowment for the Arts grant, 1976. Agent: Dorothy Pittman, Illington Road, Ossining, New York 10562. Address: P.O. Box 63, Poolville, New York, 13432, U.S.A.

PUBLICATIONS

Novels

I Wanted a Year Without Fall. London, Calder and Boyars, 1971.
Manual Labor. New York, New Directions, 1974.
The Mutual Friend. New York, Harper, and Hassocks, Sussex, Harvester Press, 1978.
Rounds. New York, Farrar Straus, and London, Hamish Hamilton, 1980.

Short Stories

Breathing Trouble and Other Stories. London, Calder and Boyars, 1974.
Domestic Particulars: A Family Chronicle. New York, New Directions, 1976; Hassocks, Sussex, Harvester Press, 1979.
Hardwater Country. New York, Knopf, 1979.

Other

Hawkes: A Guide to His Fictions. Syracuse, New York, Syracuse University Press, 1973.

*

Frederick Busch comments:

It is difficult for me to make a prefatory statement about my own work—there's too much to say, and probably very little of it actually needs to be said. I write about characters who I want to matter more than my own theories (as if I really had any) and more than my own delights. The great problem is to be brave enough to face the fullest implications of one's visions, insights, fears—and to sustain the energy to make a usable shape from those visions. No: the great problem is to sit and write something worthy of the people on the page, and the good reader.

* * *

Imagine the sincerity of Thomas Wolfe and the cynicism of the Scott Fitzgerald who wrote the Pat Hobby stories rolled into one and blessed with perfect pitch in the matter of dialogue, and you have an idea of the potential displayed to date by the young American novelist Frederick Busch. His first novel, highly amusing and beautifully written, *I Wanted a Year Without Fall*, is an adventure with words and speech rhythms. It is also an updating of the Old English poem *Beowulf*—flotsam and jetsam of that mythology float on the surface of Busch's narrative and his characters clutch at them in search of a meaning for what they say and do. It is above all a very well observed *visual* comedy about modern manners—it would make a splendid film, not least because some of its techniques (and Busch has this in common with Joyce) seem to be derived from the cinema.

Busch's second novel, *Manual Labor*, has so far appeared only in an American edition. (In passing one might add a note that this is disgraceful when so much trash is peddled one way or the other by publishers holding hands across the Atlantic.) It is a dry, grim, chilling book, more powerful and painful than *I Wanted a Year Wihtout Fall*, but again something of a stylistic *tour de force*. Everything is seen coldly and from outside; there are many precise and desperate descriptions of physical activity; the rhythms of people working with their hands dictate the sentence rhythms of the prose. The setting is New Hampshire. The people described are Anne and Phil Sorenson, mother and father of a child lost in the ninth month of Anne's pregnancy. The describing voice is in the most moving passages the voice of that child, although the section comprising Anne's monologue—a rambling letter to her mother—is also well achieved. Phil's part in the telling of the story provides the book's prescription for itself, for he writes: "What I must do is be simple and clear. I'm sure that narrative leads to sanity, and slowly, carefully, chiseling the details, I must make what's happening come from what's happened."

He succeeds, and Busch succeeds, because here is a young writer not trying to push thoughts or advertise feelings, or demonstrate his own originality, nor even derange, rearrange, or otherwise bugger up sensibility. Busch follows instead what Auden recommended as the only true path for a young poet: he hangs around words, he listens to hear what they have to say. With the difference that he is very much a prose writer, a storyteller, a syncopater of narratives.

—Robert Nye

BYATT, A(ntonia) S(usan). British. Born in Sheffield, Yorkshire, 24 August 1936; sister of Margaret Drabble, *q.v.* Educated at Newnham College, Cambridge, B.A. (honours) in English, 1957; Bryn Mawr College, Pennsylvania (English Speaking Union Fellowship), 1957-58; Somerville College, Oxford, 1958-59, B.A. Married 1) C.R. Byatt in 1959; 2) Peter J. Duffy in 1969; three children. Taught at Westminster Tutors, 1962-65; part-time lecturer, Central School of Art and Design, London, 1965-69. Extra-Mural Lecturer, 1962-71, and since 1972, Lecturer in English, University College, University of London. Regular reviewer, *The Times* and *New Statesman*, both London. Recipient: Arts Council grant, 1968. Address: 37 Rusholme Road, London S.W. 15, England.

PUBLICATIONS

Novels

Shadow of a Sun. London, Chatto and Windus, and New York, Harcourt Brace, 1964.
The Game. London, Chatto and Windus, 1967; New York, Scribner, 1968.
The Virgin in the Garden. London, Chatto and Windus, 1978; New York, Knopf, 1979.

Uncollected Short Story

"Daniel," in *Encounter* (London), April 1976.

Other

Degrees of Freedom: The Novels of Iris Murdoch. London, Chatto and Windus, and New York, Barnes and Noble, 1965.
Wordsworth and Coleridge in Their Time. London, Nelson, 1970; New York, Crane Russak, 1973.
Iris Murdoch. London, Longman, 1976.

Editor, *The Mill on the Floss*, by George Eliot. London, Penguin, 1979.

*

A.S. Byatt comments:

My novels are about habits of thought and imagination: the quartet I am writing combines a partly parodic "realist" first and last volumes, with a more experimental second and third.

* * *

Although A.S. Byatt is among the best-known literary figures in England today, she has published only three creative (as opposed to critical) books—all novels—since her writing career began nearly 20 years ago. Until the publication of her third novel, *The Virgin in the Garden*, in 1978, her reputation owed more to her scholarly and critical writing, including the first book-length study of Iris Murdoch, *Degrees of Freedom*, and to the high quality of her literary journalism and reviewing than to her fiction; this was somewhat overshadowed by the very popular output of her younger and more prolific sister, Margaret Drabble. However, with *The Virgin in the Garden*, Byatt's first novel in over a decade and one of the most impressive works of English fiction in the second half of the 1970's, she has established herself as an important novelist in her own right.

Byatt's first two novels are much less ambitious than *The Virgin in the Garden*, but both are substantial books, and they reveal a development towards the fusion of realism and symbolism in her most recent work. *Shadow of a Sun*, her first work of fiction, is essentially a straightforward piece of orthodox realism, whereas *The Game* makes extensive use of mythical and symbolic elements within a realistic framework.

The action of *Shadow of a Sun*—the title comes from a Ralegh poem—takes place in the shadow cast by Henry Severell, a major English novelist of visionary intensity who is prone to bouts of manic insanity. His teenage daughter, Anna, is the character most dominated by his overpowering personality, and the novel explores Anna's attempt to define herself as an independent being by liberating herself from parental, especially paternal, control and from her own conventionality. The book is a kind of *bildungsroman*, tracing Anna's development from a very immature schoolgirl, who makes a protest by running away from school, to a Cambridge undergraduate made pregnant by one of her father's friends and most enthusiastic critics, Oliver Canning. In the inconclusive and open-ended final chapter, Anna, having rejected the possibility of a marriage of convenience with a well-to-do, kind-hearted, and mother-dominated fellow-student, asserts her new-found independence and maturity, and confronts the future.

Despite its ample scale, *Shadow of a Sun* concentrates on a very small, tightly knit group of characters, Henry Severell and his wife, Oliver Canning and his wife, and Anna herself. Byatt's second novel, *The Game*, is less claustrophobic in this respect, taking in a much wider spectrum of characters, from academics at Oxford and a Quaker community in Northumberland to fashionable television people in London and a homeless problem family. This range is one reason for the novel being more impressive than its predecessor, although there are obvious resemblances: a novelist is again a major participant, for example, and the erosion of a marriage features prominently. At the heart of *The Game* is the complex and basically antagonistic relationship between two sisters in their thirties, the unmarried Cassandra Corbett, an Oxford don specializing in medieval romance literature, and Julia Eskelund (her husband is Norwegian), a popular novelist who writes about the problems of contemporary women. Cassandra, a convert to Anglo-Catholicism from her family's Quakerism, is other-worldly; Julia, who becomes a participant in a regular arts programme on television and also has an affair with the producer, is decidedly modish. The game that gives the book its title is their elaborate Brontë-like childhood invention, which had literary analogues and opened up an entire imaginary world. Indeed, Cassandra, unlike her much more down-to-earth sister, still lives to a considerable extent in the realm of the imagination and has only a tenuous grasp of reality; the Arthurian imagery and symbolism—she is actually editing Malory—help to convey this. It is the re-entry into their lives of another party of their shared childhood experience, the now-famous zoologist and television personality Simon Moffitt, that revitalizes their teenage conflict over him and leads to Julia rapidly writing a cruel novel based on Cassandra and Simon. This in turn precipitates the tragic denouement of Byatt's novel with a mortally humiliated Cassandra finally retreating completely from reality by killing herself. Sibling rivalry finally culminates in death 20 years later. While the surface of *The Game* is realistic, Byatt introduces a mythic level by cleverly employing the symbolism of the Garden of Eden in relation to her characters; Simon's snakes, for example, clearly bring to mind the serpent.

Although substantially larger in scale than either of its predecessors, *The Virgin in the Garden* is but the first novel in a planned tetralogy, which promises to be one of the most ambitious fictional undertakings of the postwar period, comparable to Lawrence Durrell's *Alexandria Quartet*, Doris Lessing's *The Children of Violence*, and Anthony Powell's *A Dance to the Music of Time*. The tetralogy is intended to follow the lives of a group of characters during the second Elizabethan age, from the accession of the Queen in 1952 until the major Post-Impressionist Exhibition held in London in 1980, but each novel, while advancing the chronology, is expected to be technically and stylistically distinctive.

After a short but complex and symbolically rich Prologue set in 1968, *The Virgin in the Garden* narrates events in 1952-53, with occasional and brief forward-flashes that illuminate the characters from the advantageous perspective of hindsight. The novel, set in North Yorkshire, mainly in and around a public school, concentrates on the three children of the senior English master, Bill Potter, and the person each of them is most involved with: the eldest, Stephanie, a schoolteacher, and the curate she marries, much to the annoyance of her militantly agnostic father; Frederica, a brilliant and precocious schoolgirl, and the English teacher, poet, and playwright Alexander Wedderburn she falls in love with; the strange schoolboy, Marcus, and the biology teacher, a religious maniac, with whom he indulges in a lunatic, quasi-spiritual experiment.

One of the things the novel captures best is the festive atmosphere of Coronation year with its sense of promise and rebirth, of release from postwar privations, of a new Elizabethan age with just as much potentiality as that of the first Elizabeth. A main strand of the book is the production of Alexander's verse play about the Virgin queen, *Astraea*, in the garden of an Elizabethan country house—hence the title, although it also refers to Frederica, another virgin until the closing pages. The novel is, in fact, full of quotations and literary and mythological allusions, and is concerned with both English history and the English cultural tradition, themes that will no doubt be developed in subsequent novels. While *The Virgin in the Garden* possesses an almost Victorian leisureliness in its depiction of detail and its analysis of characters, it is also a decidedly modernist work in the wake of *Ulysses*, since its meticulous realism is fused with symbolism.

—Peter Lewis

CADE, Robin. *See* **NICOLE, Christopher.**

CALDER-MARSHALL, Arthur. British. Born in Wallington, Surrey, 19 August 1908. Educated at St. Paul's School, 1920-27; Hertford College, Oxford, B.A. 1930. Married Violet Nancy Sales in 1934; two daughters. Schoolmaster, Denstone College, Staffordshire, 1931-33; Scriptwriter, MGM, Hollywood, 1937; served in the Petroleum Warfare Department, 1941, and in the Films Division of the Ministry of Information, London, 1942-45. Fellow, Royal Society of Literature, 1958. Address: c/o Elaine Greene Ltd., 31 Newington Green, London N16 9PW, England.

PUBLICATIONS

Novels

Two of a Kind. London, Cape, 1933.
About Levy. London, Cape, 1933; New York, Scribner, 1934.
At Sea. London, Cape, and New York, Scribner, 1934.
Dead Centre. London, Cape, 1935.
Pie in the Sky. London, Cape, and New York, Scribner, 1937.
The Way to Santiago. London, Cape, and New York, Reynal, 1940.
A Man Reprieved. London, Cape, 1949.
Occasion of Glory. London, Cape, 1955.
The Scarlet Boy. London, Hart Davis, 1961; New York, Harper, 1962.

Short Stories

A Crime Against Cania. London, Golden Cockerel Press, 1934.
A Pink Doll. London, Grayson, 1935.
A Date with a Duchess and Other Stories. London, Cape, 1937.

Uncollected Short Stories

"Home Is Where You Are Right Now," in *Life and Letters* (London), November 1938.
"The Cap and the Bantam," in *Horizon* (London), Spring 1940.
"Before the War," in *English Story*, edited by Woodrow and Jane Wyatt. London, Collins, 1941.
"On Account of an Overcoat," in *English Story 4*, edited by Woodrow Wyatt. London, Collins, 1943.
"The Return to the Insect World," in *Modern Reading 15*, edited by Reginald Moore. London, Phoenix House, 1947.
"Now It Is the World," in *The Pick of Today's Short Stories*, edited by John Pudney. London, Odhams Press, 1950.
"El Bobito," in *Pick of Today's Short Stories 4*, edited by John Pudney. London, Putnam, 1953.
"Iain of the Islands," in *Pick of Today's Short Stories 10*, edited by John Pudney. London, Putnam, 1959.

Plays

Screenplays and Commentary (documentaries): *To-day and Tomorrow*; *The Nine Hundred*; *Broken Dykes*; *The Last Shot*; *The Star and the Sand*; *The Bridge*; *The World Is Rich*; *The Miner's Window*.

Other

Challenge to Schools: A Pamphlet on Public School Education. London, Hogarth Press, 1935.
The Changing Scene. London, Chapman and Hall, 1937.
Glory Dead (travel). London, Joseph, 1939.
The Watershed (travel). London, Contact, 1947.
The Book Front. London, Lane, 1947.
The Magic of My Youth (autobiography). London, Hart Davis, 1951.
No Earthly Command, Being an Enquiry into the Life of Vice-Admiral the Reverend Alexander Riall Woodham Woods. London, Hart Davis, 1957.
The Man from Devil's Island (juvenile). London, Hart Davis, 1958.
The Fair to Middling (juvenile). London, Hart Davis, 1959.
Havelock Ellis: A Biography. London, Hart Davis, 1959; as *The Sage of Sex: A Life of Havelock Ellis*, New York, Putnam, 1960.
Lone Wolf: The Story of Jack London (juvenile). London, Methuen, 1961; New York, Duell, 1962.
The Enthusiast: An Enquiry into the Life of the Rev. Joseph Leycester Lyne, alias Fr. Ignatius. London, Faber, 1962.
The Innocent Eye: The Life of Robert J. Flaherty. London, W.H. Allen, 1963; New York, Harcourt Brace, 1966.
Wish You Were Here: The Art of Donald McGill. London, Hutchinson, 1966.
Lewd, Blasphemous and Obscene: Being the Trials and Tribulations of Sundry Founding Fathers of Today's Alternative Societies. London, Hutchinson, 1972.
The Grand Century of the Lady 1720-1820. London, Gordon and Cremonesi, and New York, Atheneum, 1976.
The Two Duchesses. London, Hutchinson, and New York, Harper, 1978.

Editor, *Selected Writings*, by Smollett. London, Falcon Press, 1950.
Editor, *The Bodley Head Jack London.* London, Bodley Head, 4 vols., 1963-66; as *The Pan Jack London*, London, Pan, 2 vols., 1966-68.
Editor, *Prepare to Shed Them Now: The Ballads of George R. Sims.* London, Hutchinson, 1968.

*

Arthur Calder-Marshall comments:

I regard myself as an author rather than as a novelist, who writes other things on the side. At least for me, my work is a whole, part of an attempt to understand the nature, meaning and purpose of the universe in which we live. The course I have taken has been tortuous, and since I have never written two books about the same subject or with the same object, my work may appear contradictory to others, though to me it is psychologically consistent, and even logically defensible.

The older I grow, the more conscious I become of the enormous amount there is to learn and the impossibility of saying anything that can be regarded as absolutely true. Rather than finding this cause for pessimism, which I might have when young, I am consoled by the thought that if I can either create or discover something which now or later will give someone pleasure, amusement or food for thought, I can be pardoned the self-indulgence of my greatest delight, putting words on paper.

* * *

Arthur Calder-Marshall's work has ranged from a pamphlet on public school education to the four volume Bodley Head edition of Jack London. He is representative of the best characteristics of the professional writer; his work as a writer of fiction is only a part—in fact a rather small part—of his whole list of publications, titles which include biography, criticism, books of travel, and a series of juveniles, as well as the fiction designed for adults. Over a period of 30 years, from 1932 to 1961, he published nine novels and three collections of short stories, using a wide variety of techniques to set out an equally wide variety of themes and characters.

In general, Calder-Marshall presents his characters as exploring their own individual needs and values in the context of the conventional English social structure. In *Two of a Kind* both father and daughter misjudge the people they fall in love with because neither father nor daughter can reconcile passion with idealism. The characters in *About Levy* condemn him not by the establishment of abstract justice but by the way they respond to him and the account of his trial. The young couple in *At Sea* are on their honeymoon, and the lonely and frightening hours they spend together become for them a review of their past life, an attempt to realize themselves as unique, and at the same time to become one as man and wife. Their failure to do any of these things creates within them despair amounting to spiritual death and rebirth as they are rescued.

Dead Centre, *Pie in the Sky*, and *A Man Reprieved* are directly concerned with the familiar structure of English society. *Dead Centre* examines the world of the small public school from some sixty different points of view, showing clearly the pettiness, the shoddiness, the inefficiency, indeed downright hypocrisy, of the masters and the utter confusion of their charges. The very slight series of incidents—the homesickness of the younger boys; the death of Jeffers, killed on the "tackling machine"; the terror of George who runs away because he thinks he has got the servant girl pregnant—serve as a frame for a number of memorable characterizations. *Pie in the Sky* includes a cross section of several groups of contrasting English character types. There is the mill owner, Carder Yorke, and his two sons, Bernard, weak and ineffectual, and Fenner, a dabbler in socialism and journalism. All three, Carder and his two sons, share an interest in Wynne Morris, an honest and forthright barmaid. There are the Boltons—mother, father and daughter. They represent the best of the working-folk tradition even though the father has lost his job as the daughter loses her school teaching post. Along with these there are the party leaders and members in the communist party of post-World War I in England. The elaborate scheme of the relationship of these various characters makes up the theme of the novel. At the conclusion whatever their adventures have been the characters all settle into the usual middle-class system of their world. The whole of the novel is presented in a kind of gentle, ironic fashion. *A Man Reprieved*, set in London just after the second World War, is about people with somewhat more education and financial security, but the structure of society is as rigid as that in *Pie in the Sky*. Julius Akens, a journalist returning to London quite disillusioned about war, does manage to become "a man reprieved" from his stuffy middle-class marriage but not without much uncertainty.

Two of the novels are set in Mexico. *The Way to Santiago* takes place just before the beginning of the second World War and is the story of the murder of a journalist and the curious fanaticism of a dedicated German fascist. Lionel Transit, the German, remarks that "journalists are the yeast of life. They leaven the dough of common events into the bread which is news." This quotation, in fact, describes the novel. *Occasion of Glory* is set in an imaginary Mexican tourist resort. It spans the week of Easter and suggests a kind of parallel to the sacrifice and death of Christ in the death of Alberto Rivera, whose story and that of his family is told in a chapter entitled "An Indian Who Might Be Jesus." The suggested modern myth is in no way successful, however, and the symbols are meaningless. In fact the book is so obviously "message"-filled that it is difficult to fit into a discussion of the other complex, sophisticated novels Calder-Marshall has done.

Perhaps the most notable characteristic of Calder-Marshall as a writer of fiction is his dramatic and skillful use of various techniques to present his material. *Dead Centre, About Levy*, and *At Sea* are all three highly unconventional in their use of point of view. *Dead Centre* is divided into sixty-seven sections, each told in first person point of view, thus leaving the reader to draw his own conclusions from a point at "dead centre." Levy never appears in the novel about his trial and conviction for murder. *At Sea* employs a modified stream of consciousness technique to advance the plot as well as set out character and theme.

Arthur Calder-Marshall is distinguished as a writer, not merely as a novelist. His fiction is an important part of his work as a whole, however, especially as it gives the reader, interested in the novel from 1930 onwards in our century, the opportunity to examine a master craftsman at work.

—Annibel Jenkins

CALDWELL, Erskine (Preston). American. Born in Moreland, Georgia, 17 December 1903. Educated at Erskine College, Due West, South Carolina, 1920-21; University of Virginia, Charlottesville, 1922, 1925-26; University of Pennsylvania, Philadelphia, 1924. Married 1) Helen Lannigan in 1925 (divorced), two sons and one daughter; 2) the photographer Margaret Bourke-White in 1939 (divorced, 1942); 3) June Johnson in 1942, one son; 4) Virginia Moffett in 1957. Reporter, *Atlanta Journal*, Georgia, 1925; screenwriter in Hollywood, 1930-34, 1942-43; foreign correspondent in Mexico, Spain, Czechoslovakia, Russia, and China, 1938-41; Editor, American Folkways series, 1941-55. Recipient: *Yale Review* award, 1933. Member, American Academy. Agent: McIntosh and Otis, 475 Fifth Avenue, New York, New York 10017. Address: P.O. Box 4550, Hopi Station, Scottsdale, Arizona 85258, U.S.A.

PUBLICATIONS

Novels

The Bastard. New York, Heron Press, 1930.
Poor Fool. New York, Rariora Press, 1930.
Tobacco Road. New York, Scribner, 1932; London, Cresset Press, 1933.
God's Little Acre. New York, Viking Press, and London, Secker, 1933.
Journeyman. New York, Viking Press, 1935; revised edition, Viking Press, and London, Secker, 1938.
Trouble in July. New York, Duell, and London, Cape, 1940.
All Night Long: A Novel of Guerrilla Warfare in Russia. New York, Duell, 1942; London, Cassell, 1943.
Tragic Ground. New York, Duell, 1944; London, Falcon Press, 1947.
A House in the Uplands. New York, Duell, 1946; London, Falcon Press, 1947.
The Sure Hand of God. New York, Duell, 1947; London, Falcon Press, 1949.
This Very Earth. New York, Duell, 1948; London, Falcon Press, 1949.
Place Called Estherville. New York, Duell, 1949; London, Falcon Press, 1951.
Episode in Palmetto. New York, Duell, 1950; London, Falcon Press, 1951.
A Lamp for Nightfall. New York, Duell, and London, Falcon Press, 1952.
Love and Money. New York, Duell, 1954; London, Heinemann, 1955.
Gretta. Boston, Little Brown, 1955; London, Heinemann, 1956.
Claudelle Inglish. Boston, Little Brown, 1959; as *Claudell*, London, Heinemann, 1959.
Jenny by Nature. New York, Farrar Straus, and London, Heinemann, 1961.
Close to Home. New York, Farrar Straus, and London, Heinemann, 1962.
The Bastard, and Poor Fool. London, Bodley Head, 1963.
The Last Night of Summer. New York, Farrar Straus, and London, Heinemann, 1963.
Miss Mamma Aimee. New York, New American Library, 1967; London, Joseph, 1968.
Summertime Island. Cleveland, World, 1968; London, Joseph, 1969.
The Weather Shelter. Cleveland, World, 1969; London, Joseph, 1970.
The Earnshaw Neighborhood. Cleveland, World, 1971; London, Joseph, 1972.
Annette. New York, New American Library, 1973; London, Joseph, 1974.

Short Stories

American Earth. New York, Scribner, 1931; London, Secker, 1935; as *A Swell-Looking Girl*, New York, New American Library, 1951.
Mama's Little Girl. Privately printed, 1932.
A Message for Genevieve. Privately printed, 1933.
We Are the Living: Brief Stories. New York, Viking Press, 1933; London, Secker, 1934.
Kneel to the Rising Sun and Other Stories. New York, Viking Press, 1935; London, Heinemann, 1961.
The Sacrilege of Alan Kent. Portland, Maine, Falmouth Book House, 1936.
Southways. New York, Viking Press, 1938; London, Falcon Press, 1953.
Jackpot: The Short Stories of Erskine Caldwell. New York, Duell, 1940; London, Falcon Press, 1950; abridged edition, as *Midsummer Passion*, New York, Avon, 1948.
Georgia Boy. New York, Duell, 1943; London, Falcon Press, 1947.
A Day's Wooing and Other Stories. New York, Grosset and Dunlap, 1944.
Stories by Erskine Caldwell: 24 Representative Stories, edited by Henry Seidel Canby. New York, Duell, 1944; as *The Pocket Book of Erskine Caldwell*, New York, Pocket Books, 1947.
A Woman in the House. New York, New American Library, 1949.
The Humorous Side of Erskine Caldwell, edited by Robert Cantwell. New York, Duell, 1951; as *Where the Girls Are Different and Other Stories*, New York, New American Library, 1962.
The Courting of Susie Brown. New York, Duell, and London, Falcon Press, 1952.
The Complete Stories. New York, Duell, 1953.
Gulf Coast Stories. Boston, Little Brown, 1956; London, Heinemann, 1957.
Certain Women. Boston, Little Brown, 1957; London, Heinemann, 1958.
When You Think of Me. Boston, Little Brown, 1959; London, Heinemann, 1960.
Men and Women: 22 Stories. Boston, Little Brown, 1961; London, Heinemann, 1963.

Plays

Screenplays: *A Nation Dances* (documentary), 1943; *Volcano*, 1953.

Other

In Defense of Myself. Privately printed, 1930.
Tenant Farmer. New York, Phalanx Press, 1935.
Some American People. New York, McBride, 1935.
You Have Seen Their Faces, photographs by Margaret Bourke-White. New York, Viking Press, 1937.
North of the Danube, photographs by Margaret Bourke-White. New York, Viking Press, 1939.
Say! Is This the U.S.A.?, photographs by Margaret Bourke-White. New York, Duell, 1951.
All-Out on the Road to Smolensk. New York, Duell, 1942; as *Moscow Under Fire: A Wartime Diary, 1941*, London, Hutchinson, 1942.
Russia at War, photographs by Margaret Bourke-White. New York and London, Hutchinson, 1942.
The Caldwell Caravan: Novels and Stories. Cleveland, World, 1946.
Call It Experience: The Years of Learning How to Write. New York, Duell, 1951; London, Hutchinson, 1952.
Molly Cottontail (juvenile). Boston, Little Brown, 1958; London, Heinemann, 1959.
Around About America. New York, Farrar Straus, and London, Heinemann, 1964.
In Search of Bisco. New York, Farrar Straus, and London, Heinemann, 1965.
The Deer at Our House (juvenile) New York, Collier, and London, Collier Macmillan, 1966.
In the Shadow of the Steeple. London, Heinemann, 1966.
Writing in America. New York, Phaedra, 1967.
Deep South: Memory and Observation (includes *In the Shadow of the Steeple*). New York, Weybright and Talley, 1968.
Afternoons in Mid-America: Observations and Impressions. New York, Dodd Mead, 1976.

*

Manuscript Collection: Baker Library, Dartmouth College, Hanover, New Hampshire.

Critical Studies: *The Southern Poor White from Lubberland to Tobacco Road* by Shields McIlwaine, Norman, University of Oklahoma Press, 1939; *Erskine Caldwell* by James Korges, Minneapolis, University of Minnesota Press, 1969; *Black Like It Is/ Was: Erskine Caldwell's Treatment of Racial Themes* by William A. Sutton, Metuchen, New Jersey, Scarecrow Press, 1974.

* * *

Balzac notoriously claimed that anyone wanting to know trades, manners, or business in the France of his time could learn about them by reading his novels. Erskine Caldwell, good as some of his novels are, is not Balzac's equal; precious few writers are. Yet the social historian as well as the literary critic will in the future turn to Caldwell's novels finding in them a representation of the Southern region of the United States, a representation in its own way unequalled by the other great writers of the region—Flannery O'Connor, William Faulkner, R. P. Warren, Eudora Welty, and others. For Caldwell has been observing and writing for longer than any other great writer in the region, his novels taken as a whole coming to produce one of the most fascinating measures of the life and times, attitudes and temperaments of the area. One has only to set the recent *The Weather Shelter* beside the earlier *Trouble in July* to have one of the most graphic and moving indications of the changes taking place in the Southern region of the United States. Indeed, in his autobiography of his public career, *Call It Experience*, Caldwell suggests that his novels form a "cyclorama of the South." To argue for long in this manner, however, would seem to indicate that Caldwell's novels are a mere adjunct to social studies (sometimes called "science"). Caldwell closely observes the social scene, but he is also a literary artist of high quality and the author of some splendid novels.

This brief essay is not the place to consider the wide range of his achievements as a writer—and indeed as editor of the invaluable *American Folkways* series of regional books. His achievements in reporting and analysis would alone place him in the front rank of contemporary prose writers in the English language. I have written elsewhere (*Erskine Caldwell*, University of Minnesota Press) about Caldwell's tact and his success in the forms of biography and autobiography. In each mode he undertook a very difficult subject. His biographical writing ranges from scaldingly satirical chapters in, especially, his early political, social, and economic commentary, to the tender and affecting memoir of his father, a well-known Presbyterian minister, which is full of sentiment without being sentimental—surely one of the most difficult kinds of writing. In the autobiographical mode, Caldwell undertook to write about the most banned and censored writer of his time, without being vindictive; and at the same time about the most financially successful writer of his time, without being pompous. As in his autobiography he keeps this perilous balance between self-justification and righteous scorn, so in his travel books he is both objective in his reports yet compassionate; and his eye for detail is shrewdly discerning. These qualities which mark his non-fiction are abundantly clear also in his best novels, as is his prose style which remains one of the most outstanding in this period of American literature. Every reader is impressed by the rich evocativeness of Faulkner's style, and the stylistic tension which contributes such force to Flannery O'Connor's great stories; yet not enough readers have noticed and praised the great lucid "plain" style of Erskine Caldwell. Some of his best writing is in his non-fiction, especially the Swiftian commentaries in *Some American People* (including Tenant Farmers) as well as the later and gentler *In Search of Bisco and Deep South*. And I will argue again while I have the opportunity for the great text-picture books he brought back into print, as the Agee-Walker *Let Us Now Praise Famous Men*; for the books Caldwell created with Margaret Bourke-White are among the greatest of the genre, especially *You Have See Their Faces, North of the Danube*, and *Say! Is This the U.S.A.?* These are masterpieces in an art form too often ignored. It required the happy conjuction of writer and photographer working as one author, not as one illustrating or explaining the work of the other.

When one considers Caldwell's prose fiction, one is confronted with a huge body of work; and as with all prolific writers, literary quality has ebbed and flowed in the novels and stories. Some of the novels are best read as groups or variations on themes. And despite his reputation as a writer of sexy and violent novels, Caldwell is often in the novels concerned with family relations, often tested by ideological or social conflicts. He presents resulting actions often in a comic way, which of course has the unfortunate tendency to make some readers suppose that the actions are therefore not "serious." The novels also disappoint readers who suppose that the "serious" novel must of necessity explore characters psychologically in the manner of Dostoevsky, James, or Faulkner, if the novel is to be given critical attention. Yet as Restoration comedy was once dismissed because it was not Shakespearean (and because it is sexy), and Joyce scorned because he did not write real novels as obviously Galsworthy did, so recently some simplistic notions about "the novel" have tended to lead critics to dismiss Caldwell's work because he does not write like Faulkner of Flannery O'Conner. Faulkner himself annoyed Hemingway no end by remarking his failure to risk much in his novels; and irritated his own admirers by placing himself second in achievement to Thomas Wolfe. Yet Faulkner's much publicised list of the five greatest American novelists of his generation has another surprise, for the currently much patronized Caldwell is on it: Wolfe, Faulkner, Dos Passos, Caldwell, Hemingway. (He was right about Dos Passos, also currently out of critical fashion.)

Though the whole of Caldwell's production—in fiction and non-fiction—will continue to be valuable to the student of Southern society and to the literary historian, the books that will survive as works of literary art are relatively few—as in the case of, say, Scott. Caldwell has in a way chronicled the South; his books if read in chronological succession show not just the author's mellowing into compassionate old age, but a South that slowly changes in mood and attitude. Yet Caldwell also produced three books of fiction that are masterpieces: *Tobacco Road, God's Little Acre*, and *Georgia Boy*. With these novels, 20 or 30 of his best short stories (some of this century's finest) will form a lasting body of prose fiction which, when set beside his considerable achievement in non-fiction, will clearly mark him one of the most important writers of our time.

Perhaps Caldwell's best-known work, *Tobacco Road* almost failed to survive its initial publication. Sales were so small that Caldwell's advance was barely covered. Some time later Jack Kirkland dramatized the story; but the play almost closed after two weeks. By chance, the play survived, to run longer than any previous play; and *Tobacco Road* became a best-seller book, second only to the Bible. These curiosities of publishing history are not in themselves important to literary criticism; though in this case the history of the book is especially ironic, since one of the themes of the novel is human tenacity in the face of rejection and failure. The physical hunger of Jeeter, the sexual appetites of Ellie May and Sister Bessie, the sterile marriage of Pearl and Tom, all are more than a comic presentation of low-life characters on land made sterile by culivation of tobacco that once made the region's owners rich. The deformed characters (some physically, some mentally or spiritually) wait for God; as Jeeter says: "Him and me has always been fair and square with each other....I don't know nothing else to do, except wait for Him to take notice." And they seem to act out a superior will, suggested more strongly in some of the later books.

God's Little Acre is a masterpiece. If, as many critics argue, it is less than *Absalom! Absalom!*, then it is less in the way that *Dead Souls* is less than *War and Peace*, or *Volpone* less than *King Lear*; but clearly at this level of literary competence, ranking becomes the parlor game of bored professors. Unfortunately all the censorship and banning gained *God's Little Acre* a reputation for being comic pornography; and some critics have continued to see the book as merely a comic exposé of Southern local color. The book is about southern mentality in about the same way the typist at tea-time section of *The Waste Land* is about unfair labor practices in London. I do not make the comparison lightly; for *God's Little Acre* is a novel about sterility; it is a comic presentation of one of the most ancient moral problems, here stated in low country terms by Ty Ty Walden, the digger after gold: "There was a mean trick played on us somewhere. God put us in the bodies of animals and tried to make us act like people. That was the beginning of trouble." The book itself is structured on contrasts of characters, and on a progression of scenes alternating between farm and town and building to a climax of great technical brilliance.

Georgia Boy, on the other hand, is episodic, a series of closely related incidents narrated by a 12-year-old boy. It is equalled by only two other works in recent American fiction: Wright Morris's *My Uncle Dudley* and Faulkner's *The Reivers*. The earnestly innocent reports of adult behavior tend to transform what is said and done in the books, so that fictional strategy is itself a criticism of life.

The short stories present a problem by their very number; but a reader attempting to see Caldwell for the various and talented fictionist he is may be helped by this list of some of the best stories: "Country Full of Swedes," "The People v. Ake Lathan, Colored," "Candy-Man Beechum," "After-Image," "An Evening in Nuevo Leon," "We Are Looking at You, Agnes," "An Autumn Courtship," "A Swell-looking Girl," and "Meddlesome Jack." There are many other stories as good, or almost as good, in Caldwell's collections; and one suspects that we would have to go back to Maupassant to find his equal in short story writing.

—James Korges

CALISHER, Hortense. American. Born in New York City, 20 December 1911. Educated at Barnard College, New York, A.B. 1932. Married Curtis Harnack in 1959; two children by a previous marriage. Adjunct Professor of English, Barnard College, 1956-57; Visiting Professor, University of Iowa, Iowa City, 1957, 1959-60, Stanford University, California, 1958, Sarah Lawrence College, Bronxville, New York, 1962, and Brandeis University, Waltham, Massachusetts, 1963-64; Adjunct Professor of English, Columbia University, New York, 1968-70; Clark Lecturer, Scripps College, Claremont, California, 1969; Visiting Professor, State University of New York, Purchase, 1971-72; Regents' Professor, University of California, Irvine, 1975; Visiting Writer, Bennington College, Vermont, 1977; Hurst Professor, Washington University, St. Louis, 1979. Recipient: Guggenheim Fellowship, 1952, 1955; Department of State American Specialists grant, 1958; American Academy grant, 1967; National Endowment for the Arts grant, 1967. D.Litt.: Skidmore College, Saratoga Springs, New York, 1980. Member, American Academy, 1977. Lives in New York City. Agent: Candida Donadio and Associates, 51 East 42nd Street, New York, New York 10017, U.S.A.

PUBLICATIONS

Novels

False Entry. Boston, Little Brown, 1961; London, Secker and Warburg, 1962.
Textures of Life. Boston, Little Brown, 1961; London, Secker and Warburg, 1963.
Journal from Ellipsia. Boston, Little Brown, 1965; London, Secker and Warburg, 1966.
The Railway Police, and The Last Trolley Ride. Boston, Little Brown, 1966.
The New Yorkers. Boston, Little Brown, 1969; London, Cape, 1970.
Queenie. New York, Arbor House, 1971; London, W.H. Allen, 1973.
Standard Dreaming. New York, Arbor House, 1972.
Eagle Eye. New York, Arbor House, 1973.
On Keeping Women. New York, Arbor House, 1977.

Short Stories

In the Absence of Angels. Boston, Little Brown, 1951; London, Heinemann, 1953.
Tale for the Mirror: A Novella and Other Stories. Boston, Little Brown, 1962; London, Secker and Warburg, 1963.
Extreme Magic: A Novella and Other Stories. Boston, Little Brown, and London, Secker and Warburg, 1964.
The Collected Stories of Hortense Calisher. New York, Arbor House, 1975.

Other

What Novels Are (lecture). Claremont, California, Scripps College, 1969.
Herself (memoir). New York, Arbor House, 1972.

*

Critical Studies: in *Don't Never Forget* by Brigid Brophy, London, Cape, 1966, New York, Holt Rinehart, 1967; Cynthia Ozick in *Midstream* (New York), 1969; "Ego Art: Notes on How I Came to It" by the author, in *Works in Progress*, New York, Doubleday, 1971.

Hortense Calisher comments:

(1972) *False Entry* and *The New Yorkers* are connected novels; either may be read first; together they are a chronicle perhaps peculiarly American, according to some critics, but with European scope, according to others. *Journal from Ellipsia* was perhaps one of the first or the first serious American novel to deal with "verbal" man's displacement in a world of the spatial sciences; because it dealt with the possibility of life on other planets it was classed as "science fiction" both in the USA and in England. The *Dublin Times* understood it; its review does well by it. It also satirizes male-female relationships, by postulating a planet on which things are otherwise. In category, according to some, it is less an ordinary novel than a social satire akin to *Erewhon, Gulliver's Travels, Candide*, etc. *The Railway Police* and *The Last Trolley Ride*—the first is really a long short story of an individual, the second a novella built around an environs, a chorale of persons really, with four main parts, told in the interchanging voice of two men.

I usually find myself alternating a "larger" work with a smaller one, a natural change of pace. *Textures of Life*, for instance, is an intimate novel, of a young marriage, very personal, as *Journal* is not. After the latter, as I said in an interview, I wanted to get back to people. *The New Yorkers* was a conscious return to a "big" novel, done on fairly conventional terms, descriptive, narrative, leisurely, and inclusive, from which the long monologue chapters of the two women are a conscious departure. Its earlier mate, *False Entry*, has been called the only "metaphysical" novel in the America of its period—I'm not sure what that means, except perhaps that the whole, despite such tangible scenes as the Ku Klux Klan and courtroom episodes, is carried in the "mind" of one man. It has been called Dickensian, and in its plethora of event I suppose it is; yet the use of memory symbols and of psyche might just as well be French (Proust and Gide)—by intent it does both, or joins both ways of narration. *The New Yorkers* is more tied to its environs in a localized way; part of its subject *is* the environs.

Queenie is a satire, a farce on our sexual mores, as seen through the eyes of a "modern" young girl. As it is not yet out at this writing, I shall wait to be told what it is about.

* * *

In spite of her zest, intelligence, humor and general readability, Hortense Calisher makes life difficult for critics who like to pigeonhole authors. She will not stay put in any of their categories. During the years when she was first appearing in print it was easier for them to classify her, simply because writers of short stories are allowed unusual latitude: the tag is enough. Even in this field, however, she exhibits scope and imagination, and is impishly fugitive. Not that she is thoroughly inconsistent. One quality is common to her stories whether they treat of school, loneliness, or the supernatural—love of the English language. Calisher can manage the medium. She uses words carefully, thoughtfully, and in fresh ways, as a graphic artist might use unexpected shapes and colors. If this seems an obvious and unnecessary comment on an American modern, read some of the others and ask yourself to how many the same truth applies.

Most writers with stamina go the other way about their work, first attempting to write enormous novels and later trying short stories—possibly because students of writing are so often told that short stories are harder to produce. (Incidentally, that is a statement I have never accepted.) Though I am Hortense's friend, I do not know if she did begin, tentatively, on a novel which she later dropped. I doubt it, because at the age when most university graduates try such ambitious experiments her energies were diverted. In turn, she took a job in a department store and then was a social worker; she married, had children, published a few stories, taught, and held an editorial post on a girls' magazine. This was all experience, of course, but it hardly contributed to the tranquillity one should have for sustained writing. When, awarded a Guggenheim Fellowship on the strength of her published stories, she was asked what she intended to do as a project, she replied that she wanted to go to England, sit there for a year, and just think.

Her first published novel, *False Entry*, has much of England in it as a result, but there is much else as well. Woven through the story, among the threads that tie together Europe, New York, and the South—this last-named locale providing one of the most haunting episodes I can recall reading anywhere—are accounts of characters we meet again in a much later novel, *The New Yorkers*. It is typical of Hortense Calisher that she should do this unconventional thing, picking up a group of people who were not her main actors in the first book and writing in depth about them in a totally new story which could not in any respect be called a sequel to *False Entry*. I find it absorbing to contrast the two books if only because they are so widely different in treatment. Even in these circumstances Calisher refuses to be typed. Hers is a world of varying climates.

Between these two long novels she has produced other works—collections of short or shorter stories and two novels, *Textures of Life* and *Journal from Ellipsia*. *Textures* has been accepted as her most nearly run-of-the-mill tale, dealing as it does with a young couple and their problems with their child. Described in these words the story sounds commonplace, but is is not. The reader remembers the young people in their New York loft, the little girl struggling with asthma, and somehow it becomes a new story about contemporary crises. At the other end of the scale is *Journal from Ellipsia* in a completely different genre, which I find wildly funny. Reviewers had an especially hard time with the *Journal* because, like the author, it is so hard to classify. One critic, in despair, ended by listing it as science fiction. Whatever one calls it, I like it—perhaps more than any of her other books—but I reserve the right to change my mind. Already I find myself wondering. There are many ways to read Hortense Calisher, and she creates many moods in the reader.

Her novel *Queenie* is another romp, about a girl who grows up among a weirdly out-of-time group of aging demi-mondaines in New York. Cherished, sheltered, and totally unprepared for life as it is today, Queenie goes out to grapple with reality in an up-to-the-minute progressive college. I say "reality," but...but what is the use of outlining plots? It is what Calisher does with them that counts.

—Emily Hahn

CALLAGHAN, Morley (Edward). Canadian. Born in Toronto, 22 September 1903. Educated at St. Michael's College, University of Toronto, B.A. 1925; Osgoode Hall Law School, Toronto, LL.B. 1928; admitted to the Ontario Bar, 1928. Worked with the Royal Canadian Navy on assignment for the National Film Board during World War II; travelled across Canada as Chairman of the radio forum "Of Things to Come," 1944. Married Lorette Florence Dee in 1929; two sons. Worked on the Toronto *Star* while a student; full-time writer since 1928; lived in Paris, 1928-29. Recipient: Governor-General's Award, 1952; Lorne Pierce Medal, 1960; Canada Council Medal, 1966, prize, 1970; Molson Prize, 1969; Royal Bank of Canada Award, 1970. LL.D.: University of Western Ontario, London, 1965. Address: 20 Dale Avenue, Toronto, Ontario, Canada.

PUBLICATIONS

Novels

Strange Fugitive. Toronto, Macmillan, and New York, Scribner, 1928.
It's Never Over. Toronto, Macmillan, and New York, Scribner, 1930.
A Broken Journey. New York, Scribner, 1932.
Such Is My Beloved. Toronto, Macmillan, and New York, Scribner, 1934.
They Shall Inherit the Earth. Toronto, Macmillan, and New York, Random House, 1935; London, Chatto and Windus, 1936.
More Joy in Heaven. Toronto, Macmillan, and New York, Random House, 1937.
The Varsity Story. Toronto and London, Macmillan, and New York, Macmillan, 1948.
The Loved and the Lost. New York, Macmillan, 1951; London, MacGibbon and Kee, 1961.
The Many Coloured Coat. Toronto, Macmillan, and New York, Coward McCann, 1960; London, MacGibbon and Kee, 1963.
A Passion in Rome. Toronto, Macmillan, and New York, Coward McCann, 1961; London, MacGibbon and Kee, 1964.
An Autumn Penitent (includes *In His Own Country*). Toronto, Macmillan, 1973.
A Fine and Private Place. New York, Mason Charter, 1975.
Close to the Sun Again. Toronto, Macmillan, 1977; New York, St. Martin's Press, 1978.

Short Stories

A Native Argosy. Toronto, Macmillan, and New York, Scribner, 1929.
No Man's Meat. Paris, Titus, 1931.
Now That April's Here and Other Stories. Toronto, Macmillan, and New York, Random House, 1936.
Stories. Toronto, Macmillan, 1959; London, MacGibbon and Kee, 2 vols., 1963-64.
No Man's Meat, and The Enchanted Pimp. Toronto, Macmillan, 1978.

Plays

Turn Again Home (produced New York, 1940; as *Going Home*, produced Toronto, 1950).
To Tell the Truth (produced Toronto, 1949).

Other

Luke Baldwin's Vow (juvenile). Philadelphia, Winston, 1948.
That Summer in Paris: Memories of Tangled Friendships with Hemingway, Fitzgerald, and Some Others. New York, Coward McCann, and London, MacGibbon and Kee, 1963.
Winter, photographs by John de Visser. Toronto, McClelland and Stewart, and Boston, New York Graphic Society, 1974.

*

Critical Studies: *Morley Callaghan* by Brandon Conron, New York, Twayne, 1966, and *Morley Callaghan* edited by Conron, New York, McGraw Hill, 1975; *Morley Callaghan* by Victor Hoar, Toronto, Copp Clark, 1969; *The Style of Innocence: A Study of Hemingway and Callaghan* by Fraser Sutherland, Toronto, Clarke Irwin, 1972.

* * *

The capacity which could produce Morley Callaghan's clipped, significant short stories, studies of the mysteriousness of the ordinary and the bewildering discrepancies of human fact, is not very evident in the early novels, *Strange Fugitive, It's Never Over*, and *A Broken Journey*, which are muddy in texture and melodramatic in action. It revealed itself first in *Such Is My Beloved*, a novel of which the whole air and idiom belong to the 1930's, the 1930's of the depression, of insecurity, unemployment, malnutrition, meanness.

The separation of two worlds, Christian and bourgeois, is the initiating contrast of the novel. Father Dowling speaks of it in his sermon in a lofty, generalising way. The novel shows it becoming biting and personal—"inevitable" in this way—in his own life. For all his spiritual and social conviction, and in spite of his working-class origins, he himself, because of his education, his status, his looks, his popularity with the parishioners, has a recognised position in the bourgeoisie. Officially he is on the side of religion against bourgeois convention; in reality he has at least one foot in both camps. The point at which the antagonism of the two orders becomes incorporated into his own life, the point at which he starts to be harrowed by the necessity for deciding between them, comes when he meets the two young prostitutes, Ronnie and Midge.

The economy of naturalness characteristic of Morley Callaghan—which is a reconstruction of movement rather than a Zolaesque realism of detail—is best realised in this between Father Dowling and the prostitutes. Its growth, like that of all complex human feeling, is checked, troubled, backsliding, never wholly smooth or continuous; and yet it moves irresistibly onward, obeying and balancing an inward initiative as well as outer circumstances. At first, it is sympathetic but embarrassed on one side, suspect and then irritated on the other. As the priest begins to understand the economic forces beating on the young women his attention is less firmly concentrated on the rescue from prostitution and more on bringing a spontaneous human response from them. The contradiction between the donors and the deniers of life is at the heart of *Such Is My Beloved*. It is the conclusion to which the original division between the religious and the bourgeois worlds finally leads. Father Dowling in his efforts to be as richly a donor as he can becomes a scandal to the deniers. The novel makes it quite clear why; and not only clear but convincing. It has nothing to do with any sentimental falsification of the girls or of prostitution.

Poetry and religion have a universalising effect in *Such Is My Beloved*, making it appear to the British reader more accessible and less off-puttingly embedded in alien ground than, say, *More Joy in Heaven*, which wears an aspect—I can only put it like this—of continental parochialism. *More Joy in Heaven* is irremediably indigenous, North American in a limiting way. It is the story of a paroled criminal's effort to re-enter the society which has first punished and then forgiven him. Behind it stands an ethos of violence and the myth of the heroic gangster. Its setting is the brutal North-American city, ugly and unhistorical and very much "a machine for living," the sense of which is conveyed with confident incisiveness.

The paradox of one's reaction to *More Joy in Heaven* is that while its pure Americanism is so remote (it is, it seems to me, markedly more American than Canadian, unlike *Such Is My Beloved*) its cinematic conception, technique, imagery and characterisation are intimately familiar, part indeed of the history of one's own life. So much so that it is impossible to think about *More Joy in Heaven* without seeing it as a film and without casting its characters from those familiar names: Victor McLaglen, William Bendix, Janet Gaynor, Veronica Lake, Humphrey Bogart, Richard Widmark, Sidney Greenstreet, Franchot Tone, Edwin Arnold, Edward G. Robinson. *More Joy in Heaven* would make—perhaps, for all I know, it has already made—a superb film script.

I have stressed what I take to be the essential limitation in *More Joy in Heaven*, but it remains a strong piece of work and an impressive example of its genre. It is solid, vigorous, lean, and precise, the product of a serious mind. It has more weight than the documented but insubstantial study of a university institution, *Varsity Story*, more bite than the more vaguely organised *A Passion in Rome*. *More Joy in Heaven* is a member of the group of novels which includes *Such Is My Beloved, The Many Coloured Coat*, and *The Loved and the Lost* to which I turn now. These novels, different in theme and setting, have in common a preoccupation with what I should like to call self-preservation, as long as I may remove from the term any hint of selfishness or over-personal concern. Callaghan is fascinated by what Henry James in the Preface to *What Maisie Knew* called a character's "truth of resistance," the gift or genius that some have for preserving intact the lineaments of their nature. It is a power which has at its heart a certain insistent simplicity: not self-confidence but trust in self. In Father Dowling it shows itself as a steady flame of goodness impervious even to the most high-minded opposition; in Kip Caley as the persistent, and finally desperate, trust of an abrasively independent identity. In *The Loved and the Lost* it is the girl Peggy Sanderson who possesses this faculty. It reveals itself in conduct which ignores or evades—rather than defies—the acceptable canons of behaviour in her world. The well-disposed think her capricious, the suspicious perverse. Her strangeness lies in her unpredictability, in her assumption that she is not caught in the same net as everybody else. She is described by his friend Foley to James McAlpine, a university teacher and would-be newspaper columnist, who is our source of awareness during this novel, in a fumbling conversation which tries to define her strangeness, as a blue jay, a bird which flies off at crazy and unpredictable angles.

The substance of the novel is the search for the true nature of the girl's odd, disconcerting individuality. It is conducted against the quietly insinuated but effectively established presence of Montreal. In no other novel of Callaghan is the city context so significantly part of the story and—at least to a British reader—so attractive. Incidentally, unobtrusively and, at every point, relevantly, the dimensions of the city appear.

The Many Coloured Coat is one of the finest of Callaghan's novels, and the one I take to represent his latest, and most developed work. The medium is in the same mode, quiet, unpretentious, close to speech and movement and with much of the flexibility and versatility of the spoken language. The medium, at once masculine and unpretentious, is in accord with Callaghan's attitude, which is, characteristically, both self-effacing and positive. The theme of *The Many Coloured Coat* is that of Joseph, the gifted and beloved young man. The novel rehearses the theme of the fortunes of the fortunate man. The biblical reference comes through, as the novel unfolds, without the least touch of impropriety or tactlessness, and it testifies to the steadiness Callaghan sees in human nature and to his perception of the permanent content of the varying crises it has to face.

The importance attributed in this novel to pride, not in any doctrinal way but by suggestive, concrete pointing, is justified not only by the facts of the case in this novel and the intelligent psychological investigation of them, but by a certain habit of sensibility in Callaghan himself. He has as Edmund Wilson pointed out in a perceptive an sympathetic essay, *O Canada*, "an intuitive sense of the meaning of Christianity." The human vision of these novels depends on a Christian style of feeling, of a particular tradition of religious sensibility which is present not as dogma or metaphysics but as a mode of perception and reaction.

I speak of Callaghan's Christian response, but, of course, that response and the whole economy of feeling of which it is a part, are sunk deep in the constitution of the novelist. If Callaghan is a Christian novelist, this is the way in which he is one. He is not the spokesman of religion, but the artist who possesses it as part of his personal nervous equipment. This traditional steadiness blends in Callaghan with that acute feeling for contemporary society, which, to a European at least, seems very natural to an artist working in the New World, and the combination makes him a novelist of an impressively serious quality. The contemporary flavour appears everywhere in his work, in themes, situations, characters and procedures. A single notable example of it in *The Many Coloured Coat* is his treatment of the life of the streets. The street in a modern industrial society presents itself to him as an image of that society and its experience. His skill in rendering the flow of life through the street, the brutality and ugliness, the glimpses the street provides of other, less tangible experiences, the altercations, the moments of communication, show the street not only as a place but as the analogue of human vitality and representativeness. "That night," he writes of Harry Lane after his fall, in words which are apt to describe the impression all Morley Callaghan's best work makes, "he walked through the streets for hours feeling he was wandering through his own life."

—William Walsh

CALLOW, Philip (Kenneth). British. Born in Birmingham, Warwickshire, 26 November 1924. Educated at Coventry Technical College, 1937-39; St. Luke's College, Exeter, Devon, 1968-70, Teacher's Certificate 1970. Married 1) Irene Vallance in 1953 (marriage dissolved, 1973), one daughter; 2) Penelope Jane Newman in 1974. Engineering apprentice and toolmaker, Coventry Gauge and Tool Company, 1940-48; Clerk, Ministry of Works and Ministry of Supply, 1949-51; Clerical Assistant, South West Electricity Board, Plymouth, 1951-66; Arts Council Fellow, Falmouth School of Art, 1977-78; Creative Writing Fellow, Open University, 1979. Recipient: Arts Council bursary, 1966, 1970, 1973, 1979; Society of Authors Traveling Scholarship, 1973; C. Day Lewis Fellowship, 1973; Southern Arts Association Writer's Fellowship, 1974. Agent: Christopher Busby, 27 Southampton Street, London WC2E 7JA. Address: Little Thatch, Haselbury, near Crewkerne, Somerset, England.

PUBLICATIONS

Novels

The Hosanna Man. London, Cape, 1956.
Common People. London, Heinemann, 1958.

A Pledge for the Earth. London, Heinemann, 1960.
Clipped Wings. Douglas, Isle of Man, Times Press, 1964.
Going to the Moon. London, MacGibbon and Kee, 1968.
The Bliss Body. London, MacGibbon and Kee, 1969.
Flesh of Morning. London, Bodley Head, 1971.
Yours. London, Bodley Head, 1972.
The Story of My Desire. London, Bodley Head, 1976.
Janine. London, Bodley Head, 1977.
The Subway to New York. London, Martin Brian and O'Keeffe, 1979.
The Black Rainbow. London, Martin Brian and O'Keeffe, 1980.

Short Stories

Native Ground. London, Heinemann, 1959.

Uncollected Short Story

"Merry Christmas," in *New Statesman* (London), 22 December 1961.

Plays

The Honeymooners (televised, 1960). Published in *New Granada Plays*, London, Faber, 1961.

Television Play: *The Honeymooners*, 1960.

Radio Plays: *The Lamb*, 1971; *On Some Road*, 1979.

Verse

Turning Point. London, Heinemann, 1964.
The Real Life: New Poems. Douglas, Isle of Man, Times Press, 1964.
Bare Wires. London, Chatto and Windus-Hogarth Press, 1972.

Other

In My Own Land, photographs by James Bridgen. Douglas, Isle of Man, Times Press, 1965.
Son and Lover: The Young D.H. Lawrence. London, Bodley Head, and New York, Stein and Day, 1975.

*

Manuscript Collection: University of Texas Library, Austin.

Critical Study: by the author, in *Vogue* (New York), 1 September 1969.

* * *

In all his work Philip Callow is telling the same story—his life-story. His "autobiography" *In My Own Land* confirms a close approximation between himself and the "I" of the novels and the short stories in *Native Ground*. In his earlier novels he was seeking an idiom, which he found triumphantly in the freewheeling colloquialism of the trilogy *Going to the Moon*, *The Bliss Body*, and *Flesh of Morning*.

Callow's material is his working-class adolescence in the Midlands, the experience of factory and clerical work there and in the West country, his artistic leanings and adult relationships. Louis Paul, Nicky Chapman, and Alan Lowry, the narrators respectively of *The Hosanna Man*, *Common People*, and *Clipped Wings*, and Martin Satchwell, the central character of *A Pledge for the Earth*, are prototypes for the Colin Patten of the trilogy, and its sequel *The Story of My Desire*, when Patten has qualified as a teacher. Parallels exist in the earlier books for the trilogy's other important characters, while in subsequent work the lecturer David Lowry, the central figure in *Janine*, and the poet and writer-in-residence Jacob Raby, the narrator of *The Subway to New York*, recall Patten.

Callow gives a full account of adolescence, describing the development of sexuality—more freely in the later books—as the boy grows up at the end of the war when "there was a ration even on questions." Then he has to adjust to life on the factory floor. Patten's painting and writing lead him into provincial artistic circles, amateur or bohemian and anarchic—the "city nomads." Callow's outstanding portrayal is Jack Kelvin, "the hosanna man" himself, a drop-out like Albert Dyer in *Clipped Wings*, who "sits up on a cliff like a dirty old monk"; in *Common People* there is the drunken Sunday painter, Cecil Luce, leader of the "Birmingham Twelve." With the public poetry-readings by the "Callow-figure" Jacob Raby, in *The Subway to New York*, the wheel has come full circle.

A Pledge for the Earth was the earlier of Callow's two third-person novels. The most overtly structured of his novels, it describes two generations of Satchwells, in a framework of natural imagery, and culminates in 20-odd pages in the first person written by Martin Satchwell. In *Clipped Wings* Callow returned to first-person narration: "I decided that the only way is to plant yourself down in the very centre of things, and then set out. In the same railway carriage, with all the others." With its new, forceful, colloquial idiom, *Clipped Wings* is the key book in Callow's stylistic development, and made possible the trilogy. At the same time, he'd begun to publish a good deal of poetry, which perhaps cross-fertilized his prose.

In the trilogy, Callow ranged over his experiences freely with only a rough chronological surge onward: "Going back is pure instinct with me." The rationale of his method is in a sense anti-art: "Who believes in a book cut away from its writer with surgical scissors? I don't, I never did. I don't believe in fact and fiction, I don't believe in autobiography, poetry, philosophy, I don't believe in chapters, in a story." Callow's refusal to categorize is also embodied in his non-fiction *In My Own Land*, differentiated from his novels only by the use of real names.

Yours is an extended letter written by a young girl to her ex-lover, recalling that first unhappy love-affair. In *The Story of My Desire* Callow continued the trilogy, with Colin's affair with the married Lucy, both cause and effect of the breakdown of his own marriage, in turn inextricably linked in a nexus of guilt with his mental breakdown. *Janine* describes the middle-aged David Lowry's relationship with the mixed-up young girl of the title. It's written in the third person, and from the opening sentence, "His name was Lowry," the man is referred to throughout by surname. Until a key moment late in the novel, Janine never calls David by name, so that the third-person narration has an active structural role.

The structural rationale in *The Subway to New York* is circular: "always with a woman you go in circles." Thus Marjorie of *The Story of My Desire*, already resurrected as Kate in *Janine*, reappears as Carmel in *The Subway to New York*, and Lucy of *The Story of My Desire* is Nell in *Subway*. Sexuality runs all through Philip Callow's work, rooted in an understanding of life that he derives from D.H. Lawrence, but some readers may feel an insensitivity, especially in his two most recent novels.

—Val Warner

CANAWAY, W(illiam) H(amilton). British. Born in Altrincham, Cheshire, 12 June 1925. Educated at Altrincham Grammar School; University College, Bangor, Wales, B.A. (honours) 1948, Dip. Ed. 1949, M.A. 1951. Served in the Queen's Royal Regiment and Intelligence Corps, in Italy and the Middle East, 1943-46.

Married to Pamela Mary Burgess; five children. Lecturer in technical colleges, 1949-62. Recipient: Welsh Arts Council bursary, 1973. Lives in Wales. Address: c/o Curtis Brown Ltd., 1 Craven Hill, London W2 3EP, England.

PUBLICATIONS

Novels

The Ring-Givers. London, Joseph, 1958.
The Seal. London, Joseph, 1959.
Sammy Going South. London, Hutchinson, 1961; as *Find the Boy*, New York, Viking Press, 1961.
The Hunter and the Horns. London, Hutchinson, and New York, Harper, 1962.
My Feet upon a Rock. London, Hutchinson, 1963.
Crows in a Green Tree. London, Hutchinson, and New York, Doubleday, 1965.
The Grey Seas of Jutland. London, Hutchinson, 1966.
The Mules of Borgo San Marco. London, Hutchinson, 1967.
A Moral Obligation. London, Hutchinson, 1969.
A Declaration of Independence. London, Hutchinson, 1971.
Harry Doing Good. London, Hutchinson, 1973.
The Glory of the Sea. London, Hutchinson, 1974; Indianapolis, Bobbs Merrill, 1975.
The Willow-Pattern War. London, Hutchinson, 1976.
The Solid Gold Buddha. London, Hutchinson, 1979.

Plays

Horse on Fire (produced Hawkesyard Priory, 1961).
Roll Me Over (produced Birmingham, 1971).

Screenplays: *The Ipcress File*, with James Doran, 1965; *Rendezvous in Black*, 1972.

Television Play: *Dan, Badger, and All the Coal*, 1977.

Other

A Creel of Willow (on fishing). London, Joseph, 1957.
A Snowdon Stream: The Gwyrfai and How to Fish It. London, Putnam, 1958.

* * *

A novelist who writes a best seller early in his career is both lucky and limited; lucky for obvious reasons, limited, to some extent, by its success. For ever after it he tends to be known as "Author of Such-and-such"; however hard he may try to write something different, it dogs him. This happened to W.H. Canaway after he published *Sammy Going South* in 1961, and it was successfully filmed, Penguinised, and made famous over the next few years.

There is no "typical" Canaway novel, however, and if he has been typed as an adventure story writer it is mostly the fault or the merit of *Sammy Going South*. Two early novels, *The Seal* and *My Feet upon a Rock*, are set in modern Wales; *The Ring-Givers*, about Beowulf, in the 6th century A.D. Later, the novels seem to fit into familiar slots but never quite do so. *Crows in a Green Tree* is almost domestic rural comedy, but too bleak and bitter to qualify exactly; *The Mules of Borgo San Marco*, fast moving and energetic and full of Latin low life, is almost wartime farce; *The Grey Seas of Jutland* is almost a family saga—English and German cousins whose lives interweave before, then during, the First World War. And in the adventure stories there is almost, though again not quite, a common situation—some quest, chase, or trial through danger and difficulty, an ordinary character tested through extraordinary circumstances.

In *Sammy Going South* the ten-year-old hero makes his way down the whole continent of Africa, starting alone and penniless and in danger at Port Said, ending triumphantly in Durban. In *The Hunter and the Horns* a greenhorn schoolmaster finds himself facing the terrors of the desert, the intense loneliness of life among Arabs who despise him, and whom he mistrusts. In *A Moral Obligation* a young officer in the Far East at the end of the war finds himself involved in panicky wanderings through a jungle in which enemies, though he does not know it, have overnight become allies. In each case the hero has to face, not just physical dangers—though these are hair-raising enough, and described with an exactness that makes one really credit them, live through them—but the dangers inherent in himself, in his own outlook, spirit, and limitations. In writing of spiritual as well as physical adventure, Canaway becomes much more than a realistic writer of exciting stories.

There is a particular quality about his realism, too, that makes him go beyond "mere" adventure, a quality one might call over-realism, or "going too far": the ability to face what is almost unfaceable, to produce a moment of vivid physical horror that stays in the mind as a kind of photographic flash: the arm in *The Grey Seas of Jutland*, with the woollen sleeve impacted into it by blast; the beggar in *Sammy Going South* when the stones of the camp fire explode in his face; the casual shooting of the hero's knee at close range in *A Moral Obligation*—the sense of his appalling pain, his total panic.

In the same way, realism extends to ordinary life, not just to moments of danger. Even when Canaway writes about children, an uncosy sense of adult evil lies about them, and at his quietest there is a sense of violence, even when it is subdued—violence of feeling, reaction, and spirit. His characters are not likeable, on the whole, and this includes his child characters; but one is never sure if he himself dislikes them. This ambiguity is a proof of his ability to lose himself, as narrator, in his characters, to take on their presence, their standards, and not to show his own. The spirit of places, particularly of the country—outdoor life all over the place, from Wales to Vietnam—he catches remarkably well. But where people are concerned he is a chameleon novelist, taking the spirit, as well as the colour, of his characters.

—Isabel Quigly

CANTWELL, Robert (Emmett). American. Born in Little Falls (now Vader), Washington, 31 January 1908. Educated at the University of Washington, Seattle, 1924-25. Served in the 248th Coast Artillery of the Washington State National Guard, 1925-26. Married Mary Elizabeth Chambers in 1931; three children. Veneer Clipperman, Harbor Plywood Company, Hoquiam, Washington 1925-29; Literary Editor, *New Outlook*, New York, 1931-35; Literary Editor, *Time* magazine, New York, 1935-37; Member of the Editorial Board, *Fortune* magazine, New York, 1937-38; Foreign News and National Affairs Editor, 1939-43, on special assignments, 1943-45, *Time*; Literary Editor, *Newsweek* magazine, New York, 1949-54; Editor, Limited Editions Club, New York, 1956-57. Associate Editor, 1957-61, and Senior Editor, 1961-73, *Sports Illustrated* magazine, New York. Address: Box 552, Gambier, Ohio 43022, U.S.A.

PUBLICATIONS

Novels

Laugh and Lie Down. New York, Farrar and Rinehart, 1931.
The Land of Plenty. New York, Farrar and Rinehart, and London, Bell, 1934.

Uncollected Short Stories

"Hanging by My Thumbs," in *New American Caravan.* New York, Macaulay, 1929.
"Under Every Green Tree," in *The Miscellany* (New York), March 1930.
"Babe Foley," in *The Miscellany* (New York), July 1930.
"Never Mind," in *American Caravan 4.* New York, Macaulay, 1931.
"The Wreck of the Gravy Train," in *New Republic* (New York), January 1932.
"East of the Mountains," in *Pagany: A Native Quarterly* (Boston), April-June 1932.
"A Little Reality," in *Hound and Horn* (New York), April-May 1934.
"Hills Around Centralia," in *Proletarian Literature in the United States*, edited by Granville Hicks and others. New York, International Publishers, 1935; London, Lawrence, 1936.

Other

Nathaniel Hawthorne: The American Years. New York, Rinehart, 1948.
Famous American Men of Letters (juvenile). New York, Dodd Mead, 1956.
Alexander Wilson, Naturalist and Pioneer. Philadelphia, Lippincott, 1961.
The Real McCoy: The Life and Times of Norman Selby. Princeton, New Jersey, Auerbach, 1971.
The Hidden Northwest. Philadelphia, Lippincott, 1972.

Editor, *The Humorous Side of Erskine Caldwell.* New York, Duell, 1951; as *Where the Girls Are Different and Other Stories*, New York, New American Library, 1962.

Translator, *The Charterhouse of Parma*, by Stendhal. New York, Heritage Press, 1956.

*

Manuscript Collection: University of Oregon, Eugene.

Critical Studies: *The Radical Novel in the United States* by Walter Rideout, Cambridge, Massachusetts, Harvard University Press, 1956; *The American Writer and the Great Depression* by Harvey Swados, Indianapolis, Bobbs Merrill, 1966; by Jack Conroy, in *Proletarian Writers of the Thirties* edited by David Madden, Carbondale, Southern Illinois University Press, 1968.

* * *

Although Robert Cantwell continues to write, he has not published any fiction since 1935; indeed, virtually all his stories and novels were published in the brief period from 1929 to 1935. His work during this time has led to his being identified as a "proletarian novelist," and while the term is not invalid as it applied to Cantwell, it is too restrictive adequately to define the range and quality of his art.

In "Hanging by My Thumbs," for example, which Alfred Kreymborg included in the 1929 *New American Caravan*, Cantwell evinces no concern for those matters which in the ensuing years were to dominate the writings of the literary Left. The story is a first-person account of the failure of love, and Cantwell's interest is in his narrator's inability to accept this failure. (It was to this story that F. Scott Fitzgerald alluded when, on 21 January 1930, he wrote to Maxwell Perkins of Scribners, "In the new *American Caravan* amid much sandwiching of Joyce and Co. is the first work of a 21 year old named *Robert Cantwell.* Mark it well, for my guess is that he's learned a better lesson from Proust than Thornton Wilder did and has a destiny of no mean star.") So, too, in such stories as "Under Every Green Tree" and "Never Mind," Cantwell is not at all concerned with social issues: the awkwardness of a youth in love and the break-up of a marriage are his respective subject matters in these two stories. And even in a story published in *Pagany* as late as 1932, Cantwell wrote about a frightening encounter between two young boys and the father of a retarded child; the sense of terror which dominates the story calls to mind not the proletarian works of the 1930's but a novel such as Harper Lee's *To Kill a Mockingbird.*

All this, however, is not to suggest that Cantwell's fiction is devoid of social involvement. "Babe Foley," for example, which was published in *The Miscellany* just four months after "Under Every Green Tree," is another of Cantwell's stories which deals with the confused sensibility of a young man. But in this story the narrator's intense anxiety is not the result of his love for a woman; rather, it stems from his admiration on the one hand for Babe Foley, the crude "head dogger" of his father's lumbermill, and from his desire, at the same time, to share the world of his fraternity brother, Harold Ainsley, whose very clothing gives him "an almost aristocratic appearance, a careless look suggesting an indifferent and unconscious superiority." Yet even here, where Babe Foley represents "everything in the world that seemed attractive and impossible to achieve," Cantwell's ironic viewpoint prevents the story from becoming a paean to the working class. Similarly, in his first novel, *Laugh and Lie Down*, Cantwell uses the mill as the backdrop for his tale. But again, though he is most sympathetic towards his characters, the novel is dominated by what Horace Gregory once referred to as an original tone of half-ironic terror; it is a story, that is, which is primarily concerned not with the economic conditions of mill workers but with the disillusionment and psychic disassociation of three young people.

There are, in fact, only four works of fiction by Cantwell which clearly may be designated as "proletarian": "The Wreck of the Gravy Train"; "The Land of Plenty," a powerful story about the pressures of working in a plywood factory, which was included in Edward J. O'Brien's *The Best Stories of 1933*; "Hills Around Centralia," which deals with the Wobblies and the lynching of Wesley Everett; and *The Land of Plenty*, Cantwell's second and last novel. It is for this last work that Cantwell is best known, and rightly so. He had spent most of his childhood in Washington, and for many years had worked in a lumber mill. To varying degrees, most of his fiction makes use of the experience he had as a youth. The factory Cantwell describes in *The Land of Plenty*, however, is entirely fictional, for the plant in which he worked had none of the oppressive qualities of the mill in his novel. Yet the book is permeated with an extraordinary sense of factory life; as Jack Conroy recently wrote of *The Land of Plenty*: "it has...no close rival for authenticity and accuracy. For one who has worked in a factory from necessity, as I have, it rings as true as a well-tempered bell and is as fresh and strong as it was more than 30 years ago." The workers who go out on strike in *The Land of Plenty* are brutally defeated, yet Cantwell had clearly achieved his purpose in writing the novel. He had wanted to give the "working class people a sense of their own dignity" (as he quoted one of André Malraux's characters), and in *The Land of Plenty* he did just that. It is without question one of the finest novels to come out of the left-wing movement in the United States.

—Jack Salzman

CAPOTE, Truman. American. Born in New Orleans, Louisiana, 30 September 1924. Educated at Trinity School and St. John's Academy, New York; Greenwich High School, Connecticut. Worked in the Art Department, also wrote for "Talk of the Town," *The New Yorker* magazine; now a full-time writer. Recipient: O. Henry Award, 1946, 1948, 1951; American Academy grant, 1959; Mystery

Writers of America Edgar Allan Poe Award, 1966; Emmy Award, for television adaptation, 1967. Member, American Academy. Address: 870 United Nations Plaza, New York, New York 10017, U.S.A.

PUBLICATIONS

Novels

Other Voices, Other Rooms. New York, Random House, and London, Heinemann, 1948.
The Grass Harp. New York, Random House, 1951; London, Heinemann, 1952.

Short Stories

A Tree of Night and Other Stories. New York, Random House, 1949; London, Heinemann, 1950.
Breakfast at Tiffany's: A Short Novel and Three Short Stories. New York, Random House, and London, Hamish Hamilton, 1958.
A Christmas Memory. New York, Random House, 1966.

Uncollected Short Stories

"Mojave," in *Esquire* (New York), June 1975.
"Unspoiled Monsters," in *Esquire* (New York), May 1976.
"Kate McCloud," in *Esquire* (New York), December 1976.

Plays

The Grass Harp (produced New York, 1952). New York, Random House, 1952.
House of Flowers, music by Harold Arlen (produced New York, 1954). New York, Random House, 1968.
The Thanksgiving Visitor. New York, Random House, 1968; London, Hamish Hamilton, 1969.
Trilogy (screenplay; with Eleanor Perry), in *Trilogy*, 1969.

Screenplays: *Beat the Devil*, with John Huston 1953; *Indiscretion of an American Wife*, with others, 1954; *The Innocents*, with William Archibald and John Mortimer, 1961; *Trilogy*, with Eleanor Perry, 1969.

Television Plays (with Eleanor Perry): *A Christmas Memory*, from his own story, 1966; *Among the Paths to Eden*, from his own story, 1967.

Other

Local Color. New York, Random House, 1950; London, Heinemann, 1955.
The Muses Are Heard: An Account of the Porgy and Bess Tour to Leningrad. New York, Random House, 1956; London, Heinemann, 1957.
Observations, photographs by Richard Avedon. New York, Simon and Schuster, and London, Weidenfeld and Nicolson, 1959.
Selected Writings, edited by Mark Schorer. New York, Modern Library, and London, Hamish Hamilton, 1963.
In Cold Blood: A True Account of a Multiple Murder and Its Consequences. New York, Random House, and London, Hamish Hamilton, 1966.
Trilogy: An Experiment in Multimedia, with Frank and Eleanor Perry. New York, Macmillan, 1969.
The Dogs Bark: Public People and Private Places. New York, Random House, 1973; London, Weidenfeld and Nicolson, 1974.
Then It All Came Down: Criminal Justice Today Discussed by Police, Criminals, and Correction Officers with Comments by Truman Capote. New York, Random House, 1976.
Music for Chameleons. New York, Random House, 1980; London, Hamish Hamilton, 1981.

Bibliography: *Truman Capote: A Primary and Secondary Bibliography* by Robert J. Stanton, Boston, Hall, 1980.

Manuscript Collection: Library of Congress, Washington, D.C.

Critical Studies: *The Worlds of Truman Capote* by William L. Nance, New York, Stein and Day, 1970, London, Calder and Boyars, 1973; *Truman Capote* by Helen S. Garson, New York, Ungar, 1980.

* * *

Among postwar American writers, few came to be known so young as Truman Capote; literary glamor of a certain kind came to him early to stay. There is no elegant way to summarize his work. His styles vary too much, though style itself remains a central part of his achievement. Born and raised in the deep south, Capote is his earliest fiction develops some mannerisms of the region. Yet the legacy of Faulkner affects Capote in a peculiar way, less gothic than exotic, less elemental than oneiric. An ethereal sexuality, often homoerotic, suffuses his fiction. Nor does the southern manner cling to him for long. He says: "I have lived in many places besides the South and I don't like to be called a Southern writer." There is the crackling travelogue, from Ischia to Haiti, of *Local Color*. There is the hilarious account of a trip to Russia, with the cast of *Porgy and Bess*, in *The Muses Are Heard*. There is the New York or Kansas setting of his later novels.

As the locale of Capote's work changes, so do the forms of his fiction open. His preciosity gives way to social curiosity, to laughter; witness the zany film script, *Beat the Devil*. Intelligence inhabits his fantasies. Behind the frills and fashions of his prose, one senses the tenacity of some purpose. It is as if the solitary gaze of Narcissus, watery, vague, could in time sharpen enough to discern contours of reality rising beneath the surface.

Already in the first stories of Capote, collected in *A Tree of Night*, a distinction may be observed between his nocturnal and daylight styles, the nightmares and reveries of Narcissus. A sense of dread attends "the instant of petrified violence," the locked dream, the disintegrating psyche, in such stories as "Miriam," "The Headless Hawk," "A Tree of Night." Symbol and metaphor dredge the unconscious; animism and fable meet. Yet if terror and the preternatural define the nocturnal mode, comedy and social manners characterize the daylight view of "My Side of the Matter," "Jug of Silver," "Children on Their Birthdays." The tone is chatty, admits of first-person anecdotes; the characters engage concrete realities in a small southern town rather than abstract horrors in a northern metropolis. For Capote, then, dreams contain the destructive element of the isolated soul but also express the creative element of life; their release is a prerequisite of love.

His first two novels heighten this contrast, though both are still romances, that "neutral territory," Hawthorne once said, "somewhere between the real world and fairy-land, where the Actual and the Imaginary may meet, and each imbue itself with the nature of the other." *Other Voices, Other Rooms* remains a *tour de force* of the dark, mythic sensibility which the southern formalist critics helped to make fashionable in the 1940's and early 1950's. The book enfolds the reader in its poetic language, original and also over-wrought, enfolds him in an inscape and perversion. The action centers on the boy, Joel Knox, whose initiation leads him through many mysteries, to the spectral Cloud Hotel where he is finally confirmed in his identity. The quest for the Other—be he god, father, seducer, or mirror image—ends in a hallucination of self-knowledge, a vision of love, loneliness, and mutability. Set also in the south, *The Grass Harp* deals similarly with the end of boyhood innocence, though its tone is far less eerie than nostalgic. As Collin Fenwick hears the voice of the wind through a field of Indian grass, he recovers a crisis of his youth among elderly women, besieged in a tree-house by the wicked World which, sooner than later, must storm the Heart. Yet song and memory redeem present, adult, realities by releasing the impulses of love.

Here ends the southern phase of Capote's fiction, his prepossession for the fantastic, the monstrous, the bizarre. A new kind of whimsy or camp affects his next work, *Breakfast at Tiffany's*, set mainly in New York, which celebrates headlong Holly Golightly. Bitter-sweet in its naive abandon, current with chic *argot*, the narrative suggests the interest of the times in neo-picaresques, in open forms. Thus the bruised innocence of Holden Caulfield returns in Holly who is more frivolous, but also passionately honest and free. "I'd rather have cancer than a dishonest heart," she cries.

Less than a decade later, Capote once again changes his role. We see him *In Cold Blood* as herald of a new genre, "the non-fiction novel," which recognizes the convergence of fiction and fact in times of outrage, the insane surrealism of daily life. Based upon accounts of grisly Kansas murders of a wealthy farmer and his entire family, the book ends by raising vast questions about American society, the anger and deprivation of men, the workings of justice. Years of research, mounds of tapes and notes, endless interviews are compelled into form. With covert art, Capote selects, organizes, juxtaposes; he draws nets of animal imagery around his characters; he manages to keep the violence controlled. His sympathy for stunted life quickens the work with life of its own. The fierce controversy which greeted the work centered on two issues: the authenticity of the "non-fiction" form as a medium of narrative, and the authenticity of the author in his relation to the two killers, waiting execution on death row.

Capote survives controversy, though he may not thrive on it as Mailer does. He has endurance as well as wit. He projects many images of himself—the aesthete, the terrorist, the humorist, the jet-setter, the social critic—and his mastery of language is clear. Yet, with the possible exception of *In Cold Blood*, he has failed to provide the age with some compelling image of itself. Readers do not turn to him as they do to other writers who, in their inventions, reveal more about the world in which we live. If this is no final criterion of a novelist's measure, it is an increasingly significant one. We do well to remember, though, that Capote has the special gift of surprise; and he is still in mid-career.

—Ihab Hassan

CARTER, Angela (Olive, née Stalker). British. Born in Eastbourne, Sussex, 7 May 1940. Educated at the University of Bristol, 1962-65, B.A. in English 1965. Married Paul Carter in 1960 (divorced, 1972). Journalist, Croydon, Surrey, 1958-61. Arts Council Fellow in Creative Writing, University of Sheffield, 1976-78; Visiting Professor of Creative Writing, Brown University, Providence, Rhode Island, 1980-81. Recipient: Rhys Memorial Prize, 1968; Maugham Award, 1969; Cheltenham Festival prize, 1979. Agent: Deborah Rogers Ltd., 5-11 Mortimer Street, London W1N 7RH, England.

PUBLICATIONS

Novels

Shadow Dance. London, Heinemann, 1966; as *Honeybuzzard*, New York, Simon and Schuster, 1967.
The Magic Toyshop. London, Heinemann, 1967; New York, Simon and Schuster, 1968.
Several Perceptions. London, Heinemann, 1968; New York, Simon and Schuster, 1969.
Heroes and Villains. London, Heinemann, 1969; New York, Simon and Schuster, 1970.
Love. London, Hart Davis, 1971.
The Infernal Desire Machines of Dr. Hoffman. London, Hart Davis, 1972; as *The War of Dreams*, New York, Harcourt Brace, 1974.
The Passion of New Eve. London, Gollancz, and New York, Harcourt Brace, 1977.

Short Stories

Fireworks: Nine Profane Pieces. London, Quartet, 1974; New York, Harper, 1981.
The Bloody Chamber and Other Stories. London, Gollancz, 1979; New York, Harper, 1980.

Plays

Radio Plays: *Vampirella*, 1976; *Come unto These Yellow Sands*, 1979; *The Company of Wolves*, from her own story, 1980.

Verse

Unicorn. Leeds, Location Press, 1966.

Other

Miss Z, The Dark Young Lady (juvenile). London, Heinemann, and New York, Simon and Schuster, 1970.
The Donkey Prince (juvenile). New York, Simon and Schuster, 1970.
Comic and Curious Cats, illustrated by Martin Leman. London, Gollancz, and New York, Crown, 1979.
The Sadeian Woman: An Exercise in Cultural History. London, Virago, 1979; as *The Sadeian Woman and the Ideology of Pornography*, New York, Pantheon, 1979.

Translator, *The Fairy Tales of Charles Perrault*. London, Gollancz, 1977; New York, Avon, 1978.

* * *

Angela Carter's work reveals a notable energy, a flair for the comic, and an unusual diversity of imagination. Her style, with its emphasis on visual detail and imagery, is often poetic in effect. Vividly rendered sense impressions and purposefully distorted patterns of space and time account, in large part, for the strong effects produced in her tales (*Fireworks* and *The Bloody Chamber*) and in those novels laid in the future (*Heroes and Villains*, *The Infernal Desire Machines of Dr. Hoffman*, and *The Passion of New Eve*). She reveals her fascination with violence in scenes of mutilation, murder, rape, castration, cannibalism, incest, and flagellation, but at times she can also evoke the subtlest of psychological nuances.

Certain elements recur in her work: a claustrophobic enclosure of action in a small area; a charisma exerted by a demonic figure; a perverse need felt by an individual to cling tenaciously to another who both attracts and repels; and a discordant intermingling of horror and comedy.

Her books show her preoccupation with the frankly erotic, with the sadistic linking of sex with pain, and with the struggles for mastery between the powerful individual and the vulnerable. In *The Sadeian Woman* she finds in the Marquis de Sade's depiction of the tyrannical Juliette an anticipation of a "new pornography" in which women may be portrayed as dominant in a sexual relationship. On the other hand, she identifies his victimized Justine as the prototype of Marilyn Monroe, the Good-Bad Girl—innocent, very young, and comically surprised at her own sexual force. By implication, Carter's comments on de Sade interpret her own fiction, in which most of the female protagonists are Good-Bad Girls and in which the Amazons of *The Passion of New Eve* are Juliettes.

Shadow Dance has as its milieu a British slum where streets smell of urine, vomit, and stale beer. Here the beautiful and satanic

Honeybuzzard and his woman, Ghislaine, have tyrannized over each other and over their associates, who regard them with admiration, dread, and resentment. The childlike Ghislaine with her "long yellow milkmaid hair...like moonlight on daisies" has moved from man to man like an exotic moth, but at the beginning of this novel the flamboyant Honeybuzzard, with a long slash of his knife, has, on impulse, mutilated her face. In pubs, junk shops, and abandoned building, all of the other characters—each one a comic grotesque marked by a single dominant characteristic—await her return, because they know she will return for vengeance.

In *The Magic Toyshop*, the most intense and claustrophobic of the novels, three orphaned children are sent to live with their cruel uncle above his dark London toyshop. Melanie, 15, through whose eyes the action is seen, is introduced in a superb comic prologue (laid in the country just before the parents' death) in which as an innocent she discovers the full range of her sexuality. In contrast, when she is virtually imprisoned for a year in the London shop, where even mirrors are forbidden and where her aunt was struck dumb on her wedding night, Melanie gradually loses her self-identity. Suspicion, guilt, cruelty, incestuous intrigue, and imminent rape become her realities. She finally escapes her prison by running through the flames which destroy the shop. She triumphs over malevolence, but that malevolence almost corrupts her in the process.

Love and *Several Perceptions*, two lesser novels, satirize aimlessness in British youth, the latter focusing on artists and students in a bohemian conclave.

Carter's other three novels are laid in the future. In *Heroes and Villains* she portrays Marianne, a 16-year-old runaway from the Land of the Professors, who finds herself—a century after the atomic holocaust—living in a bombed-out building and married to Jewel, a Barbarian marauder who years before killed her brother and who more recently has raped her. The decor emphasizes the macabre and the horrible, and the desolation of the Land of the Barbarians is reflected in the barrenness of the human relationships between Jewel and a magician (his master) and between Jewel and Marianne. Horrible indeed are the dying infants, the pots of excrement, the lice women comb from the hair of their lovers, the cats grown monstrous, the graves to be dug at midnight, the roofs and walls half gone, the smokey fireplaces, and the floors oozing with filth.

As in *The Magic Toyshop* and *Heroes and Villains*, Carter thoroughly convinces the reader of the reality of her grotesque and macabre fable in *The Infernal Desire Machines of Dr. Hoffman*. The protagonist, Desiderio, journeys in search of Hoffman's secret for continuous generation of energy, a secret which will enable him to replace reality with ephemeral illusion. Hoffman's power, for example, allows him to create a cathedral in one instant and destroy it in the next; to transform an audience at the opera to a flock of peacocks; and to make pigeons atop a chimney quote Hegel. After many bizarre adventures, Desiderio discovers the secret in a huge laboratory where Hoffman has assembled wire cages from floor to ceiling in each of which a pair of lovers endlessly copulate. Sardonic and grotesque humor underlines the dehumanization of intimate relationships wherever these are exploited, as in this novel, for ulterior motives.

In *The Passion of New Eve* an arrogant man, stranded in the Arizona desert, encounters sophisticated Amazons who with their advanced technology change him into a woman in order that he may experience rape and unwanted pregnancy and understand the implications of his casual exploitation of women. The book closes with a bizarre orgy and massacre at the Hollywood mansion of an elderly film actress.

Carter's books for children again reveal her talent for fantasy, for recording visual detail, and for comic dialogue. Adults must ordinarily read these books to children because of their sophisticated vocabulary and involved sentence structure.

Angela Carter's popularity has grown more rapidly in England than in America, although nearly all her books have been quickly reprinted in American editions. In her brief career, she has published prolifically. Her continued use of horror fantasy with an erotic and violent emphasis may limit her readership, but she is an author whose imaginative artistry is strong and whose literary future is by no means predictable.

—Margaret B. McDowell

CASSILL, R(onald) V(erlin). American. Born in Cedar Falls, Iowa, 17 May 1919. Educated at the University of Iowa, Iowa City, B.A. 1940, M.A. 1947; the Sorbonne, Paris, 1952-53. Served in the United States Army, 1942-46. Married Karilyn Kay Adams in 1956; three children. Instructor, University of Iowa, 1948-52; Editor, *Western Review*, Iowa City, 1951-52; Lecturer, Columbia University, New York, and the New School for Social Research, New York, 1957-59, and the University of Iowa, 1960-65; Writer-in-Residence, Purdue University, Lafayette, Indiana, 1965-66. Since 1966, Associate Professor of English, and since 1967, President of the Associated Writing Programs, Brown University, Providence, Rhode Island. Also a painter and lithographer. Recipient: *Atlantic* "Firsts" prize, for short story, 1947; Rockefeller grant, 1954; Guggenheim grant, 1968. Address: 22 Boylston Avenue, Providence, Rhode Island, U.S.A.

PUBLICATIONS

Novels

The Eagle on the Coin. New York, Random House, 1950.
Dormitory Women. New York, Lion, 1954.
Left Bank of Desire, with Eric Protter. New York, Ace, 1955.
A Taste of Sin. New York, Ace, 1955; London, Digit, 1959.
The Hungering Shame. New York, Avon, 1956.
The Wound of Love. New York, Avon, 1956.
An Affair to Remember (novelization of screenplay; as Owen Aherne). New York, Avon, 1957.
Naked Morning. New York, Avon, 1957.
Lustful Summer. New York, Avon, 1958.
Nurses' Quarters. New York, Fawcett, 1958; London, Muller, 1962.
Tempest. New York, Fawcett, 1959.
The Wife Next Door. New York, Fawcett, 1959; London, Muller, 1960.
Clem Anderson. New York, Simon and Schuster, 1961.
My Sister's Keeper. New York, Avon, 1961.
Night School. New York, New American Library, 1961.
Pretty Leslie. New York, Simon and Schuster, 1963; London, Muller, 1964.
The President. New York, Simon and Schuster, 1964.
La Vie Passionée of Rodney Buckthorne: A Tale of the Great American's Last Rally and Curious Death. New York, Geis, 1968.
Doctor Cobb's Game. New York, Geis, 1970.
The Goss Women. New York, Doubleday, 1974; London, Hodder and Stoughton, 1975.
Hoyt's Child. New York, Doubleday, 1976.
Labors of Love. New York, Arbor House, 1980.
Flame. New York, Arbor House, 1980.

Short Stories

15 x 3, with Herbert Gold and James B. Hall. New York, New Directions, 1957.
The Father and Other Stories. New York, Simon and Schuster, 1965.

The Happy Marriage and Other Stories. West Lafayette, Indiana, Purdue University Studies, 1966.

Uncollected Short Stories

"The Rationing of Love," in *New American Review 13*, edited by Theodore Solotaroff. New York, Simon and Schuster, 1968.
"The Gadfly," in *Jeopardy* (Bellingham, Washington), Spring 1969.
"The Invention of the Airplane," in *The Best Literary Magazine Fiction 1971*, edited by Curt Johnson and Alvin Greenberg. New York, New York University Press, 1971.

Other

Writing Fiction. New York, Pocket Books, 1963; revised edition, Englewood Cliffs, New Jersey, Prentice Hall, 1975.
In an Iron Time: Statements and Reiterations: Essays. West Lafayette, Indiana, Purdue University Studies, 1967.

Editor, *Intro 1, 2, 3.* New York, Bantam, 3 vols., 1968-70.
Editor, *Norton Anthology of Short Fiction.* New York, Norton, 1968.

*

Manuscript Collection: Sugarman Library, Boston University.

R.V. Cassill comments:

(1972) My most personal statement is probably to be found in my short stories. If few of them are reliably autobiographical at least they grew from the observations, moods, exultations, and agonies of early years. If there is constant pattern in them, it is probably that of a hopeful being who expects evil and finds worse.

From my first novel onward I have explored the correspondences between the interior world—of desire and anxiety—and the public world of power—extra-social violences and politics. In *The Eagle on the Coin* I wrote of the ill-fated attempt of some alienated liberals, including a compassionate homosexual, to elect a Negro to the schoolboard in a small mid-western city. In *Doctor Cobb's Game* I used the silhouette of a major British political scandal as the area within which I composed an elaborate pattern of occult-sexual-political forces weaving and unweaving. Between these two novels, almost 20 years apart, I have played with a variety of forms and subject matter, but the focus of concern has probably been the same, under the surface of appearances. In *Clem Anderson* I took the silhouette of Dylan Thomas's life and within that composed the story of an American poet's self-destructive triumph. It probably is and always will be my most embattled work, simply because in its considerable extent it replaces most of the comfortable or profitable clichés about an artist's life with tougher and more painful diagrams.

But then perhaps my whole productive life has been a swimming against the tide. A Midwesterner by origin, and no doubt by temperament and experience, I worked through decades when first the Southern and then the urban-Jewish novel held an almost monopolistic grip on the tastes and prejudices of American readers. In my extensive reviewing and lecturing I have tried more to examine the clichés, slogans, and rallying cries of the time than to oppose or espouse them—thus leaving myself without any visible partisan support from any quarter. To radicals I have appeared a conservative, to conservatives a radical—and to both a mystification or, I suppose, I would not have been tolerated as long as I have been. As I grow older I love the commonplace of traditional thought and expression with a growing fervor, especially as their rarity increases amid the indoctrinating forces that spoil our good lives.

* * *

From the first novel, *The Eagle on the Coin*, and the early stories, R.V. Cassill's art shows a steady development from the autobiographical and the imitative to the fully dramatic capabilities of the mature novelist and short story writer. The range of his talent is wide: from near-pastoral impressions of midwestern America, to urban life in Chicago and New York, to his most technically accomplished work, *Doctor Cobb's Game*, based on the Profumo scandals in London.

Cassill's most complex work relies on four broad kinds of material: stories and novels about the midwest, most notably Iowa as in *Pretty Leslie*; stories and novels concerning academic life, as in "Larchmoor Is Not the World" and *The President*; materials about art and the artist's life (*Clem Anderson*); and finally materials of a less regional nature which may be called the vision of modernity found in the short story "Love? Squalor?" and *Doctor Cobb*. A second lesser known order of Cassill's work consists of a dozen novels, "paperback originals" so-called because of the contractual circumstances of their first publication. For the most part *The Wound of Love*, *Dormitory Women*, and others await sophisticated literary evaluation. These shorter, often more spontaneous novels also exploit the same kinds of material. It should be well understood that these categories are intended to be only suggestive; the most ambitious work, for example, displays all these materials.

Beyond the technical accomplishments of any professional novelist, Cassill's most noteworthy literary quality is the "visual" nature of his prose fiction. There is a steady exploitation of color, of the precise, telling, visual detail, a sensitivity to proportion, and to the architectonics of scene. In fact Cassill began his artistic career as a painter, a teacher of art; from time-to-time he still exhibits his work. His fiction shows some of the same qualities as the Impressionists, the Post-Impressionists, and the German Expressionistic painters.

The literary influences are wide-ranging and interestingly absorbed. In general these influences are evoked when necessary rather than being held steadily as "models" in any neo-classic sense. Specifically, Cassill values Flaubert, James, Joyce, and especially D.H. Lawrence. Of a different order of specific influence would be *Madam Bovary*, Gissing's *New Grub Street*, and Benjamin Constant's *Adolphe* (1815). It is interesting that Cassill has written the best extant appreciation of *Adolphe*. Thus Cassill is a highly literary writer, with a broad, useful knowledge of American and European literatures; for many years he has been a teacher of contemporary literature and a writer-in-residence at universities, a professional reviewer, essayist, a discerning cultural commentator and critic.

The governing themes of Cassill's work are less easy to identify. A recurring situation is the nature and the resultant fate of a human pair, the destiny of a man or woman in the throes of new love, old love, marriage, or adultery. Closely bound to these concerns is the nature of love and responsibility; the implications of choice, loyalty, and liberty. Often there are conflicts generated between rationality and a merely emotional yearning—real or imagined—genuine affection as against the implied necessity of sexual aggression or the ironies of "modern love." At times these relationships are between teacher and pupil, lovers, man and wife; between artist and patron, mistress, or the world "out there."

A fascination with these and other difficult themes places a heavy obligation on the novelist, especially in the matter of plot-structures and the handling of sex scenes. Throughout Cassill's work there is the insistence on the centrality of the sexual aspect of all human relationships. If in real life such concerns are seldom finally resolved, so is it in many novelistic structures which tend to rely on sexual involvements as a central motivation. Often, therefore, a story or a novel will begin with a vivid, strong situation which in the end is obscured or vague rather than suggestive or resolved. The reliance on the sexual drive as a compelling motive becomes more insistent in the later work.

Although he is primarily a novelist, Cassill's most sustained work is often in the short fiction, of which he is a master. The best stories focus on domestic scenes, memories of youth, the pathos of age, the casual lost relationship, conversations on art, ideas, literature, and the meaning of life itself.

Taken together, the stories, novels, and criticism show a strongly unified sensibility, a dedicated, energetic artist, a man in a modern world imaginatively and at times romantically comprehended, a man whose powerful gifts are his best protection against his own vision of America and of the midwest where modernity is rampant and the end is nowhere in sight.

—James B. Hall

CAUTE, (John) David. British. Born in Alexandria, Egypt, 16 December 1936. Educated at Edinburgh Academy; Wellington College; Wadham College, Oxford, M.A. in modern history, D. Phil. 1962; Harvard University, Cambridge, Massachusetts (Henry Fellow), 1960-61. Served in the British Army, in Africa, 1955-56. Married 1) Catherine Shuckburgh in 1961 (divorced, 1970), two sons; 2) Martha Bates in 1973, two daughters. Fellow, All Souls College, Oxford, 1959-65; Visiting Professor, New York University and Columbia University, New York, 1966-67; Reader in Social and Political Theory, Brunel University, Uxbridge, Middlesex, 1967-70; Regents Lecturer, University of California, 1974. Since 1979, Literary and Arts Editor, *New Statesman*, London. Deputy Chairman, Writers Guild of Great Britain, 1979-80. Recipient: London Authors' Club Award, 1960; Rhys Memorial Prize, 1960. Address: 41 Westcroft Square, London W6 OTA, England.

PUBLICATIONS

Novels

At Fever Pitch. London, Deutsch, 1959; New York, Pantheon, 1961.
Comrade Jacob. London, Deutsch, 1961; New York, Pantheon, 1962.
The Decline of the West. London, Deutsch, and New York, Macmillan, 1966.
The Occupation. London, Deutsch, 1971; New York, McGraw Hill, 1972.
The Baby Sitters (as John Salisbury). London, Secker and Warburg, and New York, Atheneum, 1978.
Moscow Gold (as John Salisbury). London, Futura, 1980.

Plays

Songs for an Autumn Rifle (produced Edinburgh, 1961).
The Demonstration (produced Nottingham, 1969; London, 1970). London, Deutsch, 1970.
The Fourth World (produced London, 1973).

Radio Play: *Fallout*, 1972.

Television Documentary: *Brecht & Co.*, 1979.

Other

Communism and the French Intellectuals, 1914-1960. London, Deutsch, and New York, Macmillan, 1964.
The Left in Europe since 1789. London, Weidenfeld and Nicolson, and New York, McGraw Hill, 1966.
Fanon. London, Fontana, and New York, Viking Press, 1970.
The Illusion. London, Deutsch, 1971; New York, Harper, 1972.
The Fellow-Travellers. London, Weidenfeld and Nicolson, and New York, Macmillan, 1973.
Collisions: Essays and Reviews. London, Quartet, 1974.
Cuba, Yes? London, Secker and Warburg, and New York, McGraw Hill, 1974.
Great American Families, with others. New York, Norton, and London, Times Books, 1977.
The Great Fear: The Anti-Communist Purge under Truman and Eisenhower. New York, Simon and Schuster, and London, Secker and Warburg, 1978.

Editor, *Essential Writings*, by Karl Marx. London, MacGibbon and Kee, 1967; New York, Macmillan, 1968.

*

Critical Studies: by Dennis Potter, in *The Times* (London), 22 July 1971; *The Listener* (London), 22 July 1971; *The Guardian* (London), 22 July 1971; by Benedict Nightingale, in *New Statesman* (London), 23 July 1971; *Sunday Telegraph* (London), 25 July 1971; David Jay, in *Times Educational Supplement* (London), 27 August 1971; *Times Literary Supplement* (London), 2 December 1971.

David Caute comments:

Ten years have passed since I wrote a word of fiction, apart from two pseudonymous thrillers. It would be idle to reflect upon a craft one is not practising. But if I have an ambition for the 1980's, it is to write good novels.

* * *

David Caute is a rare breed among contemporary English novelists. Indeed, he is probably unique. For his novels are written out of a deep ideological commitment to Marxism, and they are thus attempts to explore and account for the nature of imperialism, bourgeois capitalism and Western liberal democracy. To say as much is to indicate how extraordinarily at odds they are with the customary modest scope and intention of the contemporary English novel.

It is a generally accepted, if unwritten, rule for the novelist that he can only write well about what he knows from first-hand experience. The raw material out of which he fashions his art must, that is, be familiar enough to him for him to be able to handle it with confidence and authority. In other words, one wants the "ring of truth" in all that is depicted, one expects authenticity of detail and verification of fact that will allow us as readers to have confidence that the author quite simply knows what he is talking about.

In so far as this is a demand we make of the novel, it is clear that David Caute frequently falls short of meeting it. To look at his first novel is to see this. The handling of the African colonial life in *At Fever Pitch* quite lacks the kind of grasp of the sweaty actual that we find in the work of a master journalist-novelist like Graham Greene, for example, or that is so vividly present in Anthony Burgess's early and brilliant *Malayan Trilogy*. Caute very obviously cannot match their keenness of eye and ear for local colour, for realistic exactness. Yet he would no doubt reply that such veracity is unimportant for him and is finally unimportant to the novel as such. For what essentially matters is not how minutely you can detail all aspects of a way of life, but what deep and penetrative understanding you have of it; and for Caute such understanding can come only through Marxism. His novels are therefore living histories, analyses of societies which try to define their true nature through the historical and economic arguments of Karl Marx.

So far, so good. But then it may be argued, and indeed frequently *is*, that Caute's fictional writing is so much arid didacticism, a dressing-up of Marxist orthodoxy which succeeds only in suffocating the poor life of the novel itself. Caute, the argument runs, attempts to put a covering of skin over the bones of his theory, with the result that his novels can very clearly be seen to be skeletons, lifeless, inert, crucially artificial. None of his novels has suffered more from this criticism than the third one, *The Decline of the West*, and of none, perhaps, is the criticism more just. For as the un-ironic use of Oswald Spengler in the title implies, Caute is out to ram a thesis about capitalism in decay down our throats, and the consequence is that we turn away in irritation.

Yet to say this is not to question the validity of the novel of ideas.

Sartre is an obvious and distinguished example of a novelist whose ideology is present in his fiction without constricting it, and what is true of him is true of others. But the difference between Sartre and Caute, at least in his early work, is that Sartre understands that to write a novel of ideas does not require the novelist to be impatient of anything *but* ideas. "No ideas but in things" the great American poet, William Carlos Williams said, and there is heartening evidence that David Caute is beginning to realise as much. Certainly *The Occupation* suggests that he has become aware of the problem that George Eliot formulated over a hundred years ago, when she remarked that her prime difficulty was "to make certain ideas incarnate, as if they had revealed themselves to me first in the flesh." On the evidence of David Caute's work, he, too, has seen the need to provide an ampler covering for the bones of his theory.

—John Lucas

CHAPLIN, Sid(ney). British. Born in Shildon, Durham, 20 September 1916. Attended the Workers' Educational Association, University of Durham, 1932-46; Fircroft College for Working Men, Birmingham, 1939. Married Irene Rutherford in 1941; one son and two daughters. Miner, 1931-50; Branch Secretary, Miners Federation of Great Britain, 1943-45. Writer for various coal industry publications and Public Relations Officer for the Northern Division of the National Coal Board, 1950-71. Member, Northern Region Advisory Council, BBC, 1963-68. President, Mid-Northumberland Arts Group. Recipient: Rockefeller Atlantic Award, 1946. M.A.: University of Newcastle upon Tyne, 1978. Honorary Fellow, Sunderland Polytechnic. O.B.E. (Officer, Order of the British Empire), 1977. Agent: David Higham, 5-8 Lower John Street, London W1R 3PE, England.

PUBLICATIONS

Novels

My Fate Cries Out. London, Phoenix House, 1949.
The Thin Seam. London, Phoenix House, 1950.
The Big Room. London, Eyre and Spottiswoode, 1960.
The Day of the Sardine. London, Eyre and Spottiswoode, 1961.
The Watchers and the Watched. London, Eyre and Spottiswoode, 1962.
Sam in the Morning. London, Eyre and Spottiswoode, 1965.
The Mines of Alabaster. London, Eyre and Spottiswoode, 1971.

Short Stories

The Leaping Lad and Other Stories. London, Phoenix House, and New York, Dent, 1946; revised edition, London, Longman, 1970.
The Thin Seam and Other Stories. Oxford, Pergamon Press, 1968.
On Christmas Day in the Morning. Manchester, Carcanet Press, 1978; New York, Persea, 1979.
The Bachelor Uncle and Other Stories. Manchester, Carcanet Press, 1980.

Plays

The Big Room, with Jeremy Kingston (produced Billingham, County Durham, 1969).
The Day of the Sardine, with David Illingworth and Alex Glasgow (produced Billingham, County Durham, 1973).

Television Plays: *When the Boat Comes In* series (2 episodes), 1976; *Paper Round* series (1 episode), 1978; *Funny Man* series (2 episodes), 1980.

Other

The Lakes of Tyneside. London, Collins, 1951.
The Smell of Sunday Dinner. Newcastle upon Tyne, Frank Graham, 1971.
A Tree with Rosy Apples. Newcastle upon Tyne, Frank Graham, 1972.
Geordie Pride, with Frank Graham. Newcastle upon Tyne, Frank Graham, 1974.

Editor, with Arthur Wise, *Us Northerners.* London, Harrap, 1970.

*

Bibliography: "Sid Chaplin," by George Stephenson, in *Newcastle Life*, January 1969.

Manuscript Collections: University of Durham Library; Northern Arts Collection, Literary and Philosophical Society of Newcastle upon Tyne.

Critical Study: "Prodigal Sons" by Michael Standen, in *Stand* (Newcastle upon Tyne), x, 3, 1969.

Sid Chaplin comments:

My earlier work was strongly influenced by early experiences in workshops and mines—an environment often strained and always exacting and one in which the born story-teller was at a premium. It was probably the discovery that I was a failure in the latter role that started me writing. Naturally I have also been concerned with man's running battle with the intolerable conditions of modern industrial society—and his own conscience. It is this area I wish to depict—and occasionally celebrate.

* * *

Sid Chaplin's first book of short stories, *The Leaping Lad*, established him almost immediately as a regional writer of talent and potential. His intimate understanding of the Durham mining community comes out very well in these stories. This book was followed by *My Fate Cries Out*, a historical novel about the Weardale district of the 1740's, that perhaps owes something in inspiration to Stevenson and Meade Faulkener. It certainly conveys a very special feeling the author has for the moorscape of this part of Durham.

It was with his third book, however, *The Thin Seam*, that Sid Chaplin came to maturity as a writer. It is a novella with a coalmine as setting. The chief character, Chris, is a young man raised in a mining village who has aspired to a wider horizon through a working-men's college before deciding to return to the life in the pit he thought he had left for good. He is one of a team, and the story takes us with Matty, Art, Daniel, and Andrews through the labour and travail of one shift underground. A short space of time, a single setting, a handful of characters suffice to reveal the inner nature of the hero to the reader. The exploratory nature that is given us of Chris is a masterly one. Moorscape also lays a part in *The Big Room*, a family drama, again revolving round a mine, but with the characterisation deepened and the conflict heightened. The economy of the setting is such that it is not surprising that it was dramatised for the stage.

His work is a gradual progress, a continuing broadening of the regional base, so that each novel develops out of its predecessor. Newcastle and "the big city" were themes that he explored next in *The Watchers and the Watched* and *The Day of the Sardine*. His own experience as always gives the satisfactory solidity of factory and excavation-site locales in these two lively and exciting books. In

Sam in the Morning he deals with a different aspect of cityscape: the fascination with the monolithic building that houses the corporate enterprise, and the managerial society, cut off from both the workers and the boardroom in their own quest for power. In this novel his Northeast hero is placed in a metropolitan setting. He keeps in touch with his regional roots while expanding his scale. It is as though by this stage he can leave the immediate Tyneside scene confident that it is always there to come back to if he needs it.

His latest novel, *The Mines of Alabaster*, continues this expansion. He now moves with ease whatever the setting, be it London, East Anglia, or Italy. His main character, Harry John Brown, has problems which are not those of an expatriate Geordie, but the more universal concerns of any human being in trouble.

Critics are sometimes inclined to put regional writers into a second division. Sid Chaplin confounds the critics by his continuing and changing variety. The regional theme is still there but it is one on which he can now play infinite variations.

—George Stephenson

CHARLES, Gerda. British. Born in Liverpool, Lancashire. Educated in Liverpool schools. Free-lance writer: television critic, *Jewish Chronicle*, London, 1978-79. Recipient: Black Memorial Prize, 1964; Arts Council grant, 1970; Whitbread Literary Award, 1971. Address: 22 Cunningham Court, London W9 1AE, England.

PUBLICATIONS

Novels

The True Voice. London, Eyre and Spottiswoode, 1959.
The Crossing Point. London, Eyre and Spottiswoode, 1960; New York, Knopf, 1961.
A Slanting Light. London, Eyre and Spottiswoode, and New York, Knopf, 1963.
A Logical Girl. London, Eyre and Spottiswoode, and New York, Knopf, 1967.
The Destiny Waltz. London, Eyre and Spottiswoode, 1971; New York, Scribner, 1972.

Uncollected Short Stories

"The Staircase," in *Vanity Fair* (London), April 1956.
"Rosh Hashanah in Five Weeks," in *Pick of Today's Short Stories 11.* London, Putnam, 1960.
"The Czech-Slovakian Chandelier," in *Modern Jewish Stories.* London, Faber, 1963; Englewood Cliffs, New Jersey, Prentice Hall, 1965.
"A Mixed Marriage," in *Quest* (London), 1965.
"The Difference," in *Jewish Chronicle* (London), 24 November 1967.
"The Mitzvah," in *Jewish Chronicle* (London), March 1978.

Other

Editor, *Modern Jewish Stories.* London, Faber, 1963; Englewood Cliffs, New Jersey, Prentice Hall, 1965.

*

Critical Studies: "The World of Gerda Charles," in *Jewish Quarterly* (London), Summer 1967; "Facing the Music" by C.P. Snow, in *Financial Times* (London), 15 April 1971; "Revenge Is Sour," in *Guardian* (London), 27 May 1971; "Gerda Charles: A Visionary Realist," in *Jewish Quarterly* (London), Summer 1971.

Gerda Charles comments:

Though I am known primarily as an Anglo-Jewish writer, my five novels all deal in general with what I have described (in my third book, *A Slanting Light*) as "the region of everyday hurt." My books are not concerned with extremes—which I believe to be largely unrelated to the real problems of living. They are not concerned with madness but rather with the job of maintaining sanity, dignity, and order. They advocate the unfashionable virtues of delicacy, tact, and generosity of heart within the context of day-to-day life.

* * *

The True Voice is an excellent first novel in which Gerda Charles develops a principal theme—the alienation felt by a person of talent when he is unable to articulate his aspirations and to communicate his inner intensities to others. After two disillusioning experiences with men, Lindy Frome finds that her only valid resource is the self, as she attains awareness of "the compassionate irony with which it was necessary to confront life; how flexibility, awareness and forgiveness were all."

With *The Crossing Point* Miss Charles wrote her best book. She asserts through Rabbi Leo Norberg that Judaism is the most viable of religions for human beings since it is at "the crossing point" where opposites such as asceticism and sensuousness, mysticism and secularism, idealism and practicality converge. Boruch Gabriel is imposing as a presence but not as an influence since his conception of religion is literal and monolithic. His daughter, Sara, illustrates the true strength of Judaism as it gives her courage to face her father and her own life of impaired fulfilment. Rabbi Norberg is the novel's intellectual center. Humane and imaginative, he sometimes lacks the courage to act upon his insights. Knowing the best in Sara Gabriel, he chooses, out of a certain perversity and false pride, the second best, a calculating and fourth-rate woman, for wife. The characters, big with life, give the book its stature. They are human beings who also happen to be Jews, as they falter or triumph in achieving their destinies.

A Slanting Light is a notable if less arresting book. A psychically immolated American playwright, Bernard Zold, is protagonist. His chief antagonist is a power-hungry mother; his wife is superficial and his child unloving. He is a sufferer rather than a doer, a man of sympathetic imagination rather than of active confidence. For the narrator he is emblematic of "the whole role of the Jew in the historic life of the world's soul" and exemplifies "the human nature of society." Zold hardly achieves this archetypal dimension, and Charles's analysis of Zold as artist lacks immediacy and exactitude. But as a novel exploring entangled relationships it has distinction and force.

In *A Logical Girl*, Charles's best book since *The Crossing Point*, Rose Morgan's views of what ought to be are in abrupt contrast with the way things are. In World War II in a seaside town, she develops from naive adolescence to maturity while the town is "invaded" by European and American troops. Her sensitivity allows her to see how selfish, impersonal, and degrading her associates and family often are, while they impress the world as models of virtue and propriety. The elements of deceit, inconsiderateness, and cruelty which all too often determine human relationships are the reflection in little of the injustices and sadism in the Nazi regime on the continent. Rose learns that human beings do not behave consistently and logically, that impulse is often triumphant over honesty. Charles finely controls her irony as she demonstrates in Rose how the individual who sees the truth is disregarded by most other people in their reverence for the flashy, the meretricious, and the materialistic.

The Destiny Waltz is Charles's longest and least satisfactory novel. It concerns the surviving influence of Paul Salomon, a great poet from the 1920's who had been passed over in his lifetime. At the instigation of a television company, Jimmy Marchant, a retired band leader and Paul's closest friend, meets Michele Sandburg, a college teacher in her forties who has written the best life of the poet. They are to help make a documentary film about Salomon's life. Much pathos and intense feeling develop when Jimmy realizes that in Michele he may yet find the happiness that eluded him in his marriage and sexual affairs. Yet Jimmy lacks interest and presence, and his moralizing, while genuine, is frequently labored. Again, Charles fails to make her artist believable; we have, in short, little idea of what Salomon's poetry was like. She does depict with assuredness the studio milieu, wherein prudential motives and the requirements of art are in locked conflict. In sum, Charles has overextended her materials for the value which accrues to them.

Gerda Charles has analyzed with sympathy and comprehension the spiritual misfit in modern life. Her insight into human nature is penetrating; and her eccentrics, as well as her fully developed figures, are authentic. She establishes the outlines of her characters economically by concentrated analysis and persuasive dialogue. As a stylist her prose is always perspicuous and perfectly modulated to convey a sense of Jamesian complexities in character and situation. Her main preoccupation is with the painful incursion of moral knowledge. The process whereby her protagonists determine "how to be" is fraught with anguish, on occasion with muted triumph, always with the ring of truth.

—Frederick P.W. McDowell

CHARYN, Jerome. American. Born in New York City, 13 May 1937. Educated at Columbia University, New York, B.A. (cum laude) 1959. Former Recreation Leader, New York City Department of Parks. English Teacher, High School of Music and Art and School of Performing Arts, New York, 1962-64; Assistant Professor of English, Stanford University, California, 1965-68. Assistant Professor, 1968-72, Associate Professor, 1972-78, and since 1978, Professor of English, Herbert Lehman College of the City University of New York. Mellon Visiting Professor of English, Rice University, Houston, 1979; Visiting Professor, Princeton University, New Jersey, 1980. Since 1970, Founding Editor, *Dutton Review*, New York; since 1972, Executive Editor, *Fiction*, New York. Recipient: Rosenthal Foundation Award, 1981. Address: 39 West 67th Street, Apartment 802, New York, New York 10023, U.S.A.

PUBLICATIONS

Novels

Once Upon a Droshky. New York, McGraw Hill, 1964.
On the Darkening Green. New York, McGraw Hill, 1965.
Going to Jerusalem. New York, Viking Press, 1967; London, Cape, 1968.
American Scrapbook. New York, Viking Press, 1969.
Eisenhower, My Eisenhower. New York, Holt Rinehart, 1971.
The Tar Baby. New York, Holt Rinehart, 1973.
Blue Eyes. New York, Simon and Schuster, 1975.
Marilyn the Wild. New York, Arbor House, 1976.
The Education of Patrick Silver. New York, Arbor House, 1976.
The Franklin Scare. New York, Arbor House, 1977.
Secret Isaac. New York, Arbor House, 1978.
The Seventh Babe. New York, Arbor House, 1979.
The Catfish Man: A Conjured Life. New York, Arbor House, 1980.
Darlin' Bill. New York, Arbor House, 1980.
Pinocchio's Nose. New York, Arbor House, 1981.
Panna Maria. New York, Arbor House, 1981.

Short Stories

The Man Who Grew Younger and Other Stories. New York, Harper, 1967.

Other

Editor, *The Single Voice: An Anthology of Contemporary Fiction.* New York, Collier, 1969.
Editor, *The Troubled Vision.* New York, Collier, 1970.

*

Critical Studies: reviews in *Life* (New York), 6 June 1969; *Newsweek* (New York), 9 June 1969; *Time* (New York), 4 July 1969; *Christian Science Monitor* (Boston), 24 July 1969; *Saturday Review* (New York), 23 August 1969; *Midstream* (New York), October 1969; introductions by the author to *The Single Voice*, 1969, and *The Troubled Vision*, 1970; *New York Times Book Review*, 28 March 1971; "Notes on the Rhetoric of Anti-Realist Fiction" by Albert Guerard, in *Tri-Quarterly* (Evanston, Illinois), Spring 1974.

* * *

One of our most prolific young novelists, Jerome Charyn is at his best when describing the contemporary urban scene. His prose then moves at the frantic pace of city life, his eccentric characters at home in the bizarre world of city streets. Charyn's people are civilization's cast-offs—emotional, physical, or intellectual misfits—in whose attempts to understand themselves and their environment Charyn finds both comedy and poetry.

Charyn's earliest novels, *Once Upon a Droshky* and *On the Darkening Green*, are set in New York City in the 1930's and 1940's. Each has a first-person narrator whose simple, coarse, and yet melodic language accounts for much of the merit in the stories they tell. *Once Upon a Droshky* concerns a group of Jewish tenants fighting modern society in the form of an eviction notice. Their struggle is doomed from the start, but Charyn avoids depicting their ultimate defeat; instead he ends the novel just before their final confrontation with the authorities. The victims in *On the Darkening Green* are not the very old but the very young. The narrator, an Italian tenement dweller from the Bronx, accepts a position as counsellor at the Blattenburg Home for Wayward Jewish Boys, but his natural instincts align him with the boys, and he even joins them in a futile rebellion against their oppressors.

In his next group of novels Charyn unfortunately broke away from the big city setting. *Going to Jerusalem* begins at the South Brooklyn Military Academy, but the chief characters soon leave Brooklyn for a series of chess exhibitions across America, ending on Crazy Day in Yell County, Arkansas. The story is told through the eyes and mind of an epileptic undergoing a breakdown, so the reader does not always know whether the outlandish incidents he describes are meant to be real or imaginary. *American Scrapbook* presents an equally unsavory view of America, but the setting at least is decidedly real: a detention camp for Japanese-Americans during World War II. Some of the inmates choose to cooperate with the authorities; others form an organization of terrorists. The atmosphere is unreal, even surreal, but the conditions described are historically authentic. Charyn takes more liberties with history in *The Franklin Scare*, a novel about the Roosevelts, J. Edgar Hoover, Churchill, and Stalin in the closing days of the war, all as viewed through the eyes of FDR's personal barber, a Candide-like figure observing great events with wide-eyed innocence and incomprehension.

Violence is again pervasive in Charyn's second string of novels on urban life. After *Eisenhower, My Eisenhower*, an allegory set in a city called Bedlam, Charyn turned to a cycle of novels about an unorthodox police inspector fighting a crime family in Manhattan and the Bronx. There is an overall coherence in *Blue Eyes*, *Marilyn the Wild*, *The Education of Patrick Silver*, and *Secret Isaac* not to be found in any of the books individually. The series is reminiscent of Charyn's earliest works, and some of his most colorful characters flit in and out of these stories: an Ivy-league cop, a teenage porno queen, a detective living in a ping-pong parlor, gypsies, an albino, a seemingly endless supply of grotesques.

Charyn's views about the literary world come through in two less successful novels, *The Tar Baby*, a satire on the academic community in general, literary scholarship in particular, and *The Catfish Man*, a self-consciously autobiographical book whose principal virtue is once again the evocation of the New York scene.

The most interesting of Charyn's non-urban novels may well be his recent *The Seventh Babe*, a baseball story steeped in Americana. The hero, the son of a business tycoon, rejects his father's wealth and presents himself to the fans as an orphan from Baltimore, just like the other Babe. As a left-handed third baseman, Babe Ragland already defies tradition, but he fits thereby the Charyn mold perfectly. When banned from the majors by the powers of baseball for accepting money from gamblers, he and a hunchback batboy move to the Negro League and barnstorm America. Like so many other Charyn characters, the Babe is happiest when surrounded by other homeless victims of social oppression.

The recurring Charyn themes may seem simplistic, but he presents them with persuasive charm in almost every one of his many books: that power over others inevitably corrupts, that the only ones free of corruption are the powerless, that human decency is invariably and exclusively the single possession of the dispossessed.

—Robert E. Lynch

CHEEVER, John. American. Born in Quincy, Massachusetts, 27 May 1912. Educated at the Thayer Academy. Served in the United States Army in World War II. Married Mary M. Winternitz in 1941; one daughter and two sons. Taught at Barnard College, New York, 1956-57; Visiting Professor of Creative Writing, Boston University, 1974-75. Recipient: Guggenheim Fellowship, 1951; Benjamin Franklin Award, 1955; O. Henry Award, 1956, 1964; American Academy grant, 1956, and Howells Medal, 1965; National Book Award, 1958; National Book Critics Circle Award, 1979; Pulitzer Prize, 1979; Edward MacDowell Medal, 1979. Member, American Academy. Address: Cedar Lane, Ossining, New York 10562, U.S.A.

PUBLICATIONS

Novels

The Wapshot Chronicle. New York, Harper, and London, Gollancz, 1957.
The Wapshot Scandal. New York, Harper, and London, Gollancz, 1964.
Bullet Park. New York, Knopf, and London, Cape, 1969.
Falconer. New York, Knopf, and London, Cape, 1977.

Short Stories

The Way Some People Live: A Book of Stories. New York, Random House, 1943.
The Enormous Radio and Other Stories. New York, Funk and Wagnalls, and London, Gollancz, 1953.
Stories, with others. New York, Farrar Straus, 1956; as *A Book of Stories*, London, Gollancz, 1957.
The Housebreaker of Shady Hill and Other Stories. New York, Harper, 1958; London, Gollancz, 1959.
Some People, Places, and Things That Will Not Appear in My Next Novel. New York, Harper, and London, Gollancz, 1961.
The Brigadier and the Golf Widow. New York, Harper, 1964; London, Gollancz, 1965.
The World of Apples. New York, Knopf, 1973; London, Cape, 1974.
The Stories of John Cheever. New York, Knopf, 1978; London, Cape, 1979.

Uncollected Short Story

"The Night Mummy Got the Wrong Mink Coat," in *New Yorker*, 21 April 1980.

*

Critical Studies: *John Cheever* by Samuel Coale, New York, Ungar, 1977; *John Cheever* by Lynne Waldeland, Boston, Twayne, 1979.

* * *

John Cheever has been a consistently successful writer of short stories, as the collected edition of these stories so amply demonstrates, but his four ventures into the more ambitious form of the novel have been, with the possible exception of *The Wapshot Chronicle*, far less satisfying. He is a shrewd observer of the manners and morals of American middle-class life, especially in the suburbs. He is also, rather unexpectedly, a keen and appreciative observer of light and shadow, sea foam and cloud; he has a sensuous rapport with the world of nature. His work reveals a sensibility that has retained a certain naive faith and romantic glow despite a recognition of man's capacity for error and sin and despite a conviction that things are growing steadily worse in contemporary society.

The sprightly social comedy that Cheever writes cannot hide, and is not intended to hide, the fact that Cheever is delivering judgments on his characters as they blunder or claw their way through life. And he judges them, in their modern folly, by conventional and traditional standards. If he is amused by the carnal anarchy that he records as the characteristic sexual pattern of suburban life, he is also likely to punish those who engage in it. He records the disintegration of the middle class in America with the accuracy and detachment of the sociologist, but he is in reality concerned and disapproving. When he shows that people cannot maintain their marriages intact, the thrust of the story clearly indicates Cheever's sense of their inadequacy. When, in a story like "The Cure," a divorced couple comes together again in a moving moment, Cheever is triumphant in the affirmation of domestic stability and the sanctity of marriage. Like most other social observers, Cheever knows that Americans cannot cope with love, which he unabashedly if not profoundly celebrates. He does not abjure the discussion of sex, but he treats the matter with dignity and, except in *Falconer*, with a rather old-fashioned reticence. He portrays his sophisticated characters as failures in parenthood who either abuse or neglect their children; the people in "The Sutton Place Story" see their child only at the cocktail hour and can know neither the joys nor the sorrows of raising her. Cheever's protagonists, his modern anti-heroes, are frequently immoral, lecherous, frightened, fraudulent, empty, and failing human beings.

It is the note of failure that says so much for Cheever's penetration to the realities of American society. He has seen beneath the glossy surface—he himself makes the conventional distinction between the appearance and reality of things—of prosperous America where the imminent possibility of failure lies like lead in the heart of the suburbanite as he lolls at poolside or plans his bomb shelter. Cheever's people know that they must scramble for success and that some of them will not reach it. They know they must cling to respectability, and some of them will fail. Cheever recognizes the dynamic quality of American society, but he takes a dim view of it because change can mean lack of community or downward mobility. In Cheever's stories change can be for the worse, and frequently is, because no one has a fixed place or a fixed identity. The class lines are always shifting. The irony of Cheever's fiction is that behind the bright surfaces presented by the station wagon and the Georgian home of the suburbs are the tensions of lives in disorder and the fears of losing one's place.

In a few stories dealing with the international theme, Cheever has been critical of expatriates, whose efforts to adopt another culture constitute another kind of failure. He rejects the international experience out of a view, again old-fashioned and unashamed, that his own country, flawed as it is, is superior to others. *The Wapshot Chronicle* reveals the nature of Cheever's engagement with America, which is a nostalgic and romantic attachment to its past. Successfully skirting sentimentality, Cheever re-creates a dying fishing village in Massachusetts. The quality of life in the past here stands as a rebuke to the shabby present. The hero of the novel possesses virtues and vitality derived from the past; they are living criticism of life in the present. Leander Wapshot loves his sons, he loves the rituals of life, especially those pertaining to manliness, he loves his native place, and he recognizes a compelling urge to come into a right relation with the world of nature. He rejects modern skepticism and despair. The dignity, compassion, courage, and trust that he brings to the world make him an anachronism. The contrast between the present and the past to which he belongs is summed up in the loss of his job. He is the skipper of a ferry boat which he loses to his wife, who converts it into New England's only floating gift shoppe. Leander commits suicide by swimming off into the sea.

The Wapshot Scandal, which deals with the lives of Leander's sons, is a thesis-ridden novel in which Cheever mounts a predictable attack upon contemporary American life. He laments its failure of community; its science, which creates weapons but tells us nothing about lust and pain; its plastic and glass environments. In short, he protests against all the forces of modern culture that make us less than human. *Bullet Park*, which considers familiar Cheever subjects like the suburbs and failure, is so feeble a novel that the less said about it the better.

Falconer, much more effective, deals with prison life as a metaphor for human degradation. The protagonist, descendant of a patrician Yankee family, is a victim and participant in a crumbling marriage, sexual deviation, dope addiction, and violence. He demonstrates that it is virtually impossible for traditional attitudes and persons to survive in our time. But he refuses to surrender, and against all reason, does survive and gains his freedom under the open sky. The novel is unsteady in tone and marred by stereotype and sentimentality. Cheever does not have the intensity of imagination to sustain a long fiction. But he does have the courage to assert the validity of the old virtues and the rhetoric to move us to admiration for them. In our dreary time he speaks unblushingly of loving, gentle women, of stout-hearted friends, of admiring the world, of the bread and wine of life. He almost persuades us that these goods are still available.

—Chester E. Eisinger

CLARK, Eleanor. American. Born in Los Angeles, California, 6 July 1913; grew up in Roxbury, Connecticut. Educated at Vassar College, Poughkeepsie, New York, B.A. 1934. Married Robert Penn Warren, *q.v.*, in 1952; two children. Editorial Staff Member, W.W. Norton and Company, publishers, New York, 1936-39. Worked for the United States Office of Strategic Services, Washington, D.C., 1943-45. Recipient: American Academy grant, 1947; Guggenheim Fellowship, 1947, 1949; National Book Award, for non-fiction, 1965. Member, American Academy. Address: 2495 Redding Road, Fairfield, Connecticut 06430, U.S.A.

PUBLICATIONS

Novels

The Bitter Box. New York, Doubleday, 1946; London, Joseph, 1947.
Baldur's Gate. New York, Pantheon, 1970.
Gloria Mundi. New York, Pantheon, 1979.

Short Stories

Dr. Heart: A Novella and Other Stories. New York, Pantheon, 1974.

Uncollected Short Stories

"Zoysia Grass," in *Yale Review* (New Haven, Connecticut), October 1977.
"Chains of Loches," in *Southern Review* (Baton Rouge, Louisiana), October 1977.

Other

Rome and a Villa. New York, Doubleday, 1952; London, Joseph, 1953; revised edition, New York, Pantheon, 1975; Henley on Thames, Ellis, 1976.
The Song of Roland (juvenile). New York, Random House, 1960; London, Muller, 1962.
The Oysters of Locmariaquer. New York, Pantheon, 1964; London, Secker and Warburg, 1965.
Eyes, Etc.: A Memoir. New York, Pantheon, 1977; London, Collins, 1978.

Editor, with Horace Gregory, *New Letters in America*. New York, Norton, 1937.

Translator, *The Dark Wedding*, by Ramón Sender. New York, Doubleday, 1943; London, Grey Walls Press, 1948.

*

Eleanor Clark comments:

(1972) I do not feel it is wise or in most cases helpful for writers to analyze their own work. In any case, I find it impossible, except to remark that, concerning impulse, motive and kind of personal involvement, I find no clear line of demarcation between my novels and nonfiction books (*Rome* and *Oysters*). This does not of course refer to essays—a different job altogether.

Can a woman be a good writer (artist) and a good mother? I have no idea. Are the two in conflict? Of course—so is art and everything else. Do I love and value my two children above my books? Certainly. Would I have stopped writing altogether if necessary for the children's happiness? Well, yes, but it would perhaps not have been physically possible—in the sense that one eats when hungry and scratches when itching—and with a little sleight-of-hand it was never quite necessary for too fatally long at a time. However, these facts do relate to *Baldur's Gate* having been written over a period of many years. It was in gestation, with false starts, long before that, but the home-town scene (the usual first novel) was too close. I disposed of it when young in a story, "Hurry, Hurry," found a built-in distance for my first published novel, *The Bitter Box*, and came to the perspective for the original one only years later, possibly through the fact of having children.

* * *

Twenty-four years separate Eleanor Clark's first novel and her second and in comparison one gives the impression of looking backward and the other of looking forward. *The Bitter Box*, though published in 1946, reflects the leftist social ferment of the 1930's. The novel's center is a timid, punctilious bank clerk named Mr.

Temple who in his teller's cage serves efficiently, almost worshipfully, the symbol of capitalism until driven by a sense of oppression to search out and embrace another god vaguely defined as "the party," the official organ of which is the *Word*. His ultimate realization that both gods are false and corrupt is accompanied by an awakening to the redemptive influences of suffering and love. By painfully relinquishing the safety of a life of order and obedience he gradually learns to trust and to give of himself in concern for others. This theme of surrender into life, present also in *Baldur's Gate*, fails of effect in *The Bitter Box* largely because of a patronizing, detached point of view which creates a curiously remote and improbable hero whose political activism seems arbitrary rather than necessary and probable.

Baldur's Gate, an ambitious work rich in symbol and allusion, deals with a wealth of themes: the preservation of tradition, the search for values, the function of art, commercialism, ecology, among others. Eva Buckingham Hines relates the events in a complex style—disordered chronology, internal monologue, depth analysis—which complements her personal tortuous course out of the often painful and sometimes alluring memories of the past toward acceptance of the present and courage for the future. The memories derive from growing up in Jordan, an old Connecticut town rich in tradition and in the history of human weakness and error. And though she seems to be committed to the future, having married Lucas Hines and borne a son, in reality she is hostage to her past: to the pain and frustration of an indifferent and alcoholic mother, an ineffectual father, a corrupt brother, a once proud family socially disgraced, and to the memory of a love betrayed.

Her futile attempt to renew this early love affair with Jack Pryden and thus redeem the past is the motivating force behind many of the events, but it is the presence of the 70-year-old sculptor, Baldur Blake (the name suggesting his role as demi-god and mystic), which lifts the novel above this rather trivial love affair. Having himself fought the battle of disillusionment with the heritage of the past, he returns to vision and creativity, like a fertility god in spring, revitalizing the whole community with promise that the future which destroys the past can also generate new beauty and harmony.

In the closing scene as Eva stands in the falling snow viewing the town dump, symbol of waste but also of change, the fundamental law of things, she reflects that his message had been "not to kid ourselves, about what art, home, love, Jordan, anything could ever mean to us again, and yet to keep capable of love, of work, of hope." The dream of a new community fails of realization, but the vision of the gate model Baldur never lived to complete remains, the "imitation of some large serenity always in the act of rising out of torment." The novel captures that torment and the courage to master it, but more frequently in the rhetoric than in the characters and situations. In the final analysis the plot and characters seem not quite the equal of the novel's deep philosophical vision.

—Dale K. Doepke

CLARKE, Arthur C(harles). British. Born in Minehead, Somerset, 16 December 1917. Educated at Huish's Grammar School, Taunton, Somerset, 1927-36; King's College, London, B.Sc. (honours) in physics and mathematics 1948. Flight Lieutenant in the Royal Air Force, 1941-46; served as Radar Instructor, and Technical Officer on the first Ground Controlled Approach radar; originated proposal for use of satellites for communications, 1945. Married Marilyn Mayfield in 1954 (divorced, 1964). Assistant Auditor, Exchequer and Audit Department, London, 1936-41; Assistant Editor, *Physics Abstracts*, London, 1949-50. Since 1954, engaged in underwater exploration and photography of the Great Barrier Reef of Australia and the coast of Sri Lanka. Director, Rocket Publishing, London, Underwater Safaris, Colombo, and Spaceward Corporation, New York. Has made numerous radio and television appearances, and has lectured widely in Britain and the United States; commentator, for CBS-TV, on lunar flights of Apollo 11, 12, and 15. Recipient: International Fantasy Award, 1952; Hugo Award, 1956, 1974, 1980; Unesco Kalinga Prize, 1961; Boys' Clubs of America award, 1961; Franklin Institute Ballantine Medal, 1963; Aviation-Space Writers Association Ball Award, 1965; American Association for the Advancement of Science Westinghouse Award, 1969; *Playboy* award, 1971; Jupiter Award, 1973; Nebula Award, 1973, 1974, 1980; Campbell Memorial Award, 1974; American Institute of Aeronautics and Astronautics award, 1974; Boston Museum of Science Washburn Award, 1977. D.Sc.: Beaver College, Glenside, Pennsylvania, 1971. Chairman, British Interplanetary Society, 1946-47, 1950-53. Fellow, Royal Astronomical Society; Fellow, King's College, London, 1977; Chancellor, Moratuwa University, Sri Lanka, 1979. Agent: David Higham Associates Ltd., 5-8 Lower John Street, London W1R 4HA, England. Address: 25 Barnes Place, Columbo 7, Sri Lanka.

PUBLICATIONS

Novels

Prelude to Space. New York, Galaxy, 1951; London, Sidgwick and Jackson, 1953; as *Master of Space*, New York, Lancer, 1961; as *The Space Dreamers*, Lancer, 1969.
The Sands of Mars. London, Sidgwick and Jackson, 1951; New York, Gnome Press, 1952.
Against the Fall of Night. New York, Gnome Press, 1953.
Childhood's End. New York, Ballantine, 1953; London, Sidgwick and Jackson, 1954.
Earthlight. London, Muller, and New York, Ballantine, 1955.
The City and the Stars. London, Muller, and New York, Harcourt Brace, 1956.
The Deep Range. New York, Harcourt Brace, and London, Muller, 1957.
Across the Sea of Stars (omnibus). New York, Harcourt Brace, 1959.
A Fall of Moondust. London, Gollancz, and New York, Harcourt Brace, 1961.
From the Oceans, From the Stars (omnibus). New York, Harcourt Brace, 1962.
Glide Path. New York, Harcourt Brace, 1963; London, Sidgwick and Jackson, 1969.
Prelude to Mars (omnibus). New York, Harcourt Brace, 1965.
2001: A Space Odyssey (novelization of screenplay). New York, New American Library, and London, Hutchinson, 1968.
The Lion of Comarre, and Against the Fall of Night. New York, Harcourt Brace, 1968; London, Gollancz, 1970.
Rendezvous with Rama. London, Gollancz, and New York, Harcourt Brace, 1973.
Imperial Earth. London, Gollancz, 1975; New York, Harcourt Brace, 1976.
The Fountains of Paradise. London, Gollancz, and New York, Harcourt Brace, 1979.

Short Stories

Expedition to Earth. New York, Ballantine, 1953; London, Sidgwick and Jackson, 1954.
Reach for Tomorrow. New York, Ballantine, 1956; London, Gollancz, 1962.
Tales from the White Hart. New York, Ballantine, 1957; London, Sidgwick and Jackson, 1972.
The Other Side of the Sky. New York, Harcourt Brace, 1958; London, Gollancz, 1961.
Tales of Ten Worlds. New York, Harcourt Brace, 1962; London, Gollancz, 1963.
The Nine Billion Names of God: The Best Short Stories of Arthur C. Clarke. New York, Harcourt Brace, 1967.

The Wind from the Sun: Stories of the Space Age. New York, Harcourt Brace, and London, Gollancz, 1972.
Of Time and Stars: The Worlds of Arthur C. Clarke. London, Gollancz, 1972.
The Best of Arthur C. Clarke 1937-1971, edited by Angus Wells. London, Sidgwick and Jackson, 1973.

Uncollected Short Story

"Quarantine," in *Isaac Asimov's Science Fiction Magazine* (New York), Spring 1977.

Play

Screenplay: *2001: A Space Odyssey*, with Stanley Kubrick, 1968.

Other

Interplanetary Flight: An Introduction to Astronautics. London, Temple Press, 1950; New York, Harper, 1951; revised edition, 1960.
The Exploration of Space. London, Temple Press, and New York, Harper, 1951; revised edition 1959.
Islands in the Sky (juvenile). London, Sidgwick and Jackson, and Philadelphia, Winston, 1952.
The Young Traveller in Space (juvenile). London, Phoenix House, 1954; as *Going into Space*, New York, Harper, 1954; as *The Scottie Book of Space Travel*, London, Transworld, 1957; revised edition, with Robert Silverberg, as *Into Space*, New York, Harper, 1971.
The Exploration of the Moon. London, Muller, 1954; New York, Harper, 1955.
The Coast of Coral. London, Muller, and New York, Harper, 1956.
The Making of a Moon: The Story of the Earth Satellite Program. London, Muller, and New York, Harper, 1957; revised edition, Harper, 1958.
The Reefs of Taprobane: Underwater Adventures Around Ceylon. London, Muller, and New York, Harper, 1957.
Voice Across the Sea. London, Muller, 1958; New York, Harper, 1959; revised edition, London, Mitchell Beazley, and Harper, 1974.
Boy Beneath the Sea (juvenile). New York, Harper, 1958.
The Challenge of the Spaceship: Previews of Tomorrow's World. New York, Harper, 1959; London, Muller, 1960.
The First Five Fathoms: A Guide to Underwater Adventure. New York, Harper, 1960.
The Challenge of the Sea. New York, Holt Rinehart, 1960; London, Muller, 1961.
Indian Ocean Adventure. New York, Harper, 1961; London, Barker, 1962.
Profiles of the Future: An Enquiry into the Limits of the Possible. London, Gollancz, 1962; New York, Harper, 1963; revised edition, Harper, 1973; Gollancz, 1974.
Dolphin Island (juvenile). New York, Holt Rinehart, and London, Gollancz, 1963.
The Treasure of the Great Reef. London, Barker, and New York, Harper, 1964; revised edition, New York, Ballantine, 1974.
Indian Ocean Treasure, with Mike Wilson. New York, Harper, 1964; London, Sidgwick and Jackson, 1972.
Man and Space, with the editors of Life. New York, Time, 1964.
Voices from the Sky: Previews of the Coming Space Age. New York, Harper, 1965; London, Gollancz, 1966.
The Promise of Space. New York, Harper, and London, Hodder and Stoughton, 1968.
First on the Moon, with the astronauts. London, Joseph, and Boston, Little Brown, 1970.
Report on Planet Three and Other Speculations. London, Gollancz, and New York, Harper, 1972.
The Lost Worlds of 2001. London, Sidgwick and Jackson, and New York, New American Library, 1972.
Beyond Jupiter: The Worlds of Tomorrow, with Chesley Bonestell. Boston, Little Brown, 1972.
Technology and the Frontiers of Knowledge (lectures), with others. New York, Doubleday, 1975.
The View from Serendip (on Sri Lanka). New York, Random House, 1977; London, Gollancz, 1978.

Editor, *Time Probe: Sciences in Science Fiction*. New York, Delacorte Press, 1966; London, Gollancz, 1967.
Editor, *The Coming of the Space Age: Famous Accounts of Man's Probing of the Universe*. London, Gollancz, and New York, Meredith, 1967.
Editor, *Science Fiction Hall of Fame 4*. London, Gollancz, 1981.

*

Manuscript Collection: Mugar Memorial Library, Boston University.

Critical Studies: "Out of the Ego Chamber" by Jeremy Bernstein, in *New Yorker*, 9 August 1969; *Arthur C. Clarke* edited by Joseph D. Olander and Martin H. Greenberg, New York, Taplinger, and Edinburgh, Harris, 1977; *The Space Odysseys of Arthur C. Clarke* by George Edgar Slusser, San Bernardino, California, Borgo Press, 1978; *Arthur C. Clarke* (includes bibliography) by Eric S. Rabkin, West Linn, Oregon, Starmont House, 1979.

Arthur C. Clarke comments:

I regard myself primarily as an entertainer and my ideals are Maugham, Kipling, Wells. My chief aim is the old SF cliché, "The search for wonder." However, I am almost equally interested in style and rhythm, having been much influenced by Tennyson, Swinburne, Housman, and the Georgian poets.

My main themes are exploration (space, sea, time), the position of Man in the hierarchy of the universe, and the effect of contact with other intelligences. The writer who probably had most influence on me was W. Olaf Stapledon (*Last and First Men*).

* * *

Arthur C. Clarke writes adventures of the near and far future, in which men seek knowledge and explore new environments. The most notable aspect of his fiction is the perfect welding of the expository passages, containing accurate but clear scientific explanations of how the adventures will sooner or later become possible, to the narrative passages.

Several of the adventures occur at or near the beginnings of exploration of a new environment. *Prelude to Space* fictionalizes what leads up to the first trip to the moon. *Earthlight* depicts the workings of the lunar colony, and *The Sands of Mars* does the same for that planet. *Islands in the Sky* explores the uses of space stations, and *The Deep Range* and *Dolphin Island* explore the uses of the sea, such as whale farming and cooperation with dolphins.

Three of Clarke's novels are primarily religious and philosophical. *Against the Fall of Night*, completed in 1946 and published in 1953, was rewritten as *The City and the Stars*. Diaspar, a city of the remote future, has (to paraphrase a favorite Clarke generalization) a technology so advanced that it cannot be distinguished from magic. But the city is a womb from which none of its citizens dare to escape until one courageous explorer goes on a quest for knowledge of the past, which opens up a new future for his society. In *Childhood's End* alien "Overlords" stop man's development of space travel until man, remade by his own unsuspected psychic powers, rises to a new level of childhood and moves toward the stars. The quest of David Bowman in *2001: A Space Odyssey* transforms him into Star-Child, who will "think of something" to move man up the ladder of evolution.

Clarke does in his short stories (such as those collected in *Reach for Tomorrow*, *The Other Side of the Sky*, *Tales of Ten Worlds*, and *Tales from the White Hart*) what he does elsewhere—plus some things which he does not do elsewhere. "Breaking Strain," for example, is a study of contrasting personalities in crisis; "Hate" is a moral fable; "Transcience" is a nearly plotless poem written in prose which compares and contrasts three stages of man's existence.

Rendezvous with Rama, about an alien spaceship's mysterious visit to the solar system, is in some ways unique among Clarke's novels in that it allows the mystery to remain unexplained. Astronauts from Earth visit the vast ship, which is apparently now devoid of intelligent life and acting automatically; but they never do discover its origin and purpose. This is in contrast to *2001: A Space Odyssey*, in which the alien purpose is perhaps explained too thoroughly. Clarke's descriptive powers come marvellously to bear on the vast interior of the ship and the strange robotic forms which inhabit it.

What could Clarke do after *2001: A Space Odyssey* and *Rendezvous with Rama*? There is some, perhaps inevitable, deflation in *Imperial Earth*, a novel about the American Quincentennial in 2276. Clarke assumes an Americanized world—indeed, solar system—after a rather vague "time of troubles." The prestige of the MacKenzie family, derived from centuries of prominence in diplomacy, is more significant than any remaining national power. Duncan MacKenzie's visit to earth from his native Titan fails to provide enough plot to sustain a novel. There are only technological bits and pieces of interest, such as an excursion on the raised ship *The Titanic*.

Clarke's full imaginative powers return with *The Fountains of Paradise*. Clarke fuses a general technical idea of much interest—the space ladder as an alternative to rocketry—with the spirit of a particular place, a thinly disguised version of his homeland, Sri Lanka. A religious sect has inhabited the site of the space ladder for thousands of years, and Clarke lightly suggests a connection between their ancient presence and the scientific innovation which threatens them. If this novel marked the end of Clarke's career, as he says, he ended with one of his best novels.

Although Clarke's style can be wordy and pedestrian at times (as when he overexplains), at other times it is sparse and poetic. His typical mode of narration—focusing all data through a first or second-person persona—generally facilitates his effective presentation of the concrete.

The universe challenges us, Clarke believes, by its inexhaustible beauty, strangeness, and richness. Unless we rise to the challenge by keeping our curiosity and extending our environment, both our art and our science will stagnate. The scientist is as likely to lack the necessary vision and spirit of adventure as the humanist; the romantic maverick is Clarke's protagonist. The eternal renewal of childhood in a never-ending expansion into the unknown is Clarke's theme.

—Curtis C. Smith

CLARKE, Austin C(hesterfield). Barbadian. Born in Barbados, 26 July 1934. Educated at Combermere Boys' School, Barbados; Harrison's College, Barbados; Trinity College, University of Toronto. Married Betty Joyce Reynolds in 1957; three children. Hoyt Fellow, 1968, and Visiting Lecturer, 1969, 1970, Yale University, New Haven, Connecticut; Fellow, Indiana University School of Letters, Bloomington, 1969; Margaret Bundy Scott Visiting Professor of Literature, Williams College, Williamstown, Massachusetts, 1971; Lecturer, Duke University, Durham, North Carolina, 1971-72; Visiting Professor, University of Texas, Austin, 1973-74. Currently, Cultural and Press Attaché, Embassy of Barbados, Washington, D.C. Member, Board of Trustees, Rhode Island School of Design, Providence, 1970. Recipient: Belmont Short Story Award, 1965; President's Medal, University of Western Ontario, 1966; Canada Council Senior Arts Fellowship, 1967, 1970, and grant, 1977. Address: 432 Brunswick Avenue, Toronto 4, Ontario, Canada.

PUBLICATIONS

Novels

The Survivors of the Crossing. Toronto, McClelland and Stewart, and London, Heinemann, 1964.
Amongst Thistles and Thorns. Toronto, McClelland and Stewart, and London, Heinemann, 1965.
The Meeting Point. Toronto, Macmillan, and London, Heinemann, 1967; Boston, Little Brown, 1972.
Storm of Fortune. Boston, Little Brown, 1973.
The Bigger Light. Boston, Little Brown, 1975.
The Prime Minister. Toronto, General, 1977; London, Routledge, 1978.

Short Stories

When He Was Free and Young and He Used to Wear Silks. Toronto, Anansi, 1971; revised edition, Boston, Little Brown, 1973.

Uncollected Short Stories

"I Hanging On, Praise God," in *From the Green Antilles*, edited by Barbara Howes. New York, Macmillan, 1966; London, Souvenir Press, 1967.
"The Woman with the BBC Voice," in *Tamarack Review* (Toronto), 1966.
"Why Didn't You Use a Plunger," in *Tamarack Review* (Toronto), 1969.
"The Collector," in *Stories from the Tamarack Review*, edited by Joseph F. McCrindle. New York, Holt Rinehart, 1970.
"A Wedding in Toronto," in *Tamarack Review* (Toronto), 1970.
"What Happened?," in *Prejudice*, edited by Charles R. Larson. New York, New American Library, 1971.
"They Heard the Ringing of Bells," in *Toronto Short Stories*, edited by Morris Wolfe and Douglas Daymond. New York, Doubleday, 1977.

Other

The Confused Bewilderment of Martin Luther King and the Idea of Non-Violence as a Political Tactic. Burlington, Ontario, Watkins, 1968.
Growing Up Stupid under the Union Jack: A Memoir. Toronto, McClelland and Stewart, 1980.

*

Critical Studies: "The West Indian Novel in North America: A Study of Austin Clarke" by Lloyd W. Brown, in *Journal of Commonwealth Literature* (Leeds), July 1970; interview with Graeme Gibson, in *Eleven Canadian Novelists*, Toronto, Anansi, 1974.

Austin C. Clarke comments:

Whenever I am asked to give a statement about my work I find it difficult to do. All I can say in these situations is that I try to write about a group of people, West Indian immigrants (to Canada), whose life interests me because of the remarkable problems of readjustment, and the other problems of ordinary living. The psychological implications of this kind of life are what make my work interesting and I hope relevant to the larger condition of preservation. The themes are usually those of adjustment, as I have said, but this adjustment is artistically rendered in the interrelationship of the two predominant groups of which I write: the host Jewish-Anglo Saxon group, and the black group (West Indian and expatriate black American).

* * *

Generally the discussion of West Indian fiction tends to focus exclusively on work written in England and the Caribbean. But the growing number of West Indian immigrants in Canada, especially over the last two decades, has given rise to a small but increasingly significant body of West Indian literature in that country. On the whole, West Indian literature in Canada is dominated by the predictable and familiar themes of exile, but the theme is integrated here with the West Indian's response to Canada's much-touted ideal of a cultural mosaic—the notion that the country is, or ought to be, a harmonious aggregation of distinctive cultures which maintain their distinctiveness while blending with each other to create a diversified cultural whole.

But for West Indians the ideal of a cultural mosaic is not quite as simple as it sounds to the Anglo-Canadians who often espouse it. Given the usual disadvantages of being black in a predominantly white society, West Indians must choose between being integrated into a strange culture—at the cost of their cultural uniqueness and racial integrity—or being so dedicated to maintaining their black, West Indian identity that they risk being cultural and economic outsiders in their adopted homeland. This dilemma, one that is explored by the growing number of writers in Canada, dominates the writings of Austin C. Clarke, unquestionably the major West Indian writer in Canada at this time.

These Canadian issues are not the major concern in his earliest novels, or in his most recent. *The Survivors of the Crossing* and *Amongst Thistles and Thorns* are set in Barbados and they explore the twin evils of colonial self-hatred and Caribbean poverty. *The Prime Minister* is centered on the experiences of a West Indian writer, John Moore, who has returned to Barbados, to a government appointment, after 20 years in Canada. Significantly, Moore does not stay in Barbados: he returns to his Canadian home after discovering, to his mortification, that he no longer has a real place in Barbados.

Moore's experiences can be viewed as a paradigm of West Indians including Clarke himself, now living and writing in Canada. And it is logical enough that the Canadian presence dominates Clarke's fiction as a whole. His collection of short stories includes works which take a close look at Canada as the West Indians' El Dorado. In "They Heard a Ringing of Bells" a group of West Indians discuss their experiences as immigrants—delighting in the sense of being released from Caribbean poverty while lambasting the hostility and indifference of white Canada to the West Indian presence. "Waiting for the Postman to Knock" is less ambivalent, more openly hostile to the adopted homeland. Enid, the heroine, is one of the most typical and enduring symbols of West Indian life in Canada—the lonely and isolated West Indian domestic servant who feels equally exploited by her white employer and by her West Indian lover (if she is lucky enough to find a lover). For other West Indians in Clarke's short fiction the problems of loneliness are compounded by racial self-hatred, especially in the lives of those who are achieving some degree of economic success at the cost of their racial pride or cultural integrity ("Four Stations in His Circle" and "The Motor Car").

These related themes of loneliness, self-hatred, and cultural exclusion are the main concerns of Clarke's Canadian trilogy, *The Meeting Point*, *Storm of Fortune*, and *The Bigger Light*. The three works center on the lives of a group of West Indians in Toronto—especially Bernice Leach, her sister Estelle, Boysie Cumberbatch, his wife Dots, and Henry White. *The Meeting Point* concentrates on Bernice's experiences as a maid in the home of the wealthy Burrmann family, and emphasizes the usual themes of sexual loneliness, cultural isolation, and the sense of economic exploitation.

Storm of Fortune shifts the focus to Estelle and her somewhat uneven struggle to gain a toehold in Canada. The novel also traces the failures of Henry White and his subsequent death, and, most important of all, it depicts the gradual emergence of Boysie Cumberbatch, from shiftless *bon vivant* to ambitious small businessman with his own janitorial company. His success-story is continued in *The Bigger Light* which, despite some uneven writing, remains Clarke's most ambitious novel to date. Having devoted much of the preceding novels to the failures and half-successes in the West Indian community, Clarke concentrates here on a successful man, but one whose economic successes have not protected him from emotional failure (the gradual breakdown of his marriage and his increasing isolation from his less fortunate West Indian friends). And in fact his success as a *Canadian* businessman, in the Anglo-Saxon mould, has had the effect of encouraging a certain snobbery and a marked reserve towards matters of cultural and racial significance. In short he becomes increasingly hostile towards the issue of racial identity.

But in spite of his extreme and increasing isolation in the novel, Boysie is not an entire failure as a human being. His very isolation becomes a catalyst for a certain perceptiveness which allows him to recognize the real nature of his choices and the limitations of the world in which he has chosen to live. And as a consequence he remains the typical Austin Clarke protagonist, one whose failures—economic and moral—are counterbalanced by a persistent ability to perceive their own lives, without self-deception or self-pity, as they really are. Given the persistent hostilities of the world in which they live, this kind of honest self-awareness is the most important quality of all—and Austin Clarke invariably presents and invites judgements on his characters on the basis of their ability to achieve such an awareness.

—Lloyd W. Brown

CLEARY, Jon (Stephen). Australian. Born in Sydney, New South Wales, 22 November 1917. Educated at Marist Brothers School, Randwick, New South Wales, 1924-32. Served in the Australian Imperial Forces in the Middle East and New Guinea, 1940-45. Married Constantine Lucas in 1946; two children. Prior to 1939 worked as a commercial traveller, bush worker, and commercial artist. Since 1945, full-time writer. Journalist, Government of Australia News and Information Bureau, in London, 1948-49, and in New York, 1949-51. Recipient: Australian Broadcasting Commission Prize, for radio drama, 1944; Australian Section Prize, *New York Herald Tribune* World Short Story Contest, 1950; Mystery Writers of America Edgar Allan Poe Award, 1974. Lives in New South Wales. Address: c/o John Farquharson Ltd., 8 Bell Yard, London WC2A 2JU, England.

PUBLICATIONS

Novels

You Can't See Around Corners. New York, Scribner, 1947; London, Eyre and Spottiswoode, 1949.
The Long Shadow. London, Laurie, 1949.
Just Let Me Be. London, Laurie, 1950.
The Sundowners. New York, Scribner, and London, Laurie, 1952.
The Climate of Courage. London, Collins, 1954; as *Naked in the Night*, New York, Popular Library, 1955.
Justin Bayard. London, Collins, 1955; New York, Morrow, 1956; as *Dust in the Sun*, New York, Popular Library, 1957.
The Green Helmet. London, Collins, 1957; New York, Morrow, 1958.

Back of Sunset. New York, Morrow, and London, Collins, 1959.
North from Thursday. London, Collins, 1960; New York, Morrow, 1961.
The Country of Marriage. New York, Morrow, and London, Collins, 1962.
Forests of the Night. New York, Morrow, and London, Collins, 1963.
A Flight of Chariots. New York, Morrow, 1963; London, Collins, 1964.
The Fall of an Eagle. New York, Morrow, 1964; London, Collins, 1965.
The Pulse of Danger. New York, Morrow, and London, Collins, 1966.
The High Commissioner. New York, Morrow, and London, Collins, 1966.
The Long Pursuit. New York, Morrow, and London, Collins, 1967.
Season of Doubt. New York, Morrow, and London, Collins, 1968.
Remember Jack Hoxie. New York, Morrow, and London, Collins, 1969.
Helga's Web. New York, Morrow, and London, Collins, 1970.
The Liberators. New York, Morrow, 1971; as *Mask of the Andes*, London, Collins, 1971.
The Ninth Marquess. New York, Morrow, 1972; as *Man's Estate*, London, Collins, 1972.
Ransom. New York, Morrow, and London, Collins, 1973.
Peter's Pence. New York, Morrow, and London, Collins, 1974.
The Safe House. New York, Morrow, and London, Collins, 1975.
A Sound of Lightning. New York, Morrow, and London, Collins, 1976.
High Road to China. New York, Morrow, and London, Collins, 1977.
Vortex. London, Collins, 1977; New York, Morrow, 1978.
The Beaufort Sisters. New York, Morrow, and London, Collins, 1979.
A Very Private War. New York, Morrow, and London, Collins, 1980.
The Golden Sabre. New York, Morrow, and London, Collins, 1981.

Short Stories

These Small Glories. Sydney, Angus and Robertson, 1946.
Pillar of Salt. Sydney, Horwitz, 1963.

Plays

Strike Me Lucky (produced Bromley, Kent, 1963).

Screenplays: *The Siege of Pinchgut*, with Harry Watt and Alexander Baron, 1959; *The Green Helmet*, 1961; *The Sundowners*, 1961; *The Sidecar Boys*, 1975.

Radio Play: *Safe Horizon*, 1944.

Television Play: *Just Let Me Be*, 1957 (UK).

*

Jon Cleary comments:

I write primarily to entertain, but, having stated that, I also write to inform about the world we live in. I have no overall theme, unless it is to affirm my belief that Man can, somehow, overcome the effects of his own disasters. I do my best not to be categorised, mainly because I want to keep fresh my enthusiasm for writing; but I'm afraid critics tend to overlook those books in which I do not write about adventure in exotic places (such as *The Country of Marriage* and *Remember Jack Hoxie*), and I'm resigned now to being classified as an "adventure" writer. I have a principle that I will not write about a place I have not visited—this involves me in a lot of travel and is, I hope, opening me up for a book or two of wider scope in the future. I am, I supose, an old-fashioned story-teller—but I feel that stories, combining action with character, will always be read. I hope so—the job opportunities for out-of-work novelists in their sixties are not too numerous.

* * *

Jon Cleary's conviction that he has been virtually "classified as an 'adventure' writer" despite books like *The Country of Marriage* and *Remember Jack Hoxie* should not come as a surprise. The great bulk of his work does, after all, invite such a classification: his characters confront ill-fortune, the elements, physical dangers, and personal ordeals in places as separated and contrasting as Bhutan and the Australian outback, New Guinea and Beirut. Yet it is in those relatively few novels in which neither locale nor the pace and excitement of suspenseful action are paramount that Cleary does some of his best work.

He has a sensitive understanding of the fractional shifts in mood, the alterations in psychological atmosphere, the delicacy of the thread of communication that characterize—yet also in certain circumstances bedevil—the relationship between man and woman and, more particularly, husband and wife. Equally, he seems intuitively to grasp, and to be able to evoke with tact and controlled inference, that sense of the enduringly passionate undercurrent in successful love relationships; a passion which persists despite tangible and external vicissitudes. These are qualities which make *The Country of Marriage* such an impressive achievement; they also contribute significantly to the impact of *The Sundowners* which, for all its picaresque and unsophisticated sprawl, remains one of Cleary's most engaging successes—a Lawsonian picture of, among other things, a marriage weathering crises which are partly induced by the very nature of the "place," the bush environment.

But the full range of Cleary's work reveals emphatically that action not only suits his pen—he describes scenes of action with enormous zest and tough economy—but also his temperament. He is attracted to movement, suspense, resolution through decisive action. And it is this preoccupation which comes to predominate in his work. *Justin Bayard* is one of several novels in which conflicting forces in Cleary's artistic sensibility become evident: on the one hand there is a concern with marital tension, with the power of love and sexual passion to surmount external difficulties and with the alienating, corrosive effect of the outback upon the personality. On the other hand, the book is a disguised "country house thriller": the protagonists are virtually marooned in a homestead while evil and ultimately murder work among them. Violent action decides or overwhelms most of the personal dilemmas in Cleary's novels and resolves the human issues not by allowing them to be worked out but, as it were, by default.

Action and adventure, flavoured by exotic or dramatic geographical settings, thus emerge as important distinguishing features of Cleary's growing output. A characteristic Cleary "hero" evolves: a man of action plagued by an inner tentativeness, a fear of decision and responsibility. Paddy Carmody (*The Sundowners*), Vern Radcliffe (*The Climate of Courage*), Justin Bayard, Paul Tancred (*Season of Doubt*), Jack Marquis (*The Pulse of Danger*), Adam Nash (*The Country of Marriage*) are all recognizably in this mould. Scobie Malone, however—the hero of *The High Commissioner*, *Helga's Web* and *Ransom*—is not. And perhaps this is as good a way as any of pointing to the change that has come over Cleary's work in the last half dozen years. He has dropped into his stride as a fully equipped writer of popular fiction. He is skilful in the economical creation of character, his plots are inventive without being outlandish, and he knows how to manipulate narrative pace. He is also very witty on occasions. Equally, he has an eye for the world stage as a source for fiction: the IRA (*Peter's Pence*), third world tensions (*The Liberators*), political kidnap (*Ransom*), the resurgent interest in surviving Nazis (*Safe House*)—these are some of the topicalities which Cleary turns into superbly managed, gripping tales.

What *might* have been (recalling *The Country of Marriage*, *The Sundowners*, and *Remember Jack Hoxie*) is now a throroughly hypothetical proposition. Jon Cleary is well established in the forefront of modern adventure writers.

—Brian E. Matthews

COHEN, Leonard (Norman). Canadian. Born in Montreal, Quebec, 21 September 1934. Educated at McGill University, Montreal, B.A. 1955; Columbia University, New York. Composer and Singer: has given concerts in Canada, the United States, and Europe. Artist-in-Residence, University of Alberta, Edmonton, 1975-76. Recipient: McGill University Literary Award, 1956; Canada Council Award, 1960; Quebec Literary Award, 1964. D.L.: Dalhousie University, Halifax, Nova Scotia, 1971. Lives in Montreal and Greece. Address: c/o Magna Artists, 1370 Avenue of the Americas, New York, New York 10019, U.S.A.

PUBLICATIONS

Novels

The Favorite Game. New York, Viking Press, and London, Secker and Warburg, 1963.
Beautiful Losers. Toronto, McClelland and Stewart, and New York, Viking Press, 1966; London, Cape, 1970.

Uncollected Short Stories

"Luggage Fire Sale, " in *Parallel 2* (Montreal), May-June 1966.
"Charles Axis," in *The Single Voice*, edited by Jerome Charyn. New York, Collier, 1969.

Plays

The New Step (produced London, 1972).
Sisters of Mercy: A Journey into the Words and Music of Leonard Cohen (produced Niagara-on-the-Lake, Ontario, and New York, 1973).

Verse

Let Us Compare Mythologies. Montreal, Contact Press, 1956.
The Spice-Box of Earth. Toronto, McClelland and Stewart, 1961; New York, Viking Press, 1965; London, Cape, 1971.
Flowers for Hilter. Toronto, McClelland and Stewart, 1964; London, Cape, 1973.
Parasites of Heaven. Toronto, McClelland and Stewart, 1966.
Selected Poems 1956-1968. Toronto, McClelland and Stewart, and New York, Viking Press, 1968; London, Cape, 1969.
Leonard Cohen's Song Book. New York, Collier, 1969.
Five Modern Canadian Poets, with others, edited by Eli Mandel. Toronto, Holt Rinehart, 1970.
The Energy of Slaves. Toronto, McClelland and Stewart, and London, Cape, 1972; New York, Viking Press, 1973.

Recordings: *The Songs of Leonard Cohen*, Columbia, 1968; *Songs from a Room*, Columbia, 1969; *Songs of Love and Hate*, Columbia, 1971; *Live Songs*, Columbia, 1973; *New Skin for the Old Ceremony*, Columbia, 1974; *Death of a Lady's Man*, Warner Brothers, 1977; *Recent Songs*, CBS, 1979.

Other

Death of a Lady's Man. Toronto, McClelland and Stewart, 1978; London, Deutsch, and New York, Viking Press, 1979.

*

Critical Studies: *Leonard Cohen* by Michael Ondaatje, Toronto, McClelland and Stewart, 1970; *The Immoral Moralists: Hugh MacLennan and Leonard Cohen* by Patricia Morley, Toronto, Clarke Irwin, 1972; *Leonard Cohen: The Artist and His Critics* edited by Michael Gnarowski, Toronto, McGraw Hill, 1976.

* * *

Few modern authors have presented critics so clearly as Leonard Cohen does with the problem of how to regard the writer who personifies the Zeitgeist. With astonishing rapidity, in the mid-1960's, Cohen passed from the obscurity of a romantic Canadian poet into the celebrity of an international pop singer who seemed to exemplify the decade's popular culture.

Time will decide how far, when fashion abandons him, Cohen's real qualities will sustain his standing as a writer. What the critic perceives even now is that the factors which made Cohen popular are those he shares with modish culture: conventionalism masquerading as independence; a slightly acrid romanticism merging into a solipsistic sentimentality; an echoing of past movements like the Decadence, Art Nouveau and Dada, which elevated style above substance. The fiction such movements have produced has usually been strained and eccentric. *The Picture of Dorian Gray*, the novels of Huysmans and, later, Raymond Queneau, are examples.

Cohen stands in this company; his novels, *The Favorite Game* and *Beautiful Losers*, are interesting examples of black romance, and though *Beautiful Losers* projects a bizarre kind of splendour, as the novels of poets often do, it is a work of solitary fantasy that stands apart from the main stream of fiction in our time.

A shallowness of feeling, a solipsistic passionlessness masquerading as stylized passion, infects almost all of Cohen's writings. It is linked with the Pygmalion urge that is a dominant theme in his novels, exemplified in F.'s delusions of godly creativeness in *Beautiful Losers* and in the fantasies of occult power that haunt Breavman throughout *The Favorite Game*. "I want to touch people like a magician," he says to one of his mistresses, "to change them or hurt them, leave my brand, make them beautiful."

To be beautiful, and to be a loser; both desires find their places in the romantic fancy; their juxtaposition in the title of Cohen's second novel is neither accidental nor inappropriate. The solipsist creates beauty within the mind and that is his only real world; he loses because the actual world does not correspond with his visionary world yet impinges on his life. F., the quasi-hero of *Beautiful Losers*, lives in flamboyant style; he is killed, in true decadent tradition, by syphilis.

Cohen's first novel, *The Favorite Game*, tells the development of a rich Montreal Jewish boy into a poet and folk singer; the resemblances to Cohen's life are close enough to justify an assumption that this is the autobiographical novel with which many writers make their finest sacrifice to the muse of fiction. *The Favorite Game* is an episodic work, its shuffled time sequences strung along the thread of Breavman's affair with the all-American girl, Shell, most recent of his mistresses; the account of his experience becomes a kind of dialogue with Shell, from whom in the end he parts, as he has parted from her predecessors. His life has been measured off by relationships with girls, yet in none has Breavman been able to evade in passion that observing mind which is the alien participant.

Parallel to these uninvolved liaisons runs the continuing current of Breavman's friendship with Krantz, which survives all the broken love affairs. But the moment of real involvement comes when, working as a staff member in a Jewish summer camp, Breavman encounters the boy Martin, "a divine idiot" with a mathematical mania who spends his time counting grass blades and pine needles, and dies grotesquely when he is crushed by a bulldozer while killing and counting mosquitoes in a marsh.

Martin represents the other pole in Cohen's world to profane love. He is—albeit in disguise—of the company of saints, those exalted and obsessed ones to whom Cohen is always drawn. Destroyed saints appear often in his poems; Martin is one of them. Yet he dies at the peak of joy, rating his days at "98 percent"—and the joyful saint is always present in Cohen's world:

> Something about him so loves the world that he gives himself to the laws of gravity and chance. Far from flying with the angels, he traces with the fidelity of a seismograph needle the state of the solid bloody landscape. His house is dangerous and finite, but he is at home in the world. He can love the shapes of human beings, the fine and twisted shapes of the human heart.

To the Cohen alive to the call of sainthood as the complement of earthly love, the world takes on dual aspects. Breavman, inexperienced, sees decay everywhere. "The works themselves were corruption, the monuments were made of worms." But in *Beautiful Losers*, when "I" puts the classic decadent point about "the diamonds in the shit," F. replies, "It's all diamond."

It is the unity in duality of the erotic and the spiritual that provides the bridge from *The Favorite Game* to *Beautiful Losers*. But, though there are many ways in which—in details of plot and imagery—the earlier novel anticipates its more ambitious successor, *Beautiful Losers* moves into a quite different category. Young artist novels can only be written once, and Cohen makes his escape in the same direction as Joyce, in the aestheticist reconstruction of life. *Beautiful Losers* is very much a work of artifice, and makes no concession to verisimilitude.

Of the three parts into which this novel is divided, the first contains the erratic musings of the onanist "I." Edith, his wife who has committed bizarre suicide, and F., the megalomaniac lover of them both, move in memory within a pattern which F. describes when he declares, "I was your journey and you were my journey and Edith was our holy star." Whether they have ever existed is not important, since they are absorbed in a timeless dream continuum where they are no more and no less real, no more and no less distant, than the Mohawk saint, Catherine Tekakwitha, three centuries dead, whose monumental holy masochism fascinates both F. and "I." F. becomes an industrialist who uses his unmanned factory for playing games, a member of Parliament quickly discredited, a leader of the Quebec underground, but these achievements are no more substantial than the grandiose fantasies which, one eventually realises, are the products of a brain rotted by the pox.

This becomes evident in the wild inventions of the "Long Letter from F." In the central episode described in this document, F. and Edith, after packing "I" off on an absurd research assignment, set off for Argentina with a bag of erotic devices, and indulge in a long orgy in which they are ravished in turn by the "Danish vibrator" (a machine that develops and fulfils desires of its own) and finally bathe "three in a tub" with a waiter who provides human soap and turns out to be Hitler in exile.

Book III, an "Epilogue in the Third Person," closes with a description of the last dissolving days of "I," who has learnt to combine F.'s debauchery and Catherine Tekakwitha's self-mortifications in a regressive tree-house existence; he is saint and sinner, at once himself and F. and Edith, and he disappears in a puff of ambiguity.

Beautiful Losers is filled with interesting experiments, some of which belong to poetry rather than fiction; indeed there are passages which are actually concealed verse. But the burlesque element is overdone and the savage sexual comedy quickly palls. As a novel the book has no functioning unity; Cohen lacks the architectonic power with which Céline, for example, transformed similar material into self-consistent and convincing works of fiction.

—George Woodcock

COHEN, Matt(hew). Canadian. Born in Kingston, Ontario, 30 December 1942. Educated at the University of Toronto, M.A. in political science. Has taught at McMaster University, Hamilton, Ontario, the University of Alberta, Edmonton, and the University of Victoria, British Columbia. Lives near Kingston, Ontario. Address: c/o Mc Clelland and Stewart, 25 Hollinger Road, Toronto, Ontario M4B 3G2, Canada.

PUBLICATIONS

Novels

Korsoniloff. Toronto, Anansi, 1969.
Johnny Crackle Sings. Toronto, McClelland and Stewart, 1971.
The Disinherited. Toronto, McClelland and Stewart, 1974.
Wooden Hunters. Toronto, McClelland and Stewart, 1975.
The Colours of War. Toronto, McClelland and Stewart, 1977; New York, Methuen, 1978.
The Second Sweet Summer of Kitty Malone. Toronto, McClelland and Stewart, 1979.

Short Stories

Columbus and the Fat Lady and Other Stories. Toronto, Anansi, 1972.
Too Bad Galahad. Toronto, Coach House Press, 1972.
Night Flight: Stories New and Selected. New York, Doubleday, 1978.

Uncollected Short Stories

"Pat Frank's Dream," in *Aurora: New Canadian Writing 1978*, edited by Morris Wolfe. New York, Doubleday, 1979.
"Summer Crossing," in *Sewanee Review* (Tennessee), Winter 1979.

Verse

Peach Melba. Toronto, Coach House Press, 1974.

Other

The Leaves of Louise (juvenile). Toronto, McClelland and Stewart, 1978.

Editor, *The Story So Far 2.* Toronto, Coach House Press, 1973.

*

Manuscript Collection: Mills Memorial Library, McMaster University, Hamilton, Ontario.

* * *

In Matt Cohen's first book, *Korsoniloff*, a narrator possessed of dual consciousness confronts the reader with themes taken up and variously treated in Cohen's later work: that of the opacity of a character with little or no self-knowledge, and whose inner forces have been "misaligned." The novella is the journal of a schizophrenic professor of philosophy, Andre Korsoniloff, whose surname represents his alter ego. He does not yet "exist in the world," since his opposing selves together form a man who is essentially "unwhole and without judgement"; a man who is, however, wittily aware of this division within himself. We see Korsoniloff in the same way that he sees other characters, as being self-possessed and without need, but his one violent act—disturbing the peace at his mistress's wedding—renders credible his subsequent fantasies of suicide and murder.

Korsoniloff's potential for eruption also underscores the pop-hero of *Johnny Crackle Sings*, a star who cultivates "condition zero," his personal term for a state approaching Nirvana, as a retreat from pressure and decision. Rock idol of screaming school children, Johnny Crackle, born Johnny Harper, moves aimlessly, withdrawing into drug-induced illusions rather than reacting, another Cohen character "born without any destiny at all." He seems only subliminally aware that the rural landscape to which he continually returns has a calming effect upon him. When he moves to urban environments or travels abroad, he sinks back into his state of suspended animation. He and his girl-friend Jenny are finally married, and have a son, also Johnny. Crackle, in describing his reaction to the birth, sums himself up too: "Afterwards it was almost like I hadn't been there except like watching a movie."

Characters of Cohen's other books suffer from an uncultivated "condition zero," or (if one takes seriously *Too Bad Galahad*, distinguished more by Margaret Hathaway's illustrations than Cohen's literary merits), admit the quest for a Holy Grail of one sort or another, though they must perish finding it.

Cohen's short stories collected in *Columbus and the Fat Lady* can be whimsical, self-conscious, or embarrassingly weak. He is at his best with acutely observed psychological detail, as in "Janice"; stories with magical or fantastic elements are his least successful.

The Disinherited states what, in embryonic form, other books and characters have pointed to. The title applies to most of the characters in this novel, in which various forces of dispossession are at work. While it concentrates on the slow death of farmer Richard Thomas, and the alienation felt by his city-dwelling son, the novel flashes continually back and forth through four generations: young Erik Thomas and his adopted brother Brian, his father, his grandfather Simon Thomas, and his great-grandfather Richard, whose relative, a poet from England, had come to Canada as though to Canaan, like "Abraham being sent to father a new race of men." But those who came after him have been unable to accept the vision he wished them to inherit. The poet's son is mentally retarded and an outcast in the same way that other characters have been cast out, through human inadequacy or legal disheritance, from real and metaphoric promised lands. Richard is dying, Erik is not fully alive. With Erik begins the new breed; unlike his father, uncle or grandfather there is no heroic stance for him to assume: "A man has to know his own destiny," says Richard. Erik replies: "No-one has destinies any more. They live in apartments and breed goldfish."

The first and last chapters are the most successful of this book; here the basic dichotomy between the two generations and kinds of men stands out most clearly. As the book opens, Richard Thomas begins to succumb to the illness that kills him in the last pages, and is for the first time aware of the microscopic unknown workings of his body, an experience he explores in seemingly timeless detail throughout the rest of the book. Nature is revealed to him in an immediate and alarming fashion as he lies on the ground integrated into the landscape—a position symbolic of what Cohen makes him stand for in the book; and Richard Thomas has recurring dreams of being rooted in earth, hands and arms as branches growing up and out from soil. In the final chapter Erik returns to Toronto after his father's death, forcibly struck by the extent of his alienation from the city, sucking in peripheral lives like his. From his high-rise apartment he looks down aimlessly on the city, dispossessed of the farm, indispensable to no-one, not in pain, not even searching, but beginning to believe in the need for something other. *The Disinherited* is Cohen's most accomplished book, but he has not yet achieved balance, the kind of perspective that would allow him, instead of insisting on obscure eddies, to concentrate on the main currents he is obviously equipped to handle.

—Barrie Davies

COLE, Barry. British. Born in Woking, Surrey, 13 November 1936. Served in the Royal Air Force for two years. Married Rita Linihan in 1958; three daughters. Worked in the Central Office of Information, London, 1965-70. Northern Arts Fellow in Literature, universities of Newcastle upon Tyne and Durham, 1970-72. Address: 68 Myddelton Square, London E.C.1, England.

PUBLICATIONS

Novels

A Run Across the Island. London, Methuen, 1968.
Joseph Winter's Patronage. London, Methuen, 1969.
The Search for Rita. London, Methuen, 1970.
The Giver. London, Methuen, 1971.
Doctor Fielder's Common Sense. London, Methuen, 1972.

Verse

Blood Ties. London, Turret, 1967.
Ulysses in the Town of Coloured Glass. London, Turret, 1968.
Moonsearch. London, Methuen, 1968.
The Visitors. London, Methuen, 1970.
Vanessa in the City. London, Trigram Press, 1971.
Pathetic Fallacies. London, Eyre Methuen, 1973.
The Rehousing of Scaffardi. Richmond, Surrey, Keepsake Press, 1976.
Dedications. Nottingham, Byron Press, 1977.

*

Barry Cole comments:

I have no general statement to make about my novels, but the epigraphs which precede *The Giver* may say more than any collected exegeses:

And down I set, abruptly I believe; what I had heard all in my head. (Fielding).

Aesthetics cannot exist because an artist never solves any problems except those which are entirely of his own creation. (Jean-François Revel).

The thought of the epistolary diary had long interested and troubled me. (Nabokov).

Everyone should read a book; to read two books shows intelligence; to read three is showing off. (Rita Linihan, 15).

A poet is the most unpoetical of anything in existence, because he has no identity; he is continually in for, and filling, some other body...(Keats).

No Costaguanero had ever learned to question the eccentricities of a military force. (Conrad).

He spoke in English and pronounced even the name "Boris" as if it were English. (Turgenev).

...getting the disorder of one's own mind in order...(Yeats).

Let not the critic ask how Corporal Trim could come by all this...(Sterne).

The Commissioner gazed at them with suspicion, almost with revulsion. Then he fell to laughing. (Jorge Luis Borges).

There is something funny about the human condition, and civilized intelligence makes fun of its own ideas. (Saul Bellow).

But Hetty's face had a language that transcended her feelings. (George Eliot).

Is it only that? said the willow-wren;
It's that as well, said the stars. (W.H. Auden).

Themes and thimes and habit reburns. To flame in you. (Joyce).

"Were you drunk?" asked Pleasant. (Dickens).

* * *

Barry Cole's novels have one striking thing in common. They are extremely well-written. It may, of course, be said that to write well is not so much a virtue in a novelist as a necessity. Yet the fact is that the majority of novelists lack Barry Cole's gifts of verbal precision, wit, exact ear for conversation, and his feeling for the elastic possibilities of language, the way it can be stretched and twisted to provide unexpected meanings and insights. No doubt the fact that he is also a very fine poet accounts for much of his virtue as a writer of prose, but this should not be taken to mean that he writes poetic prose. On the contrary: his style is as free as possible from those encrustations of adjective and epithet that identify "fine" writing.

A Run Across the Island is a brilliant *tour de force* and for it Cole invented a form that he has found it possible to use for all his subsequent novels. Although by far the larger part of the novel is seen through the eyes of its hero, Robert Haydon, there is no straightforward narrative or division into chapters. Instead, we move about in time, each remembered detail or incident given a section, small or large, that is juxtaposed against others. By the end of the novel, however, the different incidents have been worked out and together compose one man's life, and it has been so resourcefully done that we have a much more *real* sense of a man's identity than we would have through a straightforward narrative.

The major theme of *A Run Across the Island* is, perhaps, of loneliness, of the difficulties of establishing relationships, of the slippery impermanence of friendship and love. And this theme is also present in the next novel. *Joseph Winter's Patronage* is, however, very different from *A Run Across the Island* in that its characters are almost exclusively old people. Indeed, the novel is mostly set in an Old People's Home, and the novelist manages with great sensitiveness to create the feeling of the Home itself and of its inhabitants. *Joseph Winter's Patronage* is the most touching and warmly sympathetic novel that Barry Cole has so far written.

By contrast, *The Search for Rita* is the most glittering. It is an extremely elegant novel, but the elegance is not one that marks how far its author stands fastidiously aloof from life. It is rather that the mess of life is met by a keen-eyed wit that can be ironic, self-deprecatory, satiric, and bawdy by turns. Style means everything in a novel of this kind, and the novelist's style does not let him down.

Barry Cole has been called one of the most promising of our younger novelists. It seems better to adapt a line of Robert Graves and say that already there is nothing promised he has not performed.

—John Lucas

COLTER, Cyrus. American. Born in Noblesville, Indiana, 8 January 1910. Educated in Noblesville public schools; Youngstown University, Ohio; Ohio State University, Columbus; Kent College of Law of the Illinois Institute of Technology, Chicago, J.D. 1940: admitted to the Illinois Bar, 1940. Served as a Captain in the United States Army Field Artillery, Italy, 1942-46. Married Imogene Mackay Colter in 1943. Worked for the YMCA, Youngstown, 1932-34, and Chicago, 1934-40; United States Government Deputy Collector of Internal Revenue, 1940-42; in private practice of law, Chicago, 1946-51; Commissioner, Illinois Commerce Commission, Chicago, 1951-73. Professor of Creative Writing, 1973-76, and since 1976, Chester D. Tripp Professor of Humanities, Northwestern University, Evanston, Illinois. Recipient: Iowa School of Letters Award, 1970. D.Litt: University of Illinois, Chicago, 1977. Address: 601 East 32nd Street, Apartment PH-2, Chicago, Illinois 60616, U.S.A.

PUBLICATIONS

Novels

The Rivers of Eros. Chicago, Swallow Press, 1972.
The Hippodrome. Chicago, Swallow Press, 1973.
Night Studies. Chicago, Swallow Press, 1980.

Short Stories

The Beach Umbrella. Iowa City, University of Iowa Press, 1970.

Uncollected Short Stories

"The Amoralists," in *University Review* (Kansas City), June 1971.
"Frog Hunters," in *Chicago Review*, xxv, 1, 1973.

* * *

In his first volume of fiction, the stories collected as *The Beach Umbrella*, Cyrus Colter reveals a high purpose. The subject of each story, often an apparently small event, Colter recounts in the style of modern realism, keeping his authorial self unobtrusive while exploiting colloquial dialogue and entering briefly into the conscious minds of characters in order to develop the subject into a story intending no less than a dramatic *exemplum* of life in general. "The Lookout," for example, records the painful jealousy of a woman who discovers the frailty of what she had taken to be friendships; "Rescue," which tells of a woman finding herself unable to get out of a loveless relationship with a man agrees to marry him, has as a counterpart "Overnight Trip" in which a man becomes aware that he has lost his wife's love by sensing the joy she feels in going away from him ever so briefly. "An Untold Story" and "Moot" tell of death, one in violence and the other by natural causes, but though the subject is larger than in the other stories, these do not differ in suggesting the essential human condition is isolation and powerlessness before fate.

The Rivers of Eros introduces into Colter's writing a wider variety of characters, and the greater length of the novel form permits him to range more widely in time. His theme also undergoes some development. Set in a Chicago rooming house, *The Rivers of Eros* is presided over by an aging woman named Clotilda and, more importantly, by an act of adultery she committed many years before. The granddaughter living with her is the offspring of the child she conceived in adultery, and the environment of Clotilda's house can offer no alternative when the girl becomes involved in dangerous love affairs herself. The other people in Clotilda's world, with the exception of a promising grandson, are eccentric outsiders, inadequate to mitigate a situation that drives the granddaughter to attempt suicide and Clotilda to insanity as a result of guilt for her sexual transgression and for the fact that it seemed to set in motion a series of events that caused her daughter to be murdered. The last link in the chain Clotilda forges by murdering her grandchild. The development of Colter's theme in this book amounts to a broadening of fate into a conception of determinism (he says that Hobbes has especially influenced him). Evidently Colter is agnostic about the possibility of a purpose in the deterministic universe, but he is sure that the pattern of living once set in the personalities and characters of human beings is irreversible and normally painful. Though the situations he describes occur in the humanly constructed world of social and personal relationships, Colter's determinism allows no modification through social change or human will, because he finds neither social status and its consequent material environment nor any historical experience to be the source of life's direction. One is tempted to say that, though Colter's deterministic view of human life appears to be metaphysical, he bases it upon empirical observation. Realist that he is in style, he could deny any selectiveness in his choice of fictional material and say that he only shapes the truth into an exemplary tale.

In his second novel, *The Hippodrome*, an additional factor appears to be suggested by epigraphs taken from Dostoevsky's "The Man Who Lived Underground," Sartre's *La Nausée*, and Genet's *Miracle of the Rose*. That factor is an interest in the emotions of fear and anguish which he describes in the mind of a man who brutally murders his wife in jealousy and through curious circumstances becomes imprisoned in a house (the hippodrome) engaged in the business of providing sex shows for a voyeuristic clientele. The peculiar setting, the alienating effect it has on characters, and the protagonist's obsession with his macabre crime provide an effective representation of human extremity. Again, however, the accomplishment occurs within the style of realism. The suggestions of philosophical reflection result in a scene of elementary pondering on such ideas as motives as always selfish and the appropriateness of uncertainty as a way of life.

In his chosen style Colter is masterly. His imagination for situation is fertile, and his representation of characters instills them with interest. Thematically, however, his conceptions offer no challenge. Many sources outside literature are available to assert the popular "wisdom" of restricted determinism. Like the traditional tale-teller Colter renders consensual views in narrative, but the view of fate held by this tale-teller is insufficiently complex for a world as fluid as ours has become.

—John M. Reilly

COMFORT, Alex(ander). British. Born in London, 10 February 1920. Educated at Highgate School, London; Trinity College, Cambridge (Styring Scholar; Senior Scholar), M.B., B.Ch. 1944, M.A. 1945; London Hospital (Scholar), D.C.H. 1945, Ph.D. (biochemistry) 1949, D.Sc. (gerontology) 1963; M.R.C.S., L.R.C.P. Married 1) Ruth Muriel Harris in 1943 (marriage dissolved, 1973), one son; 2) Jane Tristram Henderson in 1973. House Physician, London Hospital, 1944; Resident Medical Officer, Royal Waterloo Hospital, 1944-45; Lecturer in Physiology, 1945-51, Honorary Research Associate, Department of Zoology, 1951-73, Director of Research on the Biology of Ageing, 1966-73, University College, London; Professor of Pathology, University of California School of Medicine, Irvine, 1976-78. Since 1974, Lecturer in Psychiatry, Stanford University, California; since 1975, Senior Fellow, Institute for Higher Studies, Santa Barbara, California; since 1978, Consultant Psychiatrist, Brentwood Hospital, Los Angeles; since 1980, Associate Professor, Neuropsychiatric Institute, University of California, Los Angeles. Editor, Poetry Folios, 1942-46. President, British Society for Research on Ageing, 1967. Recipient: Ciba Foundation Prize, 1958; Karger Memorial Prize in Gerontology, 1969. Address: 683 Oak Grove Drive, Santa Barbara, California 93108, U.S.A.

PUBLICATIONS

Novels

The Silver River, Being the Diary of a Schoolboy in the South Atlantic, 1936. London, Chapman and Hall, 1938.
No Such Liberty. London, Chapman and Hall, 1941.
The Almond Tree: A Legend. London, Chapman and Hall, 1942.
The Power House. London, Routledge, 1944; New York, Viking Press, 1945.
On This Side Nothing. London, Routledge, and New York, Viking Press, 1949.
A Giant's Strength. London, Routledge, 1952.
Come Out to Play. London, Eyre and Spottiswoode, 1961.
Tetrarch. Boulder, Colorado, Shambhala, 1980; London, Wildwood House, 1981.

Short Stories

Letters from an Outpost. London, Routledge, 1947.

Plays

Into Egypt: A Miracle Play. Billericay, Essex, Grey Walls Press, 1942.
Cities of the Plain: A Democratic Melodrama. London, Grey Walls Press, 1943.

Television Play: *The Great Agrippa*, 1968.

Verse

France and Other Poems. London, Favil Press, 1941.
Three New Poets, with Roy McFadden and Ian Serraillier. Billericay, Essex, Grey Walls Press, 1942.
A Wreath for the Living. London, Routledge, 1942.
Elegies. London, Routledge, 1944.
The Song of Lazarus. Barnet, Hertfordshire, Poetry Folios, and New York, Viking Press, 1945.
The Signal to Engage. London, Routledge, 1946.
And All But He Departed. London, Routledge, 1951.
Haste to the Wedding. London, Eyre and Spottiswoode, 1962; Chester Springs, Pennsylvania, Dufour, 1964.
All But a Rib: Poems Chiefly of Women. London, Mitchell Beazley, 1973; as *Coming Together: Poems Chiefly about Women*, New York, Crown, 1975.
Poems for Jane. London, Mitchell Beazley, 1978; New York, Crown, 1979.

Other

Peace and Disobedience. London, Peace News, 1946.
Art and Social Responsibility: Lectures on the Ideology of Romanticism. London, Falcon Press, 1946.
The Novel and Our Time. Letchworth, Hertfordshire, Phoenix House, and Denver, Swallow, 1948.
Barbarism and Sexual Freedom: Six Lectures on the Sociology of Sex from the Standpoint of Anarchism. London, Freedom Press, 1948.
First-Year Physiological Techniques. London, Staples Press, 1948.
The Pattern of the Future. London, Routledge, and New York, Macmillan, 1949.
The Right Thing to Do, Together with the Wrong Thing to Do. London, Peace News, 1949.
Authority and Delinquency in the Modern State: A Criminological Approach to the Problem of Power. London, Routledge, 1950.
Sexual Behaviour in Society. London, Duckworth, and New York, Viking Press, 1950; revised edition, as *Sex in Society*, Duckworth, 1963; New York, Citadel Press, 1966.
Delinquency (lecture). London, Freedom Press, 1951.
Social Responsibility in Science and Art. London, Peace News, 1952.
The Biology of Senescence. London, Routledge, and New York, Rinehart, 1956; revised edition, as *Ageing: The Biology of Senescence*, 1964; revised edition, Edinburgh, Churchill Livingston, 1979.
Darwin and the Naked Lady: Discursive Essays on Biology and Art. London, Routledge, 1961; New York, Braziller, 1962.
The Process of Ageing. New York, New American Library, 1964; London, Weidenfeld and Nicolson, 1965.
The Nature of Human Nature. New York, Harper, 1965; as *Nature and Human Nature*, London, Weidenfeld and Nicolson, 1966.
The Anxiety Makers: Some Curious Preoccupations of the Medical Profession. London, Nelson, 1967.
What Rough Beast? and What Is a Doctor? (lectures). Vancouver, Pendejo Press, 1971.
The Joy of Sex: A Gourmet's Guide to Love Making. New York, Crown, and London, Quartet, 1973.
More Joy: A Sequel to "The Joy of Sex." London, Mitchell Beazley, and New York, Crown, 1974.

A Good Age. New York, Crown, 1976; London, Mitchell Beazley, 1977.
A Practise of Geriatric Psychiatry. New York, Elsevier, 1979.
The Facts of Love: Living, Loving, and Growing Up (juvenile), with Jane Comfort. New York, Crown, 1979; London, Mitchell Beazley, 1980.
I and That: Notes on the Biology of Religion. London, Mitchell Beazley, and New York, Crown, 1979.
The Education of a Doctor. New York, Van Nostrand Reinhold, 1980.
What Is a Doctor? Essays on Medicine and Human Natural History. Philadelphia, Stickley, 1980.
Practice of Geriatric Psychiatry. New York, Elsevier, 1980.

Editor, with Robert Greacen, *Lyra: An Anthology of New Lyric.* Billericay, Essex, Grey Walls Press, 1942.
Editor, with John Bayliss, *New Road 1943* and *1944: New Directions in European Art and Letters.* London, Grey Walls Press, 2 vols., 1943-44.
Editor, *History of Erotic Art, I.* London, Weidenfeld and Nicolson, and New York, Putnam, 1969.
Editor, *Sexual Consequences of Disability.* Philadelphia, Stickley, 1978.

Translator, with Allan Ross Macdougall, *The Triumph of Death,* by C.F. Ramuz. London, Routledge, 1946.
Translator, *The Koko Shastra.* London, Allen and Unwin, 1964; New York, Stein and Day, 1965.

*

Bibliography: "Alexander Comfort: A Bibliography in Progress" by D. Callaghan, in *West Coast Review* (Burnaby, British Columbia), 1969.

Critical Studies: *The Freedom of Poetry* by Derek Stanford, London, Falcon Press, 1947; "The Scientific Humanism of Alex Comfort," in *The Humanist* (London), November-December 1951, and "Kafka and Alex Comfort," in *Arizona Quarterly* (Tucson), Summer 1952, both by Wayne Burns; "The Anarchism of Alex Comfort" by John Ellerby, "Sex, Kicks and Comfort" by Charles Radcliffe, and "Alex Comfort's Art and Scope" by Harold Drasdo, all in *Anarchy* (London), November 1963; "Alex Comfort as a Novelist" by John Doheny, in *Limbo* (Vancouver), November 1964; *Alex Comfort* by Arthur E. Salmon, Boston, Twayne, 1978.

* * *

During the Second World War Alex Comfort established a name for himself as a critic, poet, and playwright concerned with expounding an ethic and aesthetic of freedom, a morality of the Good Samaritan, and a policy of "direct action" and "mutual aid." The leading anarcho-pacifist of his own generation in letters, he presented his ideas through his fiction in such novels as *No Such Liberty*, *The Power House*, and *On This Side Nothing*. Since his pacifism and anarchism, however, derive from prior attitudes of pessimism and idealism, and since these latter attitudes are fully expressed in his early novel *The Almond Tree*, it is as well to consider this first.

For a certain type of mind, the pathos of life resides in recognizing the unattainable while helplessly committed, for all time, to the finite; and *The Almond Tree* may be regarded as an illustrated thesis upon this theme. Then, too, idealism in this novel is powerfully linked with pessimism, and references to *Ecclesiastes* and Solomon's doctrine of the vanity of all things are quite explicit. The story (like most of the author's fiction) has a European setting. Pyotr, the patriarch, is very old and dying. Through the death of his son, his grape-farm has passed to his grand-daughter Teresa and her German husband—a fact which Pyotr resents but cannot alter. A family tyrant, though often kindly, Pyotr has constricted and warped the lives of his children who have found it difficult to break away from his parental possessiveness and authority. One by one they make their bid for freedom and independence, all of them in some sense failing. And, along with old Pyotr, all of them regard, or remember, the almond tree as a fixed symbol of beauty, the one constant in their world of flux, a visual—almost metaphysical—absolute. In this novel time and experience are seen as diminishing or destroying factors, giving rise to the pessimism which the characters respectively feel. On the other hand, the almond tree is equated with a feeling of idealism, a transcendental feature acting as a magnet or focus above the currents of mutability in which men's lives pass and flounder. In the vicious circle this novel traces—with its final return to the inevitable—there are certain parallels with Flaubert's great chronicle of emotional vanity, *Sentimental Education*. There is, though, one difference in the conclusions of these novels. The defeatism in Flaubert implies a cynicism whereas defeat in Alex Comfort's fiction never quite severs the connection which its characters maintain—through the tree—with the ideal.

Of his anarcho-pacifist novels *The Power House* is the most important. Set in occupied France, it preaches, through the words and actions of four young men, a message of civil disobedience and non-cooperation. "We are," remarks one of the characters, "the enemies of society, and we must learn disobedience. Then we shall probably inherit the earth by default when the maniacs have burnt each other to a cinder"; "The weak do a great deal—every woman who hides a deserter, every clerk who doesn't scutinize a pass, every worker who bungles a fuse saves somebody's life for a while." Seven years later, *On This Side Nothing* again chose a wartime setting, and argued, in dramatic terms, the uncertain ethics of—in Auden's words—"the necessary murder."

In more recent years, Alex Comfort's libertarianism has operated in the field of sexological writing, and his novel *Come Out to Play* reflects this interest in terms of a satirical fantasy about a biologist, Dr. George Goggins, deeply learned in the knowledge of human mating habits.

—Derek Stanford

CONDON, Richard (Thomas). American. Born in New York City, 18 March 1915. Educated in public schools in New York. Served in the United States Merchant Navy. Married Evelyn Hunt in 1938; two daughters. Worked briefly in advertising; publicist in the American Film industry for 21 years: worked for Walt Disney Productions, Hal Horne Organization, Twentieth-Century Fox, Richard Condon Inc., and other firms; theatrical producer, New York, 1951-52. Agent: Harold Matson Company Inc., 22 East 40th Street, New York, New York 10016, U.S.A.; or, A.D. Peters Ltd., 10 Buckingham Street, London WC2N 6BU, England. Address: 3436 Asbury Avenue, Dallas, Texas 75205, U.S.A.

Publications

Novels

The Oldest Confession. New York, Appleton Century Crofts, 1958; London, Longman, 1959; as *The Happy Thieves*, New York, Bantam, 1962.
The Manchurian Candidate. New York, McGraw Hill, 1959; London, Joseph, 1960.
Some Angry Angel: A Mid-Century Faerie Tale. New York, McGraw Hill, 1960; London, Joseph, 1961.
A Talent for Loving; or, The Great Cowboy Race. New York, McGraw Hill, 1961; London, Joseph, 1963.

An Infinity of Mirrors. New York, Random House, and London Heinemann, 1964.
Any God Will Do. New York, Random House, and London Heinemann, 1966.
The Ecstasy Business. New York, Dial Press, and London, Heinemann, 1967.
Mile High. New York, Dial Press, and London, Heinemann, 1969.
The Vertical Smile. New York, Dial Press, 1971; London, Weidenfeld and Nicolson, 1972.
Arigato. New York, Dial Press, and London, Weidenfeld and Nicolson, 1972.
The Star-Spangled Crunch. New York, Bantam, 1974.
Winter Kills. New York, Dial Press, and London, Weidenfeld and Nicolson, 1974.
Money Is Love. New York, Dial Press, and London, Weidenfeld and Nicolson, 1975.
The Whisper of the Axe. New York, Dial Press, and London, Weidenfeld and Nicolson, 1976.
The Abandoned Woman: A Tragedy of Manners. New York, Dial Press, and London, Hutchinson, 1977.
Bandicoot. New York, Dial Press, and London, Hutchinson, 1978.
Death of a Politician. New York, Marek, 1978; London, Hutchinson, 1979.
The Entwining. New York, Marek, 1980; London, Hutchinson, 1981.

Plays

Men of Distinction (produced New York, 1953).

Screenplays: *A Talent for Loving*, 1965; *The Summer Music*, 1969; *The Long Loud Silence*, 1969.

Other

And Then We Moved to Rossenarra; or, The Art of Emigrating. New York, Dial Press, 1973.
The Mexican Stove: What to Put on It and in It, with Wendy Bennett. New York, Doubleday, 1973.

Editor, with Burton O. Kurth, *Writing from Experience.* New York, Harper, 1960.

*

Manuscript Collection: Mugar Memorial Library, Boston University.

Richard Condon comments:

A writer may call himself an artist but he cannot sit down and consciously create art. What is art is not likely to be decided for decades or longer after the work has been produced—and then is often redecided—so we must not feel badly if we think of literature as entertainment rather than as transcendent enlightenment. The truest banner leading such a Children's Crusade should be blazoned: ENTERTAINMENT FOR THE SAKE OF LITERATURE. Any designation of any author's work as art, either by himself (shyly) or by his peers, is merely the kiss of a wish. Readers buy novels to be entertained, to be taken out of their own lives for a few hours, not to purchase the awe of the ages which will follow.

* * *

Richard Condon published his first novel, *The Oldest Confession*, at the age of 42; he had previously spent more than 20 years working as a publicist for the American film industry. Perhaps his fiction is best viewed in light of his prior Hollywood connection, for Condon is known primarily as the author of entertaining novels, novels that are what the public would term "good reads." Some of his more famous books (*The Manchurian Candidate* and *Winter Kills*, for example) have been made into successful movies, furthering Condon's own claim of "What I *am* is a professional entertainer."

Condon's first novel defines many of the trademarks of his later works. Although the characters are involved in a highly unlikely plot of art theft and intrigue and the book lacks a certain depth, the author's fine writing and the book's sheer readability save it from the dismal fate of many first novels. Condon proves himself a very able, if not excellent, satirist, parodying everything from the art world to American politics. His subtlest, yet most significant, satire, however, is that of the thriller novel itself. It would seem as if the author sets out to parody the very genre in which he is working; such is the humor and ingenuity of the early Condon.

With the publication of his second novel, *The Manchurian Candidate*, Condon gained an even larger readership, one which was drawn to his eccentric brand of satire and espionage. This novel of political intrigue, brainwashing, murder, and incest is perhaps the best of the author's earlier works. The plot centers around the brainwashing by the Chinese of Richard Shaw, an American GI during the Korean War. Upon returning to the United States, Shaw is recommended for a Medal of Honor, not realizing that he has been the victim of an international plot. He is now the pawn in a dangerous game of political murder. As if he didn't have enough problems, he is also faced with an incestuous relationship with his mother, and a step-father who bears a striking resemblance to Senator Joe McCarthy.

Condon's taking the absurd in any given situation to the extreme and examing the foibles and paranoia of modern American society soon won him wide public and critical acclaim. He became a type of cult novelist, being likened to Kerouac and Kafka. The novels published in the 1960's, although they still were read by avid fans, were greeted with less enthusiasm by critics. With each ensuing book, the mania and early satire gives way to an ever-increasing paranoia, a love of the too-grotesque, and an obsession with minute facts and statistics. This seeming divergence from his promising first novels lends credence to Condon's view of himself as the entertainer. Although the novels written in mid-career are neither satirical masterpieces nor realistic thrillers, they do combine moments of enjoyment with suspense.

Winter Kills re-established Condon's critical appeal. His best book since *The Manchurian Candidate*, *Winter Kills*, with its plot centering around the assassination of the wealthy, liberal Irish President Tim Kegan in 1960, could have back-fired in the hands of a less skillful novelist. The headline plot, as well as Condon's handling of it, raises paranoia to a high art, but Condon controls it to a much better extent in *Winter Kills* than in any of his more recent works.

—Sally H. Bennett

CONNELL, Evan S(helby), Jr. American. Born in Kansas City, Missouri, 17 August 1924. Educated at Dartmouth College, Hanover, New Hampshire, 1941-43; University of Kansas, Lawrence, 1946-47, A.B. 1947; Stanford University, California, 1947-48; Columbia University, New York, 1948-49. Served in the United States Navy, 1943-45. Editor, *Contact* magazine, Sausalito, California, 1960-65. Recipient: Saxton Fellowship, 1952; Guggenheim Fellowship, 1962; Rockefeller grant, 1967. Address: 487 Sherwood Drive, Apartment 310, Sausalito, California 94965, U.S.A.

PUBLICATIONS

Novels

Mrs. Bridge. New York, Viking Press, 1958; London, Heinemann, 1960.
The Patriot. New York, Viking Press, 1960; London, Heinemann, 1961.
The Diary of a Rapist. New York, Simon and Schuster, 1966; London, Heinemann, 1967.
Mr. Bridge. New York, Knopf, and London, Heinemann, 1969.
The Connoisseur. New York, Knopf, 1974.
Double Honeymoon. New York, Putnam, 1976.

Short Stories

The Anatomy Lesson and Other Stories. New York, Viking Press, 1957; London, Heinemann, 1958.
At the Crossroads: Stories. New York, Simon and Schuster, 1965; London, Heinemann, 1966.
St. Augustine's Pigeon: The Selected Stories. Berkeley, California, North Point Press, 1980.

Uncollected Short Stories

"A Cross to Bear," in *Foreign Service* (Kansas City), April 1947.
"The Flat-Footed Tiger," in *American Mercury* (New York), May 1949.
"The Most Beautiful," in *Tomorrow* (New York), September 1949.
"Filbert's Wife," in *Today's Woman* (New York), Summer 1950.
"Cocoa Party," in *Paris Review*, Autumn 1953.
"The Succubus," in *Gent* (New York), August 1957.
"Death and the Wife of John Henry," in *Transatlantic Review* (London), Spring 1960.
"The End of Summer," in *Premiere 1* (Mobile, Alabama), n.d.
"Leon and Bebert Aloft," in *Carolina Quarterly* (Chapel Hill, North Carolina), Winter 1966.
"Puig's Wife," in *New Mexico Quarterly* (Albuquerque), Summer 1967.
"The Voyeur," in *Lillabulero* (Chapel Hill, North Carolina), Winter 1967.
"Undersigned, Leon and Bebert," in *Esquire* (New York), December 1969.
"The Caribbean Provedor," in *Southern Review* (Baton Rouge, Louisiana), Winter 1970.
"Neil Dortu," in *Boston University Journal*, xxv, 1, 1977.
"The Palace of the Moorish Kings," in *Denver Quarterly*, Fall 1977.

Verse

Notes from a Bottle Found on the Beach at Carmel. New York, Viking Press, 1963; London, Heinemann, 1964.
Points for a Compass Rose. New York, Knopf, 1973.

Other

A Long Desire. New York, Holt Rinehart, 1979.
The White Lantern. New York, Holt Rinehart, 1980.

Editor, *I Am a Lover*, by Jerry Stoll. Sausalito, California, Angel Island, 1961.
Editor, *Woman by Three*. Menlo Park, California, Pacific Coast Publishers, 1969.

*

Manuscript Collection: Boston University Library.

Critical Studies: "After Ground Zero" by Gus Blaisdell, in *New Mexico Quarterly* (Albuquerque), Summer 1966.

* * *

In a short story, "The Trellis" (*The Anatomy Lesson*), a murder suspect, in the course of talking rings around a bewildered and suspicious police inspector, observes of the dead man, "He felt that time was passing and he seemed vaguely baffled and resentful of the fact, for he knew he had not done much." The observation might be made of almost any of Evan S. Connell's characters who lead generally privileged but ineffectual lives in the almost hermetic worlds of their private preoccupations.

Connell's reputation rests principally on *Mrs. Bridge* and *Mr. Bridge*, tales of an affluent couple who live in the Country Club district of Kansas City, Missouri, where Connell grew up. The Bridges appeared first in several short sketches collected in *The Anatomy Lesson*; and the two books about them are in no sense traditional novels, but rather montages of many short sketches out of which the reader gradually constructs his own portraits. While they are comfortably wealthy and enjoy an unruffled family life, the Bridges are indeed "vaguely baffled" by life, which the husband has dealt with by following formulas while his wife has floundered around. Their story is summed up by the final episode of *Mrs. Bridge*, in which one December morning the now widowed wife finds herself stuck in her Lincoln, half-out of the garage, so that she cannot open the car doors. She calls, "Hello out there"; but no one answers, "unless it was the falling snow." The Bridges are the kind of earnest, upper-middle-class suburbanites found especially in the American midwest (and probably any provincial culture without a strong local tradition) who have become wealthy without achieving the sophistication to enjoy their lives. One inquiring why so many talented young Americans flee to New York and San Francisco need only read the Bridges' story to find out. (Connell himself now lives near San Francisco and writes mostly about New York.)

Between the Kansas City novels, Connell published *The Patriot*, a *bildungsroman* about a young man from Kansas City who becomes a Naval air cadet during World War II and at least breaks free of the suffocating obligations he feels to family and country. Though published after the success of *Mrs. Bridge*, the novel is so much more traditional in form than his others and so much in the convention of first novels by sensitive young Americans, it seems surely an early work.

Connell's most remarkable achievement is *The Diary of a Rapist*, a tour de force in the form of a calendar year's diary entries in which 26-year old Earl Summerfield, alienated by his ambitious wife and spiteful fellow Civil Service bureaucrats, is "tempted to keep a scrapbook of monstrous events," occurring daily in San Francisco. Ultimately, he is tempted also to commit monstrous acts and finally, as he has observed others do, to betray himself in his pathetic quest for attention. The disconcerting novel is limited only by the usual problems of a work limiting the reader's perspective to the paranoid revelations of an unreliable narrator.

Since abandoning the Bridges, Connell has focused on Muhlbach, a New York insurance executive (though with a name borrowed—like others in the books—from those prominent in Kansas City). Like the Bridges, Muhlbach—a widower with a young son and daughter and a domineering housekeeper—first appears in short stories (collected in *At the Crossroads*). The first novel about him, *The Connoisseur*, is, in fact, hardly more than a long short story about Muhlbach's developing an obsession for pre-Columbian art, extended to book length by virtuoso passages displaying the author's vast erudition about folk arts. *Obsession* is indeed the theme of all the Muhlbach stories (perhaps of all Connell's work), as this anti-hero realizes when he thinks, "I can't distinguish reality any longer, I'm gripped by an obsession. I suppose I should be alarmed, but as a matter of fact I'm not." Pre-Columbian art is entirely forgotten, however, in *Double Honeymoon*, in which Muhlbach becomes obsessed with an exotic young girl named Lambeth, whose erratic behavior culminates in suicide after she appears in the pornographic motion picture that gives the novel its title. The Muhlbach story—unlike the Bridges—remains unresolved as he disappears into a crowd.

Connell's book-length poems defy summary because, like most of the novels, they are a montage of fragments drawn from the author's vast readings about ancient peoples and their cultures that show how he shares the skill of his dazzling speaker in "The Trellis."

—Warren French

CONROY, Jack (John Wesley Conroy). American. Born in Moberly, Missouri, 5 December 1899. Attended the University of Missouri, Columbia, 1920-21. Married Gladys Kelly in 1922; one living child. Migratory worker in the 1920's. Editor, *The Rebel Poet*, Moberly, 1931-32; *The Anvil*, Moberly, 1933-37; with Nelson Algren, *The New Anvil*, Chicago, 1939-41; Literary Editor, Chicago *Defender*, 1946-47, Chicago *Globe*, 1950. Associate Editor, Nelson's Encyclopedia, and Universal World Reference Encyclopedia, Chicago, 1943-47; Senior Editor, New Standard Encyclopedia, Chicago, 1947-66; Director, Standard Information Service, Chicago, 1949-52. Instructor in Creative Writing, Columbia College, Chicago, 1962-66; Lecturer, University of Connecticut, Storrs, 1969. Recipient: Guggenheim Fellowship, 1935; Society of Midland Authors Dow Award, 1967; *Literary Times* Award, 1967; Louis M. Rabinowitz Foundation grant, 1968; National Endowment for the Arts grant, 1977. L.H.D.: University of Missouri, Kansas City, 1975. Address: 701 Fisk Avenue, Moberly, Missouri 65270, U.S.A.

PUBLICATIONS

Novels

The Disinherited. New York, Covici Friede, 1933; London, Wishart, 1934.
A World to Win. New York, Covici Friede, 1935.

Uncollected Short Stories

"Bun Grady," in *Pagany* (Boston), July-September 1932.
"Pipe Line," in *American Mercury* (New York), September 1932.
"Siren," in *American Mercury* (New York), May 1933.
"Coal Miner's Widow," in *Proletarian Literature in the United States*, edited by Granville Hicks and others. New York, International Publishers, 1935; London, Lawrence, 1936.
"Happy Birthday to You," in *North, East, South, West,* edited by Charles Lee. San Francisco, Howell, 1945.
"The High Divers," in *The Family Book of Humor*, edited by Helen Hoke. New York, Hanover House, 1957.
"Lute Goins' Sawmill," in *A Treasury of American Anecdotes*, edited by B.A. Botkin. New York, Random House, 1957.
"Boyhood in a Coal Town," in *Missouri Reader*, edited by Frank Luther Mott. Columbia, University of Missouri Press, 1964.

Other

The Fast Sooner Hound (juvenile), with Arna Bontemps. Boston, Houghton Mifflin, 1942.
They Seek a City: A Study of Negro Migration, with Arna Bontemps. New York, Doubleday, 1945; revised edition as *Anyplace But Here*, New York, Hill and Wang, 1966.
Slappy Hooper: The Wonderful Sign Painter (juvenile), with Arna Bontemps. Boston, Houghton Mifflin, 1946.
Sam Patch: The High, Wide and Handsome Jumper (juvenile), with Arna Bontemps. Boston, Houghton Mifflin, 1951.
The Jack Conroy Reader, edited by Jack Salzman and David Ray. New York, Burt Franklin, 1980.

Editor, with Ralph Cheyney, *Unrest 1929.* London, Stockwell, 1929.
Editor, with Ralph Cheyney, *Unrest 1930.* London, Studies Publications, 1930.
Editor, with Ralph Cheyney, *Unrest 1931.* New York, Henry Harrison, 1931.
Editor, *Midland Humor: A Harvest of Fun and Folklore.* New York, Wyn, 1947.
Editor, with Curt Johnson, *Writers in Revolt: The Anvil Anthology, 1933-1940.* New York, L. Hill, 1973.

*

Bibliography: "A Preliminary Checklist of the Writings of Jack Conroy" by John Gordon Burke, in *American Book Collector* (Chicago), Summer 1971.

Manuscript Collection: University of Wyoming, Laramie.

Critical Studies: *American Novelists of Today* by Harry Werfel, New York, American Book Company, 1951; introduction by Daniel Aaron to *The Disinherited*, New York, Hill and Wang, 1963; "Versatile Performer" by Hoke Norris, in *Chicago Sun-Times*, 14 April 1963; Warren Beck, in *Chicago Tribune Magazine of Books*, 12 May 1963; radio interview printed in *Chicago Daily News*, 18 May 1963; Erling Larsen, in *Proletarian Writers of the Thirties*, edited by David Madden, Carbondale, Southern Illinois University Press, 1968; "Home to Moberly" by the author, in *Missouri Library Association Quarterly* (Columbia), March 1968; "Jack Conroy Issue" of *New Letters* (Kansas City), Fall 1972; "Charley Was Our Darlin' " by the author, and "Conroy, Mencken and *The American Mercury*" by Jack Salzman, in *Journal of Popular Culture* (Bowling Green, Ohio), Winter 1973; "The Literary Underworld of the Thirties" by the author, in *New Letters* (Kansas City), Spring 1974; "Jack Conroy's Return," in *Newsletter of the Society for the Study of Midwestern Literature* (East Lansing, Michigan), Summer 1974.

Jack Conroy comments:

The Disinherited isn't really a novel—as some critics have said. I agree with that. Novel or not, just so it tells the truth. I describe myself as a witness to the times, not as a novelist. And that's what I prefer to be known as. If I succeeded in conveying something of the times, something of the terror and the uncertainty and the actual desperation, then I'm content.

* * *

Despite the fact of an extensive and variegated literary career, Jack Conroy's reputation is associated primarily with his first novel, *The Disinherited.* The novel was published in 1933, in a moment when "proletarian literature" was a prominent cause and an occasion for debate. It was obviously autobiographical—indeed, Conroy had written it as an essay in autobiography originally, only later and by order of his publisher transforming it into fiction. The hero of the novel is the son of a coal miner, and therefore he is of the family of America's "disinherited." He tells the story of his boyhood in a company-owned coal town, and then the story of his young manhood during the first years of the Great Depression, spent pursuing laboring jobs and wandering when there are no jobs. All of his experiences present evidence of a conspiracy against ordinary workers. The coal company places profits above safety; two of his brothers and his father are killed in the mine. Government connives with industry to break strikes, and union leaders are corrupted. The interests of laboring men are defeated by the technique of anti-Communist hysteria. The hero discovers that nonetheless there exists a latent unity among workers. The novel ends with the double event of a group of farmers resisting the eviction of a debtor from his home, and the hero's resolve to become an active agent in the class struggle.

Marxist criticism tended to be virtually scholastic in its discriminations, and it was objected that Conroy's hero had inclinations towards poetry. The novel was, however, almost unimpeachable: it was written by a genuine proletarian, it touched upon all of the proper themes, and it ended in polemic. Conroy's book secured great reputation for its purity. It has remained a primary document of the social literature of the 1930's.

That historical judgment has perhaps obscured the fact that the novel—and Conroy's ambitions in general—were much less ideological than they appeared to be. Conroy has himself, in later years, expressed skepticism about the place of ideology in literature. (See his essay "Home to Moberly," 1968.) His novel in fact engaged dramatically materials which were quite unproletarian, and developed themes much more in the tradition of American pastoral. The novel begins and ends with scenes of the Missouri mining town of the hero's boyhood, and in spite of the record of capitalist tyrannies which the hero recounts, the novel presents the town in terms of a pervading loveliness. There are woods nearby, where the young bucks play their accordians and flutes. The youngsters have Indian games, the plot and even the vocabulary of which seem to come from the novels of James Fenimore Cooper. The boy falls in love with a girl who is a farmer's daughter, who has all of the flouncing and charming righteousness of Becky Thatcher in *Tom Sawyer*. The novel dwells on such materials for almost a third of its length. In another large part, as the hero moves from job to job, the novel dwells on the craft that is in industry—the workman's requisite skills in the making of steel, rubber, automobiles, etc. It is these credibilities—the small town, the woods, the sense of individual craft—from which the hero will be disinherited, and the novel is its own social action, rather than a call to social action, by the amount that it vivifies them. By that amount also it testifies to the implication of American "proletarian literature" in a much broader American myth.

—Marcus Klein

COOPER, Lettice (Ulpha). British. Born in Eccles, Lancashire, 3 September 1897. Educated at St. Cuthbert's School, Southbourne; Lady Margaret Hall, Oxford, 1916-18, B.A. Editorial Assistant and Drama Critic, *Time and Tide*, London, 1939-40. Public Relations Officer, Ministry of Food, London, 1940-45. President, Robert Louis Stevenson Club, 1958-74; Vice Chairman, 1975-78, and President, 1979-81, English P.E.N. Club. Recipient: Arts Council bursary, 1968; Eric Gregory Travelling Scholarship, 1977. Agent: A.P. Watt and Son, 26-28 Bedford Row, London WC1R 4HL. Address: 95 Canfield Gardens, London NW6 3DY, England.

PUBLICATIONS

Novels

The Lighted Room. London, Hodder and Stoughton, 1925.
The Old Fox. London, Hodder and Stoughton, 1927.
Good Venture. London, Hodder and Stoughton, 1928.
Likewise the Lion. London, Hodder and Stoughton, 1928.
The Ship of Truth. London, Hodder and Stoughton, and Boston, Little Brown, 1930.
Private Enterprise. London, Hodder and Stoughton, 1931.
Hark to Rover. London, Hodder and Stoughton, 1933.
We Have Come to a Country. London, Gollancz, 1935.
The New House. London, Gollancz, and New York, Macmillan, 1936.
National Provincial. London, Gollancz, and New York, Macmillan, 1938.
Black Bethlehem. London, Gollancz, and New York, Macmillan, 1947.
Fenny. London, Gollancz, 1953.
Three Lives. London, Gollancz, 1957.
A Certain Compass. London, Gollancz, 1960.
The Double Heart. London, Gollancz, 1962.
Late in the Afternoon. London, Gollancz, 1971.
Tea on Sunday. London, Gollancz, 1973.
Snow and Roses. London, Gollancz, 1976.
Desirable Residence. London, Gollancz, 1980.

Uncollected Short Stories

"Frowning Caryatid," in *London Calling*, edited by Storm Jameson. New York, Harper, 1942.

Other

Robert Louis Stevenson. London, Home and Van Thal, 1947; Denver, Swallow, 1948.
Yorkshire: West Riding. London, Hale, 1950.
George Eliot. London, Longman, 1951; revised edition, 1960, 1964.
Great Men of Yorkshire (West Riding) (juvenile). London, Lane, 1955.
The Young Florence Nightingale (juvenile). London, Parrish, 1960; New York, Roy, 1961.
Blackberry's Kitten (juvenile). Leicester, Brockhampton Press, 1961; New York, Vanguard Press, 1963.
The Young Victoria (juvenile). London, Parrish, 1961; New York, Roy, 1962.
The Bear Who Was Too Big (juvenile). London, Parrish, 1963; Chicago, Follett, 1966.
Bob-a-Job (juvenile). Leicester, Brockhampton Press, 1963.
James Watt (juvenile). London, Black, 1963.
Garibaldi (juvenile). London, Methuen, 1964; New York, Roy, 1966.
The Young Edgar Allan Poe (juvenile). London, Parrish, 1964; New York, Roy, 1965.
Contadino (juvenile). London, Cape, 1964.
The Fugitive King (juvenile). London, Parrish, 1965.
The Twig of Cypress (juvenile). London, Deutsch, 1965; New York, Washburn, 1966.
We Shall Have Snow (juvenile). Leicester, Brockhampton Press, 1966.
A Hand upon the Time: A Life of Charles Dickens (juvenile). New York, Pantheon, 1968; London, Gollancz, 1971.
Robert Louis Stevenson (juvenile). London, Burns and Oates, 1969.
Gunpowder, Treason, and Plot (juvenile). London and New York, Abelard Schuman, 1970.
Robert the Spy Hunter (juvenile). London, Kaye and Ward, 1973.
Parkin (juvenile). London, Harrap, 1977.

*

Manuscript Collection: The Public Library, Eccles, Lancashire.

Critical Study: "Lettice at 70" by Francis King, in *Sunday Telegraph* (London), 1967.

Lettice Cooper comments:

I want to write stories about people in depth, using the traditional form, but hoping to show how the unconscious pressures and situations are always there beneath the conscious pattern. I want to indicate both the inner and outer life of my characters, and to "explore the truth of the human situation."

* * *

Lettice Cooper has been writing novels for many years, and social historians of the future may well study them for their careful reflection of middle-class English life at various stages of this century. The worlds she described in her younger days may have gone, but this does not mean that the novels themselves have dated: technically and psychologically they still stand up well. Their settings are domestic, though their domesticity varies. In *Fenny*, one of the most ambitious and successful, we see some grandish Italian interiors; in *National Provincial*, lower middle-class North Country life; in *The Ship of Truth*, a young clergyman's home, penny-pinching through necessity; in *The New House*, an upper-middle-class family, suffocatingly cosy and financially quite secure; in *The Double Heart*, more townish and trendy people; in *Late in the Afternoon*, a smartish background in the main characters, very different ones in the others, who include a wandering hippy.

In some of the novels institutions stand behind the domesticity. In *Three Lives* it is an adult education college; in *We Have Come to a Country* an "occupational centre for unemployed men" (the time is the mid-1930's). In these cases, the institutions are not just decorative backgrounds, realistically painted flats; we get inside them, learn how they work. Nothing, in Cooper's novels, is put in without a point or a place in the action, without being properly inserted and made familiar. Cooper is always professional, a writer whose care, and whose respect for her readers, deserve respect.

Two places are of primary importance in her novels—her native Yorkshire, standing rocklike and immoveable, often a symbol of stability in a shifting world, sometimes of narrowness in a wider one (London beckons the young); and the country for which she feels the deep love of the enchanted (though knowledgeable) outsider: Italy, and more specifically Tuscany. Again and again the novels are set in, or have excursions to, one or other of these places. Both, in a sense, seem to represent homecoming.

If the settings of the novels are domestic, the action, as a rule, is unadventurous, in the sense of undramatic—except in terms of feelings and personalities. But this might be said, of course, of the majority of English fiction written by women, from *Middlemarch* downwards, and implies no narrowness of outlook. Cooper has kept fairly firmly within the worlds she knows and understands, but that they have opened out with the years is clear from *Late in the Afternoon*, in which, from the standpoint of an elderly woman, she deals sympathetically with the new young, and makes a splendidly unpatronising excursion into a working-class household touched but not radically altered by the new prosperity. From her domestic settings she deals, in fact, with the basic issues and problems: love and indifference, parental selfishness, the young's longing for escape, moral dilemmas, varying standards of behaviour, of loyalty and truth. In what seems a straightforward way she concentrates much into seemingly simple scenes and passages; her strength lying in an intelligent understanding of human nature, in warmth tempered with briskness and humour, and in an intuitive interpretation of events, psychological and spiritual. At its simplest this concentration appears in her children's books, outstandingly good among which is *Bob-a-Job*, a small masterpiece of insight on that attractive menace, the predatory wolf-cub, out to help.

—Isabel Quigly

COOPER, William. Pseudonym for Harry Summerfield Hoff. British. Born in Crewe, Cheshire, 4 August 1910. Educated at Christ's College, Cambridge, M.A. 1933. Served in the Royal Air Force, 1940-45. Married Joyce Barbara Harris in 1950; two daughters. Schoolmaster, Leicester, 1933-40; Assistant Commissioner, Civil Service Commission, London, 1945-58. Part-time Personnel Consultant, for the United Kingdom Atomic Energy Authority, 1958-72, the Central Electricity Generating Board, 1960-72, and the Commission of European Community, 1972-73; Staff Director, Civil Service Selection Board, 1973-75; Member of the Board, Crown Agents, 1975-77; Adviser, Millbank Technical Services, 1975-77. Since 1977, Adjunct Professor of English, Syracuse University, London Center. Address: 22 Kenilworth Court, Lower Richmond Road, London S.W. 15, England.

PUBLICATIONS

Novels

Trina (as H.S. Hoff). London, Heinemann, 1934; as *It Happened in PRK*, New York, Coward McCann, 1934.
Rhéa (as H.S. Hoff). London, Heinemann, 1937.
Lisa (as H.S. Hoff). London, Heinemann, 1937.
Three Marriages (as H.S. Hoff). London, Heinemann, 1946.
Scenes from Provincial Life. London, Cape, 1950.
The Struggles of Albert Woods. London, Cape, 1952; New York, Doubleday, 1953.
The Ever-Interesting Topic. London, Cape, 1953.
Disquiet and Peace. London, Macmillan, 1956; Philadelphia, Lippincott, 1957.
Young People. London, Macmillan, 1958.
Scenes from Married Life. London, Macmillan, 1961.
Scenes from Life (includes *Scenes from Provincial Life* and *Scenes from Married Life*). New York, Scribner, 1961.
Memoirs of a New Man. London, Macmillan, 1966.
You Want the Right Frame of Reference. London, Macmillan, 1971.
Love on the Coast. London, Macmillan, 1973.
You're Not Alone: A Doctor's Diary. London, Macmillan, 1976.

Uncollected Short Stories

"Ball of Paper," in *Winter's Tales 1*. London, Macmillan, and New York, St. Martin's Press, 1955.
"A Moral Choice," in *Winter's Tales 4*. London, Macmillan, and New York, St. Martin's Press, 1958.

Plays

High Life (produced London, 1951).
Prince Genji (produced Oxford, 1958). London, Evans Brothers, 1959.

Other

C.P. Snow. London, Longman, 1959; revised edition, 1971.
Shall We Ever Know? The Trial of the Hosein Brothers for the Murder of Mrs. McKay. London, Hutchinson, 1971; as *Brothers*, New York, Harper, 1972.

*

Manuscript Collection: Humanities Research Center, University of Texas, Austin.

Critical Studies: *Tradition and Dream* by Walter Allen, London, Phoenix House, 1964; Introduction by Malcolm Bradbury to *Scenes from Provincial Life*, London, Macmillan, 1969.

William Cooper comments:

(1972) I don't know that I specially believe in artists making statements about their own work. An artist's *work* is *his* statement. And that's that. The rest is for other people to say. Perhaps a writer whose original statement has turned out obscure may feel it useful to present a second that's more comprehensible—in that case I wonder why he didn't make the second one first.

Speaking for myself, *Scenes from Provincial Life* seems to me so simple, lucid, attractive, and funny that anyone who finds he can't read it probably ought to ask himself: "Should I be trying to read books at all? Wouldn't it be better to sit and watch television or something?" I write about the real world and real people in it. And I stick pretty close to what I've had some experience of. That's why *Scenes from Metropolitan Life*, which is also simple, lucid, attractive and funny, was suppressed. *Scenes from Married Life*, makes the third of a trilogy. *Albert Woods* and *Memoirs of a New Man* are about goings-on in the world of science and technology; *You Want the Right Frame of Reference* in the world of arts—they have an added touch of wryness and malice. An unusual marriage is the core of *Young People* and *Disquiet and Peace*, the former set in the provinces in the '30's, the latter in Edwardian upperclass London—its small group of admirers think it's a beautiful book. *The Ever-Interesting Topic* is about what happens when you give a course of lectures on sex to a board-school full of boys: what you'd expect. *Shall We Ever Know?* is a day-by-day account of a most surprising and mystifying murder trial, a kidnapping for ransom in which no trace whatsoever of the body was ever found, and two men were found guilty of murder.

(1981) *Love on the Coast*, my only novel to be set outside England, is about some former "flower children" in San Francisco who are working their way back into society by running an "experimental" theatre. And *You're Not Alone*, one of my best and wisest books, is the diary of a London doctor, a retired GP of some distinction, to whom people come to confide their sexual quirks—as a start he tells them they are not alone. He is a widower, and touchingly the youngest daughter of one of his friends falls in love with him and he with her.

* * *

William Cooper is the pen-name of an author who had already published four novels under his own name, H.S. Hoff, when in 1950 he emerged with a new literary identity, and won a new literary reputation, with *Scenes from Provincial Life*—a novel which quickly became a classic of a new kind of realism and undoubtedly had a significant influence on the general development of the English novel in the 1950's and since. A delightful, tough-minded story set among young provincial intellectuals, in a midlands town suspiciously like Leicester, over the months just before the outbreak of the Second World War, and dealing with their mores and emotions, *Scenes from Provincial Life* was the forerunner of a sequence of books which, in the postwar years, were to treat local English life, the familiar and ordinary experience of recognizable people, with a youthful, fresh, exploratory, critical curiosity. There can be little doubt that the book did help encourage, if not directly influence, a number of younger writers like John Braine, David Storey, Stanley Middleton, and Stan Barstow, some of whom have directly expressed indebtedness to Cooper's work; and it certainly helped postwar writers to find a sense of direction. Its force was strengthened by the fact that Cooper—along with C.P. Snow, Pamela Hansford Johnson, and some other rather younger writers like Kingsley Amis and John Wain—was deliberately, and in obvious reaction against the Bloomsbury-dominated climate of "cultured" experimentalism, seeking out a form of fiction much more social, detailed, empirical, realistic, and humanly substantial in character, concerned with the felt sense of contemporary life. This spirit in writing has been characterized by some critics as middlebrow, and its spirit has been seen as banal, but it retained a humanist vigour and a closeness to familiar life in the practice of serious English writing at a time when, in literary traditions in other countries, deeper signs of strain were obviously being felt. Cooper's book had a general influence on that, the more important because it was not only one of the first, but also one of the best, of the kind.

Cooper has since produced ten more novels, all marked by the same commitment to familiar life and all marked with the same qualities of luminosity and delicacy. One of them, *Disquiet and Peace*, is an historical novel, set in the high society milieu of political and drawing-room life in the Edwardian England when the period of Liberal domination was ending. The rest are all in a sense banal novels—concerned with the world of day-to-day social experience, under the conditions we most of us know. Set in the provinces, the suburbs, or the world of the urban middle-classes, a slice of social experience which Cooper knows and details very well, they represent ordinary things happening to intelligent, sceptical people: they have affairs, get married, breed families, and they work in schools and offices. The stratum in question is usually that of the new men of the pre- and post-war meritocratic world. Most of them are rising toward social and intellectual possession, and part of their realistic pleasure in the world around comes from the fact that it is obviously open to their mobility and talents. In form and content, Cooper's world is not a world of the exceptionable or the unexpected; even *Disquiet and Peace* is a study in depth of marriage, that institution and area of emotional and psychic activity of which Cooper is among the best modern analysts.

But if one of Cooper's striking qualities is his realism, another is his comedy. The life in which he deals may be familiar, but he lights it up with a remarkable sense of human oddity, and of the quirkiness and extremity that exist within his dense and recognizable characters. Ordinariness is set off against outrage, often deriving from the cool, undercutting tone of the narrator himself. Like Muriel, who in *Disquiet and Peace* brings disorder into the world of the book by donning an eyeglass and dropping it into her soup, Cooper, or his surrogate Joe Lunn, enters his fictional world to introduce the oblique vision. Most of the struggles and desires of the characters, desires for social, material or sexual success, become matters for very cool irony. His plots often seem to be about moral conflicts, between liberal and traditional values, but Cooper by the end seems to move lightly away from the conflict, leaving the entire experience ridiculous. Such is the case with *The Ever-Interesting Topic*, dealing with a headmaster who tries to introduce lectures on sex education into his public school. Cooper has always a buoyant, vitalist view of sexuality and a sense of the way it renders most human pretensions ridiculous. Comedy in his books serves to show up ridiculousness and peculiarity, and helps make his realism into a writing of surprise. As a result the books have a sharp revealing clarity which is part of his distinctive style, and which distinguishes his work from that of, say, C.P. Snow—about whom he has written warmly—who writes about a somewhat similar world, and who shares his interest in those in the field of administration and technology, in the struggles of the new men, in the Albert Woods and Joe Lunns of modern society. Comedy too makes his heroes attractive centres of vision. This is especially true of the most successful of all, Joe Lunn, the first-person narrator of both *Scenes from Provincial Life* and *Scenes from Married Life*. Lunn, being both a performer in the action and the artistic observer recalling and shaping it, neatly shows off the writer's balance between sympathy and irony, fact and fiction. In other books, other narrative techniques are used, but the result is usually an adept mixture of sympathetic identification with characters and an ironic distance from them.

As a result, Cooper's novels do possess a distinctive style and vision. Nonetheless, they vary somewhat in quality; and his luminous delicacy, his gift for catching the flavour and quality of the right, revealing scene, for cutting deep into life, is more apparent in some than others. What distinguishes his work at best from other writing superficially like it is a very precise artistic control. It is most evident when he is catching at the flavour of a distinctive ethos and time and catching the behaviour of vital people in it (e.g., as in *Young People*). The comparison with H.G. Wells is not inexact; he has the same gift for conveying hopeful, buoyant contingency, youthful pleasure in life. But there is also at times (as in *Scenes from Provincial Life*) a balance of reminiscence, irony and sentiment so carefully composed as to recall the "artistic" realism of, say, Turgenev. His technique is not always particularly noticeable (except when the narrator, as occasionally happens, intrudes very self-consciously on the action to comment) but it is self-conscious and adept. The result is that his work is not only socially and humanely dense and comically and morally illuminating, but is also shot through with literary perspectives. It is this that has helped to give *Scenes from Provincial Life*—which remains probably his best novel—the status of a small modern classic which it now possesses.

—Malcolm Bradbury

COOVER, Robert (Lowell). American. Born in Charles City, Iowa, 4 February 1932. Educated at Southern Illinois University, Carbondale, 1949-51; Indiana University, Bloomington, B.A. 1953; University of Chicago, 1958-61, M.A. 1965. Retired Lieutenant in the United States Navy; on active duty, 1953-57. Married Pilar Sans-Mallafré in 1959; three children. Taught at Bard College, Annandale on Hudson, New York, 1966-67; University of Iowa, Iowa City, 1967-69; Writer-in-Residence, Wisconsin State University, Superior, 1968, Washington University, St. Louis, 1969, Columbia University, New York, 1972, Princeton University, New Jersey, 1972-73, Virginia Military Institute, Lexington, 1976, and University of Maine, Orono, 1979. Since 1979, Writer-in-Residence, Brown University, Providence, Rhode Island. Fiction Editor, *Iowa Review*, Iowa City, 1974-77. Recipient: Faulkner Award, 1966; Brandeis University Creative Arts Award, 1969; Rockefeller Fellowship, 1969; Guggenheim Fellowship, 1971, 1974; American Academy award, 1976. Agent: Georges Borchardt, 136 East 57th Street, New York, New York 10022, U.S.A.

PUBLICATIONS

Novels

The Origin of the Brunists. New York, Putnam, 1966; London, Barker, 1967.
The Universal Baseball Association, Inc., J. Henry Waugh, Prop. New York, Random House, 1968; London, Hart Davis, 1970.
The Public Burning. New York, Viking Press, 1977; London, Allen Lane, 1978.

Short Stories

Pricksongs and Descants. New York, Dutton, 1969; London, Cape, 1971.
The Water Pourer (unpublished chapter from *The Origin of the Brunists*). Bloomfield Hills, Michigan, Bruccoli Clark, 1972.
Hair o' the Chine. Bloomfield Hills, Michigan, Bruccoli Clark, 1979.
After Lazarus. Bloomfield Hills, Michigan, Bruccoli Clark, 1980.
Charlie in the House of Rue. Lincoln, Massachusetts, Penmaen Press, 1980.
A Political Fable. New York, Viking Press, 1980.

Uncollected Short Stories

"Blackdamp," in *Noble Savage* (Cleveland), October 1961.
"Dinner with the King of England," in *Evergreen Review* (New York), November-December 1962.
"D.D., Baby," in *Cavalier* (New York), July 1963.
"The Duel," in *Evergreen Review* (New York), June 1967.
"The Square-Shooter and the Saint," in *Evergreen Review Reader*, edited by Barney Rosset. New York, Grove Press, 1968.
"Some Notes about Puff," in *Iowa Review* (Iowa City), Winter 1970.
"The Reunion," in *Iowa Review* (Iowa City), Winter 1971.
"McDuff on the Mound," in *Iowa Review* (Iowa City), Fall 1971.
"Beginnings," in *Harper's* (New York), January 1972.
"Lucky Pierre and the Music Lesson," in *New American Review 14*, edited by Theodore Solotaroff. New York, Simon and Schuster, 1972.
"The Dead Queen," in *Quarterly Review of Literature* (Princeton, New Jersey), 1973.
"Whatever Happened to Gloomy Gus of the Chicago Bears?," in *American Review 22*, edited by Theodore Solotaroff. New York, Bantam, 1974.
"In Bed One Night," in *Playboy* (Chicago), January 1980.
"A Working Day," in *Iowa Review* (Iowa City), Spring 1980.

Plays

The Kid (produced New York, 1972; London, 1974). Included in *A Theological Position*, 1972.
A Theological Position (includes *A Theological Position*, *The Kid*, *Love Scene*, *Rip Awake*). New York, Dutton, 1972.
Love Scene (as *Scène d'amour*, produced Paris, 1973; as *Love Scene*, produced New York, 1974). Included in *A Theological Position*, 1972.
Rip Awake (produced Los Angeles, 1975). Included in *A Theological Position*, 1972.
A Theological Position (produced Los Angeles, 1977; New York, 1979). Included in *A Theological Position*, 1972.

Other

Editor, with Kent Dixon, *The Stone Wall Book of Short Fiction*. Iowa City, Stone Wall Press, 1973.
Editor, with Elliott Anderson, *Minute Stories*. New York, Braziller, 1976.

*

Critical Studies: *Fiction and the Figures of Life* by William Gass, New York, Knopf, 1970; "Robert Coover's Fiction" by Jackson I. Cope, in *Iowa Review* (Iowa City), ii, 4, 1971; *Black Humor Fiction of the Sixties* by Max Schulz, Athens, Ohio University Press, 1973; "Robert Coover and the Hazards of Metafiction" by Neil Schmitz, in *Novel 7* (Providence, Rhode Island), 1974; "Humor and Balance in Coover's *The Universal Baseball Association, Inc.*" by Frank W. Shelton, in *Critique 17* (Atlanta), 1975; "Robert Coover, Metafictions, and Freedom" by Margaret Heckard, in *Twentieth Century Literature 22* (Los Angeles), 1976; "The Dice of God: Einstein, Heisenberg, and Robert Coover" by Arlen J. Hansen, in *Novel 10* (Providence, Rhode Island), 1976; "Structure as Revelation: Coover's *Pricksongs and Descants*" by Jessie Gunn, in *Linguistics in Literature*, ii, 1, 1977.

* * *

The change that has overtaken American fiction, Robert Coover has said, came about for two reasons. One is the familiar notion that the novel as a literary form is exhausted. We therefore need new ideas concerning what story writing is about, and we must search for new principles of fiction. The other is equally familiar: we have been pushed, in the modern world, to a state of extremity in which we face the obliteration of the race. This condition raises questions about the value of religion and of history. If these are meaningless, as now appears to be the case, then writers have recourse to the grotesque or to a nightmarish fiction or to a form of comedy, but not to tragedy, which is an "adolescent response to the universe."

In his own fiction Coover has accordingly turned away from traditional realism. What he demonstrates in *Pricksongs and Descants*, which represents his earliest writing although published subsequent to his first novel, and in everything written since, is the conviction that reality, history, and truth are "made" or invented, that appearances are everything, that forms are really substance, that poetry is the art of subordinating facts to the imagination, and that objectivity is an impossible illusion. These are matters that he actually discusses, in the self-reflexive mode of modernist fiction, in his novels; all the above come specifically from *The Public Burning*. Coover's aim is to dis-establish dogmatic confidence in the nature of reality, as his well-known story, "The Babysitter," so clearly demonstrates. It is a goal which rests on the premise, to which both Vladimir Nabokov and William Gass have given voice, that the author is a dictator or a god. In "The Magic Poker" the authorial voice announces that *I* have invented these characters, have dressed them and may well undress them, have endowed them with physical attributes but need not be bound by any anatomical reality: they will have or not have organs exactly as I decree. Despite these assertions, however, Coover cannot altogether free himself in his fiction from the sense-apprehensible reality which most of us acknowledge.

An alternative to the realistic novel which attempts to mirror life is a fiction which centers its attention upon language and technique. Language is a form of play, an expression of wit, and a source of joy. Language is an end in itself, rather than a means of expressing the ideas and feelings of characters and the culture. The magic of language becomes the supreme ordering principle of our existence. When Coover pushes these matters far enough, language transcends itself and becomes the culture. The play of language opens us to the literary strategies that are the means of defining and knowing the culture. The variety of techniques in *The Public Burning* offers the readiest example of Coover's conviction in this matter: he uses here, among others, the techniques of the drama, collage, montage, surrealism, opera, farce and slap-stick, the absurd, parody, and satire.

So much for Coover's version of the new ideas about fiction. Now as to history and religion, which are meaningless. Assuming the problematic nature of reality, Coover turns to myth in each of the three novels he has published to date. In *The Origins of the Brunists* a rational editor cynically invents a miracle which becomes the basis for a system of religious belief. This novel is an exercise in the creation of "truth"; the Brunist religion as an act of creation is a mirror-reflection of Coover's own creation of the novel itself. Coover is a myth-maker demonstrating how myth is made. In *The Universal Baseball Association, Inc., J. Henry Waugh, Prop.*, Coover's most successful book, "real" events pass into myth and are expressed in recurring ritual. The primacy of the imagined world is established as a result of conflict with the "real" world, which is Coover's way of asserting the primacy of fiction. "The world itself being a construct of fictions," he has said, "I believe the fiction maker's function is to furnish better fictions with which we can re-form our notions of things." In this novel, both real and invented realms are merged and coalesce in time; a system of belief emerges which passes into myth or religion. The reality upon which Coover builds here is the history of baseball. The reality in *The Public Burning* is the espionage trial of Ethel and Julius Rosenberg, which Coover transmutes by way of folklore and history into the myth of America. He provides initiation into evil and the threat of evil in the conflict with the Phantom; sacrifices of the victims, who are to be executed; spectacle and saturnalia, since the execution, an orgasmic occasion, is staged by Cecil B. De Mille and others in Times Square; purification by fire; and rescue and preservation of the sacred flame—the atomic bomb—by Uncle Sam, the archetypal American hero. But Uncle Sam is also Sam Slick, the Yankee Peddler, who has his dark side. And much of the novel is narrated by Vice-President Richard Nixon, portrayed as treacherous, cunning, ruthless, paranoid, mean-spirited, vengeful, repressed, self-pitying, sentimental, lonely, and alienated. The mythic world is a self-encapsulated fiction. The judgment about the American myth and American heroes—real or symbolic—takes us out of the hermetic world of myth. In this novel, Coover validates equally the two realms and thus undercuts his expressed belief in the supremacy of fiction and the imagination.

—Chester E. Eisinger

COPE, Jack (Robert Knox Cope). South African. Born in Mooi River, Natal, 3 June 1913. Educated at Durban High School. Married Lesley de Villiers in 1942 (divorced, 1956); two children. Reporter, *Natal Mercury*, Durban, 1930-35; Correspondent in London for South African Morning Newspapers, 1936-40; Farmer in Natal, 1941-42; engaged in shark-fishing enterprise, Cape Town, 1943-45; Director, South African Association of the Arts, Cape Town, 1946-48. Since 1949, free-lance writer and reporter: since 1960, Founding Editor, *Contrast*, Cape Town; Editor, Mantis Editions in the 1970's. Recipient: South African Arts and Sciences Prose Prize, 1959; British Council travel grant, 1960; Carnegie Travel Fellowship, 1966; South African Festival of the Soil Award, 1970. Address: Sea Girt, Second Beach, Clifton, Cape Town, South Africa.

PUBLICATIONS

Novels

The Fair House. London, MacGibbon and Kee, 1955.
The Golden Oriole. London, Heinemann, 1958.
The Road to Ysterberg. London, Heinemann, 1959.
Albino. London, Heinemann, 1964.
The Dawn Comes Twice. London, Heinemann, 1969.
The Rain-Maker. London, Heinemann, 1971.
The Student of Zend. London, Heinemann, 1972.
My Son Max. London, Heinemann, 1977.

Short Stories

The Tame Ox. London, Heinemann, 1960.
The Man Who Doubted. London, Heinemann, 1967.
Alley Cat and Other Stories. London, Heinemann, 1973.

Uncollected Short Story

"Drinker of the Bitter Water," in *Paris Review*, Winter 1974.

Verse

Lyrics and Diatribes. Cape Town, Stewart, 1948.
Marie: A South African Satire (as R.K. Cope). Cape Town, Stewart, 1949.

Other

Comrade Bill (biography). Cape Town, Stewart, 1943.

Editor, with Uys Krige, *The Penguin Book of South African Verse*. London, Penguin, 1968.
Editor, *Seismograph: Best South African Writing from Contrast*. Cape Town, Reijger, 1970.

Translator, with William Plomer, *Selected Poems of Ingrid Jonker*. London, Cape, 1968.

*

Jack Cope comments:

(1972) Raised by a farming family on the South African veld a long way from anywhere, I had made up my mind at about 10 years of age that I was going to be a writer. How to do it was another thing. I am still on that search. It has been said that the art of writing lies in the struggle against the inability to write. I was a third generation from settlers in a practically empty region of Natal; white, English-speaking. Zulus came up from the warm bush country to work on the cold high-veld and they were often the only playmates I and my brothers had. We got to know them, liked them, learnt from them.

In the old stone farmhouse there were thousands of books—sermons, religious tracts and poetry, Victorian novels by "Ouida," Disraeli, Mrs. Gaskell, Wilkie Collins, Mrs. Henry Wood, etc. But there were also Fenimore Cooper, Kingsley, Defoe, Mark Twain, Dickens, Ruskin, Scott, William Morris, Thackeray; there were Shakespeare and all the English poets up to Browning. The Bible was part of one's life, though we were too far away to go to church more than a few times. I knew that I couldn't model myself on any of the writers I read—we had no Redskins, no sea or pirates, no rivers, lakes, forests, no cities, no factories, no art, no stage. Living in a mental desert, what did one specially see and feel, let alone write about? We hunted and had guns and dogs and horses, but it was all so ordinary. At 12 I was sent 100 miles to boarding school in Durban, a seaport which seemed duller, more lonely even than the farm.

Then I left school, refused to enter university and went instead into a newspaper in Durban as an "apprentice." A mistake. I was ten years in journalism and never liked it. Learnt how not to write. One thing the newspaper business did for me—it got me out of South Africa and to London. I worked in Fleet Street. In four years I was almost flattened out into an Englishman. But there's the paradox, the nearer you are, the further you are away from a thing. Anyway I remained African. Language, blood, family, tradition were all on one side; but the break of nearly a century was too long. I belonged to Africa or to nowhere.

Of course I had long since made a mental holocaust of *white* race attitudes as no-one can like somebody born into them. Mad about Shaw and Morris, Russell, Marx, Ibsen, Pound (!), Eliot and O'Casey, I cultivated a polyglot creed, a sort of anarcho-social-communonihilist with a strong dash of pacifism. Wrote bad verse with an admiring eye on Yeats, Lawrence, or Pound, and my stories limped on crutches of Gorky, Bunin, Hemingway. No nationalism, no dogma, no traditionalism, I thought myself a citizen of that other country, The World. My time—the coming apocalypse.

The war drove me morosely from England home to Natal, to the farm, the loneliness. I tried to start writing consistently, seriously. To my astonishment and disgust I found I just couldn't. The novel I started with a family-historical background went through four rewrites over a period of 12 years—all torn up or burnt. Friends used to put down my typescript in embarrassment. The book was *The Fair House*. The fifth script I sent to London. Back came a cable from a young publisher, James MacGibbon: "Fair House is magnificent." I got very drunk. I'd like to believe it was true. But I know: it was shaky but a beginning. Meanwhile I was suddenly writing short stories that got accepted.

That was the break-out. I stumbled about after that but have made it a point not to get frozen into a "manner" (substitute for style) or be carried away by form. In each story and novel, as in my poems, I wanted all the elements; rhythm, structure, tone, to work separately and together within a different context and to be ruled by it. Each book, I hope, shifts a peg on. Seven novels so far, two books, and a lot of uncollected stories—the objective is still to produce one good book by the time I pack in, and then I'll feel there was something in my dreams at the age of ten.

Writing in South Africa is not easy. There's a high voltage of tension. There's Censorship, intimidation; one's books get banned. But I don't believe in quitting; you can't see things straight from too great a distance, from exile. I am against writing dirt for sales or for its own sake. Life's full enough of dirt and if it gets into a book the context must give it an absolute necessity. I remain an African, and Africa somehow keeps a certain innocence, a certain newness and strength. It's not a political slogan. Or a garbage dump.

To fight against isolation I've always tried to work back from my own experience and to draw together the younger writers, raise critical standards, demand sound craftsmanship. I make translations from Afrikaans, Zulu, Sotho, Xhosa, and this I feel helps create links in a multi-national society. Writers cannot get a wide enough readership in the developing languages and therefore aim to master English or Afrikaans. To command a new language and learn to write in it is a mammoth task—one can be helped or encouraged, but there are no short cuts. In 1960 I took part in starting a two-language literary quarterly, *Contrast*, and still edit it. The magazine has been a mouthpiece as well as workshop for many promising young poets, fiction writers, dramatists, artists.

South Africa still has a small enough population for writers living even thousands of miles apart to get to know each other. They come from every nationality, race, belief, outlook. Many are banned, exiled. But they form a kind of republic of talent rising above the jargon and propaganda, throwing shadows ahead.

*   *   *

As his novels, and even more his short stories, show, Jack Cope is not only a skilled writer, but one whose range—as regards character, setting, and plot—is greater than that of many South African novelists. His work has moved from the historical and purely regional approach of *The Fair House* (based on an armed rising of the Zulu in 1902) and *Albino* (life in rural Natal), through a consideration of general moral issues (*The Road to Ysterberg*), to a fairly optimistic appraisal of the black resistance movement in *The Dawn Comes Twice*. Cope's characters include black politicians and intellectuals (notably in *The Golden Oriole*, which offers a fascinating glimpse into the world of black politics 40 years ago); people on the fringes of society, both black and white; and ordinary South Africans of all races and of all classes. Bushmen, *trekboers* (nomadic farmers), "poor whites," and bewildered immigrants have all claimed his sympathetic attention, and he invests these less well-known South African types with a humanity denied them by most previous writers. In two of his novels, *The Road to Ysterberg* and *The Dawn Comes Twice*, a Coloured (i.e., a half-caste) woman is given a central role, and it must be recognised that Cope is one of the very few white South African writers who is able to present such characters simply and credibly as human beings. His characters are always intimately related to their background, and in his detailed evocations of the South African landscape—desert, mountain, subtropical farmland, or uncultivated bush—he has produced some of his most impressive writing.

What one may, however, find disturbing in Cope's work, in spite of its undeniable competence and authenticity, is his tendency to romanticise the real and unpleasant issues which dominate contemporary South African life: the inequality and injustice of *apartheid* (racial segregation); the powerlessness of the black majority; the callousness of most whites. As his novels show, Cope is not unaware of these issues; but, by focussing his attention on tribal Africans, by suggesting that underground resistance movements are fairly well-organised, and, most of all, by a deliberate and too-often melodramatic manipulation of plot to avoid embarrassing personal confrontations (between, for instance, a white man and a black woman), Cope distinctly blurs the edges of his realism, and presents his readers with an attractive but subtly distorted version of South Africa. The reason for this is not hard to find. Unlike many of his contemporaries, who have in recent years chosen to live abroad, Cope lives and works within a South African context. This means, among other things, that he is subject to the increasingly complex network of censorship legislation which has, under the present government, come to affect not only the literature which may be distributed inside the country, but that which is being produced as well. Cope's own awareness of the effect of this deliberate clamp on imagination is shown in his story "A Face of Stainless Steel," which offers a poignant glimpse into the mind of a sensitive man who feels himself trapped and bound by a society he knows to be evil, but to which he is committed. The glittering mask of "Steel" (a party disguise) symbolises the emotional sterility which is the inevitable concomitant of such knowledge. In some ways, Cope's choice is an admirable one: he, at least, can and does write from *within* a tortured society: his voice is still a rational one. But, ultimately, the price exacted by this society, from a writer of integrity, may come to seem inordinately high.

—Ursula Laredo

COWAN, Peter. Australian. Born in Perth, Western Australia, 4 November 1914. Educated at the University of Western Australia, Nedlands, B.A. 1940, Dip.Ed. 1946. Served in the Royal Australian Air Force, 1943-45. Member of the faculty of the University of Western Australia, 1946-50; Senior English Master, Scotch College, Swanbourne, Western Australia, 1950-62. Since 1964, Senior Tutor, English Department, University of Western Australia. Recipient: Commonwealth Literary Fund Fellowship, 1963; Australian Council for the Arts Fellowship, 1974, 1980. Address: Department of English, University of Western Australia, Nedlands, Western Australia 6009, Australia.

PUBLICATIONS

Novels

Summer. Sydney and London, Angus and Robertson, 1964.
Seed. Sydney and London, Angus and Robertson, and San Francisco, Tri-Ocean, 1966.

Short Stories

Drift: Stories. Melbourne, Reed and Harris, 1944.
The Unploughed Land: Stories. Sydney, Angus and Robertson, 1958.
The Empty Street: Stories. Sydney and London, Angus and Robertson, and San Francisco, Tri-Ocean, 1965.
The Tins and Other Stories. Brisbane, University of Queensland Press, 1973.
New Country, with others, edited by Bruce Bennett. Fremantle, Western Australia, Fremantle Arts Centre Press, 1976.
Mobiles. Fremantle, Western Australia, Fremantle Arts Centre Press, 1979.

Other

A Unique Position: A Biography of Edith Dircksey Cowan 1861-1932. Nedlands, University of Western Australia Press, 1978.
A Colonial Experience: Swan River 1839-1888. Privately printed, 1979.

Editor, *Short Story Landscape: The Modern Short Story*. Melbourne, Longman, 1964.
Editor, with Bruce Bennett and John Hay, *Spectrum 1* and *2*. Melbourne, Longman, 2 vols., 1970; London, Longman, 2 vols., 1971.
Editor, *A Faithful Picture: The Letters of Eliza and Thomas Brown at York in the Swan River Country 1841-1852*. Fremantle, Western Australia, Fremantle Arts Centre Press, 1977.

*

Critical Studies: "The Short Stories of Peter Cowan" by John Barnes, in *Meanjin* (Melbourne), 1960; "New Tracks to Travel: The Stories of White, Porter and Cowan" by John Barnes, in *Meanjin* (Melbourne), 1966; essay by Grahame Johnston in *Westerly* (Perth), 1967; "Cowan Country" by Margot Luke, in *Sandgropers*, edited by Dorothy Hewett, Nedlands, University of Western Australia Press, 1973; "Behind the Actual" by Bruce Williams, in *Westerly* (Perth), no. 3, 1973; "Regionalism in Peter Cowan's Short Fiction" by Bruce Bennett, in *World Literature Written in English* (Guelph, Ontario), 1980.

Peter Cowan comments:

Up to the present time writing has been for me as much something I wanted to do to please myself as something aimed solely at publication and any kind of wide audience. Now, I don't think this kind of attitude is any longer possible, and the chances for this kind of fiction have greatly diminished.

My writing may have been concerned as much with place as with people, though I have tried to see people against a landscape, against a physical environment. If isolation is one of the themes that occur frequently, particularly in the short stories, this is perhaps enforced by the Australian landscape itself. I am deeply involved in everything to do with the physical Australia, the land, its shapes and seasons and colors, its trees and flowers, its birds and animals. And its coast and sea.

I have been more interested in the short story than the novel. The technical demands of a short story are high, and seldom met, and through the short story a writer has perhaps a better chance of trapping something of the fragmentary nature of today's living.

* * *

Peter Cowan is a quietly introspective writer, and consequently his intensity of vision and his scrupulous craftsmanship can easily be under-rated. Although he has written novels, his talent appears to be most suited to the short story or novella, in which he can focus on a single relationship and explore a single line of feeling. His stories, written in a spare, taut style, have as a recurring theme the relationship of a man and a woman seeking relief from their loneliness in sexual love. Cowan is intent upon an inner reality: his characters are seldom individualized very far, they seem almost anonymous, and the sensuous reality of the external world is only faintly felt. His imagination is compelled by a painful awareness of the feelings of loneliness and alienation that lie beneath the surface of commonplace lives; and in exploring this territory he has become, more than is generally recognized, a significant interpreter of Australian realities, the realities portrayed by an Australian painter like Robert Dickerson (whose painting, *Boy in a Street*, Cowan chose for the dustjacket of his volume *The Empty Street*).

In Cowan's first collection of stories, *Drift*, the preoccupations of his mature work are merely sketched in. Uneven in quality and stylistically in debt to Hemingway, the book nevertheless has a coherence and a unity of impression unexpected in the work of a young writer. Cowan has known his subject right from the start. Most of these early stories are set in the poor farming country of southwestern West Australia before the Second World War, and they centre on the lives of people who are emotionally unfulfilled or unable to express themselves in normal relationships.

Over the next 14 years Cowan wrote little. In his second collection, *The Unploughed Land*, he reprinted seven of his stories from *Drift*, along with six new stories, which represent a distinct advance in technique. These new stories include the much-anthologized "The Redbacked Spiders," a powerful story of a boy whose resentment at his brutal father leads to the man's death. The title story is an extended treatment of that pre-war country life about which he writes in his first volume. In its evocation of that life it is one of his finest pieces, and it marks the end of the first phase of his development.

From this point onward Cowan has been more prolific and more varied—though compared with most writers he has a small and narrow output. In his third collection, *The Empty Street*, there is a noticeable shift in setting. Cowan now writes of people in suburbia, for whom the country is a refuge. The sense of being caught in an irresistible and disastrous historical process is expressed in a story like "The Tractor," which concerns the efforts of a hermit to stop the clearing of the land. Cowan's sympathies are with those who oppose "progress," but he sees their dilemma truly. "The Empty Street," a novella, is an impressive study of an unhappy middle-aged clerk, whose marriage is now a mere shell, and whose children are strangers to him: desperate to escape the pressures of a life that is meaningless to him, he collapses into schizophrenia and turns murderer. Cowan is especially responsive to the theme of the middle-aged, defeated and desolate in marriage, groping for a way out. *The Tins and Other Stories* confirms the achievement of the earlier volumes, with stories like "The Rock" and "The Tins," in which Cowan is seen at his characteristic best.

Peter Cowan's two attempts at novels have not been very successful. *Summer* is a short novel, more like two short stories that have been expanded and linked together. A businessman whose marriage has failed takes a job on the wheat bins, and in this lonely setting forms a relationship with the wife of the nearby storekeeper. The violent resolution is not well managed, and the central character tends to be a mouthpiece for Cowan's reflections on the spoiling of the natural environment. Yet there are some fine sequences establishing the relationship of the two lonely people in a solitary landscape.

In *Seed* Cowan set out to portray a group of middle-class families living in Perth. An Australian reader feels the force of his thesis about the boredom and frustration of suburban living, but it remains a thesis and seldom quickens into drama. It is a disappointing work, the result of Cowan's trying to write against the grain of his talent. He is not skilled at creating personalities or at suggesting the social facts of life, but in this rather old-fashioned, realistic novel the emphasis falls on just those aspects of his writing where he is weakest.

The distinction of Peter Cowan's stories rests on his insight into what Yeats once called "the quarrel with ourselves." He writes of a character in *Seed*:

> At such times he knew a strange duality, as if he were at the edge of two kinds of life, one of people, their buildings, of the work he did all day, the other his interest in the places where people did not go and where other forms of life took on an increasing reality, a significance, that at times he found hard to return from, not easily displaced by what others regarded, and would assure him, was the normal world of human beings. It was as if he belonged nowhere. An emptiness, an uncertainty, displaced the simple affirmation of life, creating an ambivalence he supposed people sensed in some of his painting. And which he supposed was why they did not like it.

Substituting "writing" for "painting," we have an interpretation of Peter Cowan more acute than that any critic could hope to offer.

—John Barnes

CREWS, Harry (Eugene). American. Born in Alma, Georgia, 6 June 1935. Educated at the University of Florida, Gainesville, B.A. 1960, M.S.Ed., 1962. Served in the United States Marine Corps, 1953-56: Sergeant. Married Sally Ellis in 1960; two sons. English teacher, Broward Junior College, Fort Lauderdale, Florida, 1962-68. Associate Professor, 1968-74, and since 1974, Professor of English, University of Florida. Recipient: Bread Loaf Writers Conference Atherton Fellowship, 1968; American Academy award, 1972; National Endowment for the Arts grant, 1974. Address: 1800 N.W. 8th Avenue, Gainesville, Florida 36201, U.S.A.

PUBLICATIONS

Novels

The Gospel Singer. New York, Morrow, 1968.
Naked in Garden Hills. New York, Morrow, 1969.
This Thing Don't Lead to Heaven. New York, Morrow, 1970.
Karate Is a Thing of the Spirit. New York, Morrow, 1971; London, Secker and Warburg, 1972.
Car. New York, Morrow, 1972; London, Secker and Warburg, 1973.
The Hawk Is Dying. New York, Knopf, 1973; London, Secker and Warburg, 1974.
The Gypsy's Curse. New York, Knopf, 1974; London, Secker and Warburg, 1975.
A Feast of Snakes. New York, Atheneum, 1976; London, Secker and Warburg, 1977.

Uncollected Short Stories

"The Player Piano," in *Florida Quarterly* (Gainesville), Fall 1967.
"The Unattached Smile," in *Craft and Vision*, edited by Andrew Lytle. New York, Delacorte Press, 1971.

Other

A Childhood: The Biography of a Place (on Bacon County, Georgia). New York, Harper, 1978; London, Secker and Warburg, 1979.
Blood and Grits. New York, Harper, 1979.

* * *

Harry Crews's eight novels establish him as the most astringent observer of contemporary good-old-boy culture, the grass roots of the South. An outrageous satirist of U.S. life in general, Crews pits the empty materialism of our mainstream society against deep-South grotesques and misfits with results at once comic and horrific.

Beginning with *The Gospel Singer*, which probes the psychology of show-biz fundamentalism, Crews has invented a gallery of social, sexual, and spiritual outcasts who seek salvation in a civilization which offers them only *things*. The theme is expanded in *Naked in Garden Hills.* Fat Man, the six-hundred-pound protagonist, lives in an abandoned phosphorus mine, where the earth has been eaten away, and he tries to eat the world itself. This is echoed in *Car*, in which Herman Mack vows to eat an entire 1971 Ford Maverick. A refugee from a junkyard, Mack revenges himself on the world by trying to consume and defecate it. *This Thing Don't Lead to Heaven* caricatures the old-folks industry, in which people are the used-up detritus of our society. In this novel, Jefferson Davis Munroe, a midget who works for a "graveyard chain," competes with Axel's Senior Club for the bodies (if not souls) of the dying.

In *Karate Is a Thing of the Spirit* Crew deals with the fads and obsessions of contemporary trendy culture. John Kaimon, its central character, wears a tee-shirt stenciled with William Faulkner's face and tries to find himself through an outlaw karate group. The story develops our sick fascination with sex and violence and the fear of love and belief which Crews sees as being at the focus of our lives. *The Hawk Is Dying* portrays a more positive, even heroic, obsession, George Gattling's desire to "man" (train) a hawk in the prescribed medieval ritual. His attempt to fuse his soul with the raptor's is another way out of the stylized hell of a technologically focused world. George's need for belief is satisfied by the vitality of his hawk, its innate freedom and dignity.

The Gypsy's Curse returns to a world of physical violence and action with Marvin Molar, born with stunted legs, who walks on his hands and develops his upper body through exercise. In his upside-down world, he becomes sexually obsessed with Hester, a normal woman. The connection between possessiveness, "normality," sexuality, and strength is a basic Crews theme. It appears also in the savage burlesque of *A Feast of Snakes*, in which high school football, baton-twirling, weightlifting, moonshine selling and rattlesnake hunting are intermixed as American rituals. The story ends, like *The Gospel Singer*, in an explosion of mortal violence, as Joe Lon Mackey, ex-state-champ quarterback, loses his slender grip on his own life.

Crews's satire is directed toward the triviality and rootlessness of our culture, its lack of belief. His characters search frantically for salvation through money, sex, social status, physical strength, mystical rites, through sheer acquisitiveness. Crews shows how these are false paths, failures. John Kaimon, in *Karate Is a Thing of the Spirit*, thinks:

> ...he also knew he did not believe. The breath of little children would leave his flesh only flesh.
>
> Belief could see through glass eyes, could turn flesh to stone or stone to flesh. But not for him. He would walk through the world naked. He would bruise and bleed. He saw it clearly.

Crews sees clearly, through his scathing satire, that the absence of faith leads to violence, madness, death. His creatures search through a world of junkyards and abandoned mines and prisons for their authenticity through belief, and our world fails and maims them in savage ways.

—William J. Schafer

CRICHTON, (John) Michael. American. Born in Chicago, Illinois, 23 October 1942. Educated at Harvard University, Cambridge, Massachusetts, A.B. (summa cum laude) 1965 (Phi Beta Kappa); Harvard Medical School, M.D. 1969; Salk Institute, La Jolla, California, 1969-70. Married 1) Joan Radam in 1965 (divorced, 1971); 2) Kathleen St. Johns in 1978 (divorced, 1980). Recipient: Mystery Writers of America Edgar Allan Poe Award, 1968, 1980; Association of American Medical Writers Award, 1970. Agent: International Creative Management, 8900 Beverly Boulevard, Los Angeles, California 90048. Address: 9348 Santa Monica Boulevard, Beverly Hills, California 90210, U.S.A.

PUBLICATIONS

Novels

Odds On (as John Lange). New York, New American Library, 1966.
Scratch One (as John Lange). New York, New American Library, 1967.
Easy Go (as John Lange). New York, New American Library, 1968; London, Sphere, 1972; as *The Last Tomb*, as Michael Crichton, New York, Bantam, 1974.
A Case of Need (as Jeffery Hudson). Cleveland, World, and London, Heinemann, 1968.
The Venom Business (as John Lange). Cleveland, World, 1969.
Zero Cool (as John Lange). New York, New American Library, 1969; London, Sphere, 1972.
The Andromeda Strain. New York, Knopf, and London, Cape, 1969.
Drug of Choice (as John Lange). New York, New American Library, 1970; as *Overkill*, New York, Centesis, 1970.
Grave Descend (as John Lange). New York, New American Library, 1970.
Dealing; or, The Berkeley-to-Boston Forty-Brick Lost-Bag Blues (as Michael Douglas, with Douglas Crichton). New York, Knopf, 1971; London, Talmy Franklin, 1972.
Binary (as John Lange). New York, Knopf, and London, Heinemann, 1972.
The Terminal Man. New York, Knopf, and London, Cape, 1972.
The Great Train Robbery. New York, Knopf, and London, Cape, 1975.
Westworld. New York, Bantam, 1975.
Eaters of the Dead. New York, Knopf, and London, Cape, 1976.
Congo. New York, Knopf, 1980; London, Allen Lane, 1981.

Plays

Screenplays: *Westworld*, 1973; *Coma*, 1978; *The First Great Train Robbery*, 1978; *Looker*, 1981.

Other

Five Patients: The Hospital Explained. New York, Knopf, 1970; London, Cape, 1971.
Jasper Johns. New York, Abrams, and London, Thames and Hudson, 1977.

Theatrical Activities:

Director: **Films**—*Westworld*, 1973; *Coma*, 1978; *The First Great Train Robbery*, 1978. **Television**—*Pursuit*, 1972.

* * *

Prefacing his novel *Drug of Choice*, John Lange, one of the pseudonyms used by the young American novelist Michael Crichton, quotes Karl Jaspers's frightening realization that "The beginning of modern science is also the beginning of calamity." Living as he did in this century of applied science, when so much of the calamity already was manifest, Jaspers merely was acknowledging the truth of communiques encoded centuries before. In 1726 Jonathan Swift in his third book of *Gulliver's Travels* imagined a trope for science, the Flying Island, the mordant vision of the concentration of power in the hands of a clique remote from human needs, motivated by pure theory, and dedicated to experiment and improvisation. Approximately a century later, Dostoevsky's lonely underground man also took violent opposition, this time to Chernyskevsky's rationalistic utopia, where the Crystal Palace (that better ant hill) already was constructed. Thus did Swift accurately conclude that men who governed scientifically, not morally, were mad, and underground man observed that science in its axiomatically progressive march was driving him mad.

The fictional world of Michael Crichton, while not a vision, is a reproduction of our world of science and technology sometimes gone mad but more often appropriated by madmen. In *Easy Go* a brilliant but corrupt archeologist leads a team of international adventurers to unearth and rob the tomb of Rekhmire in Egypt's Valley of the Kings. In *Drug of Choice* a biosystems research institute (Advance Inc.) develops and dispenses a mind controlling drug of frightening potential. The villain of *Binary* is a deranged right-wing mathematician who attempts to poison the San Diego area and thereby assassinate the President. And in *Westworld*, the automata of an electronic entertainment center turn against their guests and creators.

But the genius of characterization and the complexities of personality are absent. For Crichton's characters who operate by a simpler law, Newtonian mechanics, do what they are programmed to do. As a medical doctor, Crichton approaches men and women as case studies; the essence of much that is human is irrelevant when diagnosing. So if a doctor-hero suffers a set-back, he invariably will rely on his reason, return his memory tape, and come up with the logical deduction. And if he blunders, he does so out of no deeply rooted propensity but because he is momentarily exhausted. Simply, his is a world without evil and therefore without tragedy: machines run amok, a man's mind blows a resistor, and neither is reprehensible. Nevertheless, there is near-catastrophe or the potentiality for catastrophe, occasioned by an agency's failure to implement an adequate failsafe system or because someone carelessly pushed the wrong button, dispensed the wrong drug, entered the wrong input, played the wrong tape.

The merit of Crichton's fiction is best revealed in the dexterity with which a situation is quickly established and developed, and in the superabundance of scientific information. A Crichton plot begins with a problem to be solved, necessarily in a few hours or a few days, otherwise a fabulous facility, a city, a nation, or the world is fated. In *The Andromeda Strain* five men in five days define a rapidly growing lethal organism brought accidentally to earth from outer space. Frequently, however, the drama is not sustained through the denouement because of a too heavy reliance on describing scientific processes, or details; and the catastrophe is avoided because of a fortuitous and unscientific bit of human reserve, surprising, if not delightful, because unexpected. Every melody is ended but the author's failure to exclude good fortune and to step back and sum up the more meaningful implication of the man/machine interface lingers on. The end of *The Andromeda Strain* is a good example. The organism is indeed characterized and understood, but it has mutated to a benign form because, fortuitously, our atmosphere contains oxygen. However, the five-man team feels triumphant, whereas they should profoundly realize their impotence. As we are with the characters in Camus's *The Plague*, we should be made to feel that their work in concert, the re-establishment of the diffident brotherhood of man, caused that tyranny of death momentarily to recede.

Fortunately for Crichton's characters, they generally work in teams (*The Andromeda Strain, Zero Cool, Binary, Five Patients, The Terminal Man, Train Robbery*); but they embody collectively only the data that is scientifically organizable and therefore which allows them to operate inside a matrix with its own check-and-balance system and a feedback informational loop that corrects any one unit of the mechanism from drifting too far towards error or entropy. It is not surprising, therefore, that in *The Terminal Man* the conflict between two cross-talking computers—Martha and George—is more dramatically explosive and interesting than between hero and villain, lover and beloved, agency and agent, members of the team. In *Binary*, the better psychological tension results when the hero has to fight, and only at the end of the novel, to overcome a personality defect in himself, revealed when he reads, without authorization, his own classified personality file. Character is rarely densely psychological: it is automization in the trial and error mode.

The novels are full of high-density scientific data, for Crichton is enamored of details, details in the form of glossaries, annotated bibliographies, computer print-outs, output maps, transcripts, formulae, graphs, charts, photographs, x-rays. And the arenas in which the real action takes place are research institutes, government laboratories, information agencies, operating rooms, military installations, filled with intricate and expensive electronic devices that when operated by highly skilled, but less intricate and expensive, technicians probe the mysteries of the phenomenological universe, in which unfortunately man is the guinea pig. The ending of *The Terminal Man* is a case in point. Because the implantation of a computer into the brain of Harry Benson ultimately fails to control the violent behavior caused by his epileptic seizures, the man/machine must be destroyed. And all the reader is led to feel is the loss of an experimental model, led to accept that science in this particular case had merely made a mistake. Of course, Harry Benson expresses his fear that machines are taking over the world, and his psychologist (and a member of the surgical research team), Janet Ross, who is herself under psychiatric care, is dimly aware that some larger moral question looms over them. But Harry Benson's thesis is not fully articulated throughout the novel.

The Great Train Robbery makes it clear that Michael Crichton is not becoming a serious writer or novelist. The plot, based on the 1855 robbery of gold bullion being shipped by train to Paris for the British soldiers fighting in the Crimea, is similar to the master-plan-unfolding technique that he used in *Easy Go*; coincidentally the slightly Machiavellian ring leader is also named Pierce. The team character is composed of never-changing types collectively engaged in an elementary form of group dynamics. Carefully researched documentary information proliferates.

It must be admitted that Crichton has and will continue to achieve success in two branches of American fiction, the Movelists (money, movie novelists such as Harold Robbins) and the Factionists (Arthur Hailey). And he certainly has attracted a public—the Dell paperback edition of *The Andromeda Strain* is into its 26th printing—but let no man's epitaph be: "I read the complete works of Michael Crichton and was satisfied."

—Chet Leach

CROSS, Ian (Robert). New Zealander. Born in Wanganui in 1925. Educated at Wanganui Technical College. Married to Tui Tunnicliffe; four sons. Associate Nieman Fellow in Journalism, Harvard University, Cambridge, Massachusetts, 1954-55; Robert Burns Fellow, Otago University, Dunedin, 1959. Currently, Editor, *New Zealand Listener*, Wellington. Address: 6 Blackbridge Road, Wellington, New Zealand.

PUBLICATIONS

Novels

The God Boy. New York, Harcourt Brace, 1957; London, Deutsch, 1958.
The Backward Sex. London, Deutsch, 1960.
After Anzac Day. London, Deutsch, 1961.

Uncollected Short Stories

"Love Affair," in *Atlantic* (Boston), January 1958.

Play

Television Play: *The City of No*, 1970.

* * *

Ian Cross has written three novels of social concern, which explore the tensions in personal relationships, especially those given emphasis by the narrow experience of small communities. *The God Boy* presents this material through the eyes of a 13-year-old boy who has, two years previously, been a participant in a family tragedy which he observed but did not understand, and which has left its mark upon him. Torn between his father and his mother, young Jimmy reacts with violence and obsession, a classic case history. A clever child who has thought of himself as "chosen," he expects God to give him a helping hand, but no aid comes. He therefore sets up his own private "mutiny against God." The book is notable for its skilful handling of a difficult narrative mode, and for its successful evocation of the speech and ways of an average New Zealand boy. Irony thickens the texture. The reader is closely involved with Jimmy, and like the social worker whose concern this kind of situation so often becomes, begins to comprehend the disaster from within, with sympathetic insight.

The Backward Sex disappoints by being too similar in both manner and material. Raggleton, the coastal settlement of *The God Boy*, has become Albertville, but is otherwise the same place, with a wider range of wharves, sandhills, lupins, and suburban lives as befits the older teller, this time a boy of 17. The topic is the fumbling sexuality of adolescence, but the theme does not seem serious, and the novel is not far above the level of melodrama.

After Anzac Day is wider in both scope and narration. Four people share the telling: The Girl, whose life is going wrong (she is pregnant but unmarried); The Woman, wife of Rankin, ex-soldier and public servant, whose marriage has become a prison with "solitary cells" where the inmates do not even attempt to communicate; The Man, her husband; and The Old Man, her father. These four play out a domestic drama springing from the presence in The Woman's expensive well-oiled home of Jennie, The Girl, to whom her husband has unexpectedly extended a helping hand. Each narrator is given a short turn, which allows Ian Cross to weave four different attitudes and backgrounds into the texture of his fictional world. Clearly, he means to raise wide social, personal, and even historical issues in the New Zealand of 1960. Had he succeeded fully, the elaborate narrative apparatus would have been justified, perhaps. But the problems of John and Margaret Rankin seldom lift above the level of private affairs; the story remains a family drama, without any transfer of significance to the wider issues. *The God Boy*, however, the best of these three novels, is a remarkable little work.

—Joan Stevens

CUNNINGHAM, E.V. *See* **FAST, Howard.**

DAHL, Roald. British. Born in Llandaff, Glamorgan, 13 September 1916. Educated at Repton School, Yorkshire. Served in the Royal Air Force, 1939-45: in Nairobi and Habbanyah, 1939-40; with a Fighter Squadron in the Western Desert, 1940 (wounded); in Greece and Syria, 1941; Assistant Air Attaché, Washington, D.C., 1942-43; Wing Commander, 1943; with British Security Co-ordination, North America, 1943-45. Married the actress Patricia Neal in 1953; one son and four daughters (one deceased). Member of the Public Schools Exploring Society expedition to Newfoundland, 1934; Member of the Eastern Staff, Shell Company, London, 1933-37, and Shell Company of East Africa, Dar-es-Salaam, 1937-39. Recipient: Mystery Writers of America Edgar Allan Poe Award, 1953, 1959, 1980. Agent: Murray Pollinger, 4 Garrick Street, London WC2E 9BH. Address: Gipsy House, Great Missenden, Buckinghamshire HP16 0PB, England.

PUBLICATIONS

Novels

Sometime Never: A Fable for Supermen. New York, Scribner, 1948; London, Collins.
My Uncle Oswald. London, Joseph, 1979; New York, Knopf, 1980.

Short Stories

Over to You: 10 Stories of Flyers and Flying. New York, Reynal, 1946; London, Hamish Hamilton, 1947.
Someone Like You. New York, Knopf, 1953; London, Secker and Warburg, 1954; revised edition, London, Joseph, 1961.
Kiss, Kiss. New York, Knopf, and London, Joseph, 1960.
Twenty-Nine Kisses. London, Joseph, 1969.
Selected Stories. New York, Random House, 1970.
Penguin Modern Stories 12, with others. London, Penguin, 1972.
Switch Bitch. New York, Knopf, and London, Joseph, 1974.
The Best of Roald Dahl. New York, Vintage, 1978.
Tales of the Unexpected. London, Joseph, and New York, Vintage, 1979.
More Tales of the Unexpected. London, Joseph, 1980.

Plays

The Honeys (produced New York, 1955).

Screenplays: *You Only Live Twice*, with Harry Jack Bloom, 1967; *Chitty-Chitty-Bang-Bang*, with Ken Hughes, 1968; *The Night-Digger*, 1970; *The Lightning Bug*, 1971; *Willy Wonka and the Chocolate Factory*, 1971.

Other (fiction for children)

The Gremlins. New York, Random House, 1943; London, Collins, 1944.
James and the Giant Peach. New York, Knopf, 1961; London, Allen and Unwin, 1967.
Charlie and the Chocolate Factory. New York, Knopf, 1964; London, Allen and Unwin, 1967.
The Magic Finger. New York, Harper, 1966; London, Allen and Unwin, 1968.
Fantastic Mr. Fox. New York, Knopf, and London, Allen and Unwin, 1970.
Charlie and the Great Glass Elevator. New York, Knopf, 1972; London, Allen and Unwin, 1973.
Danny, The Champion of the World. London, Cape, and New York, Knopf, 1975.
The Wonderful Story of Henry Sugar and Six More. London, Cape, 1977; as *The Wonderful World of Henry Sugar,* New York, Knopf, 1977.
The Enormous Crocodile. London, Cape, and New York, Knopf, 1978.
The Twits. London, Cape, 1980; New York, Knopf, 1981.
George's Marvellous Medicine. London, Cape, 1981.

*

Critical Studies: in *New York Herald-Tribune*, 7 February 1960; *Wilson Library Bulletin* (New York), February 1962; *Saturday Review* (New York), 17 February 1962.

Roald Dahl comments:

(1972) I am primarily a short-story writer. But a good plot is hard to find, and it gets harder all the time. No short-story writer should continue in this field when he has run out of plots, otherwise he finishes up producing indifferent work, as well as "mood-pieces" and essays all labelled "short stories"—which they are not.

I now write books for children. It gives me great pleasure. Sometimes I write screenplays for my wife, who is an actress.

* * *

Conventional human responses to bizarre circumstances domesticate Roald Dahl's carefully detailed, grotesque world. This shock of the familiar makes credible the logic of a cautionary tale in a universe that initially seems devoid of guidelines. "An African Story," which only tangentially develops the theme of Dahl's first adult book, *Over to You: Ten Stories of Flyers and Flying*, foreshadows the pattern dominating his later work. A neurotic's sensitivity to unpleasant animal habits causes an elderly Englishman to sacrifice him to a deadly Mamba snake that can, in a characteristic Dahl touch, drink milk from a cow. Though the neurotic is punished rather more severely than he might be at home, the vengeful old man emerges as a champion of the typical English dedication to animals which operates even in the jungle. The snake's contented sip of milk after the killing produces a simultaneous effect of horror and conventional moral righteousness; in "The Visitor" (*Switch Bitch*) the discovery by Oswald, an antithetical blend of hypochondria and satyriasis, that an unscrupulous seduction has exposed him to leprosy produces a similar moral frisson.

Dahl's adult novel *Sometime Never: A Fable for Supermen*, which attempts to raise the war horrors and hallucinations of *Over to You* to the mythic level, effectively details some deadpan accounts of the discovery of gremlins, who "scraped platinum off the points and put it carefully into small leather purses which had zip-fasteners on them." However, Dahl's whimsical treatment of these creatures undercuts their lethal activities, which are "a bit too much like death to be funny...far too ridiculous to be amusing." And an atomic holocaust, that familiar feature of post-World War II novels, turns the gremlins of the second half of the book into rational thinkers contemptuous of the insanity of human war-making, though Dahl gives them Thurberish names like Snogs, Bogglers, and Hornswogglers. The final irony that equates total disappearance of human beings, an event long awaited by the gremlins, with the vanishing of these creatures themselves, since they are merely projections of the human imagination, does not resolve the contradictory roles of the gremlins and the resulting confusion in tone. The structural problems of this novel, and the only sporadic effectiveness of the long stories in *Switch Bitch*, suggest that Dahl's talent works best within the tightly plotted *short* story. Though he can create brilliant moments in which disturbed narrators reveal their lunatic obsessions, he seems unable to develop a consistent character who might unify a series of incidents. While Oswald's personality contributes to the atmosphere of "The Visitor," in his other appearance in "Bitch" he fades into a faceless, quirkless narrator whose part in the sexual climax would suit any non-senescent male.

The quintessential pattern of domesticated (often in both senses) horror was firmly established in the stories Dahl collected as *Someone Like You* and *Kiss, Kiss.* Frequently these stories focus on a bet or competition, usually rigged, and the perverse morality of Dahl's universe causes the dishonest victor to lose his status as a gourmet in "Taste," a Chippendale commode in "Parson's Pleasure," his money *and* his life in "Dip in the Pool," and the title of "Champion of the World" among partridge poachers. (Conversely, the juvenile novel *Charlie and the Chocolate Factory* utilizes the contest motif to stress the rewards of virtuous triumph.) Dahl gives verisimilitude to these situations by bombarding the reader with a wealth of detail involving such disciplines as wine lore, period furniture, and partridge trapping. Often, this almost statistical documentation simultaneously reinforces otherwise improbable anecdotes and ridicules self-styled expertise.

The many stories involving mutilation, either real or threatened, also depend on factual data both to mitigate and substantiate the horror. "Skin" seems so knowledgeable about the details of Soutine's life and technique, and so deadpan in its dialogue, that negotiations for the picture Soutine inconveniently painted on the back of an elderly beggar seem at once utterly absurd and frighteningly realistic. Apparently factual data similarly buttress Dahl's treatment of experiments in the monstrous, whether the sinister effects of feeding a sickly baby on "Royal Jelly," or a downtrodden wife's reaction to the survival of her dead husband's brain in "William and Mary." Her practical wifely stance parallels a husband's malevolently commonsense response in "Edward the Conqueror" to his wife's ecstatic discovery that a stray cat houses the soul of Liszt.

Such mismatches occur frequently in Dahl's fiction and are often symbolized by the disproportionate physical dimensions of the partners: the diminutive husband and his "big rather than tall wife" in "My Lady Love, My Dove"; the tiny, repressed clergyman of "Georgy Porgy" and his amorous female parishioners, notably Miss Roach, "...a striking person—unusually muscular for a woman, with broad shoulders and powerful arms and a huge calf bulging on each leg." Dahl also stresses physiognomy, especially the mouth, as an index to character. People with "salmon" mouths ("Nunc Dimittis") and "caterpillar" mouths ("Mr. Hoddy") display the appropriate traits, and the gourmet's mouth in "Taste" functions not merely as the key to his character, but as the character itself: "...all mouth—mouth and lips—the full, wet lips of the professional gourmet, the lower lip hanging downward in the center, a pendulous, permanently open taster's lip, shaped open to receive the rim of a glass or a morsel of food. Like a keyhole, I thought, watching it; his mouth is like a large wet keyhole."

The symbolic possibilities of the mouth achieve fullest development in "Georgy Porgy," the title itself suggesting Dahl's gift for playing with the perverse implications of the childlike. The sex education given the protagonist by his progressive mother goes awry when the boy, witnessing the birth of rabbits, sees that the fondling, kissing mouth of the mother rabbit is devouring its offspring. Immediately, the child perceives his own mother's "huge red mouth opening wider and wider until it is just a great big round gaping hole with a black black centre...." This regrettable epiphany foreshadows his response years later when Miss Roach attempts to kiss him: "I saw this great mouth of hers coming slowly down on top of me, starting to open, and coming closer and closer, and opening wider and wider...I had never in all my life seen anything more terrifying than that mouth...." The clergyman's final insane conviction that he has been swallowed and now inhabits the woman's interior is made credible by his matter-of-fact tone: "It is all a trifle bizarre for a man of conservative tastes like myself. Personally, I prefer oak furniture and parquet flooring...." Though Dahl avoids underlining the ultimate significance of his key symbol, he illuminates it obliquely through the clergyman's wonderfully detailed experiments with the sex drives of rats. In blending the ordinary and the grotesque, in ballasting both with convincing details and, especially, in preserving a delightfully ambivalent attitude toward the reader's credulity, "Georgy Porgy" might serve as the archetype for Dahl's fiction.

—Burton Kendle

DATHORNE, O(scar) R(onald). British. Born in Georgetown, Guyana, 19 November 1934. Educated at the University of Sheffield, Yorkshire, 1955-58, B.A. 1958, M.A. 1960, Ph.D. 1966; University of London, 1958-59, Cert.Ed. 1959, Dip.Ed. 1967. Married Hildegard Ostermaier in 1959; two children. Lecturer, Ahmadu Bello University, Zaria, Nigeria, 1959-63, and University of Ibadan, Nigeria, 1963-66; UNESCO Consultant to the Government of Sierra Leone, 1967-68; Professor of English, Njala University College, University of Sierra Leone, Freetown, 1968-69; Professor, Afro-American Studies Department, University of Wisconsin, Madison, 1970, and Ohio State University, Columbus, 1971-77. Since 1977, Professor of English and Director of American Studies, University of Miami. Editor, *Journal of Caribbean Studies.* Address: Department of English, University of Miami, Coral Gables, Florida 33124, U.S.A.

PUBLICATIONS

Novels

Dumplings in the Soup. London, Cassell, 1963.
The Scholar-Man. London, Cassell, 1964.

Uncollected Short Stories

"The Wintering of Mr. Kolawole," in *Stories from the Caribbean*, edited by Andrew Salkey. London, Elek, 1965; as *Island Voices*, New York, Liveright, 1970.
"Hodge" and "The Nightwatchman and the Baby Nurse," in *Nigerian Radio Times* (Ibadan), 1967.
"Constable," in *Political Spider.* London, Heinemann, 1969.

Verse

Kelly Poems. Privately printed, 1977.

Other

The Black Mind: A History of African Literature. Minneapolis, University of Minnesota Press, 1974; abridged edition, as *African Literature in the 20th Century*, University of Minnesota Press, and London, Heinemann, 1976.
Dark Ancestors. Baton Rouge, Louisiana State University Press, 1980.

Editor, with others, *Young Commonwealth Poets '65.* London, Heinemann, 1965.
Editor, *Caribbean Narrative.* London, Heinemann, 1966.
Editor, *Caribbean Verse.* London, Heinemann, 1967.
Editor, with Willfried Feuser, *Africa in Prose.* London, Penguin, 1969.
Editor, *African Poetry for Schools and Colleges.* Yaba, Nigeria, Macmillan, 1969.
Editor, *Selected Poems*, by Derek Walcott. London, Heinemann, 1977.

*

Critical Studies: "Guyanese Writers" by Wilfred Cartey, in *New World* (Georgetown, Guyana), 1966; *The Islands in Between* by Louis James, London, Oxford University Press, 1968; *The Chosen Tongue* by Gerald Moore, London, Longman, 1969; *Homecoming* by James Ngugi, London, Heinemann, 1972, New York, Hill, 1973.

O.R. Dathorne comments:

(1972) My work has in general utilized situations which seemed near enough for me to handle. Black immigration in England, a black man's quest for identity in Africa have been the starting points for what I hope have been larger involvements of the protagonist's new understanding of the world. Frequently, the "new" contact with reality cannot be resolved on a rational level and this is why in plays and poetry I have moved towards an intentionally "irrational" approach which expresses bewilderment.

I lived for ten years in Africa; they taught me to be wary of novelty, as did the creative urges of young African writers like myself. Only incidentally, I became a "critic" of the new African literature; only incidentally, I was forced to learn about a man's world-view (which I had to understand) before I spoke. Only incidentally this led me back to myself and the large interrogatives concerning my history. Now I am aware of the manifestations of curious parallels in cultural experience and it is this I proclaim.

* * *

O.R. Dathorne as a novelist has two characteristics—an eye for comic idiosyncrasy, in particular African and West Indian, and a concern for the predicament of the expatriate. The first is uppermost in *Dumplings in the Soup*. Here John Jiffey Jacket gets a room in a London tenement crowded with immigrant lodgers. They are dominated by Boffo, a genial non-rent-paying confidence man who enlivens the religious devotions of the local Shakers club with strong drinks, and lets his landlord's cellar to a newcomer from Africa for fifty pounds in advance. The book is lively and readable, but the comic exaggeration undermines the more serious undertones, and, ultimately, some of the comedy itself.

The Scholar-Man is a more complex and successful book. Adam Questus, a West Indian, goes in search of Egor, an English-born mulatto who has had such a strong impression on his childhood that Adam looks to him for a meaning for his life. He teaches English at a University in an African state on the brink of independence. In his quest he visits a village where cult-drumming induces a trance in which he glimpses his slave-ancestry: at the same time the cult-whip inflicts a blow that would have been fatal but for the self-sacrifice of a University servant. He finds Egor has vanished, but making love to the mentally deficient girl Egor had run away with, he glimpses the highly ambiguous "reality" he had been seeking.

The search, with its echoes of Conrad's *Heart of Darkness*, is interwoven with satirical comedy about expatriate academic life and the political turmoil of a country exchanging one set of superstitions for another in its own search for identity. Some of the humour is again too forced, but the comedy also touches the wider theme, the absurdities of reality.

—Louis James

DAVENPORT, Guy (Mattison, Jr.). American. Born in Anderson, South Carolina, 23 November 1927. Educated at Duke University, Durham, North Carolina, B.A. 1948; Merton College, Oxford (Rhodes Scholar), 1948-50, B.Litt. 1950; Harvard University, Cambridge, Massachusetts, Ph.D. 1961. Served in the United States Army Airborne Corps, 1950-52. Instructor, Washington University, St. Louis, 1952-55; Assistant Professor, Haverford College, Pennsylvania, 1961-63. Since 1963, Professor of English, University of Kentucky, Lexington. Since 1962, Contributing Editor, *National Review*. Also book and magazine illustrator and designer. Recipient: Blumenthal-Leviton Prize (*Poetry*, Chicago), 1967; American Academy Morton Dauwen Zabel Award, 1981. Address: 621 Sayre Avenue, Lexington, Kentucky 40508, U.S.A.

PUBLICATIONS

Short Stories

Tatlin! New York, Scribner, 1974.
Da Vinci's Bicycle: Ten Stories. Baltimore, Johns Hopkins University Press, 1979.
Eclogues: Eight Stories. Berkeley, California, North Point Press, 1981.
Trois Caprices. Louisville, Weng, 1981.

Verse

Flowers and Leaves: Poema vel Sonata, Carmina Autumni Primaeque Veris Transformationum. Highlands, North Carolina, Jargon, 1966.

Other

Cydonia Florentia. Cambridge, Massachusetts, Lowell Adams House Printers, 1966.
Pennant Key-Indexed Guide to Homer's Iliad [and *Odyssey*]. Philadelphia, Educational Research Associates, 2 vols., 1967.
Do You Have a Poem Book on E.E. Cummings? Highlands, North Carolina, Jargon, 1969.
Jonathan Williams, Poet. Cleveland, Asphodel Book Shop, 1969.
The Geography of the Imagination: Forty Essays. Berkeley, California, North Point Press, 1981.

Editor, *The Intelligence of Louis Agassiz: A Specimen Book of Scientific Writings.* Boston, Beacon Press, 1963.

Translator, *Carmina Archolochi: The Fragments of Archilochos.* Berkeley, University of California Press, 1964.
Translator, *Sappho: Songs and Fragments.* Ann Arbor, University of Michigan Press, 1965.
Translator, *Archilochos, Sappho, Alkman: Three Lyric Poets of the Late Greek Bronze Age.* Berkeley, University of California Press, 1980.
Translator, *Herakleitos and Diogenes.* Berkeley, California, Grey Fox Press, 1980.
Translator, *The Mimes of Herondas.* Berkeley, California, Grey Fox Press, 1981.

*

Critical Studies: "*Tatlin!*; or, The Limits of Fiction" by Richard Pevear, Spring 1975, and "Guy Davenport in Harmony," Autumn 1980, both in *Hudson Review* (New York).

Guy Davenport comments:

My talent is minor, my prose unskilled and contrived, my ideas derivative. In my stories I shape anecdotes about real people much as Parson Weems made a folktale hero of George Washington. This is not my intention: it is what happens when anybody writes about things in ignorance and from a distance. I have Panait Istrati wearing a flowery embroidered shirt; Marguerite Dorian tells me that he wouldn't be caught dead in one. In spite of doing research, this wrong-shirt effect usually turns up in every detail. I read some 40 books about prehistory to write the story "Robot," visited the site of Lascaux, talked with Jacques Marsal, have heard first-hand accounts of refugees fleeing the Germans across that part of France; and yet my story (which is about the discovery of the prehistoric cave at Lascaux in 1941) could not possibly have a single sentence of truth in it. From five to ten years of such research go into every story; for one, fifteen. The stories are not what they seem to be about (what story is?), but I don't have any interpretation up my sleeve that I would insist on. My ambition is solely to get some effect, as of light on stone in a forest on a September day, that seems to me to be a duty to preserve, as a quality of our world, in a rhythm of words. I cannot write about myself or of emotions with which I am familiar. Fiction's essential activity is to imagine how others feel, what a Saturday afternoon in an Italian town in the second century looked like. I trust the world to speak for itself. If I write *rose*, there are roses to stand me good. When Louis Zukofsky wrote his *Eighty Flowers*, he went to the trouble to see each flower. Picture and description would not do. I have stood on my toes and touched Blériot's *Antoinette*, I've held Shelley's snuffbox in my hands, and have sat on the chair of Gertrude Stein's that Ezra Pound broke; I'll find a place for these encounters. I mention them because some such haptic event authenticates every detail in my writing. But for this invisible substantiality I would not write at all. In a sense my texts are translations of an obliterated original that can never be reconstituted. The story "Robot," for instance, is an afternoon looking for Indian arrowheads with my father in South Carolina (I feel certain). "The Dawn in Erewhon" is a translation and elaboration of a split second of a sunny morning in Amsterdam. "A Field of Snow on a Slope of the Rosenberg" is of course not about Robert Walser, but about Christopher Middleton's Robert Walser, and probably a translation of a moment in Paris 30 years ago, sitting in one of Joyce's *brasseries* (on the street where Rimbaud wrote *Les Illuminations*) when Chris and I saw a horse wearing a hat that made our day. "C. Musonius Rufus" is about Ezra Pound, or perhaps Vergil. "Au Tombeau de Charles Fourier" began in my head when I was reading Fourier on a bluff of the Ohio River and encountered the unknown word *quagga*. My feeling is that my stories just might, with luck, be included in the corporate attempt of writing in our time to understand how so hopeful a century as ours blundered so tragically as to be the most inhuman of them all.

* * *

Guy Davenport's a critic, poet, classicist, translator, teacher, and book illustrator who with the publication of *Tatlin!* and *Da Vinci's Bicycle* has become a master fictionist as well. These collections include novellae treating the Soviet constructivist V. Tatlin, the Dutch philosopher Adriaan van Hovendaal and friends, and the Modernist circle surrounding Stein and Picasso. Other stories feature Leonardo Da Vinci inventing a bicycle (to be ridden in battle, "a phalanx of these *due rote* bearing lancers at full tilt"), Kafka and Max Brod attending an air show where they brush shoulders with Wittgenstein, and most remarkably (and fictionally) "A photograph of Lenin reading *Iskra* at a Zurich cafe" which "accidentally includes over to the left James and Nora Joyce haggling with a taxi driver about the fare."

What strange yet telling juxtapositions of the Moderns, the very makers of our century. The fact that half of them are made up takes nothing from Davenport's achievement; indeed, he considers such combinations of fact and fantasy "necessary fictions" which in their very form of delight tell us much about our Postmodern selves. Ezra Pound spinning a fable about Yeats's body lost at sea by a drunken navy crew? Nietzsche signing the guestbook at a Rapallo inn with the caution, "Beware the beefsteak"? These are snapshots of the Modern, crafted by the same aesthetic in which, as part of an early photographic plate of fossils at the Museum of Natural History, "two gentlemen stand in the background, spectators at the museum. One wears a top hat and looks with neurotic intelligence at the camera. He is Edgar Allan Poe. The other gentleman is cross-eyed and wears a beret. God knows who he is."

History is a dream that strays into innocent sleep. This motto, from the heart of Davenport's fiction, helps tell why he feels the two modes must be mixed. "The mind is what it knows!" one of his characters insists. "It is nothing else at all, at all." Can our very nature be formed by the way we view history? Consider how that relatively new and most typically Modern of aesthetic media, the camera, composes things for us. Poe caught posing with a dinosaur, Lenin and Joyce so casually compared in their own worlds of economics, all recorded by the chance photograph—"for the first time in the history of art," Davenport's story explains, "the accidental became the controlling iconography of a representation of the world."

Therefore *Tatlin!* and *Da Vinci's Bicycle* present imaginative exercises on characters who do not completely match up with our conventional readings of the past. The camera, by its very rigidity, rattles our perception and makes us see things we never knew were there; and so Davenport's fiction, using many of the same accidental and juxtapositional methods, attempts to do the same thing. Gertrude Stein is seen reading the Sunday comics to Picasso; ancient Greek philosophers invent a mechanical pigeon; President Richard Nixon, impressed by the Great Wall of China, bombs the DMZ to similarly impress his host. If any of these events did indeed happen, it was probably in other people's imaginations, for if history is a dream which strays into innocent sleep, so too may dreams contaminate (or perhaps enrich) history. In any event, Davenport concludes, we know reality only through our fictions, and his stories and novellae are attempts to structure those fictions according to the photographic, cinematic, and collagist natures of our time.

—Jerome Klinkowitz

DAVIES, Robertson. Canadian. Born in Thamesville, Ontario, 28 August 1913. Educated at Upper Canada College; Queen's University, Kingston, Ontario; Balliol College, Oxford, 1936-38, B.Litt. 1938. Married Brenda Mathews in 1940; three children. Teacher and Actor, Old Vic Theatre School and Repertory Company, London, 1938-40; Literary Editor, *Saturday Night*, Toronto, 1940-42; Editor and Publisher, *Examiner*, Peterborough, Ontario, 1942-63. Since 1960, Profesor of English, and since 1962, Master of Massey College, University of Toronto. Formerly, Governor, Stratford Shakespeare Festival, Ontario; Member, Board of Trustees, National Arts Centre. Recipient: Louis Jouvet Prize, Dominion Drama Festival, for directing, 1949; Leacock Medal, 1955; Lorne Pierce Medal, 1961; Governor-General's Award, 1973. LL.D.: University of Alberta, Edmonton, 1957; Queen's University, 1962; University of Manitoba, Winnipeg, 1972; D.Litt.: McMaster University, Hamilton, Ontario, 1959; University of Windsor, Ontario, 1971; York University, Toronto, 1973; Mount Allison University, Sackville, New Brunswick, 1973; Memorial University of Newfoundland, St. John's 1974; University of Western Ontario, London, 1974; McGill University, Montreal, 1974; Trent University, Peterborough, Ontario, 1974; D.C.L.: Bishop's University, Lennoxville, Quebec, 1967; D.Univ.: University of Calgary, Alberta, 1975. Fellow, Royal Society of Canada, 1967. Companion of the Order of Canada, 1972. Agent: Curtis Brown Ltd., 575 Madison Avenue, New York, New York 10022, U.S.A. Address: Massey College, 4 Devonshire Place, Toronto, Ontario M5S 2E1, Canada.

PUBLICATIONS

Novels

Tempest Tost. Toronto, Clarke Irwin, 1951; London, Chatto and Windus, and New York, Rinehart, 1952.

Leaven of Malice. Toronto, Clarke Irwin, 1954; London, Chatto and Windus, and New York, Scribner, 1955.

A Mixture of Frailties. Toronto, Macmillan, London, Weidenfeld and Nicolson, and New York, Scribner, 1958.

Fifth Business. Toronto, Macmillan, and New York, Viking Press, 1970; London, Macmillan, 1971.
The Manticore. Toronto, Macmillan, and New York, Viking Press, 1972; London, Macmillan, 1973.
World of Wonders. Toronto, Macmillan, 1975; New York, Viking Press, 1976; London, W.H. Allen, 1977.

Plays

Overlaid (produced Peterborough, Ontario, 1947). Included in *Eros at Breakfast and Other Plays*, 1949.
The Voice of the People (produced Montreal, 1948). Included in *Eros at Breakfast and Other Plays*, 1949.
At the Gates of the Righteous (produced Peterborough, Ontario, 1948). Included in *Eros at Breakfast and Other Plays*, 1949.
Hope Deferred (produced Montreal, 1948). Included in *Eros at Breakfast and Other Plays*, 1949.
Fortune, My Foe (televised; produced Ottawa, 1948). Toronto, Clarke Irwin, 1949.
Eros at Breakfast (produced Ottawa, 1948). Included in *Eros at Breakfast and Other Plays*, 1949.
Eros at Breakfast and Other Plays (includes *Hope Deferred, Overlaid, At the Gates of the Righteous, The Voice of the People*). Toronto, Clarke Irwin, 1949.
At My Heart's Core (produced Peterborough, Ontario, 1950). Toronto, Clarke Irwin, 1950.
King Phoenix (produced Peterborough, Ontario, 1950). Included in *Hunting Stuart and Other Plays*, 1972.
A Masque of Aesop (produced Toronto, 1952). Toronto, Clarke Irwin, 1952; in *Five New One-Act Plays*, edited by J.A. Stone, London, Harrap, 1954.
A Jig for the Gypsy (broadcast; produced Toronto and London, 1954). Toronto, Clarke Irwin, 1954.
Hunting Stuart (produced Toronto, 1955). Included in *Hunting Stuart and Other Plays*, 1972.
Love and Libel; or, The Ogre of the Provincial World, adaptation of his own novel *Leaven of Malice* (produced Toronto and New York, 1960).
A Masque of Mr. Punch (produced Toronto, 1962). Toronto, Oxford University Press, 1963.
Hunting Stuart and Other Plays (includes *King Phoenix* and *General Confession*). Toronto, New Press, 1972.
Question Time (produced Toronto, 1975). Toronto, Macmillan, 1975.

Radio Plays: *A Jig for the Gypsy*, and others.

Television Plays: *Fortune My Foe*, *Brothers in the Black Art*, and others.

Other

Shakespeare's Boy Actors. London, Dent, 1939; New York, Russell, 1964.
Shakespeare for Young Players: A Junior Course. Toronto, Clarke Irwin, 1942.
The Diary of Samuel Marchbanks (essays). Toronto, Clarke Irwin, 1947.
The Table Talk of Samuel Marchbanks (essays). Toronto, Clarke Irwin, 1949; London, Chatto and Windus, 1951.
Renown at Stratford: A Record of the Shakespeare Festival in Canada 1953, with Tyrone Guthrie. Toronto, Clarke Irwin, 1953.
Twice Have the Trumpets Sounded: A Record of the Stratford Shakespearean Festival in Canada 1954, with Tyrone Guthrie. Toronto, Clarke Irwin, 1954; London, Blackie, 1955.
Thrice the Brinded Cat Hath Mew'd: A Record of the Stratford Shakespearean Festival in Canada 1955, with Tyrone Guthrie. Toronto, Clarke Irwin, 1955.
A Voice from the Attic. New York, Knopf, and Toronto, McClelland and Stewart, 1960.
The Personal Art: Reading to Good Purpose. London, Secker and Warburg, 1961.
Marchbanks' Almanack. Toronto, McClelland and Stewart, 1967.
Stephen Leacock. Toronto, McClelland and Stewart, 1970.
The Revels History of Drama in English, vol. 7, with others. London, Methuen, 1975.
One Half of Robertson Davies: Provocative Pronouncements on a Wide Range of Topics. Toronto, Macmillan, 1977; New York, Viking Press, 1978.
The Enthusiasms of Robertson Davies, edited by Judith S. Grant. Toronto, McClelland and Stewart, 1979.

Editor, *Feast of Stephen: An Anthology of Some of the Less Familiar Writings of Stephen Leacock.* Toronto, McClelland and Stewart, 1970.

*

Manuscript Collection: Massey College, University of Toronto.

Critical Studies: *Conversations with Canadian Novelists 1* by Donald Cameron, Toronto, Macmillan, 1975; "Robertson Davies Issue" of *Journal of Canadian Studies* (Peterborough, Ontario), February 1977; *Robertson Davies* by Judith S. Grant, Toronto, McClelland and Stewart, 1978; *Here and Now 1*, edited by John Moss, Toronto, NC Press, 1979; "The Master of the Unseen World" by Judith Finlayson, in *Quest* (Toronto), viii, 4, 1979.

Theatrical Activities:

Actor: **Plays**—Lord Norfolk in *Traitor's Gate* by Morna Stuart, London, 1938; Stingo in *She Stoops to Conquer* by Oliver Goldsmith, London, 1939; roles in *The Taming of the Shrew* by Shakespeare, London, 1939.

Robertson Davies comments:

The theme which lies at the root of all my novels and several of my plays is the isolation of the human spirit. This sounds somewhat gloomy but I have not attempted to deal with it in a gloomy fashion but rather to demonstrate that what my characters do that might be called really significant is done entirely on their own volition and usually contrary to what is expected of them. This theme, which might be called in C.G. Jung's phrase "The Search for the Self," is worked out in terms of characters, usually young, who are trying to escape from early influences and find their own place in the world, but who are reluctant to do so in a way that will bring pain and disappointment to others, and particularly to people of the previous generation. As I say, this may not look like a theme for comedy but I find it so, and many readers of my books have assured me that they agree.

* * *

Much that is best in the attempt to create a Canadian personality in literature has been satirical and self-denigrating. A nation that has as yet produced little that is memorable in lyrical or contemplative poetry has as its prized literary possession a superb anthology of sharp comic verse and among its poets at least one, F.R. Scott, who, though seldom noticed outside Canada, deserves to take his place among the few considerable satirical poets of this century.

Robertson Davies is in some senses the Frank Scott of Canadian prose. Like Scott he is cultivated, irascible, unbending, a relentless persecutor of the bourgeois mentality, the provincialism and the pretentiousness of his countrymen, and yet, in the last resort, proudly patriotic and intensely optimistic that his scalpel-pen will remove the ulcers that inhibit the growth of a culture that is both truly Canadian and of international worth. And like so many of the leading Canadian writers—like Scott, MacLennan, and A.J.M. Smith—Davies acquired his intellectual and artistic standards in part at least outside Canada. Even more than MacLennan, Scott, or Smith, in middle-age he remains quintessentially the product of a British education. He is, again like so many Canadian authors, also an academic but in Davies's case, though his career has been set in

Kingston and Toronto, he seems to dance still to tunes that are played at ancient universities and the wit, stylishness, and *hauteur* of his essays and his novels seem to be accompanied by the sound of donnish gossip and the port-decanter sliding across well-polished tables.

High-toned critics have attempted to read into Davies's work some grandiose purpose: generally, a parable of the conflict between the lovely and lovable powers of the imagination and the hideous and pervasive forces of materialism. Such purpose it is not difficult to construct from the evidence of Davies's novels, but the effort reduces to pomposity the ingenuity of Davies's comedy. Because it blows him up to the level of universal genius, it tends to make Davies himself appear as one of those Canadian minnows whose whale-pretensions he is so eager to reduce to true scale. Because it aspires to place him in a very small group of grand masters whose achievements are beyond him it blunts the sharp edge of his satire on the hard stone of a *tu quoque*.

Enough to accept that Davies writes brilliantly, with a sense of comedy that is not often found in Canadian novels, and that, despite his superficial conservatism, he is at heart a reformer, his cause limited (but none the worse for that)—the destruction of the provincialism that is the canker of Canadian society.

Davies's fiction is a comparatively small part of his total work. He has written much for the theatre, a literary form in which Canada's achievement is remarkably slight and to which Davies has added little of lasting quality. He has been prolific as critic and essayist, but the prelude and in many ways the preliminary exposition of his novels is in two collections of newspaper columns: *The Diary of Samuel Marchbanks* and *The Table Talk of Samuel Marchbanks*, for in these there first appeared the satirical themes which were to be elaborated and given substance in his Salterton trilogy.

Marchbanks, a character who was unashamedly a Canadian and 20th-century reincarnation of Samuel Johnson, abused in caustic fury the pettiness of Canadian life, laying about him with such uncompromising brutality that it is a miracle that he was allowed to practise his severe wit in the pages of a Canadian newspaper.

The novels that followed are superficially both more gentle—and certainly far more comic. In them Davies seems to have abandoned the sharpness of Samuel Johnson for the quiet satire of Anthony Trollope and though he hardly troubles to hide the fact that Salterton, the city of his fiction, is in fact Kingston, Ontario, it is not difficult to think of it as Barchester transplanted—and (because Davies sees the outmodishness of so much in Canada) a Barchester not much modernised.

But for all the comedy, in the novels, Davies's knife pierces the skin and gets to work on the very vitals of Canadian existence. Salterton-Kingston is plush with opportunities for a satirist. It has its university, its military college, its industries, its old families rich in dollars and eager for traditions that are not theirs. The middle-class Saltertonians look with eyes full of envy towards the United States and spike their conversation with malice about all things American. Britain has for them a fascination that is equalled only by their insistence that the British are decadent. Salterton seldom looks at itself but Davies looks and sees balloons pretending to be human-beings.

The first of Davies's novels, *Tempest Tost*, is an uproarious travesty of Shakespeare's play in which Prospero, Miranda, Ferdinand, Caliban, and Ariel are each given a Salterton and distorted-mirror image. The other novels in the Salterton trilogy, *Leaven of Malice* and *A Mixture of Frailties*, have some of the same qualities, and reveal the same skill in plotting romance to satirical purpose. *Leaven of Malice* is less comic than *Tempest Tost*, *A Mixture of Frailties* more serious than *Leaven of Malice*. The comedy is spasmodic and where it has been excised its place is taken by melodrama. Davies has come to believe that Canada is close to achieving an integrity of culture. A satirist who has lost his satirical purpose is like the vanishing Fool in *King Lear*. He has gone to bed at noon.

Davies seems to have recognised what had happened. He roused himself and found it midnight. The three linked novels of the 1970's, *Fifth Business*, *The Manticore*, and *World of Wonders*, are scarcely satirical at all, though Davies's capacity for donnish humour is unquenchable, and, even if their roots are set still in small-town Ontario and the narrator is a growling Canadian schoolmaster, the trilogy represents a deliberate attempt by the author to enlarge his horizons, to settle himself in European culture, to release himself from the task of satirising provincialism and to move instead into the vast realms of myth, magic, Jungian psychology, of God and the Devil.

Davies's genius for characterisation is undiminished. His plotting is as ingenious as ever and even more elaborate, and he writes with a deliberate elegance that is rare among contemporaries. The trilogy is an achievement on a grand scale and yet one is left with the feeling that the significance of Davies's literary contribution was more certain when he was less obviously determined to make his novels significant.

—J.E. Morpurgo

DAVIN, Dan(iel Marcus). British. Born in Invercargill, New Zealand, 1 September 1913. Educated at Marist Brothers' School, Invercargill; Sacred Heart College, Auckland; Otago University, Dunedin, M.A., Dip.M.A. 1936; Balliol College, Oxford (Rhodes Scholar), B.A. 1939, M.A. 1945. Served in the Royal Warwickshire Regiment, 1939-40, and in the New Zealand Division, 1940-45; M.B.E. (Member, Order of the British Empire), 1945. Married Winifred Gonley in 1939; three daughters. Junior Assistant Secretary, 1946-48, and Assistant Secretary, 1948-69, Clarendon Press, Oxford; Deputy Secretary to the Delegates, 1970-78, and Director of the Academic Division, 1974-78, Oxford University Press: retired 1978. Fellow of Balliol College, 1965, Emeritus since 1978. Fellow, Royal Society of Arts. Address: 103 Southmoor Road, Oxford, England.

PUBLICATIONS

Novels

Cliffs of Fall. London, Nicholson and Watson, 1945.
For the Rest of Our Lives. London, Nicholson and Watson, 1947.
Roads from Home. London, Joseph, 1949.
The Sullen Bell. London, Joseph, 1956.
No Remittance. London, Joseph, 1959.
Not Here, Not Now. London, Hale, 1970.
Brides of Price. London, Hale, 1972; New York, Coward McCann, 1973.

Short Stories

The Gorse Blooms Pale. London, Nicholson and Watson, 1947.
Breathing Spaces. London, Hale, 1975.
Selected Stories. London, Hale, 1981.

Other

An Introduction to English Literature, with John Mulgan. London, Oxford University Press, 1947; New York, Oxford University Press, 1948.
Crete. Wellington, New Zealand Government War History Department, and London and New York, Oxford University Press, 1953.
Writing in New Zealand: The New Zealand Novel, with W.K. Davin. Wellington, School Publications Board, 1956.
Katherine Mansfield in Her Letters. Wellington, School Publications Board, 1959.

Closing Times (memoirs). London, Oxford University Press, 1975.

Editor, *New Zealand Short Stories.* Wellington and London, Oxford University Press, 1953.
Editor, *Selected Stories*, by Katherine Mansfield. Wellington and London, Oxford University Press, 1953.
Editor, *English Short Stories of Today, Second Series.* London, Oxford University Press, 1958.

*

Critical Studies: *New Zealand Literature* by Eric McCormick, London, Oxford University Press, 1959; in *Landfall* (Christchurch), September 1970; "Dan Davin, Novelist of Exile" by James Bertram, in *Meanjin* (Melbourne), June 1973.

Dan Davin comments:

(1972) *Not Here, Not Now* more of less concluded, as far as I can at present project, a sequence of novels that I had in mind as long ago as 1939. The war and the turn my career subsequently took gave the novels I intended to write a different cast and brought in new themes and substance. Thus *Not Here, Not Now*, the last of the sequence, is the one I originally intended to have done first.

My work has suffered and gained from the fact that so large a share of my energies has had to go into an exacting and very responsible job.

My most recent novel, *Brides of Price*, makes a new departure (for me) in subject and technique.

*   *   *

On the evidence of his short stories and novels, Dan Davin might well echo Katherine Mansfield's nostalgic cry: "New Zealand is in my very bones." Despite his long residence as an expatriate in England, he returns continually to the haunts of his childhood and youth. As a New Zealander who has left his country, an Irish Catholic who has lost both creed and community, as a soldier in the New Zealand Division who cannot retain the comradeship he found in the service, he has kept faith with his memories, relives his estrangement from early allegiances and, with sympathetic if critical understanding, contemplates his fellow-countrymen wherever they may be found. By so doing he has discovered a starting-point for much wider human explorations than the search for national identity, a starting-point not an anchorage.

Yet the anchorage is suggested if only because no writer has walked more consistently on his own shadow and in the places where that shadow has appeared. It is tempting, but inaccurate, to describe him as a regional novelist or perhaps as the historian and cartographer of a small enclave of Irish Catholics, farming and labouring within the confines of Southland and sending some of their children northwards as far as the University of Otago. His characters bear such names as Mark Burke, Ned Hogan, Tom O'Dwyer, Frank Fahey, Hugh Egan and Martin Cody; they have an assortment of qualities and fortunes that are not very dissimilar to Davin's. Whether they are in London, North Africa, or more commonly in New Zealand, their Southland backgrounds travel with them and are described with loving care and great accuracy; their experiences and conflicts provide material for discussion and meditation; but the shadow of Dan Davin is always present, and his *Roads from Home* turn back towards the homeland that fires his imagination.

Nevertheless, that much of Davin's writing is comprised of incidents, places, and people recollected in tranquillity is less important than his possession of the historian's eye for the appropriate detail and the artist's instinct for a workable situation. By remaining true to his memories he is able to give authenticity to his glimpses of provincial life, and by remaining true to himself fits them into a pattern of human change and struggle. His collection of short stories *The Gorse Blooms Pale* contains clear and vivid evidence both of his biographical dependence and of his ability to recreate and select from the local minutiae those features that best serve his purpose, for it is not the scene but the aim of his endeavour that becomes significant. Davin's provincial studies of an earlier Southland have not been undertaken as a simple act of piety of former days, but because he had discovered the fascination that the retracing of steps holds for those who are more than usually conscious of the continuity of life and know that the future is contained in the womb of the past.

It is in *Roads from Home* rather than in his earlier or later novels dedicated to his memories of Southland that the thematic structure rivets attention and indicates some of his major preoccupations. The plot serves, but no more than serves, the purpose. Davin is concerned with the implications of his title—the roads down which men travel from youth to age, the many roads they might have taken, the changing ways of the world, the old paths followed by established traditions and the new that excite the young and disturb their seniors. Southland has provided him with a microcosm of community life and aspiration, and with provincial material sufficient to reanimate old themes. Family relationships, complicated by a protestant daughter-in-law, unsettled by a son's loss of faith, the slow secularisation of life, the pathos of the clash between generations, the failure of communications between parents and children, husbands and wives, together with the threats of separation and departure, are unified by recurrent imagery associated with the walls that divide human beings and the roads that lead in different directions.

A characteristic feature of Davin's writing, not unconnected with his biography, is his ability to switch from a simple and unaffected language which catches the casual accents and speech habits of New Zealanders to a more complex and literary style. In his use of the interior monologue he combines the inward thoughts with indirect authorial elaboration that becomes metaphorical and allusive, and is able to suggest wider implications than the bare narrative can supply. This is most apparent in his fictional record of the New Zealand Division in North Africa. Some have been inclined to dismiss *For the Rest of Our Lives* because it attempts, in the author's words, "to combine history and fiction in order to produce the illusion of reality," but fails to give that illusion through defects in its rendering of the fragments of dislocated lives and in the creation of character. It remains, however, an impressive novel, not because it achieves aims imposed on the writer from outside, but because its thematic structure serves another function, prescribed by its subject of war for the rest of our lives. By imagery, related episodes, by description and meditation, the emphasis is placed on the appalling insignificance of the individual in the immensity of time, on his feelings of helplessness and guilt in the midst of heroic exploits and the unbreakable unity of the Division, on the centuries-old martyrdom of man and the frightful continuity of history in pain and suffering.

Davin has not always done justice to his capabilities as a novelist. He has tended to rely too heavily on reflective monologue and dramatised discussions about "things that matter" at the cost of plot structure and character portrayal. His preoccupation with Southland memories has given his work an air of provinciality, in keeping with his themes, but ill-adapted to the exercise of his gifts as a writer. However his latest novel, *Brides of Price*, is a much more sophisticated narrative, both in matter and manner. He seems to have freed himself from the burden of memories and produced a witty, ironic comedy of contemporary life in which plot, character, and style are in harmony with the theme. The first-person narrator is a middle-aged anthropologist who, in his involvement with a series of women and his desire to escape appointment to a University Chair, comes no nearer to Southland than Sydney and Auckland. Whereas in his earlier novels, Davin was concerned with memories of "a man young," he is now intent on "a man old," continually surprised that experience has not enabled him to overcome the deficiencies of his own character, and increasingly conscious that communication with a younger generation is more difficult than he had imagined.

Brides of Price only emphasises at a more sophisticated level that Davin's "period pieces" were not the result of nostalgia but rather an outcome of his wish to explore all the roads down which men pass as they seek to know and understand "the warp and woof of things."

—H. Winston Rhodes

DAWSON, Jennifer. British. Educated at Mary Datchelor School, London; St. Anne's College, Oxford, B.A. 1952. Has worked for the Clarendon Press, Oxford, as a social worker in a mental hospital, and as a teacher. Recipient: Black Memorial Award, 1962; Cheltenham Festival Award, 1963. Address: c/o Quartet Books, 27 Goodge Street, London W1P 1FD, England.

PUBLICATIONS

Novels

The Ha-Ha. London, Blond, and Boston, Little Brown, 1961.
Fowler's Snare. London, Blond, 1962.
The Cold Country. London, Blond, 1965.
Strawberry Boy. London, Quartet, 1976.
A Field of Scarlet Poppies. London, Quartet, 1979.

Short Stories

Penguin Modern Stories 10, with others. London, Penguin, 1972.
Hospital Wedding. London, Quartet, 1978.

*

Jennifer Dawson comments:

My greatest passion in life has always been music. I regard writing as a last resort, a *faute de mieux* for me. In a world where language has been eroded, gutted ("pre-emptive strike," "take-out" for the murder of eight million civilians, etc.) all art "aspires to the condition of music," which cannot be exploited, interpreted, which explores the lost places of the heart, which makes all things new. Two of my novels have had musicians as their main characters—studies of the composer/musician who for social and political reasons experiences dryness, aridity, and cannot play any more. Politics creep, burst inevitably into my novels. They then become shrill, rhetorical, routine, etc.

One feeling that has haunted me all my life is that life, social life as we know it, is a kind of game with correct moves, correct remarks and replies, correct procedures. I do not know the rules. I have struggled in vain to solve this problem, the real life as opposed to the game of men-and-women.

But the thing that obsesses me most, and which I feel I shall never put into language, is the strangeness of life, its accidentalness. Here we all are on a tiny, precious blue-green balloon in the midst of space, naked gases, chambers of violence. The planet as an accident that has produced music, literature, art, and the extraordinary theme-and-variations of religions. Here we are, with our fitted carpets and Mixmasters and spin-dryers, stilted above the world, talking about mock O-levels, who is to be next Master of St. Judas's, how all the cars in St. John's Street seemed badly parked today. Here we are in the midst of nothingness, in the midst of a mystery, accidental and yet behaving politically and socially as though the bizarre nature of our life on this planet has not hit us yet. To me this freak of life (like a purple flower growing out of the dumped tippings of a hoover-bag) is the invitation to a new kind of freedom. Only art can introduce us to this. But my art? *No!* It must be someone else's. I shall never succeed in saying what I want to say.

* * *

Novels which explore madness have certain qualities in common. They describe a world which is enclosed, static and ruled by obsessions; they are vivid, fragmented, highly personal documents in which only one character can be fully realised. This intensity is double-edged. It can exclude, and ultimately bore, the reader or it can provide him with a vision of life which has a relevance beyond the barriers of mental illness. Kafka's metaphors have been readily accepted and understood. Jennifer Dawson's *The Ha-Ha* is one of the few contemporary novels significant enough to deserve the appellation Kafkaesque.

The Ha-Ha is set in a mental hospital where the narrator, Jean, is slowly recovering from a breakdown. She has progressed from the ward and the company of the irretrievably mad; she is now allowed her own room and promised a suitable job, an eventual regrading. Even as the nurse explains these steps towards freedom, we see their sad irrelevance. Jean's private world is ready to obtrude at any moment; her existence is precarious, threatened by the anarchy in her own imagination. One of the most moving illustrations of her plight is given in the description of her work as a librarian. She happily catalogues books for an elderly couple in the nearby town but is nonplussed by their casual, friendly conversation. When fine weather is mentioned she remarks "I wonder whether the monkeys would be better at the tops or the bottoms of the trees." Her own company of animals, spotted, sleek, furred and quilled, wait relentlessly for the time when she will step back into their universe.

The inevitable relapse is brought about by her first real relationship, a love relationship, a love affair with another patient. Alastair is critical of doctors and routines; he alarms Jean by telling her the true nature of her illness and she panics when he leaves the hospital. She runs away, is picked up by the police and brought back to face "the black box crashing down around my head." It is at this point that the novel changes direction. Jean remembers Alastair for his anger; she begins to share his indignation, rejects the doctors and escapes for good, feeling that her own identity is worth more than any medical tag of health.

Schizophrenia is a disease that has received much attention from modern writers. It has been used to symbolise the artist's alienation from society and, by extension, presented as the condition of modern man, lost, lonely, unable to communicate. The schizophrenic is sometimes hailed as a prophet, whose view of life is not only as valid as that of his doctors but also morally superior to the standards they uphold. Jennifer Dawson shares this fashionable, essentially romantic, attitude but her writing is without the stridency of propaganda. The parallels with Sylvia Plath's *The Bell Jar* are many and the prose is equally fine. Miss Dawson has written further explorations of her subject but has not yet matched the sustained brilliance of this first novel.

—Judy Cooke

DEIGHTON, Len (Leonard Cyril Deighton). British. Born in London, 18 February 1929. Educated at Marylebone Grammar School, St. Martin's School of Art, and Royal College of Art, all London. Served in the Royal Air Force. Married Shirley Thompson in 1960. Has worked as a railway lengthman, pastry cook, dress factory manager, waiter, illustrator, teacher, and photographer; art director of advertising agencies in London and New York; steward, British Overseas Airways Corporation, 1956-57; wrote a weekly comic strip on cooking for *The Observer*, London, in the 1960's; founder of Continuum One literary agency, London. Lives in Ireland. Address: c/o Jonathan Cape Ltd., 30 Bedford Square, London WC1B 3EL, England.

PUBLICATIONS

Novels

The Ipcress File. London, Hodder and Stoughton, 1962; New York, Simon and Schuster, 1963.
Horse under Water. London, Cape, 1963; New York, Putnam, 1968.
Funeral in Berlin. London, Cape, 1964; New York, Putnam, 1965.
Billion-Dollar Brain. London, Cape, and New York, Putnam, 1966.
An Expensive Place to Die. London, Cape, and New York, Putnam, 1967.
Only When I Larf. London, Joseph, 1968.
Bomber. London, Cape, and New York, Harper, 1970.
Close-Up. London, Cape, and New York, Atheneum, 1972.
Spy Story. London, Cape, and New York, Harcourt Brace, 1974.
Yesterday's Spy. London, Cape, and New York, Harcourt Brace, 1975.
Twinkle, Twinkle, Little Spy. London, Cape, 1976; as *Catch a Falling Spy*, New York, Harcourt Brace, 1976.
SS-GB: Nazi-Occupied Britain 1941. London, Cape, 1978; New York, Knopf, 1979.
XPD. London, Hutchinson, and New York, Knopf, 1981.

Short Stories

Declarations of War. London, Cape, 1971; as *Eleven Declarations of War*, New York, Harcourt Brace, 1975.

Plays

Screenplay: *Oh! What a Lovely War*, 1969.

Television Plays: *Long Past Glory*, 1963; *It Must Have Been Two Other Fellows*, 1977.

Other

Action Cook Book: Len Deighton's Guide to Eating. London, Cape, 1965; as *Cookstrip Cook Book*, New York, Geis, 1966.
Où Est le Garlic; or, Len Deighton's French Cook Book. London, Penguin, 1965; New York, Harper, 1977; revised edition as *Basic French Cooking*, London, Cape, 1978.
Len Deighton's Continental Dossier: A Collection of Cultural, Culinary, Historical, Spooky, Grim and Preposterous Fact, compiled by Victor and Margaret Pettitt. London, Joseph, 1968.
Fighter: The True Story of the Battle of Britain. London, Cape, 1977; New York, Knopf, 1978.
Airshipwreck, with Arnold Schwartzman. London, Cape, 1978; New York, Holt Rinehart, 1979.
Blitzkrieg: From the Rise of Hitler to the Fall of Dunkirk. London, Cape, 1979; New York, Knopf, 1980.
Battle of Britain. London, Cape, and New York, Coward McCann, 1980.

Editor, *London Dossier.* London, Cape, 1967.
Editor, with Michael Rund and Howard Loxton, *The Assassination of President Kennedy.* London, Cape, 1967.
Editor, *Tactical Genius in Battle*, by Simon Goodenough. London, Phaidon Press, 1979.

* * *

Partly as a result of the work of Len Deighton, the spy story has replaced the formal detective novel as the relevant thriller for its time. While continuing the tradition of literary excellence that has distinguished espionage fiction since the days of Somerset Maugham, Eric Ambler, and Graham Greene, both he and his gifted contemporary John le Carré have contributed a new energy, intelligence, and meaning to the novel of espionage. Ever since his first novel, *The Ipcress File*, Deighton has instructed a large reading public in some of the factual and emotional realities of the modern business of espionage and counterespionage. Writing with a lively wit, a keen eye for the surfaces of modern life, a convincing sense of authenticity, and a genuine intellectual concern for what the dark side of governmental practice can mean, Deighton has revealed some of the sham and self-delusion of contemporary politics in all of his novels.

In his spy novels Deighton employs a nameless first person narrator who owes something to Raymond Chandler's Philip Marlowe in his breezy wisecracks and his sometimes strained metaphors; beneath the wiseguy surface, however, he possesses also some of Marlowe's decency and compassion. Resolutely working class in background, education, and point of view, Deighton's hero is a professional spy who must do constant battle with the forces of the British Establishment in their full and whinnying glory as well as with whatever is on the other side. Frequently, in fact, his spy never knows precisely which side he is on, and is so often betrayed by his colleagues and superiors that it sometimes doesn't matter.

Accompanying the energetic style and disillusioned outlook is a complicated sense of novelistic architecture. Deighton's books frequently reveal, at their conclusion, both their method and their meaning. As the protagonist solves whatever mystery that has been confronting him, or wraps up a long and entangled investigation, the book shows the conclusion to a usually puzzling and elliptical narrative structure. The complications of its subject and of its fictional development appear to mesh perfectly; the construction becomes, very artfully, an emblem of the meaning of espionage, as much as the anonymity of the narrator suggests something about the problem of identity in this troubled world. The author's concern for both authenticity and ingenuity appear in his war novel, *Bomber*, as well, in which he mingles a love for the great machines of World War II, admiration for the brave men who operated them, and a moving realization of the horror and futility of war itself.

Like John le Carré again, Deighton has done much to advance our knowledge of the way spies and spying work and what they really mean in our time. For both writers the novel of expionage serves an emblematic function. It shows, all too convincingly, the sad history of treason that marks the real battle in the shadows—a spy seems always to betray one cause, one country, one person or another in order to do his task. The contemporary reality of the Western world provides the necessary historical context for Deighton's novels of espionage; daily headlines indicate the truth of his fictional perceptions, and the Kafkaesque quality of international politics and modern life itself reflects the deeper truth of his books.

Because Deighton's novels invariably show the folly, imbecility, and corruption of the wealthy and privileged classes in England, they have some of the flavor of the satiric works of the Angry Young Men, and his hero is somewhat of a Lucky Jim of espionage. Because they present a labyrinthine picture of undeclared war, conflicting loyalties, multiple betrayals, and complicated national alignments, they provide a useful image of the world we all inhabit. Their dominant ideas and emotions are those of our time—puzzlement, anxiety, cynicism, and guilt. They recognize, further, one of the major lessons of the English spy novel in this age, that an entire class, long protected by its own sense of unity and privilege, has sold its birthright, as the sordid history of Burgess, Maclean, Philby, and Blunt have proved.

In his own flip, entertaining, and exciting style, Deighton treats essentially the same problem that haunts a great deal of English fiction, the timeless question of who will inherit the virtue of the nation, who will save England from itself. Oddly enough, his works, therefore, show some connection with such books as *Adam Bede* and *Tess of the D'Urbervilles*, carrying on in a highly unlikely form the theme of a nation and a class that, ultimately, has betrayed itself. His novels indicate that the continuing vitality of the English novel may very well derive from the popular and often subliterary genres. As a spy novelist, and as a British writer of fiction, he deserves sympathetic reading and consideration with some of the better writers of the time.

—George Grella

DELANY, Samuel R(ay). American. Born in New York City, 1 April 1942. Educated at the Bronx High School of Science, New York; City College of New York (Poetry Editor, *The Promethean*), 1960, 1962-63. Married the poet Marilyn Hacker in 1961 (separated, 1974), one daughter. Butler Professor of English, State University of New York, Buffalo, 1975; Fellow, Center for Twentieth Century Studies, University of Wisconsin, Milwaukee, 1977. Recipient: Nebula Award, 1966, 1967 (two awards), 1969; Hugo Award, 1970. Address: c/o Bantam Books Inc., 666 Fifth Avenue, New York, New York 10019, U.S.A.

PUBLICATIONS

Novels

The Jewels of Aptor. New York, Ace, 1962; revised edition, Ace, and London, Gollancz, 1968.
The Fall of the Towers. London, Sphere, 1971; New York, Ace, 1972.
Captives of the Flame. New York, Ace, 1963; revised edition, as *Out of the Dead City*, London, Sphere, 1968; Ace, 1977.
The Towers of Toron. New York, Ace, 1964; London, Sphere, 1968.
City of a Thousand Suns. New York, Ace, 1965; London, Sphere, 1969.
The Ballad of Beta-2. New York, Ace, 1965.
Empire Star. New York, Ace, 1966.
Babel-17. New York, Ace, 1966; London, Gollancz, 1967.
The Einstein Intersection. New York, Ace, 1967; London, Gollancz, 1968.
Nova. New York, Doubleday, 1968; London, Gollancz, 1969.
The Tides of Lust. New York, Lancer, 1973; Manchester, Savoy, 1979.
Dhalgren. New York, Bantam, 1975.
Triton. New York, Bantam, 1976; London, Corgi, 1977.
The Ballad of Beta-2, and Empire Star. London, Sphere, 1977.
Empire: A Visual Novel, illustrated by Howard V. Chaykin. New York, Berkley, 1978.

Short Stories

Driftglass: 10 Tales of Speculative Fiction. New York, Doubleday, 1971; London, Gollancz, 1978.
Tales of Nevèrÿon. New York, Bantam, 1979.

Other

The Jewel-Hinged Jaw: Notes on the Language of Science Fiction. Elizabethtown, New York, Dragon Press, 1977.
The American Shore: Meditations on a Tale of Science Fiction by Thomas M. Disch—"Angouleme." Elizabethtown, New York, Dragon Press, 1978.
Heavenly Breakfast: An Essay on the Winter of Love (memoir). New York, Bantam, 1979.
Editor, with Marilyn Hacker, *Quark 1-4.* New York, Paperback Library, 4 vols., 1970-71.
Editor, *Nebula Award Winners 13.* New York, Harper, 1980.

*

Critical Studies: *The Delany Intersection* by George Edgar Slusser, San Bernardino, California, Borgo Press, 1977; *World Out of Words: The SF Novels of Samuel R. Delany* by Douglas Barbour, Frome, Somerset, Bran's Head, 1979.

* * *

Unlike many science-fiction authors, Samuel R. Delany shows little sign of wishing to repeat themes and settings in his novels, or to organise consistently his history of the future. His central concerns are, instead, the nature of myth, and the limits of perception. In some ways these spring naturally out of traditional topics in science fiction, as for instance in the relatively early book *Empire Star.* Here, as in many novels since *Huckleberry Finn*, a boy brought up in a rigid and unquestioning cultural setting moves out of it, and slowly learns that his values are not those of the entire universe. To describe the transition Delany coins the terms simplex, complex, multiplex, and in many comic scenes shows Comet Jo learning his own simplexity, as well as others' false multiplexity (for multiplexity is gained neither by travel, nor knowledge, nor even intelligence). The individual twist which Delany gives to this theme, however, is to insist that multiplexity is not only moral, but real: there are characters literally able to participate in the story at different ages, with different roles and levels of insight. One of these, Jewel, a "crystallised Tritovian" whom Jo carries as a talisman, in fact tells the story.

Empire Star ends abruptly and confusedly. It is mentioned as a work of fiction in *Babel-17* (though there it is not by Samuel R. Delany but by his anagram Muels Aranlyde, also a character in *Empire Star*), but this is more to blur the line between fact and fiction than to link the two stories. *Babel-17* is in fact strikingly different from *Empire Star* in that its protagonist, Rydra Wong, "the most famous poet in five explored galaxies," is a sophisticate from the start. Once again, however, Delany writes about the relativity of perception, as Rydra succeeds in breaking the code, or rather learning the language called Babel-17: a language which like all languages (Delany repeats the thesis advanced by Wittgenstein, B.L. Whorf, et al.) contains an entire world-view, in its case a particularly true and successful one. By learning the language Rydra Wong becomes almost superhuman in her capacity to see things as they are, though she also finds Babel-17 insidiously booby-trapped.

Up to this point Delany's works had contained mythical suggestions only peripherally. But an author's note on and in *The Einstein Intersection* says: "The central subject of the book is myth." Delany returns to the apparent setting of *The Jewels of Aptor* and the "Toromon" trilogy, a world riddled with radiation and mutants which seems to have undergone a nuclear war; and in it once more allows a naive protagonist, Lo Lobey, to venture into a wider culture. The difference is that Lo Lobey recreates the myths handed down by his people's defective history. He is the singer (Orpheus, Ringo) searching for his dead love (La Friza, Eurydice) killed by Bonny William, alias Kid Death, who is also evidently Satan and Pluto. The stories of Orpheus and Theseus, the Crucifixion, and the Temptation in the Wilderness, are mixed with the Hollywood western, romance, or "cliff-hanger," in such a way as to imply the essential unity of many experiences. But there is a literal explanation as well as a mythical one. Lo Lobey's world is not in fact a devastated Earth of the near future, but one of the far future in which an alien race has taken over human shapes and is trying to identify itself with its predecessors. The myths are recreated half-deliberately, and the "Einstein Intersection" of the title is, interestingly, an almost mathematical one: the intersection of the curves of influence of Einstein (who gave limits to man's perception) and

Goedel (who eradicated them by indicating the extent of the imperceptible).

In *Nova* also, Delany seeks to combine the attractiveness and elemental significance of ancient story (in this case the Grail story) with the deep-rooted rationalism of modern times. One of the protagonists, Mouse, an Earthman, shows the 20th-century scepticism mocked at, in the future, as old-fashioned; the rest, including Katin (another Delany-figure), accept the guidance of fortune-telling and the Tarot pack. In this novel Delany combines his own strengths, wide suggestion and preoccupation with the craft of writing, with those of the traditional science-fiction novel—fertility of invention, skill at analysing political, social, and technological factors. Simply in describing his crew of questers, Delany shows his gift for making highly abstract points without losing the sense of individual reality: in William James's terms, he is both tough- and tender-minded.

—T.A. Shippey

DeLILLO, Don. American. Born in New York City, 20 November 1936. Educated at Fordham University, Bronx, New York, 1954-58. Recipient: Guggenheim Fellowship, 1979. Agent: Wallace and Sheil Agency, 177 East 70th Street, New York, New York 10021, U.S.A.

PUBLICATIONS

Novels

Americana. Boston, Houghton Mifflin, 1971.
End Zone. Boston, Houghton Mifflin, 1972; London, Deutsch, 1973.
Great Jones Street. Boston, Houghton Mifflin, 1973; London, Deutsch, 1974.
Ratner's Star. New York, Knopf, 1976.
Players. New York, Knopf, 1977.
Running Dog. New York, Knopf, 1978; London, Gollancz, 1979.

Uncollected Short Stories

"Spaghetti and Meatballs," in *Epoch* (Ithaca, New York), Spring 1965.
"Take the 'A' Train," in *Stories from Epoch*, edited by Baxter Hathaway. Ithaca, New York, Cornell University Press, 1966.
"Coming Sun. Mon. Tues.," in *Kenyon Review* (Gambier, Ohio), June 1966.
"Baghdad Towers West," in *Epoch* (Ithaca, New York), Spring 1968.
"Game Plan," in *New Yorker*, 27 November 1971.
"In the Men's Room of the Sixteenth Century," in *The Secret Life of Our Times*, edited by Gordon Lish. New York, Doubleday, 1973.
"The Uniforms," in *Cutting Edges*, edited by Jack Hicks. New York, Holt Rinehart, 1973.
"Showdown at Great Hole," in *Esquire* (New York), June 1976.
"The Network," in *On the Job*, edited by William O'Rourke. New York, Random House, 1977.
"Creation," in *Antaeus* (New York), Spring 1979.

Play

The Engineer of Moonlight, in *Cornell Review* (Ithaca, New York), Winter 1979.

* * *

> What writing means to me is trying to make interesting, clear, beautiful language. Working at sentences and rhythms is probably the most satisfying thing I do as a writer. I think after a while a writer can begin to know himself through his language. He sees someone or something reflected back at him from these constructions. Over the years it's possible for a writer to shape himself as a human being through the language he uses. I think written language, fiction, goes that deep. He not only sees himself but begins to make himself or remake himself. Of course this is mysterious and subjective territory. Writing also means trying to advance the art. Fiction hasn't quite been filled in or done in or worked out. We make our small leaps (unpublished interview, September 1979).

Of American novelists who began publishing in the 1970's, Don DeLillo is one of the most prolific and compelling. DeLillo believes, with his subway inspector in *Ratner's Star*, that existence is "nourished from below, from the fear level, the place of obsession, the starkest tract of awareness." His six novels are a spelunker's guide to American life, cool explorations of undergrounds and subcultures where the powers once housed in churches may now exist; football, rock music, film, terrorism, espionage, pure mathematics. His characters experiment with crime and violence, burrow into bat caves and esoterica, travel to deserts and shut themselves in empty rooms to seek what can be called "subcendence," a private being far beneath the strictures, conditioning, and boredom of ego and ordinary life. Paralleling their quest is DeLillo's experiment with specialized languages, his search for a precision of style that will imply what he quotes Hermann Broch as calling "the word beyond speech."

Consistent in motive and theme, DeLillo's work has a virtuoso variety of subject, form, and style. Like Pynchon, DeLillo knows the new modular man, component of large systems, consumer of banalities enlarged and projected by electronic media. His features are boredom, game-playing, narcissism, paranoia. Like Barth, DeLillo turns popular forms—the thriller, science fiction, the sports novel—against themselves and the reader's expectations. His books move toward vanishing points, not conclusions. Like Barthelme, DeLillo records the babble of jargons—scientific, military, entertainment, and many others—that compete for power over silent reality. He can do aphorisms and slapstick, irony and meditation, linear plots and recursive structures. But for DeLillo, learning and craft are always the means to mystery, ways to manifest and pass through filters and occlusions, manufactured passions and trained gestures toward "the starkest tract of awareness," the primal and unnameable.

DeLillo thinks of his work as two parts: *Ratner's Star* and the five realistic novels preceding and following this hybrid of *Alice in Wonderland* and science fiction. The five are data, and *Ratner's Star* their formula; they are texts and commentary. *Americana* is an extravagant, yet rather conventional, first novel, an on-the-road book full of observation and notebook philosophizing. Its protagonist, David Bell, leaves the politics of the New York City television industry to tour his small-town past and to cross the continent. As he travels, he both stores up and empties out experience, a signature of the DeLillo hero. In *End Zone* Gary Harkness, like Bell, moves West, away from civilization and towards an atavistic existence playing football for Logos College. The novel becomes a struggle between word (logos) and act, symbol systems and signal behavior, as the characters who surround Harkness try to claim him within their very different discourses. Probably DeLillo's best-known work, *End Zone* skillfully compresses into its football metaphor social, linguistic, and religious themes. *Great Jones Street* completes the protagonist's retreat. Bucky Wunderlick, a Mick Jagger-like rock star, drops out of his group to become "the least of what he was." Although *Great Jones Street* was largely unnoticed by reviewers, I think DeLillo's presentation of rock music, its motives, excesses, and voids, compares with West's treatment of the movies in *Day of the Locust*.

Ratner's Star, like other encyclopedic novels of the 1970's—

Barth's *Letters*, Gaddis's *JR*, Coover's *The Public Burning*—is more about processes than people, the paradoxical process of learning uncertainty. Trying to decipher a message from space, mathematical prodigy Billy Twillig finds that all abstract structures must be thought through and that a meta-language ("Have you emptied your system of meaning?" one character asks him) must be constructed. Dervish philosophers, inhabitants of holes, and other Alice-like creatures rise up to give the reader a history of mathematics and a Gödelian lesson: in "our press to measure and delve...we implicate ourselves in endless uncertainty." A fiction about all fiction-making, *Ratner's Star* is a conceptual monster, a tail- and tale-eating beast worthy of Sterne, Carroll, or Escher.

DeLillo's recent novels—*Players* and *Running Dog*—are more modest, scaled down to show the meager ways contemporaries try to fill up rather than map out voids. Conspirators in excitement, the protagonists hunt extremity in terrorism, sexual adventure, and pornography. The books, though, are subtracting machines: they show how little becomes less, not the mysterious "least" of Wunderlick and other early DeLillo characters but a gradual divestment of humanness. While these books lack the energy and inventiveness of *End Zone* and *Ratner's Star*, the subtlety of observation and control in the later fiction have prompted John Leonard to call DeLillo "our wittiest writer." It is a wit without nostalgia, detached and elegant in its clarity yet finally humane because DeLillo drills through both traditional consolations and their fashionable substitutes.

—Thomas LeClair

DENNIS, Nigel (Forbes). British. Born in Bletchingley, Surrey, 16 January 1912. Educated at Plumtree School, Southern Rhodesia; Odenwaldschule, Germany. Married 1) Mary-Madeleine Massias; 2) Beatrice Ann Hewart Matthew in 1959; two daughters. Secretary, National Board of Review of Motion Pictures, New York, 1935-36; Assistant Editor, and Book Reviewer, *New Republic*, New York, 1937-38; Staff Book Reviewer, *Time*, New York, 1940-59. Since 1960, Drama Critic, and Joint Editor, 1967-70, *Encounter*, London; since 1961, Staff Book Reviewer, *The Sunday Telegraph*, London. Recipient: Houghton Mifflin-Eyre and Spottiswoode Award, for fiction, 1950; Heinemann award, for non-fiction, 1966. Fellow, Royal Society of Literature, 1966. Address: c/o A.M. Heath and Company, 40-42 William IV Street, London WC2N 4DD, England.

PUBLICATIONS

Novels

Boys and Girls Come Out to Play. London, Eyre and Spottiswoode, 1949; as *A Sea Change*, Boston, Houghton Mifflin, 1949.
Cards of Identity. London, Weidenfeld and Nicolson, and New York, Vanguard Press, 1955.
A House in Order. London, Weidenfeld and Nicolson, and New York, Vanguard Press, 1966.

Uncollected Short Stories

"Poor Signora," in *New Yorker*, 13 May 1961.
"Blocked Feed," in *Harper's* (New York), December 1961.
"The Pukey," in *Anti-Story*, edited by Philip Stevick. New York, Free Press, 1971.

Plays

Cards of Identity, adaptation of his own novel (produced London, 1956). Included in *Two Plays and a Preface*, 1958.
The Making of Moo (produced London, 1957; New York, 1958). Included in *Two Plays and a Preface*, 1958.
Two Plays and a Preface (includes *Cards of Identity* and *The Making of Moo*). London, Weidenfeld and Nicolson, 1958; New York, Vanguard Press, 1959.
August for the People (produced Edinburgh and London, 1961). London, French, 1962.

Verse

Exotics: Poems of the Mediterranean and the Middle East. London, Weidenfeld and Nicolson, 1970; New York, Vanguard Press, 1971.

Other

Dramatic Essays. London, Weidenfeld and Nicolson, 1962; Westport, Connecticut, Greenwood Press, 1978.
Jonathan Swift: A Short Character. New York, Macmillan, 1964; London, Weidenfeld and Nicolson, 1965.
An Essay on Malta. London, Murray, 1972; New York, Vanguard Press, 1974.

* * *

Although Nigel Dennis has published only three novels, their quality is high enough to give him a place as one of the best English novelists of his generation. He lived in America for many years and in fact the principal characters of his first novel, *Boys and Girls Come Out to Play*, are all American. It is set in the summer of 1939, on the eve of the Second World War, and the action takes place partly in America and partly in Poland. A liberal journalist, Max Divver, goes to Poland to report on the political situation for a progressive magazine, accompanied by Jimmy Morgan, the adolescent son of the rich woman who owns and edits the magazine. Jimmy is a difficult boy, who is liable to fits, but the visit proves the making of him, whereas it is the undoing of Max, a forceful but insecure character, who is consumed by self-loathing. Nigel Dennis develops the relationship between them in a leisurely fashion that allows for much indulgence in psychological nuance but results in a long book that has rather a lot of static passages. There is a slightly uneasy contrast between the reflective sections and the element of adventure that builds up as Max and Jimmy try to escape from Poland just before the German invasion. The interest is essentially in the characters and the Polish setting never really seems convincing. The novel leaves no doubt, however, of the quality of Dennis's writing, shown for instance in the dazzling account of the attempts by a mechanic to start a large and ancient car (a vehicle which much later comes to play a crucial part in the plot). It also shows a satirical inclination, and a tendency to allegory or fable in that Max Divver is clearly meant to embody the insufficiencies of the liberal intellectual at a time of great historical crisis.

These tendencies were fully developed in Dennis's next novel, *Cards of Identity*, which established his reputation and remains one of the most brilliant works of post-war English fiction. It is about the "problem of identity" which is so much discussed in the modern world, and the essence of the novel lies in the characters' difficulty in knowing who they are supposed to be. Yet *Cards of Identity* also indicates the time and place of its composition. The setting is an English country house where a body called the Identity Club is holding its annual meeting, at which the members listen to papers describing the case-histories of interesting identity problems. Much of the detail reflects English life in the late 1940's and early 1950's, a period of ration-books and identity cards and continuing post-war privations. One of the case-histories is about an ex-communist turned monk who is writing his memoirs in a monastery, all of whose inmates have had a similar communist past; it is very entertaining, but inevitably seems rather dated now. On the other hand, the story of the Co-Wardens of the Badgeries, and the sad farcical events that took place while ceremoniously leading a symbolic stuffed badger across London in the funeral procession of the Lord Royal, is still a valid satire on the more absurd manifestations of English public traditionalism. The case histories are told with great verve and are full of Dennis's imaginative exuberance. But where *Cards of Identity* transcends the treatment of individual forms of identity crisis and looks at the problem of English cultural identity as a whole, is not in the separate case-histories but in the narrative framework of the novel. The setting of the events is a traditional country house of the kind familiar in innumerable English novels. But it has been empty for a long time, and in order to find staff for it the local representatives of the Identity Club abduct various of the local inhabitants and by unspecified but infallible means transform them into typical denizens of the English country house, such as the butler, the cook and the eccentric gardener. In fact they construct, specially for the Club, a model of the comfortable timeless milieu of much traditional English fiction, though it proves in the end no more than a house of cards, and identity-cards at that. In this brilliantly comic and ingenious novel Nigel Dennis probes at many contemporary problems. The satirical examination of the way in which the familiar symbols of English cultural identity have been losing their validity is an important part of the meaning of *Cards of Identity*.

Dennis's third novel, *A House in Order*, also dwells on the question of identity, though it is more personal and less culturally specific than its predecessor. The subject is deliberately narrow and intensely treated: during a war between two unnamed powers a prisoner is kept confined in a greenhouse by the soldiers of one side. He cannot be moved as he is an object of contention between two branches of the military establishment, though neither of them is interested in his personal welfare. With enormous patience the man cultivates the small plants he finds in the greenhouse and in the yard outside where he is allowed to exercise; he thereby keeps not only his house but his mind in order, and preserves his sense of self. At the end of the story, when he has been released and returned to his own country and a greenhouse of his own, he even looks back nostalgically to the days of his imprisonment as to some vanished ideal order. The story has of course many obviously allegorical implications about the human condition, but Dennis embodies them in a detailed convincing narrative that never becomes thinly symbolic, and where the humour that distinguished *Cards of Identity* is still noticeable. *A House in Order* is remarkable for the way in which it works as a novel, even while being an evident moral fable.

—Bernard Bergonzi

DESAI, Anita (née Mazumdar). Indian. Born in Mussoorie, 24 June 1937. Educated at Queen Mary's Higher Secondary School, Delhi; Miranda House, Delhi University, B.A. in English literature 1957. Married Ashvin Desai in 1958; four children. Since 1972, Member of the Sahitya Akademi English Board. Recipient: Royal Society of Literature Winifred Holtby Prize, 1978; Indian National Academy of Letters Award, 1979. Fellow, Royal Society of Literature, 1978. Address: c/o Hind Pocket Books, G.T. Road, Shahdara, Delhi 32, India.

PUBLICATIONS

Novels

Cry, The Peacock. London, Peter Owen, 1963.
Voices in the City. London, Peter Owen, 1965.
Bye-Bye, Blackbird. Delhi, Hind, and Thompson, Connecticut, InterCulture, 1971.
Where Shall We Go This Summer? New Delhi, Vikas, 1975.
Fire on the Mountain. London, Heinemann, and New York, Harper, 1977.
Clear Light of Day. London, Heinemann, and New York, Harper, 1980.

Short Stories

Games at Twilight and Other Stories. London, Heinemann, 1978; New York, Harper, 1980.

Uncollected Short Stories

"Circus Cat, Alley Cat," in *Thought* (Delhi), 1957.
"Tea with the Maharani," in *Envoy* (London), 1959.
"Grandmother," in *Writers Workshop* (Calcutta), 1960.
"Mr. Bose's Private Bliss," in *Envoy* (London), 1961.
"Ghost House," in *Quest* (Bombay), 1961.
"Descent from the Rooftop," in *Illustrated Weekly of India* (Bombay), 1970.

Other

The Peacock Garden (juvenile). Bombay, India Book House, 1974; London, Heinemann, 1979.
Cat on a Houseboat (juvenile). New Delhi, Orient Longman, 1976.

*

Critical Studies: *Indian Writing in English* by Paul Verghese, Bombay, Asia Publishing House, 1970; *Anita Desai* by Meena Belliappa, Calcutta, Writers Workshop, 1971; *The Twice-Born Fiction* by Meenakshi Mukherjee, Delhi, Arnold-Heinemann, 1972; *Indian Writing in English* by Srinivas Iyyengar, Bombay, Asia Publishing House, 1972.

Anita Desai comments:

I have been writing, since the age of 7, as instinctively as I breathe. It is a necessity to me: I find it is in the process of writing that I am able to think, to feel, and to realize at the highest pitch. Writing is to me a process of discovering the truth—the truth that is nine-tenths of the iceberg that lies submerged beneath the one-tenth visible portion we call Reality. Writing is my way of plunging to the depths and exploring this underlying truth. All my writing is an effort to discover, to underline and convey the true significance of things. That is why, in my novels, small objects, passing moods and attitudes acquire a large importance. My novels are no reflection of Indian society, politics, or character. They are part of my private effort to seize upon the raw material of life—its shapelessness, its meaninglessness, that lack of design that drives one to despair—and to mould it and impose on it a design, a certain composition and order that pleases me as an artist and also as a human being who longs for order.

While writing my novels, I find I use certain images again and again and that, although real, they acquire the significance of symbols. I imagine each writer ends by thus revealing his own mythology, a mythology that symbolizes his private morality and philosophy. One hopes, at the end of one's career, to have made some significant statement on life—not necessarily a water-tight, hard-and-fast set of rules, but preferably an ambiguous, elastic, shifting, and kinetic one that remains always capable of further change and growth.

Next to this exploration of the underlying truth and the discovery of a private mythology and philosophy, it is style that interests me most—and by this I mean the conscious labour of uniting language and symbol, word and rhythm. Without it, language would remain a dull and pedestrian vehicle. I search for a style that will bring it to vivid, surging life. Story, action, and drama mean little to me except insofar as they emanate directly from the personalities I have chosen to write about, born of their dreams and wills. One must find a way to unite the inner and the outer rhythms, to obtain a certain integrity and to impose order on chaos.

* * *

Of Anita Desai's novels, the first two—*Cry, The Peacock* and *Voices in the City*—deal with spiritual collapse among upper-class Indians whose traditional religion and manner of life have been undermined by modern concepts and ways. In *Cry, The Peacock* the heroine, who is the daughter of a wealthy, dilettantish Brahmin, has acquired by her upbringing a hypersensitivity to the arts and the beauties of nature. After her marriage she retains her aesthetic attachments, but she finds her husband unresponsive to her affection. As a result she pours out her love on her dog and her flowers. *The Bhagavad-Gita*, which she quotes at length, warns against strong attachments. Nature, art, animals, human beings are illusions or maya (this unhappy woman's name is Maya); and undue dependence on them can bring misery or disaster. If Maya at times seems to forget this doctrine so central to her ancestral religion, her husband reminds her of it. A successful lawyer, he has himself achieved non-attachment, as his name, Gautama (one of the Buddha's names), suggests.

Mainly through Maya's stream of consciousness is unfolded the tragic story of a woman almost completely misunderstood by her husband, who regards her as little more than a household ornament. To a degree, her situation illustrates many of Simone de Beauvoir's points concerning the plight of women in a male-dominated society. But Maya's problem is more than a socio-cultural one. It is deeply rooted in the spirit, and it is incurable. Starting as mildly hysterical, she becomes fully psychotic. In this state she murders her husband.

In her second novel, *Voices in the City*, Desai traces the disintegrative effects of residence in Calcutta on three talented young people—two sisters and a brother—who come to the metropolis from the hills. Calcutta, indeed, in this story lives up to its name, which derives from Kali, the black Goddess of Death. The brother sinks into a life of squalid dissipation. One of the sisters, married to a crassly bourgeois and dominating husband, dies—first spiritually, and then physically as a suicide. The other sister attempts a career as a commercial artist, but ends in desolate disillusionment.

Desai's later novels focus on similar intellectual and spiritual stresses experienced by modern educated Indians. *Bye-Bye, Blackbird* deals with the conflicting loyalties of Indians who, living in London, are attracted to Western culture but are reluctant to let it supplant their Eastern heritage. *Where Shall We Go This Summer?* relates the struggles of a woman who tries, unsuccessfully, to escape from a meaningless life as wife of a Bombay businessman. Her flight to a nearby island where she had lived as a girl provides no remedy for her misery; and, defeated, she permits her husband to lead her back to the city. *Fire on the Mountain* has as its chief character an aged woman who, after a lifetime as the wife of a university official, has sought solitude in a Himalayan hill station, only to have her peace shattered by the arrival of a mentally disturbed great-granddaughter. Desai's handling of the relationship between the two is penetrating, convincing, and extremely moving. *Fire on the Mountain* is remarkable for its psychological insights and its emotional power. It is her most impressive novel.

In all her writing, including her collection of short stories, *Games at Twilight*, Desai's style is rich, sensuous, sometimes truly lyrical. As a creator of atmosphere, whether of the squalor and turmoil of Calcutta, of a monsoon-drenched island off the Malabar Coast, or of the airy isolation of a hill station, she is unsurpassed.

—Perry D. Westbrook

DESANI, G(ovindas) V(ishnoodas). British. Born in Nairobi, Kenya, 8 July 1909. Correspondent, Reuters and Associated Press, 1935-45; Lecturer for the British Ministry of Information and the Imperial Institute, and BBC broadcaster during World War II. After the war, lived in monasteries in India, Burma, and Japan, for 19 years. Special Contributor, and Columnist ("Very High and Very Low"), *Illustrated Weekly of India*, Bombay, 1960-68. Fulbright-Hays Lecturer, 1968, and since 1969, Professor of Philosophy, University of Texas, Austin. Address: Department of Philosophy, University of Texas, Austin, Texas 78712, U.S.A.

PUBLICATIONS

Novel

All about Mr. Hatterr: A Gesture. London, Francis Aldor, 1948; as *All about H. Hatterr: A Gesture*, London, Saturn Press, 1949; New York, Farrar Straus, 1951; revised edition, London, Bodley Head, and Farrar Straus, 1970; revised edition, New York, Lancer, 1972; London, Penguin, 1973.

Uncollected Short Stories

"A New Bridge of Plenty," "Mephisto's Daughter," "The Lama Arupa," "Trade Winds," "A Border Incident," "The Fall of G.M. Haii, In Memoriam," "The Sticky Affair," "Goan, Meet a Samoan," "With Malice Aforethought," "The Second Mrs. Was Wed in a Nightmare," "Sutta Abandoned," "The Last Long Letter," "The Fiend Screams 'KYA CHAHATE HO?,' " in *Illustrated Weekly of India* (Bombay), 1957-67.
"The Explanation," in *Hindi Review* (Benares), July 1959.
"Mephisto's Daughter," in *Noble Savage 4* (Cleveland), 1961.
"With Malice Aforethought," in *Noble Savage 5* (Cleveland), 1962.
"The Second Mrs. Was Wed in a Nightmare," in *Transatlantic Review 9* (London), Spring 1962.

Play

Hali. London, Saturn Press, 1950; revised edition, Calcutta, Writers Workshop, 1967.

*

Critical Study: "The Dialogue in G.V. Desani's *All about H. Hatterr*" by D.M. Burjorjee, in *World Literature Written in English* (Arlington, Texas), November 1974.

* * *

G.V. Desani's published fiction consists of a small number of short stories and one novel, *All about H. Hatterr*. In addition, he has published a prose poem, in dramatic form, titled *Hali*, which some critics consider his most significant work. *Hali* has also been called a "story of passion"; but whatever its classification, it serves as companion piece for Desani's novel. In both works the author is taking the measure of man—in *Hali*, ideal man, and in *All about H. Hatterr*, everyman or man as he really is in a far-from-perfect world. *Hali* is written in the prophetic and exalted style that its subject demands. In it the young hero, Hali, passes through fear, defeat, and sorrow to achieve a selfless, changeless, Christlike love for all humanity. Discarding deities that he had revered earlier, he now worships only his newly found God of Love, who is "eternally incarnated" in the human form.

H. Hatterr in *All about H. Hatterr* has accurately been described as "the mathematical opposite of Hali." The same may be said of the styles and the tones of the two works. A Eurasian born in Penang but a resident for long periods in India and England, H. Hatterr is indeed fitted for the role of everyman that Desani intends him to fill. The language employed by H. Hatterr as he narrates his "Autobiographical" is a mixture, wholly unique in literature, of cockney and babu English with liberal infusions of American slang, the argot of criminals, the jargon of the medical and legal professions, and literal translations from Hindi, the whole being sprinkled with quotations and misquotations from Shakespeare and other poets. Desani has aptly been called "a playboy of the English language, a juggler with words." His virtuosity in this respect is one of the chief pleasures and wonders of his novel: e.g., "Only a few days ago...I was sitting in my humble belle-vue-no view, cul-de-sack-the-tenant, a landlady's up-and-do-'em opportunity apartment-joint in India." H. Hatterr's incessant flow of vulgarisms, cynicisms, sarcasms, and malapropisms reflects the vulgarity-cum-naivety of his character as a 20th-century everyman. In contrast to Hali's religion of selfless love, H. Hatterr phrases his philosophy as follows: "To be easy and comfortable appears to be the aim of all man: even at the expense of the other feller." H. Hatterr's application of this simple rule of conduct in seven "life-encounters" supplies the action of the novel. Each of the "encounters" is preceded by a humorous "Instruction," in which an eccentric guru voices some general truth about the human condition, and a "Presumption," which presents H. Hatterr's distortion of this truth. The "encounters" themselves are absurd and fantastic, and from each of them H. Hatterr emerges rather badly battered. But he always bounces back for more. "*Life*," he avers, "is no one-way pattern. It's *contrasts* all the way. And *contrasts* by Law!...I am not fed up with *Life*...." The fact that H. Hatterr enjoys the absurdity of life, at least as he leads it, serves to raise him somewhat above the stature of a mere buffoon and to give the reader the sense that the author's purpose is one of life-affirmation.

In his short fiction, G.V. Desani writes in one or other of the two contrasting veins of *Hali* and *All about H. Hatterr*. Thus "The Last Long Letter" records the ecstatic visions of a young man, a suicide, who casts his soul back into the opaque void of the universe, where it had been a light, as he has previously cast his jeweled ring into the depths of the sea to symbolize his belief that from time to time spirit illuminates matter but then withdraws, leaving all in chaos and darkness until its next coming. Other stories—"Mephisto's Daughter," "With Malice Aforethought," and "The Second Mrs. Was Wed in a Nightmare"—are fantasies, sometimes with a satiric sting, which further exemplify the talent that made *All about H. Hatterr* one of our century's major contributions to the literature of the absurd.

—Perry W. Westbrook

DE VRIES, Peter. American. Born in Chicago, 27 February 1910. Educated at Calvin College, Grand Rapids, Michigan, A.B. 1931; Northwestern University, Evanston, Illinois, 1931. Married Katinka Loeser in 1943; four children. Editor of community newspapers, Chicago, 1931; candy vending machine operator, and radio actor, Chicago, 1931-38; Associate Editor, 1938-42, and Co-Editor, 1942-44, *Poetry* magazine, Chicago. Since 1944, Staff member of *The New Yorker* magazine. Recipient: American Academy grant, 1946. Member, American Academy, 1969. Address: 170 Cross Highway, Westport, Connecticut 06880, U.S.A.

PUBLICATIONS

Novels

But Who Wakes the Bugler? Boston, Houghton Mifflin, 1940.
The Handsome Heart. New York, Coward McCann, 1943.
Angels Can't Do Better. New York, Coward McCann, 1944.
The Tunnel of Love. Boston, Little Brown, 1954; London, Gollancz, 1955.
Comfort Me with Apples. Boston, Little Brown, and London, Gollancz, 1956.
The Mackerel Plaza. Boston, Little Brown, and London, Gollancz, 1958.
The Tents of Wickedness. Boston, Little Brown, and London, Gollancz, 1959.
Through the Fields of Clover. Boston, Little Brown, and London, Gollancz, 1961.
The Blood of the Lamb. Boston, Little Brown, and London, Gollancz, 1962.
Reuben, Reuben. Boston, Little Brown, and London, Gollancz, 1964.
Let Me Count the Ways. Boston, Little Brown, and London, Gollancz, 1965.
The Vale of Laughter. Boston, Little Brown, 1967; London, Gollancz, 1968.
The Cat's Pajamas and Witch's Milk. Boston, Little Brown, 1968.
Mrs. Wallop. Boston, Little Brown, and London, Gollancz, 1970.
Into Your Tent I'll Creep. Boston, Little Brown, 1971; London, Gollancz, 1972.
Forever Panting. Boston, Little Brown, and London, Gollancz, 1973.
The Glory of the Hummingbird. Boston, Little Brown, 1974; London, Gollancz, 1975.
I Hear America Swinging. Boston, Little Brown, and London, Gollancz, 1976.
Madder Music. Boston, Little Brown, 1977; London, Gollancz, 1978.
Consenting Adults; or, The Duchess Will Be Furious. Boston, Little Brown, 1980; London, Gollancz, 1981.

Short Stories

No, But I Saw the Movie. Boston, Little Brown, 1952; London, Gollancz, 1954.
Without a Stitch in Time: A Selection of the Best Humorous Short Pieces. Boston, Little Brown, 1972; London, Gollancz, 1974.

Uncollected Short Stories

"Come Down to Queue," in *New Yorker*, 11 March 1974.
"The Iridescence of Mrs. Pulsifer," in *New Yorker*, 26 March 1979.

Play

The Tunnel of Love, with Joseph Fields, adaptation of the novel by De Vries (produced New York and London, 1957). Boston, Little Brown, 1957.

*

Bibliography: *Peter De Vries: A Bibliography 1934-1977* by Edwin T. Bowden, Austin, University of Texas Humanities Research Center, 1978.

Manuscript Collection: Boston University Library.

Critical Studies: *Peter De Vries* by Roderick Jellema, Grand Rapids, Michigan, Eerdmans, 1967; interviews with Roy Newquist in *Counterpoint*, Chicago, Rand McNally, 1964, and Richard B. Sale in *Studies in the Novel* (Denton, Texas), Fall 1969; *Shriven Selves* by Wesley A. Kort, Philadelphia, Fortress Press, 1972; William Walsh, in *Encounter* (London), January 1973; *An Anatomy of Laughter* by Richard Boston, London, Collins, 1974; "The Case for Comic Seriousness" by Craig Challender, in *Studies in American Humor* (San Marcos, Texas), April 1974; "Peter De Vries: The Vale of Laughter" by Calvin De Vries, in *Theology Today* (Princeton, New Jersey), April 1975; "Tragicomedy and Saving Grace" by John

Timmerman, in *Christian Century* (Chicago), 26 November 1975; by Max Byrd, in *New Republic* (Washington, D.C.), 23 October 1976; *Peter De Vries* by James H. Bowden, Boston, Twayne, 1980.

* * *

Peter De Vries is a wit who writes humorous, often very funny, moral fables that look like novels but are in reality just vehicles for his comic energies. His sense of play tends to overwhelm his plot, which frequently suffers from discontinuity and misplaced emphasis. His characters generally lack size and complexity; they exist more as De Vries's witty and insouciant mouthpieces than as individualized fictional creations. Not that De Vries is incompetent in plotting a novel: when he puts his mind to it, as *Comfort Me with Apples* illustrates, he contrives an action as satisfyingly complicated as the Cretan maze. And not that he is without imagination in the handling of character. De Vries has great skill with role-playing. When his characters indulge in it, he uses this device with the joy of a writer dedicated to the exploitation of fantasy and self-delusion. In many of the books in which he uses a first person narrator, De Vries himself seems to play a role, ranging, in his virtuoso way, from that of a shrewd Connecticut Yankee to that of a Polish piano mover in Indiana. He has certain technical skills in fiction, then, but he applies them haphazardly to his work. It is not the craft of fiction that is of real interest in his work but the nature of his humor, his religious and moral attitudes, and his social commentary.

De Vries is like a precocious child at play—word play, of course, which seems to flow spontaneously from his pen. His novels are packed with pun and parody, with solecism and epigram, with caricature, and with sheer, delightful idiocy. He is dedicated to nonsense, which he regards as a lowly but tricky art, because the penalty for its failure is silliness. His skills are largely verbal, but he can do situation comedy too, in the zany mode of the Marx Brothers. But of course he goes beyond play to assume the traditional burden of the humorist as critic. As a novelist of manners, his mode is satire. His literary criticism is expressed mostly in parody; *The Tents of Wickedness* is the outstanding example among his books, with its laughing attack on Faulkner's style, on the excessive depravity of Erskine Caldwell's characters and on the excessive guilt of Graham Greene's. De Vries humor also has a dark side. He knows that a joke may be a device for resolving fear. He knows that the "real" world is mad and that it makes men desperate. One of his humorous devices is to permit his characters to escape to fantasy; another, as in the Tom Waltz section of *Let Me Count the Ways*, is to counter the world's madness with the most extravagant and wildest kind of individual action. Like any good humorist, De Vries knows that the vale of laughter is not far from the vale of tears.

The religious and moral problems in his fiction certainly owe much to his Dutch Calvinist background. The general movement of his fiction is from a youthful total rejection of Calvinism to a hard-won agnosticism. The novels are full of guilt, especially with respect to religion and sexual behaviour, as De Vries works to liberate himself from his heritage. It is not always clear whether it is the characters' guilt as they move toward fornication or adultery or the author's, but De Vries is certainly pre-occupied with sex and unsure of the morality that should govern it. One of the characters in *The Mackerel Plaza* says we do not know how to cope with guilt because we have done away with the concept of sin. De Vries seems to want freedom from sin, but he has contempt for atheism, which would abolish the idea. Stein, the atheist in *The Blood of the Lamb*, enjoys the deprivations of faith that are self-inflicted and cannot forgive God for not existing. De Vries also has contempt for liberal Christianity and for its ministers who are ignorant of theology and preach in splitlevel churches. In *The Blood of the Lamb*, a semi-documentary novel about a father and his daughter who dies of leukemia, De Vries has made his most painful and most incisive statement about agnosticism. The child reveals to the father that human beings have only the human trinity to fall back upon: reason, courage, and grace. And this is the view, tentatively and skeptically entertained, that De Vries seems in his maturity to have adopted.

De Vries's social comment, a part of his humor and implicit in his attitude toward religion and morality, deals largely with the middle and upper middle classes in suburbia. He has a keen ear for the linguistic pretentions of this class and a keen eye for its yearning for factitiously "gracious" living. He observes America as an anthropologist or as a witty foreign writer might, and he directs his ridicule and laughter at everything from aptitude tests for corporation personnel to the generation gap, always making fun of the maniacal zeal for sociological research into their own lives that Americans habitually reveal. In *The Vale of Laughter* the take-off on the Masters-Johnson investigation into sexual behaviour is perhaps the high point of this kind of hi-jinks. The apostles of behaviorism, like the child psychologist or the marriage counsellor, are a constant butt of his humor. He is overwhelmed by the excesses of people who have unlimited opportunities for consumption in an affluent society: they not only have too much of everything but most of what they buy is synthetic. The protest he makes is easily recognizable as that of a traditionalist and humanist who regrets that men and women are foolish, greedy, gullible, lecherous, and essentially incompatible. De Vries is a humorist like so many others who have made laughter out of the failure of human beings to live up to the moral and social standards that the society has set for itself. His difficulty is that he is unsure of these standards himself and full of a sense of his own failings and guilt. Yet it is this condition which enables his reader to identify with him and enables him to speak so persuasively to the reader.

—Chester E. Eisinger

DICK, Philip K(indred). American. Born in Chicago, Illinois, 16 December 1928. Educated at Berkeley High School, California, graduated 1945. Married five times; two daughters and one son. Has worked as a record store manager and an announcer on KSMO-AM radio, Berkeley. Recipient: Hugo Award, 1963; Campbell Memorial Award, 1975. Agent: Scott Meredith Literary Agency, 845 Third Avenue, New York, New York 10022. Address: 408 East Civic Center Drive, Apartment 301, Santa Ana, California 92701, U.S.A.

PUBLICATIONS

Novels

Solar Lottery. New York, Ace, 1955; as *World of Chance*, London, Rich and Cowan, 1956.
The World Jones Made. New York, Ace, 1956; London, Sidgwick and Jackson, 1968.
The Man Who Japed. New York, Ace, 1956; London, Eyre Methuen, 1978.
Eye in the Sky. New York, Ace, 1956; London, Arrow, 1971.
The Cosmic Puppets. New York, Ace, 1957.
Time Out of Joint. Philadelphia, Lippincott, 1959; London, Sidgwick and Jackson, 1961.
Dr. Futurity. New York, Ace, 1960; London, Eyre Methuen, 1976.
Vulcan's Hammer. New York, Ace, 1960; London, Arrow, 1976.
The Man in the High Castle. New York, Putnam, 1962; London, Penguin, 1965.
The Game-Players of Titan. New York, Ace, 1963; London, Sphere, 1969.
Martian Time-Slip. New York, Ballantine, 1964; London, New English Library, 1976.

The Simulacra. New York, Ace, 1964; London, Eyre Methuen, 1977.
The Penultimate Truth. New York, Belmont, 1964; London, Cape, 1967.
Clans of the Alphane Moon. New York, Ace, 1964; London, Panther, 1975.
The Three Stigmata of Palmer Eldritch. New York, Doubleday, 1965; London, Cape, 1966.
Dr. Bloodmoney; or, How We Got Along after the Bomb. New York, Ace, 1965; London, Arrow, 1977.
The Crack in Space. New York, Ace, 1966; London, Eyre Methuen, 1977.
Now Wait for Last Year. New York, Doubleday, 1966; London, Panther, 1975.
The Unteleported Man. New York, Ace, 1966; London, Eyre Methuen, 1976.
Counter-Clock World. New York, Berkley, 1967; London, Sphere, 1968.
The Zap Gun. New York, Pyramid, 1967; London, Panther, 1975.
The Ganymede Takeover, with Ray Nelson. New York, Ace, 1967; London, Arrow, 1971.
Do Androids Dream of Electric Sheep? New York, Doubleday, 1968; London, Rapp and Whiting, 1969.
Ubik. New York, Doubleday, 1969; London, Rapp and Whiting, 1970.
Galactic Pot-Healer. New York, Doubleday, 1969; London, Gollancz, 1971.
A Maze of Death. New York, Doubleday, 1970; London, Gollancz, 1972.
Our Friends from Frolix 8. New York, Ace, 1970; London, Panther, 1976.
We Can Build You. New York, DAW, 1972; London, Fontana, 1977.
Flow My Tears, The Policeman Said. New York, Doubleday, and London, Gollancz, 1974.
Deus Irae, with Roger Zelazny. New York, Doubleday, 1976; London, Gollancz, 1977.
A Scanner Darkly. New York, Doubleday, and London, Gollancz, 1977.
Confessions of a Crap Artist. Glen Ellen, California, Entwhistle, 1978; London, Magnum, 1979.
The Divine Invasion. New York, Simon and Schuster, 1981.
Valis. New York, Bantam, 1981.

Short Stories

A Handful of Darkness. London, Rich and Cowan, 1955; Boston, Gregg Press, 1978.
The Variable Man and Other Stories. New York, Ace, 1956; London, Sphere, 1969.
The Preserving Machine and Other Stories. New York, Ace, 1969; London, Gollancz, 1971.
The Book of Philip K. Dick. New York, DAW, 1973; as *The Turning Wheel and Other Stories,* London, Coronet, 1977.
The Best of Philip K. Dick, edited by John Brunner. New York, Ballantine, 1977.
The Golden Man. New York, Berkley, 1980; London, Eyre and Methuen, 1981.

*

Bibliography: in *Science-Fiction Studies* (Terre Haute, Indiana), March 1975.

Manuscript Collection: California State University, Fullerton.

Critical Studies: *The Shape of Future Things,* London, Faber, 1970, New York, Doubleday, 1971, and *Billion Year Spree,* London, Weidenfeld and Nicolson, and New York, Doubleday, 1973, both by Brian Aldiss; "Can God Fly?," in *Foundation 4* (London), July 1973, and *Philip K. Dick and the Umbrella of Light,* Baltimore, T-K Graphics, 1975, both by Angus Taylor; *Modern Science Fiction* edited by Norman Spinrad, New York, Doubleday, 1974; "The Great Tradition of Proto SF" by Peter Nicholls, in *Foundation 5* (London), January 1974; interview with Arthur Bryon Cover, in *Vortex* (New York), February 1974; *Phillip K. Dick: Electric Shepherd* (includes bibliography) edited by Bruce Gillespie, Melbourne, Norstrilia Press, 1975; *Phillip K. Dick* edited by Martin H. Greenberg and Joseph D. Olander, New York, Taplinger, 1981.

Philip K. Dick comments:

Using science fiction as a framework, I attempt to cut through the layers of quasi-reality, finding in the process that the elliptical viewpoints of psychosis act as starting points. Although I have been able to determine and then represent in my fiction many private universes, differing from one personality type to the next, I am in no sense trying to state what in the final analysis is "real." It is, rather, the search which interests me; perhaps the outcome is not the same for all of us. In my early novels and stories I often used sociological and political themes; later I branched into drug trips and also theological trips, sometimes combining both (which angered many readers, both those who used drugs as well as those who used God). However, out of this I have recently come to sense a new level of feeling rather than intuition or reasoning. It is perhaps possible that when all the layers of the mind are stripped away the reality of the heart remains, or anyhow some organ more vital than the brain. In my work-in-progress I seek to contact some vein of cognition, some perceptual entity outside myself, outside our own race...where this entity would be, if anywhere at all, I can't say. Still, I think it exists, and, having helped me in my work throughout my career, perhaps it will guide me toward itself during the remaining part of my professional and creative life.

* * *

Because Philip K. Dick embraces the unpredictable, his fiction is more easily experienced than described. He has written a very large number of novels (probably too many), almost all of them shorter than two hundred pages. Typically, he manages to cram a dozen characters and an unbelievably elaborate plot into each one.

Dick's science fiction situations and devices allow him to express a radical 1960's sensibility. Frequently, his scene is a postwar U.S., thinly populated with humans and various non-humans (aliens, robots, and androids). The human protagonist struggles against an alien or human establishment that is nowhere and everywhere. Indeed, the cues shift rapidly as to what is "reality." The reader suddenly realizes that the entire situation is directly the opposite of what he thought it was. Yet Dick preserves thematic consistency from book to book. Events in his universe are linked by the Jung-Pauli principle of "synchronicity" rather than by cause and effect. Random actions succeed best; dogmatic predictions are unreliable. In *Our Friends from Frolix 8* Amos Ild, the world's most intelligent human mutation, uses all available data to make a prediction which turns out to be completely incorrect. A 16-year-old girl named Charley makes the correct prediction, based on no data at all.

Dick is opposed to all self-stabilizing systems and homeostatic devices. All of Dick's environment is quasi-alive, and none of it can be trusted. In *The Game-Players of Titan* elevators and automatic cabs talk back to their human operators and may or may not obey the orders given to them. Dick distrusts all politics, too. He is obsessed with German fascism. *The Man in the High Castle* concerns an alternate universe in which Germany and Japan won World War II. In *The Unteleported Man* New Germany controls the U.N., and unsuspecting emigrants are being teleported to an interstellar concentration camp. Dick is also anti-communist. In "Faith of Our Fathers" the reality cues shift, and the Chairman Mao figure, the Absolute Benefactor, is no longer a politician appearing on TV every night but a God of disorder and death. Yet in *The Game-Players of Titan* the most dangerous alien antagonists are the moderates rather than the extremists. Dick, in fact, tends to distrust all groups, placing his reliance on individuals and their ability to empathize with a few others near them.

Dick also distrusts categories and the classifications that people presume to put upon other people. In *Clans of the Alphane Moon* Earth classifies certain people as "insane" and ships them off to a satellite, where they form clans according to their type of mental illness. The conflicts between schizophrenics, paranoics, and melancholics are bizarre, but these people are sane in comparison with the social workers sent to examine them. Dick joins the skepticism of the radical psychologists in questioning whether there is such a thing as mental illness.

All of Dick's judgments, positive and negative, are placed in ironic or humorous settings. Empathy can be dialed on a machine in *Do Androids Dream of Electric Sheep?* and empathy for animals, all species of which are nearly extinct and hence enormously expensive, blocks out empathy for "chickenheads," human beings below a certain I.Q. level. Conversely, Dick often reminds us that there were good Germans, and he extends his own empathy to the establishment as well as to the oppressed, giving extensive consideration to the points of view of the Japanese Trade Minister in *The Man in the High Castle* and Council Chairman Gram in *Our Friends from Frolix 8*.

All of Dick's novels are, in a sense, parts of a single work. We tend to remember brilliant, surreal bits and pieces rather than particular novels. We may remember the security officer in *Eye in the Sky*, a solid American Legionaire who makes accusations of communism but is himself a communist. We may remember the "padre-booth" in *Galactic Pot-Healer*, in which one can dial Zen, Puritan Ethic, Roman Catholic, Allah, or Judaism. We may remember that drugs are legal but alcohol is "alc" in *Our Friends from Frolix 8*, with sips of beer cherished as if they were reefer puffs. No one is more fearsome or potentially violent that the alc addict. We may remember, in the same book, that God is indeed dead—a carcass of Being once able to create worlds and endow them with life has been discovered floating in outer space. Most of all, perhaps, we may remember the novelist secluded in the Rockies in *The Man in the High Castle*, doing the I Ching to construct a subversive novel in which Germany and Japan lost the war.

Dick remains a prolific writer of science-fiction stories and novels. Increasingly of late he has let his irony drop. In *A Scanner Darkly* Dick's only futuristic device is a scramble suit to change the identity of police agents, and this is little more than a correlative for schizophrenia. Previously in his fiction Dick had implied sympathy for the drug culture, but *A Scanner Darkly* delivers an overt polemic against drug abuse. In his recent collection, *The Golden Man*, Dick also moves away from irony by including notes to each story which explain his meaning. "Pre-Persons," the last story in the collection, is another diatribe without irony, this time against abortion. In his short stories Dick often stays closer to science-fiction convention, with space wars and Mars colonization. On the other hand, some of his best stories, such as "The King of the Elves" and "Small Town," are not science fiction at all but fantasy. "Mold of Yancy" is Dick at his satirical best, exposing the mechanism of social control through bland paternalism. In "Not by Its Cover" the living fur on book covers is able to change the contents of the books.

A major value of Dick's is empathy, even for his villains; but he seems unable to extend empathy to his women characters, who are characteristically either nagging housewives or sex symbols, but who in either case lack independent consciousness.

There is no mistaking a Philip K. Dick novel. To be sure, there are echoes of Pirandello and Kafka. But Dick has done more than translate their themes to an American setting. To Dick, American life is a paranoid game with unknown but unfair rules. Yet it is possible to win this game, by bluffing and cheating and riding chance. Dick himself has said that his credo is contained in this paragraph, from *The Three Stigmata of Palmer Eldritch*: "I mean, after all; you have to consider we're only made out of dust. That's admittedly not much to go on and we shouldn't forget that. But even considering, I mean it's sort of a bad beginning, we're not doing too bad. So I personally have faith that even in this lousy situation we're faced with we can make it. You get me?"

—Curtis C. Smith

DICKENS, Monica (Enid). British. Born in London, 10 May 1915. Educated at St. Paul's Girls' School, London. Married Commander Roy Olin Stratton, U.S. Navy, in 1951; two daughters. Worked as a maid and cook in private houses; as a factory worker, nurse, and with the Samaritans. Columnist, *Woman's Own*, London, 1946-65. M.B.E. (Member, Order of the British Empire), 1981. Address: 237 Main Street, Post Office Box 386, North Falmouth, Massachusetts 02556, U.S.A.

PUBLICATIONS

Novels

Mariana. London, Joseph, 1940; as *The Moon Was Low*, New York, Harper, 1940.
The Fancy. London, Joseph, 1943; as *Edward's Fancy*, New York, Harper, 1944.
Thursday Afternoons. London, Joseph, 1945.
The Happy Prisoner. London, Joseph, 1946; Philadelphia, Lippincott, 1947.
Joy and Josephine. London, Joseph, 1948; as *Portobello Road*, Toronto, Joseph, 1948.
Flowers on the Grass. London, Joseph, 1949; New York, McGraw Hill, 1950.
No More Meadows. London, Joseph, 1953; as *The Nightingales Are Singing*, Boston, Little Brown, 1953.
The Winds of Heaven. London, Joseph, and New York, Coward McCann, 1955.
The Angel in the Corner. London, Joseph, 1956; New York, Coward McCann, 1957.
Man Overboard. London, Joseph, 1958; New York, Coward McCann, 1959.
The Heart of London. London, Joseph, and New York, Coward McCann, 1961.
Cobbler's Dream. London, Joseph, and New York, Coward McCann, 1963.
Kate and Emma. London, Heinemann, 1964; New York, Coward McCann, 1965.
The Room Upstairs. London, Heinemann, and New York, Doubleday, 1966.
The Landlord's Daughter. London, Heinemann, and New York, Doubleday, 1968.
The Listeners. London, Heinemann, 1970; as *The End of the Line*, New York, Doubleday, 1970.
Last Year When I Was Young. London, Heinemann, 1974.

Other

One Pair of Hands (autobiography). London, Joseph, and New York, Harper, 1939.
One Pair of Feet (autobiography). London, Joseph, and New York, Harper, 1942.
Yours Sincerely (*Woman's Own* articles), with Beverley Nichols. London, Newnes, 1949.
My Turn to Make the Tea (autobiography). London, Joseph, 1951.
My Fair Lady (juvenile). New York, Four Winds, 1967.
The Great Fire (juvenile). London, Kaye and Ward, 1970; New York, Doubleday, 1973.
The House at World's End (juvenile). London, Heinemann, 1970; New York, Doubleday, 1971.
The Great Escape (juvenile). London, Kaye and Ward, 1971.
Summer at World's End (juvenile). London, Heinemann, 1971; New York, Doubleday, 1972.
Follyfoot (juvenile). London, Heinemann, 1971.
World's End in Winter (juvenile). London, Heinemann, 1972; New York, Doubleday, 1973.
Dora at Follyfoot (juvenile). London, Heinemann, 1972.
Cape Cod. New York, Viking Press, 1972.
Follyfoot Farm (omnibus; juvenile). London, Heinemann, 1973.

Spring Comes to World's End (juvenile). London, Heinemann, 1973.
Talking of Horses. London, Heinemann, 1973; Boston, Little Brown, 1974.
The Heroes of Follyfoot (juvenile). London, Heinemann, 1975.
Stranger at Follyfoot (juvenile). London, Heinemann, 1976.
An Open Book (autobiography). London, Heinemann, and New York, Mayflower, 1978.

Editor, with Rosemary Sutcliff, *Is Anyone There?* (on the Samaritans). London, Penguin, 1978.

*

Monica Dickens comments:

(1972) My novels are mostly based on my own firsthand experience. Before I was married and had children, I used to go and do the jobs or join the communities in which I was interested. Now, not being able to throw up everything for an idea and start a new chapter of life every few years, I work more like a journalist, and research by observing and listening. Perhaps it will be helpful to name the backgrounds which led to each book:

Mariana. The first novel everyone writes sooner or later, about one's own childhood and growing up.

The Fancy. I worked in a factory that repaired Spitfires during the Battle of Britain.

Thursday Afternoons. I was a hospital nurse for most of the war.

The Happy Prisoner. I nursed a patient who was adjusting to amputation.

Joy and Josephine. I used my own background of Notting Hill and the Portobello road where I was born and brought up.

Flowers on the Grass. I did many of the various jobs that the central character tries (holiday camp, companion to sick boy, teaching, etc.)

No More Meadows. I used my own experiences in marrying into the US Navy and joining Washington Service society.

The Winds of Heaven. Observation of changing family patterns in which there is no room for the ageing parent.

Man Overboard. Observation of forcibly retired Service people.

The Heart of London. My own background again, of Notting Hill, plus months of research among the black community, social workers, police, teachers, churches, road construction gangs, midwives.

Cobbler's Dream. My own experiences with horses. Plus extensive work with the RSPCA.

Kate and Emma. Extensive field work with the NSPCC and juvenile courts.

The Room Upstairs. My own family experiences with the problems and terrors of an old lady, and with a nearby house in Massachusetts, USA, bisected by a highway.

The Listeners. My own experiences as a Samaritan.

My aim is to entertain, rather than instruct. I want readers to recognize life in my books, either as they know it, or as they are able to understand it, however alien the situation.

Increasingly, as I grow more prolific, my writing is for me the greater part of life. I live fully, surrounded by people and animals, but find more and more reality and interest in the people and worlds I create. Writing is a cop-out. An excuse to live perpetually in fantasy land, where you can create, direct and watch the products of your own head. Very selfish.

* * *

Monica Dickens's autobiographical books belong to a genre popular in the late 1930's and 1940's: amusing, mildly satiric, loosely organized personal experiences, usually written by a woman, a shrewd observer of the eccentricities of commonplace people, adroit at illuminating character with sudden flashes of insight, never herself top girl in any group, but always more radical and socially-conscious than most of the people she works or lives among. Thus, the heroine of *One Pair of Hands*, after picaresque adventures as a cook-general for a Dickensian series of employers, originally ended by making a speech at a Household Fair, suggesting improvements in the treatment of servants. With rueful irony she reports audience reaction: " 'Words, words, words, and when you think of it, what did all that talk amount to?' "

This book gave Dickens the episodic structure for later plots as in *Flowers on the Grass*, *Man Overboard*, and *Last Year When I Was Young*, whose low-key heroes go from job to job, each with a cluster of satirically sketched personalities. Another favourite, closely related pattern, the concurrent picaresque, so to speak, is an intercutting from group to group of persons tenuously related by a common character as in *The Heart of London* and *The Listeners*. The incidents of these plots are often conventionally melodramatic, although they seem less stereotypic in her later novels where violence arises from urban slums and is the self-damage of the life-damaged.

Dickens, while prodigal in characterisation, has always been economical in subject matter. Her own experience while training as a nurse has, for example, produced both the autobiographical *One Pair of Feet* and the novel *Thursday Afternoons*, in which Dr. Sheppard, trapped by his own bedside manner, longs for active naval duty in the imminent Second World War. In *Flowers on the Grass* Daniel's rebellious adventures include a hospital episode in which Nurse Saunders recalls Nurse Dickens. Elizabeth (*The Happy Prisoner*) is a private nurse who married her patient; May (*The Heart of London*) is a district midwife who saves her best friend's premature illegitimate baby; the central character of *Last Year When I Was Young* is a male nurse. Even when it serves no useful plot function, a hospital may be a part of a character's background as it is in Christine Cope's (*No More Meadows*).

Likewise Dickens's wartime factory work provided material for *The Fancy* and for a long episode in *Joy and Josephine*, whose heroine prefers making airplanes to dilettante canteen service. Other books draw on Dickens's experiences as a reporter and as a Samaritan. Readers interested in seeing the facts of her fictions will find a great deal of material in Dickens's recent unfictionalized autobiography, *An Open Book*.

Certain characters also reappear: e.g., the slightly feeble-minded spinster, the married man with an affair, and especially the one-legged or lame man, who may be as engaging as Oliver (*Happy Prisoner*) or as selfish as David (*The Fancy*). In another group of novels these cripples become girls in wheelchairs or crippled boys. Naval officers recur, sometimes as minor as Uncle Tim (*Mariana*), married to "a walking Gieve's," or as crucial as Commander Vinson Gaegler, who inflicts American naval protocol on his English bride (*No More Meadows*). In *Man Overboard*, Commander Ben Francis, R.N., dismissed as redundant in postwar cutbacks, tries to find a civilian career. From this novel on, Dickens has generally turned more explicitly to social or socio-psychological themes: racial tension, schools, urban redevelopment, perversion, alcoholism (*Heart of London*); child abuse (*Kate and Emma*); old age (*The Winds of Heaven* and *The Room Upstairs*); the feeble-minded, the suicidal, the alone (*The Listeners*). Here she is interested in strange emotional liaisons, often touching but also grotesque. Emma Bullock, daughter of a Children's Court Magistrate, becomes the "blood comrade" of Kate, a mistreated adolescent who in turn beats and chains her own scapegoat child. The vulgarly sinister Dorothy Grue (*Room Upstairs*) adores Roger, a budgerigar. Charlotte (*The Landlords's Daughter*) welcomes Peter as a lover although he has killed and dismembered a former love, whose incriminating hank of hair Charlotte hides.

These books are grim, unlike the earlier, overflowing novels for which Dickens drew most heavily on family personalities and experiences. Minor personages of the later books are still likely to be humour characters, but their ruling passions lack ebullience—perhaps because the eccentricities of urban poverty, however compassioned, are rarely amiable ones. Still, all her novels show her eye for visual detail, her understanding of absurdities and values, petty satisfactions and hugged-tight rancors, and her assumption that not even the most minor and peripheral characters need lack identity and idiosyncrasy.

—Jane W. Stedman

DIDION, Joan. American. Born in Sacramento, California, 5 December 1934. Educated at the University of California, Berkeley, B.A. 1956. Married the writer John Gregory Dunne in 1964; one daughter. Associate Feature Editor, *Vogue* magazine, New York, 1956-63; Columnist, *Saturday Evening Post*, Philadelphia; Contributing Editor, *National Review*, New York. Recipient: *Vogue* Prix de Paris, 1956; Bread Loaf Writers Conference Fellowship, 1963; American Academy Morton Dauwen Zabel Award, 1979. Agent: Wallace and Sheil Agency, 177 East 70th Street, New York, New York 10021, U.S.A.

PUBLICATIONS

Novels

Run River. New York, Obolensky, 1963; London, Cape, 1964.
Play It As It Lays. New York, Farrar Straus, 1970; London, Weidenfeld and Nicolson, 1971.
A Book of Common Prayer. New York, Simon and Schuster, and London, Weidenfeld and Nicolson, 1977.

Uncollected Short Stories

"Coming Home," in *Saturday Evening Post* (Philadelphia), 11 July 1964.
"The Welfare Island Ferry," in *Harper's Bazaar* (New York), June 1965.
"When Did the Music Come This Way? Children Dear, Was It Yesterday?," in *Denver Quarterly*, Winter 1967.
"California Blue," in *Harper's* (New York), October 1976.

Plays

Screenplays, with John Gregory Dunne: *Panic in Needle Park*, 1971; *A Star Is Born*, 1977.

Other

Slouching Towards Bethlehem (essays). New York, Farrar Straus, 1968; London, Deutsch, 1969.
The White Album. New York, Simon and Schuster, and London, Weidenfeld and Nicolson, 1979.

*

Critical Study: *Joan Didion* by Katherine Usher Henderson, New York, Ungar, 1981.

* * *

Though very much a California writer, Joan Didion is not provincial. She uses her immediate milieu to envision, simultaneously, the last stand of America's frontier values pushed insupportably to their limits and the manifestations of craziness and malaise which have initiated their finale. And while her novels invite a feminist critique, her understanding of sexual politics is beyond ideology. Each of her major characters struggles with a demonic nihilism which is corroding the individual, the family, and the social organism. Affluent and glib, her people endure a relatively privileged despair which may initially suggest a narrow purview. But a considerable ability to render social and physical environment broadly is saving.

In addition to dialogue which rivals Albee's, Didion's finest gifts are her talents for keeping clean of self-indulgence and for realizing a moral dimension in lives veering *inevitably* out of control. Certain recurring features of her work constitute leitmotifs germane to their interpretation. These include newspaper headlines, phrases from popular ballads, cinematic jargon, snakes, and the genteel Christian educations of her females. All pertain to the disintegration of an orderly past into a chaotic present, perhaps Didion's most irreducible theme.

Run River follows the eroding marriage of Everett and Lily (Knight) McClellan through 20 years. Concomitantly, it chronicles the collapse of a way of life and the betrayal of the land which had given an epoch its apparent order. Ryder Channing enters the McClellans' lives when he courts Everett's sister. Though Martha never misconceives his selfishness and venality, she kills herself when Channing quits her. Lily's many unfeeling liaisons express her isolation from her husband and fatally draw her into Channing's increasingly nihilistic orbit. In his futile attachment to their Northern California ranch, Everett lives at a tangent to Lily's very genuine crises. When Everett kills Channing, it is not simply because Channing and his sleazy economic machinations are the wave of California's future, the perverse energy which turns redwoods to taco stands. Everett's suicide ends an era. But Lily's justifiable conclusion that Channing is guiltless, because he is a "papier-mâché Mephistopholes," implies Didion's conviction that, however tawdry this interloper, he has only played upon a native tendency to ruin. Lily's survival implies her relatively greater, if tainted, adaptability and strength.

Play It As It Lays presents a culture beyond this metamorphosis. Consequently, it is set in Los Angeles where those tacky schemes of Ryder Channing are a *fait accompli* defining a whole state of being. Maria Wyeth's past is utterly disintegrated, her childhood home in Nevada having been detonated to oblivion by nuclear testing. Moribund, her marriage thins to extinction. With her brain-damaged daughter institutionalized and herself facing an abortion, Maria aimlessly drives the freeways to evade a ubiquitous dread.

Though Didion never politicizes abortion, she is morally obsessed with it. Lily and Maria endure the experience, but the treatment is fuller and more alarming here. A last straw, it pushes Maria closer to her counterpart and nemesis, B Z, another instance of the modern demonic. Associated throughout with the serpent, this Hollywood Beelzebub tries with conscious nihilism to exploit Maria's drinking and sexual looseness. Maria's father, taking life as a crap game, had offered his case as a gambler and a cynic: "it goes as it lays, don't do it the hard way"; "overturning a rock [is] apt to reveal a rattlesnake." For Maria, this worldview is an affliction of passivity and anxiety, until she finally manages the small victory of rejecting B Z's invitation to join him in his successful suicide.

With *A Book of Common Prayer*, Didion suggests that the country is in the throes of metastisized California. So she invents an archetypal banana republic devoid of history. Boca Grande ("big mouth") yaps chamber of commerce propaganda and ingests North American residue. Charlotte Douglas, a San Francisco Pollyanna, weathers two difficult marriages: to a brilliant, callous and cynical opportunist, and to a well-heeled radical lawyer. What she doesn't quite weather is the loss (à la Patty Hearst) of her daughter, Marin, "to history." Marin's situation is really very simple. She suffers from severe cases of banality and political jargon. But her new way of life tests to the limit Charlotte's too selective memory of the girl in Easter dresses. With the FBI agents who litter her house and the futility of her marriages at her back, she makes it to Boca Grande and a marginal life of good works for the suffering masses. She continues to put the best light on dark matters: stateside things like her brother's miserable existence on the old homestead in Hollister; Grande things like the Army's confiscation, for profit, of the people's cholera serum. She becomes oddly Sisyphean but holds out for the idea that we all remember what we need. Charlotte dies in the crossfire between Army and revolutionary forces, the guerilleros having decided that for once their insurrection is not going to be a State-sponsored melodrama. We come to like her and to wonder about the future of such folks as the Simbianese Liberation Army.

—David M. Heaton

DOCTOROW, E(dgar) L(aurence). American. Born in New York City, 6 January 1931. Educated at Kenyon College, Gambier, Ohio, A.B. (honors) in philosophy 1952; Columbia University, New York, 1952-53. Served in the United States Army, 1953-55. Married Helen Setzer in 1954; two daughters and one son. Editor, New American Library, New York, 1960-64; Editor in Chief, 1964-69, and Publisher, 1969, Dial Press, New York. Since 1971, Member of the Faculty, Sarah Lawrence College, Bronxville, New York. Writer-in-Residence, University of California, Irvine, 1969-70; Creative Writing Fellow, Yale School of Drama, New Haven, Connecticut, 1974-75. Director, Authors Guild of America, and American P.E.N. Recipient: Guggenheim Fellowship, 1972; Creative Artists Public Service grant, 1973; National Book Critics Circle Award, 1976; American Academy award, 1976. L.H.D.: Kenyon College, 1976. Address: 170 Broadview Avenue, New Rochelle, New York 10804, U.S.A.

PUBLICATIONS

Novels

Welcome to Hard Times. New York, Simon and Schuster, 1960; as *Bad Man from Bodie*, London, Deutsch, 1961.
Big as Life. New York, Simon and Schuster, 1966.
The Book of Daniel. New York, Random House, 1971; London, Macmillan, 1972.
Ragtime. New York, Random House, and London, Macmillan, 1975.
Loon Lake. New York, Random House, and London, Macmillan, 1980.

Uncollected Short Stories

"The Songs of Billy Bathgate," in *New American Review 2*, edited by Theodore Solotaroff. New York, New American Library, 1968.
"The Pyramid Club," in *American Review 21*, edited by Theodore Solotaroff. New York, Bantam, 1975.

Play

Drinks Before Dinner (produced New York, 1978). New York, Random House, 1979; London, Macmillan, 1980.

* * *

E. L. Doctorow cannot be readily assimilated to any single school of contemporary fiction; rather, his works synthesize various important strains in post-modernist writing. Doctorow's formal inventiveness, wit, and covertly apocalyptic philosophy link him with such practitioners of metafiction as Pynchon, Barthelme, and Barth; his fascination with "facts"—invented or real—links him with new journalists and nonfiction novelists. But Doctorow decries the privatism of much contemporary fiction, which, he says, is lacking in "social reverberation." He is a serious historical novelist who weds experimental techniques with strong political convictions in an exploration of the historical roots of contemporary America.

Welcome to Hard Times, Doctorow's first novel, adopts the format of the Western to examine the illusory foundations of the American myth of progress. The town of Hard Times, devastated in one day by the rampaging Bad Man from Bodie, rebuilds itself and looks forward to a thriving future—only to be destroyed once again by its implacable antagonist. While in one sense the Bad Man exemplifies an archetypal evil that triumphs over weak humanity, in another sense the parable's judgments are specifically historical. Insofar as the town—read, the nation—is animated primarily by mutual exploitation, competition, and dreams of "hitting pay dirt," it is disarmed in its struggle with time and nature. Doctorow's implied critique of American false consciousness is reinforced by the first-person narration of Blue, the well-intentioned but shallow mayor, who chronicles the town's fate in his bookkeeping ledgers. Profit and loss, it would seem, provide no framework for grasping the realities of historical process. In *Big as Life*, a science-fiction satire, Doctorow restates this apocalyptic theme: New York City is shown in the grip of Brobdignagian monsters that threaten it with extinction, and the question of nuclear holocaust hovers in the not too distant background.

The Book of Daniel explores the recent past in greater depth and specificity and with greater formal complexity: it is Doctorow's first major work. Revolving around the fates of a family named the Isaacsons—who clearly resemble the Rosenbergs—the novel examines the lies, myths, and historical realities that shaped American consciousness from the McCarthy period to the 1960's. Structurally and thematically, the novel probes the relationship between past and present, as the Old Left is compared with the New, the parents with the children. Daniel Lewin/Isaacson's search for the truth about his parents is at once personal and general; his dissertation ("book") is an anatomy of contemporary culture and an exorcism of his own tortured past. The novel's form aptly bears out this dialectical theme: the blend of first-and third-person narration and the shifts in chronology underline the interplay of past and present, public and private, while the finale—which draws together Susan Isaacson's death in 1968, the parents' electrocution a decade and a half before, and Daniel's confrontation with his parents' betrayer in the mindless wilderness of Disneyland—effectively conveys the human cost of American historical myopia.

Ragtime is generally acknowledged to be Doctorow's tour de force. While Doctorow recreates the atmosphere of the Ragtime era with wit, accuracy, and a winsome nostalgia, he also examines its legacy for the present. Like the invented characters in much 19th-century historical fiction, Doctorow's invented characters represent social types who signal the dominant historical movements of the age—and thus undercut sentimental and complacent myths about American democracy and justice. The anonymous immigrant family reveals the harsh realities of working-class oppression. The anonymous middle-class WASP family exemplifies the impact of historical change upon the "mainstream" of American life—one direction represented by Mother's growing sexual liberation, another by Father's development of his fireworks factory into a munitions plant. Coalhouse Walker, a black ragtime pianist who is the novel's central character, confronts the racist establishment and is executed for his pride: his tale not only exposes some roots of contemporary racism but also (through its ingenious parallel with Kleist's *Michael Kohlhaas*) demonstrates the clashes that inevitably erupt when power relations are challenged by rising social forces. The public historical figures who appear in the novel—Emma Goldman, Evelyn Nesbit, Harry K. Thaw, Freud, Jung, Morgan, and Ford, to name a few—underline Doctorow's satire and introduce a note of hilarity. By placing real people in patently invented situations, indeed, Doctorow intentionally blurs the line between fact and fiction and thus leads us to question not only the content of the nation's historical myths but also the means by which these myths are constituted. In response to a fetishistic society that, Doctorow says, "deifies facts," he wittily proclaims the superiority of the imagination in arriving at a comprehensive vision of historical truth. Asked whether Morgan and Ford ever met, Doctorow has replied, "They have now."

While Doctorow's audacious confrontation with the substance and method of history is impressive, this last remark suggests the basis upon which his work is open to criticism: if historical truth is chimerical, then change is merely epiphenomenonal, and progress is only a bourgeois myth that must be lampooned. Does Doctorow's breezy cynicism thus undercut the force of his social and historical critique? *Welcome to Hard Times* and *The Book of Daniel* can be seen as expressions of a cyclical and absurdist view of history, while *Ragtime* can be accused of reducing history to pastiche—as Doctorow puts it, "a tune on a player piano." Certainly Doctorow's intense awareness of historical injustice and obfuscation may yet take him to the threshhold of absurdism, as is indicated in his recent play *Drinks Before Dinner*, where he examines the intense alienation and hollow liberalism of a group of middle-class intellectuals.

In *Loon Lake* Doctorow steps back somewhat from the threshold of the absurd and re-enters the realm of concrete historicity; but is is questionable whether this return is accompanied by a revived grasp of essential social realities. Returning to the themes of class struggle and economic and political injustice that animated *The Book of Daniel* and *Ragtime*, Doctorow proposes a biting portrait of the United States during the Depression. His ruthless and manipulative hero, Joseph Korzeniowski (shades of Joseph Conrad?), exemplifies the human cost that is involved in the capitalist scramble from rags to riches; his hero's counterpart, the failed poet Warren Penfield, poses an unflattering image of the romantic alternative. The novel's hybrid locale—part grim mining towns, part the rich man's Adirondack paradise of Loon Lake—underlines the breadth of Doctorow's social critique. Indeed, in one sense *Loon Lake* undertakes a more comprehensive exploration of the nation's past than any of the earlier novels, insofar as Doctorow refrains from the easier strategies of parodying national myth, evoking historical echoes, or playing fast and loose with facts, and instead fleshes out a past era by creating a microcosmic fictive world. *Loon Lake* also expands upon the technical achievement of Doctorow's earlier work, combining the rapid stylistic pace of *Ragtime* with the complex alternation of chronology and point of view of *The Book of Daniel*. Where *Loon Lake* does not represent a movement ahead for Doctorow is in its essential failure of moral energy. While the novel is an exploration of national ethics that relies upon characterization to achieve its ends, Joe Korzeniowski and Warren Penfield constitute a composite protagonist with whom it is impossible to feel sympathy or even concern; Daniel Lewin/Isaacson and Coalhouse Walker involve the reader much more fully in Doctorow's implied system of beliefs. This weakness of characterization corresponds to another problem in *Loon Lake*—namely, its lack of a grand theme or even of a grand moment. The novel reveals a multitude of social ills rife with novelistic possibilities; but the suspenseful ending is contrived, and the hero's moral erosion is fundamentally uninteresting. The book's breathtaking style and complicated temporal structure cannot compensate for what we sense as an ethical absence: like the expanding circles produced by a loon's predatory descent into a lake, the novel's concentric circles of chronology and perspective ripple outward from a center that is disturbingly calm.

—Barbara Foley

DONLEAVY, J(ames) P(atrick). Irish. Born in Brooklyn, New York, United States, 23 April 1926; became an Irish citizen, 1967. Educated at preparatory school, New York, Trinity College, Dublin. Served in the United States Navy during World War II. Married 1)Valerie Heron (divorced), one son and one daughter; 2)Mary Wilson Price in 1970, one daughter. Recipient: *Evening Standard* award, for drama, 1961; Brandeis University Creative Arts award, 1961; American Academy award, 1975. Address: Levington Park, Mullingar, County Westmeath, Ireland.

PUBLICATIONS

Novels

The Ginger Man. Paris, Olympia Press, and London, Spearman, 1955; New York, McDowell Obolensky, 1958; complete edition, London, Corgi, 1963; New York, Delacorte Press, 1965.

A Singular Man. Boston, Little Brown, 1963; London, Bodley Head, 1964.

The Saddest Summer of Samuel S. New York, Delacorte Press, 1966; London, Eyre and Spottiswoode, 1967.

The Beastly Beatitudes of Balthazar B. New York, Delacorte Press, 1968; London, Eyre and Spottiswoode, 1969.

The Onion Eaters. New York, Delacorte Press, and London, Eyre and Spottiswoode, 1971.

A Fairy Tale of New York. New York, Delacorte Press, and London, Eyre Methuen, 1973.

The Destinies of Darcy Dancer, Gentleman. New York, Delacorte Press, 1977; London, Allen Lane, 1978.

Schultz. New York, Delacorte Press, 1979; London, Allen Lane, 1980.

Short Stories

Meet My Maker the Mad Molecule. Boston, Little Brown, 1964; London, Bodley Head, 1965.

Uncollected Short Stories

"A Friend" and "In My Peach Shoes," in *Queen* (London), 7 April 1965.

"Rite of Love," in *Playboy* (Chicago), October 1968.

"A Fair Festivity," in *Playboy* (Chicago), November 1968.

"A Small Human Being," in *Saturday Evening Post* (Philadelphia), 16 November 1968.

Plays

The Ginger Man, adaptation of his own novel (produced London and Dublin, 1959; New York, 1963). New York, Random House, 1961; as *What They Did in Dublin, with The Ginger Man: A Play*, London, MacGibbon and Kee, 1962.

Fairy Tales of New York (produced Croydon, Surrey, 1960; London, 1961). London, Penguin, and New York, Random House, 1961.

A Singular Man, adaptation of his own novel (produced Cambridge and London, 1964; Westport, Connecticut, 1967). London, Bodley Head, 1965.

The Plays of J.P. Donleavy (includes *The Ginger Man, Fairy Tales of New York, A Singular Man, The Saddest Summer of Samuel S*). New York, Delacorte Press, 1972; London, Penguin, 1974.

Radio Play: *Helen*, 1956.

Other

The Unexpurgated Code: A Complete Manual of Survival and Manners, drawings by the author. New York, Delacorte Press, and London, Wildwood House, 1975.

*

Critical Studies: *J.P. Donleavy: The Style of His Sadness and Humor* by Charles G. Masinton, Bowling Green, Ohio, Popular Press, 1975.

* * *

J.P. Donleavy, perhaps because of his Transatlantic and multinational character, defies easy classification and suffers from a certain critical neglect. His books blend some of the special literary qualities of all three—American, English, Irish—national traditions. He has a typically American zaniness, an anarchic and sometimes lunatic comic sense mingled with an undertone of despair. He possesses an English accuracy of eye and ear for the look and sound of things, for the subtle determinants of class in appearances and accents, a Jamesian grasp of density of specification. Finally, his novels display an Irish wit, energy, and vulgarity as well as a distinctly Irish sense of brooding and melancholy. Like any Irish writer, he is inevitably compared to Joyce, but in this case the comparison is appropriate—his tone, voice, and prose style have the comic brevity and particularity of many of Leopold Bloom's sections in *Ulysses*.

Ever since his great success with *The Ginger Man*, Donleavy has followed a sometimes distressing sameness of pattern and subject in his books, whatever their individual differences may be. Roughly, they are serio-comic picaresques which mix a close attention to verifiable reality with an increasingly outrageous sense of fantasy. Although the fantasy is always strongly sexual—and Donleavy writes about sex with refreshingly carnal gusto—it also dwells on the sensuousness, even perhaps the eroticism, of all materiality. When he sinks his teeth into the dense texture of life, Donleavy imparts an almost sexual appetite to his prose, glorying in the things of this world, to the virtual exclusion of all else. He writes with the same zest about such matters as gentlemen's clothing, liquor, food, tobacco, women's bodies, the interior and exterior decorations of luxurious homes, all of the lovingly itemized concretions that represent the good life. In his most recent novel, *Schultz*, Donleavy records, with no diminution in his sense of awe, the dithyrambic praise of the appetitive view of life as fully and joyously as in *The Ginger Man*.

Because of the basic similarity of characters, events, and structures of his books, they often seem at first a mere continual rewriting of the first and most famous novel. They pile, often rather randomly and plotlessly, episode upon outrageous episode, repeat the scenes of sex, of comic violence, of pratfalls and ridicule, and often appear to run out of steam rather than end. Few of his books seem to have a real sense of closure: the protagonist most often is left, like the Ginger Man, suspended midway between triumph and ignominy, humor and sadness, still completely himself but also touched by despair and defeat. Their constant, most powerful note is elegiac—the protagonist may continue on his crazy way but he inevitably recognizes the most final and undeniable fact of all, the fact of death. The last perception of Sebastian Dangerfield in *The Ginger Man* is a vision of horses: "And I said they are running out to death which is with some soul and their eyes are mad and teeth out." In *The Destinies of Darcy Dancer, Gentleman*, the fox hunt, which runs throughout the book, provides the final metaphors of mortality—"Till the Huntsman's blowing his long slow notes. Turn home. At end of day." The one book that mixes the perception of death with some of the jaunty, lifeloving energy that pervades all of his novels is *Schultz*, Donleavy's "Jewish" novel about a theatrical producer in London that caps the entire canon of Henry James in its portrait of an innocent American abroad. Contemplating the wreckage of all his lunatic schemes, Schultz contemplates what is, for him, the structure of the universe. Out of his recognition of an enigma of infinitude and fatality, he concludes, "But if you can balance on top. You can not only scratch your fanny but touch the moon. But don't count on anything."

Like all good comic writers, Donleavy's vision is embedded in a dark view of the world; amid all his embracing vitality lies a perception of the need for comedy. His art derives from that perception—under the fully realized surfaces of life lie fear, guilt, and the dread of death. His books quite properly partake of the three traditions with which he has associated himself; all three converge in his mixture of solemnity and humor and in the same mixture of resolution and disintegration which invariably forms his conclusions. Life loving and deathfearing, his novels end, at best, in a resounding "if." You may touch the moon, but don't count on anything. As Schultz responds to that notion, "You bet / Your sweet / Rabbi ass / I won't." Good advice from a widely celebrated but insufficiently known novelist, and entirely appropriate as a commentary on the body of his works.

—George Grella

DRABBLE, Margaret. British. Born in Sheffield, Yorkshire, 5 June 1939; sister of A.S. Byatt, *q.v.* Educated at the Mount School, York; Newnham College, Cambridge, B.A. (honours) 1960. Married Clive Swift in 1960 (divorced, 1975), two sons and one daughter. Deputy Chairman, 1979-80, and since 1980, Chairman, National Book League. Recipient: Rhys Memorial Prize, 1966; Black Memorial Prize, 1968; E.M. Forster Award (USA), 1973. D.H.L.: University of Sheffield, 1976. C.B.E. (Commander, Order of the British Empire), 1980. Lives in London. Agent: A.D. Peters, 10 Buckingham Street, London WC2N 6BU, England.

PUBLICATIONS

Novels

A Summer Bird-Cage. London, Weidenfeld and Nicolson, 1963; New York, Morrow, 1964.
The Garrick Year. London, Weidenfeld and Nicolson, 1964; New York, Morrow, 1965.
The Millstone. London, Weidenfeld and Nicolson, 1965; New York, Morrow, 1966; as *Thank You All Very Much*, New York, New American Library, 1969.
Jerusalem the Golden. London, Weidenfeld and Nicolson, and New York, Morrow, 1967.
The Waterfall. London, Weidenfeld and Nicolson, and New York, Knopf, 1969.
The Needle's Eye. London, Weidenfeld and Nicolson, and New York, Knopf, 1972.
The Realms of Gold. London, Weidenfeld and Nicolson, and New York, Knopf, 1975.
The Ice Age. London, Weidenfeld and Nicolson, and New York, Knopf, 1977.
The Middle Ground. London, Weidenfeld and Nicolson, and New York, Knopf, 1980.

Short Stories

Penguin Modern Stories 3, with others. London, Penguin, 1969.

Uncollected Short Stories

"Hassan's Tower," in *Winter's Tales 12*, edited by A.D. Maclean, London, Macmillan, and New York, St. Martin's Press, 1966.
"A Voyage to Cytherea," in *Mademoiselle* (New York), December 1967.
"The Reunion," in *Winter's Tales 14*, edited by Kevin Crossley-Holland. London, Macmillan, and New York, St. Martin's Press, 1968.
"The Gifts of War," in *Winter's Tales 16*, edited by A.D. Maclean. London, Macmillan, 1970; New York, St. Martin's Press, 1971.
"Crossing the Alps," in *Mademoiselle* (New York), February 1971.
"A Successful Story," in *Spare Rib* (London), 1973.
"A Day in the Life of a Smiling Woman," in *In the Looking Glass*, edited by Nancy Dean and Myra Stark. New York, Putnam, 1977.

Plays

Bird of Paradise (produced London, 1969).

Screenplays: *Isadora*, with Melvyn Bragg and Clive Exton, 1969; *A Touch of Love*, 1969.

Television Play: *Laura*, 1964.

Other

Wordsworth. London, Evans, 1966; New York, Arco, 1969.
Arnold Bennett: A Biography. London, Weidenfeld and Nicolson, and New York, Knopf, 1974.

For Queen and Country: Britain in the Victorian Age (juvenile). London, Deutsch, 1978; New York, Seabury Press, 1979.
A Writer's Britain: Landscape in Literature. London, Thames and Hudson, and New York, Knopf, 1979.
Virginia Woolf: A Personal Debt. New York, Aloe, 1973.

Editor, with B.S. Johnson, *London Consequences* (a group novel). London, Greater London Arts Association, 1972.
Editor, *Lady Susan, The Watsons, Sanditon*, by Jane Austen. London, Penguin, 1974.
Editor, *The Genius of Thomas Hardy.* London, Weidenfeld and Nicolson, and New York, Knopf, 1976.
Editor, with Charles Osborne, *New Stories 1.* London, Arts Council, 1976.

*

Manuscript Collections: Boston University; University of Tulsa, Oklahoma.

Critical Studies: *Margaret Drabble: Puritanism and Permissiveness* by Valerie Grosvenor Myer, London, Vision Press, 1974; *The Novels of Margaret Drabble: Equivocal Figures* by Ellen Cronan Rose, London, Macmillan, 1980.

Margaret Drabble comments:

My books are I think mainly concerned with privilege, justice, and salvation. Equality and egalitarianism preoccupy me constantly, and not very hopefully. None of my books is about feminism, because my belief in the necessity for justice for women (which they don't get at the moment) is so basic that I never think of using it as a subject. It is part of a whole.

* * *

Margaret Drabble began novel writing early, after a brilliant undergraduate career at Cambridge and a short period as an actress. She is a deliberately conventional novelist who likes to write what she calls "a good traditional tale" and has no time for avant-garde innovations. Her principal model is George Eliot, and she writes in the tradition of English moral seriousness, of which George Eliot was such a distinguished exponent. The narrators of her novels, and the other characters in them, are constantly alert for signs of self-deception in themselves and of insincerity in other people; there is a prevalent atmosphere of sharp intelligence and of probing into motives. Drabble can display an agreeably incisive wit but rather little sense of humour. Her language is always sensitive to moral nuance, and its flexibility and subtlety are clearly indebted to Henry James.

Her first novel, *A Summer Bird-Cage*, was characteristically intelligent and witty, a study of two sisters, one clever and just down from Oxford, the other beautiful and on the point of marrying a fashionable novelist, and of the tensions between them. For a first novel, it was immensely accomplished though the moral sharpness often declined into a rather brittle cynicism. In *The Garrick Year* Drabble, who was married to an actor and lived for some time in Stratford-on-Avon, wrote entertainingly about actors and worked off some of her own ambivalent feelings about theatrical life. But more importantly she began to develop themes which have a genuine newness about them, despite her conservative attitudes to form and technique. The heroine of *The Garrick Year*, Emma, has two small children; at a crucial moment in the story she is suddenly distracted from her conversation with the theatrical producer with whom she is having a remarkably half-hearted affair, and plunges into a river to rescue one of her children. It is a vivid piece of writing, showing how a basic maternal instinct suddenly asserts itself through the more trivial sentiments that lie closer to the surface of Emma's life.

It is Drabble's particular contribution to the contemporary novel to have devised a genuinely new kind of character and predicament. There are, of course, innumerable women novelists who write from a feminine viewpoint, but Drabble differs from them in writing about young women who are not merely intelligent, educated, more or less attractive, and sharply observant. They are also mothers, and their involvement with their children cuts sharply across their concern with a career, and their desire for emotional freedom. For many novelists the emancipated woman and the mother are two sharply different types; Drabble has shown that in the modern world the two roles are often combined in the same person. Her third novel, *The Millstone*, is a lucid and moving exploration of this problem. Her heroine, Rosamund Stacey, is a dedicated scholar completing a Ph.D. thesis on Elizabethan poetry. After a single brief encounter with a young man she has no particularly strong feelings about, she becomes pregnant. She decides to have the baby and to keep it, to the general astonishment of her friends. Drabble gives a compelling account of the complexities of pregnancy, as they impinge on a young woman who is psychologically quite unprepared for them. In encounters with gynaecologists and midwives at an ante-natal clinic in a poor area of London, Rosamund not only discovers unexpected things about her own physical and psychological make-up, but by meeting the other expectant mothers who attend the clinic she is forced into an awareness of ordinary life and its attendant suffering, from which she had been cut off in the enclosed world of scholarship. After the sharpness and detachment of Drabble's first two novels there is a remarkable compassion and humanity in *The Millstone*.

Its successors, *Jerusalem the Golden* and *The Waterfall*, are disappointing. As attempts at revealing the consciousness of intelligent young women in love with more or less unsuitable men they have moments of psychological insight, but they tend also to be embarrassing and unconvincing over long stretches. They represent that aspect of Drabble's art which is closer to women's magazine fiction than to George Eliot or Henry James.

But her next work, *The Needle's Eye*, made a decisive and welcome advance. If the setting and subject—the difficulties of marriage and family life in an unglamorous North London environment—were by now recognisably Drabble material, there was a new breath and confidence in the treatment. The heroine, Rose, has as a very young heiress married a Greek, who was generally regarded as a fortune-hunter, and been disinherited by her family. The marriage had not endured but it had not decisively ended either, and the novel shows Rose's situation about ten years later. In Simon Camish, the shy, self-doubting lawyer, himself unhappily married, who takes a professional interest in Rose's troubles and then falls in love with her, we have this author's most successful portrayal of a male character.

Drabble's later novels show a widening range, in variety of human type and social observation. At the same time, the author persists in keeping a firm control over characters and events; the authorial tone is omniscient and manipulative, disturbingly so at times. *The Realms of Gold* is an accomplished and satisfying novel; it takes as its central figure a successful professional woman, the archaeologist Frances Wingate, who has achieved much freedom but whose life is still complicated by a long-drawn out love affair, and her dealings with her extensive and difficult family of origin.

In *The Ice Age* Drabble projected a panoramic novel about British society permeated with a panicky sense of crisis in a particular phase of recent history, 1975-76. The novel is lively and full of incidental interest, but it is probably too reportorial and tied to its period to endure. *The Middle Ground* is disappointing and indeed boring. Here the author returns to more familiar and domestic subjects, focussing on another successful though problem-beset middle-aged heroine, the journalist Kate Armstrong. The intention is to present a study of the difficulties of contemporary professional people in their forties, under pressure from both their children and their own parents, in the brittle, threatening London scene of the late 1970's. The novel is, however, deeply deficient in narrative and dramatic interest, and the reader is bogged down for long periods in Kate's slow ruminations. But with so conscious an author we have to assume that this is the way she wanted to tell it.

—Bernard Bergonzi

DRIVER, C(harles) J(onathan). British. Born in Cape Town, South Africa, 19 August 1939. Educated at St. Andrews College, Grahamstown; University of Cape Town, B.A. (honours) in English, and B.Ed. 1962; Trinity College, Cambridge, B.Phil. 1967. Married Anne Hoogewerf in 1967; two sons and one daughter. President, National Union of South African Students, 1963-64; detained in 1964 under the "90 Day Law"; South African passport revoked in 1966. Housemaster, International Sixth Form Centre, Sevenoaks School, Kent, 1968-73. Since 1973, Director of Studies, Matthew Humberstone Comprehensive School, Humberside. Agent: John Johnson, 45-47 Clerkenwell Green, London EC1R 0HT. Address: 11 Rowston Street, Cleethorpes, South Humberside, Lincolnshire, England.

PUBLICATIONS

Novels

Elegy for a Revolutionary. London, Faber, 1969; New York, Morrow, 1970.
Send War in Our Time, O Lord. London, Faber, 1970.
Death of Fathers. London, Faber, 1972.
A Messiah of the Last Days. London, Faber, 1974.

Short Story

Penguin Modern Stories 8, with others. London, Penguin, 1971.

Uncollected Short Story

"Impossible Cry," in *London Magazine*, February 1966.

Other

Patrick Duncan, South African and Pan-African. London, Heinemann, 1980.

Editor, with H.B. Joicey, *Landscape and Light: Photographs and Poems of Lincolnshire and Humberside.* Lincoln, Lincolnshire and Humberside Arts, 1978.

*

C.J. Driver comments:

(1976) I am a writer and a teacher; the order depends on whether I am writing or teaching, but I am a full-time teacher in a fairly senior position in a very big comprehensive school. I write poems, though I do little about publishing them these days; I do quite a bit of reviewing, partly for the money, but more for my own enjoyment; I plan to spend much of the next two years writing the biography of Patrick Duncan, one of the tragic heroes of recent South African history—I have recently been appointed his official biographer; and I write novels. I believe profoundly that the novel is the "great book of life," and I hope that all my concerns as a human being enter my work as a novelist—love, marriage, children, homes, money, food, work, leisure—though at the moment my predominant concerns are with politics—in the widest sense—the relation of self and society, and the relation of conscious and unconscious minds.

* * *

C.J. Driver is a South African writer whose four novels, all published since 1969, have already earned him a considerable reputation. Not exclusively South African in setting or in theme, the novels concentrate on issues which are both topical and popular, and offer a sometimes challenging and always recognisable view of contemporary society.

Elegy for a Revolutionary, the first and least satisfactory of the novels, utilizes Driver's own experience of underground political action in South Africa during the early 1960's. Like Nadine Gordimer's *The Late Bourgeois World*, it is an attempt to examine the motives and the fate of a group of young white "liberals" who turned to violence as a means of opposing the repressive Nationalist Government. Driver's analysis centres on the personality of the student leader, Jeremy, whom he sees as both traitor and, paradoxically, hero. The weakness of the novel lies in its excessively uncritical view of Jeremy. Unlike Nadine Gordimer, who presents her revolutionary as an integral part of a wider social setting, Driver fails to create a context in which Jeremy's actions can be understood. And, although he is much concerned with psychological motivation, the discussion of Jeremy's peculiar family relationships and obscure guilts remains too abstract to be really credible.

In *Send War in Our Time, O Lord* Driver's main theme is the examination of the liberal conscience under stress. His portrayal of Mrs. Allen, a middle-aged white widow, discovering the inadequacy of her life-long moral code based on decency and tolerance, demonstrates his ability to create a convincing character. The setting (an isolated missionary settlement on South Africa's northern border) is also well-presented. The major weakness of this novel lies in its melodramatic and somewhat far-fetched plot, which involves terrorist activity, much police brutality, madness and two or three suicides, all graphically described. In the welter of violent action, the central issues (the failure of liberal values, the need for dynamic leadership, the nature of political commitment) are almost submerged.

Death of Fathers and *A Messiah of the Last Days* are both set in England, and show a much surer grasp of technique and theme than the earlier books. Driver's interest in details of violence and suffering are still in evidence, but now become part of a general vision of modern life. *Death of Fathers* has a close affinity with *Elegy for a Revolutionary*, although it is set in the confines of an English public school. Its central character is a schoolmaster, and, as in the earlier novel, he is both "heroic" (larger in every way than his colleagues) and "treacherous" (he betrays the confidence of his most brilliant and difficult pupil, in an attempt to "save" him). Again, Driver explores the nature of guilt, and the concept of betrayal, which appears, in his view, to be an inherent part of human experience. Friendship between two different but complementary male characters forms another strand in the novel, and is more competently handled here than in the earlier book.

In *A Messiah of the Last Days* Driver returns to a contemplation of political action. This time he makes his anti-establishment figures a group of idealistic young anarchists, the Free People, who set up a commune in a disused warehouse in London. Their leader, charismatic John Buckleson, projects such a powerful and attractive vision of a new society that he wins the allegiance of a number of eminently respectable people, as well as exciting the younger members of society. The most ambitious of the four novels, *A Messiah of the Last Days* contrasts a number of different life styles, and presents a complex image of contemporary Britain. Through the fast-moving story runs what is clearly, by now, Driver's most persistent theme: the need society has for a "leader" with a compelling vision, and its equal need to destroy him. Buckleson, who ends his life as a "vegetable" in a psychiatric ward, having been shot at close range by a former follower of his, is the latest version of Jeremy, sentenced to death for sabotage; of the terrorist leader, gunned down by the police; and of Nigel, the schoolboy who hanged himself. Skilled as Driver undoubtedly is in contriving variations on his theme, one hopes that his interest in leadership and betrayal will not become obsessive.

—Ursula Laredo

DRURY, Allen (Stuart). American. Born in Houston, Texas, 2 September 1918. Educated at Stanford University, California, B.A. 1939. Served in the United States Army, 1942-43. Editor, Tulare, California, *Bee*, 1940-41; County Editor, Bakersfield *Californian*, 1941-42; Member, United Press Senate Staff, Washington, D.C., 1943-45; National Editor, *Pathfinder* magazine, Washington, D.C., 1947-53; Member, Congressional Staff, *Washington Evening Star*, 1953-54, and *New York Times*, 1954-59; Political Correspondent, *Reader's Digest*, 1959-63. Recipient: Sigma Delta Chi award, for journalism, 1941; Pulitzer Prize, for fiction, 1960. Lit.D.: Rollins College, Winter Park, Florida, 1961. Address: c/o Doubleday, 245 Park Avenue, New York, New York 10017, U.S.A.

PUBLICATIONS

Novels

Advise and Consent. New York, Doubleday, 1959; London, Collins, 1960.
A Shade of Difference. New York, Doubleday, 1962; London, Joseph, 1963.
That Summer. London, Joseph, 1965; New York, Coward McCann, 1966.
Capable of Honor. New York, Doubleday, 1966; London, Joseph, 1967.
Preserve and Protect. New York, Doubleday, and London, Joseph, 1968.
The Throne of Saturn. New York, Doubleday, and London, Joseph, 1971.
Come Nineveh, Come Tyre: The Presidency of Edward M. Jason. New York, Doubleday, 1973; London, Joseph, 1974.
The Promise of Joy: The Presidency of Orrin Knox. New York, Doubleday, and London, Joseph, 1975.
A God Against the Gods. New York, Doubleday, and London, Joseph, 1976.
Anna Hastings: The Story of a Washington Newspaperperson. New York, Morrow, 1977; London, Joseph, 1978.
Return to Thebes. New York, Doubleday, and London, Joseph, 1977.
Mark Coffin, U.S.S.: A Novel of Capitol Hill. New York, Doubleday, and London, Joseph, 1979.
The Hill of Summer. New York, Doubleday, 1981.

Uncollected Short Stories

"Something," in *The Best from Fantasy and Science Fiction 10*, edited by Robert P. Mills. New York, Doubleday, 1961; London, Gollancz, 1963.
"No More Tears," in *Good Housekeeping* (New York), February 1971.

Other

A Senate Journal 1943-1945. New York, McGraw Hill, 1963.
Three Kids in a Cart: A Visit to Ike and Other Diversions. New York, Doubleday, 1965.
"A Very Strange Society": A Journey to the Heart of South Africa. New York, Simon and Schuster, 1967; London, Joseph, 1968.
Courage and Hesitation: Notes and Photographs of the Nixon Administration. New York, Doubleday, 1971; as *Courage and Hesitation: Inside the Nixon Administration*, London, Joseph, 1972.
Egypt: The Eternal Smile, photographs by Alex Gotfrydx. New York, Doubleday, 1980.

*

Manuscript Collection: Hoover Institution, Stanford, California.

* * *

Allen Drury's experiences as a journalist, especially as a political correspondent in Washington, D.C., have left their mark, for better or worse, on his novels and non-fiction. Almost all his fiction is concerned with political warfare in the United States, with attacks by the media upon politicians when in power and opposition, and with the external enemies of the United States. These enemies are shown as unprincipled, ungrateful, and malicious both when making their verbal assaults in the United Nations, an institution that is rarely shown in a flattering light, and when physically attacking American installations. Communist Russia, the arch-foe, is made completely villainous, particularly in *The Throne of Saturn* and *Come Nineveh, Come Tyre.* In the former, Russian astronauts try to destroy American space craft far above the earth; in the latter, Russia invades Alaska and humiliates a foolishly idealistic left-wing president.

Of his novels, *Advise and Consent* is the first published and the best. It would undoubtedly benefit from severe pruning, but there is a momentum built upon a melodramatic presentation of events that carries the reader along, even if he is wary of the hysterical undertone of the book. In the detailing of Congressional infighting and the tension of significant debates in the Senate, Drury is at his strongest. Here his years as a member of the United Press Senate Staff are effectively used. He is not so strong, however, when presenting the actions of the president or the left-wingers. As in later books, many characters are stereotypes. Even in this book, a Pulitzer prize winner, he uses a plot that appears contrived (even though it has real life counterparts) and characters that are mere puppets.

Subsequent novels carry on the story of political struggles and national alarums through outbreaks of "liberal"-inspired violence and presidential assassination. Instead of refining and subtilizing the promising material and fictional technique of *Advise and Consent*, he seems to have been pushed by an increasing fear for the preservation of traditional American values and institutions into composing novels that are more overtly propagandistic statements of his conservative political beliefs than aesthetically pleasing books. Readers who share his deep distrust of liberals and his hatred of Communism may accept his fiction more readily, but they too probably find his prose heavy and his plots excessively sensational. Even characters such as Orrin Knox, who are interestingly depicted in the early novels, begin to pall in the later works. The use of melodramatic incident (often to compensate for feeble characterization) is strikingly exemplified in *Preserve and Protect*, which opens with the death of President Harley M. Hudson in a fiery plane crash and (on the last page) concludes with the assassination before a huge crowd of either the presidential or the vice-presidential nominee—in movie-serial fashion we are not told which one. The failure to identify the victims is deliberate since Drury is thereby able to give us two novels as sequels. In *Come Nineveh, Come Tyre*, Orrin Knox, the stalwart conservative, is identified as the victim. Thus Edward Montoya Jason, the liberal but too-malleable vice-presidential nominee assumes the highest office; but, exploited by NAWAC (National Anti-War Activities Congress) and Communist imperialists, he brings the country to abject international defeat. The alternative, with Jason dead and Knox alive, is given in *The Promise of Joy.*

Non-American readers are probably irritated by the obstrusive patriotism and the condescension shown for foreigners. Drury seems unable or unwilling to present foreigners with sympathy or in depth. Too often he resorts to stereotypes or caricatures in his fiction. Lord Claude Maudulayne, the British Ambassador, is an example. In addition, by failing to develop credible characters for the ambassadors at the UN or in Washington, he loses the chance to utilize them as a kind of Greek chorus commenting on American tragedies. On the other hand, a moderate and balanced view of foreigners is given in *"A Very Strange Society": A Journey to the Heart of South Africa.* Perhaps he is too ready to depreciate the achievements of black African nations, but he acknowledges the complex problems of a multi-racial society.

His main claim to fame, however, is his series of political novels, structured around the beliefs and actions of Americans during the sixties and seventies—some of the novels might indeed be read as *romans à clef.* Yet recent American history has betrayed Allen Drury: his right-wing heroes—at least their equivalents in real life—have been found guilty through such investigations as Watergate of the very crimes he attributes in recent novels to his left-wing villains. He has been equally unfortunate in his non-fiction. *Courage and Hesitation: Notes and Photographs of the Nixon Administration* (1971) is a tribute, with only a few cautionary statements, to "a decent and worthy man, leading an Administration composed, for the most part, of decent and worthy men." To overcome the unkind cuts of history, Drury must either develop a greater political sensitivity or take more seriously his role as a creator of fiction.

—James A. Hart

DUFFY, Maureen (Patricia). British. Born in Worthing, Sussex, 21 October 1933. Educated at Trowbridge High School for Girls, Wiltshire; Sarah Bonnell High School for Girls; King's College, London, 1953-56, B.A. (honours) in English 1956. School teacher for five years. Co-Founder, Writers Action Group, 1972; Joint Chairman, Writers Guild, 1977-78. Recipient: City of London Festival Playwright's Prize, 1962; Arts Council bursary, 1963, 1966, 1975; Society of Authors Travelling Scholarship, 1976. Agent: Jonathan Clowes Ltd., 19 Jeffrey's Place, London NW1 9PP. Address: 14-A Richmond Mansions, Old Brompton Road, London S.W.5, England.

PUBLICATIONS

Novels

That's How It Was. London, Hutchinson, 1962.
The Single Eye. London, Hutchinson, 1964.
The Microcosm. London, Hutchinson, and New York, Simon and Schuster, 1966.
The Paradox Players. London, Hutchinson, 1967; New York, Simon and Schuster, 1968.
Wounds. London, Hutchinson, and New York, Knopf, 1969.
Love Child. London, Weidenfeld and Nicolson, and New York, Knopf, 1971.
I Want to Go to Moscow: A Lay. London, Hodder and Stoughton, 1973; as *All Heaven in a Rage*, New York, Knopf, 1973.
Capital. London, Cape, 1975; New York, Braziller, 1976.
Housespy. London, Hamish Hamilton, 1978.

Uncollected Short Story

"The Happy Bastard," in *One Parent Families.* London, Davis Poynter, 1975.

Plays

The Lay Off (produced London, 1962).
The Silk Room (produced Watford, Hertfordshire, 1966).
Rites (produced London, 1969). Published in *New Short Plays 2*, London, Methuen, 1969.
Solo, Olde Tyme (produced Cambridge, 1970).
A Nightingale in Bloomsbury Square (produced London, 1973). Published in *Factions*, edited by Giles Gordon and Alex Hamilton, London, Joseph, 1974.

Television Play: *Josie*, 1961.

Verse

Lyrics for the Dog Hour: Poems. London, Hutchinson, 1968.
The Venus Touch. London, Weidenfeld and Nicolson, 1971.
Actaeon. Rushden, Northamptonshire, Sceptre Press, 1973.
Evesong. London, Sappho, 1975.
Memorials of the Quick and the Dead. London, Hamish Hamilton, 1979.

Other

The Erotic World of Faery. London, Hodder and Stoughton, 1972.
The Passionate Shepherdess: Aphra Behn 1640-1689. London, Cape, 1977; New York, Avon, 1979.
Inherit the Earth: A Social History. London, Hamish Hamilton, 1980.

Editor, with Alan Brownjohn, *New Poetry 3.* London, Arts Council, 1977.

Translator, *A Blush of Shame*, by Domenico Rea. London, Barrie and Rockliff, 1963.

*

Critical Study: by Dulan Barber, in *Transatlantic Review 45* (London), Spring 1973.

* * *

Maureen Duffy is a prolific novelist, poet, and playwright whose work has developed rapidly in range and importance. *That's How It Was* won her immediate acclaim for its simplicity and forcefulness. It is a moving account of the relationship between a mother and daughter; their existence is poor, insecure, even brutal, but transcended by mutual love. "I grew six inches under the light touch of her hand," explains the narrator. The little girl has an acute sense of social isolation and a fierce loyalty to the one constant figure in her universe; her mother's death is thus cause for more than grief, it brings total despair. The loneliness, restlessness, and sexual hunger which spring from the situation are the dominating themes of each subsequent novel.

Realism is the touchstone of Duffy's style; like many other observers of working-class life, she is at her best when she relies on accurate, detailed reportage and at her weakest when tempted by sentiment. *The Paradox Players* is an example of her writing at its most compelling. It describes a man's retreat from society to live for some months in a boat moored on the Thames. The physical realities of cold, snow, rats, and flooding occupy him continually and the hardship brings him peace. He is a novelist, suffering from the hazards peculiar to that profession and has some pertinent comments to make about the vulnerability of the writer. "When I saw the reviews I could have cut my throat. You see they're very kind to first novels for some mistaken reason but when the poor bastard follows it up with a second and they see he really means it they tear its guts out." The experience of winter on the river restores his faith in his own ability to survive.

Duffy's observations are acute, her use of dialogue witty and direct; this authenticity is complemented by an interest in the bizarre, the fantastic. Her best-known book uses these qualities to great effect in a study of Lesbian society which is both informative and original. *The Microcosm* begins and ends in a club where the central characters meet to dance, dress up, and escape from the necessity of "all the week wearing a false face." Their fantasies are played out in front of the juke box; then the narrative follows each woman back into her disguise, her social role. Steve is Miss Stephens, a schoolmistress; Cathy is a bus conductress; Matt works in a garage. Their predictament as individuals, the author suggests, extends beyond the interest of their own minority group. A plea is made for tolerance, understanding, and that respect without which the human spirit must perish. "Society isn't a simple organism with one nucleus and a fringe of little feet, it's an infinitely complex structure and if you try to suppress any part...you diminish, you mutilate the whole." *Wounds* and *Love Child* reaffirm this belief.

—Judy Cooke

---

du MAURIER, Daphne. British. Born in London, 13 May 1907; daughter of the actor/manager Sir Gerald du Maurier; granddaughter of the writer George du Maurier. Educated privately and in Paris. Married Lieutenant-General Sir Frederick Browning in 1932 (died, 1965); two daughters and one son. Recipient: Mystery Writers of America Grand Master Award, 1977. Fellow, Royal Society of Literature, 1952. D.B.E. (Dame Commander, Order of the British Empire), 1969. Address: Kilmarth, Par, Cornwall, England.

PUBLICATIONS

Novels

The Loving Spirit. London, Heinemann, and New York, Doubleday, 1931.
I'll Never Be Young Again. London, Heinemann, and New York, Doubleday, 1932.
The Progress of Julius. London, Heinemann, and New York, Doubleday, 1933.
Jamaica Inn. London, Gollancz, and New York, Doubleday, 1936.
Rebecca. London, Gollancz, and New York, Doubleday, 1938.
Frenchman's Creek. London, Gollancz, 1941; New York, Doubleday, 1942.
Hungry Hill. London, Gollancz, and New York, Doubleday, 1943.
The King's General. London, Gollancz, and New York, Doubleday, 1946.
The Parasites. London, Gollancz, 1949; New York, Doubleday, 1950.
My Cousin Rachel. London, Gollancz, 1951; New York, Doubleday, 1952.
Mary Anne. London, Gollancz, and New York, Doubleday, 1954.
The Scapegoat. London, Gollancz, and New York, Doubleday, 1957.
Castle Dor, with Arthur Quiller-Couch, completed by du Maurier. London, Dent, and New York, Doubleday, 1962.
The Glass-Blowers. London, Gollancz, and New York, Doubleday, 1963.
The Flight of the Falcon. London, Gollancz, and New York, Doubleday, 1965.
The House on the Strand. London, Gollancz, and New York, Doubleday, 1969.
Rule Britannia. London, Gollancz, 1972; New York, Doubleday, 1973.

Short Stories

Happy Christmas (story). New York, Doubleday, 1940; London, Todd, 1943.
Come Wind, Come Weather. London, Heinemann, 1940; New York, Doubleday, 1941.
Nothing Hurts for Long, and Escort. London, Todd, 1943.
Consider the Lilies (story). London, Todd, 1943.
Spring Picture (story). London, Todd, 1944.
Leading Lady (story). London, Vallancey Press, 1945.
London and Paris (two stories). London, Vallancey Press, 1945.
The Apple Tree: A Short Novel, and Some Stories. London, Gollancz, 1952; as *Kiss Me Again, Stranger: A Collection of Eight Stories, Long and Short*, New York, Doubleday, 1953; as *The Birds and Other Stories*, London, Penguin, 1968.
Early Stories. London, Todd, 1954.
The Breaking Point: Eight Stories. London, Gollancz, and New York, Doubleday, 1959; as *The Blue Lenses and Other Stories*, London, Penguin, 1970.
The Treasury of du Maurier Short Stories. London, Gollancz, 1960.
Not after Midnight and Other Stories. London, Gollancz, 1971; as *Don't Look Now*, New York, Doubleday, 1971.
Echoes from the Macabre: Selected Stories. London, Gollancz, 1976; New York, Doubleday, 1977.
The Rendezvous and Other Stories. London, Gollancz, 1980.

Plays

Rebecca, adaptation of her own novel (produced Manchester and London, 1940; New York, 1945). London, Gollancz, 1940; New York, Dramatists Play Service, 1943.
The Years Between (produced Manchester, 1944; London, 1945). London, Gollancz, 1945; New York, Doubleday, 1946.
September Tide (produced Oxford and London, 1948). London, Gollancz, 1949; New York, Doubleday, 1950.

Screenplay: *Hungry Hill*, with Terence Young and Francis Crowdry, 1947.

Television Play: *The Breakthrough*, 1976.

Other

Gerald: A Portrait (on Gerald du Maurier). London, Gollancz, 1934; New York, Doubleday, 1935.
The du Mauriers. London, Gollancz, and New York, Doubleday, 1937.
The Infernal World of Branwell Brontë. London, Gollancz, 1960; New York, Doubleday, 1961.
Vanishing Cornwall, photographs by Christian Browning. London, Gollancz, and New York, Doubleday, 1967.
Golden Lads: Sir Francis Bacon, Anthony Bacon, and Their Friends. London, Gollancz, and New York, Doubleday, 1975.
The Winding Stair: Francis Bacon, His Rise and Fall. London, Gollancz, 1976; New York, Doubleday, 1977.
Growing Pains: The Shaping of a Writer (autobiography). London, Gollancz, 1977; as *Myself When Young*, New York, Doubleday, 1977.
The Rebecca Notebook and Other Memories (includes short stories). New York, Doubleday, 1980; London, Gollancz, 1981.

Editor, *The Young George du Maurier: A Selection of His Letters 1860-1867.* London, Davies, 1951; New York, Doubleday, 1952.
Editor, *Best Stories*, by Phyllis Bottome. London, Faber, 1963.

* * *

Daphne du Maurier's enormous popularity can be traced in large part to extremely well-made plots, crammed with action, suspense, and mystery; she is also very adroit at capturing the atmosphere of her settings whether they be her beloved Cornwall or an imaginary but sharply rendered Italian city. Details of architecture, significant information about professions, chronicles of great historical events are combined with brief but telling identification of the flora of the area and particularly effective descriptions of weather. Frequently presented as the observations of her narrator and/or of her protagonist, these comments not only vivify the settings but also contribute to characterization.

Characterization is, in fact, of major interest in du Maurier's oeuvre. Her people seem breathtakingly vital during the course of the reading, but in retrospect are, often, almost unknowable. This seeming paradox arises from the types of personalities du Maurier explores and from the situations in which she examines them. Frequently she depicts men and women undergoing significant changes of personality and of life style, sometimes against their wills. Other characters display a startling duality of nature, seeming to some observers good and attractive, to others evil and corrupt.

Not surprisingly, the characters displaying this duality are the most fascinating. Rebecca de Winter (*Rebecca*) is known to most acquaintances as the brilliant, capable, perfect chatelaine of the family estate, but actually she leads a promiscuous, exploitative secret life. Rachel Ashley (*My Cousin Rachel*) is an even greater puzzle. She may be a loving, gentle, dreadfully unfortunate woman; she may also be a conniving fortune-hunting poisoner; du Maurier maintains that even she doesn't know the truth. Aldo Donati (*The Flight of the Falcon*) may be a murderer and is certainly engaged in an alarmingly successful attempt at manipulating the students in the local university; his intentions may be noble or destructive. The action arises from other characters' attempts to understand, judge, and counter the behavior of these puzzling major figures, and in these three novels the plots are further complicated by the late maturation of the protagonist-narrators. In each instance, the action, centering on the paradoxical characters, is firmly resolved, yet the books are open-ended, for the newly emerged personalities of the protagonist-narrators are not fully dramatized, leaving the powerfully ironic conclusions deeply satisfying on one level, endlessly titillating on another.

In *The Scapegoat* du Maurier rings a change on the duality motif; the central characters, John, an indecisive Englishman, and Jean, a domineering Frenchman, represent the passive-innocent and the active-corrupt sides of one personality. It is a tribute to du Maurier's narrative skill that the improbable premise (that John can substitute for Jean in the midst of his family) proves viable, and the novel's theme, the effect of personal power upon its wielder, is neatly done. This theme is also apparent in *Hungry Hill* and *The Progress of Julius*, but each novel takes a different perspective, raises and suggests answers to slightly different questions.

Political power is a theme of some of du Maurier's historical novels—*The Glass Blowers* (the French Revolution), *The King's General* (the Cromwellian era)—and of *Rule Britannia* (set in a U.S.-dominated future). Like *The Glass Blowers*, *Mary Anne* and *The du Mauriers* depict the author's ancestors as well as their historical periods and are both fictional and biographical. *Jamaica Inn* and *Frenchman's Creek* highlight adventure and romance over history and are also notable because their female protagonists deny their vibrant personalities because of the men they love. Both Mary Yellan and Dona St. Columb make their decisions consciously; both know exactly what they are sacrificing, and each understands her motivations fully. The novels' thrilling climaxes leave the viability of the heroines' choices unresolved, their development unevaluated. These characters contrast sharply with the strong female protagonists of *The Loving Spirit* (like *Hungry Hill*, a family saga) and *The King's General*, women who behave consistently throughout. More contemporary settings figure in *I'll Never Be Young Again*, *The Progress of Julius*, and *The Parasites* which examine their protagonists' capacities to surmount or to be warped by personal error and cultural stress. *The House on the Strand* borders on science fiction, for its hero lives in both the present and the past. Like *Rebecca* and *Jamaica Inn*, it is a triumph of setting and mood.

Also a productive biographer, short story writer, and dramatist, Daphne du Maurier has successfully experimented with characterization and setting in her memorable novels.

—Jane S. Bakerman

DUNDY, Elaine. American. Born in New York City, in 1927. Educated at Sweet Briar College, Virginia. Married the writer Kenneth Tynan in 1951 (marriage dissolved, 1964); one daughter. Actress; worked for the BBC, London; directed the Winter Workshop of the Berkshire Festival; also journalist. Agent: Patricia White, Deborah Rogers Ltd., 5-11 Mortimer Street, London W1N 7RH. Address: 570 Kings Road, London S.W.6, England.

PUBLICATIONS

Novels

The Dud Avocado. London, Gollancz, and New York, Dutton, 1958.
The Old Man and Me. London, Gollancz, and New York, Dutton, 1964.
The Injured Party. London, Joseph, 1974.

Uncollected Short Stories

"The Sound of a Marriage," in *Queen* (London), 1965.
"Death in the Country," in *Vogue* (New York), 1974.

Plays

My Place (produced London, 1962). London, Gollancz, 1962; New York, French, 1963.
Death in the Country, and The Drowning (produced New York, 1976).

Screenplay: *Life Sign*, 1975.

Other

Finch, Bloody Finch (biography of Peter Finch). London, Joseph, and New York, Holt Rinehart, 1980.

* * *

In *The Dud Avocado* and *The Old Man and Me*, Elaine Dundy employs first-person, reflective narrators who self-consciously and self-indulgently record and evaluate their experiences in Paris and Soho. The narrators relate their stories in a candid, energetic, witty style, spiced with parenthetical revelations, word association games, and sensory impressions. Their language is often the jargon of the Beat-hipster: audacious, flippant, nervous, saucy. Their tone is the good-humored self-mockery of the cocktail party confession, the stage whisper, the open diary. The narrators are deliberate storytellers, replaying moments from their pasts, exposing their naivety and limitations, and benefiting from hindsight.

Sally Jay in *The Dud Avocado* is the contemporary American innocent abroad, superficially hip to the decadent Left Bank and "running for her life." Caught in the ambiguity between naivety and sophistication, she is in pursuit of "freedom" and the ability "to be so sharp that I'll always be able to guess right...on the wing." She expends her time and innocence in a disorganized, impulsive debauch with the avant-garde of Paris.

Through a series of wrong guesses, she eventually is schooled in the ways of the world. The glamorous, daring, free world of Paris is revealed as pretentious, opportunistic, grotesque. Her romantic vision of the rebellious life is destroyed when she understands that her would-be lover is a pimp and that her life in Paris has exposed her to "too much prostitution." She declares herself a dud avocado—a seed without life potential.

In flight to Hollywood, the narrator confronts her runaway life strategy and determines that some "unrunning" is called for to "[lay] the ghost once and for all." She seeks out the role of librarian and schools herself in cynicism until she recognizes the life which she wishes to embrace. Giddy with optimism, she accepts the love and marriage proposal of a famous photographer and embarks on a new life with "an entirely new passport," the new self emerging from the old like the growth of an avocado seedling from the stone of the old fruit: "It's zymotic!" The narrator survives her initiation experience ready to "Make voyages. Attempt them. That's all there is."

Betsy Lou in *The Old Man and Me* is older and more experienced than Sally Jay, but like Sally Jay, she is on a quest which leads to greater self-knowledge. Motivated by puerile revenge, she journeys to London to recover her "stolen" inheritance from C.D. McKee. As his unknown heir, she plans to hasten the recovery of her money by any means necessary—lying, cheating, masquerading, or attempting murder. She partially achieves her declared end, and in the process realizes her injustice to those in her past, the reasons for the loss of her father's love, and her love for C.D. despite his age and possession of her money. Thus she corrects her mistaken view of her past and sees the futility of trying to salve emotional loss with money.

Betsy Lou's relationship to C.D. is never linear and controllable. The very complexity of the relationship betrays her ambiguity over her past, her present motives, and her unconscious needs. She loves/hates him, recognizes that he is/is not a father figure, accepts/rejects him as teacher, is repulsed/excited by his lust, and wishes him dead/fears for his life. This confusion drives her to abandonment in jazz, drink, dope, and sex, which results in C.D.'s collapse and her self-confrontation and confession.

Betsy Lou's declaration of her identity, her deceit, and her desire for C.D. comes too late. He rejects the contrite Betsy Lou, gives her fifty percent of her money, and leaves her with the advice that she "use it. See its power to corrupt or save....Learn from our stupidities." She is left with what she initially wanted "only...because it was mine."

In both novels the narrators are left at the point of departure. For Sally Jay the future appears glorious with possibility. She sees her new life as "the end. The end. The last word." However, the author implies that Sally Jay has ended one cycle of learning experiences and is beginning another with her marriage. One is reminded of Stefan's description of the Typical American Girl as the avocado, "So green—so eternally green." She has experienced growth and is more worldly wise, but her final pronouncement indicates that her maturation is not complete. The process has just begun. Similarly, Betsy Lou is left facing her future. She hasn't Sally Jay's confidence of joy, but rather experiences a sense of unreality. She has no delusions about the future, and the past "seems (to) never really (have) happened." She is no longer directed by spurious monetary goals; instead she suffers the bewilderment of a hollow victory. Thus, while both narrators experience an epiphany, that moment of awareness is tinged with irony.

Elaine Dundy is an entertaining novelist who rehearses the familiar theme of initiation with adeptness and flair. However, her craftsmanship and energy do not always compensate for her characters' lack of psychological depth nor for her rather formulaic situations. Her novels do not provoke new or refined insights, but they do provide moments of engaging and refreshing humor.

—Deborah Duckworth

DUNN, Nell (Mary). British. Born in London, in 1936. Educated at a convent school. Married the writer Jeremy Sandford in 1956; three children. Recipient: Rhys Memorial Prize, 1964. Address: 10 Bell Lane, Twickenham, Middlesex, England.

PUBLICATIONS

Novels

Poor Cow. London, MacGibbon and Kee, and New York, Doubleday, 1967.
The Incurable. London, Cape, and New York, Doubleday, 1971.
I Want, with Adrian Henri. London, Cape, 1972.
Tear His Head off His Shoulders. London, Cape, 1974; New York, Doubleday, 1975.
The Only Child: A Simple Story of Heaven and Hell. London, Cape, 1978.

Short Stories

Up the Junction. London, MacGibbon and Kee, 1963; Philadelphia, Lippincott, 1966.

Plays

Steaming (produced London, 1981).

Screenplay: *Poor Cow*, with Ken Loach, 1967.

Other

Talking to Women. London, MacGibbon and Kee, 1965.
Freddy Gets Married (juvenile). London, MacGibbon and Kee, 1969.

Editor, *Living Like I Do.* London, Futura, 1977; as *Different Drummers*, New York, Harcourt Brace, and London, Lorrimer, 1977.

* * *

Nell Dunn begins with vignettes or fragmental episodes to build a picture of British urban life. Much like Charles Dickens, with his newspaper sketches and small portraits of London street life, she began her career with a set of brilliant realistic snapshots of the mod world. In *Up the Junction* she collected these sketches, which in effect are much like the 17th-century Theophrastan "character." They deal primarily with young working-class Britons in their milieu, incised in photographic reportage, built on their dialect, street signs, bits of popular music, the clichés and repetitious folk-wisdom of ghetto life. The feeling for the nagging, obstinate details of daily life is very strong—the sketches demonstrate how complex yet unrewarding most of these lives can be.

In *Poor Cow* Dunn develops the same method of terse, richly detailed sketches into a more unified form, a novel centering on the life of one young woman. Ironically named Joy, she becomes a "poor cow" through the constant erosion of her life. At 22 she has gone through one luckless marriage, and her life moves certrifugally around Jonny, her son. Joy drifts into casual prostitution, random affairs with anchorless men. She worries constantly about her looks, her body, her sexual responsiveness, the prospects of aging. Life is intractable, and wishes evaporate in the face of simple necessities. Joy's role as a mother is a transference of her egocentrism to Jonny, as an extension of her former hopes for herself. Her own life has run down a blind alley, but her son's life may be different. As she clings to Jonny, Joy invents a bitter epitaph for her youth: "To think when I was a kid I planned to conquer the world and if anyone saw me now they'd say, 'She's had a rough night, poor cow.' "

A vision of the confusion and oppressiveness of modern life is extended in *The Incurable*, which deals with a middle-class woman, Maro, whose life collapses in crisis. Maro's husband develops multiple sclerosis, and her formerly orderly and manageable existence is destroyed. She falls into a state of anomie which, like her husband's progressive disease, eats up her life. She too is "incurable," although her malaise is mental and spiritual. Her children's cannibalistic demands and the relentless pressure of everyday routine erode her will and energy: "She felt like some country that had been oppressed for a long time and was slowly rising up and throwing over its oppressors. She was making a revolution but the bloodshed was horrifying and how many lives would be lost and when was it going to end and would she ever make the country of the free spirits?

Tear His Head off His Shoulders is another set of related vignettes and episodes in the lives of women. The narrative revolves around the sexual obsessions and conflicts of women, viewed in retrospect. The vernacular style and the complex combination of nostalgia and revulsion give a bittersweet flavor to the work. A strong "fascination of the abomination" feeling makes the stories of sexual compulsion convincing.

In *The Only Child* Dunn constructs a novel again focused on sexual obsession and possessiveness—of a mother for her son. We follow Esther Lafonte through Dunn's careful sensual details as she drifts from her over-comfortable marriage to a search for her identity—sexual and spiritual—in her 19-year-old son, Piers. At one point she speaks for all of Dunn's lost women: "I want to get in, I want to be somebody, I have a feeling that I could have done very much more with my life, that I could be doing more now, I want to be a part of things."

Nell Dunn's special province is the mind and spirit of the beleaguered woman—a view from the "oppressed country" of the woman trapped by circumstances. The vignettes she presents deal with developing sexuality, the allure of the pop world, the deadly immobility of domestic responsibilities. Her recent fiction extends this vision to the perimeters of middle-class life.

—William J. Schafer

DURRELL, Lawrence (George). British. Born in Julundur, India, 27 February 1912. Educated at the College of St. Joseph, Darjeeling, India; St. Edmund's School, Canterbury, Kent. Married 1) Nancy Myers in 1935 (divorced, 1947); 2) Eve Cohen in 1947 (divorced); 3) Claude Durrell in 1961 (died, 1967); 4) Ghislaine de Boysson in 1973 (divorced, 1979); two children. Has had many jobs, including jazz pianist (Blue Peter nightclub, London), automobile racer, and real estate agent. Lived in Corfu, 1934-40. Editor, with Henry Miller and Alfred Perlès, *The Booster* (later *Delta*), Paris, 1937-39; Columnist, *Egyptian Gazette*, Cairo, 1941; Editor, with Robin Fedden and Bernard Spencer, *Personal Landscape*, Cairo, 1942-45; Special Correspondent in Cyprus for *The Economist*, London, 1953-55; Editor, *Cyprus Review*, Nicosia, 1954-55. Taught at the British Institute, Kalamata, Greece, 1940. Foreign Press Service Officer, British Information Office, Cairo, 1941-44; Press Attaché, British Information Office, Alexandria, 1944-45; Director of Public Relations for the Dodecanese Islands, Greece, 1946-47; Director of the British Council Institute, Cordoba, Argentina, 1947-48; Press Attaché, British Legation, Belgrade, 1949-52; Director of Public Relations for the British Government in Cyprus, 1954-56. Andrew Mellon Visiting Professor of Humanities, California Institute of Technology, Pasadena, 1974. Recipient: Duff Cooper Memorial Prize, 1957; Prix du Meilleur Livre Etranger, 1959. Fellow, Royal Society of Literature, 1954. Has lived in France since 1957. Address: c/o Grindlay's Bank, 13 St. James's Square, London S.W.1, England.

PUBLICATIONS

Novels

Pied Piper of Lovers. London, Cassell, 1935.
Panic Spring (as Charles Norden). London, Faber, and New York, Covici Friede, 1937.
The Black Book: An Agon. Paris, Obelisk Press, 1938; New York, Dutton, 1960; London, Faber, 1973.
Cefalû. London, Editions Poetry London, 1947; as *The Dark Labyrinth*, London, Ace, 1958; New York, Dutton, 1962.
White Eagles over Serbia. London, Faber, and New York, Criterion, 1957.
The Alexandria Quartet. London, Faber, and New York, Dutton, 1962.
  Justine. London, Faber, and New York, Dutton, 1957.
  Balthazar. London, Faber, and New York, Dutton, 1958.
  Mountolive. London, Faber, 1958; New York, Dutton, 1959.
  Clea. London, Faber, and New York, Dutton, 1960.
The Revolt of Aphrodite. London, Faber, 1974.
  Tunc. London, Faber, and New York, Dutton, 1968.
  Nunquam. London, Faber, and New York, Dutton, 1970.
Monsieur; or, The Prince of Darkness. London, Faber, 1974; New York, Viking Press, 1975.
Livia; or, Buried Alive. London, Faber, 1978; New York, Viking Press, 1979.

Short Stories

Zero, and Asylum in the Snow. Privately printed, 1946; as *Two Excursions into Reality*, Berkeley, California, Circle, 1947.
Esprit de Corps: Sketches from Diplomatic Life. London, Faber, 1957; New York, Dutton, 1958.
Stiff Upper Lip: Life among the Diplomats. London, Faber, 1958; New York, Dutton, 1959.
Sauve Qui Peut. London, Faber, 1966; New York, Dutton, 1967.
The Best of Antrobus. London, Faber, 1974.

Plays

Sappho: A Play in Verse (produced Hamburg, 1959; Edinburgh, 1961; Evanston, Illinois, 1964). London, Faber, 1950; New York, Dutton, 1958.
Acte (produced Hamburg, 1961). London, Faber, and New York, Dutton, 1965.
An Irish Faustus: A Morality in Nine Scenes (produced Sommerhausen, Germany, 1966). London, Faber, 1963; New York, Dutton, 1964.

Screenplays: *Cleopatra*, with others, 1963; *Judith*, with others, 1966.

Radio Script: *Greek Peasant Superstitions*, 1947.

Television Scripts: *The Lonely Roads*, with Diane Deriaz, 1970; *The Search for Ulysses* (USA); *Lawrence Durrell's Greece*; *Lawrence Durrell's Egypt*.

Recording: *Ulysses Come Back: Sketch for a Musical* (story, music, and lyrics by Durrell), 1971.

Verse

Quaint Fragment: Poems Written Between the Ages of Sixteen and Nineteen. London, Cecil Press, 1931.
Ten Poems. London, Caduceus Press, 1932.
Ballade of Slow Decay. Privately printed, 1932.
Bromo Bombastes: A Fragment from a Laconic Drama by Gaffer Peeslake. London, Caduceus Press, 1933.
Transition. London, Caduceus Press, 1934.
Mass for the Old Year. Privately printed, 1935.
Proems: An Anthology of Poems, with others. London, Fortune Press, 1938.
A Private Country. London, Faber, 1943.
The Parthenon: For T.S. Eliot. Privately printed, 1945(?).
Cities, Plains, and People. London, Faber, 1946.

On Seeming to Presume. London, Faber, 1948.
A Landmark Gone. Privately printed, 1949.
Deus Loci. Ischia, Italy, Di Mato Vito, 1950.
Private Drafts. Nicosia, Cyprus, Proodos Press, 1955.
The Tree of Idleness and Other Poems. London, Faber, 1955.
Selected Poems. London, Faber, and New York, Grove Press, 1956.
Collected Poems. London, Faber, and New York, Dutton, 1960; revised edition, 1968.
Penguin Modern Poets 1, with Elizabeth Jennings and R.S. Thomas. London, Penguin, 1962.
Poetry. New York, Dutton, 1962.
Beccafico Le Becfigue (English, with French translation by F.-J. Temple). Montpellier, France, La Licorne, 1963.
A Persian Lady. Edinburgh, Tragara Press, 1963.
Selected Poems 1935-1963. London, Faber, 1964.
The Ikons and Other Poems. London, Faber, 1966; New York, Dutton, 1967.
The Red Limbo Lingo: A Poetry Notebook for 1968-1970. London, Faber, and New York, Dutton, 1971.
On the Suchness of the Old Boy. London, Turret, 1972.
Vega and Other Poems. London, Faber, 1973.
Lifelines. Edinburgh, Tragara Press, 1974.
Selected Poems, edited by Alan Ross. London, Faber, 1977.
Collected Poems 1931-1974, edited by James Brigham. London, Faber, and New York, Viking Press, 1980.

Other

Prospero's Cell: A Guide to the Landscape and Manners of the Island of Corcyra. London, Faber, 1945; with *Reflections on a Marine Venus*, New York, Dutton, 1960.
Key to Modern Poetry. London, Peter Nevill, 1952; as *A Key to Modern British Poetry*, Norman, University of Oklahoma Press, 1952.
Reflections on a Marine Venus: A Companion to the Landscape of Rhodes. London, Faber, 1953; with *Prospero's Cell*, New York, Dutton, 1960.
Bitter Lemons (on Cyprus). London, Faber, 1957; New York, Dutton, 1958.
Art and Outrage: A Correspondence about Henry Miller Between Alfred Perlès and Lawrence Durrell, with an Intermission by Henry Miller. London, Putnam, 1959; New York, Dutton, 1960.
Groddeck (on Georg Walther Groddeck). Wiesbaden, Limes, 1961.
Briefwechsel über "Actis", with Gustaf Gründgens. Hamburg, Rowohlt, 1961.
Lawrence Durrell and Henry Miller: A Private Correspondence, edited by George Wickes. New York, Dutton, and London, Faber, 1963.
La Descente du Styx (English, with French translations by F.-J. Temple). Montpellier, France, La Murène, 1964; as *Down the Styx*, Santa Barbara, California, Capricorn Press, 1971.
Spirit of Place: Letters and Essays on Travel, edited by Alan G. Thomas. London, Faber, and New York, Dutton, 1969.
Le Grand Suppositoire (interview with Marc Alyn). Paris, Belfond, 1972; as *The Big Supposer*, London, Abelard Schuman, and New York, Grove Press, 1973.
The Happy Rock (on Henry Miller). London, Village Press, 1973.
The Plant-Magic Man. Santa Barbara, California, Capra Press, 1973.
Blue Thirst. Santa Barbara, California, Capra Press, 1975.
Sicilian Carousel. London, Faber, and New York, Viking Press, 1977.
The Greek Islands. London, Faber, and New York, Viking Press, 1978.
A Smile in the Mind's Eye. London, Wildwood House, 1980.
Literary Lifelines: The Richard Aldington-Lawrence Durrell Correspondence, edited by Harry T. Moore and Ian S. McNiven. New York, Viking Press, and London, Faber, 1981.

Editor, with others, *Personal Landscape: An Anthology of Exile.* London, Editions Poetry London, 1945.
Editor, *A Henry Miller Reader.* New York, New Directions, 1959; as *The Best of Henry Miller*, London, Heinemann, 1960.
Editor, *New Poems 1963.* London, Hutchinson, 1963.
Editor, *Lear's Corfu: An Anthology Drawn from the Painter's Letters.* Corfu, Corfu Travel, 1965.
Editor, *Wordsworth.* London, Penguin, 1973.

Translator, *Six Poems from the Greek of Sikelianos and Seferis.* Privately printed, 1946.
Translator, with Bernard Spencer and Nanos Valaoritis, *The King of Asine and Other Poems*, by George Seferis. London, Lehmann, 1948.
Translator, *The Curious History of Pope Joan*, by Emmanuel Royidis. London, Verschoyle, 1954; revised edition, as *Pope Joan: A Romantic Biography*, London, Deutsch, 1960; New York, Dutton, 1961.

*

Manuscript Collections: University of California, Los Angeles; University of Illinois, Urbana.

Critical Studies: *The World of Lawrence Durrell* edited by Harry T. Moore, Carbondale, Southern Illinois University Press, 1962; *Lawrence Durrell* by John Unterecker, New York, Columbia University Press, 1964; *Lawrence Durrell* by John A. Weigel, New York, Twayne, 1966; *Lawrence Durrell: A Critical Study* (includes bibliography by Alan G. Thomas), London, Faber, 1968, New York, Dutton, 1969, and *Lawrence Durrell*, London, Longman, 1970, both by G.S. Fraser; *Sensation, Vision, and Imagination: The Problem of Unity in Lawrence Durrell's Novels* by Hartwig Isernhagen, Bamberg, Bamberger Fotodruck, 1969; *Lawrence Durrell and the Alexandria Quartet* by Alan Warren Friedman, Norman, University of Oklahoma Press, 1970; *Alexandria Still: Forster, Durrell, and Cavafy* by Jane Lagoudis Pinchin, Princeton, New Jersey, Princeton University Press, 1977; *Lawrence Durrell Newsletter* (Kelowna, British Columbia).

* * *

Prolific since writing his first novel, *Pied Piper of Lovers* (1935), Lawrence Durrell suddenly achieved commercial and critical success with *The Alexandria Quartet* in the late 1950's. Though protean and eclectic, Durrell displays a consistency of concerns and techniques: a lush, baroque style; a rich patterning of ideas (about personal relationships, politics, mysticism, relativity, etc.) and ideas about ideas; a multidimensional universe and vision transcending temporal and spatial barriers; an aesthetic dependent on personal mythos, on felt reality, on narrative perspectives and deceptions, on the interplay of art, love, and death. Also central to Durrell's writing are a sense of deracination and a concomitant need to belong somewhere (perhaps his most revealing book is a collection entitled *Spirit of Place*); for like most placeless men, Durrell worships place: his landscapes embody, parallel, even motivate and control the workings of his characters. Their individuality seems often suffused, subordinated to some *deus loci*—as, on the largest scale, Alexandria dominates the *Quartet*: "Only the city is real." Durrell's writing is pervaded by the evanescent glow of place that functions as central metaphor, as touchstone, for the individual maturing into meaningful human involvement. Further, Durrell's early fiction, poetry, verse plays, and island books all anticipate the *Quartet's* theme of isolation and the individual's attaining full potential in both art and life only through total, active commitment to the creative process: art for love's sake. Thus, Justine associates work with love; Mountolive's failures in love are correlatives of his hating his work; Darley and Clea become lovers and artists only after long struggle. Most of Durrell's successful protagonists create an internal deity of selfhood, an analogue of the external *deus loci*.

In both *The Black Book* and *The Revolt of Aphrodite* demonically named protagonists reach beyond defining constrictions toward freedom and creativity. In *The Black Book* Lawrence Lucifer struggles to escape the spiritual sterility embodied by smug, dying England; he finally emerges into creative affirmation symbolized by Greece's warmth, color, and fertility. The book's style, like that of the contemporaneous *Zero, and Asylum in the Snow*, anticipates that of the *Quartet*, for its rich interweaving of naturalistic and poetic narratives transforms language into something fluid, unstructured, atemporal. In *Revolt*—a satire on science-fiction, gothic, romantic, and business exposé novels—a master inventor, Felix Charlock, becomes ensnared in the international cartel Merlin. He sells, and sells out, his work; love consequently becomes horrific, for, in Durrell, to deny the validity of one's work is to negate love. Charlock's ultimate task is to fashion an exact, "living" replica of the beautiful Greek Io, deceased ex-prostitute and world-famous actress. But the wholly successful product (able even to copulate) cannot bear the world's reality and climactically "commits suicide."

Most of Durrell's protagonists ultimately flee inhospitable surroundings, and, as his poems suggest, seek meaning and selfhood in landscape and language. Durrell's series of island books most successfully represents his love of place, of landscape corresponding and responding to man's needs and proportions without dominating him, of what he here calls islomania. Pre-war Corfu, war-devastated Rhodes, the incipient civil war of Cyprus, and the invader-dominated Sicily are concomitants of failures in art and love. Yet the permanence and strength of Durrell's Greek pattern undergird and inspirit his island books, making them not only fine travel reportage but also extended prose/poems.

Durrell's current work in progress is a series of five novels, which Blanford (his writer/protagonist) refers to as "Q novels written in a highly elliptical quincunxial style invented for the occasion." Since only two have been published, it is not yet possible to take their measure, but they contain several memorable characters and scenes; complex narrative layering (including some intense exchanges between writer and characters); fine descriptions of Provence, Paris, and Egypt; and rich discussion of such ideas and historical moments as gnosticism and the destruction of the Knights Templar in the early 14th century. One significant difference between these two books and most of Durrell's other writings is that in them death occurs at the beginning rather than at the end, so that *Monsieur* and *Livia* are, in part, a working out of accommodations to that fact.

All four books of the *Quartet* climax in death—which is almost always equivocal, other than what it seems. Durrell, among the most death-haunted and self-reflexive of contemporary novelists, is obsessed with death's creative, vitalizing power. In the *Quartet*, which was entitled "The Book of the Dead" during its genesis, death is incident, theme, motif, character, and setting. In Alexandria, city of death, virtually all its inhabitants, like those in *The Black Book*, are dead and kicking from the first. They are "playing-card characters of the living," shades partaking of the city's "obsessive rhythms of death." When Darley, the main narrator and maturing writer and lover, returns, it is "like a summons back to the Underworld," for "the dead are everywhere," he says.

Numerous characters disappear, then re-emerge in altered form. Chief among them is Pursewarden, Durrell's speaker for artistic vision and dedication *despite* his being a suicide of apparently minor significance in *Justine*. Pursewarden's death is equivocal because much of the *Quartet* attempts in various ways to explain its motivation; because large chunks of his posthumous papers are included and many characters quote him verbatim; and because he embodies the central themes of art, love, and death, as well as the *Quartet's* ultimate focus on "resurrection from the dead." And so one character dies for another, a third apparently dies but returns after another is buried for him; one is resurrected as a saint, others as characters who seemed someone else, or they grow new parts to replace worn out ones.

In Durrell character becomes, in effect, anti-character: less imposing itself upon its surroundings than imposed upon, will-less, subordinated to such forces as Alexandria itself. Conventional distinctions—major/minor characters, main/sub plots, protagonist/antagonist—are denied. Every character becomes an independent fountainhead of actions multiplying in consequence and impact. For Durrell what man knows remains elusive, incessantly becoming; truth lacks validity unless and until someone responds and interprets it. Thus, the *Quartet* is simultaneously promise and fulfillment, culmination and prophecy, a finished work of art and one prematurely made public with scaffolding still lying about, a vast, complex genre bearing the signs of an enduring and proliferating achievement.

Discussing the differences between Victorianism and modernism, Durrell in *Key to Modern Poetry* provides a "key" to himself. He maintains that human possibility, personality, values, validity, and time were transformed by Darwin, Einstein, and Freud, among others. Certainty's rock foundation has revealed itself as restive sand blown by winds of pluralism, relativity, subjectivity, indeterminacy. Like other impressionist novels, the *Quartet* dramatizes a limited narrator who seeks to understand a complex sequence of events. Yet truth's core remains forever elusive; everything is susceptible of, and receives, contradictory interpretations. In such novels the more "facts" we learn, the less significant they become; not despite but because *Mountolive* tells us most, depicts an "objective" reality, it says least about truth itself, the essence of reality captured, if anywhere, in the heart and mind of the interpreter. An early poem, "Eight Aspects of Melissa" (1946), anticipates the central devices of the *Quartet*—mirrors, prisms, lake water—and expresses Durrell's continuing concern with multifaceted personality, love, landscape, time. Both "Melissa" and the *Quartet*, like virtually all of Durrell's writings, are open-ended, implying that all aspects examined are equally valuable and that an indeterminate number of additional aspects await the seeker after truth. Neither pretends to exhaust the many questions it raises; each answer contains both additional questions and a proliferating chain of "truths." The open-endedness of the *Quartet* suggests not that all has been arranged but that, past and present having somehow accommodated themselves to each other, the future can begin to begin. Pathways now exist where there had seemed only dead ends. With "Once upon a time..."—the ending of the *Quartet*—all avenues are open; no visionary world of man's imagination remains artificially precluded. At least for the moment—and therefore for all time, since each moment contains all time—impeding checks are removed; art and life are dynamically possible.

Durrell does not claim mastery of Einsteinian relativity or Freudian psychology, but he recognizes their radical influence upon literature; ranging widely, he has made uniquely his own and his art's all he has read and experienced. His finest achievement, despite much successful poetry, drama, and travel books, lies in experimental fiction. For like this century's supreme novelists, Durrell seeks both to create art of lasting significance and to proclaim new modes of thought, new ways of envisaging a world he too has helped imagine. He has assisted in our becoming what he says we must: our own contemporaries.

—Alan Warren Friedman

DUTTON, Geoffrey (Piers Henry). Australian. Born in Anlaby, South Australia, 2 August 1922. Educated at Geelong Grammar School, Victoria, 1932-39; University of Adelaide, 1940-41; Magdelen College, Oxford, 1946-49, B.A. 1949. Served in the Royal Australian Air Force, 1941-45: Flight Lieutenant. Married Ninette Trott in 1944; three children. Senior Lecturer in English, University of Adelaide, 1954-62; Visiting Lecturer in Australian Literature, University of Leeds, 1960; Visiting Professor, Kansas State University, Manhattan, 1962. Editor, Penguin Australia, Melbourne, 1961-65. Since 1965, Editorial Director of Sun Books Pty. Ltd.,

Melbourne. Co-Founder, *Australian Letters*, Adelaide, 1957, and *Australian Book Review*, Kensington Park, 1962. Member of the Australian Council for the Arts, 1968-70, Commonwealth Literary Fund Advisory Board, 1972-73 and Australian Literature Board, 1973-78. Address: Piers Hill, Williamstown, South Australia 5351, Australia.

PUBLICATIONS

Novels

The Mortal and the Marble. London, Chapman and Hall, 1950.
Andy. Sydney and London, Collins, 1968.
Tamara. Sydney and London, Collins, 1970.
Queen Emma of the South Seas. Melbourne and London, Macmillan, 1976; New York, St. Martin's Press, 1978.

Short Stories

The Wedge-Tailed Eagle. Melbourne, Macmillan, 1980.

Verse

Night Flight. Melbourne, Reed and Harris, 1944.
Antipodes in Shoes. Sydney, Edwards and Shaw, 1955.
Flowers and Fury. Melbourne, Cheshire, 1963.
On My Island: Poems for Children. Melbourne, Cheshire, 1967.
Poems Soft and Loud. Melbourne, Cheshire, 1968.
Findings and Keepings: Selected Poems 1940-1970. Adelaide, Australian Letters, 1970.
New Poems to 1972. Adelaide, Australian Letters, 1972.
A Body of Words. Sydney, Edwards and Shaw, 1977.

Other

A Long Way South (travel). London, Chapman and Hall, 1953.
Africa in Black and White. London, Chapman and Hall, 1956.
States of the Union (travel). London, Chapman and Hall, 1958.
Founder of a City: The Life of William Light. Melbourne, Cheshire, and London, Chapman and Hall, 1960.
Patrick White. Melbourne, Lansdowne Press, 1961; revised edition, London and New York, Oxford University Press, 1971.
Walt Whitman. Edinburgh, Oliver and Boyd, and New York, Grove Press, 1961.
Paintings of S.T. Gill. Adelaide, Rigby, 1962.
Russell Drysdale (art criticism). London, Thames and Hudson, 1962; revised edition, Sydney, Angus and Robertson, 1981.
Tisi and the Yabby (juvenile). Sydney and London, Collins, 1965.
Seal Bay (juvenile). Sydney and London, Collins, 1966.
The Hero as Murderer: The Life of Edward John Eyre, Australian Explorer and Governor of Jamaica, 1815-1901. Melbourne, Cheshire, and London, Collins, 1967.
Tisi and the Pageant (juvenile). Adelaide, Rigby, 1968.
Australia's Last Explorer: Ernest Giles. London, Faber, 1970.
Australia since the Camera: From Federation to War 1901-14. Melbourne, Cheshire, 1972.
White on Black: The Australian Aborigine Portrayed in Art. Melbourne, Macmillan, 1974.
A Taste of History: Geoffrey Dutton's South Australia. Adelaide, Rigby, 1978.
Patterns of Australia, photographs by Harri Peccinotti. Melbourne, Macmillan, 1979.
Impressions of Singapore, photographs by Harri Peccinotti. Melbourne and London, Macmillan, 1981.

Editor, *The Literature of Australia.* Melbourne, Penguin, 1964; revised edition, 1976.
Editor, *Modern Australian Writing.* London, Fontana, 1966.
Editor, *Australia and the Monarchy: A Symposium.* Melbourne, Sun, 1966.
Editor, with Max Harris, *The Vital Decade: 10 Years of Australian Art and Letters.* Melbourne, Sun, 1968.
Editor, with Max Harris, *Sir Henry Bjelke, Don Baby, and Friends.* Melbourne, Sun, 1971.
Editor, *Republican Australia?* Melbourne, Sun, 1977.

Translator, with Igor Mezhakoff-Koriakin, *Bratsk Station*, by Yevgeny Yevtushenko. Melbourne, Sun, 1966; New York, Doubleday, 1967; London, Hart Davis, 1968.
Translator, with Igor Mezhakoff-Koriakin, *Fever and Other New Poems*, by Bella Akhmadulina. Melbourne, Sun, 1968; New York, Morrow, 1969; London, Peter Owen, 1970.
Translator, *Kazan University and Other New Poems*, by Yevgeny Yevtushenko. Melbourne, Sun, 1973.

*

Geoffrey Dutton comments:

(1972) My three novels, although completely different in characters and in settings, have all basically dealt with the same theme, that of Australian innocence as against the experience of "older" countries. In more detail, *The Mortal and the Marble* deals with the impact of European migrants on Australia after the second world war; *Andy* with the idiocy of war, especially in a country on whose soil it is never fought; *Tamara* with the impact on an intelligent but relatively unsophisticated Australian scientist of the complex world of Soviet Russian poetry.

* * *

Geoffrey Dutton's reputation is that of an accomplished all-round man of letters—poet and critic, biographer and cultural historian, publisher, editor, and journalist—and his entertaining novels contribute to this general reputation. Although they vary widely in their settings and development, the four novels have some structural similarities, and all are concerned with conflicts between local and European values, individual freedom and social restriction, and the natural and the civilized worlds.

His first novel, *The Mortal and the Marble*, reveals its period by exhibiting what the Australian critic A.A. Phillips has called the "cultural cringe." With an eye on the overseas market, it explains local folkways in the obtrusive way that has characterized "colonial novels" for over a century, and even such hallowed clichés as the incongruity of eating Christmas pudding in the middle of summer find their place. The theme of the novel is Mark Vaughan's ambivalence towards two conflicting sets of values—the traditional culture of the Europe he has never seen and the material comfort and natural beauty of his own "uncultured" country. And, the reader feels, *The Mortal and the Marble* is itself the author's attempt to resolve a similar conflict between his own "literary" notions of the novel and the incongruous, because "unliterary," actuality of his experiences in Australia.

Dutton attempts not only to work out dramatically the concern of the Australian novelist who feels his "complex fate" but also a more fundamental theme. As well as the encounters between the Vaughans and such representatives of European culture (and of the post-World War II immigration to Australia) as their Russian friend Alexey and the Germans Paul, Willi, and Professor Klein, there is contrast between personal and social life. The aridity of ordinary suburbia and the frigidity of Melbourne "Society" are both contrasted with the Vaughans' escapes to the bush. When the characters go to an island for a holiday the conflicts between Australian and European values and between the "natural" and the civilized life are explored in almost fable form, and action, rather than dialogue, becomes the vehicle of the theme.

The author is more successful with his description of the young married lovers in the bush than he is with them in Society, where his concerns become too overtly stated through the dialogue. Dutton has talents for describing action and natural setting (as his *The Hero as Murderer* reveals), and the passages of natural description draw with ease and enthusiasm on the English Romantic poetic tradition, while the most memorable sections of this first novel are accounts of body surfing and an interpolated story of stunt flying.

The resolution of Mark Vaughan's conflict is curious. His European friends, as in much New World writing, prove to be corrupt and degenerate beneath their charm and erudition. Dinkum Aussie values are finally vindicated but Mark also secures his ticket to the Europe he has idealized. The ending does not resolve his conflicts so much as allow him to have the best of both worlds. It is a novelettish ending to a book in which what is happening at the level of the author's own involvement with his characters (especially the impossibly stereotyped Professor Klein, embodiment of European degeneracy) proves more interesting than their involvement with each other.

In Dutton's second novel, *Andy*, nostalgia for the old Australia before the American alliance eroded the national virtues of independence and self-reliance lurks beneath the comic picaresque story of a young R.A.A.F. pilot's conflicts with authority. *Andy* is deliberately freer in form and more comic than the first novel, but again one senses personal experiences and responses to social change are being worked out through fantasies that are indistinguishable from those of the novelette. Andy, however, is not unequivocally an autobiographical projection. The author's merging with his hero is balanced by his merging with other characters as well—with the virginal and intellectual Ian Almond and with the idealized Tasmanian squire John Lydford.

More thematically than structurally organized, *Andy* is a free-wheeling comedy of the moral education of a pilot during World War II; but is is impossible to say what his moral education consists of because of a complete surrender to fantasy at the end. Like the first novel, *Andy* contains too much to be controlled and directed. It seems, appropriately for its hero, a cavalier enterprise, a deliberately off-handed indulgence in irresponsible *joie-de-vivre* accompanied by a nostalgia for youth and the past with which it is associated.

Dutton's third novel, *Tamara*, is his most satisfactory to date. Like the works of others, e.g., Malamud and Updike, who have visited the U.S.S.R. and attempted to come to grips with their own confused impressions through fiction, it presents the contradictions perceived in contemporary Russian society—warm humanity and cold bureaucracy, technological advance and bad plumbing, a national passion for literature and rigorous political censorship. Such contradictions offer possibilities for both social comedy and serious social concern and Dutton blends the two more successfully in this novel than in its predecessors. He is a fine travel writer and his descriptive powers are seen at their best in the scenes which present Russian, especially Georgian, life.

The story is one of a simple soil scientist from Kangaroo Island who is invited to Russia as Australian delegate to a literary conference and who falls in love with Russia's leading poetess. Through this romantic and not very probable story is expressed a serious concern with the position of the writer in the Soviet Union as a critical point for evaluating the whole direction of post-Stalinist Russia. The presentation of Russian society is vivid and sympathetic and, although it is a romantic comedy, *Tamara* avoids the wish-fulfilment endings of the earlier novels.

The most recent novel, *Queen Emma of the South Seas*, is a documentary fiction that presents, through multiple points of view, the life of the historical figure Emma Coe. The daughter of a U.S. commercial agent and one of his Samoan wives, she was educated in Australia and became unofficial queen of her island and a prosperous trader. The novel's early chapters evoke the lush natural setting and innocent Samoan life. With all of his romantic sympathies, Dutton presents Emma as beautiful, intelligent, and amorous, and his basic theme of innocence conflicting with experience is elaborated through the contrast between Samoan hedonism and the "civilization" brought by European colonizers and missionaries.

—Brian Kiernan

EASTLAKE, William (Derry). American. Born in New York City, 14 July 1917. Educated at Bonnie Brae School; Caldwell High School, New Jersey; Alliance Française, Paris, 1948-50. Served in the United States Army in World War II. Married Martha Simpson in 1943. Writer-in-Residence, Knox College, Galesburg, Illinois, 1967-68; Lecturer, University of New Mexico, Albuquerque, 1968-69; Writer-in-Residence, University of Southern California, Los Angeles, 1969, and University of Arizona, Tucson, 1969-71. Recipient: Ford grant, 1964; Rockefeller grant, 1966. D.Litt.: University of Albuquerque, 1970. Address: 102 Coconino Drive, Bisbee, Arizona 85603, U.S.A.

PUBLICATIONS

Novels

Go in Beauty. New York, Harper, 1956; London, Secker and Warburg, 1957.
The Bronc People. New York, Harcourt Brace, 1958; London, Deutsch, 1963.
Portrait of an Artist with Twenty-Six Horses. New York, Simon and Schuster, 1963; London, Joseph, 1965.
Castle Keep. New York, Simon and Schuster, 1965; London, Joseph, 1966.
The Bamboo Bed. New York, Simon and Schuster, 1969; London, Joseph, 1970.
Dancers in the Scalp House. New York, Viking Press, 1975.
The Long, Naked Descent into Boston: A Tricentennial Novel. New York, Viking Press, 1977.

Uncollected Short Stories

"Ishimoto's Land," in *Essai* (Geneva, Switzerland), Summer 1952.
"Two Gentlemen from America," in *Hudson Review* (New York), Fall 1954.
"Homecoming," in *Quarto* (New York), Fall 1954.
"The Barfly and the Navajo," in *Nation* (New York), 12 September 1959.
"A Long Day's Dying," in *The Best American Short Stories 1964*, edited by Martha Foley and David Burnett. Boston, Houghton Mifflin, 1964.
"Little Joe," in *The Best American Short Stories 1965*, edited by Martha Foley and David Burnett. Boston, Houghton Mifflin, 1965.
"Something Big Is Happening to Me," in *New American Story*, edited by Robert Creeley and Donald Allen. New York, Grove Press, 1965.
"What Nice Hands Held," in *Gallery of Modern Fiction*, edited by Robie Macauley. New York, Salem Press, 1966.
"There's a Camel in My Cocktail," in *Harper's* (New York), April 1966.
"Jack Armstrong in Tangiers," in *Evergreen Review* (New York), August 1966.
"The Last Frenchman in Fez," in *Evergreen Review* (New York), December 1967.
"Three Heroes and a Clown," in *Evergreen Review Reader 1957-1967*, edited by Barney Rosset. New York, Grove Press, 1968.
"Now Lucifer Is Not Dead," in *Evergreen Review* (New York), November 1968.
"The Message," in *New Mexico Quarterly* (Albuquerque), Winter 1968.
"The Hanging at Prettyfields," in *Evergreen Review* (New York), February 1969.
"A Dead Man's Guide to Mallorca," in *New Mexico Quarterly* (Albuquerque), Winter-Spring 1969.
"The Biggest Thing Since Custer," in *Prize Stories 1970: The O. Henry Awards*, edited by William Abrahams. New York, Doubleday, 1970.

"The Dancing Boy," in *The Best American Short Stories 1971*, edited by Martha Foley and David Burnett. Boston, Houghton Mifflin, 1971.

"The Death of Sun," in *The Best American Short Stories 1973*, edited by Martha Foley. Boston, Houghton Mifflin, 1973.

"Mrs. Gage in Her Bed of Pain with a Nice Cup of Gin," in *Ms* (New York), March 1977.

Verse

A Child's Garden of Verses for the Revolution (verse and essays). New York, Grove Press, 1971.

*

Critical Studies: "The Novels of William Eastlake" by Delbert W. Wylder, in *New Mexico Quarterly* (Albuquerque), 1965; "Of Cowboys, Indians and the Modern West" by Peter M. Kenyon, in *Sage Magazine* (Las Vegas, Nevada), Winter 1969; *William Eastlake* by Gerald Haslam, Austin, Texas, Steck Vaughn, 1970.

William Eastlake comments:

(1972) As long as we are serving a life sentence on this earth there has got to be something to make the time go easy. The thing to work at is to be the best writer on earth, or the best magician, for writing is magic, and like all the things that are important you do it all alone. As I expressed it in *The Bronc People*:

> "You can't give anyone anything."
> "You mean I've got to do it alone?"
> "Yes."
> "But the missionary says no man is an island."
> "Well, he is."
> "You think the missionary got that saying from another preacher?"
> "Yes."
> "We've got to go it all alone?"
> "Yes, we do."

My last book, *A Child's Garden of Verses for the Revolution*, is a comment on the end of America and the west, the only part of the earth I really know. But the artist is sentenced and elected as medicine man because he holds out hope. That is his job. That is what he was hired for. My hope is in the youth of the world. The people of the earth turn more and more to the writer, the medicine man, as their tribal leaders fail them. And as our present tribal leaders are unworthy even of the dignity of death, the medicine man, through his novels, fulfills man through artistic re-enactment.

> Once upon a time there was a time. The land here in the Southwest had evolved slowly and there was time and there were great spaces. Now a man on horseback from atop a bold mesa looked out over the violent spectrum of the Indian Country—into a gaudy infinity where all the colors exploded soundlessly. "There is not much time," he said.

The death of all of us worthy of death is enacted by the Indian medicine man. Death he calls "Something big is happening to me." Any place the writer, the medicine man, the shaman, lives is the center of the earth.

> Below at the post, the exact center and the capital of the world for The People, two Indians crouched at the massive stone root of the petrified-wood house where it made its way into the ground.
>
> "This crack," the Indian said, tracing it with his brown finger.
>
> "They can fix it," Rabbit Stockings said.
>
> "No. And perhaps even The People cannot stop something coming apart and beginning here at the center of the world."

The artist's job is to hold the world together. What the politicians cannot do with reality the artist does with magic, even if the artist is an epileptic Dostoievsky, a failed Melville working in a customs house, a wandering Walt Whitman peddling his *Leaves of Grass* from door to door. The artist finds life everlasting in his magic. William Shakespeare is still very much alive. God is pronounced dead.

* * *

At first glance William Eastlake appears to be America's most paradoxical literary artist. Although he was born in New York and grew up in New Jersey and although he traveled widely in Europe after World War II and for some years lived and worked in Los Angeles, he purchased land in an isolated, remote area of New Mexico and there for some years lived the life of the small-spread rancher and literary man. Eastlake thereby became a strongly committed regionalist and one of the most astute observers of present-day American Indian life. Although isolated, Eastlake's concerns were always with national policy, our establishment in Washington and in Vietnam, or the significance of American poverty at home as against American explorations of outer space. On the one hand he appears to seek a kind of peace in a remote area, yet he remains angry at fellow provincials of limited vision, the rednecks and unenlightened army colonels. If Eastlake protests the fate of Mexican, Indian, and Black persons in America, he cannot defend, in the name of a beloved democracy, the violence and the turmoil in our urban centers and on the country roads of out-yonder America. His life-style suggests the pursuit of calm by association with Nature; yet the work presents a sharp focus on the evils of modernity in an idiom which combines the sardonic and the realistic along with an acceptance of the implied values of both ritual and myth. If these paradoxes are real, then their resolution in Eastlake's work suggests an artist of uncommon personal stability and unusual dedication to his own view of the world. If there is tension implicit in these paradoxical roles, the result is artistic production of a high order.

From the centers of these contradictive conflicts emerge his most significant works. Ostensibly the materials are Indians and tourists; cattlemen and brute geography; the neon market towns and the sagebrush. Beneath this closely observed, naturalistic surface, however, the concern is the modes of right conduct, the moral propositions implicit in actions, the attitudes toward life of the protagonists. Irony, humor, and fantasy are everywhere, and thus the true position of the authorial voice behind the prose fictions is not always easy to discern. In moral considerations a continued reliance on irony is no position at all.

Nevertheless, the pervading irony—and compassion—suggest Eastlake's American literary tradition and major influence. His overt search for materials (the move to New Mexico), his stints as war correspondent in Vietnam, his running commentary on cultural and political policy suggest the tradition of the 19th-century correspondent/writer: Stephen Crane, Jack London, and more recently Hemingway. Likewise, the concern for a "moral center," for Justice, for the destiny of America and its people suggests Walt Whitman, poet, editor, "correspondent" of an earlier age. Of the direct literary influences, however, Hemingway is the most significant: the terse understatement, the stripped-down dialogue, the concept of the character, the close focus on the details of war, the sometimes anti-intellectual, anti-bookish, anti-cultural stances strongly suggest the Hemingway of the early novels and the war-correspondent years. Many commonplaces from the criticism of Hemingway, for example, the kind of commentary which identifies the strong romantic element in his work, could be applied as well to Eastlake. If the two men in a great many ways are comparable literary talents, Eastlake's exemplary management of his own talent may prove ultimately the more productive. Eastlake is a model of affirmative experience in the matter of attaining a balance between artistic necessity and humanitarian concern.

Of the novels *The Bronc People* and the short fictions in the same vein attract the most critical attention. Although *Castle Keep* became a successful film and was widely translated, the novel increasingly becomes an example of a book less effective as a whole than the sum of its sometimes brilliant episodes. The Vietnam materials, the journalistic snap shots and quasi-interviews, are repetitive and are less effective together than when they appeared singly in the *Nation*. The poetry of *A Child's Garden of Verses for the Revolution* purports to be "revolutionary" but on balance fails either to move the reader or to offer an effective program beyond the necessity of mutual respect, a change of heart, or other humanistic concerns. While the work varies in quality, the commitment is always firm, and a strong sensibility is apparent everywhere.

If Eastlake's artistic concerns appear now somewhat resolved, this condition is probably a prelude to the continuing search for new materials.

—James B. Hall

EKWENSI, Cyprian (Odiatu Duaka). Nigerian. Born in Minna, Northern Nigeria, 26 September 1921. Educated at Government College, Ibadan; Achimota College, Ghana; School of Forestry, Ibadan; Higher College, Yaba; Chelsea School of Pharmacy, University of London. Married to Eunice Anyiwo; five children. Lecturer in Biology, Chemistry and English, Igbodi College, Lagos, 1947-49; Lecturer in Pharmacognosy and Pharmaceutics, School of Pharmacy, Lagos, 1949-56; Pharmacist, Nigerian Medical Service, 1956; Head of Features, Nigerian Broadcasting Corporation, 1957-61; Director of Information, Federal Ministry of Information, Lagos, 1961-66. Since 1966, Director of Information Services in Enugu. Travelled to the United States, with Chinua Achebe and Gabriel Okara, to seek help for Biafra, 1969. Chairman, East Central State Library Board, Enugu, 1971; Member, Nigerian Arts Council. Recipient: Dag Hammarskjöld International Award, 1968. Address: 50 Ogbete Street, P. O. Box 317, Enugu, Nigeria.

PUBLICATIONS

Novels

People of the City. London, Dakers, 1954; revised edition, London, Heinemann, 1963; New York, Fawcett, 1969.
Jagua Nana. London, Hutchinson, 1961; New York, Fawcett, 1969.
Burning Grass: A Story of the Fulani of Northern Nigeria. London, Heinemann, 1962.
Beautiful Feathers. London, Hutchinson, 1963.
Iska. London, Hutchinson, 1966.
Survive the Peace. London, Heinemann, 1976.

Short Stories

The Rainmaker and Other Stories. Lagos, African Universities Press, 1965.
Lokotown and Other Stories. London, Heinemann, 1966.
Restless City and Christmas Gold with Other Stories. London, Heinemann, 1975.

Other (juvenile)

When Love Whispers. Onitsha, Nigeria, Tabansi Bookshop, 1947.
Ikolo the Wrestler and Other Ibo Tales. London, Nelson, 1947.
The Leopard's Claw. London, Longman, 1950.
The Drummer Boy. London, Cambridge University Press, 1960.
The Passport of Mallam Ilia. London, Cambridge University Press, 1960.
An African Night's Entertainment: A Tale of Vengeance. Lagos, African Universities Press, and London, Deutsch, 1962.
Yaba Roundabout Murder. Lagos, Tortoise, 1962.
The Great Elephant-Bird. London, Nelson, 1965.
Trouble in Form Six. London, Cambridge University Press, 1966.
The Boa Suitor. London, Nelson, 1966.
Juju Rock. Lagos, African Universities Press, 1966.
Coal Camp Boy. Lagos, Longman, 1973.
Samankwe in the Strange Forest. Lagos, Longman, 1973.
The Rainbow-Tinted Scarf and Other Stories. London, Evans, 1975.
Samankwe and the Highway Robbers. London, Evans, 1975.

Editor, *Festac Anthology of Nigerian New Writing* (for adults). Lagos, Federal Ministry of Information, 1977.

*

Critical Study: *Cyprian Ekwensi* by Ernest Emenyona, London, Evans, 1974.

* * *

Granted much mawkish sentiment, an eye for the sensational, a technical naivety that allows abrupt transitions and unlikely coincidences, and a frequently banal use of English, yet Cyprian Ekwensi cannot be lightly dismissed as a Nigerian writer. His career began in the Onitsha market in Eastern Nigeria, where cheap, sentimental, moralistic stories in English catered for readers with an English-type primary education obtained in mission schools—and this Onitsha ethos can be detected in all his writings. Yet there are other characteristics also, chiefly a vivid sense of actuality, especially when he places his characters on the street and in the night clubs and slums of Lagos. Except for *Burning Grass* and stories written for children, Ekwensi's writings convey the heady experience of young Africans from the country being attracted, excited, bemused, usually destroyed by the glitter of city lights. Passing fashions of dress and undress are catalogues, highlife rhythms pulsate in the background, hips wiggle, and bosoms quiver alluringly, but with real understanding Ekwensi evokes the frustration, inner unhappiness, restlessness, and rootlessness of a new urbanized African generation. There is also a muted satirical tone. He attacks political jobbery and public scandal. He invents a Nigerian Ministry of Consolation to epitomize all that is corrupt and inefficient.

These qualities together suggest that Ekwensi's talent is that of a good journalist rather than a novelist, that he is the chronicler of modern West African urbanization. He clearly disapproves of much that he reports but, like a journalist, is so involved in the reporting that he also becomes excited by the things he would condemn. The banal dialogue of characters in moments of emotional intensity is the banality of the everyday speech of ordinary people—a dedication to the actual precludes any attempt at a literary artefact that would suggest the "real" and yet transcend it. He has claimed that he is no "artist," simply a teller of entertaining tales. His historical position is clear enough: with *People of the City* he became the first Anglophone African writer who tried to present in fictional terms the human problems that confronted individuals in a time of rapid social and political change in Africa, as the mores of village culture came into conflict with westernized city life.

Though *Jagua Nana* is still episodic in construction, it gains from being a character-study in depth of a Lagos prostitute desperately trying to find stability before she has worked herself out. The book also probes the thuggery of Nigerian politics in the old Federation. *Beautiful Feathers* is the most successfully satirical of Ekwensi's books, with its wry treatment of politicians and civil servants. Its symbolic big-game hunt, when white observers get away with the quarry while the African delegates to a Conference on African solidarity squabble among themselves, points to one of Ekwensi's genuine strengths—his sensitiveness to the larger political issues of the day. Despite its lingering Onitsha qualities, *Iska* warns with prophetic insistence of the dangers of tribal factionalism in Nigeria on the eve of the Biafran war, and shows a serious social purpose in its treatment of the 1966 Igbo massacres in Northern Nigeria. Ekwensi's role as vivid chronicler of change is confirmed in *Survive the Peace*, set in war-torn Eastern Nigeria as the Civil War ends.

—Arthur Ravenscroft

ELKIN, Stanley (Lawrence). American. Born in New York City, 11 May 1930. Educated at the University of Illinois, Urbana, 1948-60, B.A. 1952, M.A. 1953, Ph.D. 1961. Served in the United States Army, 1957-59. Married Joan Jacobson in 1953; three children. Since 1960, Member of the English faculty, and since 1968, Professor of English, Washington University, St. Louis. Visiting Lecturer, Smith College, Northampton, Massachusetts, 1964-65; Visiting Professor, University of California at Santa Barbara, Summer 1967, University of Wisconsin, Milwaukee, Summer 1969, and Yale University, New Haven, Connecticut, 1975. Recipient: Longview Foundation Award, 1962; *Paris Review* prize, 1965; Guggenheim Fellowship, 1966; Rockefeller Fellowship, 1968; National Endowment for the Arts grant, 1971; American Academy grant, 1974; Rosenthal Foundation award, 1980. Address: Department of English, Washington University, St. Louis, Missouri 63130, U.S.A.

PUBLICATIONS

Novels

Boswell. New York, Random House, and London, Hamish Hamilton, 1964.
A Bad Man. New York, Random House, 1967; London, Blond, 1968.
The Dick Gibson Show. New York, Random House, and London, Weidenfeld and Nicolson, 1971.
The Franchiser. New York, Farrar Straus, 1976.
The Living End. New York, Dutton, 1979; London, Cape, 1980.

Short Stories

Criers and Kibitzers, Kibitzers and Criers. New York, Random House, 1966; London, Blond, 1968.
The Making of Ashenden. London, Covent Garden Press, 1972.
Searches and Seizures. New York, Random House, 1973; as *Eligible Men*, London, Gollancz, 1974; as *Alex and the Gypsy*, London, Penguin, 1977.

Uncollected Short Stories

"A Sound of Distant Thunder," in *Epoch* (Ithaca, New York), 1957.
"The Party," in *Views* (Louisville, Kentucky), 1958.
"Fifty Dollars," in *Southwest Review* (Dallas), 1959.
"The Graduate Seminar," in *Fiction* (New York), i, 1, 1972.
"The Conventional Wisdom." in *American Review 26*, edited by Theodore Solotaroff. New York, Bantam, 1977.

Play

The Six-Year-Old Man (filmscript), in *Esquire* (New York), 1969.

Other

Stanley Elkin's Greatest Hits (omnibus). New York, Dutton, 1980.
Editor, *Stories from the Sixties.* New York, Doubleday, 1971.
Editor, with Shannon Ravenel, *The Best American Short Stories 1980.* Boston, Houghton Mifflin, 1980.

*

Manuscript Collection: Washington University Library, St. Louis.

Critical Studies: *Humanism and the Absurd* by Naomi Lebowitz, Evanston, Illinois, Northwestern University Press, 1971; *City of Words* by Tony Tanner, London, Cape, 1971; *The Jewish Writer in America* by Allen Guttman, New York, Oxford University Press, 1971; *Beyond the Wasteland* by Raymond Olderman, New Haven, Connecticut, Yale University Press, 1972.

Stanley Elkin comments:

I don't know what to say about my work. What I like best about it, I suppose, are the sentences. What I like least about it is my guess that probably no one is ever moved by it.

* * *

> [Writing] is a matter of feeling one's way. It is not instinctive. It's a question of using a pencil, erasing, creating a palimpsest of metaphor right there on the page. One gets a notion of the conceit and one is inspired to work with it as a draftsman might work with some angle that he is interested in getting down correctly. That's where all the fun of writing is for me. I don't read much non-fiction because the non-fiction I do read always seems to be so badly written. What I enjoy about fiction—the great gift of fiction—is that it gives language an opportunity to happen. What I am really interested in after personality are not philosophic ideas or abstractions or patterns, but this superb opportunity for language to take place (interview with Thomas LeClair, in *Paris Review*, Summer 1976).

"Surely the point of life was the possibility it always held out for the exceptional. The range of the strange," says Dick Gibson, Stanley Elkin's disc jockey and fellow word man. The point, too, of Elkin's fiction which is exceptional because sentence for sentence, metaphor for metaphor, no novelist in America writes as energetically and musically as Elkin. His books display the "range of the strange": not the exotic or esoteric, but ordinary life made extraordinary by his imaginative participation in it, the usual seen and said with unusual clarity. "The world is a miracle," adds franchiser Ben Flesh, but, he goes on for himself and for Elkin, you have to "Drive up and down in it.... Look close at it. See its moving parts, its cranes and car parks and theater districts." Elkin has pressed his nose to the American showcase, heard all the sellers of self and thing, has eaten Colonel Sanders chicken and slept in Holiday Inns. Everything—and this is the secret of Elkin's prose—is available for the sentences that turn us back to our franchised and media-furrowed land with new apprehension and appreciation.

"Drive drives the world," to quote Dick Gibson again. Elkin's heroes are obsessives, common men with uncommon appetites, bad men because they refuse to compromise, good men for the same reason. The professional wrestler in *Boswell*, Elkin's first novel, is obsessed with death and with what he calls "The Great." Like his predecessor James, Boswell seeks out the exceptional. Feldman, entrepreneur hero of *A Bad Man*, is driven to make the ultimate sale, either in his bargain basement or in the prison to which he is sent. Dick Gibson of *The Dick Gibson Show* and Ben Flesh of *The Franchiser* must have destinies, must feel chosen for the services they render: Gibson as a late-night Miss Lonelyhearts of the air, Flesh as provider of the goofy comfort of familiar franchises. For these characters, fixation turns an occupation into a life, and Elkin turns their lives into success stories for a shrinking America: modest means transformed by the gaiety of will.

Like his characters, Elkin's prose is willful, obsessive, omnivorous. Here is Dick Gibson describing quiet: "I was in a trance, a catalepsy, a swoon, a brown study, a neutral funk. I was languid, gravid, the thousand-pound kid in Miriam's room, sensitized as human soup. And if I heard her at all it was in my ilium I listened—as deep as that—harkened in my coccyx, my pajama strings all ears, and my buttons and the Kleenex under my pillow." The series of synonyms tries to exhaust meaning as the extravagant metaphors, hyperbole, and refurbished clichés try to extend it. Elkin's models are oral and colloquial—the pitch of his salesman father, the oratory he wrote about in Faulkner's work, the shop talk he collects. His purposes are performance—Elkin loves the comic high-wire—and defamiliarization, the artistic recovery of "all the derelict and marooned, the ditched and scavenged. Debris, dregs, lees. Dregs addicts. All the multitudinous slag of the ordinary."

While Elkin's stories in *Criers and Kibitzers, Kibitzers and Criers* are widely anthologized, and the three novellas in *Searches and Seizures* are much admired, Elkin's gifts are those of the novelist. He describes himself as a "putter-inner." Because shorter forms do not allow Elkin room for the accretion of character that marks the novels, situations and people in the stories can seem simply eccentric. In the novels, repetition of image and action, rhetorical intensity, even digressions and included tales, have a cumulative effect. A whole world is created, laced and grained with detail. Some readers complain that not enough happens, and critics worry Elkin about structure, but for him action is language working on the world and the reader. The books have fairy-tale skeletons and the page-to-page metaphoric order of poetry. *Boswell* and *A Bad Man* do conclude with the fantastic. In *The Dick Gibson Show* and *The Franchiser* Elkin's sensibility has deepened, giving the books a Siamese connection of pain and the ecstasy of ego.

Always a writer's writer, Elkin has with *The Living End*, a triad of long stories about heaven and hell, attracted a larger readership. Widely and favorably reviewed, *The Living End* is Elkin at his best: ranging from the life of a Minneapolis-St. Paul liquor salesman to the secrets God held back from man ("why dentistry was a purer science than astronomy, biography a higher form than dance" and more), encompassing the banalities of conventional wisdom and the profundities of last things. Not since Melville shook Ahab's fist at heaven has an American novelist written so affectingly about the problem of Evil, the bugs in the divine "state of the art." *The Living End* also furnishes an epigraph for all of Elkin's fiction: "Anything could happen, everything is true."

—Thomas LeClair

ELLISON, Ralph (Waldo). American. Born in Oklahoma City, Oklahoma, 1 March 1914. Educated at a high school in Oklahoma City, and at Tuskegee Institute, Alabama, 1933-36. Served in the United States Merchant Marine, 1943-45. Married Fanny McConnell in 1946. Writer from 1936; Lecturer, Salzburg Seminar in American Studies, 1954; Instructor of Russian and American Literature, Bard College, Annandale-on-Hudson, New York, 1958-61; Alexander White Visiting Professor, University of Chicago, 1961; Visiting Professor of Writing, Rutgers University, New Brunswick, New Jersey, 1962-64; Whittall Lecturer, Library of Congress, Washington, D.C., 1964; Ewing Lecturer, University of California at Los Angeles, 1964; Visiting Fellow in American Studies, Yale University, New Haven, Connecticut, 1966. Since 1970, Albert Schweitzer Professor in the Humanities, New York University. Chairman, Literary Grants Committee, American Academy, 1964-67; Member, National Council on the Arts, 1965-67; Member, Carnegie Commission on Educational Television, 1966-67; Member of the Editorial Board, *American Scholar*, Washington, D.C., 1966-69; Honorary Consultant in American Letters, Library of Congress, Washington, D.C., 1966-72. Trustee, John F. Kennedy Center of the Performing Arts, Washington, D.C., New School for Social Research, New York, Bennington College, Vermont, Educational Broadcasting Corporation, and the Colonial Williamsburg Foundation. Recipient: Rosenwald Fellowship, 1945; National Book Award, 1953; National Newspaper Publishers Association Russwarm Award, 1953; American Academy Prix de Rome, 1955, 1956; United States Medal of Freedom, 1969. Ph.D. in Humane Letters: Tuskegee Institute, 1963; Litt.D.: Rutgers University, 1966; University of Michigan, Ann Arbor, 1967; Williams College, Williamstown, Massachusetts, 1970; Long Island University, New York, 1971; College of William and Mary, Williamsburg, Virginia, 1972; Wake Forest College, Winston-Salem, North Carolina, 1974; Harvard University, Cambridge, Massachusetts, 1974; L.H.D.: Grinnell College, Iowa, 1967; Adelphi University, Garden City, New York, 1971; University of Maryland, College Park, 1974. Chevalier de l'Ordre des Arts et Lettres, France, 1970. Member, American Academy, 1975. Agent: Owen Laster, William Morris Agency, 1350 Avenue of the Americas, New York, New York 10019. Address: 730 Riverside Drive, New York, New York 10031, U.S.A.

PUBLICATIONS

Novel

Invisible Man. New York, Random House, 1952; London, Gollancz, 1953.

Excerpts from novel-in-progress: "The Roof, the Steeple and the People," in *Quarterly Review of Literature* (Princeton, New Jersey), 1960; "And Hickman Arrives," in *The Noble Savage* (Cleveland), March 1960; "It Always Breaks Out," in *Partisan Review* (New Brunswick, New Jersey), Spring 1963; "Juneteenth," in *Quarterly Review of Literature 13*, 1965; "Night-Talk," in *Quarterly Review of Literature 16*, 1969; "Song of Innocence," in *Iowa Review* (Iowa City), Spring 1970.

Uncollected Short Stories

"Slick Gonna Learn," in *Direction* (Darien, Connecticut), September 1939.
"Afternoon," in *American Writing*. Prairie City, Illinois, James A. Decker, 1940.
"The Birthmark," in *New Masses* (New York), 2 July 1940.
"Mister Toussan," in *New Masses* (New York), 4 November 1941.
"That I Had the Wings," in *Common Ground* (New York), Summer 1943.
"Flying Home," in *Cross Section*, edited by Edwin Seaver. New York, Fischer, 1944.
"In a Strange Country," in *Tomorrow* (New York), July 1944.
"King of the Bingo Game," in *Tomorrow* (New York), November 1944.
"Did You Ever Dream Lucky?," in *New World Writing 5*. New York, New American Library, 1954.
"A Coupla Scalped Indians," in *New World Writing 9*. New York, New American Library, 1956.
"Out of the Hospital and under the Bar," in *Soon, One Morning: New Writing by American Negroes, 1940-62*, edited by Herbert Hill. New York, Knopf, 1963.
"The Death of Clifton," in *Brothers and Sisters*, edited by Arnold Adoff. New York, Macmillan, 1970.
"Cadillac Flambé," in *American Review 16*, edited by Theodore Solotaroff. New York, Bantam, 1973.
"Backwacking: A Plea to the Senator," in *Massachusetts Review* (Amherst), Autumn 1977.

Other

The Writer's Experience, with Karl Shapiro. Washington, D.C., Library of Congress, 1964.
Shadow and Act (essays). New York, Random House, 1964; London, Secker and Warburg, 1967.

The City in Crisis, with Whitney Young and Herbert Gnas. New York, Randolph Educational Fund, 1968.

*

Bibliography: "A Bibliography of Ralph Ellison's Published Writings" by Bernard Benoit and Michel Fabre, in *Studies in Black Literature* (Fredericksburg, Virginia), Autumn 1971; *The Blinking Eye: Ralph Waldo Ellison and His American, French, German and Italian Critics, 1952-1971* by Jacqueline Covo, Metuchen, New Jersey, Scarecrow Press, 1974.

Critical Studies: *The Negro Novel in America*, revised edition, by Robert A. Bone, New Haven, Connecticut, Yale University Press, 1958; "The Blues as a Literary Theme" by Gene Bluestein, in *Massachusetts Review* (Amherst), Autumn 1967; *Five Black Writers: Essays* by Donald B. Gibson, New York, New York University Press, 1970; *Twentieth-Century Interpretations of "Invisible Man"* edited by John M. Reilly, Englewood Cliffs, New Jersey, Prentice Hall, 1970; "Ralph Ellison Issue" of *C.L.A. Journal* (Baltimore), March 1970; interview in *Atlantic* (Boston), December 1970; *The Merrill Studies in "Invisible Man"* edited by Ronald Gottesman, Columbus, Ohio, Merrill, 1971; *Ralph Ellison: A Collection of Critical Essays* edited by John Hersey, Englewood Cliffs, New Jersey, Prentice Hall, 1973; *The Craft of Ralph Ellison* by Robert G. O'Meally, Cambridge, Massachusetts, Harvard University Press, 1980.

* * *

From the fact that he has published a single novel and that some 30 years ago, Ralph Ellison's reputation as a major American novelist seems phenomenal, but then his novel is a remarkable work. On one level the nameless protagonist of *Invisible Man* is a modern *picaro* moving through the realms of the Southern American black bourgeosie, Northern industrial society, and the radical political movement learning to survive the bewildering contradictions of racial stereotype and reality by converting the instability of personal identity, which he finds to be the normal state of a black person in the white world, into a condition for freedom. His triumph is less than the classical *picaro*'s, for it is conscious knowledge of the absurdity of the situations he has experienced that sustains him after his American progress rather than a tested capacity to determine his fate. In that fact, however, lies both Ellison's commentary on freedom in the modern world and his understanding of a philosophical role for fiction. The self-aware figure of the invisible man is liberated from external sanctions and, in the imagery of Camus, having seen the stage sets collapse knows there is no just authority to support the human inventions of caste. Crouched in his hole in the ground, mentally journeying through time and space while deliberating a responsible plan for living he gathers all of his being into potentiality. Only potentiality, though, because *Invisible Man*, published in 1952, announces the prerequisite mind set for liberation, not the tactics of the struggle.

The philosophical dynamics of Ellison's novel are embodied in its structure. The narrative of absurd experiences bound between a prologue and epilogue makes clear that the events have already happened to the invisible spokesman and are thus contained within his consciousness where he is free to shape them into significance as he wills. Where the realist or naturalist stresses the clarity of perception, saying he will record only what objectively happens in the world, the surrealist Ellison considers his tale to be an epistemological drama in which the active forces are the conceptions of race and society that determine what each character will perceive. Consequently, the stress upon sight in the title of the novel points not only to stereotypes that obscure our social vision but indicates as well the power of imagination to create a habitable reality.

Ellison's modernist esthetics have earned his novel high critical estimation. In 1965 *Book Week*, then a leading American weekly book review, conducted a poll of critics and found them choosing *Invisible Man* as the most distinguished American fiction of the post-war period. While the book undoubtedly merits its critical distinction, the nearly unanimous approval it receives from white critics often carries the implication that Ellison's universal *picaro*—"Who knows," he says, "but that I speak for you"—represents the transcendence of the invariable concerns of black writers. Clearly such sentiment is less an evaluation of Ellison's work than it is a product of the wish that the divisive issue of race could be verbally resolved without disturbing social arrangements or cultural commonplaces. Certainly, from the time of his earliest published writing Ellison has been interested in the universal theme of identity, but he has always conceived the theme in the context of black culture. "Did You Ever Dream Lucky?," which elaborates the story of Mary Rambo, and "Slick Gonna Learn," which tells of an aborted beating of a black workingman, describe experiences typifed by their occurrence in the special circumstances of Afro-American life. Several stories ("Afternoon," "That I Had the Wings," "Mister Toussan," "A Coupla Scalped Indians") representing young black boys contending with fear and guilt, learning of sex, and fantasizing retaliation on whites who despise them might be tales of the invisible protagonist in adolescence, while the discovery by a young black aviator in "Flying Home" of his kinship to a black peasant employs race and culture as the basic terms for self discovery. If anything the attention to black life evident in these stories is more marked in *Invisible Man*, where the narrator's consciousness is provided substance by orations and jive sayings, Toms and race men, dreams and behavior from popular black culture.

So, too, does the surreal quality of the narrative manifest black experience. Caste restrictions seem reasonable perhaps to those who enforce them, but for those who experience them they are literally absurd. A society ordered by caste, therefore, can only be described adequately in narrative that departs from the decorum of rationality and insinuates that insanity is perceptive response, or a dream of anxiety a sound analysis.

Growing up in a black culture, and relishing it as he demonstrably does, Ellison found ready-to-hand the premise that would lead to the philosophical position of his invisible man; yet, his application of imagination to the story of the modern *picaro* is, in fact, a major achievement, for he has done nothing less than bring to its culmination a period of Afro-American literary history that had as its motif the sensation described by W.E.B. Du Bois in 1903 as a double-consciousness wherein "one ever feels his twoness,—an American, a Negro...two warring ideals in one dark body." By liberating his invisible protagonist of the ideals that, like an alien force, had invaded his ego, Ellison has prepared his narrator and those who, through influence, sympathy, or coincidence, will follow him to live with a unitary consciousness of themselves in the world.

—John M. Reilly

ELY, David. American. Born in Chicago, Illinois, 19 November 1927. Educated at the University of North Carolina, Chapel Hill, 1944-45; Harvard University, Cambridge, Massachusetts, 1947-49, B.A. 1949; St. Antony's College, Oxford (Fulbright Scholar), 1954-55. Served in the United States Navy, 1945-46, and the United States Army, 1950-52. Married Margaret Jenkins in 1954; four children. Reporter, *St. Louis Post-Dispatch*, 1949-50, 1952-54, 1955-56. Administrative Assistant, Development and Resources Corporation, New York, 1956-59. Address: Via de' Serragli 126, Florence, Italy.

PUBLICATIONS

Novels

Trot. New York, Pantheon, 1963; London, Secker and Warburg, 1964.
Seconds. New York, Pantheon, 1963; London, Deutsch, 1964.
The Tour. New York, Delacorte Press, and London, Secker and Warburg, 1967.
Poor Devils. Boston, Houghton Mifflin, 1970.
Walking Davis. New York, Charterhouse, 1972.
Mr. Nicholas. New York, Putnam, 1974; London, Macmillan, 1975.

Short Stories

Time Out. New York, Delacorte Press, 1968; London, Secker and Warburg, 1969.

Uncollected Short Stories

"The Wizard of Light," in *Amazing* (New York), 1961.
"The Alumni March," in *Cosmopolitan* (New York), 1962.
"McDaniel's Flood," in *Elks Magazine* (Chicago), 1963.
"The Captain's Boarhunt," in *Saturday Evening Post* (Philadelphia), 1963.
"The Assault on Mount Rushmore," in *Cavalier* (New York), July 1966.
"The Language Game," in *Playboy* (Chicago), 1970.
"The Knave of Hearts," in *Ellery Queen's Mystery Magazine* (New York), 1971.
"The Carnival," in *Antaeus* (New York), 1971.
"The Gourmet Hunt," in *Best Detective Stories of the Year 1973*, edited by Allen J. Hubin. New York, Dutton, 1973.
"The Many Faces of John Dobbler," in *Gallery* (Chicago), 1973.
"A Middleaged Nude," in *Cosmopolitan* (New York), 1974.
"A Place to Avoid," in *Playboy* (Chicago), 1974.
"The Light in the Cottage," in *Playboy* (Chicago), 1974.
"The Prince," in *Redbook* (New York), February 1974.
"Always Home," in *Playboy* (Chicago), 1975.
"Rockefeller's Daughter," in *Redbook* (New York), August 1975.
"Starling's Circle" and "The Running Man," in *Ellery Queen's Mystery Magazine* (New York), 1976.
"Last One Out," in *Playboy* (Chicago), 1976.
"The Squirrel," in *Penthouse* (New York), 1976.
"The Weed Killer," in *Ellery Queen's Mystery Magazine* (New York), 1977.
"The Partisan," in *Atlantic* (Boston), February 1977.
"Counting Steps" and "Going Backward," in *Ellery Queen's Mystery Magazine* (New York), 1978.
"The Temporary Daughter," in *Seventeen* (New York), April 1978.
"The Rich Girl," in *Seventeen* (New York), July 1978.
"Remember Me," in *Redbook* (New York), 1979.
"Methuselah," in *Atlantic* (Boston), March 1980.

* * *

David Ely's fiction describes the cost and conditions of freedom—what an ordinary man must do to understand himself and his world. His novels are shaped like thrillers; in each a man is driven onto a quest (initially for the wrong motives) which ultimately leads him to himself, to his unconscious mind, his heart. The novels describe with remarkable sensitivity individuals coping with worlds that are alien, inimical and all-powerful. The triumph of the individual spirit in a hostile modern milieu is accompanied by pain and sorrow, loss of innocence and simple comfort, but it brings both self-knowledge and peace.

Trot, Ely's first novel, is subtitled "A Novel of Suspense" and predicates the world of all of Ely's fiction: an alien, minatory and hostile environment, in this case the Paris underworld after World War II. An Army CID man, Sergeant Trot, abruptly becomes the victim in a case on which he is assigned. Suspected of corruption and murder, he hides with the criminals he has stalked. The inversion of his world causes him to reassess his concepts of justice and freedom. Finally he is able to reinstate himself by breaking an extortion-murder plot by escaped Nazis. But the significant victory is Trot's own self-revelation.

In *Seconds*, probably Ely's best-known novel, a Babbitt-like man, a cipher known only by the code name "Wilson," abandons his comfortable but aimless upper-middle-class existence when a mysterious corporation offers him a new life, a second chance. He is surgically rehabilitated and supplied a total identity as a successful artist, but the new freedom proves too painful and challenging. Wilson disintegrates under the stress of his open and unfamiliar world of freedom and nonconformity. "I never had a dream," he says when he returns to the corporation to be erased.

The Tour deals with the same theme in a more terrifying form. A parable of American imperialism and military-scientific manipulation of other cultures, it describes a "tour" designed to provide jaded bourgeois travelers with ultimate thrills in a mythical central American banana republic. The tour includes episodes of sex, jungle survival and guerilla fighting, carefully staged for the fuddled gringos. Behind the scenes a test is made on an automated counter-insurgency weapon, a robot tank which wipes out a starveling guerilla band (and its builders) and nearly decimates the tour. The novel develops as an analogue for U.S. involvement in Southeast Asia and for other paramilitary "tours" of policy. It is similar in shape to Peter Matthiessen's important *At Play in the Fields of the Lord.*

Poor Devils attacks the sociological concepts of poverty and its alleviation. Another parable, it describes the slow education of a history professor, Aaron Bell, who stumbles onto a Project Nomad, a genocidal agency for a "final solution" to poverty, a technological bureau that fights poverty with coldly mechanical games theory and supertechnology. Bell's education leads him to discover the futility of his life and his career, the absurdity of history and ideals faced with amoral technology. The old man he has pursued, Lundquist, a "picaresque saint," teaches him finally that he must discover (or invent) his values himself. Bell opts out of the system of research and manipulation to become a Whitmanesque wanderer, following the "Lindquist heresy, the preamble written short for men in too big a hurry to read much: *Life, liberty, and the pursuit.*"

An allegorical study of personality in existentialist terms, *Walking Davis* describes Pierce Davis, who decides to walk around the world. Setting out from Spark, Iowa, Davis makes a Robinson Crusoe voyage of survival and self-discovery, finally plumbing all his human resources and learning that "You can't build a monument to a hero. If a man's a hero, he builds his own." His walk leads him into a strange union with nature and himself, stripped of all pretense like Camus's Sisyphus, reduced to one essential human function—questing.

Mr. Nicholas describes the complete symptomology of paranoia, centering on an executive in the surveillance industry who becomes convinced that "He was being watched everywhere and all the time." The protagonist, Henry Haddock, eventually adjusts to a life without privacy, wherein his public function subsumes his whole personality, and he becomes reconciled to a world without privacy, without self. The story develops allegorically in that it describes a whole world pressed and overcrowded, when personal rights are lost to the pressure of the many.

Ely's novels are all parables of the New Babbitt redeemed, the affluent and self-satisfied "Executive Man" freed to make real, life-or-death decisions, to direct his life and test the morality of his society. The transformations are costly, painful and sometimes tragic, but they are real and significant actions, leaps of faith which give meaning to the small existences Ely depicts.

—William J. Schafer

ENGEL, Marian (Ruth). Canadian. Born in Toronto, Ontario, 24 May 1933. Educated at McMaster University, Hamilton, Ontario, B.A. 1955; McGill University, Montreal, M.A. 1957; University of Aix-en-Provence. Married Howard Engel in 1962 (divorced); twin daughter and son. Taught at the University of Montana, Missoula, 1957-58; The Study School, Montreal, 1958-60; St. John's RAF School, Nicosia, Cyprus, 1964; Writer-in-Residence, University of Alberta, Edmonton, 1978-79, and University of Toronto, 1980-81. Recipient: Rotary Foundation Fellowship, 1961; Governor-General's Award, 1976. Agent: Timothy Seldes, 551 Fifth Avenue, New York, New York 10017, U.S.A. Address: 70 Marchmont Road, Toronto, Ontario M6G 2A9, Canada.

PUBLICATIONS

Novels

No Clouds of Glory. Toronto, Longman and New York, Harcourt Brace, 1968; as *Sarah Bastard's Notebook*, Toronto, Paperjacks, 1974.
The Honeyman Festival. Toronto, Anansi, 1970; New York, St. Martin's Press, 1972.
Monodromos. Toronto, Anansi, 1973; as *One Way Street*, London, Hamish Hamilton, 1975.
Joanne. Toronto, Paperjacks, 1975.
Bear. New York, Atheneum, 1976; London, Routledge, 1977.
The Glassy Sea. Toronto, McClelland and Stewart, 1978; New York, St. Martin's Press, 1979.
The Year of the Child. New York, St. Martin's Press, 1981.

Short Stories

Inside the Easter Egg. Toronto, Anansi, 1975.

Other

Adventure at Moon Bay Towers (juvenile). Toronto, Clarke Irwin, 1974.
My Name Is Not Odessa Yarker (juvenile). Toronto, Kids Can Press, 1977.

* * *

In Marian Engel's recent novel *The Glassy Sea* her leading character, the on-and-off nun, Sister Mary Pelagia, alias Rita Heber, says that her "life has always been a quest for simplifications, patterns, stylizations...," and one can gain a great deal of insight into Engel's novels by applying this remark to them. For I suspect the main reason why they have not received the critical attention they deserve is that they are so clearly written, so simply formed, so deftly patterned and rendered in window-pane prose, that they appear to be more transparent and more obvious than in fact they are.

They are all, to begin, small books, as unupholstered as Shaker furniture. The shortest, *The Honeyman Festival*, set in a single night of incident and recollection, is a mere 131 pages; the longest, *Monodromos*, though it spends more space on background detail (the background being Cyprus) still comes only to 250 pages. They are really not novels in the expansive Anglo-Saxon sense, nor are they quite so uncomplicated as to be novellas, and perhaps the best term to describe them is *récit*, the word so often used by Gide for his fictions. Engel's fictions are indeed as simple, patterned, stylized, and also moralist as the masterpieces of short French fiction have been in our time—and as Sister Mary Pelagia saw her life.

In terms of the typology of situations, one can see Engel's novels as a gallery of feminine roles in late 20th-century western society. *No Clouds of Glory* presents the woman as academic, challenging man in the career world; *The Honeyman Festival* the woman as quintessential earth mother; *Monodromos* the woman as divorced wife moving back through surrogate sisterhood to renewed individuality; *Joanne* the woman as wife and mother finding her way through the ruins of a failed marriage; *Bear* the woman as humanity recognizing and seeking unity with its animal nature; *The Glassy Sea* the woman as nun—humanity uniting reluctantly with its angelic nature.

Interesting as each of the earlier novels is in its own terms, and pleasing as all of them are in their evocation of setting—rural, smalltown, and city Ontario, the Europe of the 1950's where living was a *rite de passage* for Canadian intellectuals—there is no doubt that the last two, *Bear* and *The Glassy Sea*, are far more mature and finished works of fictional art than Engel's first books. Both are written with a brilliance of craftsmanship so sustained and so spare that they emerge as marvellously luminous and self-sufficient artifacts.

Bear's audacity is to bring primitive legends into the modern Canadian world, and this essentially is what makes it a fable rather than a novel in the ordinary sense. It is a tale, told with impeccable plausibility, about an improbable encounter between a human being and a beast, when an archivist sent to catalogue the library of a remote country house falls in love with a pet bear who lives there and by his violent and literally wounding rejection finds that, having pushed herself to the edge of human possibilities and survived, she is in a sense reborn. At the end, when the bear has been taken away by his Indian friends and Lou departs:

> She went up the river slowly. She felt tender, serene. She remembered evenings of sitting by the fire with the bear's head in her lap. She remembered the night the stars fell on her body and burned and burned. She remembered guilt, and a dream she had had where her mother made her write letters of apology to the Indians for having to do with a bear, and she remembered the claw that had healed guilt. She felt strong and pure.

But pure, one feels inclined to emphasize, because of the rejecting claw that maintained the proper distances in an ordered ecology. In *Bear* the earthy and the fantastic dance in proper harmony.

Though in appearance The *Glassy Sea*'s story of an Anglican nun's withdrawal into secular life and marriage, and her eventual return to conventual religion may seem very different from *Bear*, it does in fact complement the earlier novel in the sense of going back to the dual basic nature of man, and if *Bear* is a fable of reconciliation with the natural world to which by origin we belong, *The Glassy Sea* is a psychological novel about the search for spiritual perfection to which we aspire. Rita Bowen as Sister Mary Pelagia has sought faith through the aesthetic route, the way of taste, and found herself forced to return and relive the secular life; when she re-enters the religious order, it is not even with manifest faith, but with a plain sense of duty.

If *Bear* showed humanity's need to recognize its oneness with the natural world, *The Glassy Sea* movingly shows how the spiritual life gives meaning to the brutal chaos of existence. For passionately as Mary Pelagia in the end seems to reject everything aesthetic, the pattern is still there, to be known through endurance and understanding if not through poetry and good taste. In this beautifully concise novel where every word tells and adds, the compassion, the lyricism, the resonance of prose that characterize Engel's novels throughout are brought together in their most powerful expression.

—George Woodcock

ENGLISH, Isobel. British. Born in London, 9 June 1923. Educated at a convent school in Somerset. Recipient: Katherine Mansfield Prize, 1974. Address: Grove House, Castle Road, Cowes, Isle Wight, England.

PUBLICATIONS

Novels

The Key That Rusts. London, Deutsch, 1954.
Every Eye. London, Deutsch, 1956; New York, Crowell, 1959.
Four Voices. London, Longman, 1961.

Short Stories

Life after All and Other Stories. London, Martin Brian and O'Keeffe, 1973.

Uncollected Short Stories

"Cousin Dot," in *Christian Century* (Chicago), 9 November 1977.

Play

Meeting Point, in *New Review* (London), 1976.

Other

The Gift Book, illustrations by Barbara Jones. London, Parrish, 1964.

*

Critical Study: interview in *Friends and Friendship* by Kay Dick, London, Sidgwick and Jackson, 1974.

* * *

Isobel English's particular angle of vision, focusing on the various implications of an action and intricate suppositions of hidden motivation, inclines her naturally towards first-person narration. For her, experience must necessarily be filtered through the eye of one particular observer, with an implicit question as to the nature of the filter in each case.

The Key That Rusts deals with the love-affair of the narrator's married step-brother and a friend, culminating in the latter's madness. The narrator both reveals much of herself in her account of this, and is insidiously affected by the action. The flashbacks to her childhood, as she revisits her old convent school, introduce another scale of values, though without necessarily any acceptance of "the security of faith," and complicated by the implications of the metamorphosis of her schoolgirl love, Felicity, into Mother Peter.

Confusion of time sequences to bring out thematic continuity is taken further in the more stylized *Every Eye*, with its exploitation of photographic imagery. Here, the narrator's holiday journey across Europe is accompanied by a journey through her memory, reconstructing her youthful love-affair with the middle-aged Jasper. Although in these memories the narrator is ostensibly one of the two chief protagonists, it yet seems appropriate for the journey through place to reveal that her role in Jasper's life was subsidiary to Cynthia's, whose presence has permeated the book. The closing factual substantiation of the relationship between Jasper and Cynthia is a highly skilful sleight-of-hand. Isobel English's quirky phrasing is well suited both to the piquant past and the contented present which her narrator juxtaposes; the style has shed the occasional overselfconsciousness of her previous book.

Middle-class characters similar to those of the earlier books reappear in *Four Voices*, but here Isobel English introduces the middle-class failures, Mona and Penry. Penry has sunk to the level of a men's hostel, though the exigencies of the plot keep the setting mostly middle-class. In fact, the accidents of marriage unite the characters in the same family—an institution which fascinates English in all three novels. However, it is doubtful whether the slightly clumsy narrative technique—inspired by the radio?—justifies the wider range of characterization. In any case the technique of blending monologues "spoken" by the main characters, once used, is probably a dead end for this author.

Isobel English's stories, collected in *Life after All*, show an individual and accomplished use of the form. In general she dispenses with the first-person narrator on the smaller scale of the short story. An exception, "Running Away," describes a convent school childhood, while Sebastian's mother in "The Crucifix after Cellini" is cast in the same mould as the Catholic *dévoté* in *Four Voices*. English's preoccupation with the extended family runs through several stories, including the longest, "One of the Family," which like *The Key That Rusts* confronts mental illness. Her material ranges from the Jewish background of this story to an evocation of an American academic's homosexual haunts and cronies in "Saying Goodbye." Only one story, "Nobody Came," is unsuccessful, failing to avoid cliché in its treatment of lonely old age; but "Cousin Dot," partly in verse, is an interesting if light-weight attempt to handle a similar subject.

The middle-class ambience of Isobel English's work recalls Elizabeth Bowen and Elizabeth Taylor. Her power lies in her ironic control of nuance: "She frayed away the edges of her last days in the flat in a sadly distracted manner, that had behind it a great strength of purpose." There is a rare but all the more effective grotesqueness in her humor: "Then he said 'Granny,' and two heads reared up off their pillows like old tortoises, but fell back again when they saw him." This highly individual voice is only occasionally blurred by imprecision.

—Val Warner

EVERETT, Peter. British. Born in Hull, Yorkshire, 1 June 1931. Educated at Thorne College; Hull Grammar School. Has worked in a foundry, on a barge, selling electric signs, as a market gardner and labourer, in a wine merchant's, as a toy maker and as a furniture salesman. Recipient: ITV Award, for drama, 1962; Maugham Award, 1965; Arts Council grant, 1970. Address: 9 Laitwood Road, London S.W.12; or, c/o Jonathan Cape Ltd., 30 Bedford Square, London WC1B 3EL, England.

PUBLICATIONS

Novels

A Day of Dwarfs. London, Spearman, 1962.
The Instrument. London, Hutchinson, 1962.
Negatives. London, Cape, 1964; New York, Simon and Schuster, 1965.
The Fetch. London, Cape, 1966; New York, Simon and Schuster, 1967.
Visions of Heydrich. London, W.H. Allen, 1979.
A Death in Ireland. Boston, Little Brown, 1981.

Plays

Day at Izzard's Wharf (broadcast, 1959; produced Canterbury, 1962).
The Daguerrotypes (produced London, 1963).

Screenplays: *Negatives*, with Roger Lowry, 1968; *The Last of the Long-Haired Boys*, 1971.

Radio Plays: *Night of the March Hare*, 1959; *Day at Izzard's Wharf*, 1959; *Private View*, 1966; *The Cookham Resurrection*,

1975; *Buffo*, 1976; *Me and Mr. Blake*, 1977; *Harmonium*, 1978; *Martyr of the Hive*, 1980; *Over the Rainbow*, 1980.

Television Plays: *The Girl Who Loved Robots*, 1965; *Hurt Hawks*, 1974; *Hoodwink*, 1975; *Freedom of the Dig*, 1978.

*

Peter Everett comments:

How much freedom is there? I mean: what is available to us to question? I mean: what are the possible questions still open to us when we've been stitched-up by childhood hang-ups, life's bias, education and tradition? Having tried to sort this out—to hang oneself by one's bookstraps, as it were—how is it possible to ask the question in a form that is the question itself, since I do not seem able to divorce any question I pose from the density of the actuality in which I find it?

Therefore, to make a form, a shape, with its shift of colours, weathers, shades of meaning, I always start with people in an actual setting: a room, a field, a garden. I move only with what I hear said, what I see, what I smell and taste. Into this, I "edit-in" speculation and ambiguity by juxtaposition, as I live out the uncertainty or certainty of these people in their particular milieu.

One always fails. Whatever form one arrives at in order to show the "thing" extorts its own payment. Wanting to deal with the nub and quick of things conflicts with a need in me to state the obvious flatly, without simile or metaphor; it still involves me in the blatant rhetoric of form ...Blatant rhetoric of form? Hamlet's poisoned cups, Claudius' foils and ruses. What the greatest rhetoric does is to contain and permit a moment of impact, the sudden electric shock of reality. The documentary aspect of *Wuthering Heights*, its realism, is haunted by ghosts. Pinter's realistic idiom suffers a sea-change in the final precipitate, just as Kafka's business letter to the world defines the real nature of the company.

No form is inevitable, since it is only a shape articulating many possibilities. At every twist and turn of plot, a fresh aspect can present itself. Character is bias—but to deal truthfully with the absurdity of being is difficult when one is involved in structure. Characters in fiction must in continuum read Blackpool Blackpool Blackpool, as in a stick of rock when cut at any point—if they don't, if their behaviour patterns shift—they are open to question. At this intersection, certainty of being and new action, the novel is attempted.

It is no longer possible to deal with reality as the traditional novelist dealt with it. Honest as such novels are, often luminous with insight, they reassure as mirrors do; they protect us from our uncertainty. Hence the novel must be concerned with identity; what we become when our lives meet crises which force us to question our norms, attitudes, and fixed attributes.

* * *

Peter Everett shares the concern of many 20th-century writers with the destruction of Western man's confident 19th-century image of himself. Everett, in seeing what can be made from the pieces, has been led to explore the conventional frontiers between the sane and the insane and towards a curt, rather disjointed technique that reflects his subject matter and may perhaps be likened to a heap of strangely angled, deeply shadowed still photographs flicked on to the table by an apparently ironic photographer.

In *The Instrument* tormentor and tormented confront each other like cat and mouse in a bare room. Madison, the unfrocked policeman, plans to murder his wife and use as his instrument Helm, an agonised schizophrenic, who has killed once already and now, released from prison, is struggling vainly to achieve identity as a writer. Madison, deeply involved with Helm from the past, urges him with deadly plausibility that he will find reality not as a writer but as a killer. Helm struggles to escape this deterministic trap but in the end falls into it. In doing so, however, he betrays Madison. The latter, driving into the arms of the police, feels cheated. It is Helm who, by achieving what Madison falsely believes to be his real identity, has found freedom. It is the ruthless, rational Madison who has entered a world of permanent unreality, where the game has become everything.

The Fetch, published after but written before *Negatives*, continues Everett's exploration of the private worlds of the sensitive, the lonely, the neurotic, all those shut off from everyday experience by deep-seated emotional disturbance. Bruno, a young cinema projectionist, suspended uneasily between reality and the fantasy world of motion-picture images, inherits the family house on the death of his father. Moving in, he finds himself surrounded by menacing figures: Childers, the gardener-handyman, Jane, his granddaughter, alias Elf, and Uncle Elia. Secluded in his stinking attic, Uncle Elia bombards Bruno with cryptic notes. Gradually he swells, in Bruno's eyes, into a doppelganger or "fetch" of his dead brother, Bruno's father, whose domineering personality has made Bruno the timid, emotionally crippled creature that he is. Elf, with whom Bruno falls in love, proves to be not a refuge but a further threat to his stability, encouraging him (as Reingard does Theo in *Negatives*) to don a mask, to act out roles, pushing him further from reality. In the end Bruno achieves release by shooting and wounding Uncle Elia, the symbolic attack he should have made but never did upon his father. But it is too late. Bruno falls back into the world of unreality, of cinema images.

In *Negatives*, Everett's best-known novel, the borders between fantasy and reality become even more blurred. Everett's preoccupation with the search for personal identity becomes stylised into an overt role- and game-playing situation. Written, like *The Fetch*, in the present tense, it is less obsessive in tone, with more feeling for the comic and grotesque. Theo, the antique-dealer, is not, we feel, mad, but inhabiting a contemporary world of super-sanity where personal identity is not a unique inalienable attribute but an ever-changing sequence of masks, do-it-yourself disposable kits, to be used for as long as the mood takes one. Theo and Vivien begin by playing the game of Crippen and/or his wife and mistress, but the arrival of the German photographer Reingard on the scene changes everything. Gradually Reingard asserts a power over Theo, seduces him from his Crippen role to that of Von Richthofen, the First World War air ace, with, in the end, fatal consequences. There are a detachment and irony about this work missing from the earlier novels. Everett's vision has grown sharper and colder. Theo, Vivien, and Reingard are all puppets. Artistically the book is an advance, being more fluid and imaginative, but it has lost in compassion and involvement with its characters.

—Keith Walker

FAST, Howard (Melvin). Pseudonym: **E.V. Cunningham.** American. Born in New York City, 11 November 1914. Educated at George Washington High School, New York, graduated 1931; National Academy of Design, New York. Served with the Office of War Information, 1942-43, and the Army Film Project, 1944. Married Bette Cohen in 1937; one daughter and one son. War Correspondent in the Far East for *Esquire* and *Coronet* magazines, 1945. Taught at Indiana University, Bloomington, Summer 1947. Imprisoned for contempt of Congress, 1947. Founder of the World Peace Movement, and member of the World Peace Council, 1950-55. Operated Blue Heron Press, New York, 1952-57. Currently, Member of the Fellowship for Reconciliation. American-Labor Party candidate for Congress for the 23rd District of New York, 1952. Recipient: Bread Loaf Writers Conference Award, 1933; Schomburg Race Relations Award, 1944; Newspaper Guild Award, 1947; Jewish Book Council of America Award, 1948; Stalin International Peace Prize (now Soviet International Peace Prize), 1954; Screenwriters Award, 1960; National Association of Independent

Schools Award, 1962. Agent: Sterling Lord Agency, 660 Madison Avenue, New York, New York 10021. Address: 1401 Laurel Way, Beverly Hills, California 90210, U.S.A.

PUBLICATIONS

Novels

Two Valleys. New York, Dial Press, 1933; London, Dickson, 1934.
Strange Yesterday. New York, Dodd Mead, 1934.
Place in the City. New York, Harcourt Brace, 1937.
Conceived in Liberty: A Novel of Valley Forge. New York, Simon and Schuster, and London, Joseph, 1939.
The Last Frontier. New York, Duell, 1941; London, Lane, 1948.
The Unvanquished. New York, Duell, 1942; London, Lane, 1947.
The Tall Hunter. New York, Harper, 1942.
Citizen Tom Paine. New York, Duell, 1943; London, Lane, 1946.
Freedom Road. New York, Duell, 1944; London, Lane, 1946.
The American: A Middle Western Legend. New York, Duell, 1946; London, Lane, 1949.
The Children. New York, Duell, 1947.
Clarkton. New York, Duell, 1947.
My Glorious Brothers. Boston, Little Brown, 1948; London, Lane, 1950.
The Proud and the Free. Boston, Little Brown, 1950; London, Lane, 1952.
Spartacus. Privately printed, 1951; London, Lane, 1952.
Fallen Angel (as Walter Ericson). Boston, Little Brown, 1952; as *The Darkness Within*, New York, Ace, 1953; as *Mirage*, as Howard Fast, New York, Fawcett, 1965.
Silas Timberman. New York, Blue Heron Press, 1954; London, Lane, 1955.
The Story of Lola Gregg. New York, Blue Heron Press, 1956; London, Lane, 1957.
Moses, Prince of Egypt. New York, Crown, 1958; London, Methuen, 1959.
The Winston Affair. New York, Crown, 1959; London, Methuen, 1960.
The Golden River, in *The Howard Fast Reader*. New York, Crown, 1960.
April Morning. New York, Crown, and London, Methuen, 1961.
Power. New York, Doubleday, 1962; London, Methuen, 1963.
Agrippa's Daughter. New York, Doubleday, 1964; London, Methuen, 1965.
Torquemada. New York, Doubleday, 1966; London, Methuen, 1967.
The Hunter and the Trap. New York, Dial Press, 1967.
The Crossing. New York, Morrow, 1971; London, Eyre Methuen, 1972.
The Hessian. New York, Morrow, 1972; London, Hodder and Stoughton, 1973.
The Immigrants. Boston, Houghton Mifflin, 1977; London, Hodder and Stoughton, 1978.
Second Generation. Boston, Houghton Mifflin, and London, Hodder and Stoughton, 1978.
The Establishment. Boston, Houghton Mifflin, 1979; London, Hodder and Stoughton, 1980.
The Legacy. Boston, Houghton Mifflin, 1981.

Novels as E.V. Cunningham

Sylvia. New York, Doubleday, 1960; London, Deutsch, 1962.
Phyllis. New York, Doubleday, 1962; London, Deutsch, 1963.
Alice. New York, Doubleday, and London, Deutsch, 1963.
Lydia. New York, Doubleday, 1964; London, Deutsch, 1965.
Shirley. New York, Doubleday, and London, Deutsch, 1964.
Penelope. New York, Doubleday, 1965; London, Deutsch, 1966.
Helen. New York, Doubleday, 1966; London, Deutsch, 1967.
Margie. New York, Morrow, 1966; London, Deutsch, 1968.
Sally. New York, Morrow, and London, Deutsch, 1967.
Samantha. New York, Morrow, 1967; London, Deutsch, 1968.
Cynthia. New York, Morrow, 1968; London, Deutsch, 1969.
The Assassin Who Gave Up His Gun. New York, Morrow, 1969; London, Deutsch, 1970.
Millie. New York, Morrow, 1973; London, Deutsch, 1974.
The Case of the One-Penny Orange. New York, Holt Rinehart, and London, Deutsch, 1978.
The Case of the Russian Diplomat. New York, Holt Rinehart, 1978; London, Deutsch, 1979.
The Case of the Poisoned Eclairs. New York, Holt Rinehart, 1979; London, Deutsch, 1980.

Short Stories

Patrick Henry and the Frigate's Keel and Other Stories of a Young Nation. New York, Duell, 1945.
Departures and Other Stories. Boston, Little Brown, 1949.
The Last Supper and Other Stories. New York, Blue Heron Press, 1955; London, Lane, 1956.
The Edge of Tomorrow. New York, Bantam, 1961; London, Corgi, 1962.
The General Zapped an Angel. New York, Morrow, 1970.
A Touch of Infinity. New York, Morrow, 1973; London, Hodder and Stoughton, 1975.
Time and the Riddle: Thirty-One Zen Stories. Pasadena, California, Ward Ritchie Press, 1975.

Plays

The Hammer (produced New York, 1950).
Thirty Pieces of Silver (produced Melbourne, 1951). New York, Blue Heron Press, and London, Lane, 1954.
General Washington and the Water Witch. London, Lane, 1956.
The Crossing (produced Dallas, 1962).
The Hill (screenplay). New York, Doubleday, 1964.

Screenplay: *The Hessian*, 1971.

Verse

Never to Forget the Battle of the Warsaw Ghetto, with William Gropper. New York, Jewish Peoples Fraternal Order, 1946.

Other

The Romance of a People (juvenile). New York, Hebrew Publishing Company, 1941.
Lord Baden-Powell of the Boy Scouts. New York, Messner, 1941.
Haym Salomon, Son of Liberty. New York, Messner, 1941.
The Picture-Book History of the Jews, with Bette Fast. New York, Hebrew Publishing Company, 1942.
Goethals and the Panama Canal. New York, Messner, 1942.
The Incredible Tito. New York, Magazine House, 1944.
Intellectuals in the Fight for Peace. New York, Masses and Mainstream, 1949.
Tito and His People. Winnipeg, Contemporary Publishers, 1950.
Literature and Reality. New York, International Publishers, 1950.
Peekskill, U.S.A.: A Personal Experience. New York, Civil Rights Congress, and London, International Publishing Company, 1951.
Korean Lullaby. New York, American Peace Crusade, n.d.
Tony and the Wonderful Door (juvenile). New York, Blue Heron Press, 1952; as *The Magic Door*, Culver City, California, Peace Press, 1979.
Spain and Peace. New York, Joint Anti-Fascist Refugee Committee, 1952.
The Passion of Sacco and Vanzetti: A New England Legend. New York, Blue Heron Press, 1953; London, Lane, 1954.

The Naked God: The Writer and the Communist Party. New York, Praeger, 1957; London, Bodley Head, 1958.
The Howard Fast Reader. New York, Crown, 1960.
The Jews: Story of a People. New York, Dial Press, 1968; London, Cassell, 1970.
The Art of Zen Meditation. Culver City, California, Peace Press, 1977.

Editor, *The Selected Work of Tom Paine.* New York, Modern Library, 1946; London, Lane, 1948.
Editor, *Best Short Stories of Theodore Dreiser.* Cleveland, World, 1947.

Manuscript Collection: University of Pennsylvania Library, Philadelphia.

*

Howard Fast comments:

(1972) From the very beginning of my career as a writer, my outlook has been teleological. Since my first work was published at a very early age—my first novel at the age of eighteen—my philosophical position was naturally uncertain and in formation. Yet the seeds were there, and by the end of my first decade as a writer, I had clearly shaped my point of view. In the light of this, both my historical and modern novels (excepting the entertainments I have written under the name of Cunningham) were conceived as parables and executed as narratives of pace and, hopefully, excitement. I discovered that I had a gift for narrative in the story sense; but I tried never to serve the story, but rather to have it serve my own purpose—a purpose which I attempted in a transcendental sense.

In other words, I was—and am—intrigued by the apparent lunacy of man's experience on earth; but at the same time never accepted a pessimistic conclusion or a mechanical explanation. Thereby, my books were either examinations of moments or parables of my own view of history. As a deeply religious person who has always believed that human life is a meaningful part of a meaningful and incredibly wonderful universe, I found myself at every stage in my career a bit out of step with the current literary movement or fashion. I suppose that this could not have been otherwise, and I think I have been the most astounded of any at the vast audiences my work has reached.

Since I also believe that a person's philosophical point of view has little meaning if it is not matched by being and action, I found myself willingly wed to an endless series of unpopular causes, experiences which I feel enriched my writing as much as they depleted other aspects of my life. I might add that the more I have developed the parable as a form of literature, the more convinced I become that truth is better indicated than specified.

All of the above is of course not a critical evaluation of my work; and I feel that a writer is the last person on earth capable of judging his own work as literature with any objectivity. The moment I cease to feel that I am a good writer, I will have to stop writing. And while this may be no loss to literature, it would be a tragic blow to my income.

As for the dozen books I have written under the name of E.V. Cunningham, they are entertainments, for myself primarily and for all others who care to read them. They are also my own small contribution to that wonderful cause of women's liberation. They are all about wise and brave and gallant women, and while they are suspense and mystery stories, they are also parables in their own way.

* * *

Howard Fast has written in virtually every genre—novels, plays, poems, filmscripts, critical essays and short stories—and in a number of subgenres of fiction, including science fiction, social satire, historical and contemporary novels, spy thrillers and moral allegories. He began publishing novels at the age of eighteen and has kept up a brisk pace of production.

His strongest fictional gifts are a talent for swift, interesting narrative, the vivid portrayal of scenes of action, especially of violence, and an uncluttered style only occasionally marred by sentimental lapses. Although he became identified in the 1940's as a publicist for the Communist Party line, his novels reveal an intensely emotional and religious nature which eventually clashed with his left-wing allegiances. His ideals reflect a curious compound of slum-culture courage, Jewish concern for social justice, self-taught history, Cold-war Stalinism and, in his later years, Zen Buddhism. His entire literary career embodies his deepest beliefs: that life has moral significance, that the writer must be socially committed, that literature should take sides.

After two youthful blood-and-thunder romances, Fast found his métier in a series of class-conscious historical novels of the American Revolution. *Conceived in Liberty* heralded the loyalty of the common soldier; *The Unvanquished* celebrated the dogged persistence of George Washington (despite his aristocracy and wealth, Fast's favorite hero); and *Citizen Tom Paine* glorified our first professional revolutionary. Fast then championed anonymous heroes of other races: *The Last Frontier* is a spare but moving account of the heroic flight in 1878 of the Cheyenne Indians to their Powder River home in Wyoming; *Freedom Road* recounts the amazing social experiments of black Southern legislatures in the Reconstruction era. The best selling of the popular novels of the early 1940's, *Freedom Road* shows great power in its scenes of violent conflict but it is melodramatic and tendentious. By contrast, the poetically evocative *Last Frontier*, perhaps his best novel, enlists profound sympathy through great control and objectivity, and evades the pitfalls of "noble redskin" sentimentality.

In 1946 *The American* detailed the rise and fall of Illinois Governor John Peter Altgeld, who was politically defeated after he pardoned three anarchists convicted of bomb-throwing in Haymarket Square in 1886. Although Fast's novels had reflected Marxist thought since his youthful conversion to socialism, his propagandizing became too obtrusive with *Clarkton* in 1947. This proletarian strike novel of life in the Massachusetts textile mills revealed his inability to maintain the necessary distance to interpret contemporary events soundly. He returned in 1948 to the historical novel with *My Glorious Brothers*, a stirring account of the Maccabees and the 30-year Jewish resistance to Greek-Syrian tyranny. This success was duplicated with *Spartacus*, the largely imagined story of the gladiatorial revolt against Rome in 71 BC. *Spartacus* was self-published in 1951 after the author was blacklisted for Communist activities and had spent three months in federal prison for contempt of Congress. But, predictably, Fast's other works of the early 1950's were failures in proportion to their nearness to the present day: *The Passion of Sacco and Vanzetti* recounted sentimentally the last hours of the doomed Italian anarchists; *Silas Timberman* depicted an academic victim of a McCarthyite witchhunt; and *The Story of Lola Gregg* described the FBI pursuit and capture of a heroic Communist labor leader. These self-published works of imprisoned martyrs, abounding in Christ-figures and symbolic Judases, reflect their author's bitter sense of entrapment and isolation, for he could neither publish with established houses nor leave the country.

In 1957 Fast publicly quit the Communist Party after the Hungarian revolution and then described his tortured apostasy in *The Naked God.* He soon revisited Jewish history as a favored novelistic subject with *Moses, Son of Egypt*; *Agrippa's Daughter*; and *Torquemada.* He returned, with a more mature vision, thrice more to the American revolution in *April Morning*, *The Crossing*, and *The Hessian.* In other historical novels he continued to re-examine earlier themes: *The Winston Affair* deals with the court-martial of an American murderer, homosexual and anti-Semite who nevertheless deserves and wins justice in a military court, while *Power* shows the corruption by power by a John L. Lewis-type of labor leader; *Agrippa's Daughter* rejects the "just-war" theory of *My Glorious Brothers* in favor of Rabbi Hillel's pacifism.

Most readers saw Fast in two new guises (or disguises), as author of science-fiction stories and as a writer of "entertainments" in the manner of Graham Greene. These late science fiction or "Zen stories" include stories in *The Edge of Tomorrow*, *The Hunter and the Trap* and *The General Zapped an Angel* (later gathered into one volume, *Time and the Riddle*). The dozen or so "entertainments" are written under the pseudonym E.V. Cunningham, most built around the female title characters. Both the science fiction and the women-novels criticize American institutions and values with wit and humor, and all show the deft hand of the professional storyteller at work. A newer series of Cunningham thrillers stars Masao Masuto, a Japanese-American detective of the Beverly Hills Police Department and a Zen Buddhist. In these, character holds the main appeal, especially that of family-man Masuto.

Recently, Fast has achieved repeated bestsellerdom with an immigrant-saga that has grown to four large novels: *The Immigrants*, *Second Generation*, *The Establishment*, and *The Legacy*. These volumes trace the Italian, Dan Lavette, and his family while newly arrived Italians, Jews, Orientals, and others struggle against the entrenched wealth and prejudice of old-line Americans. Beginning with the San Francisco earthquake of 1906, the series energetically sweeps across 20th-century American history and recent world events. No longer axe-grinding, Fast uses well his own rich experiences for the first time, and here he is at the top of his admirable narrative form.

—Frank Campenni

FAUST, Irvin. American. Born in New York City, 11 June 1924. Educated at City College of New York, B.S. 1949; Columbia University, New York, M.A. 1952, D.Ed. 1960. Served in the United States Army, 1943-46. Married Jean Satterthwaite in 1959. Teacher, Manhattanville Junior High School, New York, 1949-53; Guidance Counselor, Lynbrook High School, Long Island, 1956-60. Since 1960, Director of Guidance and Counseling, Garden City High School, Long Island. Taught at Columbia University, Summer 1963, and University of Rochester, New York, Summer 1978. Address: 417 Riverside Drive, New York, New York 10025, U.S.A.

PUBLICATIONS

Novels

The Steagle. New York, Random House, 1966.
The File on Stanley Patton Buchta. New York, Random House, 1970.
Willy Remembers. New York, Arbor House, 1971.
Foreign Devils. New York, Arbor House, 1973.
A Star in the Family. New York, Doubleday, 1975.
Newsreel. New York, Harcourt Brace, 1980.

Short Stories

Roar Lion Roar and Other Stories. New York, Random House, and London, Gollancz, 1965.

Uncollected Short Stories

"The Dalai Lama of Harlem," in *Sewanee Review* (Tennessee), 1964.
"Operation Buena Vista," in *Paris Review*, Fall 1965.
"The Double Snapper," in *Esquire* (New York), December 1965.
"Simon Girty Go Ape," in *Transatlantic Review* (London), Summer 1966.
"Gary Dis-donc," in *Northwest Review* (Seattle), Summer 1967.

Other

Entering Angel's World: A Student-Centered Casebook. New York, Columbia Teachers College Press, 1963.

Critical Studies: by Richard Kostelanetz in *The New America Arts*, New York, Horizon Press, 1965, in *Tri-Quarterly* (Evansto Illinois), Winter 1967, and in *On Contemporary Literature*, Ne York, Avon, 1967; by R.V. Cassill, in *New York Times Boo Review*, 29 August 1971; interview with Matthew Bruccoli, in *Conversations with Writers 2*, Detroit, Gale, 1978.

Irvin Faust comments:

(1972) It seems to me that thus far my work has dealt with th displacement and disorganization of Americans in urban life; wit their attempt to find adjustments in the glossy attractions of th mass media—movies, radio, t.v., advertising, etc.—and in th image-radiating seductions of our institutions—colleges, sport teams, etc. Very often this "adjustment" is to the "normal" percep tion a derangement, but perfectly satisfying to my subjects.

Recently my work has moved out to include suburban Americ and also back in historical directions. My characters to this da have been outside of the white anglo-saxon milieu, but hav included Jews, Blacks, Puerto Ricans and the so-called Ethni Americans.

Both *Roar Lion Road* and *The Steagle* were published in Franc (Gallimard) and I feel the reviews were most perceptive, leading m to muse that perhaps, unbeknownst to me, I am quite close to th French literary sensibility.

* * *

In six novels and a volume of short stories, Irvin Faust ha attempted (as he said of one novel), "to show the rise and fall of th nation over the last forty years." Were this all, he would be essen tially a social historian disguised as fictional chronicler of our time Faust, however, has managed to weave together a substantia number of additional themes, drawing upon his background as Jew New Yorker, veteran, husband, and professional guidance counse lor. The integration of these materials, when successful, produces rich tapestry of life in contemporary urban America, especiall when played off against the past, both mythicized and actual.

His first fictional book, *Roar Lion Roar*, treated with sensitiv compassion the interior lives of disturbed adolescents of minorit backgrounds. In the title story, Ishmael Ramos, a janitor at Colum bia University, so identifies with the "ivory leak" school that he kil himself when the football team loses. Most of the protagonists c these stories are insane but even the sane have been mind-molded b the mass media or warped by the pressures of recent history. Indeec Faust's major theme of the forming and deforming of personality b an empty culture in a violent, chaotic world may here have found it most solid embodiment.

The broader canvas of the novel form permitted Faust th breadth and depth needed to convey the specificity of a conflicte culture in its dizzying impact upon the individual. In Faust's firs novel, *The Steagle*, English Professor Harold Weissburg develops multiple personality while his sense of self disintegrates during th Cuban missile crisis. The title is a composite-name formed from tw football teams, the Steelers and the Eagles. Thus, as the Unite States shifts from "good neighbor" to threatening nuclear powe Weissburg, in desperate flight across the country, becomes Bo Hardy (brother of Andy, of the wholesome movie family), gangste Rocco Salvato, a football hero, a flying ace, and, finally Humphre Bogart. In *The File on Stanley Buchta* his protagonist is an under cover policeman, Vietnam veteran, and college graduate who infil trates both a para-military rightist group within the police depart ment and a New Left organization. He is further divided in romanti loyalty to an all-American blonde beauty and a black militant o whom he is spying. Perhaps because the hero is not fully realized, o because the material lacks the historical density which the autho prefers, this fairly conventional novel lacks impact.

Faust's next two novels, however, are probably his best to date *Willy Remembers* features the redoubtable Willy Kleinhans, who a 93 is an embodiment and archive of America in the 19th century The history he recalls is badly scrambled but curiously apt: Grove Cleveland is confused with baseball-pitcher Grover Clevelan

Alexander; John F. Kennedy melds with McKinley, another assassinated President; Admiral and Governor Dewey, Franklin and Teddy Roosevelt likewise interchange. The Haymarket Riot, the frame-up of Tom Mooney, prohibition, and T.R. at San Juan Hill all whiz by as kaleidoscopic snapshots. Despite Willy's anti-Semitism, curmudgeonly judgments and angry confusion, he is a likable and likely representative of his time and place. Although critic R.V. Cassill rightly praised *Willy Remembers* for its "overlapping stereotypes of urban and national memory" and the novel's "Joycean complexity," Faust does not always guide the reader adequately along these high-speed, involuted memory-trips. The novel does display, nevertheless, a marked advance in control of point-of-view and the blend of fantasy and realism. With *Foreign Devils* Faust achieves mastery in weaving together the items of popular culture, the myths by which many Americans live, and the disintegrating personality of a Jewish writer. His hero, Sidney Benson (born Birnbaum), is separated from his wife and living partly off his mother's earnings from a candy store. Inspired by President Nixon's trip to China, Benson, who has suffered from writer's block, begins a novel about the Boxer rebellion. This melodrama, or novel-within-the novel, is an exquisite parody of the swashbuckling accounts of Richard Harding Davis, and is perhaps the chief attraction of *Foreign Devils*. The action in the present, except for Benson's reunion at the end with his father (who had deserted his family years ago), is cluttered with topical references, both a shortcoming and an attraction in Faust's fiction.

Faust's two most recent novels, *A Star in the Family* and *Newsreel*, show flashes of power as each book scans recent American history, but he is in danger of repeating himself. The tale of vaudevillian Bart Goldwine, protagonist of *Star in the Family*, consists of interviews conducted by Goldwine's biographer, plus longer memoiristic accounts by Goldwine. The reproduction of show-business patter, street talk, fan magazine prose, courtship, and family discussions is flawless in evoking the cynicism and innocence of the last generation. Showman Goldwine's impression of John F. Kennedy is abruptly ended by the assassination; his long decline thereafter is symbolically entwined with the decline of American vitality and national will. In *Newsreel* former Army Captain Manny "Speed" Finestone, is again the victim of his times. Linked spiritually with his wartime "chief," Dwight Eisenhower, Speed cannot escape contrasting the purity of the great crusade against Hitler with the materialism of the affluent 1950's, the cold war mentality, and the slaying of President Kennedy (Chapter 29 is simply "11/22/63"). Finestone's inability to write, his failed romances with two Jewish women and an Irish girl, his unraveling into psychosis are all played against national deterioration in a cultural wasteland. Other previous themes and motifs are also present: sex and sports, the abandoning father, the Jew fighting his ethnic identity, the writer supported by his mother, the use of dialogues with other selves or fantasy-heroes. Although their repeated use suggests personal concerns that are insufficiently integrated into fiction, Faust continues to portray both interior individual lives and cultural tension with skill and sincerity.

—Frank Campenni

FEDERMAN, Raymond. American. Born in Paris, France, 15 May 1928; emigrated to the United States in 1947. Educated at Columbia University, New York, 1954-57, B.A. (cum laude) 1957 (Phi Beta Kappa); University of California, Los Angeles, 1957-63, M.A. 1958, Ph.D. in French 1963. Served in the United States Army 82nd Airborne Division in Korea, 1951-54: Sergeant. Married Erica Hubscher in 1960; one daughter. Jazz saxophonist, 1947-50; Lecturer and Assistant Professor, University of California, Santa Barbara, 1959-64. Associate Professor of French, 1964-68, Professor of French and Comparative Literature, 1968-73, and since 1973, Professor of English and Comparative Literature, State University of New York, Buffalo. Visiting Professor, University of Montreal, 1970. Editor, *Mica* magazine, Santa Barbara, 1959-64. Director, Fiction Collective, 1977-80. Recipient: Guggenheim Fellowship, 1966; *Panache* Experimental Fiction Prize, 1971; Steloff Prize, 1972. Agent: Charles Neighbors, 240 Waverley Place, New York, New York 10014. Address: 46 Four Seasons West, Eggertsville, New York 14226, U.S.A.

PUBLICATIONS

Novels

Double or Nothing: A Real Fictitious Discourse. Chicago, Swallow Press, 1971.
Amer Eldorado (in French). Paris, Stock, 1974.
Take It or Leave It. New York, Fiction Collective, 1976.
The Voice in the Closet (bilingual edition), with *Echos à Federman*, by Maurice Roche. Madison, Wisconsin, Coda Press, 1979.

Uncollected Short Stories

"The Man on the Bridge" (as Robin St. Gill), in *Mica*, i, 1, 1960.
"False Evidence," in *Kolokon*, Summer 1966.
"Histoire du Ballon," in *West Coast Review* (Burnaby, British Columbia), Fall 1969.
"The Captain and the Kids," in *Assembling*, edited by Richard Kostelanetz. New York, Assembling Press, 1970.
"Suspension," in *UCLAN Review Magazine*, Winter 1970.
"Au pied du Livre," in *Sub-Stance 5-6* (Madison, Wisconsin), Summer 1973.
"An Impromptu Swim," in *Out of Sight* (Wichita, Kansas), April 1974.
"Inside the Thing," in *Oyęz Review* (Berkeley, California), Fall 1974.
"Setting and Tripping," in *Statements*, edited by Jonathan Baumbach. New York, Braziller, 1975.
"Self-Plagiaristic Autobiographical Poem in Form of a Letter from Here and Elsewhere," in *Oyez Review* (Berkeley, California), n.s., 5, 1977.
"Hat Missive," "Questionnaire," and "Hats Hats Hats," in *Milk 11-12*, 1978.
"Premembrance," in *Mississippi Review* (Hattiesburg), Fall 1978.
"Parcifal in Hamburg," in *Chicago Review*, Spring 1980.

Verse

Among the Beasts (bilingual edition). Paris, Millas Martin, 1967.
Me Too. Reno, Nevada, West Coast Poetry Review Press, 1976.

Other

Journey to Chaos: Samuel Beckett's Early Fiction. Berkeley, University of California Press, 1965.
Samuel Beckett: His Works and His Critics: An Essay in Bibliography, with John Fletcher. Berkeley, University of California Press, 1970.

Editor, *Cinq Nouvelles Nouvelles*. New York, Appleton Century Crofts, 1970.
Editor, *Surfiction: Fiction Now and Tomorrow*. Chicago, Swallow Press, 1975; revised edition, Athens, Ohio University Press, 1981.
Editor, with Tom Bishop, *Samuel Beckett*. Paris, L'Herne, 1976.
Editor, with Lawrence Graver, *Samuel Beckett: The Critical Heritage*. London, Routledge, 1979.

Translator, *Temporary Landscapes* (bilingual edition), by Yvonne Caroutch. Venice, Mica, 1965.

*

Critical Studies: *The End of Intelligent Writing* by Richard Kostelanetz, New York, Sheed and Ward, 1974; "The Choice of Invention" by Harris Dienstfrey, in *Fiction International 2* (Canton, New York), 1974; *Literary Disruptions* by Jerome Klinkowitz, Urbana, University of Illinois Press, 1975, revised edition, 1980; *American Fiction* by Melvin J. Friedman, Boston, Northeastern University Press, 1977; "Flushing Out 'The Voice in the Closet' " by Charles Caramello, in *Sub-Stance 20* (Madison, Wisconsin), 1978.

Raymond Federman comments:

Although my work has been labelled "experimental" and "avant-garde," and it is true my fiction departs radically from conventional narrative forms, I do believe that it speaks to the reality of our modern times. That does not mean it is realistic; on the contrary, I am not interested in writing fiction which represents the world, but which improves reality. My main concern is with language, but not a language which reproduces meaning but which produces new meaning. I have expressed my position on fiction in several theoretical essays, in particular the essay/manifesto "Surfiction" (*Partisan Review*, 1973), and more recently in "Imagination as Playgiarism" (*New Literary History*, 1977). I believe that my novels form a coherent project which is an effort on my part to come to terms with both my personal experiences (especially during World War II, and as an immigrant in America) and the recent historical events in which I have participated as a writer and a human being. The distinction I make, however, is that I do not think that my life and history are the sources of my fiction, but that in fact my fiction is what invents my life and history. In other words, the stories I write are my life.

* * *

Raymond Federman established himself as a critic before he turned to novel-writing. His books and essays about Samuel Beckett seem to have shaped his career as a novelist just as surely as Beckett's early criticism on Joyce and Proust pointed the way to his fiction from *More Pricks Than Kicks* to the *Molloy* trilogy. Federman once called Beckett's fiction "le roman du langage." He was trying on this occasion to distinguish between André Gide's *Counterfeiters*, which he saw as "primarily a reflection on fiction by fiction," and Beckett's work, which is more "a reflection on fiction by its own language."

Federman's novels are, among other things, showcases for "linguistic play" and "narrative joy" (as Jerome Klinkowitz points out in his *Literary Disruptions*). Like Beckett, Federman is enviably bilingual and moves with ease between English and French. His novels seem to profit from experiments—verbal, visual, and narrative—he has observed on both the American and French fictional scenes.

Double or Nothing, his first novel, is described on the dustjacket as "a *concrete* novel—*concrete*, as in *concrete poetry*." Each page seems to go its own visual and verbal way. All classical distinctions between image and word appear to be rendered obsolete. *Double or Nothing* is what the French might call a "roman-en-train-de-se-faire." We witness the growing pains of writing a novel while we see the grudging, halting fleshing-out of a story which involves the arrival in America of a 19-year-old immigrant. Everything is tentative, every detail of the story is subject to the caprices of the narrator. Hence names change as they do in Beckett ("In fact I'll change all the names eventually. Has to be"), situations alter on retelling, digressions wear down the narrative at every turn. It seems to take the immigrant as long to disembark from his boat as it does Tristram Shandy to get born. Catalogues, inventories, all sorts of spatial devices slow down time and arrest any kind of forward movement.

The same complex, digressive, unlinear telling characterizes *Take It or Leave It*. This novel is more completely "a reflection on fiction by its own language" than *Double or Nothing*. This "exaggerated second-hand tale," as it is called on the title page, seems less eccentric typographically than its predecessor but much denser verbally and narratively. In a certain sense it is part of the tradition of the French voyage-of-discovery-of-America, a tradition which includes Céline's *Journey to the End of the Night* and Butor's *Mobile*. (There are even references to Céline in the text, such as "here go back and reread the arrival of Bardamu in New York in le Voyage.")

The telling of *Take It or Leave It* has more than its share of exhilaration (a word used appropriately as the title for the sixth chapter of the novel). Words seem to explode on the page as Frenchy's adventures are recounted from his days with the 82nd Airborne Division in North Carolina through his trip north to Camp Drum in early 1951. These adventures, which offer something of a narrative line, are eclipsed at every turn by an elaborate series of subtexts which comment on such unrelated matters as the differences between French and English, the theories of Derrida and the terrible legacy of the Holocaust. There is room in this unpaginated novel for almost anything its creator chooses to place within its covers. Titles of Federman's earlier works are paraded before us as well as a brief biographical sketch of the author when he retreats behind the mask of Hombre De La Pluma. This *opera aperta* (Umberto Eco's words) keeps opening-out and breaking down the walls of conventional fiction. The novelist freely enters the frame of his novel and creator and creatures come to confront one another on equal terms.

Even on this crowded canvas, with its "story that cancels itself as it goes," the presence of Beckett is unmistakable. Federman at one point embellishes a line from *Murphy*: "MUST I BITE THE HAND THAT STARVES ME SO THAT IT CAN STRANGLE ME BETTER?" At another he nods fondly to his mentor: "In complete LESSNESSness my friend Sam would say where nothing is even less than nothing."

Federman's latest fiction, *The Voice in the Closet*, seems to honor Beckett at every turn. Just as the Irish writer achieved such remarkable economy of means in his recent prose, so has Federman realized a startling process of reduction here. *The Voice in the Closet* which looks more like an art book than fiction, contains three texts parallel English and French versions of a work by Federman (*The Voice in the Closet/La Voix dans le Cabinet de Débarras*), with a piece by Maurice Roche, *Echos* (dedicated to Federman), sandwiched in between. The Federman work, with its disturbing hermetic words and cadences, is unpunctuated and unparagraphed in both languages. Here is the way the author described *The Voice in the Closet* in a recent letter: "A complex double book—system of mirrors, echoes, boxes within boxes to accommodate my plural voice."

Federman's career as writer and critic seems reduced to a few words and images in this latest text. A reading of the two earlier novels as well as a knowledge of his criticism and poetry would seem a prerequisite for any understanding of *The Voice in the Closet*. A forbidding Mallarméan density should keep away all but the most serious students of recent Franco-American literature. While the author hid behind a series of masks or disguises in *Double or Nothing* and *Take It or Leave It*, he emerges here as "federman" (or as "namredef" or "featherman") and Beckett quite simply as "sam." The matters of Jewishness ("the yellow star on my chest") and the experience of the Holocaust ("the empty skins already remade into lampshades") are perhaps more sharply focused here than anywhere else in Federman's work.

—Melvin J. Friedman

FEIKEMA, Feike. *See* **MANFRED, Frederick.**

FEINSTEIN, Elaine. British. Born in Bootle, Lancashire, 24 October 1930. Educated at Wyggeston Grammar School, Leicester; Newnham College, Cambridge. Married Dr. Arnold Feinstein in 1956; three sons. Editorial Staff Member, Cambridge University Press, 1960-62; Lecturer in English, Bishop's Stortford Training College, Hertfordshire, 1963-66; Assistant Lecturer in Literature, University of Essex, Wivenhoe, 1967-70. Recipient: Arts Council grant, 1970; Daisy Miller Award, for fiction, 1971; Kelsus Prize, 1978. Agent: (verse) Olwyn Hughes, 100 Chetwynd Road, London N.W.5; (fiction) Hilary Rubinstein, A.P. Watt Ltd., 26-28 Bedford Row, London WC1R 4HL. Address: c/o Hutchinson Publishing Group Ltd., 3 Fitzroy Square, London W1P 6JD, England.

PUBLICATIONS

Novels

The Circle. London, Hutchinson, 1970.
The Amberstone Exit. London, Hutchinson, 1972.
The Glass Alembic. London, Hutchinson, 1973; as *The Crystal Garden*, New York, Dutton, 1974.
Children of the Rose. London, Hutchinson, 1975.
The Ecstasy of Dr. Miriam Garner. London, Hutchinson, 1976.
The Shadow Master. London, Hutchinson, 1978; New York, Simon and Schuster, 1979.

Short Stories

Matters of Chance. London, Covent Garden Press, 1980.
The Silent Areas. London, Hutchinson, 1980.

Plays

Radio Play: *Echoes*, 1980.

Television Play: *Breath*, 1975.

Verse

In a Green Eye. London, Goliard Press, 1966.
The Magic Apple Tree. London, Hutchinson, 1971.
At the Edge. Rushden, Northamptonshire, Sceptre Press, 1972.
The Celebrants and Other Poems. London, Hutchinson, 1973.
Some Unease and Angels: Selected Poems. London, Hutchinson, and University Center, Michigan, Green River Press, 1977.

Other

Editor, *Selected Poems of John Clare.* London, University Tutorial Press, 1968.
Editor, with Fay Weldon, *New Stories 4.* London, Hutchinson, 1979.

Translator, *The Selected Poems of Marina Tsvetayeva.* London, Oxford University Press, 1971.
Translator, *Three Russian Poets: Margarita Aliger, Yunna Moritz, Bella Akhmadulina.* Manchester, Carcanet Press, 1978.

*

Manuscript Collection: Cambridge University.

Elaine Feinstein comments:

My earliest fiction was very much an extension of my poetry, but as the novels have moved away from a single narrative voice to explore a wider territory, I have largely abandoned those rhythms and have come to prefer the traditional clarity of prose.

* * *

Lena, the central character in Elaine Feinstein's first novel, *The Circle*, comes to realize *à propos* her husband "that she would have to take it up again. Her separate life. Her lonely life, the music of words to be played with, the books;...they would be her refuge; her private world. As his was this of the laboratory. And she must now move as securely into that as he into his cold room, and find magic." However, in the general context of Feinstein's work, which shows a progressive widening of focus, this is broader than a feminist prescription. Her later novels are dominated by men and women involved in the search for "magic," partly via illegitimate means in *The Ecstasy of Dr. Miriam Garner*, and both actively and contemplatively through religion in *The Shadow Master.* "Magic" may be partially embodied in people, as in *The Amberstone Exit*, with Emily's fascination with the glamorous Tyrenes, the local rich family, and in *The Ecstasy of Dr. Miriam Garner*, with Miriam's fascination with the brilliant but brutal Stavros; in both novels there's a strong erotic element in the fascination, and Emily's youthful hunger for sexual experience, which comes to focus on Max Tyrene, anticipates Miriam's more sophisticated desire for Stavros.

The fundamental source of "magic" is inevitably "the music of words," and Feinstein's definition of this develops. For Lena and Emily it's joy in intoxicating language, but in the little story of *The Silent Areas* poetry must be "the words that ran in the blood of freezing men without food. Or the minds of the half-mad in lonely cells." (This is an Englishman's thought in Russia; Feinstein, herself a poet, has translated Marina Tsvetayeva.) The widening of her range globally across the human condition is climaxed in her most recent novel, *The Shadow Master*, where before the closing religious acceptance, the search for magic meant apocalyptic action. Thus, unfashionably, Feinstein is concerned with validation for people's lives outside as well as inside human relationships.

The Circle has vivid scenes, especially with children. Perhaps transposing from her experience as a poet, in this first novel she used technical devices, notably spaces within paragraphs, intended for immediacy but in practice often distracting, and later abandoned. Her staple technique through her work is the juxtaposition of different time sequences. In *The Circle* this is unstructured, while *The Amberstone Exit* opens in a maternity ward where Emily is having her baby and swings back over the events bringing her there, with the two time sequences run together towards the end.

The Amberstone Exit covers ground in a woman's life prior to *The Circle*, while in *The Glass Alembic* Feinstein takes a more mature woman, Brigid, and for the first time focuses on a group. Two passages from this novel are reworked with different names and alternative endings in the stories "Complicity" and "Strangers" (*The Silent Areas*). Brigid's husband is a biochemist working in Basel, and with air-fare mysteriously paid by one of his colleagues—which?—she flies out to join him with their virtually grown-up children. Her presence is a catalyst for various human reactions in the scientific community. The setting of Paracelsus-haunted Basel is merely coincidentally metaphoric of the action. By contrast, the settings are integral in *Children of the Rose*, which evokes Collaborationist tensions in present-day Provence and the reactions of Jews, once refugees, on revisiting Poland. Feinstein always writes effectively about illness, and a character's transformation by illness into a near-saintly image memorably concludes this novel.

In *The Ecstasy of Dr. Miriam Garner* Feinstein plaits a strand of narrative from medieval Toledo with a glamorous female academic's life into a mystery story with spiritual sidelights. *The Shadow Master* is her most ambitious novel, set mainly in Turkey, where an international religious and political apocalyptic movement begins, leading indirectly to the explosion of "a small nuclear device." But despite juxtaposition of different tones and the final gravity, some readers may prefer Feinstein's first novel, for its characterization. She's moved away from the humanistic novel, where characterization is everything, though by eschewing this she risks failing to involve the reader's emotions. Yet with a poet's use of language and myth, interlocking ideas and strong dialogue, and historical, religious, and occult elements, frequently fused with an exoticism reminiscent of Lawrence Durrell, Elaine Feinstein's vision is distinctive and refreshing.

—Val Warner

FIEDLER, Leslie A(aron). American. Born in Newark, New Jersey, 8 March 1917. Educated at New York University, B.A. 1938; University of Wisconsin, Madison, M.A. 1939, Ph.D. 1941; Harvard University, Cambridge, Massachusetts (Rockefeller Fellow), 1946-47. Served in the United States Naval Reserve, 1942-46: Lieutenant. Married 1) Margaret Ann Shipley in 1939 (divorced, 1973), six children; 2) Sally Smith Andersen, 1973, two foster children. Assistant Professor, 1947-48, Associate Professor, 1948-52, Professor of English, 1953-64, and Chairman of the Department, 1954-56, Montana State University, Missoula. Since 1965, Professor of English, currently Samuel Clemens Professor, State University of New York at Buffalo. Fulbright Lecturer, University of Rome, 1951-52, University of Bologna and Ca Foscari University, 1952-53, and University of Athens, 1961-62; Gauss Lecturer in Criticism, Princeton University, New Jersey, 1956-57; Lecturer, University of Sussex, Brighton, and University of Amsterdam, 1967-68; Visiting Professor, University of Vincennes, Paris, 1970-71. Fellow, Indiana University School of Letters, Bloomington, 1953; Associate Fellow, Calhoun College, Yale University, New Haven, Connecticut, 1969. Advisory Editor, *Ramparts* magazine, New York, 1958-61; Literary Adviser, St. Martin's Press, New York, 1958-61. Recipient: *Furioso* poetry prize, 1951; *Kenyon Review* Fellowship, for non-fiction, 1956; American Academy grant, 1957; American Council of Learned Societies grant, 1960, 1961; Guggenheim Fellowship, 1970. Address: 154 Morris Avenue, Buffalo, New York 14214, U.S.A.

PUBLICATIONS

Novels

The Second Stone: A Love Story. New York, Stein and Day, 1963; London, Heinemann, 1966.
Back to China. New York, Stein and Day, 1965.
The Messengers Will Come No More. New York, Stein and Day, 1974.

Short Stories

Pull Down Vanity and Other Stories. Philadelphia, Lippincott, 1962; London, Secker and Warburg, 1963.
The Last Jew in America. New York, Stein and Day, 1966.
Nude Croquet and Other Stories. New York, Stein and Day, 1969; London, Secker and Warburg, 1970.

Other

An End to Innocence: Essays on Culture and Politics. Boston, Beacon Press, 1955.
The Jew in the American Novel. New York, Herzl Press, 1959.
Love and Death in the American Novel. New York, Criterion, 1960; London, Secker and Warburg, 1961; revised edition, New York, Stein and Day, 1966; London, Cape, 1967.
No! In Thunder: Essays on Myth and Literature. Boston, Beacon Press, 1960; London, Eyre and Spottiswoode, 1963.
The Riddle of Shakespeare's Sonnets. New York, Basic, 1962.
Waiting for the End. New York, Stein and Day, 1964; as *Waiting for the End: The American Literary Scene from Hemingway to Baldwin*, London, Cape, 1965.
The Return of the Vanishing American. New York, Stein and Day, and London, Cape, 1968.
Being Busted. New York, Stein and Day, and London, Secker and Warburg, 1970.
The Collected Essays of Leslie Fiedler. New York, Stein and Day, 2 vols., 1971.
The Stranger in Shakespeare. New York, Stein and Day, 1972; London, Croom Helm, 1973.
To the Gentiles. New York, Stein and Day, 1972.
Cross the Border, Close the Gap. New York, Stein and Day, 1972.
A Fiedler Reader. New York, Stein and Day, 1977.
Freaks: Myths and Images of the Secret Self. New York, Simon and Schuster, 1978.
The Inadvertent Epic: From Uncle Tom's Cabin to Roots. Toronto, Canadian Broadcasting Corporation, 1979; New York, Simon and Schuster, 1980.

Editor, *The Art of the Essay.* New York, Crowell, 1958; revised edition, 1969.
Editor, *Selections from "The Leaves of Grass,"* by Walt Whitman. New York, Dell, 1959.
Editor, with Jacob Vinocur, *The Continuing Debate: Essays on Education.* New York, St. Martin's Press, 1965.
Editor, with Arthur Zeiger, *O Brave New World.* New York, Dell, 1968.
Editor, with Houston A. Baker, Jr., *English Literature: Opening Up the Canon.* Baltimore, Johns Hopkins University Press, 1981.

Leslie A. Fiedler comments:

My chief interest in the field of fiction has always been the exploration of the comic possibilities inherent in the elusive distinctions between races and generations, as well as between East and West, and Europe and America. I have also been deeply concerned with the difficulties of knowing who is one's father, or is not, for that matter. None of this, however, has seemed to me a proper occasion for tears.

* * *

There is no doubt that Leslie A. Fiedler aimed from his professional beginnings to be not just a critic but a genuine all-round man-of-letters, publishing not only controversial essays but also poetry and fiction soon after his literary debut; and he has followed all these muses, as well as a powerful one for public speaking, throughout his career. His fiction is, by common consent, less interesting and less original than his criticism (and his poetry even less substantial); and few critics of conscience have ever honored his imaginative work in print. In his opening critical essays, eventually collected as *An End to Innocence*, Fiedler established a knack for controversial argument, full of far-fetched connections and exaggerated remarks, all expressed in equally provocative prose; few since Mencken have provoked so much outrage. Rejecting the simple sentence along with the simplistic idea, Fiedler concocted a robust style composed of long and convoluted clause-compounded sentences riddled by paradoxes, parentheses, and charming self-ironies. However, only the tough-minded intelligence behind this forceful style, rather than the characteristic language, informs his fictions, which nonetheless reflect certain ideas in his criticism (which, in turn, sometimes mentions, if not quotes, his fiction!). The key theoretical text is the brilliant title essay opening his second collection, *No! In Thunder*, where Fiedler argues that the great modern writers have responded to ideals, institutions, and even people with uncompromised negation—the Melvillian cry of "No! in Thunder" indicating a complete stripping down that reveals inadequacy, deceit, failure, and the impossibility of perfection. "The No! in Thunder is never partisan," Fiedler writes, "it infuriates Our

Side as well as Theirs, reveals that all Sides are one, insofar as they are all yea-sayers and hence all liars."

The title of his first collection of stories, *Pull Down Vanity*, announces the characteristic strategy of his fiction, for most of the pieces here are shaped around the uncovering of illusory images presented by a person or group; and in this stripping away of human artifice is unveiled another favorite Fiedler theme of universal culpability. Thus, these stories are structured around actions of exposure and embarrassment—a technique admittedly indebted to Nathanael West's *The Day of the Locust* (1939). Thus, should readers come to believe that one of Fiedler's characters might be honest and good, the rug is pulled out before the story is done, leaving that character too sprawled in the fundamental mud. In "Nude Croquet" a busty young thing darkens a party's room and then leads a group of middle-aging "intellectuals" in playing croquet in the buff. Not at all uncomfortable, she flaunts her fresh figure, forcing the others to uncover both their masked bodily defects and, then, their spiritual vanities. One has body hair different in color from that on her head, another a withered leg, a third is flat-chested, while on another level one is insanely jealous, another has never completed his projected and much-announced masterpiece, a third has "sold out" to the commercial theater. When the group's slightly older idol collapses from over-exertion and dies of a heart attack, the girl screams a long blast as the lights go on. "Molly-o," Fiedler writes, "confronted them in the classic pose of nakedness surprised, as if she knew for the first time what it meant to be really nude." Discovering one's nudity is, symbolically, recognizing comparable inadequacies and culpability.

Fiedler's first and best novel takes for its unusual subject the demonic attachment of unrelated twins who, once childhood friends, re-encounter each other over a dozen years. One character speaks of "a comedy of confused identities," and these confusions are not only witty, but also difficult to summarize. The novel's protagonist, Clem Stone, is an unsuccessful writer, while his friend is Mark Stone, an eminent TV intellectual and existentialist rabbi. In the past, Clem was named Mark Stone, and the present Mark's last name was Stein. But as the present Mark changed his surname, Clem, overshadowed by the most successful Mark, became known as Mark the second, or Mark Twain. As the historical author Twain's real identity was Samuel Clemens, Stone takes the first name of Clem. The two Stones have always competed for the same goals, and before the novel is over, Clem seduces Mark's pregnant wife. The novel is similarly erudite in its joking, as in one scene Mark pummels his wife with a rolled-up copy of a magazine entitled *Thou*; and he is described, of course, as unable to stop stuttering "I-I-I-I." Long on such literary gags and arch symbols, *The Second Stone* is also short on credible surface and literary importance.

The protagonist of Fiedler's second novel, *Back to China*, is a college teacher in Montana, whose career in some respects parallels Fiedler's own—a Jew from the East teaching in the West, with a reputation for being the most famous radical on campus, the author of several books, a former wartime Japanese interpreter in the Far East; but whereas Fiedler himself has been a father several times over, Baro Finklestone's main problem is that he and his wife are childless. The reason, as we learn through a series of flashbacks, is that Finklestone's life, as well as the book's plot, turned upon a vasectomy, an irreparable voluntary sterlization, that he underwent in China. His reasons for doing this are never made entirely clear—indeed, the act itself is barely credible—and the novel never quite emerges from a mire of absurdities. Indeed, this slide toward preposterousness, which comes from mixing too much realistic, highly detailed, almost pedantic satire with more wholly symbolic fantasy—a mismating of Sinclair Lewis with Franz Kafka—becomes even more pronounced in the three novellas collected as *The Last Jew in America*; and Fiedler's next book of fiction, *Nude Croquet*, adds four slighter stories to those previously collected. A more suggestive step comes in *Being Busted*, an autobiographical memoir devoid of proper names, that successfully elevates to imaginative myth not only Fiedler's 1967 arrest on a marijuana related charge but also his responses to the life-styles of his children; for Fiedler ranks among the few writers of his post-fifty generation to suffer genuine confrontation and rebirth.

If Fiedler the critic is ambitious and original, as well as appreciative of eccentricity, the novelist is rather conventional in style, structure, and subject-matter—his own fiction scarcely acknowledging the innovative literature praised in his criticism; and the impact of his recent rebirth has so far been more intellectual than artistic. A truth of literature's past apparently unremembered in all this effort is that critics as major as Fiedler have rarely produced consequential fiction, try as much as they otherwise might. With his encompassing theme of deflation, Fiedler's fiction suggests that marriage is insufferable, that adultery is inevitable and just as inevitably disappointing; and his fictions deal as well with ambivalent attitudes toward paternity, slavish obsessions with seduction's ulterior motives, and the terrors of American professors and intellectuals. This rather limited range is, needless to say perhaps, closer to more prosaic writing than to what Fiedler the critic has defined as the great tradition of American imaginative prose.

—Richard Kostelanetz

FIELDING, Gabriel. Pseudonym for Alan Gabriel Barnsley. British. Born in Hexham, Northumberland, 25 March 1916. Educated at The Grange, Eastbourne, Sussex; Llangefni County School, Anglesey, Wales; St. Edward's, Oxford; Trinity College, Dublin, B.A. 1940; St. George's Hospital, London; Member of the Royal College of Surgeons, and Licentiate of the Royal College of Physicians, 1941. Served in the Royal Army Medical Corps, 1942-46. Married Edwina Eleanora Cook in 1943; three sons and two daughters. General Medical Practitioner, Maidstone, Kent, 1946-66. Author-in-Residence, 1966-67, and since 1967 Professor of English, Washington State University, Pullman. Recipient: St. Thomas More Association Gold Medal, 1963; Smith Literary Award, 1963; National Catholic Book Award, 1964. D.Litt.: Gonzaga University, Spokane, Washington, 1967. Address: 945 Monroe Street, N.E., Pullman, Washington 99163, U.S.A.

PUBLICATIONS

Novels

Brotherly Love. London, Hutchinson, 1954; New York, Morrow, 1961.

In the Time of Greenbloom. London, Hutchinson, 1956; New York, Morrow, 1957.

Eight Days. London, Hutchinson, 1958; New York, Morrow, 1959.

Through Streets Broad and Narrow. London, Hutchinson, and New York, Morrow, 1960.

The Birthday King. London, Hutchinson, 1962; New York, Morrow, 1963.

Gentlemen in Their Season. London, Hutchinson, and New York, Morrow, 1966.

Pretty Doll Houses. London, Hutchinson, 1979.

Short Stories

Collected Short Stories. London, Hutchinson, 1971.

New Queens for Old: A Novella and Nine Stories. London, Hutchinson, and New York, Morrow, 1972.

Verse

The Frog Prince and Other Poems (as Alan Barnsley). Aldington, Kent, Hand and Flower Press, 1952.
XXVIII Poems. Aldington, Kent, Hand and Flower Press, 1955.

*

Manuscript Collection: McMaster University, Hamilton, Ontario.

Critical Studies: interview in *Counterpoint*, edited by Roy Newquist, Chicago, Rand McNally, 1964; *Gabriel Fielding* by Alfred Borrello, New York, Twayne, 1974.

Gabriel Fielding comments:

I am not a prolific writer, writing only where an obsession leads me. So far I have been led through the intricacies of family life in post-Evangelical northern England, to North Africa where the international drinking set settled for a while, to Germany during the Second World War and to England again where a restless postwar world was unsettling the old guard.

My short stories cover much the same ground: the alchemy of childhood, international and domestic misunderstandings and, again, the impact of the New Morality on the old middle and upper middle classes in England.

* * *

Gabriel Fielding's growing reputation as a major serious novelist rests, in the main, on three of his novels—*In the Time of Greenbloom*, *The Birthday King*, and *Gentlemen in Their Season*. Throughout these novels, Fielding explores the theme of individual responsibility which has attracted European writers like Camus, Sartre, and Hesse, but which has been largely neglected by English novelists.

The narrative of *Greenbloom*, which forms, with *Brotherly Love* and *Through Streets Broad and Narrow*, a trilogy of the Blaydon family, concerns John Blaydon's growth to adolescence through a period of undeserved blame for the death of his friend Victoria Blount. Fielding presents a world devoted to finding sin in the young and innocent as a means of relieving its own sense of guilt. John only escapes acquiescence in a guilt which the world has persuaded him to own, through the intervention of Horat Greenbloom, an eccentric Jewish undergraduate follower of Wittgenstein and Sartre. Greenbloom's sympathetic interest is that of one scapegoat for another; his therapy, which is explicitly existential, subjective, and counter-abstractive, is to make John see that the empty categorizations of adult society lead to personal irresponsibility and consequent feelings of guilt which have to be transferred to the innocent and vulnerable for punishment.

The same theme is further explored in *The Birthday King* which chronicles the rise and fall of Nazi Germany through the history of two Jewish brothers, Alfried and Ruprecht Waitzmann, co-directors of a large industrial group. The brothers are contrasted to present contrary reactions to the mechanistic Hitler society. Ruprecht chooses survival at all costs, running the factories on forced labour for the Nazi regime, betraying Alfried but preserving the family inheritance; Alfried, on the other hand, deliberately and ostentatiously ridicules the system, is imprisoned in a concentration camp and tortured to be "cured" of his eccentricity. Together, the brothers present the two faces of Jewishness, survival and sacrifice, and through them Fielding explores the extremes of human response to the absurdity of the world. Of all Fielding's novels, *The Birthday King* comes nearest to the work of Camus in its investigation of individual choice in a society dehumanized and wholly objective. Alfried's response is that of the mystic innocent whose honesty makes him rebel against the "rectitudes, mad superstitions and madder certainties" of romantic Nazism; he consciously and literally makes himself the scapegoat which might liberate others from their guilt. Ruprecht's response, which is that of the opportunist, aggressive, shrewd, and lucky, is just as "existential" as Alfried's, but takes the form of an unflamboyant endurance which makes him see Alfried's heroism as a luxury: "What difference does it make that he's in a camp when the whole country's a camp?" So Fielding's theme is no simple contrast between the kind of individual choice made in the face of Nazism; rather it is that the *fact* of choosing is important because we are still free to choose. In this, he echoes Sartre's "We were never more free than under the Nazi occupation. The choice that each of us made of his life and his being was a genuine choice because it was made in the presence of death." Both Ruprecht and Alfried make authentic decisions; they are contrasted with characters like the Kommandent, Baron von Hoffbach, Alexandra von Boehling, and Herr Grunwald who sleepwalk through the Hitler-time: "They must have been bored for years without ever knowing it and there must have been thousands like them, practically a whole generation."

Boredom provides the focus of analysis in *Gentlemen in Their Season*, but here it is the less dramatic though no less deadly boredom of marriage and adultery. The novel is, in many ways, more disturbing than either *Greenbloom* or *The Birthday King*: issues no longer look quite as clear-cut and the setting is too proximate to allow the reader to be uninvolved. The action concerns two middle-aged, middle-class men, Randell Coles and Bernard Presage, whose marriages (to a brisk humanist and devout Catholic, respectively) have entered the dark night of aimless stagnation and dishonest intellectualism which is characterized by "clever" parties, self-conscious devotion to the Third Program, unmotivated religious retreats, and rigorous partner criticism. Each of them drift into affairs which have disastrous consequences for an uninvolved third party, Hotchkis, who before finishing his sentence for the manslaughter of his wife's lover, breaks from prison to protect his marriage once more and is killed by the police.

Although the scapegoat figure appears, he is not given the centre of the novel. Fielding instead probes into the lives of the bystanders whose guilt causes, and is atoned by, Hotchkis's death; Coles and Presage are the von Hoffbachs and Grunwalds of the novel, somnambulistic puppets of their wives and of their own abstract preconceptions of marriage which prevent them from acting decisively. Hotchkis's night ends by his triumphant decision to break out of prison and force events by his own action. The dark night of Coles and Presage never ends and they remain hollow drifters, unable even to conduct their extra-marital affairs with pleasure or humanity.

Thus in all his major novels, Fielding presents the admonition that we are all, as humans, involved in the total of human activity; a man's choice is a choice for all men. But if this account might seem to imply that Fielding merely dramatizes a "message," the implication must be dispelled. The didactic conclusions drawn by the reader come not from editorial commentary but from the compelling narrative and evocative imagery which support each other so intimately that the novels transcend their parts to become themselves images of ideas which act on the reader directly, rather than merely persuade by explicit argument and apt illustration. Indeed, the texture of Fielding's novels is akin to that of good dramatic poetry; images cluster and iterate to form a depth of reference which sets up unconscious associations with the reader's conscious awareness of plot and character. The movement of his novels strongly recalls symphonic structure in its series of statements, repetitions, modifications, and juxtapositions of action and imagery.

It is on grounds of both thematic force and artistic integrity that one must claim for Fielding a position in the forefront of English novelists.

—Frederick Bowers

FIGES, Eva. British. Born in Berlin, 15 April 1932. Educated at Kingsbury Grammar School, 1943-50; Queen Mary College, University of London, 1950-53, B.A. (honours) in English, 1953. Married John George Figes in 1954 (divorced); one daughter and one son. Free-lance editor and translator, London, 1955-67. Recipient: *Guardian* Fiction Prize, 1967; C. Day Lewis Fellowship, 1973; Arts Council Fellowship, 1977-79. Agent: Deborah Rogers, 5-11 Mortimer Street, London W1N 7RH. Address: 24 Fitzjohn's Avenue, London, N.W.3, England.

PUBLICATIONS

Novels

Equinox. London, Secker and Warburg, 1966.
Winter Journey. London, Faber, 1967; New York, Hill and Wang, 1968.
Konek Landing. London, Faber, 1969.
B. London, Faber, 1972.
Days. London, Faber, 1974.
Nelly's Version. London, Secker and Warburg, 1977.
Waking. London, Hamish Hamilton, 1981.

Uncollected Short Story

"Obbligato, Bedsitter," in *Signature Anthology.* London, Calder and Boyars, 1975.

Plays

Radio Plays: *Time Regained*, 1980; *Days*, from her own novel, 1981.

Other

The Musicians of Bremen: Retold (juvenile). London, Blackie, 1967.
The Banger (juvenile). London, Deutsch, and New York, Lion Press, 1968.
Patriarchal Attitudes: Women in Society. London, Faber, and New York, Stein and Day, 1970.
Scribble Sam (juvenile). London, Deutsch, and New York, McKay, 1971.
Tragedy and Social Evolution. London, Calder, and New York, Riverrun Press, 1976.
Little Eden: A Child at War (autobiography). London, Faber, 1978.

Editor, *Classic Choice 1.* London, Blackie, 1965.
Editor, *Modern Choice 1* and *2.* London, Blackie, 2 vols., 1965-66.
Editor, with Abigail Mozley and Dinah Livingstone, *Women Their World.* Gisburn, Lancashire, Platform Poets, 1980.

Translator, *The Gadarene Club*, by Martin Walser. London, Longman, 1960.
Translator, *The Old Car*, by Elisabeth Borchers. London, Blackie, 1967.
Translator, *He and I and the Elephants*, by Bernhard Grzimek. London, Deutsch-Thames and Hudson, and New York, Hill and Wang, 1967.
Translator, *Little Fadette*, by George Sand. London, Blackie, 1967.
Translator, *A Family Failure*, by Renate Rasp. London, Calder and Boyars, 1970.
Translator, *The Deathbringer*, by Manfred von Conta. London, Calder and Boyars, 1971.

* * *

One of the most important jobs a novelist does—often to the useful discomfort of his readers—is surely to create *the moment from inside*, vividly, patiently, admitting every ounce of its current ambiguity, so that his sentences read like heart-beats. Such a richness of life going on, actually being lived from one word to another, is well approached in *Winter Journey*, Eva Figes's second novel, which won the *Guardian* Fiction Prize in the year of its publication and which remains her most notable achievement to date. Figes in all her work goes beyond gesture to fix the most fugitive movements of existence in a pattern true to themselves—the best critical commentary on her fiction is probably to be found quite accidentally in Nathalie Sarraute's essays in the volume published in English as *Tropisms and The Age of Suspicion*, where such movements are perceived as the source of creative energy. Figes's own texts, like Sarraute's, tend to be short and sharp—nothing distracts her attention from what she considers to be essential. She is, like her French contemporary, a real realist—and offers much thereby that seems threatening or disconcerting to one's necessarily limited experience of "reality."

Winter Journey, which has a form inspired by Schubert's *Winterreise*, takes shape in the mind of old man, Janus, living out the last days of his life in a London house. Janus is ignorant and bitter: "a dull head among windy spaces." Elliot's "Gerontion" makes a pertinent point of reference, as does that empathy for the impotence of extreme age found in some of Beckett's finest writing. Figes gives us a man who has unearthed no peace in the accumulation of experience; his thoughts are stupid, his feelings flow or dribble in a cloudy stream of images inspired by needs he has never satisfied. Women, the war, the state of his bowels, figments of impossible adventure, the remorseless tick of the clock, snow, woodworm, the warmth of the reading room in the public library, remembered tags of nursery advice and admonition, all the odds and sods of Janus's pointless existence are drawn together in a jerky, rambling style that is again reminiscent of Beckett in that it makes a kind of poetry of the inarticulate.

Yet *Winter Journey* does not rely, for its total effect, on the mere depiction of a sequence of psychological states designed to engender pity in the reader. Janus is rich in character because he is not a simple personality; his memories cancel each other out; his only abiding passion is the constantly reiterated wish to "keep moving forever" because "if you could keep moving forever you would keep alive forever, it stands to reason." Out of the conflict between this ancient adolescent reduction of his existence to crazy going-on, pathetic endurance, and the deathward drag of all his memories, Figes fashions a detailed and compelling verbal substance. One feels in the presence of a person stripped to what he is, and records gratitude for a 119-page experience that might otherwise have taken a lifetime.

—Robert Nye

FINLAYSON, Roderick (David). New Zealander. Born in Auckland, 26 April 1904. Educated at Ponsonby School; Seddon Memorial Technical College, 1918-21, diploma in engineering 1922; Auckland University School of Architecture 1922-24. Served in the New Zealand Home Guard, 1940-45. Married Ruth Evelyn Taylor in 1936; three daughters and three sons. Architectural draftsman, 1922-28; writer, Department of Education School Publications Branch, Wellington, 1950-60; printing-room assistant, Auckland City Council, 1958-66. Recipient: New Zealand Centennial Prize, 1940. Address: 46 McLeod Road, Weymouth, Manurewa, New Zealand.

PUBLICATIONS

Novels

Tidal Creek. Sydney and London, Angus and Robertson, 1948; revised edition, Auckland, Auckland University Press-Oxford University Press, 1979.
The Schooner Came to Atia. Auckland, Griffin Press, 1953.

Short Stories

Brown Man's Burden. Auckland, Unicorn Press, 1938.
Sweet Beulah Land. Auckland, Griffin Press, 1942.
Brown Man's Burden and Later Stories, edited by Bill Pearson. Auckland, Auckland University-Oxford University Press, 1973.
Other Lovers. Dunedin, McIndoe, 1976.

Uncollected Short Stories

"Mr. Hake's Joyous Quest," in *Bulletin* (Sydney), 13 December 1944.
"A Nice Little Nest of Eggs," in *Bulletin* (Sydney), 30 April 1947.
"Mr. Stoke Had No Complaints," in *Bulletin* (Sydney), 5 November 1947.
"The Girl at the Golden Gate," in *Bulletin* (Sydney), 29 December 1948.
"The Secret," in *New Zealand Listener* (Wellington), 23 May 1952.
"Fuel for the Fires of Love," in *New Zealand Listener* (Wellington), 18 July 1952.
"The Whole Mean Trick," in *New Zealand Listener* (Wellington), 24 October 1952.
"The Morning for a Bargain," in *Arena 31* (Wellington), 1952.
"Sunday Outing," in *Arena 37* (Wellington), 1954.
"The Bulls," in *Landfall* (Christchurch), March 1956.
"A Nice Girl," in *Thursday* (Auckland), 1 May 1975.
"The Gift," in *Thursday* (Auckland), 22 March 1976.
"The Boomerang Boy," in *New Zealand Listener* (Wellington), 14 July 1979.

Other

Our Life in This Land (essay). Auckland, Griffin Press, 1940.
The Coming of the Maori [Musket, Pakeha]. Wellington, Department of Education School Publications Branch, 3 vols., 1955-56.
The Golden Years. Wellington, Department of Education School Publications Branch, 1956.
The Return of the Fugitives. Wellington, Department of Education School Publications Branch, 1957.
Changes in the Pa. Wellington, Department of Education School Publications Branch, 1958.
The Maoris of New Zealand, with Joan Smith. London, Oxford University Press, 1959.
The New Harvest. Wellington, Department of Education School Publications Branch, 1960.
The Springing Fern (juvenile). Christchurch, Whitcombe and Tombs, 1965; San Francisco, Tri-Ocean Books, 1967.
D'Arcy Cresswell. New York, Twayne, 1972.

*

Manuscript Collection: Hocken Library, University of Otago, Dunedin.

Critical Studies: introduction to *Brown Man's Burden and Later Stories,* 1973, "The Maori and Literature 1938-1965," in *Essays in New Zealand Literature* edited by Wystan Curnow, Auckland, Heinemann, 1973, and "Attitudes to the Maori in Some Pakeha Fiction," in *Fretful Sleepers and Other Essays,* Auckland, Heinemann, 1974, all by Bill Pearson; "Narrative Stance in the Early Short Stories of Roderick Finlayson" by John Muirhead, in *World Literature Written in English 14* (Arlington, Texas), April 1975.

Roderick Finlayson comments:

(1976) From the time I left school I had done occasional journalistic writing, mainly articles descriptive of the country and Maori traditions. But I suppose my work as a serious writer began when, after young manhood days among the Maori people of the Bay of Plenty, I found myself separated by city life from those friends. To give a more lasting form to my memories I began to embody them in short stories. The attention these attracted when published encouraged me to go on and to broaden the scope of my writing and to touch on all aspects of life in New Zealand. If, besides the literary, there is a social aim in my work, it could be said to be the hope to promote understanding between the races in New Zealand, and to take a hard look at our way of life in this land. I am now taking a new look at the relationship between the sexes, and am working on another series of short stories and two works of novella length.

* * *

When Roderick Finlayson began writing in the mid-1930's, the image of the Maori in Pakeha fiction was still confined to stereotypes which included the shiftless and unreliable native of the early settlers, the noble savage of romantic Victorians, and the comic foil to white superiority. He was exploited in fiction as well as in fact. At best he was patronised; at worst treated with contempt or open hostility. It is to Finlayson's credit that he was the first Pakeha writer to reveal the Maori as a human being with an identity that was both racial and individual, to reveal him with understanding, with sympathy, and with a determination to grasp the contemporary truth and not the historical illusion.

In this self-appointed task he was helped by an unusual combination of circumstances. As he has recorded, while still in his teens he rejected "our ruthless technological society," and sought the company of Maoris in remote country and coastal areas. He was accepted by them in their homes and became increasingly identified with their way of life. The depression of the 1930's only strengthened his attitudes both to the aggressive Pakeha world bent on self-destruction and to the dispossessed inheritors of ancient traditions, inheritors whose close relationship with the natural environment enabled them to survive in the present while cherishing their past. The desire to write about them was always uppermost in Finlayson's mind and, again as he records, his accidental discovery of Verga's Sicilian stories provided him with a convenient if distant model for his experiments. Their unaffected simplicity of style and vivid but unsentimental portrayal of peasant life admirably suited his purpose without tempting him to substitute imitation for observed experience. Moreover the beginning of his friendship with the New Zealand poet and prose-writer, D'Arcy Cresswell, who published *Eena Deena Dynamo; or, The Downfall of Modern Science* in 1936, reinforced his antagonism to civilised gadgetry, and gave him a sympathetic critic for his manuscript stories.

The title of his first collection of short stories drew attention to an important aspect of his writing. *Brown Man's Burden* suggested both an underlying theme and an authorial attitude. Nevertheless, Finlayson was always aware of the dangers of didacticism to artistic integrity and, although he could be described as a writer with a thesis, the thesis itself is the outcome of close observation and intense human experience among people whose customs and mode of existence have been sacrificed, as he believed, to the needs of a decadent civilisation and its idea of progress. The reader of *Brown Man's Burden and Later Stories,* which includes stories from his early collections together with a number written at various times through the last 40 years, will soon discover that he has kept in touch with the changing Maori world, and has continued with humour and insight, with sorrow as well as anger, to demonstrate the effects of that social pollution which sometimes goes under the name of race relations.

Finlayson is more concerned with the dramatic structure of his stories than with stylistic devices and the subtleties of language. As author he is aloof but compassionate, a master of ceremonies who takes no part in the proceedings, observant but uninvolved. The episode is chosen and so shaped that it generates its own ironies and moves swiftly to a climax without irrelevance or descriptive interruptions; and yet the reader is always made aware of implications that are likewise generated by action and setting. It would be a pity to use such well-worn phrases as "the cultural clash" or "the generation gap" to describe the major themes, because the incidents are brought to life in such a human way that sociological concepts seem to have no place in their development. The different values of Maori and Pakeha are laid bare by the logic of the narrative; and changes occurring as one set of values is more and more eroded by association with the other are revealed through character and circumstance. No attempt is made to idealise the Maoris, but the culture of traditional rural communities is keenly observed as it becomes submerged in the impoverished culture of cities.

Finlayson the novelist is less impressive than the short story writer. *Tidal Creek* is little more than a loosely strung series of humorous episodes and eccentric characters, among whom an elderly subsistence farmer exemplifies some of the rural virtues which Finlayson had stressed in his contentious *Our Life in This Land. The Schooner Came to Atia* is a slightly melodramatic tale of Europeans and Polynesians on a Pacific island, but its emphasis is not on the clash of cultures but on the soul-searching and vacillations of a missionary who has lost his faith. In some ways Finlayson has not fulfilled the expectations that his earlier work raised. Dependent on free-lance journalism, writing for School Publications and, latterly, on work for a City Council, he has found that time and energy have been insufficient to produce other than a handful of short stories which are not included in *Brown Man's Burden and Later Stories.* Nevertheless, such books as his account of the history of the Maoris in *The Springing Fern* and his critical biography of his friend, the poet D'Arcy Cresswell, are useful contributions to the literature of New Zealand.

Of greater significance in relation to his earlier imaginative work has been the appearance of three novellas under the title *Other Lovers.* Finlayson's preoccupations here, as elsewhere, revolve around ways of living and ways of loving in an environment where differing life-styles exert their pressures. His "other lovers" are by no means the usual protagonists of romantic fiction, for they include an elderly, disreputable tramp and a rebellious schoolgirl, a land-developer's agent seeking to purchase tribal land who becomes emotionally involved with a young Maori woman, and two frequenters of a small town milk-bar, one of whom is the daughter of an Island woman. From such unpromising material Finlayson is able to create a group of narratives in which the focus of his attention remains on the land and the people, on innocence and corruption, and on the social pollution that destroys or hinders spontaneous relationship. A sensitivity to change and difference in traditional modes of life together with the effects these have on individual attitudes and incentives cannot fail to give far more than romantic interest to these stories. The reappearance of imaginative work by an author who in the past has contributed so much is, therefore, of some consequence.

—H. Winston Rhodes

FITZGERALD, Penelope (Mary, née Knox). British. Born in Lincoln, 17 December 1916. Educated at Wycombe Abbey; Somerville College, Oxford, B.A. (honours) in English 1939. Married Desmond Fitzgerald in 1941 (died, 1976); one son, two daughters. Teacher with Westminster Tutors, London. Recipient: Booker Prize, 1979. Address: c/o William Collins and Company Ltd., 14 St. James's Place, London SW1A 1PS, England.

PUBLICATIONS

Novels

The Golden Child. London, Duckworth, 1977; New York, Scribner, 1978.
The Bookshop. London, Duckworth, 1978.
Offshore. London, Collins, 1979.
Human Voices. London, Collins, 1980.

Uncollected Short Story

"The Axe," in *The Times Anthology of Ghost Stories.* London, Cape, 1975.

Other

Edward Burne-Jones: A Biography. London, Joseph, 1975.
The Knox Brothers: Edmund ("Evoe") 1881-1971, Dillwyn 1883-1943, Wilfred 1886-1950, Ronald 1888-1957. London, Macmillan, and New York, Coward McCann, 1977.

*

Penelope Fitzgerald comments:

I've done short novels so far because I like economy and compression; I don't think long novels are necessarily better than short ones, any more than tall men are necessarily better than short men—it's a different form, that's all. Tolstoy's *Master and Man* is the great example.

I try to get the movement and counter-movement of the novel and its background to go together. *Offshore* was set in the Thames houseboat community and I wanted the movement of the novel to rise and ebb like the tidal river. *Human Voices* was set in Broadcasting House in the old days of wartime radio, and the narration as far as possible is through voices and music.

I write from my own experience and places where I've worked and from what I can judge of the feelings of other people, particularly when they are quiet by nature and prefer not to give away too much. Sometimes readers write and ask why I can't manage to produce a happy ending, but I don't see where to find one except in the considerate endurance of the human beings I have known.

* * *

Penelope Fitzgerald's first novel, *The Golden Child*, was a delightful, intelligent, and witty detective story. Even in a genre which does not call for such qualities, her characters are wholly believable—kind, vain, ambitious, or suffering. Her second, *The Bookshop*, was a "straight" novel, very short but beautifully composed and filled with flashing insights into the concealed, shaping currents of human behaviour. Her third novel, *Offshore*, equally short and memorable though not quite as outstanding as *The Bookshop* won the Booker Prize. But for this award and its attendant and focussing publicity, many people would never have discovered her, the best possible argument for the awarding of literary prizes, despite the absurdity of so many choices.

Before the novels, however, there were biographies of Edward Burne-Jones, the Victorian painter, and of the four famous Knox brothers, one of whom, Evoe (who became editor of *Punch*), was Fitzgerald's father. Both volumes were competently written, well researched, smoothly put together, and, above all, accurate. The author has that rare quality of engaging the reader's absolute trust. And though the biographies lack the acute and astonishing insights of the novels, Fitzgerald makes up for this by a brilliant ability to select other people's words: marvellously apt quotations which strikingly illuminate the narrative. Just one example from *Burne-Jones*, perfectly placed in context, is from a letter from his wife to George Eliot: "My heart smites me that I have somewhat resembled those friends who talk only of themselves to you." How revealing of the Victorian concept of good behaviour. That one phrase, in its delicacy, its self-accusation, is like a gleam of light shed on the entire English, upper-middle-class sensibility of the time.

It is, nevertheless, said by someone else. Fitzgerald's real talents only begin to reveal themselves in the novels. She evidently needs the imaginative freedom of fiction before she can take wing—though perhaps "plunge" would be a better word since she goes so deep. Give someone an enviably cultivated and civilised background, a First at Somerville, what seems to have been a wonderfully lively and interesting life, marriage and three bright children, and what kind of novels would one expect? Clever-academic? Grand-historical? The novel of manners? Even polished Women's Rights? Not a bit of it. Even in *The Golden Child*, for all its wit in portraying the jockeying for position of scholarly men in museums, she has an eye for the uncertainties which govern all our lives. She sees the tiny sources of terrible distress. In *The Bookshop*, about a pleasant, intelligent widow trying to run a bookshop in a small town, the theme is betrayal—sometimes from spite, sometimes from the baffling resentment always aroused by intelligence allied to modesty, sometimes from the equally inexplicable fury felt by the well-placed towards the less lucky, and sometimes from pure laziness. She sees the vast importance of small truths. Human beings, she says, are "divided into exterminators and exterminatees with the former, at any given moment, dominating." The book is a sad little masterpiece yet it sparkles with wit. And who could not admire a writer who can speak of an M.P. as "a brilliant, successful and stupid young man"?

Offshore deals with the fortunes, or rather misfortunes, of a variety of people living on houseboats on a stretch of the Thames. There are children who speak in a curiously formalised, almost Ivy Compton-Burnett style; their mother, beautiful and incapable; a stiff, competent, unhappily married man; and many others, all struggling to find a degree of fullness in their lives. Faced with the possibility of finally losing her estranged husband, the beautiful Nenna says: "I feel unemployed. I don't know what I'm going to think about if I'm not going to worry about him all the time." Fitzgerald sees with extraordinary perception what all our other women novelists, however famous, do not—that the root of love is not sex but occupation, the having something to do.

It is, again, startling to find that such a privileged life and nurturing should produce such understanding of what it is like to live on infinitely lower levels, socially, intellectually, and even emotionally. How did she manage to create a character like ten-year-old Christine, the working-class child in *The Bookshop*; perky, helpful, shrewd, impatient, and, in the end, like everyone else, a betrayer? Perhaps partly because, like her heroine in the same book: "In the end she valued kindness above everything."

—Gerda Charles

FLANAGAN, Thomas (James Bonner). American. Born in Greenwich, Connecticut, 5 November 1923. Educated at Amherst College, Massachusetts, B.A. 1945; Columbia University, New York, M.A. 1948, Ph.D. in English 1958. Instructor and Assistant Professor, Columbia University, 1952-60; Assistant Professor and Associate Professor, 1960-73, Professor, 1973-78, and Chairman of the Department of English, 1973-76, University of California, Los Angeles. Since 1978, Professor of English, State University of New York, Stony Brook. Recipient: American Council of Learned Societies grant, 1962; Guggenheim Fellowship, 1962; National Book Critics Circle Award, 1979. Address: Department of English, State University of New York, Stony Brook, New York 11794, U.S.A.

PUBLICATIONS

Novel

The Year of the French. New York, Holt Rinehart, and London, Macmillan, 1979.

Other

The Irish Novelists 1800-1850. New York, Columbia University Press, 1959.

* * *

Thomas Flanagan spent 30 years researching and developing *The Year of the French*, his only novel to date. This narrative was based on an actual historical event in which a French military force landed at Killala, County Mayo, Ireland on August 22, 1798. The French, who came ostensibly to free Ireland from British rule, were apparently more interested in embarrassing and harassing the English than in actually aiding the Irish. The French troops were joined by many peasants and various Irish rebel organizations. After marching through much of western and central Eire and winning several battles, they were eventually badly defeated at Ballinamuck, near Longford, by a vastly superior army led by Lord Cornwallis, whose success redeemed his tarnished experience in America. One of the most fascinating aspects of Flanagan's novel, which gives it an epic quality, is his attempt to portray in depth all sides and viewpoints in the conflict: the high born and the peasants, the Catholics and the Protestants, the French, Irish, and British military units, the clergy, the schoolmasters, the merchants—these and other groups are delineated with flesh and blood realization. At one point Flanagan even switches the scene to England and conveys a memorable portrait of an absentee landlord. Among the personages who beguile the reader are Arthur Broome, the local Anglican clergyman in Killala; Owen MacCarthy, the heavy drinking itinerant poet and hedgerow schoolmaster; Jean-Joseph Humbert, the wily, pragmatic French general; Malcolm Elliott, an upper-class Protestant estate holder committed to a more equitable economic order; and Captain Ferdy O'Donnell, a courageous, sensitive rebel leader.

Fictional characters are interrelated with real-life figures such as Wolfe Tone, George and John Moore, Dennis Browne, and Maria Edgeworth. The social, political, economic, and historical background and climate are presented and examined in thorough detail. Flanagan effectively intersperses dialogue and description with numerous imaginary diaries and memoirs of the era, and this technique adds immeasurably to the verisimilitude.

The novel is also distinguished by capturing the scene with marvelously rendered poetic lyricism exemplified in both the written and spoken language of the period. The book is a mellifluous delight—many of the pages are sheer poetry glowing with beauty and picturesque phrasing. Further, *The Year of the French* possesses considerable narrative drive. Although the use of journals and memoirs, frequent shifting from one character to another, and many scenic changes render the novel episodic, the pace never slows, and the movement is dynamic and pervasive.

The book's deficiencies center on three points. Flanagan presents a biased, hostile view of the Roman Catholic clergy (for example, if Flanagan's portrait of Father Murphy is compared with Liam O'Flaherty's Father Geelan in *Famine*, Flanagan's slant is evident; O'Flaherty too is anti-clerical, but his analysis of Geelan is balanced). On the other hand, Flanagan's Protestant clergymen appear to be wonderful, decent fellows. Secondly, Flanagan too often de-emphasizes the sufferings and oppression which the common people endured; he strikes an unhealthy and distasteful note in describing the uneducated peasants. Thirdly, he fantasizes too unrealistically about a humanitarian union between Catholics and Protestants which could have somehow magically come about and solved all the country's problems. While this solution would have been highly desirable, Flanagan attempts unsuccessfully to make it appear within the realm of possibility.

Aside from these weaknesses, *The Year of the French* is an epic saga of living history. It gives a panoramic view of one episode in the tragedy of English-Irish relations, reflected even today in the agony of Ulster. Flanagan is presently at work on another novel focusing on the late 19th-century Fenian Brotherhood era. If he can retain his combination of perceptive character portrayal, keen poetic sensibility, and gripping narrative force, and avoid his oversimplifications and a kind of upper-class long nose snobbism, he could secure for himself an important niche in the field of historical fiction.

—Paul A. Doyle

FOOTE, Shelby. American. Born in Greenville, Mississippi, 17 November 1916. Educated at the University of North Carolina, Chapel Hill, 1935-37. Served in the United States Army, 1940-44, and Marine Corps, 1944-45. Married Gwyn Rainer in 1956; two children. Novelist-in-Residence, University of Virginia, Charlottesville, November 1963; Playwright-in-Residence, Arena Stage, Washington, D.C., 1963-64; Writer-in-Residence, Hollins College, Virginia, 1968. Recipient: Guggenheim Fellowship, 1955, 1956, 1957; Ford Fellowship, for drama, 1963; Fletcher Pratt Award, for non-fiction, 1964, 1974; University of North Carolina award, 1975. Address: 542 East Parkway South, Memphis, Tennessee 38104, U.S.A.

PUBLICATIONS

Novels

Tournament. New York, Dial Press, 1949.
Follow Me Down. New York, Dial Press, 1950; London, Hamish Hamilton, 1951.
Love in a Dry Season. New York, Dial Press, 1951.
Shiloh. New York, Dial Press, 1952.
Jordan County: A Landscape in Narrative (includes stories). New York, Dial Press, 1954.
September September. New York, Random House, 1978.

Play

Jordan County: A Landscape in the Round (produced Washington, D.C., 1964).

Other

The Civil War: A Narrative:
I. *Fort Sumter to Perryville.* New York, Random House, 1958.
II. *Fredericksburg to Meridian.* New York, Random House, 1963.
III. *Red River to Appomattox.* New York, Random House, 1974.

*

Bibliography: in *Mississippi Quarterly* (State College), October 1971.

Manuscript Collection (non-fiction): Southern Historical Collection, Chapel Hill, North Carolina.

Critical Studies: *South* edited by Louis D. Rubin, Jr., and R.D. Jacobs, New York, Doubleday, 1961; "Shelby Foote Issue" of *Mississippi Quarterly* (State College), October 1971; "Shelby Foote's *Iliad*" by Helen White and Reading Sugg, in *Virginia Quarterly Review* (Charlottesville), Spring 1979.

* * *

Shelby Foote appears to succeed as a historian, not as a novelist; his multi-volume history *The Civil War: A Narrative* shows his ability to best advantage. However, one should remember that his entree into the literary world came as a promising novelist. His novels show a serious craftsman at work.

Foote experimented with technique. *Tournament* is a character study—approaching biography—with an objective omniscient point of view. *Follow Me Down* takes a single plot but incorporates a multiple point of view. This method is interesting because it allows eight characters—including protagonist and minor characters—to comment in a limited first person viewpoint on their reactions to a violent murder. *Love in a Dry Season* is a *tour de force* in which the author links two separate stories centered on the subject of money by a character who tries and fails to obtain a place in the financial elite of a small delta town. *Shiloh* enters the domain of historical fiction as the author recreates that Civil War battle through the eyes of six soldiers from both camps. Unlike the viewers in *Follow Me Down*, these narrators describe different aspects of the three-day confrontation, and only by adroit maneuvering does the author bring the respective narratives into contact. The battle, therefore, becomes the hero of the novel. *Jordan County* is a collection of seven tales or episodes ranging from 1950 backward to 1797. In each case the locale is Bristol, Jordan County, Mississippi. As his previous novel focused on a single battle, so this chronicles human drama of a fictional area, which becomes the only constant in a world of flux.

With the exception of his historical novel, all of Foote's novels are located in his microcosm, the delta country around Lake Jordan. This fictive locale includes two counties, Issawamba and Jordan, Solitaire Plantation, and the town of Bristol on the Mississippi River. Through a habit of cross reference, Foote links episodes from one novel to another. For instance, the novella "Pillar of Fire" (*Jordan County*) relates the story of Isaac Jameson, founder of Solitaire Plantation and a patriarch of the delta, while *Tournament* supplies information about the man, Hugh Bart, who brought Solitaire back from devastation by war and reconstruction.

Foote's use of setting, as well as style, subject matter, themes, and characterization, invites comparison with his geographical neighbor, Faulkner, but Foote's accomplishments suffer thereby. Foote is competent, not great. Normally his style is simple, lean, and direct; it seldom takes on richly suggestive qualities. Most of his themes move in the negative, anti-social direction: violence instead of peace; lust rather than love; avarice, power, and pride instead of self-sacrifice; and loneliness rather than participation in community. At his best Foote deals effectively with dramatic situations and characterizations, for example, the concatenation of episodes in the life of Hugh Bart or Luther Eustis's murder (*Follow Me Down*); however, Harley Drew's career (*Love in a Dry Season*) of lust and avarice seems an exploitation of violence rather than art. In general, Foote chronicles events in the realistic tradition without conveying a larger insight than the particular. Foote's method is a competent beginning beyond which he must go in order to achieve a significant place in Southern literature.

—Anderson Clark

FORD, Jesse Hill (Jr.). American. Born in Troy, Alabama, 28 December 1928. Educated at Vanderbilt University, Nashville, B.A. 1951; University of Florida, Gainesville, M.A. 1955; University of

Oslo (Fulbright Fellow), 1961. Served in the United States Navy, in the Far East, 1951-53. Married 1)Sally David in 1951 (divorced, 1975), four children; 2)Lillian Chandler in 1975. Reporter, *Nashville Tennesseean*, 1950-51; Editorial News Writer, University of Florida, 1953-55; Medical News Writer, Tennessee Medical Association, Nashville, 1955-56; Public Relations Executive, American Medical Association, Chicago, 1956-57. Fellow, Center for Advanced Study, Wesleyan University, Middletown, Connecticut, 1965. Founder, Yellow Rose Productions, Los Angeles, 1969. Trustee, Reelfoot Regional Libraries, Tennessee. Recipient: *Atlantic* "Firsts" Award, 1959; Guggenheim Fellowship, 1966. D.Litt.: Lambuth College, Jackson, Tennessee, 1966. Address: Winter Island, St. Thomas, Virgin Islands 00801, U.S.A.

PUBLICATIONS

Novels

Mountains of Gilead. Boston, Little Brown, 1961.
The Liberation of Lord Byron Jones. Boston, Little Brown, 1965; London, Bodley Head, 1966.
The Feast of Saint Barnabas. Boston, Little Brown, and London, Bodley Head, 1969.
The Raider. Boston, Little Brown, 1975.

Short Stories

Fishes, Birds, and Sons of Men: Stories. Boston, Little Brown, 1967; London, Bodley Head, 1968.

Uncollected Short Stories

"Collector," in *Atlantic* (Boston), February 1968.
"Doctor," in *Atlantic* (Boston), June 1969.
"Destruction," in *Esquire* (New York), July 1969.
"Debt," in *Atlantic* (Boston), June 1972.
"Big Boy," in *Atlantic* (Boston), 1974.
"The Jail," in *Playboy* (Chicago), April 1975.

Plays

The Conversion of Buster Drumwright: The Television and Stage Scripts. Nashville, Tennessee, Vanderbilt University Press, 1964.

Screenplay: *The Liberation of L.B. Jones*, 1969.

Other

Mister Potter and His Bank. Nashville, McDonald, 1977.

*

Bibliography: *Jesse Hill Ford: An Annotated Check List* by Helen White, Memphis, Tennessee, Memphis State University, 1974.

Manuscript Collection: Memphis State University, Tennessee.

Jesse Hill Ford comments:

In 1963 I found to my surprise that I had been working on the same story for ten years and that bits and pieces of it had by then appeared in several short stories, one play, and one novel. The second novel continued the story. In the third novel, *The Feast of St. Barnabas*, I tried, but failed to escape the one long story I began in 1953, the story I have, fitfully to be sure, been writing ever since. If one reads all my books and stories the pattern will emerge in tenuous connections sometimes indicated only by the appearance of a name carried forward, or backward, from one generation into another. The story begins in the western district of Tennessee in the American South and it probably will end there someday, far off in the future I hope, even though I am now 51 years old and still attempting to write it all down, not just the tragic events, but also the happy ones, and not just the earth-shaking things, but also the small moments that have been of such singular importance to the people I work to portray.

* * *

One generation removed from the modern Southern Renaissance, Jesse Hill Ford has begun to establish his legitimate place in that literary heritage. He has shown ability to treat universal themes embodied in the subjects—people, attitudes, events—of a particular geographical region, the American South. The greater portion of Ford's work—including two novels, *The Liberation of Lord Byron Jones* and *Mountains of Gilead*, and several short stories collected in *Fishes, Birds, and Sons of Men*—is set in the author's fictional 20th-century microcosm, Somerton, Sligo County, Tennessee. Through the continuity of locale and the cross reference to particularly prominent families and community events, the reader of Ford's fiction absorbs one writer's observation of the diversified southern consciousness.

Ford's observation covers an impressive range of themes. For example, the theme of innocence to experience has several dimensions. Simple childhood reminiscences in "The Cave" and "The Cow" respectively lead a child to intuit the fact of evil and of death, although the child can not articulate these experiences. In another short story, "A Strange Sky," Ford deals directly with the effects of this progression to experience in the life of his adult protagonist, Patsy Jo. She examines her past life, especially the seduction and manipulation by her irresponsible childhood lover, who has continually postponed marriage. Now past her marriageable prime, Patsy Jo reaches a point of maturity by severing her relationship as mistress. In the hunting story, "Savage Sound," the same theme is used differently. The protagonist does not move from innocence to experience; rather, he is responsible for teaching his young whippets to kill rabbits and, thereby, for changing the dogs' loving natures to that of vicious predators.

Violence as a theme pervades all of Ford's fiction. A catalogue of physical violence includes assault and battery, automobile wrecks, arson, rape, adultery, rusty coat hanger abortion, castration, cattle-prodding humans, drowning, man-slaughter in self-defense, premeditated murder, and even a bizaare homicide effected by the chomping jaws of a hay-bailing machine. Psychological violence, often a concomitant of the physical, makes Ford's characters also an emotionally mangled humanity. Both facets of violence show that in Ford's chaotic world ego-centric modern man chooses to satisfy his own desires at the expense of his fellow man.

The violence in Ford's fiction is often an adjunct of the revenge theme. His drama, *The Conversion of Buster Drumwright*, produced first as a television play and later expanded for the stage, links murder, a desire for blood revenge, and religion. Ford's plot functions in such a way as to discredit the impulse toward revenge and sanction the worth, if not the authenticity, of the Christian message of repentance, forgiveness, and salvation. *Mountains of Gilead*, Ford's first novel, artistically uneven, offers a perceptive characterization of a Southern father caught in the dilemma of avenging his daughter's violated honor while remembering the unhappy consequences of his own early marital infidelity. That the father follows the code of revenge, despite his own moral inconsistency, allows the plot to resolve—after a blood bath, suicide, and time interval—in a melodramatic reunion and marriage of the estranged youthful lovers.

Another significant theme is racial injustice, prejudice, and discrimination in Ford's South. The short story "Bitter Bread" recounts the agony and humiliation of a black man whose wife dies in a hospital corridor because they have no money for admission. Ford continues this theme of racial injustice in his second novel, *The Liberation of Lord Byron Jones*. Somerton's respectable black mortician, L.B. Jones, in seeking a divorce from his young, promiscuous wife, precipitates his own violent "liberation," his murder by the white policeman involved in the miscegenous affair. Jones is a believably tragic character as well as a representative of the oppressed southern Negro. Other characters—with varying degrees of success—demonstrate typical attitudes including that of White Citizens' agitator, socially conservative and moderate whites, and simple and militant blacks. Ford takes another viewpoint in the third novel, *The Feast of Saint Barnabas*, by focusing on the forces operating in a southern racial riot. He shows a rich black man manipulating the violent elements in the community for selfish gains. While this novel contains plenty of action, it lacks dimensions of characterization and even psychological suffering which underscore themes of the two earlier impressive works.

As an imaginative craftsman, Ford writes especially well in the short story genre. In this particular genre, in contrast to a drift in his longer works toward the melodramatic or the maudlin, Ford welds dramatic action, effective characterization, and vivid imagery into a thematic unity. His talents in the short story are in the best of Southern Renaissance literary tradition. His narration is simple; his style is clear and direct. In the shorter pieces he handles point of view with strict control, and while *The Liberation* offers a multiple point of view, Ford uses his short story technique of control from section to section. Of primary importance are his vivid eye for details, which often function both literally and symbolically, and his fine ear for dialogue. His sense of humor moves from the rockingly jovial to the grimly ironic, and his best characters possess the complexity and vitality of a gifted artist's imagination.

—Anderson Clark

FORSYTH, Frederick. British. Born in Ashford, Kent, in 1938. Educated at Tonbridge School, Kent. Served in the Royal Air Force. Married; has children. Journalist: with *Eastern Daily* Press, Norwich, and later in King's Lynn, Norfolk, 1958-61; reporter for Reuters, London, Paris, and East Berlin, 1961; reporter, BBC Radio, London, 1965-67; Assistant Diplomatic Correspondent, BBC Television, 1967; free-lance journalist in Nigeria, 1967-68. Recipient: Mystery Writers of America Edgar Allan Poe Award, 1971. Lives in Ireland. Address: c/o Hutchinson Publishing Group Ltd., 3 Fitzroy Square, London W1P 6JD, England.

PUBLICATIONS

Novels

The Day of the Jackal. London, Hutchinson, and New York, Viking Press, 1971.
The Odessa File. London, Hutchinson, and New York, Viking Press, 1972.
The Dogs of War. London, Hutchinson, and New York, Viking Press, 1974.
The Shepherd. London, Hutchinson, 1975; New York, Viking Press, 1976.
The Devil's Alternative. London, Hutchinson, 1979; New York, Viking Press, 1980.

Uncollected Short Stories

"No Comebacks," in *Best Detective Stories of the Year 1974*, edited by Allen J. Hubin. New York, Dutton, 1974.

Other

The Biafra Story. London, Penguin, 1969; as *The Making of an African Legend: The Biafra Story*, 1977.

*   *   *

Frederick Forsyth achieved considerable commercial success with his first book, *The Day of the Jackal*, and in each of his three subsequent novels has followed the same basic formula. Start with a plausible international crisis, mix real historical personages with fictional characters, scatter violent and/or erotic incidents liberally through the story, explain the secrets of criminal activity in minute detail, build toward an explosive climax, end with an unexpected twist of plot. The formula has produced best sellers at least one notch above standard popular fare, all already made or likely soon to be made into profitable feature films.

The Day of the Jackal still represents the finest product of the Forsyth formula. The main plot seems simple enough: a group of disgruntled army veterans of the Algerian War hire a professional assassin from England, code named the jackal, to kill President De Gaulle for betraying the French cause in North Africa. Forsyth complicates the story by adding an abundance of peripheral plots and characters, many based on actual events of the time. We are jolted back and forth between two centers of intrigue—the solitary assassin meticulously planning each step of the murder and the special police unit trying to track him down. It is Forsyth's fascination with detail which draws the reader into the story, details such as how to acquire false passports, how to obtain a custom-made rifle, how to travel around Europe under a variety of identities, and how, on the other hand, police forces of different nations communicate in the effort to locate the assassin. Despite, or because of, the multitude of characters, we see action without really understanding the human motives behind it. But though we do not feel any understanding of the main figure, the jackal, we are willing to ascribe it to the nature of the character: a professional assassin keeps his own counsel, revealing little or nothing of himself to anyone. Thus a fundamental flaw in Forsyth's work, his inability to create convincing characters, can be seen as a virtue in his first novel.

No such mitigating circumstance applies to his subsequent books, however. *The Odessa File* concerns a young German journalist's attempt to infiltrate an organization of influential former SS officers and to locate one war criminal in particular. The theme of hunter and hunted is repeated from the earlier book, but the lack of characterization is more apparent and less excusable. So too with *The Dogs of War*, a novel about mercenaries overthrowing an African dictator, and *The Devil's Alternative*, about a series of international events taking place in the near future which bring the world to the brink of nuclear war. All have a wealth of incidents, a surprising denouement, and a continuing preoccupation with detail. We learn in these books how to plant bombs, smuggle guns through customs, plan assassinations; we learn how terrorists operate, how world leaders confer and conspire. But all of this detail does not produce a single convincing character. The events seem real, at least plausible, but not the people.

Forsyth himself is entirely candid about the strengths and weaknesses of his work. He recognizes the need for thorough research into his material knowing that the credibility of his plots lies in his attention to detail, not in his characters. He sees himself, moreover, as a strictly commercial writer, and his language is crisp and direct, without grace or pretention. Proficient within his genre, Forsyth has the intelligence and good taste not to stray beyond his metier.

—Robert E. Lynch

FOSTER, David (Manning). Australian. Born in Sydney, 15 May 1944. Educated at the University of Sydney, B.Sc., 1967; Australian National University, Canberra, Ph.D. 1970. Research Fellow, U.S. Public Health Service, Philadelphia, 1970-71; Senior

Research Officer, University of Sydney Medical School, 1971-72. Recipient: Australian Literature Board Fellowship, 1973, 1975, 1979; *The Age* award, 1974; Marten Bequest award, 1978. Address: Ardara, Bundanoon, New South Wales, Australia.

PUBLICATIONS

Novels

The Pure Land. Melbourne, Macmillan, 1974.
The Empathy Experiment, with D.K. Lyall. Sydney, Wild and Woolley, 1977.

Short Stories

North South West: Three Novellas. Melbourne, Macmillan, 1973.
Escape to Reality. Melbourne, Macmillan, 1977.

Verse

The Fleeing Atalanta. Adelaide, Maximus, 1975.

* * *

David Foster has established for himself a reputation as one of Australia's most promising and wide-ranging prose writers, drawing not only on a large social range but also on concepts derived from his early years as a research chemist both in Sydney and the U.S.A. His work has won much local praise and Nobel Laureate Patrick White has stated that: "It is a long time since a work of Australian fiction impressed me as much as D.M. Foster's *North South West*. Foster's wit and vision are all his own, and very Australian. He is particularly good at ugly suburban interiors, trains, country towns, the sticks and stones of introspection, and the bitterly hilarious unreason of life."

While White's praise is strong and his isolation of the physical elements of Foster's world accurate, most of the interest in the novellas in *North South West* is to be found in the concept of entropy in the third, "Time's Arrow." Entropy is a complex concept, and not one to which readers of fiction other than Pynchon's are often exposed. But in "Time's Arrow" an anonymous narrator, writing in a loosely connected and scarcely punctuated prose that is both energetic and formless, becomes obsessed with it, and the fact that "the entropy of the world tends to a maximum entropy times arrow a powerful concept is everywhere folks you cannot escape it most people have never even heard of entropy although you will find mention of it here and there increasingly...." He researches the concept only to find himself fighting against its implications, facing negentropy, turning, but hopelessly, away from the fall into the social chaos Nathanael West called entropy, and the narrator's own possible contribution to it.

The other novellas in *North South West* are considerably less interesting and more doggedly plotted and styled. But in *The Pure Land* concerns similar to those of "Time's Arrow" are run through a more complex situation covering three generations and, again, a hunt for meaning and comprehension in the face of forces that seem to preclude chances of success. "i ache to see the sun rise again the clouds materialize above the mountains!—but it won't last...it can't last...law of entropy...just a pocket an inversion..." (Foster's eclipses) writes the narrator of "Time's Arrow." And the third-generation narrator of *The Pure Land* finishes up gaining incorrect information from his quest for "My Land of Purity." Drunk, he has sifted through documents that should explain his mother and grandfather more clearly and finished in a shambles: "I have decided there are no implications....I've let facts lead me astray too long to take any notice of them now.... I don't know how to end this—I can't believe it's really ended."

In *The Pure Land* these burnt-out conclusions are at the end of a strong and forceful narrative. The grandfather, a shy Jewish photographer named Mainwaring, who is separated from his wife and lives in the Blue Mountains outside Sydney, stumbles across a market for pornography and abducts his daughter and settles in Jersey City. His life is sad and aimless and leads to an increasingly lachrimose self-pity. The daughter Janet is similarly aimless and unsettled and it is eventually her son, Danny, who turns his back on a career as a scientist and returns to the Australia of his immediate forebears hunting for the pure land of the title and of his obsessions. But hunting in the past seems to be all wrong, and certainly leads Danny astray and into a sense of personal disintegration.

It is this shaping concept, this obsession with the forces that break down spirit and body while the mind aches for coherence and the next sunrise that is Foster's most fruitful area of concern. His prose is often rather lax and slack, as is his poetry, but his ability to forge a new awareness of aspects of social pressures, and to do so through scientific analogy that, to the extent of my limited comprehension, is neither forced nor made too schematically exact is a major asset, and one that gives his fiction a demanding and experimental freshness.

—Carl Harrison-Ford

FOWLES, John (Robert). British. Born in Leigh-on-Sea, Essex, 31 March 1926. Educated at Bedford School, 1940-44; Edinburgh University, 1944; New College, Oxford, B.A. (honours) in French 1950. Served in the Royal Marines, 1945-46. Married Elizabeth Whitton in 1956. Lecturer in English, University of Poitiers, 1950-51; Taught at Anargyrios College, Spetsai, Greece, 1951-52, and in London, 1953-63. Recipient: Silver Pen Award, 1969; Smith Literary Award, 1970. Agent: Anthony Shiel Associates, 2-3 Morwell Street, London WC1B 3AR, England.

PUBLICATIONS

Novels

The Collector. London, Cape, and Boston, Little Brown, 1963.
The Magus. Boston, Little Brown, 1965; London, Cape, 1966; revised edition, Cape, 1977; Little Brown, 1978.
The French Lieutenant's Woman. London, Cape, and Boston, Little Brown, 1969.
Daniel Martin. Boston, Little Brown, and London, Cape, 1977.

Short Stories

The Ebony Tower: Collected Novellas. London, Cape, and Boston, Little Brown, 1974.

Plays

Don Juan, adaptation of the play by Molière (produced London, 1981).

Screenplay: *The Magus*, 1968.

Verse

Poems. New York, Ecco Press, 1973.
Conditional. Northridge, California, Lord John Press, 1979.

Other

The Aristos: A Self-Portrait in Ideas. Boston, Little Brown, 1964; London, Cape, 1965; revised edition, London, Pan, 1968; Little Brown, 1970.

Shipwreck, photographs by the Gibsons of Scilly. London, Cape, 1974; Boston, Little Brown, 1975.
Islands, photographs by Fay Godwin. London, Cape, 1978; Boston, Little Brown, 1979.
The Tree, photographs by Frank Horvat. London, Aurum Press, 1979; Boston, Little Brown, 1980.
The Enigma of Stonehenge, photographs by Barry Brukoff. London, Cape, and New York, Summit, 1980.

Editor, *Steep Holm: A Case History in the Study of Evolution*. Sherborne, Dorset, Allsop Memorial Trust, 1978.
Editor, with Rodney Legg, *Monumenta Britannica*, by John Aubrey. Sherborne, Dorset Publishing Company, 1980.

Translator, *Cinderella*, by Perrault. London, Cape, 1974; Boston, Little Brown, 1975.
Translator, *Ourika*, by Claire de Durfort. Austin, Texas, Thomas Taylor, 1977.

*

Bibliography: "John Fowles: An Annotated Bibliography 1963-76" by Karen Magee Myers, in *Bulletin of Bibliography* (Boston), xxxiii, 4, 1976.

Critical Studies: *Possibilities* by Malcolm Bradbury, London and New York, Oxford University Press, 1972; *The Fiction of John Fowles: Tradition, Art, and the Loneliness of Selfhood* by William J. Palmer, Columbia, University of Missouri Press, 1974; *John Fowles, Magus and Moralist* by Peter Wolfe, Lewisburg, Pennsylvania, Bucknell University Press, 1976; *Etudes sur "The French Lieutenant's Woman" de John Fowles* by Jean Chevalier, Caen, University of Caen, 1977; *John Fowles* by Barry N. Olshin, New York, Ungar, 1978.

* * *

John Fowles is a highly allusive and descriptive novelist. In all his fictions, situations and settings are carefully and lavishly done; the French country landscape of "The Cloud" (*The Ebony Tower*), or the blues and purples of the stark New Mexican mountains or the soft rainy contours of Devon in various greens and greys or the bleak and menacing deserts of Syria, all in *Daniel Martin*. Most frequently, Fowles's richly painted settings conceal a mystery, as in the title story of *The Ebony Tower*, in which an old English painter has created his "forest" in France, like that of the legendary Chrétien de Troyes, a "mystery island" to break away from the closed formal island into "love and adventure and the magical." Similarly, the lush Greek island of *The Magus* conceals mystery and magic, a stage for the complicated and elaborate series of theatricals that enchant, enslave, and instruct a young Englishman who has taken a teaching job there. Fowles's central characters, like Nicholas Urfe in *The Magus*, try to solve the mysteries, to make sense of what happens as they are initiated into new worlds, but they are not entirely successful. Most often, as in the short story "The Enigma," in which a solid, stable, middle-aged Tory M.P. simply disappears, Fowles never resolves the mystery and concentrates on the implications for others in living in terms of what is finally unknown.

In staging his mysteries, in choosing what to reveal and what to conceal, Fowles has often been seen by readers as manipulative. Such manipulation, however, is not merely a matter of tricks, ingenious switches, or "the God-game." Rather, the sense of "reality" as something that has to be manipulated, rearranged, in order to be understood is central to Fowles's conception of both the nature and the function of fiction. When victimized by a mock trial in the culminating theatrical invented for him, Nicholas Urfe realizes that he is only getting what he has deserved, for "all my life I had tried to turn life into fiction, to hold reality away." The novelist's manipulation is even more open, more immediately recognizable, in *The French Lieutenant's Woman*, which is full of parodies of old novelistic devices, switches in time and history, and frequent interruptions of the Victorian narrative that acknowledge the author's deliberate arrangements. The reader is constantly led to question what "Victorian" means, to recognize the texture of anachronism, parody, research, quotations from Marx, Darwin, Victorian sociological reports, Tennyson, Arnold, and Hardy as various means of demonstrating the conditional nature of time and history, the necessity of locating oneself in the present before one can understand anything of the nature of the past. The novel also has three endings, not simply as a form of prestidigitation, but as a demonstration that three different possible resolutions, each characterizing a different possible perspective itself historically definable toward the events of the novel, is consistent with the issues and characters Fowles has set in motion. Only in *Daniel Martin* do all Fowles's speculations about the nature of fiction become both modish and arid rather than intrinsically connected with the nature of the particular novel.

The allusive references of Fowles's ingenious fictions have widened and deepened over the course of his development. In his first novel, *The Collector*, more sensational than those that followed, Fowles attempted to probe psychologically and sociologically on a single plane of experience, to demonstrate what in a young man of one class caused him to collect, imprison, and dissect the girl from another class he thought he loved. This interest in the English class system is also echoed in a story like "Poor Koko," in which the "words" of an old writer are unavailing in preventing or assuaging needless cruelty by a young thief, a representative of a newer England. The fabrications of *The Magus* extend further into history, legend, and myth, exploring various kinds of Gods, of perspectives "real" and imaginary (one can never finally draw a line between the two) that negate human freedom. A number of the long stories of *The Ebony Tower*, like "Eliduc," re-tell ancient myths or recreate them in contemporary terms. *The French Lieutenant's Woman*, with all its literary, historical, and artistic allusions, shows what of the story is of the past, what of the present, and what indeterminate, for history, for Fowles, invariably includes much of the time and perspective of the historian. Thematically, *Daniel Martin* is, in some ways, an expansion of *The French Lieutenant's Woman*, an analysis of Fowles's own generation, the last in England that might still be characterized as Victorian, "brought up in some degree of the nineteenth century since the twentieth did not begin until 1945." *Daniel Martin* also makes explicit a theme implicit in Fowles's earlier fiction, the paralyzing and complicated effects of all the guilts originating in the Victorian past, what he calls "a pandemic of self-depreciation" that leads to emotional insularity and to the capacity to live gracefully with loss rather than trying to overcome it. In this novel, which ranges geographically (America, Italy, and the Middle East, as well as England) and historically (past wars and cultural legends), the guilt and self-depreciation are also attached to attractions to lost civilizations, the American Indians, the Minoans, the Etruscans, and the contemporary English.

All Fowles's central characters are isolated, rational, self-punishing males who attempt to join with independent, passionate, and enigmatic women. As the voice of the author in *The French Lieutenant's Woman* claims, he may be simply transferring his own inabilities to understand the enigmatic female into the safety of his historically locatable Victorian story. This sexual focus, however, with its attendant guilts and metaphorical expansions, is characteristic, and all the novels develop the rational and sometimes manipulative means the male uses to try to understand and control the amorphous and enigmatic female. The male is always limited, his formulations and understandings only partial. And, in his frustration, the necessity that he operate in a world where understanding is never complete, he acts so as to capture (*The Collector*), desert (*The Magus*), betray (*The French Lieutenant's Woman*), or both betray and finally recover (*Daniel Martin*) the female he can only partially comprehend. Fowles develops and metaphorically expands this constant focus with growing insight, sympathy, and intelligence, as well as with a fascinating complexity of sociological, historical, and psychological implications of the incessant human effort involved.

—James Gindin

FRAME, Janet. New Zealander. Born in Dunedin, 28 August 1924. Educated at Oamaru North School; Waitaki Girls' High School; Otago University Teachers Training College, Dunedin. Recipient: Church Memorial Award, 1951, 1954; New Zealand Literary Fund Award, 1960; New Zealand Scholarship in Letters, 1964; Robert Burns Fellowship, Otago University, 1965. D.Litt.: Otago University, 1978. Address: c/o Brandt and Brandt, 1501 Broadway, New York, New York 10036, U.S.A.

PUBLICATIONS

Novels

Owls Do Cry. Christchurch, Pegasus Press, 1957; New York, Braziller, 1960; London, W.H. Allen, 1961.
Faces in the Water. Christchurch, Pegasus Press, and New York, Braziller, 1961; London, W.H. Allen, 1962.
The Edge of the Alphabet. Christchurch, Pegasus Press, New York, Braziller, and London, W.H. Allen, 1962.
Scented Gardens for the Blind. Christchurch, Pegasus Press, and London, W.H. Allen, 1963; New York, Braziller, 1964.
The Adaptable Man. Christchurch, Pegasus Press, New York, Braziller, and London, W.H. Allen, 1965.
A State of Siege. New York, Braziller, 1966; London, W.H. Allen, 1967.
The Rainbirds. London, W.H. Allen, 1968; as *Yellow Flowers in the Antipodean Room*, New York, Braziller, 1969.
Intensive Care. New York, Braziller, 1970; London, W.H. Allen, 1971.
Daughter Buffalo. New York, Braziller, 1972; London, W.H. Allen, 1973.
Living in the Maniototo. New York, Braziller, 1979.

Short Stories

The Lagoon: Stories. Christchurch, Caxton Press, 1952; revised edition, as *The Lagoon and Other Stories*, 1961.
The Reservoir: Stories and Sketches. New York, Braziller, 1963.
Snowman, Snowman: Fables and Fantasies. New York, Braziller, 1963.
The Reservoir and Other Stories. Christchurch, Pegasus Press, and London, W.H. Allen, 1966.

Uncollected Short Stories

"You Are Now Entering the Human Heart," in *New Yorker*, 29 March 1969.
"The Birds of the Air," in *Harper's Bazaar* (New York), June 1969.
"Winter Garden," in *New Yorker*, 31 January 1970.

Verse

The Pocket Mirror. New York, Braziller, and London, W.H. Allen, 1967.

Other

Mona Minim and the Smell of the Sun (juvenile). New York, Braziller, 1969.

*

Bibliography: by John Beston, in *World Literature in English* (Arlington, Texas), November 1978.

Critical Studies: *An Inward Sun: The Novels of Janet Frame*, Wellington, New Zealand University Press, 1971, and *Janet Frame*, Boston, Twayne, 1977, both by Patrick Evans.

* * *

"All dreams," Janet Frame writes in her 1970 novel *Intensive Care*, "lead back to the nightmare garden." And all nightmares lead circuitously into truth. In all her novels, the looming threat of disorder, violent and disrupting, persistently attracts those that it frightens, for it proves more fertile, more imaginatively stimulating, more genuine, and more real than the too-familiar world of daily normality. The tension between safety and danger recurs as her characters—voyaging into strange geographies (like the epileptic Toby Withers in *The Edge of the Alphabet*), or madness (like Daphne in *Owls Do Cry*, or Istina Mavet in *Faces in the Water*), or other people's identities (like Ed Glace in *Scented Gardens for the Blind*), or mirrors (like Vic in *The Adaptable Man*), or death (like Godfrey Rainbird in *The Rainbirds*)—discover both the mental debilitation that the safe state, in oxymoronic creativity, engenders, and the disembodying that danger contrives. The opening of *Faces in the Water* demonstrates the author's thematic density and sardonic touch:

> They have said that we owe allegiance to Safety, that he is our Red-Cross God who will provide us with ointment and...remove the foreign ideas, the glass beads of fantasy, the bent hair-pins of unreason embedded in our minds. On all the doors which lead to and from the world they have posted warning notices and lists of safety measures to be taken in extreme emergency.... Never sleep in the snow. Hide the scissors. Beware of strangers.... But for the final day...they have no slogan. The streets throng with people who panic, looking to the left and the right, covering the scissors, sucking poison from a wound they cannot find, judging their time from the sun's position in the sky when the sun itself has melted and trickles down the ridges of darkness into the hollows of evaporated seas.

Nightmares and madness, the education in the nature of Apocalypse and survival, become not mere metaphors of sanity, but direct training in the reactivation of the mind's perceiving eyes.

By "shipwrecking" oneself in mad geographies, however (Frame speaks in one novel of "an affliction of dream called Overseas"—as in another she observes that OUT is in man, is what he fears, "like the sea"), one places oneself on "the edge of the alphabet," in possession perhaps of insight, but no longer capable of communicating with the people who stay within regulated boundaries. Malfred Signal, in Janet Frame's weakest novel, *A State of Siege*, for example, leaves her old self to live on an island and to find the perspectives of "the room two inches behind the eyes." What she discovers, when the elements besiege her, is fear, but all she can do then is silently utter the strange new language that she clutches, alone, into seacalm and death. Like Ed Glace in *Scented Gardens*, who researches the history of the surname *Strang* and (discovering *Strong, Strange*, and *Danger* along the way) wonders if people are merely anagrams, Malfred lives in a mad mirror world of intensely focused perception that anagrammatic Joycean punning—distorting day-to-day language—tries to render. As *Owls Do Cry* had earlier specified, in the shallow suburban character of Chicks, the "safe" world deals in language, too, as a defence against upset, hiding in the familiarity of conventional clichés and tired similes. What the brilliant punning passages of *The Rainbirds* show is what the title poem of *The Pocket Mirror* implies: that convention will not show ordinary men the "bars of darkness" that are optically contained within the "facts of light"; "To undeceive the sight a detached instrument like a mirror is necessary." Or her narratives. But even that vantage point is fraught with deceit. Superstition, like convention, and Platonic forms, like safe order, can all interfere with true interpenetration with "actuality." And to find the live language—the "death-free zone" of Thora Pattern, in *Edge of the Alphabet—as a novelist inevitably dealing with day-to-day words* becomes an increasingly difficult task the stronger the visionary sense of the individual mind on its own. Turnlung, the aging New Zealand writer in New York, in *Daughter Buffalo*, finds the challenge particularly acute; his exile to "a country of death" brings him into bizarrely creative contact with a young doctor, but in the epilogue to the story, he wonders if he has dreamed everything. What matters, as Turnlung puts it, is that "I have what I gave." To conceive is to create some kind of reality, however unconventional the act, the result, and the language of rendering the experience may seem.

There are passages in Frame that are reminiscent of Doris Lessing—like the apocalyptic scenes of *Scented Gardens* and *Intensive Care*, the one anticipating the atomic destruction of Britain and the birth of a new language, the other observing the destruction of animals in Waipori City (the computerized enactment of the Human Delineation Act which will identify the strong normal law-abiding "humans" and methodically, prophylactically, eliminate the rest), and the ironic intensification of a vegetable human consciousness. In the earlier novel, particularly, the author emphasizes the relationship between the "safety dance of speech" and a kind of Coleridgean death-in-life, and that between winter (the gardenless season) and madness, life-in-death, "Open Day in the factory of the mind." *The Rainbirds*, the writer's gentlest, most comic (however hauntingly, macabrely, relentlessly discommoding) book, takes up the metaphor in its story of a man *pronounced* dead after a car accident. Though Godfrey Rainbird lives, the official pronouncement, the conventional language, the public utterance, takes precedence over the individual spiritual actuality, depriving him of his job, his children, public acceptance, and so on. Indeed, he only becomes acceptable when he has "died" a second time, when his story is sufficiently distanced into legend and into the past to become a tourist attraction. But if you visit the grave in the winter, Janet Frame adds, you must create the summer flowers within yourself. Summer gardens are openly available even to the spiritually blind; winter gardens are not. Her quiet acceptance, however, of that (mad, winter) power to change seasons within the mind expresses her most optimistic regard of humanity. And as *Living in the Maniototo* reaffirms, there is an ordering potentiality in the recognition of any person's several selves.

Intensive Care more broodingly evokes the same theme and provokingly points out the difference between the hospitalization of the body and the intensive care required to keep the mind truly alive. When the second world war is long over and the computer mentality takes over after the next impersonal War, all fructifying abnormality seems doomed; Deciding Day will destroy that which is not *named* human. Through the sharp memory of the supposedly dull Milly Galbraith, who is one of the few to appreciate an ancient surviving pear-tree, and the damningly conciliatory (and then expiatory) attitudes of Colin Monk, who goes along with the system, valuing Milly too late to save her, the apocalyptic days of Waipori City are told. Behind them both looms the mythical presence of Colin's twin Sandy, the Reconstructed Man, made of metal and transplanted parts, who is also the Rekinstruckdead Man, a promise of technological finesse and an accompanying sacrifice of man's animal warmth and spiritual being. Milly is exterminated; Sandy is myth; Colin, declared human, breathes:

> I was safe. I had won.
>
> I had lost. I began losing the first day, when the news of the Act came to me and I signed the oath of agreement. Why of course, I said, I'll do anything you ask, naturally, it's the only way, the only solution, as I see it, to an impossible situation, as if situations needed solving, I mean, looked at objectively, as it must be seen to be....
>
> The skimming words and phrases that need leave no footprints; one might never have been there, but one had spoken; and the black water lay undisturbed beneath the ice; and not a blade of grass quivered or a dead leaf whispered; a race of words had lived and died and left no relic of their civilization.
>
> As it must be seen to be, looked at objectively....

The ironies multiply around each other. Language reasserts its fluid focus; the Society for the Prevention of Cruelty to Vegetation plants new pear trees on the Livingstone estate; the computer (not having been programmed for nostalgia) fails to account for the new enthusiasm for old abnormalities; and the Sleep Days cannot erase the time of the fires from the mind of Colin Monk. The mind survives. That her commitment to the spiritual independence of such perception is made so provocative is a tribute to Janet Frame's arresting skill with images. She has an uncanny ability to arouse the diverse sensibilities of shifting moods and to entangle in language the worldless truths of her inner eye.

—W.H. New

FRANCIS, Dick (Richard Stanley Francis). British. Born in Tenby, Pembrokeshire, 31 October 1920. Educated at Maidenhead County Boys' School, Berkshire. Served as a Flying Officer in the Royal Air Force, 1940-45. Married Mary Margaret Brenchley in 1947; two sons. Amateur National Hunt (steeplechase) Jockey, 1946-48; Professional, 1948-57; National Hunt Champion, 1953-54. Racing Correspondent, *Sunday Express*, London, 1957-73. Recipient: Crime Writers Association Silver Dagger, 1965, Golden Dagger, 1980; Mystery Writers of America Edgar Allan Poe Award, 1969. Agent: John Johnson, 45-47 Clerkenwell Green, London EC1R 0HT. Address: Penny Chase, Blewbury, Didcot, Oxfordshire OX11 9NH, England.

PUBLICATIONS

Novels

Dead Cert. London, Joseph, and New York, Holt Rinehart, 1962.
Nerve. London, Joseph, and New York, Harper, 1964.
For Kicks. London, Joseph, and New York, Harper, 1965.
Odds Against. London, Joseph, 1965; New York, Harper, 1966.
Flying Finish. London, Joseph, 1966; New York, Harper, 1967.
Blood Sport. London, Joseph, 1967; New York, Harper, 1968.
Forfeit. London, Joseph, and New York, Harper, 1969.
Enquiry. London, Joseph, and New York, Harper, 1969.
Rat Race. London, Joseph, 1970; New York, Harper, 1971.
Bonecrack. London, Joseph, 1971; New York, Harper, 1972.
Smokescreen. London, Joseph, and New York, Harper, 1972.
Slay-Ride. London, Joseph, 1973; New York, Harper, 1974.
Knock-Down. London, Joseph, 1974; New York, Harper, 1975.
High Stakes. London, Joseph, 1975; New York, Harper, 1976.
In the Frame. London, Joseph, 1976; New York, Harper, 1977.
Risk. London, Joseph, 1977; New York, Harper, 1978.
Trial Run. London, Joseph, 1978; New York, Harper, 1979.
Whip Hand. London, Joseph, 1979; New York, Harper, 1980.
Reflex. London, Joseph, 1980; New York, Putnam, 1981.

Uncollected Short Stories

"A Day of Wine and Roses," in *Sports Illustrated* (New York), May 1973.
"The Gift," in *Winter's Crimes 5*, edited by Virginia Whitaker. London, Macmillan, 1973.
"A Carrot for a Chestnut," in *Stories of Crime and Detection*, edited by Joan D. Berbrich. New York, McGraw Hill, 1974.
"The Big Story," in *Ellery Queen's Crime Wave*. New York, Putnam, 1976.
"Nightmare," in *Ellery Queen's Searches and Seizures*. New York, Davis, 1977.

Play

Screenplay: *Dead Cert*, 1974.

Other

The Sport of Queens: The Autobiography of Dick Francis. London, Joseph, 1957; revised edition, 1968, 1974; New York, Harper, 1969.

Editor, with John Welcome, *Best Racing and Chasing Stories 1-2.* London, Faber, 2 vols., 1966-69.
Editor, with John Welcome, *The Racing Man's Bedside Book.* London, Faber, 1969.

* * *

Wasting no time in a literary apprenticeship, Dick Francis established himself with *Dead Cert* as a master of action narrative, memorable characterization, and authentically detailed settings. Variations on character and milieu in subsequent novels have only freshened the curious pleasure we feel when our nerves are strained in the vicarious experiences of literature.

The only problem Francis provides his fans, and it appears to be a small problem indeed, is how to label his works. Does he write mysteries or novels of detection? His books have been featured by the Detective Book Club and the Mystery Guild, and he has won an award given to outstanding detective works. Is he a serious writer, then, or an entertainer? Various reviewers call him an outstanding author of suspense, mystery, or thriller writing, while others choose to say he writes bona fide novels. Of course determining a "correct" category for his works could never affect his reputation or our pleasure in his writing. Nevertheless, insisting that Dick Francis writes adventure stories as serious entertainment and not detective or mystery fiction has a critical point to it, because it clarifies the esthetic effect of his writing.

A threat to order jeopardizing life and honor forms the heart of each Francis novel. The order is usually associated with the sport of horse racing menaced by unscrupulous gamblers, as in *Dead Cert*, *Forfeit*, and *For Kicks*; hijacking of thoroughbreds as in *Blood Sport*, or those who would use the sport for their own psychological aggrandizement as in *Nerve* and *Bonecrack*. In other novels proper business operation, whether of races tracks as in *Odds Against*, sportsmen's insurance as in *Rat Race*, or international petroleum development as in *Slay-Ride* represents the order besieged. Though the threats to order link the novels to all of crime literature, the stress in a Francis novel falls lightly upon ingenuity of method for commission of crime. Nor is the method by which the central character, who usually narrates the story, given special significance. He reasons and follows leads but never takes on the manner of a literary detective, because he is the person—and here is the chief point—to whom things happen rather than the ordained sleuth. Consequently, the focus is upon his overcoming adversity not merely to restore order but to survive.

The relative absence of the literary imperatives that would face him as the "rules of the game" if he were writing within the framework of detective or mystery stories permits Francis a wide range in which to develop narrative tensions. Often they are psychological and the result of a freedom to use varied characters: Sid Hally's struggle in *Odds Against* to regain his will to compete as a jockey, the conflicts between pairs of fathers and sons in *Bonecrack*, the identity problem of Henry Guy in *Flying Finish*, the difficulties of a chronic loser in *Rat Race*, or the compulsions of persecution complexes and megalomania among secondary characters. The greatest opportunity for narrative tension results, however, from Francis's concentration on external action rather than puzzle solving. The narrators' occupations as jockeys, pilots, investigators, or stars of action films necessarily require them to relate the regular adventures of their work. Then, their involvement in criminal plots subject them to assault, torture, and murder attempts, so that finally the highpoint of nearly every novel combines occupational skill with the dangers caused by the criminal plot in top-flight scenes of chases and endurance of danger leading to a conclusive resolution. The very severity of others' hostility, and even the plausible weaknesses of the narrators' own personalities, strongly enforces the fact that the hero has survived to set things right and to go on to new life.

Francis briefly provides in his novels what we may take as personal views about the world and society. He is, for example, apologetic about the class system. On the whole, though, unlike detective story writers and most novelists in forms other than adventure fiction, he intrudes very little to espouse a world view. His decision to write in the adventure story mode frees him from the implication that he describes a social microcosm, and his disposition seems to be to concentrate upon the experience of individuals who take the world stoically day to day. A code of honor inheres in them but so deeply that it rarely comes to consciousness. Surviving adverse circumstances and antagonists they serve their sport or their employers; yet, after all it is the process not the end that engages them and gratifies us.

Seeking to entertain rather than to comment, Francis applies his talents to writing thrilling variations upon a basic story. Our dreams, if not enough of our lives, are much of the time devoted to the same theme of confronting danger, so the fantasy of the Francis novels resonates with deeply felt experiences in his audience. The adventure plots simplify our familiar experience of tension by representing it in external form. The stories entertain by giving us detail we readily accept as realistic in time and place and by offering the pleasure of positive resolution. Dick Francis has the wide readership of a popular novelist, because in the sequence of narrative events that only a few people might undergo in actuality he embodies experience so popular that nearly everyone has it in the mind.

—John M. Reilly

FRAYN, Michael. British. Born in London, 8 September 1933. Educated at Kingston Grammar School, Surrey; Emmanuel College, Cambridge, B.A. 1957. Served in the Royal Artillery and Intelligence Corps, 1952-54. Married Gillian Palmer in 1960; three children. Reporter, 1957-59, and Columnist, 1959-62, *The Guardian*, Manchester and London; Columnist, *The Observer*, London, 1962-68. Recipient: Maugham Award, 1966; Hawthornden Prize, 1967; National Press Award, 1970; *Evening Standard* award, for play, 1976; Society of West End Theatre Award, 1977; *New Standard* award, for play, 1981. Address: c/o Elaine Greene Ltd., 31 Newington Green, London N16 9PU, England.

PUBLICATIONS

Novels

The Tin Men. London, Collins, 1965; Boston, Little Brown, 1966.
The Russian Interpreter. London, Collins, and New York, Viking Press, 1966.
Towards the End of the Morning. London, Collins, 1967; as *Against Entropy*, New York, Viking Press, 1967.
A Very Private Life. London, Collins, and New York, Viking Press, 1968.
Sweet Dreams. London, Collins, 1973; New York, Viking Press, 1974.

Plays

Zounds!, with John Edwards, music by Keith Statham (produced Cambridge, 1957).
The Two of Us (includes *Black and Silver*, *The New Quixote*, *Mr. Foot*, *Chinamen*) (produced London, 1970; Ogunquit, Maine, 1975; *Chinamen* produced New York, 1979). London, Fontana, 1970; *Chinamen* published in *The Best Short Plays 1973*,

edited by Stanley Richards, Radnor, Pennsylvania, Chilton, 1973.
The Sandboy (produced London, 1971).
Alphabetical Order (produced London, 1975; New Haven, Connecticut, 1976). Included in *Alphabetical Order and Donkeys' Years*, 1977.
Donkeys' Years (produced London, 1976). Included in *Alphabetical Order and Donkeys' Years*, 1977.
Clouds (produced London, 1976). London, Eyre Methuen, 1977.
Alphabetical Order and Donkeys' Years. London, Eyre Methuen, 1977.
The Cherry Orchard, adaptation of a play by Chekhov (produced London, 1978). London, Eyre Methuen, 1978.
Balmoral (produced Guildford, 1978).
The Fruits of Enlightenment, adaptation of a play by Tolstoy (produced London, 1979). London, Eyre Methuen, 1979.
Liberty Hall (produced London, 1980).
Make and Break (produced London, 1980). London, Eyre Methuen, 1980.

Television Plays and Documentaries: *Jamie, On a Flying Visit*, 1968; *One Pair of Eyes*, 1968; *Birthday*, 1969; *Imagine a City Called Berlin*, 1975; *Making Faces*, 1975; *Vienna: The Mask of Gold*, 1977; *Three Streets in the Country*, 1979.

Other

The Day of the Dog (*Guardian* columns). London, Collins, 1962; New York, Doubleday, 1963.
The Book of Fub (*Guardian* columns). London, Collins, 1963; as *Never Put Off to Gomorrah*, New York, Pantheon, 1964.
On the Outskirts (*Observer* columns). London, Collins, 1964.
At Bay in Gear Street (*Observer* columns). London, Fontana, 1967.
Constructions (philosophy). London, Wildwood House, 1974.

Editor, *The Best of Beachcomber*, by J.B. Morton. London, Heinemann, 1963.

* * *

Three of Michael Frayn's novels, the first, fourth, and fifth, are highly original, a satire and fantasies; the second and third, on the other hand, are conventional. The second, *The Russian Interpreter*, concerns an English research student in Moscow who serves as interpreter for a mysterious businessman (he seeks ordinary Russians for exchange visits), and the pair become involved with a Russian girl. Though Moscow's streets and weather are described, soon the action is moving swiftly. Books are stolen and sought, somebody is tricking somebody, espionage or smuggling is occurring, and we read on eagerly, awaiting explanations. Even when the student is imprisoned, Frayn focuses on his comic efforts to obtain a towel, and the novel remains a good, cheerful read.

The American title of the third novel points to opposing inertia and conformity; the English one, only a little more relevantly, to the subject of being in the mid-thirties (the hero "had spent his youth as one might spend an inheritance, and he had no idea of what he had bought with it"). Frayn's 37-year-old is a Features Editor, worrying about repairs to his Victorian house with West Indian neighbours in S.W.23 and dreaming of escape, hopefully through appearance on a television panel. The plot is vehicle for comedy about a newspaper office, with a few shrewd observations, as when a girl reflects: "She wasn't a girl at all, in any sense that the fashion magazines would recognize. She was just a young female human being, fit only to be someone's cousin or aunt." Some passages suggest Frayn intends more, a fuller study of his hero's marriage and serious focus on the future of newspapers (a cynical, pushful graduate challenges the office's ways), but these are not pursued.

The Tin Men, the first book, is about the William Morris Institute of Automation Research and its eccentric scientists. A thin plot-line turns on a new wing, the arrangements for the Queen to open it, and the TV company that plans to finance it. Most of the fun is about computers: the automating of football results because the Director believes "the main object of organised sports and games is to produce a profusion of statistics," the programmed newspaper, which prints the core of familiar stories such as "I Test New Car" and "Child Told Dress Unsuitable by Teacher," and Delphic I, the Ethical Decision Machine, which expresses its moral processes in units called pauls, calvins, and moses. Amid clever jokes, Frayn shows anxiety about the dangerous possibilities of computers and the limitations of the men responsible for them.

A Very Private Life begins "Once upon a time there will be a little girl called Uncumber." In her world, "inside people" remain all their lives in windowless houses, supplied by tube and tap and using drugs—Pax, Hilarin and Orgasmin—for every experience. In very brief chapters, Frayn explains how life has grown more private, first physically, then through drugs to cope with anger and uncertainty. Dissatisfied Uncumber meets a man through a wrong number on "holovision" and goes to the other side of the world to visit him. The compelling story is part fairy tale, part fantasy, part morality, so that we ask "Is it plausible?" and "What is the moral?" Frayn's inspiration was contemporary America, where he noticed dark glasses used to hide feelings, and city people buying disused farmhouses to be alone in. He touches on penology, longevity, the treatment of personality, but concentrates on technology making possible a new kind of isolation which excludes uncomfortable realities. And Frayn the moralist never dominates Frayn the story-teller.

Even better is *Sweet Dreams*—clever, entertaining, dazzling. A typical middle-aged, middle-class Londoner is killed and finds himself in a Heaven where he can fly, speak any language, change his age, and retrieve long-lost possessions. He is set to invent the Matterhorn, returns to England and writes an official report on its condition, drops out to the simple country life and bounces back as righthand man to God (who proves to be a blend of Freddie Ayer and A.J.P. Taylor, and says "To get anything done at all one has to move in tremendously mysterious ways"). Slowly we realise the hero's Heavenly evolution is markedly similar to his earthly one. Frayn tells with wit and flourish his shrewd, sardonic and deceptively charming fable.

—Malcolm Page

FREELING, Nicolas. British. Born in London in 1927. Educated in local primary and secondary schools. Served in the British military forces. Married Cornelia Termes in 1954; four sons and one daughter. Worked as a hotel and restaurant cook, throughout Europe, 1945-60. Recipient: Crime Writers Association Golden Dagger, 1964; Grand Prix de Roman Policier, 1964; Mystery Writers of America Edgar Allan Poe Award, 1966. Address: 28 Rue de Fréland, 67100 Strasbourg, France.

PUBLICATIONS

Novels

Love in Amsterdam. London, Gollancz, and New York, Harper, 1962; as *Death in Amsterdam*, New York, Ballantine, 1964.
Because of the Cats. London, Gollancz, 1963; New York, Harper, 1964.
Gun Before Butter. London, Gollancz, 1963; as *Question of Loyalty*, New York, Harper, 1963.
Valparaiso (as F.R.E. Nicolas). London, Gollancz, 1964; as Nicolas Freeling, New York, Harper, 1965.

Double-Barrel. London, Gollancz, 1964; New York, Harper, 1965.
Criminal Conversation. London, Gollancz, 1965; New York, Harper, 1966.
The King of the Rainy Country. London, Gollancz, and New York, Harper, 1966.
The Dresden Green. London, Gollancz, 1966; New York, Harper, 1967.
Strike Out Where Not Applicable. London, Gollancz, and New York, Harper, 1967.
This Is the Castle. London, Gollancz, and New York, Harper, 1968.
Tsing-Boum. London, Hamish Hamilton, 1969; as *Tsing-Boom!*, New York, Harper, 1969.
Over the High Side. London, Hamish Hamilton, 1971; as *The Lovely Ladies*, New York, Harper, 1971.
A Long Silence. London, Hamish Hamilton, 1972; as *Auprès de ma Blonde*, New York, Harper, 1972.
Dressing of Diamond. London, Hamish Hamilton, and New York, Harper, 1974.
What Are the Bugles Blowing For? London, Heinemann, 1975; as *The Bugles Blowing*, New York, Harper, 1976.
Lake Isle. London, Heinemann, 1976; as *Sabine*, New York, Harper, 1977.
Gadget. London, Heinemann, and New York, Coward McCann, 1977.
The Night Lords. London, Heinemann, and New York, Pantheon, 1978.
The Widow. London, Heinemann, and New York, Pantheon, 1979.
Castang's City. London, Heinemann, and New York, Pantheon, 1980.
One Damn Thing after Another. London, Heinemann, 1981; as *Arlette*, New York, Pantheon, 1981.

Uncollected Short Stories

"Van der Valk and the Beach Number," in *Ellery Queen's Mystery Magazine* (New York), May 1969.
"Van der Valk and the Old Seaman," in *Ellery Queen's Mystery Magazine* (New York), August 1969.
"Van der Valk and the Four Mice," in *Ellery Queen's Mystery Magazine* (New York), November 1969.
"Van der Valk and the Young Man," in *Ellery Queen's Mystery Magazine* (New York), December 1969.
"Van der Valk and the High School Riot," in *Ellery Queen's Mystery Magazine* (New York), March 1970.
"Van der Valk and the Great Pot Problem," in *Ellery Queen's Mystery Magazine* (New York), April 1970.
"Van der Valk and the Wolfpack," in *Ellery Queen's Mystery Magazine* (New York), August 1970.
"Van der Valk and the False Caesar," in *Ellery Queen's Mystery Magazine* (New York), February 1972.
"Van der Valk and the Man from Nowhere," in *Ellery Queen's Mystery Magazine* (New York), May 1972.
"Van der Valk and the Cavalier," in *Ellery Queen's Mystery Magazine* (New York), January 1974.
"Van der Valk and the Spanish Galleon," in *Ellery Queen's Mystery Magazine* (New York), August 1975.
"Van der Valk and the Two Pigeons," in *Ellery Queen's Magicians of Mystery.* New York, Davis, 1976.

Other

Kitchen Book. London, Hamish Hamilton, 1970; as *The Kitchen*, New York, Harper, 1970.
Cook Book. London, Hamish Hamilton, 1971.

*

Nicolas Freeling comments:

I am known as a crime novelist, an expression meaningless unless preceded by the word "commercial," meaning one who writes a series on a similar theme purely for entertainment value and to make a living. This describes my activities accurately enough, but not my ideas, nor my ambitions.

The advantages of this method—to a writer with a large dependent family, like myself, very great—is that the public for crime novels is large, appreciative, faithful, and generous. For this I am extremely grateful. There is a corresponding large disadvantage: that one is held to and bound by a rigid formula. Any originality or variation in theme is severely discouraged by a sharp drop in sales; this rigidity is the enemy of progress and growth. The writer is expected to concentrate exclusively upon telling an entertaining story, which is indeed the first basic element of the novelist's craft, and to introduce elements of mystery and suspense, melodramatic and largely artificial. The crime novelist who attempts art, his natural function and legitimate ambition, is asking for trouble.

Few commercial crime novelists make the attempt. Most are content to work in purely mechanical fashion, with no artistic or literary pretension whatever. The result is that they receive no critical attention—indeed they need none, for their public rarely bothers with book reviews and has small interest in literary effort—and have small ambition, being content with a commercial operation and financial success.

It does not seem to me that the "crime" novelist should have such limited and materialistic ambitions.

Raymond Chandler agreed. He thought that it should be possible to write a crime "entertainment" which would rejoin the main stream of fiction. It would be about basic human themes and predicaments, of which crime, obviously a phenomenon of much social importance, with increasing impact upon the lives of any and all of us, would be the predominant subject, not necessarily the only subject.

I wish to attempt this ambitious design.

So far I have failed, and am not much ashamed because the ambition is high and the technical problems posed very considerable. Only the best European novelists—Stendhal, Dostoievsky, Conrad are the examples which come first to mind—have succeeded, and then often partially or imperfectly. A real human being, when involved in a traumatic situation such as a crime creates, behaves destructively—towards himself, towards society, and towards I may add the structure and coherence of a novel. This creates pitfalls for the novelist, the most obvious being to fall into mere sociological observation, documentary journalism in the interests of veracity. Also the behaviour of a criminal (a man by definition set at odds with his society) raises wide moral, metaphysical, and philosophic problems. To disregard these is to write a play with no third act. Many technically accomplished writers dodge ethical problems of right and wrong on the ground of "tolerance" and because their own ethical, not to say religious beliefs are vague and often because they are frightened to appear unfashionable.

It has become too fashionable to disregard the craftsmanship of form, shape, and rhythm, on the ground that this is mere artificial mechanical contrivance. Such a notion is both immature and superficial: without form there is no art. The public insists, rightly, that a crime novel shall rebound continually in interest and excitement, and shall culminate, that is to say end in a climax.

I intend to keep trying.

* * *

Love in Amsterdam began Nicolas Freeling's career as a writer of novels which have an almost startling verisimilitude: their dialogue, setting, and action convey a feeling of exact observation at work. Freeling's Van der Valk is a Dutch detective who is human, individual, unorthodox. He has both compassion and a stern compulsion to solve the puzzles that are presented to him. His thoughts as he proceeds in his investigations are shown clearly to us; we share in his intellectual unravelling of problems of human behaviour; and we believe in the reflections and the actions because the characters are real and the locale so effectively re-created. The flavour of Dutch life, the tempo of Amsterdam, the attitudes of the Dutch emerge convincingly in *Love in Amsterdam*; they are consolidated in *Because of the Cats*, an unfolding of the terrifying ruthlessness displayed by a gang of Dutch teenagers, morally corrupted and warped. This story is set partially in a seaside town of about sixty thousand people, half an hour by train from Amsterdam, "a new town, the pride of Dutch building and planning." Here is where Van der Valk displays his intuition, becomes friendly with the local whore, and understands the parents' relations with their children as he probes into their activities. The tempo of the novel is skilfully varied, and the final speeding up comes with an inevitability which holds the reader's horrified attention. The effect of Freeling's narration is heightened by the sceptical comments, the iconoclastic attitude with which he invests his policeman. Van der Valk's humanity gains by his lack of illusion.

This Is the Castle showed a deepening in Freeling's powers of characterization. The story revolves around the Swiss menage of a successful novelist, a neurotic yet likeable man, whose tensions and foibles are seen through his own eyes and his wife's. The relationship between the novelist and his wife (to whom he is God), his secretary-mistress, his Spanish servants, his sons and, above all, his teenage daughter are unfolded with skill and sympathy; the visiting publisher and the American journalist arrive in time for a shooting of a macabre kind. This novel explores the blurred edges between the writer's imagination and the real events of his life: it does much to convey the effort of writing, the nervous strain between books, the dangerous seductiveness of the daydream. It moves away from the genre of *roman policier*.

Freeling's next *roman policier*, *Tsing-Boum*, carries on this deeper interest in human nature. The parallel with Simenon's writing becomes clearer, and indeed Van der Valk mentions Maigret twice in this story of the murder of the wife of a dull Dutch sergeant. She is machine-gunned in her dull municipal flat during a television gangster serial. She leaves behind a daughter whose father is unknown, and as Van der Valk investigates he finds himself puzzling out the connections between this Mevrouw Zomerlust and Dien Bien Phu. This allows Freeling to explore the French surrender there and the complex aftermath: a case of cowardice, revenge, blackmail, jealousy, violence. The Dutch police Commissaire, older now (and suffering from wounds incurred in an earlier novel), regards his quarry with sympathy as well as severity, and the pathos of the story is effectively built up, with constant reminders of humanity's frailties as well as moments of bravery.

In *Valparaiso* Freeling develops further his uniting of person and place. Into Porquerolles he brings a second rank Parisian film star. Her coming has an explosive effect upon Raymond, who has drifted around the Mediterranean for years, nourishing a dream of crossing the Atlantic in his boat the *Olivia*. The need to refit the *Olivia* tempts Raymond into crime. The story has a seeming inexorability. The slow lazy tempo of life in Porquerolles gives way to an equally Mediterranean urgency, and the narrative tautens as Raymond becomes more deeply enmeshed in the consequences of what seemed a perfect plan for the quick acquisition of the money which would enable him to act out his dream. In *Valparaiso* Freeling again shows his Simenon-like capacity to absorb atmosphere, to assess how far it is created by and how much it affects the human beings whose lives he presents in such concentrated description, such revealing action and inaction.

After ten novels centering on Van der Valk, Freeling developed a French equivalent, Henri Castang. The new setting is an imaginary French city, and in *The Night Lords* Freeling explored differences between French and British legal institutions, for a British High Court Judge and his family on holiday in France are caught up in the machinery of the law when their Rolls-Royce is found to have a naked female corpse in its boot.

Strasbourg is the scene for *The Widow* in which Van der Valk's widow Arlette, now married to an Englishman, becomes a private detective, and tumbles into a narcotics racket. The suspense is, as usual, well maintained and Arlette's mental processes deftly sketched in, amid the continuous and sinister action. Freeling manages to mix the detail well; his city is alive, Arlette and her husband lucky to be so. *Castang's City*, however, is deliberately not Strasbourg: but it is a convincing French provincial city, in which Freeling's Commissaire Richard is an elegant foil to Castang, and his Colette Delavigne, the judge of instruction, a charming, intelligent French woman. There is a good deal of instruction in this novel about French provincial life, and French ways of dealing with crime; but this does not intrude unduly on the action. The action requires the detailed information supplied copiously in dialogue for the story to come alive, which, thanks to the careful creation not only of inanimate detail but of human idiosyncracies, it does, most convincingly too. Freeling's own attitudes burst out of his narration from time to time, and this gives his story an extra credibility since we are asked to share in his detached examination of characters who move through the novel with an apparent reality of their own.

—A. Norman Jeffares

FREEMAN, Gillian. British. Born in London, 5 December 1929. Educated at the University of Reading, 1949-51, B.A. (honours) in English literature and philosophy 1951. Married Edward Thorpe in 1955; two children. Copywriter for C.J. Lytle Ltd., London, 1951-52; schoolteacher in London, 1952-53; reporter, *North London Observer*, 1953; literary secretary to Louis Golding, 1953-55. Address: c/o Curtis Brown Ltd., 1 Craven Hill, London W2 3EP, England.

PUBLICATIONS

Novels

The Liberty Man. London, Longman, 1955.
Fall of Innocence. London, Longman, 1956.
Jack Would Be a Gentleman. London, Longman, 1959.
The Leather Boys (as Eliot George). London, Blond, 1961; New York, Guild Press, 1962.
The Campaign. London, Longman, 1963.
The Leader. London, Blond, 1965; Philadelphia, Lippincott, 1966.
The Alabaster Egg. London, Blond, 1970; New York, Viking Press, 1971.
The Marriage Machine. London, Hamish Hamilton, and New York, Stein and Day, 1975.
Nazi Lady: The Diaries of Elisabeth von Stahlenberg 1933-1948. London, Blond and Briggs, 1978; as *The Confessions of Elisabeth von S.*, New York, Dutton, 1978; as *Diary of a Nazi Lady*, New York, Ace, 1979.
An Easter Egg Hunt. London, Hamish Hamilton, 1981.

Uncollected Short Stories

"The Souffle," in *Courier* (London and New York), May 1955.
"Pen Friend," in *Woman's Own* (London), December 1957.
"The Changeling," in *London Magazine*, April 1959.
"The Polka (Come Dance with Me)," in *Woman's Own* (London), December 1962.
"Kicks," in *Axle Quarterly* (London), Summer 1963.
"Dear Fred," in *King* (London), June 1965.
"Venus Unobserved," in *Town* (London), July 1967.

Plays

Pursuit (produced London, 1969).

Screenplays: *The Leather Boys*, 1963; *Cold Day in the Park*, 1968; *I Want What I Want*, 1970.

Radio Plays: *Field Day*, 1974; *Commercial Break*, 1974.

Television Play: *The Campaign*, 1965.

Ballet Scenarios: *Mayerling*, 1978; *Intimate Letters*, 1978; *Isadora*, 1981.

Other

The Story of Albert Einstein (juvenile). London, Vallentine Mitchell, 1960.
The Undergrowth of Literature. London, Nelson, 1967; New York, Delacorte Press, 1969.
The Schoolgirl Ethic: The Life and Work of Angela Brazil. London, Allen Lane, 1976.

*

Manuscript Collection: University of Reading, Berkshire.

Critical Study: *Don't Never Forget* by Brigid Brophy, London, Cape, 1966.

Gillian Freeman comments:

(1972) I have always been concerned with the problems of the individual seen in relation to society and the personal pressures brought to bear because of moral, political or social conditions and the inability to conform. This is reflected in all my work to date, although I have never set to propound themes, only to tell stories. After seven novels I am able to make my own retrospective assessment, and I find recurring ideas and links of which I was unconscious at the time of writing.

My first six novels are in some way concerned with the class system in England, either as a main theme (*The Liberty Man*, *Jack Would Be a Gentleman*) or as part of the background (*The Leather Boys*). Although the rigid class patterns began to break up soon after the last war and have changed and shifted, they still retain subtle delineations that I find absorbing. In *The Liberty Man* there is the direct class confrontation in the love affair between the middle-class school teacher and the cockney sailor. In *Fall of Innocence* I was writing about the sexual taboos of the middle class attacked by an outsider, a young American girl. This element, the planting of an alien into a tight social structure, reappears constantly in the novels—atheist Harry into the Church of England parish in *The Campaign*; the Prossers in *Jack Would Be a Gentleman* from one class area into an elevated one in the same town; the cross-visiting of Freda and Derek in *The Liberty Man*; and, strongest of all, Hannah in *The Alabaster Egg*, transplanted from Munich in the 1930's to post-war London. This is the theme I want to pursue in my next novel, with a heroine from rural England unable to adapt completely to life in the United States of America. In *Jack Would Be a Gentleman* the theme is the sudden acquisition of money without the middle or upper-middle class conditioning which makes it possible to deal with it. *The Campaign* has the background of a seedy seaside parish, against which the personal problems of a cross section of individuals (all involved with a fund-raising campaign) are exacerbated; God and Mammon, the permissive society, the Christian ethics. *The Leather Boys* is the story of two working-class boys who have a homosexual affair; *The Leader* explores fascism in a modern democracy, which, on both sides of the Atlantic, throws up a sufficient number of people who are greedy, ruthless, intolerant, bigoted and perverted enough to gravitate towards the extreme right.

Some of these themes reappear in *The Alabaster Egg*, which I consider my best work to date—fascism, homosexuality, the main characters all victims of the prevailing political scenes. This novel deals with Munich in the 1930's, and, with the device of a fictitious diary, finds parallels between Hitler's Germany and Bismarck's reflecting in two love affairs which end in betrayal. I used real as well as imaginary characters, linking fiction and reality closely. The heroine meets Hitler briefly at a party, for instance, and the diarist is a lover of King Ludwig II.

My choice of Einstein for a children's biography—a highly individual man whose life was spent in trying to eliminate frontiers of prejudice—and the thesis of *The Undergrowth of Literature* (the need for fantasy in the sexually disturbed) illustrate my interest in and compassion for those unable to conform to the accepted social mores. To some extent my film writing has also dealt with social and sexual distress, as did my short play, *Pursuit*.

* * *

Since her first novel, *The Liberty Man*, Gillian Freeman has shown an outstanding ability to get inside the skin of characters from very different social backgrounds. It should be remembered that *The Liberty Man* was considerably in advance of its time in its truly empathic conveyance of a working-class character (Derek, a naval rating) who becomes involved in an affair with an intellectual and middle-class woman. This book appeared when the prevailing literary method of portraying working-class people still tended to be by projecting the image of the well-intentioned but clumsy, scruffy, and inarticulate "little man." The unusual power of *The Liberty Man*, however, does not rest only in its portrait of Derek, but in his relationship with Freda, the middle-class school teacher, through which Freeman analyses resonances between people from extremely diverse social groups, and between the inner experiences of the individual and the externals that he sees in operation around him.

Freeman is, in a sense, the writer of the archetypal anti-Cinderella story. She has acute honesty and a flair for precise, almost wickedly unerring observation of detail and motive. In her novels, despite changes of fortune (*Jack Would Be a Gentleman* is a good example) people's lives are *not* transformed, and their basic inadequacies remain. Her novels are preoccupied with frustration and fallibility; she frequently manages, however, by well-timed injections of compassion, to lift a book's mood of inadequacy and doubt into warmth and well-being that are almost physical in the strength of their expression.

Freeman observes and analyses the vagaries of human nature but rarely makes moral judgements. She highlights complexities in apparently "ordinary" or superficial characters, and makes her jaded sophisticates capable of sudden deep and challenging emotions. She explores conflicts between ambition and conscience, and the primitive feelings that underlie the veneer of our civilization. Permeating some of her narratives is a sense that the protective social structure we strive to perpetuate is deeply flawed. She is, in this context, extremely concerned with nonconformity—the healthily truculent attitudes of the working classes; the bewildered responses of the unconscious homosexual; the rootlessness of the young that can sometimes find expression only in violence (*The Leather Boys*).

Freeman's novels are synonymous with power and panache, though these qualities are often expressed in low-key and even throwaway language. She is in this respect quintessentially English, and until *The Alabaster Egg* her preoccupations were with issues particularly pertinent to English society. *The Alabaster Egg* is her most trenchant and telling work. It is about the pursuit of political power, and this is counterpointed by a probing of the exploitation of human beings at the personal level. Her setting is wider than in the earlier novels; it is no longer England but Europe—or the world—and the focus, significantly, is Germany—the vortex of 20th-century "civilization," corruption, and decay.

Her earlier stories were concerned wih displacement, in particular with the catalytic effect of an alien presence in a close-knit and apparently secure social structure (*Fall of Innocence*, *The Campaign*). *The Alabaster Egg* highlights an ironic reversal of this theme of dissociation; Hannah, the book's heroine, has the misfortune to be a Jew in Nazi Germany. She does not, however, see herself as an alien. In her own estimation she is as much a German as a Jew. Her situation, of course, stresses one of the most pernicious effects of

Nazi racist policies—the enforced separation of certain people from their own communities, from the only group to which they had felt a sense of belonging. Hannah's tragic but resilient story has parallels with happenings in the time of Bismarck. Her love affair with a "real" German is illuminated by her readings from the diary of the homosexual lover of King Ludwig II. This affair—like Hannah's—ends in bewilderment and betrayal.

Having written compellingly from the viewpoint of a sensitive and intelligent Jewish woman caught up in the hideousness of fascism, Freeman goes on to write as if from the inside about a passionate supporter of Hitler's ideologies in *Nazi Lady*. This originally appeared as a factual diary; it was so convincing that one critic pronounced it "unquestionably genuine." Genuineness, of course, does not have to be a matter of fact but of mood, and in this sense *Nazi Lady* is genuine, although it is a work of fiction. Freeman says that it was inspired by her publisher's observations on the extraordinary dichotomy between the anguishes of the battles of Stalingrad and the "good life" enjoyed at the same time by influential civilians in Germany.

In *Nazi Lady* the heroine's initial enthusiasm for Nazism is presented with subtlety and conviction. Elisabeth is German; to English readers she is possibly a slightly glamorized amalgam of Marlene Dietrich, Irma Greeser, and whatever the Nazi slogan "Strength Through Joy" suggested. As well as being brittle she is beautiful, and her experiences are macabrely fascinating.

Freeman combines fact and fiction with aplomb. (For example, Elisabeth has to accept expert but distasteful seduction by Goebbels in order to save her husband from the rigours of the Russian Front.) In the end, all her convictions are reduced to ashes, as both her son and her husband become victims of Nazi ruthlessness and fanaticism. But she survives—and marries an American from the liberating forces.

Freeman's most recent novel, *An Easter Egg Hunt*, is set in a girls' school during the First World War, and it is not only an intriguing mystery story on its own account but memorable for its evocation of Angela Brazil's schoolgirl adventures. School was, of course, regarded by Angela Brazil as the (essentially neatly ordered) world in microcosm; but Freeman recognizes bizarre and eccentric elements even in the innately conservative and sheltered confines of school life. She adeptly creates and manipulates her adolescent characters without excesses or sentimentality, and they are in fact far removed from Brazil's colourful but artless embodiments of schoolgirlishness.

The narrative style of all Freeman's novels is perfectly suited to her sensitive but down-to-earth approach. Her prose is robust and direct; her plots are constructed with economy and excellence, and the stories seem to vibrate with energy and insight.

—Mary Cadogan

FRIEDMAN, Bruce Jay. American. Born in New York City, 26 April 1930. Educated in New York public schools, and at the University of Missouri, Columbia, 1947-51, Bachelor of Journalism 1951. Served in the United States Air Force, 1951-53: Lieutenant. Married Ginger Howard in 1954 (divorced, 1977); three children. Editorial Director, Magazine Management Company, publishers, New York, 1953-66. Visiting Professor of Literature, York College, City University, New York, 1974-76. Address: 430 East 63rd Street, New York, New York 10021, U.S.A.

PUBLICATIONS

Novels

Stern. New York, Simon and Schuster, 1962; London, Deutsch, 1963.
A Mother's Kisses. New York, Simon and Schuster, 1964; London, Cape, 1965.
The Dick. New York, Knopf, 1970; London, Cape, 1971.
About Harry Towns. New York, Knopf, 1974; London, Cape, 1975.

Short Stories

Far from the City of Class and Other Stories. New York, Frommer-Pasmantier, 1963.
Black Angels. New York, Simon and Schuster, 1966; London, Cape, 1967.

Uncollected Short Stories

"The Scientist," in *Esquire* (New York), April 1967.
"The Pledges," in *Esquire* (New York), September 1967.
"Car Lover," in *Esquire* (New York), June 1968.
"The Partners," in *Esquire* (New York), August 1969.
"Just Back from the Coast," in *Harper's* (New York), March 1970.
"High, Wide, and Handsome," in *Esquire* (New York), October 1971.
"Lady," in *The Secret Life of Our Times*, edited by Gordon Lish. New York, Doubleday, 1973.
"Blind Side," in *All Our Secrets Are the Same*, edited by Gordon Lish. New York, Norton, 1977.

Plays

23 Pat O'Brien Movies, adaptation of his own short story (produced New York, 1966).
Scuba Duba: A Tense Comedy (produced New York, 1967). New York, Simon and Schuster, 1968.
A Mother's Kisses, music by Richard Adler, adaptation of the novel by Friedman (produced New Haven, Connecticut, 1968).
Steambath (produced New York, 1970). New York, Knopf, 1971.
First Offenders, with Jacques Levy (also co-director: produced New York, 1973).
A Foot in the Door (produced New York, 1979).

Screenplay: *Stir Crazy*, 1980.

Other

The Lonely Guy's Book of Life. New York, McGraw Hill, 1978.

Editor, *Black Humor.* New York, Bantam, and London, Corgi, 1965.

*

Critical Study: *Bruce Jay Friedman* by Max F. Schulz, New York, Twayne, 1974.

Theatrical Activities:

Director: **Play**—*First Offenders* (co-director, with Jacques Levy), New York, 1973.

* * *

With his first novel, *Stern*, Bruce Jay Friedman established himself as a wildly comic chronicler of the agonies of the Jewish neurotic, buffeted and flayed by gentile America. He followed, diminishingly, with *A Mother's Kisses* and *The Dick*, along with two short story collections, *Far from the City of Class* and *Black Angels*. He has also authored several plays (produced off-Broadway), including *Scuba Duba* and *Steambath*. To each of these genres, Friedman brings unusual gifts for comic simile, the creation of unpredictable dilemmas and a biting sympathy for his trapped characters. He tends to repeat situations, character types, and even favorite images, and he seems inhibited in developing or climaxing the black humor of his plots.

The titular hero of *Stern* is a remarkably successful invention, a tall, fearful man with "pale, flowing hips," who is obsessed with his own cowardice, with a sense of sexual inadequacy, and with a deep suspicion that the gentile world waits to do him in. The plot turns on a trivial incident when an insensitive neighbor calls Stern's wife a Kike and pushes her to the ground so that the pantsless woman is exposed. Stern's inability to respond lands him, ulcered and guilt-ridden, in a bizarre rest-home. But everything happens to Stern no matter where he is: dogs seize his wrists and lead him on forced walks; his mother takes him in the shower with her; he vomits on trains; trees suddenly die when he acquires property. What doesn't happen, he fears will; that he will die of frostbite within yards of his home, that his son will die and he will be unable to cry convincingly, that each time Stern ogles a woman, a stranger simultaneously retaliates by raping Stern's distant wife.

In *A Mother's Kisses* Friedman creates the ultimate Jewish Mom: sexy, domineering Meg takes her son Joseph to the only college that will admit him—and then she refuses to leave. In *The Dick* Kenneth Sussman, public relations man for the homicide bureau, changes his name to LePeters, and tries, like Stern, to save his wife sexually from aggressive gentiles. In the title short story of *Black Angels* a crew of Negro carpenter-gardeners do cheap but splendid home-repair work for a middle-class neurotic, only to charge him four hundred dollars an hour for psychotherapy. Thus Friedman everywhere offers variations on the themes of *Stern*: violence, sexuality, racism, identity-crises, abnormal family relationships, and mental breakdown.

Most of Friedman's main characters are timid schlemiels who suffer from dread and guilt while failing to cope with a callous, demanding society. But the protagonist of *About Harry Towns* is a successful screenwriter with a steel-and-glass apartment, many willing girlfriends, and a son who dotes on him. Despite these apparent switches, Harry, like Stern, is lonely and desperate; he is a compulsive gambler and cocaine sniffer who fails in love-relationships as husband, father, and son. Carried over from earlier work are Friedman's brilliant flair for sight gags, the outlandish incongruities, and his black-humor irreverence (Towns suffers when his parents die "back-to-back" but not close enough in time for one funeral).

Yet, *About Harry Towns* adds new dimensions and sounds deeper notes; in Harry's frantic gaiety there is genuine terror, so that Friedman's stand-up comedy now elicits our pity as well as our laughter.

—Frank Campenni

FUCHS, Daniel. American. Born in New York City, 25 June 1909. Educated at Eastern District High School, Brooklyn; City College of New York, B.A. 1930. Married Susan Hessen in 1932; two sons. Taught elementary school, New York, 1930-37. Since 1937, scriptwriter. Recipient: Oscar, for screenplay, 1956; American Academy award, 1962; National Jewish Book award, 1980. Agent: Irving Paul Lazar Agency, 211 South Beverly Drive, Beverly Hills, California 90212. Address: 430 South Fuller Avenue, Apartment 9-C, Los Angeles, California 90036, U.S.A.

PUBLICATIONS

Novels

The Williamsburg Trilogy. New York, Avon, 1972.
Summer in Wiliamsburg. New York, Vanguard Press, 1934; London, Constable, 1935.
Homage to Blenholt. New York, Vanguard Press, and London, Constable, 1936.
Low Company. New York, Vanguard Press, 1937; as *Neptune Beach*, London, Constable, 1937.

West of the Rockies. New York, Knopf, and London, Secker and Warburg, 1971.

Short Stories

Stories, with others. New York, Farrar Straus, 1956; as *A Book of Stories*, London, Gollancz, 1957.

The Apathetic Bookie Joint. New York, Methuen, 1979; London, Secker and Warburg, 1980.

Plays

Screenplays: *The Day the Bookies Wept*, with Bert Granet and George Jeske, 1939; *The Big Shot*, with Bertram Millhauser and Abem Finkel, 1942; *The Hard Way*, with Irwin Shaw and Jerry Wald, 1942; *Between Two Worlds*, 1944; *The Gangster*, 1947; *Hollow Triumph*, 1948; *Criss Cross*, 1949; *Panic in the Streets*, with others, 1950; *Storm Warning*, with Richard Brooks, 1951; *Taxi*, with others, 1952; *The Human Jungle*, with William Sackheim, 1954; *Love Me or Leave Me*, with Isobel Lennart, 1955; *Interlude*, with Franklin Coen and Inez Cocke, 1957; *Jeanne Eagels*, with Sonya Levien and John Fante, 1957.

* * *

Of the young Jewish novelists who came of age in the 1930's, none depicted ghetto life more effectively than Daniel Fuchs, a Brooklyn schoolteacher who produced three novels in four years. *Summer in Williamsburg*, appearing when Fuchs was 24, was followed by *Homage to Blenholt* and *Low Company*. Each is given over more to private neuroses than public disorders; Fuchs touches rarely on politics—and then only to laugh. Even sex provides less motivation than does the obsessive desire for dignity, success, money.

All three are summer novels. Life then is more exposed, emotions more volatile, uncertainty more evident. Fuchs's hunched little people are not symbols or folk heroes enacting tribal myths; they are clamoring, sweating, lower-middle-class Jews who have inched from Ellis Island to Brooklyn across the East River's Williamsburg Bridge. There, locked into stifling little rooms, they are torn between Judaism's high principles and life's low facts. Most are natural losers attaining only anxiety and pain. *Summer in Williamsburg* catches the cosmic absurdity of their lives. Rejecting a linear narrative for a melange of contrapuntal scenes, Fuchs explores the moral choices confronting a dozen Ripple Street eccentrics during eight sweltering, explosive weeks. He focuses most clearly upon a young would-be writer, Philip Hayman, his family and friends. For Philip, at twenty, the summer is a time of choice and exploration. For several of his neighbors its proves life's end.

Even as a new novelist Fuchs opts for cinematic narrative; to avoid undue literary influence, he derives his structure less from Dos Passos's "Camera Eye" than from actual film-editing techniques. Leaning heavily upon dialogue, gesture, and setting, he bridges his imagistic scenes by a quick dissolve at points of greatest stress. Such mechanical crosspatching has its dangers; a sense of incompletion, fragmentary profiles rather than rounded portraits, characters abandoned with emotions exposed not explained, actions left dangling in mid-gesture. Yet his resolve to look anew at people and events too often glazed by familiarity and sentiment enables Fuchs to infuse *Summer in Williamsburg* with a self-sustaining vitality. It remains a hard, convincing montage of a Brooklyn summer.

Homage to Blenholt is an even more mocking commentary on the American dream. Here again, amid the airless redbrick tenements, are self-pitying little people shouting, slamming doors, overflowing kitchen and flat to cover fire-escape, sidewalk, and alley. Gleaning dreams from movie and tabloid, they suffer from barren delusions, bad luck, and crushing conditions. The sad-funny narrative is spun of two hectic days in the lives of three young misfits—Max Balkan, Mendel Munves, and Coblenz—who, striving mightily to enrich their lives, only make them more frantic, comic, and pitiable. Yet each, by accepting without whining his inevitable fate, attains a measure of dignity. In Depression America few can expect much more.

Homage to Blenholt evoked charges of cynicism, but Fuchs's cynicism is that of the committed moralist or frustrated idealist who doubts man's ability to control his destiny. Life seems a cosmic burlesque comprised equally of the tragic and comic, sublime and ridiculous. With an eye for every reflex and ambiguity, an ear for every sigh, Fuchs shapes nuance, slang, gesture into telling revelations of character; in the process, he deftly fuses Yiddish-English and Brooklyn patois into a vernacular as idiomatic as Hemingway's, as native as Faulkner's or O'Hara's.

Low Company is the most somber and violent of the novels. It is also the best constructed, with plotting tighter, incidents more revealing, and characters more fully realized. Intensifying his caricatures, Fuchs moves from sour humor to greed and brutality, and from Williamsburg to Brooklyn's soggy fringe. Neptune Beach (a composite of Brighton Beach and Coney Island) is a marginal world of squalid beach cottages, sand, weeds, and flimsy boardwalk gaiety. Sun-soaked concessions hide a struggling, embittered world verging always on violence and disaster. Its human flotsam have been cast up on the sands by an inability to cope with city complexities. Maimed, brutalized, rejected, the Neptuners here spend three days messing-up their lives. Most damaged is Shubunka, the ugly, fat brothel operator; a childhood fall had bent both legs, heightened his apelike appearance, and rendered him a lonely grotesque. Intelligent, sensitive, and gentle, he arouses in those about him disgust and suspicion. Yet in the confused reader he evokes not only compassion but guilt for misplaced sympathy. Shubuanka at least recognizes his own evil, the peculiar justice of his pathetic fate, and his need for atonement.

Thus Fuchs touches notes long sounded by tragic poets, naturalists, and existentialists: the individual discovers little from experience but to exist and endure. He learns that all prayers are to a God indifferent to individual loss and collapse. Before such cosmic indifference, Fuchs insists, man can rely on what he can grab, steal or find. He himself neither condemns nor judges.

Time has not changed his ideas. *West of the Rockies*, Fuchs's long-awaited fourth novel, is a vigorous, but formless, distillation of three decades of accumulated movieland impressions. But despite the California locale, his scurrying hyperactives seem as scarred and self-pitying as their older New York cousins; caught up in the same savage ritual (the need to "make it"), they are propelled by similar anxieties and compulsions. Each is a survivor, with a proved ability to claw a limited victory from any defeat.

To Fannie Case's Palm Springs hotel, in the late 1950's, comes high-strung movie queen Adele Hogue, with three small children, a nervous skin disorder, an imperiled career, and a trail of scandals, broken marriages, and operations. In pursuit is a familiar Hollywood pack: her sinking producer, a torch-carrying ex-racketeer, and assorted talent agents. Among the last is Burt Claris, Fuchs's wry observer and commentator. A no-talent ex-athlete, a loser and "grifter," Burt, clinging desperately to the movie crowd's fringe, is now sexually involved with Adele. Also concerned for the actress is ex-rackets muscle man Harry Case; years back he had deserted his wife Fannie for Adele who, at the last moment, had spurned him.

Fuchs's style is still "cinematic," with characters moving forward, speaking, dissolving. Their talk is the hard, stiff jabs of seasoned winners who suddenly find themselves slipping and, fearing the slide, strike out at those nearest. With Burt watching and waiting, Harry and Adele repeatedly cut and slash at each other; moving back and forth between them is Fannie Case, loving and hating them both. Tough, generous Fannie is the classic Hollywood first wife, the one discarded when the ambitious husband, finally hitting it big, goes after a younger woman. Pugnacious Harry Case, a Catskills-rackets veteran with a strong resemblance to Philip Hayman's gangster uncle, Papravel, still lusts for Adele. But, at story's end, Adele and Burt decide that together they can better confront their harsh, tinsel world.

For all its vivid, quick-paced truths, *West of the Rockies* is not vintage Fuchs. Shorter than his previous novels, with thoughts and deeds summarized rather than acted out, it seems a condensed version of a much longer work, more screenplay synopsis than novel. It hardly matters—Daniel Fuchs, after all, is writing again.

—Ben Siegel

FULLER, Roy (Broadbent). British. Born in Failsworth, Lancashire, 11 February 1912. Educated at Blackpool High School, Lancashire; qualified as a solicitor, 1933. Served in the Royal Navy, 1941-46; Lieutenant, Royal Naval Volunteer Reserve. Married Kathleen Smith in 1936; one son, the poet John Fuller. Assistant Solicitor, 1938-58, Solicitor, 1958-69, and since 1969, Director, Woolwich Equitable Building Society, London. Chairman of the Legal Advisory Panel, 1958-69, and since 1969, a Vice-President, Building Societies Association. Professor of Poetry, Oxford University, 1968-73. Chairman, Poetry Book Society, London, 1960-68; Governor, BBC, 1972-79; Member, Arts Council of Great Britain, and Chairman of the Literature Panel, 1976-77 (resigned). Recipient: Arts Council Poetry Award, 1959; Duff Cooper Memorial Prize, for poetry, 1968; Queen's Gold Medal for Poetry, 1970; Cholmondeley Award, for poetry, 1980. M.A.: Oxford University. Fellow, Royal Society of Literature, 1958. C.B.E. (Commander, Order of the British Empire), 1970. Address: 37 Langton Way, Blackheath, London S.E.3, England.

PUBLICATIONS

Novels

The Second Curtain. London, Verschoyle, 1953; New York, Macmillan, 1956.
Fantasy and Fugue. London, Verschoyle, 1954; New York, Macmillan, 1956.
Image of a Society. London, Deutsch, 1956; New York, Macmillan, 1957.
The Ruined Boys. London, Deutsch, 1959; as *That Distant Afternoon*, New York, Macmillan, 1959.
The Father's Comedy. London, Deutsch, 1961.
The Perfect Fool. London, Deutsch, 1963.
My Child, My Sister. London, Deutsch, 1965.
The Carnal Island. London, Deutsch, 1970.

Verse

Poems. London, Fortune Press, 1940.
The Middle of a War. London, Hogarth Press, 1942.
A Lost Season. London, Hogarth Press, 1944.
Epitaphs and Occasions. London, Lehmann, 1949.
Counterparts. London, Verschoyle, 1954.
Brutus's Orchard. London, Deutsch, 1957; New York, Macmillan, 1958.

Collected Poems 1936-1961. London, Deutsch, and Chester Springs, Pennsylvania, Dufour, 1962.
Buff. London, Deutsch, and Chester Springs, Pennsylvania, Dufour, 1965.
New Poems. London, Deutsch, and Chester Springs, Pennsylvania, Dufour, 1968.
Pergamon Poets 1, with R.S. Thomas, edited by Evan Owen. Oxford, Pergamon Press, 1968.
Off Course. London, Turret, 1969.
Penguin Modern Poets 18, with A. Alvarez and Anthony Thwaite. London, Penguin, 1970.
To an Unknown Reader. London, Poem-of-the-Month Club, 1970.
Song Cycle from a Record Sleeve. Oxford, Sycamore Press, 1972.
Tiny Tears. London, Deutsch, 1973.
An Old War. Edinburgh, Tragara Press, 1974.
Waiting for the Barbarians: A Poem. Richmond, Surrey, Keepsake Press, 1974.
From the Joke Shop. London, Deutsch, 1975.
The Joke Shop Annexe. Edinburgh, Tragara Press, 1975.
An Ill-Governed Coast. Sunderland, Ceolfrith Press, 1976.
Re-treads. Edinburgh, Tragara Press, 1979.
The Reign of Sparrows. London, London Magazine Editions, 1980.

Other

Savage Gold (juvenile). London, Lehmann, 1946.
With My Little Eye (juvenile). London, Lehmann, 1948; New York, Macmillan, 1957.
Catspaw (juvenile). London, Alan Ross, 1966.
Owls and Artificers: Oxford Lectures on Poetry. London, Deutsch, and La Salle, Illinois, Library Press, 1971.
Seen Grandpa Lately? (juvenile). London, Deutsch, 1972.
Professors and Gods: Last Oxford Lectures on Poetry. London, Deutsch, 1973; New York, St. Martin's Press, 1974.
Poor Roy (juvenile). London, Deutsch, 1977.
The Other Planet (juvenile). Richmond, Surrey, Keepsake Press, 1979.
Souvenirs (memoirs). London, London Magazine Editions, 1980.

Editor, *Byron for Today.* London, Porcupine Press, 1948.
Editor, with Clifford Dyment and Montagu Slater, *New Poems 1952.* London, Joseph, 1952.
Editor, *The Building Societies Acts 1874-1960: Great Britain and Northern Ireland,* 5th edition. London, Frayney, 1961.
Editor, *Supplement of New Poetry.* London, Poetry Book Society, 1964.

*

Critical Study: *Roy Fuller* by Allen E. Austin, Boston, Twayne, 1979.

* * *

Roy Fuller is a leading contemporary British poet. He is also a prolific writer of fiction; his production to date includes eight novels, as well as three book-length tales for children. For many poets the novel is in a double sense a sport: a *tour de force* in an unaccustomed medium written to pass the time when verse is hard to compose. Fuller has committed himself more seriously to fiction. There is not, in his work, any capricious alternation between verse-writing and prose-writing, and the art of the novel has always held for him a particular fascination. He was, long before he began to publish fiction in the 1950's, an ardent student of Henry James; he was interested in the contributions which the socially conscious crime novelists of the 1930's had made to the wider techniques of fiction; later he was one of a group of English writers, including also Angus Wilson, Walter Allen, and George Woodcock, who critically reinstated William Godwin's great novel, *Caleb Williams*, as the true precursor of the modern novel of pursuit and persecution, with its attendant ambiguities.

All these influences can be found reflected in Fuller's own novels which, like his poetry, proceed by a process of refinement from a concern for man in his relationship to society and its demands, to a preoccupation with the narrowing world of the human being who advances out of youth towards age and death.

If one takes an early Fuller novel, like *The Second Curtain*, the whole Godwinian paradox of the individual and his sense of justice, pitted against a society inevitably inhuman, seems to be re-stated in modern terms. Like Caleb Williams, the solitary writer George Garner finds himself involved in a criminal conspiracy. A friend of his dies mysteriously, and Garner is horrified to discover that the very men who are proposing to establish him as editor of a literary magazine are in fact responsible for his friend's death. Their organization, formed to protect wealthy manufacturers against indiscreet inventors who may render their products obsolete, is to be seen as a microcosm of the unregenerate society we inhabit, and Garner becomes the type of the well-intentioned intellectual, anxious to struggle for what is true, but susceptible to fear if not bribery, and, by a positively Godwinian twist, feeling guilty towards those who are his enemies and whom he knows to be evil.

The equivocal relationship between the individual—particularly the intellectual or the artist—and the collectivity is further developed in Fuller's later novels, one of which is significantly entitled *Image of a Society*, the Building Society whose affairs form the background to the shifting relationships of the characters is in fact a metaphysical substitute for society as a whole, containing all its moral sanctions, all its possibilities for tyranny and injustice. In *The Ruined Boys* the collectivity is a private school on the edge of failure, and the spurious loyalties which the Headmaster tries to induce seem to be merely the emanations of more real loyalties that make tenuous but irresistible demands. A further variation of the social frame occurs in *The Father's Comedy*, where the leading figure, a successful and ambitious civil servant, finds his future in "the Authority" (a mysterious corporation which again is an image of society as a whole) threatened by both the past (his own radical youth) and the present (his son's rebellion against a repressive army). It is only in his late novel, *My Child, My Sister*, that Fuller follows in fiction the move he had made in poetry a decade before, and narrows but at the same time widens his focus to embrace the individual and ageing man grappling with his own nature and by the same token with the generalized horror of the human condition.

Of course, that struggle of the individual with himself and with his human destiny had been present in all the novels, and in a sense the social dimension has acted merely as a frame of the moral core of each book, since what the contest with society shows most clearly is the degree of courage, sensitivity, and adaptability in the individual. It is in the solitude of his own weakness that George Garner in *The Second Curtain* has to consider his defeat by the evil forces of the Power Industries Protection Corporation. And if, at the end of *The Father's Comedy*, Harold Colmore feels—after he has revealed all the secrets of his left-wing past in order to secure his son's acquittal in a court martial—that he must return "to show himself to the Authority and to Dorothy, to find out what his character and his career had become," the significance of the novel to the reader lies not in what will happen to Colmore's career in the future, but in the fact that in the present he has been able to ignore such possibilities and to commit what may well be a sacrifice of his planned future out of love for his son.

For it is ultimately in the validity of human relationships that the characters of Fuller's novels are tested, and here it is—rather than in any stylistic shaping—that the effects of his early Jamesian enthusiasms may be detected. For the rigid forms of society are complemented by the fragile links that bind human beings in a web of indestructible gossamer, and perhaps Fuller's best achievement as a novelist lies in the restraint and sureness with which he establishes this network of relationships. The relationships may be ambiguous: an elderly man, like Albert Shore in *My Child, My Sister*, feeling sexually stirred by his wife's daughter by a second marriage; Harold Colmore in *The Father's Comedy* clandestinely meeting a girl in whom his conscript son had been interested; Gerald Bracher in *The Ruined Boys* sensing all at once the epicene charms of a younger boy who plays a female part in a school play. Nothing happens in a physical sense; Fuller's novels are almost completely lacking in the scenes of sexual action that figure in so many contemporary novels, and even scenes of violence are rare, petty, and dependent on the imperatives of the plot; there is no gratuitous sensationalism of any kind. But the very scantiness of outward action tends to heighten the inward intensity of the relationships.

Almost always, in such relationships, the attraction-repulsion between the young and the ageing is involved, and, as a corollary, the sense in one partner of the loss of a beauty and an innocence that he is trying to regain. It is not merely a sentimental nostalgia that is involved, for often the young seem hardly worthy of the love directed towards them and the person who directs it is at least partly conscious of this fact; the central feeling is rather—less crudely and directly expressed than by the existentialists—of the inexorable progress of every life towards decay.

The tone of Fuller's novels, like the tone of his poetry, is restrained and undramatic; he recognizes that each man to himself is a failure, and it is the inner voice expressing this recognition that he uses. His world is not without fear; indeed, fear pervades it, but it is expressed most often in such forms as anxiety and apprehension. His heroes are of human dimensions, and the whole landscape is that of a normal world which breeds its own terrors, shames, and victories without any need to import disaster or false passion from outside. The consequence is that, while so many novels written out of bogus anger in Britain during the 1950's and early 1960's have become as dated as their years of publication, Fuller's have outlived their time, and if they are too muted to survive in detailed memory, they project, on re-reading, an unblurred freshness of tone and sharpness of outline.

—George Woodcock

GADDIS, William. American. Born in New York City in 1922. Educated at Harvard University, Cambridge, Massachusetts. Has two children. Recipient: American Academy grant, 1963; National Endowment for the Arts grant, 1966, 1974; National Book Award, 1976. Agent: Candida Donadio and Associates, 51 East 42nd Street, New York, New York 10017, U.S.A.

PUBLICATIONS

Novels

The Recognitions. New York, Harcourt Brace, 1955; London, MacGibbon and Kee, 1962.
JR. New York, Knopf, 1975; London, Cape, 1976.

*

Critical Study: *City of Words* by Tony Tanner, London, Cape, and New York, Harper, 1971.

* * *

John W. Aldridge well described *The Recognitions* (in the *Saturday Review*) as an attempt to create "a satirical portrait of no less than the entire modern world...through a most intricate 956-page exploration of such arcane matters as art forgery, counterfeiting, false religious rhetoric, ambidextrous sexuality, the fraudulence of political life, and the masquerades of intellectual and artistic society." As one might suspect—given the fact the novel is dense in style, has little plot, and is encyclopedic in scope (treating in Joycean fashion everything from the origins and varieties of religious belief to every major period in human history)—it was greeted with a mixed reception. Even today, while it is regarded by an impressive group of prominent and respected critics as one of the most brilliant works of our century, it has a small reading public. *JR*, Gaddis's second novel, also difficult to read and gargantuan in size, with multiple levels of meaning and the intentional obscurity between characters, has led many of Gaddis's (also highly respected) detractors to question if the effort in reading his books is equal to their rewards.

In both novels, Gaddis focuses his vast erudition and epistemologic questions upon the corrupt contemporary world. It is a world overwhelmed by technology and big business—the money (and efficiency) ethic—and characterized by the demise of human relationships. This he mirrors in the corruption of language and all apparent communicative patterns—from art to a telephone call. Gaddis focuses upon human suffering and the almost universal alienation that exists in a society of hypocrisy, greed, and fraudulence. He searches for redemption with the recurrent question of whether or not the individual can assert some control within such a world, as well as within a universe that may lack design or purpose. Beneath all of society's counterfeit structures, after all, may lie chaos, rather than order and the simplicity of basic form.

Although Gaddis's vision is often grim and his satire black, he implies in both novels the power of human love, and perhaps even the transcending possibilities of artistic creation. The acceptance of self and the *effort* to create or extend toward some fundamental unity, may at least set in balance the chaotic and entropic universe.

The Recognitions—with its 50 characters and dozen or so minor ones (whose paths cross throughout, and who contrast, echo, and parallel one another within a vast number of subplots), and with its echoes from Joyce, Rilke, Dante, Eliot, Augustine, Melville, and dozens more—covers a 30-year period and takes place in New York, New England, Paris, Italy, and Spain. Its central figure is Wyatt Gwyon, the son of an eccentric clergyman, who rejects the ministry to become an artist, and who then rejects his own original work (his aunt had accused him years before of trying to assume God's creative function) to copy the Old Flemish Masters who "found God everywhere." Although he leaves his father and wife to become the counterfeit artist and is exploited by a series of people (like Rectall Brown), his is a pilgrimage to discover the counterfeits of contemporary life. He ultimately arrives at a Spanish monastery and (in blinding insight or madness?) goes beyond copying the "falsifications" of the Masters to arrive at final truth—by erasing their canvases. He departs, presumably having had the ultimate epiphany, having "seen" the simple truth behind all artifice and structure.

The novel is filled with recognitions and failed recognitions—of forgeries on every conceivable level—social, aesthetic, scientific, sexual, religious, political. Throughout is the sense that man has surrendered all sense of mystery, wonder, feeling, and belief to science, technology, psychology, and commerce. Wyatt tries to get beyond the contemporary disease of ego to original truths, as Gaddis pursues the distinctions between the real and fictional. What lies behind all human enterprise (a forgery), he asks throughout—form, chaos, or God? In the end it may be that art and reality are, after all, the same—both constructs over and against chaos.

What Wyatt accomplishes finally is a spatial, spiritual, and truly creative experience, a "recognition" of the unity of all living and nonliving things. He goes beyond art, which like life (and all human relationships and systems) separates ("afraid of spaces") to gain a sense of even the intermingling of life and death (in a bizarre scene where he eats bread mistakenly made of his father's ashes).

Although *JR* is also vast in scope, its most immediate focus is the corruptive power of money in our society with its scores of wasted human relationships and aborted creative potentiality. Beneath Gaddis's concentration upon the immediate and topical is his sense of cosmic meaninglessness. The novel lacks any formal organization. It has no chapter divisions; sentences often do not finish; it utilizes minimum punctuation. The book consists of uninterrupted speech, in dialogues and monologues. Its minimal plot centers on an 11-year-old boy, rejected by both his family and society, who is a student at a modern (computerized) school on Long Island. An emblem of his society, which teaches wheeling and dealing rather than thinking and feeling, the illiterate JR—with torn sweater, open sneakers, and running nose—having mastered Wall Street jargon, puts into practice the lessons of his time and place. Horatio Alger magnified (and satirized) a hundred-fold, he builds a paper empire that touches the political, cultural, and social power bases of our society. Gaddis focuses on the decadence of the people involved in all his maneuvering. In their midst, however, is the "hero" Edward Bast, the one-time composer at the school (fired for sneaking some truths about Mozart into his TV lesson). Bast is taken over by JR and becomes his business agent. At the end Bast gives up financial security to return to art, and JR, who has never actually realized (i.e., cashed in on) his paper empire, pleads for the respect of personal values. One's worth, it appears, depends upon his acts—in an existential sense.

Although *JR*'s canvas appears smaller than that of *The Recognitions* (the story takes place in New York and Long Island during a few months), it is even more difficult to read. With little description, narrative, or characterization (which is handled through dialect variations), one has a difficult time assigning speeches, even though Gaddis utilizes a remarkable variety of spoken styles. But one has no difficulty focusing upon his predominant image of American life—as one of corruption, lovelessness, and easy surrender. This is an insane world where friendship and love, on any level, are betrayed. Language mirrors the separation of the individual from his world and the entropy of that very world. One no longer listens, or if he does, he doesn't hear what is said. Language so studded with bureaucratic and political jargon has lost any "meaning."

Beneath Gaddis's scathing portrait of education, big business, government, the arts, human relationships—virtually every area of human experience—are his humor and good sense regarding what has gone awry. One always feels his compassion toward his suffering people, no matter how grotesque or foolish their vision or behavior. Tony Tanner, looking ahead to a writer like Pynchon, says that Gaddis inaugurated "a new period of American fiction in which the theme of fictions/recognitions has come to occupy the forefront of the American writer's consciousness."

—Lois Gordon

GAINES, Ernest J. American. Born in Oscar, Louisiana, 15 January 1933. Educated at San Francisco State College, 1955-57, B.A. 1957; Stanford University, California, 1958-59. Served in the United States Army, 1953-55. Writer-in-Residence, Denison University, Granville, Ohio, 1971, and Stanford University, Spring 1981. Recipient: Wallace Stegner Fellowship, 1958; San Francisco Foundation Joseph Henry Jackson Award, 1959; National Endowment for the Arts grant, 1966. D.Litt.: Denison University, 1980. Agent: Dorothea Oppenheimer Literary Agency, 866 United Nations Plaza, Room 471, New York, New York 10017. Address: 988 Divisadero Street, San Francisco, California 94115, U.S.A.

PUBLICATIONS

Novels

Catherine Carmier. New York, Atheneum, 1964; London, Secker and Warburg, 1966.
Of Love and Dust. New York, Dial Press, 1967; London, Secker and Warburg, 1968.
The Autobiography of Miss Jane Pittman. New York, Dial Press, 1971; London, Joseph, 1973.
In My Father's House. New York, Knopf, 1978.

Short Stories

Bloodline. New York, Dial Press, 1968.

Uncollected Short Stories

"The Turtles," in *Transfer* (San Francisco), 1956.
"Boy in the Doublebreasted Suit," in *Transfer* (San Francisco), 1957.
"My Grandpa and the Haint," in *New Mexico Quarterly* (Albuquerque), Summer 1966.

Other

A Long Day in November (juvenile). New York, Dial Press, 1971.

*

Critical Studies: "Human Dignity and Pride in the Novels of Ernest Gaines" by Winifred L. Stoelting, in *C.L.A. Journal* (Baltimore), March 1971; "Ernest J. Gaines: Change, Growth, and History" by Jerry H. Bryant, in *Southern Review* (Baton Rouge, Louisiana), October 1974; "Bayonne ou le Yoknapatawpha d'Ernest Gaines" by Michel Fabre in *Recherches Anglaises et Américaines 9* (Strasbourg), 1976; "To Make These Bones Live: History and Community in Ernest Gaines's Fiction" by Jack Hicks, in *Black American Literature Forum*, Spring 1977; "Ernest Gaines: 'A Long Day in November' " by Nalenz Puschmann, in *The Black American Short Story in the 20th Century* edited by Peter Bruck, Amsterdam, Grüner, 1978.

Ernest J. Gaines comments:

I have tried to show you a world of my people—the kind of world that I came from.

* * *

The fictive world of Ernest J. Gaines, as well as certain technical aspects of his works, might be compared to that of William Faulkner. But useful as such a comparison may be, it should not be pursued to the point of obscuring Gaines's considerable originality, which inheres mainly in the fact that he is Afro-American and very much a spiritual product, if no longer a resident, of the somewhat unique region about which he writes: south Louisiana, culturally distinguishable from the state's Anglo-Saxon north, thus from the nation as a whole, by its French legacy, no small part of which derives from the comparative ease with which its French settlers and their descendants formed sexual alliances with blacks.

Gaines's Afro-American perspective enables him to create, among other notable characters both black and white, a Jane Pittman (*The Autobiography of Miss Jane Pittman*) whose heroic perseverance we experience, rather than a housekeeping Dilsey (*The Sound and the Fury*) for whom we have little more than the narrator's somewhat ambiguous and irrelevant assurance that "She endured." In general, Gaines's peculiar point of view generates a more complex social vision than Faulkner's, an advantage Gaines has utilized with increasing dramatic force and artistic promise. The society of which he writes consists of whites, blacks, and creoles, a traditionally more "favored" class ("shade" is perhaps more appropriate) of Afro-American given to fantasies of racial superiority of the kind Frantz Fanon explores in *Black Skin, White Masks*, in terms of Martinican society.

The Gainesian counterparts of the Sartorises and Snopeses (the moribund aristocracy and parvenu "poor white trash" of Faulkner's mythical Mississippi county) are the south Louisiana plantation owners, mostly of French extraction, and the cajuns, of French extraction but of lesser "quality." The cajuns are inheriting and spoiling the land and displacing the creoles and blacks, the former tragically though not irrevocably doomed by a persistent folly, the latter a people of promise who have never really betrayed their Africanness.

All Gaines's works reflect the inherent socio-economic intricacy of this quadruplex humanity, though we are never allowed to lose sight of its basic element of black and white. In the apprentice first novel *Catherine Carmier*, for instance, we see the sickly proscribed love of Jackson, who is black, and Catherine, daughter of an infernally proud creole farmer, as a perverted issue of the miscegenation that resulted from the white male's sexual exploitation of black people. This mode of victimization assumes metaphoric force in Gaines's works, figuring forth in historical perspective the oppression of black people generally. The fictive plantation world, then, is uniquely microcosmic. It is south Louisiana, the south, the nation as a whole. This aspect is explored, for example, in the title story of *Bloodline*. Copper, a character of mythopoeic proportion, the militant young son of a now deceased white plantation owner and a black woman field hand, stages a heroic return, presumably from his education in school and in the world at large, to claim his heritage: recognition of kinship by an aristocratic white uncle and his rightful share of the land. In *In My Father's House*, and for the first time, Gaines deals with the black father-son relationship, and explores a neglected aspect of Afro-American life: the perplexities of the public vs. private person relative to individual responsibility. The Reverend Phillip Martin, a grass roots Civil Rights leader in the fictional south Louisiana town of St. Adrienne, is forced to confront his wayward past when his estranged son Etienne, reminiscent of Copper, comes to claim paternal recognition and redress of grievances.

—Alvin Aubert

GALLANT, Mavis. Canadian. Born in Montreal, 11 August 1922. Agent: Georges Borchardt, 136 East 57th Street, New York, New York 10022, U.S.A. Address: 14 rue Jean Ferrandi, 75006 Paris, France.

PUBLICATIONS

Novels

Green Water, Green Sky. Boston, Houghton Mifflin, 1959; London, Deutsch, 1960.

A Fairly Good Time. New York, Random House, and London, Heinemann, 1970.

Short Stories

The Other Paris. Boston, Houghton Mifflin, 1956; London, Deutsch, 1957.

My Heart Is Broken: 8 Stories and a Short Novel. Toronto and New York, Random House, 1964; as *An Unmarried Man's Summer*, London, Heinemann, 1965.

The Pegnitz Junction: A Novella and Five Short Stories. New York, Random House, 1973; London, Cape, 1974.

The End of the World and Other Stories. Toronto, McClelland and Stewart, 1974.

From the Fifteenth District: A Novella and Eight Short Stories. New York, Random House, 1979; London, Cape, 1980.

Other

The Affair of Gabrielle Russiter, with others. New York, Knopf, 1971; London, Gollancz, 1973.

*

Critical Studies: "Mavis Gallant Issue" of *Canadian Fiction 28* (Prince George, British Columbia), 1978; *Mavis Gallant: Narrative Patterns and Devices* by Grazia Merler, Ottawa, Tecumseh Press, 1978.

Mavis Gallant comments:

I was born in Montreal. My father was English, my mother German-Rumanian-Breton. My father died when I was still a small child (an only child) and I spent a great deal of time being shifted about here and there and from school to school. I went to seventeen schools in all, beginning with a prison-like French-Canadian convent at the age of four. These schools, all recalled with horror, were in two provinces and two states, Catholic and Protestant, French and English speaking, co-educational and segregated, and this constant shifting and changing made it virtually impossible for me to obtain any education at all.

I have not had "jobs," but have lived entirely on my writing, except for a few years in my twenties when I worked for a newspaper in Montreal. This paper no longer exists.

I live with writing exactly as an architect lives with design or a doctor with medicine. I knew from the beginning that I was a slow writer and would probably not produce much, and I arranged my life around my work. A girl I knew when we were both fifteen in New York told me recently that I had told her then exactly how and where I would live.

Nothing is as obnoxious to me as a writer talking about himself and his aims and theories. These things should be evident in the work (I am talking about serious writers). I have noticed that what interests people is irrelevant. Whenever I have been interviewed I have been asked if I write on a typewriter, if I work in the morning or the afternoon, and how I first sold a story to *New Yorker*. My answer to the last of these—that I typed a story and sent it in—never seems satisfactory, yet that is all there was to it.

The beginning is easy; what happens next is much harder.

* * *

The characters who move through the fiction of Mavis Gallant are unwilling exiles and victims, born or made. Her first collection of short stories, *The Other Paris*, clearly sets the tone of her work: in a series of impersonal, almost clinical sketches the lonely and displaced struggle against an indifferent or hostile world. A naive American girl, engaged to a dull American in Paris, wonders why her colorless days have no connection with the legendary "other Paris" of light and civility; a pathetic American army wife in Germany faces her stale marriage and a rootless future; a bitter, unforgiving set of brothers and sisters gathers after the funeral of their mother, a dingy Roumanian shopkeeper in Montreal; a cow-like Canadian girl with Shirley Temple curls is repeatedly deceived by seedy fiancés; a traveler staying in a Madrid tenement watches a petty bureaucrat trying to justify the new order "to which he has devoted his life and in which he must continue to believe." These anti-romantic glimpses of dislocation and despair are rendered in deliberately hard, dry prose, reminiscent, like their subject matter, of Joyce's *Dubliners*. The narrative manner is flat, unadorned, without any relieving touches of wit—or, it seems, compassion (save for the best of the stories, "Going Ashore," in which a sensitive child is dragged from port to port by a desperate, amoral mother). Although there are an admirable consistency of theme and feeling in these stories, and a high degree of professional skill, there is little here to suggest the brilliance of Miss Gallant's later work and her gradual mastery of longer, more demanding fictional forms.

The title of the next collection, *My Heart Is Broken*, reveals a continuation of the same concerns. Yet there is a good deal more vigor here, and an indication as well that the author, if not her characters, may be taking some pleasure in the sharpness of her perceptions. There is also the first clear suggestion of a problem which is to become of major importance in Miss Gallant's later work: the eccentricity and near-madness to which her losers may be driven by want or isolation. Gallant has an appallingly accurate eye for the desperation of the shabby genteel, the Englishwomen who live at the edge of poverty in unfashionable pensions out of season, and a shrewd eye as well for the vulgarities of those who try to keep up the pretense of well being. And there is at least one completely successful story, "An Unmarried Man's Summer" which manages to combine many of the earlier preoccupations with a degree of wit and energy not present before.

Gallant's first experiment with longer fiction, *Green Water, Green Sky*, despite a vivid central section, suffers from an uncertainty of focus. Three of the four parts of the novella offer peripheral views of the breakdown of a young American wife, raised abroad and now living in Paris. The reasons for her drift into madness are never fully explained, although the blame must in part rest with a vain and foolish mother. Florence remains an intriguing and pathetic puzzle; our questions are unanswered, our sympathies largely unresolved. A second short novel, "Its Image on the Mirror" (*My Heart Is Broken*), is an unqualified success, partly because the point of view is strictly limited to one character—a device which is the source of some ambiguity here as well as consistency. The faintly repressed family hostilities which have appeared in various guises in the earlier work are now given sustained treatment. The narrator, Jean, who has always suffered from a sense of drabness and compromise in contrast to her beautiful younger sister, tries to come to terms with her ambivalent feelings. After years of apparent freedom and romance the spoiled Isobel makes what seems to be an unhappy and confining marriage; looking back, Jean is able to move towards compassion and acceptance. But to what degree is she using the narrative as a kind of revenge for the years she was forced to take second place? Is her sympathy finally untainted by satisfaction? The reader has no means of deciding, precisely because the author makes no comments on Jean's reminiscences. The uncertainty we feel at the end of the work, however, is entirely appropriate: Jean herself is still divided between love, pity and jealousy.

A Fairly Good Time is a splendidly complex full-length novel. Again the plot is familiar and simple in outline: a well-off, still young Canadian woman passes over the borders of sanity as her second marriage, to a Parisian journalist, dissolves. The reasons for her collapse, again, are hinted at rather than developed: an eccentric, domineering mother, a happy first marriage cruelly ended by a freak accident, the frustrating sense of isolation in a foreign world of would-be intellectuals and amoral opportunists—all of these play a partial role. This time, however, Gallant operates directly inside the mind of her heroine, and the result is a spectacular tour de force: the writing is disconcertingly vivid, full of the unmediated poetry of near-hallucination, yet nothing is irrelevant or misplaced. Shirley's madness has a kind of honesty about it which attracts the users and manipulators around her. The sane world of her husband's family and the Maurel family, into whose civil wars she is thrust, seems finally to offer much less integrity than her own world of memories and fantasies. At the conclusion there is just a hint that Shirley may be returning to reality, as she learns to moderate her hopes: "if you make up your mind not to be happy," runs the epigraph from Edith Wharton, "there's no reason why you shouldn't have a fairly good time."

There are no ideas in Gallant's work, no set of theses. The strong and willful may or may not succeed; the sensitive will almost certainly pay for their gifts. And if they endure, as Shirley may, or as Jean does in "Its Image on the Mirror," the only wisdom is a kind of expensive stoicism:

> We woke from dreams of love remembered, a house recovered and lost, a climate imagined, a journey never made.... We would waken thinking the earth must stop now, so that we could be shed from it like snow. I knew, that night, we would not be shed, but would remain, because that is the way it was. We would survive, and waking—because there was no help for it—forget our dreams and return to life.

This is not exactly hopeful, but neither is it completely despairing: perhaps if we learned to moderate our hopes we might have a fairly good time. But Gallant's recent collections *The Pregnitz Junction* and *From the Fifteenth District* seem to deny even this modest possibility. The mood here is that of *The Other Paris*; the effect is considerably more oppressive, however, since Gallant has extended the range of her style. The relatively dry, understated manner of the first books has now been replaced by a highly poetic technique in which feelings are conveyed by sudden, uncanny, and yet astonishingly precise images. Yet as before, her characters do not act, they are acted upon; they suffer, but in the end it hardly seems to matter. Life dwindles away and with it everything which gave pleasure, so perhaps nothing had much substance to begin with. The conclusion of "An Autobiography" (*The Pegnitz Junction*) is typical. A middle-aged woman thinks about her failure to hold onto the love of a shiftless young man called Peter (the cause of the failure is left undefined, these things just "happen"):

> These are the indecisions that rot the fabric, if you let them. The shutter slams to in the wind and sways back; the rain begins to slant as the wind increases. This is the season for mountain storms. The wind rises, the season turns; no autumn is quite like another. The autumn children pour out of the train, and the clouds descend upon the mountain slopes, and there we are with walls and a ceiling to the village. Here is the pattern on the carpet where he walked, and the cup he drank from. I have learned to be provident. I do not waste a sheet of writing paper, or a postage stamp, or a tear. The stream outside the window, deep with rain, receives rolled in a pellet the letter to Peter. Actually, it is a blank sheet on which I intended to write a long letter about everything—about Véronique. I have wasted a sheet of paper. There has been such a waste of everything; such a waste.

"The only way to be free," reflects one of the battered characters in *From the Fifteenth District*, "is not to love." This is the freedom of isolation, madness, and death, but perhaps any escape from being is preferable to the pain of living. Thus Piotr, for example, the central figure in the novella "Potter," welcomes the imagined prospect of his death: "Oh, to be told that there were only six weeks to live! To settle scores; leave nothing straggling, to go quietly." Yet even death may offer no release. In "From the Fifteenth District," a truly harrowing prose-poem—it can hardly be called a story—the pathetic ghosts of the dead complain to the "authorities" that the memories of life and the intrusions of the still-living make any final rest impossible.

—Elmer Borklund

GARDNER, John (Champlin, Jr.). American. Born in Batavia, New York, 21 July 1933. Educated at DePauw University, Greencastle, Indiana, 1951-53; Washington University, St. Louis, A.B. 1955; University of Iowa (Woodrow Wilson Fellow, 1955-56), M.A. 1956, Ph.D. 1958. Married 1) Joan Louise Patterson in 1953, two children; 2) Liz Rosenberg in 1980. Taught at Oberlin College, Ohio, 1958-59; California State University, Chico, 1959-62, and San Francisco, 1962-65; Southern Illinois University, Carbondale, 1965-74; Bennington College, Vermont, 1974-76; Williams College, Williamstown, Massachusetts, and Skidmore College, Saratoga Springs, New York, 1976-77; George Mason University, Fairfax,

Virginia, 1977-78. Since 1978, Member of the English Department, State University of New York, Binghamton. Visiting Professor, University of Detroit, 1970-71, and Northwestern University, Evanston, Illinois, 1973. Editor, *MSS*, and Southern Illinois University Press Literary Structures series. Recipient: Danforth Fellowship, 1970; National Endowment for the Arts grant, 1972; American Academy award, 1975. Address: R.D.1, Susquehanna, Pennsylvania 18847, U.S.A.

PUBLICATIONS

Novels

The Resurrection. New York, New American Library, 1966.
The Wreckage of Agathon. New York, Harper, 1970.
Grendel. New York, Knopf, 1971; London, Deutsch, 1972.
The Sunlight Dialogues. New York, Knopf, 1972; London, Cape, 1973.
Jason and Medeia (novel in verse). New York, Knopf, 1973.
Nickel Mountain: A Pastoral Novel. New York, Knopf, 1973; London, Cape, 1974.
October Light. New York, Knopf, 1976; London, Cape, 1977.
In the Suicide Mountains. New York, Knopf, 1977.
Freddy's Book. New York, Knopf, 1980.
Vlemk, The Box-Painter. Northridge, California, Lord John Press, 1980.

Short Stories

The King's Indian: Stories and Tales. New York, Knopf, 1974; London, Cape, 1975.
The Art of Living and Other Stories. New York, Knopf, 1981.

Plays

William Wilson (libretto). Dallas, New London Press, 1978.
Three Libretti (includes *William Wilson*, *Frankenstein*, *Rumpelstiltskin*). Dallas, New London Press, 1979.

Verse

Poems. Northridge, California, Lord John Press, 1978.

Other

The Gawain-Poet. Lincoln, Nebraska, Cliff's Notes, 1967.
Le Mort Darthur. Lincoln, Nebraska, Cliff's Notes, 1967.
The Construction of the Wakefield Cycle. Carbondale, Southern Illinois University Press, 1974.
Dragon, Dragon and Other Timeless Tales (juvenile). New York, Knopf, 1975.
The Construction of Christian Poetry in Old English. Carbondale, Southern Illinois University Press, 1975.
Gudgekin the Thistle Girl and Other Tales (juvenile). New York, Knopf, 1976.
A Child's Bestiary (juvenile). New York, Knopf, 1977.
The Poetry of Chaucer. Carbondale, Southern Illinois University Press, 1977.
The Life and Times of Chaucer. New York, Knopf, and London, Cape, 1977.
The King of the Hummingbirds and Other Tales (juvenile). New York, Knopf, 1977.
On Moral Fiction. New York, Basic, 1978.

Editor, with Lennis Dunlap, *The Forms of Fiction.* New York, Random House, 1962.
Editor, *The Complete Works of the Gawain-Poet in a Modern English Version with a Critical Introduction.* Chicago, University of Chicago Press, 1965.
Editor, with Nicholas Joost, *Papers on the Art and Age of Geoffrey Chaucer.* Edwardsville, Southern Illinois University Press, 1967.
Editor, *The Alliterative Morte Arthure, The Owl and the Nightingale, and Five Other Middle English Poems, in a Modernized Version, with Comments on the Poems, and Notes.* Carbondale, Southern Illinois University Press, 1971.

*

Bibliography: *John Gardner: A Bibliographical Profile* by John M. Howell, Carbondale, Southern Illinois University Press, 1980.

Critical Study: *John Gardner: An Interview* with Joyce Renwick and Howard Smith, Dallas, New London Press, 1980.

* * *

John Gardner's canon divides into three modes: what he calls "the older literature," that is, his scholarly studies of medieval and classical works, and, secondly, contemporary fictions, that is, his New England novels and stories, plus a third domain comprising his own fictive creations on the older literary models. As well as one of the most prominent novelists of his generation in America, Gardner is an accomplished and respected medieval scholar, literary critic, and historian, and, of late, spokesman for the moral responsibilities of modern art.

To Gardner the medieval and modern periods are similar ages of ambiguity and uncertainty, of non-communication, notably "the paradox of speech denying speech," and of menace to traditional values from crumbling ethical standards. He has said that in writing medieval biography he uses novelistic techniques to heighten effects, but as a critic "writing about Chaucer's poetry, on the other hand, I use the second side of a novelist's brain—the lobe that calculates and squints, studies older literature in hopes of understanding its methods and purposes with the greatest possible accuracy, perhaps so that someday, when it seems convenient, the novelist can steal them" (preface to *The Poetry of Chaucer*). His thefts are frequent and often brilliant enrichments of modern fiction with medieval, especially Chaucerian, techniques of structure, paradox, verbal characterization, and allusive reflexivity.

Often irradiated with the myths and the heroic ethos of the medievals, every Gardner work is built upon a dualism that slowly either unravels or fuses, ending on one or more flawed samaritans doing their best to act responsibly in an incomprehensible world. Relative to that world, there is true moral grandeur in their pained discovery that the only answer to their many questions is somehow themselves, their individual response to their own perplexity. The pervasiveness of the Gardner dualism is apparent in his titles, obvious in *Jason and Medeia* and *The Sunlight Dialogues* wherein two characters begin in opposition but gradually exchange attributes, more subtle in *Grendel* and "The King's Indian" wherein the monster assimilates many of Beowulf's qualities like the "indian" his king's. The dissolving dualisms (culture and anarchy, youth and age, saintliness and criminality, desire and fear, wisdom and madness, ethics and amorality) seem designed to undermine easy certainties, forcing his characters to recognize their common humanity and mortality when faced with "emptiness," the bewildering and often frightening "painful universe" devoid of permanence, structure, and absolutes. Their courage and compassion save them, indeed ennoble them, in the brutal social and natural worlds whose cruelty only moral decency and the redemptive power of art can withstand.

The first novels concern a lone figure facing his nemesis (often death) in near solitude, in a room or a cell from which he rarely wanders. Gardner unpacks this tight structure in the works of the early 1970's, extending it into whole social panoramas of characters. He returns to it in the later works, wherein the social extension enters through intercalated novels being read or written by his solitaries in flight from the world that continues to fascinate them.

Increasingly divided in their assessment of his works since 1972, a division deepened by Gardner's recent long essay *On Moral Fiction*, almost all his readers nevertheless agree that *The Resurrection* and *The Wreckage of Agathon* are flawed beginnings of the novelistic mastery achieved in *Grendel* and *The Sunlight Dialogues*.

The first two novels exhibit Gardner's two creative modes: *The Resurrection* a contemporary fiction in what was to become his typical harsh New England landscape, *The Wreckage of Agathon* a virtuoso's tour de force in classical Greek history. James Chandler, Yankee philosopher facing death as mortal illness, and Agathon, Greek philosopher facing death as political imprisonment while dying, both reconsider their lives and question whether there is any cause for which they lived or now die. Through stages of, respectively, rather ponderous pessimism dwelling on the dehumanizing effects of technology without conscience, and a bawdy cynicism enraged at the trampling of humanistic values by the imperialistic police state (sometimes awkward metaphors for Gardner's America of 1966 and of 1970), both philosophers pass from thinking themselves wasted dupes to affirming the values their society abuses, vaguely humanistic ones of compassion and charity that appear "frail" and the already distinct treasure of humanizing art. These are the works of a young man already sure of his thematic concerns and commanding an awesome knowledge of western cultural history, which, as yet, remains something of the scholar's encrustation on the novelist's work.

No such disjunction remains in *Grendel*, Gardner's second tour de force in historical literary imagination but a fully achieved monologue presenting "the other side of the story" of the Beowulf epic. There remains some metaphorical relevance to America's "civilizing" of the Vietnam barbarian, but Gardner's primary emphasis is upon history, the Beowulf-Grendel contest as the keystone of Anglo-Saxon literary and, he infers, ethical traditions. It is a superb conception, effected with flawless control of technique, rhetorical range, tonal shadows and rhythms. That classic monster of western civilization, Grendel emerges in monologue as an endearingly haunted and sorrowing beast fascinated with the agile articulations of human speech and song, and with his own innate need to kill it or make it kill him in celebration of its stupid ignorance of him: "'Theories,' I whisper to the bloodstained ground." Grendel is the first victim of civilization's "progress," the sacrificial animal in whose slaughter we try as a society to eradicate our primitive being so splendidly outlaw and naive. It is just as important to note that Grendel is *good* as to note that he is insufficient. We are Beowulf also, through his history that we inherit and re-enact every day as a soulless society, though Gardner infers that we must pause, listen to our dragons. Grendel is a heart in duel with mere mind.

The cavernous heart is Gardner's narrative field for *The Sunlight Dialogues*, as extended over dozens of characters in Batavia, New York. The placid little society is splendidly individuated, each character speaking in Chaucerian precision the language of his station or milieu. The bumbling antagonist Police Chief Fred Clumly has managed to maintain himself in ill health and ill marriage, and to preserve the public peace despite the minor infractions typical to suburban life, until the dazzling advent of the Sunlight Man. Half brilliant and half mad, part anarchist and part saint, puzzling combination of con man and magician, the Sunlight Man was born in the town and now returns "from nowhere" to wreak death and havoc. Ostensibly a political saboteur (later revealed to be the past victim of a brutal act in the town), he gradually resembles more and more—in the lengthy dialogues with Clumly—the medieval jester as professional disturber of the moral peace, stripping away masks of hypocrisy and habit and "theoretical" order, revealing bigotry, moral corruption, callous brutality, human exploitation and sufferings. When not in dialogue, the novel consists in Clumly's and the town's long hunt to imprison the Sunlight Man, who in the end—party because of a moment's panic—is shot through the heart. "God forgive us!" someone shouts, and Clumly affirms, "Correct." All return to lives indelibly altered. The Sunlight Man is another, to date the best, of Gardner's brilliant genius-philosophers, no longer in solitary retreat but brought into the midst of the society that he disrupts and instructs.

Grendel and the Sunlight Man are extraordinary creations and curiously opposite, a gentle brute crouched in shadow sorrowfully listening to human song and a mad caustic genius illumining vice and virtue with the skill of a Socrates, opposites eloquent of Gardner's protean imagination.

His finest subsequent work remains focused upon middling lives against the New England landscape, increasingly restricted to a single rural building in a cold autumn, and often to a male-female couple. *Nickel Mountain* concerns the stoic despair and rejuvenation of Henry Soames, middle-aged overweight proprietor of the diner where he meets and marries young Callie, in a samaritan act that becomes love, and tenderly devotes himself to her and her illegitimate son. The somber shadow of Nickel Mountain dominates the valley and the other, similarly quiet groping lives of minor characters, all "nicked" (thwarted, harmed, even maimed) by unaccountable chance accidents or needless misfortunes, all bound in a common struggle for calm and rest. *October Light* is the violent, raging counterweight to this "Pastoral Novel": the couple are octogenarian brother and sister in desperate, often comic grotesque struggle to smash each other to death with apple crates or rifle butts or anything else they can wield with feeble old arms and failing eyes. In recurrent ire at the modern world, cantankerous old James blasts his sister's television with his shotgun and imprisons her in her bedroom with one of her trashy novels about sexual liberation and the women's movement. Alternately, both characters rail and muse in monologue, and we learn the tragic history of guilt and suicide that links his dead son with her dead husband, and the ghastly desire for vengeance in blind expiation. Their conflict, which has been called a pschomachy of the Protestant soul, is echoed in the lives of minor characters. These are both the spurned peacemakers who visit, and especially the zany cast of the dime novel *The Lost Souls of Smuggler's Rock*, concerning three sexually liberated gangs of interracial marijuana smugglers in orgiastic outlawry—James's and Sally's unrepressed violence writ large. The lurid intercalation reflexively situate James and Sally as contemporary America's ancestors still battling away at each other in guilty rage and tears, as the younger generation in delusions of progress continues re-enacting the old tragedy of selfish and loveless lives. Though *Nickel Mountain* and *October Light* are Gardner's most naturalistic novels in conception as in technique, they are eerily pendant to one another, the first an almost serene moral odyssey through self-sacrifice and love, the second a grotesque paralysis in history and hatred.

Gardner's recent *Freddy's Book* attempts for the first time, in perhaps experimental ways, to bring together many of his anterior motifs and techniques, most notably the monster-pariah, the intercalated fiction, the mad denunciatory genius, and especially Gardner's own alternation between contemporary and historical modes. History Professor Jack Winesap recounts accepting an invitation from an old historian to visit his home where his son ("I have a son who's a monster") has locked himself in his room and writes a strange book that perhaps the professor can understand. He arrives during a blizzard, meets the obese eight-foot Freddy, and begins the manuscript, *King Gustav and the Devil*, a crowded murky tale set in 16th-century Sweden, in which an upright knight manages finally to vanquish the Devil. Gardner ends on that slaying without return to the framing tale of Winesap and Freddy, and thus without clarifying its reflexive significance.

Disappointed readers of *Freddy's Book* often allude to the essay *On Moral Fiction* by way of confirming a "slackening" of Gardner's powers as novelist and critic. But the opposite case might be made that, taken together, the two works show a gifted novelist reassessing his role and attempting finally to unite his many voices. The essay is his historical review of literature's great "moral artists" from Homer, Dante, and Tolstoy through Malamud, Bellow, Guy Davenport, Eudora Welty, that is, artists with an affirming belief in and sympathy for human possibility. The essay is marred by exaggerated counter-critiques of the "despair" promoted by Mailer, Barth, Heller, Updike, Coover, Vonnegut, Roth. "My position is not Christian," he said in a recent interview. "It's simpler than that. Art, like medicine, should support what's healthy. It shouldn't support despair. Is that old hat? Of course it is, outrageously so.

We're getting so caught up in our complete moral corruption that we can't see what's happening." Few writers write so candidly about their own contemporaries, and Gardner provoked the very arguments that undoubtedly he sought.

In one of his few purely comic works, "The King's Indian," the jaunty narrator has a somber moment: "Caught up in a destinal vortex somehow of our own mad construction we'd intellected Eden to a soot-dark Foundry...." Foundries are in the nature of modern life, knows Gardner, but it is the *intellection* of Eden into brutal exploitation that appalls him, that killed Grendel and the Sunlight Man, that menaces even Freddy's fiction neatly divided into God and Devil with man vacillating between them. In that novel, "everything's the work of the Devil," ponders a Bishop, wondering, how is it possible to obey the "commandments of a god who has not spoken to anyone sane for fifteen centuries"? Gardner's answer has always been clear: by attending "the cavernous heart," eliding intellection for the more primitive and enduring human elements of lonely compassion and quiet courageous persistence past nature's hazards and fashion's nihilism.

—Jan Hokenson

GARRETT, George (Palmer, Jr.). American. Born in Orlando, Florida, 11 June 1929. Educated at Sewanee Military Academy; The Hill School; Princeton University, New Jersey, 1947-48, 1949-52, B.A. 1952, M.A. 1956; Columbia University, New York, 1948-49. Served in the United States Army Field Artillery, 1952-55. Married Susan Parrish Jackson in 1952; three children. Assistant Professor, Wesleyan University, Middletown, Connecticut, 1957-60; Visiting Lecturer, Rice University, Houston, 1961-62; Associate Professor, University of Virginia, Charlottesville, 1962-67; Writer-in-Residence, Princeton University, 1964-65; Professor of English, Hollins College, Virginia, 1967-71; Professor of English and Writer-in-Residence, University of South Carolina, Columbia, 1971-73; Senior Fellow, Council of the Humanities, Princeton University, 1974-77; Adjunct Professor, Columbia University, 1977-78; Writer-in-Residence, University of Michigan, Ann Arbor, 1979. Since 1979, Professor of English, Bennington College, Vermont. President of Associated Writing Programs, 1971-73. United States Poetry Editor, *Transatlantic Review*, Rome (later London), 1958-71; Contemporary Poetry Series Editor, University of North Carolina Press, Chapel Hill, 1962-68; Co-Editor, *Hollins Critic*, Virginia, 1965-71. Since 1970, Contributing Editor, *Contempora*, Atlanta; since 1971, Assistant Editor, *The Film Journal*, Hollins College, Virginia; since 1972, Co-Editor, *Worksheet*, Columbia, South Carolina. Recipient: *Sewanee Review* Fellowship, 1958; American Academy in Rome Fellowship, 1958; Ford grant, in drama, 1960; National Endowment for the Arts grant, 1967; *Contempora* award, 1971; Guggenheim Fellowship, for fiction, 1974. Agent: Perry Knowlton, Curtis Brown Ltd., 575 Madison Avenue, New York, New York 10022. Address: Box 264, York Harbor, Maine 03911, U.S.A.

PUBLICATIONS

Novels

The Finished Man. New York, Scribner, 1959; London, Eyre and Spottiswoode, 1960.
Which Ones Are the Enemy? Boston, Little Brown, 1961; London, W.H. Allen, 1962.
Do, Lord, Remember Me. New York, Doubleday, and London, Chapman and Hall, 1965.
Death of the Fox. New York, Doubleday, 1971; London, Barrie and Jenkins, 1972.

Short Stories

King of the Mountain. New York, Scribner, 1958; London, Eyre and Spottiswoode, 1959.
In the Briar Patch. Austin, University of Texas Press, 1961.
Cold Ground Was My Bed Last Night. Columbia, University of Missouri Press, 1964.
A Wreath for Garibaldi. London, Hart Davis, 1969.
The Magic Striptease. New York, Doubleday, 1973.
To Recollect a Cloud of Ghosts: Christmas in England. Winston-Salem, North Carolina, Palaemon Press, 1979.

Plays

Sir Slob and the Princess: A Play for Children. New York, French, 1962.
Garden Spot, U.S.A. (produced Houston, 1962).

Screenplays: *The Young Lovers*, 1964; *The Playground*, 1965; *Frankenstein Meets the Space Monster*, 1966.

Verse

The Reverend Ghost. New York, Scribner, 1957.
The Sleeping Gypsy and Other Poems. Austin, University of Texas Press, 1958.
Abraham's Knife and Other Poems. Chapel Hill, University of North Carolina Press, 1961.
For a Bitter Season: New and Selected Poems. Columbia, University of Missouri Press, 1967.
Welcome to the Medicine Show: Postcards, Flashcards, Snapshots. Winston-Salem, North Carolina, Palaemon Press, 1978.
Love's Shining Child: A Miscellany of Poems and Verses. Winston-Salem, North Carolina, Palaemon Press, 1981.

Other

Editor, *New Writing from Virginia.* Charlottesville, Virginia, New Writing Associates, 1963.
Editor, *The Girl in the Black Raincoat.* New York, Duell, 1966.
Editor, with W.R. Robinson, *Man and the Movies.* Baton Rouge, Louisiana State University Press, 1967.
Editor, with R.H.W. Dillard and John Moore, *The Sounder Few: Essays from "The Hollins Critic."* Athens, University of Georgia Press, 1971.
Editor, with O.B. Hardison, Jr., and Jane Gelfman, *Film Scripts 1-4.* New York, Appleton Century Crofts, 4 vols., 1971-72.
Editor, with William Peden, *New Writing in South Carolina.* Columbia, University of South Carolina Press, 1971.
Editor, with John Graham, *Craft So Hard to Learn.* New York, Morrow, 1972.
Editor, with John Graham, *The Writer's Voice.* New York, Morrow, 1973.
Editor, with Walton Beacham, *Intro 5.* Charlottesville, University Press of Virginia, 1974.
Editor, with Katherine Garrison Biddle, *The Botteghe Oscure Reader.* Middletown, Connecticut, Wesleyan University Press, 1974.
Editor, *Intro 6: Life As We Know It.* New York, Doubleday, 1974.
Editor, *Intro 7: All of Us and None of You.* New York, Doubleday, 1975.
Editor, *Intro 8: The Liar's Craft.* New York, Doubleday, 1977.
Editor, with Michael Mewshaw, *Intro 9* . Austin, Texas, Hendel and Reinke, 1979.

*

Bibliography: in *Seven Princeton Poets*, Princeton, New Jersey, Princeton University Library, 1963; "George Garrett: A Checklist of His Writings" by R.H.W. Dillard, in *Mill Mountain Review* (Roanoke, Virginia), Summer 1971; "George Garrett: A Bibliographical Chronicle 1947-1980" by Stuart Wright, in *Bulletin of Bibliography* (Boston), January-March 1981.

Critical Studies: "George Palmer Garrett, Jr." by James B. Meriwether, in *Princeton University Library Chronicle* (New Jersey), xxv, 1, 1963; "George Garrett Issue" of *Mill Mountain Review* (Roanoke, Virginia), Summer 1971; "Imagining the Individual: George Garrett's *Death of the Fox*" by W.R. Robinson, in *Hollins Critic* (Hollins College, Virginia), August 1971.

George Garrett comments:

(1972) I feel I am only just beginning, still learning my craft, trying my hand at as many things, as many ways and means of telling as many stories as I'm able to. I hope that this will always be the case, that somehow I'll avoid the slow horror of repeating myself or the blind rigor of an obsession. I can't look back, I'm not ashamed of the work I've done, but it is done. And I am (I hope) moving ahead, growing and changing. Once I've seen something into print I do not re-read it. I have tried always to write out of experience, but that includes imaginative experience which is quite as "real" to me and for me as any other and, indeed, in no way divorced from the outward and visible which we often (and inaccurately) call reality. I only hope to continue to learn and to grow. And to share experience with my imaginary reader. I use the singular because a book is a direct encounter, a conversation between one writer and one reader. Though I couldn't care less how many, in raw numbers, read my work, I have the greatest respect for that one imaginary reader. I hope to manage to please that reader before I'm done, to give as much delight, or some sense of it, as I have received from reading good books by good writers.

* * *

Directness, seriousness, a Chaucerian comic sense which in no way conflicts with that seriousness, imaginative vigor, and a rich variety of matter and manner—these qualities mark the fiction of George Garrett. An American, a Southerner, Garrett has published four novels, a collection of short novels, books of stories, poems, a respectable body of critical work, and he has had three of his screenplays produced as well. These figures suggest his energy and the scope of his interests, and they offer some indication of the seriousness with which he pursues those interests, for none of that large and varied body of work is the result of hack production. Garrett approaches his world and his work with an Elizabethan forcefulness and range, directly and with all his strength. And the result is a body of literature which demands serious attention and rewards that attention when it is given.

Garrett is a Christian artist—not a pietist, but a writer whose very sense of the living world is infused with an Augustinian Christian understanding. He approaches experience directly in his work; he is a realist and not a fabulist, but, because of his Christian belief, his work is never far from parable, his direct reality always formed by the enigmas of the spirit. His four novels are very different each from each in subject, texture and form: *The Finished Man* is a novel of modern Florida politics; *Which Ones Are the Enemy?* takes place in Trieste during the American occupation following the second world war; *Do, Lord, Remember Me* concerns the shattering visit of an evangelist to a small Southern town; *Death of the Fox* is an account of the events, exterior and interior, of the last two days of Sir Walter Raleigh's life. But they are all products of the same central concerns—a blessing of the dark and fallen world, a knowledge of the power of the imagination to create and sustain values in that fallen world, a faith in the possibility of redemption and salvation even in the very process of the fall into sin and death, and a commitment to the individual moment as the sole window on eternity.

Appropriately, Garrett's major work is the large novel *Death of the Fox*, for in it all of his major thematic concerns come together in the person of Ralegh, the soldier, the politician, the sailor and explorer, the scholar, the poet, the sinner, and the morally creative man. In his imaginative union with Ralegh, Garrett fuses present and past into an artistic present which is both truth and lie—the disappointing truth which nevertheless burns ideally in the imagination and dreams of the beholder as in Garrett's earlier short story, "An Evening Performance," and the saving lie of love of his poem, "Fig Leaves," which enables us to "to live together."

George Garrett is one of the most interesting writers of his generation, for he has continued to grow and change in his work while so many of his contemporaries have faltered or simply repeated themselves book after book. His importance becomes clearer year by year, for his fiction has maintained its freshness and its vitality even as it has developed and matured.

—R.H.W. Dillard

GASS, William H(oward). American. Born in Fargo, North Dakota, 30 July 1924. Educated at Kenyon College, Gambier, Ohio, 1942-43, 1946-47, A.B. 1947; Ohio Wesleyan University, Delaware, 1943; Cornell University, Ithaca, New York, 1947-50, Ph.D. 1954. Served in the United States Navy, 1943-46: Ensign. Married 1) Mary Pat O'Kelly in 1952; 2) Mary Alice Henderson in 1969; five children. Instructor of Philosophy, College of Wooster, Ohio, 1950-54; Assistant Professor, 1955-58, Associate Professor, 1960-65, and Professor of Philosophy, 1966-69, Purdue University, Lafayette, Indiana. Since 1969, Professor of Philosophy, now David May Distinguished University Professor in the Humanities, Washington University, St. Louis. Visiting Lecturer in English and Philosophy, University of Illinois, Urbana, 1958-59. Recipient: Longview Foundation Award, 1959; Rockefeller Fellowship, 1965; Guggenheim Fellowship, 1969; American Academy award, 1975, and Medal of Merit, 1979. Address: 6304 Westminster, University City, Missouri 63130, U.S.A.

PUBLICATIONS

Novels

Omensetter's Luck. New York, New American Library, 1966; London, Collins, 1967.
Willie Masters' Lonesome Wife (essay-novella). New York, Knopf, 1971.

Short Stories

In the Heart of the Heart of the Country and Other Stories. New York, Harper, 1968; London, Cape, 1969.
The First Winter of My Married Life. Northridge, California, Lord John Press, 1979.

Uncollected Short Stories

"The Clairvoyant," in *Location 2* (New York), 1964.
"The Sugar Crock," in *Art and Literature 9* (Paris), 1966.
"We Have Not Lived the Right Life," in *New American Review 6*, edited by Theodore Solotaroff. New York, New American Library, 1969.
"Why Windows Are Important to Me," in *Tri-Quarterly 20* (Evanston, Illinois), 1971.
"The Cost of Everything," in *Fiction* (New York), i, 3, 1972.
"Mad Meg," in *Iowa Review* (Iowa City), Winter 1976.

"Koh Whistles Up a Wind," in *Tri-Quarterly 38* (Evanston, Illinois), 1977.
"Susu, I Approach You in My Dreams," in *Tri-Quarterly 42* (Evanston, Illinois), 1978.
"August Bees," in *Delta 8* (Montpelier), May 1979.
"The Old Folks," in *Kenyon Review* (Gambier, Ohio), n.s., i, 1, 1979.

Other

Fiction and the Figures of Life. New York, Knopf, 1970.
On Being Blue. Boston, Godine, 1976; London, Donker, 1978.
The World Within the Word. New York, Knopf, 1978.
The House VI Book, with Peter Eisenman. Boston, Godine, 1980.

*

Bibliography: "A William H. Gass Bibliography," by Larry McCaffery, in *Critique* (Atlanta), August 1976.

Manuscript Collection: Washington University Library, St. Louis.

Critical Studies: "Omensetter's Luck" by Richard Gilman, in *New Republic* (Washington, D.C.), 7 May 1966; "The Stone and the Sermon" by Saun O'Connell, in *Nation* (New York), 9 May 1966; "Nothing But the Truth" by Richard Howard, in *New Republic* (Washington, D.C.), 18 May 1968; interview with Thomas Haas in the *Chicago Daily News*, 1 February 1969; *City of Words* by Tony Tanner, London, Cape, and New York, Harper, 1971; "The Well Spoken Passions of William H. Gass" by Earl Shorris, in *Harper's* (New York), May 1972; "But This Is What It Is Like to Live in Hell," in *Modern Fiction Studies* (Lafayette, Indiana), Autumn 1974; "Against the Grain: Theory and Practice in the Work of William H. Gass" by Ned French, in *Iowa Review* (Iowa City), Winter 1976.

William H. Gass comments:

I think of myself as a writer of prose rather than a novelist, critic, or story-teller, and I am principally interested in the problems of style. My fictions are, by and large, experimental constructions; that is, I try to make things out of words the way a sculptor might make a statue out of stone. Readers will therefore find very little in the way of character or story in my stories. Working in the tradition of the Symbolist poets, I regard the techniques of fiction (for the contemporary artist) as in no way distinct from the strategies of the long poem.

* * *

William H. Gass, a philosopher and literary critic as well as a fiction writer, derives from and is closely allied to the *symbolistes*, Gertrude Stein, Ortega y Gasset, John Crowe Ransom and the New Critics generally, Borges, Robbe-Grillet, Sarraute, and the structuralists. He believes that language is all in all; that words are not agents to instruct or direct us in fiction but that they exist there for their own sake; that the novelist must keep us imprisoned in his language, because there is nothing beyond it; and that the only events in novels are linguistic events. Metaphor is the means by which concepts are expressed in fiction. The writer, furthermore, does not simply render a world; he makes one out of language, creating imaginary objects and imaginary lives. He works toward the purity of prose fiction and the autonomy of art. He works against the concept of mimesis, that is the imitation of "reality," partly because it is futile for the artist to strive for the illusion of life, and partly because he has no obligation to life. His commitment is to aesthetic satisfaction achieved through metaphorical language; it is to writing as process.

Omensetter's Luck is, accordingly, an exercise in the use of language, which in this instance is a prose that strives constantly to be like poetry or music. The words are better than experience, are, indeed, the experience, and the book is intended to be about language and writing. To give himself ample opportunity to exercise his writing capabilities, Gass designed the novel in three sections, each written in a different mode: the first in the narrative, the second in the lyric, and the third in the rhetorical and dramatic modes. The rhythms and images of the Bible, the baroque qualities of Sir Thomas Browne, the technical virtuosity of Flaubert, the stream of consciousness of Joyce all contribute to the writing of the novel in full freedom from the conventional principles of realism and the traditional values of humanism. Nevertheless, lurking behind this dedication to process are narrative and theme, those Gass-identified enemies to the purity of art. The novel dramatizes a conflict between Omensetter, a natural force who represents being-in-nature, and Jethro Furber, a man of religion and thought, obsessed with death and sex. Attractive as he is, Omensetter demonstrates the inadequacies of mindless and spiritless being, while Furber shows us the failure to fuse successfully word, belief, and action in such a way as to elevate the spirit. In short, Gass has drawn, perhaps despite himself, upon the mythological dimensions of Christianity.

While the title story in Gass's *In the Heart of the Heart of the Country* is confessedly modelled on reality, the collection as a whole is experimental. "The Pedersen Kid" is deliberately designed to call into question the nature of reality and the possibility of truth, matters that must live side by side with Gass's concern for the shape of his sentences and the relation of sentence to sentence in the paragraph. In the stories generally, the narrative voice struggles to get inside the characters and with words, magic words, steal their souls away and play with them.

But even more thoroughly committed to experimentalism is *Willie Masters' Lonesome Wife*, in which conventional narrative is largely discarded. The book offers instead a pastiche of various materials: reminiscences of the narrator, little essays on words and the imagination by the author, a variety of typographical play, authorial abuse of the reader, a parody of pornography, and footnotes. All this is designed to destroy the character and form of traditional fiction and to offer opportunities, once the old patterns of linear and logical thought, linear time, and linear print are broken up, for free-wheeling use of the imagination. The book is an experience in art, as Gass tells us at the end, where he inserts a motto: You have fallen into art—return to life. In *Willie Masters' Lonesome Wife* Gass gives himself to self-indulgent play, maximizing the freedom that the author, a god-like figure in Gass's view, justifiably claims in his dedication to the autonomy of art.

—Chester E. Eisinger

GEE, Maurice (Gough). New Zealander. Born in Whakatane, 22 August 1931. Educated at Avondale College, Auckland, 1945-49; University of Auckland, 1950-53, M.A. 1953; Auckland Teachers College, 1954. Married; one son and two daughters. Schoolteacher, 1955-57; held various jobs, 1958-66; Assistant Librarian, Alexander Turnbull Library, Wellington, 1967-69; City Librarian, Napier Public Library, 1970-72; Deputy Librarian, Teachers Colleges Library, Auckland, 1974-76. Since 1976, full-time writer. Recipient: New Zealand Literary Fund Scholarship, 1962, 1976, and Achievement Award, 1965, 1972; Robert Burns Fellowship, University of Otago, 1964; Hubert Church Memorial Award, 1973; New Zealand Book Award, 1976, 1979; Black Memorial Award, 1979; Sir James Wattie Award, 1979. Address: 125 Cleveland Terrace, Nelson, New Zealand.

PUBLICATIONS

Novels

The Big Season. London, Hutchinson, 1962.
A Special Flower. London, Hutchinson, 1965.
In My Father's Den. London, Faber, 1972.
Games of Choice. London, Faber, 1976.
Plumb. London, Faber, 1978.

Short Stories

A Glorious Morning, Comrade. Auckland, Auckland University Press-Oxford University Press, 1975.

Other

Under the Mountain (juvenile). London and New York, Oxford University Press, 1979.
The World Around the Corner (juvenile). Wellington, Oxford University Press, 1980; London and New York, Oxford University Press, 1981.

*

Critical Studies: "Beginnings" by the author, in *Islands* (Auckland), March 1977; *Introducing Maurice Gee* by David Hill, Auckland, Longman Paul, 1980.

* * *

Maurice Gee, as he approaches the age of 50, must now be seen as a writer who has gone on steadily refining and unfolding his creative gifts over a period of 25 years. He began with short stories which, though well-fashioned and authentic in their study of New Zealand society, do little to extend our literary boundaries. These stories, however, support one another strongly to make the collection of them in *A Glorious Morning, Comrade* a surprisingly individual account of local types and situations.

Like the early novels, the stories trace crises in the lives of commonplace people, shopkeepers, workingmen, housewives, office clerks, and school-teachers. Some of these characters, both male and female, in their vulgarity and rough appetites seem limited in their interests to beer and sport and sex. Yet certain codes and loyalties are seriously preserved among them and just as seriously recorded by their author. The Saturday afternoon football, the tug-of-war, the day at the races, the boxing match, even a game of darts, all are rendered with an almost moral earnestness which it is sometimes difficult for the reader to share.

Yet Gee always makes a distinction between self-esteem and self-righteousness. Alongside the healthily vulgar in his fiction there flourishes another group who are narrow-minded and puritanical. The pressures towards conformity which they exert are the more severe the more confined the community, and a recurrent setting for both stories and novels is the smug little town in which a rebel becomes an outcast. The dissenters, to employ a title of Gee's, are usually "The Losers." Another common theme is the incompatibility of man and woman in marriage; and here again the conflict may be between crudity (in the man) and respectability (in the woman). In this Lawrentian pattern they are often rivals for their sons' allegiance, and one son may become Mother's boy, conformist and spiteful, while the other takes after his father and is humane and rebellious. The hostility between the brothers thus becomes a metaphor for Gee's vision of a society divided against itself.

Family strife prevails throughout two later novels, *In My Father's Den* and *Games of Choice*. In these novels, however, some escape is allowed to the central figure: there is a haven of literature into which he may retire in his defeat. At the end of both novels, when the bitterness and the violence have spent themselves, the hero turns back to his books. If the first of these two novels is interesting mainly as a murder mystery, the second is a more serious and even sombre commentary on modern society. In both there are examples of well-rounded characters, and Harry, the hero's disgraceful old father in *Games of Choice*, is memorably coarse, righteous, and carnal. This power of character creation is fully released in Gee's widely acclaimed novel *Plumb*.

It is a diminution of the imaginative feat of *Plumb* to regard it as purely an historical novel. Yet much of its content does derive from real events in New Zealand during the early years of this century, and Gee's own grandfather provided in his career a model after which the fictional hero, George Plumb, is drawn. The themes of religious contention, conformity, rebellion, literary civilization, family bonds and strifes, everything in the New Zealand scene that Gee has approached hitherto is now embraced within the long view and complex character of George Plumb. By making the late 1940's the point from which the old man reviews his personal career, Gee manages an astonishingly coherent compression of the social history through which Plumb's recollections stray. And for all the vividness of separate scenes and crises the novel is always proceeding towards ends that are implicit throughout. It is the first-person delivery that gives immediacy to the events and richness to the narrating personality, one of the most substantial in contemporary fiction.

There are reasons to hope that *Plumb* will eventually become the first piece in a larger fictional design. Certainly Maurice Gee has attained the mastery of his medium that can only suggest further work of a high order.

—R.A. Copland

GELLHORN, Martha (Ellis). American. Born in St. Louis, Missouri, in 1908. Educated at the John Burroughs School, St. Louis; Bryn Mawr College, Pennsylvania. Married 1) the writer Ernest Hemingway in 1940 (divorced, 1945); 2) T.S. Matthews in 1954 (divorced, 1964); one son. War Correspondent for *Collier's Weekly* in Spain, 1937-38, Finland, 1939, China, 1940-41, England, Italy, France and Germany, 1943-45, and Java, 1946; and for *The Guardian* in Vietnam, 1966, and Israel, 1967. Recipient: O. Henry Award, 1958. Lives in London. Address: c/o Morgan Guaranty Trust Company, 31 Berkeley Square, London W.1, England.

PUBLICATIONS

Novels

What Mad Pursuit. New York, Stokes, 1934.
A Stricken Field. New York, Duell, 1940; London, Cape, 1942.
Liana. New York, Scribner and London, Home and Van Thal, 1944.
The Wine of Astonishment. New York, Scribner, 1948.
His Own Man. New York, Simon and Schuster, 1961.
The Lowest Trees Have Tops. London, Joseph, 1967; New York, Dodd Mead, 1969.

Short Stories

The Trouble I've Seen. New York, Morrow, and London, Putnam, 1936.
The Heart of Another. New York, Scribner, 1941; London, Home and Van Thal, 1946.
The Honeyed Peace: Stories. New York, Doubleday, 1953; London, Deutsch, 1954.
Two by Two. New York, Simon and Schuster, and London, Longman, 1958.

Pretty Tales for Tired People. New York, Simon and Schuster, and London, Joseph, 1965.
The Weather in Africa. London, Allen Lane, 1978; New York, Dodd Mead, 1980.

Plays

Love Goes to Press, with Virginia Cowles (produced London, 1946; New York, 1947).

Television Play: *Venus Ascendant*, 1963.

Other

The Face of War. New York, Simon and Schuster, and London, Hart Davis, 1959.
Travels with Myself and Another. London, Allen Lane, 1978; New York, Dodd Mead, 1979.

*

Manuscript Collection: Boston University.

* * *

Some novelists are born to their craft. Others are made. Among the latter kind are those who, while possessing no striking originality of gift or of vision, have nonetheless an ability to handle prose, to depict scenes, and to control narrative flow which make them very similar in kind to the good journalist (and the gifts of novelist and journalist do, after all, cross at a great many points). Martha Gellhorn is one of the better "made" writers. None of her novels can be considered a masterpiece, none has pioneered a new kind of fiction and in none do we experience that all-important shock of recognition that comes when we encounter a genuinely original voice. Yet that said it has to be added that if her novels never surprise they rarely disappoint. At the very least there is about them a cool, controlled craftsmanship that rewards our interest in them.

Martha Gellhorn is without doubt remarkable for the utterly candid manner in which she understands and makes the most of her gifts. She does not try to overreach herself; she knows, none better, what she can and what she cannot do, and she keeps her fiction within the scope of her abilities. As a result she is incapable of falling disastrously flat, as is so often the way with would-be "great" writers who lack her sure self-knowledge. On the other hand, it is no good expecting her to take the kind of dangerous risk which is perhaps necessary for the production of major art. Gellhorn is modest, efficient, clever, and above all she is content to move within limits which she knows she can encompass.

Much of her ability as novelist is bound up with her ability as a journalist, and in this respect it is worth noting that as a journalist she is first-rate. A few years ago, for example, she produced a searingly accurate and moving account of her journey to Vietnam to investigate the effect America's war was having on the unhappy people of that country. And what more than anything else comes across from her reports is her candour, her real feeling for people no matter what the colour of their skins or their political ideologies, and the openness, even perhaps acute vulnerability of her conscience. She did not produce bleeding-heart journalism—and indeed all her writing, fiction especially, is remarkable for the wry toughness of her stance towards life (a kind of controlled stoicism which it would probably be unfair to say she derived from her one-time husband, Ernest Hemingway, but which has striking affinities with his steely self-containment). But for all that, there is in her accounts of life in Vietnam a real tenderness of regard for individuals which shows how easily the novelist and journalist blend into each other. For her fiction is good in its controlled but never dispassionate observation of different people caught up in fates which they can neither control nor ignore.

In this respect I would think that *A Stricken Field* and *The Trouble I've Seen* are works in which Gellhorn's powers of judicious, sympathetic, wry, and compassionate observation of human beings are at their best. And although both suffer from what is really a muddied narrative (in neither does she manage to tell the story as well as she might), they succeed admirably in bringing home to us their touching sense of how other people live and suffer privately.

Of all her novels, however, it is *Liana* which seems to me most fully to embody her virtues and which is least marred by her faults. True, there is a suspiciously Hemingway-like handling of the dialogue—Gellhorn is always at her weakest in this area—but for the rest there is a sharpness, a truth of observation in the studies of Liana herself and of Marc that would make the novel worth reading if there were nothing else to commend it. Add to that, however, the keen feeling for atmosphere, emotional as well as environmental, and you have a fine piece of fiction. *Liana* alone assures Martha Gellhorn a respectable place among the order of good if not great novelists.

—John Lucas

GHOSE, Zulfikar. British. Born in Sialkot, Pakistan, 13 March 1935. Educated at Keele University, England, B.A. in English and philosophy 1959. Married in 1964. Cricket Correspondent for *The Observer*, London, 1960-65. Teacher in London, 1963-69. Since 1969, Lecturer in English, University of Texas, Austin. Recipient: Arts Council of Great Britain bursary, 1967. Agent: Anthony Sheil Associates Ltd., 2/3 Morwell Street, London WC1B 3AR, England. Address: Department of English, University of Texas, Austin, Texas 78712, U.S.A.

PUBLICATIONS

Novels

The Contradictions. London, Macmillan, 1966.
The Murder of Aziz Khan. London, Macmillan, 1967; New York, Day, 1969.
The Incredible Brazilian:
The Native. London, Macmillan, and New York, Holt Rinehart, 1972.
The Beautiful Empire. London, Macmillan, 1975.
A Different World. London, Macmillan, 1978.
Crump's Terms. London, Macmillan, 1975.
Hulme's Investigations into the Bogart Script. Austin, Texas, Curbstone Press, 1981.

Short Stories

Statement Against Corpses, with B.S. Johnson. London, Constable, 1964.

Uncollected Short Stories

"The Absences," in *Winter's Tales 14*, edited by Kevin Crossley-Holland. London, Macmillan, and New York, St. Martin's Press, 1968.

Verse

The Loss of India. London, Routledge, 1964.
Jets from Orange. London, Macmillan, and Chester Springs, Pennsylvania, Dufour, 1967.
The Violent West. London, Macmillan, 1972.

Penguin Modern Poets 25, with Gavin Ewart and B.S. Johnson. London, Penguin, 1974.

Other

Confessions of a Native-Alien (autobiography). London, Routledge, 1965.

Hamlet, Prufrock, and Language. London, Macmillan, and New York, St. Martin's Press, 1978.

*

Zulfikar Ghose comments:

My first novel, *The Contradictions*, begins with the words, "The Earth!" I had not thought of that during the 15 years that those words have been in print, but now, writing this in March 1981, a week before my seventh novel, *Hulme's Investigations into the Bogart Script*, is due from the printer, I realise that the earth, or, more precisely, its *landscapes*, is what I've been writing about in my fictions. *Hulme's Investigations into the Bogart Script* begins with the sentence, "Finally we arrived in the desert." And it ends with its principal character, Walt, high among the foothills of the Rockies looking down upon the land and recollecting the landscapes which constitute the idea of America in his mind.

I've tried to do different things in my several novels. In *The Murder of Aziz Khan* I was interested in writing a solid old-fashioned novel, with a strong story, to prove that I could draw so that I could be liberated from the formal constraints of the past and enjoy the freedom of creating new fictions. The next novel I wrote, *Crump's Terms* (which, however, was published eight years after it was written), was what is called "experimental" by those who believe that to give a thing a label is to have arrived at conclusive knowledge. Now, *Crump's Terms* was *about* many things; but, just as in *The Murder of Aziz Khan* I had dwelt upon the landscapes of Pakistan, so in *Crump's Terms* my obsession, in retrospect, had been the landscapes of Europe.

Then I wrote a trilogy, *The Incredible Brazilian*, which takes in 400 years of Brazilian history. But I realize now, long after having written the 1,035 pages of these three books, that it was not Brazil I was writing about so much as the idea of the land to which I myself longed to belong. Indeed, the final volume of the trilogy, *A Different World*, ends with a paragraph which begins, "come, O voyager, the voice of the tribe calls the exile home...."

It is as if I wished to discover that landscape which I could call *home*. The fact is: I was born in Pakistan when Pakistan had not been created but was part of British India; and I left that part of Pakistan-to-be to live in what was India, but ruled then by the British; that my family emigrated from there to England soon after the Empire began to disintegrate; that I emigrated to the U.S.A. from England while developing, by marrying a Brazilian, an interest in South America. In each intance, even when returning to Pakistan for a visit, I have remained an alien whose unconscious desire is to attach himself to a land with which he can claim an identity. The poems in my first collection of verse, *The Loss of India*, were written some years before *The Contradictions*; my obsession with landscapes in the subsequent novels is almost an attempt to make up for that *loss*. Of course, while writing the dozen or so books I've so far published I never knew that I was doing anything other than seeking an interesting way of completing the sentence which had somehow been begun by some obscure desire of the imagination.

* * *

Zulfikar Ghose's five stories in *Statement Against Corpses* repeatedly concern the metaphysics that unites thought with action, life with death, success with failure, aspirations with accomplishment. "The Zoo People" is the best of these. Thematically complex, linguistically assured, subtle in its evocation of character, delicate in its responses to landscape, provocative in its approach to time, it probes the mind of the English émigré Emily Minns, as she comes to terms with physical and metaphysical perception in an India alien to her upbringing. Is an animal more beautiful in the wild than in a zoo, she asks—and what happens if, taking a cage away, one discovers "primitive wildness" *instead* of beauty? Her ultimate answer arises from her increased sensitivity to Indian paradoxes and her adaptation of them to her "European Enlightenment" patterns of thought:

> Absolute barrenness was a reality with which she now felt a sympathy. There were rocks and rocks: each, whether a pebble or a boulder, was a complete, homogeneous, self-sufficient mass of matter in itself; each stood or lay in the dust at perfect peace with the universe which did no more to it than round its edges; each was there in its established place, a defiant mass of creation, magnificently aloof, without ancestry and without progeny.

Order, in other words, is within her mind's eye.

The Contradictions not only continues the metaphor of barrenness, but also structures itself on East-West logical oppositions. The "assertions" that open the book explore an Englishman's inhibited barriers against India, and India's human fecundity nonetheless. The "contradictions" that close it are set in England and pick up each theme and symbol from the first half of the book—not in order to refute them, but to complete them. The English rationalist philosophers must be blended with India's atemporality; material welfare must be glimpsed concurrently with the noumenal importance of the colour of silk squares; Sylvia's English miscarriage must encourage her to appreciate what her experience of India did not directly allow: that an "area of nothingness" might possess "an odd attraction, and in this darkness, a disturbing power."

Attached ambivalently to a landscape of heart as well as a landscape of mind, Sylvia spirals towards a point of balance between antitheses. For Ghose himself, as his autobiography clearly announces, the point of balance is representd by the tenuous hyphen in "native-alien." Pakistan, India, British India, Britain, and the USA are all part of his experience, and all necessary to him, in conjunction. In another short story, "Godbert," the antithesis is conveyed by a different metaphor: "Donald...looked at horizons whereas John examined the texture of cobblestones." Later in the story, in a similar tense vein, Ghose writes: "One chooses a way of life. Or life imposes its own pattern upon one despite oneself." Such a dilemma lies at the core of Ghose's ambitious and moving novel *The Murder of Aziz Khan*, about a peasant farmer's futile effort to preserve his traditional land from industrial expansion, political roguery, blatant thuggery, and the power of money in other people's hands.

The metaphysics of perception and cultural tension continues to preoccupy Ghose in his later novels. Though *Crump's Terms*, the reflections of a London schoolteacher, is a weak foray into wry social comedy, the three volumes of *The Incredible Brazilian* show the author at his most imaginative and successful. Influenced by Márquez and others, these three books—*The Native*, *The Beautiful Empire*, and *A Different World*—tell the marvelous, almost picaresque narratives of a single character named Gregório, who in a series of reincarnations is variously native, explorer, soldier, planter, merchant, marketeer, writer, and revolutionary. In writing out the three "lives" of the three books, Gregório confronts various ethical, historical, and mythological claims to both the territory and the idea of Brazil: native land, European colony, and new nation. Beyond the claim to the land lies the claim to the future, he writes, and he asks if cultural contact must necessitate corruption, if power is really man's only motivation, and in a closing and magnificently eloquent irony, if efforts to prevent violence inevitably prove destructive. This knot of abstract ideas gives the work its breadth of vision; its success derives also from Ghose's skill in telling a vivid, concrete narrative.

—W.H. New

GIBBONS, Stella (Dorothea). British. Born in London, 5 January 1902. Educated at North London Collegiate School for Girls; University College, London. Married Allan Bourne Webb in 1933 (died, 1959); one daughter. Cable Decoder, British United Press, Feature Writer, *Evening Standard*, London, 1926-28; Drama and Literary Critic, *The Lady*, London, 1928-31. Recipient: Femina Vie Heureuse Prize, 1933. Fellow, Royal Society of Literature, 1950. Address: 19 Oakeshott Avenue, London N6 6NT, England.

PUBLICATIONS

Novels

Cold Comfort Farm. London, Longman, 1932; New York, Longman, 1933.
Bassett. London and New York, Longman, 1934.
Enbury Heath. London and New York, Longman, 1935.
Miss Linsey and Pa. London and New York, Longman, 1936.
Nightingale Wood. London and New York, Longman, 1938.
My American: A Romance. London, Longman, 1939; New York, Scribner, 1940.
The Rich House. London and New York, Longman, 1941.
Ticky. London and New York, Longman, 1943.
The Bachelor. London, Longman, and New York, Dodd Mead, 1944.
Westwood; or, The Gentle Powers. London, Longman, 1946; as *The Gentle Powers*, New York, Dodd Mead, 1946.
The Matchmaker. London, Longman, 1949.
The Swiss Summer. London, Longman, 1951.
Fort of the Bear. London, Longman, 1953.
The Shadow of a Sorcerer. London, Hodder and Stoughton, 1955.
Here Be Dragons. London, Hodder and Stoughton, 1956.
White Sand and Grey Sand. London, Hodder and Stoughton, 1958.
A Pink Front Door. London, Hodder and Stoughton, 1959.
The Weather at Tregulla. London, Hodder and Stoughton, 1962.
The Wolves Were in the Sledge. London, Hodder and Stoughton, 1964.
The Charmers. London, Hodder and Stoughton, 1965.
Starlight. London, Hodder and Stoughton, 1967.
The Snow-Woman. London, Hodder and Stoughton, 1969.
The Woods in Winter. London, Hodder and Stoughton, 1970.

Short Stories

Roaring Tower and Other Short Stories. London and New York, Longman, 1937.
Christmas at Cold Comfort Farm and Other Stories. London and New York, Longman, 1940.
Conference at Cold Comfort Farm. London, Longman, 1949.
Beside the Pearly Water. London, Peter Nevill, 1954.

Verse

The Mountain Beast and Other Poems. London, Longman, 1930.
The Priestess and Other Poems. London and New York, Longman, 1934.
The Lowland Venus and Other Poems. London and New York, Longman, 1938.
Collected Poems. London, Longman, 1951.

Other

The Untidy Gnome (juvenile). London and New York, Longman, 1935.

*

Manuscript Collection: Boston University.

Stella Gibbons comments:

I think of myself as a poet, not a novelist, because I am not deeply interested in human beings, but in ideas and in Nature, and, above all, in the possible existence and nature of God. For what I may call ordinary purposes I think of myself as a moralist and a craftswoman, not as an artist, but I *enjoy* writing. I do not enjoy what may be called the peripheral circumstances attached to being a writer: reputation, literary life, meeting other writers, literary gossip. I love making what is arrogantly called "ordinary people" laugh, and perhaps giving them a happier turn of thought or even some hope. I have a strong distaste for drama and "scenes," which I believe has vitiated my powers as a novelist; my books are really a kind of bitter-sweet fairy story, all of them, though I sometimes flatter myself by calling them poetic realism.

I retired from writing novels in 1970.

* * *

Stella Gibbons is a prolific and talented writer whose reputation for wit was immediately established by her first novel, *Cold Comfort Farm*. This is one of the funniest examples of parody ever put into novel form; it takes on the pulp romance, the philosophy of D.H. Lawrence, the pessimism of Thomas Hardy and all those who, in praising the primitive and the rural, devalue the rational and the urbane.

Cold Comfort Farm was published in 1932. It will never date while there are literary critics of more sensibility than sense and a steady annual output of romantic novels. The heroine, Flora, encounters a Lawrence enthusiast who is writing a book to prove that Branwell Brontë is the real author of *Wuthering Heights*. Branwell's sisters, he confides, "were all drunkards, but Anne was the worst of the lot." Reluctantly, Flora accompanies him on a walk. "The stems reminded Mr. Mybug of phallic symbols and the buds made him think of nipples and virgins. Flora used sometimes to ask him the name of a tree, but he never knew." While the source material for this portrait is not known, it seems certain that Gibbons's weekly stint of book reviewing provoked such passages as the following. "Claud, who had served in the Anglo-Nicaraguan war of '46, was at his ease in the comfortable silence in which they sat, and allowed the irony and grief of his natural expression to emerge from beneath the mask of cheerful idiocy with which he usually covered his sallow, charming face."

The story of the Doom Family frequently recalls the more pessimistic episodes from the sagas of Hardy's Wessex but, at a guess, it was a novel by Mary Webb which provided the immediate inspiration. This is *Precious Bane*, a rural tale in which murder, suicide, and infanticide follow each other in quick succession. Thanks to Flora's good sense, none of these misfortunes come to the inhabitants of Cold Comfort Farm. Seth's sexual obsessions are channelled into a career in Hollywood; Elfine is dissuaded from modelling herself on St. Francis of Assisi and groomed for marriage to the local squire, Dick Hawk-Monitor. Even Aunt Ada Doom who as a child "saw something nasty in the woodshed" is restored to health and flies off to Paris in search of a wicked old age.

Since that triumph, Gibbons has sometimes returned to satire but never with such singleness of purpose; her novels are intelligent explorations of the social themes which have always provided the mainstay of English fiction. She writes about love and marriage, class, money, power, and if caricature is still a favourite method of attack, this is usually incidental to her main focus of interest. Her heroines tend to be shy single women with the selfishness that can accompany timidity. They gain self-knowledge and a greater capacity for happiness, often through contact with a group of people from a wider social circle, never without a measure of pain and disillusionment.

Society is as important in these novels as it is in the novels of Jane Austen and for the same reason; both authors believe that the most reliable assessment of character is based on close observation of social behaviour. Gibbons resembles her predecessor in many other ways. She plots her stories skilfully, allowing room for development and surprise; she enjoys putting the cat among the pigeons and confronting one set of social values with another totally opposed to it. She has a good sense of the dramatic. She has chosen one sphere of London life as a natural setting for her comedies of manners: the artistic and literary community centred on the two hills of Hampstead and Highgate. Many of her most successful novels chart this territory and its special charm, although in human terms this is shown to hide an underlying ruthlessness. The houses and streets of the area, on the other hand, provide a continuing source of pleasure. Gibbons may dislike nature worship but her evocations of Hampstead Heath in all its moods reveal her affection for London's largest stretch of countryside.

One of her best novels is *Westwood; or, The Gentle Powers*. This was published in 1946 and contains some fine descriptions of wartime London. "Weeds grew in the City itself; a hawk was seen hovering over the ruins of the Temple, and foxes raided the chicken-roosts in the gardens near Hampstead Heath." It is a dropped ration-book, appropriately enough, which provides the link between the heroine and the glamorous Niland family. Margaret is a young teacher with a great capacity for hero-worship. The ration-book which she finds and returns belongs to Hebe Niland, wife of a famous painter and daughter of a famous playwright. The Nilands exploit Maragaret from the first but at the same time they educate her; she loses much of her naivety when she discovers that a distinguished playwright can also be a lecherous old man.

Margaret's story is echoed in a later novel of Hampstead life, *Here Be Dragons*, a study of egoism which shows the author at her most perceptive. Again, the heroine enters a charmed circle, at first dazzled, later disillusioned, and ultimately gains from the experience. This time the artists are poor, young, and struggling and the heroine, Nell, is a natural mother figure for them, a kind, practical girl, not unlike the Flora of *Cold Comfort Farm*. She is fascinated by the leader of the group, a writer of genuine talent and unscrupulous charm who enjoys manipulating people for his own amusement. Nell is in some danger from his influence but is saved by one brutal act of betrayal. A similar theme is handled in *The Charmers*.

Stella Gibbons has never lost her popularity as a writer of traditional, well-constructed novels. Her success is surely based on the two qualities which most characterise her work: a strong sense of moral values and an equally strong sense of fun.

—Judy Cooke

GILL, Brendan. American. Born in Hartford, Connecticut, 4 October 1914. Educated at Yale University, New Haven, Connecticut, A.B. 1936. Married Anne Barnard in 1936; five daughters and two sons. Since 1936, regular contributor to *The New Yorker* magazine: Movie Critic, 1961-67; since 1968, Theatre Critic. President, Municipal Art Society, New York; Vice-President, Victorian Society in America, Philadelphia; Member, Board of Directors, Film Society of Lincoln Center, New York. Recipient: American Academy grant, 1951; National Book Award, 1951. Address: c/o The New Yorker, 25 West 43rd Street, New York, New York 10036, U.S.A.

PUBLICATIONS

Novels

The Trouble of One House. New York, Doubleday, 1950; London, Gollancz, 1951.

The Day the Money Stopped. New York, Doubleday, and London, Gollancz, 1957.

Short Stories

The Malcontents. New York, Harcourt Brace, 1973.

Ways of Loving: Two Novellas and Eighteen Stories. New York, Harcourt Brace, 1974; London, Joseph, 1975.

Uncollected Short Stories

"Adriance Prize," in *Saturday Evening Post* (Philadelphia), 22 February 1941.

"Together," in *Saturday Evening Post* (Philadelphia), 8 August 1941.

"Choice," in *New Yorker*, 16 August 1941.

"King Barney the First," and "All the Right People," in *Stories of School and College Life*, edited by Robert J. Cadigan. New York, Appleton, 1942.

"Scientific Mind," in *With a Merry Heart*, edited by Paul J. Phelan. New York, Longman, 1943.

"Interest in Boys," in *New Yorker*, 21 August 1943.

"Grand Old Man," in *Virginia Quarterly Review* (Charlottesville), October 1943.

"Helpmeet," in *New Yorker*, 20 November 1943.

"More Like Home," in *Cross-Section 1944*, edited by Edwin Seaver. New York, Fischer, 1944.

"Privilege," in *World's Great Tales of the Sea*, edited by William McFee. Cleveland, World, 1944.

"Will's Girl," in *Collier's* (New York), 28 October 1944.

"The Test," in *The Best American Short Stories 1945*, edited by Martha Foley. Boston, Houghton Mifflin, 1945.

"Mother Coakley's Reform," in *Our Father's House*, edited by Mariella Gable. New York, Sheed and Ward, 1945.

"The Guide," in *New Yorker*, 21 April 1945.

"Fall from Grace," in *Collier's* (New York), 20 December 1945.

"Fine Start," in *Collier's* (New York), 9 February 1946.

"A Little Rain," in *Fireside Book of Yuletide Tales*, edited by Edward Wagenknecht. Indianapolis, Bobbs Merrill, 1958.

"Night Bus to Atlanta," in *Girls from Esquire*, edited by Frederic A. Birmingham. New York, Random House, 1952.

Play

La Belle (produced Philadelphia, 1962).

Verse

Death in April and Other Poems. Windham, Connecticut, Hawthorn House, 1935.

Other

Cole: A Book of Cole Porter Lyrics and Memorabilia, with Robert Kimball. New York, Holt Rinehart, 1971; as *Cole: A Biographical Essay*, London, Joseph, 1972.

Tallulah. New York, Holt Rinehart, 1972; London, Joseph, 1973.

Happy Times, photographs by Jerome Zerbe. New York, Harcourt Brace, 1973; London, Joseph, 1974.

Here at "The New Yorker." New York, Random House, and London, Joseph, 1975.

The U.S. Custom House on Bowling Green. New York, New York Landmarks Conservancy, 1976.

Lindbergh Alone. New York, Harcourt Brace, 1977.

Summer Places, photographs by Dudley Witney. New York, Methuen, 1978.

The Dream Come True: Great Houses of Los Angeles, photographs by Derry Moore. New York, Harper, 1980.

Editor, *States of Grace: Eight Plays*, by Philip Barry. New York, Harcourt Brace, 1975.

* * *

A fly mounted a curtain in the sun, and
the fly's shadow mounted the shadow of
lace, like a dream threading a dream.
The Trouble of One House

Reversing conventional causation, Brendan Gill's novels and short stories dramatize a present that seems to create, rather than derive from, a densely textured past. Both novels ostensibly focus on immediate problems in upper-middle-class Irish Catholic families—the death of a young mother in *The Trouble of One House*, and the dispute over a father's will in *The Day the Money Stopped*. But the books reveal the past to be as alive and insistent as the present, perhaps more insistent, since in *Money* questions from the past demand solution with an urgency which transcends mere significance for the present, and the dead lawyer father compels greater interest than his son, Charlie Morrow, the protagonist. And in *House*, the nuances of the characters' previous relationships with each other not only explain their responses to Elizabeth's death, but actually seem forced into life for the first time by that death.

This creation by the present of a vital new past does not, however, totally overshadow the more conventional themes of the shaping power of the past, and its continual struggle with the present. Dependent on fragile and illusory human memory, the force of the past can nevertheless guide the present, as does the unlabelled photograph that begins and ends *House*. The last thing the dying Elizabeth sees is this picture of her children, an aid to memory at the moment her memory fades. But the photograph will dominate the father as long as his memory functions: "There was no indication of where the picture had been taken, or when, or by whom. A stranger would have been able to make nothing of it. It was just a picture of three children on a beach. But they were his children; he was theirs. From now on, he was theirs forever." Objects and places redolent with meaning from the past also stimulate conflict in the present: the dead Elizabeth's sister and mother-in-law vie for her chair at the dining table in *House*, and Charlie is intimidated by his father's office chair in *Money*. The cemetery opposite the office window has been a trysting place for as long as Charlie can remember, an image that reinforces the struggle between past and present in his own consciousness. In the story "The Cemetery" a doctor's son confronts the mingled accomplishment and futility of his father's life in a similar office opposite a symbolic cemetery. The American heroine of Gill's recent novella *The Malcontents* redefines herself through the order precariously preserved by an antique mirror, a sign of the 18th-century obsession with the elegance of a remoter past: "In the depths of the intricately carved frame of the mirror, elderly mandarins holding parasols sauntered through latticed pavilions, dreaming that they were butterflies. The mantel and the mirror—all that survived of a red-brick Georgian house in the ferny depths of Sussex—had come up at auction in London, and Claire had outbid the richest magnate in the world in order to make them hers.... Claire bowed to her image among the mandarins, and said, 'Well! So I am a nice person, after all!' "

Money is a tour de force creating past and present largely through dialogue during Charlie's brief visit to his father's office. (This abundant dialogue, concentrated time, and single setting presumably facilitated Maxwell Anderson's dramatic adaptation.) But despite the technical skill of the book, *Money* suffers from Gill's failure to endow Charlie with the charm to which the other characters unvaryingly respond. Though *House* is the better novel, the supporting characters act with a vitality denied Elizabeth, who, like Browning's Pippa, merely stimulates others without herself undergoing much change or awareness. Her sister and undertaker brother-in-law perform with an arresting combination of vulgarity and pathos; Father Degnan and Monsignor Brady are dramatized with a blend of satire and compassion that rivals the best of J.F. Powers; and Elizabeth's daughter awakens to sex on the day of her mother's death in an episode sustaining a complex tone of serious irony. But these brilliant vignettes and characterizations threaten to unbalance the novel, since Elizabeth's character fails to act as a unifying force.

Though *House* is a competent, often moving, work, Gill's major accomplishments are his short stories, which escape the structural problems of the novels. Harry Carter in "Something You Just Don't Do in a Club" is a convincing version of the successful scoundrel, a figure familiar in Gill's fiction, but, like Charlie Morrow in *House*, incapable of sustaining an entire novel. Admittedly, there are some early *Saturday Evening Post* stories, "King Barney the First," "Adriance Prize," and "All the Right People," in which prep school or Yale protagonists manage, through a series of plot contrivances and unmotivated epiphanies, to avoid becoming adult versions of Charlie Morrow. But, contemporary with these works and continuing through the present are a wealth of first-rate *New Yorker* pieces, including Gill's finest, "Triumph," which undercuts, without destroying, an impoverished dowager's distorted reminiscences of an elegant past. The couple in "Helpmeet" provide a grimmer version of the relationship between the undertaker and his wife in *House*; the episode in the novel loses some of its strength to the overall diffuseness of the work, while the story preserves its power intact. "Grand Old Man," the most effective of Gill's clerical stories, dramatizes the same ambivalent struggle between religious innocence and practicality as does *House*. "Interest in Boys" portrays a girl like Elizabeth's daughter, awakening to sexuality and learning that the object of her excitement is a young priest. As in all his best fiction, Gill uses this sudden revelation to illuminate both character and the nature of religious commitment.

Like his biographies *Cole* and *Tallulah*, Gill's recent story "Fat Girl" and novellas "Last Things" and *The Malcontents* compassionately pursue the new theme of unconventional sexuality, its attendant violence, and its occasional delicate balances: "Jack and Fletcher would go on being lovers, Laura and Harry would go on being man and wife, and Laura and Jack would be lovers in every respect except that of sex" ("Last Things"). A continuity underlies these apparent innovations, however. Although the international theme of *The Malcontents* allows Gill to chart the wanderings of the very rich, and although the protagonists of both novellas finally transcend the family or sexual relationships that dominated their early lives (and much of Gill's early fiction), ultimately these novellas seem secularized versions of "And Holy Ghost" and other religious stories. Harry, having buried his wife, escaped the ministrations of his conventional offspring, and shot his beloved, ailing dog, is apparently ready for "Last Things," while Claire, surviving the death of her antagonist mother, the independence of her son, and the waning of her sexuality "looked forward to enjoying the emptiness for a while....Long ago, she had predicted that she would be coming to the simplest things last."

—Burton Kendle

GILLIATT, Penelope (Ann Douglass). British. Born in London. Educated at Queen's College, University of London, 1942-47; Bennington College, Vermont, 1948-49. Married 1) R.W. Gilliatt in 1954; 2) the playwright John Osborne in 1963 (divorced, 1968), one daughter. Film Critic, 1961-65, 1966-67, and Theatre Critic, 1965-66, *The Observer*, London; Film Critic, *The New Yorker*, 1967-79. Recipient: American Academy award, 1971; National Society of Film Critics Award, 1971; New York Film Critics Award, 1971; British Film Academy Award, 1972. Fellow, Royal Society of Literature, 1978. Address: c/o The New Yorker, 25 West 43rd Street, New York, New York 10036, U.S.A.

PUBLICATIONS

Novels

One by One. London, Secker and Warburg, and New York, Atheneum, 1965.
A State of Change. London, Secker and Warburg, 1967; New York, Random House, 1968.
The Cutting Edge. London, Secker and Warburg, 1978; New York, Coward McCann, 1979.

Short Stories

What's It Like Out? and Other Stories. London, Secker and Warburg, 1968; as *Come Back If It Doesn't Get Better*, New York, Random House, 1969.
Penguin Modern Stories 5, with others. London, Penguin, 1970.
Nobody's Business. London, Secker and Warburg, and New York, Viking Press, 1972.
Splendid Lives. London, Secker and Warburg, 1977; New York, Coward McCann, 1978.

Uncollected Short Stories

"Catering," in *New Yorker*, 30 September 1972.
"Iron Larks," in *New Yorker*, 13 January 1973.
"The Sports Chemist," in *New Yorker*, 8 December 1973.
"Autumn of a Dormouse," in *Atlantic* (Boston), November 1974.
"Teeth," in *New Yorker*, 15 October 1979.
"As Is," in *New Yorker*, 7 April 1980.
"One Asks Oneself," in *New Yorker*, 26 May 1980.
"Seven O'Clock of a Strange Millennium and All's Well," in *New Yorker*, 28 July 1980.
"Timely Is the Hand That Winds the Clock," in *New Yorker*, 8 September 1980.

Plays

Sunday Bloody Sunday (screenplay). New York, Bantam, and London, Corgi, 1971.
Property, and Nobody's Business (produced New York, 1980). *Property* published in *The Women's Project: Seven New Plays by Women*, edited by Julia Miles, New York, Performing Arts Journal-American Place Theatre, 1980.
In Trust, in *New Yorker*, 14 January 1980.
Beach of Aurora, music by Tom Eastwood (produced London, 1981).

Screenplay: *Sunday Bloody Sunday*, 1971.

Radio Play: *In the Unlikely Event of an Emergency*, 1979.

Television Plays: *The Western* (documentary); *The Method* (documentary); *Living on the Box*; *The Flight Fund*, 1975.

Other

Unholy Fools: Wits, Comics, Disturbers of the Peace. London, Secker and Warburg, and New York, Viking Press, 1973.
Jean Renoir: Essays, Conversations, and Reviews. New York, McGraw Hill, 1975.
Jacques Tati. London, Woburn Press, 1976.
Three-Quarter Face: Reports and Reflections. London, Secker and Warburg, and New York, Coward McCann, 1980.

*

Critical Studies: by Vincent Canby, in *New York Times*, 3 October 1971; Anthony Burgess, in *New York Times Book Review*, 10 September 1972; Francis Hope, in *The Observer* (London), 24 September 1972.

* * *

Although her film reviews earned her recognition first as a critic, Penelope Gilliatt's fiction has earned her recognition as a serious writer as well. Her emergent prose style is spartan, favoring terse dialogue and spare narrative, and the bulk of her work focuses on young people in their twenties and thirties who engage in an ambivalent struggle for the moral freedom offered by their pluralistic postwar world and the moral order that they perceive to exist in the world of the preceding generation. The locus of this moral order is, for Gilliatt, marriage (or a relationship which takes the form of marriage), and thus in nearly all of her works the struggle of her characters is epitomized by and manifested in their attempt to hold together a threatened and shifting relationship which is, ironically, of their own making.

In Gilliatt's early novels, *One by One* and *A State of Change*, the struggles of the central characters play against backdrops which are obvious, if not transparent, analogues for contemporary life. The plague in *One by One*, the salient symptom of which is, appropriately enough, terminal madness, obsesses the young veterinarian Joe Talbot with the absurdity and repugnance of life, and thus prompts in Polly, his wife, a futile struggle to rescue him from his destructive obsession by her assertion of love. Though she fails, her love endures her exile from London to Joe's self-righteous mother, who urges her to leave him because of exaggerated newspaper stories of his adolescent homosexuality, then Joe's rejection when she returns to London with their newborn child, and, finally, Joe's suicide. In *A State of Change* the analogue for the moral struggle shifts from the London plague to the struggle for political freedom in postwar Europe, as Kakia Grabowska, a Polish cartoonist living in London, quests for moral and intellectual freedom while at the same time striving to maintain that which denies it, her long-term relationship with the physician Harry Clopton. The relationship, which she refuses to define as marriage, is complicated by Harry's best friend, Don Clancy, a writer-producer, whom she rejected for Harry, but who is, in Harry's words, "free of the past instead of formed and punished by it." Though the three remain friends, the relationships become increasingly ambivalent as Kakia finds in Don the freedom that her relationship with Harry denies her and Don sees in her relationship with Harry an antidote for his own rootlessness. While both novels achieve moments of brilliance and genius, especially in the neat juxtaposition and balance of opposite characters, their frequent lapses into polemics mar both the style and the credibility of the characters.

Gilliatt's most recent novel, *The Cutting Edge*, along with the collections *Nobody's Business* and *Splendid Lives* represents her finest and most significant achievement. Here she perfects both the style and characterization of the earlier novels by overcoming the tendency to shift the narrative to polemics which use the characters as mouthpieces. Through her spare, crisp narrative, frequently punctuated by wry humor, she develops marvelously unique and independent characters who, in terse, often cryptic and witty dialogue, simply *suggest* subjects for debate or speculation. Resolutions, elusive even in the earlier novels, often remain a secret known only by the characters, and are further obfuscated by their cryptic remarks or an equally cryptic narrative comment. We wait through "Splendid Lives" for the radical, ruggedly independent, 92-year-old Bishop Hurlingham to identify his interest in the young Ridgeway as intellectual or physical, only to hear him remark, "One gathers the mind to a point and other things pass us by." In *The Cutting Edge* we follow the peripatetic searches of the flamboyant radical Peregrine Corbett, a barrister-turned-writer, and his brother Benedick, a musician, as each struggles to find the identity denied him by his father and the world his father represents. The struggles span the two decades of their lives between twenty and forty and are accompanied by a number of vicissitudes, including Peregrine's loss of repute as a barrister and his hardships as a writer, Benedick's failure first in his career then in his marriage, and the estrangement of the two brothers, caused by Peregrine's romantic relationship with Joanna, Benedick's ex-wife. At the end of the quest, where we see the three living together in Paris, each brother having changed his appearance to that of the other, the narrator, having anticipated our obvious question, remarks that Joanna loved "Both, in both cases, it seemed, as is the way of things."

Though Penelope Gilliatt's work may be of special interest to the academic reader, there is much in it to recommend it to the general reading public as well.

—Tom Nelson

GLANVILLE, Brian (Lester). British. Born in London, 24 September 1931. Educated at Newlands School; Charterhouse School, Surrey, 1945-49. Married Pamela de Boer in 1959; two sons and two daughters. Literary Adviser, Bodley Head, publishers, London, 1958-62. Since 1958, Sportswriter for *The Sunday Times*, London. Recipient: Berlin Film Festival Documentary Award, 1963; British Film Academy Documentary Award, 1967; Thomas Coward Memorial Award, 1969. Address: 160 Holland Park Avenue, London W.11, England.

PUBLICATIONS

Novels

The Reluctant Dictator. London, Werner Laurie, 1952.
Henry Sows the Wind. London, Secker and Warburg, 1954.
Along the Arno. London, Secker and Warburg, 1956; New York, Crowell, 1957.
The Bankrupts. London, Secker and Warburg, and New York, Doubleday, 1958.
After Rome, Africa. London, Secker and Warburg, 1959.
Diamond. London, Secker and Warburg, and New York, Farrar Straus, 1962.
The Rise of Gerry Logan. London, Secker and Warburg, 1963; New York, Delacorte Press, 1965.
A Second Home. London, Secker and Warburg, 1965; New York, Delacorte Press, 1966.
A Roman Marriage. London, Joseph, 1966; New York, Coward McCann, 1967.
The Artist Type. London, Cape, 1967; New York, Coward McCann, 1968.
The Olympian. New York, Coward McCann, and London, Secker and Warburg, 1969.
A Cry of Crickets. London, Secker and Warburg, and New York, Coward McCann, 1970.
The Financiers. London, Secker and Warburg, 1972; as *Money Is Love*, New York, Doubleday, 1972.
The Comic. London, Secker and Warburg, 1974; New York, Stein and Day, 1975.
The Dying of the Light. London, Secker and Warburg, 1976.
Never Look Back. London, Joseph, 1980.

Short Stories

A Bad Streak and Other Stories. London, Secker and Warburg, 1961.
The Director's Wife and Other Stories. London, Secker and Warburg, 1963.
Goalkeepers Are Crazy: A Collection of Football Stories. London, Secker and Warburg, 1964.
The King of Hackney Marshes and Other Stories. London, Secker and Warburg, 1965.
A Betting Man. New York, Coward McCann, 1969.
Penguin Modern Stories 10, with others. London, Penguin, 1972.
The Thing He Loves and Other Stories. London, Secker and Warburg, 1973.
A Bad Lot and Other Stories. London, Penguin, 1977.

Uncollected Short Stories

"The Child in the Basement," in *Punch* (London), December 1973.
"Up She Jolly Goes," broadcast on BBC 4, March 1974.
"Footballers Don't Cry," in *Winter's Tales 21*, edited by A.D. Maclean. London, Macmillan, 1975; New York, St. Martin's Press, 1976.
"Noblesse Oblige," in *Winter's Tales 24*, edited by A.D. Maclean. London, Macmillan, 1978; New York, St. Martin's Press, 1979.

Plays

Television documentaries: *European Centre Forward*, 1963; *Goal!*, 1967.

Other

Cliff Bastin Remembers, with Cliff Bastin. London, Ettrick Press, 1950.
Arsenal Football Club. London, Convoy, 1952.
Soccer Nemesis. London, Secker and Warburg, 1955.
World Cup, with Jerry Weinstein. London, Hale, 1958.
Over the Bar, with Jack Kelsey. London, Stanley Paul, 1958.
Soccer round the Globe. London, Abelard Schuman, 1959.
Know about Football. London, Blackie, 1963.
World Football Handbook (annual). London, Hodder and Stoughton, 1964; London, Mayflower, 1966-72; London, Queen Anne Press, 1974.
People in Sport. London, Secker and Warburg, 1967.
Soccer: A History of the Game, Its Players, and Its Strategy. New York, Crown, 1968; as *Soccer: A Panorama*, London, Eyre and Spottiswoode, 1969.
The Puffin Book of Football. London, Penguin, 1970.
Goalkeepers Are Different (juvenile). London, Hamish Hamilton, 1971; New York, Crown, 1972.
Brian Glanville's Book of World Football. London, Dragon, 1972.
The Sunday Times History of the World Cup. London, Times Newspapers, 1973; as *History of the Soccer World Cup*, New York, Macmillan, 1974; revised edition, as *The History of the World Cup*, London, Faber, 1980.
Soccer 76. London, Queen Anne Press, 1975.
Target Man (juvenile). London, Macdonald and Jane's, 1978.
The Puffin Book of Footballers. London, Penguin, 1978.
A Book of Soccer. New York, Oxford University Press, 1979.
Kevin Keegan (juvenile). London, Hamish Hamilton, 1981.

Editor, *Footballer's Who's Who*. London, Ettrick Press, 1951.
Editor, *The Footballer's Companion*. London, Eyre and Spottiswoode, 1962.

*

Critical Study: "Khaki and God the Father" in *A Human Idiom* by William Walsh, London, Chatto and Windus, 1965.

Brian Glanville comments:

(1972) There has, I suppose, been some tendency to categorise my work under three headings; that which deals with Italy (*Along the Arno*, *A Cry of Crickets*, *A Roman Marriage*), that which deals with Jewish life (*The Bankrupts*, *Diamond*), and that which deals with professional football (*The Rise of Gerry Logan* and many of the short stories). I think I might accept the categorisation of the two Jewish novels, but it scarcely places *The Olympian*, which uses an athlete as its figure, athletics as its theme, or rather as its metaphor; or *A Second Home*, which is narrated in the first person by a Jewish actress—and has been bracketed with *A Roman Marriage*, itself narrated by a young girl. Again, one can, and does, use similar material for widely different purposes.

A large disenchantment with the conventional novel and its possibilities has, I think, led one gradually away from it, to more experimental methods. Like many novelists of serious intentions, one lives uneasily from one novel to the elusive next, always questioning and trying to establish the validity of the form.

* * *

Brian Glanville has written of his novels that "large disenchantment with the conventional novel...has, I think, led one gradually away from it, to more experimental methods." Each novel from this prolific writer has demonstrated that impatience; his need to break away from the manners of the traditional novel and from its central narrative line to a more fluid exposition of his thought has meant that the action frequently unfolds through his characterisation instead of through the plot. In *A Roman Marriage* the story is told by the young English girl who has allowed herself to be trapped into a futile, claustrophobic marriage to a handsome young Italian; and through her outraged consciousness we experience, too, the suffocation of her husband's clinging, over-protective mother as the tentacles of family life cut the girl off from reality and draw her in to nightmare. Similarly the tensions and cabalistic integrity of the family are strikingly unfolded in his Jewish novels such as *The Bankrupts*, *Diamond*, and *A Second Home*.

A further strength of the novels in this latter group is Glanville's sure ear for the cadences of everyday speech. The Jewish patois is never forced to gain its effect through comic music hall over-indulgence but is allowed to expose itself through Glanville's feeling for the poetic possibilities of the spoken language. Although the unforced ease of his dialogue gives it a down-to-earth integrity, Glanville never allows it to become mundane or demeaning, and the simplicity of effect is a structural strength of all his writing.

As a commentator on professional sport Glanville has also written several novels about the stamina and passion that make up the modern athlete. In *The Olympian* a young miler, Ike Low, is torn between his passion for his wife Jill and the almost sexual release that he finds in winning races. Against their uneasy relationship stands the ambiguous figure of Sam Dee, Ike's trainer, who acts as both agent provocateur and chorus over their slowly disintegrating marriage. The narrative is broken up with journalese and taut, film-like dialogue as the drama of Ike's racing career draws to an unexpected climax. *The Dying of the Light* is perhaps Glanville's most profound and satisfying sporting novel to date. Although it is described as "a football novel," it is in effect a parable of contemporary life. Len Rawlings, a footballing hero in the post-war years, slumps gradually to the bottom of the ladder in a world where the aged and the losers are quickly forgotten. In desperation he turns to petty crime but finds salvation in the love of his daughter, so unlike him in character, but the only one to understand the terrifying loneliness of his personal predicament. As in all Glanville's novels, the moralising is made manifest by its absence—Rawlings may have broken the law but it is the law of the jungle that is at fault, the "sporting" code that allows a talented man to be driven to despair through no fault of his own.

Contemporary obsessions of another kind are examined in *Never Look Back*, a novel that explores the world of rock and roll bands and the attitudes of its denizens: the stars, their managers and hangers-on, the agents and the crooks. The documentary detail is impressive but Glanville's mastery of language and skillful handling of dialogue convey subtle shifts of feeling, and they also constantly change his and the reader's focus on this kaleidoscopic world. Above all, Brian Glanville shows that he is one of the few contemporary novelists capable of tackling and expressing the values, or lack of them, in our rapidly changing society.

—Trevor Royle

GLOAG, Julian. British. Born in London, 2 July 1930; son of the writer John Gloag. Educated at Rugby School; Magdalene College, Cambridge. Served in the British Army. Married Danielle Haase-Dubosc in 1968; two children. Fellow, Royal Society of Literature, 1970. Address: c/o M. Lapautre, 6 rue Jean Carriès, 75007 Paris, France.

PUBLICATIONS

Novels

Our Mother's House. New York, Simon and Schuster, and London, Secker and Warburg, 1963.
A Sentence of Life. New York, Simon and Schuster, and London, Secker and Warburg, 1966.
Maundy. New York, Simon and Schuster, and London, Secker and Warburg, 1969.
A Woman of Character. New York, Random House, and London, Weidenfeld and Nicolson, 1973.
Sleeping Dogs. London, Secker and Warburg, and New York, Dutton, 1980.
Lost and Found. New York, Linden Press, 1981.

Other

Editor, *The American Nation: A Short History of the United States*, by John Gloag. London, Cassell, 1954.

* * *

Julian Gloag is a writer of diverse talents: he can bring the reader into close contact with a variety of characters through the precise creation of patterns of speech and thought; he has a wit that shows itself not only verbally—"I been livin' in a foolish paradise"—but in the choice of extraordinary incident and the use of ironic juxtaposition; he can handle interweaving threads of narrative skilfully, giving each one room to tug at our moral and emotional sympathies. He keeps us alert and busy, and as a result most of his books are extremely readable.

His first novel, *Our Mother's House*, is in many ways his most successful, having a form of its own, something that the later novels fail to achieve. The book is shaped and dominated by the contrast between the delicate morbidity of its opening chapters, in which a family of children bury their mother's body secretly in the garden, and the subsequent cheerful, only gradually suspicious, homecoming of their long absent father. The book's main impact is in line with this contrast. We are made to see the children as both peculiar and normal, their father as repellent yet, on his own terms, justified. We ourselves are manoeuvred into an ambiguous position by the novel's tone: it encourages us to sympathize yet establishes us as adult and therefore hostile.

A Sentence of Life is given external shape and purpose by its association with the traditional forms of murder enquiry and trial, but the important movement of the book is introspective and fluid as the suspect pursues private definitions of guilt by remembering and reinterpreting his past. Looked at coolly, the lines of the book don't converge as neatly as its final pages, which use the warmth of selected memories to promote an optimistic conclusion, suggest. The novel's discussion of responsibility and its imaginative range are nevertheless good. Again the reader is not permitted to sympathise or dislike too easily and judgment remains uncertain.

Maundy is uncertain in a different way. Maundy is a smooth young banker who goes off the rails: whether this is due to psychological stress or actual devils is one of the things we are left to decide for ourselves. Unfortunately no way of looking at the book makes sense of it. Whereas Gloag's other books present conflicting accounts of reality, this one presents a chaos heavy with sex and violence and lumpy with significance. It's a tale of sound and fury that's not much fun to read.

With *A Woman of Character* Gloag returns to familiar ground. A corpse gets things off to a brisk start and financial negotiations, detective elements and the bereaved fiancée's search for consolation keep up the pace. The book is again concerned with the distribution of sympathy and guilt; it has a sense of some of the ways women feel and a warming portrayal of the rich life. Gloag's work remains interesting, intelligent, and inventive but one cannot see it as important.

—Mary Conroy

GODDEN, (Margaret) Rumer. British. Born in Sussex, 10 December 1907. Educated privately and at Moira House, Eastbourne, Sussex. Married 1) Laurence Sinclair Foster in 1934, two daughters; 2) James Lesley Haynes Dixon in 1949 (died, 1973). Former director of a children's ballet school, Calcutta. Recipient: Whitbread Award, for children's book, 1973. Agent: Curtis Brown Ltd., 1 Craven Hill, London W2 3EP, England. Address: The Small House, Tundergarth, Lockerbie, Dumfriesshire DG11 2PU, Scotland.

PUBLICATIONS

Novels

Chinese Puzzle. London, Davies, 1936.
The Lady and the Unicorn. London, Davies, 1937.
Black Narcissus. London, Davies, and Boston, Little Brown, 1939.
Gypsy, Gypsy. London, Davies, and Boston, Little Brown, 1940.
Breakfast with the Nikolides. London, Davies, and Boston, Little Brown, 1942.
A Fugue in Time. London, Joseph, 1945; as *Take Three Tenses: A Fugue in Time*, Boston, Little Brown, 1945.
The River. London, Joseph, and Boston, Little Brown, 1946.
A Candle for St. Jude. London, Joseph, and New York, Viking Press, 1948.
A Breath of Air. London, Joseph, 1950; New York, Viking Press, 1951.
Kingfishers Catch Fire. London, Macmillan, and New York, Viking Press, 1953.
An Episode of Sparrows. New York, Viking Press, 1955; London, Macmillan, 1956.
The Greengage Summer. London, Macmillan, and New York, Viking Press, 1958.
China Court: The Hours of a Country House. London, Macmillan, and New York, Viking Press, 1961.
The Battle of the Villa Fiorita. London, Macmillan, and New York, Viking Press, 1963.
In This House of Brede. London, Macmillan, and New York, Viking Press, 1969.
The Peacock Spring. London, Macmillan, 1975; New York, Viking Press, 1976.
Five for Sorrow, Ten for Joy. London, Macmillan, and New York, Viking Press, 1979.

Short Stories

Mooltiki and Other Stories and Poems of India. London, Macmillan, and New York, Viking Press, 1957.
Swans and Turtles: Stories. London, Macmillan, 1968; as *Gone: A Thread of Stories*, New York, Viking Press, 1968.

Plays

Screenplays: *The River*, with Jean Renoir, 1951; *Innocent Sinners*, with Neil Patterson, 1958.

Verse (juvenile)

In Noah's Ark. London, Joseph, and New York, Viking Press, 1949.
St. Jerome and the Lion. London, Macmillan, and New York, Viking Press, 1961.

Other

Rungli-Rungliot (Thus Far and No Further). London, Davies, 1943; as *Rungli-Rungliot Means in Paharia, Thus Far and No Further*, Boston, Little Brown, 1946; as *Thus Far and No Further*, London, Macmillan, 1961.
Bengal Journey: A Story of the Part Played by Women in the Province 1939-1945. London, Longman, 1945.
The Doll's House (juvenile). London, Joseph, 1947; New York, Viking Press, 1948.
The Mousewife (juvenile). London, Macmillan, and New York, Viking Press, 1951.
Impunity Jane: The Story of a Pocket Doll (juvenile). New York, Viking Press, 1954; London, Macmillan, 1955.
Hans Christian Andersen: A Great Life in Brief. London, Hutchinson, and New York, Knopf, 1955.
The Fairy Doll (juvenile). London, Macmillan,and New York, Viking Press, 1956.
Mouse House (juvenile). New York, Viking Press, 1957; London, Macmillan, 1958.
The Story of Holly and Ivy (juvenile). London, Macmillan, and New York, Viking Press, 1958.
Candy Floss (juvenile). London, Macmillan, and New York, Viking Press, 1960.
Miss Happiness and Miss Flower (juvenile). London, Macmillan, and New York, Viking Press, 1961.
Little Plum (juvenile). London, Macmillan, and New York, Viking Press, 1963.
Home Is the Sailor (juvenile). London, Macmillan, and New York, Viking Press, 1964.
Two under the Indian Sun (autobiography), with Jon Godden. London, Macmillan, and New York, Knopf, 1966.
The Kitchen Madonna (juvenile). London, Macmillan, and New York, Viking Press, 1967.
Operation Sippacik (juvenile). London, Macmillan, and New York, Viking Press, 1969.
The Tale of the Tales: The Beatrix Potter Ballet. London, Warne, 1971.
Shiva's Pigeons: An Experience of India, with Jon Godden. London, Chatto and Windus, and New York, Viking Press, 1972.
The Old Woman Who Lived in a Vinegar Bottle (juvenile). London, Macmillan, and New York, Viking Press, 1972.
The Diddakoi (juvenile). London, Macmillan, and New York, Viking Press, 1972.
Mr. McFadden's Hallowe'en (juvenile). London, Macmillan, and New York, Viking Press, 1975.
The Rocking Horse Secret (juvenile). London, Macmillan, 1977; New York, Viking Press, 1978.
The Butterfly Lions: The Story of the Pekingese in History, Legend, and Art. London, Macmillan, 1977; New York, Viking Press, 1978.
A Kindle of Kittens (juvenile). London, Macmillan, 1978; New York, Viking Press, 1979.
Gulbadan: Portrait of a Rose Princess at the Mughal Court. London, Macmillan, 1980; New York, Viking Press, 1981.
The Dragon of Og (juvenile). London, Macmillan, 1981.

Editor, *Round the Day, Round the Year, The World Around: Poetry Programmes for Classroom or Library*. London, Macmillan, 6 vols., 1966-67.
Editor, *A Letter to the World: Poems for Young Readers*, by Emily Dickinson. London, Bodley Head, 1968; New York, Macmillan, 1969.
Editor, *Mrs. Manders' Cookbook*, by Olga Manders. London, Macmillan, and New York, Viking Press, 1968.
Editor, *The Raphael Bible*. London, Macmillan, and New York, Viking Press, 1970.

Translator, *Prayers from the Ark* (verse), by Carmen de Gasztold. New York, Viking Press, 1962; London, Macmillan, 1963.
Translator, *The Creatures' Choir* (verse), by Carmen de Gasztold. New York, Viking Press, 1965; as *The Beasts' Choir*, London, Macmillan, 1967.

*

Critical Studies: by Marshall A. Best, in *Book-of-the-Month Club News* (New York), 1969; *Rumer Godden* by Hassell A. Simpson, New York, Twayne, 1973.

* * *

Rumer Godden inherited a love of language from her philologist father. In whatever vein of fiction she writes—and there have been several—her work is informed with a loving sense of the color and shape and rhythm of the words she chooses. It is not surprising that she is also a poet and has published two narratives in verse: *In Noah's Ark* and *St. Jerome and the Lion*.

The traditional novel of individual lives, however, is her natural medium. She thinks as a novelist. When she came to collect some of her short stories (*Swans and Turtles*), she chose to string them together as a "thread," with notes to tell how they had arisen from remembered incidents in her own life. In this sense her novels, too, can be seen to reflect her autobiography.

Three themes, which sometimes interweave, have predominated in the novels and stories: the lives of foreigners in an exotic land (she grew up in India and has often returned there); the religious life (paralleling her own conversion to Roman Catholicism); and the secret lives and thoughts of children viewing their elders through their own fresh eyes. From the latter grows a fourth theme, of imaginative and playful fantasy, which is particularly evident in her many books for children but also occurs in such a novel as *A Breath of Air*, her modern version of *The Tempest*.

In evaluating her novels, one is inclined to give most critical weight, in the Indian group, to *Breakfast with the Nikolides*, a poignantly perceptive study of inter-racial relations, and the beautiful short novel, *The River*, about a childhood tragedy in the mysterious aura of Indian tradition (which she helped Jean Renoir to make into an exceptional motion picture). Experimentally, *China Court*, evoking an English household through several generations with its sense of past and present running concurrently, is perhaps the most interesting. She had earlier tried a similar experiment, less successfully, in *A Fugue in Time*, set in wartime London. Among the books with a religious theme, *In This House of Brede* has the peculiar fascination of a special way of life (a contemporary English Catholic nunnery) shown in intimate detail. She completed it in Lamb House at Rye, the long-time home of Henry James where she lived for some years by invitation of its owners, the British National Trust. She now lives in Scotland.

The public at large has most loved *Black Narcissus*, about an Anglican sisterhood in India, written before her conversion; *An Episode of Sparrows*, a tender story of street-urchins in London; and *The Greengage Summer*, a mystery involving a family of English children on their own in a French hotel. All three became successful motion pictures.

She writes her adult novels at long intervals, with time for reflection while children's books and lesser writings continue. More recently, *The Peacock Spring* was a shorter work of young love between an English girl and a native boy in India. Her latest novel, *Five for Sorrow, Ten for Joy*, came ten years after *Brede*. It renewed the theme of devoted convent life, but in another country, France, and with something quite unexpected added: before the convent came life in a Paris brothel, a murder that might appear as a crime of passion, and years of penitence in a women's prison. In terms of rather ordinary humans, though often in unusual situations, Rumer Godden wins sympathy by dealing thoughtfully and hopefully with some persistent verities.

—Marshall A. Best

GODFREY, Dave. Canadian. Born in Winnipeg, Manitoba, 9 August 1938. Educated at Harvard University, Cambridge, Massachusetts, 1957; University of Toronto, 1957-58; University of Iowa, Iowa City, 1958-60, 1963, 1965-66, B.A. 1960, Ph.D. 1966; Stanford University, California, 1960-61, M.A. 1963; University of Chicago, 1965. Married Ellen Swartz in 1963; three children. Acting Head of the English Department, Adisadel College, Cape Coast, Ghana, 1963-65; Assistant Professor of English, Trinity College, University of Toronto, 1966-71. Co-Founder, House of Anansi, publishers, Toronto, 1967-69; Co-Founder, New Press, Toronto. Recipient: President's Medal, University of Western Ontario, 1965; Canada Council Award, 1969; Governor-General's Award, 1971. Address: Maple Lane Farm, R.R. 1, Erin, Ontario NOB 1TO, Canada.

PUBLICATIONS

Novel

The New Ancestors. Toronto, New Press, 1970.

Short Stories

Death Goes Better with Coca-Cola. Toronto, Anansi, 1967.
Dark Must Yield. Erin, Ontario, Press Porcépic, 1978.

Other

I Ching Kanada. Erin, Ontario, Press Porcépic, 1976.

Editor, with Bill McWhinney, *Man Deserves Man*. Toronto, Ryerson Press, 1967.
Editor, *Gordon to Watkins to You*. Toronto, New Press, 1970.
Editor, with others, *Read Canadian: A Book about Canadian Books*. Toronto, Lorimer, 1972.
Editor, with Douglas Parkhill, *Gutenberg Two*. Toronto, Press Porcépic, 1979.

*

Critical Studies: "Dave Godfrey" by Dorah Hood, in *Oxford Companion to Canadian Literature*, Toronto, Oxford University Press, 1967; by Margaret Laurence, in *Ellipse Magazine* (Quebec), Fall 1970, and in *The Mysterious East* (Fredericton, New Brunswick), December 1970; by Phyllis Grosskurth, in *Canadian Forum* (Toronto), April 1971; *Sex and Violence in the Canadian Novel*, Toronto, McClelland and Stewart, 1977.

Dave Godfrey comments:

I am most interested in that portion of literature where myth meets social realities; literary dogma concerning the purity of fantasy or of realism does not interest me. The Canadian environment has influenced me greatly although I write mainly about people from cultures other than my own. A good part of my twenties was spent travelling about the U.S. and Africa. I strive for great complexity in my writing because that is how I find life; I do not believe the writer has a duty to simplify or interpret life for his readers; his major tasks are to be as intelligent as possible and to take flights of imagination into bodies, minds, and situations other than his own.

* * *

Although Dave Godfrey's novel, *The New Ancestors*, is set in West Africa, and most of his short stories are set in Canada, similar themes appear in both. One of his main themes is expressed with precision and irony in the title of his collection *Death Goes Better with Coca-Cola*. The influence of one culture on another, in what can be termed the colonizing process, ends by destroying the original fabric of the taken-over society. In his stories, this theme often appears in relation to American influence in Canada, whereas in the novel it is seen as the destructive effect of the great powers on African countries, even after independence.

Godfrey's writing is in no sense narrowly or exclusively political. His social analyses are always done through individual character portrayals, and his ability to create complex and vivid characters is quite exceptional. Michael Burdener, the maverick Englishman in *The New Ancestors*, his African wife Ama, the brave and misguided drummer Gamaliel who has his life torn away in his attempt to believe in the necessary dream of a new and perfect Africa—all these are splendidly realized, as the novel assumes the narrative voice of one after another.

Godfrey's second recurring theme is the linkage of past and future, the ways in which archetypal patterns appear in human life and mythology. Our ancestors are reborn, with variations, in us. We, too, are in the process of becoming legendary; we are the "new ancestors" of the novel's title. This theme takes Godfrey deeply into the realm of myth, and some of his writing is an attempt to express our vital mythology in contemporary terms. In his finest story, "The Hard-Headed Collector," Godfrey gives shape to Canadian myth in the form of such men as Piet Catogas, André Mineur, Scrop Calla, and Looky McLaww, who represent the many races and cultures which make up the country.

In *The New Ancestors* Lost Coast is an imaginary West African country with a strong resemblance to Nkrumah's Ghana. It is a land of intrigue, suspicion, bribery, and brutality beneath the drums and the laughter. It is also the dark continent of the mind, where the eternal stuggles take place between fathers and sons, matriarchs and their children, the living and the dead but ever-present ancestors, man and his gods, that area of the mind in which we are all forever seeking to re-film in fantasy our own pasts.

Radical in content and frequently in form as well, Godfrey's writing is never propagandist. He is involved with the social scene; he is concerned about man's survival on this planet. His writing, at the same time, is very cool and incisive, moving and entertaining. It is to be hoped that his work will soon become available to a wider readership, as he is undoubtedly the most talented young prose writer in Anglophone Canada, and one of the most interesting anywhere.

—Margaret Laurence

GODWIN, Gail (Kathleen). American. Born in Birmingham, Alabama, 18 June 1937. Educated at Peace Junior College, Raleigh, North Carolina, 1955-57; University of North Carolina, Chapel Hill, 1957-59, B.A. in journalism 1959; University of Iowa, Iowa City, 1967-71, M.A. 1968, Ph.D. in English 1971. Reporter, Miami *Herald*, 1959-60; consultant, U.S. Travel Service, United States Embassy, London, 1962-65; researcher, *Saturday Evening Post*, New York, 1966; Instructor in English, 1967-70, and lecturer at the Writers Workshop, 1972-73, University of Iowa; Instructor and Fellow, Center for Advanced Studies, University of Illinois, Urbana, 1971-72; American Specialist, United States Information Service, Brazil, 1976; lecturer, Vassar College, Poughkeepsie, New York, 1977, and Columbia University, New York, 1978. Recipient: National Endowment for the Arts grant, 1974, and Fellowship, for libretto, 1978; Guggenheim Fellowship, 1975; St. Lawrence Award, 1976; American Academy Award, 1981. Agent: John W. Hawkins, Paul R. Reynolds Inc., 12 East 41st Street, New York, New York 10017, U.S.A.

PUBLICATIONS

Novels

The Perfectionists. New York, Harper, 1970; London, Cape, 1971.
Glass People. New York, Knopf, 1972.
The Odd Woman. New York, Knopf, 1974; London, Cape, 1975.
Violet Clay. New York, Knopf, and London, Gollancz, 1978.

Short Stories

Dream Children. New York, Knopf, 1976; London, Gollancz, 1977.

Uncollected Short Stories

"A Cultural Exchange," in *Atlantic* (Boston), February 1978.
"Fate of Fleeing Maidens," in *Mademoiselle* (New York), May 1978.
"A Father's Pleasures," in *Cosmopolitan* (New York), January 1979.
"The Unlikely Family," in *Redbook* (New York), August 1979.
"Amanuensis: A Tale of the Creative Life," in *Prize Stories 1980: The O. Henry Awards*, edited by William Abrahams. New York, Doubleday, 1980.

Plays

The Last Lover, music by Robert Starer (produced Katonah, New York, 1975).
Journals of a Songmaker, music by Robert Starer (produced Philadelphia, 1976).
Apollonia, music by Robert Starer (produced Minneapolis, 1979).

Recording: *Anna Margarita's Will* (song cycle), music by Robert Starer, C.R.I., 1980.

*

Critical Studies: "*The Odd Woman*: Literature and the Retreat from Life" by Susan E. Lorsch, in *Critique* (Atlanta), xx, 2, 1978; "Reaching Out: Sensitivity and Order," in *Recent American Fiction by Women* by Anne Z. Mickelson, Metuchen, New Jersey, Scarecrow Press, 1979.

Gail Godwin comments:

Since I began writing fiction I have been most interested in creating characters who operate at a high level of intelligence and feeling as they go about trying to make sense of the world in which they find themselves, and as they make decisions about how to live their lives.

* * *

Gail Godwin is a serious, probing novelist. Her concern in all four of her novels is what it is that will make a contemporary woman happy and content. How much dependence, independence, or merging? The answer, of course, will vary from woman to woman. But the most satisfying novel will be the one that attempts to find the answer for the most complex, demanding woman. It is in the third of her four novels, *The Odd Woman*, that Godwin has created the woman of the most heightened consciousness and least susceptibility to easy answers.

The Odd Woman is Godwin's best novel. It is not only a comprehensive, in-depth portrayal of a contemporary woman but a suspenseful, well-structured novel, with an impressive cast of minor characters, all of whom have a relevant thematic function. Jane Clifford is a woman whose mind is seldom at rest. She is even an insomniac. Her mind monitors and questions everything. No nuance escapes her. She wonders about all her activities, all her feelings. This, however, does not make her grotesque; she is attractive and pleasant, modest and considerate.

Jane is a college English instructor, trying to put together a career out of a series of one-year appointments. She does her work conscientiously, and does not leave herself much opportunity for dalliance. She does, however, initiate an affair with an older man, a married professor of art history at a college four hours off. Their 14 trysts over a period of two years have been momentous events in Jane's lonely scholar's life, for Gabriel is attractive, pleasant, considerate, loving. But he is also very much the academic—cautious and restrained and given to equivocation. Jane tries to assess the depth of his feeling for her and her feeling for him. Does she really love him, or is she in love with the *idea* of loving him? Could he absorb the change that really committing himself to her would involve?

Jane's notion of love is an exalted one. She aspires to the kind of love that Marian Evans (George Eliot) and George Henry Lewes had for each other, a love that for years provided both partners sustenance and delight. Jane wonders whether in reality such love is possible; if it is not, she would be more sensible and stop wanting the impossible for herself. That is exactly what her mother has done. After being widowed quite young, Jane's mother married pragmatically. Jane's arch-feminist friend, Gerda, has only contempt for women who enter such marriages, who willingly foreclose on all possibilities for themselves simply for the sake of having a man. Gerda wants Jane to accept her belief that ultimately men are destructive to the woman who would preserve her own identity and her dignity; men use, betray, discard. Jane, then, aware of the extremities, hopes Gabriel will rise to her highest expectations. When she is forced to recognize that he will not, courageously she leaves him. That means, however, that she must retreat back into loneliness and fantasy.

At the very end of *The Odd Woman*, we are told of this moment of Jane's insomniac awareness: "From the little concrete house behind came the barely audible tinkle of a soul at the piano, trying to organize the loneliness and the weather and the long night into something of abiding shape and beauty." That is what Jane will struggle to do with her life. The protagonist of *Violet Clay* also hopes to make something abiding out of the sparse materials of her life. Because she is an artist, Violet has more of an opportunity than Jane; if she cannot succeed in love, she still can succeed as an artist. She, though, must face the question whether she really has it in her to make first-rate art. Is she a truly committed artist, or just a more skilled and clever dilettante?

At the end of her novel, Violet is not in retreat, as Jane is. She has proved herself with at least one outstanding painting. What lies ahead for Violet is not clear, but out of her anguish and struggle and the unfavorable omens something worthwhile has been produced. And also she has achieved her success despite a precursor's shadow. Ambrose Clay, her youngish uncle, had aspired to be a novelist of consequence. When he abandons his hopes and commits suicide, he leaves behind a note that says, "Violet, honey, I'm sorry, there's nothing left."

For a while, Violet, too, after giving herself totally to art could find nothing, nothing within her, no source of enduring art. Ambrose's death, ironically, gave her the opportunity and means with which to test herself. She can work in the Adirondack cabin where he worked—and failed. She accepts the challenge, and is plunged into despair. Like Ambrose, she is unable to find within her the inspiration for an important work. She lies down, gun in hand, where Ambrose did, feeling her way into his suicide; it is the book's finest scene. She is not yet at the point Ambrose was. She gets up, and through chance there enters into her life a very unusual woman—earthy, totally independent, goddess-like in her special beauty. This woman has a profound affect upon Violet's feelings, and becomes the inspiration for the painting that lets Violet know that as an artist she does have a unique sensibility and vision. *Violet Clay* and *The Odd Woman* are significant achievements. They are sensitive, sophisticated novels of character. While the pace of both books is rather slow, they both are enriched by the frequent and extensive backward looks that interrupt the unfolding of the plots.

The protagonists of Godwin's last two novels are heroic. The young women of her earlier two, Dane of *The Perfectionists* and Francesca of *Glass People*, are not. They are women who surrender themselves to be shaped by their husbands. Although written by a feminist, neither novel is angry or bitter in tone; both women willingly have submitted to be molded. Indeed in *Glass People*, Francesca leaves her husband and makes an attempt at being independent and developing her own identity, but being free is too painful and she returns to a life in which she can be little more than her husband's most-prized possession.

Dane's husband, unlike Francesca's, wants his young wife fully merged into his own life. That two souls can be merged into "our universe" is the romantic fantasy of Dr. Empson, the deluded and fatuous philosopher-psychiatrist. Young, innocent, and impressed, Dane has allowed herself to be swept into the fantasy. But she comes to see through Empson and rejects the closeness and mutual dependence he has envisioned for them. She wants an identity of her own, and will soon break away, stronger, wiser, and knowing more about herself than her guru husband knows about himself.

—Paul Marx

GOLD, Herbert. American. Born in Cleveland, Ohio, 9 March 1924. Educated at Columbia University, New York, B.A. 1946, M.A. 1948; the Sorbonne, Paris (Fulbright Scholar), 1949-51. Served in the United States Army, 1943-46. Married 1) Edith Zubrin in 1948 (divorced, 1956); 2) Melissa Dilworth, 1968; five children. Lecturer in Philosophy and Literature, Western Reserve University, Cleveland, 1951-53; Lecturer in English, Wayne State University, Detroit, 1954-56. Visiting Professor, Cornell University, Ithaca, New York, 1958, University of California, Berkeley, 1963, Harvard University, Cambridge, Massachusetts, 1964, and Stanford University, California, 1967. Recipient: Inter-American Cultural grant, to Haiti, 1950; *Hudson Review* Fellowship, 1956; Guggenheim Fellowship, 1957; American Academy grant, 1958; Longview Foundation Award, 1959; Ford Fellowship, for drama, 1960. Address: 1051-A Broadway, San Francisco, California 94133, U.S.A.

PUBLICATIONS

Novels

Birth of a Hero. New York, Viking Press, 1951.
The Prospect Before Us. Cleveland, World, 1954; as *Room Clerk*, New York, New American Library, 1955.

The Man Who Was Not with It. Boston, Little Brown, 1956; London, Secker and Warburg, 1965.
The Optimist. Boston, Little Brown, 1959.
Therefore Be Bold. New York, Dial Press, 1960; London, Deutsch, 1962.
Salt. New York, Dial Press, 1963; London, Secker and Warburg, 1964.
Fathers: A Novel in the Form of a Memoir. New York, Random House, and London, Secker and Warburg, 1967.
The Great American Jackpot. New York, Random House, 1970; London, Weidenfeld and Nicolson, 1971.
Swiftie the Magician. New York, McGraw Hill, 1974; London, Hutchinson, 1975.
Waiting for Cordelia. New York, Arbor House, 1977; London, Hutchinson, 1978.
Slave Trade. New York, Arbor House, 1979.
He/She. New York, Arbor House, 1980.
Family: A Novel in the Form of a Memoir. New York, Arbor House, 1981.

Short Stories

15 x 3, with R.V. Cassill and James B. Hall. New York, New Directions, 1957.
Love and Like. New York, Dial Press, 1960; London, Deutsch, 1961.
The Magic Will: Stories and Essays of a Decade. New York, Random House, 1971.

Uncollected Short Stories

"The Smallest Part," in *Prize Stories 1979: The O. Henry Awards*, edited by William Abrahams. New York, Doubleday, 1979.
"The Urban Cowboy and the Stranger," in *Atlantic* (Boston), May 1980.

Other

The Age of Happy Problems (essays). New York, Dial Press, 1962.
Biafra Goodbye. San Francisco, Twowindows Press, 1970.
My Last Two Thousand Years (autobiography). New York, Random House, 1972; London, Hutchinson, 1973.
The Young Prince and the Magic Cone (juvenile). New York, Doubleday, 1973.
A Walk on the West Side: California on the Brink (stories and essays). New York, Arbor House, 1981.

Editor, *Fiction of the Fifties: A Decade of American Writing.* New York, Doubleday, 1959.
Editor, with David L. Stevenson, *Stories of Modern America.* New York, St. Martin's Press, 1961; revised edition, 1963.
Editor, *First Person Singular: Essays for the Sixties.* New York, Dial Press, 1963.

*

Herbert Gold comments:

Subjects: Power, money, sex and love, intention in America.
Themes: The same.
Moral: Coming next time.

* * *

In Herbert Gold's introduction to *Fiction of the Fifties*, he makes a distinction between fiction which *avows* and fiction which *controls.* The fiction which avows is a rather faithful transcription of the immediate and personal experience of the writer; such fiction makes use of the writer's own experience of his past and the section of social life where that experience took place. The other sort of fiction makes an attempt to present the experiences of persons who indeed are not the writer; these experiences are given clarity by an effort of the imagination which takes the writer outside himself and immerses him in circumstances that are not his own. All this is done by the exercise of *control.*

These interesting categories can be used to classify Gold's own fiction. A great deal of that fiction falls into the first category, that of avowal, as one can see from an inspection of his autobiographical *My Last Two Thousand Years.* This book is a narrative of Gold's own life, a life that finds its way into several of his novels. It was a life in which, as the son of a Jewish immigrant who settled in Cleveland, Gold experienced a difficult youth, in the shadow of a strong father who had found a place for himself in an alien society. Gold's narrative relates his own struggles to detach himself from his father's ambitions for his son, and to achieve his own goals, in New York and elsewhere, as student, critic, and novelist. All this was a process of self-discovery that demanded acts of will and personal heroism. This self-discovery, as Gold relates it, also involved a succession of painful relationships: marriage, parenthood, divorce, and a second marriage, with various temporary relationships along the way.

These are all matters that various other novelists would regard as private. So are they for Gold. But they are also the stuff of much of his fiction. These are the novels which *avow* (or assert) the essentials of the writer's own life. Such fiction contrasts with other novels in which Gold borrows and reshapes elements of other lives; it is in these latter novels that Gold *controls* the experiences other persons and also depicts social patterns which the writer does not know directly and immediately.

Gold's frequent adherence to the dictum of Sir Philip Sidney's muse—"Fool...look in thy heart and write"—is illustrated by an excellent novel, *Fathers*, which is subtitled "A Novel in the Form of a Memoir." The novel tells of the relation between an immigrant father and his son; it is a vivid recollection of matters that Gold also puts down in *My Last Two Thousand Years. Fathers* offers homage to a courageous father and to the equally courageous son who chooses to turn aside from his father. The novel offers a convincing texture of loyalty and enmity. The same section of Gold's life appears in *Therefore Be Bold* which, however, centers attention on "Daniel Berman's" adolescent years in Cleveland: his encounters with poetry and sex and his bitter first experience of anti-Semitism.

Other novels, one can judge, are transcriptions of Gold's own experience of self-assertion and self-discovery in the New York literary world. Thus, *Swiftie the Magician* displays Gold's creative imagination moving onwards from his youth and assessing a man's attempts to find his own way through the jungles of professional and emotional life that surround a person in the second half of the 20th century. The novel relates the involvement of a writer with three women: an East Coast innocent, a West Coast "experienced" young woman, and the hard-bitten Swiftie, a "magician" who knows what the score is in a rough world. *Salt* gives the reader a more complex version of such pursuits of identity. Two men—one a complacent Wasp and the other once more an alter ego for Gold—move from woman to woman, the Wasp learning little and the young Jew from Cleveland a great deal.

Such are the novels in which Gold reworks the stuff of his own life. But there are other novels in which Gold is exercising *control*—is, in more conventional literary language, inventing persons not himself and following the courses of their experiences. *Birth of a Hero* follows the attempts of a middle-aged business man, Reuben Flair, a faceless cypher, to become a man fully aware of what he has done, in marriage and beyond marriage. As in other novels by Gold, the outlines of Reuben's achievement are cloudy, but a sense of travel and change is conveyed. In *The Prospect Before Us* Gold moves still farther afield. In this novel the chief person is Harry Bowers, manager of a run-down motel in Cleveland. A level of life—low, raunchy, and cruel, and quite different from the world of the novels of avowal—is presented in colors that convince. And there is no touch of the frequent father-son situation; Harry Bowers allows a black woman to rent a room in his motel and is hounded for what he has done. *The Man Who Was Not With It* allows us to inhabit the awareness of a carnival worker. Here, however, there is an approach to the themes of the novels of avowal. Bud, the carnie, is saddled with two fathers: one, his real one in Pittsburgh, and the other a carnival barker. The barker delivers Bud from his drug habit (and falls foul of it himself) and hovers like a threatening cloud over the early weeks of Bud's marriage: a relation that links this novel with other work of Gold. In *The Great American Jackpot* the persona is also not Gold's own (the hero is a Berkeley student of the 1960's), but the student's preoccupations are not unfamiliar. Al Dooley loves and hates his teacher, a black sociologist; Dooley tries to find out who he is in the arms of two girls; and, finally, he asserts his identity by breaking out: in this instance, by robbing a bank and experiencing the farce of American justice. Dooley reappears in *Waiting for Cordelia* where he is doing a thesis on prostitution in the San Francisco area. A madam (Cordelia) and Marietta, a woman eager to become a reforming mayor of San Francisco, enrich Dooley's research. In the course of writing his study, Dooley faces Gold's usual questions about the nature of love and the sadness and the loneliness which hamper its realization. Similar preoccupations mark the early novel, *The Optimist*, in which Burr Fuller makes his way through a failed marriage and achieves some mastery of the mysteries of love and career.

In all, a considerable variety. It is a variety bound together by a style that is generally pervasive save for variations that reflect the different social levels reproduced. A certain vigor results from the determined contemporary quality of Gold's references, including commercial products and public diversions, and even turns of speech. What usually holds this variety together is Gold's own sense of the worth of what he is doing. The language of the novels is a considerable support to the portions of wisdom that appear in the novels.

—Harold H. Watts

GOLDING, William (Gerald). British. Born in St. Columb Minor, Cornwall, 19 September 1911. Educated at Marlborough Grammar School; Brasenose College, Oxford, B.A. 1935. Served in the Royal Navy, 1940-45. Married Ann Brookfield in 1939; one son and one daughter. Writer, actor, and producer in small theatre companies, 1934-40, 1945-54; schoolmaster, Bishop Wordsworth's School, Salisbury, Wiltshire, 1939-40, 1945-61; Visiting Professor, Hollins College, Virginia, 1961-62. Recipient: Black Memorial Award, 1980; Booker Prize, 1980. M.A.: Oxford University, 1961; D.Litt.: University of Sussex, Brighton, 1970. Honorary Fellow, Brasenose College, 1966. Fellow, Royal Society of Literature, 1955. C.B.E. (Commander, Order of the British Empire), 1966. Address: Ebble Thatch, Bowerchalke, Wiltshire, England.

PUBLICATIONS

Novels

Lord of the Flies. London, Faber, 1954; New York, Coward McCann, 1955.
The Inheritors. London, Faber, 1955; New York, Harcourt Brace, 1956.
Pincher Martin. London, Faber, 1956; as *The Two Deaths of Christopher Martin*, New York, Harcourt Brace, 1957.
Free Fall. London, Faber, 1959; New York, Harcourt Brace, 1960.
The Spire. London, Faber, and New York, Harcourt Brace, 1964.
The Pyramid. London, Faber, and New York, Harcourt Brace, 1967.
Darkness Visible. London, Faber, and New York, Farrar Straus, 1979.
Rites of Passage. London, Faber, and New York, Farrar Straus, 1980.

Short Stories

The Scorpion God. London, Faber, 1971; New York, Harcourt Brace, 1972.

Uncollected Short Stories

"Miss Pulkinhorn," in *Encounter* (London), August 1960.
"On The Escarpment," in *Kenyon Review* (Gambier, Ohio), June 1967.
"The Anglo-Saxon," in *Winter's Tales 16*, edited by A.D. Maclean. London, Macmillan, 1970; New York, St. Martin's Press, 1971.

Plays

The Brass Butterfly, adaptation of his story "Envoy Extraordinary" (produced London, 1958). London, Faber, 1958; Chicago, Dramatic Publishing Company, n.d.

Radio Plays: *Miss Pulkinhorn*, 1960; *Break My Heart*, 1962.

Verse

Poems. London, Macmillan, 1934; New York, Macmillan, 1935.

Other

The Hot Gates and Other Occasional Pieces. London, Faber, 1965; New York, Harcourt Brace, 1966.
Talk: Conversations with William Golding, with Jack I. Biles. New York, Harcourt Brace, 1970.

*

Critical Studies: (selection): *William Golding* by Samuel Hynes, New York, Columbia University Press, 1964; *William Golding: A Critical Study* by James R. Baker, New York, St. Martin's Press, 1965; *The Art of William Golding* by Bernard S. Oldsey and Stanley Weintraub, New York, Harcourt Brace, 1965; *William Golding* by Bernard F. Dick, New York, Twayne, 1967; *William Golding: A Critical Study* by Mark Kinkead-Weekes and Ian Gregor, London, Faber, 1967, New York, Harcourt Brace, 1968; *William Golding* by Leighton Hodson, Edinburgh, Oliver and Boyd, 1969, New York, Putnam, 1971; *The Novels of William Golding* by Howard S. Babb, Columbus, Ohio State University Press, 1970; *William Golding: The Dark Fields of Discovery* by Virginia Tiger, London, Calder and Boyars, and Atlantic Highlands, New Jersey, Humanities Press, 1974; *William Golding* by Stephen Medcalf, London, Longman, 1975; *William Golding: Some Critical Considerations* edited by Jack I. Biles and Robert O. Evans, Louisville, University Press of Kentucky, 1978; *Of Earth and Darkness: The Novels of William Golding* by Arnold Johnston, Columbia, University of Missouri Press, 1980.

* * *

The fame of the English novelist William Golding rests on his early novel, *Lord of the Flies*. It is a novel which takes place in the near-future: a future too near to be read about with anything but horrid fascination. As an incident in a world-wide war a company of boys—the oldest only in their early teens—are isolated on a tropical island and must make the best of their painful situation. They have brought with them imprecise insights of what civilization—English civilization, in particular—was. At the outset of their stay, they set up a social organization, complete with a deliberative assembly and an assignment of the duties that will be necessary for survival: fruit-gathering, shelter construction, hunting of boar-meat, and—most important of all—the feeding of a fire that will send up a pillar of smoke and alert passing ships. Eventual rescue is at the outset the raison d'être of all the boys' activity. But gradually the belief in rescue wanes, and the mass of the exiles falls into savagery and the life of primitive fear. They paint their bodies, propitiate a nameless numen that haunts the island, and can hardly remember the civilization that, in the early stages of their stay, they aspired to return to. Indeed, just before the actual rescue at the end of the novel, they are hunting down the one boy who has the courage and resistance to remember what the rest are determined to forget. They have not, in the phrase of their British rescuer, put up a "good show."

For a good many readers, this novel of Golding's was a haunting portent; it spoke not so much of island survival as of the chancy conditions of all human survival in decades to come. It reminded readers of the quick lapse into savagery that all men might soon experience. It suggested that the web of human culture was gossamer and that the only reality that would remain after wide destruction was the animating and savage will of the nameless "god" of the island. Thus, Golding's novel was taken by many to be an uncompromising handwriting on a wall. Its texture of compelling excitement and adventure was the Crusoe experience without the comforts that Defoe presented. Human culture—justice, order, "basic decency"—was but a weak reed and would quickly collapse beneath the hands that touched it for support. That Golding's novel was not unique—that there is, in the 20th century, a considerable tradition of such works as his—can come as a significant afterthought to one's reading of *Lord of the Flies*. Other works as various as Aldous Huxley's *Ape and Essence* and Robert Heinlein's *Stranger in a Strange Land* make some of the points so tellingly offered in Golding's novel. All these novels suggest that modern man is living on borrowed time.

This is the point made by *Lord of the Flies* considered in isolation from the rest of Golding's work. When it is read in conjunction with the later novels, its meaning is qualified if not greatly altered. For the other novels, in terms of subject matter at least, present us Golding laboring at tasks somewhat unlike those of a tale in which the harrowing experiences of castaway boys are civilization writ small. *The Inheritors* is perhaps as fanciful as *Lord of the Flies*; it too is a flight in time, though the flight is to ages before the beginning of civilization rather than to a period when civilization is on its way out. For *The Inheritors* tells of the last days of a small group of humanoid beings who go down in defeat before another—and superior—group of fire-builders, who, in the last chapter of the novel, are revealed as mankind's not very admirable progenitors; they are the "inheritors" whose violence takes over the cave and the forest that the humanoid group had regarded as their own. *Pincher Martin* is a kind of flight to the immediate present; it concerns the efforts of a seaman to survive on a rocky islet during World War II.

Quite different in subject-matter and tone are two other novels: *Free Fall* and *The Pyramid*. *Free Fall* is the rather soberly told story of a young Englishman's coming to maturity; the young man recalls his lower-class childhood, his education, his first serious love affair, and the testing of his resolution at the hands of a Nazi inquisitor. Throughout, the first person narrator is engaged in an assessment of his responsibility for his action: how was he free, how bound? *The Pyramid* is concerned with a middle-class hero who resembles the narrator of *Free Fall* in that he too—with an accent of irony that is absent from *Free Fall*—is assessing elements in his rather protected youth; he measures the amatory and artistic encounters that have shaped the mature consciousness with which the past is scanned. These two novels belong to a very common genre in English fiction: tales which relate the experiences of mastery and defeat which young men undergo in the course of their entrance into a real social world.

One other novel, *The Spire*, moves in a quite different direction. It is the tale of the efforts of a medieval priest to crown his cathedral with a 400 foot spire, an effort that encounters the scepticism of other men and the grim opposition of the law of gravity itself. Yet, despite the opposition of society and nature, the tower is built, at a human cost that is dreadful. Jocelin, the priest-builder of the novel, is subject to divine guidance or obsession, as one will; angels inspire him at his work, and demons seduce him. The temptations of the flesh dog Jocelin at every step of his work, and yet he finally transcends them.

An effort to see an organizing unity in the novels of Golding is not only troubled by the sheer variety of subject-matter presented. The style of presentation varies from novel to novel. The style of *Lord of the Flies* is dramatic, spare, relentless; the experience of the lost boys is reported, not analyzed, and comment and interpretation are the province of the reader. Contrastingly, in *The Inheritors*, *Pincher Martin*, and *The Spire*, the texture of Golding's prose and the accompanying narrative movement are leisurely, involved, and even nebulous and imprecise. One can understand why these variations occur. Golding, in *The Inheritors*, faces the almost impossible task of rendering the humanoid consciousness which, in theory, is almost pre-verbal. Analogous difficulties mark the reproduction of the World War II castaway in *Pincher Martin*. The style of *The Spire* repeats the qualities of diffuseness and tedium, but for different reasons. Jocelin, as well as his recording author, is trying to find expression for impulses that are either satanic or divine. The consequence is, once again, a texture of language that is neither dramatic nor direct; the prose follows the wanderings of the priest up and down his spire with an oppressive abundance that, in this instance, aims at the trascendent. Somewhere between the extremes of expression just cited falls the prose of *Free Fall* and *The Pyramid*, whose recording personae, adults remembering their adolescent experience and understanding it in part, have some chance of mastering what they present. As noted earlier, *Free Fall* is a sober recreation of adolescent hope, whereas *The Pyramid* is a half-serious, half-ironic recreation of the physical and artistic passions that once swept through the mind of Golding's hero. In *Darkness Visible*, the novelist catches up some of the grimmest themes. *Darkness Visible* is a reiteration of the dark visions that have haunted other novels.

Darkness Visible—the phrase comes from Milton's description of Satanic regions—is Golding's often repeated account of the threats by which mankind is surrounded or, better, animated. The threats lie not in the external world but within each psyche which Golding draws out from the outwardly placid English world. There is a perverse English schoolmaster who is almost helpless as he watches the ebb and flow of his desires. Lovely twin girls are corroded by the darkness that is, they believe, the reality at the centers of their lives; when they love, the ultimate intent is destruction. One of these girls, Sophie, finds at the center of her being only a dark tunnel—a "black hole"—into which sink and disappear all the social forms by which she is surrounded. Most of the other characters share her vertigo. Only a boy—Matty, a victim of the London blitz—endures his repulsive disfigurement with heroism and keeps asking such questions as "Who am I?" and "What am I for?" Even he is surrounded by evil pressures—Sophie's tunnel made visible—and tries to exorcise them with Scriptural aid. His attempts have value for himself but count for little in the lives of the other characters. As Matty himself feels, everything is going under or winding down. The result is a novel which presents a merging of nullities or near-nullities that, in their negation, surpass the wordless ur-men of *The Inheritors* and the destructive children of *Lord of the Flies*. But, once again, human sentience is undergoing threat if not dissolution.

However, a more positive comment about the bulk of Golding's work is possible. That a significant hub or center exists—a hub from which the various novels extend like spokes—is suggested by a passage early in *Free Fall*. The hero—or Golding—writes, justifying his meditation on his past: "I have hung all systems on the wall like a row of useless hats. They do not fit. They come in from outside, they are suggested patterns, some dull and some of great beauty. But I have lived enough of my life to require a pattern that fits over everything I know; and where shall I find that?" Slightly later Golding adds: "The mind cannot hold more than so much; but understanding requires a sweep that takes in the whole of remembered time and then can pause." The body of Golding's work suggests that the "hats" are not altogether useless. Each novel represents a "pause" in the presence of "the whole of remembered time." Golding has worn a series of hats, not always consonant with each other but all expressive of certain ranges of human aspiration. One hat—the humanoid one of *The Inheritors*—makes the whole civilized enterprise look like a betrayal of the chance to exist. Another—the hat of *The Spire*—suggests that civilized enterprise always falls short of what is possible for man. And a third hat—the hat assumed by the heroes of *Free Fall* and *The Pyramid*—indicates, if only temporarily, that the gossamer web of civilized life is worth cherishing. It should not be torn asunder as it is by the thoughtless boys of *Lord of the Flies*.

—Harold H. Watts

GOLDMAN, William. American. Born in Chicago, Illinois, 12 August 1931. Educated at Oberlin College, Ohio, B.A. 1952; Columbia University, New York, M.A. 1956. Served in the United States Army, 1952-54. Married Ilene Jones in 1961; two children. Recipient: Oscar, for screenplay, 1970, 1977. Address: 740 Park Avenue, New York, New York 10021, U.S.A.

PUBLICATIONS

Novels

The Temple of Gold. New York, Knopf, 1957.
Your Turn to Curtsy, My Turn to Bow. New York, Doubleday, 1958.
Soldier in the Rain. New York, Atheneum, and London, Eyre and Spottiswoode, 1960.
Boys and Girls Together. New York, Atheneum, 1964; London, Joseph, 1965.
No Way To Treat a Lady (as Harry Longbaugh). New York, Fawcett, 1964; as William Goldman, New York, Harcourt Brace, 1968.
The Thing of It Is.... New York, Harcourt Brace, and London, Joseph, 1967.
Father's Day. New York, Harcourt Brace, and London, Joseph, 1971.
The Princess Bride: S. Morgenstern's Classic Tale of True Love and High Adventure: The "Good Parts" Version, Abridged. New York, Harcourt Brace, 1973; London, Macmillan, 1975.
Marathon Man. New York, Delacorte Press, 1974; London, Macmillan, 1975.
Magic. New York, Delacorte Press, and London, Macmillan, 1976.
Tinsel. New York, Delacorte Press, and London, Macmillan, 1979.

Uncollected Short Stories

"Something Blue," in *Rogue* (New York), 1958.
"Da Vinci," in *New World Writing 17.* Philadelphia, Lippincott, 1960.
"Till the Right Girls Come Along," in *Transatlantic Review 8* (London), Winter 1961.
"The Ice Cream Eat," in *Stories from the Transatlantic Review*, edited by Joseph F. McCrindle. New York, Holt Rinehart, 1970.

Plays

Blood, Sweat and Stanley Poole, with James Goldman (produced New York, 1961). New York, Dramatists Play Service, 1962.
A Family Affair, with James Goldman and John Kander (produced New York, 1962).
Butch Cassidy and the Sundance Kid (screenplay). New York, Bantam, and London, Corgi, 1969.
The Great Waldo Pepper (screenplay). New York, Dell, 1975.

Screenplays: *Masquerade*, with Michael Relph, 1964; *Harper* (*The Moving Target*), 1966; *Butch Cassidy and the Sundance Kid*, 1969; *The Hot Rock* (*How to Steal a Diamond in Four Uneasy Lessons*), 1972; *The Great Waldo Pepper*, 1974; *The Stepford Wives*, 1975; *A Bridge Too Far*, 1976; *Marathon Man*, 1976; *All the President's Men*, 1976; *Magic*, 1978; *Mr. Horn*, 1978.

Other

The Season: A Candid Look at Broadway. New York, Harcourt Brace, 1969.
Wigger (juvenile). New York and London, Harcourt Brace, 1974.
The Story of "A Bridge Too Far." New York, Dell, 1977.

*

Critical Study: *William Goldman* by Richard Andersen, Boston, Twayne, 1979.

* * *

William Goldman is a successful novelist, film scenarist, playwright, critic, and children's book author who focuses much of his attention on the illusions by which men and women live. These illusions often make existence more miserable than it need be and provide a core from which all of Goldman's protagonists seek to escape. Ironically, what they escape to is more often than not other illusions, which, because of the artificial distinctions society attaches to them, rarely satisfy their human needs.

When Raymond Trevitt's desperate attempts to protect the ideals of his childhood from adult realities in *The Temple of Gold* inadvertently cause the deaths of his closest friends, he leaves his home, but discovers only frustration and intolerance elsewhere. In *Your Turn to Curtsy, My Turn to Bow*, Chad Kimberly is driven by his ambitious illusions into believing he is a new Messiah, whose schizophrenic demands frighten the novel's protagonist, Peter Bell, into a life of escapist daydreaming. Ambition is not the only illusion that drive the characters of *Boys and Girls Together* to New York; most of them are escaping from the unbearable circumstances of their home lives. Nevertheless, their hopes for self-improvement are dashed by unsuccessful love affairs, domineering parents, professional failures, embarrassing social exposures, and suicide. In *Soldier in the Rain*, Eustis Clay and Maxwell Slaughter cannot free themselves from the military-economic complex of which they are so much a part.

The great American illusions about success are the central concerns of *The Thing of It Is...* and *Father's Day*, in which the talented, rich, but quirky Amos McCracken spends a tremendous amount of money trying to save his marriage and then his relationship with his daughter. In the end, his guilt-ridden personal failures lead him to create fantasies that enable him to fulfill the images he has of himself but that also pose a serious threat to the safety and well-being of others.

Unlike Amos McCracken or Kit Gil of *No Way to Treat a Lady*, Westley and Buttercup of *The Princess Bride*, Babe Levy of *Marathon Man*, and Corky Withers of *Magic* cannot retreat to a fabulous land to try to make themselves whole; they already live in a fabulous land, where they are constantly assaulted by its empirical and psychological facts. Forced to encounter a vast confusion of fact and fiction, to deal with pain and death, and to seek power against forces that are difficult to pinpoint and consequently understand, the protagonists of these three novels must stay rooted in social systems that attempt to deny their vitality while creating illusions that life is what it should be.

Combining the everyday reality of Goldman's early novels with the fabulous reality of his later works, *Tinsel* tells the story of three women who desperately try to escape from the boredom of their daily lives to the fame and fortune of movie stardom, which, like all illusions, eludes them. As he did in *Marathon Man* and *Magic*, Goldman divides this into many chapters, so short and so different from any other in terms of setting and action that they flash by the reader like scenes in a movie. Because of their length, Goldman can keep simultaneously occurring stories running vividly in the reader's imagination without making any significant connections between them. When the individual stories eventually come together, Goldman continues flashing different scenes containing markedly different actions at such a pace that reading Goldman's story about the film industry becomes as close to a cinematic experience as literature can provide.

Perhaps because of his popularity or the reputation he has established in Hollywood (many of his novels have been adapted to the screen), many critics have misunderstood or underrated Goldman's works. Perhaps these critics have been confused by Goldman's use of multiple modes—novel of manners, confessional journal, psychological novel, social satire, romantic parody, black humor novel, detective story, spy novel, radical protest novel, soap opera, absurdist novel, and more—within a wide frame of genres. Whatever the reason, Goldman is an extraordinarily talented and prolific writer whose incorporation of cinematic techniques with conventional narrative forms mark a significant contribution to the novel tradition.

—Richard Andersen

GORDIMER, Nadine. South African. Born in Springs, Transvaal, 20 November 1923. Educated at a convent school, and the University of the Witwatersrand, Johannesburg. Married 1) G. Gavron in 1949; 2) Reinhold Cassirer in 1954; one son and one daughter. Visiting Lecturer, Institute of Contemporary Arts, Washington, D.C., 1961, Harvard University, Cambridge, Massachusetts, 1969, Princeton University, New Jersey, 1969, Northwestern University, Evanston, Illinois, 1969, and the University of Michigan, Ann Arbor, 1970; Adjunct Professor of Writing, Columbia University, New York, 1971. Recipient: Smith Literary Award, 1961; Thomas Pringle Award, 1969; Black Memorial Prize, 1972; Booker Prize, 1974; Grand Aigle d'Or Prize, France, 1975; CNA Literary Award, 1975. Address: 7 Frere Road, Parktown West, Johannesburg, South Africa.

PUBLICATIONS

Novels

The Lying Days. London, Gollancz, and New York, Simon and Schuster, 1953.
A World of Strangers. London, Gollancz, and New York, Simon and Schuster, 1958.
Occasion for Loving. London, Gollancz, and New York, Viking Press, 1963.
The Late Bourgeois World. London, Gollancz, and New York, Viking Press, 1966.
A Guest of Honour. New York, Viking Press, 1970; London, Cape, 1971.
The Conservationist. London, Cape, 1974; New York, Viking Press, 1975.
Burger's Daughter. London, Cape, and New York, Viking Press, 1979.
July's People. New York, Viking Press, 1981.

Short Stories

Face to Face: Short Stories. Johannesburg, Silver Leaf, 1949.
The Soft Voice of the Serpent and Other Stories. New York, Simon and Schuster, 1952; London, Gollancz, 1953.
Six Feet of the Country. London, Gollancz, and New York, Simon and Schuster, 1956.
Friday's Footprint and Other Stories. London, Gollancz, and New York, Viking Press, 1960.
Not for Publication and Other Stories. London, Gollancz, and New York, Viking Press, 1965.
Penguin Modern Stories 4, with others. London, Penguin, 1970.
Livingstone's Companions: Stories. New York, Viking Press, 1971; London, Cape, 1972.
Selected Stories. London, Cape, 1975; New York, Viking Press, 1976; as *No Place Like*, London, Penguin, 1978.
Some Monday for Sure. London, Heinemann, 1976.
A Soldier's Embrace. London, Cape, and New York, Viking Press, 1980.

Play

Television Documentary: *A Terrible Chemistry* (*Writers and Places* series), 1981 (UK).

Other

African Lit. (lectures). Cape Town, University of Cape Town, 1972.
On the Mines, photographs by David Goldblatt. Cape Town, Struik, 1973.
The Black Interpreters: Notes on African Writing. Johannesburg, Spro-Cas Ravan, 1973.

Editor, with Lionel Abrahams, *South African Writing Today.* London, Penguin, 1967.

*

Bibliography: *Nadine Gordimer, Novelist and Short Story Writer: A Bibliography of Her Works* by Racilia Jilian Nell, Johannesburg, University of the Witwatersrand, 1964.

Manuscript Collection: University of Texas, Austin.

Critical Studies: *Nadine Gordimer* by Robert F. Haugh, New York, Twayne, 1974; *Nadine Gordimer* by Michael Wade, London, Evans, 1978.

* * *

Nadine Gordimer occupies a prominent place among the handful of novelists who have begun, in recent decades, to create a distinctive South African literary tradition. Her fiction, like that of Alan Paton, Dan Jacobson, and Jack Cope, presents and critically explores many areas of contemporary life, and accurately reflects the tensions inherent in South Africa's white-dominated, multiracial society. Where her contemporaries occasionally allow sentiment or humour to blur the edges of their realism, Nadine Gordimer's vision of life in South Africa is uncompromising and has grown steadily bleaker over the years. Focussing on the experience of white South Africans, she implies that the price one pays for living in a colour-bar society and accepting the dubious privilege of belonging to the "master-race" is high: a kind of creeping paralysis of the feelings. She shows a numbing fear underlying all relationships, which destroys love affairs, blights friendship, and eventually induces a kind of terror of the unknown. "Afraid, alive," is the refrain ticked out on the narrator's clock at the end of *The Late Bourgeois World*, as she lies awake, remembering her deliberate refusal to help a black friend. "Run," Mehring, the "conservationist" tells himself as he flees from the need to acknowledge the uglier facts of South African life.

The setting of most of the novels and short stories is Johannesburg, South Africa's "golden city." For Gordimer, as for a number of other South African writers, Johannesburg is a microcosm of modern South Africa: a place where the very rich and the very poor live and work almost side by side; where black and white come into daily contact with one another; where sophisticated Europe rubs shoulders with tribal Africa. It is a cosmopolitan city where loneliness can be a matter of being white in a black crowd. The characters who interest Gordimer, and whose lives she meticulously examines, are, in the main, sensitive, cultivated men and women. Sometimes they are politically conscious, more often they are simply anxious to enjoy a comfortable life. All of them are engaged in the same kind of quest: a search for satisfactory personal relationships, in which differences of class and colour will be forgotten. The first four novels are a record of the increasing difficulty of this quest, hampered as it necessarily is in South Africa by restrictive legislation and social taboo. *The Lying Days* is perhaps the most optimistic of the novels. Helen Shaw, the central character, is young enough not to be daunted by the signs of violence and unpleasantness she can so easily see in her society. She cherishes a belief in what Gordimer calls "the phoenix illusion," hope for a future in which she will find a place in South African society, and where her personal happiness and that of others will be secure. Toby Hood, the narrator and central character in *A World of Strangers*, is less certain about his ability to live in Johannesburg. His world seems split in two: a white half and a black one. In spite of his efforts to unite the two fragments, there seems, in the end, no possibility of introducing the "strangers" to one another. Both these novels are full of brilliantly observed and recorded scenes: childhood and adolescence in *The Lying Days*, and township and urban life in *A World of Strangers*. Scenes such as these established Gordimer very early in her career as one of the most accurate and credible commentators on South African life. Ironically, it is this same facility for detailed observation which may be seen as the source of her major weakness. In her desire to record accurately, to convey the exact feel, the smell, the taste of an experience, the episode itself sometimes tends to lose its outlines; the plot, particularly in *The Lying Days*, seems to vanish behind details.

The two early novels are concerned very largely with representative South African types and with typical South African scenes. *Occasion for Loving* and *The Late Bourgeois World*, and, more recently, *The Conservationist*, explore in considerable depth and with increasing complexity, the effect of life in a colour-bar society on individuals who are fundamentally decent and humane. With a depressing and logical clarity, Gordimer portrays the slow but inevitable withering of the heart. In a tortured society neither love nor passion can survive, and even the bought caress of a prostitute can induce terror. *Occasion for Loving* is based on a triangular relationship. An older woman observes and helps, as far as she is able, a love affair between two of her friends, a black man and a white woman. When the affair ends, all three have clearly lost something valuable. *The Late Bourgeois World* takes as its starting point the political trials of 1964, when a number of white intellectuals were found guilty of sabotage. Examining the "case" of one such would-be revolutionary, in the context of his family, his friends and his political associates, Gordimer evokes with considerable power the sterility and fear which increasingly make the "bourgeois world" of the middle-class whites irrelevant and, in a metaphorical sense, dead.

Against this background of hopelessness and gloom, *A Guest of Honour* comes as something of a surprise. In this book about the trials of a newly independent African country, Gordimer focusses on a character who knows very clearly what he is about. James Bray, a middle-aged Englishman who has spent most of his life in Africa, is the "guest of honour" at the independence celebrations, and later becomes a "special adviser" to the government. Although there is little he can do to avert the strife which neo-colonial tensions make inevitable, or even to create a better educational system, he nevertheless knows that what he does do is right and necessary. Neither his death, nor his love for the South African girl, Bekky, can be seen as wrong, or completely futile. Impressive both in its analysis of political cross-currents, and in its complex presentation of the country and its inhabitants, *A Guest of Honour* is easily Gordimer's finest novel. Even her occasional coldness towards her own characters seems missing here, and the love affair is treated with warmth and sympathy.

The Conservationist returns to a contemplation of the South African scene, and to an analysis of a wealthy industrialist turned farmer. Through Mehring's keenly observant eyes, we see both black and white South Africans, and are drawn into the uneasy world of the white businessmen who sit in boardrooms buying and selling on international markets, but living always on the fringe of real experience, and in the shadow of fear. The novel cleverly exploits a number of paradoxes peculiarly pertinent to the South African situation: the man who owns the land because he has paid for it, can never own it in the way the African squatters do, because they belong to the land in a way he does not. Yet they, having no rights of ownership, can never really own it either. Perhaps only the dead man, buried and rotting in the ground, truly "owns" the farm, of which he has become an actual "living" part. In the juxtaposition of two widely differing ways of life (big business and rural African), Gordimer once again encapsulates a characteristic area of South African experience, and, as always, faces her central character with the almost unanswerable problem of survival in a deeply divided society.

—Ursula Laredo

GORDON, Giles (Alexander Esme). British. Born in Edinburgh, 23 May 1940. Educated at Edinburgh Academy, 1948-57. Married Margaret Anna Eastoe in 1964; two sons and one daughter. Advertising Executive, Secker and Warburg, publishers, London, 1962-63; Editor, Hutchinson Publishing Group, London, 1963-64, and Penguin Books, London, 1964-66; Editorial Director, Victor Gollancz, publishers, London, 1967-72. Since 1972, Partner, Anthony Sheil Associates, literary agents, London. Lecturer in Creative Writing, in London, for Tufts University, Medford, Massachusetts, 1971-76; C. Day Lewis Fellow in Writing, King's College, London, 1974-75. Member, Arts Council of Great Britain Literature Panel, 1966-69; Member, Society of Authors Committee of Management, 1973-75. Member of the Governing Board, Writers' Guild of Great Britain. Recipient: *Transatlantic Review* prize, 1966; Scottish Arts Council grant, 1976. Address: 9 St. Ann's Gardens, London NW5 4ER, England.

PUBLICATIONS

Novels

The Umbrella Man. London, Allison and Busby, 1971.
About a Marriage. London, Allison and Busby, and New York, Stein and Day, 1972.
Girl with Red Hair. London, Hutchinson, 1974.
100 Scenes from Married Life: A Selection. London, Hutchinson, 1976.
Enemies: A Novel about Friendship. Hassocks, Sussex, Harvester Press, 1977.

Ambrose's Vision: Sketches Towards the Creation of a Cathedral. Hassocks, Sussex, Harvester Press, 1980.

Short Stories

Pictures from an Exhibition. London, Allison and Busby, and New York, Dial Press, 1970.
Penguin Modern Stories 3, with others. London, Penguin, 1970.
Farewell, Fond Dreams. London, Hutchinson, 1975.
The Illusionist and Other Fictions. Hassocks, Sussex, Harvester Press, 1978.
Couple. Knotting, Bedfordshire, Sceptre Press, 1978.

Uncollected Short Stories

"The Line-up on the Shore," in *Mind in Chains*, edited by Christopher Evans. London, Panther, 1970.
"The Partition," in *Triangles*, edited by Alex Hamilton. London, Hutchinson, 1973.
"Crampton Manor," in *The Ninth Ghost Book*, edited by Rosemary Timperley. London, Barrie and Jenkins, 1973.
"Peake," in *The Eleventh Ghost Book*, edited by Aidan Chambers. London, Barrie and Jenkins, 1975.
"Morning Echo," in *The Sixteenth Pan Book of Horror Stories*, edited by Herbert Van Thal. London, Pan, 1975.
"In Spite of Himself," in *The Twelfth Ghost Book.* London, Barrie and Jenkins, 1976.
"Nineteen Policemen Searching the Solent Shore," in *Scottish Short Stories 1976.* London, Collins, 1976.
"Horses of Venice," in *The Thirteenth Ghost Book*, edited by James Hale. London, Barrie and Jenkins, 1977.
"The Necessary Authority," in *The Midnight Ghost Book*, edited by James Hale. London, Barrie and Jenkins, 1978.
"Room, With Woman and Man," in *New Stories 3*, edited by Francis King and Ronald Harwood. London, Hutchinson, 1978.
"Liberated People," in *Modern Scottish Short Stories*, edited by Fred Urquhart and Giles Gordon. London, Hamish Hamilton, 1978.
"The Red-Headed Milkman," in *The Punch Book of Short Stories*, edited by Alan Coren. London, Robson, 1979.
"Screens," in *Labrys 4* (Hayes, Middlesex), 1979.
"Mask," in *The After Midnight Ghost Book*, edited by James Hale. London, Hutchinson, 1980.
"Drama in Five Acts," in *New Terrors 2*, edited by Ramsey Campbell. London, Pan, 1980.
"Madame Durand," in *Punch* (London), 19 November 1980.
"The Indian Girl," in *Winter's Tales 27*, edited by Edward Leeson. London, Macmillan, 1981.
"Three Resolutions to One Kashmiri Encounter," in *Scottish Short Stories 1981.* London, Collins, 1981.

Plays

Radio Plays: *Nineteen Policemen Searching the Sedway Shore*, 1976; *The Jealous One*, 1979; *Birdy*, from the novel by William Wharton, 1980.

Verse

Landscape Any Date. Edinburgh, M. Macdonald, 1963.
Two and Two Make One. Preston, Lancashire, Akros, 1966.
Two Elegies. London, Turret, 1968.
Eight Poems for Gareth. Frensham, Surrey, Sceptre Press, 1970.
Between Appointments. Frensham, Surrey, Sceptre Press, 1971.
Twelve Poems for Callum. Preston, Lancashire, Akros, 1972.
One Man Two Women. London, Sheep Press, 1974.
Egyptian Room, Metropolitan Museum of Art. Rushden, Northamptonshire, Sceptre Press, 1974.
The Oban Poems. Knotting, Bedfordshire, Sceptre Press, 1977.

Other

Book 2000: Some Likely Trends in Publishing. London, Association of Assistant Librarians, 1969.
Walter and the Balloon (juvenile). London, Heinemann, 1973.

Editor, with Alex Hamilton, *Factions: Eleven Original Stories.* London, Joseph, 1974.
Editor, with Michael Bakewell and B.S. Johnson, *You Always Remember the First Time.* London, Quartet, 1975.
Editor, *Beyond the Words: Eleven Writers in Search of a New Fiction.* London, Hutchinson, 1975.
Editor, with Dulan Barber, *"Members of the Jury—": The Jury Experience.* London, Wildwood House, 1976.
Editor, *Prevailing Spirits: A Book of Scottish Ghost Stories.* London, Hamish Hamilton, 1976.
Editor, *A Book of Contemporary Nightmares.* London, Joseph, 1977.
Editor, with Fred Urquhart, *Modern Scottish Short Stories.* London, Hamish Hamilton, 1978.

*

Manuscript Collection: National Library of Scotland, Edinburgh.

* * *

Relationships lie at the root of Giles Gordon's novels and short stories, relationships between man and woman, woman and woman, man and man, husband and wife, lover and lover—and also the relationship between the writer and the reader. In his first novel, *The Umbrella Man*, Gordon was content to view the burgeoning affair between Felix and Delia from the outside, using the technique that a film director might bring to bear in building up a scene from different camera angles. This is a device of which Gordon is particularly fond, and its exposition is seen to good effect in his story "Nineteen Policemen Searching the Solent Shore."

About a Marriage is a more straightforward narrative in which the seeming detritus of modern married life assumes a form that the protagonists, the husband and wife, can understand. A reasonably well-off couple, Edward and Ann, move from a bland acceptance of their marriage to a blazing revelation of the strengths of their relationship and of the bond that exists between them. Their love is based not so much on a romantic attachment, although that is also present, as on the many-sided passions and frustrations that ultimately give each partner a vivid insight into their own strengths and weaknesses. Of growing importance in this novel is Gordon's mastery of dialogue and his relaxed ability to enter the minds of his characters who cease to exist as mere cyphers and have grown into stark, living creatures.

Enemies ("A Novel about Friendship") is in the now-familiar Gordon mould of a terse examination of how people relate to each other in familiar and not so familiar circumstances, but its stylistic achievement lies in his ability to strip the central narrative line to a series of scenes which embody sharp dialogue with an internalisation of the characters' thoughts and emotions. The Hiltons live in an unspecified European country, and the action centres on the events of a few days while they are being visited by their parents and friends from England. Events outside their house, which at the beginning of the novel seems to be so secure against outside interference, threaten the fabric of their cosy world as it becomes a microcosm of a beleaguered society with all its concomitant stresses. Faced with the centre falling away, the adults find their relationships shifting uneasily before they reach the triumphant conclusion of the salving power of their own friendships.

100 Scenes from Married Life picks up again the story of Edward and Ann. The intensity of their love for each other is still apparent, but growing self-doubt and encroaching middle age, with its sense of the loss of youth and vitality, gnaw at Edward's vitals. Interestingly, as if to prove the security of their marriage, Gordon disconcertingly opens the first scene with Edward returning from a week in

Venice with his mistress. The novel's title reflects Gordon's debt to Ingmar Bergman's *Scenes from a Marriage*, and in a series of 18 scenes he has captured the warm, womblike, yet claustrophobic story of a close relationship. The inscription is from Philip Roth's *My Life as a Man*: "You want subtlety, then read *The Golden Bowl*. This is life, bozo, not high art." And there are many echoes from Roth's and John Updike's style in Gordon's low-key examination of the matter of middle-class life.

With those two American writers he also shares an interest in language and the economy of its use. At his best he is able to strip his sentences to an almost surreal invisibility which is allied disconcertingly to a lively, sparkling wit. His first collection of what Gordon calls "short fictions," *Pictures from an Exhibition*, was stylistically naive but there was a sense of innovatory excitement as he adopted the attitude of the detached observer in his frequently startling revelations. *Farewell, Fond Dreams* continued many of the same conventions but it showed a surer touch as Gordon risked some breathtaking conceits in his mixture of fact and fantasy, as in the sequence "An attempt to make entertainment out of the war in Vietnam." *The Illusionist and Other Fictions* showed a return to calmer waters, with Gordon seeming to take a fresh interest in the traditional structure of the short story, although he can never lose sight completely of their liquid, three-dimensional possibilities. Critics have been frequently exasperated by the audacious verve of much of Gordon's writing, but he remains one of the few British writers interested in pushing the possibilities of the novel to their outer limits.

—Trevor Royle

GOVER, (John) Robert. American. Born in Philadelphia, Pennsylvania, 2 November 1929. Educated at the University of Pittsburgh, B.A. in economics 1953. Married 1) Mildred Vitkovich in 1955 (divorced, 1966); 2) Jeanne-Nell Gement in 1968; one son. Held a variety of jobs, including that of reporter on various newspapers, in Pennsylvania and Maryland, until 1961. Address: 20 Paradise Road, Star Route, Santa Barbara, California 93105, U.S.A.

PUBLICATIONS

Novels

One Hundred Dollar Misunderstanding. New York, Grove Press, and London, Spearman, 1962.

The Maniac Responsible. New York, Grove Press, 1963; London, MacGibbon and Kee, 1964.

Here Goes Kitten. New York, Grove Press, 1964; London, Mayflower, 1965.

Poorboy at the Party. New York, Simon and Schuster, 1966.

J.C. Saves. New York, Simon and Schuster, 1968; London, Arrow, 1979.

Going for Mr. Big. New York, Bantam, 1973.

To Morrow Now Occurs Again (as O. Govi). Santa Barbara, California, Ross Erikson, 1975.

Getting Pretty on the Table (as O. Govi). Santa Barbara, California, Capra Press, 1975.

Other

Editor, *The Portable Walter: From the Prose and Poetry of Walter Lowenfels.* New York, Grove Press, 1968.

*

Manuscript Collection: Boston University.

Robert Gover comments:

His trilogy, *One Hundred Dollar Misunderstanding*, *Here Goes Kitten*, and *J.C. Saves*, captures in two characters relations between Black and White in America, especially as it evolved during the 1960's.

J.C Holland first meets Kitten while he is a university sophomore and she a 13-year-old prostitute. In the second book, J.C. is public relations director of the local political party in power and encounters Kitten as a nightclub singer, or "B-girl." In the third, he finds her ducking police gunfire during a "race riot."

The Maniac Responsible examines the *why* of a rape-murder case. The protagonist, Dean, becomes so involved in the invisible mental process that led to the brutal slaying that he becomes "possessed." Gover uses Joycean techniques to vivify his character's mental world.

Poorboy at the Party mythologizes the split between rich and poor in America. Randy, the main character, goes with his wealthy friend to a party in a large old mansion containing art treasures. Conflicting emotions and values plant seeds of frustration and the party erupts into a violent orgy of destruction.

Going for Mr. Big is the tale of a pimp and his two ladies and a millionaire and his wife. Luke Small is a self-styled revolutionary with a lust to pull down the rich and powerful, but his "campaign" to conquer Malcolm McMasters first backfires, then resolves itself in a meaningful togetherness that is outside the prevailing economic system.

To Morrow Now Occurs Again, published under Gover's pen-name, O. Govi, is a surrealist romp through a mythical land called all Damnation, which is one big Plantation where Big Money is the Holy Spirit. The protagonist, Big I and little me, soul and ego of one entity, is baffled by the situation he finds himself in. The Rat Doctor, whose experimental maze of millions of rats is periodically studied to show the workings of society and shed light on the religion of Big Money, does not deter Big I from asserting that His currency is eternal.

Victor Versus Mort, a novella published only in Portuguese, pits two archtypal forces against each other in an American social setting. In the end, the main character's worldly successes are eclipsed by death.

Getting Pretty on the Table, also a novella, carries into a suburban orgy a game played by pimps and prostitutes. The game combines psychic therapy and spiritual cleansing.

* * *

In the "After Words" to *J.C. Saves* (the last volume of the trilogy begun with *One Hundred Dollar Misunderstanding* and *Here Goes Kitten*), Robert Gover tells us that at the beginning "I had no preconceived idea where these two characters would lead me, their author." Unfortunately, the reader's sharing of that aimlessness is such that he arrives at the last page of the last volume with the sense that the trilogy is completed only because the author has told him so. There is no reason why the characters might not go on in book after book, *ad infinitum*, like the Rover Boys. When J.C. Holland, the white middle-class protagonist, and Kitten, his black prostitute love, achieve their partial understanding at the end of *J.C. Saves*, it is clear that the slightest alteration provided by another time and other circumstances will be enough to set another story in motion. For the fact is that this is formula fiction: shake up the characters, move them to a new starting point, put them in motion, follow the formula, and you have another book. The other works, from *Poorboy at the Party* through *Getting Pretty on the Table*, play variations on the same basic themes.

Yet there is an honesty in Gover, a vision of the life about him, and a quality of writing that raises him above the level of either the pulp pornographer or the slick composer of best sellers. However much he taxes the reader's impatience with shallow characterizations, absurd plot manipulations, gratuitous sex, and moral implications that are occasionally downright silly, he is at times an accomplished satirist. One must only imagine his books in the form of Classic Comics, illustrated by cartoonists for *Mad Magazine*, to be made aware how sure is his touch for the particular grotesque exaggeration that comically, or cruelly, reveals a specific truth. His are not realistic novels, but verbal comic strips, sharing a good many of the virtues and faults of such a paradigm of the genre as Norman Mailer's *An American Dream*.

In large measure he is a moralist—disgusted at times, bitter and angry at others, but always subordinating the matter to the message. And the message is always the same: the Anglo-Saxon American power structure has created a society in which sex and violence are so perversely twisted together that there is no place for honest respect and affection between individuals, classes, or races. Never showing what society might be, he concentrates his attention on the extremes of actuality that he sees as emblematic of the whole. In some respects his most memorable statement is *The Maniac Responsible*, where he parallels the movements of a reporter covering a brutal sex murder with the man's movements while attempting to seduce his teasingly voluptuous neighbor. Finally driven by circumstances (the natural circumstances, the author suggests, of the American way of life) and his own sensitivity, he becomes a suspect in the murder and breaks down into an admission that he, himself, is the maniac responsible (as we all are) for the rape and murder of the girl.

Sex is in the forefront of all of Gover's novels. However, the human failures he depicts are not to be blamed on sex, but rather on the failure of its right use, the tendency to treat the other human being as a means rather than an end. Significantly, in the twisted world of Gover's vision the individual who seems best to know how to use her sex is Kitten, the Negro prostitute. Significantly, too, the Kitten trilogy, *Poorboy at the Party*, and *The Maniac Responsible* all end in rejections of the middle-class societies they have portrayed.

—George Perkins

GOYEN, (Charles) William. American. Born in Trinity, Texas, 24 April 1915. Educated at Rice University, Houston, B.A. 1937, M.A. 1939. Served in the United States Navy, 1940-45. Married Doris Roberts in 1963. Critic and Reviewer, *New York Times*, 1950-65. Taught at the New School for Social Research, New York, 1955-60, Columbia University, New York, 1964-66, Brown University, Providence, Rhode Island, 1973-75, and Princeton University, New Jersey, 1976-78. Senior Editor, McGraw Hill, publishers, New York, 1966-72. Recipient: Guggenheim Fellowship, 1950, 1952; Ford grant, for theatre, 1963; ASCAP award, for musical compositions, 1965, 1966, 1968, 1969, 1970; O. Henry award, 1976; Rice University Award, 1977. Address: 6225 Quebec Drive, Los Angeles, California 90068, U.S.A.

PUBLICATIONS

Novels

The House of Breath. New York, Random House, 1950; London, Chatto and Windus, 1951.
In a Farther Country. New York, Random House, 1955; London, Owen, 1962.
The Fair Sister. New York, Doubleday, 1962; as *Savata, My Fair Sister*, London, Owen, 1963.
Come, The Restorer. New York, Doubleday, 1974.
Arcadio. New York, Farrar Straus, 1981.

Short Stories

Ghost and Flesh: Stories and Tales. New York, Random House, 1952.
The Faces of Blood Kindred: A Novella and 10 Stories. New York, Random House, 1960.
The Collected Stories of William Goyen. New York, Doubleday, 1975.
Arthur Bond. Winston-Salem, North Carolina, Palaemon Press, 1979.

Uncollected Short Stories

"Simon's Castle" and "The Storm Doll," in *Ontario Review* (Windsor), 1977-78.
"Right Here at Christmas," in *Redbook* (New York), December 1977.
"Precious Door," in *Southwest Review* (Dallas), Autumn 1978.

Plays

The House of Breath, adaptation of his own novel (produced New York, 1956).
The Diamond Rattler (produced Boston, 1960).
Christy (produced New York, 1964).
Aimee, music by Worth Gardner, lyrics by Goyen (produced Providence, Rhode Island, 1973).

Screenplay: *The Left Handed Gun* (lyrics only), 1958.

Verse

Nine Poems. New York, Albondocani Press, 1976.

Other

Ralph Ellison's Invisible Man. New York, American R.D.M., 1966.
A Book of Jesus. New York, Doubleday, 1973.
Selected Writings of William Goyen. New York, Random House, 1974.
While You Were Away. Houston, Houston Public Library, 1978.

Translator, *The Lazy Ones*, by Albert Cossery. New York, New Directions, and London, Owen, 1952.

*

Manuscript Collections: Fondren Library, Rice University, Houston; Humanities Research Center, University of Texas, Austin.

Critical Studies: "The House of Breath" by Katherine Anne Porter, in *New York Times Book Review*, 20 August 1950; "The First Novel of a Young American" by Ernst Robert Curtius, in *Neue Schweize Rundschau* (Zurich), March 1952; Lon Tinkle, in *Dallas Morning News*, October 1955; Granville Hicks, in *Saturday Review* (New York), 5 October 1963; *The Poetics of Space* by Gaston Bachelard, New York, Orion Press, 1964; *The Novel of the Future* by Anaïs Nin, New York, Macmillan, 1966; Clyde Grimm, Jr., in *Studies in South-Western Literature* (Austin, Texas), 1971; interview in *Paris Review 68*, 1976; *William Goyen* by Robert Phillips, Boston, Twayne, 1979; "William Goyen Issue" of *Delta* (Montpelier), 1979.

William Goyen comments:

My birthplace, once a thriving railroad and sawmill town by the Trinity River, is Trinity, located in the soft woods-and-meadows area of East Texas. My father's family brought him as a young man to Trinity from Mississippi. They were sawmill people. My mother's family, native Texans, was made up of carpenters, railroad men (there was a prominent roundhouse in Trinity), but her father was Postmaster of the town for many years. We lived in Trinity until I was seven. The world of that town, its countryside, its folk, its speech and superstition and fable, was stamped into my senses during those first seven years of my life; and I spent the first twelve years of my writing life reporting it and fabricating it in short fiction. In my seventh year we moved to Shreveport, Louisiana, lived there a year, thence to Houston. I was educated, from the third grade, in that city: grammar school, Junior High School, High School, Rice University. As a child I was quick and scared; serving; secretly unsettled; imaginative and nervous and sensual. When I reached Sam Houston High School, I thought surely I would be a composer, actor, dancer, singer, fantastico. My mother and father were embarrassed by such ambitions. Nevertheless, I found a way to study dancing, music composition, singing, clandestinely. When this was found out by my parents, who were outraged by the extents of my determination, I did not run away from home to a city. I decided to go underground at home, and write. No one could know that I was doing that. It was my own. This was in my sixteenth year, and what I wrote was lyrical, melancholy, yearning, romantic and sentimental. Above all, it was homesick, and written at home.

College for me was intolerable. I hated the classes, the courses, the students. I refused to study Mathematics, and so failed the required Freshman course in Mathematics for three straight years. I wanted to make up new things, not "study" what had already been made. In my Junior year, the thunderstrike came. I discovered Shakespeare, Chaucer, Milton, Yeats, Joyce, the French Symbolists, Flaubert, Turgenev, Balzac, Melville, Hawthorne. I was at literature, insatiable, for the next three years, reading, and writing under the glow and turmoil of what I was reading. Suddenly—it seemed—I had accomplished the Masters Degree in Comparative Literature (1939). I had been writing plays and stories, and in my Junior and Senior years I took all the prizes in both forms.

Leaving Rice University, I took a teaching position at the University of Houston in its first year. Near the end of that year, I was drafted; it was 1939. I joined the Navy as an enlisted man, worked a year in the local Recruiting Office of Houston, then was sent to Midshipman School in New York City for Officer Training at Columbia University. It was my first exposure to city life and culture, and I was in uniform, preparing to go to sea and war. After three months of indoctrination, I went off to the war, and I served five years in it, mostly on an aircraft carrier in the South Pacific. During the war, I determined to write as a way of life; and at the end of war, I went to New Mexico (El Prado, above Taos) and began to write from myself. There I met Frieda Lawrence and Dorothy Brett who became the first real influences on my life as artist. I built a little adobe house in El Prado on land given to me by Frieda and began my first novel, *The House of Breath*, in that mud house. I worked close to two years on it there, then finished it in London. It was clear to me now: I saw my life as a writing life, a life of giving shape to what happened, of searching for meanings, clarification, Entirety. It was my Way: expression in words. From then on, I managed to write, with little or no money, with growing distinction—which, I have come to see, brings little usable reward—awards, honors, little money. What I wanted was to make splendor. What I saw, felt, knew was real, was bigger than what I could make of it. That made it a lifetime task, I saw that.

I have felt nagged to write for the theatre from time to time, craving theatricality, collaborative fanfare, and show; have written very scarcely for the films and for television. All forms of writing excite me and pain me and labor me; but the printed word, the Book—especially the short narrative form—most challenges and most frees me.

* * *

The literary position of the state of Texas has always been dubious in the spectrum of the Southern Literary Renaissance, that remarkable florescence of literary genius in 20th-century American writing which matches and in some ways surpasses the great 19th-century Flowering of New England. Much of the literary production of Texas seems to belong to a category best labeled "South-Western" rather than "Southern," whereas some novels are obviously closer to the fiction of the South and Border States. Whatever the labels, the literary record of Texas is more impressive than is generally assumed, ranging as it does from the celebrated books of folklorist J. Frank Dobie (such as *Apache Gold and Yaqui Silver*, and *Tales of Old Texas*) and George Sessions Perry's famous novel *Hold Autumn in Your Hand* (1941) to the now almost forgotten novels *The Devil Rides Outside* by John Howard Griffin and *Summer on the Water* by David Westheimer, but also including the works of Katherine Anne Porter, William Humphrey, Walter Clemons and William Goyen. An attempt to "locate" a body of fiction by state or region may, finally, be misleading. When Goyen's first novel, *House of Breath*, appeared in 1950, reviewers tended to see it in terms of William Faulkner and Thomas Wolfe, and in terms of clichés about the "Southern" novel. To those early reviewers, the richness of image, some eccentricities of syntax (parentheses within parentheses), the occasional violence, the hurt, and other such elements seemed to indicate a novel in the Southern mode; and certainly East Texas where the action takes place is closer in heritage to the Southern border states than to the wild west stereotypes. But, with the passage of time it has become increasingly apparent that Goyen's themes and fictional strategies are closer to those of Virginia Woolf than to Thomas Wolfe or Faulkner or even Anderson's *Winesburg, Ohio*.

Like the work of Flannery O'Connor, John Hawkes, and the later Mailer, Goyen's fiction is deliberately outside the realist traditions. Virginia Woolf in a review of Dorothy Richardson's *Revolving Lights* pointed out that Richardson was concerned "with states of being and not with states of doing." The violent activity in these writers' stories is often the outward sign for psychic states, so that Mailer in *An American Dream* seems finally uninterested in the murder, but rather more interested in the states of being of his characters—something quite different from Dreiser's treatment of the murder in *An American Tragedy*. Whether concerned with religion, sex, or politics the works are Romance. Hawthorne, after all, defined the word "Romance" at the beginning of *The House of the Seven Gables*—and despite Hemingway's brave assertion in *Green Hills of Africa* that all American literature comes from Twain's *Huckleberry Finn*, it is apparent that almost all major American novels can, in their theoretical basis, be traced back to Hawthorne's preface to his novel. William Goyen and a few other contemporary American novelists have taken the process a step further with their increasing reliance on a poetic prose to evoke deep psychic states, and their increasing abandonment of traditional realist themes and strategies: these novels are closer to *Cymbeline* and *A Winter's Tale* than to *Tom Jones* or *Bleak House*.

This particular sort of Romance has been distinguished in Ralph Freedman's important study *The Lyrical Novel*. The lyrical novel he defines as "concentration on the inner life and on its distillation in spiritual or aesthetic forms. The passive hero, recreating his perceptions symbolically, dominates the world of images for whose existence he is responsible." Further, "the lyrical novel assumes a unique form which transcends the causal and temporal movement of narrative within the framework of fiction." Though Freedman centers his examination on European writers of "the lyrical novel" (Rilke, Hesse, Woolf, Gide), that examination might be extended to Anaïs Nin, John Hawkes, Flannery O'Connor, and William Goyen. I have labored this theoretical point because Goyen's work has been constantly overlooked or even dismissed, since its aim and strategies have been overlooked or mistaken by critics and other readers.

Faces of Blood Kindred, for example, is a collection of brilliant "lyrical" stories, in Freedman's sense of the word. In many of them nothing much happens in the sense of external "doing." Yet states of being are evoked, or explored. The stories bear down on moments of revelation, when ties of family or kinship are revealed, usually by chance incidents. The consequences of the revelation or discovery seem less important than the moment of perception itself: in a 19th century English novel, a boy might discover who his parents were, and he would automatically fit into a family structure; but in Goyen's work, the old stable family units have broken down, so that kinship tends to be spiritual rather than social, tends to an archetypal relationship beyond the social world.

To many readers, expecting a different sort of fiction, the stories seem vague, seeking to evoke more than they say, something beyond language at which language can only offer hints and guesses. "There are, indeed, things that cannot be put into words. They *make themselves manifest.* They are what is mystical." These words are not Goyen's but Wittgenstein's in his supposedly "positivist" *Tractatus* (6.522).

Like Carson McCullers, whose stories are also often ostensibly violent yet internalized, Goyen is a true extension of the Transcendental strain in American fiction. The rude, scarred, outcast people of the stories are manifestations of spiritual conditions. In his second novel, *In a Farther Country*, the narrator says: "Here, again, was the frail artifice built by the world that dreamt the solid other, the marriage and mixture of dream and circumstance that breeds back daily the pure race...." His novels and stories are collections of voices (compare Wallace Stevens's great line in "The Woman That Had More Babies Than That": "The self is a cloister full of remembered sounds") each trying to tell of some hidden sort of Platonic other-world of forms or ideal states, or the truth of a life.

The stories and tales collected in *Ghost and Flesh* all concern characters whose telling of their lives, as in conversation, lead Goyen to deal with intermediate states, to the struggles between body and soul, ghost and flesh, the frustrated search of each for the other in a total communion that can at best be only momentary. The intermediacy is also temporal; for as in *House of Breath* the narrator recounts stories that do not happen in the present, yet are not entirely in the past: they are part of what the narrator thinks he might blow away (the house, or family, of the book is, after all, the creation of the telling, the boy-man's breath) yet cannot since it all exists like "a fresco on the wall of [his] skull." The permanence of the fleeting moment, in altered lives as in a single man's memory, constitutes one of the recurring themes. Yet reality always seems to lie elsewhere, somewhere toward which the tensions between ghost and flesh may lead. It is strange to hear Mailer apparently so different from Goyen, now saying in *Maidstone* (1971): "You can't say that this is real now, what we're doing. You can't say what we were doing last night is real; the only thing you can say is that the reality exists somewhere in the extraordinary tension between the extremes."

This questioning of reality is one of the central themes in Goyen's books. *The Fair Sister*, for example, is a shrewd, witty, and revealing study of religious feeling. The first person narrator, Ruby Drew, tells (or seems to tell) about the Light of the World Holiness Church, her fair sister Savata, and Canaan Johnson who tempted and won. The story of two sisters, one dark and one light, gives us the struggle of ugliness (self-concealed) and devotion (self-congratulated), of holiness and sensuality, cast in the diction and rhythms of a revivalism which is finally ambiguous: who can say what is being revived, or what the truth of the situation is? Or, another example from *In a Farther Country*, the setting in Woolworth's to which the central character returns "every day to smell and touch" the things of this world within the other world of New York City. "She seemed unhurried, unenthusiastic. She asked the same question every day, 'Where is the lunch counter?' as though Woolworth's were a vast uncharted country...." When she gains entry to the store at night, she asks, "But where is Woolworth's?" The counters have been covered with dustcloths, so that the store of the nightwatchman is not the same as the store of the salesgirls. The eccentric behaviour of the woman and her apparently simple questions raise issues of appearance and reality which become central in later chapters, as each character in his telling of his life arrives at some moment of communal insight: "Confusion seeks confusion to clarify itself before falling to confusion again." And the novel rises to a visionary denouement.

I have not dealt with Goyen's superb first novel, *House of Breath*, since it has received ample critical commentary already; nor with his classic stories, "The White Rooster" and "Letter in the Cedar Chest," well known through anthologies. For it seems to me crucial that we begin to see the work of this fine literary artist not in terms of the southern gothic novel of violence and race, but in larger terms.

—James Korges

GRAHAM, Winston. British. Born in Victoria Park, Manchester, Lancashire, in 1909. Married Jean Mary Williamson in 1939; one son and one daughter. Chairman, Society of Authors, London, 1967-69. Recipient: Crime Writers Association prize, 1956. Fellow, Royal Society of Literature, 1968. Address: Abbotswood House, Buxted, East Sussex, England.

PUBLICATIONS

Novels

The House with the Stained-Glass Windows. London, Ward Lock, 1934.
Into the Fog. London, Ward Lock, 1935.
The Riddle of John Rowe. London, Ward Lock, 1935.
Without Motive. London, Ward Lock, 1936.
The Dangerous Pawn. London, Ward Lock, 1937.
The Giant's Chair. London, Ward Lock, 1938.
Strangers Meeting. London, Ward Lock, 1939.
Keys of Chance. London, Ward Lock, 1939.
No Exit: An Adventure. London, Ward Lock, 1940.
Night Journey. London, Ward Lock, 1941; New York, Doubleday, 1968.
My Turn Next. London, Ward Lock, 1942.
The Merciless Ladies. London, Ward Lock, 1944; revised edition, London, Bodley Head, 1979.
The Forgotten Story. London, Ward Lock, 1945; as *The Wreck of The Grey Cat*, New York, Doubleday, 1958.
Ross Poldark: A Novel of Cornwall 1783-1787. London, Ward Lock, 1945; as *The Renegade*, New York, Doubleday, 1951.
Demelza: A Novel of Cornwall 1788-1790. London, Ward Lock, 1946; New York, Doubleday, 1953.
Take My Life. London, Ward Lock, 1947; New York, Doubleday, 1967.
Cordelia. London, Ward Lock, 1949; New York, Doubleday, 1950.
Night Without Stars. London, Hodder and Stoughton, and New York, Doubleday, 1950.
Jeremy Poldark: A Novel of Cornwall 1790-1791. London, Ward Lock, 1950; as *Venture Once More*, New York, Doubleday, 1954.
Warleggan: A Novel of Cornwall 1792-1793. London, Ward Lock, 1953; as *The Last Gamble*, New York, Doubleday, 1955.
Fortune Is a Woman. London, Hodder and Stoughton, and New York, Doubleday, 1953.
The Little Walls. London, Hodder and Stoughton, and New York, Doubleday, 1955; abridged edition, as *Bridge to Vengeance*, New York, Spivak, 1957.
The Sleeping Partner. London, Hodder and Stoughton, and New York, Doubleday, 1956.
Greek Fire. London, Hodder and Stoughton, and New York, Doubleday, 1958.
The Tumbled House. London, Hodder and Stoughton, 1959; New York, Doubleday, 1960.
Marnie. London, Hodder and Stoughton, and New York, Doubleday, 1961.
The Grove of Eagles. London, Hodder and Stoughton, 1963; New York, Doubleday, 1964.

After the Act. London, Hodder and Stoughton, 1965; New York, Doubleday, 1966.
The Walking Stick. London, Collins, and New York, Doubleday, 1967.
Angell, Pearl and Little God. London, Collins, and New York, Doubleday, 1970.
The Black Moon: A Novel of Cornwall 1794-1795. London, Collins, 1973; New York, Doubleday, 1974.
Woman in the Mirror. London, Bodley Head, and New York, Doubleday, 1975.
The Four Swans: A Novel of Cornwall 1795-1797. London, Collins, 1976; New York, Doubleday, 1977.
The Angry Tide: A Novel of Cornwall 1798-1799. London, Collins, 1977; New York, Doubleday, 1978.
The Merciless Ladies. London, Bodley Head, 1979; New York, Doubleday, 1980.

Short Stories

The Japanese Girl and Other Stories. London, Collins, 1971; New York, Doubleday, 1972.

Uncollected Short Story

"The Circus," in *Winter's Crimes 6*, edited by George Hardinge. London, Macmillan, 1974.

Plays

Shadow Play (produced Salisbury, 1978).
Circumstantial Evidence (produced Guildford, Surrey, 1979).

Screenplays: *Take My Life*, with Valerie Taylor, 1947; *Night Without Stars*, 1951.

Radio Play: *Little Walls*, 1956.

Other

The Spanish Armadas. London, Collins, and New York, Doubleday, 1972.

*

Winston Graham comments:

I look on myself simply as a novelist. I have written—always—what I wanted to write and not what I thought people might want me to write. Reading for me has always been in the first place a matter of enjoyment—otherwise I don't read—and therefore I would expect other people to read my books for the enjoyment they found in them—or not at all. Profit from reading a novel should always be a by-product. The essence to me of style is simplicity, and while I admit there are depths of thought too complex for easy expression, I would despise myself for using complexity of expression where simplicity will do.

If there has been a certain dichotomy in my work, it is simply due to a dichotomy in my own interests. I am deeply interested in history and deeply interested in the present; and I find a stimulus and a refreshment in turning from one subject and one form to another.

I like books of suspense at whatever level they may be written, whether on that of Jane Austen or of Raymond Chandler; so I think all my books of whatever kind contain some of that element which makes a reader want to turn the page—the "and then and then" of which E.M. Forster speaks. This can be a liability if over-indulged in; but so of course can any other preference or attribute.

Although I have always had more to say in a novel than the telling of a story, the story itself has always been the framework on which the rest has depended for its form and shape. I have never been clever enough—or sufficiently self-concerned—to spend 300 pages dipping experimental buckets into the sludge of my own subconscious. I have always been more interested in other people than in myself—though there has to be something of myself in every character created, or he or she will not come to life. I have always been more interested in people than in events, but it is only through events that I have ever been able to illuminate people.

* * *

Of the 30-odd novels Winston Graham has published over nearly 50 years, many of the modern ones are in some way concerned with crime. But they are not, in the usual sense of the term, "crime stories." In them, crime is a kind of catalyst speeding and provoking action, rather than an end in itself or a sufficient reason for the story, as it is in thrillers. It is seen as an aberration in otherwise normal lives, something non-criminal people, generally respectable and middle-class, may slip into or become involved with, gradually, almost imperceptibly, for all kinds of reasons—greed, love, loyalty, even a sudden impulse, but not through a "professional" criminal background. It is not surprising that his novel *Marnie* became one of Hitchcock's most successful films—since Hitchcock too is interested in the way ordinary people may become entangled in the bizarre.

Graham has written straighforward thrillers, and what Michael Gilbert wrote in choosing *The Little Walls* for his "classics of detection and adventure" series applies to the other novels equally well. It was, he says, "the very best of those adventure stories which introduce what has come to be known in critical jargon as the anti-hero...a useful portmanteau expression to describe someone who undertakes the hero's role, without the hero's normal equipment." The characters in all Graham's novels are, in fact, floundering and all-too-human amateurs, realistically placed in a present-day life that includes jobs and domesticity well observed, and with a normal proneness to fear, indiscretion and lack of nerve; caught in the end by their moral attitudes, by those who love them, by grief, conscience, and the realistic eye of their creator, who knows that their amateur status fails to give them the professional's coolness, his moral indifference.

Graham's sinners are nearly all racked by their sins, and he is fascinated both by the "congenital" liars and outsiders (Marnie, or the crook-lover in *The Walking Stick*), who are conditioned by their past yet devotedly loved in the present, and by their victims, or the victims of circumstances, mistakes, impulses, devotions: the narrator of *After the Act*, for instance, who pushes his ailing wife off a balcony, then finds he cannot face the mistress he ostensibly did it for. Graham values suspense; and, for his own fiction, at least, believes in action rather than analysis as the means to bring his characters to life.

His novels can roughly be divided into two, the modern and the historical. To the historical novels he brings the same *kind* of realism that he does to the present day. Through *Cordelia*, the Poldark novels set in 18th-century Cornwall, or *The Forgotten Story*, another tale about ordinary people involved in murder, this time at the turn of the last century, one walks familiarly. Graham has the good historical novelist's ability to suggest, rather than describe, the physical surroundings; above all to avoid gadzookery and picturesqueness. As he can get the feel of an insurance office, a printing works, or an auctioneer's, so he can walk into the past, giving the sense and atmosphere of it rather than the physical detail, making one breathe its air.

—Isabel Quigly

GRANGE, Peter. *See* **NICOLE, Christopher.**

GRAU, Shirley Ann. American. Born in New Orleans, Louisiana, 8 July 1929. Educated at Tulane University, New Orleans, B.A. 1950. Married James Kern Feibleman in 1955; four children. Recipient: Pulitzer Prize, 1965. Lives in Metairie, Louisiana. Address: c/o Brandt and Brandt, 1501 Broadway, New York, New York 10036, U.S.A.

PUBLICATIONS

Novels

The Hard Blue Sky. New York, Knopf, 1958; London, Heinemann, 1959.
The House on Coliseum Street. New York, Knopf, and London, Heinemann, 1961.
The Keepers of the House. New York, Knopf, and London, Longman, 1964.
The Condor Passes. New York, Knopf, 1971; London, Longman, 1972.
Evidence of Love. New York, Knopf, and London, Hamish Hamilton, 1977.

Short Stories

The Black Prince and Other Stories. New York, Knopf, 1955; London, Heinemann, 1956.
The Wind Shifting West. New York, Knopf, 1973; London, Chatto and Windus, 1974.

* * *

Shirley Ann Grau may be described as a Southern writer, whose range is sometimes narrowly regional. She may also, therefore, be described as a local colorist whose observations of custom and character suggest an anthropologist at work in a fictional mode. She is a white author who deals with blacks and the black sub-culture, which makes her an anomaly in a period of black militancy. And she is finally a novelist of manners who is sharply aware of the collapse of conventional behaviour patterns in modern life. The pervasive style and mood of her work may be summed up best in the terms tough, cold, and realistic. The toughness and the apparent realism seem to reveal a debt to Hemingway. She is never sentimental, and almost always she maintains sufficient distance from her characters to depict them with an objectivity that is sometimes little short of chilling. At her best she displays a kind of cold power. But she is, in general, a limited writer. She lacks originality, especially in her treatment of Negroes and of the South. More seriously, she lacks the complex vision that enables her both to see around and to penetrate deeply into her subject. She is a competent writer who stands at some distance from the center of the Southern Renaissance.

Her best work to date is *The Keepers of the House*, a novel about a Southern family. The story concerns Will Howland who inherits a great deal of land and acquires more. After the death of his wife, he brings a Negro girl into his house and has by her three children who survive. Late in the book, it is revealed that Will had secretly married the Negro girl. He is portrayed as a good, compassionate man whose miscegenation arose out of love. His white granddaughter marries a man who enters politics, joins the Klan, runs for governor, and makes anti-Negro speeches. One of Will's children by the Negro woman reveals that his father is related to a racist politician. As a result of the revelation, the latter is ruined and the Howland family estate attacked. The estate endures, and the daughter revenges herself upon the town.

Grau is fully aware that the glamourous past may be a trap, as one of her short stories reveals. But she also knows that family traditions which are rooted in the past may endow life in the present with an illuminating sense of time and a stabilizing sense of place; in these ways the past provides a sense of continuity which enriches life in the present. This novel centers on these conceptions of life, which are characteristically Southern and which mark the work of other contemporary Southern writers as different as Robert Penn Warren and Eudora Welty. The treatment of inter-racial love here, made acceptable by marriage, appears to be an apologia for Southern miscegenation, which is, of course, usually conceived in much harsher terms. The same is true of the manipulation of racial animosities in politics, which in itself is authentic enough in the novel. But in depicting the defeat of the racist, Grau seems to depart from her characteristically objective stance.

That stance she had maintained in *The Hard Blue Sky*, which reveals her talent for local color. The scene is an island in the Gulf of Mexico inhabited by characters of French and Spanish descent. The principal conflict is between them and the inhabitants of another island who are Slavic in descent. A boy from one island marries a girl from another; the marriage precipitates a feud. Added to the violence of men is the violence of nature, displayed when a hurricane sweeps through the Gulf. Miss Grau does not dwell on the quaintness of character or place in her novel, and she does not patronize her characters, although the temptation to do so must have been quite real, since she conceives them as primitives. She looks at them coldly and clearly, dramatizing their attitudes toward life but passing no judgment on their behaviour. These are people who recognize no canons of respectability, who admit of no restraints on their passions, and who recognize no guilt. Their sexual attitudes are thus quite free, sex being simply in the natural order of things, and their tendency toward violence is always close to the surface, since they believe that a good fight is healthy. Their life is hard and the hazards of nature, whether snakes or wind, make it harder.

Her treatment of the characters in this novel is the same, generally speaking, as her treatment of Negroes throughout her fiction. Her composite Negro lives an unstructured life in which he obeys appetite and impulse in a naturally selfish movement toward gratification. His morality is virtually non-existent, but casual if apparent at all. His capacity for violence is like that of the islanders. This Negro does not rise to the level of self-consciousness. Ralph Ellison might say that he is a stereotype, perceived because the white writer suffers from a psychic-social blindness caused by the construction of the inner eye; that is, either Grau is blind or the real Negro is invisible.

Grau's chief contribution to the novel of manners is *The House on Coliseum Street.* Although it is an inferior work, it demonstrates, as some of her short stories have, that she understands the various kinds of moral corruption that mark modern life. She knows that the contemporary world is without values, and she makes divorce and sexual promiscuity the obvious signs, in this novel, of the disintegration of well-to-do society.

The Condor Passes is another family novel, melodramatic in plot but of interest for its method: much of the story is told from the five points of view of the five major characters. *Evidence of Love*, like James Gould Cozzens's *By Love Possessed*, concerns the varieties of love, some a burdensome chore, as Grau shows in the sensitive and effective section on the old mother who, content in her loneliness, awaits the coming of death. The title story of her collection *The Wind Shifting West* displays Grau's feel for water and sky, but only occasionally do the other stories reveal the detachment and power which distinguish her fictional voice at its best.

—Chester E. Eisinger

GRAVES, Robert (Ranke). British. Born in London, 24 July 1895. Educated at Charterhouse School, Surrey; St. John's College, Oxford, B. Litt. 1926. Served with the Royal Welch Fusiliers in World War I; was refused admittance into the armed forces in World War II. Married 1)Nancy Nicholson, one son and two daughters; 2)Beryl Pritchard, three sons and one daughter. Professor of English, Egyptian University, Cairo, 1926. Settled in Deyá, Mallorca, in 1929; with the poet Laura Riding established the Seizin Press and *Epilogue* magazine. Clark Lecturer, Trinity College, Cambridge, 1954; Professor of Poetry, Oxford University, 1961-66; Arthur Dehon Little Memorial Lecturer, Massachusetts Institute of Technology, Cambridge, 1963. Recipient: Bronze Medal for Poetry, Olympic Games, Paris, 1924; Hawthornden Prize, 1935; Black Memorial Prize, 1935; Femina Vie Heureuse-Stock Prize, 1939; Russell Loines Poetry Award, 1958; National Poetry Society of America Gold Medal, 1960; Foyle Poetry Prize, 1960; Arts Council Poetry Award, 1962; Italia Prize, for radio play, 1965; Queen's Gold Medal for Poetry, 1968; Gold Medal for Poetry, Cultural Olympics, Mexico City, 1968. M.A.: Oxford University, 1961. Honorary Member, American Academy of Arts and Sciences, 1970. Address: c/o A.P. Watt Ltd., 26-28 Bedford Row, London WC1R 4HL, England.

PUBLICATIONS

Novels

No Decency Left (as Barbara Rich, with Laura Riding). London, Cape, 1932.
The Real David Copperfield. London, Barker, 1933; as *David Cooperfield by Charles Dickens, Condensed by Robert Graves,* edited by Merrill P. Paine, New York, Harcourt Brace, 1934.
I, Claudius.... London, Barker, and New York, Smith and Haas, 1934.
Claudius the God and His Wife Messalina.... London, Barker, 1934; New York, Smith and Haas, 1935.
"Antigua, Penny, Puce." Deyá, Mallorca, Seizin Press, and London, Constable, 1936; as *The Antigua Stamp*, New York, Random House, 1937.
Count Belisarius. London, Cassell, and New York, Random House, 1938.
Sergeant Lamb of the Ninth. London, Methuen, 1940; as *Sergeant Lamb's America*, New York, Random House, 1940.
Proceed, Sergeant Lamb. London, Methuen, and New York, Random House, 1941.
The Story of Marie Powell: Wife to Mr. Milton. London, Cassell, 1943; as *Wife to Mr. Milton*, New York, Creative Age Press, 1944.
The Golden Fleece. London, Cassell, 1944; as *Hercules, My Shipmate*, New York, Creative Age Press, 1945.
King Jesus. New York, Creative Age Press, and London, Cassell, 1946.
Watch the North Wind Rise. New York, Creative Age Press, 1949; as *Seven Days in New Crete*, London, Cassell, 1949.
The Islands of Unwisdom. New York, Doubleday, 1949; as *The Isles of Unwisdom*, London, Cassell, 1950.
Homer's Daughter. London, Cassell, and New York, Doubleday, 1955.

Short Stories

The Shout. London, Mathews and Marrot, 1929.
¡Catacrok! Mostly Stories, Mostly Funny. London, Cassell, 1956.
Collected Short Stories. New York, Doubleday, 1964; London, Cassell, 1965; as *The Shout and Other Stories*, London, Penguin, 1978.

Plays

John Kemp's Wager: A Ballad Opera. Oxford, Blackwell, and New York, Edwards, 1925.

Radio Play: *The Anger of Achilles*, 1964.

Verse

Over the Brazier. London, Poetry Bookshop, 1916; New York, St. Martin's Press, 1975.
Goliath and David. London, Chiswick Press, 1916.
Fairies and Fusiliers. London, Heinemann, 1917; New York, Knopf, 1918.
Treasure Box. London, Chiswick Press, 1919.
Country Sentiment. London, Secker, and New York, Knopf, 1920.
The Pier-Glass. London, Secker, and New York, Knopf, 1921.
Whipperginny. London, Heinemann, and New York, Knopf, 1923.
The Feather Bed. Richmond, Surrey, Hogarth Press, 1923.
Mock Beggar Hall. London, Hogarth Press, 1924.
Welchman's Hose. London, The Fleuron, 1925; Folcroft, Pennsylvania, Folcroft Editions, 1971.
(Poems). London, Benn, 1925.
The Marmosite's Miscellany (as John Doyle). London, Hogarth Press, 1925.
Poems (1914-1926). London, Heinemann, 1927; New York, Doubleday, 1929.
Poems (1914-1927). London, Heinemann, 1927.
Poems 1929. London, Seizin Press, 1929.
Ten Poems More. Paris, Hours Press, 1930.
Poems 1926-1930. London, Heinemann, 1931.
To Whom Else? Deyá, Mallorca, Seizin Press, 1931.
Poems 1930-1933. London, Barker, 1933.
Collected Poems. London, Cassell, and New York, Random House, 1938.
No More Ghosts: Selected Poems. London, Faber, 1940.
(Poems). London, Eyre and Spottiswoode, 1943.
Poems 1938-1945. London, Cassell, and New York, Creative Age Press, 1946.
Collected Poems (1914-1947). London, Cassell, 1948.
Poems and Satires 1951. London, Cassell, 1951.
Poems 1953. London, Cassell, 1953.
Collected Poems 1955. New York, Doubleday, 1955.
Poems Selected by Himself. London, Penguin, 1957; revised edition, 1961, 1966, 1972.
The Poems of Robert Graves. New York, Doubleday, 1958.
Collected Poems 1959. London, Cassell, 1959.
More Poems 1961. London, Cassell, 1961.
Collected Poems. New York, Doubleday, 1961.
New Poems 1962. London, Cassell, 1962; as *New Poems*, New York, Doubleday, 1963.
The More Deserving Cases: Eighteen Old Poems for Reconsideration. Marlborough, Marlborough College Press, 1962; Folcroft, Pennsylvania, Folcroft Editions, 1978.
Man Does, Woman Is 1964. London, Cassell, and New York, Doubleday, 1964.
Love Respelt. London, Cassell, 1965.
Collected Poems 1965. London, Cassell, 1965.
Seventeen Poems Missing from "Love Respelt." Privately printed, 1966.
Collected Poems 1966. New York, Doubleday, 1966.
Colophon to "Love Respelt." Privately printed, 1967.
(Poems), with D.H. Lawrence, edited by Leonard Clark. London, Longman, 1967.
Poems 1965-1968. London, Cassell, 1968; New York, Doubleday, 1969.
Poems about Love. London, Cassell, and New York, Doubleday, 1969.
Love Respelt Again. New York, Doubleday, 1969.
Beyond Giving. Privately printed, 1969.
Poems 1968-1970. London, Cassell, 1970.
Advice from a Mother. London, Poem-of-the-Month Club, 1970.
The Green-Sailed Vessel. Privately printed, 1971.
Corgi Modern Poets in Focus 3, with others, edited by Dannie Abse. London, Corgi, 1971.

Poems 1970-1972. London, Cassell, 1972; New York, Doubleday, 1973.
Deyá. London, Motif Editions, 1973.
Timeless Meeting: Poems. London, Rota, 1973.
At the Gate. London, Rota, 1974.
Collected Poems 1975. London, Cassell, 2 vols., 1975.
New Collected Poems. New York, Doubleday, 1977.

Recordings: *Robert Graves Reading His Own Poems,* Argo and Listen, 1960; *Robert Graves Reading His Own Poetry and The White Goddess*, Caedmon; *The Rubaiyat of Omar Khayyam*, Spoken Arts.

Other

On English Poetry. New York, Knopf, and London, Heinemann, 1922.
The Meaning of Dreams. London, Cecil Palmer, 1924; New York, Greenberg, 1925.
Poetic Unreason and Other Studies. London, Cecil Palmer, 1925.
My Head! My Head! Being the History of Elisha and the Shunamite Woman; With the History of Moses as Elisha Related It, and Her Questions to Him. London, Secker, and New York, Knopf, 1925.
Contemporary Techniques of Poetry: A Political Analogy. London, Hogarth Press, 1925; Folcroft, Pennsylvania, Folcroft Editions, 1977.
Another Future of Poetry. London, Hogarth Press, 1926.
Impenetrability; or, The Proper Habit of English. London, Hogarth Press, 1926.
The English Ballad: A Short Critical Survey. London, Benn, 1927; revised edition, as *English and Scottish Ballads*, London, Heinemann, and New York, Macmillan, 1957.
Lars Porsena; or, The Future of Swearing and Improper Language. London, Kegan Paul Trench Trubner, and New York, Dutton, 1927; revised edition, as *The Future of Swearing and Improper Language*, Kegan Paul Trench Trubner, 1936.
A Survey of Modernist Poetry, with Laura Riding. London, Heinemann, 1927; New York, Doubleday, 1928.
Lawrence and the Arabs. London, Cape, 1927; as *Lawrence and the Arabian Adventure*, New York, Doubleday, 1928.
A Pamphlet Against Anthologies, with Laura Riding. London, Cape, 1928; as *Against Anthologies*, New York, Doubleday, 1928.
Mrs. Fisher; or, The Future of Humour. London, Kegan Paul Trench Trubner, 1928; Folcroft, Pennsylvania, Folcroft Editions, 1974.
Goodbye to All That: An Autobiography. London, Cape, 1929; New York, Cape and Smith, 1930; revised edition, New York, Doubleday, and London, Cassell, 1957; London, Penguin, 1960.
T.E. Lawrence to His Biographer Robert Graves. New York, Doubleday, 1938; London, Faber, 1939.
The Long Week-end: A Social History of Great Britain 1918-1939, with Alan Hodge. London, Faber, 1940; New York, Macmillan, 1941.
Work in Hand, with others. London, Hogarth Press, 1942.
The Reader over Your Shoulder: A Handbook for Writers of English Prose, with Alan Hodge. London, Cape, 1943; New York, Macmillan, 1944.
The White Goddess: A Historical Grammar of Poetic Myth. London, Faber, and New York, Creative Age Press, 1948; revised edition, Faber, 1952, 1966; New York, Knopf, 1958.
The Common Asphodel: Collected Essays on Poetry 1922-1949. London, Hamish Hamilton, 1949; Folcroft, Pennsylvania, Folcroft Editions, 1971.
Occupation: Writer. New York, Creative Age Press, 1950; London, Cassell, 1951.
The Nazarene Gospel Restored, with Joshua Podro. London, Cassell, 1953; New York, Doubleday, 1954.
The Crowning Privilege: The Clark Lectures 1954-1955; Also Various Essays on Poetry and Sixteen New Poems. London, Cassell, 1955; as *The Crowning Privilege: Collected Essays on Poetry*, New York, Doubleday, 1956.
Adam's Rib and Other Anomalous Elements in the Hebrew Creation Myth: A New View. London, Trianon Press, 1955; New York, Yoseloff, 1958.
The Greek Myths. London and Baltimore, Penguin, 2 vols., 1955.
Jesus in Rome: A Historical Conjecture, with Joshua Podro. London, Cassell, 1957.
They Hanged My Saintly Billy. London, Cassell, 1957; as *They Hanged My Saintly Billy: The Life and Death of Dr. William Palmer*, New York, Doubleday, 1957.
Steps: Stories, Talks, Essays, Poems, Studies in History. London, Cassell, 1958.
5 Pens in Hand. New York, Doubleday, 1958.
Food for Centaurs: Stories, Talks, Critical Studies, Poems. New York, Doubleday, 1960.
The Penny Fiddle: Poems for Children. London, Cassell, 1960; New York, Doubleday, 1961.
Greek Gods and Heroes. New York, Doubleday, 1960; as *Myths of Ancient Greece*, London, Cassell, 1961.
Selected Poetry and Prose, edited by James Reeves. London, Hutchinson, 1961.
The Siege and Fall of Troy (juvenile). London, Cassell, 1962; New York, Doubleday, 1963.
The Big Green Book. New York, Crowell Collier, 1962; London, Penguin, 1978.
Oxford Addresses on Poetry. London, Cassell, and New York, Doubleday, 1962.
Nine Hundred Iron Chariots: The Twelfth Arthur Dehon Little Memorial Lecture. Cambridge, Massachusetts Institute of Technology, 1963.
The Hebrew Myths: The Book of Genesis, with Raphael Patai. New York, Doubleday, and London, Cassell, 1964.
Ann at Highwood Hall: Poems for Children. London, Cassell, 1964.
Majorca Observed. London, Cassell, and New York, Doubleday, 1965.
Mammon and the Black Goddess. London, Cassell, and New York, Doubleday, 1965.
Two Wise Children (juvenile). New York, Harlin Quist, 1966; London, W.H. Allen, 1967.
Poetic Craft and Principle. London, Cassell, 1967.
Spiritual Quixote. London, Oxford University Press, 1967.
The Poor Boy Who Followed His Star (juvenile). London, Cassell, 1968; New York, Doubleday, 1969.
The Crane Bag and Other Disputed Subjects. London, Cassell, 1969.
On Poetry: Collected Talks and Essays. New York, Doubleday, 1969.
Poems: Abridged for Dolls and Princes (juvenile). London, Cassell, and New York, Doubleday, 1971.
Difficult Questions, Easy Answers. London, Cassell, 1972; New York, Doubleday, 1973.
An Ancient Castle (juvenile). London, Owen, 1980.

Editor, with Alan Porter and Richard Hughes, *Oxford Poetry 1921.* Oxford, Blackwell, 1921.
Editor, *John Skelton (Laureate), 1460(?)-1529.* London, Benn, 1927.
Editor, *The Less Familiar Nursery Rhymes.* London, Benn, 1927.
Editor, *The Comedies of Terence.* New York, Doubleday, 1962; London, Cassell, 1963.

Translator, with Laura Riding, *Almost Forgotten Germany*, by Georg Schwartz. Deyá, Mallorca, Seizin Press, London, Constable, and New York, Random House, 1936.
Translator, *The Transformations of Lucius, Otherwise Known as The Golden Ass*, by Apuleius. London, Penguin, 1950; New York, Farrar Straus, 1951.

Translator, *The Cross and the Sword*, by Manuel de Jésus Galván. Bloomington, Indiana University Press, 1955; London, Gollancz, 1956.
Translator, *The Infant with the Globe*, by Pedro Antonio de Alarcón. London, Trianon Press, 1955; New York, Yoseloff, 1958.
Translator, *Winter in Majorca*, by George Sand. London, Cassell, 1956.
Translator, *Pharsalia: Dramatic Episodes of the Civil Wars*, by Lucan. London, Penguin, 1956.
Translator, *The Twelve Caesars*, by Suetonius. London, Penguin, 1957.
Translator, *The Anger of Achilles: Homer's Iliad*. New York, Doubleday, 1959; London, Cassell, 1960.
Translator, with Omar Ali-Shah, *Rubaiyat of Omar Khayyam*. London, Cassell, 1967; New York, Doubleday, 1968.
Translator, *The Song of Songs*. New York, Clarkson Potter, and London, Collins, 1973.

*

Bibliography: *A Bibliography of the Works of Robert Graves* by Fred H. Higginson, London, Nicholas Vane, 1966.

Manuscript Collections: Lockwood Memorial Library, State University of New York at Buffalo; New York City Public Library; University of Texas Library, Austin.

Critical Studies (selection): *Robert Graves* by Martin Seymour-Smith, London, Longman, 1956, revised edition, 1965, 1970; *Robert Graves* by J.M. Cohen, Edinburgh, Oliver and Boyd, 1960, New York, Barnes and Noble, 1965; *Robert Graves* by George Stade, New York, Columbia University Press, 1967; *Robert Graves* by Katherine Snipes, New York, Ungar, 1979; *Robert Graves* by Robert H. Canary, Boston, Twayne, 1980.

* * *

The critic who sets out to comment upon Robert Graves the novelist by considering first his work in other literary forms is not taking an unnecessary detour but the high road to understanding. It is not merely that Graves is a most versatile writer—perhaps more versatile than any of his contemporaries—but that his writing of fiction has been notably affected by his literary interests outside the novel and that those interests illuminate the style, the *mores*, and the subject matter of his novels.

Graves has been biographer, autobiographer, translator, critic, mythologist, biblical commentator, essayist, polemicist, and, above all other things, poet, as well as novelist. He has infused many of these roles into his work as a novelist, and in all of them he has shown himself to be flamboyant, original sometimes to the point of eccentricity, and always superbly competent.

If it is possible to forecast the judgement of posterity then it is likely that he will come to be regarded finally and highly as a poet, but it is as a novelist, and particularly as a historical novelist, that he has won and holds affection among the widest range of contemporary readers. Yet the two novels that are, at least in the mundane sense, his most successful, *I, Claudius* and *Claudius the God and His Wife Messalina*, are palpable extensions of his work as a classical scholar though neither of them is in any sense a scholar's novel. Graves seizes upon a central figure—Claudius, the bumbling, near-lunatic nonentity of the history books—and settles the patterns of his career to fit a subtle psychological interpretation that is history only as Graves would have had it. The background to the novels, of brutality, sensuality, and superstition in Rome of the first century, is custom-built for Graves's robust skill.

Similarly, his classical and his biblical scholarship establishes an authority for *King Jesus*, but it is an unorthodox, even a perverse authority. His Jesus like his Claudius is a god, just as Belisarius in *Count Belisarius* and Jason in *The Golden Fleece*, being myth-heroes, are close to being gods, but these gods and myth-heroes he drags from their pedestals, not because he despises the gods themselves but because, by revealing the fallibility of generally accepted mythology, by reducing to the level of everyday human behaviour, he hopes to undermine the power of those—the latter-day priests—who have made myth into religion. "The true fiend governs in God's name."

Paradoxically, Graves is seldom interested in the ordinary. His god-heroes are extraordinary mortals and immortals; even while they move and speak in a superficially ordinary way they are larger than life. His few seemingly contemporary novels such as *"Antigua, Penny, Puce"* are equally unconnected with reality and almost as fantastical as his novels based on history and mythology. Most of his characters are larger than life, as close to caricature as is myth itself, and in this tendency there is a hint of the autobiographer, the self-revealer, at work, for Graves is himself larger than life—and one suspects that he knows it and revels in the knowledge.

Only one novella, *The Shout*, is more patently written in response to personal experience, though it is not difficult to read even into an ostensibly historical novel, *Wife to Mr. Milton*, something of the same confessional quality that is obvious in much of Graves's love poetry, and to see in the novel as in the poems the conflict between ardour and squeamishness which appears to have disrupted his own life. *The Shout*, however, despite its supernatural theme, is founded substantially upon Graves's recollections of the effects of shell-shock and is, as it were, a codicil to his autobiography, *Goodbye to All That*, one of the best autobiographies of this century.

To assert that *Count Belisarius*, *Sergeant Lamb of the Ninth*, *Proceed, Sergeant Lamb*, as well as the many and fine military passages in other novels, are also autobiographies may seem ridiculous and certainly involves the critic in anachronism, yet Graves the soldier is intrinsic to Graves the novelist. Like so many of his literary contemporaries Graves suffered from his experiences in the First World War and seems never to have shaken off the nightmare of the trenches. Like many of them—and notably his friends Sassoon and Blunden—he had been a good front-line soldier, with all that implies of staunchness and courage, and he is at his best when he writes of war, sensitive to its horrors but revelling in the ingenuity, bravery, and comradeship that it inspires.

Graves is not in the fullest sense an original writer of fiction. He seldom "creates" plots, characters, or situations. His is the genius that uses what was or what might have been, twists it and moulds it to suit his own polemical and narrative purposes. It is no mean genius.

> Assemble first all casual bits and scraps
> That may shake down into a world perhaps.
> Sigh then, or frown, but leave (as in despair)
> Motive and end and moral in the air:
> Nice contradiction between fact and fact
> Will make the whole read human and exact.
>
> "The Devil's Advice to Story-tellers"

—J.E. Morpurgo

GRAY, Simon (James Holliday). British. Born on Hayling Island, Hampshire, 21 October 1936. Educated at a school in Montreal; Westminster School, London; Dalhousie University, Halifax, Nova Scotia, 1954-57, B.A. (honours) in English 1957; Trinity College, Cambridge, 1958-61, B.A. (honours) in English 1961, M.A. Married Beryl Mary Kevern in 1965; one son and one daughter. Harper-Wood Student, St. John's College, Cambridge, 1961-62; Research Student, Trinity College, Cambridge, 1962-63; Lecturer in English, University of British Columbia, Vancouver, 1963-64; Supervisor in English, Trinity College, Cambridge, 1964-66. Sinc

1966, Lecturer in English, Queen Mary College, London. Since 1964, Editor of *Delta* magazine, Cambridge. Recipient: *Evening Standard* award, 1972, 1976; New York Drama Critics Circle Award, 1977. Agent: Judy Daish Associates, Globe Theatre, Shaftesbury Avenue, London W.1. Address: 70 Priory Gardens, London N6, England.

PUBLICATIONS

Novels

Colmain. London, Faber, 1963.
Simple People. London, Faber, 1965.
Little Portia. London, Faber, 1967.
A Comeback for Stark (as Hamish Reade). London, Faber, 1968.

Uncollected Short Story

"Le Grand Carcenac" (as James Holliday), in *Delta* (Cambridge), February 1960.

Plays

Wise Child (produced London, 1967; New York, 1972). London, Faber, 1972.
Molly (as *Death of a Teddy Bear*, televised, 1967; revised version, as *Molly*, produced Watford, Hertfordshire, and London, 1977; New York, 1978). Included in *The Rear Column and Other Plays*, 1978; in *The Rear Column, Dog Days, and Other Plays*, 1979.
Sleeping Dog (televised, 1967). London, Faber, 1968.
Spoiled (televised, 1968; produced Glasgow, 1970; London, 1971). London, Methuen, 1971.
Dutch Uncle (produced Brighton and London, 1969). London, Faber, 1969.
Pig in a Poke (televised, 1969). Included in *Close of Play and Pig in a Poke*, 1979.
The Idiot, adaptation of a novel by Dostoevsky (produced London, 1970). London, Methuen, 1971.
Butley (produced Oxford and London, 1971; New York, 1972). London, Methuen, 1971; New York, Viking Press, 1972.
Man in a Side-Car (televised, 1971). Included in *The Rear Column and Other Plays*, 1978; in *The Rear Column, Dog Days, and Other Plays*, 1979.
Dog Days (produced Watford, Hertfordshire, 1975). London, Eyre Methuen, 1976; in *The Rear Column, Dog Days, and Other Plays*, 1979.
Otherwise Engaged (produced Oxford and London, 1975; New York, 1977). Included in *Otherwise Engaged and Other Plays*, 1975.
Plaintiffs and Defendants (televised, 1975). Included in *Otherwise Engaged and Other Plays*, 1975.
Two Sundays (televised, 1975). Included in *Otherwise Engaged and Other Plays*, 1975.
Otherwise Engaged and Other Plays (includes *Two Sundays* and *Plaintiffs and Defendants*). London, Eyre Methuen, 1975; New York, Viking Press, 1976.
The Rear Column (produced London and New York, 1978). Included in *The Rear Column and Other Plays*, 1978; in *The Rear Column, Dog Days, and Other Plays*, 1979.
The Rear Column and Other Plays (includes *Molly* and *Man in a Side-Car*). London, Eyre Methuen, 1978.
The Rear Column, Dog Days, and Other Plays (includes *Molly* and *Man in a Side-Car*). New York, Viking Press, 1979.
Close of Play (produced London, 1979). Included in *Close of Play and Pig in a Poke*, 1979.
Close of Play and Pig in a Poke. London, Eyre Methuen, 1979.
Stage Struck (produced London, 1979). London, Eyre Methuen, 1979; New York, Seaver, 1981.
Quartermaine's Terms (produced London, 1981).

Screenplay: *Butley*, 1975.

Television Plays: *The Caramel Crisis*, 1966; *Death of a Teddy Bear*, 1967; *A Way with the Ladies*, 1967; *Sleeping Dog*, 1967; *Spoiled*, 1968; *Pig in a Poke*, 1969; *The Dirt on Lucy Lane*, 1969; *Style of the Countess*, 1970; *The Princess*, 1970; *Man in a Side-Car*, 1971; *Plaintiffs and Defendants*, 1975; *Two Sundays*, 1975.

Other

Editor, with Keith Walker, *Selected English Prose.* London, Faber, 1967.

*

Theatrical Activities:

Director: **Play**—*Dog Days*, Vienna, 1980.

Simon Gray comments:

I really can't write anything useful about the themes or subjects of my novels—I'm not sure I know what "themes" are, except that students get asked about them in examinations on Shakespeare. I'm not conscious, when I'm writing, of having a subject—just a few people in a distinct place having, or failing to have, to do with each other. Of course I begin to get a suspicion when I read the proofs, but I never follow it up and have recently taken to asking my wife to look after proofs for me. I expect that if I could bear to read through anything I've published or had performed on the stage, I could come up with a few phrases and what in the critical/academic professions are called insights, but it would only be patter. I'm not in the slightest interested in what I've *done*; it seems to me in recollection to have been done by somebody else for reasons I can't guess at.

* * *

Colmain is the capital of the mythical province of New Thumberland, Canada's least progressive province, which actually sounds remarkably like Halifax, Nova Scotia. Readers who know the Canadian maritimes would enjoy the novel most. Simon Gray is satirical about the blacks, Indians, and especially the English element in the province. Of the English, "All the attitudes and performances that had merged so inevitably into the harmonious atmosphere of Kensington or Wembley Park or Reigate became, in Colmain's harsher, less-textured atmosphere, almost stark. The afternoon tea-taking and the tricks of speech seemed matters of calculation almost, little but explicit testimonies to a world that had been left but would never be forgotten." Gray jokes about tactlessness: "'And where is Mrs. Weatherby? I hope that she's enjoying it.' Mr. Weatherby positively loomed. 'Mrs. Weatherby is in Holyoke Cemetery,' he said very distinctly. 'I don't know whether she's enjoying it.'"

The date is 1936, and a new, young Lieutenant-Governor's role is learning his job and about Colmain. (In fact, I have no very clear idea of a Lieutenant-Governor's role after finishing the book.) He is faced with Mrs. Tennant who, like Jane Austen's Mrs. Bennett, makes the business of her life getting her daughter married—preferably to the uneasy Lieutenant-Governor. Mrs. Tennant is obsessed with the importance of good breeding: "It *is* a question of breeding and Myra Davis, although she is a Canadian, is very well-bred, with her husband a judge, you know. Everything in the end comes to that. If we discipline ourselves in private then we appear well-bred in public, and people notice it." The parallel to Trollope is closer, with society in Colmain revolving round the Lieutenant-Governor's residence. Gray refers to the problems of newcomers entering society and the crucial importance of receiving invitations, together with a subplot about shady business which the Lieutenant-Governor cannot begin to comprehend. The novel is gently entertaining, with only a touch of astringency toward a society which is so much more decadent and fatuous than it realises.

Simple People takes Logan, a young Canadian, who is smug,

serious, rich, polite, earnest, and moralistic, to Cambridge University as a research student. The book begins with the big subject of the impact of England on Logan: a nice awareness of the exact uses of "Great!" "I guess" and "Is that right?" is shown, and their incongruity in Cambridge. His caricature academics—the translator of Rumanian epics and the student of Shakespeare's dolphin imagery—are amusing. But soon Logan is involved with Joey, a novelist's mistress, and the subject becomes much narrower. Joey is volatile and unpredictable, startling to the upright Nova Scotian with his own clear idea of how boy-meets-girl has to operate. The novelist lives in a picturesque row off Kings Parade, but otherwise the bulk of the novel does not have much to do with Cambridge or a Candadian's discovery of it. A subplot around some tiresome characters, with hints of mystery around Maria Hodges and her activities, is tedious. Gray's special talent here is for awkward conversations, where the presuppositions are different and the unstated nuances mutually confusing. Finally the novel is neither a slapstick view of university life nor a subtle account of England through a foreigner's eyes, but something much more limited, a mild, quite clever, little comedy.

Gray writes entirely of English characters in *Little Portia*, a rambling account of a youth's experiences from early childhood to early twenties: he is named from Shakespeare's Portia by a homosexual teacher. We read briefly of the unsympathetic maiden aunt who brings up the boy and his sister, their governess, the local private school and the public school where he is briefly a footballing success. His years at Cambridge are described at greater length, with informed discriminations between his clever, fashionable friends and the ordinary ones: he begins as a brilliant scholar, then abandons studying in his final weeks. He has an affair with a young Cockney art student and is going to marry her, fastidiously rejects her, falls in love with her memory, then sees her again. At the end he may be free, but it is inconclusive.

Some observation is neat, for instance, of finding "the proper tone" for scholarship exams: " 'It would seem,' 'it could be said,' 'it might be argued,' instead of the 'I think,' 'I feel,' 'I believe' which the History Fifth Master had preferred." Gray's account of the Cambridge "Academy" where the hero teaches English to foreigners is amusing satire, and the Christmas party scene there, with the principal as Santa Claus, is funny. But such set-pieces are few, and coherence is lacking: I cannot see how the experiences described shape the young man. The relationship to the sister remains puzzling, and references to Pip and Estella in *Great Expectations* hint at some buried parallel here: the account of this, too, is abandoned incomplete at the end.

Since 1967 Gray's work has been stage and TV plays, and his accomplishment here is greater than his novels, which lack the originality of *Sleeping Dog*, the psychological subtlety of *Spoiled*, and the epigrammatic wit of *Butley*.

—Malcolm Page

GREENE, Graham. British. Born in Berkhamsted, Hertfordshire, 2 October 1904. Educated at Berkhamsted School; Balliol College, Oxford. Served in the Foreign Office, London, 1941-44. Married Vivien Dayrell-Browning in 1927; one son and one daughter. Staff Member, *The Times*, London 1926-30; Movie Critic, 1937-40, and Literary Editor, 1940-41, *Spectator*, London. Director, Eyre and Spottiswoode, publishers, London, 1944-48, and The Bodley Head, publishers, London, 1958-68. Member, Panamanian Canal Treaty Delegation to Washington, 1977. Recipient: Hawthornden Prize, 1941; Black Memorial Prize, 1949; Shakespeare Prize, Hamburg, 1968; Thomas More Medal, 1973; Jerusalem Prize, 1981. Litt.D.: Cambridge University, 1962; D. Litt.: Edinburgh University, 1967; Oxford University, 1979. Honorary Fellow, Balliol College, 1963. Honorary Citizen, Anacapri, 1978. Companion of Honour, 1966. Chevalier of the Legion of Honour, 1967. Address: c/o The Bodley Head, 9 Bow Street, London WC2E 7AL, England.

PUBLICATIONS

Novels

The Man Within. London, Heinemann, and New York, Doubleday, 1929.

The Name of Action. London, Heinemann, 1930; New York, Doubleday, 1931.

Rumour at Nightfall. London, Heinemann, 1931; New York, Doubleday, 1932.

Stamboul Train: An Entertainment. London, Heinemann, 1932; as *Orient Express: An Entertainment*, New York, Doubleday, 1933.

It's a Battlefield. London, Heinemann, and New York, Doubleday, 1934; revised edition, London, Heinemann, 1948; New York, Viking Press, 1952.

England Made Me. London, Heinemann, and New York, Doubleday, 1935; as *The Shipwrecked*, New York, Viking Press, 1953.

A Gun for Sale: An Entertainment. London, Heinemann, 1936; as *This Gun for Hire: An Entertainment*, New York, Doubleday, 1936.

Brighton Rock. London, Heinemann, 1938; as *Brighton Rock: An Entertainment*, New York, Viking Press, 1938.

The Confidential Agent. London, Heinemann, and New York, Viking Press, 1939.

The Power and the Glory. London, Heinemann, 1940; as *The Labyrinthine Ways*, New York, Viking Press, 1940.

The Ministry of Fear: An Entertainment. London, Heinemann, and New York, Viking Press, 1943.

The Heart of the Matter. London, Heinemann, and New York, Viking Press, 1948.

The Third Man: An Entertainment. New York, Viking Press, 1950.

The Third Man, and The Fallen Idol. London, Heinemann, 1950.

The End of the Affair. London, Heinemann, and New York, Viking Press, 1951.

Loser Takes All: An Entertainment. London, Heinemann, 1955; New York, Viking Press, 1957.

The Quiet American. London, Heinemann, 1955; New York, Viking Press, 1956.

Our Man in Havana: An Entertainment. London, Heinemann, and New York, Viking Press, 1958.

A Burnt-Out Case. London, Heinemann, and New York, Viking Press, 1961.

The Comedians. London, Bodley Head, and New York, Viking Press, 1966.

Travels with My Aunt. London, Bodley Head, 1969; New York, Viking Press, 1970.

The Honorary Consul. London, Bodley Head, and New York, Simon and Schuster, 1973.

The Human Factor. London, Bodley Head, and New York, Simon and Schuster, 1978.

Doctor Fischer of Geneva; or, The Bomb Party. London, Bodley Head, and New York, Simon and Schuster, 1980.

Short Stories

The Basement Room and Other Stories. London, Cresset Press, 1935.

The Bear Fell Free. London, Grayson, 1935; Folcroft, Pennsylvania, Folcroft Editions, 1977.

Twenty-four Stories, with James Laver and Sylvia Townsend Warner. London, Cresset Press, 1939.

Nineteen Stories. London, Heinemann, 1947; New York, Viking Press, 1949; augmented edition, as *Twenty-one Stories*, Heinemann, 1954; Viking Press, 1962.
A Visit to Morin. Privately printed, 1959.
A Sense of Reality. London, Bodley Head, and New York, Viking Press, 1963.
May We Borrow Your Husband? and Other Comedies of the Sexual Life. London, Bodley Head, and New York, Viking Press, 1967.
The Collected Stories of Graham Greene. London, Bodley Head-Heinemann, 1972; New York, Viking Press, 1973.

Uncollected Short Story

"Church Militant," in *Critic* (Chicago), January 1974.

Plays

The Living Room (produced London, 1953; New York, 1954). London, Heinemann, 1953; New York, Viking Press, 1954.
The Potting Shed (produced New York, 1957; London, 1958). New York, Viking Press, 1957; London, Heinemann, 1958.
The Complaisant Lover (produced London, 1959; New York, 1961). London, Heinemann, 1959; New York, Viking Press, 1961.
Carving a Statue (produced London, 1964; New York, 1968). London, Bodley Head, 1964.
The Third Man: A Film, with Carol Reed. New York, Simon and Schuster, 1968; London, Lorrimer Films, 1969.
Alas, Poor Maling, adaptation of his own story (televised, 1975). Published in *Shades of Greene*, London, Bodley Head-Heinemann, 1975.
The Return of A.J. Raffles: An Edwardian Comedy Based Somewhat Loosely on E.W. Hornung's Characters in "The Amateur Cracksman" (produced London, 1975). London, Bodley Head, 1975; New York, Simon and Schuster, 1976.
Yes and No, and For Whom the Bell Chimes (produced Leicester, 1980).

Screenplays: *The First and the Last (21 Days)*, 1937; *The New Britain*, 1940; *Brighton Rock (Young Scarface)*, with Terence Rattigan, 1947; *The Fallen Idol*, with Lesley Storm and William Templeton, 1958; *The Third Man*, with Carol Reed, 1950; *The Stranger's Hand*, with Guy Elmes and Giorgino Bassani, 1954; *Loser Takes All*, 1956; *Saint Joan*, 1957; *Our Man in Havana*, 1960; *The Comedians*, 1967.

Radio Play: *The Great Jowett*, 1980.

Television Play: *Alas, Poor Maling*, 1975.

Verse

Babbling April: Poems. Oxford, Blackwell, 1925.
For Christmas. Privately printed, 1951.

Other

Journey Without Maps: A Travel Book. London, Heinemann, and New York, Doubleday, 1936.
The Lawless Roads: A Mexican Journey. London, Longman, 1939; as *Another Mexico*, New York, Viking Press, 1939.
British Dramatists. London, Collins, 1942; included in *The Romance of English Literature*, New York, Hastings House, 1944.
The Little Train (juvenile). London, Eyre and Spottiswoode, 1946; New York, Lothrop, 1958.
Why Do I Write: An Exchange of Views Between Elizabeth Bowen, Graham Greene, and V.S. Pritchett. London, Marshall, and New York, British Book Centre, 1958.
After Two Years. Privately printed, 1949.
The Little Fire Engine (juvenile). London, Parrish, 1950; as *The Little Red Fire Engine*, New York, Lothrop, 1952.
The Lost Childhood and Other Essays. London, Eyre and Spottiswoode, 1951; New York, Viking Press, 1952.
The Little Horse Bus (juvenile). London, Parrish, 1952; New York, Lothrop, 1954.
The Little Steam Roller: A Story of Mystery and Detection (juvenile). London, Parrish, 1953; New York, Lothrop, 1955.
Essais Catholiques, translated by Marcelle Sibon. Paris, Editions de Deuil, 1953.
In Search of a Character: Two African Journals. London, Bodley Head, 1961; New York, Viking Press, 1962.
The Revenge: An Autobiographical Fragment. Privately printed, 1963.
Victorian Detective Fiction: A Catalogue of the Collection Made by Dorothy Glover and Graham Greene, Introduced by John Carter. London, Bodley Head, 1966.
Collected Essays. London, Bodley Head, and New York, Viking Press, 1969.
A Sort of Life (autobiography). London, Bodley Head, and New York, Simon and Schuster, 1971.
The Pleasure-Dome: The Collected Film Criticism, 1935-40, of Graham Greene, edited by John Russell Taylor. London, Secker and Warburg, 1972; as *The Pleasure-Dome: Graham Greene on Film: Collected Film Criticism, 1935-40*, New York, Simon and Schuster, 1972.
The Portable Graham Greene, edited by Philip Stratford. New York, Viking Press, 1973; London, Penguin, 1977.
Lord Rochester's Monkey, Being the Life of John Wilmot, Second Earl of Rochester. London, Bodley Head, and New York, Viking Press, 1974.
Ways of Escape. London, Bodley Head, 1980; New York, Simon and Schuster, 1981.

Editor, *The Old School: Essays by Divers Hands.* London, Cape, and New York, Peter Smith, 1934.
Editor, *The Best of Saki.* London, British Publishers Guild, 1950.
Editor, with Hugh Greene, *The Spy's Bedside Book: An Anthology.* London, Hart Davis, 1957.
Editor, *The Bodley Head Ford Madox Ford.* London, Bodley Head, 4 vols., 1962, 1963.
Editor, *An Impossible Woman: The Memories of Dottoressa Moor of Capri.* London, Bodley Head, 1975; New York, Viking Press, 1976.

*

Bibliography: *Graham Greene: A Checklist of Criticism* by J.D. Vann, Kent, Ohio, Kent State University Press, 1970; *Graham Greene: A Descriptive Catalog* by Robert H. Miller, Lexington, University Press of Kentucky, 1978; *Graham Greene: A Bibliography and Guide to Research* by R.A. Wobbe, New York, Garland, 1979.

Manuscript Collection: Humanities Research Center, University of Texas, Austin.

Critical Studies (selection): *Graham Greene and the Heart of the Matter* by Marie Mesnet, London, Cresset Press, 1954; *Graham Greene* by Francis Wyndham, London, Longman, 1955, revised edition, 1958; *Graham Greene* by John Atkins, London, Calder, and New York, Roy, 1957, revised edition, London, Calder and Boyars, 1966, New York, Humanities Press, 1967; *The Labyrinthine Ways of Graham Greene* by Francis Leo Kunkel, New York, Sheed and Ward, 1960, revised edition, Mamaroneck, New York, Appel, 1973; *Graham Greene* by David Pryce-Jones, Edinburgh, Oliver and Boyd, 1963, New York, Barnes and Noble, 1968; *Graham Greene: Some Critical Considerations* (includes bibliography by N. Brennan) edited by Robert O. Evans, Lexington, University of Kentucky Press, 1963; *Graham Greene* by A.A. DeVitis, New York, Twayne, 1964; *Graham Greene* by David Lodge, New York, Columbia University Press, 1966; *Graham Greene: A Critical Essay* by Martin Turnell, Grand Rapids, Michigan, Eerdmans, 1967; *Graham Greene: The Aesthetics of Exploration* by Gwenn R. Boardman, Gainesville, University of Florida Press, 1971; *Graham Greene the Entertainer* by Peter Wolfe, Carbondale, Southern Illinois University Press, 1972; *Graham Greene: A Collection of Critical Essays* edited by Samuel Hynes, Englewood Cliffs, New Jersey, Prentice Hall, 1973; *Graham Greene the Novelist* by J.P. Kulshrestha, Delhi, Macmillan, and Atlantic Highlands, New Jersey, Humanities Press, 1977.

* * *

Graham Greene himself indicates the nature of his achievement as a novelist when he writes, in the preface to the 1971 edition of *The Confidential Agent*, that he began the novel "with a certain vague ambition to create something legendary out of a contemporary thriller." At the centre of all his novels, from the first, *The Man Within*, onwards, is a man on the run—from society or from the police, from himself or his conscience, or from God. He has, in other words, claimed a popular and often largely disregarded fictional genre for the purposes of serious art in order to express a deeply felt and deeply idiosyncratic view of man's condition. The ambition is perhaps not new: Greene has obvious affinities with novelists of action like Stevenson, a kinsman, and Conrad, by whom he has been much influenced; but the achievement can be measured by the comparison with the admirable novels of "serious" thriller-writers like Eric Ambler and Patricia Highsmith. The difference is precisely one of ambition, the imparting to the basic thriller situation of the "something legendary" which makes Greene's novels paradigms of the human condition as he sees it.

Greene is of course a Roman Catholic convert, but the explicitly Catholic novels, *Brighton Rock, The Power and the Glory, The Heart of the Matter, The End of the Affair*, and *A Burnt-Out Case*, do not differ in essence or in point of view from the secular novels. Indeed, it is clear that for Greene Catholicism is a religion of desperation, and, a natural nonconformist, he is, one feels, as much against the Roman Catholic Establishment as he is against any other Establishment. Nor, in what may be called his religious novels, do the spokesmen for the Church necessarily get the best of the argument. The last words in *A Burnt-Out Case*, the action of which is set in a leper-colony run by monks in the Congo, are those of the atheist doctor, Colin. For there is another aspect of Greene, what has been called the romantic anarchist. The words seem as good as any to denote a passionate sympathy for the poor and oppressed which goes hand in hand with a distrust of authority, of the established, which is seen in his ambiguous attitude towards Communism. Sometimes his Catholicism, or his religious sense, and his romantic anarchism exist in polarity, as in his most famous and probably his finest novel *The Power and the Glory*. Set in a state in Mexico in which the Church is outlawed, the action dramatises the pursuit and in the end the capture by a police lieutenant of the last priest in the state. The policeman, incorruptible, devoted to the moral and material betterment of his fellows, is the representative of secular idealism; the priest, on the face of it a bad priest, the father of a child and able to keep himself going only by resort to the brandy-bottle, is still the representative of the other-worldly, the divine, God, in whose grace, Greene claims in this novel, man's one hope lies. In *The Power and the Glory* God wins; but what is impressive is Greene's fairness: the policeman is presented as a good man: if the priest attains to something like sanctity, the policeman is something like a secular saint.

In this novel Greene seems to have dramatised two sides of his nature. In the much later novel, *The Comedians*, on the other hand, both sides come together. The setting is Haiti under the Duvalier tyranny, and the spokesmen for Greene's values, the Communist Dr. Magiot, writes to the narrator towards the end of the novel:

> Communism, my friend, is more than Marxism, just as Catholicism—remember I was born a Catholic too—is more than the Roman Curia. There is a *mystique* as well as a *politique*....Communists have committed great crimes, but at least they have not stood aside, like an established society, and been indifferent. I would rather have blood on my hands than water like Pilate.... I implore you—a knock on the door may not allow me to finish this sentence, so take it as the last request of a dying man—if you have abandoned one faith, do not abandon all faith. There is always an alternative to the faith we lose. Or is it the same faith under another mask?

Greene's abiding view of man is stated in some words of Newman's which he prefixes to his Mexican travel book *The Lawless Roads*: "...either there is no Creator, or this living society of men is in a true sense discarded from His presence...*if* there be a God, *since* there is a God, the human race is implicated in some terrible aboriginal calamity." Greene's theme, then, is alienation. It is, throughout the world, the great theme of the contemporary novel, and it is obviously one reason for Greene's immense reputation throughout the world; without question, internationally he is the most seriously regarded of living English novelists. But the theme is one thing: equally important is his treatment of it. For he is an international novelist in a quite other sense than that he commands a worldwide readership, as the settings of his novels show: Sweden in *England Made Me*, Mexico in *The Power and the Glory*, West Africa in *The Heart of the Matter*, Vietnam during the war against the French in *The Quiet American*, Cuba on the eve of the Castro revolution in *Our Man in Havana*, the Congo just before the Belgian withdrawal in *A Burnt-Out Case*, in Haiti in *The Comedians*. He seems to have an unerring eye for the trouble spots of the world just as they are on the verge of erupting. This means that the novels when first published have an immediate topical interest, and this is an aspect of fiction never to be despised. Greene is a great journalist in his own right, and this is part of his strength as a novelist. But he is not simply the special correspondent as novelist. The violent places of the earth attract him for an especial reason; in them the ingredients of the normal world are caught in sharper perspective; the violence that lurks just below the surface of the London of *It's a Battlefield*, of the English seaside resort of *Brighton Rock*, or of the English Midlands city of *Gun for Sale* is the overt and accepted condition of life in Haiti. In Greene's fiction it is London, Brighton, and Nottingham, with their relative temperateness of life, that are distortions of the norm, not Saigon and Haiti. The effect is one of universalisation: men are the same everywhere: "Why this is hell, nor am I out of it."

But there is something else, without which all would be nothing. This is Greene's art. He is, to begin with, a superb story-teller, perhaps the best alive, in the simple and fundamental sense that he immediately captures the reader's appetite for excitement and sustains it by his use of detail, his manipulation of suspense, and his unceasing invention. One recalls the opening sentences of his novels, of *Brighton Rock*, for instance: "Hale knew they meant to murder him before he had been in Brighton three hours." But one might just as well write, "He is, to end with, a superb story-teller," for his stories are the fruits of his great range of technical skills and resources. There are those novelists who can be called learned novelists, as some painters are called painterly. Greene is one of them. He is learned in the works of the masters and he has made what he has learned from them his own. His most obvious masters are Henry James and Conrad, not least in his ambition to make of a novel a self-contained work of art. But he has also learned from the films. It is not for nothing that for some years as a young man he was a film critic and became a distinguished writer of film-scripts. He uses the image and the cutting from image to image very much as the film-director does, in order to give his action pace, diversity, contrast, and immediate impact on the reader; witness, as an obvious instance, the first two paragraphs of *The Power and the Glory*. The result is concision, compactness, intensity of focus, and it is something for which Greene has not been given sufficient credit.

All this may be seen in his extraordinarily idiosyncratic prose style, with its use of the unexpected, sometimes bizarre image, a prose that in its imagery is often strikingly like the early poetry of W.H. Auden. He is, it is difficult not to think, at times the prisoner of his own penchant for the bizarre or melodramatic image. Then he seems to be parodying himself, as in *The Heart of the Matter* in which the thoughts of the central character, Scobie, are given us in a manner stylistically too close to the language of the anonymous narrator. Nevertheless, at its best his style is the perfect, i.e., it seems the only possible, medium of expression for his attitude towards and analysis of the human state.

Something else remains to be said. In recent years Greene has shown himself an admirable and original comic writer; in *Our Man in Havana*, the volume of short stories *May We Borrow Your Husband?*, and *Travels with My Aunt*. But the comedy still exists in the realm of Greene's abiding preoccupations.

—Walter Allen

GROSSMAN, Alfred. American. Born in New York City, 14 May 1927. Educated at Haverford College, Pennsylvania, 1944-48, B.A. 1948; Harvard University, Cambridge, Massachusetts, 1948-49, M.A. 1949. Served in the United States Navy, 1945-46. Married Althea Eudora Van Boskirk in 1971. Editor, *East Europe Magazine*, New York, 1954-61. Since 1968, Editor of the *New York Times Almanac*. Address: 54 Riverside Drive, Apartment 14-A, New York, New York 10024, U.S.A.

PUBLICATIONS

Novels

Acrobat Admits. New York, Brazilier, 1959; London, Heinemann, 1960.
Many Slippery Errors. London, Heinemann, 1963; New York, Doubleday, 1964.
Marie Beginning. London, Heinemann, 1964; New York, Doubleday, 1965.
The Do-Gooders. New York, Doubleday, and London, Heinemann, 1968.

Uncollected Short Stories

"The Big Girls," in *Rogue* (Evanston, Illinois), 1963.
"The Gobbitch Men," in *Amazing Stories* (New York), 1965.
"The Beauty Contest," in *Transatlantic Review* (London), Winter 1966-67.

*

Manuscript Collection: Mugar Memorial Library, Boston University.

* * *

At his best Alfred Grossman is his own acrobat; putting on disguises, slipping effortlessly from one style to another (the barracks monologue of Sarge, the poor-white-trash dialect of the yokel in *Acrobat Admits*), parodying and punning in a zany show of life's lunacy; at his worst, he is the acrobat tripped, caught in his own trick, unable to disentangle himself, finally resorting to any device to take him off-stage. When his performance is deft, he writes in the ironic mode, exposing man's emotional and spiritual impoverishment, his desperate attempts to make contact through sex, the failure of these attempts to do anything but that. When he flounders, he denies the contradictions which sustain his irony and turns his satire on man's hapless attempts to give life meaning into an insignificant story of the disintegration of a neurotic personality.

New York is Grossman's circus with a publishing house (*Acrobat Admits*), the United Nations Secretariat (*Many Slippery Errors*), or a shoe manufacturing corporation (*Marie Beginning*) as the arena. The time is the 1960's with the radical right and left battling. His theme is that modern, urban life is insupportable—that the only relief from boredom will come from an action. The possibilities for action vary in Grossman's novels, but in no case does Grossman, a comedian of black humor, allow the action to be positive. In *Acrobat Admits* destruction of another is the central action. Kennan attempts self-destruction in both *Marie Beginning* and again in its self-contained sequel, *Do-Gooders*, and Dicherty succeeds in *Many Slippery Errors*. Finally, in Grossman's most recent novel, *The Do-Gooders*, the act that brings the novel to its conclusion is not murder, or suicide, but the destruction of some part of the System. In Grossman's second novel, Dicherty's dream of blowing-up Con-Ed is only a dream; in *The Do-Gooders* the dream is fulfilled when Marie, Spider, and Kennan blow up the connecting link of a twelve-lane expressway. This reliance on a sophomoric solution diminishes Grossman's art: after sensing the nihilistic vision that lies beneath an often hilarious, but always troubling, surface, the audience expects more from him. Perhaps Grossman's next novel will offer it.

In his arena are his characters: men, imperfectly synchronized with their time—intelligent, restive, bored with the banalities of their jobs and marriages, but always insecure and dependent; and women, of two types, either middle-class and insecure, cloaking that insecurity with the conventions of marriage (Cairo Joy in *Acrobat Admits*, Sally in *Many Slippery Errors*, and Sheila in *Marie Beginning*) or working-class and secure (the typists from Brooklyn: taciturn Pia [*Many Slippery Errors*] or candid Marie [*Marie Beginning*] refreshingly blunt with a flawless sense of the possibilities of a moment). The plot revolves around the adventures of these men and women and their constant attempts to couple, which are described in a fashion reminiscent of the rituals in the writings of the Marquis de Sade.

Grossman's strengths lie in his comic voice and his ability to caricature. Few of his characters are deeply motivated; even Marie for whom Grossman has a respect and affection which are lacking in his other portraits, falls short of the mark. But a number of his caricatures are excellent. There are Alexander Forbes, the wealthy playboy who locks women in his padded one-room apartment and subjects them to innumerable indignities as he feeds all his sadistic yearnings and his contempt for his sister; and Dicherty, the aged, wandering lecher who garrulously talks of the vanity of human wishes while he provides a clubhouse for the initiation rites of the toreador-pants set in Brooklyn; and Spider, a mafioso-type with a nice sense of retributive justice; and also Cairo Joy, the embodiment of middle-class consciousness.

His style is often facile, but marred by a self-consciousness which makes much of his dialogue inauthentic. The strained imitation of Hamlet's words in the opening chapter of *Acrobat Admits* provides ample evidence of this defect: "The problem: to start clean, where I am unknown. Self-protection, the bubble that I may burst if needs must, the escape gear of ultimate anonymity, shelter from my own grenades. I intend to complicate, I do not intend to brick myself into a cellar wall. George must not be George."

To complicate life in order to penetrate its banalities is the *raison d'être* of all the antics and pursuits in Grossman's novels. Often the complications are outrageous, occasionally they are hilarious, sometimes, as in his all-too-frequent episodes of amorous impertinences varied with exercises in sadism, they are tedious and without point. A dextrous style saves the superficiality of the characters; a weird but limited imagination creates the lively episodes that carry his art; but until more of Grossman's work emerges, it will not be clear whether he can outgrow his forced service to masters as diverse as Joyce, Shakespeare, and Max Shulman, exercise a care with dialogue which will eliminate the inconsistent images and figures that so often make his parodies inauthentic, and perfect the vehicle which will simultaneously express his moral outrage and convince his readers of the substance and importance of both his characters and themes.

—Carol Simpson Stern

GUERARD, Albert (Joseph). American. Born in Houston, Texas, 2 November 1914. Educated at Stanford University, California, B.A. 1934, Ph.D. 1938; Harvard University, Cambridge, Massachusetts, M.A. 1936. Served in the Psychological Warfare Branch of the United States Army, 1943-45. Married Mary Maclin Bocock in 1941; three children. Instructor in English, Amherst College, Massachusetts, 1935-36; successively Instructor, Assistant Professor, and Associate Professor of English, 1938-54, and Professor of English, 1954-61, Harvard University. Since 1961, Professor of Literature, Stanford University. Recipient: Rockefeller Fellowship, 1946; Fulbright Fellowship, 1950; Guggenheim Fellowship, 1956; Ford Fellowship, 1959; *Paris Review* Fiction Prize, 1963; National Endowment for the Arts grant, 1967, 1974. Member, American Academy of Arts and Sciences. Address: 635 Gerona Road, Stanford, California 94305, U.S.A.

PUBLICATIONS

Novels

The Past Must Alter. London, Longman, 1937; New York, Holt, 1938.
The Hunted. New York, Knopf, 1944; London, Longman, 1947.
Maquisard: A Christmas Tale. New York, Knopf, 1945; London, Longman, 1946.
Night Journey. New York, Knopf, 1950; London, Longman, 1951.
The Bystander. Boston, Little Brown, 1958; London, Faber, 1959.
The Exiles. London, Faber, 1962; New York, Macmillan, 1963.

Uncollected Short Stories

"Miss Prindle's Lover, " in *The Magazine* (Beverly Hills, California), 1932.
"Davos in Winter," in *Hound and Horn* (Cambridge, Massachusetts), October-December 1933.
"Turista," in *The Best American Short Stories of 1947*, edited by Martha Foley. Boston, Houghton Mifflin, 1947.
"The Incubus," in *The Dial* (New York), i, 2, 1960.
"The Lusts and Gratifications of Andrada," in *Paris Review*, Summer-Fall 1962.
"On the Operating Table," in *Denver Quarterly*, Autumn 1966.
"The Journey," in *Partisan Review* (New Brunswick, New Jersey), Winter 1967.
"The Rabbit and the Tapes," in *Sewanee Review* (Tennessee), Spring 1972.
"The Pillars of Hercules," in *Fiction* (New York), December 1973.
"Bon Papa Reviendra," in *Tri-Quarterly* (Evanston, Illinois), Spring 1975.
"Post Mortem: The Garcia Incident," in *Southern Review* (Baton Rouge, Louisiana), Spring 1978.

Other

Robert Bridges: A Study of Traditionalism in Poetry. Cambridge, Massachusetts, Harvard University Press, and London, Oxford University Press, 1942.
Joseph Conrad. New York, New Directions, 1947.
Thomas Hardy: The Novels and Stories. Cambridge, Massachusetts, Harvard University Press, 1949; London, Oxford University Press, 1950.
André Gide. Cambridge, Massachusetts, Harvard University Press, and London, Oxford University Press, 1951; revised edition, 1969.
Conrad the Novelist. Cambridge, Massachusetts, Harvard University Press, 1958; London, Oxford University Press, 1959.
The Triumph of the Novel: Dickens, Dostoevsky, Faulkner. New York, Oxford University Press, 1976; London, Oxford University Press, 1977.
The Touch of Time: Myth, Memory, and the Self. Stanford, California, Stanford Alumni Association, 1980.

Editor, *Prosateurs Américains du XXe Siècle.* Paris, Laffont, 1947.
Editor, *The Return of the Native*, by Thomas Hardy. New York, Holt Rinehart, 1961.
Editor, *Hardy: A Collection of Critical Essays.* Englewood Cliffs, New Jersey, Prentice Hall, 1963.
Editor, *Perspective on the Novel*, special issue of *Daedalus* (Boston), Spring 1963.
Co-Editor, *The Personal Voice: A Contemporary Prose Reader.* Philadelphia, Lippincott, 1964.
Editor, *Stories of the Double.* Philadelphia, Lippincott, 1967.

*

Manuscript Collection: Stanford University Library.

Critical Studies: *The Modern Novel in America* by Frederick Hoffman, Chicago, Regnery, 1951; *The Hero with the Private Parts* by Andrew Lytle, Baton Rouge, Louisiana State University Press, 1966; "The Vanishing Anarchists," in *Sewanee Review* (Tennessee), Summer 1969, "Was Lya de Putti Dead at 22?" in *Tri-Quarterly* (Evanston, Illinois), Autumn 1970, and "My Grande Naufrage," in *Southern Review* (Baton Rouge, Louisiana), Winter 1972, all by the author.

Albert Guerard comments:

My work has been notably affected by wartime experience (political intelligence work in France) and by the pressures and ambiguities of the subsequent cold war. I have tried without success to put the political subject aside; thousands of unpublished pages, many of them angry, testify to inescapable contemporary pressures.

Maquisard, written immediately after the 1944 events it describes, is an affectionate record of wartime comradeships among men who had been in the underground. Apologetically subtitled *A Christmas Tale*, it is the slightest of my novels and was the most warmly received. *Night Journey*, my most complex and most substantial novel, is more truthful in its picture of the political and moral devastation caused by American-Soviet rivalries in a world as deceptive, and as self deceptive, as that of *1984*. It was, on publication, repeatedly compared to Orwell's book. The confession of Paul Haldan (wandering and evasive, with his final crime left undescribed, and indeed undetected by most readers) is that of a liberal "innocent" who can accept neither his mother's sexual betrayals nor his country's systematic abuse of power and liberal ideology, nor its threatened use of germ warfare. Haldan's night journey into temporary regression takes him into the middle European city of his childhood, disrupted by the two great powers and betrayed by both. The ambiguities of an undeclared war are internalized by Paul Haldan, and his psycho-sexual anxieties projected onto the screen of public conflict. *The Exiles* (based on a journey to Cuba, Haiti, and Santo Domingo during the turmoil of 1959) explores deception and self-deception in the tragi-comic context of Caribbean propaganda and political intrigue. It dramatizes the conflict of a quixotic Trujillo assassin incorrigibly drawn to the exiled statesman he is supposed to destroy. Manuel Andrada appears to be the most winning of my fictional creations.

In *The Hunted*, an earlier novel and conventionally realistic in technique, psycho-sexual anxieties and monumental vanities reflect public disorders in a small New England college just before World War II. Oedipal conflicts and fantasies, dramatized fairly unconsciously in *The Past Must Alter*, are central to *Night Journey* and to *The Bystander*, another story of romantic love vitiated by immaturity and regression. The technique of *The Bystander* is that of the French *récit*, with the motives either concealed or distorted by the narrator-protagonist. But the story is also of a collision between American "innocence" and European compromise. One of my central aims has been to avoid, while writing fairly complex psychological novels, the deadening burden of explicit and accurate analysis *The Bystander*—very easy to read, perhaps too easy to read—requires, to be truly understood, the closest attention to hint, to image, to nuance of voice and style.

My fiction-writing has undoubtedly been affected by the work done on my critical books. Conrad is the most obvious of my masters, as Graham Greene remarked. But Hardy and Gide Also helped me overcome, to some extent, the realistic documentary impulses of my first three novels.

* * *

Of Albert Guerard's six novels, four are primarily of political or social significance—*The Exiles, Night Journey, Maquisard*, and *The Hunted*—and two are psychological studies involving the necessity of recovery and re-evaluation of one's personal past—*The Bystander* and *The Past Must Alter*. A preoccupation with the psychology of divided loyalties and of fear of betrayal is recurrent throughout Guerard's fiction as well as the theme of recovery of the past.

The Exiles, which best exemplifies what the author has called subjective or visionary fiction as opposed to journeyman realism, was suggested by the situation in the Dominican Republic (Santa Isabella) under Trujillo (the Protector). Manuel Andrada, Guerard's most fully realized character, agent and loyal supporter of the Protector, is assigned the task of bringing the exile Justo de Villamayor, a great poet, back to his homeland and, failing that, to kill him. The tormented conscience of the agent, divided between loyalty to the Protector and admiration for Villamayor, is rendered with dramatic and visionary intensity. *Night Journey* presents a nightmare Europe of the future, divided between the dictatorship of the East and the so-called Democracy of the West, engaged in endless, indecisive, and undeclared border warfare. Paul Haldan, an idealistic socialist from England, abandons his superior officer, Philip Montalva, to enemy capture because of Montalva's supposed betrayal of the socialist cause. But Montalva's eventual heroic death in a one man machine gun stand reveals his integrity and the difficulty of making moral judgments in a bleak and dehumanized world. The action of *Maquisard* occurs near a French seaside town during World War II where the Ruc Brigade, composed of former Maquis, is attempting to wipe out a pocket of Germans. Interest centers on Jean Ruyader's attempt to return to a normal life of love and a new marriage after the execution of his wife by the Nazis. The toughness and heroism of the Maquis fighting in the depths of a biting French winter are unforgettably portrayed. *The Hunted*, a novel of social criticism, is the story of an imprudent marriage between a self-centered romantically tempered college English teacher and a beautiful waitress with no social background. Their marriage goes to pieces under the pressure of the snobbish and petty faculty of a small New England town. In *The Bystander* Anthony eventually meets and has an affair with his dream girl, Christiane Mondor, but the liaison ends in Anthony's humiliation when he cannot develop his adolescent concept of a grand passion into mature companionship and love. In *The Past Must Alter* young Jim Simmons witnesses the breakup of the marriage of his gambling journalist father and his passive and conventional mother. As a result of the boy's terror and isolation, a new and presumably successful marriage of the mother is temporarily prevented until the boy, as a result of meeting a beautiful young actress, breaks the oedipal bond.

Guerard's social and political views are those of a humane liberal. His highly literate and perceptive style, counter-realist and counter-naturalist, is reminiscent of but not imitative of Conrad. His psychological complexity appears to owe much to Gide and Freud.

—Donald E. Stanford

GUTHRIE, A(lfred) B(ertram), Jr. American. Born in Bedford, Indiana, 13 January 1901. Educated at schools in Choteau, Montana; University of Washington, Seattle, 1919-20; University of Montana, Missoula, A.B. in journalism 1923. Married 1) Harriet Larson in 1931 (divorced, 1963), one son and one daughter; 2) Carol B. Luthin in 1969. Worked for the Choteau *Acantha*, 1915-19; Reporter, 1926-29, City Editor and Editorial Writer, 1929-45, and Executive Editor, 1945-47, *Leader*, Lexington, Kentucky. Fellow, and Lecturer, Bread Loaf Writers Conference, Vermont, 1945-47. Professor of Creative Writing, University of Kentucky, Lexington, 1947-52. Recipient: Nieman Fellowship, 1944; Pulitzer Prize, 1950; Boys' Clubs of America Junior Book Award, 1951; National Association of Independent Schools Award, 1961. Litt.D.: University of Montana, 1949. Agent: Brandt and Brandt, 1501 Broadway, New York, New York 10036. Address: The Barn, Choteau, Montana 59422, U.S.A.

PUBLICATIONS

Novels

Murders at Moon Dance. New York, Dutton, 1943; as *Trouble at Moon Dance*, New York, Popular Library, 1951; London, Long, 1961.
The Big Sky. New York, Sloane, and London, Boardman, 1947.
The Way West. New York, Sloane, 1949; London, Boardman, 1950.
These Thousand Hills. Boston, Houghton Mifflin, 1956; London, Hutchinson, 1957.
Arfive. Boston, Houghton Mifflin, 1971; London, Eyre Methuen, 1972.
Wild Pitch. Boston, Houghton Mifflin, 1973; London, David Bruce and Watson, 1974.
The Last Valley. Boston, Houghton Mifflin, 1975.
No Second Wind. Boston, Houghton Mifflin, 1980.

Short Stories

The Big It and Other Stories. Boston, Houghton Mifflin, 1960; London, Hutchinson, 1961; as *Mountain Medicine*, New York, Pocket Books, 1961.

Uncollected Short Stories

"Loco," in *Esquire* (New York), November 1967.
"Posse on the Marsh," in *Saturday Evening Post* (Philadelphia), September 1976.

Plays

Screenplays: *Shane*, with Jack Sher, 1951; *The Kentuckian*, 1955.

Other

The Blue Hen's Chick (autobiography). New York, McGraw Hill, 1965.
Once upon a Pond (juvenile). Missoula, Montana, Mountain Press, 1973.

*

Bibliography: in *Western American Literature* (Fort Collins, Colorado), Summer 1969.

Manuscript Collection: University of Kentucky, Lexington.

Critical Study: *A. B. Guthrie, Jr.* by Thomas W. Ford, Austin, Steck Vaughn, 1968.

* * *

The attempt to create fiction out of one of the central facts of American experience, the existence of the Frontier, is as old as

American history. John Smith added a gloss of romance to his geographical and autobiographical ramblings and cast himself as hero of a book that is as much a western as the novels of Zane Grey. Fenimore Cooper set his mark upon the whole future of American mythology by the selection as prime theme for his novels of the conflict between a sophisticated, sometimes decadent but essentially Christian ethos of European culture transplanted and the unsophisticated, sometimes savage, but often wonderfully primitive morality of the wild forests. But just about the time when American historians began to comprehend the influence that the Frontier had exerted upon the whole cultural history of their nation, the Frontier was officially closed, and from the last decade of the 19th century almost until the opening of the Second World War the life of the Frontier was for the American people little more than a folk-memory, and even that folk-memory was rapidly perverted by the crude exploitation of the authors of dime novels, Hollywood "B" films, and, finally, television serials.

In the late 1930's and early 1940's a new school of Western authors (Western in both senses of the word) began to emerge, among them two, Walter Van Tilburg Clark and A.B. Guthrie, Jr., outstanding, who put fact back into fiction. Guthrie in particular is a scholarly historian who adds the accuracy of his research to a novelist's power for creating character, to an artist's eye for scenery, and to a Montanan's affection for his home country.

His first novel, *Murders at Moon Dance*, transcends the conventional melodramatic form of the gun-toting Western only insofar as the action explodes with more than ordinary literary force, but his three major novels, *The Big Sky*, *The Way West*, and *These Thousand Hills*, together form a persuasive, sensitive and substantial history of the spirit of the West, free from the stereotypes of the Western.

Arfive, the fourth novel in the sequence, is a more contrived attempt to add a rich cloak of fiction to historical fact—this time the historical facts of the homesteading period—but in the fifth, *The Last Valley*, which takes the story of the West on through the Second World War, Guthrie's miraculous gifts are at work yet again and his sympathy for rural and hitherto isolated communities forced to come to terms with a structured, urbanised and industrialised society is as apparent, and almost as vivid, as Faulkner's.

Guthrie insisted that this novel was his last essay in his account of America's westering and he took to writing mystery-novels. *Wild Pitch* is adroit if slight and it is only the clarity of the Montana setting which sets it above most books in this *genre* but his autobiography *The Blue Hen's Chick*, his closely written short stories and his screenplays—above all, that Hollywood classic *Shane*—fill in the interstices in his vast historical reconstruction of the American West.

Even so it remains that the claim that Guthrie be considered in the front rank of contemporary American novelists must rest largely on the achievement of *The Big Sky*, *The Way West*, and *These Thousand Hills*.

—J.E. Morpurgo

HAGGARD, William. Pseudonym for Richard Henry Michael Clayton. British. Born in Croydon, Surrey, 11 August 1907. Educated at Lancing College, Sussex; Christ Church, Oxford, B.A. 1929. Served in the Indian Army, 1939-45: Lieutenant Colonel, General Staff. Married Barbara Myfanwy Sant in 1936; one son and one daughter. Served in the Indian Civil Service, 1931-39; worked for the Board of Trade, 1947-69: Controller of Enemy Property, 1965-69. M.A.: Oxford University, 1947. Address: 15 Court Gardens, Firlands Avenue, Camberley, Surrey GU15 2HY, England.

PUBLICATIONS

Novels

Slow Burner. London, Cassell, and Boston, Little Brown, 1958.
The Telemann Touch. London, Cassell, and Boston, Little Brown, 1958.
Venetian Blind. London, Cassell, and New York, Washburn, 1959.
Closed Circuit. London, Cassell, and New York, Washburn, 1960.
The Arena. London, Cassell, and New York, Washburn, 1961.
The Unquiet Sleep. London, Cassell, and New York, Washburn, 1962.
The High Wire. London, Cassell, and New York, Washburn, 1963.
The Antagonists. London, Cassell, and New York, Washburn, 1964.
The Powder Barrel. London, Cassell, and New York, Washburn, 1965.
The Hard Sell. London, Cassell, 1965; New York, Washburn, 1966.
The Power House. London, Cassell, 1966; New York, Washburn, 1967.
The Conspirators. London, Cassell, 1967; New York, Walker, 1968.
A Cool Day for Killing. London, Cassell, and New York, Walker, 1968.
The Doubtful Disciple. London, Cassell, 1969.
The Hardliners. London, Cassell, and New York, Walker, 1970.
The Bitter Harvest. London, Cassell, 1971; as *Too Many Enemies*, New York, Walker, 1972.
The Protectors. London, Cassell, and New York, Walker, 1972.
The Old Masters. London, Cassell, 1973; as *The Notch on the Knife*, New York, Walker, 1973.
The Kinsmen. London, Cassell, and New York, Walker, 1974.
The Scorpion's Tail. London, Cassell, and New York, Walker, 1975.
Yesterday's Enemy. London, Cassell, and New York, Walker, 1976.
The Poison People. London, Cassell, 1978; New York, Walker, 1979.
Visa to Limbo. London, Cassell, 1978; New York, Walker, 1979.
The Median Line. London, Cassell, 1979.
The Money Men. London, Hodder and Stoughton, 1980.

Uncollected Short Stories

"Night Train to Milan," in *Best Secret Service Stories 2*, edited by John Welcome. London, Faber, 1965.
"Madam," in *Welcome Aboard* (London), 1971.
"Why Beckett Died," in *Blood on My Mind*. London, Macmillan, 1972.
"The Hirelings," in *Winter's Crimes 4*, edited by George Hardinge. London, Macmillan, 1972.
"Timeo Danaos," in *Winter's Crimes 8*, edited by Hilary Watson. London, Macmillan, 1976.

Other

The Little Rug Book. London, Cassell, 1972.

*

Critical Studies: in *Sunday Times* (London), 12 May 1963; by Robin W. Winks, in *New Republic* (Washington, D.C.), 30 July 1977.

William Haggard comments:

I write suspense stories with a political background.

* * *

William Haggard builds his stories around Colonel Charles Russell, head of the Security Executive. He is about 60, an Anglo-Irishman who looks at the English impersonally. His thoughts are put crisply; what he finds contemptible about the establishment isn't

> its power but its inefficiency. The supine respect for precedent, the passion for soldiers in fancy dress. The leathery clubs and the squalid canteens. Industrial bigwigs talking on telly in terms of economics a generation out of date. Pompous trade unionists as startlingly antique. Compromise. Keep it clean. Russell had once told an eminent journalist that he was an old-fashioned radical. The man had blinked then changed the subject. Russell has known he's been misunderstood.

Russell is a gentleman in a tough job which he handles with some intuition and considerable scrupulosity. He has a touch of Edwardian courtesy, a sense of what is proper and becoming.

And so he is hurled into the chessboard puzzles of modern diplomatic, industrial, political struggles. He uncovers and sometimes covers up again the seamier side of public and private life. He has his unofficial contacts with the other side of the curtain, as in *The Antagonists* where his friendship with the "Confederate Republic," an independent satellite, pays off. Again in *The Powder Barrel* he and the (Russian) General share information where their interests are common. Colonel Russell is an individual who appreciates other individuals and his is an unusual, strong character, though paradoxically enough he tends to achieve his ends by inaction rather than action. He waits for others to commit their treacheries, peccadillos, plain mistakes. In Russell's world there are Ministers of the Crown, efficient in some cases, less so in others; there is a crafty Prime Minister, a brilliant study; there is the worried director of a Merchant Bank struggling with diabetes. The range is wide but it is largely drawn from the establishment. There are women who are powerful—and dangerous, such as Sheila Raden in *A Cool Day for Killing* or Madam, the weak Sheik's sister, in *The Powder Barrel*. There are men who are weak and blackmailable, men who are vicious, men who are idealistic. Some become stock types—Mortimer the loyal subordinate, Professor Waserman the German-Jewish refugee now Chairman of Amalgamated Steel, and Lord Normer, a C.P. Snow-like character, who advises Russell on radar matters. There are the classic traitors, and these are often self-deluding, weak left-wing intellectuals, such as Margaret Palfrey in *The Antagonists*. There are also ruthless industrialists or the selfish and sophisticated engineers of whom Gervase Leat in *Venetian Blind* is a good example.

The complicated nexus between characters is well handled. Haggard enjoys the interplay of his characters; his dialogue can be lively and is at its best when sophisticated men and women are engaged in conversations, the serious import of which is lightly conveyed. Colonel Russell himself can be surprising in his unorthodoxies: he is careful not to overstep what he thinks are the proper limits of his difficult, dangerous post. He emerges as very human indeed.

The dangers are given full treatment. The action is crisp; there is suspense in plenty—the waiting after a decision is taken, then the action described with sufficient detail to be convincing, with sufficient speed to remain exciting. The backgrounds are sketched in with small touches of accuracy; the atmosphere of a gulf sheikdom, a Malayan state under British protection, an Italian aircraft factory, a London pub, a country house are all evoked with equal skill. The pattern of modern life evolves in all its complexity: not least in the relationships between men and women, where Russell often throws a cool, tolerant, yet interested eye on intrigues or relationships which affect the action of the characters. In marriages breaking up—the Leggatts' in *The Unquiet Sleep* or the Lowe-Andersons' in *Venetian Blind* are cases in point—Haggard can capture nuances and clashes and the odd mixtures of loyalty and disloyalty with considerable economy. He can show the complexities of racial differences at times as in the Deshmukhs in *The Conspirators*, he Indian, she an Irish nationalist (yet related, way back, to Colonel Russell). *Visa to Limbo* illustrates Haggard's capacity to write a cool account of crisis: the attempted highjack of an Israeli aircraft. He places this in the centre of a story of a coup in a small arab state occurring when Colonel Russell is visiting Israel, though to the distaste of Israeli Intelligence. The threads are neatly tangled and untangled for us, and the violence erupts, though the danger of a large flare-up is avoided. The terror, the tension, the tightrope walking are conveyed delicately but very convincingly.

The element of chance is something Haggard understands. In *The Median Line*, up-to-date as ever, he explores the Mediterranean Island's relationship with the wealthy Arab Oil State. Irony plays through the account; it is steeped with mellow Mediterranean sunshine, and the clash of human greed and envy, personal and national, echoes in the narrow streets, spreads by the rocky fields and over the distant desert. Russell, on a visit to the island and caught up to his disgust in the quarrel, is wily; he admires the place and its people, but is glad to escape the politicians' blackmail, the pressures and violence of the rulers of both countries.

Perhaps Haggard's chief virtue is that he conveys a sense to the reader of being allowed to know it all works, it being the world as seen by an intelligence service chief. It is not the whole world, but a sophisticatedly stylised one, where an occasional comment—on, say, the reduced role played by a modern head of Mission; or on the restricted options open to a politician, or captain of industry, or chief of police, or diplomat—strikes home with a dash of devastating reality which helps to carry forward the strange doings of Colonel Russell, his helpers and the enemies he often respects.

—A. Norman Jeffares

HAILEY, Arthur. Canadian. Born in Luton, Bedfordshire, England, 5 April 1920; emigrated to Canada in 1947: Canadian citizen, 1952. Served as a pilot in the Royal Air Force, 1939-47: Flight Lieutenant. Married 1) Joan Fishwick in 1944 (divorced, 1950), three sons; 2) Sheila Dunlop in 1951, one son and two daughters. Worked as an office boy and clerk, London, 1934-39. Editor, MacLean Hunter, publishers, Toronto, 1947-53; Sales Promotion Manager, Trailmobile Canada, Toronto, 1953-56. Since 1956, free-lance writer. Recipient: Canadian Council of Authors and Artists Award, 1956; Best Canadian TV Playwright Award, 1957, 1958; Doubleday Prize Novel Award, 1962. Address: Lyford Cay, P.O. Box N.7776, Nassau, Bahamas.

PUBLICATIONS

Novels

Flight into Danger, with John Castle. London, Souvenir Press, 1958; as *Runway Zero-Eight*, New York, Doubleday, 1959.

The Final Diagnosis. New York, Doubleday, 1959; London, Joseph-Souvenir Press, 1960; as *The Young Doctors*, London, Corgi, 1962.

In High Places. London, Doubleday, and London, Joseph-Souvenir Press, 1962.

Hotel. London, Doubleday, and London, Joseph-Souvenir Press, 1965.

Airport. London, Doubleday, and London, Joseph-Souvenir Press, 1968.

Wheels. London, Doubleday, and London, Joseph-Souvenir Press, 1971.

The Moneychangers. London, Doubleday, and London, Joseph-Souvenir Press, 1975.

Overload. London, Doubleday, and London, Joseph-Souvenir Press, 1979.

Plays

Flight into Danger (televised, 1956). Published in *Four Plays of Our Time*, London, Macmillan, 1960.
Close-up on Writing for Television. New York, Doubleday, 1960.

Screenplays: *Zero Hour*, with Hall Bartlett and John Champion, 1958; *The Moneychangers*, 1976; *Wheels*, 1978.

Radio Play: *Time Lock*, 1962 (UK).

Television Plays: *Flight into Danger*, 1956 (USA); *Course for Collision*, 1962 (UK); and plays for *Westinghouse Studio One*, *Playhouse 90*, *U.S. Steel Hour*, *Goodyear-Philco Playhouse*, and *Kraft Theatre* (USA).

*

Critical Studies: interview with Frank Cameron, in *Writer's Yearbook '67*, Cincinnati, F. and W., 1967; "Arthur Hailey: Novelist at Work," in *Manuscripts* (Carbondale, Illinois), xxii, 1, 1970; "The Hailey Papers," in *Maclean's* (Toronto), lxxxiv, 10, 1971; *Sunday Times Magazine* (London), 27 February 1972.

Arthur Hailey comments:

My novels are the end product of my work and are widely available. Therefore I see no reason to be analytical about them.

Each novel takes me, usually, three years: a year of continuous research, six months of detailed planning, then a year and a half of steady writing, with many revisions.

My only other comment is that my novels are the work of one who seeks principally to be a storyteller but reflect also, I hope, the excitement of living here and now.

* * *

Arthur Hailey has developed and virtually perfected a highly efficient and extremely successful (and profitable) process of novel writing. Whether he is writing about doctors (*The Final Diagnosis*) or airline pilots (*Flight into Danger*), hotels (*Hotel*) or airports (*Airport*), government (*In High Places*) or industry (*Wheels*), he follows the same formula. Each of his novels is filled with enough information about the subject of his exhaustive research to satisfy the most curious reader; there are enough character types to appeal to the widest possible audience; everything is interwoven into a complex web of plots and sub-plots to satisfy every reader's desire for a good, suspenseful story.

Hailey writes documentary fiction, or what has been called "faction," that is, a mixture of the real and the fictitious. After spending a year of research for each novel, Hailey is prepared to give his reader as much factual information as he can work into the novel. Consequently, only his characters and situations are imaginary, and they are sometimes only slightly fictitious.

To speak of any Hailey novel is to speak of every Hailey novel for there is little to distinguish one from the rest except subject matter. Each novel shares the same characteristic strengths and weaknesses. *Airport* is a typical example. The action of the novel is centered at a fictitious Chicago airport during one of the worst blizzards in the city's history. To give his reader an inside look at the operations of a major airport and into the lives of the people responsible for its existence, Hailey devises several plots; an airliner is stuck in the snow, blocking a runway and causing emergency situations in the air; an air-traffic controller is planning suicide; a trans-Atlantic airliner is about to take off with a bomb aboard; a stewardess has discovered she is pregnant; a group of local citizens is demonstrating against the excessive noise of the airport. The novel follows each plot to its conclusion, but not before the reader's intellectual curiosity about airports and his emotional curiosity about the characters are satisfied.

The narrative is slick and fast-moving, the information is interesting, the prose is readable, but the seams in Hailey's fabric too often show through. In order to introduce all his researched information into the novel, he is frequently forced to construct irrelevant sub-plots or to break the flow of the narrative for a lecture on such things as the safety records of commercial airlines or the pressures suffered by air-traffic controllers. To manage all his characters, he is forced into a "holding pattern" of his own. The focus of the novel shifts from one character to another as Hailey abandons characters temporarily only to return to them later when their number in the rotation comes up again. Consequently what unity there is in the book is provided only by the subject matter. The characters themselves are paper thin, reduced to simple dimensions; they are so typical that they could be interchanged from one novel to the next with little difficulty.

Wheels is much like *Airport* in its intention and its execution. The main difference is its lack of dramatic suspense; there is less drama to be derived from the introduction of a new car, the primary plot device in the novel, than from the naturally more exciting subjects of the earlier novels.

Hailey is a good popular novelist. He has learned what his audience expects and his audience knows what to expect from him; the reciprocal arrangement ought to ensure a continuing place for Hailey's novels on the best seller lists for years to come.

—David J. Geherin

HALE, Nancy. American. Born in Boston, Massachusetts, 6 May 1908. Educated at Winsor School, Boston; Boston Museum (Art) School. Married Fredson Bowers in 1942; two children from previous marriages. Assistant Editor, *Vogue*, New York, 1928-32, and *Vanity Fair*, New York, 1932-33; Reporter, *The New York Times*, 1935. Lecturer, Bread Loaf Writers Conference, Vermont, 1957-62; Phi Beta Kappa Visiting Scholar, 1971-72. Recipient: O. Henry Award, 1933; Benjamin Franklin Citation, 1948; Bellaman Award, 1968; Sarah Josepha Hale Award, 1974. Address: Woodburn, Route 8, Charlottesville, Virginia 22901, U.S.A.

PUBLICATIONS

Novels

The Young Die Good. New York, Scribner, 1932.
Never Any More. New York, Scribner, 1934.
The Prodigal Women. New York, Scribner, 1942.
The Sign of Jonah. New York, Scribner, 1950; London, Heinemann, 1952.
Dear Beast. Boston, Little Brown, 1959; London, Macmillan, 1960.
Black Summer. Boston, Little Brown, 1963; London, Gollancz, 1964.
Secrets. New York, Coward McCann, 1971.

Short Stories

The Earliest Dreams. New York, Scribner, 1936; London, Dickson and Davies, 1937.
Between the Dark and the Daylight. New York, Scribner, 1943.
The Empress's Ring. New York, Scribner, 1955.
Heaven and Hardpan Farm. New York, Scribner, 1957.
The Pattern of Perfection: Thirteen Stories. Boston, Little Brown, 1960; London, Macmillan, 1961.

Uncollected Short Stories

"Handful of r's," in *Vogue* (New York), 1 November 1961.

"In a Word," in *New Yorker*, 27 July 1963.
"Girl with the Goat-Cart," in *New Yorker*, 30 November 1963.
"An Age for Action," in *Ladies' Home Journal* (Des Moines, Iowa), March 1965.
"The Signorina," in *Transatlantic Review* (London), Autumn 1965.
"Sunday Lunch," in *Prize Stories 1966: The O. Henry Awards*, edited by Richard Poirier and William Abrahams. New York, Doubleday, 1966.
"All Anybody," in *Georgia Review* (Athens), Spring 1966.
"Family Ties," in *Southern Review* (Baton Rouge, Louisiana), April 1966.
"Animals in the House," in *Harper's* (New York), September 1966.
"Waiting," in *Virginia Quarterly Review* (Charlottesville), Autumn 1966.
"The Innocent," in *Virginia Quarterly Review* (Charlottesville), Spring 1967.
"The Most Elegant Drawing Room in Europe," in *Prize Stories 1968: The O. Henry Awards*, edited by William Abrahams. New York, Doubleday, 1968.
"Mr. Hamilton," in *Michigan Quarterly Review* (Ann Arbor), April 1970.
"Dreams of Rich People," in *McCall's* (New York), August 1972.

Plays

The Best of Everything (produced Charlottesville, Virginia, 1951).
Somewhere She Dances (produced Charlottesville, Virginia, 1953).

Other

A New England Girlhood. Boston, Little Brown, and London, Gollancz, 1958.
The Realities of Fiction: A Book about Writing. Boston, Little Brown, 1962; London, Macmillan, 1963.
The Life in the Studio. Boston, Little Brown, 1969.
Mary Cassatt. New York, Doubleday, 1975.
The Night of the Hurricane (juvenile). New York, Coward McCann, 1977.

Editor, *New England Discovery: A Personal View.* New York, Coward McCann, 1963.
Editor, *Daughter of Abolitionists*, by Ellen Wright. Northampton, Massachusetts, Smith College, 1964.

*

Manuscript Collection: Smith College Library, Northampton, Massachusetts.

Nancy Hale comments:

I am averse to making statements on my work because I have found by experience that fiction is so protean that today's aim can be tomorrow's anathema. But I may make the comment that in general I have striven to conceal the purpose underlying my work with "the light touch" since nothing seems to me so self-defeating as overt earnestness. Yet I can assure readers of my work that its purpose is earnest, indeed painful.

* * *

For almost four decades Nancy Hale has depicted varying aspects of the changing American social scene in terms of what for a more precise label must still be called the American upper and upper-middle class. Her fiction—some dozen novels and collections of short stories—ranges from recollections of family life in Massachusetts where she was born and raised to the pseudo-sophisticated intellectual circles of New York City where she lived relatively early in her career and the Virginia Piedmont which has been her home for many years. From the beginnings Hale (in private life the wife of a University professor) has been a witty and perceptive observer of individual and societal foibles which she recreates with admirably disciplined craftsmanship.

Hale's fiction has evoked widely different opinions, although even her least understanding critics have been impressed by the artistry and technical expertise which have been her hallmarks. And as her career progressed Hale's compassion deepened, or perhaps it was the other way around. In either case, *A New England Girlhood*, published rather beyond the midpoint of her career, is described as *An Affectionate Re-creation of Things Past* (some sixty years after her grandfather, Edward Everett Hale, had published his *A New England Boyhood*). And affectionate it is, without slopping into bathos or sentimentality: in her subsequent work the author's concern with stupidity, grossness, absurdity—and their opposites—is constantly alive, constantly keen, but she has learned, as has been observed, to shed the blood without disfiguring the bodies of her subjects.

Hale's characters fight no great battles to reform society or change the world. Their stories, as is inevitable in the fiction of manners, are extremely personal, involving relations between parents and children, husbands and wives, individuals versus individuals: the growing antagonism between the three teenage girls of *Never Any More* during a summer holiday; the searing problems of their adult counterparts in Hale's best-known and most commercially-successful novel *The Prodigal Women*, a book about the disorders of love and the warfare between men and women which has been aptly described as a depiction of "one kind of Hell...the Gulf of Self-tormenters"; the experiences of the group of emotionally disturbed women and their psychiatrist of *Heaven and Hardpan Farm*; the situation stories from what is perhaps her best collection, *The Empress's Ring*, which center around incidents no more dramatic than a mother's experiences with a sick child or a quiet day at the beach.

The theater of Nancy Hale's fiction is relatively limited, but she works within it with skill, precision, and a high awareness. And it is in the field of what she has called "Autobiographical Fiction" that she displays a wizardry uniquely her own, manifested in many stories and novels and in such recent books as *The Life in the Studio*, recollections of her painter mother, or *Secrets*, an autobiographical memoir. In such work Hale has captured—as she comments in *The Realities of Fiction*—"the atmosphere of the past...less by remembering than by inventing; less by calling up than by making up. It is as if to capture that atmosphere I have to create it, because in fact it never was on land or sea, least of all in my own childhood."

—William Peden

HALL, James B(yron). American. Born in Midland, Ohio, 21 July 1918. Educated at Miami University, Oxford, Ohio, 1938-39; University of Hawaii, Honolulu, 1938-40; University of Iowa, Iowa City, B.A. 1947, M.A. 1948, Ph.D. 1953; Kenyon College, Gambier, Ohio, 1949. Served in the United States Army, 1941-46. Married Elizabeth Cushman in 1946; five children. Writer-in-Residence, Miami University, 1948-49; Instructor, Cornell University, Ithaca, New York, 1952-53; Writer-in-Residence, University of North Carolina, Greensville, 1954; Assistant Professor, 1954-57, Associate Professor, 1958-60, and Professor of English, 1960-65, University of Oregon, Eugene; Director of the Writing Center, and Professor of English, University of California, Irvine, 1965-68. Since 1968, Professor of Literature, and Provost of College V, University of California, Santa Cruz. Writer-in-Residence, University of British Columbia, Vancouver, Summer 1956; Guest Artist, Pacific Coast Festival of Art, Reed College, Portland, 1958; Writer-in-Residence, University of Colorado, Boulder, 1963. Co-Founding Editor,

Northwest Review, Eugene, Oregon, 1957-60; Founder and Director, University of Oregon Summer Academy of Contemporary Arts, Eugene, 1959-64. Editorial Consultant, Doubleday and Company, publishers (West Coast staff), 1960; Cultural Specialist, United States Department of State, Washington, 1964. Recipient: Yaddo grant, 1952; Chapelbrook Fellowship, 1967; Institute of Creative Arts Fellowship, 1967; Balch Fiction Prize, 1967. Address: College V, University of California, Santa Cruz, California 95060; or, 31 Hollins Drive, Santa Cruz, California 95060, U.S.A.

PUBLICATIONS

Novels

Not by the Door. New York, Random House, 1954.
TNT for Two. New York, Ace, 1956.
Racers to the Sun. New York, Obolensky, 1960; London, Corgi, 1962.
Mayo Sergeant. New York, New American Library, 1967.

Short Stories

15 x 3, with Herbert Gold and R.V. Cassill. New York, New Directions, 1957.
Us He Devours. New York, New Directions, 1964.
The Short Hall: New and Collected Stories. Athens, Ohio University Press, 1980.

Verse

The Hunt Within. Baton Rouge, Louisiana State University Press, 1973.

Other

Editor, with Joseph Langland, *The Short Story.* New York, Macmillan, 1956.
Editor, *The Realm of Fiction: 61 Short Stories.* New York, McGraw Hill, 1965; revised edition, 1970, 1977.
Editor, with Barry Ulanov, *Modern Culture and the Arts.* New York, McGraw Hill, 1967; revised edition, 1972.

*

James B. Hall comments:

Although the novels are interesting, the central significance of the work resides largely in the short stories; the poetry is various, and by intention ancillary to the prose.

The novels, short stories, and poetry are thematically interrelated. The re-occurring motifs are the effects of competition on individuals in a system of modified capitalism such as obtains in the United States. Thus acquisitive, frustrated, evasive protagonists re-occur, some of them mad or nearly so. Extreme conduct in a hostile world is not infrequent; the adjustments which protagonists make vary from callous acceptance or the exploitation of others to withdrawal, revenge, and self-destruction. In general, the work shows the difficulty of remaining human in a competitive, non-Darwinian world fashioned in large part by a democratic society. Specifically, *Racers to the Sun* traces the "rise" and fall of a motorcycle racer who builds his own machine; the hero is injured (used up), and then is dropped by those who exploited his talent for machinery and speed. Likewise, in the typical short stories, "Us He Devours" and "The Claims Artist," the protagonists are in some ways laudable, but in the end are victims of their own and of society's demands. A typical poem, "Pay Day Night," treats the counter-productive nature of experience in another bureaucracy, the Army.

The short stories are experimental, highly compressed, and exploit language poetically for artistic effect. They are condensed statements that very often extend the possibilities of the genre. Many of the stories are anthologized; because they are complex they apparently "teach well" in classrooms.

* * *

James B. Hall, like Fitzgerald, Lewis, perhaps most of the important American writers of this century, sees the American dream as a combination of an ethic once moral and humane, and a goal of success that inevitably corrupts the ethic and so the dream. This is the theme he began to delineate in 1954 with the publication of *Not by the Door*, and continued to explore in subsequent novels. Howard Marcham, the protagonist of the first novel, is an Episcopal clergyman in a middle American town, "an American priest, with no real background of the spirit." Marcham is not an evil man, Hall is saying; but it is difficult for an American to hear a higher call over the rustle of money and the clink of cocktail glasses.

Racers to the Sun is an absorbing novel that examines the almost sexual mystique of machinery and speed—particularly of motorcycle racing—in America. The main character, Harold Hill, is practically raised in an automobile graveyard in Ohio, from where it seems perfectly natural for him to move into the world of the motorcycle track, the world of a worshipper of speed and success named "Gunner," who has transformed herself into a trophy for winners. He understands his motorcycle clearly as "a naked force...a dance step which would take him from Savile, Ohio, to the salt flats of Bonneville or to Daytona Beach where demi-gods in leather riding breeches flashed through the electric timers to the immortality of record books." It is a strength of the novel that Hall causes his spokesman to recognize the essence of his life and not give way to adolescent bleating about it.

Hall really hit his stride as a novelist in *Mayo Sergeant*. It is clear from the beginning with the appearance of red, white, and blue sails on the sea, that sailing is in some way symbolic of America; sailing vessels and the code the sport imposes (like the hunting code of Hemingway or Faulkner) are a metaphor of the business ethic and morality in America. The graceful old *Indus* is being replaced by the new *Tektra*, even as whatever was human in Industry has yielded to the unfeeling force of Technocracy. Or is the new order in America actually much different, the new businessman less human, or the new real-estate man more rapacious than the old, as Roberte Glouster, the easy-going narrator with ties to California history, likes to suppose? The conclusion can only be left in doubt.

The resemblance of Mayo Sergeant to Fitzgerald's Gatsby is unmistakable. Both, for example, come from obscure origins in the Midwest; both depend in part on an awkward personal attractiveness and win material success. But Gatsby never comes into harmony with the American dream, and it destroys him. Mayo Sergeant, who may seem more contemptible than Gatsby because Hall makes him more familiar than Gatsby, succeeds because the dream has become as venal as he is. Hall has more in common with Fitzgerald than character and theme: in one of the most successful broad comic chapters in American fiction, Hall, with a satiric sense no less acute than Fitzgerald's, illuminates the sanctimonious greed of land developers. If *Mayo Sergeant* falls short of *The Great Gatsby*, it is because Hall does not sustain the satire, and because he scatters the sympathy of the audience among several important characters.

—Alan R. Shucard

HANLEY, Clifford (Leonard Clark). Pseudonym: Henry Calvin. British. Born in Glasgow, Scotland, 28 October 1922. Educated at Eastbank School, Glasgow. Conscientious Objector in World War II. Married Anna E. Clark in 1948; three children. Reporter, Scottish Newspaper Services, Glasgow, 1940-45; Sub-Editor, *Scottish Daily Record*, Glasgow, 1945-57; Feature Writer, *TV Guide*, Glasgow, 1957-58; Columnist, *Glasgow Evening Citizen*, 1958-60. Visiting Professor, Glendon College, York University, Toronto, 1979-80. Member, Close Theatre Management Committee, Glasgow, 1965-71, Inland Waterways Council, 1967-71, and Scottish Arts Council, 1967-74; Vice-President, 1966-73, and President, 1974-77, Scottish P.E.N.; Scottish Chairman, Writers Guild of Great Britain, 1968-73. Agent: Curtis Brown Ltd., 1 Craven Hill, London W2 3EP, England. Address: 36 Munro Road, Glasgow 3, Scotland.

PUBLICATIONS

Novels

Love from Everybody. London, Hutchinson, 1959; as *Don't Bother to Knock*, London, Digit, 1961.
The Taste of Too Much. London, Hutchinson, 1960.
Nothing But the Best. London, Hutchinson, 1964; as *Second Time Round*, Boston, Houghton Mifflin, 1964.
The Hot Month. London, Hutchinson, and Boston, Houghton Mifflin, 1967.
The Red-Haired Bitch. London, Hutchinson, and Boston, Houghton Mifflin, 1969.
Prissy. London, Collins, 1978.

Novels as Henry Calvin

The System. London, Hutchinson, 1962.
It's Different Abroad. London, Hutchinson, and New York, Harper, 1963.
The Italian Gadget. London, Hutchinson, 1966.
The DNA Business. London, Hutchinson, 1967.
A Nice Friendly Town. London, Hutchinson, 1967.
Miranda Must Die. London, Hutchinson, 1968; as *Boka Lives*, New York, Harper, 1969.
The Chosen Instrument. London, Hutchinson, 1969.
The Poison Chasers. London, Hutchinson, 1971.
Take Two Popes. London, Hutchinson, 1972.

Plays

The Durable Element (produced Dundee, Scotland, 1961).
Saturmacnalia, music by Ian Gourlay (produced Glasgow, 1965).
Oh for an Island, music by Ian Gourlay (produced Glasgow, 1966).
Dick McWhittie, music by Ian Gourlay (produced Glasgow, 1967).
Jack o' the Cudgel (produced Perth, 1969).
Oh Glorious Jubilee, music by Ian Gourlay (produced Leeds, 1970).
The Clyde Moralities (produced Glasgow, 1972).

Television Play: *Alas, Poor Derek*, 1976.

Other

Dancing in the Streets (autobiography). London, Hutchinson, 1958.
A Skinful of Scotch (travel). London, Hutchinson, and Boston, Houghton Mifflin, 1965.
Burns Country: The Travels of Robert Burns. Newport, Isle of Wight, Dixon, 1975.
The Unspeakable Scot. Edinburgh, Blackwood, 1977.
Poems of Ebenezer McIlwham. Edinburgh, Gordon Wright, 1978.
The Biggest Fish in the World (juvenile). Edinburgh, Chambers, 1979.
A Hypnotic Trance. Edinburgh, BBC Scotland, 1980.
The Scots. Newton Abbot, Devon, David and Charles, and New York, Times, 1980.

*

Clifford Hanley comments:

(1972) *Dancing in the Streets*, my first published book, was written at the suggestion of my publisher, who wanted a book about the city of Glasgow. At the time I thought it a rather pedestrian recital of childhood memories and was taken aback by its critical and commercial success (it is still used as background reading in schools of social studies and urbanology). My first novel, *Love from Everybody*, written previously but published later, was frankly intended as a light entertainment, to make money, and was later filmed as *Don't Bother to Knock*. Having then retired from journalism, I wrote what I considered my first serious work, *The Taste of Too Much*, as a study of "ordinary" adolescence, without crime and adventitious excitement, and it may well be my most successful book in the sense of fully achieving the author's original conception. In the subsequent novels under my own name, I think my intention was to look at some areas of life—a businessman's troubles, the family situation, the agonies of work in the theatre—simply in my own way, without reference to fashionable literary conceptions. I have often been surprised when people found the novels "funny" because their intention was serious; but an author can't help being what he is. I do see the human condition as tragic (since decay and death are the inevitable end), but I don't distinguish between comedy and tragedy. Funerals can be funny too, and life is noble and absurd at the same time. I also insist on distinguishing between seriousness and solemnity, which are opposite rather than similar. On looking back, I realise that the tone of the novels tends to be affirmation rather than despair. This may be a virtue or a fault, or an irrelevance—a novelist should probably leave such judgments to critics and simply get on with what he must do. Maybe they also betray some kind of moral standpoint of which I was unconscious. This was explicit, in fact, in my first professionally produced play, *The Durable Element*, which was a study of the recurrent urge to crucify prophets. It was also deliberate in *The Chosen Instrument*, a pseudonymous Henry Calvin ten years later, in which a contemporary thriller mode was used to do a sort of feasibility study on the New Testament mythology. (The intention was so well disguised that no critic noticed it.)

But I suppose cheerfulness keeps breaking through. I am an entertainer as well as novelist, and the two may be compatible. My first commandment as a writer is not at all highfalutin. It is Thou Shalt Not Bore. *A Skinful of Scotch* is an irreverent guide to one man's Scotland and was written for fun. So, originally, were the Henry Calvin thrillers. I enjoy reading thrillers and I adopted the pen-name simply to feel uninhibited. The thriller too is a morality, but the morality is acceptable only if it has character and pace. These are not intellectual mysteries but tales of conflict between good and evil. My later work for the theatre was exclusively devoted to calculated entertainment and I am glad that people were actually entertained. I find now that I see life in more sombre terms, but whether this will show in future novels is hard to tell. It may even be a temporary condition.

* * *

Clifford Hanley is by far the funniest of the novelists now writing from and about Scotland. Like the character in the song, he "belongs to Glasgow," and from there, after some twenty years in journalism, he produced his fantasticated autobiography, *Dancing in the Streets*, where the facts are often more fantastically comic than the craziest of fictions. A year later his first novel, *Love from Everybody*, a confection concerned—or unconcerned—with the Edinburgh Festival, revealed his command of witty invention, and then with *The Taste of Too Much* he created a novel about adolescence in and around Glasgow which is as true in feeling as it is funny.

His most hilarious work to date is *The Hot Month*, a deliciously devilish presentation of the wildest and most wicked of all Highland holidays. Fully to enjoy this continuously entertaining work, however, the reader must join the author in making an assumption of the highest improbability—that Scotland might enjoy a whole summer month of unbroken sunshine—and anyone unable to contemplate even the remotest possibility of such a miracle may fail to appreciate the finer flights of Hanley's impish fancy. For the reader who can summon up sufficient suspension of disbelief, the dead-pan humour is irresistible. Yet Hanley achieves long and frequent laughter without ever allowing his characterisation to sink to the low level of farce. As a Highland holiday, *The Hot Month* is also a vacation from the puritanical-Presbyterian view that "sex is no joke," and its laughing liberalism is at the opposite pole from the sexlessness of most recent fiction about the Celtic scene. Unlike much of that fiction, again, Hanley deals with the present, and with people like ourselves—and that, in provincialised Scotland, is dynamite.

Equally dynamic, *The Red-Haired Bitch* is more analytical in its characterisation of the ambiguities of human relationships, either in the Glasgow theatre—the rocky pivot about which most of the action revolves—or anywhere. The problems arising from the production of a musical comedy about hag-ridden Scotland's most celebrated hag, Mary Queen of Scots, have results which are both dramatic in the wider sense and theatrical in the narrower, and Hanley's intimate acquaintance with the Glasgow scene beyond—as well as on—the stage enables him to paint the back-cloth to his story with as much subtlety as complexity.

Under the puckish pseudonym of Henry Calvin, Hanley has also written some highly entertaining who-dun-its, among which one, *The Chosen Instrument*, is a remarkable *tour de force*, the re-telling of the gospel story in the guise of a contemporary thriller. That these entertainments have not reached the heights—or depths—of popularity achieved by some other modern Scottish adventure stories can be attributed only to the fact that their heroes are fallible human beings rather than indestructible supermen.

—Alexander Scott

HANLEY, Gerald (Anthony). British. Born 17 February 1916; brother of James Hanley, *q.v.* Served with the Royal Irish Fusiliers for seven years. Lives in Ireland. Address: c/o Gillon Aitken, 17 Belgrave Place, London SW1X 8BS, England.

PUBLICATIONS

Novels

Monsoon Victory. London, Collins, 1946.
The Consul at Sunset. London, Collins, and New York, Macmillan, 1951.
The Year of the Lion. London, Collins, 1953; New York, Macmillan, 1954.
Drinkers of Darkness. London, Collins, and New York, Macmillan, 1955.
Without Love. London, Collins, and New York, Harper, 1957.
The Journey Homeward. London, Collins, and Cleveland, World, 1961.
Gilligan's Last Elephant. London, Collins, and Cleveland, World, 1962.
See You in Yasukuni. London, Collins, 1969; Cleveland, World, 1970.

Plays

Screenplay: *The Blue Max*, with others, 1966.

Radio Play: *A Voice from the Top*, 1962.

Other

Warriors and Strangers. London, Hamish Hamilton, and New York, Harper, 1971.

* * *

The principal themes of Gerald Hanley's novels are the dissolution of the British Empire and the impact of that dissolution on the relationships of individuals of different races, creeds and religions. He also explores subsidiary themes to illuminate these main preoccupations—the nature of courage, the wielding of power, and especially the public results of personal inadequacy on the part of those responsible for exercising power.

Gerald Hanley has lived through these themes and scenes himself and writes of what he knows; but although this makes him an interesting and distinctive writer he falls short of outstanding distinction as a novelist. His plots are sometimes rather obviously contrived in their resolution; the structural balance from chapter to chapter of interior monologue and dramatic dialogue is often repetitive; and when this lack of diversification is compounded with a failure to deepen and intensify the psychological development of his characters, the total effect is a little monotonous. One can see why he remains in the second rank of contemporary novelists, despite the intrinsic interest of his subject-matter and the clarity of his prose style.

Before the war Gerald Hanley farmed in Kenya, of all the East and Central African colonies the one in which the divisions between the hierarchy of colonial administrators, British settlers, missionaries, Levantine and Indian merchants, and the various African tribes were most strongly contrasted. Wartime Army service took him through the Somaliland campaign, another formative experience on which his imagination could later draw.

After *Monsoon Victory* he reached a wide public with *The Consul at Sunset*, the best introduction to his work. The novel is set in sunbaked African terrain where there is a tribal dispute over the use of water-holes. Responsibility for maintaining peace and justice rests with a handful of white men whose ability to discharge it successfully demands political realism, understanding of an alien culture, self-confidence, and personal integrity. The political officer dominated by an African mistress and the well-meaning but weak liberal both fail on some counts, while the discipled army officers, a Captain risen from the ranks and a Colonel of the old school, measure up to the situation. But as he stands bare-headed before the Union Jack at sunset the Colonel is uneasy about the adequacy of his kind in the changes that must lie ahead beyond the coming war.

In *Year of the Lion* again the seeds of racial, social and political conflict are seen to be germinating in African soil, even though British, African, and Dutch all unite to fight the lions and herds of zebra that threaten their farms and grazing, while in *Drinkers of Darkness* the slightly odd tensions of the white settlers have been developed into a crazed blindness to political realities as they struggle to assert their prestige. *The Journey Homeward* turns to the politics of a princely state in the Himalayas after partition, and explores further the political failure of leaders whose private lives are tortured, seedy or corrupt. But Africa is Gerald Hanley's proper milieu, revisited in his clear-eyed travel-book *Warriors and Strangers*.

—Stewart F. Sanderson

HANLEY, James. British. Born in Dublin, in 1901; brother of Gerald Hanley, *q.v.* Served in the Canadian Navy during World War I. Married to Dorothy Enid Heathcot; one son. Merchant seaman and journalist. Recipient: Welsh Arts Council Award, 1979. Agent: David Higham Associates, 5-8 Lower John Street, London W1R 3PE, England.

PUBLICATIONS

Novels

Drift. London, Partridge, 1930.
Boy. London, Boriswood, 1931; New York, Knopf, 1932.
Ebb and Flood. London, Lane, 1932.
Captain Bottell. London, Boriswood, 1933.
Resurrexit Dominus. Privately printed, 1934.
The Furys:
The Furys. London, Chatto and Windus, and New York, Macmillan, 1935.
The Secret Journey. London, Chatto and Windus, and New York, Macmillan, 1936.
Our Time Is Gone. London, Lane, 1940; with *The Furys* and *The Secret Journey*, New York, Dent, 1949.
Winter Song. London, Phoenix House, 1950.
An End and a Beginning. London, Macdonald, and New York, Horizon Press, 1958.
Stoker Bush. London, Chatto and Windus, 1935; New York, Macmillan, 1936.
Hollow Sea. London, Lane, 1938.
The Ocean. London, Faber, and New York, Morrow, 1941.
No Directions. London, Faber, 1943.
Sailor's Song. London, Nicholson and Watson, 1943.
What Farrar Saw. London, Nicholson and Watson, 1946.
Emily. London, Nicholson and Watson, 1948.
The House in the Valley (as Patric Shone). London, Cape, 1951.
The Closed Harbour. London, Macdonald, 1952; New York, Horizon Press, 1953.
The Welsh Sonata: Variations on a Theme. London, Verschoyle, 1954; New York, Horizon Press, 1978.
Levine. London, Macdonald, and New York, Horizon Press, 1956.
Say Nothing. London, Macdonald, and New York, Horizon Press, 1962.
Another World. London, Deutsch, and New York, Horizon Press, 1972.
A Woman in the Sky. London, Deutsch, and New York, Horizon Press, 1973.
A Dream Journey. London, Deutsch, and New York, Horizon Press, 1976.
A Kingdom. London, Deutsch, and New York, Horizon Press, 1978.

Short Stories

The German Prisoner. Privately printed, 1930.
A Passion Before Death. Privately printed, 1930.
The Last Voyage. London, W. Jackson-Joiner and Steele, 1931.
Men in Darkness: Five Stories. London, Lane, 1931; New York, Knopf, 1932.
Stoker Haslett. London, Joiner and Steele, 1932.
Aria and Finale. London, Boriswood, 1932.
Quartermaster Clausen. London, Arlan, 1934.
At Bay. London, Grayson, 1935.
Half an Eye: Sea Stories. London, Lane, 1937.
People Are Curious. London, Lane, 1938.
At Bay and Other Stories. London, Faber, 1944.
Crilley and Other Stories. London, Nicholson and Watson, 1945.
Selected Stories. Dublin, Fridberg, 1947.
A Walk in the Wilderness. London, Phoenix House, 1950.
Don Quixote Drowned. London, Macdonald, 1953.
Collected Stories. London, Macdonald, 1953.
The Darkness. London, Covent Garden Press, 1973.

Plays

Say Nothing (broadcast, 1961; produced London, 1962; New York, 1965). Published in *Plays of the Year 27*, London, Elek, 1963.
The Inner Journey (produced Hamburg, 1967; New York, 1969). London, Black Raven Press, and New York, Horizon Press, 1965.
Forever and Ever (produced Hamburg, 1966).
Plays One (includes *The Inner Journey* and *A Stone Flower*). London, Kaye and Ward, 1968.
Leave Us Alone (produced London, 1972).

Radio Plays: *S.S. Elizabethan*, 1941; *Freedom's Ferry* series, 1941; *Open Boat* series, 1941; *Return to Danger*, 1942; *A Winter Journey*, 1958; *I Talk to Myself*, 1958; *A Letter in the Desert*, 1958; *Gobbet*, 1959; *The Queen of Ireland*, 1960; *Miss Williams*, 1960; *Say Nothing*, 1961; *A Pillar of Fire*, 1962; *A Walk in the World*, 1962; *A Dream*, 1963; *The Silence*, 1968; *Sailor's Song*, 1970; *One Way Only*, 1970; *A Terrible Day*, 1973; *A Dream Journey*, 1974; *Another World*, from his own novel, 1980.

Television Plays: *The Inner World of Miss Vaughan*, 1964; *Another Port, Another Town*, 1964; *Mr. Ponge*, 1965; *Day Out for Lucy*, 1965; *A Walk in the Sea*, 1966; *That Woman*, 1967; *Nothing Will Be the Same Again*, 1968; *It Wasn't Me*, 1969.

Other

Broken Water: An Autobiographical Excursion. London, Chatto and Windus, 1937.
Grey Children: A Study in Humbug and Misery. London, Methuen, 1937.
Between the Tides. London, Methuen, 1939; as *Towards Horizons* (as James Bentley), London, Mellifont Press, 1949.
John Cowper Powys: A Man in the Corner. Loughton, Essex, Ward, 1969.
The Face of Winter (sketch). Loughton, Essex, Ward, 1969.
Herman Melville: A Man in the Customs House. Loughton, Essex, Dud Noman Press, 1971.

Editor, with Nina Froud, *Chaliapin: An Autobiography as Told to Maxim Gorky*, London, Macdonald, and New York, Stein and Day, 1967.

*

Critical Study: *The Novels of James Hanley* by Edward Stokes, Melbourne, Cheshire, 1964.

* * *

James Hanley is one of the most prolific of contemporary novelists; between 1930 and 1962 he published 22 novels, as well as seven volumes of short stories (and four works of non-fiction). But, though praised by leading writers and critics (including W.H. Auden, E.M. Forster, Herbert Read, and C.P. Snow) as "one of the most important of living writers," Hanley has been little read, and has received little critical notice.

Hanley's work is undeniably uneven, and the nature of his subject-matter (usually the world of the urban and sea-going proletariat) has probably had little popular appeal. But the main reason for the neglect of his work may be the mistaken assumption that he is a realist, in a period when realism has been generally considered an inferior fictional mode. "Realist," however, is a no more adequate label for Hanley than for Faulkner, whom he resembles in his selective and prevailingly sombre but compassionate vision of human life; in his power to create larger-than-life characters which achieve an almost mythic stature; and in his surrealistic experiments with language, especially in some of the shorter novels, like *Sailor's Song*, *No Directions*, and *The Welsh Sonata*. Even in the longer novels like *The Furys* and *Hollow Sea*, with their masses of realistic detail, Hanley's primary interest is always in what goes on in the minds of his characters, in their private dreams, fantasies, obsessions, and nightmare dreads.

Hanley is usually thought of as a novelist of the sea, but in fact only half-a-dozen of his books are sea-novels. His earliest novels were concerned with youths in the slums of Liverpool; his most ambitious project was a five-volume saga of working-class life centered on the Fury family; and much of his best work is concerned with the Second World War and its aftermath in the lives of war-shattered people.

Of the three earliest novels—*Drift*, *Boy*, and *Ebb and Flood*—the second, praised by Faulkner as "a damn fine job," is the most important. An angry and appalling study of outraged, humiliated and victimized adolescence, it is also Hanley's first novel of the sea.

Dennis Fury, a main character in the Fury saga, has also been a seaman for most of his life. But it is his wife, Fanny, who is the most memorable figure in this gargantuan cycle. One of the great characters in contemporary fiction, she is both prosaic and legendary, at once a middle-aged, dowdy, toil-worn, intensely respectable, and bigoted housewife, and a creature as vital, passionate, and amoral as a heroine of Celtic myth. Despite faults of diffuseness and melodrama, the first four novels, held together by the domineering central figure of Mrs. Fury, have an impressive sweeping movement, through growing conflict within the family to the climax in the murder of a lustful money-lender, by the son, Peter, a failed priest, then through the fragmentation of the family to the slow knitting together of the surviving parents and their achievement of some degree of tranquility. The final volume, centred on Peter Fury, released after 15 years in prison, is one of Hanley's most successful technical experiments in the fusing of past and present; it really belongs with other studies of loneliness, unfulfillment, and inability to communicate written in the 1950's.

Hanley began as a sea-writer with two volumes of stories, *Men in Darkness* and *Aria and Finale*; the two most memorable stories are, probably, "The Last Voyage" (which has a close resemblance to O'Neill's *S.S. Glencairn* plays) and "Narrative," which contains the seeds of three later novels of war at sea—*Hollow Sea*, *The Ocean*, and *Sailor's Song*. Compared with these, the two other sea-novels, *Captain Bottell* (in which Hanley seems to have deliberately challenged Conrad) and *Stoker Bush*, are relatively unimportant.

The three novels about sailors, ships and the sea in time of war represent one of the peaks of Hanley's creative achievement. (No doubt Henry Green was thinking mainly of them when he described Hanley as "far and away the best writer of the sea and seafaring men since Conrad.") Though published within five years (1938-43) they are very different in scale, subject, and treatment. The formidably long *Hollow Sea*, concerned with the 1914-18 war, depends far more heavily on Hanley's memories of his own experiences than does the novella *The Ocean*, concerned with the 1939-45 war. *Sailor's Song*, by a remarkable feat, brings into the compass of a short novel the two wars at sea, and the quarter-century between. The first two are, in the main, straightforwardly realistic, but *Sailor's Song* is one of Hanley's most experimental novels, in language and technique.

Hollow Sea, in the grand simplicity of its conception, is potentially a great novel. The power of Hanley's imaginative treatment makes the story of a single voyage of a troop-ship into a double parable—a parable of the futility, absurdity, and waste of war, and a parable of the conflict between ordinary, decent humanity and impersonal, omnipotent authority. But it loses some of its force by being unnecessarily protracted. In *Sailor's Song* the immediate setting, a raft on which four seamen—one the injured and delirious Manion, whose name is almost an anagram of "any man"—drift helplessly after their ship has been torpedoed, serves mainly as a springboard from which, through Manion's confused and chaotic memories, we plunge back into the past. Hanley was aiming not at individual portraiture, but at a representation of the course of England's maritime history over a quarter of a century, as reflected in the lives, and especially the emotions, of a typical sailor and his family. The experiments in prose-poetry are sometimes unsuccessful, but, at worst, the novel in its intensity, its impassioned striving to give memorable expression to a great theme, is a magnificent failure.

The Ocean is one of Hanley's best three or four novels. In outline it is austerely simple—a war-time survival story. It has complete unity of place, the open boat in which the five survivors suffer unnumbered days of hunger, thirst, and exposure; in a sense it has unity of time, for the days are almost identical; it has complete unity of action and atmosphere. Man's struggle against nature in the form of the indifferent but ever-threatening sea could hardly be reduced to simpler or starker terms; but especially in the seaman, Curtain (who has been described as "one of the great figures of the English novel"), the novel presents a vision of the human spirit that refuses to be broken—a vision of meanness, selfishness, and weakness redeemed by charity, humility, and strength.

Hanley's only novel of the war on land, *No Directions*, has some similarity to *The Ocean* and in quality ranks with it. The setting is a single Chelsea house, divided into five flats; the time-scheme is restricted to a single evening during the blitz. But it is more like *Sailor's Song* in its fusion of realism and fantasy; it is a haunting fantasia rather than a story. The reality that Hanley sought to present was itself a nightmare, and his mingling of wild poetry and bleak naturalism conveys the terror, the macabre confusion, and the horrifying grandeur of the blitz with superb effectiveness.

Of Hanley's post-war novels two (apart from *An End and a Beginning*) are particularly impressive—*The Closed Harbour* and *Levine*. They are very different in tone and atmosphere (the sticky heat of Marseilles is as important in *The Closed Harbour* as the wintry bleakness of northern England in *Levine*) but they are alike in that their chief characters are war-scarred ex-sailors who are obsessed by the desire to get back to sea. Both the French merchant captain, Eugene Marius, and the Polish ordinary seaman, Felix Levine, are sole survivors of ships sunk during the war, and both are distrusted outcasts—Marius because he is suspected of the murder of his nephew, Levine because he has no probable past or identity. The end for Marius is insanity, for Levine the murder of the English woman who marries him, and stifles him by the devouring possessiveness of her devotion. These two novels embody, in a pure form, Hanley's vision of human beings as solitary, unable to communicate with one another, the victims of obsessions and compulsive drives. But, psychically self-imprisoned as they are, his people lack neither humanity and compassion (Levine, careless of the consequences to himself, returns to the hospital); nor proud grandeur (his wife, questioned about Levine on her death-bed, will answer nothing). Tragic vision, masterful technical control, and the sheer distinction of the writing combine to make these two of the finest English works of the 1950's.

James Hanley developed strikingly during his career as a novelist, though his Hardyesque vision—bleak but never misanthropic—remained essentially the same. The melodramatic violence of his earlier work was eliminated without any loss of real power; its clumsiness, crudity, and turgidity give way to a style spare, strong, disciplined but flexible, evocative, and individual. Despite the neglect of his work, few of his British contemporaries have equalled his achievement.

—Edward Stokes

HARDWICK, Elizabeth (Bruce). American. Born in Lexington, Kentucky, 27 July 1916. Educated at the University of Kentucky, Lexington, A.B. 1938, M.A. 1939; Columbia University, New York, 1939-41. Married the poet Robert Lowell in 1949 (divorced, 1972); one daughter. Adjunct Associate Professor, Barnard College, New York. Founder and Advisory Editor, *New York*

Review of Books. Recipient: Guggenheim Fellowship, 1948; George Jean Nathan Award, for criticism, 1966; American Academy award, 1974. Address: 15 West 67th Street, New York, New York 10023, U.S.A.

PUBLICATIONS

Novels

The Ghostly Lover. New York, Harcourt Brace, 1945.
The Simple Truth. New York, Harcourt Brace, and London, Weidenfeld and Nicolson, 1955.
Sleepless Nights. New York, Random House, and London, Weidenfeld and Nicolson, 1979.

Uncollected Short Stories

"People on the Roller Coaster," in *O. Henry Memorial Award Prize Stories of 1945.* New York, Doubleday, 1945.
"Saint Ursula and Her Eleven Thousand Virgins," in *Yale Review* (New Haven, Connecticut), March 1945.
"The Mysteries of Eleusis," in *The Best American Short Stories 1946*, edited by Martha Foley. Boston, Houghton Mifflin, 1946.
"What We Have Missed," in *O. Henry Memorial Award Prize Stories of 1946.* New York, Doubleday, 1946.
"The Temptations of Dr. Hoffman," in *Partisan Review* (New Brunswick, New Jersey), Fall 1946.
"The Golden Stallion," in *The Best American Short Stories 1947*, edited by Martha Foley. Boston, Houghton Mifflin, 1947.
"Evenings at Home," in *The Best American Short Stories 1949*, edited by Martha Foley. Boston, Houghton Mifflin, 1949.
"The Friendly Witness," in *Partisan Review* (New Brunswick, New Jersey), April 1950.
"A Florentine Conference," in *Partisan Review* (New Brunswick, New Jersey), May-June 1951.
"A Season's Romance," in *New Yorker*, 10 March 1956.
"The Oak and the Axe," in *New Yorker*, 12 May 1956.
"The Classless Society," in *Stories from The New Yorker 1950-1960.* New York, Simon and Schuster, 1960.
"The Purchase," in *The Best American Short Stories 1960*, edited by Martha Foley and David Burnett. Boston, Houghton Mifflin, 1960.
"Two Recent Triumphs," in *Gallery of Modern Fiction*, edited by Robie Macauley. New York, Salem Press, 1966.
"The Faithful," in *New Yorker*, 19 February 1979.

Other

A View of My Own: Essays in Literature and Society. New York, Farrar Straus, 1962; London, Heinemann, 1964.
Seduction and Betrayal: Women and Literature. New York, Random House, and London, Weidenfeld and Nicolson, 1974.

Editor, *Selected Letters*, by William James. New York, Farrar Straus, 1961.

* * *

For over two decades, Elizabeth Hardwick's reputation as a tough-minded, occasionally wry, critic has been secure. Her career as a novelist has been less certain. Her first novel, *The Ghostly Lover*, published in 1945, was promising, but its early feminist slant was not rightly appreciated. A novel about Marian Coleman who learns that she cannot settle for the comforts of a man, it offers telling glimpses into her life, the life of her restless parents, the hot, lazy days in the South, the grubby days studying in New York, and the dreams of the ghostly men who pursue her. Marian knows the value of concealment; the book confirms her suspicion that love is not "the hard, demanding surrender she had imagined." Marian suffers from a peculiar emptiness, one that comes from knowing that what men want from her is not in her, but is "tuned to a certain imaginary pitch in women" that men have invented. The novel closes with Marian's act of independence: she walks unseen away from her lover who has come to the station to meet her. She knows that to accept him would be to accept marriage and not to care about motives. Hardwick's next novel, *The Simple Truth*, appeared a decade later. Tightly plotted, probing the motives behind a frightful act, the novel examines the death of a beautiful college girl, Betty Jane Henderson, who died in her boyfriend's rooming-house, after hours. The trial of the boyfriend, Rudy, dominates the book. It is examined from numerous perspectives, most important those of two curious onlookers, the affable, married Mr. Parks and the middle-aged, married Anita Mitchell who is drawn to the case to investigate the working of the unconscious. The truth about the act, late at night, in a rooming-house where two lovers frolicked and struggled, ultimately emerges, but equally as interesting is the picture of the psyches of the characters who become caught up in the trial. These two early novels were competent—the writing was careful; the characters, ordinary, but true, surprisingly often; the plots were slightly thin.

Sleepless Nights appeared in 1979 and broke a silence of more than 20 years. It should make Hardwick's name. Its form is novel, daringly breaking the strictures of her earlier narrative style. The autobiographical component of the novel is openly confronted, and handled affectively. Roaming like an insomniac from one recollection to another, the book continually surprises us with its fleeting memories of rooms we have all known, feelings we have felt, losses we have never remedied. In retrospect, Hardwick's earlier novels show a niggling regret on the author's part that the story is not a little more important, that life for women is not a little more adventuresome. *Sleepless Nights* reflects a more mature sensibility—one that has learned that ordinary experience needs no apology.

Sleepless Nights offers a record of life's obscenities. The insomniac narrator is identified as "Elizabeth" in the novel. The book is a queer blend of autobiography and fiction. Hardwick's decision to create a persona with her own name heightens our sense of how life informs fiction. The Elizabeth of this book is very nearly the Elizabeth Hardwick who lives, the woman who is a career journalist, writer, reviewer for *Partisan Review* and the *New York Review of Books*, and the ex-wife of the poet Robert Lowell. The memories and imaginings of the persona curl about the lives of deprived souls, of which Elizabeth is one. There is Josette, the Boston cleaning-lady, a victim of "unfair diseases," with her "breasts hacked off by cancer." There is Billie Holiday, self-destructive, haunting, pure style, who died in agony, with the police at her bedside, denied in her last hours the drugs her body craved. Elizabeth wonders at the "sheer enormity" of Holiday's vices. There is Alex A., Elizabeth's bachelor friend, an intellectual and failed academic who does not marry the woman who might have made his life different. There is her other half, the partner of the "we" she alludes to. She complains of his tyranny by the weak, women. He reads and writes all day, drinks quarts of mild, smokes cigarettes, and complains when she plays jazz records. There is her mother, bearer of nine children; childbearing is "what she was always doing, and in the end what she had done." There is the neighborhood prostitute, Juanita, who died of "prodigious pains and sores." This is a bitter, troubling book of memories to keep us all awake. But if the dose is bitter, it is also life. The laundress, the cleaning-lady, the Boston spinster, the middle-aged persona whose divorce has brought her back to her old territory, the talk of a mother, troubled that her son cannot cope and the complaints of a couple too long married are all authentic. The style is often sparse; the details are selected with startling directness and simplicity; yet the whole is very full.

—Carol Simpson Stern

HARRIS, Mark. American. Born in Mount Vernon, New York, 19 November 1922. Educated at the University of Denver, B.A. in English 1950, M.A. in English 1951; University of Minnesota, Minneapolis, Ph.D. in American Studies 1956. Served in the United States Army, 1943-44. Married Josephine Horen in 1946; one daughter and two sons. Reporter, *Daily Item*, Port Chester, New York, 1944-45, *PM*, Long Island, New York, 1945, and International News Service, St. Louis, 1945-46; Writer for the *Negro Digest* and *Ebony*, Chicago, 1946-51. Taught at San Francisco State College, 1954-68, Purdue University, Lafayette, Indiana, 1967-70, California Institute of the Arts, Valencia, 1970-73, Immaculate Heart College, Los Angeles, 1973-74, and University of Southern California, Los Angeles, 1973-75. Since 1975, Professor of English, University of Pittsburgh. Fulbright Professor, University of Hiroshima, 1957-58; Visiting Professor, Brandeis University, Waltham, Massachusetts, 1963. Member, San Francisco Art Commission, 1961-64; U.S. Delegate, Dartmouth Conference, Kurashiki, Japan, 1964. Recipient: Ford grant, for theatre, 1960; American Academy grant, 1961; Guggenheim Fellowship, 1965, 1974; National Endowment for the Arts grant, 1966. D.H.L.: Illinois Wesleyan University, Bloomington, 1974. Agent: A.L. Hart, Fox Chase Agency, 419 East 57th Street, New York, New York 10022. Address: Department of English, University of Pittsburgh, Pittsburgh, Pennsylvania 15260, U.S.A.

PUBLICATIONS

Novels

Trumpet to the World. New York, Reynal, 1946.

City of Discontent: An Interpretive Biography of Vachel Lindsay, Being Also the Story of Springfield, Illinois, USA, and of the Love of the Poet for That City, That State, and That Nation, by Henry W. Wiggen. Indianapolis, Bobbs Merrill, 1952.

The Southpaw, by Henry W. Wiggen: Punctuation Inserted and Spelling Greatly Improved. Indianapolis, Bobbs Merrill, 1953.

Bang the Drum Slowly, by Henry W. Wiggen: Certain of His Enthusiasms Restrained. New York, Knopf, 1956.

A Ticket for a Seamstitch, by Henry W. Wiggen: But Polished for the Printer. New York, Knopf, 1957.

Something about a Soldier. New York, Macmillan, 1957; London, Deutsch, 1958.

Wake Up, Stupid. New York, Knopf, 1959; London, Deutsch, 1960.

The Goy. New York, Dial Press, 1970.

Killing Everybody. New York, Dial Press, 1973.

It Looked Like Forever. New York, McGraw Hill, 1979.

Plays

Friedman & Son (produced San Francisco, 1962). New York, Macmillan, 1963.

Screenplay: *Bang the Drum Slowly*, 1973.

Television Play: *The Man That Corrupted Hadleyburg*, from the story by Mark Twain, 1980.

Other

Mark the Glove Boy; or, The Last Days of Richard Nixon (autobiography). New York, Macmillan, 1964.

Twentyone Twice: A Journal (autobiography). Boston, Little Brown, 1966.

Public Television: A Program for Action, with others. New York, Harper, 1967.

Best Father Ever Invented: The Autobiography of Mark Harris. New York, Dial Press, 1976.

Short Work of It: Selected Writing. Pittsburgh, University of Pittsburgh Press, 1980.

Saul Bellow, Drumlin Woodchuck. Athens, University of Georgia Press, 1980.

Editor, *Selected Poems*, by Vachel Lindsay. New York, Macmillan, 1963; London, Collier Macmillan, 1965.

Editor, with Josephine and Hester Harris, *The Design of Fiction.* New York, Crowell, 1976.

Editor, *The Essential Boswell: Highlights from the Journals.* New York, McGraw Hill, 1980.

*

Critical Study: *Mark Harris* by Norman Lavers, Boston, Twayne, 1978.

Mark Harris comments:

(1972) I have written eight novels. I think that a constant line travels through them. I didn't know this was happening while it was happening, but I can see it now, looking back after a quarter of a century since my first novel was published.

They are about the writer. That is, if you will, they are about the artist. Which is to say, if you will, they are about the one man against his society and trying to come to terms with his society, and trying to succeed within it without losing his own identity or integrity.

My novels are always very carefully written. Since hard work makes the writing look easy, there exist stupid reviewers and critics who think I (and others) just slam these writings out. My books are all constructed with great care. Nothing is missing from any of them in the way of plot. I forget nothing.

Of course, although I am spiritually at the center of my novels (every novel is mainly about one man), I am disguised as poet or baseball player or professor or historian. I am always a minority person in some sense, either because I am fictionally left-handed or, most recently, Gentile in a Jewish milieu. (My first book was about a black man in a white milieu.) I don't know why this is so. I believe that it is most deeply the result of being a Jew, but it may be attributable to other things I am not fully aware of. Maybe I was just born that way. It is a mystery.

Subject and theme: sometimes these aren't really stated in the works, and people feel disappointed. They want to know what they shouldn't: where does the author stand? In my heart, if not always dogmatically in my books, I stand for human equality and peace and justice.

I also stand for writing well: I don't believe that good ends can come of false or shoddy or hasty means. Books must be beautiful so that the world is put into a mood of beauty. Books mustn't merely *say* but must, on the other hand, *exist* as beauty.

I am opposed to the reduction or paraphrase of works of art. Thus I feel that I may on this page already have written more than I should.

* * *

Mark Harris's fiction and autobiography share several themes: the problems of racism and racial justice, the dilemma of violence and pacifism, the price of individualism and the forms of democracy and social justice. His work is dominated by genial comedy, a gently optimistic view of man's possibilities and capacities, and Mark Harris has pursued his own life through this fiction. His journal-autobiographies *Mark the Glove Boy* and *Twentyone Twice* complement fictionalized self-portraits like pitcher-author Henry Wiggen (*The Southpaw*, *Bang the Drum Slowly*, *A Ticket for a Seamstitch*), boxer-novelist-teacher Lee Youngdahl (*Wake Up, Stupid*), soldier-pacifist Jacob Epstein (*Something about a Soldier*) and historian-diarist Westrum (*The Goy*).

Harris's novels depict individuals in pursuit of themselves, discovering through self-analysis, experience, and observation who they are and what their lives mean. His first novel, *Trumpet to the World*, follows a black man through self-discovery and self-education to his rejection of war and violence and his attempts to reach the world through writing. He suffers poverty, hatred, and violence but also discovers friendship and love. Through determination and courage, he overcomes dehumanizing conditions to become fully alive, a fully functioning man. The baseball trilogy (*The Southpaw*, *Bang the Drum Slowly*, *A Ticket for a Seamstitch*) describes the career of Henry W. Wiggen, a young man who succeeds in big-league baseball. In a Lardneresque style, Wiggen writes the journal of his maturity as an athlete and a man. Wiggen grapples with the mysteries of love, the problem of hatred and violence, becomes reconciled with the finality of death. Each story shows Wiggen's growth, mentally and spiritually, and his progress down a road to self-understanding and reconciliation. Overtly a comedy of athletics and folk-hero rambunctiousness, the three books also form a study of pacifism, love and justice.

Something about a Soldier turns explicitly to the problems of violence and nonviolence which appear in the earlier novels. In it Jacob Epp (Epstein) discovers the importance of his identity, the meaning of love and loyalty, and the relationship between violence and justice. A young, very bright, but naive recruit, Jacob rejects the Army and the war (WW II), militantly works for justice and equality for black people and begins to understand love and friendship. He rejects death for life, war for peace, goes AWOL, and through meditation in prison comes to self-reconciliation.

In *Wake Up, Stupid* Harris uses the epistolary form to follow a crisis of insecurity in the life of a man who is successful as an athlete, teacher, and writer. Lee Youngdahl, during a lull in artistic creativity, takes up letter-writing to occupy his imagination. Comic crises of his fantasy life involve all his friends and enemies and lead him to a final understanding of his needs and desires, the sources of his imagination.

The Goy continues this theme of self-discovery. In it, Westrum, a midwestern gentile who has married an eastern Jew, pursues his identity through a massive, life-long journal. He comes to understand, through the journal, his relationship with the Jews in his life, his father's virulent anti-semitism, his own obsession with history, his relationship with his son, his wife and his mistress. The past, through his journal and his study of history, ultimately explains his present.

In *Killing Everybody* Harris explores opposing passions of love and rage, life-giving and death. The novel deals with the madness of the world and of individuals caught up in its madness. It studies revenge and charity, physical love and sexual fantasy, a dialectic skilfully developed as a complex dance between four central minds. The story moves more deeply into the roots of modern psychic life than Harris's earlier fiction, and he confronts a massive theme—civilization and its discontents.

All of Mark Harris's fiction is comic in conception, and sports and games are at the center of the work, especially the social games which are the substance of comedy of manners. Lee Youngdahl, in *Wake Up, Stupid*, analyzes American literature in a statement epitomizing Harris's own work:

> What is it that thrusts Mark Twain and Sherwood Anderson into one stream, and Henry James into another?...It has so much to do with a man's early relationship to the society of boys and games—that miniature of our larger society of men and business, with its codes and rules, its provision for imagination within these rules, with winning, losing, timing, bluffing, feinting, jockeying, with directness of aim and speech and with coming back off the floor again.

Harris's fiction is solidly within this tradition which translates social games into comedy, a comedy which explains our secret lives more clearly than any social or psychological theory.

—William J. Schafer

HARRIS, (Theodore) Wilson. British. Born in New Amsterdam, British Guiana, now Guyana, 24 March 1921. Educated at Queen's College, Georgetown. Married 1) Cecily Carew in 1945; 2) Margaret Whitaker in 1959. Government Surveyor in the 1940's, and Senior Surveyor, 1955-58, Government of British Guiana. Visiting Lecturer, State University of New York at Buffalo, 1970; Writer-in-Residence, Scarborough College, University of Toronto, 1970; Commonwealth Fellow in Caribbean Literature, Leeds University, Yorkshire, 1971; Visiting Professor, University of Texas, Austin, 1972, University of Mysore, 1978, and Yale University, New Haven, Connecticut, 1979. Delegate to the National Identity Conference, Brisbane, 1968; to UNESCO Symposium on Caribbean Literature, Cuba, 1968. Recipient: Arts Council grant, 1968, 1970; Guggenheim Fellowship, 1973; Henfield Writing Fellowship, 1974; Southern Arts Writing Fellowship, 1976. Address: c/o Faber and Faber Ltd., 3 Queen Square, London WC1N 3AU, England.

PUBLICATIONS

Novels

The Guiana Quartet:
  Palace of the Peacock. London, Faber, 1960.
  The Far Journey of Oudin. London, Faber, 1961.
  The Whole Armour. London, Faber, 1962.
  The Secret Ladder. London, Faber, 1963.
Heartland. London, Faber, 1964.
The Eye of the Scarecrow. London, Faber, 1965.
The Waiting Room. London, Faber, 1967.
Tumatumari. London, Faber, 1968.
Ascent to Omai. London, Faber, 1970.
Black Marsden: A Tabula Rasa Comedy. London, Faber, 1972.
Companions of the Day and Night. London, Faber, 1975.
Da Silva da Silva's Cultivated Wilderness, and Genesis of the Clowns. London, Faber, 1977.
The Tree of the Sun. London, Faber, 1978.

Short Stories

The Sleepers of Roraima. London, Faber, 1970.
The Age of the Rainmakers. London, Faber, 1971.

Verse

Fetish. Privately printed, 1951.
The Well and the Land. Georgetown, Magnet, 1952.
Eternity to Season. Privately printed, 1954; revised edition, London, New Beacon, 1979.

Other

Tradition, The Writer, and Society: Critical Essays. London, New Beacon, 1967.
History, Fable, and Myth in the Caribbean and Guianas. Georgetown, National History and Arts Council, 1970.
Fossil and Psyche (lecture on Patrick White). Austin, University of Texas, 1974.
Explorations: A Selection of Talks and Articles, edited by Hena Maes-Jelinek. Aarhus, Denmark, Dangaroo Press, 1981.

*

Manuscript Collections: University of the West Indies, Mona, Kingston, Jamaica; University of Texas, Austin; University of Indiana, Bloomington; University of Guyana, Georgetown.

Critical Studies: *The Novel Now* by Anthony Burgess, London, Faber, and New York, Norton, 1967, revised edition, 1971; essay by John Hearne, in *The Islands in Between* edited by Louis James, London, Oxford University Press, 1968; introduction by Kenneth

Ramchand to *Palace of the Peacock*, London, Faber, 1968; *Wilson Harris and the Caribbean Novel* by Michael Gilkes, Trinidad and London, Longman, 1975; *Enigma of Values* edited by Kirsten Holst Petersen and Anna Rutherford, Aarhus, Denmark, Dangaroo Press, 1975; *The Naked Design* by Hena Maes-Jelinek, Aarhus, Denmark, Dangaroo Press, 1976; *West Indian Literature* edited by Bruce King, London, Macmillan, 1979; "The Eternal Present in Wilson Harris's *The Sleepers of Roraima* and *The Age of the Rainmakers*" by Gary Crew, in *World Literature Written in English* (Arlington, Texas), Autumn 1980; "Limbo, Dislocation, Phantom Limb" by Nathaniel Mackey, in *Criticism* (Detroit), Winter 1980.

Wilson Harris comments:

(1972) *Palace of the Peacock* through *The Guiana Quartet* and successive novels up to *The Sleepers of Roraima* and *The Age of the Rainmakers* are related to a symbolic landscape-in-depth—the shock of great rapids, vast forests and savannahs—playing through memory to involve perspectives of imperilled community and creativity reaching back into the Pre-Columbian mists of time.

I believe that the revolution of sensibility in defining community towards which we may now be moving is an extension of the frontiers of the alchemical imagination beyond an *opus contra naturam* into an *opus contra ritual*. This does not mean the jettisoning of ritual (since ritual belongs in the great ambivalent chain of memory; and the past, in a peculiar sense, as an omen of proportions, shrinking or expanding, never dies); but it means the utilisation of ritual as an ironic bias—the utilisation of ritual, not as something in which we situate ourselves absolutely, but as an unravelling of self-deception with self-revelation as we see through the various dogmatic proprietors of the globe within a play of contrasting structures and anti-structures: a profound drama of consciousness invoking contrasting tones is the variable phenomenon of creativity within which we are prone, nevertheless, to idolise logical continuity or structure and commit ourselves to a conservative bias, or to idolise logical continuity or anti-structure and commit ourselves to a revolutionary bias. Thus we are prone to monumentalise our own biases and to indict as well as misconceive creativity. A capacity to digest as well as liberate contrasting figures is essential to the paradox of community and to the life of the imagination.

* * *

It is becoming clear that, viewed together, Wilson Harris's short and complex novels form one of the major fictional achievements in English in this century. His works are experimental and revolutionary. The boldness of his vision, the terseness and accumulated depths of his symbolical language, the progression of the narratives through significant moments of intuition and the metamorphosis of "images in space" rather than through plot, and his conception of characters as a nucleus of selves or "community of being" rather than a sharply defined entity—these are some of the elements that set the novel once more on the path of discovery and renewal. To the traditional novel, which, in his eyes, consolidates a world view and presents it as inevitable, Harris opposes the "drama of consciousness" which involves his characters in a process of breaking down biases and self-deceptions as a preliminary to re-discovery and fulfilment. His work is a focus of cross-cultural traditions (English, South American, Caribbean) but its distinctive character emerges from his confrontation with, and immersion in, the Guyanese landscapes and from his re-interpretation of the basic facts of Caribbean history. Harris sees the Guyanese psyche as a "spatial" reality equivalent to the phenomenal world. Both are the receptacle of lost generations of victims (historically, Amerindians and runaway slaves). Hence the exploration in his novels of hidden densities in both outer and inner landscape. Harris's characters search for a nameless eclipsed dimension of being inspired by the void-like condition experienced in the past by Caribbean peoples but seen now as a way out of polarizations inherited from the complex circumstances of conquest and colonization. This explains their "double vision," the constant interplay in the narratives between material shapes and the immaterial perspectives with which the oppressed are associated. It also accounts to a large extent for the texture of the narratives, the fusion between the animate and inanimate, between the sensuous and the "abstract," and the startling juxtapositions or associations of contrary images.

Harris's fictional work to date can be divided into three major phases. In the first, *The Guiana Quartet* creates a composite picture of Guyana, revealing the specific character of its contrasting landscapes and its various racial communities. A journey (at once historical conquest and individual expedition) into the Guyanese interior, the harsh lives of East Indian labourers in the savannahs, a tragedy of guilt and innocence on the coast, and the scientific measuring of the rise and fall of a river in the heartland provide the narrative framework for the protagonist's encounter in each novel with a terrible past that needs to be re-interpreted. The originality of Harris's approach lies in his discovering in the very traumas of history neglected possibilities of fulfilment for both the conquerors and the conquered of Guyana. Catastrophe need never be final but offers an occasion for change and renewal when re-lived and "digested." Though a sense of social justice may be responsible for the protagonist's change of attitude towards victimized people, this does not stem from a social or political ideal but rather illustrates a need for individual regeneration as a prelude to a new conception of community. The emphasis in the *Quartet* is on unity and interrelatedness between all forms of being, on spiritual freedom, responsibility and genuine authority, all of which are envisaged through the recognition of the alien and weak element in the community as its true roots and therefore springhead of change. Also paramount is the possiblility of unlocking a fixed order of things and eroding the certainties in which the characters are self-imprisoned. Hence the crumbling rather than "consolidation" of personality. Even the characters' mode of apprehension is shattered and reshaped.

This shattering of rigid ways of being leads to partial and unfinished reconstructions in the protagonist's consciousness, unfinished because the dynamic tension between dissolution and rebirth is, according to Harris, in the very nature of existence and because he refuses to invest absolutely in one way of being. In his second cycle of novels (from *The Eye of the Scarecrow* to *Ascent to Omai*) the main character moves towards an "other," who is the object of his exploration, without ever finally identifying with that "other." There is a double preoccupation in these novels with the creation of genuine, though never wholly achieved, community and the art of fiction Harris (and the narrator or protagonist within the novels) attempts to create. Their subject-matter is, even more specifically than in the earlier fiction, the subjective imagination, its working on memory and its transformation of the raw material of experience, which is wholly internalized. The protagonist is an "agent of personality" through which the past re-enacts itself as a free and living "construction of events." The result is a fragmentation of the surface reality (and of the narrative structure) concomitant with an accumulation of motifs and images, which are so many partial ways of approaching an underlying wholeness.

Between his second and third cycles of novels Harris wrote two collections of stories, *The Sleepers of Roraima* and *The Age of the Rainmakers*, in which he re-interprets Amerindian myths and shows that they can elicit a wholly new conception of life. The novels that follow are no longer set in Guyana (except *Genesis of the Clowns*) but in Scotland (*Black Marsden*), Mexico (*Companions of the Day and Night*) and London (*Da Silva da Silva's Cultivated Wilderness* and its sequel *The Tree of the Sun*). Experience is still wholly perceived through the individual consciousness of the protagonist, but one of his major concerns is to bridge the gap between civilizations and bring to light the mutation by which eclipsed people(s) are beginning to emerge from their buried condition. Another aspect of these latest novels is the way in which Harris uses painting as an exploratory metaphor to grasp the "inimitable." In the da Silva novels particularly the main character is a painter whose visionary canvases are "doorways" into an inner reality or light that can never be wholly unearthed. Existences on these canvases reveal unpredictable resources that modify the two faces of tradition, one assertive and oppressive, the other immaterial and hardly perceptible, growing out of unacknowledged sacrifice. The need for an imaginative balance between the two underlies the painter's effort to create a "middle ground" between the contrasting figures he paints, people whom he sees as resurrected selves moving in and out of his consciousness.

Throughout his fiction Harris's major concern is with both the creation of a "new architecture of consciousness" and the nature of creativity itself. His belief that form is prior to content is illustrated in his use of language as a means to develop awareness and stimulate a renewal of sensibility in modern man. With each new novel the extraordinary possibilities of aesthetic and spiritual renascence he discovers in the individual's dialogue with outer and inner world are a challenge to the reader to probe with him into man's genius for recovery and change.

—Hena Maes-Jelinek

HARROWER, Elizabeth. Australian. Born in Sydney, New South Wales, 8 February 1928. Worked for the Australian Broadcasting Commission, Sydney, 1959-60; Reviewer, *Sydney Morning Herald*, 1960; worked for Macmillan and Company Ltd., publishers, Sydney, 1961-67. Recipient: Commonwealth Literary Fund Fellowship, 1968; Australian Council for the Arts Fellowship, 1974. Address: c/o Macmillan Company of Australia, 107 Moray Street, South Melbourne, Victoria 3205, Australia.

PUBLICATIONS

Novels

Down in the City. London, Cassell, 1957.
The Long Prospect. London, Cassell, 1958.
The Catherine Wheel. London, Cassell, 1960.
The Watch Tower. London and Melbourne, Macmillan, 1966.

Uncollected Short Stories

"Lance Harper—His Story," in *Australian Letters* (Adelaide), 1961.
"The Cost of Things," in *Summer's Tales 1*, edited by Kylie Tennant. Sydney, Macmillan, 1964.
"English Lesson," in *Summer's Tales 2*, edited by Kylie Tennant. Sydney, Macmillan, 1965.
"The Beautiful Climate," in *Modern Australian Writing*. London, Fontana, 1968.

*

Manuscript Collection: Mitchell Library, Library of New South Wales, Sydney.

Critical Studies: "The Novels of Elizabeth Harrower" by Max Harris, in *Australian Letters* (Adelaide), December 1961; *Forty-Two Faces* by John Hetherington, Melbourne, Cheshire 1962; "Elizabeth Harrower's Novels: A Survey" by R.G. Geering, in *Southerly* (Sydney), no. 2, 1970; *Recent Fiction* by R.G. Geering, Melbourne, Oxford University Press, 1974.

* * *

An ideal introduction to Elizabeth Harrower's work is the short story "The Beautiful Climate," since it provides a paradigm of her fictional universe. It is a world in which selfish men manipulate their women and material possessions in a vain attempt to achieve happiness; frustrated by their blind male egotism, they become subject to fits of smouldering violence and frequent relapses into bouts of alcoholism and morbid self-pity. The woman's role is to suffer, to pity, and to provide the innocent seeing eye for the narrative. In "The Beautiful Climate" the paranoiac male is Mr. Shaw, who secretly buys a holiday island, reduces his wife and daughter to domestic slavery there, then sells the place behind their backs. The consciousness that develops from innocent passivity to partial sad wisdom is the daughter's, who reflects her creator in turning from psychology to literature as a guide to truth. The same basic situations and characters recur throughout the novels; and the tormented relationship between father and daughter in this short story might seem to offer a psychological clue to the novelist's preoccupation with male domination.

In *Down in the City*, a very remarkable first novel, Harrower traces the disenchantment that follows when the heroine exchanges the empty security of her wealthy bay-side suburb in Sydney for the puzzling ups and downs of her husband's shady business world. In describing the characteristic claustrophobia of the flat-dwelling city wife, she succeeds wonderfully well in evoking the typical sights and sounds of Sydney and in establishing a connection between climate and states of mind. And the hero, who oscillates between his classy wife and his obliging mistress, reflects the conflicting drives and split personality of many an Australian business man.

What distinguishes Harrower's second novel, *The Long Prospect*, from all her others is that the malevolent main character is a woman not a man. But once again the viewpoint is through an innocent seeing eye; in this case, it is a child's. By the end of the novel, she has plumbed the seedy adult world to its depths. The scene in which four irredeemably corrupt adults spy on the 12-year-old and her middle-aged friend, transferring their own "atmosphere of stealth" onto the innocent pair, is only one of many pieces of superb psychological drama in this accomplished novel.

While the third novel, *The Catherine Wheel*, laudably attempts to extend the range of the fictional world by having its setting in London bed-sitter-land, it is a somewhat disappointing work that hardly prepares the reader for the splendid fourth novel, *The Watch Tower*. The conspicuous success in *The Watch Tower* lies in the creation of Felix Shaw, the Australian business man, who climaxes a series of similar portraits and shares the surname of the father in "The Beautiful Climate." But equally subtle is the analysis of pity, through the contrasted characters of Shaw's two victims, who show that pity may enslave as well as ennoble (this a continuous preoccupation in the novels). Shaw's capriciousness, his bursts of petty pique and rage, his resentment at others' success, his dark nihilism, brutal aggression, unrecognised homosexuality and alcoholism, all point to a profound psychic disorder. But it is the novelist's triumph to suggest that this disorder is at least partly the product of a society that worships materialism and masculinity.

In most of her work, Elizabeth Harrower combines sharp observation of individual life with a searching critique of Australian society. Although she lacks the resilient vitality of such English novelists as Margaret Drabble, her vision of a male-dominated society is depressingly authentic. She has been highly praised and compared favourably with Patrick White, but her unflattering, somewhat drab and disenchanted view of Australian life is unlikely to win her the wide local readership her work certainly deserves.

—John Colmer

HAWKES, John (Clendennin Burne, Jr.). American. Born in Stamford, Connecticut, 17 August 1925. Educated at Trinity School, 1940-41; Pawling High School, 1941-43; Harvard University, Cambridge, Massachusetts, 1943-49, A.B. 1949. Served as an ambulance driver with the American Field Service in Italy and Germany, 1944-45. Married Sophie Goode Tazewell in 1947; three sons and one daughter. Assistant to the Production Manager, Harvard University Press, 1949-55; Visiting Lecturer, 1955-56, and Instructor in English 1956-58, Harvard University. Assistant Professor, 1958-62, Associate Professor, 1962-67, Professor of English, 1967-73, and since 1973, T.B. Stowell University Professor, Brown University, Providence, Rhode Island. Special Guest, Aspen Institute for Humanistic Studies, Colorado, 1962; member of the staff of the Utah Writers Conference, summer 1962, and Bread Loaf Writers Conference, Vermont, summer 1963; Visiting Professor of Creative Writing, Stanford University, California, 1966-67; Visiting Distinguished Professor of Creative Writing, City College of the City University of New York, 1971-72. Member, Panel on Educational Innovation, Washington, D.C., 1966-67. Recipient: American Academy grant, 1962; Guggenheim Fellowship, 1962; Ford Fellowship, for drama, 1964; Rockefeller Fellowship, 1968; Prix du Meilleur Livre Etranger, 1973. Member, American Academy of Arts and Sciences, 1973; Member, American Academy, 1980. Agent: Lynn Nesbit, International Creative Management, 40 West 57th Street, New York, New York 10019. Address: 18 Everett Avenue, Providence, Rhode Island 02906, U.S.A.

PUBLICATIONS

Novels

The Cannibal. New York, New Directions, 1949; London, Spearman, 1962.
The Beetle Leg. New York, New Directions, 1951; London, Chatto and Windus, 1967.
The Lime Twig. New York, New Directions, 1961; London, Spearman, 1962.
Second Skin. New York, New Directions, 1964; London, Chatto and Windus, 1966.
The Blood Oranges. New York, New Directions, and London, Chatto and Windus, 1971.
Death, Sleep, and the Traveler. New York, New Directions, 1974; London, Chatto and Windus, 1975.
Travesty. New York, New Directions, and London, Chatto and Windus, 1976.
The Passion Artist. New York, Harper, 1979.

Short Stories

The Goose on the Grave, and The Owl: Two Short Novels. New York, New Directions, 1954.
Lunar Landscapes: Stories and Short Novels 1949-1963. New York, New Directions, 1969; London, Chatto and Windus, 1970.
The Universal Fears. Northridge, California, Lord John Press, 1978.

Uncollected Short Stories

"Two Shoes for One Foot," in *Tri-Quarterly* (Evanston, Illinois), Fall 1979.

Plays

The Wax Museum (produced Boston, 1966; New York, 1977). Included in *The Innocent Party*, 1966.
The Questions (produced Stanford, California, 1966). Included in *The Innocent Party*, 1966.
The Innocent Party: Four Short Plays (includes *The Wax Museum. The Questions, The Undertaker*). New York, New Directions, 1966; London, Chatto and Windus, 1967.
The Undertaker (produced Boston, 1967). Included in *The Innocent Party*, 1966.
The Innocent Party (produced Boston, 1968). Included in *The Innocent Party*, 1966.

Verse

Fiasco Hall. Privately printed, 1943.

Other

Editor, with others, *The Personal Voice: A Contemporary Prose Reader.* Philadelphia, Lippincott, 1964.
Editor, with others, *The American Literary Anthology 1: The 1st Annual Collection of the Best from the Literary Magazines.* New York, Farrar Straus, 1968.

*

Bibliography: *Three Contemporary Novelists: An Annotated Bibliography* by Robert M. Scotto, New York, Garland, 1977; *John Hawkes: An Annotated Bibliography* by Carol A. Hryciw, Metuchen, New Jersey, Scarecrow Press, 1977.

Manuscript Collection: Houghton Library, Harvard University, Cambridge, Massachusetts.

Critical Studies: *The Fabulators* by Robert Scholes, New York, Oxford University Press, 1967; *Hawkes: A Guide to His Fictions* by Frederick Busch, Syracuse, New York, Syracuse University Press, 1973; *Comic Terror: The Novels of John Hawkes* by Donald J. Greiner, Memphis, Memphis State University Press, 1973; *John Hawkes and the Craft of Conflict* by John Kuehl, New Brunswick, New Jersey, Rutgers University Press, 1975; *A John Hawkes Symposium* edited by Anthony C. Santore and Michael N. Pocalyko, New York, New Directions, 1977.

* * *

John Hawkes, perhaps the most original American novelist since Faulkner, bears only superficial resemblances to other contemporary innovators. His work is distinctly less philosophical and less parodic than that of Barth, Nabokov, Pynchon, Durrell, Borges. And if he chooses to create fictional worlds, rather than represent ours—fictional worlds in which one man on a motorcycle may occupy a third of Germany, or a Caribbean island wander in space and time—these visionary landscapes yet seem genuine dynamic projections of our real underground lives. Childhood terror, oral fantasies and castration fears, fears of regression and violence, profound sexual disturbances—these (rather than the spatial inventions of science fiction or of Nabokov's *Ada*) are the components of Hawkes's myths and of the "places" he calls Germany or America or England.

Hawkes claims to have recognized at the outset of his career four enemies: plot, character, setting, theme. Haunting chordal insistences and recurring images replace plot; the symbols of nightmare and neurosis and of the preconscious serve for character; a general vision of deterioration and collapse offers a semblance of theme. All these, and the dark hallucinatory landscapes, are redeemed by humor and by what Tony Tanner calls the "complicated and wrought fabric of his style." To a degree rare even in contemporary literature ugly materials—violence, suffering, deliberately reversed sympathies, magnified obscenities of landscape or human form—become things of beauty. Are the visions of violence and collapse prompted, as the author has occasionally insisted, by a belief in order and love? These stylized, distanced enormities maintain a very powerful hold on us, even as we enjoy them aesthetically, in part because they are rarely explained. This is the one thing Hawkes has in common with Robbe-Grillet; his world is unexplained. Hawkes's fictional world simply and dynamically, even magically, *is*.

Such originality and uncompromising difficulty long restricted

Hawkes to an underground audience. *The Cannibal*, written as a Harvard undergraduate, drew some attention because it appeared to be a powerful symbolic commentary on the American occupation of a diseased, deteriorated Germany. The ruined landscape of 1945 is juxtaposed against a Germany of 1914, already doomed; there is a vision of history as fated yet inconsecutive and absurd. But at least a few readers were drawn rather by powerful scenes of grotesque transformation and psychic substitution (as cannibalism for homosexual assault) and by the nervous, exceptionally brilliant phrasing. *The Cannibal* is, for some readers, the masterpiece of American avant-garde fiction.

The Beetle Leg is a cooler vision, at times parodic, often comic, of a mythical American west and sexless wasteland in which helpless persons somnambulistically wander. This excellent novel had few readers at first; *The Goose and the Grave* (a volume containing also *The Owl*) was also almost completely ignored. It has been reissued, with several stories added, as *Lunar Landscapes*. These darkly playful short novels are laid in 20th-century Italy and in a fictionized San Marino locked in medieval legend and ritual: "two sides of a single dream," Tony Tanner has remarked, "centering on human violence in a hostile terrain—sudden deaths in still squares." (Tanner's essay in *City of Words* is one of the best brief introductions to Hawkes's work.)

By 1961, with *The Lime Twig*, a number of major writers and critics had discovered Hawkes, and this novel has become a favorite in American college classrooms. Moreover, Hawkes had by now moved to a more conscious understanding of his own materials and methods, and even some distance toward realism and narrative suspense. Parody of the detective novel form is merely the thin surface or pretext, in *The Lime Twig*, for another powerful vision of violence and tormented sexuality, this time laid in a bleakly plausible wartime and post-war England. Freudian substitutions and displacements are clearly evident as such, and are therefore oddly comic (an injection in the place of sexual penetration, or beating by a truncheon as rape). Yet the writing is so powerful that we continue to experience fascination and terror, even as we coolly watch the author's game. Few novels have dramatized so powerfully ultimate threats to identity.

With *Second Skin*, which lost the National Book Award to Saul Bellow's *Herzog* by one vote, Hawkes reached a much larger audience. And now for the first time the concealed affirmations and sympathies of the earlier books come to the surface in a vision of death and disaster (in America and on a north Atlantic island) succeeded by pastoral bliss on a wandering southern island. The narrator has survived the suicide of father, wife, daughter, and, escaped from a world of impotence, has become an artificial inseminator of cows. He is also, possibly, the father of the child of the black Catalina Kate, whom he shares with his messboy Sonny. Some of the dark materials of Hawkes's earlier fiction are present, even on that lush tropical island—a monstrous iguana, for instance, clinging to Catalina Kate's back. But the final vision of equanimity is genuine, reinforced by a conversational style of Nabokovian loveliness.

Hawkes has clearly moved from the brilliant groping of a wholly original, half-conscious, at times primitive visionary to the wholly conscious artistry and calculated rhetoric of a novelist who is also a gifted literary critic and professor of English (at Brown University). The writing of several tightly constructed plays, collected as *The Innocent Party*, may have contributed to Hawkes's development toward a more open and public art. *The Blood Oranges* has only a few scenes of wildly antirealist invention, though it has many moments of original and exquisite writing. Its comic treatment of two couples who have exchanged partners, yet still live together, often seems both to parody Ford's *The Good Soldier* and to satirize the gravity with which middle-class Americans, in the 1960's, contemplated their sexual anxieties. In one respect *The Blood Oranges* is like its predecessors. The Mediterranean world of "Illyria"—recalling *Twelfth Night* as *Second Skin* evoked *The Tempest*—is absolutely plausible, and absolutely Hawkes's own.

Hawkes's later fictions reveal a more and more conscious and suave art. *Death, Sleep, and the Traveler* is perhaps the slightest of the later novels, and in its ambiguities and comic sexuality is even closer than *The Blood Oranges* to Nabokovian fictional games. In place of a quaternion of lovers there are now three sexual triangles, with the pleasures of "sharing" and complicity, and those of fellatio, even more overt than before. *Travesty*, on the other hand, is a masterpiece of first-person narration, though the very existence of the narrator's interlocutors remains problematic. The *données* of the fiction, while superficially melodramatic, invite a teasing, speculative, even philosophical voice reminiscent of Clamence's voice in Albert Camus's *The Fall*: the narrator and only speaker driving fast toward a deliberate murder and suicide that will crash the car against an already designated wall far ahead; beside him "Henri," who has been the lover of both the narrator's wife and his daughter, who is riding in the back seat. In a statement of cosmic skepticism as absolute as Camus's the car's journey becomes, metaphorically, that of the earth's "progress through the fortress of space." Between the Creation (the mechanic's last adjustments) and "the life of the mind that holds the moving car to the road there is nothing, nothing at all"; or there is only "design and debris."

With *The Passion Artist* Hawkes returned deliberately to the fictional world of *The Cannibal*, its bleak city and devastated landscape reflecting the psychic impotence of its protagonist, its gratuitous violence stemming from a revolt in a penal institution for women. The misogynous imagination evident in powerful pages throughout Hawkes's fiction is now allowed altogether free play; the familiar sexual materials (castration fear and fear of engulfment, Oedipal configurations, etc.) are wholly unrepressed and virtually undisplaced. The first 50 or 60 pages of *The Passion Artist* may seem disappointingly methodical and realistic to the lover of the audacities of *The Cannibal*. But the later portions of the novel, energized by a remarkable dream sequence, recover the tension and terror, the dynamic fantasies and stylistic beauties of the best earlier work. The circumstance is virtually unique in modern literature: that of a suave, immensely skilled conscious artist in his mid-fifties remanipulating the powerful dreams and atavistic energies of 30 years before.

—Albert Guerard

HAZZARD, Shirley. Australian. Born in Sydney, 30 January 1931. Educated at Queenwood School, Sydney. Married the writer Francis Steegmuller in 1963. Worked in Combined Services Intelligence, Hong Kong, 1947-48; United Kingdom High Commissioner's Office, Wellington, New Zealand, 1949-50; United Nations Headquarters, New York (General Service Category), 1951-61. Recipient: American Academy award, 1966; Guggenheim Fellowship, 1974; O. Henry Award, 1977; National Book Critics Circle Award, 1981. Address: 200 East 66th Street, New York, New York 10021, U.S.A.

PUBLICATIONS

Novels

The Evening of the Holiday. New York, Knopf, and London, Macmillan, 1966.

People in Glass Houses: Portraits from Organization Life. New York, Knopf, and London, Macmillan, 1967.

The Bay of Noon. Boston, Little Brown, and London, Macmillan, 1970.

The Transit of Venus. New York, Viking Press, and London, Macmillan, 1980.

Short Stories

Cliffs of Fall and Other Stories. New York, Knopf, and London, Macmillan, 1963.

Uncollected Short Stories

"The Flowers of Sorrow," in *Winter's Tales 10*, edited by A.D. Maclean. London, Macmillan, and New York, St. Martin's Press, 1964.
"Forgiving," in *Ladies' Home Journal* (Des Moines, Iowa), August 1964.
"Comfort," in *New Yorker*, 24 October 1964.
"The Evening of the Holiday," in *New Yorker*, 17 April 1965.
"Out of Itea," in *New Yorker*, 1 May 1965.
"Nothing in Excess," in *New Yorker*, 26 March 1966.
"The Meeting," in *New Yorker*, 23 July 1966.
"A Sense of Mission," in *New Yorker*, 4 March 1967.
"Swoboda's Tragedy," in *New Yorker*, 20 May 1967.
"Story of Miss Sadie Graine," in *New Yorker*, 10 June 1967.
"Official Life," in *New Yorker*, 24 June 1967.
"The Separation of Dinah Delbanco," in *New Yorker*, 22 July 1967.
"The Everlasting Delight," in *New Yorker*, 19 August 1967.
"Statue and the Bust," in *McCall's* (New York), August 1971.
"Sir Cecil's Ride," in *Winter's Tales 21*, edited by A.D. Maclean. London, Macmillan, 1975; New York, St. Martin's Press, 1976.
"A Long Story Short," in *Prize Stories 1977: The O. Henry Awards*, edited by William Abrahams. New York, Doubleday, 1977.
"A Crush on Doctor Dance," in *Winter's Tales 24*, edited by A.D. Maclean. London, Macmillan, 1978; New York, St. Martin's Press, 1979.
"Something You'll Remember Always," in *New Yorker*, 17 September 1979.
"She Will Make You Very Happy," in *New Yorker*, 26 November 1979.

Other

Defeat of an Ideal: A Study of the Self-Destruction of the United Nations. Boston, Little Brown, 1972; London, Macmillan, 1973.

*

Critical Studies: "Patterns and Preoccupations of Love: The Novels of Shirley Hazzard" by John Colmer, in *Meanjin* (Melbourne), December 1970; *Recent Fiction* by R.G. Geering, Melbourne, Oxford University Press, 1974; "Shirley Hazzard: Dislocation and Continuity" by Robert Sellick, in *Australian Literary Studies* (Hobart), October 1979.

* * *

Shirley Hazzard was born and spent her early years in Australia, but she is essentially an expatriate cosmopolitan writer, deeply rooted in the European literary tradition, much travelled, acutely sensitive to the spirit of place, with a keen eye for national differences, and an acute ear for the words that express and unconsciously betray human values. So far she has drawn mainly on experiences gained from foreign travel, ten years employment in UNO, and residence in America for the material of her fiction. However, the brilliant short story "Woollahra Road," which holds in poignant juxtaposition a child's eye and an adult's eye view of Australia during the Depression, suggests that there is a store of memories belonging to the first 15 years of her life that has only partly found fictional expression. And the portrait in *People in Glass Houses* of the Australian UNO official, Mervyn, protected alike from disenchantment and beauty by his "defensive scepticism," establishes her skill in getting under the skin of certain Australian types.

The publication of *Cliffs of Fall*, a collection of short stories that had already appeared in *The New Yorker*, drew enthusiastic and discriminating praise from reviewers in America and Britain. It did not require the photograph of the author holding a copy of *Madame Bovary* on the dust-jacket to establish her admiration for Flaubert and other continental masters: Maupassant, Chekhov, and Turgenev, for example. Her insight into the paradoxes of love, her power to render moments of unspoken anguish (as in "The Worst Moment of the Day"), the combination of reticent suggestion and poetic resonance, the extraordinary economy of means in creating character and situation, and the unerring feel for the *mot juste*, all these qualities link her writing to the continental masters. In several of the stories, especially those set in an Italian pensione, the contrast between true and false values and the concern with sudden moments of illumination is reminiscent of E.M. Forster, without in any way being derivative. Of all the stories, the longest, called "A Place in the Country," is the best and foreshadows the author's later work. And the fact that "The Picnic" deals with the same characters suggests that the material might once have been intended for a novel. The central character in each, Nettie, come to realise that there is balance but no fairness in life and that the claims of humanity are prior to the demands of reason. These two ideas inform and control Hazzard's fictional universe.

In *The Evening of the Holiday* the promise of the Italian short stories is fulfilled, but the work is still only a novella rather than a full length novel. For the experience explored, the form is perfect. Each situation is exactly placed; the relationship between the half-English half-Italian heroine, Sophie, and the Italian architect Tancredi slowly unfolds towards its moment of piercing illumination and sad climax. It is not only Tancredi's married state that stands in the way of happiness; masculine pride and Sophie's reluctance to commit herself play their part. Sophie, like many of Hazzard's heroines, is an expatriate of the heart, in search of her spiritual home abroad, but forced to look for it within herself. In some respects *The Bay of Noon* is the natural extension and development of that search, but in between come the dazzlingly witty portraits from organization life called *People in Glass Houses*.

The "Portraits," like the short stories in *Cliffs of Fall*, first appeared in *The New Yorker*. Each could be read as a separate study, but because similar characters recur and a single controlling vision illuminates each, they cohere into an amusing but highly serious work of satirical fiction. Two related paradoxes bring the portraits into a single focus. The first is that the attempt to bring new life to the peoples of the undeveloped countries often destroys not only them but the bureaucrats and technologists themselves, who become the maimed and inhuman servants of a great impersonal machine. The second is that language and reason, the two great sources of truth and reality, become translated into the instruments of power, self-deception, and unreality. The irony, which in the other works controls and profoundly modifies the poetic vision, bites deeper here, producing an astringent but still deeply compassionate view of life. And the sensitivity to language, the source of the marvellous evocation of person and place in *Cliffs of Fall* and *The Evening of the Holiday*, becomes one of the main weapons in the author's satiric armoury. What gives *People in Glass Houses* its special power is the author's perception that the debasement of language and the dehumanising of man are but different aspects of a single process. Because the cast of characters is representatively cosmopolitan and because even love affairs are moulded by the great administrative machine, no corner of life seems untouched; the political and social implications of this for the whole world are startlingly revealed in Hazzard's historical study of the United Nations, *Defeat of an Ideal*.

Although *The Bay of Noon* develops naturally from *The Evening of the Holiday*, it is much more of a Proustian exercise in fiction than the earlier novella. The story is simple, but the pattern of relationships is intricate and subtle. In essence it deals with the experiences of a young girl, Jenny, a secretary-translator at a NATO base at Naples. In seeking to escape from a triangular affair involving her brother and her brother's wife, she finds herself enmeshed within an intricate web spun by a beautiful Italian novelist and her film-producer lover. The novel seems to suggest that one escapes from one pattern of relationships only to recreate a similar pattern elsewhere. It is centrally concerned with two themes: the achievement of happiness and the search for one's true home. Jenny finds momentary happiness in her flat at Naples, where as a convalescent she looks out on the tranquil bay, but the quest remains. At the end of the novel, Jenny revisits Italy. Whereas once she had expected to find the object of her pilgrimage in people and places, she has come to realize that the pilgrims of the heart must learn to take their inward bearings if they are to know the meanings of the outward journeys. Memory supplies the signposts. But which point home and which point elsewhere? Through its superbly controlled composition, *The Bay of Noon* invites the reader to bring Jenny's remembered images into final focus. For her, as for the reader, the images, so tinted by sadness and irradiated by hope, serve "not to direct, but to solace us; not to fix our positions, but show us how we came." This is a wise and beautiful novel that shows equal understanding of male pride and female need.

The Transit of Venus marks a striking expansion and deepening of the novelist's vision. Concerned with the lives of two Australian sisters who go to England after the death of their parents, the novel evokes an acute sense of time and place, as it moves, through action and through Proustian flights of memory, from country to country and from past to present, covering the period from World War I to the present. In this first full-length novel, the minor characters are as firmly and memorably created as the major ones and contribute as significantly to the thematic pattern, which is woven out of the threads of loyalty and abnegation. The moral issues affect public and private life and involve the consciences of scientists, artists, and lovers. Appropriately, the novelist's prose acquires a deeper resonance than in earlier works as she condenses her mature, George Eliot-like, reflections on chance and human fallibility. Yet for all the sudden shocks and disasters that befall the characters, the novel finally affirms that in spite of the malignities of fate truth has a life of its own.

In Shirley Hazzard's fiction, as in the mind of one of her fictional characters, "poetry and reason meet without the customary signs of struggle." This accounts for her classic beauty of form. With exquisite delicacy and restraint, she reveals the coexistence of happiness and sorrow in love, the poignancy of misunderstanding and regret, and the consolations of memory. Through the eyes of her very different heroines, all of whom combine intellectual toughness and extreme vulnerability, she presents a world that immediately strikes the reader as both beautiful and true.

—John Colmer

HEAD, Bessie. Citizen of Botswana. Born in Pietermaritzburg, South Africa, 6 July 1937. Educated at Umbilo Road High School. Married Harold Head in 1961; one son. Teacher in primary schools in South Africa and Botswana, for four years; Journalist, Drum Publications, Johannesburg, for two years. Private and unpaid work in agriculture in Botswana. Address: P.O. Box 15, Serowe, Botswana.

PUBLICATIONS

Novels

When Rain Clouds Gather. New York, Simon and Schuster, and London, Gollancz, 1969.
Maru. London, Gollancz, and New York, McCall, 1971.
A Question of Power. London, Davis Poynter, 1973; New York, Pantheon, 1974.

Short Stories

The Collector of Treasures and Other Botswana Village Tales. London, Heinemann, 1977.

Other

Serowe: The Village of the Rain Wind. London, Heinemann, 1981.

*

Manuscript Collection: Mugar Memorial Library, Boston University.

Critical Studies: "The Novels of Bessie Head" by Arthur Ravenscroft, in *Aspects of South African Literature* edited by Christopher Heywood, London, Heinemann, 1976.

Bessie Head comments:

I call myself—The New African. It is an extremely painful title full of sudden and disastrous changes of fortune and a sort of mental tight-rope walk with an abyss beneath. The abyss seems to be un-African and to belong to my soul. It is an almost violent urge to make gigantic moral abdications for the sake of mankind. What is African in the urge is the process of learning how to make these abdications in the face of human weakness. I do not believe African society caters for the superman. Other societies do and that is why their Gods are clothed in so much mumbo jumbo and hazy mysticism and dubious holiness. (People in India were angered by a biography about Gandhi which stated that he found celibacy extremely difficult. Gandhi was their God and presumably a superman and they did not care to examine *his* abyss, his humanity, though he clearly stated that celibacy was a mistake for him, I think in a letter to Tolstoy.)

Now, in Africa you have to be pretty clear about what you are thinking and feeling. NO ONE is going to set you up as a God. People are too human, too deep in their understanding of human nature. Therefore, my men—Makhaya and Maru—I first created majestic, with vast, straddling personalities and set them on a tightrope of my own abyss. It is always touch and go. There is really no God in Africa or a feeling of assurance that one would make it to the end of the tightrope and find eternal salvation and perfection, like Buddha, Gandhi and Jesus. The devil is equally paramount but his thought processes can be explained just as much as God's can. This means they are equals here and forced to think things over together. These themes are the basis of my preoccupations, the equality of man, the equality of God and the devil in Africa.

* * *

Bessie Head's three novels set in Botswana together form a cohesive treatment of the experience of national, racial, and religious displacement through a coming to terms with strange surroundings and with alienation that shades into mental illness, and finally acceptance of physical and moral discomforts and a delicate equilibrium between scepticism and a humanist faith. Despite similarity of setting and, superficially, of narrative, her novels chart different psychological and moral landscapes. But their cohesion is revealed in the frequent, perhaps not entirely conscious, use of words, phrases, and images connoting "control" and "prison." The former usually convey the idea of necessary restraint upon an individual's own disruptive appetites no less than upon those with which people exercising political power mangle the lives of others. "Prison" tends to be applied to a state of escape from the pressures of reality, but more often in order to find refreshment before a more vital engagement in communal affairs. The action in Bessie Head's novels takes place against a vivid rendering of Botswana landscape and climate; nevertheless, the issues, worked out unobtrusively, are not merely regional but radiate, politically and morally, across Africa, and sometimes beyond.

The central character in *When Rain Clouds Gather* is Makhaya, a black South African who enters Botswana on the run from apartheid and his own inner "jumble of chaotic discord." In the village of Golema Mmidi he almost casually joins other exiles from past pain in a co-operative farming venture under the guidance of an expatriate expert, himself in flight from a middle-class English background. The novel abounds in detail about such mundane matters as crops and agricultural methods but Bessie Head invests it all with a strange drama, for beneath the back-breaking labour in reluctant soil the characters learn how to intermesh their raw, damaged personalities in the attainment of a restorative communal self-sufficiency, both economic and human. This creative process is under constant threat from self-indulgent traditional chiefs and from new demogogic politicians. Golema Mmidi is no pastoral retreat, for it makes insatiable demands upon their physical energy and wrenches away their tightly clutched individualism. Gradually they take on new shared responsibilities of the very kind they had fled from in seeking the seclusion of Golema Mmidi.

The second novel, *Maru*, is more complex and adventurous in technique. That the opening projects two of the characters into a situation timed after the events of the story is no mere clever quirk but a necessary mechanism to provide insight into the humane motives behind Maru's seemingly selfish use of power. He is a paramount-chief elect who manipulates his sister's marriage with his friend Moleka so that he himself can marry the racially outcast, half-Bushman or Masarwa woman, Margaret, whom Moleka also loves. Maru's methods seem unscrupulous, smacking of the cynicism of political manoeuvering, but he knows that his kingdom is of love and that, because Moleka's is of power, Moleka would be unable to live with the social consequences of marrying a Masarwa. Maru renounces his chieftaincy when he marries Margaret, and, although he loves her dearly, the marriage to a Masarwa has also a symbolic meaning for the status of the Masarwa people in Botswana.

Much more than *When Rain Clouds Gather*, *Maru* is about interior experience, though that experience is closely related to political behaviour. *A Question of Power* moves even more deeply and disturbingly into the recesses of personality. From the engagement, there emerges a clearly shaped integration of the personal and social levels of experience. Like Makhaya, Elizabeth, the heroine of *A Question of Power*, has sought political refuge from apartheid, and, like Margaret, has endured the ignominy of being regarded as a half-caste. Even in Botswana she feels so racially alienated that she suffers nightmares of mental torture which later affect her waking life, where, in a co-operative gardening enterprise she is, ironically, being fully accepted as a member of the community. The frighteningly vivid, cinema-like world of her nightmares is dominated by Sello who enacts her lust for moral powers and Dan who exhibits the full propensities of her carnal appetites. The tussle for her allegiance constitutes also a debate about the present and future of Africa, so that it is no mere personal agony that we witness. The novel is a profoundly honest, courageous confrontation of the horrors of 20th-century existence that every news bulletin gives us a glimpse of.

—Arthur Ravenscroft

HEARNE, John. Jamaican. Born in Montreal, Canada, 4 February 1926. Educated at Edinburgh University, 1947-49, M.A. 1949; London University, 1949-50, T.D. 1950. Served in the Royal Air Force as an Air Gunner, 1943-46. Married 1)Joyce Veitch in 1947; 2)Leeta Hopkinson in 1955; two children. Teacher in London and Jamaica, 1950-59; Information Officer, Government of Jamaica, 1962; Resident Tutor, Department of Extra-Mural Studies, 1962-67, and since 1968, Head of the Creative Centre, University of the West Indies, Kingston. Visiting Fellow in Commonwealth Literature, University of Leeds, Yorkshire, 1967; O'Connor Professor in Literature, Colgate University, Hamilton, New York, 1969-70. Recipient: Rhys Memorial Prize, 1956; Institute of Jamaica's Silver Musgrave Medal, 1964. Address: c/o Creative Arts Centre, University of the West Indies, Kingston 7, Jamaica.

PUBLICATIONS

Novels

Voices under the Window. London, Faber, 1955.
Stranger at the Gate. London, Faber, 1956.
The Faces of Love. London, Faber, 1957; as *The Eye of the Storm*, Boston, Little Brown, 1958.
Autumn Equinox. London, Faber, 1959; New York, Vanguard Press, 1961.
Land of the Living. London, Faber, 1961; New York, Harper, 1962.
Fever Grass (as John Morris, with Morris Cargill). London, Collins, and New York, Putnam, 1969.
The Candywine Development (as John Morris, with Morris Cargill). London, Collins, 1970; New York, Stuart, 1971.
The Sure Salvation. London, Faber, 1981.

Uncollected Short Stories

"The Wind in This Corner" and "At the Stelling," in *West Indian Stories*, edited by Andrew Salkey. London, Faber, 1960.
"A Village Tragedy" and "The Lost Country," in *Stories from the Caribbean*, edited by Andrew Salkey. London, Elek, 1965; as *Island Voices*, New York, Liveright, 1970.

Plays

The Golden Savage (produced London, 1965).

Television Plays: *Soldiers in the Snow*, with James Mitchell, 1960 (UK); *A World Inside*, 1962 (UK).

Other

Our Heritage, with Rex Nettleford. Mona, University of the West Indies, 1963.

Editor, *Carifesta Forum: An Anthology of 20 Caribbean Voices*. Kingston, Carifesta 76, 1976.

*

John Hearne comments:

My first concern has been to try to say something about the way we live now that could not be said except by the use of fiction.

When I first started to write I had the feeling that the novel and the short story are the forms that keep the individual most alive in the necessary but increasing synonymity of the industrial and post-industrial world.

Themes, as such, don't interest me much—only a gesture, made by some unsolicited person, that suddenly seizes the imagination and which must be finally explained.

Style and technique are very important, but if the gesture that comes to you when you're not looking for it really needs explanation, then you'll find the style and technique to work it out.

* * *

John Hearne is essentially a West Indian novelist: at the same time he lies outside the main stream of the Caribbean novel. Where this has focussed characteristically on the peasant experience, Hearne has explored the predicament of the middle-class intellectual, who can be twice an exile in the largely black developing nations. In *Voices under the Window* it is Mark Lattimer, a "white" Jamaican lawyer, who has devoted himself to the people, but is cut down pointlessly by a marijuana-smoking peasant in a city riot. In *Stranger at the Gate* the hero is Roy McKenzie, again a lawyer who becomes a communist and dies ramming a police car to allow a communist ex-president of a neighbouring island to escape. In *Autumn Equinox* Jim Diver, a young American of Cuban origin, attempts to run a communist paper on a noncommunist island.

These novels do not suggest political solutions; indeed the sketchy treatment of political themes only suggests their irrelevance to his real concern, which is with the difficulty and importance of individual relationships, in particular between men and women. This emerges overtly in *The Faces of Love* and his best novel to date, *Land of the Living*. In the latter the love theme is related to recognisable Caribbean social issues through the involvement of Mahler, a German Jew lecturing at a Caribbean university, with Joan Culpepper, a middle-class "white," and Brysie, a "black" bar servant with paternal links with a politico-religious cult.

Hearne's third concern is with the physical experience of the Caribbean, showing a gift for description and narrative put to vivid use also in his "James Bond" type thrillers (with Morris Cargill) *Fever Grass* and *The Candywine Development*. They have helped him create a fictional world, Cayuna, an island closely resembling Jamaica. While unlikely to be placed in the small top group of Caribbean novelists, Hearne has made an individual and important contribution to the mapping of the West Indian experience.

—Louis James

HEATH, Roy A(ubrey) K(elvin). Guyanese. Born in British Guiana, now Guyana, 13 August 1926. Educated at Central High School, Georgetown; University of London, 1952-56, B.A. (honours) in French 1956. Married to Hemilia Oberli-Heath; three children. Treasury clerk, Georgetown, 1944-51; worked in London, 1951-58; primary school teacher, Inner London Education Authority, 1959-68. Since 1968, French and German teacher, Barnet Borough Council, London. Recipient: Guyana Theatre Guild Award, 1972; *Guardian* Fiction Prize, 1978. Address: c/o Allison and Busby Ltd., 6-A Noel Street, London W1V 3RB, England.

PUBLICATIONS

Novels

A Man Come Home. London, Longman, 1974.
The Murderer. London, Allison and Busby, 1978; New York, Schocken, 1981.
From the Heat of the Day. London, Allison and Busby, 1979; New York, Schocken, 1981.
One Generation. London, Allison and Busby, and New York, Schocken, 1981.

Uncollected Short Stories

"Miss Mabel's Burial," in *Kaie* (Georgetown, Guyana), 1972.
"The Wind and the Sun," in *Savacou* (Kingston, Jamaica), 1974.

Play

Inez Combray (produced Georgetown, Guyana, 1972).

*

Roy A.K. Heath comments:

A Man Come Home relates the story of a large working-class Guyanese family whose mores provide a striking contrast to those of their middle-class brethren. *From the Heat of the Day* and *One Generation* are the first two parts of a trilogy treating the condition of the middle classes in Guyana in the 20th century. I see myself as a chronicler of Guyanese life in this century.

* * *

Roy A.K. Heath's novels are set in his native Guyana, and deal with life in, or on the fringes of, the slums of the city of Georgetown. Money and class are important in all his books because of their effect on people's relationships, and on the opinions individuals have of themselves. Heath is especially concerned with the influence of such external pressure on the human personality. His people live on the brink of insanity, and some occasionally fall over the edge.

To escape from the slum conditions in which he lives, Bird Foster, the central character of Heath's first novel, *A Man Come Home*, offers himself in return for wealth as a lover to a Fairmaid, a supernatural creature of the Guyanese rivers. The easy money which he introduces into the world of his family and friends creates bitterness and tension where cordiality had existed. Unpleasant aspects of their characters emerge. Bird dies as a result of the Fairmaid's jealousy and becomes the man come home of the novel's title, but his money continues to create enmity after his death. Although Heath explores interestingly the dilemma of those who yearn to escape from the grip of poverty but find themselves unable to deal with the social and psychological problems which the acquisition of money thrusts on them, there is some technical uncertainty which undermines the book's impact. For example, the Fairmaid and many of the minor characters are never thoroughly integrated into the plot.

The Murderer, a much more tightly organized book, describes the gradual disintegration into insanity of the personality of Galton Flood. Steeped as a child in the values of middle-class respectability by his mother, whom unconsciously he grows to hate for her tyranny over him and her humiliating treatment of his father, Galton feels compelled to desecrate her memory after her death by going to live in the slums and by taking a menial job. Intense though his hatred is of her, his attitude towards his mother predetermines much of his behaviour in later life and controls his relationship with his wife who confuses him when she is compliant and submissive at times and at others talks about her independence. He claims to hate domineering women but yearns to be dominated. Incapable of reconciling these tendencies in his personality his mind snaps and he kills his wife. It is not enough, however, to label Galton Flood a murderer. Society, which has imposed on him a burden he cannot be expected to bear, is his accomplice in the act. Galton's intense paranoia and self-centeredness make his breakdown thoroughly convincing, though sometimes they make it difficult for the reader to empathize with him.

From the Heat of the Day, the first novel of a projected trilogy, deals with a marriage that fails. The husband and wife cannot communicate with each other because he is inhibited by the fact that his social background is inferior to hers. It fails also because of lack of money. The wife, Gladys, is reduced to relating her masochistic fantasies to her servants, and the husband to trying to find escape from his problems in drink and whores. Preoccupied with his own sense of inadequacy he never understands or shows concern for his wife's suffering until after her death.

Heath's characters are not a match for the problems they encounter. Life degrades them even in the means they use to try to escape: the vast quantities of rum they consume, and the sordid encounters they have with prostitutes, which Heath makes both vivid and revolting with such grotesque touches as an aging prostitute offering a shrivelled breast to Galton, and a whore going into an epileptic fit as she gets ready to entertain a customer.

Heath is not a typical Guyanese writer. The landscape of Guyana is not evoked in the manner of Wilson Harris, Jan Carew, Christopher Nicole, or Edgar Mittelholzer. However, his concern with the psychological scars created by social pressure is reminiscent of Mittelholzer, even though race is never as important in his work as it is in Mittelholzer's.

—Anthony Boxill

HEINLEIN, Robert A(nson). American. Born in Butler, Missouri, 7 July 1907. Educated at Central High School, Kansas City; University of Missouri, Columbia, one year; United States Naval Academy, Annapolis, Maryland, B.S. 1929. Served in the United States Navy, 1929 until retirement because of physical disability, 1934. Married 1) Leslyn McDonald; 2) Virginia Gerstenfeld in 1948. Worked in mining and real estate, 1934-39; civilian engineer, Philadelphia Navy Yard, 1942-45. Recipient: Hugo Award, 1956, 1960, 1962, 1967; Boys' Clubs of America Award, 1959; Grand Master Nebula Award, 1975. Guest of Honor, World Science Fiction Convention, 1941, 1961, 1976. Agent: Blassingame McCauley and Wood, 60 East 42nd Street, New York, New York 10017, U.S.A.

PUBLICATIONS

Novels

Beyond This Horizon. Reading, Pennsylvania, Fantasy Press, 1948; London, Panther, 1967.
Sixth Column. New York, Gnome Press, 1949; as *The Day after Tomorrow*, New York, New American Library, 1951; London, Mayflower, 1962.
Waldo, and Magic Inc. New York, Doubleday, 1950.
The Puppet Masters. New York, Doubleday, 1951; London, Museum Press, 1953.
Double Star. New York, Doubleday, 1956; London, Joseph, 1958.
The Door into Summer. New York, Doubleday, 1957; London, Panther, 1960.
Methuselah's Children. New York, Gnome Press, 1958; London, Gollancz, 1963.
Stranger in a Strange Land. New York, Putnam, 1961; London, New English Library, 1965.
Glory Road. New York, Putnam, 1963; London, New English Library, 1965.
Farnham's Freehold. New York, Putnam, 1964; London, Dobson, 1965.
The Moon Is a Harsh Mistress. New York, Putnam, 1966; London, Dobson, 1967.
A Heinlein Triad (includes *The Puppet Masters*, *Waldo*, *Magic Inc.*). London, Gollancz, 1966.
I Will Fear No Evil. New York, Putnam, 1971; London, New English Library, 1972.
Time Enough for Love: The Lives of Lazarus Long. New York, Putnam, 1973; London, New English Library, 1974.
The Number of the Beast. New York, Fawcett, and London, New English Library, 1980.
Expanded Universe. New York, Grosset and Dunlap, 1980.

Short Stories

The Man Who Sold the Moon. Chicago, Shasta, 1950; London, Sidgwick and Jackson, 1953.
Universe. New York, Dell, 1951.
The Green Hills of Earth. Chicago, Shasta, 1951; London, Sidgwick and Jackson, 1954.
Revolt in 2100. Chicago, Shasta, 1953; London, Digit, 1959.
Assignment in Eternity. Reading, Pennsylvania, Fantasy Press, 1953; London, Museum Press, 1955; abridged edition, as *Lost Legacy*, London, Digit, 1960.
The Menace from Earth. New York, Gnome Press, 1959; London, Dobson, 1966.
The Unpleasant Profession of Jonathan Hoag. New York, Gnome Press, 1959; London, Dobson, 1964; as *6 x H: Six Stories*, New York, Pyramid, 1961.
Orphans of the Sky. London, Gollancz, 1963; New York, Putnam, 1964.
The Worlds of Robert A. Heinlein. New York, Ace, 1966; London, New English Library, 1970.
The Past Through Tomorrow: Future History Stories. New York, Putnam, 1967; London, New English Library, 2 vols., 1977.
The Best of Robert Heinlein 1939-1959, edited by Angus Wells. London, Sidgwick and Jackson, 1973.

Plays

Screenplays: *Destination Moon*, with Rip Van Ronkel and James O'Hanlon, 1950; *Project Moonbase*, with Jack Seaman, 1953.

Other

The Discovery of the Future (address). Los Angeles, Novacious, 1941.
Rocket Ship Galileo (juvenile). New York, Scribner, 1947; London, New English Library, 1971.
Space Cadet (juvenile). New York, Scribner, 1948; London, Gollancz, 1966.
Red Planet (juvenile). New York, Scribner, 1949; London, Gollancz, 1963.
Farmer in the Sky (juvenile). New York, Scribner, 1950; London, Gollancz, 1962.
Between Planets (juvenile). New York, Scribner, 1951; London, Gollancz, 1968.
The Rolling Stones (juvenile). New York, Scribner, 1952; as *Space Family Stone*, London, New English Library, 1971.
Starman Jones (juvenile). New York, Scribner, 1953; London, Sidgwick and Jackson, 1954.
The Star Beast (juvenile). New York, Scribner, 1954; London, New English Library, 1971.
Tunnel in the Sky (juvenile). New York, Scribner, 1955; London, Gollancz, 1965.
Time for the Stars (juvenile). New York, Scribner, 1956; London, Gollancz, 1963.
Citizen of the Galaxy (juvenile). New York, Scribner, 1957; London, Gollancz, 1969.
Have Space Suit—Will Travel (juvenile). New York, Scribner, 1958; London, Gollancz, 1970.
Starship Troopers (juvenile). New York, Putnam, 1959; London, New English Library, 1961.
Podkayne of Mars: Her Life and Times (juvenile). New York, Putnam, 1963; London, New English Library, 1969.
The Notebooks of Lazarus Long. New York, Putnam, 1978.

Editor, *Tomorrow, The Stars: A Science Fiction Anthology.* New York, Doubleday, 1951.

*

Bibliography: *Robert A. Heinlein: A Bibliography* by Mark Owings, Baltimore, Croatan House, 1973.

Manuscript Collection: University of California Library, Santa Cruz.

Critical Studies: *Seekers of Tomorrow* by Sam Moskowitz, Cleveland, World, 1966; *Heinlein in Dimension: A Critical Analysis* (includes bibliography) by Alexei Panshin, Chicago, Advent, 1968;

Robert A. Heinlein, Stranger in His Own Land, San Bernardino, California, Borgo Press, 1976, and *The Classic Years of Robert A. Heinlein*, Borgo Press, 1977, both by George Edgar Slusser; *Robert A. Heinlein* edited by Martin H. Greenberg and Joseph D. Olander, New York, Taplinger, and Edinburgh, Harris, 1978; *Robert A. Heinlein: America as Science Fiction* by H. Bruce Franklin, New York, Oxford University Press, 1980.

Robert A. Heinlein comments:

I got into writing because I was unexpectedly disabled and retired from my chosen profession, the Navy. Like many others in precarious health I turned to what I was physically able to do. Writing is, and has been for 30 years, my only profession and my livelihood. But I have never devoted as much as half my time to it: Mrs. Heinlein and I have traveled much of the time—three times around the world and to about 80 countries, in long, leisurely trips. (I have a smattering of several languages; she speaks eight—no, she's not a linguist, she's a chemist and engineer—and a Fellow of the British Royal Horticulturist Society; she experiments in plant genetics.) I am a member of many scientific, engineering, and military associations, plus the Authors League of America, but am not very active in them, as we prefer a quiet life and avoid publicity as much as we can. We are country people, living 15 miles from the nearest town, almost 100 miles from a city. My study faces the Pacific Ocean, past a heated pool and through some of my wife's gardens—I don't work very hard when the weather is good; life is too short and too sweet.

My stories have been mostly speculations about the future and what mankind may make of it. I am hopelessly old-fashioned in many of my opinions and this annoys some people. My writing has been strongly affected by Rudyard Kipling, Winston Churchill, H.G. Wells, et al. My interests and hobbies are catholic, ranging from stone masonry, cats, sculpture, ballistics, fiscal theory, figure skating, to figure drawing. I enjoy life and believe that Man will live forever and spread out through the universe.

*   *   *

At any one time there have never been more than a dozen or so writers working at the very core of the science-fiction field, a handful of innovators who to greater or lesser extent influence all other practitioners. It is a measure of Robert A. Heinlein's success that he has been among the leaders of this select band almost since the publication of his first story in 1939.

"Innovator" is the key word if we wish to measure Heinlein's contributions to science-fiction writing. His innovations have been in ideas, in storytelling techniques, but most importantly of all in *attitudes*. In this respect he is responsible more than any other for establishing the methods and traditions of modern science fiction.

To understand fully his achievement we must look at science fiction as it was, an ingrown species of category fiction confined almost entirely to the American pulp magazines. The vitality and literacy of earlier pioneers such as Wells had been lost, and science fiction was, quite simply, fiction *about* science, with the occasional space operatics for good measure. Heinlein picked up the field and shook it until it rattled. By his example he changed that definition to mean instead "fiction written according to the scientific method," and there is a vast difference between the two. Almost for the first time there began to appear stories in which the marvel of technology was a beginning rather than an end in itself.

Once this bridge had been crossed science fiction could take a large stride towards maturity, and others besides Heinlein started to stress characterisation and the treatment of human responses to new situations. In the three years between 1939 and 1942 Heinlein himself wrote 22 stories for the leading magazine, *Astounding*, including most of his "Future History" series and three major novels, *Sixth Column*, *Beyond This Horizon*, and *Methuselah's Children*. Had he stopped then his name would have been one of the "greats" of the science-fiction field. But after the Second World War Heinlein returned with stories which concentrated even more upon human values than on science for science's sake. Quite deliberately he wrote to "make the American public think about the future," and the medium he chose was the *Saturday Evening Post*. Stories such as "Columbus Was a Dope" and "It's Great to Be Back" are skilfully written and topical today, and the complete series is available in the collection *The Green Hills of Earth*. He also commenced the famous juvenile series which eventually was to amount to 13 novels in 13 years. Here again the aim was similar—to "educate" the growing generation, although the books have tremendous appeal to all ages. Several, such as *Have Space Suit—Will Travel* and *Citizen of the Galaxy*, were initially published in adult magazines.

During the 1950's Heinlein produced few short stories and only four adult novels, of which three—*The Pupper Masters*, *Double Star*, and *The Door into Summer*—may prove to be among his most well-rounded work. The fourth, *Starship Troopers*, marked the beginning of Heinlein's final period. This and four subsequent long novels (*Stranger in a Strange Land*, *Glory Road*, *Farnham's Freehold*, *The Moon Is a Harsh Mistress*) provoked more controversy than any of Heinlein's earlier work. *Stranger* became a "hippie" cult-book, much to the author's dismay, one imagines, and all have showed some flaws in construction, in particular the loss of Heinlein's former economy of words.

Nonetheless they have a fascination of their own, through the inventiveness and narrative power of the writer. The same can not be said of *I Will Fear No Evil* and *Time Enough for Love*, which have almost no redeeming virtues and can only be regarded as over-wordy and fatuous. They mark a sad ending to a truly great writing career.

So perhaps they should be ignored when considering the splendid record from 1939 to 1969 (and fittingly the anniversary coincided with the landing of Apollo 11 upon the Moon)—30 years in which the name of Robert Heinlein dominated the entire field of science fiction. His gift has been to combine a truly compulsive storytelling power with a disciplined, brilliant imagination.

—Peter R. Weston

HELLER, Joseph. American. Born in Brooklyn, New York, 1 May 1923. Educated at New York University, B.A. 1948; Columbia University, New York, M.A. 1949; Oxford University (Fulbright Scholar), 1949-50. Served in the United States Army Air Force in World War II: Lieutenant. Married Shirley Held in 1945; one son and one daughter. Instructor in English, Pennsylvania State University, University Park, 1950-52; Advertising Writer, *Time* magazine, New York, 1952-56, and *Look* magazine, New York, 1956-58; Promotion Manager, *McCall's* magazine, New York, 1958-61. Recipient: American Academy grant, 1963. Member, American Academy, 1977. Address: 390 West End Avenue, New York, New York 10024, U.S.A.

PUBLICATIONS

Novels

Catch-22. New York, Simon and Schuster, 1961; London, Cape, 1962.

Something Happened. New York, Knopf, and London, Cape, 1974.

Good as Gold. New York, Simon and Schuster, and London, Cape, 1979.

Uncollected Short Stories

"I Don't Love You Anymore," in *Story* (New York), September-October 1945.

"Castle of Snow," in *Atlantic* (Boston), May 1947.
"Bookies, Beware!," in *Esquire* (New York), March 1948.
"Girl from Greenwich," in *Esquire* (New York), June 1948.
"A Man Named Flute," in *Atlantic* (Boston), August 1948.
"Nothing to Be Done," in *Esquire* (New York), August 1948.
"MacAdam's Log," in *Gentlemen's Quarterly* (New York), December 1959.
"World Full of Great Cities," in *Nelson Algren's Own Book of Lonesome Monsters*, edited by Algren. New York, Lancer, 1962; London, Panther, 1964.
"Love, Dad," in *Playboy* (Chicago), December 1969.

Plays

We Bombed in New Haven (produced New Haven, 1967; New York, 1969; London, 1971). New York, Knopf, 1968; London, Cape, 1969.
Catch-22, adaptation of his own novel. New York, Delacorte Press, and London, French, 1973.
Clevinger's Trial, adaptation of chapter 8 of his novel *Catch-22* (produced London, 1974). New York, French, 1973; London, French, 1974.

Screenplays: *Sex and the Single Girl*, with David R. Schwartz, 1964; *Casino Royale* (uncredited), 1967; *Dirty Dingus Magee*, with Tom and Frank Waldman, 1970.

*

Bibliography: *Three Contemporary Novelists: An Annotated Bibliography* by Robert M. Scotto, New York, Garland, 1977; *Joseph Heller: A Reference Guide* by Brenda M. Keegan, Boston, Hall, 1978.

Critical Studies: "Joseph Heller's *Catch-22*" by Burr Dodd, in *Approaches to the Novel* edited by John Colmer, Edinburgh, Oliver and Boyd, 1967; "The Sanity of *Catch-22*" by Robert Protherough, in *Human World* (Swansea), May 1971; *A Catch-22 Casebook* edited by Frederick T. Kiley and Walter McDonald, New York, Crowell, 1973; *Critical Essays on Catch-22* edited by James Nagel, Encino, California, Dickinson Seminar Series, 1974; "*Something Happened*: A New Direction" by George J. Searles, in *Critique* (Atlanta), xviii, 3, 1977.

* * *

Joseph Heller has a better claim than any other American writer to having written the definitive novel of modern warfare—if universal response to his definition is any measure. People now know as "catch-22" the circular bureaucratic formula they had learned from experience. In Heller's book the "catch" is the bombing unit's regulation based on the knowledge that "a concern for one's own safety in the face of dangers that were real and immediate was the process of a rational mind." Anyone who is crazy can be grounded; all he has to do is ask. If he asks, he can't possibly be crazy. Heller's routine remains as true of Flanders and Vietnam as of the air war in Europe that was the setting of his novel, and it seems, moreover, to characterize civilian bureaucracies as well as military organizations.

Catch-22 is a burlesque epic built upon the "catch-22" routine. Vaudeville, comic strips, and animated cartoons provide its basic structure and pace, which is not to say that Heller is flippant or callous. Far from it. It is his special talent to render the horrors of war in the formats of popular culture and then juxtapose them with the feelings they provoke in such men as his hero, Yossarian—feelings also bordered in film frames and comic strip panels. Yossarian is determined "to live forever or die in the attempt." Almost as often as assorted characters perform the catch-22 routine, he relives the moment in the air over Avignon when the wounded gunner, Snowden, lay "spilling his secret all over the back of the plane." "Ou sont les neige-dens..." Yossarian begins to recite over his crewman's body, touching the secret with a wisecrack.

Yossarian's struggle to survive is waged against a system in which a Lieutenant Scheisskopf necessarily moves through the ranks to become the commanding officer. Another name from the folklore of humor is Captain Aardvark, "Good Old Arfie," who can ignore the suffering he sees because he can't quite hear what the sufferer is saying. The chaplain is an Anabaptist. The Soldier in White is a plaster-cast embodiment of the system with a circuit of tubes running into and out of what is assumed to be his body. There is the Unknown Soldier killed on his first mission before he has a chance to unpack his bags and get to meet anyone. His name is Mudd. In the world of *Catch-22*, a conversation begins with someone inventing the rumor that the Germans are now using the LePage anti-aircraft gun to spray webs of mucilage over formations of Allied planes and ends with official confirmation that LePage guns at Bologna have inflicted losses on the squadron by shooting webs of mucilage over formations of its planes. Yossarian is briefly "in love with the one woman he could make love to without falling in love with." *Catch-22* is a brilliant, if exhausting, mosaic of comic invention.

Something Happened seems to be the effort to write as complicated a book as *Catch-22* about the mean, narrow life of a New York corporation executive. Bob Slocum is an insensitive man who knows himself quite well. "A friend in need is no friend of mine," he says, and in every relationship of his life he comes slowly or never. His "Snowden" is the older girl who teased him when he was an office boy and left the rest of his agitated sex life short of fulfillment. Slocum is a mimic and an echolalic who cannot resist imitating the defects of those who most suffer at his hands. One recognizes the comic techniques of *Catch-22* grimly transformed in a claustrophobic, introverted structure. *Something Happened* is deadlier and more polished than Heller's undoubted masterpiece.

After these two extraordinarily ambitious books, critics were harsh with *Good as Gold*. This novel is often funnier than *Catch-22* and always livelier than *Something Happened*, but it is also an uneasy mixture of two comic inspirations. One was to have Bruce Gold try to write about "the Jewish Experience in America," despite his headlong efforts to reject that experience for all tokens of assimiliation. The other was to satirize the career of Henry Kissinger. Accordingly, Gold is a plodding intellectual who covets power in Washington and lusts after tall gentile girls. His father bullies him, and his prospective father-in-law addresses him with anti-semitic epithets; his closest gentile friend admits that if worst came to worst he wouldn't hide him. The Washington fantasies are less effective than the bitter comedy involving Gold and his father, which is a little surprising given the similarities between Heller's top brass in government and the military. Gold admires his recently deceased brother as "a wonderful person." "You don't know," his father snaps. "Not like you." In his most lightly regarded books, Heller is still capable—repeatedly—of stating the essence of the matter. That and his mastery of comic improvisation are indisputable after the first 25 years of his career.

—David Sanders

HERBERT, (Alfred Francis) Xavier. Australian. Born in Murchison District, Western Australia, 15 May 1901. Educated in local schools and at Christian Brothers College, Fremantle; Technical College, Perth; University of Melbourne, diploma in pharmacy. Served in the Australian Imperial Forces in the Pacific, 1942-44. Began career as a hospital pharmacist; has also worked as a deep-sea diver, sailor, miner, stock rider, and aviator. Superintendent of Aborigines, Darwin, 1935-36. Writer-in-Residence, University of Newcastle, New South Wales, 1975, and University of Queensland, Brisbane, 1976; Visiting Fellow, Australian National University,

Canberra, 1978, and James Cook University, Townsville, Queensland, 1979. Recipient: Commonwealth Sesqui-Centenary Prize, 1938; Australia Literary Society Gold Medal, 1939; Miles Franklin Award, 1976. D.Litt.: University of Newcastle, 1975; University of Queensland, 1976. Address: Redlynch, via Cairns, Queensland 4870, Australia.

PUBLICATIONS

Novels

Capricornia. Sydney, Publicist, 1938; London, Rich and Cowan, 1939; New York, Appleton Century, 1943.
Seven Emus. Sydney and London, Angus and Robertson, 1959.
Soldiers' Women. Sydney, Angus and Robertson, 1961; London, Angus and Robertson, 1962.
Poor Fellow, My Country. Sydney, Collins, 1975; London, Pan, 1977; New York, St. Martin's Press, 1980; excerpt, as *Dream Road*, illustrated by Ray Crooke, Sydney, Collins, 1977.

Short Stories

Larger Than Life: Twenty Short Stories. Sydney, Angus and Robertson, 1963; London, Angus and Robertson, 1964.

Other

Disturbing Element (autobiography). Melbourne, Cheshire, and London, Angus and Robertson, 1963.

*

Manuscript Collection: Fryer Memorial Library, University of Queensland, Brisbane.

Critical Study: *Xavier Herbert* by Harry Heseltine, Melbourne, Oxford University Press, 1973.

Xavier Herbert comments:

(1972) All the work I've done so far will become irrelevant with publication of my latest and final *Poor Fellow My Country.* I'm not a professional writer. I mean I've never done it as a means of livelihood, although I have long made a living from it. My aim has been, through my literary work, to discover whatever is possible of the reality of my own existence...and self-discovery means discovery of the world.

* * *

Xavier Herbert is somewhat of a maverick in the world of Australian letters. His first novel, *Capricornia*, is an Australian classic. Set in the northern parts of Australia, this long novel is a passionate study of whites' callous and often lethal mistreatment of Aborigines, documenting specific social abuses and injustices and focusing especially on the ambigious position of half-castes, displaced from the blacks' culture but refused a decent position in society by whites. It is also, however, much more than that. For Herbert goes far beyond mere social protest to offer, in a style that is a curious mixture of indignation and exuberance, a metaphysical vision of a universe that is anarchic and irrational and in which men and women become the helpless playthings of Nature and Destiny. Herbert mocks the attempts of human beings to impose their will on the universe and create a semblance of "civilization," a word that recurs again and again in the novel with increasingly resonant irony.

At the centre of *Capricornia* is a vision of man (or at least white man) as an aggressive, anomalous being, alienated from a Nature which is above all bountiful, and although sometimes violent and apparently treacherous, also ethically neutral, dispassionate, dangerous mostly to those who do not accept its objective existence but attempt to subvert it or conquer it. Man is a "disturbing element" in Nature, at war with his kind and environment, yet although some passages and incidents in the novel (the death of an Aborigine girl from starvation, a series of train accidents which wipe out several Capricornians) are somber, others are wildly funny and anarchic. The novel is what its author called it, "A hymn-book in adoration of Australia," and one of the greatest as well as most nationalistic of Australian novels.

Herbert's second book, the novella-length *Seven Emus*, is a slight and wordy account of two men who attempt to steal a precious Aboriginal artifact, the dreaming-stone of the now lost Emu Tribe; they at first appear to be successful but are finally defeated in ironical fashion by Fate. It was written primarily to demonstrate the efficacy of a somewhat eccentric mode of punctuation which Herbert himself devised (in this it was a signal failure).

Soldiers' Women, the second of the three long novels, is in the words of one critic "an appalling and embarrassing flop." This story of women, freed of their marital commitments, on the loose in wartime Sydney, reeks of sensationalism and lurid melodrama and seems written primarily to demonstrate Herbert's extraordinary theories about female sexuality and the readiness with which women, once freed from societal restraints, gratify their sexual impulses. Herbert is never at ease in writing about urban life and though the novel is packed with detail of Sydney wartime life this has very much the appearance of having been "got up." *Disturbing Element* is an engaging and frank account of the first 24 years of the author's life, and *Larger Than Life* collects the best of the numerous early short stories Herbert wrote while struggling to live off his earnings as a writer.

But it is on *Poor Fellow, My Country* that most discussion of his work has focused recently. If *Capricornia* is a hymn-book to Australia, *Poor Fellow, My Country* is a dirge in lament for the kind of Australia Herbert wished to see occur and the one that actually has, and from which he turns in revulsion. It is an extraordinary book by any standards, 850,000 words in length, a sprawling, embittered, agonised behemoth of a novel that attempts to sum up and crystallize all the concerns—which by now have become obsessions—that are apparent in the author's earlier work. Though the novel deeply divided critics and though Herbert believes that is has dwarfed and even made obsolescent all his earlier work in fact it is sprawling where *Capricornia* was tightly disciplined and structured, garrulous and didactic, dominated by the torrent of bitterness and bile that is spewed forth by its main character and Herbert's spokesman, Jeremy Delacy. Though it has many fine things in it, notably an astonishing degree of familiarity with Aboriginal customs and modes of living, the real novel that is buried somewhere inside the book is never allowed to emerge. It is an unhappy climax to a long, distinguished, and courageous career.

—Laurie Clancy

HERLIHY, James Leo. American. Born in Detroit, Michigan, 27 February 1927. Educated at Black Mountain College, North Carolina, 1947-48; Pasadena Playhouse, California, 1948-50; Yale University Drama School, New Haven, Connecticut. Served in the United States Navy, 1945-46. Taught playwriting at City College of New York, 1967-68. Agent: Jay Garon-Brooks Associates, Inc., 415 Central Park West, New York, New York 10025, U.S.A.

PUBLICATIONS

Novels

All Fall Down. New York, Dutton, 1960; London, Faber, 1961.

Midnight Cowboy. New York, Simon and Schuster, 1965; London, Cape, 1966.
The Season of the Witch. New York, Simon and Schuster, and London, W.H. Allen, 1971.

Short Stories

The Sleep of Baby Filbertson and Other Stories. New York, Dutton and London, Faber, 1959.
A Story That Ends with a Scream and Eight Others. New York, Simon and Schuster, 1967; London, Cape, 1968.

Plays

Streetlight Sonata (produced Pasadena, California, 1950).
Moon in Capricorn (produced New York, 1953).
Blue Denim, with William Noble (produced New York, 1958; Swansea, Wales, 1970). New York, Random House, 1958.
Crazy October (also director: produced New Haven, Connecticut, 1958).
Stop, You're Killing Me (includes *Terrible Jim Fitch*; *Bad Bad Jo-Jo*; *Laughs, Etc.*) (produced Boston, 1968; New York, 1969; *Terrible Jim Fitch* and *Laughs, Etc.*, produced London, 1973). New York, Simon and Schuster, 1970.

*

Theatrical Activities:

Director: **Play**—*Crazy October*, New Haven, Connecticut, 1958.

Actor: **Plays**—roles at the Pasadena Playhouse, California; in *The Zoo Story* by Edward Albee, Boston and Paris, 1961. **Film**—*In the French Style*, 1963.

* * *

In the seven bizarre stories which comprise *The Sleep of Baby Filbertson* James Leo Herlihy first made clear his interest in the themes of loneliness, crippled emotions, and physical debility. The themes converge in his work to create a picture of the modern urban world as a purgatory, but a purgatory lightened somewhat by the pathos and respect with which the author presents his twisted characters. Readers of this collection frequently linked Herlihy's name with such gifted contemporaries as Truman Capote, James Purdy, and Flannery O'Connor.

All Fall Down, Herlihy's remarkable first novel, widely extended the dimensions of his ironic humor in chronicling the misadventures and the disintegration of a middle-class family. The father, a disillusioned socialist, declines into alcoholism and the mother into helpless inaction. One son has become a vagabond and petty criminal, and the other is a 16-year-old drop-out who imagines his older brother a great romantic rebel against bourgeois convention. Clinton, the younger son, eventually frees himself not only from his family but also from the projections of his own imagination, a process recorded in graphic detail in lengthy extracts from his journal. The very commonplace nature of Herlihy's characters lends an air of authenticity to the novel and intensifies the horror of their dilemmas by making them seem so constant and unavoidable.

This sense of horror was more intensely explored in *Midnight Cowboy*, the story of a simple-minded cowboy, Joe Buck, who travels to New York in the hope of making his fortune as a hustler. Instead, he is cast adrift on a sea of grotesques, eventually casting his lot with that of a crippled pickpocket, with whom he creates a community of love and grudging respect against the hostile world outside. When Ratso becomes ill, Joe cares for him, steals for him, and undertakes a quixotic journey to Florida in the hope that his friend may recover. *Midnight Cowboy* is a grim novel in which the author repeatedly exploits his own talent for depicting the grotesque. Nonetheless, because the central characters' needs are so basic and so human, they rise above the fashions of alienation, urban malaise, and sexual degeneracy which are often the gratuitous complements of contemporary fiction.

Gloria Random, the heroine of Herlihy's third novel, *The Season of the Witch*, runs away from home with a friend, a homosexual draft-evader. The novel records their adventures in New York City, Gloria's reunion with her father, and her eventual return to her mother. As a study of the geography of the generation gap, the novel oversimplifies and glamorizes the essential cultural schism which that term loosely designates. Nonetheless, *The Season of the Witch* is a memorable exploration of the growth of a sensitive, troubled consciousness as it struggles to find some correlation between revolutionary hope and quotidian realities.

Herlihy is fascinated by society's rejects, by men and women whose lives seem doomed by their emotional needs and their longing, but who struggle to maintain some shred of human dignity in a world which seems remorseless in its devices for destroying the self. Such themes are also explored in Herlihy's plays, where the raucous spirit of black humor is even more pervasive than in the novels.

—David Galloway

HERSEY, John (Richard). American. Born in Tientsin, China, 17 June 1914. Educated at Hotchkiss School; Yale University, New Haven, Connecticut, B.A. 1936; Clare College, Cambridge (Mellon Fellow), 1936-37. Married 1) Frances Ann Cannon in 1940 (divorced, 1958), three sons and one daughter; 2) Barbara Day Kaufman in 1958, one daughter. Secretary to Sinclair Lewis, 1937; Writer and Correspondent, in China, Japan, the South Pacific, the Mediterranean and Russia, for *Time*, New York, 1937-45, *Life*, New York, 1944-46, and *The New Yorker*, 1945-46; Editor and Director of the writers' cooperative magazine *'47*, 1947-48; Fellow of Berkeley College, 1950-65, and Master of Pierson College, 1965-70, Lecturer, 1971-76, Visiting Professor, 1976-77, and since 1977, Adjunct Professor, Yale University: Member of the Yale University Council Committee on the Humanities, 1951-56, and Member, 1959-64, and Chairman, 1964-69, Yale University Council Committee on Yale College. Writer-in-Residence, American Academy in Rome, 1970-71. Member, National Citizens' Commission for the Public Schools, 1954-56; Consultant, Fund for the Advancement of Education, 1954-56; Chairman, Connecticut Committee for the Gifted, 1954-57; Delegate, White House Conference on Education, 1955; Trustee, National Citizens' Council for the Public Schools, 1956-58; Trustee, National Committee for Support of the Public Schools, 1962-68. Chairman, Connecticut Volunteers for Stevenson, 1952; Member, Stevenson Campaign Staff, 1956. Member of the Council, 1946-71, and Vice-President, 1949-55, Authors League of America; Delegate, P.E.N. Congress, Tokyo, 1958. Since 1946, Member of the Council, and President, 1975-80, Authors Guild. Recipient: Pulitzer Prize, 1945; Anisfield-Wolf Award, 1950; Daroff Memorial Award, 1950; Sidney Hillman Foundation Award, 1950; Yale University Howland Medal, 1952; Tuition Plan Award, 1961; Sarah Josepha Hale Award, 1963. LL.D.: Washington and Jefferson College, Washington, Pennsylvania, 1946; University of New Haven, West Haven, Connecticut, 1975; M.A.: Yale University, 1947; L.H.D.: New School for Social Research, New York, 1950; D.H.L.: Dropsie College, 1950; Litt.D.: Wesleyan University, Middletown, Connecticut, 1957; Bridgeport University, Connecticut, 1959; Clarkson College of Technology, Potsdam, New York, 1972. Member, 1953, and Secretary, 1961-76, American Academy. Honorary Fellow, Clare College, Cambridge, 1967. Address: 420 Humphrey Street, New Haven, Connecticut 06511, U.S.A.

PUBLICATIONS

Novels

A Bell for Adano. New York, Knopf, 1944; London, Hamish Hamilton, 1945.
The Wall. New York, Knopf, and London, Hamish Hamilton, 1950.
The Marmot Drive. New York, Knopf, and London, Hamish Hamilton, 1953.
A Single Pebble. New York, Knopf, and London, Hamish Hamilton, 1956.
The War Lover. New York, Knopf, and London, Hamish Hamilton, 1959.
The Child Buyer. New York, Knopf, 1960; London, Hamish Hamilton, 1961.
White Lotus. New York, Knopf, and London, Hamish Hamilton, 1965.
Too Far to Walk. New York, Knopf, and London, Hamish Hamilton, 1966.
Under the Eye of the Storm. New York, Knopf, and London, Hamish Hamilton, 1967.
The Conspiracy. New York, Knopf, and London, Hamish Hamilton, 1972.
My Petition for More Space. New York, Knopf, 1974; London, Hamish Hamilton, 1975.
The Walnut Door. New York, Knopf, 1977; London, Macmillan, 1978.

Uncollected Short Stories

"Joe Is Home Now," in *Life* (New York), 3 July 1944.
"The Breadline," in *Taken at the Flood*, edited by Ann Watkins. New York, Harper, 1946.
"The Death of Buchan Walsh," in *Atlantic* (Boston), April 1946.
"Pen," in *Atlantic* (Boston), June 1946.
"Short Wait," in *New Yorker*, 14 June 1947.
"The Woman Who Took Gold Intravenously," in *Cosmopolitan* (New York), 1947.
"In Touch," in *Cosmopolitan* (New York), 1947.
"Why Were You Sent Here?," in *The Best American Short Stories 1948*, edited by Martha Foley. Boston, Houghton Mifflin, 1948.
"Moment of Judgment," in *World's Best*, edited by Whit Burnett. New York, Dial Press, 1950.
"Peggety's Parcel of Shortcomings," in *Prize Stories 1951: The O. Henry Awards*, edited by Herschel Brickell. New York, Doubleday, 1951.
"Bridge over Dry Creek Bed," in *Sports Illustrated* (New York), 1972.

Other

Men on Bataan. New York, Knopf, 1942.
Into the Valley: A Skirmish of the Marines. New York, Knopf, 1943.
Hiroshima. New York, Knopf, and London, Penguin, 1946.
Here to Stay: Studies in Human Tenacity. London, Hamish Hamilton, 1962; New York, Knopf, 1963.
The Algiers Motel Incident. New York, Knopf, and London, Hamish Hamilton, 1968.
Robert Capa, with others. New York, Paragraphic, 1969.
Letter to the Alumni. New York, Knopf, 1970.
The President. New York, Knopf, 1975.
Aspects of the Presidency: Truman and Ford in Office. New Haven, Connecticut, Ticknor and Fields, 1980.

Editor, *Ralph Ellison: A Collection of Critical Essays.* Englewood Cliffs, New Jersey, Prentice Hall, 1973.
Editor, *The Writer's Craft.* New York, Knopf, 1974.

*

Manuscript Collection: Yale University Library, New Haven, Connecticut.

Critical Study: *John Hersey* by David Sanders, New York, Twayne, 1967.

John Hersey comments:

I believe that a writer should be reticent about himself and his work. Ideally he should, I feel, appear in his books and nowhere else in public. Each of his works entails a double act of creation: he makes one part of the finished work, but until the reader brings his imagination and experience to bear on it, the book does not come to life, does not even *exist* as a book. I do not think that the writer should attempt to influence the second half of this partnership of makers by stating intentions, his "meaning." The writing process is a mysterious one; the writer works within a magic circle—and his intentions, if indeed he understands them himself, may not have much to do with the effect he produces. If he is honest and at all able, the work speaks his deepest self, its themes derive from his view of humanity, its style comes from the cadences and vibrations of his innermost voice. The work interprets him better than he can interpret the work.

* * *

John Hersey, who once described himself as a novelist of contemporary history, began his writing career as a reporter for *Time* and *Life* with his earliest dispatches forming such volumes of wartime journalism as *Men on Bataan* and *Into the Valley*. His first novel, *A Bell for Adano*, was a simple, vivid story based on incidents he had observed in Sicily. It became widely read and won Hersey a Pulitzer Prize on V-E Day. In 1946 he visited Hiroshima, interviewed survivors of the first atomic bomb attack, and wrote the *New Yorker* article that had an extraordinary impact as the first personal—and, therefore, comprehensible—account of the event.

In *Hiroshima* and later in his greatest novel, *The Wall*, Hersey drew from the victims themselves the understanding of history that neither he nor anyone else had gained in reporting the war. The six Hiroshima residents told him how they had lived before the bomb struck, why they were not killed, and precisely how illness, exhaustion, and sorrow had accompanied their survival. He had no comparable opportunity to interview participants in the Warsaw ghetto uprisings, but this holocaust obsessed him as much as the other. He read such documentary evidence as *The Black Book of the Polish Jewry*, listened to victims' eyewitness accounts as sight-translated by Polish Jews who had escaped to America, and created a story in the form of Noach Levinson's archive. This fictional scholar records not merely the events that lead through four years to the uprisings, but also every occurrence that he feels may help to explain the culture under attack. The result is an achievement that defines the novel of contemporary history: the narrative of an event with its full historic implications and without any melodramatic action or a single sentimental cliché.

Hersey's novels since *The Wall* have in common chiefly the author's constant attention to large social issues. In most of these books he attempts some experiment in narrative form as appropriate as Noach Levinson's archive was to *The Wall*. He failed in *The Marmot Drive*, a dim allegory about witch-hunting in the heyday of Senator Joseph McCarthy. *A Single Pebble*, a short novel reaching into his Chinese background, beautifully illuminates the limitations of technology as the way to happiness. In *The War Lover* Hersey's narrator, an American bombardier, notices psychotic changes in his pilot, yearns for survival himself, and somewhat contradicts Hersey's own earlier accounts in *Life* of the necessarily impersonal perspective that flyers developed through their bombsights.

The Child Buyer, an extended irony, is Hersey's attack on an educational system he accuses of neglecting the bright child. A whole town acquiesces in selling ten-year-old Barry Rudd to a "defense" firm, which, by tying off his senses, will try to turn him into a human computer capable of reaching an I.Q. of 1000. The story, told in the form of the record of a legislative committee hearing, is often awkward, but it is luminous at the moment when the child himself joins the conspiracy "because life at U Lympho might at least be *interesting*." In *White Lotus* Hersey's intention was nothing less than to make white readers feel what it would be like if they were members of an oppressed race taken as slaves from America after a late 20th-century conquest by the Chinese. The author's admiration for Ralph Ellison's *Invisible Man* is apparent, but, unfortunately, his narrative cannot, like Ellison's, encompass the whole history of a culture.

With less poetry or humor than Ellison's narrator, White Lotus, still a young woman as she ends her story, must account for the full outline of parallels from her capture as a teen-ager up to her celebrity as a civil rights leader.

Too Far to Walk employs the Faust legend in describing college unrest of the late 1960's, and may be seen as a further ironic reflection on themes from *The Child Buyer. Under the Eye of the Storm* opposes the behavior of two yachtsmen, a technologist and a humanist, struggling to bring their boat in from the sea. These comparatively slight books were followed in the 1970's by three remarkable allegories that recall *The Single Pebble* and *The Child Buyer* in lucidity and feeling. *The Conspiracy*, an account of a plot to overthrow Nero, states not only that a writer's responsibility is to write, but that he most nearly overcomes his enemies when he is lost to any other purpose but his work. Lucan, the poet, and Tigellinus, the secret policeman, are among Hersey's strongest and subtlest characterizations. The narrator of *My Petition for More Space* tells his story in the time that it takes him to move in a line of human beings, four abreast, three-quarters of a mile long to the window where he will have his only chance to tell authorities why he should be granted more than his allotted cubicle. The credibility that had eluded Hersey in *White Lotus* is immediate and painful in this novel, although he is again on the edge of being trapped by the very ingenuity of his conception—here, a story as bleak and cramped as its premise. The hero and heroine of *The Walnut Door* are isolated drop-outs who meet after years of drifting through the wreckage of the student revolution. Without denying the sympathies he had expressed in *Letter to the Alumni*, the report based on his term as a college master at Yale, Hersey develops a plot in which erotic discoveries rescue his characters from the empty failure of their early ideals.

Hersey's typical novel is an allegory. He is a reporter addicted to fiction, not only to the indirection of allegory but also to a life-long variety of narrative techniques. He is most faithful to his apprenticeship at *Time* and *Life* in being among the least autobiographical of American novelists. His work is about what he has seen and studied, and it refers faintly, if ever, to the story of his own education except when the power of *Hiroshima* or *The Wall* compels a reader to consider the imagination that stirs before him.

—David Sanders

HICKS, Granville. American. Born in Exeter, New Hampshire, 9 September 1901. Educated at Harvard University, Cambridge, Massachusetts, A.B. 1923, M.A. 1929. Married Dorothy Dyer in 1925; one child. Instructor in Biblical Literature, Smith College, Northampton, Massachusetts, 1925-28; Assistant Professor of English, Rensselaer Polytechnic Institute, Troy, New York, 1929-35; Counselor in American Civilization, Harvard University, 1938-39; Instructor in Novel Writing, New School for Social Research, New York, 1955-58; Berg Visiting Professor, New York University, 1959; Visiting Professor, Syracuse University, New York, 1960, McGuffey Visiting Professor, Ohio University, Athens, 1967-68, and Chatham College, Pittsburgh, 1973. Literary Adviser, Macmillan Company, New York, 1930-65; Member, Editorial Staff, *New Masses*, New York, 1934-39; Literary Consultant, *The New Leader*, New York, 1951-58; Contributing Editor, *Saturday Review*, New York, 1958-69; Books Editor, *The American Way* magazine, San Antonio, Texas. Acting Executive Director, Corporation of Yaddo, Saratoga Springs, New York, 1970-71. Recipient: Guggenheim Fellowship, 1936; Rockefeller Fellowship, 1945. D.H.L.: Skidmore College, Saratoga Springs, New York, 1968; Ohio University, 1969; Litt.D.: Siena College, Loudonville, New York, 1971. Address: Box 144, Grafton, New York 12082, U.S.A.

PUBLICATIONS

Novels

The First to Awaken, with Richard M. Bennett. New York, Modern Age, 1940.
Only One Storm. New York, Macmillan, 1942.
Behold Trouble. New York, Macmillan, 1944.
There Was a Man in Our Town. New York, Viking Press, 1952.

Verse

New Light, music by Stuart B. Hoppin. Boston, Birchard, 1932.

Other

Eight Ways of Looking at Christianity. New York, Macmillan, 1926.
The Great Tradition: An Interpretation of American Literature since the Civil War. New York, Macmillan, 1933; London, Macmillan, 1934; revised edition, New York, Macmillan, 1935, Chicago, Quadrangle, 1969.
One of Us: The Story of John Reed. New York, Equinox Press, 1935.
John Reed: The Making of a Revolutionary, with John Stuart. New York, Macmillan, 1936.
I Like America. New York, Modern Age, 1938.
Catholics, Communists, and Democracy. Boston, Communist Party of Massachusetts, 1939.
Figures of Transition: A Study of British Literature at the End of the Nineteenth Century. New York, Macmillan, 1939.
Small Town. New York, Macmillan, 1946.
Where We Came Out. New York, Viking Press, and London, Gollancz, 1954.
James Gould Cozzens. Minneapolis, University of Minnesota Press, 1958.
Part of the Truth (autobiography). New York, Harcourt Brace, 1965.
Literary Horizons: A Quarter Century of American Fiction. New York, New York University Press, 1970.
Granville Hicks in "The New Masses," edited by Jack Alan Robbins. Port Washington, New York, Kennikat Press, 1974.

Editor, with others, *Proletarian Literature in the United States: An Anthology.* New York, International Publishers, 1935; London, Lawrence, 1936.
Editor, with Ella Winter, *The Letters of Lincoln Steffens.* New York, Harcourt Brace, 2 vols., 1938.
Editor, *The Living Novel: A Symposium.* New York, Macmillan, 1957.

*

Bibliography: "Granville Hicks: An Annotated Bibliography, February 1927 to June 1967, with a Supplement to June 1968" by Robert J. Bicker, in *Emporia State Research Studies* (Kansas), 1968.

Manuscript Collection: Syracuse University Library, New York.

Granville Hicks comments:

Although I started out as a critic, I always had an urge to write novels. *The First to Awaken* was not a serious novel, but a kind of utopian game I played with a friend, Richard Bennett, artist and architect. *Only One Storm* was serious, an attempt to portray realistically the crisis of America between Munich and Pearl Harbor. It was reasonably successful, but I was never satisfied with it as a piece of fiction. *Behold Trouble* came closer to what I wanted both in style and characterization, but 1944 was no year for a novel about a conscientious objector. *There Was a Man in Our Town* (for which my working title was *The Prickly Pear*) was worked over many times—too many I came to think. I decided that I couldn't be the kind of novelist I wanted to be unless I devoted full time to the job, and that I couldn't afford.

Although I gave up novel-writing, I continued to find the novel an absorbing literary form, and I wrote often about fiction, especially the work of young writers, in my regular column in *The New Leader* and *Saturday Review*. (For the latter I wrote a weekly page for eleven years.) Some of my pieces have been collected in *Literary Horizons*. In *The Living Novel* I gathered original essays by younger writers.

* * *

Granville Hicks has taken a goodly share of abuse from people who interpret his famous work *The Great Tradition* as a radical and possibly a Marxist interpretation of American literature, but in fact that study can best be understood as an explication of American writers' continuing awareness of the moral contradictions of an economic and political system that requires exploitation to produce wealth. During the period of the Popular Front in America Hicks's brand of moral humanism was consistent with left wing political activity, for then the Communist Party offered its program as "good Americanism," which by anybody's definition should not require massive exploitation.

The startling development of the Soviet-Nazi Pact of 1939 ended Hicks's involvement in left-wing politics. While it can easily be maintained that Socialism is basically humanistic, for Hicks the Pact could not possibly be good even for Russian Socialism and it represented for him a repudiation of his good intentions. He had no choice but to assert his independence of the left. Much to his credit he never has felt the need to "rehabilitate" himself by engaging in the polemics of the domestic anti-Communist crusade. Rather, he has gone along independently espousing his views in critical essays and the book reviews he contributed over the years to *The New Leader* and *Saturday Review*.

Perhaps to gain a broader scope of expression (perhaps, too, because one tires of writing always about other people's books) Hicks also has written four novels.

With Richard M. Bennett, whom he acknowledges as contributing a stimulus in discussion as well as drawings for the volume, Hicks made his first published entry into fiction with a utopia entitled *The First to Awaken*. The pattern is that of Bellamy's *Looking Backward:* George Swain having received cryogenic treatments awakens in 2040 after a century's events have transformed his native town of Braxton into one of the many self-governing regional cooperatives in a world that has arrived at democratic socialism after major wars, civil strife, and periods of technological experimentation. The historical information Swain gains about the development of the new society is far more plausible than the rationalist fantasy of Bellamy. So, too, is Hicks's departure from the Utopian formula to the extent that he describes a society that has not done away with problems but rather has raised them to a new level of human consideration. For all its technological detail, though, the novel reveals its inspiration to be Jeffersonian democracy and its explicit model the traditional democracy of the New England town.

Only One Storm, Hicks's most popular and widely reviewed novel, has the same model, and while the setting is contemporary, the style that of realism, and the development of the book includes considerable discussion derived from Hicks's own experience of the possibility of fulfilling moral commitment within the Communist Party, this novel also suggests the awakening of its protagonists to the values of the humane life that can be led in a small New England town.

Behold Trouble is the most tightly structured of Hicks's novels, because it attempts to be less panoramic than the others. Also it poses issues differently, as it does on the experience of Pierre Mason, a neurotic young man who flees his assignment to a work camp for conscientious objectors because he believes government agents are persecuting him. Hicks has said (in *Part of the Truth*) that the story resembles his own to the extent that Mason is betrayed by good intentions into actions that have unforeseen consequences. In the novel he is careful to avoid taking a position for or against his young protagonist, so careful that many reviewers were baffled by the book; yet, his testimony about personal involvement in the moral dilemma and the abundance of detail of the Berkshire community that is its setting demonstrates again Hicks's fundamental belief that the humane life can only be achieved in a face-to-face community.

His final assertion in fiction of this belief, *There Was a Man in Our Town*, cannot really be said to add anything new. Once again it is evident that autobiography is at the core of the story of a retired professor who after originally trying to shape a small town in accordance with theoretical views eventually learns that a town consists of inviolable and somewhat unpredictable people.

None of Hicks's novels is exceptional. Despite his experience with Communism he tells us less about the moral issues of left politics than Dos Passos or Farrell, to name only anti-Communists. And in each of his novels it is hard to separate his humanistic view of social relationships from the anachronistic theme of a return to the village, but perhaps that is because the importance of Hicks's novels after all is not in what they have to tell us about our lives but in what they record of the author's own struggle to live consistently.

—John M. Reilly

HIGGINS, Aidan. Irish. Born in County Kildare, 3 March 1927. Educated at Celbridge Convent; Killashee Preparatory School; Clongowes Wood College. Married Jill Damaris Anders in 1955; three sons. Worked as a copywriter for Domas Advertising, Dublin, in the early 1950's; as a factory hand, extrusion moulder, and storeman, London, in the mid-1950's; as a puppet-operator for John Wright's Marionettes, in Europe, South Africa and Rhodesia, 1958-60; Script-Writer for Filmlets (advertising films), Johannesburg, 1960-61. Recipient: British Arts Council grants; Black Memorial Prize, 1967; German Academy stipend, Berlin, 1969; Irish Academy of Letters award, 1970. Lives in London. Address: c/o John Calder, 18 Brewer Street, London W1R 4AS, England.

PUBLICATIONS

Novels

Langrishe, Go Down. London, Calder and Boyars, and New York, Grove Press, 1966.

Balcony of Europe. London, Calder and Boyars, and New York, Delacorte Press, 1972.

Scenes from a Receding Past. London, Calder, and New York, Riverrun Press, 1977.

Short Stories

Felo de Se. London, Calder, 1960; as *Killachter Meadow*, New York, Grove Press, 1961; revised edition, as *Asylum and Other Stories*, Calder, 1978; New York, Riverrun Press, 1979.

Plays

Radio Plays: *Franz Ferdinand*, 1973; *Imperfect Sympathies*, 1977.

Other

Images of Africa: Diary 1956-60. London, Calder and Boyars, 1971.

Editor, *A Century of Short Stories.* London, Cape, 1977.
Editor, *Colossal Gongorr and the Turkes of Mars*, by Carl, Julien, and Elwin Higgins. London, Cape, 1979.

*

Manuscript Collection: University of Victoria, British Columbia.

Critical Studies: by David Holloway, in *The Bookman* (London), December 1965; "Maker's Language" by Vernon Scannell, in *Spectator* (London), 11 February 1966; *New Leader* (London), 25 September 1967; Morris Beja, in *Irish University Review* (Dublin), Autumn 1973.

* * *

Aidan Higgins made the clasic debut of an Irish prose writer, a volume of stories. But in sharp contrast to his predecessors of the 1930's, like Frank O'Connor and Sean O'Faolain, he was not a regionalist. Even in those stories which have an Irish background, the pressure of the outside world is always felt; one of the spinster sisters of "Killachter Meadow" has a brief, violent affair with a German student. And in the longest story, "Asylum" (Higgins can let his material exfoliate to *nouvelle* length), the country bumpkin Eddy Brazill makes his way to London. But perhaps the most typical are the two stories with German backgrounds, especially "Winter Offensive" where another lecher, Herr Willie Bausch, follows "wherever his cupidity led him."

Such buoyant lubricity contrasts with the melancholy self-destructiveness of the other characters. *Langrishe, Go Down*, Higgins's first novel, is a re-working of "Killachter Meadow" into a definitive statement of these early themes. On the one hand you have provincial Ireland, or the part of it represented by the genteel Langrishes, with their country home in Kildare. On the other hand, you have the pressures of contemporary history as the world lurches towards the second world war.

The link between them is Otto Beck, a German student who takes over the lodge at Springfield, as well as the youngest daughter, Imogen. Their affair is a kind of symbolic rape of all the frail Langrishes represent, but it is also a brief triumph, for at least one of the family discovers physical passion. And behind the lovers stretches the lugubrious beauty of the Irish countryside, a tapestry woven from the thousand details of Higgins's imagistic style. "The fox covert. Acrid smell of the foxes, bitter scattered bones, rabbit and hen bones, fowl. Plover passing overhead. Dempsey's land. Mournful cries."

Two elements go to the making of this style, which is the outstanding feature of Higgins's work so far: an extension of the Joycean technique of juxtaposed epiphanies and a strong visual sense. He writes, as it were, in pictures, held in stereoscopic depth. Exact, but static, the faults of the style are reflected in the exposition: *Langrishe, Go Down* is often baffling, like a marriage between Maria Edgeworth and Robbe-Grillet. But part of its melancholy power undoubtedly springs from such abrupt contrasts between Ireland and the outside world, between passive introversion and energy.

At the end of the novel, the Germans have invaded Austria, and Springfield recedes. Since *Langrishe*, Higgins has published a long novel, *Balcony of Europe*, and its afterthought, *Scenes from a Receding Past*, as well as *Images of Africa*, a diary of the four years he spent in the southern part of that continent. "Things seen but not judged" is the declared intention (*Guardian*, 11 October 1971) but it is not hard to hear the drumbeat of menace. And the emotional climax of the book is Sharpeville, which as in a Greek tragedy happens off-stage. Carefully, Higgins searches for the image to link this contemporary disaster to his own world. "A Johannesburg *Star* photograph of the 'weapons' used by the African insurgents at Sharpeville. In 40-45 seconds of firing, so many killed, so many wounded, so much blood. A pile of knobkerries, sticks, stones. Like what? Windfalls in a winter wood."

After long gestation, *The Balcony of Europe* came as a puzzling disappointment. It was as if Higgins had allowed it to be accumulated rather than created. The main character is a painter, Dan Ruttle (a thinly disguised portrait of the author) whose mother is dying in a Dublin suburb. In true Irish style, this is perhaps the most moving passage in the book, one long tug at the heartstrings, beautifully controlled.

But the main subject of the novel appears when the protagonist moves, with his wife and family, to Spain. There Ruttle falls violently in love with a Jewish-American girl. This classic rectangle (she is married as well) is analysed in a welter of allusion and comment since most of the characters are expatriate writers. When, scruples overcome, the lovers embrace, the novel comes briefly alive: there is an underwater love scene, the literary equivalent of Esther Williams in its virtuosity. But they soon separate and the novel falls apart rather than ends, with a few sour scenes in Dublin, including a gratuitously hostile portrait of the dying Brendan Behan.

Scenes from a Receding Past fills in some of the chronological gaps, with snapshots of Ruttle as a boy in a composite landscape of Sligo and Kildare. This time it is the central character's brother, Wally, whose tongue-tied plight exacts our pity, his inflexibility leading him to a mental institution. But there is warmth in the glimpses of Ruttle's young wife, whom he meets and woos in gloomy London. More pieced than planned, the book still poses the same problem; caught between an old-fashioned gift for scene and character, and a relentless urge to be modern, Higgins falls back on style, so far his most certain strength, distinctive and detailed.

—John Montague

HIGGINS, George V(incent). American. Born in Brockton, Massachusetts, 13 November 1939. Educated at Rockland High School, Massachusetts; Boston College, A.B. in English 1961; Stanford University, California, 1961-62, M.A. 1965; Boston College Law School, Brighton, Massachusetts, J.D. 1967: admitted to the Massachusetts Bar, 1967. Divorced; two children. Reporter, *Journal* and *Evening Bulletin*, Providence, Rhode Island, 1962-63; Bureau Correspondent, Springfield, Massachusetts, 1963-64, and Newsman, Boston, 1964, Associated Press; Researcher, Guterman Horvitz and Rubin, attorneys, Boston, 1966-67; Legal Assistant, Administrative Division and Organized Crime Section, 1967, Deputy Assistant Attorney General, 1967-69, and Assistant Attorney General, 1969-70, Commonwealth of Massachusetts; Assistant U.S. Attorney for the District of Massachusetts, 1970-73, and Special Assistant U.S. Attorney, 1973-74; President, George V. Higgins Inc., Boston, 1973-78. Since 1978, Partner, Griffin and Higgins, Boston. Consultant, National Institute of Law Enforcement and Criminal Practice, Washington, D.C., 1970-71; Instructor in Trial Practice, Boston College Law School, 1973-74 and 1978-79; Columnist, Boston *Herald American*, 1977-79. Address: 50 Staniford Street, Boston, Massachusetts 02114, U.S.A.

PUBLICATIONS

Novels

The Friends of Eddie Coyle. New York, Knopf, and London, Secker and Warburg, 1972.
The Digger's Game. New York, Knopf, and London, Secker and Warburg, 1973.
Cogan's Trade. New York, Knopf, and London, Secker and Warburg, 1974.
A City on a Hill. New York, Knopf, and London, Secker and Warburg, 1975.
The Judgment of Deke Hunter. Boston, Little Brown, and London, Secker and Warburg, 1976.
Dreamland. Boston, Little Brown, and London, Secker and Warburg, 1977.
A Year or So with Edgar. New York, Harper, and London, Secker and Warburg, 1979.
Kennedy for the Defense. New York, Knopf, and London, Secker and Warburg, 1980.
The Rat on Fire. New York, Knopf, and London, Secker and Warburg, 1981.

Uncollected Short Stories

"All Day Was All There Was," in *Arizona Quarterly* (Tucson), Spring 1963.
"Something of a Memoir," in *Massachusetts Review* (Amherst), Summer 1969.
"Mass in Time of War," in *Cimarron Review* (Stillwater, Oklahoma), September 1969.
"Something Dirty You Could Keep," in *Massachusetts Review* (Amherst), Autumn 1969.
"Dillon Explained That He Was Frightened," in *North American Review* (Cedar Falls, Iowa), Fall 1970.
"The Habits of Animals, The Progress of the Seasons," in *The Best American Short Stories 1973*, edited by Martha Foley. Boston, Houghton Mifflin, 1973.
"Two Cautionary Tales: Donnelly's Uncle and The Original Watercourse," in *North American Review* (Cedar Falls, Iowa), Winter 1974.
"The Judge Who Tried Harder," in *Atlantic* (Boston), April 1974.
"Warm for September" and "A Place of Comfort, Light, and Hope," in *North American Review* (Cedar Falls, Iowa), Spring 1977.
"Dublin Coat," in *Harper's* (New York), August 1980.

Other

The Friends of Richard Nixon. Boston, Little Brown, 1975.

* * *

Whatever other merits they possess, best-sellers rarely deserve attention as literary experiments. Their stock-in-trade, after all, is the popular topic represented through familiar conventions. George V. Higgins varies the rule by writing best-sellers that may attract readers because of the prevalent interest in crime but achieve their popular and critical success through stylized restriction of technique to simulation of speech.

In a sense Higgins's novels are reminiscent of the popular newspaper sketches that prepared the American vernacular for adaptation to the novel. Like his 19th-century predecessors Higgins uses characters' speech to provide all the essential information about personality and incident and allows their talk to retain the form of oral delivery with its digressions and incremental movement. Yet, these 20th-century novels are written in the knowledge that American oral language has already been thoroughly assimilated to the purposes of the novel. Like Twain or Hemingway, Higgins concentrates upon syntactic patterns and rhythms in speech, rather than the specificities of pronunciation or vocabulary that intrigued the sketch writers.

Higgins has a marvelous ear for cadence and verbal tone, so his talky novels appeal to us first of all because they promise to satisfy our inherent interest in story-telling. Communicative creatures that we are, we love the relation of anecdotes, for in the sound and manner of a voice there exists a person. The story need not be new, or even have a point; it is the act of communication itself that attracts us.

There is somewhat more to Higgins's stories, though, since it is the underlying premise of his development of vernacular fiction that talk discloses a culture as well as a person. In *The Digger's Game* and *Cogan's Trade* we discover the system of specialization and division of labor in the contemporary criminal world. Loan sharking, fraudalent travel agencies, robbery, and fencing of stolen goods from dogs to TV's have their peculiar principles of operation and their particular practitioners. Similarly conversation among these specialists reveals the violent means by which a scheme of order is enforced in the predatory criminal environment. On a more subtle level the manner of talk communicates style and values. *The Friends of Eddie Coyle* adumbrates criminal activity as a distorted mirror image of American social mobility, and like the other novels focused on criminals, demonstrates the fact that a desire for commodity-based living and sensual gratification is as central to underworld life as it is to respectable bourgeois culture.

It might be expected that amoral frankness about the ways of the underworld might appear attractive in contrast to the hypocrisy in the legitimate world, but it is not so. Neither do we find that the amusing passages of sarcastic or wise-guy dialogue endear the characters to us. They all live sleazy lives, sometimes pathetic ones, in no way glamorous. On the other hand, Higgins makes no effort to represent hoods as social victims either. Nearly all have spent time in prison, lost opportunities, and experienced failure in personal relationships. It is clear, though, that they have chosen, more or less, to live as they do. Their desires and mistakes, bigotry and predaciousness are traits of characters. That's all.

With *A City on a Hill* Higgins tried his narrative technique in a new area, the realm of political insiders, and in the process revealed a limitation to his vernacular experiment. The connecting thread among the dialogues is the entirely legitimate effort to advance the candidacy of a politician who might restore credibility to national government in the aftermath of Watergate. The effort fails ostensibly for lack of interest among potential supporters, but the whole attempt is pervaded by the failure of character Higgins reveals in his leading figures' speech. Like their counterparts in the previous novels, they too live deracinated lives while waiting for the big hit. The point may be accurate, but the convoluted dialogue overheard among speechwriters and advance men reminds us how static the technique of stylized conversation really is. The illusion of unshaped speech permits us to consider characters as authentically human as they speak, but Higgins's unwillingness to draw conclusions—to provide characters a thematic significance—leaves a void too readily filled with cynicism.

The same charge can be leveled against *Dreamland* and *A Year or So with Edgar.* In the latter novel, for example, the title character is an alcoholic newspaper reporter whose rambling talk cannot conceal his stereotypic features. Still, the prolific Higgins has begun to add a dimension to his stories. It appears first in a formal shift to the use of first-person narration. This speaker necessarily must be more reflective than other characters have been, because he has a privileged vantage point and an inevitable designation as the reader's norm. The second alteration Higgins has made in recent works is the selection of narrators whose occupations require at least a sidelong glance at ethical issues.

The Judgment of Deke Hunter, a novel concerning the career of a plainclothes officer in the Massachusetts State Police, thus, involves an exploration of Deke's discovery of the will to become the best cop he can be, regardless of personal disappointments and without exceptional compromise with a frustratingly imperfect criminal justice system. *Kennedy for the Defense* continues in this promising direction by introducing as narrator a man characterized by his wife as Boston's "classiest, sleazy criminal lawyer." Kennedy—no relation to the famous ones—handles the cases of such small time criminals as populate Higgins's first novels, so there is plenty of opportunity for the revealing talk of the hoods. But there is in addition Kennedy himself who is without illusions, rather than disillusioned. He knows what sort of people he has to talk to, and his own aggressive talk is his means of sustaining control over the situations he finds himself in so that he can accomplish the not inconsiderable task of providing clients their Constitutional right to the best possible defense. Most of us, even Kennedy, would prefer a neater, cleaner way of life, but in reconciling the demands of reality and integrity the counsellor for the defense engages in authentic ethical drama. With Jerry Kennedy, Higgins provides us with reference to the world that exists outside his fiction. He seems to have become a serious novelist as well as first-rate storyteller.

—John M. Reilly

HIGHSMITH, (Mary) Patricia (née Plangman). American. Born in Fort Worth, Texas, 19 January 1921; grew up in New York. Educated at Barnard College, New York, B.A. 1942. Has lived in Europe since 1963. Recipient: Grand Prix de Littérature Policière, 1957; Crime Writers Association Silver Dagger, 1964. Address: 21 Boissière, 77 880 Moncourt, France.

PUBLICATIONS

Novels

Strangers on a Train. New York, Harper, and London, Cresset Press, 1950.
The Blunderer. New York, Coward McCann, 1954; London, Cresset Press, 1956; as *Lament for a Lover*, New York, Popular Library, 1956.
The Talented Mr. Ripley. New York, Coward McCann, 1955; London, Cresset Press, 1957.
Deep Water. New York, Harper, 1957; London, Heinemann, 1958.
A Game for the Living. New York, Harper, 1958; London, Heinemann, 1959.
This Sweet Sickness. New York, Harper, 1960; London, Heinemann, 1961.
The Cry of the Owl. New York, Harper, 1962; London, Heinemann, 1963.
The Two Faces of January. New York, Doubleday, and London, Heinemann, 1964.
The Glass Cell. New York, Doubleday, 1964; London, Heinemann, 1965.
The Story-Teller. New York, Doubleday, 1965; as *A Suspension of Mercy*, London, Heinemann, 1965.
Those Who Walk Away. New York, Doubleday, and London, Heinemann, 1967.
The Tremor of Forgery. New York, Doubleday, and London, Heinemann, 1969.
Ripley under Ground. New York, Doubleday, 1970; London, Heinemann, 1971.
A Dog's Ransom. New York, Knopf, and London, Heinemann, 1972.
Ripley's Game. New York, Knopf, and London, Heinemann, 1974.
Edith's Diary. New York, Simon and Schuster, and London, Heinemann, 1977.
The Boy Who Followed Ripley. New York, Lippincott, and London, Heinemann, 1980.

Short Stories

The Snail-Watcher and Other Stories. New York, Doubleday, 1970; as *Eleven*, London, Heinemann, 1970.
Little Tales of Misogyny (in German). Zurich, Diogenes Verlag, 1974; (in English) London, Heinemann, 1977.
The Animal Lover's Book of Beastly Murder. London, Heinemann, 1975.
Slowly, Slowly in the Wind. London, Heinemann, 1979.
The Black House. London, Heinemann, 1981.

Other

Miranda the Panda Is on the Veranda (juvenile), with Doris Sanders. New York, Coward McCann, 1958.
Plotting and Writing Suspense Fiction. Boston, The Writer, 1966.

*

Critical Study: by Julian Symons, in *London Magazine*, June 1969.

Patricia Highsmith comments:

I am said to write stories of psychological terror and suspense, but as I think all novels are psychological I cannot understand why this quality is so often singled out in my writing. My main characters, or heroes, are often the culprits, and murderers, and so my books have never any element of mystery. On the contrary, my chief goal is clarity, and if possible an explanation of criminal behaviour.

* * *

Patricia Highsmith's long career has been as a writer of unique fiction, usually about crime, often murder; but her novels transcend the usual categories into which such fiction is placed. Her interest consistently lies with people involved in violent and extreme situations, and she exhibits their portraits with great skill. Her theme is the psychology of crime explored through the creation of believable, ordinary characters who seem slightly out of focus. Since the criminal is already known, her books center upon the why and the how, rather than the who of most crime fiction.

Reviewing *The Cry of the Owl* in *New Statesman*, Francis Wyndham writes: "Guilt is her theme, and she approaches it through two contrasting heroes. These may be simplified as the guilty man who has justified his guilt and the innocent man who feels himself to be guilty." Throughout her fiction, Highsmith returns again and again to these two figures. In her first novel, *Strangers on a Train* (filmed by Alfred Hitchcock), she uses both characters and explores the symbiosis as they act on each other. In *The Talented Mr. Ripley* (filmed as *Purple Noon*) she introduces her most enduring character, Tom Ripley, an amoral killer drawn into successive acts of violence. Ripley appears in four of her books, most recently in 1980.

In the past decade, Highsmith's fiction has moved slightly beyond her earlier themes. Her collection *The Snail-Watcher and Other Stories* explores the ironies of success. *A Dog's Ransom* returns to the exploration of evil; but, in 1977, in *Edith's Diary* she moved away from the psychology of crime to an examination of a deserted woman's paranoiac retreat into a fantasy diary.

All of Highsmith's novels are written in a flat, realistic style that implies a certain detached view of the private worlds she creates; and the very lack of emphasis upon the events of her plots increases the horror of her characters' irrationality and moral ambiguity. Some reviewers have found her unemotional prose somewhat mechanical, but most have suggested that it adds to the tone of quiet tension, persistent apprehension, under the surface plausibility of the characters' actions.

—Kay J. Mussell

HILL, Carol (née Dechellis). American. Born in New Jersey, 20 January 1942. Educated at Chatham College, Pittsburgh, 1957-61, B.A. 1961. Divorced. Publicist, Crown Publishers, 1965-67, and Bernard Geis Associates, 1967-69; Publicist, 1969-71, and Editor, 1971-73, Pantheon Books; Publicity Manager, Random House, 1973-74; Senior Editor, William Morrow, 1974-76. Since 1976, Senior Editor, Harcourt Brace Jovanovich. Formerly, actress in the Judson Poets Theatre, New York, and in summer stock at the Gateway Playhouse, New Jersey. Agent: Lynn Nesbit, ICM, 40 West 57th Street, New York, New York 10019. Address: 2 Fifth Avenue, Apartment 19-U, New York, New York 10011, U.S.A.

PUBLICATIONS

Novels

Jeremiah 8:20. New York, Random House, 1970.
Let's Fall in Love. New York, Random House, 1974; London, Quartet, 1975.
An Unmarried Woman (novelization of screenplay). New York, Avon, and London, Coronet, 1978.

Uncollected Short Stories

"The Shameless Shika," in *Playboy* (Chicago), 1969.
"Gone," in *Viva* (New York), November 1974.
"Lovers," in *Viva* (New York), April 1975.

Play

Mother Loves (produced New York, 1967).

Other

Subsistence U.S.A., photographs by Bruce Davidson, edited by Jamie Shalleck. New York, Holt Rinehart, 1973.

*

Critical Studies: by Christopher Ricks, in *New York Review of Books*, July 1970; Annie Gottleib, in *New York Times Book Review*, 14 April 1975.

Carol Hill comments:

I shall have to leave the introduction to my fiction to someone else. For me the narrative is the statement.

* * *

Versatility is an asset in an author; but in Carol Hill's case, the contrast between her first and second novels—her only published original novels so far—verges on the incredible. The first, *Jeremiah 8:20*, was a lumpy pudding, heavy, tasteless, almost impossible to finish and digest—while the second, *Let's Fall in Love*, is a fluff of spun sugar, delightful, often bizarre, melting in your mouth—and turning into thin air.

The degree of bewilderment with which the two novels have been received may be illustrated by two quotes about *Jeremiah 8:20*. John Leonard, in the *New York Times*, declares: "this remarkable novel moves from the particular to the prophetic, from man to metaphor to myth....If you can't identify with him [the hero], you probably can't identify with yourself." A huge overstatement at best. Reviewer Thompson, on the other hand, writing in *Harper's*, sums up his reactions to the book in the chilly phrase, "It is strange that books like this are published." Between these two extreme opinions the reader is free to stake out a reasonable area of compromise. The title, to be sure, is intriguing. The "8:20" refers, first, to the prophet Jeremiah's warning (Jeremiah 8:20), "The harvest is past, the summer is ended, and we are not saved." A potential for profundity. "8:20" also happens to refer to the time of day when the main character, whose first name just happens to be Jeremiah, started his new life in New York City. A portent for adventure, or enlightenment, or something. But this anti-hero, Jeremiah Francis Scanlon, "fat, balding, and thirty-nine," is just about the least interesting and least attractive character imaginable, and anyone who follows him through dreams, daydreams, interior monologs, dull dialogs, etc. through the first 300-odd pages, will be relieved to be rid of him on page 371 and good riddance.

All this does not mean that the book does not deal with interesting issues—there is a surfeit of them on the novel's pages. There is racism, police brutality, sex, power, physical culture, money, and—on the final pages—the combined madness of electronic eavesdropping gadgetry and Jeremiah's riding a motorcycle through the night. There is one stunning scene of a senseless murder. The best summary of the plot, however, appeared in *Time*: "The plot proceeds with the authority of a three-year-old dressing himself."

Then came *Let's Fall in Love*. At first, it seems like a wild combination of Wilder's *Cabala* (a cabab of power centered in Rome) with Durrell's *Justine* ("more than five sexes" written about torridly). But it becomes also "a spoof of pornography, pornography, a spoof of espionage thrillers, an espionage thriller" (*New Yorker*). Chiefly, it is a fantasy about Superwoman, one woman's answer to James Bond and all male chauvinists since the beginning of time. The heroine, Anna—she has no family name—is an oversexed predator who, in a typical scene, allows herself to be raped, turns aggressor, and then charges (and collects) $10,000 for her services. She is everything a woman isn't supposed to be: bank president and bank robber, high diver and deep-sea diver. She plays billiards with four oil wells for stakes and wins. In one of the funniest scenes of the book, she is on her way to the airport but stops to help a truck driver fix his engine and, while she is at it, changes a tire too. She is admonished by her priest-confidant for showing off and is told to review the conditions for hubris.

There are many such absurdly funny passages. Lola, another main character, cultivates rumors that she had slept with Kissinger; she hopes to gain prestige from this. A live cat is used as a clandestine radio transmitter; near the body of a murder victim, Latin clues from Juvenal are found in a Chinese fortune cookie. Whole pages are reproduced from the *New York Times* and from classical erotica. The War Office has a "Department 008," the fog comes on little cat feet, and we read that one of the minor characters, "Nude, descended staircase."

Occasionally the author attempts serious and/or philosophical moods—these don't come off nearly as well. Neither do the really fantastic episodes such as the big rescue scene from the burning building by a woman and man on a swinging rope. Jókai had done it much better in *A Hungarian Nabob* (1853). At the bottom, Hill wants to work out a serious conflict involving father-daughter incest. Its surface statement, involving a beauty queen and her adoptive father, is mainly silly. The deeper one, that involving Anna and her real father, has potential and the scene in which Anna's search for the father culminates is the only truly chilling moment of the book. What is Anna's object? Murder or incest? It's left up to the reader.

There is much else in the book, including a narrator of indeterminate sex whose ultimate destiny is unclear. There is murder and rape and spy business and a million-dollar art theft. There is sex, lots of it. There is Martin Borman, the Nazi chieftain, hiding in Brazil. Of the total effect of the book one of the minor characters makes the best comment, "Well, it all fits somehow, we just don't know how." For all that, it is a most entertaining novel.

How could one author have written two such widely dissimilar books? A neat question. In effecting the shift from obese Jeremiah's obscure stumbling through Harlem to the comic-strip adventures of glamorous Anna and her jet-set playmates, Carol Hill also changed her photographic image of herself. On the cover of *Jeremiah 8:20*, she appears Sphinx-like and demure, with a Mona Lisa smile. By contrast, the sleek, sexy dame on the cover of *Let's Fall in Love* smirks just like the alley cat who swallowed the canary.

—Dalma H. Brunauer

HILL, Susan (Elizabeth). British. Born in Scarborough, Yorkshire, 5 February 1942. Educated at grammar schools in Scarborough and Coventry; King's College, University of London, B.A. (honours) in English 1963. Married Stanley Wells in 1975; one daughter. Since 1963, full-time writer: since 1977, monthly columnist, *Daily Telegraph*, London. Recipient: Maugham Award, 1971; Whitbread Literary Award, 1972; Rhys Memorial Prize, 1972. Fellow, King's College, 1978. Fellow, Royal Society of Literature, 1972. Address: Midsummer Cottage, Church Lane, Beckley, Oxfordshire, England.

PUBLICATIONS

Novels

The Enclosure. London, Hutchinson, 1961.
Do Me a Favour. London, Hutchinson, 1963.
Gentleman and Ladies. London, Hamish Hamilton, 1968; New York, Walker, 1969.
A Change for the Better. London, Hamish Hamilton, 1969.
I'm the King of the Castle. London, Hamish Hamilton, and New York, Viking Press, 1970.
Strange Meeting. London, Hamish Hamilton, 1971; New York, Saturday Review Press, 1972.
The Bird of Night. London, Hamish Hamilton, 1972; New York, Saturday Review Press, 1973.
In the Springtime of the Year. London, Hamish Hamilton, and New York, Saturday Review Press, 1974.

Short Stories

The Albatross and Other Stories. London, Hamish Hamilton, 1971; New York, Saturday Review Press, 1975.
The Custodian. London, Covent Garden Press, 1972.
A Bit of Singing and Dancing. London, Hamish Hamilton, 1973.

Uncollected Short Story

"Kielty's," in *Winter's Tales 20*, edited by A.D Maclean. London, Macmillan, 1974; New York, St. Martin's Press, 1975.

Plays

The Cold Country and Other Plays for Radio (includes *The End of Summer, Lizard in the Grass, Consider the Lilies, Strip Jack Naked*). London, BBC Publications, 1975.
On the Face of It (broadcast, 1975). Published in *Act 1*, edited by David Self and Ray Speakman, London, Hutchinson, 1979.
The Ramshackle Company (juvenile; produced London, 1981).

Radio Plays: *Taking Leave*, 1971; *The End of Summer*, 1971; *Lizard in the Grass*, 1971; *The Cold Country*, 1972; *Winter Elegy*, 1973; *Consider the Lilies*, 1973; *A Window on the World*, 1974; *Strip Jack Naked*, 1974; *Mr. Proudham and Mr. Sleight*, 1974; *On the Face of It*, 1975; *The Summer of the Giant Sunflower*, 1977; *The Sound That Time Makes*, 1980; *Here Comes the Bride*, 1980; *Chances*, 1981.

Television Play: *The Blackness Within Them*, 1980.

Other

Editor, *The Distracted Preacher and Other Tales*, by Thomas Hardy. London, Penguin, 1979.
Editor, with Isabel Quigly, *New Stories 5*. London, Hutchinson, 1980.

* * *

Susan Hill's protagonists typically are caught in desperate struggles for self-justification, which has been denied them by selfish parents and an unfeeling society that pays no attention to their essential needs. In trying to escape the pain of alienation many experience what seems to them the brink of madness. Those who escape do so at enormous cost; the others choose the safety of their predictable, unfulfilled lives.

They are never pitiable. Hill's writing does not allow pity. They are too intensely alive, involved with their own survival, their deep hatreds. Her style is powerful in its simplicity and seductive in its intimate detail and unexpected juxtaposition of images.

In "The Albatross" Duncan is a boy who is different, and, as a result, locked within himself, tormented with fears of inadequacy, dreaming of escape. He lives with his invalid mother, who fosters his feelings of impotence in order to keep him at home with her. The only person who tries to help Duncan is Ted Flint, a fisherman who has lived the independent life Duncan fantasizes. Flint offers him work on his boat, invites him to the local pub to drink with the other men, gives him a chance to belong. Duncan's mother throws Flint out of the house and tells Duncan, "Nobody could trust you in any boat....You stay as you are." When Flint dies at sea Duncan is left without hope; and hopeless, he resolves to be free. "I can do anything," he tells himself. For the first time he buys himself a pint at the pub. Then he goes home, drugs his mother, pushes her in her wheelchair over a cliff, sets fire to the house, and runs away—gaining a few hours of freedom before he is found.

A Change for the Better explores much the same theme. Deirdre Fount, dominated by a selfish mother, is prevented from a life of her own by mother-inspired feelings of inadequacy. Unable to establish other relationships, fearful of what people will think, she tries to gain her son's dependence by smothering him, with predictable results. When her mother dies she makes a brief, doomed attempt at a new life; failing, she resigns herself to the life her mother designed for her.

A happier, more humorous version of this theme occurs in the delightful short story "A Bit of Singing and Dancing." Esme Fanshaw, a middle-aged woman, takes in a boarder, Mr. Curry, when her mother dies. He becomes increasingly important to her until, curious about what he does for a living, she goes into the town and sees him at work. There on a streetcorner "he was singing, in a tuneful, but rather cracked voice, and doing an elaborate little tap dance on the spot, his rather small feet moving swiftly and daintily in time with the music." Her humiliation (she hears her mother's "I told you so") is overcome by her need and when he comes home that night she tells him "I always like a little singing and dancing.... It takes you out of yourself." He bows.

In *Strange Meeting* Hilliard, who comes from a reserved, ungiving family, meets Barton, his opposite. Barton's gregariousness and genuine warmth allow Hilliard to open himself. This intimacy is gained, however, against the background of trench warfare in World War I, and probably could not have been reached had destruction not been imminent. Insanity is the medium that makes a relationship possible in *The Bird of Night*. Lawson, an introverted scholar, is able to allow himself to love Francis Croft, a poet whose life vacillates between intense creativity, despair, and potential homicidal tendencies. Lawson is perhaps able to accept this degree of intimacy because it has parental, and therefore more acceptable, overtones. Their lives together are convincing because of Susan Hill's matter-of-fact treatment of bizarre and frightening events, and she provides an unforgettable experience of madness in everyday life.

In the Springtime of the Year shows a young woman fighting madness after the senseless death of her husband. She isolates herself from all company except that of her husband's younger brother, whose gentleness is similar to her husband's. Methodically she finds objects instead of people to make sense of her days. "...burying her hands deep into the soil, feeling about until she found a potato, and then another, she would cook them, perhaps, make a small fire and bake them and eat them with butter, it would be a treat. It would be something." Her life, told in rich unsentimental detail, is a series of day-to-day triumphs or setbacks, as she tries to reaffirm her connection with the world. In "The Peacock" a married woman is forced to suddenly confront an isolation she has been unaware of. Newly returned from Africa, where the clearly defined boundaries of colonial life had provided a sure course for her, enabled her to ignore her deeper needs, she finds herself living with a husband she does not know. Her state of mind is reflected when she accidentally locks herself in a summerhouse. She panics, then hears "a sound inside the close, dark space, a scratching noise underneath the slatted bench. She looked down. A peacock was there, cornered and bright-eyed."

The depth of childhood terror is laid bare in *I'm the King of the Castle*. Two children, Kingshaw and Hooper, are thrown together against their will when Kingshaw's mother comes to act as housekeeper for Hooper's father. Gradually the parents become absorbed with each other, oblivious to the torment that exists in the children. Hooper, a compulsive boy whose isolation has led him to deep hatred and periods of near-madness, sets out to establish his supremacy by terrorizing Kingshaw. He threatens him, locks him in a dark cellar, taunts him until Kingshaw decides to run away to preserve himself. Hooper follows, and in the woods that they must cross Kingshaw learns of Hooper's fears, which makes him for the moment feel superior to Hooper. Nature is itself a character in this book, a pagan, frightening Nature that reflects the terror in which the boys live. When Kingshaw, determined to be brave, first walks alone through the cornfields of the Hooper estate, he finds that "for a moment he could only hear the soft thudding of his own footsteps, and the silky sound of the corn, brushing against him. Then, there was a rush of air, as the great crow came beating down, and wheeled about his head. The beak opened and the hoarse caaw came out again and again, from inside the scarlet mouth." Gradually Hooper and Kingshaw are drawn into a malevolent pattern too strong for them to cope with, and death results.

The psychic world in which Susan Hill's protagonists live is evoked with great strength and careful observation. They are real people, usually in fairly conventional situations, to whom something unexpected seems always about to happen, a feeling that allows the reader to live with them, in anticipation or dread.

—Barbara Hults

HILLIARD, Noel (Harvey). New Zealander. Born in Napier, Hawke's Bay, 6 February 1929. Educated at Gisborne High School, 1942-45; Victoria University, Wellington, 1946-50; Wellington Teachers College, 1954-55. Married Kiriwai Mete in 1954; four children. Journalist, *Southern Cross*, Wellington, 1946-50; Teacher, Khandallah School, Wellington, 1955-56, and District High School, Mangakino, 1956-64; Chief Sub-Editor, *New Zealand Listener*, Wellington, 1965-70; Sub-Editor, *New Zealand's Heritage* and *New Zealand Today*, 1972-73; Deputy Editor, *New Zealand's Nature Heritage*, 1973-74; full-time writer, 1974-77. Since 1977, sub-editor, Wellington *Evening Post*. Robert Burns Fellow at the University of Otago, Dunedin, 1971. Chairman, Mangakino-Pouakani Maori Executive Committee, and Delegate to the Waiariki District Council of Maori Executive Committees, 1962-64. Recipient: Hubert Church Memorial Award, 1960; New Zealand Literary Fund Scholarship, 1963, 1975. Address: 28 Richard Street, Titahi Bay, Wellington, New Zealand.

PUBLICATIONS

Novels

Maori Girl. London, Heinemann, 1960.
Power of Joy. Christchurch, Whitcombe and Tombs, and London, Joseph, 1965; Chicago, Regnery, 1966.
A Night at Green River. Christchurch, Whitcombe and Tombs, and London, Hale, 1969.
Maori Woman. Christchurch, Whitcombe and Tombs, and London, Hale, 1974.
The Glory and the Dream. London, Heinemann, 1978.

Short Stories

A Piece of Land. Christchurch, Whitcombe and Tombs, and London, Hale, 1963.
Send Somebody Nice: Stories and Sketches. Christchurch, Whitcombe and Tombs, and London, Hale, 1976.
Selected Stories. Dunedin, McIndoe, 1977.

Other

We Live by a Lake (juvenile), photographs by Ans Westra. Auckland, Heinemann, 1972.
Wellington: City Alive, photographs by Ans Westra. Christchurch, Whitcoulls, 1976.

*

Bibliography: *Noel Hilliard: A Preliminary Bibliography* by Jeffrey Downs, Wellington, National Library of New Zealand, 1976.

Critical Studies: *The New Zealand Novel 1869-1965*, Wellington, Reed, 1966, and *New Zealand Short Stories*, Wellington, Price Milburn, 1968, both by Joan Stevens; *New Zealand Fiction since 1945*, Dunedin, McIndoe, 1968, and *New Zealand Novels*, Wellington, New Zealand University Press, 1969, both by H. Winston Rhodes; "The Maori and Literature 1938-65" by Bill Pearson, in *The Maori People in the Nineteen-Sixties*, Auckland, Paul, 1968; *A Descriptive Account of Social Attitudes in the Fiction of Noel Hilliard* by T.J. Mullinder, Christchurch, University of Canterbury, 1974; "The Persistence of Realism: Dan Davin, Noel Hilliard, and Recent New Zealand Short Stories" by Lawrence Jones, in *Islands 20* (Auckland), December 1977.

Noel Hilliard comments:

My principal area of interest has been life in New Zealand today, and particularly how Maori and Pakeha view and behave towards each other. All my writing has been about working people.

* * *

Maori Girl, Noel Hilliard's first novel, made an immediate impact on its readers. It appeared at a time when many New Zealanders were becoming uncomfortably aware that all was not well with race relations in their country; and the story of Netta Samuel's early life in a Maori farming community, together with her painful experiences when she arrived alone in the city, were as disturbing as they were impressive. The competence and sincerity of the author could hardly be questioned. Yet the realistic portrayal and unrelenting exposure of discriminatory practices caused some to disparage the novel as mere documentary and to complain that Hilliard was too obviously writing to a thesis.

Although complete in itself, *Maori Girl* proved to be the prelude to a theme. It was the first of a series of novels that can be said to be without parallel in New Zealand fiction. When *Power of Joy* appeared and was followed at intervals by *Maori Woman* and *The Glory and the Dream*, it became apparent that the whole tetralogy had been devised and orchestrated to give life and form to a much more complex theme than had been surmised. If the first novel had evoked the childhood and youth of a Maori girl, forced to endure the pressures of a bi-racial society, *Power of Joy* followed the development of a Pakeha or European boy who almost unconsciously discovers his sense of identity in the spirit of earth, in tree and river and hill, in all his natural New Zealand surroundings, and is forced to resist the traditional pressure of his conventional but poverty-stricken family background. Both are significant variations of the theme of growing up in New Zealand. With *Maori Woman* the lives of these two become interwoven and entangled in a harsh city-world of dominant pakehas and under-privileged Maoris. In the final book of the tetralogy Maori girl and Pakeha boy have come together, to find unity through a process of adjustment, to discover harmony in difference.

Hilliard has certainly been intent on exploring relations between Maoris and Pakehas, and unmasking discriminatory practices, but his aim has been far more comprehensive. He has been even more intent on revealing the human implications of cultural diversity, on identifying his leading characters with the spirit of place and with their inherited but distinctive traditions. He has attempted to reveal and dramatise the tensions that are produced in the community at large and in the unitary family of mixed race from the different ways of life of Maori and Pakeha. However, the major difficulty in such an ambitious undertaking is that of achieving both individuality and typicality, of avoiding the special case and of refraining from the temptation to stereotype characters and their responses to particular situations. This must always be a daunting task for any writer whose aim is not confined to entertainment of a trivial kind. The measure of Hilliard's achievement is that he succeeds not only in establishing his leading characters in an authentic setting and involves the reader in their problems of adjustment, but also in introducing subsidiary themes and characters to illuminate and give further meaning to his many-sided treatment of human relations in a bi-racial community.

In the midst of writing this quartet of novels Hilliard produced a number of short stories. A group of these shorter pieces contains episodes in the lives of two Maori children, and the involvement of the whole family in the simple rhythms of work, play, and ceremonial occasions; but other stories touch on Maori-Pakeha relations and on aspects of the ordinary life of ordinary New Zealanders, generally with implications that have some social significance. Hilliard has always shown his preference for dealing with subjects and people that are of the earth.

Besides these stories Hilliard has written *A Night at Green River*, a novel with the very simple theme of a Pakeha farmer's need for assistance in stacking his hay. Its patterned development emphasises the different values of Pakeha and Maori, especially in relation to material wealth and possessions, to the gospel of work and to human dignity. *A Night at Green River* becomes a comic parable that has relevance to the human predicaments caused when two races with different life-styles and aspirations attempt to mingle. As a lively parable it achieves a rare distinction and enhances Hilliard's reputation for providing valuable insights to the mental and emotional processes that collide when European and Polynesian come together.

—H. Winston Rhodes

HIMES, Chester (Bomar). American. Born in Jefferson City, Missouri, 19 July 1909. Educated at Glenville High School, Cleveland, graduated 1926; Ohio State University, 1926-28. Married 1) Jean Lucinda Johnson in 1937; 2) Lesley Packard. Imprisoned for armed robbery, Ohio State Penitentiary, 1928-36; worked for the Works Progress Administration (WPA) Writers Project in Ohio, 1938-41. Since 1953, has lived in Europe. Recipient: Rosenwald Fellowship, 1944; Grand Prix de Littérature Policière, 1958. Agent: Rosalyn Targ Literary Agency, 250 West 57th Street, New York, New York 10019, U.S.A.

PUBLICATIONS

Novels

If He Hollers Let Him Go. New York, Doubleday, 1945; London, Falcon Press, 1947.
Lonely Crusade. New York, Knopf, 1947; London, Grey Walls Press, 1950.
Cast the First Stone. New York, Coward McCann, 1952.
The Third Generation. Cleveland, World, 1954.
The Primitive. New York, New American Library, 1955.
For Love of Imabelle. New York, Fawcett, 1957; as *A Rage in Harlem*, New York, Avon, 1965; London, Panther, 1969.
The Crazy Kill. New York, Avon, 1959; London, Panther, 1968.
The Real Cool Killers. New York, Avon, 1959; London, Panther, 1969.
All Shot Up. New York, Avon, 1960; London, Panther, 1969.
The Big Gold Dream. New York, Avon, 1960; London, Panther, 1968.
Pinktoes. Paris, Olympia Press, 1961; New York, Putnam, and London, Barker, 1965.
Cotton Comes to Harlem. New York, Putnam, and London, Muller, 1965.
The Heat's On. New York, Putnam, and London, Muller, 1966; as *Come Back, Charleston Blue*, New York, Berkley, 1970.
Run Man Run. New York, Putnam, 1966; London, Muller, 1967.
Blind Man with a Pistol. New York, Morrow, and London, Hodder and Stoughton, 1969; as *Hot Day, Hot Night*, New York, Dell, 1970.
A Case of Rape. New York, Targ Editions, 1980.

Uncollected Short Stories

"Crazy in the Stir," in *Esquire* (New York), August 1934.
"To What Red Hell," in *Esquire* (New York), October 1934.
"The Visiting Hour," in *Esquire* (New York), September 1936.
"Every Opportunity," in *Esquire* (New York), May 1937.
"Salute to the Passing," in *Opportunity* (New York), March 1939.
"Face in the Moon," in *Coronet* (New York), February 1941.
"The Things You Do," in *Opportunity* (New York), May 1941.
"Two Soldiers," in *Crisis* (New York), January 1943.
"So Softly Smiling," in *Crisis* (New York), October 1943.
"Money Don't Spend in the Stir," in *Esquire* (New York), April 1944.
"The Song Says 'Keep on Smiling,' " in *Crisis* (New York), April 1945.
"The Something in a Colored Man," in *Esquire* (New York), January 1946.
"To End All Storms," in *Crisis* (New York), July 1948.
"The Snake," in *Esquire* (New York), October 1959.
"Marihuana and a Pistol," in *The Best Short Stories by Negro Writers*, edited by Langston Hughes. Boston, Little Brown, 1967.
"Life Everlasting," in *First World* (Atlanta), Spring 1978.

Other

The Quality of Hurt (autobiography). New York, Doubleday, 1972; London, Joseph, 1973.
Black on Black: Baby Sister and Selected Writings. New York, Doubleday, 1973; London, Joseph, 1975.
My Life of Absurdity (autobiography). New York, Doubleday, 1976.

*

Critical Studies: "Chester Himes Issue" of *Black World* (Chicago), March 1972; *Chester Himes* by James Lundquist, New York, Ungar, 1976; *Chester Himes* by Stephen F. Milliken, Columbia, University of Missouri Press, 1976; *Too Close to the Truth: The*

American Fiction of Chester Himes by Melvin Troy Peters, unpublished dissertation, East Lansing, Michigan State University, 1978.

* * *

Whether writing about convicts or police detectives, industrial workers or a bourgeois family, Chester Himes has been concerned throughout his productive career to express the dynamic relationship between social environment and individual personality. Taking up his authorial position within the consciousness of oppressed characters, Himes makes what one has learned to think of, too abstractly, as "the race problem" an experience of psychic conflict: Bob Jones in *If He Hollers Let Him Go* exists mentally on the borderline between fierce hatred, fed by a thousand and one indignities he experiences in a wartime industrial plant, and ego collapse; the career of Lee Gordon, confronted by racism within the union in his "lonely crusade" for black workers' rights, is reduced to a moment in which he braves reprisal for a gratuitous act of defiance; the members of the black bourgeois family of *The Third Generation* turn the hostility generated by caste barriers toward themselves; personally based relationships in *The Primitive* are contaminated by socially conditioned fears; and the white prisoner in *Cast the First Stone* finds love impossible among men, like himself, who have been brutalized.

Himes's vision of the psychic conflicts is naturalistic. Rather than plot the growth of his characters' hostilities or fears of reprisal were they to resist discrimination openly, he records the presence of these feelings as given aspects of personality. Psychic conflicts, thus, replicate the primary reality of social caste conflicts, and each character's mental struggle to survive represents the options of accomodation, flight, or resistance which appear in the collective experience of all black Americans.

Shortly after he chose to exile himself from the United States in 1953 Chester Himes began a series of Harlem crime stories, which, with the exception of the most recent—*Blind Man with a Pistol*—have been originally published in French and subsequently translated for American paperback distribution. These nine novels constitute an adaptation of the tough guy detective genre into a cycle that explores the unique experience of the capital of black America. In the cycle white society is evidently the cause of oppressive social conditions but as the detectives, settings, plots, and viewpoint are all black, the Harlemites live under less psychic tension than characters in Himes's earlier novels. In effect, they have the room to determine in a limited way their own values and social relations. Himes's police detectives, Coffin Ed Johnson and Grave Digger Jones, who ruthlessly hunt down crooks that deceive the poor but yet tolerate organized vice, therefore, serve as enforcers of Harlem's specialized justice. Willing to bend the white man's law and regarding his abstract categories of morality as irrelevant to the survival of their people, the tough guys express a humanism decidedly black.

Recently critics have begun to acknowledge the presence in Afro-American writing of an intuitive existentialism. Chester Himes's work might well serve as illustration. Consistently naturalistic, his documentation of the experience of oppression repudiates the bad faith of white American culture, while his portrayal of black culture asserts that people can freely choose in a world of absurd social practice to survive with principle.

—John M. Reilly

HINDE, Thomas. Pseudonym for Sir Thomas Willes Chitty, Baronet. British. Born in Felixstowe, Suffolk, 2 March 1926; succeeded father to the baronetcy, 1955. Educated at Winchester School, Hampshire; University College, Oxford. Served in the Royal Navy, 1944-47. Married Susan Elspeth (i.e., the writer Susan Chitty) in 1951; one son and three daughters. Worked for Inland Revenue, London, 1951-53; for Shell Petroleum Company, in England, 1953-58, and in Nairobi, Kenya, 1958-60. Granada Arts Fellow, University of York, 1964-65; Visiting Lecturer, University of Illinois, Urbana, 1965-67; Visiting Professor, Boston University, 1969-70. Fellow, Royal Society of Literature. Address: Bow Cottage, West Hoathly, near East Grinstead, Sussex RH19 4QF, England.

PUBLICATIONS

Novels

Mr. Nicholas. London, MacGibbon and Kee, 1952; New York, Farrar Straus, 1953.
Happy as Larry. London, MacGibbon and Kee, 1957; New York, Criterion, 1958.
For the Good of the Company. London, Hutchinson, 1961.
A Place Like Home. London, Hodder and Stoughton, 1962.
The Cage. London, Hodder and Stoughton, 1962.
Ninety Double Martinis. London, Hodder and Stoughton, 1963.
The Day the Call Came. London, Hodder and Stoughton, 1964; New York, Vanguard Press, 1965.
Games of Chance: The Interviewer, The Investigator. London, Hodder and Stoughton, 1965; New York, Vanguard Press, 1967.
The Village. London, Hodder and Stoughton, 1966.
High. London, Hodder and Stoughton, 1968; New York, Walker, 1969.
Bird. London, Hodder and Stoughton, 1970.
Generally a Virgin. London, Hodder and Stoughton, 1972.
Agent. London, Hodder and Stoughton, 1974.
Our Father. London, Hodder and Stoughton, 1975; New York, Braziller, 1976.
Daymare. London, Macmillan, 1980.

Other

Do Next to Nothing: A Guide to Survival Today, with Susan Chitty. London, Weidenfeld and Nicolson, 1976.
The Great Donkey Walk, with Susan Chitty. London, Hodder and Stoughton, 1977.
The Cottage Book: A Manual of Maintenance, Repair, and Construction. London, Davies, 1979.
Sir Henry and Sons: A Memoir. London, Macmillan, 1980.

Editor, *Spain: A Personal Anthology.* London, Newnes, 1963.

*

Manuscript Collection: University of Texas, Austin.

Critical Studies: in *New York Herald Tribune*, 24 May 1953; *The Angry Decade* by Kenneth Allsop, London, Owen, 1958; *The Times Literary Supplement* (London), 26 May 1961, 27 October 1966, 7 November 1968, 11 September 1970; *The Observer* (London), 7 June 1964; *The New York Times*, 9 August 1967; *Books and Bookmen* (London), September 1974.

Thomas Hinde comments:

I write novels because I like novels and I like trying to make my own. These aim to be—but unfortunately hardly every succeed in being—the novels I will like best of all. Just as my taste in novels changes, so the sort of novel I try to write changes. I also believe in the importance of the novel—one of the few places where individual art as opposed to script-conference art can still flourish. I believe that it can and will change and develop, however fully explored it seems at present. I believe that people will go on wanting to read novels. But however much I am convinced by these logical arguments of the vitality, value, and survival of the form, the real reason why I go on writing novels remains personal: despite its anxiety and difficulties, I like the process, and, despite disappointments, I am still excited by the results which I aim for.

* * *

When, in 1957, American popular journalism first discovered the "Angry Young Men," Thomas Hinde was listed, in articles in *Time* and *Life*, along with Kingsley Amis, John Wain, and John Braine, as one of the principal progenitors of the "Movement." *Happy as Larry*, Hinde's second novel, had just been published and the novel's protagonist was a rather feckless young man who lost menial jobs, was vaguely trying to write, and irresponsibly drifted away from his wife. Yet the designation of "Angry Young Men," over-generalized and inappropriate as it was for all the writers to whom it was applied, was particularly inappropriate for Hinde. Far from "angry" or defiantly rebellious, Hinde's protagonist wanders about apologetically, full of guilt, trying to help a friend recover a lost photograph that might be used for blackmail. His indecision, inhibitions, and constant self-punishment characterize him far more consistently than do any articulate attitudes toward society. In addition, Hinde's point of view in the novel is far from an unqualified endorsement of his protagonist's actions and attitudes. The ending, like the endings of most of Hinde's novels, is left open, without any definitive or summarizable statement. And the kind of judgment frequently assumed in popular accounts of novelists, the clarion call for a new way of life or the castigation of depraved contemporary morality, is entirely absent.

At the same time, however, in other terms, *Happy as Larry* is a novel of the 1950's. The protagonist's wandering, his lack of certainty, his allegiance only to close personal friends, his inhibitions and apologies, his insistence on self as a starting point for value, are all characteristic of much of the serious fiction of the decade. London, too, shrouded in rain, and gloom, spotted with crowded pubs that provide the only refuge, is also made the grim post-war city. In addition, Hinde uses a frequent symbol in fiction, the photograph, as central to the plot of his novel. In a world in which identity was regarded as shifting, unreliable, unknowable, only the photograph, the fixed and permanent image, could give identity any meaning, although that meaning, far more often than not, was itself a distortion, an over-simplification, occasion for blackmail. In fact, Hinde's novels most characteristically begin with categories definable in terms of other novels and novelists, with genres to which the reader is accustomed.

His first novel, *Mr. Nicholas*, chronicles the struggles of a young Oxonian, home on holidays, to define himself against his domineering and insensitive father. Another novel, *For the Good of the Company*, deals with the struggles for definition and power within the business combine, the complex organization that seemed a microcosm to depict human efforts to maintain a sense of rational control. *The Cage* and *A Place Like Home* are Hinde's African novels, *The Cage* a particularly sensitive and effective treatment of a young British colonial girl in Kenya attempting to retain her ties to the world of her parents while simultaneously understanding sympathetically the emerging black society. *The Village* establishes, without sentimentality or nostalgia, the world of the small English village about to be levelled by bulldozers and flooded for a new reservoir. *High* is Hinde's American visit novel, an account of the 40-year-old British writer teaching at an American university, including the familiar device of a novelist character writing a novel which is itself partly reproduced within the novel. In other words, the themes, techniques, concerns, and atmosphere of Hinde's novels are all familiar, all representative of their time and place—the heroine of *The Cage* often sounds like a more restrained Doris Lessing heroine, the protagonist of *High* is well established in a lineage that stretches back to Eric Linklater—yet Hinde is also an individual novelist of great skill with an individual sense of texture and intelligence.

Hinde is frequently at his best in describing the sensitivities of his young characters—their introspections, their naivety, their commitments to attitudes and to people they cannot entirely understand. The heroine of *The Cage*, unable to untangle the racial antagonisms she does not entirely understand, thinks her young colonial boyfriend will kill the black man he thinks she's been sleeping with, over-dramatizing a conflict she cannot solve. The young budding capitalist in *For the Good of the Company* makes love to the boss's daughter but cannot really fathom all the perplexities of her emotions. He is loyal to the enigma he has partially observed and partially constructed, always wondering how much he has made up himself. A similarly intelligent sensitivity characterizes the love affair in *The Village* between the harassed local doctor and the opportunistic young stockbroker's wife, an affair in which love is created out of mutual desperation. Hinde's sensitivity is applied not only to personal relationships, but to exterior atmospheres as well. Each novel contains many descriptions of weather, rich and subtle evocations of different climates and seasons—equally acute whether England, America or Africa—that are shaped carefully to suit the emotions or the problems of the characters. Weather is both the material for physical description and a principal means of controlling the atmosphere of the novel.

Hinde's novels are also full of action, concerned with plot. Yet the plots never reach definitive conclusions, never entirely resolve the issues they present. The protagonist of *Happy as Larry* finally finds the photograph, but may or may not become a solid citizen and create a home for his faithful wife. The young capitalist in *For the Good of the Company* is enmeshed in the system and, at the end, like his boss, is about to live his past over again. But whether or not he will be any wiser is an open question. *The Village* ends with the feeling that the old English village is probably doomed, as much from its own hypocrisies and inadequacies as from an insensitive "urban bureaucracy," but the fight to save the village is not completely finished. Hinde's novels are, in a way, slices of recognizable contemporary life, a life in which people live and react, in which things happen although those things are not irremediably conclusive, and in which judgment is superficial or irrelevant. And these slices, communicated with a rich sense of personal and historical atmosphere, are never distorted by conversion into an object lesson or part of a message. In fact, Hinde, as author, keeps his distance. He can use familiar themes effectively because he treats them from a distance, stands far enough away to demonstrate a compassionate irony or an intelligent sympathy with his fictional world, a world effectively communicated because, like our larger world, it is one not easily reduced to understandable principles or judgments.

—James Gindin

HOAGLAND, Edward. American. Born in New York City, 21 December 1932. Educated at Harvard University, Cambridge, Massachusetts, 1950-54, A.B. 1954. Served in the United States Army, 1955-57. Married 1)Amy Ferrara in 1960; 2)Marion Magid in 1968; one child. Since 1963, part-time teacher at Rutgers University, New Brunswick, New Jersey, Sarah Lawrence College, Bronxville, New York, City College of New York, New School for Social Research, New York, University of Iowa, Iowa City, and Columbia University, New York. Recipient: Houghton Mifflin Literary Fellowship, 1956; Longview Foundation Award, 1961; Guggenheim Fellowship, 1964, 1975; American Academy Traveling Fellowship, 1964, and Vursell Memorial Award, 1981; O. Henry Award, 1971; New York State Council on the Arts Fellowship, 1972; Brandeis University Citation in Literature, 1972. Address: Westbeth, 463 West Street, New York, New York 10014, U.S.A.

PUBLICATIONS

Novels

Cat Man. Boston, Houghton Mifflin, 1956.

The Circle Home. New York, Crowell, 1960.
The Peacock's Tail. New York, McGraw Hill, 1965.

Uncollected Short Stories

"Cowboys," in *Noble Savage 1* (New York), 1960.
"The Last Irish Fighter," in *Esquire* (New York), August 1960.
"The Colonel's Power," in *New American Review 2*, edited by Theodore Solotaroff. New York, New American Library, 1967.
"The Witness," in *Paris Review*, Summer-Fall 1967.
"Kwan's Coney Island," in *New American Review 5*, edited by Theodore Solotaroff. New York, New American Library, 1969.
"A Fable of Mammas," in *Transatlantic Review* (London), Summer 1969.
"The Final Fate of the Alligators," in *Prize Stories 1971: The O. Henry Awards*, edited by William Abrahams. New York, Doubleday, 1971.

Other

Notes from the Century Before: A Journal from British Columbia. New York, Random House, 1969.
The Courage of Turtles: Fifteen Essays about Compassion, Pain, and Love. New York, Random House, 1970.
Walking the Dead Diamond River (essays). New York, Random House, 1973.
The Moose on the Wall: Field Notes from the Vermont Wilderness. London, Barrie and Jenkins, 1974.
Red Wolves and Black Bears (essays). New York, Random House, 1976.
African Calliope: A Journey to the Sudan. New York, Random House, 1979.
The Edward Hoagland Reader, edited by Geoffrey Wolff. New York, Random House, 1979.

*

Critical Studies: by R.W. Flint, in *New York Review of Books*, 11 September 1969; Alfred Kazin, 25 March 1973, and Diane Johnson, 16 September 1979, both in *New York Times Book Review*.

* * *

So far Edward Hoagland has not achieved through his novels and non-fiction a secure or influential place as an important American writer, even though his circus and boxing novels have been labelled required reading for those interested in these activities, and his prose style is distinctively his own. It is perhaps this distinctiveness that may disappoint readers who expect an author to be a virtuoso. Hoagland enjoys travelling in relatively primitive areas of North America and detailing life in occupations where brawn or physical skills are more important than intellect. His essay, "Big Cats," is a deft description of the cat family; *Cat Man* is a novel of circus life that contains sordid but not unrealistic detail about the human struggles unseen by the spectators; and *The Circle Home* is a novel full of information about the training of boxers and life among the destitute. In his third but not best novel, *The Peacock's Tail*, he still shows an interest in the lower classes, for the protagonist is a young white man who gradually loses cultural and racial prejudice as he works among the urban poor.

Throughout his works there is a uniformity of prose style. He is fond of an unembellished, staccato prose that at times is reminiscent of Hemingway, yet because his narrators and protagonists are usually lower-class men, relatively uneducated and inarticulate, the direct, colloquial, often simple, prose is not inappropriate. In its direct, deflationary tone, the beginning of his short story, "The Final Fate of the Alligators," is a succinct introduction to most of his main characters: "In such a crowded, busy world the service each man performs is necessarily a small one. Arnie Bush's was no exception." Yet the lack of subtle, intellectual prose does not mean that the author offers no insights. A description of leopards in motion ends, for example, with a deft comment: "Really, leopards are like machines. They move in a sort of perpetual motion. Their faces don't change; they eat the same way, sleep the same way, pace much the same as each other. Their bodies are constructed as ideally as a fish's for moving and doing, for action, and not much room is left for personality." Regrettably, the final cause may aptly be applied to his characters, for many of them are so busy learning survival techniques in an uncaring world that their personalities are never fully developed. We may believe in them, but we are not always interested in them. The lack of interest sometimes results from the brevity of a character's role or the analysis devoted to it. Thus when characters fall back into self-destructive habits such as self-pity or alcoholism, we feel little sympathy. We impatiently dismiss them as born losers.

An accurate and just sense of Hoagland's strengths and weaknesses in prose style, narrative technique, characterization, and thought may be obtained from *The Circle Home*, the story of Denny Kelly, an irresponsible 29-year-old who has failed and continues to fail as a prize fighter and husband. In prose direct and at times colourful, the author demonstrates a close knowledge of the world of third-rate boxers:

> A lively fight: One-hand found occasion to manoeuver into every foot the ring provided. He'd be close, mining in the belly, and spring back with a lithe light antelope-type movement. Often when his left returned from thrusts his arms dropped by his sides to balance him. Those leaps, narrow body straight upright and turning in the air to face the way he wanted, were the essence of his style....

The author seems intent, not upon muckraking, but upon having readers understand the world of boxers and boxing. The reader comes to know Denny through the straight chronological flow of his attempted comeback, and through a series of flashbacks that chronicle his irresponsible and immature behaviour as a husband and father. In re-creating the flow of events Hoagland shows a keen ear for dialogue. The ending of the novel, however, is weak: Denny, contrite yet once more, phones to inform his wife that he is determined (because of *his* miseries) to return and to be henceforth a good family man. The title, *The Circle Home*, suggests that at last he will be truly home, but because he has failed so often before and has shown no true deep reformation, the reader may prophesy further backsliding. If we are meant to view Denny's future optimistically, the author's compassion for the dwellers in the "lower depths" has led him to a sentimental conclusion.

From his works as a whole, Hoagland appears as a careful writer who, steeped in firsthand knowledge of his material, attempts with some humour and considerable compassion to show us men and women struggling first to survive and then to improve themselves or the world. Because life embraces much that is sordid, he utilizes it in his works; but he is neither a muckraker nor a sensationalist.

—James A. Hart

HOBSON, Laura Z(ametkin). American. Born in New York City, 18 June 1900. Educated at Cornell University, Ithaca, New York, B.A. 1921. Married Thayer Hobson in 1930 (divorced, 1935); two children. Worked as an advertising copywriter until 1934, except for one year as a reporter for the *New York Post*; Promotion Writer, later Copy Chief of all magazine promotion, Time Inc., then Director of Promotion for *Time* magazine, New York, 1934-40. Since 1941, full-time writer: Columnist ("Trade Winds"), *Saturday Review of Literature*, 1952-56, and for International News Service, 1953-54, and *Good Housekeeping*, 1953-56; consultant, Time Inc.,

1956-62; since 1960, consultant, as puzzle editor, *Saturday Review*. Member of the National Council, Authors League of America P.E.N., 1947-75. Address: c/o Harper and Row, 10 East 53rd Street, New York, New York 10022, U.S.A.

PUBLICATIONS

Novels

The Trespassers. New York, Simon and Schuster, 1943; London, Gollancz, 1944.
Gentleman's Agreement. New York, Simon and Schuster, 1947; London, Cassell, 1948.
The Other Father. New York, Simon and Schuster, and London, Cassell, 1950.
The Celebrity. New York, Simon and Schuster, 1951; London, Cresset Press, 1953.
First Papers. New York, Random House, 1964; London, Heinemann, 1965.
The Tenth Month. New York, Simon and Schuster, and London, Heinemann, 1971.
Consenting Adult. New York, Doubleday, and London, Heinemann, 1975.
Over and Above. New York, Doubleday, 1979.

Other

A Dog of His Own (juvenile). New York, Viking Press, and London, Hamish Hamilton, 1941.
"I'm Going to Have a Baby" (juvenile). New York, Day, and London, Heinemann, 1967.

*

Manuscript Collection: Columbia University, New York.

* * *

Laura Z. Hobson is best known for her competent thesis fiction on current social problems. Her most singular success was her 1947 bestseller, *Gentleman's Agreement*. The film version received the Academy Award for best picture of the year.

Gentleman's Agreement details the experiences of a New York journalist who pretends to be Jewish for several months in order to gain inside information for a series on anti-semitism for his magazine. Hobson's target in this novel is not the professional bigot, but those well-meaning people who acquiesce in prejudice not realizing how deeply it exists in daily life. Her protagonist finds anti-semitism in the employment practices of his own liberal magazine and in his fiancée, who had suggested the series to him. Although the novel was criticized for its cardboard characters and contrived plot, most critics agreed that it performed a needed service in alerting readers to the existence of widespread prejudice in American life.

Hobson has frequently been ahead of the public debate in her choice of unpopular and emotional issues. Her first novel, published during World War II, is a well-documented indictment of the United States' failure to help European refugees before the war. *The Tenth Month* is about a 40-year-old unwed mother who wants to keep her baby. *Consenting Adult* details the internal struggle of a mother whose son admits he is a homosexual. Always, Hobson takes a liberal view of the issue, researches it well, and dramatizes it in a form accessible to readers of light fiction. Many reviewers have criticized Hobson's writing style and her didacticism, but most have approved of her commitments and ideals; and many have praised her for daring fictional treatment of subjects other authors prefer to ignore.

—Kay J. Mussell

HOLMES, John Clellon. American. Born in Holyoke, Massachusetts, 12 March 1926. Educated at Columbia University, New York, 1943, 1945-46; New School for Social Research, New York, 1949-50. Served in the Hospital Corps of the United States Navy, 1944-45. Married Shirley Allen in 1953. Lecturer, Yale University, New Haven, Connecticut, 1959; Visiting Lecturer, Writers Workshop, University of Iowa, Iowa City, 1963-64; Writer-in-Residence, University of Arkansas, Fayetteville, 1966; Visiting Professor, Bowling Green State University, Ohio, 1968, and Brown University, Providence, Rhode Island, 1971-72. Since 1977, Professor of English, University of Arkansas. Member of the Executive Board, Associated Writing Programs of America. Recipient: *Playboy* award, for non-fiction, 1964, 1970, 1971, 1972, 1973; Guggenheim Fellowship, 1976; Alexander Capon Prize (*New Letters*, Kansas City), 1978. Address: Box 75, Old Saybrook, Connecticut 06475, U.S.A.

PUBLICATIONS

Novels

Go. New York, Scribner, 1952; as *The Beat Boys*, London, Ace, 1959.
The Horn. New York, Random House, 1958; London, Deutsch, 1959.
Get Home Free. New York, Dutton, 1964; London, Corgi, 1966.

Uncollected Short Stories

"Tea for Two," in *Neurotica* (St. Louis), Spring 1948.
"A Length of Chain," in *Nugget* (New York), August 1960.
"The Next to the Last Time," in *Escapade* (New York), September 1967.
"The Manifest Destiny of Mrs. Polk's Sudie," in *Penthouse* (New York), February 1977.
"Night-Blooming Cereus," in *Black Warrior Review* (Birmingham, Alabama), Spring 1978.

Verse

The Bowling Green Poems. California, Pennsylvania, Unspeakable Visions, 1977.
Death Drag: Selected Poems 1948-1979. Pocatello, Idaho, Limberlost Press, 1979.

Other

Nothing More to Declare. New York, Dutton, 1967; London, Deutsch, 1968.
Visitor: Jack Kerouac in Old Saybrook. California, Pennsylvania, Unspeakable Visions, 1981.

*

Bibliography: *An Annotated Bibliography of the Works of John Clellon Holmes* by Richard Ardinger, Pocatello, University of Idaho Press, 1979.

Manuscript Collection: Boston University Library.

Critical Studies: *Radical Innocence* by Ihab Hassan, Princeton, New Jersey, Princeton University Press, 1961; *The Erotic Revolution* by Lawrence Lipton, Los Angeles, Sherbourne Press, 1965; *Voices from the Love Generation* by Leonard Wolf, Boston, Little Brown, 1968; *Naked Angels* by John Tytell, New York, McGraw Hill, 1976; interview with Tim Hunt, in *Quarterly West* (Salt Lake City), 1978; *Jack's Book* by Barry Gifford, New York, St. Martin's Press, 1979.

John Clellon Holmes comments:

I take as my working-rule D.H. Lawrence's statement: "Man is a great venture in consciousness." To me, this venture into new areas of awareness is the underlying theme of most important 20th-century work.

The rebel, the outcast, the artist, the young—all those whose extremes of consciousness match their extremes of experience—are my subjects. The single recurring theme of my work so far has been a concern with the origins and effects of contemporary uprootedness—particularly its psychological and spiritual aspects. The search for new continuities to replace those of the family, religious faith, and social idealism—continuities in comradeship, passional love, and artistic creation—occurs again and again in my work.

As a novelist, I find myself wedded to the idea that the building of living characters is the first essential for enduring fiction, and so I tend to work outward, from character toward events, instead of vice versa. The power of the novel to illuminate our lives lies precisely in its ability to convince us that others live as intensely as ourselves.

* * *

John Clellon Holmes writes novels that one would find easy to praise extravagantly if they were written by a friend. He is an alert and intelligent observer of the public and private life about him. His prose is precise, his images clearly etched and accurate in detail, his novels carefully structured. Whenever he sits down to write he has a subject squarely in front of him, and for the most part he gives every evidence of knowing precisely what he wants to do with it. Yet his novels are good primarily in the sense that they are pedestrian, workmanlike, and completely serious. He has not yet broken throught to the BIG novel he might one day write.

Much of his later performance is an extension of what was begun in his first novel, *Go*, where he recorded the life style of his friends in the late 1940's in New York, and because two of those friends were Jack Kerouac and Allen Ginsberg (fictionalized as Gene Pasternak and David Stofsky) the novel has acquired an interest for literary historians that it did not have on its initial appearance. Firmly entrenched as a chronicler of his times after the appearance of *Go* and the fine essay "This Is the Beat Generation," he turned to the world of jazz—told from the perspective if its Negro performers—in *The Horn*. Again the interest is not solely novelistic; the reader's affection for such musicians as Lester Young and Billie Holiday adds a dimension not generally present in the fictional characters who serve as their surrogates. Only in *Get Home Free*, where the life of Holmes himself seems more central than it does in the earlier novels, does he begin to create characters who are asked to exist firmly on their own, without the support of the reader's outside knowledge and interest. (This last statement must be qualified by the recognition that when Holmes began *Go* he could not have known of the fame later to be attained by Kerouac and Ginsberg and when he got into the last hundred pages of *The Horn* he did much to lift his horn player out of the world of fact and into the world of fictional reality.)

One thinks in terms of a BIG novel for Holmes primarily because he has tried to force bigness upon each one that he has thus far written. In *Go* he spread the action north to Connecticut and south to Louisiana in search of a geographic definition for the rootlessness of Americans making it in Manhattan. An old-fashioned novelist in some ways, he displays an old-fashioned desire to write the Great American Novel. One of his most annoying traits is his habit of assigning SIGNIFICANCE to the actions of his characters, so that it comes as a relief when an individual scatches his nose without the author informing us that the action is a peculiarly American one, with Freudian overtones, dating from Cotton Mather's investigations of the psychology of the invisible world. His structure, too, can be burdensome, as it is in *The Horn*, where he selects an American literary figure to associate, for reasons not usually clear, with each of his characters.

In *Nothing More to Declare* he informs us that he has less desire now than he once had to classify, to generalize. Whether that also means that he has less urge to write novels is not clear; perhaps it means that if he does write them he will allow the meanings to grow from within rather than imposing them from without. If he does that he may yet write a better book than those he has given us to date.

—George Perkins

HOOD, Hugh (John Blagdon). Canadian. Born in Toronto, Ontario, 30 April 1928. Educated at the University of Toronto, 1947-55, B.A. 1950, M.A. 1952, Ph.D. 1955. Married Ruth Noreen Mallory in 1957; four children. Teaching Fellow, University of Toronto, 1951-55; Associate Professor, St. Joseph College, West Hartford, Connecticut, 1955-61. Since 1961, Professeur titulaire, University of Montreal. Recipient: President's Medal, University of Western Ontario, 1961, 1967; Beta Sigma Phi Sorority Prize, 1965; Canada Council Senior Arts Fellowship, 1971, 1974, and grant, 1977. Address: 4242 Hampton Avenue, Montreal, Quebec H4A 2K9, Canada.

PUBLICATIONS

Novels

White Figure, White Ground. Toronto, Ryerson Press, and New York, Dutton, 1964.
The Camera Always Lies. Toronto, Longman, and New York, Harcourt Brace, 1967.
A Game of Touch. Toronto, Longman, 1970.
You Can't Get There from Here. Ottawa, Oberon Press, 1972.
The Swing in the Garden. Ottawa, Oberon Press, 1973.
A New Athens. Ottawa, Oberon Press, 1977.
Reservoir Ravine. Ottawa, Oberon Press, 1979.

Short Stories

Flying a Red Kite. Toronto, Ryerson Press, 1962.
Around the Mountain: Scenes from Montreal Life. Toronto, Peter Martin, 1967.
The Fruit Man, The Meat Man, and The Manager. Ottawa, Oberon Press, 1971.
Dark Glasses. Ottawa, Oberon Press, 1976.
Selected Stories. Ottawa, Oberon Press, 1978.
None Genuine Without This Signature. Toronto, ECW Press, 1980.

Other

Strength Down Centre: The Jean Beliveau Story. Toronto, Prentice Hall, 1970.
The Governor's Bridge Is Closed: Twelve Essays on the Canadian Scene. Ottawa, Oberon Press, 1973.
Scoring: The Art of Hockey, with Seymour Segal. Ottawa, Oberon Press, 1979.

*

Critical Studies: "Line and Form" by Dave Godfrey, in *Tamarack Review* (Toronto), Spring 1965; "Grace: The Novels of Hugh Hood" by Dennis Duffy, in *Canadian Literature* (Vancouver), February 1971; *Before the Flood* edited by J.R. Struthers, Toronto, ECW Press 1979 (includes bibliography).

Hugh Hood comments:

(1972) An interviewer recently asked me why all my fiction began with an appearance of realism and then almost always merged into a dream or reverie or fantasy. I thought that this was a very astute question, because this is exactly how I design my work. I consider it as both realist and super-realist, somewhat like the movies of Fellini or the paintings of Stanley Spencer or Alex Colville—where a pertinacious imitation of the appearance of social reality turns without much warning into a very curious and private vision. I couldn't answer the interviewer's question "why?" I just know that this is how I do it. I might add that I do not think that the Romantic Movement failed, nor do I think that it is over. It seems to me that I, at least, am still in the middle of it.

* * *

Hugh Hood is a writer in whom pedantry wars with creative gifts of a high order. His best work so far occurs in his short stories which demonstrate his mastery at revealing what is immense through what is small. He is an indefatigable explorer of human aspiration, conveying much of its mystery, heroism, and comedy. An impassioned drive towards some symbolic victory is celebrated seriously or gaily in such stories as "Silver Bugles, Cymbals, Golden Silks" (*Flying a Red Kite*), "The Pitcher" (*Dark Glasses*), and "Le Grand Déménagement" (*Around the Mountain*). His art is at its finest in "Looking Down from Above" (*Around the Mountain*), where separate characters connect in a visionary moment of great beauty, crowded like a medieval tapestry with life: "inscrutable but undeniable."

Hood's earlier novels have something of this imaginative intensity, as in the burning warehouse scene (*A Game of Touch*), an incident pivotal to the hero's fate and a keystone in the novel's structure. However, Hood is unable to control the tone of his prose over the long course of a novel. When the painter in *White Figure, White Ground* retreats to the safety of his old manner and family life, Hood's point of view is unclear. Although the hard urbanity and narrow sympathies of the wife offend, it is uncertain whether the artist's glorification of her is to be received with irony or approval. In *The Camera Always Lies*, a romance, Hood's continuing problem with creating likeable characters re-emerges. A romance requires archetypal figures on whom fantasies can be projected: yet "virtuous" Rose Leclair, suffering through near-death and rebirth, is a bore, the hero who saves her an overbearing prig. Precise detail of film financing, production, and costume design merely throws into relief Hood's difficulty with his characters. *You Can't Get There from Here*, set in an imaginary African nation, is both a study of struggle in a new society and "Christological [except]...that the Christ figure does not rise again...." Because he is writing satire and allegory, Hood must be excused for missing opportunities of further defining the two tribes, and of describing the personal history of his sketchy hero; but his Cabinet villains need sharper outlines to succeed either as allegory or satire.

When Hood attempts in *The New Age*, a serial novel in twelve volumes of which three have been completed, to work on the scale of "Coleridge, Joyce, Tolstoy, and Proust," his inadequacies become obvious. He is striving for "a very wide range of reference without apparent connection on the surface which nonetheless will yield connections and networks and links and unities if you wait and allow them to appear." Moving back and forth through time, the huge project includes passages of philosophy, social history, topography, and lectures on a broad variety of topics, as well as the fictionalized incidents of his own life.

As a simultaneous "realist and transcendental allegorist" (his admitted aim), Hood falls short in these novels, for although characters and events have a formal importance, they rarely achieve emotive significance. The marriage in *A New Athens*, for instance, is never felt as the redemptive force intended, because Edie is no more than a shadow, and Matt Goderich remains, as one character observes, "a pompous ass." Too often Hood offers neither psychological nor pictorial realism, but the factuality of an encyclopaedia or a catalogue. Obsessive lists of, for example, baseball players (*The Swing in the Garden*) suggest an inability to select. Local history and neighbourhood cartography too often supply the substance rather than the raw material of these fictions. Pedantic tenacity in description cannot of itself invest places or objects with meaning, nor is Hood's style sufficiently adept, usually, to produce this result by its own power. He even slips into bathos with the showpiece engagement scenes in *A New Athens* and *Reservoir Ravine*. His uninspired prose has created a bland, provincial world where values do not develop organically, but are imposed from without. Only when he writes of marvels does the reader's interest freshen, as with the appearance of the visionary painter (*A New Athens*). Striving to write a masterpiece, Hood is so concerned with large patterns and themes that he fails to breathe life into the material of which these patterns are composed. Heterogeneity can succeed only for the writer gifted enough to consume disparate material in the unifying fire of his art; but, with nine novels still to come, Hood may yet produce work on a level comparable to that of the short stories.

—Margaret Keith

HORGAN, Paul. American. Born in Buffalo, New York, 1 August 1903. Educated at Nardin Academy, Buffalo; Albuquerque public schools; New Mexico Military Institute, Roswell, 1920-23. Served in the United States Army as Chief of the Army Information Branch, 1942-46: Lieutenant Colonel; Legion of Merit; recalled to active duty, 1952. Member of the Production Staff, Eastman Theatre, Rochester, New York, 1923-26; Librarian, 1926-42, and Assistant to the President, 1947-49, New Mexico Military Institute (the Institute library is named for him); Lecturer, University of Iowa, Iowa City, 1946. Senior Fellow, 1959-61, and Director, 1962-67, Center for Advanced Studies, and Adjunct Professor of English and Author-in-Residence, 1967-71, and since 1971, Professor Emeritus and permanent Author-in-Residence, Wesleyan University, Middletown, Connecticut. Hoyt Fellow, 1965, and since 1967, Associate Fellow, Saybrook College, Yale University, New Haven, Connecticut. President, Roswell Museum, 1946-52; Member of the Board, Roswell Public Library, 1958-62; Chairman of the Board, Santa Fe Opera, New Mexico, 1958-62. President, American Catholic Historical Association, 1960. Member, National Council on the Humanities, 1966-71. Scholar-in-Residence, 1968, 1970, 1972, 1973, and since 1974, Fellow, Aspen Institute, Colorado. Member of the Editorial Board, 1969-72, and since 1972, Associate, Book of the Month Club, New York. Recipient: Harper Prize Novel Award, 1933; Guggenheim Fellowship, 1945, 1958; Pulitzer Prize, for history, 1955, 1976; Bancroft Prize, for history, 1955; Catholic Book Club Campion Award, 1957; Catholic Book Award, 1965, 1969; Christopher Award, 1976; Western Writers of America Award, for non-fiction, 1976. D.Litt.: Wesleyan University, 1956; Southern Methodist University, Dallas, 1957; University of Notre Dame, Indiana, 1958; Boston College, 1958; New Mexico State University, Las Cruces, 1961; College of the Holy Cross, Worcester, Massachusetts, 1962; University of New Mexico, Albuquerque, 1963; Fairfield University, Connecticut, 1964; D'Youville College, Buffalo, New York, 1965; Pace College, New York, 1968; Loyola College, Baltimore, 1968; Lincoln College, Illinois, 1969; St. Bonaventure University, New York, 1969; La Salle College, Philadelphia, 1971; Yale University, 1978; D.H.L.: Canisius College, Buffalo, 1960; Georgetown University, Washington, D.C., 1963. Knight of St. Gregory, 1957. Address: 77 Pearl Street, Middletown, Connecticut 06457, U.S.A.

PUBLICATIONS

Novels

The Fault of Angels. New York, Harper, 1933; London, Hamish Hamilton, 1934.

No Quarter Given. New York, Harper, and London, Constable, 1935.
Mountain Standard Time (trilogy). New York, Farrar Straus, and London, Macmillan, 1962.
Main Line West. New York, Harper, and London, Constable, 1936.
Far from Cibola. New York, Harper, and London, Constable, 1938.
The Common Heart. New York, Harper, 1942.
A Lamp on the Plains. New York, Harper, and London, Constable, 1937.
The Devil in the Desert: A Legend of Life and Death in the Rio Grande. New York, Longman, 1952.
The Saintmaker's Christmas Eve. New York, Farrar Straus, 1955; London, Macmillan, 1956.
Give Me Possession. New York, Farrar Straus, 1957; London, Macmillan, 1958.
A Distant Trumpet. New York, Farrar Straus, and London, Macmillan, 1960.
Things as They Are. New York, Farrar Straus, 1964; London, Bodley Head, 1965.
Everything to Live For. New York, Farrar Straus, 1968; London, Bodley Head, 1969.
Whitewater. New York, Farrar Straus, 1970; London, Bodley Head, 1971.
The Thin Mountain Air. New York, Farrar Straus, 1977; London, Bodley Head, 1978.

Short Stories

The Return of the Weed. New York, Harper, 1936; as *Lingering Walls*, London, Constable, 1936.
Figures in a Landscape. New York, Harper, 1940.
One Red Rose for Christmas. New York, Longman, 1952.
Humble Powers: 3 Novelettes. London, Macmillan, 1954; New York, Doubleday, 1956.
The Peach Stone: Stories from Four Decades. New York, Farrar Straus, 1967; London, Bodley Head, 1968.

Plays

A Tree on the Plains: A Music Play for Americans, music by Ernst Bacon (produced Spartanburg, South Carolina). Published in *Southwest Review* (Dallas), Summer 1943.
Yours, A. Lincoln (produced New York, 1942).

Verse

Lamb of God. Privately printed, 1927.
Songs after Lincoln. New York, Farrar Straus, 1965.

Other

Men of Arms (juvenile). Philadelphia, McKay, 1931.
From the Royal City of the Holy Faith of Saint Francis of Assisi, Being Five Accounts of Life in That Place. Santa Fe, Villagra Bookshop, 1936.
The Habit of Empire. Santa Fe, Rydal Press, and New York, Harper, 1938.
Look at America: The Southwest, with the editors of Look. Boston, Houghton Mifflin, 1947.
Great River: The Rio Grande in North American History. New York, Rinehart, 2 vols., 1954.
The Centuries of Santa Fe. New York, Dutton, 1956; London, Macmillan, 1957.
Rome Eternal. New York, Farrar Straus, 1957.
One of the Quietest Things (address). Los Angeles, University of California School of Library Service, 1960.
Citizen of New Salem. New York, Farrar Straus, 1961; as *Abraham Lincoln: Citizen of New Salem*, London, Macmillan, 1961.
Toby and the Nighttime (juvenile). New York, Farrar Straus, and London, Macmillan, 1963.
Conquistadors in North American History. New York, Farrar Straus, 1963; as *Conquistadors in North America*, London, Macmillan, 1963.
Peter Hurd: A Portrait Sketch from Life. Austin, University of Texas Press, 1965.
Memories of the Future. New York, Farrar Straus, and London, Bodley Head, 1966.
The Heroic Triad: Essays in the Social Energies of Three Southwestern Cultures. New York, Holt Rinehart, 1970; London, Heinemann, 1971.
Encounters with Stravinsky: A Personal Record. New York, Farrar Straus, and London, Bodley Head, 1972.
Approaches to Writing. New York, Farrar Straus, 1973; London, Bodley Head, 1974.
Lamy of Santa Fé: His Life and Times. New York, Farrar Straus, 1975; London, Faber, 1977.
Josiah Gregg and His Vision of the Early West. New York, Farrar Straus, 1979.

Editor, with M.G. Fulton, *New Mexico's Own Chronicle: Three Races in the Writings of Four Hundred Years.* Dallas, Upshaw, 1937.
Editor, *Maurice Baring Restored: Selections from His Work.* New York, Farrar Straus, and London, Heinemann, 1970.

*

Manuscript Collection: Yale University, New Haven, Connecticut.

Paul Horgan comments:

In my fiction I hope to enclose in a precisely appropriate and thus beautiful form a story which rises from the interaction of characters brought alive through understanding of human life, in settings which are evocative in atmosphere, set forth in language interesting for its own sake as well as for its suitability to the subject matter.

In my non-fiction—history, biography, other forms—I hope to tell the truth of actual events while retelling them in such a manner that the resources of the novelist in presenting scene and character allow the reader a sense of experiencing the past rather than simply hearing about it.

* * *

One literary legend has it that as an orphan Paul Horgan was standing on a Buffalo, New York, street corner singing to passersbys; by chance, and attracted by the quality of the song, a wealthy gentleman befriended the waif and among other things later sponsored professional vocal training at a conservatory. Precisely true or not, this legend gives certain insights into Horgan's life and work.

The Horatio Alger implication of Horgan's career is manifest in steady production and wide variety: novels, short stories, plays; opera, biography, cultural reportage, national, regional, and church history. Among other things, he is an acknowledged national authority on Lincoln, Beethoven, the conquistadors, the cultures and history of the Great Southwest in America, most notably the regions of the Rio Grande River. Horgan brings to all his work an artistic integrity of a very high order. The style is supple and clean; the attitude towards all materials is broadly humanistic. The history and the cultural reportage are remarkable for the visual quality, scrupulous attention to detail, and the exploitation of symbolic incident or encounter. Horgan's talent is fully dramatic in nature; his responses to materials is symphonic in scale. Industry for its own sake, however, is not implied for the author's concept of work is of an order which in fact tends to enrich the writer's life. Thus Horgan's well-known gift for friendship is another facet of a productive, well-integrated personality of great warmth and charm. These things are even more remarkable when it is understood that Horgan taught himself to write while serving as a librarian in a boy's school in the Southwest; only after a long literary apprenticeship of frustration and isolation was his talent recognized when he won a major American literary prize for his novel *The Fault of Angels*.

Paul Horgan is a deeply committed Catholic and is America's foremost writer of that conviction at the present time. This fact has several literary implications. Although *Rome Eternal* may suggest a thoroughly Catholic point of view, Horgan is much too deeply committed as an artist to become merely a "spokesman" for the Church. Doubtless he would concur with the suggestion that he is an artist who happens to be a Catholic; yet, presumably, he would not seriously imagine writing to greater advantage from any other viewpoint. Actually the weight of his very personal kind of commitment varies a great deal. When handling church-connected subject matter he treats the theme sympathetically, urbanely, and with great delicacy; when writing on materials less specifically Catholic he displays a characteristic optimism, a charity, a softening of certain reoccurring realities of life. In turn this softening of the hard edge of reality is not so much sentiment as it is an awareness of spiritual forces in the world which may be registered as ultimately harmonious. Whether or not these fundamentally optimistic attitudes are to be equated with either the more fortuitous aspects of his own life and/or his spiritual training is a question too complex for brief analysis.

Ultimately, Horgan's literary significance will rest less with a commitment to Catholicism and much more with his stature as a regional writer. America's literature is a regional literature, and Horgan already is the Master of the Great Southwest. In comparison with Faulkner (of the same literary generation) Horgan's clarity, objectivity, and consistency are the greater; on the other hand, Horgan is the less experimental and is less inclined to focus on the more pervasive, sordid aspects of modernity. Unlike Faulkner, Horgan probably makes more concessions to the genteel audience, the literary passersby of America. In any event, the comparison as regionalists of the two talents reflects no discredit on either artist.

Horgan continues to be vital and productive. His life itself is a meaningful, artistic statement of what a gifted writer in America may accomplish even though the odds were great beyond calculation.

—James B. Hall

HOUSEHOLD, Geoffrey (Edward West). British. Born in Bristol, 30 November 1900. Educated at Clifton College, Bristol, 1914-19; Magdelen College, Oxford, 1919-22, B.A. (honours) in English 1922. Served in the Intelligence Corps, 1939-45: Lieutenant Colonel; Territorial Decoration; mentioned in despatches. Married Ilona M.J. Zsoldos-Gutmán in 1942; one son and two daughters. Engaged in commerce abroad, 1922-35. Address: Church Headland, Whitchurch, Aylesbury, Buckinghamshire, England.

PUBLICATIONS

Novels

The Third Hour. London, Chatto and Windus, 1937; Boston, Little Brown, 1938.
Rogue Male. London, Chatto and Windus, and Boston, Little Brown, 1939; as *Man Hunt*, New York, Triangle, 1942.
Arabesque. London, Chatto and Windus, and Boston, Little Brown, 1948.
The High Place. London, Joseph, and Boston, Little Brown, 1950.
A Rough Shoot. London, Joseph, and Boston, Little Brown, 1951.
A Time to Kill. Boston, Little Brown, 1951; London, Joseph 1952.
Fellow Passenger. London, Joseph, and Boston, Little Brown 1955; as *Hang the Man High*, New York, Spivak, 1957.
Watcher in the Shadows. London, Joseph, and Boston, Little Brown, 1960.
Thing to Love. London, Joseph, and Boston, Little Brown, 1963.
Olura. London, Joseph, and Boston, Little Brown, 1965.
The Courtesy of Death. London, Joseph, and Boston, Little Brown, 1967.
Dance of the Dwarfs. London, Joseph, and Boston, Little Brown, 1968.
Doom's Caravan. London, Joseph, and Boston, Little Brown, 1971.
The Three Sentinels. London, Joseph, and Boston, Little Brown, 1972.
The Lives and Times of Bernardo Brown. London, Joseph, 1973; Boston, Little Brown, 1974.
Red Anger. London, Joseph, and Boston, Little Brown, 1975.
Hostage—London: The Diary of Julian Despard. London, Joseph, and Boston, Little Brown, 1977.
The Last Two Weeks of Georges Rivac. London, Joseph, and Boston, Little Brown, 1978.
The Sending. London, Joseph, and Boston, Little Brown, 1980.
Summon the Bright Water. London, Joseph, 1981.

Short Stories

The Salvation of Pisco Gabar and Other Stories. London, Chatto and Windus, 1938; augmented edition, Boston, Little Brown, 1940.
Tales of Adventurers. London, Joseph, and Boston, Little Brown, 1952.
The Brides of Solomon and Other Stories. London, Joseph, and Boston, Little Brown, 1958.
Sabres on the Sand and Other Stories. London, Joseph, and Boston, Little Brown, 1966.
The Cats to Come. London, Joseph, 1975.
The Europe That Was. Newton Abbot, Devon, David and Charles, and New York, St. Martin's Press, 1979.
Capricorn and Cancer. London, Joseph, 1981.

Other

The Terror of Villadonga (juvenile). London, Hutchinson, 1936; revised edition, as *The Spanish Cave*, Boston, Little Brown, 1936; London, Chatto and Windus, 1940.
The Exploits of Xenophon (juvenile). New York, Random House, 1955; as *Xenophon's Adventure*, London, Bodley Head, 1961.
Against the Wind (autobiography). London, Joseph, 1958; Boston, Little Brown, 1959.
Prisoner of the Indies (juvenile). London, Bodley Head, and Boston, Little Brown, 1967.
Escape into Daylight (juvenile). London, Bodley Head, and Boston, Little Brown, 1976.

*

Manuscript Collection: Lilly Library, Indiana University, Bloomington.

Critical Studies: "The Governance of Geoffrey Household" by L.E. Sissman, in *New Yorker*, 1 May 1971; "The Lives and Times of Geoffrey Household" by Michael Barber, in *Books and Bookmen* (London), January 1974.

Geoffrey Household comments:

My first concern is with the English I write, simple, evocative, and therefore enabling me to produce the required impact on the reader without any obscurity. I cannot estimate its literary worth, but I suggest that if there is any permanent value in my work it is to be found in my short stories.

My novels are all suspense novels and deal with the individual trapped in an unwelcome or thoroughly dangerous environment. Only one is a "spy" story and none is a "crime" story. I am told that they seem to be written on two levels—which may mean that in order to create the illusion of reality I have to examine the political, ethical, or religious motives of the characters.

By and large the books fall into two classes. *The Third Hour, Arabesque, The High Place, Thing to Love*, and *The Three Sentinels* are fairly straight novels, though certainly depending on action and the development of plot. The rest are unashamed "thrillers" with the possible exception of *Olura, Dance of the Dwarfs*, and *Doom's Caravan*, which are less conventional in form or subject or both and may be defined as the reader likes.

Pedigree: a good, working strain directly descended from Defoe, with a dash of thoroughbred blood from Stevenson and Conrad.

* * *

Geoffrey Household came slowly to prominence as a novelist by way of banking, business, and war-time Intelligence Service. His first notable success, *Rogue Male*, was published in 1939. He had already placed a number of short stories in the upper reaches of the magazine market, written radio plays for children, and published one novel and a collection of his stories. With *Rogue Male* his career as a professional author was finally consolidated though the war years were to interrupt his output.

He specialises in what used to be called "thrillers" or "suspense stories"—action stories with a strong narrative line, unexpected turns and checks of plot, and on the whole rather slight attention to the portrayal and development of character. Probably the best-known of his books in this genre, after *Rogue Male*, are *A Rough Shoot, Watcher in the Shadows*, and *Sabres on the Sand*. This is John Buchan-Richard Hannay territory, complete with officers and gentlemen, foreign agents and manhunts, sketchily realised and subordinate female characters, tweeds, shot-guns and sporting rifles whose telescopic sights are suddenly put to use on more sinister targets than red deer.

It is easy to register a sneer at some aspects of Buchan's Hannay novels today—the blatant snobbery, the imperialist ethno-centrism, the toadying to the pre-war "establishment" and monarchy; but one can never fault Buchan's sure-footed narrative pace. It is a tribute to Geoffrey Household's excellence that his Buchanesque novels stand comparison with his master's in this last respect and do very much better in the others.

The main themes he explores are courage and endurance on the extreme edge of danger and at the limits of human survival, the discharge of obligation and duty, loyalty, and personal honour. The best of his man-hunts take place in the English West Country, about which he writes with affection and the kind of knowledge which comes only to those who stalk wild life with field-glasses and camera or gun. The rogue male's survival in his hideout in a thicket-choked lane; the hunt through the Cotswolds by the shadowy watcher; the hero's frenzied tunnelings in the Mendips in *The Courtesy of Death* (a novel whose donnée of a cult dedicated to killing is less credible than the author's usual contrivances); and the dirty work in the hedgerows and rabbit-warrens of *A Rough Shoot*, are stamped with authenticity.

There is a change of milieu to South America in *Thing to Love*, which portrays the conflict between technologically based progress and a romantic attachment to the traditional way of life, but continues to examine the theme of divided loyalty and an officer's personal honour.

Geoffrey Household has also published children's books. *Xenophon's Adventure*, his retelling of the *Anabasis*, maintains a characteristically swift pace; while *Prisoner of the Indies*, also based on a factual account, tells the story of a cabin-boy on a slave-ship who is captured by the Spaniards, tortured by the Inquisition, and consigned to a monastery before finally escaping.

—Stewart F. Sanderson

HOWARD, Elizabeth Jane. British. Born in London, 26 March 1923. Educated privately; trained as an actress at the London Mask Theatre School and with the Scott Thorndyke Student Repertory; played at Stratford-upon-Avon, and in repertory theatre in Devon. Served as an Air Raid Warden in London during World War II. Married 1) Peter M. Scott in 1941, one daughter; 2) James Douglas-Henry in 1959; 3) Kingsley Amis, *q.v.*, in 1965. Worked as a model, and in radio and television broadcasting, 1939-46; Secretary, Inland Waterways Association, London, 1947-50; Editor, Chatto and Windus Ltd., London, 1953-56, and Weidenfeld and Nicolson Ltd., London, 1957; Book Critic, *Queen* magazine, London, 1957-60. Honorary Artistic Director, Cheltenham Literary Festival, 1962. Recipient: Rhys Memorial Prize, 1951. Address: Gardnor House, Flask Walk, London N.W.3, England.

PUBLICATIONS

Novels

The Beautiful Visit. London, Cape, and New York, Random House, 1950.
The Long View. London, Cape, and New York, Reynal, 1956.
The Sea Change. London, Cape, 1959; New York, Harper, 1960.
After Julius. London, Cape, 1965; New York, Viking Press, 1966.
Something in Disguise. London, Cape, 1969; New York, Viking Press, 1970.
Odd Girl Out. London, Cape, and New York, Viking Press, 1972.

Short Stories

We Are for the Dark: Six Ghost Stories, with Robert Aickman. London, Cape, 1951.
Mr. Wrong. London, Cape, 1975; New York, Viking Press, 1976.

Plays

Screenplay: *The Very Edge*, 1963.

Radio Plays: *Make Thee an Ark*, 1969; *Wife Swapping 7-10:30 P.M.*, 1970.

Television Plays: *The Glorious Dead* (*Upstairs, Downstairs* series), 1974; *Skittles* (*Victorian Scandals* series), 1976; *Sight Unseen* (*She* series), 1977; *After Julius*, from her own novel, 1979; *Something in Disguise*, 1980.

Other

Bettina: A Portrait, with Arthur Helps. London, Chatto and Windus, and New York, Reynal, 1957.

Editor, *The Lover's Companion: The Pleasure, Joys, and Anguish of Love*. Newton Abbot, Devon, David and Charles, 1978.

*

Elizabeth Jane Howard comments:

I consider myself to be in the straight tradition of English novelists. I do not write about "social issues or values"—I write simply about people, by themselves and in relation to one another. The first aim of a novel should be readability. I do not write (consciously, at least) about people whom I know or have met.

My methods are to be able to write in one sentence what my novel is to be about, to test this idea for several months, and then to invent situations that will fit the theme. I make the people last—to suit the situations. I write only one draught and rarely make any alterations to it. Occasional cutting has sometimes seemed necessary. I write about 300 words a day with luck and when I am free to do so. I do it chiefly because it is the most difficult thing that I have ever tried to do.

I began by writing plays when I was 14. Before that I wrote 400 immensely dull pages (since destroyed) about a horse. I have also written a film script of *The Sea Change* with Peter Yates, but this has not yet been produced. I would very much like to write a good play, and, indeed, come to that, a first rate novel.

* * *

All Elizabeth Jane Howard's novels are distinguished by sharp and sensitive perceptions about people—their loves, their guilts, the damage they wittingly or unwittingly do to others. Sometimes, the perceptions are worked into satirical set pieces, like the treatment of a group of feckless post-Oxford young people sponging in London in *Something in Disguise*. Often the satire is more gentle and generous, like that of the patriotic major in *After Julius* who combines long, boring speeches about the past with silent sensitivity to the human dramas around him. Howard's heroines, generally simple, gentle young girls, from a variety of different backgrounds, are treated with a great deal of sympathy, with respect for their quiet intelligence and their capacity to feel for others. Any tendency toward the mawkish or sentimental is carefully controlled by a prose that works on sharp and often comic juxtapositions of images from contemporary experience. The heavy-handed Colonel, trying to appear sympathetic to others in *Something in Disguise*, is seen as "about as jocular and useless as the Metro-Goldwyn-Mayer Lion." In *The Sea Change*, a young actress tries desperately to impress a playwright by showing a knowledge of his plays, "broadcasting her innocuous opinions like weed killer on a well kept lawn."

The careful control visible in Howard's prose is also apparent in the structure of her novels. Sometimes, as in all of *The Sea Change* and most of *After Julius*, the novel consists of alternate narrations from the point of view of a small number of closely connected characters. Each episode is seen from at least two points of view, started by one character, taken up by the next who then moves the narrative on a little further until a third character takes it up. In *After Julius* the action of the novel is even confined to a three-day week-end, although most of the characters are engaged in sorting out causal connections of current problems to the heroic death of Julius at Dunkerque 20 years earlier. *Something in Disguise* compresses action into three segments: April, August, and December of a single year. *The Long View* begins with a marriage breaking up in 1950 and its consequences for the couple's children, then traces the marriage back, through several precisely dated stages of problem and uneasy reconciliation, to its desperate origin in 1926. The past inevitably leads to the present in Howard's fictional world, and the structural control often indicates both a working out of causation in human affairs and a kind of moral control, an insistence on a combination of awareness, responsibility, and refusal to hurt others in order to end the painful isolation of contemporary dilemmas.

More tightly controlled, and showing the characters able to resolve their dilemmas more positively than do the other novels, *After Julius* depends, to some extent, on a rather striking coincidence. A young woman, visiting her mother for the week-end, finds her London lover, whom she had thought in Rome, arriving, with his wife, for dinner, and the affair explodes in a scene where fireworks are literal as well as symbolic. The structured plot shapes a novel in which moral or immoral actions eventually reveal themselves, in which moral judgment insists that characters take publicly visible responsibility for their actions. Similarly, in *Odd Girl Out*, the young girl, amoral from a conventional point of view, who visits a young couple who have established a self-sufficient "island" in ten years of marriage and, in turn, sleeps with each of the partners, refuses to lie and insists on confronting both together to try to establish the "truth" of a three-way love that could nourish a child. Although the *ménage à trois* cannot, in this novel, full of ironic parallels and other forms of structural compression, work for these three characters, the young girl who proposes it is seen as more moral, more willing to face the consequences of her actions and her emotions, than is the superficially more respectable couple. Virtue, in Howard's world, is not fragmented or buried, never the private gesture of an alienated sensibility; rather, more actions have consequences, visible and direct, on the people closest to one.

Knowing and facing the past allows all three of the central women in *After Julius* some kind of resolution of their current dilemmas, but Howard's endings are not always so positive. In *The Sea Change* an aging playwright, who has longed for a renewal of youth in loving a young girl brought up in a village parsonage, and his wife who has lost her only child, can understand and forgive each other in an acknowledgment of mutual pain and loss. The acknowledgment, the assumption of responsibility, allows them to survive although it is far from a triumphant resolution. In *Something in Disguise* the resolution is melodramatic. The mother, a war widow who has raised her children alone, finally marries a retired army colonel to whom both her children object. Underneath the colonel's blunt, dull, insensitive exterior, the author slowly reveals, is the criminal heart of a man who tries gradually to poison his wife for her money, as he has poisoned two previous wives. And the daughter who unpredictably marries a man who is both exciting and considerate, both a successful man of the world and a paragon of simple understanding and virtue, is desolate when the man is killed in an auto accident, having been sent on a fool's errand by one of the inconsiderate. Although moral judgment on each of the characters is clear enough, the plot punishes with an intensity that seems, somewhat sensationally, to detract from the emphasis on moral choice in some of the other novels.

Howard's carefully shaped moral tales are also dense with descriptions and references that convey the social texture of the times. *The Long View* is skillful in recreating both the sense of the wealthy English in southern France between the wars and the austerely genteel dinner party of 1950. *The Sea Change* contrasts the conventional life in the village parsonage with that of the fifties' playwright conveying a young girl to London, New York, and a Greek Island. *After Julius* is brilliant with settings: the tiny attic office of the editorial staff of an old, respectable publishing firm; the spacious chintzy Tudor of the mother's house in Sussex; the cheerful chaos of a young doctor and his family's crowded flat. *Something in Disguise* contains a terrifying portrait of daily life in the pseudo-Spanish surroundings of the "distinguished" house on a new suburban housing estate. Within these tartly observed and wholly recognizable environments, certain types appear in novel after novel. The apparently dull retired Army officer, either basically sensitive and kindly or basically cruel and criminal, represents an older England, an irrelevant survival. The confident man of the world, playwright in *The Sea Change*, doctor in *After Julius*, international business-man in *Something in Disguise*, has not allowed charm, success, or the modern world to distort his basically simple sense of responsibility. But all these men are seen from the point of view of women, and the novels reiterate a constant sense, made explicit in *Odd Girl Out*, that women are more responsible, more affectionate, more genuinely concerned with others than men are. After the dinner party that opens *The Long View*, the men rejoin the women "having discussed the fundamentals as superficially as the women in the drawing room discussed the superficialities fundamentally."

Howard's intelligent and sensitive heroines are, however, far from independent. They invariably regret or seek to rediscover the wise father lost. The benign and revered village parson father in *The Sea Change* is killed in a bicycle accident; fathers in other novels are killed in the Second World War; still other fathers, like the one in *The Long View*, are remote and indifferent or, like the actor who deserts his family in a melodramatic sub-plot in *Odd Girl Out*, completely irresponsible. The heroines seek protection, look for the man who might replace the absent father and make smoothly decisive all the hard and complex edges of a difficult world. They want to be safe and cosseted, a desire that can lead to the aridity of *The Long View*, the self-discovery of *After Julius*, the impossible fantasy of *Something in Disguise*, or the bizarre plan for sharing love that, in turn, is rejected in *Odd Girl Out*. The complexities of the search for protection are stated explicitly near the end of *Odd Girl Out*, when the couple turns the amoral young girl who proposed it into a scapegoat who can be exorcised. Yet they cannot return to their "island:" "Both felt that they were there to protect the other: neither anted the results of the protection. Each thought of what he had to o to sustain life for the other; each considered his efforts and anslated them into nobility and unselfish determination." The oles are not equivalent, for, a few pages later, at the very end of the ovel, the wife realizes that she, who had thought herself protected riginally, must now become the principal protector. And they will ot have a child. In Howard's fictional world sympathetic and ompetent mothers, who abound, are not enough. The heroines eed the wisdom, the control, and the safety of the responsible and aring father, a safety dimly seen, always lost, and invariably overompensated for. Looking for the safety, always precarious in a 'orld of airplanes and betrayals, requires a great deal of sensitivity nd control. Elizabeth Jane Howard's great distinction is that the earch for safety is presented with such rare and intelligent iscrimination.

—James Gindin

IUIE, William Bradford. American. Born in Hartselle, Alaama, 13 November 1910. Educated at the University of Alabama, A.B. 1930 (Phi Beta Kappa). Served as a Lieutenant in the United States Navy, 1943-45. Married Ruth Pucket in 1934. Reporter, *Birmingham Post*, Alabama, 1932-34; Associate Editor, 1942-43, and Editor and Publisher, 1945-52, *American Mercury*, New York. Address: P.O. Box 248, Hartselle, Alabama 35640, U.S.A.

PUBLICATIONS

Novels

Mud on the Stars. New York, Fischer, 1942; London, Hutchinson, 1944.
The Revolt of Mamie Stover. New York, Duell, 1951; London, W.H. Allen, 1953.
The Americanization of Emily. New York, Dutton, 1959; London, W.H. Allen, 1960.
Hotel Mamie Stover. London, W.H. Allen, 1962; New York, Potter, 1963.
The Klansman. New York, Delacorte Press, 1967; London, W.H. Allen, 1968.
In the Hours of the Night. New York, Delacorte Press, 1975.

Short Stories

Wolf Whistle and Other Stories. New York, New American Library, 1959.
The Hero of Iwo Jima and Other Stories. New York, New American Library, 1962.

Other

The Fight for Air Power. New York, Fischer, 1942.
Seabee Roads to Victory. New York, Dutton, 1944.
Can Do! The Story of the Seabees. New York, Dutton, 1944.
From Omaha to Okinawa: The Story of the Seabees. New York, Dutton, 1946.
The Case Against the Admirals: Why We Must Have a Unified Command. New York, Dutton, 1946.
The Execution of Private Slovik: The Hitherto Secret Story of the Only American Soldier since 1864 to Be Shot for Desertion. New York, Duell, and London, Jarrolds, 1954.
Ruby McCollum: Woman in the Suwannee Jail. New York, Dutton, 1956; revised edition, New York, New American Library, 1964; as *The Crime of Ruby McCollum*, London, Jarrolds, 1957.
The Hiroshima Pilot. New York, Putnam, and London, Heinemann, 1964.
Three Lives for Mississippi. New York, Whitney Communication Corporation, and London, Heinemann, 1965.
He Slew the Dreamer: My Search with James Earl Ray for the Truth about the Murder of Martin Luther King. New York, Delacorte Press, and London, W.H. Allen, 1970; revised edition, as *Did the FBI Kill Martin Luther King?*, Nashville, Nelson, 1977.
It's Me, O Lord! (on Dan Ronsisvalle). Nashville, Nelson, 1979.

* * *

William Bradford Huie is primarily a journalist, and his fiction shows that in two ways—by his being able to turn out a light, popular novel, and by his recourse to fiction to present a situation of controversy which he could not prove well enough to present as fact. His non-fiction, however, can be read as a novel, for his books are always structured well, and the subjects he chooses are dramatic to the point of being shocking. Only once has he failed to build horrendous suspense in a story, and that was when he was let down in his interviews with James Earl Ray, the convicted murderer of Martin Luther King, by Ray's persisting that he had no accomplices. *The Revolt of Mamie Stover* and *Hotel Mamie Stover* are lusty stories carried by the character of the title figure. *The Americanization of Emily* is a sentimental story of a love affair between an English girl and an American soldier during the war. Although highly popular, these are ephemeral works, and if Huie had written nothing but this kind of thing and his short stories he would not be the important figure that he is in American writing.

Huie soon became interested in lost, forgotten, or obscured causes. He came across the fact that only one American soldier had been executed for desertion during the second World War; and in *The Execution of Private Slovik* he not only presented a thorough and understanding biography and analysis of that pathetic slum boy, who was chosen out of many deserters as an example because he seemed worthless to the reviewing officers, but made the point of view of all such people come clear. Huie's book is essential to the understanding of a book like Nelson Algren's *The Man with the Golden Arm.*

The Hiroshima Pilot blasts the myth that the man who dropped the first atom bomb was consumed by conscience over it—he wasn't the pilot who carried the bomb out but flew a weather plane. Huie is a native Southerner, and lives in Alabama, so he has written extensively about the injustices of his region, especially toward Blacks. When three young civil rights workers were murdered in Mississippi in 1964, with at least the connivance of the county sheriff, he investigated deeply and produced *Three Lives for Mississippi.*

Unable to tell all he knew, not only about this atrocity, Huie produced a novel, *The Klansman*, that although too melodramatic and journalistic to be considered a fine novel, is certainly more polished than that earlier polemic, *Uncle Tom's Cabin.* His villain is the system, not people. His sheriff, although a racist, is above the average. His hero, a descendent of the old southern aristocracy, and his victim, a Negro girl with a good job in Chicago, back in Mississippi, are too good to be true. Huie uses fiction, but he uses it to good effect.

—William Bittner

HUMPHREY, William. American. Born in Clarksville, Texas, 18 June 1924. Educated at Southern Methodist University, Dallas; University of Texas, Austin. Married. Recipient: American Academy award, 1962. Lives in Lexington, Virginia. Address: c/o William Koshland, Alfred A. Knopf, 201 East 50th Street, New York, New York 10022, U.S.A.

PUBLICATIONS

Novels

Home from the Hill. New York, Knopf, and London, Chatto and Windus, 1958.
The Ordways. New York, Knopf, and London, Chatto and Windus, 1965.
Proud Flesh. New York, Knopf, and London, Chatto and Windus, 1973.

Short Stories

The Last Husband and Other Stories. New York, Morrow, and London, Chatto and Windus, 1953.
A Time and a Place: Stories. New York, Knopf, 1968; as *A Time and a Place: Stories of the Red River Country*, London, Chatto and Windus, 1969.

Uncollected Short Story

"Mrs. Shumlin's Cow Trixie," in *Esquire* (New York), December 1969.

Other

The Spawning Run: A Fable. New York, Knopf, and London, Chatto and Windus, 1970.
Ah, Wilderness! The Frontier in American Literature. El Paso, Texas Western Press, 1977.
Farther Off from Heaven. New York, Knopf, and London, Chatto and Windus, 1977.
My Moby Dick. New York, Doubleday, 1978; London, Chatto and Windus, 1979.

*

Critical Study: *William Humphrey* by James W. Lee, Austin, Texas, Steck Vaughn, 1967.

* * *

Locale is a potent force in all of William Humphrey's best work. His three novels and his most successful short stories are all set in the Red River country of northeast Texas. Humphrey should not, however, be dismissed as nothing more than a regionalist. Like Faulkner, with whom he is often compared, Humphrey uses locale as a framework for discussion of universal issues.

Home From the Hill, Humphrey's first and certainly his best novel, is both a first-class *Bildungsroman* and a family tragedy of mythic dimensions. Much of the novel concerns young Theron Hunnicutt's passage to manhood, a journey largely related to his hunting experiences. The most powerful force in the novel, however, is Theron's father Captain Wade—wealthy cotton planter, legendary hunter, notorious philanderer, more an embodiment of Texas myth than an actual flesh-and-blood man. The House of Hunnicutt is destined to have the father's sins visited upon it. The captain is murdered by the crazed father of a pregnant teenage girl in a highly ironic case of mistaken identity. Following the primitive code of manhood learned from his father and other hunting men, Theron pursues the murderer and eventually kills him. Theron then retreats to the recesses of Sulpher Bottom, an almost impenetrable swamp, presumably to die alone. Hannah Hunnicutt, the long-suffering wife, is taken away to a Dallas asylum where she spend the last 15 years of her life. *Home From the Hill* contains more tha a touch of melodrama, and the last third of the novel is too much series of coincidences.

While Humphrey's first novel is a melodramatic tragedy, hi second is a mock epic. *The Ordways* is a panoramic novel spannin four generations. Its first section largely concerns the journey of th wounded, blinded Civil War veteran Thomas Ordway and his wif Ella, along with both the remains and the tombstones of thei kindred, from eastern Tennessee to northeast Texas. Most of th rest of the novel concerns the 1898 journey of Sam Ordway, wh traverses much of Texas in an attempt to find his kidnapped son Despite his solemn oath to search to the ends of the earth if neces sary, Sam Ordway is no avenging western hero, no believer in th primitive code of manhood that governs the life of Theron Hunni cutt and, for that matter, the lives of Sam's own Texas neighbors His quest becomes picaresque and includes such events as a politica rally in the small town of Paris, Texas, a jailing in Dallas on charge of intent to commit murder, and a stint with a traveling circus. In th best picaresque tradition, *The Ordways* ends happily, though in thi case the hero fails in his quest. The reunion of father and son take place some 30 years after Sam's journey. The strength of the novel i in its evocation of late 19th-century Texas. The author also include an enlightening discourse on the relationship of the Southerner t his past. The book's major weakness is in the extent of the episodi account of Sam's travels. Though highly entertaining at points, thi segment often seems like nothing more than a collection of inci dents. One wishes for an end to the sequence long before it comes

Humphrey has written of the Southerner: "Clannishness was an is the key to his temperament." *Proud Flesh*, his third novel, i about clannishness gone berserk. Centering on the death of matri arch Edwina "Ma" Renshaw, the novel is highly grotesque an often hilarious. Grotesquerie piles upon grotesquerie. When th family physician pronounces Edwina dead, he is forced to spend ar additional three-day vigil at her bedside, just to make sure that hi judgment has not been premature. An irrationally guilt-ridden old est daughter entombs herself in the storm cellar, vowing never to emerge—an event which leads to the formation of a new religiou cult. Finally, the dead matriarch's body is stored in a local cold storage plant while two Renshaws are dispatched to New York City to search for the family "black sheep," Edwina's favorite, who mus return home before the funeral takes place. The novel's weakness i the same as that of *The Ordways* and even more apparent. More a collection of incidents than a coherent novel, *Proud Flesh* is allowed to continue far too long.

Most of Humphrey's short stories are competent, and some o them are first rate. The best stories in *The Last Husband* include "The Shell," an account of a young man's growth to self-awarenes as he struggles to free himself from the shadow of his deceased father, a legendary hunter; "Quail for Mr. Forester," a young narrator's recollection of an evening spent in the presence of a member o "the old order," a remnant of the vanishing aristocracy of a smal Texas town; and "A Fresh Snow," a sensitive sketch of a lonely southern girl in a northern industrial city. *A Time and a Place*, stories of Depression-era Red River country, includes such masterpieces as "The Ballad of Jesse Neighbors," an account of an ill-fated "poreboy" who, as a victim of society and circumstance, reminds one of Hardy's Tess; "A Good Indian," the reminiscence of a former car salesman who made much of his money during the Depression by callously selling Cadillacs to suddenly rich, uneducated Indians; and "Mouth of Brass," perhaps Humphrey's best story, a sensitive young narrator's recounting of his first experience with racial prejudice and small town cowardice.

In addition to his fiction, Humphrey has written two slender volumes on fishing, *The Spawning Run* and *My Moby Dick*, as well as a poignant autobiographical work, *Farther Off From Heaven*. Though uneven, his work is quite readable. In his ability to evoke his native region, Humphrey has few if any equals.

—Craig Hudziak

UMPHREYS, Emyr (Owen). British. Born in Prestatyn, lwyd, Wales, 15 April 1919. Educated at University College of 'ales, Aberystwyth, 1937-39; University College of North Wales, angor, 1946-47. Served as a Relief Worker in the Middle East and e Mediterranean during World War II. Married Elinor Myfanwy ones in 1946; three sons and one daughter. Teacher, Wimbledon echnical College, London, 1948-50; Pwllheli Grammar School, orth Wales, 1951-54; Producer, BBC Radio, Cardiff, 1955-58; rama Producer, BBC Television, 1958-62; free-lance writer and rector, 1962-65; Lecturer in Drama, University College of North /ales, 1965-72. Since 1972, free-lance writer. Recipient: Maugham ward, 1953; Hawthornden Prize, 1959; Welsh Arts Council ward, 1972, 1975, 1979; Gregynog Fellowship, 1974; Society of uthors Travelling Scholarship, 1979. Agent: Richard Scott Simon td., 32 College Cross, London N1 1PR, England. Address: 13 fordd Llangors, Cyncoed, Cardiff CF2 6PF, Wales.

UBLICATIONS

Novels

The Little Kingdom. London, Eyre and Spottiswoode, 1946.
The Voice of a Stranger. London, Eyre and Spottiswoode, 1949.
A Change of Heart. London, Eyre and Spottiswoode, 1951.
Hear and Forgive. London, Gollancz, 1952; New York, Putnam, 1953.
A Man's Estate. London, Eyre and Spottiswoode, 1955; New York, McGraw Hill, 1956.
The Italian Wife. London, Eyre and Spottiswoode, 1957; New York, McGraw Hill, 1958.
Y Tri Llais (in Welsh). Llandybie, Dyfed, Llyfrau'r Dryw, 1958.
A Toy Epic. London, Eyre and Spottiswoode, 1958.
The Gift. London, Eyre and Spottiswoode, 1963.
Outside the House of Baal. London, Eyre and Spottiswoode, 1965.
National Winner. London, Macdonald, 1971.
Flesh and Blood. London, Hodder and Stoughton, 1974.
The Best of Friends. London, Hodder and Stoughton, 1978.
The Anchor Tree. London, Hodder and Stoughton, 1980.

Short Stories

Natives. London, Secker and Warburg, 1968.

Uncollected Short Stories

"Down in the Heel on Duty," in *New English Review* (London), 1947.
"Michael Edwards," in *Wales* (London), vii, 26, 27, 1947.
"A Girl in the Ice" and "The Obstinate Bottle," in *New Statesman* (London), 1953.
"Mrs. Armitage," in *Welsh Short Stories.* London, Faber, 1959.
"The Arrest," in *Madog 3* (Barry), 1977.

Plays

King's Daughter, adaptation of a play by Saunders Lewis (produced London, 1959; as *Siwan*, televised, 1960). Published, as *Siwan*, in *Plays of the Year, 1959-60*, London, Elek, 1960.
Dinas, with W.S. Jones. Llandybie, Dyfed, Llyfrau'r Dryw, 1970.

Radio Plays: *A Girl in a Garden*, 1963; *Reg*, 1964; *The Manipulator*, 1970.

Television Play: *The Shining Pyramid*, from a novel by Arthur Machen, 1979.

Verse

Roman Dream, music by Alun Hoddinott. London, Oxford University Press, 1968.
An Apple Tree and a Pig, music by Alun Hoddinott. London, Oxford University Press, 1969.
Ancestor Worship: A Cycle of 18 Poems. Denbigh, Gwasg Gee, 1970.
Landscapes, music by Alun Hoddinott. London, Oxford University Press, 1975.
Penguin Modern Poets 27, with John Ormond and John Tripp. London, Penguin, 1979.
The Kingdom of Bran. London, Keith Holmes, 1979.

*

Bibliography: in *A Bibliography of Anglo-Welsh Literature, 1900-1965* by Brynmor Jones, Swansea, Library Association, 1970.

Critical Studies: *The Novel 1945-1950* by P.H. Newby, London, Longman, 1951; *Y llenor a'i Gymdeithas* by A. Llewelyn Williams, London, BBC, 1966; *The Dragon Has Two Tongues* by Glyn Jones, London, Dent, 1969; *Ysgrifau Beirniadol VII* by Derec Llwyd Morgan, Denbigh, Gwasg Gee, 1972; Jeremy Hooker and André Morgan, in *Planet 39*, 1977; *Emyr Humphreys* by Ioan Williams, Cardiff, University of Wales Press, 1980.

* * *

The preoccupations of Emyr Humphreys are peculiarly Welsh, and since there are very few Welsh novelists writing in English who spring from or have assimilated the Welsh Nonconformist heritage, his work has few parallels in that of his contemporaries. Emyr Humphreys manifests in his novels a Puritan seriousness about the purpose of living, about the need for tradition and the understanding of it, and about the future of the community (usually seen as Wales) as well as the good of the individual. Welsh Nationalist as well as Christian, he re-emphasised in 1953 that "personal responsibility is a Protestant principle" and saw himself as engaged in writing the *Protestant novel.* His interest in the non-realist novel is minimal and his technical experimentation is limited to the use, in *A Man's Estate*, of a number of narrators and, in *Outside the House of Baal*, to an interleaving of narratives in which the past rapidly catches up with the present.

His first two novels, *The Little Kingdom* and *The Voice of a Stranger*, are concerned respectively with idealism betrayed by false leadership and idealism bludgeoned by knavery. Their conclusions are pessimistic. The earlier of those themes appears again in *A Toy Epic*. But with *A Change of Heart* begins Emyr Humphreys's concern with the Christian belief in the gradual progress of society towards *the good* and the means by which *good* is transmitted from generation to generation. Heredity is soon discarded in favour of answers more complex. Perhaps the finest of the earlier novels which pursue this theme is *Hear and Forgive*, and of the later, *Outside the House of Baal*. In this book Emyr Humphreys faces the apparently total defeat of his Calvinistic Methodist minister with no more than the silence of faith. Since the problems involved plainly need the longest time-scale possible, Emyr Humphreys's more recent novels (with the exception of *The Anchor Tree*, which is a digression, with the same preoccupations, into his recent Welsh-American experience) are intended as a quartet, the fourth of which, *National Winner*, he wrote first. The first and second, *Flesh and Blood* and *The Best of Friends*, complete the first half of the plan, but the absence of the third so far makes the full meaning difficult to penetrate. The honesty and seriousness of these concerns are shot with humour, but the seeing eye is so utterly unsentimental as to strike some critics as cold. Two of the novels are set in Italy, two mostly in London, one in Pennsylvania, and the rest in Wales.

—Roland Mathias

HUNTER, Evan. Pseudonym: **Ed McBain.** American. Born S.A.Lombino in New York City, 15 October 1926. Educated at Cooper Union, New York, 1943-44; Hunter College, New York, B.A. 1950 (Phi Beta Kappa). Served in the United States Navy, 1944-46. Married 1) Anita Melnick in 1949 (divorced), three sons; 2) Mary Vann Finley in 1973, one step-daughter. In the early 1950's taught in vocational high schools, and worked for Scott Meredith Literary Agency, in New York. Recipient: Mystery Writers of America Edgar Allan Poe Award, 1957. Agent: Owen Laster, William Morris Agency, 1350 Avenue of the Americas, New York, New York 10019, U.S.A.; or, Ed Victor Ltd., 27 Soho Square, London W1V 6AY, England.

PUBLICATIONS

Novels

The Big Fix. N.p., Falcon, 1952; as *So Nude, So Dead* (as Richard Marsten), New York, Fawcett, 1956.
Don't Crowd Me. New York, Popular Library, 1953; London, Consul, 1960; as *The Paradise Party*, London, New English Library, 1968.
Cut Me In (as Hunt Collins). New York, Abelard Schuman, 1954; London, Boardman, 1960; as *The Proposition*, New York, Pyramid, 1955.
The Blackboard Jungle. New York, Simon and Schuster, 1954; London, Constable, 1955.
Runaway Black (as Richard Marsten). New York, Fawcett, 1954; London, Red Seal, 1957.
Murder in the Navy (as Richard Marsten). New York, Fawcett, 1955; as *Death of a Nurse* (as Ed McBain), New York, Pocket Books, 1968; London, Hodder and Stoughton, 1972.
Second Ending. New York, Simon and Schuster, and London, Constable, 1956; as *Quartet in H*, New York, Pocket Books, 1957.
The Spiked Heel (as Richard Marsten). New York, Holt, 1956; London, Constable, 1957.
Tomorrow's World (as Hunt Collins). New York, Avalon, 1956; as *Tomorrow and Tomorrow*, New York, Pyramid, 1956; (as Ed McBain), London, Severn House, 1980.
Vanishing Ladies (as Richard Marsten). New York, Permabooks, 1957; London, Boardman, 1961.
Even the Wicked (as Richard Marsten). New York, Permabooks, 1958; (as Ed McBain), London, Severn House, 1979.
Strangers When We Meet. New York, Simon and Schuster, and London, Constable, 1958.
I'm Cannon—For Hire (as Curt Cannon). New York, Fawcett, 1958; London, Fawcett, 1959.
Big Man (as Richard Marsten). New York, Pocket Books, 1959; (as Ed McBain), London, Penguin, 1978.
A Matter of Conviction. New York, Simon and Schuster, and London, Constable, 1959; as *The Young Savages*, New York, Pocket Books, 1966.
Mothers and Daughters. New York, Simon and Schuster, and London, Constable, 1961.
Buddwing. New York, Simon and Schuster, and London, Constable, 1964.
The Paper Dragon. New York, Delacorte Press, 1966; London, Constable, 1967.
A Horse's Head. New York, Delacorte Press, 1967; London, Constable, 1968.
Last Summer. New York, Doubleday, 1968; London, Constable, 1969.
Sons. New York, Doubleday, 1969; London, Constable, 1970.
Nobody Knew They Were There. New York, Doubleday, and London, Constable, 1972.
Every Little Crook and Nanny. New York, Doubleday, and London, Constable, 1972.
Come Winter. New York, Doubleday, and London, Constable, 1973.
Streets of Gold. New York, Harper, 1974; London, Macmilla 1975.
Doors (as Ezra Hannon). New York, Stein and Day, 1975; Lo don, Macmillan, 1976.
The Chisholms: A Novel of the Journey West. New York, Harpe and London, Hamish Hamilton, 1976.
Walk Proud. New York, Bantam, 1979.
Love, Dad. New York, Crown, 1981.

Novels as Ed McBain

Cop Hater. New York, Simon and Schuster, 1956; Londo Boardman, 1958.
The Mugger. New York, Simon and Schuster, 1956; Londo Boardman, 1959.
The Pusher. New York, Simon and Schuster, 1956; Londo Boardman, 1959.
The Con Man. New York, Simon and Schuster, 1957; Londo Boardman, 1960.
Killer's Choice. New York, Simon and Schuster, 1958; Londo Boardman, 1960.
Killer's Payoff. New York, Simon and Schuster, 1958; Londo Boardman, 1960.
April Robin Murders, with Craig Rice (completed by McBain New York, Random House, 1958; London, Hammond, 1959.
Lady Killer. New York, Simon and Schuster, 1958; Londo Boardman, 1961.
Killer's Wedge. New York, Simon and Schuster, 1959; Londo Boardman, 1961.
'Til Death. New York, Simon and Schuster, 1959; Londo Boardman, 1961.
King's Ransom. New York, Simon and Schuster, 1959; Londo Boardman, 1961.
Give the Boys a Great Big Hand. New York, Simon and Schuste 1960; London, Boardman, 1962.
The Heckler. New York, Simon and Schuster, 1960; Londo Boardman, 1962.
See Them Die. New York, Simon and Schuster, 1960; Londo Boardman, 1963.
Lady, Lady, I Did It! New York, Simon and Schuster, 196 London, Boardman, 1963.
Like Love. New York, Simon and Schuster, 1962; London, Han ish Hamilton, 1964.
Ten Plus One. New York, Simon and Schuster, 1963; Londo Hamish Hamilton, 1964.
Ax. New York, Simon and Schuster, and London, Hamis Hamilton, 1964.
The Sentries. New York, Simon and Schuster, and London, Han ish Hamilton, 1965.
He Who Hesitates. New York, Delacorte Press, and Londo Hamish Hamilton, 1965.
Doll. New York, Delacorte Press, 1965; London, Hamish Hami ton, 1966.
Eighty Million Eyes. New York, Delacorte Press, and Londo Hamish Hamilton, 1966.
Fuzz. New York, Doubleday, and London, Hamish Hamilto 1968.
Shotgun. New York, Doubleday, and London, Hamish Hami ton, 1969.
Jigsaw. New York, Doubleday, and London, Hamish Hamilto 1970.
Hail, Hail, The Gang's All Here! New York, Doubleday, an London, Hamish Hamilton, 1971.
Sadie When She Died. New York, Doubleday, and Londo Hamish Hamilton, 1972.
Let's Hear It for the Deaf Man. New York, Doubleday, an London, Hamish Hamilton, 1973.
Hail to the Chief. New York, Random House, and London, Ham ish Hamilton, 1973.
Bread. New York, Random House, and London, Hamish Hami ton, 1974.

Where There's Smoke. New York, Random House, and London, Hamish Hamilton, 1975.
Blood Relatives. New York, Random House, 1975; London, Hamish Hamilton, 1976.
Guns. New York, Random House, 1976; London, Hamish Hamilton, 1977.
So Long as You Both Shall Live. New York, Random House, and London, Hamish Hamilton, 1976.
Long Time No See. New York, Random House, and London, Hamish Hamilton, 1977.
Goldilocks. New York, Arbor House, 1977; London, Hamish Hamilton, 1978.
Calypso. New York, Viking Press, and London, Hamish Hamilton, 1979.
Ghosts. New York, Viking Press, and London, Hamish Hamilton, 1980.
Rumpelstiltskin. New York, Viking Press, and London, Hamish Hamilton, 1981.
Heat. New York, Viking Press, and London, Hamish Hamilton, 1981.

Short Stories

The Jungle Kids. New York, Pocket Books, 1956; augmented edition, as *The Last Spin*, London, Constable, 1960.
I Like 'em Tough (as Curt Cannon). New York, Fawcett, 1958.
The Empty Hours (as Ed McBain). New York, Simon and Schuster, 1962; London, Boardman, 1963.
Happy New Year, Herbie, and Other Stories. New York, Simon and Schuster, 1963; London, Constable, 1965.
The Beheading and Other Stories. London, Constable, 1971.
The Easter Man (a Play) and Six Stories. New York, Doubleday, 1972; as *Seven*, London, Constable, 1972.

Uncollected Short Stories

"Chinese Puzzle" (as Richard Marsten) and "Ticket to Death," in *Best Detective Stories of the Year 1955*, edited by David Coxe Cooke. New York, Dutton, 1955.
"A Very Small Homicide," in *The Saint* (New York), July 1959.
"Classification: Dead" (as Richard Marsten), in *Dames, Danger, and Death*, edited by Leo Margulies. New York, Pyramid, 1960.
"Easy Money," in *Ellery Queen's Mystery Magazine* (New York), September 1960.
"Nightshade" (as Ed McBain) in *Ellery Queen's Mystery Magazine* (New York), August 1970.
"Someone at the Door," in *Ellery Queen's Mystery Magazine* (New York), October 1971.
"Sympathy for the Devil," in *Seventeen* (New York), July 1972.
"Weeping for Dustin," in *Seventeen* (New York), July 1973.
"The Analyst," in *Playboy* (Chicago), December 1974.
"Dangerous Affair," in *Good Housekeeping* (New York), March 1975.
"Eighty Million Eyes" (as Ed McBain), in *Ellery Queen's Giants of Mystery.* New York, Davis, 1976.
"What Happened to Annie Barnes?," in *Ellery Queen's Mystery Magazine* (New York), June 1976.
"Stepfather," in *Ladies' Home Journal* (Des Moines), June 1976.

Plays

The Easter Man (produced Birmingham and London, 1964; as *A Race of Hairy Men*, produced New York, 1965). Included in *The Easter Man (a Play) and Six Stories*, 1972.
The Conjuror (produced Ann Arbor, Michigan, 1969).

Screenplays: *Strangers When We Meet*, 1960; *The Birds*, 1963; *Walk Proud*, 1979.

Other

Find the Feathered Serpent (juvenile). Philadelphia, Winston, 1952.
Rocket to Luna (juvenile; as Richard Marsten). Philadelphia, Winston, 1952; London, Hutchinson, 1954.
Danger: Dinosaurs! (juvenile; as Richard Marsten). Philadelphia, Winston, 1953.
The Remarkable Harry (juvenile). New York and London, Abelard Schuman, 1961.
The Wonderful Button (juvenile). New York, Abelard Schuman, 1961; London, Abelard Schuman, 1962.
Me and Mr. Stenner (juvenile). Philadelphia, Lippincott, 1976; London, Hamish Hamilton, 1977.

Editor (as Ed McBain), *Crime Squad.* London, New English Library, 1968.
Editor (as Ed McBain), *Homicide Department.* London, New English Library, 1968.
Editor (as Ed McBain), *Downpour.* London, New English Library, 1969.
Editor (as Ed McBain), *Ticket to Death.* London, New English Library, 1969.

*

Manuscript Collection: Mugar Memorial Library, Boston University.

Evan Hunter comments:

(1972) The novels I write under my own name are concerned mostly with identity, or at least they have been until the most recent book. (I cannot now predict what will interest or concern me most in the future.) I change my style with each novel, to fit the tone, the mood, and the narrative voice. I have always considered a strong story to be the foundation of any good novel, and I also apply this rule to the mysteries I write under the Ed McBain pseudonym. Unlike my "serious" novels, however, the style here is unvaried. The series characters are essentially the same throughout (although new detectives appear or old ones disappear from time to time, and each new case involves a new criminal or criminals), the setting is the same (the precinct and the city), and the theme is the same—crime and punishment. (I look upon these mysteries, in fact, as one *long* novel about crime and punishment, with each separate book in the series serving as a chapter.) I enjoy writing both types of novels, and consider each equally representative of my work.

* * *

The vividness and immediacy of the author's prose, coupled with the timeliness of his subject, drew considerable attention to Evan Hunter's novel *Blackboard Jungle.* This story of a young teacher confronting the brutal realities of a big city vocational high school was praised for its realism and for opening to fiction an area of public concern that had begun to attract national attention in the United States. *Second Ending* was an even more aggressively topical novel, tracing the effects of drugs on four young New Yorkers. The central character, a young trumpet player who has been addicted for two years, draws the other characters together, and they are all altered in some way by his descent toward death. Some of the novel's episodes, which were termed "sensational" at the time of publication, now no longer seem so unique, and despite the awkwardness with which portions of the novel are narrated, Hunter's power as a storyteller moved his characters unerringly toward the slough of mutual desparation.

In *Strangers When We Meet* Hunter elected to describe a more muted kind of action in which a young architect, happily married and the father of two children, drifts into an affair with a suburban neighbor. Hunter showed a keen eye for the minute details which slowly gather round the illicit relationship, creating a highly realistic impression of a young man unable to cope with conflicting loyalties.

Nonetheless, his characters finally seem insignificant—certainly not sufficiently strong to carry the philosophical baggage which the author gives them in an improbable conclusion.

A Matter of Conviction was a return to the mode of social protest which Hunter had developed so successfully in his two earlier novels. A polemic against the forces in society that make young men into killers, it was too contrived to offer more than passing interest. *Mothers and Daughters*, which chronicles the youth and maturity of four middle-class women—their dreams and their loves—is a more substantial work, despite its occasional melodrama.

Much of Hunter's fiction is over-written: striving for a realistic thickness, it bogs down in minutiae, and while the author writes with a high and consistent degree of professionalism, his vision rarely penetrates beneath the elaborate surfaces which his prose projects. *Last Summer* is a major exception to this adroit verbosity. It is told with an unforgettable simplicity and directness which nonetheless conveys the author's own highly sophisticated point of view. During a summer holiday two teenage boys and a girl explore an Atlantic island, tell each other the "truth," and dominate a shy young girl. Their experiences end in violence which vividly symbolizes the moral degeneracy of their society.

Few contemporary writers can match the versatility and consummate professionalism of Evan Hunter. His work includes a highly successful series of detective novels published under the pseudonym of Ed McBain; a science-fiction novel for children; a comic cops-and-robbers novel, *A Horse's Head*, written with great inventiveness and wit; and a spirited children's book in verse, illustrated by his own sons. *Sons* tells the story of three generations of a Wisconsin family, powerfully challenging some of the basic presumptions of the American Dream; *The Paper Dragon* is a densely plotted, intriguing story of a five-day plagiarism trial; and *Buddwing* plunges its amnesiac hero into the heart of a Washington Square riot, a hold-up, and a crap game. *Nobody Knew They Were There* takes a futuristic look at the innate forces of violence that assail man's attempt to achieve world peace. Throughout a varied and highly prolific career, Hunter has produced a body of work distinguished for its sound craftsmanship, although only one of his novels, *Last Summer*, clearly demonstrates the art which such craft should sustain.

—David Galloway

HUNTER, Kristin. American. Born in Philadelphia, Pennsylvania, 12 September 1931. Educated at the University of Pennsylvania, Philadelphia, 1947-51, B.S. in education 1951. Married John I. Lattany in 1968. Teacher, Camden, New Jersey public schools, 1951; Copywriter, Lavenson Bureau of Advertising, Philadelphia, 1952-59; Research Assistant, School of Social Work, University of Pennsylvania, 1961-62; Copywriter, Wermen and Schorr, Philadelphia, 1962-63; Information Officer, City of Philadelphia, 1963-64, 1965-66. Lecturer in Creative Writing, 1972-79, and since 1980, Adjunct Professor of English, University of Pennsylvania. Writer-in-Residence, Emory University, Atlanta, 1980. Recipient: Fund for the Republic Prize, for television documentary, 1955; Whitney Fellowship, 1959; Sigma Delta Chi Award, for reporting, 1968; National Council on Interracial Books for Children Award, 1968; National Conference of Christians and Jews Brotherhood Award, 1969; *Book World* Festival award, 1973; Christopher Award, 1974. Agent: Harold Matson Company, 22 East 40th Street, New York, New York 10016. Address: 366 Fountain Avenue, Camden, New Jersey 08105, U.S.A.

PUBLICATIONS

Novels

God Bless the Child. New York, Scribner, 1964; London, Mull[e]
1965.
The Landlord. New York, Scribner, 1966; London, Pan, 1970.
The Survivors. New York, Scribner, 1975.
The Lakestown Rebellion. New York, Scribner, 1978.

Uncollected Short Stories

"To Walk in Beauty," in *Sub-Deb Scoop* (Philadelphia), 1953.
"Supersonic," in *Mandala* (Philadelphia), i, 1, 1956.
"There Was a Little Girl," in *Rogue* (New York), 1959.
"An Interesting Social Study," in *The Best Short Stories by Neg[ro] Writers*, edited by Langston Hughes. Boston, Little Brow[n] 1967.
"Debut," in *Negro Digest* (Chicago), June 1968.
"Honor among Thieves," in *Essence* (New York), April 1971.
"The Tenant," in *Pennsylvania Gazette* (Philadelphia).

Plays

The Double Edge (produced Philadelphia, 1965).

Television Play: *Minority of One*, 1956.

Other (juvenile)

The Soul-Brothers and Sister Lou. New York, Scribner, 196[8]; London, Macdonald, 1971.
Boss Cat. New York, Scribner, 1971.
The Pool Table War. Boston, Houghton Mifflin, 1972.
Uncle Daniel and the Raccoon. Boston, Houghton Mifflin, 197[2].
Guests in the Promised Land: Stories. New York, Scribner, 197[3].

*

Critical Studies: reviews in *Saturday Review* (New York), 14 Ma[y] 1966, *New Yorker*, 10 July 1978, and *Philadelphia Magazin[e]*, October 1978.

Kristin Hunter comments:

The bulk of my work has dealt—imaginatively, I hope—wit[h] relations between the white and black races in America. My ear[ly] work was "objective," that is, sympathetic to both whites an[d] blacks, and seeing members from a perspective of irony and humo[r] against the wider backdrop of human experience as a whole. Sinc[e] about 1968 my subjective anger has been emerging, along with m[y] grasp of the real situation in this society though my sense of humo[r] keeps cropping up like an uncontrollable weed.

* * *

In her first two novels Kristin Hunter played upon the contradic[-] tions between reality as it is experienced by the black urban poo[r] and the false optimism of popular story. *God Bless the Chil[d]* parodies the tale of the enterprising but low-born youngster who, since the origins of middle-class fiction, has set out to achieve [a] place in society by the application of nerve and energy. In the case o[f] Rosie Fleming, however, her vitality leads to failure, for by settin[g] up as a small entrepreneur in the numbers game she earns the enmit[y] of the white men who manage the poor people's version of financ[e] capitalism. Despite her portrayal of the relentless power that des[-] troys Rosie, Hunter is not resigned to a sense of human powerless[-] ness. A sympathetic and complex portrayal of three generations o[f] black women conveys an intensely humanistic conception of char[-] acter, which in her second novel, *The Landlord*, becomes the basi[s] for an optimistic theme. The formal foundation of this book is the novel of maturation. Its main character, determined to "become a man" by exercising mastery over his tenants, is frustrated and tricked at every turn as they disabuse him of the mythology of white male dominance. Against his will, and contrary to the assumptions of middle-class convention the landlord forms an admiration and appreciation for the diverse styles by which blacks cope with life's troubles, large and small.

Following publication of *The Landlord* Hunter occupied herself with stories of ghetto life directed toward "younger readers." Like the adult novels that preceded them these juvenile publications reject the idealizations of popular genres while preserving a belief in the capacity of the black underclass to transform their lives by the power of their spirit. In both the adult and juvenile works the message has been that society's "victims" refuse the dehumanization which either social relations or a literature of pity would assign them.

This insider's view, informed by Hunter's commitment to the verve and quality of black life, has led her in the past five years to write two additional adult novels that must be termed celebrations. The first signifies by its title, *The Survivors*, its author's devotion to the rendition of character traits that enable a middle-aged dressmaker and a street kid to form an emotional and practical alliance that enables them both to overcome the predacious circumstances of the neighborhood. There are more than enough coincidence and pathos in the plot, but that is a small price to pay for the vibrancy of humor and characterization.

It is with *The Lakestown Rebellion*, however, that Hunter achieves the fulfillment of her craft. This story of a small black township, originally settled by fugitive slaves, battling against plans to build a highway that will destroy their homes, renews the tradition of the folk tricksters. A range of ingenious, zany, and simply unusual characters play the entire repertory of stereotypical roles popularly assumed to be black in order to stop the encroachment of "progress" upon their lives. The wit of the novel's conception perfectly suits Hunter's optimistic humanism. The book is so enjoyable one is almost unaware that it is also a symbolic reenactment of cultural history, but there can be no missing the fact that it places Kristin Hunter squarely in the tradition of Afro-American fiction at one of its best moments.

—John M. Reilly

HUTCHINS, Maude (Phelps McVeigh). Born in New York City. Educated at St. Margaret's School, Waterbury, Connecticut; Yale University, New Haven, Connecticut, B.F.A. 1926. Married the educator Robert Maynard Hutchins in 1921 (divorced, 1948); three children. Sculptor: one-man shows in New York, Chicago, St. Louis, Toledo, and San Francisco; works exhibited at the Paint and Clay Club, New Haven, Connecticut, the Brooklyn Museum, the National Association of Woman Painters and Sculptors, and the Chicago World's Fair Show of Modern Art; represented the State of Illinois at the 3rd annual National Exhibition of American Art, American Fine Arts Society Galleries, New York. Address: 1046 Pequot Road, Southport, Connecticut 06490, U.S.A.

PUBLICATIONS

Novels

Georgiana. New York, New Directions, 1948.
A Diary of Love. New York, New Directions, 1950; London, Spearman, 1953.
My Hero. New York, New Directions, and London, Spearman, 1953.
The Memoirs of Maisie. New York, Appleton Century Crofts, 1955.
Victorine. Denver, Swallow, and London, Spearman, 1959.
Honey on the Moon. New York, Morrow, 1964; London, Blond, 1965.
Blood on the Doves. New York, Morrow, 1965.
The Unbelievers Downstairs. New York, Morrow, 1967.

Short Stories

Love Is a Pie: Stories and Plays. New York, New Directions, 1952.
The Elevator: Stories. New York, Morrow, 1962.

Other

Diagrammatics, with Mortimer J. Adler. New York, Random House, 1932.

* * *

The first book of Maude Hutchins, then the handsome aloof wife of the President of the University of Chicago, and a sculptor of repute, was *Diagrammatics*, in which her own line-drawing collocations of female forms were complemented by similarly abstract logical forms, in double-talk, by Mortimer Adler, her husband's Great Books partner. Her foreword expounded artistic abstraction in a witty, figurative style which she trusted would not be intelligible, since if it were her art would be superfluous.

But she soon took up verbal art, first poems, then fiction. Stories and "plays," collected in *Love Is a Pie*, ranged from memoirs of a male amorist to the love-life of a gorilla. Some played irreverently with Christianity: Mary, on Easter Eve, ecstatically recalling her "affair" with the Heavenly Messenger, but glad Jesus is dead; Jesus—the Wandering Jew—as the cranky inmate of an Old People's Home.

Eight slim novels deal mostly with love—hence sex—in adolescent New England girls resembling herself: slender, dark, attractive, sensorily acute, intelligent, great readers and day-dreamers. Parents are lacking or ineffective, but grand-parents are strong-willed gentry, often in financial decay, with large old houses, Irish or Swedish maids, a farm, a pond, Southern connections, resident relatives, and a doctor as intimate friend. The girls are not sexually precocious or promiscuous, but, as Hutchins once remarked, sex seems to be what she has to write about. A woman's story, she says, is necessarily a love story, because "a woman knows what comes first," and physical sex (however sublimated or censored) is the basis of "all affection between persons of all sexes." But significant experiences happen in the mind, not the body, and raise emotion-charged questions about free will and passion, or about "innocence"—naive acceptance—and defensive "guilt."

Hutchins is not re-telling one story. She perhaps draws discreetly on autobiography, but her job as an artist is, she believes, to "intuit" others' feelings and actions, make a "spare choice" among her materials, then throw them into various perspectives, on various organizing principles. Her style alternates brisk narrative, involuted thought-streams, wicked satire, and the darting imagery of a well-stocked, wildly associative mind (often, a yeasty *id* seems to be bubbling through a Great Books-saturated *ego*), in sentences where a qualification may hang from every joint: "And I, without portfolio, as it were, in secret, I watch and observe and peek through keyholes, you might say, to solve, being curious and alert, a problem."

Georgiana is a Freudianly organized (first, formative girlhood influences; last, Georgiana, adult, unconsciously searching in successive lovers for her dominating, perfectionist grandfather) and is at times unreadably quirky, except in the mid-section, Georgiana's Colette-ish diary as a lively, amusing school-girl. The more successful *A Diary of Love* is all journal," but Noel is, even at 13, more educated in sex (which got the book banned in Chicago and burned in England) and she goes off, not to school but to an unforgettable desert sanitarium. *My Hero* ventured, unconvincingly, into non-genteel life—a mechanically minded boy who grows into a truck-driver. But it has two genuinely comic creations (an entomologist enthralled by insect sex, and his social-climbing wife), plus Hutchins-eye sketches of Chicago, from strip joints to the University.

Beginning with *Memoirs of Maisie*—the recollections, real and imaginary, of a centenarian, fusing oddly with current happenings—life frequently appears in mental distorting-mirrors, comic, grim, or surreal. In *Victorine* a pubescent girl, sexually responsive to church services, finally rejects them for chaste love with a half-wit who makes her see visions of a mystic stallion. A bride, in *Honey on the Moon*, goes from sexual initiation to schizophrenia as her adored older mate turns out to be a homosexual and then shoots himself. In a second short-story collection, *The Elevator*, passengers on an elevator "to Japan" prove to be stock characters in the romances of a negro novelist, who himself sounds like a white-man's cliché. A woman finds time so accelerated cigarettes burn her fingers before she can puff; a youth murders from respect for the meanings of words. Most of *Blood on the Doves* transpires, Faulknerianly, in the mind of a lunatic mountain boy with ESP who mingles past, present, and visualized future in obsessively recurring patterns as he strangles a girl and castrates himself; his brother engages in rape and in World War I battles in similarly ghastly style. The incredibly but hilariously precocious 8-year-old narrator of *The Unbelievers Downstairs* (who at times believes she is invisible) reports with naïve knowingness on the scrambled sex-lives of her elders.

Critically, Hutchins has always fared best abroad, but her American reception has improved as fashions caught up with her frankness and experimental techniques. Despite her intelligence and wide knowledge she correctly calls herself "no scholar, no historian, no thinker"—that is, no systematic philosopher. But each work is shaped by an idea, paradoxical, perverse, or arrestingly insightful. The short pieces are as economically modelled as her sculptures; in a novel, the idea may wear thin, but the development (which always includes amusing minor "humour" characters) is distinctive and usually interesting.

—George McElroy

IHIMAERA, Witi (Tame). New Zealander. Born in Gisborne, 7 February 1944. Educated at Te Karaka District High School, 1957-59; Church College of New Zealand, 1960-61; Gisborne Boys High School, 1962; University of Auckland, 1963-66; Victoria University, Wellington, 1968-72, B.A. 1972. Married Jane Cleghorn in 1970. Cadet Reporter, *Gisborne Herald*, 1967; Journalist, Post Office Headquarters, Wellington, 1968-72; Information Officer, 1973-74, Third Secretrary, Wellington, 1975-78, and Second Secretary, Canberra, New Zealand Ministry of Foreign Affairs. Recipient: Freda Buckland Literary Award, 1973; James Wattie Award, 1974; Robert Burns Fellowship, University of Otago, 1974. Address 11 Hungerford Road, Wellington 3, New Zealand.

PUBLICATIONS

Novels

Tangi. Auckland and London, Heinemann, 1973.
Whanau. Auckland, Heinemann, 1974; London, Heinemann, 1975.

Short Stories

Pounamu, Pounamu. Auckland, Heinemann, 1972; London, Heinemann, 1973.
The New Net Goes Fishing. Auckland, Heinemann, 1977; London, Heinemann, 1978.

Other

Maori. Wellington, Government Printers, 1975.

Editor, with D.S. Long, *Into the World of Light* (anthology of Maori writing). Auckland, Heinemann, 1980.

*

Critical Studies: "Participating" by Ray Grover, in *Islands* (Auckland), Winter 1973; "Tangi" by H. Winston Rhodes, in *Landfall* (Christchurch), December 1973; "Maori Writers," in *Fretful Sleepers and Other Essays* by Bill Pearson, Auckland, Heinemann, 1974; *The Maoris of New Zealand* by Joan Metge, London, Routledge, 1977.

Witi Ihimaera comments:

There are two cultural landscapes in my country, the Maori and the Pakeha (European), and although all people, including Maori, inhabit the Pakeha landscape, very few know the Maori one. It is important to both Maori and Pakeha that they realize their dual cultural heritage, and that is why I began to write. Not to become the first Maori novelist but to render my people into words as honestly and as candidly as I could; to present a picture of Maoritanga which is our word for the way we feel and are, in the hope that our values will be maintained. I like to think that I write with both love—aroha—and anger in the hope that the values of Maori life will never be lost. So far I have written about exclusively Maori people within an exclusively Maori framework, using our own oral tradition of Maori literature, our own mythology, as my inspiration. Cultural difference is not a bad thing, it can be very exciting and it can offer a different view of the world, value system, and interpretation of events. This is what I would like to offer: a personal vision of Maori life as I see it, the Maori side of New Zealand's dual heritage of culture.

* * *

With Ihimaera's collection of short stories, *Pounamu, Pounamu*, together with his novels, *Tangi* and *Whanau*, each with its appropriate Maori title, have given shape and significance to his people's traditional but rapidly disappearing life in village and rural settings. He has written "both with anger and with love"; but although as the first Maori novelist he is proudly conscious that he is conducting what amounts to a crusade, he has not allowed any missionary zeal to corrupt his artistic integrity.

In his unusual narratives human experience is not distorted. Maori characters act, feel and speak as authentic human beings, not as the formalised or picturesque figures of some romantic tale. They do not become inverted stereotypes, nor is their behaviour marred by false emotionalism. As author, Ihimaera does not pretend to be superior to his creations but, without a trace of irony, he joins in their gaiety, shares in their sorrows, accepts their shortcomings and participates in their traditional ceremonies. He identifies himself with old and young: laments with his elders because so many of a later generation have gone the Pakeha way, and sympathises with those who cannot resist the attraction of the city lights and are forgetful of their Maoritanga. Yet such sympathy and such authorial fellowship cannot conceal that a serious purpose lies behind his artistic endeavours or that he is deeply concerned with those values which too often have been ignored or derided.

If there is a central theme running through his short stories and novels, it is one related to the title of his third book. "Whanau" refers to the enlarged family community of the Maori village, held together not only by tradition but by bonds of relationship and love that are not easily comprehended by the sophisticated Pakeha. "Aroha" is used to imply something more than individual love; it includes that warmth of human affection that subsists within and through the whole whanau. Both relationship and love are vitally important elements of Maoritanga, a word that suggests all those customs and qualities regarded as specifically Maori. The conception of the enlarged family community therefore gives a very different flavour to the narratives of Ihimaera because, even in many of his short stories, the reader is continually aware of a complex pattern of relationships uniting the whanau and of an indescribable warmth of feeling that should not be confused with sexual love. His central characters are not and cannot be isolated. However different their personalities may be, however far they may roam, they remain members of the extended family, and sooner or later they will return, for the deep sense of belonging to the whanau is part of their heritage. The literary consequence of this is that each of Ihimaera's narratives may be recognised as a fragment of a contemporary saga, and "character in action" becomes less than an adequate description of his dramatic method.

Although at times the reader of *Whanau* may be disconcerted by the number of village people that together constitute the whole group, by their interconnections and by the variety of their fortunes and aspirations, it would be wrong to suggest that the novel is merely episodic or that it is a series of loosely linked short stories. With remarkable success the author has devised a form suitable to his dominant theme and, without loss of individuality or neglect of personal drama, has given life, substance, and meaning to the whanau itself. *Tangi*, as its name implies, is concerned with death, the death of a father, and its effect on the son and all the members of the extensive Maori family. It is a journey of self-discovery in which the present reality of the funeral rites and the expression of uninhibited grief are intertwined with personal memories, with the life of the whanau and the beginning of a journey to the future. In his less ambitious and more accessible short stories, Ihimaera demonstrates his talent for finding and moulding those significant incidents that reveal the life-style and attitudes of the Maori people. His lightness of touch and his ability to alternate between humour, tenderness, and pathos are more effective and more powerful as a commentary on race-relations than undue emphasis or stridency of tone could possibly be.

Pounamu, Pounamu and the two novels are not linked together, but they, nevertheless, form something in the nature of a trilogy. An ancient mythology, time-honoured traditions, and the values inherent in Maoritanga are woven into the texture of narratives that record the community life and rural setting of the older generation of Maoris. Even here, the whanau, the family, and the aroha which binds them are being increasingly disrupted by the alien culture, by the pale stranger with his "you got to get on" way of living. The younger people in particular are departing from their villages, lured by the bright lights of the city and the attractions of a pakeha world.

Ihimaera has already begun a second trilogy with the publication of *The New Net Goes Fishing*—a title borrowed from a Maori proverb which implies that a new generation takes the place of the old. The short stories contained in this volume should be regarded as a prelude to the urban novels which will follow; and the published collection has its own prelude in "Yellow Brick Road," and its own envoy, "Return from Oz." The former is concerned with the hopes and expectations of a Maori family as adults and children travel from their ancestral home to the Emerald City; and the latter with the return of the grandfather to Waituhi in the hope that he will draw his descendants back there again. Between Prelude and Envoy are 15 short stories that recount episodes in the lives of those who in the city environment still retain some of the values of Maoritanga, of those who are lost and discarded, of those who succeed or fail or rebel. Without enhancing or typifying his Maori characters Ihimaera reveals the mental and emotional turmoil experienced by so many of his people. He has said, "Te taha Maori [the Maori side] belongs to us all," and in this conviction he has written from a point of view that with insight interprets the meaning of Maoritanga and the meaning of its loss to Maori and Pakeha alike.

—H. Winston Rhodes

INNES, (Ralph) Hammond. British. Born in Horsham, Sussex, 15 July 1913. Educated at Cranbrook School, Kent, graduated 1931. Served in the British Army Artillery, 1940-46: Major. Married Dorothy Mary Lang in 1937. Staff Member, *Financial News*, London, 1934-40. C.B.E. (Commander, Order of the British Empire), 1978. Address: Ayres End, Kersey, Ipswich, Suffolk IP7 6EB, England.

PUBLICATIONS

Novels

The Doppelganger. London, Jenkins, 1937.
Air Disaster. London, Jenkins, 1937.
Sabotage Broadcast. London, Jenkins, 1938.
All Roads Lead to Friday. London, Jenkins, 1939.
Wreckers Must Breathe. London, Collins, 1940; as *Trapped*, New York, Putnam, 1940.
The Trojan Horse. London, Collins, 1940.
Attack Alarm. London, Collins, 1941; New York, Macmillan, 1942.
Dead and Alive. London, Collins, 1946.
The Killer Mine. London, Collins, and New York, Harper, 1947; as *Run by Night*, New York, Bantam, 1951.
The Lonely Skier. London, Collins, 1947; as *Fire in the Snow*, New York, Harper, 1947.
Maddon's Rock. London, Collins, 1948; as *Gale Warning*, New York, Harper, 1948.
The Blue Ice. London, Collins, and New York, Harper, 1948.
The White South. London, Collins, 1949; as *The Survivors*, New York, Harper, 1950.
The Angry Mountain. London, Collins, 1950; New York, Harper, 1951.
Air Bridge. London, Collins, 1951; New York, Knopf, 1952.
Campbell's Kingdom. London, Collins, and New York, Knopf, 1952.
The Strange Land. London, Collins, 1954; as *The Naked Land*, New York, Knopf, 1954.
The Mary Deare. London, Collins, 1956; as *The Wreck of the Mary Deare*, New York, Knopf, 1956.
The Land God Gave to Cain. London, Collins, and New York, Knopf, 1958.
The Doomed Oasis. London, Collins, and New York, Knopf, 1960.
Atlantic Fury. London, Collins, and New York, Knopf, 1962.
The Strode Venturer. London, Collins, and New York, Knopf, 1965.
Levkas Man. London, Collins, and New York, Knopf, 1971.
Golden Soak. London, Collins, and New York, Knopf, 1973.
North Star. London, Collins, 1974; New York, Knopf, 1975.
The Big Footprints. London, Collins, and New York, Knopf, 1977.
The Last Voyage: Captain Cook's Lost Diary. London, Collins, 1978; New York, Knopf, 1979.
Solomons Seal. London, Collins, and New York, Knopf, 1980.

Plays

Screenplay: *Campbell's Kingdom*, with Robin Estridge, 1957.

Television Play: *The Story of Captain James Cook*, 1975.

Other

Cocos Gold (juvenile; as Ralph Hammond). London, Collins, and New York, Harper, 1950.
Isle of Strangers (juvenile; as Ralph Hammond). London, Collins, 1951; as *Island of Peril*, Philadelphia, Westminster Press, 1953.
Saracen's Tower (juvenile; as Ralph Hammond). London, Collins, 1952; as *Cruise of Danger*, Philadelphia, Westminster Press, 1954.
Black Gold on the Double Diamond (juvenile; as Ralph Hammond). London, Collins, 1953.
Harvest of Journeys. London, Collins, and New York, Knopf, 1960.
Scandinavia, with editors of Life. New York, Time, 1963.
Sea and Islands. London, Collins, and New York, Knopf, 1967.
The Conquistadors. London, Collins, and New York, Knopf, 1969.
Hammond Innes Introduces Australia, edited by Clive Turnbull. London, Deutsch, and New York, McGraw Hill, 1971.

Editor, *Tales of Old Inns*, by Richard Keverne, revised edition. London, Collins, 1947.

*

Critical Study: in *Sunday Telegraph Magazine* (London), 10 August 1980.

Hammond Innes comments:

Writing and travelling can be kept in separate compartments of time. But the organisation and preparation for journeys and voyages cannot. And this is a major problem, for I need the familiarity of my own home and the peace of the country in order to write. I need my books and my maps and charts around me. I also need to live with it seven days a week, for I am a painfully slow writer, usually discarding far more than appears in the final work.

I find it very difficult to be certain at what point I became conscious of the role travel was to play in my writing. I think probably after the war. I had cut my writing teeth in the great depression of the early 1930's, a particularly insular period that I believe to have been the result of the mud and blood of Flanders. To earn my living, however, I worked as a journalist on a London daily. My starting wage was a now unbelievable 17s. 6d. a week, and at the time I counted myself fortunate to get the job, for most newspapers were firing, not hiring, staff. All through the 1930's I had to be content to discover my own country, so that when I finally did go abroad it was at H.M.'s expense—a voyage round the Cape, my destination the Western Desert.

I was 27 when I joined the Services. I felt the best years of my life were being wasted. It was only when I was demobilised, and had taken the plunge and abandoned journalism for full-time writing, that I realised what a wealth of experience I had been soaking up.

As a youngster, my imagination had been fired by geography almost as much as by literature. On my return to England after the war, I was made strongly aware that, whilst I had been absorbing the atmosphere of the old world of the Mediterranean, the vast majority of the British people had been locked up in their island fortress for six long years. I had characters and backgrounds that seemed to interest them. There is always an element of luck in everything, and in writing the luck is to find that what you want to write, and therefore what you write best, is what people happen to want to read.

I wanted to write about far-off places and people. Because of that I determined to plough back as much of my royalties as possible into travel. And looking back now, how glad I am that I did. A writer has no business, no land, no factory that he can call his own. His capital assets are all in his head, and one of the very few things that can't be taxed, expropriated, or in any way filched by others, is personal experience.

This was a conscious decision, the only one I have ever made about my writing. The rest has developed in the normal haphazard way of things. I cannot even say what it is that draws me at a certain period of time to a certain part of the world. The choice would appear to be intuitive. But I can say that, as with the voyages under sail, a lot of preparation is necessary. The research, the books, the maps, the visits to London to seek out the right contacts. This is all necessary, so that when one arrives in the country itself there is a sense of familiarity; by which I mean that the people and their way of life are at least within one's comprehension. And the journey itself needs to be planned—meetings with ministers, industrialists, writers to get the overall picture, and then, with the country's problems clear in mind, a prolonged stay in one area so that one gets to grips with the people themselves.

Returning, one begins a long, slow process of rendering down. The mind is too often overflowing with all that one has absorbed, and the only way I know to rid oneself of this embarrassment of riches is to write a travel piece—hence my two books in search of background. Even then, it may be two or three years before I am ready to start on the novel, for if it is to be real, the story has to grow out of the background. And in the case of remote areas like the Labrador, or Addu Atoll in the Indian Ocean, there is probably only one real story line that will achieve my purpose and show what the country and the people are really like.

It may appear from this that I am a highly organised writer. I wish this were so. It would make my life a lot easier if it were. But at least by building on a background of very personal travel I know what I am trying to achieve. And whether I succeed or not, it is at least a start to have the goal clear in mind.

* * *

Reading the novels of Hammond Innes as they appeared, one forms the opinion that they display great versatility. His settings range from Greece to Western Canada and from North Africa to the Labrador. He displays expertise on flying, sailing, mining, skiing, engineering, and now even archaeology. His situations include German espionage in Britain during the last war, the problems of veterans just beyond the law, the toughest kind of free enterprise from the Berlin airlift to the Maldive Islands, and the continual conflict between the crooked and the straight.

Yet re-read one after the other, these books show a remarkable sameness. His heroes seem all the same, but getting older. His heroines are all resourceful, courageous, and ready to lend a hand when the going gets tough. There is almost always a companion to share the hero's burden—and to provide an excuse for dialogue to salt the long introspective explanations that lend authenticity to the tales. The other side—usually self-made businessman—are single-minded and ruthless, and with assistants who are downright evil.

It is impossible to divide these works into groups with great ease. *Attack Alarm* and *The Trojan Horse* concern the infiltration of German agents into the defense establishment. *Dead and Alive*, *The Killer Mine*, *The Lonely Skier*, *The Blue Ice*, and *The Angry Mountain* deal with various aspects of the aftermath of the war, as does *Maddon's Rock*, although the latter introduces the theme of man against the sea continued in *The Mary Deare*, *Atlantic Fury*, and *The Strode Venturer*. *The White South* shifts from this theme to man against the Antarctic. *The Strange Land* and *The Doomed Oasis* pose North African and Arabian problems, *Campbell's Kingdom* and *The Land God Gave to Cain* those of the Canadian frontier. *Air Bridge* stands by itself as does *Levkas Man*. The latter also has no real villain, but a dedicated archaeologist who will go to any lengths to prove his theory about the migration of prehistoric man.

If Innes's books are mere entertainment, they are very good entertainment indeed. The characters and basic situations are introduced deftly and quickly. There is always a series of suspense-creating surprises. The hero is inevitably carried through a physical ordeal, often in competition with the villain. Always at some point all seems lost. The stories end quickly with the resolution of the conflict. Characterisation is stereotyped as it might be in an adventure film, where the type-cast actor plays himself, but the narrative pace alleviates this.

Levkas Man was a new departure for Innes in a literary sense as well as a new area for his erudition. It is more complex, less sensational, and the characters are more finely shaded. Both sides in the conflict are well-intentioned although both are on the wrong side of the law.

—William Bittner

INNES, Michael. *See* **STEWART, J.I.M.**

IRELAND, David. Australian. Born in Lakemba, New South Wales, 24 August 1927. Married Elizabeth Ruth Morris in 1955; two sons and two daughters. Recipient: *Adelaide Advertiser* Literary Award, 1966; Miles Franklin Award, 1972, 1976, 1979; *The Age* Award, 1980. Agent: Curtis Brown (Australia) Pty. Ltd., 86 William Street, Paddington, New South Wales 2021. Address: Box 101, Darlinghurst, New South Wales 2010, Australia.

PUBLICATIONS

Novels

The Chantic Bird. London, Heinemann, and New York, Scribner, 1968.
The Unknown Industrial Prisoner. Sydney and London, Angus and Robertson, 1971.
The Flesheaters. Sydney and London, Angus and Robertson, 1972.
Burn. Sydney and London, Angus and Robertson, 1975.
The Glass Canoe. Melbourne and London, Macmillan, 1976.
A Woman of the Future. New York, Braziller, 1979.

Play

Image in the Clay (produced Sydney, 1962). Brisbane, University of Queensland Press, 1964.

* * *

David Ireland is Australia's most astute political novelist and one of the nation's more innovative prose stylists. His immediate concerns are the treatment of the poor and unemployed, the plight of the worker, the dangers of foreign ownership of Australian resources. But he does not see political questions simply in terms of certain isolated issues: his is a commandingly total vision, encompassing the whole fabric of society.

Ireland's first three novels depict a world that is in its "industrial adolescence," obsessed with profit and production to the point where those who do not contribute to industry (the poor, the aged, the unemployed) are treated as failures, misfits—lepers. In his masterpiece, *The Unknown Industrial Prisoner*, Ireland sketches the life of workers in a foreign-owned Sydney oil refinery, examining their plight piece by piece and layer by layer, until the fragmented mosaic builds into an image of a whole society. The novel records the dehumanisation of the work force—but it also acknowledges the laziness and the stupidity of the workers. Thus, far from adopting a "leftist" or "right-wing" attitude to industrial relations, Ireland attempts to view the problem honestly and objectively—though with compassion. The novel's analytic quality, and its characteristic use of language and imagery, are seen in the repeated references to the workers as "the soil" in which "the money tree" of industry is growing. This is primarily an image of protest at exploitation and degradation—but it can also be seen as a wholly natural organic image, for if there is to be a "money tree" then there must be "soil" in which it can grow. Instead of accepting social realities at face value, Ireland digs for the underlying assumptions and implications.

Monotonous conformity is the keynote of Ireland's vision of Australian society. He sees Australians as tame and insipid, bowed in philistine worship to the god of materialism. (At night the people of Sydney sit at home, "filling in insurance policies on their fowls, their wrought-iron railings, concrete paths, light globes, their health, funeral expenses, borers, carpets," and so on.) In *The Chantic Bird*—the story of a teenage delinquent who escapes the social system by becoming unemployed—the pressures to conform are shown to come not only from the outside (as social rules and customs) but also from inside (as an inherent conservatism).

The Flesheaters and *Burn* deal with the outcasts of Australian society. Written in the absurdist-surrealist mode, *The Flesheaters* offers a vision of the world as "a madhouse without walls," using a boarding-house for the poor and unemployed as a microcosm of society as a whole. These "terminal cases" of industrial uselessness are forced to live in trees, tin sheds, or even dog kennels. (Old Granny Upjohn is the one in the kennel: an emblem of society's treatment of the aged, she is fitted with collar and chain and kept under sedation.) By contrast, *Burn* is written largely in the realist mode. Based upon Ireland's play, *Image in the Clay*, it documents a day in the life of an Aboriginal dwelling on the fringe of white society. Though the moving finale to the novel laments the white man's treatment of the Aborigines, the account of the central character's life makes it clear that the Aborigines have been too complacent in accepting their plight.

Ireland's two most recent novels have explored new territory. *The Glass Canoe* is a bawdy and violent celebration of life in a Sydney pub, offering the view that the cheery brawling drinkers are the last of a colourful "tribe" that preserves values (such as mateship and brawniness) from Australia's past. Unlike Ireland's earlier works, *The Glass Canoe* is descriptive and evocative rather than persistently analytical. *A Woman of the Future* represents Ireland's first attempt to create a full-scale female character. By setting the novel in the future, Ireland allows himself to extrapolate the effects of current social problems (especially unemployment), but the novel's chief concern is to draw a parallel between the young heroine, stepping out into life, and her country—Australia—stepping out into nationhood. Praised by some critics and damned by others, *A Woman of the Future* is Ireland's most controversial work to date. It signifies his willingness to turn to new material, yet it also reaffirms his interest in man's socio-political plight.

Ireland's novels have their foundation in the tradition of Australian social realism, but they transcend the restrictions of that tradition because of Ireland's pressing need to *rouse* his reader. His writing is zany, witty, fraught with black humour and tortured ironies, his novels peopled with obsessives, homosexuals, failed artists, morbid children. Provocative material—but never sensational, for Ireland's writing, despite its effervescence, runs dark and deep with detail. His madhouse world is painstakingly scrutinised, its details transcribed with almost documentary care, and brilliantly used to serve thematic ends. By the very blackness of their cramped and complex intensity, David Ireland's novels create a yearning for a radically freer way of life.

—Van Ikin

IRVING, John (Winslow). American. Born in Exeter, New Hampshire, 2 March 1942. Educated at the University of Pittsburgh, 1961-62; University of Vienna, 1963-64; University of New Hampshire, Durham, B.A. (cum laude) 1965; University of Iowa, Iowa City, M.F.A. 1967. Married Shyla Leary in 1964; two sons. Assistant Professor, 1967-72 and since 1975, Member of the Department of English, Mount Holyoke College, South Hadley, Massachusetts. Writer-in-Residence, University of Iowa, 1972-75. Recipient: Rockefeller grant, 1971; National Endowment for the Arts grant, 1974; Guggenheim Fellowship, 1976; American Book Award, 1980. Address: Department of English, Mount Holyoke College, South Hadley, Massachusetts 01075, U.S.A.

PUBLICATIONS

Novels

Setting Free the Bears. New York, Random House, 1969; London, Corgi, 1979.
The Water-Method Man. New York, Random House, 1972; London, Corgi, 1980.
The 158-Pound Marriage. New York, Random House, 1974; London, Corgi, 1980.
The World According to Garp. New York, Dutton, and London, Gollancz, 1978.
The Hotel New Hampshire. New York, Dutton, 1981.

Uncollected Short Stories

"A Winter Branch," in *Redbook* (Dayton, Ohio), November 1965.
"Almost in Iowa," in *The Secret Life of Our Times*, edited by Gordon Lish. New York, Doubleday, 1973.
"Lost in New York," in *Esquire* (New York), March 1973.
"Dog in the Alley, Child in the Sky," in *Esquire* (New York), June 1977.

* * *

The publication of *The World According to Garp* was an important event in contemporary American literature. For John Irving himself, of course, the novel's reception must have been extremely gratifying; the author of three previous books which rapidly sought the remainder lists—*Setting Free the Bears*, *The Water-Method Man*, and *The 158-Pound Marriage*—he suddenly found himself inundated by critical superlatives and, no doubt, positively drenched in money. He achieved the rare combination of literary acclaim and wide readership that every writer dreams of. The success of *Garp*, along with the previous popularity of E.L. Doctorow's *Ragtime*, indicated that fiction, after more than a decade of stifling academicism, may have finally graduated from college and gone out into the arena of ordinary life. Because many professors seem to believe that literature was written to be studied in their courses and because probably far too many writers receive their training at their hands, a great deal of contemporary American writing has been marked by a sterile obsession with technique for its own sake, a conscious avoidance of traditional subjects, and a perverse desire to appeal only to a coterie of initiates.

Irving's works, and *Garp* most spectacularly, signal the return of fiction to its proper and honorable concerns—a close engagement with the stuff of real life, a profound compassion for humanity and—inextricably and possibly even causally connected to these qualities—great dedication to the narrative process, to storytelling itself. Irving cares very much about his characters and their stories and he makes his readers care about them as well; in doing so he places his work in the greatest traditions of the novel. Only a bold and innovative writer could venture so daringly backward into the literary past.

In addition to his refreshingly old-fashioned qualities, Irving also demonstrates his appropriateness to his own time and place. His novels in many ways are as contemporary as the works of any of his peers. They possess all the familiar elements we have learned t recognize as landmarks of the American literary countryside: violence, grotesquerie, a certain craziness, a racy energetic style, powerful interest in the fiction-making process. All of his work differ from one another in manner, matter, and even in merit—*The 158-Pound Marriage* seems his weakest performance—but the also share certain peculiarly Irvingesque subjects that help to give them their special zany charm. In no particular order of importance his books all deal with such matters as academia, art, writers marital triangles and quadrangles, children, and especially wrestling, mutilation, Vienna, and bears. His curious and reiterated fondness for bears is most evident in the title of his first novel and i the long story, "The Pension Grillparzer," that appears within *The World According to Garp*; it comes as no surprise that his forthcoming novel, as he has described it in a recent *New York Times Book Review* piece, begins "The summer my father bought the bear...."

Irving's early work is lively, comic, whimsical, written with confidence, a kind of assured easiness unusual in a young beginner, an therefore beyond the usual condescending critical clichés abou promise. *Setting Free the Bears* is a kind of revitalized America picaresque set improbably (but not incredibly) against the landscape of Austria; the goal of its protagonist's lunatic quest is suggested in its title and works out to be as unusual and improbable a its setting. *The Water-Method Man* deals with the sexual escapades personal failures, and professional problems of a more or les lovable rogue with the wonderful name of Bogus Trumper; explores, with rich glee, some fascinating notions about the creation of art from the chaos of Trumper's life, all of this through the medium of *avant garde* filmmaking and Trumper's absurd doctora dissertation. Moving gradually and partially out of the comic real and clearly beginning to catch sight of *Garp* on the horizon, Irvin considers in *The 158-Pound Marriage* some of the painful an potentially tragic consequences of complicated marital entanglements, the punishing psychic displacements of the sexual guilt h has been writing about in the past.

Whatever the value of his earlier work, however, in retrospect a least it now seems a preliminary for the main event, *The Worl According to Garp*. That novel is a remarkable performance, written with enormous energy and strength, and clearly the work of a important writer in full command of his material and his method Although the style presents no particular problems and the book plot moves in a straightforward linear way, the novel seems a radically experimental within its temporal and cultural context a anything published in the last ten years. Its generally simple narrative of the life of T.S. Garp from conception to death is interrupte by a number of other fictions, from "The Pension Grillparzer" (ful as Garp's teacher says, of "lunacy and sorrow") to a horribly violer account of rape, murder, and despair, Garp's novel, *The Worl According to Bensenhaver*; the book also encompasses a few bi from Garp's mother's autobiography, *A Sexual Suspect*, and som lines from the biography of Garp that will only be written after h life and the book are over. Garp, incidentally, is one of the mo convincing portraits of a writer in the history of fiction, in pa because we are allowed to see his work in all its horror and beaut In an action that must have called for some courage, Irving eve includes an epilogue, detailing the lives of his characters—all them—after the main events of his major fiction have concluded; once again, in reverting to the habits of the past the author seems daringly innovative.

The actual subjects and events of *Garp* are as unusual as its attention to narrative archaism. Although the novel was almost universally regarded as comic and, in Irving's words, "life affirming," it is also a book haunted by violence, savagery, fear, horror, and despair, an immensely sad and troubling work. From beginning to end a bleeding wound of mutilation gapes across the book: Garp's mother slashes a soldier in a theater; his father (who exists only to provide his mother with a child) dies of a terrible war wound; his wife bites her lover's penis off; one of Garp's sons is killed and the other maimed in an automobile accident; Garp's novel, *The World According to Bensenhaver*, presents one of the most vivid and frightening rape scenes in all of literature; and so on. The relationship between sexuality and mutilation is emphasized in virtually every major character—Roberta Muldoon is a former football player who has elected to become a transsexual; a cult of feminists called the Ellen Jamesians cut out their own tongues to commemorate the rape and maiming of a young girl; Garp himself is assassinated by one of them, who is also the sister of the girl with whom he has experienced his first sexual act.

Along with the zany and horrific narrative and the close attention to the character and life of the artist, the theme of sexual maiming suggests something about the creative act itself. Throughout the novel, art is generated out of fear, pain, blood, and guilt; experiencing all these, Garp creates his fictions, which also make up a large part of the book about him. Art, life, and the interpretation of both provide the novel's rich and often puzzling structure, sometimes causing it to roam far off its initial simple narrative line—into horror, grotesquerie, craziness, and myth.

The World According to Garp appears to be a truly major work of art with a rare combination of elements; despite its great success and its intrinsic charm, the book is also quite a difficult and often puzzling work. Irving has achieved a great deal in his book and will undoubtedly accomplish more in the future. His wonderful mixture of accessibility and complexity, of clarity and confusion, of strong narrative with compassionate vision, of horrified despair and life affirming comedy seems somehow perfectly suited to the present state of our culture and literature. The responsive chord his novel struck in a large and varied reading public indicated how timely and appropriate *Garp* is; it also shows how a vast readership, despite the pronouncements about their illiteracy from highbrow commentators, will recognize and read a novel that happens to be a work of art.

—George Grella

ISHERWOOD, Christopher (William Bradshaw). American. Born in High Lane, Cheshire, England, 26 August 1904; emigrated to the United States, 1939; naturalized, 1946. Educated at Repton School, 1919-22; Corpus Christi College, Cambridge, 1924-25; King's College, London, as a medical student, 1928-29. Private Tutor, and Secretary to André Mangeot and his Music Society String Quartet, London, 1926-27; taught English in Berlin, 1930-33; travelled in Europe, 1933-37, and in China, with W.H. Auden, 1938; reviewer, *The Listener*, London, 1935-37; screenwriter, in Hollywood, from 1939; worked with the American Friends Service Committee, Haverford, Pennsylvania, 1941-42; Resident Student, Vedanta Society of Southern California: Editor, with Swami Prabhavananda, *Vedanta and the West*, Hollywood, 1943-44; Guest Professor of Modern English Literature, Los Angeles State College, and the University of California at Santa Barbara, 1959-62; Regents Professor, University of California at Los Angeles, 1965-66, and University of California at Riverside, 1966-67. Recipient: Brandeis University Creative Arts Award, 1975. Member, American Academy, 1949. Address: 145 Adelaide Drive, Santa Monica, California 90402, U.S.A.

PUBLICATIONS

Novels

All the Conspirators. London, Cape, 1928; New York, New Directions, 1958.
The Memorial: Portrait of a Family. London, Hogarth Press, 1932; New York, New Directions, 1946.
Mr. Norris Changes Trains. London, Hogarth Press, 1935; as *The Last of Mr. Norris*, New York, Morrow, 1935.
Sally Bowles. London, Hogarth Press, 1937.
Goodbye to Berlin. London, Hogarth Press, and New York, Random House, 1939.
Prater Violet. New York, Random House, 1945; London, Methuen, 1946.
The Berlin Stories (includes *Mr. Norris Changes Trains*, *Sally Bowles*, and *Goodbye to Berlin*). New York, New Directions, 1946, as *The Berlin of Sally Bowles*, London, Hogarth Press, 1975.
The World in the Evening. New York, Random House, and London, Methuen, 1954.
Down There on a Visit. New York, Simon and Schuster, and London, Methuen, 1962.
A Single Man. New York, Simon and Schuster, and London, Methuen, 1964.
A Meeting by the River. New York, Simon and Schuster, and London, Methuen, 1967.

Plays

The Dog Beneath the Skin; or, Where Is Francis?, with W.H. Auden (produced London, 1936; revised version, produced London, 1937). London, Faber, and New York, Random House, 1935.
The Ascent of F6, with W.H. Auden (produced London, 1937; New York, 1939). London, Faber, 1936; revised version, New York, Random House, and Faber, 1937.
On the Frontier, with W.H. Auden (produced Cambridge, 1938; London, 1939). London, Faber, 1938; New York, Random House, 1939.
The Adventures of the Black Girl in Her Search for God, adaptation of the novel by G.B. Shaw (produced Los Angeles, 1969).
A Meeting by the River, with Don Bachardy, adaptation of the novel by Isherwood (produced Los Angeles and New York, 1972).
Frankenstein: The True Story (screenplay), with Don Bachardy, based on the novel by Mary Shelley. New York, Avon, 1973.

Screenplays: *Little Friend*, with Margaret Kennedy, 1934; *Rage in Heaven*, with Robert Thoeren, 1941; *Forever and a Day*, with others, 1944; *Adventure in Baltimore*, with Lionel Houser and Lesser Samuels, 1949; *The Great Sinner*, with Ladislas Fodor and Rene Fulop-Miller, 1949; *Diane*, 1955; *The Loved One*, with Terry Southern, 1965; *The Sailor from Gibraltar*, with Don Magner and Tony Richardson, 1967; *Frankenstein: The True Story*, with Don Bachardy, 1972.

Other

Lions and Shadows: An Education in the Twenties. London, Hogarth Press, 1938; New York, New Directions, 1947.
Journey to a War (on China), with W.H. Auden. New York, Random House, and London, Faber, 1939.
The Condor and the Cows: A South American Travel Diary. New York, Random House, and London, Methuen, 1950.
An Approach to Vedanta. Hollywood, Vedanta Press, 1963.

Ramakrishna and His Disciples. New York, Simon and Schuster, and London, Methuen, 1965.
Exhumations: Stories, Articles, Verses. New York, Simon and Schuster, and London, Methuen, 1966.
Essentials of Vedanta. Hollywood, Vedanta Press, 1969.
Kathleen and Frank (autobiographical). London, Methuen, 1971; New York, Simon and Schuster, 1972.
Christopher and His Kind: 1929-1939 (autobiography). New York, Farrar Straus, 1976; London, Eyre Methuen, 1977.
An Isherwood Selection, edited by Geoffrey Halson. London, Longman, 1979.
My Guru and His Disciple (on Swami Prabhavananda). New York, Farrar Straus, and London, Eyre Methuen, 1980.

Editor, *Vedanta for the Western World*. Hollywood, Marcel Rodd, 1945; London, Allen and Unwin, 1948.
Editor, *Vedanta for Modern Man*. New York, Harper, 1951; London, Allen and Unwin, 1952.
Editor, *Great English Short Stories*. New York, Dell, 1957.

Translator, *Intimate Journals*, by Charles Baudelaire. London, Blackamore Press, and New York, Random House, 1930.
Translator (verse only), *A Penny for the Poor*, by Bertolt Brecht. London, Hale, 1937; New York, Hillman Curl, 1938; as *Threepenny Novel*, New York, Grove Press, 1956.
Translator, with Swami Prabhavananda, *Bhagavad-Gita: The Song of God*. Hollywood, Marcel Rodd, 1944; London, Phoenix House, 1947.
Translator, with Swami Prabhavananda, *Crest-Jewel of Discrimination*, by Shankara. Hollywood, Vedanta Press, 1947.
Translator, with Swami Prabhavananda, *How to Know God: The Yoga Aphorisms of Patanjali*. New York, Harper, and London, Allen and Unwin, 1953.

*

Bibliography: *Christopher Isherwood: A Bibliography, 1923-1967* by Selmer Westby and Clayton M. Brown, Los Angeles, California State College, 1968; *Christopher Isherwood: A Reference Guide* by Robert W. Funk, Boston, Hall, 1979.

Critical Studies: *Christopher Isherwood* by Carolyn G. Heilbrun, New York, Columbia University Press, 1970; *Christopher Isherwood* by Alan Wilde, New York, Twayne, 1971; *Christopher Isherwood* by Francis King, London, Longman, 1976; *Isherwood: A Biography* by Jonathan Fryer, London, New English Library, 1977, New York, Doubleday, 1978; *Christopher Isherwood: Myth and Anti-Myth* by Paul Piazza, New York, Columbia University Press, 1978; *Christopher Isherwood: A Critical Biography* by Brian Finney, London, Faber, 1979; *Christopher Isherwood* by Claude J. Summers, New York, Ungar, 1980.

Christopher Isherwood comments:

(1972) All my writing is fundamentally autobiographical—that is to say, I write about experiences I myself have had, at first or second hand. (What I mean by "second hand" is that the attempted suicide in *The Memorial*, for example, was actually experienced and described to me by a friend.) In my novels, much of the action and the dialogue is fictitious and many of the characters are composites; but the experience upon which the scenes and characters are founded is my own.

I write because I am trying to study my life in retrospect and find out what it is, what it is made of, what it is all about. The attempt to do this is ultimately frustrating, of course, but nevertheless the most fascinating occupation I can imagine. At present (aged 67) it seems to me that I would prefer to write direct autobiography, as frank as possible, rather than any more fiction.

*   *   *

Near the opening of his finest novel thus far, *Down There on a Visit*, the Christopher Isherwood of 1962 looks back critically at the young Isherwood of 1928. Despite his anxieties and untested arrogance, the young man had his points: "Perhaps his strongest negative emotion is ancestor hatred. He has vowed to disappoint, disgrace and disown his ancestors. If I were sneering at him I should suggest that this is because he fears he will never be able to live up to them; but this would be less than half true. His fury is sincere. He is genuinely a rebel. He knows instinctively that it is only through rebellion that he will ever learn and grow." There are a number of valid ways of describing Christopher Isherwood's achievements over the past 40 years, but it is this theme of rebellion and growth which dominates everything he has written. The early novels, *All the Conspirators* and *The Memorial*, the autobiographical *Lions and Shadows*, and to a lesser extent *The Berlin Stories*, record stages of revolt against the false and dying cultures through which Isherwood and his characters move; the problem is that of finding an authentic self which can avoid compromise and resist destruction. The later work, beginning with *Prater Violet*, gradually questions the earlier goal of self-development—so much so that readers may wonder if Isherwood's final spiritual commitments may not prove incompatible with the kind of egoism which is one of the chief sources of creative energy: to question the value of the ego as radically as Isherwood has done in *Down There on a Visit* and *A Meeting by the River* may be a crucial step in the quest for purity, but it may also be fatal to the artistic projections of the ego. Beyond conversion and renunciation—which is the point towards which Isherwood has been propelling his recent heroes—there can be only the silence of meditation and self-discipline. Isherwood's fiction should be seen in this light, then, as an initial series of movements towards selfhood, rendered with extraordinary clarity, followed by a countermovement of spiritual rebellion against egoism.

The conspirators of *All the Conspirators* are the perpetual enemies of youthful freedom and expression—the family, the job, the routine obligations of living, everything which the older generation represents—and the motto of his first hero is, as Isherwood puts it, "My generation—right or wrong." The record of Philip Lindsay's two abortive rebellions against his family and class is the record of a "trivial but furious battle which the combatants fight out passionately and dirtily to a finish, using whatever weapons come to their hands" ("tribal" here rather than tragic because Lindsay is no Stephen Dedalus, but merely a suffocated only son with a vague desire to "paint and write"). Nevertheless, Lindsay's weak campaigns and pathetic defeat are rendered in a series of sharp, economical scenes of remarkable skill for so young a writer; Isherwood, at least, is no Philip Lindsay. *The Memorial*, a far more ambitious novel, fails, despite brilliant passages, because one of Isherwood's central preoccupations is insufficiently dramatized. The novel was conceived as a bitter memorial to the first World War and its casualties among the living. Those who have survived, if not physically wounded, find themselves "living on in a new world, unwanted among enemies," while the young must grow up under the shadow of an unmet challenge. In *Lions and Shadows* Isherwood remarks that *The Memorial* was to be "about war," which for his generation meant "the test of your courage, of your maturity, of your sexual prowess. Are you really a man?... We young writers of the twenties were all suffering, more or less, from a feeling of shame that we hadn't been old enough to take part in the European War." The dislocation of the older generation is sympathetically presented (Isherwood reveals a good deal of sympathy for at least some members of the older generation who would have been categorically dismissed a few years before), but the uneasiness and mild hysteria of the young are dramatically puzzling and finally inexplicable in terms of the novel as we have it, without the helpful gloss of *Lions and Shadows*.

The Berlin Stories (1935-39), Isherwood's most directly autobiographical work, is already something of a modern classic, largely because of two superbly realized characters, Sally Bowles and Arthur Norris. The retiring narrator refers to himself, the young novelist barely making ends meet as an English teacher in Berlin during the rise of Hitler, as simply a "camera," recording the troubled scenes around him. But the image is misleading: cameras don't of themselves select and focus, whereas Isherwood in cool, understated terms carefully selects and focuses on those "small" incidents which will reveal and stand for the greater historical upheavals going on around them.

Prater Violet, Isherwood's first book after coming to America, looks back to pre-war London—and Germany—and at the same time introduces, however tentatively, the author's new mistrust of "personality." The narrator describes his growing attachment to a refugee film-maker, a man of great power and charm who is to preside over the next stage of young Isherwood's education. Bergman is a commanding father figure, as well as an archetype of the artist, but in the splendid climax of this short novel something else is at work. Beyond a series of shadowy lovers the narrator senses for a moment, "but how infinitely faint, how distant, like the far high glimpse of a goat track through the mountains between clouds ...something else"—something other, that is, than passing attractions and involvements of the superficial, narcissistic self:

> the way that leads to safety. To where there is no fear, no loneliness, no need of J., K., L., or M. For a second, I glimpse it. For an instant, it is even quite clear. Then the clouds shut down, and a breath off the glacier, icy with the inhuman coldness of the peaks, touches my cheek. "No," I think, "I could never do it. Rather the fear I know, the loneliness I know.... For to take that other way would mean that I would lose myself. I should no longer be a person. I should no longer be Christopher Isherwood. No. No. That's more terrible than having no lover. That I can never face."

The World in the Evening is the weakest of Isherwood's novels. Here the central figure (no longer so clearly a projection of Isherwood himself) uses his money, his considerable charm and sensitivity tyrannically, if half-unconsciously, as a means of confirming his ego: he will exist if others can be made to respond. An apparent accident forces him to review his life and admit his manipulation of others, but the ending is inconclusive, perhaps deliberately so. Is there to be any new growth now that the past has been understood? At the end of the novel Stephen claims that he can forgive anything, even himself: "Do you know," he concludes, "I really do forgive myself, from the bottom of my heart." This knowing self-indulgence is, however, only a version of the sin of pride. "We must overcome this terrible desire to luxuriate in our guilt and our scruples," warns Augustus, the Gerald Heard-like teacher in Isherwood's next novel, *Down There on a Visit*: "as long as we're going to indulge in that sort of vanity, well, it's just hopeless." The novel fails, not because Stephen may still be unable to overcome his egoism, but rather because of Isherwood's uncertainty in handling the American scenes and idioms, and because of a quite uncharacteristic idealization and finally sentimentalization of Stephen's saintly wife and his Quaker friends.

Down There on a Visit dramatizes four critical stages in the career of Isherwood's narrative self: in "Mr. Lancaster" and "Ambrose" the young observer watches the destructive power of the ego at work in two radically different kinds of characters; in "Waldemar" the young novelist watches Europe plunging into war; and in "Paul" the now older writer watches the perilous spiritual experiments of a magnetic young man with equal capacity for damnation or sainthood. In each of the episodes the narrator himself moves a little closer to participation and commitment: negatively, he leaves the old world and its claims; positively, he reaches towards Paul and his desperate attempts to find release from the prison of selfhood. *A Single Man* is a moving account of an aging man, a survivor of his own past, drifting towards death, recalling the comforts and pains of his past and trying to make some tentative connection with the young. But it is his most recent novel, *A Meeting by the River*, which provides the clearest indication of the path Isherwood has been travelling: here a young Englishman, a searcher in the earlier Isherwood tradition, is preparing to join a Hindu religious order based on the extinction of the individual ego and its attachments to the material world (Isherwood has described the doctrine of renunciation at length in his biography, *Ramakrishna and His Disciples*). Oliver's older brother, a splendid instance of a man caught hopelessly in his own vanity, appears to tempt the novitiate but fails, and in the course of failing comes to realize some of his own evasions. Just possibly he too may be preparing for the state of grace.

At the conclusion of *Down There on a Visit* Paul lashes out at the uneasy, observing Isherwood: "You know, you really are a tourist, to your bones. I bet you're always sending postcards with 'down here on a visit' on them. That's the story of your life." This self-criticism has all the power of a shrewd half-truth. Isherwood's career has been spent in the service of sending extraordinary, synoptic postcards from crucial places at crucial times. But more than that, the messages inscribed offer a symbolic account of the quest for self-purification.

—Elmer Borklund

ISRAEL, Charles (Edward). American. Born in Evansville, Indiana, 15 November 1920. Educated at the University of North Carolina, Chapel Hill, 1937-39; University of Cincinnati, Ohio, B.A. 1952; Hebrew Union College, Los Angeles, B.H.L. 1943. Served in the United States Merchant Marine, 1943-45. Married Verna Margaret Sweezey in 1950. Deputy Chief of Repatriation, then Deputy Chief of the Voluntary Societies Division, United Nations Relief and Rehabilitation Administration (UNRRA) International Refugee Organization, in Munich, Heidelberg and Bad Kissingen, Germany, 1946-50. Radio and television playwright, in Hollywood, 1950-53, and since 1953 in Canada. Member of the Executive Board, 1957-59, and of the Board of Directors, 1965-66, Association of Canadian Radio and Television Artists. Recipient: Genoa Prize, for television film, 1964. Address: c/o Simon and Schuster, 630 Fifth Avenue, New York, New York 10020, U.S.A.

PUBLICATIONS

Novels

How Many Angels. Toronto and London, Macmillan, 1956.
The Mark. New York, Simon and Schuster, and London, Macmillan, 1958.
Rizpah. New York, Simon and Schuster, and London, Macmillan, 1961.
Who Was Then the Gentleman? New York, Simon and Schuster, and London, Macmillan, 1963.
Shadows on a Wall. New York, Simon and Schuster, and London, Macmillan, 1965.
The Hostages. Toronto and London, Macmillan, and New York, Simon and Schuster, 1966.

Plays

The Labyrinth: A Play for Television (televised, 1964). Toronto, Macmillan, 1969; New York, St. Martin's Press, 1970.

500 radio and television plays and documentaries produced in the United States and Canada, and *The Labyrinth*, 1964 (UK).

Other

The True North: The Story of Captain Joseph Bernier, with T.C. Fairley. Toronto and London, Macmillan, and New York, St. Martin's Press, 1957.
Five Ships West: The Story of Magellan (juvenile). New York, Macmillan, 1966; London, Collier Macmillan, 1967.

The Newcomers: Inhabiting a New Land. Toronto, McClelland and Stewart, 1979.

* * *

The novels of Charles Israel reflect a mind with an extraordinarily wide range of knowledge. So varied are the settings and the subjects of these books that one can find no linking thematic patterns among them: *Rizpah*, a sprawling biblical romance; *Who Was Then the Gentleman?*, the story of Wat Tyler and the peasant revolt of 1381; *The Mark*, contemporary California and the difficulties of a paroled sex offender in adjusting to society; *Shadows on a Wall*, a complex narrative centering on black-white relationships, disparate ethnic values, with action in Europe, Africa and the United States; *The Hostages*, the story of a group of United Nations members' children who are kidnapped in New York and held as hostages.

Perhaps the most impressive thing about this varied subject matter is Israel's command of detail. In rendering accurately and convincingly the surface of things, the particular feel of a place and time through the careful accumulation of facts, Israel is a master. Perhaps it is a mark of his concern with such detail that, though he has lived in Canada since 1953, he has not yet written a novel with a Canadian setting.

Israel's novels are so strongly oriented toward the surfaces of reality that frequently the fictional structure seems a mere facade that falls away to reveal a kind of semi-documentary or perhaps a social worker's case study. Something of this sort happens in *The Mark* in which the internal conflicts of the central character are never quite convincing; we are told of his tensions and his fears, but we cannot truly feel them ourselves. We are led to view him as a kind of specimen or sample to be studied but the study is cold.

The feeling of a case study is equally strong in *The Hostages*; the book is even structured in a kind of documentary form. Even at his fictional best, as in *Shadows on a Wall* where Israel almost succeeds in bringing out the contradictions deep within a human personality and the contradictions and differences within and between two cultures, the visual orientation rules. Perhaps the difficulty in these books is that we are told that the characters are emotional, tense, impulsive. Indeed they frequently act on feeling or impulse. But we seldom see far enough into them to understand why they feel the way they do. They are like strangers observed at a party, people whom we will never get to know, people about whom we are told scraps of gossip. Adam, the sophisticated black journalist in *Shadows on a Wall*, is incapable of making love to a white woman. The scene is a village in Africa. "But oh, Nancy, I can't. Understand, understand, will you please? I can't!" We are told that his impotence stems from experiences a few years before with "those rich tramps who came to Harlem for kicks." Here, as in many other such situations in Israel's novels, the explanation seems too thin.

Unlike a writer like Robbe-Grillet, Israel cannot move smoothly from the surface to the interior. But that is a most subtle art, one found only in the best of novelists. Probably Israel is not of the absolute best, but he is a skilful observer and craftsman, an extraordinarily facile and knowing writer, whose range and versatility alone are sufficient to merit him rank among contemporary writers.

—Leo J. Hertzel

JACOBSON, Dan. British. Born in Johannesburg, South Africa, 7 March 1929. Educated at the University of the Witwatersrand, Johannesburg, 1946-49, B.A. 1949. Married Margaret Pye in 1954; four children. Public Relations Assistant, South African Jewish Board of Deputies, Johannesburg, 1951-52; Correspondence Secretary, Mills and Feeds Ltd., Kimberley, South Africa, 1952-54. Fellow in Creative Writing, Stanford University, California, 1956-57; Visiting Professor, Syracuse University, New York, 1965-66; Visiting Fellow, State University of New York, Buffalo, 1971. Lecturer, 1976-80, and since 1980, Reader in English, University College, London. Recipient: Rhys Memorial Prize, 1959; Maugham Award, 1964; H.H. Wingate Award (*Jewish Chronicle*, London), 1978. Agent: A.M. Heath and Company, 40-42 William IV Street, London WC2N 4DD, England.

PUBLICATIONS

Novels

The Trap. London, Weidenfeld and Nicolson, and New York, Harcourt Brace, 1955.

A Dance in the Sun. London, Weidenfeld and Nicolson, and New York, Harcourt Brace, 1956.

The Price of Diamonds. London, Weidenfeld and Nicolson, 1957; New York, Knopf, 1958.

The Evidence of Love. London, Weidenfeld and Nicolson, and Boston, Little Brown, 1960.

The Beginners. London, Weidenfeld and Nicolson, and New York, Macmillan, 1966.

The Rape of Tamar. London, Weidenfeld and Nicolson, and New York, Macmillan, 1970.

The Wonder-Worker. London, Weidenfeld and Nicolson, 1973; Boston, Little Brown, 1974.

The Confessions of Josef Raisz. London, Secker and Warburg, 1977; New York, Harper, 1979.

Short Stories

A Long Way from London. London, Weidenfeld and Nicolson, 1958.

The Zulu and the Zeide. Boston, Little Brown, 1959.

Beggar My Neighbour. London, Weidenfeld and Nicolson, 1964.

Through the Wilderness. New York, Macmillan, 1968.

Penguin Modern Stories 6, with others. London Penguin, 1970.

A Way of Life and Other Stories, edited by Alix Pirani. London, Longman, 1971.

Inklings: Selected Stories. London, Weidenfeld and Nicolson, 1973; as *Through the Wilderness*, London, Penguin, 1977.

Play

Television Play: *The Caves of Adullan*, 1972.

Other

No Further West: California Visited. London, Weidenfeld and Nicolson, 1959; New York, Macmillan, 1961.

Time of Arrival and Other Essays. London, Weidenfeld and Nicolson, and New York, Macmillan, 1963.

*

Bibliography: *Dan Jacobson: A Bibliography* by Myra Yudelman, Johannesburg, University of the Witwatersrand, 1967.

Critical Studies: "The Novels of Dan Jacobson" by Renee Winegarten, in *Midstream* (New York), May 1966; "Novelist of South Africa" by Midge Decter, in *The Liberated Woman and Other Essays*, New York, Coward McCann, 1971; "The Gift of Metamorphosis" by Pearl K. Bell, in *New Leader*(New York), April 1974; "Apollo, Dionysus, and Other Performers in Dan Jacobson's Circus" by Michael Wade, in *World Literature Written in English* (Arlington, Texas), April 1974; "A Somewhere Place" by Jonathan Driver, in *New Review* (London), October 1977.

Dan Jacobson comments:

My novels and stories up to and including *The Beginners* were naturalistic in manner an were written almost entirely about life in South Africa. This is not true of the novels I have written subsequently.

*   *   *

Dan Jacobson's first two novels, *The Trap* and *A Dance in the Sun*, marked him as a writer of considerable ability, with an interest in typically South African "problems." Since then, he has developed rapidly to become one of South Africa's best known and most interesting novelists.

The two early novels are both concerned with the tensions inherent in the extremely close, almost familial, relationships between white employer and black employee, which tend to develop in the particular kind of farm community Jacobson describes. Both embody what might be described as allegorical statements about the South African situation. Jacobson implies that the inhabitants of the country are trapped in their own environment and condemned to perform a ritualistic "dance in the sun." To an outsider this can only appear to be a form of insanity. This vision of South Africa leaves out of account, or, at best, finds irrelevant, the group (English speaking, liberal, white) to which Jacobson himself belongs, and it is, therefore, not surprising that he should have chosen to live and work abroad.

For some years, however, his novels continued to deal with South African themes: the "colour problem" in *The Evidence of Love*; illicit diamond buying in *The Price of Diamonds*; and major social and political attitudes in *The Beginners*. *The Price of Diamonds* reveals a gift for comedy, and is altogether more successful than *The Evidence of Love*, which centres rather uneasily on a black-white love affair.

The Beginners, which together with the collection of stories *A Long Way from London* and the essays *Time of Arrival*, firmly established Jacobson's position as a writer of stature, is an ambitious and substantial novel. The story of three generations of an immigrant Jewish family, it offers a penetrating, subtle, and complex analysis of what it means to be a "demi-European at the foot of Africa" and a "demi-Jew" in the modern world. Ranging over the entire fabric of contemporary South African life, and free from any obvious political or humanitarian bias, it must rank as one of the finest South African novels yet produced.

The Beginners ends with a new "beginning" in London, and it is, therefore, perhaps not surprising that in his next two novels Jacobson turns completely away from South Africa. *The Rape of Tamar*, a witty and sophisticated reconstruction of an episode at the court of King David, is a political allegory, focussing on the power-struggle. *The Wonder-Worker* is set in contemporary working-class London, and shows Jacobson at his best, both in observing and in interpreting details of behaviour with an unerring and compassionate eye. The novel explores the world of a sensitive and lonely character whose inability to establish meaningful relationships with anyone around him leads inevitably to complete alienation, and, paradoxically, to complete understanding.

Like other contemporary South African novelists, Jacobson has produced some excellent short stories. Most of them probe the guilts and fears of white South Africans, revealing the irrational impulses which govern the lives of a people who feel themselves perpetually threatened by the surrounding, and, for the most part, black masses. Two stories which are among the best things he has done are "The Zulu and the Zeide" and "Beggar My Neighbour." "The Zulu and the Zeide" ironically counterpoints the hard-headed acquistiveness of a successful Jewish businessman with the humanity of a "raw" (i.e., tribal) African. Half deliberately, Harry Grossman delegates his filial obligation to Paulus, his black servant, whose tenderness and understanding finally shame him into a belated and futile recognition of his own callousness. "Beggar My Neighbour," an apparently simple story, nevertheless encapsulates an entire South African way of life. A chance acquaintance between three children, one white and two black, gradually forces an awareness—on the white child as well as on the reader—of the intricate connections between people in a colour-bar society, even when prejudice has all but destroyed any meaningful contact. In these stories, as in all his work, Jacobson's special skills are displayed: detailed observation, economic presentation, and a compassionate but objective analysis of the varieties of human behaviour.

—Ursula Laredo

JAMES, C(yril) L(ionel) R(obert). West Indian. Born in Trinidad, 4 January 1901. Educated at Queen's Royal College, Port of Spain, Trinidad, 1911-18. Married Selma Jones in 1955; one child by a previous marriage. Journalist and Teacher in the West Indies until 1932, when he moved to England; Press Correspondent, chiefly on cricket, in England, until 1938; went to the United States in 1938, and remained there, lecturing on politics and literature, until 1953; has lived in England since 1953, except for two years in the West Indies, 1958-60, when he worked as Secretary of the West Indian Federal Labour Party. Address: c/o Hutchinson and Company, 3 Fitzroy Square, London W1P 6JD, England.

PUBLICATIONS

Novel

Minty Alley. London, Secker, 1936.

Uncollected Short Stories

"La Divina Pastora," in *The Best Short Stories of 1928*, edited by Edward J. O'Brien. London, Cape, 1928.

"Triumph," in *Stories from the Caribbean*, edited by Andrew Salkey. London, Elek, 1965; as *Island Voices*, New York, Liveright, 1970.

Play

Toussaint L'Ouverture (produced London, 1936). One scene published in *Life and Letters* (London), Spring 1936.

Other

The Life of Captain Cipriani. Privately printed, 1933; abridged as *The Case for West Indian Self-Government*, London, Hogarth Press, 1933; New York, University Place Book Shop, 1967.

Cricket and I, with L.N. Constantine. London, Allan, 1933.

World Communism 1917-1936: The Rise and Fall of the Communist International. London, Secker and Warburg, and New York, Pioneer, 1937.

A History of Negro Revolt. London, Fact, 1938; revised edition, as *A History of Pan-African Revolt*, Washington, D.C., Drum and Spear Press, 1969.

The Black Jacobins: Toussaint Louverture and the San Domingo Revolution. London, Secker and Warburg, and New York, Dial Press, 1938; revised edition, New York, Random House, 1963.

My Friends: A Fireside Chat on the War (as Native Son). New York, Workers Party, 1940.

Mariners, Renegades, and Castaways: The Story of Herman Melville and the World We Live In. Privately printed, 1953.

Modern Politics (lectures). Port of Spain, Trinidad Public Library, 1960.

Party Politics in the West Indies. Privately printed, 1962.

Marxism and the Intellectuals (as J.R. Johnson). Detroit, Facing Reality, 1962.

Beyond a Boundary. London, Hutchinson, 1963.
Lenin, Trotsky, and Vanguard Party. Detroit, Facing Reality, 1964.
Marxism for the Sixties. Detroit, Facing Reality, 1965.
Wilson Harris: A Philosophical Approach (lecture). St. Augustine, Trinidad, University of the West Indies, 1965.
West Indians of East Indian Descent. Port of Spain, Ibis, 1965(?).
Perspectives and Proposals. Detroit, Facing Reality, 1966.
Education, Propaganda, Agitation. Detroit, Facing Reality, 1968.
State Capitalism and World Revolution. Detroit, Facing Reality, 1969.
Black Studies and the Contemporary Student. Detroit, Facing Reality, 1969(?).
Notes on Dialectics: Hegel and Marxism. Detroit, Facing Reality, 1971; London, Allison and Busby, 1980.
Nkrumah and the Ghana Revolution. London, Allison and Busby, 1977.
The Future in the Present: Selected Writings. London, Allison and Busby, and Westport, Connecticut, L. Hill, 1977.
Black Nationalism and Socialism, with Tony Bogues and Kim Gordon. London, Socialists Unlimited, 1979.
Spheres of Existence: Selected Writings. London, Allison and Busby, 1980.

Translator, *Stalin: A Critical Survey of Socialism*, by Boris Souvarine. New York, Alliance, and London, Secker and Warburg, 1939.

* * *

C.L.R. James shocked the middle-class Trinididian readers of the late 1920's and early 1930's with short stories that explored the manners and morals of the indigenous population. For while everyone knew of them, this central area of Caribbean experience was kept out of "respectable" literature. Today levels of moral acceptance, not only in Trinidad, have drastically changed, and the work of writers such as V.S. Naipaul and Samuel Selvon in the same area makes part of James's explorations of lower-class Caribbean life colourless; nevertheless James's qualities of human compassion in an area land-mined with prejudices of class and colour have not been superseded, and will never be irrelevant.

Minty Alley, James's only full-length novel, tells how a young office-worker, Haynes, is forced by poverty to live in the unfamiliar surroundings of a lower-class tenement. It is run by a Mrs. Rouse and her man Benoit, who is also carrying on an affair with a powerful and somewhat sinister woman known only as "the nurse." The community is violent and unstable in its relationships, lit with sudden moments of tenderness, and Haynes quickly becomes involved in it, in particular through his liaison with the servant Maisie, Mrs. Rouse's niece. Although at first Haynes appears a "superior" figure by class and education, by the end he can begin to realise that he came as an immature person, and has been mothered into manhood by the little community. Benoit dies, and, although he has deserted Mrs. Rouse for the nurse, Mrs. Rouse loses all desire to run the house, and Haynes leaves as its inhabitants disperse.

James hoped that a second novel would be his major work, but this never appeared. *Minty Alley*, however, assures him a place in Caribbean fiction.

—Louis James

JAMESON, (Margaret) Storm. English. Born in Whitby, Yorkshire, 8 January 1891. Educated at Leeds University, Yorkshire, 1909-12, B.A. (1st class honours) in English language and literature 1912; King's College, London, 1912-13, M.A. 1914. Married Guy Patterson Chapman in 1924 (second marriage; died, 1972); one son from first marriage. Formerly Copywriter, Carlton Agency, advertising firm, London; Editor, *New Commonwealth*, London, 1919-21; English Representative, and later London Co-Manager, Alfred A. Knopf, publishers, New York, 1925-28; Reviewer, *New English Weekly*, London, 1934. President, English Centre of P.E.N., 1938-45. Recipient: Calabrian International Prize, 1972; P.E.N. Award, 1974. D.Litt.: Leeds University, 1943. Honorary Member, American Academy, 1978. Address: c/o Macmillan and Company, 4 Little Essex Street, London WC2R 3LF, England.

PUBLICATIONS

Novels

The Pot Boils. London, Constable, 1919.
The Happy Highways. London, Heinemann, and New York, Century, 1920.
The Clash. London, Heinemann, and Boston, Little Brown, 1922.
Lady Susan and Life: An Indiscretion. London, Chapman and Hall, and New York, Dodd Mead, 1923.
The Pitiful Wife. London, Constable, 1923; New York, Knopf, 1924.
Three Kingdoms. London, Constable, and New York, Knopf, 1926.
The Triumph of Time: A Trilogy. London, Heinemann, 1932.
  The Lovely Ship. London, Heinemann, and New York, Knopf, 1927.
  The Voyage Home. London, Heinemann, and New York, Knopf, 1930.
  A Richer Dust. London, Heinemann, and New York, Knopf, 1931.
Farewell to Youth. London, Heinemann, and New York, Knopf, 1928.
That Was Yesterday. London, Heinemann, and New York, Knopf, 1932.
The Single Heart. London, Benn, 1932.
A Day Off. London, Nicholson and Watson, 1933.
Women Against Men (includes *A Day Off*, *The Delicate Monster* and *The Single Heart*). New York, Knopf, 1933.
The Mirror in Darkness:
  Company Parade. London, Cassell, and New York, Knopf, 1934.
  Love in Winter. London, Cassell, and New York, Knopf, 1935.
  None Turn Back. London, Cassell, 1936.
In the Second Year. London, Cassell, and New York, Macmillan, 1936.
Delicate Monster. London, Nicholson and Watson, 1937.
The Moon Is Making. London, Cassell, 1937; New York, Macmillan, 1938.
The World Ends (as William Lamb). London, Dent, 1937.
Loving Memory (as James Hill). London, Collins, 1937.
No Victory for the Soldier (as James Hill). London, Collins, 1938
Here Comes a Candle. London, Cassell, 1938; New York, Macmillan, 1939.
Farewell, Night: Welcome Day. London, Cassell, 1939; as *The Captain's Wife*, New York, Macmillan, 1939.
Europe to Let: The Memoirs of an Obscure Man. London, Macmillan, and New York, Macmillan, 1940.
Cousin Honoré. London, Cassell, 1940; New York, Macmillan, 1941.
The Fort. London, Cassell, and New York, Macmillan, 1941.
Then We Shall Hear Singing: A Fantasy in C Major. London, Cassell, and New York, Macmillan, 1942.
Cloudless May. London, Macmillan, 1943; New York, Macmillan, 1944.
The Journal of Mary Hervey Russell. London, Macmillan, and New York, Macmillan, 1945.

The Other Side. London, Macmillan, and New York, Macmillan, 1946.
Before the Crossing. London, Macmillan, and New York, Macmillan, 1947.
The Black Laurel. London, Macmillan, 1947; New York, Macmillan, 1948.
The Moment of Truth. London, Macmillan, and New York, Macmillan, 1949.
The Green Man. London, Macmillan, 1952; New York, Harper, 1953.
The Hidden River. London, Macmillan, and New York, Harper, 1955.
The Intruder. London, Macmillan, and New York, Macmillan, 1956.
A Cup of Tea for Mr. Thorgill. London, Macmillan, and New York, Harper, 1957.
A Ulysses Too Many. London, Macmillan, 1958; as *One Ulysses Too Many*, New York, Harper, 1958.
Last Score; or, The Private Life of Sir Richard Ormston. London, Macmillan, and New York, Harper, 1961.
The Road from the Monument. London, Macmillan, and New York, Harper, 1962.
A Month Soon Goes. London, Macmillan, and New York, Harper, 1963.
The Aristide Case. London, Macmillan, 1964; as *The Blind Heart*, New York, Harper, 1964.
The Early Life of Stephen Hind. London, Macmillan, and New York, Harper, 1966.
The White Crow. London, Macmillan, and New York, Harper, 1968.
There Will Be a Short Interval. London, Harvill Press, and New York, Harper, 1973.

Short Stories

A Day Off: Two Short Novels and Some Stories. London, Macmillan, 1959.

Plays

Full Circle (produced Liverpool, 1928). Oxford, Blackwell, 1928.
William the Defeated (televised). Published in *The Book of the P.E.N.*, edited by Hermon Ould, London, Barker, 1950.

Television Plays: *William the Defeated*; *The Commonplace Heart*, 1953.

Other

Modern Drama in Europe. London, Collins, and New York, Harcourt Brace, 1920.
The Georgian Novel and Mr. Robinson. London, Heinemann, and New York, Morrow, 1929.
The Decline of Merry England. London, Cassell, and Indianapolis, Bobbs Merrill, 1930.
No Time Like the Present (autobiography). London, Cassell, and New York, Knopf, 1933.
The Soul of Man in the Age of Leisure. London, Nott, 1935.
The Novel in Comtemporary Life. Boston, The Writer, 1938.
Civil Journey. London, Cassell, 1939.
The End of This War. London, Allen and Unwin, 1941.
The Writer's Situation and Other Essays. London, Macmillan, and New York, Macmillan, 1950.
Morley Roberts: The Last Eminent Victorian. London, Unicorn Press, 1961.
Journey from the North (autobiography). London, Collins-Harvill Press, 2 vols., 1969-70; New York, Harper, 1 vol., 1971.
Parthian Words. London, Collins-Harvill Press, 1970; New York, Harper, 1971.
Speaking of Stendhal. London, Gollancz, 1979.

Editor, *Challenge to Death.* London, Constable, 1934; New York, Dutton, 1935.
Editor, *London Calling.* New York, Harper, 1942.
Editor, *A Kind of Survivor: The Autobiography of Guy Chapman.* London, Gollancz, 1975.

Translator, *Mont-Oriol*, by Guy de Maupassant. New York, Knopf, 1924.
Translator, *Horla and Other Stories*, by Guy de Maupassant. New York, Knopf, 1925.
Translator, with Ernest Boyd, *88 Short Stories*, by Guy de Maupassant. London, Cassell, and New York, Knopf, 1930.

*

Manuscript Collections: University of Texas, Austin; Wellesley College, Massachusetts; other libraries have single manuscripts.

Storm Jameson comments:

My earliest novels are not worth reading. Nor are all of the later ones. It took me some years to learn how to write. A short list of those novels worth looking at might run: *That Was Yesterday*; *A Day Off*; *Company Parade*, *Love in Winter*, *None Turn Back*—three novels of an unfinished series; *Farewell, Night: Welcome, Day*; *Europe to Let*; *Cousin Honoré*; *Cloudless May*; *The Journal of Mary Hervey Russell*; *Before the Crossing* and *The Black Laurel*—two novels which are really one; *The Green Man*; *The Hidden River*; *A Cup of Tea for Mr. Thorgill*; *The Road from the Monument*; *The Early Life of Stephen Hind*; *The White Crow*; *There Will Be a Short Interval.*

Of more lasting value is my autobiography: *Journey from the North.* It says all that needs to be said about my novels, myself and my life.

My last but one book, *Parthian Words*, contains my declaration of faith as a writer.

Readers of *Journey from the North* will discover that I have written three novels under other names. One of these, *The World Ends*, by William Lamb, is good, I think.

* * *

Storm Jameson was born in Whitby, Yorkshire, into a family of shipbuilders in 1891; and these basic facts are relevant for both her outlook and writing. Three of her novels—*The Lovely Ship*, *The Voyage Home*, and *A Richer Dust*—form a trilogy in which the author chronicles the fortunes of a shipbuilding family and its Victorian matriarch. Some of her later novels have continued the story of Mary Hervey's descendants, and one may suppose that Jameson drew freely on personal contacts and memories, as well as on records, of her own family.

Storm Jameson has told us much—and told it memorably—about her own life in her autobiography, *Journey from the North*, so it is clear that her own life and her family background have provided a great deal of her subject matter. After reading English at Leeds University she did post-graduate research for her M.A. degree at King's College, London, and her thesis appeared in book form as *Modern Drama in Europe.* Already, then, one notes her interest in European literary art and ideas. Despite her consciousness of and pride in her Yorkshire roots, she is the least insular of writers. As President of the English Centre of P.E.N. she revealed herself as an outspoken liberal and anti-Nazi, and a hard-working friend to refugee writers.

"I have every talent of the good businessman," Jameson has said of herself, "shrewdness, persistence, a talent for strategy—except a talent for enjoying business." More pertinent, perhaps, in considering her fiction is her statement, "My mother was a Congregationalist and what religion I got in youth was coloured by that stiff, self-regarding faith. It would be no use for me to deny to myself my

Nonconformist upbringing." There one finds both her strength and her limitation, for she appears to have retained the Nonconformist "narrow ideas of right and wrong, its distrust of enjoyment." Few writers can have been so honest as to declare bluntly: "I am not what you may call a born writer, and I should have been much happier as an engineer."

Born writer or not, Jameson has proved herself a prolific writer. She has been candid enough to admit that her earliest novels are not very good; and few critics would wish to dispute the author's own judgment. Out of a great mass of fiction only a handful of novels are worth attention. Those that may be singled out for scrutiny and some praise are *Cousin Honoré*, *The Road from the Monument*, *The White Crow*, and *A Cup of Tea for Mr. Thorgill.*

Cousin Honoré, possibly the most satisfying novel Jameson has written, draws the portrait not only of Honoré Burckheim but of the province of Alsace. She brings out splendidly the flavour of an area which is partly French in character and partly German, but yet remains stubbornly itself. Burckheim is the owner of the family ironworks in the village that bears their name but his real interest—almost to the point of obsession—is his vineyards and the fine Alsatian wine they produce. He likes to turn over in his mind the old rhyme: "Burckheim, Burckheim, A little town, a great wine." The "Nonconformist" Storm Jameson appears to have been fascinated by her own creation: a wily, yet fundamentally sound, old sensualist. The period of time covered runs from 1918 to 1939, and this gives Jameson the opportunity to reveal her love of France and her contempt for the aggressive, boorish aspect of the German national character that found its ultimate expression in Nazi brutality and hysteria. She also flays those Frenchmen whose corruption and inertia led to the defeat of France in 1940.

Burckheim is studied in depth. A self-willed not to say selfish man, a greedy, self-indulgent man, he nevertheless represents much that is good in the French tradition. But it is Berthelin who stands for the true élite of France: intelligent, honourable, responsible. Siguenau, a schemer and liar, stops short of treachery to his country if not to his friends. Eschelmer, the son of Burckheim's illegitimate daughter and a half-German, works as a German agent; he is hysterical in nature, driven by self-pity and vanity, and ends up as a murderer. Reuss, while not pro-German, does not appreciate that saving Alsace from destruction is too narrow an objective when the West is faced with the destruction of its values.

But *Cousin Honoré* does not consist simply of men and ideas. Jameson explores—and with great sensitivity—the feminine world. She brings to life for us Caroline, Burckheim's second wife, who comes from Boston and assesses her husband as being "as naturally honest as a child and completely unmanageable"; the English Blanche Siguenau who "rode, gardened, dried herbs for the different teas"; and eager young Fanny Siguenau who watches her fiancé go off to fight the incorrigible Boche from across the Rhine.

Cousin Honoré is an Englishwoman's tribute to French civilisation. It can also be enjoyed for the skilful way in which Jameson builds up her situations and characters. Perceptive, witty, generous, it is vintage Jameson.

A question Storm Jameson often tries to answer is this: are people really, at bottom, what they seem to others or even to themselves? This theme runs through *The Road from the Monument* and *The White Crow.* In the first of these Gregory Mott comes under the microscope. On the surface his life seems happy and assured; but religious faith and the support of friends fail him when he comes face to face with his real self. Reality is also explored in *The White Crow.* Here, the setting runs from 1890 to 1942, so Jameson takes the opportunity not only to probe into her main character but to underline the social changes of that half-century.

A Cup of Tea for Mr. Thorgill satirises the self-consciously clever academic world. She lashes the "profound frivolity—frivolity at a deep level, below whatever you like of scholarship, sophistication, wit" that can be found in the inbred society of an Oxford college. She brings to her task delicacy and irony and not a little feminine malice. Yet, as in all her work, she is a committed writer: one to whom the integrity of the human personality and freedom of individual action are of supreme importance. Had she been less prolific, Storm Jameson's reputation on the literary stock exchange would undoubtedly be quoted as a much higher figure than it is today. Her best work assures her a place among the significant English novelists of our time.

—Robert Greacen

JENKINS, (John) Robin. British. Born in Cambuslang, Lanarkshire, Scotland, 11 September 1912. Educated at Hamilton Academy; Glasgow University, 1931-35, B.A. (honours) in English 1935, M.A. 1936. Married Mary McIntyre Wyllie in 1937; one son and two daughters. Taught at Dunoon Grammar School; Ghazi College, Kabul, 1957-59; the British Institute, Barcelona, 1959-61; Gaya School, Sabah, 1963-68. Recipient: Frederick Niven Award, 1956. Address: Fairhaven, Toward, by Dunoon, Argyll, Scotland.

PUBLICATIONS

Novels

So Gaily Sings the Lark. Glasgow, Maclellan, 1951.
Happy for the Child. London, Lehmann, 1953.
The Thistle and the Grail. London, Macdonald, 1954.
The Cone-Gatherers. London, Macdonald, 1955; New York, Taplinger, 1981.
Guests of War. London, Macdonald, 1956.
The Missionaries. London, Macdonald, 1957.
The Changeling. London, Macdonald, 1958.
Love Is a Fervent Fire. London, Macdonald, 1959.
Some Kind of Grace. London, Macdonald, 1960.
Dust on the Paw. London, Macdonald, and New York, Putnam, 1961.
The Tiger of Gold. London, Macdonald, 1962.
A Love of Innocence. London, Cape, 1963.
The Sardana Dancers. London, Cape, 1964.
A Very Scotch Affair. London, Gollancz, 1968.
The Holy Tree. London, Gollancz, 1969.
The Expatriates. London, Gollancz, 1971.
A Toast to the Lord. London, Gollancz, 1972.
A Figure of Fun. London, Gollancz, 1974.
A Would-Be Saint. London, Gollancz, 1978; New York, Taplinger, 1980.
Fergus Lamont. Edinburgh, Canongate, and New York, Taplinger, 1979.

Short Stories

A Far Cry from Bowmore and Other Stories. London, Gollancz, 1973.

* * *

Robin Jenkins achieved an early success with *Happy for the Child*, an evocative re-creation of a Scottish childhood, but later novels on his native scene, although incisively written, suffered from plots which carried too heavy a weight of symbolic interpretation and broke down into melodramatic situations jarring against the nicely-observed backgrounds. It appeared that his leaning towards the strikingly significant action required a wider stage than the narrow bounds of a provincialised Scotland. This he eventually discovered in Afghanistan, which became the "Nurania" of *Dust on the Paw*.

Here Jenkins presents a country trying to wrench itself up out of medievalism by its own sandalstraps, a society half-fascinated by modernity and half-afraid of it, with intellectuals and administrators uprooted from ancestral traditions which they despise and yet fiercely defend against criticism from the outside world. Whether Jenkins's picture of Afghanistan is wholly accurate, fair, impartial, and unbiased can be judged only by those who have lived there, but to the foreign reader it seems entirely convincing—the alpine sunshine, the dust and the dirt, the peasants dignified in their old poverty and the westernised middle class desperate in their new, the idealism and the corruption, the blind fanaticism and the wary self-seeking, above all the sheer muddle out of which nevertheless some kind of pattern does appear to emerge as the various characters struggle "between two worlds, one dead, the other powerless to be born."

This pattern suggests that the two worlds are in fact one, in which we all share, whatever our creeds or colours. If this is a platitude, the erstwhile dominant minority of Europeans find it hard to accept and even harder to live up to. One of the books's two heroes is the poet Harold Moffat, whose intellectual assent to the idea of racial equality is undermined by a deep-rooted emotional prejudice which compels him to deny motherhood to his Chinese wife. The characterisation of Moffat, whose self-loathing sours into hatred of the men and women around him who challenge those aspects of his personality most distasteful to himself, searches deep but never becomes unsympathetic.

At least equally successful is the characterisation of the other hero, the Afghan Abdul Wahab whose engagement to an Englishwoman sparks off the action of the book. A patriot divided from his own people by his English university education, Wahab lives on a see-saw of ideas and emotions, one eye on his ideals and the other on the main chance—a man with all his qualities, noble and ignoble, forced into play by the precariousness of his situation as a focal point of change in a society undergoing a revolution. The powers of mature insight and imagination revealed in this character-study, and throughout the book as a whole, have created a work which ranks high among British novels on the Asian scene. It remains Jenkins's most impressive creation, although a more recent work, *The Holy Tree*, a bittersweet tragi-comedy of life in colonial Malaya, comes close to its unblinking awareness of the wide differences which divide the races of mankind and its profound appreciation of the fundamental sympathies which unite us all.

—Alexander Scott

JHABVALA, Ruth Prawer. British. Born in Cologne, Germany, of Polish parents, 7 May 1927; emigrated to England, as a refugee, 1939; naturalized, 1948. Educated at Hendon County School, London; Queen Mary College, University of London, 1945-51, M.A. in English literature 1951. Married the architect C.S.H. Jhabvala in 1951; three daughters. Lived in India, 1951-75. Since 1975 has lived in New York City. Recipient: Booker Prize, 1975; Guggenheim Fellowship, 1976; Neil Gunn International Fellowship, 1978. Address: c/o Harper and Row Publishers, 10 East 53rd Street, New York, New York 10022, U.S.A.

PUBLICATIONS

Novels

To Whom She Will. London, Allen and Unwin, 1955; as *Amrita*, New York, Norton, 1956.
The Nature of Passion. London, Allen and Unwin, 1956; New York, Norton, 1957.
Esmond in India. London, Allen and Unwin, and New York, Norton, 1958.
The Householder. London, Murray, and New York, Norton, 1960.
Get Ready for Battle. London, Murray, 1962; New York, Norton, 1963.
A Backward Place. London, Murray, and New York, Norton, 1965.
A New Dominion. London, Murray, 1972; as *Travelers*, New York, Harper, 1973.
Heat and Dust. London, Murray, 1975; New York, Harper, 1976.

Short Stories

Like Birds, Like Fishes and Other Stories. London, Murray, 1963; New York, Norton, 1964.
A Stronger Climate: Nine Stories. London, Murray, 1968; New York, Norton, 1969.
An Experience of India. London, Murray, 1971; New York, Norton, 1972.
Penguin Modern Stories 11, with others. London, Penguin, 1972.
How I Became a Holy Mother and Other Stories. London, Murray, and New York, Harper, 1976.

Uncollected Short Stories

"Parasites," in *New Yorker*, 13 March 1978.
"A Summer by the Sea," in *New Yorker*, 7 August 1978.
"Commensurate Happiness," in *Encounter* (London), January 1980.

Plays

Shakespeare Wallah: A Film, with James Ivory, with *Savages*, by James Ivory. London, Plexus, and New York, Grove Press, 1973.
Autobiography of a Princess, Also Being the Adventures of an American Film Director in the Land of the Maharajas, with James Ivory and John Swope. London, Murray, and New York, Harper, 1975.

Screenplays: *The Householder*, 1963; *Shakespeare Wallah*, with James Ivory, 1965; *The Guru*, 1968; *Bombay Talkie*, 1970; *Autobiography of a Princess*, with James Ivory and John Swope, 1975; *Roseland*, 1976; *Hullabaloo over Georgie and Bonnie's Pictures*, 1978; *The Europeans*, 1979; *Quartet*, 1981.

Television Plays: *The Place of Peace*, 1975; *Jane Austen in Manhattan*, 1980.

Other

Meet Yourself at the Doctor (published anonymously). London, Naldrett Press, 1949.

*

Critical Studies: *The Fiction of Ruth Prawer Jhabvala* by H.M. Williams, Calcutta, Writer's Workshop, 1973; "A Jewish Passage to India" by Renee Winegarten, in *Midstream* (New York), March 1974; *Ruth Prawer Jhabvala* by Vasant A. Shahane, New Delhi, Arnold-Heinemann India, 1976.

Ruth Prawer Jhabvala comments:

(1972) The central fact of all my work, as I see it, is that I am a European living permanently in India. I have lived here for most of my adult life and have an Indian family. This makes me not quite an insider but it does not leave me entirely an outsider either. I feel my position to be at a point in space where I have quite a good view of both sides but am myself left stranded in the middle. My work is an attempt to charter this unchartered territory for myself. Sometimes

I write about Europeans in India, sometimes about Indians in India, sometimes about both, but always attempting to present India to myself in the hope of giving myself some kind of foothold. My books may appear objective but really I think they are the opposite: for I describe the Indian scene not for its own sake but for mine. This excludes me from all interest in all those Indian problems one is supposed to be interested in (the extent of Westernisation, modernity vs. tradition, etc! etc!). My work can never claim to be a balanced or authoritative view of India but is only one individual European's attempt to compound the puzzling process of living in it.

(1981) In 1975 I left India, and am now living in and writing about America—but not for long enough to be able to make any kind of comment about either of these activities.

* * *

The unique character of the novels and short stories of Ruth Prawer Jhabvala is related to her unusual position as an outsider able to take an inside view of Indian society. Her marriage to an Indian architet in 1951 brought her into the intimate life of an Indian family, and she has been able to delineate with great insight the stresses of contemporary Indian society. At the same time she retains the background of a European, particularly rootless as a Polish emigre who was educated in Britain, and this deep sense of alienation from society is explored in several characters in her novels. The position of Westerners confronting Indian culture is also developed in her successful screenplays, particularly *Shakespeare Wallah*, *Autobiography of a Princess*, and *Hullaballoo over Georgie and Bonnie's Pictures*, all directed by the distinguished film-maker James Ivory, with whom she has worked for many years. Her short stories, widely published in American and English magazines as well as in collections, also reveal her preoccupation with the tensions and complexities of Indian life.

The term "comedy of manners" is often used in connection with this writer because of her domestic settings and her witty observation of the social interplay of New Delhi. There is, however, much more of her than that; the corruption, snobbery, and hypocrisy of the upper and middle classes in Delhi are certainly very efficiently exposed but there is also a deep understanding of the unhappiness of men and women who find themselves locked in a role, whether of concubine or clerk or wealthy princess, and are unable to escape from its restrictions.

Her first two novels, *To Whom She Will* and *The Nature of Passion*, remain narrow in scope, dealing with marriage and the pressures in a society that is torn between ancient customs and modern western ideas. *Esmond in India* develops themes that are to become typical of the author, examining as it does the Englishman Esmond whose love/hate relationship with India is clearly revealed. His Indian wife represents the sensual side of India; its smells, its relaxed lifestyle, its passion that once made Esmond decide to stay in India and to delight in his dark son. Now he is disgusted with these very features, and wants to leave India which he now sees as representing only "boredom and futility." Another strand in the novel is concerned with a restless, educated Indian girl who aspires to a life beyond the confines of her well-run, luxurious home, with an arranged marriage in the offing; yet she is unable to define her dissatisfaction or her ideals. She drifts, as do her father's old friends, middle-aged idealists who battled for Indian independence and now feel out of place in the prosperous consumer society that engulfs them.

The Householder is a deceptively simple tale using almost entirely Indian characters, and in its restricted canvas it develops several themes that are to recur in Jhabvala's work: the difficulties of arranged marriages, the gap between westernized Indians and those who refuse to change, the attractions of the swami, the ludicrous enthusiasms of the Europeans who peck at the surface of Indian life. The early married days of Prem and Indu, and Prem's not very successful experience as a young teacher in his first post, are treated with considerable warmth and sympathy, and although many of the problems of the young couple are particularly Indian, many are also universal, such as the visit of the disapproving mother-in-law, and the hideously awkward tea-party given by the headmaster for his staff and their wives.

The chief character in *Esmond in India* resembles another Englishman, Raymond, who is central to *A New Dominion*, a much more profound novel that again explores the effect that India has on the European visitor. The figure of the swami has by now become a familiar satirical target for Ruth Prawer Jhabvala; obviously she has observed many examples of young Europeans seeking the world of Hindu transcendentalism who attach themselves to a mystic, usually an avaricious sham, and mislead themselves into becoming dedicated disciples. Her long story "How I Became a Holy Mother" deals humorously with such a situation, but in *A New Dominion* the exploitation of three young English girls by a swami ends in tragedy. Raymond, like Esmond, retains his essential English attitudes; although fascinated by India he cannot bear Indian food and prefers to stay in air-conditioned hotels. This novel employs a form of omniscient narration, but shifts the viewpoint from one character to another until gradually, as the plot develops, all the characters are linked together.

Technical innovation is also notable in *Heat and Dust* (Booker Prize, 1975). Although it is a slender novel, the historical dimension adds considerably to the rather enclosed interiors that characterised much of her early work. Structurally, *Heat and Dust* is a brilliant inter-weaving of contemporary observations by a young English visitor, juxtaposed with the events of 1923 when Olivia, the young wife of a District Officer, falls in love with an Indian prince and runs away with him. Using Olivia's letters as a basis for her own journal, the contemporary traveller who is in fact grand-daughter of the deserted District Officer, visits the town and even the bungalow where Olivia used to live. By filtering the past through the present we are able to share the complicated attitudes held by the English civilian and military staff in 1923, and although background details are suggested rather than described, the reactions of the two races are totally convincing, even as cameo studies.

Ruth Prawer Jhabvala's most recent work for films includes the screenplays for *The Europeans*, *Roseland*, and *Jane Austen in Manhattan*, revealing a shift away from Indian themes now that she is not permanently resident in India.

—Margaret Lewis

JOHNSON, Josephine (Winslow). American. Born in Kirkwood, Missouri, 20 June 1910. Educated at Washington University, St. Louis. Married Grant G. Cannon in 1941 (died); three children. Taught at the University of Iowa, Iowa City, 1942-45. Recipient: O. Henry Award, 1934, 1935, 1942-45; Pulitzer Prize, 1935; Alumnae Citation, Washington University, 1955; Cincinnati Institute of Fine Arts Award, 1964; American Academy award, 1974. D.H.L.: Washington University, 1970. Address: 4907 Klatte Road, Cincinnati, Ohio 45244, U.S.A.

PUBLICATIONS

Novels

Now in November. New York, Simon and Schuster, 1934; London, Gollancz, 1935.
Jordanstown. New York, Simon and Schuster, and London, Gollancz, 1937.
Wildwood. New York, Harper, 1946; London, Gollancz, 1947.
The Dark Traveler. New York, Simon and Schuster, 1963.

Short Stories

Winter Orchard and Other Stories. New York, Simon and Schuster, 1935.
The Sorcerer's Son and Other Stories. New York, Simon and Schuster, 1965.

Verse

Unwilling Gypsy. Dallas, Kaleidograph, 1936.
Year's End. New York, Simon and Schuster, 1937.

Other

Paulina: The Story of an Apple-Butter Pot. New York, Simon and Schuster, 1939.
The Inland Island (essays). New York, Simon and Schuster, 1969.
Seven Houses: A Memoir of Time and Places. New York, Simon and Schuster, 1973.
Circle of Seasons, photographs by Dennis Stock. New York, Viking Press, and London, Secker and Warburg, 1974.
Florence Farr: Bernard Shaw's "New Woman." Totowa, New Jersey, Rowman and Littlefield, and Gerrards Cross, Buckinghamshire, Colin Smythe, 1975.

* * *

The world of Josephine Johnson's fiction is circumscribed and quiet, but not untroubled and not without echoes of the wider and more troubled outer world. The affairs in her books are affairs of jealousy, rejection, disappointment, and frustration, relieved on every page by the beauty of nature and the music of breath and blood. Larger affairs are not so much shut out as reflected and symbolized. "Salamanders and fungus seem more exciting to me than war or politics," she wrote early in her career, "but it is cowardly and impossible to ignore them or try to escape."

She was prodigious enough to receive the Pulitzer Prize for her first novel, *Now in November*, published when she was 24 years old. It came out of a time when the whole of the economy of the United States was in crisis, and when the agricultural economy was still in the throes of an even older crisis. It tells the story of small farmers in Missouri. A pall of doom is made to hang over every turn of every season, culminating in disastrous fire. And the emotional patterns within the family she depicts are far from idyllic. Yet somehow it is more a celebration of rural life than a denunciation. It has more bitterness than anger, more resignation than protest. It is certainly not the masterpiece some eager reviewers proclaimed it. But the significant view it gave of a part of American life was odd at the time and is still almost entirely unique.

Jordanstown was an attempt to increase the proportion of anger and protest in her fiction, in step with the movement for the "proletarian novel" of that time. It was by far less successful than her initial effort, and bears the marks of having been nurtured in a publisher's office rather than in an author's heart.

Wildwood and *The Dark Traveler* are novels of terror and disturbance in the young, followed by some degree of resolution and hope. Neither has the unity of conception and execution to be found in *Now in November*; indeed, these later books have the exploratory and tentative qualities which are usually found in a novelist's earliest projects. Furthermore, there are a preoccupation with neurosis and phantasm, and an absence of real harshness and deprivation, that deny to these works the steadiness and balance to be found in the earliest book. She shows that only perfect love casteth out fear, but in showing it she somehow makes the flavor of fear stronger than the flavor of love.

Like many American writers who have turned away from fiction to journalism, memoirs, and diaries as a means of expression, Josephine Johnson has most recently tried to give her vision through a calendar of rural life. *The Inland Island* is divided into twelve sections for the months of the year, and records not only the naturalist's findings in the field but the philosopher's accompanying thoughts, in a tradition that goes back to Thoreau's *Walden*. The book came at the beginning of the recent American preoccupation with ecology. Here again, her pessimism seems to have outlasted her love of life: "democracy becomes less and less capable to cope as the numbers increase. If we want to save law, we shall have to stop our lawless, fertile sprawl." She has given up, it would seem, any hope that man can order his affairs in such a way as to accommodate more and more human life upon the planet Earth.

—Richard Greenleaf

JOHNSON, Pamela Hansford. British. Born in London, 29 May 1912. Educated at Clapham County Secondary School, London. Married 1) Gordon Neil Stewart in 1936, one son and one daughter; 2) the writer C.P. Snow (Lord Snow) in 1950 (died, 1980), one son. Fellow, Center for Advanced Studies, Wesleyan University, Middletown, Connecticut, and Honorary Fellow, Dwight College, Yale University, New Haven, Connecticut, 1961. D. Litt.: Temple University, Philadelphia, 1963; York University, Toronto, 1967; Widener College, Chester, Pennsylvania, 1970; D.H.L.: University of Louisville, Kentucky. Fellow, Royal Society of Literature, 1951. C.B.E. (Commander, Order of the British Empire), 1975. Address: c/o Macmillan and Company, 4 Little Essex Street, London WC2N 3LF, England. *Died 19 June 1981.*

PUBLICATIONS

Novels

This Bed Thy Centre. London, Chapman and Hall, and New York, Harcourt Brace, 1935.
Blessed above Woman. London, Chapman and Hall, and New York, Harcourt Brace, 1936.
Here Today. London, Chapman and Hall, 1937.
World's End. London, Chapman and Hall, 1937; New York, Carrick and Evans, 1938.
The Monument. London, Chapman and Hall, and New York, Carrick and Evans, 1938.
Girdle of Venus. London, Chapman and Hall, 1939.
Too Dear for My Possessing. London, Collins, and New York, Carrick and Evans, 1940.
Tidy Death (as Nap Lombard, with Neil Stewart). London, Cassell, 1940.
The Family Pattern. London, Collins, 1942.
Winter Quarters. London, Collins, 1943; New York, Macmillan, 1944.
Murder's a Swine (as Nap Lombard, with Neil Stewart). London, Hutchinson, 1943; as *The Grinning Pig*, New York, Simon and Schuster, 1943.
The Trojan Brothers. London, Joseph, 1944; New York, Macmillan, 1945.
An Avenue of Stone. London, Joseph, 1947; New York, Macmillan, 1948.
A Summer to Decide. London, Joseph, 1948; New York, Scribner, 1975.
The Philistines. London, Joseph, 1949.
Catherine Carter. London, Macmillan, and New York, Knopf, 1952.
An Impossible Marriage. London, Macmillan, 1954; New York, Harcourt Brace, 1955.
The Last Resort. London, Macmillan, 1956; as *The Sea and the Wedding*, New York, Harcourt Brace, 1957.
The Humbler Creation. London, Macmillan, 1959; New York, Harcourt Brace, 1960.

The Unspeakable Skipton. London, Macmillan, and New York, Harcourt Brace, 1959.
An Error of Judgement. London, Macmillan, and New York, Harcourt Brace, 1962.
Night and Silence, Who Is Here? An American Comedy. London, Macmillan, and New York, Scribner, 1963.
Cork Street, Next to the Hatter's: A Novel in Bad Taste. London, Macmillan, and New York, Scribner, 1965.
The Survival of the Fittest. London, Macmillan, and New York, Scribner, 1968.
The Honours Board. London, Macmillan, and New York, Scribner, 1970.
The Holiday Friend. London, Macmillan, 1972; New York, Scribner, 1973.
The Good Listener. London, Macmillan, and New York, Scribner, 1975.
The Good Husband. London, Macmillan, 1978; New York, Scribner, 1979.
A Bonfire. London, Macmillan, and New York, Scribner, 1981.

Uncollected Short Stories

"Sanctuary," in *English Review* (London), February 1937.
"Altarwise by Owl-light," in *English Review* (London), June 1937.
"Scrap-book for 1938," in *Spectator* (London), 16 December 1938.
"The Swan," in *Stories of the Forties*, edited by Reginald Moore and Woodrow Wyatt. London, Nicholson and Watson, 1945.
"My Books Are My Children," in *Winter's Tales 1.* London, Macmillan, and New York, St. Martin's Press, 1955.
"Death of a Duchess," in *Winter's Tales 3.* London, Macmillan, and New York, St. Martin's Press, 1957.
"The Empty Schoolroom," in *Some Things Strange and Sinister*, edited by Joan Kahn. New York, Harper, 1973.

Plays

Corinth House (produced London, 1948; revised version, produced London, 1951). London, Macmillan, and New York, St. Martin's Press, 1954.
Six Proust Reconstructions (broadcast, 1948-56). London, Macmillan, 1958; as *Proust Recaptured: Six Radio Sketches, Based on the Author's Characters*, Chicago, University of Chicago Press, 1958.
The Supper Dance, with C.P. Snow. London, Evans, 1951.
Family Party, with C.P. Snow. London, Evans, 1951.
Spare the Rod, with C.P. Snow. London, Evans, 1951.
To Murder Mrs. Mortimer, with C.P. Snow. London, Evans, 1951.
The Pigeon with the Silver Foot, with C.P. Snow. London, Evans, 1951.
Her Best Foot Forward, with C.P. Snow. London, Evans, 1951.
The Rehearsal, with Kitty Black, adaptation of a play by Jean Anouilh (produced London, 1961; New York, 1963). London, Methuen, 1961; New York, Coward McCann, 1962.
The Public Prosecutor, with C.P. Snow, adaptation of a play by Georgi Dzhagarov, translated by Marguerite Alexieva (produced London, 1967). London, Peter Owen, 1969.

Radio Plays: *Six Proust Reconstructions: The Duchess at Sunset*, 1948, *Swann in Love*, 1952, *Madame de Charlus*, 1954, *Albertine Regained*, 1954, *Saint-Loup*, 1955, and *A Window at Montjaurain*, 1956.

Verse

Symphony for Full Orchestra. London, Sunday Referee-Parton Press, 1934.

Other

Thomas Wolfe: A Critical Study. London, Heinemann, 1947; as *Hungry Gulliver: An English Critical Appraisal of Thomas Wolfe*, New York, Scribner, 1948; as *The Art of Thomas Wolfe*, Scribner, 1963.
I. Compton-Burnett. London, Longman, 1951.
On Iniquity: Some Personal Reflections Arising Out of the Moors Murder Trial. London, Macmillan, and New York, Scribner, 1967.
Important to Me: Personalia. London, Macmillan, 1974; New York, Scribner, 1975.

Editor, with C.P. Snow, *Winter's Tales 7: Stories from Modern Russia.* London, Macmillan, and New York, St. Martin's Press, 1961.

*

Manuscript Collection: University of Texas, Austin.

Critical Study: *Pamela Hansford Johnson* by Isabel Quigly, London, Longman, 1968.

Pamela Hansford Johnson comments:

(1972) I am primarily a novelist, though I have written one stage and many radio scripts, and much criticism.

I suppose I might call myself a psychological novelist. I have written two trilogies, *An Avenue of Stone*, *Too Dear for My Possessing*, *A Summer to Decide* (no overall title) and the "Dorothy Merlin Comedies," i.e., *The Unspeakable Skipton*, *Night and Silence, Who Is Here?*, and *Cork Street, Next to the Hatter's.* My novels vary much in kind and in background.

* * *

Pamela Hansford Johnson has been writing novels at a fairly regular rate since 1935; but the real date of her debut as a serious novelist was 1940. The six years before this have a curious literary history. Her first book, a volume of verse called *Symphony for Full Orchestra*, appeared in 1934, when she was twenty-two. Then came the first novel, *This Bed Thy Centre*, a vigorous and promising story about the shabby gentility of some parts of Clapham, the extreme shabbiness of others, and in particular about a local girl who married a local boy but without at all the expected happy ending. This had a good deal of success, both critical and popular, and seemed, above all, to be full of vitality that suggested there was much more to be written, a kind of headlong, overflowing talent. But after it came five novels (five in only four years, and fairly long novels at that) which failed to fulfill its promise. All of them were set in the present, two at least gave a vivid impression of contemporary life among people politically involved in it; they are readable, have dated remarkably little, even at this distance, and to the student of Pamela Hansford Johnson's work they are of course interesting. But they marked no advance, said little that the first novel had not said, seemed to be going nowhere in particular. This brought her up to 1940, when, quite suddenly, her gifts seemed to fall into place, her style to take the right direction. *Too Dear for My Possessing* is the first of the "full-grown" novels, the first to speak with a mature voice, to flow confidently, fully and satisfactorily. A standard, though not a tone or a pattern, was set for the novels she was to write over the next 30 years.

She was to write more than fiction: works of criticism, essays and studies of various kinds, a play, and some remarkable radio programmes that have been published in book form. But it is as a novelist that she is chiefly known; as the writer, not of one particular novel, of a single, outstanding best-seller, but of an impressive body of work that must be seen as a whole, though it is anything but monolithic. Each novel goes its own way, seeking a new direction: she hardly ever repeats a method, never sticks to a formula. The novels vary in method, tone, situation, even in style; in social level and atmosphere, even more in social outlook. They have no common pattern, no repetition of effects; each is individual, unpredictable, and the characters, too, their situations and ways of life, are unpredictable and untypical. Her people never behave as fictional characters are expected to, loving the right person at the right moment, for instance, and so tying their lives in satisfactory knots at the end of the story. Almost every novel ends in an open, inconclusive way, with little that is knotted or neat about it, but plenty of possibilities and available futures. They are "social" novels in the sense that they are closely tied to a particular time and place and social milieu, to particular groups of people, ways of life; anyone seeking to know how life felt in the 1940's, 1950's, or 1960's should look at them for a view that is both panoramic and detailed. And this external world really counts, pressing on its people and making them responsible to one another. Work, outside interests, friends, background, loyalties, politics, community feelings, all weigh upon the characters, helping to form them and to shape their destinies. Yet, more than this, they are novels of character, in which primary importance is given to individual people rather than to their surroundings; although, as it is one of Pamela Hansford Johnson's main gifts to be able to balance one with the other, to deal with the inner and outer lives simultaneously, one does not divide the two in considering her books, or consider one without the other.

Untypically for a woman, she is able to enter all kinds of social situations as well as all kinds of characters. There is a sense of breadth about her novels, of a vigorous, far-ranging intellect, reflected in the strong, transparent style, informal, functional and unfrilly. She is not confined by the usual limitations of her sex—the trilogy that begins with *Too Dear for My Possessing* and goes on with *An Avenue of Stone* and *A Summer to Decide*, one of her most successful works, has a man for narrator without any sense of strain; and, more generally, she is not confined by what is often, in women writers, a narrowness of feeling as well as of experience, an inability or unwillingness to go outside a subjective, feminine world. She is not, in fact, subjective in the way that most women writers are, even at a high level; does not reveal her own personality, background, or opinions; keeps her artistic distance, and uses time and memory as integral parts of the action, so that, in some of the novels at least, one has a sense of double attitudes towards what happens—the attitude of the time, the retrospective judgement.

In 1959, there was an interesting and highly successful turnabout in manner (rather than method); from "straight" novels, the best of which so far were the trilogy, *Catherine Carter*, *An Impossible Marriage*, and *The Last Resort*, Pamela Hansford Johnson moved to satire with *The Unspeakable Skipton*, first and best of a group of three comedies (the others were *Night and Silence*, *Who Is Here?* and *Cork Street, Next to the Hatter's*), in which the same characters keep recurring. *The Humbler Creation*, in 1959, went back to the earlier manner, and was her most successful attempt to enter a small community—the (movingly created) world of a London clergyman, vicar of a rundown parish, domestically wretched and confined. *The Survival of the Fittest* was a very long, ambitious novel covering the adult years of a number of interconnected middle-aged characters. *The Honours Board* took another small community, a boys' preparatory school in Sussex. This is a novelist who fits no school or formula, whose past cannot be pigeon-holed, whose future cannot be foreseen.

—Isabel Quigly

JONES, (Morgan) Glyn. Welsh. Born in Merthyr Tydfil, Glamorgan, 28 February 1905. Educated at Castle Grammar School, Merthyr Tydfil; St. Paul's College, Cheltenham. Married Phyllis Doreen Jones in 1935. Formerly a schoolmaster in Glamorgan; now retired. Vice-President, Yr Academi Gymreig (English Section). Recipient: Welsh Arts Council Prize, for non-fiction, 1969, and Premier Award, 1972. D.Litt.: University of Wales, 1974. Address: 158 Manor Way, Whitchurch, Cardiff, Wales.

PUBLICATIONS

Novels

The Valley, The City, The Village. London, Dent, 1956.
The Learning Lark. London, Dent, 1960.
The Island of Apples. London, Dent, and New York, Day, 1965.

Short Stories

The Blue Bed. London, Cape, 1937; New York, Dutton, 1938.
The Water Music. London, Routledge, 1944.
Selected Short Stories. London, Dent, 1971.
Welsh Heirs. Llandysul, Dyfed, Gomer, 1978; Chicago, Academy Chicago, 1979.

Play

The Beach of Falesá, music by Alun Hoddinott (produced Cardiff, 1974). London, Oxford University Press, 1974.

Verse

Poems. London, Fortune Press, 1939.
The Dream of Jake Hopkins. London, Fortune Press, 1954.
Selected Poems. Llandysul, Dyfed, Gomer, 1975.

Other

The Dragon Has Two Tongues: Essays on Anglo-Welsh Writers and Writing. London, Dent, 1968.

Editor, *Poems '76.* Llandysul, Dyfed, Gomer, 1976.

Translator, with T.J. Morgan, *The Saga of Llywarch the Old.* London, Golden Cockerel Press, 1955.
Translator, *What Is Worship?*, by E. Stanley John. Swansea, Wales for Christ Movement, 1978.
Translator, *When the Rose-bush Brings Forth Apples* (Welsh folk poetry). Gregynog, Powys, Gregynog Press, 1980.

*

Manuscript Collection: National Library of Wales, Aberystwyth.

Critical Study: *Glyn Jones* by Leslie Norris, Cardiff, University of Wales Press, 1973.

Glyn Jones comments:

I began my literary life as a poet. In 1934 I first became friendly with Dylan Thomas, who suggested I should write short stories, as he himself was doing then. My first published book was a volume of short stories, *The Blue Bed.* This was written when the great industrial depression was at its most intense in South Wales and the longest story in the book takes this for its subject. South Wales, industrial and agricultural—this is the theme in all the stories in *The Blue Bed.* Indeed, all my prose, and much of my poetry, is concerned with this region. The novel *The Valley, The City, The Village*, which is partly autobiographical, tries to convey what it was like to grow up in South Wales; *The Learning Lark* deals with learning and teaching in the area; *The Island of Apples* describes childhood and its fantasies in a closely knit community in the Welsh valleys.

The Water Music has stories about both the industrial east of South Wales (Glamorgan) and the agricultural west (Carmarthen, Pembroke, Cardigan). To quote my publisher—I have "carried the medium [i.e., the imaginative short story] to an unexcelled synthesis of realism and fantasy, magic and humour. From the regional contrasts of industrialism and pastoralism, modernity and tradition, he builds up a world of convincing beauty, and expresses himself in a prose style of unusual poetic vitality." I would accept this as a statement of what I have *tried* to do in my short stories. Whether I've done it is of course quite another question.

* * *

"While using cheerfully enough the English language, I have never written in it a word about any country other than Wales, or any people other than Welsh people," wrote Glyn Jones in *The Dragon Has Two Tongues*. This deliberate limitation of his material is the only reason I can suggest for any kind of restriction to the general recognition his gifts deserve.

Certainly his stories and novels, although they share a Welsh background, are set in widely separate countries of the mind, pose different problems, and offer to us recognisable human situations. His prose, too, is very much more than the "cheerful use" of the English language. Always exuberant and seemingly spendthrift ("I fancy words," he says in his poem, "Merthyr"), it is also exact, muscular, very energetic. He can range from elegant and mannered writing—and the use of a vocabulary so exotic that it upset some reviewers of his first novel, *The Valley, The City, The Village*—to the direct, racy, almost physical style, the true, idiosyncratic speaking voice we find in some of the stories and in the two later novels.

His Wales commonly has two contrasting faces, that of the idyllic land of country happiness opposing the suppurating mining towns where the ugly, comical people are unfailingly kindly. But it also exists as a metaphysical universe, and the young people who are to be found in almost everything Jones writes are given early experience of both Heaven and Hell. To some extent this duality reflects Glyn Jones's own early life; during his impressionable boyhood he lived in the grimy steel and coal town of Merthyr Tydfil, but spent significant periods in Llanstephan, a beautiful Carmarthenshire village.

His identification with the scenes and characters of his imagination is absolutely complete, and it is noticeable that many of these stories and all three of his novels are told in the first person. Many critics, indeed, thought *The Valley, The City, The Village* largely autobiographical, although this story of a young painter, aware of his vocation but forced by the obstinate love of his grandmother to go to university to train as a preacher, has only tenuous links with Jones's own life. It is the quality of Glyn Jones's visual imagination and the unjudging tolerance that lies behind his observation that make his young artist credible.

For in the end Glyn Jones's love of his people is the illuminating quality of his work. He has created a whole gallery of memorable characters, some of them fully realised, some of whom enter his pages but once. He sees their blemishes, particularly their physical shortcomings, as clearly as their virtues, but to him they are loveable because their faults are the faults of human beings. Even in *The Learning Lark*, that picaresque send-up of the state of education in a corrupt mining valley where teachers have to bribe their way to headships, there is no scalding satire. Both bribed and bribers are seen as only too human and the book is full of gargantuan laughter.

The world of childhood and adolescence, that magical period when the real and the imagined are hardly to be distinguished, has been a particularly fertile area of Glyn Jones's concern. *The Water Music*, for example, is a collection of stories about young people: of his three novels only one is set entirely in the world of adults, and even that one has some very realistic schoolboys in it.

The Island of Apples is a full-scale exploration of the world of adolescence, seen through the eyes of the boy Dewi. It is a remarkable novel, using a prose which is obviously the boy's voice, yet flexible and powerful enough to describe an enormous range of events and emotions. Its sensitivity, its combination of dreamlike confusion and the clear, unsentimental observation which is the adolescent state of mind, the excitement with which the boy invests the commonplace with the exotic, are perfectly balanced attributes of a work which is as individual and complete as *Le Grand Meaulnes*, that other evocation of vanishing youth.

Perhaps the greatest of Glyn Jones's qualities is that of delight in the created world and the people who inhabit it. If he writes of a small and often shabby corner of that world—the first story in *The Blue Bed* is called "I Was Born in the Ystrad Valley" and it is to Ystrad that he returns for *The Island of Apples*—yet his writing is a celebration, an act of praise. To this end he has shaped his craftsmanship and inspiration, and his achievement is permanent and real.

—Leslie Norris

JONES, Gwyn. British. Born in Blackwood, Monmouthshire, 24 May 1907. Educated at Tredegar Grammar School; University College, Cardiff, 1924-29, B.A. 1927, M.A. 1929. Married 1) Alice Rees in 1928 (died, 1979); 2) Mair Sivell in 1979. Schoolmaster, 1929-35; Lecturer, University College, Cardiff, 1935-40; Professor of English Language and Literature, University College of Wales, Aberystwyth, 1940-65; Professor of English Language and Literature, University College, Cardiff, 1965-75. Editor, *Welsh Review*, Cardiff and Aberystwyth, 1939-48; Director, Penmark Press, Cardiff, 1939-60. President, Viking Society for Northern Research, 1951-52; Chairman, Welsh Arts Council, 1957-67. Recipient: Welsh Arts Council award, 1973; Christian Gauss Award, for non-fiction, 1973. D.Litt.: University of Wales, Cardiff, 1977; University of Nottingham, 1978. Knight of the Order of the Falcon, Iceland, 1963. C.B.E. (Commander, Order of the British Empire), 1965. Address: Department of English, University College, Cardiff CF1 1XL, Wales.

PUBLICATIONS

Novels

Richard Savage. London, Gollancz, and New York, Viking Press, 1935.
Times Like These. London, Gollancz, 1936.
The Nine-Days' Wonder. London, Gollancz, 1937.
Garland of Bays. London, Gollancz, and New York, Macmillan, 1938.
The Green Island. London, Golden Cockerel Press, 1946.
The Flowers Beneath the Scythe. London, Dent, 1952.
The Walk Home. London, Dent, 1962; New York, Norton, 1963.

Short Stories

The Buttercup Field and Other Stories. Cardiff, Penmark Press, 1945.
The Still Waters and Other Stories. London, Davies, 1948.
Shepherd's Hey and Other Stories. London, Staples Press, 1953.
Selected Short Stories. London, Oxford University Press, 1974.

Other

A Prospect of Wales. London, Penguin, 1948.
Welsh [and *Scandinavian*] *Legends and Folk-Tales Retold* (juvenile). London, Oxford University Press, 2 vols., 1955-56; New York, Walck, 2 vols., 1965.
The First Forty Years: Some Notes on Anglo-Welsh Literature (lecture). Cardiff, University of Wales Press, 1957.

The Norse Atlantic Saga, Being the Norse Voyages of Discovery and Settlement to Iceland, Greenland, America. London and New York, Oxford University Press, 1964.
The Legendary History of Olaf Tryggvason (lecture). Glasgow, Jackson, 1968.
A History of the Vikings. London and New York, Oxford University Press, 1968.
Kings, Beasts, and Heroes. London and New York, Oxford University Press, 1972.

Editor, with E.M. Silvanus, *Narrative Poems for Schools.* London, Rivingtons, 3 vols., 1935.
Editor, *Prose* [and *Poems*] *of Six Centuries.* London, Rivingtons, 2 vols., 1935-36.
Editor, *Welsh Short Stories.* London, Penguin, 1940.
Editor, with Gweno Lewis, *Letters from India*, by Alun Lewis. Cardiff, Penmark Press, 1946.
Editor, *Salmacus and Hermaphroditus.* London, Golden Cockerel Press, 1951.
Editor, *Circe and Ulysses: The Inner Temple Masque*, by William Browne. London, Golden Cockerel Press, 1954.
Editor, *Welsh Short Stories.* London, Oxford University Press, 1956.
Editor, *Songs and Poems of John Dryden.* London, Golden Cockerel Press, 1957.
Editor, *The Metamorphosis of Publius Ovidius Naso.* London, Golden Cockerel Press, 1958.
Editor, *The Poems and Sonnets of Shakespeare.* London, Golden Cockerel Press, 1960.
Editor, with Islwyn Ffowc Elis, *Twenty-Five Welsh Short Stories.* London, Oxford University Press, 1971.
Editor, *The Oxford Book of Welsh Verse in English.* London and New York, Oxford University Press, 1977.

Translator, *Four Icelandic Sagas.* London, Allen and Unwin, and Princeton, New Jersey, Princeton University Press, 1935.
Translator, *The Vatnsdalers' Saga.* London, Oxford University Press, and Princeton, New Jersey, Princeton University Press, 1944.
Translator, with Thomas Jones, *The Mabinogion.* London, Golden Cockerel Press, 1948; New York, Dutton, 1950; revised edition, London, Dent, 1975.
Translator, *Sir Gawain and the Green Knight.* London, Golden Cockerel Press, 1952.
Translator, *Egil's Saga.* Syracuse, New York, Syracuse University Press, 1960.
Translator, *Eirik the Red and Other Icelandic Sagas.* London and New York, Oxford University Press, 1961.

*

Bibliography: in *A Bibliography of Anglo-Welsh Literature, 1900-1965* by Brynmor Jones, Swansea, Library Association, 1970.

Critical Study: *Gwyn Jones* by Cecil Price, Cardiff, University of Wales Press, 1976.

* * *

Gwyn Jones did not begin as an "Anglo-Welsh" writer—that is, as a Welshman writing in English about Wales; his first book was a weighty historical novel, *Richard Savage*, in which he traced the decline of the 18th-century poet against a richly described background peopled with a large number of real and imaginary characters. The same ability to conjure up the very smell of a bygone age is apparent in his *Garland of Bays*, an even longer, picaresque, novel in which the story of Robert Greene is used to link striking pictures of Elizabethan life—in country and city, in university and prison, at home and abroad. In between these considerable undertakings he produced a Manchester novel—*The Nine-Days' Wonder*—in which there is an attempt to depict part-time criminals living otherwise ordinary lives, and his first book with a Welsh background—*Times Like These*, a novel of the General Strike of 1926 as it affected life in a South Wales mining valley.

All Gwyn Jones's fiction after 1938 is set in Wales, but he seems to have largely avoided the themes most immediately associated with Anglo-Welsh writers from South Wales. It is true that a part of *The Flowers Beneath the Scythe* recalls pit disasters, unemployment, and poverty in the Welsh valleys between the wars, but the filter is the middle-class guilt-feelings of the hero, and the novel is equally concerned with the horrors of trench warfare, the rise of the dictators, the debate about pacifism, the challenge of the Second World War—in short, it looks retrospectively at some of the major preoccupations of the period covered. *The Walk Home*, too, reaches out to more general themes; here Gwyn Jones returns to the historical novel, though this time the place is 19th-century Wales and the hero the victim not of his own folly and weakness but of Evil incarnate in experienced, ruthless men.

Of the volumes of short stories, *The Buttercup Field* is the most conventionally "Anglo-Welsh" and it sounds notes of comedy and whimsy heard more rarely in the two later collections. The dominant features of the more impressive stories in this and the later volumes are strong story-lines, dramatic—even melodramatic—situations, and that acceptance of the importance and dignity of ordinary people which so often informs serious regional fiction. The characters and settings are Welsh, certainly, but the Welshness is taken for granted as the elemental situations take hold of the author's imagination.

Orthodox in structure, Gwyn Jones's fiction has been notable for the energy of its narrative style, the vividness of its descriptive passages, and the boldness of its characterisation; it has been most successful when the material has been sufficiently distanced in the exercise of an outstanding talent for research, whether historical or cultural. Many readers will find it interesting to note the tensions between the writer's fascination with crime and violence and his tacit acceptance of the most humane standards of his time, between the shrewdness of his even-toned reflections on human nature and a strain of romanticism not always held in check, between occasional self-indulgence and a strong, versatile prose style rooted in detailed observation and firm self-discipline.

—Roy Thomas

JONES, LeRoi. *See* **BARAKA, Amiri.**

JONES, Madison (Percy, Jr.). American. Born in Nashville, Tennessee, 21 March 1925. Educated at Vanderbilt University, Nashville, A.B. 1949; University of Florida, Gainesville, A.M. 1951. Served in the United States Army in the Corps of Military Police, Korea, 1945-46. Married Shailah McEvilley in 1951; five children. Farmer in Cheatham County, Tennessee, in the 1940's; Instructor in English, Miami University, Oxford, Ohio, 1953-54, and University of Tennessee, Knoxville, 1955-56. Since 1956, Member of the English Department, since 1967, Writer-in-Residence, and since 1968, Professor of English, Auburn University, Alabama. Recipient: *Sewanee Review* Fellowship, 1954; Rockefeller Fellowship, 1968; Guggenheim Fellowship, 1973. Address: 800 Kuderna Acres, Auburn, Alabama 36830, U.S.A.

PUBLICATIONS

Novels

The Innocent. New York, Harcourt Brace, and London, Secker and Warburg, 1957.
Forest of the Night. New York, Harcourt Brace, 1960; London, Eyre and Spottiswoode, 1961.
A Buried Land. New York, Viking Press, and London, Bodley Head, 1963.
An Exile. New York, Viking Press, 1967; London, Deutsch, 1970; as *I Walk the Line*, New York, Popular Library, 1970.
A Cry of Absence. New York, Crown, 1971; London, Deutsch, 1972.
Passage Through Gehenna. Baton Rouge, Louisiana State University Press, 1978.

Uncollected Short Stories

"The Homecoming," in *Perspective* (St. Louis), Spring 1952.
"Dog Days," in *Perspective* (St. Louis), Fall 1952.
"The Cave," in *Perspective* (St. Louis), Winter 1955.
"Home Is Where the Heart Is," in *Arlington Quarterly* (Texas), Spring 1968.
"A Modern Case," in *Delta Review* (Memphis, Tennessee), August 1969.
"The Fugitive," in *Craft and Vision*, edited by Andrew Lytle. New York, Delacorte Press, 1971.

Other

History of the Tennessee State Dental Association. Nashville, Tennessee Dental Association, 1958.

*

Critical Studies: by Ovid Pierce, in *New York Times Book Review*, 4 July 1971; Joseph Cantinella, in *Saturday Review* (New York), 9 July 1971; Reed Whittemore, in *New Republic* (Washington, D.C.), July 1971; *Separate Country* by Paul Binding, London and New York, Paddington Press, 1979.

Madison Jones comments:

Generally, on a more obvious level, my fiction is concerned with the drama of collision between past and present, with emphasis upon the destructive elements involved. More deeply, it deals with the failure, or refusal, of individuals to recognize and submit themselves to inevitable limits of the human condition.

* * *

There is a homogeneity of theme which links together into a coherent body the published fiction of Madison Jones. The setting of these books is invariably Jones's native South. But whether their time be late 18th-century settlement days or the region's more recent past, his unvarying song is abstraction, ideology, and its consequences. *The Innocent*, his first novel, set in rural Tennessee immediately after the coming of modernity, treats of the attempts by a young Southerner, Duncan Welsh, to repent of earlier impiety and re-establish himself upon inherited lands in inherited ways. The enterprise is a failure because of Duncan's deracinated preconception of it. Welsh "sets up a grave in his house." Soon he and his hopes are buried in another.

A Cry of Absence again focuses on a fatal archaist, a middle-aged gentlewoman of the 1960's who is anything but innocent. Hester Glenn finds an excuse for her failures as wife, mother and person in a self-protective devotion to the tradition of her family. But when her example proves, in part, responsible for her son's sadistic murder of a Negro agitator, Hester is driven to know herself and, after confession, to pay for her sins with suicide.

A kind of Puritanism distorts Mrs. Glenn. In *The Innocent* the error is a perversion of the Agrarianism of Jones's mentors (Lytle, Davidson). But in his other novels the informing abstractions are not so identifiably Southern. Jones's best, *A Buried Land*, is set in the valley of the Tennessee River during the season of its transformation. Percy Youngblood, the heir of a stern hill farmer (and a central character who could be any young person of our century), embraces all of the nostrums we associate with the futurist dispensation. He attempts to bury the old world (represented by a girl who dies aborting his child) under the waters of the TVA; but its truths (and their symbol) rise to haunt him back into abandoned modes of thought and feeling. In *An Exile* Hank Tawes, a rural sheriff, is unmanned by a belated explosion of passion for a bootlegger's daughter. His error has no date or nationality, but almost acquires the force of ideology once Tawes recognizes that, because he followed an impulse to recover his youth, his "occupation's gone." *Forest of the Night* tests out an assumption almost as generic, the notion that man is inherently good. An interval in the Tennessee "outback" is sufficient to the disabusement of Jonathan Cannon. There is no more telling exposé of the New Eden mythology.

In all of Jones's fiction there operates an allusive envelope embodied in a concrete action and supported by an evocative texture. That action is as spare as it is archetypal; and in every case its objective is to render consciousness. Jones is among the most gifted of contemporary American novelists, a craftsman of tragedy in the great tradition of his art.

—M.E. Bradford

JONES, Marion (Patrick). Citizen of Trinidad and Tobago. Address: c/o Columbus Publishers, 64 Independence Square, Port of Spain, Trinidad.

PUBLICATIONS

Novels

Pan Beat. Port of Spain, Columbus, 1973.
J'Ouvert Morning. Port of Spain, Columbus, 1976.

* * *

The relatively limited contributions of women writers to Caribbean literature has been one of the long-standing curiosities about the region. In the area of prose fiction there has been a small handful of women novelists, and from the English-language Caribbean in particular there have only been Sylvia Wynter of Jamaica, the Barbados-born Paule Marshall of the United States, and Merle Hodges and Marion Jones of Trinidad. Jones therefore belongs to a rather small circle in Caribbean literature, one that has unfortunately been slow—with the exception of Paule Marshall—to attract significant attention from students and teachers of the literature. And on the basis of her published works it is clear that Jones has already carved out a distinctive niche for herself within that small circle.

Thus far, at any rate, she has chosen to concentrate on domestic drama as the main staple of her novels. For example, both *Pan Beat* and *J'Ouvert Morning* center on middle-class marriages in Port of Spain, Trinidad, each work concentrating on not one but several couples, on the quality of the marriages (invariably bad and getting worse), on the circle within which the couples move (usually since their childhood), and on a social background that is experiencing the growing pains of new nationhood. And in the case of *J'Ouvert Morning* this all spans three generations. As this synopsis is intended to imply, Jones's fiction usually borders on soap opera. Her plots are endless strands of unrelieved misery that are interwoven in a pattern of endless conflicts and unmitigated wretchedness.

In *Pan Beat*, for example, the narrative events are sparked by Earline MacCardie's return home to Trinidad for a holiday visit. As a high-schooler she was associated with the Flamingoes steel band. After high-school she and David Chow, a member of the band, emigrated to England. He committed suicide after their estrangement, and she promptly turned to prostitution to assuage her grief—and to express her resentment at his suicide. Then she had subsequently married a British homosexual in New York (where she has been "passing" as a white Brazilian). Now that she is in Trinidad her husband breaks off the marriage, and she discovers that her former friends have been just as unhappy as she has been abroad: another old boyfriend, Louis Jenkins, is a futile, left-wing radical who is eventually killed in a gang war during Earline's visit; Louis's wife, Denise, enjoys some success, but merely as an insipid, commercially popular artist; Alan Hastings is a highly paid oil refinery worker who divides his time between a disastrous marriage and an affair with Earline herself. Of the two persons who have managed to avoid the endemic miseries of marriage, Tony Joseph is a desperately lonely prude of a civil servant, while Leslie Oliver, a Roman Catholic priest, is tormented by his sexual passion for Denise Jenkins.

The middle-class miseries of *J'Ouvert Morning* are less convoluted, largely because Jones mercifully concentrates on a smaller, more tightly knit group of sufferers in this novel—the Grant family. But their collective wretchedness is no less acute. Helen and Mervyn Grant have worked hard to secure a good education and middle-class affluence for their children. But one daughter, Elizabeth, is a well-known city drunk whom everyone knows as "Stinking Fur Liz." Their son, John, is a wealthy Port-of-Spain doctor with an unhappy marriage and a rebellious son, John Jr. Eventually John Jr.'s rebelliousness leads to an anti-government, left-wing plot that ends in his death at the hands of the police. The novel itself ends with the abortive suicide attempt by John Jr.'s distraught mother.

In spite of the soap operatic quality of her narrative materials, Jones's novels succeed as riveting documents of a troubled society in a state of transition. Jones's Trinidad has left official colonialism behind, but it has not yet discovered a vital sense of its own direction and purpose. It is soulless, without a driving motive, except the predictable trappings of neo-colonial values and the second-hand middle-class aspirations that have been handed down from Europe and the United States. The present tragedies and failures of her characters therefore reflect the unfulfilled promise of a generation that grew up in the years before independence. The empty successes of her achievers demonstrate the limitations of the neocolonial imitativeness that too often thwarts the growth of a healthy national consciousness. The radical dissidents like Louis Jenkins or John Jr. are equally failures in their own way: their radicalism is too often a self-destructive aimlessness that merely underscores their irrelevance in a society which is completely indifferent to them and their revolutionary messages.

Moreover, all of this remains convincing in the long run, because, despite Jones's melodramatic tendencies, the characters are vividly drawn and the language—especially in *J'Ouvert Morning*—is original and invigorating. Thus far she has demonstrated considerable promise, one that should be fulfilled to a significant degree if she continues to integrate an engaging narrative language with both disturbing social insights and a formidable grasp of the human personality.

—Lloyd W. Brown

JONES, Mervyn. British. Born in London, 27 February 1922. Educated at Abbotsholme School, Derbyshire; New York University, 1939-41. Served in the British Army, 1942-47. Married Jeanne Urquhart in 1948; one son and two daughters. Assistant Editor, 1955-60, and Dramatic Critic, 1958-66, *Tribune*, London; Assistant Editor, *New Statesman*, London, 1966-68. Address: 10 Waterside Place, Princess Road, London N.W.1, England.

PUBLICATIONS

Novels

No Time to Be Young. London, Cape, 1952.
The New Town. London, Cape, 1953.
The Last Barricade. London, Cape, 1953.
Helen Blake. London, Cape, 1955.
On the Last Day. London, Cape, 1958.
A Set of Wives. London, Cape, 1965.
John and Mary. London, Cape, 1966; New York, Atheneum, 1967.
A Survivor. London, Cape, and New York, Atheneum, 1968.
Joseph. London, Cape, and New York, Atheneum, 1970.
Mr. Armitage Isn't Back Yet. London, Cape, 1971.
Holding On. London, Quartet, 1973; as *Twilight of the Day*, New York, Simon and Schuster, 1974.
The Revolving Door. London, Quartet, 1973.
Strangers. London, Quartet, 1974.
Lord Richard's Passion. London, Quartet, and New York, Knopf, 1974.
The Pursuit of Happiness. London, Quartet, 1975; New York, Mason Charter, 1976.
Nobody's Fault. London, Quartet, and New York, Mason Charter, 1977.
Today the Struggle. London, Quartet, 1978.
The Beautiful Words. London, Deutsch, 1979.
A Short Time to Live. London, Deutsch, 1980; New York, St. Martin's Press, 1981.

Short Stories

Scenes from Bourgeois Life. London, Quartet, 1976.

Uncollected Short Stories

"The Foot," in *English Story 8*, edited by Woodrow Wyatt. London, Collins, 1948.
"The Bee-Keeper," in *English Story 10*, edited by Woodrow Wyatt. London, Collins, 1950.
"Discrete Lives," in *Bananas* (London), 1978.
"Five Days by Moonlight," in *Encounter* (London), November 1978.
"Living Together," in *Woman* (London), 1979.

Other

Guilty Men, 1957: Suez and Cyprus, with Michael Foot. London, Gollancz, and New York, Rinehart, 1957.
Potbank (documentary). London, Secker and Warburg, 1961.
Big Two: Life in America and Russia. London, Cape, 1962; as *The Antagonists*, New York, Potter, 1962.
Two Ears of Corn: Oxfam in Action. London, Hodder and Stoughton, 1965; as *In Famine's Shadow: A Private War on Hunger*, Boston, Beacon Press, 1967.
Life on the Dole. London, Davis Poynter, 1972.
Rhodesia: The White Judge's Burden. London, Christian Action, 1972.
The Oil Rush, photographs by Fay Godwin. London, Quartet, 1976.

Editor, *Kingsley Martin: Portrait and Self-Portrait.* London, Barrie and Rockliff, and New York, Humanities Press, 1969.
Editor, *Privacy.* Newton Abbot, Devon, David and Charles, 1974.

Translator, *The Second Chinese Revolution*, by K.S. Karol. New York, Hill and Wang, 1974.

*

Mervyn Jones comments:

(1981) I have become known as a political novelist, although only two of my books—*Joseph* and *Today the Struggle*—could be defined strictly as political novels, and some others are deliberately limited to the study of personal relationships. Probably, this reveals how rarely most British novelists concern themselves with the political framework of life. Taking account of that framework does, I think, extend the novel's range. But I also think, decidedly, that a novel ceases to be a novel when it does not have human character and human experience at its centre. Those interested in my views on the matter are referred to a *Guardian* interview, 9 July 1979.

I have never planned a recurrent theme in my writing, but when I consider it I believe that there is one: the nobility and irony of idealism. I take both the nobility and the irony to be realities. This is the subject of *Strangers*, the novel with which I am least dissatisfied and by which I should wish to be judged.

* * *

Some writers leap to fame and achievement with their first novel, and then face the problem of avoiding an anti-climax with their next. Others climb the ladder slowly but steadily: Mervyn Jones clearly belongs to the latter category. In his early books he showed himself a first-class reporter with a flair for discovering topical subjects and the knack of familiarising himself with an astonishingly wide range of jobs, classes, and walks of life. Since then he has developed his gifts as a creator of character while remaining a keen observer of social experiment and a connoisseur of sharply differing life-styles. The breadth of his interests has opened up to him an exceptionally large range of themes, and the diversity of his subject matter is matched by the versatility of his technique. This has enabled him to write books as different as *The New Town* (documentary-style naturalism), *On the Last Day* (politically flavoured prophecy), *Joseph* (a historical novel on Stalin), *John and Mary* (a novel *à deux*) and many more.

His first substantial novel was *The New Town*, a study of a community born in the idealistic atmosphere of the late 1940's. The strength of the book lies in the accuracy of the reporting and in the author's grasp of the forces which are in conflict from the start—the idealism of the general manager, the competing interests of new arrivals and established residents, the rival demands of industry and Whitehall. There followed two novels dominated by political themes, *The Last Barricade*, a sympathetic study of the exiled president of a Central European state, and *On the Last Day*, a disturbingly plausible projection of a third world war, with an émigré British government quartered on reluctant French Canadian hosts in Quebec.

His next novel, *A Set of Wives*, signalled a great advance in terms of characterisation: there is a tragi-comic chronicle of three sisters, all members of the liberal establishment, married respectively to a barrister, a television commentator and a Labour MP. The plot is set during the run-up to the General Election of 1964, and if the tragic denouement seems a shade contrived, the portraits of the three sisters are brilliantly sketched, and the balance between public and private life perfectly held.

John and Mary is an entertaining, slightly artificial tour de force, told by the two protagonists in alternating narratives. The pair meet at a party, are strongly attracted, and wake up in John's room the next morning, sexual intimates but social and emotional strangers. The rest of the Sunday is spent in a mating ritual of approach and retreat, as each in turn seeks or evades commitment, but by the end of the day they are planning to spend the rest of their lives together.

Joseph is a fictional reconstruction of the life of Stalin, an ambitious conception backed by plenty of solid research. Although Mervyn Jones writes from a strongly left wing standpoint, this is by no means a work of idolatry. But it is written in a dead-pan style, the uniformity of which contrasts so sharply with the exuberance and paradox of his normal manner as to leave the impression that his critical intelligence has been lulled, stunned, or suspended. *A Survivor* is the most accomplished but at the same time the most enigmatic of his books to date: it is also arguably the one which has extended him most fully. The "survivor" is a wartime airman who becomes a successful novelist. He survives his closest friend and wartime comrade and marries the girl they have both loved, knowing that his feelings are never fully returned. He survives her, and survives a succession of affairs, in the sense that none of them can replace the love he has lost, unrequited though it was. The pattern of these relationships resembles a perspective of mutually reflecting mirrors: the novelist reveals much about his mistresses and they about him, but always there is a side which is turned away. He remains a man hard to know and a writer who is unable to communicate all that he wishes to tell. *Mr. Armitage Isn't Back Yet* is an entertaining and again a highly topical fable. A middle-aged business man, a perfect specimen of the self-made apostle of private enterprise, is amicably kidnapped by a quartet of drop-outs, who spirit him off to a deserted Scottish island and explain that he is the subject of a study-project: they want to discover what makes him tick. Amid the mutual confessions and couplings that follow, Mr. Armitage finds his ideals of self-reliance dissolving, and although his hosts do not arrive at any alternative formula for running society, he returns to civilisation a changed man.

Mervyn Jones's fiction occupies a territory where the work of the novelist shades imperceptibly into that of the publicist. He is keenly aware of the mood and climate of the moment, and if some of his work has the ephemerality of good journalism, he has never ceased to develop and he has always had something new to say.

—Ian Scott-Kilvert

JONG, Erica (née Mann). American. Born in New York City, 26 March 1942. Educated at Barnard College, New York (George Weldwood Murray Fellow, 1963), 1959-63, B.A. 1963 (Phi Beta Kappa); Columbia University, New York (Woodrow Wilson Fellow, 1964), M.A. 1965; Columbia School of Fine Arts, 1969-70. Married 1) Michael Werthman; 2) Allan Jong in 1966 (divorced, 1975); 3) the writer Jonathan Fast in 1977, one daughter. Lecturer in English, City College of New York, 1964-66, and University of Maryland European Division, Heidelberg, Germany, 1967-68; Instructor in English, Manhattan Community College, New York, 1969-70. Since 1971, Instructor in Poetry, YM-YWHA Poetry Center, New York. Recipient: Bess Hokin Prize (*Poetry*, Chicago), 1971; New York State Council on the Arts grant, 1971; Madeline Sadin Award (*New York Quarterly*), 1972; Alice Fay di Castagnola Award, 1972; National Endowment for the Arts grant, 1973. Agent: Sterling Lord Agency, 660 Madison Avenue, New York, New York 10021. Address: P.O. Box 1034, Weston, Connecticut 06883, U.S.A.

PUBLICATIONS

Novels

Fear of Flying. New York, Holt Rinehart, 1973; London, Secker and Warburg, 1974.

How to Save Your Own Life. New York, Holt Rinehart, and London, Secker and Warburg, 1977.
Fanny, Being the True History of Fanny Hackabout-Jones. New York, New American Library, and London, Granada, 1980.

Uncollected Short Stories

"From the Country of Regrets," in *Paris Review*, Spring 1973.
"Take a Lover," in *Vogue* (New York), April 1977.

Verse

Fruits and Vegetables. New York, Holt Rinehart, 1971; London, Secker and Warburg, 1973.
Half-Lives. New York, Holt Rinehart, 1973; London, Secker and Warburg, 1974.
Here Comes and Other Poems. New York, New American Library, 1975.
Loveroot. New York, Holt Rinehart, 1975; London, Secker and Warburg, 1977.
The Poetry of Erica Jong. New York, Holt Rinehart, 1976.
Selected Poems. London, Panther, 1977.
At the Edge of the Body. New York, Holt Rinehart, 1979.
Witches. New York, Abrams, 1981.

Other

Four Visions of America, with others. Santa Barbara, California, Capra Press, 1977.

* * *

Erica Jong is an impressive poet of the confessional school (Sexton, Lowell, Plath, Berryman) who writes an energetic, garrulous, witty, and tender verse, both erudite and earthy, about the conflict between sexuality and inhibiting intelligence, about death (and one's impulse to and away from suicide), the problems of sexual and creative energy (which both consumes and propels), the hunger for love, knowledge, and connecting. Although she has been embraced by every denomination of the Feminist movement (and has aligned herself with it), her poetry goes beyond the dilemma of being a woman in a male-dominated world, or a Jew in an urban culture—to the ubiquitous need for human completeness in a fiercely hostile social and cosmic world.

Jong distinguishes her poetic and fictional forms: "In poetry I could be pared down, honed, minimal. In the novel what I wanted was excess, digression, rollicking language, energy, and poetry." Jong's preference was always for the novel that made one believe "it was all spilled truth." It is in this matter of "truth" that the novelist runs into problems. First, one questions if her very earthy language is in fact true to experience. Second, although *Fear of Flying* may well be a female's *Portnoy's Complaint*, it is not clear if Jong's playing out of her heroine's extravagant sexuality is intended as a reflection of concrete female experience—universal and realistic—or merely as fantasy—elaborated and heightened through the creative imagination.

One would not argue with Jong that the problem for the woman reading or writing about women is that there are no adequate role models: "Until women started writing books there was only one side of the story." "Where," Jong properly asks, "was the female Chaucer? One lusty lady who had juice and joy and love and talent too?" Yet, when she writes "throughout all of history, books were written with sperm, not menstrual blood," there is something self-consciously petulant, let alone reductive and offensive about her remark.

Quoting Kosinski, Jong reaffirms that art is a structure that distorts experience, that it is life edited. If then she edits experience through a textured prose laced with literary references, or a variety of poetic techniques, why must she maintain such a strict adherence to what she calls the veracity of women's language ("I saw no reason why the same liberties with language should not belong to women since women take them in life")? The reader questions whether women—or men—use her language. And even if they do, within this novel such language often jars with her frequently more poetic forms. Moreover, one soon becomes tired, if not offended, by the numerous references to Isadora's insatiable "unfillable cunt."

Having said this—with the admission that it may be due to lingering prudishness (which may account for why this book reads better nearly ten years after its publication)—one should applaud Jong for the honesty of her statement (and her very lively and appealing prose). *Fear of Flying* is moving, thought-provoking, and deeply serious. "Nothing human was worth denying," her character says, "and even if it was unspeakably ugly, we could learn from it, couldn't we?" The heroine, a picaresque figure, is the bright, pretty, Jewish, guilt-ridden (a redundancy) writer, Isadora Wing, who accompanies her Chinese-American, child-psychiatrist husband, Bennett Wing, to a psychoanalytic congress in Vienna. Torn between the stability of marriage and her sexual fantasies (for the "zipless fuck"), she abandons Bennett for a selfish, pompous bully, a rather illiterate and sadistic but very sexy London psychiatrist (Adrian Goodlove), whose words arouse her as much as his sexual promise. (Bennett, though often "wordless," is a far better lover.) Her excursions through her past, where we meet her family and childhood world, her brilliant but sad and insane first husband, her series of lovers (or at least sexual partners) before her present, second husband, are all drawn in a racy and ebullient fashion. But beneath all the bravura is Isadora's basic unfulfillment. Sex is only the apparent means toward connecting and feeling alive, the means through which one confuses desperation with freedom. It is only a temporary departure from guilt—an illusory means of "flying." It is a barely understood psychological mechanism that permits her to defy and escape her family, after which she is driven back—with only deeper guilt and despair. Isadora's life (until the novel's end, which only half-heartedly suggests some sort of insight and the half-believed "People don't complete us. We complete ourselves") remains tortured. She has struggled to write as a means of self-discovery and as a sublimated fulfillment for the frustrations of the real world. (Only in her art can people—indeed the world—be under her control.) But she lives with an unremitting sense of guilt, vulnerability, childish impulsiveness, and romanticism.

Jong announces her real subject throughout, both here and in the less successful "sequel," *How to Save Your Own Life*, which focuses on Isadora's literary success, on her divorce from Bennett, and on her subsequent move to Hollywood with its virtually limitless number of disappointments, sexual and otherwise. As Jong portrays it, the plight of woman is to be torn between her own restlessness and the bourgeois virtues of marriage. She illustrates poignantly and powerfully how the woman's greatest fear is being alone, how one's deepest wish is to break free as "hostage" to her own "fantasies," her "fears," and "false definitions."

"Women are programmed for suffering," she writes, adding, "I feel guilty for *every*thing," and as a result have to be "the greatest in everything," making life "a test of stamina." She adds: "Women are their own worst enemies. And guilt is the main weapon of self-torture." Near the end of *Fear of Flying*, Isadora admits that her ideal woman is a "Ruth and Esther and Jesus and Mary rolled into one...a vehicle, a vessel, with no needs or desires of her own...capable of everything except self-preservation." Despite all of her sex, success, and apparent freedom, she admits "[and] I am always ashamed of myself for not being her."

—Lois Gordon

JOSEPH, M(ichael) K(ennedy). New Zealander. Born in Chingford, Essex, England, 9 July 1914. Educated at Auckland University College, B.A. 1933, M.A. 1934; Merton College, Oxford, B.A. 1938,

B.Litt. 1939, M.A. 1945. Served in the British Army in the Royal Artillery, 1940-46. Married Mary Julia Antonovich in 1947; five children. Lecturer in English, 1945-49, and Senior Lecturer, 1950-59, Auckland University College; Associate Professor, 1960-69, and Professor of English, 1970-79, University of Auckland; now retired. Recipient: Hubert Church Prose Award, 1958; Jessie Mackay Poetry Award, 1959; Sir James Wattie Prize, 1976; National Book Award, for fiction, 1978. Address: 185 Victoria Avenue, Auckland 5, New Zealand.

PUBLICATIONS

Novels

I'll Soldier No More. Auckland, Paul's Book Arcade, and London, Gollancz, 1958.
A Pound of Saffron. Auckland, Paul's Book Arcade, and London, Gollancz, 1962.
The Hole in the Zero. London, Gollancz, 1967; New York, Dutton, 1968.
A Soldier's Tale. Auckland and London, Collins, 1976.
The Time of Achamoth. Auckland and London, Collins, 1977.

Verse

Imaginary Islands. Privately printed, 1950.
The Living Countries. Auckland, Paul's Book Arcade, 1959.
Inscription on a Paper Dart. Auckland, Auckland University Press-Oxford University Press, 1974.

Other

Charles Aders: A Biographical Note. Auckland, Auckland University Press, 1954.
Byron the Poet. London, Gollancz, 1964.

Editor, *Frankenstein*, by Mary Shelley. London, Oxford University Press, 1969.

*

M.K. Joseph comments:

I have published five novels at fairly long intervals, and if they have anything in common it is the attempt to write in a fairly traditional way, to tell a story and create characters, with as much originality as I can manage. I admire contemporary novelists like Graham Greene, William Golding, and Anthony Burgess, who seem to me to display a wide variety of subject matter, formal inventiveness without being *avant-garde*, and moral concern without didacticism.

* * *

M.K. Joseph is one of the most sophisticated artists in New Zealand fiction. He is keenly aware of the problems of form, which he confronts with a wise urbanity, and his subject-matter is more diverse and his range of intellectual interests wider than those of almost all his contemporaries. While he is seriously concerned with exploring man's nature and his destiny, he also delights in the curious and the unexpected. A gentle irony irradiates the play of ideas in his novels. The general impression they leave is of an exercise of "wit" in its several 18th-century senses.

This does not mean that the novels are academic or lacking in sensitivity. On the contrary, it is Joseph's human compassion which removes his fiction from the area of literary exercise. His Catholic sense of an extra dimension to reality and a moral sensibility certainly help to condition his characterisation and, at times, the novels reveal a tension between the hypothetical "freedom" of fictional characters and the way in which ideas manoeuvre them. But Joseph's endeavor to understand his fellow-men makes this tension a creative element in his work.

I'll Soldier No More, a war novel without anger or hysteria, treats of the lengthy training period in England, the soul-destroying boredom of "the waiting war" and its effects on, in the main, three members of the same unit. As they move into Germany as part of the army of occupation, they react, in one case tragically, to their environment in terms of their character and values. This semi-documentary novel, which contains a splendid picture of Germany in defeat, explores man's capacity to accept and endure, with mature understanding.

In *A Pound of Saffron* the scene is a New Zealand university and the plot turns on the machinations of an academic Machiavelli whose attempt to manipulate people's lives in pursuit of his own ambition leads to tragedy. Certain elements of melodrama infect the story, and possibly the novel a shade too insistently illustrates a theme. Yet a wide range of New Zealand social attitudes are skilfully exposed, the common-room atmosphere is finely realised, and the limitations of conventional academic positivism shrewdly defined.

Joseph's most surprising and original novel is *The Hole in the Zero*. A science-fiction framework provides the entry into a complex pattern of myth and archetype, in which moral and philosophical concepts are deftly and imaginatively handled. Four people in a deep-space rocket journey beyond the end of the universe and plunge into a series of strange planes of reality and non-reality, during which a struggle develops between philosophical man and sensual man. There are calculated echoes here of a variety of writers, from Milton to C.S. Lewis, yet the book has its own fascinating individuality and the characters do not become mere types. The fusion of fantasy and reality convinces, and Joseph's poetic skill raises some passages to a high pitch of sensitivity.

—J.C. Reid

JOSIPOVICI, Gabriel (David). British. Born in Nice, France, 8 October 1940. Educated at Victoria College, Cairo, 1950-56; Cheltenham College, Gloucestershire, 1956-57; St. Edmund Hall, Oxford, B.A. 1961. Lecturer, 1963-74, Reader, 1974-80, and since 1981, part-time Reader in English, University of Sussex, Brighton. Northcliffe Lecturer, University College, London, 1981. Recipient: *Sunday Times* Award, for play, 1970. Agent: John Johnson, 45-47 Clerkenwell Green, London EC1R OHT. Address: Department of English, University of Sussex, Falmer, Brighton, Sussex BN1 9RH, England.

PUBLICATIONS

Novels

The Inventory. London, Joseph, 1968.
Words. London, Gollancz, 1971.
The Present. London, Gollancz, 1975.
Migrations. Hassocks, Sussex, Harvester Press, 1977.
The Echo Chamber. Hassocks, Sussex, Harvester Press, 1980.
The Air We Breathe. Hassocks, Sussex, Harvester Press, 1981.

Short Stories

Mobius the Stripper: Stories and Short Plays (includes the plays *One*, *Dreams of Mrs. Fraser*, *Flow*). London, Gollancz, 1974.
Four Stories. London, Menard Press, 1977.

Plays

Dreams of Mrs. Fraser (produced London, 1972). Included in *Mobius the Stripper*, 1974.
Evidence of Intimacy (produced London, 1972).
Flow (produced Edinburgh and London, 1973). Included in *Mobius the Stripper*, 1974.
Echo (produced London, 1975).
Marathon (produced London, 1977).
A Moment (produced London, 1979).
Vergil Dying (broadcast, 1979). Windsor, SPAN, 1981.

Radio Plays: *Playback*, 1973; *A Life*, 1974; *Ag*, 1976; *Vergil Dying*, 1979.

Other

The World and the Book: A Study of Modern Fiction. London, Macmillan, and Stanford, California, Stanford University Press, 1971.
The Lessons of Modernism and Other Essays. London, Macmillan, and Totowa, New Jersey, Rowman and Littlefield, 1977.

Editor, *The Modern English Novel: The Reader, The Writer, and the Work*. London, Open Books, and New York, Barnes and Noble, 1976.

*

Critical Studies: interview with Bernard Sharratt, in *Orbit* (Tunbridge Wells, Kent), December 1975; "True Confessions of an Experimentalist" by the author, in *Granta* (Cambridge), 1981.

* * *

"Modern art," says Gabriel Josipovici in *The Lessons of Modernism*, "moves between two poles, silence and game." In his own novels the game is that of verbal art; the silence is that of unanswered questions. Conversations abound, explanations are sought, inquiries are pursued, but answers are always lacking. Characters experience an overwhelming pressure to speak, like a weight on the chest. But there is no narrator with authority to pronounce on the truth. The reader is drawn into puzzled involvement, impotent attentiveness, and pleasure in the play of the text.

In *The Inventory* a young man is constructing a list of the contents of a flat in which an old man and his son Sam used to live. They are both now dead. The precision of the inventory contrasts with the uncertainty of what he hears about their lives from Susan who tells him stories about her experiences of the two men. Why did Sam suddenly leave? Was he in love with Susan? Did she love him? Are her stories based on memory or invention? The novel is almost entirely in dialogue form and its effect depends on the author's precise control of rhythm, pace, and tone. It demonstrates his fascination with the musical, kinaesthetic, and dramatic aspects of speech which he has explored equally in his work for radio and theatre.

In *Words* Louis and his wife Helen are visited by Jo, who was once Louis's girlfriend and who may or may not also have had an affair with his brother Peter. The reader learns about the characters only through what they say to each other. Conversations return again and again to certain nagging questions. What happened years ago when Louis and Jo separated? Are either of them in earnest now when they talk about going away together? Are they serious or are they playing games? We only have their words to go on and words always leave open a variety of possible interpretations: cheerful banter or wounding aggression, flirtation or contempt, honesty or evasion?

The Present represents a change in fictional technique, for in this novel even the basic narrative situation is left undecided. The narrative, in the present tense, simultaneously develops stories in a number of different possible directions. The present leaves the future open. Reg and Minna share a flat with Alex; Minna is in hospital after a breakdown and dreams or imagines her life with Reg; Minna is married to Alex and they live with their two daughters in the country; Alex is dead having thrown himself from the window of Reg and Minna's flat. The stories interweave, each compelling but inconclusive.

Since 1977 Gabriel Josipovici has written his most ambitious and accomplished work, including the major radio play *Vergil Dying* and the novels *Migrations* and the forthcoming *The Air We Breathe*. In these novels he moves further away from the conventions of realist narrative. Whereas the early novels (and *The Echo Chamber*) are constructed around inconclusive stories and are primarily in dialogue form the later novels are constructed around multiple repetitions of fragmentary scenes and haunting images.

In *Migrations* a man lies on a bed in an empty room; a man collapses in an urban street; an autistic child fails to communicate with uncomprehending adults; a man talks in an overfurnished room with an unsympathetic woman, and so on. The text migrates restlessly from scene to scene: "You try to find a place to stop, roots...attempt to find a resting place for the imagination." "A series of places. Each must be visited. In turn. Then it will be finished. Then they will disappear." Temporary stillness and a disturbing sense of the physicality of speech, of words in the mouth, are achieved as the narrative voice repeats certain rhythms, images, and sound patterns and occasionally settles on certain sensuous sentences: "The black sky presses on his face like a blanket." "The sun streams in through the closed panes." "Silence drains away from him in dark streams." There is a poetic preoccupation with certain elemental forces, water and light, motion and rest, air and breath, which are to become an explicit theme of inquiry in *The Air We Breathe*.

One central image from *Migrations* can serve as an index of Gabriel Josipovici's concerns as a novelist. The friends and relations of Lazarus wait outside the tomb, excited, anticipating a miracle. Lazarus emerges and slowly unwinds the linen cloth. He unwinds and unwinds and when he is finished there is nothing there, nothing but a little mound of dust. There is nothing in the centre. There is no central meaning. As Josipovici says in *The Lessons of Modernism* the modern writer, like Eliot's Prufrock, rejects the role of Lazarus, "come back from the dead, come back to tell you all."

—John Mepham

KARP, David. American. Born in New York City, 5 May 1922. Educated at the City College of New York, 1940-42, 1946-48, B.S.Sc. 1948. Served in the United States Army in the South Pacific and Japan, 1943-46. Married Lillian Klass in 1944; two sons. Continuity Director, Radio Station WNYC, New York, 1948-49. Since 1949, free-lance writer. Since 1968, President of Leda Productions Inc., Los Angeles. Member, Executive Board, Writers Guild of America East, 1963-66. Since 1967, Member of the Executive Council, and President of the Television-Radio Branch, 1969-71, Writers Guild of America West. Member of the Editorial Board of *Television Quarterly*, 1966-71, and since 1972. Recipient: Guggenheim Fellowship, 1956; Ohio State University Award, for drama, 1948, and for television drama, 1958; *Look Magazine* Award, for television drama, 1958; Mystery Writers of America Edgar Allan Poe Award, for television drama, 1959; American Bar Association Gavel Award, for television documentary, 1963; Emmy Award, 1965. Address: 1116 Corsica Drive, Pacific Palisades, California 90272; or, c/o Robinson-Weintraub and Associates Inc., 554 South San Vicente Boulevard, Los Angeles, California 90048, U.S.A.

PUBLICATIONS

Novels

The Big Feeling. New York, Lion, 1952.
The Brotherhood of Velvet. New York, Lion, 1952.
Cry, Flesh. New York, Lion, 1953; as *The Girl on Crown Street*, 1956.
Hardman. New York, Lion, 1953.
Platoon (as Adam Singer). New York, Lion, 1953.
One. New York, Vanguard Press, 1953; London, Gollancz, 1954; as *Escape to Nowhere*, New York, Lion, 1955.
The Charka Memorial (as Wallace Ware). New York, Doubleday, 1954.
The Day of the Monkey. New York, Vanguard Press, and London, Gollancz, 1955.
All Honorable Men. New York, Knopf, and London, Gollancz, 1956.
Leave Me Alone. New York, Knopf, 1957; and London, Gollancz, 1958.
Enter, Sleeping. New York, Harcourt Brace, 1960; as *The Sleep-Walkers*, London, Gollancz, 1960.
The Last Believers. New York, Harcourt Brace, 1964; London, Cape, 1965.

Uncollected Short Stories

"All American," in *Argosy* (New York), October 1950.
"Life of the Party," in *American Magazine* (New York), January 1951.
"Wait for Her Laughter," in *Esquire* (New York), January 1952.
"The Red-Necked Peasant from Dubuque," in *Esquire* (New York), October 1952.
"The Lady With the French Ideas," in *Park East* (New York), February 1953.
"Blood Money," in *Collier's* (New York), 7 August 1953.
"Death Warrant," in *Saturday Evening Post Stories 1954*. New York, Random House, 1954.

Plays

Cafe Univers (produced New York, 1967).

Screenplays: *Sol Madrid*, 1967; *Che!*, 1968; *Tender Loving Care*, 1972.

Radio Plays: *House I Live In* series (2 plays), 1946; *One Step Forward* series (21 plays), 1946-47; *A Day to Remember* series (4 plays), 1947; *Famine Relief* series (3 plays), 1947; *Unsung Heroes* series (5 plays), 1947; *People, Unlimited* series (5 plays), 1947; *Grand Central Station* series (3 plays), 1948-49; *Aunt Jenny* series (64 programs), 1950-56; *City Hospital* series (3 plays), 1957; and other plays for *Skippy Hollywood Theatre*, *American Bible Society*, and *CBS Radio Workshop*, 1948-60.

Television Plays: *The Defenders* series (10 plays), 1961-64; *Saints and Sinners* series (3 plays), 1962; *Profiles in Courage* series (5 plays), 1963-65; *The Brotherhood of the Bell*, 1971; *The Family Rico*, 1972; *Hawkins on Murder*, 1973; *W.E.B.*, 1978; and other plays.

Verse

The Voice of the Four Freedoms. Privately printed, 1942.

Other

Vice-President in Charge of Revolution (biography), with Murray D. Lincoln. New York, McGraw Hill, 1960.

*

Manuscript Collection: Mugar Memorial Library, Boston University.

David Karp comments:

(1972) If there is such a thing as a moralist novelist I am probably in that class or genre. I am a didactic writer. My first teacher was Upton Sinclair. I devoured all of his works and learned my liberalism from this impassioned teacher. Poverty was given to me by the world into which I was born. I was poor, I was ambitious, I was filled with outrage against injustice and yet I inherited from my mother, I guess, a pragmatism which I have never forgotten. I am, in many ways, the product of the Depression, Judaism, American liberalism and idealism, and Jewish middle class pragmatism and ambition. What kind of an odd bird does that make me? I know it isn't a common species—because I have been shut out of the literary establishment, the avant-garde (which is another kind of establishment) and the "mainstream" (what an awful description) of American letters. I have nothing but contempt for most academic critics and the literary games they play. I do not really write short fiction and will not write criticism and do not share the cheap and easy self-hating liberalism which is so fashionable these days. I am isolated by my politics, my tastes, my pragmatism (I think a writer is entitled to earn every bit as much as a movie star), and my belief that clear thinking and clear writing are two beautiful pure fluids which need no adulteration or coloring. I do my work (such as it is) with all the attention and integrity and passion that I can—whatever the work is. I do not disdain writing for television or motion pictures (or radio)—a writer's first responsibility is to survive and to be self-sufficient. I don't think a writer is entitled to be a mendicant on the grounds that his art prevents him from being self-supporting. Nor do I think he should become a freak to exploit his position. A writer has the right to do his work and if it gains acceptance to be modestly grateful and if it is rejected to be immodestly contemptuous but to go on. I will not compromise to be successful, I will not kiss asses to be accepted and I will not give up being a writer because I am ignored. I have written many things—many of them (too many of them) to maintain myself and my family and to maintain my pride in being self-sufficient. I am active in union affairs of a writer's organization because I believe no writer should be exploited by an employer. But I also believe writers should not exploit one another for professional self-aggrandizement. I have too much pride to elbow my way into the public glare. I leave that game to the publicity-seeking wretches whose names I am sure you know so well. Newspaper clippings rot—good work does not.

* * *

The world of David Karp's fiction is one of fairly predictable ironies, most often involving the biter bit, the spider snared in its own web, the bomber hoist with his own petard. Frank Ames, for example, in *The Big Feeling*, is just insane enough to botch up his own insanity plea; and his escape is ruined by the same traits of character that made his robberies successful. Similarly, James Watterson (in *The Brotherhood of Velvet*) and Professor Burden (in *One*) are driven out of jobs, families, and ultimately, out of personal identity itself by the same conspiracies they have served so well. The ironies are doubled in *Cry, Flesh*, in which Rose Genovese, mercy killer, is herself killed by her lover, Cheval, whose motives are those of compassion and pity; and in which Cheval himself is saved from the consequences of that killing by the same sort of understanding tainted with moral corruption that brought about his own attempt to save Rose from the consequences of *her* killings.

This love of poetic justice, Karp's deft touches of conventional psychological insight, and his careful attention to the working details of plot—particularly those pertaining to crime—do not, however, distinguish his work from that of half-a-hundred other more or less competent writers of sensational fiction. The qualities which are particularly Karp's are, first, a deep moral sense of the integrity of the individual, and, second, his ability to touch those hideous fantasies that are common to all of us.

At times the individual whom Karp pits against the group is

clearly mad, like Frank Ames; at other times he gives us a Rose Genovese, whose madness is a saintly one. But whether the opposition is the police or the *1984*-like organizations of *One* or *The Brotherhood of Velvet*, the individual must lose, the principle of the individual must be vindicated.

Sometimes Karp's fantasies are those common to much police fiction (that of Richard Stark comes to mind)—the perfect bank robbery, for example. More often they are more nightmarish—discovering that the loved one is a killer, killing the loved one. These nightmares are perhaps most successful when they awaken in the reader the latent paranoia of our century—they are after me.

Karp draws these threads together most successfully in *One* (later reissued as *Escape to Nowhere*), which enjoyed some success in the 1950's and was favorably compared to *1984*. Its prose is not, of course, as skilful as that of Orwell, but almost nobody's is; nor does Karp work out the details of his future society with the same care. But Lark, his chief inquisitor and ex-heretic, is a walking embodiment of the ironies and contradictions with which Karp loves to deal, and his confrontation with Burden, a victim with whom the reader can identify more readily, perhaps more readily than with Orwell's, is loaded with the ultimate moral implications which preoccupy Karp.

One's nightmare is, I think, more nightmarish than Orwell's, because it is less complicated, less gimmicked, and because, finally, the threat of breaking (as in *1984*) is not as horrid as the threat of having one's identity destroyed. Finally, Karp achieves his most successful irony at the end of *One* in the simultaneous triumph and death of Burden.

—Irving F. Foote

KELLEY, William Melvin. American. Born in New York City in 1937. Educated at Harvard University, Cambridge, Massachusetts (Reed Prize, 1960). Married Karen Gibson in 1962; two children. Writer-in-Residence, State University College, Geneseo, New York, Spring 1965; taught at New School for Social Research, New York, 1965-67. Recipient: Bread Loaf Writers Conference grant, 1962; Whitney Foundation Award, 1963; Rosenthal Foundation Award, 1963; *Transatlantic Review* Award, 1964. Address: c/o Doubleday and Company Inc., 245 Park Avenue, New York, New York 10017, U.S.A.

PUBLICATIONS

Novels

A Different Drummer. New York, Doubleday, 1962; London, Hutchinson, 1963.
A Drop of Patience. New York, Doubleday, 1965; London, Hutchinson, 1966.
Dem. New York, Doubleday, 1967.
Dunsfords Travels Everywheres. New York, Doubleday, 1970.

Short Stories

Dancers on the Shore. New York, Doubleday, 1964; London, Hutchinson, 1965.

Uncollected Short Stories

"Jest, Like Sam," in *Negro Digest* (Chicago), October 1969.
"The Dentist's Wife," in *Women and Men, Men and Women*, edited by William Smart. New York, St. Martin's Press, 1975.

* * *

William Melvin Kelley's novels to date have dealt with interracial conflict, but the emphasis has been on the examination of characters, black and white, and the myths with which they delude themselves. His novels pose no "solutions" to the conflict but the solution of self-understanding, and his depiction of the relationships—loving and competitive—between men and women and blacks and whites combines compassion, objectivity, and humor.

His first novel, *A Different Drummer*, set realistically rendered characters in a fantasy plot. From multiple points of view he displayed the reactions of the whites of a fictional Southern state to the spontaneous, grass-roots emigration of the state's blacks. A minor incident in *A Different Drummer* concerns Wallace Bedlow, who is waiting for a bus to take him to New York City, where he plans to live with his brother, Carlyle. Bedlow appears only that one time, but he surfaces again in "Cry for Me," probably the best short story in *Dancers on the Shore*, in which he becomes a famous folk singer. In that story the themes of one's public image versus the true self and commercialism versus art are explored.

These themes are developed further in Kelley's second novel, *A Drop of Patience*. The protagonist is a blind, black jazz musician, whose intuitive experimentation is contrasted to the intellectualization of critics, and whose love of music comes into conflict with the commercialization of music. More important than these themes, however, is the development of the character himself, who passes through various rites of passage as he learns to deal with sex, love, racism, and fame.

Carlyle Bedlow, who appeared in several of the stories in *Dancers on the Shore*, reappears in *Dem*, Kelley's third novel. "Lemme tellya how dem folks live," the novel begins. It goes on to show dem white folks living out their myths of white superiority, masculine prerogative, and soap-opera escapism. They are such victims of the pernicious myths of their culture that they are no longer even a threat to black people.

Racial conflict nearly disappears amidst the experimentation and fantasy of *Dunfords Travels Everywheres*, Kelley's own clever and original permutation of *Finnegans Wake*. A tryptich in plot, style, and character, *Dunfords Travels Everywheres* is an ambitious short novel; it succeeds in being clever, but as an exploration into character it's less satisfying that his earlier novels.

Kelley has shown himself a skillful craftsman in a variety of styles and approaches. In his stories and in his first three novels his exploration of character develops as the character seeks—or refuses to seek—a unity between the person he feels he is and the personality he or society thinks he should be. This is true also in one of the three interwoven stories of *Dunfords Travels Everywheres*. In the other two stories a playful fantasy dominates. If Kelley's fiction has a direction, it's one that moves from seriousness and psychological probing to fantasy, playfulness, and comedy.

—William Borden

KENEALLY, Thomas (Michael). Australian. Born in Sydney, New South Wales, 7 October 1935. Educated at St. Patrick's College, Strathfield, New South Wales; studied for the priesthood and studied law. Served in the Australian Citizens Military Forces. Married Judith Martin in 1965; two daughters. High school teacher in Sydney, 1960-64; Lecturer in Drama, University of New England, Armidale, New South Wales, 1968-70. Recipient: Commonwealth Literary Fund Fellowship, 1966, 1968, 1972; Miles Franklin Award, 1967, 1968; Captain Cook Bi-Centenary Prize, 1970. Fellow, Royal Society of Literature, 1973. Address: c/o William Collins Ltd., 14 St. James's Place, London SW1A 1PS, England.

PUBLICATIONS

Novels

The Place at Whitton. Melbourne and London, Cassell, 1964; New York, Walker, 1965.
The Fear. Melbourne and London, Cassell, 1965.
Bring Larks and Heroes. Melbourne, Cassell, 1967; London, Cassell, and New York, Viking Press, 1968.
Three Cheers for the Paraclete. Sydney, Angus and Robertson, 1968; London, Angus and Robertson, and New York, Viking Press, 1969.
The Survivor. Sydney, Angus and Robertson, 1969; London, Angus and Robertson, and New York, Viking Press, 1970.
A Dutiful Daughter. Sydney and London, Angus and Robertson, and New York, Viking Press, 1971.
The Chant of Jimmie Blacksmith. Sydney and London, Angus and Robertson, and New York, Viking Press, 1972.
Blood Red, Sister Rose. London, Collins, and New York, Viking Press, 1974.
Moses the Lawgiver (novelization of TV play). London, Collins-ATV, and New York, Harper, 1975.
Gossip from the Forest. London, Collins, 1975; New York, Harcourt Brace, 1976.
Season in Purgatory. London, Collins, 1976; New York, Harcourt Brace, 1977.
A Victim of the Aurora. London, Collins, 1977; New York, Harcourt Brace, 1978.
Passenger. London, Collins, and New York, Harcourt Brace, 1979.
Confederates. London, Collins, 1979; New York, Harper, 1980.

Uncollected Short Story

"The Performing Blind Boy," in *Festival and Other Stories*, edited by Brian Buckley and Jim Hamilton. Melbourne, Wren, 1974; Newton Abbot, Devon, David and Charles, 1975.

Plays

Halloran's Little Boat, adaptation of his novel *Bring Larks and Heroes* (produced Sydney, 1966). Published in *Penguin Australian Drama 2*, Melbourne, Penguin, 1975.
Childermass (produced Sydney, 1968).

Screenplay: *The Priest* (episode in *Libido*), 1973.

Television Plays (UK): *Essington*, 1974; *The World's Wrong End* (documentary; *Writers and Places* series), 1981.

Other

Ned Kelly and the City of Bees (juvenile). London, Cape, 1978; Boston, Godine, 1981.

*

Thomas Keneally comments:

(1972) I would like to be able to disown my first two novels, the second of which was the obligatory account of one's childhood—the book then that all novelists think seriously of writing.

I see my third novel as an attempt to follow out an epic theme in terms of a young soldier's exile to Australia.

The fourth and fifth were attempts at urbane writing in the traditional mode of the English novel: confrontations between characters whose behaviour shows layers of irony and humour, in which all that is epic is rather played down.

For *A Dutiful Daughter*, the best novel I have written (not that I claim that matters much), I have turned to myth and fable, as many a novelist is doing, for the simple reason that other media have moved into the traditional areas of the novel.

* * *

Thomas Keneally has been quoted by the *Guardian* as "the leading Australian novelist of his generation, with an international reputation second only to Patrick White." Keneally had chosen to desert a life in the Church, and then a life in the Law, in order to devote himself to fiction. It has been a productive devotion.

After disowning his first two published novels—trial flights—he settled down to a rare eclecticism—novels both historical and contemporary, increasingly skilled in narrative, yet weighted with problems of conscience: problems of morals and of principle, of which he had already found himself an individualist. From his first historical novel, on the early Australian penal colony (*Bring Larks and Heroes*), to his contemporary theme of a man in search of self and love against the background of the Church (*Three Cheers for the Paraclete*), he was a sympathetic questioner of orthodoxy. Later, he branched out into the social question of the Abo—or particularly the half-caste (*The Chant of Jimmie Blacksmith*)—ending in a wild pursuit that ironically echoes the legend of Australia's famous white outlaw, Ned Kelly.

Meanwhile he had tried a domestic drama of conscience (*The Survivor*) in which the head of a South Polar expedition had risked the life of a colleague whose wife he craved. He then wrote his only fantasy (*A Dutiful Daughter*), a modern-dress realistic parable in which people become animals. Psychology and moral subtleties are its point: "The only way for [a prideful family] to get humility is by learning that they are beasts." Though suspension of disbelief may not be quite willing, this is original and touching.

He returned to history in his next book with a new interpretation of Joan of Arc (*Blood Red, Sister Rose*). Though imaginative and skillful, this is full of difficult subtleties for the unwary. It had been foreshadowed in *Dutiful Daughter*, in which the unfortunate girl tending the "beasts" was attempting to write a similar history. In a way they supplement each other, centuries apart.

Writing fiction, not history, Keneally need not be held accountable for the facts, but only for the semblance of truth that comes through to us convincingly from his characters. He has since turned most often to fiction arising from history, and the discrepancies between his own view and the conventional view tend more and more to set him apart.

In *Gossip from the Forest*, his grimly comical story of the conclave in the railway car which set up the 1919 Armistice, he damns the British admirals and double-damns Foch for his arrogance and self-glory, leaving only the second-rate German representatives as defenders of a better world future—as his hindsight seems to believe. But the imaginary dialogue is an ironic delight, and his reconstruction of the motives is telling. *Season in Purgatory*, set during World War II, tells of a British hospital for Tito's partisans while the Nazis were still in Yugoslavia. This is almost non-political: the partisans appear to be about as vicious as the Nazis, though more inviting as individuals. The young English medic's love affair with an older partisan heroine is attractive. The interest, however, lies with the medical expertise under extreme stress—the skill for detail that Keneally knows how to use well.

More recently Keneally has tried his hand in the manner of the expert British mystery writers. He stands up well in that fraternity. In *Victim of the Aurora* a fictional South Polar Expedition of 1910 offers us 20 Englishmen not only trying to reach the Pole but becoming involved in the murder of one of their fellows in which all the others are legitimate suspects. As usual, Keneally has his own point to make. His 82-year-old Edwardian narrator closes his nostalgic record by saying that this 1910 murder and its punishment, strictly on a point of honour, made it "the act that rendered the condition of the century terminal" and added: "Nothing ever since has surprised me."

Turning swiftly from his 82-year-old Edwardian, he has chosen to make his next narrator, in *Passenger*, a foetus in the womb of an illegitimate mother—a subject that the present commentator feels incompetent to deal with. The "Right to Life" controversy seems beyond his means at that level, though the book has been highly praised in the *New York Times* and other periodicals.

Now the author has tackled the American Civil War. *Confederates* gives him the opportunity, perhaps a little late, to defend the

American South. Burke Davis in the *Washington Post* has called this an "intricately structured book, awash in battle and athrob with sexuality," and that can hardly be bettered. One wonders how four such solid novels, with their totally different backgrounds, could have come forth from the same writer in four successive years. True to his leaning for the underdog against the Establishment, going from Jimmie Blacksmith through Joan of Arc to the Germans at Compiegne and Tito's guerillas, he now gives a sympathetic picture of Dixie in its heyday, 1862. When he comes to the Emancipation Proclamation, it appears as nothing more than a Yankee dirty trick to thwart the heroic Rebs. While admiring his independence, we have to conclude that he is not a serious historical novelist. But he is wonderfully entertaining, full of believable characters both fictional and real—Stonewall Jackson is one of his best—and worthy of the *Washington Post*'s assertion that "*Gone with the Wind* is a soap opera in comparison." He now belongs in the class of his more established and popular compatriot, Morris West.

—Marshall A. Best

KESEY, Ken (Elton). American. Born in La Junta, Colorado, 17 September 1935. Educated at the University of Oregon, Eugene, B.A. 1957; Stanford University, California (Woodrow Wilson Fellow), 1958-59. Married Norma Faye Haxby in 1954; four children. Has worked as a ward attendant in a mental hospital; President of Intrepid Trips Inc., a motion picture company; Publisher, *Spit in the Ocean* magazine, Eugene, Oregon, 1974. Recipient: Saxton Memorial Trust Award, 1959. Address: 85829 Ridgeway Road, Pleasant Hill, Oregon 97401, U.S.A.

PUBLICATIONS

Novels

One Flew over the Cuckoo's Nest. New York, Viking Press, 1962; London, Methuen, 1963.
Sometimes a Great Notion. New York, Viking Press, 1964; London, Methuen, 1966.

Uncollected Short Stories

"The First Sunday in October," in *Northwest Review* (Seattle), Fall 1957.
"McMurphy and the Machine," in *Stanford Short Stories 1962*, edited by Wallace Stegner and Richard Scowcroft. Stanford, California, Stanford University Press, 1962.
"Letters from Mexico," in *Ararat* (New York), Autumn 1967.
"Excerpts from Kesey's Jail Diary,"in *Ramparts* (Berkeley, California), November 1967.
"Correspondence," in *Tri-Quarterly* (Evanston, Illinois), Spring 1970.
"Once a Great Nation," in *Argus* (College Park, Maryland), April 1970.
"Dear Good Dr. Timothy," in *Augur* (Eugene, Oregon), 19 November 1970.
"Cut the Motherfuckers Loose," in *The Last Whole Earth Catalog*. San Francisco, Straight Arrow, 1971.
"The Bible," "Dawgs," "The I Ching," "Mantras," "Tools from My Chest," in *The Last Supplement to the Whole Earth Catalog-The Realist* (New York), March-April 1971.
"Over the Border," in *Oui* (Chicago), April 1973.
"Tranny-Man" and " 'Seven Prayers' by Grandma Whittier," in *Spit in the Ocean* (Eugene, Oregon), i, 1, 1974.
"The Day after Superman Died," in *Esquire* (New York), October 1979.

Other

Kesey's Garage Sale (miscellany). New York, Viking Press, 1973.

*

Manuscript Collection: University of Oregon, Eugene.

Critical Studies: *The Electric Kool-Aid Acid Test* by Tom Wolfe, New York, Farrar Straus, 1968; *Ken Kesey* by Bruce Carnes, Boise, Idaho, Boise State College, 1974.

* * *

Ken Kesey's critical reputation rests for the time being on his two novels. The first, *One Flew over the Cuckoo's Nest*, was a widely popular success which has been adapted for performance as a play. The second novel, *Sometimes a Great Notion*, has received relatively little attention. Since finishing it, Kesey has announced a shift from "literature" to "life," and has achieved a great deal of public notoriety in the process of making the change. He was public news during the late 1960's forming a band of "Merry Pranksters" (reported on at length in Tom Wolfe's *Electric Kool-Aid Acid Test*) who attempted to live life as a work of comic fiction. Stray pieces of notebooks have been published in the last few years, suggesting that eventually a new work, perhaps a new kind of work, will emerge. Until then, Kesey followers will have to content themselves with *The Last Supplement to the Whole Earth Catalog*. This volume has more of Kesey's writing in it (mostly reviews and articles) than anything published since his second novel.

Both of Kesey's novels are richly northwestern and regional in quality, with a strong sense of the impingement of the white man on the Indian's land and way of life. The emphasis is a bit one-sided in *Cuckoo's Nest*, which has for its stream-of-consciousness center and narrator-observer an Indian named Chief, whose father was in fact the last chief of his tribe. The novel could be read as an allegory of how the white man is driven to subjugate and eliminate the Indian because he is a reminder to him of those parts of himself he has lost through a conquest of the will over the passions. More basically, however, the novel reveals the power struggle between man's desire to be free and his fears of the consequence of that freedom. Most of the characters in the mental institution could leave if they wished; but their fear of the outside is more intense than their hatred of the inside. The novel tempts one to allegorical generalities because the institution in which it is set becomes increasingly recognizable as a microcosm of the world we all live in. Recognizable, but comically exaggerated, as are the main characters who represent general qualities and attitudes towards life and humanity. The book captures and reflects the reality of a "Walt-Disney world," as perceived by the "Big Chief" who used to be on our childhood writing tablet covers but is now pretending to be a vegetable in a nut house. What he sees is "Like a cartoon world, where the figures are flat and outlined in black, jerking through some kind of goofy story that might be real funny if it weren't for the cartoon figures being real guys...." The comic-book quality has lent itself nicely to dramatic production, as have the compactness and wild humor of the novel. These qualities also tempt one to allegorize, but at the same time mock the attempt as absurd. For the work is not itself allegorical; it is a report or presentation of the way people see themselves and their world in allegorical or comic-book fashion, yet without being able to laugh at what they see. The reality of the villain, "Big Nurse," is as exaggerated by the characters who fear and hate her as it is by the novelist. The institution, with its equipment and routines, is a focus for sociological and psychological myths and techniques pushed to an illogical but all-too-plausible extreme. The prefrontal lobotomy performed on McMurphy at the end is *any* operation on or treatment of or way of seeing a man, that decides to limit and dehumanize him for his own sake. The Big Nurse is that spirit which loves the "idea" of man so much it can't allow individual men to exist.

Sometimes a Great Notion deserves more attention than *Cuckoo's Nest*, and much more than I can give it here. I can indicate its ambition, by pointing out that it is in considerable part an *Absalom, Absalom!* set in Oregon. I pick this example not only to suggest the intense regionalism of the book, but to indicate the intricate complexities of the narrative structure which Kesey has attempted. After the second reading, what at first seem like gratuitous confusions and exploitations of "the miracle of modern narrative technique," begin to emerge as the necessary supports for a novelistic structure which doesn't quite get brought into finished shape. In this novel Kesey has aimed higher than many of his contemporaries, and he has come impressively close to his traget.

—Thomas A. Vogler

KHAN, Ismith (Mohamed). American. Born in Port of Spain, Trinidad, 16 March 1925; became American citizen in 1958. Educated at Queen's Royal College, Port of Spain; Michigan State University, East Lansing, 1948-51; New School for Social Research, New York, 1951-54, B.A. in social sciences 1954; Johns Hopkins University, Baltimore, 1969-70, M.A. in creative writing 1970. Married 1) Mariam Ghose in 1949 (marriage dissolved, 1966); 2) Vera Simon in 1966; two children. Research assistant, Department of Far Eastern Studies, Cornell University, Ithaca, New York, 1955-56; library assistant, New York Public Library, 1956-61; Instructor in Creative Writing, New School for Social Research, 1959-69, and Great Neck public schools, Long Island, New York, 1963; Visiting Professor of English, University of California, Berkeley, 1970-71; Assistant Professor of Caribbean and Comparative Literature, University of California, San Diego, 1971-74; Senior Lecturer, University of Southern California, Los Angeles, 1977, and California State University, Long Beach, 1978, 1980. Agent: John Schaffner, Suite 6-D, 425 East 51st Street, New York, New York 10022. Address: 539 South Clementine Street, Anaheim, California 92805, U.S.A.

PUBLICATIONS

Novels

The Jumbie Bird. London, MacGibbon and Kee, 1961; New York, Obolensky, 1963.
The Obeah Man. London, Hutchinson, 1964.

Uncollected Short Stories

"In the Subway," in *New Voices 2*, edited by Don M. Wolfe. New York, Hendricks House, 1955.
"A Day in the Country," in *From the Green Antilles*, edited by Barbara Howes. New York, Macmillan, 1966; London, Souvenir Press, 1967.
"The Red Ball," in *New Writing in the Caribbean*, edited by A.J. Seymour. Georgetown, Government of Guyana, 1972.
"The Village Shop," in *Lambailey*, edited by Ron Heapy and Anne Garside. London, Oxford University Press, 1980.
"Shadows Move in the Bratania Bar," in *Sunlight and Shadows*. London, Cassell, 1980.

*

Ismith Khan comments:

All of my novels and short stories are set in the Caribbean. This has necessitated certain choices, questions, and considerations: 1) what language to write in, pidgin or Standard English; 2) how well can an expatriate writer, despite frequent visits to his area, speak for and about its times; 3) which audience to write for, local or international, bearing in mind the size and literacy of the local audience, and the prohibitive cost of books.

Despite the drawbacks, I have opted to write for a local audience in an attempt to revivify the cultural milieu from which my work derives its inspiration, because the writer from the Caribbean has to assume the responsibility of "teacher" and "historian" in order to record periods of history not normally found in history books. It is the long view, the long term that is of importance. There should be a body of literature written by Caribbean authors that will fill the literary vacuum for the younger generation, and other generations to come, so that they will be able to come to grips with their "identity" in what has become a world of rapid change where the sense of intrinsic values and the importance of traditions are lost, swallowed up by international values that seem to mitigate the breakdown of culture and human personality. This is the material from which the "drama" of the Caribbean and its people is made.

My work is an attempt to confront "culture shock," to resurrect a sense of self, to look at values and traditions in the period of bewildering change that our independence has brought with it, changes not necessarily of our own making but which nonetheless affect our lives directly.

* * *

Ismith Khan's fiction takes the Indian community of Trinidad as its starting point, analyzing the special features of that community at the same time that the writer explores the Indian experience as a microcosm of the West Indian experience as a whole. In his two published novels this exploration centers on the theme of exile and isolation: the historical exile of Indians, Africans, and Europeans to the Caribbean has resulted in a culture that is simultaneously linked with and isolated from its original sources.

In the first novel, *The Jumbie Bird*, the narrative plot centers on three generations of the Khan family—Kale, his son Rahmin, and his grandson Jamini. Kale is one of the original migrants from India, those who first came to Trinidad and other islands in the British Caribbean colonies as contract labourers. But he is a lifelong malcontent, always busy with plans to return to India from a world in which he has never really felt at home. Rahmin shares some of his father's revulsion at Trinidad, but having grown up in the Caribbean he does not identify as strongly with the Indian homeland or with Kale's perennial back-to-India schemes. And in the third generation Jamini is even further removed from the Indian memories of his grandfather, even though he is very fond of old Kale himself.

The theme of isolation in the novel—especially Kale's isolation—is therefore integrated with the migrant's sense of dislocation and cultural exile. The fact that the old man lives alone, in a separate room of the Khan house, emphasizes the degree to which he is alienated from the family while belonging to it. Similarly, he belongs to Trinidad to the extent that, willy-nilly, it is his permanent home; but he is wholly alienated from the society—its colonial heritage, its Western trappings, and, quite simply, the fact that it is not India. But although he is a prime mover of local repatriation politics, he really hates India itself—it is the place that forced him into exile in the first place because it had nothing to offer him by way of socioeconomic survival.

The tragedy of Kale's isolation is that it is so complete. His profound dissatisfaction with the world around him leads to a deep-seated revulsion at people in general. His alienation is not just the migrant's usual nostalgia: it is also a form of isolation from the human condition in general. And in fact his involvement with the repatriation movement is really a desperate attempt to provide himself with a sense of belonging. When the movement fails, when the official representative from India makes its futility quite clear,

Kale literally has nothing to live for, and he dies shortly afterwards. His grandson is left to carry the burden of isolation, but when the novel ends the reader is left with the assurance that Jamini can cope. He recognizes that isolation is not simply a cultural condition imposed by the circumstances of (West Indian) history: it is also an integral part of the human condition. His early, and abortive, sexual experience demonstrates to him that even in moments of intimacy human beings usually manage to remain "locked up within themselves and quite alone." And paradoxically enough this recognition of the nature of isolation prepares him to deal with people, and with his culture, on a much more substantial basis than his grandfather ever could.

In *Obeah Man* Khan returns to the theme of individual loneliness, by emphasizing once again that individual feelings and identity are often "locked up" from others as a normal course of events, and that this prevailing human tendency usually thwarts or dilutes attempts to formulate patterns of cultural solidarity or sexual intimacy. In the first novel Jamini learns that even in intimate relationships we see only the "outer surfaces" of others. In this second novel the hero, Zampi the obeah man, sees the masks of carnival as symbols of those outer surfaces. Thus when he removes a grinning mask from a carnival reveller's face he discovers a face that's sweaty, tearful, and pathetic.

Zampi himself is a mixture of several races on the island, and to this degree he represents the history of synthesis and fusion that has been characteristic of Caribbean culture. And on another level his role as obeah man, or healer, represents a certain commitment to the well-being of his community. But at the same time that role requires a certain distance from others—hence he lives as a hermit, away from the city and—except for this carnival—away from its festivals and flesh-pots. And this isolation reflects his scepticism about the possibility of maintaining really enduring relationships based on complete knowledge of the other. In turn this scepticism has led to his estrangement from his girlfriend Zolda. Finally, his private estrangement, and the jealousies and social divisions that he discovers underneath the joyous masks of carnival, all counteract the sense of cultural and social fusion that his own ethnic heritage represents. As in *Jumbie Bird* Khan offers no sweeping, transcendental solutions to all of this. At best we are left with Zampi's ability to survive, emotionally and physically, precisely because he refuses to take the "outer surfaces" of human behaviour at face value. And this is the lesson that Zolda is beginning to learn at the end of the novel when she agrees to join him in his hermit's exile from the city.

It is a central paradox of Ismith Khan's fiction, and one of its major achievements, that he is able to explore the social milieu of his characters in convincing detail—at the same time that he insists on the prevailing isolation of individuals from each other and from their social milieu as a whole. The world of the Indian in Trinidad is painted in painstaking detail in *Jumbie Bird*; and in *Obeah Man* the carnival is not only a picturesque celebration as such, it is also a microcosm of Trinidad society as the novelist envisions it. As a result Khan's fiction occupies a rather special, though too often neglected niche in Caribbean literature: it celebrates the special vitality of the region's culture without romanticizing it, allowing writer and reader alike to remain painfully aware of the degree to which a sense of social or ethnocultural belonging is often counterbalanced, even thwarted, by persistent isolation and divisiveness between individuals.

—Lloyd W. Brown

KIELY, Benedict. Irish. Born in Dromore, County Tyrone, 15 August 1919. Educated at Christian Brothers' schools, Omagh; National University of Ireland, Dublin. Married Maureen O'Connell in 1944; four children. Journalist in Dublin, 1939-64. Writer-in-Residence, Hollins College, Virginia, 1964-65; Visiting Professor, University of Oregon, Eugene, 1965-66; Writer-in-Residence, Emory University, Atlanta, Georgia, 1966-68. Since 1970, Visiting Lecturer, University College, Dublin. Recipient: American-Irish Foundation Award, 1980; Irish Academy of Letters Award, 1980. Member of the Council, and President, Irish Academy of Letters. Address: c/o The Irish Times, Westmoreland Street, Dublin, Ireland.

PUBLICATIONS

Novels

Land Without Stars. London, Johnson, 1946.
In a Harbour Green. London, Cape, 1949; New York, Dutton, 1950.
Call for a Miracle. London, Cape, 1950; New York, Dutton, 1951.
Honey Seems Bitter. New York, Dutton, 1952; London, Methuen, 1954.
The Cards of the Gambler: A Folktale. London, Methuen, 1953.
There Was an Ancient House. London, Methuen, 1955.
The Captain with the Whiskers. London, Methuen, 1960; New York, Criterion, 1961.
Dogs Enjoy the Morning. London, Gollancz, 1968.
Proxopera. London, Gollancz, 1977.

Short Stories

A Journey to the Seven Streams: Seventeen Stories. London, Methuen, 1963.
Penguin Modern Stories 5, with others. London, Penguin, 1970.
A Ball of Malt and Madame Butterfly: A Dozen Stories. London, Gollancz, 1973.
A Cow in the House and Nine Other Stories. London, Gollancz, 1978.
The State of Ireland: A Novella and Seventeen Stories. Boston, Godine, 1980.

Other

Counties of Contention: A Study of the Origins and Implication of the Partition of Ireland. Cork, Mercier Press, 1945.
Poor Scholar: A Study of the Works and Days of William Carleton, 1794-1869. London, Sheed and Ward, 1947; New York, Sheed and Ward, 1948.
Modern Irish Fiction: A Critique. Dublin, Golden Eagle, 1950.
All the Way to Bantry Bay and Other Irish Journeys. London, Gollancz, 1976.

Editor, *The Various Lives of Keats and Chapman and The Brother*, by Flann O'Brien. London, Hart Davis MacGibbon, 1976.

*

Critical Studies: *Benedict Kiely* by Daniel J. Casey, Lewisburg, Pennsylvania, Bucknell University Press, 1974; *Benedict Kiely* by Grace Eckley, New York, Twayne, 1974.

* * *

Myth and legend, the heroic and the mock-heroic, form the central strands to the short stories of Benedict Kiely. He relies heavily on the Irish genius for creating epic myths about man, his heroic deeds and his human frailties. Although his fiction is largely set in the County Tyrone of his boyhood, a landscape that he knows intimately and with a sense of delight, it is transformed in a story like "A Journey to the Seven Streams" to a land of eternal and universal childhood. The trip to the stone-fiddle beside Lough Erne in Hookey Baxter's whimsical motor car takes on the aspect of a pilgrimage to a shrine or the tale of travellers in a magic, dreamlike land who have to face numerous adventures and dangers. And Kiely's language, too, is finely honed to a mock-serious note, with elegy never far away, reflecting both the absurdity of the journey and its underlying comic pathos: "White cottages far away on the lower slopes of Dooish could have been in another country."

Kiely's reputation has been somewhat retarded by what many critics dismiss as a narrow provincialism but what is also a source of joy to his readers. In a second collection, *A Ball of Malt and Madame Butterfly*, Kiely confirmed that although his work continues to be rooted in the Ireland that he knows so well, it has a breadth of vision and humanity in its subject matter and literary style that raises it above the merely provincial. The Tyrone of his childhood and the Dublin of his formative years are favourite backdrops for his novels where the mood changes from the mock-epic to the mock-gothic romance in a work like *The Captain with the Whiskers* with its memorable scene of the mad captain drilling his three sons in Boer War uniforms in the doomed big house; and in *Dogs Enjoy the Morning* with its satirical mixture of pub gossip and idle anecdote in the grotesque, but finely drawn, village of Cosmona where a newspaper reporter remarks, aptly enough, that "all human life is here."

A new note in Keily's work was struck with the publication of *Proxopera* in 1977, a savagely indignant novel with its anger directed against all men of violence in Ireland. The title comes from an "operation proxy" when an elderly grandfather, Binchey, is forced by three terrorists holding his family ransom to take a bomb into the neighbouring town. The background is again Tyrone, but the mood is at once savage in Binchey's outrage at the terrorism that Ireland has helped to spawn, and at once an elegy for the non-sectarian, chivalrous past of his own childhood. Everything is seen through the enraged consciousness of Binchey and his sense of loss that nothing, his past, his family, the countryside and his relationship to them, will ever be the same again. *Proxopera* is a bold and courageous work, a lament for the injuries perpetrated on the Ireland that the author obviously holds so dear.

—Trevor Royle

KILLENS, John Oliver. American. Born in Macon, Georgia, 14 January 1916. Educated at Edward Waters and Morris Brown colleges, Atlanta; Atlanta University; Howard University, Washington, D.C.; Terrel Law School; Columbia University, New York. Served in the United States Army during World War II. Married Grace Killens; one son and one daughter. Worked for the National Labor Relations Board, Washington, 1936-42, and after 1946; Writer-in-Residence, Howard University, 1971-72, and at other universities. Address: 1392 Union Street, Brooklyn, New York 11213, U.S.A.

PUBLICATIONS

Novels

Youngblood. New York, Dial Press, 1954; London, Bodley Head, 1956.
And Then We Heard the Thunder. New York, Knopf, 1963; London, Cape, 1964.
'Sippi. New York, Simon and Schuster, 1967.
Slaves. New York, Pyramid, 1969.
The Cotillion; or, One Good Bull Is Half the Herd. New York, Simon and Schuster, 1971.
Great Gittin' Up Morning. New York, Doubleday, 1972.

Uncollected Short Stories

"God Bless America," in *American Negro Short Stories*, edited by John Henrik Clarke. New York, Hill and Wang, 1966.
"The Stick Up," in *The Best Short Stories by Negro Writers*, edited by Langston Hughes. Boston, Little Brown, 1967.

Plays

Lower than the Angels (produced New York, 1965).
Cotillion, adaptation of his own novel (produced New York, 1975).

Screenplays: *Odds Against Tomorrow*, with Nelson Gidding, 1959; *Slaves*, with Herbert J. Biberman and Alida Sherman, 1969.

Other

Black Man's Burden (essays). New York, Simon and Schuster, 1965.
A Man Ain't Nothin' But a Man (juvenile). Boston, Little Brown, 1975.

* * *

Born in Macon, Georgia, in 1916, John Oliver Killens grew up in his native town and there received his early schooling. Though he worked for the National Labor Relations Board before and after World War II, his true and permanent interest was writing. By 1954 he was able to witness publication of *Youngblood*, his first novel. Other novels have followed, with, also, an important book of essays, *Black Man's Burden*, and contributions to the movies and television, notably the script for the film *Odds Against Tomorrow*. For years now a resident of Brooklyn, with his wife and their two children, Killens has occasionally interrupted his absorption in creative literature to serve as writer-in-residence on various academic campuses. But such interruptions obviously constitute no actual deviation from his devotion to letters. There was a time when Negro writers almost exclusively tended to be of some non-literary vocation first and writers only in their leisure time. Not so with Killens. He has pursued the craft of fiction as his first love and, given his obvious conception of the poet not only as seer but also as obligated, almost surely because of his superior capacities for ascertaining truth, to involve himself personally in attempts at the improvement of society, the very active roles Killens has played with organizations themselves as active or as "political" as the American Society for African Culture and the Harlem Writers Guild become only additional dimensions of his commitment to the arts.

At the beginning of his career as an author Killens was very clearly an advocate of integration. No message, other than the sheer iniquity of race prejudice, comes so unequivocally out of his novel *Youngblood*, as the message of the necessity for white and black workers to unite. But, also, a high point in *Youngblood*, an episode in which Negro school children in a Georgia town, under the direction of one of their teachers, convert a concert of Negro spirituals from a submissive gesture to the local whites into a respectful rendering of the meaning of their own past, affirms the theme which now is often represented in the phrase "black is beautiful." Increasingly, it does seem, it has been the "black is beautiful" theme, even to the extreme of Black Separatism, which has governed Killens in his affirmation of his art, as well as, indeed, in his conduct as a citizen of the world.

—Blyden Jackson

KIM, Richard E(unkook). American. Born in Hamhung City, Korea, 13 March 1932; became a United States citizen, 1964. Educated at primary and secondary schools in Korea; Middlebury College, Vermont, 1955-59; Johns Hopkins University, Baltimore, 1959-60, M.A. in writing 1960; University of Iowa, Iowa City, 1960-62, M.F.A. in writing 1962; Harvard University, Cambridge, Massachusetts, 1962-63, M.A. in Far Eastern literature 1963. Served in the Korean Army and Marines, 1950-54: First Lieutenant. Married Penelope Anne Groll in 1960; two children. Instructor in English, California State College, Long Beach 1963-64. Assistant Professor, 1964-68, Associate Professor, 1968-69, and since 1969, Adjunct Associate Professor of English, University of Massachusetts, Amherst; also, Director, University of Massachusetts Imaginative Writers' Workshop, Nantucket, Summers 1967-69. Visiting Writer, Mediterranean Institute, Mallorca, 1969; Visiting Professor of English, Syracuse University, New York, 1970-71. Member of the Board of Directors of the American-Korean Foundation, New York. Recipient: Mary Roberts Rinehart Foundation Fellowship, 1961; Ford Foreign Area Fellowship, 1962; Guggenheim Fellowship, 1965; National Endowment for the Arts grant, 1977. Address: Leverett Road, Shutesbury, Massachusetts 01072, U.S.A.

PUBLICATIONS

Novels

The Martyred. New York, Braziller, and London, Hutchinson, 1964.
The Innocent. Boston, Houghton Mifflin, 1968; London, Hutchinson, 1969.
Lost Souls. Boston, Houghton Mifflin, 1974.

Short Stories

Lost Names: Scenes from a Korean Boyhood. New York, Praeger, 1970; London, Deutsch, 1971.

* * *

Richard E. Kim's fiction deals with war's effect on private morality. Using an inexperienced first person narrator—an unnamed child in *Lost Names* and a young officer named Lee in *The Martyred* and *The Innocent*—he sensitively delineates questions of bravery, patriotism, humaneness, and even the nature of truth as they are clouded by violence and made more complex by despair.

Periods of national crisis in recent Korean history provide a background against which are focused the moral crises of individuals. Love of country, despair over the suffering of its people, and pride in their resilience are recurring themes. The forbidding Korean countryside, especially the winter scenery of North Korea, is used to underscore the characters' anguish. At the end of each book, the narrator's education—though incomplete—leads him to hope for Korea's future despite the suffering and death he has seen.

Lost Names is a collection of stories dealing with the ordeal of a single family during the last 13 years of the 36 year Japanese occupation. The book is thematically unified by the child's growing awareness that the mere survival of his father is significant heroism. Although the stories vary in weight, the best of them, such as the title story, are taut and powerful. Natural imagery is skillfully used, and the maturation process of a child is well suited to the thematic development.

The Innocent treats a compelling question; how much bloodshed can an individual justify by patriotism? The focal character, Colonel Min, is struggling for his soul while leading a *coup d'état*. There is some fine descriptive writing in this book, too, and characters such as Min and Chaplain Koh are strikingly alive, but it does not have the solid power one might wish for. The complexity of the plot detracts from the moral drama, and the large cast of conspirators requires too much sorting out, especially when they are all men designated by military titles and similar monosyllabic Korean names. There is special difficulty with the three characters opposing the coup: General Mah, General Ahn and General Ham.

Kim's best book, *The Martyred*, is uniformly fine. It is tightly plotted, austere in style, and moving in subject matter. The tone of passion never approaches bathos; the people are believable and their struggles compelling. Economy of incident and explication heightens the drama. The writing is smooth and strong; necessary information about the movement of armies is worked in unobtrusively and does not detract from the focus on a single moral drama and the half dozen characters intimately concerned with its unfolding. Brutality and helplessness are effectively portrayed without sensational description. *The Martyred* deserves a wide readership.

Though each of these books draws heavily upon the tragic history of Korea, the reader feels that Kim is equipped to deal sensitively with the human condition wherever he finds it. These are not ethnic novels; they simply utilize a compelling historical situation with which the novelist is familiar. Future works by Kim may use different milieux, but one would hope they convey the same awareness of the dramatic, the same moral cogency and keen sense of selectivity he shows in the best passages of these books.

—Barbara M. Perkins

KING, Francis (Henry). British. Born in Adelboden, Switzerland, 4 March 1923. Educated at Shrewsbury School; Balliol College, Oxford, B.A. 1949, M.A. 1951. Poetry Reviewer, *The Listener*, London, 1945-50; worked for the British Council, 1949-63: Lecturer in Florence, 1949-50, Salonika, 1950-52, and Athens 1953-57; Assistant Representative, Helsinki, 1957-58; Regional Director, Kyoto, 1959-63. Literary reviewer, 1964-78, and since 1978, theatre reviewer, *Sunday Telegraph*; since 1978, fiction reviewer, *Spectator*, London. Member of the Executive Committee, 1969-73, Vice-President, 1977, and President, 1978, P.E.N., London. Since 1974, Member of the Executive Committee, and Chairman, 1975-77, Society; since 1977, Member of the Committee, Royal Literary Fund; since 1980, Member of the Executive Committee, National Book League. Recipient: Maugham Award, 1952; Katherine Mansfield Prize, 1965; Arts Council bursary, 1966. Fellow, Royal Society of Literature, 1952; resigned, then re-elected, 1967. O.B.E. (Officer, Order of the British Empire), 1979. Address: 19 Gordon Place, London W8 4JE, England.

PUBLICATIONS

Novels

To the Dark Tower. London, Home and Van Thal, 1946.
Never Again. London, Home and Van Thal, 1948.
An Air That Kills. London, Home and Van Thal, 1948.
The Dividing Stream. London, Longman, and New York, Morrow, 1951.
The Dark Glasses. London, Longman, 1954; New York, Pantheon, 1956.
The Firewalkers: A Memoir (as Frank Cauldwell). London, Murray, 1956.
The Widow. London, Longman, 1957.
The Man on the Rock. London, Longman, and New York, Pantheon, 1958.
The Custom House. London, Longman, 1961; New York, Doubleday, 1962.

The Last of the Pleasure Gardens. London, Longman, 1965.
The Waves Behind the Boat. London, Longman, 1967.
A Domestic Animal. London, Longman, 1970.
Flights (2 novellas). London, Hutchinson, 1973.
A Game of Patience. London, Hutchinson, 1974.
The Needle. London, Hutchinson, 1975; New York, Mason Charter, 1976.
Danny Hill: Memoirs of a Prominent Gentleman. London, Hutchinson, 1977.
The Action. London, Hutchinson, 1978.

Short Stories

So Hurt and Humiliated and Other Stories. London, Longman, 1959.
The Japanese Umbrella and Other Stories. London, Longman, 1964.
The Brighton Belle and Other Stories. London, Longman, 1968.
Penguin Modern Stories 12, with others. London, Penguin, 1972.
Hard Feelings and Other Stories. London, Hutchinson, 1976.
Indirect Method and Other Stories. London, Hutchinson, 1980.

Plays

Far East (produced Coventry, 1980).

Radio Plays: *The Prisoner*, 1967; *Corner of a Foreign Field*, 1969; *A Short Walk in Williams Park*, from a story by C.H.B. Kitchin, 1972; *Death of My Aunt*, from the novel by C.H.B. Kitchin, 1973; *Desperate Cases*, 1975.

Verse

Rod of Incantation. London, Longman, 1952.

Other

Japan, photographs by Martin Hürlimann. London, Thames and Hudson, and New York, Viking Press, 1970.
Christopher Isherwood. London, Longman, 1976.
E.M. Forster and His World. London, Thames and Hudson, and New York, Scribner, 1978.

Editor, *Introducing Greece*. London, Methuen, 1956; revised edition, 1968.
Editor, *Collected Short Stories*, by Osbert Sitwell. London, Duckworth, 1974.
Editor, with Ronald Harwood, *New Stories 3*. London, Hutchinson, 1978.

Translator, *An Angel in Sodom*, by Saint Ours. London, Quartet, 1977.

*

Manuscript Collection: University of Texas, Austin.

Critical Studies: essay by the author, in *Leaving School*, London, Phoenix House, 1957; "Waves and Echoes: The Novels of Francis King" by John Mellors, in *London Magazine*, December 1975-January 1976.

Francis King comments:

Except for the period of my schooling and the war, mine has always been an itinerant life. As a child, I was brought up alternately in India and Switzerland (the country of my birth); subsequently I worked for the British Council in Italy, Greece, Egypt, Finland and Japan. After a maximum of three years in any one house or even any one city, I want to move on. This desire always to set off for another destination is reflected in my novels. Of course, certain themes in them are constant; but I have never wished to be identified with only one type of fiction. Perhaps this has harmed me in popular esteem; the public tends to like its novelists to write the same novel over and over again.

Foreign places have always provided me with imaginative stimulation and the majority of my books have foreign settings. Most English novelists, like the society from which they derive, seem to me to be too much preoccupied with differences of class, which obscure for them differences more profound between human beings. In choosing so often to write about "abroad," I have, perhaps subconsciously, attempted to avoid this class-obsession.

I believe strongly in national character, and a recurrent theme of my books is the way in which people struggle to break out of the patterns of national behaviour in which they have been imprisoned since birth.

Critics sometimes say that they find my work "depressing" and my readers sometimes ask why I never write about "nice" people or "normal" people—not surprisingly perhaps, since mine is an attitude of profound, if resigned, pessimism about the world. I do not expect people to behave consistently well, and my observation is that few of them do. But I should like to think that the tolerance and compassion that I genuinely feel are also reflected in my writing.

I have always been preoccupied with style and form. I feel that I am most successful in achieving both if the reader is unconscious of any straining for them.

In my early books, written at a period of loneliness in my own life, isolation is a recurrent theme; in my later books I see now that envy and jealousy—to my mind the least attractive of human traits—have taken over.

My biggest and most successful novel was *The Custom House*. The novel that comes nearest to saying what I wanted to say—and that cost me most—was *A Domestic Animal*.

* * *

Francis King's first novel, *To the Dark Tower*, is his most experimental. In some of the stories in *The Japanese Umbrella* he adopts Isherwood's trick of using a narrator to whom he gives his own name, and *The Firewalkers*, subtitled "a memoir," was first published under the pseudonym of Frank Cauldwell, who is also the narrator, and who first appeared as a novelist in *To the Dark Tower*. King's stress on the plurality of truth, as formulated in the early story "A True Story" (*So Hurt and Humiliated*), led him to write from both first- and third-person angles in *The Custom House* and *The Last of the Pleasure Gardens*. *The Action*, actually about a novel, seems redolent with echoes from King's previous work. A new departure, *Danny Hill* purports to be an 18th-century text by John Cleland and is written by King in that idiom, modernized.

The themes of separation and loss recurring throughout his work may be traced to his second novel, *Never Again*, a moving evocation of childhood and adolescence in India and at an English prep school. In King's third novel, *An Air That Kills*, there is a rare lyricism, often negated, in the spirit of Housman's poem whence the title comes. *The Dividing Stream*, a complex novel set in Florence, is imbued with a sense of decay and the melancholy that pervades much of King's work. These moods are articulated in the stark ending of *The Dark Glasses*, as Patrick recognizes "the terrible, morbid beauty of this world." Yet the Greek setting seems to make for an easier sensual acceptance; in *The Dark Glasses* King evokes the natural beauty of Corfu, while *The Firewalkers* is a mainly happy reminiscence of a group of friends in Athens centred on the dilettante and metaphorical firewalker, Colonel Grecos. In *The Man on the Rock*, King succeeds in impersonating as narrator the parasitic Spiro, a character utterly removed from the self-effacing King/Cauldwell persona. King is as skilful with the short story form as the novel, and some of the stories in his first collection *So Hurt and Humiliated* are set in Greece. So is the second short novel in *Flights*, "The Cure," which like the other, "The Infection," set in Hungary, has political overtones.

King's most ambitious book to date, *The Custom House*, also has political implications. In this long, complex novel he focuses on a cross-section of Japanese society, both from within and through

Western eyes. King's writing is always rich in ambivalence; he found congenial material in Japanese formalism, recording "the echoes which surround events, not merely after they have taken place but also before them." Yet the novel has his characteristic intense sensualism hedged with negatives. Like the collection of short stories *The Japanese Umbrella*, *The Waves Behind the Boat* is set in Japan, though its theme of incest and dishonesty concerns expatriates, one of whom, a woman, tells the story.

Christine Cornwell in *The Widow* is outstanding among King's female portraits. This novel's opening illustrates his skill in manipulating the reader's sympathy in a few pages as he highlights alternately her unlikeable and likeable traits; he can also play on the reader's response during a single paragraph. His evocation of wartime London in Part II of *The Widow* is complemented by his account of civilian rural experience, chiefly through the eyes of a 17-year-old land-girl, in *A Game of Patience*. In *The Last of the Pleasure Gardens*, King shows how an idiot child exacerbates beyond endurance the weaknesses in a marriage. Most of the short stories in *The Brighton Belle* are studies in decay, symbolized in the town itself. *A Domestic Animal*, about unreciprocated homosexual love, is a poignant and powerful study of sexual jealousy; the narrator's attitude to Pam recalls the narrator's attitude to Anne in *An Air That Kills*, although the novels are different in tone.

The darkness of *The Needle*, about a doctor's love for her weak brother, is expressed too in some of the stories in *Hard Feelings*, where King breaks new ground with two stories about the supernatural. King's recent work also includes the bawdy *Danny Hill*, drawing not least on linguistic humour. *The Action*, focussing on the libel action threatened against Hazel's novel by a female acquaintance on the eve of publication, incidentally reveals much about King's understanding of the novel form; the ending, as Hazel begins a new story, is something of a writer's *credo*. Francis King is a master of implication, in the Forsterian tradition, and writes with outstanding precision, strength, and sensitivity.

—Val Warner

KNEBEL, Fletcher. American. Born in Dayton, Ohio, 1 October 1911. Educated at Miami University, Oxford, Ohio, B.A. 1934. Served in the United States Navy in World War II. Married Laura Bergquist in 1965; two children by a previous marriage. Reporter, *Coatesville Record*, Pennsylvania, 1934, *Chattanooga News*, Tennessee, 1934-35, and *Toledo News-Bee*, Ohio, 1935; Reporter, 1936, and Washington Correspondent, 1937-50, *Cleveland Plain Dealer*; Washington Correspondent, Cowles Publications, 1950-64, and columnist ("Potomac Fever"), 1951-64; Writer for *Look* magazine, New York, 1950-71. Recipient: Sigma Delta Chi award, for reporting, 1955. D.L.: Miami University, 1964; D.LL.: Drake University, Des Moines, Iowa, 1968. Address: 208 Edgerstoune Road, Princeton, New Jersey 08540, U.S.A.

PUBLICATIONS

Novels

Seven Days in May, with Charles W. Bailey II. New York, Harper, and London, Weidenfeld and Nicolson, 1962.
Convention, with Charles W. Bailey, II. New York, Harper, and London, Weidenfeld and Nicolson, 1964.
Night of Camp David. New York, Harper, and London, Weidenfeld and Nicolson, 1965.
The Zinzin Road. New York, Doubleday, 1966; London, W.H. Allen, 1967.
Vanished. New York, Doubleday, and London, W.H. Allen, 1968.
Trespass. New York, Doubleday, and London, W.H. Allen, 1969.
Dark Horse. New York, Doubleday, 1972; London, Hodder and Stoughton, 1973.
The Bottom Line. New York, Doubleday, 1974; London, Hodder and Stoughton, 1975.
Dave Sulkin Cares! New York, Doubleday, 1978.

Other

No High Ground, with Charles W. Bailey II. New York, Harper, and London, Weidenfeld and Nicolson, 1960.

*

Manuscript Collection: Mugar Memorial Library, Boston University.

Critical Study: in *New York Times Book Review*, January 1968.

Fletcher Knebel comments:

My novels are basically suspense stories with a major social or political theme in the background. The first aim is always to tell a good story, but I hope the message comes through.

* * *

Fletcher Knebel, a former Washington, D.C., journalist, has written several political novels since 1962, the first two co-authored by Charles W. Bailey, a former colleague. He is recognized as one of the foremost writers of the political suspense thriller, combining his journalistic skill with well-constructed plots to produce popular and entertaining accounts of fictionalized but plausible crises in American politics. Knebel is at his best in the depiction of behind-the-scenes action, and the vivid immediacy of his plots must be accounted as a main element of appeal to his audience. His extensive knowledge of the Washington scene gives him the ability to delineate the surface details of his stories with verisimilitude, and his journalistic experience has aided him in developing a direct descriptive prose style. His characters are often vividly drawn, particularly members of the press or professional politicians, although some reviewers have criticized him for over-dependence upon the stock characters or for caricaturing those characters, such as military or intelligence chiefs, that he does not like.

Knebel's plots consistently portray his liberal political views, particularly in his protagonists' dependence upon rational problem-solving and his antagonists' Machiavellian disregard for democratic procedures. His books are concerned with such problems as a projected military takeover of the government, a utopian Presidential plan for peace, mental illness as a Presidential disability, black terrorism, and the political nomination process. He is consistently interested in such issues as the acquisition and maintenance of power, the Presidency as an institution, and conspiracy as a political tool. In his books both protagonists and antagonists conspire secretly to accomplish their aims, indicating to the reader that this is the way goals are reached in American politics.

The major shortcomings of his novels are inherent in their conception. If Knebel sincerely believes in the dangers that he warns against and desires to alert his readers to possible pitfalls in the present system, as he has indicated he does, then his choice of the political thriller as the vehicle for his jeremiads renders those warnings, to some extent, hollow. Because he relies, somewhat simplistically, upon the rationality and good will of his main characters to solve the significant and overwhelming problems with which they are faced, he runs the risk of trivializing those problems for the purpose of fictional excitement. Ultimately, it is difficult to see the seriousness of the threats when the books ritually exorcise them in the resolution of the action, reassuring the reader of the essential soundness of his political system. Knebel does well in reporting the events of his stories; he is too competent a journalist to do otherwise. But in his attempts to explore the dilemma of the sensitive man of good will in the face of political apocalypse, he succumbs to the essential optimism of popular fiction, and, in so doing, succeeds in entertaining but fails to develop the ultimate implications of the messages he professes to deliver.

—Kay J. Mussell

KNOWLES, John. American. Born in Fairmont, West Virginia, 16 September 1926. Educated at Phillips Exeter Academy, New Hampshire; Yale University, New Haven, Connecticut, B.A. 1949. Reporter, *Hartford Courant*, Connecticut, 1950-52; free-lance writer, 1952-56; Associate Editor, *Holiday* magazine, Philadelphia, 1956-60. Recipient: Rosenthal Foundation Award, 1961; Faulkner Foundation Award, 1961; National Association of Independent Schools Award, 1961. Address: Box 939, Southampton, New York, 11968, U.S.A.

PUBLICATIONS

Novels

A Separate Peace. London, Secker and Warburg, 1959; New York, Macmillan, 1960.
Morning in Antibes. New York, Macmillan, and London, Secker and Warburg, 1962.
Indian Summer. New York, Random House, and London, Secker and Warburg, 1966.
The Paragon. New York, Random House, 1971.
Spreading Fires. New York, Random House, 1974.
Vein of Riches. Boston, Little Brown, 1978.
Peace Breaks Out. New York, Holt Rinehart, 1981.

Short Stories

Phineas: Six Stories. New York, Random House, 1968.

Other

Double Vision: American Thoughts Abroad. New York, Macmillan, and London, Secker and Warburg, 1964.

*

Manuscript Collection: Beinicke Library, Yale University, New Haven, Connecticut.

* * *

John Knowles writes, in general, not about his home turf but about New England or Europe. Only one novel, *Vein of Riches*, and that not his best, is about West Virginia, his childhood home. His fictional world is a cultivated, cosmopolitan, somewhat jaded world. He is a fine craftsman, a fine stylist, alert to the infinite resources and nuances of language. Yet, as he says, he is one of the live-around-the-world people, rootless, nomadic, and making a virtue of that rootlessness. He is a connoisseur of different cultures but master of none—or perhaps of one only, the sub-culture of the New England prep school. One defect of this very cosmopolitanism is the feeling of alienation that Knowles feels from his fictional world. As a veteran of many cultures he finds this trait an advantage when he writes graceful travel essays for *Holiday* magazine. He finds it a disadvantage when he wishes to create for his most recent novel, *Vein of Riches*, a thoroughly credible fictional character.

A Separate Peace, his first novel, is also by far his most important novel. It is a prep school novel about Gene Forrester and his close friend, Finney, and the studied set of ambiguities and ambivalences arising from the intense and complex relationship between the two. Gene, beset by a love-hate attitude toward Finney, causes Finney to suffer a serious injury and still later is the putative cause of his death from a second injury. But Finney's death is preceded by Gene's reconciliation with him, a redemptive act which to some degree assuages his feeling of guilt. Thus, the novel recounts Gene's initiation into manhood and into both worldly and moral maturity. Fifteen years after Finney's death, Gene returns to Devon to conclude the novel by thinking—"Nothing endures, not a tree, not love, not even a death by violence." What does endure is the extraordinary popularity of this novel with prep school and college students.

Knowles's later books display his writing grace but not the inner strength of *A Separate Peace*. His second novel, *Morning in Antibes*, has a pot-pourri of comatose characters revolving about the deracinated Nicholas Petrovich Bodine in a kind of latter day *The Sun Also Rises*; it lacks, however, the Hemingway tone, atmosphere, and taut dialogue. The people are phony and maybe the novel is too. The long passivity of Nick makes him seem to move under water. The novel fails in characterization.

His third novel, *Indian Summer*, follows Cleet Kinsolving, World War II vet, in his jousting with his friend, Neil Reardon, Irish Catholic and heir to multi-millions (seemingly modelled on John Kennedy). Cleet's conviction, which he shares with T.S. Eliot's Sweeney, is that each man needs to do someone in. A good deal of cultural primitivism is spread about, but again the characters are unconvincing. His next novel, *The Paragon*, describes Lou Colfax, a brilliant, handsome sophomore in love with a beautiful actress four years older than he. In spite of the Yale ambience and a plethora of cocktail parties and beautiful people the intended "Gatsby glamour" never comes to this novel. Perhaps because we miss the "yellow cocktail music" of *Gatsby*, perhaps because the characters remain partially developed. *Spreading Fires*, a brief novel of decadence and homosexual vagaries set in the south of France, deals with madness, potential madness, and the low life of the upper class.

Knowles's recent novel *Vein of Riches* is a study of the great coal boom of 1910-1924 in a West Virginia town. He shows a house, a family, and an industry, and the interactions of the three; he employs one of the central themes of American fiction, money versus land. It is a pleasant novel but the characters again are given perfunctory treatment. We do not have the empathy and zest that bubbled up from *A Separate Peace*. Coal does not interest Knowles the way New England prep school life did.

In summary, Knowles is intelligent, highly literate, a skilled and sensitive craftsman and stylist. He is knowledgeable of the world, tolerant, a connoisseur of many cultures. He possesses in his own person that bifocal vision which he praises in *Double Vision*. He has created one extraordinary novel, *A Separate Peace*, which for many young people has truly caught the *zeitgeist*. There is also a negative side. Every novel but his first suffers from one fundamental defect—the characters are not plausible. There is not a single memorable woman character in his fiction and only two male characters—Gene Forrester and Phineas—that stay in our memory. The result is an imperfect empathy and a resultant lack of reader interest. In general his male protagonists are inert, deracinated, ambivalent, depersonalized, dehumanized. Why does Knowles create such types? Only he can answer this definitively, but perhaps he gives us the answer in his book *Double Vision* where he argues *against roots* and for rootlessness, the new form of nomadism. "We need to be nomadic and uprooted today," he maintains. As he says, he is not regional, does not come from a town or a city. He is one of the live-around-the-world people. So he is and so are the characters in his books. This is his fundamental failure and it is a major one. He may yet overcome this and give us again a convincing, brilliant novel as was *A Separate Peace*.

—Ruel E. Foster

KOCH, C(hristopher) J(ohn). Australian. Born in Hobart, Tasmania, 16 July 1932. Educated at Clemes College; St. Virgil's Christian Brothers College; Hobart State High School, 1946-50; University of Tasmania, Hobart, 1951-54, B.A. 1954. Married; one son. Until 1972, radio producer, Australian Broadcasting Commission, Sydney. Recipient: Melbourne *Age* Award, 1978; Australian National Book Award, 1979. Agent: Bolt and Watson Ltd., 8-12 Queen Street, Storey's Gate, London SW1H 9HP, England. Address: 192 Lenah Valley Road, Hobart, Tasmania 7008, Australia.

PUBLICATIONS

Novels

The Boys in the Island. London, Hamish Hamilton, 1958; revised edition, Sydney, Angus and Robertson, 1974.
Across the Sea Wall. London, Heinemann, 1965; revised edition, Sydney, Angus and Robertson, 1981.
The Year of Living Dangerously. Melbourne, Nelson, and London, Joseph, 1978; New York, St. Martin's Press, 1979.

*

Critical Studies: "In the Shadow of Patrick White" by Vincent Buckley, in *Meanjin* (Melbourne), no. 2, 1961; "The Novels by C.J. Koch" by Robyn Claremont, in *Quadrant* (Sydney), 1980.

C.J. Koch comments:

I began by writing verse, but gave my main attention to the novel from the age of 19. I believe that the novel can be a poetic vehicle, and that it has taken over the function of narrative poetry in this century. By this I do not mean that it uses the techniques of verse; nor do I mean that it can replace the lyric. But I would place such works as *Heart of Darkness*, *A Passage to India*, and *The Alexandria Quartet* in a class of their own—what I am forced to call "poetic novels"—in that they work through metaphor as much as through narrative: their metaphor and symbolism being more extended than that of verse. To such novels the same amount of time and reworking must be given as a poet gives to verse. Where a poet concentrates on metre, the poetic novelist concentrates on cadence and response. To me this is the summit of the novelist's art, the only goal worth aiming for.

My first two novels were youthful and over-written. I have cut and revised both, and am now more satisfied with them. I don't expect to do this again, since I feel that I reached the stage of mastering my craft with *The Year of Living Dangerously*. Poets and some novelists have reserved the right to revise youthful work, and I see no reason why a novelist should not do the same, if he thinks the work worth preserving. I admire John Fowles for doing this with *The Magus*.

Two things preoccupy me as a novelist: the way in which many people search for a world just outside normal reality; and dualities: the dualities that run through both the human spirit and the world itself. It is the effort to reconcile these contradictions that makes for the pathos and drama I am interested in. Perhaps an Australian is attuned to duality more than some other writers, since he comes from a country born of Europe, but lying below Asia.

* * *

C.J. Koch (who originally signed himself Christopher Koch) had his first poem accepted when he was 17 and still at school and began his first novel when he was only 19. In 1972, at the age of 40, he left his position in order to devote himself to writing. The result was his third and by far his most accomplished novel, *The Year of Living Dangerously*, which immediately placed him in the front rank of contemporary Australian novelists. Koch has heavily revised his two early novels and believes that he only really mastered his craft with his third. He sees the other two as being marred by youthful over-writing and has trimmed and cut them. These second versions are the only ones the author wishes to survive.

Whatever the changes made to *The Boys in the Island*, the novel still retains very much the feel of a young man's book. It tells the story of a sensitive young boy from the age of six (in 1936) through his school days and adolescence to his final, reluctant initiation into early manhood. Francis falls in love with a young girl who suddenly, heartbreakingly, abandons him. He fails his exams and travels from Tasmania to Melbourne where he becomes involved in a meaningless life of petty crime. Then the suicide of a friend and his own near-death in a car crash send him back to his home to reassess his life and accept unprotestingly what the author calls "the iron bonds of his imminent adulthood." Despite the familiarity of the material, Koch's keen ear for colloquial speech, his sensuous command of natural detail, and the delicate restraint with which his understated prose conveys the boy's confusion and distress give the novel a fresh and poignant flavour.

Across the Sea Wall opens with Robert O'Brien, a 29-year-old journalist, looking back over an affair he had had six years ago. Fleeing from an imminent marriage and the terrors of the life of a staid suburbanite working for his future father in law, O'Brien and a schoolhood friend take a boat to Naples. En route he falls in love with Ilsa Kalnins and they skip the boat at Ceylon. But eventually O'Brien discovers that he is a suburbanite after all. He cannot accept the challenge of Ilsa's love or believe in its sincerity against the facts which his friends bring against Ilsa's character and returns to Australia. Two years later she turns up in Sydney and they make plans to marry but once again O'Brien abandons her. In its original form *Across the Sea Wall* is over-written—the descriptions of India in particular, finely done though they are, go on much too long. But the novel has many shrewd touches of characterisation and the same sensitivity in dealing with the impact of love on the uninitiated that marked Koch's first novel.

The Year of Living Dangerously is set in Indonesia in 1965, the last year of Sukarno's regime. The Sukarno of this novel is a man who seemed originally to embody the hopes and dreams of his people (as well as in particular an Australian-Chinese dwarf named Billy Kwan who is in the country as a press photographer) but who now has lost himself in grandiose schemes and the pursuit of private gratification. Unknowingly, a coup is being prepared against him and it is this that provides the spectacular climax to the novel. Slowly, as Billy begins to see through Sukarno, his idealistic allegiance to and hope in a saviour begin to switch towards Guy Hamilton, the journalist who has been sent out to replace Billy's previous boss. Once again, the novel is told in the first person, this time by a narrator identified only as "Cookie" or by the initials he supplies to his occasional footnotes, R.J.C. Through the use of diaries, speaking through the voices of various characters, using purloined documents from Billy Kwan's private files, speculating and inventing when he cannot know for certain, the narrator builds up layer upon layer of texture upon the basic structure of the narrative. At the end Koch tries, unfashionably and audaciously, to suggest Hamilton's final redemption and capacity to love as he ascends into insight via partial blindness.

The Year of Living Dangerously is thoughtful, intelligent, and beautifully written; it captures the sense of Indonesia in the mid-1960's convincingly, and has a narrative that is unfailingly compelling. Like Graham Greene, Koch invests the semi-popular form of the political thriller with depth through the ideas and moral issues he explores.

—Laurie Clancy

KOESTLER, Arthur. British. Born in Budapest, Hungary, 5 September 1905; became a British subject 1948. Educated at the University of Vienna, 1922-26. Married 1) Dorothy Asher in 1935 (divorced, 1950); 2) Mamaine Paget in 1950 (divorced 1953); 3) Cynthia Jefferies in 1965; one daughter. Foreign Correspondent for the Ullstein chain, Berlin, in the Middle East, 1927-29, and in Paris, 1929-30; Foreign Editor, *B.Z. am Mittag*, and Science Editor, *Vossische Zeitung*, Berlin, 1930-32; member of the Graf Zeppelin polar expedition, 1931; travelled in Russia, 1932-33; member of the Communist Party, 1932-38; free-lance writer, in Paris, London, and Zurich, 1933-36; War Correspondent for the *News Chronicle*, London, in Spain, 1936-37; imprisoned by the Nationalists, then exchanged through intervention of the British government; imprisoned in France, 1939-40, then joined the French Foreign Legion, 1940-41, escaped to Britain, and served in the British Pioneer Corps, 1941-42; after discharge, worked for the Ministry of Information, London, and as a night ambulance driver; Special Correspondent, in Palestine, for *The Times*, London, 1945, and for the *Manchester Guardian* and *New York Herald Tribune*, 1948; Visiting Chubb Fellow, Yale University, New Haven, Connecticut, 1950; Fellow, Center for Advanced Study in the Behavioral Sciences, Stanford University, California, 1964-65. Recipient: Sonning Prize, University of Copenhagen, 1968. LL.D.: Queen's University, Kingston, Ontario, 1968; D.Lit.: Leeds University, 1977. Fellow, 1957, and Companion of Literature, 1974, Royal Society of Literature; Fellow, Royal Astronomical Society, 1976. C.B.E. (Commander, Order of the British Empire), 1972. Address: c/o A.D. Peters and Company Ltd., 10 Buckingham Street, London WC2N 6BU, England.

PUBLICATIONS

Novels

The Gladiators, translated by Edith Simon. London, Cape, and New York, Macmillan, 1939.

Darkness at Noon, translated by Daphne Hardy. London, Cape, 1940; New York, Macmillan, 1941.

Arrival and Departure. London, Cape, and New York, Macmillan, 1943.

Thieves in the Night: Chronicle of an Experiment. London, Macmillan, and New York, Macmillan, 1946.

The Age of Longing. London, Collins, and New York, Macmillan, 1951.

The Call-Girls: A Tragi-Comedy with Prologue and Epilogue. London, Hutchinson, 1972; New York, Random House, 1973.

Uncollected Short Stories

"The Mixed Transport," in *Horizon* (London), October 1943.

"Les Temps Heroiques," in *Occident* (Paris), March 1948.

"Apage Satanas," in *World's Best*, edited by Whit Burnett. New York, Dial Press, 1950.

"Pythagoras and the Psychoanalyst," in *Fantasia Mathematica*, edited by Clifton Fadiman. New York, Simon and Schuster, 1958.

"Tell Me More about Jerusalem," in *Yisröel* (revised edition), edited by Joseph Leftwich. New York, Yoseloff, 1963.

"Confrontation," in *Harper's* (New York), December 1978.

Plays

Twilight Bar: An Escapade in Four Acts (produced Paris and Baltimore, 1946). London, Cape, and New York, Macmillan, 1945.

Screenplay: *Lift Your Head, Comrade* (documentary), 1944.

Other

Von Weissen Nächten und Roten Tagen. Kharkov, Ukrainian State Publishers for National Minorities, 1933.

Encyclopédie de la Vie Sexuelle, with Ludwig Levy-Lenz and A. Willy. Paris, Aldor, 1934.

Menschenopfer Unerhört. Paris, Carrefour, 1937.

Spanish Testament (autobiography). London, Gollancz, 1937; excerpt, as *Dialogue with Death*, translated by Phyllis and Trevor Blewitt, London, Macmillan, 1938; New York, Macmillan, 1942.

Scum of the Earth (autobiography). London, Cape, and New York, Macmillan, 1941.

The Yogi and the Commissar and Other Essays. London, Cape, 1945; New York, Macmillan, 1946.

Sexual Anomalies and Perversions: A Summary of the Works of Magnus Hirschfeld. London, Torch, 1946; revised edition edited by Norman Haire, London, Encyclopaedic Press, 1952.

L'Encyclopédie de la Famille, with Manes Sperber. Paris, n.d.

Insight and Outlook: An Inquiry into the Common Foundations of Science, Art, and Social Ethics. London, Macmillan, and New York, Macmillan, 1949.

Promise and Fulfillment: Palestine 1917-1949. London, Macmillan, and New York, Macmillan, 1949.

Arrow in the Blue (autobiography). London, Collins-Hamish Hamilton, and New York, Macmillan, 1952.

The Invisible Writing (autobiography). London, Collins-Hamish Hamilton, 1954; Boston, Beacon Press, 1955.

The Trail of the Dinosaur and Other Essays. London, Collins, and New York, Macmillan, 1955.

Reflections on Hanging. London, Gollancz, 1956; New York, Macmillan, 1957.

The Sleepwalkers: A History of Man's Changing Vision of the Universe. London, Hutchinson, and New York, Macmillan, 1959; section published as *The Watershed: A Biography of Johannes Kepler*, New York, Doubleday, 1960; London, Heinemann, 1961.

The Lotus and the Robot. London, Hutchinson, 1960; New York, Macmillan, 1961.

Hanged by the Neck: An Exposure of Capital Punishment in England, with C.H. Rolph. London, Penguin, 1961.

The Act of Creation. London, Hutchinson, and New York, Macmillan, 1964.

The Ghost in the Machine. London, Hutchinson, 1967; New York, Macmillan, 1968.

Drinkers of Infinity: Essays 1955-1967. London, Hutchinson, 1968; New York, Macmillan, 1969.

The Case of the Midwife Toad. London, Hutchinson, 1971; New York, Random House, 1972.

The Roots of Coincidence. London, Hutchinson, and New York, Random House, 1972.

The Lion and the Ostrich (lecture). London, Oxford University Press, 1973.

The Challenge of Chance: Experiments and Speculations, with Alister Hardy and Robert Harvie. London, Hutchinson, 1973; New York, Random House, 1975.

The Heel of Achilles: Essays 1968-1973. London, Hutchinson, 1974; New York, Random House, 1975.

The Thirteenth Tribe: The Khazar Empire and Its Heritage. London, Hutchinson, and New York, Random House, 1976.

Janus: A Summing Up. London, Hutchinson, and New York, Random House, 1978.

Bricks to Babel (selections). London, Hutchinson, 1980; New York, Random House, 1981.

Editor, *Suicide of a Nation? An Enquiry into the State of Britain Today*. London, Hutchinson, 1963; New York, Macmillan, 1964.

Editor, with J.R. Smythies, *Beyond Reductionism: New Perspectives in the Life Sciences: The Alpbach Symposium*. London, Hutchinson, 1969; New York, Macmillan, 1970.

*

Bibliography: *Arthur Koestler: An International Bibliography* by Reed Merrill and Thomas Frazier, Ann Arbor, Michigan, Ardis, 1979.

Critical Studies (selection): "Arthur Koestler" by Derek Stanford, in *Writers of Today*, London, Sidgwick and Jackson, 1946; *Arthur Koestler* by J. Nedava, London, Anscombe, 1948; "Arthur Koestler: The Russian Myth" by J.B. Coates, in *The Crisis of the Human Person*, London, Longman, 1949; "The Art of Koestler," in *Books in General* by V.S. Pritchett, London, Chatto and Windus, and New York, Harcourt Brace, 1953; *Arthur Koestler* by John Atkins, London, Spearman, and New York, Roy, 1956; *Arthur Koestler: Das Literarische Werk* by Peter Alfred Zuber, Zurich, Fretz und Wasmuth, 1962; *Chronicles of Conscience: A Study of George Orwell and Arthur Koestler* by Jenni Calder, London, Secker and Warburg, 1968, Pittsburgh, University of Pittsburgh Press, 1969; *Arthur Koestler* by Wolfe Mays, Guildford, Surrey, Lutterworth Press, and Valley Forge, Pennsylvania, Judson Press, 1973; *Astride the Two Cultures: Arthur Koestler at 70* edited by Harold Harris, London, Hutchinson, 1975, New York, Random House, 1976; *Arthur Koestler: A Collection of Critical Essays* edited by Murray A. Sperber, Englewood Cliffs, New Jersey, Prentice Hall, 1977; *Arthur Koestler* by Sidney A. Person, Jr., Boston, Twayne, 1978.

Arthur Koestler comments:

(1972) Out of the twenty-five books that I have published to date—1971—only five are novels; thus I can call myself only one-fifth of a novelist. On the other hand, one of the novels, *Darkness at Noon*, has sold more copies than all my other books put together, which somehow redresses the balance. It also makes some of my friends feel that I am wasting my time by not sticking to fiction. I do not agree with them. From my school-days onward, my interests have been divided, and sometimes rather painfully torn, between the two cultures. Out of my quarrels with the human condition I made my novels; the other books are attempts to analyse that same condition in scientific terms. In my more optimistic moments it seems to me that the two add up to a whole. At any rate, without both media I would feel only half alive.

The five novels have one basic theme in common: whether, or to what extent, and in what circumstances, a noble end justifies the use of ignoble means. Whether, when, how far it is justified to inflict pain on individuals in the higher interests of humanity. At what point the surgeon's lancet turns into the butchers' hatchet. How the love of mankind in the abstract can engender contempt for man in the flesh. How movements for gradual reform go off the boil; how revolutionary movements start like fresh mountain springs and end up as polluted rivers strewn with corpses.

The problem of Ends and Means sounds theoretical but for my generation of Europeans it has a concrete, bloody meaning. We have lived through 1914-18, the War to end all Wars; listened to the rival promises of the Classless Society and the Thousand Years Reich, and witnessed the holocausts they brought in their wake with relentless logic. Most of my erstwhile friends were sacrificed to that logic in the death factories of Utopia.

The Gladiators, *Darkness at Noon*, and *Arrival and Departure* can be read as a trilogy. The first has as its subject the abortive revolt of the Roman Slaves in 73-71 B.C. The slave army, let by Spartacus, defeated one Roman general after another and very nearly conquered the capital, but went to pieces—because its leaders did *not* accept that the end justifies the means and rejected revolutionary terror.

In *Darkness at Noon* we witness the opposite tragedy—reason running amok in the great Russian Purges, where the victims concurred with their executioners that expediency must come before morality, and the revolution must be allowed to devour its own children if it is to triumph in the end. In *Arrival and Departure* the same problem is transferred from the historical plane to that of individual psychology. Its hero suffers a nervous breakdown and comes out of it with a tentative solution of the dilemma that haunted him—and the author.

If the theme of the trilogy is the ethics of revolution, the theme of *Thieves in the Night* is the ethics of survival—as reflected in the tangled events that preceded the birth of the State of Israel. Lastly, *The Age of Longing*, written at the height of the Cold War, can be read as a kind of parable or warning—a companion piece to *Nineteen Eighty-Four.*

Two of the novels—*Darkness at Noon* and *Thieves in the Night*—had unexpected political repercussions which I have described in *The Invisible Writing* (p. 464, pp. 490ff.). These two incidents are to me the most satisfactory rewards a writer can hope for.

My first two novels I wrote in German, but collaborated on their English translations. Since 1940 I have written only in English.

(1976) Since the above was written I have added one more volume to the fiction list: *The Call-Girls*, a satire on academic symposia which are meant to provide solutions and produce puffs of hot air.

* * *

As a novelist, Arthur Koestler belongs to that phase of Western culture which reflects the abandonment and destruction of blind faith in Russian Communism that distinguished the 1930's and 1940's. Koestler had himself been a member of the Communist Party for seven years—from 1932 to 1938—and like many others (Max Eastman, say, in the U.S. and Douglas Hyde in Britain) in his reversion he was as emphatic and adamant as he had earlier been in his adherence. But whereas Eastman and Hyde were publicists, theorists, and commentators, expressing their position in critical terms, Koestler (besides performing these roles also) added through his fictional writing a creative and imaginative wing to this phase of psychological and political withdrawal. Readable as his four main novels remain, it was their topicality at the time of publication which focussed so much attention upon them. As imaginative expositions, in terms of human drama, of this particular moment of history they have a permanent value. Compared with such a political novel as H.G. Wells's *The New Machiavelli*, these fictions of Koestler are more immediately informed of the facts and forces operating in their field. As a committed long-acquainted member, he was familiar with the behaviour and procedure of the Communist Party. Wells—apart from his meeting with Lord Curzon in a London club—knew little of the structure and hierarchy of the Conservative Party.

But it was not this political inside information solely which made Koestler the imaginative chronicler of "the dying god" Communism. Fiction, as an art-form, has its own obligations and needs; and the person who would write a good novel must feel a duty to both his subject and his medium. Unlike so many novelists dealing with polemical issues, Koestler recognised this double observance called for from him. Some of the ideas which he held regarding the function of the modern novel may be found by referring to an article "Les Tentations du Romancier" in *La France Libre* which was later reprinted in his critical book *The Yogi and the Commissar*. In it, he envisages the author as a figure looking at the world from behind a window. The first temptation which visits him—at a time when the scene grows riotous, when truncheons are drawn and stones thrown in the street—is to close the curtains and settle to work by artificial light. This is a return to the ivory tower. The second temptation which the author may feel is an urge to throw the window up, leap upon the sill and there participate in the struggle by exhorting the side whose cause he favors. This is the position of the propagandist. With neither of these roles does Koestler agree. The author must master the art of mental balance; achieve by discipline a kind of nervous patience. He must learn how to stand before the open window; controlled though not indifferent, sympathetic but not a partisan. A strong-point of intelligence and imagination between two magnetic tensions—such is Koestler's idea of what the political novel should be; and such, in fact, within reasonable limits, his own works of fiction are.

The Gladiators was the book with which Koestler made his debut as a novelist in England. Its subject was the rebellion of Spartacus, known in Roman history as the Slave War. In this book the invoice of hope is matched by a crippling bill of disappointment. At first, the gladiators, slaves, and under-dogs are successful in their venture against tyranny and officialdom. Spartacus founds a Sun State and allies himself with powerful enemies of the Empire. But the revolutionary spirit of his followers becomes corrupt and withers, and in the end they are massacred by the cohorts under Crassus who lines the Appian Way to Rome with the crucified bodies of these pioneers of equality. The inward corruption of the revolutionary ideal, in this phase of Roman history, constituted a topical parallel with the corruption of Soviet Communism under Stalin.

This was a theme which Arthur Koestler's most famous novel, *Darkness at Noon*, was to explore, but another train of thought in the novel which he was subsequently to develop was the conflict between ends and means. "He who yearns for the Sun State and the Realm of Goodwill should not use political wiles and sinister facetious tricks," declares one character, to which another—intimating that there is no short cut to Utopia—replies: "The law of detours. None can act outside it. Everyone with a goal in front is forced to its baleful track," a conclusion which the first speaker will not accept. "Many a man," he says, "has strutted the road of tyranny, at the outset solely with the purpose of serving his lofty ideals, and in the end the road alone has made him carry on."

Darkness at Noon presents us with an old-guard Bolshevik deciding to make a public confession to the Party Torquemadas of political crimes he has never committed. The "crimes" in question constitute not actions but errors (if indeed they be errors) of judgment. The trial, we see, is a trial for heresy—for thinking for oneself, out of prescribed limits. Like Nicolas Berdyaev's book *Origins of Russian Communism*, this novel shows the essentially theological nature of Soviet thinking—its bigotry and crusading ardour, its unreality and ruthless inhumanity.

Arrival and Departure, his next published novel, may be regarded as the continuation of the debate between Political Man and Ethical Man which made up the drama of *Darkness at Noon*. Instead of listening to the brief of the political sense (whose canons are necessity and expediency) and the ethical sense (whose canon is conscience), here we witness the tug-of-war between the dictates of psychology (whose canons are pleasure and self-fulfilment) and the plea of the spirit (whose proof and goal are the sense of glory). The questions raised by this story are of the deepest importance. Sonia, the psychologist, suggests that all who oppose society—reformers, rebels, revolutionaries—do so out of a sense of guilt: neurosis. She traces the zeal for violent change in Peter—an ex-martyr in the cause of revolution—to a subconscious desire to expiate, by hard endurance, a sin committed in early childhood. Acceptance, she tells him, is the secret of "the good life." At first, Peter is deeply impressed and prepares to leave Europe to rejoin his hedonistic girl-friend in America. At the last moment, however, he gives up this bright lure of pleasure to return to the dangerous political struggle in his own country. The dictates of the spirit have triumphed.

Thieves in the Night again shows Arthur Koestler fixing his attention upon one of those contemporary situations in which a group or party of people are trying to interpret moral concepts in political terms. In it we see the Palestinian Jews (before the foundation of the State of Israel) "trying," as Anthony Burgess puts it, "to build a society in the face of injustice and their own awareness of how suffering may corrupt rather then ennoble. " Professor Harold Fisch describes it as "probably the best novel in English so far to deal with the new reality," and goes on to consider how well the author—a sympathetic observer—has none the less eschewed Zionist blinkers in describing the complex field of forces. "What Koestler discerns," he writes, "is a human structure still marked by duality and paradox. He praises the courage of the new fighters and settlers but smiles at what he feels is the absurdity of their brand of religious mysticism and the quixoticism of their practical socialism. Past and present have not (for him) convincingly joined hands: romance and realism have not been made one."

British Communists and their fellow-travellers powerfully attacked Koestler, ostensibly for his political pessimism, but actually for his devastating exposure of Party-line tyranny in the Soviet. They claimed that his "thesis [had] no relevance to the English scene," which might partly be allowed to be true, largely because the machinations of Communism in Britain were comparatively without due effect.

—Derek Stanford

KOPS, Bernard. British. Born in London, 28 November 1926. Educated in London elementary schools to age 13. Married Erica Gordon in 1956; four children. Has worked as a docker, chef, salesman, waiter, lift man, and barrow boy. Writer-in-Residence, London Borough of Hounslow, 1980-82. Recipient: Arts Council bursary, 1957, 1975; C. Day Lewis Fellowship, 1980. Agent: David Higham Associates, 5-8 Lower John Street, London W1R 4HA. Address: Flat 1, 35 Canfield Gardens, London N.W.6, England.

PUBLICATIONS

Novels

Awake for Mourning. London, MacGibbon and Kee, 1958.
Motorbike. London, New English Library, 1962.
Yes from No-Man's Land. London, MacGibbon and Kee, 1965; New York, Coward McCann, 1966.
The Dissent of Dominick Shapiro. London, MacGibbon and Kee, 1966; New York, Coward McCann, 1967.
By the Waters of Whitechapel. London, Bodley Head, 1969; New York, Norton, 1970.
The Passionate Past of Gloria Gaye. London, Secker and Warburg, 1971; New York, Norton, 1972.
Settle Down Simon Katz. London, Secker and Warburg, 1973.
Partners. London, Secker and Warburg, 1975.
On Margate Sands. London, Secker and Warburg, 1978.

Plays

The Hamlet of Stepney Green (produced Oxford, 1957; London and New York, 1958). London, Evans, 1959.
Goodbye World (produced Guildford, Surrey, 1959).
Change for the Angel (produced London, 1960).
The Dream of Peter Mann (produced Edinburgh, 1960). London, Penguin, 1960.
Enter Solly Gold, music by Stanley Myers (produced Wellingborough, Northamptonshire, and Los Angeles, 1962; London, 1970). Published in *Satan, Socialites, and Solly Gold: Three New Plays from England*, New York, Coward McCann, 1961; in *Four Plays*, 1964.
Home Sweet Honeycomb (broadcast, 1962). Included in *Four Plays*, 1964.
The Lemmings (broadcast, 1963). Included in *Four Plays*, 1964.
Stray Cats and Empty Bottles (televised, 1964; produced London, 1967).
Four Plays (includes *The Hamlet of Stepney Green*, *Enter Solly Gold*, *Home Sweet Honeycomb*, *The Lemmings*). London, MacGibbon and Kee, 1964.
The Boy Who Wouldn't Play Jesus (juvenile; produced London, 1965). Published in *Eight Plays: Book 1*, edited by Malcolm Stuart Fellows, London, Cassell, 1965; Chicago, Dramatic Publishing Company, n.d.
David, It is Getting Dark (produced Rennes, France, 1970). Paris, Gallimard, 1970.
It's a Lovely Day Tomorrow, with John Goldschmidt (televised, 1975; produced London, 1976).
More Out Than In (produced on tour and London, 1980).

Ezra (produced London, 1981).

Radio Plays: *Home Sweet Honeycomb*, 1962; *The Lemmings*, 1963; *Born in Israel*, 1963; *The Dark Ages*, 1964; *Israel: The Immigrant*, 1964; *Bournemouth Nights*, 1979; *I Grow Old, I Grow Old*, 1979; *Over the Rainbow*, 1980.

Television Plays: *I Want to Go Home*, 1963; *Stray Cats and Empty Bottles*, 1964; *The Lost Years of Brian Hooper*, 1967; *Alexander the Greatest*, 1971; *Just One Kid*, 1974; *Why the Geese Shrieked*, and *The Boy Philosopher*, from stories by Isaac Bashevis Singer, 1974; *It's a Lovely Day Tomorrow*, 1975; *Moss*, 1975; *Rocky Marciano Is Dead*, 1976.

Verse

Poems. London, Bell and Baker Press, 1955.
Poems and Songs. Lowestoft, Suffolk, Scorpion Press, 1958.
An Anemone for Antigone. Lowestoft, Suffolk, Scorpion Press, 1959.
Erica, I Want to Read You Something. Lowestoft, Suffolk, Scorpion Press, and New York, Walker, 1967.
For the Record. London, Secker and Warburg, 1971.

Other

The World Is a Wedding (autobiography). London, MacGibbon and Kee, 1963; New York, Coward McCann, 1964.

*

Manuscript Collections: University of Texas, Austin; Indiana University, Bloomington.

* * *

The novels of Bernard Kops may be taken as studies in the disintegration of those exclusive closed Jewish communities which were a feature of English society before the Second World War. It is particularly London Jewish life which Kops presents: that of the poor East End or prosperous, quietly ostentatious Golders Green. The tone of his fiction begins as tragic and elegiac in the novel *Yes from No-Man's Land* and becomes wildly, sometimes preposterously, comic in *The Dissent of Dominick Shapiro* and *By the Waters of Whitechapel.*

Yes from No-Man's Land is largely a stream-of-consciousness novel. Joe Levene, dying in Hackney Hospital, recapitulates his past experience of pogrom and persecution in Eastern Europe and poverty in the East End of London in the 1930's. Thoughts on existence in Israel combine with these recollections to constitute a sort of history of his race in terms of the last two generations. Joe's lamentations are the more pathetic since he knows his son Barry will not follow in his footsteps or beget a child to continue the tradition. Professor Harold Fisch has described this work as "ultimately an elegy for the passing of the Jew and his faith."

The same authority has characterised Kops's play *The Dream of Peter Mann* as an illustration of the "radical revolt against the Jewish mother [which] has been building up in the mid-twentieth century in Jewish writing on both sides of the Atlantic." The author's portrait of Sonia, the mother, shows her as bullying and assertive, not from any sadistic tendency but from an over-riding force of otherwise unchannelled affection. The bearing of this work upon Kops's fiction is readily apparent. He is one of those authors—Philip Roth and Montagu Haltrecht are two others—who have written novels with a central theme of the Jew as drop-out figure. The tone of the most outstanding of these fictions is richly humorous, and the conformity from which the characters seek to release themselves is familial rather than religious.

Whereas it is the mother who is seen as the obstacle in *The Dream of Peter Mann*, it is the father in *The Dissent of Dominick Shapiro* who features the more largely. But both the parents of the young 16-year-old Dominick have helped to create confusion in their son not through oppressive authority so much as excessive indulgence. Dominick's revolt, in which he runs away to join what his father terms "a Hippie Kibbutz," is therefore just an aspect of adolescent pyrotechnics and no carefully cogitated protest-gesture at all. It is, in fact, partially a satire on hipster social theories (one of Dominick's young protesting friends describing himself as "a Nothingist").

By the Waters of Whitechapel is probably Kops's masterpiece. Aubrey, at 35, is still tied to his mother's apron-strings. He lives mostly in fantasy and when those fantasies impinge, in action, upon the outward world, the comic dimensions of the novel receive an additional inflation. Aubrey's mother keeps a little sweet-shop in a street off the Commercial Road, but Aubrey—all-but-unemployed and living on his mother's charity—dreams of himself as a rich barrister and seeks to make others accept this dream. Aubrey's fantasies of material wealth and power are, of course, the engines of his own drop-out impulses—a further ironical and paradoxical feature in a wonderfully ironical fantasy. Kops has, deservedly, a reputation as a poet, and the inventive and colourful use of language in *By the Waters of Whitechapel* proves that a transition to prose cannot dampen or diminish the author's fervid verbal imagination.

—Derek Stanford

KOSINSKI, Jerzy (Nikodem). American. Born in Lodz, Poland, 14 June 1933; emigrated to the United States, 1957; naturalized, 1965. Educated at the University of Lodz, 1950-55, M.A. in history 1953, M.A. in political science 1955; Columbia University, New York, 1958-64; New School for Social Research, New York, 1962-65. Married Mary Hayward Weir in 1962 (died, 1968). Aspirant (Associate Professor), Polish Academy of Sciences, Warsaw, 1955-57; Fellow, Center for Advanced Studies, Wesleyan University, Middletown, Connecticut, 1968-69; Senior Fellow, Council for the Humanities, and Visiting Lecturer in English Prose, Princeton University, New Jersey, 1969-70; Professor of English Prose and Criticism, School of Drama, and Resident Fellow, Davenport College, Yale University, New Haven, Connecticut, 1970-73. President, American P.E.N. Club, 1973-75. Member of the Executive Board, National Writers Club; Director, International League for the Rights of Man. Recipient: Polish Academy of Sciences grant, 1955; Ford Fellowship, 1958; Prix du Meilleur Livre Etranger, France, 1966; Guggenheim Fellowship, 1967; National Book Award, 1969; American Academy grant, 1970; John Golden Fellowship in Playwriting, 1970; Brith Sholom Humanitarian Freedom Award, 1974. Address: c/o S.F. Inc., 60 West 57th Street, Suite 18-K, New York, New York 10019, U.S.A.

Publications

Novels

The Painted Bird. Boston, Houghton Mifflin, 1965; London, W.H. Allen, 1966; revised edition, New York, Modern Library, 1970.
Steps. New York, Random House, 1968; London, Bodley Head, 1969.
Being There. New York, Harcourt Brace, and London, Bodley Head, 1971.
The Devil Tree. New York, Harcourt Brace, and London, Hart Davis MacGibbon, 1973; revised edition, New York, St. Martin's Press, 1981.
Cockpit. Boston, Houghton Mifflin, and London, Hutchinson, 1975.
Blind Date. Boston, Houghton Mifflin, 1977; London, Hutchinson, 1978.

Passion Play. New York, St. Martin's Press, 1979; London, Joseph, 1980.

Play

Being There (screenplay). Los Angeles, Lorimar, 1980.

Screenplay: *Being There*, 1980.

Other

Dokumenty Walki o Czlowieka. Lodz, Scientific Society of Lodz, 1955.
Program Rewolucji Ludowej Jakoba Jaworskiego. Lodz, Scientific Society of Lodz, 1955.
The Future is Ours, Comrade: Conversations with the Russians (as Joseph Novak). New York, Doubleday, and London, Bodley Head, 1960.
No Third Path (as Joseph Novak). New York, Doubleday, 1962.
Notes of the Author on "The Painted Bird" 1965. New York, Scientia Factum, 1965.
The Art of the Self: Essays à propos "Steps." New York, Scientia Factum, 1968.

Editor, *Socjologia Amerykánska*. New York, Polish Institute of Arts and Sciences in America, 1962.

*

Bibliography: *John Barth, Jerzy Kosinski, and Thomas Pynchon: A Reference Guide* by Thomas P. Walsh and Cameron Northouse, Boston, Hall, 1977.

Critical Studies: "The End of Humanism" by Don Anderson, in *Quadrant* (New York), December 1976; "Horatio Algers of the Nightmare" by Elizabeth Stone, in *Psychology Today* (New York), December 1977; "Life at a Gallop" by Daniel J. Cahill, in *Washington Post*, 16 September 1978; "The Moral Universe of Jerzy Kosinski" by Lawrence S. Cunningham, in *America* (New York), 11 November 1978; "Jerzy Kosinski: Passionate Player" by Christopher Evans, in *Minneapolis Star Magazine*, 22 September 1979.

* * *

Trained as a sociologist and the author of two studies of collective behavior (*The Future Is Ours, Comrade* and *No Third Path*), Jerzy Kosinski turned to fiction as the most appropriate form to express his ideas about individuality and the human imagination.

His first novel, *The Painted Bird*, is an imaginative response to his childhood in Poland during and immediately following the Second World War. Its protagonist, simply called "The Boy," is separated from his parents in Warsaw, and wanders the war-torn countryside for five years as an orphan. Brutalized by all factions, who by reason of their superstition or ideology see him as a threatening outsider, The Boy learns that the power of his own imagination is all that can protect him from the ravages of these collectivized herds. He admires models of superior power and especially of silent revenge, of which he becomes a master. After the war, he is unable to adapt himself to the collectivized order of the new social world; the scenes of unmatched brutality he has survived by his own ingenuity and daring have shaped him as a superior individual, who by the greater power (and freedom) of his imagination transcends society. In 1975, for a new edition of *The Painted Bird*, Kosinski prepared a revealing foreword, clarifying his own relationship to the fictional events his novel describes.

Kosinski's subsequent novels expand and explore the theme of the individual versus society, and the imagination as pitted against the quotidian reality of social life. *Steps*, the author's most experimental work, consists of fragmentary independent narratives linked together by brief italicized conversations, usually of two lovers discussing the themes emerging from these narrative sections. The predominant topic is that of love—how one is most attracted to the reflection of one's self, and how fear, rivalry, and the inclination to dominate often destroys any chance for a full relationship. "Meet me within your own self," the true lover urges; only in this way can there be a true union of selves.

Being There is a short parable illustrating just how dangerous this fascination with self-image can be. Chance, a retarded gardener whose only contact with the world has been through television, is suddenly shoved out into the social mainstream. Unable to communicate except by repeating the tag ends of his listener's conversation and speaking in utterly bland metaphors (for which references can be supplied at will), Chance becomes an instantaneous media celebrity and likely Vice-Presidential candidate. He succeeds as everyone's favorite person simply by reflecting back a flattering image of themselves.

This third novel is Kosinski's first work set entirely in the United States (to which he emigrated from Poland in 1957), and reflects his own fear that mass media and commercialization have created a collectivism no less oppressive than in the Communist countries. His subsequent novels describe the attempts of various protagonists to overcome this collective impulse by asserting their singular imaginative wills. In *The Devil Tree* the young man Jonathan Whalen struggles to assert his own identity within the strangling branches of his family tree; he survives only by drowning his godparents. Tarden, the retired secret agent of *Cockpit*, finds full security only by isolating himself from human relations within his manipulative "cockpit" of intellectual and emotional controls. A God who variously rewards or punishes individuals for their actions, he succeeds only in alienating himself from life. *Blind Date* and *Passion Play* construct elaborate parallels to Kosinski's own life as a novelist: Levanter, the speculative investor, and Fabian, the professional polo player, live by their wits—more specifically, by constructing lives of fiction around themselves so that nothing and nobody can penetrate to their personal beings. Their virtues are a professional facility; but in the process they, like Tarden, isolate themselves from life and love.

As a writer of fiction, Jerzy Kosinski has been most widely praised for the clear and lucid quality of his prose. Writing in an adopted language learned in adulthood, free from the traumatizing obstacles of his native Polish and Russian, Kosinski claims he is in full rational control of the words he uses, immune to any conditional response or phobia. His success is evident in *The Painted Bird* and in certain grisly passages from *Blind Date*, where the most exceptional violence is described in unrelenting, spellbinding detail, with no lapses into the all-too-possible titillation or farce. A peasant is eaten alive in a cistern literally boiling with voracious rats; a band of mass murderers slaughter a group of the narrator's closest friends (an incident recalling the Sharon Tate / Charles Manson murders, to which Kosinski was a tardy guest). In each case his precise and unrelenting prose fastens the reader's attention to a reality our culture has otherwise found to be unimaginable—Kosinski's own measure of the writer's greatest success.

—Jerome Klinkowitz

KRIGE, Uys. South African. Born in Swellendam, Cape Province, 4 February 1910. Educated at Paul Roos Gymnasium; Stellenbosch University, 1927-29, B.A. in law 1929. Married Lydia Pindeque in 1937; two children. Reporter, *Rand Daily Mail*, Johannesburg, 1930; Lived in France and Spain, 1931-36; correspondent, *Die Suiderstem*, Cape Town, 1936; broadcaster, Bureau of Information, 1939; war correspondent in Egypt and Abyssinia during World War II: prisoner of war in Italy, 1941-43; Founding

Editor, *Vandag* (Today), Johannesburg, 1949. Recipient: French government bursary, 1952; Carnegie grant, 1959. Honorary doctorate: University of Natal, 1958. Address: P.O. Box 25, Onrust, Cape Province, South Africa.

PUBLICATIONS

Short Stories

Die Palmboom (The Palm Tree). Pretoria, Van Schaik, 1940.
The Dream and the Desert. London, Collins, 1953; Boston, Houghton Mifflin, 1954.
Orphan of the Desert. Cape Town, John Malherbe, 1967.

Plays

Binnenshuis, adaptation of a play by Maeterlinck, in *Huiggenoot*, 14 August 1931.
Magdalena Retief (in Afrikaans). Cape Town, Unie Volkspers, 1938; revised edition, 1948.
Die Wit Muur (includes *Die Wit Muur* [The White Wall], *Die Skaapwagters van Bethlehem* [The Shepherds of Bethlehem], *Die Arrestasie* [The Arrest]). Cape Town, Unie Volkspers, 1940.
All Paaie Gaan na Rome (All Roads Go to Rome). Cape Town, Unie Volkspers, 1949.
Die Twee Lampe (The Two Lamps), adaptation of a story by Sannie Uys. Johannesburg, Afrikaanse Pers, 1951.
Die Sluipskutter (The Sniper) (includes *Die Gees van die Water* [The Spirit of the Water]). Johannesburg, Afrikaanse Pers, 1951.
Die Ryk Weduwee (The Rich Widow) (produced 1950). Johannesburg, Afrikaanse Pers, 1953.
Die Goue Kring (The Golden Circle) (produced Johannesburg, 1950's). Cape Town, Balkema, 1956.
The Sniper and Other One-Act Plays (includes *The Arrest*, *Fuente Sagrada*, *All Roads Lead to Rome*). Cape Town, Hollands-Afrikaanse Uitwegers Maatskappy, 1962.
Yerma (in Afrikaans), adaptation of the play by Lorca. Cape Town, Hollands-Afrikaanse Uitwegers Maatskappy, 1963.
The Two Lamps, and The Big Shots. Cape Town, Hollands-Afrikaanse Uitwegers Maatskappy, 1964.
Twaalfde Nag, adaptation of the play *Twelfth Night* by Shakespeare (produced Transvaal, 1965[?]).
Muur van die Dood (Wall of Death). Cape Town, Constantia, 1968.
Die Grootkanome (The Big Shots). Johannesburg, Dramatiese Artistieke en Letterkundige Regte Organisasie, 1969.
Die Ongeskrewe Stuk (The Unwritten Play). Johannesburg, Dramatiese Artistieke en Letterkundige Regte Organisasie, 1970.

Verse

Kentering (Turning Point). Pretoria, Van Schaik, 1935.
Rooidag (Daybreak). Pretoria, Van Schaik, 1940.
Ooclogsgedigte. Pretoria, Van Schaik, 1942.
Die Einde van die Pad (The End of the Road). Pretoria, Van Schaik, 1947.
Hart Sonder Hawe (Heart Without Haven). Cape Town, Unie Volkspers, 1949.
Vir die Luit en die Kitaar (For the Lute and the Guitar). Johannesburg, Afrikaanse Pers, 1950.
Ballade van die Groot Begeer (Ballad of the Great Desiring). Cape Town, Balkema, 1960.
Gedigte 1927-1940 (Poems). Pretoria, Van Schaik, 1961.
Eluard en die Surrealisme (Eluard and Surrealism). Cape Town, Hollands-Afrikaanse Uitwegers Maatskappy, 1962.
Vooraand (Eve). Johannesburg, Afrikaanse Pers, 1964.

Other

Vanguard of Victory: A Short Review of the South African Victories in East Africa 1940-1941, with Conrad Norton. Pretoria, Bureau of Information, 1941.
The Way Out: Italian Intermezzo. London, Collins, 1946; revised edition, Cape Town, Maskew Miller, 1955.
Sol y Sombra (in Afrikaans). Pretoria, Unie Volkspers, 1948; revised edition, Pretoria, Van Schaik, 1955.
Ver in die Wereld (Far in the World). Johannesburg, Afrikaanse Pers, 1951.
Sout van die Aarde (Salt of the Earth). Cape Town, Hollands-Afrikaanse Uitwegers Maatskappy, 1961.

Editor, *Poems of Roy Campbell.* Cape Town, Maskew Miller, 1960.
Editor, *Olive Schreiner: A Selection.* Cape Town and London, Oxford University Press, 1968; New York, Oxford University Press, 1969.
Editor, with Jack Cope, *The Penguin Book of South African Verse.* London, Penguin, 1968.
Editor, *Spaans-Amerikaanse Keuse* (Spanish-American Verse). Cape Town, Human and Rousseau, 1969.

*

Critical Study: *Uys Krige* by Christina Van Heyningen and Jacques Berthoud, New York, Twayne, 1966.

* * *

Uys Krige is one of the very few white South African writers who have established a literary reputation in both the official languages of the country: English and Afrikaans. Of Afrikaner descent, and brought up in an Afrikaans environment, Krige's first allegiance is, naturally, to Afrikaans; and his contribution to its rapidly growing literature is considerable, comprising poetry, plays and criticism. Characteristic of his work is an obvious delight in exploring the nuances of a relatively new and constantly changing language. His linguistic facility is seen to good advantage in his successful comedy, *Die Ryk Weduwee*, in much of his recent poetry, and in his translations from Spanish, notably Lorca's play *Yerma.* He has also successfully translated *Twelfth Night*, adapting Shakespeare's verse patterns into idiomatic and colourful Afrikaans.

Krige's interest in English, consciously developed throughout his writing career, was stimulated by his extensive pre-war travels in Europe, and by his experience during the Second World War, first as a war correspondent in Africa, later as a prisoner of war in Italy. Contact with Europe sharpened his awareness of European civilization, and contact with Englishmen stimulated his desire to write for an English audience. On his return to South Africa in 1946, he began not only to write in English, but to translate some of his own work, in an attempt to bridge the language barrier which, traditionally, separates the white races in South Africa. His work has thus become available to a much wider audience than that reached by most Afrikaans authors, and has opened hitherto largely inaccessible areas of experience to the non-Afrikaans reader. Krige, that is, writes as an Afrikaner, about Afrikaners, and his work is valuable for its patently honest, consistently realistic account of a people who, more often than not, have been portrayed as conscienceless, narrow-minded white supremacists. Krige's Afrikaners are ordinary people, involved in the common human experiences of birth, love, and death. He is particularly conscious of Afrikaner traditions, which both link the people with, and separate them from their European ancestors. He is aware, too, of their limitations, as well as justly proud of their achievements. His poetic sensibility enables him to see his characters in a close and living relationship with the peculiar South African landscape, which has always had a strong fascination for him, and which he presents with accuracy and deep feeling, disguising neither its harshness nor its great beauty.

"The Coffin" and "The Dream," both of which appear in *The*

Dream and the Desert, demonstrate one side of Krige's awareness. "The Coffin" is a story about a kindly Afrikaner patriarch, living life to the full though always conscious of death, and prepared to meet it, with his coffin standing ready in the loft. "The Dream" is a delightful evocation of a half-rural South African childhood, in which humorous irony controls but does not destroy the deliberately romantic nostalgia for a way of life which is rapidly disappearing. *The Two Lamps* displays another facet of the Afrikaner personality, and of Krige's talent. This play, which has received much critical acclaim in America as well as in South Africa, dramatises, in a typically South Africa version, the conflict between father and sons. It presents an uncompromising study of the Calvinist conscience, which is powerless, finally, to avert overwhelming tragedy. Set against a haunting background of mist, marsh and farmland, *The Two Lamps* is possibly Krige's finest achievement.

An important part of Krige's work is not confined exclusively to South Africa. Much of this is criticism, translation (from French and Spanish), and a popular genre in South Africa, travel literature. In addition however, there is some fine war writing, in which Krige's talent for objective reportage is seen to good advantage. *The Way Out* is an account of Krige's escape from an Italian prison camp, but it is more than a simple escape story. The narrative develops into a penetrating psychological study of men under stress, and at the same time celebrates the loyalty and courage of the impoverished Italian partisans who risked their lives to help the escapers. "The Death of the Zulu," also based on his war experiences, is one of the few stories in which Krige attempts to deal with black characters. Although it is very slight, being hardly more than the description of a single incident (one man's death in the desert), the story shows Krige's ability to present all his characters, whatever their race, with genuine sympathy.

Where many South African writers succumb to a self-conscious humanitarianism, understandable in the present political context, but often destructive of literary merit, it is Krige's distinctive achievement to write without any obvious bias: his work thus reflects the reality of the South Africa he knows, and of which he is part. Although this reality is limited (to the extent that it virtually excludes black South Africa, and includes "non-whites" only as servants and inferiors), it is a reality which is a living part of the South African experience, and deserves recognition as such.

—Ursula Laredo

KROETSCH, Robert (Paul). Canadian. Born in Heisler, Alberta, 26 June 1927. Educated at the University of Alberta, Edmonton, B.A. 1948; McGill University, Montreal, 1954-55; Middlebury College, Vermont, M.A. 1956; University of Iowa, Iowa City, Ph.D. 1961. Married Mary Jane Lewis in 1956; two daughters. Laborer and purser, Yellowknife Transportation Company, Northwest Territories, 1948-50; Information Specialist (civilian), United States Air Force Base, Goose Bay, Labrador, 1951-54; Assistant Professor, 1961-65, and Associate Professor of English, 1965-75, State University of New York, Binghamton; Artist-in-Residence, Calgary University, Alberta, Fall 1975, and University of Lethbridge, Alberta, Spring 1976. Artist-in-Residence, University of Manitoba, Winnipeg, 1976-78, and since 1980. Recipient: Bread Loaf Writers Conference grant, 1966; Governor-General's Award, 1970. Address: Department of English, University of Manitoba, Winnipeg, Manitoba R3T 2N2, Canada.

PUBLICATIONS

Novels

But We Are Exiles. London, Macmillan, and New York, St. Martin's Press, 1966.
The Words of My Roaring. London, Macmillan, and New York, St. Martin's Press, 1966.
The Studhorse Man. Toronto, Macmillan, and London, Macdonald, 1969; New York, Simon and Schuster, 1970.
Gone Indian. Toronto, New Press, 1973.
Badlands. Toronto, New Press, 1974.
What the Crow Said. Toronto, General Publishing, 1978.

Verse

The Stone Hammer Poems 1960-1975. Lantzville, British Columbia, Oolichan, 1975.
The Ledge. London, Ontario, Applegarth Follies, 1975.
Seed Catalogue. Winnipeg, Turnstone Press, 1977.
The Sad Phoenician. Toronto, Coach House Press, 1979.

Other

Alberta. Toronto, Macmillan, and New York, St. Martin's Press, 1968.

Editor, with James Bacque and Pierre Gravel, *Creation* (interviews). Toronto, New Press, 1970.

*

Manuscript Collection: University of Calgary Library, Alberta.

* * *

The setting of Robert Kroetsch's *Gone Indian* is depicted as the "far, last edge of our civilization," and, both geographically and metaphorically, this phrase suggests the limits and nature of Kroetsch's fictional worlds. Rural Alberta and the Mackenzie River valley, scenes that shaped his own upbringing, are vividly and realistically evoked in his novels, but the fictional situations within these settings are subjected to a mythical transmutation so that the ultimate effect is much closer to allegory than to literal realism. In his various literary activities over the past decade—as critic, editor, poet, as well as novelist—Robert Kroetsch has been in the forefront of the revolt against realism in Canadian literature, a position he affirmed in a recent interview with Donald Cameron: "I'm fascinated right now by the effects of moving away from realism—the kinds of freedom you get, and the kinds of truth you get at, by departing from the sterner varieties of realism."

To this aesthetic concern he has been increasingly faithful in his fiction, and perhaps only in his first novel, *But We Are Exiles*, did he fail to weld successfully the realistic and the surrealistic elements. There is a somewhat awkward relationship here between the day to day log-book detail of the *Nahanni Jane*'s voyages down and up the Mackenzie River, and the mythical journey that Peter Guy is embarked upon in his quest for expiation and re-birth. *But We Are Exiles* is the only one of his novels which reflects a tragic vision of life, and in it Kroetsch seems to miss his later broad and flexible vision which allows for an organic fusion between the physical landscape and the inner landscape. As a "stern variety of realism" it is a remarkable first novel, however, and Kroetsch's depictions of the riverboat men, the natives of the lower Mackenzie River, and his feeling for this "far edge" of Canada give this novel a solid authenticity.

Beyond these qualities, however, the novel also adumbrates the mythical concerns which constitute the substance of his later trilogy—*The Words of My Roaring*, *The Studhorse Man*, and *Gone Indian*. A narcissistic concern with one's identity, the death-rebirth pattern, an obsession with the dead and the dying, the vast, cosmic jokes—all these elements reappear in various forms throughout these novels. The trilogy is informed by a comic vision of experience, with the result that the fusion of the realistic and the allegorical is consistently successful, particularly in *The Studhorse Man* and *Gone Indian*. In all three of these novels the landscape of the Canadian prairie, though geographically the same as that exploited by such traditional realists as Robert Stead and Frederick Philip Grove, becomes essentially a surrealistic world in which there are, to use Malcolm Lowry's words, "strange trafficking and curious merchandise" indeed.

The Words of My Roaring is in this sense the most restricted of these novels, in that it is essentially a parable of the political upheaval that took place during Alberta's depression years. But because it is so firmly rooted in tangible social reality, its rich comic texture does not become strained by some of the fanciful and at times unchecked imagination which characterizes the other two novels. The Johnnie Backstrom-Doc Murdoch conflict reflects the political, generational, and Oedipal situations which essentially obtain in our society, and on this level the novel is skilfully executed. But Backstrom is not only an opponent of tangible authority, as it were, for as a lover, as an undertaker, as a political prophet tricked into promising rain, he is also a protagonist within the irrational, cosmic order, and it is the depiction of his survival here which attracts Kroetsch's special talents and which allows him to exploit the absurd elements of this world.

The Studhorse Man carries this obsession with survival into a completely surrealistic world, and here the richness and chaos of event and character almost distract us from the grim point that Kroetsch is making: the tenuousness of survival. Specifically, this comic odyssey is about the survival of a species—of the last of a line of breed stallions, but the survival of the studhorse *man*, which by extension means the sexual or life force itself, is an inseparable part of this. The spectre of the gaunt and ailing Hazard Lepage, leading his stallion Poseidon on an endless quest for the perfect mare, constitutes one of the most vivid images in recent Canadian fiction, and Kroetsch reinforces the absurdity of this spectacle by having the entire chronicle narrated by a madman sitting naked in his empty bathtub.

That Hazard Lepage fails in his primary quest is, given the imminent total mechanization of the farms, inevitable; but aesthetically, too, the possibilities of the comic mode not only allow for, but in a sense require, a compromising of original ideals. Hazard is killed by his stallion, but not before he impregnates his fiancée; Poseidon is pressed into service in the production of PMU, a vital ingredient in the artificial controlling of life. Thus, the life force continues, but not as rampantly as it would have had Hazard and Poseidon been granted free rein to their prowess and lust.

Kroetsch's concern with the sexual force takes a more consistently comic turn in *Gone Indian*, where the protagonist, Jeremy Sadness, has a peculiar sexual problem: he cannot make love in a prone position. Sadness is a graduate student who, after nine years of study, still has only the first sentence of his dissertation completed, so it is clear that in this book long-time English professsor Robert Kroetsch is getting something else off his chest. Sexual prowess diminishes in proportion to academic prone-ness, presumably, so the obvious solution is to walk abroad and procreate oneself. All this is perhaps a rather fanciful way of getting Sadness out of a New York university into Edmonton, where he has come for an interview. But as with Hazard Lepage, complications, cosmic and otherwise, confound his plans, and he is soon caught up in an absurd series of events which allow Kroetsch full vent to his rich, comic imagination. Most important for Sadness, he was finally able to emulate his lifelong idol, Grey Owl, "a man who died into a new life," a fate which also overtook Jeremy shortly after his new found mistress had cured him of his sexual problem.

What Robert Kroetsch has done in his novels is to transform historical, cultural, and psychological "truths" into mythical possibilities by exploiting settings and materials which contain within them both realistic and surrealistic dimensions. He has on the whole achieved a very satisfactory synthesis of these elusive elements, and has demonstrated the rich possibilities inherent in the "far, last edges of our civilization."

—Hallvard Dahlie

LA GUMA, (Justin) Alex(ander). South African. Born in Cape Town, 20 February 1925. Educated at Trafalgar High School, Cape Town; Cape Technical College, Cape Town; London School of Journalism. Married Blanche Valerie in 1954; two children. Staff Writer, *New Age Weekly*, Cape Town, 1955-62. Active in political movement in South Africa; arrested for treason, 1956, acquitted, 1960; proscribed under Suppression of Communism Act, 1962; under house arrest, Cape Town, 1962-66, and detained in solitary confinement, 1963 and 1966; journalist in London, 1966-78. Since 1978, official representative of the African National Congress of South Africa, Havana. Address: Calle 21-A, No. 20617, Esq. 214, Atabey, Havana 16, Cuba.

PUBLICATIONS

Novels

A Walk in the Night. Ibadan, Mbari, 1962.
And a Threefold Cord. Berlin, Seven Seas, 1964.
The Stone-Country. Berlin, Seven Seas, 1967; London, Heinemann, 1974.
In the Fog of the Season's End. London, Heinemann, 1972; New York, Third Press, 1973.
Time of the Butcherbird. London, Heinemann, 1979.

Short Stories

Quartet: New Voices from South Africa, with others. New York, Crown, 1963; London, Heinemann, 1965.
A Walk in the Night and Other Stories. London, Heinemann, 1967; Evanston, Illinois, Northwestern University Press, 1968.

Other

A Soviet Journey. Moscow, Progress, 1978.

Editor, *Apartheid: A Collection of Writings on South African Racism by South Africans.* New York, International Publishers, 1971; London, Lawrence and Wishart, 1972.

*

Critical Studies: *The African Image* by Ezekiel Mphahlele, London, Heinemann, 1962; "Tribute to Alex La Guma" by Ezekiel Mphahlele, in *Sechaba* (London), February 1971; *Standpoints on African Literature* by C.L. Wanjala, Nairobi, East African Literature Bureau, 1973.

Alex La Guma comments:

All my works are concerned with the contemporary South African scene, particularly the experiences of the non-White population.

* * *

In manner the most realistic of South African novelists, Alex La Guma is also the most politically convinced and articulate. His first novel, *A Walk in the Night*, is so entitled (from *Hamlet*, I, v) because he presents the people of District Six, Cape Town's former "Coloured" slum, as inhabitants of a social hell; David Rabkin writes that the "characters...are there not for their 'foul crimes' but as a consequence of the social and political systems....Hell is not a state of mind, but a system of legislation." All La Guma's fiction shows in concrete detail how that system blights the lives of black South Africans and distorts the humanity of both white and black. In narrative terms *A Walk in the Night* projects in accelerated motion the transformation of a legitimately aggrieved worker into a murderer by chance and gangster from choice, while the police pursue another man, shoot him, and callously leave him to die in their vehicle. The dilapidated, overcrowded, unsanitary conditions of District Six are described with great physical clarity, and the imagery (pustules of anger, cockroaches slithering in darkness) provides a grim commentary upon the overall sordidness. Yet the novel is not oppressively determinist: there is tenderness within the Lorenzo family, and the gentle, simple-minded Joe responds to the "beauty of starfish and anemone" along the seashore.

La Guma's settings are always precise and authentic, and he uses characterization less to analyse individuality than to exemplify the human wastage of South Africa's social and economic policy. *And a Threefold Cord* is about the inhabitants of a shanty town on the sandy Cape Flats, who improvise scanty shelter from white South Africa's cast-off rubbish, but it also celebrates their warm community spirit, which attracts a lonely white man while his upbringing prevents him from entering into it. In *The Stone-Country* an unusual blending of realism and symbolism enables La Guma to render very powerfully the hopelessness experienced by the victims of apartheid: the action takes place within a prison, the outward appearance of which (with lawns and flower beds to soften the approach), together with its internal organizations of warders and different categories of prisoners, neatly mirrors South Africa's social and economic structure. The role of the educated political prisoner is that of a black intellectual identifying himself with both the workers and those who are criminals by circumstance.

In the Fog of the Season's End is devoted to the underground resistance to apartheid, but the usual richness of background detail fails to sustain the attempted note of individual heroism, and La Guma's own unease is betrayed by an excessively adjectival style and a surfeit of far-fetched, obtrusive similes. In *Time of the Butcherbird* his sympathies with communal hardship are fully engaged again with the theme of the South African government's forcible removal of tribal people from their ancestral soil to distant wastelands. The shift from urban to rural and a fuller treatment of white characters mark a broadening of La Guma's range.

—Arthur Ravenscroft

LAMMING, George (Eric). Barbadian. Born in Barbados in 1927. Taught school in Trinidad and Venezuela; host of a book review programme for the West Indian Service of the BBC, London, 1951; Member of the Faculty, University of the West Indies, Kingston, Jamaica, 1968. Recipient: Guggenheim Fellowship, 1954; *Kenyon Review* Fellowship, 1954; Maugham Award, 1957. Address: 14-A Highbury Place, London N.5, England.

PUBLICATIONS

Novels

In the Castle of My Skin. London, Joseph, and New York, McGraw Hill, 1953.

The Emigrants. London, Joseph, 1954; New York, McGraw Hill, 1955.

Of Age and Innocence. London, Joseph, 1958; New York, Schocken, 1981.

Season of Adventure. London, Joseph, 1960; New York, Schocken, 1980.

Water with Berries. London, Longman, 1971; New York, Holt Rinehart, 1972.

Natives of My Person. London, Longman, and New York, Holt Rinehart, 1972.

Uncollected Short Stories

"David's Walk," in *Life and Letters* (London), November 1948.

"Of Thorns and Thistles" and "A Wedding in Spring," in *West Indian Stories*, edited by Andrew Salkey. London, Faber, 1960.

"Birds of a Feather," in *Stories from the Caribbean*, edited by Andrew Salkey. London, Elek, 1965; as *Island Voices*, New York, Liveright, 1970.

Other

The Pleasures of Exile. London, Joseph, 1960.

Editor, *Cannon Shot and Glass Beads: Modern Black Writing.* London, Pan, 1974.

* * *

The critical reception of George Lamming's first four novels has fallen short of their real merits and originality. It is often said that Lamming demands too much of the reader; it might be truer to say that the reader demands too little of Lamming. West Indian fiction has often been distinguished by a certain energy and rhetorical glow but not, except in the work of Lamming and Wilson Harris, by much complexity of form or texture. Right from his first book, *In the Castle of My Skin*, Lamming made it clear that the real complexity of West Indian experience demanded some adequate response of its writers. He has since elaborated this view in an important essay called "The Negro Writer and His World," where he wrote: "To speak of his [the Negro Writer's] situation is to speak of a general need to find a centre as well as a circumference which embraces some reality whose meaning satisfies his intellect and may prove pleasing to his senses. But a man's life assumes meaning first in relation to other men...."

In the Castle of My Skin may at first appear to be an autobiography of childhood, but it soon becomes apparent that the book is also the collective autobiography of a Barbadian village moving through the break-up of the old plantation system dominated by the Great House and into the new age of nationalism, industrial unrest and colonial repression. The four boys who stand at the centre of the book are given a more or less equal importance though it is "George" who ultimately registers the meaning of their disparate experiences as they are driven asunder by education, travel, and emerging social distinctions.

The collective quality already evident in this, the most personal of all Lamming's books, is more strongly present in *The Emigrants*. Here the portrait is of one boatload of the black emigrants (the title is significant, for it stresses what they leave as well as what they find) who flocked from the Caribbean to Britain between 1950 and 1962. On the boat the emigrants discover a new identity as "West Indians," only to lose it again as they fly centrifugally apart under the stresses of life in an alien culture.

The Emigrants is the saddest of all Lamming's books, because there is almost no focus of hope amid so much disillusionment and despair. By contrast both *Of Age and Innocence* and *Season of Adventure* are powerfully positive books in which what is shed is a set of values adhering to the older generation, those who are unable to match the pace and tendency of the times. *Of Age and Innocence* is set in San Cristobal, a fictional Caribbean island colony rapidly approaching independence. The dominant generation of islanders is unable to break away from its class and racial identities to work together for a new society which will redeem the past of slavery and colonialism, but it is throughout juxtaposed to the generation of its children, who struggle towards that meaning which the nationalist leader Shepherd has glimpsed and then lost again:

> I had always lived in the shadow of a meaning which others had placed on my presence in the world, and I had played no part at all in making that meaning, like a chair which is wholly at the mercy of the idea guiding the hand of the man who builds it.... But like the chair, I have played no part at all in making that meaning which others use to define me completely.

Shepherd is destroyed by the forces of the past, but the children look out through the flames of destruction which end the novel towards a future they have already presaged in their games. At the centre of *Season of Adventure* stands another unawakened character, the "big-shot coloured" girl Fola, whose father is a West Indian police officer imbued with all the old ideas of order, dominance, and segregation. A visit to a Voduñ ceremony awakens her to the real capacity of her nature for self-discovery and self-renewal. This awakening by ancestral drums is in itself a cliché of Caribbean literature, but here it escapes banality by the intensity of Lamming's lyrical style and the bizarre violence of much of the action. *Season of Adventure* is in some ways the finest of his novels, just as *The Emigrants* is certainly the weakest. Yet the hesitancy which overtakes the drums at the end of the novel, in the very moment of their triumph as the expression of popular values, is analogous to the problem of language Lamming faces in projecting a West Indian culture which will be truly united, consistent and free: "But remember the order of the drums...for it is the language which every nation needs if its promises and its myths are to become a fact."

After a silence of more than ten years, Lamming published two new novels within a year. These were powerfully contrasted in style and theme. *Water with Berries* is superficially a naturalistic novel about three West Indian artists living difficult and ever more lonely lives in modern London. Gradually, however (and the quotation of Caliban in the title gives a clue), the reader becomes aware that this is a study of what happens when Caliban comes to Prospero's original home. The revenges of history work themselves out through characters who are helpless to prevent completing the bizarre and violent patterns of the past. Each of the friends is an aspect of Caliban and each passes through an extreme personal crisis at the novel's end. But Derek, erect upon the stage before a howling audience, having completed the rape of Miranda at last, or Teeton, erect upon a northern island after destroying his last links with the racial past, have at least sketched the possibilities of freedom from these tyrannies of history.

Natives of My Person is more of an extended reverie upon certain dominant themes in Atlantic mythology—the demonic captain, the slave-ship, the imprisoned Amerindian prince, the crew variously haunted by tragedy and terror—which are treated like themes in music. The style is deliberately wrought from the timbers of 17th-century maritime prose, in which this mythology finds its roots. Hence the novel voyages freely in the dimension of space-time, deriving its structure simply from the musical resolution of its dominant themes. This is a work of great beauty, originality, and difficulty, which may finally prove to be Lamming's most important achievement.

—Gerald Moore

LAURENCE, (Jean) Margaret. Canadian. Born in Neepawa, Manitoba, 18 July 1926. Educated at the University of Manitoba, Winnipeg, B.A. 1947. Married John F. Laurence in 1947 (divorced, 1969); one son and one daughter. Lived in Somali and Ghana, 1950-57, and in England; Writer-in-Residence, University of Toronto, 1969-70. Recipient: Beta Sigma Phi award, 1960; President's Medal, University of Western Ontario, 1961, 1962, 1964; Governor-General's Award, 1967, 1975; Canada Council Senior Fellowship, 1967, 1971; Molson Prize, 1974. Address: Elm Cottage, Beacon Hill, Penn, Buckinghamshire, England.

PUBLICATIONS

Novels

This Side Jordan. Toronto, McClelland and Stewart, London, Macmillan, and New York, St. Martin's Press, 1960.
The Stone Angel. Toronto, McClelland and Stewart, London, Macmillan, and New York, Knopf, 1964.
A Jest Of God. Toronto, McClelland and Stewart, London, Macmillan, and New York, Knopf, 1966; as *Rachel, Rachel*, New York, Popular Library, 1968; as *Now I Lay Me Down*, London, Panther, 1968.
The Fire-Dwellers. Toronto, McClelland and Stewart, London, Macmillan, and New York, Knopf, 1969.
The Diviners. Toronto, McClelland and Stewart, London, Macmillan, and New York, Knopf, 1974.

Short Stories

The Tomorrow-Tamer. Toronto, McClelland and Stewart, and London, Macmillan, 1963; New York, Knopf, 1964.
A Bird in the House. Toronto, McClelland and Stewart, London, Macmillan, and New York, Knopf, 1970.
The Olden-Days Coat. Toronto, McClelland and Stewart, 1979.

Other

The Prophet's Camel Bell (travel). Toronto, McClelland and Stewart, and London, Macmillan, 1963; as *New Wind in a Dry Land*, New York, Knopf, 1964.
Long Drums and Cannons: Nigerian Novelists and Dramatists 1952-1966. London, Macmillan, and New York, Praeger, 1968.
Jason's Quest (juvenile). Toronto, McClelland and Stewart, London, Macmillan, and New York, Knopf, 1970.
Heart of a Stranger (essays). Toronto, McClelland and Stewart, 1976; Philadelphia, Lippincott, 1977.
Six Darn Cows (juvenile). Toronto, Lorimer, 1979.
The Christmas Birthday Story (juvenile). New York, Knopf, 1980.

Editor, *A Tree for Poverty: Somali Poetry and Prose*. Nairobi, Eagle Press, 1954.

*

Bibliography: "Margaret Laurence: An Annotated Bibliography" by Susan J. Warwick, in *The Annotated Bibliography of Canada's Major Authors 1*, edited by Robert Lecker and Jack David, Downsview, Ontario, ECW Press, 1979.

Manuscript Collection: McMaster University, Hamilton, Ontario.

Critical Studies: "The Maze of Life" by S.E. Read, in *Canadian Literature* (Vancouver), Winter 1966; "Geographer of Human Identities" by Walter Swayze, in *A.C.U.T.E.* (Ottawa), 1967; *Margaret Laurence*, Toronto, McClelland and Stewart, 1969, and *The Manawaka World of Margaret Laurence*, McClelland and Stewart, 1975, both by Clara Thomas; "Ten Years' Sentences" by the author, in *Canadian Literature* (Vancouver), Summer 1969; "Sources" by the author, in *Mosaic* (Winnipeg), April 1970; *Margaret Laurence: The Writer and Her Critics* edited by W.H. New, Toronto, McGraw Hill Ryerson, 1977.

* * *

Margaret Laurence's first novel, *This Side Jordan*, is set in the Gold Coast, some months before it became Ghana, the first British colony in Africa to gain independence. The novel deals with conflicting pulls of tribal and urban ways, misunderstandings between Europeans and Africans, and between Africans and Africans. Nathaniel Amegbe, a schoolmaster, experiences many of these pressures; he rejects the older pattern of life, yet he constantly feels its influence on him, finally deciding, despite severe setbacks, that his work must be undertaken in the new life of the city. This novel is fundamentally concerned with change; its texture is sufficiently complex to give depth to its picture of rapidly altering Ghananian life. The characters emerge convincingly, and the novel has a pulsating sense of immediacy about it.

Laurence's collection of Somali folk tales and poetry, *A Tree for Poverty*, was followed by an account of her life in British Somaliland, *The Prophet's Camel Bell*; and her study of Nigerian literature, *Long Drums and Cannons*, rounds off the picture we form of an author who is sensitive to oral and written literature, but, above all, to human beings.

A rich pattern of African life was exhibited in her early stories, published in book form in *The Tomorrow-Tamer*. In these, too, we see her preoccupation with people rather than background, however successful her portrayal of the contrasts of the African scene. For her characters have humour and pathos, strength and weakness, and a capacity for increasing self knowledge which involves the reader in their fortunes, in their development as human beings. Her further volume, *A Bird in the House*, reinforced the success of *The Tomorrow-Tamer*; Hagar in *The Stone Angel* is a character who reveals herself freely, and continues to hold the reader's attention. In *A Jest of God* Laurence developed further a capacity to invest an introspective character's account of her own life with increasing interest as the story develops. In this case it is the sterile life of Rachel Cameron, a spinster schoolteacher of 34 living with her mother in a small provincial Canadian town. The story of sudden awakening and incautious love is unfolded with skill and great sensitivity. The crippling conventionalism of a small community is a suitable background for this study, which is ultimately focussed on Rachel Cameron's escape from this stifling environment into a new and freer life, away from the pain of her past experience. Rachel's relationships with her colleagues, with her friend, and with neighbours, are the punctuation in her story, the pauses for breath in her long monologue with herself.

Laurence has a capacity for conveying the intensity of emotion which racks her characters; she chooses detail illuminatingly and economically; and she develops her human sympathies steadily from book to book. The reader is left with a comforting sense of architectonic control at work, however uncontrolled the actions of the characters may seem at some crucial point of story or novel.

—A. Norman Jeffares

LAVIN, Mary. Irish. Born in East Walpole, Massachusetts, 11 June 1912; moved with her family to Ireland as a child. Educated at East Walpole schools; Loreto Convent, Dublin; National University of Ireland, Dublin, M.A. (honours) 1938. Married 1) William Walsh in 1942 (died, 1954), three daughters; 2) Michael MacDonald Scott in 1969. President, Irish P.E.N., 1964-65. Recipient: Black Memorial Prize, 1944; Guggenheim Fellowship, 1959, 1961, 1962; Katherine Mansfield Prize, 1962; Ella Lynam Cabot Fellowship, 1971; Eire Society Gold Medal (U.S.A.), 1974; Gregory Medal, 1974. D.Litt.: National University of Ireland, 1968. President, Irish Academy of Letters, 1971-73. Address: The Abbey Farm, Bective, Navan, County Meath; or, Mews 11, Lad Lane, Rere Fitzwilliam Place, Dublin, Ireland.

PUBLICATIONS

Novels

The House in Clewe Street. Boston, Little Brown, and London, Joseph, 1945.

Mary O'Grady. Boston, Little Brown, and London, Joseph, 1950.

Short Stories

Tales from Bective Bridge. Boston, Little Brown, 1942; London, Joseph, 1943.

The Long Ago and Other Stories. London, Joseph, 1944.

The Becker Wives and Other Stories. London, Joseph, 1946; as *At Sallygap and Other Stories*, Boston, Little Brown, 1947.

A Single Lady and Other Stories. London, Joseph, 1951.

The Patriot Son and Other Stories. London, Joseph, 1956.

Selected Stories. New York, Macmillan, 1959.

The Great Wave and Other Stories. London, Macmillan, and New York, Macmillan, 1961.

The Stories of Mary Lavin. London, Constable, 2 vols., 1964-74.

In the Middle of the Fields and Other Stories. London, Constable, 1967; New York, Macmillan, 1969.

Happiness and Other Stories. London, Constable, 1969; Boston, Houghton Mifflin, 1970.

Collected Stories. Boston, Houghton Mifflin, 1971.

A Memory and Other Stories. London, Constable, 1972; Boston, Houghton Mifflin, 1973.

The Shrine and Other Stories. London, Constable, and Boston, Houghton Mifflin, 1977.

Uncollected Short Story

"Face of Hate," in *Southern Review* (Baton Rouge, Louisiana), January 1979.

Other (juvenile)

A Likely Story. New York, Macmillan, 1957.

The Second-Best Children in the World. London, Longman, and Boston, Houghton Mifflin, 1972.

*

Bibliography: by Paul A. Doyle, in *Papers of the Bibliography Society of America 63* (New York), 1969.

Manuscript Collections: Southern Illinois University, Carbondale; Mugar Memorial Library, Boston University.

Critical Studies: Preface by the author to *Selected Stories*, 1959, and by V.S. Pritchett to *Collected Stories*, 1971; *Mary Lavin* by Zack Bowen, Lewisburg, Pennsylvania, Bucknell University Press, 1975; *Mary Lavin* by Richard Peterson, Boston, Twayne, 1978. *Mary Lavin, Quiet Rebel: A Study of Her Short Stories* by A.A. Kelly, New York, Barnes and Noble, 1980.

* * *

Mary Lavin has obvious gifts for fiction: she can tell a story, invent characters and give them vivid speech, a life of their own, settings described economically yet evocatively. But she has more also, a capacity for selecting those moments of crisis when the world passes by but time stops still as the meaning of life is suddenly crystalised for some person. She first showed this gift in her short stories, which are Chekhovian in scope. *Tales from Bective Bridge* contained "Love Is for Lovers" where Mathew, an elderly bachelor, is attracted and then repelled by Mrs. Cooligan, a widow. His sudden nausea at the thought of her, of her love of warmth, of her dog, of cushions, of her orange dress, occurs one summer day in her garden. She tips a half dead fly out of her tea: the fly shakes the liquid out of his wings, as though celebrating his release. But the lazy fat dog swallows him. The whole Saturday afternoon's lesson is there, and we are prepared for Mathew's thoughts that evening: he had been trying to go back, to his dreams of a slender girl, a sweet cool fragrant marriage: "But you couldn't go back, ever."

These sudden moments of perception enrich her stories, which also explore the differences between dream and reality. The story "Magenta," for instance, in *The Becker Wives* builds slowly and remorselessly up to a climax where the girl's quickly invented stories about the supposed actress who employs her, lending her her clothes, are punctured by the small mistake of her being 20 minutes too late for the train back, so that she cannot replace the clothes she has stolen.

There is a remorseless quality about Lavin's fiction which marks her two major novels, *The House in Clewe Street* and *Mary O'Grady*. In both she displays an impressive skill in handling different ages in family groupings. *The House in Clewe Street* explores a boy's growing up under the care of two aunts, and his sudden rebellion and running away with the servant girl. In this story Lavin explores the tyranny given by the possession of both money and ruthless self-confidence and shows its crippling effect upon Gabriel, the protagonist. The story is, in essence, about the gradual undermining of his innocence. He does not question or rebel, without the outside stimulus given by his friend Sylvester. The exploration of his school, his growing interest in Onny the servant, his jealousy of her friendships in Dublin are all unfolded with the precision of a surgeon's skill. Yet this is no clinical novel, for we are aware of a compassionate attitude on the part of the authoress towards her characters. They have choice, they even enjoy the after effects of making a wrong choice. They are indeed children to whom Yeats's lines might well apply: "young/We loved each other and were ignorant."

In *Mary O'Grady* we are given the history of a family living in a Dublin suburb: a devoted husband and wife, their children growing up, and becoming adults, one going to America and eventually returning, one studying to become a priest, the girls finding husbands. The emotional content is rich and varied, the mother's strength impressive, the children's development into adults charted with convincing knowledge.

If the reader were to concentrate upon one specific aspect of Lavin's story-telling capacity and the subtle human understanding which informs all her fiction it might well be upon that delicate stage where adolescence asserts independence, is critical of parents while half ashamed of being so, yet determined to escape from the round of accustomed family life. In *Mary O'Grady*, for instance, there is the brilliantly evoked evening when the daughters are visited for the first time by the two engineering students who fall in love with them. The shyness, the gaucherie, the gradually developing friendliness of the family are handled with an assurance which not only encourages the reader to accept the narrator's unobtrusive, tactful guidance, but reinforces the sympathetic interest created from the beginning of the novel.

The secret of Lavin's success is, perhaps, to be found in that ability she possesses of taking her readers into her confidence, sharing with them her panoptic survey of those characters whom she regards in a kindly yet detached fashion. She has an awareness of the comedy as well as the tragedy of human life. She relishes its absurdities, weaves them into the tapestry, and keeps her proportions right. Her stories are set in Ireland, but her characters are universal. They may speak with the accents of the Irish countryside or of the city of Dublin, their particular modes of tact or forthrightness may be Irish in emphasis or accent, but these are people who exist anywhere in the world, given the author's ability to see them with insight, and, like Lavin, to portray them with realistic compassion, in their actions and in their self-revealing speech. She believes a writer distills the essence of his thought in a short story, that this kind of writing is only looking closer into the human heart. Her themes are loneliness, despair, escape, paralysis, and frustration: her strength comes from the impersonal objectivity with which she depicts unhappy characters. Ultimately she is an enduring writer, because the irony which is the mainstay of her technique is matched by penetrating insight into human thought and its effect on behaviour.

—A. Norman Jeffares

---

le CARRÉ, John. Pseudonym for David John Moore Cornwell. British. Born in Poole, Dorset, 19 October 1931. Educated at Sherborne School, Dorset; St. Andrew's Preparatory School; Berne University, Switzerland, 1948-49; Lincoln College, Oxford, B.A. (honours) in modern languages 1956. Married 1) Alison Ann Veronica Sharp in 1954 (divorced, 1971), three sons; 2) Valerie Jane Eustace in 1972, one son. Tutor at Eton College, 1956-58; Member of the British Foreign Service, 1959-64: Second Secretary, Bonn Embassy, 1961-64; Consul, Hamburg, 1963-64. Recipient: British Crime Novel Award, 1963; Maugham Award, 1964; Mystery Writers of America Edgar Allan Poe Award, 1965; Crime Writers Association Golden Dagger, 1978; Black Memorial Award, 1978. Agent: John Farquharson Ltd., 8 Bell Yard, London WC2A 2JU, England.

PUBLICATIONS

Novels

Call for the Dead. London, Gollancz, 1961; New York, Walker, 1962; as *The Deadly Affair*, London, Penguin, 1966.
A Murder of Quality. London, Gollancz, 1962; New York, Walker, 1963.
The Spy Who Came In from the Cold. London, Gollancz, 1963; New York, Coward McCann, 1964.
The Looking-Glass War. London, Heinemann, and New York, Coward McCann, 1965.
A Small Town in Germany. London, Heinemann, and New York, Coward McCann, 1968.
The Naive and Sentimental Lover. London, Hodder and Stoughton, 1971; New York, Knopf, 1972.
Tinker, Tailor, Soldier, Spy. London, Hodder and Stoughton, and New York, Knopf, 1974.
The Honourable Schoolboy. London, Hodder and Stoughton, and New York, Knopf, 1977.
Smiley's People. London, Hodder and Stoughton, and New York, Knopf, 1980.

Uncollected Short Stories

"Dare I Weep, Dare I Mourn," in *Saturday Evening Post* (Philadelphia), 28 January 1967.
"What Ritual Is Being Observed Tonight?," in *Saturday Evening Post* (Philadelphia), 2 November 1968.

* * *

Though John le Carré had written two thrillers, *Call for the Dead* and *A Murder of Quality*, it was when *The Spy Who Came In from the Cold* was published that it became obvious that a new talent for writing a different kind of spy story had emerged. Le Carré caught a new mood of chilling horror in this picture of the beastliness underlying the espionage of the cold war, for this is a novel which shows how man's capacity for inhumanity to man and woman is heightened through the process of espionage. The style matches the material. The moods evoked are of grey despair. The tone is cold, almost clinical. The conversations convince; they have the authentic texture of contemporary speech. And the details of the British, Dutch, and German background are painted in with a casual assurance. The story is unfolded, given fresh twists, until the reality of life itself becomes warped. Leamas, the British agent, is created convincingly; he carries out his role of defector only to find that his own people have framed him, in order to frame Fiedler, an East German who has discovered the truth about Mundt, his chief.

This is a world of intellectual skills applied arbitrarily, of brilliance without scruple, of brutality without restraint. The inexorable march of the story continues: its destiny is disaster, the same kind of disaster which opens its account of the effects of treason and betrayal. And yet in the final moment Leamas returns for Liz, the English communist party member who befriended him in London, who has been brought to East Germany to testify against him. Before their final moments, before they attempt to cross the Berlin wall, he makes his apology to her. To him it seems the world has gone mad. His life and hers, their dignity, are a tiny price to pay. They are, ultimately, the victims of a temporary alliance of expediency. His people save Mundt because they need him, "so that," he says to her, "the great moronic mass that you admire can sleep soundly in their beds at night. They need him for the safety of ordinary crummy people like you and me." He sees the loss of Fiedler's life as part of the small-scale war which is being waged, with a wastage of innocent life sometimes, though it is still smaller than other wars. Leamas doesn't believe in anything, but he sees people cheated, misled, lives thrown away, "people shot and in prison, whole groups and classes of men written off for nothing." Her party, he remarks, was built on the bodies of ordinary people, and she remembers the German prison wardress describing the prison as one for those who slow down the march, "for those who think they have the right to err."

Le Carré's next book, *The Looking-Glass War*, carries his exploration of the work of intelligence services further. This story opens impressively, with the death of a courier who has gone to Finland to pick up films made by the pilot of a commerical flight apparently off course over Eastern Germany. An unconfirmed report indicates the likelihood of a rocket site there. Then a small intelligence unit is authorized to put an agent into the area. The preparations are described in detail: the recruiting and training of the agent, the ineptitude involved, and the rivalry among the different agencies—and ultimately the schooled indifference with which the older professionals see their scheme fail abysmally. They are already planning the future, disowning the agent whose slow broadcasting on single frequencies on an obsolete radio has doomed him to capture. The story is well told; it explores the stresses and the vanities, the dangerous risks, even delusions, which beset the world of intelligence; it has a curious pathos, accentuated by the naivety and decency of the young man Avery which is opposed in fury by Haldane, who has become a technician: "We sent him because we needed to; we abandon him because we must."

In *A Small Town in Germany* there is an enlarging of scope. Here is a story of the British Embassy in Bonn, from which secret files—and Leo Harting—have vanished. Turner comes from London to investigate. His interrogations of some of the Embassy staff are brilliant. The pattern of thieving, of treachery, of insinuation, of making himself indispensable, of using others, emerges slowly as Turner tries to build up his picture of Leo Harting. The contrasts of personalities as Turner painstakingly pursues his enquiries give this picture depth, and yet the nature of the vanished man remains elusive. The complications of the British negotiations in Brussels where German support is necessary, the student riots, and the ugly neo-nazism give the man-hunt an extreme urgency. The attitude of the German authorities, and that of the Head of Chancery, surprise Turner. And the events he unravels surprise the reader.

The novel has a continuous tension; the discoveries of the investigator are cumulative; and finally his aggressive desire to hunt out the missing man turns to a sympathetic understanding of just what Harting has been doing. At this point his attitude differs markedly from that of the Head of Chancery. To a certain extent his reactions are parallel to those of Avery in *The Looking-Glass War*. Both are younger men, outside the orthodoxies of their elders, possessed ultimately of more humanity, though they have no capacity to influence the final stages of the story. The difference lies between the character who professes to control the processes of his own mind and the character who believes we are born free, we are not automatons and cannot control the processes of our minds. The novel is, in fact, about the problems of forgetting, and about the problems of idealism, innocence, and practical politics; and the incidental picture it gives of the complex working life of an Embassy provides a very suitable background against which political issues can be spotlit.

The Naive and Sentimental Lover lacks the punch and energy of his earlier works. In them the tendency of the characters to be warped, maimed, frustrated men and women mattered little because the action backed by skilful description carried the plot forward at such headlong speed that analysis of character *per se* was less important than the actions taken by the participants. In this novel there is a need for a deeper analysis of character, and this does not seem to have been fully achieved, while the story does not move with the same sureness. However, it is likely that le Carré was experimenting with a new genre, and just as *The Spy Who Came In from the Cold* needed preliminary studies this may herald a development in character depiction similar to his earlier advances in technique and architectonic power in *The Spy Who Came In from the Cold*, which will remain as a chilling exposé of the continuous underground battle of intelligence services.

Tinker, Tailor, Soldier, Spy and *The Honourable Schoolboy* are both surpassed by *Smiley's People*, the narrative art of which is combined with a sympathetic compassion for its characters. Here le Carré shows Smiley torn by loyalties, uncovering instead of covering up the murder of an ex-agent, and in the process peeling layer after layer from the mystery of betrayal, getting steadily closer to his old enemy the Russian Karla. The story moves deliberately, the details are amassed, but the tension is maintained right to the climax. This is a tour de force because its present action demands an understanding of the past, and that past is revealed so skilfully that its actions live as a pressing part of the present. The reader is involved in the characters' memories, their evasions and searchings.

—A. Norman Jeffares

LEE, John A(lexander). New Zealander. Born in Dunedin, 31 October 1891. Educated in local schools. Served as a sergeant in the New Zealand Expeditionary Forces in World War I, 1915-18: lost an arm in combat; Distinguished Conduct Medal. Married Marie E. Guy in 1919 (died); three children. Farm and factory worker until 1909; joined the New Zealand Public Works Department, 1910; Labour Member of Parliament for Auckland East, 1922-28, and for Grey Lynn, 1931-43: Under-Secretary to the Minister of Finance, 1936-39; Comptroller of the State Housing Department, 1939-40; expelled from the Labour Party, 1940; Director, Printing Service Ltd., and Democratic Property Ltd., Auckland, 1940-46; Managing Director, Vital Books Ltd., Auckland, from 1950. President, Auckland Rugby League, 1935-40; Member of the Council, New Zealand Booksellers Association, 1959-61; Honorary President, New Zealand Branch, P.E.N., 1969. Recipient: Book Publishers Association Award, 1978; LL.D.: University of Otago, Dunedin, 1965. Address: Box 8601, Symonds Street, Auckland, New Zealand.

PUBLICATIONS

Novels

Children of the Poor (published anonymously). New York, Vanguard Press, 1934; as John A. Lee, London, Laurie, 1934.
The Hunted. London, Laurie, 1936.
Civilian into Soldier. London, Laurie, 1937.
The Yanks Are Coming. London, Laurie, 1943.
Shiner Slattery. Auckland, Collins, 1964.
Mussolini's Millions. London, Baker, 1970.
Soldier. Wellington, Reed, 1976.

Short Stories

Shining with the Shiner. Hamilton, New Zealand, Mead, 1944; London, Henry, 1950.

Other

Four Years from Failure: A History of the Smash-and-Grab Government. Wellington, New Zealand Labour Party, 1935.
Labour and Prosperity. Auckland, Worker Printery, 1935.
Labour Has a Plan. Wellington, Labour Bookroom, 1935.
Returned Soldiers—Vote Labour, with W.E. Barnard and W.J. Jordan. Wellington, New Zealand Worker, 1935.
Banking and the New Zealand Labour Government. Privately printed, 1937.
Money Power for the People. Auckland, Grey Lynn Branch of the New Zealand Labour Party, 1937.
Socialism in New Zealand. London, Laurie, 1938.
A Letter Which Every New Zealander Should Read (the "Lee Letter"). Auckland, Parker, 1939.
Debt-Hold, Leasehold, Bankhold, or Prosperityhold. Privately printed, 1940.
The Democratic Labour Party in Business and the Home. Wellington, Earle, 1940.
Expelled from the Labour Party for Telling the Truth. Auckland, Grey Lynn Democratic Labour Party, 1940.
Hitler. Privately printed, 1940.
I Fight for New Zealand. Privately printed, 1940.
Mussolini, Apostle of Violence. Privately printed, 1940.
This Debt Slavery, with Harry Atmore. Privately printed, 1940.
Manufacture or Perish. Auckland, Service Printery, 1941.
Resist Peace-Time Conscription, with Jock Barnes. Wellington, Universal, 1949.
Simple on a Soap-Box (autobiography). Auckland, Collins, 1963; London, Collins, 1964.
Rhetoric at the Red Dawn. Auckland, Collins, 1965.
The Lee Way of Speech Training. London, Collins, 1965; as *The Lee Way to Public Speaking*, Auckland, Collins, 1965.
Delinquent Days (autobiography). Auckland, Collins, 1967.
Political Notebook. Wellington, Taylor, 1973.
For Mine Is the Kingdom. Martinborough, New Zealand, Taylor, 1975.
The Scrim-Lee Papers: C.G. Scrimgeour and John A. Lee Remember the Crisis Years 1930-1940, edited by Tony Simpson. Wellington, Reed, 1976.
Roughnecks, Rolling Stones, Rouseabouts, With an Anthology of Early Swagger Literature. Christchurch, Whitcoulls, 1977.
Early Days in New Zealand. Martinborough, New Zealand, Taylor, 1977.

*

Manuscript Collection: Auckland Library.

Critical Study: *John A. Lee* by Erik Olssen, Dunedin, University of Otago Press, 1977.

* * *

In his novels and short stories, John A. Lee has always been less concerned with impeccable craftsmanship and the artistic conscience than with vigorous communication and the social conscience. He has been a maverick among creative writers who have built reputations on imaginative work and sought to free themselves from autobiographical dependence. Without apology he has walked unwaveringly on his own shadow, knowing full well that his own stormy career has been an inalienable part of the social and political history of New Zealand. He has always refused to observe a becoming reticence about his personal background or about those with whom he has had dealings in his wandering days and political life. He has been a child of the poor, familiar with back streets and sordid tenements. He has been a delinquent boy pursued by the police. He has been an itinerant worker and a war-hero, a parliamentarian and a propagandist; and he has worn his past as well as his present as a badge of honour, transmuting both into fiction and memoir.

His first novel, praised by Bernard Shaw and Upton Sinclair, and based on his childhood, was regarded as an outrageous challenge to the refinements of respectability. No one, it was maintained, should rattle the skeletons in his cupboard with such energy. His book was dedicated provocatively but with passionate earnestness to "Daughters of the poor. To errant brats and guttersnipes. To eaters of left-overs, the wearers of cast-offs. To slaves of the wash-tubs and scrub-brush, whose children, nevertheless, go to hell...." *Children of the Poor* may not be autobiography in every page and scene, but an abrasive memory is present throughout. It is told as the personal reminiscences of Albany Porcello struggling to survive in a Dunedin slum where his sister is forced into prostitution, but the voice is that of John A. Lee, and the anger, the bitter commentary, the stress on the social implications of the narrative belong equally to Albany and to the author. Despite the artlessness of the writing, despite the absence of any attempt to achieve formal perfection, Lee's ebullience and dramatic sense, his sympathetic understanding of what it means to be a social outcast, his power to identify himself with character and scene, so pervade his writing that the reader shares the intensity of experience with which the book was written.

Albany Porcello is also the central figure in *The Hunted*, a sequel to the earlier book, but, although third-person narration replaces the reminiscent mode, Lee's own period of detention in a borstal, of escape, pursuit, and capture provide the substantial material of which it is composed. *The Hunted*, described as a novel, was followed 30 years later by *Delinquent Days*, described as an autobiography, so that once again readers of Lee's books find difficulty in determining when and how the recording memory is transformed or modified by the creative imagination. Nevertheless, because the novel is more tightly constructed, and because its theme has such dramatic possibilities of which Lee took full advantage, it has proved more acceptable than *Children of the Poor* to those with a more formal approach to literature.

Both these novels appeared when Lee had become a Labour member of parliament and was already Under-Secretary to the Minister of Finance. *Civilian into Soldier*, although probably written earlier, appeared when he was Comptroller of the State Housing Department. It covered the years of World War I and, in particular, the seamier sides of military life, but cannot bear comparison with most other novels about the same period. Not until after Lee had been expelled from the Labour Party and had lost his seat in parliament did he return to reminiscences of former days. *Shining with the Shiner*, a series of short stories or sketches, told with zest, centres on the disreputable but remarkable character of another social outcast, a rebel and "professional" swagman, and indirectly recalls the days when Lee was carrying his swag up and down New Zealand. Twenty years later the novel, *Shiner Slattery*, supplemented the short stories and was published almost simultaneously with *Simple on a Soap-Box*. If one turns from this autobiographical work, or from *Rhetoric at the Red Dawn* and *Delinquent Days*, both of which appeared later, to the books that are described as novels, the boundaries between fiction, memoir, and autobiography begin to fade. What remains, and it is an impressive remainder, is the flamboyant personality of John A. Lee, an actor in every sense of the word, who has first acted out his fiction and then dramatised his life with a purposefulness and a forthrightness that cannot be dismissed or ignored as mere flamboyance.

—H. Winston Rhodes

LE GUIN, Ursula K(roeber). American. Born in Berkeley, California, 21 October 1929. Educated at Radcliffe College, Cambridge, Massachusetts, A.B. 1951 (Phi Beta Kappa); Columbia University, New York (Faculty Fellow; Fulbright Fellow, 1953), M.A. 1952. Married Charles A. Le Guin in 1953; two daughters and one son. Instructor in French, Mercer University, Macon, Georgia, 1954, and University of Idaho, Moscow, 1956; former department secretary, Emory University, Atlanta; has taught writing workshops at Pacific University, Forest Grove, Oregon, 1971, University of Washington, Seattle, 1971-73, Portland State University, Oregon, 1974, 1977, 1979, in Melbourne, Australia, 1975, and at the University of Reading, England, 1976. Recipient: *Boston Globe-Horn Book* Award, for children's book, 1969; Nebula Award, 1969, 1974 (twice); Hugo Award, 1970, 1973, 1974, 1975; National Book Award, for children's book, 1972; Jupiter Award, 1974 (twice); Gandalf Life Award, 1979. Guest of Honor, World Science Fiction Convention, 1975. D.Litt.: Bucknell University, Lewisburg, Pennsylvania, 1978; honorary degree: Lawrence University, Appleton, Wisconsin. Lives in Portland, Oregon. Agent: Virginia Kidd, Box 278, Milford, Pennsylvania 18337, U.S.A.

PUBLICATIONS

Novels

Rocannon's World. New York, Ace, 1966; London, Tandem, 1972.
Planet of Exile. New York, Ace, 1966; London, Tandem, 1972.
City of Illusions. New York, Ace, 1967; London, Gollancz, 1971.
The Left Hand of Darkness. New York, Walker, and London, Macdonald, 1969.
The Lathe of Heaven. New York, Scribner, 1971; London, Gollancz, 1972.
The Dispossessed: An Ambiguous Utopia. New York, Harper, and London, Gollancz, 1974.
The Word for World Is Forest. New York, Putnam, 1976; London, Gollancz, 1977.
Malafrena. New York, Putnam, 1979; London, Gollancz, 1980.
The Beginning Place. New York, Harper, 1980; as *Threshold*, London, Gollancz, 1980.

Short Stories

The Wind's Twelve Quarters. New York, Harper, 1975; London, Gollancz, 1976.
Orsinian Tales. New York, Harper, 1976; London, Gollancz, 1977.
The Eye of the Heron and Other Stories. London, Panther, 1980.

Play

No Use to Talk to Me, in *The Altered Eye*, edited by Lee Harding. Melbourne, Norstrilia Press, 1976; New York, Berkley, 1980.

Verse

Wild Angels. Santa Barbara, California, Capra Press, 1975.
Hard Words and Other Poems. New York, Harper, 1981.

Other (juvenile)

A Wizard of Earthsea. Berkeley, California, Parnassus Press, 1967; London, Gollancz, 1971.
The Tombs of Atuan. New York, Atheneum, 1971; London, Gollancz, 1972.
The Farthest Shore. New York, Atheneum, 1972; London, Gollancz, 1973.
Very Far Away from Anywhere Else. New York, Atheneum, 1976; as *A Very Long Way from Anywhere Else*, London, Gollancz, 1976.
Leese Webster. New York, Atheneum, 1979; London, Gollancz, 1981.

Other

From Elfland to Poughkeepsie (lecture). Portland, Pendragon Press, 1973.
Dreams Must Explain Themselves. New York, Algol Press, 1975.
The Water Is Wide. Portland, Pendragon Press, 1976.
The Language of the Night: Essays on Fantasy and Science Fiction, edited by Susan Wood. New York, Putnam, 1979.

Editor, *Nebula Award Stories 11.* London, Gollancz, 1976; New York, Harper, 1977.
Editor, with Virginia Kidd, *Interfaces.* New York, Ace, 1980.
Editor, with Virginia Kidd, *Edges.* New York, Pocket Books, 1980.

*

Bibliography: by Jeffrey Levin, in *The Language of the Night*, 1979.

Critical Studies: "Wholeness and Balance" by Douglas Barbour, in *Science-Fiction Studies* (Terre Haute, Indiana), Spring 1974; "The Good Witch of the West" by Robert Scholes, in *Hollins Critic* (Hollins College, Virginia), April 1974; *The Farthest Shores of Ursula K. Le Guin* by George Edgar Slusser, San Bernardino, California, Borgo Press, 1976; *Ursula Le Guin* by Joseph D. Olander and Martin H. Greenberg, New York, Taplinger, and Edinburgh, Harris, 1979; *Ursula K. Le Guin: Voyager to Inner Lands and to Outer Space* edited by Joseph W. De Bolt, Port Washington, New York, Kennikat Press, 1979; *Ursula K. Le Guin* by Barbara J. Bucknall, New York, Ungar, 1981.

* * *

Ursula K. Le Guin's earliest works attracted, almost exclusively, the devoted audience of science-fiction readers. *Rocannon's World*, *Planet of Exile*, and *City of Illusions* are interconnected novels which depict a situation entirely familiar to such readers. Earth and other planets of a far-future "League of All Worlds" are peopled by "human" races which must struggle to recognize one another as such. The League prepares to meet a rather vaguely defined invasion from afar. Heroes out of touch with lost civilization undertake quests of self-discovery, or get the enemy's location through to headquarters just in time to repel the invasion. In short, Le Guin offers us space opera, although the delicate tone, the theme of communication, and the imagery of light and darkness suggest her future development.

With *The Left Hand of Darkness*, "The Word for World Is Forest," her "Earthsea" fantasy trilogy, and *The Dispossessed*, Le Guin has moved to another level, and has begun, deservedly, to attract an audience outside the science-fiction ghetto. The treatment of Androgyny in *The Left Hand of Darkness* has made the book into a minor classic. The League of All Worlds has been succeeded by a non-imperialistic "Ekumen," which sends a lone envoy, Genly Ai, to make an alliance with the isolated planet Winter (Gethen). The Ekumen has no wish to subdue Winter but to extend "the evolutionary tendency inherent in Being; one manifestation of which is exploration." Subverting the stock situation of civilization brought to the savages, Le Guin has Ai learn at least as much from the relatively primitive Gethenians as they from him. Gethenians mate only once a month, and they may adopt alternately male and female roles. We hear at one point that "the King is pregnant." Ai, a male chauvinist, learns how difficult it is to think of our fellow humans as people rather than as men and women. When he forms an alliance with a Gethenian called Estraven, Ai learns how close together the words "patriot" and "traitor" can be. Ai's loyalty begins to shift from the Ekumen to Gethen, but this shift is a precondition of his mission's success. Conversely, Estraven's loyalty shifts to Ai, but only because he loves his country well enough to want Ai to succeed.

Although Ai and Estraven grow closer to one another, a vast distance also remains between them. Humans are alienated from one another in a wintry universe. But hope springs from the melancholy. The universe is dark but young, and spring will follow winter. The book reverberates with a nontheistic prayer: "Praise then darkness and Creation unfinished."

Although they meet as equal individuals, Ai and Estraven are members of differing societies. Le Guin would insist on Aristotle's definition of people as social animals. In her ambivalent utopia *The Dispossessed*, Le Guin preserves this insistence—while making it equally clear that anarchism is one of her centers of value. The book is an important break in science fiction's anti-utopian trend. A scientist, Shevek, moves to and fro between an anarchist utopia which is becoming middle-aged, and a world—obviously analogous to our own—that is divided between propertarian (capitalist) and statist (communist) countries. Nowhere does he find full self-expression; conversely, full self-expression requires one's participation in a society. In alternating chapters which disrupt sequential chronology, Shevek moves both away from the anarchist utopia and back toward it. Le Guin identifies herself both as a stylistic artist and as a thinker. Her stark, wintry worlds are philosophically rich with dialectic Taoism and the co-reality of such opposites as light and darkness, religion and politics, and language and power. In *A Wizard of Earthsea* the magician has power over things when he knows their true names, so that his power is the artist's power. Le Guin plays with the notion, in "The Author of the Acacia Seeds and Other Extracts from *The Journal of the Association of Therolinguistics*," that ants, penguins, and even plants might be producing what could be called language and art.

Since writing *The Dispossessed*, Le Guin has been turning in the direction of fantasy. *Malafrena* is a compelling mixture of fantasy and historical fiction. Le Guin sets the imaginary country of Orsinia into central Europe in the 19th century. It is Itale Sorde's story: he rejects the ease of an inherited landed estate (Malafrena) to work for revolution against Orsinia's domination by the Austrian Empire. After being jailed for several years and after a failed insurrection in 1830, he returns to Malafrena, but there are hints that will leave again. True voyage is return, and structure and theme coalesce, as in *The Dispossessed*.

In her recent works Le Guin often presents us with the ambiguity of revolution, once again the theme of a long short story, "The Eye of the Heron." A colony of young counter-culturalists attempt to break away from their elders, with typically ambiguous results. A central paradox in Le Guin's fiction is her simultaneous recognition of the need for harmony and the need for revolt.

Praise for Le Guin has been high—too uniformly high. Her style is unexceptional and her desire for peace and harmony borders on sentimentality at times. But she has taken important steps toward blending politics and art in her novels, and she is still experimenting with both form and content.

—Curtis C. Smith

LEHMANN, Rosamond (Nina). British. Born in Bourne End, Buckinghamshire, 3 February 1901; sister of the writer John Lehmann and the actress Beatrix Lehmann. Educated at Girton College, Cambridge (scholar). Married 1) Leslie Runciman (marriage dissolved); 2) the Honorable Wogan Philipps, later Lord Milford, in 1928 (marriage dissolved), one daughter (deceased) and one son. Co-Director, John Lehmann Ltd. Past President, P.E.N. English Centre, and International Vice-President, International P.E.N.; Member of the Council, Society of Authors. Commandeur dans l'Ordre des Arts et Lettres. Address: 70 Eaton Square, London S.W.1, England.

PUBLICATIONS

Novels

Dusty Answer. London, Chatto and Windus, and New York, Holt, 1927.
A Note in Music. London, Chatto and Windus, and New York, Holt, 1930.
Invitation to the Waltz. London, Chatto and Windus, and New York, Holt, 1932.
The Weather in the Streets. London, Collins, and New York, Reynal, 1936.
The Ballad and the Source. London, Collins, 1944; New York, Reynal, 1945.
The Echoing Grove. London, Collins, and New York, Harcourt Brace, 1953.
The Sea-Grape Tree. London, Collins, 1976; New York, Harcourt Brace, 1977.

Short Stories

The Gipsy's Baby and Other Stories. London, Collins, 1946; New York, Reynal, 1947.

Play

No More Music (produced London, 1938). London, Collins, 1939.

Other

A Letter to a Sister. London, Hogarth Press, 1931; New York, Harcourt Brace, 1932.
A Man Seen Afar, with W. Tudor Pole. London, Spearman, 1965.
The Swan in the Evening: Fragments of an Inner Life. London, Collins, 1967; New York, Harcourt Brace, 1968.
Letters from Our Daughters, with Cynthia Hill Sandys. London, College of Psychic Studies, 2 vols., 1972.

Editor, with others, *Orion: A Miscellany 1-3.* London, Nicholson and Watson, 3 vols., 1945-46.
Editor, with Cynthia Hill Sandys, *The Awakening Letters.* London, Spearman, 1978.

Translator, *Geneviève*, by Jacques Lemarchand. London, Lehmann, 1947.
Translator, *Children of the Game*, by Jean Cocteau. London, Harvill Press, 1955; as *The Holy Terrors*, New York, New Directions, 1957.

*

Bibliography: "Rosamond Lehmann: A Bibliography" by M.T. Gustafson, in *Twentieth Century Literature 4* (Hempstead, New York), 1959.

Manuscript Collection: University of Texas, Austin.

Critical Study: *Rosamond Lehmann* by Diana E. Le Stourgeon, New York, Twayne, 1965.

* * *

Rosamond Lehmann's distinctive gift as a novelist lies in her sympathetically realistic depiction of the intimate psychology of young girls. This won her instant critical recognition in her first novel, *Dusty Answer*, a portrayal of childhood and adolescence, set partly in Cambridge, which anticipates several of her favourite later themes. *Invitation to the Waltz* explores, with a delicacy of perception reminiscent of Elizabeth Bowen's *The Death of the Heart*, a girl's growth in insight and understanding—during a single evening, that of her first dance—of the hitherto unintelligible and intimidating adult world. Eighteen-year-old Olivia, gauche, naive, and pitifully over-exposed to the chill of unconscious or imagined snubs which cause her "to bleed in her self-esteem," is shown gradually turning her gaze outward from the adolescent agonies of self to participate in the problems and perplexities of others. In this process of quickening comprehension, she achieves a new confidence and readiness for the future adventures of living related in the book's sequel, *The Weather in the Streets*. Here experience has replaced innocence, but beneath superficial sophistication the old, painful vulnerability remains. Ten years later *The Ballad and the Source* was also presented through the awakening consciousness of a girl, fascinated by the personality of a dominating old woman whose story powerfully compels her imagination. The characters of girls likewise play an important part in the collection of short stories entitled *The Gipsy's Baby*.

The complex narrative structure of *The Ballad and the Source*, as the listening child comments and questions, sometimes only half understanding what she hears, is handled with a Jamesian subtlety of technique. So, too, is the unfolding of relationships in *The Echoing Grove*, Lehmann's most intricately constructed, accomplished, and perhaps most satisfying novel, which skilfully interweaves the experience of three characters helplessly embroiled in a mutually tormenting passion. The conflict of emotions suffered by two sisters, divided yet finally united by their love for the same man—a character whose charm and weakness are presented with relentless feminine penetration—evoked the tribute from Marghanita Laski that "no English writer has told of the pains of women in love more truly or movingly...of what it felt like to be a woman." It is probably this novel, more than any other, which reveals a strong affinity between Lehmann's deliberately wrought prose and finely attuned sensibility and those of Virginia Woolf.

But *The Echoing Grove* is not only a tale of personal exaltations and miseries: it is also a vivid portrait of the era immediately preceding and during the last war. The restless turbulence of private lives, chronicled with such intensity and compassion, is mirrored and echoed in the upheavals of the social and political scene. The characters are firmly established as recognizable products of their generation, class, and background; and the disintegration of the old order and of the stability of its values is acutely anatomized through the musings of the Marxist daughter, Dinah, on "the contemporary situation, the crack-up." Lehmann has, in fact, a keen eye for the detail of a period, particularly in the life of the upper middle classes. *The Ballad and the Source* communicates an indefinable sense of "a defeat somewhere, a failure of the vital impulse" undermining comfortable patrician security in the years leading into the First World War. *Invitation to the Waltz* recreates with nostalgic precision the atmosphere—old family servants, the rituals of nursery tea, "finishing" in Paris, and country-house balls—of a safe and sheltered childhood between the wars. The self-consciously cynical stance of the older, bohemian Olivia of *The Weather in the Streets* conveys something of the disenchanted climate of living—adultery, back-street abortion, divorce—among the fashionable young during the mid-1930's.

For all the accuracy of her social observation, however, it is finally as a delineator of the inner world of feeling, and in her subtle investigation of the nuances of personal relationship, that Rosamond Lehmann excels, and for which she will be remembered.

—Margaret Willy

LEIBER, Fritz (Reuter, Jr.). Born in Chicago, Illinois, 25 December 1910. Educated at the University of Chicago, Ph.B. 1932; Episcopal General Theological Seminary, Washington, D.C. Married Jonquil Stephens in 1936 (died, 1969); one son. Episcopal minister at two churches in New Jersey, 1932-33; actor, 1934-36; Editor, Consolidated Book Publishers, Chicago, 1937-41; Instructor in Speech and Drama, Occidental College, Los Angeles, 1941-42; precision inspector, Douglas Aircraft, Santa Monica, California, 1942-44; Associate Editor, *Science Digest*, Chicago, 1944-56. Lecturer, Clarion State College, Pennsylvania, summers 1968-70. Recipient: Hugo Award, 1958, 1965, 1968, 1970, 1971, 1976; Nebula Award, 1967, 1970, 1975; Ann Radcliffe Award, 1970; Gandalf Award, 1975; World Fantasy Award, 1976, 1978. Guest of Honor, World Science Fiction Convention, 1951. Address: 565 Geary Street, Apartment 604, San Francisco, California 94102, U.S.A.

PUBLICATIONS

Novels

Gather, Darkness! New York, Pellegrini and Cudahy, 1950; London, New English Library, 1966.
Conjure Wife. New York, Twayne, 1953; London, Penguin, 1969.
The Sinful Ones. New York, Universal, 1953; as *You're All Alone*, New York, Ace, 1972.
The Green Millennium. New York, Abelard Press, 1953; London, Abelard Schuman, 1960.
Destiny Times Three. New York, Galaxy, 1957.
The Big Time (includes stories). New York, Ace, 1961; published separately, London, New English Library, 1965.
The Silver Eggheads. New York, Ballantine, 1961; London, New English Library, 1966.
The Wanderer. New York, Ballantine, 1964; London, Dobson, 1967.
Tarzan and the Valley of Gold. New York, Ballantine, 1966.
The Swords of Lankhmar. New York, Ace, 1968; London, Hart Davis, 1969.
A Specter Is Haunting Texas. New York, Walker, and London, Gollancz, 1969.
Swords and Deviltry. New York, Ace, 1970; London, New English Library, 1971.
Our Lady of Darkness. New York, Berkley, 1977; London, Millington, 1978.

Short Stories

Night's Black Agents. Sauk City, Wisconsin, Arkham House, 1947; London, Spearman, 1975.
The Girl with the Hungry Eyes and Other Stories. New York, Avon, 1949.
Two Sought Adventure: Exploits of Fafhrd and the Gray Mouser. New York, Gnome Press, 1957.
Shadows with Eyes. New York, Ballantine, 1962.
A Pail of Air. New York, Ballantine, 1964.
Ships to the Stars. New York, Ace, 1964.
The Night of the Wolf. New York, Ballantine, 1966; London, Sphere, 1976.
The Secret Songs. London, Hart Davis, 1968.
Swords Against Wizardry. New York, Ace, 1968; London, Prior, 1977.
Swords in the Mist. New York, Ace, 1968; London, Prior, 1977.
Night Monsters. New York, Ace, 1969; revised edition, London, Gollancz, 1974.
Swords Against Death. New York, Ace, 1970; London, New English Library, 1972.
The Best of Fritz Leiber, edited by Angus Wells. London, Sidgwick and Jackson, and New York, Ballantine, 1974.
The Book of Fritz Leiber. New York, DAW, 1974.
The Second Book of Fritz Leiber. New York, DAW, 1975.
The Worlds of Fritz Leiber. New York, Ace, 1976.

Swords and Ice Magic. New York, Ace, and London, Prior, 1977.
Rime Isle. Browns Mills, New Jersey, Whispers Press, 1977.
Bazaar of the Bizarre. West Kingston, Rhode Island, Grant, 1978.
Heroes and Horrors. Browns Mills, New Jersey, Whispers Press, 1978.
The Change War. Boston, Gregg Press, 1978.
Ship of Shadows. London, Gollancz, 1979.

Verse

The Demons of the Upper Air. Glendale, California, Squires, 1969.
Sonnets to Jonquil and All. Glendale, California, Squires, 1978.

Other

Editor, with Stuart David Schiff, *The World Fantasy Awards 2.* New York, Doubleday, 1980.

*

Bibliography: *Fritz Leiber: A Bibliography 1934-1979* by Chris Morgan, Birmingham, Morgenstern, 1979.

* * *

Uncommonly elegant, rich in wit and ideas value, Fritz Leiber's fiction is unusual in its appeal to lovers of science fiction and fantasy alike. Arguably he is the field's finest stylist; certainly a man who has played every part. One can almost imagine the anguish of historians in years to come as they try to classify the unclassifiable: "Primarily a fantasy writer"; "no, a great satirist"; "far more concerned with serious social and technological extrapolation." For Fritz Leiber has done the lot, and done it superbly.

His very first sales in 1939 introduced Fafhrd the Barbarian and his cosmopolitan colleague the Gray Mouser, two of the most unusual swashbucklers ever to emerge from the realms of swordplay and sorcery. Over the years he has woven a tangled web of the adventures of these two fine rogues in the fabled land of Nehwon, and recently the author has put them into chronological order in the five books of the "Swords of Lankhmar" series.

Many readers seem to enjoy these stories while generally disliking most other heroic fantasies. Probably the reason is that Leiber never lets his heroes take themselves too seriously; the sardonic humour and writing skill are entirely above the level of usual epics of blood and gore or supernatural mystery.

This first active period from 1939-43 culminated in two novels, *Gather, Darkness!* and *Conjure Wife* (later filmed as *Burn, Witch, Burn!*), both juxtaposing the trappings of witchcraft against technological or contemporary settings to produce original and memorable results. Then came a dry spell, and Leiber did not return to science fiction until the early 1950's. His new work was mostly in a biting, satiric vein, almost more so than the market dared to handle in the age of McCarthyism. The novelette "Coming Attraction" is a frightening glimpse of a psychotic America, and the two stories "The Night He Cried" and "Poor Superman" are superb take-offs of Mickey Spillane and L. Ron Hubbard respectively. *The Green Millennium* is similarly outrageous but equally ingenious and soundly constructed.

Once again Leiber stopped writing, this time until 1958 when he made a triumphant return with *The Big Time*, one of the most unusual of all science-fiction novels and which won him his first Hugo Award. With this story something became apparent which had been there all along if anyone had looked for it; Leiber writes *plays* rather than stories, even in his fantasies. His works are scripts, acted out by characters in settings suited to a restricted theatrical stage (in *Big Time*, one room throughout). There are some superb lines, superbly delivered; one whole chunk of this particular novel is delivered by a girl of Bronze Age Crete in perfectly-scanning iambic pentameter.

Another novel, *The Silver Eggheads*, was not well received; in 1963 the author decided to try something different, and after a year of effort the result was *The Wanderer*, a long, incredible "catastrophe" novel which simultaneously does more things than can easily be recounted. It won a Hugo for 1965, and Fritz Leiber never looked back. He has at last been recognised as one of the truly major talents in science fiction, while publishers too have suddenly woken up and are issuing his stories in new form for the enjoyment of an entirely new generation of readers.

Perhaps the most revealing test of all is this. Science fiction nearly always dates very rapidly, and yet Leiber's earliest stories are in print alongside his most recent work, and they read as well as ever. His fiction has a timeless quality that will endure long after the arbitrary divisions between "literature" and "science fiction" have disappeared.

—Peter R. Weston

LELCHUK, Alan. American. Born in Brooklyn, New York, 15 September 1938. Educated at Brooklyn College, B.A. 1960; University College, London, 1962-63; Stanford University, California, M.A. 1963, Ph.D. in English 1965. Married Barbara Kreiger in 1979. Since 1966, Assistant Professor of English, and since 1975, Writer-in-Residence, Brandeis University, Waltham, Massachusetts. Associate Editor, *Modern Occasions* quarterly, Cambridge, Massachusetts, 1970-72. Guest, Mishkenot Sha'Ananim, Jerusalem, 1976-77. Recipient: Yaddo Foundation grant, 1968, 1971, 1973; MacDowell Colony Fellowship, 1969; Guggenheim Fellowship, 1976. Agent: Georges Borchardt, 136 East 57th Street, New York, New York 10022. Address: RFD 2, Canaan, New Hampshire 03741, U.S.A.

PUBLICATIONS

Novels

American Mischief. New York, Farrar Straus, and London, Cape, 1973.
Miriam at Thirty-Four. New York, Farrar Straus, 1974; London, Cape, 1975.
Shrinking: The Beginning of My Own Ending. Boston, Little Brown, 1978.

Uncollected Short Stories

"Sundays," in *Transatlantic Review 21* (London), Summer 1966.
"Of Our Time," in *New American Review 4*, edited by Theodore Solotaroff. New York, New American Library, 1968.
"Winter Image," in *Transatlantic Review 32* (London), Summer 1969.
"Cambridge Talk," in *Modern Occasions 1* (Cambridge, Massachusetts), Fall 1970.
"Hallie of the Sixties," in *Works in Progress 6* (New York), 1972.

Play

Screenplay: *Tippy*, with Jiri Weiss, 1978.

*

Manuscript Collection: Mugar Memorial Library, Boston University.

Critical Studies: by Philip Roth in *Esquire* (New York), September

1972; "Lelchuk's Inferno" by Wilfrid Sheed, in *Book-of-the-Month Club News* (New York), March 1973; "The Significant Self" by Benjamin DeMott, in *Atlantic Monthly* (Boston), October 1974.

Alan Lelchuk comments:

Some points about my fiction:

A realism of extreme sensibilities and modernism of content...the intensity and ambiguity of sensual moments...a blurring of the line between the comic and the serious...vibrating the odd strings of obsession...character through sexuality, and sexuality as (native) social gesture...a mingling of lofty thought and contemporary vulgarity...playing out the deep comic disorders of our culture...some unnerving fables and sweet myths of our time camouflaged by realistic garb and inhabited by real souls....

* * *

Alan Lelchuk's novels recreate that rich American intellectual life which synthesizes John Garfield with Bakunin. These cautionary tales dramatize the self-destructiveness inherent in political, artistic, and sexual revolt, the three frequently fused, as an academician (*American Mischief*), a woman photographer (*Miriam at Thirty-four*), and a novelist (*Shrinking*) painfully test the boundaries of contemporary experience. *American Mischief*, Lelchuk's version of *The Possessed*, explores 1960's campus upheaval through the contrapuntal voices of a radical student, Lenny Pincus ("Not the son of Harry and Rose Pincus of Brooklyn, but a boy with fathers like Reston and Cronkite, mothers such as Mary McCarthy and Diana Trilling"), and a liberal dean, Bernard Kovell ("a kind of Americanized version of Romanov-Quixote, a European Liberal-Idealist turned Massachusetts sensualist, tilting simultaneously at foolish theories and female bodies"). A wealth of political and literary theories and allusions threatens to overwhelm the novel, as the protagonists share both their private agonies and extensive bibliographies with the reader. But the novel impresses with its vivid style, ultimately sane perspective, and frequently brilliant imagination: the notorious episode detailing Norman Mailer's symbolically appropriate bloody end manages to outdo an already bizarre reality (Lelchuk often seems to be challenging such contemporaries as Mailer and Roth). Like Lelchuk's other novels, *American Mischief* attempts narrative complexity by telling its story through a variety of "documents": Lenny's preface; Kovell's journal focusing on his six mistresses; his lengthy speech during a campus uprising, interlarded with Lenny's comments; Lenny's "Gorilla Talk," his account of radical activities that occupies more than half the book. This attempt to heighten the dialectical tension between the two men fails because their voices sound so alike from the beginning that the fusion of their ideologies into a compassionate, ultimately victimized, humanity seems predictable.

Victimization goes even further in *Miriam at Thirty-four*. The heroine's sexual experimentation (three lovers with a variety of tastes) parallels her exploration of the Cambridge setting, which was "a male with secrets..., one whom she could arouse by uncovering different parts of his anatomy and photographing them." This obsession with exposing truth leads Miriam to take sexually revealing pictures of herself and exhibit them at a prestigious gallery to the sound of "early Dylan, trio sonatas (Tartini? Bach?), the Beatles." Miriam's final breakdown results from the uncomprehending responses of her audience: "they were cannibals who had just feasted on human flesh with no time yet for digestion. And the flesh was herself, Miriam." To provide multiple views of Miriam, Lelchuk supplements the narrative with her letters, and notebook ("her self-therapy kit, her doctor-between-covers, her book of reason, reflection, questions..."). Shorter and less ambitious than *American Mischief*, the novel conveys merely Miriam's pathos and leaves the sources of her disaster uncertain: a society that simultaneously seeks and savages the new, or the destructive urges that accompany Miriam's authentic artistry?

A similar uncertainty pervades *Shrinking*, which chronicles the breakdown of novelist/academician Lionel Solomon, victimized by both inner doubts and a hostile world epitomized by Tippy, a predatory young woman who humiliates him sexually, reveals his inadequacies in an *Esquire* exposé, and leads him on a strange journey into Hopi country. Elaborately narrated, *Shrinking* includes a foreword and afterword by Solomon's psychiatrist, letters from other characters, and the text of Tippy's article with Solomon's comments and marginalia. The article forces a comparison of Tippy's version with the "real" experience, a contrast that underscores the novel's obsession with truth: "what happens in life, when put into fiction, can sound 'in poor taste' and be near impossible to write about." This apologia and Lelchuk's witty parodies of foolish reviewers almost disarm criticism, but do not blind the reader to the catch-all quality of the book: essays on Hopi culture and Melville, however they reflect the workings of Solomon's mind, are too long for the effects they achieve, and Lelchuk's wit seems more forced, less outrageous than in *American Mischief*. Despite these weaknesses, *Shrinking*, like Lelchuk's other fiction, conveys a real voice that is often brilliant, often loquaciously irrelevant, and more often suggests an underlying despair that the writing can only imperfectly duplicate.

—Burton Kendle

LESSING, Doris (May). British. Born in Kermansha, Persia, 22 October 1919; moved with her family to Southern Rhodesia, 1924. Educated at Girls High School, Salisbury. Married 1) Frank Charles Wisdom in 1939 (divorced, 1943), one son and one daughter; 2) Gottfried Lessing in 1945 (divorced, 1949), one son. Lived in Southern Rhodesia, 1924-49, then settled in London. Recipient: Maugham Award, 1954; Médicis Prize, 1976. Associate Member, American Academy, 1974; Honorary Fellow, Modern Language Association (USA), 1974. Agent: Curtis Brown Ltd., 1 Craven Hill, London W2 3EP, England.

PUBLICATIONS

Novels

The Grass Is Singing. London, Joseph, and New York, Crowell, 1950.

Children of Violence:

- *Martha Quest.* London, Joseph, 1952.
- *A Proper Marriage.* London, Joseph, 1954; with *Martha Quest*, New York, Simon and Schuster, 1964.
- *A Ripple from the Storm.* London, Joseph, 1958.
- *Landlocked.* London, MacGibbon and Kee, 1965; with *A Ripple from the Storm*, New York, Simon and Schuster, 1966.
- *The Four-Gated City.* London, MacGibbon and Kee, and New York, Knopf, 1969.

Retreat to Innocence. London, Joseph, 1956.

The Golden Notebook. London, Joseph, and New York, Simon and Schuster, 1962.

Briefing for a Descent into Hell. London, Cape, and New York, Knopf, 1971.

The Summer Before the Dark. London, Cape, and New York, Knopf, 1973.

The Memoirs of a Survivor. London, Octagon Press, 1974; New York, Knopf, 1975.

Canopus in Argos: Archives:

- *Shikasta.* London, Cape, and New York, Knopf, 1979.
- *The Marriages Between Zones Three, Four, and Five.* London, Cape, and New York, Knopf, 1980.
- *The Sirian Experiments.* London, Cape, 1981.

Short Stories

This Was the Old Chief's Country. London, Joseph, 1951; New York, Crowell, 1952.
Five: Short Novels. London, Joseph, 1953.
No Witchcraft for Sale: Stories and Short Novels. Moscow, Foreign Languages Publishing House, 1956.
The Habit of Loving. London, MacGibbon and Kee, 1957; New York, Crowell, 1958.
A Man and Two Women. London, MacGibbon and Kee, and New York, Simon and Schuster, 1963.
African Stories. London, Joseph, 1964; New York, Simon and Schuster, 1965.
Winter in July. London, Panther, 1966.
The Black Madonna. London, Panther, 1966.
Nine African Stories. London, Longman, 1968.
The Story of a Non-Marrying Man and Other Stories. London, Cape, 1972; as *The Temptation of Jack Orkney and Other Stories*, New York, Knopf, 1972.
Collected African Stories:
1. *This Was the Old Chief's Country.* London, Joseph, 1973.
2. *The Sun Between Their Feet.* London, Joseph, 1973.

Collected Stories:
1. *To Room Nineteen.* London, Cape, 1978.
2. *The Temptation of Jack Orkney.* London, Cape, 1978.

Stories. New York, Knopf, 1978.

Plays

Before the Deluge (produced London, 1953).
Mr. Dolinger (produced Oxford, 1958).
Each His Own Wilderness (produced London, 1958). Published in *New English Dramatists*, London, Penguin, 1959.
The Truth about Billy Newton (produced Salisbury, Wiltshire, 1960).
Play with a Tiger (produced London, 1962; New York, 1964). London, Joseph, 1962.
The Storm, adaptation of a play by Alexander Ostrowsky (produced London, 1966).
The Singing Door, in *Second Playbill 2*, edited by Alan Durband. London, Hutchinson, 1973.

Television Plays: *The Grass Is Singing*, from her own novel, 1962; *Please Do Not Disturb*, 1966; *Care and Protection*, 1966; *Between Men*, 1967.

Verse

Fourteen Poems. Northwood, Middlesex, Scorpion Press, 1959.

Other

Going Home. London, Joseph, 1957.
In Pursuit of the English: A Documentary. London, MacGibbon and Kee, 1960; New York, Simon and Schuster, 1961.
Particularly Cats. London, Joseph, and New York, Simon and Schuster, 1967.
A Small Personal Voice: Essays, Reviews, Interviews, edited by Paul Schlueter. New York, Knopf, 1974.

*

Bibliography: *Doris Lessing: A Bibliography* by Catharina Ipp, Johannesburg, University of the Witwatersrand Department of Bibliography, 1967; *Doris Lessing: A Checklist of Primary and Secondary Sources* by Selma R. Burkom and Margaret Williams, Troy, New York, Whitston, 1973; *Doris Lessing: An Annotated Bibliography of Criticism* by Dee Seligman, Westport, Connecticut, Greenwood Press, 1981.

Critical Studies (selection): *Doris Lessing* by Dorothy Brewster, New York, Twayne, 1965; *The Novels of Doris Lessing* by Paul Schlueter, Carbondale, Southern Illinois University Press, 1973; *Doris Lessing*, London, Longman, 1973, and *Doris Lessing's Africa*, London, Evans, 1978, both by Michael Thorpe; *Doris Lessing: Critical Studies* edited by Annis Pratt and L.S. Dembo, Madison, University of Wisconsin Press, 1974; *The City and the Veld: The Fiction of Doris Lessing* by Mary Ann Singleton, Lewisburg, Pennsylvania, Bucknell University Press, 1976; *The Novelistic Vision of Doris Lessing: Breaking the Forms of Consciousness* by Roberta Rubenstein, Urbana, University of Illinois Press, 1979.

* * *

Doris Lessing is one of the most impressive women authors writing today; she is also one of the most unpredictable. Over the past 20 years, she has published more than 20 books. Some are over-written; many express, a little too insistently, a rather thin, and naive, political philosophy. I suspect this is even more true in her most recent books, *Shikasta* and *The Marriages Between Zones Three, Four, and Five*, in which the higher truth grasped by the Chronicler of the latter book is that "everyone of us anywhere is what we think and imagine. No more and no less": and that we are all part of a whole, a "we," not an "I." Nonetheless, if some of the ideas are simplistic, Lessing often makes them tantalizing in her fictional contexts. Her books have always articulated her ideas, whether they be about women's orgasms, Armageddon, or utopia. More often than one would expect from so prolific a writer, she is sufficiently imaginative to integrate smoothly her ideas into her narrative. Even more to her credit is that her writing is continually evolving and is unusual in its breadth. Her recent plunge into science fiction seemed entirely unexpected. In its incipient stages, in *Briefing for a Descent into Hell*, it was startling and seemed to mark a change as radical as Picasso's when he moved from the Blue Period to Abstract Cubism. With more reflection, one can discover the thread that connects *The Golden Notebook* to her trilogy *Canopus in Argos: Archives*; but it is hard to think of a writer of her caliber in the past half-century who has demonstrated such range.

Her career began with *The Grass Is Singing*, a gem of a book. Set in Rhodesia, it charts with an economy rare in Lessing's works the dissolution of a couple's relationship. After Lessing left Africa in 1949, she devoted ten years to the *Children of Violence* series which explored exhaustively the theme of the "free woman" long before it was fashionable. It also displayed Lessing's preoccupation with politics which many have criticized as tedious. 1962 saw the publication of *The Golden Notebook*, the best of her works from this period despite its obvious flaws. It was greeted with an ecstatic response from the Women's Movement; scholarly critics were more grudging in their admiration. *The Golden Notebook* is as much a book about writing as it is an exploration of women's relationships with each other and men. In many ways, it ought to be compared to Gide's *The Counterfeiters*: the writer's quest to capture the self intended in fiction, not a different, diminished, or enhanced self; the journey through madness that this task requires; the visions of violence it calls up are integral to both books. Both descend from Joyce; both require a sophisticated audience which enjoys unravelling puzzles, putting together fragmented parts. Both mirror an age when the Heisenberg Uncertainity Principle threatens the reliability of all narrators and estranges the artist from the world he makes and the self he is.

In the 1970's Lessing's works took an unexpected turn. She began to experiment with science fiction. Her interest in extra-sensory perception first emerged in *Landlocked.* Madness had been seen as a state offering Anna Wulf a respite from the obsessional insistence upon the self, the ego, the "I,I,I,I" that Saul Green spattered out like machine-gun bullets in *The Golden Notebook*. In *Briefing for a Descent into Hell* Lessing took her interest in madness a step further. Calling the book a work of "inner space fiction," she built a story around Charles Watkins, a 50-year-old classics professor who is found wandering on Waterloo Bridge and is confined for a stay in a psychiatric hospital. There, two doctors, of conflicting views, struggle to bring back his memory while he follows a visionary journey in which he enjoys a different, higher identity—one conferred upon him by the Crystal—and one that ordained that he enter earth, hell, as part of a Descent Team whose mission is to show the mad, I-ridden humans that they are part of a larger harmony, "we" not "I." Lessing, following R.D. Laing, explores the possibility that only the mad are sane. But much more intriguing than this idea is Lessing's decision to fashion the language and metaphors of madness from the idiom of science fiction and the visions experienced through ESP. The inner journey of this modern Odysseus is travelled on the space-time warp of science fiction. The regions he visits are vividly depicted, sometimes reminding one of Rousseau's lion in the desert, sometimes recalling Swift's *Gulliver's Travels* in the way that animals, rat-dogs, monkeys, and a great white bird are imagined. The language which attempts to capture the visions Watkins is experiencing is one where words are understood by their sounds, not their denotative meanings. "I" glides into "aye" and "eye" as Watkins's mind seems to float in limbo, carrying his body through an unfamiliar medium, revealing images from the visionary realm. Lessing sustains this style, interrupted by only the curt notations of the two psychiatrists, for over a hundred pages. The effect is startling. At times one almost drowns in her verbiage, but somehow she then manages to interrupt the flow of the vision, interject it with the banal observations of the doctors, or the staccato questioning of the patient, and carries the reader on. Undoubtedly, Lessing's style will cost her some readers, but those who bear with her will find themselves caught up in this bizarre account and caring very much whether this amnesiac will tenaciously hang on to his visionary self or succumb to the pressures of the doctors and society and return to the ordinary realm where he is merely a slightly eccentric don. Watkins's hold on the link between the two ways of seeing is most precarious. Lessing, feeding her usual appetite to perplex the reader, makes us try to decide whether Felicity, Constancia, and Nancy, creatures in his visions, correspond with his wife, Felicity, his mistress, Constance, and the wife of his friend. We are also left puzzling whether Miles and Watkins are at some level identical, and whether the loss of Watkins's higher self is total, or whether it matters at all since others in the Descent Team seem still to be around. Also, of course, there is the possibility that Watkins is nothing more than temporarily schizophrenic, though the weight of the story seems to negate this alternative. This book introduces all the ideas and the paraphernalia of science fiction that dominate Lessing's recent trilogy.

Shikasta and *The Marriages Between Zones Three, Four, and Five* are works of science fiction. In the first a compilation of reports, historical documents, letters, and psychiatric diagnoses is used to unfold the story of Johor's three visits to Shikasta (Earth), the last taking place in the final phase just following the Third World War. Johor is an emissary from the galactic Empire of Canopus, sent to Shikasta to report on the colony. It is Johor's task to educate those who survive the Third World War to their true place in a larger planetary System, where cosmological accidents have heavily contributed to the blighted human condition, and where Shammat, the criminal planet of another galactic empire, has temporarily obstructed the Lock that will connect Shikasta to Canopus. A Chronicler from Zone Three is the narrator of the second book in the trilogy. He tells one of the myths that accounts for man's fallen state and reveals the will of the Powers that the potentates of three hitherto separate zones are to marry and so hasten the evolutionary design that governs the six zones encircling Earth. The myth he tells is of the marriage of Al-Ith, Queen of Zone Three, to Ben Ata, ruler of Zone Four, and, later, the marriage of Ben Ata to Vahshi, ruler of Zone Five. Two births follow. The marriages alter the Zones, estrange their monarchs from the old dispensation, and bring about alterations which enable all the peoples to move between the Zones and fulfill the will of the Powers. Both books allow Lessing to explore again, in new metaphors, the human qualities responsible for the catastrophic happenings in this century, and the nature of the kinds of relationships men and women must make and the kinds of societies that must be constructed to move humans to a higher consciousness. *The Marriages Between Zones Three, Four and Five* is far more lyrical than *Shikasta*. The Chronicler uses songs and pictures to capture the mythic dimension of the story he tells. The third book projected in this series will tell of the Sirian Empire, that, along with Canopus, carried on colonial experiments on Shikasta and contributed to the events that took the Shikastians to their 20th century of Destruction.

While Lessing's most recent work has been in this realm of science fiction, she published two other books in the years between *Briefing for a Descent into Hell* and the *Canopus* series. *The Summer Before the Dark* is one of Lessing's more perfect works. Compact, tightly constructed, it tells the moving story of a woman's coming to terms with aging. Kate Brown, the 45-year-old mother of four children, all grown, and the wife of a neurologist of some standing, is a woman who has lived her married years making accomodations, to her husband's choices, to the needs of her children. In the summer of the story, events unexpectedly leave Kate Brown without family responsibilities and alone in London for the first time since her marriage. She holds a job briefly, depending again on the talents that the sympathetic understanding of mothering taught her. Then she has a brief affair with a young man on the continent. Both fall sick; Kate returns to London where she lies ill, preoccupied with a recurring dream of a seal which she must complete. She loses weight; her brightly tinted red hair becomes brassy, then banded in grey. In the last phase of the story, she shares quarters with a young woman who is struggling with her own coming of age. The two women work upon each other; Kate's dream is completed; both separate to enter another stage of their lives—the young woman choosing marriage, children, even respectability; Kate, returning to her husband, with her hair grey, as a woman who acts for her own reasons, not merely to please others.

The Memoirs of a Survivor is an even more remarkable book, and equally as mature. It is the memoirs of a nameless woman who has survived "it," a nameless war that has left the cities of England nearly empty shells, with conclaves of people living nearly barricaded in their apartments while gangs of youths roam the streets and the air is so polluted that hand-driven machines are necessary to purify it. The narrator retells how she lived through this period; how she came by a child, Emily, who was entrusted to her care; how she entered a space behind the white walls of her living-room, and inhabited other rooms, from earlier times, and witnessed the traumatic moments of Emily's youth spent with her real parents. She struggles to tell in words how the two worlds, at first so different, began to impinge upon one another. She contrasts what she calls "personal" moments of experience with others that she labels "impersonal." Both reside in the world behind the wall. The story blends the dreamy, prophetic, timeless moments behind the wall where some heightened consciousness, some visionary powers, exists with a dispassionate, often chilling, realistic account of "ordinary" life in a ravaged London apartment. Always, when the narrator goes behind the wall, she seeks, with a sense of urgency, the inhabitant of that other house, those other gardens. The protagonist's memoirs end with her account of how they somehow came through the darkest times, and realized that the worst was over, that something new would be built. The final paragraphs describe the moment when the walls opened again, and she saw the face she had sought so long, the inhabitant of that hidden world. And that presence takes the hands of Emily, her boyfriend, and the evil child who had terrorized the London streets and leads them into the garden. It is a mystical moment, transfiguring, mysterious, and a consummate end for this exquisitely crafted book.

It is too early to assess Lessing's place in literary history. Her imagination is too rich; her fiction is going in new directions. What can be said is that she is deeply concerned with the human condition, hungry to explore new dimensions, to redefine relationships. All in a nearly obsessive effort to find a way through the historical ravages of this century to a condition beyond the one of personal unhappiness that plagues so many human relationships.

—Carol Simpson Stern

LEVIN, Ira. American. Born in New York City, 27 August 1929. Educated at Drake University, Des Moines, Iowa, 1946-48; New York University, 1948-50, A.B. 1950. Served in the United States Army Signal Corps, 1953-55. Married Gabrielle Aronsohn in 1960 (divorced, 1968); three children. Recipient: Mystery Writers of America Edgar Allan Poe Award, 1954, and Special Award, 1980. Agent: Harold Ober Associates, 40 East 49th Street, New York, New York 10017, U.S.A.

PUBLICATIONS

Novels

A Kiss Before Dying. New York, Simon and Schuster, 1953; London, Joseph, 1954.
Rosemary's Baby. New York, Random House, and London, Joseph, 1967.
This Perfect Day. New York, Random House, and London, Joseph, 1970.
The Stepford Wives. New York, Random House, and London, Joseph, 1972.
The Boys from Brazil. New York, Random House, and London, Joseph, 1976.

Plays

No Time for Sergeants, adaptation of the novel by Mac Hyman (produced New York, 1955; London, 1956). New York, Random House, 1956.
Interlock (produced New York, 1958). New York, Dramatists Play Service, 1958.
Critic's Choice (produced New York, 1960; London, 1961). New York, Random House, 1961; London, Evans, 1963.
General Seeger (produced New York, 1962). New York, Dramatists Play Service, 1962.
Drat! The Cat!, music by Milton Schafer (produced New York, 1965).
Dr. Cook's Garden (also director: produced New York, 1967). New York, Dramatists Play Service, 1968.
Veronica's Room (produced New York, 1973). New York, Random House, 1974; London, Joseph, 1975.
Deathtrap (produced New York and London, 1978). New York, Random House, 1979.
Break a Leg (produced New York, 1979).

Theatrical Activities:

Director: **Play**—*Dr. Cook's Garden*, New York, 1967.

* * *

The heroine of *Rosemary's Baby* is overwhelmed by the "elaborate...evil" of the witches' coven through whose agency she has unknowingly borne Satan's child, which now lies in a black bassinet with an inverted crucifix for a crib toy. Elaborateness is, indeed, the chief characteristic of both evil and good in Ira Levin's novels. Bud Corliss of *A Kiss Before Dying* makes neat lists of ways to arrange his pregnant girlfriend's "suicide" and to win her eldest sister's love. In *This Perfect Day* all human actions are ostensibly directed by a world computer and everyone must touch his identification bracelet to scanners before he can do anything, go anywhere, or receive any supplies. The novel's hero, Chip (or Li RM35M4419, to give him his "nameber") fights system with system in a complicated expedition to disable UniComp's memory banks. The first dozen pages of *The Boys from Brazil* describe, course by course, Dr. Mengele's dinner party-*cum*-briefing for the assassination of 94 retired civil servants, each of whom has unwittingly adopted a clone of Hitler, produced by the Doctor, who now intends to recreate Hitler's family environment.

Such procedures provide the sustaining interest and suspense of Levin's novels, combining neatness and system with Satanism, secrets, universal surveillance, violence, and death. Rosemary uses a scrabble set to work out the anagram which identifies her friendly neighbor Roman Castevet as devil-worshipping Steven Marcato. In *A Kiss Before Dying* Dorothy's provision of "Something old, Something new, Something borrowed, And something blue" enables her sister to deduce that Dorothy intended marriage, not suicide. The husbands of *The Stepford Wives* make speaking, moving replicas of their spouses. They begin with seemingly innocuous sketches of each real wife and tape recordings of her voice; they end by killing her off-stage. Levin increases the "reality" of such sinister processes by mingling them with ordinary routines or eating, pregnancy, moving to a new house, etc.

Both good and bad characters must, at times, revise their elaborate plans on the spur of the crisis. Their expedients are ingenious, often complex, and the pleasure of following Levin's details is enough to make some of his novels re-readable when their surprise is over.

The forward movement and acceleration of the plots are further complicated by sudden reversals, single or double, overt or psychological, in which characters (and often readers) are temporarily disoriented. For example, Rosemary, arriving at the logical conclusion that her husband had joined the coven, "didn't know if she was going mad or going sane." Joanna cannot tell if her best friend is still a person or has become an automaton. (She *is* an automaton, and stabs Joanna.) Although the reader is sometimes prepared for these discoveries, there are also unexpected shocks as when Rosemary, thinking herself safe, sees her witch-obstetrician enter, or when Chip, suddenly taken prisoner by a trusted team-member, discovers that betrayal is really recruitment by the elite subterranean programmers. The effect on the reader of such continual reversals and realignments is a constant uneasiness as to his personal safety and moral identity, which produces horror very successfully in *Rosemary's Baby*, but rather mechanically in *This Perfect Day* and *The Stepford Wives*. No doubt Levin's constant readers now anticipate his surprises, which may account for his increasing detail of violence as excitement in *The Boys from Brazil*.

Occasionally, and chiefly in *This Perfect Day*, Levin's literary antecedents are apparent. His shock techniques are essentially those of Ambrose Bierce and Villiers de l'Isle Adam. Bud's slow plunge into a vat of molten copper recalls H.G. Wells's "The Cone" with its archetypal death by blast furnace. The world of UniComp is essentially a Brave New World with a Big Brother mentality, but controlled by a mad scientist out of Edgar Rice Burroughs, who rejuvenates through body transference. In short, Levin has drawn upon the almost inescapable traditional materials of his genre, but he uses them intelligently and individually.

Increasingly, Levin's novels imply larger significances. Looking at the copper smelter, the murderer says seriously, "It makes you realize what a great country this is." Rosemary's subtly evil apartment house is owned by the church next door, and there are seemingly casual references to the Death of God. An ideal universe of "the gentle, the helpful, the loving, the unselfish" is the vision of a power-joyful egoist. Even the intelligent Stepford husbands in a strange feminist fable want only big-breasted, floor-waxing, mindless wives. A wise old Nazi-hunter, clashing with a radical rabbi, refuses to let 94 teenage Hitlers be exterminated for the sake of future Jewish safety, saying, "This was *Mengele's* business, killing children. Should it be ours?" These moral paradoxes, undeveloped though they are, both extend and intensify the disquieting uncertainty which is Levin's chief characteristic.

—Jane W. Stedman

LEVIN, Meyer. American. Born in Chicago, Illinois, 8 October 1905. Educated at the University of Chicago, Ph.B. 1924. Writer-Director of documentary films for the United States Office of War Information, 1942-44. Married 1) Mabel Schamp in 1933 (divorced, 1942); 2) Thereska Szarc Torres in 1948; four children. Reporter and Writer for the *Chicago Daily News*, 1922-28, and the Jewish Telegraphic Agency, Palestine and New York, 1929-31; opened experimental marionette theatre in Chicago, 1929, and taught puppet-theatre production at the New School for Social Research, New York, 1932; Associate Editor, 1933-38, and Film Critic, 1933-39, *Esquire* magazine, Chicago; writer in Hollywood, 1939-41; War Correspondent in Europe for the Overseas News Agency and the Jewish Telegraphic Agency, 1944-45. After the war, lived and worked in Palestine and France, writing and making films, until 1952; lived in New York, 1952-57, and since 1957 in Israel and America. Recipient: Bensonhurst Award, 1966; Daroff Memorial Award, 1966; Baltimore Hebrew College Award, 1980. D.H.L.: Hebrew Union College, New York, 1977. Agent: Scott Meredith Literary Agency, 580 Fifth Avenue, New York, New York 10036, U.S.A. Address: Street of the Blue Waves, Herzlia-on-Sea, Israel. *Died 9 July 1981.*

PUBLICATIONS

Novels

Reporter. New York, Day, 1929.
Frankie and Johnny: A Love Story. New York, Day, 1930; as *The Young Lovers*, New York, New American Library, 1952.
Yehuda. New York, Cape and Smith, and London, Cape, 1931.
The New Bridge. New York, Covici Friede, and London, Gollancz, 1933.
The Old Bunch. New York, Viking Press, 1937.
Citizens. New York, Viking Press, 1940.
My Father's House. New York, Viking Press, 1947.
Compulsion. New York, Simon and Schuster, 1956; London, Muller, 1957.
Eva. New York, Simon and Schuster, and London, Muller, 1959.
The Fanatic. New York, Simon and Schuster, 1964.
The Stronghold. New York, Simon and Schuster, and London, W.H. Allen, 1965.
Gore and Igor: An Extravaganza. New York, Simon and Schuster, and London, W.H. Allen, 1968.
The Settlers. New York, Simon and Schuster, and London, W.H. Allen, 1972.
The Obsession. New York, Simon and Schuster, 1974.
The Spell of Time: A Tale of Love in Jerusalem. New York, Praeger, 1974.
The Harvest. New York, Simon and Schuster, 1978.

Uncollected Short Stories

"The Sold Sin," in *This Quarter* (Paris), July 1931.
"Israel and the Enemy," in *Jewish Caravan*, edited by Leo W. Schwarz. New York, Rinehart, 1935.
"The Upturn," in *Story* (New York), July 1935.
"Love Note," "Love Made Simple," "Glamor Girl in Your Home," "No Excuse for Ace," "Plenty of Experience," "Night Work," "Idea Man," "Faith in Humanity," "Big Winner," "Private Argument," "If We'd Only Met Ten Years Ago," "Open: Come In," "To Fire the Wife," "And on the Double," in *Collier's* (Springfield, Ohio), 1937-44.
"The System Was Doomed," in *The Best Short Stories 1941*, edited by Edward J. O'Brien. Boston, Houghton Mifflin, 1941.
"Maurie Finds His Medium," in *This Land, This People*, edited by Harold U. Ribalow. New York, Beechhurst Press, 1950.
"After All I Did for Israel," in *These Your Children*, edited by Harold U. Ribalow. New York, Beechhurst Press, 1952.
"The Dance," in *Feast of Leviathan*, edited by Leo W. Schwarz. New York, Rinehart, 1956.
"Pick Up," in *Good Housekeeping* (New York), September 1957.
"Marry a Million," in *Cosmopolitan* (New York), September 1957.
"His Clever Wife," in *Anthology of Best American Short Stories 7*, edited by Robert Oberfirst. New York, Fell, 1959.
"The Water Spirit," in *A Treasury of Jewish Sea Stories*, edited by Samuel Sobel. New York, David, 1965.
"Chicago, America," in *The American Judaism Reader*, edited by Paul Kresh. New York, Abelard Schuman, 1967.
"The Boy's Song," in *The Yom Kippur Anthology*, edited by Philip Goodman. Philadelphia, Jewish Publication Society of America, 1971.

Plays

Compulsion (produced New York, 1957; Croydon, Surrey, 1960). New York, Simon and Schuster, 1959.
The Diary of Anne Frank. Privately printed, 1967.

Screenplays: *My Father's House*, 1947; *The Illegals*, 1947; *Bus to Sinai*, 1968; *The Falashas*, 1970; *The Mountain of Moses*, 1973.

Other

The Golden Mountain: Marvellous Tales of Rabbi Israel, Baal Shem, and of His Great-Grandson, Rabbi Nachman, Retold from Hebrew, Yiddish, and German Sources. New York, Cape and Ballou, 1932; revised edition, as *Classic Hassidic Tales*, New York, Citadel Press, 1966; London, Penguin, 1975.
If I Forget Thee: A Picture History of Modern Palestine (juvenile). New York, Viking Press, 1947.
In Search: An Autobiography. New York, Horizon Press, 1950; London, Vallentine Mitchell, 1951.
The Story of the Synagogue, with Toby Kurzband. New York, Behrman, 1957.
The Story of the Jewish Way of Life, with Toby Kurzband. New York, Behrman, 1959.
God and the Story of Judaism, with Dorothy Kripke. New York, Behrman, 1962.
The Story of Israel (juvenile). New York, Putnam, 1966.
An Israel Haggadah for Passover. New York, Abrams, 1970.
Beginnings in Jewish Philosophy. New York, Behrman, 1971.

Editor, and Translator, *Kibbutz Buchenwald: Selections from the Kibbutz Diary.* New York, Zionist Organization, 1946.
Editor, *Diary*, by David S. Kogan. New York, Beechhurst Press, 1955.
Editor, *Golden Egg*, by Arthur D. Goldhaft. New York, Horizon Press, 1957.
Editor, with Charles Angoff, *The Rise of American Jewish Literature.* New York, Simon and Schuster, 1970.

Translator, *Tales of My People*, by Sholom Asch. New York, Putnam, 1948.
Translator, *The Dangerous Games*, by Tereska Torres. New York, Dial Press, 1957; London, W.H. Allen, 1958.
Translator, *Not Yet*, by Tereska Torres. New York, Crown, 1957; London, W.H. Allen, 1959.
Translator, *The Golden Cage*, by Tereska Torres. New York, Dial Press, 1959; London, W.H. Allen, 1961.
Translator, *Women's Barracks*, by Tereska Torres. London, W.H. Allen, 1960.
Translator, *The Only Reason*, by Tereska Torres. London, W.H. Allen, 1962.

*

Manuscript Collections: Boston University; New York University; Brandeis University, Waltham, Massachusetts; Hebrew University, Jerusalem.

Critical Study: "The Haunting of Meyer Levin" by Benno Weiser, in *Midstream* (New York), August 1976.

Meyer Levin comments:

(1972) Of the American-Jewish authors of my time, many of the most prominent prefer to be viewed as American authors who "write Jewish" because of the happenstance of their background. Though I started with this attitude, I found myself drawn more and more to self-recognition as a Jewish rather than an American author, with deeper roots in Jewish culture, and with the portrayal of the Jewish ethos as the dominant theme in my continuing work.

Thus, my first novel, *Reporter*, was a reaction to the Chicago scene of the Twenties, and my second novel, *Frankie and Johnny*, was an attempt at an urban love story with an American folk quality, in which I erased or transmuted the Jewish quality of my characters. But from the very first, I had been deeply affected by that quality; my earliest serious piece of publication was a sketch of a ghetto group of garment workers listening to a street-corner orator, which appeared in the *Menorah Journal* (predecessor to *Commentary*) while I was at college. Just after graduation, I ended a wander-year in Palestine, and became profoundly affected by the revival of the Jewish spirit among the socialist pioneers. This resulted in many returns to that land, with *Yehuda*, a novel of life in a kibbutz, as a first product.

By chance or by the need to find this material, I stumbled on the folk-lore of Hasidism in this same period, for my American Jewish upbringing had been void of either Zionist or traditional religious orientation. I adapted the Hasidic tales into *The Golden Mountain*, my next book. From then on, I increasingly saw the continuing Jewish consciousness as affected by these sources: life in the dispersion (for me, America); life in the religious tradition (though I was far from orthodox); and life in the Jewish renewal in its source-land.

Three of my novels may be grouped together as impregnated with the American as well as the American-Jewish experience. They are the Chicago novels, *The Old Bunch*, *Citizens*, and *Compulsion*. It is significant that when *The Old Bunch* was completed the publisher who had contracted for it asked me to change the characters to a "melting pot" group and rejected the book when I refused. And though when published by Viking Press it was hailed as a breakthrough in fiction about American Jews, this same publisher then attempted to de-Judaize my next novel, *Citizens*, by asking me to change the Jewish doctor in the steel-strike story to a non-Jew. However, he did not reject the book when I was uncompliant.

The Second World War had begun, and my experience as a correspondent specializing in the death-camps has profoundly affected all that I have written since. I feel that every living Jew bears in his consciousness at every moment the knowledge of the holocaust, the awareness of Israel (even if he is one who is uneasy with it), and the sense of his place as a Jew in the particular society in which he happens to live. This three-stream formation corresponds to the three sources I have discerned for myself as a writer, and virtually all of my post-war novels reflect it—*Eva*, *My Father's House*, *The Fanatic* in particular.

In connection with *The Fanatic* I should explain a career difficulty that has beset me in these post-war years. The novel tells the story of the distortion on Broadway of a manuscript left by a victim of the death camps. It follows quite closely my own sickening history with *The Diary of Anne Frank*, and illuminates an area of politics in literature, even outside the Soviet Union, that is little known.

My dramatization of *The Diary of Anne Frank* was rejected and suppressed through the influence of an acknowledged Stalinist, an American Jewish playwright of high achievement, who persuaded Mr. Frank that it was "unstageworthy" because I was "a novelist and novelists can't write plays." Eventually, another dramatization was produced to world-wide success, but a jury in the New York State Supreme Court found that it was largely derived from my earlier play. The single production of my version, in Israel, was suppressed on the question of rights, but not until the critics had hailed it as "infinitely superior" to the Broadway play, theatrically as well as in literary quality. The crux of the matter was that my play had preserved the full Jewish content, the avowals of faith in Anne Frank's diary, and even the desire of her sister to live in Palestine if she lived. Anti-Zionists who interfered with its production and turned Mr. Frank against me were carrying out the same Stalinist opposition to Jewish writing that was at that very time (1952) resulting in the liquidation of scores of Jewish authors in the Soviet Union. Though since then there have been continuous requests for the presentation of my play, and though Albert Camus, Norman Mailer, Elie Wiesel, Bruno Bettelheim, I.B. Singer and many others signed appeals for its production, it is still forbidden. In two decades of battle over this question, I learned that I had indeed even before the *Diary* episode been under anti-Zionist attack, that my novel *My Father's House* had been sabotaged on publication by a Stalinist assigned to do public relations on the book, that my autobiography *In Search* had been turned back under the influence by a publisher who had accepted it, and that negative reviews, particularly on *The Fanatic*, had been planted by literary-political anti-Zionists in important media. Smears, whispering campaigns labelling me a "trouble maker," and literary denigration have proven a great professional handicap. Much of this has spread far beyond the original political sources. Because of it, I believe, there has been no proper evaluation of my work, whatever may be its quality.

* * *

In an introductory note to one of his most celebrated novels, *Compulsion*, Meyer Levin defines his attitude towards its writing and, the evidence of the other novels suggests, the writing of fiction in general. *Compulsion*, it can be noted, is a treatment of the celebrated Loeb-Leopold case in which two privileged Jewish boys murdered a much younger boy, Bobby Franks. The deed was done not out of malice but was an expression of the alienation, arrogance, and elitism of the two young killers. It was a case that stirred the horror and curiosity of a wide public. Levin had particular reasons for keeping the case in mind for more than two decades; as a young man he had covered the case for a Chicago paper. When Levin measured what he had done in *Compulsion*—in a way an anticipation of the literary kind that Truman Capote produced in his "true" narrative of another pair of criminals, *In Cold Blood*—he made these remarks: remarks that provide an entry into nearly all Levin's other work.

> Because of this identification [between the "reporter" of the novel and one of the killers, Judd Steiner] it sometimes becomes difficult to tell exactly where my imagination fills in what were gaps in the documents and in the personal revelations. In some instances, the question arises: Is this true; did this actually happen? And my answer is that it needed to happen; it needed to happen in the way I tell it or in some similar way, or else nothing can be explained for me. In the last analysis, I suppose it will have to be understood that what I tell is the reality for me. For particularly where emotions must be dealt with, there is no finite reality; our idea of actuality always has to come through someone, and this is the reality through me.

This is a passage which defines the kind of confidence in the art of fiction that informs not only *Compulsion* but the other voluminous work of Levin. Whether he is narrating the behavior of a couple of young murderers or the collective efforts of a group of Jewish immigrants to establish settlements in Israel in the first half of the century, as in *The Settlers* and *The Harvest*, Levin has an attitude toward the writing of fiction that is not everywhere found. There are now many writers for whom the creation of novels is an exercise in self-discovery or a chance to display wit and ingenuity at the expense of a chosen subject matter. Thus, with writers like Barth and Pynchon, less important is the *what* (the chosen subject) than the *how* of the subject's presentation; techniques of presentation and refinements of style draw a reader's attention away from the narrative itself and make the reader think about the writer's own sensibility.

Levin, as the quoted passage suggests, is not such a writer. For Levin, a novelist's prime duty is, so far as possible, that of getting his story straight, to recreate, as in the instance of *Compulsion*, the essential narrative as it "actually" happened. Or, as in the case of *The Settlers* and *The Harvest*, to provide a representative course of events, so that the reader will close the book with factual knowledge and more: a correct view of the early clashes between Jew and Arab, Jew and Turk, and Jew and English, and also a sense of the psychological and social tensions the settlers faced. In short, Levin can be thought of as a conscientious and sensitive reporter of a chosen subject, a subject which finds both its outlines and its essence exactly presented in a certain work. All this amounts to a subordination of the novelist to the truth that is "outside" him. He serves his subject rather than his own sensibility.

Brief inspection of Levin's novels displays Levin at work in this fashion. In *Compulsion* the facts and the inner psychological realities of two murderers are traced. In *The Settlers* and *The Harvest*, novels as vast and panoramic as the subject they treat, the heroism and the pettiness, the betrayals and the great faith involved in the taking-over of part of the promised land, are represented with unfaltering energy and, so far as may be in a work of fiction, truthfulness.

And so it happens in Levin's other novels. Levin's fifth novel, *The Old Bunch*, traces the destinies of a group of high school graduates as they work out their adult lives in the Chicago of the 1920's and early 1930's. *The Stronghold* is an analysis of various responses of Germans to the "fact" of the Jewish holocaust of World War II. A Nazi, reminiscent of Eichmann, simply tries to protect himself from the victorious Allies, whereas an old-style German aristocrat experiences guilt for the crimes performed by fellow Germans. In *The Fanatic*, as an autobiographical work, *The Obsession*, allows us to see, Levin gives novelistic form to the problem of a writer who tries to give dramatic shape to the life and death of a World War II victim. *The Fanatic* is essentially the same tale that Levin sets down in *The Obsession* where he tells of the literary politics that frustrated the production of his play about Anne Frank. Another novel, *Eva*, is the first-person account of a young woman who has gone through the Nazi terrors and finally reaches Israel. *Gore and Igor* is the somewhat picaresque tale of two young Jews—one from America and one from Russia—who manage to survive, by energy and wit, in the newly emerging state of Israel.

A bit to one side of these many conscientious recreations of sections of the real world—of the world that is "out there"—is a brief tale called *The Spell of Time*. Two men, one elderly and famous, the other young and relentlessly ambitious, are in contest for the love of a young woman. The men, with the aid of ancient Jewish mysticism, exchange personalities; the woman wisely chooses the young man whose inner being now contains the gentleness and sweetness of the old man. This tale, however, is not entirely to one side of Levin's many reports on the world that is "outside" and awaits the novelist's reporting. For, as in *Compulsion* and elsewhere, Levin is recurrently concerned with the springs of human action, action that is base and action that is, as in *The Settlers*, noble and beyond the call of duty.

This survey presents a writer who has been a servant of realities external to himself: realities that are challenges to fact-finding and interpretive ability. In consequence, the reader of Levin acquires much information of specific sorts. The reader is also shown, with care and with frequent energy, how this particular information may be understood. All this is done in a style that is plain and direct. The novelist lets us hear actual voices from the near or distant past, and we are caught up in the events to which those voices respond. The combined work of Levin is an act of faith: that a reality external to both author and reader exists and waits for the acts of knowing that take place in novel after novel from the writer's desk.

—Harold H. Watts

LEVINE, (Albert) Norman. Canadian. Born in Ottawa, Ontario, 22 October 1923. Educated at McGill University, Montreal, 1946-49, B.A. 1948, M.A. 1949; King's College, London, 1949-50. Served as a Flying Officer in the Royal Canadian Air Force, 1942-45. Married Margaret Payne in 1952; three daughters. Employed by the Department of National Defence, Ottawa, 1940-42; Head of the English Department, Barnstaple Boys Grammar School, Devon, 1953-54; Resident Writer, University of New Brunswick, Fredericton, 1965-66. Recipient: Canada Council Fellowship, 1959, and Arts Award, 1969, 1971, 1974. Has lived in England since 1949. Address: 45 Bedford Road, St. Ives, Cornwall, England.

PUBLICATIONS

Novels

The Angled Road. Toronto, McClelland and Stewart, and London, Werner Laurie, 1952.
From a Seaside Town. Toronto and London, Macmillan, 1970; as *She'll Only Drag You Down*, Toronto, Paperjacks, 1975.

Short Stories

One Way Ticket. Toronto, McClelland and Stewart, and London, Secker and Warburg, 1961.
I Don't Want to Know Anyone Too Well: 15 Stories. Toronto and London, Macmillan, 1971.
Selected Stories. Ottawa, Oberon Press, 1975.
Thin Ice. Ottawa, Reneau and Greenberg, 1980.

Verse

Myssium. Toronto, Ryerson Press, 1948.
The Tight-Rope Walker. London, Totem Press, 1950.
I Walk by the Harbour. Fredericton, New Brunswick, Fiddlehead, 1976.

Other

Canada Made Me. London, Putnam, 1958.

Editor, *Canadian Winter's Tales.* Toronto and London, Macmillan, 1968.

*

Manuscript Collection: University of Texas, Austin; York University, Toronto.

Critical Studies: "The Girl in the Drugstore" by the author, in *Canadian Literature 41* (Vancouver), 1969; interview in *Canadian Literature 45* (Vancouver), 1970; Philip Oakes, in *Sunday Times* (London), 19 July 1970; Alan Heuser, in *Montreal Star*, 26 September 1970; *Times Literary Supplement* (London), 3 December 1971; Maurice Capitanchik, in *Books and Bookmen* (London), September 1972.

Norman Levine comments:

(1972) For anyone who wants to know where to begin, I suggest that the start would be *From a Seaside Town*, the three short stories, then *Canada Made Me*.

Writing in the *Atlantic Advocate*, I said: "When you go to a writer's work—it is into his personal world that you enter. What he is doing is paying, in his own way, an elaborate tribute to people and places he has known."

* * *

Norman Levine has always been remarkable for the reserve of his writing; but it has taken him some years to learn what best to withhold and what to reveal. In his early autobiographical stories and novel, *The Angled Road*, he was "trying to cut out [his] past, to cover...up" his origins as the Canadian-bred son of a Jewish street-peddler. As if to compensate for this leaching of colour from his material, he was also experimenting with patches of vulgar prose-poetry. While teaching himself to write simply and directly, he came to terms with his personal history. Now, in *Thin Ice*, although his range is narrow, he shapes his stories with the unmistakable authority of a writer who has found his subject and style.

Speaking for the most part in the first person, Levine relates in neutral prose incidents from his Canadian upbringing and his years in England. Certain worlds are revealed which he leaves and is drawn back to: Jewish society, life at McGill University, summer cottages by the Richelieu, the tourist villages of Cornwall, poverty in a small town. He has achieved the outsider's vantage point from which he turns a telephoto lens on ordinary people and events. The danger of his method is that when it miscarries, as sometimes it does, the reader is left with a commonplace, colourless anecdote that adds up to nothing. His later stories and novel do not differ greatly from his travel-narrative, *Canada Made Me*, except in being increasingly crafted, concise, and superficially detached. Although he has escaped the heavy cold of Montreal and the intimate squalor of lower Ottawa, he takes with him wherever he goes his Canadian melancholy and taste for failure.

In drawing on his personal past, Levine often returns to the same scenes, characters, and even fragments of conversation, as if he were unable to invent afresh or to leave behind any of his life. An Englishman awaiting the flowering of a large cactus, a woman without a nose, a prowling man whom a couple nicknames "the house detective," are only a few of many recurrent elements in the work of this man who mines his own writings, word for word, as well as his past. The friction of repeated use has polished his memories until all that is inessential has worn away, leaving a smooth pebble of experience.

Levine consistently avoids evocative vocabulary, choosing instead to make a plain statement of fact in language so empty of implication that it becomes mysterious. It is as if he is trying to create prose as objective as the reality he perceives. Yet, in his best work, when everything possible has been jettisoned, a core of emotion remains. He writes in short, often broken, sentences that correspond to the fragmentary moments of human contact in his tales. Sometimes an ugly expression such as "less worse" (*Canada Made Me*) has been selected as the only way of expressing what he means, but at other times a sentence muddles into ambiguity that adds nothing, or an angularity almost illiterate. Except for brief periods, Levine has lived in England since 1949; so it is not surprising that he has somewhat lost his grasp of Canadian idiom and fact. His use of such expressions as "the School of Seven," "motorways," "left luggage," and "do some walks" is evidence of the distance he has travelled from his native speech. Even his distinguished German translator, Heinrich Böll, the Nobel prize-winner, must feel it a hopeless task to convey in all its aspects Levine's continual shuttling between England and Canada.

Although Levine says little about his feelings, one cannot miss the passion that concentrates his prose and sends him back to places and people he cannot forget. His journeys are the counterpart of the sexual hunger that runs through *From a Seaside Town*. His appetite for experience and his enjoyment of the grotesque have so far saved him from the sterility that threatens autobiographical writers in middle age. In his low-keyed world even tiny incidents stand out like figures against a landscape of snow. They may mean nothing or anything, but to him they have an importance which the reader feels, but never entirely understands.

—Margaret Keith

LEWIS, Janet. American. Born in Chicago, Illinois, 17 August 1899. Educated at the Lewis Institute, Chicago, A.A. 1918; University of Chicago, Ph.B. 1920. Married the writer Yvor Winters in 1926 (died, 1968); one daughter and one son. Passport Bureau Clerk, American Consulate, Paris, 1920; Proofreader, *Redbook* magazine, Chicago, 1921; English Teacher, Lewis Institute, 1921-22. Lecturer, Writers Workshop, University of Missouri, Columbia, 1952, and University of Denver, 1956; Visiting Lecturer, then Lecturer in English, Stanford University, California, 1960, 1966, 1969, 1970. Recipient: Friends of American Literature award, 1932, Shelley Memorial Award, for poetry, 1948; Guggenheim Fellowship, 1950. Address: 143 West Portola Avenue, Los Altos, California 94022, U.S.A.

PUBLICATIONS

Novels

The Invasion: A Narrative of Events Concerning the Johnston Family of St. Mary's. New York, Harcourt Brace, 1932.
The Wife of Martin Guerre. San Francisco, Colt Press, 1941; London, Rapp and Carroll, 1967.
Against a Darkening Sky. New York, Doubleday, 1943.
The Trial of Sören Qvist. New York, Doubleday, 1947; London, Gollancz, 1967.
The Ghost of Monsieur Scarron. New York, Doubleday, and London, Gollancz, 1959.

Short Stories

Goodbye, Son, and Other Stories. New York, Doubleday, 1946.

Uncollected Short Stories

"At the Swamp," in *The Best Short Stories of 1930*, edited by Edward J. O'Brien. Boston, Houghton Mifflin, 1930.
"La Pointe Chegiomegon," in *Hound and Horn* (Portland, Maine), October-December 1931.
"A Still Small Voice," in *McCall's* (New York), 1946.
"The Breakable Cup," in *Saturday Evening Post* (Philadelphia), 27 February 1965.

Play

The Wife of Martin Guerre, music by William Bergsma, adaptation of the novel by Lewis (produced New York, 1956). Denver, Swallow, 1958.

Verse

The Indians in the Woods. Bonn, Germany, Monroe Wheeler, 1922.
The Wheel in Midsummer. Lynn, Massachusetts, Lone Gull Press, 1927.
The Earth-Bound 1924-1944. Aurora, New York, Wells College, 1946.
The Hangar at Sunnyvale 1937. San Francisco, Book Club of California, 1947.
Poems 1924-1944. Denver, Swallow, 1950.
The Ancient Ones. Portola Valley, California, No Dead Lines, 1979.
Poems Old and New 1918-1978. Athens, Ohio University Press, 1981.

Other

The Friendly Adventures of Ollie Ostrich (juvenile). New York, Doubleday, 1923.
Keiko's Bubble (juvenile). New York, Doubleday, 1961; Kingswood, Surrey, World's Work, 1963.

The U.S. and Canada, with others. Green Bay, University of Wisconsin Press, 1970.

*

Manuscript Collection: Stanford University Library, California.

Critical Studies: by Richard F. Goldman, in *Musical Quarterly* (New York), July 1956; "The Legacy of Fenimore Cooper" by Donald Davie, in *Essays in Criticism* (Brill, Buckinghamshire), July 1959; "The Historical Novels of Janet Lewis" by Donald Davie, in *Southern Review* (Baton Rouge, Louisiana), January 1966; "Genius Unobserved" by Evan S. Connell, Jr., in *Atlantic* (Boston), December 1969; "Patriarchal Women: A Study of Three Novels by Janet Lewis" by Ellen Killoh, in *Southern Review* (Baton Rouge, Louisiana), Spring 1974.

Janet Lewis comments:

It is difficult to know what to say about my own work. Most of it needs little if any explanation. In regard to *The Invasion* I can state that I meant to write history as if I were writing fiction. It is in every way, in so far as I could manage, faithful to the facts and the events. When it comes to the three novels based on the famous cases of circumstantial evidence, I can only state again that I intended to write history as if it were fiction. I remained in each case as faithful to the facts as I could, but I was so far from them in time and space that I needed to invent rather freely, in order to clothe the facts with life. In the case of *Martin Guerre* I began with a very brief account of the events, and have learned bit by bit since the day the book was first published more and more about the truth of the matter, so that now, thirty years later, I have at hand the ultimate source for the story, the account by one of the judges, Jean de Coras. My story of Martin Guerre is fiction, but it is very close indeed to the known facts.

* * *

Janet Lewis, widow of the poet and critic Yvor Winters, and herself a distinguished poet, is admired as one of the purest stylists in contemporary fiction, and as a novelist who continued to write quietly probing dramas of psycho-moral ambiguity with almost total disregard for the changing fashions of American fiction. She is to be compared, in the quiet integrity of her art, with Willa Cather, Caroline Gordon, and her friend Elizabeth Madox Roberts. Only her modest volume of short stories (*Goodbye, Son*) and the slow-paced, intelligent, at times dreary *Against a Darkening Sky* are contemporary in scene. Her reputation rests instead on her four historical novels, one related to her own part-Indian background, the others laid in remote European times.

The Invasion occupies a surprisingly satisfying border region between fiction and history, and contains some of the loveliest prose in modern American literature. Its singular achievement is to present without pretentiousness or strain an Indian culture from within (the Ojibway of the Lake Superior area), and its gradual change and slow obliteration over a century and a half. The family chronicle extends from 1791, when we meet the 14-year-old Woman of the Glade, who married the trader John Johnston, to the death in 1944 of Anna Maria Johnston, the Red Leaf. The novel is the work of a poet recording delicate nuances of landscape and mood, and of a scrupulous historian contemplating with equanimity the inevitable outrages of human passion and eroding time. It combines with remarkable success an intimate immersion in scene (a succession of lived moments) and a flow of time that is calm as well as swift. The chronicle's exceptional authenticity is strengthened by the fact that the famous ethnologist, linguist, and Indian agent Henry Rowe Schoolcraft is a central figure in the family history.

Three very different historical novels are based on incidents recorded in Phillips's *Famous Cases of Circumstantial Evidence*, an early 19th-century work. *The Trial of Sören Qvist*, laid in 17th-century Denmark, is the story of a saintly pastor executed for a crime he did not commit. This is a spare and dramatic novel, but meditative too, like everything Janet Lewis has written. *The Ghost of Monsieur Scarron* is the product of years of research, some of it in a part of Paris that has not greatly changed since 1694. It is the minutely realistic story of a bookbinder falsely accused of authoring a libelous pamphlet directed against Louis XIV and Madame de Maintenon. The evocation of the Paris of that time is remarkable.

The best of these novels, one of the greatest short novels in American literature, is *The Wife of Martin Guerre*, a quietly authentic, immaculately written story of a man whose physical "double" (but far more considerate and more loving than the original) returns to claim the wife of a soldier supposed dead in the wars of 16th-century France. Here as in her other two novels of ambiguous crime and punishment Janet Lewis dramatizes, always calmly, situations exerting extreme pressure on her characters. The marriage of Martin Guerre and Bertrande de Rols, at 11, is of its time, and so too the execution 21 years later. A sentence from Janet Lewis's "Foreword" suggests the human understanding underlying all her work. "The rules of evidence vary from century to century, and the morality which compels many of the actions of men and women varies also, but the capacities of the human soul for suffering and for joy remain very much the same."

—Albert Guerard

LINDSAY, Jack. Australian. Born in Melbourne, Victoria, 20 October 1900; son of the writer and artist Norman Lindsay. Educated at Brisbane Grammar School; University of Queensland, Brisbane, 1918-21, B.A. (honours) in classics 1921. Served in the British Army, 1941-45, in the Royal Corps of Signals, 1941-43, and as a scriptwriter in the War Office, 1943-45. Married Meta Waterdrinker in 1956; one son and one daughter. Editor, with Kenneth Slessor and F. Johnson, *Vision*, Sydney, 1923-24; settled in England, 1926; Proprietor and Director, Fanfrolico Press, London, 1927-30; Editor, with P.R. Stephensen, *London Aphrodite*, 1928-29; Editor, *Poetry and the People*, London, 1938-39; Editor, *Anvil*, London, 1947; Editor, with John Davenport and Randall Swingler, *Arena*, London, 1949-51. Recipient: Australian Literature Society Couch Gold Medal, 1960; Order of Merit, U.S.S.R., 1968. D.Litt.: University of Queensland. Fellow of the Royal Society of Literature, 1945, and of the Ancient Monuments Society, 1961; Member, Order of Australia, 1981. Address: 40 Queen Street, Castle Hedingham, Essex, England.

PUBLICATIONS

Novels

Cressida's First Lover: A Tale of Ancient Greece. London, Lane, 1931; New York, Long and Smith, 1932.
Rome for Sale. London, Mathews and Marrot, and New York, Harper, 1934.
Caesar Is Dead. London, Nicholson and Watson, 1934.
Last Days with Cleopatra. London, Nicholson and Watson, 1935.
Despoiling Venus. London, Nicholson and Watson, 1935.
Storm at Sea. London, Golden Cockerel Press, 1935.
The Wanderings of Wenamen: 1115-1114 B.C. London, Nicholson and Watson, 1936.
Shadow and Flame (as Richard Preston). London, Chapman and Hall, 1936.
Adam of a New World. London, Nicholson and Watson, 1936.
Sue Verney. London, Nicholson and Watson, 1937.
End of Cornwall (as Richard Preston). London, Cape, 1937.
1649: A Novel of a Year. London, Methuen, 1938.

Brief Light: A Novel of Catullus. London, Methuen, 1939.
Lost Birthright. London, Methuen, 1939.
Giuliano the Magnificent, adapted from a work by D. Johnson. London, Dakers, 1940.
Light in Italy. London, Gollancz, 1941.
Hannibal Takes a Hand. London, Dakers, 1941.
The Stormy Violence. London, Dakers, 1941.
We Shall Return: A Novel of Dunkirk and the French Campaign. London, Dakers, 1942.
Beyond Terror: A Novel of the Battle of Crete. London, Dakers, 1943.
The Barriers Are Down: A Tale of the Collapse of a Civilisation. London, Gollancz, 1945.
Hullo Stranger. London, Dakers, 1945.
Time to Live. London, Dakers, 1946.
The Subtle Knot. London, Dakers, 1947.
Men of Forty-Eight. London, Methuen, 1948.
Fires in Smithfield. London, Lane, 1950.
The Passionate Pastoral. London, Lane, 1951.
Betrayed Spring: A Novel of the British Way. London, Lane, 1953.
Rising Tide. London, Lane, 1953.
The Moment of Choice. London, Lane, 1955.
A Local Habitation: A Novel of the Brtish Way. London, Bodley Head, 1957.
The Great Oak: A Story of 1549. London, Bodley Head, 1957.
The Revolt of the Sons. London, Muller, 1960.
All on the Never-Never: A Novel of the British Way of Life. London, Muller, 1961.
The Way the Ball Bounces. London, Muller, 1962.
Masks and Faces. London, Muller, 1963.
Choice of Times. London, Muller, 1964.
Thunder Underground: A Story of Nero's Rome. London, Muller, 1965.

Short Stories

Come Home at Last and Other Stories. London, Nicholson and Watson, 1936.
Death of a Spartan King and Two Other Stories of the Ancient World. London, Inca Books, 1974.

Plays

Marino Faliero: A Verse-Play. London, Fanfrolico Press, 1927.
Helen Comes of Age: Three Original Plays in Verse (includes *Ragnild* and *Bussy d'Amboise*). London, Fanfrolico Press, 1927.
Hereward: A Verse Drama, music by J. Gough. London, Fanfrolico Press, 1930.
The Whole Armour of God (produced London, 1944).
Robin of England (produced London, 1945).
The Face of Coal, with B. Coombes (produced London, 1946).
Iphigeneia in Aulis, adaptation of a play by Euripides (produced London, 1967).
Hecuba, adaptation of a play by Euripides (produced London, 1967).
Electra, adaptation of a play by Euripides (produced London, 1967).
Orestes, adaptation of a play by Euripides (produced London, 1967).
Nathan the Wise, adaptation of a play by Lessing (produced London, 1967).

Verse

Fauns and Ladies. Sydney, Kirtley, 1923.
The Pleasante Conceited Narrative of Panurge's Fantastic Ally Brocaded Codpiece. Sydney, Panurgean Society, 1924.
The Spanish Main and Tavern. Sydney, Panurgean Society, 1924.
The Passionate Neatherd. London, Fanfrolico Press, 1926.
Into Action: The Battle of Dieppe. London, Dakers, 1942.
Second Front: Poems. London, Dakers, 1944.
Clue of Darkness. London, Dakers, 1949.
Peace Is Our Answer. London, Collet, 1950.
Three Letters to Nikolai Tikhonov. London, Fore, 1951.
Three Elegies. Sudbury, Suffolk, Myriad Press, 1957.
Faces and Places. Toronto, Basilike, 1974.

Other

William Blake: Creative Will and the Poetic Image. London, Fanfrolico Press, 1927; revised edition, 1929; New York, Haskell House, 1971.
Dionysos; or, Nietzsche contra Nietzsche: An Essay in Lyrical Philosophy. London, Fanfrolico Press, 1928.
The Romans. London, Black, 1935.
Runaway (juvenile). London, Oxford University Press, 1935.
Rebels of the Goldfields (juvenile). London, Lawrence and Wishart, 1936.
Marc Antony: His World and His Contemporaries. London, Routledge, 1936; New York, Dutton, 1937.
John Bunyan: Maker of Myths. London, Methuen, 1937; New York, Kelley, 1969.
The Anatomy of Spirit: An Enquiry into the Origins of Religious Emotions. London, Methuen, 1937.
To Arms! A Story of Ancient Gaul (juvenile). London, Oxford University Press, 1938.
England, My England. London, Fore, 1939.
A Short History of Culture. London, Gollancz, 1939; revised edition, London, Studio Books, 1962; New York, Citadel Press, 1964.
The Dons Sight Devon: A Story of the Defeat of the Invincible Armada (juvenile). London, Oxford University Press, 1942.
Perspective for Poetry. London, Fore, 1944.
British Achievement in Art and Music. London, Pilot Press, 1945.
Mulk Raj Anand: A Critical Essay. Bombay, Hind Kitabs, 1948; revised edition, as *The Elephant and the Lotus*, Bombay, Kutub Popular, 1954.
Song of a Falling World: Culture During the Break-up of the Roman Empire (A.D. 350-600). London, Dakers, 1948; Westport, Connecticut, Hyperion Press, 1979.
Marxism and Contemporary Science; or, The Fulness of Life. London, Dobson, 1949.
A World Ahead: Journal of a Soviet Journey. London, Fore, 1950.
Charles Dickens: A Biographical and Critical Study. London, Dakers, and New York, Philosophical Library, 1950.
Byzantium into Europe: The Story of Byzantium as the First Europe (362-1204 A.D.) and Its Further Contribution till 1453 A.D. London, Lane, 1952.
Rumanian Summer, with M. Cornforth. London, Lawrence and Wishart, 1953.
Civil War in England: The Cromwellian Revolution. London, Muller, 1954; New York, Barnes and Noble, 1967.
George Meredith: His Life and Work. London, Lane, 1956; New York, Kraus, 1973.
The Romans Were Here: The Roman Period in Britain and Its Place in Our History. London, Muller, 1956; New York, Barnes and Noble, 1969.
After the Thirties: The Novel in Britain and Its Future. London, Lawrence and Wishart, 1956.
Life Rarely Tells: An Autobiographical Account Ending in the Year 1921 and Situated Mostly in Brisbane, Queensland. London, Bodley Head, 1958.
Arthur and His Times: Britain in the Dark Ages. London, Muller, 1958; New York, Barnes and Noble, 1966.
The Discovery of Britain: A Guide to Archaeology. London, Merlin Press, 1958.
1764: The Hurly-Burly of Daily Life Exemplified in One Year of the 18th Century. London, Muller, 1959.
The Writing on the Wall: An Account of Pompeii in Its Last Days. London, Muller, 1960.

The Roaring Twenties: Literary Life in Sydney, New South Wales, in the Years 1921-26. London, Bodley Head, 1960.
Death of the Hero: French Painting from David to Delacroix. London, Studio, 1960.
William Morris: Writer. London, William Morris Society, 1961.
Our Celtic Heritage. London, Weidenfeld and Nicolson, 1962.
Fanfrolico and After (autobiography). London, Bodley Head, 1962.
Daily Life in Roman Egypt. London, Muller, 1963; New York, Barnes and Noble, 1964.
Nine Days' Hero: Wat Tyler. London, Dobson, 1964.
The Clashing Rocks: A Study of Early Greek Religion and Culture, and the Origins of Drama. London, Chapman and Hall, 1965.
Leisure and Pleasure in Roman Egypt. London, Muller, 1965; New York, Barnes and Noble, 1966.
Our Anglo-Saxon Heritage. London, Weidenfeld and Nicolson, 1965.
J.M.W. Turner: His Life and Work: A Critical Biography. London, Adams and MacKay, and Greenwich, Connecticut, New York Graphic Society, 1966.
Our Roman Heritage. London, Weidenfeld and Nicolson, 1967.
Meetings with Poets: Memories of Dylan Thomas, Edith Sitwell, Louis Aragon, Paul Eluard, Tristan Tzara. London, Muller, 1968; New York, Ungar, 1969.
Men and Gods on the Roman Nile. London, Muller, and New York, Barnes and Noble, 1968.
The Ancient World: Manners and Morals. London, Weidenfeld and Nicolson, and New York, Putnam, 1968.
Cézanne: His Life and Art. London, Adams and MacKay, and Greenwich, Connecticut, New York Graphic Society, 1969.
The Origins of Alchemy in Graeco-Roman Egypt. London, Muller, and New York, Barnes and Noble, 1970.
Cleopatra. London, Constable, and New York, Coward McCann, 1971.
Origins of Astrology. London, Muller, and New York, Barnes and Noble, 1971.
Gustave Courbet: His Life and Work. Bath, Adams and Dart, 1973; New York, Harper, 1974.
Helen of Troy: Woman and Goddess. London, Constable, and Totowa, New Jersey, Rowman and Littlefield, 1974.
Blast-Power and Ballistics: Concepts of Force and Energy in the Ancient World. London, Muller, and New York, Barnes and Noble, 1974.
The Normans and Their World. London, Hart Davis MacGibbon, 1974; New York, St. Martin's Press, 1975.
William Morris: His Life and Work. London, Constable, 1975; New York, Taplinger, 1979.
Decay and Renewal: Critical Essays on Twentieth Century Writing. Sydney, Wild and Woolley, 1976; London, Lawrence and Wishart, 1977.
The Troubadours and Their World of the Twelfth and Thirteenth Centuries. London, Muller, 1976.
Hogarth: His Art and World. London, Hart Davis MacGibbon, 1977; New York, Taplinger, 1979.
William Blake: His Life and Work. London, Constable, 1978; New York, Braziller, 1979.
The Monster City: Defoe's London 1688-1730. London, Hart Davis MacGibbon, and New York, St. Martin's Press, 1978.
Thomas Gainsborough: His Life and Art. London, Granada, 1981.
The Crisis in Marxism. Bradford on Avon, Wiltshire, Moonraker Press, and New York, Barnes and Noble, 1981.

Editor, with Kenneth Slessor, *Poetry in Australia*. Sydney, Vision Press, 1923.
Editor, with P. Warlock, *Loving Mad Tom: Bedlamite Verses of the XVI and XVII Centuries*. London, Fanfrolico Press, 1927; New York, Kelley, 1970.
Editor, *The Metamorphosis of Aiax*, by Sir John Harington. New York, McKee, 1928.
Editor, *Parlement of Pratlers*. London, Fanfrolico Press, 1928.
Editor (as Peter Meadows), *Delighted Earth*, by Robert Herrick. London, Fanfrolico Press, 1928.
Editor, *Inspiration*. London, Fanfrolico Press, 1928.
Editor, *Letters of Philip Stanhope, Second Earl of Chesterfield*. London, Fanfrolico Press, 1930.
Editor, with Edgell Rickword, *A Handbook of Freedom: A Record of English Democracy Through Twelve Centuries*. London, Lawrence and Wishart, and New York, International Publishers, 1939.
Editor, with others, *New Lyrical Ballads*. London, Editions Poetry, 1945.
Editor, *Anvil: Life and the Arts: A Miscellany*. London, Meridian, and New York, Universal Distributors, 1947.
Editor, *New Development Series*. London, Lane, 1947-48.
Editor, *Herrick: A Selection*. London, Grey Walls Press, 1948.
Editor, *William Morris: A Selection*. London, Grey Walls Press, 1948.
Editor, with Randall Swingler, *Key Poets*. London, Fore, 1950.
Editor, *Barefoot*, by Z. Stancu. London, Fore, 1950.
Editor, *Paintings and Drawings of Leslie Hurry*. London, Grey Walls Press, 1952.
Editor, *The Sunset Ship: Poems of J.M.W. Turner*. Lowestoft, Suffolk, Scorpion Press, 1966.
Editor, *The Autobiography of Joseph Priestley*. Bath, Adams and Dart, 1970; Teaneck, New Jersey, Fairleigh Dickinson University Press, 1971.

Translator, *Lysistrata*, by Aristophanes. Sydney, Kirtley, 1925; London, Fanfrolico Press, 1926.
Translator, *Satyricon and Poems*, by Petronius. London, Fanfrolico Press, 1927; revised edition, London, Elek, 1960.
Translator, *Homage to Sappho*. London, Fanfrolico Press, 1928.
Translator, *Complete Poems of Theocritus*. London, Fanfrolico Press, 1929.
Translator, *Hymns to Aphrodite*, by Homer. London, Fanfrolico Press, 1929.
Translator, *Women in Parliament*, by Aristophanes. London, Fanfrolico Press, 1929.
Translator, *The Mimiambs of Herondas*. London, Fanfrolico Press, 1929.
Translator, *The Complete Poetry of Gaius Catullus*. London, Fanfrolico Press, 1930; revised edition, London, Sylvan Press, 1948.
Translator, *Sulpicia's Garland: Roman Poems*. New York, McKee, 1930.
Translator, *Patchwork Quilt: Poems by Ausonius*. London, Fanfrolico Press, 1930.
Translator, *The Golden Ass*, by Apuleius. New York, Limited Editions Club, 1931; revised edition, London, Elek, and Bloomington, Indiana University Press, 1960.
Translator, *I Am a Roman*. London, Mathews and Marrot, 1934.
Translator, *Medieval Latin Poets*. London, Mathews and Marrot, 1934.
Translator, *Daphnis and Chloe*, by Longus. London, Daimon Press, 1948.
Translator, with S. Jolly, *Song of Peace*, by V. Nezval. London, Fore, 1951.
Translator, *Poems of Adam Mickiewicz*. London, Sylvan Press, and New York, Transatlantic Arts, 1957.
Translator, *Russian Poetry 1917-1955*. London, Lane, 1957; Chester Springs, Pennsylvania, Dufour, 1961.
Translator, *Asklepiades in Love*. Twinstead, Essex, Myriad Press, 1960.
Translator, *Modern Russian Poetry*. London, Vista, 1960.
Translator, *Cause, Principle, and Unity: 5 Dialogues*, by Giordano Bruno. London, Daimon Press, 1962; New York, International Publishers, 1964.
Translator, *Ribaldry of Ancient Greece*. London, Elek, and New York, Ungar, 1965.
Translator, *Ribaldry of Ancient Rome*. London, Elek, and New York, Ungar, 1965.

ranslator, *The Elegy of Haido*, by Teferos Anthias. London, Anthias Publications, 1966.

ranslator, *The Age of Akhenaten*, by Eleonore Bille-de-Mot. London, Adams and MacKay, 1967; New York, McGraw Hill, 1968.

ranslator, *Greece, I Keep My Vigil for You*, by Teferos Anthias. London, Anthias Publications, 1968.

ranslator, *The Twelve*, by Aleksandr Blok. London, Journeyman Press, 1981.

*

ritical Studies: *Mountain in the Sunlight* by Alick West, London, awrence and Wishart, 1958.

ack Lindsay comments:

I began as a poet and feel that my devotion to poetry has deter-nined my writing career in all its aspects. First as poet and classical cholar I turned to translating Greek and Latin poetry; then as critic eeking to understand the ancient poets I worked at history, needing o grasp their world and find out how far the poems were linked with hat world's workings; out of concern for the nature of poetry I urned to philosophy, especially Plato and Nietzsche though also to oet-philosophers like Blake; later the same interests drew me to ultural anthropology and to psychoanalysis. Thus out of various isciplines, which I approached always from the angle of poetry and s nature, I expanded my interests and the range of my work.

A friend and I hand-printed my *Lysistrata* in Sydney, Australia, 924-25, with illustrations by my father Norman Lindsay. The book vas well received and he asked me to come to London to start a fine ress, the Fanfrolico (a name devised by my father in *contes drola-iques* he had written for an Abbey of Thelema): we used that name o express the aesthetic we had devised in Australia. The friend anded the press over to me, as he wanted to return to Australia; I vas thus involved in much typographical, editing, translating work, nd did much literary research at the B.M. Reading Room, as well s writing poetry. When the press ended in 1930 I went to Cornwall n an effort to find a new basis for work, and lived in extreme ardship till 1934 when I managed to synthesise my interests (as utlined above) in the historical novel. I had translated and anno-ated Catullus, and I now developed a picture of his world in a Roman trilogy.

My method was thus derived wholly from poetry and my quest nto its nature as the highest point of human consciousness. It ought to bring together the following elements: (a) the element of ensuous immediacy in experience, the timeless present of the poetic mage; (b) the tragic pattern of conflict, breakdown, recognition, riumph as I had learned it from the Greeks, Nietzsche, and Freud-an technique, and from my broodings over Shakespeare and Dos-oevsky; (c) the related pattern of death-rebirth which was revealed n tribal ritual (especially of the initiation-ceremony) and carried on y the mystery-religions of the ancient world and by Christianity. I hen attempted to make a dynamic synthesis of all these elements in n interpretation of the structure of development in history and of he dialectical relation of individual and social whole. I was (and ave continued to go on) seeking to grasp in a single conception or mage a largescale moment of life, especially a moment of revolu-ionary change when all the issues come together in full force, and at he same time to realise the situation at a multiple series of levels personal, social, aesthetic, philosophic, legal, religious, etc.).

This has continued to be my method, with varying emphases—hough I soon turned to English history as well as to ancient, and hen moved on to the contemporary situation. I have tried to grasp he particular forms of death-rebirth in every period, to grasp both he total movement and the individual refractions. In turn I have xpanded this method to deal directly with many periods of history especially Graeco-Roman Egypt), with problems of anthropology, with the biographies of writers and artists, and so on. I think I can hen claim a definite unity in all my work despite its very multifar-ous nature. The novels have been especially recognized in the Soviet Union, where over a million copies have been sold in translation and *Betrayed Spring* has been printed in its English form as a textbook. Versions have also appeared in Chinese and Mongolian, as well as in German, Polish, Hungarian, Czech, Romanian, Bulgarian. I believe that this wide interest has been because of the fusion I have attempted of a poetic and an historical vision—the way in which my method seeks to grasp the patterns of change in a perspective of all that constitutes the human universal.

* * *

Jack Lindsay divides his many novels into two groups: "Historical Novels" and "Contemporary Novels of the British Way." These two groups are closely linked by an overwhelming concern for the socialist ideal in its purist form. What interests this writer primarily is the moment of revolutionary stuggle when the forces working for the good life for every human being rise up against the apathy and de-humanisation caused by an out-of-control capitalist system. This moment of change may take place in Rome in 63 B.C., as it does in the early novel *Rome for Sale*, or in the formation of a branch of the Campaign for Nuclear Disarmament in a small midland town, as it does nearly 30 years later in *The Way the Ball Bounces*.

It is no doubt because of this strong political bias that Lindsay's novels are so widely read in the Soviet Union and the Eastern bloc. But political propaganda and the art of the novelist are two separate activities. One must look beyond the unvarying message, however much one may agree or disagree with it, to discover how these novels take shape and live. The first thing one notices after reading several of them from any period is how strongly they are influenced by Elizabethan drama. These novels are structured as plays, the reader being given a list of the main characters. The plot is almost invariably of a strong and definite nature involving events of life and death; and the action is divided into contrasting scenes, with comic relief supplied in an almost Shakespearean manner in the Roman novels by the most bawdy of the common soldiers and their prostitutes.

As for love, as distinct from lust, that is an emotion that for Lindsay is very strongly linked with political ideals. Catalina in *Rome for Sale* owes the deep love he has for his wife Orestilla to the knowledge that they are both working for the same cause, the prosperity of the common citizens of Rome. In a much later novel, *Revolt of the Sons*, Chris, the youngest of Samuel Todd's five sons, realises his love for his cousin Rebecca at the same time that he becomes convinced of the need to break free of the tyranny of private family capitalism in which he and his brothers are locked. The case of Alan Horton, the young solicitor in *The Way the Ball Bounces*, is somewhat different. A withdrawn young man, he was so emotionally shattered by his experiences in the Korean war that he successfully immured himself against any form of feeling apart from a mild delight in the verbal logic of the law. It takes a short, sincere, and slightly desperate affair with a young West Indian girl to batter these defences down.

Lindsay is above all a very conscious novelist. He does not expect the reader totally to suspend disbelief. So in the historical novels he keeps very closely to the actual recorded events, and in the contemporary novels in imagined settings he often lets the reader observe how the characters are being handled. Francis Musgrave, one of the main characters in *A Local Habitation*, acts as a sort of chorus in *The Revolt of the Sons*. He and his friend Roland have been discussing old Todd, his five sons and the wives of the three older ones. He reports "You might say that family represents our world in miniscule.... I said it was a Balzacian theme: the power of money and its ubiquitous tendrils of distortion. He said it was Dostoevskian: the fascination and hatred of authority, the jealous sons surrounding the father-god." In fact, as in so many of these novels, it is both.

—Shirley Toulson

LITVINOFF, Emanuel. British. Born in London, 30 June 1915. Served as a Major in the Royal West African Frontier Force, 1940-46. Married Cherry Marshall in 1942 (divorced); three children. Before World War II, worked in tailoring, cabinet-making, and the fur trade; after the war worked as a journalist and broadcaster, and founded the journal, *Jews in Eastern Europe*, London. Since 1958, Director of the Contemporary Jewish Library, London. Recipient: Wingate Award (*Jewish Chronicle*, London), 1979. Address: c/o David Higham Associates, 5-8 Lower John Street, London W1R 4HA, England.

PUBLICATIONS

Novels

The Lost Europeans. New York, Vanguard Press, 1959; London, Heinemann, 1960.
The Man Next Door. London, Hodder and Stoughton, 1968; New York, Norton, 1969.
A Death Out of Season. London, Joseph, 1973; New York, Scribner, 1974.
Blood on the Snow. London, Joseph, 1975.
The Face of Terror. London, Joseph, and New York, Morrow, 1978.

Short Stories

Penguin Modern Stories 2, with others. London, Penguin, 1969.
Journey Through a Small Planet. London, Joseph, 1972.

Uncollected Short Stories

"The God I Failed," in *The Guardian* (London), 1966.
"Call Me Uncle Solly," in *The Listener* (London), 1967.

Plays

Magnolia Street Story, adaptation of a novel by Louis Golding (produced London, 1951).

Television Plays: *Another Branch of the Family*, 1967; *Marriage and Henry Sunday*, 1967; *A Dream in the Afternoon*, 1967; *A Foot in the Door*, 1969; *The World Is a Room*, 1970; *Warm Feet, Warm Heart*, 1970.

Verse

Conscripts: A Symphonic Declaration. London, Favil Press, 1941.
The Untried Soldier. London, Routledge, 1942.
A Crown for Cain. London, Falcon Press, 1948.
Notes for a Survivor. Newcastle upon Tyne, Northern House, 1973.

Editor, *Soviet Anti-Semitism: The Paris Trial.* London, Wildwood House, 1975.
Editor, *The Penguin Book of Jewish Short Stories.* London, Penguin, 1979.

*

Emanuel Litvinoff comments:

(1976) My novel *The Lost Europeans* is haunted by the Holocaust. It describes the morbid psychological obsessions of victim and persecutor in a situation where former German Jews return to Germany after the war and confront their erstwhile neighbours.

The Man Next Door is, in a sense, related to this theme. Its central character is a conventional suburban Englishman of the middle-class whose personality begins to disintegrate under the encroachments of middle-age, accompanied by a sense of social and sexual failure. In the process, a mild and commonplace xenophobia turns to rabid hatred of Jews and Negroes of the kind so hideously expressed by the Nazis.

A Death Out of Season and *Blood on the Snow* are two novels of a trilogy following the fortunes of a group of young revolutionaries in the early years of the century, through the Russian Revolution, civil war and famine, to their final disillusion and bitterness in the Stalinist purges of the mid-1930's.

My short stories, set in the milieu of the London Jewish East End, celebrate the idealism, pain, and promise of adolescence.

* * *

Emanuel Litvinoff's short stories describe the atmosphere of a close Jewish community in London's East End where he grew up between the wars. The stories contain some poignant and sometimes verbose semi-autobiographical sketches of adolescence, as in "A View from the Seventh Floor":

> "What do you do on week-ends?" I stammered.
> "On Saturday," she whispered, without lifting her head, "I go to the synagogue with my aunt."
> Soft black hair curled on the nape of her slender neck and I was tormented by her narrow, sleepy Russian eyes. I wanted to say something miraculous and unforgettable, or so sharp, cruel and eloquent it would remain a fresh wound all of her life. But instead I said: "Does your aunt shave on Shabbos?"

In the same story, Litvinoff mentions his early feelings of rootlessness which inform much of his later work: "In those days I had the shadowy premonition that unless my life was shattered to pieces and I could put it together differently, I'd never, never be myself."

As Litvinoff approaches maturity, he becomes increasingly aware of his "ancestry of misfortune." He regards it as mere chance that he was born in Whitechapel. His home could as easily have been in Hitler's Germany or Stalin's Russia. Litvinoff's first novel, *The Lost Europeans*, develops this idea and examines the restless lives of a few World War II survivors. The novel is set in post-war Berlin where ex-nazis and communists, hedonistic young Aryans, whores, and a few Jews live in awkward peace. Martin Stone, a London accountant, takes time off to visit the city of his childhood and claim the legal restitution of his family's fortune. The war-blighted Berliners whom Martin meets involuntarily inflame his smouldering bitterness. There is Hugo Krantz, a fellow Jew, once the witty doyen of Berlin's theatre circles, now a fat businessman in relentless pursuit of sensual pleasures, and the friend who betrayed him to the S.S. Hugo arranges accommodation for Martin in the guesthouse of his oldest friend, Frau Goetz. Her gothic hair-do and bird-like charm cannot conceal the marks of Auschwitz. Every Berliner is a victim. In the parks and pastryshops and honky tonk bars, Martin feels once more "the poisons moving in the bloodstream, the familiar throbbing of the diseased night." But it is in this city that Martin meets Karin, a docile factory worker from the eastern sector. She too is a victim—raped in childhood by conquering Russian soldiers. In order to offer her his love, Martin must expiate Karin's years of numbness and resolve his own haunting resentments.

Litvinoff's descriptions of the strange personal lives of Hugo and Frau Goetz are especially good, and Hugo's foray into the ambiguous and dangerous world of intelligence agents has all the atmosphere of a first-rate spy thriller. But just as the pace is getting really hot, we are back with the dour, curiously faceless Martin. The impact of each story—Martin's and Hugo's—is reduced rather than enhanced by its entanglement with the other. Nevertheless, *The Lost Europeans* is a very readable and frequently compelling account of the obsessions of German Jews and their former persecutors.

The Man Next Door focuses on Harold Bollam, a man who blossomed early in life. Boarding school, the army, and a spell as a store manager in West Africa supported and strengthened his hawkish sentiments on class and race. Back in England he finds life somewhat bewildering:

> The country had gone mad for gimmicks. Young smart alecks were getting in everywhere. Long-haired pop-singers bought up the stately homes, public opinion media were in the hands of queers and sensation-mongers who made England look cheap in the eyes of the world. Cheap, indeed, when black college boys became prime ministers of ridiculous "independent" states, dined with the Queen and lectured the British on the what's-what of democracy.

Middle-age does not mellow a man like Bollam; failures and frustrations pile upon him. Relations with his fretful wife Edna are bleak; prospects for promotion at International Utilities dwindle daily; sex is a combat between flesh and despair; his children, away at boarding school, are strangers. When the Winstons (born Weinsteins) move in next door, Bollam's resentments and fears become obsessions. His wife, his colleagues, the Blacks, the Jews, and especially the Jews next door, are all conspiring to degrade and defeat him. Obsession turns to paranoia and Bollam seeks insane revenge. "...as soon as the Winstons arrived he'd guessed it would end badly. They didn't fit. Apart from being Jews, there was something alien and disruptive about them. They were the kind who carried the germ of misfortune wherever they went, like spores of an invisible cancer...."

The Man Next Door has a certain morbid fascination, but it lacks the authenticity of Litvinoff's first novel. Most of the characters are incredibly stereotyped, and his portrayal of Bollam's grim, neurotic life is often glib. The analogy between Bollam's retrogression and the rise of nazism is obvious but rarely effective.

Litvinoff writes about people whose painful history has left them bitter, tormented, and potentially destructive. But he does not have the sheer grasp or the calm incisiveness that characterizes the best writing of this kind.

—Roland Turner

LODGE, David (John). British. Born in London, 28 January 1935. Educated at St. Joseph's Academy, London; University College, London, 1952-55, 1957-59, B.A. (honours) in English 1955, M.A. 1959; University of Birmingham, Ph.D. 1967. Served in the Royal Armoured Corps, 1955-57. Married Mary Frances Jacob in 1959; two sons and one daughter. Assistant, British Council, London, 1959-60. Assistant Lecturer, 1960-62, Lecturer, 1963-71, Senior Lecturer, 1971-73, Reader, 1973-76, and since 1976, Professor of Modern English Literature, University of Birmingham. Visiting Associate Professor, University of California, Berkeley, 1969. Recipient: Harkness Commonwealth Fellowship, 1964; *Yorkshire Post* Award, 1975; Hawthornden Prize, 1976; Whitbread Award, for fiction and for book of the year, 1980. Fellow, Royal Society of Literature, 1976. Address: Department of English, University of Birmingham, Birmingham B15 2TT, England.

PUBLICATIONS

Novels

The Picturegoers. London, MacGibbon and Kee, 1960.
Ginger, You're Barmy. London, MacGibbon and Kee, 1962; New York, Doubleday, 1965.
The British Museum is Falling Down. London, MacGibbon and Kee, 1965; New York, Holt Rinehart, 1967.
Out of the Shelter. London, Macmillan, 1970.
Changing Places: A Tale of Two Campuses. London, Secker and Warburg, 1975; New York, Penguin, 1979.
How Far Can You Go? London, Secker and Warburg, 1980.

Uncollected Short Stories

"The Man Who Couldn't Get Up," in *Weekend Telegraph* (London), 6 May 1966.

Plays

Between These Four Walls, with Malcolm Bradbury and James Duckett (produced Birmingham, 1963).
Slap in the Middle, with others (produced Birmingham, 1965).

Other

About Catholic Authors (juvenile). London, St. Paul Publications, 1958.
The Language of Fiction. London, Routledge, and New York, Columbia University Press, 1966.
Graham Greene. New York, Columbia University Press, 1966.
The Novelist at the Crossroads and Other Essays on Fiction and Criticism. London, Routledge, and Ithaca, New York, Cornell University Press, 1971.
Evelyn Waugh. New York, Columbia University Press, 1971.
The Modes of Modern Writing: Metaphor, Metonymy, and the Typology of Modern Literature. London, Arnold, and Ithaca, New York, Cornell University Press, 1977.
Modernism, Antimodernism, and Postmodernism (lecture). Birmingham, University of Birmingham, 1977.
Working with Structuralism: Essays and Reviews on Nineteenth and Twentieth-Century Literature. London, Routledge, 1981.

Editor, *Jane Austen: "Emma": A Casebook.* London, Macmillan, 1968; Nashville, Aurora, 1970(?).
Editor, with James Kinsley, *Emma*, by Jane Austen. London, Oxford University Press, 1971.
Editor, *Twentieth Century Literary Criticism: A Reader.* London, Longman, 1972.
Editor, *Scenes of Clerical Life*, by George Eliot. London, Penguin, 1973.
Editor, *The Woodlanders*, by Thomas Hardy. London, Macmillan, 1974.

*

Critical Studies: Interview with Bernard Bergonzi, in *The Month* (London), February 1970; "The Novels of David Lodge" by Michael Parnell, in *Madog* (Barry, Wales), Summer 1979.

David Lodge comments:

(1972) My novels belong to a tradition of realistic fiction (especially associated with England) that tries to find an appropriate form for, and a public significance in, what the writer has himself experienced and observed. In my case this experience and observation include such things as: lower-middle-class life in the inner suburbs of South East London; a wartime childhood and a post-war "austerity" adolescence; Catholicism; education and the social and physical mobility it brings; military service, marriage, travel, etc. My first, second, and fourth novels are "serious" realistic novels about such themes, the last of them, *Out of the Shelter*, which is a kind of *Bildungsroman*, being, as far as I am concerned, the most inclusive and most fully achieved.

My third novel, *The British Museum Is Falling Down*, was something of a departure in being a comic novel, incorporating elements of farce and a good deal of parody. I plan to write more fiction in the comic mode, as I enjoy the freedom for invention and stylistic effect it affords. On the other hand, I have not (like many contemporary writers) lost faith in traditional realism as a vehicle for serious fiction. The writer I admire above all others, I suppose, is James Joyce, and the combination one finds in his early work of ealistic truthtelling and poetic intensity seems to me an aim still worth pursuing.

As an academic critic and teacher of literature with a special interest in prose fiction, I am inevitably self-conscious about matters of narrative technique, and I believe this is a help rather than a hindrance. I certainly think that my criticism of fiction gains from my experience of writing it.

(1981) Since writing the above I have come to have less faith in the viability of the traditional realistic novel of the kind that seeks, by suppressing the signs that it is written, and narrated, to give the illusion of being a transparent window upon the real. This shift of attitude does not entail abandoning the novel's traditional function of engaging with, organizing, and interpreting social-historical experience—merely being open about the necessarily conventional and artificial ways in which it does so. My last two works of fiction, therefore, have a prominent "metafictional" thread running through them, through which the self-consciousness about fictional technique referred to above is allowed some play in the texts themselves—licenced by comedy in *Changing Places*, but with more serious thematic intent in *How Far Can You Go?*

* * *

David Lodge combines the writing of fiction with a keen interest in its theory, as is shown in his books of criticism *The Language of Fiction* and *The Modes of Modern Writing*. As a critic he is sympathetic to literary experiment and the kind of fiction that probes the problematical relations between art and reality, though as a novelist he still finds the realistic tradition viable and continues to write within it, drawing in large measure on autobiographical material.

Lodge is a Roman Catholic by birth and upbringing. His basic milieu is shabby-genteel Catholic family life in South London, whose nearest literary equivalent lies in the domestic scenes of Joyce's *Portrait of the Artist*. His first novel, *The Picturegoers*, was set against this background, which was treated in a warm and even sentimental manner; he returned to it ten years later in *Out of the Shelter*, where it was regarded with a cool but not contemptuous eye, and with a much greater sense of its narrowness and limitations.

The Picturegoers was an ambitious novel, focused on a suburban cinema and showing a broad range of contrasted characters, though it was rather lacking in dramatic movement and interplay. It suggested that despite a speculative interest in the hero's religious struggles, Lodge's basic talent was as a comic novelist. It was followed by *Ginger, You're Barmy*, an obsessively realistic story of army life that was clearly a working-off of unassimilated resentments about the author's military service. *The British Museum Is Falling Down* represented a real development. It was a comic novel on a serious topic, the Roman Catholic ban on contraception. The central character is an anxious Catholic graduate student, married with three children and the nagging possibility that a fourth might be on the way; he spends his days working on a literary thesis at the British Museum, which Lodge presents as an area for farcical happenings of all kinds. The hero's professional interest in literary style is worked into the fabric of the novel in recurring passages of accomplished parody of distinguished modern novelists.

Out of the Shelter is, in all senses, a serious novel, though often showing its author's humorous bias. It is a *Bildungsroman* that traces its hero's childhood in wartime London up to a point in his mid-teens when he spends a holiday with his sister who is a secretary with the American army of occupation in Germany. After the deprivations of English life the boy is overwhelmed by the riches of the American Way of Life: the story, as Lodge tells it, is both an account of individual sensibility, and a representative treatment of a significant Anglo-American cultural encounter. Clashes between English and American attitudes are further exploited in *Changing Places*, an unreserved and satisfying return to comic fiction. It traces the fortunes of two university teachers of English, one from the English Midlands, one from the American West Coast, who exchange jobs and, eventually, wives. It is both a compellingly funny story and an intelligent expression of Lodge's interests in the nature of fictional form.

How Far Can You Go? is Lodge's most ambitious novel to date. It follows the lives of a group of English Catholics, from their student days in the early 1950's to the crises of impending middle age in the late 1970's. It shows their personal and professional struggles the successes or failures of their marriages, and their problems with contraception (by the end of the novel most of them have rejected the continuing official Catholic ban on it). Lodge registers the rapid changes in English society over a quarter of a century in an excellent novel that, though sometimes unconvincing in characterization, is faultlessly observant and readable.

—Bernard Bergonzi

LOGAN, Mark. *See* **NICOLE, Christopher.**

LOOS, Anita. American. Born in Sissons, now Mt. Shasta, California, 26 April 1893. Educated at schools in San Francisco. Married 1) Frank Pallma, Jr. in 1915 (marriage dissolved); 2) the writer and film director John Emerson in 1919 (died, 1956). Address: 506 Ocean Front, Santa Monica, California 90402, U.S.A. *Died 18 August 1981.*

PUBLICATIONS

Novels

A Mouse Is Born. New York, Doubleday, and London, Cape, 1951.

No Mother to Guide Her. New York, McGraw Hill, and London, Barker, 1961.

Short Stories

Gentlemen Prefer Blondes: The Illuminating Diary of a Professional Lady. New York, Boni and Liveright, 1925; London, Brentano's, 1926.

But Gentlemen Marry Brunettes. New York, Boni and Liveright, and London, Bretano's, 1928.

Plays

The Love Expert (screenplay), with John Emerson. Included in *How to Write Photoplays*, 1920.

Red Hot Romance (screenplay), with John Emerson. Included in *Breaking into the Movies*, 1921.

The Whole Town's Talking, with John Emerson (produced New York, 1923; London, 1926). New York, Longman, 1925; London, French, 1928.

The Fall of Eve (produced New York, 1925).

Gentlemen Prefer Blondes, with John Emerson, adaptation of the stories by Loos (produced New York, 1926; London, 1928). New York, Century Play Company, 1926; revised version, with Joseph Fields, music by Jule Styne and Leo Robin (produced New York, 1949; London, 1962).

The Social Register, with John Emerson (also co-director: produced New York, 1931).

The Women (screenplay), with Jane Murfin, in *Twenty Best Film Plays*, edited by John Gassner and Dudley Nichols. New York, Crown, 1943.

A Tree Grows in Brooklyn (screenplay), with Tess Slesinger and

Frank Davis, in *Best Film Plays 1945*, edited by John Gassner and Dudley Nichols. New York, Crown, 1946.
Happy Birthday (produced New York, 1946). New York, French, 1947.
Gigi, adaptation of the novel by Colette (produced New York, 1951; London, 1956). New York, Random House, 1952; London, French, 1957.
Intolerance (screenplay), with D.W. Griffith, edited by Theodore Huff. New York, Museum of Modern Art, 1955.
The Amazing Adele, adaptation of a play by Pierre Barrillet and Jean-Pierre Grédy (produced Philadelphia, 1955).
Chéri, adaptation of two novels by Colette (produced New York, 1959).
Gogo Love You (produced New York, 1964).
The King's Mare, adaptation of a play by Jean Canolle (produced London, 1966). London, Evans, 1967.
San Francisco (screenplay), edited by Matthew J. Bruccoli. Carbondale, Southern Illinois University Press, 1978.

Screenplays and scenarios: beginning with *The New York Hat*, 1912, wrote many short subjects; also wrote *The Widow's Kids*, 1913; *Oh, Sammy!*, 1913; *Pa Says*, 1913; *The Power of the Camera*, 1913; *The Suicide Pact*, 1913; *The Wedding Gown*, 1913; *Bink's Vacation*, 1913; *A Cure for Suffragettes*, 1913; *A Fallen Hero*, 1913; *The Hicksville Epicure*, 1913; *Highbrow Love*, 1913; *His Hoodoo*, 1913; *A Horse on Bill*, 1913; *The Lady in Black*, 1913; *False Colors*, 1914; *When Roads Part*, 1914; *Billy's Rival*, 1914; *A Bunch of Flowers*, 1914; *Gentleman or Thief*, 1914; *Manhattan Madness*, 1916; *The Wild Girl of the Sierras*, 1916; *Little Liar*, 1916; *The Half-Breed*, 1916; *American Aristocracy*, 1916; *His Picture in the Papers*, with John Emerson, 1916; *Intolerance*, with D.W. Griffith, 1916; *The Americano*, 1917; *Wild and Woolly*, 1917; *Reaching for the Moon*, with Emerson, 1917; *Down to Earth*, with Emerson, 1917; *In Again-Out Again*, 1917; *Under the Top*, 1918; *Come On In*, 1918; *Good-Bye, Bill*, 1918; *Hit-the-Trail Holiday*, with Emerson, 1918; *Let's Get a Divorce*, with Emerson, 1918; *Oh, You Women!*, with Emerson, 1919; *A Temperamental Wife*, with Emerson, 1919; *The Virtuous Vamp*, with Emerson, 1919; *Getting Mary Married*, with Emerson, 1919; *The Isle of Conquest*, with Emerson, 1919; *The Love Expert*, with Emerson, 1920; *In Search of a Sinner*, with Emerson, 1920; *Woman's Place*, with Emerson, 1921; *The Perfect Woman*, with Emerson, 1921; *The Branded Woman*, 1921; *Hold Your Man*, 1921; *Dangerous Business*, with Emerson, 1921; *Mama's Affair*, with Emerson, 1921; *Polly of the Follies*, with Emerson, 1922; *Red Hot Romance*, with Emerson, 1922; *Dulcy*, with Emerson and C. Gardner Sullivan, 1923; *Three Miles Out*, with Emerson and Neysa McMein, 1924; *The Social Secretary*, 1924; *Learning to Love*, with Emerson, 1925; *Stranded*, with Wyndham Gittens and Frances Guihan, 1927; *Publicity Madness*, with Andrew Bennison and Malcolm Stuart Boylan, 1927; *Gentlemen Prefer Blondes*, with Emerson and Herman Mankiewicz, 1928; *The Fall of Eve*, with others, 1929; *The Struggle*, with Emerson and D.W. Griffith, 1931; *Ex-Bad Boy*, 1931; *Red-Headed Woman*, 1933; *The Girl from Missouri*, with Emerson, 1934; *Biography of a Bachelor Girl*, 1934; *Riffraff*, with Francis Marion and H.W. Hanemann, 1935; *San Francisco*, 1936; *Saratoga*, with Robert Hopkins, 1937; *Mama Steps Out*, 1937; *The Women*, with Jane Murfin, 1939; *Susan and God*, 1940; *Blossoms in the Dust*, 1941; *They Met in Bombay*, with Edwin Justus Mayer and Leon Gordon, 1941; *When Ladies Meet*, with S.K. Lauren, 1941; *I Married an Angel*, 1942; *A Tree Grows in Brooklyn*, with Tess Slesinger and Frank Davis, 1945.

Other

How to Write Photoplays (includes *The Love Expert*), with John Emerson. New York, McCann, 1920.
Breaking into the Movies (includes *Red Hot Romance*), with John Emerson. New York, McCann, 1921.
A Girl Like I (autobiography). New York, Viking Press, 1966; London, Hamish Hamilton, 1967.
Twice Over Lightly: New York Then and Now, with Helen Hayes. New York, Harcourt Brace, 1972.
Kiss Hollywood Good-by. New York, Viking Press, and London, W.H. Allen, 1974.
Cast of Thousands. New York, Grosset and Dunlap, 1977.
The Talmadge Girls: A Memoir. New York, Viking Press, 1978.

*

Theatrical Activities:

Director: **Play**—*The Social Register* (co-director, with John Emerson), 1931. **Film**—*Mama's Affair*, 1921.

Actress: **Plays**—roles in *Little Lord Fauntleroy, East Lynne, On the Yukon, The Prince Chap, The Jewess*, and *Mary Jane's Pa*, all in San Diego, California, and in *An Evening of Theatrical Reminiscences*, New York, 1963.

* * *

One of Anita Loos's four books of fiction, *Gentlemen Prefer Blondes*, brought her international fame and, as a stage play, a musical comedy, and on the screen—in several versions each—made her a millionaire. Her other novels and plays and her many photoplays have kept her in the public eye, but it is *Gentlemen Prefer Blondes* that has attracted most attention to her work. The rest of her fiction is lightly amusing, but her first book remains her most attractive and most admired. *But Gentlemen Marry Brunettes* carries on with the characters introduced in the earlier volume, yet as the attention swings away from the blonde Lorelei Lee to her friend Dorothy, the interest diminishes somewhat, although Lorelei continues as narrator, with her breezy style, which occasionally uses a long word correctly and often blunders over a shorter one.

To say that the last three books are not so good as the first is not to suggest that they are not amusing; *A Mouse Is Born* and *No Mother to Guide Her* are both built around the film colony, and the outstanding American critic Edmund Wilson noted that the latter book is "the novel about Hollywood with most teeth in it."

Anita Loos has attracted the favourable attention of many intellectuals (Aldous Huxley and H.L. Mencken were among her closest friends). She has written of them entertainingly in her autobiographical writings; Mencken asked her, after *Gentlemen Prefer Blondes* appeared, "Do you realize, young woman, that you're the first American writer ever to poke fun at sex?"

Anita Loos is herself an intellectual, despite her lack of formal, higher education: in her adolescence she read Schopenhauer and Kant. Lorelei Lee is in no way her author's counterpart. A girl from Little Rock, Arkansas, she has a brief career on the screen before moving to New York and then on to Paris, which she finds "devine." In what she calls "The Central of Europe" she goes to Vienna and astonishes "Dr. Froyd" by revealing that she does not dream. The doctor talks "to his assistance quite a lot in the Viennese landguage" and eventually tells Lorelei "to cultivate a few inhibitions and get some sleep." At the end of this book, which was a favorite of Sir Winston Churchill's, Lorelei marries a wealthy Philadelphian who has been "entreeged" by her. As have two generations of readers, for in creating Lorelei and her environment, Anita Loos has provided a memorable picture of the 1920's and flappers with cloche hats, abbreviated skirts, and rolled stockings. As Lorelei chirps the idiom of the time, the precisely comic and neatly satiric story moves through its entertaining situations that capture and perpetuate the spirit of what another of its recorders, F. Scott Fitzgerald, christened the Jazz Age.

—Harry T. Moore

LOVELACE, Earl. Trinidadian. Born in Trinidad in 1935. Married. Civil servant: agricultural assistant in Jamaica. Recipient: B.P. Independence Award, 1965. Address: c/o André Deutsch Ltd., 105 Great Russell Street, London WC1B 3LJ, England.

PUBLICATIONS

Novels

While Gods Are Falling. London, Collins, 1965; Chicago, Regnery, 1966.
The Schoolmaster. London, Collins, and Chicago, Regnery, 1968.
The Dragon Can't Dance. London, Deutsch, 1979.

*   *   *

Earl Lovelace's most recent novel, *The Dragon Can't Dance*, like his first, *While Gods Are Falling*, is set in the slums of "that big, fast and terrible city that is Port-of-Spain." The squalor and confusion of life in these areas, and the inability of the slum dwellers to control their destinies and to lift themselves out of this environment, encourage the characters of Lovelace's novels to conclude that life is meaningless, and therefore that religious faith and constructive action are pointless. Bewildered by the injustices of life, Walter Castle, the central character of the first novel, thinks only of escaping to a remote rural area where social pressures are less severe. Eventually he comes to realize that real fulfilment and meaning can only be derived from responsible individual action, action which both expresses the individual's personality and puts it at the disposal of the community.

Lovelace's second novel, *The Schoolmaster*, examines in some detail the kind of escape to a remote innocent place that Walter Castle had considered. Kumaca, a small village in the mountains of Trinidad, has little contact with the outside world. Its inhabitants lead simple lives, and are on intimate terms with their landscape and their religion. Against the advice of Father Vincent, who wishes to keep them innocent, they persist in building a school in their village, and pressing for the construction of a road. Although these facilities bring tragedy and disaster, Lovelace makes it clear that Father Vincent is wrong and the villagers right in their aspirations for Kumaca. One cannot come to terms with the complexity of the world or find meaning in life by hiding from change, which is inevitable. The novel also contrasts the actions of the villagers which are motivated by their sense of themselves as part of a community, with the actions of the schoolmaster which are the result of greed and the desire for power. It is their sense of identity which gives the villagers the strength to deal with their temptations and to begin again after misfortune has struck. *The Schoolmaster* is a less sentimental and less preachy novel than *While Gods Are Falling*, which is too obviously influenced by Alan Paton's *Cry, The Beloved Country*.

In *The Dragon Can't Dance* Lovelace intensifies and complicates the exploration of his themes. The inhabitants of the slum, Calvary Hill, make carnival the focus of their lives. They convince themselves that it gives purpose and drama to their otherwise empty existence. Furthermore they connect carnival to their African past. The violence associated with the steelbands, the frightening costumes are blatant signs of their protest against the system which exploits them. But carnival, as Lovelace suggests, has its shortcomings as a means of effecting change. It deludes the slum dwellers into believing too easily that "All of we is one," while at the same time it is one of the grounds on which Paraig, an Indian slum dweller, is ostracized. Carnival also has the effect of reducing real life to the level of playing mas'. When a group of "Bad Johns" seizes a police jeep and drives about the city, this gesture, this dragon's dance, is perceived as a kind of masquerade. As far as Lovelace is concerned actions in which the individual is content to appeal to someone else to relieve him of his problems and is not prepared to act constructively on his own behalf are never going to bring about the profound social changes that will allow people to live together in harmony and with dignity.

All three of Lovelace's novels insist upon the responsibility of the individual to himself and to his fellow man, but technique grows more confident with each new novel, and the interpretation of life becomes correspondingly less sentimental, more complex, and more powerful.

—Anthony Boxill

LOWRY, Robert (James Collas). American. Born in Cincinnati, Ohio, 28 March 1919. Educated at Withrow High School, Cincinnati; University of Cincinnati, 1937-38. Served in the United States Army Air Force, in Tunisia and Italy, 1942-45. Married four times; three children. Publisher, The Little Man Press, Cincinnati; Production Manager and Editor, New Directions, publishers, New York, 1945-46; Book Reviewer, *Time* magazine, New York, 1949-50, and the *New York Times*, 1950-56; Staff Writer, *American Mercury*, New York, 1951-53. Address: 3747 Hutton Street, Cincinnati, Ohio 45226, U.S.A.

PUBLICATIONS

Novels

Casualty. New York, New Directions, 1946.
Find Me in Fire. New York, Doubleday, 1948.
The Big Cage. New York, Doubleday, 1949.
The Violent Wedding. New York, Doubleday, 1953; London, Barker, 1954.
What's Left of April. New York, Doubleday, 1956.
The Prince of Pride Starring. Cincinnati, Haine, 1959.
That Kind of Woman. New York, Pyramid, 1959.

Short Stories

Trip to the Bloomin' Moon. Cincinnati, Little Man Press, 1939.
Defense in University City (as James Caldwell). Cincinnati, Little Man Press, 1939.
I'll Never Be the Same. Cincinnati, Little Man Press, 1939.
Murderpie. Cincinnati, Little Man Press, 1939.
Hutton Street. Cincinnati, Little Man Press, 1940.
The State of the Nation, with 9 Interludes, with others. Cincinnati, Little Man Press, 1940.
Gup: 3 Adventures. Cincinnati, Little Man Press, 1942.
The Bad Girl Marie. Cincinnati, Little Man Press, 1942.
The Blaze Beyond the Town, The Toy Balloon. Bari, Italy, Piccolo Uomo, 1945.
The Journey Out. Bari, Italy, Piccolo Uomo, 1945.
The Wolf That Fed Us. New York, Doubleday, 1949.
Happy New Year, Kamerades! New York, Doubleday, 1954.
The Last Party: A Memorable Collection of Short Stories. New York, Popular Library, 1956.
New York Call Girl. New York, Doubleday, 1958.
The Knife. Privately printed, 1959.
Party of Dreamers. New York, Fleet, 1962.

Uncollected Short Stories

"The Kiss," in *Carleton Miscellany* (Northfield, Minnesota), Fall 1965.
"A Lively Museum of Youth and Desire," in *Carleton Miscellany* (Northfield, Minnesota), Spring 1967.

Play

The Violent Wedding, in *Poet Lore* (Boston), 1961.

Verse

Feelthy Pomes. Bari, Italy, Piccolo Uomo, 1945.
New Poems. Cincinnati, Little Man Press, 1959.

Other

Pip Pap Po: A Book of Many Things, with others. Cincinnati, Little Man Press, 1940.
Literature and the Communist State. Cincinnati, Little Man Press, 1959.
Dreams. Cincinnati, Little Man Press, 1976.
The Nut. Cincinnati, Little Man Press, 1976.
A Chronology of My Life since 1952. Cincinnati, Little Man Press, 1979.
Robert Lowry Diary. Cincinnati, Little Man Press, 1979.

Editor, *Narration with a Red Piano*, by J. Calder Joseph. Cincinnati, Little Man Press, 1940.
Editor, with Robert B. Goldman, *Hey Joe: A Book Recording the History and Activities of the Fourth Photographic Technical Squadron.* Rome, Fourth Photographic Technical Squadron, 1945.

*

Manuscript Collections: Boston University; University of Southern California, Los Angeles; Kent State University, Ohio.

Robert Lowry comments:

I am a realist in my novels. And a trance realist at that—meaning that I wrote and rewrote them until I could almost see and hear the events recorded. You will find fantasy only in my short stories—and most of these fantastic stories have been collected in *Party of Dreamers*.

My first-published novels were war novels. *Casualty* is about Italy in World War II; and the short novel *The Wolf That Fed Us* is about American-occupied Rome in wartime. The novel of mine that bridges the war and the peace is *Find Me in Fire*, about an American solider and what he finds America is really like when he returns from World War II. *The Violent Wedding* (about a world-champion boxer and an artist in Greenwich Village), *What's Left of April* (about an American fashion model who becomes a movie star), and *The Prince of Pride Starring* (about the nervous breakdown of a magazine editor) are all novels about American careers. So, in its way, is *The Big Cage*, the story of the childhood and adolescence of a literary genius.

And so the pattern my novels follow is the heartbreak of war, the disillusionment of the peace, and the morality of American life after the war. My short stories recreate all areas of American life, from the very rich to the very poor.

* * *

A boyhood in Cincinnati, Ohio, service on European battlefields during World War II, and the life of an artist in Greenwich Village are the major private experiences which Robert Lowry has translated into a series of novels and short stories. While he has never enjoyed wide commercial success, Lowry has remained, often against considerable odds, the consummate professional, and his writing constitutes a continuing *Bildungsroman*—the semi-autobiographical story of his own emergence and development as a writer. Lowry has, at various times, worked as a book reviewer and editor, and some of his work has been published by his own Little Man Press in Cincinnati.

Casualty, Lowry's first, short novel, was singled out for special attention by numerous reviewers despite the fact that it was one of a great number of protest novels to follow the Second World War. The novel traces the catastrophic chain of events that follow the hero's broken engagement, and at the same time indicts the culture which forced him to don a uniform. *Casualty* is a bitter novel, but powerfully convincing in its tone, and memorable for the way in which detail accumulates to create a vivid sense of atmosphere and mood.

Find Me in Fire records the experiences of a soldier who returns to the small Ohio town where he had grown up and makes an abortive attempt to live his old life there again. Despite the familiarity of the basic material, Lowry was able to suggest that his hero's struggle represented the struggle of all men to gain a sense of belonging, and how their frustration can lead inexorably to violence.

The Big Cage is even more explicitly autobiographical than Lowry's first two novels. It follows the life of Dick Black from a Cincinnati childhood to his arrival in New York, armed with the firm ambition to become a writer. Nelson Algren recommended the book for its swift technique and emotional candor, but most reviewers found the hero's adventures rather routine, despite their immediacy. *Violent Wedding* was a more unique conception, the story of a Negro prize fighter and the white girl whom he loved, yet the novel lacked depth of insight in the handling of the central characters.

Lowry early established his reputation as a writer of spare, clean prose that vividly recreated milieu in the best naturalistic tradition. At a time when many writers were directing their attention to the inner workings of personality, he was creating sound, well-disciplined works in the best Hemingway tradition. Fashion in a sense passed Lowry by, but in doing so it overlooked the sardonic humor which often plays just beneath the surface of his writing. It is a quality best realized in his shorter fiction, where the author occasionally feels secure in abandoning his allegiance to naturalism and exercising a sense of the whimsical and the bizarre which also reveals itself in his drawings. "A Roar in the Village" sacrifices no depth of perception or feeling in its elaborate joking, and like most of the stories in *Party of Dreamers* it reveals an aspect of Lowry's talent not immediately visible in his longer fiction.

—David Galloway

LUDWIG, Jack (Barry). Canadian. Born in Winnipeg, Manitoba, 30 August 1922. Educated at the University of Manitoba, Winnipeg, B.A. 1944; University of California, Los Angeles, Ph.D. 1953. Married Leya Lauer in 1946; two children. Taught at Williams College, Williamstown, Massachusetts, 1949-53; Bard College, Annandale-on-Hudson, New York, 1953-58; University of Minnesota, Minneapolis, 1958-61. Since 1961, Professor of English, State University of New York, Stony Brook. Co-Editor, *The Noble Savage*, New York, then Cleveland, 1960-62. Chairman, Humanities Group, International Seminar, Harvard University, Cambridge, Massachusetts, Summers 1963-66. Writer-in-Residence, University of Toronto, 1968-69; Playwright-in-Residence, Stratford Shakespeare Festival Workshop, Ontario, 1970; Writer-in-Residence, Banff Centre, Alberta, Summer 1974; Visiting Professor, University of California, Summer 1976. Recipient: Longview Foundation Award, 1960; *Atlantic* "Firsts" Award, 1960; O. Henry Award, 1961, 1965; Canada Council award, 1962, and Senior Arts Fellowship, 1967, 1975. Address: P.O. Box A, Setauket, Long Island, New York 11733, U.S.A.

PUBLICATIONS

Novels

Confusions. Greenwich, Connecticut, New York Graphic Society, and London, Secker and Warburg, 1963.
Above Ground. Toronto and Boston, Little Brown, 1968.
A Woman of Her Age. Toronto, McClelland and Stewart, 1973.

Short Story

Requiem for Bibul. Agincourt, Ontario, Book Society of Canada, 1967.

Uncollected Short Stories

"Orlick Miller and Company," in *Commentary* (New York), January 1960.
"Thoreau in California," in *Noble Savage 1* (New York), April 1960.
"Meesh," in *Tamarack Review* (Toronto), Autumn 1961.
"Death Was the Glass," in *Midstream* (New York), Winter 1961.
"Celebration on East Houston Street," in *Tamarack Review* (Toronto), Spring 1963.
"Einstein and This Admirer," in *London Magazine*, September 1965.
"A Death of One's Own," in *Tamarack Review* (Toronto), Winter 1968.
"Shirley," in *Tamarack Review* (Toronto), Spring 1969.

Plays

The Alchemist, adaptation of the play by Ben Jonson (produced Stratford, Ontario, 1969).
Bustout, with Peter Scupham (produced Stratford, Ontario, 1969).
Ubu Rex, adaptation of a play by Alfred Jarry (produced Stratford, Ontario, 1970).

Television Play: *Hedda Gabler*, from the play by Ibsen, 1979.

Verse

Homage to Zolotova. Banff, Alberta, Banff Centre Press, 1974.

Other

Recent American Novelists. Minneapolis, University of Minnesota Press, 1962.
Hockey Night in Moscow. Toronto, McClelland and Stewart, 1972; revised edition, as *The Great Hockey Thaw; or, The Russians Are Here*, New York, Doubleday, 1974.
Games of Fear and Winning: Sports with an Inside View. New York, Doubleday, 1976.
The Great American Spectaculars: The Kentucky Derby, Mardi Gras, and Other Days of Celebration. New York, Doubleday, 1976.
Five-Ring Circus: The Montreal Olympics. New York, Doubleday, 1977.

Editor, with Richard Poirier, *Stories: British and American.* Boston, Houghton Mifflin, 1953.
Editor, with Andy Wainwright, *Soundings: New Canadian Poets.* Toronto, Anansi, 1970.

*

Jack Ludwig comments:

Winnipeg, Los Angeles, New York, London were for me never centres of abstraction. Doubtless each city had its moral paralytics; doubtless I didn't run into them often. A liar and a truth-teller have always been equally fascinating to me. The imagination's scale of values is not easily coerced. When I look at Brueghel's paintings I see life without categories, without underlined morals, without tilting: the paltry and exalted, the sleazy and the grand are great challenges to the image that alone makes for realization. Comedy and tragedy are different, but, to the imagination, equal. I reject the Eliot and Pound notions about the past giving shape to the formless present. Whether literature rises out of Dublin or Rome, New York or London, it begins, as Yeats finally recognized, in "A mound of refuse or the sweepings of a street."

* * *

Taken together, all of Jack Ludwig's several voices are the voice of a civilized North American; also the voice of a cultured man. His culture, a culture he wears with ease, comes more from the roots of things genuine than from the academy alone. It comes from underground. Ludwig was born into the Jewish community of Winnipeg. He knows it in North America and in its European roots; his own, in Odessa; he knows much of its rich Yiddish and Hasidic backgrounds. In reading him one may think of Mordecai Richler or Philip Roth or I.B. Singer.

To a degree all his writing voices one central, pervasive concern. With his emphasis included, it reads: "...*re-educate yourself, kid, but do it with ebullience*" (*Recent American Novelists*, 1962). Was he advising then, in the early '60's, what the '70's have taken as the quest; namely, alternative modes of doing almost everything in everyday life, alternative modes to those which have come to threaten everyday life on almost every hand? The difference would lie with the rarity of ebullience in much of that quest. But in Ludwig it carries the reader joyously, if he be willing and aware. As it does, even in such a short story as "Meesh" in which the hero, in that poignant Yiddish mode, is forced daily to sacrifice himself for *un*worthy kin with hardly a murmur of dissent. And as it carries the reader, even when he is telling of his summer spent on the vacant floor of the old Ryan Building in downtown Winnipeg where he wrote *Confusions*.

So in *Confusions*, Ludwig celebrates life and vitality. Even the mock epic hero Joe Galsky (a Roxbury Jew)/Joseph Gillis (a Harvard graduate) does so in his confusions ("confissions"), troubled as he is by trying to follow what his creator refers to as a kind of North American credo, the putting of "Second Things First," second things such as "status-establishing, career-making and image-projecting." Galsky/Gillis will need to admit, "I am confused, therefore I am." One wonders if Ludwig may intend this to mean in part somewhat what Alan Watts means about the wisdom of insecurity in his book of that title. At any rate, Galsky/Gillis refuses to accept mephistophelean aid. He will not seek success as a novelist, if it means creating the kind of book he could not believe in. His closing words echo: "Look on me, ye unmighty, and live a little." Rabbinical spirit prevails.

In *Above Ground*, Ludwig celebrates life and vitality, more in a lyric than a satiric way, not the least sexual vitality, even though, or perhaps because, the hero, Joshua, has had to spend almost all his formative years in hospital rooms due to a crippling ailment of the hip-bone. And that sexual vitality appeals. It has been suggested (by D.O. Spettique, in *Queen's Quarterly*, 1968) that the women in Joshua's life may be "death-figures," especially since two of them, his dying mother and an amazing, neurotic mistress, pose "threats to his living integrity." But one wonders. The novel carries such a constant lyricism.

In his extended essay *Recent American Novelists*, Ludwig writes as though he were already thinking of the form this second of his novels would take. "Serious fiction shows definite signs of turning from Kafkaesque 'Underground Man' to Tolstoian or Conradian 'Aboveground Man,' the hero who breaks out of his real or symbolic, sealed-off rooms to re-enter the world of action and history..." (*The New Romans*, 1968). At any rate, when his hero Joshua does find himself free of those "symbolic" (at least) "sealed-off rooms," he "re-enters" a world of vital sexual activity which Ludwig celebrates without self-consciousness. Again, in praising Saul Bellow's *The Adventures of Augie March* in *The New*

Romans, Ludwig says, "history becomes a dimension of a hero's awareness—if not yet his acts." And he seems to describe the kind of novel *Above Ground* was going to become, one in which the sexual could find honest expression in the hero's awareness. Lastly, *Above Ground* seems to be a novel written in the open form as he had earlier conceived it: "...an open form, a way of writing *about* almost anything with almost unlimited scope—i.e.; the limits are imposed not by the chosen form of the novel, but rather, as they should be, by the author's own limitations of talent, imagination, and knowledge." Two simple sentences from this same essay seem to define Joshua's growing consciousness. "He lives as an aware Aboveground Man. The man aware knows there is limitless fiction in the fall of a sparrow." And now the woman becoming aware in *A Woman of Her Age* shows that life at 85 years can crowd limitless fiction into the span of a single Friday—*shabbes*—of a single spring day between Montreal's Westmount and Saint Lawrence Main.

In the dozen dazzling and discontinuous chapters of *A Woman of Her Age*, Ludwig brings together within the same pages, although not within the same dramatic scenes, two of his most unforgettable short story characters. They are Doba Goffmann, a now-85-year-old ex-radical, displaced from the Montreal Jewish community of the Main to Westmount and pampering wealth; and "the chicken-slaughterer's daughter Shirley," similarly displaced, but also disoriented by a second marriage and motherhood, and estranged from Doba Goffmann since the death of Jimmy, her first husband, and Doba's favorite among her devoted sons. Ludwig's almost breathless shifts of focus among memory, fantasy, and present event give effects in his narrative resembling as much as anything perhaps the fluid, fantastic, and comic imagery in many a Chagall canvas of Jewish subject. As he draws his interlocking dramatic portraits of Doba and Shirley, and of the various men in their present lives, Ludwig undercuts the confusions and hypocrisies of "success" while again finding stature in the comic vitality of the seemingly anti-heroic. As Dave Godfrey has suggested, "It's life on every page."

What better way to bring this to a stop than to hear Ludwig speak again: "...the novel has broken through, and broken out. Liberated from the tyranny of symbolic smallness it has attempted to become *the* literary form to catch the visible world in all its complexity, clangor, and untriumphant celebration. Our times have a tonality the novel cannot ignore."

Ludwig's is a voice true to his convictions. I like and admire its sound and its sense.

—Herbert C. Burke

LURIE, Alison. American. Born in Chicago, Illinois, 3 September 1926. Educated at Radcliffe College, Cambridge, Massachusetts, A.B. 1947. Married Jonathan Peale Bishop, Jr., in 1948; three children. Since 1968, Lecturer in English, Cornell University, Ithaca, New York. Recipient: Yaddo Foundation Fellowship, 1963, 1964, 1966; Guggenheim Fellowship, 1965; Rockefeller grant, 1968; New York State Council on the Arts grant, 1972; American Academy award, 1979. Address: c/o Department of English, Cornell University, Ithaca, New York 14850, U.S.A.

PUBLICATIONS

Novels

Love and Friendship. London, Heinemann, and New York, Macmillan, 1962.
The Nowhere City. London, Heinemann, 1965; New York, Coward McCann, 1966.
Imaginary Friends. London, Heinemann, and New York, Coward McCann, 1967.
Real People. New York, Random House, 1969; London, Heinemann, 1970.
The War Between the Tates. New York, Random House, and London, Heinemann, 1974.
Only Children. New York, Random House, and London, Heinemann, 1979.

Uncollected Short Story

"Hansel and Gretel," in *New Story 2* (New York), 1951.

Other

V.R. Lang: A Memoir. Privately printed, 1959; in *Poems and Plays*, by V.R. Lang, New York, Random House, 1975.
The Heavenly Zoo: Legends and Tales of the Stars (juvenile). London, Eel Pie, 1979; New York, Farrar Straus, 1980.
Clever Gretchen and Other Forgotten Folk Tales (juvenile). New York, Crowell, and London, Heinemann, 1980.

*

Manuscript Collection: Radcliffe College Library, Cambridge, Massachusetts.

* * *

Alison Lurie has the unfortunate habit of telling the truth, but only parts thereof. In her beautifully crafted novels, she continues the great English tradition of the comedy of manners. With the incisive wit, precision, and economy of Jane Austen, she surveys the groves of Academe, ever-abundant field of wise fools, depicting folly and self-deception which unexpected change reveals beneath the facade of intellect and respectability. However, though clearly, and devastatingly, drawn from life, most of her characters do not truly exist as human beings but as specimens, coolly dissected. Despite her subtle psychological probing, cunning tracing of transformations in marital relationships, we remain near the surface still. For all their complexities, her subjects finally stand unmasked, almost stock figures, or are reduced to Jonsonian humours, cleverly laid bare for our ridicule. Were Alison Lurie merely a competent writer and her works simply skilful examples of satire and manners comedy, this would not be criticism but praise. Of narrative technique alone she is a modern master, in both genres. Her inventive and artfully constructed plots, her descriptive powers and realistic dialogue, her delightful facility with language (particularly ambiguous words whose several opposite meanings she simultaneously exploits), and her sophisticated sense of irony, all place her near the major figures of the English novel. But, because of her insight and depth of understanding, she cannot create, in her major protagonists, mere comic stereotypes. Despite remarkable rhetorical control, she cannot prevent an empathetic response to her disillusioned characters. Thus, her comic treatment produces mixed emotions, and ultimately it seems cavalier and inadequate; the very brilliance of her technique becomes cause for dissatisfaction.

Love and Friendship, in theme, characterization, and structure, typifies Lurie's approach. Set at prestigious Convers College, the novel exposes in vivid detail the intricate, petty, and pretentious social rituals of academic life through the gradual collapse of a young couple's marriage. Holman Turner, an ambitious new English instructor of lower-middle-class origin, becomes absorbed in teaching Convers' much-touted Humanities course and in finishing his dissertation, while his beautiful, rich, and rather sheltered wife, Emmy, grows bored. Enter libertine Will Thomas, a lazy composer-in-residence, who easily "seduces" Emmy. After several passionate and imaginative escapades about the countryside (Emmy's high-class education and hum-drum marriage have neglected the fine points of sexual technique), she realizes that Holman is "a cold, selfish, opinionated academic booby who had never really loved her." While Emmy renews Will's creative powers—or so she believes—Holman's paranoia and confusion increase to enormous proportions, until, during a campus demonstration, he pushes a gay activist whom he suspects into a bonfire. Though these and other incidents verge on the pathetic, if not tragic, Lurie treats them comically. In the end, poetic justice is done, though for Emmy, over-conscious of familial and social pressures, the ultimate decisions are left ambiguous.

Throughout the novel Professor Lurie paints a gallery-full of satiric portraits of vindictive, pompous, and eccentric academic types: Dean Lumkin and his spiteful wife, crafty old McBane, and the unpredictable Fenns. Here and in the other novels, the Jonsonian tags reinforce their humours treatment. Further distancing and commentary (as well as plot connectives) are provided by Allen Ingram's letters to his friend in New York, which end each chapter. Ingram, a novelist-in-residence and homosexual, uses his "tourist's position" to achieve, as he says, "the necessary interested detachment." And he suggests a key to Lurie's work: "But comedy does not consist only of exaggeration; it can well be an imbalance of end and means."

Though its pat conclusion may make a reader skeptical, *The Nowhere City* does illustrate Lurie's comic theory of imbalance. Transported from Harvard Yard to sprawling Los Angeles, athletic Paul Cattleman is first enchanted, while his neurotic wife, Katherine, is disgusted by its superficial, wasteful, and unconventional life-styles. Though he is dismayed that his history of the Nutting Research and Development Corporation is for naught and his dissertation has not progressed, the philandering Paul is delighted by the easy, seemingly uninvolved sex with Ceci, a beatnik waitress, and with Glory Green, an uneducated but glamorous starlet. Appalled by California and by Paul's blatant infidelities, Katherine suffers raging psychosomatic symptoms, until Dr. Isidore ("call me Iz") Einsam, her employer (and Glory's estranged husband), reads her obvious subconscious desires and forcibly induces the soothing remedy of multiple orgasms. By novel's end, the initial responses are reversed: newly "liberated" (i.e., having become what she first despised), "Kay" decides to stay in L.A., in teased blond hair and toreador pants; while Paul's true nature (stuffy, "Establishment," and snobbish) reasserts itself, and he leaves timeless and amoral Lotus-land for the East and propriety. Though Lurie's vision is not as trenchant as Nathanael West's, her sketch is telling, and amusing, especially in the Hollywood and somewhat dated beatnik scenes.

Sociology and academic in-fighting are Lurie's targets in *Imaginary Friends*. Young Roger Zimmern and once-famous Thomas McMann infiltrate a bizarre religious cult called the Seekers to do a small-group study; but, despite "non-directive" techniques, Roger fears the theatrical McMann has skewed the results. Roger himself nearly destroys their meticulous efforts through ineptitude and infatuation for the young semi-psychic leader, Verena. The detailed record of their manipulative methodology, of their class-consciousness (Roger begins to lose his condescension when he discovers several parallels between fanatics and scholars), and of nasty competition among "colleagues" is damning but sometimes dull, because Roger narrates in sociologese. The surprise ending is ambiguous and contrived but singularly apropos.

In *Real People*, the novelist examines modern American life in the arts. On her third trip to Illyria, a luxurious retreat for artists, writers, and musicians, Janet Smith, a sensitive "lady writer," records in her diary her steady disillusionment. At first, the comfortable housewife-authoress believes here "one becomes one's *real* self, the person one would be in a decent world." Then she makes several unsettling discoveries: class-structure is even more rigid among the "creative"; her dear friend Kenneth Foster is homosexual; Teddy Berg, the greatest living American composer, and others, cowtow to rich philistines; most of these imaginative men (and women) make fools of themselves over a silly, callous, fame-chasing young "chick." Back-biting, egocentric, and childish, the great, nearly-great, and once-great compete shamelessly. Worst, however, is Janet's personal enlightenment: she is sexually attracted and capitulates to a boorish, lower-class, junk sculptor, who finally makes her realize her work is a sham, self-censored to "protect" family and friends. Resolving to mend her ways, she leaves a disappointed but wiser writer. Often parodic (Janet's jottings are banal and overwrought by turns), Lurie points her message through the delights of the *roman à clef*.

With *The War Between the Tates*, Lurie approaches the summit of her art. Using the Vietnam War and campus unrest as metaphor and backdrop, she portrays the dissolution of middle-aged Brian and Erica's marriage and its complicated aftermath. Short in stature, fame, and sexual apparatus, Professor Tate compensates belatedly with a comic-pathetic affair with an implausibly stupid and "helpless" grad student. Guilty over her assumed failure with The Children, who have become hateful strangers, and hurt, the proud Erica overreacts. The wounded vanity and marvelous rationalization of both compound a commonplace error into a string of ever more ludicrous and convoluted dilemmas. Reduced to the decidedly unfunny realities of separation—relative poverty, social unease, psychic upheaval—Erica and Brian eventually tire of face-saving and destructive retaliation. By now, Erica has learned her morality is selfish strategy, and Brian has achieved undesirable fame. The recently independent woman and the foiled political scientist may reunite, not so much for love as lack of alternatives. Neither a consistently comic nor a genuinely thorough, serious critique, the brilliant novel reflects the inconsistencies and imperfections of life.

—Joseph Parisi

LYTLE, Andrew (Nelson). American. Born in Murfreesboro, Tennessee, 26 December 1902. Educated at Sewanee Military Academy, Tennessee; Exeter College, Oxford, 1920; Vanderbilt University, Nashville, B.A. 1925; Yale University School of Drama, New Haven, Connecticut, 1927-29. Married Edna Langdon Barker in 1938 (died, 1963); three daughters. Professor of History, Southwestern College, Memphis, Tennessee, 1936; Professor of History, University of the South, Sewanee, Tennessee, and Managing Editor of the *Sewanee Review*, 1942-43; Lecturer, 1946-48, and Acting Head, 1947-48, University of Iowa School of Writing, Iowa City; Lecturer in Creative Writing, University of Florida, Gainesville, 1948-61; Lecturer in English, 1961-67, and Professor of English, 1968-73, University of the South, Sewanee, and Editor of the *Sewanee Review*, 1961-73. Recipient: Guggenheim Fellowship, 1940, 1941, 1960; National Endowment for the Arts grant, 1966. Litt.D.: Kenyon College, Gambier, Ohio, 1965; University of Florida, 1970; University of the South, 1973. Address: Department of English, University of the South, Sewanee, Tennessee 37375; or, Log Cabin, Monteagle, Tennessee 37356, U.S.A.

PUBLICATIONS

Novels

The Long Night. Indianapolis, Bobbs Merrill, 1936; London, Eyre and Spottiswoode, 1937.
At the Moon's Inn. Indianapolis, Bobbs Merrill, 1941; London, Eyre and Spottiswoode, 1943.
A Name for Evil. Indianapolis, Bobbs Merrill, 1947.
The Velvet Horn. New York, McDowell Obolensky, 1957.

Short Stories

A Novel, A Novella and Four Stories. New York, McDowell Obolensky, 1958.

Uncollected Short Story

"Old Scratch in the Valley," in *Virginia Quarterly Review* (Charlottesville), 1935.

Other

Bedford Forrest and His Critter Company (biography). New York, Minton Balch, 1931; London, Eyre and Spottiswoode, 1939; revised edition, New York, McDowell Obolensky, 1960.
The Hero with the Private Parts: Essays (literary criticism). Baton Rouge, Louisiana State University Press, 1966.
A Wake for the Living: A Family Chronicle. New York, Crown, 1975.

Editor, *Craft and Vision: The Best Fiction from "The Sewanee Review."* New York, Delacorte Press, 1971.

*

Bibliography: *An Andrew Lytle Checklist* by Jack De Bellis, Charlottesville, Bibliographical Society of the University of Virginia, 1960.

Manuscript Collection: Joint University Libraries (Vanderbilt University), Nashville, Tennessee; University of Florida Library, Gainesville.

Critical Studies: "Andrew Lytle Issue" of *Mississippi Quarterly* (State College), Fall 1970 (includes bibliography); *The Form Discovered: Essays on the Achievement of Andrew Lytle*, edited by M.E. Bradford, Jackson, University and College Press of Mississippi, 1973.

Andrew Lytle comments:

My work is best described in the rendition of the fiction I have done and in the critical reading of other books. An artist is not a scientist. He discovers his theme and subject as he writes. When he has dealt totally with either, and brought it all out, he is done for.

* * *

The art of Andrew Lytle is clearly within the tradition of Flaubert, James, and Joyce. It is the work of a man who has thought carefully about what a novel is supposed to be, a gifted critic, editor, and advisor to many younger novelists who have honored his example in their own best production. Lytle's novels are dramatic in the modern sense. They render from within a felt life gathered to some central image or cluster of images, and project that life from the post of observation where resides "the author's seeing eye." The result of this procedure in Lytle's reader in something like a shock, a full and simultaneous engagement of all the faculties in a moment of illumination.

His first novel, *The Long Night*, is a powerful evocation of the character of ante-bellum Southern society. Yet is is not *about* history—except as his times can be said to converge upon Pleasant McIvor, the central character. The plot here is Celtic in overtone and the issue revenge. But the Civil War interrupts the enactment of McIvor honor, reminding Pleasant that it is possible to offend his own dignity by pursuing it privately in a time when the future survival of such values is very much at stake. Pleasant's extravagance is perceived and judged by a younger kinsman who refuses to extend it into later days.

Lytle's *At the Moon's Inn* (and the related novella "Alchemy") discover form and meaning in the Spanish conquest of Eldorado. Both novel and novella "occur" from the viewpoint of an engaged spectator who, after being overcome by the vital presence of a conquistador, sees in his captain the Promethean pride which dissolved Christendom. In *At the Moon's Inn* Tovar draws back from the delusion of a worldly beatitude at the behest of De Soto's ghost. The nameless speaker in "Alchemy" retreats from Pizarro after years of reflection on the adventure in Peru. The two conquerors are counters for modernity in being representative of Columbus, their prototype of feudal Spain gone awry.

A Name for Evil is Lytle's Tennessee revelation of abstract and self-delusive traditionalism. It is, for an Agrarian, a contributor to the Southern manifesto *I'll Take My Stand*, and devoted champion of the "landed interest," an amazing book. Henry Brent attempts to restore the patriarchy on land cursed by the self-centered severity of his ancestor, Major Brent. As in James's *The Turn of the Screw*, a wicked history prevails over him. Henry hates the Major too much. The "why" of his ruin is revealed ironically in his account of its unfolding. His Eden is too private for an Eve. Wife, unborn child, and therefore the entire enterprise, are the victims.

The Velvet Horn is Lytle's masterpiece. Again the scene is the Tennessee of his fathers. The Fall of Man is there re-enacted in the context of another excessive isolation. Years later, Lucius Cree is compelled by ostensible father and by mother and uncle to learn of it. First Captain Cree and then the Cropleighs "pay" for the boy's education. Yet (thanks to them) he comes forth complete from his own loss of innocence to seek a "Paradise within, greater by far." The book is, as Caroline Gordon has written, a "landmark in American fiction."

—M.E. Bradford

LYTTON, David. South African. Born in South Africa in 1927. Married; four children. Emigrated to England in 1949. Actor, 1949-50, and Box Office Manager, 1952-54, Shakespeare Memorial Theatre, Stratford-upon-Avon. School Teacher, 1950-52. Writer and Producer, BBC, 1954-56. Since 1957, free-lance writer. Address: c/o The Bodley Head, 9 Bow Street, London WC2E 7AL, England.

PUBLICATIONS

Novels

The Goddam White Man. London, MacGibbon and Kee, 1960; New York, Simon and Schuster, 1961.
A Place Apart. London, MacGibbon and Kee, 1961.
The Paradise People. London, MacGibbon and Kee, and New York, Simon and Schuster, 1962.
The Grass Won't Grow Till Spring. London, Bodley Head, 1965.
The Freedom of the Cage. London, Bodley Head, 1966.

Short Stories

A Tale of Love, Alas, and Other Episodes. London, Bodley Head, 1969.

Plays

Radio Plays: *Episodes of an Easter Rising*, 1968; *Itami for the Wheel*, 1969.

Television Play: *Cruel Necessity*, 1962.

* * *

In his five novels and one volume of short stories, David Lytton has shown himself to be not only an acute observer of the South African scene, but also a satirist of considerable talent. South African fiction has always tended towards seriousness: writers have been intimately concerned with the very real social and political problems which have grown rather than lessened in the years since Union (1910); and South African novels have reflected this concern. With the exception of *Turbott Wolfe*, William Plomer's satirical novel published in 1924, and Roy Campbell's poetry of the same period, satire—and indeed humour of any kind—has been almost totally absent from the South Africn literary scene. Lytton, whose tone ranges from the near tragic, through various degrees of satire to compassionate and decidedly humorous irony, may therefore be regarded as something of an innovator. Writing with a detached but imaginative perception, sharpened possibly by his long residence in Britain, away from day to day involvement with the morally corrupting influence of *apartheid* (racial segregation as practised in South Africa), Lytton is able to pinpoint not only the tragedy and nastiness inherent in much contemporary South African life, but also to underline its absurdity. In this respect, his fourth novel, *The Grass Won't Grow Till Spring*, is his best and most savagely funny book. Based on South Africa's notorious "Immorality Law" which forbids miscegenation, the novel delineates the predicament of a white "liberal" caught in a veritable sexual wilderness, from which the only escape, ultimately, is into despair.

Lytton's earlier *The Goddam White Man* and *A Place Apart* are attempts to deal sympathetically with the experience of black and half-caste South Africans. Like most such attempts by white writers these novels are limited: life seen from the outside only must confine itself to easily observable data. *The Paradise People*, a romanticised account of Boer life, brings Lytton to more familiar ground, though his version of the growth of the Afrikaner personality, and his belief that these people instinctively know that they do not really belong to Africa, is more literary than real. *The Freedom of the Cage* seeks to analyse the mind of a contemporary Afrikaner. The central character is a man who first accepts, and later begins to question, the ideology and way of life which he and his ancestors have helped to create. His growing frustration leads him to attempt a symbolic "assassination" of the Prime Minister (the gun is not loaded), for which he is, inevitably, imprisoned. The "villain" in this novel is an English-speaking liberal and Lytton's sympathies are with the Afrikaner "victim": a neat reversal of the usual South African fictional pattern.

Lytton's most recent book is a collection of short stories, *A Tale of Love, Alas*, which centre on the experiences of a blind white man. Through his contact with a number of representative figures (a humanitarian priest, a Coloured woman, a rural Afrikaner, colonial English ladies), the hero is gradually brought to "see" that there is virtually no place for him in contemporary South Africa. This regretful insight (for his own relationship with his country is also "a tale of love, alas") appears to be Lytton's own view, and is a logical conclusion to his first series of novels.

—Ursula Laredo

MACAULEY, Robie (Mayhew). American. Born in Grand Rapids, Michigan, 31 May 1919. Educated at Kenyon College, Gambier, Ohio, A.B. 1941; University of Iowa, Iowa City, M.F.A. 1950. Served in the United States Army, in the Counter Intelligence Corps, 1942-46. Married 1) Anne Draper in 1948 (died, 1973), one child; 2) Pamela Painter in 1979. Instructor in English, Bard College, Annandale-on-Hudson, New York, 1946-47, and University of Iowa, 1947-50; Assistant Professor, Woman's College of the University of North Carolina, Greensboro, 1950-53; teacher, Kenyon College, 1953-66, and Editor on the *Kenyon Review*, 1959-66; Fiction Editor, *Playboy*, Chicago, 1966-77. Since 1978, Senior Editor, Houghton Mifflin, publishers, Boston. United States Delegate, P.E.N. Conference, Tokyo, 1957, and Brazil, 1960; State Department Lecturer, Australia, 1962. Recipient: *Furioso* prize, 1949; Guggenheim Fellowship, 1964; Fulbright Research Fellowship 1964; O. Henry Award, 1967. Agent: ICM, 40 West 57th Street New York, New York 10019. Address: c/o Houghton Mifflin Company, 2 Park Street, Boston, Massachusetts 02107, U.S.A.

PUBLICATIONS

Novels

The Disguises of Love. New York, Random House, 1952; London, Harrap, 1954.
A Secret History of Time to Come. New York, Knopf, 1979.

Short Stories

The End of Pity and Other Stories. New York, McDowell Obolensky, 1957; London, Harrap, 1958.

Uncollected Short Stories

"Dressed in Shade," in *Prize Stories 1967: The O. Henry Awards*, edited by William Abrahams. New York, Doubleday, 1967.
"For Want of a Nail," in *Cosmopolitan* (New York), October 1967.
"That Day," in *Playboy* (Chicago), November 1967.
"Ellen's Dream" (as A. Dumbarton), in *Playboy* (Chicago), July 1971.
"The Barrington Quality," in *Ellery Queen's Aces of Mystery.* New York, Davis, 1975.

Other

Technique in Fiction, with George Lanning. New York, Harper, 1964.

Editor, *Gallery of Modern Fiction: Stories from the Kenyon Review.* New York, Salem Press, 1966.
Editor, with Larzer Ziff, *America and Its Discontents.* Waltham, Massachusetts, Xerox College Publishing Company, 1971.

* * *

Robie Macauley's prose, like the best poetry, has a startling economy of means and precision of language. Macauley seems to have applied certain poetic theories of his teacher at Kenyon College, John Crowe Ransom, to the demands of fiction. It is not surprising that a writer so attentive to technique should have produced his own poetics of the novel. The book which Robie Macauley wrote with George Lanning, *Technique in Fiction* (appropriately dedicated to Ransom), serves as an addendum to his own practices as a novelist and story writer and asserts his feelings about the importance of craft. The introduction points to the inseparability of the functions of critic and creator, distantly echoing a famous remark of Charles Baudelaire: "The best modern critics of fiction, from the standpoint of technique, and probably the only critics that the beginning writer will find of any specific help, are those who write fiction themselves."

Macauley's *The Disguises of Love* is the enviable product of years spent in close and sympathetic relationship with the best novels from Jane Austen through Joyce. Several reviewers were disturbed at certain things they saw and expressed mild discomfort. Thus Anthony West, writing in *The New Yorker*, saw in the novel the "reversal of masculine and feminine roles" which gives it, in the end, "a nonsensical quality." Stanley Edgar Hyman (*Hudson Review*) started with West's argument and proceeded to find "accounts of homosexual relations...disguised as accounts of heterosexual relations" in good Proustian fashion. Macauley roundly expressed his disapproval of this reading by turning Hyman's evidence from the text against him to assure us that he had in no sense tampered with gender.

Indeed, Macauley's temptress Frances (a name which Hyman

suggests should more accurately be spelled "Francis") has very little in common with Albertine, Gilberte, Andrée, or Proust's other men-women. In accustomed heterosexual fashion she manages to take to bed with her the straight-laced college professor and paterfamilias Howard Graeme. The novel is shaped by the twists and turns of their love affair. Macauley sets up three "successive centres" (Henry James's expression in his preface to *The Wings of the Dove*) who alternate in the telling of the story; they are: Howard, his wife Helen, and their son Gordon. Howard's voice is stuffy and pedantic; Helen's has the unmistakable ring of the soap opera; Gordon's is precocious, mischievous, and ironical. The tellings have in common an unreliability. Howard mistakenly believes Gordon is "in fact pretty much an average boy with all the insensitivity of the average boy...." Helen accepts Howard's pretense that he is writing a book and resists the notion that he is carrying on a love affair. Gordon believes that it is his mother rather than his father who has a lover. The unravelling of the various threads of misunderstanding is performed by outsiders.

The Disguises of Love, in a sense, is an academic novel. It has in common with the best examples of the genre, like Kingsley Amis's *Lucky Jim* and Mary McCarthy's *The Groves of Academe*, the uncomfortable feeling that "teaching is the one job where you can hang on for years after you go completely bad" (Howard's words). Macauley knows the precise cadence of academic exchange and reproduces it convincingly at a musical gathering at Professor Lleweilen's house and again at a party of the U.F.W.G. (University Faculty Wives' Group), with Helen Graeme acting as one of the hostesses. Three of the eleven stories in Macauley's *The End of Pity* are also concerned with academics. "The Academic Style" and "The Chevigny Man" are set on college campuses while "A Guide to the Muniment Room" involves a professor in England on "a literary pilgrimage." Stuffiness, phoniness, the narrow devotion to one's "special subject" are exposed in all three.

The first four stories in *The End of Pity* have to do with military experiences, removed from the front lines, involving Counter-Intelligence Corps personnel. Macauley mentions in his superb introduction to Ford's *Parade's End* that "some of us went to war ourselves"; these stories seem to represent a glance over his left shoulder at the absurdities and ironies of his own World War II encounters. The remaining four stories have fairly little in common. Two, "The Invaders" and "The Wishbone," end in moments of violence. "Legend of the Two Swimmers" is faintly reminiscent of Katherine Anne Porter's "Old Mortality" with its family secrets and legends. "Windfall" involves the unexpected gesture of another of Macauley's heroes overwhelmed by events; the difference is, however, that Vanderbilt acts with a decisiveness and affirmation which elude most of the other characters in *The Disguises of Love* and *The End of Pity*.

After a long stint as fiction editor of *Playboy*, Macauley returned to novel-writing with *A Secret History of Time to Come*. The humanistic soundings of *The Disguises of Love* have been replaced by the technological rumblings of this second novel. Just as Macauley suffered at the hands of certain reviewers with his first novel, so in periodicals as dissimilar as *The New York Times Book Review* and *The Magazine of Fantasy and Science Fiction* his credentials as a science-fiction writer were placed seriously in doubt. In this "post-holocaust novel," as one reviewer called it, we are confronted with a landscape of the future which resembles the frontier of much 19th-century American literature. Like a good many philosophers of history—Vico immediately comes to mind—Macauley appears to accept a cyclical view of human endeavor, with its inevitable *ricorso*. He expresses this position structurally by beginning and ending his novel with the same words. The book begins with the diary notations ("my recollective therapy") of a black newspaperman-turned-revolutionary in Chicago. His writing is charged with elegance and a sense of mission: "All revolutions must have the same standard footage and stock shots, I think. The vehicles and the clothes are different, but Paris in 1789, Moscow in 1917, Johannesburg in 1986 must have told the same stories to the eye." These journal entries at first alternate with the third-person account of a traveler named Kinkaid; then the diary stops and Kinkaid's story becomes the only narrative. It is all an account of "time to come," but Kinkaid's adventures occur far in the future while the diarist's jottings are close to our own period.

Macauley links up the journal with the account of Kinkaid's adventures by having the traveler see the black diarist "on the horizon of his dreams" and finally, at the end of his journey, uncover "a dusty book" which turns out to be that journal itself. *A Secret History of Time to Come*, like so many novels with an apocalyptic bent, walks a thin line between dream and reality.

—Melvin J. Friedman

MACDONALD, Ross. Pseudonym for Kenneth Millar. American. Born in Los Gatos, California, 13 December 1915. Educated at the University of Western Ontario, London, 1933-38, B.A. 1938; University of Toronto, 1938-39; University of Michigan, Ann Arbor, 1941-44, 1948-49 (Graduate Fellow, 1941-42; Rackham Fellow, 1942-43), M.A. 1942, Ph.D. 1951. Served in the United States Naval Reserve, 1944-46: Lieutenant Junior Grade. Married Margaret Sturm, i.e., Margaret Millar, *q.v.*, in 1938; one child (deceased). Teacher of English and History, Kitchener-Waterloo Collegiate Institute, Ontario, 1939-41; Teaching Fellow, University of Michigan, 1942-44, 1948-49; book reviewer, San Francisco *Chronicle*, 1957-60. Member, Board of Directors, 1960-61, 1964-65, and President, Mystery Writers of America. Recipient: Crime Writers Association Silver Dagger, 1965; University of Michigan Outstanding Achievement Award, 1972; Mystery Writers of America Grand Master Award, 1973; Popular Culture Association Award of Excellence, 1973. Address: 4420 Via Esperanza, Santa Barbara, California 93105, U.S.A.

PUBLICATIONS

Novels

The Dark Tunnel (as Kenneth Millar). New York, Dodd Mead, 1944; as *I Die Slowly*, London, Lion, 1955.
Trouble Follows Me (as Kenneth Millar). New York, Dodd Mead, 1946; as *Night Train*, London, Lion, 1955.
Blue City (as Kenneth Millar). New York, Knopf, 1947; London, Cassell, 1949.
The Three Roads (as Kenneth Millar). New York, Knopf, 1948; London, Cassell, 1950.
The Moving Target (as John Macdonald). New York, Knopf, 1949; London, Cassell, 1951; as *Harper*, New York, Pocket Books, 1966.
The Drowning Pool (as John Ross Macdonald). New York, Knopf, 1950; London, Cassell, 1952.
The Way Some People Die (as John Ross Macdonald). New York, Knopf, 1951; London, Cassell, 1953.
The Ivory Grin (as John Ross Macdonald). New York, Knopf, 1952; London, Cassell, 1953; as *Marked for Murder*, New York, Pocket Books, 1953.
Meet Me at the Morgue (as John Ross Macdonald). New York, Knopf, 1953; as *Experience with Evil*, London, Cassell, 1954.
Find a Victim (as John Ross Macdonald). New York, Knopf, 1954; London, Cassell, 1955.
The Barbarous Coast. New York, Knopf, 1956; London, Cassell, 1957.
The Doomsters. New York, Knopf, and London, Cassell, 1958.
The Galton Case. New York, Knopf, 1959; London, Cassell, 1960.
The Ferguson Affair. New York, Knopf, 1960; London, Collins, 1961.

The Wycherly Woman. New York, Knopf, 1961; London, Collins, 1962.
The Zebra-Striped Hearse. New York, Knopf, 1962; London, Collins, 1963.
The Chill. New York, Knopf, and London, Collins, 1964.
The Far Side of the Dollar. New York, Knopf, and London, Collins, 1965.
Black Money. New York, Knopf, and London, Collins, 1966.
The Instant Enemy. New York, Knopf, and London, Collins, 1968.
The Goodbye Look. New York, Knopf, and London, Collins, 1969.
The Underground Man. New York, Knopf, and London, Collins, 1971.
Sleeping Beauty. New York, Knopf, and London, Collins, 1973.
The Blue Hammer. New York, Knopf, and London, Collins, 1976.
Archer in Jeopardy (omnibus). New York, Knopf, 1979.

Short Stories

The Name Is Archer (as John Ross Macdonald). New York, Bantam, 1955; London, Fontana, 1976.
Lew Archer, Private Investigator. Yonkers, New York, Mysterious Press, 1977.

Other

On Crime Writing. Santa Barbara, California, Capra Press, 1973.

Editor, *Great Stories of Suspense.* New York, Knopf, 1974.

*

Bibliography: *Kenneth Millar/Ross Macdonald: A Checklist* by Matthew J. Bruccoli, Detroit, Gale, 1971.

Manuscript Collection: University of California Library, Irvine.

Critical Study: *Ross Macdonald* by Jerry Speir, New York, Ungar, 1978.

* * *

In many ways, although too few critics and reviewers realize it, Ross Macdonald is one of the central authors of his time and place. Inheriting a wide variety of influences from a number of different sources in the past, his works provide an accurate and fascinating chronicle of the major preoccupations of contemporary America; it seems likely that future generations will read his fiction as we read, for example, the works of Conan Doyle—to discover some important facts and truths about a bygone age. The complicated elements of his complicated books reveal a spider web of connections with literature and history, with the cultures of past and present, and with some timeless themes and patterns of human behavior.

Initially, as all readers of detective fiction must know, Macdonald's novels grew out of the hard-boiled fiction of the 1930's and 1940's, more specifically, from the powerful traditions established by Dashiell Hammett and Raymond Chandler. (The author himself has characterized his first novel as "Chandler with onions.") He named his private detective Lew Archer, after Sam Spade's murdered partner in *The Maltese Falcon*, and endowed him with some of the wit and compassion of Chandler's Philip Marlowe. Although his early books displayed some interesting prose, a sure sense of scene and atmosphere, and an ability to sketch out character, Macdonald came into his own when he stopped merely trying to improve upon Chandler and Hammett and began to stake out his own territory in detective fiction. His humor and toughness always had the forced, false ring of a toy telephone and his style sometimes bordered on the self-consciously literary; what changed Macdonald's books was his own recognition of his real strengths—complexity and sorrow.

Starting—by his own reckoning—with *The Galton Case*, Macdonald began the creation of that tangled wilderness of the human heart that he embodies in the landscape of Southern California. His novels depart radically from the tough fiction of his original inspiration in their curiously static sense of action; instead of representing human behavior in moments of sequential violence, they generally demonstrate the continuing mysteries of the past. The most notable element in all of Macdonald's fiction is its obsessive preoccupation with the sources of human evil. Lew Archer invariably discovers that whatever crime or problem he confronts in the present has its real meaning in some previous—almost always perverse or shocking—event many years before. The immensely complicated plots of the Macdonald novels are not so much chronicles of actions as retracings of interlocking histories and personalities.

In their profuse ramifications, the plots—along with other important aspects of his fiction—demonstrate the author's important links with a variety of writers and modes far removed from the usual backgrounds of detective stories. Like his illustrious predecessors in the form, he creates yet another important version of the chivalric romance, which has always been submerged but visible beneath the dark waters of the private eye novel. Like previous American writers, Hawthorne and Melville especially, his chief concern is not so much with the fact of crime as with its sources and effects. Like Dickens, whom he resembles in his penchant for intricate stories and surprising connections, he frequently builds his work around the image and reality of a betrayed, neglected, abandoned, and suffering child.

Out of his knowledge of psychology and his interest in figures as diverse as Homer, Sophocles, Coleridge, and Freud, and perhaps out of the painful personal life which he has occasionally discussed with interviewers, Macdonald has also made the most powerful use of the normal materials of mystery fiction. With a structure and texture derived from romance, folklore, fairy tale, and myth, he confronts the age-old problems that also, quite unsurprisingly, turn out to be the major difficulties of our time: paternity, identity, the powerful chains forged by violence, by sex, by blood, by guilt. The body of his fiction forms a complex picture of our world and its tensions and anxieties. Those who see his work as a sort of Southern California sociology miss the point; that is merely the place where his subject surfaces. Those who consider him a useful reporter of the rapid changes in contemporary American society catch a bit more, but all the descriptions of aimless youths, drug users, the decadent rich and the corrupted bourgeoisie, the destruction of the environment, and so forth are only the necessary context for more permanent concerns. Those who read his works in the future may find some accurate creation of a special time and place, but it is more likely that in Ross Macdonald's fiction they will be instructed in the harsh lessons of an inner reality. They will discover in the novel of crime, violence, and detection, a sense of the mystery and sadness of human action, a dark and troubled picture of a dark and troubled age. Like Freud, Wordsworth, Coleridge, and other great Romantics, Macdonald shows us that reality can reside in dreams, especially bad dreams, and that the child is father to the man. Finally, his novels may be the truest of any, in his lifetime, in America.

—George Grella

MacLENNAN, (John) Hugh. Canadian. Born in Glace Bay, Nova Scotia, 20 March 1907. Educated at Halifax Academy; Dalhousie University, Halifax, B.A. 1928; Oriel College, Oxford (Rhodes Scholar), B.A., M.A. 1932; Princeton University, New Jersey, Ph.D. 1935. Married 1) Dorothy Duncan in 1936 (died,

1957); 2) Frances Walker in 1959. Classics Master, Lower Canada College, Montreal, 1935-45; full-time writer, 1945-51; Associate Professor, 1951-67, and Professor of English, 1967-79, McGill University, Montreal; now Professor Emeritus. Recipient: Guggenheim Fellowship, 1943; Governor-General's Award, 1948, 1949 and 1954 (for non-fiction), 1959; Lorne Pierce Medal, 1952; Quebec Prize, 1952; Critics Circle Award, 1959; Alberta Medal, 1960; Canada Council grant, 1963; Molson Award, 1966; Royal Bank Award, 1967. D.Litt.: University of New Brunswick, Fredericton, 1952; University of Western Ontario, 1952; University of Manitoba, Winnipeg, 1953; Waterloo Lutheran University, Ontario, 1961; McMaster University, Hamilton, Ontario, 1964; University of Sherbrooke, Quebec, 1967; University of British Columbia, Vancouver, 1968; University of Waterloo, Ontario, 1977; LL.D.: Dalhousie University, 1955; University of Saskatchewan, Saskatoon, 1959; University of Toronto, 1965; Laurentian University, Sudbury, Ontario, 1966; Carleton University, Ottawa, 1967; St. Mary's University, Halifax, Nova Scotia, 1968; Mount Allison University, Sackville, New Brunswick, 1969; D.C.L.: Bishop's University, Lennoxville, Quebec, 1965. Fellow, Royal Society of Canada, 1952; Fellow, 1956, and Companion of Literature, 1967, Royal Society of Literature. C.C. (Companion, Order of Canada), 1967. Address: 1535 Summerhill Avenue, Montreal 25, Quebec, Canada.

PUBLICATIONS

Novels

Barometer Rising. Toronto, Collins, and New York, Duell, 1941; London, Harrap, 1942.
Two Solitudes. Toronto, Collins, and New York, Duell, 1945; London, Cresset Press, 1946.
The Precipice. Toronto, Collins, and New York, Duell, 1948; London, Cresset Press, 1949.
Each Man's Son. Toronto, Macmillan, and Boston, Little Brown, 1951; London, Heinemann, 1952.
The Watch That Ends the Night. New York, Scribner, and London, Heinemann, 1959.
Return of the Sphinx. New York, Scribner, 1967.
Voices in Time. New York, St. Martin's Press, 1981.

Other

Oxyrhynchus: An Economic and Social Study. Princeton, New Jersey, Princeton University Press, 1935.
Cross-Country. Toronto, Collins, 1949.
The Present World as Seen in Its Literature (address). Fredericton, University of New Brunswick, 1952(?).
Thirty and Three (essays), edited by Dorothy Duncan. Toronto, Macmillan, 1954; London, Macmillan, 1955.
The Future of the Novel as an Art Form (lecture). Toronto, University of Toronto Press, 1959(?).
Scotchman's Return and Other Essays. Toronto, Macmillan, and New York, Scribner, 1960; as *Scotsman's Return and Other Essays*, London, Macmillan, 1961.
Seven Rivers of Canada. Toronto, Macmillan, 1961; as *The Rivers of Canada*, New York, Scribner, 1962; revised edition, Toronto, Macmillan, 1974; London, Macmillan, 1975.
The History of Canadian-American Relations (lecture). Plainfield, Vermont, Goddard College, 1963.
The Colour of Canada. Toronto, McClelland and Stewart, 1967; Boston, Little Brown, 1968; revised edition, 1972, 1978.
The Other Side of Hugh MacLennan: Selected Essays Old and New, edited by Elspeth Cameron. Toronto, Macmillan, 1978.

Editor, *McGill: The Story of a University.* London, Allen and Unwin, 1960.

*

Bibliography: "Hugh MacLennan: An Annotated Bibliography" by Elspeth Cameron, in *The Annotated Bibliography of Canada's Major Authors 1*, edited by Robert Lecker and Jack David, Downsview, Ontario, ECW Press, 1979.

Manuscript Collections: McGill University Library, Montreal; University of Calgary Library, Alberta; Fisher Library, University of Toronto.

Critical Studies: *O Canada* by Edmund Wilson, New York, Farrar Straus, 1965, London, Hart Davis, 1967; *Hugh MacLennan* by Peter Buitenhuis, Toronto, Forum House, 1969; *Hugh MacLennan* by George Woodcock, Toronto, Copp Clark, 1969; *Hugh MacLennan* by Alec Lucas, Toronto, McClelland and Stewart, 1970; *The Novels of Hugh MacLennan* by Robert H. Cockburn, Montreal, Harvest House, 1971; *The Immoral Moralists: Hugh MacLennan and Leonard Cohen* by Patricia Morley, Toronto, Clarke Irwin, 1972; *Hugh MacLennan* edited by Paul Goetsch, Toronto, McGraw Hill Ryerson, 1973; *Hugh MacLennan: A Writer's Life* by Elspeth Cameron, Toronto, University of Toronto Press, 1981.

Hugh MacLennan comments:

Nearly all of my published non-fiction has been in the form of personal essays. However, I must have published more than 60 pieces over the years dealing with various contemporary situations and problems, many connected with Canada.

As for my novels, after two unpublished books, I discovered that I had as a Canadian a special technical problem. I was writing out of a country at that time unknown even to itself, to say nothing of the rest of the world. All Canadian stereotypes were false. As drama depends upon recognitions, I was forced in my earlier fiction to explore many aspects of the Canadian character and experience in a detail no longer necessary. I always tried to turn this work into as universal a statement as possible, and must to some extent have succeeded because by this time I have been translated into 12 different languages—though not all books were so translated. The most successful translations were in German, but my last novel, *Return to the Sphinx*, seems to have done well in Poland. I have been told that at least one of my books is in Russian but I never saw a copy of it or a confirmation that it is.

* * *

Since the First World War Canadian writing—and especially Canadian writing in English—has been in much the same condition as American literature a century earlier. Working in the midst of a people who were discovering for the first time the pangs and delights of nationhood, Canadian authors have too often concerned themselves with the need to give literary expression to the Canadian identity and, frequently, have been so much involved with Canadianism that they have let slip the artist's prime duty: to establish his own literary personality. More even than the Founding Fathers of American literature they have been plagued by external influences, by history, which linked them almost irrevocably to the substantial tradition of London, by geography, which set them virtually inescapably in the suburbs of New York, by language which gave them two giant brothers, and by economics which committed them to a minuscule circulation unless they were prepared to commit the treason of making themselves comprehensible and acceptable in the huge market-places of Britain and the United States.

The analogy between Canada in the 50 years since the end of the First World War and the United States a century earlier is, of course, both incomplete and deceptive, the more so because Canada has produced no unquestionable masters of the order of Melville or Whitman who could transpose national characteristics into the magnificence of universality, nor a Canadian Emerson who could lead rebellion against the courtly and uncourtly muses of the greater literary nations while borrowing the philosophical inheritance that they provided, nor even a Canadian Fenimore Cooper who could create an intrinsically Canadian mythology.

Some Canadian writers, Mazo de la Roche, Thomas Costain,

even, in a more subtle, less popular, and more truly artistic manner, Morley Callaghan, Malcolm Lowry, and John Glassco, have on occasion solved the problem of their Canadianism by ignoring it, by writing as if the world is their country. Others of a meaner sort have been persistently parochial and are in consequence acceptable only in the tiny confines of the parish or else, outside it, as folklorish curiosities. Only one Canadian novelist, Hugh MacLennan, has been consistent in his efforts to represent the Canadian character both as something quintessentially idiosyncratic and as a parable to the human condition.

It is no paradox but in itself typical of the Canadian ethos that MacLennan is himself in so many ways an untypical Canadian. For all that he is a fourth generation Nova Scotian, MacLennan is the son of a man who spoke Gaelic or a lilting Highland English and who held to the Calvinist ways of the Scots and their superstition. His son has inherited the religiosity, something of the fatalism, and much of the Scotsman's not unjustified conceit in the pioneering achievements of his race, so that several of his novels—and above all *Each Man's Son* and *Return of the Sphinx*—can be regarded as transatlantic epilogues to the history of Scottish literature, as the records of a pastoral people battered and bewildered by urban society, rather than as the opening chapters of the glorious literary enterprise of an ebullient new nation.

Yet for all his urgent Canadianism and for all his inescapable Scottishness the most obvious influences on MacLennan are cosmopolitan and urbane. True, when he moves outside the Canadian setting, as in parts of *The Precipice* and *Return of the Sphinx*, his novelist's confidence falters, but in everything that he writes, whether fiction or non-fiction, his style is overtly the product of the two great civilised institutions (some would say over-civilised) in which he was educated. His literary manners are set to the precepts of Oxford and Princeton, and fashioned by communities that are centuries and worlds away from the Canada he describes. A classical scholar of repute, he creates characters who move to patterns that were fashioned long ago by Greek mythology.

To argue that an author's first novel is also his most successful would seem to imply a lack of development, and in one sense this claim for *Barometer Rising* does reduce the stature of all that has come from MacLennan since 1941. Certainly never again has MacLennan achieved an equivalent synthesis of theme and narrative without that constant interruption of didactic exposition which is the prime fault in most of MacLennan's books. But the entire success of *Barometer Rising* is almost an accident; it could hardly be repeated for MacLennan is deliberately both chronicler and creator of parables and there have been few other incidents in Canadian history so significant to Canadian development as the First World War and no event so open to translation into parable as the Halifax explosion of 1917. The First World War, the foreground and the background of *Barometer Rising*, was the time when Canada discovered its identity, and the explosion is at once a moment from history and an inescapable symbol of the end of the colonial era and the true beginning of nationhood.

Almost all of MacLennan's later work attempts in one form or another a similar fusion of realism and symbolism and always he is concerned not so much with narrative, plot, or setting (though with all these elements in the writing of novels MacLennan is a master) as with laying bare one or the other of the major impulses that lie behind the peculiarly Canadian nature of Canada. In *Two Solitudes*, for example, it is the schism between French and English Canadians. In *The Precipice* and *Each Man's Son* the puritanical sense of guilt that Puritanism has inflicted upon Canadian life, "the belief that man has inherited from Adam a nature so sinful that there is no hope for him and that, furthermore, he lives and dies under the wrath of an arbitrary God who will forgive only a handful of his elect on the Day of Judgment."

Archie MacNeil, the shabby decaying boxer of *Each Man's Son*, is the most complete character in all MacLennan's work, and the book as a whole contrives well two seemingly disparate themes, the gentleness of a man who lives by violence, and a threnody for the rural culture of Highlanders condemned by a cynical society to live by coal-mining.

The Watch That Ends the Night shows MacLennan as superb craftsman, handling with extraordinary skill a complicated time-sequence and with remarkable vividness the life of English Montreal, but because it is constructed on a grand scale it reveals in broad terms weaknesses which are less palpable in most of the other novels. MacLennan in all his books, but in *The Watch That Ends the Night* (and in *Return of the Sphinx*) more than in the others, is oppressively didactic. He is also an essayist almost more than he is a novelist. His expository asides and his descriptive vignettes though in themselves powerful and often elegant give to the book a stammering indecisiveness in which the hesitations become more compelling and sometimes more substantial than the fiction itself.

With courage beyond that of any other Canadian author, and to-day rare in all literatures, MacLennan writes on a grand scale. *Barometer Rising* and *The Watch That Ends the Night* are not masterpieces of the order of *War and Peace* but MacLennan has attempted to be Canada's Tolstoy and in doing so has disgraced neither himself nor Canada.

—J.E. Morpurgo

MADDEN, (Jerry) David. American. Born in Knoxville, Tennessee, 25 July 1933. Educated at the University of Tennessee, Knoxville, B.S. 1957; San Francisco State College, M.A. 1958; Yale Drama School (John Golden Fellow), New Haven, Connecticut, 1959-60. Served in the United States Army, 1955-56. Married Roberta Margaret Young in 1956; one daughter. Instructor in English, Appalachian State Teachers College, Boone, North Carolina, 1958-59, and Centre College, Danville, Kentucky, 1960-62; Lecturer in Creative Writing, University of Louisville, Kentucky, 1962-64; Member of the English Department, Kenyon College, Gambier, Ohio, and Assistant Editor, *Kenyon Review*, 1964-66; Lecturer in Creative Writing, Ohio University, Athens, 1966-68. Since 1968, Writer-in-Residence, Louisiana State University, Baton Rouge. Recipient: Rockefeller grant, 1969; National Endowment for the Arts Prize, 1970; Bread Loaf Writers Conference William Raney Fellowship, 1972. Address: 614 Park Boulevard, Baton Rouge, Louisiana 70806, U.S.A.

PUBLICATIONS

Novels

The Beautiful Greed. New York, Random House, 1961.
Cassandra Singing. New York, Crown, 1969.
Brothers in Confidence. New York, Avon, 1972.
Bijou. New York, Crown, 1974.
The Suicide's Wife. Indianapolis, Bobbs Merrill, 1978.
Pleasure-Dome. Indianapolis, Bobbs Merrill, 1979.
On the Big Wind. New York, Holt Rinehart, 1980.

Short Stories

The Shadow Knows. Baton Rouge, Louisiana State University Press, 1970.

Uncollected Short Stories

"My Name Is Not Antonio," in *Yale Literary Magazine* (New Haven, Connecticut), March 1960.
"Hair of the Dog," in *Adam* (Los Angeles), April-November 1967.
"The Master's Thesis," in *Fantasy and Science Fiction* (New York), July 1967.

"Nothing Dies But Something Mourns," in *Carleton Miscellany* (Northfield, Minnesota), Fall 1968.
"A Voice in the Garden," in *English Record* (Oneonta, New York), October 1969.
"On Target," in *December* (Western Springs, Illinois), xi, 1-2, 1969.
"The Day the Flowers Came," in *The Best American Short Stories 1969*, edited by Martha Foley and David Burnett. Boston, Houghton Mifflin, 1969.
"Home Comfort," in *Jeopardy* (Bellingham, Washington), March 1970.
"The House of Pearl," in *Twigs 6* (Pikeville, Kentucky), 1970.
"Traven," in *Short Stories from the Little Magazines*, edited by Jarvis Thurston and Curt Johnson. Chicago, Scott Foresman, 1970.
"No Trace," in *The Best American Short Stories 1971*, edited by Martha Foley and David Burnett. Boston, Houghton Mifflin, 1971.
"A Secondary Character," in *Cimarron Review* (Stillwater, Oklahoma), July 1972.
"A Part in Pirandello," in *North American Review* (Mt. Vernon, Iowa), Summer 1972.
"The Spread-Legged Girl" (as Jack Travis), in *Knight* (Los Angeles), October 1972.
"Looking at the Dead," in *Minnesota Review* (Minneapolis), Fall 1972.
"Night Shift," in *Playboy's Ribald Classics 3*. Chicago, Playboy Press, 1972.
"The Singer," in *Scenes from American Life: Contemporary Short Fiction*, edited by Joyce Carol Oates. New York, Random House, 1972.
"Lindberg's Rival," in *Quartet* (College Station, Texas), Spring-Summer 1973.
"Here He Comes! There He Goes!," in *Contempora* (Atlanta, Georgia), Summer 1973.
"Wanted: Ghost Writer," in *Epoch* (Ithaca, New York), Fall 1973.
"The World's One Breathing," in *Appalachian Heritage* (Pippa Passes, Kentucky), Winter 1973.
"Hurry Up Please, It's Time," in *The Botteghe Oscure Reader*, edited by George Garrett and Katherine Garrison Biddle. Middletown, Connecticut, Wesleyan University Press, 1974.
"The Hero and the Witness," in *New Orleans Review*, iv, 3, 1974.
"In the Bag," in *Southern Review* (Baton Rouge, Louisiana), 1977.
"Putting an Act Together," in *Southern Review* (Baton Rouge, Louisiana), 1980.

Plays

Call Herman in to Supper (produced Knoxville, Tennessee, 1949).
They Shall Endure (produced Knoxville, Tennessee, 1953).
Cassandra Singing (produced Knoxville, Tennessee, 1955). Published in *New Campus Writing 2*, edited by Nolan Miller, New York, Putnam, 1957; (expanded version, produced Albuquerque, New Mexico, 1964).
From Rome to Damascus (produced Chapel Hill, North Carolina, 1959).
Casina, music by Robert Rogers, lyrics by Joseph Matthewson (produced New Haven, Connecticut, 1960).
In My Father's House, in *First Stage* (Lafayette, Indiana), Summer 1966.
Fugitive Masks (produced Abingdon, Virginia, 1966).
The Day the Flowers Came (produced Baton Rouge, Louisiana, 1974). Chicago, Dramatic Publishing Company, 1975.
Three Mean Fairy Tales, with Thomas Newman, music by Newman (produced Washington, D.C., 1979).

Other

Wright Morris. New York, Twayne, 1965.
The Poetic Image in Six Genres. Carbondale, Southern Illinois University Press, 1969.
James M. Cain. New York, Twayne, 1970.
Harlequin's Stick, Charlie's Cane: A Comparative Study of Commedia dell'Arte and Silent Slapstick Comedy. Bowling Green, Ohio, Popular Press, 1975.
A Primer of the Novel, For Readers and Writers. Metuchen, New Jersey, Scarecrow Press, 1980.
Writer's Revisions, with Richard Powers. Metuchen, New Jersey, Scarecrow Press, 1980.

Editor, *Tough Guy Writers of the Thirties*. Carbondale, Southern Illinois University Press, 1968.
Editor, *Proletarian Writers of the Thirties*. Carbondale, Southern Illinois University Press, 1968.
Editor, *American Dreams, American Nightmares*. Carbondale, Southern Illinois University Press, 1970.
Editor, *Rediscoveries: Informal Essays in Which Well-Known Novelists Rediscover Neglected Works of Fiction by One of Their Favorite Authors*. New York, Crown, 1971.
Editor, with Ray B. Browne, *The Popular Cultural Explosion: Experiencing Mass Media*. Dubuque, Iowa, William Brown, 2 vols., 1972.
Editor, *Nathanael West: The Cheaters and the Cheated*. Deland, Florida, Everett Edwards, 1973.
Editor, *Remembering James Agee*. Baton Rouge, Louisiana State University Press, 1974.
Editor, *Creative Choices: A Spectrum of Quality and Technique in Fiction*. Chicago, Scott Foresman, 1975.
Editor, with Virgil Scott, *Studies in the Short Story*. New York, Holt Rinehart, 1975.

*

Manuscript Collection: University of Tennessee Library, Knoxville.

Critical Studies: "A Conversation with David Madden," and "The Mixed Chords of David Madden's *Cassandra Singing*" by Sanford Pinsker, in *Critique* (Atlanta), xv, 2, 1973; "An Interview with David Madden," in *The Penny Dreadful* (Bowling Green, Ohio), iii, 3, 1974; "The Story Teller as Benevolent Con Man" by the author, in *Appalachian Heritage* (Pippa Passes, Kentucky), Summer 1974; interview in *Southern Review* (Baton Rouge, Louisiana), xi, 1, 1975.

David Madden comments:

I've been trying all my life to pass the test F. Scott Fitzgerald set for himself. "The test of a first-rate intelligence is the ability to hold two opposed ideas in the mind at the same time and still retain the ability to function." Camus's concept of the absurd helped clarify Fitzgerald's: one's life should be a self-created contradiction of the fact that life is basically absurd. A similar polarity has given some form to my art as well as my life. It was not books but my grandmother's story-telling and the movies' charged images that inspired me to write. My first literary hero was the Dionysican Thomas Wolfe; then came the Apollonian James Joyce. In the tensions between those two extremes I have tried to shape my own work. I have practiced for a long time now the concept that it is between the limitations externally imposed by the form I'm working in and limitations I imposed on myself in the writing of a specific work that I experience genuine and productive freedom. Two metaphors of the artist (and the teacher) are useful for me: the magician and the con man. As with the magician's techniques of illusion, art works by a phantom circuit; and the relationship between writer and reader is like that between the con man and his mark, except that the climax (the sting) is beneficial for both . For me, the function of fiction is to create imaginary worlds; discipline and technique enable me to cause that to happen. And in that process I consider my reader as an active collaborator.

* * *

Three groups, not in any way organized, have in recent years dominated American fiction: the Jewish novelists (Bellow, Heller, Malamud), the fantasists (Barth, Pynchon, Vonnegut), and the Southern writers (Faulkner, Flannery O'Connor, Welty). By birth, early environment, and subject matter, David Madden belongs to the third group, and he admits it, but points out that the Southern writers make use of universal themes: the scenery may be local, but the vision can be limitless. Madden's own range is indicated in the urban, mountain, and university settings of his novels and prize-winning book of short stories. Most of his work has a breadth and depth which invite serious critical consideration.

Madden is, among other things, a born story-teller. The first voice he remembers is that of his grandmother, a "Homeric" figure who looked like Wallace Beery. By the time he was three years old, his stories were entertaining his friends: "It's always been play—in many guises, through many stages, all my writing is play." He became aware, even as a child, "of the dynamic interplay between teller and listener"—and it is his perpetuation of this relationship that makes his stories so gripping. Madden has long been an admirer of Joseph Conrad, and even before his own experience in the merchant marine in the early 1950's, he had thought of the novel that was to become *The Beautiful Greed*, which, though it takes its title from a phrase in *Lord Jim*, shows that Madden was speaking with his own voice. Similarly, he early cast off the influence of Thomas Wolfe; although he sometimes deals with Wolfean themes, his writing avoids Wolfe's often pompous rhetoric. Madden's style is simple, but vivid, and careful of the right word to convey thought and action.

His novels are significant contributions to contemporary American fiction. *Cassandra Singing*, the least autobiographical of Madden's works, is a neat combination of the realistic and the fanciful-romantic, which at the same time is a Southern family-story about the tense relationship between the semi-invalid Cassie and her brother Lone, a ferocious motorcyclist. Madden labored over this story, as a one-act play and a three-act play—both produced—and, in various literary journals, as a piece of narrative fiction. After finally putting together all the material as a novel which won some critical but not popular acclaim, he was invited to Hollywood to write the film script and came out with three different versions.

Although *Cassandra Singing*, an essentially serious book, has some irony and comedy, Madden's writing did not reach its full comic potentiality until his short novel *Brothers in Confidence*, the story of a graduate student whose older and younger brothers are confidence men, in and out of jails but making even the prosecuting attorneys fond of them. These con-men brothers are a small part of *Bijou*, which is autobiographical in scenery and circumstance, but is in larger part effectively inventive. As a Book-of-the-Month Club alternate selection it has reached a wider audience than any of his other works.

In addition to his fiction, Madden has produced several critical books, of which *The Poetic Image in Six Genres* is the most personal; it discusses a number of current (in some cases quite recent) American novelists, particularly Joyce Carol Oates and Madden's own favorite contemporary author, Wright Morris. The book also contains a number of useful comments by the author on his own writings.

So far, *Bijou* is the finest of them. It takes its name from a familiar one in American cinema history, for in the early days of film, the theatres were often looked upon as "gems." In Madden's story, young Lucius Hutchfield is an usher who is fascinated by the screen stars of the 1940's. Madden deals with all aspects of movie-going in *Bijou*—he once said we ourselves are the movies—but he also treats other phases in the life of an adolescent. Altogether, *Bijou* is an important event in today's American literature.

—Harry T. Moore

MAILER, Norman. American. Born in Long Branch, New Jersey, 31 January 1923. Educated at Boys' High School, Brooklyn, New York, graduated 1939; Harvard University, Cambridge, Massachusetts, 1939-43, S.B. in aeronautical engineering 1943; the Sorbonne, Paris, 1947. Served in the United States Army, 1944-46. Married 1) Beatrice Silverman in 1944 (divorced, 1952), one daughter; 2) Adèle Morales in 1954 (divorced, 1962) two daughters; 3) Lady Jean Campbell in 1962 (divorced, 1963), one daughter; 4) Beverly Bentley in 1963 (divorced, 1971), two sons; 5) Carol Stevens in 1971, one daughter; 6) Norris Church. Co-Editor, *Dissent*, New York, 1953-63; co-founding editor, *Village Voice*, New York, 1954; columnist, *Esquire*, New York, 1962-63. Independent Candidate for Mayor of New York City, 1969. Recipient: *Story* magazine prize, 1941; American Academy grant, 1960; Pulitzer Prize, for non-fiction, 1969; National Book Award, for non-fiction, 1969; MacDowell Medal, 1973; National Art Club Gold Medal, 1976. Member, American Academy, 1967. D.Litt.: Rutgers University, New Brunswick, New Jersey, 1969. Lives in Brooklyn, New York. Address: c/o Molly Malone Cook, P.O. Box 338, Provincetown, Massachusetts 02657, U.S.A.

PUBLICATIONS

Novels

The Naked and the Dead. New York, Rinehart, 1948; London, Wingate, 1949.
Barbary Shore. New York, Rinehart, 1951; London, Cape, 1952.
The Deer Park. New York, Putnam, 1955; London, Wingate, 1957.
An American Dream. New York, Dial Press, and London, Deutsch, 1965.
Why Are We in Vietnam? New York, Putnam, 1967; London, Weidenfeld and Nicolson, 1969.
A Transit to Narcissus: A Facsimile of the Original Typescript, edited by Howard Fertig. New York, Fertig, 1978.

Short Stories

New Short Novels 2, with others. New York, Ballantine, 1956.
Advertisements for Myself (includes essays and verse). New York, Putnam, 1959; London, Deutsch, 1961.
The Short Fiction of Norman Mailer. New York, Dell, 1967.

Plays

The Deer Park, adaptation of his own novel (produced New York, 1959). New York, Dial Press, 1967; London, Weidenfeld and Nicolson, 1970.
A Fragment from Vietnam (as *D.J.*, produced Provincetown, Massachusetts, 1967). Included in *Existential Errands*, 1972.
Maidstone: A Mystery (screenplay and essay). New York, New American Library, 1971.

Screenplays: *Wild 90*, 1967; *Beyond the Law* (two versions), 1968; *Maidstone*, 1970.

Verse

Deaths for the Ladies and Other Disasters. New York, Putnam, and London, Deutsch, 1962.

Other

The White Negro. San Francisco, City Lights, 1957.
The Presidential Papers. New York, Putnam, 1963; London, Deutsch, 1964.
Cannibals and Christians. New York, Dial Press, 1966; London, Deutsch, 1967.
The Bullfight. New York, Macmillan, 1967.

The Armies of the Night: The Novel as History, History as a Novel. New York, New American Library, and London, Weidenfeld and Nicolson, 1968.

Miami and the Siege of Chicago: An Informal History of the Republican and Democratic Conventions of 1968. New York, New American Library, and London, Weidenfeld and Nicolson, 1968.

The Idol and the Octopus: Political Writings on the Kennedy and Johnson Administrations. New York, Dell, 1968.

Of a Fire on the Moon. Boston, Little Brown, 1970; as *A Fire on the Moon*, London, Weidenfeld and Nicolson, 1970.

The Prisoner of Sex. Boston, Little Brown, and London, Weidenfeld and Nicolson, 1971.

The Long Patrol: 25 Years of Writing from the Works of Norman Mailer, edited by Robert F. Lucid. Cleveland, World, 1971.

King of the Hill: On the Fight of the Century. New York, New American Library, 1971.

Existential Errands. Boston, Little Brown, 1972.

St. George and the Godfather. New York, New American Library, 1972.

Marilyn: A Novel Biography. New York, Grosset and Dunlap, and London, Hodder and Stoughton, 1973.

The Faith of Graffiti, with Mervyn Kurlansky and Jon Naar. New York, Praeger, 1974; as *Watching My Name Go By*, London, Mathews Miller Dunbar, 1975.

The Fight. Boston, Little Brown, 1975; London, Hart Davis MacGibbon, 1976.

Some Honorable Men: Political Conventions 1960-1972. Boston, Little Brown, 1976.

Genius and Lust: A Journey Through the Major Writings of Henry Miller, with Henry Miller. New York, Grove Press, 1976.

The Executioner's Song: A True Life Novel (on Gary Gilmore). Boston, Little Brown, and London, Hutchinson, 1979.

Of Women and Their Elegance, photographs by Milton H. Greene. New York, Simon and Schuster, and London, Hodder and Stoughton, 1980.

*

Bibliography: *Norman Mailer: A Comprehensive Bibliography* by Laura Adams, Metuchen, New Jersey, Scarecrow Press, 1974.

Critical Studies (selection): *Norman Mailer* by Richard Foster, Minneapolis, University of Minnesota Press, 1968; *The Structured Vision of Norman Mailer* by Barry H. Leeds, New York, New York University Press, 1969; *Norman Mailer: The Man and His Work* edited by Robert F. Lucid, Boston, Little Brown, 1971; *Norman Mailer* by Richard Poirier, London, Collins, and New York, Viking Press, 1972; *Norman Mailer: A Collection of Critical Essays*, edited by Leo Braudy, Englewood Cliffs, New Jersey, Prentice Hall, 1972; *Down Mailer's Way* by Robert Solotaroff, Urbana, University of Illinois Press, 1974; *Norman Mailer: A Critical Study* by Jean Radford, London, Macmillan, and New York, Barnes and Noble, 1975; *Existential Battles: The Growth of Norman Mailer* by Laura Adams, Athens, Ohio University Press, 1976; *Mankind in Barbary: The Individual and Society in the Novels of Norman Mailer* by Stanley T. Gutman, Hanover, New Hampshire, University Press of New England, 1976; *Norman Mailer* by Philip Bufithis, New York, Ungar, 1978; *Acts of Regeneration: Allegory and Archetype in the Work of Norman Mailer* by Robert J. Begiebing, Columbia, University of Missouri Press, 1980; *An American Dreamer: A Psychoanalytic Study of the Fiction of Norman Mailer* by Andrew M. Gordon, Rutherford, New Jersey, Fairleigh Dickinson University Press, 1980.

Theactrical Activities:

Director and Actor: **Films**—*Wild 90*, 1967; *Beyond the Law* (two versions), 1968; *Maidstone*, 1970.

* * *

A formal distinction between fiction and non-fiction, or between fiction and journalism, is not the most helpful way to approach either the direction or the value of Norman Mailer's work. Involving himself directly with public events as well as private concerns, reporting on activities as diverse as protest marches, prizefights, the moon landing, political conventions, and the life of the first man executed for murder in America for more than ten years, Mailer characteristically blurs, argues about, and plays with the conventional categories of fiction and non-fiction. The public events he reports become metaphors that clarify and demonstrate the issues he sees as significant, apocalyptic, or destructive about contemporary America. This combination of reporting with a personal fictive vision underlies some of Mailer's best and most searching prose, like *The Armies of the Night* or much of *The Executioner's Song*. Mailer began his career with a much more conventional idea of the difference between fiction and non-fiction, for, in the early novel *The Deer Park*, he had Sergius O'Shaugnessy, the young Air Force veteran trying to become a writer in the "new" Hollywood off-shoot of Desert D'Or, smugly certain that "a newpaperman is obsessed with finding the facts in order to tell a lie, and a novelist is a galley-slave to his imagination so he can look for the truth." More central to Mailer's later, more complicated, fiction and reporting is another statement from the same novel, the remark by Charles Eitel, the failed and (in the 1950's) politically suspect Hollywood writer and director, musing that "the artist was always divided between his desire for power in the world and his desire for power over his work." This emphasis on power, on the capacity to change both public and private circumstances, is never far from the center of Mailer's consciousness.

Rather than using any formal means of distinguishing one example of Mailer from another, the reader recognizes that a problem of selectivity, of what to include and what to exclude, is always visible. At times, Mailer seems to concentrate too repetitiously for too long on the relatively trivial or excessively personal, as in the rather stereotyped and remote satire of Hollywood in *The Deer Park*, all the legalisms of the last third or so of *The Executioner's Song*, or the defense of his own part in literary squabbles at the beginning of *The Prisoner of Sex*. Frequently, as he recognized himself in *The Presidential Papers*, he lacks a sense of proportion, is not sure about "how to handicap the odds."

Mailer's considerable literary ambition and the popular success of his first novel, *The Naked and the Dead*, published when he was just 25, placed his own development as a writer in a highly public focus. In spite of all the claims (many of them not from Mailer himself) about the "new" voice of his generation, his first three novels were somewhat literary and derivative. *The Naked and the Dead*, the novel about the platoon fighting both the Japanese and its own Army on a Pacific island during World War II, shows considerable allegiance to the fiction of both Hemingway and Dos Passos, as well as deference to the ethnic mix visible in Hollywood films made during the war. *Barbary Shore*, probably the best of the three novels, taking place in a Brooklyn rooming house after the war, using characters to debate all the various perspectives of radical politics in the 1930's and ending with no resolution for the young alienated writer, is reminiscent of James T. Farrell. And *The Deer Park*, depicting the Hollywood world of drugs, pimps, mate-swapping, and politics, contains echoes of both Fitzgerald and Nathanael West without the force or originality of either, all seen at a great distance, as if the chronicle of events could shock with nothing of the feelings rendered. Although interesting, often competent, and (particularly *Barbary Shore*) full of excellent description, this fiction was more distinctive in aim than in achievement. Mailer's perspective, however, changed considerably in the middle and late 1950's, a change first visible in the 1957 essay *The White Negro*, a recognition of the clash of cultures and the violence endemic in American life. In that essay, as well as in the work that followed, Mailer began to associate imagination and creativity with the position of a sociological minority, a potentially healthy underside of American life. As he later, in *The Presidential Papers*, explained, he had not earlier acknowledged his own secret admiration for his violent characters in *The Naked and the Dead*, his own obsession with violence. From *The White Negro* on, although still disapproving strongly of "inhuman" or abstract violence, of the violence of technology, Mailer recognized the possibilities of creative change through violence, both in himself and in others. He also began to probe himself more consciously as a metaphor for the larger world he described.

Mailer regards his central characters, whether in the persona of himself in works like *The Armies of the Night* or *Miami and the Siege of Chicago* or through fictional personae in the novels *An American Dream* or *Why Are We in Vietnam?*, as "existential" heroes who constantly test the possible edges of human experience. Always in conflict, within themselves and with others, they dare, like Rojack walking around the parapet of the terrace high above New York, possible destruction in order to live all the possibilities of the self. Through action, they create the self, as Rojack does through murder, varieties of sexual experience, escape, criminality, and understanding. This self-creation involves a good deal of fear, as well as overcoming fear, for the hero must break away from the safe and familiar, acknowledging violence and destruction within himself. In *Why Are We in Vietnam?*, the novel of Texans on a bear hunt in Alaska, a metaphor that coalesces all those attitudes, tests, totems, and taboos that explain the American presence in Vietnam, the young voice, D.J., must create himself by recognizing and overcoming his own fear of the bear. The most frequent action, in Mailer's work, which overcomes stasis, safety, and fear, is sex, the direct relationship with another being. Each sexual encounter is a victory over isolation and abstraction, and, as Mailer explains in *The Prisoner of Sex*, he objects to masturbation and contraception because, in different ways, they prevent the fullest exploration of direct physical relationship. Mailer has always implicitly thought of sex in these terms, ending *The Dear Park* with a God-like voice intoning "think of Sex as Time, and time as the connection of new circuits." Yet the full development of self-creation through sexual experience, the sense of the orgasm as "the inescapable existential moment," detailed variously and explicitly, is in the work that follows *The White Negro*.

Mailer's "existentialism" is not simply private self-definition. In the first place, he frequently argues that existentialism is rootless unless one hypothesizes death as an "existential continuation of life," so that how one dies, how one faces destruction, matters. In addition, and emphasized much more frequently, Mailer's "existential" values are also social, the public consequences of definitions at the edges of experience. Social conflict is always visible, men defining themselves through the active public and social metaphors of parties, prize-fights, and wars. War (and Mailer frequently distinguishes "good" wars from "bad") has the possibility, seldom actually achieved, of changing the consciousness of a sufficient number of people to alter the whole society. Mailer began his definition of "existential politics" in 1960, with his essay called "Superman Comes to the Supermarket," on the nomination of John Kennedy for president at the convention in Los Angeles. He called Kennedy an "existential" leader because he displayed the capacity to commit himself to the "new" when "the end is unknown," a contrast to the safety and public predictability of the Eisenhower years, although Mailer doubted that Kennedy had the "imagination" to create a wholly beneficial revolution. Yet, for Mailer, the potentiality for change and revolution, for self-creation on a public scale, is always there, a human impulse that if repressed or thwarted causes "cancer" on either the individual or social level. In these terms, Mailer, through subsequent "reports" on protests, political conventions, and public events, propounds both a vision and an analysis of contemporary American society.

In rather undiscerning popular terms, Mailer is often accused of a monstrous ego. Yet, the persona of "Norman Mailer," as it develops through many of the "journalistic" works, is highly complicated and self-critical, a metaphor for all the possibilities in contemporary man that the author can visualize and understand. As he explains in *The Armies of the Night*, he can accept the ambivalences of all the personae he adopts, "warrior, presumptive general, ex-political candidate, embattled aging enfant terrible of the literary world, wise father of six children, radical intellectual, existential philosopher, hard-working author, champion of obscenity, husband of four battling sweet wives, amiable bar drinker, and much exaggerated street fighter, party giver, hostess insulter." But the one persona he finds "insupportable" is that of "the nice Jewish boy from Brooklyn," the one with which he began, which would deny his possibility to change and create himself. The personae of his later fiction are also complicated and carefully structured voices: the violent explosions, sensitivities, challenges, and social concerns of Rojack in *An American Dream* (still, to some extent, literary, as one critic, Richard Poirier, has explained, "both a throwback to Christopher Marlowe and...a figure out of Dashiell Hammett"); the scatology, sensitivity, fear, bravery, and self-recognition of D.J. in *Why Are We in Vietnam?* These voices, rhetorical and linguistic creations of a point of view, effectively express much of Mailer's complexity, although they lack something of the arch self-criticism (though not the humor) and the multiplicity of the persona of Norman Mailer who enriches *The Armies of the Night* and *Of a Fire on the Moon*, and whose implicit and more self-abnegating presence created *The Executioner's Song*. As personae, creative and capacious as they are, Rojack and D.J. can sound slightly more insistent, missing something of the "Norman Mailer" acknowledged incapacity to represent immediately all of America.

As a writer, Norman Mailer is variously talented. He is a superb journalist, always aware of the differences between what an observer sees directly and what he creates. He is an excellent literary critic, as in his attack on Kate Millett and his defenses of Henry Miller and D.H. Lawrence in *The Prisoner of Sex*. He can describe pictorially and movingly, as in *Of a Fire on the Moon*, or select brilliantly to chronicle American life, as in most of *The Executioner's Song*. More than any of these, he is consciously, seriously, humorously, and often convincingly, the heir to a tradition of American visionaries, the writer who can create, in terms of the imagination, a new consciousness for his time and his country. In spite of his prolixity, his repetition, his occasional tendency to simplify polarities (his arguments against "technology" can become rant that denies his own understanding of science), and his occasional insistence on the literal applications of his own metaphors (as in parts of *The Prisoner of Sex*), Mailer has achieved something of his own revolutionary form in transforming the consciousness of others.

—James Gindin

MAJOR, Clarence. American. Born in Atlanta, Georgia, 31 December 1936. Educated at the Art Institute, Chicago (James Nelson Raymond Scholar), 1952-54; Armed Forces Institute, 1955-56; New School for Social Research, New York, 1972. Served in the Unted States Air Force, 1955-57. Married Joyce Sparrow in 1958 (divorced 1964). Research Analyst, Simulmatics, New York, 1967. Taught in the Harlem Education Program Writers Workshop, New York, 1967, and the Teachers and Writers Collaborative, New York, 1967-72. Since 1972, Member of the Faculty, Sarah Lawrence College, Bronxville, New York. Associate Editor, *Proof Magazine*, Chicago, 1959-60; Editor, *Coercion Review*, Chicago, 1958-65; Associate Editor, *Caw!* magazine, 1967-68, and *Journal of Black Poetry*, 1967-70. Recipient: National Endowment for the Arts grant, 1970; New York Cultural Foundation grant, 1971. Agent: Howard Moorepark, 444 East 82nd Street, New York, New York, 10028, U.S.A.

PUBLICATIONS

Novels

All-Night Visitors. New York, Olympia Press, 1969.

NO. New York, Emerson Hall, 1973.
Reflex and Bone Structure. New York, Fiction Collective, 1975.
Emergency Exit. New York, Fiction Collective, 1979.

Uncollected Short Stories

"Church Girl," in *Human Voices 3* (Homestead, Florida), Summer-Fall 1967.
"An Area in the Cerebral Hemisphere," in *Statements*, edited by Jonathan Baumbach. New York, Braziller, 1975.
"Dossy O," in *Writing under Fire*, edited by Jerome Klinkowitz and John Somer. New York, Dell, 1978.

Verse

The Fires That Burn in Heaven. Privately printed, 1954.
Love Poems of a Black Man. Omaha, Nebraska, Coercion Press, 1965.
Human Juices. Omaha, Nebraska, Coercion Press, 1965.
Swallow the Lake. Middletown, Connecticut, Wesleyan University Press, 1970.
Symptoms and Madness. New York, Corinth, 1971.
Private Line. London, Paul Breman, 1971.
The Cotton Club: New Poems. Detroit, Broadside Press, 1972.
The Syncopated Cakewalk. New York, Barlenmir House, 1974.

Other

Dictionary of Afro-American Slang. New York, International, 1970; as *Black Slang: A Dictionary of Afro-American Talk*, London, Routledge, 1971.
The Dark and Feeling: Black American Writers and Their Work. New York, Third Press, 1974.

Editor, *Writers Workshop Anthology.* New York, Harlem Education Project, 1967.
Editor, *Man Is Like a Child: An Anthology of Creative Writing by Students.* New York, Macomb's Junior High School, 1968.
Editor, *The New Black Poetry.* New York, International, 1969.

*

Bibliography: "Clarence Major: A Checklist of Criticism" by Joe Weixlmann, in *Obsidian* (Fredonia, New York), iv, 2, 1978; "Toward a Primary Bibliography of Clarence Major" by Joe Weixlmann and Clarence Major, in *Black American Literature Forum* (Terre Haute, Indiana), Summer 1979.

* * *

In a novel, the only thing you have is words," Clarence Major told the interviewer John O'Brien. "You begin with words and you end with words. The content exists in our minds. I don't think it has to be a reflection of anything. It is a reality that has been created inside of a book." Clarence Major's fiction exists as a rebellion against the stereotype of mimetic fiction—that telling a story, one of the things fiction can do, is the only thing fiction can do.

His first novel, *All-Night Visitors*, is an exercise in the imaginative powers of male sexuality. Major takes the most physical theme—the pleasure of the orgasm—and lyricizes it, working his imagination upon the bedrock world of sense not customarily indulged by poetry. The pre-eminence of the imagination is shown by blending Chicago street scenes with fighting in Vietnam—in terms of the writing itself, Major claims that there is no difference. His second novel, *NO*, alternates narrative scenes of rural Georgia life with a more disembodied voice of fiction, and the action advances as it is passed back and forth, almost conversationally, between these two fictive voices. In both books, language itself is the true locus of action, as even the most random and routine development is seized as the occasion for raptures of prose (a fellatio scene, for example, soon outstrips itself as pornography and turns into an excuse for twelve pages of exuberant prose).

Clarence Major's best work is represented in his third and fourth novels, *Reflex and Bone Structure* and *Emergency Exit*. In the former, he describes an action which takes place legitimately within the characters' minds, as formed by images from television and film. "We're in bed watching the late movie. It's 1938. *A Slight Case of Murder*. Edward G. Robinson and Jane Bryan. I go into the bathroom to pee. Finished, I look at my aging face. Little Caesar. I wink at him in the mirror, He winks back. / I'm back in bed. The late show comes on. It's 1923. *The Bright Shawl*. Dorothy Gish. Mary Astor. I'm taking Mary Astor home in a yellow taxi. Dorothy Gish is jealous." Throughout this novel, which treats stimuli from social life and the output of a television set as equally informative, Major insists that the realm of all these happenings is in language itself. "I am standing behind Cora," he writes. "She is wearing a thin black nightgown. The backs of her legs are lovely. I love her. The word standing allows me to watch like this. The word nightgown is what she is wearing. The nightgown itself is in her drawer with her panties. The word Cora is wearing the word nightgown. I watch the sentence: the backs of her legs are lovely."

Emergency Exit is Clarence Major's most emphatic gesture toward pure writing, accomplished by making the words of his story refer inward to his own creative act, rather than outward toward the panoramic landscape of the socially real. The novel's structure makes this strategy possible. *Emergency Exit* consists of elementary units of discourse: words, sentences, paragraphs, vignettes, and serial narratives. The novel is composed of equal blocks of each, spread out and mixed with the others. At first, simple sentences are presented to the reader. Then elements from these same sentences (which have stood in reference-free isolation) recur in paragraphs, but still free of narrative meaning. The plan is to fix a word, as word, in the reader's mind, apart from any personal conceptual reference—just as an abstract expressionist painter will present a line, or a swirl of color, without any reference to figure. Then come a number of narratives, coalescing into a story of lovers and family. When enough sections of the serial narrative have accumulated to form a recognizable story, we find that the independent and fragmentary scenes of the sentences and paragraphs have been animated by characters with whom we can now empathize. Forestalling any attempt to rush off the page into incidental gossip is the memory and further repetition of these words—whether they be of black mythology, snatches of popular song, or simply brilliant writing—all within Major's arresting sentences and paragraphs. A word, an image, or scene which occurs within the narrative leads the reader directly back to the substance of Major's writing. All attention is confined within the pages of the book.

—Jerome Klinkowitz

MALAMUD, Bernard. American. Born in Brooklyn, New York, 26 April 1914. Educated at Erasmus Hall, New York; City College of New York, 1932-36, B.A. 1936; Columbia University, New York, 1937-38, M.A. 1942. Married Ann de Chiara in 1945; one son and one daughter. Teacher, New York high schools, evenings 1940-49; Instructor to Associate Professor of English, Oregon State University, Corvallis, 1949-61. Since 1961, Member of the Division of Language and Literature, Bennington College, Vermont. Visiting Lecturer, Harvard University, Cambridge, Massachusetts, 1966-68. President, P.E.N. American Center, 1979-80. Recipient: Rosenthal Award, 1958; Daroff Memorial Award, 1958; Ford Fellowship, 1959, 1960; National Book Award, 1959, 1967; Pulitzer Prize, 1967; O. Henry Award, 1969, 1973; Jewish Heritage Award, 1977.

Member, American Academy, 1964, and American Academy of Arts and Sciences, 1967. Lives in New York City. Agent: Russell and Volkening, 551 Fifth Avenue, New York, New York 10017, U.S.A.

PUBLICATIONS

Novels

The Natural. New York, Harcourt Brace, 1952; London, Eyre and Spottiswoode, 1963.
The Assistant. New York, Farrar Straus, 1957; London, Eyre and Spottiswoode, 1959.
A New Life. New York, Farrar Straus, 1961; London, Eyre and Spottiswoode, 1962.
The Fixer. New York, Farrar Straus, 1966; London, Eyre and Spottiswoode, 1967.
Pictures of Fidelman: An Exhibition. New York, Farrar Straus, and London, Eyre and Spottiswoode, 1969.
The Tenants. New York, Farrar Straus, 1971; London, Eyre Methuen, 1972.
Dubin's Lives. New York, Farrar Straus, and London, Chatto and Windus, 1979.

Short Stories

The Magic Barrel. New York, Farrar Straus, 1958; London, Eyre and Spottiswoode, 1960.
Idiots First. New York, Farrar Straus, 1963; London, Eyre and Spottiswoode, 1964.
Penguin Modern Stories 1, with others. London, Penguin, 1969.
Rembrandt's Hat. New York, Farrar Straus, and London, Eyre Methuen, 1973.

Uncollected Short Stories

"An Exorcism," in *Harper's* (New York), December 1968.
"God's Wrath," in *Atlantic* (Boston), February 1972.
"Home Is the Hero," in *The Best American Short Stories 1979*, edited by Joyce Carol Oates and Shannon Ravenel. Boston, Houghton Mifflin, 1979.
"A Wig," in *Atlantic* (Boston), January 1980.

Other

A Malamud Reader. New York, Farrar Straus, 1967.

*

Bibliography: *Bernard Malamud: An Annotated Checklist* by Rita N. Kosofsky, Kent, Ohio, Kent State University Press, 1969.

Manuscript Collection: Library of Congress, Washington, D.C.

Critical Studies: *Bernard Malamud* by Sidney Richman, New York, Twayne, 1967; *Bernard Malamud and Philip Roth: A Critical Essay* by Glenn Meeter, Grand Rapids, Michigan, Eerdmans, 1968; *Bernard Malamud and the Critics*, New York, New York University Press, and London, University of London Press, 1970, and *Bernard Malamud: A Collection of Critical Essays*, Englewood Cliffs, New Jersey, Prentice Hall, 1975, both edited by Leslie A. and Joyce W. Field; *Art and Idea in the Novels of Bernard Malamud* by Robert Ducharme, The Hague, Mouton, 1974; *Bernard Malamud and the Trial by Love* by Sandy Cohen, Amsterdam, Rodopi, 1974; *The Fiction of Bernard Malamud* edited by Richard Astro and Jackson J. Benson, Corvallis, Oregon State University Press, 1977 (includes bibliography); *Bernard Malamud* by Sheldon J. Hershinow, New York, Ungar, 1980.

* * *

Since *The Assistant* in 1957, Malamud has easily maintained his rank with Bellow as one of the leading novelists of contemporary America and especially of his generation of "urban Jewish-American writers." Since the 1970's, readers of Malamud, Bellow, Roth, Salinger, Mailer, have been less attentive to the ethnic hyphen that links them and more concerned with their wide divergence as literary artists. Benefitting from this enlarged focus, Malamud's work is seen as that of "an American novelist in the tradition of Hawthorne," drawing upon Jewish material as component elements of his larger design and achievement. Malamud himself has said that "as a writer, I've been influenced by Hawthorne, James, Mark Twain, Hemingway, more than I have by Sholem Aleichem and I.L. Peretz." Malamud's self-mocking irony, comic caricatures redolent of Yiddish folktales, his urban ghetto heroes struggling for maturity in the shadow of immigrant families, indeed his whole fictional populace of characters and motifs familiar from Aleichem and Peretz, interweave in fictions superficially resembling much naturalistic work of the hyphenated school but profoundly kindred to symbolic moral romance in the Hawthorne manner.

Concerning pursuit of the American dream of money and fame as played out in the national sport of baseball, Malamud's first novel *The Natural* is clearly the work of a moral fabulist. In the extended metaphor of life-as-game, Roy Hobbs's baseball career would have been spectacular were it not for the moral concerns that intrude onto the playing field and destroy him, a disgraced failure who—partly from desire for his rival's mistress—throws a playoff game and ends sobbing in the street. Hobbs was a "natural," naturally gifted in the physical skills of the game, but those are insufficient to Malamud. Whatever its exterior form, the elemental contest in Malamud's people is played out in narrated monologues, in the long haunted questionings and discoveries of self. Hobbs is the first and least adroit of these auto-interrogators, whom readers variously describe as Jewish self-examiners tracking their own mysterious inadequacy and guilt, or existential solitaries in quest of self-knowledge and certitude, and who are undoubtedly both. To themselves they are all qualified failures, failing to attain the norm of human dignity that they either discern in the social world or unwittingly inherit from lineage or (in the late works) literature. As in Hobbs's disgrace, many adverse elements come into the play (bad luck, flawed friends, pressure of debts) but the failure is a personal one, a flaw in the moral character of the protagonist who is seen to be weak or fearful, paralyzed in the face of what he knows to be a right action. In later novels the pained intensity of the moral struggle transcends the hero's own negative assessment of himself, and affirms value in his small, contingent victories. Though *The Natural* inaugurates this pattern of self-confrontation, discovery, and judgement, it is not satisfying, primarily because of the simplicity of the ethical failure as "the champ" degenerates into crime. After *The Natural* Malamud modifies the proportions, locating the climax of his drama in emotional rather than public events and focusing in finer detail upon subtle shifts of mood and nuance that constitute emotion, as well as concentrating exclusively on characters signifying Jew-Gentile interrelations.

The Assistant brought Malamud national acclaim and introduced his claustral immigrant world of dark tenement houses and dim shops. Deft caricatural figures such as Breitbart the lightbulb peddler flesh out Malamud's symbolic society, whose primary figures are an old grocer, Morris Bober, and his young assistant Frank Alpine. Frank is a thieving drifter and anti-Semite whom the good-hearted Morris rescues and employs in his shop, only to discover him rifling the till and insulting his daughter. Malamud traces the emergent self of the youth against the diminishing powers of the old man. Frank works his way from cynicism through uncertainties to grace, which in Malamud always means moral commitment to others, and after Bober's death stays on to run the store. In the bleak misery to which these lives are bound, small objects have a grotesque edge to them, and large ones seem like open mouths or tombs devouring the living ("the blood-sucking store"). But with misery comes the clarity won through great suffering and the frail victory of "a little peace, a little order" won in common struggle. Just as the Bober characterization threatens to dissolve in sentimentality but does not because subsumed into the contest with the cynical youth, so the events of plot threaten to collapse into simplistic fable but do not because of the fabulist's subtle orchestration of symbolic narrative, daring even to end on the youth's conversion to the old man's religion.

In setting and tone, each of Malamud's novels is an abrupt *volte-face* away from the last one, recasting the moral quest and menaced values in wholly new ways. *A New Life* opens far from the ghetto in mountainous western America, where Seymour Levin arrives at a small college to take up teaching duties and seek happiness. Levin's comic rounds of ecstasy and despair, as he discards one romantic and humanist ideal after the other, are often amusing, and it is a measure of the novel's density that it has been called both an academic satire and a mock pastoral. Counterpointed in comic grotesque with the public events of the 1950's (Korea, the Cold War, McCarthyism), Levin's personal crisis of humanism seems ended in dismal defeat when he is dismissed from the college. But as the novel ends, in startling reversal Levin offers to marry a woman he no longer loves and to adopt her whining children. Malamud protagonists must fail the social tests of success (solid employment, marriage, income) in order to reach the rockbed of solitude, self-discovery, candor, and courage from which they can accede to the moral heights of true manhood and humanism (elements and process impacted in the name Frank Alpine) through commitment of self to others similarly deprived. The comical sufferings of Levin the zany idealist cannot bear such moral weight, and *A New Life* reveals Malamud's satirical skills without transposing the moral quest onto a new or greater scale. Like *Pictures of Fidelman* five years later, and many of the short stories of the 1950's and 1960's, *A New Life* is light metaphysical fiction, often wondrously funny as the comic loser reaches for infinity (a great love to Levin, a great painting to Fidelman) only to fall back into mortal finitude, sympathetic to human frailties.

The Fixer is a somber historical fiction set in Tsarist Russia, where persecution of the Jews echoes Biblical events and foreshadows modern genocide. Yakov Bok is a "fixer," a repairman, and what he fixes—as well as how—are the paramount concerns of the novel. This gentle bookish idealist is falsely imprisoned as a scapegoat, and the moral dilemma is clear; sign a false confession, freeing oneself while contributing to the historical scapegoating of the Jews, or refuse, accept persecution as an innocent man suddenly swept out of books into the bigotted cruelty of the historical moment. In the end he does "fix" (in the dual sense of to mend and to set firmly in the mind) his identity as Yakov and as a Jew through anguished analysis of himself as Everyman. Freed when another Jew is arrested, Yakov knows that "the purpose of freedom is to create it for others," and that no one is ever free of history and ethical imperatives. It is a searing novel, constructed with self-deprecating humor and some of the finest narrated monologues Malamud has ever crafted.

Without literary pretensions, both Yakov and Levin record their "insights," in a diaristic mode of self-exploration. In *The Tenants* and *Dubin's Lives* Malamud's protagonists are professional writers, novelist and biographer respectively. Harry Lesser writes his novel in a crumbling tenement he thinks abandoned, only to discover the presence of another novelist also completing a manuscript. Harry seems to be a modernist in the tradition of Flaubert and Joyce ("Once I hit it right—it's a matter of stating the truth in unimpeachable form"), but Willie Spearmint is a militant Black writing appalling social truths in jived prose. In irritation, then fear, then terror for his life and above all his manuscript, each writer stalks the other and by night accelerates the writing, in the belief that whichever novel is finished first effectively slays the other. The prose art of two New York City generations collides in these last tenants of a crumbling building. Though they slowly understand that as writers they both falsify the "self" expressed, and that as men they are more alike than different in experience, neither will yield to the other. They kill each other with ax and razor ("Each, thought the writer, feels the anguish of the other") as the novel ends on the slumlord's scream "mercy," the word repeated over eighty times until the reader sees it as mere ink on the page. The moral fable moves from light farce into bloody grotesque, and any humorous nostalgia for the 1950's heyday of Jewish-American art dies in the apocalyptic damning of all such ethnic hyphens in art as in life.

One of the unanswered questions in *The Tenants* was whether art does indeed help people to be free. The answer appears in *Dubin's Lives* and, though qualified, is positive. A prominent biographer of literary lives (Thoreau, Emerson), William Dubin knows the vicarious nature of his craft ("One writes lives he can't live") but does not know why he is drawn to a life of D.H. Lawrence. His own life becomes a Lawrentian odyssey through various liberations, not always his: his affair with a sexually liberated woman half his age causes him untold confusion and pain, while his wife finds satisfaction in her first job, his daughter finds fulfillment in having an illegitimate child, and even his son as a Vietnam deserter in Sweden finally achieves personal peace, while Dubin the self-appointed center of their lives disintegrates in self-discovery ("My God, what else am I capable of that I didn't know? How many more hollows will I uncover in myself?") His manuscript at a standstill, Dubin must learn to live the truths that art discovers. He is Malamud's most articulate self-interrogator, as a literary man in full command of verbal expression, and one of the most amusing. He is astonished to find that his Lawrentian liberation seems only to free his three women from their orbit round him. Once he learns what an unstructured muddle real life and true emotion actually are, and appreciates that "one's essential loneliness" is more than a literary cliché, Malamud seems fondly to rescue him: his mistress suddenly reappears to buy a farm near his and he is saved, as wife and mistress agree to share him, in an ending that suggests Lawrentian fantasia.

Dubin's Lives and *The Tenants* are as distinct in their handling of similar themes as are all of Malamud's works from one another. His canon spans not only a remarkable variety of settings and modes, but one of the most diverse assortments of literary heroes in modern fiction. Moving through their moral odysseys, they suggest prismatic reflections of one essential odyssey through self-discovery to the humanistic life.

—Jan Hokenson

MALGONKAR, Manohar (Dattatray). Indian. Born in Bombay, 12 July 1913. Educated at Karnatak College, Dharwar; Bombay University, B.A. (honours) in English and Sanskrit 1936. Served in the Maratha Light Infantry, 1942-52: Lieutenant Colonel. Married Manorama Somdutt in 1947; one daughter. Professional big-game hunter, 1935-37; Cantonment Executive Officer, Government of India, 1937-42. Owner, Jagalbet Mining Syndicate, 1953-59. Since 1959, self-employed farmer in Jagalbet. Independent candidate for Parliament, 1957, and Swatantra Party candidate, 1962. Address: P.O. Jagalbet, Londa, Belgaum District, India.

PUBLICATIONS

Novels

Distant Drum. Bombay, Asia Publishing House, 1960; London and New York, Asia Publishing House, 1961.
Combat of Shadows. London, Hamish Hamilton, 1962; Thompson, Connecticut, InterCulture, 1968.
The Princes. London, Hamish Hamilton, and New York, Viking Press, 1963.
A Bend in the Ganges. London, Hamish Hamilton, 1964; New York, Viking Press, 1965.
The Devil's Wind: Nana Saheb's Story. New York, Viking Press, and London, Hamish Hamilton, 1972.

Krishna Shah's Shalimar. New Delhi, Vikas, 1978.

Short Stories

A Toast in Warm Wine. Delhi, Hind, 1974.
In Uniform. Delhi, Hind, 1975.

Play

Spy in Amber (screenplay). Delhi, Hind, 1971.

Other

Kanhoji Angrey, Maratha Admiral: An Account of His Life and His Battles with the English. Bombay, London, and New York, Asia Publishing House, 1959; as *The Sea Hawk*, New Delhi, Vision, 1978.
The Puars of Dewas Senior. Bombay, Orient Longman, 1963.
Chhatrapatis of Kolhapur. Bombay, Popular Prakashan, 1971.
Bombay Beware. New Delhi, Orient, 1975.
Rumble-Tumble. New Delhi, Orient, 1977.
The Men Who Killed Gandhi. Madras, Macmillan, 1978; London, Macmillan, 1979.
Cue from the Inner Voice: The Choice Before Big Business. New Delhi, Vikas, 1980.

*

Critical Studies: *An Area of Darkness* by V.S. Naipaul, London, Deutsch, 1964, New York, Macmillan, 1965; "Purdah and Caste Marks" by the author, in *Times Literary Supplement* (London), 4 June 1964; *Eating the Indian Air* by John Morris, London, Hamish Hamilton, 1968; *Manohar Malgonkar* by G.S. Amur, New Delhi, Arnold-Heinemann India, and New York, Humanities Press, 1973; *Manohar Malgonkar* by James Y. Dayananda, New York, Twayne, 1974.

Manohar Malgonkar comments:

Praise can embarrass but it does not call for a rejoinder. Censure often does, so here goes. Those who disparage my work think that (1) I write with one eye on Hollywood, (2) my writing is "withdrawn" from the reality of my country's poverty as well as the reality of the four-letter word, and (3) I inject my values and politics and prejudices into my writings.

Well, I do strive to write the sort of novel I also like to read, full of meat, exciting, well-constructed, plausible and with a lot of action—in short, to tell a good story. If this is what Hollywod also likes, good for Hollywood and, I hope, some day for me too. I know one admits this rather shamefacedly, as one might say "I'm afraid I do chew paan," or "Yes, I do use a night shirt." At the same time, I often think of myself as belonging to the advance guard in the swing back of the romantic novel. The pedlars of erotica and drug dreams may churn out best sellers, but these are not novels; and the interminable ramblings about a day in the life of somebody or the other are like dissecting the veins in every single leaf of a cabbage. All this was a phase and it has had too long a run, but you cannot go on playing with a cabbage forever. The novel will be back, plot, action and all; the signs are already there.

Withdrawn? I maintain that my novels are close enough to the ground to pass off for straight history. The withdrawal is seen in my refusal to be trapped in the dirt and misery of India. The social life of millions of Indians centres around the dustbins of cities. Granted. But mine doesn't, and for me to write about it would be as insincere as a white man writing about Harlem life. And this is perhaps related to my other "withdrawal"—the disrelish for the language of graffiti. For two years during my army service, I was in daily contact with British and other ranks and can thus claim to have acquired a fairly full vocabulary of raw words which I can use far more naturally than those who discovered a handful of them since *Fanny Hill* came out as a paperback. I don't use them for the same reason that I don't have my characters talking in local accents: they would show up as being utterly false to my style.

But the third point of criticism I accept as a kind of compliment. I believe that it is the thinking man's business to influence. In a country such as ours, where democracy itself is threatening to throttle individual freedom, it is the duty of every writer to do so.

* * *

Essentially a romantic novelist of action, Manohar Malgonkar adds the freshness of an exotic scene and the novelty of a bi-focal viewpoint to an expert use of tried and true Western techniques. English is his own first language and his life style is westernized (unlike his compatriot R.K. Narayan, for example). He had a university education and is a man of cosmopolitan culture, widely read; but he has lived for the past many years on a remote estate in the heart of India. He commands a lively and colloquial English, full of vivid metaphors. He uses dialogue fluently. One thinks of affinities to Conrad on the one hand and John Masters on the other.

In the earliest of his novels first published in the West, *Combat of Shadows*, he writes of British tea planters in the last years of the British Raj, somewhat in the vein of a disillusioned Kipling; he is able to mock the pukka-sahib Establishment by letting the reader see it through the eyes of its own cynics and outcasts. But it is primarily a story of love and derring-do rather than social comment. *The Princes*, on the other hand, deals with the old Indian aristocracy before the Princely States were absorbed into the new India, and with the painful transition. This has been his most widely read, most thoughtful, and perhaps most distinguished work. Here E.M. Forster comes to mind.

A Bend in the Ganges, though politically objective, echoes recent history in its personal love story set against the cruelty of a great civil disaster—the Indian-Pakistani split of 1947. Two other novels of post-Independence days, still unpublished in the West, reflect his involvement with current Indian politics, in which he has participated from a minority position to the right of the dominant Congress Party. One is an adventure story of the Indian take-over of Goa; the other a character study of a land-owning politician in a country district.

The Devil's Wind goes back a century to the so-called "Indian Mutiny," never before presented from the Indian point of view. He narrates it in the person of Nana Saheb, an actual princely leader of the rebellion and a notorious villain in British eyes. Neither a hero nor an anti-hero, he is the kind of ambiguous character that Malgonkar delights in. In being a historical novel, and in its marked change of sympathy toward the British, this is a new departure; but in style and in story-telling qualities, particularly its violence, it has the characteristics of his other best novels.

While Malgonkar's books all have thoughtful overtones, he is first of all the story teller. He enjoys heroic characters fighting the odds and struggling with inner conflicts. He understands how to stretch the reader's willing suspension of disbelief for the sake of a dramatic confrontation. He makes graphic the hunt for a rogue elephant or a tiger; the crude violence of a human massacre; the tragic dislocations of civil war, from the burning of a single house to bombers over a great city. He bridges the nostalgia of India's past with the turbulence of her present.

—Marshall A. Best

MALOUF, David. Australian. Born in Brisbane, Queensland, 20 March 1934. Educated at Brisbane Grammar School, 1947-50; University of Queensland, Brisbane, 1951-54, B.A. (honours) in English 1954. Lecturer, University of Sydney, 1968-77. Recipient:

Australian Literature Society Gold Medal, 1974; Grace Leven Prize, for verse, 1974; James Cook Award, 1975; Australia Council Fellowship, 1978; New South Wales Premier's Prize, 1979. Agent: Curtis Brown (Australia) Pty. Ltd., 89 William Street, Paddington, New South Wales 2021, Australia; or, Curtis Brown Ltd., 1 Craven Hill, London W2 3EP, England.

PUBLICATIONS

Novels

Johnno. Brisbane, University of Queensland Press, 1975; New York, Braziller, 1978.
An Imaginary Life. New York, Braziller, and London, Chatto and Windus, 1978.

Verse

Four Poets, with others. Melbourne, Cheshire, 1962.
Bicycle and Other Poems. Brisbane, University of Queensland Press, 1970; as *The Year of the Foxes and Other Poems*, New York, Braziller, 1979.
Neighbours in a Thicket. Brisbane, University of Queensland Press, 1974.
Poems 1975-76. Sydney, Prism, 1976.
Wild Lemons. Sydney, Angus and Robertson, 1980.

Other

Editor, with others, *We Took Their Orders and Are Dead: An Anti-War Anthology.* Sydney, Ure Smith, 1971.
Editor, *Gesture of a Hand* (anthology of Australian poetry). Artarmon, New South Wales, Holt Rinehart, 1975.

* * *

When *Johnno* appeared, David Malouf was already a poet with two well-respected book publications—*Bicycle and Other Poems* and *Neighbours in a Thicket*. In them, Malouf's places and preoccupations had been announced: Brisbane and Europe, especially Italy; and the persisting presence of the past. There is even an early poem, "Wolf-boy," which prefigures a motif in *An Imaginary Life*, but broaches the subject by making a point entirely consonant with others in *Bicycle*.

Johnno tells of the youth and early manhood of two Brisbane boys. Dante (a nick-name) is the narrator. A "well-brought-up" boy, he is attracted to the other's wildness, which is ascribed partly to the death of a father in the Second World War. The relationship progresses despite jolts and absences. Dante shows Johnno's formative influence on his reading and ideals, and forms a conviction of Johnno's generosity and boyish punctilio behind the facade of drunkenness, japes, and fecklessness. His own quickly shamed attempt to imitate Johnno's shop-lifting panache is succeeded by sharing long rambling conversations on ritualized city pub-crawls. Before the departure of Johnno—his farewell gesture, the burning of several churches—for the Congo, Dante indicates his recognition of difference between them by refusing to follow Johnno on a swim in the flooded Brisbane River. In Paris, Dante is once more under the spell of Johnno's personality, but Johnno is unstable, his plans are fantasies, his relationships botched or shady. The plot ends with Dante and a now-seedy Johnno back in Australia. A suspicion of Johnno's intention to commit suicide comes simultaneously with news of his drowning. A posthumously delivered note reveals Johnno's despair, his feeling of emotional dependence, and his blame of Dante's restraint and ambivalence.

Although Johnno is viewed directly and a correction administered to his early glamour, the predominant insight is into the deeply susceptible narrator. The reader sees Dante's excited devotion veer through impatience to a still emotionally informed observation. His preoccupation is such that potentially interesting minor characters like Johnno's mother are passed over, a girl-friend who clearly forms part of the apparatus for assessment of both young men fails to claim attention, and mates such as the "young Nachaev," Bill Mahoney, are immediately forgotten. The strength of the novel is the richly evoked presence of Brisbane before and after the War, and of the War itself in the imaginative life of Dante. This aspect has drawn most favourable comment on the book. Though it is causally related to the plot and what Johnno calls his need "to shit this bitch of a country right out of my system," it is most easily grouped as "local colour" with the idyllic description of Dante's early family life in South Brisbane, with remarkably vivid sections on his mother and father. These sections, early in the book, make the latter half read less memorably despite the identification of directions and the sudden fathoming of the reciprocal stresses of the Dante-Johnno pairing.

An Imaginary Life is a daringly poetic realization of the life in exile of the Roman poet Ovid. In the Getic village Tomis, Ovid glimpses the wild boy, raised by wolves, who has already been present to him in his own childhood. Over a period of five years Ovid's absorption into the language and ways of the village, under the tutelage of the headman Ryzak, is followed by the long process of teaching and being taught by the wolf-child. As the relationship develops, he rediscovers the significant turns of his own life—especially the knowledge of the life and death of his favoured twin, the heir—and with that wholeness, a direction towards the unknown future. When the headman dies during the boy's first winter in the family hut, Ovid and the boy flee from the villagers' probable retribution out on to the steppe, till the failing and aging poet finds the spot where he is to die.

The indelibly realized half-dozen subsidiary characters, and scenes in both worlds—for instance, the ceremony in the Getic horseman-cemetery, and the Parilia where the young Ovid realises his participation involves his brother's death—and the cunning sequence of events and thoughts represent an enormous advance in Malouf's skill. The prose is of richly distinctive poetic quality. As with many cherished novels, the voice outlasts in the mind the happenings which call it into existence, but not the area in which it re-echoes, of conjecture about civilization and destiny.

The theme of learning to know a hidden part of oneself constitutes a link between the two novels. Apart from this, their topics are startlingly different and alert readers for Malouf's next departure.

—Judith Rodriguez

MALTZ, Albert. American. Born in Brooklyn, New York, 28 October 1908. Educated at Erasmus High School, Brooklyn, graduated 1926; Columbia University, New York, A.B. 1930 (Phi Beta Kappa); Yale University Drama School, New Haven, Connecticut, 1930-32. Married 1) Margaret Larkin in 1937 (divorced, 1964); 2) Rosemary Wylde in 1964 (died, 1968); 3) Esther Engelberg in 1969; one son and one daughter. Instructor in Playwriting, New York University, 1937-41, and Writers Conference in the Rocky Mountains, Boulder, Colorado, 1939, 1940. Editor, *Equality* magazine, New York, 1939-40. Co-Founder, and Member of the Executive Board, Theatre Union, 1933-37; Member of the Council, Authors League of America, 1936-41. Recipient: O. Henry Award, for short story, 1938, 1941; Oscar, for screenplay, 1946. Agent: Roslyn Targ Literary Agency, 250 West 57th Street, New York, New York 10019. Address: 9120 St. Ives Drive, Los Angeles, California 90069, U.S.A.

PUBLICATIONS

Novels

The Underground Stream: An Historical Novel of a Moment in the American Winter. Boston, Little Brown, 1940.
The Cross and the Arrow. Boston, Little Brown, 1944; London, Harrap, 1946.
The Journey of Simon McKeever. Boston, Little Brown, and London, Gollancz, 1949.
A Long Day in a Short Life. New York, International Publishers, and London, John Calder, 1957.
A Tale of One January. London, Calder and Boyars, 1967.

Short Stories

The Way Things Are and Other Stories. New York, International Publishers, 1938.
Afternoon in the Jungle: The Selected Short Stories of Albert Maltz. New York, Liveright, 1970.

Plays

Merry-Go-Round (as Eric Trent), with George Sklar (produced New York, 1932).
Peace on Earth: An Anti-War Play, with George Sklar (produced New York, 1933; London, 1934). New York, French, 1934.
Black Pit (produced New York, 1935). New York, Putnam, 1935.
Private Hicks (produced New York, 1935; London, 1936). Published in *The Best Short Plays of the Social Theatre*, edited by William Kozlenko, New York, Random House, 1939.
Red-Head Baker (broadcast, 1937). Published in *100 Non-Royalty Radio Plays*, edited by William Kozlenko, New York, Greenberg, 1941.
Rehearsal (produced New York and London, 1938). Published in *One-Act Play Magazine* (New York), March 1938.
Mr. Tojo and His Friends, in *Plays* (New York), December 1942.
The Naked City (screenplay), with Malvin Wald. Carbondale, Southern Illinois University Press, 1979.

Screenplays: *This Gun for Hire*, with W.R. Burnett, 1941; *Moscow Strikes Back* (commentary), 1942; *Destination Tokyo*, with Delmer Daves, 1943; *Seeds of Freedom* (commentary), 1943; *Pride of the Marines*, 1945; *The House I Live In*, 1945; *Cloak and Dagger*, with others, 1946; *The Naked City*, with Malvin Wald, 1948; *Two Mules for Sister Sara*, 1970; *Scalawag*, with Sidney Fleischman, 1973.

Radio Play: *Red-Head Baker*, 1937.

Other

The Writer as the Conscience of the People. Hollywood, Progressive Citizens of America, 1947.
The Citizen Writer: Essays in Defense of American Culture. New York, International Publishers, 1950.

*

Manuscript Collections: Columbia University, New York; Boston University; University of Wisconsin, Madison.

Critical Studies: *Creative Differences* by David Talbot and Barbara Zheutlin, Boston, South End Press, 1978; *Albert Maltz* by Jack Salzman, Boston, Twayne, 1979.

* * *

Like so many writers of the Left who came to prominence during the 1930's, Albert Maltz is little read these days. When he is remembered—when he is written about—it is primarily because of his political commitments. Maltz is best known as one of the Hollywood Ten: a writer who defied the notorious House Un-American Activities Committee, was sentenced to prison, was blacklisted, and who, for almost 20 years, was unable to put his name on his own work. But Maltz's significance in the history of American letters must not be limited to his role in the fight against the insidious power of HUAC. Not only was he one of the pivotal figures in many of the crucial controversies that dominated the literary class wars of the 1930's; more importantly, he was—and remains—a writer of great talent. Several of his short stories are classic examples of protest writing; and much of his fiction retains a vitality and compassion absent in the works of writers of far greater reputation.

Maltz's first writings were for the stage. While still a student at Yale, he and a fellow student, George Sklar, wrote *Merry-Go-Round*, a play about corruption in city government. Two more plays quickly followed: *Peace on Earth* (also with Sklar) and *Black Pit*, which was produced in 1935. Thereafter, Maltz's main concern was with fiction; and from 1935-1940, it was with the short story in particular. In 1938, he published his first collection of stories, *The Way Things Are*. Although not all the stories are of equal excellence, at least three are remarkable achievements: "The Way Things Are," "Season of Celebration" (one of the few stories in American literature to deal with the "bottom dogs" of society), and the justly famous "Man on a Road"—which is said to have been reprinted in more trade union and labor papers in the United States than any other story, and which reputedly was responsible for a Congressional investigation into silicosis.

Even more powerful than "Man on a Road" is a story also published in 1938 but not included in *The Way Things Are*, "The Happiest Man on Earth." This taut, terrifying, and bitterly ironic story, which deals with an unemployed man's happiness at obtaining a job driving a truck filled with nitroglycerin, received the O. Henry Award as the best short story of 1938. It may well be the single most effective piece of writing Maltz has produced. And, taken together with the stories in *The Way Things Are*, it certainly justifies Michael Gold's comment that Maltz's stories are written with such a deep and brooding pain that he may well be regarded as "a nerve along which crept all the vast sufferings of the poor."

Although Maltz has continued to write short stories, from 1940 on his focus of artistic expression has been the novel. *The Underground Stream*, his first novel, is a work that grew out of the attempt to unionize the automotive industry in Detroit. Maltz has at the center of *The Underground Stream* the struggle between the Communists who wanted to organize the unions and the incipient fascist forces of management which tried to destroy both the unions and their organizers. At a time when many writers on the Left had suddenly turned apologist, Maltz's novel was written out of an obvious faith in the Communist Party. It argued, and argued with considerable force, that fascism in the United States could only be defeated by the "underground stream" in American life—the Communist Party.

Despite its political character, however, the real "motor power" of *The Underground Stream*, as Maltz has stated, is supplied by a moral quest. This is equally true of his next novel, *The Cross and the Arrow*. Maltz wrote this work largely in response to the increasingly influential doctrine of Vansittartism, which contended that the German people as a race were addicted to war. Maltz argued in the novel that the human being is born neither good nor evil, but can, by circumstances or pressures, be led in various directions. His hero is a trusted German factory worker, Willi Wegler, who suddenly betrays the Nazis by directing British planes to a camouflaged tank factory. It is Willi's courage and simple humanity that ultimately define the essence of *The Cross and the Arrow*, and which offer Maltz's refutation of all racist theories of history.

Maltz's third novel, *The Journey of Simon McKeever*, is at once the least political and most exhilarating of his works. (Some critics even see it as a modern *Pilgrim's Progress*.) What dominates the novel is Simon McKeever's extraordinary spirit, his determination not to spend empty hours in a rocking chair. At the end of the harrowing yet exciting journey which makes up most of the novel, Simon is tired and "really and truly old." But he is not despondent; he will write a book and help to move the world one inch forward.

He is a great "yea-sayer," and he is perhaps Maltz's greatest creation.

Shortly after the publication of *The Journey of Simon McKeever*, Maltz was sent to prison for his refusal to answer questions before the House Un-American Activities Committee. When he was released he moved to Mexico, and there he wrote *A Long Day in a Short Life*, a book based on his prison experience. The events in the novel occur within a 24-hour period and focus upon two characters, Floyd Varney and Huey Wilson. Maltz's concern here is not only with political injustice and racial discrimation; but, like Theodore Dreiser in *An American Tragedy*, he contends that the judicial system is incapable of adequately responding to certain crimes. It is, as one reviewer noted, a book which is both tough and tender; above all, *A Long Day* is a work marked by enormous compassion for those who are victimized by the failure of the judicial system.

Compassion is also the touchstone of *A Tale of One January*, the last novel Maltz has published to date. It is a sensitively told story about ex-Auschwitz inmates who escape from a column of prisoners as it withdraws before the invasion of the Russians. Maltz seldom has been more effective than he is in this short novel; and it is ironic that despite the favorable reviews the book has received in Great Britain, it still has not been published in the United States. Maltz simply has not received the recognition which is due him. He is one of the finest writers of social protest literature the United States has ever produced; unlike too many writers of the 1930's, Maltz was capable of transcending the limitations of social proselytizing. Upon the publication of *The Way Things Are*, Alfred Kazin wrote: "It is because [Maltz] writes out of a hot, lacerating fury that never rises to a scream that these few stories are so effective." It is a judgment which, I think, applies equally to almost all of Maltz's work.

—Jack Salzman

MANFRED, Frederick (Feikema). Pseudonym (1944-1951): Feike Feikema. American. Born near Doon, Rock Township, Iowa, 6 January 1912. Educated at Western Academy, Hull, Iowa; Calvin College, Grand Rapids, Michigan, 1930-34, B.A. 1934; Nettleton Commercial College, Sioux Falls, South Dakota, 1937; correspondence courses, University of Minnesota, Minneapolis, 1941-42. Married Maryanna Shorba in 1942; three children. Worked as a filling-station attendant, harvest and factory hand, salesman, etc., 1934-37; Reporter, *Minneapolis Journal*, 1937-39; Interviewer, Minnesota Opinion Poll, St. Paul, 1939-40; patient in a tuberculosis sanitarium, 1940-42; Abstract Writer, *Modern Medicine*, Minneapolis, 1942-43; Reporter, *East Side Argus*, Minneapolis, 1943-44; Writer-in-Residence, Macalester College, St. Paul, Minnesota, 1949-52. Since 1958, Writer-in-Residence, University of South Dakota, Vermillion. Recipient: Rockefeller Fellowship, 1944, 1945; American Academy grant, 1945; Field Fellowship, 1948; Andreas Fellowship, 1949, 1952; McKnight Fellowship, 1959; Huntington Hartford Fellowship, 1963, 1964; National Endowment for the Arts grant, 1976. Agent: Curtis Brown Ltd., 575 Madison Avenue, New York, New York 10022. Address: Roundwind, R.R.3, Luverne, Minnesota 56156, U.S.A.

PUBLICATIONS

Novels (as Feike Feikema)

The Golden Bowl. St. Paul, Minnesota, Webb, 1944; London, Dobson, 1947.
Boy Almighty. St. Paul, Minnesota, Itasca Press, 1945; London, Dobson, 1950.
This Is the Year. New York, Doubleday, 1947.
The Chokecherry Tree. New York, Doubleday, 1948; London, Dobson, 1950; revised edition, Denver, Swallow, 1961.
World's Wanderer, revised edition, as *Wanderlust*, Denver, Swallow, 1962.
  The Primitive. New York, Doubleday, 1949.
  The Brother. New York, Doubleday, 1950.
  The Giant. New York, Doubleday, 1951.

Novels (as Frederick Manfred)

Lord Grizzly. New York, McGraw Hill, 1954; London, Corgi, 1957.
Morning Red: A Romance. Denver, Swallow, 1956.
Riders of Judgment. New York, Random House, 1957.
Conquering Horse. New York, McDowell Obolensky, 1959.
Scarlet Plume. New York, Simon and Schuster, 1964.
The Man Who Looked Like the Prince of Wales. New York, Simon and Schuster, 1965.
King of Spades. New York, Simon and Schuster, 1966.
Eden Prairie. New York, Simon and Schuster, 1968.
Milk of Wolves. Boston, Avenue Victor Hugo, 1976.
The Manly-Hearted Woman. New York, Crown, 1976.
Green Earth. New York, Crown, 1977.
Sons of Adam. New York, Crown, 1980.

Short Stories

Arrow of Love. Denver, Swallow, 1961.
Apples of Paradise and Other Stories. New York, Simon and Schuster, 1968.

Verse

Winter Count: Poems 1934-1965. Minneapolis, Thueson, 1966.

Other

Conversations with Frederick Manfred, edited by John R. Milton. Salt Lake City, University of Utah Press, 1974.
The Wind Blows Free: A Reminiscence. Sioux Falls, South Dakota, Augustana College Center for Western Studies, 1979.

*

Bibliography: *Frederick Manfred: A Bibliography* by George Kellogg, Denver, Swallow, 1965.

Manuscript Collection: University of Minnesota, Minneapolis.

Critical Studies: "Writing in the West and Midwest Issue" of *Critique* (Minneapolis), Winter 1959; "The Novel in the American West" by John R. Milton, in *South Dakota Review* (Vermillion), Autumn 1964; "Sinclair Lewis-Frederick Manfred Issue" of *South Dakota Review* (Vermillion), Winter 1969-70; *The Literature of the American West* by J. Golden Taylor, Boston, Houghton Mifflin, 1971; *Frederick Manfred* by Joseph M. Flora, Boise, Idaho, Boise State College 1973; "An Interview in Minnesota with Frederick Manfred" by James W. Lee, in *Studies in the Novel* (Denton, Texas), Fall 1973; *Frederick Manfred* by Robert C. Wright, Boston, Twayne, 1979.

Frederick Manfred comments:

It has been my dream for many years to be able to finish a long hallway of pictures in fiction dealing with the country I call Siouxland (located in the center of the Upper Midlands, USA) from 1800 and on to the day I die. Not only must the history be fairly accurate, and the description of the flora and fauna fairly precise, and the use of the language of the place and time beautiful, but the delineation of the people by way of characterization living and illuminating. It has long been my thought that a "place" finally selects the people who best reflect it, give it voice, and allow it to make a cultural contribution to the sum of all world culture under the sun. In fact, it is the sun beating on a certain place in a certain time that at last causes that place to flower into literature, the highest expression of intelligence (and not necessarily human intelligence).

It has been my feeling for some time that Middle America is more apt to speak with a clear voice from this continent than are either of the two American seaboards, the East with New York as the center and the West with Los Angeles as the center. The East in New York (and Boston and Washington, etc.) still speaks in part with an alien voice. It is not clear. It is muddy. It is as polluted with foreign sounds as is the air with foreign particles. And the West in Los Angeles (and all other California points) speaks with a most artificial voice, that of Hollywood, of the sudden uncultured rich. Only the Upper Midlands (and in my case, only my Siouxland) has a chance to speak with as clear a separate voice within the whole Western Culture complex as say Madrid for Spain and Paris for France and London for England.

The final test of good fiction rests with how well the characters come through, their reality, their meaning, their stature, their durability, no matter what the situation may be. The characters should be so well done that the reader should not be aware of plot or the unraveling of time in the work. The reader should be lost in the story. The plot should be hidden like a skeleton is in a flying eagle.

If a "place" truly finds voice at last the ultimate sacred force speaks.

And in the USA, Western American literature does this the best.

* * *

The author was born Frederick Feikema; later as Feike Feikema he changed his name again (1951) and thereafter is Frederick Feikema Manfred. The final name-taking is apparently of literary impulse, for in the most characteristic early novels the main protagonist is Thurs Manfred Wrâldsoan, an orphan, a wanderer, a reader of Lord Byron. Thus an invented character's name becomes in fact the author's name. This literary anomoly, with its strong implication of continuing self-analysis, indicates that questions of identity indeed are central to a full appreciation of the most significant prose fiction.

For example, *The Primitive*, *The Brother*, and *The Giant* constitute a trilogy wherein the main protagonist embarks on a journey of dual intention: a literary journey from a "Siouxland" college of fundamentalist persuasion to New York City and return. This is a quest for identity, for a viable past, for meaningful human relationships; by parallel, although not always comprehended by Wrâldsoan, himself, there is an inner quest for spiritual enlightenment, psychic resolutions, for means of artistic expression, for adulthood, for wisdom. In *Conquering Horse*, a characteristic later work of considerably higher literary quality, the quest for identity is dramatized in the emergence from adolescence of an American Indian. A comparison and contrast of the supportive institutions shown in the mid western trilogy in contrast to parallel institutions in an Indian culture is instructive and—incidentally—suggests one measure of Manfred's artistic growth.

The breadth of the subject matter of the novels is greater than the reoccurring thematic concerns might suggest. The early *Golden Bowl* dramatizes the conflict between two generations of midwest "Siouxland" farmers; *Boy Almighty* is the semi-autobiographical tale of a writer's life as a patient in a mid-western tuberculosis sanitarium; *This Is the Year* concerns a wilful Frisian-American farmer; *Morning Red* treats politics and journalism in a small Minnesota town; "Arrow of Love" and *Scarlet Plume* are best described as Romance; *Lord Grizzly* and *Riders of Judgment* exploit materials of the American past, the mountain men, and the cattle wars in Wyoming in the 1890's. The poetry in *Winter Count* is of little technical interest and suffers from a rhetoric which is often inappropriate for the subject matter; the two irregular short story collections command discerning approval. On balance, possibly because of his unswerving commitment to a midwestern, American region "Siouxland" where the literary audience is notoriously few and unfit, Manfred's work remains not much appreciated at the present time.

By no means, however, can it be said that Manfred's work is an example of isolated literary genius. Far from it. The novels are very much a part of a little explored sub-genre of American literature: those works of "epic" vision, of great vigor and industry by writers who value a direct rendering of their own life-experience; from one point-of-view those writers may be seen in contrast to the more cloistered, the merely "literary" artists who rely on the received virtues of consistency, of well-wrought structure, the "fully dramatic" posture. Aside from the controversial implications of the suggested sub-genre of American literature, Manfred's materials, themes, scope, "giantism," reliance on autobiography—and an inevitable redundancy of effect—suggest a close alignment with the novels of Thomas Wolfe (d. 1938). In the use of dialect, "down-home folks" protagonists, and a stubborn, at times anti-intellectual concern with "Truth," Manfred's work also suggests the tone and the strengths of Sherwood Anderson (d. 1941). In Manfred's intensity of attitude towards materials—though not always in erudition—the work also suggests the novels of Vardis Fisher (d. 1968). All of these writers, including possibly Upton Sinclair, are to be distinguished from the American naturalistic school. Manfred and the others are more consciously democratic, in the Whitmanesque sense of that word; more empirical in their methods. As a matter of literary principle they remain unreconstructed by continental or British literary conventions. The price paid for this fierce, regional independence is high: critical acclaim comes slowly, if at all; the weakest fictions teeter on the edge of literary disaster. Yet the best novels, by force of authorial energy alone, appear to sweep all merely literary reservations aside.

Presently this sub-genre of American literature is insufficiently explored possibly because it represents an old-fashioned, limited concept of the novel form. Understandably, the present age does not much approve of a reoccurring, implied didacticism, or of authorial voices behind the works which freely elected the novel form and then declined to assume the full obligations of the totally aware literary artist.

Manfred continues to live and to work near Luverne, Minnesota. The literary community of America and Britain deserves a more readily available, artistically arranged collection of his prose fiction. With that impressive panoply of work at hand, the novels may well attain the monumental effect which is everywhere present, for each chapter has the great, good quality of fidelity to a vision stoutly defended.

—James B. Hall

MANGIONE, Jerre (Gerlando Mangione). American. Born in Rochester, New York, 20 March 1909. Educated at Syracuse University, New York, B.A. 1931. Married Patricia Anthony in 1957. Staff Writer, *Time* magazine, New York, 1931; Book Reviewer, *New York Herald Tribune*, 1931-35, and the *New Republic*, New York, 1931-37; Book Editor, Robert M. McBride Company, New York, 1934-37; National Coordinating Editor, Federal Writers' Project, 1937-39; Information Specialist, 1940-42, Special Assistant to the United States Commissioner, 1942-48, and Editor-in-Chief of the *Monthly Review*, 1945-48, Immigration and Naturalization Service of the United States Department of Justice; advertising and public relations writer for various firms in New York and Philadelphia, 1948-61. Lecturer, 1961-63, Associate Professor, 1963-68, Professor of English and Director of the Writing Program, 1968-78, Acting Director, Italian Studies Center, 1978-80, and since 1978,

Emeritus Professor of American Literature, University of Pennsylvania, Philadelphia. Visiting Lecturer, Bryn Mawr College, Pennsylvania, 1967-68; Visiting Professor, Queens College, City University of New York, Flushing, 1980. Editor-in-Chief, *WFLN Philadelphia Guide*, 1959-61; Advisory Editor, *The Humanist*, 1979. National President, Friends of Danilo Dolci Inc., New York, 1969-71; Member of the Executive Council, American Italian Historical Association, 1980. Recipient: Guggenheim Fellowship, 1946; Fulbright Research Fellowship, 1965; Rockefeller grant, 1968; American Philosophical Society grant, 1971. D.Lit.: University of Pennsylvania, 1980. Commander, Order of the Star of Italian Solidarity, 1971; Fellow, Society of American Historians, 1974. Address: 1901 Kennedy Boulevard, No. 2404, Philadelphia, Pennsylvania 19103, U.S.A.

PUBLICATIONS

Novels

Mount Allegro. Boston, Houghton Mifflin, 1943.
The Ship and the Flame. New York, Wyn-Current, 1948.
Night Search. New York, Crown, 1965; as *To Walk the Night*, London, Muller, 1967.

Short Stories

Life Sentences for Everybody (fables). New York and London, Abelard Schuman, 1966.

Other

Reunion in Sicily. Boston, Houghton Mifflin, 1950.
A Passion for Sicilians: The World Around Danilo Dolci. New York, Morrow, 1968; as *The World Around Danilo Dolci*, New York and London, Harper, 1972.
America Is Also Italian. New York, Putnam, 1969.
The Dream and the Deal: The Federal Writers' Project 1935-1943. Boston, Little Brown, 1972.
Mussolini's March on Rome (juvenile). New York, Watts, 1975.
An Ethnic at Large: A Memoir of America in the Thirties and Forties. New York, Putnam, 1978.

*

Manuscript Collection: University of Pennsylvania, Philadelphia.

Critical Studies: *Current Biography* (New York), 1943; *The Italian in America* by Lawrence Frank Pisani, New York, Exposition Press, 1957.

Jerre Mangione comments:

As a writer I am motivated by the need to understand myself and the world around me. This need was first nourished by the circumstance of being born and raised among Sicilian relatives in an urban American environment. That experience, which is the substance of my first book, *Mount Allegro*, accentuated for me the sharp contrast between the philosophical values of the old world and those of the new. It also succeeded in casting me in the role of the outsider who, belonging to neither world, tries to create his own world by the writing of fiction. Two of my novels, *The Ship and the Flame* and *Night Search*, are efforts in that direction, and for that reason may be more truly autobiographical than the four books I have written in the first person, namely *Mount Allegro, Reunion in Sicily, A Passion for Sicilians*, and *An Ethnic at Large*. Although *Mount Allegro* is somewhat fictional in content, it is a basic part of this series which extends over a span of 50 years and deals largely with my public identity as a Sicilian-American observing the people and places he knows best.

My other books are more simply explained.

Life Sentences for Everybody consists of fables dealing with contemporary characters. "Life Sentences" were inspired by the challenge of telling a story within the confines of a single sentence. These are, frankly, exercises in procrastination (I was trying to work on a novel when I wrote the first batch), which gave me more pleasure than I usually derive from the act of writing. At least two critics have written that "Life Sentences" represent a new genre. And that too is pleasurable, for who doesn't enjoy being an innovator?

I have also written two social histories: *America Is Also Italian*, a brief telling of the Italian-American immigrant saga; and *The Dream and the Deal*, an account of the Federal Writers' Project of the thirties. These two histories were written because I was personally involved in both of them and felt that they needed to be told.

* * *

Jerre Mangione's prose style is straightforward and lively. Because he often employs a first person narration his work conveys the impression of conversation liberally sprinkled with anecdote and description. Much of it is factual or semi-fictional accounting of the author's experiences. The ordering of this material is subtle and it is only at the end of the book such as *Mount Allegro* or *A Passion for Sicilians* that one sees the cumulative effect of the massing of seemingly unrelated detail.

At the heart of Mangione's prose are the mountains, temples, and people of Sicily. He draws from his Sicilian relatives, his acquaintances in all levels of Sicilian society, and his extensive travels on the island a wealth of fascinating detail. On one level the last chapters of *Mount Allegro, Reunion in Sicily*, and *A Passion for Sicilians* function as travel books to introduce the reader to a land, comparatively untouched by tourism, which has fascinated and lured observers like D.H. Lawrence by its forbidding beauty. The ruined Greek temples of Agrigento, the hilltop castle of Mussolmeli built atop a Saracen fortification, the beautiful fishing village of Scopello are tantalizingly described. But the slums of Palermo are not forgotten. Villages with beautiful mountain views but no water, and hovels where ten people live in one room are painted with the same force and clarity.

His presentation of people is no less effective. The transplanted families of the Mount Allegro section of Rochester, New York, who try to keep Sicily alive there with their gregariousness, their intimate brand of Catholicism, their devotion to food, and their resignation to *destinu* are presented with warmth and vitality. Their Sicilian counterparts are also sympathetically and clearly drawn, but the author's partisanship is not blind. Danilo Dolci, for instance, who is studied at length in *A Passion for Sicilians*, is presented as a complex man who desires approval but sometimes courts dissension, who attracts and alienates followers. The reader is allowed to sort out for himself the powers and foibles of this pacifist and his programs for economic and social reform.

Mangione displays similar talents in his fiction. In the novel, *The Ship and the Flame*, which deals with the development of the will to act in Stiano Argento, a Sicilian refugee from fascism, we are presented with the action as Stiano experiences it and we see his need to act taking shape. He is a passenger, with his wife and daughter, on a Portuguese ship filled with people fleeing several European countries. Although they have been issued entrance visas to Mexico, they find when they arrive there that these visas are not authentic and that Mexican officials will not allow them to land. Goaded to action by the suicide of his friend Josef Renner, the love of Tereza Lenska, and the bravery of Peter Sadona, Stiano helps secure permission for most of them to land in the United States. If there are problems with Mangione's method in this book they are shown in Stiano's frustrated love affair with Tereza. Although reviewers at the time seem to have found it torrid, the effect today is quite the opposite. The limits permissible for sexual description have changed so much in the intervening years that a reader now finds it hard to believe in the force of this passion.

Books like *Mount Allegro* and *A Passion for Sicilians* fare better. In these the material remains interesting even though not current. The process of assimilation in America is a fascinating one and the stories of *Mount Allegro* enliven our understanding of what has happened and is occurring. Social action is a continuing interest to us: Dolci's work goes on and it is important to be shown that imperfect people can accomplish much and a single life can affect the lives of others.

—Barbara M. Perkins

MANKOWITZ, (Cyril) Wolf. British. Born in London, 7 November 1924. Educated at East Ham Grammar School, London; Downing College, Cambridge, M.A. in English 1946. Married Ann Margaret Seligmann in 1944; four sons. Film producer, 1955-72. Honorary Consul to the Republic of Panama in Dublin, 1971. Recipient: Society of Authors Award, for verse, 1946; Venice Film Festival prize, 1955; British Film Academy Award, 1955, 1961; Oscar, for screenplay, 1957; Film Council of America Golden Reel, 1957; *Evening Standard* award, for drama, 1959; Cork Film International Critics Prize, 1972; Cannes Film Festival Grand Prix, 1973. Address: The Bridge House, Ahakista, Durrus, near Bantry, County Cork, Ireland.

PUBLICATIONS

Novels

Make Me an Offer. London, Deutsch, 1952; New York, Dutton, 1953.
A Kid for Two Farthings. London, Deutsch, 1953; New York, Dutton, 1954.
Laugh Till You Cry: An Advertisement. New York, Dutton, 1955; included in *The Penguin Wolf Mankowitz*, 1967.
My Old Man's a Dustman. London, Deutsch, 1956; as *Old Soldiers Never Die*, Boston, Little Brown, 1956.
Cockatrice. London, Longman, and New York, Putnam, 1963.
The Biggest Pig in Barbados: A Fable. London, Longman, 1965.
Raspberry Reich. London, Macmillan, 1979.
Abracadabra! London, Macmillan, 1980.

Short Stories

The Mendelman Fire and Other Stories. London, Deutsch, and Boston, Little Brown, 1957.
Expresso Bongo: A Wolf Mankowitz Reader. New York, Yoseloff, 1961.
The Blue Arabian Nights: Tales of a London Decade. London, Vallentine Mitchell, 1973.
The Day of the Women and the Night of the Men: Fables. London, Robson, 1977.

Plays

Make Me an Offer, adaptation of his own novel (televised, 1952; revised version, music and lyrics by Monty Norman and David Heneker, produced London, 1959).
The Bespoke Overcoat (produced London, 1953). London, Evans, 1954; New York, French, n.d.
The Baby, adaptation of a work by Chekhov (televised, 1954). Included in *Five One-Act Plays*, 1955.
The Boychik (produced London, 1954).
It Should Happen to a Dog (televised, 1955; produced Princeton, New Jersey, 1967; London, 1977). Included in *Five One-Act Plays*, 1955.
Five One-Act Plays (includes *The Bespoke Overcoat, The Baby, It Should Happen to a Dog, The Last of the Cheesecake, The Mighty Hunter*). London, Evans, 1955; New York, French, n.d.
The Mighty Hunter (produced London, 1956). Included in *Five One-Act Plays*, 1955.
The Last of the Cheesecake (produced London, 1956). Included in *Five One-Act Plays*, 1955.
Expresso Bongo, with Julian More, music and lyrics by David Heneker and Monty Norman (produced London, 1958). London, Evans, 1960.
Belle; or, The Ballad of Doctor Crippen, with Beverley Cross, music by Monty Norman (produced London, 1961).
Pickwick, music and lyrics by Cyril Ornadel and Leslie Bricusse, adaptation of the novel by Dickens (produced London, 1963).
Passion Flower Hotel, music and lyrics by Trevor Peacock and John Barry, adaptation of the novel by Rosalind Erskine (produced London, 1965).
The Samson Riddle (produced Dublin, 1972). London, Vallentine Mitchell, 1972.
Jack Shepherd, music by Monty Norman (produced Edinburgh, 1972; as *Stand and Deliver*, produced London, 1972).
Dickens of London (televised, 1976). London, Weidenfeld and Nicolson, 1976; New York, Macmillan, 1977.
The Hebrew Lesson (screenplay). London, Evans, 1976.
Samson and Delilah (produced London, 1978).
The Irish Hebrew Lesson (produced London, 1978; New York, 1980).

Screenplays: *Make Me an Offer*, with W.P. Lipscomb, 1954; *A Kid for Two Farthings*, 1955; *The Bespoke Overcoat*, 1955; *Trapeze*, 1955; *Expresso Bongo*, 1959; *The Two Faces of Dr. Jekyll* (*House of Fright*), 1960; *The Millionairess*, with Ricardo Aragno, 1960; *The Long and the Short and the Tall*, with Willis Hall, 1961; *The Day the Earth Caught Fire*, with Val Guest, 1961; *Waltz of the Toreadors*, 1962; *Where the Spies Are*, with James Leasor and Val Guest, 1965; *Casino Royale*, with John Law and Michael Sayers, 1967; *The Twenty-fifth Hour*, 1967; *The Assassination Bureau*, with Michael Relph, 1969; *Bloomfield*, with Richard Harris, 1970; *Black Beauty*, 1970; *Treasure Island*, 1971; *The Hebrew Lesson*, 1972; *The Hireling*, 1973; *Wah-hoo-Wah!*, 1980.

Television Plays: *Make Me an Offer*, 1952; *The Baby*, 1954; *The Girl*, 1955; *It Should Happen to a Dog*, 1955; *The Killing Stones*, 1958; *Love Is Hell*, 1966; *Dickens of London* series, 1976.

Verse

XII Poems. London, Workshop Press, 1971.

Other

The Portland Vase and the Wedgwood Copies. London, Deutsch, 1952.
Wedgwood. London, Batsford, and New York, Dutton, 1953.
Majollika and Company (juvenile). London, Deutsch, 1955.
ABC of Show Business. London, Oldbourne Press, 1956.
A Concise Encyclopaedia of English Pottery and Porcelain, with R.G. Haggar. London, Deutsch, and New York, Hawthorn, 1957.
The Penguin Wolf Mankowitz. London, Penguin, 1967.
The Extraordinary Mr. Poe: A Biography of Edgar Allan Poe. London, Weidenfeld and Nicolson, and New York, Summit, 1978.

*

Theatrical Activities:

Director: **Film**—*The Hebrew Lesson*, 1972.

* * *

Wolf Mankowitz writes in the tradition of the Yiddish storyteller, holding his audience by a powerful blend of cynicism and sentiment. His narration is simple and direct; his subject matter ranges from life in London's East End to the manipulations of the antique trade and show business. This material gives him a scope for satire which he exploits to the full. He pokes gentle fun at the characters of whom he is fond and tears the others apart. Above all, he cares that people should care, whether for 18th-century English pottery or for their religion or for the happiness of their children. His villains are those with no emotions to hide.

Make Me an Offer is about a man who cares obsessively for Wedgwood and is both lucky and unscrupulous enough to track down the object of his passion, an early copy of a Portland vase. It is a fantasy rooted in the reality of double dealing, bluff, and auction rigging. The central character knows all the tricks he needs and has no illusions about his profession; Mankowitz makes him attractive for his humour, his knowledge, and his genuine love of beauty. "Who knew better than he that nothing is given, that everything passes, the woods decay. He was the ultimate human being. He resigned himself to making a profit."

The immediate success of this novella, which was made into a prize-winning musical, is paralleled by the acclaim given to *A Kid for Two Farthings*. This is a celebration of the author's Cockney childhood, told with a warmth and pathos that are wholly irresistible. "Life is all dreams—dreams and work," says the tailor Kandinsky to his six-year-old friend Joe. Joe's dream comes true: he goes to the market to buy a unicorn and finds one, the kid of the title and of the Passover song.

Mankowitz conveys the flavour of Jewish life in anecdote and dialogue; he lets moral values and social attitudes emerge out of business confrontations and family relationships. "The Mendelman Fire" is a particularly fine treatment of paternal love, told by Mr. Mendelman's admiring accountant, a man who "could make a company for twelve pounds and liquidate it for five." Many of the stories in this collection are set in Russia and have the charm of folk-tale, a form which, transposed to the West Indies, is used in *The Biggest Pig in Barbados*.

Perhaps the most original of the novels is *My Old Man's a Dustman*, a study of survival and friendship at the lowest levels of human experience. It takes place in a Beckett-like landscape of shacks and rubbish-tips but is lightened by Cockney songs and Cockney cheek. *Cockatrice* is a far more bitter book in a far plushier setting. We meet the hero, Daniel Pisarov, in "a Regency bed with swans' heads": like everything else, this belongs to his boss, the film producer whom he is vainly trying to double-cross. Mankowitz takes a grim pleasure in putting Danny through the hoops of ambition and corruption; in the film industry, the story suggests, no dreams are realised, only the nightmares come true.

—Judy Cooke

MANN, Leonard. Australian. Born in Melbourne, Victoria, 15 November 1895. Educated at Wesley College, Melbourne; University of Melbourne, LL.B. 1920. Served in the Australian Army, Infantry, and Engineers, in France and Flanders, during World War I. Married Florence Eileen Archer in 1926; two children. President, 1938, 1941, and Honorary Life Member, 1967, Fellowship of Australian Writers. Since 1963, Member of the Council, Australian Society of Authors, Sydney. Recipient: Australian Literary Society award, 1932; Crouch Award, for poetry, 1941; Grace Leven Award, for poetry, 1957.

PUBLICATIONS

Novels

Flesh in Armour. Melbourne, Robertson and Mullens, 1932.
Human Drift. Sydney, Angus and Robertson, 1935.
A Murder in Sydney. London, Cape, and New York, Doubleday, 1937.
Mountain Flat. London, Cape, 1939.
The Go-Getter. Sydney, Angus and Robertson, 1942.
Andrea Caslin. London, Cape, 1959.
Venus Half-Caste. London, Hodder and Stoughton, 1963.

Verse

The Plumed Voice. Sydney, Angus and Robertson, 1938.
Poems from the Mask. Melbourne, Hawthorn Press, 1941.
The Delectable Mountains. Sydney, Angus and Robertson, 1944.
Elegiac and Other Poems. Melbourne, Cheshire, 1957.

*

Critical Studies: "A Double Life" by the author, in *Southerly* (Sydney), 1969; "Leonard Mann's *A Murder in Sydney*" by Maurice Vintner, in *Overland* (Melbourne), Winter 1970.

Leonard Mann comments:

In the 1920's and 1930's Australian writing suddenly grew up, adult in age, vigour, and content. It was considerably nationalistic. The Australian people were then become aware of their own individuality. They were already become politically one nation. The experience of the Australian soldiery in the war of 1914-18, in which they had shown themselves second to none, asserted that awareness.

The new writers were, therefore, much concerned to show the Australian people to themselves, as not only in a different physical environment but as different within a new nation from the British peoples from which they were derived. The British past, including its literature, belongs also to Australia, but its present, from the beginning of this century, became quite rapidly not much more than an influence, for good and ill, so that now it is only a part, though a major one, of the influences from the world at large, in literature and in other affairs. In my own case, for instance, the influence of the French writers of the last century, and to some extent of the present, has been much greater than that of British writers.

Another, not unrelated, opinion of mine is that all discussion, all dialogue, that is, all talk should so far as possible be excluded from the novel except it be part of the *res gestae*. And further, that the novel should not be a forum for the author's self-display, not for smartness, not for instruction, but be rather an incitement and provocation of the reader's own mind, thinking and feeling, within himself. At any rate that has always been my intention: any debate a debate by the reader with himself.

* * *

The fiction of Leonard Mann is not remarkable for any great formal accomplishment. It offers little in the way of structural subtlety or stylistic virtuosity. What does command respect in his work is the penetrating honesty with which he scrutinizes some of the most important areas of 20th-century Australian social experience. His first book, *Flesh in Armour*, records a decisive phase in the country's growth: its patricipation in the First World War. Concentrating on the activities of men in one platoon of an A.I.F. battalion, Mann shows a sense of community, of distinctive Australianity, developing in this motley group of soldiers. The writing has dull patches and is sometimes even clumsy, but without detracting from the strong impression of authenticity. Then, having observed the emergence of a national spirit, Mann attempted in his next novel to uncover the roots of that spirit in the Victorian goldfields of the 1850's. *Human Drift* is less an examination of personal relationships than an evocation of life in the diggings, and its central narrative event is the celebrated fight at the Eureka Stockade, when about 30 diggers were killed in a dispute with police over mining licences.

A Murder in Sydney is a crime story, but of a more complex sort than its title seems to suggest. The reader is in no doubt about who the murderer is, so interest derives not from whodunit suspense but from the interaction of personalities seen against background patterns of urban life. That is to say, it is essentially a city novel; and indeed Mann was one of the earliest writers to turn his attention to the specifics of urbanization. Like that of *A Murder in Sydney*, the action of *The Go-Getter* takes place during the Great Depression, and again a large city provides the conditioning environment—this time Melbourne. By tracing the main character's search for self-respect to the point where he decides to resist involvement in a shady political deal, Mann is able to comment incisively on the values that the modern city lives by. Between these two city novels came *Mountain Flat*, a study of claustrophobic tensions in a small rural community of mixed ethnic character. Particular emphasis falls on the economic rivalry which exists between two farming families and which is complicated by sexual jealousies.

The gap of 17 years between *The Go-Getter* and *Andrea Caslin* is explained by the fact that a huge novel dealing with the conditions of Australian society during the Second World War was written and rewritten during those years but failed to find a publisher. Its length was a difficulty, but there is also reason to think that publishers found it too outspoken; during the 1930's Mann's political position had moved steadily to the left.

While all his novels show a sure grasp of social realities, they are notable too for their psychological insights. The hypersensitive self-analysis of Frank Jeffreys in *Flesh in Armour*, the moral conflicts experienced by Chris Gibbons in *The Go-Getter*, the varieties of greed among the characters in *Mountain Flat*—all these are memorably represented. But Mann's finest achievement as an analyst of personality is in his conception of the title character in *Andrea Caslin*, a woman who hardens herself emotionally as a defensive measure, and who becomes in consequence impervious to healing influences. *Venus Half-Caste*, his last book, is a compassionate account of a girl adrift between two cultures—her dissolving aboriginal heritage and the society confronting her in modern Melbourne—and of two men who are attracted to her, one white and the other half-caste like herself. There is some treatment of inter-racial friction, but this is not a novel of social protest; as in *Andrea Caslin*, the primary focus is psychological.

—Ian Reid

MANNIN, Ethel (Edith). British. Born in London, in 1900. Educated at a local council school. Married 1) J.A. Porteous in 1920 (marriage dissolved), one daughter; 2) Reginald Reynolds in 1938 (died, 1958). Associate Editor, *The Pelican* magazine, 1918; freelance writer. Address: Overhill, Brook Lane, Shaldon, Teignmouth, Devon TQ14 0AW, England.

PUBLICATIONS

Novels

Martha. London, Leonard Parsons, and New York, Duffield, 1923; revised edition, London, Jarrolds, 1929.
Hunger of the Sea. London, Jarrolds, and New York, Duffield, 1924.
Sounding Brass. London, Jarrolds, 1925; New York, Duffield, 1926.
Pilgrims. London, Jarrolds, and New York, Doran, 1927.
Green Willow. London, Jarrolds, and New York, Doubleday, 1928.
Crescendo, Being the Dark Odyssey of Gilbert Stroud. London, Jarrolds, and New York, Doubleday, 1929.
Children of the Earth. London, Jarrolds, and New York, Doubleday, 1930.
Ragged Banners: A Novel with an Index. London, Jarrolds, and New York, Knopf, 1931.
Linda Shawn. London, Jarrolds, and New York, Knopf, 1932.
Love's Winnowing. London, Wright and Brown, 1932.
Venetian Blinds. London, Jarrolds, and New York, Knopf, 1933.
Men Are Unwise. London, Jarrolds, and New York, Knopf, 1934.
Cactus. London, Jarrolds, 1935; revised edition, 1944.
The Pure Flame. London, Jarrolds, 1936.
Women Also Dream. London, Jarrolds, and New York, Putnam, 1937.
Rose and Sylvie. London, Jarrolds, 1938.
Darkness My Bride. London, Jarrolds, 1938.
Julie: The Story of a Dance-Hostess. London, Jarrolds, 1940.
Rolling in the Dew. London, Jarrolds, 1940.
Red Rose: A Novel Based on the Life of Emma Goldman ("Red Emma"). London, Jarrolds, 1941.
Captain Moonlight. London, Jarrolds, 1942.
The Blossoming Bough. London, Jarrolds, 1943.
Proud Heaven. London, Jarrolds, 1944.
Lucifer and the Child. London, Jarrolds, 1945.
The Dark Forest. London, Jarrolds, 1946.
Comrade, O Comrade; or, Low-Down on the Left. London, Jarrolds, 1947.
Late Have I Loved Thee. London, Jarrolds, and New York, Putnam, 1948.
Every Man a Stranger. London, Jarrolds, 1949.
Bavarian Story. London, Jarrolds, 1949; New York, Appleton Century Crofts, 1950.
At Sundown the Tiger.... London, Jarrolds, and New York, Putnam, 1951.
The Fields at Evening. London, Jarrolds, 1952.
Lover under Another Name. London, Jarrolds, 1953; New York, Putnam, 1954.
The Living Lotus. London, Jarrolds, and New York, Putnam, 1956.
Pity the Innocent. London, Jarrolds, and New York, Putnam, 1957.
Fragrance of Hyacinths. London, Jarrolds, 1958.
The Blue-Eyed Boy. London, Jarrolds, 1959.
Sabishisa. London, Hutchinson, 1961.
Curfew at Dawn. London, Hutchinson, 1962.
The Road to Beersheba. London, Hutchinson, 1963; Chicago, Regnery, 1964.
The Burning Bush. London, Hutchinson, 1965.
The Night and Its Homing. London, Hutchinson, 1966.
The Lady and the Mystic. London, Hutchinson, 1967.
Bitter Babylon. London, Hutchinson, 1968.
The Midnight Street. London, Hutchinson, 1969.
Free Pass to Nowhere. London, Hutchinson, 1970.
The Curious Adventure of Major Fosdick. London, Hutchinson, 1972.
Mission to Beirut. London, Hutchinson, 1973.
Kildoon. London, Hutchinson, 1974.
The Late Miss Guthrie. London, Hutchinson, 1976.

Short Stories

Forbidden Music, with *Martyrdom* by Warwick Deeping, and *The House Behind the Judas Tree*, by Gilbert Frankau. London, Readers' Library, 1929.
Green Figs. London, Jarrolds, 1931.
The Tinsel Eden and Other Stories. London, Wright and Brown, 1931.
Bruised Wings and Other Stories. London, Wright and Brown, 1931.

Dryad. London, Jarrolds, 1933.
The Falconer's Voice. London, Jarrolds, 1935.
No More Mimosa. London, Jarrolds, 1943.
Selected Stories. Dublin, Fridberg, 1946.
The Wild Swans and Other Tales Based on the Ancient Irish. London, Jarrolds, 1952.
So Tiberius.... London, Jarrolds, 1954.

Other

Confessions and Impressions. London, Jarrolds, 1930.
Common-Sense and the Child: A Plea for Freedom. London, Jarrolds, 1931; Philadelphia, Lippincott, 1932.
All Experience (travel). London, Jarrolds, 1932.
Forever Wandering. London, Jarrolds, 1934; New York, Dutton, 1935.
South to Samarkand. London, Jarrolds, 1936; New York, Dutton, 1937.
Common-Sense and the Adolescent. London, Jarrolds, 1937; revised edition, 1945.
Women and the Revolution. London, Secker and Warburg, 1938; New York, Dutton, 1939.
Privileged Spectator: A Sequel to "Confessions and Impressions." London, Jarrolds, 1939; revised edition, 1947.
Christianity—or Chaos? A Re-Statement of Religion. London, Jarrolds, 1941.
Castles in the Street. London, Dent, 1942.
Commonsense and Morality. London, Jarrolds, 1942.
Bread and Roses: An Utopian Survey and Blue-print. London, Macdonald, 1944.
Connemara Journal. London, Westhouse, 1947.
German Journey. London, Jarrolds, 1948.
Jungle Journey. London, Jarrolds, 1950.
This Was a Man: Some Memories of Robert Mannin by His Daughter. London, Jarrolds, 1952.
Moroccan Mosaic. London, Jarrolds, 1953.
Two Studies in Integrity: Gerald Griffin and the Rev. Francis Mahony ("Father Prout"). London, Jarrolds, and New York, Putnam, 1954.
Land of the Crested Lion: A Journey Through Modern Burma. London, Jarrolds, 1955.
The Country of the Sea: Some Wanderings in Brittany. London, Jarrolds, 1957.
Ann and Peter in Sweden (juvenile). London, Muller, 1959.
Brief Voices: A Writer's Story. London, Hutchinson, 1959.
The Flowery Sword: Travels in Japan. London, Hutchinson, 1960.
Ann and Peter in Japan (juvenile). London, Muller, 1960.
Ann and Peter in Austria (juvenile). London, Muller, 1962.
With Will Adams Through Japan (juvenile). London, Muller, 1962.
A Lance for the Arabs: A Middle East Journey. London, Hutchinson, 1963.
Rebel's Ride: A Consideration of the Revolt of the Individual. London, Hutchinson, 1964.
Aspects of Egypt: Some Travels in the United Arab Republic. London, Hutchinson, 1964.
The Lovely Land: The Hashemite Kingdom of Jordan. London, Hutchinson, 1965.
Loneliness: A Study of the Human Condition. London, Hutchinson, 1966.
An American Journey. London, Hutchinson, 1967.
England for a Change (travel). London, Hutchinson, 1968.
The Saga of Sammy-cat (juvenile). Oxford, Pergamon Press, 1969.
Practitioners of Love: Some Aspects of the Human Phenomenon. London, Hutchinson, 1969; New York, Horizon Press, 1970.
England at Large (travel). London, Hutchinson, 1970.
Young in the Twenties: A Chapter of Autobiography. London, Hutchinson, 1971.
My Cat Sammy. London, Joseph, 1971.
England My Adventure. London, Hutchinson, 1972.
Stories from My Life. London, Hutchinson, 1973.
An Italian Journey. London, Hutchinson, 1974.
Sunset over Dartmoor: A Final Chapter of Autobiography. London, Hutchinson, 1977.

* * *

In *Young in the Twenties* Ethel Mannin described her contemporaries as becoming politically conscious: "by the mid-Thirties we were beginning to be that." Throughout her 50 years of writing Mannin has faithfully reflected the preoccupations of the age—perhaps all too faithfully, where another mind would have imposed its own order. Yet, just as she brought an independent and ironic eye to the "gay twenties," her later books reflect several unpopular political alignments.

Mannin herself has discounted as immature the novels written before *Linda Shawn*, but her third book, *Sounding Brass*, a satire on the advertising world, fully deserved its success. These early novels have the fluency which distinguishes all her writing. Their passionate convictions about personal relationships represent her initial commitment, which widened into her use of the sociological novel, involved her in ideological and international issues, and finally led her to lend her pen to the Arab cause.

Mannin's interest in children and progressive education is prominent in *Green Willow* and many of the stories in *Green Figs*. *Linda Shawn* is a careful study of the farming family of Shawns, centred on the child Linda, whose development is followed to puberty. It was immediately followed by the "proletarian" novel *Venetian Blinds*, whose tripartite division into "Ledstock Street," "Rinscombe Road," and "Acacia Avenue" plots the hero's rise up the social scale, with an implicit question as to its value.

In *Cactus* and even more in its sequel, *The Pure Flame*, the author's socialist convictions sound a didactic note. But *Cactus*, portraying the English heroine's love for two "enemy" Germans in succession during the First World War, remains one of her best novels, and is highly topical in its discussion of the attitude of women to war. *Red Rose*, based on the life of Emma Goldman, the anarchist, is also topical in its treatment of this woman of action. Since 1939, Mannin herself has held a consistent anarchist and pacifist position, reflected in her political and ethical studies.

She reacted against the revolutionary progagandist note of *The Pure Flame* in later works, but as she has written: "I am of those who believe that the writer should concern himself with current affairs, be of his times, concerned with its problems, social and political." Some of her novels written during and soon after the Second World War, though not her most popular, are arguably her best, particularly *The Dark Forest*, about the invasion of a neutral country by a Fascist power—both given imaginary names—and *Every Man a Stranger*, with its traitor anti-hero from an imaginary neutral country; in both these novels, an element of fable makes for easier acceptance of her habitually simplistic characterization. Yet *Bavarian Story*, with an authentic setting in prewar and wartime Germany, is also among her best.

Inevitably, themes of war and "the after-war" permeate many of Mannin's books which, like *Proud Heaven*, are not primarily political. In these middle years she handled a characteristic diversity of material, ranging from *Captain Moonlight*, a 19th-century rural story, and one of a number of books reflecting her attachment to Ireland, to *Lucifer and the Child*, about witchcraft in a contemporary setting of London's dockland. Her constant concern with social issues prompted books like *Pity the Innocent*, focusing on the effect on her child of a mother's execution for murder. Her highly successful Catholic novel, *Late Have I Loved Thee*, is a remarkable feat from a rationalist pen, though her volumes of autobiography—invaluable for their insights into her work—reveal that the book was written under strong, if temporary, Catholic influence.

Just as many of Mannin's books of the interwar period reflect her European travels, many of her later novels have Asian settings, sometimes paralleling her travel books, as with the novel *The Living*

Lotus and the travel book *Land of the Crested Lion*, both about Burma. An important group reflects her support for the Arab cause. *The Road to Beersheba* was conceived as an "answer" to Leon Uris's *Exodus*, while *The Night and Its Homing* was "designed to speak for the [Palestine] Resistance." Of *The Midnight Street*, inspired by the assassination of General Abdel Karim Qassim of Iraq, the author has written that it "is virtually straight biography, with very little invented." *Free Pass to Nowhere* and *Mission to Beirut* share the same settings and some of the same characters.

Ethel Mannin has constantly updated her material. The characterization of her recent novel *Kildoon* is among her best, avoiding facility. In contrast to this tendency, the structuring of her novels is invariably firm and sometimes daring, especially in those of her middle period; in *The Dark Forest* she successfully achieves a tricky division into sections, chronologically simultaneous, devoted to the two main characters before their paths converge. Elsewhere, a favourite method of narration which focuses chronologically on different characters in succession is equivalent to the topographical structuring of *Venetian Blinds*.

Ethel Mannin's realism precludes many happy endings. The youthful insistence on "the pure flame of life" in the early books will be found exhilarating or naive according to taste. Yet the motif of "the pattern in the carpet" runs through all her work; her later stress on *karma* reframes her earlier conviction, "We are what we are by what we have experienced."

—Val Warner

MARKANDAYA, Kamala. Pseudonym for Kamala Purnaiya Taylor. Indian. Born in 1924. Educated at Madras University. Married; one daughter. Journalist, now full-time writer. Recipient: National Association of Independent Schools Award (USA), 1967; English-Speaking Union Award, 1974. Lives in London. Address: c/o Barclays Bank, 5 Oxford Street, London W1R 2DH, England.

PUBLICATIONS

Novels

Nectar in a Sieve. London, Putnam, 1954; New York, Day, 1955.
Some Inner Fury. London, Putnam, 1955; New York, Day, 1956.
A Silence of Desire. London, Putnam, and New York, Day, 1960.
Possession. Bombay, Jaico, London, Putnam, and New York, Day, 1963.
A Handful of Rice. London, Hamish Hamilton, and New York, Day, 1966.
The Coffer Dams. London, Hamish Hamilton, and New York, Day, 1969.
The Nowhere Man. New York, Day, 1972; London, Allen Lane, 1973.
Two Virgins. New York, Day, 1973; London, Chatto and Windus, 1974.
The Golden Honeycomb. London, Chatto and Windus, and New York, Crowell, 1977.

* * *

Kamala Markandaya is one of the best of contemporary Indian women novelists. Her novels are remarkable for their range of experience. *Nectar in a Sieve* is set in a village and examines the hard agricultural life of the Indian peasant; *Some Inner Fury*, which includes a highly educated young woman and her English lover who are torn apart by the Quit India campaign of the time, has to do with the quarrel between Western and Indian influences, as they are focussed in a marriage; *A Silence of Desire* deals with the middle class, and *A Handful of Rice* with the city poor; *Possession* moves from the West End of London to a South Indian village, and is centred on the conflict of Eastern spirituality with Western materialism; *The Coffer Dams* is a highly contemporary examination of the activities of a British engineering firm which is invited to build a dam in India. She has not the same intimacy and familiarity with all these areas of life, and she has indeed been criticised by Indian critics for a certain lack of inwardness with the life of the indian poor. Her particular strength lies in the delicate analysis of the relationships of persons, particularly when these have a more developed consciousness of their problems, and particularly when they are attempting to grope towards some more independent existence. She has, too, the genuine novelist's gift for fixing the exact individuality of the character, even if she is less successful at establishing it in a reasonably convincing social context. She has been most successful and at her best, an impressive best, in dealing with the problems of the educated middle class, and she has a gift in particular for delineating the self-imposed laceration of the dissatisfied.

Perhaps her most achieved and characteristic work is *A Silence of Desire*. It is a delicate, precise study of husband and wife, although the wife has less actuality than the husband, Dandekar, a nervy, conscientious, petty government clerk. He is rocked off his age-old balance by his wife's strange absences, excuses, and lies. It turns out that she has a growth and is attending a Faith Healer. The husband is by no means a westernised person, but he is to some degree secular and modern, and the situation enables the author to reflect on the tensions, the strength and the inadequacies and aspirations of middle-class Indian life. The book is gentle in tone but sharp in perception, and the mixture of moods, the friction of faith and reason, the quarrel of old and young, are beautifully pointed. There are conventional, perfunctory patches in the novel, but Markandaya shows very high skill in unravelling sympathetically but unflinchingly the structure of the protagonist's motives and the bumbling and stumbling progress of his anxieties.

Towards the end of *A Silence of Desire* there occurs a suggestion in an encounter between Sarojini and Dandekar, the husband and wife, of a theme which clearly much engages Markandaya. The wife reverences the tulasi tree as embodying the divine spirit, whereas the husband understands its purely symbolic function. "You with your Western notions, your superior talk of ignorance and superstition...you don't know what lies beyond reason and you prefer not to find out. To you the tulasi is a plant that grows in earth like the rest—an ordinary common plant...." She is preoccupied with the opposition between a cerebral, Western—and she seems to be suggesting, a narrowly Benthamite—habit of mind and the more inclusive, the more ancient and ritualistic Indian sensibility. This is a theme which works its way in and out of *Possession*, in which the artist Valmiki is discovered and taken over by Lady Caroline Bell, a relationship which appears to offer itself as a tiny image of India's being taken over by Britain. Neither Valmiki nor Lady Caroline is irresistibly convincing. There is a certain put-up, slightly expected, air about them. The novel's merit lies in the clarity and point of the prose, in an unusual metaphorical capacity and in a gift for the nice discrimination of human motives.

Kamala Markandaya's failure as yet is to establish a context as impressively real and as sympathetically grasped as her central characters. She is very much more conscious in *A Handful of Rice* of the context, in this case an urban one, which nevertheless still suffers from a lack of solidity. Ravi, on the other hand, the central character, an educated peasant, is seen with the coolest and most accurate eye and realised with a very considerable creative skill. Nor does this novel offer any easy solution or any obvious superiority of one side of a spiritual dilemma over the other. The novel ends flatly and hopelessly but rightly in a way which suggests the achievement by the author of a bleaker and more necessary kind of wisdom.

—William Walsh

MARKFIELD, Wallace (Arthur). American. Born in Brooklyn, New York, 12 August 1926. Educated at Brooklyn College, B.A. 1947; New York University, 1948-50. Married Anna May Goodman in 1949; one child. Film Critic, *New Leader*, New York, 1954-55. Recipient: Guggenheim Fellowship, 1965; National Endowment for the Arts grant, 1966. Address: 15 Vista Way, Port Washington, New York 11050, U.S.A.

PUBLICATIONS

Novels

To an Early Grave. New York, Simon and Schuster, 1964; London, Cape, 1965.
Teitlebaum's Window. New York, Knopf, 1970; London, Cape, 1971.
You Could Live If They Let You. New York, Knopf, 1974.

Short Story

Multiple Orgasms. Bloomfield Hills, Michigan, Bruccoli Clark, 1977.

Uncollected Short Stories

"Notes on the Working Day," in *Partisan Review* (New Brunswick, New Jersey), September-October 1946.
"Ph.D.," in *These Your Children*, edited by Harold U. Ribalow. New York, Beechhurst Press, 1952.
"The Patron," in *Partisan Review* (New Brunswick, New Jersey), January 1954.
"The Country of the Crazy Horse," in *Commentary* (New York), March 1958.
"The Decline of Sholem Waldman," in *My Name Aloud*, edited by Harold U. Ribalow. New York, Yoseloff, 1969.
"Under the Marquee," in *Jewish-American Stories*, edited by Irving Howe. New York, New American Library, 1977.

*   *   *

Philip Roth has helped enormously, if inadvertently, to make people conscious of Wallace Markfield by referring to him in *Portnoy's Complaint*. "The novelist, what's his name, Markfield, has written in a story somewhere that until he was fourteen he believed 'aggravation' to be a Jewish word." Roth is referring to "The Country of the Crazy Horse," which sets the tone and milieu of New York Jewish life that carries through all of Markfield's work: the story begins in this way, "As the train began the long crawl under the tunnel to Brooklyn...." Markfield's characters travel by subway or Volkswagen as they negotiate the impossible distances separating the boroughs of New York City and encounter the unique kind of aggravation which is part of their Jewish vantage point.

Stanley Edgar Hyman spoke of Markfield's first novel, *To an Early Grave*, as a more modest *Ulysses* and as "Mr. Bloom's Day in Brooklyn." The part of *Ulysses* it most nearly resembles is the sixth episode, "Hades." Joyce's "creaking carriage" has been replaced by a Volkswagen; Paddy Dignam has turned into a young writer named Leslie Braverman; and the four mourners who attend the Dignam funeral, Martin Cunningham, Leopold Bloom, John Power, and Simon Dedalus, give way to the more literary foursome of Morroe Rieff, Holly Levine, Felix Ottensteen, and Barnet Weiner. The Jew, Leopold Bloom, feels uncomfortable and unwanted among his Christian companions during the ride to the cemetery. Braverman and his mourners are Jews, as are the other characters who figure prominently in *To an Early Grave*. Their conversation on the way to the cemetery reflects the urban chic of New York City, with its literary quarterlies, its literary critical conscience ("And he hissed softly, 'Trilling...Leavis...Ransom...Tate...Kazin...Chase...' and saw them, The Fathers, as though from a vast amphitheater, smiling at him, and he smiled at them"), its intellectual's obsession with popular culture, its carefully placed Yiddishisms.

Wallace Markfield has been fascinated by Joyce since his early story "Notes on the Working Day"; there are nods here toward the Joyce of *Finnegans Wake* (There goes Everyman, Here Comes Everybody, the H.C.E. of our culture-lag") and toward the Joyce of *Ulysses* ("Leopold Bloom of the garment center" and "Leopold fat-belly Bloom"). When the Volkswagen of *To an Early Grave* arrives at a chapel, Braverman's four friends are treated to an elaborate funeral oration by a rabbi, which seems indeed to be the Jewish equivalent of the terrifying sermons which dominate chapter three of Joyce's *A Portrait of the Artist as a Young Man*. Here is a sample of the rabbi's language: "*That* on the Day of of Judgment *in* the Valley of Jehoshaphat you'll be called up. *Either* to everlasting life *or* to such a shaming there's no imagining *how* terrible." Markfield manages to turn this into a wonderfully comic scene when the four mourners discover on examining the corpse that they have attended the wrong funeral. The novel ends with the most sympathetic of the four mourners, Morroe Rieff, finally breaking into tears—the only genuine tears shed in all of *To an Early Grave*—but the humorous and satirical effects in character and situation linger on; the comic survives the fleeting attempts at tragedy.

Teitlebaum's Window is the Brighton Beach-Coney Island version of the *Bildungsroman*, the Jewish boy, Simon Sloan, coming of age between the Depression years and the beginnings of World War II. *To an Early Grave* takes place during a single day, a Sunday, while *Teitlebaum's Window* covers a ten-year period. Joyce continues to be very much on Markfield's mind in this novel, especially in the use of certain impressionistic techniques and symbolic patterns. The narrative proceeds in a vastly complicated way, with traditional storytelling methods giving way frequently to diary notations, letters, classroom notes, and snatches of monologue. Many of the chapters begin with a single convoluted sentence which may go on for several pages: dating the events, reintroducing characters, referring to celebrities in the political, film and comic book worlds, and quoting the signs in Teitlebaum's store window (for example, "There will always be an England but there will not always be such a low low price on belly lox"). These long sentences act rather like the interchapters in Virginia Woolf's *The Waves*. The references to Teitlebaum's window offer the novel a symbolic design and supply the reader with a useful *point de repère*.

Teitlebaum's Window is a vintage American-Jewish novel. Here the mother-son confrontation is quite as convincingly realized as it was in *Portnoy's Complaint*. Markfield's Jewish mother, with her "dropped stomach," gargantuan stutter, constant aggravation, and dislocated syntax, is quite as believable in her own way as Sophie Portnoy.

You Could Live If They Let You continues Markfield's concern with Jewish subjects, but is less closely plotted than either of the previous novels. It offers what is probably, according to reviewers, another version of the Lenny Bruce saga, following closely on the heels of Albert Goldman's book *Ladies and Gentlemen, Lenny Bruce!!* and Bob Fosse's film *Lenny*. The Lenny Bruce character appears under the name Jules Farber and he has a Boswell in the person of Chandler Van Horton (whom one is tempted to think of as a non-Jewish Albert Goldman). The novel is dedicated to "the wisest men of our time—the stand-up comics" and indeed its narrative procedures often remind us of the staccato verbal habits of a Lenny Bruce or a Woody Allen.

Farber's stand-up comic delivery favors the incongruous, the unexpected: "Plehnt hah tree in Eretz Yisroel for Norman Vincent Peale"; "Readings from Kierkegaard, Kafka and Julia Child"; "it's Bobby Fischer's end game and Thomas Aquinas quoting from William Buckley and Bella Abzug buying two-and-a-half pounds of the best flanken...." It is consistently irreverent as it takes on such formidable adversaries as the Anti-Defamation League, American rabbis, the Modern Language Association of America, and the world of popular culture. There is seemingly no end to the literary echoes and allusions: "cold, iron-hard epiphany which Farber favored"; "because every carhop and every checkout girl and every chippy and every cellar-club thumper is Molly Boom and Madeline [*sic*] Herzog." (Joyce is unmistakably a presence here as he was in Markfield's earlier fiction!)

We not only hear the voice of Farber, the "vertical monologist," but also that of Chandler Van Horton and that of Farber's sister, Lillian Federman. Farber's life story is eventually fleshed out in bits and pieces as we find out about his autistic son, Mitchell, and his Christ Therapist estranged wife, Marlene. We find Markfield's latest hero to have the same Jewish awareness and identity as the characters in *To an Early Grave* and *Teitlebaum's Window*. He shares with them the assurance that "there are certain things only a Jewish person can understand" and that "when you're in love the whole world is Jewish; and perhaps, in fact, even when you're not in love." We recognize the Markfield touch most emphatically when Farber proclaims: "I got a terminal case of aggravation."

—Melvin J. Friedman

MARSH, (Edith) Ngaio. New Zealander. Born in Christchurch, 23 April 1899. Educated at St. Margaret's College, Christchurch, 1910-14; Canterbury University College School of Art, Christchurch, 1915-20. Actress in New Zealand, 1920-23; Theatrical Producer, New Zealand, 1923-27; Interior Decorator, in partnership with Mrs. Tahu Rhodes, London, 1928-32. Served in a New Zealand Red Cross transport unit during World War II. Producer for D.D. O'Connor Theatre Management, New Zealand, 1944-52. Honorary Lecturer in Drama, Canterbury University, 1948. Ngaio Marsh Theatre founded at Canterbury University, 1962. Recipient: Mystery Writers of America Grand Master Award, 1977. D.Litt.: Canterbury University, 1963. Fellow, Royal Society of Arts. O.B.E. (Officer, Order of the British Empire), 1948; D.B.E. (Dame Commander, Order of the British Empire), 1966. Agent: Hughes Massie Ltd., 69 Great Russell Street, London WC1B 3DH, England. Address: 37 Valley Road, Cashmere, Christchurch 2, New Zealand.

PUBLICATIONS

Novels

A Man Lay Dead. London, Bles, 1934; New York, Sheridan, 1942.
Enter a Murderer. London, Bles, 1935; New York, Pocket Books, 1941.
The Nursing-Home Murder, with Henry Jellett. London, Bles, 1935; New York, Sheridan, 1941.
Death in Ecstasy. London, Bles, 1936; New York, Sheridan, 1941.
Vintage Murder. London, Bles, 1937; New York, Sheridan, 1940.
Artists in Crime. London, Bles, and New York, Furman, 1938.
Death in a White Tie. London, Bles, and New York, Furman, 1938.
Overture to Death. London, Collins, and New York, Furman, 1939.
Death at the Bar. London, Collins, and Boston, Little Brown, 1940.
Death of a Peer. Boston, Little Brown, 1940; as *Surfeit of Lampreys*, London, Collins, 1941.
Death and the Dancing Footman. Boston, Little Brown, 1941; London, Collins, 1942.
Colour Scheme. London, Collins, and Boston, Little Brown, 1943.
Died in the Wool. London, Collins, and Boston, Little Brown, 1945.
Final Curtain. London, Collins, and Boston, Little Brown, 1947.
Swing, Brother, Swing. London, Collins, 1949; as *A Wreath for Rivera*, Boston, Little Brown, 1949.
Opening Night. London, Collins, 1951; as *Night at the Vulcan*, Boston, Little Brown, 1951.
Spinsters in Jeopardy. Boston, Little Brown, 1953; London, Collins, 1954; as *The Bride of Death*, New York, Spivak, 1955.
Scales of Justice. London, Collins, and Boston, Little Brown, 1955.
Death of a Fool. Boston, Little Brown, 1956; as *Off with His Head*, London, Collins, 1957.
Singing in the Shrouds. Boston, Little Brown, 1958; London, Collins, 1959.
False Scent. Boston, Little Brown, and London, Collins, 1960.
Hand in Glove. Boston, Little Brown, and London, Collins, 1962.
Dead Water. Boston, Little Brown, 1963; London, Collins, 1964.
Killer Dolphin. Boston, Little Brown, 1966; as *Death at the Dolphin*, London, Collins, 1967.
Clutch of Constables. London, Collins, 1968; Boston, Little Brown, 1969.
When in Rome. London, Collins, 1970; Boston, Little Brown, 1971.
Tied Up in Tinsel. London, Collins, and Boston, Little Brown, 1972.
Black as He's Painted. London, Collins, and Boston, Little Brown, 1975.
Last Ditch. Boston, Little Brown, and London, Collins, 1977.
Grave Mistake. Boston, Little Brown, and London, Collins, 1978.
Photo-Finish. London, Collins, and Boston, Little Brown, 1980.

Uncollected Short Stories

"I Can Find My Way Out," in *Queen's Awards 1946*, edited by Ellery Queen. Boston, Little Brown, and London, Gollancz, 1946.
"Death on the Air," in *Anthology 1969*, edited by Ellery Queen. New York, Davis, 1968.
"Chapter and Verse," in *Ellery Queen's Murdercade*. New York, Random House, 1975.
"A Fool about Money," in *Ellery Queen's Crime Wave*. New York, Putnam, 1976.

Plays

The Nursing-Home Murder, with Henry Jellett, adaptation of their own novel (produced Christchurch, 1936).
False Scent, adaptation of her own novel (produced Worthing, Sussex, 1961).
The Christmas Tree (juvenile). London, S.P.C.K., 1962.
A Unicorn for Christmas, music by David Farquhar (produced Sydney, 1965).
Murder Sails at Midnight (produced Bournemouth, Hampshire, 1972).

Television Play: *Evil Liver* (*Crown Court* series), 1975.

Other

New Zealand, with Randal Matthew Burdon. London, Collins, 1942.
A Play Toward: A Note on Play Production. Christchurch, Caxton Press, 1946.
Perspectives: The New Zealander and the Visual Arts. Auckland, Auckland Gallery Associates, 1960.
New Zealand. New York, Macmillan, 1964; London, Collier Macmillan, 1965.
Black Beech and Honeydew: An Autobiography. Boston, Little Brown, 1965; London, Collins, 1966.

*

Manuscript Collections: Mugar Memorial Library, Boston University; Alexander Turnbull Library, Wellington.

Critical Studies: *Bloody Murder* by Julian Symons, London, Faber, 1972, as *Mortal Consequences*, New York, Harper, 1972; *Murderess Ink* edited by Dilys Winn, New York, Workman, 1979.

Ngaio Marsh comments:

(1972) The earliest books were written in the style of their time—post-Dorothy Sayers—and had perhaps some affinity with Marjorie Allingham rather than with Agatha Christie. They have developed, I hope, into stories of crime and its detection in which the emphasis is on style and character rather than on mechanics. The latest, *When in Rome*, was reviewed by *The Times* as a "novel of place."

I began as a painter, became a professional actress and later a director. I still work as a director. These activities have strongly influenced my choice of subject-matter and background. Six of the books are about people of the theatre. A portrait painter, Troy Alleyn, appears in many of them while *Artists in Crime* concerns itself with a group of painters. Most of the stories are set in England. Three have a New Zealand background, one concerns a sea voyage, and *When in Rome* is where you'd expect it to be. I have dramatized, in collaboration, some of the books, but so far, although one was brought by a London management, none has been produced there.

* * *

With some exceptions (e.g., *Death and the Dancing Footman, Final Curtain, Clutch of Constables*), Ngaio Marsh's novels centre around her detective, Roderick Alleyn. He combines being a good policeman (like French) with being an extremely cultured (M.A., Oxon.; marriage with painter Agatha Troy) as well as socially privileged gentleman (mother: Lady Alleyn, brother George: an ambassador; compare Wimsey, Campion, Appleby) and *not* being a one-sided eccentric (like Holmes or Poirot), but still a strong personality (not quite a Maigret). There is little intellectual or social snobbery about him; he is thoroughly normal, humane, intelligent, sober, yet not over-serious. Surprisingly, he hardly ages: 42 around 1937 (*Vintage Murder*) he still performs strenuous activities 20 years later. This static quality (from which his private life is partly exempt) he shares, by and large, with his friends and helpers such as detective-sergeants Bailey and Thomson and the invaluable "Br'er" Fox, doomed to eternal inspectordom for all his progress in French and his ingratiating ways with parlour-maids. All this (as also Alleyn's moderate promotion to superintendent) is of course essential to the performance of *their* particular duties with verisimilitude.

Their creator has likewise adhered to her manner since *A Man Lay Dead*, although she has expanded and refined it. She has kept (with exceptions like *Singing in the Shrouds*) to relatively few environments—New Zealand, London, the English countryside—and social strata—the upper classes generally, artists and actors, with a sprinkling of rustics and low cockneys. She has also kept to the conventions of firm social and cultural scales of value and the feeling of security that goes with them, as well as to her narrative technique and the interweaving of a love story into the main action. Guided by a comparatively unobtrusive third-person narrator we mostly follow the events, while perceiving the thoughts and emotions of other characters, with Alleyn—or, sometimes, Troy. Towards the end, however, we are left through information gaps to do some brainwork ourselves and check it against the inevitable, but nicely varied final elucidation. Unhampered by too much physical action or personal danger threatening the detective (one exception is the finale of *Dead Water*) we can concentrate on the lives—or comments, reflections, and often quite demanding descriptions of landscape, buildings, and interiors; enjoy, too, the lucid, expressive language with its striking imagery. The eccentricity lacking in Alleyn is amply provided by many people he deals with (see notably the Lampreys, *Death of a Peer*, and the Ancreds, *Final Curtain*).

The later novels, including *When in Rome*, tend to abandon such families along with the overcrowding of the "cast" and the over-intricacy of plot which although amusing slightly fatigue in some earlier books. The later books also tend to move from the private murder puzzle towards collective crime involving murder as a corollary. But Ngaio Marsh never loses the one quality which informed her fiction from the beginnings: the placing of what perforce is a sensational and melodramatic story in a solid background of human lives, experiences, desires, and failings. There are limits to the genre, but within them she has very evenly achieved a great deal. None of her numerous tableaux of this "rum life" are facilely thrilling. A certain amount of intellectual and emotional engagement is needed to appreciate them fully. There are very few reasons for saying "t'uh" and very many for saying "good-oh."

—H.M. Klein

MARSHALL, Bruce. British. Born in Edinburgh, 24 June 1899. Educated at Edinburgh Academy, 1906-09; Trinity College, Glenalmond, 1909-15; St. Andrews University, 1916-17; Edinburgh University, 1922-25, M.A. 1924, B. Com. 1925; Admitted a Member of the Society of Accountants, Edinburgh, 1926. Served in the Royal Irish Fusiliers, 1918-20 (lost a leg in action); served in the Royal Army Pay Corps and Intelligence, 1940-46. Married Mary Pearson Clark in 1928; one child. Chartered Accountant with Peat Marwick Mitchell Ltd., Paris, 1926-40. Recipient: Wlodimierz Petrzak Prize, Warsaw, 1959. Lives in Antibes, France. Address: c/o Lloyds Bank Ltd., 6 Pall Mall, London S.W. 1, England.

PUBLICATIONS

Novels

This Sorry Scheme. London, Harrap, 1924; New York, Harcourt Brace, 1925.
Teacup Terrace. London, Hurst and Blackett, 1926.
The Stooping Venus. London, Hurst and Blackett, and New York, Dutton, 1926.
The Other Mary. London, Hurst and Blackett, 1927.
And There Were Giants. London, Jarrolds, 1927.
The Little Friend. London, Jarrolds, 1928; New York, Macaulay, 1929.
High Brows: An Extravaganza of Manners—Mostly Bad. London, Jarrolds, 1929.
The Rough House: A Possibility. London, Jarrolds, 1930.
Children of This Earth. New York, Macaulay, 1930.
Father Malachy's Miracle. London, Heinemann, and New York, Doubleday, 1931; revised edition, London, Constable, 1947.
Prayer for the Living. London, Gollancz, and New York, Knopf, 1934.
The Uncertain Glory. London, Gollancz, 1935.
Canon to Right of Them. London, Gollancz, 1936.
Luckypenny. London, Gollancz, 1937; New York, Dutton, 1938.
Delilah Upside Down: A Tract with a Thrill. London, Heinemann, 1941.
Yellow Tapers for Paris: A Dirge. London, Constable, 1943; Boston, Houghton Mifflin, 1946.
All Glorious Within. London, Constable, 1944; as *The World, The Flesh, and Father Smith*, Boston, Houghton Mifflin, 1945.
George Brown's Schooldays. London, Constable, 1946.
The Red Danube. London, Constable, 1946; as *Vespers in Vienna*, Boston, Houghton Mifflin, 1947.
To Every Man a Penny. Boston, Houghton Mifflin, 1949; as *Every Man a Penny*, London Constable, 1950.
The Fair Bride. London, Constable, and Boston, Houghton Mifflin, 1953.
Only Fade Away. London, Constable, and Boston, Houghton Mifflin, 1954.

Girl in May. London, Constable, and Boston, Houghton Mifflin, 1956.
The Bank Audit. London, Constable, 1958; as *The Accounting*, Boston, Houghton Mifflin, 1958.
A Thread of Scarlet. London, Collins, 1959; as *Satan and Cardinal Campbell*, Boston, Houghton Mifflin, 1959.
The Divided Lady. London, Collins, and Boston, Houghton Mifflin, 1960.
A Girl from Lübeck. London, Collins, and Boston, Houghton Mifflin, 1962.
The Month of the Falling Leaves. London, Constable, and New York, Doubleday, 1963.
Father Hilary's Holiday. London, Constable, and New York, Doubleday, 1965.
The Bishop. London, Constable, and New York, Doubleday, 1970.
The Black Oxen. London, Constable, 1972.
Urban the Ninth. London, Constable, 1973.
Operation Iscariot. London, Constable, 1974.
Marx the First. London, Constable, 1975.
Peter the Second. London, Constable, 1976.
The Yellow Streak. London, Constable, 1977.
Prayer for a Concubine. London, Hale, 1978.

Short Stories

As a Thief in the Night and Other Stories. Amersham, Buckinghamshire, Morland, and London, Foyle, 1919.

Other

The White Rabbit. London, Evans, 1952; Boston, Houghton Mifflin, 1953.
Thoughts of My Cats. London, Constable, and Boston, Houghton Mifflin, 1954.

*

Bruce Marshall comments:

I started out by writing very bad religious novels which I prefer to forget. In all my novels the real drama will be found, I think, in the acceptance or rejection of the dictates of conscience for which the theological and, I think, the most accurate term is grace. It is perhaps for this reason that my books have been more widely read in Germany and in Italy than in my own country, because both those countries touched bottom at the end of the war and were therefore more percipient.

None of my novels is as good as I should have wished it, but *The Bishop* is not, I think, in spite of a Jesuit's sneer in *The Sign*, a badly written book. *Father Malachy's Miracle*, almost unnoticed in Britain, was very popular in America in 1931 and, in proof of what I have said above, became a bestseller both in Italy and Germany in 1949 and 1950.

* * *

Bruce Marshall is a vastly underestimated author largely because he is a Catholic writer and as such he is expected to deal in matters of less than compelling interest to most of us. He is inevitably compared to Graham Greene and found to be pallid by comparison, less richly rounded, almost superficial. But to the common reader, though Marshall would doubtless disagree, his Catholicism might appear to be a red herring and his main talents to lie not in apologetics but in the realm of high farce. The enormous output of this author falls into four chronologically indistinct categories. They can be divided into novels dealing with the individual, with international politics, with farcical situations, and with the church in the modern world.

Some of the earlier, simpler novels pursue the development of character to a more successful degree than their later counterparts. The faith of a simple priest is convincingly described in *All Glorious Within; George Brown's Schooldays* explores the feelings of the average man in time of war, while *Father Malachy's Miracle* makes a specifically Catholic point. Then Marshall branches out into international politics. *The Red Danube* is set in Vienna at the end of the war, while a viewpoint that is neither pro-Falangist, nor pro-Communist in the Spain of 1938 is put forward in *The Fair Bride*. The international cultural bureaucracy is satirised in *A Girl from Lübeck*. This group of novels is extremely professional though the characterisation is becoming shallower and the treatment of the issues involved is on a fairly simple level. They might be described as lightly dramatised essays on various subjects, designed for the man in the street.

The farcical novels are more slick and amusing: improbable situation is piled upon improbable reunion in *Father Hilary's Holiday* set in a quasi-revolutionary neo-Cuba, and in *The Divided Lady* Marshall takes his readers to Catholic headquarters, Rome. The technique of hustling the cast on and off the stage is excellent in all but the occasional flashback, but as characters they have now become eroded into mere lay figures. Finally, in his latest works, Marshall shows a wish to return to an exploration of the individual mind in, needless to say, a Catholic setting. Ambition within the church is analysed in *A Thread of Scarlet*, and *The Bishop* deals with the burning contemporary issues of birth control and priestly celibacy. The inclusion of an eloping nun is a disaster as the theme emphasises the lack of flesh and blood with which Marshall clothes his men and women. Indeed it would be true to say that successful and highly workmanlike as entertainments as some of Marshall's books are, the success of the majority is, sadly, in inverse proportion to the seriousness of their intent.

—Anastasia Leech

MARSHALL, Paule. American. Born in Brooklyn, New York, 9 April 1929. Educated at Brooklyn College, B.A. (cum laude) 1953 (Phi Beta Kappa); Hunter College, New York, 1955. Married Kenneth E. Marshall in 1950 (divorced, 1963); one son. Librarian, New York Public Library; staff writer, *Our World*, New York, 1953-56. Recipient: Guggenheim Fellowship, 1961; Rosenthal Award, 1962; Ford grant, for drama, 1964; National Endowment for the Arts grant, 1966, 1977; Creative Arts Public Service Fellowship, 1974. Address: 407 Central Park West, New York, New York 10025, U.S.A.

PUBLICATIONS

Novels

Brown Girl, Brownstones. New York, Random House, 1959; London, W.H. Allen, 1960.
The Chosen Place, The Timeless People. New York, Harcourt Brace, 1969; London, Longman, 1970.

Short Stories

Soul Clap Hands and Sing. New York, Atheneum, 1961; London, W.H. Allen, 1962.

Uncollected Short Stories

"Reena," in *American Negro Short Stories*, edited by John Henrik Clarke. New York, Hill and Wang, 1966.

"To Da-duh, in Memoriam," in *Afro-American Writing 2*, edited by Richard Long and Eugenia Collier. New York, New York University Press, 1972.

* * *

From the beginning of slavery times West Indian character and experience have figured prominently in the popular imagination of North Americans. Servile insurrections in British Guiana, Jamaica, Saint Domingue, and the smaller islands played their part inspiring the similar though less successful uprisings of the Carolinas and Virginia. More recently charismatic West Indian nationalists of the likes of Marcus Garvey have carried a vision of black autonomy directly to the masses of blacks whose arrival in the Northern cities provide conditions for a new consciousness. Yet, with the exception of the works of Claude McKay and a few others who contributed to the Harlem Renaissance of the 1920's the self-conscious literature of North America has scarcely remarked the significance of the black West Indies. That is until Paule Marshall, whose powerful imagination has raised to the highest levels of art a sensitive perception of the West Indian place in modern life.

Her major novel, *The Chosen Place, The Timeless People*, records the encounter of an American research development team with the "backward" people inhabiting Bournehills, the wasted corner of an island resembling perhaps Barbados but signifying the entire Caribbean. Out of sympathy for the human predicament she portrays both aliens and natives in terms of the motives of guilt and frustration by which they comprehend their personal lives. The North Americans' desire to be useful and to alleviate their pain by working in Bournehills she considers genuine, because they do. Similarly, Marshall permits the cane workers and native families to reveal themselves through their most immediate feelings. Only with opportunists, those who readily do the work of the neo-colonial system, does she allow a distance that encourages readers to doubt their personal sincerity, but even there the readers' urge to mock can be no greater than the characters' own. As the narrative progresses Merle Kinbona, a woman of Bournehills whose residence in England included schooling in painfully exploitive relationships as well as professional training, assumes a predominance that translates personal drama into general social meaning. A native of the island despite her "modernization," Merle shares the timelessness of the people to whom the experience of slavery and particularly the momentary success of the rebellion of Cuffee Ned remains palpably present. On a level as deep as culture and as unavailable to scientific measurement as the subconscious, they know that technological change is nothing compared to the redemption presaged in Cuffee's rebellion, and in their integrity they will settle for nothing less. Ultimately, the theme of *The Chosen Place, The Timeless People* is political. Not the politics of parliaments, nor even of parties, but the politics that grows from knowledge that the configurations of character and the complex relationships of love or resentment gain their shape from historical cultures.

Thematically less comprehensive than *The Chosen Place, The Timeless People*, Marshall's two earlier works also display the interweaving narrative and organically conceived meaning of her masterpiece.

Brown Girl, Brownstones traces the maturation of young Selina Boyce beyond a loving father, whose incapacity for the get-ahead life of New York City issues in romantic dreams of a big-paying job or self-sufficiency on two acres of inherited land home in Barbados, and beyond, as well, the equally deadening illusions of her mother who sacrifices her being to the successful Bajan's goal of property ownership. The heroine's autonomy is welcome, but, through her delightful rendition of Barbados English and folk say, Marshall makes it clear that Selina's necessary sacrifice of community with the transplanted islanders tragically likens her to the mass of other rootless Americans.

In the light of her two novels each of the four stories in *Soul Clap Hands and Sing* may be considered Marshall's portrayal of the ways individual animation so frequently is replaced in modern life by a protective but deadening routine. Whether in "Barbados," "Brooklyn," "British Guiana," or "Brazil" an aged man discovers that in seeking ease he has in fact lost the surety of self-hood, so that, as the volume's Yeatsian epigraph puts it, he is "a paltry thing."

Simply put, Paule Marshall's art is remarkable. She manages the often summoned but rarely arriving synthesis of the particular and universal, for in revealing the rich texture of West Indian life within her fiction she also constructs a microcosm of the contemporary struggle to be free at last.

—John M. Reilly

MASTERS, John. British. Born in India, 26 October 1914. Educated at the Royal Military College, Sandhurst. Married Barbara Allcard; one son and one daughter (and one daughter deceased). Served in the British Army, 1934 until his retirement as Lieutenant Colonel in 1948: commissioned 2nd Lieutenant, Indian Army, 1934; served in the 2nd Battalion, 4th Prince of Wales's Own Gurkha Rifles, 1935; served on the North West Frontier, 1936-37; Adjutant, 1939; served in Iraq, Syria and Persia, 1941; Brigade Major, 114th Indian Infantry Brigade, 1942, and 111th Indian Infantry Brigade, 1943; Commandant, 3rd Battalion, 1944; served in Burma, 1944-45; General Staff Officer-1, 19th Indian Division, 1945; General Staff Officer-2, Staff College, Camberley, Surrey, 1947: D.S.O. (Companion, Distinguished Service Order), 1944; O.B.E. (Officer, Order of the British Empire), 1945. Agent: Brandt and Brandt, 1501 Broadway, New York, New York 10036, U.S.A.

PUBLICATIONS

Novels

Nightrunners of Bengal. London, Joseph, and New York, Viking Press, 1951.

The Deceivers. London, Joseph, and New York, Viking Press, 1952.

The Lotus and the Wind. London, Joseph, and New York, Viking Press, 1953.

Bhowani Junction. London, Joseph, and New York, Viking Press, 1954.

Coromandel! London, Joseph and New York, Viking Press, 1955.

Far, Far the Mountain Peak. London, Joseph, and New York, Viking Press, 1957.

Fandango Rock. London, Joseph, and New York, Harper, 1959.

The Venus of Konpara. London, Joseph, and New York, Harper, 1960.

To the Coral Strand. London, Joseph, and New York, Harper, 1962.

Trial at Monomoy. London, Joseph, and New York, Harper, 1964.

Fourteen Eighteen. London, Joseph, 1965; New York, British Book Centre, 1966.

The Breaking Strain. London, Joseph, and New York, Delacorte Press, 1967.

The Rock. London, Joseph, and New York, Putnam, 1970.

The Ravi Lancers. London, Joseph, and New York, Doubleday, 1972.

Thunder at Sunset. London, Joseph, and New York, Doubleday, 1974.

The Field-Marshal's Memoirs. London, Joseph, and New York, Doubleday, 1975.

The Himalaya Concerto. London, Joseph, and New York, Doubleday, 1976.

Loss of Eden trilogy:

Now, God Be Thanked. London, Joseph, and New York, McGraw Hill, 1979.

Heart of War. London, Joseph, and New York, McGraw Hill, 1980.

Other

The Compleat Indian Angler. London, Country Life, 1938.
Bugles and a Tiger: A Personal Adventure. London, Joseph, and New York, Viking Press, 1956.
The Road Past Mandalay (autobiography). London, Joseph, and New York, Viking Press, 1961.
Casanova. London, Joseph, and New York, Geis, 1969.
Pilgrim Son: A Personal Odyssey. London, Joseph, and New York, Putnam, 1971.

* * *

While John Masters has received deserved acknowledgement as an accomplished narrator of dramatic and exciting stories, it would seem to me that he has not received his full due as a novelist *per se.* There is much more to Masters than the superb story teller. This may have been overlooked because the stories he tells are adventure stories in the old fashioned sense. Heroes stand alone against physical dangers and desperate odds in *Nightrunners of Bengal* and *The Deceivers*; the hero redeems himself after accusations of cowardice in *The Lotus and the Wind.* But these heroes are much more complex than the usual run of romantic adventurers. They suffer doubts and heart searchings as well as fears and privations; their quest is often as much for identity or relationships as for the enemy or the spy.

When William Savage in *The Deceivers* sets out to track down and disband the Thugs by joining them and entering their mysteries, he becomes aware of spiritual dangers as acute as the more obvious physical ones. The struggle is with the worshippers of Kali and within himself; and while Captain Rodney Savage in *Nightrunners of Bengal* has to overcome every danger and hardship to rescue himself and his son from the perils and horrors ensuing from the Indian mutiny, he has also to rescue himself from the bitterness of heart and mind which these experiences engender in him. In *Far, Far the Mountain Peak* Peter Savage has to wrestle not only with the almost daemonic urge to prove himself, but with the temptation to take others with him. It is not just a superb story of mountaineering and soldiering, but that of spiritual redemption and of relationships which have parallels with Lawrence's *Women in Love*, and it is at this level Masters's novels ought to be discussed. The peculiar affinity which develops between Robin Savage and his adversaries makes *The Lotus and the Wind* much more than a story about the pursuit of spies in Afghanistan. It is this ability to probe deep into motivation, and to engage our sympathy and interest in the internal struggles of characters not immediately likeable or even admirable, which raises Masters above the level of a mere narrator of adventure stories.

In *Bhowani Junction*, where the narrative is divided between the three main protagonists—Patrick Taylor and Victoria Jones, both Anglo-Indians, and Colonel Savage—a story of sabotage and political intrigue, exciting in itself, serves as a background for their search for identity in a rapidly changing India. It would be difficult to find in fiction a more thoroughly sympathetic understanding of the situation of the Anglo-Indian at that time, which brings us to a consideration of these works as historical novels. The history of the Savage family, as told in this series of novels, is closely interwoven with the history of British India, from the seventeenth century in *Coromandel!* to the time of partition in *Bhowani Juntion.* It is an India for which Masters has an immense sympathy and understanding, and of which he has an intimate and often firsthand knowledge. When John Raymond described *Nightrunners of Bengal*, as the best historical novel about the Indian mutiny he was not exaggerating, and *The Deceivers* displays a knowledge of Thuggee which can be the result only of thorough scholarship, and an understanding which displays a remarkably imaginative insight. There is considerable skill, too, in the way Masters organizes his material. Indeed, it is this and his remarkable qualities of imaginative understanding that make him a novelist who deserves our serious attention.

In his more recent work Masters has undertaken in *Now, God Be Thanked* a novel of epic scope, in which the events of the first years of the first World War are related through the experiences of a number of interlinked families encompassing a broad spectrum of English society, from the family of the squire to that of the local poacher, taking in factory workers and an American manager on the way. Here he breaks new ground and employs new techniques. The fictional episodes are glossed by extracts from the newpapers of the time. This tends to break up Masters's usual narrative flow, and the foresight of some of his more knowledgeable characters is sometimes difficult to accept. Nevertheless it is a courageous attempt, painstakingly researched. With *The Himalayan Concerto* he returns to more familiar territory and theme, a spying expedition in the countries north of India. The use of musical analogies (the hero is a composer) is sometimes overworked, but the narrative, full of tensions, and the atmosphere of place approach those of the vintage Masters.

—John Cotton

MATHERS, Peter. British. Born in England, in 1931; emigrated to Australia as an infant. Educated at Sydney Technical College. Married in 1961; two daughters. Recipient: Miles Franklin Award, 1967. Lives in Melbourne. Address: c/o Cassell Australia Ltd., 44 Waterloo Road, North Ryde, New South Wales 2113, Australia.

PUBLICATIONS

Novels

Trap. Melbourne, Cassell, 1966; London, Sphere, 1970.
The Wort Papers. Melbourne, Cassell, 1972; London, Penguin, 1973.

* * *

Peter Mathers is the author of only two novels, *Trap* and *The Wort Papers*, yet he is undoubtedly one of the best of the so-called second generation of contemporary Australian novelists—those who followed Patrick White, Christina Stead, and Xavier Herbert. He is also, with White (who has publicly expressed admiration for his work), one of the few writers possessed of genuinely mythic aspirations—whose work is not merely intelligent and talented but ambitious enough to attempt to capture archetypal truths about Australian experience.

Trap, for instance, commences with the story of the central figure, Jack Trap, a part-Aboriginal, but as it continues the area it covers steadily widens until finally it takes in, with the discussion of Trap's forebears, the whole savage history of the Aboriginal race: the shooting down and poisoning by white settlers; exploitation by businessmen and missionaries; abuse and mistreatment by foremen and fellow-workers; and finally, assaults by police and jailings by magistrates. If the novel is dominated by the angry, ebullient presence of its central character, the author makes it clear nevertheless that Jack is the product of a whole history of cruelty, exploitation, and contemptuous indifference on the part of white people. He is a misfit—neither craven nor surly, neither in society nor wholly out of it. Although he schools himself constantly to patience, he undergoes violent eruptions at periodic intervals and the consequence is always "six months from an understanding magistrate." He is resentful of his Aboriginal features and hopes they will not be recognized: "There was little resemblance between the Traps, father and son. The father, Wilson, wished he could resemble the son, Jack. The son, Jack, sought the anonymity of the father, Wilson. Pale father—dark son. The unfairness of it all pained them both." But at the same time Jack "marries" an Aboriginal girl and his final scheme is to lead a part of followers across the continent to the Naraki Mission.

In his second novel, Mathers maintains some of the concerns of *Trap* but takes the stylistic experiments of that novel a great deal further, virtually out of the realms of social realism altogether. Style in *The Wort Papers* is not merely the means of recording the rebellious and independent freedom to which the protagonist aspires, but is also the means of achieving and demonstrating it. The last word in the novel is MATTERS, the name of the protagonist's alter ego and the mysterious writer who has hovered on the outskirts of the narrative throughout.

Although it is concerned with a smaller area of time than *Trap*—roughly from the 1930's onwards—*The Wort Papers* is also concerned with questions of identity and of journeys inland, except that there are two journeys (or series of journeys) and both are seen in comic and parodic terms. The first third of the novel is taken up with the various expeditions of William Wort, and his attempt to define himself in terms of his sense of Englishness. Like his son later William is constantly "In Flight"; Mathers's awareness that William's peregrinations carry him over territory already covered by White and other writers is shown by the heading of one section: "Journey and Employers (& obligatory bushfire)." However, once the attention of the novel shifts to Percy and his series of nomadic expeditons the preoccupation with the English fades and Percy hints strongly from his cave that it has ceased to trouble his father, as if exorcized by his wanderings.

Percy himself is an explorer, like his father, but whereas earlier explorers and even his father travelled on foot or on horseback, Percy mounts a 500 c.c. Norton motor-bike. Whereas they travelled inland, to the Kimberleys or Northern Queensland, he sticks mostly to the cities, and his predicaments are mostly urban ones, often taking a farcical form. Where their enemies were droughts or hostile natives, Percy's are figures of bureaucratic authority—policemen, mysterious representatives of A.S.I.O., and recalcitrant bosses and bar-keepers.

The freedom envisaged in *Trap* was still a relatively limited and conventional one, the rebellion against the restrictions of a stifling society by specifically anti-social gestures: at the end of the novel Jack's timid, white biographer and counterpart, David David, has been moved by Jack's fate to smash aluminium and glass doors worth £10,000 in a wanton act of vandalism which Jack would have called "unchannelled dissent," and we leave him muttering "I must, must, must, must, beware." In *The Wort Papers*, on the other hand, the gesture of rebellion is a deliberately symbolic one, useless in terms of social efficacy. The real acts of insurrection are embodied in the language of the novel itself. Wort's words are exuberant, hilariously funny, and finally surreal weapons fired by his "sturdy, 350 shot Remington." At the end Percy dies but his doppelganger Matters is still around. It is the artist, the word-maker, who in Mathers's view survives.

—Laurie Clancy

MATTHEWS, Jack (John Harold Matthews). American. Born in Columbus, Ohio, 22 July 1925. Educated at Ohio State University, Columbus, 1945-49, B.A. in classics and English 1949, 1952-54, M.A. in English 1954. Served in the United States Coast Guard, 1943-45. Married Barbara Jane Reese in 1947; two daughters and one son. Associate Professor, 1959-62, and Professor of English, 1962-64, Urbana College, Ohio. Associate Professor, 1964-70, and since 1971, Professor of English, Ohio University, Athens. Distinguished Writer-in-Residence, Wichita State University, Kansas, 1970-71. Recipient: Florence Roberts Head Award, 1967; Quill Award (*Massachusetts Review*, Amherst), 1967; Guggenheim grant, 1974. Agent: Ann Elmo Agency Inc., 60 East 42nd Street, New York, New York 10017. Address: 24 Briarwood Drive, Athens, Ohio 45701, U.S.A.

PUBLICATIONS

Novels

Hanger Stout, Awake! New York, Harcourt Brace, 1967.
Beyond the Bridge. New York, Harcourt Brace, 1970.
The Tale of Asa Bean. New York, Harcourt Brace, 1971.
The Charisma Campaigns. New York, Harcourt Brace, 1972.
Pictures of the Journey Back. New York, Harcourt Brace, 1973.

Short Stories

Bitter Knowledge: Short Stories. New York, Scribner, 1964.
Tales of the Ohio Land. Columbus, Ohio Historical Society, 1978.

Uncollected Short Stories

" 'When the Shark, Babe,' "in *North American Review* (Mt. Vernon, Iowa), January 1966.
"The Names of My Brothers," in *Georgia Review* (Athens), Spring 1966.
"My Son," in *Prairie Schooner* (Lincoln, Nebraska), Spring 1966.
"Night" and "A Fire on the Hill," in *North American Review* (Mt. Vernon, Iowa), May 1966.
"Inviolate on Shawnee Street," in *North American Review* (Mt. Vernon, Iowa), July 1966.
"The Strong One," in *University Review* (Kansas City, Missouri), Autumn 1966.
"A Slightly Different World," in *North American Review* (Mt. Vernon, Iowa), March 1967.
"Schlachner, The Hero," in *December 9* (Western Springs, Illinois), 1967.
"The Hotel," in *Massachusetts Review* (Amherst), Autumn 1967.
"In the Neighborhood of Dark," in *North American Review* (Mt. Vernon, Iowa), September 1967.
"The Knife," in *Yale Review* (New Haven, Connecticut), December 1968.
"The Betrayal," in *Malahat Review* (Victoria, British Columbia), April 1969.
"Another Story," in *The Best American Short Stories 1970*, edited by Martha Foley and David Burnett. Boston, Houghton Mifflin, 1970.
"Love Song for Doris Ballinger," in *Short Stories from the Little Magazines*, edited by Jarvis Thurston and Curt Johnson. Chicago, Scott Foresman, 1970.
"A Genealogy of Trees and Flesh," in *Iowa Review* (Iowa City), Spring 1971.
"The Colonel's Birthday Party," in *Ohio Review* (Athens), Spring 1972.
"The Stone in the Path," in *Sewanee Review* (Tennessee), Summer 1972.
"A Questionnaire for Emilio Roszas," in *Malahat Review* (Victoria, British Columbia), July 1972.
"On Chad Creek," in *Prize Stories 1972: The O. Henry Awards*, edited by William Abrahams. New York, Doubleday, 1972.
"Invaders of the Fields," in *Yale Review* (New Haven, Connecticut), Autumn 1973.
"Questionnaire for T.M. Connolly," in *Salmagundi* (Flushing, New York), Spring 1974.
"Who Is Who and When Will We Be Real?," in *Yale Review* (New Haven, Connecticut), Winter 1978.
"The Execution," in *Ohio Review* (Athens), Winter 1978.
"Eternal Mortgage," in *Southwest Review* (Dallas), Spring 1979.
"Muerte, Nada, and Bradley Jones," in *Malahat Review* (Victoria, British Columbia), July 1979.

"The Last Abandonment," in *Georgia Review* (Athens), Fall 1979.
"Tableau with Three Ghostly Women," in *Chariton Review* (Kirksville, Missouri), Fall 1979.

Verse

An Almanac for Twilight: Poems. Chapel Hill, University of North Carolina Press, 1966.
In a Theater of Buildings. Marshall, Minnesota, Ox Head Press, 1970.

Other

Collecting Rare Books for Pleasure and Profit. New York, Putnam, 1977.

Editor, with Elaine Gottlieb Hemley, *The Writer's Signature: Idea in Story and Essay.* Chicago, Scott Foresman, 1972.
Editor, *Archetypal Themes in the Modern Story* (anthology). New York, St. Martin's Press, 1973.

*

Manuscript Collection: Ohioana Library, Ohio Departments Building, Columbus.

Critical Study: "Jack Matthews and the Shape of Human Feelings" by Elmer F. Suderman, in *Critique* (Atlanta), xxi, 1, 1979.

Jack Matthews comments:

I think of every literary work as a place where three classes of people come together: the author, the reader, and the characters. The work is importantly, if not solely, definable in terms of these three classes and their relationships to one another and to the story (or poem) which is the arena of their convention. Thus, every story can be viewed as, in varying degrees, an occasion and ceremony of passionate learning.

All stories are philosophical probes, hypotheses, heuristic journeys, maps of powerful and conceivable realities, speculations, ceremonies of discovery. All these, every one. Some attempts to write a good story work beautifully; others prove sadly unworthy, false, flat, silly. Nevertheless, an author should have the courage and energy to experiment constantly and knowledgeably (i.e., remembering and adding to his craft), even in his awareness that he will often miss whatever mark is there, and knowing also that whatever can conceivably happen to him and come out of him will ultimately be found to have taken place within his signature.

Man's character is his fate, but he should never let this fact inhibit his real freedom of the real moment. I celebrate this truth in my stories, as well as in the act of writing them.

* * *

Many contemporary fiction writers—especially in America—are displaced persons: they don't really live *in* any particular place, they merely reside there. But Jack Matthews's mature imagination *lives* in the American heartland where it was shaped. In fact, Matthews is at his best when he is taking the pulse of Middle America (not merely a geographical area, of course, but a state of consciousness extending far beyond Matthews's native Ohio). In his five novels (and in many of his published short stories) the reader can sense the wide open spaces of the midwest, the relatively closed minds of its inhabitants, the limitless possibilities of success and failure, the comic and the tragic in ironic balance. Like Sinclair Lewis, Matthews captures the essence of Middle America. He does so, however, without the didacticism of Lewis and with more of the comic and a surer control of the dramatic.

Matthews's novels are all rather short, but they are richly developed and populated with authentic and memorable characters—originals with far more than mere literary validity, ranging from gas-station attendants and warehouse laborers to used-car salesmen and battered cowboys. Most of them are relative innocents, viewed with unsentimental compassion as they try to cope with what they see of the confusion around them, but they carry their innocence in interestingly differing ways.

The most openly naive of his characters is "Hanger" Stout, the narrator of Matthews's first novel, who relates a poignant but truly funny account of how he was tricked into competing for the championship of a nonexistent sport ("free-hanging" by one's hands). Genuinely unaware of how much others are using him, and often unaware of the refreshing comedy in his tale, Hanger emerges from his experiences relatively untouched, still kind and trusting, a most convincing original.

Less convincing is the more self-conscious narrator of *Beyond the Bridge*, a middle-aged man who narrowly escapes death when the Silver Bridge collapses into the Ohio River, and who recognizes the unique chance he now has to shed previous responsibilities and begin a new life elsewhere. Such a break with one's past is not so easy, as Matthews demonstrates, and the novel offers some nicely detailed moments in the mind of the neurotic narrator. But the action here seems excessively internalized, for the most part, and the symbolism often too overt. It remains the least successful of Matthews's novels.

Matthews's ironic sense of humor surfaces as witty sexual satire in *The Tale of Asa Bean*, where the innocent is a former Ph.D. candidate in philosophy now working in an A & P grocery warehouse. Asa, burdened with an IQ of more than 170 and an overactive libido, is a compulsive verbalist with a tendency to drop recondite phrases (often in Latin) at inappropriate moments—a habit that regularly scares off the women he so desperately wants. "What ironic man can make love?" Asa agonizes, "And yet, how can man achieve truth, understanding, humor, manhood, without irony?" But Asa's hilarious misadventures end in ultimate triumph—despite himself—in a brilliant demonstration of wit and verbal precision, a winning performance.

In *The Charisma Campaigns* Matthews takes a calculated risk in creating a character who is announced as possessing magnetic charisma—and, indeed, convincingly does. A used-car dealer in a small Ohio town, Rex McCoy plays with a full deck of corny sales slogans and gimmicks, but like nearly all of Matthews's characters he moves far beyond any stereotyped model. His cunning machinations and energetic naivety, his success in selling cars and his failures in other aspects of life, all blend into a fascinating portrait. It is easy to agree with Anthony Burgess when he writes, "This book already has the feel of an American classic." It's a superb novel—Matthews's finest accomplishment to date.

In his most recent novel, *Pictures of the Journey Back*, Matthews portrays a trip from Kansas to Colorado by three disparate characters: a weathered ex-rodeo hand, a confused college girl estranged from her mother, and the girl's hippie lover, an aspiring film-maker. The cowboy insists upon returning the girl to her dying mother because, he argues, it is "only right," and the boy friend accompanies them to make a film of the total experience. Here is the vehicle for the unending dialectics of youth vs. age, freedom vs. tradition, appearance vs. reality, etc. More ambitious technically than his earlier work, *Pictures* employs a shifting point of view to examine a concern that, although usually more subordinate, occupies much of Matthews's fiction—a sense that something is slowly being lost: "the sacred ideals of one's family and culture," as Matthews sees it, "what the Romans termed *Pietas*." Although these values are being eroded, however, their presence is still a felt factor—and *Pictures of the Journey Back* dramatizes this with sensitive power.

All of Matthews's novels invite and sustain additional readings, and—despite limited publisher promotion—they appear to be winning a steadily enlarging audience. Moreover, as his distinctive fusion of the regional and the archetypal continues to be recognized and appreciated, critical acclaim is slowly catching up with Jack Matthews. That acclaim has been well earned.

—Stanley W. Lindberg

MATTHIESSEN, Peter. American. Born in New York City, 22 May 1927. Educated at Hotchkiss School, Connecticut; Yale University, New Haven, Connecticut, B.A. 1950; the Sorbonne, Paris, 1948-49. Married Deborah Love in 1963 (died); four children. Commercial fisherman, 1954-56. Has made anthropological and natural history expeditions to Alaska, the Canadian Northwest Territories, Peru, New Guinea (Harvard-Peabody Expedition, 1961), Africa, Nicaragua, and Nepal. Founder, 1952, and Editor, *Paris Review*. Trustee of the New York Zoological Society, 1965-79. Recipient: *Atlantic* "Firsts" Award, 1951; American Academy award, 1963; National Book Award, for non-fiction, 1979; Brandeis University Creative Arts Award, 1979; American Book Award, for non-fiction, 1980. Address: Bridge Lane, Sagaponack, Long Island, New York 11962, U.S.A.

PUBLICATIONS

Novels

Race Rock. New York, Harper, 1954; London, Secker and Warburg, 1955.
Partisans. New York, Viking Press, 1955; London, Secker and Warburg, 1956; as *The Passionate Seekers*, New York, Avon, n.d.
Raditzer. New York, Viking Press, 1961; London, Heinemann, 1962.
At Play in the Fields of the Lord. New York, Random House, 1965; London, Heinemann, 1966.
Far Tortuga. New York, Random House, 1975; London, Bantam, 1976.

Uncollected Short Stories

"Sadie," in *Atlantic* (Boston), January 1951.
"Fifth Day," in *Atlantic* (Boston), September 1951.
"A Replacement," in *Paris Review 1*, Spring 1953.
"Lina," in *Cornhill* (London), Fall 1956.
"Travelin' Man," in *Prize Stories 1958: The O. Henry Awards*, edited by Paul Engle. New York, Doubleday, 1958.
"Midnight Turning Gray," in *Saturday Evening Post* (Philadelphia), 28 September 1963.

Other

Wildlife in America. New York, Viking Press, 1959; London, Deutsch, 1960.
The Cloud Forest: A Chronicle of the South American Wilderness. New York, Viking Press, 1961; London, Deutsch, 1962.
Under the Mountain Wall: A Chronicle of Two Seasons in the Stone Age. New York, Viking Press, 1962; London, Heinemann, 1963.
The Shorebirds of North America. New York, Viking Press, 1967; as *The Wind Birds*, 1973.
Oomingmak: The Expedition to the Musk Ox Island in the Bering Sea. New York, Hastings House, 1967.
Sal Si Puedes: Cesar Chavez and the New American Revolution. New York, Random House, 1970.
Blue Meridian: The Search for the Great White Shark. New York, Random House, 1971.
Everglades: Selections from the Writings of Peter Matthiessen, edited by Patricia Caulfield. New York, Ballantine, 1971.
Seal Pool (juvenile). New York, Doubleday, 1972; as *The Great Auk Escape*, London, Angus and Robertson, 1974.
The Tree Where Man Was Born: The African Experience, photographs by Eliot Porter. New York, Dutton, and London, Collins, 1972.
The Snow Leopard. New York, Viking Press, 1978; London, Chatto and Windus, 1979.
Sand Rivers (on the Selous Game Reserve). New York, Viking Press, and London, Aurum Press, 1981.

* * *

Peter Matthiessen has a dream of mankind living gracefully in the world, one species of many in an organic relationship. Unlike earlier American authors given to a version of this dream, Matthiessen can have no illusions. He writes with our contemporary knowledge that the "natural man," whose free application of energy to the environment was for earlier Americans to be the means of achieving a paradise, has wrought ecological disaster. Materially that disaster derives from the rapacious application of technology to the subjugation of nature, and Matthiessen's works of non-fiction are its historical record reporting the extinction and threatened destruction of animal species, the fateful meetings of representatives of industrial society with people yet to experience even the agricultural revolution, and the desperate resistance of American farm workers to the culminating stage of exploitation. Philosophically, the disastrous consequences of the traditional American dream result from the theoretical separation of society, usually conceived of as oppressive, and the individual, always assumed to be noble; thus, people celebrating individualism but nonetheless required to construct a social system find that their rejection of the claims of fraternity does not foster sturdy independence but merely produces anomie. The counterpart of his historical record of the destruction of the natural environment, Matthiessen's first novels are a representation of this disabled American character.

Writing evocatively of his own generation and social class in *Race Rock*, he links four young Americans in exploring the directions their lives have taken since their adolescence in the same seacoast setting. The shifting viewpoint and intermingling of recollection and present event provide the sense of movement we associate with growth, but it is ironic since there has been no growth. Two of the male characters—George and Sam—are the ineffectual products of middle-class culture: uncertain of vocation, implausible in deeds, in short unable to complete the arc between thought and action because they doubt the efficacy of their thought. Providing the apex of a triangle is a woman who, though female and, therefore, less intensively drawn by the romance of achievement, is herself ungratified. Her fulfillment must come through the ineffectual males to one of whom she has been married and with the second of whom she is involved in a love affair. The point of reference for all three is Cady, a man whose natural capacity to act let him bully them in childhood. As adults these four are bound as they were in adolescence into personally destructive relationships. Cady's irresponsible brutishness has merely become more lethal. He still seeks to get what he wants according to a base code of individual force, while George, Sam, and Eve ambivalently resent and admire his dominance. For Matthiessen the behavior of the characters has explanation, but no excuse. Carefully avoiding extenuating circumstances that would lift their personal responsibility, he shows that they have neither the direction nor the will to exist in other than an unjustifiably predatory arrangement.

In *Partisans* Matthiessen again focuses upon an ineffectual son of the American bourgeoisie. Barney Sand, alienated from family and culture, proceeds on a search for a revolutionary who had befriended him as a child. By means of a descent into Parisian working class life on which Barney is led by a Stalinist Party functionary named Marat, Matthiessen parallels the physical search with an inquiry into the motives for revolutionary action. The Brechtian portrayal of proletarian conditions denies Barney the clarity available to those who think in the abstract. The bestial lives of the poor make sympathy, or even the belief in their natural rectitude, impossible for Barney, and a politics without idealism is beneath his consideration. All that Matthiessen permits Barney to grasp is that revolutionaries have strong convictions for which they will sacrifice everything—the man for whom he searches gives life and reputation. But since there can be no doubt that revolutionary forces are in motion, the failure to comprehend must lie in Barney. Matthiessen seems to be suggesting that so long as thought and action are held to be categorically separate, as they are in Barney's mind, no motive will be sufficient for action and no action entirely justifiable. It is integration of both in practice that makes a revolutionary and comprehension of that fact that is necessary for modern men to make their lives adequately human.

Technically Matthiessen's neatest explication of character occurs in *Raditzer*. The figure who gives his name to the book is a passive-aggressive, physically weak and socially a parasite, yet able to strike through the mask of civilized respectability and mastery to reveal in those he victimizes a deep-seated guilt and bewildering remorse. The kinship Raditzer insists he shares with the respectable Navy men whose tenuous security he undermines conveys, as in *Race Rock*, Matthiessen's perception of the split between thought and action that manifests itself in the indecisiveness of American men. The tight narrative construction enforcing psychological parallels goes beyond the earlier novel, however, making it evident in *Raditzer* through the substance of style that the leading characters of the book amalgamate into a general type.

Successful though he has been in the manner of psychological realism, Matthiessen's developing vision has required that he exceed the form of his first three novels, and in *At Play in the Fields of the Lord* he introduces to fiction the comprehensiveness of philosophical anthropology. Carrying the ineffectual civilized types he has previously described into the jungle of South America, Matthiessen strips away the protective coloration they gain from their native culture; thus, they are as exposed as the jungle Indians to the test of survival. As the narrative increasingly centers upon the grand attempt of a reservation trained North American Indian to reclaim his past by immersing himself in the natural and cultural world of the primitive South American Indians, three levels of meaning emerge. The first concerns the historical conflict between modern technological civilization and the less developed societies whose destruction is only a matter of time. Through imaginative sympathy with both Indians and whites Matthiessen, then, establishes a second theme of the unity of desire to humanize the world. For the Indians this involves a balanced relationship to nature that yet allows a sense of trascendence. For the North Americans sharing the same impulse the desire is domination. Certainly their technology will eventually dominate but for the time being they are alone with only personal resources inadequate to sustain their sanity. Finally, on a third level of meaning he reveals both Indians and whites to be lonely beings who must find salvation through development of community that embraces the total material and social world.

Thematically more spare than the previous novels, *Far Tortuga* embodies in literary technique itself the forces of the natural and human world that might make community. The crew of a Grand Cayman fishing boat going about the business of sailing to the turtle banks off Nicaragua communicates in dialogue detached from expository context. Their speech, afloat as they are, concerns the specifics of job and personality but is imbued with the sense that fishing has come upon hard times. Tales of past voyages, former captains, and historical events imply the decline their way of life has suffered because excessive fishing has depleted marine life. Impressionistic description of sea and weather and time dominates the narrative just as natural forces dominate the watery world. There is no significant plot to the narrative, for at sea the men cannot be a cause of their destiny, and, for the same reason, narrative movement is simply temporal. Human purpose appears in the novel's title, which refers to a legendary cay where fishing is eternally good, but that very purpose has sustained material nature as the ultimate force in human life.

Peter Matthiessen's fiction and non-fiction are one. As he writes in *Sal Si Puedes*: "In a damaged human habitat, all problems merge." The good life will be achieved, if at all, only when man and society and nature are equally nurtured and cherished.

—John M. Reilly

MAVOR, Elizabeth (Osborne). British. Born in Glasgow, Lanarkshire, in 1927. Educated at St. Leonard's School, St. Andrews, Scotland; St. Anne's College, Oxford. Married to Haro Hodson; two sons. Address: Home Close, Garsington, Oxfordshire, England.

PUBLICATIONS

Novels

Summer in the Greenhouse. London, Hutchinson, 1959; New York, Morrow, 1960.
The Temple of Flora. London, Hutchinson, 1961.
The Redoubt. London, Hutchinson, 1967.
A Green Equinox. London, Joseph, 1973.

Other

The Virgin Mistress: A Study in Survival: The Life of the Duchess of Kingston. London, Chatto and Windus, and New York, Doubleday, 1964.
The Ladies of Llangollen: A Study in Romantic Friendship. London, Joseph, 1971.

* * *

Elizabeth Mavor's forte is the combination of different—often incongruous—tones in a single novel. Each of her four novels centres on a woman in love, around whom revolve questions of the justification of adultery, and who pits herself against time, past or future.

In Mavor's first novel, *Summer in the Greenhouse*, the predominant mood of lyrical reminiscence contrasts with the stylized and fantastic plotting on which it is hinged. The middle-aged Claire Peachey recounts the sad love-affair of her youth to a child and a young man who see "not so much Mrs. Peachey's house and the walks and flower-beds about it as the buildings and monuments of Florence beneath an identical burning sky in that June of 1895." Mrs. Peachey is observed through the grand-daughter of her old admirer; the child's quest for the Fra Angelico painting of "the face," which she has seen reproduced, brings the adults together after 45 years. Though anticipated throughout the book, this encounter remains a *tour de force*, upstaged by the radio announcement of Britain's entry into the Second World War.

Mavor boldly extends the range of broad comedy in *The Temple of Flora*, which switches from rural fun reminiscent of *Cold Comfort Farm* to sometimes serious theology. Dinah Gage's aspirations to reform the semi-pagan village of Thrussel are complicated by her tangling with a local youth. In a heavily symbolic but hilarious climax, a bull disrupts the harvest festival, which has already transformed the church into the temple of the title. The novel shifts to a consideration of the eternal triangle in which Dinah now involves herself. In the closing farewell scenes, as she decides to renounce her married lover, Mavor successfully treads a dizzy tightrope between poignance and ridicule, with Dinah's wish for "a sacramental relationship between him and me so that I could live apart from him with courage and a belief that I was doing something true and creative."

In *The Redoubt* Mavor broke away from the third-person narration of her two previous novels for a mixture of first- and third-person narration which she retained in *A Green Equinox*, though in both books the potentialities of this freedom are left unexplored. In *The Redoubt*, too, she extended her range of characterization with the publican Lil, who is her only fullscale lower-class portrait. The novel is set over the weekend of the 1953 East Coast floods, as Eve gives birth to a child. Through flashbacks grafted on to the chaos of the floods and the proverbial reliving of the past before drowning, the flickering validity of a childhood friendship comes across, "a kind of marriage in that childhood moment." But the book's ending is facile as Eve, who wishes that the father of her child were not her abandoned husband, but Faber, her rediscovered—married—and now drowned childhood friend, resolves that "it is out of his death that my own life must be remade somehow."

A Green Equinox ranges even wider than *The Temple of Flora*, and fuses its diverse material better in an ironical circular structure. It follows Hero Kinoull's search for "Heaven now" in her successive loves for Hugh Shafto, the Rococo expert, his wife and his mother, in Beaudesert—to be found on the same allegorical map as Thrussel. The novel partially resolves itself into a meditation on age, as Hero's third love is seen as the most lyrical; old Mrs. Shafto's gardens and model boats—"a love for the miniature"—recall Faber's in *The Redoubt. A Green Equinox* combines the bathetic comedy of saving the Bunyan Elm with a plethora of dramatic disasters—car accident, typhoid epidemic, near-drowning, drowning, and fire. Complete with metaphysical overtones, all this is crammed into six months which culminate in Hero's defiance of time; the reader has been initially forewarned to her "love affair, sexual almost, with the lost past." The Rococo, "the worst and most provocative of all styles," subsumes all the ramifications of this tale under its imagery.

In *The Virgin Mistress*, the first of her two historical biographies, Mavor affirmed that "a human personality is not mewed up in its own life-span." She has an antiquarian fascination with objects, just as Imogen in *In the Greenhouse* listening to Mrs. Peachey's story was spellbound by "all the props of the play that had been." *A Green Equinox* is Elizabeth Mavor's most ambitious and best novel because the extended metaphor of Rococo frivolity permits her even greater licence for lyricism and satire.

—Val Warner

MAXWELL, William (Keepers). American. Born in Lincoln, Illinois, 16 August 1908. Educated at the University of Illinois, Urbana, B.A. 1930; Harvard University, Cambridge, Massachusetts, M.A. 1931. Married Emily Gilman Noyes in 1945; two children. Member of the English Department, University of Illinois, 1931-33. Since 1936, in the art department, then fiction editor, *New Yorker*; retired 1976. Recipient: Friends of American Writers Award, 1938; American Academy award, 1958, and Howells Medal, 1980. President, National Institute of Arts and Letters, 1969-72. Address: 544 East 86th Street, New York, New York 10028, U.S.A.

PUBLICATIONS

Novels

Bright Center of Heaven. New York, Harper, 1934.
They Came like Swallows. New York, Harper, and London, Joseph, 1937.
The Folded Leaf. New York, Harper, 1945; London, Faber, 1946.
Time Will Darken It. New York, Harper, 1948; London, Faber, 1949.
The Château. New York, Knopf, 1961.
So Long, See You Tomorrow. New York, Knopf, 1980.

Short Stories

Stories, with others. New York, Farrar Straus, 1956; as *A Book of Stories*, London, Gollancz, 1957.
The Old Man at the Railroad Crossing and Other Tales. New York, Knopf, 1966.
Over by the River and Other Stories. New York, Knopf, 1977.

Other

The Heavenly Tenants (juvenile). New York, Harper, 1946.
The Writer as Illusionist (lecture). New York, Unitelum Press, 1955.
Ancestors. New York, Knopf, 1971.

* * *

The subjects of William Maxwell's major novels vary, but the sensibility that informs them is a midwestern one. In both *They Came like Swallows* and *The Folded Leaf*, for example, the novelist is reworking and focusing his recollections of an Illinois boyhood and college experience. The materials he draws on in these novels he thus shares with somewhat older writers like Sinclair Lewis and Sherwood Anderson. But these novelists were involved in labors of repudiation; their work was marked by what has been called the "revolt from the village," by a keen sense that the midwestern setting was a stultifying one from which the writer, by a satirical and unflattering report, had to separate himself. This accent of mockery and dismissal is absent from Maxwell's novels, which render the texture of midwestern life in the early decades of this century. It is an accent which is absent from Maxwell's *Ancestors*, a work of non-fiction which gives an attentive account of the writer's forebears.

In general, then, there is a cherishing of the provincial limitations that other writers have found galling. There is, in most of the novels, a precise if not loving recollection of the diversions and the limited esthetic taste that created upper-class, prosperous sensibility in "downstate" Illinois towns. *They Came like Swallows*, for example, tells of the impact of a mother's death on a decent and conventional Illinois household. *Time Will Darken It* is an account of a protracted visit which Southern relatives pay and the disruption that the visitors bring to what was a moderately happy family. *The Folded Leaf*, which the French critic Maurice Coindreau has referred to as the best novel about college experience, tells of the adolescent and college experiences of two young midwestern men; it leaves them on the threshold of an uneasy maturity, a maturity far short of ideal, but the only maturity that is open to them under midwestern conditions.

The clearest indications of Maxwell's attitude toward his American materials appears in two novels; *The Folded Leaf* and *So Long, See You Tomorrow. The Folded Leaf* is about the "coming of age" of two boys; the author draws explicit parallels between the boys' rather casual passage from youth to maturity and the "rites of passage" that anthropologists and students of comparative religion describe in the tradition-oriented societies they study. *So Long, See You Tomorrow* also deals with the friendship of two boys. It is friendship terminated by the sensational crime and death of the father of one of the boys. Here also Maxwell deals with studious attention to matters that other writers handle sensationally or ironically. Maxwell even allows us to see how he has collected his materials—old newspapers—as a first step to his imaginative reconstruction. Both novels contain controlled attention, free of animus.

The same sort of attention is offered adult experience in *The Château*. The American travellers at the center of this novel undergo contacts with an enigmatic culture—that of the French—which are a series of challenges that are neither mockingly presented, as in Sinclair Lewis's *Dodsworth*, nor offered as proof of American superiority, as in Booth Tarkington's *The Plutocrat*. Rather is Maxwell's prevailing note that of detached comprehension, the same sort of comprehension that the anthropologist offers the alien culture that he wishes to grasp. The anthropologist does not question the values of his "informants"; he reports those values. Such is also the attitude of Maxwell toward the aspirations of the characters he creates.

—Harold H. Watts

MAYFIELD, Julian. American. Born in Greer, South Carolina, 6 June 1928. Educated at Dunbar High School, Washington, D.C.; Lincoln University, Pennsylvania. Served in the United States Army, 1946-47. Married 1) Ana Livia Cordero in 1954, two children; 2) Joan Luisa Cambridge in 1972. Writer and Editor in the office of President Kwame Nkrumah, Ghana, 1962-66; Founding Editor, *The African Review*, Accra, 1964-66; Fellow, Society for the Humanities, Cornell University, Ithaca, New York, 1967-68; Lecturer, Schweitzer Program in the Humanities, New York University, 1968-70; W.E.B. Du Bois Visiting Fellow, Cornell University, 1970-71; Senior Political Adviser to the Prime Minister of Guyana, 1971-74; Fulbright Lecturer in West Germany, 1976-77; Lecturer, University of Maryland, College Park, 1977-78. Since 1978, Writer-in-Residence, Howard University, Washington, D.C. Recipient: Rabinowitz Fellowship, 1967. Address: 1814 Metzerott Road, Adelphi, Maryland 20783, U.S.A.

PUBLICATIONS

Novels

The Hit. New York, Vanguard Press, 1957; London, Joseph, 1959.
The Long Night. New York, Vanguard Press, 1958; London, Joseph, 1960.
The Grand Parade. New York, Vanguard Press, 1961; London, Joseph, 1962.

Uncollected Short Story

"Black on Black," in *Ten Times Black*, edited by Mayfield. New York, Bantam, 1972.

Plays

A World Full of Men, and The Other Foot (produced New York, 1952).
417, in *Contemporary Reader* (New York), 1954.
Fount of the Nation (produced Baltimore, 1978).

Screenplay: *Uptight*, with Ruby Dee and Jules Dassin, 1968.

Other

Editor, *The World Without the Bomb: The Papers of the Accra Assembly.* Accra, Ghana Government Press, 1963.
Editor, *Ten Times Black: Stories from the Black Experience.* New York, Bantam, 1972.

*

Manuscript Collection: Schomburg Collection, New York Public Library.

Critical Studies: *Black Literature in America* by Houston A. Baker, Jr., New York, McGraw Hill, 1971; *From the Dark Tower: Afro-American Writers 1900 to 1960* by Arthur P. Davis, Washington, D.C., Howard University Press, 1974; "The Goal of Julian Mayfield: Fusing Art and Politics" by Hollie I. West, in *Washington Post*, 7 July 1975; interview with Harriet Scarupa, in *New Directions* (Washington, D.C.), April 1979.

* * *

In his ironically titled first novel, *The Hit*, Julian Mayfield guides most of his characters into impasses in which they realize that "the hit," the lucky break, will not come to fulfill their hopes. The exception is the most persistent dreamer, Hubert Cooley, the Black superintendent of four Harlem tenements who bets heavily on the numbers to win the money to go to San Francisco, far from his bothersome wife Gertrude. At the end of the novel, his son James Lee uselessly informs him about John Lewis, the numbers runner who has fled without paying Cooley his forty-two hundred dollars: "He never comes, pop. Don't you see that? John Lewis never really comes." Cooley will not believe that Lewis and Number 417, the hit, are only symbols of the dream deferred.

The widow Sister Clarisse finds that she cannot run away with Cooley, and Gertrude accepts the apparent fact that she will remain unloved by both husband and son. Her son James Lee, too, faces hard reality in his girlfriend Essie's prudent decision—the breakup of her own dream—to end their affair. Weaknesses in character, not just ghetto-narrowed destiny, propel events, and some are related to racial attitudes. Gertrude's selfishness and masochism, for example, contrast with her husband's delusion that being white would eradicate his problems. Generally, people in *The Hit*, trying to escape "the locks and chains of definitions," become "enmeshed by [their] personal Me" (phrases that begin the book) and must emerge into an acceptance of life-without-luck.

In *The Long Night* a numbers hit is again important: sent by his mother to collect her winnings, ten-year-old Steely spends a long night trying to recover the 27 dollars stolen from him by gang members. After failing to get the money through honest work, borrowing, and theft, he gets it from his estranged father, whom he mistakes for a sleeping drunk whose wallet can be lifted. The novel, the simple story of a boy in simple trouble, is able in characterization and in descriptions of Harlem and Manhattan seen through Steely's eyes.

Another ironically named novel, *The Grand Parade*, unfolding complicated machinations by a selfish parade of town officials in fictional Gainesboro, climaxes in Southern-style violence and death at a newly integrated school. Naturalistic and sometimes humorous in its panorama of sex, corruption, betrayals, and bombings, this novel of practical politics has, among its many characters, several that are thematically important. Randy Banks, City Councilman from the Black district, has used politics to escape the powerlessness of his slum origins. Joe Weeks, a skilful behind-the-scenes opportunist and image maker, furnishes Banks's political brains. Their white counterparts are Mayor Douglas Taylor and his mentor, Alex Kochek. The author uses the mayor's ethical ambivalence centrally: to Taylor politics is "the deal forever brewing...climbing forever toward a place, any place, from which one could look down"; yet he considers himself an upright liberal who now and then compromises to pass good laws. Alex, his brilliant adviser known as a "crusader for honesty in government," typically reminds him: "There are no great moral issues in American life today. Only political issues and power struggles."

Mayfield uses some stock figures: Ralph Blackburn, the government agent; Patty Speed, the numbers queen; Reverend Mathews, president of the Negro Progress Association; J.D. Carson, the bold, unscrupulous seeker of power; and Hank Dean, the misfit whose racism partakes of hysteria. Two others, however, are more than types. Clarke Bryant, certain that God and history have made him a racist, rationalizes his exploitations with perverse intelligence. Banks's moral brother Lonnie, expelled from the Communist Party for having expressed his independence and belief in the goodness of man in a "dangerous and counter-revolutionary" paper, ends up friendless and alienated from America, where he "can't get a cup of coffee in most restaurants, can't get a job and can only live in certain areas."

In this political novel (a genre that increasingly attracts Black authors), Mayfield has characters turn their cynicism satirically upon themselves; human rights are no more than a clever insertion into a speech; and the mayor is shot dead for his peace-making remarks outside the school inside which children are singing "My Country 'Tis of Thee." A few years after its publication, the author was at work on another novel whose tentative title, *Look Pretty for the People*, has political overtones. In his novel of 1961, then, his best, Mayfield might have found the mode in which he will excel himself.

—James A. Emanuel

McBAIN, Ed. *See* **HUNTER, Evan.**

McCARTHY, Mary (Therese). American. Born in Seattle, Washington, 21 June 1912. Educated at Forest Ridge Convent, Seattle; Annie Wright Seminary, Tacoma, Washington; Vassar College, Poughkeepsie, New York, A.B. 1933 (Phi Beta Kappa). Married 1) Harold Johnsrud in 1933; 2) the writer Edmund Wilson in 1938, one son; 3) Bowden Broadwater in 1946; 4) James Raymond West in 1961. Editor, Covici Friede, publishers, New York, 1936-38; Editor, 1937-38, and Drama Critic, 1937-62, *Partisan Review*, New Brunswick, New Jersey; Instructor, Bard College, Annandale on Hudson, New York, 1945-46, and Sarah Lawrence College, Bronxville, New York, 1948; Northcliffe Lecturer, University College, London, 1980. Recipient: Guggenheim Fellowship, 1949, 1959; *Horizon* prize, 1949; American Academy grant, 1957. Member, American Academy. D.Let.: Syracuse University, New York, 1973; D.Litt.: University of Hull, Yorkshire, 1974; LL.D.: Aberdeen University, 1979. Address: Castine, Maine 04421, U.S.A.

PUBLICATIONS

Novels

The Company She Keeps. New York, Simon and Schuster, 1942; London, Nicholson and Watson, 1943.
The Oasis. New York, Random House, 1949; as *A Source of Embarrassment*, London, Heinemann, 1950.
The Groves of Academe. New York, Harcourt Brace, 1952; London, Heinemann, 1953.
A Charmed Life. New York, Harcourt Brace, 1955; London, Weidenfeld and Nicolson, 1956.
The Group. New York, Harcourt Brace, and London, Weidenfeld and Nicolson, 1963.
Birds of America. New York, Harcourt Brace, and London, Weidenfeld and Nicolson, 1971.
Cannibals and Missionaries. New York, Harcourt Brace, and London, Weidenfeld and Nicolson, 1979.

Short Stories

Cast a Cold Eye. New York, Harcourt Brace, 1950; London, Heinemann, 1952.

Uncollected Short Stories

"The Company Is Not Responsible," in *New Yorker*, 22 April 1944.
"The Unspoiled Reaction," in *Modern Short Stories*, edited by Marvin Felheim and others. New York, Oxford University Press, 1951.
"The Appalachian Revolution," in *New Yorker*, 11 September 1954.
"Yellowstone Park," in *Prize Stories 1957: The O. Henry Awards*, edited by Paul Engle. New York, Doubleday, 1957.
"Ask Me No Questions," in *Stories from the New Yorker 1950-1960.* New York, Simon and Schuster, 1960.
"The Hounds of Summer," in *Prize Stories 1965: The O. Henry Awards*, edited by Richard Poirier and William Abrahams. New York, Doubleday, 1965.
"Artists in Uniform," in *Modern Short Stories* (revised edition), edited by Arthur Mizener. New York, Norton, 1967.

Other

Sights and Spectacles 1937-1956. New York, Farrar Straus, 1956; as *Sights and Spectacles: Theatre Chronicles 1937-1958*, London, Heinemann, 1959; augmented edition, as *Theatre Chronicles 1937-1962*, Farrar Straus, 1963.
Venice Observed: Comments on Venetian Civilization. Paris, Bernier, and New York, Reynal, 1956; London, Heinemann, 1961.
Memories of a Catholic Girlhood. New York, Harcourt Brace, and London, Heinemann, 1957.
The Stones of Florence. New York, Harcourt Brace, and London, Heinemann, 1959.
On the Contrary (essays). New York, Farrar Straus, 1961; London, Heinemann, 1962.
The Humanist in the Bathtub (essays). New York, New American Library, 1964.
Vietnam. New York, Harcourt Brace, and London, Weidenfeld and Nicolson, 1967.
Hanoi. New York, Harcourt Brace, and London, Weidenfeld and Nicolson, 1968.
The Writing on the Wall and Other Literary Essays. New York, Harcourt Brace, and London, Weidenfeld and Nicolson, 1970.
Medina. New York, Harcourt Brace, 1972; London, Wildwood House, 1973.
The Mask of State: Watergate Portraits. New York, Harcourt Brace, 1974.
The Seventeenth Degree. New York, Harcourt Brace, 1974; London, Weidenfeld and Nicolson, 1975.
Can There Be a Gothic Literature? (lecture). Amsterdam, Harmonie, 1975.
Ideas and the Novel. New York, Harcourt Brace, 1980; London, Weidenfeld and Nicolson, 1981.

Translator, *The Iliad; or, The Poem of Force*, by Simone Weil. New York, Politics, 1948.
Translator, *On the Iliad*, by Rachel Bespaloff. New York, Pantheon, 1948.

*

Bibliography: *Mary McCarthy: A Bibliography* by Sherli Goldman, New York, Harcourt Brace, 1968.

Critical Studies: "Mary McCarthy," in *A View of My Own* by Elizabeth Hardwick, New York, Farrar Straus, 1962, London, Heinemann, 1964; interview with Elisabeth Niebuhr, in *Paris Review*, Winter-Spring 1962; *Mary McCarthy* by Barbara McKenzie, New York, Twayne, 1966; *The Company She Kept* by Doris Grumbach, New York, Coward McCann, and London, Bodley Head, 1967; *Mary McCarthy* by Irvin Stock, Minneapolis, University of Minnesota Press, 1968.

* * *

Mary McCarthy's America is a remarkably small country, inhabited by that equally small group of people she considers worth describing, or since it amounts to the same thing, worth ridiculing. Her young women never seem to go further north than Wellfleet or further south than Washington Square. They come from well-off families, have been expensively educated in the east, and now live in New York or the Connecticut suburbs. They came of age—it would be misleading to say they "grew up"—during the middle years of the Depression, and were married young (and often unhappily) to men whose schools, professions, and attitudes are generally as predictable as their own. Of course a severely limited range of persons and places is not necessarily a handicap; but if a writer is to win anything like the respect and success Mary McCarthy has been enjoying for over 40 years, he needs some collateral virtues. In McCarthy's case, as everyone recognized from the start, the strength comes from her unerring gift for social satire, that species of comedy which thrives on recording the follies of groups rather than stray individuals. This placing of McCarthy works well enough—up to a certain point.

McCarthy's comments about the "comic" are useful here. In

"Characters in Fiction" (*On the Contrary*) she asks, "Who would deny that Stephen Dedalus...seems less 'real' than Mr. Bloom and Molly, less 'real' than his father? In what does this 'reality' consist?" Her answer is as curious as it is revealing: Leopold and Molly Bloom, Falstaff and Mr. Micawber are "real" because of their "incorrigibility and changelessness." By some extraordinary sleight-of-hand McCarthy then makes the "real" and the "comic" synonymous. Heroes and heroines, she maintains, can learn their lessons and change, but "the comic element is the incorrigible element in every human being; the capacity to learn, from experience or instruction, is what is forbidden to all comic creations and to what is comic in you and me." This comic inability to learn and grow is thus more "real," more typical of the way the world is, than any heroic capacity to develop. What is involved here, then, is not simply a literary distinction but a whole set of assumptions about human nature itself. When we do encounter a hero in fiction, we "identify" with him and

> follow him with all our hopes, i.e., with our subjective conviction of human freedom; on the comic characters we look with despair, in which, though, there is a queer kind of admiration—we really, I believe, admire the comic characters *more* than we do the hero or the heroine, because of their obstinate power to do-it-again, combined with a total lack of self-consciousness and shame.

The comic mode is thus "the subjective as opposed to the objective"; but "subjective," for McCarthy, comes perilously close to meaning simply "egotistical," and as she soon suggests, we are left with an all too familiar paradox: we are subjects to ourselves, objects to others. Moreover, we are subjects to ourselves because of our own vanity; we need to *feel* we are free and able to change, whereas in fact we are largely what others see us as being, fixed comic "objects."

An important part of McCarthy's aim as a writer has always been to demonstrate that however free her characters may think they are, they are not free at all, and especially not free of that "subjective" self-love—here she is as obsessed as La Rochefoucauld—which makes them, in their own eyes, capable of growth and therefore some dignity. In passing she concedes that "the principle of growth is as real, of course (though possibly not so common), as the principle of eternity or inertia represented by the comic," but the concession is purely theoretical. No one in her world is free; and her claim that we "admire" the "power" of such characters to "do-it-again" could hardly be more deceptive. We are amused, as she means us to be, by, for example, the pathetic inability of Margaret Sargent, Henry Mulcahy, and Martha Sinnott, *not* to lie (and come to believe the lies), *not* to cheat, and *not* to pick, once again, the fatally wrong lover. Finally McCarthy's conception of comedy seems to have a firm classical basis; it is essentially the revelation of human failings, though not failings so extreme that they arouse in us complete disgust or contempt.

It is easy enough to list the comic objects in McCarthy's fiction. In *The Company She Keeps* and *Cast a Cold Eye* they are the bright young New Yorkers mentioned before; in *A Charmed Life* "creative" upper-Bohemians; in *The Oasis* self-righteous liberals and leftists; in *Cannibals and Missionaries* a deluded group of do-gooders hijacked en route to a futile humanitarian enterprise in Iran. The satire is all the more intriguing when McCarthy lets us glimpse, behind these figures, "real" people—Edmund Wilson, Dwight Macdonald, Philip Rahv, Eugene McCarthy, a good many others, and, always, McCarthy herself. *The Group*, which remains her best-known novel, is no different in kind. It is, she has explained, "a kind of mock-chronicle novel...about the idea of progress...seen in the female sphere": "home economics, architecture, domestic technology, contraception, child-bearing, the study of technology in the home, in the play-pen, in the bed. It's supposed to be the history of the loss of faith in progress, in the idea of progress, during that twenty-year period." "Idea of progress" is perhaps too resounding a phrase: loss of faith in the possibility of fulfillment and, once again, growth would be more accurate. Even so, it is the author and her readers and not the characters themselves who come to realize what has become, on the verge of World War II, of the hopeful, energetic young Vassar graduates, Class of '33.

There is a good deal of cruelty in *The Group*, possibly more than McCarthy intended. And by this time attentive readers should have recognized that "satire" was no longer a very precise label for her art. Traditionally, or at least academically, satire has always been regarded as a kind of comedy which has as its goal the amendment of human folly. By definition, then, the satirist believes he has a remedy, some way of correcting the vices he records, either by urging a return to old values or by proposing a new set of standards. And it is precisely here that McCarthy is silent. She never suggests that things could be changed, never offers any prescriptions for amendment; the alternatives are no better than things she mocks. The fact that she fails to conform to an academic definition is of course irrelevant; but her unwillingness or inability to imagine something better makes her a writer considerably more despairing than readers seem to have realized. In this respect *Birds of America* is her most moving and revealing novel. An engaging young American, Peter Levi, intent on living by the Kantian ethic (treat others as ends in themselves, not as objects or means), encounters a series of rebuffs and disappointments during his junior year abroad. At the close of the novel he is recovering from one of these adventures when he sees a "tiny man" with "something to tell him" by his hospital bed:

> He spoke in a low thin voice. "God is dead," Peter understood him to say. "I *know* that," he protested. "And you didn't say that anyway. Nietzsche did." He felt put upon, as though by an imposter. Kant smiled. "Yes, Nietzsche said that. And even when Nietzsche said it, the news was not new, and maybe not so tragic after all. Mankind can live without God." "I agree," said Peter. "I've always lived without him." "No, what I say to you is something important. You did not hear me correctly. Listen now, carefully and remember." Again he looked Peter steadily and searchingly in the eyes. "Perhaps you have guessed it. Nature is dead, *mein kind*."

There is muted anger in *Birds of America*, and despair, but eloquence as well, and no gratuitous cruelty. For the first time McCarthy has created a completely believable male character and given him the kind of humane sympathy she has always withheld from her central figures and the company they keep.

—Elmer Borklund

McELROY, Joseph. American. Born in Brooklyn, New York, 21 August 1930. Educated at Williams College, Williamstown, Massachusetts, 1947-51, B.A. 1951; Columbia University, New York, 1951-52, 1954-56, M.A. 1952, Ph.D. in English 1961. Served in the United States Coast Guard 1952-54. Married Joan Leftwich in 1961; one daughter. Instructor and Assistant Professor of English, University of New Hampshire, Durham, 1956-61. Since 1964, Professor of English, Queens College, City University of New York. Visiting Professor, Johns Hopkins University, Baltimore, 1976, and Columbia University, 1978; Writer-in-Residence, Northwestern University, Evanston, Illinois, 1977; Hurst Professor, Washington University, St. Louis, 1979. Recipient: Rockefeller grant, 1968; Ingram Merrill Foundation grant, 1970; Creative Artists Public Service grant, 1973; National Endowment for the Arts Fellowship, 1973; Guggenheim Fellowship, 1976; American Academy award, 1977. Agent: Georges Borchardt, 136 East 57th Street, New York, New York 10022, U.S.A.

PUBLICATIONS

Novels

A Smuggler's Bible. New York, Harcourt Brace, 1966; London, Deutsch, 1968.
Hind's Kidnap: A Pastoral on Familiar Airs. New York, Harper, 1969; London, Blond, 1970.
Ancient History. New York, Knopf, 1971.
Lookout Cartridge. New York, Knopf, 1974.
Plus. New York, Knopf, 1977.

Uncollected Short Stories

"The Accident," in *New American Review 2*, edited by Theodore Solotaroff. New York, New American Library, 1967.
"The Future," in *New Yorker*, 22 December 1980.

* * *

I hope that I am writing for readers who would be willing to commit themselves to a strenuous, adventurous fiction, but I don't write fiction of deliberate difficulty. What I believe I am doing is being, possibly in some new way I'm not sure about, a realist. In the collaboration between the syntax of my sentences and the observation of phenomena that is contained in my sentences, I think that I am being faithful as much as I can be to the world that I find with my senses and feel in the forms that are in my mind. I have a choice between going on as I have been or leavening and loosening and to some extent dissolving the surface obstacles that a reader finds reading me. I am trying to write easier prose because I don't think people have time for long books and I am not even sure the human race has a great deal of time. So I want to write easier prose, but what comes out continues to be a sentence which is packed and convoluted (interview with Thomas LeClair, in *Chicago Review*, Spring 1979).

From Melville and James to Faulkner and Pynchon, the most important American novelists have practiced the art of excess, have used mass and multiplicity to present new versions of complexity. Joseph McElroy has extended this tradition to bring into fiction the Age of Information, the world of cybernetics, computers, and space technology. McElroy loads, even overloads, his books with information and techniques that resist the reader to create what he calls "models," fictions that offer systems of relation more congruent with contemporary science than with the mechanism that one finds in most fiction. This description of McElroy's ambition—and achievement—is rather abstract, but the novels are specifically located in recent American life, rich in character and memory, feeling and concern for human survival. Information is used to provide new metaphors, microscopic and macroscopic ways of measuring family experience. While McElroy's originality and intelligence have unfortunately intimidated some readers, his is the kind of work, a fiction of the true leading edge, that seems bound to be valued as more readers come to know what McElroy knows and reflects in his five books.

The complexities of McElroy's first three novels, which lead up to the major achievement of *Lookout Cartridge*, can be suggested by comparing them with the works of writers McElroy discusses in his remarkable autobiographical/critical essay "Neural Neighborhoods and Other Concrete Abstracts" (*Tri-Quarterly 34*, 1975). *A Smuggler's Bible* is an exhaustive novel, similar to Gaddis's *The Recognitions*, about recovering and avoiding the past. McElroy's writer-hero attempts to smuggle himself across boundaries of time and temperament to his dead father, whom he both loves and fears. Like the Bible, the novel is composed of different books and styles; it is an imitative form of continuities and discontinuities, authentic acts and apocryphal gestures. In *Hind's Kidnap* McElroy returns to the search-for-a-father theme, this time using extreme Nabokovian word play to express the difficulty of connecting with the past. The novel's hero, Jack Hind, is a pastoral figure in an urban landscape who realizes, as he attempts to find a kidnapped boy and his own father, that the duplicity of language disallows him a detective's certainty. The languages of city and country, which Hind has used as clues, interpenetrate, foiling both separation and simple unity.

A Smuggler's Bible and *Hind's Kidnap* are ambitious and sophisticated, yet finally exploratory, books. *Ancient History* is less derivative and literary, more confident in the uses to which scientific language and abstract structures can be put. As the anthropologist Cy meditates on his relationship with the polymath Dom, Cy also considers his childhood friends Al and Bob. These A,B,C, D characters are presented as points in space, figures in a field composition influenced by physics. The various languages of space McElroy employs—historical, mathematical, astronomical—give vitality to the familiar materials of friendship and childhood.

Lookout Cartridge is, I think, one of the most underrated books of the decade. It does not humor the reader as Pynchon's *Gravity's Rainbow* does, but McElroy's novel equals that book in its awareness of power and "the great multiple field of impinging informations" in which we make our lives. The novel begins as a linear detective pursuit—the hero Cartwright's trying to locate a stolen film he has shot—and turns into a circling model of collaborating systems as Cartwright has to find his way through natural, political, technological, and spiritual networks of relation. Several dozen British and American characters, pipelines and capillaries of plot, Stonehenge, liquid crystals, cartography, cartridges, and much more combine for a new planetary realism, the plenitude of a fine-linked chain of being. Because McElroy seems to find the world's intricate connections—rather than arbitrarily invent them—*Lookout Cartridge* has the force of fact and the economy of fiction. The style of impacted homologies that McElroy has created is both illustrated and commented on in the following passage: "So much more: not only the idea of the sun cutting across the eyeball as if its vitreous arc were a gate giving a million alignments to that other energy the brain—oh not only the hot god or mere star or grid-fixed force passing from parallel to parallel across that useful fiction the celestial sphere...each day each year each 26,000-year cycle of the whole solar system."

McElroy's most recent novel, *Plus*, is a short tour de force that brings together a stock science-fiction situation—a disembodied brain sent into space—and a radical experiment with language. As the brain, called Imp Plus, begins to grow, it develops its own singular consciousness, a hybrid of neuro-physiology and Gertrude Stein. A moving story of recovery, *Plus* is also a coda to McElroy's career, for this orbiting consciousness Plus, like McElroy, sends back to earth original and large visions of human possibility few other minds have ventured. Plus means positive, and plus means more, and these two meanings also apply to McElroy's art of excess.

—Thomas LeClair

McEWAN, Ian. British. Born in Aldershot, Hampshire, 21 June 1948. Educated at the University of Sussex, Brighton, B.A. (honours) 1970; University of East Anglia, Norwich, M.A. 1971. Recipient: Maugham Award, 1976. Address: c/o Jonathan Cape Ltd., 30 Bedford Square, London WC1B 3EL, England.

PUBLICATIONS

Novels

The Cement Garden. London, Cape, and New York, Simon and Schuster, 1978.

The Comfort of Strangers. London, Cape, and New York, Simon and Schuster, 1981.

Short Stories

First Love, Last Rites. New York, Random House, and London, Cape, 1975.
In Between the Sheets. London, Cape, 1978; New York, Simon and Schuster, 1979.

Uncollected Short Stories

"Intersection," in *Tri-Quarterly* (Evanston, Illinois), Fall 1975.
"Untitled," in *Tri-Quarterly* (Evanston, Illinois), Winter 1976.
"Deep Sleep, Light Sleeper," in *Harpers and Queen* (London), 1978.

Plays

The Imitation Game: Three Plays for Television (includes *Solid Geometry* and *Jack Flea's Birthday Celebration*). London, Cape, 1981.

Radio Play: *Conversation with a Cupboardman*, 1975.

Television Plays: *Jack Flea's Birthday Celebration*, 1976; *The Imitation Game*, 1980.

* * *

During the 1970's, two British prose writers in their twenties established literary reputations for themselves with extraordinary rapidity, both winning the Somerset Maugham Award for their first books, and both achieving a *succès de scandale* as well as critical acclaim. One is Martin Amis; the other, Ian McEwan. Appearing at a time when the media were glibly purveying the modish idea of an unshockable, permissive society, both writers acquired notoriety as "shocking sensationalists" on the basis of work neither shocking nor sensational—except, it appears, in England. Admittedly, McEwan's subject matter is often potentially lurid and pornographic, with sex, perversion, and bodily functions featuring frequently, but his actual treatment of these is highly controlled and even reticent. It is easy to damn McEwan as obscene or praise him as liberated by isolating the "dirty" bits, but both responses reveal more about the commentators than about McEwan since they are based on misrepresentation.

Nevertheless, there is something obsessional in his work, a quality not evident when his stories are read separately, but conspicuous enough when encountered in a collection. Several stories in his first book, *First Love, Last Rites*, include scenes of male masturbation, and the title story involves copulation during menstruation. "Homemade" is about a teenage boy, determined to lose his virginity, who seduces his ten-year-old sister during a game of Mummies and Daddies; "Disguises" treats a teenage boy forced to dress as a girl; "Solid Geometry" features a pickled penis; "Butterflies" concerns a lonely man who almost inadvertently becomes the sex killer of a nine-year-old girl. McEwan's second collection, *In Between the Sheets*, is similar in this respect, featuring bondage, bestiality, a sex doll, and teenage lesbianism, while the first story, actually called "Pornography," culminates in a penis amputation performed as an act of revenge. Although *The Cement Garden* is less replete with the more bizarre and deviant aspects of sexuality, it still contains incest, adolescent sex games, and childhood transvestism. Again there is a considerable emphasis on the sexually confused world of adolescents and teenagers, one of McEwan's favourite subjects and the impulse behind some of his best work.

Yet obsessional as he is, McEwan is no more a pornographer than T.S. Eliot is in that poem full of gloomy sexuality, *The Waste Land.* In a number of his stories, McEwan, too, is depicting an existential void, an emotional and spiritual waste land of frustration, lovelessness, non-communication, isolation, and *la nausée*, and he finds some of his objective correlatives in sexual behaviour. His reputation as a "shocking" writer has probably arisen not because he writes about sex and perversion but because he deals with them in such an anti-romantic and unerotic way. When he focuses on masturbation, or love-making with non-human substitutes, or the link between disease and sex, McEwan severs the connection between sex and meaningful fulfilment and is therefore radically undermining the importance sex has assumed in Western society as a substitute for religion, with orgasm replacing God. One thing McEwan most decidedly is not is titillating.

Sex is an important source of objective correlatives for McEwan, as it was for Eliot, but it is far from being the only one. It is significant that in the first paragraph of *First Love, Last Rites* the narrator of "Homemade" says, "this story is about Raymond and not about virginity, coitus, incest and self-abuse," suggesting that the sex, prominent though it is, is not there just for its own sake. In the ironically entitled "Butterflies" the images of widespread industrial decay, the "brown stinking water" of the canal, and the boys torturing a cat in a scrap yard, all correspond to the emotional sterility, stifled passion, and inner waste land of the narrator himself. The futuristic and dystopian "Two Fragments: March 199-" (*In Between the Sheets*), which is strongly reminiscent of Doris Lessing's *The Memoirs of a Survivor* in its prophetic portrayal of a disintegrating civilization, employs similar imagery to convey McEwan's bleak, joyless vision of the human condition. The house occupied by the orphaned children in *The Cement Garden*, a fable about the fallen and apparently irredeemable world of adolescence and therefore bearing some resemblance to Golding's *Lord of the Flies*, is an island in a sea of demolition and desolation, and the symbolism of this urban wilderness, like that of the nature-destroying cement garden itself, is as clear as those of the polluted Thames and the dust heaps in Dickens's *Our Mutual Friend*, to take an example other than *The Waste Land*.

On the evidence of his three books so far, McEwan seems to be a natural story writer rather than a novelist, although this frequently seems to be the case with writers in their twenties. The outstanding story in his first collection is the title story, "First Love, Last Rites," a complex study of adolescence on the verge of adulthood, awakening to the potency of sexual love, the possibility of parenthood, and the reality of death. This compact and electrifying story builds up to a horrific climax with the brutal killing of a pregnant rat, an event that has a profound effect on the narrator—and on many readers too. The story that stands out in his second collection, on the other hand, is the longest and the only American one, "Psychopolis," a word summing up the city where it is set, Los Angeles, the symbolic "unreal city" of many writers' waste land. While containing an abundance of the "outrageous" ingredients for which he is famous, this story is really about dislocation, incoherence, futility, and the impossibility of achieving wholeness in the pluralist, multi-faceted psychopolis we have created for ourselves where truth is so ambiguous and uncertain. The admirable technical control of his stories is not so evident in *The Cement Garden*, where the first-person narration by a teenager is less consistently sustained than it might be, the adolescent consciousness sometimes appearing to have an adult awareness of the situation.

In devising his own variant of the grotesque, partly by redeeming aspects of sub-literary pulp for serious fiction, McEwan has expanded the parameters of the English short story, taking it into normally taboo areas. At its best, McEwan's writing is powerful, poetic, and original—most reviewers have emphasized the stylishness of his prose—yet he is not altogether immune to the charge that there is something intellectually modish in his underlying nihilism, morbidity, and gothicism. It is possible that he has exhausted a creative vein, and perhaps his next novel will continue the change of direction evident in his impressive television play, *The Imitation Game*.

—Peter Lewis

McGAHERN, John. Irish. Born in Dublin, 12 November 1934. Educated at St. Patrick's, Dublin; University College, Dublin. Married Madeline Green in 1973. Primary School Teacher. Research Fellow, University of Reading, Berkshire, 1968; Visiting O'Connor Professor of Literature, Colgate University, Hamilton, New York, 1969, 1972, 1978, 1980; Northern Arts Fellow, University of Newcastle, 1974-76. Recipient: A E Memorial Award, 1962; Macauley Fellowship, 1964; Arts Council Award, 1966, 1968, 1971, 1978; Society of Authors Travelling Scholarship, 1975. Address: c/o Faber and Faber Ltd., 3 Queen Square, London WC1N 3AU, England.

PUBLICATIONS

Novels

The Barracks. London, Faber, 1963; New York, Macmillan, 1964.
The Dark. London, Faber, 1965; New York, Knopf, 1966.
The Leavetaking. London, Faber, 1974; Boston, Little Brown, 1975.
The Pornographer. London, Faber, and New York, Harper, 1979.

Short Stories

Nightlines. London, Faber, 1970; Boston, Little Brown, 1971.
Getting Through. London, Faber, 1978; New York, Harper, 1980.

Uncollected Short Story

"The Gold Watch," in *New Yorker*, 17 March 1980.

Plays

Sinclair (broadcast, 1971; produced London, 1972).

Radio Play: *Sinclair*, 1971.

Television Play: *Swallows*, 1975.

* * *

John McGahern achieved immediate fame with his first novel, *The Barracks*. The opening scene—a kitchen interior with a woman darning in the dying twilight, surrounded by her stepchildren—seemed as comfortable as the first act of an old Abbey play. What was new and startling was the quality of the writing; Irish provincial life had never been transcribed with such exactness before. Lovingly recorded, the details are yet presented without any protective sentimentality. Regionalists like Francis MacManus and Michael MacLaverty had evoked the details of Irish country life as part of a pattern, a way of belief, suggesting that unhurriedness was all. But McGahern rips all this away, showing that man, as well as nature, was as "red in tooth and claw" in Ireland as elsewhere: "They all lived on each other and devoured each other as they themselves were devoured, who would devour whom the first was the one question."

So Elizabeth Regan reflects at the end of her life, the end of the book. This brilliant study (especially for a young writer in his mid-twenties) of the mind of a dying woman inevitably recalls *Madame Bovary*, both in its subject-matter and the poetic detail of its style. But if McGahern's work is technically anachronistic there is a dimension of sympathy which is absent in Flaubert. Emma Bovary's death is recorded with clinical distaste; although there is a brief look of peace on her face when she receives the Last Sacraments, she never breaks through to the almost mystical acceptance of Elizabeth Regan: "All real seeing grew into smiling and if it moved to speech it must be praise."

The other main character in *The Barracks* is not a seducer but a police sergeant, more pathetic even than his sick wife in his baffled, male violence. This dominant figure appears again in *The Dark* where the ebb and flow of his struggle with his eldest son provide most of the structure of the book. Now all feminine gentleness has disappeared, and McGahern's keening rage against the emptiness of life takes over. Like the adolescent hero we are soiled and insulted by the ordeal of growing up under the double pressures of poverty and piety. Short chapters and flowing, often punctuationless sentences, leave no escape: we have moved from the calm detail of Flaubert to the involving claustrophobia of a Mauriac. But we are not allowed the grim consolations of Jansenism: it is not evil which rules the world but the hopeless clash of our needs. "It seemed that the whole world must turn over in the night and howl in its boredom...."

There is no alleviation of this vision in his collection of stories, *Nightlines*, but there are some extensions of theme and background. "Summer in Strandhill," "Bomb Box," "Korea," still focus on the narrow world of childhood, with its humiliations and adult enforced boredom. There is, however, a more varied treatment of sex; the stories move from the familiar initiation theme of "Coming into His Kingdom," through the youthful frustration of "My Love, My Umbrella," to the analysis of a disintegrating marriage in "Peaches." The latter is set in Spain, but neither travel nor love can finally dissolve childhood patterns of guilt and conflict, and we are left with the crude message of the story about building site labourers in London, "Lungs of Oak and Bellies of Brass": "pork chops, pints of bitter and a good old ride before you sleep, that's fukken ambition." McGahern's stripped style, his emotional honesty, and his ear for dialogue make him a harrowing witness of the void which underlies a good deal of Irish, and perhaps modern, life.

To redeem that void there is only the meaning which memory can draw from the past, and the search for love in the present. "If I was lucky I'd find someone I liked as well as loved, the dream of a friend and a beloved in one, a person as well as a body." In *The Leavetaking* the protagonist has suffered a great hurt in his youth, the death by cancer of his beloved mother. Years later he discovers a love to redeem the old but because she is a divorcée he will have to leave his job as a teacher in a Catholic school. The book is structured around the ebb and flow of his thoughts, which later join or parallel those of his beloved. Only those who have been hurt, the implication is, can solace each other; she is guarded by a gigolo father whom, like the school authorities, the main character has to face down. It is a relatively slight novel, and the international world of the divorcée and her parasite father are more exhibited than felt, but there are tenderness and honesty in the love scenes—a new note in McGahern.

Getting Through again shows that McGahern can ring changes on the traditional Irish short story, but it is *The Pornographer*, a novel which seems to guy his twin obsessions with death and sex, which represents a real advance. "Write it like a life, but with none of life's unseemly infirmities," prescribes his editor, a failed poet, to the pornographer narrator. Meanwhile the latter's aunt is dying of cancer, and he gets involved with a woman, who gets pregnant and flees to London. This tragicomedy of "life's unseemly infirmities" ends with a funeral, like *The Barracks*, but the wild dance of opposites, country and town, love and death, Dublin and London, makes for a harsher, more ironic statement.

—John Montague

McGUANE, Thomas (Francis, III). American. Born in Michigan, 11 December 1939. Educated at Michigan State University, East Lansing, B.A.; Yale University, New Haven, Connecticut, M.F.A.; Stanford University, California (Wallace Stegner Fellow), 1965. Since 1968, free-lance writer and film director. Recipient: Rosenthal Foundation Award, 1972. Agent: John Hawkins, Paul R. Reynolds Inc., 12 East 41st Street, New York, New York 10017. Address: Route 38, Livingston, Montana 59047, U.S.A.

PUBLICATIONS

Novels

The Sporting Club. New York, Simon and Schuster, 1968; London, Deutsch, 1969.
The Bushwhacked Piano. New York, Simon and Schuster, 1971.
Ninety-Two in the Shade. New York, Farrar Straus, 1973; London, Collins, 1974.
Panama. New York, Farrar Straus, 1978.

Uncollected Short Story

"Another Horse," in *Atlantic* (Boston), October 1974.

Plays

Screenplays: *The Bushwhacked Piano*, 1970; *Rancho Deluxe*, 1973; *The Missouri Breaks*, 1975; *Ninety-Two in the Shade*, 1975; *Tom Horn*, with Bud Shrake, 1980.

Other

An Outside Chance: Essays on Sport. New York, Farrar Straus, 1980.

*

Manuscript Collection: University of Rochester, New York.

Theatrical Activities:

Director: **Film**—*Ninety-Two in the Shade*, 1975.

Thomas McGuane comments:

I write fiction in the hope of astounding myself. I am seldom successful, and have long ago lost interest in the rest of my audience.

* * *

Mortality, madness, and merry diversion abound in Thomas McGuane's work. *The Sporting Club* depicts the destruction of a fish and game preserve owned by wealthy weekend sportsmen. The club's members (especially Spengler) are convinced of its noble heritage; but, during their centennial celebration—a parody of American's past glories—they discover that their predecessors were perverts. Witnesses to the club's demise are James Quinn, a Detroit businessman who visits the club to relax, and Vernor Stanton, an eccentric who will not permit the club any self-delusion. A literary descendant of Donleavy's Ginger Man, Stanton treats the world "like the shit it is." He suffers from boredom and a sense of doom, which he repels with plenty of hell-raising, pistol-dueling, role-playing, travel, and inanity.

To disrupt the club Stanton gets its superior but resented sportsman-manager fired. The new manager, Earl Olive, is a sloppy bait (not fly) fisherman whose motorcycling, fornicating friends rut around the preserve, upsetting the old guard. Challenged to a mock, wax-ball duel with Stanton, Olive loses but begins dynamiting the preserve out of revenge. Stanton is delighted. But for him and Quinn there is no transcending the muck. Vernor ends the novel insane and "compromised," the "happy" new owner of the preserve but without his pistols.

Whereas *The Sporting Club* ends with the insanity of its main character, *The Bushwhacked Piano* begins with the "lunacy" of Nicholas Payne—a lunacy stemming from his recognition of mortality and suggested by his youthful gunning (bushwhacking) of a neighbor's piano. Partly recuperated from his malaise, Nick lives a *non-serviam* life of silliness, lousing up "monuments," inventing himself "*ab ovo*" because that is the "only crack at release from the bondage of time." With Ann Fitzgerald, a rich Detroit girl, he falls in love. She is a photography enthusiast (oblivious to the industrial ugliness around her), preferring for a time Payne's irrationality to her other boyfriend's G.M. "calculations."

Money-minded and "fussy," Ann's parents don't like Payne; and so they take her off to a Montana ranch. Nick pursues, traveling digressively like a caromed billiard ball (a favorite image of McGuane's), becoming a bronco rider, teaming up with one C.J. Clovis to build a tower for mosquito-eating bats, and finally reaching Ann's place. After upsetting the elder Fitzgeralds with his philosophy of "fun," Payne runs off to Key West, Florida, with Ann and Clovis—there to build another bat tower. In Key West, Nick has a bizarre hemorrhoidectomy; and Ann leaves for her G.M. boyfriend. At the dedication of the bat tower, Payne confesses its inflated price; and Clovis dies mysteriously with a heart on the "fritz." Nick is arrested for fraud and forced to enact his trial on *Night Court*, a television program. Exhibited in Ann's first photography show as "a cautionary monument of the failed life," this anti-hero thinks he is finally understood.

Like *The Bushwhacked Piano*, *Ninety-Two in the Shade* begins with a half-crazy character, Tom Skelton. Tom has never acted instinctively or "followed through." As a marine biology student, he lost the sense of life's mystery; and so he decides to become a fishing guide. Like Nick Payne, Skelton is inventing himself. He has learned from his father that the "general view [of experience] is tragic; but...the trick" is "to become interested in something else. Look askance and it all shines." Unfortunately, Tom's career choice conflicts with a gun-toting guide named Nichol Dance, whom Skelton admires for the ability to follow through. Not wanting extra competition, Dance tells Tom to forget guiding or else. Again using the image of billiard balls but in a new way, McGuane suggests that certain lives are bound to collide. As the butt of a practical joke by Dance, Skelton responds by burning Nichol's skiff and resolving to guide. Like Vernor Stanton, Tom does not wish to die but instead give life meaning by raising its tension. During his last few days, he enjoys his girlfriend more than ever and learns from his father that the greatest "power," more heroic than the financial empire built by Tom's grandad, is to face life's abyss, laugh, and follow through. Thus, "on the margin of a horselaugh magnanimity that reveals new things under heaven," Skelton follows through with Dance; and "the question of his courage...was answered.... It was the discovery of his life."

Through wit, parody, and ridiculous but ultimately sobering practical jokes, McGuane bursts many contemporary delusions about individuality and American "snivelization." His fiction is a humorous and sometimes meaningful extension of Anna Wulf's assessment of today's malaise (in Doris Lessing's *The Golden Notebook*): "...sometimes I meet people and...the fact they are cracked across, they're split, means they are keeping themselves open for something."

—Dennis M. Welch

McHALE, Tom. American. Grew up in Scranton, Pennsylvania. Educated at Jesuit schools; Temple University, Philadelphia, B.S. 1963; University of Pennsylvania, Philadelphia; University of Iowa, Iowa City. Since 1971, Writer-in-Residence, Monmouth College, West Long Branch, New Jersey. Recipient: Guggenheim Fellowship, 1974; Thomas More Association Medal, 1976. Address: 40 Mt. Vernon Street, Boston, Massachusetts 02108, U.S.A.

PUBLICATIONS

Novels

Principato. New York, Viking Press, 1970; London, Joseph, 1971.
Farragan's Retreat. New York, Viking Press, and London, Joseph, 1971.
Dooley's Delusion. Atlanta, Droke Hallux, 1971.
Alinsky's Diamond: A Love Story. Philadelphia, Lippincott, 1974.
School Spirit. New York, Doubleday, 1976.
The Lady from Boston. New York, Doubleday, 1978.

* * *

Joseph Heller's *Catch-22* established the popularity of the absurdist novel for the 1960's. Among the lesser writers who explored this position in the 1970's is Tom McHale, whose first two novels are tragi-comic, nihilistic, yet sympathetic to the pains of the protagonists. Both Angelo Principato of *Principato* and Arthur Farragan of *Farragan's Retreat* are destroyed by their growing ability to see through the categories of presumed reality, and by their half optimistic, half mindless decency.

The treatment of these Candides, however, is Rabelaisian. A host of absurdly cruel, crass, and improbable incidents contrive to teach them that everything is the opposite of what it seems. The Mother Superior encourages Principato's nun-sister to meet her lover in the convent, and Farragan's frigid, pious, loony wife swings with a supposedly castrated lifeguard. Both protagonists are men who too rapidly begin seeing these impossible realities. However, in *Principato* we are given a man who is disillusioned as the accidents of life and the manipulations of his father show him the truth behind appearances, while Arthur Farragan's existential sufferings derive, the end reveals, from his own actions.

"The church," Nick tells Principato, "is a frigging cancer. You're either with it all the way like you, or limping along outside within shouting distance like me. But you never really get free of it." McHale himself is not limping, but vigorously running in a ring around the rosary. The Catholic motif is everywhere, the Catholicism of the characters essentially informs their actions, and yet the novels are remote from the Catholic novel of Evelyn Waugh and Graham Greene. These are not crises of soul and self, but pseudo-involvements with the symbols of the matter. Principato's wife lusts unashamedly after her young neighbor while staring at the four-foot tall luminescent statue of the Virgin Mary he has given her. Farragan's sister Anna keeps a rosary wrapped around the pistol she carries, to insure perfect aim on the inevitable day a black rapist attacks her. Flocks of St. Christopher's medals and flocks of avaricious priests suggest the cancerous pervasiveness of the Church.

Nevertheless, it is not the often pointed-up corruptions of the Church, but those of the people which are significant. And in many cases the point is not that the Church has corrupted them, but that it can be used as an excuse for their brutal behaviour. McHale's families are pious, rich, shanty Irish Philadelphians. Mother Corrigan of *Principato* is echoed in "the one, true Mother" Farragan, and her clan's primal devotion to her, a devotion little changed by their discovery that she sent one brother to death in the war, not because she believed in patriotism (like the Church, patriotism is an excuse), but because she had caught him in a homosexual act. These mothers, like the police, "have the key to everything."

McHale's characterizations are brutal, multi-dimensional caricatures; the children of the weak Angelo Principato are so lifeless they literally shun the sun like moles; his crippled brother is both childishly and sexually sadistic. These characters are frequently discovered by the protagonists in scenes which fix into tableaus and which they watch with a hypnotized terror.

McHale's later novels are less impressive, though still concerned with some of the themes of his first two novels. *Alinsky's Diamond* is a caper novel involving a religious pilgrimage to Jerusalem. *School Spirit* is a thriller mixed with Catholic black humor, and *The Lady from Boston* mixes a wild plot with a political theme.

—Jeanne Desy

McMURTRY, Larry (Jeff). American. Born in Wichita Falls, Texas, 3 June 1936. Educated at North Texas State College, Denton, B.A. 1958; Rice University, Houston, M.A. 1960; Stanford University, California (Wallace Stegner Fellow). Married Josephine Ballard in 1959; one son. Formerly, Lecturer in English, Rice University. Recipient: Guggenheim grant, 1964. Agent: Dorothea Oppenheimer, 52 Wall Street, Room 1052, New York, New York 10005. Address: P.O. Box 126, Waterford, Virginia 24450, U.S.A.

PUBLICATIONS

Novels

Horseman, Pass By. New York, Harper, 1961; as *Hud*, New York, Popular Library, 1963; London, Sphere, 1971.
Leaving Cheyenne. New York, Harper, 1963; London, Sphere, 1972.
The Last Picture Show. New York, Dial Press, 1966; London, Sphere, 1972.
Moving On. New York, Simon and Schuster, 1970; London, Weidenfeld and Nicolson, 1971.
All My Friends Are Going to Be Strangers. New York, Simon and Schuster, 1972; London, Secker and Warburg, 1973.
Terms of Endearment. New York, Simon and Schuster, 1975; London, W.H. Allen, 1977.
Somebody's Darling. New York, Simon and Schuster, 1978.

Uncollected Short Story

"There Will Be Peace in Korea," in *Texas Quarterly* (Austin), Winter 1964.

Other

In a Narrow Grave: Essays on Texas. Austin, Texas, Encino Press, 1968.
It's Always We Rambled: An Essay on Rodeo. New York, Frank Hallman, 1974.
Larry McMurtry: Unredeemed Dreams, edited by Dorey Schmidt. Edinburgh, Texas, Pan American University, 1980.

*

Critical Studies: *Larry McMurtry* by Thomas Landess, Austin, Texas, Steck Vaughn, 1969; *The Ghost Country: A Study of the Novels of Larry McMurtry* by Raymond L. Neinstein, Berkeley, California, Creative Arts, 1976; *Larry McMurtry* by Charles D. Peavy, Boston, Twayne, 1977.

* * *

The literature of the American West that most of us know (those stories of peace officers and outlaws) is inspired by nostalgia and aims to give heroic dimensions to characters and events. The elegiac titles of Larry McMurtry's early novels reveal their link to the popular genre, but in their development they are founded upon such detail of foreground landscape, vascular spoken language, vital character description, and realistic conception as make fictional events memorable for their authenticity rather than mythic effect.

McMurtry's first two novels present the distinctly contrasting lives of cowboys and ranchers. In *Horseman, Pass By* he uses the perspective of a 17-year-old boy to record the calamitous season when disease infects his elderly grandfather's herd of cattle. The boy does not reflect upon the drama, but it is clear that its theme is the passing of a way of ranching that had begun in the previous century. The cattle are destroyed by order of government agricultural agents acting to protect the commercial investment of the region, and Homer Bannon, too old to start anew, can do nothing but retreat mentally into his past. Arrogant, amoral "Hud," Homer's stepson, speaks of resistance to the government as if he were a plains anarchist. Calamity, however, is simply an opportunity he grasps for gaining control of the ranch. Hud is a man of the future despite his cowboy's style.

Leaving Cheyenne pairs a genuine cowboy, Johnny, with another rancher, Gid, in a tale of the way their lives from boyhood to old age interweave through work and their mutual devotion to the spontaneous Molly. Johnny, the free worker, moves as he wishes, always content to be the hired hand, while Gid, despite unusual skills as a bronc buster, cannot help but be entranced by the thought of the money to be made dealing in cattle and land. Each man lives as a unique personality; yet the casual joy experienced by the one and the guilt felt by the other in loving Molly urge the reader to understand them also as psycho-historical types. The rancher loves the land, but the desire to be its respectable master foreshadows eventual conversion to big business ranching. The cowboy acts as the complete individualist but is anachronistic almost from the start, since his way of life is dependent upon the ranchers.

The tone of each of McMurtry's works is carefully located in the range of comic distance, and the compelling expressions of particularity in character behavior keep our attention upon immediate events. Thus, *The Last Picture Show* evokes first of all recognition of the foolish-serious ways high-school-age boys center their lives upon gratification of their sexual desires. The lives of adults appearing also in terms of their intimate relationships enter the story first as backdrop then gradually become future options, but ones poorly understood. People describe the good and bad breaks in their lives, while all the time fate is beyond them in the impersonal forces that determine the lives of whole towns.

In his novels published during the 1970's McMurtry focuses upon the present that once was future. As regional life no longer provides definition he relates the tales of people moving about in the medium of cities and mass culture. Restless characters pair briefly until they change their lives by acquiring new sexual partners and irresolutely devote themselves to role after role. Passing through the concretely realized settings of the rodeo circuit and the graduate student community Pete and Patsy Carpenter of *Moving On* speak a language reminiscent of the source of their affluence in an older Texas, but each of the cultural orbits into which they veer is a second-hand interpretation of reality. The rodeo, which Pete wishes to capture in a book of photographs, is a ritualization of cowboy skill; a motion picture he works on idealizes a rodeo celebrity; and the graduate study of literature consists of boning up on criticism and making fetishes of first editions. The memorialized past no longer has use; it has become currency of exchange among the alienated.

A character named Danny Deck who is briefly introduced in *Moving On* as a sort of tragic hero for the rootless young people becomes the main figure in *All My Friends Are Going to Be Strangers*. His story bluntly presents the dilemma of the new free-floating culture. Deck, as restless as his contemporaries, nevertheless attains the control to complete a novel, but the achievement is insufficient to give him security. He wades into a river, like a land-locked Martin Eden, destroying his work and himself. The act is both an assertion of residual individualism and evidence of hopelessness before the task of discovering what values might be created in the new America.

Though integrity eludes his characters, it is present in the formal development of McMurtry's fictional project. In a culture bereft of fixed roles to define character, the self must rely on personality, so it is necessary that the self-centered Aurora Greenway—a woman who capitalizes the promise of sexuality—should dominate the narrative in *Terms of Endearment* just as she seeks to prevail over the lives of her daughter and suitors. So, too, the fluidity of self-definition requires the shifting perspectives with which Jill Peel's nervous advancement as a film artist is related in *Somebody's Darling*. Finally the cross-references among the 1970's novels, and their portrayal of a loosely acquainted and large cast of contemporary figures who surface in each others' picaresque lives, show McMurtry taking on the production of a chronicle of our times as the imperative of his narrative.

—John M. Reilly

McNEISH, James (Henry Peter). New Zealander. Born in Auckland, 23 October 1931. Educated at the University of Auckland, B.A. in languages 1953. Served in the Territorial Army, 1954-55. Married 1) Felicity Wily in 1960 (divorced, 1964), one daughter; 2) Helen Schnitzer in 1968, one son. Arts Editor, *New Zealand Herald*, Auckland, 1955-58; teacher, Peckham Manor School, London, 1959-60; sociologist, Danilo Dolci Organization, Sicily, 1961-64. Since 1960, free-lance producer for BBC Radio, Radio New Zealand, and Canadian Broadcasting Corporation. Recipient: Katherine Mansfield Fellowship, 1973; New Zealand Government Scholarship, 1979. Agent: George Greenfield, John Farquharson Ltd., 8 Bell Yard, London WC2A 2JU, England. Address: Private Bag, Kawhia, New Zealand.

PUBLICATIONS

Novels

Mackenzie. London, Hodder and Stoughton, 1970.
The Mackenzie Affair. Auckland, Hodder and Stoughton, 1972.
The Glass Zoo. London, Hodder and Stoughton, and New York, St. Martin's Press, 1976.

Plays

The Rocking Cave (produced Auckland, 1973).
The Mouse Man (produced Auckland, 1975).
1 8 9 5 (produced Auckland, 1975).

Radio Plays and Documentaries: *Diary of a Fast*, 1963 (UK); *Power Is Sweeter Than Love*, 1965 (UK); *The Black Madonna*, 1966 (UK); *To the End of the Earth*, 1968 (Canada); *The Last Colony*, 1974 (Canada); *A Great War in Miniature*, 1975 (UK).

Other

Tavern in the Town (social history). Wellington, Reed, 1957.
Fire under the Ashes: The Life of Danilo Dolci. London, Hodder and Stoughton, 1965; Boston, Beacon Press, 1966.
Larks in a Paradise: New Zealand Portraits, photographs by Marti Friedlander. Auckland and London, Collins, 1974.
As for the Godwits (autobiography). Auckland and London, Hodder and Stoughton, 1977.
Art of the Pacific, with David Simmons, photographs by Brian Brake. Wellington, Oxford University Press, and New York, Abrams, 1980.
Belonging: Conversations with Men and Women Who Have Chosen to Make Israel Their Home. New York, Holt Rinehart, and London, Collins, 1980.

James McNeish comments:

What interests me is: minorities in society; the underdog in society; isolation; pressures on the individual by the community to conform.

What concerns me is: the levelling effect of modern egalitarianism; alienation; waste; injustice.

I hope that these interests and concerns are reflected in my novels and plays.

* * *

In his three novels James McNeish has demonstrated rare artistic vigour and precision. A major source of his strength as a writer rests on a paradox: he is a distinctly New Zealand artist because of the influence European culture has on his craft. One can discern in his novels a strong dichotomy and tension between two worlds, the uncompromised natural world rich with the passion and imponderables of life, and an opposite mundane world of civilized rationality and entrenched values.

Just as this relationship in McNeish's novels is not a simple contrast between New Zealand and Europe, neither is McNeish content to exalt the natural over the mundane world. Herein lies both the particularity and universality of his fiction. The characters and situations, regardless of their physical setting, often seem to crystallize the ambivalent and divided loyalties of a writer like McNeish—or for that matter, Katherine Mansfield—who feels not only the power and timelessness of the land, and the deep human emotions this implies, but also the stimulation of the European corpus of knowledge and tradition, however decadent and ossified this may be. This dynamic interaction gives McNeish's novels a breadth and clarity of vision, accentuated by his skilful prose and authoritative command of detail.

"You are a bloody Kiwi, you haf not such rules," says Stepan to Ralph Stanton in *The Glass Zoo*, referring to England's social mores. Stanton is isolated in London, teaching at a comprehensive school, and recalling the lupins and equinoctial gales of his homeland. In *Mackenzie*, set in the New Zealand of 1855, this sense of the Old World's hidebound code is no less apparent. The three pillars of English society—"nepotism, hypocrisy, and public piety"—are disparaged, and Sparrow, the missionary, implicitly provides Christianity with a rival by saying that the Maoris' system of cosmic order rivals Genesis. Yet it is significant that Sparrow falls back on the Bible, for he attempts to convert the natives after all. The Old World is building itself anew. Polson considers he has burnt his boats with England, but he keeps up his ties with Europe in buying old copies of *The Times*. Amidst this natural world, with its "Rousseau-like landscape," the settlers plot further land-grabbing expeditions, and the governor tells Polson that even here "honesty and self-criticism are the last requirements of a public man."

In many ways the settlers are serpents in Paradise but the experience does not leave them untouched. Frances, Polson's daughter, does not occupy a traditional feminine role. She is independent and assertive as well as practical; after riding she declares, "I've never been more filthy in my life and yet I feel somehow *cleansed*." Like her, Ralph Stanton is partially altered by an alien environment. "You have no code. It's a colonial thing possibly," the deputy headmaster tells him, but Stanton has the knowledge of the Old World as well, and this potentiality is activated in successfully helping the schoolboy Marsh.

In fact, it is Marsh who stands as a pure symbol of the natural world. Together with James Mackenzie of the first novel, he is McNeish's evocation of the uncompromised flame of life. Their unalloyed essence prevents them from adapting to societies which are kaleidescopes of variegated greys, and their talents are wasted. Marsh, a genius, escapes being convicted of murder, but even with his ability recognized family and class prevent him from realizing himself. He remains "just another casualty, a case of the damage education can do to the intelligence." Mackenzie, a shepherd without a home but able to straddle all cultures—the Maoris call him the Dreamer—discovers a new land beyond the New Zealand alps, but mercifully dies through nature before he sees his Erewhon turned into a "little English garden." Throughout, Mackenzie remains incorruptible amid injustice and waste.

In his fiction, then, James McNeish clearly articulates the tragedy of human society unable to rise above the ashes of its own condition and consuming those rare individuals not of this Earthly City. McNeish is comparable to the New Zealander in Macaulay's prophecy, who sketches the ruins of St. Paul's from a broken arch of London Bridge and in doing so thereby perpetuates the efficacy of the Old World and the continued postponement of a truly uncompromised way of life.

—Paul F. Field

McPHERSON, James A(lan). American. Born in Savannah, Georgia, 16 September 1943. Educated at Morgan State College, Baltimore, 1963-64; Morris Brown College, Atlanta, B.A. 1965; Harvard University, Cambridge, Massachusetts, LL.B. 1968; University of Iowa, Iowa City, M.F.A. 1969. Instructor, University of Iowa Law School, 1968-69; member of the faculty, University of California, Santa Cruz, 1969-70. Since 1969, Contributing Editor, *Atlantic Monthly*, Boston. Recipient: American Academy Award, 1970; Guggenheim Fellowship, 1972; Pulitzer Prize, 1978. Agent: Carl Brandt, Brandt and Brandt Inc., 101 Park Avenue, New York, New York 10017. Address: c/o Little Brown and Company, 34 Beacon Street, Boston, Massachusetts 02106, U.S.A.

PUBLICATIONS

Short Stories

Hue and Cry. Boston, Little Brown, and London, Macmillan, 1969.
Elbow Room. Boston, Little Brown, 1977.

Other

Railroad: Trains and Train People in American Culture, with Miller Williams. New York, Random House, 1976.

* * *

In two collections of brilliant short fiction, James A. McPherson has surveyed contemporary black American culture and defined its sensibility. His work, sharply realistic and dramatic, focuses on the connections and abrasions of black and white individuals in our time. The insights accumulated in the stories form a comprehensive mosaic of U.S. life as viewed by black citizens.

Hue and Cry, McPherson's first collection, revolves around the world of work and black positions in it. The stories deal with "traditional" black occupations—waiter, Pullman porter, stockboy, janitor—from the inside, where each position is a window on the white world. McPherson's controlled, incisive style offers shrewdly defined character-types almost mythic in proportion. Stories like "A Solo Song: For Doc," which describes the end of a man's lifelong career as a railroad waiter, offer important illuminations on daily life for black people in America. "Gold Coast" and "Hue and Cry," two of the best-known stories of the book, deal directly with the tensions and tragic ironies of black-white sexual relationships.

The stories in *Elbow Room* are more complex extensions of McPherson's concerns. His narrative style is often dense and subtle, but his focus is still on archetypal characters and situations. "The Story of a Dead Man," for example, is a kind of bad-man ballad contrasting a near-mythic "bad nigger" with his educated, upwardly mobile nephew. This "Railroad Bill" character is a fighting, lying wanderer whose existence embarrasses blacks aspiring to gentility in white middle-class terms. The same theme emerges in "Elbow Room," which describes the marriage of a young white draft-resister to a sharp, urbane black woman. It is narrated by a black consciousness tormented with problems of definition. The young white man is obsessed with the question "What is a nigger?" He finally bursts out:

> "At *least* I tried! At *least* I'm *fighting!* And I know what a *nigger* is, too. It's what you are when you begin thinking of yourself as a work of art!"
> I did not turn to answer, although I heard him clearly. I am certain there was no arrogance at all left in his voice.

James McPherson has used the medium of the short story to extend the intense meditations on black Americans begun by Ralph Ellison in *Invisible Man*. McPherson's stories are carefully crafted, subtle and penetrating observations of the range and variety of the contemporary black experience. His characters are vivid storytellers, too, and he captures their inflections and idioms precisely. His people—black and white—struggle to know themselves and each other, to penetrate the barriers of appearances to the central mysteries of being. As the narrator of "Just Enough for the City" expresses it:

> I think love must be the ability to suspend one's intelligence for the sake of something. At the basis of love therefore must be imagination. Instead of thinking always "*I am I*," to love one must be able to feelingly conjugate the verb *to be*. Intuition must be part of the circuitous pathway leading ultimately to love.

This seeking for love and identity, love for self and others, the world itself, is at the center of McPherson's stories. His people become visible to others because they learn to see themselves.

—William J. Schafer

MENEN, (Salvator) Aubrey (Clarence). British. Born in London, 22 April 1912. Educated at University College, London, 1930-32. Drama Critic, *The Bookman*, London, 1934; Director, The Experimental Theatre, London, 1935-36; worked for Personalities Press Service, London, 1937-39. Head of the English Drama Department, All-India Radio, 1940-41; Script Editor, Information Films, Government of India, 1943-45; Education Officer, Backward Tribes, Indian Political Department, 1946; Head of the Motion Picture Department, J. Walter Thompson Company, London, 1947-48. Now lives in Italy. Address: c/o Peggy Tsukahira, McGraw-Hill Book Company, 1221 Avenue of the Americas, New York, New York 10020, U.S.A.

PUBLICATIONS

Novels

The Prevalence of Witches. London, Chatto and Windus, 1947; New York, Scribner, 1948.
The Stumbling-Stone. London, Chatto and Windus, and New York, Scribner, 1949.
The Backward Bride: A Sicilian Scherzo. London, Chatto and Windus, and New York, Scribner, 1950.
The Duke of Gallodoro. London, Chatto and Windus, and New York, Scribner, 1952.
Rama Retold. London, Chatto and Windus, 1954; as *The Ramayana*, New York, Scribner, 1954.
The Abode of Love: The Conception, Financing and Daily Routine of an English Harem in the Middle of the Nineteenth Century Described in the Form of a Novel. New York, Scribner, 1956; London, Chatto and Windus, 1957.
The Fig Tree. London, Chatto and Windus, and New York, Scribner, 1959.
SheLa: A Satire. New York, Random House, 1962; London, Hamish Hamilton, 1963.
A Conspiracy of Women. New York, Random House, 1965; London, Hamish Hamilton, 1966.
Fonthill: A Comedy. New York, Putnam, 1974; London, Hamish Hamilton, 1975.

Play

The Mysterious Universe, music and lyrics by Peter Mendoza and Reginald Barstow, adaptation of the book by Sir James Jeans (also director: produced London, 1935).

Other

Dead Man in the Silver Market. New York, Scribner, 1953; as *Dead Man in the Silver Market: An Autobiographical Essay on National Prides*, London, Chatto and Windus, 1954.
Rome for Ourselves. New York, McGraw Hill, 1960; as *Rome Revealed*, London, Thames and Hudson, 1960.
Speaking the Language Like a Native: Aubrey Menen on Italy. New York, McGraw Hill, 1962; London, Hamish Hamilton, 1963.
India. New York, McGraw Hill, and London, Thames and Hudson, 1969.
The Space Within the Heart (autobiography). New York, McGraw Hill, and London, Hamish Hamilton, 1970.
Upon This Rock (on St. Peter's). New York, Saturday Review Press, 1972.
Cities in the Sand. London, Thames and Hudson, 1972; New York, Dial Press, 1973.
The New Mystics and the True Indian Tradition, with Graham Hall. London, Thames and Hudson, 1974; as *The Mystics*, New York, Dial Press, 1974.
London, with the editors of Time-Life Books, photographs by Brian Seed. New York, Time Life, 1976.
Venice, with the editors of Time-Life Books, photographs by Ernst Haas. New York, Time Life, 1976.
Four Days of Naples. New York, Seaview, 1979.
Art and Money: An Irreverent History. New York, McGraw Hill, 1980.

*

Manuscript Collection: Boston University.

Aubrey Menen comments:

My novels are not of this world: my characters actually talk to one another and exchange ideas, instead of sitting in front of the television. Any real, sound, and solid reader who wishes to succeed in life is advised to dismiss them as witty. The late President Kennedy used to engrave one of my remarks on the silver mugs he gave to his staff—and look what happened to him.

Editorial note: the quotation came at the end of *Rama Retold*, and is as follows: "There are three things which are real: God, human folly, and laughter. Since the first two pass our comprehension, we must do what we can with the third."

* * *

Aubrey Menen is perhaps the finest satirist writing in English today, and it is strongly to his credit that he is more concerned with amusing than he is with reforming. Satirists fare better in more simple eras, and the present cynical age has shown little appreciation for satirical writing. Aubrey Menen reminds one of Aldous Huxley or of Norman Douglas, except that he does not possess their mastery of social comedy. Nor is he as viciously humorous as Evelyn Waugh. As he himself put it, "The message of at least one kind of satirist is that human nature is corrupt, but that this is not necessarily either a disastrous or a melancholy thing." He seems to be especially equipped for his amusing forays upon human foibles by virtue of his parentage of an Indian father and an Irish mother. Nor should it be any surprise that Menen was discovered by H.G. Wells, himself a social satirist who wrote novels of ideas in a sophisticated manner. What has most hurt the critical reputation of Menen is that the novel of ideas has not had a fair reading in the post-Freudian age in which the psychological novel reigns supreme. Menen, without apology, uses the novel as a vehicle for his ideas, and in the process he employs but shallow characterization and sketchy psychological description. At the same time, his works hardly follow the traditional novel form. The essays that appear within the novels are always witty and entertaining, showing little use for false intellectual obscurity. In addition, the dialogue of his characters is invariably lively and sophisticated.

Menen uses a wide-angle lens when he chooses subjects for attack. The Devil in *SheLa* might be speaking for the author in explaining the need to laugh at man's stupidity: "If anyone could recall all the collective idiocies that had taken place in his own lifetime, he would go out of his mind." Menen's most persistent theme is the sickness of modern nationalism, from the absurd posturing of supposedly advanced nations like the United States to the ridiculous pretentions of the new African nations. His special quality is that he is not afraid to attack sacred cows. In *The Backward Bride* false intellectualism is made the butt of his scorn. In a more wide-ranging attack, *The Abode of Love*, the story of a harem in Victorian England, makes fun of conventional religion, morality, and economics. The author has a rare quality for a satirist, and that is his sympathy with his characters. While he might despise pretentious intellectuals and blundering politicians, he shows warm feeling towards those who are victims of powers larger than themselves. The native Indians in *The Prevalence of Witches* are victims of the British law; the heroine of *The Backward Bride* is under attack for her simple beliefs by exponents of modern intellectualism, from existentialism to psychoanalysis. In *SheLa* two innocent Dalai Lamas, one male (HeLa) and one female (SheLa), are used as pawns to attain influence in the Far East by the great powers, the United States and Russia. The focus of attack is Western rationalism which is mirrored in the talk of God and his angels. Menen undoubtedly sympathizes with the Devil and Buddha whose intuitive thought and relativism are the antithesis of the rationalism and power he is attacking. Again, Menen might himself be speaking through the Devil to make a comment on his total work: "I have no interest in people who feel themselves wicked. I am fascinated, on the other hand, by people who are sure that they are good. I set them a little trap to prove that they are not....As I always say, think what conceited opinions people would have of themselves if it were not for the Devil."

—Lawrence Ries

MICHAELS, Leonard. American. Born in New York City, 2 January 1933. Educated at the High School for Music and Art, New York, graduated 1949; New York University, 1949-53, B.A. 1953; University of Michigan, Ann Arbor, M.A. 1956, Ph.D. 1967. Married 1) Priscilla Older in 1966 (divorced), two sons; 2) Brenda Hillman in 1976, one daughter. Taught at Paterson State College, New Jersey, 1961-62; Assistant Professor of English, University of California, Davis, 1967-69. Since 1970, Professor of English, University of California, Berkeley. Since 1977, Editor, *University Publishing* review, Berkeley. Recipient: National Endowment for the Arts grant, 1967; *Massachusetts Review* Award, 1969, 1970; Guggenheim Fellowship, 1970; American Academy Award, 1971. Agent: Lynn Nesbit, International Creative Management, 40 West 57th Street, New York, New York 10019. Address: 438 Beloit Avenue, Kensington, California 94708, U.S.A.

PUBLICATIONS

Novel

The Men's Club. New York, Farrar Straus, 1981.

Short Stories

Going Places. New York, Farrar Straus, 1969; London, Weidenfeld and Nicolson, 1970.

I Would Have Saved Them If I Could. New York, Farrar Straus, 1975.

Uncollected Short Stories

"Words for Penis," in *Tri-Quarterly* (Evanston, Illinois), Winter 1976.

"Pretty Women," "Imagine a Man," and "You," in *American Review 26*, edited by Theodore Solotaroff. New York, Bantam, 1977.

Other

Editor, with Christopher Ricks, *The State of the Language*. Berkeley, University of California Press, 1980.

*

Critical Studies: "A Berkeley Memoir," in *New Republic* (Washington, D.C.), October 1978, and "Legible Death," in *Antaeus* (New York), Summer 1979, both by the author.

Leonard Michaels comments:

My writing tends to be terse and quick. It is usually about urban types and the various kinds of psychological violence they inflict upon one another. I have no philosophical or political messages, though much of my work depends on traditional beliefs in regard to ethical and literary matters. I am not a modernistic writer. I write about what I know exists. Even in its most extreme moments my work is essentially realistic or descriptive. It is intended to be true in its observations and precise in its language.

* * *

Leonard Michaels's fiction is not easily described—it resists categories. It is realistic, but its dominant feature is irrationality of plot, sometimes comic, sometimes tragic, sometimes both at once. It is symbolic in its depiction of urban life, but its meanings are never reducible to messages, never allegorical. It is surreal and fragmented, but there is a consistency of viewpoint which can tie stories together and make for an overall coherence not to be found in the individual pieces. It reflects, sometimes self-consciously, the influence of such writers as Kafka, Roth, Malamud, Barthelme, and Borges, but it is nevertheless distinctive and compelling. At their best, Michaels's stories are intense, active, and imaginative; they can also be vague and even incomprehensible.

Michaels's fiction has been published in two thin volumes of stories, *Going Places* and *I Would Have Saved Them If I Could*, and one short novel, *The Men's Club*, which is also really a collection of stories. Most of the earlier pieces consist of brief glimpses of contemporary urban existence, full of bizarre incidents meant to suggest the unnatural condition of city life: a naked boy is denied entrance to the subway for lack of a token; a couple maim each other in a fight and then decide to marry; a Talmudic scholar slips on an icy street and is assumed to be a drunken derelict; by never speaking in class, a professor of philosophy wins a reputation for profundity; an honors graduate preferring to make a living by driving a cab is beaten gratuitously; a boy spying on his rabbi making love falls to his death; a telephone call to a friend's apartment reaches the burglar there. Usually some form of intense, though often anonymous, sexual encounter begins or ends the story. In all of this there is the recognition of the craziness of things and yet of their plausibility—at least so long as the setting is New York City.

The element that provides continuity in both volumes is the "central intelligence" of a recurring character, Phillip Liebowitz. Identified in many stories, present as unnamed narrator in others, he is a self-proclaimed, street-wise "city boy." In story after story he experiences strange twists of fate, absurd reversals of normal expectations, but being a New Yorker he takes all in his stride.

Michaels's stories are full of plot, but except for Phillip Liebowitz there are no real persons, and even Phillip emerges as a character not in any particular story but only in the collection as a whole. His contact with others is almost entirely in a sexual context: the women in the stories are merely objects of his lust, the other men his rivals for their favors. Through sexual conquest, Phillip asserts his existence and a degree of control over the hostile urban environment. But none of this is explicit; there are no explanations, only actions.

Although novelistic in form, *The Men's Club* is strongly reminiscent of Michaels's story collections. A group of men get together to form what might be called a consciousness-raising group. They decide that each will tell the story of his life, but what we get instead are fragments of stories, not biographical data but moments of intense self-awareness. As in a group of Chaucer tales (one of the characters is named Canterbury), there is a recurring theme: the fascinating power of women over men. These husbands who come together this evening specifically to be free of women can speak of nothing but their wives and lovers, women they have lived with for many years, women they spent a few moments with many years before. The anecdotes, like all Michaels's stories, lack endings. When one character complains that he did not get the point of another's story, the narrator expresses views which apply to all Michaels's fiction: "Doesn't matter....I don't get it either. I could tell other stories that have no point. This often happens to me. I start to talk, thinking there is a point, and then it never arrives. What is it, anyhow, this point? Things happen. You remember. That's all. If you take a large perspective, you'll realize there never is a point."

—Robert E. Lynch

MICHENER, James A(lbert). American. Born in New York City, 3 February 1907. Educated at Doylestown High School, Pennsylvania; Swarthmore College, Pennsylvania, A.B. (summa cum laude) 1929 (Phi Beta Kappa); University of Northern Colorado, Greeley, A.M. 1936; University of St. Andrews, Scotland. Served in the United States Navy, 1944-45: Lieutenant Commander. Married 1) Patti Koon in 1935 (divorced, 1948); 2) Vange Nord in 1948 (divorced, 1955); 3) Mari Yoriko Sabusawa in 1955. Master, Hill School, Pottstown, Pennsylvania, 1929-31, and George School, Newtown, Pennsylvania, 1934-36; Professor, University of Northern Colorado, 1936-40; Visiting Professor, Harvard University, Cambridge, Massachusetts, 1940-41; Associate Editor, Macmillan Company, New York, 1941-49. Since 1949, free-lance writer. Member, Advisory Committee on the Arts, United States Department of State, 1957; Chairman, President Kennedy's Food for Peace Program, 1961; Secretary, Pennsylvania Constitution Convention, 1967-68; Member of the Advisory Committee, United States Information Agency, 1970-76. Recipient: Pulitzer Prize 1948; National Association of Independent Schools Award, 1954 1958; Einstein Award, 1967; National Medal of Freedom, 1977 D.H.L.: Swarthmore College, 1954; LL.D.: Temple University Philadelphia, 1957; Litt.D.: Washington University, St. Louis 1967. Address: P.O. Box 125, Pipersville, Pennsylvania 18947 U.S.A.

PUBLICATIONS

Novels

The Fires of Spring. New York, Random House, 1949; London Corgi, 1960.

The Bridges at Toko-Ri. New York, Random House, and London, Secker and Warburg, 1953.

Sayonara. New York, Random House, and London, Secker and Warburg, 1954.

The Bridge at Andau. New York, Random House, and London Secker and Warburg, 1957.

Hawaii. New York, Random House, 1959; London, Secker and Warburg, 1960.

Caravans. New York, Random House, 1963; London, Secker and Warburg, 1964.

The Source. New York, Random House, and London, Secker and Warburg, 1965.

The Drifters. New York, Random House, and London, Secker and Warburg, 1971.

Centennial. New York, Random House, and London, Secker and Warburg, 1974.

Chesapeake. New York, Random House, and London, Secker and Warburg, 1978; selections published as *The Watermen* Random House, 1979.

The Covenant. New York, Random House, and London, Secker and Warburg, 1980.

Short Stories

Tales of the South Pacific. New York, Macmillan, 1947; London Collins, 1951.

Return to Paradise. New York, Random House, and London Secker and Warburg, 1951.

Other

The Unit in the Social Studies, with Harold M. Long. Cambridge Massachusetts, Harvard University Graduate School of Education, 1940.

The Voice of Asia. New York, Random House, 1951; as *Voices of Asia*, London, Secker and Warburg, 1952.

The Floating World (on Japanese art). New York, Random House, 1954; London, Secker and Warburg, 1955.

Rascals in Paradise, with A. Grove Day. New York, Random House, and London, Secker and Warburg, 1957.

Selected Writings. New York, Modern Library, 1957.

Japanese Prints from the Early Masters to the Modern. Rutland Vermont, Tuttle, and London, Paterson, 1959.

Report of the County Chairman. New York, Random House, and London, Secker and Warburg, 1961.

Iberia: Spanish Travels and Reflections. New York, Random House, and London, Secker and Warburg, 1968.

The Modern Japanese Print: An Appreciation. Rutland, Vermont, Tuttle, 1968.

Presidential Lottery: The Reckless Gamble in Our Electoral System New York, Random House, and London, Secker and Warburg 1969.

The Quality of Life. Philadelphia, Lippincott, 1970; London, Secker and Warburg, 1971.
Facing East: A Study of the Art of Jack Levine. New York, Random House, 1970.
Kent State: What Happened and Why. New York, Random House, and London, Secker and Warburg, 1971.
A Michener Miscellany 1950-1970, edited by Ben Hibbs. New York, Random House, 1973; London, Corgi, 1975.
About "Centennial": Some Notes on the Novel. New York, Random House, 1974.
Sports in America. New York, Random House, 1976; as *Michener on Sport*, London, Secker and Warburg, 1976.
In Search of Centennial: A Journey. New York, Random House, 1978.

Editor, *The Future of the Social Studies: Proposals for an Experimental Social-Studies Curriculum*. New York, National Council for the Social Studies, 1939.
Editor, *The Hokusai Sketch Books: Selections from the Manga*. Rutland, Vermont, Tuttle, 1958.
Editor, *Firstfruits: A Harvest of 25 Years of Israeli Writing*. Philadelphia, Jewish Publication Society of America, 1973.

*

Manuscript Collection: Library of Congress, Washington, D.C.

Critical Study: *James Michener* by A. Grove Day, New York, Twayne, 1964, revised edition, 1977.

James A. Michener comments:

I had the good fortune to arrive on the scene when America was broadening its intellectual horizons to include the entire world. Millions of our men would experience the South Pacific; millions of families would live in Japan or Germany, and countries like Great Britain and Italy became commonplace adventures. Had I written as I did twenty years earlier, I doubt seriously that I would have enjoyed much of a readership. America was not only prepared for what I had to say, but apparently eager to hear it.

Also, I came along when the television set was about to command the attention of the middle American family to the exclusion of almost all else, and I made a conscious decision: "If they look at television long enough, they will grow hungry for the more substantial experience they can get only through books," and it became evident to me that instead of abandoning reading, the people I was aiming at would demand more of it, and would be prepared to accept long and difficult books, would indeed seek them out. In this judgment I was confirmed.

I am sometimes thought of, for these reasons, as an exotic writer. On the contrary, I have worked in an unusually wide spectrum of human experience, from politics to ecology to education to Asian art to the fine arts. I have also worked in these fields, having been an active politician and a connoisseur of the arts. My life has been therefore a vain attempt to keep many interests in balance, and my books have been proof of how one or the other of those interests has run away with me from time to time.

My style has always been deceptively simple, and I have worked assiduously to keep it that way. This requires not only careful writing, but endless rewriting, redrafting, rejection, and final polishing. I find that I work principally in a Latinized vocabulary, in fairly long sentences; revision consists of going back to simpler Anglo-Saxon words and shorter sentences. My ideals have been Henry James, Gustave Flaubert and Ivan Turgenev, whom I have never tried to ape, and William Thackeray, Honoré Balzac, Leo Tolstoy and Samuel Butler, whom I have. My influences have thus been almost exclusively European rather than American, a consequence of my education, and I have always felt this to have been a pity.

* * *

No one could ever justifiably accuse James A. Michener of being intellectually stagnant or lazy. Few, if any, other contemporary American writers have dared to explore the vast territories he has covered in so much depth. No period of history or topic of social concern, it would seem, has escaped Michener's pen. From the ancient Middle East to modern-day Colorado, Michener has written the histories of places and their inhabitants, always with a sharp, clear eye for detail and description. His non-fiction work is perhaps even more impressive in scope and bulk; his subjects range from the Kent State killings and ensuing investigation to the world of Japanese art.

Michener began his writing career in 1947 with the publication of *Tales of the South Pacific*, a collection of loosely connected stories concerning the lives and loves of American soldiers stationed in that area during World War II. The book, an immediate success which was hailed as one of the most significant books to emerge from a war-time experience in decades, won the Pulitzer Prize. Against the backdrop of the lush islands and sensuous natives, Michener places a group of American military personnel. The lives and cultures of the two disparate peoples become entwined, the first of many such juxtapositions of cultures to be found in Michener's works. (A later novel, *Sayonara*, displays even more of this clash as it chronicles the tragic love affair of an American GI and his Japanese mistress.) Although a definite flair for story-telling is evident, the author does have a tendency to go into rather too much detail, causing some of the weaker stories to fall flat.

An attempt at an autobiographical novel, *The Fires of Spring*, followed. The story of a poor boy from Pennsylvania who, through academic success and help from a Quaker family, travels to New York to try his luck at writing has all the marks of a too-autobiographical work. It comes off as hastily written and lacking in perspective.

Depending upon the reader's taste, Michener is at either his best or his worst in his long historical novels. After *Sayonara* was published in 1954, Michener allowed his love of place and history to overtake his fiction. Whereas in his earlier novels he paid careful consideration to characterization and dialogue, in his later novels, he seems to believe that the sweeping historical plots will interest his readers enough to carry them through books that even his most avid fans must find too often long and sometimes dull.

Hawaii, perhaps the most famous of the historical novels, is a panoramic book that depicts the formation, development, and settlement of the islands. While rich in historical and cultural description, the book is flawed in that the characters are not well-drawn or expanded. Still, the novel is a masterful example of the genre. *Centennial* and *Chesapeake* both rival *Hawaii* as Michener's historical masterpieces, but, again, the books suffer from length, lack of characterization, and descriptive overkill. Even less successful are *Caravans* and *The Source*, in which the background and sense of history play a larger part than do essential fictional elements.

That Michener is an important and popular novelist there is no denying. He would prove himself a more capable novelist, however, if he developed his characters more fully and kept a tighter rein on his rather unwieldy historical descriptions.

—Sally H. Bennett

MIDDLETON, O(sman) E(dward Gordon). New Zealander. Born in Christchurch, 25 March 1925. Educated at New Plymouth Boys High School, 1939-41; Auckland University, 1946, 1948; the Sorbonne, Paris (New Zealand Government Bursary), 1955-56. Served in the Royal New Zealand Air Force, 1944-45. Married Maida Edith Middleton (marriage dissolved, 1970), two children. Recipient: New Zealand Literary Fund Award, 1959, and Scholarship, 1965; Hubert Church Award, 1964; Robert Burns Fellowship, University of Otago, 1970; New Zealand Prose Fiction Award, 1976. Address: 20 Clifford Street, Dunedin, New Zealand.

PUBLICATIONS

Short Stories

Short Stories. Wellington, Handcraft Press, 1954.
The Stone and Other Stories. Auckland, Pilgrim Press, 1959.
A Walk on the Beach. London, Joseph, 1964.
The Loners. Wellington, Square and Circle, 1972.
Selected Stories. Dunedin, McIndoe, 1975.
Confessions of an Ocelot, Not for a Seagull. Dunedin, McIndoe, 1978.

Verse

Six Poems. Wellington, Handcraft Press, 1951.

Other

From the River to the Tide (juvenile). Wellington, School Publications Branch, 1964.

*

Manuscript Collections: Auckland Public Library; Hocken Library, Dunedin.

Critical Studies: *New Zealand Fiction since 1945* by H. Winston Rhodes, Dunedin, McIndoe, 1968; "O.E. Middleton: Not Just a Realist" by Jim Williamson, in *Islands* (Auckland), Winter 1973; *O.E. Middleton: The Sympathetic Imagination and the Right Judgements* by Lawrence Jones, Auckland, Pilgrim Press, 1980.

O.E. Middleton comments:

My published fiction comprises two novellas, several dozen short stories and a work for children. Unpublished material includes two novels and numerous stories.

It is not my wish to explain, analyse, or otherwise obscure what I have sought to render in fictional terms. I should feel that I had failed as a writer if my work did not speak for itself.

* * *

As a short story writer primarily devoted to the New Zealand scene, O.E. Middleton remains faithful to the tradition of unsophisticated realism. He is less interested in technical innovation than in his wide experience of people and places at home and abroad, less attracted to ironic or symbolic patterns than to the rhythms of the spoken language and the texture of the workaday world. The titles of his best-known collections, *The Stone and Other Stories* and *A Walk on the Beach*, are symptomatic of an unpretentious manner and direct approach to subject matter that is rarely remote from the commonplace, but is raised to a level of significance by its truth of substance.

Unlike some writers held in greater esteem he never adopts an authorial position from which he finds it convenient to look down on the antics of his characters with fastidious disapproval or superior sensibility. On the contrary he is always democratically at ease in the scene and among the people he has created. The narrators of "The Corporal's Story" and "The Greaser's Story" are familiar with their occupations and in harmony with their backgrounds.

Middleton populates his fictional world with labourers and seamen, farmers and city-dwellers, Europeans and Maoris, children and adolescents. They are ordinary people, generally unremarkable for subtlety of thought or emotion; and the incidents related are associated with their normal activities during work and leisure. Their understanding is limited and their conversation borders on the banal; but what must be lost in felicity of expression is gained in authenticity and restraint. "A Married Man" concludes tritely with " 'Never mind,' she said, smiling and friendly, 'It will come right in the end.' " The narrator of "A Day by Itself" observes "It had been a funny day really, and there were things about it which I still didn't understand." Even when stories are based on episodes derived from the eventful years of the writer's wanderings, both language and character become absorbed into the raw material of life.

Despite the absence of any guide-lines which can be attributed to the author, a moral sensibility is distinctly present in choice of theme, development of action, and establishment of character. A particular kind of neo-colonial egalitarian humanism informs every aspect of his writing and is readily detected in what he has called "sorties into the No-man's-land of inter-racial relations." The most substantial of these stories is found in the novella *Not for a Seagull*, told by a young Maori who is continually made aware that goodfellowship often masks attitudes of racial discrimination. This has recently been republished with the addition of a later and more sophisticated work, *Confessions of an Ocelot*, which relates the experiences of a human victim innocently trapped in a city-jungle. The narrator is a withdrawn and sensitive youth whose "confessions" are intended to reveal "to any who may share a like sensibility the perils that can await its flowering." With characteristic thoroughness Middleton enters into the interior world of his guideless recorder and at the same time uncovers the external world in which he moves uncomprehendingly. Yet, surprisingly enough, the didacticism latent in this and other themes does not often obtrude. Middleton is too honest a craftsman to allow strongly held opinions to falsify his representation of the life he has both experienced and observed. His characters play their parts in the diverse activities of the communities in which they find themselves, with the result that any temptation to over-emphasise private perplexities is checked by the recognition of otherness, and Middleton is able both to explore his chosen terrain and disclose rather than publish his humane attitudes.

The measure of his work is to be found not in terms of quantity, for his output has not been large, but in the success he has achieved in responding to the epigraph from Dryden which he attached to his *Selected Stories*—"For the spirit of man cannot be satisfied but with truth or at least verisimility...." It is also to be found in the range and variety of scene, character, and situation. He moves easily from land to sea, from the Americas to Europe and back again to New Zealand, distilling fragments of his wide experiences and activity into imaginative work that attains significance from the authenticity of its treatment. Such stories as "The Crows," "For Once in Your Life," "The Doss-House and the Duchess," and "The Collector" (all in *Selected Stories*) are characterised by the same concern with variations of the human predicament as is to be found in his more frequent New Zealand narratives.

—H. Winston Rhodes

MIDDLETON, Stanley. British. Born in Bulwell, Nottingham, 1 August 1919. Educated at High Pavement School, Nottingham; University College of Nottingham, now Nottingham University, 1938-40, 1946-47, B.A. (London) 1940; M.Ed. (Nottingham) 1952. Served in the Royal Artillery and the Army Education Corps, 1940-46. Married Margaret Shirley Welch in 1951; two daughters. Since 1947, English Master, and since 1958, Head of the English Department, High Pavement College, Nottingham. Recipient: Booker Prize, 1974. M.A.: Nottingham University, 1975. Address: 42 Caledon Road, Sherwood, Nottingham NG5 2NG, England.

PUBLICATIONS

Novels

A Short Answer. London, Hutchinson, 1958.

Harris's Requiem. London, Hutchinson, 1960.
A Serious Woman. London, Hutchinson, 1961.
The Just Exchange. London, Hutchinson, 1962.
Two's Company. London, Hutchinson, 1963.
Him They Compelled. London, Hutchinson, 1964.
Terms of Reference. London, Hutchinson, 1966.
The Golden Evening. London, Hutchinson, 1968.
Wages of Virtue. London, Hutchinson, 1969.
Apple of the Eye. London, Hutchinson, 1970.
Brazen Prison. London, Hutchinson, 1971.
Cold Gradations. London, Hutchinson, 1972.
A Man Made of Smoke. London, Hutchinson, 1973.
Holiday. London, Hutchinson, 1974.
Distractions. London, Hutchinson, 1975.
Still Waters. London, Hutchinson, 1976.
Ends and Means. London, Hutchinson, 1977.
Two Brothers. London, Hutchinson, 1978.
In a Strange Land. London, Hutchinson, 1979.
The Other Side. London, Hutchinson, 1980.

Plays

Radio Plays: *The Captain from Nottingham*, 1972; *Harris's Requiem*, 1972; *A Little Music at Night*, 1972; *Cold Gradations*, from his own novel, 1973.

*

Manuscript Collection: Central Library, Nottingham.

Stanley Middleton comments:

(1972) I put down a few obvious points about my novels.

They are set mainly in the English midlands with characters drawn from the professional middle-classes (students, teachers, actors, writers, architects), though one will find labourers and factory-workers as well as businessmen of real affluence.

The action usually occupies a short period of some months only (*Wages of Virtue* is an exception), and the plot deals with people in a state of crisis or perplexity caused by illness and death, or a breakdown of personal relationships, or the difficulties of creating a work of art (which may be music, *Harris's Requiem*, or poetry, *Him They Compelled*, or a novel in *Brazen Prison*). At this time of dilemmas, friends or relatives intervene, and thus learn their own inadequacies and, sometimes, strengths. No perfect characters or solutions exist; all is difficult, compromising, but a bonus of success or joy is occasionally found.

My idea is not only to tell an interesting story but to demonstrate the complexity of human character and motive. One must not only describe what has happened to people, or what they are like; one must make the characters live out what they are said to be, and this must include deviations from normality and actions "out of character." I find this most difficult, but when I am charged, sometimes, with "mere reportage," I can see no sense at all in the accusation. My novels are imaginative attempts to write down illuminating actions and talk from the lives of fictional people, and not transcriptions of tape-recordings of real conversations or blow-by-blow commentaries on events which have really taken place. I am sometimes praised for the "realism" of my dialogue, and this makes me wonder if these critics, who may of course be using a "shorthand" dictated by the small space at their disposal, know how differently my sort of dialogue is from that of real life.

This preoccupation leads to a choice of different levels of writing. A novel cannot always be intense; both by the shape of my work and my use of language I try constantly to interfere with the reader, to rest him as well as violently assault him. Therefore it is galling when I find critics who apparently subscribe to the notion that contemporary novels are either "well-written" (i.e. in "mandarin") or dashed down without care. Mine are usually dumped by such people in the second category. Shifts on my part from the point-of-view of one character to that of another also seem to pass unnoticed.

I am often asked if my novels are didactic. I wouldn't object to that word since the greatest work of art I know—Bach's *St. Matthew Passion*—could be so described. But unless a novel is complex, memorable, capable of holding a reader and moving him deeply, I've not much time for it.

I can't think these notes very helpful. General exegesis as opposed to critical discussion of precise points in specific books has little attraction for me as a writer. A novel should be its own defence; if it does not speak for itself to a well-equipped reader, call out echoes in him, it's not properly written.

* * *

When the novels of Stanley Middleton first appeared he was grouped rather too quickly with the regional, kitchen sink novelists who set the trend in the late 1950's. Then possibly because he works and writes in and about Nottingham and realises that the act of copulation is central to human motivation, his critics started to compare him with Lawrence. However it is those who see in his novels some of the qualities of E.M. Forster who are perhaps somewhat nearer the mark, an observation supported by the fact that the novelist in *Brazen Prison* is at work on a book which has some affinities in setting and concern with *A Passage to India*.

But all these allusions really emphasise the difficulties which reviewers have in attempting to describe the individual quality of this novelist, who has the rare and surprising gift of making all his characters at the same time both unlikeable and interesting. His women for the most part are tormented frigid tormentors, while his affluent middle class men are mediocrities in their professions and indecisive shamblers in their personal lives. What he has grasped is that people at the end of their tether do not become heroic and loveable through suffering. An emotional snarl-up makes people selfish, irritable and dull. The skill of the dialogue here is that, although the first two qualities are caught, the third is avoided because the reader is held by the way the remarks of one speaker rasp on those of the other.

This is especially true when the participants in the dialogue try to meet across the gaps of generation, social class, and economic status. In *Terms of Reference* the two late-middle-aged couples are perplexed and powerless when confronted by the failure of the marriage between the son of the very wealthy pair and the daughter of the academically respectable ones. Yet although they can do nothing to hold their wayward children together, and are by no means altogether certain that it would be a good thing to do so, all four of them are too fascinated by the situation to leave it alone.

Edward Tenby, the architect hero of *Apple of the Eye*, is not only the sole moderately creative and productive character in the novel, he is also the only visible male. He becomes involved with three neurotic women, all young enough to be his daughters. One of them is of sufficient wealth to be able to indulge her sickness to its limit, while the other two are poor enough to be flattered and astounded at making any contact with a man in his position. In *Brazen Prison* the ex-grammar schoolboy novelist, Charles Stead, has to cope with the social nuances of relating to his wealthy socialite wife and her friends, while at the same time involving himself with the husband and family of the local girl he'd picked up in the dance halls of his youth.

Because all these people are caught in a crisis point of their lives, they lay aside the masks that make the usual run of social intercourse both possible and dull. They speak completely out of their personality, circumstance, and background, right down to the endless and infuriating 'er, umph, er's of Professor Dodds-Walker in *Terms of Reference*. That despite it all these people do somehow get something over to each other is the surprising optimism of these bleak novels.

—Shirley Toulson

MILLAR, Margaret (Ellis, née Sturm). American. Born in Kitchener, Ontario, Canada, 5 February 1915. Educated at Kitchener Collegiate Institute, 1929-33; University of Toronto, 1933-36. Married Kenneth Millar, i.e., Ross Macdonald, *q.v.*, in 1938; one child (deceased). Screenwriter, Warner Brothers, Hollywood, 1945-46. President, Mystery Writers of America, 1957-58. Recipient: Mystery Writers of America Edgar Allan Poe Award, 1956; Los Angeles *Times* Woman of the Year Award, 1965. Agent: Harold Ober Associates Inc., 40 East 49th Street, New York, New York 10017. Address: 4420 Via Esperanza, Santa Barbara, California 93105, U.S.A.

PUBLICATIONS

Novels

The Invisible Worm. New York, Doubleday, 1941; London, Long, 1943.
The Weak-Eyed Bat. New York, Doubleday, 1942.
The Devil Loves Me. New York, Doubleday, 1942.
Wall of Eyes. New York, Random House, 1943; London, Lancer, 1966.
Fire Will Freeze. New York, Random House, 1944.
The Iron Gates. New York, Random House, 1945; as *Taste of Fears*, London, Hale, 1950.
Experiment in Springtime. New York, Random House, 1947.
It's All in the Family. New York, Random House, 1948.
The Cannibal Heart. New York, Random House, 1949; London, Hamish Hamilton, 1950.
Do Evil in Return. New York, Random House, 1950; London, Museum Press, 1952.
Vanish in an Instant. New York, Random House, 1952; London, Museum Press, 1953.
Rose's Last Summer. New York, Random House, 1952; London, Museum Press, 1954; as *The Lively Corpse*, New York, Dell, n.d.
Wives and Lovers. New York, Random House, 1954.
Beast in View. New York, Random House, and London, Gollancz, 1955.
An Air That Kills. New York, Random House, 1957; as *The Soft Talkers*, London, Gollancz, 1957.
The Listening Walls. New York, Random House, and London, Gollancz, 1959.
A Stranger in My Grave. New York, Random House, and London, Gollancz, 1960.
How Like an Angel. New York, Random House, and London, Gollancz, 1962.
The Fiend. New York, Random House, and London, Gollancz, 1964.
Beyond This Point Are Monsters. New York, Random House, 1970; London, Gollancz, 1971.
Ask for Me Tomorrow. New York, Random House, 1976; London, Gollancz, 1977.
The Murder of Miranda. New York, Random House, 1979; London, Gollancz, 1980.

Uncollected Short Stories

"The Couple Next Door," in *Ellery Queen's Awards: Ninth Series.* Boston, Little Brown, 1954; London, Collins, 1956.
"The People Across the Canyon," in *Ellery Queen's Mystery Magazine* (New York), October 1962.
"McGowney's Miracle," in *Every Crime in the Book.* New York, Putnam, 1975.

Other

The Birds and the Beasts Were There (autobiography). New York, Random House, 1968.

* * *

Margaret Millar began her career with an effort to create a series of detection stories presided over by the symbolically named Dr. Paul Prye. His vocation as consulting psychiatrist suggested that he might become the modern version of the consulting scientists Sherlock Holmes and Dr. Thorndyke whose stories provided the basic conventions of the detection novel that Millar employed in *The Invisible Worm* and *The Weak-Eyed Bat.* As it turned out Prye's vocation had more importance than contemporaneity, for Millar changed her emphasis in later novels, reducing the process of detection until it became simply the means for exposition of her primary subject, the psychology of individuals as it has been concealed in the passage of time, obscured by the appearance of the ordinary surface of life, or distorted by stress.

Describing what he calls her "art of bamboozlement," Julian Symons writes in *Mortal Consequences* that Millar "presents us with a plausible criminal situation, builds it up to a climax of excitement, and then in the last few pages shakes the kaleidoscope and shows us an entirely different pattern from the one we have been so busily interpreting." Symons's description of Millar's structure is accurate. For example, in *Do Evil in Return* the logic of circumstantial evidence points to the guilt of Lewis Ballard for the murder of a young woman he has made pregnant, until it is revealed that in a mad attempt to keep her home intact Lewis's wife had killed the woman and attempted to place the blame on her husband's mistress; and in the remarkable *Beast in View* Millar develops readers' sympathetic participation in Helen Clarvoe's terror as she is persecuted by Evelyn Merrick, who, it turns out, is actually the malignant dimension of Helen's own split personality.

The twists of plot vary in complexity without showing any diminishment of the author's skill. *Rose's Last Summer* works through simple impersonation by an impoverished actress of an elderly dowager; *The Fiend* transfers a suspicion of guilt from a known child molester to "reputable" characters whose adulterous behavior is the actual cause of a little girl's disappearance; but in *An Air That Kills* an elaborate sequence of scandals that drive a man to suicide can never be fully explained as ruse or truth.

Were Millar concerned exclusively with the imaginative mysteries she invents for her plots, she might well have remained an author of detection stories, or if her ability to convey the sinister appearance of the abnormal in ordinary circumstances were more limited she might have indulged in the eerie atmospheric manipulations of popular gothicism. It is character, though, that interests Millar. The devices of plot and envelope of atmosphere serve to define human psychology rather than to interest for their own sakes.

Millar has accepted the idea that the truly great detective of modern times is Sigmund Freud. The problems that demand explanation are those that typify human experience within the mind, so her plots bamboozle with twists and reverses in order to represent movement within the novels from external circumstances amenable to rational ordering to the irrational internal life. Discovery of cause and effect in external circumstances could establish socially defined guilt and lead to reconstruction of social order, but revelation of the sequence of internal occurrences leads only to knowledge, gratifying in single cases but leaving a residue of uncertainty rather than optimism.

In *The Iron Gates, How Like an Angel*, and *Beyond This Point Are Monsters* events issuing from experiences long past make characters function as though fated. In books such as *Vanish in an Instant, A Stranger in My Grave, Wives and Lovers*, as well as some previously mentioned novels, the intensity of family relationships is portrayed as inevitably damaging for characters working their ways through patterns of submission and dominance. The evidence of fated behavior or the harm done in the most fundamental personal relationships is fascinating as psychiatric anecdote, but related in fiction with its means of dramatization it is unsettling. Relieved as we may be by a story's resolution, we are shocked by its revelation and carry away with us a nagging sense of identification with characters or recognition in ourselves of some aspect of their psychology.

Taking this effect as Millar's serious purpose, we must recognize that she has been devoting her mature novels to the general project of describing the reciprocity of events and personal experiences. At the core of her works, since she abandoned the novel of detection, lies the observation that people may not be able to change the events which shape them, but people can alter their experience of events. We are all familiar with simple illustrations of the point: The elongation of time before an auto accident or the tendency to speed up time by sleeping excessively when we feel depressed. Millar's project establishes a continuum from these relatively ordinary experiences to the mysterious transformations of perception that distinguish psychological abnormality.

We can admire Margaret Millar for her clever mastery of the technique of popular mystery. We praise her, though, because she provides what we still expect to find in the novel—some news about life.

—John M. Reilly

MIRSKY, Mark (Jay). American. Born in Boston, Massachusetts, 11 August 1939. Educated at Harvard University, Cambridge, Massachusetts, B.A. (magna cum laude) 1961 (Phi Beta Kappa); Stanford University, California, M.A. 1962. Served in the United States Air Force Reserve. School teacher, Boston, 1962; Staff Writer, *American Heritage* magazine, New York, 1964; Lecturer in English, Stanford University, 1966. Lecturer, 1967-70, and since 1970, Assistant Professor of English, City College of New York. Editor, *Fiction* magazine, New York. Member of the Board, Teacher-Writers Collaborative, New York. Recipient: Bread Loaf Writers Conference grant. Address: Box 112, New York, New York 10009, U.S.A.

PUBLICATIONS

Novels

Thou Worm, Jacob. New York, Macmillan, and London, Collier Macmillan, 1967.
Proceedings of the Rabble. Indianapolis, Bobbs Merrill, 1970.
Blue Hill Avenue. Indianapolis, Bobbs Merrill, 1972.

Short Stories

The Secret Table. New York, Fiction Collective, 1975.

Uncollected Short Stories

"Swapping," in *Statements 1.* New York, Braziller, 1975.
"The Last Lecture," in *Tri-Quarterly* (Evanston, Illinois), Spring 1976.

Other

My Search for the Messiah: Studies and Wanderings in Israel and America. New York, Macmillan, 1977.

* * *

A catalogue of Mark Mirsky's fictional liabilities in his early work is short and bittersweet: he reworks worn material; he cannot resist dreamworld and fantasyland scenes; he is too delighted with royal-purple prose and "experimentalism"; finally he breaks himself up with broad ethnic humor that often offends. Yet he has such large talent that he skillfully turns each of these faults to advantage even when he does not transcend them.

His first volume of fiction seemed partly to be a parodic melange of Aleichem, Singer, and Malamud. The inversions of Yiddish, the barrage of exclamation and interrogation points, the spread-finger resignation of the Jewish immigrant, all knotted and clotted the young writer's style and suggested the bar mitzvah school of cheap Catskill entertainment. Thus, the "Introduction" begins:

> "I've got the whole state of Jewish affairs right between my fingers!
>
> "What? You don't understand? Take a seat. Don't worry, it won't break. A bit cracked but it's had a rest. Watch out! Watch out for that pile of books. Knock one over, my whole place is on your head. Pages, dust, dirty yarmulkes. Eh! Let it fall."

In spite of such false starts, Mirsky knows and loves his "material" and manages to move us to both laughter and pity in this collection of tales about East European immigrants struggling to remain Jews in their new homeland. The familiar figure of the schlemiel hero is brilliantly renewed in the collection's finest story, "The Shammos from Aroostook County." Five years later, Mirsky returned to the struggling Jews of the old towns near Boston with *Blue Hill Avenue.* Although he labeled his tale "vaudeville," he writes here with more control, except for an inappropriate slapstick ending. Four of the characters are superbly drawn: Rabbi Lux, who is "a little to good, too pious for much of Dorchester"; the rabbi's wife, once timid and passionate, now a loving, lunatic protectress; Simcha Tanzenn, a canny, lisping politician who collects on favors rarely delivered; and a demented Jewish mother, who uses the telephone like a mortar and wills her war-lost (and worthless) son back to safety. Mirsky's latest treatment of Jewish traditions, *The Secret Table,* is more serious in tone and, despite some obscurity of form, marks another fictional advance for the author in portraying his fierce bookish forebears. The first novella depicts the search through memory of 30-year-old Maishe for the womb-security now lacking in the decayed streets of Blue Hill Avenue; the companion novella, "Onan's Child," builds upon Genesis to explore, through Jacob, Isaac, Joseph, and Onan, the terrible contradictions of man's nature and Jewish history. In both stories, past and present, subjective and objective worlds, the Jew and the universal man, are blended into a believable, densely-textured reality.

Mirsky's second novel, *Proceedings of the Rabble,* may be his most ambitious to date. Anticipating Robert Altman's film, *Nashville,* in an urban locale, Mirsky uses the evangelical right-wing political crusade of William Starr to portray the murderous impotence moving American democracy toward rage, outrage, and self-destruction. Despite the straining interior-cinema technique employed, Mirsky's apocalyptic ending matches the final upheaval of West's *Day of the Locust.* Indeed, in all four "novels," Mirsky renews such staple items of contemporary American fiction as violence, sexual sickness, and the Jew as representative sufferer, so that they still serve to tell us about ourselves.

—Frank Campenni

MITCHELL, Adrian. British. Born in London, 24 October 1932. Educated at Dauntsey's School, Wiltshire; Christ Church, Oxford (Editor, *Isis* magazine, 1954-55), 1952-55. Served in the British Army, 1951-52. Reporter, *Oxford Mail*, 1955-57, and *Evening Standard*, London, 1957-59; Columnist and Reviewer, *Daily Mail*, *Woman's Mirror*, *The Sun*, *The Sunday Times*, *Peace News*, *The Black Dwarf*, and *The Guardian*, all in London. Instructor, University of Iowa, Iowa City, 1963-64; Granada Fellow in the Arts, University of Lancaster, 1967-69; Fellow, Wesleyan University

Center for the Humanities, Middletown, Connecticut, 1971; Resident Writer, Sherman Theatre, Cardiff, 1974-75; Visiting Writer, Billericay Comprehensive School, Essex, 1978-80; Judith E. Wilson Fellow, Cambridge University, 1980-81. Recipient: Eric Gregory Award, 1961; P.E.N. Translation Prize, 1966; Tokyo Festival Television Film Award, 1971. Agent: Fraser and Dunlop Scripts Ltd., 91 Regent Street, London W1R 8RU, England.

PUBLICATIONS

Novels

If You See Me Comin'. London, Cape, 1962; New York, Macmillan, 1963.
The Bodyguard. London, Cape, 1970; New York, Doubleday, 1971.
Wartime. London, Cape, 1973.
Man Friday. London, Futura, 1975.

Plays

The Ledge (libretto), music by Richard Rodney Bennett (produced London, 1961).
The Persecution and Assassination of Jean-Paul Marat as Performed by the Inmates of the Asylum of Charenton under the Direction of the Marquis de Sade, adaptation of the play by Peter Weiss (produced London, 1964; New York, 1965). London, Calder, 1965; New York, Atheneum, 1966.
The Magic Flute, adaptation of the libretto by Schikaneder and Giesecke, music by Mozart (produced London, 1966).
US, with others (produced London, 1966). Published as *US: The Book of the Royal Shakespeare Production US/Vietnam/US/Experiment/Politics...*, London, Calder and Boyars, 1968; as *Tell Me Lies*, Indianapolis, Bobbs Merrill, 1968.
The Criminals, adaptation of a play by José Triana (produced London, 1967; New York, 1970).
Tyger: A Celebration of the Life and Work of William Blake, music by Mike Westbrook (produced London, 1971). London, Cape, 1971.
Tamburlane the Mad Hen (for children; produced Devon, 1971).
Man Friday music by Mike Westbrook (televised, 1972; produced London, 1973). Included in *Man Friday, and Mind Your Head*, 1974.
Mind Your Head, music by Andy Roberts (produced Liverpool, 1973; London, 1974). Included in *Man Friday, and Mind Your Head*, 1974.
The Inspector General, adaptation of a play by Gogol (produced Nottingham, 1974).
Man Friday, and Mind Your Head. London, Eyre Methuen, 1974.
A Seventh Man, music by Dave Brown, adaptation of the book by John Berger and Jean Mohr (produced London, 1976).
White Suit Blues, music by Mike Westbrook, adaptation of works by Mark Twain (produced Nottingham and London, 1977).
Houdini: A Circus-Opera, music by Peter Schat (produced Amsterdam, 1977). Amsterdam, Clowns, 1977(?).
Uppendown Mooney (produced Welwyn Garden City, Hertfordshire, 1978).
The White Deer (juvenile), adaptation of the story by James Thurber (produced London, 1978).
Hoagy, Bix, and Wolfgang Beethoven Bunkhaus (produced London, 1979; Indianapolis, 1980).

Screenplays: *Marat/Sade*, 1966; *Tell Me Lies* (lyrics only), 1968; *The Body* (commentary), 1969; *Man Friday*, 1976.

Radio Play: *The Island* (libretto), music by William Russo, 1963.

Television Plays: *Animals Can't Laugh*, 1961; *Alive and Kicking*, 1971; *William Blake* (documentary), 1971; *Man Friday*, 1972; *Somebody Down There Is Crying*, 1974; *Daft as a Brush*, 1975; *The Fine Art of Bubble Blowing*, 1975; *Silver Giant, Wooden Dwarf*, 1975; *Glad Day*, 1979.

Initiated and helped write student shows: *Bradford Walk*, Bradford College of Art; *The Hotpot Saga*, *The Neurovision Song Contest*, and *Lash Me to the Mast*, University of Lancaster; *Move Over Jehovah*, National Association of Mental Health; *Poetry Circus*, Wesleyan University; *Mass Media Mash* and *Mud Fair*, Dartington College of the Arts, 1976 and 1977.

Verse

(Poems). Oxford, Fantasy Press, 1955.
Poems. London, Cape, 1964.
Peace Is Milk. London, Peace News, 1966.
Out Loud. London, Cape Goliard Press, and New York, Grossman, 1968; revised edition, London, Writers and Readers, 1976.
Ride the Nightmare: Verse and Prose. London, Cape, 1971.
Cease-Fire. London, Medical Aid Committee for Vietnam, 1973.
Penguin Modern Poets 22, with John Fuller and Peter Levi. London, Penguin, 1973.
The Apeman Cometh. London, Cape, 1975.
For Beauty Douglas: Collected Poems and Songs. London, Allison and Busby, 1981.

Recording: *Poems*, with Stevie Smith, Argo, 1974.

Other

Naked in Cheltenham (miscellany). Cheltenham, Gastoday, 1978.

Editor, with Richard Selig, *Oxford Poetry 1955.* Oxford, Fantasy Press, 1955.
Editor, *Jump, My Brothers, Jump: Poems from Prison*, by Tim Daly. London, Freedom Press, 1970.

Translator, with Joan Jara, *Victor Jara: His Life and Songs.* London, Hamish Hamilton, 1976.

*

Adrian Mitchell comments:

I am outraged by the cruelty of man to man and especially by the criminal record of the rich white nations. I write out of this outrage. If I tell of my horror with jokes often, it's in order to make it bearable. Viva Cuba! Viva Fidel!

* * *

Adrian Mitchell is best-known as a "committed" poet, his verse serving his fiery Far Left views, but his novels are not narrowly political. The first, *If You See Me Comin'*, springs in part from his participation in various experiments in the late 1950's in putting together jazz and poetry. The book is a first person account of six days in the life of Johnny Crane, a blues singer, in an English provincial town. The days include some singing and eating, a rehearsal and a civic ball, with thoughts alternating with the actual sequence of events. His brother, on the run from gangsters, breaks up his room while Johnny, finding himself, rather to his surprise, falling in love with a girl, moves in with her. Some actions are stranger; he gets into a tiny concealed space in a museum and cuts down the flagpost on top of the town hall at night. Finally a girl is murdered and her fiancé kills himself.

The novel's features include "poetic" touches ("Morning sun has the hand of a woman," "His face was obscure and slick as the numberless plastic stopped clock on the wall beyond his shoulder") and some comedy, often irrelevant: parodies of a children's television show about animals and of the country-house murder play, and the sick park-keeper who waylays you with "I shouldn't be doing this, with my chest, everyone says I shouldn't."

Johnny is the kind of man who buys a car when he has money on Wednesday, travels by train that night, and sells the car on Thursday. We read of his response to music, and the ways he feels when he sings, Mitchell giving the words of several of the songs he likes. Equally important is his intense response to suffering and death: he has buried corpses in the Korean War and is obsessed with an approaching execution, so that half-heartedly he collects signatures on a petition for a reprieve. Johnny seems to be made unbalanced by over-sensitivity to the world's pain and horror. But primarily this is a psychological study. His is a mind close to the end of its tether.

The novel overflows with half-disciplined talent, a little incoherent, imaginative, spiky and unsettling.

The second novel, *The Bodyguard*, is more unusual. The time is the mid-1980's, when Britain has an All-Party government operating a police state, which is ineffective in combatting the Resistance. Facets of 1980's life include frequent nudity on Saturday mornings in Ladbroke Grove and black Africans kept in a zoo at New Johannesburg in Surrey, with visitors free to do what they like with them.

Mitchell's subject, however, is Len Rossman, whose tape-recorded life story this is. He is "the best-known bodyguard in the British Isles," uncritically serving several masters. In a rapid and varied sequence of adventures, we find him trapping "subverts" as an undercover agent at Oxford University, and plotting an ingenious mock-killing as a training exercise. Mitchell diverts us, too, with the comic rebel whose only weapon is custard and the nudist bridal party Rossman must guard. On one level, Mitchell seems to enjoy writing of violence, with a little crude sex. But among these diversions, we see Rossman as the violent Fascist: "I have dreamed of an England and a Europe which are both strong and clean," he says. While another bodyguard explains: "In the city you can forget all that neighbour stuff. Nobody has to be friends. You're competing, you're struggling, you're using your eyes and your brain and your body. Nobody's equal, ever, in the city. Any city is just a series of little battlefields. Win or lose. I like that. And I don't want either the city or the country to change. Yes, that's why I hate subverts." Mitchell shows in an original, half-amusing, half-frightening way how sterile a policy of more repression towards crime and dissent is, and where it leads.

Wartime is also about Fascism, and more successful. An eccentric colonel catches three teenage boys on his estate and forces them to shoot at each other with airguns. Then one is blinded, and the colonel kills himself. His daughter, more arrogantly upper-class Fascistic than he was, spends the next ten years trying to destroy the youths. She marries one, ruining his talents and depriving him of his ideals, and keeps the second locked up as a slave, ostensibly training him to survive nuclear war. The third, however, an independent radical, escapes her. The long central section is a deliberately uncontrolled and disordered vision, incorporating a speech, dreams, a television interview, a madman's letter about London, and news items of 5 December 1963. *Wartime* is, in the *TLS* reviewer's words, "a parable of destructive Toryism nearly doing in the spontaneous and beneficial, political, artistic and sexual life of the masses," a strange and disturbing fantasy.

—Malcolm Page

MITCHELL, Joseph. American. Born in Fairmont, North Carolina, 27 July 1908. Educated at the University of North Carolina, Chapel Hill, 1925-29. Married Therese Dagny Jacobsen in 1931; two daughters. Reporter, New York *World*, 1929-30, New York *Herald Tribune*, 1929-31, and New York *World Telegram*, 1931-38. Since 1938, Staff Writer for *The New Yorker* magazine. Recipient: American Academy award, 1965. Vice-President, 1971, and Secretary, 1972-74, National Institute of Arts and Letters. Address: c/o The New Yorker, 25 West 43rd Street, New York, New York 10036, U.S.A.

PUBLICATIONS

Short Stories

McSorley's Wonderful Saloon. New York, Duell, 1943; London, Porcupine Press, 1946.
Old Mr. Flood. New York, Duell, 1948.
The Bottom of the Harbor. Boston, Little Brown, 1959; London, Chatto and Windus, 1961.
Joe Gould's Secret. New York, Viking Press, 1965.

Other

My Ears Are Bent (collection of newspaper articles). New York, Sheridan House, 1938.

*

Critical Studies: "The Grammar of Facts" by Malcolm Cowley, in *New Republic* (New York), 26 July 1943; "The Art of Joseph Mitchell" by Stanley Edgar Hyman, in *New Leader* (New York), 6 December 1965.

* * *

Throughout his works Joseph Mitchell places himself in the tradition of the tall tale in America and reveals why he can say in *McSorley's Wonderful Saloon* to the "Gifted Child" that Mark Twain's *Life on the Mississippi* is the one book he likes above all others. He walks in wonder and records what he sees. All of his central figures emerge as larger-than-life people, yet there is almost always a quality of reflection and tone-setting that makes them believable as well as memorable.

In an author's note to *McSorley's Wonderful Saloon* Mitchell concludes with, "There are no little people in this book. They are as big as you are, whoever you are." And he then works with a fine eye, ear, and hand to give profile to such "little" people as John McSorley, president of "an organization of gluttons called the Honorable John McSorley Pickle, Beefsteak, Baseball Nine and Chowder Club"; Mazie P. Gordon, owner of, ticket seller, and bouncer at the Venice theater in the Bowery; King Cockeye Johnny Nikanov, a Russian and King of the Gypsies in New York; Lady Olga Jane Bardwell, the freak show bearded lady, with a fourteen-and-a-half inch beard, mustache, and her fourth husband; and various others. His favorite setting is lower Manhattan, and his stories become urban pastorals, strongest when he focuses with care on his people: Mr. Hugh G. Flood, in *Old Mr. Flood*, and Joe Gould, in *Joe Gould's Secret*, exemplify best Mitchell's role as profilist-story teller.

Mr. Flood, age 93 to 95, wants to live to be 115, is a "seafoodetarian," and can eat bushels of clams and consume large quantities of whiskey. From the many scenes and wild anecdotes of "Old Mr. Flood," "The Black Clams," and "Mr. Flood's Party" comes a man whom the narrator obviously loves, one who, as Mr. Mitchell says, is not one man but "several old men, who work or hang out in Fulton Fish Market." He's too big to exist, but he is nonetheless there, and the *I* of the story penetrates his moods—from extreme loneliness to convivial joy—with touching sensitivity. One feels that Mr. Flood will indeed live to age 115.

Joe Gould, on the other hand, is, as the author says in a note, "a lost soul." As Professor Sea Gull in *McSorley's Wonderful Saloon*, he is a tall-tale character too—a blithe and emaciated little man who has been a notable in the cafeterias, diners, barrooms, and dumps of Greenwich Village for a quarter of a century. A Harvard alumnus, class of 1911, he sometimes brags that he is the last of the bohemians. Of chief interest to Mitchell is Gould's *An Oral History of Our*

Time—a document eleven times as long as the *Bible*, over 9,000,000 words in longhand and still unfinished. As a solitary nocturnal wanderer he talks much of his *Oral History* and at his ability, among other things, to translate Longfellow's "Hiawatha" into sea gull. Here he shouts to a Village waitress: "I'm Joe Gould, the poet; I'm Joe Gould, the historian; I'm Joe Gould, the wild Chippewa Indian dancer; and I'm Joe Gould, the greatest authority in the world on the language of the sea gull."

Joe Gould's secret, however, discovered by Mitchell years later, is that there is no *Oral History*. Gould has not only duped Mitchell and the people but has duped himself. He can recite it but cannot put it down. Mitchell keeps the secret until he writes it down in his story, stepping out of, as he says, "the role I had stepped into the afternoon I discovered that the *Oral History* did not exist."

My Ears Are Bent and *The Bottom of the Harbor* show Mitchell's consistency throughout his career in reporting on but also building on the people and places of his world, from Sloppy Louie's, the old Fulton Ferry Hotel, and the "Baymen" to the rats on the waterfront. When he writes of his home country in rural North Carolina he uses his same profilist's eye and feeling for his "people" to bring to life such characters as Mrs. Copenhagen Calhoun in "I Blame It All on Mama," Uncle Dockery in "Uncle Dockery and the Independent Bull" and Mr. Catfish Giddy in "The Downfall of Fascism in Black Ankle County." Mitchell is the country boy who went to the city to find his way—and found it in *The New Yorker* where he perfected the urban tall-tale pastoral.

—Frank T. Phipps

MITCHELL, (Charles) Julian (Humphrey). British. Born in Epping, Essex, 1 May 1935. Educated at Winchester College, 1948-53; Wadham College, Oxford, B.A. 1958; St. Antony's College, Oxford, M.A. 1962. Served as a Midshipman in the Royal Naval Volunteer Reserve, 1953-55. Member of the Arts Council Literature Panel, 1966-69. Governor, Chelsea School of Art, London. Recipient: Harkness Fellowship, 1959; Rhys Memorial Prize, 1965; Maugham Award, 1966; International Critics Prize, for television play, 1977; Christopher Award, for television play, 1977 (USA). Address: 16 Ovington Street, London SW3 2JB, England.

PUBLICATIONS

Novels

Imaginary Toys. London, Hutchinson, 1961.
A Disturbing Influence. London, Hutchinson, 1962.
As Far As You Can Go. London, Constable, 1963.
The White Father. London, Constable, 1964; New York, Farrar Straus, 1965.
A Circle of Friends. London, Constable, 1966; New York, McGraw Hill, 1967.
The Undiscovered Country. London, Constable, 1968; New York, Grove Press, 1970.

Short Stories

Introduction, with others. London, Faber, 1960.

Plays

A Heritage and Its History, adaptation of the novel by Ivy Compton-Burnett (produced London, 1965). London, Evans, 1966.
Shadow in the Sun (televised, 1971). Published in *Elizabeth R*, edited by J.C. Trewin, London, Elek, 1972.
A Family and a Fortune, adaptation of the novel by Ivy Compton-Burnett (produced Seattle, 1974; Bath and London, 1975). London, French, 1976.
Half-Life (produced London, 1977). London, Heinemann, 1977.
Henry IV, adaptation of the play by Pirandello. London, Eyre Methuen, 1979.
The Enemy Within (produced Leatherhead, Surrey, 1980).

Screenplay: *Arabesque*, with Stanley Price and Pierre Marton, 1966.

Radio Documentary: *Life and Deaths of Dr. John Donne*, 1972.

Television Plays: *Persuasion*, from the novel by Jane Austen, 1971; *The Man Who Never Was*, 1972; *A Perfect Day*, 1972; *Fly in the Ointment*, 1972; *A Question of Degree*, 1972; *Rust*, 1973; *Jennie*, 1974; *Abide with Me*, from the novel *A Child in the Forest* by Winifred Foley, 1976; *Staying On*, from the novel by Paul Scott, 1980; *The Good Soldier*, from the novel by Ford Madox Ford, 1981; and other adaptations.

Other

Truth and Fiction (lecture). London, Covent Garden Press, 1972.
Jennie, Lady Randolph Churchill: A Portrait with Letters, with Peregrine Churchill. London, Collins, 1974; New York, St. Martin's Press, 1975.

Editor, with others, *Light Blue, Dark Blue: An Anthology of Recent Writing from Oxford and Cambridge Universities*. London, Macdonald, 1960.

* * *

Julian Mitchell's books reveal a remarkably talented writer, whose work is consistently fluent, witty and ingenious. But they do leave a doubt in the mind whether his literary gifts are, in the last analysis, those of a natural novelist. He began his career precociously early, and published four novels before he was thirty. The first of them, *Imaginary Toys*, is, like many other first novels, a partly sentimental, partly satirical recreation of university life. It covers a small group of young people during a few days in one summer term at Oxford; the story is of the slightest, but Mitchell uses it as the vehicle for some serious disquisitions on sexual and social problems. The novel is at its most engaging, though, in its fanciful, essay-like speculations, which make it a little reminiscent of the early Aldous Huxley. Mitchell is like Huxley, too, in his acute sense of period; *Imaginary Toys* effectively catches the feel of the late 1950's, though this responsiveness to contemporary atmosphere inevitably made the book seem dated after a few years. His next novel, *A Disturbing Influence*, was not a particularly exciting development, though it was a smoothly written narrative. It described the impact on a complacent, even sleepy Berkshire village of a strange, destructive, amoral young man, the "disturbing influence" of the title. Such types evidently have a particular fascination for Mitchell, for they tend to recur in his fiction. This book was followed by a more substantial and interesting work, *As Far As You Can Go*, in which Mitchell drew on some of his own recent experience to write the kind of novel that was to become increasingly common in England in the 1960's—the account of a peripatetic Englishman's adventures in America. Harold Barlow, the central character, is a typical Mitchell hero—intelligent, amiable, rather inept—and he conveys a tourist's eye view of life in the hipster sub-culture of California.

The White Father, which won Mitchell the Somerset Maugham Award, was a more determinedly ambitious novel than its predecessors. The narrative is divided between London and a remote African territory, and Mitchell shows much of the action through the eyes of Hugh Shrieve, a district officer in Africa who has come to London to plead for his tribe at a conference to arrange independence for the territory. Shrieve has been out of England for years, and he is unprepared for what he finds when he arrives: the frenetic beginnings of the "Swinging London" cult. Mitchell looks satirically though tolerantly at the world of pop music, and there is a powerful imaginative touch in his portrayal of the megalomaniac Mr. Brachs, head of a vast commercial empire catering to the youth cult, who is going steadily mad in his inaccessible penthouse on top of the London skyscraper that houses all his many enterprises. *The White Father* is one of Mitchell's best novels, which makes some sharp observations about life in a high-consumption society, as well as telling an entertaining story. The novelist and the essayist are more closely fused than is usual in his fiction. Two years later Mitchell published an extremely thin novel, *A Circle of Friends*, which moves between New York and the English Home Counties, showing how one of his characteristically weak young men gets unhappily entangled with a wealthy Anglo-American family, culminating in a wholly undeserved position as co-respondent in a divorce action.

All these novels present, at varying levels of literary achievement, some recurring characteristics: a tendency to draw fairly directly on personal experience and to use the novel as a vehicle for airing ideas, a taste for likeable but weak central characters, and a generally relaxed and good-humoured tone. In *The Undiscovered Country*, which is Mitchell's most striking contribution to recent English fiction, all these qualities are present in a new combination. Unlike his previous novels, it is a deliberately experimental work, which plays with the conventions of fiction writing, and the relations between art and reality, in the manner of Nabokov or Borges. The first part is, on the face of it, undisguised autobiography, where Mitchell writes in his own person about his friendship with an enigmatically attractive young man, Charles Humphries, who dies at an early age. He leaves behind the fragmentary manuscript of a novel called "The New Satyricon," which Mitchell edits with introduction and commentary, and presents as the second part of *The Undiscovered Country*. Undoubtedly "Humphries" is an alter ego for "Mitchell" (whose full Christian names are Charles Julian Humphrey), though the relation between them remains teasing. *The Undiscovered Country* is a generally entertaining novel, and the second part is full of pleasant literary jokes, where Mitchell engages to the full his essayistic tendencies. It is also a watershed in his development as a novelist, and marks his dissatisfaction with his more conventional earlier novels. Indeed, at the end of part one, before he introduces "The New Satyricon," Mitchell observes, "I think it unlikely that I shall write another book of my own for a long time, with the fact of this one before me. Charles said that all art comes from an inner need. He said that I began to write because I wanted to be a writer, and that was the wrong kind of need."

—Bernard Bergonzi

MITCHELL, W(illiam) O(rmond). Canadian. Born in Weyburn, Saskatchewan, 13 March 1914. Educated at the University of Manitoba, Winnipeg, 1932-34; University of Alberta, Edmonton, B.A. 1942. Married Merna Lynne Hirtle in 1942; two sons and one daughter. Has worked as a seaman, salesman, teacher, and high school principal. Writer-in-Residence, University of Calgary, Alberta, 1968-71. Recipient: Maclean's Novel Award, 1953; President's Medal, University of Western Ontario, 1953; Leacock Medal, 1962. Address: 3031 Roxboro Glen Road, Calgary, Alberta, Canada.

PUBLICATIONS

Novels

Who Has Seen the Wind. Boston, Little Brown, 1947; London, Macmillan, 1948.
Jake and the Kid. Toronto, Macmillan, 1961.
The Kite. Toronto, Macmillan, 1962.
The Vanishing Point. Toronto, Macmillan, 1973.

Short Story

The Black Bonspiel of Wullie MacCrimmon. Calgary, Alberta, Frontiers Unlimited, 1965.

Uncollected Short Stories

"The Owl and the Bens," in *The Best American Short Stories 1946*, edited by Martha Foley. Boston, Houghton Mifflin, 1946.
"Saint Sammy," in *Book of Canadian Stories*, edited by Desmond Pacey. Toronto, Ryerson Press, 1950.
"The Princess and the Wild Ones," in *Cavalcade of the North*, edited by G.E. Nelson. New York, Doubleday, 1958.

Plays

The Black Bonspiel of Wullie MacCrimmon, adaptation of his own story (produced Calgary, 1979). Published in *Three Worlds of Drama*, Toronto, Macmillan, 1966.
Ladybug, Ladybug (radio play), in *Edge 5* (Edmonton), Fall 1966.
The Devil's Instrument (produced Ottawa, 1972). Toronto, Simon and Pierre, 1973.
Back to Beulah (produced Vancouver, 1976).
The Day Jake Made 'er Rain (produced Winnipeg, 1979).

Radio Plays: *Ladybug, Ladybug* and other plays for CBC since 1947.

* * *

W.O. Mitchell, generally considered a "regional humourist," perhaps himself encourages such a reputation. In the guise of the homespun philosopher he finds a traditional folk identity with which to meet contemporary life and a literary format which matches his penchant for the humour of understatement, wise saws, tall tales, and home truths. But this is not to say that he spurns sophistication, progress, or the 20th century. His stories constantly ask blunt questions about reality and values, probing "sophistication" to see if it isn't hypocrisy by a different name, and reducing contemporary problems to domestic proportions in order to reveal the lineage of human foible which the present has inherited.

Most clearly illustrative of such a technique are the wry though somewhat dated stories of Jake and the Kid, which were written first as dramas and were performed on the Canadian Broadcasting Corporation as a continuing radio series in the 1940's. Set in the ranching country of the Alberta foothills which Mitchell knows well, they detail the laconic education in the vagaries of life which Jake, a hired hand, gives to the young son of his employers—and incidentally, always ironically, to himself. They seldom directly invoke contentious social issues—indeed, when Mitchell does contend head-on with such matters as race relations, as in his serialized novel *The Alien*, the result is more melodramatic than provocative. In rewritten form, *The Alien* was published as *The Vanishing Point* in 1973, but the radical structural changes do not alter its central weakness. Despite Mitchell's wit, his capacity for creating lively scenes and clever caricatures, his central characters here do not develop. Accordingly, their reflections on life seem to lack substance.

One of Mitchell's most successful uses of anecdote occurs in his novel *The Kite*, when the centenarian central character, Daddy Sherry, irrepressibly individual (particularly when officialdom dictates prudence to him), accepts a flooding river as an invitation to a

South Seas cruise and sails his uprooted house matter-of-factly away, at dark of night, across the American border. The wit is paramount, but incidentally Mitchell manages bemused swipes at customs regulations and bureaucratic nervousness, and builds up the engagingly exaggerated personalities of his cast. The book as a whole celebrates the virtue of living life fully, of engaging oneself in the *process* of living, of which the cruise incident is merely a genial sign.

The developing spiritual affinity between Daddy and a young boy varies the Jake-Kid relationship, and adds a Wordsworthian dimension to Mitchell's world that is more readily seen in his best book, *Who Has Seen the Wind.* In it, the young Brian O'Connal is broken out of his innocent childhood oneness with the world (into the imperfect loves and prejudices of ordinary humanity) by his increasingly adaptive encounters with death and disorder. The "sleep and forgetting" that marks his growth are accompanied by a developing social conscience, however, revealed ultimately in his "mature" child's commitment to agricultural science, and counter-pointed by the novel's subplots. Their exploration of institutional hypocrisy, educational rigidity, race prejudice, and religious intemperance tends sometimes towards the maudlin, but in the characters of Saint Sammy and the Young Ben, "naturals" whose oneness with the prairie and the wind serves as a kind of true spiritual example to Brian, Mitchell has created unforgettable animated forces. With Brian's renegade Uncle Sean, they together fill the "Jake" role to Brian's "kid" and widen rather than reduce the intensity of the effect Jake was meant to exert. For a generation of radio listeners Jake was a shrewd observer of daily life; Brian's relationship with the world of the Young Ben appeals to rather more, for the imaginative experience it represents transcends place and time. Tracing the loss of a child's self and the gain of a man's, the book probes the many dimensions of reality—raising Berkeleyan dilemmas, countering them with Wordsworthian intuitions—and covering all with the gentle humour of a man in love with life whose acute eyes remind him constantly of the failings of mankind as well as of its humane possibilities.

—W.H. New

MITCHISON, Naomi (Margaret). British. Born in Edinburgh, 1 November 1897; sister of the writer J.B.S. Haldane. Educated at Dragon School, Oxford; St. Anne's College, Oxford. Served as a volunteer nurse, 1915. Married G.R. Mitchison (who became Lord Mitchison, 1964) in 1916 (died, 1970); three sons and two daughters. Labour Candidate for Parliament, Scottish Universities constituency, 1935; Member, Argyll County Council, 1945-66; Member, Highland Panel, 1947-64, and Highland and Island Advisory Council, 1966-76. Tribal Adviser, and Mmarona (Mother), to the Bakgatla of Botswana, 1963-73. Recipient: Palmes de l'Académie Française, 1921. D.Univ.: University of Stirling, Scotland, 1976. Honorary Fellow, St. Anne's College, 1980. Address: Carradale, Campbeltown, Argyll, Scotland.

PUBLICATIONS

Novels

The Conquered. London, Cape, and New York, Harcourt Brace, 1923.
Cloud Cuckoo Land. London, Cape, 1925; New York, Harcourt Brace, 1926.
The Corn King and the Spring Queen. London, Cape, and New York, Harcourt Brace, 1931; as *The Barbarian*, New York, Cameron, 1961.
The Powers of Light. London, Cape, and New York, Smith, 1932.
Beyond This Limit. London, Cape, 1935.
We Have Been Warned. London, Constable, 1935; New York, Vanguard Press, 1936.
The Blood of the Martyrs. London, Constable, 1939; New York, McGraw Hill, 1948.
The Bull Calves. London, Cape, 1947.
Lobsters on the Agenda. London, Gollancz, 1952.
Travel Light. London, Faber, 1952.
To the Chapel Perilous. London, Allen and Unwin, 1955.
Behold Your King. London, Muller, 1957.
Memoirs of a Spacewoman. London, Gollancz, 1962.
When We Become Men. London, Collins, 1965.
Cleopatra's People. London, Heinemann, 1972.
Solution Three. London, Dobson, and New York, Warner, 1975.

Short Stories

When the Bough Breaks and Other Stories. London, Cape, and New York, Harcourt Brace, 1924.
Black Sparta: Greek Stories. London, Cape, and New York, Harcourt Brace, 1928.
Barbarian Stories. London, Cape, and New York, Harcourt Brace, 1929.
The Delicate Fire: Short Stories and Poems. London, Cape, and New York, Harcourt Brace, 1933.
The Fourth Pig: Stories and Verses. London, Constable, 1936.
Five Men and a Swan: Short Stories and Poems. London, Allen and Unwin, 1958.
Images of Africa. Edinburgh, Canongate, 1980.

Uncollected Short Stories

"After the Accident," in *The Year 2000*, edited by Harry Harrison. New York, Doubleday, 1970; London, Faber, 1971.
"Mary and Joe," in *Nova 1*, edited by Harry Harrison. New York, Delacorte Press, 1970; London, Sphere, 1975.
"Death of a Peculiar Boar," in *Worlds of Fantasy* (New York), Winter 1970.
"Miss Omega Raven," in *Nova 2*, edited by Harry Harrison. New York, Walker, 1972; London, Sphere, 1975.
"The Factory," in *Nova 3*, edited by Harry Harrison. New York, Walker, 1973; London, Sphere, 1975.
"Out of the Waters," in *Nova 4*, edited by Harry Harrison. New York, Walker, 1974; London, Sphere, 1976.
"Valley of the Bushes," in *Andromeda 1*, edited by Peter Weston. London, Futura, 1976; New York, St. Martin's Press, 1979.

Plays

Nix-Nought-Nothing: Four Plays for Children. London, Cape, 1928; New York, Harcourt Brace, 1929.
The Price of Freedom, with L.E. Gielgud (produced Cheltenham, 1949). London, Cape, 1931.
Full Fathom Five, with L.E. Gielgud (produced London, 1932).
An End and a Beginning and Other Plays. London, Cape, 1937; as *Historical Plays for Schools*, London, Constable, 2 vols., 1939.
As It Was in the Beginning, with L.E. Gielgud. London, Cape, 1939.
The Corn King, music by Brian Easdale, adaptation of the novel by Mitchison (produced London, 1950).
Spindrift, with Denis Macintosh (produced Glasgow, 1951). London, French, 1951.

Verse

The Laburnum Branch. London, Cape, 1926.
The Alban Goes Out. Harrow, Middlesex, Raven Press, 1939.
The Cleansing of the Knife and Other Poems. Edinburgh, Canongate, 1978.

)ther (juvenile)

'he *Hostages and Other Stories.* London, Cape, 1930; New York, Harcourt Brace, 1931.
loys and Girls and Gods. London, Watts, 1931.
'he Big House. London, Faber, 1950.
iraeme and the Dragon. London, Faber, 1954.
'he Swan's Road. London, Naldrett Press, 1954.
'he Land the Ravens Found. London, Collins, 1954.
.ittle Boxes. London, Faber, 1956.
'he Far Harbour. London, Collins, 1957.
udy and Lakshmi. London, Collins, 1959.
'he Rib of the Green Umbrella. London, Collins, 1960.
'he Young Alexander the Great. London, Parrish, 1960; New York, Roy, 1961.
.arensgaard: The Story of a Danish Farm. London, Collins, 1961.
'he Young Alfred the Great. London, Parrish, 1962; New York, Roy, 1963.
'he Fairy Who Couldn't Tell a Lie. London, Collins, 1963.
lexander the Great. London, Longman, 1964.
lenny and the Crispies. Wellington, New Zealand School Publications, 1964.
.etse and the Chief. London, Nelson, 1965.
'riends and Enemies. London, Collins, 1966; New York, Day, 1968.
'he Big Surprise. London, Kaye and Ward, 1967.
lighland Holiday. Wellington, New Zealand School Publications, 1967.
lfrican Heroes. London, Bodley Head, 1968; New York, Farrar Straus, 1969.
)on't Look Back. London, Kaye and Ward, 1969.
'he Family at Ditlabeng. London, Collins, 1969; New York, Farrar Straus, 1970.
un and Moon. London, Bodley Head, 1970; Nashville, Nelson, 1973.
'unrise Tomorrow. London, Collins, and New York, Farrar Straus, 1973.
'he Danish Teapot. London, Kaye and Ward, 1973.
'nake! London, Collins, 1976.
'he Brave Nurse and Other Stories. Cape Town, Oxford University Press, 1977.
'he Two Magicians, with Dick Mitchison. London, Dobson, 1979.
'he Vegetable War. London, Hamish Hamilton, 1980.

)ther

lnna Comnena. London, Howe, 1928.
'omments on Birth Control. London, Faber, 1930.
'he Home and a Changing Civilisation. London, Lane, 1934.
'ienna Diary. London, Gollancz, and New York, Smith and Haas, 1934.
'ocrates, with Richard Crossman. London, Hogarth Press, 1937; Harrisburg, Pennsylvania, Stackpole, 1938.
'he Moral Basis of Politics. London, Constable, 1938; Port Washington, New York, Kennikat Press, 1971.
'he Kingdom of Heaven. London, Heinemann, 1939.
len and Herring, with Denis Macintosh. Edinburgh, Serif, 1949.
)ther People's Worlds (travel). London, Secker and Warburg, 1958.
'resenting Other People's Children. London, Hamlyn, 1961.
l Fishing Village on the Clyde, with G.W.L. Paterson. London, Oxford University Press, 1961.
leturn to the Fairy Hill (autobiography and sociology). London, Heinemann, and New York, Day, 1966.
'he Africans: A History. London, Blond, 1970.
'mall Talk: Memories of an Edwardian Childhood. London, Bodley Head, 1973.
l Life for Africa: The Story of Bram Fischer. London, Merlin Press, and Boston, Carrier Pigeon, 1973.
Oil for the Highlands? London, Fabian Society, 1974.
All Change Here: Girlhood and Marriage (autobiography). London, Bodley Head, 1975.
Sittlichkeit (lecture). London, Birkbeck College, 1975.
You May Well Ask: A Memoir 1920-1940. London, Gollancz, 1979.
Mucking Around: Five Continents over Fifty Years. London, Gollancz, 1981.

Editor, *An Outline for Boys and Girls and Their Parents.* London, Gollancz, 1932.
Editor, *Re-Educating Scotland.* Glasgow, Scoop, 1944.
Editor, *What the Human Race Is Up To.* London, Gollancz, 1962.

*

Manuscript Collections: National Library of Scotland, Edinburgh; University of Texas, Austin.

Naomi Mitchison comments:

I write a number of different kinds of books, as you see. When I began writing this was possible because at that time books were written because the authors had something they wanted to say; today books are a commodity like other commodities. What is important is whether publishers think they can sell them. Most publishers have definite selling plans and if a given book does not fit into this, the author has little chance of getting it published. Today, if one wants to write about something special, one has to try and persuade a publisher that this was something he had already thought of. I like writing children's books because one has to write absolutely straight, without playing any of the stylistic or literary tricks which will take in an adult audience. I like digging out the facts of history and seeing what they will add up to. I like thinking what people do in strange situations, for instance in the past, in Africa or India, or in imaginary but possible situations in science fiction. This may enable one—or other people—to make some contribution towards a happier world.

* * *

In Naomi Mitchison's historical novels and short stories, with which she established her earliest reputation, an essential theme is conflict of loyalties, whether in Gaul at the time of Caesar's conquest, as in her first novel, *The Conquered*, or among the people of a small Aegean island who are dragged willy-nilly, on one side or another, into the bitter fratricidal battle between Athens and Sparta in the 4th century B.C.—the subject of her ironically entitled *Cloud Cuckoo Land*. Her major work in this genre is *The Corn King and the Spring Queen*, a study in the relationships between the people of three different societies—an agricultural community in the Crimea where the old fertility religion still remains strong enough to provide the folk with purposive unity; a decadent Greece where religious belief has broken down and the struggle to create a just society is conducted—and fails—on a secular basis; and an imperial Egypt where despotism has led to political apathy, disillusion, cynical hedonism, and a frantic search for religious consolation. At once a presentation of personal breakdown and reintegration, a picture of the stresses between idealism and expediency involved in the rise and fall of a revolutionary movement, and an exploration of the relationship between religious conviction and communal solidarity, between scepticism and the loosening of social cohesion, this novel is unsurpassed in 20th-century British historical fiction for range and variety of scene and characterisation, for political awareness, and for religious depth.

On Scottish subjects, Lady Mitchison is at her best in *The Big House*, a children's fairytale which is also a tragi-comedy expressing a profound understanding of the intermingled light and darkness of the human situation, a book where the natural magic of childhood, the terrible charm of the supernatural, the dark power of history, and a vision of life as at once dreadful and sublime, are all woven together. From the fairytale she has gone on to science-fiction fantasy with *Memoirs of a Spacewoman*, where she shows—in three related chapters about a world inhabited by butterflies and their larvae—a deep imaginative comprehension of extra-terrestrial modes of existence, and a compassionate reverence for life, even at its most remote and mysterious, which lift her work out of the category of the merely inventive and fanciful to give it something of the universality of legend. A poet as well as a prose-writer, Lady Mitchison has written a futuristic story about the exploration of space which is itself a myth, a concentrated symbolical expression of generations of experience.

Alongside fantasy, Lady Mitchison has also written "documentary" novels on contemporary social experience, some with a Scottish location and some set in Africa, where she has worked in Botswana. In these, characterisation tends to be subordinated to background detail. Perhaps the finest of her contemporary studies is the title-story of her collection *Five Men and a Swan*, a modern Scottish folk-tale which combines tenderness, brutality, humour, beauty, and sheer magic in a parable on the theme of human greed and stupidity. While the detail of this story is exactly in period, the writing has a quality of timelessness before which criticism must needs be silent.

—Alexander Scott

MOMADAY, N(avarre) Scott. American. Born in Lawton, Oklahoma, 27 February 1934. Educated at the University of New Mexico, Albuquerque, A.B. 1958; Stanford University, California (Creative Writing Fellow, 1959), A.M. 1960, Ph.D. 1963. Married 1) Gaye Mangold in 1959 (divorced), three daughters; 2) Regina Heitzer. Assistant Professor, 1963-67, and Associate Professor, 1967-69, University of California, Santa Barbara; Professor of English and Comparative Literature, University of California, Berkeley, 1969-72. Since 1973, Professor of English, Stanford University. Professor, University of California Institute for the Humanities, 1970; Visiting Professor, New Mexico State University, Las Cruces, 1972-73, State University of Moscow, Spring 1974, Columbia University, New York, 1979, and Princeton University, New Jersey, 1979. Recipient: Guggenheim grant, 1966; Pulitzer Prize, 1969; American Academy award, 1970; Western Heritage Award, 1974. D.H.L.: Central Michigan University, Mt. Pleasant, 1970; University of Massachusetts, Amherst, 1975; D.Litt.: Lawrence University, Appleton, Wisconsin, 1971; College of Ganado, 1979. Address: 1690 Beach Street, San Francisco, California 94123, U.S.A.

PUBLICATIONS

Novel

House Made of Dawn. New York, Harper, 1968; London, Gollancz, 1969.

Verse

Angle of Geese and Other Poems. Boston, Godine, 1974.
The Gourd Dancer. New York, Harper, 1976.

Other

The Journey of Tai-me (Kiowa Indian tales). Privately printed, 1967; revised edition, as *The Way to Rainy Mountain*, Albuquerque, University of New Mexico Press, 1969.
Colorado: Summer, Fall, Winter, Spring, photographs by Davi Muench. Chicago, Rand McNally, 1973.
The Names: A Memoir. New York, Harper, 1976.

Editor, *The Complete Poems of Frederick Goddard Tuckerma* New York, Oxford University Press, 1965.

* * *

The Rainy Mountain that is central to both of N. Scott Moma day's major works is the lost Eden of the Kiowa Indians. In *Th Way to Rainy Mountain* it haunts the narrator's memory and is th still point around which the complex chronology of myth, tellin and recollection is woven. Like a piece of Renaissance typograph the text is differentiated by typefaces into the myth, the history the tribe that the narrator's grandmother remembers, and the mor lyrical Wordsworthian recollections of a land of lost content tha are the narrator's own observations. And in this fiction Momada gives us the American equivalent of a whole tradition of Englis writing that runs from Hardy and Jefferies and Hudson to Ronal Blythe and Peter Laslett.

What is strikingly different in Momaday is the central symbol myth—the Tai-me image of the human in white feathers, fo instance. The government's prohibition of the ritual of the Su Dance, to which this image of the tribe's ancient power of surviv was central, spelled the end of the Kiowa as a people who knew wh they were and why. No one knows better than Momaday that " people without history is not redeemed from time, for history is pattern of timeless moments." And it is that pattern that his triads myth, history, and recollection present again and again, almo musically, the significance of the myth finding itself felt upon th narrator's pulses as uncorrupted spectator.

In this sense Momaday becomes the voice of the past but in n merely nostalgic way, rather its literal discoverer in the prese world of drab that looks for roots. "What the dead had no speec for when living, they can tell you, being dead," might also be h text, for the world of myth and history belongs to an oral cultu that had no need for the dead letters of the printed page and written down only when it has been forgotten.

So the Abel of Momaday's *House Made of Dawn* is paradox cally Cain—the outcast, the man running forever to find the wor that was lost almost before he began. There are echoes of Fitzgera in him—perhaps he might run a little faster, and one fine day..., there are echoes of Faulkner's Christmas in the outcast who runs a circle never breaking out or being understood. And like the figur in Faulkner's landscapes the distance seems never to diminish. I the prologue Abel, running against the wintry sky and the long, lig landscape of the valley at dawn, "seemed almost to be standing sti very little and alone." Above all the landscape is important in a wa that a post-ecology generation has only begun to discover—th Indians' incomprehension of the white man's desire to possess th land that, like the air, is everyone's legacy.

Abel's experience is increasingly of the starvation of that life the sterility of LA. Perhaps partly because Momaday is less effecti writing about the white demi-monde into which Abel stumbles—h momentary stasis of love is never satisfactory and curiously thir hand—the images of his dissolution are the more telling—broke like a bird against a fence, his hands swollen useless under th violence of meaningless attack.

One sees him at this moment close-up as if the runner we passing. Increasingly he recedes as a figure in a landscap running—the sound of the feet and the breathless runner. But one sense is also of a rhythm in that, the beat of the heart that measur terror, loneliness, and hope—always winning near the goal, nev achieving. The land of lost content is lost even though Abel has come home to find it so. But even in his dying there is a haunting eloquent evocation of myths that are truer than those of Faulkne Sartorises, felt at last, wordlessly, only at the moment of death.

—D.D.C. Chambe

MOORE, Brian. Canadian. Born in Belfast, Northern Ireland, 25 August 1921; moved to Canada in 1948 and to the United States in 1959. Educated at Saint Malachi's College, Belfast. Served in the Belfast Fire Service, 1942-43, and with the British Ministry of War Transport, in North Africa, Italy, and France, 1943-45. Married 1) Jacqueline Sirois in 1951; 2) Jean Denney in 1966; one son. Served with United Nations Relief and Rehabilitation Administration (UNRRA) Mission to Poland, 1946-47; Reporter, Montreal *Gazette*, 1948-52. Regents' Professor, 1974-75, and since 1976, Professor, University of California, Los Angeles. Recipient: Authors Club of Great Britain Award, 1956; Beta Sigma Phi Award, 1956; Quebec Literary Prize, 1958; Guggenheim Fellowship, 1959; Governor-General's Award, 1961, 1975; American Academy grant, 1961; Canada Council Fellowship, 1962; Smith Literary Award, 1973; National Catholic Book Award, 1973; Black Memorial Award, 1976. Agent: Curtis Brown Ltd., 575 Madison Avenue, New York, New York 10022, U.S.A.

PUBLICATIONS

Novels

The Executioners (as Michael Bryan). Toronto, Harlequin, 1951.
Wreath for a Redhead (as Michael Bryan). Toronto, Harlequin, 1951.
Judith Hearne. Toronto, Collins, and London, Deutsch, 1955; as *The Lonely Passion of Judith Hearne*, Boston, Little Brown, 1956.
Intent to Kill (as Michael Bryan). New York, Dell, and London, Eyre and Spottiswoode, 1956.
Murder in Majorca (as Michael Bryan). New York, Dell, 1957; London, Eyre and Spottiswoode, 1958.
The Feast of Lupercal. Boston, Little Brown, 1957; London, Deutsch, 1958; as *A Moment of Love*, London, Panther, 1965.
The Luck of Ginger Coffey. Boston, Little Brown, and London, Deutsch, 1960.
An Answer from Limbo. Boston, Little Brown, 1962; London, Deutsch, 1963.
The Emperor of Ice-Cream. New York, Viking Press, 1965; London, Deutsch, 1966.
I Am Mary Dunne. New York, Viking Press, and London, Cape, 1968.
Fergus. New York, Holt Rinehart, 1970; London, Cape, 1971.
Catholics. London, Cape, 1972; New York, Harcourt Brace, 1973.
The Great Victorian Collection. New York, Farrar Straus, and London, Cape, 1975.
The Doctor's Wife. New York, Farrar Straus, and London, Cape, 1976.
The Mangan Inheritance. New York, Farrar Straus, and London, Cape, 1979.
The Temptation of Eileen Hughes. New York, Farrar Straus, 1981.

Short Stories

Two Stories. Northridge, California, Santa Susana Press, 1978.

Plays

Catholics, adaptation of his own novel (produced Seattle, 1980).

Screenplays: *The Luck of Ginger Coffey*, 1964; *Torn Curtain*, 1966; *The Slave*, 1967; *Catholics*, 1973.

Other

Canada, with the editors of Life. New York, Time, 1963.
The Revolution Script. New York, Holt Rinehart, 1971; London, Cape, 1972.

Critical Studies: "The Simple Excellence of Brian Moore" by Christopher Ricks, in *New Statesman* (London), 18 February 1966; "Crisis and Ritual in Brian Moore's Belfast Novels" by John Wilson Foster, in *Eire-Ireland* (St. Paul, Minnesota), Autumn 1968; *Brian Moore* by Hallvard Dahlie, Toronto, Copp Clark, 1969; *Odysseus Ever Returning* by George Woodcock, Toronto, McClelland and Stewart, 1970; "The Novels of Brian Moore" by Michael Paul Gallagher, S.J., in *Studies (Ireland)* (Dublin), Summer 1971; "The Crisis of Identity in the Novels of Brian Moore" by Murry Prosky, in *Eire-Ireland* (St. Paul, Minnesota), Summer 1971; *Brian Moore* by Jeanne Flood, Lewisburg, Pennsylvania, Bucknell University Press, 1974; "Brian Moore: Private Person" by Bruce Cook, in *Commonweal* (New York), 23 August 1974; "The Novels of Brian Moore: A Retrospective" by DeWitt Henry, in *Ploughshares* (Boston), Fall 1974; "Webs of Artifice" by Derek Mahon, in *New Review* (London), October 1975; "Brian Moore: Past and Present" by Kerry McSweeney, in *Critical Quarterly* (Manchester), 1976; "Portrait of the Artist as Emigré" by Philip French, in *Observer* (London), October 1977; "The Calligraphy of Pain" by Hubert de Santana, in *Maclean's* (Toronto), September 1979.

* * *

Highly praised by reviewers and critics, Brian Moore's compressed and effective fiction has not always achieved the wide popular acclaim it merits. His subjects indicate an extraordinary diversity of interest and sympathy: the lonely spinster who drinks while she longs for contacts with others she cannot sustain in *Judith Hearne*, Moore's first novel; the young Canadian newspaperman who returns to the Ireland his grandfather migrated from to try to find whether or not he is descended from the famous Irish poet, James Clarence Mangan, in *The Mangan Inheritance*; the contemporary women uneasy about their sexuality and their marriages, in America in *I Am Mary Dunne* and in Northern Ireland in *The Doctor's Wife*. Moore doesn't repeat themes, metaphors, and subjects from novel to novel. Similarly, his settings (always almost immediately contemporary, but with frequent reference to the past) vary from Belfast to Montreal to California to New York to southern Ireland and England, paralleling Moore's own migration from Belfast to Canada to California.

Moore's best-known novel, made into a popular film, and the one that can be most easily attached to a popular genre of fiction, is *The Luck of Ginger Coffey*. An Irish immigrant to Canada whose dreams of business success are at odds with his shabby reality, as his small green feathered fedora is out of place in Montreal in the late 1950's, Ginger is forced to accept jobs as a night-shift proof-reader for a newspaper and a driver for a diaper service rather than the entrepreneurial positions of his imagination. In the difference between Ginger's vision of himself and reality, Moore manages a brisk and highly comic version of the contemporary picaresque, the estranged hero wandering about the modern world. But, unlike some of his contemporaries, Moore combines this satirical distance with a respect for Ginger, a sympathy with this aging displaced man who would do anything to give his wife and daughter the kind of life he assumes they ought to have. Finally, when arrested for drunkenness and indecent exposure, Ginger gives the police a false name and is willing to accept further punishment just to protect his family. His wife recognizes, in a moving and understated conclusion, the concern for others and the humanity that propel Ginger's feeble self-deceptions.

In Moore's fiction the alienation of the central characters is often, in part, the result of internalized clashes between cultures dramatized with considerable sensitivity. Young Gavin Burke in *The Emperor of Ice-Cream* is growing up as a Catholic in Belfast at the beginning of the Second World War, experiencing all the religious and national divisions involved, and rebelling from his family by working for the Home Guard instead of following his elder brother to the university. When the Germans bomb Belfast, Gavin is publicly vindicated, but vindication is less the issue than Gavin's realization of his own identity, his capacity to resolve the dualisms of his childhood, in which he had always a "white" angel contending with a "black," and recognize his own responsibility for what he is. In a much later novel, *The Doctor's Wife*, the "troubles" of Northern Ireland are also visible as constantly present background, handled with skill and subtlety, in the story of Sheila Redden, married to a Belfast doctor for 16 years, who runs off with a young American she meets in Paris. Again, the issue is self-definition far more than cultural conflict or victimization. Another novel, *Catholics*, deals with a young American priest of Irish descent who is sent by Rome to gain the obedience of a remote abbey on the rocky west coast of Ireland to the new order for the secular mass. He is successful, yet the novel concludes with a powerful and understated sense that the remote community, which had resisted despoliation by Henry VIII and by Cromwell will never be the same again, another inevitable sacrifice to the historical process in which "yesterday's orthodoxy is today's heresy."

Always treating his central characters with considerable respect, no matter how comic or ludicrous the dilemmas in which they involve themselves, Moore sometimes writes from the point of view of female characters. He is, in his own way, sensitive to changes in the general perception of female consciousness. In his 1960's novel from the female point of view, Mary Dunne, presented on a single day, rather like that of *Mrs. Dalloway*, that recalls all her other days and her two earlier marriages as well as her present successful one, marriages that parallel her migration from the Canadian maritimes to Montreal to New York, is likely to attribute too much of her uneasiness to pre-menstrual tension. In his 1970's novel, *The Doctor's Wife*, such an explanation is part of the impercipient doctor's point of view and Sheila Redden, finally, must work out what she is independently, not through marriage or an affair. In spite of this difference in contemporary fashion, both novels maintain a combination of sympathy and distance, convincingly show a character coming to terms with both her past and her present, as, in Mary Dunne's terms, 'Memento ergo sum" ("I remember, therefore I am").

Moore's plots are frequently highly inventive. *The Great Victorian Collection* begins with a young history professor from Montreal temporarily in Carmel, California, who wakes to find that a full collection of Victoriana he has just dreamed really exists in a motel parking lot. The complications of his strange creation are comically fascinating, although the novel, perhaps Moore's least effective, does not sustain the interest initially generated by the metaphor and the fantasy. The search for the Irish poetic past in *The Mangan Inheritance* is also highly inventive, propelled by young Jamie Mangan's resemblance to a photograph he finds of his famous ancestor, a physical similarity as well as a similarity in poetic talent and a tendency toward self-destruction. The novel proceeds through a gradual revelation of mystery, sometimes with touches of the macabre. Yet, in this novel, revelation of the past yields some similarities and some differences for the central character. Identity is a complicated mixture of acting out what one has inherited and consciously working out what one wants to be. In this kind of complexity, in depicting characters living both what of themselves they can change and what of themselves they must accept, Brian Moore, writing always with economy and understatement, is at his very best.

—James Gindin

MOORHOUSE, Frank. Australian. Born in Nowra, New South Wales, 21 December 1938. Educated at the University of Queensland, Brisbane. Served in the Australian Army and Reserves, 1957-59. Divorced. Journalist, *Sydney Telegraph*, 1956-59; Editor, *Lockhart Review*, New South Wales, 1960, and *Australian Worker*, Sydney, 1962; assistant secretary, Workers' Educational Association, Sydney, 1963-65; union organiser, Australian Journalists Association, 1966; contributor and columnist, 1970-79, and night club writer, 1980, *Bulletin*, Sydney; Co-Founding Editor, *Tabloid Story*, Sydney, 1972-74. Vice President, Australian Society of Authors, 1978-80. Recipient: Lawson Short Story Prize, 1970; National Award for Fiction, 1975; Senior Literary Fellowship, 1976. Address: G.P.O. Box 4430, Sydney, New South Wales 2001, Australia.

Publications

Short Stories

Futility and Other Animals. Sydney, Powell, 1969.
The Americans, Baby. Sydney and London, Angus and Robertson, 1972.
The Electrical Experience. Sydney, Angus and Robertson, 1974.
Conference-ville. Sydney, Angus and Robertson, 1976.
Tales of Mystery and Romance. London, Angus and Robertson, 1977.
The Everlasting Secret Family and Other Secrets. Sydney, Angus and Robertson, 1980.

Play

Screenplay: *Between Wars*, 1974.

Other

Editor, *Coast to Coast.* Sydney, Angus and Robertson, 1973.
Editor, *Days of Wine and Rage.* Melbourne, Penguin, 1980.

*

Manuscript Collections: Fryer Library, University of Queensland, Brisbane; National Library of Australia, Canberra.

Critical Studies: "The Short Stories of Wilding and Moorhouse" by Carl Harrison-Ford, in *Southerly* (Sydney), vol. 33, 1974; "Frank Moorhouse's Discontinuities" by D. Anderson, in *Southerly* (Sydney), vol. 35, 1975; interview with J. Davidson, in *Meanjin* (Melbourne), no. 2, 1977.

Frank Moorhouse comments:

Futility and Other Animals, *The Americans, Baby*, *The Electrical Experience*, and *The Everlasting Secret Family* are described as "discontinuous narratives" and are experiments with interlocked and overlapped short stories. The individual books also overlap and characters recur.

* * *

In the stories of Frank Moorhouse Australian life has nothing to do with Jackeroos, kangaroos, or desert places. The Australians of whom he writes are a "modern, urban tribe which does not recognize itself as a tribe," he says in introductory comments for the first collection, *Futility and Other Animals.* The tribe in *Futility* weave love affairs around knives, walk "vehicle-stewing" streets, are lectured in pubs and tutored in beds. Whatever their niche in the city they share in the common futility. Moorhouse doesn't seem to like these animals, this tribe, and after a while the limited emotional range of the stories begins to pall. This doesn't happen in *The Electrical Experience.* Here Moorhouse is at his best, still lucidly satirical but this time with some affection, playful and inventive. The stories centre around George McDowell, who grows and ages with the century. George is an earnest manufacturer of aerated waters, a Rotarian *par excellance* (nothing thrills him like the 192[illegible] Rotary Convention in St. Louis), an inveterate talker and sometimes bully who worries about being shy (but manages to "diminish" his shyness when he burns down Charles Crowhurst's house—

legally, of course). Detail by detail, McDowell's life and mind accrue mythological stature. Moorhouse has created with wit and intelligence the Australian companion to that American archetype, Sinclair Lewis's Babbitt. Through McDowell, Moorhouse dramatizes his country's political conservatism and its 20th-century subservience to American ideas and products.

In *The Americans, Baby* the milieu is a Sydney confused by the enervating enthusiasm and precarious sexuality of the 1960's. Here are the under-40's who hope that by being either earnest or outrageous, they will turn out to be real. Demonstrations provide religious training mixed with summer camp. They seem more self-conscious than self-fulfilling. If there should happen to be a moment of ease, something will quickly ruin it. Carl will move "of his own free volition" into the arms of the American journalist, Paul Jonson, but afterwards will feel guilty and humiliated and trapped—and will return to the flat again. Throughout these stories dramatic tension develops between impulse, which is associated with sex in various avatars, and an egregiously cerebral approach to life, an approach which suffocates physicality and seems to offer nothing much more appealing than baked potatoes with lemon for dinner, even though the potatoes are served in "a beautiful dark wooden bowl" with "a pile of coarse black bread." The virtue of it all scarcely seems worth the trouble.

Both *The Electrical Experience* and *The Americans, Baby* are sub-titled "a discontinuous narrative." The phrase suggests that each collection is held together as a definable fictional world but that the world is created episodically through an accretion of incident rather than linearly through the chronological narrative traditional to novels. When Moorhouse began publishing his collections, Australian fiction was still heavily bound to the conventions of realism. Few writers had experimented with altering forms to enact experience. Moorhouse did. There was nothing formalistic or sterile about his experiments. He needed a notion of narrative which would suit his vision of what life has become in an Australia where almost a quarter of the country's population was born overseas. As he has said in an interview, "The discontinuous narrative and the fragmented view that come out in the structure of my books" is "a map of how the world—Australia—seems to appear to me. I don't see any underlying harmonies.... That old homogeneity through Anglo-Saxon dominance has gone."

The three most recent collections are further evidence of this view but none of them is quite as satisfying as *The Electrical Experience* and *The Americans, Baby*. *Tales of Mystery and Romance* circles around the intricacies of a relationship between two men, the writer-narrator and an academic named Milton. The social vision has contracted to the literary-bohemian life which swirled around the Libertarian Society in the Sydney suburb of Balmain. The stories don't overcome the claustrophobia of that world. The same is true of *Conference-ville*. There Moorhouse uses the conference as a social ritual which detaches people from their ordinary life and makes them vulnerable to the pressures of ideas and personalities. As in *Tales of Mystery and Romance* the narrator is so given to ironic detachment, self-deprecation, and world-weariness that the stories lack vividness and energy. Aridity spreads from the conference to the prose. The most recent collection, *The Everlasting Secret Family*, contains four separate story sequences. The first, "Pacific City," returns to George McDowell's world but this time focuses on the much shadier, gloomier Irving Bow, proprietor of the Odeon Cinema and of a world of darkness where he entertains and seduces children, where illusion is reality and fantasy, where the imagination incurs guilt and runs a business. The second and third sequences are again conference stories in a quasi-documentary vein, but the final section, which gives the collection its title, is something rather different. Political allegory is fused with pornography in the story of a politician who seduces a schoolboy to whom years later he brings his own son for initiation into a secret and unrecognized family with full membership in that urban Australian tribe whose lives are the stories in Moorhouse's fiction.

—Lucy Frost

MORRIS, Wright (Marion). American. Born in Central City, Nebraska, 6 January 1910. Educated at Lakeview High School, Chicago; Crane College, Chicago; Pomona College, Claremont, California, 1930-33. Married 1) Mary Ellen Finfrock in 1934 (divorced, 1961); 2) Josephine Kantor in 1961. Has lectured at Haverford College, Pennsylvania, Sarah Lawrence College, Bronxville, New York, and Swarthmore College, Pennsylvania; Professor of English, California State University, San Francisco, 1962-75. Also a photographer. Recipient: Guggenheim Fellowship, 1942, 1946, 1954; National Book Award, 1957; American Academy grant, 1960; Rockefeller grant, 1967; American Book Award, 1981. Honorary degrees: Westminster College, Fulton, Missouri, 1968; University of Nebraska, Lincoln, 1968; Pomona College, Claremont, California, 1973. Member, American Academy, 1970. Address: 341 Laurel Way, Mill Valley, California 94941, U.S.A.

PUBLICATIONS

Novels

My Uncle Dudley. New York, Harcourt Brace, 1942.
The Man Who Was There. New York, Scribner, 1945.
The World in the Attic. New York, Scribner, 1949.
Man and Boy. New York, Knopf, 1951; London, Gollancz, 1952.
The Works of Love. New York, Knopf, 1952.
The Deep Sleep. New York, Scribner, 1953; London, Eyre and Spottiswoode, 1954.
The Huge Season. New York, Viking Press, 1954; London, Secker and Warburg, 1955.
The Field of Vision. New York, Harcourt Brace, 1956; London, Weidenfeld and Nicolson, 1957.
Love among the Cannibals. New York, Harcourt Brace, 1957; London, Weidenfeld and Nicolson, 1958.
Ceremony in Lone Tree. New York, Atheneum, 1960; London, Weidenfeld and Nicolson, 1961.
What a Way to Go. New York, Atheneum, 1962.
Cause for Wonder. New York, Atheneum, 1963.
One Day. New York, Atheneum, 1965.
In Orbit. New York, New American Library, 1967.
Fire Sermon. New York, Harper, 1971.
War Games. Los Angeles, Black Sparrow Press, 1972.
A Life. New York, Harper, 1973.
The Fork River Space Project. New York, Harper, 1977.
Plains Song: For Female Voices. New York, Harper, 1980.

Short Stories

Green Grass, Blue Sky, White House. Los Angeles, Black Sparrow Press, 1970.
Here Is Einbaum. Los Angeles, Black Sparrow Press, 1973.
The Cat's Meow. Los Angeles, Black Sparrow Press, 1975.
Real Losses, Imaginary Gains. New York, Harper, 1976.

Other

The Inhabitants (photo-text). New York, Scribner, 1946.
The Home Place (photo-text). New York, Scribner, 1948.
The Territory Ahead (essays). New York, Harcourt Brace, 1958; London, Peter Smith, 1964.
A Bill of Rites, A Bill of Wrongs, A Bill of Goods (essays). New York, New American Library, 1968.
God's Country and My People (photo-text). New York, Harper, 1968.
Wright Morris: A Reader. New York, Harper, 1970.
Love Affair: A Venetian Journal (photo-text). New York, Harper, 1972.
About Fiction: Reverent Reflections on the Nature of Fiction with Irreverent Observations on Writers, Readers, and Other Abuses. New York, Harper, 1975.

Structure and Artifacts: Photographs 1933-1954. Lincoln, University of Nebraska Press, 1976.
Conversations with Wright Morris: Critical Views and Responses, edited by Robert E. Knoll. Lincoln, University of Nebraska Press, 1977.
Earthly Delights, Unearthly Adornments: American Writers as Image Makers. New York, Harper, 1978.
Will's Boy: A Memoir. New York, Harper, 1981.

Editor, *The Mississippi River Reader.* New York, Doubleday, 1962.

*

Manuscript Collection: Bancroft Library, University of California, Berkeley.

Critical Studies: *Wright Morris* by David Madden, New York, Twayne, 1965; *Wright Morris* by Leon Howard, Minneapolis, University of Minnesota Press, 1968; *The Novels of Wright Morris: A Critical Interpretation* (includes bibliography) by G.B. Crump, Lincoln, University of Nebraska Press, 1978.

* * *

No contemporary American novelist has managed to be so persistently unfashionable as Wright Morris. Despite his many books, and despite both occasional public honors and a continuous critical assent to his talents, intelligence, integrity, and seriousness, he has never commanded a general attention. His work has resisted categories and obvious affiliations, while in its uniqueness it has prevented imitation. Morris is now an undeniable literary fact, without ever having been an event.

It is in part strange that this should be the case, because no other contemporary American novelist has been so diligently or sensitively in touch with the manners, voices, and things of American civilization. Morris's knowledge has led him, however, to an effort which prohibits ideological assertion for the reason that it prevents final judgements. Narrative line in Morris's fiction is seldom forthright. Thematic development is always subject to new doubts and allurements. The prose is elliptical, allusive, punning, to so great an extent as to seem sometimes incapable of statement. Indeed, language itself seems to be for Morris one more of those mysterious objects produced by the American civilization, which is to be explored for the hint of a revelation rather than be exploited. And the individual novels are not even discrete episodes of realization. Morris borrows freely from himself from book to book, re-using not only characters and events but lengthy passages of narration and reflection. He seems to have been long engaged in thinking through a single work—consisting of fiction, photographs, and an amount of literary and cultural criticism—the end of which is not yet in sight.

He has been so engaged for more than 30 years and through more than 25 books. In this time his single subject has been American nativity, and, if he has been influenced by any literary or cultural movement, it is that new nationalism which was being predicated in the 1910's and 1920's by Van Wyck Brooks, Lewis Mumford, Waldo Frank, Sherwood Anderson, the photographer Alfred Stieglitz, and others. Brooks had made a case for what he called the "usable past." More particularly, he had called upon American writers and critics to seek their own—American—literary past in such a way as to discover a cultural coherence, in which they then might participate. The invitation had itself become a part of the past by the time that Morris began to write, but he seems to have been impressed by some of the later nationalists, notably James Agee and Walker Evans. In any event, quite like those artists who participated in Brooks's enterprise, Morris has made his field of endeavor the American folk past and its relationship to the American present. The subject is the continuity of the American character, sought in its typicality and in its everydayness.

Despite the continuousness—indeed, the circularity—of effort proposed to Morris by his subject, the subject has also commanded a distinguishable progress in his thinking. He began with a commitment to discovery of the past, and he repeated that commitment without qualification, though with varying kinds of cunning, in the five books which he published in the 1940's. In the first, *My Uncle Dudley*, he composed a narrative which would ironically recapitulate the American past of the early middle 19th century. The time present of the novel is the 1920's. Uncle Dudley and his sidekick, the boy who tells the story, do a stint of vagabondage, which secures its significance because it simulates pioneering. In this day and age, the pursuit of the frontier must go from west to east, from Los Angeles to Chicago, and the pretence of the vagabonds to a covered wagon is an ancient touring car. They are assaulted on all sides by contemporary materialism, timidity, and restrictiveness, but they thereby are able to prove the older ways and virtues. And they succeed in their pretence until, just like Huckleberry Finn before them, they are incarcerated in a small town in Missouri. In the succeeding books in this period, Morris reversed his strategy for recovery of the past. *My Uncle Dudley* accepts a conventional myth of the older America and imposes it upon the present. The next books—a volume of novellas, two photo-texts, and a novel—have protagonists who, from their vantage in the present, come upon suggestive, buried, and ambiguous mementos of the past. As is usually the case in Morris's work, the locus of the past is the rural or small-town midwest. The protagonists of these books find a beckoning but elusive vitalism in occasional survivors from the past, and in such artifacts as peeling Mail Pouch signs on old barns, the fading pages of the old mail order catalogue, or an old and sputtering Model T. The process of apprehension is the area of Morris's concern.

This process seems finally, however, to have borne malign implications for Morris. With *The World in the Attic* he began to explore another realization, to the effect that the past was also potentially imprisoning, and the books thereafter become progressively less retrospective. The protagonists are not at home in the present, which is seen to be a spiritual wasteland, but they avoid regressive nostalgia. The intent of the books of the 1950's—novels and one volume of literary criticism—is recovery into the present not of the past but of a native American character, which is seen to be at once conservative, practical, desperate for spiritual liberation, and audacious. Salvation, if there is to be any, is in the occasional gesture on the part of the protagonists which combines past and present, transcending both.

In these books there was an implication of an astonishing persistence of the rural, frontiering American past, symbolized perhaps most aptly by a character who appeared first in *The World in the Attic* and who becomes the protagonist of *Ceremony in Lone Tree.* Tom Scanlon is the one remaining inhabitant of the town of Lone Tree, Nebraska. Lone Tree is a ghost town in which there is a life, which if solitary and ancient is yet imperative.

In likely response to a more anarchic climate in American society, in recent novels Morris has begun to explore still another realization within his general subject. That audacity which had been proposed as one of the resources of heroism in the American character, might well be criminal in this time. In *One Day* he speculates on the native American character as it emerges in the American boy who killed President Kennedy. The novel *In Orbit* speculates, not quite so harshly, on the nativity of those randomly violent American boys who are to be seen crossing the landscape on their motorcycles, in perpetual flight. In still more recent novels, stories, and photo-texts the area of discovery has again been broadened, now to include speculation on the qualities of resiliency or merely quirky defiance that may be the secret direction of seemingly feckless lives in America. In the title story of the collection *Here Is Einbaum* the protagonist survives wars and insults by the strategem of refusing usual commitments. (In this instance the protagonist, for once, is not a midwestern American. He is an Austrian-Jewish refugee living in New York, but he is nonetheless clearly related to Morris's usual characters, as may be indicated by the fact that a credible translation of "Einbaum" would be "Lone Tree.") In the paired novels *Fire Sermon* and *A Life*, Morris repeats the plot lineaments of his first novel, *My Uncle Dudley*, but now both the mode and the objects of the defiance which is the old man's legacy to the young boy are more complex and more desperate. Defying God, Heaven, and progress, the old man manages to be murdered by a surviving American Indian. In such seemingly topical novels as *The Fork River Space Project* and *Plains Song: For Female Voices*, which find their subject matters alternately in space landings and in Women's Liberation, Morris's protagonists again discover the true sources of their defiant knowledge in their inheritance of the rural American past. In the severity and loneliness of that past is the origin of the imaginative independence with which they can confront a crowded and demanding contemporary civilization.

These latter novels, too, fail to make final assertions. Like all of Morris's novels, they are populated by characters who confess themselves to be frustrated and bewildered, thereby providing opportunity for other and continuous reaches of realization.

—Marcus Klein

MORRISON, Toni (Chloe Anthony Morrison, née Wofford). American. Born in Lorain, Ohio, 18 February 1931. Educated at Howard University, Washington, D.C., B.A. 1953; Cornell University, Ithaca, New York, M.A. 1955. Has two sons. Instructor in English, Texas Southern University, Houston, 1955-57, and Howard University, 1957-64. Since 1965, Senior Editor, Random House, publishers, New York. Visiting Lecturer, Yale University, New Haven, Connecticut, 1976-77. Currently, Visiting Lecturer, Bard College, Annandale on Hudson, New York. Agent: Lynn Nesbit, International Creative Management, 40 West 57th Street, New York, New York 10019. Address: c/o Random House, 201 East 50th Street, New York, New York 10022, U.S.A.

PUBLICATIONS

Novels

The Bluest Eye. New York, Holt Rinehart, 1970; London, Chatto and Windus, 1980.
Sula. New York, Knopf, and London, Allen Lane, 1974.
Song of Solomon. New York, Knopf, 1977; London, Chatto and Windus, 1978.
Tar Baby. New York, Knopf, and London, Chatto and Windus, 1981.

* * *

A comparison of Toni Morrison with Joyce and Faulkner is irresistible. One dominant aspect of her work is an exhaustive, mythical exploration of place. Another is the search for the nexus of past and present. She is to the black milieu of Lorain what Joyce and Faulkner are to Dublin and Oxford, and her Medallion is as curiously fascinating as Anderson's Winesburg. Her stories translate a multiplicity of places, often superficially tawdry, into a rich cultural matrix. Likewise, the times of her forbears and herself in Ohio are a duration, not a chronology. She thus makes the legendary altogether new, and discovers in colloquial habit and naming the altogether legendary. Legend includes not only the tales of her black folk, but the myths of world literature. She has excluded Caucasians from her fiction more than Joyce and Faulkner have excluded ethnic "others" from theirs. But her focus on personality and character (in the moral sense) is indisputably universal. Her pervasive irony and paradox are not merely adroit but ethically motivated. At times they accentuate an erosion of the dignified, reliable courtliness of ancestral blacks, the more profound because it was maintained through the grossest depredations in American history. She is able to say of her contemporaries: "We raised our children and reared our crops; we let infants grow, and property develop." It is a deep regard for craft—for verbal nuance, metaphor, image, point of view—that enables Toni Morrison not merely to discourse upon but to animate social process and existential crisis.

The Bluest Eye tells of the incestuous rape of 11-year-old Pecola Breedlove by her father. The girl's need to be loved (pushed to the extreme when she observes her mother, a "domestic," heaping upon a little white girl affections Pecola has only dreamed of) takes the doomed form of a yearning for blue eyes. The insanity of this flight from reality comes to fruition after the death of the baby, when she actually believes herself to have acquired them. With her ubiquitous metaphor of flight, Morrison sums up this personal fate and the novel's powerful theme:

> The damage done was total. She spent her days...walking up and down, up and down, her head jerking to the beat of a drummer so distant only she could hear. Elbows bent, hands on shoulders, she flailed her arms like a bird in an eternal, grotesquely futile effort to fly. Beating the air, a winged but grounded bird, intent on the blue void it could not reach—could not even see—but which filled the valleys of the mind.

We are led to conclude that the narrator, Claudia Macteer, and her sister Frieda probably dodged this perversion by directing an ordinate malice at their Shirley Temple dolls and by being born to a family that, though rough and austere, did know how to breed love.

Sula explores equally an extraordinary consciousness and the gap between generations. Sula Mae Peace and her grandmother, Eva, share a great deal in common. Both left the same home in Medallion's "Bottom" only to return and inhabit it in willful isolation. Both shun tender expressions of love. Both have authored another's death. But in her indifference to family bonds, Sula is her grandmother's opposite. Where Eva left to save her family, Sula left to indulge her fancy. Where Eva returned for her children (though only content alone on the second floor), Sula returned from boredom and put her grandmother in a home. Where Eva, with tragic awareness, ignited her son's drug-addicted body, Sula dropped the little boy "Chicken" to his death with a weird inadvertence. And where Eva maimed herself trying to save her flaming daughter Hannah, Sula watched her mother's immolation with distant curiosity.

Yet this portrait is not simply a paean to the old ways. There is sympathy for Sula because as a child she had misconceived Hannah's remark about her, "I love her, I just don't like her," and because of her vain effort to save "Chicken." Of that the narrator remarks that it has exorcised "her one major feeling of responsibility." Moreover, her temperament blends "Eva's arrogance and Hannah's self indulgence" in an "experimental life" which itself seems a precondition for seeing and acting upon hard social truths. And finally, she seems like Pecola Breedlove, whose "guilt" mysteriously sanctified those around her. Sula performs the original Eve's purpose; as a community "witch," she provides others with a scapegoat, a model of such evil conduct that their own is actually elevated thereby.

Song of Solomon is a work of enormous breadth. Macon and Ruth Dead complete an often devastating characterization of genteel blacks begun with Geraldine and Helene in the earlier novels. Self-serving and cool, their son "Milkman" has given full life to the family name. Burdened by his parents' merciless marriage and prompted by his saintly aunt, Pilate, he sets out for Virginia and the skeletons in his family closet. But lore steadily leads and yields to more interesting truth, in the form of persons who correct his myopic view. He discovers his dead grandmother, Sing, so called because she was half Indian, Singing Bird, but also the daughter of a white Virginian named Byrd. And he discovers his great grandfather, Solomon, who once proudly flew the coop of slavery and about whom the country black kids still sing: "O Solomon don't leave me." Song and flight make life endurable and beautiful in Morrison's world. Having discovered these true ancestors, Milkman forgets the mundane, taking his best friend Guitar's advice to heart: "[If you] wanna fly, you got to give up the shit that weighs you down." The murderous conflict that had developed between the two (Guitar is a consummate study of an extremist racial approach toward which the novel displays both sympathy and disgust) is ended: "For now [Milkman] knew what Shalimar knew: If you surrendered to the air, you could *ride* it."

—David M. Heaton

MORTIMER, Penelope (Ruth, née Fletcher). British. Born in Rhyl, Flint, 19 September 1918. Educated at Croydon High School; New School, Streatham; Blencathra, Rhyl; Garden School, London; St. Elphin's Clergy Daughters School; Central Educational Bureau for Women; University College, London. Married 1) Charles Dimont in 1937 (divorced, 1949), four daughters; 2) the playwright John Mortimer in 1949 (divorced, 1971), one son and one daughter. Free-lance writer and journalist: movie critic, *The Observer*, London, 1967-70. Recipient: Whitbread Award, for non-fiction, 1979. Address: The Old Post Office, Chastleton, Moreton-in-Marsh, Gloucestershire, England.

PUBLICATIONS

Novels

Johanna (as Penelope Dimont). London, Secker and Warburg, 1947.
A Villa in Summer. London, Joseph, 1954; New York, Harcourt Brace, 1955.
The Bright Prison. London, Joseph, 1956; New York, Harcourt Brace, 1957.
Daddy's Gone A-Hunting. London, Joseph, 1958; as *Cave of Ice*, New York, Harcourt Brace, 1959.
The Pumpkin Eater. London, Hutchinson, 1962; New York, McGraw Hill, 1963.
My Friend Says It's Bullet-Proof. London, Hutchinson, 1967; New York, Random House, 1968.
The Home. London, Hutchinson, 1971; New York, Random House, 1972.
Long Distance. London, Allen Lane, and New York, Doubleday, 1974.

Short Stories

Saturday Lunch with the Brownings. London, Hutchinson, 1960; New York, McGraw Hill, 1961.

Uncollected Short Stories

"Philpot," in *New Yorker*, 25 August 1962.
"The Skylight," in *Tales of Unease*, edited by John Burke. London, Pan, 1966; New York, Doubleday, 1969.
"Love Story," in *New Yorker*, 15 July 1974.
"Curriculum Vitae," in *New Yorker*, 26 May 1975.
"In the First Place," in *New Yorker*, 22 December 1975.
"Granger's Life So Far," in *New Yorker*, 22 March 1976.
"Diver," in *Encounter* (London), February 1978.

Plays

Screenplay: *Bunny Lake Is Missing*, with John Mortimer, 1965.

Television Plays: *The Renegade*, from her own story, 1961; *Ain't Afraid to Dance*, 1966; *Three's One*, 1973.

Other

With Love and Lizards (travel), with John Mortimer. London, Joseph, 1957.
About Time: An Aspect of Autobiography. London, Allen Lane, and New York, Doubleday, 1979.

*

Penelope Mortimer comments:

(1972) My father was a C. of E. clergyman and I was brought up in Buckinghamshire, Thornton Heath, and Belper in Derbyshire. For various reasons (my father's changing theories as well as residences) I went to seven schools, ending up at a School for the Daughters of the Clergy (disaster). Did a secretarial course in London at the age of 17, hated it, went to London University, left after a year because my father said he was broke, took a job as a secretary to the Publicity Manager of Butlins Holiday Camp, decided after three weeks that marriage was preferable, married, had four children, wrote the odd piece for the *New Statesman* and *Our Time* and spent four years writing *Johanna*, which sank like a stone in 1947.

As well as the 8 books and 2 Mortimer children, I wrote a lot for the *New Yorker*, did fiction reviews for the *Sunday Times*, wrote a Lonely Hearts column under the pseudonym of Ann Temple for the *Daily Mail* (2 ghastly years), and did a considerable amount of other journalism.

The canvas of my fiction is narrow—domestic, mainly concerned with sexual and parental relationships—but I hope makes up in depth what it lacks in breadth. So far, I am almost entirely concerned with individuals' motives (i.e. what "makes them tick") and the development of their personalities from an early age (*Pumpkin Eater* and *The Home* particularly). Rather obviously (though not necessarily) I write through the eyes and ears of a woman. My men, I think, are getting better, and maybe I will someday venture to try to put myself inside a man's head and write from there. I believe that comedy is absolutely essential to tragedy, and I hope my books are almost as funny as they are (I'm told) sad or depressing. I would like to enlarge my scope, but not if it's at the expense of depth. Once my characters are established psychologically—heredity, environment, the lot—they take over their own growth and perform their own actions; I have very little to do with it.

* * *

The themes of popular fiction remain what they have always been: sex and marriage, class, money, and power. What has changed is the writer's attitude towards this material. A Victorian novel in this genre ended with a wedding; nowadays the plot tends to begin with an unhappy marriage, trace the course of the more or less unhappy affairs and end where it began, in sexual stalemate.

Of the many English novelists who have explored this territory, none has more sheer ability to write than Penelope Mortimer. She catalogues the debris of failure: the repetitive rows, the broken resolutions, the betrayals which would exact revenge had they not paralysed their victim. In each book the central relationship is destructive; only the children survive "sitting in a patient row on the sofa...their eyes restless as maggots, expecting us to bring them up." This description from *The Pumpkin Eater* is an example of her writing at its best, candid and original.

Villa in Summer is an accomplished study of corruption, a portrait of a couple who cling together out of habit as much as out of love. Emily has drifted so far from her husband that he feels "there were two species: Emily and women." Their marriage is vulnerable enough and easily shaken by a predatory pair of adulterers, teachers from the local progressive school.

Emily is the first in a string of lost innocents, heroines who are aware of the truth but unable to act on it. The central character in *Daddy's Gone A-Hunting* is shut off from potential pleasure, experiencing life in waves of guilt and pain. She cannot use her suffering to change her own situation but is able to protect her daughter against their common enemy, Rex, the unfaithful husband and callous father. Rex is typical of the men in Mortimer's fiction, drifting in and out of the story, excluded, pacified, accused. Only occasionally does the implicit violence break through into an open declaration of war. "A man has to be drunk, insane or unbalanced by talent before he'll behave like a woman," comments the heroine of *The Pumpkin Eater*, begging an awful lot of questions.

It is ironic that Penelope Mortimer has been both praised and criticised for her analysis of modern marriage. She keeps a witty and compassionate eye on that institution, it is true, but her observations do not set out to be objective. She is not a satirist, nor does her writing reflect the struggles of that old phenomenon, the new woman. Society is of secondary importance in her novels, which are intense, imaginative explorations of an inner world. It is an enclosed world, dominated by fear, in which physical experiences such as sterilisation and abortion isolate her characters from their fellow beings and are metaphors for a deeper spiritual isolation. Her most recent work shows an intensification of this mood. *My Friend Says It's Bullet-Proof* and *Home* are about women at the edge, held from destruction by an obsessive need to record and understand their own despair.

—Judy Cooke

MOSLEY, Nicholas (Lord Ravensdale). British. Born in London, 25 June 1923; eldest son of Sir Oswald Mosley; became 3rd Baron Ravensdale on the death of his aunt, Baroness Ravensdale, 1966. Educated at Eton College, 1937-42; Balliol College, Oxford, 1946-47. Served as Captain in the Rifle Brigade, 1942-46: Military Cross, 1944. Married 1) Rosemary Laura Salmond in 1947 (marriage dissolved, 1974), three sons and one daughter; 2) Verity Elizabeth Bailey in 1974, one son. Address: 9 Church Row, London N.W.3, England.

PUBLICATIONS

Novels

Spaces of the Dark. London, Hart Davis, 1951.
The Rainbearers. London, Weidenfeld and Nicolson, 1955.
Corruption. London, Weidenfeld and Nicolson, 1957; Boston, Little Brown, 1958.
Meeting Place. London, Weidenfeld and Nicolson, 1962.
Accident. London, Hodder and Stoughton, 1965; New York, Coward McCann, 1966.
Assassins. London, Hodder and Stoughton, 1966; New York, Coward McCann, 1967.
Impossible Object. London, Hodder and Stoughton, 1968; New York, Coward McCann, 1969.
Natalie Natalia. London, Hodder and Stoughton, and New York, Coward McCann, 1971.
Imago Bird. London, Secker and Warburg, 1980.

Plays

Catastrophe Practice: Plays for Not Acting, and Cypher: A Novel (includes *Skylight, Landfall, Cell*). London, Secker and Warburg, 1979.

Screenplays: *The Assassination of Trotsky*, 1973; *Impossible Object*, 1975.

Other

Life Drawing, with John Napper. London, Studio, 1954.
African Switchback (travel). London, Weidenfeld and Nicolson, 1958.
The Life of Raymond Raynes. London, Faith Press, 1961.
Experience and Religion: A Lay Essay in Theology. London, Hodder and Stoughton, 1965; Philadelphia, United Church Press, 1967.
The Assassination of Trotsky. London, Joseph, 1972.
Julian Grenfell: His Life and the Times of His Death 1888-1915. London, Weidenfeld and Nicolson, and New York, Holt Rinehart, 1976.

Editor, *The Faith: Instructions on the Christian Faith*, by Raymond Raynes. London, Faith Press, 1961.

* * *

An approach to the work of Nicholas Mosley might be made by considering the reply made to a question asked by a character in *Accident*: "Why is it that modern novels have to be different, cannot just be stories of characters, action and society?" The reply was: "We know too much about characters, action, and society,...we can now write about people *knowing*." Certainly Mosley's first three competent and straightforward novels of the 1950's made it plain that he was thoroughly at home in the genre and could produce a convincing picture of life in the post war period. It is with the fourth novel, *Meeting Place*, that the first hint comes that the author might not be content with the novel as a mere chronological narration of events. In the fragmented and impressionistic story of a social worker and the relationships of varying depths he makes with the people around him, Mosley is clearly making an attempt to expand the limits of what he might require a novel to do.

There is a strong philosophical element in all Mosley's work. The title *Accident* indicates a random event as well as referring to the car crash which resolves the coming together of a particular group of people in academic Oxford. One of the characters says: "We imagine we move according to cause and effect but in reality we are particles with velocity but no location." *Accident* is a successful blend of ideas, impressionistically presented visual lushness, and a delicately explored nexus of relationships around the central character of Anna, the catalyst, about whom as a person we are told nothing. Like *Accident*, *Assassins* is "a good story." The daughter of the British Foreign Secretary is abducted from his country house where he is engaged in delicate negotiations with the leader of a communist country. The relationship of the teenage girl with her youthful kidnapper is an example of the kind of writing at which Mosley excels.

The seventh novel, *Impossible Object*, has been described as like a crossword puzzle, or like a Royal Academy problem picture. The average reader might be tempted not to try to hammer out the solution. In form it is eight short stories which switch from one narrator to another to present a central relationship. Interspersed with the narrative are surrealistic essays which, however elusive in meaning, serve to heighten the total impact. This novel is successful in maintaining a balance between what the author has proved he can do so well, and the extension of the techniques of novel writing which, it has become plain, is now his aim. *Natalie Natalia* concerns a politician who leaves a maritally complex situation to go to Africa where he has a nervous breakdown. Although the form is looser than in the previous novel, in it Mosley attempts the same thing on a greater scale with less success. It is paradoxical that the diversions from the narrative in *Natalie Natalia* are less opaque and more of a piece than those in *Impossible Object* and yet in some way they dilute it.

It is tempting to speculate about the direction Mosley's future development as a writer might take. Certainly the later novels have a smoothness of style which acquit him of earlier infelicities which caused a reviewer to describe him as a literary grocer dropping dried peas into a bag until he has half a pound or so of paragraph. The reader may still be snatched from one idea to another but he is no longer jerked from word to word. Mosley as a writer is supremely good when he is exploring the relationship of one person to another: the married couple in *Accident*, the lovers in *Impossible Object*, the young girl and her abductor in *Assassins*. He is an interesting writer and difficult to assess because he is not content just to do what he can do well.

—Anastasia Leech

MPHAHLELE, Ezekiel (Es'kia Mphahlele). South African. Born in Pretoria, 17 December 1919. Educated at St. Peter's Secondary School, Johannesburg; Adam's College, Natal, 1939-40; University of South Africa, Pretoria, 1946-49, 1953-54, 1956, B.A. (honours) 1949, M.A. in English 1956; University of Denver, 1966-68, Ph.D. in English 1968. Married Rebecca Mochadibane in 1945; five children. Clerk in institution for the blind, 1941-45; English and Afrikaans teacher, Orlando High School, Johannesburg, 1945-52; Lecturer in English Literature, University of Ibadan, Nigeria, 1957-61; Director of African Programmes, International Association for Cultural Freedom, Paris, 1961-63; Director of ChemiChemi Creative Centre, Nairobi, Kenya, 1963-65; Lecturer, University College, Nairobi, 1965-66; Senior Lecturer in English, University of Zambia, Lusaka, 1968-70; Associate Professor of English, University of Denver, 1970-74; Professor of English, University of Pennsylvania, Philadelphia, 1974-77; Inspector of Education, Lebowa, Transvaal, 1978-79. Since 1979, Professor of African Literature, University of the Witwatersrand, Johannesburg. Fiction Editor, *Drum*, Johannesburg, 1955-57; Editor, *Black Orpheus*, 1960-66, and *Journal of New African Literature and the Arts*. Address: African Studies Institute, University of the Witwatersrand, Johannesburg 2001, South Africa.

PUBLICATIONS

Novels

The Wanderers. New York, Macmillan, 1971; London, Macmillan, 1972.
Chirundu. Johannesburg, Ravan Press, 1979; Walton on Thames, Surrey, Nelson, 1980.

Short Stories

Man Must Live and Other Stories. Cape Town, African Bookman, 1947.
The Living and Dead and Other Stories. Ibadan, Black Orpheus, 1961.
In Corner B and Other Stories. Nairobi, East African Publishing House, 1967.

Other

Down Second Avenue (autobiography). London, Faber, 1959; New York, Doubleday, 1971.
The African Image (essays). London, Faber, and New York, Praeger, 1962; revised edition, Faber and Praeger, 1974.
A Guide to Creative Writing. Nairobi, East African Literature Bureau, 1966.
Voices in the Whirlwind and Other Essays. New York, Hill and Wang, 1972; London, Macmillan, 1973.
Editor, with Ellis Komey, *Modern African Stories*. London, Faber, 1964.
Editor, *African Writing Today*. London, Penguin, 1967.

*

Critical Studies: *Seven African Writers* by Gerald Moore, London, Oxford University Press, 1962; *The Chosen Tongue* by Gerald Moore, London, Longman, 1969; "The South African Short Story," by the author in *Kenyon Review* (Gambier, Ohio), 1969; *Ezekiel Mphahlele* by Ursula A. Barnett, Boston, Twayne, 1976.

Ezekiel Mphahlele comments:

(1972) I began my writing career as a short-story writer during World War II. I wrote for *Drum* magazine in Johannesburg, *Fighting Talk* and *New Age* in Johannesburg, and *Africa South* in Cape Town (the last 3 journals since banned by the South African Government). My earliest stories, i.e., *Man Must Live*, were escapist stuff which came spontaneously. I moved on to vitriolic protest fiction. I left South Africa as an exile in September 1957 to teach in Nigeria where I finished the second half of *Down Second Avenue*, my autobiography. Even in exile my fictional themes have always been South Africa. But *In Corner B*, which I wrote in Paris in 1963, has two stories set in Nigeria: "The Barber of Bariga" and "The Ballad of Oyo." The rest are set in South Africa. I wrote these Nigerian stories and "Mrs. Plum" in Paris. The rest had appeared in Johannesburg journals. "Mrs. Plum" in that volume was my first attempt at the long short-story. I have often thought of fiction as my specific commitment; when I am still composing such a work in my mind, I write critical essays—such as *The African Image* and *Voices in the Whirlwind*. *The Wanderers* has an autobiographical outline but the incidents are fictional. I am planning a novel set in Zambia. I am trying to come to terms with the greater Africa as a setting, but I know the South African in me will accompany me to the grave.

* * *

Ezekiel Mphahlele has been one of the most versatile and influential of African authors. As literary critic, autobiographer, journalist, short story writer, novelist, dramatist, and poet, he has probably contributed more than any other individual to the growth and development of an African literature in English. Since leaving South Africa he has travelled widely, stopping to teach for a year or two in at least five different countries—Nigeria, Kenya, Zambia, France and the United States.

In South Africa Mphahlele wrote mainly short stories about life in the urban black ghettos where he had grown up and spent most of his adult years. The events in these stories were based on his personal experiences and reflected a wide variety of responses to the people and places he knew best. There were humorous sketches and satirical vignettes as well as more serious stories about human or social problems. Later, as stringent apartheid legislation made life more difficult for urban blacks, Mphahlele began to write angry protest fiction. By the mid-1950's he felt stifled in his home country and applied for an "exit permit," a document allowing him to leave South Africa on the condition that he never return. The South African government granted his request in 1957 and he has lived in exile ever since.

His first major piece of writing abroad was an autobiography, *Down Second Avenue*, in which he tried to work off the emotional steam and creative energy that had been building up inside him during his last years in South Africa. It is a moving story, told with candour and compassion for his people. In 1962 he published a pioneering work of literary criticism, *The African Image*, part of which had been written in South Africa as an M.A. thesis. He also brought out two collections of his short stories and produced a manual for aspiring fiction writers. His first novel, *The Wanderers*, examined the plight of the black South African intellectual in exile, a depressing tale constructed out of the debris of his own personal life.

In most of his recent writing Mphahlele has been able to arrive at the kind of emotional balance and aesthetic distance from his subject matter that he found impossible to achieve while living in South Africa. The element of protest is still strong in his fiction but it is now under much firmer artistic control. Exile, though a painful and frustrating experience, has made Mphahlele a more accomplished literary craftsman.

—Bernth Lindfors

MUNONYE, John (Okechukwu). Nigerian. Born in Akokwa, 28 April 1929. Educated at Christ the King College, Onitsha, 1943-47; University College, Ibadan, 1948-52, B.A. in classics and history 1952; Institute of Education, University of London, 1952-53, diploma in education. Married Regina Nwokeji in 1957; one daughter and one son. Education Officer, 1954-57, and Provincial Education Officer and Inspector of Education, 1958-70, Nigerian Ministry of Education; Principal, Advanced Teachers College, Oweri, 1970-73; Chief Inspector of Education, East Central State, 1973-76, and Imo State, 1976-77. Member of the Board of Directors, East Central State Broadcasting Service, Enugu, 1974-76. Member, Order of the Niger, 1980. Agent: David Higham Associates Ltd., 5-8 Lower John Street, London W1R 4HA, England. Address: P.O. Box 23, Akokwa, Orlu, Imo State, Nigeria.

PUBLICATIONS

Novels

The Only Son. London, Heinemann, 1966.
Obi. London, Heinemann, 1969.
Oil Man of Obange. London, Heinemann, 1971.
A Wreath for Maidens. London, Heinemann, 1973.
A Dancer of Fortune. London, Heinemann, 1974.
Bridge to a Wedding. London, Heinemann, 1978.

Uncollected Short Stories

"Silent Child," in *Okike 4* (Amherst, Massachusetts), December 1973.
"Pack Pack Pack" in *Festac Anthology of Nigerian New Writing.* Lagos, Ministry of Information, 1977.

Other

Drills and Practice in English Language (textbook), with J. Cairns. Lagos, African Universities Press, 1966.

*

John Munonye comments:

All six of my novels are children of the land. Set in the Igbo area of Nigeria, they draw from the experiences of ordinary men and women, children too. The motif is the processes of change that started with the arrival of Christian missionaries some 60 years ago. Culture ("all the arts, beliefs, social institutions...characteristic of a community") had to shift ground. And the environment, sensitive in its own way, was transformed too. How did our ordinary men and women fare in it all? Is there anything of their authentic nature that could be said to have survived the stress? The earliest experiences, which are depicted in *The Only Son* and *Obi*, were severe and traumatic. Later, people came to live with the new state of things, and the result is *Bridge to a Wedding*, a novel of accomodation and reconciliation between traditional and modern. We do indeed need the bridge.

Oil Man of Obange is a relentless tragedy, a novel of confrontation on an individual scale. The Oil Man musters all his energy, zeal, optimism, and integrity towards improving his low social status. But did he consult the god of success? *A Wreath for Maidens* also deals with moral issues—on a wider canvas. The blood shed in the end is not, unfortunately, that of the protagonists: it is a novel of futility. *A Dancer of Fortune* proceeds on much lighter feet.

What next? The beautyful ones are not yet born—yes. But hope is one of man's sustaining gifts, a gift of the spirit. With it goes vision (without which a people perish) and commitment. Nothing shrill or didactic; no sermons; no protest.

* * *

As the author of six novels within 12 years, John Munonye has attracted surprisingly little critical attention. The reason is not far to seek: despite the intrinsically interesting material he works on, his craftsmanship and command of English have flagged noticeably since his earliest books. Yet, as a compassionate chronicler of the ways in which ordinary Eastern Nigerian people have been affected by historical and social change, he is a writer well worth reading. In his first and third novels, *The Only Son* and *Oil Man of Obange*, theme and treatment interlock admirably and reveal his competence at its best. Jeri, the petty trader in palm oil of *Oil Man of Obange*, pits his own elemental resources of courage, devotion, and physical strength against fate, accident, and malice to raise money for his children's schooling; Munonye subdues the narration rigorously to a stark recording of the everyday hardships of bare human existence that is still the lot of most Nigerians, indeed of the peoples of the Third World in general. With similar, though slightly less stringent, narrative austerity, *The Only Son* presents the privations of a self-reliant widow whose humble, sparse life is touched into tragic proportions by her simple courage and steadfastness: the relationship between Chiaku and her son is tenderly but unsentimentally handled, and, in their estrangement, when he seeks western and Christian education, Munonye achieves a sympathetic insight into both sides of an irreconcilable clash of aspirations.

The Only Son is the first novel in Munonye's trilogy about the fortunes of one family, the 20th-century descendants of the legendary Udemezue of Burning Eyes in the community of Umudiobia of ten villages and two. In *Obi* the fully Christianized son and his Christian wife return to Umudiobia to re-establish his father's *obi* or homestead, but the tensions between traditional custom and their new faith culminate in their flight into exile in a distant town. *Bridge to a Wedding* introduces them as the materially prosperous parents of six children and traces the patient and successful efforts of a highly respected Umudiobian to heal the feud between them and their village kinsfolk so that his son can marry their daughter. While these two novels share the attractive unifying theme of how African custom still operates upon the lives of ordinary Nigerians, for good and for ill, Munonye's very concern with this theme, especially in *Bridge to a Wedding*, leads him into an often irritating discursiveness.

The virtue of Munonye's civil-war novel, *A Wreath for the Maidens*, rests upon his intimate knowledge of how the common people are affected for the worse by large historical events, despite the public rhetoric that accompanies them. Poor characterization and a tendency to wordiness do not vitiate the sombre moral concern at the heart of this book. That it could so soon be followed by *A Dancer of Fortune*, with its apparent endorsement of mere individualist opportunism, is a disturbing measure of Munonye's increasing lack of self-criticism as a writer.

—Arthur Ravenscroft

MUNRO, Alice. Canadian. Born in Wingham, Ontario, 10 July 1931. Educated in Wingham public schools; University of Western Ontario, London, 1949-51. Married 1) James Armstrong Munro in 1951, three children; 2) Gerald Fremlin in 1976. Artist-in-Residence, University of Western Ontario, 1974-75, and University of British Columbia, Vancouver, 1980. Recipient: Governor-General's Award, 1969, 1978; Canada-Australia Literary Prize, 1977. Lives in Clinton, Ontario. Address: c/o Macmillan Company of Canada, 70 Bond Street, Toronto M5B 1X3, Canada

PUBLICATIONS

Novel

Lives of Girls and Women. Toronto, McGraw Hill Ryerson, 1971; New York, McGraw Hill, 1972; London, Allen Lane, 1973.

Short Stories

Dance of the Happy Shades. Toronto, Ryerson Press, 1968; New York, McGraw Hill, 1973; London, Allen Lane, 1974.
Something I've Been Meaning to Tell You. Toronto, McGraw Hill Ryerson, and New York, McGraw Hill, 1974.
Who Do You Think You Are? Toronto, Macmillan, 1978; as *The Beggar Maid: Stories of Flo and Rose*, New York, Knopf, 1979; London, Allen Lane, 1980.

Uncollected Short Stories

"Dulse," in *New Yorker*, 21 July 1980.
"Word," in *New Yorker*, 29 November 1980.

* * *

In her novel and short stories Alice Munro concerns herself largely with the small town or rural scene, but she is no mere singer of the pastoral virtues. The world she depicts is seemingly orderly and uneventful, but its inhabitants characteristically are at the edge of some discovery or revelation which threatens not only their tenuous day to day values and ideas, but in a sense the very cosmic order itself. On the surface, this recurring tension appears to be between certainty and uncertainty, or between innocence and experience, but it is really an opposition between the many facets of uncertainty. The past, for example, or childhood, or a strong code of morality or progress—qualities which the world at large tends to regard favourably—these forces in Alice Munro's works are as threatening and unsettling as the undefined dimensions against which they are juxtaposed.

Munro's special talent is reflected in the manner in which she dramatizes the conjunction of her characters with these threatening and dimly understood encroachments. In *Dance of the Happy Shades* and *Lives of Girls and Women* the emphasis was on the youthful character trying to come to terms with the world of adulthood and experience. In *Something I've Been Meaning to Tell You* it is frequently the other way around: grandmothers trying to understand granddaughters, elderly sisters trying to make sense out of their common past, a sensitive old man just failing to come to terms with the younger generation around him. In all cases, however, Munro unfolds her confrontations in a tangible and recognizable sociological world, where social issues or social behaviour frequently generate the impulse towards rebellion. In "The Shining Houses," from her first collection, it is the spectacle of physical urbanization and its accompanying dehumanizing conformity which is central to this conflict; in "Walking on Water," from her second, Munro expresses a similar kind of bitterness against unfeeling conformity, but this time directed against the hippy individuals constantly and selfishly proclaiming the virtues of their life style in complete disregard of the community's established citizens.

But Munro's resolution of these issues is not so much sociological as it is moral and psychological, and her characters seem to drift into salvation rather than consciously elect it. Del Jordan, throughout all the episodes of *Lives of Girls and Women*, is in a state of incipient rebellion against the values of Jubilee, but it is not a conflict where she obviously assumes a consciously superior stance towards her fellow townspeople. On the contrary, she is a very ordinary individual, as susceptible to the sordid experiences of falsity as her companions, who, as Del later recalled, "faded into jobs or marriage." That she is ultimately saved from a similar fate derives from something other than overt rebellion or extraordinary talents, though she does possess a quality of orthodoxy which separates her from even her closest companions. Throughout Munro's fiction, we are constantly reminded of how thin the line is between succumbing and salvation, and of how normally only the sensitive and curious of her characters have any chance at all to make the right moves.

In a very real sense, what Munro does in her fiction is to dramatize the conjunction of existential terror and existential possibility. Her sensitive characters all come to somewhat the same realization that the narrator of "Dance of the Happy Shades" articulates: "Things are getting out of hand, anything may happen," but at the same time they reflect Del Jordan's belief that they can do what the men in her world do: "go out and take on all kinds of experiences and shuck off what they didn't want and come back proud." An awareness of these existential possibilities makes control of one's life and the act of survival a challenge, as it were. "The world that we accept—you know, external reality," asserts a character in "Walking on Water," "is nothing like so fixed as we have been led to believe. It responds to more methods of control than we are conditioned to accept." In her explorations and manipulations of the various shapes and dimensions of external reality, Alice Munro reflects a metaphysical and aesthetic perception that has made her one of the most satisfying writers in Canada today.

—Hallvard Dahlie

MURDOCH, (Jean) Iris. British. Born in Dublin, Ireland, 15 July 1919. Educated at the Froebel Education Institute, London; Badminton School, Bristol; Somerville College, Oxford, 1938-42, B.A. (honours) 1942; Newnham College, Cambridge (Sarah Smithson Student in philosophy), 1947-48. Married the writer John Bayley in 1956. Assistant Principal in the Treasury, London, 1942-44; Adminstrative Officer with the United Nations Relief and Rehabilitation Administration (UNRRA) in London, Belgium, and Austria, 1944-46; Fellow, St. Anne's College, Oxford, and University Lecturer in Philosophy, Oxford University, 1948-63; Honorary Fellow of St. Anne's College since 1963; Lecturer, Royal College of Art, London, 1963-67. Recipient: Black Memorial Award, 1974; Whitbread Literary Award, 1974; Booker Prize, 1978. Member, Irish Academy, 1970. Honorary Member, American Academy, 1975. Honorary Fellow, Somerville College, 1977. C.B.E. (Commander, Order of the British Empire), 1976. Address: Cedar Lodge, Steeple Aston, Oxford, England.

PUBLICATIONS

Novels

Under the Net. London, Chatto and Windus, and New York, Viking Press, 1954.
The Flight from the Enchanter. London, Chatto and Windus, and New York, Viking Press, 1956.
The Sandcastle. London, Chatto and Windus, and New York, Viking Press, 1957.

The Bell. London, Chatto and Windus, and New York, Viking Press, 1958.
A Severed Head. London, Chatto and Windus, and New York, Viking Press, 1961.
An Unofficial Rose. London, Chatto and Windus, and New York, Viking Press, 1962.
The Unicorn. London, Chatto and Windus, and New York, Viking Press, 1963.
The Italian Girl. London, Chatto and Windus, and New York, Viking Press, 1964.
The Red and the Green. London, Chatto and Windus, and New York, Viking Press, 1965.
The Time of the Angels. London, Chatto and Windus, and New York, Viking Press, 1966.
The Nice and the Good. London, Chatto and Windus, and New York, Viking Press, 1968.
Bruno's Dream. London, Chatto and Windus, and New York, Viking Press, 1969.
A Fairly Honourable Defeat. London, Chatto and Windus, and New York, Viking Press, 1970.
An Accidental Man. London, Chatto and Windus, 1971; New York, Viking Press, 1972.
The Black Prince. London, Chatto and Windus, and New York, Viking Press, 1973.
The Sacred and Profane Love Machine. London, Chatto and Windus, and New York, Viking Press, 1974.
A Word Child. London, Chatto and Windus, and New York, Viking Press, 1975.
Henry and Cato. London, Chatto and Windus, 1976; New York, Viking Press, 1977.
The Sea, The Sea. London, Chatto and Windus, and New York, Viking Press, 1978.
Nuns and Soldiers. London, Chatto and Windus, 1980; New York, Viking Press, 1981.

Uncollected Short Story

"Something Special," in *Winter's Tales 3.* London, Macmillan, and New York, St. Martin's Press, 1957.

Plays

A Severed Head, with J.B. Priestley, adaptation of the novel by Murdoch (produced Bristol and London, 1963; New York, 1964). London, Chatto and Windus, 1964.
The Italian Girl, with James Saunders, adaptation of the novel by Murdoch (produced Bristol, 1967; London, 1968). London, French, 1969.
The Servants and the Snow (produced London, 1970). Included in *The Three Arrows and The Servants and the Snow*, 1973.
The Three Arrows (produced Cambridge, 1972). Included in *The Three Arrows and The Servants and the Snow*, 1973.
The Three Arrows, and The Servants and the Snow: Two Plays. London, Chatto and Windus, 1973; New York, Viking Press, 1974.
Art and Eros (produced London, 1980).

Verse

A Year of Birds. Tisbury, Wiltshire, Compton Press, 1978.

Other

Sartre, Romantic Rationalist. Cambridge, Bowes, and New Haven, Connecticut, Yale University Press, 1953.
The Sovereignty of Good over Other Concepts (lecture). Cambridge, University Press, 1967.
The Sovereignty of Good (essays). London, Routledge, 1970; New York, Schocken, 1971.
The Fire and the Sun: Why Plato Banished the Artists. London and New York, Oxford University Press, 1977.

Bibliography: *Iris Murdoch and Muriel Spark: A Bibliography* by Thomas T. Tominaga and Wilma Schneidermeyer, Metuchen, New Jersey, Scarecrow Press, 1976.

Manuscript Collection: University of Iowa, Iowa City.

Critical Studies: *Degrees of Freedom: The Novels of Iris Murdoch*, London, Chatto and Windus, and New York, Barnes and Noble, 1965, and *Iris Murdoch*, London, Longman, 1976, both by A.S. Byatt; *The Disciplined Heart: Iris Murdoch and Her Novels* by Peter Wolfe, Columbia, University of Missouri Press, 1966; *Iris Murdoch* by Rubin Rabinovitz, New York, Columbia University Press, 1968; *Iris Murdoch* by Frank Baldanza, New York, Twayne, 1974; *Iris Murdoch* by Donna Gerstenberger, Lewisburg, Pennsylvania, Bucknell University Press, 1974; *Iris Murdoch: The Shakespearian Interest* by Richard Todd, New York, Barnes and Noble, 1979.

* * *

Most of her readers are aware, often a little uneasily, that Iris Murdoch is a professional philosopher, but remain uncertain as to the exact nature of her philosophic commitments and the degree to which some knowledge of them is essential to an understanding of her densely populated, intricately plotted novels. Critical summaries such as this which approach Murdoch's fiction primarily in terms of her intellectual position have the virture of orderliness, perhaps, and yet should not imply that the novels demand familiarity with the purely philosophic work. Murdoch herself has stated that the novel should be "an art of image," not merely an instrument of analysis and reflection; and the questions she asks of Sartre's work—has a certain transmutation of ideas taken place, has the philosophy been fused completely with the image constituted by the story—are questions she would presumably agree must be asked of her own efforts. In many instances the answer is a positive one: *Under the Net*, *The Bell*, *A Severed Head*, and at least a few of the later novels do in fact embody a moving and wholly intelligible view of life. Moreover, it would be a mistake to conclude that the fiction is primarily a simplification of ideas developed elsewhere, for more than once Murdoch has complained of "those exasperating moments in philosophy when one seems to be relentlessly prevented from saying something which one is irresistibly impelled to say." Murdoch's activity as a novelist should be seen in part as an implied criticism of the limits of philosophic discourse: "A moral philosophy," she remarks, "should be inhabited."

At the center of Murdoch's work there is a pessimism which may startle her more casual readers. "We are anxiety-ridden animals," she writes; "Our minds are continually active, fabricating an anxious, usually self-protective, often falsifying *veil* which partially conceals the world....We are largely mechanical creatures, the slaves of relentlessly strong selfish forces the nature of which we scarcely comprehend." Although these crucial qualifications, "largely" and "scarcely," save her thought from the blank determinism and inconsistently romantic nihilism she criticizes in Freud and the existentialists, Murdoch nevertheless accepts the definition of man as an accidental creature briefly adrift in a contingent universe:

> That human life has no external point...is a view as difficult to argue as its opposite, and I shall simply assert it. I can see no evidence to suggest that human life is not something self-contained. There are properly many patterns and purposes within life, but there is no general and as it were guaranteed pattern or purpose of the kind for which philosophers and theologians used to search. We are what we seem to be, transient mortal creatures subject to necessity and chance....Our destiny can be examined but it cannot be justified or totally explained. We are simply here.

These denials prepare the way for Murdoch's persistent concern as a philosopher and novelist, the nature of ethical behavior. She is finally a kind of modern non-transcendental Platonist for whom freedom, knowledge, and virtue are ultimately one, forming the human goal which art is especially potent to depict.

"The world is aimless, chancy, and huge, and we are blinded by self": true knowledge involves the difficult task of coming to see things as they are, without the consoling fantasies of the "fat relentless ego" which longs for a more commanding place and destiny. Murdoch's tactic in her philosophical essays is to point out the inadequacies of two of the conceptions of man which dominate modern thought. Both the existentialist and the linguistic philosopher, she argues, present a shallow view of human nature, a "simplified and impoverished inner life." For Sartre the individual is the center, but "a solipsistic center," a thin blade of pure will in a world where human relationships become impossible, whereas the world of the Oxford philosophers is "a world in which people play cricket, cook cakes, make simple decisions, remember their childhood and go to the circus; not the world in which they commit sins, fall in love, say prayers or join the Communist Party." What is lacking above all in these influential models of human nature is a genuine conception of love and freedom, beginning with a respect for—rather than a hatred or dismissal of—the contingency and final "pointlessness" of life. For Murdoch freedom is not mere exercise of the will, but rather "the experience of accurate vision...a disciplined overcoming of self"; virtue, which pre-supposes objective vision, is concerned with "apprehending that other people exist...knowing and understanding and respecting things other than ourselves." Thus goodness means knowledge and so "connects us with reality"; and the chief human virtue, love, is finally the exercise of "the extremely difficult realization that something other than oneself is real," manifesting itself as patient, attentive respect for others as separate beings and not merely objects to be grasped and used. The novel proper is "about people's treatment of each other" and the creation and enjoyment of works of art promote that "unselving" which is the beginning of virtue: "What is learnt here is something about the real quality of human nature, when it is envisaged, in the artist's just and compassionate vision, with a clarity which does not belong to the self-centered rush of ordinary life." Art may delineate the good with a fullness denied to philosophy: "we know that the real lesson to be taught is that the human person is precious and unique; but we seem unable to set it forth except in terms of ideology and abstraction."

If the reader has a grasp of what Murdoch means by contingency, freedom, knowledge, and love, the most intricate of her plots and the most puzzling of her characters' motivations become readily intelligible, even predictable. There is an archetypal plot at work in each of the novels in which a character is forced by some event, often violent or irrational in nature, to realize his lack of freedom, his inability to know or to love; he may stop at this insight or he may pass beyond, into that difficult-to-dramatize area in which love can be exercised. The complexities of Murdoch's plots usually spring from her trick of surrounding the central action of discovery with a host of variations, comic or serious, in which other characters learn or fail to learn the same lesson. The formal ancestor of Murdoch's novels turns out to be *Point Counter Point*.

At the opening of the first novel, *Under the Net*, for example, Jake Donaghue "hates contingency" and "hates solitude but is afraid of intimacy." After undergoing a series of brilliantly inventive comic adventures, Jake becomes free, able to work and to accept the reality of others. In her study of Sartre Murdoch repeats Gabriel Marcel's question, why does Sartre "find the contingent overabundance of the world nauseating rather than glorious?" At the end of *Under the Net* Jake is happily marvelling at the inexplicable appearance of a siamese kitten in a brood of tabbies: "I don't know why it is....It's just one of the wonders of the world." No other small incident illustrates so well the particular tone and attractiveness of Murdoch's best work—a kind of joyous but far from complacent acceptance of things as they are and as they must be respected for being.

The Flight from the Enchanter dramatizes the interlocking efforts of several characters to cope with the domineering Mischa Fox—or some version of what he stands for, the manipulation of others as objects. The central figure, Rosa, escapes, to return to a life clarified but hardly simplified by the knowledge of what Fox represents. The quasi-hero of *The Sandcastle*, Mor, is tempted to escape from a sour marriage and routine career into a romantic dream of freedom and happiness, only to realize the egotism of his temptation; like Rosa he returns to a prosaic world of tasks and obligations. In these early novels, as in most of those which follow, Murdoch seems to agree completely with Sartre's assertion that the writer "has only one subject—freedom."

The Bell, perhaps the finest of the novels, traces the disintegrating relationships between a set of characters who seek in a Benedictine lay community "a retreat from human frailty." They represent "a kind of sick people, whose desire for God makes them unsatisfactory citizens of an ordinary life, but whose strength or temperament fails them to surrender the world completely." Their failures are inevitable, and inevitably involve the failure to love: "Imperfect love must not be condemned and rejected, but made perfect." ("Imperfect love" appears emblematically in many of the novels as incest or homosexuality.) As Murdoch observes elsewhere, "it is an empirical fact about human nature that this attempt [to love] cannot be entirely successful....In the practical world there may only be mourning and the final acceptance of the incomplete." The most one can hope for, as often as not, is "a fairly honourable defeat." *A Severed Head* is a splendid comic version of the quest for liberation and maturity, while *An Unofficial Rose* is a muted, almost Jamesian study of an elderly man's final recognition of the meaning of his past and his deeply equivocal attempt to let his son "live." The symbolism of the earlier novels is restrained; much of the action is now conveyed by scene and dialogue, as is to be the case with most of the later novels.

Between 1963 and 1969 Murdoch published no less than six novels, five of them dark, troubling and often obscure in detail. *The Unicorn* is a gothic "fantasy of the spiritual life"—an instructive parody, perhaps, rather than mere fantasy—in which allegory finally overwhelms plausibility. *The Italian Girl*, the briefest and least consequential of the novels, was followed by the cruelly effective *The Red and the Green*, in which unsuccessful attempts to work out individual freedom are ironically mirrored in the abortive Irish uprising of Easter, 1916. (Something affirmative emerges here, however: the doomed actions of "inconceivably brave men...saved from the corruption of time and from those ambiguous second thoughts which dim the brightest face of youth.") *The Time of the Angels* fails almost entirely to fuse the image and idea (a much put-upon serving girl, for example, literally stumbles over a copy of Heidegger, the Lucifer behind the evil genius of the book, Carel Fisher). *Bruno's Dream* is, finally, a nightmarish account of a grotesque old man's dying attempts to establish bonds of knowing and loving with the world.

Fortunately the virtues of the earlier novels return in *The Nice and the Good* and the other books published after 1968, although there is nothing particularly new in any of them (save perhaps for the slight formal experiments in *The Black Prince*). Drawn from the interlocking worlds of civil servants, dons, and the *haute bourgeoisie* whose tone Murdoch has mastered so completely, an enormous cast of characters continues to struggle with the ethical problems which suddenly break up the conventional surface of their lives. There are the usual comic and tragic consequences of imperfect love and the renewed efforts of the battered survivors to make the best of a bad job. The view of love summarized above tends toward a certain kind of sentimentality. Murdoch may be aware of this; and if it troubles her, it may also account for the increasing role which malice and violence play—as balancing agents in the service of an uncompromising "realism"—in the later novels. Or it may be simply that she is now rather less optimistic about the chances of taming the ego. Murdoch may be writing too much too quickly, but for moral intensity and apparently endless inventive skill there is really no one writing now who can approach her.

—Elmer Borklund

NAIPAUL, Shiva. British. Born in Port of Spain, Trinidad, in 1945. Educated at Oxford University, degree in Chinese. Recipient: Royal Society of Literature Winifred Holtby Memorial Prize, 1970; Rhys Memorial Prize, 1970; Jock Campbell Award (*New Statesman*, London), 1970; Guggenheim Fellowship, 1978. Address: c/o Hamish Hamilton Ltd., 57-59 Long Acre, London WC2E 9JZ, England.

PUBLICATIONS

Novels

Fireflies. London, Deutsch, 1970; New York, Knopf, 1971.
The Chip-Chip Gatherers. London, Deutsch, and New York, Knopf, 1973.

Short Stories

Penguin Modern Stories 4, with others. London, Penguin, 1970.
The Adventures of Gurudeva. London, Deutsch, 1976.

Other

North of South: An African Journey. London, Deutsch, 1978; New York, Scribner, 1979.
Black and White. London, Hamish Hamilton, 1980; as *Journey to Nowhere: A New World Tragedy*, New York, Simon and Schuster, 1981.

* * *

Shiva Naipaul's fiction is sombre, serious, and shrewd. It shows a society in transition from one undesirable *modus vivendi* in rural Trinidad to another, no more desirable, in urban Trinidad. The sombre power of the fiction stems in no small part from the fact that he surveys a great range of affluence, education and ambition, and offers us little that is either beautiful, admirable or hopeful in any of the individuals or sections of the community. Environmental determinism and naturalistic motivations seem to prevail; and in forceful prose Naipaul indicates his dislike of these conditions and his even stronger dislike of impotent or quiescent people.

Fireflies is a remarkably coherent first novel, mixing as it does psycho-sociological observations, humor, and an extremely deft plot structure. The novel describes the virtual demise of the acknowledged leaders of the Hindu community in Trinidad, the Khoja dynasty. It focusses on two sections of the Khoja family: one ruled by Govind, the recently elevated head of the family following the paralysis of his mother, and the other by Baby, the old lady's great-niece. The way in which Baby is married off and subsequently treated by Govind mirrors the fluxional state of things. A husband is found for her, Ram Lutchman, a driver for the Central Trinidad Bus Company. Thus a poor girl is married to an even poorer man; and the logical corollary of her marriage should be no help from the Khojas, who traditionally believed that "the rich were automatically good; the poor must look after their souls....An ill-conceived, unhappy marriage was nectar to the undisciplined soul. Thus, with an unruffled conscience, could the young girl with the fine nose be consigned to the tenderness of an alien family." The fine nose which distinguishes Baby makes it impossible for Govind, who also has some distinction, to ignore her or her problems. Distinction is disastrous for them both. Baby developes a riotous imagination, all the more powerfully fuelled because, nose apart, she is fat and ordinary. Her ambitions for her son are tremendous. The good-looking Romesh will become a film-star; the moderately intelligent Bhaskar is sent to India to study medicine. But the vessels are too frail. Romesh becomes a drop-out and Bhaskar has a nervous breakdown. Govind's distinction and downfall are a vague belief in progress, a vague impulse to generosity. Traditions are modified or are allowed to slip; he dabbles in politics, fails, and next tries to set up a Rousseauesque educational experiment. His stature in the community at large, and his grip on the family, disintegrate.

Naipaul's characterization of Govind's wife and Baby's husband accentuates the theme of change that is only partly willed, often unwelcome, and usually disastrous. Govind finds Ram a job as a clerk in the Ministry of Education, a job which effectively displaces and disorientates Ram, who strives inconsistently and with a lazy desperation for the fulfilment he thinks he should feel. He has an affair with an American anthropologist and develops unrewarded passions for gardening and photography. Sumintra, Govind's wife, who is allowed to keep Christian texts on her bedroom wall, and who loves best the six dolls which are her vicarious children, is an even more pathetic figure. Her ideal is a tiled dining-room; Ram's a soft, buttery avocado of his own growing.

Naipaul's second novel lacks the comic relief, the pathos, and the resonances of *Fireflies*. The settings are sordid, and so, on the whole, are the characters. Only the fittest survive; and the fittest of all is Egbert Ramsaran, who emerged from the backwoods "Settlement" (alternately squelchy swamp and caked earth) "much like the first adventurous sea-creature who had crawled out of the primeval waters and taken to the land, a mutant in whom implacable urges had been implanted," whose "cold-bloodedness was as tangible a trait as his well-developed muscles." His son Wilbert and his illegitimate son Singh are reflections of their father; and even those young people with whom Naipaul seems more in sympathy, whose ambitions are intellectual, lack passion, warmth, and humanity. Everyone in and out of the Settlement, irrespective of age and sex, lives for himself, even Ramsaran's second wife, the volptuous Sushila: "No man was too old, too young, too ugly, too inaccessible...for her to bring her talents into play. It was a pursuit dictated by her own needs and convenience and there was neither tenderness nor regard for her prey. She aroused desire to no purpose beyond desire itself. It was a callous, cynical and selfish deployment of her powers." The atmosphere of the book is as fetid and oppressive as Sushila's cheap scent and pancake cosmetics. The characters merely succeed in degrading each other. Like the chip-chip gatherers the effort they expend "is meaningless....Inside each chip-chip shell was the sought-after prize: a minuscule kernel of insipid flesh."

—Ann Massa

NAIPAUL, V(idiadhar) S(urajprasad). Trinidadian. Born in Trinidad, 17 August 1932. Educated at Queen's Royal College, Port of Spain, Trinidad, 1943-48; University College, Oxford, 1950-54, B.A. (honours) in English 1953. Married Patricia Ann Hale in 1955. Settled in England, 1950; Editor, "Caribbean Voices," BBC, London, 1954-56; Fiction Reviewer, *New Statesman*, London, 1957-61. Recipient: Rhys Memorial Prize, 1958; Maugham Award, 1961; Phoenix Trust Award, 1962; Hawthornden Prize, 1964; Smith Literary Award, 1968; Arts Council grant, 1969; Booker Prize, 1971; Bennett Award (*Hudson Review*, New York), 1980. Address: c/o André Deutsch Ltd., 105 Great Russell Street, London WC1B 3LJ, England.

PUBLICATIONS

Novels

The Mystic Masseur. London, Deutsch, 1957; New York, Vanguard Press, 1959.
The Suffrage of Elvira. London, Deutsch, 1958.
Miguel Street. London, Deutsch, 1959; New York, Vanguard Press, 1960.

A House for Mr. Biswas. London, Deutsch, 1961; New York, McGraw Hill, 1962.
Mr. Stone and the Knights Companion. London, Deutsch, 1963; New York, Macmillan, 1964.
The Mimic Men. London, Deutsch, and New York, Macmillan, 1967.
In a Free State. London, Deutsch, and New York, Knopf, 1971.
Guerrillas. London, Deutsch, and New York, Knopf, 1975.
A Bend in the River. London, Deutsch, and New York, Knopf, 1979.

Short Stories

A Flag on the Island. London, Deutsch, 1967; New York, Macmillan, 1968.

Other

The Middle Passage: Impressions of Five Societies—British, French and Dutch—in the West Indies and South America. London, Deutsch, 1962; New York, Macmillan, 1963.
An Area of Darkness: An Experience of India. London, Deutsch, 1964; New York, Macmillan, 1965.
The Loss of El Dorado: A History. London, Deutsch, 1969; New York, Knopf, 1970; revised edition, London, Penguin, 1973.
The Overcrowded Barracoon and Other Articles. London, Deutsch, 1972; New York, Knopf, 1973.
India: A Wounded Civilization. London, Deutsch, and New York, Knopf, 1977.
The Return of Eva Perón, with the Killings in Trinidad (essays). London, Deutsch, and New York, Knopf, 1980.

*

Critical Studies: *V.S. Naipaul: An Introduction to His Work* by Paul Theroux, London, Deutsch, and New York, Africana, 1972; *V.S. Naipaul* by Robert D. Hamner, New York, Twayne, 1973, and *Critical Perspectives on V.S. Naipaul* edited by Hamner, Washington, D.C., Three Continents, 1977, London, Heinemann, 1978; *V.S. Naipaul* by William Walsh, Edinburgh, Oliver and Boyd, and New York, Barnes and Noble, 1973; *V.S. Naipaul: A Critical Introduction* by Landeg White, London, Macmillan, and New York, Barnes and Noble, 1975; *Paradoxes of Order: Some Perspectives on the Fiction of V.S. Naipaul* by Robert K. Morris, Columbia, University of Missouri Press, 1975; *V.S. Naipaul* by Michael Thorpe, London, Longman, 1976.

V.S. Naipaul comments:
I feel that any statement I make about my own work would be misleading. The work is there: the reader must see what meaning, if any, the work has for him. All I would like to say is that I consider my non-fiction an integral part of my work.

* * *

V.S. Naipaul is the most accomplished novelist yet to emerge from the English-speaking Caribbean. This definition, however, can limit his achievement, which stands in the main stream of the modern English novel. Similarly, although it is impossible to discuss his work without seeing it as a progressive exploration of an awareness based in the Caribbean, his concern is with the universal human predicament.

His work to date falls into three phases. His first-written (though third-published) work is *Miguel Street*. It consists of sketches of life in a lower-class area of Trinidad. The focus is that of a child, but although this changes as the boy grows older and more comprehending, Naipaul omitted the story intended to show the boy's own involvement in its frustrated and inherently tragic world. (Reprinted as "The Enemy" in *A Flag on the Island.*) The child's point of view can therefore avoid adult implications: in spite of the plots of the stories—which include a prostitute Laura driving her daughter to commit suicide when in her time she also has an illegitimate child, and Man Man, who wants to be crucified as Christ until the villagers throw too large rocks—the tone is one of delicately balanced humour. This is both its achievement and its limitation.

The Mystic Masseur achieves a greater complexity. On one hand there is the narrator who views the story from a changing perspective as he grows up; on the other there is use of the main protagonist's own suppressed autobiography, significantly called "The Years of Guilt." The hero moves from humble beginnings as Pundit Ganesh Ramsummair, an incompetent Trinidad masseur, through assumption of powers as a mystic and writer, to the position of G. Ramsay Muir, Esq., M.B.E., member of the Legislative Council. It is at once a satire on the roots of power that lie in popular superstition and apparent education, and of a figure driven by the forces he himself exploits. Ganesh provides a human centre lacking in *The Suffrage of Elvira*, another satire on popular political power in the Caribbean.

These three novels led George Lamming in *The Pleasures of Exile* (1960) to attack Naipaul's work as "castrated satire," an attempt to take a superior ironic stance avoiding full involvement in the Caribbean predicament. Whatever truth lies behind Lamming's criticism, it is not applicable to *A House for Mr. Biswas*, a major novel spanning three generations of life in Trinidad. There is satire on Caribbean ways of life, from the West Indian social structure to such facets as popular journalism. But the satire itself is mediated through the particular sensibility of the ever-present Mohun Biswas. Biswas, born with an extra finger which shows both his endemic bad luck and the effects of malnutrition, reacts to his world with an artist's fastidious consciousness, although in Trinidad the only outlets he can find for his creative imagination are sign-writing and the reporting of sensational episodes for the Trinidad *Sentinel*. Of Brahmin caste, he is seized in marriage by the merchant family of Tulsis, who are hungry for every bit of status they can get, to bolster up their own immigrant insecurity. Everything in the commercial vulgarity and oppressive clannishness revolts Biswas, who struggles to get free of them, while needing (and taking) the home they offer. Mr. Biswas's quest for a house of his own is an attempt to find both independence and some place that he can imbue with meaning. Surrounding this overt theme is Naipaul's sense of the inherent loneliness of man himself—the darkness both physical and spiritual that Biswas faces when a hurricane blows his house from around him causing him a nervous breakdown. But by the end Biswas has his own precarious house, while the Tulsi family is disintegrating. A tender tragi-comedy, in scope and theme the book approaches epic proportions.

With *Mr. Stone and the Knights Companion*—about a middle-class Englishman coming to terms with old age—Naipaul's work begins to look more deliberately outward from the Caribbean. *The Mimic Men* is set largely on the fictional West Indian Island of Isabella, and explores the rise to power of Ralph Kriplesingh, building on fortunes from Coca Cola and real estate. It follows up many of the questions *Elvira* poses about the roots of political power in the Caribbean, brought up to date with the advent of Black Power. One possibility for a meaningful society is offered in Ralph's father who becomes a *sunyasi* (holy man), but the novel questions whether any actions in the contemporary island predicament can have meaning. Partly because he too is a "mimic man," Ralph cannot see any. The novel opens and closes in England, and Ralph's vision comes in a moment of existential desolation at the end.

In a Free State is a thematically united trio of stories, set between two factual diary entries of a Middle East tour. They concern an Indian servant in the United States, West Indians in England, and an Englishman in an African state at time of revolution. Action and description are stripped to the nerve, and slight actions, such as an image in a television set, or a blank stare, take on momentous impact. The cutting away of the rich detail that characterised *Miguel Street* to elements of consciousness, here reaches a brilliant stage of development. It is the logical progression of both Naipaul's style and themes.

Naipaul has noted above that his non-fiction and fiction form an integral whole. As *The Middle Passage* is essential background to *A*

House for Mr. Biswas and *The Mimic Men*, other journalistic work, including *The Killings in Trinidad*, has laid the groundwork for his more recent novels. *Guerrillas* is set on a Caribbean island smouldering on the brink of revolution. Jimmy Ahmed, Afro-Chinese, Muslim, and English educated, attempts to organise a socialist commune, but is defeated by his own illusions and the futile racial and social conflicts of the island. So also is Roche, a hero of the South African freedom struggle, who is finally trapped into confessing his political disillusionment. Jane, an English girl, pays for her shallow attempts to relate to both Roche and Ahmed by being brutally murdered. As objective analysis, the novel is sharper than *The Mimic Men*, but the cold despair impairs the book's imaginative impact. Focused through the character of Selim, an East African merchant, *A Bend in the River* is a more emphatic work. It masterfully recreates the experience of living in a contemporary central African state under dictatorship, where the political struggle is complicated by race, education, and modern ideologies awkwardly coexisting with traditional society. Those in power one day may be prey to others the next, while, underlying all, the jungle, river, and forest people remain impervious to the vagaries of history. Complex, objective, yet emotively powerful, the novel is arguably Naipaul's finest since *A House for Mr. Biswas*.

—Louis James

NARAYAN, R(asipuram) K(rishnaswami). Indian. Born in Madras, 10 October 1906. Educated at Maharaja's College, Mysore, graduated 1930. Owner, Indian Thought Publications, Mysore. Recipient: Indian Literary Academy National Prize, 1958; Padma Bhushan, India, 1964; National Association of Independent Schools Award (USA), 1965; English-Speaking Union Award, 1975; Royal Society of Literature Benson Medal, 1980. Litt.D.: University of Leeds, Yorkshire, 1967; D.Litt.: University of Delhi; Sri Venkateswara University; University of Mysore. Fellow, Royal Society of Literature, 1980. Agent: Anthony Sheil Associates Ltd., 2-3 Morwell Street, London WC1B 3AR, England. Address: 15 Vivekananda Road, Yadavagiri, Mysore 2, India.

PUBLICATIONS

Novels

Swami and Friends: A Novel of Malgudi. London, Hamish Hamilton, 1935; with *The Bachelor of Arts*, East Lansing, Michigan State College Press, 1954.
The Bachelor of Arts. London, Nelson, 1937; with *Swami and Friends*, East Lansing, Michigan State College Press, 1954.
The Dark Room. London, Macmillan, 1938.
The English Teacher. London, Eyre and Spottiswoode, 1945; as *Grateful to Life and Death*, East Lansing, Michigan State College Press, 1953.
Mr. Sampath. London, Eyre and Spottiswoode, 1949; as *The Printer of Malgudi*, East Lansing, Michigan State University Press, 1957.
The Financial Expert. London, Methuen, 1952; East Lansing, Michigan State College Press, 1953.
Waiting for the Mahatma. London, Methuen, and East Lansing, Michigan State College Press, 1955.
The Guide. Madras, Higginbothams, London, Methuen, and New York, Viking Press, 1958.
The Man-Eater of Malgudi. New York, Viking Press, 1961; London, Heinemann, 1962.
The Vendor of Sweets. New York, Viking Press, 1967; as *The Sweet-Vendor*, London, Bodley Head, 1967.
The Painter of Signs. New York, Viking Press, 1976; London, Heinemann, 1977.

Short Stories

Cyclone and Other Stories. Mysore, Indian Thought Publications, n.d.
Malgudi Days. Mysore, Indian Thought Publications, 1943.
An Astrologer's Day and Other Stories. London, Eyre and Spottiswoode, 1947.
Dodu and Other Stories. Mysore, Indian Thought Publications, 1950(?).
Lawley Road. Mysore, Indian Thought Publications, 1956.
A Horse and Two Goats. London, Bodley Head, and New York, Viking Press, 1970.

Uncollected Short Stories

"Naga," in *New Yorker*, 26 August 1972.
"The Cobbler and the God," in *Playboy* (Chicago), 1975.

Other

Mysore. Mysore, Government Branch Press, 1939.
My Dateless Diary (travel in America). Mysore, Indian Thought Publications, 1960.
Next Sunday: Sketches and Essays. Bombay, Pearl, 1960.
Gods, Demons, and Others. New York, Viking Press, 1964; London, Heinemann, 1965.
The Ramayana: A Shortened Modern Prose Version of the Indian Epic. New York, Viking Press, 1972; London, Chatto and Windus, 1973.
Reluctant Guru (essays). Delhi, Hind, 1974.
My Days: A Memoir. New York, Viking Press, 1974; London, Chatto and Windus, 1975.
The Emerald Route. Bangalore, Government of Karnataka, 1977.
The Mahabharata: A Shortened Modern Prose Version of the Indian Epic. New York, Viking Press, and London, Heinemann, 1978.

*

Manuscript Collection: Mugar Memorial Library, Boston University.

Critical Studies: *R.K. Narayan: A Critical Study of His Works* by Harish Raizada, New Delhi, Young Asia, 1969; *R.K. Narayan* by William Walsh, London, Longman, 1971; *The Novels of R.K. Narayan* by Lakshmi Holmstrom, Calcutta, Writers Workshop, 1973; *R.K. Narayan* by P.S. Sundaram, New Delhi, Arnold-Heinemann India, 1973.

* * *

No other 20th-century novelist besides William Faulkner has so well succeeded in creating through a succession of novels an imagined community that microcosmically reflects the physical, intellectual, and spiritual qualities of a whole culture as has R.K. Narayan in his tales of the South Indian community of Malgudi. His stories have made a naive, highly emotional society half a world away as much a part of a reader's experience as Faulkner's novels have made the mad, decadent world of the red hills of Mississippi.

Narayan took longer than Faulkner to discover his metier, though all the Indian writer's novels have been largely set in Malgudi. With his third novel, *Sartoris* (1929), published when he was 32, Faulkner laid the cornerstone for his Yoknapatawpha saga of pride-doomed families. Narayan published four apprentice works based largely on reminiscences before producing, at the age of 43,

Mr. Sampath, the first of the five most remarkable studies of flamboyant characters who electrified the sleepy city of Malgudi.

It is unlikely that anyone would have guessed that Narayan's first two novels were the work of a major artist. *Swami and Friends* is a kind of charming Indian *Penrod and Sam*, an episodic account of the adventures of two cricket-playing chums as they start high school. *The Bachelor of Arts* is another episodic account of a young man's graduating from college, experiencing a frustrating love affair, wandering about the country disconsolately, returning home to become agent for a big city newspaper, and finally marrying under family auspices. His third novel, *The Dark Room*, he describes as dealing with a Hindu wife who submitted passively to an overbearing husband.

His work changed drastically with *The English Teacher*, a thinly veiled account of his own marriage and the event that most matured and shaped his character, the early death of his beloved wife. This novel begins like Narayan's earlier ones with episodic sketches of a young preparatory school teacher's relationships with his students, colleagues, and family. After the tragic death of the wife while househunting, however, the novel becomes a much deeper and more tightly unified work.

With his next novel, Narayan settled upon the kind of characters and narrative patterns that he was to employ in his five remarkable explorations of the fantastic agitations beneath the enervating surface of the life of Malgudi. Near the end of *Mr. Sampath*, Narayan observes of Srinivas, the principal character, that "he felt he had been involved in a chaos of human relationships and activities."

Nearly all of Narayan's subsequent novels involve characters and readers in such chaos. Srinivas is a rather aimless young man who has finally been driven by his family to choose a profession and who comes to Malgudi in 1938—when war clouds hang over the whole world—to found a newspaper that has "nothing special to note about any war, past or future," but is "only concerned with that war that is always going on—between man's inside and outside." He falls into the hands of a printer, Mr. Sampath, who takes a proprietary interest in the success of the paper, but who is lured from his printing trade into a film-producing venture. Even Srinivas is briefly tempted to abandon his paper and take up script writing. Despite frantic activity and great expenditures, however, the movie-making venture collapses. Only Srinivas emerges unscathed. He finds another printer and returns to publishing his paper, reflecting on one of the men involved in the catastrophe he has witnessed:

> throughout the centuries...this group was always there: Ravi with his madness, his well-wishers with their panaceas and their apparatus of cure. Half the madness was his own doing, his lack of self-knowledge, his treachery to his own instincts as an artist, which had made him a battle-ground. Sooner or later he shook off his madness and realized his true identity—though not in one birth, at least in a series of them.

The passage is a key to understanding Narayan's major works and their relationship to Hindu philosophy; for the characters he focuses upon are those who are "mad" as a result of their lack of self-knowledge. Some must await another reincarnation; but some manage to shake off the madness and find their true identities.

One who must wait is the title character of *The Financial Expert*, Margayya, whom we meet sitting under a banyan tree assisting peasants in obtaining loans from a co-operative banking institution. The society's officers resent Margayya's activities, but his business flourishes until his spoiled young son throws into a sewer the book in which all accounts are kept. During a trip to collect a red lotus needed for a penitential ritual, Margayya meets Dr. Pal, a self-styled sociologist, who has written a pornographic manuscript based on the *Kama Sutra*. Margayya recoups his fortune by publishing it under the title *Domestic Harmony*; then, embarrassed by the source of his new wealth, he goes back into a money-lending business that is based on withholding the interest from the first installment on the loan. He becomes so successful that he achieves an honored position in the community and recruits Dr. Pal to attract investors. The scheme collapses, however, when the son, who has been gambling with Dr. Pal, demands a share in the business; Margayya assaults Dr. Pal, who in turn discredits the money-lender with his investors. When investors demand their money back, both Margayya and his son are ruined and driven back into dealings with the peasants beneath the banyan tree.

Narayan's next novel, *Waiting for the Mahatma*, is one of his most noble-minded, but least successful. It tells, in the episodic manner of his earlier books, of the misadventures of two young disciples of Mahatma Gandhi during the master's long effort to free his native land. Written after Gandhi's assassination, the book is an admirable tribute, but the fictional characters are too sketchily developed to make it of more than historical interest.

Narayan next turned to the work that has generally been recognized as his most outstanding, *The Guide*, an extremely complicated tale of a confidence man turned saint. In flashbacks, we learn of the rise of Raju from food-seller in the Malgudi railroad station to manager and apparent husband of Rose, who becomes an extremely popular dancer, and his quick fall when he is jailed for forging her signature to a package of jewels. We meet him first, however, when he has installed himself in an abandoned temple after his release from jail and has begun to play the role of spiritual advisor to a peasant community that accepts him as a Mahatma. Gradually he comes to believe in the role he has created, and to relieve a drought he feels compelled to make a 15-day fast that he has suggested as an appropriate penance. As a great crowd gathers, he gains "a peculiar strength" from, for the first time in his life, "learning the thrill of full application, outside money and love." Despite grave peril to his health he continues to fast until he feels that the rain is falling in the hills. The ending of this novel like that of *The English Teacher* is ambiguous: does Swami Raju die? do the rains come? Narayan tells us only, "He sagged down"; but he has transcended the madness that once affected him and found a fulfillment denied the printer of Malgudi and the financial expert.

Such fulfillment is denied also Vasu, the fanatical taxidermist of *The Man-Eater of Malgudi*, Narayan's greatest picture of the madness that leads to self-destruction. After successfully flaunting his great strength about the community unchecked through a series of outrageous incidents, he finally devises a plot against Malgudi's beloved temple elephant. The beast seems doomed, but Vasu dies instead; and in one of the most spectacular conclusions to any of Narayan's works, the almost incredible but carefully foreshadowed way in which he destroyed himself is disclosed.

The complementary *The Vendor of Sweets* is Narayan's most mellow portrayal of the man who discovers at last his true identity. Jagan had been freed from patriarchal thralldom when he broke with his orthodox family and went to jail in support of Mahatma Gandhi's program. His experiences, however, are of no help to him in dealing with another of the spoiled, insolent, uncommunicative sons that appear in many of Narayan's works. The son prefers American "get-rich-quick" ideas to the simple, self-sacrificial life recommended by Gandhi, and Jagan indulges the boy's whims by selling sweetmeats to the luxury-loving community. When the son begins to get into serious troubles, however, Jagan decides that there is nothing he can do. He abandons his business and retires to a decrepit garden of meditation, explaining to one of the protesting opportunists who has fattened on him, "I am going to watch a Goddess come out of a stone." He has freed himself from the successive bondages to parents, hero, and child and has found a tranquility unique in Narayan's tales.

Only confusion, however, awaits the protagonist of Narayan's most recent novel, *The Painter of Signs*, in which the novelist also moves with the times by dealing maturely from many viewpoints with India's urgent and controversial problem of population control. Raman, a highly traditional 30-year-old bachelor, who took up signboard painting because he "loved calligraphy," is cared for by his devoted aunt until he meets Daisy, a dynamic zealot who propagandizes for birth control in remote villages. When the aunt learns that Raman has induced Daisy to marry him, the older woman departs on a religious pilgrimage from which she does not expect to return. When Daisy, however, also discovers that she cannot give up her missionary work for marriage, hapless Raman finds that he has destroyed his old life without creating a new one.

The major Malgudi novels can thus be read not only individually as remarkable character studies, but as a unit describing the soul's progress—despite setbacks—from fanaticism towards serenity and the transcendence of the grimy chaos of the Malgudi railroad station.

—Warren French

NATHAN, Robert (Gruntal). American. Born in New York City, 2 January 1894. Educated at Public School 6 and the Collegiate School, New York; Ethical Culture School, Geneva; Phillips Exeter Academy, New Hampshire, 1910-12; Harvard University, Cambridge, Massachusetts, 1912-15. Married 1) Dorothy Michaels in 1915 (divorced, 1922); 2) Nancy Wilson in 1930 (divorced, 1936); 3) Lucy Lee Hall Skelding in 1936 (divorced, 1939); 4) Janet McMillen Bingham in 1940 (divorced, 1951); 5) Clara May Blum Burns in 1951 (divorced, 1955); 6) Shirley Kneeland in 1955 (died, 1969); 7) Joan Winnifrith in 1970; one child. Advertising Solicitor, New York, 1916-18; Lecturer, New York University School of Journalism, 1924-25; Screenwriter, Metro-Goldwyn-Mayer, Hollywood, 1943-49. Composer and illustrator. President, United States P.E.N., 1940-42; Chancellor, Academy of American Poets. Member, American Academy, 1935. Address: 1240 North Doheny Drive, Los Angeles, California 90069, U.S.A.

PUBLICATIONS

Novels

Peter Kindred. New York, Duffield, 1919.
Autumn. New York, McBride, 1921.
The Puppet Master. New York, McBride, 1923; London, Lane, 1924.
Jonah. New York, McBride, 1925; as *Son of Amittai*, London, Heinemann, 1925.
The Fiddler in Barley. New York, McBride, 1926; London, Heinemann, 1927.
The Woodcutter's House. Indianapolis, Bobbs Merrill, 1927; London, Mathews and Marrot, 1932.
The Bishop's Wife. Indianapolis, Bobbs Merrill, and London, Gollancz, 1928.
There Is Another Heaven. Indianapolis, Bobbs Merrill, 1929.
The Orchid. Indianapolis, Bobbs Merrill, 1931; London, Mathews and Marrot, 1932.
One More Spring. New York, Knopf, and London, Cassell, 1933.
Road of Ages. New York, Knopf, and London, Constable, 1935.
The Enchanted Voyage. New York, Knopf, 1936; London, Constable, 1937.
The Barly Fields: A Collection of Five Novels (includes *The Fiddler in Barly*, *The Woodcutter's House*, *The Bishop's Wife*, *The Orchid*, *There Is Another Heaven*). New York, Knopf, 1938; London, Constable, 1939.
Winter in April. New York, Knopf, and London, Constable, 1938.
Journey of Tapiola. New York, Knopf, and London, Constable, 1938.
Portrait of Jennie. New York, Knopf, and London, Heinemann, 1940.
They Went On Together. New York, Knopf, and London, Heinemann, 1941.
Tapiola's Brave Regiment. New York, Knopf, 1941.
The Sea-Gull Cry. New York, Knopf, 1942.
But Gently Day. New York, Knopf, 1943.
Mr. Whittle and the Morning Star. New York, Knopf, and London, Low, 1947.
Long after Summer. New York, Knopf, 1948; London, Low, 1949.
The River Journey. New York, Knopf, 1949.
The Married Look. New York, Knopf, 1950; as *His Wife's Young Face*, London, Staples Press, 1951.
The Innocent Eye. New York, Knopf, 1951.
Nathan 3 (includes *The Sea-Gull Cry*, *The Innocent Eye*, *The River Journey*). London, Staples Press, 1952.
The Train in the Meadow. New York, Knopf, 1953.
Sir Henry. New York, Knopf, 1955; London, Barker, 1956.
The Rancho of the Little Loves. New York, Knopf, 1956.
So Love Returns. New York, Knopf, 1958; London, W.H. Allen, 1959.
The Color of Evening. New York, Knopf, and London, W.H. Allen, 1960.
The Wilderness-Stone. New York, Knopf, and London, W.H. Allen, 1961.
A Star in the Wind. New York, Knopf, and London, W.H. Allen, 1962.
The Devil with Love. New York, Knopf, and London, W.H. Allen, 1963.
The Fair. New York, Knopf, 1964.
The Mallot Diaries. New York, Knopf, 1965.
Stonecliff. New York, Knopf, 1967.
Mia. New York, Knopf, 1970; London, W.H. Allen, 1971.
The Elixir. New York, Knopf, 1971.
The Summer Meadows. New York, Delacorte Press, 1973.
Heaven and Hell and the Megas Factor. New York, Delacorte Press, 1975.

Plays

Music at Evening (produced White Plains, New York, 1937).
Jezebel's Husband; or, Jonah in Zebulon (produced Mountainholm, Pennsylvania, 1952). Included in *Jezebel's Husband, and The Sleeping Beauty*, 1953.
Jezebel's Husband, and The Sleeping Beauty. New York, Knopf, 1953.
Juliet in Mantua. New York, Knopf, 1966.
Susan and the Stranger (produced Los Angeles, 1979).

Screenplays: *The White Cliffs of Dover*, with others, 1944; *The Clock*, with Joseph Schrank, 1945; *Pagan Love Song*, with Jerry Davis, 1950.

Verse

Youth Grows Old. New York, McBride, 1922.
A Cedar Box. Indianapolis, Bobbs Merrill, 1929.
Selected Poems. New York, Knopf, 1935; London, Constable, 1936.
A Winter Tide: Sonnets and Poems. New York, Knopf, 1940.
Dunkirk: A Ballad. New York, Knopf, 1942.
Morning in Iowa. New York, Knopf, 1944.
The Darkening Meadows. New York, Knopf, 1945.
The Green Leaf: The Collected Poems. New York, Knopf, 1950.
The Married Man. New York, Knopf, 1962.
Evening Song: Selected Poems 1950-1973. Santa Barbara, California, Capra Press, 1973.

Other

The Concert. New York, House of Books, 1940.
Journal for Josephine (memoirs). New York, Knopf, 1943.
The Snowflake and the Starfish (juvenile). New York, Knopf, 1959.
The Weans (archaeology). New York, Knopf, 1960.
Tappy (juvenile). New York, Knopf, 1968.

Bibliography: *Robert Nathan: A Bibliography* by Dan H. Lawrence, New Haven, Connecticut, Yale University Press, 1960.

Manuscript Collection: Yale University, New Haven, Connecticut.

Critical Studies: *The Work of Robert Nathan* by Louis Bromfield, Indianapolis, Bobbs Merrill, 1927; *American Literature* by Russell Blankenship, New York, Holt, 1931; Introduction by Stephen Vincent Benét to *The Barly Fields*, 1938; *Robert Nathan* by Clarence Sandelin, New York, Twayne, 1969.

Robert Nathan comments:

I have tried—as far as I could—to be a comforter in the world ...not through what I know, but what I don't—and cannot—know. I have tried to suggest the mystery and the magic.

* * *

A traditionalist in that good sense which describes most popular writers of merit, Robert Nathan has written more than 50 books of fiction, verse, drama, and gently ironic speculation—not to mention the songs, screenplays, essays, and obiter dicta which remain uncollected.

In his work he regularly invokes the piety of Hebrew prophets, the skepticism of Roman stoics, the absolute awe of medieval mystics, and the consternation of contemporary scientists as evidence of the mystery of our being. He recommends a non-sectarian, private, humble faith in God as the best hope of surviving our modern anomie. In his best early treatment of this theme, *Jonah*, there is a lyric balance of humor, earnestness, and hope. By 1962, when he wrote *Star in the Wind*, the humor and hope had all but disappeared, his plea for love and faith grown urgent.

Yet his humor remains as essential ingredient of all his work. *Sir Henry* is a delightful parody of the White Knight we first met in the pages of Lewis Carroll, and *The Weans* is a mock essay in archeology that provides a startling indictment of contemporary morals and manners by means of ironic perspective. Often as not, his novels include worldly dogs, philosophical horses, communistic ants, capitalistic cockroaches, an insecure fox or narcissistic whale, as actors and sooth-sayers, the distorted but essentially honest projections of our own frail humanity, the humorous versions of the truth we can accept in laughter.

Nathan's forte is the short novel of ironic fantasy, employing a melodic prose, relying upon traditional argument, evoking a mood of sympathy and wonder for the everyday miracle of existence. His most popular story, *Portrait of Jennie*, uses a double time pattern to suggest how "fated" lovers can meet as kindergarten child and adult man in the winter of 1938, and then suffer a traumatic separation as lovers, both 28 years of age, in the following autumn of 1939. The man lives through one year of experience, in this interval, but the woman lives through more than 20. And this mixture of ordinary and accelerated time is but one game Nathan plays with our arbitrary notions of reality. He also has stories that depend on suspended time, reversed time, impressionistic time, and expressionistic time. The very mystery of time suggests, indeed, our human limitations in a multiverse beyond comprehension.

Of course his fantasy involves other elements as well, such as the displacement of characters from expected into unexpected circumstances, the substitution of place or circumstance to achieve ironic contrasts—as in *There Is Another Heaven* where a Jew who has converted to Christianity arrives in the Protestant heaven defined in accordance with popular convictions and practice, only to find Jesus is not in residence—and the employment of characters and attitudes in bizarre ways, as when the demons of Hell are obsessed with man's self-destruction because, since they must take on the form of those who succeed him as denizens of Earth, they fear they will all turn into cockroaches.

But it is as a man of feeling that Nathan should be remembered. All of his wit and humor, all of his deft fantasy, all of his pellucid prose are secondary to the central function of his work, which is to evoke the sentiment of love. Most of his stories deal with the passionate awakening of young lovers, but the implications go beyond the physical and psychological gratifications this involves. In Nathan's work the mortal love of man and woman, the enfolding love of man for other men, the sympathy of man for the mystery of God's infinite works, all combine at last in a mystical conviction that love is the access to God. It is quite appropriate, therefore, that the principal character in *Stonecliff*—a fictional representation of Nathan himself—insists that "a wizard does things with the heart," for he thus describes in cryptic fashion how all the verbal skill, the imaginative reversals, the rich traditions, and the brilliant commonsense of this particular author are made to serve the ultimate goal of generating and sustaining in his readers the joy and hope that comes through every kind of love.

—Clarence Sandelin

NAUGHTON, Bill. British. Born in Ballyhaunis, County Mayo, Ireland, 12 June 1910; grew up in Lancashire, England. Educated at St. Peter and St. Paul School, Bolton, Lancashire. Civil Defence Driver in London during World War II. Married to Ernestine Pirolt. Has worked as a lorry driver, weaver, and coal-bagger. Recipient: Screenwriters Guild Award, 1967, 1968; Prix Italia, for radio play, 1974; Other Award, for children's book, 1978. Agent: Dr. Jan Van Loewen Ltd., 81-83 Shaftesbury Avenue, London W1V 8BX, England. Address: Kempis, Orrisdale Road, Ballasalla, Isle of Man, United Kingdom.

PUBLICATIONS

Novels

Rafe Granite. London, Pilot Press, 1947.
One Small Boy. London, MacGibbon and Kee, 1957.
Alfie. London, MacGibbon and Kee, and New York, Ballantine, 1966.
Alfie Darling. London, MacGibbon and Kee, 1970; New York, Simon and Schuster, 1971.

Short Stories

Late Night on Watling Street and Other Stories. London, MacGibbon and Kee, 1959; New York, Ballantine, 1966.
The Goalkeeper's Revenge. London, Harrap, 1961.
The Goalkeeper's Revenge and Spit Nolan. London, Macmillan, 1974.
The Bees Have Stopped Working and Other Stories. Exeter, Wheaton, 1976.

Plays

My Flesh, My Blood (broadcast, 1957). London, French, 1959; revised version, as *Spring and Port Wine* (produced Birmingham, 1964; London, 1965; as *Keep It in the Family*, produced New York, 1967), London, French, 1967.
She'll Make Trouble (broadcast, 1958). Published in *Worth a Hearing: A Collection of Radio Plays*, edited by Alfred Bradley, London, Blackie, 1967.
June Evening (broadcast, 1958; produced Birmingham, 1966). London, French, 1973.
Alfie (as *Alfie Elkins and His Little Life*, broadcast 1962; as *Alfie*, produced London, 1963). London, French, 1964.
All in Good Time (produced London, 1963; New York, 1965). London, French, 1964.

He Was Gone When We Got There, music by Leonard Salzedo (produced London, 1966).
Annie and Fanny (produced Bolton, Lancashire, 1967).
Lighthearted Intercourse (produced Liverpool, 1971).

Screenplays: *Alfie*, 1966; *The Family Way*, with Roy Boulting and Jeffrey Dell, 1966; *Spring and Port Wine*, 1970.

Radio Plays: *Timothy*, 1956; *My Flesh, My Blood*, 1957; *She'll Make Trouble*, 1958; *June Evening*, 1958; *Late Night on Watling Street*, 1959; *The Long Carry*, 1959; *Seeing a Beauty Queen Home*, 1960; *On the Run*, 1960; *Wigan to Rome*, 1960; *'30-'60*, 1960; *Jackie Crowe*, 1962; *Alfie Elkins and His Little Life*, 1962; *November Day*, 1963; *The Mystery*, 1973.

Television Plays: *Nathaniel Titlark* series, 1957; *Starr and Company* series 1958; *Yorky* series, with Allan Prior, 1960; *Looking for Frankie*, 1961; *Somewhere for the Night*, 1962; *It's Your Move*, 1967.

Other

A Roof over Your Head (autobiography). London, Pilot Press, 1945.
Pony Boy (juvenile). London, Pilot Press, 1946.
A Dog Called Nelson (juvenile). London, Dent, 1976.
My Pal Spadger (juvenile). London, Dent, 1977.

* * *

Bill Naughton's first book, *A Roof over Your Head*, was written while he was working as a Civil Defence driver in London during the War. This book, a blend of fiction and autobiography, deals with working-class life in Lancashire where Naughton, the son of Irish immigrants, grew up. For background, there is the unplanned industrial jungle of the 1920's and 1930's, the grimy, crumbling factories and the monotonous rows of brick houses that L.S. Lowry has so accurately depicted.

A Roof over Your Head is artlessly constructed as a series of short sketches: a naive yet oddly moving and direct account of what life was like under the shadow of the dole queue. Childhood, elopement, married life, a first baby, efforts to find work, a job as a coalman, and finally, extracts from a war-time diary: these form the subject matter that is narrated unsentimentally and without self-pity. Naughton writes frankly but undepressingly about poverty and hardship, and shows how these were made more endurable by the good-hearted camaraderie of Lancashire's ordinary people.

Pony Boy is a novel for boys. In it, two Pony Boys—Corky and Ginger—set out to discover "the world." Here is a rollicking, picaresque tale that indicates how well Naughton remembers what boyhood was like. In the 1940's and 1950's Naughton was busy writing short stories for magazines, the best of which were collected in *Late Night on Watling Street*. In these stories, descriptive writing is kept to a minimum and Naughton reveals his gift for dialogue that explains situation and illuminates character. He keeps the narrative on the move like a true storyteller. His title story emphasises the solidarity of lorry-drivers, especially in their dealings with bosses and the police, and brings out their sense of right and wrong. They ostracise a man who has committed murder but will not "split" on him: "He might have got one across the law, but he hadn't got one across Watling Street." Of this collection Naughton has said: "This book includes stories I heard people tell and I just 'put together,' as they say. ...I write mostly about the life I have known."

More cross-sections of the life Naughton actually experienced may be found in *The Goalkeeper's Revenge*, a collection of stories mainly about but not written specifically for boys. One of these stories, "Gift of the Gab," tells the reader what can happen when a deaf-and-dumb boy is taught to speak. The result is both prosaic and humorous. The boy returns to his home town and at first seems as silent as ever. But he readily bursts into speech when questioned about food in the "institution": "Cold suet pud! Morning, noon and ruddy night—nothing but cold suet pud!"

One Small Boy is a novel in which a family—like Naughton's own—leave the West of Ireland for Lancashire's milltowns. A boy grows up and the author explores his relationship with parents and girls. *Alfie*—and Alf is a recurrent name in Naughton's work—was first a radio play called "Alfie Elkins and His Little Life," then a stage play, a film, and a novel. Here, too, one finds the usual understated humor, the eye for detail, and the tolerant good humour. Yet *Alfie*, despite its sophisticated finish, lacks the urgency and freshness of *A Roof over Your Head* and the best of the short stories.

—Robert Greacen

NEMEROV, Howard (Stanley). American. Born in New York City, 1 March 1920. Educated at Fieldston School, New York; Harvard University, Cambridge, Massachusetts, A.B. 1941. Served in the Royal Canadian Air Force and the United States Air Force, 1941-45: First Lieutenant. Married Margaret Russell in 1944; three children. Instructor in English, Hamilton College, Clinton, New York, 1946-48; Member of the Literature Faculty, Bennington College, Vermont, 1948-66; Professor of English, Brandeis University, Waltham, Massachusetts, 1966-69. Professor of English, 1969-76, and since 1976, Edward Mallinckrodt Distinguished University Professor, Washington University, St. Louis. Visiting Lecturer, University of Minnesota, Minneapolis, 1958-59; Writer-in-Residence, Hollins College, Virginia, 1962-64; Consultant in Poetry, Library of Congress, Washington, D.C., 1963-64. Associate Editor, *Furioso*, Madison, Connecticut, later Northfield, Minnesota, 1946-51. Recipient: *Kenyon Review* Fellowship, 1955; Oscar Blumenthal Prize, 1958, Harriet Monroe Memorial Prize, 1959, Frank O'Hara Prize, 1971, and Levinson Prize, 1975 (*Poetry*, Chicago); *Virginia Quarterly Review* Short Story Award, 1958; American Academy grant, 1961; New England Poetry Club Golden Rose, 1962; Brandeis University Creative Arts Award, 1962; National Endowment for the Arts grant, 1966; Theodore Roethke Award, 1968; Guggenheim Fellowship, 1968; St. Botolph's Club Prize, 1968; Academy of American Poets Fellowship, 1970; Pulitzer Prize, for poetry, 1978; National Book Award, for poetry, 1978; Bollingen Prize, 1981. D.L.: Lawrence University, Appleton, Wisconsin, 1964; Tufts University, Medford, Massachusetts, 1969; Washington and Lee University, Lexington, Virginia, 1976; University of Vermont, Burlington, 1977. Fellow, American Academy of Arts and Sciences, 1966; Member, American Academy, 1976; Chancellor, Academy of American Poets, 1977. Address: Department of English, Washington University, St. Louis, Missouri 63130, U.S.A.

PUBLICATIONS

Novels

The Melodramatists. New York, Random House, 1949.
Federigo; or, The Power of Love. Boston, Little Brown, 1954.
The Homecoming Game. New York, Simon and Schuster, and London, Gollancz, 1957.

Short Stories

A Commodity of Dreams and Other Stories. New York, Simon and Schuster, 1959; London, Secker and Warburg, 1960.
Stories, Fables and Other Diversions. Boston, Godline, 1971.

Verse

The Image and the Law. New York, Holt, 1947.
Guide to the Ruins. New York, Random House, 1950.
The Salt Garden. Boston, Little Brown, 1955.
Small Moment. Los Angeles, Ward Ritchie Press, 1957.
Mirrors and Windows. Chicago, University of Chicago Press, 1958.
New and Selected Poems. Chicago, University of Chicago Press, 1960.
The Next Room of the Dream: Poems and Two Plays. Chicago, University of Chicago Press, 1962.
Five American Poets, with others, edited by Ted Hughes and Thom Gunn. London, Faber, 1963.
The Blue Swallows. Chicago, University of Chicago Press, 1967.
A Sequence of Seven. Roanoke, Virginia, Tinker Press, 1967.
The Winter Lightning: Selected Poems. London, Rapp and Whiting, 1968.
The Painter Dreaming in the Scholar's House. New York, Phoenix Book Shop, 1968.
Gnomes and Occasions. Chicago, University of Chicago Press, 1972.
The Western Approaches: Poems 1973-1975. Chicago, University of Chicago Press, 1975.
The Collected Poems of Howard Nemerov. Chicago, University of Chicago Press, 1977.
Sentences. Chicago, University of Chicago Press, 1980.

Other

Poetry and Fiction: Essays. New Brunswick, New Jersey, Rutgers University Press, 1963.
Journal of the Fictive Life. New Brunswick, New Jersey, Rutgers University Press, 1965.
Reflexions on Poetry and Poetics. New Brunswick, New Jersey, Rutgers University Press, 1972.
Figures of Thought: Speculations on the Meaning of Poetry and Other Essays. Boston, Godine, 1978.

Editor, *Longfellow*. New York, Dell, 1959.
Editor, *Poets on Poetry*. New York, Basic Books, 1966.

*

Manuscript Collection: Olin Library, Washington University, St. Louis.

Critical Studies: *Howard Nemerov* by Peter Meinke, Minneapolis, University of Minnesota Press, 1968; *The Critical Reception of Howard Nemerov: A Selection of Essays and a Bibliography* edited by Bowie Duncan, Metuchen, New Jersey, Scarecrow Press, 1971; *The Shield of Perseus* by Julia Bartholomay, Gainesville, University of Florida Press, 1972; *The Stillness in Moving Things: The World of Howard Nemerov* by William Mills, Memphis, Memphis State University Press, 1975; *Howard Nemerov* by Ross Labrie, Boston, Twayne, 1980.

* * *

In *Journal of the Fictive Life*, which is something like a novel about not being able to write a novel, Howard Nemerov records this meditation: "Of course! To write a work of fiction is essentially to tell a story. And to tell a story is to tell a lie, because a lie was a story." It is the words—*story/lie*—that engage his attention, and appropriately so, for Nemerov principally and most notably is a poet, not a novelist. The novel form, however, has enabled him to explore, in successive stages of authorship, the doubleness of life and art, as exemplified in the imagination that both lives and creates. He has thus written four (if one counts *Journal of the Fictive Life*) novels, and two volumes of shorter pieces. All involve, in one way or another, the theme of doubleness. His first novel, *The Melodramatists*, is set in Boston in the early years of the Second World War, and describes the separate paths toward self-discovery taken by two sisters. One chooses the Roman Church, and at the end finds it without use as a method of living in the world itself. The other elects psychoanalysis and sensuality, and finds these even more unsatisfactory; she manages to kill herself in the process. The approach throughout is satirical; it is almost as if a cosmic skeptic had produced, one year before Eliot, a Beacon Street version of *The Cocktail Party*.

In Nemerov's second novel, *Federigo; or, The Power of Love*, the two personalities of the first novel become one—or, rather, become opposite halves of man and döppelgänger. The interaction of Federigo, the double, with an advertising man, Julian Ghent, turns into not merely a witty satire on sophisticated New Yorkers in search of sexual identity, but a mordant examination of human identity in general, as seen from either side of the looking glass.

The third novel, *The Homecoming Game*, subsequently turned into a play and a motion picture, has an academic setting, and probes into the way that reality intrudes upon intellectual contemplation. The intrusion takes the form of a history professor finding that he is about to give a failing grade to the college's star football player. The "double" is here, too; it turns out that the young athlete has failed *two* courses, and the other is likewise taught by a Jew, not one who is thoroughly middle-class American in upbringing and attitudes like the history professor, but a contentious, not-so-assimilated, idea-ridden firebrand from the big city ghetto. Before all is resolved, raw power and atavistic violence get thoroughly mixed in with the pursuit of truth and goodness, and the history professor, to his chagrin, learns that "it is commonly allowed that you may more easily call the things of this world symbolical than say what they are symbolical of."

Eight years intervened before Nemerov turned to novel-length prose fiction again. *Journal of the Fictive Life*, not only utterly unlike his earlier books but resembling almost no other book ever written, presents the ruthlessly honest progression of the thoughts, dreams, and interpretations of dreams of a man trying to write fiction after eight years of mostly poetry. In a very real sense it isn't "fiction" at all (and it is not put forward as such). For though the authorial persona starts out with a name, Felix Ledger, the "pretence" is abandoned halfway through. Yet as the meditation develops, it turns out to have a plot after all; the author is searching for the explanation of his unwilling renunciation of novel writing, and in the process he also discovers what his father's life and death meant for him, and what the imminent arrival of a new child signifies. The story ends with the birth a son and the making of a poem. Is it fiction? Yes and no; that is the point. "It is, in effect," the narrator declares at one point, "as though I were covertly writing, not my life, but a novel about a life rather like mine, conforming to certain conventions of psychoanalysis." Thus in *Journal of the Fictive Life* the theme of the double becomes that of the author and his persona, the son and the father, the poet and the story-teller. Whether fiction, memoir, or both, *Journal of the Fictive Life* is a remarkable revelation of the creative process, in which notable intellectual perception is turned upon a gifted imagination.

—Louis D. Rubin, Jr.

NEUGEBOREN, Jay. American. Born in Brooklyn, New York, 30 May 1938. Educated at Columbia University, New York, B.A. 1959 (Phi Beta Kappa); Indiana University, Bloomington, M.A. 1963. Married Betsy Bendorf in 1964; three children. Junior Executive Trainee, General Motors Corporation, Indianapolis, 1960; English Teacher, Saddle River Country Day School, New Jersey,

1961-62; High School and Junior High School Teacher, New York City public schools, 1963-66; Preceptor in English, Columbia University, 1964-66; Lecturer, Stanford University, California, 1966-67; Assistant Professor, State University of New York, Old Westbury, 1968-69. Since 1971, Writer-in-Residence, University of Massachusetts, Amherst. Recipient: Bread Loaf Writers Conference Fellowship, 1966; *Transatlantic Review* Novella Award, 1969; National Endowment for the Arts grant, 1973; Guggenheim Fellowship, 1977; Massachusetts Council on the Arts Fellowship, 1978. Address: Department of English, University of Massachusetts, Amherst, Massachusetts 01002, U.S.A.

PUBLICATIONS

Novels

Big Man. Boston, Houghton Mifflin, 1966.
Listen Ruben Fontanez. Boston, Houghton Mifflin, and London, Gollancz, 1968.
Sam's Legacy. New York, Holt Rinehart, 1974.
An Orphan's Tale. New York, Holt Rinehart, 1976.
The Stolen Jew. New York, Holt Rinehart, 1981.

Short Stories

Corky's Brother and Other Stories. New York, Farrar Straus, 1969; London, Gollancz, 1970.
Penguin Modern Stories 3, with others. London, Penguin, 1970.

Uncollected Short Stories

"My Son, The Freedom Rider," in *Colorado Quarterly* (Boulder), Summer 1964.
"Connorsville, Virginia," in *Transatlantic Review* (London), Winter 1969.
"My Life and Death in the Negro American Baseball League: A Slave Narrative," in *Massachusetts Riview* (Amherst), Summer 1973.
"The Place Kicking Specialist," in *Transatlantic Review* (London), 1975.
"Monkeys and Cowboys," in *Present Tense* (New York), Summer 1976.
"A Worthy Cause," in *Willmore City 6-7* (Carlsbad, California), 1978.
"Uncle Nathan," in *Ploughshares* (Cambridge, Massachusetts), iv, 4, 1978.
"His Violin," in *Atlantic* (Boston), November 1978.
"Kehilla," in *Present Tense* (New York), Winter 1978.
"Star of David," in *Tri-Quarterly* (Evanston, Illinois), Spring 1979.
"The St. Dominick's Game," in *Atlantic* (Boston), December 1979.
"Poppa's Books," in *Atlantic* (Boston), May 1980.
"Bonus Baby," in *John O'Hara Journal*, Fall 1980.
"Jonathan," in *Tri-Quarterly* (Evanston, Illinois), Fall 1980.
"Noah's Song," in *Present Tense* (New York), Winter 1980.

Play

Radio Play: *The Stolen Jew*, 1980.

Other

Parentheses: An Autobiographical Journey. New York, Dutton, 1970.

Editor, *The Story of "Story" Magazine: A Memoir*, by Martha Foley. New York, Norton, 1980.

*

Critical Studies: statement by Ian Watt, in *Listen Ruben Fontanez*, London, Gollancz, 1968; "Parentheses" by Charles Moran, in *Massachusetts Review* (Amherst), Fall 1970; "From Kerouac to Koch" by Michael Willis, in *Columbia College Today* (New York), Winter-Spring 1971; "A Decade of the Ethnic Fiction of Jay Neugeboren" by Cordelia Candeleria, in *Melus* (Los Angeles), Winter 1978; interview with Steven Goldleaf, in *Columbia College Today* (New York), December 1979.

* * *

A deep imaginative compassion would appear to be the motive force behind the writing of the American author Jay Neugeboren. For all those who live precariously on the margins of economic, social, or psychological safety he has an immediate, instinctive subtle pity. Nor is there the slightest note of emotional patronage about his attitude. First, the pity which he feels is expressed only objectively in terms of artistic distancing; and secondly, it is constituted of understanding and self-identification.

Thus, whether he is writing, in his novel *Listen Ruben Fontanez*, of poor Puerto Ricans in New York or of the Chassidic Jews (at whose singular dress the gentiles laugh) in that city, he is close to them with a sympathetic sixth sense which excludes any chance of superiority in his role as an observer. His approach and technique are largely the same in his book of 13 shorter tales, *Corky's Brother and Other Stories*, though the earliest of these pieces dates from 1962, and the volume as a whole does not reveal the consistently sure deftness and balance which distinguish *Listen Ruben Fontanez*. The catalysts (rather than objects) of his compassion here include the tough kids of Brooklyn with their obsessive baseball addiction, a young drop-out delinquent negro, and men who are lonely or isolated not through race or social position but through their individual circumstance. It is age (bringing with it the loss of a wife) which creates the loneliness of the two men—a professor and a janitor—in "Finkel," and it is mental instability, on the part of a teen-ager in an institution, in the desperate but beautifully controlled sketch "The Pass."

Compassion may have the first and last word in Jay Neugeboren's writing but it is a sentiment totally removed from the sentimental. Indeed, in between this first and last compassion other states of mind enjoy a field-day, the most prominent of which are humor, hopelessness, and despair. *Listen Ruben Fontanez* might indeed be described as *King Lear* written in prose by James Thurber with contemporary settings. Next go on to make King Lear himself Jewish, and one may possess a zany formula for this strange, deeply moving work of fiction. Old Harry Myers, a Jewish teacher in New York, seeks to keep his heart in cold storage, feeling that sympathetic involvement would dangerously impair his very existence. Like the two old men in the short story "Finkel," Myers's wife has died, leaving him lost, deprived, and lonely. The last of six brothers, Myers has only one old friend of his boyhood left. Teaching his Skid Row kids, he is less than a year from retirement, asking only his pension and tail-end peace from life. Concealed but deep-rooted, however, his humanity has got the better of his fear-ridden nature. Against all counsels of prudence and caution, he acts heroically and is saved from the consequence of his gesture by a group of poor Puerto Rican street arabs whom he once taught.

If the last word in this novel is not "love" at least it is one which points to the promise of a release, for the aged protagonist, from the doubt and withdrawal which have him in their grip. Imagine a Kafka writing of the literally rotting tenements of New York, its polyglot children and over-crowded schools. But this Kafka, with a Kafka-like despair, is possessed of another resonance as well: the gift of laughter. And that is Jay Neugeboren.

—Derek Stanford

NEWBY, P(ercy) H(oward). British. Born in Crowborough, Sussex, 25 June 1918. Educated at Hanley Castle Grammar School, Worcester; St. Paul's College, Cheltenham, 1936-38. Served in the Royal Army Medical Corps, in France and Egypt, 1939-42. Married Joan Thompson in 1945; two daughters. Lecturer in English Language and Literature, Fouad I University, Cairo, 1942-46; free-lance writer and journalist, 1946-49; joined the BBC, London, 1949: Producer, Talks Department, 1949-58; Controller of the Third Programme, subsequently Radio 3, 1958-71; Director of Programmes, Radio, 1971-75; Managing Director of Radio, 1975-78. Since 1978, Chairman, English Stage Company. Recipient: Atlantic Award, 1946; Maugham Award, 1958; Smith-Mundt Fellowship, 1952; Booker Prize, 1969. C.B.E. (Commander, Order of the British Empire), 1972. Address: Upton House, Cokes Lane, Chalfont St. Giles, Buckinghamshire HP8 4TX, England.

PUBLICATIONS

Novels

A Journey to the Interior. London, Cape, 1945; New York, Doubleday, 1946.
Agents and Witnesses. London, Cape, and New York, Doubleday, 1947.
Mariner Dances. London, Cape, 1948.
The Snow Pasture. London, Cape, 1949.
The Young May Moon. London, Cape, 1950; New York, Knopf, 1951.
A Season in England. London, Cape, 1951; New York, Knopf, 1952.
A Step to Silence. London, Cape, 1952.
The Retreat. London, Cape, and New York, Knopf, 1953.
The Picnic at Sakkara. London, Cape, and New York, Knopf, 1955.
Revolution and Roses. London, Cape, and New York, Knopf, 1957.
A Guest and His Going. London, Cape, 1959; New York, Knopf, 1960.
The Barbary Light. London, Faber, 1962; Philadelphia, Lippincott, 1964.
One of the Founders. London, Faber, and Philadelphia, Lippincott, 1965.
Something to Answer For. London, Faber, 1968; Philadelphia, Lippincott, 1969.
A Lot to Ask. London, Faber, 1973.
Kith. London, Faber, and Boston, Little Brown, 1977.

Short Stories

Ten Miles from Anywhere and Other Stories. London, Cape, 1958.

Other

The Spirit of Jem (juvenile). London, Lehmann, 1947; New York, Delacorte Press, 1967.
The Loot Runners(juvenile). London, Lehmann, 1949.
Maria Edgeworth. London, Barker, and Denver, Swallow, 1950.
The Novel 1945-1950. London, Longman, 1951; Folcroft, Pennsylvania, Folcoft Editions, 1970.
The Third Programme. London, BBC Publications, 1965.
The Egypt Story: Its Art, Its Monuments, Its People, photographs by Fred J. Maroon. London, Deutsch, and New York, Abbeville Press, 1979.
Warrior Pharaohs. London, Faber, 1980.

Editor, *A Plain and Literal Translation of the Arabian Nights' Entertainments*, by Sir Richard Burton. London, Barker, 1950; as *Tales from the Arabian Nights*, New York, Pocket Books, n.d.

*

Critical Studies: "Portrait of the Artist as a Jung Man" by Lucia Dickerson, in *Kenyon Review* (Gambier, Ohio), Winter 1959; "A Novelist on His Own," in *Times Literary Supplement* (London), 6 April 1962; *The Fiction of P.H. Newby* by F.X. Mathews, Madison, University of Wisconsin Press, 1964; *Identity in Four of P.H. Newby's Novels* by M.G. St. Leger, unpublished master's thesis, The American University, Beirut, 1969; *P.H. Newby* by G.S. Fraser, London, Longman, 1974; *P.H. Newby* by E.C. Bufkin, Boston, Twayne, 1975.

P.H. Newby comments:

In common with many English novelists my preoccupations have always been with what seems and what is. Many of my novels have been set in the Middle East but that is only because I spent some years there; it does not mean that I regard myself as particularly knowledgable about that part of the world, only that I used this part of my experience to say what I would otherwise have said out my English background—that the most interesting problem is the relationship between innocence and knowledge.

* * *

The lengthy series of novels by P.H. Newby can, with some justice, be assigned to two categories. There are novels which represent Newby's assessment of the contacts of two cultures; *Revolution and Roses*, *The Picnic at Sakkara*, and *Something to Answer For* are examples of these. And there are novels like *A Season in England*, *The Barbary Light*, and *One of the Founders* which abandon the fascinating game of assessing sharp cultural differences and that instead take up an analysis of a single culture: the texture of middle- and lower-class British life. The center of awareness in the novels which specialize in cultural clash is always that of some British traveller or teacher who has been thrust into an alien world, usually Arab but in one instance—*Revolution and Roses*—Greek. The center of awareness in novels that take up a specifically British theme is usually that of a fairly well-educated person who can assess the clash and diversity inherent in a society that, to the careless viewer, is or should be homogeneous.

Both varieties of subject matter have long been worked on by writers of British fiction. Alien cultural contacts experienced in the course of Britain's bearing "the white man's burden" are the stock-in-trade of writers as various as Kipling, E.M. Forster, and Joyce Cary. And novels which relate the maturing of an English hero in his own environment abound. But it is not just to Newby to suggest that he works in two traditions only loosely related to each other. For he brings to either tradition a variation that is his own. Moreover, this variation appears in almost every novel and effects a unity of tone that pervades the novels despite the variety of subject-matter. That tone is the tone of farce.

It is a tone that separates the novels that represent contact with an alien culture from Forster's *A Passage to India* in which the English characters achieve some kind of understanding of the world they visit. Newby's English visitors begin in incomprehension and end there; at certain moments they indeed think they grasp the mystery of Arab or Greek temperament, but later turns of event and later deeds of the "natives" indicate that the comprehension of the English visitor rests on an insecure basis or no basis at all.

Newby's tone of farce also separates his novels with an English setting from the "coming of age" category they may seem to belong to. For in novels like *The Barbary Light* the characters only seem to "come of age"; new events and new potentialities within the hero's own nature give the lie to stances that had seemed final. Only in *A Season in England* and *One of the Founders* do the heroes finally transcend the texture of farce and achieve positions that are crypto-Christian. More usually, the heroes of the English novels just move through a succession of attitudes—attitudes that are related to each other only in that they flow in upon the same person. They do not come to compose a character, a fixed personality, a settled body of convictions. The attitudes simply overtake the hero, temporarily overwhelm him, and presently give way to other emotions and impressions thrust upon him by new events or by discovery of new potentialities within himself. The character lives in a society which is far from unified; this being so, how can he arrive at any consistency of gesture and aspiration? He has no more chance to arrive at a consistent view of his own motives than does the English visitor in *The Picnic at Sakkara.* He will fall in and out of love, will alter his purposes from year to year. Just as will the travelling Englishmen impose one revision after another on their impressions about "natives."

If a discrimination can indeed be made between the two groups of novels, it is this one. The farce of *The Picnic at Sakkara* and *Revolution and Roses* is overt and often violent. The farce of the British novels—which on the surface seem to be more serious—is covert. If one defines farce as existence seen under the sign of radical inconsequence, the definition is easily applied to the non-British novels, which despite the acuteness of Newby's notations on foreign customs and sensibilities are rich in the traditional pleasures of farce: the pleasures that come to us from events that are unpredictable and utterly disconcerting. A "native" who has seemed to be a friend, in *The Picnic at Sakkara,* turns into a bitter foe—and yet gives the English visitor a farewell gift. A man spits in an English woman's face (*Revolution and Roses*) and yet later turns up in London as a suitor. The pleasures of such foreign contacts are not much more predictable than entrance into a lion's cage; docility or murderous assault is equally likely. Such experience cannot be expected to yield a steady meaning; in its presence the visitor can brace himself to offer resignation and, at the worst, amused contempt. The safest course, in such farcically operating worlds, is to keep one's distance and expect very little in the way of fixed and dependable certainties.

One might expect a diminution of these farcical inconsequences when the hero of a novel is living in a world that is culturally his own. But this is not so of Newby's novels that represent the English world. The farcical texture of that world is simply more difficult to bear just because it is indeed one's own world. Gestures of kindness that ought to yield happy results beget unforeseen consequences—consequences that disconcert because of the unpredictable choices of other characters and, most painfully, because of changes in one's own wishes. For the British world of Newby is, in large part, that of Kingsley Amis's *Lucky Jim,* where farce is the product of an endemic British hypocrisy and, still worse, of a lack of any fixed values that could support social consensus. Farce experienced at one remove, in a visit to a foreign country, has become, in novels like *One of the Founders* and *The Barbary Light,* farce experienced at the very center of the culture one belongs to and, indeed, at the very center of one's own nature. Both tragedy and comedy, in varying ways, presuppose a society of shared values. Farce, instead, invites one to the fashioning of a detached, self-protective monologue that celebrates, as do the novels of Newby, the lack of consequence and coherence. It is a lack that just as strongly marks one's own culture and, if sharply inspected, one's own nature. If farce is to be left behind, this must be done by religious gesture (as in *One of the Founders*) which is private and quite incommunicable. Or by religious gesture, as in *A Lot to Ask,* that when it comes to the surface finally reveals itself as not notably unlike hopes for identity and meaning that are both commonplace and important in our time.

—Harold H. Watts

NEWHOUSE, Edward. American. Born in Budapest, Hungary, 10 November 1911; emigrated to the United States in 1923. Educated at Townsend Harris Hall Preparatory School, New York, 1926-29. Served in the United States Army Air Force, 1942-46: Major; Legion of Merit; Conspicuous Service Cross. Married Dorothy DeLay in 1941; two children. Since 1936 has been affiliated with *The New Yorker* magazine. Address: Upper Nyack, New York 10960, U.S.A.

PUBLICATIONS

Novels

You Can't Sleep Here. New York, Macaulay, 1934.
This Is Your Day. New York, Furman, 1937.
The Hollow of the Wave. New York, Sloane, 1949; London, Reinhardt and Evans, 1950.
The Temptation of Roger Heriott. Boston, Houghton Mifflin, 1954; London, Gollancz, 1955.

Short Stories

Anything Can Happen. New York, Harcourt Brace, 1941.
The Iron Chain. New York, Harcourt Brace, 1946.
Many Are Called. New York, Sloane, 1951; London, Gollancz, 1952.

Uncollected Short Stories

"The Bromley Touch," in *New Yorker,* 18 May 1957.
"Howard and Dinah," in *New Yorker,* 23 November 1957.
"The Ambassador," in *Prize Stories 1958: The O. Henry Awards,* edited by Paul Engle. New York, Doubleday, 1958.
"Lead, Damsel, and I Follow," in *New Yorker,* 8 March 1958.
"Debut Recital," in *New Yorker,* 26 April 1958.
"Hungarians," in *New Yorker,* 27 November 1966.

* * *

The hero of Edward Newhouse's third novel, *The Hollow of the Wave,* is a commercial artist who once painted many canvases. The first few pages of the book show this young man, Neil Miller, destroying all his paintings because now he finds them bad. When he is finished, he feels cleansed.

This passage is perhaps the most autobiographical in the work of Newhouse, for, if published books were as easy to incinerate as canvases, he would have destroyed his first two novels. And it would have been a pity.

Following his disillusionment with the Communist Party in 1937, Newhouse no longer saw any merit in his work done under the influence of the dream of the revolution to come. Yet, we who are now removed from the anti-Communist hysteria of the late 1940's and 1950's can once more look at those early books with something approaching the wonder which accompanied their original publication.

You Can't Sleep Here was published early in 1934, when the author had barely passed his 22nd birthday. It was an astonishingly precocious work. The hero, Eugene Marsay, a young reporter of Hungarian background, is struggling with the woes of unemployment during the depression. His problems are the simple ones of where to sleep and what to eat, but they are complicated by an intense pride which forbids him to accept charity or even the love of a rich girl; instead, Gene is driven into more and more conscious identification with the hungry, unemployed masses. His path leads to a shanty colony in Queens, to Party work, and to imprisonment. Throughout, the dialog is crackling with wit, and the action fast-moving. The hero's struggles seem so timely as to give the reader a feeling of *déjà vu,* while his vision of a better America to come is almost surrealistic.

Its sequel, *This Is Your Day,* follows Gene Marsay's career as a Communist organizer. Most of the action takes place in a Pennsylvania farming region. The book's greatest triumph is the characterization of Gene's mother-in-law, a Mrs. Darvas, perhaps the most moving, most authentic portrait of a working woman in American letters. Her figure alone would make the novel worth reading. Newhouse dedicated this book to his own mother.

Twelve years elapsed until the next novel was brought out, but the fictional time of *The Hollow of the Wave* takes up soon after the other left off, on the eve of Dunkirk. Paralleling the author's own development, this book's heroes have moved away from revolutionary ideals into disillusionment with Communism; Party members and fellow travelers are seen largely as shams or dupes. Symbolically, Neil Miller is the illegitimate son of a Communist whom he never knew and who became the victim of a purge. Neil's vague search for this unreal father sets the tone for much of the book. The other hero, Larry Holland, born to great wealth, is skillfully drawn—a man who can bloom only under the special stresses of a challenge called war—in everything else, he is a failure. When the war is over, he is caught "in the hollow of the wave," and asks Neil "savagely," "What are we doing here, you and I?"

His fourth and to date last novel, *The Temptation of Roger Heriott*, comes closest to the classical mold. In a two-week period, Roger Heriott, an executive for a musical scholarship foundation, is faced with a number of circumstances which threaten to upset the equilibrium of his life-style. He may lose his job or he may inherit a sizable sum. The second is the greater threat. In a manner reminiscent of Gene Marsay, Roger Heriott remains true to himself. The global struggle has become a very private one—Gene fought for the masses, against kings and dominions; Roger fights against his temptations, and preserves his integrity. In a style that is always lively and with a structure which is always taut, Newhouse brings his book to a satisfactory conclusion.

On his return from his 20,000 mile freight-hopping jaunt, the 24-year-old author sold five stories to *The New Yorker*. That magazine has continued, throughout the years, to be the chief publisher of his short fiction. Three collections of these have appeared so far: *Anything Can Happen*, *The Iron Chain*, and *Many Are Called*.

In the eyes of many critics, Newhouse is primarily a short story writer. His strengths lie in what Richard Harrity has described as "an accurate ear, an infallibility of character, and a discerning eye for telling incident." Lincoln Steffens called him "the first authentic and eloquent literary voice of America's next generation." Struthers Burt, writing in *The Saturday Review of Literature*, said of *The Iron Chain*, "So far as I'm concerned, they are by long odds the best American short stories I have read in a long while. The reading of this volume was an event in my life."

In recent years, his only major work has been a long story, "Hungarians." Full of revealing incidents about himself, his family, and Hungarians in general, it caps his achievement as the foremost American literary voice to have come from a Hungarian background.

—Dalma H. Brunauer

NEWMAN, C(oleman) J(oseph). Canadian. Born in Montreal, Quebec, 17 February 1935. Educated at Sir George Williams University, Montreal (Woodrow Wilson Fellow), 1954-59, B.A. in English 1959; University of Toronto, 1959-60; Marianopolis College, Montreal, 1967-68. Married Frances Margaret Newman in 1962 (separated, 1977); two sons and one daughter. Lecturer, 1960-66, and Assistant Professor of English, 1971-72, Sir George Williams University; Assistant Professor, Macdonald College, McGill University, Montreal, 1966-71. Since 1972, Assistant Professor of Creative Writing, University of British Columbia, Vancouver. Recipient: Canada Council bursary, 1966, and grant, 1968, 1969. Agent: Russell and Volkening Inc., 551 Fifth Avenue, New York, New York 10017, U.S.A. Address: Department of Creative Writing, University of British Columbia, Vancouver, British Columbia V6T 1W5, Canada.

PUBLICATIONS

Novels

We Always Take Care of Our Own. Toronto, McClelland and Stewart, and London, Gollancz, 1965.

A Russian Novel. Toronto, New Press, and London, Gollancz, 1973.

Short Stories

New Canadian Writing 1969, with John Metcalf and D.O. Spettigue. Toronto, Clarke Irwin, 1969.

Uncollected Short Stories

"A Time To Heal," in *Canadian Genesis* (Toronto), 1971.

"That Old David Copperfield Kind of Crap," in *Canadian Fiction* (Prince George, British Columbia), Winter 1973.

"Your Green Coast," in *Malahat Review* (Victoria, British Columbia), 1973.

"Falling in Love, Again," in *Fiddlehead* (Fredericton, New Brunswick), Fall 1974.

"The Best Lay I Ever Had," in *Journal of Canadian Fiction* (Fredericton, New Brunswick), iii, 3, 1974.

"The Game of Limping," in *Prairie Schooner* (Lincoln, Nebraska), Winter 1974-75.

"The Last Beginning. The Last! The Last!" in *Canadian Fiction* (Prince George, British Columbia), Winter 1975.

Plays

Radio Plays: *All the State Children Got Shoes*, *The Jam on Gerry's Rocks*, *A Work of Art*, *The Last Potato*, and *The Haunted House of Capuscins*, 1959-63.

Television Plays: *The Birth of a Salesman*; *A Bottle of Milk for Mother*.

* * *

C.J. Newman's first novel, *We Always Take Care of Our Own*, is a *bildungsroman* in which the protagonist Meyer Rabinovitch seeks an identity independent of the series of roles offered him by his parents, his rich relatives, and the Jewish community of Montreal as a whole. The family and the community, dedicated to the North American ideal of material success, are self-enclosing and self-absorbed. Meyer, in such an atmosphere, suffocates, but he is primarily motivated by a need to replace the deadening material conformity with values he believes to be essentially spiritual and peculiarly Jewish, values which derive from a Jewish past of suffering and humility. Hence his decision to be the only Jewish beggar in Montreal. Much of the novel is devoted to Meyer's droll and sometimes grotesque attempts to remain a beggar in face of the family's and the Jewish community's attempts to return him to a conformity more North American than Jewish; or more exactly because the Jewish community strives neurotically to be accepted, even more North American than the North Americans themselves. The simple plot is complicated by Meyer's disturbance at his father's business inability, by his socialistic uncle's approval which becomes disapproval, and his love for Rachel, the daughter of the crass *nouveau riche* Eli Echenberg. During the latter's decline and eventual death Meyer becomes indispensable to the family and almost weds the pregnant Rachel. She, however, marries into an even richer Jewish family and the abandoned and disillusioned Meyer is left at the end of the book contemplating the image of his earlier self, this time in the form of another young man who has also decided to be the only Jewish beggar in Montreal. Reflecting on the young man's triumphant hopelessness and smug humility Meyer decides that it is not enough to be Jewish, that the self-definition he seeks must lie in areas beyond the mere inversion of the acceptable patterns of the Jewish and North American community.

Newman's short stories have appeared in many Canadian and American little magazines. Only three so far have been collected, in *New Canadian Writing 1969*. The first two, "Yenteh" and "Everything Must Be Sold," are set in contemporary Montreal and the third, "An Arab Up North," though set in the Canadian Arctic is paradoxically intensely aware of the international situation in the Middle East. The first two stories have in common a strong sense of an urban setting in transition from the small, intimate, and dilapidated to the large, impersonal, and modern. These settings are important inasmuch as they emphasize Newman's apparent theme of the loss of humane warmth in face of a world increasingly materialistic, insecure, and either suspicious of, or hostile to, the idiosyncrasies of being. Mrs. Klein may well be a *yenteh*, but energetic vulgarity is preferable to the deadly gentility of the ironically named Wisemans and the dis-ease of the Schachters who trail after the Wisemans of this world. Likewise the aged owner of the store which is about to be demolished so that the neighbourhood may be "renewed" arouses the malice of the two young men—a malice obscurely motivated by the rootlessness and depersonalization which such renewal seems to breed. Again in the third story it is the claims of history, race, religion, or class which blind the central characters, Arab and Jew, to the important realization that they have more in common with each other than with the rest of the men in the camp. It is because the recognition of each other's humanity is finally less important than a situation seemingly so remote from the Canadian Arctic that the story ends in death and desperate isolation.

A Russian Novel is a much more ambitious book than Newman's first one, and also a less successful one. The protagonist, David Miller, like Meyer Rabinovitch, is Jewish-Canadian and this novel too, appears to be concerned with an identity quest. Miller's mother emigrated many years ago from Russia, and after her death he decides to go there. It is only at the beginning, however, that the quest theme is emphasized. Much of the book is concerned with the love affair between Miller and the wife of the Russian novelist he is supposed to be studying, and with the political complexities surrounding Mikhali Ratin. It is especially in these areas that the novel becomes more of a tract than anything else and the didactic and documentary interests which have always been present in Newman's work usurp narrative, dramatic, and character emphases. One's final impression is of a novel which lacks both direction and linguistic vigour.

—Barrie Davies

NEWMAN, Charles (Hamilton). American. Born in St. Louis, Missouri, 27 May 1938. Educated at North Shore Country Day School, Winnetka, Illinois, graduated 1956; Yale University, New Haven, Connecticut (Editor, *Criterion* magazine), B.A. (summa cum laude) in American Studies 1960 (Phi Beta Kappa); Balliol College, Oxford (Woodrow Wilson Fellow, Fulbright Fellow), 1960-62. Served in the United States Air Force Reserve. Administrative Assistant to Congressman Sidney R. Yates (Democrat, Illinois), 1962-63. Instructor, 1964-65, Assistant Professor, 1965-68, Associate Professor, 1968-73, and Professor of English, 1974-75, Northwestern University, Evanston, Illinois. Since 1975, Professor of English, and Chairman of the Writing Seminars, Johns Hopkins University, Baltimore, Founding Editor, 1964-75, and since 1975, Advisory Editor, *Tri-Quarterly*, Evanston, Illinois. Director, Coordinating Council of Literary Magazines, National Endowment for the Arts, Washington, D.C., 1968-74. Since 1976, Director, P.E.N., American Center. Recipient: National Endowment for the Arts grant, for editing, 1966, and Fellowship, 1973; Rockefeller grant, 1967; Bread Loaf Writers Conference John Atherton Fellowship, 1969; Society of Midland Authors Award, 1973; Friends of Literature Award, 1973; Ingram Merrill Foundation grant, 1974; Guggenheim grant, 1974; American Academy Morton Dauwen Zabel Award, 1975. Agent: Georges Borchardt Inc., 143 East 52nd Street, New York, New York 10022. Address: P.O. Box 65, Volney, Virginia 24379, U.S.A.

PUBLICATIONS

Novels

New Axis; or, The Little Ed Stories: An Exhibition. Boston, Houghton Mifflin, 1966; London, Calder and Boyars, 1968.

The Promisekeeper: A Tephromancy. New York, Simon and Schuster, 1971.

Short Stories

There Must Be More to Love Than Death: Three Short Novels. Chicago, Swallow Press, 1976.

Uncollected Short Stories

"That's the Way the American People Like to Do," in *Tri-Quarterly* (Evanston, Illinois), Spring 1964.

"The Scavengers," in *Vogue* (London), 1968.

"Eclipse, Etc.," in *Chicago Review*, Spring 1971.

"Comprehensive Development Project for These United States...," in *Tri-Quarterly* (Evanston, Illinois), Winter 1976.

"Age of Art," in *Paris Review*, Winter 1976.

"The Woman Who Thought Like a Man," in *The Best American Short Stories 1977*, edited by Martha Foley. Boston, Houghton Mifflin, 1977.

Other

A Child's History of America: Some Ribs and Riffs for the Sixties. Chicago, Swallow Press, 1973.

Editor, with George Gomori, *New Writing from East Europe.* Chicago, Quadrangle, 1968.

Editor, *The Art of Sylvia Plath: A Symposium.* Bloomington, Indiana University Press, and London, Faber, 1970.

Editor, with William A. Henkin, Jr., *Under 30: Fiction, Poetry, and Criticism of the New American Writers.* Bloomington, Indiana University Press, 1970.

Editor, *For Edward Dahlberg.* Evanston, Illinois, Northwestern University Press, 1970.

Editor, with Alfred Appel, Jr., *Nabokov: Criticism and Reminiscences, Translations and Tributes.* Evanston, Illinois, Northwestern University Press, 1970; London, Weidenfeld and Nicolson, 1971.

Editor, with George Abbott White, *Literature in Revolution.* New York, Holt Rinehart, 1972.

Editor, with Mary Kinzie, *Prose for Borges.* Evanston, Illinois, Northwestern University Press, 1974.

* * *

Charles Newman, probably best known as the editor of several anthologies of criticism on Plath, Borges, and the literature of revolution, is also a gifted, richly comic writer. His subjects are varied and numerous. In *A Child's History of America* he charts with colloquial ease his travels through Haight-Ashbury when the

Hippies were confronting the "pigs," on to Paris during the May revolt of the students, and ending in Czechoslovakia during the Russian invasion. The margins of his book are cluttered with aptly chosen quotes from such notables as Trotsky and Marx, Bergson and Merleau-Ponty, Locke and Thoreau, and a gentleman who left graffiti on a lavatory wall. The book offers a disarming and refreshingly original portrait of the confusion of 1968. In *New Axis* Little Ed narrates a series of stories about the life of the affluent D family and their neighbours in a wealthy suburb, King's Kove, situated in Middle-America. Little Ed's world is one of diminished, ordinary pleasures. There is no passion, only adolescent lust and paternal, well-meaning affection. It is also a world of automation: Vibrolators restore the circulation and make plump, curved women trim. *The Promisekeeper* is a "Tephromancy." Auguries of the future are found by reading the ashes of Chicago. Super-elegant, suave, executive Sam Hooper climbs the ladder of success at Management Concerns (pun on emcee is intended). Hooper, the technocrat's dream of efficiency and success, is a promisekeeper who only pledges what he can deliver; he is only victor when he relinquishes his limited powers and lets himself be killed. Hooper's relaxation takes the form of reading the journal of Captain Fuess, a millionaire mariner who voyages around the world in ever smaller ships crafted by his own hands. The narrative is interspersed with Captain Fuess's tale, relics of Sam's past, his report cards, his Christmas market analysis, and other diverse odds and ends. In *There Must Be More to Love Than Death* Newman presents three novelettes. The first tells the story of Gee Patek of the 121st Air Dispensary Unit. Gee is personally in charge of loading and unloading HRCs, human remains containers, from planes arriving from Vietnam; his pal, Gonzales, unloads buckets of feces and wishes he were a woman. Never seeing active duty, Patek manages to be accused of sexual deviancy and of attacking Commander Pompillo with a hypodermic needle filled with morphine. The story recounts the events that lie behind these accusations. The second short novel, a masque, is a "hopelessly confused affair in which everyone feels neglected." Gerald Fox, the protagonist, is a burgeoning young baritone who sells Cranachware cutlery employing techniques similar to those he uses during his vocal recitals when he delivers Purcell's *Dido and Aeneas* to the dutiful applause of the audience at the university's organ recital. The third short novel is the narrative of a thirteen year old boy who possesses a photographic memory and perfect recall of all he hears. He admonishes the reader to "please remember that what I'm saying is what other people said—something I've read or heard somewhere—and a lot of the time I honestly don't understand it myself." The story is allegorical. It tells of a trip the narrator takes with his imaginary brother into the forest and back home. But it is not an ordinary tale of initiation. It is not the entrance into the forest that matters, or even the discovery that at its heart is the wreck of a broken-down machine. What matters, and what is difficult to tell, is the story of how one comes out of the forest and survives.

Newman is a writer who delights in language and its deceptions. Intrigued and disturbed by our highly technological society where print services the hard sell, Newman in all his books manipulates words and assaults his reader with the startling immediacy and variety of his often convoluted prose. He has an encyclopedic mind and the ability to recall and select exactly the word his subject requires. He never lacks the technical term required, be it from army manuals, musical scores, advertising copy, graffiti, or ordinary speech. Like Barth and Nabokov, Newman is a virtuoso of words. His books are full of lists, exhibits, marginalia, questionnaires, snippets of song lyrics, and letters. He imitates the mechanical, bureaucratic language of army manuals, describing latrines, their size, depth, capacity, and location with a fine, latinate precision. He mimics the programmed patter of sales dialogues, or the practiced spontaneity of a Mozart aria. His style ranges from studied, ornate sentences to the ease of colloquial speech. He has a keen ear for tempo. He can imitate the speech impediment of a stutterer, the rapid talk of a salesman whose sentences have to carry him through the door, or the uneducated speech of a military recruit who punctuates all his impoverished ideas with four-letter words.

So far, with one exception, Newman has not attempted a full-scale novel. His works are short, clever, teasing, and fresh. He continually experiments with language and form. Perhaps his next book will find a subject that will exercise the full range of his gifts.

—Carol Simpson Stern

NGUGI wa Thiong'o. Formerly wrote as James T. Ngugi. Kenyan. Born in Limuru in 1938. Educated at Alliance High School; University College, Makerere (Editor, *Penpoint*), B.A. 1963; Leeds University, Yorkshire, B.A. 1964. Married; five children. Teacher in East Africa, 1964-67; Lecturer, University College, Nairobi, 1967-70; Visiting Lecturer, Northwestern University, Evanston, Illinois, 1970-71; Senior Lecturer and Chairman of the Department of Literature, University of Nairobi, 1972-77. Imprisoned under Public Security Act, 1977-78. Editor, *Zuka*, Dar es Salaam, 1965-70; regular contributor, *Sunday Nation*, Nairobi. Recipient: East African Literature Bureau award, 1964. Address: c/o William Heinemann Ltd., 10 Upper Grosvenor Street, London W1X 9PA, England.

PUBLICATIONS

Novels

Weep Not, Child. London, Heinemann, 1964; New York, Collier, 1969.
The River Between. London, Heinemann, 1965.
A Grain of Wheat. London, Heinemann, 1967.
Petals of Blood. London, Heinemann, 1977; New York, Dutton, 1978.
Caitaani Mutharaba-ini (in Kikuyu). Nairobi, Heinemann, 1980; as *Devil on the Cross*, London, Heinemann, 1981.

Short Stories

Secret Lives and Other Stories. London, Heinemann, and New York, Hill, 1975.

Plays

The Black Hermit (produced Nairobi, 1962). Kampala, Makerere University Press, 1963; London, Heinemann, 1968.
This Time Tomorrow (broadcast, 1967). Included in *This Time Tomorrow*, 1970.
This Time Tomorrow (includes *The Rebels* and *The Wound in the Heart*). Nairobi, East African Literature Bureau, 1970.
The Trial of Dedan Kimathi, with Micere Mugo. Nairobi, Heinemann, 1976; London, Heinemann, 1977.
Ngahika Ndenda (in Kikuyu), with Ngugi wa Mirii (produced Nairobi, 1977). Nairobi, Heinemann, 1980.

Radio Play: *This Time Tomorrow*, 1967.

Other

Homecoming: Essays on African and Caribbean Literature, Culture, and Politics. London, Heinemann, 1972; New York, Hill, 1973.
Writers in Politics. London, Heinemann, 1980.
Detained: A Writer's Prison Diary. London, Heinemann, 1981.

*

Critical Study: *Ngugi wa Thiong'o* by Clifford Robson, London, Macmillan, 1979.

* * *

Ngugi wa Thiong'o was a Gikuyu adolescent in Kenya during the Mau Mau Rebellion, and the events of those years, of the larger issues of Black dispossession by white settlers, and of the history of the Gikuyu from pre-colonial times to the present, lie at the centre of his novels and most of his short stories. He was the first Anglophone African writer to give in fiction a Gikuyu view of the bitter colonial war that the British called the Mau Mau Emergency—a healthy corrective to other fictional accounts, like Robert Ruark's, from a white man's point of view. Ngugi's attitudes to larger political questions are by no means unambiguous in his first two novels (hence some considerable uncertainty of craftsmanship in them) but what emerges clearly from *The River Between* (the first to be written, but the second published) is a deep sense of African deprivation and of the desire to win back a lost heritage. It is expressed in *Weep Not, Child* through Ngotho's religious attachment to the land of his ancestors taken from him by Mr. Howlands, and through his older sons' determination to fight for their lands by joining the Mau Mau. But Ngugi is also aware of another part of the African heritage diminished by white colonialism—the Gikuyu religion and tribal culture; it is this aspect of their disinheritance that figures particularly in *The River Between*.

The river is a symbol of sustenance and growth, but it also divides the christianized half of the tribe from the adherents of the traditional tribal ways, soon after the advent of colonialism. Waiyaki, the hero, is an idealistic youth, who dreams with messianic fervour of leading his people out of colonial tutelage, peacefully, by acquiring the white man's education. He would also reconcile the two religiously divided villages; though associated with the traditionalists, he loves a daughter of the fanatical Christian Gikuyu pastor. But Waiyaki's enthusiasm for western education blinds him to political methods, and he is rejected by his people. The weakness of the novel is that Ngugi romanticizes and glamorizes Waiyaki: his tribal opponents are presented as vindictive personal enemies; their different political approach is not seriously considered.

Njoroge in *Weep Not, Child* is another self-centred youth with mission-school education and messianic ambitions, whose hopes are destroyed when his brothers' involvement in Mau Mau forces him out of school, but again self-centredness is not part of any ironic regarding of the hero by the novelist. Yet *Weep Not, Child* is a better novel, for Ngugi develops some complexity of structure. There are ironic parallels between the African devotion to ancestral lands and the white settler's love of the soil he has acquired, with the opposed characters oblivious to their common human suffering. Such ironical treatment is a great advance in Ngugi's technique, as are the convincing portraits of subsidiary characters who betray the very values they struggle to achieve, or who suffer constant frustration.

A Grain of Wheat is a novel of mature outlook and much subtler technique. Ostensibly about the Uhuru celebrations of Kenya's independence in 1963, it keeps flashing back to individual sufferings in Mau Mau days. There is no single, central hero this time, but four major characters, each guilty of betraying himself and others when sorely tried in the Rebellion. Mugo, regarded by his people as a Mau Mau hero, has messianic visions before the Rebellion, but his jealousy of the real leader led him to betray him to the British. At last Ngugi is able to treat a messianic figure with detachment, but also with humane sympathy: the years of Mugo's lonely, conscience-ridden life are movingly conveyed. Other characters who also committed acts of betrayal painfully learn, first, the depths of utter disillusion, and then, the harrowing experience of coming to terms with their own limitations. Mugo's public confession brings *him* peace of mind, and helps *them* to face the future with some hope. A great strength of this finely orchestrated novel is Ngugi's skilful use of disrupted time sequence to indicate the interrelatedness of the characters' behaviour in the Rebellion and the state of their lives (and of the nation) at Independence. Ngugi's maturity appears also in his sober attitude both to the struggle for, and attainment of, Independence; there are signs of the new African politicians already betraying the ordinary people who suffered under colonialism. Though a disturbing novel, it proclaims hope for the regenerative capabilities of ordinary human nature.

In his critical essays in *Homecoming*, Ngugi argues the vital social function of literature in Africa, and the Third World generally. In *Petals of Blood* he impressively puts this belief into practice. A convincing attack, often Marxist in language, upon neo-colonialism in Independent Africa is achieved fictionally by indicating powerfully and affectively how the lives of dispossessed little people are all but broken by an imported capitalist system. The four major characters, each a misfit in Independent Kenyan society, have come to the distant village of Ilmorog to seek personal peace and modest new beginnings. Long associated with heroic Gikuyu legends, Ilmorog becomes a living presence in the novel. In the grip of prolonged drought, and ignored by the M.P. who had begged their votes, the desperate villagers undertake an epic march to the capital to lay their troubles before the authorities. Subsequently religious, political, and economic exploiters swarm upon Ilmorog to "develop" it, and using such devices as foreclosed loans eventually dispossess the local inhabitants and establish New Ilmorog. The ample detail with which Ngugi conveys the ruthless stripping of already deprived ordinary people gains power from a sophisticated narrative technique that enables Kenya's history since 1963 to be felt through the consciousness of its social victims. *Petals of Blood* is an angry novel but it does affirm the potentialities of native communality for a just, humane African polity.

—Arthur Ravenscroft

NICHOLSON, Christina. *See* **NICOLE, Christopher.**

NICOL, Abioseh. Pseudonym for Davidson Sylvester Hector Willoughby Nicol. Sierra Leonean. Born in Freetown, 14 September 1924. Educated at schools in Nigeria and Sierra Leone; Christ's College, Cambridge, 1943-50, B.A. 1946, M.A., M.D., Ph.D. Married Marjorie Esme Johnston in 1950; three sons and two daughters. Science Master, Prince of Wales School, Freetown, 1941-43; House Physician and Research Assistant, London Hospital Medical College, University of London, 1950-52; University Lecturer, Medical School, Ibadan, 1952-54; Beit Memorial Fellow, 1954, and Benn Levy University Student, 1956, Cambridge University; Fellow and Supervisor in Natural Sciences and Medicine, Christ's College, Cambridge, 1957-59; Senior Pathologist, Sierra Leone Government, 1958-60; Visiting Lecturer, University of California, Berkeley, and Mayo Clinic, Rochester, Minnesota, 1958; Principal, Fourah Bay College, 1960-67, and Vice-Chancellor, 1966-68, University of Sierra Leone, Freetown; Aggrey-Fraser-Guggisberg Lecturer, University of Ghana, Accra, 1963; Danforth Lecturer, Association of American Colleges, 1968-70. Ambassador of Sierra Leone to the United Nations, 1968-71; High Commissioner of the Republic of Sierra Leone to the United Kingdom, and Ambassador of Sierra Leone to Denmark, Norway, Sweden, and Finland, 1971-72. Since 1972, Executive Director, United Nations Institute for Training and Research, and Under-Secretary-General, United Nations, New York. Member, West African Council for Medical Research, 1959-62; Chairman, Sierra Leone National

Library Board, 1959-65; Member, Public Service Commission of Sierra Leone, 1960-68; President, Sierra Leone Red Cross Society, 1962-66; Delegate, UNESCO Higher Education Conference, Tananarive, 1963; President, West African Science Association, 1964-66; Delegate, Commonwealth Prime Ministers Conference, London, 1965, 1969, 1971. Director, Sierra Leone Selection Trust Ltd., 1961-71, Central Bank of Sierra Leone, 1963-68, and since 1961, Consolidated African Selection Trust Ltd., London. Recipient: Margaret Wrong Prize, 1951; Independence Medal, Sierra Leone, 1961. D.Sc.: University of Newcastle upon Tyne, 1964; Kalamazoo College, Michigan, 1964; LL.D.: University of Leeds, 1968; D.Litt.: Davis-Elkins College, Elkins, West Virginia, 1971. Honorary Fellow, Ghana Academy of Sciences, and Christ's College, Cambridge, 1972. C.M.G. (Companion, Order of St. Michael and St. George), 1964; Grand Commander, Order of Rokel, Sierra Leone, 1974; Star of Africa, Liberia, 1974. Address: UNITAR, 801 United Nations Plaza, New York, New York 10017, U.S.A.

PUBLICATIONS

Short Stories

The Truly Married Woman and Other Stories. London, Oxford University Press, 1965.
Two African Tales. London, Cambridge University Press, 1965.

Other

Alienation: An Essay. London, MacGibbon and Kee, 1960.
Africa: A Subjective View. London, Longman, 1964.
New and Modern Roles for the Empire and Commonwealth (lecture; as Davidson Nicol). London, Cambridge University Press, 1976.

Editor, *Africanus Horton: The Dawn of Nationalism in Modern Africa.* London, Longman, 1969; as *Black Nationalism in Africa 1867*, New York, Africana, 1969.

*

Bibliography: in *A Bibliography of Sierra Leone, 1925-1969*, edited by G.J. Williams, New York, Africana, 1970.

Critical Studies: *The African Image* by Ezekiel Mphahlele, London, Faber, 1962; *African-English Literature* by Anne Tibble, London, Peter Owen, 1965.

Abioseh Nicol comments:

My short stories and poetry have predominantly an African background although a few are set in Europe and America. Their characters are drawn from all levels of black and white society in Africa, and are based on observations gained by me during my work as a teacher, administrator, and doctor, plus the insight gained as a black African patriot engaged in plans towards our independence. I tried to keep an independent and non-racist outlook.

My appearance in print owes itself to the encouragement of the late Langston Hughes, the black American writer, who first included me in his anthology of African verse, and to Stephen Spender, the English poet, and Irving Kristol, the American writer, both of whom, as former editors of *Encounter*, gave me the unprecedented encouragement of publishing three of my short stories within a year in their magazine. My literary criticism was encouraged and fostered in that excellent weekly *West Africa* by its Editor, David Williams, and by Walter Allen, former Literary Editor of the *New Statesman and Nation*. Without the advice and encouragement of these writers, my publications would still have been in manuscript form, at the bottom of a drawer.

All this, of course, refers to creative writing. I have written a considerable amount also on higher education and politics over the past twenty years and have also published in professional journals the results of research carried out in Europe and Africa on medical and scientific subjects such as malnutrition, tropical diseases, endocrinology, and biochemistry.

* * *

Abioseh Nicol, one of Africa's most talented short story writers, belongs to the older generation of living African authors who wrote in the twilight of the colonial era, when Africa was still under the political thumb of Europe. Unlike many of his contemporaries, he did not write militant protest fiction but chose instead to deal with the cultural problems and moral dilemmas of Africans and Europeans who lived in this era "with its emphasis on pensionable jobs in Government service, official decorations, and black and white keeping their distance." Nicol has stated that he started writing

> partly because I wanted to and partly because I found that most of those who wrote about us seldom gave any nobility to their African characters unless they were savages or servants or faced impending destruction. I knew differently. I saw all around me worthy Africans who lived and worked with varying degrees of success, distinction, and happiness. I began to write about them.

Nicol's stories are usually set in the part of Africa under British rule and frequently describe situations in which British colonial administrators and Africans strain against each other and toward each other. Nicol, who admits he owes much to E.M. Forster, Joyce Cary, Graham Greene, and Evelyn Waugh, pictures the mutual misunderstandings, the problems of communication, the gropings toward friendship, the lapses into anger and hostility, the hopes and the fears that characterize the relationships between the colonizers and the colonized, between white and black in Africa. It is a credit to Nicol's sensitivity and literary skill that these stories paint both sides of the racial fence accurately and compassionately.

In other stories Nicol investigates the plight of westernized Africans who still cling to traditional beliefs and customs. Victims of internal culture conflict, these men and women have to struggle to maintain their equilibrium in a changing world. Sometimes their difficulties are resolved in hilarious comedy, sometimes in tender pathos. Nicol's sharp eye for human foibles and tolerance for individual eccentricities make these stories a delight to read. He is an urbane humorist with a talent for gently poking fun at some of Africa's most entertaining absurdities.

—Bernth Lindfors

NICOLE, Christopher (Robin). Pseudonyms: Leslie Arlen; Robin Cade; Peter Grange; Mark Logan; Christina Nicholson; Robin Nicholson; Alison York; Andrew York. British. Born in Georgetown, British Guiana, now Guyana, 7 December 1930. Educated at Harrison College, Barbados; Queen's College, Guyana. Married 1) Jean Barnett in 1951 (divorced), two sons and two daughters; 2) Diana de la Rue. Clerk, Royal Bank of Canada, in the West Indies, 1947-56. Lived in Guernsey for many years after 1957; now domiciled in the Bahamas. Agent: John Farquharson Ltd., 8 Bell Yard, London WC2A 2JU, England.

PUBLICATIONS

Novels

Off White. London, Jarrolds, 1959.
Shadows in the Jungle. London, Jarrolds, 1961.

Ratoon. London, Jarrolds, and New York, St. Martin's Press, 1962.
Dark Noon. London, Jarrolds, 1963.
Amyot's Cay. London, Jarrolds, 1964.
Blood Amyot. London, Jarrolds, 1964.
The Amyot Crime. London, Jarrolds, 1965; New York, Bantam, 1974.
White Boy. London, Hutchinson, 1966.
King Creole (as Peter Grange). London, Jarrolds, 1966.
The Eliminator (as Andrew York). London, Hutchinson, 1966; Philadelphia, Lippincott, 1967.
The Co-Ordinator (as Andrew York). London, Hutchinson, and Philadelphia, Lippincott, 1967.
The Predator (as Andrew York). London, Hutchinson, and Philadelphia, Lippincott, 1968.
The Self-Lovers. London, Hutchinson, 1968.
The Devil's Emissary (as Peter Grange). London, Jarrolds, 1968.
The Deviator (as Andrew York). London, Hutchinson, and Philadelphia, Lippincott, 1969.
The Thunder and the Shouting. London, Hutchinson, and New York, Doubleday, 1969.
The Dominator (as Andrew York). London, Hutchinson, 1969; New York, Lancer, 1971.
The Tumult at the Gate (as Peter Grange). London, Jarrolds, 1970.
The Longest Pleasure. London, Hutchinson, 1970.
The Infiltrator (as Andrew York). London, Hutchinson, and New York, Doubleday, 1971.
The Face of Evil. London, Hutchinson, 1971.
The Expurgator (as Andrew York). London, Hutchinson, 1972; New York, Doubleday, 1973.
The Golden Goddess (as Peter Grange). London, Jarrolds, 1973.
Lord of the Golden Fan. London, Cassell, 1973.
The Captivator (as Andrew York). London, Hutchinson, 1973; New York, Doubleday, 1974.
Caribee. London, Cassell, and New York, St. Martin's Press, 1974.
The Fear Dealers (as Robin Cade). London, Cassell, and New York, Simon and Schuster, 1974.
The Fascinator (as Andrew York). London, Hutchinson, and New York, Doubleday, 1975.
The Devil's Own. London, Cassell, and New York, St. Martin's Press, 1975.
Dark Passage (as Andrew York). New York, Doubleday, 1975; London, Hutchinson, 1976.
Mistress of Darkness. London, Cassell, and New York, St. Martin's Press, 1976.
Tricolour (as Mark Logan). London, Macmillan, and New York, St. Martin's Press, 1976.
Guillotine (as Mark Logan). London, Macmillan, and New York, St. Martin's Press, 1976.
Black Dawn. London, Cassell, and New York, St. Martin's Press, 1977.
Tallant for Trouble (as Andrew York). London, Hutchinson, and New York, Doubleday, 1977.
The Power and the Passion (as Christina Nicolson). London, Corgi, and New York, Coward McCann, 1977.
Tallant for Disaster (as Andrew York). London, Hutchinson, and New York, Doubleday, 1978.
Sunset. London, Cassell, and New York, St. Martin's Press, 1978.
Brumaire (as Mark Logan). London, Wingate, and New York, St. Martin's Press, 1978.
The Savage Sands (as Christina Nicholson). London, Corgi, and New York, Coward McCann, 1978.
The Secret Memoirs of Lord Byron. Philadelphia, Lippincott, 1978; London, Joseph, 1979; as *Lord of Sin*, London, Corgi, 1980.
The Fire and the Robe (as Alison York). London, W.H. Allen, and New York, Berkley, 1979.
The Queen of Paris (as Christina Nicholson). London, Corgi, 1979.
The Scented Sword (as Alison York). London, W.H. Allen, 1980.
The Borodins (as Leslie Arlen):
Love and Honour. New York, Jove, and London, Futura, 1980.
War and Passion. New York, Jove, and London, Futura, 1981.
Destiny and Desire. New York, Jove, and London, Futura, 1981.
Vengeance and Hope. New York, Jove, and London, Futura, 1982.
Haggard. London, Joseph, and New York, New American Library, 1980.
Haggard's Inheritance. London, Joseph, 1981.
The Friday Spy (as Christina Nicholson). London, Corgi, 1981; as *A Passion for Treason* (as Robin Nicholson), New York, Jove, 1981.

Other

West Indian Cricket. London, Phoenix House, 1957.
The West Indies: Their People and History. London, Hutchinson, 1965.
The Doom Fishermen (juvenile; as Andrew York). London, Hutchinson, 1969; as *Operation Destruct*, New York, Holt Reinhart, 1969.
Manhunt for a General (juvenile; as Andrew York). London, Hutchinson, 1970; as *Operation Manhunt*, New York, Holt Rinehart, 1970.
Where the Cavern Ends (juvenile; as Andrew York). London, Hutchinson, and New York, Holt Rinehart, 1971.
Appointment in Kiltone (juvenile; as Andrew York). London, Hutchinson, 1972; as *Operation Neptune*, New York, Holt Rinehart, 1872.
Introduction to Chess. London, Corgi, 1973.

*

Christopher Nicole comments:

I was born and largely educated in the West Indies, and my first eight novels were concerned with the West Indian Scene, five historicals, one thriller, and two serious studies of West Indian society, although I should say that the historicals are all serious commentaries on this society, and the Amyot trilogy is a history of the Bahamas from 1704 to 1956, i.e., just as the present Bahamian Government was contesting elections for the first time. During this period I also wrote a history of the area, and a history of West Indian cricket.

Since 1966 my work has become more diversified. Some novels about the Second World War were interspersed with a series of thrillers under the pseudonym of Andrew York; these included three juveniles. Happily four years ago I was encouraged to return to my favorite historical field. *Lord of the Golden Fan* was a fictional biography of Will Adams, the first Englishman to visit Japan. Since then I have written a five-volume fictional history of the West Indies, the Caribee series, several black gothics, and a wholly enjoyable "autobiography" of Byron. Now I am under a long-term contract with Jove publishers for a series of historical novels.

I have been criticised on two main counts, firstly, for preferring historical backgrounds to dealing with the problems of the present day, and, secondly, for choosing to write mainly on topics of violence and physical involvement. I happen to hold the opinion that the centuries between 1700 and 1900 formed not only English, but European and therefore, Atlantic society as we know it today; we are in a process of decline from a very high level of humanitarian self-involvement in politics and in culture, and I feel strongly that our society could only be improved by regaining some of the enthusiastic ambition which created the prosperity of Europe and America.

Secondly, I think that the Twentieth Century fascination with psychology has been allowed to over-shadow the fact that our lives are almost entirely governed by the physical events in which we are involved. I cannot believe there is anyone alive today of whatever age who has not been profoundly influenced by the brutalities, as well as the heroics, and certainly by the pure destruction of the Second World War. Historically the life of any West Indian was dominated by the yearly hurricane, by the fear of a slave up-rising if he was a planter, by the fear of a planter's brutality if he was a slave, by the constant threat of enemy action. The knowledge that disaster might occur at any moment was the very factor that made these men and women what they were.

I have also been asked why I write so very much—my output is now averaging something like four and sometimes five books a year. As nearly all of them are fairly successful, I no longer actually *have* to write that many to live. But the fact of the matter is, I love writing. I love to tell stories. I love creating characters and then placing them in genuinely exciting or different historical contexts, and I equally love investigating real historical characters and trying to decide what made them tick. I am often amazed at my good fortune in being paid for what is in any event a hobby, and which I would be doing whether it was professionally or not. And there are so very many stories to tell, so very many characters to be created and investigated. I shall never find the time to treat them all.

* * *

When one looks for the first time at the list of Christopher Nicole's novels, one is awed by his productiveness and by his versatility (his works include a book on cricket, a history of the West Indies, serious novels, historical romances, secret agent thrillers, and adventure novels for young readers; furthermore, his novels are set in places as different as the West Indies and Russia). But this awe turns to skepticism when one realizes that twenty-five of those books were written in about twelve years. Nothing, one is inclined to feel, done so rapidly can have been done well.

This initial prejudice does Nicole's work a real injustice for there is much that is worthwhile in it. His secret agent thrillers, although written to a certain formula, are well enough executed to be exciting and suspenseful. Each is distinct enough to prevent it from being completely predictable. These books share with his other novels his excellence at describing physical action and his ability to make dialogue and setting work together towards a final effect. There are a carefulness of craftsmanship and an economy of style which mark the work of the real professional.

However, if Nicole is to be taken as a serious writer, it is his books set in the West Indies which will qualify him for this title. He has written other works set in parts of the world where he has travelled, Poland for example, but these lack the intimacy of insight that he demonstrates when he is writing about the West Indies and Guyana, where he grew up.

His West Indian novels contain all the elements that make his secret agent books so entertaining. In fact, in retrospect, one can see how his earlier West Indian books prepared him for his later adventure stories. The novels about the West Indies indicate his reliance on physical action, and his fascination with the sensational. *Ratoon*, for instance, deals with a slave rebellion, and *Dark Noon* is set in St. Vincent at the time of the eruption of the volcano Soufriere. This willingness to remain on the level of the physical gives a sense of superficiality to all his work, which is only occasionally dispelled when the author's precise descriptions of the society in the West Indies produce interesting social and racial reverberations. Nicole is at his best when, in a novel like *Shadows in the Jungle*, he suggests the character of the jungle and develops the relationship between it and its inhabitants.

Much of Nicole's work reminds one of that of Mittelholzer, the older Guyanese novelist. *Off White* echoes *The Life and Death of Sylvia*, *Shadows in the Jungle* seems to have been influenced by *My Bones and My Flute* and *Shadows Move Among Them*, and Nicole's Amyot trilogy bears obvious resemblances to Mittelholzer's Kaywana trilogy. Because Nicole is white, however, he does contribute a different point of view to West Indian fiction. There are other West Indian novelists who are white (Phyllis Allfrey, Jean Rhys, and Geoffrey Drayton come immediately to mind) but these are so few when compared with the non-whites that a novelist who suggests what it is like to be white in the West Indies can make a distinctly original contribution to West Indian fiction.

Nicole's contribution is sometimes suggestive, but it is too superficial to fulfill its possibilities.

—Anthony Boxill

NYE, Robert. British. Born in London, 15 March 1939. Educated at Dormans Land, Sussex; Hamlet Court, Westcliff, Essex; Southend High School. Married 1) Judith Pratt in 1959 (divorced, 1967), three sons; 2) Aileen Campbell in 1968, one daughter, one step-daughter, and one step-son. Free-lance writer. Since 1967, Poetry Editor, *The Scotsman*; since 1971, Poetry Critic, *The Times*. Recipient: Eric Gregory Award, 1963; Scottish Arts Council bursary, 1970, 1973, and publication award, 1970, 1976; James Kennaway Memorial Award, 1970; *Guardian* fiction prize, 1976; Hawthornden Prize, 1977. Fellow, Royal Society of Literature, 1977. Address: The Anchorage, Summer Cove, Kinsale, County Cork, Ireland.

PUBLICATIONS

Novels

Doubtfire. London, Calder and Boyars, and New York, Hill and Wang, 1968.
Falstaff. London, Hamish Hamilton, and Boston, Little Brown, 1976.
Merlin. London, Hamish Hamilton, 1978; New York, Putnam, 1979.
Faust. London, Hamish Hamilton, 1980; New York, Putnam, 1981.

Short Stories

Tales I Told My Mother. London, Calder and Boyars, 1969; New York, Hill and Wang, 1970.
Penguin Modern Stories 6, with others. London, Penguin, 1970.

Uncollected Short Stories

Lines Review 38 (includes 4 stories, verse, and a film script) (Edinburgh), 1971.
"Visakha," in *Scottish Short Stories*. London, Collins, 1973.
"The Lesson," in *Scottish Short Stories 1974*. London, Collins, 1974.
"The Whole Story," in *Factions*, edited by Giles Gordon and Alex Hamilton. London, Joseph, 1974.
"Adam Kadmon," in *Beyond the Words*, edited by Giles Gordon. London, Hutchinson, 1975.
"True Thomas," in *Signature Anthology*. London, Calder and Boyars, 1975.
"Randal," in *Prevailing Spirits*, edited by Giles Gordon. London, Hamish Hamilton, 1976.
"The Barner," in *All Our Secrets Are the Same*, edited by Gordon Lish. New York, Norton, 1977.
"The Facts of Life," in *New Stories 4*, edited by Elaine Feinstein and Fay Weldon. London, Hutchinson, 1979.
"Glendower," in *The After Midnight Ghost Book*, edited by James Hale. London, Hutchinson, 1980.

Plays

Sawney Bean, with Bill Watson (produced Edinburgh, 1969; London, 1972). London, Calder and Boyars, 1970.
Sisters (broadcast, 1969; produced Edinburgh, 1973). Included in *Penthesilea, Fugue, and Sisters*, 1976.
Penthesilea, adaptation of a play by Heinrich von Kleist (broadcast, 1971). Included in *Penthesilea, Fugue, and Sisters*, 1976.
The Seven Deadly Sins: A Mask, music by James Douglas (produced Stirling, 1973). Rushden, Northamptonshire, Omphalos Press, 1974.
Mr. Poe (produced Edinburgh and London, 1974).
Penthesilea, Fugue, and Sisters. London, Calder and Boyars, 1976.

Radio Plays: *Sisters*, 1969; *Penthesilea*, 1971; *The Devil's Jig*, with Humphrey Searle, from a work by Thomas Mann, 1980.

Verse

Juvenilia 1. Lowestoft, Suffolk, Scorpion Press, 1961.
Juvenilia 2. Lowestoft, Suffolk, Scorpion Press, 1963.
Darker Ends. London, Calder and Boyars, and New York, Hill and Wang, 1969.
Agnus Dei. Rushden, Northamptonshire, Sceptre Press, 1973.
Two Prayers. Richmond, Surrey, Keepsake Press, 1974.
Five Dreams. Rushden, Northamptonshire, Sceptre Press, 1974.
Divisions on a Ground. Manchester, Carcanet Press, 1976.

Other

Taliesin (juvenile). London, Faber, 1966; New York, Hill and Wang, 1967.
March Has Horse's Ears (juvenile). London, Faber, 1966; New York, Hill and Wang, 1967.
Bee Hunter: Adventures of Beowulf (juvenile). London, Faber, 1967; New York, Hill and Wang, 1968; as *Beowulf, The Bee Hunter*, Faber, 1972.
Wishing Gold (juvenile). London, Macmillan, 1970; New York, Hill and Wang, 1971.
Poor Pumpkin (juvenile). London, Macmillan, 1971; as *The Mathematical Princess and Other Stories*, New York, Hill and Wang, 1972.
Cricket: Three Stories (juvenile). Indianapolis, Bobbs Merrill, 1975; as *Once upon Three Times*, Tonbridge, Kent, Benn, 1978.
Out of the World and Back Again (juvenile). London, Collins, 1977; as *Out of This World and Back Again*, Indianapolis, Bobbs Merrill, 1978.
The Bird of the Golden Land (juvenile). London, Hamish Hamilton, 1980.
Harry Pay the Pirate (juvenile). London, Hamish Hamilton, 1981.

Editor, *A Choice of Sir Walter Raleigh's Verse.* London, Faber, 1972.
Editor, *William Barnes: A Selection of His Poems.* Oxford, Carcanet Press, 1972.
Editor, *A Choice of Swinburne's Verse.* London, Faber, 1973.
Editor, *The Faber Book of Sonnets.* London, Faber, 1976; as *A Book of Sonnets*, New York, Oxford University Press, 1976.
Editor, *The English Sermon 1750-1850.* Manchester, Carcanet Press, 1976.

*

Manuscript Collections: University of Texas, Austin; National Library of Scotland, Edinburgh.

* * *

A hallmark of Robert Nye's fiction has been his ability to harness the imagination to his will, to take the facts of everyday history and to transform them into fantastic happenings so that myth and reality become as one. The stories in *Tales I Told My Mother* rework the lives of literary personalities, and his first novel, *Doubtfire*, ranges in time and space between different worlds with remarkable ease and fluidity of style. Equally fantastic have been his children's novels which have followed faithfully C.S. Lewis's dictum that children's stories should be equally enjoyed by adults.

In his three most recent novels, *Falstaff*, *Merlin*, and *Faust*, Nye has created a triumvirate of closely related myths from characters who exist in our collective pasts. The worlds that they people are dreamlike and fabulous, half-caught, half-forgotten by the subconscious mind. And yet their darksome existence is lightened by Nye's ability to steer away from allegory by making their worlds new again and instantly recognisable: Falstaff lives in an England that is demonstrably 14th-century, Merlin's world is one of medieval chivalry, and Faust knows a Europe shared by Luther and Calvin.

Falstaff, a novel of 100 chapters, tells the story of Sir John Fastolf—his relationship to the English aristocracy and to the giant of Cerne Abbas, his conduct at the siege of Kildare, his friendship with Prince Hal, and his prowess at the Battle of Agincourt. Much of the story is recognisable from the Falstaff of Shakespeare's plays, but Nye takes in the whole panorama of life in England at a time of cultural and economic transition. Falstaff's adventures, often unlikely and scabrous, unfold before the reader's eyes like a medieval tapestry, and by the end of the novel he has been consumed by myth, the eternal John Bull, both patriot and buffoon.

Myth of another kind lies at the heart of *Merlin* whose central character is at once the unmistakable Merlin of Sir Thomas Malory's *Le Morte Darthur* and at the same time an older, more cunning figure from Welsh vernacular literature and from the poetry of the 12th-century French poet Robert de Boron, who created a Merlin capable of seeing both past and future and thus able to connect the ancient history of the Grail with the court of King Arthur. Nye's Merlin is a nebulous figure, sired by the Devil and a virgin in an attempt to create the Anti-Christ, and a man whose sexual ambiguity is a source of good and of evil. The veiled eroticism of medieval courtly love is torn open in Nye's version of a world in which sexual deviation is more potent than chivalry and black magic more powerful than religious faith. Throughout the novel, which keeps more or less faithfully to the facts of the medieval romance, runs the seminal myth of the Quest for the Holy Grail and man's striving for the eternal.

Faust follows many of the same themes and expands on them: a delight in mixing myth with reality, an earthy eroticism, and a fast-moving dialogue that is both funny and deeply serious. The story of Faust's final 40 days on earth, having sold his soul to the devil, is seen through the excited reaction of his servant, Kit Wagner. For, unlike Marlowe's Faust, Dr. John Faust is not content to wait meekly for his damnation in the company of Helen of Troy, Mephistopheles, and his monkey Akercocke; rather he sets out with his entourage on a pilgrimage to Rome in hot pursuit of a dog called Satan. The story of the chase takes on the aspect of a thriller with supernatural overtones as the inevitable conclusion is reached in Rome during Holy Week and the outcome of Faust's pact. As in all of Nye's novels the writing is crisp and lucid, a mixture of scholarly anecdotes racily told and erudite low comedy.

Robert Nye is one of the most inventive and adventurous of contemporary novelists with an imagination of Rabelaisian proportions, capable of encapsulating different worlds so that the reader is presented not so much with a mirror image as a crystallisation of them.

—Trevor Royle

OAKLEY, Barry K. Australian. Born in Melbourne, Victoria, 24 February 1931. Educated at Christian Brothers College, St. Kilda; University of Melbourne, B.A. Married to Carmel Hart; four sons and two daughters. Secondary School Teacher, 1955-62; Lecturer in Humanities, Royal Melbourne Technical Institute, 1963; Advertising Copywriter, 1964-65. Since 1966, Writer for the Australian Department of Trade and Industry. Recipient: Captain Cook Bicentenary Award, 1970. Address: 12 Francis Street, Richmond, Victoria 3121, Australia.

PUBLICATIONS

Novels

A Wild Ass of a Man. Melbourne, Cheshire, 1967.
A Salute to the Great McCarthy. Melbourne, Heinemann, 1970.
Let's Hear It for Prendergast. Melbourne, Heinemann, 1970.

Short Stories

Walking Through Tigerland. Brisbane, University of Queensland Press, 1977.

Plays

A Lesson in English (produced Melbourne, 1967). Sydney, Currency Press, and London, Eyre Methuen, 1976.
Witzenhausen, Where Are You? (produced Melbourne, 1967).
It's a Chocolate World (produced Melbourne, 1968).
The Feet of Daniel Mannix, music by Lorraine Milne (produced Melbourne, 1970). Sydney, Angus and Robertson, 1975.
Beware of Imitations (produced Melbourne, 1972).
Bedfellows (produced Melbourne, 1975). Sydney, Currency Press, 1975; London, Eyre Methuen, 1976.

Radio Play: *The Great God Mogodan*, 1980 (UK).

Other

How They Caught Kevin Farrelly (juvenile). Melbourne, Cassell, 1973; London, Cassell, 1975.
A Letter from Hospital (juvenile). Oxford, Pergamon Press, 1975.

* * *

Barry Oakley's three novels are picaresque moralities of the vanity of human wishes in an absurd world—the author's native Melbourne. The novels comically dramatize his love-hate relationship with that city through his anti-heroes, who escape from the deadening conformity and small-mindedness of the sprawling suburbs only to blunder into a succession of other traps amidst the city's cosmopolitan sophisticates. Oakley combines fresh humorous observation of his milieu with a literary self-consciousness of his fictional mode, and his ultimate irony in his recognition of the possibility that Melbourne might simply be one version of the reality that youthful idealism must measure itself against—anywhere. Instead of savage satire railing against provincialism, the reader finds a comic delight in the foibles of a staid, smug outpost of civilization and in those who do battle with it.

A Wild Ass of a Man is likely to strike the reader as a "first novel" in that the early episodes dealing with school days at the Christian Brothers, student days at the University of Melbourne, teaching in a country Technical School and youthful love affairs seem the working up, in a comic way, of autobiographical experience. In these episodes the author is too close to his narrator Muldoon, in comparison to later events when Muldoon becomes a fashionable avant garde painter and later an evangelist railing against the wickedness of the world. The novel is too episodic, too diverse in its tones to achieve overall unity through the figure of Muldoon, but its better sections have a wit and inventiveness, in style and situation, that are not excelled in the more unified novels that follow.

A Salute to the Great McCarthy which satirically tilts at Melbourne's most sacred institution—Australian Rules football—won Oakley his reputation and popularity as a novelist. The story of the rise to fame of a country lad in the big league, and his subsequent fall, provides a much surer narrative development than the first novel. The control of the anti-hero's narration is more confident and there is a tighter thematic organization. The frenetic pace, manic inventiveness, and taut witty style with its satiric observations on society are sustained throughout a rich variety of episodes. Some of these are undeveloped, but the best of them bear on the novel's theme of hubris. In the country town he has come from, McCarthy has seen the handsome sports coach and his own father destroyed by malice and envy. But in Melbourne as a star player for the Kingswood Football Club, and a familiar figure on TV ads and chewing gum packets, McCarthy is defying the gods. His alter ego is Ackerman, a middle European Icarus who has invented a pedal plane which crashes on its test flight at the Councillor A.H. Memorial Reserve in the suburb of Oakleigh. Ackerman, like McCarthy, is a high flier doomed to crash in a society dominated by conformity, respectability, the struggle for status—and football.

In his third novel, *Let's Hear It for Prendergast* (winner of the prestigious Captain Cook Bicentenary Award), Oakley again exploits the satiric opportunities of the free-wheeling picaresque novel combined with the theme of the education of a young man in the ways of the world. Instead of the anti-hero-narrator of the two earlier novels, the decline into nihilism of Athol Prendergast, tallest and possibly worst poet in the world, is charted by his friend Morley, one of Melbourne's aspiring novelists. Prendergast invades Morley's flat to announce that he has opted out of the rat race to devote himself to the redemption of Australian society through verse. His "Australian Square" cantos are a bardic howl against the smug materialism of his society. To keep Whitmanesque soul and bean pole body together, Prendergast decides to accompany his poems with a book of unretouched nude photographs, and outrages respectable Melbourne.

The result of having the narrator play Sancho to Prendergast's Quixote (these spindly shanks are familiar) is that the characterization is more convincingly consistent than in the earlier novels. McCarthy, for example, could not help seeming too literate for a star footballer from the bush. Morley is a rather callow ex-Christian Brothers lad, like Oakley's previous heroes; Prendergast, however, is their schizoid other self, split off completely and observed with more detachment—though perhaps with too much detachment for him to engage the reader's sympathies. *Prendergast* shows a more confident overall control, but this greater craftsmanship has been gained at the expense of the denser comic textures and more sophisticated wit of *A Wild Ass of a Man*.

Barry Oakley began writing plays in the late 1960's for the alternative theatres in Melbourne and has continued, with increasing success. Today he is more prominent as a playwright than as a novelist, and his most recent play, *Bedfellows*, combines, better than any of his novels, his exuberant comic talents with an underlying seriousness.

—Brian Kiernan

OATES, Joyce Carol. American. Born in Lockport, New York, 16 June 1938. Educated at Syracuse University, New York, B.A. 1960 (Phi Beta Kappa); University of Wisconsin, Madison, M.A. in English 1961. Married Raymond Joseph Smith in 1961. Instructor, 1961-65, and Assistant Professor of English, 1965-67, University of Detroit. Since 1967, Member of the Department of English, University of Windsor, Ontario. Writer-in-Residence, Princeton University, New Jersey, 1978-81. Recipient: National Endowment for the Arts grant, 1966, 1968; Guggenheim Fellowship, 1967; O. Henry Award, 1967, and Special Award for Continuing Achievement, 1970; Rosenthal Award, 1968; National Book Award, 1970. Member, American Academy, 1978. Address: c/o Department of English, University of Windsor, Windsor, Ontario, Canada.

PUBLICATIONS

Novels

With Shuddering Fall. New York, Vanguard Press, 1964; London, Cape, 1965.
A Garden of Earthly Delights. New York, Vanguard Press, 1967; London, Gollancz, 1970.
Expensive People. New York, Vanguard Press, 1968; London, Gollancz, 1969.
Them. New York, Vanguard Press, 1969; London, Gollancz, 1971.
Wonderland. New York, Vanguard Press, 1971; London, Gollancz, 1972.
Do with Me What You Will. New York, Vanguard Press, 1973; London, Gollancz, 1974.
The Assassins: A Book of Hours. New York, Vanguard Press, 1975.
Childwold. New York, Vanguard Press, 1976; London, Gollancz, 1977.
Son of the Morning. New York, Vanguard Press, 1978; London, Gollancz, 1979.
Unholy Loves. New York, Vanguard Press, 1979; London, Gollancz, 1980.
Cybele. Santa Barbara, California, Black Sparrow Press, 1979.
Bellefleur. New York, Dutton, 1980; London, Cape, 1981.
Angel of Light. New York, Dutton, 1981.
A Sentimental Education. New York, Dutton, and London, Cape, 1981.

Short Stories

By the North Gate. New York, Vanguard Press, 1963.
Upon the Sweeping Flood and Other Stories. New York, Vanguard Press, 1966; London, Gollancz, 1973.
The Wheel of Love. New York, Vanguard Press, 1970; London, Gollancz, 1971.
Cupid and Psyche. New York, Albondocani Press, 1970.
Marriages and Infidelities: Short Stories. New York, Vanguard Press, 1972; London, Gollancz, 1974.
A Posthumous Sketch. Los Angeles, Black Sparrow Press, 1973.
The Girl. Cambridge, Massachusetts, Pomegranate Press, 1974.
Plagiarized Material (as Fernandes/Oates). Los Angeles, Black Sparrow Press, 1974.
The Goddess and Other Women. London, Vanguard Press, 1974; London, Gollancz, 1975.
Where Are You Going, Where Have You Been? Stories of Young America. Greenwich, Connecticut, Fawcett, 1974.
The Hungry Ghosts: Seven Allusive Comedies. Los Angeles, Black Sparrow Press, 1974; Solihull, Warwickshire, Aquila, 1975.
The Seduction and Other Stories. Los Angeles, Black Sparrow Press, 1975.
The Poisoned Kiss and Other Stories from the Portuguese (as Fernandes/Oates). New York, Vanguard Press, 1975.
The Triumph of the Spider Monkey. Santa Barbara, California, Black Sparrow Press, 1976.
Crossing the Border. New York, Vanguard Press, 1976; London, Gollancz, 1978.
Night-Side. New York, Vanguard Press, 1977; London, Gollancz, 1979.
All the Good People I've Left Behind. Santa Barbara, California, Black Sparrow Press, 1978.
The Step-Father. Northridge, California, Lord John Press, 1979.

Plays

The Sweet Enemy (produced New York, 1965).
Sunday Dinner (produced New York, 1970).
Ontological Proof of My Existence, music by George Prideaux (produced New York, 1972). Included in *Three Plays,* 1980.
Miracle Play (produced New York, 1974). Los Angeles, Black Sparrow Press, 1974.
Daisy (produced New York, 1980).
Three Plays (includes *Ontological Proof of My Existence, Miracle Play, The Triumph of the Spider Monkey*). Windsor, Ontario Review Press, 1980.

Verse

Women in Love and Other Poems. New York, Albondocani Press, 1968.
Anonymous Sins and Other Poems. Baton Rouge, Louisiana State University Press, 1969.
Love and Its Derangements. Baton Rouge, Louisiana State University Press, 1970.
Wooded Forms. New York, Albondocani Press, 1972.
Angel Fire: Poems. Baton Rouge, Louisiana State University Press, 1973.
Dreaming America and Other Poems. New York, Aloe Editions, 1973.
The Fabulous Beasts. Baton Rouge, Louisiana State University Press, 1975.
Women Whose Lives Are Food, Men Whose Lives Are Money. Baton Rouge, Louisiana State University Press, 1978.

Other

The Edge of Impossibility: Tragic Forms in Literature. New York, Vanguard Press, 1972; London, Gollancz, 1976.
The Hostile Sun: The Poetry of D.H. Lawrence. Los Angeles, Black Sparrow Press, 1973; Solihull, Warwickshire, Aquila, 1975.
New Heaven, New Earth: The Visionary Experience in Literature. New York, Vanguard Press, 1974; London, Gollancz, 1976.
Contraries: Essays. New York, Oxford University Press, 1981.

Editor, *Scenes from American Life: Contemporary Short Fiction.* New York, Random House, 1973.
Editor, with Shannon Ravenel, *The Best American Short Stories 1979.* Boston, Houghton Mifflin, 1979.

*

Critical Studies: *Joyce Carol Oates* by Joanne V. Creighton, Boston, Twayne, 1979; *Critical Essays on Joyce Carol Oates* edited by Linda W. Wagner, Boston, Hall, 1979; *Joyce Carol Oates* by Ellen G. Friedman, New York, Ungar, 1980.

* * *

The sheer quantity of Oates's writing is impressive: 12 novels since her first, *With Shuddering Fall,* in 1964, in addition to another 30 or more volumes of short stories, verse, plays, and criticism. Often she writes about extraordinary people, people whose will to dominate their lives, to compel life to conform to their vision of it, is all-consuming, and, finally destructive. In these books, she relentlessly charts the disintegration of the self in what appears to be her protest against the solipsistic view that underlies most of modern fiction. *Son of the Morning* offers perhaps her most shocking and gripping exploration of this theme. Here it is a pentecostal preacher,

Nathanael Vickery, who witnesses seven visitations from the Lord, each more terrifying than the last. The last shows him that God has withdrawn himself and left him, Nathanael, to sink back into oblivion and write the book of himself. Oates's appetite as a writer is as voracious as the will of her most willful protagonists. She consumes and disgorges experience, her own and that of others. She has recast the visions and stories of numerous writers. She has imaginatively entered into the lives of pentecostal preachers, children of the Detroit slums, professors in academia, and countless others. Her writing is thoroughly American, after the manner of Fitzgerald and Faulkner, Dreiser and Farrell. Her Yoknapatawpha County is Eden County, set near Millertown, New York where she lived as a child. Farrell's Chicago is her Detroit: Studs Lonigan is made over into Jules and Maureen Wendall in *Them*. Fitzgerald's Gatsby is her Jules, a man in love with the aloofness money brings, crazily hungry for Nadine, Daisy's counterpart in *Them*. Like her American ancestors, Oates is fascinated with property and the violence it engenders in those obsessed with it. She searches for the American epic, built around a dynastic family, which will place American history and American appetites, each in its true perspective. *Bellefleur* is her ambitious attempt at such an epic, an attempt which eluded the grasp of writer's whose talents dwarf hers—Melville and Twain, Faulkner and Bellow. Oates, nonetheless, is a story-teller of considerable gifts. She is also a writer's writer. Although she claims to write with a social purpose, out of concerns that are moral and political, recently she is turning more and more towards myth, and she is searching for new forms to capture her vision. Her literary borrowings are becoming more functional as they are increasingly more integrated into her works.

Childwold and *Cybele* offer the first real evidence of this shift away from naturalism, with *The Assassins* figuring as a transitional, experimental work in her evolution as a writer. The assassin who stalks Andrew Petrie, the one-time State Senator, is Andrew. The murderer in this book is monistic thinking, the willful fixation upon one idea, be it religious, philosophic, or literary, which severs the individual from the community of man, isolates him, and destroys him. The monism encases its believer in an isolation as total as that Hugh experiences as a paralytic, breathing with the aid of an iron-lung, without his sight. *Bellefleur* and *Unholy Loves*—few books could be less alike—testify to Oates's skill and range.

Bellefleur is vast, sprawling, weirdly welding the natural and supernatural together to create a psychologically and imaginatively plausible history of six generations of the Bellefleur family, from 1744 to the present. The book belongs in the tradition of American Gothic, but it has stretched the genre, bringing history into its domain. *Unholy Loves* is a tightly constructed, unified book: five chapters, five parties, it lays bare the soul of Birgit Stott, a recent divorcée, member of the English Department, and writer in a university modelled after Syracuse University where Oates earned her B.A. Oates's writings are usually humorless, but *Unholy Loves* belongs with Amis's *Lucky Jim* and Murdoch's *The Severed Head*. It still contains scenes of erupting violence, but the general atmosphere is one of forced conviviality. Oates knows intimately the scandals of the university, the ambitions, bitchiness, pomposity, petty jealousy, and colossal loneliness that are endemic to the modern university life. *Cybele* and *Childwold* are the books that mark Oates's movement away from her quasi-naturalistic fiction, preoccupied with America from the 1930's through the 1960's, and committed to a narrative line that revealed the violence-filled lives of her protagonists. The style of *Childwold* is lyrical. It is set back in Eden County, but nature is more mysterious and erotic, and, in a Faulknerian way, Oates celebrates the survivors. *Cybele* is more disturbing. Edwin Locke is the luckless victim of Cybele, the great goddess of nature who asked for nothing less than the life of this man who fell under her enchantment during his midlife crisis. She is a demanding goddess; he paid her the ultimate sacrifice when he allowed himself to be consumed by his own passions. He confuses eros with love and falls. The action of *Cybele* is typical of the action in portions of *Do with Me What You Will*. But love redeems Elena in *Do with Me What You Will*; Edwin never experiences love. But the narrative angle of *Cybele* shifts, reflecting Oates's desire to move more overtly into the realm of the demonic and the unconscious. Certainly, she embraces such terrain in *Bellefleur*.

Much has been written about Oates's obsession with violence. Rape, incest, patricide, self-mutilation, suicide, and child-abuse abound in her fiction, shocking and numbing her readers, often occasioning a shudder of recognition of the acts we want to deny. Sometimes the violence is gratuitous; too often, it is sensational; but more often than one wants to admit it demands to be confronted. Conceptions are violent in her fiction, blighting the children born of them. In *Them* Jules is conceived in a coupling that leaves his father murdered by his mother's brother, and leaves his mother bathed in blood of her dead lover and hostage to the policemen whose help she seeks. The violence that marked his conception doggedly pursues him. Hopelessly drawn to Nadine, he finds himself the target of her gun after a night of love-making in which he could not satisfy her. Later, caught up in the chaos of the Detroit fires, he kills a man and paradoxically recovers himself. Nathanael William Vickery, the pentecostal priest of *Son of the Morning*, is a child born of his mother's rape. Lacking a father, he grows up believing he is God's child and that his will is not his own. The initiation that rids him of this delusion, leaving him a nullity, is a terrifying one. When God withdraws from this man he has inhabited for 35 years, Nathanael is left without words or gestures. He crawls off the platform where he had been preaching before thousands, numbering himself among the damned. Stephen in *The Assassins* and Jebediah in *Bellefleur* are similarly abandoned by the god of their willful self-creation. In *Bellefleur* Oates is not satisfied to stop with only two or three of these familiar scenes of sensational violence. Every one of the violent acts numbered above and many more plague the lives of six generations of Bellefleurs. And this violence is not enough. Germaine is one of the Bellefleurs who survives. Her father, Gideon, wreaks his vengeance on his past and his wife when he dive-bombs his plane into the Bellefleur Mansion, destroying it, and killing himself, his wife, and her numerous followers. The special child he saves is the child whose birth chills us in the opening book. She is born a biological freak, with the genitalia of her male twin protruding from her abdomen to be sliced-off by her quick-thinking mother. (I could not read this without thinking that Judith Rossner's *Attachments* had had an unfortunate influence upon the already sufficiently grotesque imagination of Oates.)

At this stage in Oates's career it is difficult to know what finally to say about her reliance on violence. It is integral to her vision. It rivets her action and often constellates her characters. And it does not go away. Often it seems to mar her characterization, leaving motives ill-defined or murky. The tensions unleashed by the violence threaten the boundaries of her art. But the violence is often believable and it does not let us forget. It stuns us; makes us wonder how the imagination that so clear-sightedly depicts it can remain intact. Some would say that Oates is monstrously consumed with self-hatred; that it is her imagination that is the nightmare. I think not. She is touching something little understood, but now that she is tunnelling behind it, letting us glimpse its mainsprings more fully, I think she may in the end justify the experience she forces us to endure.

—Carol Simpson Stern

O'BRIEN, Edna. Irish. Born in Tuamgraney, County Clare, 15 December 1932. Attended National School, Scariff; Convent of Mercy, Loughrea; Pharmaceutical College of Dublin: Licentiate, Pharmaceutical Society of Ireland; practiced pharmacy briefly. Married Ernest Gebler in 1952 (marriage dissolved); two sons. Recipient: Kingsley Amis Award, 1962; *Yorkshire Post* Award, 1971. Agent: A.M. Heath, 40-42 William IV Street, London WC2N 4DD, England.

PUBLICATIONS

Novels

The Country Girls. London, Hutchinson, and New York, Knopf, 1960.
The Lonely Girl. London, Cape, and New York, Random House, 1962; as *Girl with Green Eyes*, London, Penguin, 1964.
Girls in Their Married Bliss. London, Cape, 1964; New York, Simon and Schuster, 1968.
August Is a Wicked Month. London, Cape, and New York, Simon and Schuster, 1965.
Casualties of Peace. London, Cape, 1966; New York, Simon and Schuster, 1967.
A Pagan Place. London, Weidenfeld and Nicolson, and New York, Knopf, 1970.
Night. London, Weidenfeld and Nicolson, 1972; New York, Knopf, 1973.
Johnny I Hardly Knew You. London, Weidenfeld and Nicolson, 1977; as *I Hardly Knew You*, New York, Doubleday, 1978.

Short Stories

The Love Object. London, Cape, 1968; New York, Knopf, 1969.
A Scandalous Woman and Other Stories. London, Weidenfeld and Nicolson, and New York, Harcourt Brace, 1974.
Mrs. Reinhardt and Other Stories. London, Weidenfeld and Nicolson, 1978; as *A Rose in the Heart*, New York, Doubleday, 1979.

Uncollected Short Stories

"Ghosts," in *New Yorker*, 9 April 1979.
"Violets," in *New Yorker*, 5 November 1979.
"Doll," in *Redbook* (Des Moines, Iowa), December 1979.
"Call," in *New Yorker*, 3 December 1979.
"Plan," in *New Yorker*, 25 February 1980.

Plays

A Cheap Bunch of Nice Flowers (produced London, 1962). Published in *Plays of the Year 1962-1963*, London, Elek, 1963.
Zee and Co. (screenplay). London, Weidenfeld and Nicolson, 1971.
A Pagan Place, adaptation of her own novel (produced London, 1972; New Haven, Connecticut, 1974). London, Faber, 1973.
The Gathering (produced Dublin, 1974; New York, 1977).
The Ladies (produced London, 1975).
Virginia (produced Stratford, Ontario, 1980; London and New York, 1981). London, Hogarth Press, 1981.

Screenplays: *Girl with Green Eyes*, 1964; *I Was Happy There* (*Time Lost and Time Remembered*), with Desmond Davis, 1965; *Three into Two Won't Go*, 1969; *Zee and Co.*, 1971.

Television Plays: *The Wedding Dress*, 1963; *The Keys of the Cafe*, 1965; *Give My Love to the Pilchards*, 1965; *Which of These Two Ladies Is He Married To?*, 1967; *Nothing's Ever Over*, 1968.

Other

Mother Ireland. London, Weidenfeld and Nicolson, and New York, Harcourt Brace, 1976.
Arabian Days, photographs by Gerard Klijn. New York, Horizon Press, and London, Quartet, 1977.
The Collected Edna O'Brien (miscellany). London, Collins, 1978.
The Dazzle (juvenile). London, Hodder and Stoughton, 1981.

Editor, *Some Irish Loving: A Selection.* London, Weidenfeld and Nicolson, and New York, Harper, 1979.

*

Critical Study: *Edna O'Brien* by Grace Eckley, Lewisburg, Pennsylvania, Bucknell University Press, 1974.

Edna O'Brien comments:

I quote from two critics: William Trevor and John Berger.

A Pagan Place: "Constitutes a reconstruction of a childhood experience which so far as I know, is unique in the English language. In this respect, though otherwise it is different, it invites comparison with Proust; a book whose genius is memory" (Berger).

The Love Object: "Rarely has a woman protested as eloquently as Edna O'Brien. In sorrow and compassion she keens over the living. More obviously now, despair is her province" (Trevor).

My aim is to write books that in some way celebrate life and do justice to my emotions as well as form a connection with the reader, the unknown one.

* * *

When John Millington Synge's *Playboy of the Western World* was first produced in the Abbey Theatre, Dublin, in 1907, there were riots because Synge told too much of the truth. His detractors fumed because he depicted, so they said, his fellow-countrymen as peasants whose main characteristic was a compound of gormlessness and cunning. More than half a century later *The Playboy of the Western World* is the Abbey's proudest classic. Voices are raised only in admiration when it's staged; and without qualification it's recommended to Ireland's tourist millions.

Ireland, new in its national fulfilment and with the sensitivity of a small nation, jealously guards the voices that speak for it. Synge, Yeats, Joyce, O'Casey, Shaw are recent figures: revered they may be now, but the reverence cannot be the same as that accumulated over centuries by a Shakespeare or a Molière. In Ireland time has hallowed no long and ordered tradition of literature: there is instead the confusion of two languages, of the imposed Ascendancy, of a culture shared between London and Dublin and then suddenly seeming suspect. In spite of the literary flowering at the beginning of this century, and the pride now found in it, Ireland is still as nervously uncertain in a cultural sense as it was when the crowds howled down the *Playboy*. The old, with the achievements of a lifetime tucked away, can take criticism without too much flinching. The adolescent becomes shrill.

In the new, liberated Republic the voice of Edna O'Brien is not widely heard: her books are banned. Other Irish writers who have suffered that indignity, like Joyce and Frank O'Connor, may be read in Ireland now, and sooner or later Edna O'Brien will in the same way come into her own. But it's significant that O'Brien today persists in giving offence, because she writes occasionally about sex.

Contemporary novels and plays tend to treat of sexual matters in much the same tone of voice as they do any other subject: this in itself is something of a novelty, but one that has by now lost a lot of its original glamour. What is still new, however, is that, where sex on the page is concerned, women are making the running: women novelists, once famous for romance and happy endings, have profitably taken over the male province of exploring the sexual side of their characters. Edna O'Brien has been at the forefront of that change and has become a best-selling novelist not because she is one of the most talented writers of her generation but because she writes frankly about women's desire for, and response to, sexual attention. From the horse's mouth she corroborates the suggestions on this subject made by Joyce and O'Connor and many another Irish male, and finds herself plunged into a Celtic darkness for her pains. Irish women, it is almost said, should be above such things.

Yet sex, or the lack of it, is only a single aspect of the obsession that powers O'Brien's fiction. Solitude has always been her subject and it remains so: in *The Country Girls* and *The Lonely Girl*, through the less successful, more sophisticated novels of life in London and holidaying abroad, in the stories of *The Love Object*, in *A Pagan Place*.

The O'Brien girls, from Cathleen and Baba of the early novels to the sharp heroine in the story "Paradise," are lost in a desperation of loneness. They long to belong, to find a land they feel has been promised to them, in which there is the comfort of easy communication, in which men are different from the men they know. Rarely does their dream come true, and though she has lost none of her comic inventiveness, Edna O'Brien increasingly writes now with despair.

In *The Country Girls* Mr. Gentleman isn't at all like the crude boozers of the pitch-and-toss schools of Co. Clare. He's a cultured man, of French descent, an older man who in theory at least seems to offer Cathleen the chance of the escape she prays for. But Mr. Gentleman is married: he fades away as a Prince Charming, as does the gentleman who is *The Love Object*. He, too, isn't so young: "The hair was greying on the outside and he had spread the outer grey ribs across the width of his head....He had what you'd call a very religious smile." But behind the smile lay the treachery of ineffectiveness, and weakness when it came to the point. The nice artistic Englishman in the story called "Irish Revel" is younger, but little better. With more of a dash than Mr. Gentleman, he makes his way out of a shy girl's life—on a motor-bike that was once romantic. Such girls are left to fall into the arms of the Hickeys and O'Tooles at dances in Mrs. Rodgers' Commercial Hotel, or to be filled with gin by Dublin jackeens who know all about seizing what chances distress offers them. Pregnant, one of them returns to the family farmhouse: "Your father told her to speak up, to give the man's name, occupation, earnings and character. Your mother said not to use the word context in that context. Your father told your mother to keep out of it, that it was business between men, and he and the doctor hefted Emma on to the leather pouffe....Your father said did she want grub."

Again and again, in seeking the roots of Edna O'Brien's talent, one is driven back to the country that has in a sense rejected her, to the pillars of the Church on which modern Ireland rests, to the harsh country background that isn't at all like the tourist posters. She is rebellious, she states herself; she comes of a rebellious country. And yet few other women have been as rebellious there, preferring to wait for the honour of motherhood, settling for the affection of sons when the love of men fails them. In her novels and stories—and the best ones erupt from her Irishness—a husband may take, quite naturally, a pitchfork to his wife, and a handsome priest may leave a girl emotionally crippled by his seduction, and a father may savage a daughter with words. Such women weep, accepting their lot, knowing no other; for Ireland—lost for so long in struggles with invaders, with poverty and with the land—has had too little time for delicacy of polite society and leisurely relationships.

The novels of Edna O'Brien are haunted by this hard Ireland of the past, which often she uses as a microcosm of the world as it always is. The violence, the toughness, the separation of man and woman, the Establishments that breed hypocrisy, the falsehoods that pass for honesty, the stones that remain unturned: all this is grist in a mill that grinds out, with its despair, reality and truth.

—William Trevor

O'FAOLAIN, Julia. Irish. Born in London; daughter of Sean O'Faolain, *q.v.* Educated at the Sacred Heart Convent, Dublin; University College, Dublin, B.A. and M.A.; University of Rome; the Sorbonne, Paris. Married Lauro Martines; one son. Has worked as a language teacher and translator. Agent: A.P. Watt Ltd., 26-28 Bedford Row, London WC1R 4HL, England.

Publications

Novels

Godded and Codded. London, Faber, 1970; as *Three Lovers*, New York, Coward McCann, 1971.
Women in the Wall. London, Faber, and New York, Viking Press, 1975.
No Country for Young Men. London, Allen Lane, 1980.

Short Stories

We Might See Sights! and Other Stories. London, Faber, 1968.
Man in the Cellar. London, Faber, 1974.
Melancholy Baby and Other Stories. Dublin, Poolbeg Press, 1978.

Other

Editor, with Lauro Martines, *Not in God's Image: Women in History from the Greeks to the Victorians.* London, Temple Smith, and New York, Harper, 1973.

Translator (as Julia Martines), *Two Memoirs of Renaissance Florence: The Diaries of Buonaccorso Pitti and Gregorio Dati*, edited by Gene Brucker. New York, Harper, 1967.
Translator, *A Man of Parts*, by Piero Chiara. Boston, Little Brown, 1968.

*

Critical Studies: *Two Decades of Irish Writing* edited by Douglas Dunn, Manchester, Carcanet Press, and Philadelphia, Dufour, 1975; "The Irish Novel in Our Time" edited by Patrick Rafroidi and Maurice Harmon, in *Publications de l'Université de Lille 3*, 1975-76.

* * *

Broad but darkening comedy characterizes Julia O'Faolain's concern with social issues, especially the position of women. However, there is something *déjà vu* about her novel *Godded and Codded*, centring on the innocent Irish Sally's further education—in several senses—in Paris, not wholly redeemed by the book's uproarious comedy. The inevitably pregnant Sally's equally inevitable Christmas visit to her parents in Ireland covers even more familiar ground, as we are shown the circumstances that have made Sally what she is—that is, what she must react against. O'Faolain's earlier story "A Pot of Soothing Herbs" encapsulated this—the archetypal Irish virginal dilemma; the later story "Lots of Ghastlies" more adroitly transplants to an English bourgeois setting the theme of a return visit to the parental home. More interesting in *Godded and Codded* than the "innocents abroad" theme is the peripheral description of the underground activities of a group of Algerian students in Paris shortly before Independence. Irish expatriates provide much of the novel's burlesque comedy, in the persons of the painter Fintan McCann (first glimpsed in the story "Turkish Delight"), one of Sally's *Three Lovers* of the American title, and of the ageing and amorous Letty Murray O'Keefe. Fintan's "spontaneous picture," created before a respectable bourgeois audience, is a comic *tour de force*, though, as with the sexual comedy, the situation is somewhat clichéd.

O'Faolain's best short stories not only handle situations more skilfully but also eschew the mock-Joycean interior monologue, which put into the minds of the main characters in *Godded and Codded* is the chief vehicle for its tumultuous progress. When this device is used in a story, as in "Chronic," it is less effective than on the larger scale of the novel, where the sheer verve of its rumbustious bawdiness maintains a momentum. The use of letters as the narrative device in the long story "Man in the Cellar" (anticipated in "A

Pot of Soothing Herbs") permits much of the freedom of interior monologue, while structuring this story temporally.

The stories in her first collection, *We Might See Sights!*, are divided by O'Faolain, who is a professional Italian translator, into Irish and Italian stories. The latter are superior, perhaps because the author finds it easier to distance their material. Against a background of the poorer sections of Italian society she focuses on the small shopkeeper, "Mrs. Ross," while in the Italian setting of 'Death Duties" she airs the problem of abortion, sparing the clinical details of *Godded and Codded*. The outstanding story is "Dies Irae," set in a hairdresser's saloon and perhaps influenced by Colette; to pacify an elderly Russian princess, the hairdresser points out signs of decay in the narrator, for whom a normally pleasant occasion becomes her *dies irae*. "An Afternoon on Elba" is a more direct exploration of the position of women, whose difficulties Sally personifies in the novel; this is also the main concern of *Man in the Cellar*.

The didactic element is stronger in this later collection of stories, but is offset by the use of out-of-the-way situations; "This Is My Body," for instance, set in a 6th-century convent, handles the female Irish writer's stock-in-trade of convent material from a new angle, which her *Women in the Wall* also exploits. This collection draws less frequently but more effectively on Irish material. An aggressive note in O'Faolain's full-blooded humour has become more dominant, in stories like "A Travelled Man," which transplants "Lucca's last scribe" to the sexual hotbed of a Los Angeles college campus. There is black, rather than burlesque comedy in the plight of the husband chained in the cellar by his wife, in the title story "Man in the Cellar," and the final surprisingly affectionate letter from the decamped and mentally disturbed wife reveals how securely the invisible chains are fastened on her. O'Faolain's thoughtful involvement with female liberation, demonstrated in her editing of a collection of texts on the position of women in European society throughout history, *Not in God's Image*, helps to make this story her outstanding achievement.

—Val Warner

O'FAOLAIN, Sean. Irish. Born in Cork, 22 February 1900. Educated at University College, Cork, M.A. 1925; Harvard University, Cambridge, Massachusetts (Commonwealth Fellow, 1926-28; John Harvard Fellow, 1928-29), 1926-29, M.A. 1929. Served in the Irish Republican Army. Married Eileen Gould in 1928; two children, including Julia O'Faolain, *q.v.* Lecturer in English, Boston College, 1929, and St. Mary's College, Strawberry Hill, Twickenham, Middlesex, 1929-33. Full-time writer from 1933: Editor of *The Bell*, Dublin, 1940-46. Director, Arts Council of Ireland, 1957-59. Address: 17 Rosmeen Park, Dunlaoire, County Dublin, Ireland.

PUBLICATIONS

Novels

A Nest of Simple Folk. London, Cape, 1933; New York, Viking Press, 1934.
Bird Alone. London, Cape, and New York, Viking Press, 1936.
Come Back to Erin. London, Cape, and New York, Viking Press, 1940.
And Again? London, Constable, 1979.

Short Stories

Midsummer Night Madness and Other Stories. London, Cape, and New York, Viking Press, 1932; as *Stories of Sean O'Faolain*, London, Penguin, 1970.
There's a Birdie in the Cage. London, Grayson, 1935.
A Born Genius. Detroit, Schuman's, 1936.
A Purse of Coppers: Short Stories. London, Cape, 1937; New York, Viking Press, 1938.
Teresa and Other Stories. London, Cape, 1947; as *The Man Who Invented Sin and Other Stories*, New York, Devin Adair, 1948.
The Finest Stories of Sean O'Faolain. Boston, Little Brown, 1957; as *The Stories of Sean O'Faolain*, London, Hart Davis, 1958.
I Remember! I Remember! Boston, Little Brown, 1961; London, Hart Davis, 1962.
The Heat of the Sun: Stories and Tales. Boston, Little Brown, and London, Hart Davis, 1966.
The Talking Trees. Boston, Little Brown, 1970; London, Cape, 1971.
Foreign Affairs and Other Stories. Boston, Little Brown, and London, Constable, 1976.
Selected Stories. Boston, Little Brown, and London, Constable, 1978.
The Collected Stories of Sean O'Faolain 1. London, Constable, 1980.

Plays

She Had to Do Something (produced Dublin, 1937; London, 1954). London, Cape, 1938.
The Train to Banbury (broadcast, 1947). Published in *Imaginary Conversations*, edited by Rayner Heppenstall, London, Secker and Warburg, 1948.

Radio Play: *The Train to Banbury*, 1947.

Other

The Life Story of Eamon De Valera. Dublin, Talbot Press, 1933.
Constance Markievicz; or, The Average Revolutionary: A Biography. London, Cape, 1934; revised edition, London, Sphere, 1968.
King of the Beggars: A Life of Daniel O'Connell. London, Nelson, and New York, Viking Press, 1938.
De Valera: A Biography. London, Penguin, 1939.
An Irish Journey. London and New York, Longman, 1940.
The Great O'Neill: A Biography of Hugh O'Neill, Earl of Tyrone 1550-1616. London, Longman, and New York, Duell, 1942.
The Story of Ireland. London, Collins, 1943.
The Irish: A Character Study. London, Penguin, 1947; New York, Devin Adair, 1949; revised edition, Penguin, 1969.
The Short Story. London, Collins, 1948; New York, Devin Adair, 1951.
A Summer in Italy. London, Eyre and Spottiswoode, 1949; New York, Devin Adair, 1950.
Newman's Way: The Odyssey of John Henry Newman. London, Longman, and New York, Devin Adair, 1952.
South to Sicily. London, Collins, 1953; as *An Autumn in Italy*, New York, Devin Adair, 1953.
The Vanishing Hero: Studies in Novelists of the Twenties. London, Eyre and Spottiswoode, 1956; Boston, Little Brown, 1957.
Vive Moi! (autobiography). Boston, Little Brown, 1964; London, Hart Davis, 1965.

Editor, *Lyrics and Satires from Tom Moore*. Dublin, Cuala Press, 1929.
Editor, *The Autobiography of Theobald Wolfe Tone*. New York and London, Nelson, 1937.
Editor, *The Silver Branch: A Collection of the Best Old Irish Lyrics*. London, Cape, and New York, Viking Press, 1938.

Editor, *Short Stories: A Study in Pleasure*. Boston, Little Brown, 1961.

*

Manuscript Collection: Bancroft Library, University of California, Berkeley.

Critical Studies: *Sean O'Faolain: A Critical Introduction* by Maurice Harmon, Notre Dame, Indiana, University of Notre Dame Press, 1966; *Sean O'Faolain* by Paul A. Doyle, New York, Twayne, 1968; *The Short Stories of Sean O'Faolain: A Study in Descriptive Techniques* by Joseph Storey Rippier, Gerrards Cross, Buckinghamshire, Smythe, and New York, Barnes and Noble, 1976.

* * *

Emerging at a period in Irish history when the passionate man cannot identify with any particular group, Sean O'Faolain remains in fundamental discord with society and has to work out his own destiny by relying on his own intense demand for a rich and varied existence, and for a background appropriate to his imagination's image of life. Each of his three novels contains a central figure who abides at first the canons of respectability that govern the lower middle class to which he belongs, but rebels in favour of more liberal, less restrictive ways and in search of a more desirable vision of life than is available to him in his own class. That rebellion affects all of his subsequent life, cutting him off from the familiar moral and social patterns of his childhood and early life and propelling him in quest of a more congenial and more satisfying adult existence. It is his fate however to be forever denied a happy solution to his search for fulfillment. *And Again?*, a playful treatment of memory and of human nature, is free of social problems.

O'Faolain's short stories reflect a similar concern. It is through them that his development as a writer may be most fully seen. Beginning with romantic stories that try to deal objectively with his experience as a revolutionary, he moved on to stories that reveal the emergence of a distinctive, pessimistic point of view. The central issue is the plight of the individual in a stagnant, post-revolutionary society. In his second collection, *A Purse of Coppers*, his characters experience an alienation so complete that it becomes an impasse beyond which there seems to be no accessible line of development. But gradually O'Faolain discovered a less rigid response. Instead of portraying the sensitive, intelligent man, struggling against insurmountable social conditions, he treats, gently and humorously, of the ambivalent man, who is not particularly concerned with social or moral issues. In this figure he wanted to express the contradictory forces in Irish life at a time when the country was emerging into a modern civilisation but was moulded instinctively by forces from the past. In the process of describing the contradictory nature of the modern Irishman, O'Faolain came to appreciate the power and the value of the various influences on thought and behaviour that lie beneath the conscious or rational part of the individual. With his greater respect for the deeper psychological experiences, he began to concentrate on the universal themes of time and change, the impermanence of youth and age, and the accomodations of middle age.

No account of O'Faolain's fiction should ignore his other prose, in particular his historical biographies which also study the relation of the individual to his society. Each attempts to understand how a great figure emerges from his background, to calculate to what degree he personifies his people's needs, and to determine the nature of the heritage he created for subsequent Irishmen. Nor should one ignore his work as editor of *The Bell*, in which he sought to stimulate Irish writers and in which he spoke out clearly in favour of liberal values. His many articles in Irish, English, and American journals, his literary criticism, and even his travel books are all part of the picture of a man of letters, and one who was deeply engaged as an intellectual and creative writer with the whole range of Irish life. "There is," he said, "only one admirable form of the imagination—the imagination that is so intense that it creates a new reality, that it makes things happen, whether it be a political thing, or a social thing, or a work of art."

—Maurice Harmon

O'FLAHERTY, Liam. Irish. Born in the Aran Islands, County Galway, 28 August 1896. Educated at Rockwell College, Cashel, 1908-12; Blackrock College, 1912-13; University College, Dublin, 1913-14. Organized a Republican corps in 1913, and fought for the Republicans in the Irish Civil War; served with the British Army during World War I; invalided out of service, 1918. Travelled around the world, working as a deckhand, porter, filing clerk, and farm labourer, in Asia, South America, the United States, and Canada, 1918-21; returned to Ireland, and settled in Dublin; full-time writer from 1922. Recipient: Black Memorial Prize, 1926; Allied Irish Banks-Irish Academy of Letters Award, 1979. Agent: A.D. Peters and Company, 10 Buckingham Street, London WC2N 6BU, England.

PUBLICATIONS

Novels

Thy Neighbour's Wife. London, Cape, 1923; New York, Boni and Liveright, 1924.
The Black Soul. London, Cape, 1924; New York, Boni and Liveright, 1925.
The Informer. London, Cape, and New York, Knopf, 1925.
Mr. Gilhooley. London, Cape, 1926; New York, Harcourt Brace, 1927.
The Assassin. London, Cape, and New York, Harcourt Brace, 1928.
The House of Gold. London, Cape, and New York, Harcourt Brace, 1929.
Return of the Brute. London, Mandrake Press, 1929; New York, Harcourt Brace, 1930.
The Puritan. London, Cape, 1931; New York, Harcourt Brace, 1932.
Skerrett. London, Gollancz, and New York, Long and Smith, 1932.
The Martyr. London, Gollancz, and New York, Macmillan, 1933.
Hollywood Cemetery. London, Gollancz, 1935.
Famine. London, Gollancz, and New York, Random House, 1937.
Land. London, Gollancz, and New York, Random House, 1946.
Insurrection. London, Gollancz, 1950; Boston, Little Brown, 1951.
The Wilderness. Dublin, Wolfhound Press, 1978.

Short Stories

Spring Sowing. London, Cape, 1924; New York, Knopf, 1926.
Civil War. London, Archer, 1925.
The Terrorist. London, Archer, 1926.
The Child of God. London, Archer, 1926.
The Tent and Other Stories. London, Cape, 1926.
The Fairy-Goose and Two Other Stories. London, Faber and Gwyer, and New York, Gaige, 1927.
Red Barbara and Other Stories. London, Faber and Gwyer, and New York, Gaige, 1928.
The Mountain Tavern and Other Stories. London, Cape, and New York, Harcourt Brace, 1929.

The Ecstasy of Angus. London, Joiner and Steele, 1931.
The Wild Swan and Other Stories. London, Joiner and Steele, 1932.
The Short Stories of Liam O'Flaherty. London, Cape, 1937.
Two Lovely Beasts and Other Stories. London, Gollancz, 1948; New York, Devin Adair, 1950.
Dúil. Dublin, Sáirséal and Dill, 1953.
The Stories of Liam O'Flaherty. New York, Devin Adair, 1956.
Selected Stories, edited by Devin A. Garrity. New York, New American Library, 1958.
Irish Portraits: 14 Short Stories. London, Sphere, 1970.
More Short Stories of Liam O'Flaherty. London, Sphere, 1971.
The Wounded Cormorant and Other Stories. New York, Norton, 1973.
The Pedlar's Revenge and Other Stories, edited by A.A. Kelly. Dublin, Wolfhound Press, 1976.

Plays

Darkness. London, Archer, 1926.

Screenplays: *The Devil's Playground,* with others, 1937; *Last Desire,* 1939; *Jacqueline,* with others, 1956.

Other

The Life of Tim Healy. London, Cape, and New York, Harcourt Brace, 1927.
A Tourist's Guide to Ireland. London, Mandrake Press, 1929.
Two Years. London, Cape, and New York, Harcourt Brace, 1930.
Joseph Conrad: An Appreciation. London, Lahr, 1930; New York, Haskell House, 1973.
I Went to Russia. London, Cape, and New York, Harcourt Brace, 1931.
A Cure for Unemployment. London, Lahr, and New York, Julian Press, 1931.
Shame the Devil (autobiography). London, Grayson, 1934.
All Things Come of Age: A Rabbit Story (juvenile). Dublin, Wolfhound Press, 1977.
The Test of Courage (juvenile). Dublin, Wolfhound Press, 1977.

*

Bibliography: *Liam O'Flaherty: An Annotated Bibliography* by Paul A. Doyle, Troy, New York, Whitston, 1972.

Manuscript Collection: University of Texas, Austin.

Critical Studies: *The Literary Vision of Liam O'Flaherty* by John Zneimer, Syracuse, New York, Syracuse University Press, 1970; *Liam O'Flaherty* by Paul A. Doyle, New York, Twayne, 1971; *Liam O'Flaherty* by James H. O'Brien, 1973; *The Novels of Liam O'Flaherty: A Study in Romantic Realism* by Patrick F. Sheeran, Dublin, Wolfhound Press, and Atlantic Highlands, New Jersey, Humanities Press, 1976; *Liam O'Flaherty: The Storyteller* by A.A. Kelly, London, Macmillan, 1976, New York, Barnes and Noble, 1977.

* * *

Most of Liam O'Flaherty's novels follow a recurring pattern. The books' protagonists are usually lonely, melancholy, and tormented individuals who are intensely emotional. The hero will be depressed and disillusioned with life and its apparent meaninglessness; he will utter wild sentiments, aspire to herculean achievement, and find solace rarely. When security is obtained, it is usually through a brief unification with the forces of nature. While often beautiful and inspiring, nature can also be hostile and destructive, and O'Flaherty readily demonstrates the ambivalence which nature holds. *The Black Soul, Thy Neighbour's Wife, The Martyr,* and *Skerrett* best exemplify these aspects in which exuberant Romanticism and a glorification of primitive instincts play a dominant role.

The Informer and *Mr. Gilhooley* stand as important achievements. The former book is raised above the rank of a mere effective suspense-thriller by a penetrating analysis of Gypo Nolan as a symbol of suffering humanity caught amid the handicaps of physical strength without intelligence and the sordid pervasiveness of the Dublin slums. *Mr. Gilhooley* is one of the most heartrending and realistic studies ever attempted of a middle-aged man trapped in the despair of loneliness and emptiness.

O'Flaherty's strengths as a novelist especially involve three qualities: 1) he is a gifted storyteller whose dynamic sweep and flow capture reader interest; 2) he presents scenes with a compelling pictorial vividness; 3) he possesses a Dostoevsky-like talent for digging deeply into the psychological and emotional turmoil experienced by his principal characters. These talents mingle with several weaknesses. Episodes of genius are interspersed with ordinary pedestrian prose. While at times O'Flaherty's lyricism is extremely effective, his style is too often heavy-handed, flat, and merely utilitarian. Further, his philosophizing becomes jejune and unconvincing; and, frequently, he is not intellectually equal to his themes, which in themselves are of vital importance. Melodrama is common since he deals with highly temperamental figures and very emotional situations. At times he lets excessive emotionalism distract him both from narrative verisimilitude and character plausibility. He rarely resists parading his own neurasthenic feelings so that both omniscient author and the characters continually wear their hearts on their sleeves.

Famine, O'Flaherty's finest novel, is strikingly unlike his other fiction. In this saga he eschews the melodramatic approach and the emphasis on one protagonist and concentrates on heavily naturalistic social documentary in which feelings are kept subdued. Even the narrator stands apart from the starvation and death portrayed and allows the individual tragic episodes to speak for themselves. So balanced is O'Flaherty's handling that he presents deficiencies in the people as well as in the governing groups. Thus, this novel has a balanced comprehensiveness and an artistic profundity which his other long narratives lack.

O'Flaherty has received considerable praise for his numerous short stories, which are of two types: 1) vignettes of rural scenes and people; 2) sketches of animal life in its physical aspects, such as a wild goat defending its kid from a dog, or an eel struggling to escape a fisherman's net. Such stories are characterized by an acute awareness of nature's power, grim realism focusing on the tragic aspects of existence, and a perceptive attention to closely observed detail. "Going into Exile," "Red Barbara," and "The Cow's Death" are illustrative of O'Flaherty's most impressive work in the genre of the brief narrative.

—Paul A. Doyle

OLSEN, Tillie. American. Born in Omaha, Nebraska, 14 January 1913. High school education. Married Jack Olsen in 1936; four daughters. Has worked in the service, warehouse, and food processing industries, and as an office typist. Visiting Professor, Amherst College, Massachusetts, 1969-70; Visiting Instructor, Stanford University, California, Spring 1971; Writer-in-Residence, Massachusetts Institute of Technology, Cambridge, 1973; Visiting Professor, University of Massachusetts, Boston, 1974; Visiting Lecturer, University of California, San Diego, 1978. Creative Writing Fellow, Stanford University, 1956-57; Fellow, Radcliffe Institute for Independent Study, Cambridge, Massachusetts, 1962-64. Recipient: Ford Grant, 1959; O. Henry Award, 1961; National Endowment for the Arts grant, 1966; American Academy Award, 1975; Guggenheim Fellowship, 1975. Doctor of Arts and Letters: University of

Nebraska, Lincoln, 1979. Agent: Russell and Volkening Inc., 551 Fifth Avenue, New York, New York 10017. Address: 1712 West Cliff, Santa Cruz, California 95060, U.S.A.

PUBLICATIONS

Novel

Yonnondio: From the Thirties. New York, Delacorte Press, 1974; London, Faber, 1975.

Short Stories

Tell Me a Riddle: A Collection. Philadelphia, Lippincott, 1961; enlarged edition, London, Faber, 1964.

Uncollected Short Story

"Requa: Part One," in *The Best American Short Stories 1971*, edited by Martha Foley and David Burnett. Boston, Houghton Mifflin, 1971.

Other

Silences. New York, Delacorte Press, 1978; London, Virago, 1980.

*

Manuscript Collection: Berg Collection, New York Public Library.

Critical Studies: "The Short Stories of Tillie Olsen" by William Van O'Connor, in *Studies in Short Fiction* (Newberry, South Carolina), Fall 1963; Annie Gottlieb, in *New York Times Book Review*, 31 March 1974; "Fragments of Time Lost" by Jack Salzman, in *Washington Post Book World*, 7 April 1974; "Tillie Olsen: The Weight of Things Unsaid" by Sandy Boucher, in *Ms* (New York) September 1974; "De-Riddling Tillie Olsen's Writings" by Selma Burkom and Margaret Williams, in *San Jose Studies 2* (California), 1976.

* * *

Tillie Olsen repeatedly expresses her conviction that literature is impoverished to the degree that creativity is not nourished and sustained in women and in people of the working class. Her speeches and essays on the waste of talent and on periods of aridity in the lives of authors, her long treatise on Rebecca Harding Davis's thwarted career following marriage, and her notes and quotations on this theme—collected over a period of 15 years—constitute *Silences*. Her own artistic recognition was postponed by the exigencies of making a living for herself and her children. She "mislaid" a novel for 35 years and wrote no story she thought worthy of publication until she was 43.

Tell Me a Riddle includes the three stories and the novella published between 1956 and 1960. "Tell Me a Riddle" centers on the antagonism which arises between two Jewish immigrants after their 37 years of marriage. In this novella Olsen reflects also upon the embarrassment and bewilderment of their married children as the "gnarled roots" of this marriage split apart. The wife's slow death from cancer greatly intensifies the conflict, but also dramatizes the love that remains only because it has become a habit. The wife returns in her delirium to their 1905 revolutionary activism, as her husband sighs, "how we believed, how we belonged." Almost without plot, this novella demonstrates Olsen's artistry in characterization, dialogue, and sensory appeal, and it fully displays, as does all her fiction, her highly rhythmic and metaphorical use of language. In the monologue "I Stand Here Ironing" a woman reviews the 19 years of her daughter's life and mourns those days which blighted the daughter's full "flowering." Most intense are the mother's memories of being torn away from her infant in order to support her after they were abandoned. In "Hey Sailor, What Ship?" Whitey, a sailor, is given to drink and to buying admiration from the children of Lennie and Helen by giving them expensive gifts. Here he endures his last visit with his adopted family, with whom he has spent San Francisco shore leaves for years. The oldest daughter, embarrassed before her friends, turns in judgment upon the man who has brought a sense of adventure and romance to the family, while they have provided him some understanding and security over the years. In the elegiac close, Whitey pauses at the top of the third of seven hills to look back through the fog to the house with "its eyes unshaded." In the story "O Yes" a 12-year-old black girl invites her white friend to her baptism. As the throb of voices and clapping and the swaying of bodies intensifies the congregation's religious fervor, the white child feels her senses assailed and faints. The next year in junior high, as rigid social patterns separate the two friends, she mourns the warmth and openness she felt momentarily at the baptism.

The novel *Yonnondio: From the Thirties*, which Olsen began at the age of 19 (when she was already a mother), she abandoned five years later, a few pages short of its close. The manuscript was found 35 years later, and in 1973, in "arduous partnership" with her younger self, Olsen selected, edited, and organized the fragments, but she could not write the ending or rewrite sections. The novel significantly adds to American fiction of the Depression years, and it provides remarkable evidence of Olsen's artistry in her early youth. Greatly impressive are the imagery, the use of smells and sounds, the rhythms which shift notably between the first two sections written from the view of the child Mazie, and the third section which emerges from the narrative consciousness of the mother, Mary Holbrook, dying gradually of exhaustion, childbearing, and malnutrition. The title of this novel is taken from Walt Whitman's "Yonnondio" and in Iroquois means a lament for the aborigines—the authors mourn the common folk who suffered greatly but left "No picture, poem, statement, passing them to the future." During the course of the novel, Jim Holbrook moves from a Wyoming mine to a North Dakota tenant farm and finally to a Chicago or Omaha meat-packing plant with his wife and family. The zestful and imaginative Mazie in the early months of their life on the farm becomes ecstatically pantheistic in the style of Whitman's nature poetry, but in the city, in section three, she has lost her aspiration and much of her sensitivity and moves into the background in her bewilderment at her mother's illness and her father's increasing bad temper and dependence on alcohol. Critics generally acclaimed the novel, but several complained that Olsen gives her readers no mercy and that her work may be too painful for sustained reading and too unrelenting in its despair to allow characters to triumph through suffering.

—Margaret B. McDowell

OWEN, Guy (Jr.). American. Born in Clarkton, North Carolina, 24 February 1925. Educated at the University of North Carolina, Chapel Hill, B.A. 1947, M.A. 1949, Ph.D. 1955. Served in the United States Army. Married Dorothy Jennings in 1952; two sons. Formerly, Teaching Assistant, University of North Carolina, Chapel Hill; Instructor, Davidson College, North Carolina, and Elon College, North Carolina; Associate Professor of English, Stetson College, DeLand, Florida. Currently, Professor of English, North Carolina State University, Raleigh. Formerly, Writer-in-Residence, University of North Carolina, Greensboro, and Appalachian State University, Boone, North Carolina. Founding Editor, *Impetus*, Raleigh, North Carolina, 1958-64; Contributing Editor, *Books Abroad*, Norman, Oklahoma, 1963-67; Editor, with Leonides Betts, *North Carolina Folklore*, Raleigh, 1966-72; Advisory Editor, *Pembroke Magazine*, *Appalachian Journal*, and *This Issue*, Atlanta. Since 1964, Editor, *Southern Poetry Review*, Raleigh. Recipient: Bread Loaf Writers Conference grant, 1960; Henry Bellamann Foundation Award, 1964; Yaddo grant, 1968; National Endowment for the Arts grant, for editing, 1969. Address: 107 Montgomery Street, Raleigh, North Carolina 27607, U.S.A.

PUBLICATIONS

Novels

Season of Fear. New York, Random House, 1960; London, Gollancz, 1962.
The Ballad of the Flim-Flam Man. New York, Macmillan, 1965; revised edition, New York, Pocket Books, 1967.
Journey for Joedel. New York, Crown, 1970.
The Flim-Flam Man and the Apprentice Grifter. New York, Crown, 1972.

Short Stories

The Flim-Flam Man and Other Stories. Durham, North Carolina, Moore, 1980.

Verse

Cape Fear Country and Other Poems. Lake Como, Florida, New Athenaeum Press, 1958.
The Guilty and Other Poems. Lanham, Maryland, Goosetree Press, 1964.
The White Stallion and Other Poems. Winston-Salem, North Carolina, Blair, 1969.

Other

Editor, with William E. Taylor, *Southern Poetry Today*. DeLand, Florida, Owen and Taylor, 1962.
Editor, *Essays in Modern American Literature*. DeLand, Florida, Stetson University Press, 1962.
Editor, *Modern American Poetry: Essays in Criticism*. DeLand, Florida, Everett Edwards, 1972.
Editor, with Mary C. Williams, *New Southern Poets: Selected Poems from Southern Poetry Review 1959-1974*. Chapel Hill, University of North Carolina Press, 1975.
Editor, with Mary C. Williams, *Contemporary Poetry of North Carolina*. Winston-Salem, North Carolina, Blair, 1977.
Editor, with Mary C. Williams, *Contemporary Southern Poetry: An Anthology*. Baton Rouge, Louisiana State University Press, 1979.

*

Manuscript Collection: University of North Carolina, Chapel Hill.

Critical Studies: "Guy Owen Issue" of *Pembroke Magazine 13* (North Carolina), 1981.

* * *

"All his life there had been one chain or another holding him back," reflects slow-witted Clay Hampton, as this doomed central figure of Guy Owen's first novel, *Season of Fear*, struggles toward the snuffing out of his frustrated life. He speaks for all the residents of the Ku Klux Klan-infested country around the decaying village of Ellers Bend in the Cape Fear tobacco-growing country of southeastern North Carolina that the novelist has endowed with a cautionary significance that would escape the casual tourist.

Clay Hampton is a 40-year-old bachelor who has dragged out his days propping up a deteriorating home for a nagging mother and kindly but ineffectual aunt, while teased by invitations to a sunlit life in Florida by a fast-talking brother who escaped the dreary round of marginal farming. Plagued by sexual and religious torments for which his restrictive culture affords no outlets, Clay convulsively tightens his chains in attempting to break them. When in fits of sexual jealousy he has one neighboring family driven out by the Klan and then gruesomely murders the son-in-law of their replacements, he triggers his own fate—himself his worst enemy in a neighborhood of few well-wishers except a Negro share-cropper who provides Clay's epitaph, "He done wrong, but there was a heap of good in that man."

This tragic tale told, Owen demonstrated his ability to change pace in the hilarious *The Ballad of the Flim-Flam Man*, about the legendary Mordecai Jones and his guitar-playing apprentice, Army deserter Curley Treadaway, whose outrageous confidence games exploit the province's credulous and avaricious. What might have become aimless slapstick, Owen turns into a lyric account of near-mythical figures, who for all their tricks cannot break the chains of the unrewarding province that hypnotically holds them in order to take their chances in the legendary city of Wilmington where national fame beckons.

In what many consider Owen's finest novel, *Journey for Joedel*, he mingles pathos and lyric humor to narrate a single crucial day in the life of a 13-year-old boy who is taking his first batch of tobacco to the annual market at which his father hopes to make the money that will free the family from share-cropping. The boy Joedel's struggle for identity is handicapped because he is a half-breed in a region whose narrow people will not even recognize the claim of his Croatan Indian mother's people to proud tradition. As Owen observes, Joedel's journey is not just geographical but spiritual: "what takes place in the novel is an awareness on the part of the boy of the moral ambiguity of the world around us," that it becomes a kind of downbeat Eastern analogue to Steinbeck's *The Red Pony*.

In *The Flim-Flam Man and the Apprentice Grifter*, Jones and Treadaway take to the road once more, but after exhausting a picked-over region, the partners this time at length reach the illusory Wilmington, where Curley—transformed into rock singer Stud Galleon—does triumph and seems bound for even greater fame in New York, when he abandons his new image because, as he muses, "I'd had more fun in the skin game, and I reckon I did less harm, in the long run, since I was only biking a few people then." He rejects the promised escape for "a new life" in the old chains because Owen's baroque vision is that freedom means not the fulfillment of dreams but only greater nightmares in a larger sphere.

—Warren French

OZICK, Cynthia. American. Born in New York City. Educated at New York University, B.A. (cum laude) 1949 (Phi Beta Kappa); Ohio State University, Columbus, M.A. 1951. Married Bernard Hallote in 1952; one daughter. Instructor in English, New York University, 1964-65. Stolnitz Lecturer, Indiana University, Bloomington, 1972. Recipient: National Endowment for the Arts grant, 1967; Wallant Award, 1972; B'nai B'rith Award, 1972; Jewish Book Council Epstein Award, 1972, 1977; American Academy Award, 1973; Hadassah Myrtle Wreath Award, 1974; O. Henry Award, for short story, 1975, 1980; Lamport Prize, 1980. Agent: Theron Raines, Raines and Raines, 475 Fifth Avenue, New York, New York 10017, U.S.A.

PUBLICATIONS

Novel

Trust. New York, New American Library, 1966; London, MacGibbon and Kee, 1967.

Short Stories

The Pagan Rabbi and Other Stories. New York, Knopf, 1971; London, Secker and Warburg, 1972.
Bloodshed and Three Novellas. New York, Knopf, and London, Secker and Warburg, 1976.
Levitation; Five Fictions. New York, Knopf, 1981.

Uncollected Short Story

"The Shawl," in *Prize Stories 1981: The O. Henry Awards*, edited by William Abrahams. New York, Doubleday, 1981.

* * *

Cynthia Ozick is a writer of uncommon talent and commitment. Her conscientious approach to her craft and subject matter places her in a small select group of American writers who, although they probably will never top the bestseller lists, continue to publish fiction of the highest quality.

Although an American, Ozick does not limit her themes to problems of her country in the late 20th century, as do many of her contemporaries. She is first and foremost a Jewish intellectual who has a deep concern for the problems of acceptance of Hebrew culture and tradition by modern Jews. The bulk of her work reflects the conflict faced by Jews living in an alien, Christian world. In what is perhaps Ozick's best short story, "Envy" (*The Pagan Rabbi*), a Yiddish poet laments the decline of an audience for his work. He feels that it marks not only the passing of the language but also the loss of a way of life and communication.

The author herself questions the validity of a Jew writing in English rather than in Yiddish: "English is a Christian language. When I write in English, I live in Christendom." She further probes the problem as she wonders whether or not a Jew is capable of writing fiction at all without breaking the Second Commandment against idol worship, "the point being that the story-making faculty itself can be a corridor to the corruptions and abominations of idol-worship, of the adoration of the magical event." This ambivalent attitude is one that Ozick never fully reconciles in her writing, for her fiction is rich, in symbolism and magical elements.

Trust, her first and largest book, is a long, complex novel. Caught up in a world of money and prestige, Allegra Vand is a woman haunted by her past. The plot centers around Allegra's nameless daughter's search for a biological and psychological father. Although a first novel, *Trust* received a tremendously positive response from critics and readers alike. Ozick displays none of the apparent traits of a novice in this work. The style is assured, the writing is fluent, and the plot is well-constructed.

The novel was followed by *The Pagan Rabbi and Other Stories*, a collection of psychologically demanding tales peopled by a strange succession of characters, all of whom are searching for themselves, trying to discover reasons for their existence. The rabbis, poets, and fellow seekers who long to find meaning in their lives never, for the most part, actually achieve their goals; they find themselves confronted with frustration and the dangers inherent in getting what one thinks he would like to obtain.

In *The Pagan Rabbi and Other Stories*, Ozick makes use of the fantasy and supernatural of which she is admittedly so wary. The title story contains a tree nymph, while a ship's figurehead comes to life in "The Dock-witch." Both of these phantasms work well in their respective tales, but it is not until her next book, *Bloodshed and Three Novellas*, that the author fully realizes her power with symbols and magic. Real and toy guns become metaphors for a psychological struggle between a worldly and an Orthodox Jew. An animated goat and the ghost of a dead writer figure into another story. Although the collection tends to be somewhat inaccessible upon the first reading, it may actually be considered Ozick's best work to date.

Critics have compared Ozick's style to that of Conrad, Lawrence, and Henry James. She is, indeed, a serious stylist. She compromises nothing in her art, thereby raising her work to first-rate fiction.

—Sally H. Bennett

PALEY, Grace. American. Born in New York City, 11 December 1922. Educated at Hunter College, New York, 1938-39. Married 1)Jess Paley in 1942, one daughter and one son; 2)Robert Nichols in 1972. Has taught at Columbia University, New York, and Syracuse University, New York. Currently, Member of the Faculty, Sarah Lawrence College, Bronxville, New York. Recipient: Guggenheim grant, 1961; National Endowment for the Arts grant, 1966; American Academy award, 1970. Address: 126 West 11th Street, New York, New York 10011, U.S.A.

PUBLICATIONS

Short Stories

The Little Disturbances of Man: Stories of Men and Women in Love. New York, Doubleday, 1959; London, Weidenfeld and Nicolson, 1960.
Enormous Changes at the Last Minute. New York, Farrar Straus, 1974; London, Deutsch, 1975.

Uncollected Short Stories

"Dreamers in a Dead Language," in *American Review 26*, edited by Theodore Solotaroff. New York, Bantam, 1977.
"Somewhere Else," in *New Yorker*, 23 October 1978.
"Friends," in *New Yorker*, 18 June 1979.
"Love," in *New Yorker*, 8 October 1979.

* * *

"All that is really necessary for survival of the fittest, it seems, is an interest in life, good, bad, or peculiar." The individuality of Grace Paley's voice—warm, comic, defensive, and without illusions—and the sophistication of her technique led to the reissue of her first collection of short stories, *The Little Disturbances of Man*, ten years after it first appeared. Her stories, invariably set in New York and often with a Jewish background, depend especially on her ear for dialogue. Her realism admits sudden surrealistic perceptions: "A Subject of Childhood" ends as the sun comes out above a woman being comforted by her child for the desertion of her lover: "Then through the short fat fingers of my son, interred forever, like a black and white barred king in Alcatraz, my heart lit up in stripes." Paley's stories have equally arresting openings, and in between these given points of opening and ending she moves, frequently in the first person, with a concision sometimes deliberately telescoped into the absurd, paradoxically reflecting the conviction that "the shortest distance between two points is a great circle."

According to one character, who has risen above the slums of his childhood, the difficulties of a woman bringing up four children on her own in the New York slums are merely "the little disturbances of man" beside the real cataclysms of existence. All the stories in *Enormous Changes at the Last Minute* are set in these slums, but in *The Little Disturbances of Man* Paley ranges over the wider social strata, probing similar preoccupations of loneliness, lust, and escapism. "An Irrevocable Diameter" relates the forced marriage of Charles C. Charley to a rich teenager, less than half his age, who claimed to have seduced him. "The Pale Pink Roast" swings between farce and lyricism in a picture of a woman going to bed with her ex-husband immediately after her new marriage to a richer man. In "In Time Which Made a Monkey of Us All" a slum boy's homemade laboratory experiments lead to his permanent mental breakdown.

Grace Paley's chief concern in *The Little Disturbances of Man* with broken and shifting relationships where the women are dominant is even more important in *Enormous Changes*. For each of the unmarried or separated mothers, it is a question of whether her "capacity for survival has not been overwhelmed by her susceptibility to abuse." Though Paley's strength remains a necessary blend of involvement and detachment, there is a new sense of commitment. The key story is "Faith in a Tree"; when the police break up a tiny demonstration against napalm-bombing in Vietnam, Faith's son defiantly writes up the demonstrators' slogan again. The story concludes: "And I think that is exactly when events turned me around,...directed...by my children's heartfelt brains, I thought more and more and every day about the world."

Earlier in this story, Faith says of some of her neighbours, "our four family units, as people are now called, are doomed to stand culturally still as this society moves on its caterpillar treads from ordinary affluent to absolute empire." These tenants crop up in other stories, some reappearing from *The Little Disturbances of Man*. "An Interest in Life" in the earlier book is retold from another character's angle as "Distance" in the later one: "There is a long time in me between knowing and telling." The last story in *Enormous Changes*, "The Long-Distance Runner," in which Faith literally runs back to her childhood home in Coney Island and stays there for three weeks with the current Black tenants, is a kind of surrealistic finale for both books.

Similarly undermining the illusion of fiction, Paley introduces as first-person narrator a female short-story writer, notably in "Debts," which mentions the Yiddish theatre subject-matter of "Goodbye and Good Luck" in the earlier volume. A father-daughter relationship is important in several stories in *Enormous Changes*; in an introductory note the author states: "Everyone in this book is imagined into life except the father. No matter what story he has to live in, he's my father..." Though these structural tricks point up "the open destiny of life," several stories must end in death. *Enormous Changes at the Last Minute* is altogether darker in tone than *The Little Disturbances of Man*. The interplay of two generations is used to show the long shadow of "the cruel history of Europe" continuing to darken second-generation immigrant lives, while the "last minute" of the title refers to the nuclear threat.

—Val Warner

PATON, Alan (Stewart). South African. Born in Pietermaritzburg, Natal, 11 January 1903. Educated at Maritzburg College, University of Natal, B.Sc. 1923, B.Ed. 1966. Married 1) Doris Francis in 1928 (died, 1967), two sons; 2) Anne Hopkins in 1969. Schoolteacher in Natal, in a native school and at Pietermaritzburg College, 1925-35; Principal, Diepkloof Reformatory, Johannesburg, 1935-48; full-time writer since 1948. Honorary Commissioner, Toc H Southern Africa, Botha's Hill, Natal, 1949-58; President of the Convocation, University of Natal, 1951-55, 1957-59; Founder and President, Liberal Party of South Africa, 1958-68; Chubb Fellow, Yale University, New Haven, Connecticut, 1973. Since 1969, Honorary President, South African National Union of Students. Recipient: Anisfield-Wolf Award, 1948; Newspaper Guild of New York Award, 1949; Freedom House Award, 1960; Free Academy of Arts Medal, Hamburg, 1960; National Conference of Christians and Jews Brotherhood Award, 1962; International League for Human Rights prize, 1977. L.H.D.: Yale University, 1954; D.Litt.: Kenyon College, Gambier, Ohio, 1962; University of Natal, 1968; Harvard University, Cambridge, Massachusetts, 1971; Trent University, Peterborough, Ontario, 1971; Rhodes University, Grahamstown, South Africa, 1972; Willamette University, Salem, Oregon, 1974; University of Michigan, Flint, 1977; D.D.: University of Edinburgh, 1971; LL.D.: University of the Witwatersrand, Johannesburg, 1975. Fellow, Royal Society of Literature, 1961; Honorary Member, Free Academy of Arts, Hamburg, 1961. Address: P.O. Box 278, Hillcrest, Natal, South Africa.

PUBLICATIONS

Novels

Cry, The Beloved Country. London, Cape, and New York, Scribner, 1948.
Too Late the Phalarope. London, Cape, and New York, Scribner, 1953.

Short Stories

Meditation for a Young Boy Confirmed. London, National Society-S.P.C.K., 1944; Cincinnati, Forward Movement, 1954.
Debbie Go Home: Stories. London, Cape, 1961; as *Tales from a Troubled Land*, New York, Scribner, 1961.

Plays

Sponono, with Krishna Shah, adaptation of stories by Paton (produced New York, 1964). New York, Scribner, 1965.

Screenplay: *Cry, The Beloved Country* (*African Fury*), 1952.

Other

Freedom as a Reformatory Instrument. Pretoria, Penal Reform League of South Africa, 1948.
Christian Unity: A South African View. Grahamstown, Rhodes University, 1951.
South Africa Today. New York, Public Affairs Committee, 1951; London, Lutterworth Press, 1953.
Salute to My Great Grandchildren. Johannesburg, St. Benedict's House, 1954.
The Land and People of South Africa. Philadelphia, Lippincott, 1955; as *South Africa and Her People*, London, Lutterworth Press, 1957; revised edition, Lippincott, 1965, 1972; Lutterworth Press, 1970.
South Africa in Transition. New York, Scribner, 1956.
Hope for South Africa. London, Pall Mall Press, 1958; New York, Praeger, 1959.
The People Wept. Privately printed, 1959(?).
The Charlestown Story. Pietermaritzburg, Liberal Party of South Africa, 1961 (?).
Hofmeyr. Cape Town, Oxford University Press, 1964; London, Oxford University Press, 1965; abridged edition, as *South African Tragedy: The Life and Times of Jan Hofmeyr*, New York, Scribner, 1965.
The Long View, edited by Edward Callan. New York, Praeger, and London, Pall Mall Press, 1968.
Instrument of Thy Peace: The Prayer of St. Francis. New York, Seabury Press, 1968; London, Collins, 1970.
Civil Rights and Present Wrongs. Johannesburg, South African Institute of Race Relations, 1968.
Kontakion for You Departed. London, Cape, 1969; as *For You Departed*, New York, Scribner, 1969.
Case History of a Pinky. Johannesburg, South African Institute of Race Relations, 1972.

Apartheid and the Archbishop: The Life and Times of Geoffrey Clayton, Archbishop of Cape Town. Cape Town, Philip, 1973; New York, Scribner, and London, Cape, 1974.
Knocking at the Door: Shorter Writings, edited by Colin Gardner. Cape Town, Philip, and London, Collings, 1975; New York, Scribner, 1976.
Towards the Mountain: An Autobiography. New York, Scribner, 1980; London, Oxford University Press, 1981.

*

Critical Studies: Introduction by Lewis Gannet to *Cry, The Beloved Country*, New York, Scribner, 1950; *Alan Paton* by Edward Callan, New York, Twayne, 1968 (includes bibliography).

Alan Paton comments:

I would not really regard myself as a contemporary novelist. In the fifties I turned to the writing of biography, and at the moment (1980) I am engaged on my autobiography.

* * *

Alan Paton's growing concern with enlightened penology and his personal harassment by compatriots resentful of his unflattering picture of his native South Africa have limited the production of one of the most gifted and compassionate 20th-century fiction writers to two novels and a slender collection of short stories. In *Cry, The Beloved Country* and *Too Late the Phalarope*, however, Paton succeeds in baring to the world the tragic effects and deep-rooted causes of his country's repressive racist policies. Paton's writings are powerful modern renderings of one of the great tragic themes of art through the ages—the contrast between the beauty of the natural world as man found it and the ugly place that his greed and narrow mindedness have made of it.

Cry, The Beloved Country begins "There is a lovely road that runs from Ixopo into the hills. These hills are grass-covered and rolling, and they are lovely beyond any singing of it." From them, "if there is no mist, you look down on one of the fairest valleys in Africa." But this affectionate note cannot be sustained, for all is not well in the valley. Paton himself speaks of the novel as describing "a process of deterioration" and identifies its theme as the change in the black natives' characters as, envious of the white man's world, they leave their tribal lands and discipline to huddle in the slums of the white man's cities.

The novel follows the Reverend Stephen Kumalo of Ndotsheni, Natal, as he searches in "the great city," Johannesburg, for his son Absalom. He discovers that the boy—who has been in a reformatory—has shot and killed during a robbery attempt a white man, Arthur Jarvis, the son of a wealthy landowner who lives in the hills above Ndotsheni. Ironically, Arthur Jarvis has been one of the most courageous white fighters for justice for the African blacks. At the time of his death, he had been working on a paper called "The Truth about Native Crime."

Although Absalom pleads that he shot in fear and did not intend to kill Jarvis, he is sentenced to be hanged. His father takes home the pregnant girl that the boy marries after he is condemned; but the preacher is unsuccessful in bringing home also his errant sister Gertrude. As a result of Arthur Jarvis's young son's visiting Kumalo's church, the elder Jarvis and the black minister are brought together and measures are taken to rehabilitate the black farming community. Thus Jarvis helps realize his dead son's dream of setting up "another system of order and tradition and convention" to replace the old tribal system that the white man has thoughtlessly destroyed, so that at last out of the evil spawned by fear comes a promise of good for the community.

Too Late the Phalarope deals only secondarily with racial problems and focuses primarily on the tragic consequences of the austere, loveless way of life of the Afrikaans-speaking descendants of the Dutch settlers in South Africa. Pieter van Vlaanderen has been a heroic soldier in World War II and is a police lieutenant and rugby player whom both black and white communities hold in almost god-like respect. Yet there is a dark, secret side to the young man that is revealed by the distraught, sympathetic aunt who tells his story. Although always respectful, Pieter has been alienated from his father since the boy at the age of 14 was deprived of his stamp collection for failing to be at the top of his class. When at 17 he received first-class marks in his Matriculation Examination, the collection was restored, but the boy did not thank the father nor would he ever speak about the stamps again. He has also become alienated from his shy, fearful wife because she cannot respond adequately to his demands for love. A dispute over the identification of a bird called the *phalarope* in a book of South African birds that Pieter gives his father promises to bring the two men into the kind of joyous relationship that they had lost long ago; but the novel's title stresses that the older man's overture comes too late. Pieter has already been driven by his strong passions into an illicit affair with a black woman. Terror assails Pieter as he begins to receive anonymous messages intimating that his liaison has been observed and as the black girl—out of work—begins to beg for money. Pieter is entrapped by a jealous, self-righteous police sergeant; and the news of his crime results in his father's death, his family's ostracism, and the termination of his sister's engagement. The aunt prophesies that after Pieter is released from jail, he and his family will be obliged to leave the country that he has served with such distinction. *Too Late the Phalarope* is not simply a South African tragedy, however. While Pieter van Vlaanderen is a victim of the fear and ignorance of his fellow countrymen, he symbolizes all those extraordinary men everywhere who demand a more dynamic life than their pusillanimous societies can provide and thus must suffer for their honesty, enlightenment, and irrepressible human desires.

The title of *Tales from a Troubled Land*, Paton's collection of short stories, suggests the contents. Perhaps the most memorable, "The Waste Land," epitomizes Paton's ironic view of the South African situation and relates it—through the use of the title of T.S. Eliot's famous poem—to the condition of 20th-century man generally. The brief tale tells of a frightened black man killing one of three young robbers who are pursuing him across a junkyard and then discovering when the boy's companions shove his body under the same truck chassis that hides the man that the boy is his own son.

—Warren French

PATTERSON, (Horace) Orlando (Lloyd). Jamaican. Born in Jamaica, 5 June 1940. Educated at the University of the West Indies, Kingston, 1959-62 (Jamaica Government Exhibition Scholar), B.Sc. in economics 1962; London School of Economics (Commonwealth Scholar), Ph.D. in sociology 1965. Married Nerys Wyn in 1963; two children. Assistant Lecturer in Sociology, London School of Economics, 1965-67; Consultant and Tutor in Sociology, Hawker Siddeley Dynamics, London, 1966-67; Lecturer in Sociology, University of the West Indies, 1967-70; Associate Professor of Afro-American Studies, 1970-71, and Professor of Sociology and Allston Burr Senior Tutor, 1971-73, Harvard University, Cambridge, Massachusetts. Since 1972, Special Advisor, Prime Minister's Office, Jamaica. Member of the Editorial Board, *New Left Review*, London, 1965-66. Recipient: Dakar Festival Prize, 1966. M.A.: Harvard University, 1971. Address: 15 Shepard Street, Cambridge, Massachusetts 02138, U.S.A.

PUBLICATIONS

Novels

The Children of Sisyphus. London, Hutchinson, 1964; Boston, Houghton Mifflin, 1965.

An Absence of Ruins. London, Hutchinson, 1967.
Die the Long Day. New York, Morrow, 1972; London, Mayflower, 1973.

Uncollected Short Stories

"The Very Funny Man: A Tale in Two Moods" and "One for a Penny," in *Stories from the Caribbean*, edited by Andrew Salkey. London, Elek, 1965; as *Island Voices*, New York, Liveright, 1970.
"The Alien," in *New Left Review* (London), September-October 1965.
"Into the Dark," in *Jamaica Journal* (Kingston), i, 2, 1968.

Other

The Sociology of Slavery: An Analysis of the Origins, Development, and Structure of Negro Slave Society in Jamaica. London, MacGibbon and Kee, 1967; Rutherford, New Jersey, Fairleigh Dickinson University Press, 1968.
Ethnic Chauvinism: The Reactionary Impulse. New York, Stein and Day, 1977.

*

Manuscript Collection: University of the West Indies, Kingston.

Critical Studies: reviews by Robert Baldick, in *Daily Telegraph* (London), 20 March 1964; in *Times Literary Supplement* (London), 2 April 1964; by Robert Nye in *The Guardian* (London), 25 June 1965 and 7 April 1967.

Orlando Patterson comments:
My main concern is with the theme of survival on all levels—physical, emotional, moral. Also concerned with related themes of isolation and exile.

* * *

Jamaican fiction is marked by its "realistic" examination of the local social scene. Though this reduces neither its technical range nor its emotional potency—the prose tone poems of Roger Mais, the imaginative adventures of Andrew Salkey, and the mythmaking of Vic Reid and Lindsay Barrett offer ready evidence to the contrary—it does mean that its central concern for the sociological exigencies of daily life often overcomes the urge to use words to build worlds rather than to analyze them. Of the contemporary analytic writers, three stand out as particularly shrewd observers/participators: John Hearne, whose austere novels explore the political impact of race and class; Sylvia Wynter, whose Marxist economic observations underlie her interpretation of Jamaican history; and Orlando Patterson, the sociologist, whose sense of individual potential is informed and guided always by his understanding of class structure and slave heritage.

Patterson's treatise *The Sociology of Slavery*, an analysis of the patterns of negro slave society in Jamaica, supplies an intelligent background to his novels, considering both the subservient and the resistant responses of the slave population to white society, and the social institutions—sorcery, religion, folk song and story, and so on—that provided some way of contending with life. To Patterson's mind, those responses and institutions continue to exert their effect, and in his novels he has attempted to demonstrate the inhibition that such a history casts over the lives of people today. Freedom in such a world is a watchword and a dream, always urging individuals into open acts of defiance, and always thwarted by the dead weight of the past.

The Children of Sisyphus is set in the slum world of Kingston, and traces the attempts that the prostitute Dinah makes to break out of the Dungle, to flee her surroundings and the course of life that circumstance has forced her into, and to find happiness, order, peace. Paralleling her search is the back-to-Africa quest of the Rastafarian movement, seeking its heritage and home in Ethiopia—"the soil...so fertile with everything that's joy back home in Zion"—and a different dream of freedom. But just as that dream is denied by deceit within Rastafarian ranks, so inside Dinah's experience is the Dungle that she cannot altogether leave. Drawn back to it and destroyed, she is typical of not only *her* world, but in Patterson's view *the* world. The suicide that closes the novel, the "soul-consuming" mockery of the shanty surroundings and the universal void, and the attempt thus to reach paradise wilfully supply an ironic perspective towards man's lot. The human ritual of striving for order appears as nothing so much as flight from uncertainty—a negative rather than a positive action—and because it is founded in emptiness and need, it lacks the self-possession that might make it anything but futile. Hence the circle back to the Dungle, like Dinah's, is closed, and absurd. For Alexander Blackman, in *An Absence of Ruins*, the discovery of such a relationship with futility voids his attempts not only to enunciate his identity but also to believe in his possession of one. Walking in London at the end, he recognizes himself only as an absence, the nothingness that a cipher concretely and phenomenally represents: "I cannot say whether I am civilized or savage, standing as I do outside of race, outside of culture, outside of history, outside of any value that could make your question meaningful. I am busy going nowhere, but I must keep up the appearance of going in order to forget that I am not." Thus the dilemma of existentiality—the conflict involved between intention, desire, history, and circumstance—is taken from Camus and given Caribbean voice. As Patterson realized, freeing the mind from slavery is a greater task than freeing the body, for it cannot be enacted by law. When people do not even believe in their capacity to attain freedom, however, the knowledge of the absurdity of their actions offers little comfort and no cure, and becomes their only reality.

—W.H. New

PEARSON, Bill (William Harrison Pearson). New Zealander. Born in Greymouth, 18 January 1922. Educated at Greymouth Technical High School; Canterbury University College, Christchurch, 1939, 1947-48; University of Otago, Dunedin, 1940-41, B.A., M.A.; King's College, London, 1949-51, Ph.D. 1952. Served in the New Zealand forces, in Fiji, Egypt, Italy, and Japan, 1942-46. Student Teacher, Dunedin Teachers Training College, 1940-41; Teacher, Blackball School, 1942, Oxford District High School, 1949, and in London County Council schools, 1952-53; Lecturer in English, University of Auckland, 1954-66; Senior Research Fellow, Department of Pacific History, Australian National University, Canberra, 1967-69. Since 1970, Associate Professor of English, University of Auckland. Closely associated with Maori students at the University of Auckland, 1956-66, and was Patron of their Club for some of those years; internal rapporteur at several Maori Leadership Conferences, 1959-63. Recipient: *Landfall* Readers' Award, for non-fiction, 1960; New Zealand Prose Award, for non-fiction, 1975. Address: Department of English, University of Auckland, Private Bag, Auckland, New Zealand.

PUBLICATIONS

Novel

Coal Flat. Hamilton, Paul's Book Arcade, and London, Angus and Robertson, 1963; revised edition, Auckland, Longmans Paul, 1970.

Uncollected Short Stories

"The Sins of the Fathers," in *Canterbury University College Review* (Christchurch), 1947.

"Indemnity," in *Canterbury Lambs* (Christchurch), 1947.
"Social Catharsis," in *Landfall* (Christchurch), December 1947; as "Purge," in *New-Story* (Paris), January 1952.
"At the Leicesters'," in *Canterbury Lambs* (Christchurch), 1948.
"Babes in the Bush," in *New-Story* (Paris), May 1951.

Other

Henry Lawson among Maoris. Canberra, Australian National University Press, and Wellington, Reed, 1968.
Fretful Sleepers and Other Essays. Auckland, Heinemann, 1974.

Editor, *Collected Stories, 1935-63*, by Frank Sargeson. Auckland, Blackwood and Janet Paul, 1964; London, MacGibbon and Kee, 1965.
Editor, *Brown Man's Burden and Later Stories*, by Roderick Finlayson. Auckland, Auckland University Press-Oxford University Press, 1973.

*

Critical Studies: "*Coal Flat*: The Major Scale, The Fine Excess," in *Comment* (Wellington), October 1963, and "*Coal Flat* Revisited," in *Critical Essays on the New Zealand Novel* edited by Cherry Hankin, Auckland, Heinemann, 1976, both by Allen Curnow; *The New Zealand Novel 1860-1965* by Joan Stevens, Wellington, Reed, 1966; "Conversation on a Train" by Frank Sargeson, in *Landfall* (Christchurch), December 1967; *New Zealand Fiction since 1945* by H. Winston Rhodes, Dunedin, McIndoe, 1968.

Bill Pearson comments:

Some commentators have seen a correspondence between my aims in *Coal Flat* and my analysis of the motifs of New Zealand behaviour and the implications for the artist which I wrote in 1951, "Fretful Sleepers."

While it has been said that a traditional structure, with subplots and a wide range of characters, is appropriate to a social novel set in a community whose attitudes and aspirations and social relations were rooted in 19th-century Britain, it has sometimes been a matter of objection that I chose a structure and style that appeared to take no cognisance of the developments in the form of the novel since Joyce. Yet I think that those commentators who stress the social realism or what they miscall "sociology" have been thrown off by a distaste for what they mistake for an outmoded technique, appropriate to *New Writing* reportage. The writers in the light of whose practice my aspirations as a writer developed were those that in common with young men of my time I read with sympathy and a deep respect, Lawrence, Joyce, Forster, Faulkner, Hemingway, Koestler; and I had a series of passions for the novels of Virginia Woolf and John Dos Passos and Thomas Hardy. At the time of my novel's first conception in 1946, the novelist who most excited me was Graham Greene. What I hoped to do when I was writing it (mostly in 1952 and 1953) was to devise a traditional structure that would be large enough to comprehend a community and sensitive enough to reflect the crises of feeling and conscience that might come to a man who was out of sympathy with the materialist values of the community. The plot would grow easily from the initial situation and by its own logic would reach a satisfying outcome without recourse to any of the tricks and evasions or improbabilities by which some of the 19th-century English novelists reached their answers. I had found, I thought, theoretical justification in Aristotle's conception of the plot as the probable and necessary consequence of certain initial acts and I conceived it as having the shape of the noble symmetrical curve that I saw in the plots of *Troilus and Criseyde* and *Wuthering Heights* and the great 19th-century Russian novels. This was not a scale that I pretended my ability or the comparatively pedestrian quality of New Zealand life would allow me to reach. But my concern for probability was necessary as a check against the rhetorical falsification that would be the risk of writing in the awareness of such examples, created from other communities and other times. My hope was to achieve an imaginative authenticity that my countrymen would immediately recognise as true, and which at the same time would be sufficiently clear of the accidents of parochiality to translate into human experience recognisable to readers from other societies. Whether I succeeded in this I cannot tell; but no one but an expatriate knows the pleasure of imaginatively recreating one's country in its detail, without sentimentality. It has often surprised me that some New Zealand commentators have seen sourness and "unappeased resentment" in a work that was written with love.

Since the moral meaning of the novel was to be in the sequence or consequence of events and their outcome, it was this rather than diction or characters or setting that demanded most thought. In its 13 years between conception and the last version, the novel survived a number of re-thinkings and radical overhauls, by which I think it gained. The last major revision was the discarding of a superficially optimistic ending, in keeping with a broadly Marxist literary theory hardly tenable after the events of 1956.

When I am moved to write fiction again, however, it is likely to be different in treatment.

* * *

Bill Pearson, essayist, critic, and scholar, has edited Frank Sargeson's *Collected Stories*, written about the impact of Western society on the Polynesian as reflected in literature, investigated in *Henry Lawson among Maoris* a little known area of the Australian writer's life, and produced a number of short stories together with a long novel, *Coal Flat*. Novels are sometimes written with a thesis. This may be religious or sociological but, whichever it is, the thesis may too easily destroy those qualities we have a right to expect in any attempt to create a life-like representation.

Coal Flat contains a thesis but survives as a novel. In "Fretful Sleepers," described as "a sketch of New Zealand behaviour and its implications for the artist," Pearson suggested that "our job is to penetrate the torpor and out of meaningless make a pattern that means something." *Coal Flat*, with its depressing but significant title, became not only a demonstration of the difficulties involved in such an attempt, but also as a novel partially fulfilled the aim that had been proposed for at least some artists.

Without allowing it to turn into satire or degenerate into a sociological survey, Pearson chose a small coal-mining and gold-dredging settlement on the West Coast of New Zealand in order to chart the course of family and community life; and by close attention to naturalistic detail evoked its oppressive narrowness, puritanism, and smugness. At one level the reader is introduced to a wide range of provincial characters, including the publican, parson, policeman, and visiting politicians, to miners, dredgers and their officials, to schoolteachers and children, to the doctor and priest, all firmly established in their local setting that combines natural grandeur with human inadequacy. The shriek of the dredge echoes and re-echoes through the book and acts as an inhuman accompaniment to the bitter animosities, perverted affections, and destructive behaviour of the people of Coal Flat. At another and perhaps more significant level these become signs and portents of a wider deterioration in the quality of life, extending well beyond its confines. Nevertheless, Coal Flat is by no means an inferno of lost souls. There are kindness, comradeship, and loyalty in abundance; there is not even a complete absence of sweetness and light; there are moments of idyllic charm and many good intentions. It is New Zealand, the world, reduced to Coal Flat.

Because its pitfalls cannot always be avoided, a close adherence to the slightly outmoded method of naturalism is liable to provoke criticism that is seldom without justification. *Coal Flat* is not a faultless novel, but it is a valuable one and especially for New Zealand. By the accumulation of detail relevant to the settlement and its inhabitants, by involving the central character, a young teacher of liberal instincts, in a mesh of conflicting loyalties, Pearson is able to dramatise the struggle between the individual conscience and the collective will, explore personal and family relationships in the broader context of the community and reveal distortions of sexual, parental, and social love. *Coal Flat* is neither a blueprint for future novels about New Zealand, nor is it an imitation of earlier novels in the naturalistic mode; but its achievement is such that it becomes an anatomy of social and spiritual decline, an exploration of the impoverishment of life, and a melancholy comment on thwarted but confused idealism unable to make headway against the conventional attitudes and mental lethargy of the majority.

—H. Winston Rhodes

PERCY, Walker. American. Born in Birmingham, Alabama, 28 May 1916. Educated at the University of North Carolina, Chapel Hill, B.A. 1937; Columbia University, New York, M.D. 1941; intern at Bellevue Hospital, New York, 1942. Married Mary Bernice Townsend in 1946; two daughters. Contracted tuberculosis, gave up medicine, and became a full-time writer, 1943. Recipient: National Book Award, 1962; American Academy grant, 1967; National Catholic Book Award, 1972. Address: P.O. Box 510, Covington, Louisiana 70433, U.S.A.

PUBLICATIONS

Novels

The Moviegoer. New York, Knopf, 1961; London, Eyre and Spottiswoode, 1963.
The Last Gentleman. New York, Farrar Straus, 1966; London, Eyre and Spottiswoode, 1967.
Love in the Ruins: The Adventures of a Bad Catholic at a Time Near the End of the World. New York, Farrar Straus, and London, Eyre and Spottiswoode, 1971.
Lancelot. New York, Farrar Straus, and London, Secker and Warburg, 1977.
The Second Coming. New York, Farrar Straus, 1980; London, Secker and Warburg, 1981.

Other

The Message in the Bottle: How Queer Man Is, How Queer Language Is, and What One Has to Do with the Other. New York, Farrar Straus, 1975.

*

Critical Studies: *The Sovereign Wayfarer: Walker Percy's Diagnosis of the Malaise* by Martin Luschei, Baton Rouge, Louisiana State University Press, 1972; *Walker Percy: An American Search* by Robert Coles, Boston, Little Brown, 1978; *The Art of Walker Percy: Strategems for Being* edited by Panthea Broughton, Baton Rouge, Louisiana State University Press, 1979; *Walker Percy: Art and Ethics* edited by Jac Tharpe, Jackson, University Press of Mississippi, 1980.

* * *

Walker Percy is that rare phenomenon of American letters: a philosophical novelist. He is a Catholic and a Southerner and his novels, firmly grounded in social observation, are a working out of his own special version of the problem of being. Percy finds the modern world in a state of moral confusion; the values of the past no longer hold, and the majority of men are spiritually dead, abstracted, cut off from life outside themselves. Percy's protagonists to some extent share in this confusion but are set apart by their awareness of the problem and, especially, by their ability to love. While that ability raises them above the general spiritual deadness, it also creates a special kind of problem which, simply stated, is: How can a man find his way in a world that regards love as a mechanical act, particularly when the traditional view he has to fall back on treats love as a set of grand ideals having little to do with physical reality? Each novel explores this dilemma.

The Moviegoer concludes with the protagonist, a lusty 30-year-old bachelor, failing in his latest sexual escapade and marrying a neurotic young woman of his own class, apparently out of affection, a feeling of kinship, and a sense of *experienced* responsibility. In *The Last Gentleman* the hero, who suffers from abstraction and the modern malaise of detachment, cures himself through his personal devotion to a dying youth and, in turn, helps cure a confused and beautiful young woman and her older brother, a cynical, corrupt doctor. *Love in the Ruins*, which is set in the future ("at a time near the end of the world") deals with the collapse of modern technology and concludes with the responsible marriage of the protagonist who had tried to save his mad world but, failing at that, had given himself up to whisky and lust for three beautiful women. Significantly he marries the most responsible and moral of the three and begins to live a simple, natural, and properly lustful life. *Lancelot* considers the problem from the point of view of a self-deceived moralist, a kind of latter-day gnostic who demands perfection of everyone but himself and ends by committing murder and arson. In *The Second Coming* Percy takes up again the story of Will Barrett of *The Last Gentleman* and shows how his hero's love for the fugitive from a mental asylum becomes the means of combatting alienation and despair.

While the philosophical and moral bases of Percy's novels are familiar enough, his rendering of characters and scenes is strikingly fresh, vivid, and bitingly satirical. He is a moral and, ultimately, a religious writer, but he is also a novelist of manners who can delineate with remarkable skill the contrast between certain kinds of Northerners, Southerners, and Midwesterners. Also, though he confines himself for the most part to the region around New Orleans, Percy is able to extend the implications of his material by creating characters and events obviously derived from the national scene, such as the white man who, some time back, went about the country masquerading as a Negro, and the Masters-Johnson studies in sexual response. Percy's style, which is sensitive and poetic, elevates material that less subtly treated might have seemed contrived and even moralistic.

—W.J. Stuckey

PERUTZ, Kathrin. American. Born in New York City, 1 July 1939. Educated at Barnard College, New York, B.A. 1960; New York University, M.A. 1966. Married Michael Studdert-Kennedy in 1966; one child. Lived in London, 1960-64. Executive Director, Contact Programs Inc., New York. Address: 16 Avalon Road, Great Neck, Long Island, New York 11021, U.S.A.

PUBLICATIONS

Novels

The Garden. London, Heinemann, and New York, Atheneum, 1962.
A House on the Sound. London, Heinemann, 1964; New York, Coward McCann, 1965.
The Ghosts. London, Heinemann, 1966.

Mother Is a Country: A Popular Fantasy. New York, Harcourt Brace, and London, Heinemann, 1968.
Reigning Passions: Leopold von Sacher-Masoch and the Hapsburg Empire. Philadelphia, Lippincott, and London, Weidenfeld and Nicolson, 1978.

Uncollected Short Story

"An American Success," in *Voices 2*, edited by Michael Ratcliffe. London, Joseph, 1965.

Other

Beyond the Looking Glass: America's Beauty Culture. New York, Morrow, 1970; as *Beyond the Looking Glass: Life in the Beauty Culture*, London, Hodder and Stoughton, 1970.
Marriage Is Hell: It's Better to Burn Than to Marry. New York, Morrow, 1972; as *The Marriage Fallacy: It's Better to Burn Than to Marry*, London, Hodder and Stoughton, 1972; as *Liberated Marriage*, New York, Pyramid, 1973.
I'd Love To, But What'll I Wear?, with Polly Bergen. New York, Wyden, 1977.

*

Critical Studies: "K. Perutz," in *Don't Never Forget* by Brigid Brophy, London, Cape, 1966; "The Truth about Fiction" by George P. Elliott, in *Holiday* (New York), March 1966.

Kathrin Perutz comments:

(1972) The only general theme (or background) of my books is America. *Mother Is a Country* is a direct parody of certain American dreams (the acquisition of power and the desire to become a commodity); *A House on the Sound* charts the distance from reality to where rich liberals have their camp. *Beyond the Looking Glass*, a non-fiction book often fictionalized, examines preoccupation with appearance in America, where people have the hope of seeming what they have not yet become, and where self-knowledge is replaced by concern over minutiae of deception.

My first three novels also concern sub-rosa relationships, the area of self that is undeveloped or suppressed. *The Garden* presents a love affair between two girls, not Lesbian (both girls are young and boy-crazy), but of an essential intensity to contradict fears of not existing. *A House on the Sound* shows different manifestations of embryonic love—homosexuality, incest, masochism—never acknowledged by the characters. The two main characters of *The Ghosts* have not reconciled themselves to the sexual roles, male and female, they are supposed to play, and often parody or pervert these roles.

But mainly, each book has been my attempt to learn more of the craft. The first was a simple diary; the second tried, in six hours, to cut through time past and present, more similar to movie techniques than traditional flashbacks. The third book tried to give a sense of development, over the space of a year. The fourth, a satire, was deliberately "surface," a board game played over true but generalized emotions. My fifth book presented problems of journalism, in organization of material, tone, pace, and the creation of a personal, but abstracted, narrator.

(1975) My last book, *Marriage Is Hell*, is an essay on the institution of marriage as it exists today in the West, particularly in America. It deals with the anachronism of marriage, its false expectations, its imprisonment of personality and distortion of both privacy and personal liberty. The book, which is strongly opinionated, attacks marriage from many perspectives—legal, historical, anthropological, sexual—and then goes on to suggest reform and finally a turning that will make marriage possible again. I consciously tried to keep the style loose and colloquial, the better to let readers argue with me, and literary experiment is superseded in this book by political, or pragmatic, aims.

* * *

Kathrin Perutz has a baroque spider-web sensibility; it is as exquisite as it is tough, and permits her to explore such matters as incest, sadomasochism, homosexuality, suicide, and murder with the delicacy of an appropriate dinner wine. It is the most pervasive force in her novels and the one that diminishes the importance of whatever flaws may appear in them as a consequence of her experimentation with form and theme.

The first novel, *The Garden*, is a straightforward first-person narrative of life at a small women's college in Massachusetts. Its treatment of the urge to put aside the burden of virginity becomes tedious, and the book is marked with jejune expressions ("O.K., Pats, shoot") that may be true to dormitory life but are vexatious in a novel. Perutz handles the garden symbolism of the novel well, however; describes a memorably tender, vivacious relationship between Kath and the Blossom, the two principal characters; and, with perfect briskness of pace and lightness of tone, captures the banal essence of a party weekend at an American men's college probably better than any other writer has.

The Ghosts, Perutz's third novel, walks the maze of a love affair in which the participants—or combatants—Luke, an excessively cerebral writer, and Judith, an undercerebral but sensitive hairdresser, are haunted chiefly by Luke's dead father and an assortment of cast-off lovers. The deficiency of the volume is that there is no one with whom an audience would much care to identify. Luke is insatiably clinical toward the involvement, and he and Panda, a deep platonic love of his who befriends Judith, are sometimes mouthpieces discussing their actions and Judith's, and examining one of the immediate themes of the novel, abortion, and, of more general metaphysical interest, the nature of human action. The conception of the characters is acute; their mechanism, however, is too much exposed and not enough is left for the reader to infer. They are often pieces of an essay rather than people in a work of fiction. Judith is too pliable, too much prop for Luke, until the end, when she takes control of herself and Luke becomes more human. But that occurs too late to place the novel in balance.

Mother Is a Country is a satiric fantasy that strikes at the mass-produced, antiseptic, Saran-wrapped materialism in American life. That quality accounts for the death of the three main characters, and the most palpable reaction in the cosmically unfeeling nation is that "a mother eagle in her nest flapped powerful wings and laid another egg." Though the book has been criticized for its superficiality of characterization, it can be argued that since superficial consumerism is primarily what the satire is about, John Scudley (a hero with much of the feeling of a Bellow character, but without the profundity) and the other characters are properly shallow. *Reigning Passions*, Perutz's latest novel, has done nothing to enhance her reputation. It is a fictionalized account of the complex man who gave his name to masochism, and so flat are the nuances of his life made to seem that to get through the book it helps to have a fair dose of the affliction.

It was Perutz's second novel, *A House on the Sound*, that proved her excellence. She paints a dinner party of sham liberals on a small canvas with precise detail, probing through the word, the facial expression, the gesture, the nuance of conversation the variety of characters present and their secret relationships. In this and in her control of time through brief, illuminating flashbacks and staging of the moments of her characters, there is the clear echo—but just the echo—of Virginia Woolf. When the experimentation ends, as far as it ever does, it is to be hoped that Perutz will return to a place like the house on the Sound and give full voice to her sensibility.

—Alan R. Shucard

PETERKIEWICZ, Jerzy (Michal). British. Born in Fabianki, Poland, 29 September 1916; emigrated to England in 1940. Educated at Dlugosz School, Wloclawek; University of Warsaw; University of St. Andrews, Scotland, M.A. 1944; King's College, London, Ph.D. 1947. Married Christine Brooke-Rose, *q.v.*, in 1948 (divorced, 1975). Lecturer, 1950-64, Reader, 1964-72, and Professor of Polish Language and Literature, 1972-79, School of Slavonic and East European Studies, University of London. Address: 7 Lyndhurst Terrace, London N.W.3, England.

PUBLICATIONS

Novels

Umarli nie są Bezbronni. Glasgow, Książnica, 1943.
The Knotted Cord. London, Heinemann, 1953; New York, Roy, 1954.
Loot and Loyalty. London, Heinemann, 1955.
Future to Let. London, Heinemann, 1958; Philadelphia, Lippincott, 1959.
Isolation: A Novel in Five Acts. London, Heinemann, 1959; New York, Holt Rinehart, 1960.
The Quick and the Dead. London, Macmillan, 1961.
The Angel Burning at My Left Side. London, Macmillan, 1963.
Inner Circle. London, Macmillan, 1966.
Green Flows the Bile. London, Joseph, 1969.

Plays

Sami Swoi (produced London, 1949).
Scena Ma Trzy Sciany. London, Wiadomości, 1974.
The Third Adam, music by Panufnik (broadcast, 1978). London, Oxford University Press, 1975.

Radio Play: *The Third Adam*, 1978.

Verse

Prowincja. Warsaw, 1936.
Wiersze i Poematy. Warsaw, Prosto z Mostu, 1938.
Pokarm Cierpki. London, Myśli Polskiej, 1943.
Piaty Poemat. Paris, Instytut Literacki, 1950.
Poematy Londynskie i Wiersze Przedwojenne. Paris, Kultura, 1965.

Other

Znaki na Niebie. London, Przyjaciot, 1940.
Po Chlopsku: Powieść. London, Mildner, 2 vols., 1941.
Pogrzeb Europy. London, Mildner, 1946.
The Other Side of Silence: The Poet at the Limits of Language. London and New York, Oxford University Press, 1970.

Editor, *Polish Prose and Verse.* London, Athlone Press, 1956.
Editor and Translator, *Antologia liryki angielskiej 1300-1950.* London, Veritas, 1958.
Editor and Translator, with Burns Singer, *Five Centuries of Polish Poetry 1450-1950.* London, Secker and Warburg, 1960; Philadelphia, Dufour, 1962; revised edition, with Jon Stallworthy, as *Five Centuries of Polish Poetry 1450-1970*, London and New York, Oxford University Press, 1970.

Translator, *Easter Vigil and Other Poems*, by Karol Wojtyla. London, Hutchinson, and New York, Random House, 1979.

*

Critical Studies: in *New Statesman* (London), 10 October 1959; *Sunday Times Magazine* (London), 10 June 1962; "Speaking of Writing" by the author, in *The Times* (London), 9 January 1964; *Le Monde* (Paris), 28 June 1967; *The Novel Now* by Anthony Burgess, London, Faber, 1968; by the author, in *Times Literary Supplement* (London), 30 July 1971.

Jerzy Peterkiewicz comments:

If titles are significant, *Isolation* and *Inner Circle* seem to be my representative novels, both structurally and thematically.

* * *

Three of Jerzy Peterkiewicz's last six novels are comic entertainments of a high order of literary craftsmanship; three others show a marked falling-off of standards. His first novels have little bearing on the later work. *The Knotted Cord* is a genuinely moving account of a peasant boyhood in Poland; its hero has to escape from many things, but particularly from the "cord" of the scratchy brown cassock that his pious mother has thrust him into, and from all that cord represents. The work is a "first novel" of promise, and it is a pity the Peterkiewicz has chosen not to develop or integrate into his later work a mode which might have provided a carbohydrate counterbalance to the sometimes too frothy champagne of the books which follow. *Loot and Loyalty* is a trivial and poorly constructed historical novel about a 17th-century Scots soldier of fortune exiled in Poland, and his connection with the "false Dmitri."

Future to Let, the first of the really successful books, is less "mannerist" by far than its successors. It is a very funny roman à clef on the tortured loves, English, plots, and politics of contemporary Polish emigrés, chief among them Julian Atrament ("ink" in Polish), quite unidentifiable, of course, but almost recognizable, whose "escape to freedom" by means of his St. Bernard dog is Peterkiewicz's finest comic turn. *Isolation*, probably his best book, parodies the erotic mystifications of a modern spy story with a skill that even the suggestions of deep meanings about the mutual isolation of sexuality, etc., cannot spoil. The Powell-esque (or Waugh-like) Commander Shrimp (alias Pennyworthing), faded semi-spy and bathetic con-man, is a great comic creation. *That Angel Burning at My Left Side* has some of the virtues of *The Knotted Cord*; it is realism with a light touch, of a boy growing up through the Second World War and post-war refugeehood, looking for father, country, and self. The gimmick of the "angels" grows tiresome, but descriptions of place and event and the hero himself are vivid and concrete—until the hero gets to England, and everything, including him, suddenly (and apparently inadvertently on the author's part) becomes less real.

The three unsuccessful works include *The Quick and the Dead*, a spoof ghost-story and fantasy of serio-comic realism, involving among other things the amorous relations of the dead in Limbo, the suffering and repentance of ghosts (a somewhat Golding-like concept), with significance, apparently, but the coy handling of its basic situation makes for heavy reading. Still harder to read, but even more significant, is *Inner Circle*, in which a three-layered story of Surface (the far future), Underground (present-day sub-Firbankian London), and Sky (a version of the Eden story), is held together by repeated "circle" and "underground" image patterns, and by analogous destinies. The themes and point-of-view games again make it seem almost like a collaboration between Golding, Burgess, and Arthur C. Clarke. Peterkiewicz's most recent novel, *Green Flows the Bile*, is as tastelessly affected a social satire as its title would suggest. It recounts the last journey together of two "fellow-travellers" (in all senses), the Secretary, a "political gigolo," and his employer, the "senior prophet of the age...the travelling peace salesman." The comic travelogue is passable in places, but the political satire is either painfully obvious or intensely private; the two pitfalls that await the topical roman à clef have caught Peterkiewicz this time.

Peterkiewicz's heroes are almost all coyly hollow semi-comic shadow-men, pretending to contain abysses and seeking with morose jocularity for an "identity" to which they are fundamentally indifferent. Their human relationships are sketched with equal shallowness. Even the intrigues are lower Greene-land, territory more powerfully explored by Burgess, though at times Peterkiewicz is clearly aiming for the playful, complex "meanings" of a Chesterton, or a Woolf (*Orlando*), or a Nabokov, or for the light, horrid satire of a Waugh (*Scott-King's Modern Europe*). Stage-metaphors, mirrors, masks, costumes, photographs, cute but pallid versions of Nabokovian artifices, crowd the pages of *Isolation*, in which mock-pornography and reciprocal voyeuristic spyings, slowly building up a posthumous portrait, bring to mind *Lolita* (courteously, or perhaps coincidentally, acknowledged in a parrot of that name) or *The Real Life of Sebastian Knight*. These are samples of tone, not assertions of source; but even the best of Peterkiewicz's work is marred by hearing continually whispered chords made up of the murmurs of other men's voices, almost as if he were unwilling to hear his own voice. His real talent for language and comedy is almost swamped by his need to be terribly à la mode in these six novels, and it is a pity, for, to paraphrase a comment he makes on one of his characters, "his anonymous extraterritorial aura predicts at every step a possible eruption of personality."

It may be that, for all the polished virtues and assurance of his better novels, Peterkiewicz will be remembered longest and known most widely for his critical essays and anthologies, and for his book *The Other Side of Silence*, in which he sensitively discusses some intricacies of modern literature and places Polish literature in their context. One would like, however, to have as well his views on his own Polish contemporaries, who are giving us one of the most flourishing of modern minor literatures. Perhaps in his criticism he has more truly earned the right than he has in his fiction, to the inevitable, and specious, comparison with Conrad, that other Polish man of letters who turned himself, in adult life, and not without success, into an English writer.

—Patricia Merivale

PETRAKIS, Harry Mark. American. Born in St. Louis, Missouri, 5 June 1923. Educated at the University of Illinois, Urbana, 1940-41. Married Diane Perparos in 1945; three children. Has worked in steelmills, as a real-estate salesman, truck driver, and sales correspondent. Since 1960, free-lance writer and lecturer. Taught at the Indiana University Writers Conference, Bloomington, 1964-65, 1970, 1974; McGuffey Visiting Lecturer, Ohio University, Athens, 1971; Writer-in-Residence, Chicago Public Library, 1976-77, and for the Chicago Board of Education, 1978-80; taught at workshops at University of Wisconsin, Rhinelander, 1978-80, and University of Rochester, New York, 1979-80. Recipient: *Atlantic* "Firsts" Award, 1957; Benjamin Franklin Citation, 1957; Friends of American Writers Award, 1964; Friends of Literature Award, 1964. D.H.L.: University of Illinois, 1971. Address: 80 East Road, Dune Acres, Chesterton, Indiana 46304, U.S.A.

PUBLICATIONS

Novels

Lion at My Heart. Boston, Little Brown, and London, Gollancz, 1959.
The Odyssey of Kostas Volakis. New York, McKay, 1963.
A Dream of Kings. New York, McKay, 1966; London, Barker, 1967.
In the Land of Morning. New York, McKay, 1973.
The Hour of the Bell. New York, Doubleday, 1976.
Nick the Greek. New York, Doubleday, 1979; London, New English Library, 1980.

Short Stories

Pericles on 31st Street. Chicago, Quadrangle, 1965.
The Waves of Night and Other Stories. New York, McKay, 1969.
A Petrakis Reader. New York, Doubleday, 1978.

Plays

Screenplays: *A Dream of Kings*, with Ian Hunter, 1969; *In the Land of Morning*, 1974.

Television Play: *The Blue Hotel*, from the story by Stephen Crane, 1978.

Other

The Founder's Touch: The Life of Paul Galvin of Motorola. New York, McGraw Hill, 1965.
Stelmark: A Family Recollection (autobiography). New York, McKay, 1970.

*

Critical Studies: in *Old Northwest* (Oxford, Ohio), December 1976; interview in *Chicago Review*, Winter 1977.

Harry Mark Petrakis comments:

(1972) Reaching the half-century point in my life, I am grateful for having survived this long to write my stories and novels. An immense amount of work ahead that grows harder to accomplish each year, because the spirit demands new challenges and because time diminishes the reserves of energy and health. Yet I cannot conceive of living without writing. On writing as a profession, one might aptly quote Thucydides writing of the Athenians captured in war and set to labor in the stone quarries of Syracuse. "Having done what men could, they suffered what men must."

* * *

In a book of personal recollections, *Stelmark*, Harry Mark Petrakis confirms what the reader of his novels would guess; that Petrakis is the son of Greek immigrants to the United States. He is in fact a second generation man who is intent on estimating the meaning of his presence in a country that is far from the Crete of his ancestors. To the territory of South Chicago, Petrakis's father, a Greek Orthodox priest, brought the recollections of a strange and noble sort of life where poverty was the foreground of an existence lived in an awesome setting of mountains and an equally demanding texture of ancient custom and suffering. As a young man, Petrakis was impressed by the interplay of his inheritance and the sections of American culture that he came into contact with in the land of promise: the narrow opportunities of a great and indifferent city, the materialism of midwestern life as the immigrants encountered it and the continuation of the pride and violence that crossed the Atlantic with the Greek immigrants. It is this basic contrast between America as dreamed in the Cretan valleys and American as experienced by an ethnic minority that gives Petrakis his subject.

It is a subject full of challenges to Petrakis's novelistic imagination. And that imagination is equal to the passions, the disappointments, and the envies of the newcomers among whom, as a meditator and creator, Petrakis has lived his artistic life. He has created a striking company of persons who are, as Kurt Vonnegut has observed, at least 14 feet tall. These persons are swept by passions that are awesome when they are compared with the feebler desires and lesser dignities of men and women who have had several generations to adapt to the conditions of American life. The male figures still know the Greek versions of omertà, the Sicilian code of honor. These men act on the basis of personal pride and have loyalties that bind them less to American society than to family and a few close acquaintances. They have a sentimental vision of the cruel and impoverished land they—or their parents—fled. There is a dual center to their lives. One center is the church, whose ministers they respect, but whose teachings they put aside as having little to do with the lives of Greeks in South Chicago. The other center, more compulsive for them, is the world of cheap restaurants, back-room gambling dens that are full of con men and bookies, and seedy offices above grocery stores where, as in *A Dream of Kings*, palms are read and advice is given to clients who do not know where to turn in a society that has scant tolerance for new arrivals. This male world has, in large part, a cold indifference for wives and mistresses; women are tolerated because men must have sons or because sexual desires must find expression. Sincere and deep affection is known to some of the men, as in *The Odyssey of Kostas Volakis*. But even so, the hopes of women remain alien to male concerns and are seldom respected or shared.

Mention of particular novels fills out this general description. *Lion at My Heart*, Petrakis's first novel, rehearses the fortunes of an immigrant household made up of a father and two sons. The father, with pride and suspicion, watches over the education and the marriages of his two sons, esteeming the son who takes a Greek wife and repudiating the son who marries "outside." A priest, a familiar figure in the novels, intervenes to mollify the father's harshness. *The Odyssey of Kostas Volakis* tells a similar story. Kostas is a young Cretan man who married a slightly older woman for her dowry, which pays for the passage to America. The novel traces stages in Kostas's adjustment to his new land: his struggle as a restaurant owner, his overcoming of his illiteracy, and—most important—his final forgiveness of his murderer-son who has disgraced his family.

A Dream of Kings explores a slightly higher social level and tells of the life of Masoukas the palm-reader and consultant, half charlatan and half concerned adviser, by turns a compulsive gambler and adulterer. But Masoukas's dreams are fixed on an ailing son, for whose cure everything must be sacrificed. A journey to the sacred land of Greece will restore the health of the child and, perhaps, of the father. In another novel with a Chicago setting, *In the Land of Morning*, Petrakis moves into the post-Vietnam American world where the shock of a veteran's return is gradually merged with the on-going tumult of life in the community. All this is a passionate and sad human encounter which the reader can find elsewhere in Petrakis, as in the collections of short stories, *Pericles on 31st Street* and *The Waves of Night*.

A bit to one side is *The Hour of the Bell*. This novel is an account of the revolution that commenced in Greece in 1820 when a confused but finally successful revolt against Turkish power began. Instead of finding the usual cultural enclave in South Chicago, the reader moves back and forth over the tumultuous Greek landscape, which is seen through various eyes: those of military leaders, some savage, some resigned to years of violence; those of a priest who respects the humanity of the slaughtered Turks; and those of an educated young man who is trying to write the history of the confusion that surrounds him. With his usual power, Petrakis, as it were, adds the completing piece to the Greek-American puzzle that is his concern. *The Hour of the Bell* is the "explanation" of the pride and the harsh tauntings and the intermittent tenderness that the novels about South Chicago record.

It is a record that is made up of prose of varying textures: realistic and poetically fierce by turns. The result is an indispensable report and also an imaginative world that takes its place along with the works of fiction—Chekhov's and others—that, Petrakis tells us, used to make him weep as a youth.

—Harold H. Watts

PETRY, Ann (Lane). American. Born in Old Saybrook, Connecticut, 12 October 1908. Educated at Connecticut College of Pharmacy, now University of Connecticut School of Pharmacy, 1928-31, Ph.G. 1931; Columbia University, New York, 1943-44. Married George D. Petry in 1938; one daughter. Pharmacist, James Pharmacy, Old Saybrook and Old Lyme, Connecticut, 1931-38; Writer and Reporter, *Amsterdam News*, New York, 1938-41; Women's Editor, *People's Voice*, New York, 1941-44; Visiting Professor of English, University of Hawaii, Honolulu, 1974-75. Secretary, Authors League of America, 1960. Recipient: National Endowment for the Arts grant, 1977. Agent: Russell and Volkening Inc., 551 Fifth Avenue, New York, New York 10017. Address: 113 Old Boston Post Road, Old Saybrook, Connecticut 06475, U.S.A.

PUBLICATIONS

Novels

The Street. Boston, Houghton Mifflin, 1946; London, Joseph, 1947.
Country Place. Boston, Houghton Mifflin, 1947; London, Joseph, 1948.
The Narrows. Boston, Houghton Mifflin, 1953; London, Gollancz, 1954.

Short Stories

Miss Muriel and Other Stories. Boston, Houghton Mifflin, 1971.

Other

The Drugstore Cat (juvenile). New York, Crowell, 1949.
Harriet Tubman: Conductor on the Underground Railroad (juvenile). New York, Crowell, 1955; as *The Girl Called Moses: The Story of Harriet Tubman*, London, Methuen, 1960.
Tituba of Salem Village (juvenile). New York, Crowell, 1964.
Legends of the Saints (juvenile). New York, Crowell, 1970.

*

Manuscript Collection: Mugar Memorial Library, Boston University.

Critical Studies: *Black on White: A Critical Study of Writing by American Negroes* by David Littlejohn, New York, Grossman, 1966; *Interviews with Black Writers* edited by John O'Brien, New York, Liveright, 1973.

Ann Petry comments:

I write short stories, novels, books for children and young people. I vary what I write even to the style, but the underlying theme deals with race relations in the U.S.A.

* * *

Ann Petry's high-school fiction and later practice whenever free from pharmaceutical chores bore fruit in three novels: *The Street*, *Country Place*, and *The Narrows*. *The Drugstore Cat* and *Tituba of Salem Village* are juveniles; but her short stories of the early 1940's in *The Crisis* and *Phylon*, as well as more recent fiction in *Redbook* and *The New Yorker*, merit attention. "On Saturday the Siren Sounds at Noon" began her career: its reception encouraged her to write *The Street*. "Like a Winding Sheet" was chosen for *The Best American Short Stories of 1946*. "Solo on the Drums," appearing in *'47 Magazine of the Year*, has a lyrical anguish that reflects her novels in theme and style.

The Street offers more than just another example of environmental determinism overshadowed by its precursor, *Native Son*. True, it opens with "a cold November wind" on 116th Street in Harlem that "did everything it could to discourage the people walking along the street" and closes with "the grime and the garbage and the ugliness" of that street as the defeated, pretty heroine-turned-murderess flees by train. Boots Smith, unscrupulous in avoiding a return to "a life of saying 'yes sir' to every white bastard who had the price of a Pullman ticket," is an older Bigger Thomas, with cash, a luxurious car, and political connections. Authorial digressions that rationalize Lutie Johnson's fear of the steet—"an evil father and a vicious mother" to Black children like her Bub—replace Boris Max's 16-page courtroom speech that blames a racist environment for Bigger's dilemma. Ann Petry's own life had verified the glum details of *The Street*, but her feminine and racial perceptions of those domestic tragedies that cluster in Black slums gave psychological sharpness to passages still alive with meaning. The Connecticut middle class with its insulting generalizations about Black women, the unemployed Harlem men reduced to loitering and philandering and desertion, the Black man with a resentment of his oppressors "so bad and so deep that I wouldn't lift a finger to help 'em stop Germans or nobody else," the tenement radios blaring to kill the feel of unbearable misery, "carrying pain and a shrinking from pain"—all these are realistic types that advance the author's theme of entrapment and resignation. The sometimes excessive description and the rather contrived plights of Lutie and Bub are redeemed by a sympathy that humanizes even the maniacally obsessed William Jones and the repulsively scarred Mrs. Hedges.

The ugliness of a small-town New England white environment, personified early by the scandalmongering cab driver "the Weasel," permeates *Country Place*. The conflict sustained between past and present is moral in the frustrations of returning war veteran Johnnie Roane and his faithless wife Glory, and philosophical in the insistence of Mrs. Gramby that her middle-aged son Mearns uphold a gracious tradition beyond his powers and desires. Sensitive to fusions of imagery, metaphor, and symbol, the author has Johnnie struggle past storm-felled trees to reach Ed Barrell's cabin and suffer disillusion in Glory's infidelity. The long storm, like the rain in which Johnnie walks after his first doubts about his wife, is emblematic of the turbulence of climactic changes forced upon the main characters. The thematic absorption of disenchantment into thinner but stronger life is presaged in Johnnie's decision not to strangle his wife and, later not to kill her lover; it is advanced—through an equally distressing decision by Mrs. Gramby—by his opportunity to become an artist in New York. *Country Place*, marred like *The Street* by seemingly thesis-conjured death at the end, continues Ann Petry's attack against a cash-and-carry society hostile to moral beauty.

The Narrows, titled after its setting, the Black neighborhood in Monmouth, Connecticut, not only has a conscience-gripping theme, but is remarkable for its vivid array of minor characters. Sexually radiant, blues-singing Mamie Powther; the frightful amputee, Cat Jimmie, who speeds on his homemade cart to peer under the dresses of women; Cesar the Writing Man, who records his sonorous prophecies on the sidewalk with colored chalk; and Weak Knees, with his collapsible limbs and innumerable gestures and mutterings ("Get away, Eddie, get away!") at the ghost of his best friend—these and others unforgettably enliven Dumble Street and the foggy dock of the River Wye. The novel is about love and its betrayal. Abbie Crunch lets puritanical snobbishness fatally betray her love for her husband, then lets grief betray her love for their adopted child, Link. Later, Link sacrifices his love for rich, white Camilo Treadway to Black pride, while she gives in to jealousy and racism. And mistakenly jealous little Malcolm Powther, having no manhood himself, betrays that of Link. "All of us," Abbie concludes, "had a hand in [Link's death], we all reacted violently...because he was coloured and she was white." Almost every character applies to himself the author's repeated refrain: "I, executioner." *The Narrows* is attuned to the 1970's in other racial themes, and it thoughtfully views the responsibilities that attend power and artistic talent. Flashbacks are excessive, sometimes confusing; but stream-of-consciousness passages are skillfully written, and the leaven of humor appears.

The craftsmanship, social truth, and humanity of Ann Petry's fiction deserve wider recognition. Her basically tragic vision, linked in some ways with themes of Lorraine Hansberry and Ralph Ellison, could culminate, if she produces more, in a distinguished, comprehensive novel.

—James A. Emanuel

PHELPS, Gilbert (Henry). British. Born in Gloucester, 23 January 1915. Educated at the Crypt School, Gloucester; Fitzwilliam College, Cambridge, B.A. (honours) in English 1937; St. John's College, Cambridge (Strathcona Research Student), 1937-39, M.A. 1941. Served in the Royal Air Force, 1940-43. Married 1) Dorothy Elizabeth Coad in 1939 (divorced), one son and one daughter; 2) Kay Batchelor in 1972, three stepsons. Assistant Supervisor of English Studies, St. John's College, 1937-40; Lecturer and Tutor, Cambridge University Board of Extra-Mural Studies, 1938-40; Lecturer in English, British Council British Institute, Lisbon, 1940-42; Senior English Master, Blundell's School, Tiverton, Devon, 1943-45; Talks Producer, BBC, Bristol, 1945-50; Supervisor, Educational Talks, 1950-52, Producer, Third Programme, 1950-53, and General Instructor, 1953-56, and Chief Instructor, 1956-60, Staff Training Department, all for BBC, London. Since 1960, free-lance writer, broadcaster, and lecturer. Recipient: Arts Council Award, 1965. Fellow, Royal Society of Literature, 1979. Agent: A.M. Heath, 40-42 William IV Street, London WC2N 4DD. Address: The Cottage, School Road, Finstock, Oxford OX7 3DJ, England.

PUBLICATIONS

Novels

The Dry Stone. London, Barker, 1953; earlier version, as *The Heart in the Desert*, New York, Day, 1954.
A Man in His Prime. London, Barker, and New York, Day, 1955.
The Centenarians: A Fable. London, Heinemann, 1958.
The Love Before the First. London, Heinemann, 1960.
The Winter People. London, Bodley Head, 1963; New York, Simon and Schuster, 1964.
Tenants of the House. London, Barrie and Jenkins, 1971.
The Old Believer. London, Barrie and Jenkins-Wildwood House, 1973; as *Mortal Flesh*, New York, Random House, 1974.
The Low Roads. London, Barrie and Jenkins, 1975.

Uncollected Short Stories

"I Have Lived a Hundred Years," in *The Pleasureground*, edited by Malcolm Elwin. London, Macdonald, 1947.
"The Guv'nor," in *Countryman* (London), 1948.
"The Corner Ghost," in *West Country Magazine* (London), 1949.
"Playing Dead," in *Cornhill* (London), 1950.
"The Loft," in *World Review* (London), 1951.
"A Body for Amsterdam," in *Cornhill* (London), 1953.
"Who Were You with Last Night?," in *The Ninth Ghost Book*, edited by Rosemary Timperley. London, Barrie and Jenkins, 1973.
"Call a Spade a Spade," in *The Twelfth Ghost Book*, edited by Rosemary Timperley. London, Barrie and Jenkins, 1976.

Plays

Radio Plays: *The Tide Comes In*, 1960; *The Spanish Cave*, from the novel by Geoffrey Household, 1960; *The Tankerdown Skull*, 1962; *The Winter People*, from his own novel, 1964; *Deliberate Adventure*, 1968.

Other

The Russian Novel in English Fiction. London, Hutchinson, 1956; St. Clair Shores, Michigan, Scholarly Press, 1971.
A Short History of English Literature. London, Folio Society, 1962; revised edition, as *A Survey of English Literature: Some of the Main Themes and Developments from Beowulf to 1939*, London, Pan, 1965.
The Last Horizon: Travels in Brazil. London, Bodley Head, 1964; as *The Green Horizons: Travels in Brazil*, New York, Simon and Schuster, 1964; revised edition, London, Charles Knight, 1971.
Latin America. London, BBC Publications, 1965.
Latin America. London, Bank of London and South America, 1970.
Romeo and Juliet. Petersfield, Hampshire, Studytapes, 1973.
Tragedy of Paraguay. London, Charles Knight, and New York, St. Martin's Press, 1975.
Squire Waterton of Walton Hall. Wakefield, Yorkshire, EP, 1976.
Story of the British Monarchy. London, Nile and Mackenzie, 1977.
An Introduction to Fifty British Novels 1650-1900. London, Pan, 1979; as *A Reader's Guide to Fifty British Novels 1650-1900*, New York, Barnes and Noble, 1979.

Editor, *Living Writers.* London, Sylvan Press, 1947.
Editor, *Vanity Fair*, by Thackeray. London, Pan, 1967.
Editor, *Question and Response: A Critical Anthology of English and American Poetry.* London, Cambridge University Press, 1969.
Editor, *The Byronic Byron: A Selection from the Poems of Lord Byron.* London, Longman, 1971.
Editor, *Villette*, by Charlotte Brontë. London, Pan, 1973.
Editor, *Wanderings in South America, the North-West of the United States, and the Antilles in the Years 1812, 1816, 1820, 1824*, by Charles Waterton. London, Charles Knight, 1973.
Editor, *The Rare Adventures and Painful Peregrinations of William Lithgow.* London, Folio Society, 1974.
Editor, *Henry Esmond*, by Thackeray. London, Pan, 1974.
Editor, *Arlott and Trueman on Cricket.* London, BBC Publications, 1977.
Editor, with John Phelps, *Animals Tame and Wild.* London, Angus and Robertson, and New York, Sterling, 1979.

*

Critical Studies: reviews by John Davenport, in *The Observer* (London), 16 February 1958; David Williams in *The Times* (London), 9 September 1971 and 30 August 1973; Jane Miller, in *Times Literary Supplement* (London), 23 May 1975; Rivers Scott, in *Sunday Telegraph* (London), 25 May 1975.

Gilbert Phelps comments:

(1976) The age-old theme in which I am most interested in my fiction is that of the intellect versus the heart and the imagination. I have attempted to explore this in two types of story: first, close studies of family life in a West Country context, especially figuring children—as in my *The Love Before the First*, which is about a boy and girl who "love" each other at a pre-adolescent stage; and second, in "fables" or allegories, sometimes with a Science Fiction element, as in *The Centenarians* and *The Winter People*. I have also experimented with the "realistic fable" in *Tenants of the House*, a story about a lodging house in London which might also be either the state of man or the layers of personality and the varying *personae* of the individual; and in *The Old Believer* I have tried the imaginary autobiography, in this case that of an old man on his death-bed who recreates the duality of sensuality and spirit in his past. *The Low Roads* seeks to explore the life of an educated man who cuts away all his old intellectual and cultural props—in order to become a tramp—and who receives "intimations" which may possibly be described as "religious." I am now beginning a family sequence.

* * *

Gilbert Phelps's work is characterized by its vitality, both in its vigorous narrative style and in the belief in "life and love" engendering basic optimism. This affirmative tone is common to the two genres of his earlier work, family studies and fantasies, and to his later attempts at their synthesis. All his novels end on a positive note.

Phelps's first novel, *The Dry Stone*, takes the form of a first-person account by Martin Crystal of a poor childhood in a West-country town, from which he wins through to Cambridge, and his subsequent career leading to success as a writer. The early part of the book is the best, and wisely Phelps returned to the theme of childhood in Cranwyck in *The Love Before the First*. In the context of what becomes in *The Dry Stone* an almost melodramatic plot, Phelps's treatment of Vera Crystal's mental breakdown and Martin's later happiness with his first love, Patricia, induces the sense of uneasiness of much of his work, as his strong narrative binds together willy-nilly different levels of perception.

A Man in His Prime, written in the third person, is less ambitious and more successful; the protagonist's rhetorical questions are redeemed by a humour absent in Crystal's turgid soul-searchings. This novel deals with the affair of William Corrie, the middle-aged man of the title, with an American girl, whom he renounces, in the context of his enduring marriage. In the lyrical family holiday scene closing the book, Corrie remains, realistically, "still rebellious at the losses."

While in *A Man in His Prime* Phelps gave affectionate thumbnail sketches of Corrie's children, in his fourth novel, *The Love Before the First*, he approached childhood subjectively, though writing in the third person. He focusses on the "no-man's-land" inhabited by Alan, "where he had to endure both the pangs of regret and those of foreboding," as he grows up and away from his constant companion and cousin, Meg, but yet remains excluded from the adults, whose preoccupations are highlighted by the arrival of debonair Uncle Hector.

The Love Before the First was written between Phelps's two fantasies. The first, the "fable" *The Centenarians*, posits a group of especially distinguished old men preserved in the future in a "beautiful retreat," while the rest of the world destroys itself. Two unprepossessing survivors reach the mountain plateau to be fêted foolishly by the old men. The tale is told by Jerrould, "court jester" to the leader, Chard, with whose wife he had been in love. In *The Old Believer* Phelps explores more fully meaning latent in lyrical memory, but here Jerrould's personal memories do not form an integral part of the fable, which by a sparing use of science-fiction props translates to laboratory conditions predominantly vain human attitudes.

In *The Winter People* "mad" Colonel John Parr's belief in his discovery of a gracious, peaceable people in an uninhabited altitude of the Andes serves to condemn by contrast the tribe of "respectable Parrs" who are merely "slowly dying." His journal, describing this people's annual winter hibernation and their "retrospective amnesia," is introduced by the lawyer, David Parr. Though he explains the Winter People in terms of his great-uncle's thwarted early love, he himself comes to believe in the discovery as one of "the miracles of Nature and of Love"; his own life will be fertilized by his great-uncle's madness, which is presented as less pernicious than the respectable Parrs' sanity.

Tenants of the House is an extended metaphor for the workings of a man's mind—perhaps at different periods in his life—into which the reader is plunged direct. Written in the third person, it is ostensibly a description of Hugo's house, inhabited by a multitude of conventional and subversive tenants, for "if the house chose to admit them, there was nothing he could do about it." The characters seem further intended to represent schizophrenia and other derangements, though the introduction of a stock "Doctor" figure to comment on Hugo's "house of many mansions" seems superfluous. The basic mental metaphor accommodates some amusing word-play, while the tenants' and squatters' antics provide the full-blooded—and sometimes black—comedy characteristic of Phelp's later work.

An integral part of Phelps's celebration of "life and love" is the recognition of death as their natural completion; the old man in *The Old Believer* becomes "proud to be dying of 'natural causes,' by the simple wearing away of time and experience." Yet his belief in the instinctive testimony of the senses, which he fully comprehends as he remembers in his hospital bed the experiences which nurtured it, seems facile. The pattern of his love for Tanya recalls *The Dry Stone*, and Phelps retains from his first novel the self-defeating trick of writing about superficial experience superficially.

In *The Low Roads* a successful cartoonist abandons his home to take to the road as a tramp, dying to his family. Coincidence, a favourite device of Phelps, comes into its own in this picaresque novel of "the episodic life" in a sub-culture of squatters, drop-outs, social workers, and the gentlemen of the road themselves. His success as a pavement artist nearly leads to his integration in "society" again, but he breaks down and undergoes electric shock treatment. Ironically, he is then overtaken by so-called fantasies of widespread pollution. The Joycean echo in the ending seems pretentious, but helps Gilbert Phelps to make even his tramps affirm ultimately.

—Val Warner

PIERCY, Marge. American. Born in Detroit, Michigan, 31 March 1936. Educated at the University of Michigan, Ann Arbor (Hopwood Award), B.A. 1957; Northwestern University, Evanston, Illinois, M.A. 1958. Member of the Visiting Faculty, Fine Arts Work Center, Provincetown, Massachusetts, 1976-77; Writer-in-Residence, College of the Holy Cross, Worcester, Massachusetts, 1976; held Butler Chair of Letters, State University of New York, Buffalo, 1977. Recipient: Borestone Mountain Poetry Award (twice); National Endowment for the Arts grant, 1977. Agent: Lois Wallace, Wallace and Sheil Agency Inc., 177 East 70th Street, New York, New York 10021. Address: Box 943, Wellfleet, Massachusetts 02667, U.S.A.

PUBLICATIONS

Novels

Going Down Fast. New York, Simon and Schuster, 1969.
Dance the Eagle to Sleep. New York, Doubleday, 1970; London, W.H. Allen, 1971.
Small Changes. New York, Doubleday, 1973.
Woman on the Edge of Time. New York, Knopf, 1976; London, Women's Press, 1979.
The High Cost of Living. New York, Harper, 1978; London, Women's Press, 1979.
Vida. New York, Summit, and London, Women's Press, 1980.

Uncollected Short Stories

"Going over Jordan," in *Transatlantic Review 22* (London), Autumn 1966.
"Love Me Tonight, God," in *The Fact of Fiction*, edited by Cyril M. Gulassa. San Francisco, Canfield Press, 1972.
"Dynastic Encounter," in *In the Looking Glass*, edited by Nancy Dean and Myra Stark. New York, Putnam, 1977.

Play

The Last White Class, with Ira Wood (produced Northampton, Massachusetts, 1978). Trumansburg, New York, Crossing Press, 1979.

Verse

Breaking Camp. Middletown, Connecticut, Wesleyan University Press, 1968.
Hard Loving. Middletown, Connecticut, Wesleyan University Press, 1969.
A Work of Artifice. Detroit, Red Hanrahan Press, 1970.
4-Telling, with others. Trumansburg, New York, Crossing Press, 1971.
When the Drought Broke. Santa Barbara, California, Unicorn Press, 1971.
To Be of Use. New York, Doubleday, 1973.
Living in the Open. New York, Knopf, 1976.
The Twelve-Spoked Wheel Flashing. New York, Knopf, 1978.
The Moon Is Always Female. New York, Knopf, 1980.

Recordings: *Laying Down the Tower*, Black Box; *At the Core*, Watershed, 1978.

Other

The Grand Coolie Dam. Boston, New England Free Press, 1970(?).

* * *

Not satisfied to be only a chronicler of social revolution in the late 1960's and 1970's, though her facts about these times are compellingly accurate, too much an artist to write the domestic melodramas that infest newsstands, Marge Piercy is first of all interested in character and the relation of the individual to society. Her fiction is a tough, courageous, yet tender representation of individuals confronting oppression. What makes Piercy a fine writer, one of the best to use the 1960's and 1970's as her milieu, is her understanding that the external world, society, is not the only oppressor. Oppression can be chosen by an act of will.

Piercy identifies the external oppressors: capitalism with its emphasis on possession of objects sets up institutions that foster objectness. For example, in marriage women are possessions to serve male needs, nuclear families are closed to sustenance from others; love is thus defined in this society as the cement that binds. Individuals in this system are powerless. Yet people can choose to be oppressed because they fear the freedom that other ways of living can bring.

Those who choose not to be oppressed in Piercy's work pay a tremendous price (a capitalist metaphor) in relation to the society they reject. Piercy's main character is the outcast, who rejects her bonds, but who then must suffer the consequences. The lesbian lovers Beth and Wanda in *Small Changes*, both fugitives from exploitative marriages, must hide from the law. Connie in *Woman on the Edge of Time* is placed in a mental hospital, as is Joanna in *Dance the Eagle to Sleep*. In *Vida* the vibrant, charismatic title character, one of Piercy's most splendid creations, has been underground for ten years. But this is not to say that Piercy's works are gloomy, naturalistic stories of defeated lives. Her novels sparkle with humor and shock with recognition; they show paths—and alley ways—to fulfillment; their intent is to give the reader the courage to try to throw off at least a small oppression or two.

Several aspects of Piercy's fiction are especially noteworthy. Her handling of contemporary settings is deft: parties bristle with the intrigue of subtle connections and betrayals; offices oppress with their hierarchies of bosses and secretaries; bedrooms too often are battlegrounds; homes are sometimes prisons where children hold moms prisoner. The utopian impulse to suggest alternative societies is strong in her work, most notably in *Woman on the Edge of Time* and *Dance the Eagle to Sleep*; in these experiments with science fiction, Piercy shows an idyllic utopia and harsh dystopia. Moreover, as a poet, Piercy reveals a sensitivity to the creative process and its ability to heal the problems she is decrying, to make "feelings real and articulate" as a character says in *Dance the Eagle*.

But it is her characterizations of men and women the reader remembers. Unlike some feminist writers, Piercy draws men who are as multi-dimensional, appealing, or odious as her women—that is, they are not stereotypes. Even her establishment men—bosses like George in *High Cost* or husbands like Leigh in *Vida* or Neil in *Small Changes*—are not entirely wicked. Three other types of men recur in her novels. One is the man whose charismatic, brooding silences attract women such as Rowley in *Going Down Fast*, Corey in *Dance the Eagle to Sleep*, Jackson is *Small Changes*, and Jackrabbit in *Woman on the Edge of Time*. The second is the counterculture activist who sells out to materialism such as Asher in *Going Down Fast* and Leigh in *Vida*. Third is the marginal man who cannot function at all such as Leon in *Going Down Fast* and Bernard in *The High Cost of Living*,

Her women are superb; few other contemporary novelists have presented the range of women Piercy has. And no one has given us a Miriam Berg or a Vida, outcasts yet free. Her other women characters are of three types. First, the victims of domesticity whose self sacrifice for the comfort of men threatens to destroy them such as Dorine and on occasion Miriam and Beth in *Small Changes*. Second, the victims of the plastic media-image of women such as Gildina in *Woman on the Edge of Time*, Caroline in *Going Down Fast*, and Honor in *The High Cost of Living*. Finally, the alternative women Beth in *Small Changes* and Luciente in *Woman on the Edge of Time* show new ways of being female.

What alternatives does Piercy offer cultural oppression and demeaning human relationships? Her work suggests that people must make their own culture, through communal living away from the nuclear family and through work that does not add to human misery. The means to these ends are as various as there are people, but the end is the same: good love and good work.

—Kathryn L. Seidel

PLANTE, David. American. Born in Providence, Rhode Island, 4 March 1940. Educated at Boston College, 1957-59, 1960-61, B.A. in French 1961; University of Louvain, Belgium, 1959-60. Teacher, English School, Rome, 1961-62; guide book writer, New York, 1962-64; Teacher, Boston School of Modern Languages, 1964-65, and St. John's Preparatory School, Massachusetts, 1965-66. Has lived in England since 1966. Recipient: Henfield Writing Fellowship, University of East Anglia, Norwich, 1977; Arts Council bursary, 1977. Agent: Deborah Rogers Ltd., 5-11 Mortimer Street, London W1N 7RH. Address: 30-A Overstrand Mansions, Prince of Wales Drive, London S.W. 11, England.

PUBLICATIONS

Novels

The Ghost of Henry James. London, Macdonald, and Boston, Gambit, 1970.
Slides. London, Macdonald, and Boston, Gambit, 1971.
Relatives. London, Cape, 1972; New York, Avon, 1974.
The Darkness of the Body. London, Cape, 1974.
Figures in Bright Air. London, Gollancz, 1976.
The Family. New York, Farrar Straus, and London, Gollancz, 1978.
The Woods. London, Gollancz, 1980.
The Country. London, Gollancz, 1981.

Short Stories

Penguin Modern Stories 1, with others. London, Penguin, 1969.

Uncollected Short Stories

"The Buried City," in *Transatlantic Review* (London), Spring 1967.
"The Tangled Centre," in *Modern Occasions* (Cambridge, Massachusetts), 1971.
"Preface," in *Beyond the Words: Eleven Writers in Search of a New Fiction*, edited by Giles Gordon. London, Hutchinson, 1975.
"This Strange Country," in *New Yorker*, 7 January 1980.
"Mr. Bonito," in *New Yorker*, 7 July 1980.

*

Manuscript Collection: University of Tulsa, Oklahoma.

David Plante comments:

One of course always writes with an intention in mind, but it is what one cannot intend that is my fascination in writing. I know, all the while I am choosing my words, making as vivid as possible my descriptions, that there is something floating beneath my words and descriptions which has a will of its own, which sometimes rises up to meet my words and most often sinks away, and one can no more intend it than one can (to borrow an image from William James) turn up a bright light to see the darkness. The best one can do is allow it to well up, to give it space.

One is or isn't in touch with this sense, and one knows one is or isn't as matter of factly, as unmysteriously, as one knows one is happy or depressed. In touch with it, one writes "Mr. Stein woke to a room of shadows," and the sentence comes to life, evokes a deep world of associations, while out of touch with it the same sentence, "Mr. Stein woke to a room of shadows," is banal, dull, dead. The difference between good and bad writing is quite as simple as that.

How does one know one is in touch or not? One knows the signs, particular enough to be recognizable. For example, walking down a street most often I am unaware of the litter that's around me, or I am aware of it only to wish it weren't there. This past afternoon, however, walking along a sidewalk, I found myself studying, on the cement, a small printed target with three or four bullet holes blown through it, a match book printed with three spades, a page torn from a magazine, a parking lot ticket, an addressed envelope, and it seemed to me that everything I saw was indicative of much more than what it was—after all, just litter—was, because of its rich suggestiveness, beyond my imaginative grasp. I wanted to *write* about that target, match book, page, ticket, letter, and I wanted to with the similarly recognizable, similarly matter of fact urge one has when one wants to sneeze. *I was in touch with something.*

One is, at various times, *aware* that one has to sneeze, one is aware that one is sexually attracted to someone, one is aware that one must work and eat and sleep, and one is aware that there is a sense, informing things yet capable of being abstracted from them, which one hopes to be the essence of one's writing, which one hopes will bring one's words and one's world to life.

Sneezing is important, and making love is important, and working and eating and sleeping are important, and something else is also important, something longed for, something which is the whole purpose of my work. William James said: "It is, the reader will see, the reinstatement, of the vague and inarticulate to its proper place in our mental life which I am so anxious to press on the attention."

* * *

David Plante's first novel was called *The Ghost of Henry James*—and, indeed, the ghost of Henry James has hovered in a rather elephantine way over all his work since. This is not to say that his work is essentially derivative or uninteresting. The best book he has published to date is probably *The Darkness of the Body*. Here he can be seen concerning himself directly with major themes of love and death, and the meaning of those only half-definable movements of unspoken significance between persons. In the earlier texts his world remained elusive and opaque. Here he takes a step into states of mind more accessible to the general reader. In this novel as in the others Plante is most successful when he indicates a pattern which he perceives as existing beyond the boundaries of behaviour, as though his people were inhabited by love as an alien ecstasy taking up residence in human forms. I am reminded of a passage in Ouspensky's *Tertium Organum* which suggests this idea directly, for it would make the perfect epigraph to any of Plante's fiction. So, for that matter, would some related lines from the poet Norman Cameron: "I fear you and I fear you, barbarous Love;/ You are no citizen of my country."

The Ghost of Henry James remains very readable, and contains clear indications of gifts which Plante has still to fulfill. It consists of a sequence of episodes in which four brothers and their sister figure over and over again in New England scenes that serve to emphasise their dependence on each other, their complex inter-relatedness as a family, and in particular the way they are haunted by the possessive presence of one brother, Henry, who is dead. Plante has great skill when it comes to itemising the trivial gesture that both reveals and conceals a world of significance. The book's ending has a sudden whiff of science fiction about it that seems even more misplaced on rereading than it did in the first place, but on the whole this is a clever and well-made novel.

Plante's prose has points in common with Nathalie Sarraute's in that it achieves maximum intensity when it rests content with drawing persons together and then making them dodge away from each other at the last moment. In at least one place he also tackles the description of sexual intercourse with more delicacy and truth than one expects to find in these days of the infinite orgasm—see pages 75 to 78 of *The Darkness of the Body*.

Here is a novelist whose analysis of the psychology of that no-man's land which lies between what we apprehend and what we understand is at best as elegant as anyone's now writing in English. The connecting principles within his narratives are not always easy to grasp, but the texts themselves have something of the coherence of dreams: things happen and you accept them before you have time to worry about what they mean. Plante's fiction is illative (in the sense defined by Newman in his *Essay in Aid of a Grammar of Assent*), intuitive, introverted, a heaping together of incidents which are sometimes obscure in themselves but which add up to something not easily forgotten.

—Robert Nye

POHL, Frederik. American. Born in New York City, 26 November 1919. Served in the United States Air Force, in the United States and Italy, 1943-45: Sergeant. Married 1) Doris Baumgardt in 1940 (divorced, 1944); 2) Dorothy DesTina in 1945 (divorced, 1947); 3) Judith Merril in 1949 (divorced, 1953), one daughter; 4) Carol Metcalf Ulf in 1952, two sons (one deceased) and one daughter. Editor, Popular Publications, New York, 1939-43; copywriter, Thwing and Altman, New York, 1946; Book Editor and Associate Circulation Manager, Popular Science Publication Company, New York, 1946-49; literary agent, New York, 1949-53; Features Editor, later Editor, *If*, New York, 1959-70; Editor, Galaxy Publishing Company, New York, 1961-69; Executive Editor, Ace Books, New York, 1971-72. Since 1973, Science Fiction Editor, Bantam Books, New York. Since 1976, Contributing Editor, *Algol*, New York. Since 1966, Member of the Executive Board, Monmouth County Civil Liberties Union, and of the Board of Directors New York City Opera. President, Science Fiction Writers of America, 1974-76. Recipient: Edward E. Smith Memorial Award, 1966 Hugo Award, 1973, 1978; *Locus* Award, 1973, 1978; Nebula Award, 1976, 1977, 1978; Campbell Memorial Award, 1978; Prix Apollo (France), 1978; American Book Award, 1980. Guest of Honor, World Science Fiction Convention, 1972. Agent: Robert P Mills Ltd., 156 East 52nd Street, New York, New York 10022 Address: 386 West Front Street, Red Bank, New Jersey 07701, U.S.A.

PUBLICATIONS

Novels

The Space Merchants, with C.M. Kornbluth. New York, Ballantine, 1953; London, Heinemann, 1955.

Search the Sky, with C.M. Kornbluth. New York, Ballantine 1954; London, Digit, 1960.

Preferred Risk (as Edson McCann, with Lester del Rey). New York, Simon and Schuster, 1955.

Gladiator-at-Law, with C.M. Kornbluth. New York, Ballantine, 1955; London, Digit, 1958.

A Town Is Drowning, with C.M. Kornbluth. New York, Ballantine, 1955; London, Digit, 1960.

Presidential Year, with C.M. Kornbluth. New York, Ballantine, 1956.

Sorority House (as Jordan Park, with C.M. Kornbluth). New York, Lion, 1956.

Edge of the City (novelization of screenplay). New York, Ballantine, 1957.

Slave Ship. New York, Ballantine, 1957; London, Dobson, 1961.

The Man of Cold Rages (as Jordan Park, with C.M. Kornbluth). New York, Pyramid, 1958.

Wolfbane, with C.M. Kornbluth. New York, Ballantine, 1959; London, Gollancz, 1961.

Drunkard's Walk. New York, Ballantine, 1960; revised edition, London, Gollancz, 1961.

The Starchild Trilogy, with Jack Williamson. New York, Pocket Books, 1977; London, Penguin, 1980.

The Reefs of Space. New York, Ballantine, 1964; London, Dobson, 1965.

Starchild. New York, Ballantine, 1965; London, Dobson, 1966.

Rogue Star. New York, Ballantine, 1969; London, Dobson, 1972.

A Plague of Pythons. New York, Ballantine, 1965; London, Gollancz, 1966.

The Age of the Pussyfoot. New York, Simon and Schuster, 1969; London, Gollancz, 1970.

Farthest Star, with Jack Williamson. New York, Ballantine, 1975; London, Pan, 1976.

Man Plus. New York, Random House, and London, Gollancz, 1976.

Gateway. New York, St. Martin's Press, and London, Gollancz, 1977.

Jem: The Making of a Utopia. New York, St. Martin's Press, and London, Gollancz, 1979.

Beyond the Blue Event Horizon. New York, Ballantine, and London, Gollancz, 1980.

The Cool War. New York, Ballantine, and London, Gollancz, 1981.

Short Stories

Danger Moon (as James MacCreigh). Sydney, American Science Fiction, 1953.

Alternating Currents. New York, Ballantine, 1956; London, Penguin, 1966.

The Case Against Tomorrow. New York, Ballantine, 1957.

Tomorrow Times Seven. New York, Ballantine, 1959.

The Man Who Ate the World. New York, Ballantine, 1960; London, Panther, 1979.
Turn Left at Thursday. New York, Ballantine, 1961.
The Wonder Effect, with C.M. Kornbluth. New York, Ballantine, 1962; London, Gollancz, 1967; revised edition, as *Critical Mass,* New York, Bantam, 1977.
The Abominable Earthman. New York, Ballantine, 1963.
The Frederik Pohl Omnibus. London, Gollancz, 1966; reprinted in part, as *Survival Kit,* London, Panther, 1979.
Digits and Dastards (includes essays). New York, Ballantine, 1966; London, Dobson, 1968.
Day Million. New York, Ballantine, 1970; London, Gollancz, 1971.
The Best of Frederik Pohl. New York, Doubleday, 1975; London, Sidgwick and Jackson, 1977.
In the Problem Pit. New York, Bantam, and London, Corgi, 1976.
The Early Pohl. New York, Doubleday, 1976; London, Dobson, 1980.

Uncollected Short Stories

"Rem the Rememberer," in *Cosmos* (New York), May 1977.
"Swanilda's Song," in *Analog* (New York), October 1978.
"Mars Masked," in *Isaac Asimov's Science Fiction Magazine* (New York), March 1979.
"Like unto the Locust," in *Isaac Asimov's Science Fiction Magazine* (New York), December, January 1979-80.

Other

Undersea Quest [*Fleet, City*] (juvenile), with Jack Williamson. New York, Gnome Press, 3 vols., 1954-58; London, Dobson, 3 vols., 1966-68.
Practical Politics 1972. New York, Ballantine, 1971.
The Way the Future Was: A Memoir. New York, Ballantine, 1978; London, Gollancz, 1979.

Editor, *Beyond the End of Time.* New York, Permabooks, 1952.
Editor, *Shadow of Tomorrow.* New York, Permabooks, 1953.
Editor, *Star Science Fiction Stories 1-6.* New York, Ballantine, 6 vols., 1953-59; vols. 1 and 2, London, Boardman, 1954-55.
Editor, *Assignment in Tomorrow.* New York, Hanover House, 1954.
Editor, *Star Short Novels.* New York, Ballantine, 1954.
Editor, *Star of Stars.* New York, Doubleday, 1960; as *Star Fourteen,* London, Whiting and Wheaton, 1966.
Editor, *The Expert Dreamers.* New York, Doubleday, 1962; London, Gollancz, 1963.
Editor, *Time Waits for Winthrop and Four Other Short Novels from Galaxy.* New York, Doubleday, 1962.
Editor, *The Seventh* [through *Eleventh*] *Galaxy Reader.* New York, Doubleday, 5 vols., 1964-69; *Seventh* through *Tenth,* London, Gollancz, 4 vols., 1965-68; *Eighth,* as *Final Encounter,* New York, Curtis, 1970; *Tenth,* as *Door to Anywhere,* New York, Curtis, 1970.
Editor, *The If Reader of Science Fiction.* New York, Doubleday, 1966; London, Whiting and Wheaton, 1967; second volume, New York, Doubleday, 1968.
Editor, *Nightmare Age.* New York, Ballantine, 1970.
Editor, *The Best Science Fiction for 1972.* New York, Ace, 1972.
Editor, with Carol Pohl, *Science Fiction: The Great Years.* New York, Ace, 1973; London, Gollancz, 1974; second volume, Ace, 1976.
Editor, with Carol Pohl, *Jupiter.* New York, Ballantine, 1973.
Editor, *The Science Fiction Roll of Honor.* New York, Random House, 1975.
Editor, with Carol Pohl, *Science Fiction Discoveries.* New York, Bantam, 1976.
Editor, *The Best of C.M. Kornbluth.* New York, Doubleday, 1976.
Editor, with Martin H. Greenberg and Joseph D. Olander, *Science Fiction of the 40's.* New York, Avon, 1978.
Editor, with Martin H. Greenberg and Joseph D. Olander, *Galaxy: Thirty Years of Innovative Science-Fiction Publishing.* Chicago, Playboy Press, 1980.
Editor, *Nebula Award Winners 14.* New York, Harper, 1980.
Editor, with Martin H. Greenberg and Joseph D. Olander, *The Great Science Fiction Series.* New York, Harper, 1980.
Editor, *Frederik Pohl's Favorite Stories: Four Decades as a Science Fiction Editor.* New York, Berkley, 1981.

*

Manuscript Collection: Syracuse University Library, New York.

Critical Study: in *New Maps of Hell* by Kingsley Amis, New York, Harcourt Brace, 1960; London, Gollancz, 1961.

Frederik Pohl comments:

My principal work has been in science fiction, and within that field in the special kind of science fiction best described as cautionary literature. Now that the world has been well alerted to such problems as pollution, overpopulation, and so on—largely, in the first instance, by science-fiction stories—it is old hat to say that we must look to the long-range consequences of our society and technology. My stories have often touched on such themes long before they were fashionable.

Apart from argument, I have been interested in exploring all the possible range of alternate futures for the human race. Some of the work in which I take most pride—short stories like *Day Million,* novels like *Wolfbane*—are not at all cautionary in the sense that they call attention to dangerous current trends; instead, they attempt to show some of the stranger, but quite possible, directions the human world-line may take.

However, no writer, myself least of all, writes very attractively when he writes according to a coldblooded plan. I don't set out to write either political agitprop or think-tank scenarios; I only attempt to think out the consequences of what seem to me to be interesting developments, to set living characters in such worlds and then to let them live their lives.

* * *

Frederik Pohl has distinguished himself both as one of the most prolific writers of science fiction and as one of its most explicit promoters. The two distinctions seem to stem from his firm didactic concern with science fiction as a social early warning system. To write science fiction, he says, "is to try to look ahead to see not only what is likely to fall upon us by way of science and technology, but to see what the side effects and the consequences and the second and third order derivatives of these things will be" (M.L.A. Forum on Science Fiction, December 1968). In a Shavian catalogue of prefaces and postcripts, Pohl repeats and amplifies his fictional purpose "to question everything...in the light of what Harlow Shepley calls the 'View from a distant star.' "

The explicit didactic purpose is borne out by his fiction, which historically falls in line with that of Wells, Huxley, and Hoyle as a kind of allegorical social satire, earth-bound rather than space-speculative. His major novels are concerned with both the special consequences of particular trends in the 20th-century and the general effects of our current population expansion and waste of natural resources. Thus, *Space Merchants* and *Gladiator-at-Law* are, respectively, biting denunciations of 20th-century commercial advertising and corporation monopoly; unrestricted expansion of advertising agencies and super-corporations permits them to become the new power blocs of the 21st century, perverting the democratic process and lowering the quality of life by pandering to society's greed for immediate physical gratification.

In *Reefs of Space* and *Starchild* Pohl looks further ahead. The earth is teeming with 13 billion human beings necessarily organised under an entire totalitarian, computer-directed Plan of Man which has the sole aim of keeping a balance of resources. Private liberty has vanished because previous centuries have wasted natural resources only to turn the earth into a closed-system in which there still "isn't enough to go round." *The Age of the Pussyfoot* takes the same distant view but focuses more closely on the quality of personal life in a society so dependent on computers that it is, in fact, symbiotic with them. Instant information and immediate self-indulgence are possible, yet no attempt has been made to solve the problems of poverty, war, and cultural triviality.

Throughout Pohl's work runs the paradoxical theme that, while we progress technologically, we don't improve the quality of living, we don't remove the inequalities of material possession, and we don't improve the prospects of human creativity and fulfilment. The only answer is the choice also expounded by Hoyle: we either stay in an entirely closed, programmed system or we evolve to another level.

Although most of Pohl's novels are written with collaborators, there is no discernible difference in the quality of writing of the collaborated and independent work. What emerges is a profoundly disturbing sense of reality, truth, and honesty which is Swiftian in its impact. In Pohl's hands, science fiction is a weapon to be used vigorously in defence of humanity. As a social critic, Pohl must rank high. In addition, however, as his *Underseas* novels indicate, he is a first-rate storyteller who never lets the message wholly take over the medium.

—Frederick Bowers

PORTER, Hal. Australian. Born in Albert Park, Melbourne, Victoria, 16 February 1911. Educated at Kensington State School, 1917; Bairnsdale State School, Victoria, 1918-21; Bairnsdale High School, 1922-26. Married Olivia Parnham in 1939 (divorced, 1943). Cadet Reporter, *Bairnsdale Advertiser*, 1927. Schoolmaster, Victorian Education Department, 1927-37, 1940; Queen's College, Adelaide, 1941-42; Prince Alfred College, Kent Town, South Australia, 1943-46; Hutchins School, Hobart, Tasmania, 1946-47; Knox Grammar School, Sydney, 1947; Ballarat College, Victoria, 1948-49; Nijimura School, Kure, Japan (Australian Army Education), 1949-50. Director, National Theatre, Hobart, 1951-53. Chief Librarian of Bairnsdale and Shepparton, 1953-61. Since 1961, full-time writer. Australian Writers Representative, Edinburgh Festival, 1962. Lecturer for the Australian Department of External Affairs, in Japan, 1967. Recipient: Sydney Sesquicentenary Prize, 1938; Commonwealth Literary Fund Fellowship, 1956, 1960, 1964, 1968, 1972, 1974, 1977, and Subsidy, 1957, 1962, 1967; *Sydney Morning Herald* Prize, 1958; Sydney Journalists' Club Prize, for fiction, 1959, for drama, 1961; *Adelaide Advertiser* Prize, for fiction, 1964, 1970, for non-fiction, 1968; *Encyclopaedia Britannica* Award, 1967; Captain Cook Bi-Centenary Prize, 1970. Address: Weroona, 504 Nicholson Street, Ballarat, Victoria 3350, Australia.

Publications

Novels

A Handful of Pennies. Sydney, Angus and Robertson, 1958; London, Angus and Robertson, 1959; revised edition in *Hal Porter*, 1980.
The Tilted Cross. London, Faber, 1961.
The Right Thing. Adelaide, Rigby, and London, Hale, 1971.

Short Stories

Short Stories. Adelaide, Advertiser Press, 1942.
A Bachelor's Children. Sydney and London, Angus and Robertson, 1962.
The Cats of Venice. Sydney, Angus and Robertson, 1965.
Mr. Butterfry and Other Tales of New Japan. Sydney, Angus and Robertson, 1970.
Selected Stories, edited by Leonie Kramer. Sydney and London, Angus and Robertson, 1971.
Fredo Fuss Love Life. Sydney, Angus and Robertson, 1974.
An Australian Selection, edited by John Barnes. Sydney, Angus and Robertson, 1974.

Uncollected Short Stories

"Frieze of Victims," in *Point* (Melbourne), 1937.
"Revenge," in *Flame* (Melbourne), 1937.
"Holiday," in *Bulletin* (Sydney), 1937.
"Hyde's Hell," in *Dit* (Sydney), 1944.
"Melbourne in the Thirties," in *London Magazine*, 1965.

Plays

The Tower (produced London, 1964). Published in *Three Australian Plays*, Melbourne and London, Penguin, 1963.
The Professor (as *Toda-San*, produced Adelaide, 1965; as *The Professor*, produced London, 1965). London, Faber, 1966.
Eden House (produced Melbourne, 1969; as *Home on a Pig's Back*, produced Richmond, Surrey, 1972). Sydney, Angus and Robertson, 1969.
Parker (produced Ballarat, Victoria, 1972). Melbourne, Arnold, 1979.

Screenplay: *The Child* (episode in *Libido*), 1973.

Verse

The Hexagon. Sydney, Angus and Robertson, 1956.
Elijah's Ravens. Sydney, Angus and Robertson, 1968.
In an Australian Country Graveyard. Sydney, Angus and Robertson, 1973.

Other

The Watcher on the Cast-Iron Balcony (autobiography). London, Faber, 1963.
Australian Stars of Stage and Screen. Adelaide, Rigby, 1965.
The Paper Chase (autobiography). Sydney, Angus and Robertson, 1966.
The Actors: An Image of the New Japan. Sydney, Angus and Robertson, 1968.
The Extra (autobiography). Melbourne, Nelson, 1975.
Bairnsdale: Portrait of an Australian Country Town. Melbourne, Ferguson, 1977.
Seven Cities of Australia. Sydney, Ferguson, 1978.
Hal Porter (selection), edited by Mary Lord. Brisbane, University of Queensland Press, 1980.

Editor, *Australian Poetry 1957*. Sydney, Angus and Robertson, 1957.
Editor, *Coast to Coast 1961-1962*. Sydney, Angus and Robertson, 1963.
Editor, *It Could Be You*. Adelaide, Rigby, 1972; London, Hale, 1973.

*

Bibliography: *A Bibliography of Hal Porter* by Janette Finch, Adelaide, Libraries Board of South Australia, 1966; "A Contribution to the Bibliography of Hal Porter" by Mary Lord, in *Australian*

Literary Studies (Hobart, Tasmania), October 1970; *Papers of Hal Porter 1924-1975*, Sydney, Mitchell Library, n.d.

Manuscript Collection: Mitchell Library, Sydney.

Critical Studies: "The Craft of Hal Porter" by Peter Ward, in *Australian Letters* (Adelaide), October 1962; "New Tracks to Travel: The Stories of White, Porter, and Cowan" by John Barnes, in *Meanjin* (Melbourne), June 1966; in *Profile of Australia* by Craig McGregor, Melbourne, Penguin, 1968; Robert Burns, in *Meanjin 1* (Melbourne), 1969; *Hal Porter* by Mary Lord, Melbourne, Oxford University Press, 1974; *Speaking of Writing* edited by R.D. Walshe and Leonie Kramer, Sydney, Reed, 1975.

Hal Porter comments:

As many Australian writers are, I am, it seems to me, *indubitably*, unavoidably Australian—in tone, attitude, sentiment, and vocabulary—all this, no doubt, because of a passionate wish to record clearly an extraordinary country and (once one is beyond the common factors of human behaviour) its unique enough inhabitants. Not only is my writing Australian: it is regionally so. Despite having dealt with 19th-century Van Diemen's Land, with Earl's Court, Venice, Occupied Japan, Milan, and so on, I see myself as a regional writer, limited, engrossed, timely, in somewhat the same way as, say, Colette is, as Eudora Welty and V.S. Pritchett are. The bulk of my work, particularly the short stories, is based on characters and landscapes of southernmost Australia, the less distraught, arid and intractable part, the greener, colder, well-combed terrain with its 19th-century provincial cities and country towns, its seaside resorts on a littoral touched by Antarctic winds.

Since I lack fictional skill and imagination my subjects are by and large shop-lifted almost directly from Life, most often directly, holus-bolus. I think I deal with these dispassionately but perceive a truth in the remarks of a critic who finds them treated with a "pitiless pity." My main aim for several decades has been to write with many-planed clarity, to achieve an incandescence, a style on the clear glass of which are visible as few of my finger-prints as possible. A perverse aim: style is, after all, the author's finger-prints.

Many of my problems stem from the curious complexities of Australian society, the infinite subtle class distinctions beneath a facade of egalitarianism, the fine-drawn sensibilities and leeriness underlying the over-all bonhomie, the shrewd ruthlessness below the love-thy-neighbourliness. I face these problems warily but with unabating fascination. Since my fervent and high-falutin desire is for an experience to reach the reader in simon-pure condition, and as though the experience has angelically magnetized to itself the most unimpeachable *mots justes*, the aptest, and therefore most pellucid and author-untainted, sentences, I am frequently disconcerted by reviewers who accuse me of "brilliant" imagination, "glittering" satire, sardonicism, irony, malice, *et tout cela*. Perhaps they read too much between the lines, or perhaps one's writing comes out not so dispassionately as one thinks. I do write my first draft, after all, headlong, in reckless long-hand. the second, and final, draft is laboriously typewritten: at this stage, I burnish and prune, intensify and high-light, and cast about for the more pungent word, the more telling clause, the nuance that helps clarify, the astringent turn of phrase that ousts fuzziness.

All in all, in spite of some strictures, I am optimistic about mankind, consider my writing ultimately compassionate, apolitical, disciplined, and as exact as it can be made within the limits I must inevitably work inside.

* * *

Hal Porter began writing fiction in the 1930's. At the time the characteristic mode of Australian fiction was realistic. Novelists tended to place more emphasis upon the substantial social realities of their fiction than upon its artistic form. From the first Porter emerged as a writer of a very different kind from most of his contemporaries—a self-conscious, mannered stylist, with an eye for the grotesque, the fantastic, and the absurd.

Porter's first novel was *A Handful of Pennies*, an allegorical satire set in Japan, and aimed at War, Peace, and Occupation Democracy, the latter being categorised as "Delusion's son...the sponsor of no Christ, but of guilds of Pontius Pilates." It is notable for its "pyrotechny of words" rather than for the intrinsic interest of its characters or situations. *The Tilted Cross* is set in 19th-century Hobart and its central character is a fictional reconstruction of the convict artist Thomas Griffiths Wainewright. Porter keeps closely to biographical and historical facts, juxtaposes the squalor of convict life and the elegant luxury of the colonial aristocracy, and brings together a set of characters whose meetings and clashes are emblems of the contradictions and hypocrisies of the society they represent. In examining the interaction between innocence and guilt he vividly and sardonically represents ugliness, impotence, perversion, and brutality. *The Right Thing* is a novel about country life in Australia. It examines the family attitudes and personal relationships of those whose loyalties are to the continuation of their landed inheritance; and it adopts a critical stance towards social and family codes of behaviour.

Porter's *Short Stories* contained, with one exception, stories not previously published, and written, according to the author, between the ages of 18 and 23. With two omissions, these were republished in a revised form, and with the addition of 16 stories from magazines and journals, in *A Bachelor's Children*. Together with *The Cats of Venice* these represent over 30 years of his work in the form. *Mr. Butterfry* contains stories set in Japan, and these show a marked change in Porter's attitude to the country since his first visit after the war. Stories from these three volumes appear in *Selected Stories*. In *Fredo Fuss Love Life* he further experiments with style and subject matter.

Porter draws heavily on his own experience as subject matter for the stories, and from them some picture of his youth, his aspirations, the beginning of his career as a writer, his friends, and his wanderings can be gained. The gift that is most clearly displayed in his three autobiographical works—a total recall of the past in fine detail—is also to be observed in the stories. He is able to recapture the flavour of a period, and to represent with absolute precision places and scenes in Australia and abroad—a country town, a city hotel, a house, a restaurant. He brings to the past and the remote a peculiar sense of present reality.

Several main themes recur in the short stories—childhood and youth, loss of innocence, the relationship between past and present, and unique moments of human experience. These, of course, are subjects not peculiar to Porter. It is in his treatment of them that his striking individuality asserts itself. There is never any sense that he is writing to a formula. He experiments freely with form, and variety of subject matter is matched by variety of approach. His style is mannered and idiosyncratic. Its virtues are sharpness, wit, and pungency; its defects a certain wilful extravagance and verbalising not always essential to or justified by his subject. Nevertheless his richness of vocabulary, range of reference, and ear for minute tonal variations make him the outstanding Australian prose stylist.

The heart of Porter's achievement can now be seen to be his three autobiographical works. They bring Porter's life story up to the 1970's. Some of the material in these works is also to be found in the short stories, and the difficulty, as so often with Porter, is to determine the boundary between fact and fiction. Therefore the autobiographies must properly be regarded also as works of fiction. In *The Watcher on the Cast-Iron Balcony* Porter places himself as an observer, regarding his world, from childhood to youth, with a curious, quizzical detachment. In *The Paper Chase* he presents his middle years as the pursuit of an uncertain trail. This volume contains a lively social commentary on Melbourne in the years 1929-49, but Porter himself remains somewhat elusive, splintered into fragments of experience as he moves in and out of the other people's lives. In *The Extra* he appears as a minor player on the stage of his later years. This volume is notable for portraits of his father, and of his literary contemporaries—Kenneth Slessor, Katherine Susannah Prichard, Eve Langley, and many others. Together these books constitute a major achievement. Social and personal history and attitudes to life and art are presented with fine artistry.

Porter's work raises basic questions about the relationship between fact and fiction, and literature and life. These questions are not canvassed in any explicit way, but they arise from his treatment of factual material, and from his determination not to "dehydrate the truth of appearances into the life of fact." If there is one impression that his fiction as a whole conveys, it is of the fragmented nature of experience. There is an air of temporariness about his characters. They are constantly on the move from place to place, cafe to cafe, party to party. His fictional world is in restless motion. It is inhabited by bizarre, pathetic, vicious, grotesque, and comic characters. It is a world firmly controlled and directed by the author, whose sharp, critical, observant eye catches the smallest details of scene and behaviour. It is essentially a product of his tireless verbal inventiveness, which brings to Australian fiction and autobiography a unique verve, wit, and polish.

—Leonie Kramer

POWELL, Anthony (Dymoke). British. Born in London, 21 December 1905. Educated at Eton College; Balliol College, Oxford, M.A. Served in the Welch Regiment, 1939-41, and in the Army Intelligence Corps, 1941-45: Major; Order of the White Lion, Czechoslovakia; Order of Leopold II, Belgium; Oaken Crown and Croix de Guerre, Luxembourg. Married the writer Lady Violet Pakenham in 1934; two sons. Worked for Duckworth, publishers, London, 1926-35; scriptwriter for Warner Brothers of Great Britain, 1936; full-time writer from 1936; Literary Editor, *Punch*, London, 1953-58; reviewer for the *Daily Telegraph*, *Times Literary Supplement*, and other London papers. Trustee, National Portrait Gallery, London, 1962-76. Recipient: Black Memorial Prize, 1958; Smith Literary Prize, 1974. D.Litt.: University of Sussex, Brighton, 1971; University of Leicester, 1976; University of Kent, Canterbury, 1976; Oxford University, 1980. Honorary Fellow, Balliol College, 1974; Honorary Member, American Academy, 1977. C.B.E. (Commander, Order of the British Empire), 1956. Address: The Chantry, near Frome, Somerset, England.

PUBLICATIONS

Novels

Afternoon Men. London, Duckworth, 1931; New York, Holt, 1932.
Venusberg. London, Duckworth, 1932; with *Agents and Patients*, New York, Periscope Holliday, 1952.
From a View to a Death. London, Duckworth, 1933; as *Mr. Zouch: Superman: From a View to a Death*, New York, Vanguard Press, 1934.
Agents and Patients. London, Duckworth, 1936; with *Venusberg*, New York, Periscope Holliday, 1952.
What's Become of Waring. London, Cassell, 1939; Boston, Little Brown, 1963.
A Dance to the Music of Time:
A Question of Upbringing. London, Heinemann, and New York, Scribner, 1951.
A Buyer's Market. London, Heinemann, 1952; New York, Scribner, 1953.
The Acceptance World. London, Heinemann, 1955; New York, Farrar Straus, 1956.
At Lady Molly's. London, Heinemann, 1957; Boston, Little Brown, 1958.
Casanova's Chinese Restaurant. London, Heinemann, and Boston, Little Brown, 1960.
The Kindly Ones. London, Heinemann, and Boston, Littl Brown, 1962.
The Valley of Bones. London, Heinemann, and Boston, Littl Brown, 1964.
The Soldier's Art. London, Heinemann, and Boston, Littl Brown, 1966.
The Military Philosophers. London, Heinemann, 1968; Boston, Little Brown, 1969.
Books Do Furnish a Room. London, Heinemann, and Boston Little Brown, 1971.
Temporary Kings. London, Heinemann, and Boston, Littl Brown, 1973.
Hearing Secret Harmonies. London, Heinemann, 1975; Boston, Little Brown, 1976.

Uncollected Short Story

"A Reference for Mellors," in *Winter's Tales 12*, edited by A.I Maclean. London, Macmillan, and New York, St. Martin's Press, 1966.

Plays

Two Plays: The Garden God, and The Rest I'll Whistle. London Heinemann, 1971; Boston, Little Brown, 1972.

Verse

Caledonia: A Fragment. Privately printed, 1934.

Other

John Aubrey and His Friends. London, Heinemann, and New York, Scribner, 1948; revised edition, Heinemann, and New York, Barnes and Noble, 1963.
To Keep the Ball Rolling (autobiography):
Infants of the Spring. London, Heinemann, 1976; New York, Holt Rinehart, 1977.
Messengers of Day. London, Heinemann, and New York, Holt Rinehart, 1978.
Faces in My Time. London, Heinemann, 1980; New York, Holt Rinehart, 1981.

Editor, *Barnard Letters 1778-1884.* London, Duckworth, 1928.
Editor, *Novels of High Society from the Victorian Age.* London, Pilot Press, 1947.
Editor, *Brief Lives and Other Selected Writings of John Aubrey* London, Cresset Press, and New York, Scribner, 1949.

*

Critical Studies: *Anthony Powell* by Bernard Bergonzi, London, Longman, 1962, revised edition, 1971; *The Novels of Anthony Powell* by Robert K. Morris, Pittsburgh, University of Pittsburgh Press, 1968; *Anthony Powell: A Quintet, Sextet, and War* by John Russell, Bloomington, Indiana University Press, 1970; "Anthony Powell Issue" of *Summary* (London), Autumn 1970; "Sisyphus Descending: Mythical Patterns in the Novels of Anthony Powell" by Frederick Karl, in *Mosaic* (Winnipeg), iv, 3, 1971; *Anthony Powell* by Neil Brennan, New York, Twayne, 1974; *The Novels of Anthony Powell* by James Tucker, London, Macmillan, and New York, Columbia University Press, 1976; *Handbook to Anthony Powell's Music of Time* by Hilary Spurling, London, Heinemann, 1977, as *Invitation to the Dance: A Guide to Anthony Powell's Dance to the Music of Time*, Boston, Little Brown, 1978.

* * *

Anthony Powell has been writing books for 50 years, though it is only in the last 20 that he has emerged as one of a small handful of contemporary British novelists who can reasonably be considered major. His reputation rests almost exclusively on *A Dance to the Music of Time*, a panoramic sequence of extraordinary scope and complexity. A work that has never relinquished its surface brilliance for portraying the insular, private, self-contained, snobbish world of the British upper and middle-classes has more latterly become a vast canvas on all English life between the wars and afterwards, and in the profoundest way no less than a comic epic on time, history, and change.

Powell's novelistic career falls into two parts with World War II as the convenient dividing line. The five novels written in the 1930's are wittily structured and skillfully textured, still of some critical interest, but hinting only imperceptibly at the great achievement to come. *Afternoon Men* is perhaps most representative of the 1930's ethos and Powell's early style. Its atmosphere is charged with the insouciance and paralysis of "the lost generation," and resonates with echoes of Waugh and Huxley, though Waugh's bright young things have become older and tarnished, some even rusty, while Huxley's windy intellectuals and poseurs have declined into frustrated, bored, laconic, loveless drifters. *From a View to a Death* is the best of the pre-war books; retrospectively it is certainly the most important, anticipating in its several character sketches the more fully realized and rounded portraits of eccentrics in *The Music of Time*, and thematically introducing a dualism of human nature that has become peculiarly associated with Powell's artistic vision and with the thrust and core of his sequence: the opposition of the man of will and the man of imagination, the power-hungry and the sensualist.

Powell began *The Music of Time* shortly after the war, projecting it initially as six volumes, then expanding the plan to twelve. In a rare aside on his work, Powell stated in 1961 that the series "is concerned with the inter-relations of individuals, their lives and love affairs, and is intended to illustrate and bring up to date considerations of the way in which the middle and upper classes live in England." This confidence proved something of a false scent to his early critics, who tended to read the series as biography or sociology with fiction as mere overlay; nor (in all fairness to them) were its intricacies and formidable design apparent even after the first trilogy: *A Question of Upbringing*, set at Eton and Oxford during the 1920's; *A Buyer's Market*, centered in a party-going ambience similar to that of *Afternoon Men*; and *The Acceptance World*, dealing with various gambits to make it both sexually and professionally in the London of the 1930's. Narrated leisurely, coolly, and at times in a way that seems maddeningly pointless by Nicholas Jenkins—the hero-narrator of the entire sequence—the first three volumes interweave his life with the lives of a growing nucleus of acquaintances, introduce almost gratuitously several amiable eccentrics, and turn potentially dramatic confrontations into low-keyed comedy of manners.

Looking back over volumes of the series, however, one realizes that Powell, from the beginning, remained consistent to his title and controlling metaphor, both inspired by the painting of Poussin in which "the seasons, hand in hand and facing outward, tread in rhythm to the notes of the lyre that the winged and naked greybeard plays." Like the Seasons, Powell's dancers step "slowly, methodically, sometimes a trifle awkwardly, in evolutions that take recognisable shape: or [break] into seemingly meaningless gyrations, while partners disappear only to reappear again, once more giving pattern to the spectacle." The world of *The Music of Time*, then, is generated through continuing change, though what Powell does with the notion is unique. By seeing all possible, shifting, interchangeable patterns, but by placing the burden of interpreting them squarely on his narrator, he makes the present the center of the novel, enlarges the most underplayed actions or contracts overblown ones without focusing on their immediate significance, integrates individual steps of the dance into the greater flux, and charts necessarily changing sensibilities against the continuum of human history.

Such is the linear movement *in* time, but there is also the vertical movement of *time*: its qualitative rather than quantitative function, the thing-in-itself that makes one "unable...to control the steps of the dance." As Nick says in *The Kindly Ones*, "Time can play within its own folds tricks that emphasize the insecurity of those who trust themselves over much to that treacherous concept." The prime mover that does not ostensibly move, does—in a sequence continually reshaping the dance—move, itself become a part of a "kaleidoscope, the colours of which are always changing, always the same." Sheer, protean, fluid, spatial, time is the backdrop for posing and transporting character, theme and plot, but also the dominating archetype embracing all of life and art and of those who would partake in them.

A dozen or more archetypal patterns throughout the sequence would confirm it as the work of a mythopoeicist rather than realist. Nevertheless, Powell has created a remarkable gallery of "real" characters: originals like Giles Jenkins, General Conyers, Lady Molly Jeavons, Lord Erridge, tinged with the harmless grotesqueries of human behaviour; men of imagination like Edgar Deacon, Hugh Moreland, Captain Rowland Gwatkin, Charles Stringham and Peter Templer, romantic transplants from another age who suffer "the strain of living simultaneously in two different historical periods"; and of men of will, cold, mechanical, disciplined, controlling the times and harmonizing with them, of which Kenneth Widmerpool is the most notorious and vital. He is certainly one of the great contemporary comic villains as well. Son of a liquid manure manufacturer, and fat-boy butt of his school fellows at Eton, Widmerpool ascends with astonishing persistence and phoenixlike regularity to positions of status and power. From a highly competent businessman to army colonel and Labour M.P., he has moved uninterruptedly and unfeelingly toward success. Yet though Widmerpool is a super-competent, specious, insensitive, self-aggrandizing, and dangerous egomaniac, one cannot dislike him. In the dance he occupies a pivotal position; and being but one more partner in the just and harmonious evolutions of time, he, like the several hundred other characters, is treated comically, not satirically. Powell accepts Widmerpool as a phenomenon of the ethos without attempting to correct the failings of either.

More importantly, perhaps, Widmerpool becomes the perfect foil for Nick Jenkins's emergent decency, dignity, and probity. Proper, fashionable, sincere, innocent, self-reliant, Nick is the above average, upper-class all-right-guy wanting to fit in and keep from becoming defeated, excessively eccentric, too ostentatiously successful, or too scandously simple. Nick operates through a comic stoicism that one feels is Powell's as well. He witnesses dissolution about him and charts a course between extremes—measuring the smallest signs or gestures against contemporary standards and holding fast to sensible and humane values. From his shadowy beginnings as narrator and his often obvious role as author-surrogate, he has blossomed into a full-blown hero; for above and beyond other things, he has learned how a student of history and society should confront the uses of the past and of men. It is the Nick of *At Lady Molly's* who finally understands that excess of either power or sensuality may become the principal destroyer of society; the Nick of *Casanova's Chinese Restaurant*, thrust into a world of decaying marriages, infidelity, frustration, failure, and suicide, whose faith in morals and ethics is shaken, but not annihilated; and the Nick of the war trilogy (*The Valley of Bones*, *The Soldier's Art*, *The Military Philosophers*) who, above all the others, remains human in the face of impersonal and fatal dehumanizing processes. It is the Nick, too, of *Temporary Kings*, who finally grasps how *The Music of Time*'s decelerating dance of death approaches the inevitable statement to which the series has long been tending. Powell's preoccupation throughout the volumes with the artist's death, and with art in general as being representative of mutability, has been transferred to the imminent death of one work of art in particular. *Temporary Kings* does not merely view the passing of friends, family, society and culture; it looks to the passing of Powell's great multi-layered novel itself. Nick, however, still survives, endures. And his growth and attitude throughout the sequence—and the added realization that through the artifice of fiction he becomes his own best example—prescribe the totally humanistic, logical and balanced perspective on the not always joyless, but admittedly unpleasant themes of change and decay.

For Nick, like Powell, is a life-affirmer, not life-denier; decay is but one part of change, growth is another. If *The Music of Time* has sustained itself over 25 years, it is because the actions of becoming—and whether one becomes a Widmerpool or a Jenkins is quite beside the point—are the most concrete ways of presenting abstract theories of time, and the comic writer, persisting in his belief that the "past, just as the present, had to be accepted for what it thought and what it was," their most balanced interpreter. Over these volumes, Powell has not only shown awareness of the ways in which the individual changes against the sameness of time, but how (in Nick's words again) "the sequence of inevitable sameness that follows a person through life" plays against time's flux. Powell's genius, it seems, lies in the ability to invert these basic conditions without sacrificing meaning or character, to make the reader realize, by means of the authorial mythic vision and comic control, that both the random movements of life and the patterned movements of the dance can be seen as the perfect movement of art.

—Robert K. Morris

POWERS, J(ames) F(arl). American. Born in Jacksonville, Illinois, 8 July 1917. Educated at Quincy College Academy, Illinois; Northwestern University, Chicago campus, 1938-40. Married the writer Betty Wahl in 1946; three daughters and two sons. Worked in Chicago, 1935-41; Editor, Illinois Historical Records Survey, 1938; worked as a hospital orderly during World War II; taught at St. John's University, Collegeville, Minnesota, 1947; Marquette University, Milwaukee, Wisconsin, 1949-51; University of Michigan, Ann Arbor, 1956-57; Writer-in-Residence, Smith College, Northampton, Massachusetts, 1955-66. Recipient: American Academy grant, 1948; Guggenheim Fellowship, 1948; Rockefeller Fellowship, 1954, 1957, 1967; National Book Award, 1963. Member, American Academy. Address: c/o Alfred A. Knopf Inc., 201 East 50th Street, New York, New York 10022, U.S.A.

PUBLICATIONS

Novel

Morte d'Urban. New York, Doubleday, and London, Gollancz, 1962.

Short Stories

Prince of Darkness and Other Stories. New York, Doubleday, 1947; London, Lehmann, 1948.
The Presence of Grace. New York, Doubleday, and London, Gollancz, 1956.
Look How the Fish Live. New York, Knopf, 1975.

Uncollected Short Stories

"Sailing Against the Wind," in *Gallery of Modern Fiction*, edited by Robie Macauley. New York, Salem Press, 1966.
"Hair Shirt," in *New Yorker*, 30 January 1978.
"Warm Sand," in *New Yorker*, 26 March 1979.

*

Critical Studies: *J.F. Powers* by John F. Hagopian, New York, Twayne, 1968; *J.F. Powers* edited by Fallon Evans, St. Louis, Herder, 1968.

* * *

When the stories of J.F. Powers first appeared in American literary magazines during the 1940's, they were welcomed by many readers with an enthusiasm perhaps even greater than their own merits would otherwise have generated, for here was a new writer—a northern writer, a midwestern writer—whose stories carried as much creative authority as did the southern writing that had dominated American fiction for three decades. Here were the same structural finesse and verbal sensitivity, but now applied to northern materials. And here was the same concern for ultimate value, now transplanted to a milieu in which some southern critics had contended it could never flourish.

In short, Powers wrote about Chicago and the small towns of Illinois and Wisconsin with skills learned essentially from such writers as Caroline Gordon, Eudora Welty, Robert Penn Warren, and other southern fictionists, and thus brought to his materials a more sensitive fictional approach than that of earlier midwestern writers, such as Sinclair Lewis, James T. Farrell, or Nelson Algren. To put it another way, a native metaphysical storywriter, using the term perhaps somewhat loosely, had appeared in the very home of American naturalism and had taken at least some of naturalism's themes for his own, with results that were stimulating to say the least.

Powers had a remarkable ear for the dialects and idioms of midwestern speech, and could put together pages of dialogue with perfect fluency, realism, and economy. At the same time he could construct stories of great significance from the smallest episodes, using reticence of symbol and event to suggest meaning and feeling. As a stylist, he was plain rather than fancy, with a classical instinct for concision and a lively sense of prose rhythm. In general, his early stories centered on two main areas of experience: social conflict in Chicago, especially between whites and blacks, and the lives of the Roman Catholic clergy in America. Both these themes appeared powerfully in his first book, *Prince of Darkness*.

The first, that of racial conflict and the misery of Negroes in northern American cities, is best developed in the story entitled "He Don't Plant Cotton," which tells about three black jazz musicians, two men and a woman, who are fired from their job in a third-rate Chicago night club after a disagreement with drunken white customers. The story is memorable on several counts. For one, Powers wrote about jazz and its place in Negro sensibility without any of the mawkishness or plain musical stupidity that has characterized most other white and even much black writing on the subject. For another, without resorting to violence of either speech or event, he conveyed the real violence of feeling that dominates the black community's response to its predicament in America, and it is worth noting that this was done a full decade before the beginning of the modern civil rights movement. Nothing since then has surpassed Powers's story in seriousness, integrity, and artistic relevance, though much recent writing has been more turbulent.

The second theme, that of Catholic religious life in America, is perhaps best exemplified in the early story called "Lions, Harts, Leaping Does," in which Powers wrote about an elderly Franciscan friar plagued by intellectual self-doubt and spiritual anxiety. As he approaches his own death, his small shortcomings seem more and more ominous to him, until in a state of demoralization he cannot experience the least impulse toward good without questioning it and reversing his motives. Very subtly Powers contrasts this spiritual finicality with the real crassness and brutishness of modern commercial civilization, showing the true value of spiritual discipline even in its own weakest condition.

These two stories, "Lions, Harts, Leaping Does" and "He Don't Plant Cotton," belong among the best short stories written in America during the years of mid-century.

In Powers's second book, *The Presence of Grace*, the religious theme became dominant, and the mood turned from that of spiritual anguish to something more objective and satirical. Some stories in the collection moved toward whimsy, including several narrated by a rectory cat, but though they won much popularity for Powers when they were first published in *The New Yorker*, in retrospect they seem comparatively insubstantial. Other stories dealt more toughly with subversion in the Church and with the restlessness of modern clerics who are drawn from true priestliness by ideas of status, power, and popular success; and these were the stories which culminated in Powers's third and most important book, the satirical novel entitled *Morte d'Urban*.

Father Urban is a proselytizing priest attached to the (fictional) Clementine Order. Beginning with the purest motives, a desire to bring renewed strength and spiritual influence to his Order, he moves more and more in the direction of a manipulator, a spiritual wheeler-and-dealer, in the most degraded American commercial tradition. In other words, he is progressively subverted by the methods and ideals of the wealthy businessmen whom he parasitizes, and though for a time his efforts, like theirs, succeed remarkably, in the end they lead to catastrophe. The novel is perfectly controlled, perfectly articulated in its elaboration of the levels of religious and lay sensibility. What saves it from being merely an "in" novel for Catholic intellectuals is its clear if indirect exposure of the broad social forces at work behind the dereliction of certain elements in the Church. *Morte d'Urban* is the best American satire of any kind in recent decades.

—Hayden Carruth

PRICE, (Edward) Reynolds. American. Born in Macon, North Carolina, 1 February 1933. Educated at Duke University, Durham, North Carolina, 1951-55 (Angier Duke Scholar), A.B. (summa cum laude) 1955 (Phi Beta Kappa); Merton College, Oxford, 1955-58 (Rhodes Scholar), B. Litt. 1958. Member of the Faculty since 1958, Assistant Professor, 1961-68, Associate Professor, 1968-72, Professor of English, 1972-77, and since 1977, James B. Duke Professor, Duke University. Writer-in-Residence, University of North Carolina, Chapel Hill, 1965, and Greensboro, 1971, and University of Kansas, Lawrence, 1967, 1969; Glasgow Professor, Washington and Lee University, Lexington, Virginia, 1971; Member of the Faculty, Salzburg Seminar on American Studies, 1977. Editor, *The Archive*, Durham, 1954-55. Since 1964, Advisory Editor, *Shenandoah*, Lexington, Virginia. Recipient: Faulkner Foundation Prize, 1963; Guggenheim Fellowship, 1964; National Association of Independent Schools Award, 1964; National Endowment for the Arts Fellowship, 1967; American Academy award, 1971; Bellamann Foundation Award, 1976; Lillian Smith Award, 1976. Litt.D.: St. Andrews Presbyterian College, Laurinburg, North Carolina, 1978; Wake Forest University, Winston-Salem, North Carolina, 1979. Agent: Russell and Volkening Inc., 551 Fifth Avenue, New York, New York 10017. Address: 4813 Duke Station, Durham, North Carolina 27706, U.S.A.

PUBLICATIONS

Novels

A Long and Happy Life. New York, Atheneum, and London, Chatto and Windus, 1962.
A Generous Man. New York, Atheneum, 1966; London, Chatto and Windus, 1967.
Love and Work. New York, Atheneum, and London, Chatto and Windus, 1968.
The Surface of Earth. New York, Atheneum, 1975; London, Arlington, 1977.
The Source of Light. New York, Atheneum, 1981.

Short Stories

The Names and Faces of Heroes. New York, Atheneum, and London, Chatto and Windus, 1963.
Permanent Errors. New York, Atheneum, 1970; London, Chatto and Windus, 1971.

Uncollected Short Stories

"Night and Day at Panacea," in *Harper's* (New York), August 1974.
"Commencing," in *Virginia Quarterly Review* (Charlottesville), Spring 1975.

Play

Early Dark (produced New York, 1978). New York, Atheneum, 1977.

Verse

Late Warning: Four Poems. New York, Albondocani Press, 1968.
Torso of an Archaic Apollo—after Rilke. New York, Albondocani Press, 1969.
Lessons Learned: Seven Poems. New York, Albondocani Press, 1977.
Christ Child's Song at the End of the Night. Privately printed, 1978.

Other

Two Theophanies: Genesis 32 and John 21. Privately printed, 1971.
Things Themselves: Essays and Scenes. New York, Atheneum, 1972.
Presence and Absence: Versions from the Bible. Bloomfield Hills, Michigan, Bruccoli Clark, 1973.
Conversations, with William Ray. Memphis, Memphis State University, 1976.
The Good News According to Mark. Privately printed, 1976.
Oracles: Six Versions from the Bible. Durham, North Carolina, Friends of the Duke University Library, 1977.
A Palpable God: Thirty Stories Translated from the Bible with an Essay on the Origins and Life of Narrative. New York, Atheneum, 1978.
Nine Mysteries (Four Joyful, Four Sorrowful, One Glorious). Winston-Salem, North Carolina, Palaemon Press, 1979.

*

Critical Studies: "A Conversation with Reynolds Price" by Wallace Kaufman, in *Shenandoah* (Lexington, Virginia), Summer 1966; "The Reynolds Price Who Outgrew the Southern Pastoral" by Theodore Solotaroff, in *Saturday Review* (New York), 26 September 1970; "Love (and Marriage) in *A Long Happy Life*," in *Twentieth Century Studies* (Los Angeles), January 1971.

* * *

Reynolds Price has moved from detailed examination of of North Carolina rural life to an intense concern with the artist's vision of reality. Beginning with the tragicomic saga of the Mustian family (*A Long and Happy Life*, *A Generous Man*, stories in *The Names and Faces of Heroes*), he has come in *Love and Work* and *Permanent Errors* to wrestle with narrative forms closer to the bone. In the preface to *Permanent Errors* Price described his work as "the attempt to isolate in a number of lives the central error of act, will, understanding which, once made, has been permanent, incurable, but whose diagnosis and palliation are the hopes of continuance."

This applies to all Price's fiction. *A Long and Happy Life* is the inside story of Rosacoke Mustian, a country girl seeking a conventional life with an unconventional young man, Wesley Beavers. Her error is that she conceives "a long and happy life" only in the clichéd terms of romance, of settled-wedded-bliss tradition. She reviews her life, her family's life, is discontent, becomes pregnant by Wesley and finally comes to see him and herself in larger terms, terms of myth, in a Christmas pageant which shows her the complete (and divine) meanings of motherhood, birth, and love.

Myth becomes the vehicle of self-understanding more overtly in *A Generous Man*, which shows the Mustian family several years earlier. It describes an allegorical search for an escaped circus python, a giant serpent named Death, and the discovery of a lost treasure. Milo Mustian describes the stifling forces of convention which circumscribe their lives: "it's what nine-tenths of the humans born since God said 'Adam!' have thought was a life, planned out for themselves—all my people, my Mama, my Daddy (it was what strangled him), Rosacoke...." Only by transcending the everyday, by seeing human life in larger terms, can the individual escape the slow strangulation of "permanent errors" and find direction and meaning in existence.

Price's fiction has become increasingly abstract and complex as he has moved to a more inward vision. From the first he has used sets of images and metaphors to suggest a mysterious or magical reality beyond his pastoral settings. He has deepened this metaphorical (and psychological) interest in *Love and Work* and *Permanent Errors*, where the protagonists are no longer the eccentric pastoral figures of the Mustian clan but are closer to Price's own viewpoint. Price's fiction has always dealt with confusion of the heart and alienation of the mind, but the recent work draws its images and symbols from Price's own experience—his family, a visit to Dachau prison camp, the writer's situation. The grotesqueness and unfamiliarity of the Mustian clan are replaced by more familiar and universal facts of contemporary life. In the massive novel *The Surface of Earth* Price is most ambitious, attempting a family saga encompassing the first half of our century. It details through letters, conversations, and lyrical soliloquies the Mayfield family and its cycle of birth, maturity, and death as seen by Rob Mayfield, who focuses the narrative. The family is more genteel than the Mustians, and their story is more concerned with the world of things and social valences. Yet Price's abiding search for wisdoms of the heart shapes the novel and controls its style.

Love and earth are polarities in Price's work—how to save life from death, how to prevent life from becoming deathly, stale, void of myth and magic? The theme appears most clearly in *A Generous Man*, when the Mustians set out to find and kill Death, the great serpent, and when they are finally told, "Death is dead." In the course of this magical hunt, Milo Mustian comes to understand what he must do to save himself from the slow death of a clichéd life; Rato Mustian, the wise fool, grapples with Death and escapes its coils through his cunning folly; Rosacoke moves from complete innocence to the dawn of maturity. In his later fiction Price has moved from symbols of external life to more internalized ones: sleep, dreams, a writer seeking a relationship between love and work, self and others, private life and shared life. Price's fiction describes the individual's perceptions of himself and of the realities around him, the uses of imagination. His characters travel on a quest for the potency of myth and the ability to transcend a closed vision of everyday reality. They move toward permanent truths through "permanent errors."

—William J. Schafer

PRIESTLEY, J(ohn) B(oynton). British. Born in Bradford, Yorkshire, 13 September 1894. Educated in Bradford schools, and at Trinity Hall, Cambridge, M.A. Served with the Duke of Wellington's and Devon Regiments, 1914-19. Married 1)Patricia Tempest (died, 1925), two daughters; 2)Mary Wyndham Lewis (divorced, 1952), two daughters and one son; 3)the writer Jacquetta Hawkes in 1953. Director, Mask Theatre, London, 1938-39; radio lecturer on BBC programme "Postscripts" during World War II; regular contributor, *New Statesman*, London. President, P.E.N., London 1936-37; United Kingdom Delegate, and Chairman, Unesco International Theatre Conference, Paris, 1947, and Prague, 1948 Chairman, British Theatre Conference, 1948; President, International Theatre Institute, 1949; Member, National Theatre Board London, 1966-67. Recipient: Black Memorial Prize, 1930; Ellen Terry Award, 1948. LL.D.: University of St. Andrews; D.Litt. University of Birmingham; University of Bradford. Honorary Freeman, City of Bradford, 1973; Honorary Student, Trinity Hall Cambridge, 1978. Order of Merit, 1977. Address: Kissing Tree House, Alveston, Stratford upon Avon, Warwickshire, England.

PUBLICATIONS

Novels

Adam in Moonlight. London, Heinemann, and New York, Harpe 1927.

Benighted. London, Heinemann, 1927; as *The Old Dark House* New York, Harper, 1928.

Farthing Hall, with Hugh Walpole. London, Macmillan, an New York, Doubleday, 1929.

The Good Companions. London, Heinemann, and New York Harper, 1929.

Angel Pavement. London, Heinemann, and New York, Harpe 1930.

Faraway. London, Heinemann, and New York, Harper, 1932.

I'll Tell You Everything: A Frolic, with Gerald Bullett. New York Macmillan, 1932; London, Heinemann, 1933.

Wonder Hero. London, Heinemann, and New York, Harpe 1933.

They Walk in the City: The Lovers in the Stone Forest. London Heinemann, and New York, Harper, 1936.

The Doomsday Men: An Adventure. London, Heinemann, an New York, Harper, 1938.

Let the People Sing. London, Heinemann, 1939; New York Harper, 1940.

Black-Out in Gretley: A Story of—and for—Wartime. London Heinemann, and New York, Harper, 1942.

Daylight on Saturday: A Novel about an Aircraft Factory. London, Heinemann, and New York, Harper, 1943.

Three Men in New Suits. London, Heinemann, and New York Harper, 1945.

Bright Day. London, Heinemann, and New York, Harper, 1946

Jenny Villiers: A Story of the Theatre. London, Heinemann, an New York, Harper, 1947.

Festival at Farbridge. London, Heinemann, 1951; as *Festival* New York, Harper, 1951.

The Magicians. London, Heinemann, and New York, Harpe 1954.

Low Notes on a High Level: A Frolic. London, Heinemann, an New York, Harper, 1954.

Saturn over the Water. London, Heinemann, and New York Doubleday, 1961.

The Thirty-First of June. London, Heinemann, 1961; New York Doubleday, 1962.

The Shapes of Sleep: A Topical Tale. London, Heinemann, ar New York, Doubleday, 1962.

Sir Michael and Sir George. London, Heinemann, 1964; Bosto Little Brown, 1965.

Lost Empires. London, Heinemann, and Boston, Little Brow 1965.

Salt Is Leaving. London, Pan, 1966; New York, Harper, 1975.

It's an Old Country. London, Heinemann, and Boston, Litt Brown, 1967.

The Image Men: Out of Town, London End. London, Heinemann, 2 vols, 1968; Boston, Little Brown, 1 vol., 1969.

Found, Lost, Found; or, The English Way of Life. London Heinemann, 1976; New York, Stein and Day, 1977.

Short Stories

The Town Major of Miraucourt. London, Heinemann, 1930.
Albert Goes Through. London, Heinemann, and New York, Harper, 1933.
Going Up: Stories and Sketches. London, Pan, 1950.
The Other Place and Other Stories of the Same Sort. London, Heinemann, and New York, Harper, 1953.
The Carfitt Crisis and Two Other Stories. London, Heinemann, 1975.

Plays

The Good Companions, with Edward Knoblock, adaptation of the novel by Priestley (produced London and New York, 1931). London and New York, French, 1935.
Dangerous Corner (produced London and New York, 1932). London, Heinemann, and New York, French, 1932.
The Roundabout (produced Liverpool, London, and New York, 1932). London, Heinemann, and New York, French, 1933.
Laburnum Grove: An Immoral Comedy (produced London, 1933; New York, 1935). London, Heinemann, 1934; New York, French, 1935.
Eden End (produced London, 1934; New York, 1935). London, Heinemann, 1934; in *Three Plays and a Preface*, 1935.
Cornelius: A Business Affair in Three Transactions (produced Birmingham and London, 1935). London, Heinemann, 1935; New York, French, 1936.
Duet in Floodlight (produced Liverpool and London, 1935). London, Heinemann, 1935.
Three Plays and a Preface (includes *Dangerous Corner, Eden End, Cornelius*). New York, Harper, 1935.
Bees on the Boat Deck: A Farcical Tragedy (produced London, 1936). London, Heinemann, and Boston, Baker, 1936.
Spring Tide (as Peter Goldsmith), with George Billam (produced London, 1936). London, Heinemann, and New York, French, 1936.
The Bad Samaritan (produced Liverpool, 1937).
Time and the Conways (produced London, 1937; New York, 1938). London, Heinemann, 1937; New York, Harper, 1938.
I Have Been Here Before (produced London, 1937; New York, 1938). London, Heinemann, 1937; New York, Harper, 1938.
Two Time Plays (includes *Time and the Conways* and *I Have Been Here Before*). London, Heinemann, 1937.
People at Sea (as *I Am a Stranger Here*, produced Bradford, 1937; as *People at Sea*, produced London, 1937). London, Heinemann, and New York, French, 1937.
The Rebels (produced Bradford, 1938).
Mystery at Greenfingers: A Comedy of Detection (produced London, 1938). London, French, 1937; New York, French, 1938.
When We Are Married: A Yorkshire Farcical Comedy (produced London, 1938; New York, 1939). London, Heinemann, 1938; New York, French, 1940.
Music at Night (produced Malvern, 1938; London, 1939). Included in *Three Plays*, 1943; in *Plays I*, 1948.
Johnson over Jordan (produced London, 1939). Published as *Johnson over Jordan: The Play, and All about It (An Essay)*, London, Heinemann, and New York, Harper, 1939.
The Long Mirror (produced Oxford, 1940; London, 1945). Included in *Three Plays*, 1943; in *Four Plays*, 1944.
Good Night Children: A Comedy of Broadcasting (produced London, 1942). Included in *Three Comedies*, 1945; in *Plays II*, 1949.
Desert Highway (produced Bristol, 1943; London, 1944). London, Heinemann, 1944; in *Four Plays*, 1944.
They Came to a City (produced London, 1943). Included in *Three Plays*, 1943; in *Four Plays*, 1944.
Three Plays (includes *Music at Night, The Long Mirror, They Came to a City*). London, Heinemann, 1943.
How Are They at Home? A Topical Comedy (produced London, 1944). Included in *Three Comedies*, 1945; in *Plays II*, 1949.
The Golden Fleece (as *The Bull Market*, produced Bradford, 1944). Included in *Three Comedies*, 1945.
Four Plays (includes *Music at Night, The Long Mirror, They Came to a City, Desert Highway*). London, Heinemann, and New York, Harper, 1944.
Three Comedies (includes *Good Night Children, The Golden Fleece, How Are They at Home?*). London, Heinemann, 1945.
An Inspector Calls (produced Moscow, 1945; London, 1946; New York, 1947). London, Heinemann, 1947; New York, Dramatists Play Service, 1948(?).
Jenny Villiers (produced Bristol, 1946).
The Rose and Crown (televised, 1946). London, French, 1947.
Ever Since Paradise: An Entertainment, Chiefly Referring to Love and Marriage (also director: produced on tour, 1946; London, 1947). London and New York, French, 1949.
Three Time Plays (includes *Dangerous Corner, Time and the Conways, I Have Been Here Before*). London, Pan, 1947.
The Linden Tree (produced Sheffield and London, 1947; New York, 1948). London, Heinemann, and New York, French, 1948.
The Plays of J.B. Priestley:
  I. *Dangerous Corner, I Have Been Here Before, Johnson over Jordan, Music at Night, The Linden Tree, Eden End, Time and the Conways*. London, Heinemann, 1948; as *Seven Plays*, New York, Harper, 1950.
  II. *Laburnum Grove, Bees on the Boat Deck, When We Are Married, Good Night Children, The Good Companions, How Are They at Home?, Ever Since Paradise*. London, Heinemann, 1949; New York, Harper, 1951.
  III. *Cornelius, People at Sea, They Came to a City, Desert Highway, An Inspector Calls, Home Is Tomorrow, Summer Day's Dream*. London, Heinemann, 1950; New York, Harper, 1952.
Home Is Tomorrow (produced Bradford and London, 1948). London, Heinemann, 1949; in *Plays III*, 1950.
The High Toby: A Play for the Toy Theatre (produced London, 1954). London, Penguin-Pollock, 1948.
Summer Day's Dream (produced Bradford and London, 1949). Included in *Plays III*, 1950.
The Olympians, music by Arthur Bliss (produced London, 1949). London, Novello, 1949.
Bright Shadow: A Play of Detection (produced Oldham and London, 1950). London, French, 1950.
Treasure on Pelican (as *Treasure on Pelican Island*, televised, 1951; as *Treasure on Pelican*, produced Cardiff and London, 1952). London, Evans, 1953.
Dragon's Mouth: A Dramatic Quartet, with Jacquetta Hawkes (also director: produced Malvern and London, 1952; New York, 1955). London, Heinemann, and New York, Harper, 1952.
Private Rooms: A One-Act Comedy in the Viennese Style. London, French, 1953.
Mother's Day. London, French, 1953.
Try It Again (produced London, 1965). London, French, 1953.
A Glass of Bitter. London, French, 1954.
The White Countess, with Jacquetta Hawkes (produced Dublin and London, 1954).
The Scandalous Affair of Mr. Kettle and Mrs. Moon (produced Folkestone and London, 1955). London, French, 1956.
Take the Fool Away (produced Vienna, 1955; Nottingham, 1959).
These Our Actors (produced Glasgow, 1956).
The Glass Cage (produced Toronto and London, 1957). London, French, 1958.
The Thirty-First of June (produced Toronto and London, 1957).
A Pavilion of Masks (produced in Germany, 1961; Bristol, 1963). London, French, 1958.
A Severed Head, with Iris Murdoch, adaptation of the novel by Murdoch (produced Bristol and London, 1963; New York, 1964). London, Chatto and Windus, 1964.

Screenplays: *Sing As We Go*, with Gordon Wellesley, 1934; *Look Up and Laugh*, with Gordon Wellesley, 1935; *We Live in Two*

Worlds, 1937; *Jamaica Inn*, with Sidney Gilliat and Joan Harrison, 1939; *Britain at Bay*, 1940; *Our Russian Allies*, 1941; *The Foreman Went to France* (*Somewhere in France*), with others, 1942; *Last Holiday*, 1950.

Radio Plays: *The Return of Jess Oakroyd*, 1941; *The Golden Entry*, 1955; *End Game at the Dolphin*, 1956; *An Arabian Night in Park Lane*, 1965.

Television Plays: *The Rose and Crown*, 1946; *Treasure on Pelican Island*, 1951; *The Stone Face*, 1957; *The Rack*, 1958; *Doomsday for Dyson*, 1958; *The Fortrose Incident*, from his play *Home Is Tomorrow*, 1959; *Level Seven*, from the novel by Mordecai Roshwald, 1966; *The Lost Peace* series, 1966; *Anyone for Tennis*, 1968; *Linda at Pulteney's*, 1969.

Verse

The Chapman of Rhymes (juvenilia). London, Alexander Moring, 1918.

Other

Brief Diversions, Being Tales, Travesties, and Epigrams. Cambridge, Bowes and Bowes, 1922.
Papers from Lilliput. Cambridge, Bowes and Bowes, 1922.
I for One. London, Lane, 1923; New York, Dodd Mead, 1924.
Figures in Modern Literature. London, Lane, and New York, Dodd Mead, 1924.
The English Comic Characters. London, Lane, and New York, Dodd Mead, 1925.
George Meredith. London and New York, Macmillan, 1926.
Talking. London, Jarrolds, and New York, Harper, 1926.
(*Essays*). London, Harrap, 1926.
Open House: A Book of Essays. London, Heinemann, and New York, Harper, 1927.
Thomas Love Peacock. London and New York, Macmillan, 1927.
The English Novel. London, Benn, 1927; revised edition, London and New York, Nelson, 1935.
Apes and Angels: A Book of Essays. London, Methuen, 1928; as *Too Many People and Other Reflections*, New York, Harper, 1928.
The Balconinny and Other Essays. London, Methuen, 1929; as *The Balconinny*, New York, Harper, 1930.
English Humour. London and New York, Longman, 1929.
Self-Selected Essays. London, Heinemann, 1932; New York, Harper, 1933.
Four-in-Hand (miscellany). London, Heinemann, 1934.
English Journey, Being a Rambling But Truthful Account of What One Man Saw and Heard and Felt and Thought During a Journey Through England During the Autumn of the Year 1933. London, Heinemann-Gollancz, and New York, Harper, 1934.
Midnight on the Desert: A Chapter of Autobiography. London, Heinemann, 1937; as *Midnight on the Desert, Being an Excursion into Autobiography During a Winter in America, 1935-36*, New York, Harper, 1937.
Rain upon Godshill: A Further Chapter of Autobiography. London, Heinemann, and New York, Harper, 1939.
Britain Speaks (radio talks). New York, Harper, 1940.
Postscripts (radio talks). London, Heinemann, 1940; as *All England Listened*, New York, Chilmark Press, 1968.
Out of the People. London, Collins-Heinemann, and New York, Harper, 1941.
Britain at War. New York, Harper, 1942.
British Women Go to War. London, Collins, 1943.
Manpower: The Story of Britain's Mobilisation for War. London, His Majesty's Stationery Office, 1944.
Here Are Your Answers. London, Socialist Book Centre, 1944.
Letter to a Returning Serviceman. London, Home and Van Thal, 1945.
The Secret Dream: An Essay on Britain, America, and Russia. London, Turnstile Press, 1946.
Russian Journey. London, Writers Group of the Society for Cultural Relations with the USSR, 1946.
The New Citizen (address). London, Council for Education i World Citizenship, 1946.
Theatre Outlook. London, Nicholson and Watson, 1947.
The Arts under Socialism (lecture). London, Turnstile Press 1947.
Delight. London, Heinemann, and New York, Harper, 1949.
The Priestley Companion: A Selection from the Writings of J.B. Priestley. London, Penguin-Heinemann, 1951.
Journey down a Rainbow (travel), with Jacquetta Hawkes. London, Cresset Press-Heinemann, and New York, Harper, 1955.
All about Ourselves and Other Essays, edited by Eric Gillett London, Heinemann, 1956.
The Writer in a Changing Society (lecture). Aldington, Kent Hand and Flower Press, 1956.
Thoughts in the Wilderness (essays). London, Heinemann, an New York, Harper, 1957.
The Art of the Dramatist: A Lecture Together with Appendices an Discursive Notes. London, Heinemann, 1957; Boston, Th Writer, 1958.
Topside; or, The Future of England: A Dialogue. London Heinemann, 1958.
The Story of Theatre (juvenile). London, Rathbone, 1959; as *Th Wonderful World of the Theater*, New York, Doubleday, 1959
Literature and Western Man. London, Heinemann, and Ne York, Harper, 1960.
William Hazlitt. London, Longman, 1960.
Charles Dickens: A Pictorial Biography. London, Thames an Hudson, 1961; New York, Viking Press, 1962; as *Charles Dicken and His World*, Thames and Hudson and Viking Press, 1969.
Margin Released: A Writer's Reminiscences and Reflections. London, Heinemann, and New York, Harper, 1962.
Man and Time. London, Aldus, and New York, Doubleday 1964.
The Moments and Other Pieces. London, Heinemann, 1966.
The World of J.B. Priestley, edited by Donald G. MacRae. London, Heinemann, 1967.
Essays of Five Decades, edited by Susan Cooper. Boston, Littl Brown, 1968; London, Heinemann, 1969.
Trumpets over the Sea, Being a Rambling and Egotistical Accoun of the London Symphony Orchestra's Engagement at Dayton Beach, Florida, in July-August 1967. London, Heineman 1968.
The Prince of Pleasure and His Regency 1811-1820. London Heinemann, and New York, Harper, 1969.
The Edwardians. London, Heinemann, and New York, Harpe 1970.
Anton Chekhov. London, International Textbook, 1970.
Snoggle (juvenile). London, Heinemann, 1971; New York, Harcourt Brace, 1972.
Victoria's Heyday. London, Heinemann, and New York, Harcourt Brace, 1972.
Over the Long High Wall: Some Reflections and Speculations o Life, Death, and Time. London, Heinemann, 1972.
The English. London, Heinemann, and New York, Viking Press 1973.
Outcries and Asides. London, Heinemann, 1974.
A Visit to New Zealand. London, Heinemann, 1974.
Particular Pleasures, Being a Personal Record of Some Varied Art and Many Different Artists. London, Heinemann, 1975.
The Happy Dream. Andoversford, Gloucestershire, Whittingto Press, 1976.
English Humour (not the same as 1929 book). London, Heinemann, 1976.
Instead of the Trees: A Final Chapter of Autobiography. London Heinemann, and New York, Stein and Day, 1977.

Editor, *Essayists Past and Present: A Selection of English Essays*

London, Jenkins, and New York, Dial Press, 1925.
Editor, *Fools and Philosophers: A Gallery of Comic Figures from English Literature.* London, Lane, and New York, Dodd Mead, 1925.
Editor, *Tom Moore's Diary: A Selection.* London, Cambridge University Press, 1925.
Editor, *The Book of Bodley Head Verse.* London, Lane, and New York, Dodd Mead, 1926.
Editor, *Our Nation's Heritage.* London, Dent, 1939.
Editor, *Scenes from London Life, From Sketches by Boz,* by Dickens. London, Pan, 1947.
Editor, *The Best of Leacock.* Toronto, McClelland and Stewart, 1957; as *The Bodley Head Leacock,* London, Bodley Head, 1957.
Editor, with Josephine Spear, *Adventures in English Literature.* New York, Harcourt Brace, 1963.

*

Bibliography: *J.B. Priestley: An Annotated Bibliography* by Alan Edwin Day, New York, Garland, 1980.

Manuscript Collection: University of Texas, Austin.

Critical Studies: *J.B. Priestley* by Ivor Brown, London, Longman, 1957, revised edition, 1964; *J.B. Priestley: An Informal Study of His Work* by David Hughes, London, Hart Davis, 1958, Freeport, New York, Books for Libraries, 1970; *J.B. Priestley: Portrait of an Author* by Susan Cooper, London, Heinemann, 1970, New York, Harper, 1971; *J.B. Priestley* by Kenneth Young, London, Longman, 1977; *J.B. Priestley* by John Braine, London, Weidenfeld and Nicolson, 1978, New York, Barnes and Noble, 1979; *J.B. Priestley* by A.A. De Vitis and Albert E. Kalson, Boston, Twayne, 1980; *J.B. Priestley: The Last of the Sages* by John Atkins, London, Calder, and New York, Riverrun Press, 1981.

Theatrical Activities:

Director: **Plays**—*Ever Since Paradise,* tour, 1946, and London, 1947; *Dragon's Mouth,* London, 1952.

J.B. Priestley comments:

(1972) When I published *The Good Companions* and *Angel Pavement* it was possible for successful novels to have enormous sales in their original clothbound editions. This has encouraged some older readers to imagine that my best work in fiction belongs to this earlier period. In my opinion—and that of many friends and critics—this is wrong. My postwar novels, notably *Bright Day* (my own favourite), *Festival at Farbridge, Lost Empires,* and *The Image Men,* are the novels I would choose to represent me. Unlike many contemporary writers, I have always believed that novels (and plays) should be entertaining. But that does not mean—as some silly reviewers, especially in America, seem to think—that my novels are entertainment and nothing else. There is always a great deal of social criticism in them, together with much symbolism, both in the action and the characters. So, for example, my last and longest novel, *The Image Men,* is not simply an elderly novelist being funny but is a sharp satire, very topical, on our ideas of education, our mass media, advertising, business expertise, etc. If at times—as in *Saturn over the Water* or *The Shapes of Sleep*—I desert the novel proper for what is really a tale, that is because I really enjoy telling a story now and again. I always write first to please myself because after all I have to spend most time with the book, so I propose to enjoy doing it. But I have almost always a serious purpose, and this is being recognised by psychologists, sociologists, publishers abroad, and the foreign students who write to tell me they are preparing theses on my work, Probably, taking me all round, I have written too much, but that is because I have always had a lot of ideas that excited me, so I always went ahead, though I knew it has been unfashionable during the last 40 years to be versatile and prolific.

* * *

To consider J.B. Priestley's novels separately from the rest of his considerable contribution to letters in the form of criticism, plays, essays, and radio scripts, is to see a diminished part of his total achievement; diminished, because the whole of Priestley seems greater than the sum of his parts. He is more of a one-man English institution than mere novelist, essayist, or dramatist. Yet, obviously he would never have become a public figure at all without his writing. The apparent paradox of the public literary figure whose work attracts less critical attention than that of many minor writers might be explained by the theory that his work in all the various genres is unified only in its role as subdominant medium for the expression of Priestley's view on just about everything; the individual novels, essays, and plays are mere messengers, not intended to be regarded as independent works of literary art.

Certainly, this seems to be the case when one considers his novels, written over a period of almost 50 years among a hectic output of plays, essays, and documentary pieces. They are so varied in kind and quality that it is difficult to discern in them any one particularly strong, concrete tendency. One feels that at heart Priestley must be the essayist and broadcaster—egocentric, journalistic, and crotchety—because his novels demonstrate the caprice and eclecticism of the bellelettrist rather than the singleminded artistry one usually associates with even minor novelists. There is no development over the years, and the whole canon has an accidental, or at least occasional, air about it.

To make a rather crude categorization, one can distinguish three groups of novels. First is that which includes all those with some claim to lasting worth—*Good Companions, Angel Pavement, Bright Day* and *Lost Empires.* Second is the group of light, almost fairytale, romance-adventures which either present what David Hughes has called "lunges out of routine" on the parts of characters whose lives hitherto have been pretty mundane, or concern the struggle between the human individual and a mechanistic establishment of science, technology, and bureaucracy: this group is represented by *Adam in Moonshine, Faraway, The Doomsday Men, The Magicians,* and *The Shapes of Sleep.* Third are the topical novels of social concern, either written to a programme of social criticism—*Wonder Hero, They Walk in the City, Low Notes on a High Level,* and *Sir Michael and Sir George*—or for particular occasions, like the war-time novels *Let the People Sing, Black-Out in Gretley, Daylight on Saturday,* and *Three Men in New Suits.*

Novels of the first group present Priestley at his best and most liked. All four novels show a real concern for humanity and the quality of individuals' lives, coupled with a vivid, panoramic picture of England. In two of the novels—*Good Companions* and *Lost Empires*—the setting is the variety theatre, and this works well at several levels; thematically, the theatre provides an image which underlies Priestley's major point that people need the right roles in life if they are to be reasonably happy; technically, the theatre provides natural and credible setting for picaresque adventures over the English provinces and, at the same time, it allows free rein to the spirit of magic, which Priestley is at pains to promote in many of his novels, without straining the reader's credulity. Further the "business" of the stage becomes the "business" of the novel, adding both interest and depth. Although they are separated by 36 years in the writing, both novels radiate similar atmospheres of human warmth without declining either to mere sentimentality or to earnest editorialising on how to be happy.

Angel Pavement and *Bright Day* are more sombre in theme and tone, but probably represent Priestley's greatest achievements in the novel. His picture of London in *Angel Pavement* has all the realism and evocativeness that Conrad manages in *The Secret Agent*; the shabby cynicism, frightening menace, and desperate alienation of the city stay long in the reader's memory. Although the reader cannot warm to the characters as he does to those in *Good Companions* he is made to share with them their helplessness in the impersonal city. A similar feeling of sadness is left by *Bright Day,* despite a tacked-on happy ending. This novel is autobiographic of at least a part of Priestley's life and character, being the first-person account by Gregory Dawson of his successful rise to eminence as a novelist and writer for the movies. The concern is with the artificiality of show-business success and its deadening effect on human relationships and artistic integrity. The sad note it strikes originates in the novel itself, but it is heightened for the reader who recalls that Dawson's final opting for artistic integrity is not necessarily Priestley's.

The romance-adventure novels of the second group are, at best, light reading for journeys, with all the elements of hero identification and wish-fulfillment that one associates with the escapist novel. They function, nevertheless, as exponents of their author's world-view by providing opportunities for much editorial comment. Unfortunately, such comment lacks both impact and subtlety, because it is not artistically supported in the novels themselves. Frequently, the mood and tone set up in the valid terms of setting, characterisation, and plot, are undermined by contrived opinionising by the author; for example, in *Faraway*, several hundred pages of well-wrought narrative culminate in an irritable attack on Americanism and the sloppiness of South Sea Islanders, which completely reverses the tone already established. In *The Magicians* and *The Shapes of Sleep* the author's opinions are so obtrusive that the novels are little more than thin allegories.

The novels of the third group are what they were, presumably, meant to be—journalistic, topical, and documentary. They do not function as anything more than transient pieces of writing to convey their author's views—encouragement and optimism in the war-time novels, prejudices and grumbles in the post-war novels. That they were written at all confirms one's suspicion that in Priestley the artist never competes with the public man; like his good companions, he is really a very talented amateur who is not willing to take the final step of commitment that the real artist must take. His writing tends to be careless, quick, and easy, as though he were not really interested in it. However, his best four novels will entertain readers for a long time after the public figure that wrote them has been forgotten.

—Frederick Bowers

PRITCHETT, V(ictor) S(awdon). British. Born in Ipswich, Suffolk, 16 December 1900. Educated at Alleyn's School, Dulwich, London. Married Dorothy Rudge Roberts in 1936; one son and one daughter. Worked in the leather trade in London, 1916-20, and in the shellac, glue, and photographic trade in Paris, 1920-32; Correspondent in Ireland and Spain for the *Christian Science Monitor*, Boston, 1923-26; Critic from 1926, Permanent Critic from 1937, and Director, 1946-78, *New Statesman*, London; Christian Gauss Lecturer, Princeton University, New Jersey, 1953; Beckman Professor, University of California, Berkeley, 1962; Writer-in-Residence, Smith College, Northampton, Massachusetts, 1966, 1970-72; Visiting Professor, Brandeis University, Waltham, Massachusetts, 1968; Clark Lecturer, Cambridge University, 1969; Visiting Professor, Columbia University, New York, 1972. President, P.E.N. Club, English Centre, 1970, and President of International P.E.N., 1974-76. Recipient: Heinemann Award, for non-fiction, 1969; P.E.N. Award, for non-fiction, 1974. D.Lit.: University of Leeds, 1972; D.Litt.: Columbia University, 1978; University of Sussex, Brighton, 1980. Fellow, Royal Society of Literature, 1969. Honorary Member, American Academy, 1971. C.B.E. (Commander, Order of the British Empire), 1968. Knighted, 1975. Address: 12 Regent's Park Terrace, London N.W.1, England.

PUBLICATIONS

Novels

Clare Drummer. London, Benn, 1929.
Shirley Sanz. London, Gollancz, 1932; as *Elopement into Exile*, Boston, Little Brown, 1932.
Nothing like Leather. London, Chatto and Windus, and New York, Macmillan, 1935.
Dead Man Leading. London, Chatto and Windus, and New York, Macmillan, 1937.
Mr. Beluncle. London, Chatto and Windus, and New York, Harcourt Brace, 1951.

Short Stories

The Spanish Virgin and Other Stories. London, Benn, 1930.
You Make Your Own Life. London, Chatto and Windus, 1938.
It May Never Happen and Other Stories. London, Chatto and Windus, 1945; New York, Reynal, 1947.
Collected Stories. London, Chatto and Windus, 1956.
The Sailor, The Sense of Humour, and Other Stories. New York, Knopf, 1956.
When My Girl Comes Home. London, Chatto and Windus, and New York, Knopf, 1961.
The Key to My Heart. London, Chatto and Windus, 1963; New York, Random House, 1964.
The Saint and Other Stories. London, Penguin, 1966.
Blind Love and Other Stories. London, Chatto and Windus, 1969; New York, Random House, 1970.
Penguin Modern Stories 9, with others. London, Penguin, 1971.
The Camberwell Beauty and Other Stories. London, Chatto and Windus, and New York, Random House, 1974.
Selected Stories. London, Chatto and Windus, and New York, Random House, 1978.
On the Edge of the Cliff. New York, Random House, 1979; London, Chatto and Windus, 1980.

Plays

The Gambler (broadcast, 1947). Published in *Imaginary Conversations*, edited by Rayner Heppenstall, London, Secker and Warburg, 1948.

Screenplays: *Essential Jobs* (documentary), 1942; *The Two Feathers*, with Anthony Asquith, 1944.

Radio Play: *The Gambler*, 1947.

Other

Marching Spain. London, Benn, 1928.
In My Good Books. London, Chatto and Windus, 1942; Port Washington, New York, Kennikat Press, 1977.
Build the Ships: The Official Story of the Shipyards in War-Time. London, His Majesty's Stationery Office, 1946.
The Living Novel. London, Chatto and Windus, 1946; New York, Reynal, 1947; revised edition, New York, Random House, 1964.
Why Do I Write: An Exchange of Views Between Elizabeth Bowen, Graham Greene, and V.S. Pritchett. London, Marshall, 1948; New York, Haskell House, 1976.
Books in General. London, Chatto and Windus, and New York, Harcourt Brace, 1953.
The Spanish Temper. London, Chatto and Windus, and New York, Knopf, 1954.
London Perceived. London, Chatto and Windus, and New York, Harcourt Brace, 1962.
Foreign Faces. London, Chatto and Windus, 1964; as *The Offensive Traveller*, New York, Knopf, 1964.
New York Proclaimed. London, Chatto and Windus, and New York, Harcourt Brace, 1965.
The Working Novelist. London, Chatto and Windus, 1965.
Dublin: A Portrait. London, Bodley Head, and New York, Harper, 1967.
A Cab at the Door: Childhood and Youth 1900-1920. London, Chatto and Windus, and New York, Random House, 1968.

George Meredith and English Comedy. London, Chatto and Windus, and New York, Random House, 1970.
Midnight Oil (autobiography). London, Chatto and Windus, 1971; New York, Random House, 1972.
Balzac: A Biography. London, Chatto and Windus, and New York, Knopf, 1973.
Great American Families, with others. New York, Norton, and London, Times Books, 1977.
The Gentle Barbarian: The Life and Work of Turgenev. London, Chatto and Windus, and New York, Random House, 1977.
Autobiography (address). London, English Association, 1977.
The Mythmakers: Essays on European, Russian, and South American Novelists. London, Chatto and Windus, and New York, Random House, 1979.
The Tale Bearers: Essays on English, American, and Other Writers. London, Chatto and Windus, and New York, Random House, 1980.

Editor, *This England.* London, New Statesman and Nation, 1938.
Editor, *Novels and Stories*, by Robert Louis Stevenson. London, Pilot Press, 1945; New York, Duell, 1946.
Editor, *Turnstile One: A Literary Miscellany from the New Statesman.* London, Turnstile Press, 1948.
Editor, *The Oxford Book of Short Stories.* London and New York, Oxford University Press, 1981.

*

V.S. Pritchett comments:

My chief interests have been: travel, specially Spanish; short stories, which I value most; literary criticism over the years for the *New Statesman*.

* * *

V.S. Pritchett is one of the most richly endowed of living men of letters and has written with equal distinction as literary critic, travel-writer, autobiographer, novelist, and short-story-writer. In whatever field he writes the work bears his thumb-print and is marked by his unfailing curiosity about the oddities and vagaries of human nature and by his exceedingly close observation of the human scene, and these are allied to a darting, idiosyncratic prose akin to brilliant talk.

If there is one subject that Pritchett has made his own and that, in one way or another, informs his writings, it is puritanism. He is, so to say, the connoisseur of puritanism in its characteristically English manifestations, which are generally lower-middle-class. As he writes in his essay on Gosse's *Father and Son*:

> Extreme puritanism gives purpose, drama and intensity to private life.... Outwardly, the extreme puritan appears narrow, crabbed, fanatical, gloomy and dull; but from the inside—what a series of dramatic climaxes his life is, what a fascinating casuistry beguiles him, how he is bemused by the comedies of duplicity, sharpened by the ingenious puzzles of the conscience, and carried away by the eloquence of hypocrisy.

Such a character is described in Matthew Burkle, the central figure in Pritchett's early novel, *Nothing like Leather*. As the title indicates, the novel is set against the background of the leather trade: though it may not be in its main interest, Pritchett's fiction is always saturated in the actual.

Burkle is a man who, hating sex, channels his energies to making money. To the extent that one feels Pritchett to be moved in his delineation by intellectual curiosity rather than by sympathy, Burkle is still a more or less conventional representation of the puritan. This is true also of the representation of Harry Johnson in *Dead Man Leading*, an explorer who deserts the scientific expedition he is with in Brazil in order to search for his father, who has disappeared in the interior. The background—the heat, damp, and squalour of the Amazon forests—is most brilliantly rendered; and so, too, is the tortured mind of Johnson, who goes up the river "with the speechless fear of a son guiltily approaching his father."

But something appears in *Dead Man Leading* that is not present in the earlier novel. Intermittently, Pritchett displays himself as a comic writer, which is how one now thinks of him, and there is, in these comic passages, a sense of liberation, of ease, a delight in human oddity for its own sake.

In Pritchett's major novel, *Mr. Beluncle*, comedy takes over completely, and comedy here is an aspect of sympathy; Beluncle is accepted totally. Beluncle, a furniture manufacturer on a small scale, during the course of life has been in turn Congregationalist, Methodist, Plymouth Brother, Baptist, Unitarian, Theosophist, Christian Scientist. All these changes are related in some way to his economic situation. When the novel begins, he is a member of an American sect called The Church of the Last Purification, Toronto, a sect that denies the objective existence of evil.

Beluncle may seem and is indeed a self-deceiver, a liar, a cheat, a hypocrite, and a domestic tyrant. But all this is not so important as the fact that he is a man who is as it were lived by a dream, the victim of a compulsive fantasy that rules his life and turns everything and everyone he meets into its accomplices, a fantasy that renders his life and those of his children who must suffer under him always dramatic. He is a character, in the tradition and even the mode of Dickens, on whom Pritchett, as literary critic, has written with such intuitive understanding. And the novel is extraordinarily faithful to and revealing of one section, which seems to be permanent, of English lower-middle-class life.

Pritchett's novels are intellectually exciting and wonderfully well-written. But they are less satisfying aesthetically. *Mr. Beluncle*, for instance, is curiously static. He is there all the time but does not develop or change in his being. The same could be said of Pecksniff, but Pecksniff, great creation though he is, is, in *Martin Chuzzlewit*, only one character among many. One feels, indeed, that for all his great knowledge of it Pritchett is not wholly at home or comfortable in the novel form. In the short story, on the other hand, he is completely at home, and it is in the short story, for which he seems to have abandoned the novel, that he had done his finest work in fiction.

Settings and characters are much the same as in the novels. Very often the scene is the south-east of England, with London and the City not far away; the characters again from the lower-middle-class, clerks and commercial travellers. It is a world closely akin to Wells's in his early novels; the characters might be the children or grandchildren of Wells's. One thinks of a story like "Many Are Disappointed," with its four characters, office-workers, on a cycling tour dreaming of beer in an inn and, in the end, settling for tea. At times, too, the matter is much the same, as in "The Saint," which might almost be an episode in *Mr. Beluncle*. The difference, however, is that in his short stories Pritchett's touch is absolutely sure; he is the complete master of the form. There are also, of course, the qualities one takes for granted in him: the swift economical language, racy, colloquial, the Dickensian eye for detail, the unerring instinct for idiosyncrasy that reveals character. There is the sense, too, that the stories are not abstractions; one feels that behind them there is a whole actual observable world which in some mysterious way they sum up in themselves. Pritchett is not a writer easily classified; his stories are his own and like no one else's. They seem very English. But each one of them, like Joyce's in *Dubliners*, is the rendering of what Joyce called an "epiphany," an incident or a sudden glimpse of a happening in which a moment of reality is made manifest. This is indeed the modern story-writer's art, and among contemporary writers no one is a greater master of it than Pritchett.

—Walter Allen

PROKOSCH, Frederic. American. Born in Madison, Wisconsin, 17 May 1908. Educated at Haverford College, Pennsylvania, 1922-25, M.A. 1926; Yale University, New Haven, Connecticut, 1930-31, Ph.D. 1933; King's College, Cambridge, 1935-37, M.A. 1937. Instructor in English, Yale University, 1932-34, and New York University, 1936-37; Printer, of modern poetry, in Bryn Mawr, Pennsylvania, Cambridge, Florence, Venice, and Lisbon, 1933-40; Cultural Attaché, American Legation, Stockholm, 1943-45; Visiting Lecturer, University of Rome, 1950-51. Squash-Racquets Champion of France, 1933-39, and of Sweden, 1944. Recipient: Guggenheim Fellowship, 1937; Harper Prize, 1937; Harriet Monroe Memorial Prize (*Poetry*, Chicago), 1941; Fulbright Fellowship, 1951; National Endowment for the Arts grant, 1977. Address: "Ma Trouvaille," Plan de Grasse, Alpes Maritimes, France.

PUBLICATIONS

Novels

The Asiatics. New York, Harper, and London, Chatto and Windus, 1935.
The Seven Who Fled. New York, Harper, and London, Chatto and Windus, 1937.
Night of the Poor. New York, Harper, and London, Chatto and Windus, 1939.
The Skies of Europe. New York, Harper, 1941; London, Chatto and Windus, 1942.
The Conspirators. New York, Harper, and London, Chatto and Windus, 1943.
Age of Thunder. New York, Harper, and London, Chatto and Windus, 1945.
The Idols of the Cave. New York, Doubleday, 1946; London, Chatto and Windus, 1947.
Storm and Echo. New York, Doubleday, 1948; London, Faber, 1949.
Nine Days to Mukalla. New York, Viking Press, and London, Secker and Warburg, 1953.
A Tale for Midnight. Boston, Little Brown, 1955; London, Secker and Warburg, 1956.
A Ballad of Love. New York, Farrar Straus, 1960; London, Secker and Warburg, 1961.
The Seven Sisters. New York, Farrar Straus, 1962; London, Secker and Warburg, 1963.
The Dark Dancer. New York, Farrar Straus, 1964; London, W.H. Allen, 1965.
The Wreck of the Cassandra. New York, Farrar Straus, and London, W.H. Allen, 1966.
The Missolonghi Manuscript. New York, Farrar Straus, and London, W.H. Allen, 1968.
America, My Wilderness. New York, Farrar Straus, and London, W.H. Allen, 1971.

Verse

Three Mysteries. New Haven, Connecticut, privately printed, 1932.
Three Sorrows. New Haven, Connecticut, privately printed, 1932.
Three Deaths. New Haven, Connecticut, privately printed, 1932.
Three Images. New Haven, Connecticut, privately printed, 1932.
The Voyage. Bryn Mawr, Pennsylvania, privately printed, 1933.
The Dolls. Bryn Mawr, Pennsylvania, privately printed, 1933.
The Grotto. Bryn Mawr, Pennsylvania, privately printed, 1933.
The Enemies. Bryn Mawr, Pennsylvania, privately printed, 1934.
The Survivors. Bryn Mawr, Pennsylvania, privately printed, 1934.
Going Southward. Bryn Mawr, Pennsylvania, privately printed, 1935.
The Red Sea. Cambridge, privately printed, 1935.
Andromeda. Cambridge, privately printed, 1935.
The Assassins. Cambridge, privately printed, 1936.
The Assassins (collection). New York, Harper, and London, Chatto and Windus, 1936.
The Sacred Wood. Cambridge, privately printed, 1936.
The Carnival. New York, Harper, and London, Chatto and Windus, 1938.
Death at Sea. New York, Harper, and London, Chatto and Windus, 1940.
Sunburned Ulysses. Lisbon, privately printed, 1941.
Among the Caves. Lisbon, privately printed, 1941.
Song. New York, privately printed, 1941.
Song. Stockholm, privately printed, 1943.
Fable. New York, privately printed, 1944.
Chosen Poems. London, Chatto and Windus, 1944; New York, Doubleday, 1947.
The Flamingoes. Rome, privately printed, 1948.
Snow Song. Paris, privately printed, 1949.
Boat Song. Venice, privately printed, 1950.
Wood Song. Florence, privately printed, 1951.
Phantom Song. Naples, privately printed, 1952.
Banquet Song. Barcelona, privately printed, 1953.
Temple Song. Stuttgart, privately printed, 1954.
Fire Song. Zurich, privately printed, 1955.
Island Song. Hong Kong, privately printed, 1956.
Jungle Song. Bangkok, privately printed, 1957.
The Death Ship. Singapore, privately printed, 1958.
The Ghost City. Antwerp, privately printed, 1959.
The Mirror. Vienna, privately printed, 1960.

Other

Translator, *Some Poems of Friedrich Hölderlin.* New York, New Directions, 1943; London, Grey Walls Press, 1947.
Translator, *Love Sonnets of Louise Labé.* New York, New Directions, 1947; London, Grey Walls Press, 1948.

*

Manuscript Collection: University of Texas, Austin.

Critical Study: *Frederic Prokosch* by Radcliffe Squires, New York, Twayne, 1964.

Frederic Prokosch comments:

It has always, it appears, been difficult, almost impossible, for English and American critics to classify or label or categorize my novels. Perhaps because an element of poetry has been infused into their themes, style, and structure; or perhaps they fall more naturally into the genre of Slavic, German, or even French styles of fiction. My influences, I should say at random, were Grimm, Cervantes, Chekov, Conrad, possibly Thomas Mann among the moderns, even Céline, in the employment of a kind of dream-picaresque form to embody certain basic themes of perpetual search, perpetual flight, multiple identities, ambiguities of destiny, and geographical symbolisms. These themes have permeated my work all the way from *The Asiatics* and *The Seven Who Fled* up through *The Missolonghi Manuscript* and *America, My Wilderness.* Thus, my commentaries on "contemporary crises" have been covert, subtle, indirect. In this aversion to purely naturalistic or overtly sociological observation I find, I suppose, a certain kinship in the work of Borges, Nabokov, I.B. Singer, Hermann Hesse, and certain Japanese writers. I pity those poor critics who might try to disentangle the Gordian knot of my obsessive symbols and images.

* * *

When Frederic Prokosch's first novel, *The Asiatics*, appeared in 1935 it immediately became clear that here was an important novelist with unique gifts. The metaphoric style touched the reader as does an intimate dream whose intensity leaves the dreamer lonely for the dream when he wakes. The tolerant, sensuous, yet ultimately mysterious young narrator who wanders through the beautifully detailed landscapes of Asia, encountering characters who are in turn vicious and virtuous, neurotic and heroic, mad and wise, enthralled a large audience. Translated into seventeen languages, the book claimed the attention of André Gide who called *The Asiatics* "an authentic masterpiece"; of Thomas Mann who wrote, "I was unable to tear myself away from this astonishing, picaresque romance, flashing with talent and an audacious, adventurous spirit. I count it among the most brilliant and original achievements of the young literary generation."

Prokosch's second novel, *The Seven Who Fled*, published as the Harper Prize novel in 1937, affirmed these impressions, and high praise continued to greet his work for the next decade. Yet it was praise that tended to dwell with the surfaces rather than the recesses of his talent. In this respect the response of Albert Camus is typical: "He has invented what might be called the geographical novel, in which he mingles sensuality with irony, lucidity with mystery. He conveys a fatalistic sense of life half-hidden beneath a rich animal energy. He is a master of moods and undertones, a virtuoso in the feeling of place, and he writes in a style of supple elegance." These words are true enough, but they neither ask nor tell the purposes of "the geographic novel."

While Frederic Prokosch's popularity as a novelist has declined, especially in America, since the end of World War II, his stature as a serious novelist, particularly in Europe, has increased. That stature rests upon stubborn teleological strengths that buttress the protean shimmer of his designs. For no aspect of Prokosch's fiction is merely what at first glance it appears to be. The vagrant drift of such novels as *Storm and Echo* contains a symbolic anthropology. The "naturalistic" or "realistic" qualities of such novels as *The Skies of Europe* contain a symbolic history. The historical aspects of such novels as *A Tale for Midnight* contain a symbolic psychology. The biographical qualities of such novels as *The Dark Dancer* or *The Missolonghi Manuscript* contain a symbolic philosophy of art.

In an anagogic sense, the nomadic novels—*The Asiatics*, *The Seven Who Fled*, *Storm and Echo*, *Nine Days to Mukalla*—contemplate man as an evolving, but not an evolved, being. Africa, vibrant with treachery and violence, chthonian gods and Promethean vision, is seen as the amoral but innocent beginning of man's emergence from the moronic babble of Nature. Asia, tricked by its own shrewdness, staggering under the burden of its exquisite civilization, is seen as decadent denouement. However, this extensive symbology is less important than the intensive symbology. The journey-novels—like the journey-poems of the Romantic poets—employ the fortuitous encounter as a means of fixing the fluctuant portrait of man's psychic being. Landscape, natural hardship—whether in Asia or Africa, Europe or America—act upon the characters as an "X-ray" to reveal what is hidden beneath the surface. The hidden self comes forth, the characters come to terms with it or else are destroyed by their fear of it.

But what does it mean, this coming to terms with the submerged atomies of self. It means at least a little more than the simple integration of personality advocated by Carl Jung, for the purpose of such integration involves for Prokosch a liberal yet austere morality. In the late novel *The Seven Sisters* Prokosch pursues the mythic rehearsals of archetypal themes in the careers of seven daughters. Ultimately one sees that these careers embody the conflicting or unmeshed elements of the hero's personality. Until he understands these elements he feels he is "dangling" in life, and his painting is a vagary of discrete daubs. Until he understands and thus reconciles these elements, he cannot love, though he is tyrannized by love; nor can he "create."

The word "create," as it involves the artist, takes us into the core of Prokosch's work. His villains (as his brief portrait of Hitler in *The Skies of Europe* makes evident) are failed artists. His ruined characters are those who, pursuing, like Rimbaud, a fanatical ideal of art, burn out and fail. But that is only the dark side of the problem. Toward the end of *The Asiatics* the narrator admonishes himself not to be

> strong; don't be alone; don't be proud; it's your only chance ever to understand anything at all. Be fragile, be tender, humiliate yourself, and let the discoloration of dream close in on you. Do that, and oddly enough, you'll remain healthy; you'll be yourself; you'll discover the best way to live in this particular most fruitless and tantalizing of possible worlds. The reality becomes a cruel dream while the dream fades into a tender man-made reality.

That rejection of strength and pride is at base a rejection of the imbalance of idealism; it parallels and equals the theme of awareness and integration of personality. Hence, from the fickle and promiscuous can come, as in *The Dark Dancer*, an eternal praise of love, the Taj Mahal. So also in *The Missolonghi Manuscript* (a novel which contains too many witty anachronisms and discrepancies for the careful reader to suppose its intent is simply a biography of Lord Byron) the Romantic ideal of "eternity" can only be attained by acceptance of decay. A susurrus of paradox articulates the resolution: to abandon idealism in life permits life to become an ideal art.

—Radcliffe Squires

PURDY, James (Otis). American. Born near Fremont, Ohio, 14 July 1923. Educated at the University of Chicago, 1941, 1946; University of Puebla, Mexico. Worked as an interpreter in Latin America, France, and Spain; taught at Lawrence College, Appleton, Wisconsin, 1949-53. Since 1953, full-time writer. Visiting Professor, University of Tulsa, Oklahoma, 1977. Recipient: American Academy award, 1958; Guggenheim Fellowship, 1958, 1962; Ford Fellowship, for drama, 1961. Address: 236 Henry Street, Brooklyn, New York 11201, U.S.A.

PUBLICATIONS

Novels

Malcolm. New York, Farrar Straus, 1959; London, Secker and Warburg, 1960.

The Nephew. New York, Farrar Straus, 1960; London, Secker and Warburg, 1961.

Cabot Wright Begins. New York, Farrar Straus, 1964; London, Secker and Warburg, 1965.

Eustace Chisholm and the Works. New York, Farrar Straus, 1967; London, Cape, 1968.

Sleepers in Moon-Crowned Valleys:

Jeremy's Version. New York, Doubleday, 1970; London, Cape, 1971.

The House of the Solitary Maggot. New York, Doubleday, 1974.

I Am Elijah Thrush. New York, Doubleday, and London, Cape, 1972.

In a Shallow Grave. New York, Arbor House, 1976; London, W.H. Allen, 1978.

Narrow Rooms. New York, Arbor House, 1978; Godalming, Surrey, Black Sheep, 1980.

Mourners Below. New York, Viking Press, 1981.

Short Stories

Don't Call Me by My Right Name and Other Stories. New York, William Frederick Press, 1956.

63: Dream Palace. New York, William Frederick Press, 1956; London, Gollancz, 1957.

Color of Darkness: Eleven Stories and a Novella. New York, New Directions, 1957; London, Secker and Warburg, 1961.
Children Is All (stories and plays). New York, New Directions, 1961; London, Secker and Warburg, 1963.
An Oyster Is a Wealthy Beast (story and poems). Los Angeles, Black Sparrow Press, 1967.
Mr. Evening: A Story and Nine Poems. Los Angeles, Black Sparrow Press, 1968.
On the Rebound: A Story and Nine Poems. Los Angeles, Black Sparrow Press, 1970.
A Day after the Fair: A Collection of Plays and Stories. New York, Note of Hand, 1977.
Lessons and Complaints. New York, Nadja, 1978.

Uncollected Short Stories

"Lily's Party," in *New Directions 29.* New York, New Directions, 1974.
"The Anonymous/Androgynous Letters of Passion," in *New Directions 38.* New York, New Directions, 1979.
"Sleep Tight," in *Antioch Review* (Yellow Springs, Ohio), Winter 1979.

Plays

Mr. Cough Syrup and the Phantom Sex, in *December* (Western Springs, Illinois), viii, 1, 1960.
Cracks (produced New York, 1963).
Wedding Finger, in *New Directions 28.* New York, New Directions, 1974.
Two Plays (includes *A Day after the Fair and True*). Dallas, New London Press, 1979.

Verse

The Running Sun. New York, Paul Waner Press, 1971.
Sunshine Is an Only Child. New York, Aloe Editions, 1973.

*

Manuscript Collection: Yale University, New Haven, Connecticut.

Critical Studies: introduction by David Daiches to *Malcolm*, 1959, by Edith Sitwell to *Colour of Darkness*, London, Secker and Warburg, 1961, and by Tony Tanner to *Color of Darkness, and Malcolm*, New York, Doubleday, 1974; *The Not-Right House: Essays on James Purdy* by Bettina Schwarzchild, Columbia, University of Missouri Press, 1968; *City of Words*, London, Cape, 1971, and "Birdsong," in *Partisan Review* (New Brunswick, New Jersey), Fall 1972, both by Tony Tanner; "James Purdy on the Corruption of Innocents" by Frank Baldanza, in *Contemporary Literature* (Madison, Wisconsin), 1974; interview with Fred Barron, in *Penthouse* (New York), July 1974; *James Purdy* by Henry Chupack, Boston, Twayne, 1975; *James Purdy* by Stephen D. Adams, London, Vision Press, and New York, Barnes and Noble, 1976; "James Purdy and the Black Mask of Humanity" by Joseph T. Skerrett, Jr., in *Melus* (Los Angeles), 1979.

James Purdy comments:

(1972) As I see it, my work is an exploration of the American soul conveyed in a style based on the rhythms and accents of American speech. From the beginning my work has been greeted with a persistent and even passionate hostility on the part of the New York literary establishment which tries to rule America's literary taste—and the world's. My early work was privately printed by friends. Dame Edith Sitwell read these works, and persuaded Victor Gollancz to publish the book in England. Without her help I would never have been published in America and never heard of. The mediocrity of the American literary scene, as is evidenced in the *New York Times* and the creatures of the vast New York establishment, has tried to reduce me to starvation and silence. Yet as a matter of fact I believe my work is the most American of any writer writing today. My subject, as I said, is the exploration of the inside of my characters, or as John Cowper Powys put it, "under the skin." The theme of American culture, American commercial culture, that is, is that man can be adjusted, that loudness and numbers are reality, and that to be "in" is to exist. My work is the furthest from this definition of "reality." All individual thought and feeling have been silenced or "doped" in America today, and to be oneself is tantamount to non-existence. I see no difference between Russia and America; both are hideous failures, both enemies of the soul, both devourers of nature, and undisciplined disciplinarians who wallow in the unnatural. Anything in America is sacred which brings in money, and the consumers can easily be persuaded to move from their old crumbling Puritan ethic to belief in things like sexual deviation and coprophilia, provided and only provided these bring in money and notoriety. The one crime is to be oneself, unless it is a "self" approved and created by the commercial forces. Beneath this vast structure of madness, money, and anaesthetic prostitution, is my own body of work.

I prefer not to give a biography since my biography is in my work, and I do not wish to communicate with anybody but individuals, for whom my work was written in the first place. I began writing completely in the dark, and so continue. Were I in a financial position to do so, I would never publish anything commercially, since the literary establishment can promote only lies, and the critics, newspapers, and public having been fed on poison so long are incapable of reading anything that is not an advertisement for their own destruction. The most applauded writers in America are those who have had no contact with native American speech, but who seem to have been born in a television studio, where words are hourly produced from baking tins. In New York City, where American speech is unknown, a writer such as myself is considered a foreigner. Clarity and idiomatic language are considered in fact mad, while the language of dope addicts and coprophiliacs is now standard "American," approved for use by the dowagers who make best-sellers.

* * *

James Purdy is fascinated by the "color of darkness." His stories and novels deal with consuming narcissism and they assume, consequently, that "normal" love is, for the most part, cruel and nightmarish.

In *Color of Darkness* he gives us many heroes who are confused, lonely, and freakish. They do not know how to love (or to be loved). They are afraid to commit themselves. We see them sitting in dark rooms or roaming city streets; we hear their silent screams. Fenton Riddleway is so tormented by love for Claire, his dying brother, in "63: Dream Palace," the most impressive story in the collection, that he must kill him. The murder is the culmination of perverse love; it is perfectly in keeping with the "not-rightness" and rot of their dream palace.

In another collection, *Children Is All*, Purdy returns to the conflicts in family relationships. Often his heroes are orphans or bachelors. The narrator of "Daddy Wolf," for example, has seen his wife and child leave him; he turns for solace to the invisible "daddy." He calls him on the "trouble phone"; he rants, confesses, and rambles. But he is, finally, alone—except for the rats which crawl near him. "Goodnight, Sweetheart," like all of the best stories, fuses the realistic (or cliché) dialogue and the fantastic incident. It begins with Pearl Miranda walking "stark naked from her class-room in the George Washington" to the house of Winston, a former pupil. Both are victims of love (or "rape"); both cannot exist in the wolfish world. Unfortunately, they cannot even live with each other. As the story ends, they "both muttered to themselves in the darkness as if they were separated by different rooms from one another." They pray for help.

Purdy's novels are more varied than his stories. (It is questionable whether they surpass the great achievement of the stories.) The hero of his first novel, *Malcolm*, searches for his father, hoping thereby to affirm his own identity and *name*. But like Fenton Riddleway, he cannot exist as a "person"—he becomes another shadow in the rotten city. He is manipulated by others; he is never understood completely, except as a mere reflection of their selfish demands. Malcolm is, to quote his lusty wife, a "little bit of this and that," and when he dies—has he ever lived?—he apparently vanishes into thin air. *Malcolm* is a wonderfully strange mixture of comedy and pathos, and it alone asserts Purdy's impressive gifts as a novelist. Although it deals with the lack of substance in relationships—between men and women; between men and men; between human beings and the cosmos—it creates its own substantial texture largely as a result of Purdy's mixed, "transformational" style.

The Nephew is set in Rainbow Center, a small American town. (It is a change from the "fairy-tale" *Malcolm*.) It delights in clichés, minor scandals, and popular holidays; it is, at least superficially, a realistic picture of the middle Americans. But it presents Boyd and Alma (and Cliff, their missing nephew) in such a deceptive, complex way that "local color" changes subtly to universal darkness. When Alma discovers that she has never known Cliff (despite having lived with him for many years) and, consequently, realizes her own needs and dreams, she is depressed *and* exalted. She grasps the hard truth; she understands that we are all "missing" shadows; we live briefly and secretly. She accepts the significance of memorial days—the novel begins and ends on this holiday—and the "faint delicious perfume" of our lives before the court house clock strikes again. Thus *The Nephew*, like all of Purdy's novels, must be read closely (as Alma reads her nephew's life)—it presents two worlds and demands the recognition that only art can reconcile their differences.

Cabot Wright Begins is a savage satire on American life. It attacks the automatic, false, and empty values which make us treat people as *valuable objects*. Cabot Wright becomes a rapist because he can assert his identity only as a vital, pumping being. Later he runs away from the others—Bernie, Zoe, and Princeton—who want to trap and use his exotic past for their narcissistic ends. Cabot Wright begins to laugh and write; he rises from the "deadly monotony of the human continuity" when he lies on the ground, "weeping a little from the pain of his laughter, a thread of drivel coming down from his mouth onto his pointed dimpled chin." Despite the cluttered sermons, this novel is brilliantly effective when it says "HA!" to the boredom of our daily routines. It is Purdy's blackest comedy.

Eustace Chisholm and the Works details the various strategies of lovers who refuse to acknowledge their own potentialities. The homosexuality which colored *Malcolm*, *The Nephew*, and "63: Dream Palace" flourishes here. Daniel Haws, for example, cannot accept his love for Amos (except at the end); he flees from it into the Army. There he is "satisfied" by sadistic Captain Stadger in a powerfully detailed execution (or embrace?). These Army scenes are perhaps the most brutal ones in all of Purdy's fiction.

Eustace Chisholm is a writer. He resembles Alma, Cabot Wright, and Bernie of *Cabot Wright Begins* in trying to solve the mysteries of love and will in the community; and like them, he discovers that he cannot get to the heart of the matter. He *abdicates*—unlike Purdy himself—and turns instead to his wife for incredible love. He warms her with "a kind of ravening love," knowing that they will probably "consume" each other in the future. He is saved only momentarily.

Jeremy's Version is the first part of an uncompleted trilogy called *Sleepers in Moon-Crowned Valleys*, but it stands alone. Jeremy is an adolescent who writes down the sermons, tales, and histories of Matthew Lacy. He is, therefore, the familiar character we have met before, but unlike the other earlier writers, he is more open, innocent, and *human* than they are. He learns as he listens and transcribes.

Jeremy moves into the past. He becomes so involved with the family conflicts of the 19th-century Fergises—he identifies especially with Jethro, another adolescent writer—that at times he becomes a free-floating *spirit*. Thus he forces us to recognize that only by giving oneself to others can we survive and create. He offers hope. His "version" is finally a mellow, full, and sunny account which indicates some new directions for Purdy's forthcoming novels.

The House of the Solitary Maggot, the second volume of the trilogy, presents different characters—Lady Bythwaite and her illegitimate sons—but it also assumes that love is a bloody mixture. The "family" is, again, a maggot-ridden, melodramatic structure. Thus this novel, a discontinuous part of the trilogy, parallels the first, implying a mythic, disturbing, general design; it offers few solutions and little hope for American society.

—Irving Malin

PUZO, Mario. American. Born in New York City in 1920. Educated at the New School for Social Research, New York; Columbia University, New York. Married; has children. Administrative Assistant in United States Government offices, in New York and overseas, for 20 years. Lives on Long Island, New York. Recipient: Oscar, for screenplay, 1975. Address: c/o William Targ, G.P. Putnam Sons Inc., 200 Madison Avenue, New York, New York 10016, U.S.A.

PUBLICATIONS

Novels

The Dark Arena. New York, Random House, 1955; London, Heinemann, 1971.
The Fortunate Pilgrim. New York, Atheneum, 1965; London, Heinemann, 1966.
The Godfather. New York, Putnam, and London, Heinemann, 1969.
Fools Die. New York, Putnam, and London, Heinemann, 1978.

Uncollected Short Stories

"Last Christmas," in *American Vanguard 1950*, edited by Charles I. Glicksberg. New York, Cambridge, 1950.
"First Sundays," in *Redbook* (Dayton, Ohio), February 1968.

Plays

Screenplays: *The Godfather*, with Francis Ford Coppola, 1972; *Godfather II*, 1974; *Earthquake*, 1974; *Superman*, with others, 1978; *Superman II*, with David Newman and Leslie Newman, 1981.

Other

The Runaway Summer of Davie Shaw (juvenile). New York, Platt and Munk, 1966; Kingswood, Surrey, World's Work, 1976.
The Godfather Papers and Other Confessions. New York, Putnam, and London, Heinemann, 1972.
Inside Las Vegas. New York, Grosset and Dunlap, 1977.

*

Manuscript Collection: Boston University.

* * *

Mario Puzo's novelistic work is in the strong, rich vein of American naturalism; his literary forebears are Frank Norris, Crane, Dreiser, Lewis, and James T. Farrell. Like Drieser, Puzo shows how institutions work, and how the individual fares in the often traumatic process; unlike Dreiser, however, Puzo seldom treats the larger social or political issues. By comparison, Puzo's vision is private; his strength is in rendering the inner working of a family in dramatizing what may constitute loyalty or right conduct in a time of crisis especially when the issue concerns either prestige or money.

As with nearly all naturalistic writers, Puzo's world is the city, the urban jungle. Here persons with power exploit without mercy the defenseless and the weak; a reoccurring motive is brute revenge. Love, loyalty, and fidelity more often than not are made viable by well-managed crime; official sentiment is expressed by ostentatious, professionally managed funerals and weddings. Typically the resolutions of human affairs remain ambivalent.

The materials of the novels are handled with great authority. In fact, Puzo was born and raised in New York's Lower East Side; his version of tenement life of that time is the most comprehensive and the most fully realized of any living American author. The language is straightforward and without pretensions; always there is a variety of lifelike characters.

Of the novels *The Dark Arena* alone takes place largely outside the U.S. The hero is an American ex-soldier who accepts civilian employment with the military government in occupied Germany. The plot is not complex, and traces two major themes: the German-American accommodation in the early years of peace and the implied emergence of a new Germany. The second theme concerns the hero, Mosca, and his attempts at emotional growth, his tragic disappointments in love, and his eventual departure from the betrayals of occupation life. The novel deserves to be better known.

The Fortunate Pilgrim is Puzo's best novel to date and traces the "rise" of an Italian peasant girl, a new bride in America, from tenement to the end of the American Dream, a bungalow of her own in Long Island. In addition to a wide variety of scenes from lower-class immigrant life and the changing mores of individuals and whole neighborhoods, this novel also presents details—and visions—of syndicate-managed crime. The episodes concerning organized crime are at once detailed and also larger than life-size; thus the episodes have a genuine mythic quality. On balance this novel is among the best two or three books ever written on American city life.

The Godfather stems directly from the passages on crime in *The Fortunate Pilgrim*. The main protagonist, Don Corleone, is a rebel-founder of a vastly influential crime syndicate. His values are at once "domestic" (he is a family man) and anti-social (he often kills off the opposition). Thus he is patron, Old Testament God, and terrible enforcer. The larger ethical, public issues are never fully dramatized; likewise, the contradictions within Don Corleone are never satisfactorily resolved. Perhaps this ambivalence accounts for its less subtle, less controlled structure. In any event, when *The Godfather* appeared it became an immediate best seller and helped revive interest in the two earlier, more interesting novels.

Puzo represents an increasingly rare type of American writer: the journeyman. Between novels he has supported a family on articles, non-fiction, and journalism. He does not teach. He lives not far from the place he was born: the City. In this and other respects his is a sturdy talent of the kind which each day meets the literary competition of a nation's literary capital.

—James B. Hall

PYNCHON, Thomas. American. Born in Glen Cove, New York, 8 May 1937. Educated at Cornell University, Ithaca, New York, 1954-58, B.A. 1958. Served in the United States Navy. Former editorial writer, Boeing Aircraft, Seattle. Recipient: Faulkner Award, 1964; Rosenthal Memorial Award, 1967; National Book Award, 1974; American Academy Howells Medal, 1975. Agent: Candida Donadio and Associates, 51 East 42nd Street, New York, New York 10017.

PUBLICATIONS

Novels

V. Philadelphia, Lippincott, and London, Cape, 1963.
The Crying of Lot 49. Philadelphia, Lippincott, 1966; London, Cape, 1967.
Gravity's Rainbow. New York, Viking Press, and London, Cape, 1973.

Short Stories

Mortality and Mercy in Vienna. London, Aloes, 1976.
Low-lands. London, Aloes, 1978.
The Secret Integration. London, Aloes, 1981.

*

Bibliography: *Three Contemporary Novelists: An Annotated Bibliography* by Robert M. Scotto, New York, Garland, 1977; *John Barth, Jerzy Kosinski, and Thomas Pynchon: A Reference Guide* by Thomas P. Walsh and Cameron Northouse, Boston, Hall, 1977.

Critical Studies: *Thomas Pynchon* by Joseph V. Slade, New York, Warner, 1974; *Mindful Pleasures: Essays on Thomas Pynchon* edited by George Levine and David Leverenz, Boston, Little Brown, 1976; *The Grim Phoenix: Reconstructing Thomas Pynchon* by William M. Plater, Bloomington, Indiana University Press, 1978; *Thomas Pynchon: A Collection of Critical Essays* edited by Edward Mendelson, Englewood Cliffs, New Jersey, Prentice Hall, 1978; *Thomas Pynchon: The Art of Allusion* by David Cowart, Carbondale, Southern Illinois University Press, 1980; *The Rainbow Quest of Thomas Pynchon* by Douglas A. Mackey, San Bernardino, California, Borgo Press, 1980; *Pynchon's Fictions: Thomas Pynchon and the Literature of Information* by John O. Stark, Athens, Ohio University Press, 1980.

* * *

Early in *V*, Thomas Pynchon's first novel, the character named Benny Profane is hunting alligators in the sewers of New York. He is hunting them on the city payroll, for a great number of baby alligators, bought as pets for children, have been flushed down toilets all over the city and are now breeding in the drainage tunnels. And as he hunts, Profane remembers the legend of Father Fairing, a Catholic priest who, during the Great Depression, decided that the rats were going to inherit the earth and went to live in the sewers, in order to convert the new chosen race to the one true faith. "At no point," Profane realized, "in the twenty or so years the legend had been handed on did it occur to anyone to question the old priest's sanity. It is this way with sewer stories. They just are. Truth or falsity don't apply."

It is a passage which says a great deal, not only about the dark and manic world of *V*, but about Pynchon's highly individual comic talent, and about the decade of the 1960's in which that talent flourished. Upon his first appearance, Pynchon was grouped by most critics with the other so-called "black humorists" of the decade: with writers like Bruce Jay Friedman, Kurt Vonnegut, and John Barth, whose satirical vision of contemporary America, with roots as diverse as Petronius, Nathanael West, and Lenny Bruce, suggested something like a new "movement" in literature, a turning away from the realistic conventions of 1950's fiction (e.g. Saul Bellow, J.D. Salinger), and from the political passivism associated with the Eisenhower era. This grouping had, indeed, some polemical point to it, in establishing the major talent and importance of some of its members. But like most other prematurely named "movements," it tended to obscure the vast differences between the writers involved, and finally to obscure even the structure of the works themselves. *V* has finally made it: reprinted as a Modern Library "Classic," it is taught in Modern Novel surveys across the country as an example of "black humor." But *V*, like *The Crying of*

Lot 49, and especially the staggering *Gravity's Rainbow*, is not an example of anything, except of its creator's unique vision. For if the "black humor" of Vonnegut consists of a series of simple, bitter parables about man's terrible need of charity, and that of Barth of an immense, baroque fantasia upon solipsism and nihilism, Pynchon's genius, neither allegorical nor epic, remains that of the teller of "sewer stories"; tales of the psychotic underground of the modern imagination, where "truth or falsity don't apply."

The image of the sewer, of the underground labyrinth, the secret network, the hidden "plot," is central to all of Pynchon's novels. But his use of this very common metaphor for modern life (one thinks of Gide, Norman Mailer, and Alain Robbe-Grillet) is a unique one. For Pynchon's labyrinths hold no mystery, and his deep dark secrets are, if anything, overillumined. Their terror, that is, is not the terror of the unknown, but precisely that of the *too well* known, of the twisted underbrush of the modern mind which has become so much our daily bread that we can never hope to see it in the full, unfamiliarized ghastliness of its reality. Another name for sewer stories, then, is perhaps "anti-Gothic romances." For Pynchon gives us an America, a world so inured to the unspeakable that one can, actually, speak about it. And his characters are somnambulists inhabiting ghost stories where their distinctive curse is to be incapacitated for horror itself.

Pynchon, while an undergraduate at Cornell, majored in English literature, but with a heavy helping of courses in modern physics: one of his former teachers still wonderingly remembers his apparently voracious appetite for the complexities of elementary particle theory. And physics, along with the myth of the labyrinth, has proved to be crucial to Pynchon's imagination. For if the modern condition may be imagined as a city honeycombed with secret subterranean passages, mind-boggling in their darkness and extensiveness, it may also be imagined as a cosmic version of that most critical quandary of contemporary physics, the so-called "Uncertainty Principle." This principle, in its baldest form, simply states that the complete description of *any* physical event is impossible—not because of the complexity of the event, but because *consciousness itself*, in attempting to examine the event, also alters the event from its "true" form into an impossible maze of self-reflexiveness. It is difficult, indeed, not to think of this principle when, in *The Crying of Lot 49*, the heroine Oedipa Maas faces the difficulty of ever discovering what, in its entirely, the mysterious "Trystero System" might mean: "Now here was Oedipa, faced with a metaphor of God knew how many parts; more than two, anyway. With coincidences blossoming these days wherever she looked, she had nothing but a sound, a word, Trystero, to hold them together." A word, a sound to resolve a metaphor which, like the "many-body" problem of physics, consists of too many parts and is therefore *intrinsically* insoluble: truth and falsity don't, cannot apply in a world where those fundamentally moral values of the reason have been reduced to the dead level of infinitely extensive "facts."

Pynchon's three novels to date are concerned, in their different ways, with the great and urgent difficulty of finding a human truth within the manifold, labyrinthine coincidences of the modern experience. In *V* the labyrinth is the gigantic one of European history since the First World War. Herbert Stencil, seeking the truth about the death of his father in 1919, is led on a crazy quest for the identity of "V," a mysterious female—seductress, hag, secret agent—who appears to have been present at every disaster which has contributed to the making of modern Europe and America. The quest for V leads to a kind of terminal despair of history, a sense that the "Plot Which Has No Name," the master diabolical plot of the Twentieth Century, is necessarily unknowable to any of its victims. (Stencil himself, who refers to himself only in the third person, is literally a "stencil," a recording instrument incapable of passing moral judgment on that which he records.) But not before Stencil and the "whole sick crew" of existential bums he gathers around him have explored what is literally an underground history of the age, from Sarajevo through the Great Depression and Nazism to the formation of "Yoyodyne," the massive munitions industry which is Pynchon's chief image of the superindustrialized death factories of modern technology. V herself, though of course ultimately unknowable, appears in one of the book's most apocalyptic moments, the bombing of Malta during World War Two, as a seductress who has been systematically replacing her living organs with pieces of precision machinery: the *femme fatale* become a shuddering *fatalité feminisée*.

After the sprawling genius of *V*, the classically spare economy of *Lot 49* seemed, in 1966, rather a terminal refinement and articulation of Pynchon's despair. Oedipa Maas searches for the clue which will reveal the meaning of "Trystero"—it is either an underground mail system which threatens the end of all civilization or an underground conspiracy which will build a new, more humane civilization—and finds the clue ungraspable. Nearly a short story compared to the length and range of *V*, *Lot 49* is nevertheless one of the most elegantly crafted nightmares of recent American fiction. And in the long, six year silence which followed its publication, many (including the present writer) felt that Pynchon's vision had grown so unrelievedly dark that there was nothing else to say. But then came *Gravity's Rainbow*.

Of *Gravity's Rainbow*, the most efficient thing that can be said is that it is one of the few truly great novels of the century, and at the same time one of the most disappointing, disturbing, maddening. Generally (and only "generally" may we summarize this immense book, nearly twice as long as *all* Pynchon's previous work), it is the story of Tyrone Slothrop, an American officer hounded into desertion at the end of the Second World War and wandering, ever losing more and more of his personality, in the area of post-War occupied Germany called "the Zone"—the greatest and most surreal of Pynchon's labyrinths. Slothrop is both archetypal man and archetypal machine—he is nearly turned into a guinea pig by British and American scientists because it is found that his erections correspond exactly and predictively to the sites of V-2 explosions in London. And as he wanders through the Zone he discovers, in the arthritic psyches of the victims of the War, the unprocreative seeds of the modern world at their most ghastly—including, of course, his own fragmented soul. A paradigm of modern man as literally in love with his own death, Slothrop's fate is complexly linked to the fate of the V-2 rockets themselves, those first mechanized versions of the Great Bombs which still terrify us, and whose graceful, deadly arc from launch to target is the "rainbow of gravity," the negative convenant of damnation, which gives the book its title. Pynchon narrates Slothrop's fate, moreover, in a language which is one of the most original fictive styles to have been developed since Joyce: a melange of scientific jargon, Gothic lyricism, and comic-book pop dialect whose range of tone and fundamental irreverence perfectly catches—with almost Swiftean efficiency—its creator's horror of and fascination with the contemporary nightmare.

Pynchon is a fanatically private man: his photograph has not been taken in 15 years, and no one knows where he lives or what he is doing at this moment. And, for a man of such deep and dark imagination, the wonder is that he has written so much: he may never write another word. But even if he does not, he has created two major novels and one incomparable one; and the strange, scandalous, absurd urge to create may overcome even a perfectly rational despair. For Pynchon's heroism, more than even his talent, is to be a matchless writer *against* the darkness, so that we might better, by talking aloud, see each other.

—Frank D. McConnell

RADDALL, Thomas Head. Canadian. Born in Hythe, Kent, England, 13 November 1903; emigrated to Canada in 1913. Educated at St. Leonard's School, Hythe; Chebucto School, Halifax, Nova Scotia; Halifax Academy. Wireless Operator, Canadian Merchant Marine, 1918-22; served in the 2nd (Reserve) Battalion, West Nova Scotia Regiment, 1942-43: Lieutenant. Married Edith Margaret Freeman in 1927; two children. Accountant in the wood pulp and paper industries in Nova Scotia, 1923-38. Full-time writer since 1938. Recipient: Governor-General's Award, 1944, for non-fiction, 1949, 1958; Boys' Club of America Junior Book Award, 1951; Lorne Pierce Medal, 1956. LL.D.: Dalhousie University, Halifax, 1949; St. Francis Xavier University, Antigonish, Nova Scotia, 1973; Litt.D.: St. Mary's University, Halifax, 1969; D.C.L.: University of King's College, Halifax, 1972. Fellow, Royal Society of Canada, 1953. Medal of Service, Order of Canada, 1970. Address: 44 Park Street, Liverpool, Nova Scotia, Canada.

PUBLICATIONS

Novels

His Majesty's Yankees. Toronto, McClelland and Stewart, and New York, Doubleday, 1942; Edinburgh, Blackwood, 1944.
Roger Sudden. Toronto, McClelland and Stewart, and New York, Doubleday, 1945; London, Hurst and Blackett, 1946.
Pride's Fancy. Toronto, McClelland and Stewart, and New York, Doubleday, 1946; London, Hurst and Blackett, 1948.
The Nymph and the Lamp. Toronto, McClelland and Stewart, and Boston, Little Brown, 1950; London, Hutchinson, 1951.
The Son of the Hawk. Philadelphia, Winston, 1950.
Tidefall. Toronto, McClelland and Stewart, and Boston, Little Brown, 1953; London, Hutchinson, 1954.
The Wings of Night. New York, Doubleday, 1956; London, Macmillan, 1957.
The Governor's Lady. New York, Doubleday, 1960; London, Collins, 1961.
Hangman's Beach. New York, Doubleday, 1966.

Short Stories

Pied Piper of Dipper Creek and Other Tales. Edinburgh, Blackwood, 1939.
Tambour and Other Stories. Toronto, McClelland and Stewart, 1945.
The Wedding Gift and Other Stories. Toronto, McClelland and Stewart, 1947.
A Muster of Arms and Other Stories. Toronto, McClelland and Stewart, 1954.
At the Tide's Turn and Other Stories. Toronto, McClelland and Stewart, 1959.
Footsteps on Old Floors: True Tales of Mystery. New York, Doubleday, 1968.

Other

The Saga of the Rover, with C.H.L. Jones and Thomas W. Hayhurst. Halifax, Royal, 1932 (?).
The Markland Sagas, with a Discussion of Their Relation to Nova Scotia, with C.H.L. Jones. Montreal, Gazette Printing, 1934.
West Novas: A History of the West Nova Scotia Regiment. Halifax, Book Room, 1948.
Halifax, Warden of the North. Toronto, McClelland and Stewart, 1948; London, Dent, 1950; New York, Doubleday, 1965; revised edition, McClelland and Stewart, 1971.
The Path of Destiny: Canada from the British Conquest to Home Rule, 1763-1850. New York, Doubleday, 1957.
The Rover: The Story of a Canadian Privateer (juvenile). London, Macmillan, 1958; New York, St. Martin's Press, 1959.
A Pictorial Guide to Historic Nova Scotia. Halifax, Book Room, 1970.
In My Time: A Memoir. Toronto, McClelland and Stewart, 1976.

*

Manuscript Collection: Killam Memorial Library, Dalhousie University, Halifax.

Critical Studies: "Thomas H. Raddall: The Man and His Work" by W.J. Hawkins, in *Queen's Quarterly* (Kingston, Ontario), Spring 1968; "Thomas Raddall: The Art of Historical Fiction" by Donald Cameron, in *Dalhousie Review* (Halifax), 1970.

Thomas Head Raddall comments:

As a youth I went to sea in Canadian ships, served in the North Atlantic for three years, and then a year as wireless operator on Sable Island, "The Graveyard of the Atlantic." Subsequently these experiences and observations gave me material for short stories and a novel, *The Nymph and the Lamp*. When I left the sea I took a job as book-keeper for a wood-pulp mill in the Nova Scotia forest. This gave me many interesting years of friendship with mill hands, loggers, river-drivers, hunters, and a band of Micmac Indians. I spent most of my spare time in the woods, exploring the Mersey River and its lakes, on foot and by canoe. On the indoor side I had a deep interest in Canadian, and especially Nova Scotian, history, and my experience of the sea and the forest gave me light on many of the old documents I found in the archives at Halifax and elsewhere. Hence, a dozen novels, many short stories of colonial times, and three books of plain history.

In all my fiction, whether historical or contemporary, I sought to inform as well as to give intelligent entertainment, and to convey in words and style my own delight in the English language.

* * *

Despite a long and distinguished career as a professional novelist, Thomas Head Raddall is curiously ignored by criticism. In part this neglect may be the result of his conservatism: he is no experimenter in either form or choice of material, he is personally retiring, and he unabashedly seeks a wide audience.

More unusually, he has achieved one. Raddall is deeply Nova Scotian, and though his novels sell well elsewhere and have been translated into several languages, perhaps the most unusual feature of his career has been his relationship with his native province. In Nova Scotia the most astonishing spectrum of people reads Raddall, from cabbies to the Cabinet. Nothing remotely parallel exists elsewhere in English Canada, and it is an inspiring example of the public uses to which the novel may still be put.

All Raddall's novels are set in Nova Scotia. Some of them are contemporary—notably *Tidefall* and *The Nymph and the Lamp*, the story of a strange love affair between a radio operator and a frustrated, lonely typist who comes to live with him amidst the collection of isolated men on thinly disguised Sable Island. Though it has done well in the bookstores, however, the novel has never found much critical favour.

Raddall points out—quite correctly—that he is not just a historical novelist, but historical fiction has yielded his greatest success. The historical passion is strong in Raddall, and his work includes a volume of Canadian history, *The Path of Destiny*, as well as perhaps the finest work of local history ever written in Canada, *Halifax, Warden of the North*.

Raddall's historical fiction includes *Roger Sudden*, *Pride's Fancy*, *The Governor's Lady*, and *Hangman's Beach*, as well as numerous short stories. Perhaps the best, however, is Raddall's first novel, *His Majesty's Yankees*, an account of the changing loyalties and fortunes of David Strang, a young Nova Scotian fired with revolutionary zeal during the American War of Independence who finally comes to accept the forces which keep his colony British. The change in David is the change in the mood of Nova Scotia itself, and the understanding he achieves of the reasons for the colony's fate is the objective of the novel.

Such a story demands precisely the gifts Raddall possesses: a strong sense of story and a flair for the description of action, a clear and muscular style, an astute awareness of the interrelation between such private concerns as sex and such public concerns as revolution. The political division separates David from part of his family and his girl, and throws him into the centre of great events. Though he is not an extraordinary young man, he is intelligent, observant, and honest, an easy man for the reader to trust.

In conversation, Raddall describes his books not as novels, but as "tales" or "romances." The terms are not ill-chosen. Northrop Frye suggests that in a romance we know at the beginning how the work will end, and in this sense historical fiction is necessarily romantic. Moreover our interest in the hero is not centred in his uniqueness, but in his typicality; he stands not for an individual ideal or value, but for a communal mode of experience.

The hero's experience, says Lukács, is the necessary prehistory of the present; understanding it, we understand our own condition. At his best, Raddall conveys just such an understanding. Because of Nova Scotia's pivotal position in both the great French-English conflict in North America and the American Revolution, his work is relevant to an audience far beyond his beloved native province.

—Donald Cameron

RAND, Ayn. American. Born in St. Petersburg, now Leningrad, Russia, 2 February 1905; emigrated to the United States in 1926; naturalized, 1931. Educated at the University of Leningrad: graduated in history 1924. Married Frank O'Connor in 1929. Screenwriter, 1932-34, 1944-49. Editor, *The Objectivist*, New York, 1962-71, and since 1971, *The Ayn Rand Letter*, New York. D.H.L.: Lewis and Clark College, Portland, Oregon, 1963. Address: P.O. Box 177, Murray Hill Station, New York, New York 10016, U.S.A.

PUBLICATIONS

Novels

We the Living. New York, Macmillan, and London, Cassell, 1936.
Anthem. London, Cassell, 1938; revised edition, Los Angeles, Pamphleteers, 1946.
The Fountainhead. Indianapolis, Bobbs Merrill, 1943; London, Cassell, 1947.
Atlas Shrugged. New York, Random House, 1957.

Plays

Night of January 16th (as *Woman on Trial*, produced Hollywood, 1934; New York, 1935; London, 1936; as *Penthouse Legend*, produced New York, 1973). New York, Longman, 1936.
The Unconquered, adaptation of her own novel *We the Living* (produced New York, 1940).

Screenplays: *You Came Along*, with Robert Smith, 1945; *Love Letters*, 1945; *The Fountainhead*, 1949.

Other

Textbook of Americanism. New York, Branden Institute, 1946.
Notes on the History of American Free Enterprise. New York, Platen Press, 1959.
Faith and Force: The Destroyers of the Modern World. New York, Branden Institute, 1961.
For the New Intellectual. New York, Random House, 1961.
The Objectivist Ethics. New York, Branden Institute, 1961.
America's Persecuted Minority: Big Business. New York, Branden Institute, 1962.
Conservatism: An Obituary (lecture). New York, Branden Institute, 1962.
The Fascist "New Frontier." New York, Branden Institute, 1963.
The Virtue of Selfishness: A New Concept of Egoism. New York, New American Library, 1965.
Capitalism: The Unknown Ideal, with others. New York, New American Library, 1966.
Introduction to Objectivist Epistemology. New York, The Objectivist, 1967.
The Romantic Manifesto: A Philosophy of Literature. Cleveland, World, 1970.
The New Left: The Anti-Industrial Revolution. New York, New American Library, 1971.

*

Manuscript Collection: Library of Congress, Washington, D.C.

Critical Study: *Who Is Ayn Rand? An Analysis of the Novels of Ayn Rand* by Nathaniel Branden, New York, Random House, 1962.

* * *

Ayn Rand has developed a considerable public, both for her novels, especially *The Fountainhead* and *Atlas Shrugged*, and for her periodical publications, *The Objectivist* and *The Ayn Rand Letter*. Her novels are meant to display her philosophical speculations; in other words, she is a novelist of "ideas." To insure that these ideas are not misinterpreted, however, she has also published several collections of essays, many of them gathered from *The Objectivist*, in which the principal premises of the novels are made explicit.

Her philosophical credo is objectivism, a peculiarly narrow and wilful form of Romanticism which holds that man is primarily a rational creature, that his happiness lies in self-fulfilment, that his only responsibility is toward himself ("the virtue of selfishness"), and that those few individuals who practice such a doctrine constitute an elite group whose function is to realize fully the rational element in man's nature. Human weakness has no place in her system, and any sympathetic regard for weakness in others is a demonstration of the philosophical bane of the modern world, altruism, which, under the guise of helping the less fortunate, has systematically eroded the artistic, political, economic, and social systems of the 20th century until we have arrived at the chaos in which we live at present. Altruism is non-productive; it takes from the producers and spreads their creativity among the non-producers until finally there is, as shown in her last novel, *Atlas Shrugged*, nothing left for anybody. Altruism is the philosophy which leads to socialism, the ultimate non-creative form of government; or, still worse, to anarchy, non-government, in which property is wrested from the weaker by the stronger by violence, the ultimate negation of reason. The only free society is capitalistic in which the individual is allowed to fulfil his rational destiny, and Rand's capitalistic Utopia is one in which self-fulfilling creativity, be it in science, art, business, or politics, results ironically in the good life which altruism promises but cannot deliver.

The difficulty with Rand's philosophical analysis, and of her applications of its results both in her fiction and in her treatment of social, artistic, and political ills in her essays, is that she is drastically simplistic. A few examples will suffice. In her series of essays on art, *The Romantic Manifesto*, she gives what surely must be one of the most uninformed definitions of Romanticism one is likely to meet. Without quite knowing it, the Romantics achieved an intellectual revolution by elevating volition (self-determinism, i.e. rationalism) to the place of prime importance in the intellectual realm. Aristotle somehow survives the reduction of previous Western civilization to intellectual limbo, but in her limbo are Plato, and by default, St. Augustine, St. Thomas Aquinas, Dante, and, one presumes, Descartes. The same is true of the arts. Shakespeare must be regarded as a failure because his tragic characters are not self-determined. One grows a bit queasy when Rand finally sets up her pantheon of artists worth regarding: Hugo, Dostoevsky, and, in the field of popular literature, Mickey Spillane and Ian Fleming. One would like to have a little more left to read.

One simply need not take Rand seriously; while her novels will not save the world, neither, we might hope, will they propel us into hers; and if one can struggle through novels as long as Dickens's with no intentional comic relief, one has done something.

—James Hill

RAO, Raja. Indian. Born in Hassan, Mysore, 5 November 1908. Educated at Madarasa-e-Aliya School, Hyderabad, 1915-25; Aligarh Muslim University, 1926-27; Nizam College, Hyderabad (University of Madras), B.A. in English 1929; University of Montpellier, France, 1929-30; the Sorbonne, Paris, 1930-33. Married 1) Camille Mouly in 1931; 2) Katherine Jones in 1965, one son. Editor, *Tomorrow*, Bombay, 1943-44. Lived in France for many years; now lives half the year in India and half in Europe and the United States. Since 1965, Professor of Philosophy, teaching one semester a year, University of Texas, Austin. Recipient: Academy of Indian Literature Prize, 1964; Padma Bhushan, 1969. Address: Department of Philosophy, University of Texas, Austin, Texas 78712, U.S.A.

PUBLICATIONS

Novels

Kanthapura. London, Allen and Unwin, 1938; New York, New Directions, 1963.
The Serpent and the Rope. London, Murray, 1960; New York, Pantheon, 1963.
The Cat and Shakespeare: A Tale of India. New York, Macmillan, 1965.
Comrade Kirillov. New Delhi, Orient, 1976.

Short Stories

The Cow of the Barricades and Other Stories. Madras and London, Oxford University Press, 1947.
The Policeman and the Rose. London, Oxford University Press, 1977.

Uncollected Short Story

"Jupiter and Mars," in *Pacific Spectator* (Stanford, California), viii, 4, 1954.

Other

The Chess Master and His Moves. New Delhi, Vision, 1978.

Editor, with Iqbal Singh, *Changing India*. London, Allen and Unwin, 1939.
Editor, with Iqbal Singh, *Whither India?* Baroda, Padmaja, 1948.
Editor, *Soviet Russia: Some Random Sketches and Impressions*, by Jawaharlal Nehru. Bombay, Chetana, 1949.

*

Critical Studies: *Raja Rao* by M.K. Naik, New York, Twayne, 1972; *Raja Rao: A Critical Study of His Work* (includes bibliography) by C.D. Narasimhaiah, Delhi and London, Heinemann, 1973.

Raja Rao comments:

(1972) Starting from the humanitarian and romantic perspective of man in *Kanthapura* and *The Cow of the Barricades*—both deeply influenced by Mahatma Gandhi's philosophy of non-violence—I soon came to the metaphysical novel, *The Serpent and the Rope*, and *The Cat and Shakespeare*, based on the Vedantic conception of illusion and reality. My main interest increasingly is in showing the complexity of the human condition (that is, the reality of man is beyond his person), and in showing the symbolic construct of any human expression. All words are hierarchic symbols, almost mathematical in precision, on and of the unknown.

* * *

In addition to two volumes of short stories, Raja Rao has published several novels. A South Indian Brahmin, Rao is chiefly concerned with religion and philosophy, not only of India but also of the West, which he has come to know through many years of residence and study in France and, more recently, in the United States. During his youth he was deeply influenced by Mahatma Gandhi; and his first novel, *Kanthapura*, testifies unmistakably to its author's intellectual involvement in the Gandhian drive for national independence—to Rao as much a religious as a political movement.

E.M. Forster considered *Kanthapura* to be the best novel ever written in English by an Indian, and indeed it has great literary strength. Not the least of its merits is the picture it gives of life in one of the innumerable villages that are the repositories of India's ancient but living culture. In vivid detail, Rao describes the daily activities, the religious observances, and the social structure of the community, and he brings to life in his pages a dozen or more unforgettable individual villagers. The novel is political on a superficial level in that it chronicles a revolt against an exploitative plantation manager and the police who support him. But more profoundly it traces the origins of the revolt more to an awakening of the long-dormant Indian soul than to the activities of the Congress party. One of the young men of the village, while away, undergoes a mystical conversion to Satyagraha, and returns to incite his fellow villagers to civil disobedience. He arouses in them not only a sense of social wrong but, more importantly, a religious fervor which proves to be the true source of their strength against the oppressors.

Kanthapura is a novel in which the reader's interest is held mainly by its action and characters. *The Serpent and the Rope* and *The Cat and Shakespeare* are unabashedly metaphysical novels in which plot, setting and even characters are of secondary interest. Semiautobiographical, *The Serpent and the Rope* records the disintegration of a marriage, mainly on philosophical grounds, of a very scholarly Indian Brahmin and a French woman professor. The union founders on the incompatibility of the Brahmin's vendantic conviction that "reality is my Self" and the wife's Western belief—even though she has become a Buddhist—that the evidence of our senses is based on an objective reality outside ourselves. "The world is either unreal or real—the serpent or the rope," the Brahmin assures his wife. "There is no in-between-the-two...." The intellectual demands that Raja Rao, roaming at large through world history and among the religions, philosophies, and literatures of Europe and Asia, makes upon his readers are unequalled in any modern novel since Thomas Mann's *The Magic Mountain*. Though he quotes at length from a bewildering assortment of languages, he provides translations in the case of only one—Sanskrit. The reader is flatteringly assumed to be fluent in Latin, Provençal, Italian, Old French, and other tongues.

The Cat and Shakespeare is much shorter and lighter in tone, though scarcely less metaphysical. The subject of its probings is the problem of individual destiny, and the solution is conveyed in an odd analogy stated by a government clerk: "Learn the way of the kitten. Then you are saved. Allow the mother cat, sir, to carry you." Critics disagree as to what the mother cat symbolizes. The most likely suggestion, made by Uma Parameswaran, is that the cat is karma, the inevitable results of our actions.

All of Rao's work is notable for seriousness of purpose, profundity of thought, a flair for vivid presentation of detail, and a distinctive and vigorous English prose. He asserts: "We cannot write like the English. We should not. We cannot write only as Indians. We have grown to look at the large world as part of us. Our method of expression therefore has to be a dialect which will some day prove to be as distinctive and colorful as the Irish or the American. Time alone will justify it." We might add that Raja Rao's books have gone far to justify it.

—Perry D. Westbrook

RAPHAEL, Frederic (Michael). American. Born in Chicago, Illinois, 14 August 1931. Educated at Charterhouse, Surrey; St. John's College, Cambridge, 1950-54 (Major Classics Scholar, 1950; Harper Wood Student, 1954), M.A. (honours) 1954. Married Sylvia Betty Glatt in 1955; two sons and one daughter. Since 1962, Contributor, and Fiction Critic, 1962-65, *Sunday Times*, London. Recipient: British Screen Writers Award, 1965, 1966, 1967; British Academy Award, 1965; Oscar, for screenplay, 1966. Fellow, Royal Society of Literature, 1964. Address: The Wick, Langham, near Colchester, Essex CO4 5PE, England; or, Lagardelle, St. Laurent-la-Vallée, 24170 Belves, France.

PUBLICATIONS

Novels

Obbligato. London, Macmillan, 1956.
The Earlsdon Way. London, Cassell, 1958.
The Limits of Love. London, Cassell, 1960; Philadelphia, Lippincott, 1961.
A Wild Surmise. London, Cassell, 1961; Philadelphia, Lippincott, 1962.
The Graduate Wife. London, Cassell, 1962.
The Trouble with England. London, Cassell, 1962.
Lindmann. London, Cassell, 1963; New York, Holt Rinehart, 1964.
Darling. New York, New American Library, 1965.
Orchestra and Beginners. London, Cape, 1967; New York, Viking Press, 1968.
Like Men Betrayed. London, Cape, 1970; New York, Viking Press, 1971.
Who Were You with Last Night? London, Cape, 1971.
April, June, and November. London, Cape, 1972; Indianapolis, Bobbs Merrill, 1976.
Richard's Things. London, Cape, 1973; Indianapolis, Bobbs Merrill, 1975.
California Time. London, Cape, 1975; New York, Holt Rinehart, 1976.
The Glittering Prizes. London, Allen Lane, 1976; New York, St. Martin's Press, 1978.
After the War. London, Cape, 1981.

Short Stories

Sleeps Six. London, Cape, 1979.
Oxbridge Blues. London, Cape, 1980.

Plays

Lady at the Wheel, with Lucienne Hill, music and lyrics by Leslie Bricusse and Robin Beaumont (produced London, 1958).
A Man on the Bridge (produced Hornchurch, Essex, 1961).
The Island (juvenile), in *Eight Plays 2*, edited by Malcolm Fellows. London, Cassell, 1965.
Two for the Road (screenplay). London, Cape, and New York, Holt Rinehart, 1967.
An Early Life (produced Leicester, 1979). London, Faber, 1977.
The Serpent Son: Aeschylus: Oresteia, with Kenneth McLeish (televised, 1979). London, Cambridge University Press, 1979.
From the Greek (produced Cambridge, 1979).

Screenplays: *Bachelor of Hearts*, with Leslie Bricusse, 1958; *Don't Bother to Knock*, with Denis Cannan and Frederic Gotfurt, 1961; *Nothing But the Best*, 1963; *Darling*, with John Schlesinger and Joseph Janni, 1965; *Two for the Road*, 1967; *Far from the Madding Crowd*, 1967; *A Severed Head*, 1970; *How About Us?*, 1971; *Daisy Miller*, 1974; *Richard's Things*, 1980.

Radio Play: *The Daedalus Dimension*, 1979.

Television Plays: *The Executioners*, 1961; *Image of a Society*, from the novel by Roy Fuller, 1963; *The Trouble with England*, from his own novel, 1964; *The Glittering Prizes*, 1975; *Rogue Male*, from the novel by Geoffrey Household, 1976; *Something's Wrong*, 1978; *The Serpent Son*, with Kenneth McLeish, 1979; *Of Mycenae and Men*, with Kenneth McLeish, 1979; *School Play*, 1979; *The Best of Friends*, 1980.

Other

W. Somerset Maugham and His World. London, Thames and Hudson, 1976; New York, Scribner, 1977.
Cracks in the Ice: Views and Reviews. London, W.H. Allen, 1979.
The List of Books: An Imaginary Library, with Kenneth McLeish. London, Mitchell Beazley, and New York, Harmony, 1981.
Byron: A Personal Tour. London, Thames and Hudson, 1981.

Editor, *Bookmarks.* London, Cape, 1975.

Translator, with Kenneth McLeish, *The Poems of Catullus.* London, Cape, 1978; Boston, Godine, 1979.

*

Critical Study: "The Varied Universe of Frederic Raphael" by Frederick P.W. McDowell, in *Critique* (Minneapolis), Fall 1965.

Theatrical Activities:

Director: **Television**—*Something's Wrong*, 1978.

Frederic Raphael comments:

Although in many ways I am the most marginal of Jews (I am agnostic in religion and wary of communities), I suppose it is honest to say that I would not be a novelist if it were not for the singular experiences of the Jewish people and for my sense of being, if not a direct participant, at least a witness, of them. My themes, if I have themes, are scarcely Jewish since I lack intimate knowledge of the practices and habits of those who live in so-called Jewish society. When I do come in contact with them I do not necessarily find them congenial. Yet, the Final Solution—its vulgarity no less than its brutality, its greedy malice no less than its murderous factories—lies always at the back of my mind even if I myself, as a child growing up in England, suffered nothing more than its bad breath blowing in my face from across the Channel. It may be an indulgence for anyone who did not have closer experience to claim personal acquaintance with the holocaust; it is equally frivolous to ignore it. It is too convenient a conclusion to dispose of the Jewish experience under the Germans (and the Australians and the Poles and the Hungarians and the Ukrainians and the Russians, and the English and the Americans) as a sort of freakish explosion, a San Francisco earthquake of an event, a once-and-for-all catastrophe after which, in the comforter's cliché, one has to "go on living." And yet, of course, one does.

For me, the novelist is, above all, the historian of conscience.

How does the individual conscience—in other words, how do I—go on living in a world which gives the clearest possible testimony of the cruelty and indifference of man? How does one continue to worry about the nuances of personal life, about love, friendship, taste, and responsibility when all the signs are that man is essentially rapacious, vindictive, and stupid? I have no answers to these questions, nor do I pretend they are in themselves new; they have been asked often enough and yet one does live at a particular time and, despite all the elegant suggestions to the contrary, it seems to me that our time is still linear. Certain things are beyond change, others lie ahead.

The problem is, in a sense, of language. Only in language is it possible to assimilate horrors and yet to achieve something which is both clear and, in a sense, pure. The way in which man remembers meaningfully is by not refusing sense in his language to those things which most profoundly influence or instruct him. This might be an argument for writing either history or philosophy and in a way I tried to do this, but I am not a historian or a philosopher. An obsession with a particular instance of the human character and a desire no less than a tendency—to show the futility of generalisation in the face of the fatuous and magnanimous individuality of human beings, lead me to examine the world through dramatic and emotional states rather than through a study of documents or the analysis of trends. Beyond and through the tragic comes the comic—the comic which does not explode the tragic but defines it—and this interpenetration is only one example of the sort of ambiguities in which the novelist finds himself at home. These ambiguities reveal themselves in drama and I have always found that, in spite of the attractions of both the theatre and the cinema, the drama can be worked out at its most personal and in the most piercing fashion in fiction. Truth may be stranger than fiction but fiction is truer.

How loftily one speaks in such generalising terms as these. The actual impulses which start a book are, of course, less grand. They spring as much from a sense of one's own contradictions as from any perception of human inadequacy or follies. When one begins to speak in the first person it sounds like conceit but it is more often confession, at least at my age. I am conscious above all of being equipped to be a novelist because it is only in a multiplicity of characters that I can reconcile my own ragbag personality. When people speak of a crisis of identity, I remind them that we know very well who we are, where we are having dinner and with whom we are sleeping, yet when I consider myself I am less commonsensical.

I was born in Chicago of a British father and an American mother. Beyond them, my grandparents and great-grandparents branched off across the world like an airline network. I was educated at Charterhouse which, I am told, is a great English Public School, and at Cambridge. I was readily influenced both by the ethos of the English middle class and by the intellectual habits of a classical education. Although I now regret much of what I was told and some of what I learned, I cannot shrug off the influence of these places, nor am I certain that I would wish to do so. The conflict of values reveals itself in fiction in the conflict of characters. I am conscious of being foreign in England and I find myself at home to some extent in many other places, yet I cannot sever myself entirely from the country where I live or from the language in which I write. I am sickened by xenophobia and yet in many ways I fear what lies beyond me. I believe that reason is better than unreason and that intelligence is better than instinct but I have not always been impressed by the decency of those who are most intelligent or by the capacity for affection and love of those who are most reasonable.

Within the nooks and crannies of the great edifices of generalisation and judgement, the innocently guilty and the guiltily innocent scurry about carrying nuts to their families, seeking their pleasures, snapping at their enemies, and providing, for those who have eyes to see, the proof of the impossibility of final solutions to the human condition.

* * *

Frederic Raphael began with a slight novel, *Obbligato*, a satiric and mock-heroic account of the rise to fame of an improvising pop-singer. Literary merit is abundant, however, in Raphael's second book, *The Earlsdon Way*, a realistic novel about the futility of British suburban life and the ineffectual revolt against its mores undertaken by Edward Keggin and his daughter Karen.

The Limits of Love gained for Raphael wide and deserved recognition. Its protagonist, Paul Riesman, is a Jew divorced by his training and inclinations from his race. Because he will not recognize what is necessity for him, his Jewishness, he becomes a selfish, life-destroying man despite his continuing efforts to achieve identity. But Paul increasingly sees that love is a defeating force if it is limited to the personal sphere and if it rejects the community; and he finds in his mother-in-law, Hannah Adler, stability that he lacks and in her daughter Julia, his wife, flexibility and depth.

In *A Wild Surmise* Raphael used a technique of montage to reveal his protagonist, Robert Carn, gradually. Carn hopes to escape British conventions in San Roque and to find genuine value through the spontaneous, impassioned, disinterested self. Ultimately, he supplements his introspective endeavors with a commitment to others in his efforts, ostensibly unsuccessful, to save some Indians from being poisoned. The novel is powerful and evocative, especially as it charts the processes of Carn's mind and the subtleties of his psychic life.

Raphael has a number of brief novels, ironically executed, which concentrate upon a moral problem and its significance for the chief characters. *The Trouble with England* develops the moral contrasts between two vacationing couples on the French Riviera; *The Graduate Wife* focuses upon the forward development of a priggish heroine to inner stability. *Who Were You with Last Night?* has, as first-person narrator, the disenchanted Charles Hanson who is amusing as he deflates bourgeois values (sometimes his own), recounts his satisfactions and frustrations with wife and mistress, and analyzes the delicate balance existing between love and hate in intimate relationships. *Richard's Things* is a tour de force, suggesting the impermanence not only of the marital relationship but of life itself, as the piquant relationship between the wife of the now dead Richard and his mistress diminishes from its first ardor to something near hatred. More recently, *The Glittering Prizes* reveals Raphael's remarkable technical expertise and depth of emotional insight as he traces the unfolding lives, after their graduation, of a group of Cambridge compatriots. The chief of these, Adam Morris, is a novelist similar in temperament to Raphael himself. He is an ironically minded but aesthetically talented Jew whose temporary foray into the world of the mass media is engaging farce, meant also to define the difficulties that the serious artist encounters in staying fast to his genuine impulses.

The peak of Raphael's achievement in writing the experimental novel is *Lindmann*. A British civil servant, James Shepherd, connived in 1942 to prevent the *SS Broda* from landing in Turkey with its Jewish refugees. Shepherd, to expiate his guilt and to achieve self-definition, assumes the identity of Jacob Lindmann, one of the two survivors from the ship who later died from exposure. A certain chastity gives Shepherd as Lindmann his moral force, since he forgoes any kind of fulfillment for himself; and he is, by his spiritual tenacity, something more than the failure he judges himself to be. Through patience and love he tries to influence others to a course of moderation, toleration, consideration, and affection.

Four more recent novels, *Orchestra and Beginners*, *Like Men Betrayed*, *April, June, and November*, and *California Time* are also works of considerable scope. In *Orchestra and Beginners* Raphael analyzes the ineffectual decency and the effete decay which characterized British upper-middle-class society just prior to World War II. Linda Strauss suffers from the moral paralysis of the class into which as an American she has married but is sympathetically seen, even if she fails her husband at his military enlistment because of her intensely personal reactions to experience. Leonard, in turn, is too impersonal toward Linda. Paradoxically, Linda's passion and Leonard's critical intelligence are both needed in confronting the complexities of modern life.

Like Men Betrayed is about Grecian and, by implication, English politics, and it is remarkable for penetrating the relationships between the individual's psyche and social institutions. Three main points in time contrapuntally organize the book: the Greece of the 1930's under the Marshal's moderate dictatorship; Greece during the Second World War when factional jealousies are only less intense than hatred for the Italians and Germans; and postwar Greece when a power struggle develops between the corrupt royalist regime and the leftist insurgents. Artemis Theodoros defects from the Royalists when government troops fail in World War II to support the leftist General Papavastrou against the Germans. The novel is subtle and complex as it traces Artemis's endeavors to reach spiritual and political truth. As the novel opens he is fleeing north to the frontier where supposedly his forces will reach asylum. Instead, he learns that they will be betrayed. He remains faithful to his inner standards, however, despite misunderstanding, violence, betrayal, imprisonment, and exile. In Artemis a deplorable waste of genius occurs. The integrity inherent in such a heroic man, however, is the resource which we will have to learn how to use to insure a revitalized polity, Raphael would seem to be saying.

April, June, and November and *California Time* are also novels about talented men whose creative energies are deflected either by weakness of will or by circumstances. In *April, June, and November* the liberal and magnetic Daniel Meyer is, in fact, capable of a heroism which he can never display to any purpose in his hedonistic, effete milieu. The football field rather than the political arena claims his intelligence and genius. In *California Time* Victor England is likewise a victim, but could he have ever achieved distinction in the cutthroat and standardless world of the motion picture studios, a world which needs his creativity but which also humiliates him to the greatest possible extent? Raphael is frankly experimental in this novel, collapsing all of Victor's experience into the ongoing present and creating doubts in him as to the reality of his perceptions of the given moment, in a milieu in which the reality and the hallucination become barely distinguishable. In these two novels Raphael develops the tragedy of the man who cannot actualize his good intentions and give free expression to his genius, with the same density, elusiveness, and complication that characterize his fiction as a whole.

—Frederick P.W. McDowell

RAVEN, Simon (Arthur Noël). British. Born in London, 28 December 1927. Educated at Charterhouse, Surrey, 1941-45; King's College, Cambridge, 1948-52, B.A. 1951, M.A. 1955. Served in the British Army, 1946-48 (commissioned in India, 1947), and 1953-57 (Captain, King's Shropshire Light Infantry). Married Susan Mandeville Kilner in 1952 (divorced, 1957); one son. Address: c/o Blond and Briggs Ltd., Victoria Works, Edgware Road, London NW2 6LE, England.

PUBLICATIONS

Novels

The Feathers of Death. London, Blond, 1959; New York, Simon and Schuster, 1960.
Brother Cain. London, Blond, 1959; New York, Simon and Schuster, 1960.
Doctors Wear Scarlet. London, Blond, 1960; New York, Simon and Schuster, 1961.
Close of Play. London, Blond, 1962.
Alms for Oblivion:
The Rich Pay Late. London, Blond, 1964; New York, Putnam, 1965.
Friends in Low Places. London, Blond, 1965; New York, Putnam, 1966.
The Sabre Squadron. London, Blond, 1966; New York, Harper, 1967.
Fielding Gray. London, Blond, 1967.
The Judas Boy. London, Blond, 1968.
Places Where They Sing. London, Blond, 1970.
Sound the Retreat. London, Blond, 1971.
Come like Shadows. London, Blond and Briggs, 1972.
Bring Forth the Body. London, Blond and Briggs, 1974.
The Survivors. London, Blond and Briggs, 1975.
The Roses of Picardie: A Romance. London, Blond and Briggs, 1980.
An Inch of Fortune. London, Blond and Briggs, 1980.

Short Stories

The Fortunes of Fingel. London, Blond and Briggs, 1976.

Plays

Royal Foundation and Other Plays (radio and television plays: *The Move Up Country*; *The Doomsday School*; *The Scapegoat*; *Panther Larkin*; *The High King's Tomb*; *The Gaming Book*; *Sir Jocelyn, The Minister Would Like a Word*). London, Blond, 1966.
The Scouncing Stoup (broadcast, 1964). Published in *New Radio Drama*, London, BBC Publications, 1966.
The Case of Father Brendan (produced London, 1968).

Screenplays: *On Her Majesty's Secret Service*, with Richard Maibaum, 1969; *Unman, Wittering, and Zigo*, 1971.

Radio Plays: *Loser Pays All*, 1961; *A Present from Venice*, 1961; *The Gate of Learning*, 1962; *A Friend in Need*, 1962; *The Doomsday School*, 1963; *The High King's Tomb*, 1964; *Panther Larkin*, 1964; *The Melos Affair*, 1965; *The Last Expedition*, 1967; *The Tutor*, 1967; *The Prisoners in the Cave*, 1968; *Salvation*, 1974; *In Transit*, 1978.

Television Plays: *The Scapegoat*, 1964; *The Gaming Book*, 1964; *Advise and Dissent*, 1965; *Sir Jocelyn, The Minister Would Like a Word*, 1965; *A Soirée at Bossom's Hotel*, 1966; *A Pyre for Private James*, 1966; *The Way We Live Now*, from the novel by Trollope; *Point Counter Point*, from the novel by Aldous Huxley, 1968; *The Human Element*, from the novel by Somerset Maugham, 1970; *The Pallisers*, from novels by Trollope, 1974; *An Unofficial Rose*, from the novel by Iris Murdoch, 1974; *Red Sky at Night* (*The Brothers* series), 1976; *Edward and Mrs. Simpson*, from a work by Frances Donaldson, 1978; *Sexton Blake* series, 1978; *Love in a Cold Climate*, from the novels *Love in a Cold Climate* and *The Pursuit of Love* by Nancy Mitford, 1980.

Other

The English Gentleman: An Essay in Attitudes. London, Blond, 1961; as *The Decline of the Gentleman*, New York, Simon and Schuster, 1962.
Boys Will Be Boys and Other Essays. London, Blond, 1963.

Editor, *The Best of Gerald Kersh*. London, Heinemann, 1960.

*

Critical Study: "The Novels of Simon Raven" by Kerry McSweeney, in *Queen's Quarterly* (Kingston, Ontario), Spring 1971.

Simon Raven comments:

My theme is the vanity of human wishes.

My object is to make money by presenting this theme in such a way as to interest and amuse intelligent readers of the upper and upper-middle classes.

* * *

Simon Raven is frequently compared to Evelyn Waugh. Yet the truth is that his novels are nearer to the spirit of P.G. Wodehouse. For all their show of satire of contemporary social *mores*, and for all their dedicated right-wing snobbishness, the fact is that one can't take them seriously. As entertainments they repay reading; as serious novels they do not. Raven would probably not mind this being said. His writing has all the marks of the good *raconteur*; it seeks to amuse and to hold the attention. All of his novels are remarkable for the ingenious sexual lives of their principal characters, yet in none are we given the sweaty detail or the naming of parts. Instead, there is hint, innuendo, suggestion. We are taken as far as the bedroom door (or more interesting doors) but not beyond. And this is not the result of prudishness, but of calculated prurience. Again, all the novels have a good deal of plot, there is much coming and going of characters, and the settings are customarily exotic, the English no less than the foreign (Raven's England tends to be bounded by seedy public schools, gambling salons, and expensive Mayfair apartments inside whose plush rooms unspeakable happenings occur). Yet it is impossible to believe in the reality of any of these places. Nor does it much matter. The pace of the narrative seldom drops below a steady gallop and we are whisked from place to place, incident to incident, in a manner that hardly allows us to question the substantiality of it all.

Yet it may perhaps be that Raven aims higher than I have suggested. In the first place there is his novel *Close of Play*, which seems to touch a darker note than is usual with him. The hero, Hugo Warren, is a person whose motto "never regret anything" carries him through a series of outrageous adventures that culminate in the murder of his sexual partner and of his own murder at the hands of relatives and former friends. And for all the high jinks, *Close of Play* is obviously meant to be a study of amorality, even of evil. Yet it is difficult to be very involved with this, because the novel's farcical elements collide so crudely with the more sombre moments.

Then again, there is the novel sequence *Alms for Oblivion*. Of these the best is probably *The Rich Pay Late*, though *The Judas Boy* runs it close. But no matter how amusing the individual novels may be, it is impossible to see the point of the sequence as a whole. It can hardly be said to provide an extended study of its central character, Fielding Gray, for he does not develop from one novel to the next. It is simply that different things happen to him. But neither can the sequence be said to build up an important study of the contemporary world (or of England), because the settings are too random for that. It is likely that *Alms for Oblivion* will be remembered for the merits of the individual novels.

—John Lucas

READ, Piers Paul. British. Born in Beaconsfield, Buckinghamshire, 7 March 1941; son of the writer Herbert Read. Educated at Ampleforth College; St. John's College, Cambridge, B.A. 1961, M.A. 1962. Married Emily Boothby in 1967; two sons and one daughter. Sub-Editor, *Times Literary Supplement*, London, 1964-65. Artist-in-Residence, Ford Foundation, Berlin, 1963-64; Adjunct Professor of Writing, Columbia University, New York, 1980. Recipient: Commonwealth Fund Harkness Fellowship, 1967; Faber Memorial Award, 1968; Hawthornden Prize, 1969; Maugham Award, 1970; Thomas More Association Medal, 1974. Fellow, Royal Society of Literature. Agent: Deborah Rogers Ltd., 5-11 Mortimer Street, London W1N 7RH. Address: Old Byland Hall, Helmsley, Yorkshire YO6 5LG, England.

PUBLICATIONS

Novels

Game in Heaven with Tussy Marx. London, Weidenfeld and Nicolson, and New York, McGraw Hill, 1966.
The Junkers. London, Secker and Warburg, 1968; New York, Knopf, 1969.
Monk Dawson. London, Secker and Warburg, 1969; Philadelphia, Lippincott, 1970.
The Professor's Daughter. London, Secker and Warburg-Alison Press, and Philadelphia, Lippincott, 1971.
The Upstart. London, Alison Press, and Philadelphia, Lippincott, 1973.
Polonaise. London, Alison Press, and Philadelphia, Lippincott, 1976.
A Married Man. London, Secker and Warburg, 1979; Philadelphia, Lippincott, 1980.

Plays

The Class War, in *Colloquialisms* (produced London, 1964).

Radio Plays: *The Family Firm*, 1970; *The House on Highbury Hill*, music by Julian Slade, 1971.

Television Plays: *Coincidence*, 1968; *The Childhood Friend*, 1974; *Margaret Clitheroe* (*Here I Stand* series), 1977.

Other

Alive! The Story of the Andes Survivors. London, Secker and Warburg, and Philadelphia, Lippincott, 1974.
The Train Robbers. London, Allen and Unwin-Alison Press, and Philadelphia, Lippincott, 1978.

* * *

Piers Paul Read is intensely concerned with moral issues. Many of his main themes are epitomized in *Monk Dawson*, the best novel he has yet written. Dissatisfied with his monastic existence, Edward Dawson enters the main stream of contemporary society—a society that is decadent, sex-obsessed, hedonistic, bored, and exceedingly materialistic. Despite sports, gambling, relaxing in the sun, and similar pleasures, Dawson finds sybaritic activities empty; life becomes painful and without meaning. Dawson's woman companion, to whom he is deeply devoted, deserts him for another lover, and qualities such as basic kindness, integrity, and good character are out of fashion. Dawson's return to monasticism is a recognition that man should possess spiritual purpose, exalt solidity in his life, and give service to moral values, which are an individual's and the world's only hope for at least partial betterment.

In Read's first novel, an extravagant fantasy in which Karl Marx's youngest daughter, Tussy, views life from an anteroom of heaven, the reader perceives that well-intentioned philosophies are marred by people who are, by their very nature, corrupt and amoral and allow the whims and blandishments of love to dominate even when love is found to be usually unstable, impermanent, and fraudulent.

Read's interest in various political theories is pervasive. In *The Professor's Daughter* Henry Rutledge is a distinguished Harvard master of political theory. Handsome, intelligent, and rich, he champions liberal and progressive ideas. His death, which results from militant revolutionary activity carried out by some of his graduate students, exposes the sharp contrast between idealistic theory and reality. Politically, Rutledge may be on the side of the angels, but he has made a wreck of his family relationships. His wife is continuously unfaithful and an alcoholic, while his oldest daughter is, successively, hippie, prostitute, and revolutionary. She is saved from suicide by the merest of accidents. She is seen not only as a casualty of a rotten society, but also as the sad victim of the breakdown of family life. Since Read stresses that the family is society's fundamental stabilizing unit, this institution must first be put in order before any significant success can be achieved outside the home.

The vicious degeneracy and animalistic cruelty of the Nazis, so expertly exposed in *The Junkers*, demonstrates anew the desperate need for moral standards in a world of treachery, SS, concentration camps, and genocide. *The Upstart* also emphasizes this theme as Hilary Fletcher commits almost every evil of which a person is capable; yet, ultimately, for Fletcher there is hope achieved by genuine repentance and atonement. Even the Communist can be applauded if morality and genuine humanitarian concerns can overcome the dominance of evil and cruelty which constantly plagues individuals.

At one point Read quotes from Julien Green's *Diary* to the effect that within each of us there is a sinner and a saint. Even though one phase dominates, the other aspect makes progress on the imaginative plane so that this mixture and conflict will cause constant turmoil, and the yearning for betterment will continue to torment. In the fiction of Read we are reminded that all too often "the devil is prince of the world....He has powers too."

Both *Polonaise* and *A Married Man* are notable examples of an increasing mastery of style and plotting. Read's earlier novels suffered from occasional stretches of pedestrian prose and a tendency to melodrama and contrived happenings. Read now demonstrates a definite growth in craftsmanship. This artistry and his perceptive and penetrating probing into crucial 20th-century moral issues demonstrate that he is a still young novelist of a considerable significance.

—Paul A. Doyle

RECHY, John (Francisco). American. Born in El Paso, Texas, 10 March 1934. Educated at Texas Western College, El Paso, B.A.; New School for Social Research, New York. Served in the United States Army. Recipient: National Endowment for the Arts grant, 1976. Lives in Los Angeles. Agent: Georges Borchardt Inc., 136 East 57th Street, New York, New York 10022, U.S.A.

PUBLICATIONS

Novels

City of Night. New York, Grove Press, 1963; London, MacGibbon and Kee, 1964.
Numbers. New York, Grove Press, 1967.
This Day's Death. New York, Grove Press, and London, MacGibbon and Kee, 1970.
The Vampires. New York, Grove Press, 1971.
The Fourth Angel. New York, Viking Press, and London, W.H. Allen, 1972.
Rushes. New York, Grove Press, 1979.

Play

Momma As She Became—Not As She Was (produced New York, 1978).

Other

The Sexual Outlaw: A Documentary of Three Days and Nights in the Sexual Underground. New York, Grove Press, 1977; London, W.H. Allen, 1978.

*

Manuscript Collection: Boston University.

* * *

John Rechy's world is the heir of Hawthorne's. His characters inhabit a moral universe whose codes are as rigorous as Calvin's and whose cops are the vigilantes of a new unmerciful Salem. The "youngmen" of *City of Night* and *Numbers* are the fallen angels of an eternally inaccessible paradise and their lives are characterised by a search for the *eros* that will at last become *agape*. That the search is frenetic is scarcely surprising; it has all the desperate urgency that characterises the role of the sensitive American—the anguish of exile within one's own country. And although in *City of Night* Rechy never quite succeeds in conveying Francis Thompson's added sense of "dreadful," it is plain that the implication is there. New York, from the first page, is a metaphor city, a fairy city—in a sense like the London of Stevenson—where anything might happen. That is not to say that Rechy's urban fantasy has the calibre of Purdy's. It is more limited in its focus. Its world is a moral world turned upside down, where the *Deus absconditus* is Priapus. The quest for that god is a never-ending and insatiable one and one in which the tyrants of the old moral order have all the destructive vindictiveness of Diocletian against the Christians.

Having said all that, one should also say that neither *City of Night* nor *Numbers* (in spite of the deliberate "allegorical" pretensions of the former) often rises above what seem to be the masturbatory fantasies of an aging queen—bad Genet. Only with his third and by far his best novel, *This Day's Death*, does Rechy get beyond the unfortunate dualisms of his earlier novels—a catalogue of well-equipped muscleboys on the one hand and a labored novelistic artifice to contain it on the other. That is not to say that *This Day's Death* does not suffer from a somewhat contrivedly concealed central event and a time scheme that is sometimes confusing and tedious. Its *à la récherche de la virginité perdue*, however, is convincing in a way that is true of neither of the earliest novels. Rechy's New Mexico, like Steinbeck's Oklahoma, is a small-town world of poverty and pain, the anguish of growth and the desire to break out. His California is the nightmare inversion of that desire—a world where the law is a monster devouring the innocents who nonetheless have a Genet-like fascination with its devious iniquities. And together these worlds, as commentaries on one another, form a larger moral universe than any Rechy has created before.

It is disenchanting then to find that in *The Vampires*, the novel that succeeds *This Day's Death*, he returns to the world of gothic fiction with an overlay of baroque Satanism—a parody of scenarios for Heliogabalus as rewritten by Albee. *The Fourth Angel* suffers less from this, being set once again in the south-west. But if its teenage characters are more "real," their problems are too much the stereotypes of the late 1960's to remain interesting, and the sentimentality of their presentation—"and so, suddenly, they're gentle children playing gentle children's games"—sounds like the worst of the Woodstock inheritance.

Rechy discovered earlier than most what Tom Wolfe has recently drawn attention to—the new reporting style of the 1960's. His first two pieces appeared in *Evergreen Review* and from one of them came *City of Night*. But journalists are as prone as anyone else to being taken over by easy "rhetoric," and the mode of confession that fascinates Rechy easily becomes trite. As Ruskin said of the first painting by Leighton, the Victorian painter, "if he does not do much better he will do worse."

—D.D.C. Chambers

REED, Ishmael (Scott). Afro-American. Born in Chattanooga, Tennessee, 22 February 1938. Educated at the University of Buffalo, New York, 1956-60. Married to Carla Blank-Reed; one daughter by a previous marriage. Co-Founder of the *East Village Other*, New York, and *Advance*, Newark, New Jersey, 1965. Since 1971, Chairman and President of Yardbird Publishing Company; since 1973, Director, Reed Cannon and Johnson Communications. Guest lecturer, University of California, Berkeley, 1968, 1969, 1974, 1976; Lecturer, University of Washington, Seattle, 1969-70; Senior Lecturer, University of California, Berkeley; Visiting Professor, Yale University, New Haven, Connecticut, Fall 1979. Recipient: National Endowment for the Arts Grant, 1974; Rosenthal Foundation Award, 1975; Guggenheim Fellowship, 1975. Address: c/o Yardbird Press, 870 53rd Street, Berkeley, California 96408, U.S.A.

PUBLICATIONS

Novels

The Free-Lance Pallbearers. New York, Doubleday, 1967; London, MacGibbon and Kee, 1968.
Yellow Back Radio Broke-Down. New York, Doubleday, 1969; London, Allison and Busby, 1971.
Mumbo-Jumbo. New York, Doubleday, 1972.
The Last Days of Louisiana Red. New York, Random House, 1974.
Flight to Canada. New York, Random House, 1976.

Verse

Catechism of d neoamerican hoodoo church. London, Paul Breman, 1970.
Conjure: Selected Poems 1963-1970. Amherst, University of Massachusetts Press, 1972.
Chattanooga. New York, Random House, 1973.
Secretary to the Spirits. New York, Nok, 1977.

Other

The Rise, Fall, and ...? of Adam Clayton Powell (as Emmett Coleman), with others. New York, Bee-Line, 1967.
Shrovetide in Old New Orleans (essays). New York, Doubleday, 1978.

Editor, *19 Necromancers from Now.* New York, Doubleday, 1970.
Editor, *Yardbird Reader.* Berkeley, California, Yardbird, 1972 (annual).
Editor, with Al Young, *Yardbird Lives!* New York, Grove Press, 1978.
Editor, *Calafia: The California Poetry.* Berkeley, California, Yardbird, 1979.

*

Bibliography: "Mapping Out the Gumbo Works: An Ishmael Reed Bibliography" by Joe Weixlmann, Robert Fikes, Jr., and Ishmael Reed, in *Black American Literature Forum* (Terre Haute, Indiana), Spring, 1978.

Critical Studies: "Robin the Cock & Doopeyduk Doing the Boogaloo in Harry Sam with Rusty Jethroe and Letterhead America..." by Lawrence Lipton, in *Cavalier* (Greenwich, Connecticut), no. 70, 1967; review by Tam Fiofori, in *Negro Digest* (Chicago), December 1969; "Blood of the Lamb" by Calvin Hernton, in *Amistad 1*, New York, Knopf, 1970.

* * *

In an introduction to an essay collection, *Shrovetide in Old New Orleans*, Ishmael Reed says: "Many people here called my fiction muddled, crazy, incoherent, because I've attempted in fiction the techniques and forms painters, dancers, film makers, musicians in the West have taken for granted for at least fifty years, and the artists of many other cultures, for thousands of years." Reed's strengths are enunciated here: flexible, vivid language ranging from street argot to lofty estheticism, experimentation with materials and means, and a deep awareness of the mythic roots of all cultures. Reed is an Afro-American ironist, but his gifts and insights are multicultural, multimedia.

Reed's early novels, *The Free-Lance Pallbearers* and *Yellow Back Radio Broke-Down*, are musical and mythical in conception and development. Using "hoodoo" as a system both of ideas and of language, Reed describes our world in terms of the hero and the prison of society. In *The Free-Lance Pallbearers* Bukka Doopeyduk is the epigonous hero fighting against HARRY SAM, which is the nation-state transformed into a monstrous personification, a dragon. In similar fashion, the Loop Garoo Kid of *Yellow Back Radio Broke-Down* is a shaman-hero (Loupe Garou = werewolf in Creole-French folklore) of a cowboy saga, in which the town of Yellow Back Radio is threatened by Drag Gibson, the stultifying force of the square world. The vaudevillian jokes, surrealism, and wordplays flow at *allegro* tempo.

In *Mumbo Jumbo* Reed concentrates on a mythic time (the 1920's) and magic places (New Orleans and Harlem) in U.S. culture. The ideas of hoodoo/voodoo and other Afro-American magic-religious cults figure in Reed's tapestry of the Jazz Age and the Harlem Renaissance. Reed describes the epic struggle between Jes Grew, the black cultural impulse, and the Atonists, i.e., the monotheistic Western tradition. In the narrative, Reed incorporates drawings, photographs, collages, and handwritten texts, along with many scholarly references.

The Last Days of Louisiana Red extends this mythology, bringing many of the same characters and ideas to Berkeley in the 1970's. "Louisiana Red" is the plague of modern technocratic-industrial culture:

> Louisiana Red was the way they related to one another, oppressed one another, maimed and murdered one another, carving one another while above their heads, fifty thousand feet, billionaires flew in custom-made jet planes equipped with saunas tennis courts swimming pools discotheques and meeting rooms decorated like the Merv Griffin show set.

In *Flight to Canada* Reed moves back to the mythos of slavery and the Civil War, applying the same wild, anachronistic expressionism to the central tragedy of black American culture. In ironic, dramatic terms, Reed answers the "cliometric" revisors of history: "Revisionists. Quantitative historians. What does a computer know? Can a computer feel? Make love? Can a computer feel passion?" Quickskill tears off his shirt. "Look at these scars. Look at them! All you see is their fruit, but their roots run deep. The roots are in my soul."

Ishmael Reed's brilliant comic vision of American history brings together the basic ingredients of black culture in a rich musical-dramatic form. His expansion of language into a radically personal style points to the richness of that culture as a storytelling source. Reed's wide interests in traditions outside the received mainstream of "Western Culture" courses, in magic, myth, and ritual, make him one of the most forceful and persuasive novelists of the past 20 years.

—William J. Schafer

REID, Vic(tor Stafford). Jamaican. Born in Jamaica, 1 May 1913. Educated in Jamaica. Married; four children. Reporter, editor, and foreign correspondent for various newspapers; worked in advertising; currently, managing director and chairman of a printing and publishing company in Kingston, Jamaica; has travelled extensively in the Americas, Africa, Europe, and the Middle East. Recipient: Guggenheim Fellowship, 1959; Canada Council Fellowship; Mexican Writers Fellowship. Address: Valley Hill Farm, Rock Hall, Jamaica.

PUBLICATIONS

Novels

New Day. New York, Knopf, 1949; London, Heinemann, 1950.
The Leopard. New York, Viking Press, and London, Heinemann, 1958.

Uncollected Short Stories

"Digging Match," in *Life and Letters* (London), November 1948.
"Waterfront Bar," in *West Indian Stories*, edited by Andrew Salkey. London, Faber, 1960.
"My Father's House," and "A Requiem for Dan'l Moore," in *From the Green Antilles*, edited by Barbara Howes. New York, Macmillan, 1966; London, Souvenir Press, 1967.

Other

Sixty-Five (juvenile). London, Longman, 1960.
The Young Warriors (juvenile). London, Longman, 1967.
Buildings in Jamaica. Kingston, Jamaica Information Service, 1970.
Peter of Mount Ephraim (juvenile). Kingston, Jamaica Publishing House, 1971.
The Sun and Juan de Bolas (juvenile). Kingston, Institute of Jamaica, 1974.

* * *

Vic Reid gives the impression of being a "loner," a man of few words. His literary out-put has not been large, but he has been an innovative and unusual novelist.

When *New Day* appeared in 1949, it proved to be innovative in two ways: in its use of a formalised Jamaican English, and in its concerns—for national growth, for the resumption and expansion of responsible government, for the role of a local family in national growth. *The Leopard*, set as it is in Kikuyu land, does not use a distinctive form of Jamaican speech, but it is structurally more interesting than *New Day*, and its concerns are not as unconnected with West Indian experience as they might seem. In fact, Reid's life as a Jamaican would have prepared him well to work out such a combination of gentleness and violence, in fact a fugue and coda, which could also be a prelude to a "new day" in Africa, and in the world.

New Day, using the flashback technique, has structural weaknesses, and from time to time its special formalised Jamaican language does not ring absolutely true. (To give two small examples: "Duppy-ghost," "congo-pea soup".) Was Reid too concerned with the fact that his Jamaican characters had to speak not only to each other, but also to a wider audience?

His historical grasp of the political and power situation in 1865 has been criticised both on ideological and historical grounds. In this connection, it should not be forgotten that Reid was very careful to say in the last paragraph of the "Author's Note" prefaced to the first edition of *New Day*: "I have not by any means attempted a history of the period from 1865 to 1944....What I have attempted is to transfer to paper some of the beauty, kindness, and humor of my people,...creating a tale that will offer as true an impression as fiction can of the way by which Jamaica and its people come to today."

There are many remarkable things in *New Day*; one notable section deals with Pastor Humphrey's sermon on "constituted authority." It starts, "Whenever we go to church...Naomi and me sit side-and-side...but when the sermon begins we close our knees tight, and then there is good space for crab-race. You know how to play crab-race?" That very Jamaican question sets the aspect of the children's presence at the service, while as Humphrey warms to his theme—"Mouth came down *snap* on authority, long neck shot out, then drew back into his cassock like iguana in stonehole"—the Stoney Gut men are about to create a groaning objection to Paul's text on obedience and the pastor's interpretation of it. The chapter ends with " 'Let us pray for rain,' says Pastor Humphrey." But we know that it is blood that will soon be quenching the long drought which had intensified, and symbolised, the disillusion and deterioration in St. Thomas Parish.

Often old John Campbell (as narrator) slips delightfully into the skin of the young boy, he had been when "in media res": "Good it is to hear her laugh but when mother says *Heh!* like that, all of your manhood is gone....Is funny how your breeches drop off anytime Mother says *heh!*" But the ably-used device of having a sleepless narrator recall his family's role in the dawning of the "new day" has its disadvantages. For one thing, John Campbell has to rush a few sequences to help us suspend, willingly, our disbelief, and it might well be this technical difficulty that tends to exaggerate a falsely Romantic view (even in Campbell's mouth) of the fighting years of Jamaican men.

The Leopard is in some ways, particularly in structure, even more noteworthy. The clean juxta-positioning of the few personae, the untransitioned switching from group to group of those concerned and then converging for the final point of the story—and meanwhile the leopard alone understands Kenya "for he avoids the strong and eats the wounded, and the weak is stalking the stalked"—all these build up into an image of sick, hunting and hunted man, not unlike Derek Walcott's in "A Far Cry from Africa." In the end the lieutenant ("robbed me of my first Kike") becomes the leopard, whom he has just deprecatingly, but more truthfully than he realises, called "Brother Leopard," and the fate long since planned for that animal becomes the lieutenant's at the hands of Nebu ("one of the loyal bucks").

Vic Reid is a flexible and varied writer, with, at times, a fist of mail beneath that gauntlet of silk. An innovator on the West Indian literary scene, he has written, besides the novels mentioned, a variety of short stories and books for young people. His work shows forth his giftedness and care, and underlines our need for more from him.

—John J. Figueroa

REID BANKS, Lynne. British and Israeli. Born in London, 31 July 1929. Educated at the Royal Academy of Dramatic Art, London. Married Chaim Stephenson in 1965; three sons. Actress in British repertory companies, 1949-53; Secretary to Wolf Mankowitz, *q.v.*, 1953-54; Interviewer, Reporter and Scriptwriter, Independent Television News, London, 1954-61; Teacher, Kibbutz Yasur School and Na'aman High School, Israel, 1962-71. Recipient: Yorkshire Arts Association award, 1977. Agent: Bolt and Watson Ltd., 8-12 Old Queen Street, Storey's Gate, London SW1H 9HP, England.

PUBLICATIONS

Novels

The L-Shaped Room. London, Chatto and Windus, 1960; New York, Simon and Schuster, 1961.
An End to Running. London, Chatto and Windus, 1962; as *House of Hope*, New York, Simon and Schuster, 1962.
Children at the Gate. London, Chatto and Windus, and New York, Simon and Schuster, 1968.
The Backward Shadow. London, Chatto and Windus, and New York, Simon and Schuster, 1970.
Two Is Lonely. London, Chatto and Windus, and New York, Simon and Schuster, 1974.
Dark Quartet: The Story of the Brontës. London, Weidenfeld and Nicolson, 1976; New York, Delacorte Press, 1977.
Path to the Silent Country: Charlotte Brontë's Years of Fame. London, Weidenfeld and Nicolson, 1977; New York, Delacorte Press, 1978.
Defy the Wilderness. London, Chatto and Windus, 1981.

Plays

It Never Rains (televised, 1954; produced Keighley, Yorkshire, 1954). London, Deane, 1954.
Miss Pringle Plays Portia, with Victor Maddern. London, Deane, 1955.
The Killer Dies Twice. London, Deane, 1956.
All in a Row. London, Deane, and Boston, Baker, 1956.
The Unborn (produced London, 1962).
Already It's Tomorrow (televised, 1962). London, French, 1962.
The Gift (produced London, 1965).

Radio Plays: *The Stowaway*, 1967; *Lame Duck*, 1978.

Television Plays: *It Never Rains*, 1954; *Already It's Tomorrow*, 1962; *The Wednesday Caller*, 1963; *The Last Word on Julie*, 1964; *The Eye of the Beholder* (*She* series), 1977.

Other

The Kibbutz: Some Personal Reflections (address). London, Anglo-Israel Association, 1972.
One More River (juvenile). London, Vallentine Mitchell, and New York, Simon and Schuster, 1973.
Sarah and After (juvenile). London, Bodley Head, and New York, Doubleday, 1975.
The Adventures of King Midas (juvenile). London, Dent, 1976.
The Farthest-Away Mountain (juvenile). London, Abelard Schuman, 1976; New York, Doubleday, 1977.
My Darling Villain (juvenile). London, Bodley Head, and New York, Harper, 1977.
Houdini: The Autobiography of a Self-Educated Hamster (juvenile). London, Dent, 1978.
Letters to My Israeli Sons: The Story of Jewish Survival. London, W.H. Allen, 1979; New York, Watts, 1980.
The Indian in the Cupboard (juvenile). London, Dent, 1980; New York, Doubleday, 1981.
The Writing on the Wall (juvenile). London, Chatto and Windus, 1981.

*

Manuscript Collection: Boston University.

Lynne Reid Banks comments:

I've never gone in much for analysing my work or my work-processes. As a writer, and as a person, I tend to be lazy and disorganised. If my characters do not "take over" and direct my typing fingers, it is nothing but drudgery for me—I write in order to have written. I find out what I had to say after I have said it. But in any case, "things to say" are not my primary driving-force. I am a story-teller. That to me is what fiction is—it is not a subtle way of communicating one's political, social, or any other opinions to a host of faceless readers. Praise, to me, is not "How I agreed with you about such-and-such!" but "How I cared about this or that character...."

Although the great rallying-cry to writers these days is "Truth for Truth's sake," objective truth, the chronicling of reality, is not my metier. If it were, I should not write fiction. Fiction means, to me, a reflection of life so "doctored" that its only relationship to truth is an illusion in the reader's mind. The reader must receive this illusion of reality, of course, or else the one binding commandment of the novel-writer—"Involve thy reader"—is broken; but this is not to say that the story need be "true" in the sense of reflecting ordinary, typical people or events.

Jane Austen is the only novelist I know whose peculiar genius lies in taking perfectly ordinary people through ordinary situations, and transmogrifying them into fascinating fiction. Every other great novelist I can think of has either created exceptional characters or has devised for them abnormal events—often both. Dickens, Tolstoi, the Brontës, Victor Hugo—all were allowed their outrageous coincidences, their larger-than life heroes, their impossible denouements and neat, incredible resolutions. Nobody in those days queried the fiction-writers' right to write *fiction*, and not fiction parading as fact.

Character in novels may not go beyond the possible. But they should—the principal ones, anyway—be exceptional people. Jane (*The L-Shaped Room*) did not behave like an ordinary girl. Her reactions and decisions were those of, let us say, one girl in ten, or fifty, or a hundred, in her situation. Perhaps the others would have liked to do what she did; perhaps that explains why the book was widely read. Her exceptional qualities made her interesting and stimulating. The same with Kofi, the Arab in *Children at the Gate*. Some Israelis complained that he was not a typical Arab. I never thought he was. He was not even a typical human being. I made him rare on purpose. I reject the criticism of those who demand that I point out his living counterpart before they will accept him.

However, themes are another matter. The themes one writes about must be true—not objectively true, but true to one's deepest convictions. My fourth novel, *The Backward Shadow*, was criticised by one American woman for its underlying assumption that women need men and cannot live full lives without them. But I believe this. It is in accordance with my own experience and observation. I doubt if I could write a convincing novel about a happy, single, "liberated" woman, not only because I have never met one but because, rightly or wrongly, deep down I don't believe they exist.

One of my recurring themes is women alone. This theme is drawn from the secret places of my own life. I was not, myself, exceptional in my reaction to singleness, but then I am an ordinary woman. My heroines may either react to loneliness with greater courage, awareness, and resourcefulness than I did, or sink to lower depths; but they must be more *extreme*, otherwise I cannot be bothered with them, nor can I see why any reader should.

In short, fiction should grow out of life; but the operative word is "out." It should be an extension, an underlining, a highlighting. Above all, it must involve the reader in a process of identification. My novels are not for everyone. They are only for those who are similar enough to me, to sympathise with the characters I create. To any reader who turns away, in boredom, irritation, or revulsion, from my heroines, however real they may seem to him, I owe an apology for failure.

* * *

The L-Shaped Room, Lynne Reid Banks's filmed and much publicised first novel, is still, if not her best book, the one by which she is most widely known. It was published in 1960, and it is easy by now to forget that it belongs to the literature of protest and outcry of that time—protest against the lot of the unmarried mother, the attitude of the medical profession, the puritanical disapproval of the heroine's father, who shows far less understanding of her situation than two total strangers, the negro jazz musician and the fledgling Jewish writer, who are her neighbours in poverty. The predicament of the unmarried mother has since become a well-worn theme and was handled with a good deal more subtlety in Margaret Drabble's *The Millstone*; it is curious that the two novels describe the child as having been conceived in almost exactly the same fashion, after an encounter so casual and meaningless that the heroine could not bear to disclose its consequences to the father. By comparison with this and with the work of other contemporaries who have specialised in the novel of domestic and personal relationships—Penelope Mortimer, Edna O'Brien, Elizabeth Jane Howard, to name a few—Lynne Reid Banks is a somewhat artless writer in terms both of style and of treatment. Much of the appeal of *The L-Shaped Room* lies in its very rawness and directness, the "look-what-happened-to-me" note which dominates it.

Its successor, *An End to Running*, is a considerably more accomplished piece of work. The heroine is engaged as secretary to a young and pampered Jewish writer who is dominated by his sister; the girl falls in love and runs away with him, and for the first half of the book tells the story in the first person: in the second part the writer become the "I," and describes their life in a kibbutz and the ultimate breakdown of their relationship. The technical demands of this device tighten the book's construction and introduces surprise and suspense into the narrative, while the contrasts of personality between the two principal characters are so sharp that their alternating moods of attraction and repulsion are thoroughly convincing. There are also some excellent descriptions of the rigours and the more comic elements of kibbutz life.

Children at the Gate introduces a new group of characters, but Israel is once more the setting, and the theme once more concerns the personal problems of a lonely woman. Gerda is a Canadian Jewess in her late thirties, who lives alone in the town of Acre and has come to the end of her tether: her marriage has broken up, she can have no more children, and she has taken to drink. She is persuaded to adopt a pair of Arab orphans and much of the plot describes the agonising experience of settling with them into kibbutz life, gradually winning their confidence and then being separated from them on legal grounds. Here the handling of the narrative reverts to the method of *The L-Shaped Room*: it is a personal account in which Gerda is present on every page, but the story is told with an eloquence and a poignancy which the earlier book does not often attain.

The Backward Shadow forms a sequel to *The L-Shaped Room*. Jane Graham has left London and settled with her baby son in the country cottage which she has inherited. The plot is mainly occupied with the problems of bringing up her child and with her relationships with the London friends who periodically descend on her. This is the weakest of the novels to date, since there is not a great deal of new material and the interest of the characters carried over from the earlier book is hardly sufficient to support a sequel.

Lynne Reid Banks relies upon experience rather than invention to a degree which makes it difficult to judge her books (with the exception of *An End to Running*) as fiction. There is no doubt that she possesses a strong impulse to write, but it is reminiscent of the Ancient Mariner's. Unmistakably as she passes from land to land the heart within her burns, and at her best the power of speech is strong, but it varies sharply from one novel to another.

—Ian Scott-Kilvert

RENAULT, Mary. Pseudonym for Eileen Mary Challans. British. Born in London, 4 September 1905. Educated at Clifton High School, Bristol; St. Hugh's College, Oxford, M.A.; Radcliffe Infirmary, Oxford, S.R.N. 1937. Writer from 1939; worked as a nurse during World War II; emigrated to South Africa, 1948. National President, P.E.N. Club of South Africa, 1961. Recipient: National Association of Independent Schools Award (U.S.A.), 1963; Silver Pen Award, 1971. Fellow, Royal Society of Literature, 1959. Address: 3 Atholl Road, Camps Bay, Cape Town 8001, South Africa.

PUBLICATIONS

Novels

Purposes of Love. London, Longman, 1939; as *Promise of Love*, New York, Morrow, 1939.
Kind Are Her Answers. London, Longman, and New York, Morrow, 1940.
The Friendly Young Ladies. London, Longman, 1944; as *The Middle Mist*, New York, Morrow, 1945.
Return to Night. London, Longman, and New York, Morrow, 1947.
North Face. New York, Morrow, 1948; London, Longman, 1949.
The Charioteer. London, Longman, 1953; New York, Pantheon, 1959.
The Last of the Wine. London, Longman, 1956; New York, Pantheon, 1959.
The King Must Die. London, Longman, and New York, Pantheon, 1958.
The Bull from the Sea. London, Longman, and New York, Pantheon, 1962.
The Mask of Apollo. London, Longman, and New York, Pantheon, 1966.
Fire from Heaven. New York, Pantheon 1969; London, Longman, 1970.
The Persian Boy. London, Longman, and New York, Pantheon, 1972.
The Praise Singer. New York, Pantheon, 1978; London, Murray, 1979.

Uncollected Short Story

"According to Celsus," in *Women Writing 3*, edited by Denys Val Baker. London, Sidgwick and Jackson, 1980.

Other

The Lion in the Gateway: The Heroic Battles of the Greeks and Persians at Marathon, Salamis, and Thermopylae (juvenile). London, Longman, and New York, Harper, 1964.
The Nature of Alexander. London, Allen Lane, and New York, Pantheon, 1975.

*

Critical Studies: by John A. Stone, in the author's *The Charioteer*, Cleveland, World, 1962; "Men Are Only Men" by Landon C. Burns, in *Critique* (Minneapolis) vi, 3, 1964; essay by the author, in *Afterwords*, New York, Harper, 1969; *Mary Renault* by Peter Wolfe, New York, Twayne, 1969; *The Hellenism of Mary Renault* by Bernard F. Dick, Carbondale, Southern Illinois University Press, 1972.

Mary Renault comments:

It has been my aim to respect the facts of history and what I believe, after careful reading, to have been the real beliefs and thought-modes, the life-style of a period. The past is a part of the human environment, and should not be polluted by falsehood. Its people should not be modernised to make an easier read, nor judged by standards irrelevant to their own day, in order to make dishonest propaganda for some modern cause: the "committed" historical novelist is of necessity a committed liar. Even the dead are entitled to justice; and the first requirements of justice is to apply to them their current moral standards, however these may differ from our own. Modernised historical characters are a bore; real ones are profoundly interesting, at least to me. I have never knowingly exploited them, but have tried to see them, as far as I am able, along the sight-lines from which they might have seen themselves.

* * *

Current esteem for the work of Mary Renault rests on the series of novels that began with *The King Must Die*. It is a series that explores with impressive vigor and learning many aspects of ancient Greek culture. The exploration extends from the mythological or quasi-mythological times of Crete into periods when gifted poets and thinkers were perfecting the modes of thought that have dominated the mental habits of much Western culture. This preoccupation with the sources of Western humanism in Greece has become intense in the 20th century and is a desperate rather than a complacent appropriation. No longer, as in the 18th century, is it assumed that the ancient Greek excellence is to be had for the taking. Instead, the questions addressed to that culture must be curious and sharp rather than, as at other Western times, bland and complacent. Thus, in the intent of her novels about the classical period, Renault joins the company of other earnest 20th-century novelists who do not take for granted that there is an easy entrance into the classic world of imagination and thought. From Caroline Gordon's *The Glory of Hera* to Robert Graves's novels about imperial Rome, there is a concentrated expenditure of imaginative energy that says something about 20th-century concerns—concerns for certain losses and degenerations of the human spirit.

It is in this perspective that the more celebrated portion of Renault's work can be discussed; her classical novels are, one and all, annotations written on the margins of a precious section of human experience. But before those annotations are inspected, it must be noted that Renault has, in the earlier portions of her career, written novels modern in setting and mainly psychological in interest: tales of well-educated English persons who are, in their contacts with others, sharply aware of class distinctions and the differences of personal history that divide one human being from another. In a novel such as *Return to Night* the physician-heroine runs a painful obstacle course; she is full of self-doubt and uncertainty about her lover for many pages. Renault's protagonist has an insatiable taste for analytical dialogue with her young lover, and both have ready access to telling passages from English literature. And when conversation fails, the characters (and Renault) retreat to extended internal analyses of motive. As do the characters in another novel, *The Charioteer*, in which the relentless observation of the social difficulties and personal dubieties of a group of modern homosexuals are displayed with sympathy and abundant detail.

When readers turn from such novels to the ones with a classic interest, they can note a growth of both authority and clarity; the human landscape is still present, but it is one that has definite outlines and direction. With Renault as guide, readers are entering times when great human values were being invented rather than, as in Renault's modern narratives, being scanned and tested with an often desperate scepticism.

Moreover, the classical novels undergo a considerable alteration of style. When she tells the tales of Theseus (a mythological figure) and of such historical figures as the rhapsodist Simonides (*The Praise Singer*), Socrates (*The Last of the Wine*), Plato (*The Mask of Apollo*), and Alexander (*Fire from Heaven* and *The Persian Boy*), Renault abandons the complex style of exposition that she uses, for example, in *The Charioteer*. In *The King Must Die* and *The Bull from the Sea* Renault is, as it were, dealing with the emergence of human consciousness rather than with its 20th-century disorder and decay. The style in which Theseus recalls his life of adventure owes a great deal to the prose of Herodotus; there are also echoes of the brutality and simplicity of Norse saga. True, Theseus is a fairly complex man, but he has less time for his complexities than for his perils and marvellous encounters. Renault's purpose is to show human sensibility (that of Theseus) introducing clarity into the realms of myth and wonder and marvel. Even the deepest mysteries, those of Crete, are brought into the light of day.

It is that daylight that shines unremittingly in the novels which deal with Greek events somewhat nearer our time. *The Last of the Wine* is an evocation of all that Socrates was as teacher and as an accused corrupter of youth. Here one of Renault's models is Platonic dialogue, with its rationality and incisiveness. Similar qualities mark the style of *The Praise Singer*, a novel about the life of a great poet, Simonides; one follows with pleasure the easy onward movement of the narrative in which the poet pursues patronage and celebrity, a pursuit that was not greatly opposed to the pursuit of art.

Ease and urbanity also mark other books to be noted here. *The Mask of Apollo* tells of Plato's involvement with the tyrant of Syracuse, but as seen through the eyes of a Greek actor, Nikeratos. Through this man's experience, the modern reader gets a keen sense of what the Greek stage was like when the plays were still being written and performed. And the two novels—*Fire from Heaven* and *The Persian Boy*—which present the career of Alexander of Macedon are essays in the understanding of the figure who has become almost as mythical as Theseus. Renault's artistic dexterity, in these novels as in others, is firm and various. *Fire from Heaven* is told from several points of view: Alexander's own, that of his strange mother, Olympias, and that of his father, Philip of Macedon. The angle of attention narrows in *The Persian Boy*; Alexander's career as a conqueror is seen through the eyes of a Persian servant, Bagoas; the result is a centering of interest that was less firm in *Fire from Heaven*.

Here, as elsewhere, whatever narrative device Renault takes up succeeds, and an aspect of the complex Greek inheritance is revealed as part of the Greek way of facing the gods and one's fellow man. The didacticism of intent is present in all that Renault does in her later work. But that didacticism merges easily with the actions and persons that exist in a particular novel.

—Harold H. Watts

RICHLER, Mordecai. Canadian. Born in Montreal, Quebec, 27 January 1931. Educated at the Montreal Hebrew Academy; Baron Byng High School, Montreal; Sir George Williams University, Montreal, 1948-50. Married Florence Wood in 1959; three sons and two daughters. Lived in Europe, 1959-72; Writer-in-Residence, Sir George Williams University, 1968-69; Visiting Professor, Carleton University, Ottawa, 1972-74. Since 1976, Member of the Editorial Board, Book-of-the-Month Club. Recipient: President's Medal, University of Western Ontario, for non-fiction, 1959; Canada Council Junior Arts Fellowship, 1959, 1960, and Senior Arts Fellowship, 1966; Guggenheim Fellowship, 1961; Governor-General's Award, 1969, 1971; Writers Guild of America award, for screenplay, 1974; Berlin Film Festival Golden Bear, 1974; Canadian Library Association English Medal Award, for children's book, 1976. Address: 1321 Sherbrooke Street, Apartment 80-C, Montreal, Quebec H3G 1JG, Canada.

PUBLICATIONS

Novels

The Acrobats. Toronto, Ambassador, London, Deutsch, and New York, Putnam, 1954; as *Wicked We Love*, New York, Popular Library, 1955.

Son of a Smaller Hero. London, Deutsch, 1955; New York, Paperback Library, 1965.
A Choice of Enemies. London, Deutsch, 1957.
The Apprenticeship of Duddy Kravitz. London, Deutsch, and Boston, Little Brown, 1959.
The Incomparable Atuk. London, Deutsch, 1963; as *Stick Your Neck Out*, New York, Simon and Schuster, 1963.
Cocksure. London, Weidenfeld and Nicolson, and New York, Simon and Schuster, 1968.
St. Urbain's Horseman. London, Weidenfeld and Nicolson, and New York, Knopf, 1971.
Joshua Then and Now. London, Macmillan, and New York, Knopf, 1980.

Short Stories

The Street. Toronto, McClelland and Stewart, 1969; London, Weidenfeld and Nicolson, 1972; Washington, D.C., New Republic Books, 1975.

Uncollected Short Story

"Manny Moves to Westmount," in *Saturday Night* (Toronto), January-February 1977.

Plays

Duddy, adaptation of his own novel (produced Stratford, Ontario, 1981).

Screenplays: *Dearth of a Salesman*, 1957; *Insomnia Is Good for You*, 1957; *No Love for Johnnie*, with Nicholas Phipps, 1961; *Tiara Tahiti*, with Geoffrey Cotterell and Ivan Foxwell, 1962; *The Wild and the Willing* (*Young and Willing*), with Nicholas Phipps, 1962; *Life at the Top*, 1965; *The Apprenticeship of Duddy Kravitz*, with Lionel Chetwynd, 1974; *Fun with Dick and Jane*, with Donald Giler and Jerry Belson, 1977.

Radio Play: *It's Harder to Be Anybody*, 1961 (UK).

Television Plays (UK): *Trouble with Benny*, 1959; *The Apprenticeship of Duddy Kravitz*, from his own novel, 1961; *The Fall of Mendel Crick*, from a story by Isaac Babel, 1963.

Other

Hunting Tigers under Glass: Essays and Reports. Toronto, McClelland and Stewart, 1968; London, Weidenfeld and Nicolson, 1969.
Shovelling Trouble (essays). Toronto, McClelland and Stewart, 1972; London, Quartet, 1973.
Notes on an Endangered Species and Others. New York, Knopf, 1974.
Jacob Two-Two Meets the Hooded Fang (juvenile). London, Deutsch, and New York, Knopf, 1975.
Creativity and the University, with André Fornier and Rollo May. Toronto, York University, 1975.
Images of Spain, photographs by Peter Christopher. New York, Norton, 1977; London, Thames and Hudson, 1978.
The Great Comic Book Heroes and Other Essays, edited by Robert Fulford. Toronto, McClelland and Stewart, 1978.

Editor, *Canadian Writing Today.* London, Penguin, 1970.

*

Bibliography: "Mordecai Richler: An Annotated Bibliography" by Michael Darling, in *The Annotated Bibliography of Canada's Major Authors 1*, edited by Robert Lecker and Jack David, Downsview, Ontario, ECW Press, 1979.

Manuscript Collection: University of Alberta, Calgary.

Critical Studies: *Mordecai Richler* by George Woodcock, Toronto, McClelland and Stewart, 1970; *Mordecai Richler* edited by G. David Sheps, Toronto, McGraw Hill Ryerson, 1971.

* * *

Mordecai Richler exemplifies one of the difficulties Canadian critics have always experienced—that of defining the Canadian novelist. Many of those who find their way into histories of Canadian writing have in fact been passing visitors like Brian Moore and Malcolm Lowry and Paul West. To an extent—to a very great extent in Lowry's case—their fiction has been affected in terms of content and even attitude by their residence in Canada. Yet their "Canadian works" constitute a mere phase in lives whose inspiration has remained mainly elsewhere.

On the other side, following the nomadic pattern of life in a great and loosely populated country, some Canadians have left their country and spent most of their writing lives abroad. Of these, Mordecai Richler is the most important. Richler left Canada in 1951, when he was 20; since then he has lived in Europe—mainly in England—and has returned to Canada only for relatively brief periods. All his novels, and most of his stories, have been written abroad. And yet, as Richler said in 1957, "All my attitudes are Canadian. I'm a Canadian; there's nothing to be done about it." Not merely are his attitudes Canadian; so are the leading figures in all his novels, whether they are shown in his native Montreal or are presented, as has been increasingly the case in recent years, as unassimilable exiles.

Even as a Canadian writer, Richler is extremely localized in his frame of reference. In this he follows the regional pattern characteristic of Canadian fiction, the pattern that makes Morley Callaghan so peculiarly the novelist of Toronto and Hugh MacLennan an unerring portrayer of the Maritimes but an unconvincing voice of Montreal. Richler, for his part, celebrates a vanished way of life in a part of Montreal that has changed completely since he knew it. It is the old Jewish ghetto, the region centred on St. Urbain Street, where Richler's heroes were born into the expatriate community of Jews who had fled from Eastern Europe under the Tsarist regime and who had brought with them a religion and a way of life which were gradually eroded by the social pressures of a city divided between English and French.

If one can isolate a theme from Richler's novels it is that of the Jew who is powerfully conscious of his people's past, and deeply nostalgic for a childhood spent in the chaotic and colourful background of the ghetto, yet who understands that in the modern world traditional Jewish attitudes have become irrelevant. Yet for Richler, in a way, the Jew is only a type of the individual set against the impersonal forces of the modern world. Three of his novels—*The Acrobats*, *A Choice of Enemies*, and *Cocksure*—are based on a deliberate inversion of the pattern of the persecuted Jew. In these the hero (or anti-hero if that seems more fitting) is a Gentile, and Jews reveal in their actions towards him that they too can be persecutors if the circumstances permit. At the end of one of these novels—*Cocksure*—we find a clue which illuminates this central Richlerian preoccupation. When Mortimer Griffin is pursued and about to be destroyed by his enemies, a Jewish intellectual remarks to him: "A Jew is an idea. Today you're my idea of a Jew."

It would be an over-simplification to suggest that embedded in Richler's fiction is the idea that the Jew has an exemplary role in the modern world. It is more accurate to say that Richler believes any writer should draw from his own experience whatever has universal significance, and shape that material into a form of social as well as aesthetic meaning. His own experience has been his childhood on St. Urbain and his expatriate life which echoes that of his grandparents. This has resulted in an alternating pattern between the early background and the land of exile. *The Acrobats*, his first novel, was set in Spain; its young Canadian hero was murdered by a psychopathic ex-Nazi. *Son of a Smaller Hero*, set in Montreal, was Richler's portrait of the artist as a young man—a story of the Montreal ghetto and the trauma of self-liberation from its moral pressures. *A Choice of Enemies*—the hero again a Canadian exile—is set in the world of film producers (expatriate from the radical America of the 1930's) with which Richler's need to earn a living as a script writer had made him familiar. Next followed what may well be Richler's best novel, *The Apprenticeship of Duddy Kravitz*, telling of the ruthless rise to wealth of a poor boy of St. Urbain Street, followed by *The Incomparable Atuk*, a fable in the manner of Voltaire on Canadian cultural pretensions. The England of the exile is again the setting in *Cocksure*, a satirical fantasy filled with monsters and hollow men in the manner of Wyndham Lewis. A collection of sketches and short stories, *The Street*, devoted entirely to the vanished past of the Montreal ghetto, completes the pattern of alternations and prepares the way for *St. Urbain's Horseman*.

In Richler's work up to the early 1970's *St. Urbain's Horseman* is the key novel, combining satire and nostalgia, and bringing the world of the exile and the world of the ghetto together in their proper and intimate relationship. Jake Hersh, a minor character in *The Apprenticeship of Duddy Kravitz*, and a film man like the victim-heroes of *Cocksure* and *A Choice of Enemies*, has reached the final stage in the classic ordeal of the pursued man; he is on trial on a morals charge, a situation brought about by police inventiveness combined with his own foolishness in associating with a blackmailing misanthrope, Harry Stein. As the trial unfolds its sinister background action, we are shown, in parallel streams of memory, Jake's life in England where a marriage that should be happy is marred by his guilts and fears, and his past life in the dense atmosphere of the Jewish family and the noisy streets of Montreal. The two lives are united by Jake's abiding obsession with his cousin, Joey Hersh, the wandering ne'er-do-well whom Jake fantasizes into an avenger seeking to destroy the destroyers of the Jews. As Jake escapes without honour at his trial, the news arrives that Joey has died as a smuggler in Paraguay. Jake is released from perils and obsessions alike, and for once a Richler novel has an ending of happiness neither unthreatened nor inappropriate.

In retrospect, the three novels by Richler that stand most securely are *Son of a Smaller Hero*, *The Apprenticeship of Duddy Kravitz*, and *St. Urbain's Horseman*, those closest to his intensely lived and remembered childhood and youth. Taken together, they form a triptych representing the difficulty of escaping from the mental chains laid on a young Jew by the rigours of his own tradition and the hostility of other traditions. Central to these novels—and indeed to all Richler's works—is the sexual encounter between Jew and Gentile, always, until the last novel, a situation of imperfectly resolved conflict. It is the steering of Jake's mixed marriage through its rapids to final success that distinguishes *St. Urbain's Horseman* and suggests that this book, which took Richler five years to write, represents a critical summation of his work up to the present.

If *St. Urbain's Horseman*, indeed, represents a thematic reconciliation, it also represents a reconciliation of the two manners that are in conflict or at least in competition in Richler's earlier writings—the fantastic and the realistic. In the vividly remembered scenes of Montreal life it is realism (not naturalism) that prevails. In the foreign scenes, the tendency is to create grotesque and implausible hollow figures of satiric fantasy, beginning with Kraus, the unlikely Nazi of *The Acrobats*, and reaching an apogee in the Starmaker, the monstrous gangster-tycoon of *Cocksure*. In *St. Urbain's Horseman* the fantasy indeed persists, but it is in Jake's mind only, where Joey the Horseman rides on his unlikely quests, and what the novel mainly explores—with much deeper satiric effect—is the fantastic nature of much that happens in the actual world, particularly if one sees with the eyes of a stranger. For Richler is still the exile, the essential Canadian, unable to render except in caricature anything outside that hypnotic circle of locality which creates what Northrop Frye has called "the garrison mentality" among Canadian writers. What his novels suggest is that "the idea of a Jew" is very much like the idea of a Canadian, for Canada is a land of minorities, regions, disguised ghettoes. In that lies Richler's appeal to his countrymen, and the reason why he is never considered as other than a Canadian writer.

—George Woodcock

ROBBINS, Tom. American. Address: c/o Bantam Books, 666 Fifth Avenue, New York, New York 10019, U.S.A.

PUBLICATIONS

Novels

Another Roadside Attraction. New York, Doubleday, 1971; London, W.H. Allen, 1973.

Even Cowgirls Get the Blues. Boston, Houghlin Mifflin, 1976; London, Corgi, 1977.

Still Life with Woodpecker. New York, Bantam, and London, Sidgwick and Jackson, 1980.

Uncollected Short Story

"The Chink and the Clock People," in *The Best American Short Stories 1977*, edited by Martha Foley. Boston, Houghlin Mifflin, 1977.

Other

Guy Anderson (exhibition catalogue), with William Ivey and Wallace S. Baldinger. Seattle, Seattle Art Museum, 1977.

* * *

Although ignored by academic critics, Tom Robbins is the only American novelist since J.D. Salinger and Jack Kerouac in the 1950's to become a cult hero among disaffected undergraduates. Paperbound editions of his novels have remained steadily in print as sales have mounted into the millions.

Like Salinger—and the even more elusive Thomas Pynchon, who has uncharacteristically publicly praised Robbins's second novel—the author lives in seclusion. He allows himself to be described only as "a student of art and religion" who "dropped out" to write fiction in a Washington state fishing village. Although Kerouac is the only author Robbins mentions in his novels, these more nearly resemble Salinger's Glass Family stories. The ostensible "author" frequently interrupts the stories; and, although the characters are more bizarre than Salinger's, they tend like his to be highly talkative, much given to self-analysis, lengthy confessions, and populist philosophical speculation. Despite mystical tendencies, they are not devoted to the specific forms of oriental mysticism that have attracted many literary members of the counter-culture.

Robbins's writing is even more bitterly anti-Establishment than Salinger's or Kerouac's; FBI and CIA violence and treachery and the conspiratorial practices of the Roman Catholic Church are his most frequent targets. Much of the action of *Another Roadside Attraction*, for example, deals with the involvement of Plucky Purcell (a renegade football player) in a secret order of monks that leads to his discovery during an earthquake of the mummified body of Jesus hidden in the Vatican catacombs. He brings his grotesque find to the "roadside attraction," a giant West Coast hot-dog stand operated by drop-out artist John Paul Ziller and his wife Amanda, an archetypal matriarchal figure. The principal movement of the story narrated by Marx Marvelous, a skeptical scientific dropout from an East Coast think tank, is toward "light," toward a physical dissolution of the individual in his reunion with the sun, which Ziller describes to Marvelous as "the source of all biological energy, and ultimately...the source of you." While Plucky debates how to use Christ's corpse to expose the hoax of Christian culture, Ziller steals it and sets off with it and his pet baboon on a space balloon for the "return to sunlight," which he had said was an "inevitability" he'd been "reckoning with." "Let Amanda be your pine cone," the novel concludes as a joyous tribute to her survival.

Even Cowgirls Get the Blues is longer, talkier, and more self-consciously whimsical than its predecessor. The first half of the novel dwells upon the picaresque adventures of Sissy Hankshaw, a born hitch-hiker with monstrous thumbs. Most of the second half is dominated by the "clock people," Indian refugees from the San Francisco earthquake, who have substituted rigid individual rituals for societal rituals. The two fantasies are united by events at the Rubber Rose Ranch, a wealthy women's retreat that is seized by insurgent cowgirls. Their brush with the government culminates in the Whooping Crane war, after the cowgirls disrupt the endangered species' migration by feeding them peyote. The convoluted story, which is related by an offbeat psychiatrist curiously named Robbins, winds up with the cranes circling the globe while Sissy is envisioned as the mother of a tribe of big-thumbed people in the "postcatastrophe" world.

Whimsy predominates again in Robbins's third comparatively short and uncomplicated tale, *Still Life with Woodpecker*, which mingles such trendy topics as deposed royalty, red-headed bombers, and pyramid power to ask the plaintive question, "Who knows how to make love stay?" Robbins despairs of an answer because he views the last quarter of the 20th century as "a time when women openly resented men, a time when men felt betrayed by women," "a severe period for lovers." An almost *Aida*-like ending hints a way out of this pit.

Although some readers will object to Robbins's fantasies as erotic and irreverent, his uninhibited celebration of man's self-conscious recognition of his place in the ecological scheme makes him the authentic fictional voice for those young Romantics who have abandoned our deteriorating urban civilization to reintegrate themselves with the mystical sources of the life force. Although he writes about the creatures of a new mythology in contemporary colloquial language, his novels are in the West Coast mystical tradition of the Vanamee subplot in Frank Norris's *The Octopus* and John Steinbeck's Monterey fables.

—Warren French

ROOKE, Daphne (Marie). British and South African. Born in Boksburg, Transvaal, South Africa, 6 March 1914. Educated at Durban Girls' High School. Married Irvin Rooke in 1937; one daughter. Has lived in Australia, 1946-53, and since 1965. Recipient: Afrikaanse Pers Beperk novel prize, 1946. Address: 34 Bent Street, Bardouroka, New South Wales 2315, Australia.

PUBLICATIONS

Novels

The Sea Hath Bounds. Johannesburg, A.P.B. Bookstore, 1946; as *A Grove of Fever Trees*, Boston, Houghton Mifflin, 1950; London, Cape, 1951.
Mittee. London, Gollancz, 1951; Boston, Houghton Mifflin, 1952.
Ratoons. London, Gollancz, and Boston, Houghton Mifflin, 1953.
Wizards' Country. London, Gollancz, and Boston, Houghton Mifflin, 1957.
Beti. London, Gollancz, and Boston, Houghton Mifflin, 1959.
A Lover for Estelle. London, Gollancz, and Boston, Houghton Mifflin, 1961.
The Greyling. London, Gollancz, 1962; New York, Reynal, 1963.
Diamond Jo. London, Gollancz, and New York, Reynal, 1965.
Boy on the Mountain. London, Gollancz, 1969.
Margaretha de la Porte. London, Gollancz, 1974.

Uncollected Short Stories

"The Deal," in *Woman* (Sydney), 26 June 1950.
"Emily," in *John Bull* (London), 1952.
"The Boundary Dog," in *John Bull* (London), 1957.
"The Friends," in *South African Stories*, edited by David Wright. London, Faber, and New York, Duell, 1960.
"Fikizolo," in *Over the Horizon.* London, Gollancz, 1960.

Other

The South African Twins (juvenile). London, Cape, 1953; as *Twins in South Africa*, Boston, Houghton Mifflin, 1955.
The Australian Twins (juvenile). London, Cape, 1954; as *Twins in Australia*, Boston, Houghton Mifflin, 1956.
New Zealand Twins (juvenile). London, Cape, 1957.
Double Ex! (juvenile). London, Gollancz, 1971.
A Horse of His Own (juvenile). London, Gollancz, 1976.

*

Bibliography: *Daphne Rooke: Her Works and Selected Criticism: A Bibliography* by Helen Camburg, Johannesburg, University of the Witwatersrand, 1969.

Manuscript Collections: Mugar Memorial Library, Boston University; National English Literary Museum, Grahamstown, South Africa.

Critical Studies: by Orville Prescott, in *New York Times*, 1 March 1950; Dorothy Canfield Fisher, in *Book-of-the-Month News* (New York), January 1952; Sylvia Stallings, in *New York Herald Tribune*, 20 December 1953; *Illustrated London News*, 21 December 1957; *Saturday Review of Literature* (New York), 7 March 1959; Chicago *Tribune*, 26 February 1961; Paul Scott, in *Country Life* (London), 24 May 1962.

Daphne Rooke comments:

The places where I have lived have been most important to my writing. My early memories of the Transvaal are reflected in *Mittee*. *Ratoons* has for background the South Coast of Natal where I lived for many years on a sugar plantation. Zululand made a most profound impression on me: I lived there for years as a girl: *A Grove of Fever Trees*, *A Lover for Estelle*, and *Wizards' Country* all have Zululand for background. *Beti* is set in India and East Africa, and *Boy on the Mountain* in New Zealand. All are written in the first person.

There is a pattern of sorts in some of the South African works: the race of the narrator has an important bearing on the story. In *Mittee* the whole story hinges on the fact that the narrator Selina is a Coloured girl; in *Ratoons* the narrator is an English-speaking South African girl who falls in love with an Afrikaner; in *Wizards' Country* the narrator is a Zulu; in *A Lover for Estelle* the narrator is an Afrikaans girl whose life is influenced by a sophisticated Englishwoman. I did not consciously set out to create this pattern; it was pointed out to me after I had written *Wizards' Country*.

All the stories, including those for children, are imaginative works but have a basis in fact. In *Wizards' Country* when writing about superstition I attempted to avoid the supernatural; for example, Benge is a hunchback and masquerades as a magic dwarf (the tokoloshi). In my short story for children, "Fikizolo," the ingredients of a fairytale were actually present in Zululand: the two children were called a prince and princess, there was a real old witch, and Fikizolo himself was like a fabled beast, a cross between a donkey and a zebra!

* * *

Recently the common verdict has been that Africa is to be written about by Africans, which has implicitly been taken to mean black male writers. And as often as not to mean black male writers preoccupied with violence and politics. Daphne Rooke, therefore, presents the critic with an interesting and not yet fashionable problem. She is a native born South African, white and female.

Racial identity and conflict do not provide the emotional power of Rooke's work. Her interests and point of view are those of a frontier woman. Set mostly on the South African frontier of the past two centuries, her works share with American fiction that sense of space, violence, and sheer physical vitality that attends the north European appetite for quest and contest. Characteristically, she writes what is commonly called women's fiction, a melodramatic form, the roots of which are firmly in the 18th-century English novels of sensibility and of gothic terror and suspense.

Rooke does not probe the past. She does not trouble to explain the present. Her narrators, secure in the present, simply recall their past. Its violence is distanced and the lessons learned do not now seem too pressing. Her narrators are each in some way oppressed, being either crippled, insane, female, or coloured. Yet social customs and institutions seem almost immaterial. Her narrators are alive. They have felt and assimilated their experience. Ideological assessment has not intervened. This is women's fiction in the very fundamental sense that the highly touted male faculties of abstraction and rationality are absent—and more ingenuously so than in the works of males who are spoken of as having a feminine sensibility.

Female culture is rich and complex. And it has been described almost exclusively in the works of women novelists because male historians and anthropologists have either been oblivious to its existence or have not deemed it of adequate importance to record. It has been left for such writers as Rooke to reveal the circumscribed but complex ambitions of women and to show how pregnancy, birth, and the management of the domestic realm are as exciting and heroic as war and politics. The richness of *The Sea Hath Bounds*, *Ratoons*, and *A Lover for Estelle* derive from her intimate awareness of the South Africa that women have experienced.

There is nothing soft and protected about the life Rooke describes. Her best effects invariably involve danger or the threat of it as when the farmer's widow and her children try to make a little egg money hatching pythons in an abandoned front bedroom. Such moments have the economy and immediacy of a treasured snapshot. Rooke has not the stature of Doris Lessing or Nadine Gordimer, but her success as a popular writer is justified. In retrospect a Rooke work is more haunting than it ought to be—an effect which depends on the part rather than the whole. When the oppressive density of events and the relentless heightening of plot and situation have faded from mind, there remain solid characters and sharp, arresting vignettes.

—Cynthia Secor

ROSS, Sinclair. Canadian. Born in Shellbrook, Sasketchewan, 22 January 1908. Served in the Canadian Army, 1942-45. With the Royal Bank of Canada: in country branches, 1924-31, in Winnipeg, 1931-42, and in Montreal, 1946-68. Address: c/o McClelland and Stewart Ltd., 25 Hollinger Road, Toronto, Ontario M4B 3G2, Canada.

PUBLICATIONS

Novels

As for Me and My House. New York, Reynal, 1941.
The Well. Toronto, Macmillan, 1958.
Whir of Gold. Toronto, McClelland and Stewart, 1970.
Sawbones Memorial. Toronto, McClelland and Stewart, 1974.

Short Stories

The Lamp at Noon and Other Stories. Toronto, McClelland and Stewart, 1968.

Uncollected Short Stories

"A Day with Pegasus," in *Queen's Quarterly* (Kingston, Ontario), Summer 1938.
"Jug and Bottle," in *Queen's Quarterly* (Kingston, Ontario), Winter 1949-50.
"Saturday Night," in *Queen's Quarterly* (Kingston, Ontario), Autumn 1951.
"The Flowers That Killed Him," in *Journal of Canadian Fiction* (Fredericton, New Brunswick), Summer 1972.

*

Critical Studies: Introduction by Roy Daniells to *As for Me and My House*, Toronto, McClelland and Stewart, 1957; "Wolf in the Snow" by Warren Tallman, in *A Choice of Critics*, Toronto, Oxford University Press, 1966; Introduction by Margaret Laurence to *The Lamp at Noon*, 1968; "Sinclair Ross's Ambivalent World" by W.H. New, in *Canadian Literature* (Vancouver), Spring 1969; "No Other Way: Sinclair Ross's Stories and Novels" by Sandra Djwa, in *Canadian Literature* (Vancouver), Winter 1971; *Patterns of Isolation* by John G. Moss, Toronto, McClelland and Stewart, 1974; "The Mirror and the Lamp in Sinclair Ross's *As for Me and My House*" by David Stouck, in *Mosaic* (Winnipeg, Manitoba), Winter 1974.

Sinclair Ross comments:

The little I have done has been spread over so many years that there is no outstanding or unifying theme. Man and nature, perhaps—especially in *The Lamp at Noon* and to some degree in *As for Me and My House*. *The Well* is a bad novel: an attempt, unsuccessful, to stretch a little the prairie and small town world of which I had been writing. *Whir of Gold* is, I suppose, another break-away attempt—or stretch; better, with some fairly good things in it, but small in range.

* * *

Sinclair Ross is primarily a chronicler of life on the Canadian prairies, and his first novel, *As for Me and My House*, seems destined to become established as a classic of prairie realism, along with the novels of Frederick Philip Grove and Margaret Laurence. Even better than his first novel are some of his short stories, such as "The Lamp at Noon," "The Painted Door," and "One's a Heifer." Ross's later novels, *The Well* and *Whir of Gold*, have some traces of the subdued intensity which makes his early work so memorable, but as wholes they are disappointing. Ross's career seems to bear out the theory that Herbert Read advanced about Wordsworth: that as his memories of his boyhood faded, his art too lost its strength. Ross lived on the prairies as a boy and young man, but his adult life has been lived mainly in Montreal, and in his later work he was too far removed from the life he once knew to write of it with continuous conviction and accuracy.

It is, then, on the early fiction that Sinclair Ross's reputation is almost certain to rest. The qualities of this early work are quite remarkable. Perhaps most remarkable of all is Ross's gift for empathy, for full identification of himself with the character he is portraying. For the boys who are the central figures of several of his short stories this is not surprising, since one is able to assume that the hero is Ross himself slightly disguised, and that he is drawing heavily upon the memories of his own boyhood. The feat is more surprising when it is applied to Philip Bentley, the clergyman and amateur artist of *As for Me and My House*, particularly since much of the tension in the novel springs from Philip's relationship with his wife: Ross is a bachelor. But what is really remarkable is that Ross is able to enter with apparently equal facility into the minds of women, as in the powerful story of a prairie dust storm, "The Lamp at Noon," and in the portrayal of Mrs. Bentley in the novel.

The special quality in the human situation which seems to attract Ross as an artist and which he treats with consummate skill is the sense of isolation and of alienation, the feeling of being trapped in a set of circumstances from which there is no apparent escape. Thus Philip Bentley finds himself trapped in a profession for which he no longer feels a vocation, in a small prairie town which seems to have no sympathy for the values he cherishes, and in a marriage which has come to be an irritant rather than an unguent. In "The Lamp at Noon" the prairie farm-wife finds herself trapped in an isolated farmhouse when she would like to be in a city, and the dust storm in which she goes mad and her baby dies becomes a symbol of the inexorable doom which is closing in upon her. Only her husband's fidelity and love stand between her and total defeat.

This use of the prairie climate and landscape both as a realistic setting and as a symbolic obbligato to the human situation is another of Ross's strengths as a writer of fiction. In words which are carefully chosen to achieve the maximum of accuracy in description, he makes vivid to us the reality of the prairie landscape with its vast distances and its overwhelming sky, and the fierce extremes of heat and cold, the long harsh winters and brief, brilliant, but often explosive summers, that mark the climate of that region. Beyond the accuracy of the descriptions, however, lie the powerful atmospheric effects which Ross achieves by relating the fluctuations of the weather to the moods and aspirations of his characters, and the way in which snow-storms and wind-storms are made to seem symbolic of the malevolence of the universe in which man finds himself a victim.

The sombreness of Ross's fiction is to some extent relieved, however, by the positive way in which he records the efforts of his characters to overcome or transcend the forbidding environment in which fate has placed them. The wife in "The Lamp at Noon" is broken, but her husband perseveres until he sees the storm go down; for all the tribulations to which the Bentleys are subjected, it is their human will which finally prevails: the last words of the novel are "I want it so." Philip's art is his means of transcending the environment: by portraying the prairie in all its harsh power he reduces it to form, transforms it by the power of the human imagination, asserts his human will in the face of its vast indifference.

Ross's own art as a novelist and writer of short stories represents a similar triumph of the human imagination. By his unremitting honesty in portraying human beings living in a physical environment which presents the maximum challenge to the instinct for survival, he has produced a small but significant volume of work which will endure.

—Desmond Pacey

ROSTEN, Leo (Calvin). American. Born in Lodz, Poland, 11 April 1908; emigrated to the United States in 1910. Educated at the University of Chicago, Ph.B. 1930 (Phi Beta Kappa), Ph.D. 1937 (Research Assistant, Political Science Department, 1933-35; Fellow, Social Science Research Council, 1934-36); London School of Economics, 1934. Married 1) Priscilla Ann Mead in 1935 (died), one son and two daughters; 2) Gertrude Zimmerman in 1960. English teacher in Chicago, 1930-32; Motion Picture Writer, 1937-38; Special Consultant to the National Defense Commission, 1939-40; Director, Motion Picture Research Project (Carnegie Foundation grant), 1939-41; Chief, Motion Picture Division, Office of Facts and Figures, Washington, D.C., 1941-42; Deputy Director, Office of War Information, Washington, 1942-43; Special Consultant to the United States Secretary of War, 1945 (Colonel, United States Army, 1945); Member, Senior Staff, RAND Corporation, Santa Monica, California, 1947-49; Editorial Adviser to *Look* magazine, New York, 1949-71. Since 1955, Lecturer, Columbia University, New York. Ford Visiting Professor of Political Science, University of California, Berkeley, 1960-61. Member of the National Board of the Authors League of America. Recipient: Rockefeller grant, 1940; George Polk Memorial Award, 1955; Freedoms Foundation Award, 1955; Professional Achievement Award, University of Chicago, 1969. D.H.L.: University of Rochester, New York, 1973; Hebrew Union College, Cincinnati, 1980. Honorary Fellow, London School of Economics, 1975. Address: 36 Sutton Place South, New York, New York 10022, U.S.A.

PUBLICATIONS

Novels

The Education of Hyman Kaplan (as Leonard Q. Ross). New York, Harcourt Brace, and London, Constable, 1937.
Dateline: Europe (as Leonard Ross). New York, Harcourt Brace, 1939; as *Balkan Express*, London, Heinemann, 1939.
Adventure in Washington (as Leonard Ross). New York, Harcourt Brace, 1940.
The Dark Corner. New York, Century, 1945; London, Edward, 1946.
Sleep, My Love. New York, Triangle, 1946.
The Return of Hyman Kaplan. New York, Harper, and London, Gollancz, 1959.
Captain Newman, M.D. London, Gollancz, 1961; New York, Harper, 1962.
A Most Private Intrigue. New York, Atheneum, and London, Gollancz, 1967.
Dear "Herm"—With a Cast of Dozens. New York, McGraw Hill, 1974; London, W.H. Allen, 1975.
O Kaplan! My Kaplan! New York, Harper, 1976; London, Constable, 1979.
Silky: A Detective Story. New York, Harper, 1979.
King Silky! New York, Harper, 1980.

Uncollected Short Stories

"Happy Was the Soldier!," in *Saturday Evening Post Stories 1956*. New York, Random House, 1956.
"Medal in the Sky," in *Atlantic* (Boston), February 1956.
"Lonely Pursuit," in *Cosmopolitan* (New York), September 1956.
"The Guy in Ward 4," in *The Best American Short Stories 1959*, edited by Martha Foley and David Burnett. Boston, Houghton Mifflin, 1959.
"The 'P' Party," "The Chaos Club," "The Happiest Couple in the World," "Freud and Monte O.," "I, The Count of Monte Cristo," and "The Cigar: A Fervent Footnote to History," in *Saturday Review/World* (New York), 1973-74.

Plays

Screenplays: *All Through the Night*, with Leonard Spigelgass and

Edward Gilbert, 1942; *The Conspirators*, with Vladimir Pozner and Jack Moffitt, 1944; *Lured*, 1947; *Sleep, My Love*, with others, 1947; *The Velvet Touch*, with others, 1948; *Where Danger Lives*, with Charles Bennett, 1950; *Whistle at Eaton Falls*, with others, 1951; *Double Dynamite*, with Mel Shavelson and Harry Crane, 1952; *Walk East on Beacon*, with others, 1952.

Other

The Washington Correspondents. New York, Harcourt Brace, 1937.
The Strangest Places (as Leonard Ross). New York, Harcourt Brace, and London, Constable, 1939.
Hollywood: The Movie Colony, The Movie Makers. New York, Harcourt Brace, 1941.
112 Gripes about the French. Washington, D.C., United States War Department, 1944.
The Story Behind the Painting. New York, Doubleday-Cowles, 1962.
The Many Worlds of Leo Rosten. New York, Harper, 1964; as *The Leo Rosten Bedside Book*, London, Gollancz, 1965.
The Joys of Yiddish. New York, McGraw Hill, 1968; London, W.H. Allen, 1970.
A Trumpet for Reason. New York, Doubleday, 1970; London, W.H. Allen, 1971.
People I Have Loved, Known, or Admired. New York, McGraw Hill, 1970; London, W.H. Allen, 1971.
Rome Wasn't Burned in a Day: The Mischief of Language. New York, Doubleday, 1972; London, W.H. Allen, 1973.
Leo Rosten's Treasury of Jewish Quotations. New York, McGraw Hill, 1972; London, W.H. Allen, 1973.
The 3:10 to Anywhere. New York, McGraw Hill, 1976.
The Power of Positive Nonsense. New York, McGraw Hill, 1977.
Passions and Prejudices; or, Some of My Best Friends Are People. New York, McGraw Hill, 1978.

Editor, *A Guide to the Religions of America.* New York, Simon and Schuster, 1955; as *Religions of America*, London, Heinemann, 1957; revised edition, as *Religions in America*, Simon and Schuster, 1963, 1975.
Editor, *The "Look" Book.* New York, Abrams, 1975.
Editor, *Infinite Riches: Gems from a Lifetime of Reading.* New York, McGraw Hill, 1979.

*

Manuscript Collection: Brandeis University, Waltham, Massachusetts.

Leo Rosten comments:

I write as my interests guide and seduce me: see the preface to *The Many Worlds of Leo Rosten*. My work ranges from political analysis to humor, from social comment to art to movie screenplays, from inquiries about science and theology to biographical vignettes of Churchill, Freud, Groucho Marx, Adam Smith—and a juicy assortment of wits, half-wits, sages, psychiatrists, and trail-blazers.

People I Have Loved, Known, or Admired suggests the range of my susceptibilities—and the varieties of techniques to which I resort. I write melodrama for pleasure, as some men play chess or go fishing. The titles of my works indicate the range of the nets I have cast into the sea of my fancies. I find writing an indescribably complex, difficult, frustrating, challenging, exhilarating, unyielding, exciting, depressing, and joyous calling, to which I commit the resources of the self. I also enjoy the play and elusiveness of my fantasies.

The only reason for being a professional writer is that you just can't help it.

* * *

Leo Rosten earned a permanent place (as Leonard Q. Ross) on the rolls of ethnic-humorists with the publication in 1937 of *The Education of Hyman Kaplan*. The title is a parody of the autobiographical "study of failure" of the patrician Henry Adams; Rosten's collection of his *New Yorker* short-stories chronicles the sharply contrasting efforts of European immigrants to learn "good English" in night school and thereby succeed in America. The brash hero of these episodes is the determined, cagey and warmly likable Kaplan, who signs his name in red crayon capitals, outlined in blue and punctuated with green stars. Kaplan innocently torments his fusspot teacher, Mr. Parkhill, with bold syntax, dazzling malapropisms, and creative mispronunciations, whereby the plural of "sandwich" is "delicatessen" and the Chinese premier becomes "Shanghai Jack." In 1959, Rosten offered a revival of the popular Kaplan-Parkhill duels, complete with familiar minor characters, but critics agreed that Rosten was too distant from the early years when he had actually taught garment workers in a Chicago night school.

Although his reputation rests on Kaplan's eager shoulders, Rosten's work has been varied, as suggested by one anthology, *The Many Worlds of Leo Rosten*. His Ph.D. thesis in sociology at the University of Chicago became *The Washington Correspondents*, followed by a Carnegie Foundation-supported study entitled *Hollywood: The Movie Colony, The Movie Makers*. Both studies are methodically sound, thorough and readable. Among his potboilers, his best is *A Most Private Intrigue*, an old-fashioned spy thriller which eschews James Bond-like violence, sex, and technology in favor of romance, plot twists, and breath-holding escapes.

Rosten's best-selling novel *Captain Newman, M.D.* illustrates his major strengths and weaknesses. As chief of the mental ward of an Air Force base in wartime, psychiatrist Newman is superhumanly insightful, while the ranking officers are as predictably arrogant as the G.I.'s are cute in their shenanigans. If the comic ethnic stereotypes in the Hyman Kaplan stories seemed embarrassing upon re-issue, Rosten nevertheless repeats them all here: the simple-minded Negro private is lovable and humble, the Italian P.O.W.'s roll their eyes and mutter "Mama Mia," the Jewish Laibowitz schemes shrewdly and parries questions with questions. The author skillfully alternates chapters of situation comedy and melodrama to suggest emotional range, but all sequences are as neatly rounded out as in a television series.

Rosten handles many genres with professional competence and intelligence but clearly prefers a light, superficial touch. *The Joys of Yiddish* displayed Rosten's impressive knowledge of the impact of English and Yiddish upon each other, as well as his familiarity with Jewish humor and history. *People I Have Loved, Known, or Admired* offers facile interpretations of public figures but is deeply moving in the author's splendid portrait of his own father. *A Trumpet for Reason* resonantly sounds off on contemporary militancy, but the author seems much more attuned to the status quo than he cares to admit. At his best, Rosten writes smooth, witty prose and wears his layers of learning with grace. At worst, he succumbs to the easy appeal of the stock character or belief and reveals the slick writer's affinity for the heart-warming cliché.

—Frank Campenni

ROTH, Henry. American. Born in Tysmenica, Austria-Hungary, 8 February 1906. Educated at the City College of New York, B.S. 1928. Married Muriel Parker in 1939; two sons. Worked for the Works Progress Administration (WPA), 1939; teacher in Roosevelt High School, New York, 1939-41; precision metal grinder in New York, Providence, Rhode Island, and Boston, 1941-46; teacher in Montville, Maine, 1947-48; attendant at the Maine State Hospital, 1949-53; waterfowl farmer, 1953-62; private tutor, 1956-65. Recipient: American Academy grant, 1965; City College of New York Townsend Harris Medal, 1965; D.H. Lawrence Fellowship, University of New Mexico, 1968. Address: Box 10160, Albuquerque, New Mexico 87114, U.S.A.

PUBLICATIONS

Novel

Call It Sleep. New York, Ballou, 1934; London, Joseph, 1963.

Uncollected Short Stories

"Broker," in *New Yorker*, 18 November 1938.
"Somebody Always Grabs the Purple," in *New Yorker*, 23 March 1940.
"Petey and Yorsee and Mario," in *New Yorker*, 14 July 1956.
"At Times in Flight," in *Commentary* (New York), July 1959.
"The Dun Dakotas," in *Commentary* (New York), August 1960.
"The Fat Guy," in *December* (Iowa City), vi, 1, 1964.
"Sam's Land," in *December* (Iowa City), vii, 1, 1965.
"The Surveyor," in *The Best American Short Stories 1967*, edited by Martha Foley and David Burnett. Boston, Houghton Mifflin, 1967.
"Final Dwarf," in *Atlantic* (Boston), July 1969.

*

Manuscript Collection: Boston University.

Critical Studies: *Bilingual Markers of a Culture in Translation* by Frances Kleederman, unpublished dissertation, New York University, 1974; *Henry Roth* by Bonnie Lyons, New York, Cooper Square Press, 1975.

Henry Roth comments:

The writing of the novel, I feel, was too long ago for me to have anything cogent to say about it now, which is not to imply that I ever did have a clear notion of what I was doing. I recall the ambience and the sensation—the affect—of the writing more than I do the "ideas" connected with it. However, one of these does persist in the memory, a kind of guide or credo: That I had no thesis whatever to advance (that I was aware of), only to convey what it felt to be alive, in my time.

I have a strong suspicion that the reason I wrote no more than I did was that I failed of maturity, lost the will to force the next stage in development at the opportune moment.

* * *

Although Henry Roth's only novel, *Call It Sleep*, received favorable reviews and sold tolerably well when it first appeared in 1934, it was known to relatively few readers until its republication in 1960. Its first paperback reprinting in 1964 was a turn in the public reception of the book. *Call It Sleep* is now recognized as one of the finest American novels of this century, perhaps the best novel about childhood ever written by an American, rivalling Dickens's or Dostoevsky's sense of the pathos of childhood.

The popularity of *Call It Sleep* during the 1960's can be explained on a number of levels. The interest in Jewish writers and the rediscovery of "ethnic identity," along with increasing curiosity about the life of the Jews in the lower East Side of New York around the turn of the century, are some of the explanations for the book's increasing readership. Also, the concern for urban experience and a renewed interest in the writers of the 1930's contributed toward a rediscovery of Roth's novel.

The vitality of the novel can be felt in the fact that it relates to and yet escapes convenient literary and social categories. A product of the 1930's, and a reflection of some of that decade's concerns, the book can hardly be categorized as a proletarian novel. A description of a Jewish family in New York City during the years preceding World War I, the book cannot be fixed by the term "Jewish novel." A keen portrayal of the mind of a boy, the book cannot quite be called a psychological novel. Yet all of these elements are vibrantly part of the novel.

Call It Sleep begins with the child David Schearl slightly less than two years old and continues to the time he is eight, concentrating on his life in the family and in the streets from his sixth to eighth year. His troubled relationships with his mother and father are keenly portrayed by Roth who describes an oedipal situation with the force of actual life and with no factitious clinical details. The novel resembles D.H. Lawrence's *Sons and Lovers* in its ability to evoke that conflict as a literary and not just a clinical event.

The image of the morose, physically powerful, and stern father is counterpointed by the characterization of the sympathetic, loving mother. The child is torn between his affection for his mother (his only security in the novel) and his secret desire to emulate and challenge the powerful and threatening stance of his father.

The scenes both in the apartment and in the street, among the family and among other children, are overwhelming experiences for David. He struggles to gain some kind of foothold by means of which he can withstand the onslaught of both his father and the gangs and friends of the street. The terrors of the family life eventually relate to the terrors and the testing of experience outside the family.

There are three levels of language in the book which Roth sometimes interweaves. First of all there is the language of narration; then there is the Yiddish spoken at home, rendered through an intelligible and confident English, unlike the broken and noisy English of the street, the third level. There is even a fourth level of language in one scene when Roth also brings into play the Hebrew of the Bible during a Hebrew class the boy attends. In that scene (in chapter IV of Book III), Roth intersperses the Biblical-ritual Hebrew of the rabbi-teacher; the angry Yiddish of that teacher as he curses his recalcitrant pupils; the puzzled, exploratory thoughts of David; and the whining, aggressive remarks of the children. It is a passage that shows to good effect Roth's absorption of Joyce and Eliot.

In an effort to match the power of his father, to meet the frustrations of his family life, to escape the puzzlements of street life, and to emulate the rabbi's description of Isaiah and the burning coal that purified his soul and burned away his sins, as well as to recover a vision he once had when staring into the light of the East River, David slips a metal milk ladle into a slot of a third rail from a trolley car line. He causes a blinding flash (the light of salvation and of authority that he longs for). He is also knocked unconscious and causes a temporary power failure in the neighborhood. In an unsuccessful effort to bring together many persons from different backgrounds in response to that power failure, Roth is forced to leave the consciousness of the child for the first time in the book and tries an unsuccessful collage of "proletarian voices" around the unconscious child in his search for light. Roth's poetic prose becomes forced at this point but regains its regular force when the novel returns to the now awakened boy who back home thinks of rest and self-possession before he falls again into sleep.

Henry Roth has not written another novel since *Call It Sleep*. A few stories have appeared over the years as Roth destroyed a second novel, imperfectly started a third, and went on to hold a number of jobs, finally becoming a raiser of waterfowl in Maine. Probably the best of those stories are "At Times in Flight" and "The Dun Dakotas." Both tales reflect Roth's difficulty in returning to writing.

An interview in the 1969 (no. 2) issue of *Partisan Review* movingly portrays Roth's situation and difficulties from the time he completed *Call It Sleep* to his new thoughts and ambition to write again following the Israeli-Arab six day war in 1967. Whether or not Roth will be able to write again at the level of *Call It Sleep*, he has accomplished in that novel one of the finest works of imagination by an American novelist in this century.

—Richard J. Fein

ROTH, Philip (Milton). American. Born in Newark, New Jersey, 19 March 1933. Educated at Newark College, Rutgers University, 1950-51; Bucknell University, Lewisburg, Pennsylvania, 1951-54, A.B. 1954; University of Chicago, 1954-55, M.A. 1955. Served in the United States Army, 1955-56. Married Margaret Martinson in 1958 (died, 1968). Instructor in English, University of Chicago, 1956-58; Visiting Writer, University of Iowa, Iowa City, 1960-62; Writer-in-Residence, Princeton University, New Jersey, 1962-64; Visiting Writer, State University of New York at Stony Brook, 1966, 1967, and the University of Pennsylvania, Philadelphia, 1967-80. Member of the Corporation of Yaddo, Saratoga Springs, New York. Recipient: Guggenheim Fellowship, 1959; National Book Award, 1960; Daroff Award, 1960; American Academy grant, 1960; O. Henry Award, 1960; Ford Foundation grant, for drama, 1965; Rockefeller Fellowship, 1966. Member, American Academy, 1970. Address: c/o Farrar Straus and Giroux, 19 Union Square West, New York, New York 10003, U.S.A.

PUBLICATIONS

Novels

Letting Go. New York, Random House, and London, Deutsch, 1962.
When She Was Good. New York, Random House, and London, Cape, 1967.
Portnoy's Complaint. New York, Random House, 1969; London, Cape, 1970.
Our Gang (Starring Tricky and His Friends). New York, Random House, and London, Cape, 1971.
The Breast. New York, Holt Rinehart, 1972; London, Cape, 1973.
The Great American Novel. New York, Holt Rinehart, and London, Cape, 1973.
My Life As a Man. New York, Holt Rinehart, and London, Cape, 1974.
The Professor of Desire. New York, Farrar Straus, 1977; London, Cape, 1978.
The Ghost Writer. New York, Farrar Straus, and London, Cape, 1979.
Zuckerman Unbound. New York, Farrar Straus, 1981.

Short Stories

Goodbye, Columbus, and Five Short Stories. Boston, Houghton Mifflin, and London, Deutsch, 1959.
Penguin Modern Stories 3, with others. London, Penguin, 1969.

Uncollected Short Stories

"The Mistaken," in *The American Judaism Reader*, edited by Paul Kresh. New York, Abelard Schuman, 1967.
"On the Air," in *New American Review 10*, edited by Theodore Solotaroff. New York, New American Library, 1970.
"Susan," in *Esquire* (New York), June 1974.

Other

Reading Myself and Others. New York, Farrar Straus, and London, Cape, 1975.
A Philip Roth Reader. New York, Farrar Straus, 1980; London, Cape, 1981.

*

Bibliography: *Philip Roth: A Bibliography* by Bernard F. Rodgers, Jr., Metuchen, New Jersey, Scarecrow Press, 1974.

Manuscript Collection: Library of Congress, Washington, D.C.

Critical Studies: *Bernard Malamud and Philip Roth: A Critical Essay* by Glenn Meeter, Grand Rapids, Michigan, Eerdmans, 1968; "The Journey of Philip Roth" by Theodore Solotaroff, in *The Red Hot Vacuum*, New York, Atheneum, 1970; *The Fiction of Philip Roth* by John N. McDaniel, Haddonfield, New Jersey, Haddonfield House, 1974; *The Comedy That "Hoits": An Essay on the Fiction of Philip Roth* by Sanford Pinsker, Columbus, University of Missouri Press, 1975; *Philip Roth* by Bernard F. Rodgers, Jr., Boston, Twayne, 1978; "Jewish Writers" by Mark Shechner, in *The Harvard Guide to Contemporary American Writing* edited by Daniel Hoffman, Cambridge, Massachusetts, Harvard University Press, 1979; introduction by Martin Green to *A Philip Roth Reader*, New York, Farrar Straus, 1980, London, Cape, 1981; *Philip Roth* by Judith Jones and Guinevera Nance, New York, Ungar, 1981.

* * *

In the title of one of the best essays on Philip Roth, Alfred Kazin used the word "toughminded." This quality pervades his novels, stories, and essays. Roth's unsparing portraits of Jews too adept at scheming and compromise have upset rabbis and Jewish organizations. His frank acknowledgment of such unmentionables as abortion, masturbation, and sexual calisthenics has alarmed the bluenoses. These irate—usually unliterary—responses have fortunately failed to unsettle him.

Until now Roth has seemed most at ease with Jewish characters and settings. His ear is especially sensitive to the verbal rhythm and pulse beat of the second-generation American Jew who has recently abandoned the inner city for the suburbs. The stories in Roth's first book, *Goodbye, Columbus*, are almost all concerned with confrontations between Jews of radically different persuasions and temperaments. Thus Neil Klugman, in the title story, confronts the Jewish society of Short Hills, as represented by Brenda Patimkin and her family, where "fruit grew in their refrigerator and sporting goods dropped from their trees!" Neil's wrong-side-of-the-track Judaism fails to make the proper concessions and adjustments. In "Eli, The Fanatic" the assimilated Jews of another suburban community, Woodenton, employ the lawyer Eli Peck to force a Yeshivah to move elsewhere or at least to "modernize." We see a skillful confrontation between the Talmudic logic of the Yeshivah's headmaster and the more worldly logic of Eli. Eli ends by donning the Hasidic garb of one of the Yeshivah instructors—which suggests to his fellow Jews of Woodenton the return of an earlier nervous breakdown. Jew is also pitted against Jew in "The Conversion of the Jews." This time the questioning Jewish schoolboy Ozzie Freedman forces embarrassing ideological concessions from Rabbi Binder and the Jewish establishment when he threatens to jump from the roof of the synagogue. The stories in *Goodbye, Columbus* are brilliantly irreverent.

Roth's heterodoxy continues into his first novel, *Letting Go.* He enlarges the focus here to include not only the idiosyncrasies of the Jewish community but also of university faculties, charlatan abortionists, and ill-suited love relationships. Very little is left out. Gabe Wallach's "I" controls the early parts of the novel; then it recedes into a kind of background first-person and finally turns into a more respectably detached third-person. Wallach is the intruder who keeps moving in and out of delicate situations—always avoiding complete involvement—and so this changing of narrative focus is especially apt. He defines his position early in the novel: "It was beginning to seem that toward those for whom I felt no strong sentiment, I gravitated; where sentiment existed, I ran." Wallach's years as a graduate student at the University of Iowa and as an instructor at the University of Chicago offer a rejection of his eastern seaboard Jewish background (born in New York, educated at Harvard). The first words of the novel are the deathbed letter of Gabe Wallach's mother. This letter, inadvertently tucked between the pages of his copy of James's *Portrait of a Lady*, starts Gabe off on the midwestern pilgrimage which involves the series of precarious relationships with Libby and Paul Herz and with Martha Reganhart. The terribly flawed Herz marriage somehow survives Gabe's "meddling"; in fact, it is strengthened by the adoption of a hild and by a spirited assertion of Judaism. Gabe Wallach's love ffair with Martha Reganhart fares less well. Gabe speaks of himself a final letter to Libby as an "indecisive man" who had had but one decisive moment."

Roth also places his next novel, *When She Was Good*, in the idwest—this time a midwest without Jews. The texture of his riting changes markedly; it seems to flatten out, to become, as heodore Solotaroff suggests, "a language of scrupulous banality." he midwestern Protestantism which underlies the novel is threa-ned only by an adolescent flirtation with the Catholic Church by e heroine Lucy Nelson; this is lightly dismissed as "all that atholic hocus-pocus." Lucy's intolerance and uncomfortable oral provincialism manage to get in the way of her own marriage nd that of her parents. She cannot put up with her husband's rather uerile brashness and incompetence or with her father's alcoholism. Just as Roth was able to capture the special quality of the conver-tion of both first and second generation American Jews in *Good-ye, Columbus* and *Letting Go*, so in *When She Was Good* he anages handsomely with the cliché-ridden language of Main treet.

Portnoy's Complaint is a return, with a vengeance, to Roth's rlier manner. It seems to come out of the best pages of *Goodbye, olumbus* and *Letting Go*. Roth has settled here on all the things he nows how to do best, especially in his creation of the urban Jewish mily with the mother at its moral center. *Portnoy's Complaint* is e staccato confession of Alexander Portnoy to his psychiatrist Dr. pielvogel (who makes another appearance in *My Life As a Man*) in avily free associative prose.

The novel begins with a section entitled "The Most Unforgettable haracter I've Met"; the reference is to Sophie Portnoy who domi-ates not only the family but also the "confessions" of her son. (She in part anticipated by Aunt Gladys in "Goodbye, Columbus" and aul Herz's mother in *Letting Go*.) She characteristically pushes to e background her perpetually constipated and henpecked hus-nd and her pathetically unendowed daughter. The confrontation between mother and son. The fiercely aggressive, domineering other seems to win out since it is the son who does the confessing om the analyst's couch. Alex, however, gains some measure of venge through seiges of masturbation in his youth and through fairs with gentiles (*shiksas*) in his more mature years. He master-lly uncovers chinks in his Jewish mother's armor by taunting her ith his conquest of Christian girls and by abusing the family rabbi, it always at the expense of his own too active feelings of guilt. verything in this novel, it would seem, "can be traced to the bonds btaining in the mother-child relationship." Jewish mothers, in the st few years, have presented a challenge to some of the best merican Jewish novelists, like Wallace Markfield, Bruce Jay riedman, and Herbert Gold. Probably the most realized and con-ncing of all is Sophie Portnoy.

Roth's versatility is very much in evidence in *Our Gang (Starring ricky and His Friends)*; he seems able to manage the rhetoric of litical corruption quite as easily as the language of the Jewish ban dweller who has recently retreated to the suburbs. In *Our ang* Roth takes on a formidable adversary, the Nixon administra-on: he carries a certain Trick E. Dixon from a press conference, an derground meeting with his "coaches," an address to his "fellow mericans," to an election speech—following his assassination—to s "fellow Fallen" in Hell. This speech ends with the revealing ntence: "And let there be no mistake about it: if I am elected Devil, intend to see Evil triumph in the end; I intend to see that our ildren, and our children's children, need never know the terrible ourge of Righteousness and Peace." Passages from Swift and rwell appropriately serve as epigraphs for this novel.

The Breast, in certain ways, marks a return to *Portnoy's Com-aint*. One might think of this novella—with its college professor rrator, David Alan Kepesh, who turns into a female breast—as a orking out of certain fantasies suggested by *Portnoy* with some lp from Kafka, Gogol, and Swift. The bookish hero cannot resist ening his peculiar condition to that of Kafka's Gregor Samsa who vakens to discover that he has turned into a huge bug or to that of ogol's Kovalyov who awakens to find that he is missing his nose; he makes reference also to Swift's "self-satisfied Houyhnhnms" and to "Gulliver among the Brobdingnags," in which country "the king's maidservants had him walk out on their nipples for the fun of it."

The Great American Novel seems to have little in common with the previous fiction. This baseball novel is Roth's contribution to a genre which has already attracted several other American Jewish writers, including Bernard Malamud and Mark Harris. It is filled with oblique references to a wide variety of literary works. Thus it begins with the sentence, "Call me Smitty." A sensational pitcher goes under the name Gil Gamesh. American literature and baseball are occasionally brought together in uneasy confrontation; they make for strange bedfellows. This mock-heroic tone reinforces the sense of caricature and pastiche which runs through the novel. Roth holds up the myth of the Great American Novel to the same ridicule as the myth of the Great American Pastime.

My Life As a Man fits snugly into place in the main line of Philip Roth's development. The Jewish ingredients are less pronounced here than in *Goodbye, Columbus, Letting Go*, and *Portnoy's Complaint*, yet the ambience is unmistakably the same. The writer-hero of the novel, Peter Tarnopol, has much in common with Gabe Wallach, Alexander Portnoy, and David Alan Kepesh. Indeed he has the same bookish tendencies as Kepesh. Roth offers a clever variation on the novel-within-the-novel device as he prefaces the main part of his latest work, "My True Story" (Tarnopol's sustained confessional), with two of his protagonist's short stories. The "useful fictions," as Roth calls these stories, have a great deal to do with Tarnopol's "true story"; truth and fiction, it would seem, are ultimately interchangeable. *My Life As a Man* reveals Roth in his dual roles as novelist and critic. The narrative strategy allows for a good deal of theorizing about the nature of novel-writing and a certain amount of literary criticism.

The Professor of Desire and *The Ghost Writer*, both first-person novels, borrow as narrators characters who appeared in the earlier fiction. *The Professor of Desire*, like *The Breast*, is told by David Kepesh while Nathan Zuckerman, the central presence in the "Useful Fictions" section of *My Life As a Man*, narrates *The Ghost Writer*. *The Professor of Desire* offers an elaborate unfolding of Kepesh's *wanderjahre* in the years preceding his metamorphosis. The restless narrative starts and ends in the Catskills—the Jewish still point of the novel. The itinerary is dotted with literary and amorous "excavations." Since his graduate school days at Stanford, Kepesh has been working intermittently on a book about romantic disillusionment in Chekhov's stories. A real and imagined Kafka occupies a central position in the Prague interlude. The amorous is even more in evidence than the literary, as Kepesh makes his way from a succession of girl friends, to a marriage and divorce, finally to a rather idyllic relationship with Claire Ovington.

The literary and the amorous are also strongly in evidence in *The Ghost Writer*. The novel turns about an odd triangular relationship, involving the narrator, Zuckerman, the renowned writer E.I. Lonoff, and a young lady who has served a kind of apprenticeship (literary and perhaps also sexual) at Lonoff's feet, Amy Bellette. Zuckerman, a youthful author, arrives at Lonoff's house at the beginning of this short novel, in retreat from his cloying Jewish parents and his Newark childhood. He is an onlooker, in much the same way as Styron's narrator in *Sophie's Choice*, as he tries to unravel the complications of a situation which couples the erotic with the literary. With some help from Henry James's "The Middle Years" and other literary texts, Zuckerman weaves a complex mosaic which turns Amy Bellette into the author of *The Diary of Anne Frank*. The mythological machinery he invents here is in a sense his work of art: the gesture which will make him worthy of becoming Lonoff's "spiritual son" and perhaps eventually Amy's sexual partner. In *The Ghost Writer* Roth seems to have moved his familiar literary baggage to a new setting, rural New England; with the change has come a minimizing of the ethnically Jewish world of the early fiction in favor of a broader Judaeo-Christian canvas.

—Melvin J. Friedman

RUBENS, Bernice (Ruth). British. Born in Cardiff, Wales, 26 July 1927. Educated at Cardiff High School for Girls; University College of South Wales and Monmouthshire, Cardiff, 1944-47, B.A. (honours) in English 1947. Married the writer Rudi Nassauer in 1947; two daughters. English Teacher, Handsworth Grammar School for Boys, Birmingham, 1947-49. Since 1950, documentary film writer and director, for the United Nations and others. Recipient: American Blue Ribbon Award, for film-making, 1968; Booker Prize, 1970; Welsh Arts Council award, 1976. Address: 89 Greencroft Gardens, London NW6 3LJ, England.

PUBLICATIONS

Novels

Set on Edge. London, Eyre and Spottiswoode, 1960.
Madame Sousatzka. London, Eyre and Spottiswoode, 1962.
Mate in Three. London, Eyre and Spottiswoode, 1965.
The Elected Member. London, Eyre and Spottiswoode, 1969; as *Chosen People*, New York, Atheneum, 1969.
Sunday Best. London, Eyre and Spottiswoode, 1971; New York, Summit, 1980.
Go Tell the Lemming. London, Cape, 1973.
I Sent a Letter to My Love. London, W.H. Allen, 1975; New York, St. Martin's Press, 1978.
The Ponsonby Post. London, W.H. Allen, 1977; New York, St. Martin's Press, 1978.
A Five Year Sentence. London, W.H. Allen, 1978; as *Favours*, New York, Summit, 1979.
Spring Sonata. London, W.H. Allen, 1979.
Birds of Passage. London, Hamish Hamilton, 1981.

Plays

I Sent a Letter to My Love, adaptation of her own novel (produced New Haven, Connecticut, 1978; London, 1979).

Television Play: *Third Party*, 1972.

*

Bernice Rubens comments:

(1972) I am never consciously aware of the actual matter of my work and never think about it unless the question is directly raised. There seems to be a terrible finality about assessing one's own work, because such an assessment might bind you to that evaluation forever. I am open to the most radical changes in my thinking and outlook. I hope it will be reflected in my work. My first four novels were essentially on Jewish themes in a Jewish environment, for in that environment I felt secure. My fifth novel, *Sunday Best*, was an attempt to challenge myself to step outside that familiarity. I noticed that my radical change of location did not involve as radical a change of style, which seems to remain simple, direct, always empty of what in school is called "descriptive passages," for these frighten me. As to the matter of what I write about, I can only be general. I am concerned with the communication, or non-communication as is more often the case, between people and families. A general enough statement, and in this general sense my books will always be about that theme.

* * *

Bernice Rubens has in the main been a chronicler of the frayed edge of middle-class Jewish life. The old sources of insecurity are gone. There is no external threat from the gentile world: the natives are friendly. And money, though not abundant, is sufficient. Nor does one find much mutual hostility. The fraying, in the main, comes from love. People are pained and give pain through the deep regard they have for one another, as can be seen in the conflicts between wife, husband, and mistress in *Mate in Three*, or at i ultimate in her accomplished novel, *The Elected Member*.

The story of *The Elected Member* suggests that within every clos group, in this case the Jewish family, one member comes forward a a sort of Jesus to atone for the sins of the others, or as a conducto for the tremors which trouble their souls. He is broken by th burden, resorts to drugs, becomes subject to horrifying hallucina tions, and ends in an asylum, while the group as a whol disintegrates.

Rubens does not try to draw a moral. These, she says, are th underlying realities of our situation; it may help to recognise then Neither does she apportion blame, though towards the end of th novel Norman, who is in fact the elected member, cries out from th depth of his anguish against God: "Your wrath, Your jealous Your expectation, Your omnipotence, Your mercy and pity, You sheer bloody mindedness." It is a cry which many a member of th Chosen Race may have made in the post-Auschwitz era. Who aske to be chosen? The story of Norman is, to an extent, the story of th Jewish people, except that even the darkest moments of Jewis history have been redeemed by Messianic hope. There is no suc optimism in Rubens's work, but on the contrary, a brooding pess mism. What redeems it, however, is the humour, which is black an ghoulish, as in her first novel, *Set on Edge*, and wryly Jewish, arisin partly from the situation, partly from the eccentricities of characte as displayed for example in *Madame Sousatzka*. Madame, teacher of pianoforte, owes something to Gogol in her makeu something to Lewis Carroll, but in the main, she is Rubens's own, memorable creation.

With four solid novels behind her one felt that Rubens wa established as the mistress of a set genre, so that one could recogni a Rubens character if one met one in the street, but her fifth, *Sunda Best*, is a complete departure, except that here too the centr character has his neurosis (you don't have to be Jewish to b neurotic, but it helps): he is a transvestite, enjoying his aberratio quietly and only on a Sunday. One day, however, he dons dra leaves home, and finds himself pursued for his own alleged murde The flavour is vintage Hitchcock, the invention unflagging, the w outrageous. It is as a result difficult to classify Rubens as this or th sort of writer. She is too versatile to be cubbyholed.

Go Tell the Lemming has all the darkness one finds in her earli work, without any of the redeeming humour, without any reli whatsoever. It is stark, a raging catharsis caught in words, about too, too understanding wife who seems to invite every calami which befalls her. But the reaction of the reader is "silly bitch" rath than "poor woman." The book displays once again Rubens's ang mastery of language and searching insights, but to no wholeso purpose, and those with happy memories of her earlier work w regard it as an aberration.

—Chaim Berma

RUMAKER, Michael. American. Born in Philadelphia, Pen sylvania, 5 March 1932. Educated at Black Mountain Colleg North Carolina, graduated 1955; Columbia University, New Yor M.F.A. 1970. Lecturer in Creative Writing, New School for Soci Research, New York, 1967-71; Writer-in-Residence and Lecture City College of New York, 1969-71. Visiting Writer-in-Residen State University of New York, Buffalo, 1967. Recipient: Dell Pu lishing Foundation Award, 1970. Agent: Harold Ober Associat 40 East 49th Street, New York, New York 10017. Address: 1 South Broadway, South Nyack, New York 10960, U.S.A.

UBLICATIONS

ovels

he Butterfly. New York, Scribner, 1962; London, Macdonald, 1968.
Day and a Night at the Baths. Bolinas, California, Grey Fox Press, 1979.

hort Stories

he Bar. San Francisco, Four Seasons, 1964.
xit 3 and Other Stories. London, Penguin, 1966; as *Gringos and Other Stories*, New York, Grove Press, 1967.

'lay

chwul (Queers), translated by Wylf Teichmann and Dirk Mülder. Frankfurt, März Verlag, 1970.

*

Ianuscript Collection: University of Connecticut, Storrs.

:ritical Study: "The Use of the Unconscious in Writing," by the uthor, in *New American Story*, edited by Donald Allen and obert Creeley, New York, Grove Press, 1965.

* * *

Michael Rumaker's coterie reputation rests upon an astonishngly small output, none of it very recent and virtually all completed y his thirtieth birthday. Yet he demonstrates virtuosity, versatility, nd sophistication, all traits which normally suggest the maturity of xperience. Rumaker must be counted among the new breed of vriters who deliberately call attention to the artifice of their writing: vith these fellow-writers he achieves his effects mostly through tyle, especially in the brilliantly clear rendering of the world of bjects, his created milieu regressing to primal states of being and nanifestations of the unconscious. What sets him off from his ounterparts is his willingness to work within the apparent contraints of traditional fiction, so that his stories may be mass-read and perhaps misread) as easily as those of Stephen Crane or Mark Twain.

Rumaker is best within the short story form, particularly when vriting of "natural" men in raw settings. His three best stories, 'Gringos," "The Pipe," and "The Desert," depict intuitive men—nisfits, cast-offs, wanderers—who create temporary "societies" with each other which threaten imminently to explode. They fight, ust, drink, and sometimes kill each other, yet at their most bizarre or violent they remain intensely human and, for that reason, are nteresting, even likable, though grotesque. In "Gringos" a young American named Jim teams up with a friendly, blustering sailor in a small Mexican town. Jim agrees to share the sailor's room and hospitality; they saunter through the streets, dodge the aggressive prostitutes, drink, turn down a young male prostitute and finally "purchase" a girl (sailor's treat). At the night's end, they are attacked by Mexicans with knives, but they beat them off and return home. Simply as experience, this account is brilliantly realized, but from the start the mutual hostility of the intruding Americans and the impoverished Mexicans, the sink-hole quality of the squalid town, the oppressive atmosphere of cripples, pornography, exploitation, and homosexuality all point a descent into the hells of our own making. "The Pipe" is even more vividly a landscape of the unconscious, projecting myth and symbol without obtruding upon the bare narrative. Five men wait by the mouth of a huge pipe. A dredgeboat anchored in mid-river will soon blow submerged waste into their midst; these scavengers will then extract the pig-iron and other "valuables" in which they trade for a livelihood. Waiting, they tease and brag, swap stories, talk sex; the idiot-boy Billy amuses his companions with an elaborate re-enactment of finding an infant's legless corpse within the muck. The "blow" comes, the men scramble among tons of oozy waste and Sam and Alex (who had found the dead baby) quarrel over a disputed find. A sudden burst of violence and Sam is dead. Bunk, who was earlier denied a drink from the common bottle because of mouth-sores, brushes the swirling flies from Sam's wound and covers his head with a sack. As the men leave, the circling chicken hawks land near the pipe and strut among the slime toward the body. Two other impressive stories, entirely different in locale and plot, deal with a group of young thieves in Camden, and suggest an incipient novel which never materialized.

In *The Butterfly*, a 28-year-old man (emotionally, a 17-year-old boy) fearfully re-enters society after two years in a mental institution. Different again from Rumaker's other fiction, the novel's cloistered atmosphere and simple story line hazard the risk on each page of descending from pathos to bathos yet rarely do so. Jim moves from the loving protection of a sensitive doctor to his love affair with a Japanese girl; the love affair fails, but only because Eiko, too, is disturbed and, unlike Jim, is fearful of loving someone. His courage in risking further disappointment is rewarded when he meets Alice and their love develops without mishap. There are perhaps too many significant, detailed dream-sequences, and the novel abounds with symbols—yellow balloons rising to the sun, birds hunted by thoughtless boys, flat rocks skipping across streams—but the sensitivity of the protagonist and the aptness of the imagery sustain a novel as delicate as haiku. Rumaker here avoids dramatizing a subject intrinsically pregnant with drama and, as with his stories, invents the form and language necessary to his ends.

—Frank Campenni

SAHGAL, Nayantara (Pandit). Indian. Born in Allahabad, 10 May 1927. Educated at Wellesley College, Massachusetts, 1943-47, B.A. in history 1947. Married Gautam Sahgal in 1949 (divorced, 1967); three children. Since 1965, has regularly contributed articles to Indian newspapers and magazines. Address: 25-C Sujan Singh Park, New Delhi 3, India.

PUBLICATIONS

Novels

A Time to Be Happy. New York, Knopf, and London, Gollancz, 1958.
This Time of Morning. London, Gollancz, 1965; New York, Norton, 1966.
Storm in Chandigarh. New York, Norton, and London, Chatto and Windus, 1969.
The Day in Shadow. New Delhi, Vikas, 1971; New York, Norton, 1972; London, London Magazine Editions, 1975.
A Situation in New Delhi. London, London Magazine Editions, 1977.

Uncollected Short Stories

"The Promising Young Woman," in *Illustrated Weekly of India* (Bombay), January 1959.
"The Golden Afternoon," in *Illustrated Weekly of India* (Bombay), February 1959.
"The Trials of Siru," in *Triveni* (Madras), January 1967.
"Crucify Me," in *Indian Horizons* (New Delhi), October 1979.

Other

Prison and Chocolate Cake (autobiography). New York, Knopf, and London, Gollancz, 1954.
From Fear Set Free (autobiography). London, Gollancz, 1962; New York, Norton, 1963.
History of the Freedom Movement. New Delhi, National Council of Educational Research and Training, 1970.
Sunlight Surround You, with Chandralekha Mehta and Rita Dar. Privately printed, 1970.
A Voice for Freedom. Delhi, Hind, 1977.
Indira Gandhi's Emergence and Style. New Delhi, Vikas, and Durham, North Carolina, Academic Press, 1978.

*

Critical Studies: *Bridges of Literature* by M.L. Malhotra, Ajmer, Sunanda, 1971; essay by the author in *Adam* (London), August 1971; *Nayantara Sahgal and the Craft of Fiction* by Suresh Kohli, New Delhi, Vikas, 1972; *Nayantara Sahgal: A Study of Her Fiction and Non-Fiction* by A.V. Krishna Rao, Madras, Seshachalam, 1976; *Nayantara Sahgal* by Jasbir Jain, New Delhi, Arnold-Heinemann India, 1978.

* * *

Most of Nayantara Sahgal's characters belong to the affluent upper class of Indian society. Sahgal scrupulously sticks to the people she knows intimately; she does not try to write about the caste-ridden middle class or the poor Indian villager just to conform with the accepted image of India. Her range of characters simplifies her technique; she does not have to struggle to present Indian conversation in English (a problem which bedevils many other Indian novelists writing in English) as most of her characters are the kind of people who would talk and think in English in real life.

Sahgal has a first-hand knowledge of politics and political figures in India, for she spent much of her childhood in Anand Bhawan, the ancestral home of the Nehrus in Allahabad. One could say that politics is in her blood—Jawaharlal Nehru was her mother's brother, while her father died because of an illness he suffered in prison when he was jailed for participating in India's freedom struggle. An important political event forms the background for each of her novels. Her first novel, *A Time to Be Happy*, presents the dawn of Indian Independence. *This Time of Morning* comes later, when the initial euphoria has worn off, and things no longer look rosy. *Storm in Chandigarh* deals with the partition of the Punjab on linguistic lines just when the state had recovered from the trauma of the 1947 Partition. *A Situation in New Delhi* presents the Indian capital faced with the After-Nehru-Who question; established politicians have given up all moral values, and the frustrated youth are becoming Naxalites (Communist extremists). But sometimes this political consciousness is not transmuted fully in artistic terms. Some of her characters are easily recognizable public figures: Kailash Sinha (Krishna Menon) in *This Time of Morning* or Shivraj (Jawaharlal Nehru) in *A Situation in New Delhi* are two examples. Her autobiographies, *Prison and Chocolate Cake* and *From Fear Set Free*, are more satisfying than her earlier novels. Her best book is *The Day in Shadow* where personal concerns take precedence over politics. The heroine Simrit Raman, a writer, is a divorcée (like Sahgal herself), and the novel shows the prejudice she faces in male-dominated Indian society. She grows close to Raj, an idealistic Member of Parliament who shares her values, unlike her husband who believes in money-making above all. Sahgal gives an authentic picture of high-level politicians and bureaucrats, wrapped up in their cocktail parties, worried more about themselves than about the problems which face the country. The mutual attraction between Simrit and Raj is not primarily sexual. As in her other novels, Sahgal suggests that marriage is not just a sexual relationship, it means companionship on equal terms. She pleads for a basic honesty in human relationships, whether they are between man and woman or the ruler and the ruled.

Because of her birth and upbringing, Shagal makes an ide[al] spokesman for the western-educated Indian who finds it difficult [to] come to terms with India. As her character Sanad in *A Time to B[e] Happy* confesses, "I don't belong entirely to India. I can't. M[y] education, my upbringing, and my sense of values have all com[-]bined to make me unIndian....Of course there can be no question [of] my belonging to any other country." Jawaharlal Nehru, too, ha[s] articulated the same problem when he wrote in his *Autobiograph[y]*: "I have become a queer mixture of the East and the West, out [of] place everywhere, at home nowhere. Perhaps my thoughts an[d] approach to life are more akin to what is called Western tha[n] Eastern, but India clings to me, as she does to all her children, i[n] innumerable ways." This realization leads to a passionate concer[n] with the Indian heritage and its meaning in the modern age; all [of] Nayantara Sahgal's novels are concerned with the present deca[-]dence of India, and how creative use can be made of its past. It is thi[s] concern with the country which led her to protest openly against th[e] Emergency imposed by her cousin Indira Gandhi when the majorit[y] of Indian writers preferred to keep silent. Her political acumen ha[s] led her to anticipate Mrs. Gandhi's action, and she had cautione[d] against it in her weekly newspaper column. Her latest books sho[w] that she deserves attention as a political commentator, not only as [a] novelist.

—Shyamala A. Naraya[n]

ST. OMER, Garth. West Indian. Born in Castries, St. Lucia. Educated at the University of the West Indies, Kingston, Jamaica, degree in French. Has lived in France, Ghana, and England. Address: c/o Faber and Faber Ltd., 3 Queen Square, London WC1N 3AU, England.

PUBLICATIONS

Novels

A Room on the Hill. London, Faber, 1968.
Shades of Grey. London, Faber, 1968.
Nor Any Country. London, Faber, 1969.
J—, Black Bam and the Masqueraders. London, Faber, 1972.

Uncollected Short Story

"Syrop," in *Introduction 2*. London, Faber, 1968.

* * *

Garth St. Omer creates in his fiction characters filled with an unrest which they themselves cannot define or explain. It is a *malaise* of the islands which makes them hesitate even before opportunities which are apparently dazzling, which makes them hurt and abandon those they love, or turn aside from courses of action they have embarked on with every sign of conviction. The immediacy of his writing springs from the fact that he is so involved himself with this unrest that he is not yet able to distance or judge his heroes. The passion and the pain of these young island lives are fully conveyed, but it is perhaps this very lack of distance that makes his writing, at present, ideally suited to the novella form. His reputation was first made with "Syrop," and the fact that he followed his first novel with a volume comprising two more novellas demonstrates his addiction to the form.

"Syrop" is a harsh, tragic story of a family blighted by inexplicable misfortune, as well as by the poverty they share with their neighbours. Syrop, the young hero, differs from other St. Omer protagonists in that he doesn't live to carry his anguish and restlessness into adult life. He is smashed by a ship's propellers, diving for pennies on the very day he has been chosen to join the fishing crews, and on the eve of his much-loved brother's return from prison. John Lestrade, in St. Omer's first novel, *A Room on the Hill*, is older and tougher, but still haunted by intimate misfortunes and early deaths in his little island circle of relatives, friends and lovers. This book ends with a hard gesture towards departure, for it is increasingly obvious that all who stay in the island are doomed or lost, and Lestrade is determined to survive and transmute grief into action.

Of the two stories in *Shades of Grey* the first, "The Lights on the Hill," is the more tightly organised. It starts at a moment of crisis in the hero's relationship with Thea, the beautiful and original girl whom he has long desired and who now loves him. Neither can explain the nature of this crisis and it can only cause pain to them both, yet Stephenson knows in his being that he must now leave her. The madman's cry from the asylum which punctuates this realisation begins and ends the story. In between these cries (or are they the same?) St. Omer cross-cuts a number of short scenes from the hero's past in Jamaica and in his native St. Lucia. We see him charcoal-burning with his father and his illiterate brother Carl in the mountains, or seeking refuge with his mother in the empty barracks on the Morne after the Castries fire of 1948, or drifting into corruption, trial and dismissal as a petty official in the Civil Service. And we see the other affairs, some furtive and bourgeois, others casual and earthy, which have preceded all the phases of his rich relationship with Thea. Through it all we are conscious of the two lovers sitting on the hillside, smoking and talking in the darkness, numbed by their awareness that some force within him is sweeping them apart. The writing is full of sharp, perfectly registered dialogue. His narrative and descriptive passages are rendered throughout in short, rather spikey paragraphs and staccato sentences, which carry the same burden of unease as the lives they describe. The effect can occasionally be irritating for the reader who longs for a deeper and more measured breath. Again, it is a style for the novella rather than the novel, but it perfectly fits the peculiar and sustained tension of this story in which jobs, lives and love affairs are all snapped off before fruition.

The second story, "Another Place Another Time," adopts a more chronological approach to a short period in the boyhood of its hero, Derek Charles. It lacks the originality and power of the first, but is full of a distinctive pain of its own. This pain stems largely from the sheer unlikeableness of this boy. He is priggish, snobbish, and jumpy, difficult to reach. He behaves brutally to Berthe, the simple girl whom he seduces and throws over. Yet we see in this society of few and roving males, of unfathered children, abortions, poverty and abandonment, how difficult it is for the growing child to find models by which to climb to maturity. It is as though leaving the island were an indispensable part of growing up, a *rite de passage* from which most of the initiates never return. The story is a cry from the forest of exile, a cry to which St. Omer fits the words of Shakespeare: "How like a winter has my absence been/From thee."

St. Omer is particularly good at rendering the speech of those who, though educated elsewhere, are still very close to the islands and unable to relate their living satisfactorily to any other place. The uncertainty of their position is registered in the groping movement of the sentences with which they seek to explain their lives. The handling of dialogue is less successful where it derives from the *patois* of St. Lucia, a dialect largely of French derivation for which St. Omer tries to find an English dialect equivalent. The shape and rhythm of this dialect are necessarily very different from those of *patois*, and the effect, despite an occasional "oui" or "non" at the end of a sentence, is vaguely West Indian rather than specifically St. Lucian. Yet it is hard to think of any more faithful alternative which would not leave most readers struggling.

To Peter Breville in *Nor Any Country*, as to all St. Omer's heroes, the memories of St. Lucia are the sore tooth which mars his enjoyment of more exotic pleasures and experiences. That nagging pain draws him at last to revisit the island in which he has left for eight years a scarcely-known wife, married only because of her pregnancy. Yet the return, which perhaps he hoped would be purgative, leads to a partial acceptance of what he is and has ever been. Phyllis is still there, still young, still open to his love and still able to awaken his lust. Peter's long-standing resentment of her existence is modified by what he sees of other lives forgotten during his absence. His brother Paul, who likewise impregnated a local girl, has become a special kind of island failure because of his refusal to marry her. The girl herself has committed suicide but her neglected son Michael has survived, whereas Peter's marriage has produced the mirror image of twins born and dead in his absence but a neglected wife who survives to challenge his egotism by her presence. At the end of his week-long visit Peter knows that he must take both Phyllis and Michael with him now. By this single gesture he will attempt to redeem the past. *Nor Any Country* thus ends on a more positive note than any of St. Omer's earlier writing. It stints nothing of the narrow fate attending those who stay in the islands. The failures lie steeped in rum and self-pity, whilst the few successes grow flashy and Americanised in their loud insecurity. Yet, when all this is said, it was the long-postponed return to the island which brought Peter Breville to his late maturity. For the last *rite de passage* is the reunification with one's origins, without which the cycle of exile can never be complete.

J—, Black Bam and the Masqueraders is a return to the themes and situations of *Nor Any Country*, with the same actors. The approach in this short novel is less naturalistic, intermingling long epistles from Paul (in St. Lucia) to Peter (in Europe), with snatches from the life of Peter in exile. There is far less memorable descriptive writing than in any of St. Omer's earlier work. The anguish of personal failure is as strong as ever, but this book gives off a powerful odour of decay. The actions, motives, and lost possibilities of the past are being raked over and examined yet again, but the novelist himself impresses us as a talent desperately in need of an entirely new subject.

—Gerald Moore

SALINGER, J(erome) D(avid). American. Born in New York City, 1 January 1919. Educated at McBurney School, New York; Valley Forge Military Academy (editor, *Crossed Sabres*), graduated 1936; New York University, 1937; Ursinus College, Collegetown, Pennsylvania, 1938; Columbia University, New York, 1939. Served in the 4th Infantry Division of the United States Army, 1942-46: Staff Sergeant. Married Claire Douglas in 1955 (divorced, 1967); one daughter and one son. Has lived in New Hampshire since 1953. Agent: Harold Ober Associates, 40 East 49th Street, New York, New York 10017, U.S.A.

PUBLICATIONS

Novel

The Catcher in the Rye. Boston, Little Brown, and London, Hamish Hamilton, 1951.

Short Stories

Nine Stories. Boston, Little Brown, 1953; as *For Esmé—With Love and Squalor and Other Stories*, London, Hamish Hamilton, 1953.

Franny and Zooey. Boston, Little Brown, 1961; London, Heinemann, 1962.

Raise High the Roof Beam, Carpenters, and Seymour: An Introduction. Boston, Little Brown, and London, Heinemann, 1963.

Uncollected Short Story

"Hapworth 16, 1924" in *New Yorker*, 19 June 1965.

*

Bibliography: *J.D. Salinger: A Thirty Year Bibliography 1938-1968* by Kenneth Starosciak, privately printed, 1971.

Critical Studies (selection): *The Fiction of J.D. Salinger* by Frederick L. Gwynn and Joseph L. Blotner, Pittsburgh, University of Pittsburgh Press, 1958, London, Spearman, 1960; *J.D. Salinger and the Critics* edited by William F. Belcher and James W. Lee, Bel mont, California, Wadsworth, 1962; *J.D. Salinger* by Warren French, New York, Twayne, 1963, revised edition, 1976; *Studies in J.D. Salinger* edited by Marvin Laser and Norman Fruman, New York, Odyssey Press, 1963; *Salinger: A Critical and Personal Portrait* edited by Henry Anatole Grunwald, New York, Harper, 1963, London, Owen, 1964; *J.D. Salinger* by James E. Miller, Minneapolis, University of Minnesota Press, 1965; *J.D. Salinger* by James Lundquist, New York, Ungar, 1978.

* * *

In terms of subject matter, the fiction of J.D. Salinger falls into two groups. His most celebrated work, *The Catcher in the Rye*, tells of several days in the life of a young man, Holden Caulfield, after he has left the school from which he has been expelled; he wanders around New York City in a late-adolescent pursuit of contacts that will have meaning for him. The novel itself is Holden's meditation on these days some months later when he is confined to a West Coast clinic. The rest of Salinger's work, with the exception of some of the stories in *Nine Stories*, has for its subject elements drawn from the experience of the Glass family who live in New York. The parents, Les and Bessie, are retired vaudeville dancers; Les is Jewish in origin, Bessie Catholic—a fact that announces the merging of religious traditions effected in the lives of their children. The children, begotten over a considerable period of time, are seven in number. There are Seymour, a gifted poet; Buddy, a writer; Walker and Wake, twins—one killed in war, the other finally a priest; Boo Boo, a happily married daughter; and two much younger children, Franny and Zooey.

The diverse subject matter of Salinger's fiction tends, in retrospect, to coalesce. Holden Caulfield's parents, less loving and concerned than the Glass couple, have also begotten several children. But in Holden's case, there is only one child—a ten-year-old girl—to whom Holden can turn in his desperation.

But it is not just the mirror-image of subject matter that binds the Caulfield narrative together with the tales of the Glass family. There are a unity of tone and a prevailing interest that inform all of Salinger's narratives and that have made them appeal deeply to readers for two decades. The tone and interest combine to produce a sad, often ironic meditation on the plight of young persons who are coming to maturity in a society where precise and guiding values are absent. This recurrent meditation, concealed in wrappings that are usually grotesque and farcical, has drawn readers to Salinger. His characters move through a "world they never made"; they address questions to that world and receive, for the most part, only a "dusty answer." Casual social contacts so nauseate Holden Caulfield, for example, that he is frequently at the point of vomiting. His quest for love is harassed by the sexual basis of love, and he is repelled. The only good relation in his life rests on the affection he feels for his younger sister; she is the one light in a wilderness of adult hypocrisy, lust, and perversion. In contrast, affection takes in a larger area in the Glass family chronicles; mutual esteem and concern bind the family together and somewhat offset the dreary vision of human relations in *The Catcher in the Rye*.

Perhaps one reason for this contrast is that, in *The Catcher in the Rye*, the narrative is presented from the point of view of Holden, a malleable, only half-conscious person. He moves in many directions, but none leads him toward the goals he aspires to. His teachers are "phonies"; the one in whom he puts some trust turns out to be a homosexual. His encounter with a prostitute gives him nothing, and his relations with girls of his class do not offer him the gift of comprehension. His parents are as deceived as he is about the proper use of the gift of life. As indicated, only his young sister can offer him the love he needs, and she is too immature to counterbalance the panorama of insincerity that unfolds before Holden's eyes. So for Holden, all is in suspense—an effect that appealed strongly to Salinger's readers.

But for members of the Glass family, all is not fully in suspense. That gifted group of young people has indeed been badly shaken by the suicide of Seymour, their most gifted sibling. Thus, the central "mystery" which they must come to terms with is not Holden's general panorama of hypocrisy; the death and even more the remembered life of Seymour contain a secret that they are haunted by. The actual death of Seymour is briefly narrated in the story, "A Perfect Day for Bananafish," in *Nine Stories*. Later work, told from various points of view, relates the efforts of members of the Glass family to grasp and apply the eclectic religious truths that the memory of Seymour reminds them of. In none of these tales is there an effort to explain the suicide; this is a fact which the brothers and sisters accept rather than assess. What they do assess, in terms of their own later experience, is the teaching presence of Seymour as they recall it. In the two sections of *Franny and Zooey*, the two youngest members of the family reach out in directions that Seymour, in effect, has already pointed out. In "Franny" the heroine is obsessed by the "Jesus prayer" which she has come across in the memoirs of a Russian monk; she does not know how to pray the prayer and is only aware that, until she does, all her other relations will be without meaning. In "Zooey" her charming brother helps her and himself to come to a grasp of what Seymour's existence had announced: repetition of the Jesus prayer transforms life that is contemptible into a constant act of love and reveals that a "fat lady" is indeed Christ—the "fat lady" and every other human being one encounters. In "Raise High the Roof Beam, Carpenters"—told from the point of view of Buddy, the writing brother—the ridiculous circumstances of Seymour's wedding day are related; Seymour and his fiancée finally elope rather than endure an elaborate and empty wedding ceremony. Finally, in "Seymour: An Introduction"—also told from the point of view of Buddy—all that can be recalled of Seymour is put down. Recalled are his mastery of the allusive oriental haiku and his even more important mastery of the process of extorting the greatest significance from trivial event (e.g., a game of marbles becomes a vehicle of Zen instruction).

It is undoubtedly the merging of Eastern and Western religious wisdom—the solution of the "mystery" of existence—that gives the work of Salinger its particular élan. In pursuit of what might be called the Seymour effect, the other Glasses consume innumerable packs of cigarettes and break out into perspiration when they find themselves in blind alleys. But the alleys occasionally open up, and fleeting vistas of human unity flash before the eyes. One can but hope that Holden Caulfield, in his later years, will meet one of the younger Glasses whose personal destinies swell to the proportions of regulative myth.

—Harold H. Watts

SALKEY, (Felix) Andrew (Alexander). Jamaican. Born in Colon, Panama, 30 January 1928. Educated at St. George's College, Kingston, Jamaica; Munro College, St. Elizabeth, Jamaica; University of London (Thomas Helmore Poetry Prize, 1955), B.A. in

English 1955. Married Patricia Verden in 1957; two sons. English teacher in a London comprehensive school, 1957-59; interviewer and scriptwriter, BBC External Services (Radio), London, 1952-76. Since 1976, Professor of Creative Writing, Hampshire College, Massachusetts. Recipient: Guggenheim Fellowship, 1960; Casa de las Americas Poetry Prize, 1979. Address: Flat 8, Windsor Court, Moscow Road, London W.2, England.

PUBLICATIONS

Novels

A Quality of Violence. London, Hutchinson, 1959.
Escape to an Autumn Pavement. London, Hutchinson, 1960.
The Late Emancipation of Jerry Stover. London, Hutchinson, 1968.
The Adventures of Catullus Kelly. London, Hutchinson, 1969.
Come Home, Malcolm Heartland. London, Hutchinson, 1976.

Short Stories

Anancy's Score. London, Bogle L'Ouverture, 1973.

Verse

Jamaica. London, Hutchinson, 1973.
Land. London, Readers and Writers Publishing Cooperative, 1976.
In the Hills Where Her Dreams Live: Poems for Chile 1973-1978. Havana, Casa de las Americas, 1979.
Away. London, Allison and Busby, 1980.

Other

Hurricane (juvenile). London, Oxford University Press, 1964; New York, Oxford University Press, 1979.
Earthquake (juvenile). London, Oxford University Press, 1965; New York, Roy, 1969.
Drought (juvenile). London, Oxford University Press, 1966.
The Shark Hunters (school reader). London, Nelson, 1966.
Riot (juvenile). London, Oxford University Press, 1967.
Jonah Simpson (juvenile). London, Oxford University Press, 1969; New York, Roy, 1970.
Havana Journal. London, Penguin, 1971.
Georgetown Journal: A Caribbean Writer's Journey from London via Port of Spain to Georgetown, Guyana, 1970. London, New Beacon, 1972.
Joey Tyson (juvenile). London, Bogle L'Ouverture, 1974.
The River That Disappeared (juvenile). London, Bogle L'Ouverture, 1980.
Danny Jones (juvenile). London, Bogle L'Ouverture, 1980.

Editor, *West Indian Stories.* London, Faber, 1960.
Editor, *Stories from the Caribbean.* London, Elek, 1965; as *Island Voices: Stories from the West Indies*, New York, Liveright, 1970.
Editor, Caribbean Section, *Young Commonwealth Poets '65.* London, Heinemann, 1965.
Editor, *Caribbean Prose.* London, Evans, 1967.
Editor, *Breaklight: An Anthology of Caribbean Poetry.* London, Hamish Hamilton, 1971; as *Breaklight: The Poetry of the Caribbean*, New York, Doubleday, 1972.
Editor, with others, *Savacou 3* and *4.* Kingston, Jamaica, and London, Caribbean Artists Movement, 1972.
Editor, *Caribbean Essays.* London, Evans, 1973.
Editor, *Writing in Cuba since the Revolution.* London, Bogle L'Ouverture, 1977.
Editor, *Caribbean Folk Tales and Legends.* London, Bogle L'Ouverture, 1980.

*

Critical Study: review by Edward Brathwaite, in *Bim* (Bridgetown, Barbados), 1959.

Theatrical Activities:

Actor: **Film**—*Reggae* (narrator), 1978.

* * *

Andrew Salkey's first novel, *A Quality of Violence*, is his best, a powerful account of savagery and superstition in a Jamaican village in 1900. Because of drought, the villagers begin to despair of reason, and turn to older, darker ways. A white cock is strangled, two men whip each other ritually till both are dead, and eventually a woman is sacrificed, stoned to death. The *obeah* cult mixes African and Christian forms, and the prologue indicates wider associations: "The drought brings a touch of madness to the land, a kind of rebellion, and a quality of compelling suicide which Calvary once witnessed. Drought first began on Calvary." Related is the conflict between old ways and new: doctors and police are imposed on this society. The hysteria and fickleness of mobs are shown, and also the oddness of children, and the strange things that are important to them. The writing is effective, jagged and unusual, but above all this is a dramatic novel, full of tension and excitement, so it is never certain what will happen next.

Escape to an Autumn Pavement takes a more familiar subject for a Caribbean book: the experiences of Johnnie, an alert West Indian in London. He works as a waiter, and learns about class and prejudice. But there is a marked sexual theme: he is torn between a demanding girl and a homosexual who tempts him. The form is disjointed thoughts passing through Johnnie's mind; such section titles as "Notes in the Present for a Time Past" suggest a sophisticated sense of time. This is Salkey's most literary book, its style the most artificial. Late evening is pictured with a kind of poetic immediacy:

> Oxford Street with its squeaking silences under shutters. Wonderland beacons continue their ogling unashamedly with the traffic lights. Sticky, biscuit-sweet, soggy lovers huddle together in a make-believe which excludes Mom and Pop. Can feel the presence of cash registers along the street. But this is different. The moment is magic. The weightiness is different. It's haunting. Metallic buddha-kind of weightiness. Plump and couchant, in a way. A threat.

Several children's books followed, all set in Jamaica, with a rich sense of atmosphere, for shops, streets, and for the weather too. While description may be central in a book like *Hurricane*, a boy's account of a 1951 disaster, usually Salkey is striving for more. In *Drought* we wonder whether the children's spells or the adults with their rational means have finally brought rain. In *Riot* we are asked to ponder whether the unionists who organize a demonstration which turns violent are heroes, unscrupulous orators, or men lacking any clear plan.

Pessimism about the role of the West Indian dominates the third and fourth adult novels. *The Late Emancipation of Jerry Stover* has a young man in Jamaica just before independence, and Salkey re-creates the social-political atmosphere of the time. Jerry seeks a purpose, but devotes energy too to girls, drinking cheap rum, and pointless trips in ancient cars into the country. He leaves his job to work full time among the poor members of the Rastafarian sect on the Dunghill, and persuades his friends, a group called the Termites because they believe they are boring at the Establishment, to assist this work. But then they are killed in a landslide, all but Jerry and an American girl, an outsider. The moral is explicit: "They had no private philosophy, no binding discipline, no real faith in anything. All they had was their freedom, an emancipation that had come much too late. They had not had the time and the kind of society in which to use it intelligently, to benefit from it, to build on it."

The Adventures of Catullus Kelly takes a young, educated Jamaican to London, a man similar to Johnnie and Jerry. The form is rambling—presumbably to echo Catullus's crumbling sanity—as his protagonist tries teaching, free-lance broadcasting, and working in a coffee bar. He is also involved with innumerable girls, at times in pairs, and once on the plinth of Nelson's Column: "he plinthed; they plinthed, like impious pigeons." The year in London results—arbitrarily, perhaps—in a mental hospital in Jamaica. Salkey sees the man as *used* in white society, as a black or as a sex object, and Catullus cannot interest other blacks in *négritude*. Catullus's two languages—received English and Caribbean dialect—are both displayed, but despite verbal flourishes, this is Salkey's weakest novel.

Anancy's Score consists of 20 fables about the traditional spiderman folk-hero of Africa and the Caribbean, told in a rich Jamaican-English dialect. Through the mythic and anarchic Anancy, Salkey provides high-spirited laughter and a dash of social comment from the Third World.

—Malcolm Page

SARGESON, Frank. New Zealander. Born in Hamilton, 23 March 1903. Educated at Hamilton High School; University of New Zealand; admitted as Solicitor of the Supreme Court of New Zealand, 1926. Estates Clerk, New Zealand Public Trust, Wellington, 1928-29; has also worked as a journalist. Recipient: Centennial Literary Competition prize, 1940; New Zealand Government literary pension, 1947-68; Hubert Church Prize, 1952, 1968; Katherine Mansfield Award, 1965. Litt.D.: University of Auckland, 1974. Address: 14 Esmond Road, Takapuna, Auckland 9, New Zealand.

PUBLICATIONS

Novels

When the Wind Blows. Christchurch, Caxton Press, 1945.
I Saw in My Dream. London, Lehmann, 1949.
I for One.... Christchurch, Caxton Press, 1954.
Memoirs of a Peon. London, MacGibbon and Kee, 1965.
The Hangover. London, MacGibbon and Kee, 1967.
Joy of the Worm. London, MacGibbon and Kee, 1969.
Man of England Now (includes *A Game of Hide and Seek* and *I for One...*). Christchurch, Caxton Press, and London, Martin Brian and O'Keeffe, 1972.
Sunset Village. London, Martin Brian and O'Keeffe, 1976.
En Route, in *Tandem*, with Edith Campion. Wellington, Reed, 1979.

Short Stories

Conversation with My Uncle and Other Sketches. Auckland, Unicorn Press, 1936.
A Man and His Wife. Christchurch, Caxton Press, 1940.
That Summer and Other Stories. London, Lehmann, 1946.
Collected Stories, 1935-1963, edited by Bill Pearson. Auckland, Blackwood and Janet Paul, 1964; London, MacGibbon and Kee, 1965; revised edition, as *The Stories of Frank Sargeson, 1935-1973*, Auckland, Longman Paul, 1973; London, Longman, 1974.
Short Stories by New Zealanders, with others, edited by P.C.N. Meikle. Auckland, Longman Paul, 1970.

Uncollected Short Stories

"Riding High," in *New Zealand Listener* (Wellington), November 1973.
"Romantic Agony," in *New Zealand Listener* (Wellington), February 1974.
"Making Father Pay," in *New Zealand Listener* (Wellington), June 1975.

Plays

A Time for Sowing (produced Auckland, 1961). Included in *Wrestling with the Angel*, 1964.
The Cradle and the Egg (produced Auckland, 1962). Included in *Wrestling with the Angel*, 1964.
Wrestling with the Angel: Two Plays: A Time for Sowing and The Cradle and the Egg. Christchurch, Caxton Press, 1964.

Other

Once Is Enough: A Memoir. Wellington, Reed, 1972; London, Martin Brian and O'Keeffe, 1973.
More Than Enough. Wellington, Reed, and London, Martin Brian and O'Keeffe, 1975.
Never Enough! Wellington, Reed, and London, Martin Brian and O'Keeffe, 1977.

Editor, *Speaking for Ourselves: A Collection of New Zealand Stories.* Christchurch, Caxton Press, 1945.

*

Bibliography: in *The Stories of Frank Sargeson*, 1973.

Manuscript Collection: Alexander Turnbull Library, Wellington.

Critical Studies: "Up onto the Roof and Down Again" by the author, in *Landfall* (Christchurch), December 1950-December 1951; *The Puritan and the Waif: A Symposium of Critical Essays on the Work of Frank Sargeson* edited by Helen Shaw, Auckland, Hoffmann, 1955; Introduction by Bill Pearson to *Collected Stories, 1935-1963*, 1964; "The Art of Frank Sargeson" by E.A. Horsman, in *Landfall* (Christchurch), 1965; *Frank Sargeson* by H. Winston Rhodes, New York, Twayne, 1969; "Wizard's Brew: Frank Sargeson's *Memoirs of a Peon*" by J.B. Ower, in *Landfall* (Christchurch), 1972; *Frank Sargeson in His Time* by Dennis McEldowney, Dunedin, McIndoe, 1976; *Frank Sargeson* by R.A. Copland, Wellington and London, Oxford University Press, 1977.

Frank Sargeson comments:

Speaking very broadly, I write my fiction out of an itch to impose some sort of order upon the chaos of existence: but more particularly, because as a schoolboy I became much aware that I was a European born in a country very remote from Europe: in the form of fiction I have *had* to say what in my view it means to be a New Zealander.

* * *

In a public tribute to Frank Sargeson on the occasion of his fiftieth birthday his fellow-craftsmen in New Zealand described him as "a liberating influence on the literature of this country," and as one who had become "a symbol in his own time." Such expressions of esteem were neither rhetorical flourishes nor casual compliments, but indicated accurately and temperately the nature both of his achievement and his influence. He had become a symbol because from an early age he had dedicated himself to the craft of fiction in a society unwilling to recognise or encourage, much less reward, artistic endeavour. Despite a formidable array of obstacles, he had succeeded in creating an imaginative world that provided an indirect commentary on human relations and attitudes.

His early reputation, endorsed not only in New Zealand but also abroad by such writers as E.M. Forster, William Plomer, John Lehmann, and Walter Allen, was established on the basis of little more than a decade of experimental work in the short story; but he had continued to extend his range and develop his techniques. Much of his early work was related to experiences during the years of depression; some of the stories were slight moral fables; but all of them revealed an extraordinary control of the medium chosen. Sargeson's habitual mode was the first person narrative which, because his central characters were usually unable to give adequate expression to their thoughts and emotions, excluded authorial comment and any kind of sophisticated analysis. Yet what was so impressive was the manner in which he could suggest through concise and colloquial language both a pattern of ironies and a pattern of values. He was able to combine an unsentimental view of the human situation with a recognition of its underlying humour and pathos. It is by means of his Teds, Bills, Toms, and Freds, the flotsam and jetsam of human society, solitary figures who have either been discarded by or opted out of the conventional community that Sargeson reveals the ambiguities and paradoxes of New Zealand, and not only New Zealand, life.

Sargeson's world has been described as "sad and savage," but such a description neglects the positive values implicit in his ironic treatment of incident and attitude. E.M. Forster chose for special praise his evident belief in "the unsmart, the unregulated and the affectionate," and in so doing directed attention to the anti-puritanism which pervades his work. Although he was not the first writer to subject to a critical examination the characteristic New Zealand ethos, based precariously on an adulterated puritanism, Sargeson has been the most successful in exposing many of its more corrosive aspects. Suburbia becomes one of the main objects of his attack, with its pseudo-respectability and artificial refinement, its concern with prohibitions and appearances, its dubious morality and the emphasis placed on "making good" and "getting on," combined with its callous disregard for the feelings and aspirations of outsiders. The destructiveness of a debased puritanism is opposed to the creative life of the senses, the desire for human fellowship and affection in the absence of high prizes.

He was already engaged in the writing of longer fictions, but with the first part of *I Saw in My Dream* (1945) Sargeson had embarked on his second career as a novelist. *I for One...*, a short novel, followed; and both of these were concerned with the inhibiting effects of a puritanical environment. The former was perhaps a more ambitious but less successful attempt to link the outward behaviour of the central character with a stream of sub-conscious thoughts and feelings. Underneath its episodic structure and abrupt transitions there is an intricate pattern of correspondences and symbolic threads providing an unorthodox unity to a narrative concerned with a quest for identity and fulfilment. Many disparate elements contribute to this endeavour to capture a significant aspect of the New Zealand scene—*Pilgrim's Progress*, *Portrait of the Artist as a Young Man* and *Huckleberry Finn*, for Sargeson's originality is displayed by a willingness to adapt to his own use whatever seems applicable to the local situation. In like manner some of his techniques are traditional, even old-fashioned, although they gain fresh vitality from their re-employment to suit different circumstances and achieve different aims. *I for One...* is written in the form of a private diary but with such concealed contrivance that without interfering with the natural outpourings of a girl communing with herself the reader is able to understand more clearly than the diarist why she seems to be "one set apart." Sargeson's next novel, *Memoirs of a Peon*, was, at one and the same time, a satirical comedy, a picaresque narrative, an exploration of the quality of life in New Zealand and an exposure of what has been called "the cultural cringe." The masks that Sargeson is able to wear with ease are many and various. This time the narrative is in the hands of a super-annuated New Zealand Casanova "stung by the snake of memory," who glories in his past achievements. The style of narration has completely deserted the bare and laconic utterance of the early short stories, the flavour of the feminine diarist's reveries, or the overwrought youth's distracted ponderings. It is mannered and literary, pedantic and involved. Excluding its array of bizarre characters and hilarious incidents, the full significance of *Memoirs of a Peon* is accessible only to those who become aware that it is an elaborate satire on a series of different levels and that the mannered style, reminiscent of the 18th century, is part of the cultural cringe that is being satirised, just as the central character is condemning himself out of his own mouth as well as exposing New Zealand manners through the very complexities in which he is entangled.

The Hangover once again indicated that Sargeson has never been a follower of social realism. His plot structure is less concerned with the probabilities of life than the implications of living and, as in *Memoirs of a Peon*, his characters may be grotesques with an uncanny resemblance to real people. He produces fictions that are imaginative analogues to the reality of human experience. *The Hangover* disconcerted some readers who, because of what seemed to be a rapidly moving and horrifying dramatic story, failed to come to terms with the agility of Sargeson's mind and deeper concern with the humanities, "that elongated hangover from Socrates and the Academy." The central character, once more an adolescent youth with a puritan background, becomes mentally and emotionally confused by the world in which he lives. His puritan heritage is at odds with the imperatives of the affluent society based on the qualified technician and the accumulation of gadgets, but equally at odds with the beatnik way of life that rejects the "establishment" of the past as well as that of the present. By means of a series of symbolic threads, literary analogues and parallels with ritual and romance Sargeson transforms a narrative that could have carried only social and psychological implications into an imaginative and philosophical commentary on modern civilisation.

A similar transformation is performed in *Joy of the Worm*. This is a richly comic novel with tragic undertones. The wry comedy is concerned with a domineering clerical father and his son who, despite a critical recognition of the defects of the Reverend's character, becomes almost a walking parody of his father; and the tragedy is one of wives reduced to silence and extinguished as a direct consequence of the rationalising indifference and wordy intellectuality of their egotistical husbands. However, the terms "comedy" and "tragedy" are not easily applicable to any of Sargeson's fictions. In *Joy of the Worm* it is by a controlled and complex use of illusion and reality, by irony, patterned loquacity, and suggestion, and above all by language that he gains his effects and achieves significance. The illusion is to be found especially in the way in which event, banal though it may be, is transformed as it passes through the crucible of human speech; and it is the relation between illusion and reality that provides depth and substance to a narrative full of incidental perceptions.

Not the least remarkable feature of Sargeson's career as a writer has been the prolonged burst of creative activity during his later years. He has not only consolidated his position as a major New Zealand novelist, but has produced three volumes of memoirs that for their literary interest, their relevance to his own development, their vivid accounts of events, places, and especially people deserve to be ranked among his best narratives. *Once Is Enough*, *More Than Enough*, and *Never Enough* are so shaped and written that they acquire the characteristics of autobiographical fiction, for Sargeson has succeeded in imposing an artistic order on the chaos of his own existence. The first of these was published in the same year as two novellas, *Man of England Now* and *A Game of Hide and Seek*. The deceptive simplicity of the former conceals a successful attempt to cover a whole period of New Zealand social history, and in a manner that dispenses with any of the masks hitherto used by the author. In contradistinction, *A Game of Hide and Seek* is a witty and outrageous story of sexual deviants which lives up to its title in every sense of the words.

Sunset Village and *En Route* indicate that in theme and narrative style there has been no slackening of creative energy. As its title suggests, *Sunset Village* is centred on the elderly inhabitants of a housing settlement for pensioners, but their personal backgrounds and idiosyncracies, the pattern of their complex relationships and emotional entanglements, and above all the characteristic Sargesonian manner of the narrative give unexpected life and vitality to this tragi-comedy of declining years. As elsewhere, what could be described as grotesquerie does not inhibit an underlying commentary on the human comedy of existence and, in particular, on prevailing attitudes to the care of the elderly in a contemporary setting. In *En Route* both scene and characters are entirely different. With comic relish Sargeson follows the excursions of two middle-aged but exceedingly liberated women whose ostensible object is to relieve the solitude of lonely bachelors living in remote farm-houses, and to give them a little sexual excitement. The underlying theme of women's lib is enriched by the introduction of a younger generation in the person of the daughter of one of the excursionists, and by scattered references to a well-known "liberationist" of an earlier generation. The result is high comedy in a semi-historical context. Once again, the Sargesonian voice, dominating but unobtrusive, can be heard through every line of this exercise in fantastic realism.

Although not far from 80, Sargeson has remained an experimenter. He has adopted many masks, including that which is veritably his own. If, many years ago, he was regarded by his contemporaries as a liberating influence in New Zealand writing, today, having achieved much that he had set out to do, he has become widely acknowledged as a master of his craft.

—H. Winston Rhodes

SARTON, May. American. Born in Wondelgem, Belgium, 3 May 1912, daughter of the historian of science George Sarton; emigrated to the United States in 1916; naturalized, 1924. Educated at the Shady Hill School and The High and Latin School, both in Cambridge, Massachusetts. Apprentice, then Member, and Director of the Apprentice Group, Eva Le Gallienne's Civic Repertory Theatre, New York, 1930-33; Founder and Director, Apprentice Theatre, New York, and Associated Actors Inc., Hartford, Connecticut, 1933-36. Taught Creative Writing and Choral Speech, Stuart School, Boston, 1937-40. Documentary Scriptwriter, Office of War Information, 1944-45. Poet-in-Residence, Southern Illinois University, Carbondale, Summer 1945; Briggs-Copeland Instructor in English Composition, Harvard University, Cambridge, Massachusetts, 1950-53; Lecturer, Bread Loaf Writers Conference, Middlebury, Vermont, 1951-52, and Boulder Writers Conference, Colorado, 1953-54; Phi Beta Kappa Visiting Scholar, 1959-60; Danforth Lecturer, 1960-61; Lecturer in Creative Writing, Wellesley College, Massachusetts, 1960-63; Poet-in-Residence, Lindenwood College, St. Charles, Missouri, 1964, 1965; Visiting Lecturer, Agnes Scott College, Decatur, Georgia, Spring 1972. Recipient: New England Poetry Club Golden Rose, 1945; Bland Memorial Prize, 1945 (*Poetry*, Chicago); American Poetry Society Reynolds Prize, 1953; Bryn Mawr College Lucy Martin Donnelly Fellowship, 1953; Guggenheim Fellowship, 1954; Johns Hopkins University Poetry Festival Award, 1961; National Endowment for the Arts grant, 1966; Sarah Josepha Hale Award, 1972. Litt.D.: Russell Sage College, Troy, New York, 1958; New England College, Henniker, New Hampshire, 1971; Bates College, Lewiston, Maine, 1974; Colby College, Waterville, Maine, 1974; Clark University, Worcester, Massachusetts, 1975; University of New Hampshire, Durham, 1976; King School of the Ministry, Berkeley, California, 1976. Fellow, American Academy of Arts and Sciences. Address: Box 99, York, Maine 04104, U.S.A.

PUBLICATIONS

Novels

The Single Hound. Boston, Houghton Mifflin, and London, Cresset Press, 1938.
The Bridge of Years. New York, Doubleday, 1946.
Shadow of a Man. New York, Rinehart, 1950; London, Cresset Press, 1952.
A Shower of Summer Days. New York, Rinehart, 1952; London, Hutchinson, 1954.
Faithful Are the Wounds. New York, Rinehart, and London, Gollancz, 1955.
The Birth of a Grandfather. New York, Rinehart, 1957; London, Gollancz, 1958.
The Small Room. New York, Norton, 1961; London, Gollancz, 1962.
Joanna and Ulysses. New York, Norton, 1963; London, Murray, 1964.
Mrs. Stevens Hears the Mermaids Singing. New York, Norton, 1965; London, Peter Owen, 1966.
Miss Pickthorn and Mr. Hare: A Fable. New York, Norton, 1966; London, Dent, 1968.
Kinds of Love. New York, Norton, 1970.
As We Are Now. New York, Norton, 1973; London, Gollancz, 1974.
Crucial Conversations. New York, Norton, 1975; London, Gollancz, 1976.
A Reckoning. New York, Norton, 1978; London, Gollancz, 1980.

Plays

The Underground River. New York, Play Club, 1947.

Screenplays: *Toscanini: The Hymn of Nations*, 1944; *Valley of the Tennessee*, 1944.

Verse

Encounter in April. Boston, Houghton Mifflin, 1937.
Inner Landscape. Boston, Houghton Mifflin, 1939; with a selection from *Encounter in April*, London, Cresset Press, 1939.
The Lion and the Rose. New York, Rinehart, 1948.
The Leaves of the Tree. Mount Vernon, Iowa, Cornell College, 1950.
The Land of Silence and Other Poems. New York, Rinehart, 1953.
In Time like Air. New York, Rinehart, 1957.
Cloud, Stone, Sun, Vine: Poems, Selected and New. New York, Norton, 1961.
A Private Mythology: New Poems. New York, Norton, 1966.
As Does New Hampshire and Other Poems. Peterborough, New Hampshire, Richard R. Smith, 1967.
A Grain of Mustard Seed: New Poems. New York, Norton, 1971.
A Durable Fire: New Poems. New York, Norton, 1972.
Collected Poems 1930-1973. New York, Norton, 1974.
Selected Poems, edited by Serena Sue Hilsinger and Lois Byrnes. New York, Norton, 1978.
Halfway to Silence. New York, Norton, 1980.

Other

The Fur Person: The Story of a Cat. New York, Rinehart, 1957; London, Muller, 1958.
I Knew a Phoenix: Sketches for an Autobiography. New York, Holt Rinehart, 1959; London, Peter Owen, 1963.
Plant Dreaming Deep (autobiography). New York, Norton, 1968.
The Poet and the Donkey (juvenile). New York, Norton, 1969.
Journal of a Solitude. New York, Norton, 1973.
Punch's Secret (juvenile). New York, Harper, 1974.
A World of Light: Portraits and Celebrations. New York, Norton, 1976.
A Walk Through the Woods (juvenile). New York, Harper, 1976.
The House by the Sea: A Journal. New York, Norton, 1977; London, Prior, 1978.
Recovering: A Journal 1978-1979. New York, Norton, 1980.

*

Bibliography: *May Sarton: A Bibliography* by Lenora P. Blouin, Metuchen, New Jersey, Scarecrow Press, 1978.

Ianuscript Collection: Berg Collection, New York Public Library.

'ritical Study: *May Sarton* by Agnes Sibley, New York, Twayne, 972.

Aay Sarton comments:

The novelists of the moderate human voice, from Trollope ırough Tchekov and Forster, are not in fashion, but I like to elieve that I am in their line of descent, for what has interested me lways is ordinary human relations, the heroism, despair, and rich omplex fibre of day to day living among the middle class. Euro-ean as I am by birth, it was natural that my first four novels should e laid in Europe, Belgium and England—my father was Belgian nd my mother English—though the important thing has never een the setting but the intimate relationships explored. Five of the ovels are centered in a marriage, from the coming of age through ıarriage of a young man (*Shadow of a Man*), to a marriage in its ıiddle years (*The Bridge of Years*), to late middle age (*The Birth of Grandfather*), and old age (*Kinds of Love*). The other major theme f my novels has been how the singular man or woman may find his lentity and/or fulfillment through an art or profession. In two ases the protagonist is homosexual, a male professor in *Faithful re the Wounds*, and a female poet in *Mrs. Stevens Hears the Aermaids Singing*. The former is a relentless exploration of the ffect of a suicide (a political suicide) on the protagonist's colleagues t Harvard University. The latter is a study of the woman as artist. nd the theme of the value of the single woman to society is touched n again in a novel, *The Small Room*, laid in a woman's college. 'inally there is a group of slighter short novels, humorous or poetic ccounts of how solitary individuals—a woman painter, a male oet—have dealt with kinds of deprivation, and triumphed.

It is my hope that all the novels, the books of poems, and the utobiographical works may come to be seen as a whole, the com-nunication of a vision of life that is unsentimental, humorous, assionate, and, in the end, timeless. We can bear any Hell if we can 'break through" to each other and come to understand ourselves.

* * *

May Sarton (also a poet and memoirist) is particularly skillful at haracter development and the examination of the pleasures and lifficulties of important human relationships, steadily analyzing er characters' simultaneous needs for independence from and nion with others.

She is also very able in the evocation of place, and setting is often entral to her novels. The physical and intellectual milieu of Boston nd Harvard in *Faithful Are the Wounds*, for example, symbolizes he characters' habits of introspection and self-analysis which gen-rate the action. *Kinds of Love* is set in Willard, New Hampshire, luring its bicentennial, and several characters have important esponsibilities for the celebration. Their researches into the vil-age's changes and consistencies parallel their serious consideration of the stable and the unstable patterns of their own lives, resulting in splendid unification of action and theme. *Kinds of Love* is also a ound portrait of modern New England village life, and, when ontrasted with the equally vivid European settings of such earlier works as *The Single Hound*, *The Bridge of Years*, and *A Shower of Summer Days*, reveals Sarton's deep love for her adopted homeland as well as her appreciation of her European heritage and roots. *Joanna and Ulysses* is set on Santorini. The Aegean island's well-endered atmosphere, its isolation, and its distance from Joanna's ıome all dramatize her growing understanding of her obligations to herself as opposed to her obligations to her father. This wedding of heme and setting is one of Sarton's greatest strengths.

One of the author's most significant themes is her protagonists' professional commitment. *Mrs. Stevens Hears the Mermaids Sing-ing* is a portrait of an elderly writer, based on Sarton herself, reflecting upon her life and work. She reconfirms the worth of her writing, recognizing and accepting the fact that professional dedica-tion often impinges upon love and friendship. In contrast, Lucy Winter, protagonist of *The Small Room*, is depicted at the outset of her career as a professor. Having undertaken her job almost acci-dentally, Lucy falls in love with her work even as she achieves a realistic understanding of it. The demands of original research are delineated in the portrayal of a highly revered senior professor, and those of the classroom are conveyed through the characterization of a brilliant but deeply troubled student. *The Small Room* offers a remarkably fair and moving analysis of the joys as well as the responsibilities of academe.

Like *Mrs. Stevens Hears the Mermaids Singing* and *Joanna and Ulysses*, *The Small Room* presents useful insights into modes of balancing human relationships against professional drive, always stressing the fact that honorable commitment to one's talent demands sacrifice and self-discipline. Sarton's belief that this level of dedication is particularly taxing for women is clearly evident in these three important works.

Some novels explore major social problems. The powerful *Faith-ful Are the Wounds* depicts anti-communist witch hunts while it examines the effect of Edward Cavan's suicide upon his circle of friends. *Crucial Conversations*, a somewhat weaker novel, incorpo-rates insights about the Viet Nam War and the Watergate scandal into the account of Poppy Whitelaw's late decision to abandon marriage to attempt a career as a sculptor. The brilliant *As We Are Now* denounces substandard care for the infirm through Caro Spencer's struggle to control her own destiny as well as to preserve her very sense of self within the debasing atmosphere of the "home" into which she has been remanded. Plot and social commentary are always firmly united, translating sweeping issues into human terms.

With Keats, Sarton believes that the fruitful life is a continuing process of "soul-making"; this theme, particularly well conveyed in *The Birth of a Grandfather*, which recounts Sprig Wyeth's devel-opment as husband, father, and friend, is almost invariably present in the author's work. Used as a positive motivation in that novel and in *A Reckoning*, the effective story of Laura Spelman's responses to cancer and approaching death, it also lends biting irony to *As We Are Now*.

Willing to confront challenging issues and basic human prob-lems, Sarton has also experimented with form; her works range from the panoramic *Kinds of Love* through the slender, delicate *Joanna and Ulysses* to *As We Are Now*, spare and incisive. She has thus won deserved respect and wide popularity.

—Jane S. Bakerman

SCHULBERG, Budd (Wilson). American. Born in New York City, 27 March 1914; son of the Hollywood film pioneer, B.P. Schulberg. Educated at Los Angeles High School, 1928-31; Deer-field Academy, 1931-32; Dartmouth College, Hanover, New Hamp-shire, 1932-36, A.B. (cum laude) 1936. Served in the United States Navy, 1943-46: Lieutenant. Married 1) Virginia Ray in 1936 (divorced, 1942); 2) Victoria Anderson in 1943 (divorced, 1964); 3) the actress Geraldine Brooks in 1964; three children. Screenwriter in Hollywood, 1936-39. In charge of photographic evidence for the Nuremberg Trials; Boxing Editor, *Sports Illustrated*, New York, 1954. Has taught writing at Columbia University, New York, Phoe-nixville Veterans Hospital, University of the Streets, New York, Douglas Creative Arts Center, New York, Southampton College, New York, and Dartmouth College. Since 1958, President, Schul-berg Productions, New York, and since 1965, President, Douglass House Foundation, Watts, Los Angeles. Member, New York Council, Authors' Guild, 1958-60. Recipient: American Library Association Award, New York Critics Award, Foreign Corres-pondents Award, Screen Writers Guild Award, and Oscar, for screenplay, 1955; Christopher Award, 1956; German Film Critics Award, for screenplay, 1958. D.Litt.: Dartmouth College, 1960. Address: c/o Alyss Dorese, 41 West 82nd Street, New York, New York 10024, U.S.A.

PUBLICATIONS

Novels

What Makes Sammy Run? New York, Random House, and London, Jarrolds, 1941.
The Harder They Fall. New York, Random House, and London, Lane, 1947.
The Disenchanted. New York, Random House, 1950; London, Lane, 1951.
Waterfront. New York, Random House, 1955; London, Lane, 1956; as *On the Waterfront*, London, Corgi, 1959.
Sanctuary V. Cleveland, World, 1969; London, W.H. Allen, 1970.
Everything That Moves. New York, Doubleday, 1980; London, Robson, 1981.

Short Stories

Some Faces in the Crowd. New York, Random House, 1953; London, Lane, 1954.

Uncollected Short Stories

"Road to Recovery," in *New Stories for Men*, edited by Charles Grayson. New York, Doubleday, 1941.
"Somebody Has to Be Nobody," in *Post Stories 1941.* New York, Random House, 1941.
"The Real Viennese Schmaltz," in *The Best American Short Stories 1942*, edited by Martha Foley. Boston, Houghton Mifflin, 1942.
"Great South Sea Story," in *Continent's End*, edited by Joseph Henry Jackson. New York, McGraw Hill, 1944.
"Passport to Nowhere," in *These Your Children*, edited by Harold U. Ribalow. New York, Beechhurst Press, 1952.
"All the Town's Talking," in *This Week's Short-Short Stories*, edited by Stewart Beach. New York, Random House, 1953.
"The Barracudas," in *Playboy* (Chicago), 1958.
"A Second Father," in *Playboy* (Chicago), 1961.
"Say Goodnight to Owl," in *Redbook* (Dayton, Ohio), August 1965.
"Señor Discretion Himself," in *Playboy* (Chicago), January 1966.
"Spotlight," in *Famous Short Stories 1*, edited by Kurt Singer. Minneapolis, Denison, 1968.
"A Latin from Killarney," in *Playboy* (Chicago), January 1968.

Plays

Hollywood Doctor (broadcast, 1941). Published in *The Writer's Radio Theatre*, edited by Norman Weiser. New York, Harper, 1941.
Tomorrow (radio play), in *Free World Theatre*, edited by Arch Oboler and Stephen Longstreet. New York, Random House, 1944.
The Pharmacist's Mate, in *The Best Television Plays 1950-1951*, edited by William I. Kauffman. New York, Merlin Press, 1952.
A Face in the Crowd: A Play for the Screen. New York, Random House, 1957.
Across the Everglades: A Play for the Screen. New York, Random House, 1958.
The Disenchanted, with Harvey Breit, adaptation of the novel by Schulberg (produced New York, 1958). New York, Random House, 1959.
What Makes Sammy Run?, with Stuart Schulberg, music by Ervin Drake, adaptation of the novel by Budd Schulberg (produced New York, 1964).
On the Waterfront: Original Story and Screenplay, edited by Ma thew J. Bruccoli. Carbondale, Southern Illinois Universi Press, 1980.

Screenplays: *Little Orphan Annie*, with Samuel Ornitz and End Bohem, 1938; *Winter Carnival*, with Maurice Rapf and Lester Col 1939; *Weekend for Three*, with Dorothy Parker and Alan Cam bell, 1941; *Government Girl*, with Dudley Nichols, 1943; *Ci Without Men*, with Martin Berkeley and W.L. River, 1943; *On th Waterfront*, 1954; *A Face in the Crowd*, 1957; *Wind Across th Everglades*, 1958.

Radio Play: *Hollywood Doctor*, 1941.

Other

Loser and Still Champion: Muhammad Ali. New York, Doubl day, and London, New English Library, 1972.
The Four Seasons of Success. New York, Doubleday, 1972; Lo don, Robson, 1974.
Swan Watch, photographs by Geraldine Brooks. New Yor Delacorte Press, and London, Robson, 1975.
Moving Pictures: Memoirs of a Hollywood Prince. New Yor Stein and Day, 1981.

Editor, *From the Ashes: The Voices of Watts.* New York, Ne American Library, 1967.

*

Manuscript Collection: Princeton University, New Jersey.

Budd Schulberg comments:

(1972) I was raised in Hollywood, in the middle of the film capita and had an early education in the vicissitudes of success and failur I became convinced, before I was out of high school, that th dynamics of success and failure were of earthquake proportions i America, and that Hollywood was only an exaggerated version o the American success drive. Undoubtedly this influenced my firs novel, *What Makes Sammy Run?*, as it did *The Harder They Fal The Disenchanted*, and many other things I have tried to write. believe it is the prime American theme, and in fact I am now in th process of publishing a study of Sinclair Lewis, Scott Fitzgerald William Saroyan, Nathanael West, Thomas Heggen, and Joh Steinbeck, all writers I knew well, because I believe that the season of success and failure are more violent in America than anywhe else on earth. Witness only Herman Melville and Jack London, t name two of the victims.

I have been influenced by Mark Twain, by Frank Norris, Jac London, Upton Sinclair, John Steinbeck, and the social novelists. believe in art, but I don't believe in art for art's sake: while despisin the Soviet official societal writing, I believe in art for people's sake. believe the novelist should be an artist cum sociologist. I think h should see his characters in social perspective. I think that is one o his obligations. At the same time, I think he also has an obligation t entertain. I think the novel should run on a double track. I am prou of the fact that *Uncle Tom's Cabin* and *The Jungle* and *The Grape of Wrath* helped to change or at least alarm society. I am proud o the fact that books of mine, *Sammy*, or *On the Waterfront*, caugh the public attention but also made it more aware of social sores, th corruption that springs from the original Adam Smith ideal o individuality. I think Ayn Rand tries to apply 18th-century ideals t 20th-century problems—and I'm not sure they worked that wel then. My flags are down: I believe in neither Smith nor Marx, i neither Nixon nor Mao nor the Soviet bureaucrats who persecut my fellow writers. There was a time when I was young when I san the "International." Who would have guessed that the "Inter national" would result in the two largest countries in the world, bot "Socialist," brandishing lethal weapons at each other? As long as w can wonder and remember, speculate and (perhaps vainly) hope, w re not dead. The non- or anti-communist humanist writer of novels nay be slightly out of style, but there are miles and decades and nany books to go before he sleeps.

* * *

Budd Schulberg earned fame with his first and best novel, *What Makes Sammy Run?*, published in 1941 on the author's 27th birthday. This narrative of an obnoxious office boy's quick rise to head of a major motion picture studio threatened to become the author's type story for all his novels. *The Harder They Fall* told the pathetic story of the rise of Toro Molina to heavy-weight boxing champion, although "El Toro" is actually the victim of an ambitious, unscrupulous fight promoter named Nick Latka. Schulberg's *The Disenchanted* traced the doomed comeback attempt of Manley Halliday, novelist and culture-hero of the 1920's now reduced to writing movie scenarios when sober. In these three early novels and many of the collected short stories of *Some Faces in the Crowd*, Schulberg is absorbed with the theme of rapid success and the psychic losses of public winners: compromise with self, betrayal by or of others, doubt, guilt, isolation, and fear haunt and shame his restless characters.

Schulberg's plots have frequently reflected the author's background as screenwriter and son of a Hollywood producer. Not surprisingly, many of his novels have been produced as movies, but his fourth novel, *Waterfront*, was a successful movie first, with the novel version a distinct improvement over the author's own scenario. After a 15 year lapse, Schulberg returned to the novel with *Sanctuary V*, a melodramatic study of a failed revolution and the ruinous effects of sudden power. In this least successful novel, Justo Suarez, the provisional president of what is obviously Cuba, has fled from the corrupted revolutionary Angel Bello to take sanctuary in a corrupt embassy among corrupt or perverted refugees and jailer-hosts.

Not only is Angel Bello clearly Fidel Castro, earlier novels just as recognizably modeled their protagonists on real-life counterparts: the hapless, peasant-fighter Toro Molina is Primo Carnera, while Manley Halliday is Scott Fitzgerald, with whom Schulberg ("Shep" in the book) had once worked on a Dartmouth winter carnival scenario. When Schulberg is not "exposing" Hollywood through memories of real-life counterparts or composites, he utilizes journalistic skill and thorough research for fictional exposés of the fight game (*Harder They Fall*) and the brutal life around New York harbor (*Waterfront*). Like most exposés, the novels exploit the most sensational elements, though Schulberg reveals an un-Hollywoodian preference for the seamy over the sexy. He does commit many other major "Hollywood" faults, employing gimmicks, stereotyped characters, sentimentality, and mechanical, reflex responses to life-situations in place of serious ideas or a personal vision.

With *Sammy*, however, even the faults seem appropriate. The snappy repartee and artificial dialogue brilliantly sum up the brittle, superficial world of 1930's Hollywood. The novel's fast pace, the picaresque audacity of the almost likable, conscienceless heel-hero, the predictable ending of the betrayer betrayed (and, implicitly, of the hunter about to be hunted) still add up, after 40 years, to one of the best Hollywood novels ever written. Like many other commercial writers, Schulberg knows that first-person is the easiest way to tell a story; he uses this form often and well, and in *What Makes Sammy Run?* he created a minor classic of this form and the Hollywood sub-genre.

—Frank Campenni

SELBY, Hubert, Jr. American. Born in Brooklyn, New York, 23 July 1928. Educated in New York City public schools, including Peter Stuyvesant High School. Served in the United States Merchant Marine, 1944-46. Married 1) Inez Taylor in 1953; 2) Judith Lumino, 1964; 3) Suzanne Shaw, 1969; four children. Hospital patient, with tuberculosis, 1946-50; held various jobs, including seaman and insurance clerk, 1950-64. Address: c/o Playboy Press, 1633 Broadway, New York, New York 10019, U.S.A.

PUBLICATIONS

Novels

Last Exit to Brooklyn. New York, Grove Press, 1964; London, Calder and Boyars, 1966.
The Room. New York, Grove Press, 1971; London, Calder and Boyars, 1972.
The Demon. New York, Playboy Press, 1976; London, Boyars, 1977.
Requiem for a Dream. New York, Playboy Press, 1978; London, Boyars, 1979.

Uncollected Short Stories

"Home for Christmas," in *Neon 2* (New York), 1956.
"Love/s Labour/s Lost," in *Black Mountain Review* (Black Mountain, North Carolina), Autumn 1957.
"Double Feature," in *Neon 4* (New York), 1959.
"Another Day, Another Dollar," in *New Directions 17*, edited by James Laughlin. New York, New Directions, 1961.
"A Penny for Your Thoughts," in *The Moderns*, edited by LeRoi Jones. New York, Corinth, 1963; London, MacGibbon and Kee, 1965.
"And Baby Makes Three," in *New American Story*, edited by Robert Creeley and Donald Allen. New York, Grove Press, 1965.
"Fat Phil's Day," in *Evergreen Review* (New York), August 1967.
"Happy Birthday," in *Evergreen Review* (New York), August 1969.

*

Hubert Selby, Jr., comments:

I write by ear. Music of line important. Want to put reader through emotional experience.

* * *

If *Last Exit to Brooklyn* and its ludicrous obscenity trial hadn't exhausted moralistic disgust, Hubert Selby, Jr.'s work could probably stand at the bench in perpetuity. The Seventh Circle of the Violent in Dante's *Inferno*; Gulliver upon the cancerous Brobdignagian breast; Genet's onanist reveries. These suggest Selby's fictive world. He is our eye-witness on the dead-ends of the daily. Stuck in the sick gut of the city, his camera fixes the disaffected masses and completes a picture begun with Crane's *Maggie*. On the other hand, his biblical epigraphs are both ironically and straightforwardly applicable. He is, then, at once a determinist and a moralist whose narratives are naturalistic fables. Consequently, his psychological landscape is more than social realism or a Hogarth satire could accommodate. It is a Bosch and Francis Bacon triptych. As the witness for the damned, Selby *is* mired in America's slime. But given a populace which could nod off on the Viet Nam War, his ability to shock may be remarkable, even morally so.

The title of his first novel is taken from an expressway sign that overlooks a cemetery of solid concrete. The work thematically connects six tales of hopeless human isolation. Its people delude themselves with faith in family and idle dreams of profound sexual communion. But Abraham's infidelity, angry remoteness, and, finally, sleep are domesticity. Tralala's rape is heterosexuality. "Georgette's" and Vinnie's bestiality is homosexuality. Casual and sadistic, the violent are little Eichmanns and Mengeles. In the background Selby works with a timeless symbology of darkness overwhelming light. This is conveyed to us by depth associations with *Ecclesiastes*, Poe's *Raven*, and our own disillusioned black "Bird," Charlie Parker. It is only by viewing Selby in this context that we can grasp his preoccupation with drugs. He knows unequivocally the life renouncing and futile lie at the heart of "kind nepenthe."

The Room shifts our focus from the sick social to the sick individual organism. Its sole province is the mind of a nameless paranoid schizophrenic, though Selby might resist terminology. The "room" is both a cell and the disconnected consciousness of the single character. Locked within each, he constructs antithetically lofty and brutal fantasies, but always out of a single-minded hatred of authority. Thus his imaginary revenges include delusions of magnanimity in which he self-sacrificially fights social injustice with the help of liberal lawyers. Conversely, they include totally dehumanizing tortures of police officers, sadistic acts which reduce his adversaries to canines. These are rendered with nauseating detail. Selby seems unwilling to attribute this state of mind to a sick society, an indifferent family, or a bad character. It is simply a *donnée*, and Selby's forte is neither sociological nor psychological reductionism but graphic presentation. The novel's unsavory force and its interest are considerably enhanced by the author's tactic of gliding constantly between an omniscient and a first person perspective.

The "demon" of Selby's third novel is sexual obsession and its mutations. It begins as womanizing so unalleviated that Harry White can sustain no connection, except tenuously to his career, with any other activity. (He cannot last out a softball game with friends or a party for his grandparents.) It ends with his murdering, on Palm Sunday, a Christlike Cardinal and his subsequent suicide. So the demoniacal obsession is larger than carnality, passing through debauchery and theft toward this ultimately exciting destructiveness which seems proof for Selby that "The wages of sin is death." The novel's complementary epigraph is from *James* 1:15. At all times, whether White is fornicating or thieving, the demon exists as a physical tension so great that Harry hates whatever stands between himself and a feeling of exhausting gratification. But all respite from enslavement, including his marriage to Linda (the healthiest person Selby has drawn), is stop-gap. Only death does the job. As a study of the connection between sex and violence in the obsessive person, the book has merit. But the conclusion is unfortunately mystical in part, especially because the only psychological perspective is provided by an arrogant neo-Freudian simpleton. This straw man certainly doesn't exhaust more modestly agnostic interpretations of the events.

Requiem for a Dream is about hope ruined by narcotic habit. It sees America in terms of a pervasive dependence upon metaphorical and literal drugs. The widow Sara Goldfarb eats compulsively and lives a stuporously vicarious life through soap operas and TV game shows. Thinking she has a chance to appear in one and wanting to be appropriately svelte, she sees a physician who addicts her to dexedrine. She ends up a skeletal and slavering schizoid in a mental hospital. Concurrently, her son Harry, his friend Tyrone Love, and Harry's lover, Marion, plot their own dreams' fulfillments. All are sad clichés. And the trio are heroine addicts. From drug profits, Harry will build a coffeehouse for sensitive artists and writers where Marion's drawings will be admired; the black Tyrone will buy into the bliss of a modest suburb. But their endeavors only increase their addiction. Marion winds up in a sort of bisexual freak show working for her portion of bliss. Harry loses his arm from an infection and sinks into oblivion in a Miami hospital. Having gone south with Harry for a big pay-off, Tyrone gets to be brutalized by rednecks and thrown in prison. By now we have to ask if Hubert Selby Jr. has anything more to tell us along these lines.

—David M. Heaton

SELVON, Samuel (Dickson). Trinidadian. Born in Trinidad, 20 May 1923. Educated at Naparima College, Trinidad, 1935-39. Served as a wireless operator with the Trinidad Royal Naval Volunteer Reserve, 1940-45. Married 1) Draupadi Persaud in 1947, one daughter; 2) Althea Nesta Daroux in 1963, two sons and one daughter. Journalist, *Trinidad Guardian*, 1946-50; civil servant, in the High Commission, London, 1950-53. Since 1954, full-time writer. Recipient: Guggenheim Fellowship, 1954, 1968; Society of Authors Travelling Scholarship, 1958; Trinidad Government Scholarship, 1962; Arts Council of Great Britain grant, 1967, 1968; Humming Bird Medal, Trinidad, 1969. Lives in London. Address: c/o Davis-Poynter Ltd., 20 Garrick Street, London WC2E 9BJ, England.

PUBLICATIONS

Novels

A Brighter Sun. London, Wingate, 1952; New York, Viking Press, 1953.
An Island Is a World. London, Wingate, 1955.
The Lonely Londoners. London, Wingate, 1956; New York, St. Martin's Press, 1957; as *The Lonely Ones*, London, Digit, 1959.
Turn Again Tiger. London, MacGibbon and Kee, 1958; New York, St. Martin's Press, 1959.
I Hear Thunder. London, MacGibbon and Kee, and New York, St. Martin's Press, 1963.
The Housing Lark. London, MacGibbon and Kee, 1965.
The Plains of Caroni. London, MacGibbon and Kee, 1970.
Those Who Eat the Cascadura. London, Davis Poynter, 1972.
Moses Ascending. London, Davis Poynter, 1975.

Short Stories

Ways of Sunlight. London, MacGibbon and Kee, and New York, St. Martin's Press, 1958.

Plays

Screenplay: *Pressure*, with Horace Ové, 1975.

Radio Plays: *Lost Property*, 1965; *A House for Teona*, 1965; *A Highway in the Sun*, 1967; *Rain Stop Play*, 1967; *You Right in the Smoke*, 1968; *Worse Than Their Bite*, 1968; *Bringing in the Sheaves*, 1969; *Perchance to Dream*, 1969; *Eldorado West One*, 1969; *Home Sweet India*, 1970; *Mary Shut Your Gate*, 1971; *The Magic Stick*, from work by Ismith Khan, 1971; *Voyage to Trinidad*, 1971; *Those Who Eat the Crocodile*, 1971; *Water for Veronica*, 1972; *Cry Baby Brackley*, 1972; *Harvest in Wilderness*, 1972; *Milk in the Coffee*, 1975; *Zeppi's Machine*, 1977.

* * *

The synthesis of oriental, African, and European elements in the Caribbean has been recent in the consciousness of the East Indian who lived for a long time in a kind of cultural cocoon (at least on the plantations), his language, religion, and ritual preserved largely intact, his experience contrasting sharply at first with that of the more deracinated African. We see the first portrayal of the East Indian community in an early novel by the Guyanese Edgar Mittelholzer, but it was in *A Brighter Sun* that an East Indian writer himself, Samuel Selvon, spoke for the first time with quiet intimate authority and simple charm about the life of the East Indian family in the Caribbean.

In this novel Selvon treats of a young Indian couple thrown together in their teens by the traditional marriage behind the veil who grow to maturity at the time of the last war on a housing settlement a few miles out of Port-of-Spain. It is written with a sensitiveness to the delicate touches of beauty in common things and through a series of commonplace events we see the Indian peasant facing crucial adjustments in the movement of the life of the land to the life of the town. The Chinese grocer, the Portuguese neighbours, the African materfamilias are drawn with an equal clarity and sureness and we get a sense of the effect of this cosmopolitan flux upon the Indian psychological fibre. In *Turn Again Tiger*, a sequel to this first novel, Selvon returns to the Indian couple, Tiger and Urmilla, and here we see the dilemma of the man who is only educated enough to be restless about his condition but can find no direction or stage for any significant extension or expression. Tiger, bewildered by the shapeless interior shadow of this restlessness, identifies it with a call to return to the life of the land, and so he journeys backwards in an attempt to feel his roots again in the virgin territory of Five Rivers. The movement back to the land culminates in a series of disillusionments and he is forced to return to suburban Barataria, but the experience brings him closer to a realisation of the true nature of himself and his predicament and an acceptance of the realities he must face in order to live.

These two novels achieve at times an almost poetic simplicity. Selvon is never intense or profoundly disturbing but his work has the freshness and tone of wide open fields and cool, noiselessly running water. There is humour too, lighter perhaps than in V.S. Naipaul's early work, but developing into pure classical farce in his novel *The Lonely Londoners*. Here Selvon, experimenting with the regional dialect with probably more success than any other Caribbean writer, gives a picture, both hilarious and pathetic, of the plight of West Indian immigrants in London. Selvon proves himself capable of handling an almost purely African cast and English landscape with the same ease and authenticity as the Indian family unit in Trinidad.

Selvon began as a short-story writer and it is as a short-story writer, perhaps, that he is best admired. In *Ways of Sunlight* one sees clearly that his gift for farce finds its happiest expression in that medium. His stories at best have a pointed finish, a rounded artistry lacking in the episodic fragmentation of the novels. In the shorter form he may be compared to his fellow Trinidadian humorist V.S. Naipaul, although Selvon's dialogue is closer to the quick of the black proletarian of the cities and the Indian peasants of the sugar plantations.

—Ivan Van-Sertima

SHADBOLT, Maurice (Francis Richard). New Zealander. Born in Auckland, 4 June 1932. Educated at Te Kuiti High School; Avondale College; University of Auckland. Married twice; three sons and one daughter. Journalist for various New Zealand publications, 1952-54; documentary scriptwriter and director for the New Zealand National Film Unit, 1954-57; full-time writer from 1957; lived in London and Spain, 1957-60, then returned to New Zealand. Recipient: Hubert Church Memorial Award, 1959; New Zealand State Literary Fellowship, 1960, 1970; Katherine Mansfield Award, 1963, 1967; Robert Burns Fellowship, Otago University, 1963; National Association of Independent Schools Award, U.S.A., 1966; Freda Buckland Award, 1969; Pacific Area Travel Association Award, for non-fiction, 1971; James Wattie Award, 1973. Address: Box 60028, Titirangi, Auckland 7, New Zealand.

PUBLICATIONS

Novels

Among the Cinders. London, Eyre and Spottiswoode, and New York, Atheneum, 1965.

This Summer's Dolphin. London, Cassell, and New York, Atheneum, 1969.

An Ear of the Dragon. London, Cassell, 1971.

Strangers and Journeys. London, Hodder and Stoughton, and New York, St. Martin's Press, 1972.

A Touch of Clay. London, Hodder and Stoughton, 1974.

Danger Zone. Auckland, Hodder and Stoughton, 1975; London, Hodder and Stoughton, 1976.

The Lovelock Version. London, Hodder and Stoughton, 1980.

Short Stories

The New Zealanders: A Sequence of Stories. Christchurch, Whitcombe and Tombs, and London, Gollancz, 1959; New York, Atheneum, 1961.

Summer Fires and Winter Country. London, Eyre and Spottiswoode, 1963; New York, Atheneum, 1966.

The Presence of Music: Three Novellas. London, Cassell, 1967.

Figures in Light. London, Hodder and Stoughton, 1979.

Other

New Zealand: Gift of the Sea, photographs by Brian Brake. Christchurch, Whitcombe and Tombs, 1963; revised edition, 1973.

The Shell Guide to New Zealand. Christchurch, Whitcombe and Tombs, 1968; London, Joseph, 1969; revised edition, Whitcombe and Tombs, 1973; Joseph, 1976.

Isles of the South Pacific, with Olaf Ruhen. Washington, D.C., National Geographic Society, 1968.

Love and Legend: Some Twentieth Century New Zealanders. Auckland, Hodder and Stoughton, 1976.

*

Critical Study: *Maurice Shadbolt* by Patrick Holland, Boston, Twayne, 1981.

Maurice Shadbolt comments:

I should like to say only that, as a man of my time and place, I have simply tried to make sense of both, in the course of a journey which allows no satisfying destination; my books might thus be seen as bottled messages tossed out at points along that journey. I know I might have been otherwise: I am frequently unsure why I write at all. But then I look from my study window out upon a bruised Eden, my country, and I begin again; there is no escape. My equivocal feeling for the country in which I happened to be born admits of no easy release in either a physical or literary sense. So I make, in diverse shapes, in stories and novels, my not always unhappy best of it. As a New Zealander, resident at the ragged edge of Western civilization, upon the last land of substance to be claimed by mankind, I often feel my involvement with the rest of the human race rather peripheral—as if upon a lonely floating raft. Yet fires lit upon the periphery may still illuminate the central and abiding concerns of man—the fires, I mean, which everywhere the human spirit ignites, and which everywhere shape the artist. So I make no apology. I might envy a Russian or an American—a Solzhenitsyn or a Mailer—his capacity to approach the giant themes of the 20th century. But I would not wish, really, to be otherwise. For I have tried, beyond the particularities of time and place, to observe and examine those hungers and thirsts which remain constant in man; those hungers and thirsts which, in my peripheral position, may sometimes be more evident than elsewhere.

* * *

In his first collection of short stories, *The New Zealanders*, Maurice Shadbolt revealed a personal identification with New Zealand which has continued to inform his fiction. The exploration of his environment in terms of its more recent history, its topographical characteristics, and its people is not, however, a mere exercise in nationalism: it exemplifies the imaginative writer's search, in a rapidly changing world, for the inner permanence afforded by conscious recognition of his roots. For Shadbolt, these roots derive chiefly from a near-emotional involvement with the land. If this preoccupation with the "spirit of place" has been remarked upon frequently, it is because the visually intense depiction of his characters' relationships with their physical surroundings is one of his major strengths. There is a suggestion, in this "painterly" approach to writing, of an affinity with New Zealand's school of landscape artists and with the similar concern of the Australian novelist, Patrick White, to delineate in words the actual appearance as well as the feeling of life in his own country.

Thematically, *The New Zealanders* foreshadows much of Shadbolt's later writing. Divided into three sections, the stories range in time from the 1920's to the late 1950's; in place from isolated farming country, small towns, and major cities to the capitals of Europe; and in character-type from dour farmers, small town adolescents, and rootless young city dwellers to expatriate artists. These short stories and those collected in *Summer Fires and Winter Country* exhibit a stylistic and formal control which renders them perhaps more satisfying artistically than the less densely written novels.

Following *The Presence of Music*, where he used the form of the novella to explore in three complementary pieces the uneasy position of the artist in New Zealand society, Shadbolt wrote his first novel. *Among the Cinders* is structurally loose and has a somewhat contrived ending; but this light-hearted account of a run-away boy's adventures in bush country with his unconventional grandfather remains one of the author's most popular books.

Shadbolt's most typical characters are aimless young adults. Torn between a desire for escape from binding commitment on the one hand and for emotional security on the other, they seek but rarely find solace in personal relationships. In *This Summer's Dolphin* a variety of narrative techniques is used to investigate the troubled inner lives of several such isolated individuals. Unifying their essentially separate stories is the novel's island setting and the appearance of a friendly dolphin who, through his temporary transcendence of the characters' self-absorption, becomes a symbol with Christlike overtones.

The incorporation of easily traceable biographical material in *An Ear of the Dragon* aroused considerable local criticism. Nevertheless, the skilful manipulation of flashbacks to illuminate the link between an immigrant writer's adolescent experiences in wartime Italy and his difficult adjustment to New Zealand life and people makes this a compelling narrative.

Strangers and Journeys, written over a period of ten years, is Shadbolt's longest and most ambitious book. Gathering together many of the themes and characters of his earlier fiction, he details in a complex pattern of social realism the contrasting lives and aspirations of two generations of fathers and sons. There is an epic sweep to the first part of the novel with its masterly evocation of the two separate working men who, in an economically harsh era, pitted themselves against their environment and survived. This is not sustained, partly because Shadbolt himself is too close to the sons. For them, external battle against the land has given way to an even more debilitating, internal struggle to find meaning in the city. It would appear that in the confused social context of the 1960's, both author and journalist-character shared a belief that "all form is crippling by nature and dishonest; only confession is honest."

—Cherry Hankin

SHARP, Margery. British. Born in 1905. Educated at Streatham Hill High School, London; Bedford College, University of London, B.A. (honours) in French. Married Major Geoffrey Castle in 1938. Army Education Lecturer in World War II. Lives in London. Address: c/o William Heinemann Ltd., 10 Upper Grosvenor Street, London W1X 9PA, England.

PUBLICATIONS

Novels

Rhododendron Pie. London, Chatto and Windus, and New York, Appleton, 1930.
Fanfare for Tin Trumpets. London, Barker, 1932; New York, Putnam, 1933.
The Nymph and the Nobleman. London, Barker, 1932.
The Flowering Thorn. London, Barker, 1933; New York, Putnam, 1934.
Sophy Cassmajor. London, Barker, and New York, Putnam, 1934.
Four Gardens. London, Barker, and New York, Putnam, 1935.
The Nutmeg Tree. London, Barker, and Boston, Little Brown, 1937.
Harlequin House. London, Collins, and Boston, Little Brown, 1939.
The Stone of Chastity. London, Collins, and Boston, Little Brown, 1940.
Three Companion Pieces: Sophy Cassmajor, The Tigress on the Hearth, and The Nymph and the Nobleman. Boston, Little Brown, 1941; London, Collins, 1955.
Cluny Brown. London, Collins, and Boston, Little Brown, 1944.
Britannia Mews. London, Collins, and Boston, Little Brown, 1946.
The Foolish Gentlewoman. London, Collins, and Boston, Little Brown, 1948.
Lise Lillywhite. London, Collins, and Boston, Little Brown, 1951.
The Gipsy in the Parlour. London, Collins, 1953; Boston, Little Brown, 1954.
The Eye of Love. London, Collins, and Boston, Little Brown, 1957; as *Martha and the Eye of Love*, London, New English Library, 1969.
Something Light. London, Collins, 1960; Boston, Little Brown, 1961.
Martha in Paris. London, Collins, 1962; Boston, Little Brown, 1963.
Martha, Eric, and George. London, Collins, and Boston, Little Brown, 1964.
The Sun in Scorpio. London, Heinemann, and Boston, Little Brown, 1965.
In Pious Memory. Boston, Little Brown, 1967; London, Heinemann, 1968.
Rosa. London, Heinemann, 1969; Boston, Little Brown, 1970.
The Innocents. London, Heinemann, 1971; Boston, Little Brown, 1972.
The Faithful Servants. London, Heinemann, and Boston, Little Brown, 1975.
Summer Visits. London, Heinemann, 1977; Boston, Little Brown, 1978.

Short Stories

The Lost Chapel Picnic and Other Stories. London, Heinemann, and Boston, Little Brown, 1973.

Plays

Meeting at Night (produced London, 1934).
Lady in Waiting, adaptation of her novel *The Nutmeg Tree* (produced New York, 1940; as *The Nutmeg Tree*, produced London, 1941). New York, French, 1941.
The Foolish Gentlewoman, adaptation of her own novel (produced London, 1949). London, French, 1950.

Television Play: *The Birdcage Room*, 1954.

Other (juvenile)

The Rescuers. London, Collins, and Boston, Little Brown, 1959.
Mélisande. London, Collins, and Boston, Little Brown, 1960.
Miss Bianca. London, Collins, and Boston, Little Brown, 1962.
The Turret. Boston, Little Brown, 1963; London, Collins, 1964.
Lost at the Fair. Boston, Little Brown, 1965; London, Heinemann, 1967.
Miss Bianca in the Salt Mines. London, Heinemann, and Boston, Little Brown, 1966.
Miss Bianca in the Orient. London, Heinemann, and Boston, Little Brown, 1970.
Miss Bianca in the Antarctic. London, Heinemann, 1970; Boston, Little Brown, 1971.
Miss Bianca and the Bridesmaid. London, Heinemann, and Boston, Little Brown, 1972.
The Children Next Door. London, Heinemann, 1974.
The Magical Cockatoo. London, Heinemann, 1974.
Bernard the Brave. London, Heinemann, 1976; Boston, Little Brown, 1977.
Bernard into Battle. London, Heinemann, and Boston, Little Brown, 1979.

*

Manuscript Collection: Houghton Library, Harvard University, Cambridge, Massachusetts.

* * *

The genre for which Margery Sharp is best known is light entertainment involving the incongruity of unclassifiable or even zany characters operating in the most conventional of settings. These off-beat characters, however, are basically sound, and the conventional persons are basically kind; all turns out well, and the satire of social assumptions lacks bitterness. Some of the books are very slightly plotted, depending for their effect on amusing conversation, while others led the reader rapidly along a zigzag path through well-planted, but not unexpected, surprises.

The novel which best realizes her comic potentialities is her seventh, *The Nutmeg Tree.* Julia, a minor vaudeville personage, plump and glowing at 39, is discovered in her usual plight of warding off bailiffs and looking for financial succor from some male source. Technically, she is also Mrs. Packett, the daughter-in-law of a conservative county family, widowed in her teens after a necessary wartime marriage. After a year with the kindly Packetts, she had fled back to the theatre. Now a letter has arrived from her daughter asking her to come to the south of France to persuade the older Mrs. Packett to assent to her marriage. Julia genuinely tries to fill her maternal, ladylike role, but since she is without resources she must use an adventuress's means. Her off-beat nature is immediately recognized by the young suitor, and a tug-of-war results, for Julia has seen that his essentially picaresque tastes, so like her own, would prove disastrous in a union with her prim, idealistic daughter. The price of the young man's renunciation is Julia's refusal, in turn, of the hand of another guest, the distinguished, elderly Sir William. Julia accepts the sacrifice, but after a paper-chase all ends well.

As an entertainer Sharp aims at readers who bring a literary background—though this is not essential—and a familiarity with the expected social niceties. These last she values, seeing their utility in easing life's relationships; but she jettisons meaningless social impositions. Of the heroine of *Cluny Brown*, a plumber's niece, everyone keeps saying, "The trouble with young Cluny is she don't know her place." For tall, loping Cluny, with her unmanageable dark hair and large features that distract the imperceptive from her fine eyes and attentive gaze, is a restless explorer, disconcertingly far from the stereotype of clerk, typist, or servant, and her class has no place for such a girl. Neither has the class of county families, but the author sends her as a parlor-maid to such a family in Devon who are harboring also a refugee Polish professor.

Of her less purely comic novels, *The Flowering Thorn* is an unsentimental account of a young London sophisticate's adoption of a little boy and her gradual acceptance of village life. Sharp has written three historical novels. The synoptic, overly thin *Britannia Mews* presents the social changes from 1865 to 1945 in a West End mews and the courageous life of a woman who, as a young girl, had naively declassed herself.

—Alice Bensen

SHAW, Irwin. American. Born in New York City, 27 February 1913. Educated at Brooklyn College, New York, B.A. in English 1934. Served in the United States Army Signal Corps, in North Africa, the Middle East, Britain, France, and Germany, 1942-45. Married Marian Edwards in 1939 (divorced); one son. Radio Writer, 1934-36; Drama Critic, *New Republic*, New York, 1947-48; taught Creative Writing, New York University, 1947-48. Has lived in Europe since 1951. Recipient: O. Henry Award, 1944, 1945; American Academy grant, 1946; *Playboy* Award, 1970, 1979. Address: P.O. Box 39, Klosters, Switzerland.

PUBLICATIONS

Novels

The Young Lions. New York, Random House, 1948; London, Cape, 1949.
The Troubled Air. New York, Random House, and London, Cape, 1951.
Lucy Crown. New York, Random House, and London, Cape, 1956.
Two Weeks in Another Town. New York, Random House, and London, Cape, 1960.
Voices of a Summer Day. New York, Delacorte Press, and London, Weidenfeld and Nicolson, 1965.
Rich Man, Poor Man. New York, Delacorte Press, and London, Weidenfeld and Nicolson, 1970.
Evening in Byzantium. New York, Delacorte Press, and London, Weidenfeld and Nicolson, 1973.
Nightwork. New York, Delacorte Press, and London, Weidenfeld and Nicolson, 1975.
Beggarman, Thief. New York, Delacorte Press, and London, Weidenfeld and Nicolson, 1977.
The Top of the Hill. New York, Delacorte Press, and London, Weidenfeld and Nicolson, 1979.
Bread upon the Waters. New York, Delacorte Press, and London, Weidenfeld and Nicolson, 1981.

Short Stories

Sailor off the Bremen and Other Stories. New York, Random House, 1939; London, Cape, 1940.
Welcome to the City and Other Stories. New York, Random House, 1942.
Act of Faith and Other Stories. New York, Random House, 1946.
Mixed Company: Collected Short Stories. New York, Random House, 1950; London, Cape, 1952.
Tip on a Dead Jockey and Other Stories. New York, Random House, and London, Cape, 1957.
Selected Short Stories. New York, Modern Library, 1961.
In the French Style (screenplay and stories). New York Macfadden, 1963.

Love on a Dark Street and Other Stories. New York, Delacorte Press, and London, Cape, 1965.
Short Stories. New York, Random House, 1966.
Retreat and Other Stories. London, New English Library, 1970.
Whispers in Bedlam: Three Novellas. London, Weidenfeld and Nicolson, 1972.
God Was Here, But He Left Early. New York, Arbor House, 1973; London, Pan, 1977.
Short Stories: Five Decades. New York, Delacorte Press, and London, Cape, 1978.

Plays

Bury the Dead (produced New York, 1936). New York, Random House, 1936; in *Famous Plays of 1936*, London, Gollancz, 1936.
Siege (produced New York, 1937).
Second Mortgage, in *One-Act Play Magazine* (New York), May 1938.
The Gentle People: A Brooklyn Fable (produced New York and London, 1939). New York, Random House, 1939.
Quiet City (produced New York, 1939).
Retreat to Pleasure (produced New York, 1940).
The Shy and the Lonely (produced Los Angeles). Published in *American Scenes*, edited by William Kozlenko, New York, Day, 1941.
Sons and Soldiers (produced New York, 1943). New York, Random House, 1944.
The Assassin (produced London and New York, 1945). New York, Random House, 1946.
The Survivors, with Peter Viertel (produced New York, 1948). New York, Dramatists Play Service, 1948.
Patate, adaptation of a play by Marcel Achard (produced New York, 1958).
Children from Their Games (produced New York, 1963). New York, French, 1962.
A Choice of Wars (produced Salt Lake City, Utah; Glasgow, 1967).

Screenplays: *The Big Game*, 1936; *The Hard Way*, with Daniel Fuchs and Jerry Wald, 1942; *The Talk of the Town*, with others, 1942; *Commandos Strike at Dawn*, 1942; *Take One False Step*, with Chester Erskine and David Shaw, 1949; *Easy Living*, with Charles Schnee, 1949; *I Want You*, 1951; *Act of Love*, 1954; *Ulysses*, with others, 1955; *Fire Down Below*, 1957; *This Angry Age*, with Rene Clement, 1958; *Desire under the Elms*, 1958; *The Big Gamble*, 1961; *In the French Style*, 1963; *Survival 1967* (documentary), 1968.

Other

Report on Israel. New York, Simon and Schuster, 1950.
In the Company of Dolphins (travel). New York, Geis, 1964.
Paris! Paris!, illustrated by Ronald Searle. New York, Harcourt Brace, and London, Weidenfeld and Nicolson, 1977.

*

Manuscript Collections: Mugar Memorial Library, Boston University; Morgan Library, Brooklyn Library, New York.

Irwin Shaw comments:

(1972) If there is one constant thread that can be shown to be woven through almost all of my work, it is that of violence—political, national, international, racial, neighborly, psychological, doctrinaire. My first play, *Bury the Dead*, was laid in the "second year of the war that is to begin tomorrow night." Another play of mine, *The Gentle People*, demonstrated the necessity of violence for peaceful folk who wished to survive in the world of that time (1939). Many of my short stories, such as "Sailor off the Bremen," "Weep in Years to Come," "Preach on the Dusty Roads," reflect the same concern. And of course my novel *The Young Lions* dealt exhaustively with the war, in America, Africa, Italy, England, France, and Germany. *Rich Man, Poor Man* is, among other things, a study of the violent climate of America since the end of World War II, and the struggle of one man to subdue the sick violence in his own soul.

At the same time, my work has been involved with the changing social scene, politics, class distinctions, sexual patterns as they form and dissolve. My attitudes have changed from work to work, but a strong streak of irony, sometimes misunderstood and not caught by the critics, has always been evident.

As for style—I have tried to keep mine flexible enough so that I can work in all mediums, the theatre, the short story, the films, the essay, the novel, and fit myself to the particular material I was working on rather than fit the material to a pre-conceived and unchanging form. My search has been for variety and I am still engaged in it.

* * *

Irwin Shaw's early fiction, both the widely known short stories and the novels, displays a quality of moral earnestness in its attempt to explore political, sociological, and historical issues in contemporary America. His first novel, *The Young Lions*, uses the alternating points of view of a cosmopolitan liberal intellectual, a naive American Jew, and a German soldier to examine the moral dilemmas involved in World War II. *The Troubled Air* deals with witch-hunting in the broadcast industry in 1950, building to the betrayal of the humane and decent man by the absolute and extreme positions of both the right, the hysterical fear of anything close to Communism, and the violent left, loyal only to its own dishonest rhetoric. *Lucy Crown*, more narrow sociologically than the other novels, chronicles the failure of a marriage and its effect, for almost 20 years, on the only child. *Rich Man, Poor Man*, following a family through three generations, and, to a much lesser extent, its sequel, *Beggarman, Thief*, question the standard American assumptions that money, physical attractiveness, and material comforts yield happiness or satisfaction.

In his early work, Shaw sometimes tended to sacrifice the credibility of his characters and situations to the thorough and fair-minded presentation of the sociological ideas and categories they represent. Particularly in *The Young Lions* and *The Troubled Air* characters shade too easily into abstractions and the moral earnestness of the novels can seem heavy and relentless. Even in *Lucy Crown*, the most dramatically effective and, unjustly, the least well-known of Shaw's early novels, characters often talk as if they believe literally in the values they are made to demonstrate. Dramatic switches are always frequent in Shaw's fiction. In *Rich Man, Poor Man* the brother originally presented as violent and destructive, rather than the apparently humane and industrious one, is finally able to give himself, to act, and to recognize the characteristically American fallacies implicit in the socially mobile family. Similarly, in its sequel, *Beggarman, Thief*, concentrating more on the next generation, the apparently feckless young man acts heroically while the young man of violent integrity seethes unproductively. Effectively ironic and dramatic as such switches are, they give the always readable and involving fiction a blocky kind of structure, a sense of one mass posed clumsily against another.

Plot and structure can seem excessively contrived or otherwise extrinsic in all Shaw's fiction. In some of the later fiction, such as *Evening in Byzantium*, which takes place at the Cannes Film Festival, and *The Top of the Hill*, set at a ski resort in Vermont, the plot is little more than an anecdotal account of alternatives thrown at the passive protagonist, a successful middle-aged American. He retreats from them all, eliminating all risk of commitment, as if they are assaults on a privacy and security he has earned. Details of setting or of tourist type are knowing and skillfully rendered, but there is little interior development of character or thoughtful social comment. More effective are those later novels propelled by action, like the violence, revenge, and contemporary terrorism in *Beggarman, Thief* or the episodic structure of *Nightwork*, in which a grounded pilot, working as a hotel nightclerk in New York, finds $100,000 in a dead man's room and is able to finance a career of investments, scams, and high-living around the resorts of Europe. The latter novel, more active and more comic than Shaw's other fiction of the last decade, succeeds in the details and the craft of its particular episodes. More in the tradition of Mann's *Confessions of Felix Krull, Confidence Man* than in the earnest social commentary of Shaw's earlier fiction, *Nightwork* represents Shaw's recent best.

Whatever artifice, theme, or structure unifies Shaw's readable fiction, his novels always contain particular scenes that combine sharp commentary and sensitive observation. *The Troubled Air* depicts an intransigent black man who defends himself in hostile white society by putting on an attitude of shuffling simplicity, a characterization now familiar but remarkable and prescient in a novel published in 1951. *Rich Man, Poor Man* contains several scenes that acutely depict the frustrations and uncertainties of the man rigidly loyal to his remote concept of his own goodness. *Lucy Crown* ends with a long and brilliant reconciliation scene between mother and son, a scene that is dramatic, moving, and without any thematic or sociological function. The same novel also contains a sharply and sympathetically observed scene of New York bars and restaurants crowded with soldiers on leave during World War II. *Nightwork* has numerous well-depicted funny treatments of American tourists on the Swiss ski slopes or justifying their choices of all the tourist traps in Rome. The most effective parts of Shaw's novels, serious, satirical, or both, often reveal the talents of the short-story writer he has so effectively been: the capacity to present, with intelligence, sensitivity, and a forceful honesty, a single scene, atmosphere, character, or relationship. Although his work is always readable, his moments of special insight and his dramatic force are sometimes blurred in the larger and more comprehensive structure of the novel.

—James Gindin

SHEED, Wilfrid (John Joseph). American. Born in London, England, 27 December 1930; emigrated to the United States in 1940. Educated at Lincoln College, Oxford, B.A. 1954, M.A. 1957. Married Maria Bullitt Darlington in 1957; three children. Film Critic, 1957-61, and Associate Editor, 1959-66, *Jubilee* magazine, New York; Drama Critic and Book Editor, *Commonweal* magazine, New York, 1964-67; Film Critic, *Esquire* magazine, New York, 1967-69; Visiting Lecturer in Creative Arts, Princeton University, New Jersey, 1970-71. Since 1971, Columnist for the *New York Times Book Review*. Agent: Candida Donadio and Associates, 51 East 42nd Street, New York, New York 10017. Address: Rysam and High Streets, Sag Harbor, New York 11963, U.S.A.

PUBLICATIONS

Novels

A Middle Class Education. Boston, Houghton Mifflin, 1960; London, Cassell, 1961.
The Hack. New York, Macmillan, and London, Cassell, 1963.
Square's Progress. New York, Farrar Straus, and London, Cassell, 1965.
Office Politics. New York, Farrar Straus, 1966; London, Cassell, 1967.
Max Jamison. New York, Farrar Straus, 1970; as *The Critic*, London, Weidenfeld and Nicolson, 1970.
People Will Always Be Kind. New York, Farrar Straus, 1973; London, Weidenfeld and Nicolson, 1974.
Transatlantic Blues. New York, Dutton, 1978; London, Sidgwick and Jackson, 1979.

Short Stories

The Blacking Factory, and Pennsylvania Gothic: A Short Novel and a Long Story. New York, Farrar Straus, 1968; London, Weidenfeld and Nicolson, 1969.

Other

Joseph. New York, Sheed and Ward, 1958.
The Morning After (essays). New York, Farrar Straus, 1971.
Vanishing Species of America. New York, Sheed and Ward, 1974.
Three Mobs: Labor, Church and Mafia. New York, Sheed and Ward, 1974.
Muhammad Ali. New York, Crowell, and London, Weidenfeld and Nicolson, 1975.
The Good Word and Other Words (essays). New York, Dutton, 1978; London, Sidgwick and Jackson, 1979.

Editor, *Essays and Poems*, by G.K. Chesterton. London, Penguin, 1958.

* * *

Wilfrid Sheed's essays on films, drama, literature, sports, and areas of Roman Catholicism display a mordant wit, revealing detail, and a strong moral sense. Sheed sees accurately what's going on and crackles in telling about it.

As a fiction writer Sheed capitalizes on his essayist talent to populate an absurd world with characters engaged in 20th-century man's chief endeavor—search for a self in an increasingly valueless world. To do this Sheed examines the soul-shriveling English public school and university system from which John Chote, a glib, shallow Oxfordian receives a scholarship to flounder around America (*A Middle Class Education*); the fatuous, self-deceiving popular Roman Catholic press which encourages Bert Flax to produce sentimental pieces for a very lowbrow parish periodical (*The Hack*); the vacuity of suburbia, the small town, Greenwich Village, and European Hippie-set playgrounds in which Fred and Alison Cope look for meaning once they have carelessly separated (*Square's Progress*); the quirky introversion of a tiny liberal journal which experiences internecine disorder when its editor suffers a heart attack (*Office Politics*); the ego-tripping atmosphere of the Broadway reviewing scene in which a powerful drama critic skirts the edge of madness (*Max Jamison*).

Sheed's style attracts the reader immediately. The accuracy of the detail creates a lively, contemporary ambiance. The increasingly supple prose reproduces the nuances of modern speech and generally scorches what it aims at. After a shaky and overlong first novel, Sheed turned to a more balanced structure. This has led sometimes to a disquieting sense of unnecessary authorial control, as in *Square's Progress* where Sheed switches the point of view between Fred Cope and his wife Alison almost metronomically. This combined with the satirist's penchant for type-casting fosters an air of contrivance and a willed conclusion. *Max Jamison* staggers because Sheed inexplicably shifts from a marvelous tour through Jamison's mind to the views of his wife and son. This appears to be Sheed's main problem as a novelist. *Office Politics*, his best novel, illustrates his mastery. Here Sheed deftly dissects his social and intellectual targets, and again tosses the point of view among a number of characters, but the shifts have causes and effects in the narrative and the characters suggest complex and compassionate insight, particularly the central figures, Gilbert Twining and George Wren. The resolutions reflect less Sheed's dicta and more the characters' desires.

Sheed's seriousness as a craftsman reflects his world view. In his chaotic world men in crisis ask: "What am I to do about my marriage, my work, my Self?" Max Jamison recognizes that the examined existence offers no easy out: " 'Why?' is a question that no man in his right mind asks himself, unless he has an answer rigged." Yet Sheed's characters embark on quests for which he offers only the mature acceptance of what a man truly is and not what an enlarged ego thinks he should be. As George Wren discovers in *Office Politics*: "It doesn't matter who edited the damn thing [*The Outsider*], it always comes out the same." With increasing verbal skill and structural control Wilfrid Sheed continues to offer variations of a modern satirist's warning: Ego, all is Ego.

—Fred Silva

SIGAL, Clancy. American. Born in Chicago, Illinois, 6 September 1926. Educated at the University of California, Los Angeles, B.A. in English 1950. Served in the United States Army Infantry, 1944-46: Staff Sergeant. Assistant to the Wage Coordinator, United Auto Workers, Detroit, 1946-47. Story Analyst, Columbia Pictures, Hollywood, 1952-54; Agent, Jaffe Agency, Los Angeles, 1954-56. Member, Citizens Committee to Defend American Freedoms, Los Angeles, 1953-56, and Group 68, Americans in Britain Against the Indo-China War. Has lived in England since 1957. Recipient: Houghton Mifflin Literary Fellowship, 1962. Agent: Elaine Greene Ltd., 31 Newington Green, London N16 9PU, England.

PUBLICATIONS

Novels

Weekend in Dinlock. Boston, Houghton Mifflin, and London, Secker and Warburg, 1960.
Going Away: A Report, A Memoir. Boston, Houghton Mifflin, 1962; London, Cape, 1963.
Zone of the Interior. New York, Crowell, 1976.

Uncollected Short Story

"Doctor Marfa," in *Paris Review 35*, Fall 1965.

* * *

Two documentary novels, *Weekend in Dinlock* and *Going Away*, have given Clancy Sigal a large reputation. These novels, imaginative fusions of autobiography, social history and fiction, convey a strong sense of time and place, a powerful feeling of reality. (A third novel, *Zone of the Interior*, is a lighter treatment of drugs and therapy in the 1960's).

Going Away (Sigal's first novel, though revised and published after *Weekend in Dinlock*) is subtitled "A Report, A Memoir." It is a compendium of significant social and political observations, an "American Studies" novel answering the question, "*What's it like in America these days?*" The time is 1956, the opening days of the Hungarian Revolt, and the autobiographical narrator drives from Los Angeles to New York with the manuscript of a confessional novel, experiencing a nervous breakdown as he passes through America and reviews his past. It is an "on-the-road" novel, a pursuit of lost time, a gathering of the narrator's experiences and a diagnosis of America's spiritual and political malaise: "for years, possibly since adolescence, I have dryly and studiously examined the indications of my own life as a clue to the country at large, as though reading a psychic thermometer."

The narrator is half-Irish, half-Jewish, a radical ex-union-organizer, an ex-Hollywood-agent, an ex-soldier in Occupied Germany; by age 29 he has led half a dozen full, complex lives and reached the end of his road in America. He realizes he must leave America in order to find it. He visits old friends and enemies, sees them in despair and collapse, so he flees his dead past encapsulated in an America of brutalizing forces—billboards, highways, movies, the blank, alienating face of capitalist culture.

Once in England, where he finished *Going Away*, Sigal also wrote a much smaller but beautifully articulated study of Yorkshire mines and miners, *Weekend in Dinlock*. A documentary study of a composite mining village in the midlands, the book compares favorably with George Orwell's classic *The Road to Wigan Pier*. It chronicles the miner's life in the nationalized mines and draws almost the same conclusion Orwell made a generation earlier—that mining is an atrocity, a deadening, dehumanizing torment on which all industrial civilization rests. The novel is also the story of Davie, a Lawrence-like young man who is both a gifted painter and a miner, caught between the need to paint, to escape Dinlock, and the powerful *machismo* ethic of the miners which demands that he stay on the job and prove himself at the coal face. Finally, the narrator leaves Davie wrestling with his irresolvable conflict, still trapped by Dinlock.

This brilliant small study is a logical extension of *Going Away*. The narrator has fled America and found in England's coal country yet another world of dehumanizing technology and alienated individuals. The wide-open feeling of crossing America (the loneliness of the land itself) is replaced by the paranoid claustrophobia of the mine shaft and the paranoid closed society of the provincial village. Both novels chronicle the pressures of modern life on the individual, both reflect Sigal's own history: "I was a member, in good standing, of the Double Feature Generation: nothing new was startling to me." Sigal, in *Going Away*, gives the intense, confessional view of the 1950's in the backwash of McCarthyism, the collapse of the old left, and draws conclusions about his own sense of self: "I see no salvation in personal relationships, in political action, or in any job I might undertake in society. Everything in me cries out that we are meaningless pieces of paste; everything in me hopes this is not the end of the story." Clancy Sigal, in two novels, has depicted America's basic contemporary dilemmas and has asked the questions we must answer to survive.

—William J. Schafer

SILLITOE, Alan. British. Born in Nottingham, 4 March 1928. Educated in Nottingham schools to the age of 14. Served as a wireless operator in the Royal Air Force, 1946-49. Married the poet Ruth Fainlight in 1959; one son and one daughter. Recipient: Authors Club prize, 1958; Hawthornden Prize, 1960. Honorary Fellow, Manchester Polytechnic, 1977; Fellow, Royal Geographical Society. Address: 21 The Street, Wittersham, Kent, England.

PUBLICATIONS

Novels

Saturday Night and Sunday Morning. London, W.H. Allen, 1958; New York, Knopf, 1959.
The General. London, W.H. Allen, 1960; New York, Knopf, 1961; as *Counterpoint*, New York, Avon, 1968.
Key to the Door. London, W.H. Allen, 1961; New York, Knopf, 1962.
The Death of William Posters. London, Macmillan, and New York, Knopf, 1965.
A Tree on Fire. London, Macmillan, 1967; New York, Doubleday, 1968.
A Start in Life. London, W.H. Allen, 1970; New York, Scribner, 1971.
Travels in Nihilon. London, W.H. Allen, 1971; New York, Scribner, 1972.

Raw Material. London, W.H. Allen, 1972; New York, Scribner, 1973; revised edition, W.H. Allen, 1979.
The Flame of Life. London, W.H. Allen, 1974.
The Widower's Son. London, W.H. Allen, 1976; New York, Harper, 1977.
The Storyteller. London, W.H. Allen, 1979; New York, Simon and Schuster, 1980.

Short Stories

The Loneliness of the Long Distance Runner. London, W.H. Allen, 1959; New York, Knopf, 1960.
The Ragman's Daughter. London, W.H. Allen, 1963; New York, Knopf, 1964.
A Sillitoe Selection, edited by Michael Marland. London, Longman, 1968.
Guzman Go Home. London, Macmillan, 1968; New York, Doubleday, 1969.
Men, Women, and Children. London, W.H. Allen, 1973; New York, Scribner, 1974.
Down to the Bone (selection). Exeter, Wheaton, 1976.
The Second Chance and Other Stories. London, Cape, and New York, Simon and Schuster, 1981.

Plays

The Ragman's Daughter (produced Felixstowe, Suffolk, 1966).
All Citizens Are Soldiers, with Ruth Fainlight, adaptation of a play by Lope de Vega (produced Stratford upon Avon and London, 1967). London, Macmillan, and Chester Springs, Pennsylvania, Dufour, 1969.
The Slot Machine (as *This Foreign Field*, produced London, 1970). Included in *Three Plays*, 1978.
Pit Strike (televised, 1977). Included in *Three Plays*, 1978.
The Interview (produced London, 1978). Included in *Three Plays*, 1978.
Three Plays (includes *The Slot Machine*, *Pit Strike*, *The Interview*). London, W.H. Allen, 1978.

Screenplays: *Saturday Night and Sunday Morning*, 1960; *The Loneliness of the Long Distance Runner*, 1961; *The Ragman's Daughter*, 1974.

Television Play: *Pit Strike*, 1977.

Verse

Without Beer or Bread. London, Outposts, 1957.
The Rats and Other Poems. London, W.H. Allen, 1960.
A Falling Out of Love and Other Poems. London, W.H. Allen, 1964.
Love in the Environs of Voronezh. London, Macmillan, 1968; New York, Doubleday, 1970.
Shaman and Other Poems. London, Turret, 1968.
Poems, with Ted Hughes and Ruth Fainlight. London, Rainbow Press, 1971.
Barbarians and Other Poems. London, Turret, 1974.
Storm: New Poems. London, W.H. Allen, 1974.
Day-Dream Communique. Knotting, Bedfordshire, Sceptre Press, 1977.
From "Snow on the North Side of Lucifer." Knotting, Bedfordshire, Sceptre Press, 1979.
Snow on the North Side of Lucifer. London, W.H. Allen, 1979.

Other

Road to Volgograd (travel). London, W.H. Allen, and New York, Knopf, 1964.
The City Adventures of Marmalade Jim (juvenile). London, Macmillan, 1967; revised edition, London, Robson, 1977.
Mountains and Caverns: Selected Essays. London, W.H. Allen, 1975.
Big John and the Stars (juvenile). London, Robson, 1977.
The Incredible Fencing Fleas (juvenile). London, Robson, 1978.
Marmalade Jim at the Farm (juvenile). London, Robson, 1980.

Editor, *Poems for Shakespeare 7*. London, Bear Gardens Museum and Arts Centre, 1979.

*

Critical Studies: *Alan Sillitoe* edited by Michael Marland, London, Times Authors Series, 1970; *Alan Sillitoe* by Allen Richard Penner, New York, Twayne, 1972; *Alan Sillitoe: A Critical Assessment* by Stanley Atherton, London, W.H. Allen, 1979.

Alan Sillitoe comments:

As one gets older there is less to say about why one writes, but at the same time there is more to write. The writing also gets more difficult, which is as it should be.

* * *

As Alan Sillitoe's fiction has developed beyond the self-contained and brilliantly presented world of *Saturday Night and Sunday Morning*, the point of view has changed from that of Arthur Seaton, the energetic, unsentimental, and superficially satisfied protagonist of the first novel, to that of his elder brother, Brian, the central figure of *Key to the Door*. Arthur, grateful for the luck involved in the contrast between his current well-paid job at the capstan lathe and his father's life on the dole before the Second World War, is relatively content so long as he can find a plentiful supply of beer and women. Sillitoe, emphasizing his perceptive intransigence in a world that is both hypocritical and hostile, makes him seem an attractive force. Brian, however, is more the intellectual, the man who questions and feels strongly, who, like Frank Dawley, the Midlands working-man in a number of the later novels, searches for a more complete life he cannot easily find. Brian is given more background, more development from childhood, than Arthur was, seen in incidents like that in which he saves pennies to buy a copy of *The Count of Monte Cristo*, his impoverished parents furious that he would waste his hard-scrounged money on a book. Part of the difference in these points of view is also apparent in the treatment of politics. For Arthur, all political systems are fraudulent rhetoric to cheat the working-man, although he has some sympathy with the Communists because, in England in the 1950's, they are so universally despised or ignored. Brian is interested in Communism as an idea, a possible transformation of the society of privilege. When conscripted after the war and sent to Malaya, Brian considers helping a Communist revolution against the establishment he now inadvertently represents. Frank Dawley, in *The Death of William Posters* and *A Tree on Fire*, running guns to the FLN in Algeria, aids the Communists directly by ideological choice, although later, back in England in *Flame of Life*, still working out his own guilt concerning the death of a comrade in Algeria, he questions the value of his revolutionary commitment.

Although these presentations of the working-class intellectual developing against strong pressures of class and society are more vulnerable to sentimentality or rhetorical rant than is Arthur Seaton's tightly controlled perspective, they are also deeper both intellectually and emotionally. Sillitoe has always been interested in abstract ideas, evident even in his early novel, *The General*, in which the symbols of music (in the form of a symphony orchestra) and mathematics (in the form of the general's focus on precise maps) contrast contradictory attitudes toward the best way of controlling the "primeval slime" of men involved in war. The structures of some later novels are similarly attached to an idea: *Travels in Nihilon* recounts the adventures of five travelers from our world who go out to the corrupt world of nihilism to write a guide-book; *A Start in Life*, in which the metaphors are more literary, follows the picaresque account of a contemporary bastard looking for where he belongs. Sillitoe is not at his best in the abstract novel, dwelling heavily on the framework of ideas as if each possible ramification of the intellectual point is a unique discovery. *Travels in Nihilon* degenerates into a kind of silly violence, as if characters from a Marx brothers film are suddenly caught in a James Bond world taken seriously, and *A Start in Life* blends the comic and picaresque techniques of the early John Wain with those of Henry Fielding, without the sense of humor of either writer. Rather, Sillitoe is at his most probing and effective in fiction, like *Key to the Door*, *The Death of William Posters*, *Flame of Life*, and *The Widower's Son*, in which the struggle to become the intellectual is part of a developing perspective and the ideas part of the attitude toward experience.

In *Key to the Door* Sillitoe depicts effectively the lives of Brian's parents: his mother's childhood as the daughter of a rural blacksmith, his father as the craftsman who slowly decays in an economy of continuous slump between the two World Wars which allows him no independent existence, and the origins of the constant emotional violence and alternations between love and hatred. The background is close to that which Sillitoe gives himself in *Raw Material*, a volume of memoirs that he claims is a fiction designed to get at the truth since "everything written is fiction" (a beginning of his speculations about the complicated nature of fiction that culminate in his recent novel *The Storyteller*). *Raw Material* details his family background, the contrast between the simple, explosive blacksmiths, "the poetry," the Burtons, his mother's family, and the dark, sallow, complex, politically rebellious Sillitoes, "the force that pushes" the poetry. Accounts of the personal past are interspersed with and connected to an argument that the social fabric of England was destroyed by the disaster of the First World War, the needless struggle in which the upper classes sent millions to their deaths in order to preserve their own mindless kind of privilege: "Before 1914 a unity could have been possible, and the men might then have tried it. Joining up to fight was, in a sense, their way of saying yes, but the old men used this affirmation to try and finish them off." Whether or not this view of social history is true (and Sillitoe argues for it cogently and knowledgeably), it provides the combination of intensity and socio-historical dimension that gives considerable richness to Sillitoe's fiction. This sense of a social past, behind descriptions like that of the Nottingham Goose Fair in *Saturday Night and Sunday Morning*, the grubby night lights and Nottingham music hall in the 1920's in *Key to the Door*, the 1972 miner's strike in "Pit Strike" (as well as descriptions in "Before Show Comes" and "The Chiker," other stories published in *Men, Women, and Children*), and the rural Lincolnshire where Albert Handley, Frank Dawley's friend, the proletarian painter, begins, helps give Sillitoe's prose a violent energy, a hard and explosive quality often absent in his more abstract or comic work.

In all Sillitoe's fiction, the world is seen as a jungle. Yet the nature of the jungle changes. In the earliest fiction, like *Saturday Night and Sunday Morning* and "The Loneliness of the Long Distance Runner," society and the exterior world are jungles in which the protagonist, himself neutral, must survive through a combination of luck and shrewd skill. But, starting with *Key to the Door*, the jungle is both the exterior worlds of Nottingham and Malaya and the questions, uncertainties, false starts, and violence within the protagonist himself. Brian has internalized all the casual violence in his background, and, unlike Arthur, cannot relegate it to a cheerful acceptance of a Saturday night punch-up. Brian begins the recognition that brutality, although endemic, can be overcome, that violence is not the "key to the door," a recognition developed further in the character of Frank Dawley through the three novels in which he is central. In the first, *The Death of William Posters*, chronicling Frank's movement away from his stifling Nottingham world, William Posters is the fictional image of the working-class man, defiant, persecuted, always hounded by society but never finally caught, using violence against others and himself indiscriminately and self-destructively. As Frank tries to move, out of Nottingham, then out of England, trying to direct his sense of violence appropriately outward and politically, he attempts to exorcise the image of Posters, leaving it moribund in Nottingham. Yet, in Sillitoe's world, Posters is never finally exorcised. Appearing as a casualty in the First World War and as a figure who casually beats his wife or his children, he is even reincarnated in *Flame of Life* as an itinerant, pot-smoking youth of the 1970's Dean William Posters, who runs off with Albert Handley's wife, just one of the gestures of irrationality and violence that destroys the community Albert and Frank Dawley have tried to establish. The theme of brutality, in Sillitoe's world, is also treated in its rationalized and institutionalized version, the military. Although many of the working-class characters deride the military and none is patriotic, Sillitoe demonstrates, particularly in an excellent recent novel, *The Widower's Son*, the use of the military career as the conscious focus for working out all the stresses of the individual and social jungles within modern man. Although unable finally to justify his interest in gunnery or the parallel war of his marriage to a general's daughter, the career soldier, heroic back at Dunkerque, an analogue for an attempted assimilation of class in England, is treated with complexity and sympathy.

Sillitoe's fiction depicts middle-class characters as well as members of the working-classes. At times, however, the middle-class characters are simple types, entirely predictable creations used as contrast for the intelligent, energetic man from the working-class world. Frank Dawley's two different middle-class mistresses seem identical, superficially placid and competent but deeply unfulfilled by their conventional marriages, apparently just waiting for authentic passion, represented by the rebellious working-man, to arrive. Their husbands are even more stereotyped, hollow, remote, educated, far from the source of life and unable to deal with violence in any form (one ignores it, the other destroys himself when confronted with it). Albert Handley becomes successful, he acquires a fat, homosexual gallery manager and a thinly elegant titled mistress, stereotypes both. These portraits seem simplified social abstraction defended by essays about the vitality of the working-class. This side of Sillitoe, most visible in *A Tree on Fire*, can sound rather silly, as in one of Frank's mistress's thoughts about men from the north: "cloth-capped, hardworking, generous, and bruto, or that was the impression she got from reading a book (or was it books?) called *Hurry on Jim* by Kingsley Wain that started by someone with eighteen pints and fifteen whiskies in him falling downstairs on his way to the top." The note of self-satire does not assuage the simplification.

In spite of such reductions, Sillitoe has always felt that the majority of whatever class is unintelligent and unresponsive. In all his fiction, he frequently refers to "rats," a term that, in his long poem called "The Rats," he uses to refer to all the agents of organized religious, political, or industrial society, a category that includes most people. Increasingly in the later fiction, he concentrates attention on the non-rat, the special person (even, as in *The Widower's Son*, the special person within an institution of "rats"), the man who attempts to challenge experience, to achieve something more than might have been expected. The special person is devoted to work, to achievement to exorcise his own brutality and that of others, and to a sense of dignity. Yet contemporary society rewards futile, parasitic, or soul-destroying work; England remains, for the most part, the land of William Posters. The special person is always posed against the society, always cares about himself and his work, rebels, burns with energy, and has roots in a more meaningful past. He is, imagistically, "a tree on fire" or "the flame of life," needing to test his specialness in some kind of vital connection with the modern world (the terms of that connection were more political in the 1960's than in the 1970's). The similarity between Sillitoe's fiction and that of D.H. Lawrence goes deeper than a common origin in the working-classes in and near Nottingham and deeper than what occasionally looks like imitation in a particular novel, as *The Death of William Posters* particularly resembles *Aaron's Rod*. Rather, as Sillitoe's concerns have widened, he has, with similar themes and attitudes, developed an authentically Lawrentian perspective of his own. The two writers are alike in their representation of the complexity of working-class experience (Albert Handley, for example, had a portrait of the Queen in his front hall when he was poor and replaced it with one of Mao Tse-tung when he became rich), in their insistence on the need to recognize violence and brutality in human experience, in their incipient romanticism, in their essays about work, in their constantly restless thoughtfulness, in their slow recognition of a need for the special person to get away from England (although this is never, finally, a panacea), and even in their occasional reductions and lack of sympathy. Sillitoe lacks Lawrence's genius, as well as his ease with theoretical and metaphysical argument, but he has the same kind of restless energy, the probing, the seriousness, and the range, all qualities that make possible the creation of unique fiction.

—James Gindin

SINCLAIR, Andrew (Annandale). British. Born in Oxford, 21 January 1935. Educated at Eton College (King's Scholar), 1948-53; Trinity College, Cambridge, 1955-58, B.A. (double 1st) in history 1958, Ph.D. in American history 1962. Served in the Coldstream Guards, 1953-55: Ensign. Married 1) Marianne Alexandre in 1960 (divorced); 2) Miranda Seymour in 1973, two sons. Harkness Fellow, Harvard University, Cambridge, Massachusetts, and Columbia University, New York, 1959-61; Fellow and Director of Historical Studies, Churchill College, Cambridge, 1961-63; Fellow, American Council of Learned Societies, 1963-64; Lecturer in American History, University College, London, 1965-67. Since 1967, Managing Director, Lorrimer Publishing Ltd., London. Recipient: Maugham Award, 1967. Fellow, Royal Society of Literature, 1972; Fellow, Society of American Historians, 1973. Address: 15 Hanover Terrace, London N.W.1, England.

PUBLICATIONS

Novels

The Breaking of Bumbo. London, Faber, and New York, Simon and Schuster, 1959.
My Friend Judas. London, Faber, 1959; New York, Simon and Schuster, 1961.
The Project. London, Faber, and New York, Simon and Schuster, 1960.
The Hallelujah Bum. London, Faber, 1963; as *The Paradise Bum*, New York, Atheneum, 1963.
The Raker. London, Cape, and New York, Atheneum, 1964.
Gog. London, Weidenfeld and Nicolson, and New York, Macmillan, 1967.
Magog. London, Weidenfeld and Nicolson, and New York, Harper, 1972.
The Surrey Cat. London, Joseph, 1976; as *Cat*, London, Sphere, 1977.
A Patriot for Hire. London, Joseph, 1978.
The Facts in the Case of E.A. Poe. London, Weidenfeld and Nicolson, 1979; New York, Holt Rinehart, 1980.

Uncollected Short Stories

"To Kill a Loris," in *Texas Quarterly* (Austin), Autumn 1961.
"A Head for Monsieur Dimanche," in *Atlantic* (Boston), September 1962.
"The Atomic Band," in *Transatlantic Review 21* (London), Summer 1966.
"Twin," in *The Best of Granta*. London, Secker and Warburg, 1967.

Plays

My Friend Judas (produced London, 1959).
Adventures in the Skin Trade, adaptation of the work by Dylan Thomas (produced London, 1966; Washington, D.C., 1969). London, Dent, 1967; New York, New Directions, 1968.
Under Milk Wood (screenplay). London, Lorrimer, and New York, Simon and Schuster, 1972.

Screenplays: *Before Winter Comes*, 1969; *The Breaking of Bumbo*, 1970; *Under Milk Wood*, 1971.

Television Plays: *The Chocolate Tree*, 1963; *Old Soldiers*, 1964; *Martin Eden*, from the novel by Jack London, 1980.

Other

Prohibition: The Era of Excess. London, Faber, and Boston, Little Brown, 1962; as *Era of Excess*, New York, Harper, 1964.
The Available Man: The Life Behind the Masks of Warren Gamaliel Harding. New York, Macmillan, 1965.
The Better Half: The Emancipation of the American Woman. New York, Harper, 1965; London, Cape, 1966.
A Concise History of the United States. London, Thames and Hudson, and New York, Viking Press, 1967; revised edition, Thames and Hudson, 1970.
The Last of the Best: The Aristocracy of Europe in the Twentieth Century. London, Weidenfeld and Nicolson, and New York, Macmillan, 1969.
Guevara. London, Fontana, and New York, Viking Press, 1970.
Dylan Thomas: Poet of His People. London, Joseph, 1975; as *Dylan Thomas: No Man More Magical*, New York, Holt Rinehart, 1975.
Inkydoo, The Wild Boy (juvenile). London, Abelard Schuman, 1976; as *Carina and the Wild Boy*, London, Beaver, 1977.
Jack: A Biography of Jack London. New York, Harper, 1977; London, Weidenfeld and Nicolson, 1978.
The Savage: A History of Misunderstanding. London, Weidenfeld and Nicolson, 1977.
John Ford: A Biography. London, Allen and Unwin, and New York, Dial Press, 1979.
Corsair: The Life of J. Pierpont Morgan. London, Weidenfeld and Nicolson, and Boston, Little Brown, 1981.

Translator, *Selections from the Greek Anthology*. London, Weidenfeld and Nicolson, 1967; New York, Macmillan, 1968.
Translator, with Carlos P. Hansen, *Bolivian Diary: Ernesto "Che" Guevara*. London, Lorrimer, 1968.
Translator, with Marianne Alexandre, *La Grande Illusion* (scenario), by Jean Renoir. London, Lorrimer, 1968.

*

Critical Study: *Old Lines, New Forces* edited by Robert K. Morris, Rutherford, New Jersey, Fairleigh Dickinson University Press, 1976.

Theatrical Activities:

Director: **Films**—*The Breaking of Bumbo*, 1970; *Under Milk Wood*, 1971.

Andrew Sinclair comments:

I work between fact and fiction: history and biography, the novel and film. The one informs the other without confusion, I hope. Aging, I find myself admiring professionals, not philosophers. Like the Victorians I have found liberty in writing and in not working for wages. Freedom is having four jobs—and only on hire. Before I die I would like to make one more good film, complete *Gog* and *Magog* with *King Ludd*, and write a trilogy on my Scots roots. That would be quite enough.

* * *

From the beginning Andrew Sinclair established himself as a writer of extraordinary fluency and copiousness, whether in fiction or in American social history. His early novels were light-hearted attempts to capture significant moments in the life of the 1950's: the misadventures of a young National Service officer in the Brigade of Guards in *The Breaking of Bumbo*, or life in Cambridge when traditional academic forms were coming apart at the seams in *My Friend Judas*. Sinclair's awareness of social nuance and his ready ear for changing forms of speech made him an effective observer, though at the cost of making these novels soon seem dated. *The Project* was a deliberate attempt to move to new ground—the moral fable and apocalyptic science fiction—but the result was wooden and contrived. In *The Hallelujah Bum* Sinclair returned to Ben Birt, the cheerfully iconoclastic hero of *My Friend Judas*, and thrust him into a thin but fast-moving narrative about driving across the United States in a stolen car. The book was partly a loving evocation of American landscape, and partly an example of a new fictional genre that emerged in the 1960's which showed the impact of America on a visiting Englishman.

Sinclair's next novel, *The Raker*, was a fresh endeavour to get away from the fictional recreation of personal experience, though it was still a projection of personal obsession, in this case what Sinclair has described as a preoccupation with death. *The Raker* is, if anything, too nakedly allegorical, with a strong flavour of Gothic fantasy about it. But it brings together the separate vision of the novelist and the historian, and it is most powerful in its superimposition of the plague-ridden London of the 17th century on the modern metropolis. The preoccupation with history and myth in *The Raker* was fully worked out in *Gog*, which is Sinclair's one outstanding contribution so far to contemporary fiction, compared with which he dismisses his previous five novels as no more than "experiments in style." "Gog" is a legendary giant of British mythology, personified in the novel by an enormous naked man washed up on the Scottish coast in the summer of 1945. The book is essentially a long picaresque account of his walk to London to claim his inheritance as a representative of the British people. On the way he has many fantastic adventures, some comic, some cruel, but all reflecting Sinclair's extraordinary imaginative exuberance. The journey takes him to many sacred places, such as York Minster, Glastonbury, and Stonehenge, and on one level the story is an exploration of the multi-layered past of England, almost like the excavation of an archaeological site. The richness of content is matched by a great variety of formal device: *Gog* draws on the techniques of the comic strip and the cinema, as well as those of the novel. It may, though, be an isolated achievement. *Magog*, its sequel, which describes the life and times of Gog's villainous brother in post-war England, is much less interesting. Although an intelligent, inventive and entertaining piece of social satire, it has little of *Gog*'s mythic power.

—Bernard Bergonzi

SINCLAIR, Jo. Pseudonym for Ruth Seid. American. Born in Brooklyn, New York, 1 July 1913. Educated at John Hay High School, Cleveland; attended night classes in playwriting, Western Reserve University, Cleveland. Has worked in a factory, in advertising, as a ghost-writer and trade magazine writer; and for the Works Progress Administration (WPA). Assistant Director, Publicity and Promotion, American Red Cross, Cleveland, 1942-46. Since 1946, free-lance writer. Recipient: Harper Prize, 1946; Daroff Memorial Award, 1956; National Conference of Christians and Jews Brotherhood Award, 1956; Fund for the Republic Prize, 1956; Wolpaw Playwriting Grant, 1969. Address: 1021 Wellington Road, Jenkintown, Pennsylvania 19046, U.S.A.

PUBLICATIONS

Novels

Wasteland. New York, Harper, 1946; London, Macmillan, 1948.
Sing at My Wake. New York, McGraw Hill, 1951.
The Changelings. New York, McGraw Hill, 1955.
Anna Teller. New York, McKay, 1960; London, W.H. Allen, 1961.

Uncollected Short Stories

"Children at Play," in *Theme and Variation in the Short Story*, edited by John de Lancey Ferguson and others. New York, Cordon, 1938.
"Red Necktie," in *America in Literature*, edited by Termaine McDowell. New York, Crofts, 1944.
"I Was on Relief," in *Social Insight Through Short Stories*, edited by Josephine Strode. New York, Harper, 1946.
"The Brothers," in *Cross Section 1947*, edited by Edwin Seaver. New York, Fischer, 1947.
"Listen to My Heart," in *Common Ground* (New York), viii, 3, 1948.
"Night Time," in *Accent* (Urbana, Illinois), x, 4, 1950.
"The Family," in *Accent* (Urbana, Illinois), xii, 2, 1952.
"Night and the General," in *Epoch* (Ithaca, New York), iv, 2, 1952.
"Curtain at Midnight," in *Saturday Evening Post* (Philadelphia), 15 November 1952.
"The Boy Who Stole Pennies," in *American Magazine* (Springfield, Ohio), December 1953.
"I Choose You," in *Collier's* (Springfield, Ohio), 23 July 1954.
"Night Club Baby," in *Cosmopolitan* (New York), February 1957.
"The Medal," in *The American Judaism Reader*, edited by Paul Kresh. New York, Abelard Schuman, 1967.

Play

The Long Moment (produced Cleveland, 1951; New York, 1952.)

*

Jo Sinclair comments:

I write because I have to; it's the only meaning I have discovered for my life. Writing is extremely hard for me, and yet nothing else draws me as a profession. I am particularly interested in the psychological aspects of man, woman, and child; in the impact of race and religion on people; and the enormous influence of love and hope on anybody and everybody.

I'd add this: Writer, get yourself a trade, profession, or job—and write, if you must, week ends and holidays. It's no fun to earn little or no money—even on what you consider in your heart a good book. The writer, at least in the United States, needs either a weekly salary or a patron of the arts!

* * *

It's not easy to remember when even enlightened people were fearful of consulting a psychiatrist lest they be considered insane or immoral. Now that seeing a "shrink" is almost as casual as going to a dentist, most of the novels which aided and abetted the shift in public opinion toward psychotherapy seem dated. The struggle to survive as reflected in contemporary fiction subsumes without fanfare psychic conflicts that were once daringly controversial.

Jo Sinclair's early fame and fortune were functions of her talent, tenacity, and timing. Back in 1946, alienated by fear and shyness from sources of help, we were ready for *Wasteland*, Jo Sinclair's first and still best-known novel. Winner of the Harper Prize, as well as enthusiastic critical notices, *Wasteland* gained its author a permanent place in that sometimes fickle sun which shines on successful novelists. It is good to be able to report that Jo Sinclair survived the dangerous aspects of these events. The three novels which ıllowed at intervals of approximately five years were spaced far ıough apart clearly to imply the kind of deliberation and concern hich results in much revising. Unlike the first work, however, they ;ver caught the same public fancy that boomed *Wasteland*.

From the first flash success in 1946 through *Sing at My Wake*, *he Changelings*, and *Anna Teller*, Sinclair's writing certainly did ɔt deteriorate, but readers' interests moved faster toward more olent resolutions than her reasonable humanity allowed for. Sinair continues to exhort human beings not to be afraid, urging them scrutinize their wastelands and to cultivate them if possible. She nflinchingly insisted on noting ghetto problems long before ggressive defenses of minorities had become fashionable. In a real nse she pioneered the so-called Jewish novel, breaking ground for ıe more sophisticated—but not necessarily more honest—works of ellow, Malamud, and Roth. Furthermore, Sinclair was virtually e first to focus on the inner conflict in minority identification as nenable to treatment.

Jake, the protagonist of *Wasteland*, was a weakling. He was ıcertain of what it meant to be a Jew, anxious and underɔtentiated as a man. Supported by his sister's enthusiasm for ychotherapy he finally agreed to consult her psychiatrist. The :count of his therapy includes flashbacks and relevant digressions, nphasizing particularly the role played in his life by his sister, ebbie. Jake's progress toward understanding is simply and clearly :lineated, and the novel possesses a classical unity that Sinclair's ter works perforce lack—as her objectives became more complex. ıke's therapy-trip, piloted by a good and wise doctor, was a bold lventure into an unknown which has only since then been arted—*ad nauseam*.

Sinclair's second novel grew out of the author's concern with ıother kind of alienation. An insecure woman, trying to adjust to ı inadequate marriage, finally settled for the mature love of a son ıe had helped liberate. The problem is personal, but it takes on eaning in the context of Sinclair's championing of all outsiders. If *'asteland* is a better novel, it is only because the problem is there nited by the structure implicit in the therapeutic process.

The Changelings is packed with desperate young people—Jews, acks, and deviants—each of whom feels as if he were "left in a ace secretly, instead of the person who's supposed to be there." he one we care most about is an outrageous tomboy, resembling ebbie in the first novel, whose experiments with sex, race relaɔns, and other existential realities, anticipate contemporary liberion movements.

Finally, in her fourth novel Sinclair engaged a big subject in the e-story of a 74-year-old woman, who, after fighting in the Hunrian uprisings, fled to America, putative land of freedom. At once wildered by those aspects of freedom that seemed to her childish, :travagant, and insincere, she eventually, like all Sinclair's protagists, helped others to transcend the sterility of their wastelands ıd the bigotries of their ghettos.

—John A. Weigel

.NGER, Isaac Bashevis. American. Born in Radzymin, Poland, July 1904; emigrated to the United States in 1935, naturalized, 43. Educated at the Tachkemoni Rabbinical Seminary, Warsaw, 20-22. Married Alma Haimann in 1940; one son. Proofreader and anslator for *Literarishe Bleter*, Warsaw, 1923-33; journalist for e *Jewish Daily Forward*, New York, from 1935. Recipient: Louis amed Prize, 1950, 1956; American Academy grant, 1959; Daroff emorial Award, 1963; two National Endowment for the Arts ants, 1966; Brandeis University Creative Arts Award, 1969; ational Book Award, for children's literature, 1970, and for ficɔn, 1974; Nobel Prize for Literature, 1978. D.H.L.: Hebrew Union ollege, Los Angeles, 1963; D.Lit.: Colgate University, Hamilton, ;w York, 1972; Litt.D.: Bard College, Annandale-on-Hudson, New York, 1974. Member, American Academy, 1965; American Academy of Arts and Sciences, 1969; Jewish Academy of Arts and Sciences; Polish Institute of Arts and Sciences. Address: 209 West 86th Street, New York, New York 10024, U.S.A.

PUBLICATIONS

Novels

The Family Moskat, translated by A.H. Gross. New York, Knopf, 1950; London, Secker and Warburg, 1966.
Satan in Goray, translated by Jacob Sloan. New York, Farrar Straus, 1955; London, Peter Owen, 1958.
The Magician of Lublin, translated by Elaine Gottlieb and Joseph Singer. New York, Farrar Straus, 1960; London, Secker and Warburg, 1961.
The Slave, translated by the author and Cecil Hemley. New York, Farrar Straus, 1962; London, Secker and Warburg, 1963.
The Manor, translated by Elaine Gottlieb and Joseph Singer. New York, Farrar Straus, 1967; London, Secker and Warburg, 1968.
The Estate, translated by Joseph Singer, Elaine Gottlieb, and Elizabeth Shub. New York, Farrar Straus, 1969; London, Cape, 1970.
Enemies: A Love Story, translated by Alizah Shevrin and Elizabeth Shub. New York, Farrar Straus, and London, Cape, 1972.
Shosha. New York, Farrar Straus, 1978; London, Cape, 1979.
Reaches of Heaven. New York, Farrar Straus, 1980.

Short Stories

Gimpel the Fool and Other Stories, translated by Saul Bellow and others. New York, Farrar Straus, 1957; London, Peter Owen, 1958.
The Spinoza of Market Street and Other Stories, translated by Elaine Gottlieb and others. New York, Farrar Straus, 1961; London, Secker and Warburg, 1962.
Short Friday and Other Stories, translated by Ruth Whitman and others. New York, Farrar Straus, 1964; London, Secker and Warburg, 1967.
Selected Short Stories, edited by Irving Howe. New York, Modern Library, 1966.
The Séance and Other Stories, translated by Ruth Whitman and others. New York, Farrar Straus, 1968; London, Cape, 1970.
A Friend of Kafka and Other Stories. New York, Farrar Straus, 1970; London, Cape, 1972.
A Crown of Feathers and Other Stories. New York, Farrar Straus, 1973; London, Cape, 1974.
Passions and Other Stories. New York, Farrar Straus, 1975; London, Cape, 1976.
Old Love. New York, Farrar Straus, 1979; London, Cape, 1980.

Uncollected Short Story

"Moon and Madness," in *New Yorker*, 6 October 1980.

Plays

The Mirror (produced New Haven, Connecticut, 1973).
Schlemiel the First (produced New Haven, Connecticut, 1974).
Yentl, The Yeshiva Boy, with Leah Napolin, adaptation of a story by Singer (produced New York, 1974). New York, French, 1977.
Teibele and Her Demon, with Eve Friedman (produced Minneapolis, 1978; New York, 1979).

Other

In My Father's Court (autobiography), translated by Channah Kleinerman-Goldstein and others. New York, Farrar Straus, 1966; London, Secker and Warburg, 1967.

Zlateh the Goat and Other Stories (juvenile), translated by the author and Elizabeth Shub. New York, Harper, 1966; London, Longman, 1970.
Mazel and Shlimazel; or, The Milk of a Lioness (juvenile), translated by the author and Elizabeth Shub. New York, Farrar Straus, 1967; London, Cape, 1979.
The Fearsome Inn (juvenile), translated by the author and Elizabeth Shub. New York, Scribner, 1967; London, Collins, 1970.
When Schlemiel Went to Warsaw and Other Stories (juvenile), translated by the author and Elizabeth Shub. New York, Farrar Straus, 1968; London, Longman, 1974.
A Day of Pleasure: Stories of a Boy Growing Up in Warsaw (juvenile), translated by the author and Elizabeth Shub. New York, Farrar Straus, 1969; London, MacRae, 1980.
Elijah the Slave: A Hebrew Legend Retold (juvenile), translated by the author and Elizabeth Shub. New York, Farrar Straus, 1970.
Joseph and Koza; or, The Sacrifice to the Vistula (juvenile), translated by the author and Elizabeth Shub. New York, Farrar Straus, 1970.
Alone in the Wild Forest (juvenile), translated by the author and Elizabeth Shub. New York, Farrar Straus, 1971; Edinburgh, Canongate, 1980.
The Topsy-Turvy Emperor of China (juvenile), translated by the author and Elizabeth Shub. New York, Harper, 1971.
An Isaac Bashevis Singer Reader. New York, Farrar Straus, 1971.
The Wicked City (juvenile), translated by the author and Elizabeth Shub. New York, Farrar Straus, 1972.
The Fools of Chelm and Their History (juvenile), translated by the author and Elizabeth Shub. New York, Farrar Straus, 1973.
The Hasidim: Paintings, Drawings, and Etchings, illustrated by Ira Moskowitz. New York, Crown, 1973.
Why Noah Chose the Dove (juvenile), translated by the author and Elizabeth Shub. New York, Farrar Straus, 1974.
A Tale of Three Wishes (juvenile), translated by the author and Elizabeth Shub. New York, Farrar Straus, 1976.
A Little Boy in Search of God: Mysticism in a Personal Light, with Ira Moskowitz. New York, Doubleday, 1976.
Naftali the Storyteller and His Horse, Sus, and Other Stories (juvenile), translated by the author and Elizabeth Shub. New York, Farrar Straus, 1976; London, Oxford University Press, 1977.
A Young Man in Search of Love, translated by Joseph Singer. New York, Doubleday, 1978.
Nobel Lecture. New York, Farrar Straus, and London, Cape, 1979.
Isaac Bashevis Singer on Literature and Life: An Interview, with Paul Rosenblatt and Gene Koppel. Tucson, University of Arizona Press, 1979.
The Power of Light: Eight Stories for Hanukkah (juvenile), translated by the author and Elizabeth Shub. New York, Farrar Straus, 1980.
Lost in America, translated by Joseph Singer. New York, Doubleday, 1981.

Editor, with Elaine Gottlieb, *Prism 2.* New York, Twayne, 1965.

Translator, *Pan*, by Knut Hamsen. Warsaw, Wilno, 1928.
Translator, *All Quiet on the Western Front*, by Erich Maria Remarque. Warsaw, Wilno, 1930.
Translator, *The Magic Mountain*, by Thomas Mann. Warsaw, Wilno, 4 vols., 1930.
Translator, *The Road Back*, by Erich Maria Remarque. Warsaw, Wilno, 1930.
Translator, *From Moscow to Jerusalem*, by Leon S. Glaser. New York, privately printed, 1938.

*

Bibliography: in *Bulletin of Bibliography* (Boston), January-March 1969.

Critical Studies: *Isaac Bashevis Singer and the Eternal Past* b Irving Buchen, New York, New York University Press, 1968; *Th Achievement of Isaac Bashevis Singer*, edited by Marcia Allentuc Carbondale, Southern Illinois University Press, 1969; *Critic Views of Isaac Bashevis Singer*, edited by Irving Malin, New Yor New York University Press, 1969, and *Isaac Bashevis Singer* b Malin, New York, Ungar, 1972; *Isaac Bashevis Singer* by Be Siegel, Minneapolis, University of Minnesota Press, 1969; *Isaa Bashevis Singer and His Art* by Askel Schiotz, New York, Harpe 1970; *Isaac Bashevis Singer, The Magician of West 86th Street* b Paul Kresh, New York, Dial Press, 1979; *Isaac Bashevis Singer* b Edward Alexander, Boston, Twayne, 1980.

Isaac Bashevis Singer comments:

I believe in story telling and dislike commentary by the autho The events must speak for themselves. A fiction writer who tries explain his story from a psychological or sociological point of vie destroys his chances to endure. I expressed this idea with the word Events never become stale; commentary is stale from the ve beginning. Commentary has almost destroyed the literature of o present century.

* * *

In the early years of the 20th century Yiddish literature w among the most active in the world and in the forefront of t development of the modern sensibility. The Jewish ghettos of Ne York and Warsaw were literary capitals, although few Genti knew it. Isaac Bashevis Singer migrated from Warsaw to New Yo in 1935 after the great days of the Yiddish literary community we over. He is the last major Yiddish writer but possibly he is t greatest (modern Jews almost all write in Hebrew). Yiddish liter ture was not provincial; on the contrary it was most cosmopolita but it was relatively uninfluenced by the modernist tradition alienation and revolution of the sensibility that began with Baud laire. Singer is the exception. He writes in the face of the full blast the contemporary apocalypse and with a mastery of all the refin ments of the 20th-century international style. His stories can compared at different levels to Bernanos's *Sous le soleil de Satan*, Céline, to Beckett, even to Artaud. Yet he is singularly independe of specific stylistic influence. His sources lie in the tangled langua of the Zohar, the Bible of the Kabbalists, and in the unearth *Märchen* of the tales of the Hasidic saints.

Martin Buber made the mystic anecdotes of the Hassids popul throughout the civilized world, but his was a sanitized Hasidism, mystical Judaism that could be assimilated by the assimilated, t Jewish communities of Dahlem and Schlactensee, the fashionab suburbs of Berlin. Singer's Hasidism is inextricably rooted in t *shtetel*, the muddy Jewish villages of Poland and the Warsa ghetto. There's none of Buber's benignity and enlightenment. The is alienation—from Western civilization, but only incidentally more fundamentally, from a cultural tradition that goes ba through the first Hebrews to be lost in the earliest records of paga Canaan—alienated but still bound, with nothing left but the witc craft, the pain, and the blood of brotherhood.

Singer's special vision is revealed most explicitly in his sho stories and the novel *Satan in Goray*, but it is there, equally powe ful but more implicit in his special handling of the tradition German and Yiddish family epic, *The Family Moskat*, *The Mano* and *The Estate*. In a sense the very subject of these novels assimilation, but it is a haunted and doomed assimilation, n primarily because we are always aware that the "final solution" assimilation is the extermination camp, but because the final co clusion is, in the words of James Baldwin, "Who needs to integrated into a burning house?" In a story based on a Chinese fo tale, the narrator goes to a highly civilized cocktail party in Ne York and, after he comes away, discovers that the people were ghosts. It's not just that the rich (Western) cultural Jewish commu ities of America are haunted by the smoke of the gas ovens. Sing has scarcely ever mentioned them. It's that life itself is haunted. T Goyim are all ghosts, too. We all live in the shadowy frivolous wor of a spiritualistic seance. An appreciable number of Singer's stories are about senility and the diseases, loneliness and hopelessness of the discarded old. They have an almost autobiographical veracity but they were written when Singer was not all that old. The point is that somewhere at the heart of reality something is running down. The crystal lattice on which everything is constructed is powdering away. Moral action is irreversible and inconvertible and Carnot's Third Law is operative in the spiritual realm as well as in thermodynamics. This is an ultimately comic vision of the world, ultimate to the point where comedy merges with tragedy into bitter compassion.

So Isaac Bashevis Singer is a writer of philosophic fictions. All too much writing of that sort is amorphous, rhetorical, and full of talk by both the author and his characters. Singer is extraordinarily precise and objective. The sensory reality of the Polish village, Warsaw bohemia, New York literary circles, or Florida hotel comes alive with the sharpest imagistic impact. His narrative is continuously dramatic, yet people seem to talk only when they have to, and Singer never talks about them. Of all Yiddish novelists he is probably the least influenced by the standard German novelists, whether Jacob Wasserman or Thomas Mann with their discursiveness, or by Dostoevsky's shameless intimacies. His people suffer the same tortures and nightmares as Dostoevsky's but he writes of them as clearly as Turgenev. Singer is probably the most specifically erotic of the major Yiddish writers, but of course by late 20th-century standards that's not very erotic. Sex seems to saturate his characters like a low-grade fever, to emerge in moments of desperation as a substitute for hope. The writer most like him in this regard is Georges Simenon. "Pity and terror," said Aristotle, taking as his model Sophocles, "are the elements of tragedy"—"and eroticism," added Euripides, and so say both Simenon and Singer. People make love in Singer's fictions as they might on a life raft, or as they might hanging all night in ropes on the north face of the Eiger in a storm. Once in a while there is total intimacy, the complete self revelation of love, but at last Carnot's Third Law takes over. Passion cools, but love runs down too. What is left is compassion and comradeship. This of course is what the two bums say at the end of *Waiting for Godot* or what Simenon's Inspector Maigret says as the killers and the dead of the Paris underworld or the bourgeois upper world go by him. So the "modernism" of Isaac Bashevis Singer is far more than a stylistic idiom learned from Stendhal and Baudelaire, James Joyce, German Expressionism, French Surrealism or Russian Futurism. It is the final modernism of the sensibility and the intellect confronted with the long drawn out apocalypse of the 20th century. He reminds us that it was the Jews who invented apocalyptic writing. Apocalypse, say the theologians, is disappointed prophecy. Singer turns that statement from the business of archangels, beasts with seven heads and chariots of fire to the commonplace relationships of ordinary people.

—Kenneth Rexroth

SINGH, Khushwant. Indian. Born in Hadali, India, now Pakistan, 2 February 1915. Educated at the Modern School, Delhi; St. Stephen's College, Delhi; Government College, Lahore, B.A. 1934; King's College, London, LL.B. 1938; called to the Bar, Inner Temple, London, 1938. Married Karal Malik in 1939; one son, one daughter. Practising lawyer, High Court, Lahore, 1939-47; Press Attaché, Indian Foreign Service, in London and Ottawa, 1947-51; member of the staff of the Department of Mass Communications, Unesco, Paris, 1954-56; Editor, *Yejna*, an Indian government publication, New Delhi, 1956-58; Visiting Lecturer, Oxford University, 1964, University of Rochester, New York, 1965, Princeton University, New Jersey, 1967, University of Hawaii, Honolulu, 1967, and Swarthmore College, Pennsylvania, 1969; Editor, *Illustrated Weekly of India*, Bombay, 1969-78. Since 1980, Editor-in-Chief, *Hindustan Times* and *Contour*, New Delhi; since 1980, Member of the Indian Parliament. Head of the Indian Delegation, Manila Writers Conference, 1965. Recipient: Rockefeller grant, 1966; Punjab Government grant, 1970; Padma Bhushan, India, 1974. Address: 49-E Sujan Singh Park, New Delhi 110 003, India.

PUBLICATIONS

Novels

Train to Pakistan. London, Chatto and Windus, 1956; New York, Grove Press, 1961; as *Mano Majra*, Grove Press, 1956.
I Shall Not Hear the Nightingale. New York, Grove Press, 1959; London, Calder, 1961.

Short Stories

The Mark of Vishnu and Other Stories. London, Saturn Press, 1950.
The Voice of God and Other Stories. Bombay, Jaico, 1957.
A Bride for the Sahib and Other Stories. Delhi, Hind, 1967.
Black Jasmine. Bombay, Jaico, 1971.

Other

The Sikhs. London, Allen and Unwin, and New York, Macmillan, 1953.
The Unending Trail. Delhi, Rajkamal, 1957.
The Sikhs Today: Their Religion, History, Culture, Customs, and Way of Life. Bombay, Orient Longman, 1959; revised edition, 1964.
Fall of the Kingdom of the Punjab. Bombay, Orient Longman, 1962.
A History of the Sikhs 1469-1964. Princeton, New Jersey, Princeton University Press, and London, Oxford University Press, 2 vols., 1963-66.
Ranjit Singh: Maharajah of the Punjab 1780-1839. London, Allen and Unwin, 1963.
Not Wanted in Pakistan. Delhi, Rajkamal, 1965.
Ghadar, 1915: India's First Armed Revolution, with Satindra Singh. New Delhi, R and K, 1966.
Homage to Guru Gobind Singh, with Suneet Veer Singh. Bombay, Jaico, 1966.
Shri Ram: A Biography, with Arun Joshi. London, Asia Publishing, 1968.
Religion of the Sikhs (lecture). Madras, University of Madras, 1968.
Khushwant Singh's India: A Mirror for Its Monsters and Monstrosities. Bombay, India Book House, 1970.
Khushwant Singh on War and Peace in India, Pakistan, and Bangladesh, edited by Mala Singh. Delhi, Hind, 1976.
Good People, Bad People, edited by Rahul Singh. New Delhi, Orient, 1977.
Khushwant Singh's India Without Humbug, edited by Rahul Singh. Bombay, India Book House, 1977.
Indira Gandhi Returns. New Delhi, Vision, 1979.

Editor, with Peter Russell, *A Note...on G. V. Desani's "All about H. Hatterr" and "Hali."* London and Amsterdam, Szeben, 1952.
Editor, with Jaya Thadani, *Land of the Five Rivers: Stories of the Punjab.* Bombay, Jaico, 1965.
Editor, *Sunset of the Sikh Empire*, by Sita Ram Kohli. Bombay, Orient Longman, 1967.
Editor, *I Believe.* Delhi, Hind, 1971.
Editor, *Love and Friendship.* New Delhi, Sterling, 1974.
Editor, with Qurratulain Hyder, *Stories from India.* New Delhi, Sterling, 1974.
Editor, *Gurus, Godmen, and Good People.* Bombay, Orient Longman, 1975.

Translator, *Jupji: The Sikh Morning Prayer.* London, Probsthain, 1959.
Translator, with M.A. Husain, *Umrao Jan Ada: Courtesan of Lucknow*, by Mohammed Ruswa. Bombay, Orient Longman, 1961.
Translator, *The Skeleton*, by Amrita Pritam. Bombay, Jaico, 1964.
Translator, *I Take This Woman*, by Rajinder Singh Bedi. Delhi, Hind, 1967.
Translator, *Hymns of Guru Nanak.* Bombay, Orient Longman, 1969.
Translator, *Dreams in Debris: A Collection of Punjabi Short Stories*, by Satindra Singh. Bombay, Jaico, 1972.
Translator, with others, *Sacred Writings of the Sikhs.* London, Allen and Unwin, 1974.

*

Critical Study: *Khushwant Singh* by V.A. Shahane, New York, Twayne, 1972.

* * *

Although Khushwant Singh is a distinguished Sikh historian, his reputation as a fiction writer rests solely upon *Train to Pakistan*, a harrowing tale of events along the borders of the newly divided nations of India and Pakistan in the summer of 1947.

The atrocities that accompanied the division of these nations had an enormously depressing effect on a world that had just fought a long, bitter war to defeat practitioners of genocide. The somewhat artificial division of the subcontinent (the boundaries remain in dispute) had been strictly along religious lines: Pakistan was to be a nation of Moslems; India, of Hindus, Sikhs, and what Singh calls "pseudo Christians." There were, however, colonies of non-coreligionists left within each nation. Rather than settle down to peaceful coexistence or permit a passive exchange of populations, partisans on both sides set out on a violent campaign of annihilating the communities that were trapped on their ancestral lands beyond friendly borders.

Train to Pakistan is laid against a background of this ruthless and senseless mass destruction. This powerful novel derives its title from a squalid border town, where a rail line crosses from India to Pakistan. At first this mixed community of Sikhs and Moslems is undisburbed by the violence that is breaking out elsewhere on the frontier, but inevitably it, too, is caught up in the mass hysteria as ominous "ghost trains" of slain Sikhs begin to arrive in town from across the border. Agitation for reprisals follows when the Moslems of the town are at last rounded up and fanatics urge the Sikhs of the community to kill their former neighbors as the train carrying them to Pakistan passes through town.

Singh's story contrasts the ineffectualness of the educated and ruling classes with the power of the violent and irrational peasants. Early in the story the town's only educated citizen, a Hindu moneylender, is gruesomely murdered by a band of Dacoity (professional bandits). Juggut Singh, a passionate Sikh farmer with a bad record, is suspected of the crime—though he played no part in it—and imprisoned; at the same time, an educated young former Sikh, Iqbal, comes to the community to agitate for a radical cause and is also imprisoned on suspicion of being a Moslem League agent. While these two are off the scene, the unlighted trains with their cargoes of dead begin to roll into town, and the agitation for reprisals begins. Both the young radical and a government commissioner, Hukum Chand, are unable to prevent the vicious plot against the fleeing Moslems from being carried out, and collapse emotionally; but in an extraordinary gesture of self-sacrifice, Juggut Singh—who had been in love with a Moslem girl—foils the plotters and allows the train to roll over his body "on to Pakistan."

Singh's terse fable suggests a profound disillusionment with the power of law, reason, and intellect in the face of elemental human passions. The philosophy that sparked his tale seems to be expressed through the thoughts of Iqbal, the young radical, as he realizes his helplessness and drifts off into a drugged sleep the night of the climactic incident of the train's passing: "If you look at things as they are...there does not seem to be a code either of man or of God on which one can pattern one's conduct.... In such circumstances what can you do but cultivate an utter indifference to all values? Nothing matters."

The same disillusioned tone characterizes Singh's second novel, *I Shall Not Hear the Nightingale*, but the rather wooden tale is almost overwhelmed by heavy-handed ironies. The action occurs about five years before that of the earlier novel, at a time when the British are expressing a willingness to get out of India once the Axis nations have been defeated in World War II. Sher Singh, the ambitious but lazy son of a Sikh senior magistrate, cannot decide between two worlds, "the one of security provided by his father...and the other full of applause that would come to him as the heroic leader of a band of terrorists." His dabblings in terrorism—actually abetted by a cynical young British civil servant—end in the pointless killing of a village leader, who has also been a political spy. Sher is suspected of the murder and imprisoned, but on the advice of his mother (when his father will not speak to him) he refuses to betray his companions. The British release him for lack of evidence, and he is honored as a kind of local hero—seemingly his political future is assured. His father is even honored by the British.

The novel takes a much dimmer view of the human capacity for compassion and self-sacrifice than *Train to Pakistan* (at one point Sher Singh reflects that "for him loyalties were not as important as the ability to get away with the impression of having them"), so that the novel ends not with the kind of thrilling gesture that its predecessor did, but with the obsequious magistrate, Sher Singh's father, sitting in the Britisher's garden observing, "As a famous English poet has said, 'All's well that ends well.'" The title of the book comes from Sher Singh's reply to his mother when she asks, "What will you get if the English leave this country?" He replies lyrically, "Spring will come to our barren land once more...once more the nightingales will sing." Khushwant Singh evidently thinks not, if the land is to fall into such self-serving hands as Sher Singh's.

His ironic short stories resemble Angus Wilson's and express a similar disillusionment about man's rationality. Singh is a brilliant, sardonic observer of a world undergoing convulsive changes; and his novels provide a unique insight into one of the major political catastrophes of this century. His difficulties in fusing his editorial comments with the action in his stories, however, cause his novels to remain principally dramatized essays.

—Warren French

SMITH, Emma. British. Born in Newquay, Cornwall, 21 August 1923. Married R.L. Stewart-Jones in 1951 (died, 1957), one son and one daughter. Recipient: Atlantic Award, 1947; Rhys Memorial Prize, 1949; Black Memorial Award, 1950. Agent: Curtis Brown Ltd., 1 Craven Hill, London W2 3EP, England.

PUBLICATIONS

Novels

Maidens' Trip. London, Putnam, 1948.
The Far Cry. London, MacGibbon and Kee, 1949; New York, Random House, 1950.
The Opportunity of a Lifetime. London, Hamish Hamilton, 1978; New York, Doubleday, 1980.

Uncollected Short Stories

"The Farmer Who Wanted Lily," in *Lilliput* (London), 1948.
"The Turning Point," in *Winter's Tales for Children 1*. London, Macmillan, 1965.
"The Boat," in *Miscellany Two*. London, Oxford University Press, 1965.

Other (juvenile)

Emily: The Story of a Traveller. London, Nelson, 1959; as *Emily: The Traveling Guinea Pig*, New York, McDowell Obolensky, 1959.
Out of Hand. London, Macmillan, 1963; New York, Harcourt Brace, 1964.
Emily's Voyage. London, Macmillan, and New York, Harcourt Brace, 1966.
No Way of Telling. London, Bodley Head, and New York, Atheneum, 1972.

*

Emma Smith comments:

What one writes for children is quite as important as what one writes for adults, and I'm not at all sure it isn't more important; because what children read can colour their feelings, and affect their behaviour, for the rest of their lives. If they are sufficiently impressed, what they read is absorbed into themselves and becomes part of their own experience to an extent that can't be so after they've grown up. Consequently, everything I write for children is really full of secret messages and exhortations and warnings of what I think the whole of life, which lies ahead waiting for them, is all about, and what I think they're going to need in the way of equipment.

* * *

Emma Smith has published three novels and several books designed for the young. In all her work there are a precise creation of character, a sensitive response to setting, and a careful attention to detail.

Her first book, *Maidens' Trip*, set in England during the second World War, is the story of three girls, Emma, Charity, and Nanette, who, during the manpower shortage, become "boaters" and guide their motorboat *Venus* and its "butty" *Adrane* over the network of locks and canals running through the heartland of the English countryside. Their adventures, observations, and problems make up the substance of the story as, without formal plot or characterizations, Smith manages to create a forward-moving, frequently suspenseful narrative. The adventures become misadventures as awkwardly at first, and later with more skill, the girls make the trip for supplies from London to Birmingham and back again. There are the physical hardships of rain and cold, blistered hands and aching backs; the hazards of machinery broken down, accidents with other boats, mud that sticks and locks that refuse to open. Charity is the housewife; Nanette, the coquette; Emma, the steady "professional" who directs the whole operation. The reality of the constant rain and cold with the contrasted coziness of the little cabin on the *Venus*, the ubiquitous steaming cups of tea, the hearty flavor of the cooking stew, and the sights and sounds of the loading docks form a background for the most memorable feature of the book—the characterization of the girls and their realization of the world of the "boaters," a world completely apart from that of a great nation at war. Even the brief appearance of a young soldier on leave is no more than a vague reminder of the danger and death in the world beyond. The other notable feature of the book is Smith's understanding of the three young girls forced by circumstances to deal with people and situations totally foreign to them. Each is a real person; not one of the three a stereotype of the adolescent. Each, however, at the same time is realized as young and immature.

Smith's second book, *The Far Cry*, is even more distinguished than *Maidens' Trip*. It is the story of an eccentric schoolmaster, Mr. Digby, who flees with his 14-year-old daughter, Teresa, to India and the sanctuary of his elder daughter, Ruth, to escape his estranged second wife, Teresa's mother. Their departure and trip across the ocean make up the first two sections of the book; the trip across India by train, the third. The fourth section is Ruth's as the reader discovers that she and her husband Edwin have not succeeded in resolving all the differences of their marriage. The last section is a kind of summary for Teresa when, confronted by the sudden horror of her father's death from a heart attack and Ruth's accidental death in Calcutta, she is obliged to become more mature than seems possible for her to be. Even at the end she "had yet to learn that the relationships of people are never established, are ever mutable...." All the principal characters are skilfully drawn: Mr. Digby, a failure as husband, father, and schoolmaster; Ruth, an exotic beauty without confidence in herself or her role as wife; Teresa, sensitive and perceptive, escaping from the repression of her unimaginative Aunt May; and Edwin, the young English tea planter who understands India and his tea workers far more than he does his beautiful wife Ruth.

The journey from England to India, the introduction of India itself, and the daily life of the tea plantation make up the chronology of the story. There is hardly a plot in the conventional definition of the term since there is little doubt from the beginning that Teresa and her father will escape her American mother. The real focus of the novel is on Teresa and her varying responses to the people she meets and the constantly shifting scenery she observes. Smith is especially good in realizing the detail of setting—the crowded life on ship board; the arresting picture of camels and their drivers at Port Suez, a kind of point in time for Teresa; the arrival at Bombay and the acquisition of their bearer, Sam; the long uncertain train trip in dirty cramped quarters; the English way of life Ruth has created in the midst of a tea plantation. The book is as full of the multitude of details as is reality itself, but each so skillfully chosen that it seems precisely right for the observation of the characters to whom it is assigned. *The Far Cry* is a beautifully sensitive novel of time, place, and character.

The Opportunity of a Lifetime, Smith's first adult novel for almost 30 years, again centers on a young girl. In this case the heroine is a 15-year-old on a summer holiday in Cornwall in 1937. And again there are many finely wrought characters, a nice sense of time and place, and moving contrasts between innocence and betrayal. If Emma Smith has chosen a rather limited range, her virtue is that she had done well what she set out to do, and her work shows an unusual sensitivity to people and a real artist's eye for detail.

—Annibel Jenkins

SMITH, Iain Crichton. British. Born on the Isle of Lewis, Outer Hebrides, Scotland, 1 January 1928. Educated at the University of Aberdeen, M.A. (honours) in English 1949. Served in the British Army Education Corps, 1950-52: Sergeant. Married. Secondary School Teacher, Clydebank, 1952-55; Teacher of English, Oban High School, 1955-77. Recipient: Scottish Arts Council Award, 1966, 1968, 1974, 1977, and Prize, 1968; BBC Award, for television play, 1970; Book Council Award, 1970; Silver Pen Award, 1971; Queen's Jubilee Medal. Fellow, Royal Society of Literature. O.B.E. (Officer, Order of the British Empire), 1980. Address: 42 Combie Street, Oban, Argyll, Scotland.

PUBLICATIONS

Novels

Consider the Lilies. London, Gollancz, 1968; as *The Alien Light*, Boston, Houghton Mifflin, 1969.
The Last Summer. London, Gollancz, 1969.
My Last Duchess. London, Gollancz, 1971.
Goodbye, Mr. Dixon. London, Gollancz, 1974.
An t-Aonaran. Glasgow, University of Glasgow Celtic Department, 1976.
An End to Autumn. London, Gollancz, 1978.
On the Island. London, Gollancz, 1979.

Short Stories

Burn is Aran (Bread and Water; includes verse). Glasgow, Gairm, 1960.
An Dubh is an Gorm (The Black and the Blue). Aberdeen, Aberdeen University, 1963.
Maighsirean is Ministearan (Schoolmasters and Ministers). Inverness, Club Leabhar, 1970.
Survival Without Error and Other Stories. London, Gollancz, 1970.
The Black and the Red. London, Gollancz, 1973.
An t-Adhar Amaireaganach (The American Sky). Inverness, Club Leabhar, 1973.
The Hermit and Other Stories. London, Gollancz, 1977.
Murdo and Other Stories. London, Gollancz, 1981.

Plays

An Coileach (The Cockerel; produced Glasgow, 1966). Glasgow, An Comunn Gaidhealach, 1966.
A' Chuirt (The Trial; produced Glasgow, 1966). Glasgow, An Comunn Gaidhealach, 1966.
A Kind of Play (produced Mull, 1975).
Two by the Sea (produced Mull, 1975).
The Happily Married Couple (produced Mull, 1977).

Radio Play: *Goodman and Death Mahoney*, 1980.

Verse

The Long River. Edinburgh, M. Macdonald, 1955.
New Poets 1959, with Karen Gershon and Christopher Levenson. London, Eyre and Spottiswoode, 1959.
Deer on the High Hills: A Poem. Edinburgh, Giles Gordon, 1960.
Thistles and Roses. London, Eyre and Spottiswoode, 1961.
The Law and the Grace. London, Eyre and Spottiswoode, 1965.
Biobuill is Sanasan Reice (Bibles and Advertisements). Glasgow, Gairm, 1965.
Three Regional Voices, with Michael Longley and Barry Tebb. London, Poet and Printer, 1968.
At Helensburgh. Belfast, Festival, 1968.
From Bourgeois Land. London, Gollancz, 1969.
Selected Poems. London, Gollancz, and Chester Springs, Pennsylvania, Dufour, 1970.
Penguin Modern Poets 21, with George Mackay Brown and Norman MacCaig. London, Penguin, 1972.
Love Poems and Elegies. London, Gollancz, 1972.
Hamlet in Autumn. Edinburgh, M. Macdonald, 1972.
Eadar Fealla-dhà is Glaschu (Between Comedy and Glasgow). Glasgow, University of Glasgow Celtic Department, 1974.
Notebooks of Robinson Crusoe. London, Gollancz, 1974.
Orpheus and Other Poems. Preston, Lancashire, Akros, 1974.
Poems for Donalda. Belfast, Ulsterman, 1974.
The Notebooks of Robinson Crusoe and Other Poems. London, Gollancz, 1975.
In the Middle—. London, Gollancz, 1977.

Other

The Golden Lyric: An Essay on the Poetry of Hugh MacDiarmid. Preston, Lancashire, Akros, 1967.
Iain Am Measg nan Reultan (Iain among the Stars; juvenile). Glasgow, Gairm, 1970.
River, River: Poems for Children. Edinburgh, M. Macdonald, 1978.
Na h-Ainmhidhean (The Animals; juvenile verse). Aberfeldy, Perthshire, Clo Chailleann, 1979.

Translator, *Ben Dorain*, by Duncan Ban Macintyre. Preston, Lancashire, Akros, 1969.
Translator, *Poems to Eimhir*, by Sorley Maclean. London and Newcastle upon Tyne, Gollancz-Northern House, 1971.

*

Bibliography: in *Lines Review 29* (Edinburgh), 1969.

Critical Study: interview in *Scottish International* (Edinburgh), 1971.

Iain Crichton Smith comments:

(1972) There is no real connection between my first two novels; one is about old age, the other about youth. However, I would like to write novels which have imagistic content, like poetry, but not "poetic" novels. I like them if possible to be generated from some kind of image or "given" imaginative fact.

* * *

With some dozen fiction works in English and in Gaelic, Iain Crichton Smith's persona and stature as a prose-writer begin to define themselves. There is a great deal of interaction between the different parts of his *oeuvre* (prose, poetry and plays; English and Gaelic), and one senses that the vital growth-points are in the poetry and the short story, with some evidence of Gaelic being his better medium for the short story.

An autobiographical shadow hangs over much of his prose work. His creative imagination does not win free of it for long, and is sometimes hesitant in this freedom. As a result Mrs. Scott is the only closely-observed character in *Consider the Lilies*, and the others—Big Betty or Donald Macleod for example—often leave a sense of uneasiness when they speak, as though their words and their minds did not mesh. *The Last Summer* is more frankly autobiographical, a re-creation of schooldays, with Malcolm, the narrator, having the greatest psychological depth and credibility. The subsidiary characters here, however, are more closely observed than those in *Consider the Lilies*. Both these novels are mainly memorable, in fact, for the skilfully-built-up mood and atmosphere.

My Last Duchess is strongly autobiographical also, at times uncritically so. Mark Simmons comes from a crofting background but seems as divorced from it as his name. The long detailed discussion of Hamlet's character, in the flashback scene in a "northern city's" cafe, is there because it looms large in the author's mind rather than in Mark Simmons'. There are many other autobiographical passages, some of them fitting well into the plot, and perhaps it is mainly in the attempts to disguise the autobiographical mainspring of the novel that dislocations occur.

This book gives the impresion of being based partly on material which had a separate existence. The first chapter, with its central theme of a disillusioning visit to a once-famous novelist, is a variant of Smith's Gaelic story "Am Bard," and it includes also some pretentious verbiage, as in the passage about the "Fortinbrases of our civilizations." The rest of Part I, set in the main in the northern University town, has a tangential relation to the theme of Part II, and it may be that earlier material has been modified slightly to fit into a new plot. Part II is much more successful, in that it is written with great pace, and is not marred by false images or gaucheries. There is a fairly steady increase of tension, as we see Lorna maturing and Mark disintegrating, and each character showing a high degree of self-observation. This developing situation is very sensitively handled, and the succession of short chapters is well designed to plot the changing irrational course of events, and their inevitable conclusion, leading to the statement in Part III: "after all this was where he must have wanted to be, in the coldness of truth."

Part II of *My Last Duchess* is Smith's most sustained achievement in prose to date, and suggests a talent which is still strongly developing. It may be, however, that his talent for writing short stories is stronger still. *Survival Without Error and Other Stories* is an uneven collection in some ways, but it has four or five stories of high quality, in which a strong sense of plot and a beautiful economy of style are brought together in a memorable way. "Survival Without Error" and "Je t'aime" and "Joseph" stand out in a collection that has much subtlety and delicacy. If we consider the variety of this collection, and add to it the still greater variety of his work in Gaelic, there is strong evidence that it is on the scale of the short story that he can best organise his insights, and best minimise the disadvantage (for a novelist) of an intense but limited range of interests.

—Derick S. Thomson

SONTAG, Susan. American. Born in New York City, 16 January 1933. Educated at the University of California, Berkeley, 1948-49; University of Chicago, 1949-51, B.A. 1951; Harvard University, Cambridge, Massachusetts, 1954-57, M.A. 1955; St. Anne's College, Oxford, 1957. Married in 1950 (divorced, 1957); one child. Instructor in English, University of Connecticut, Storrs, 1953-54; Teaching Fellow in Philosophy, Harvard University, 1955-57; Editor, *Commentary*, New York, 1959; Lecturer in Philosophy, City College of New York, and Sarah Lawrence College, Bronxville, New York, 1959-60; Instructor, Department of Religion, Columbia University, New York, 1960-64; Writer-in-Residence, Rutgers University, New Brunswick, New Jersey, 1964-65. Recipient: American Association of University Women Fellowship, 1957; Rockefeller Fellowship, 1965, 1974; Guggenheim Fellowship, 1966, 1975; American Academy award, 1976; Brandeis University Creative Arts Award, 1976. Address: c/o Farrar, Straus and Giroux, 19 Union Square West, New York, New York 10003, U.S.A.

PUBLICATIONS

Novels

The Benefactor. New York, Farrar Straus, 1963; London, Eyre and Spottiswoode, 1964.
Death Kit. New York, Farrar Straus, 1967; London, Secker and Warburg, 1968.

Short Stories

I, Etcetera. New York, Farrar Straus, 1978; London, Gollancz, 1979.

Uncollected Short Stories

"The Will and the Way," in *Partisan Review* (New Brunswick, New Jersey), Summer 1963.
"Man with a Pain," in *Harper's* (New York), April 1964.

Plays

Duet for Cannibals (screenplay). New York, Farrar Straus, 1970; London, Allen Lane, 1974.
Brother Carl (screenplay). New York, Farrar Straus, 1974.

Screenplays: *Duet for Cannibals*, 1969; *Brother Carl*, 1971; *The Spiral* (English version), 1979.

Other

Against Interpretation and Other Essays. New York, Farrar Straus, 1966; London, Eyre and Spottiswoode, 1967.
Trip to Hanoi. New York, Farrar Straus, and London, Panther, 1969.
Styles of Radical Will (essays). New York, Farrar Straus, and London, Secker and Warburg, 1969.
On Photography. New York, Farrar Straus, 1977; as *Susan Sontag on Photography*, London, Allen Lane, 1978.
Illness as Metaphor. New York, Farrar Straus, 1978; London, Allen Lane, 1979.
Under the Sign of Saturn (essays). New York, Farrar Straus, 1980.
A Susan Sontag Reader. New York, Farrar Straus, 1981.

Editor, *Selected Writings of Artaud*, translated by Helen Weaver. New York, Farrar Straus, 1976.
Editor, *A Barthes Reader.* New York, Hill and Wang, 1980; London, Cape, 1981.

*

Theatrical Activities:

Director: **Films**—*Duet for Cannibals*, 1969; *Brother Carl*, 1971; *Promised Lands* (documentary), 1974.

* * *

Traditionally readers have approached works of fiction as verbal structures which reveal and generally make statements about a pre-existing "real" subject. The writer may represent his subject directly, "imitating" in accordance with conventional understandings about the probable behavior of the human and the natural order; or he may render his subject indirectly by presenting a metaphor which stands for and usually implies a generalization about that same reality. Thus traditional criticism was designed to judge the verisimilitude of fiction and to provide a way of understanding metaphor, allegory, and parable as symbolic statements. It is impossible, however, to discuss the fiction of Susan Sontag in critical terms derived from this essentially naturalistic tradition, just as Sontag herself has attempted to construct a new critical approach to do justice to those works of *avant-garde* artists whose rendering of the modern world she finds significant.

The tough, polemical essays collected in *Against Interpretation* and *Styles of Radical Will* are more impressive than Sontag's fiction thus far, which too often seems contrived to illustrate a doctrine. For Sontag, the final "most liberating value of art" is "transparency," which means experiencing "the luminousness of the thing in itself, of things being what they are." Interpretation, which seeks to replace the work with something else—usually historical, ethical or psychological paraphrase—is essentially "revenge which the intellect takes upon art." To interpret is "to impoverish, to deplete." Sontag's chief interest as a critic is the work of artists (especially film makers) whose work is misunderstood because it resists "being reduced to a story." Thus Sontag observes that in his film *Persona* Bergman presents not a story, but "something that is, in one sense, cruder, and, in another, more abstract: a body of material, a subject. The function of the subject or material may be as much its opacity, its multiplicity, as the ease with which it yields itself to being incarnated by a determinate plot or action." Deliberately frustrating any conventional attempt to determine "what happens," the new novels and films are able, she maintains, to involve the audience "more directly in other matters, for instance in the very processes of seeing and knowing.... The material presented can then be treated as a thematic resource, from which different (and perhaps concurrent) narrative structures can be derived as variations." The artist intends his work to remain "partly encoded": the truly modern consciousness challenges the supremacy of naturalism and univocal symbolism.

While vestiges of naturalistic situations remain in Sontag's fiction (her story "The Will and the Way," for example, seems to be an allegory concerning the image of women in modern life), "interpretation" is by definition more or less irrelevant. *The Benefactor* is in its general outline a dream novel; its "thematic resource" is the problem of attaining selfhood and genuine freedom. Just as Sontag sees Montaigne's essays as "dispassionate, varied explorations of the innumerable ways of being a self," the hero of *The Benefactor* uses his dreams as a means of achieving freedom. "It seemed to me," Hippolyte concludes, that "all my life had been converging on the state of mind...in which I would finally be reconciled to myself—myself as I really am, the self of my dreams. That reconciliation is what I take to be freedom." The device which keeps the reader from treating the novel as paraphrasable allegory is the deliberate ambiguity of the narrative frame: we are left to decide whether the narrative is an account of what happened or an account which is at least in part the construction of a mad Hippolyte whose dreams are symbolic transformations, in the usual Freudian sense, of "what happened." Sontag owes a good deal to Sartre and Camus, but even more to the *auteurs* of *Last Year at Marienbad* and *L'Avventura*. *Death Kit* has as its concern the failure of a man who has no true self. "Diddy, not really alive, had a life. Not really the same. Some people are their lives. Others, like Diddy, merely inhabit their lives." Diddy commits a murder, or thinks he commits a murder; there is no way of determining this, but what matters is how Diddy handles the possibility that he is a murderer, and how he tries to appropriate the self of a blind girl whom he selfishly "loves." Out of the materials of his life Diddy assembles his death; out of his failure the reader may assemble an understanding of vanity, inauthenticity, and death. Wholly successful or not, *The Benefactor* and *Death Kit* are haunting works, effective to the degree to which the reader can accept Sontag's powerful arguments elsewhere about the exhaustion of the naturalistic tradition. As the American critic E.D. Hirsch puts it, "Knowledge of ambiguity is not necessarily ambiguous knowledge."

—Elmer Borklund

SORRENTINO, Gilbert. American. Born in Brooklyn, New York, 27 April 1929. Educated at New York public schools; Brooklyn College, 1950-51, 1955-57. Served in the Army Medical Corps, 1951-53. Married 1) Elsene Wiessner (divorced); 2) Vivian Victoria Ortiz; two sons and one daughter. Editor, *Neon* magazine, New York, 1956-60; Editor, Grove Press, New York, 1965-70. Has taught at Columbia University, New York, 1965; Aspen Writers Workshop, Colorado, 1967; Sarah Lawrence College, Bronxville, New York, 1971-72; New School for Social Research, New York, 1976-79. Since 1979, Edwin S. Quain Professor of Literature, University of Scranton, Pennsylvania. Recipient: Guggenheim Fellowship, 1973; National Endowment for the Arts grant, 1974, 1978; Fels Award, 1975; Ariadne Foundation grant, 1975; Creative Artists Public Service grant, 1975. Agent: Mel Berger, William Morris Agency, 1350 Avenue of the Americas, New York, New York 10019. Address: 463 West Street, Apartment C-614, New York, New York 10014, U.S.A.

PUBLICATIONS

Novels

The Sky Changes. New York, Hill and Wang, 1966.
Steelwork. New York, Pantheon, 1970.
Imaginative Qualities of Actual Things. New York, Pantheon, 1971.
Mulligan Stew. New York, Grove Press, 1979; London, Boyars, 1981.
Aberration of Starlight. New York, Random House, 1980; London, Boyars, 1981.

Short Story

Splendide-Hôtel. New York, New Directions, 1973.

Uncollected Short Stories

"The Moon in Its Flight," in *New American Review 13*, edited by Theodore Solotaroff. New York, Simon and Schuster, 1971.
"Land of Cotton," in *Harper's* (New York), November 1977.
"Decades," in *The Best American Short Stories 1978*, edited by Theodore Solotaroff and Shannon Ravenel. Boston, Houghton Mifflin, 1978.

Play

Flawless Play Restored: The Masque of Fungo. Los Angeles, Black Sparrow Press, 1974.

Verse

The Darkness Surrounds Us. Highlands, North Carolina, Jargon, 1960.
Black and White. New York, Totem, 1964.
The Perfect Fiction. New York, Norton, 1968.
Corrosive Sublimate. Los Angeles, Black Sparrow Press, 1971.
A Dozen Oranges. Santa Barbara, California, Black Sparrow Press, 1976.
White Sail. Santa Barbara, California, Black Sparrow Press, 1977.
The Orangery. Austin, University of Texas Press, 1978.
Selected Poems 1958-1980. Santa Barbara, California, Black Sparrow Press, 1981.

Other

Translator, *Sulpiciae Elegidia: Elegiacs of Sulpicia.* Mount Horeb, Wisconsin, Perishable Press, 1977.

*

Manuscript Collection: University of Delaware, Newark.

Gilbert Sorrentino comments:

My writing is the act of solving self-imposed problems.

* * *

Gilbert Sorrentino's novels are dedicated to several anti-traditional propositions: that space, rather than time, is the most revealing principle for narrative structure; that the physical texture of language, rather than its semantic properties, are the key to communication between a novelist and the reader; and that an awareness of the author's act of writing, rather than the willing suspension of disbelief, yields the greatest pleasure in experiencing a novel.

The Sky Changes and *Steelwork*, Sorrentino's earliest novels (from the days when he was still best known as a poet), are demonstrations of spatial order. The first is the record (told in block sections of separate narrative) of a protagonist's dissolving marriage, framed by an auto trip across the United States. Both the relationship and the journey would seem to imply a temporal order; but at several points Sorrentino self-consciously violates that order to show that the human imagination transcends simple chronology—the trip's emotional resolution comes as early as two-thirds through the cross-country journey. *Steelwork* is the spatial portrait of a Brooklyn neighborhood over two decades of human experience. On one street-corner, for example, the events of several years' distance are imaginatively rehearsed; and characters' lives are studied in a simultaneity of presence, although by the clock they have lived through much of their lives. Because space—the neighborhood—is the organizing principle, the chronology is deliberately scrambled, so that we move back and forth from 1951 to 1942 to 1949. As a result, the reader experiences the neighborhood as the spatial whole it would be for anyone who lived there all those years. Emotions and the imagination outstrip time.

Imaginative Qualities of Actual Things is Sorrentino's wildly comic exercise of his most self-apparent writing techniques. Ostensibly a *roman à clef* exposing the petty jealousies and seductions of the 1950's and 1960's New York art world, the book is in fact a demonstration of Sorrentino's pleasure in writing a novel. Characters' statements are undercut by rudely sarcastic footnotes; midway through a piece of exposition the author will stop and berate the reader for making him supply such petty details; and when the author hates a character, ludicrous scenes are devised for the unfortunate soul's humiliation and punishment. Throughout, the reader is aware that the real subject of this novel is not its mimicry of a projected real world, but is instead the process of its own composition, which the reader witnesses firsthand.

Making fiction its own subject—not a representation of an illusionary world but instead its own artifice as added to the world, an aesthetic Sorrentino learned from his mentor, William Carlos Williams—is the achievement of *Splendide-Hôtel*. Its brief chapters are named after the successive letters of the alphabet, which provide the topics for composition—the capital letter A's on the page looking like flies on a wall, breeding in decay; the letter K reminding Sorrentino of the baseball scorecard symbol for strike-out, and of a headline which spoke volumes just by saying "K-K-K-Koufax!!!!"

In his fifth and most commercially successful work of fiction, *Mulligan Stew*, Sorrentino offers a full display of novelistic talents at work. Indeed, he wishes to surpass his previous efforts by showing all aspects of fiction writing, from the novelist's act of composition to his notebooks, letters, and even the personal thoughts of his characters. Borrowing his structure from Flann O'Brien's novel *At Swim-Two-Birds* (1939), Sorrentino invents an imaginary novelist named Anthony Lamont who is struggling to shore up a sagging career with an experimental novel, a piece of "surfiction" (Sorrentino despises the term) titled *Guinea Red.* A murder mystery, it features unabashedly miserable writing; Lamont keeps losing the murdered body and forgetting where he's placed the fatal wound, and the prose itself is deadfully overwritten in a parody of low-brow style. The reader is also given access to Lamont's letters, notebooks, and journal entries. Midway through, his characters mutiny and seek ways to escape Lamont's leaden narrative and find work in a more promising repertoire. A massive novel which by its very bulk and meticulous range of styles immerses the reader in its own subject, *Mulligan Stew* is Sorrentino's fullest repertoire of writing talent.

—Jerome Klinkowitz

SOUTHERN, Terry. American. Born in Alvarado, Texas, 1 May 1924. Educated at Southern Methodist University, Dallas; University of Chicago; Northwestern University, Evanston, Illinois, B.A. 1948; the Sorbonne, Paris, 1948-50. Served in the United States Army, 1943-45. Married Carol Kaufman in 1956; one child. Recipient: British Screen Writers Award, 1965; Writers Guild of America West Award, 1965. Agent: Sterling Lord Agency, 600 Madison Avenue, New York, New York 10021. Address: c/o Arlene Donovan, 40 West 57th Street, New York, New York 10019, U.S.A.

PUBLICATIONS

Novels

Flash and Filigree. London, Deutsch, and New York, Coward McCann, 1958.
Candy (as Maxwell Kenton, with Mason Hoffenberg). Paris, Olympia Press, 1958; as Terry Southern and Mason Hoffenberg, New York, Putnam, 1964; London, Geis, 1968.
The Magic Christian. London, Deutsch, 1959; New York, Random House, 1960.
Lollipop (as Maxwell Kenton). Paris, Olympia Press, 1962.
Blue Movie. Cleveland, World, 1970; London, Calder and Boyars, 1973.

Short Stories

Red-Dirt Marijuana and Other Tastes. New York, New American Library, 1967; London, Cape, 1971.

Plays

Easy Rider (screenplay), with Peter Fonda and Dennis Hopper. New York, New American Library, 1969.

Screenplays: *Candy Kisses*, with David Burnett, 1955; *Dr. Strangelove*, with Stanley Kubrick and Peter George, 1964; *The Loved One*, with Christopher Isherwood, 1965; *The Cincinnati Kid*, with Ring Lardner, Jr., 1966; *Casino Royale* (uncredited), with others, 1967; *Barbarella*, with others, 1968; *Easy Rider*, with Peter Fonda and Dennis Hopper, 1969; *The End of the Road*, with Aram Avakian, 1969; *The Magic Christian*, with others, 1969; *Meetings with Remarkable Men*, 1979.

Other

The Journal of "The Loved One": The Production Log of a Motion Picture. New York, Random House, 1965.
The Rolling Stones on Tour. New York, Dragon's Dream, 1978.

Editor, with Richard Seaver and Alexander Trocchi, *Writers in Revolt.* New York, Fell, 1963.

* * *

Terry Southern has baffled American reviewers and annoyed critics since the appearance in 1958 of *Flash and Filigree*, which had been well received in England. This novel and subsequent efforts have variously been labeled "pointless," "pornographic," and "sick" for their thematic content or apparent lack of it. The form of Southern's fiction similarly defies easy classification: part put-on, part satire, part parody, with occasional stretches of "straight," well-written prose. Plotting is rarely conventional: *Flash and Filigree* is really two completely separate plots, while *The Magic Christian* and *Candy* are disjointedly picaresque. His recent *Blue Movie* is straightforwardly told, but conventional style and plotting seem strange indeed when used to chronicle (in living detail) the filming, and subsequent seizure by a Vatican Army, of a Hollywood-produced stag movie.

The main plot in *Flash and Filigree* centers on a dermatologist-sports car buff named Dr. Frederick Eichner, who is haunted by a prank-playing transvestite named Felix Treevly. Eichner kills his weird nemesis and is tried for murder and acquitted. Dr. Eichner is too aloofly repulsive to sustain interest, but the heroine of the sub-plot, Nurse Babs of Eichner's clinic, is just "darling," Southern's satirical tip-off word about the pretty, puerile, American Dream Girl he loves to parody. Objects of satire also include television shows ("What's My Disease?"), the medical profession, law courts, the drug scene, the American mania for gadgetry and technical data, and the crazy-culture of California. But the best scene is the seduction in a taxicab of "darling" Babs the button-nosed beauty.

Candy (co-authored with Mason Hoffenberg) was originally published pseudonymously in Paris in 1958, then published in America in 1964, by which time its shocking pornography had lost some sting. The titular heroine, a female, saccharine Candide, is reminiscent also of De Sade's Justine, Harold Gray's Little Orphan Annie, and Southern's own Nurse Babs. The book may be read equally as a satire on cherished American institutions and current delusions, or as a geography of pornography; in Southern's mind the two areas obviously blend, perhaps in their common language of cant and cliché. Candy encounters faddists and fakes in the stronghold of western culture: in academia, the mad bi-sexual Professor Mephisto; in science, the mother-ridden Irving Krankheit, author of *Masturbation Now!*; in religion, Guru Grindle, who convinces Candy of matter's unreality even as he enjoys her body. The most successful scene evolves as a psychotic, witless hunchback—whom sentimental Candy re-names Derek—copulates with the heroine ("he needs me") while he struggles to keep his half-mind on his real goal—money.

Whatever social targets the earlier works neglected, *The Magic Christian* shoots for. Guy Grand, a rich practical joker, spends ten million a year "making it hot for them": he builds superlong autos that jam up intersections; publishes a newspaper cluttered with foreign language phrases; enters a cannibalistic panther in a dog show; and goes on safari with a 75 mm. howitzer. He also inserts short pornographic scenes into film classics; in *The Best Years of Our Lives*, the war hero's hook-hands grapple under his sweetheart's skirt. Guy also opens grocery stores with preposterously low prices—then closes them the same night, to re-locate in mysterious places.

In 1967, Southern's collected short stories, published as *Red-Dirt Marijuana and Other Tastes*, revealed greater range and sympathy than suspected. Southern writes well of boys and men, of poor southern whites, of razor fights between Negro brothers, of an American in Paris who is "too hip," and of a surrealistic auto trip through Mexico. The writing is uneven and Southern's questionable taste prevails, but style and mood in the successful stories are superbly lyrical. The recent *Blue Movie* explores sexual boundaries never visited by Candy, but boredom is defeated only by Southern's fine ear for trade talk and some brilliantly awful Hollywood types. Southern is familiar with movie argot and technique, having written scenarios for *Dr. Strangelove*, *The Loved One*, and *Barbarella*. In his movies he has employed the same shock therapy by indecency and dehumanization which dominates his novelistic black comedies.

—Frank Campenni

SPARK, Muriel (Sarah, née Camberg). British. Born in Edinburgh. Educated at James Gillespie's School for Girls, Edinburgh. Married S.O. Spark in 1937 (divorced); one son. Worked in the Political Intelligence Department of the British Foreign Office during World War II. General Secretary of the Poetry Society, and Editor of the *Poetry Review*, London, 1947-49. Recipient: *The Observer* Story Prize, 1951; Italia Prize, for radio drama, 1962; Black Memorial Prize, 1966. D. Litt.: University of Strathclyde, Glasgow, 1971. Fellow, Royal Society of Literature, 1963. Honorary Member, American Academy, 1978. O.B.E. (Officer, Order of the British Empire), 1967. Lives in Rome. Address: c/o Macmillan London Ltd., 4 Little Essex Street, London WC2R 3LF, England.

PUBLICATIONS

Novels

The Comforters. London, Macmillan, and Philadelphia, Lippincott, 1957.
Robinson. London, Macmillan, and Philadelphia, Lippincott 1958.
Memento Mori. London, Macmillan, and Philadelphia, Lippincott, 1959.
The Ballad of Peckham Rye. London, Macmillan, and Philadelphia, Lippincott, 1960.
The Bachelors. London, Macmillan, 1960; Philadelphia, Lippincott, 1961.
The Prime of Miss Jean Brodie. London, Macmillan, 1961; Philadelphia, Lippincott, 1962.
The Girls of Slender Means. London, Macmillan, and New York, Knopf, 1963.
The Mandelbaum Gate. London, Macmillan, and New York, Knopf, 1965.
The Public Image. London, Macmillan, and New York, Knopf, 1968.
The Driver's Seat. London, Macmillan, and New York, Knopf, 1970.
Not to Disturb. London, Macmillan, 1971; New York, Viking Press, 1972.
The Hothouse by the East River. London, Macmillan, and New York, Viking Press, 1973.
The Abbess of Crewe. London, Macmillan, and New York, Viking Press, 1974.
The Takeover. London, Macmillan, and New York, Viking Press, 1976.
Territorial Rights. London, Macmillan, and New York, Coward McCann, 1979.
Loitering with Intent. London, Bodley Head, and New York, Coward McCann, 1981.

Short Stories

The Go-Away Bird and Other Stories. London, Macmillan, 1958; Philadelphia, Lippincott, 1960.
Voices at Play (includes the radio plays *The Party Through the Wall*, *The Interview*, *The Dry River Bed*, *Danger Zone*). London, Macmillan, 1961; Philadelphia, Lippincott, 1962.
Collected Stories I. London, Macmillan, 1967; New York, Knopf, 1968.

Plays

Doctors of Philosophy (produced London, 1962). London, Macmillan, 1963; New York, Knopf, 1966.

Radio Plays: *The Party Through the Wall*, 1957; *The Interview* 1958; *The Dry River Bed*, 1959; *The Ballad of Peckham Rye*, 1960; *Danger Zone*, 1961.

Verse

Out of a Book (as Muriel Camberg). Leith, Midlothian, Millar and Burden, 1933(?).
The Fanfarlo and Other Verse. Aldington, Kent, Hand and Flower Press, 1952.
Collected Poems I. London, Macmillan, 1967; New York, Knopf, 1968.

Other

Child of Light: A Reassessment of Mary Wollstonecraft Shelley. London, Tower Bridge, 1951.
Emily Brontë: Her Life and Work, with Derek Stanford. London, Owen, 1953; New York, British Book Centre, 1960.

John Masefield. London, Nevill, 1953.
The Very Fine Clock (juvenile). New York, Knopf, 1968; London, Macmillan, 1969.

Editor, with Derek Stanford, *Tribute to Wordsworth.* London, Wingate, 1950; Port Washington, New York, Kennikat Press, 1970.
Editor, *A Selection of Poems,* by Emily Brontë. London, Grey Walls Press, 1952.
Editor, with Derek Stanford, *My Best Mary: The Letters of Mary Shelley.* London, Wingate, 1953; Folcroft, Pennsylvania, Folcroft Editions, 1972.
Editor, *The Brontë Letters.* London, Nevill, 1954; as *The Letters of the Brontës: A Selection,* Norman, University of Oklahoma Press, 1954.
Editor, with Derek Stanford, *Letters of John Henry Newman.* London, Owen, 1957.

*

Bibliography: *Iris Murdoch and Muriel Spark: A Bibliography* by Thomas T. Tominaga and Wilma Schneidermeyer, Metuchen, New Jersey, Scarecrow Press, 1976.

Critical Studies: *Muriel Spark: A Biographical and Critical Study* by Derek Stanford, Fontwell, Sussex, Centaur Press, 1963; *Muriel Spark* by Karl Malkoff, New York, Columbia University Press, 1968; *Muriel Spark* by Patricia Stubbs, London, Longman, 1973; *Muriel Spark* by Peter Kemp, London, Elek, 1974, New York, Barnes and Noble, 1975.

* * *

"Her prose is like a bird, darting from place to place, palpitating with nervous energy; but a bird with a bright beady eye and a sharp beak as well." Francis Hope's description crystallizes one important aspect of Muriel Spark's highly idiosyncratic talent. A late starter in the field of fiction, she had until early middle age published only conventional criticism and verse which gave little hint of her real gifts and future development. These were triumphantly released with the publication of *The Comforters* in 1957, and the spate of creative activity which followed: speedily establishing her reputation as a genuine original with a style and slant on life uniquely her own.

Muriel Spark spoke in an interview of her mind "crowded with ideas, all teeming in disorder." In 1954 she had become a convert to Roman Catholicism; and she regards her religion primarily as a discipline for this prodigal fertility—"something to measure from," as she says, rather than a direct source of its inspiration. Yet her Catholicism pervasively colours a vision of life seen, in her own phrase, "from a slight angle to the universe." For all her inventive energy, verve and panache, and glittering malice, this writer is profoundly preoccupied with metaphysical questions of good and evil. Like Angus Wilson, she is a moral fabulist of the contemporary scene who works through the medium of comedy; and like him, she is often most in earnest when at her most entertaining.

Her novels abound in Catholic characters, but these are by no means always on the side of the angels. In *The Comforters* they teeter on the brink of delusion, retreating from orthodoxy into eccentric extremes of quasi-religious experience satirized with the wicked acuteness with which she later pillories spiritualism in *The Bachelors,* focusing upon the trial of a medium for fraud. Religious hypocrites such as the self-consciously progressive couple in "The Black Madonna" are quite as likely to be her targets as rationalist unbelievers. Her awareness of the powers of darkness as a palpable force at work in the world is most effectively embodied in her study of satanism in the suburbs, *The Ballad of Peckham Rye,* in the diabolic person and activities of an industrial welfare worker born with horns on his head.

Such manifestations of the supernatural in the midst of prosaic actuality are a central element in Spark's novels. Her fantasy, earthed in the everyday, is presented not as illusion but a natural extension of the material scene: the product of "that sort of mental squint," as she calls it, which perceives the credible co-existence of the uncanny with the most rational aspects of experience. Those who attempt to ignore or reject its reality—like the cynics staging their tawdry Nativity play and confounded by the avenging intervention of a real angel in "The Seraph and the Zambesi," or the sceptical George trying to explain away the flying saucer of "Miss Pinkerton's Apocalypse"—do so at their peril. Another short story, "The Portobello Road," is narrated by the ghost of a girl who materializes to her murderer in the Saturday morning street market; while *Memento Mori,* in which a number of old people are the victims of a sinister anonymous telephone caller, is a mordant exercise in the macabre. It is subtly suggested that these events might well, for those who choose to believe so, have a straightforward psychological explanation. The ghostly visitant need be no more than an externalization of the murderer's guilty conscience belatedly returned to plague him; the grim practical joker of *Memento* (never finally traced by the police) may embody the insistent reminder of imminent mortality already present within each aged subconscious mind.

Spark's work has been highly prized by Evelyn Waugh, whose influence is detectable in the quickfire satirical wit of what one critic called her "machine-gun dialogue." The savage grotesqueries of early Waugh comedy are strongly recalled, too, by the chilling vein of heartlessness, even cruelty, in the violent ends to which so many Spark characters are remorselessly doomed: Needle, smothered in a haystack; the octogenarian Dame Letty, battered in her bed; Joanna Childe, bizarrely chanting passages from the Anglican liturgy as she burns to death; and the bored and loveless office worker of *The Driver's Seat* obsessively resolved to get herself killed in the most brutal possible fashion.

Yet if disaster and death haunt the pages of Spark's novels, her piquant humours are still more abundant. Although *The Girls of Slender Means* ends in tragedy, its portrayal of the impoverished inmates of a war-time hostel for young women of good family is as delectably funny as the depiction, in *The Bachelors,* of their gossipy male counterparts in London bedsitterland; or as the intrigues among nuns at a convent besieged by the media avid for ecclesiastical scandal in *The Abbess of Crewe.* Perhaps Spark's greatest comic triumph is her creation of the exuberant Edinburgh schoolmistress Jean Brodie, grooming her girls for living through an educationally unorthodox but headily exhilarating curriculum ranging from her heroes, Franco and Mussolini, to the love-lives of remarkable women of history, including her own.

Spark's narrative expertise is best exemplified in shorter forms, where her stylistic economy so often achieves a riveting intensity of impact. By contrast a longer, more ambitious book like *The Mandelbaum Gate,* about the adventures of a half-Jewish Catholic convert caught up in the divisions of warring Jerusalem, seems laboured and diffuse. Two later novels, *The Takeover,* set during the 1970's but rooted in classical mythology, and *Territorial Rights,* have the Italian background which the author clearly finds a fruitful imaginative climate for exploring such themes as the exploitation of bogus religion and excessive wealth. Here again are illustrated those characteristic qualities of sly, deadly wit in observing human oddity and weakness, the ingenious fusion of fact with fantasy and unpredictable surprise, and the underlying moral seriousness, which make Muriel Spark one of our most stimulating and quirkily individual present-day novelists.

—Margaret Willy

SPENCER, Colin. British. Born in London, 17 July 1933. Educated at Brighton Grammar School, Selhurst; Brighton College of Art. Served in the Royal Army Medical Corps, 1950-52. Married Gillian Chapman in 1959; one son. Paintings exhibited in Cambridge and London; costume designer. Agent: (plays) Margaret Ramsey Ltd., 14a Goodwin's Court, London, WC2N 4LL; (novels) Richard Scott Simon, 32 College Cross, London N.1. Address: 44 Lonsdale Square, London N1 1EW, England.

PUBLICATIONS

Novels

An Absurd Affair. London, Longman, 1961.
Generation:
Anarchists in Love. London, Eyre and Spottiswoode, 1963; as *The Anarchy of Love*, New York, Weybright and Talley, 1967.
The Tyranny of Love. London, Blond, and New York, Weybright and Talley, 1967.
Lovers in War. London, Blond, 1969.
The Victims of Love. London, Quartet, 1978.
Asylum. London, Blond, 1966.
Poppy, Mandragora, and the New Sex. London, Blond, 1966.
Panic. London, Secker and Warburg, 1971.
How the Greeks Kidnapped Mrs. Nixon. London, Quartet, 1974.

Uncollected Short Stories

"Nightworkers," in *London Magazine*, ii, 12, 1955.
"An Alien World," in *London Magazine*, iii, 6, 1956.
"Nymph and Shepherd," in *London Magazine*, vi, 8, 1959.
"It's Anemones for Mabel," in *Transatlantic Review* (London), Spring 1963.
"The Room," in *Transatlantic Review* (London), Summer 1966.

Plays

The Ballad of the False Barman, music by Clifton Parker (produced London, 1966).
Spitting Image (produced London, 1968; New York, 1969). Published in *Plays and Players* (London), September 1968.
The Trial of St. George (produced London, 1972).
The Sphinx Mother (produced Salzburg, Austria, 1972).
Why Mrs. Neustadter Always Loses (produced London, 1972).
Keep It in the Family (also director: produced London, 1978).

Television Plays: *Flossie*, 1975; *Vandal Rule OK?* (documentary), 1977.

Other

Gourmet Cooking for Vegetarians. London, Deutsch, 1978.

*

Critical Study: interview with Peter Burton, in *Transatlantic Review 35* (London), 1970.

Theatrical Activities:

Director: **Play**—*Keep It in the Family*, London, 1978.

Colin Spencer comments:

I have the impression that my work taken as a whole can be confusing to a critic or a reader. Both the novels and the plays appear to be written in too many various styles; if this is true I make no apologies but will attempt an explanation. The main core of my work as a writer is found in the four volumes of the unfinished sequence of novels: *Generation*. This, in its simplest form is nothing but fictionalised autobiography—the line where fiction begins and reality ends is a philosophical enigma that continually fascinates me. The volumes are sagas of various families, their children and grand-children, their marriages and relationships; their social context is firmly middle-class though in later volumes some of the characters move into the upper-middle stratas while others remain socially rootless. I have struggled in these books to make the characters and their backgrounds as true to what I have observed and experienced as my perception and recollection allow. For I believe that the novel form is unique in being as exact a mirror to our experience as is afforded in the whole range of art forms. For not only can the novel communicate the great obsessive passions, frustrations, and longings of individuals, but it can also conjure up a picture of all the myriad details—quite trivial in themselves—which at certain times affect major actions. In form I based these interrelating novels on the 19th-century tradition (it is a complicated story with many characters) but I have allowed myself within that framework to use all the literary experiments forged in the first half of this century. The characters that I have created from my experience and observation are not puppets; I cannot control and guide them into some preconceived aesthetic pattern, for they exist in life and in the narration I have to pursue and relate as truthfully as possible their own tragic mistakes, their comic failures and triumphs, their self-deceit and affirmation of life.

But in my plays there is no direct autobiographical experience: they are, like some of the other novels, satires on social problems that oppress individuals. I like to entertain in the theatre, to make an audience laugh but at the same time debate at the core of the work a serious and unresolved problem. The novels *Poppy, Mandragora, and the New Sex* and *How the Greeks Kidnapped Mrs. Nixon* also use comedy to expose gross injustice. *Panic* treats another subject, that of child assault, on the surface as a murder mystery, yet its main intention was to induce the reader to understand the psychological nature of the killer. I would dismiss my first novel, *An Absurd Affair*, as merely a public rehearsal in the craft of fiction. But there is one novel that falls outside any of the above catagories—*Asylum*. The Oedipus myth has always fascinated me. (The play *The Sphinx Mother* is a contemporary account of the Jocasta figure refusing to commit suicide and struggling for final and complete possession of her son/husband.) Another myth, the Fall of Man, with its pervasive sense of original sin corroding free will seems for me with the Oedipus myth to have influenced the compulsive aspirations in Western culture for over two thousand years. In *Asylum* I created a plot, loosely based on a 19th-century American scandal, where I united both myths in the same family and set it in an hierarchic social commune, almost a science-fiction Asylum. I then tried to imply how our religious and judical structure worked through arbitrary indifference and cruel repression. I might add that for large passages of the book I allowed myself the indulgence of writing in a style akin to poetic prose.

If I may sum up I would say that I feel my job as a writer is to state the truth in as vivid a manner as is possible and to involve the reader in a celebration of life, while uncovering the injustices that as individuals and as society we impose upon each other.

* * *

Colin Spencer's novels revel in the eccentric, the bizarre, and the grotesque while tending toward social commentary. His event-filled books treat of human relationships buffeted by sexual antagonisms of various, extreme types. In depicting his frequently polymorphously perverse characters, Spencer plays a recurrent theme of protest against conventional mores and morality, although, perhaps unintentionally, the alternatives he presents hardly seem more satisfactory. With casts of almost Dickensian proportions and curiosity, he runs the gamut of sexual expression, particularly homosexual. Sympathetic understanding, graphic detail, and a fine talent for low comedy do not often, however, extend his narratives beyond the superficial or raise them from mere sensationalism to genuine significance. Nor does his tendency to have protagonist-spokesmen speechify make his arguments more appealing.

In *An Absurd Affair* Spencer sketches some telling scenes of marital dependence and oppression, but soon gives way to improbable melodrama. Conceited, petty, and dull, James dominates his immature, thoughtless child-wife, Sarah. Though he is undereducated and boring, James finds his wife inferior and her love of art beyond his comprehension. By accident, Sarah finds the negative of a "dirty" picture, and, to the prudish James's shock, she is fascinated. Undue influence by this "art," along with romantic infatuation and huge amounts of alcohol, leads the insecure woman into a ludicrous pursuit of a sadistic schoolteacher and finally into a delusory affair with a Sicilian gigolo. Though James rescues her, she finds she no longer loves him and declares her independence. For all Spencer's obvious and overdrawn psychologizing, both characters remain rather implausible caricatures in what is, indeed, an absurd affair, unredeemed by the crude poetic justice—or ladies' magazine moralizing—of its pat ending.

Of considerably more merit and interest are the volumes of the projected series *Generation*, a sizeable contribution to the large corpus of English novels examining life in reaction to post-World War II conditions, in this case a sprawling saga of the Simpson family from World War I through the 1960's. Shifting back and forth over the years, Spencer draws vivid, well-rounded portraits of several characteristic types, some of which develop into unique personalities; the ever more complicated alliances and misalliances of the heterogeneous Simpsons reveal a fascinating panorama of several social milieus. While realistic scenes are well-executed, the more emotional confrontations take on the unfortunate tone of a soap opera. And though characters occasionally mention and blame the War for their uncertain, disjointed worlds, its significance for their individual struggles is implied more than clearly stated.

Weaving in and out of the separate stories of the factional family members, friends, and lovers, Eddy Simpson's raunchy career, depicted in short, often raucous vignettes, becomes a central focus for understanding the wayward, amusing, and sometimes pathetic journeys in the novels. Crude and conscious only of his own desires, paterfamilias Eddy jokes, drinks, and womanizes. His Rabelaisian zest for life can be hilarious, but it is also ruinous for the rest of the Simpsons. Long-suffering wife Hester turns to religion, whose comforts are of little use to her artistic and volatile children Sundy and Matthew. The major portions of the novels are devoted to their painful growing up and tortured adulthood.

Hetero-, homo-, and bi-sexual roles are played out in several combinations; in the convoluted course of the interconnected plots there is more changing of partners than in a country square dance. Sundy is most original. After dallying with lesbianism, she is caught briefly in an incestuous bond. She takes up with Reg, a handsome liar, self-proclaimed anarchist, and sometime rent-boy, aborts their illegitimate child, and finally, confusedly, marries him. After losing Reg to her brother Matthew, she leads a bohemian life with an unreliable publisher. Through tumultuous years, Matthew's reactions to his father's boorishness and cruelty alternate between dejection and desire for revenge, religious fanaticism and self-hatred. His homosexuality comes slowly to consciousness but not acceptance, and his ambivalence ends in a disastrous and mutually destructive marriage to a priggish, unstable shrew.

Along the way he portrays lower-, middle-, and upper-class life, as well as the more baroque aspects of the homosexual world, with deftness and insight. Sometimes his prose sags, but generally Spencer's humor, irony, and use of contrast are skillful, allowing his themes to reveal themselves by inference. Perhaps his strongest points are made by the self-inflicted wounds of the "anarchists" whose intellectual poses ineffectually mask their adolescent, mixed-up libertinism.

Constructed in a fantastic mode, *Asylum* displays Spencer's penchant for the macabre. The patients in the ultra-modern insane asylum are prompted to act out their twisted pasts and perverse imaginings by the equally but scientifically demented psychiatrists (who are, in turn, directed by monstrous computers), before they are hunted and left to die. Spencer's surrealistic vision combines and curiously reworks *Oedipus* and the Book of Genesis through phantasmagoric permutations. In the confused dimension of illusion-reality, Cleo-Jocasta tries to work her incestuous vindicative will upon her priest-husband Max (Addams) through their dark-skinned son Carl, but Carl perfers the charms of his fair-skinned brother Angelo. While the inversions and embroidery of the Greek and Judaic myths are imaginative, their point is often as obscure as Cleo's mad history.

Perhaps Spencer's most mature work is his probing analysis of the mentality of the child molester in *Panic*. With the seamy Brighton underworld as backdrop, the novel unfolds the wretched life of Woody and his mother Saffron May and their increasingly perverted relationship, culminating in the tragic child-murders. Spencer tells the gripping story through the voices of the major characters, carefully controlling the tensions to the last climactic moments. What was once used largely for shock value in earlier books, now is integral to theme and structure. Both killer and victims are revealed with sympathy from the inside, and even the freakish characters of the lesbian burglar Trigger and the wretched dwarf Jumbo emerge as strange but human beings.

—Joseph Parisi

SPENCER, Elizabeth. American. Born in Carrollton, Mississippi, 19 July 1921. Educated at Belhaven College, Jackson, Mississippi, 1938-42, A.B. 1942; Vanderbilt University, Nashville, 1942-43, M.A. 1943. Married John Rusher in 1956. Instructor, Northwest Mississippi Junior College, Senatobia, 1943-44, and Ward-Belmont College, Nashville, 1944-45; Reporter, *The Nashville Tennessean*, 1945-46; Instructor, 1948-49, and Instructor in Creative Writing, 1949-51, 1952-53, University of Mississippi, Oxford. Donnelly Fellow, Bryn Mawr College, Pennsylvania, 1962; Creative Writing Fellow, University of North Carolina, Chapel Hill, 1969. Recipient: Women's Democratic Committee Award, 1949; American Academy grant, 1952; Guggenheim Fellowship, 1953; Rosenthal Award, 1957; *Kenyon Review* Fellowship, 1957; McGraw Hill Fiction Award, 1960; Bellamann Award, 1968. D.L.: Southwestern University, Memphis, Tennessee, 1968. Agent: Harold Ober Associates, 40 East 49th Street, New York, New York 10017. Address: 2300 St. Mathieu, Apartment 610, Montreal, Quebec H3H 2J8, Canada.

Publications

Novels

Fire in the Morning. New York, Dodd Mead, 1948.
This Crooked Way. New York, Dodd Mead, and London, Gollancz, 1952.
The Voice at the Back Door. New York, McGraw Hill, 1956; London, Gollancz, 1957.
The Light in the Piazza. New York, McGraw Hill, 1960; London, Heinemann, 1961.
Knights and Dragons. New York, McGraw Hill, 1965; London, Heinemann, 1966.
No Place for an Angel. New York, McGraw Hill, 1967; London, Weidenfeld and Nicolson, 1968.
The Snare. New York, McGraw Hill, 1972.

Short Stories

Ship Island and Other Stories. New York, McGraw Hill, 1968; London, Weidenfeld and Nicolson, 1969.
The Stories of Elizabeth Spencer. New York, Doubleday, 1981.

*

Bibliography: in *A Bibliographical Guide to the Study of Southern Literature* by Louis D. Rubin, Jr., Baton Rouge, Louisiana State University Press, 1969.

Manuscript Collection: University of Kentucky Libraries, Lexington.

Elizabeth Spencer comments:

I began writing down stories as soon as I learned how to write; that is, at about age six; before that, I made them up anyway and told them to anybody who was handy and would listen. Being a rural Southerner, a Mississippian, had a lot to do with it, I have been told, with this impulse and with the peculiar mystique, importance, which attached itself naturally thereto and enhanced it. We had been brought up on stories, those about local people, living and dead, and Bible narratives, believed also to be literally true, so that other stories read aloud—the Greek myths, for instance—while indicated as "just" stories, were only one slight remove from the "real" stories of the local scene and the Bible. So it was with history, for local event spilled into the history of the textbooks; my grandfather could remember the close of the Civil War, and my elder brother's nurse had been a slave. The whole world, then, was either entirely in the nature of stories or partook so deeply of stories as to be at every point inseparable from them. Even the novels we came later to read were mainly English 19th-century works which dealt with a culture similar to our own—we learned with no surprise that we had sprung from it.

Though I left the South in 1953, I still see the world and its primal motions as story, since story charts in time the heart's assertions and gives central place to the great human relationships. My first three novels, written or projected before I left the South, deal with people in that society who must as the true measure of themselves either alter it or come to terms with it. Years I spent in Italy and more recently in Canada have made me see the world in other than this fixed geography. The challenge to wring its stories from it became to me more difficult at the same time that it became more urgent that I and other writers should do so. A story may not be the only wrench one can hurl into the giant machine that seems bent on devouring us all, but it is one of them. A story which has been tooled, shaped, and slicked up is neither real nor true—we know its nature and its straw insides. Only the real creature can satisfy, the one that is touchy and alive, dangerous to fool with. The search for such as these goes on with me continually, and I think for all real writers as well.

* * *

"Somewhere they had shifted ground and what had at first seemed the only path now appeared as one way in a many-branched road, whose outlines were as vague as those of the sky and earth dissolving together in the rain." Thus Elizabeth Spencer provides for the pivotal situation in her first novel, *Fire in the Morning*, a description that fits all her stories of seemingly clear-cut situations grown most often unmanageably complex.

Her first three novels and early short stories portray the upper middle class of her native Mississippi trapped between the decadent planter aristocrats and politically ambitious "redneck" bigots who were William Faulkner's special province. *Fire in the Morning* (titled from Djuna Barnes's *Nightwood*) grimly depicts the effectiveness of petty greed in stifling a small community's vitality. The Gerrard family moved into Tarsus in the wake of Civil War disruptions and made themselves leading citizens through perjury and blackmail. Their machinations result, however, only in the destruction of almost everyone involved except one Gerrard son and a former schoolmate, son of one of the family's principal victims. These young men achieve a reconciliation when the Gerrard follows the many other people driven from the community and the other, Kinloch Armstrong, learns that his strength is the very "strangeness" he has always felt that allows him to transcend the squalor that engulfs the others. *This Crooked Way* is a less complex and more cynical tale about an opportunist who comes down from the hills to become a Delta planter. Through this Amos Dudley has always dreamed of seeing a ladder of angels, his inability to face reality results only in the wreckage of the lives of his family and most of those around him.

Spencer's most powerful novel, *The Voice at the Back Door*, bares the history of a well-educated and inherently decent young lawyer, Kerney Woolbright, who must sacrifice his integrity to win political perferment in his community. The novel contrasts Kerney's lying about his knowledge of an explosive situation involving a Negro in order to assure his victory at the polls with the behavior of Duncan Harper, a truculently honest athlete—once idol of the community—who sacrifices a comfortable career to protect the Negro from ignorant bigotry.

After this chilling revelation of the corruption of competence and the persecution of decency, Spencer abandoned Mississippi for Italy, which inspired two brief novels about women who escape abroad to victory, *The Light in the Piazza*, source of an unusually tasteful and subtle film, tensely relates an American mother's risky effort to marry her mentally retarded daughter to an attractive young Florentine despite her husband's misgivings and the Italian family's efforts to profit by the match. *Knights and Dragons* studies an American woman who has fled to Rome after her marriage collapse and who finds at last that human love demands too much of the individual to be worth the struggle, so that she frees herself—like Federico Fellini's Juliet of the Spirits—to become "a companion to cloud and sky."

For her most recent novels, Spencer turns to urban American backgrounds. *No Place for an Angel* traces the intricate interrelationships of two married couples and their sprawling families and a young American sculptor, who dreams like Amos Dudley of angels. One wife says of her husband, "Jerry had to be great, and he almost made it." The novel is a mature, unsentimental account of characters that almost make it, only to find—as one puts it—that "life keeps turning into a vacuum," though the author tempers the bleakness by suggesting that these people's children may find happiness by wanting less. *The Snare* concentrates on a woman who does at last "make it" by never seeking greatness. Julia Garrett's life in a New Orleans that the novelist pictures with special skill has been a search on "a many-branched road" for an identity from the time that her aimless father abandons her in the arms of better-placed relatives. Frustrated in efforts to achieve mature relationships, Julia realizes herself at last not through the vision of an angel, but the person of her own very real child.

—Warren French

STEAD, Christina (Ellen). Australian. Born in Rockdale, Sydney, New South Wales, 17 July 1902. Educated at Sydney University Teachers' College, graduated 1922. Married William James Blake in 1952 (died, 1968). Demonstrator, Sydney University Teachers' College, in Sydney schools, 1922-24; secretary in Sydney, 1925-28; moved to Europe, 1928, and worked as a clerk in offices in London, 1928-29, and in Paris, 1930-35; moved to the United States, 1935; Senior Writer, Metro-Goldwyn-Mayer, Hollywood, 1943; Instructor, New York University, 1943-44; Fellow in Creative Arts, Australian National University, Canberra, 1969-80; now emeritus. Recipient: Arts Council of Great Britain grant, 1967; Patrick White Award, 1974. Agent: Tim Curnow, Curtis Brown (Australia) Pty. Ltd., 86 William Street, Paddington, New South Wales 2021, Australia; or, Laurence Pollinger Ltd., 18 Maddox Street, London W1R 0EU, England; or, Joan Daves, 59 East 54th Street, New York, New York 10022, U.S.A. Address: 10 Donald Street, Hurstville, New South Wales 2220, Australia.

PUBLICATIONS

Novels

Seven Poor Men of Sydney. London, Davies, 1934; New York, Appleton Century, 1935.
The Beauties and Furies. London, Davies, and New York, Appleton Century, 1936.
House of All Nations. London, Davies, and New York, Simon and Schuster, 1938.
The Man Who Loved Children. New York, Simon and Schuster, 1940; London, Davies, 1941.
For Love Alone. New York, Harcourt Brace, 1944; London, Davies, 1945.
Letty Fox: Her Luck. New York, Harcourt Brace, 1946; London, Davies, 1947.
A Little Tea, A Little Chat. New York, Harcourt Brace, 1948.
The People with the Dogs. Boston, Little Brown, 1952.
Dark Places of the Heart. New York, Holt Rinehart, 1966; as *Cotters' England*, London, Secker and Warburg, 1967.
The Little Hotel. London, Angus and Robertson, 1973; New York, Holt Rinehart, 1975.
Miss Herbert (The Suburban Wife). New York, Random House, 1976; London, Virago, 1979.

Short Stories

The Salzburg Tales. London, Davies, and New York, Appleton Century, 1934.
The Puzzleheaded Girl: Four Novellas. New York, Holt Rinehart, 1967; London, Secker and Warburg, 1968.

Uncollected Short Stories

"O, If I Could But Shiver!," in *The Fairies Return.* London, Davies, 1934.
"The Personages," in *Reading I've Liked*, edited by Clifton Fadiman. New York, Simon and Schuster, 1941.
"The Hotel-Keeper's Story," in *Southerly* (Sydney), 1952.
"U.N.O. 1945," in *Southerly* (Sydney), 1962.
"A Household," in *Southerly* (Sydney), xx, 4, 1962.
"The Woman in the Bed," in *Meanjin* (Melbourne), Summer 1968.
"An Iced Cake with Cherries," in *Meanjin* (Melbourne), 1970.
"The Azhdanov Tailors," in *Commentary* (New York), 1971.
"The Milk Run," in *New Yorker*, 9 December 1972.
"I Live in You," in *Melbourne Sun*, 1973.
"The Boy," in *Meanjin* (Melbourne), March 1973.
"Fairy Child," in *Harvard Advocate* (Cambridge, Massachusetts), Winter 1973.
"Street Idyll" and "The Captain's House," in *Festival and Other Stories*, edited by Brian Buckley and Jim Hamilton. Melbourne, Wren, 1974; Newton Abbot, Devon, David and Charles, 1975.
"A View of the Homestead," in *Paris Review 14*, Spring 1974.
"The Palace with Several Sides," in *Melbourne Sun*, December 1974.
"Uncle Morgan at the Nats," in *Partisan Review* (New Brunswick, New Jersey), xliii, 1, 1976.

Other

A Christina Stead Reader, edited by Jean B. Read. New York, Random House, 1979.

Editor, with William J. Blake, *Modern Women in Love.* New York, Dryden Press, 1945.
Editor, *Great Stories of the South Sea Islands.* London, Muller, 1955.

Translator, *Colour of Asia*, by Fernand Gigon. London, Muller, 1955.
Translator, *The Candid Killer*, by Jean Giltène. London, Muller, 1956.
Translator, *In Balloon and Bathyscaphe*, by August Piccard. London, Cassell, 1956.

*

Critical Studies: "Christina Stead Issue" of *Southerly* (Sydney), 1962; *Christina Stead*, New York, Twayne, 1969, revised edition, Sydney, Angus and Robertson, 1979, and *Christina Stead*, Melbourne, Oxford University Press, 1969, both by R.G. Geering.

Christina Stead comments:

I have been interested in depicting scenes in which I myself have taken part either as actor or spectator: and in this sense, my books and stories may be called scenes from contemporary life.

* * *

For two or three decades critics and literary historians have sometimes wondered how to fit Christina Stead into their Australian scheme of things. The greater part of her life has been spent abroad and her work, naturally enough, reflects life in the many parts of the world in which she has lived. She has, now and again, drawn directly on the experiences of her early years, but not in any self-consciously Australian way. The Sydney of her first novel, though vividly recreated as an actual locale, might, for the purposes of her story, have been any other poverty-stricken city of the modern world in which people were struggling to make something of their obscure lives. The first half of *For Love Alone* is set in Australia too, but this account of a young woman's desperate search for love takes the heroine, Teresa, to England, where a different destiny from the one she expects awaits her. People are more important than places and, although the places in Stead's fiction are established with that attention to detail and atmosphere which helps us to understand the lives the characters lead, the people are her basic concern. Stead is, to put is simply, a writer absorbed in the individual experience, not an Australian novelist in the more obvious sense of the term, and the measure of her achievement is the readiness with which the sympathetic reader may enter the different worlds she creates in her books.

Though set in the depression years of the late 1920's *Seven Poor Men of Sydney* is a poetic, impressionist rather than a naturalist, sociological novel. Significantly, the characters who interest the author most are Michael Baguenault and his half-sister Catherine, both tormented, oversensitive people doomed by the very intensity of their relationship and their ill-focused strivings to frustration and defeat. *House of All Nations*, written in a quite different manner, published only four years later and the longest of all Christina Stead's novels, is a scathing account of the world of international high finance as seen in the operation of European private banks and stock exchanges of the 1930's, an account presented with an encylopaedic wealth of detail that gives to its descriptions of the most fantastic money-making exploits a ring of conviction. But even here, despite the massive documentation, the novelist's basic concern is the force of individual obsession which, under the lure of the absolute, gold, drives such misguided genuises as the banker Jules Bertillon and the merchant Henri Léon along their crazy paths.

It is, likewise, this sense of the destructive power of human obsessions that gives to *The Man Who Loved Children* and *For Love Alone* much of their dramatic impact. The ironically titled *The Man Who Loved Children*, Stead's finest novel and a book that deserves a place among the masterpieces of 20th-century fiction, depicts with a rare blend of subtlety and intensity the disastrous effects of a jocular, liberal-minded but naif scientist upon the life of his family. Sam Pollit believes the world can be saved by science and humanitarian socialism but his idealism and generosity are corrupted at their source by an incurable egoism and self-righteousness. This book traces with unsparing honesty and profound insight, which extend the artist's sympathy to all those drawn into the family conflict, the bitter, murderous feuding between Sam and his redoubtable antagonist, his wife Henny, through to its tragic and its liberating end. The self-absorption of the eldest child, the adolescent Louisa, the embryonic artist, enables her to survive and win through to the promise of freedom. In a somewhat similar manner the tenacious Teresa, obsessed by the idea of love which will free her from the simpering obscenities of suburbia, and having undergone torments in her devotion to the arrogant, cold-hearted Jonathan Crow, survives her disenchantment and steps finally across the threshold into a world that promises fulfilment for her as both woman and artist. The devastating portraits of male egoism, Sam Pollit and Crow, make the struggles depicted in these two books terrifying real.

The next three novels are, like *The Man Who Loved Children*, American in setting but fall below the high level of that book. *Letty Fox* and *A Little Tea, A Little Chat* provide, among other things, a sardonic commentary on the sexual mores and the materialism of 20th-century America; *The People with the Dogs* is an affectionate recreation of life in one of its backwaters, a country estate inhabited by descendants of 19th-century Russian liberals, the cultured and eccentric Massines, who live at a stage removed from the brashness of the modern world. Stead's sensitivity to the social and political scene is found too in *Dark Places of the Heart*, with its telling evocation of seedy Islington of the early 1950's and of the damp, dismal industrial north. The centre of the book once again (and more emphatically than ever) is character. In her presentation of the lesbian, leftist Nellie Cook (born a Cotter of a Tyneside working class family), a tyrannical, intense, self-indulgent, loquacious harpy, Stead has created another of her memorably menacing characters. The remarkable gifts for the fantastic and the grotesque which made *The Salzburg Tales* such a richly entertaining work contribute in this novel towards the deeper exploration and realization of character. In the book's central scenes Stead succeeds in fusing the commonplace and the bizarre into a single, compelling poetic vision.

Apart from a few separately published short stories and an early novel of student life in Paris, *The Beauties and Furies* (a curious and unsuccessful blend of realism and fantasy), the other fiction yet to be mentioned includes *The Puzzleheaded Girl*, *The Little Hotel*, and *Miss Herbert*. *The Puzzleheaded Girl* is a volume of four novellas. Two of these are incisive studies of addle-pated American girls at home and abroad in the post-war years; the third, "The Rightangled Creek," subtitled "A Sort of Ghost Story," is a highly successful venture in eerie atmospherics. The title story is quite different again in its slanted, indirect evocation of the strangely elusive Honor Lawrence, a wraith-like figure who seems doomed to wander lost and innocent in the indifferent world. *The Little Hotel*, Christina Stead's shortest novel, is one of her best. In a deceptively off-hand kind of way it subjects the lodgers (well-to-do expatriates living in isolation and fear of losing their money) and staff of a small Swiss hotel in the immediate post-war years to a penetrating but artistically sympathetic scrutiny. Beginning at the level of the trivial it focuses increasingly on the characters Mrs. Trollope, Mr. Wilkins, and the unattractive Blaises and works up to a strange, menacing conclusion. *Miss Herbert*, a less impressive work, is a portrait of an ordinary woman struggling (at times) against social convention but frustrated by her own inherent limitations. There are echoes here of the bourgeois traps awaiting Catherine Baguenault, Elvira (heroine of *The Beauties and Furies*), and Letty Fox. The trouble with *Miss Herbert* is that the heroine, Eleanor, for all her courage, is a rather uninteresting and irritating character.

From the work of the last two decades, *Dark Places of the Heart*, *The Puzzleheaded Girl*, and *The Little Hotel* are further proofs of the richness, variety, and originality of Christina Stead's art.

—R.G. Geering

STEGNER, Wallace (Earle). American. Born in Lake Mills, Iowa, 18 February 1909. Educated at the University of Utah, Salt Lake City, A.B. 1930; University of Iowa, Iowa City, A.M. 1932, Ph.D. 1935; University of California, Berkeley, 1932-33. Married Mary Stuart Page in 1934; one child. Instructor, Augustana College, Rock Island, Illinois, 1933-34, University of Utah, 1934-37, and University of Wisconsin, Madison, 1937-39; Faculty Instructor, Harvard University, Cambridge, Massachusetts, 1939-45. Professor of English, 1945-69, and Jackson Eli Reynolds Professor of Humanities, 1969-71, Stanford University, California. Writer-in-Residence, American Academy in Rome, 1960; Phi Beta Kappa Visiting Scholar, 1960. West Coast Editor, Houghton Mifflin Company, publishers, Boston, 1945-53. Assistant to the United States Secretary of the Interior, Washington, D.C., 1961. Member, 1962-66, and Chairman, 1965-66, National Parks Advisory Board, Washington, D.C. Editor-in-Chief, *American West* magazine, Palo Alto, California, 1966-68. Recipient: Little Brown Prize, 1937; O. Henry Award, 1942, 1950, 1954; Houghton Mifflin Life-in-America Award, 1945; Anisfield-Wolf Award, 1945; Guggenheim Fellowship, 1949-51, 1959; Rockefeller Fellowship, 1950; Wenner-Gren grant, 1953; Center for Advanced Studies in the Behavioral Sciences Fellowship, 1955; National Endowment for the Humanities Senior Fellowship, 1972; Pulitzer Prize, 1972; National Book Award, 1977; *Los Angeles Times* Kirsch Award, 1980. D.Litt.: University of Utah, 1968; Utah State University, Logan, 1972; D.F.A.: University of California, 1969; D.L.: University of Saskatchewan, Saskatoon, 1973. Member, American Academy, and American Academy of Arts and Sciences. Address: 13456 South Fork Lane, Los Altos Hills, California 94022, U.S.A.

PUBLICATIONS

Novels

Remembering Laughter. Boston, Little Brown, and London, Heinemann, 1937.
The Potter's House. Muscatine, Iowa, Prairie Press, 1938.
On a Darkling Plain. New York, Harcourt Brace, 1940.
Fire and Ice. New York, Duell, 1941.
The Big Rock Candy Mountain. New York, Duell, 1943; London, Hammond, 1950.
Second Growth. Boston, Houghton Mifflin, 1947; London, Hammond, 1948.
The Preacher and the Slave. Boston, Houghton Mifflin, 1950; London, Hammond, 1951; as *Joe Hill: A Biographical Novel*, New York, Doubleday, 1969.
A Shooting Star. New York, Viking Press, and London, Heinemann, 1961.
All the Little Live Things. New York, Viking Press, 1967; London, Heinemann, 1968.
Angle of Repose. New York, Doubleday, and London, Heinemann, 1971.
The Spectator Bird. New York, Doubleday, 1976; London, Prior, 1977.
Recapitulation. New York, Doubleday, 1979.

Short Stories

The Women on the Wall. Boston, Houghton Mifflin, 1950; London, Hammond, 1952.
The City of the Living. Boston, Houghton Mifflin, 1956; London, Hammond, 1957.
New Short Novels 2, with others. New York, Ballantine, 1956.

Uncollected Short Stories

"He Who Spits at the Sky," in *Esquire* (New York), March 1958.
"Something Spurious from the Mindanao Deep," in *Harper's* (New York), August 1958.
"The Wolfer," in *Harper's* (New York), October 1959.

"Carrion Spring," in *Prize Stories 1964: The O. Henry Awards*, edited by Richard Poirier. New York, Doubleday, 1964.

Other

Mormon Country. New York, Duell, 1942.
One Nation, with the editors of *Look*. Boston, Houghton Mifflin, 1945.
Look at America: The Central Northwest, with others. Boston, Houghton Mifflin, 1947.
The Writer in America (lectures). Tokyo, Hokuseido Press, 1952; South Pasadena, California, Perkins and Hutchins, 1953.
Beyond the Hundredth Meridian: John Wesley Powell and the Second Opening of the West. Boston, Houghton Mifflin, 1954.
Wolf Willow: A History, A Story, and A Memory of the Last Plains Frontier. New York, Viking Press, 1962; London, Heinemann, 1963.
The Gathering of Zion: The Story of the Mormon Trail. New York, McGraw Hill, 1964; London, Eyre and Spottiswoode, 1966.
The Sound of Mountain Water: The Changing American West. New York, Doubleday, 1969.
The Uneasy Chair: A Biography of Bernard De Voto. New York, Doubleday, 1974.
Ansel Adams: Images 1923-1974. Greenwich, Connecticut, New York Graphic Society, 1974.

Editor, with others, *An Exposition Workshop*. Boston, Little Brown, 1939.
Editor, with others, *Readings for Citizens at War*. New York, Harper, 1941.
Editor, with Richard Scowcroft, *Stanford Short Stories 1946*. Stanford, California, Stanford University Press, 1947 (and later volumes).
Editor, with Richard Scowcroft and Boris Ilyin, *The Writer's Art: A Collection of Short Stories*. Boston, Heath, 1950.
Editor, *This Is Dinosaur: Echo Park Country and Its Magic Rivers*. New York, Knopf, 1955.
Editor, *The Exploration of the Colorado River of the West*, by J.W. Powell. Chicago, University of Chicago Press, 1957.
Editor, with Mary Stegner, *Great American Short Stories*. New York, Dell, 1957.
Editor, *Selected American Prose: The Realistic Movement*. New York, Rinehart, 1958; London, Owen, 1963.
Editor, *The Adventures of Huckleberry Finn*, by Mark Twain. New York, Dell, 1960.
Editor, *The Outcasts of Poker Flat*, by Bret Harte. New York, New American Library, 1961.
Editor, *Report on the Lands of the Arid Region of the United States*, by J.W. Powell. Cambridge, Massachusetts, Harvard University Press, and London, Oxford University Press, 1962.
Editor, with others, *Modern Composition*. New York, Holt Rinehart, 4 vols., 1964.
Editor, *The American Novel: From Cooper to Faulkner*. New York, Basic, 1965.
Editor, *The Big Sky*, by A.B. Guthrie, Jr. Boston, Houghton Mifflin, 1965.
Editor, with others, *Twenty Years of Stanford Short Stories*. Stanford, California, Stanford University Press, 1966.
Editor, *Twice-Told Tales*, by Nathaniel Hawthorne. New York, Heritage Press, 1967.
Editor, *The Letters of Bernard De Voto*. New York, Doubleday, 1975.

*

Manuscript Collections: University of Iowa, Iowa City; Stanford University, California.

Critical Studies: *Wallace Stegner* by Merrill and Lorene Lewis, Boise, Idaho, Boise State College, 1972; "Wallace Stegner: Trial by Existence" by Robert Canzoneri, in *Southern Review* (Baton Rouge, Louisiana), Autumn 1973; *Wallace Stegner* by Forrest G. and Margaret G. Robinson, Boston, Twayne, 1977.

Wallace Stegner comments:

My subjects and themes are mainly out of the American West, in which I grew up. Because I grew up without history, in a place where human occupation had left fewer traces than the passage of buffalo and antelope herds, I early acquired the desire to find some history in which I myself belonged, and some tradition within which I might have a self-respecting part. For that reason, I suppose, I have never been a rebel against tradition in general, however much I may have resisted specific and rigid aspects of it. I have written fiction whose impulse was at least as much social as psychological. I do not think any individual, in fiction or in life, is defined except within the group life that formed him. Even *The Big Rock Candy Mountain*, which deals with a wandering, asteroid-like family on the western frontiers, is a search for a place and a stability. Even *Angle of Repose*, which likewise deals with a pioneering family of a kind, is a study in continuity.

* * *

Wallace Stegner is a writer whose sizable body of work includes not only novels and volumes of short stories but also historical works such as *Mormon Country*, *Beyond the Hundredth Meridian*, and *The Gathering of Zion: The Story of the Mormon Trail*. These latter works indicate a mind and a temperament which are profoundly stirred by elements in the American past. It is a past that has great usefulness to a writer who, in many of his works of fiction, tries to see that past as a permanent element in present American experience. This past has its beginnings in Eastern, "cultivated" experience and extends westward, in time and space, across plains and mountains, until it reaches the rich promises and frustrating ambiguities of modern California.

In his novels Stegner singles out various stages of this westward movement and attempts to assess the partial meanings that each stage offers an attentive novelist who brings to his reading of chosen subject-matter insights which he shares with social historians. Stegner's subject-matter is marked by a richness and complexity that are not easily reduced to simple patterns. Yet a kind of constant can be isolated as cropping up again and again as the novels move from New England experience of the present in *Second Growth* to various Western times and places. *On a Darkling Plain* tells of the experiment in isolation made by a young veteran of World War I in Western Canada; the young man, rather significantly in relation to Stegner's later work, feels a need to detach himself from a modern world that has distorted human promise. *The Big Rock Candy Mountain* has for its subject the wanderings of a family in Western lands: lands that offer the group a mixture of promise and defeat. In *The Preacher and the Slave* Stegner offers a fictionized account of the IWW movement of the first decades of this century. Three later novels—*A Shooting Star*, *All the Little Live Things*, and *The Spectator Bird*—move to the California of the present; they measure the sad realization of the promise inherent in the great westward movement. It is a promise badly betrayed in the experience of the neurotic heroine of *A Shooting Star*. It is a promise that is in part realized by the ability of the retired academic in *All the Little Live Things* to be a stern judge of the course that American civilization is taking. The retired academic reappears—in essence if not in fact—as the historian-hero of *Angle of Repose*, a man confined to a wheel-chair where he passes his time writing a work, part-history, part-fiction, that recreates the Western experience of his grandmother: a Western life more charged with promise than the heroes—men of the arts, one and all—find in the California present. Certainly the retired literary agent, "writer" of *The Spectator Bird* blends his personal meditation on his coming death with strictures of the emptiness of current life and literature, and meditation on a transient affair hardly offsets these. Another late novel, *Recapitulation*, is set in Utah rather than California, but its effect is much the same; once more an elderly man—in this instance a diplomat—is forced by circumstance to make a reckoning of his life, its betrayals and its small triumphs.

These brief summaries give one some idea of what one will encounter in the novels of Stegner. The subject-matter is, within the limits indicated, various. But the style and the writer's attention to his material create an effect of considerable unity in the entire body of work. The style is sober and expresses the desire of the author to reproduce the persons and the settings of their experience as, supposedly, they actually existed. The novels plainly rest at many points on careful research, as Stegner notes in prefatory remarks to *Second Growth*: "The making of fiction entails the creation of places and persons with all the seeming of reality, and these places and persons, no matter how a writer tries to invent them, must be made up piece-meal from sublimations of his own experience and his own acquaintance. There is no other material out of which fiction can be made." This is an observation that is supplemented—but not contradicted by—the "Foreword" to the IWW novel, *The Preacher and the Slave*, where Stegner defends the novelist's right to reshape what has come to him not from direct experience but from research. This is a set of remarks that express and justify the boldness with which the historian-novelist of *Angle of Repose* handles and supplements the letters, articles, and drawings out of which he reconstructs his grandmother's Western life. If there is indeed a "seeming of reality" in Stegner's fiction, it is a reality constructed by a prose that is exhaustive and faithful; there are not turns of language that, as in much modern fiction, mock the reality that the author has created only to put in question.

This style is, of course, an expression of the unfolding assessment of experience in Stegner's novels. It is an assessment that moves toward precision and some bitterness in the most recent novels. But the main outlines of this assessment are already apparent in an early work like *On a Darkling Plain*: When desperate laughter sweeps a roomful of persons suffering from influenza, Stegner indicates that there are two ways to view miserable humanity. The world may indeed by the work of a "malevolent torturer"—a reference to a dark power that is the nearest Stegner comes to theological reference, for he is the most non-theological of novelists. This "torturer" may indeed have peopled the earth with "cannibal apes." Yet Stegner qualifies this vision. "At its worst the world had that face, but at its best, in its stricken hours, one saw the reserves of nobility and endurance and high-hearted courage that kept the race alive." Stegner's hero "knew, as he had always known since Ypres, that in the comradeship of ruin there was a tempering of the spirit; the resiliency of humanity under the whip was justification for all its meannesses."

In his reading of human behavior Stegner tends to separate the "cannibal apes" from those who display "reserves of nobility and endurance and high-hearted courage." In contrast to the resilient in *On a Darkling Plain* is a low-minded, lecherous Cockney who introduces the influenza virus to his betters. *Second Growth* offers us a New England Eden—or comparative Eden—corrupted by the presence of a Lesbian. Stegner's dichotomy becomes intense in *All the Little Live Things* and *Angle of Repose*. Both novels, as noted, are told from the point of view of a meditative, scholarly, and elderly man who is able to remember and reconstruct the hopes of earlier generations. Against these hopes, both men put the current reality. It is a reality in which the privileged have lost the sense that privilege imposes obligations. It is a reality in which the underprivileged have detached themselves from the "comradeship of ruin" and seek the instant salvation that drugs and "meditation" offer. The grandmother of *Angle of Repose* accepted the "comradeship of ruin"; those who have come after her try to evade it. So doing, they turn their backs on the sort of experience that Stegner finds in the Western past. It is this keen sense of wilful modern betrayal, wilful evasion of the harsh conditions under which all men exist, that accounts for the bitter and prophetic ire that now marks Stegner's work.

—Harold H. Watts

STERN, Daniel. American. Born in New York City, 18 January 1928. Educated at the New School for Social Research, New York. Served in the United States Army, 1946-47. Married Gloria Stern in 1963; one son. Cellist, Indianapolis Symphony Orchestra, 1948-49. Senior Vice-President and Managing Director, McCann-Erickson Advertising Agency; Vice-President of Advertising and Publicity, Warner Brothers; Director of Promotion, C.B.S. Inc. Recipient: Huntington Hartford Fellowship, 1955, 1957; Wesleyan University Center for the Humanities Fellowship, 1969; Remembrance Award, 1973. Agent: Georges Borchardt, 137 East 57th Street, New York, New York 10022. Address: 1230 Park Avenue, New York, New York 10028, U.S.A.

PUBLICATIONS

Novels

The Girl with the Glass Heart. Indianapolis, Bobbs Merrill, 1953.
The Guest of Fame. New York, Ballantine, 1955.
Miss America. New York, Random House, 1959.
Who Shall Live, Who Shall Die. New York, Crown, 1963.
After the War. New York, Putnam, 1967.
The Suicide Academy. New York, McGraw Hill, 1968; London, W.H. Allen, 1969.
The Rose Rabbi. New York, McGraw Hill, 1971.
Final Cut. New York, Viking Press, 1975.
An Urban Affair. New York, Simon and Schuster, 1980.
Happiness in Cities. New York, Harper, 1980.

Uncollected Short Stories

"Conversation in Prague," in *American Vanguard*, edited by Charles I. Glicksberg and Brom Weber. New York, Dial Press, 1953.
"The Death of Isaac Mendez," in *University of Windsor Review* (Ontario).
"The Death of the Novel," in *Voyages* (Washington, D.C.).
"The Mysterious New Novel," in *Liberations: New Essays on the Humanities in Revolution*, edited by Ihab Hassan. Middletown, Connecticut, Wesleyan University Press, 1971.
"Missing the Point," in *Canto* (Cambridge, Massachusetts), 1979.
"Sacred Text," in *Confrontation* (New York), 1979.

*

Manuscript Collection: Boston University.

Critical Studies: *The Novel of the Future* by Anaïs Nin, New York, Macmillan, 1968; *Contemporary American Literature* by Ihab Hassan, New York, Ungar, 1973.

Daniel Stern comments:

Just a few words: my books have grown from a realistic novel of Jewish family life (my first book) through to two deeply experimental books (*The Suicide Academy* and *The Rose Rabbi*) in which I tried to push the novel form as far as it could go for my needs...into a kind of para-reality...retaining the essentials of character and plot, while making the over-all schema into a metaphor that would encompass the events in the story—and the larger meaning they might have (though always anchored to those concrete events).

In 1963 I published a book *Who Shall Live, Who Shall Die* which marked the beginning of my interest in Jewish themes, on a philosophical basis—as well as a fruitful source of material. The Jew as a fictional metaphor became my concern for several books—and will probably continue as such, inevitably. Though *Final Cut* is a study of power and the human motifs and relationships that color it, deny it, make it possible and, finally, unsatisfying.

Summing up: the novel of ideas expressed through concretely experienced felt life is my area of work.

* * *

Daniel Stern is a Jewish novelist whose use of the Jewish experience began realistically with a novel of family life, *The Girl with the Glass Heart*. Later novels also tended to be realistic in mode, though their subject matter was unusual—the life of a beauty queen after the contests are over in *Miss America*, and a witty combination of concentration camp and Broadway stage production in *Who Shall Live, Who Shall Die*. But his novels *The Suicide Academy* and *The Rose Rabbi* are brilliant works, a leap beyond the realistic and witty to an experimental use of the Jew as a metaphor of modern man. In fact, Stern places the hero of both novels, Wolf Walker, in such moral contexts—an institute for would-be suicides and an advertising agency—as to suggest that his interest in Wolf is less as a Jew than as a thinking, urban man.

The setting of *The Suicide Academy* is itself brilliant: a private institution (one of a world-wide group) allowing anyone who is suicidally motivated a one-day course in understanding suicide's implications. Rigorously unified in time (one bright winter day) and place (a rural estate, neither beautiful nor ugly), the novel centers on Wolf Walker, the director of the Academy. Wolf is a complex man, but absolutely devoted to making the Academy a perfect paradigm of choice.

The inscription in the "book of legends" of the Academy's founders reads: "Suicide is not to be undertaken lightly. At its best it is a life-long endeavor." (Beckett and Borges are quoted as "directors" of the French and Argentinian suicide academies.) The curriculum of the Academy is complex, and in both its layout and its specific details, Stern is always one step or even two steps ahead of the reader. The Drama Exercise consists of a harangue by Wolf's assistant: of a cancerous farmer, he asks, "Are you afraid of pain?"; of a homosexual marine, "Were you a fag before you joined up?"; of a concentration camp survivor, "Do you have fantasies of revenge?"

Wolf's nature is examined in the book in two guises—formally through his conflict with his assistant, the black Gilliatt, a "philosopher of darkness" (there are stunning exchanges here), and through his role as the middleman between his two superiors, who argue for and against life; and informally through his confrontation with his ex-wife's new husband, Max. Max has all the vitality that Wolf lacks, but it becomes apparent that the true reason Max has turned up at the Academy is not so much to make a film as to tease himself into attending the Academy as an applicant. The climax of the novel is a fire set in a suicide attempt by one of the Academy guides. As the Academy burns down, Wolf hears the voices of all the past applicants speak through the holocaust, a Babel, a burning bush, a tongue of flame: "Tonight I heard the houses, the trees, the rocks. I heard them all speak tonight from the fire. I tell you, Gilliatt, we are not here to pass judgment.... I tell you we're here to remember those who forget—we're here to let the mystery happen. To let the Bush burn—to let the voices speak. To sanctify the ground for each other and ourselves at least once before we disappear underneath it." A foreign woman applicant appears, lost after the fire, speaking a language Wolf does not understand. As Wolf leads her to safety, he plans his new Academy—to bear witness to "amnesty whole lives."

The Rose Rabbi is both a postscript and a widening-out of *The Suicide Academy*. The atmosphere and themes are similar: a search for meaning, for failure. Wolf's anxiety is part of life's complexity and contingencies; the bold decision, the strong generalization are often life-denying. Wolf *lives* his life instead of controlling it through art (in the manner of a composer); his life becomes his *Pastorale*, his opus 1 (and only). The epigraph is from Wallace Stevens: "Like a rose rabbi, I/Observed...the nature of mankind.../I pursued/...the origin and course/Of love...."

—James Vinson

STERN, James (Andrew). British. Born in Kilcairne, County Meath, Ireland, 26 December 1904. Educated at Eton College; Royal Military College, Sandhurst. Married Tania Kurella in 1935. Farmer in Rhodesia, 1925-26; bank clerk in London and Germany, 1927-29. Assistant Editor, *London Mercury*, 1929-31. Free-lance journalist, in much of Europe; lived for 16 years in the United States. Recipient: American Academy grant, 1949; Arts Council grant, 1966. Fellow, Royal Society of Literature, 1953. Address: Hatch Manor, Tisbury, Wiltshire, England.

PUBLICATIONS

Short Stories

The Heartless Land. London, Macmillan, and New York, Macmillan, 1932.
Something Wrong. London, Secker and Warburg, 1938.
The Man Who Was Loved. New York, Harcourt Brace, 1951; London, Secker and Warburg, 1952.
The Stories of James Stern. London, Secker and Warburg, 1968; New York, Harcourt Brace, 1969.

Uncollected Short Stories

"The Dunce," in *London Mercury*, July 1931.
"Strangers Defeated," in *London Mercury*, August 1933.
"The Man from Montparnasse," in *Penguin Parade 1*. London, Penguin, 1937.
"The Thief," in *New Statesman and Nation* (London), 14 September 1940.
"The Young Lady," in *Penguin Parade 7*. London, Penguin, 1940.
"The Ebbing Tide," in *Penguin New Writing*. London, Penguin, 1942.
"The Pauper's Grave," in *Harper's Bazaar* (New York), 1946.
"A Day at the Races," in *Dublin Magazine*, Winter 1970-71.
"Allergies," in *London Magazine*, June 1970.
"Bloody Monday," in *London Magazine*, June-July 1972.
"The Facts of Life," in *Winter's Tales 23*, edited by Peter Collenette. London, Macmillan, 1977; New York, St Martin's Press, 1978.
"The Terriers' Treat," in *Irish Press* (Dublin), February 1979.

Play

The Caucasian Chalk Circle, with W.H. Auden and Tania Stern, adaptation of the play by Brecht (produced London, 1962). Published in *Plays*, London, Methuen, 1960.

Other

The Hidden Damage (autobiographical). New York, Harcourt Brace, 1947.

Editor and Translator, *Grimm's Fairy Tales*. New York, Pantheon, 1944; London, Routledge, 1948; as *The Complete Grimm's Fairy Tales*, Pantheon, 1974; Routledge, 1975.

Translator (as Andrew St. James), *Brazil: Land of the Future*, by Stefan Zweig. New York, Viking Press, 1941; London, Cassell, 1942.
Translator (as Andrew St. James), *Amerigo: A Comedy of Errors in History*, by Stefan Zweig. New York, Viking Press, 1942.
Translator, *The Rise and Fall of the House of Ullstein*, by Herman Ullstein. New York, Simon and Schuster, 1943; London, Nicholson and Watson, 1944.
Translator (as Andrew St. James, with E.B. Ashton), *The Twins of Nuremberg*, by Hermann Kesten. New York, Fischer, 1946.
Translator, *Spark of Life*, by Erich Maria Remarque. New York, Appleton Century Crofts, and London, Hutchinson, 1952.

Translator, with Tania Stern, *Selected Prose*, by Hugo von Hofmannsthal. New York, Pantheon, and London, Routledge, 1952.
Translator, with Tania Stern, *Letters to Milena*, by Franz Kafka. London, Secker and Warburg, 1953; New York, Schocken, 1954.
Translator, *A Woman in Berlin* (anonymous). New York, Harcourt Brace, and London, Secker and Warburg, 1954.
Translator, with Robert Pick, *Casanova's Memoirs*. New York, Harper, 1955.
Translator, *The Foreign Minister*, by Leo Lania. Boston, Houghton Mifflin, and London, Davies, 1956.
Translator, with Tania Stern, *Description of a Struggle and Other Stories*, by Franz Kafka. New York, Schocken, and London, Secker and Warburg, 1960.
Translator, with Tania Stern, *Letters of Sigmund Freud 1873-1939*. New York, Basic, 1960; London, Hogarth Press, 1961.
Translator, with Elisabeth Duckworth, *Letters to Felice*, by Franz Kafka, edited by Erich Heller and Jurgen Born. New York, Schocken, 1973; London, Secker and Warburg, 1974.

*

Critical Study: by William Plomer, in *London Magazine*, April 1968.

James Stern comments:

The main comment I feel like making about my fiction is that it is *short*. The difference between a short story writer and a novelist is similar to that between a sprinter and a miler. Unfortunately the short story form has never been popular in England. As a result the writer of stories is frowned upon by publishers. Unless he will consent to write a novel.

*　*　*

The settings of James Stern's stories are as varied as the parts of the world in which he has travelled and lived. The Irish stories reflect the memories of his youth; those laid in South Africa (most of which were collected in his first volume, *The Heartless Land*) his life there as a farmer; there are stories from his years in France, Germany, and the United States; there are even several laid in the South Pacific.

His best work, however, is more concerned with a special time of life than a particular place. Certainly his stories of boyhood ("Our Father," "The Beginning and the End," "Under the Beech Tree," and "The Broken Leg," for instance) must be ranked high. Most of these ("The Broken Leg" is an exception) are narrated in the first person. Whether of not, therefore, they represent artistically arranged versions of events in the author's life, these stories have the mark of truth. One knows, in "The Beginning and the End," that this is exactly how a ten-year-old boy would react to the news of the death of his first "love."

The early South African stories have a special flavor quite their own—possibly because to most readers, even in this jet age, Africa is still the "mysterious continent." And, indeed, Stern catches something of the primeval force of that land in stories such as "The Cloud." Long before the racial problems of South Africa became matters of world interest, his stories were dealing with them. In fact, "The Force," a story from the 1932 collection, anticipates Alan Paton's use of the theme of miscegenation in *Too Late the Phalarope*.

Several good uncollected stories, e.g., "The Dunce" (which must be one of the earliest) and "The Thief," deal with boyhood. But it is a story with an African background, "Strangers Defeated," that one most regrets not finding in any of Stern's collections. This is the story of a spirited horse and its owner, neither of whom is accepted by the natives until their spirits are broken: the horse's by sickness and the master's by his inability to deal with the stubbornness of his workers. Seeing what happens to the horse and his owner, we are able better to understand a land and its people.

And indeed, this is what makes James Stern the fine writer that he is. It is not simply that the incidents on which his stories are based are interesting, as they surely must be for success, or that his settings give us a sense of place, or even that his characters are real and, in today's cant term, "psychologically sound." It is, rather, the fact that, in his best stories, because of what his characters do and say as they act out their little dramas in whatever setting Stern has chosen for them, we, as readers, are able to catch a momentary vision of the truth that shimmers under the surface of life. And if a storyteller can help us to do this, he had done much.

—Norman T. Gates

STERN, Richard G(ustave). American. Born in New York City, 25 February 1928. Educated at the University of North Carolina, Chapel Hill, B.A. 1947 (Phi Beta Kappa); Harvard University, Cambridge, Massachusetts, M.A. 1949; University of Iowa, Iowa City, Ph.D. 1954. Served as an Educational Adviser, United States Army, 1951-52. Married Gay Clark in 1950 (divorced, 1972); four children. Lektor, University of Heidelberg, 1950-51; Instructor, Connecticut College, New London, 1954-55. Since 1955, Member of the Faculty, and since 1965, Professor of English, University of Chicago. Visiting Lecturer, University of Venice, 1962-63; University of California, Santa Barbara, 1964; State University of New York, Buffalo, 1966; Harvard University, 1969; University of Nice, 1970; University of Urbino, 1977. Recipient: Longwood Fellowship, 1960; Friends of Literature Award, 1963; Rockefeller Fellowship, 1965; American Academy grant, 1968; National Endowment for the Arts grant, 1969; Guggenheim Fellowship, 1977; Sandburg Award, 1979. Address: Department of English, University of Chicago, 1050 East 59th Street, Chicago, Illinois 60637, U.S.A.

PUBLICATIONS

Novels

Golk. New York, Criterion, and London, MacGibbon and Kee, 1960.
Europe; or, Up and Down with Schreiber and Baggish. New York, McGraw Hill, 1961; as *Europe; or Up and Down with Baggish and Schreiber*, London, MacGibbon and Kee, 1962.
In Any Case. New York, McGraw Hill, 1962; London, MacGibbon and Kee, 1963.
Stitch. New York, Harper, 1965; London, Hodder and Stoughton, 1967.
Other Men's Daughters. New York, Dutton, 1973; London, Hamish Hamilton, 1974.
Natural Shocks. New York, Coward McCann, and London, Sidgwick and Jackson, 1978.

Short Stories

Teeth, Dying, and Other Matters, and The Gamesman's Island: A Play. New York, Harper, and London MacGibbon and Kee, 1964.
1968: A Short Novel, An Urban Idyll, Five Stories, and Two Trade Notes. New York, Holt Rinehart, 1970; London, Gollancz, 1971.
Packages. New York, Coward McCann, and London, Sidgwick and Jackson, 1980.

Other

The Books in Fred Hampton's Apartment (essays). New York, Dutton, 1973; London, Hamish Hamilton, 1974.

Editor, *Honey and Wax: Pleasures and Powers of Narrative: An Anthology.* Chicago, University of Chicago Press, 1966.

*

Manuscript Collection: Regenstein Library, University of Chicago.

Critical Studies: by Marcus Klein, in *Reporter* (Washington, D.C.), 1966; Hugh Kenner, in *Chicago Review*, Summer 1966; interview with Robert Raeder, in *Chicago Review*, Summer 1966; "Conversation with Richard Stern" by Elliott Anderson and Milton Rosenberg, in *Chicago Review*, Winter 1980; "On Richard Stern's Fiction" by G. Murray and Mary Anne Tapp, in *Story Quarterly* (Highland Park, Illinois), Winter 1980.

* * *

In a time when, serious American fiction has tended towards extreme personal assertion and extravagance of manner, Richard G. Stern has been composing a body of work which is notable for its detailed craftsmanship, its intricacy, and its reticences. His novels and stories are neither lyrically confessional nor abstractly experimental. They are processes quite in the mode of an older tradition, in which character and event discover theme. In one and another incidental observation within his fiction, Stern has rejected both the idea of the novel as "a roller coaster of distress and sympathy, love and desire," and the idea of the novel as a deliberate attack on formal expectations (*Europe*); he has addressed qualification to the view that a story is fully autonomous (see the sketch called "Introductory" in *1968*), but he has also rejected the idea of the author as solipsist (see "Story-Making" in *1968*). His own fiction accepts no extremities of technique and form. Its characteristic tone as well as its strategy of development is created by ironic modulations.

The tone and the technique are, moreover, exact functions of Stern's characteristic subject. The broad theme is the adjustment of private lives with public events. Typically, Stern's protagonist has been a passive, sensitive fellow, who is a little too old for adventuring, or a little too fat, or a little too fine-grained, but nonetheless possessing romantic inclinations. His latent disposition is tested when public event of one sort and another seeks him out. He is now forced to regard his own actions and the actions of others as moral events. And, typically, this protagonist has found himself engaged in a drama of betrayals, which have the effect of chastening his new ambitions as a public man. The end is his rather baffled, nonetheless scrupulous assessment of personal adventure. Between the beginning and the end, his motives are subjected to more and more contingencies. He has been lured from his innocent privacy into life, defined as public action which by its nature is dangerous and ambiguous. At the end he has sacrificed the self-protectedness with which he began, and he has also failed to discover an easy ground of general participation in life. His modest success is that he has become potentially moral.

Stern's first novel, *Golk*, is somewhat more spare and blatant in its actions than the fictions which follow, but it is otherwise exemplary. The hero is a 37-year-old boy, Herbert Hondorp, who lives alone with his widowed father in New York City. As he has done for most of the days of his life, he now spends his days wandering in and near Central Park, until on an occasion, abruptly, he is snared into public view and public occupation. The agent is a television program—"Golk"—which is created, precisely, by making public revelation of privacy. Ordinary, unwary people are caught by the television camera in prearranged, embarrassing situations. Stern's hero discovers that he likes not only the being caught, as do most of the Golk victims, but he also likes the catching. He takes a job with the television program, and not fortuitously at the same time he secures his first romance. Within this new situation there are moral implications, of course, but both "Golk" and Hondorp's romance are tentative and jesting. The novel then proceeds to raise the stakes of involvement: the program is transformed by its ambitious director into a device for political exposé, and Hondorp's romance becomes a marriage. This newer situation beckons and perhaps necessitates treacheries, which make it morally imperative that public involvement be terminated. Hondorp betrays the director of the program, in order to save the program—so he believes—from the fury of the political powers, and he thereby reduces it to vapidity. In a consequent narrative movement, his wife leaves him. Hondorp goes home at the end, "all trace of his ambition, and all desire for change gone absolutely and forever."

In his subsequent fictions, Stern has avoided such metaphorical ingenuity as the television program in *Golk*, and the lure to public action has been carefully limited to a matter of background or accident, but the area of his concerns has remained constant. In *Europe; or, Up and Down with Schreiber and Baggish*, the two protagonists are American civil employees in post-war occupied Germany. The pattern of their adventuring—despite the comic suggestion in the title of the novel—allows nothing implausible, and there are no sudden reversals. Realization is to be achieved, rather, through implied contrasts and comparisons. Schreiber is an aging sensitive gentleman who tries for intimate understanding of the ancient, bitter, guilty, and conquered people. Baggish is a shrewd young opportunist, who exploits the populace. Baggish succeeds, and Schreiber fails. *In Any Case* is the story of another aging American in post-war Europe, who is innocent for the reason that he has never sufficiently risked anything, his affections included. His testing comes when he is told that his son, dead in the war, was a traitor. In a belated and ironic act of love, he tries to prove that his son was really innocent, and he discovers that treachery is a vital ingredient of all social living. Although his son was indeed not guilty in the way supposed, everyone is a double agent.

His acceptance of that discovery provides the hero with the possibility of a modest participation in other people's lives. In his more recent fiction, Stern has apparently wanted to make that possibility more emphatic, by bringing historical and aesthetic confirmations to it. *Stitch* is in large part a *roman à clef* about one of the great modern traitors, Ezra Pound. The would-be disciple in the novel receives from the aged master, Stitch, lessons in the fusion of personality with civilization, and the consequence of expression in art. The background of the novel is Venice, which, from the muck of its history, raises its beauties. In the short novel *Veni, Vidi... Wendt* (included in *1968*), the protagonist is a composer who is writing an opera about modern love. The opera will extend backwards to include great love affairs of the past, which are founded on adulteries. The composer himself, meanwhile, realizes both his composition and his domestic love for wife and children only after experiments in romantic duplicity. The chief adventurer in *Other Men's Daughters* is a middle-aged professor of biology at Harvard. His life heretofore has been completely defined by such seeming ineluctabilities as filial ties, domestic habits, and the concretion of compromises, and the stern decencies of his New England ancestry. He betrays everything when he falls in love with a girl not much older than the eldest of his own children, and hopefully discovers, in nature, the justification for this treachery to nurture. In *Natural Shocks* Stern writes about a talented and successful journalist, which in this case is to say a man who with all decent good will has made a career of transforming private lives into public knowledge. The protagonist is now forced to confront the fact of death, alternately as a subject for journalism and as a domestic event, and he is thereby invited to learn the necessary treachery that is involved in his calling and also its ethical insufficiency. A true participation in life will require more strenuous sympathies, which he may or may not achieve.

The endings of Stern's fictions record an acquiescence at the most, and always something less than the assertion of a principle. The kind of realization that is in the novels makes it necessary that they be probationary and open-ended. They are by that, as well as by their detailed, persistent, and moderate account of human motives, in the great tradition of moral realism.

—Marcus Klein

STEWART, J(ohn) I(nnes) M(ackintosh). Pseudonym: Michael Innes. British. Born in Edinburgh, 30 September 1906. Educated at Edinburgh Academy; Oriel College, Oxford (Matthew Arnold Memorial Prize, 1929; Bishop Fraser's Scholar, 1930), B.A. (honours) in English 1928. Married Margaret Hardwick in 1932 (died, 1979); three sons and two daughters. Lecturer in English, University of Leeds, Yorkshire, 1930-35; Jury Professor of English, University of Adelaide, South Australia, 1935-45; Lecturer, Queen's University, Belfast, 1946-48; Student (i.e., Fellow) of Christ Church, Oxford, 1949-73, now Emeritus; Reader in English Literature, Oxford University, 1969-73. Walker-Ames Professor, University of Washington, Seattle, 1961. D.Litt.: University of New Brunswick, Fredericton, 1962; University of Leicester, 1979; University of St. Andrews, Scotland, 1980. Address: Fawler Copse, Fawler, Wantage, Oxfordshire, England.

PUBLICATIONS

Novels

Mark Lambert's Supper. London, Gollancz, 1954.
The Guardians. London, Gollancz, 1955; New York, Norton, 1957.
A Use of Riches. London, Gollancz, and New York, Norton, 1957.
The Man Who Won the Pools. London, Gollancz, and New York, Norton, 1961.
The Last Tresilians. London, Gollancz, and New York, Norton, 1963.
An Acre of Grass. London, Gollancz, 1965; New York, Norton, 1966.
The Aylwins. London, Gollancz, 1966; New York, Norton, 1967.
Vanderlyn's Kingdom. London, Gollancz, 1967; New York, Norton, 1968.
Avery's Mission. London, Gollancz, and New York, Norton, 1971.
A Palace of Art. London, Gollancz, and New York, Norton, 1972.
Mungo's Dream. London, Gollancz, and New York, Norton, 1973.
The Gaudy. London, Gollancz, 1974; New York, Norton, 1975.
Young Pattullo. London, Gollancz, 1975; New York, Norton, 1976.
A Memorial Service. London, Gollancz, and New York, Norton, 1976.
The Madonna of the Astrolabe. London, Gollancz, and New York, Norton, 1977.
Full Term. London, Gollancz, 1978; New York, Norton, 1979.
Andrew and Tobias. New York, Norton, 1980; London, Gollancz, 1981.

Novels as Michael Innes

Death at the President's Lodging. London, Gollancz, 1936; as *Seven Suspects*, New York, Dodd Mead, 1937.
Hamlet, Revenge! London, Gollancz, and New York, Dodd Mead, 1937.
Lament for a Maker. London, Gollancz, and New York, Dodd Mead, 1938.
Stop Press. London, Gollancz, 1939; as *The Spider Strikes*, New York, Dodd Mead, 1939.
The Secret Vanguard. London, Gollancz, 1940; New York, Dodd Mead, 1941.
There Came Both Mist and Snow. London, Gollancz, 1940; as *A Comedy of Terrors*, New York, Dodd Mead, 1940.
Appleby on Ararat. London, Gollancz, and New York, Dodd Mead, 1941.
The Daffodil Affair. London, Gollancz, and New York, Dodd Mead, 1942.
The Weight of the Evidence. New York, Dodd Mead, 1943; London, Gollancz, 1944.
Appleby's End. London, Gollancz, and New York, Dodd Mead, 1945.
From London Far. London, Gollancz, 1946; as *The Unsuspected Chasm*, New York, Dodd Mead, 1946.
What Happened at Hazelwood? London, Gollancz, and New York, Dodd Mead, 1946.
A Night of Errors. New York, Dodd Mead, 1947; London, Gollancz, 1948.
The Journeying Boy. London, Gollancz, 1949; as *The Case of the Journeying Boy*, New York, Dodd Mead, 1949.
Operation Pax. London, Gollancz, 1951; as *The Paper Thunderbolt*, New York, Dodd Mead, 1951.
A Private View. London, Gollancz, 1952; as *One-Man Show*, New York, Dodd Mead, 1952; as *Murder Is an Art*, New York, Avon, 1959.
Christmas at Candleshoe. London, Gollancz, and New York, Dodd Mead, 1953; as *Candleshoe*, London, Penguin, 1978.
The Man from the Sea. London, Gollancz, and New York, Dodd Mead, 1955; as *Death by Moonlight*, New York, Avon, 1957.
Old Hall, New Hall. London, Gollancz, 1956; as *A Question of Queens*, New York, Dodd Mead, 1956.
Appleby Plays Chicken. London, Gollancz, 1957; as *Death on a Quiet Day*, New York, Dodd Mead, 1957.
The Long Farewell. London, Gollancz, and New York, Dodd Mead, 1958.
Hare Sitting Up. London, Gollancz, and New York, Dodd Mead, 1959.
The New Sonia Wayward. London, Gollancz, 1960; as *The Case of Sonia Wayward*, New York, Dodd Mead, 1960; as *The Last of Sonia Wayward*, 1962.
Silence Observed. London, Gollancz, and New York, Dodd Mead, 1961.
A Connoisseur's Case. London, Gollancz, 1962; as *The Crabtree Affair*, New York, Dodd Mead, 1962.
Money from Holme. London, Gollancz, 1964; New York, Dodd Mead, 1965.
The Bloody Wood. London, Gollancz, and New York, Dodd Mead, 1966.
A Change of Heir. London, Gollancz, and New York, Dodd Mead, 1966.
Appleby at Allington. London, Gollancz, 1968; as *Death by Water*, New York, Dodd Mead, 1968.
A Family Affair. London, Gollancz, 1969; as *Picture of Guilt*, New York, Dodd Mead, 1969.
Death at the Chase. London, Gollancz, and New York, Dodd Mead, 1970.
An Awkward Lie. London, Gollancz, and New York, Dodd Mead, 1971.
The Open House. London, Gollancz, and New York, Dodd Mead, 1972.
Appleby's Answer. London, Gollancz, and New York, Dodd Mead, 1973.
Appleby's Other Story. London, Gollancz, and New York, Dodd Mead, 1974.
The Mysterious Commission. London, Gollancz, 1974; New York, Dodd Mead, 1975.

The Gay Phoenix. London, Gollancz, 1976; New York, Dodd Mead, 1977.
Honeybath's Haven. London, Gollancz, 1977; New York, Dodd Mead, 1978.
The Ampersand Papers. London, Gollancz, 1978; New York, Dodd Mead, 1979.
Going It Alone. London, Gollancz, and New York, Dodd Mead, 1980.
Lord Mullion's Secret. London, Gollancz, 1981.

Short Stories

The Man Who Wrote Detective Stories and Other Stories. London, Gollancz, and New York, Norton, 1959.
Cucumber Sandwiches and Other Stories. London, Gollancz, and New York, Norton, 1969.
Our England Is a Garden and Other Stories. London, Gollancz, 1979.

Short Stories as Michael Innes

Three Tales of Hamlet, with Rayner Heppenstall. London, Gollancz, 1950.
Appleby Talking: Twenty-Three Detective Stories. London, Gollancz, 1954; as *Dead Man's Shoes*, New York, Dodd Mead, 1954.
Appleby Talks Again: Eighteen Detective Stories. London, Gollancz, 1956; New York, Dodd Mead, 1957.
The Appleby File. London, Gollancz, 1975; New York, Dodd Mead, 1976.

Play as Michael Innes

Strange Intelligence (broadcast, 1947). Published in *Imaginary Conversations*, edited by Rayner Heppenstall, London, Secker and Warburg, 1948.

Radio Play: *Strange Intelligence*, 1947.

Other

Educating the Emotions. Adelaide, New Education Fellowship, 1944.
Character and Motive in Shakespeare: Some Recent Appraisals Examined. London, Longman, 1949; New York, Barnes and Noble, 1966.
James Joyce. London, Longman, 1957; revised edition, 1960.
Thomas Love Peacock. London, Longman, 1963.
Eight Modern Writers. London and New York, Oxford University Press, 1963.
Rudyard Kipling. London, Gollancz, and New York, Dodd Mead, 1966.
Joseph Conrad. London, Longman, and New York, Dodd Mead, 1968.
Thomas Hardy: A Critical Biography. London, Longman, and New York, Dodd Mead, 1971.
Shakespeare's Lofty Scene (lecture). London, Oxford University Press, 1971.

Editor, *Montaigne's Essays: John Florio's Translation*. London, Nonesuch Press, and New York, Random House, 1931.
Editor, *The Moonstone*, by Wilkie Collins. London, Penguin, 1966.
Editor, *Vanity Fair*, by Thackeray. London, Penguin, 1968.

* * *

Michael Innes, undoubtedly a grand-master of crime fiction, is remarkable for his wide range which extends from intricate closed-group murder cases (*The Weight of the Evidence* and *The Bloody Wood*) to fights against large-scale criminal operators (*From London Far*) and organised madness as a global menace (*Hare Sitting Up*). John Appleby, the gentleman turned policeman and rising from plain inspector to knighted commissioner until his (active) retirement, is the main detective figure. At times he is replaced by the formidable Inspector Cadover (*What Happened at Hazelwood?*), and other books manage without a detective altogether: psychological studies like *The New Sonia Wayward*, or the puzzling *Money from Holme*, or frolics like *Going It Alone*. Also the narrative technique varies. A detached third-person narrator dominates (sometimes rather obtrusively), but some stories are told by involved, highly self-conscious, and unreliable figures like Arthur Ferryman (*There Came Both Mist and Snow*).

Basic characteristics are the academic, professional, and aristocratic background, an inexhaustible knowledge of literature and the arts in most characters, which not only forms a large contents element but is frequently also functional to the plot (*The Secret Vanguard*); the skilful distribution of suspense and surprise throughout the stories, but sometimes concentrated in long, enthralling accounts of flight and pursuit (*The Journeying Boy*, *Operation Pax*, and *The Man from the Sea*); a strain of the fantastic, indeed the fairy tale (very strong in *The Daffodil Affair* and *Appleby's End*); finally, a penchant for wild comedy, manifesting itself in innumerable jokes, in prank-like interludes, in stock characters such as Hildebert Braunkopf with his "voonderable voorlt of art" as well as entire stories (*A Change of Heir*). The late works, while suggesting some fatigue (*A Family Affair*), continue to provide cultured, intelligent, and interesting—if no longer gripping—entertainment (like *The Gay Phoenix*) and evince a continued refusal to join the remorseless, bleak, and insecure world of modern British thrillers where the integrity of the police has crumbled alongside that of everybody else, where Piero, Keats, and Raeburn are totally irrelevant.

The novels and stories written as J.I.M. Stewart, by now a sizeable corpus, are set in the same academic and artistic, middle- and upper-class milieu, and show the same apt sense of people, places, of dramatic and—more recently—comic effects, as well as, likewise of late, the sustained interest in senescence, leading to an astonishing gallery of astute portraits of old age (Honeybath, Lampriere, the Mannerings, etc.). If the crime stories often turn on *objets d'art*, many novels concentrate on the creative process, on the artist and his relations to other people. The most obvious link is the quest for posthumous works of writers or painters—developing a theme from Henry James's "The Aspern Papers" (*Mark Lambert's Supper*, *The Guardians*, *An Acre of Grass*); James also provides some technical inspiration ("reflectors"—notably *The Aylwins*, *Vanderlyn's Kingdom*, *Avery's Mission*). When he makes university life the main subject—particularly in the massive Pattullo sequence—Stewart is truly covering home ground. But whereas the refined world of the Oxford don adds (along with social and intellectual snob appeal) a brilliant, strange, and often hilarious light to the world of crime, it does not easily stand up on its own, The mild perplexities and irregularities of an old college, though in themselves a pleasant variant to most, more earthy and strident "campus" literature, and though nicely presented and spiced up with modern phenomena like bed-sitters, demonstrations, and patchily educated freshmen, often seem simply too bloodless, too insubstantial.

Stewart's most important contributions to the mainstream of English fiction so far are probably *A Use of Riches* and *The Last Tresilians*. With his thrillers becoming tamer and his "serious" fiction more relaxed, this author's large and varied creative powers may yet produce something very remarkable in between the two. Among others, short, incisive sketches like "The Men" or "George" and the longer, solid "Our England Is a Garden" (a kind of *roman fleuve* in outline, and showing the pull of Hardy rather than James) could well prove points of departure in that direction.

—H.M. Klein

STIRLING, Monica. British. Born in 1916, daughter of the actor-manager Edward Stirling. Grew up in France. War Correspondent in France, for *Atlantic Monthly*, 1944. Recipient: Metro-Goldwyn award, 1946. Address: c/o Harcourt Brace Jovanovich, 757 Third Avenue, New York, New York 10017, U.S.A.

PUBLICATIONS

Novels

Lovers Aren't Company. London, Gollancz, and Boston, Little Brown, 1949.
Dress Rehearsal. London, Gollancz, 1951; New York, Simon and Schuster, 1952.
Ladies with a Unicorn. London, Gollancz, 1953; New York, Simon and Schuster, 1954.
The Boy in Blue. London, Gollancz, and New York, Coward McCann, 1955.
Some Darling Folly. London, Gollancz, and New York, Coward McCann, 1956.
Sigh for a Strange Land. London, Gollancz, 1958; Boston, Little Brown, 1959.
A Sniper in the Heart. London, Gollancz, 1960.
The Summer of a Dormouse. London, Collins, and New York, Harcourt Brace, 1967.

Short Stories

Adventurers Please Abstain: Short Stories. London, Gollancz, 1952.
Journeys We Shall Never Make: Short Stories. London, Gollancz, 1957.

Other

The Little Ballet Dancer (juvenile). New York, Lothrop, 1952.
The Fine and the Wicked: The Life and Times of Ouida. London, Gollancz, 1957; New York, Coward McCann, 1958.
A Pride of Lions: A Portrait of Napoleon's Mother. London, Collins, 1961; as *Madame Letizia*, New York, Harper, 1962.
The Wild Swan: The Life and Times of Hans Christian Andersen. London, Collins, and New York, Harcourt Brace, 1965.
The Cat from Nowhere (juvenile). New York, Harcourt Brace, 1969.
A Screen of Time: A Study of Luchino Visconti. New York, Harcourt Brace, 1979.

* * *

Monica Stirling has written some eight novels, two volumes of short stories, and several biographies and juveniles; all her work is pleasant and entertaining, designed for the general reader. From her own knowledge of Europe just after the war and her close association with the theatre Stirling has, in one novel after another, created situations and characters reflecting her background.

Her first novel, *Lovers Aren't Company*, set in Rome in 1944, tells the story of an American woman of Italian descent who returns to find her sister dead and her niece totally confused. A decade later in *Sigh for a Strange Land* there is another such situation of a girl with an Italian background who becomes much involved with the sorrows and upheavals of refugees fleeing East Europe. In both *Ladies with a Unicorn* and *Boy in Blue* there are characters whose families have been wiped out in the war. In the former, the protagonist, Françoise Jonbert, has lost her husband; in the latter, Laurent, a charming young composer, has lost mother, father, and twin brother in the deliberate destruction by the Germans of a small village in the south of France. In spite of the suggested tragedies the materials are handled in such a way that the reader is never disturbed as in smooth descriptive prose Stirling tells about the events.

In general the most attractive features of the novels are the various settings; the books could very well serve as travelogues. Stirling is obviously thoroughly familiar with Italy, France, and England. The sights and sounds, the way of life, especially the sensuous opulence of the rich and successful in France and Italy, are all a part of her work. In some of the novels these features are successful; in others, they are merely decorative, and, indeed, sometimes they serve to make serious themes trivial and heavy-handed.

Dress Rehearsal and *Some Darling Folly* are the two most successful of the novels. *Dress Rehearsal* is hardly a novel in the usual terms; it is, in fact, a series of engaging episodes, strongly autobiographical, of the boarding-school days in England of the daughter of a successful actor. The contrast of the warm family life of the past with the rather chilly properness of an English school is well done. *Some Darling Folly* is also about the world of the theatre. In this novel the traditional triangle is handled competently and wittily. It is the story of a French actor, Remy, who, intrigued by the artlessness of a lawyer's wife, is somewhat disconcerted to discover that his "interest" is quite able to discard him without tears and return to her husband.

Stirling's work for juveniles shows her charm and her smooth skill as a writer. *The Little Ballet Dancer* is an account of a little French girl who wanted to become a ballet dancer. *The Summer of a Dormouse* shows a skillful blend of sympathy and charm. It is the story of a young girl's recovery from a mental illness, reflecting perhaps Stirling's biographical study of Hans Christian Andersen.

All of Monica Stirling's work shows the hand of a competent, charming, and witty person; unfortunately this charm and wit are seldom a part of her characters, and the themes, while thoroughly admirable, are handled in an obvious and trite fashion. Someone has called her work "quality feminine fiction." If one may designate fiction as "feminine" and thereafter qualify it with any possible meaning of "quality," then perhaps this is a proper label.

—Annibel Jenkins

STIVENS, Dal(las George). Australian. Born in Blayney, New South Wales, 31 December 1911. Educated at Barker College, Hornsby, Sydney, 1927-28. Served in the Australian Army Education Service, 1943-44. Married Winifred Vera Wright in 1945; two children. Staff member, Sydney *Daily Telegraph*, 1939-42; with the Australian Department of Information, 1944-50: Press Officer, Australia House, London, 1949-50. Painter: one-man show, Sydney, 1974. Foundation President, 1963-64, Vice President, 1964-66, and President, 1967-73, Australian Society of Authors. Member, New South Wales Advisory Committee, Australian Broadcasting Commission, 1969-72. Chairman, Literary Committee, Captain Cook Bicentenary Celebrations, 1969-70. Recipient: Commonwealth Literary Fund Fellowship, 1951, 1962, 1970; Miles Franklin Award, 1970. Address: 5 Middle Harbour Road, Lindfield, New South Wales 2070, Australia.

PUBLICATIONS

Novels

Jimmy Brockett: Portrait of a Notable Australian. London, Britannicus Liber, 1951.
The Wide Arch. London, Angus and Robertson, 1959.
Three Persons Make a Tiger. Melbourne, Cheshire, 1968.
A Horse of Air. Sydney, Angus and Robertson, 1970; London, Angus and Robertson, 1971.

Short Stories

The Tramp and Other Stories. London, Macmillan, 1936.
The Courtship of Uncle Henry: Short Stories. Melbourne, Reed and Harris, 1946.
The Gambling Ghost and Other Tales. London, Angus and Robertson, 1953.
Ironbark Bill. London, Angus and Robertson, 1955.
The Scholarly Mouse and Other Tales. London, Angus and Robertson, 1958.
Selected Stories, 1936-1968. London, Angus and Robertson, 1969.
The Unicorn and Other Tales. Sydney, Wild and Woolley, 1976.
The Demon Bowler and Other Cricket Stories. Melbourne, Outback Press, 1979.

Other

A Guide to Book Contracts, with Barbara Jefferis. Sydney, Australian Society of Authors, 1967.
The Incredible Egg: A Billion Year Journey. New York, Weybright and Talley, 1974.
The Bushranger (juvenile). Sydney, Collins, 1978.

Editor, *Coast to Coast: Australian Stories 1957-1958.* Sydney, Angus and Robertson, 1959.

*

Manuscript Collections: National Library, Canberra; University of Sydney.

Critical Studies: "The Author in Search of Himself: Some Notes on Dal Stivens" by Brian Elliott, in *Australian Quarterly* (Sydney), March 1962; introduction to *Selected Stories, 1936-1968*, 1969, and article in *The Literature of Australia* edited by Geoffrey Dutton, Melbourne, Penguin, 1976, both by H.P. Heseltine.

Dal Stivens comments:

It is difficult to comment on your own work, particularly when it extends over 50 years. During that time your interest in various aspects of life, etc. has changed. But my underlying interest has been in the tension between illusion and reality, art and life. *A Horse of Air* and *The Unicorn and Other Tales* are the fruits of this preoccupation. What is the truth? Is it not relative? Importantly, a novel or a short story isn't a transcript of life. It's an art object just as a good painting should be.

My present concern is with ambiguity both in writing and in painting. (In recent years I've spent more time painting than writing.) My ambition—never to be realized!—is to write an abstract tale or novel that could be absorbed in a few seconds just as a good abstract painting is.

* * *

One remembers Dal Stivens as a small man with a bright eye under a jaunty hat, with quick movements and a more or less staccato speech. He is best known for *Jimmy Brockett*, a novel with a kind of jinx. First published in 1951, it has been variously reprinted and eventually reached a paperbook issue, yet the Australian public has consistently failed to acknowledge the brilliance of its image therein reflected. The colour and character of life in Australia have been changing so rapidly and so radically in the years since war shattered the complacency of the Pacific that a temporary neglect of satire so local is hardly remarkable. Jimmy Brockett is a character in the Falstaffian mould, conceived in terms of a richly coarse humour, an enormity of a man both mentally and physically, in whom speaks the spirit of post-colonial Australian aggressiveness and enterprise, crude, pragmatic, singleminded, and utterly philistine—and yet not without a heart, capable of tenderness in a bull-like and domineering way, and especially a conqueror of (and no less a martyr to) women. A comparison might be made with *Babbitt*; but Stivens's satire is, in the Australian way, warmer and more tolerant of human failings. The setting of the novel is Sydney and the banner it carries is for the common man—that is, the uncommon common man, the nobody of genius. Jimmy in dying crowns his career of sad triumphs with a direction which sums up his attitude to the hypocritical world: "I have asked the undertaker to put me on my face in my coffin so that anyone who doesn't like my will can kiss my arse."

The Wide Arch abandons serious portraiture and naturalism and attempts a sophisticated murder-mystery form, using as its main intellectual ingredient a scheme of *Hamlet* parallels in a Sydney setting. The book retains its interest rather as a literary experiment than as a narrative of suspense. Experiment still dominates *Three Persons Make a Tiger*, alleged to be an adaptation of a Chinese work but really a free variation on a Chinese theme with so high a degree of fantasy that its Australian satirical content tends to evaporate. It is at its best witty and clever but its successes are fragmentary. The most recent novel, *A Horse of Air*, recovers ground and is agreeably readable besides making an imaginative use of the Australian "mythical" values implicit in the journals of the explorer Giles, whose excursion into the Rawlinson Ranges provides Stivens with a "quest" theme (a search for a rare "night parrot"). However in general his novels since *Jimmy Brockett* all strive too transparently to keep up with trends.

Similarly in the short stories the pattern is one of decline. The best of all his work appears in *The Tramp* and *The Courtship of Uncle Henry*: stories and sketches of an imaginative truth and insight rare in Australian writing and not inferior to the best of Henry Lawson. In later stories he pushed spontaneous invention in the direction of a folksy style which undercut natural inspiration, with the result that, although witty and amusing at best, he lost touch with his own basic originality. He remains, however, an undervalued Australian writer who may some day yet receive the benefit of an upward reassessment.

—Brian Elliott

STONE, Irving. American. Born in San Francisco, California, 14 July 1903. Educated at Lowell High School, San Francisco; Manual Arts High School, Los Angeles; University of California, Berkeley, A.B. 1923, graduate study, 1924-26; University of Southern California, Los Angeles, M.A. 1924. Married Jean Factor in 1934; two children. Teaching Fellow in Economics, University of Southern California, 1923-24, and University of California, Berkeley, 1924-26; Visiting Lecturer in Creative Writing, University of Indiana, Bloomington, 1948, and University of Washington, Seattle, 1961; Lecturer on the writing of biography and the biographical novel, University of Southern California, 1966; Lecturer, California State Colleges, 1966. Art Critic, *Los Angeles Mirror-News*, 1959-60. United States Department of State Cultural Exchange Specialist, in the Soviet Union, Poland, and Yugoslavia, 1962. President, California Writers Guild, 1960-61; Founder, Academy of American Poets, 1962; Founder, California State Colleges Committee for the Arts, 1967; Trustee, Douglass House Foundation, Watts, Los Angeles, 1967-68; President, Dante Alighieri Society, Los Angeles, 1968-69. Since 1955, Founder and President, Fellows for Schweitzer, Southern California; since 1963, Vice-President, Eugene V. Debs Foundation, Terre Haute, Indiana, and Member, Advisory Board, University of California Institute for the Creative Arts; since 1969, President, Affiliates of the Department of English, University of California, Los Angeles. Recipient: Christopher Award, 1957. D.L.: University of Southern California, 1965; D.Litt.: Coe College, Cedar Rapids, Iowa, 1967; California State Colleges, 1971; LL.D.: University of California, Berkeley, 1968; D.H.L.: Hebrew

Union College, Cincinnati, 1978. Commendatore (Knight Commander), Republic of Italy, 1962. Lives in Beverly Hills, California. Address: c/o Doubleday and Company, 245 Park Avenue, New York, New York 10017, U.S.A.

PUBLICATIONS

Novels

Pageant of Youth. New York, King, 1933.
Lust for Life. New York, Longman, and London, Lane, 1934.
Sailor on Horseback. Boston, Houghton Mifflin, and London, Collins, 1938; as *Jack London, Sailor on Horseback*, New York, Doubleday, 1947.
False Witness. New York, Doubleday, 1940.
Immortal Wife. New York, Doubleday, 1944; London, Falcon Press, 1950.
Adversary in the House. New York, Doubleday, 1947; London, Falcon Press, 1950.
The Passionate Journey. New York, Doubleday, 1949; London, Falcon Press, 1950.
The President's Lady. New York, Doubleday, 1951; London, Lane, 1952.
Love Is Eternal. New York, Doubleday, 1954; London, Collins, 1955.
The Agony and the Ecstasy. New York, Doubleday, and London, Collins, 1961.
Those Who Love. New York, Doubleday, 1965; London, Cassell, 1966.
The Passions of the Mind. New York, Doubleday, and London, Cassell, 1971.
The Greek Treasure. New York, Doubleday, and London, Cassell, 1975.
The Origin. New York, Doubleday, 1980; London, Cassell, 1981.

Plays

The Dark Mirror (produced New York, 1928).
The White Life: A Play Based on the Life of Baruch Spinoza. New York, League of Jewish Community Associations, 1932.
Truly Valiant (produced New York, 1936).

Other

Clarence Darrow for the Defense. New York, Doubleday, 1941; as *Darrow for the Defence*, London, Lane, 1950.
They Also Ran: The Story of the Men Who Were Defeated for the Presidency. New York, Doubleday, 1943; revised edition, 1945.
The Evolution of an Idea. Privately printed, 1945.
Earl Warren. New York, Prentice Hall, 1948.
Men to Match My Mountains: The Opening of the Far West 1840-1900. New York, Doubleday, 1956; London, Cassell, 1967.
Three Views of the Novel, with John O'Hara and MacKinlay Kantor. Washington, D.C., Library of Congress, 1957.
The Irving Stone Reader. New York, Doubleday, 1963.
The Story of Michelangelo's Pietà. New York, Doubleday, 1964.
The Great Adventure of Michelangelo (juvenile). New York, Doubleday, 1965.
There Was Light: Autobiography of a University, Berkeley 1868-1968. Berkeley, University of California Press, 1970.
Mary Todd Lincoln: A Final Judgement? Springfield, Illinois, Abraham Lincoln Association, 1973.

Editor, *Dear Theo: The Autobiography of Vincent van Gogh.* Boston, Houghton Mifflin, and London, Constable, 1937.
Editor, with Richard Kennedy, *We Speak for Ourselves: Self Portrait of America.* New York, Doubleday, 1950.
Editor, with Allan Nevins, *Lincoln: A Contemporary Portrait.* New York, Doubleday, 1962.
Editor, with Jean Stone, *I, Michelangelo, Sculptor: An Autobiography Through Letters.* New York, Doubleday, 1962; London, Collins, 1963.
Editor, *Irving Stone's Jack London.* New York, Doubleday, 1977.

*

Bibliography: *Irving Stone: A Bibliography* by Lewis F. Stieg, Los Angeles, Friends of the Libraries of the University of Southern California, 1973.

Manuscript Collection: Special Collections, University of California Library, Los Angeles.

Irving Stone comments:

The biographical novel is a true and documented story of one human being's journey across the face of the years, transmuted from the raw material into the delight and purity of an authentic art form. The research must be honest and far reaching, but the result must stand as a compelling novel.

* * *

The historian in Irving Stone has cohabited with the artist through a dozen or so novels now, and although the public sanctions the arrangement by purchasing and reading the offspring books, the union is neither literarily nor historically holy. The novels that come of it suffer congenital defects; for all their broad appeal, there are problems with historical novels that are inescapable. Stone is an astute novelist, insofar as he recognizes a compelling story and can control the reader's attention for the most part, and he is a willing historian who researches his material copiously. But in the novels, the historian tends to inhibit the inventive imagination, embalming the dialogue and losing the plot for long periods in thickets of detail, while the artist always opens the history to a doubt that the most impressive bibliographical lists cannot still. This is, of course, true of all historical novelists, to an extent, but, paradoxically, the generic difficulty is more acute in the case of more serious ones, such as Stone, than in the case of slighter ones, such as Frank G. Slaughter, whose concern is entertainment and not authenticity, and whose works may be consumed like popcorn.

The point may be illustrated by any of Stone's novels. *Love Is Eternal*, for example, which treats the relationship between Mary Todd and Abraham Lincoln to the time of Lincoln's assassination, demonstrates Stone's characteristic use of the most minute details to evoke a sense of historical place. But while the setting and circumstances in which the main characters play are without doubt essentially correct, there remains the question of whether or not the conception of the characters is accurate as well. Stone is unconvincing in his attempt to restore the reputation of Mary Todd Lincoln, who has been excoriated by history. He may be right in his judgment of her, or his vindication of her may be simply an act of sentimental gallantry. There is no way to be certain; if the novel is an unfounded interpretation of her, Stone has misrepresented, and if there is historical evidence for his view, she would have been far better served by a documented history.

Stone is apparently aware, consciously or unconsciously, of the dilemma created by writing fiction that purports to echo fact, for, as in *Passionate Journey*, a fictional biography of the American painter John Noble, he is usually better when his characters act and react with each other according to the scenario provided by historical fact than when he seeks to interpret motivation. Perhaps the use of detail to the point of tediousness is an attempt to bring the problem that is imposed by the *genre* under control—an attempt to overwhelm it. *Those Who Love*, for instance, a treatment of the life and times of John and Abigail Adams, is not only lumbered with wooden dialogue, but overburdened with historical minutiae. The Michelangelo study, *The Agony and the Ecstasy*, as if to counter the effect of a great deal of love interest that smacks of modern interpolation, contains endless description of stone cutting and of anatomy, in a way that is reminiscent of Melville's whaling chapters but is less easily justifiable.

But the biographical novel does exist, of course, and Stone is undeniably one of its ablest practitioners. The history he spoon-feeds is far more palatable and interesting than popcorn, and it is no wonder that an enormous public should devour it.

—Alan R. Shucard

STOREY, Anthony. British. Born in Wakefield, Yorkshire, 10 November 1928; brother of David Storey, *q.v.* Educated at Queen Elizabeth Grammar School, Wakefield, 1939-46; Leeds University, Yorkshire, 1953-56, B.A. 1956; Cambridge University, 1966, M.A. 1969. Served in Malaya in the British Army, 1949-50, in the territorial army, 1950-66: Major; Territorial Decoration. Married 1) June Bridgewater in 1953 (divorced, 1968); 2) Anne Marie Guludec, 1969; two sons and one daughter. Schoolmaster in Wakefield, 1950-53; Psychologist for the Home Office, Newton-le-Willows, Lancashire, 1957-60, for the Armagh, Northern Ireland, County Council, 1960-62, and the Suffolk County Council, 1962-66. Since 1966, Tutor in Psychology, Cambridge University. Part-time professional rugby league player, 1947-60. Address: Beyton Cottage, Beyton, Bury St. Edmonds, Suffolk, England.

PUBLICATIONS

Novels

Jesus Iscariot. London, Calder and Boyars, 1967.
Graceless Go I. London, Calder and Boyars, 1969.
The Rector. London, Calder and Boyars, 1970.
Platinum Jag: A Psycho-Thriller. London, Calder and Boyars, 1972.
The Centre Holds. London, Calder and Boyars, 1973.
Platinum Ass. London, W.H. Allen, 1975.
Brothers Keepers. London, Boyars, 1975.
The Saviour. London, Boyars, 1978.

Plays

Television Plays: *The Plumed Serpent*, from the novel by D.H. Lawrence, 1971; *Graceless Go I*, with Lynn Hughes, from the novel by Storey, 1973; *Zulu Dawn*, with Cy Endfield, 1979.

Other

Stanley Baker: Portrait of an Actor. London, W.H. Allen, 1977.

Anthony Storey comments:

All my novels are about people trying to be whole...holy, in every case with a little, paradoxical success.

* * *

Eroticism and theology do not mix too well in English and so it happens that there is little serious precedent for the work of Anthony Storey. At his worst, he puts one in mind of an updated and psychoanalysed Marie Corelli—in his fictive world an oak tree is always liable to come crashing down at a key moment, or a girl may start dancing naked with a crucifix. In other words, tiny melodramatic or vulgar touches abound, and are allowed to spoil the general design, reducing the writing to a level of perfervid brilliance where it obviously becomes impossible for the author to realise the enormousness of his themes and he has to settle for mere enormities. To Storey's credit, though, it must be said that he engages head-on with some pretty fundamental issues; also that his world, however craftily stage-managed, is his own. His most ambitious and interesting project to date is undoubtedly the trilogy on the theme of the Second Coming.

In this work, Mary Johnson, the only daughter of a randy and intellectual overbearing North Country novelist, announces that she has "conceived of God." The news does not too much surprise her father, Tony, for it is part of his style to accept pronouncements as true, he being more than a little in love with the idea of her complete honesty, which he claims to have fostered in the way the child has been brought up. Mary, it is said more than once, has no "unconscious" because of this openness between her and her father; indeed, she is herself her own father's "immaculate conception," an unembarrassable person. It is her somewhat shadowy mother, Jane, and her fiancé, Christopher, rector of the local church—the first volume in the trilogy is called after him, *The Rector*—who are hardest hit by Mary's claim that she is pregnant yet still a virgin.

Both of them think that in some way Tony might be the father of her child, for he is indeed a man obsessed by incest and fond of relating it rather glibly to the ramifications of the Trinity, and he has brought up Mary in such a manner that she always confuses the roles of father and lover, albeit in a lucid fashion that does not allow the reader to suppose that she is mad when she makes her claim to have "conceived of God." It is Christopher, the priest, who goes mad—a process which Storey does not describe too sympathetically. This novelist is as frank as a satyr and his persistence in finding an erotic motive in nearly every relationship that transpires between his characters becomes a bit tedious. A more serious fault is the way he appears to indulge himself in the ideas of the novelist father-figure, Tony Johnson, who would have been a more interesting creation if presented critically.

—Robert Nye

STOREY, David (Malcolm). British. Born in Wakefield, Yorkshire, 13 July 1933; brother of Anthony Storey, *q.v.* Edûcated at Queen Elizabeth Grammar School, Wakefield, 1943-51; Wakefield College of Art, 1951-53; Slade School on Fine Art, London, 1953-56, diploma in fine arts 1956. Married Barbara Rudd Hamilton in 1956; two sons and two daughters. Played professionally for the Leeds Rugby League Club, 1952-56. Associate Artistic Director, Royal Court Theatre, London, 1972-74. Fellow, University College, London, 1974. Recipient: Rhys Memorial Award, 1961; Maugham Award, 1963; *Evening Standard* award, for drama, 1967, 1970; New York Drama Critics Circle Award, 1971, 1973, 1974; Faber Memorial Prize, 1973; Obie Award, for drama, 1974; Booker Prize, 1976. Lives in London. Address: c/o Jonathan Cape Ltd., 30 Bedford Square, London WC1B 3EL, England.

PUBLICATIONS

Novels

This Sporting Life. London, Longman, and New York, Macmillan, 1960.
Flight into Camden. London, Longman, 1960; New York, Macmillan, 1961.
Radcliffe. London, Longman, 1963; New York, Coward McCann, 1964.
Pasmore. London, Longman, 1972; New York, Dutton, 1974.

A Temporary Life. London, Allen Lane, 1973; New York, Dutton, 1974.
Saville. London, Cape, 1976; New York, Harper, 1977.

Plays

The Restoration of Arnold Middleton (produced Edinburgh, 1966; London, 1967). London, Cape, 1967; New York, French, 1968.
In Celebration (produced London, 1969; Los Angeles, 1973). London, Cape, 1969; New York, Grove Press, 1975.
The Contractor (produced London, 1969; New Haven, Connecticut, 1970; New York, 1973). London, Cape, 1970; New York, Random House, 1971.
Home (produced London and New York, 1970). London, Cape, 1970; New York, Random House, 1971.
The Changing Room (produced London, 1971; New Haven, Connecticut, 1972; New York, 1973). London, Cape, and New York, Random House, 1972.
The Farm (produced London, 1973; Washington, D.C., 1974; New York, 1976). London, Cape, 1973; New York, French, 1974.
Cromwell (produced London, 1973; Sarasota, Florida, 1977; New York, 1978). London, Cape, 1973.
Life Class (produced London, 1974; New York, 1975). London, Cape, 1975.
Mother's Day (produced London, 1976). London, Cape, 1977.
Sisters (produced Manchester, 1978).
Early Days (produced Brighton and London, 1980).

Screenplays: *This Sporting Life*, 1963; *In Celebration*, 1974.

Television Play: *Grace*, from the story by James Joyce, 1974.

Other

Writers on Themselves, with others. London, BBC Publications, 1964.
Edward, drawings by Donald Parker. London, Allen Lane, 1973.

*

Critical Study: *David Storey* by John Russell Taylor, London, Longman, 1974.

Theatrical Activities:

Director: **Television**—*Portrait of Margaret Evans*, 1963; *Death of My Mother* (D. H. Lawrence documentary), 1963.

* * *

David Storey's first three novels were organized around a concept. In *This Sporting Life* he attempted to show the world of the body, the atmosphere of physicality in both players and spectators, in the account of a young man from the lower middle classes who plays professional rugby. His second novel, *Flight into Camden*, is the novel depicting soul, the description of the hard spiritual independence of a miner's daughter who defies family to live with her married lover in London. *Radcliffe*, the third and most ambitious novel, portraying the troubled and violent relationship between Leonard Radcliffe, the sensitive descendant of impoverished gentility and aestheticism, and Victor Tolson, the powerful representative of the working classes, demonstrates the incompatibility of body and soul. In all the religious discussions and images in the novel, as well as in the epigraph from Yeats's "Vacillation VII," this irreconcilability between body and soul is regarded as original sin. A projected fourth novel, in which body and soul were to be reconciled, never appeared after the 1963 publication of *Radcliffe*, and more recent novels are not dependent on the concept.

Explicitly apparent in *Radcliffe*, the body-soul conflict is reflected in the conflict between the working classes and the remnants of the aristocracy in northern English society. Beaumont, the place where Leonard's family lives, his father as caretaker and restorer, represents an aesthetically and historically valuable past that cannot survive in current industrial society without special and privileged attention. Similarly, Leonard himself needs the vital and sexual connection to Tolson's physicality in order to feel "whole." Storey combines the religious, social, and personal dimensions of the body-soul controversy, keeps his metaphors consistent, and presents the issues with a fierce emotional intensity, but he also pushes his characters to the point where the intense, narrow focus and the representational quality can explode only into melodrama. Leonard kills Tolson and soon dies himself; another central character, a buffoon who also wanted Tolson, kills his family and himself. The melodrama seems to simplify the questions of class and religion presented, yet the power of the presentation itself, the intensity, invites the melodrama.

In spite of the limitations implicit in working out his concept, Storey's early fiction has considerable power, especially in dramatic scenes that come to life apart from their functions as demonstrations of an idea. Characters in revolt from the working-class origins, like Arthur Machin in *This Sporting Life* and Margaret Thorpe and her brother in *Flight into Camden*, are seen with a strong sympathy and complexity, described as partially entering a new world alien to their backgrounds and partially tied to the values and attitudes of their parents. Relationships between parents and children, the unique combinations of love and hatred bred in tidy, self-contained working-class kitchens, are particularly well done. The children, like Margaret Thorpe and her brother, or like Colin, the college teacher who deserts his wife and children in the later novel, *Pasmore*, have been educated because of their parents' effort and self-sacrifice, yet the process of education has moved them further from their parents, produced a difficult combination of independence, stubborn freedom, and guilt. For the parents, educating children had seemed the passport to the good life, to money, freedom, and release from the grinding physicality of survival in the pits, and the parents, like those in *Pasmore* or the baffled mother of Yvonne, a young wife whose incapacity to handle the strains of her life and education cause mental breakdown in *A Temporary Life*, cannot understand the complications of their educated childrens' lives. The children, too, like almost all Storey's characters, are characterized by a kind of defensive intensity, an inability to release themselves into the flux of contemporary classless experience, still carry something of the working-man's bitter intransigence, his refusal to give up the self which is the only thing he has in the difficult conditions under which he lives. Women, like the defensively unyielding Mrs. Hammond in *This Sporting Life* or the remote and incommunicative mistress of the central characters in both *Pasmore* and *A Temporary Life*, displays this imperturbable and intransigent quality more fully and honestly than men do in Storey's world; as the author comments on a character in *Pasmore*, the woman reveals "a determination, in effect, not to deny herself the pleasure as well as the security which came from holding herself apart." Relationship, in Storey's world, is difficult and dangerous, likely to lead to breakdown or dissolution, and this quality is seen, most frequently, in the more recent novels as well as the earlier ones, as part of a social and historical inheritance.

In the nine year gap between novels, Storey turned toward drama, writing eight highly praised and effective plays produced between 1967 and 1974. Often, characters and situations in the plays are similar, sometimes even identical, to those in the novels. Both *In Celebration* and *The Farm* reveal the highly charged familial emotions involved when educated children return to visit their parents in the mining or the farming village where they grew up. The parents are reminiscent of those in *Pasmore* or the Thorpes in *Flight into Camden*. *The Contractor* divides attention between the workmen setting up a large tent for a wedding and the family of the tenting company's owner, also the father of the bride. Again, family and class issues dominate the play. A similar group of workmen setting up tents is detailed in *Radcliffe*, although the dramatic version is more comic; even the name of the company's owner—Ewbank—is the same. *Life Class* depicts a simplified version of some of the events, those centering around the life model in a class in a northern art school, of *A Temporary Life*, although a full characterization of the teacher, his background, and his connection to other characters, is omitted in the play. Generally, the dramatic version of each character or incident is simpler, less complex, and more immediately communicable than is the novelistic version. Yet Storey's parallel working of themes, incidents, and characters has also given his novelistic treatments an immediacy and a force, perhaps contributed by his work in drama, that make his later novels, especially *Pasmore*, particularly effective and compelling.

Storey is also trained and talented in drawing and painting. His writing has always been characterized by an acute sense of visual imagery, apparent in descriptions of the industrial town or the rugby crowd in *This Sporting Life*. The later fiction, particularly *A Temporary Life*, in which the first person narrator, Colin Freestone, is himself a painter and a teacher of painting, exploits this sense of visual imagery even more effectively, creating descriptions that are precisely detailed and representative of the character's or observer's state of mind or emotion simultaneously. Color, shape, and landscape become terse yet rich and complex metaphors. Both of the later novels also use sharply observed short dramatic scenes to portray changing psychological patterns within characters. *Pasmore* depicts a dissolving marriage, the changes from dependence to almost comatose shock and neglect to a nervous, tenuous independence in the deserted wife, as well as the changes from concerned indifference to an artificial sense of jolly control over the situation back to indifference to passivity and guilt to jealousy and explosive fury and, finally, almost to breakdown before ultimate recovery in the erring husband. Yvonne's breakdown in *A Temporary Life* is also carefully portrayed, the alternations between withdrawal and the desperate efforts to make life and relationships around her seem "whole." The sense of breakdown, the loss of control, along with the recognition of how very difficult both control and relations are in contemporary society, is always on the edge of Storey's fictional world.

The later novels show little of the generalized concept about experience that restricted the earlier fiction, particularly *Radcliffe*. Rather, the reliance on theories about life is satirized in the treatment of theories about art in *A Temporary Life*. Both the radical art students, who refuse to learn technique and justify work that is both slovenly and unimaginative in the name of free expression and an "empirical" point of view, and the principal of the art school, who spends his time campaigning against smoking, madly collecting excreta in his locked bathroom, and painting pseudo-realistic advertising posters that proclaim the "old values," are made ludicrous. The addictive theory about art, itself a metaphor for an excessive and restrictive control over life, damages the person sensitive enough to see its limitations. Yet the human being, isolated, attempting to unify the world around him, invariably searches for intellectual and emotional forms of control. *Pasmore* and *A Temporary Life* express this dilemma with a kind of packed, potentially explosive prose, a form that dramatically conveys the pressure of experience. At its best, as in *Pasmore* and most of *A Temporary Life*, the fiction itself seems a strong and intensely human achievement just on the edge of chaos. Occasionally, however, it still drops over, as in the numerous punch-ups and the auto accident at the end of *A Temporary Life*. Even the surrealistic burning image of the town at the very end does not assuage the effect of the melodrama that has preceded it, a form of explosion that seems, conceptually and metaphorically, too easy a way to shatter the humane bastions of Storey's fiction.

—James Gindin

STOW, (Julian) Randolph. Australian. Born in Geraldton, Western Australia, 28 November 1935. Educated at Guildford Grammar School, Western Australia; University of Western Australia, Nedlands, B.A. 1956. Formerly, Anthropological Assistant, working in Northwest Australia and Papua New Guinea. Taught at the University of Adelaide, 1957; Lecturer in English Literature, University of Leeds, Yorkshire, 1962, and University of Western Australia, 1963-64; Lecturer in English and Commonwealth Literature, University of Leeds, 1968-69. Recipient: Australian Literature Society Gold Medal, 1957, 1958; Miles Franklin Award, 1958; Commonwealth Fund Harkness Travelling Fellowship, 1964-66; Britannica-Australia Award, 1966; Australia Council grant, 1973; Patrick White Award, 1979. Address: c/o Richard Scott Simon Ltd., 32 College Cross, London N1 1PR, England.

PUBLICATIONS

Novels

A Haunted Land. London, Macdonald, 1956; New York, Macmillan, 1957.
The Bystander. London, Macdonald, 1957.
To the Islands. London, Macdonald, 1958; Boston, Little Brown, 1959; revised edition, London, Secker and Warburg, 1981.
Tourmaline. London, Macdonald, 1963.
The Merry-Go-Round in the Sea. London, Macdonald, 1965; New York, Morrow, 1966.
Visitants. London, Secker and Warburg, 1979; New York, Taplinger, 1981.
The Girl Green as Elderflower. London, Secker and Warburg, and New York, Viking Press, 1980.

Plays

Eight Songs for a Mad King, music by Peter Maxwell Davies. London, Boosey and Hawkes, 1969.
Miss Donnithorne's Maggot, music by Peter Maxwell Davies (produced 1974). London, Boosey and Hawkes, 1977.

Verse

Act One. London, Macdonald, 1957.
Outrider: Poems 1956-1962. London, Macdonald, 1962.
A Counterfeit Silence: Selected Poems. Sydney and London, Angus and Robertson, 1969.
Poetry from Australia: Pergamon Poets 6, with Judith Wright and William Hart-Smith, edited by Howard Sergeant. Oxford, Pergamon Press, 1969.

Recording: *Poets on Record 11*, University of Queensland, 1974.

Other

Midnite: The Story of a Wild Colonial Boy (juvenile). Melbourne, Cheshire, and London, Macdonald, 1967; Englewood Cliffs, New Jersey, Prentice Hall, 1968.

Editor, *Australian Poetry 1964.* Sydney, Angus and Robertson, 1964.

*

Bibliography: *Randolph Stow: A Bibliography* by P.A. O'Brien, Adelaide, Libraries Board of South Australia, 1968; "A Randolph Stow Bibliography" by Rose Marie Beston, in *Literary Half-Yearly* (Mysore), July 1975.

Manuscript Collection: National Library of Australia, Canberra.

Critical Studies: "Raw Material" by the author, in *Westerly* (Nedlands, Western Australia), 1961; "The Quest for Permanence" by Geoffrey Dutton, in *Journal of Commonwealth Literature* (Leeds, Yorkshire), September 1965; "Outsider Looking Out" by W.H. New, in *Critique* (Minneapolis), ix, 1, 1967; "Waste Places, Dry Souls" by Jennifer Wightman, in *Meanjin* (Melbourne), June 1969; "Voyager from Eden" by Brandon Conron, in *Ariel (Canada)* (Calgary, Alberta), October 1970; *The Merry-Go-Round in the Sea* by Edriss Noall, Sydney, Scoutline, 1971; "The Family Background and Literary Career of Randolph Stow" by John B. Beston, in *Literary Half-Yearly* (Mysore), July 1975; *Randolph Stow* by Ray Willbanks, Boston, Twayne, 1978; "Randolph Stow's *Visitants*" by Anthony J. Hassall, in *Australian Literary Studies* (Brisbane), October 1980.

* * *

The contrast between *The Merry-Go-Round in the Sea*, with its local "realism," and *Tourmaline*, which makes a symbolic landscape out of Randolph Stow's native land, indicates the range of his fiction. *Merry-Go-Round* by no means eschews symbolic patterns, but it emerges more directly from Australian national sensibilities. The isolating impact that World War II had on the country, for example, can be appreciated not only in this book but also in works by George Turner, George Johnston, and others; what Stow's novel does is link the theme up with the older traditions of convict settlement and South Pacific paradise. (Stow is careful to debunk the easy myths which see convict and bushranger mateyness as the *sole* generative character trait *throughout* Australia; his comic children's book *Midnite*, about the triumphant adventures of a native bushranger and his gang—a cockatoo and a cat—delightfully overturns assorted local archetypes. Yet with linguistic playfulness it celebrates the spirit of the country as well, which serves as a reminder of the ambivalent blend of prison and paradise which has always provoked the Australian imagination.) For Rick Maplestead, in *Merry-Go-Round*, imprisoned in Changi and then freed only to discover his bonds to history, family, mates, and mediocrity, there is no escape but flight. But as he and his young cousin Rob Coram (whose offshore vision gives the book its title), know, glimpses of paradise are illusory and attempts to inhabit them fraught with disappointment.

By focussing ultimately on the quests of the mind, the book recapitulates many of Stow's earlier themes. His first books, full of mad characters and melodramatic incidents, are the Gothic attempts of a young novelist to record his knowledge of power and passion, of the relationship between man and landscape and the impact of belief on action. Not till these sensibilities were controlled by Stow's anthropological and historical commitments did they exert a powerful literary effect. *To the Islands* reduced the reliance on incident and traced instead the wanderings of a man through the desert of his belief, in search of the afterworld islands of aboriginal dream order. His soul, he discovers, "is a strange country"—which seems at first to be no advance on what he began by knowing. Increasingly, however, that very state of suspended apprehension becomes the world that Stow tries to explore. *Tourmaline*, about a wasteland of that name, which welcomes a stranger as a water-diviner (who begins to clothe himself in such a role), only to be desolated and turn to another authority when he fails, provides an even more archetypal canvas. Consciously symbolic and heavily mannered in style, the book tries to evoke the world of symbol, the fleeting perceptions that symbols try to convey, rather than the realities of everyday event. The reiteration on the part of Law, the narrator, that to describe a heritage as "bitter" is "not to condemn it," urges readers also to consider what it is that he does not say: what it is that he cannot say.

Tarot, Tao, and Jungian commentary become means to fathom the deep intuitive communications of silence: but wordless understandings present problems for a writer to communicate. Two later novels pursue the imaginative reaches of the reflective mind. *Visitants* explores Melanesian tribal life and traces its impact on Australians of different sensibilities; the novel is cast as a series of depositions at a legal enquiry, which prove unable entirely to explain the cultural other-worldliness. *The Girl Green as Elderflower* turns imaginative threat—the pressures of tropical disease and a foreign tongue upon a sensitive young man—into imaginative renewal; the young man, in Suffolk, reconciles himself with his heritage and his experience, and in a series of fables he writes out his recognition of the ways in which the unusual has always permeated the everyday. To admit to such flights of mind, he discovers, is to admit to a kind of health and a kind of love, and to win a "paradise" of a different, more fluid, perhaps freer, certainly more comic nature.

—W.H. New

STUART, (Henry) Francis (Montgomery). Irish. Born in Townsville, Queensland, Australia, 29 April 1902. Educated at Rugby School, Warwickshire. Married 1) Iseult Gonne in 1920 (died), one son and one daughter; 2) Gertrude Meissner in 1954. Fought on the side of the Irish Nationalists in the Civil War; imprisoned by the British, 1922. Lecturer in English and Irish literature, University of Berlin, 1940. Imprisoned by the United Nations forces, 1945-46. Founding Member, Irish Academy of Letters. Recipient: Young Poet's Prize (*Poetry*, Chicago), 1921; Royal Irish Academy Award, 1924; Northern Ireland Arts Council bursary, 1974. Address: 2 Highfield Park, Dublin 14, Ireland.

PUBLICATIONS

Novels

Women and God. London, Cape, 1931.
Pigeon Irish. London, Gollancz, and New York, Macmillan, 1932.
The Coloured Dome. London, Gollancz, 1932; New York, Macmillan, 1933.
Try the Sky. London, Gollancz, and New York, Macmillan, 1933.
Glory. London, Gollancz, and New York, Macmillan, 1933.
In Search of Love. London, Collins, and New York, Macmillan, 1935.
The Angel of Pity. London, Grayson, 1935.
The White Hare. London, Collins, and New York, Macmillan, 1936.
The Bridge. London, Collins, 1937.
Julie. New York, Knopf, and London, Collins, 1938.
The Great Squire. London, Collins, 1939.
The Pillar of Cloud. London, Gollancz, 1948.
Redemption. London, Gollancz, 1949; New York, Devin Adair, 1950.
The Flowering Cross. London, Gollancz, 1950.
Good Friday's Daughter. London, Gollancz, 1952.
The Chariot. London, Gollancz, 1953.
The Pilgrimage. London, Gollancz, 1955.
Victors and Vanquished. London, Gollancz, 1958; Cleveland, Pennington Press, 1959.
Angels of Providence. London, Gollancz, 1959.
Black List, Section H. Carbondale, Southern Illinois University Press, 1971; London, Martin Brian and O'Keeffe, 1975.
Memorial. London, Martin Brian and O'Keeffe, 1973.
A Hole in the Head. London, Martin Brian and O'Keeffe, and Nantucket, Massachusetts, Longship Press, 1977.
The High Consistory. London, Martin Brian and O'Keeffe, 1980.

Uncollected Short Stories

"Relativity," in *Lovat Dickson's Magazine* (London), November 1934.
"Isles of the Blest," in *English Review* (London), December 1934.
"Bandit," in *Cornhill* (London), February 1938.
"The Stormy Petrel," in *Paddy No More*, edited by William Vorm. Nantucket, Massachusetts, Longship Press, 1977.

Plays

Men Crowd Me Round (produced Dublin, 1933).
Glory, adaptation of his own novel (produced London, 1936).
Strange Guest (produced Dublin, 1940).
Flynn's Last Dive (produced Croydon, Surrey, 1962).
Who Fears to Speak? (produced Dublin, 1970).

Verse

We Have Kept the Faith (as H. Stuart). Dublin, Oak Leaf Press, 1923.

Other

Nationality and Culture (lecture). Dublin, Sinn Fein Ardchomahairle, 1924.
Mystics and Mysticism. Dublin, Catholic Truth Society of Ireland, 1929.
Things to Live For: Notes for an Autobiography. London, Cape, 1934; New York, Macmillan, 1935.
Racing for Pleasure and Profit in Ireland and Elsewhere. Dublin, Talbot Press, 1937.
Der Fall Casement: Das Leben Sir Roger Casement und der Verleumdungsfeldzug des Secret Service, translated by Ruth Weiland. Hamburg, Hanseatische Verlag, 1940.

Translator, *The Captive Dreamer*, by Christian de La Mazière. New York, Saturday Review Press, 1974; as *Ashes of Honour*, London, Wingate, 1975.

*

Manuscript Collections: Southern Illinois University Library, Carbondale; National Library of Ireland, Dublin.

Critical Studies: *A Festschrift for Francis Stuart on His Seventieth Birthday 29 April 1972*, Dublin, Dolmen Press, 1972 (includes bibliography); *Francis Stuart* by J.H. Natterstad, Lewisburg, Pennsylvania, Bucknell University Press, 1974.

Francis Stuart comments:

I consider myself a dissident writer, someone who is keeping flowing a countercurrent to many of the assumptions and attitudes of contemporary society. For this reason I have been called a Ghetto novelist, and several of my books have been black-listed not only in Ireland but elsewhere. For instance, *Black List, Section H.* has taken five years since its appearance in America to considerable acclaim (Lawrence Durrell in *The New York Times*, etc.) to find a publisher in England.

* * *

In the middle 1930's Francis Stuart said he was "interested in life where it is most intense," a condition he often found in races or in football matches rather than among writers and artists "with their narrow limits of the studio and library," and indeed Stuart was a practising athlete through his youth and middle years, as well as a breeder of horses and an airplane pilot. His imaginative writing reflects these activities, yet it is often introspective and psychologically motivated. And it is often, in the best sense of the word, poetic.

Stuart has published over 20 novels, but has never been so highly praised for them as for his one book of verse, *We Have Kept the Faith*, which won an award from the Royal Irish Academy, with William Butler Yeats as presiding judge. Yeats was consistent in his admiration of Stuart's work, and once said in a letter, "If luck comes to his aid he will be our great writer." Elsewhere he stated that Stuart's novel *The Coloured Dome* was "strange and exciting in theme and perhaps more personally and beautifully written than any book of our generation," and that it would work towards an understanding of "the strange Ireland that is rising up here." But not much luck came to Stuart's aid, and the new "strange Ireland" failed, for the most part, to recognise his gifts.

In marrying Iseult Gonne, he was in a sense marrying into the Irish Renaissance, and at the time of the Civil War he smuggled guns into Ireland from the Continent and was later imprisoned. Even the production of two of his plays at the Abbey Theatre did not bring him the widespread acceptance that might have been anticipated; neither did the British and American publication of his novels, which are among the finest fiction in modern Irish literature.

The second of them, *Pigeon Irish*, projects a war in the future, with the pigeons, in the best Celtic manner, somewhat symbolic creatures who in carrying messages from country to country speak slang (Pigeon Irish) and carry on love affairs and sometimes meet a grim fate. His next story, the one which won Yeats's strong admiration—*The Coloured Dome*—is another picture of war, perhaps based partly on Stuart's own 16-months' imprisonment. It was not until after the Second World War that Stuart was to write so well again, though his middle-period work won acclaim outside Ireland, by such authors as Compton Mackenzie.

Early in 1939, Stuart was invited to lecture in Berlin, and the next year he returned there to remain throughout the war, teaching modern English and Irish literature at the University of Berlin until that institution was destroyed by bombs. After the war he was imprisoned by the French forces and, after his release, lived in Paris and London, and in 1958 moved to Ireland.

Such facts are necessary in any considerations of Stuart's work, for they explain much about his work and about the response to it in Ireland. His residence in Nazi Germany was that of a neutral Irish author who, like P.G. Wodehouse, made some harmless broadcasts from Berlin; Stuart ceased this activity, however, when he discovered that he was expected to deliver Nazi propaganda. His life during those years has been examined elsewhere, and it has been established that he was never a Hitlerite or in any way antisemitic. But his willingness to stay on in Germany has been criticised, though readers must acknowledge the skillfulness of his superb (necessarily grim and appalling) pictures of a country being smashed into defeat. In *The Pillar of Cloud*, for example, he forcefully tells the story of an Irish poet in wartime Germany, and *Redemption* is the tale of a similar figure who, after the conflict, returns to his native Ireland. These are powerful books in which some critics have found almost a Dostoyevskian intensity.

These novels lead towards Stuart's twentieth, the massive and elaborate *Black List, Section H.*, an example of autobiography transformed into effective imaginative work. It deals not only with the Irish experiences of the central character H (that unused initial of Francis Stuart), but also of those connected with his travels on the Continent, before, during, and after the Second World War. It deals candidly with H's marriage and his wartime love affair in Germany, as well as with his subsequent imprisonment. The story is at once complicated and profound; and it is vividly written. It is one of the imaginative masterpieces of modern Ireland.

—Harry T. Moore

STUART, Jesse (Hilton). American. Born near Riverton, Kentucky, 8 August 1907. Educated at Lincoln Memorial University, Harrogate, Tennessee, A.B. 1929; Vanderbilt University, Nashville, Tennessee, 1931-32; Peabody College, Nashville. Served in the United States Naval Reserve, 1943-46: Lieutenant. Married Naomi Deane Norris in 1939; one child. Has worked as a farmer, newspaper editor, and schoolteacher; Superintendent, Greenup, Kentucky, city schools, 1941-43. Taught at the University of Nevada, Reno, Summer 1958, and the American University, Cairo, 1960-61; United States Department of State Lecturer in Egypt, Iran, Greece, Lebanon, Pakistan, the Philippines, Formosa, and Korea, 1962-63; Writer-in-Residence, Eastern Kentucky University, Richmond, 1965-66. American Representative, Asian Writers Conference, 1962. Recipient: Davis Poetry Prize, 1934; Guggenheim Fellowship, 1937; American Academy grant, 1941; Thomas Jefferson Southern Award, 1944; National Education Association Award, 1949; Berea College Centennial Award, 1955; Academy of American Poets Award, 1961. D.Litt.: University of Kentucky, Lexington, 1944; Marietta College, Ohio, 1952; Morris Harvey College, Charleston, West Virginia, 1959; Marshall University, Huntington, West Virginia, 1962; Northern Michigan University, Marquette, 1964; Eastern Kentucky University, 1964; D.H.L.: Lincoln Memorial University, 1950; LL.D.: Baylor University, Waco, Texas, 1954; Doctor of Pedagogy: Murray State University, Kentucky, 1968. Address: W-Hollow, Greenup, Kentucky 41144, U.S.A.

PUBLICATIONS

Novels

Trees of Heaven. New York, Dutton, 1940.
Taps for Private Tussie. New York, Dutton, 1943; as *He'll Be Comin' Down the Mountain*, London, Dobson, 1947.
Mongrel Mettle: The Autobiography of a Dog. New York, Books Inc., 1944.
Foretaste of Glory. New York, Dutton, 1946.
Hie to the Hunters. New York, Whittlesey House, 1950.
The Good Spirit of Laurel Ridge. New York, McGraw Hill, 1953.
Daughter of the Legend. New York, McGraw Hill, 1965.
My Land Has a Voice. New York, McGraw Hill, 1966.
Mr. Gallion's School. New York, McGraw Hill, 1967.
Come Back to the Farm. New York, McGraw Hill, 1971.
The Land Beyond the River. New York, McGraw Hill, 1973.

Short Stories

Head o' W-Hollow. New York, Dutton, 1936.
Tim: A Story. Cincinnati, Little Man Press, 1939.
Men of the Mountains. New York, Dutton, 1941.
Tales from the Plum Grove Hills. New York, Dutton, 1946.
Clearing in the Sky and Other Stories. New York, McGraw Hill, 1950.
Plowshare in Heaven: Stories. New York, McGraw Hill, 1958.
Save Every Lamb. New York, McGraw Hill, 1964.
A Jesse Stuart Harvest. New York, Dell, 1965.
Come, Gentle Spring. New York, McGraw Hill, 1969.
Dawn of Remembered Spring (includes verse). New York, McGraw Hill, 1972.
32 Votes Before Breakfast: Politics at the Grass Roots. New York, McGraw Hill, 1974.

Uncollected Short Stories

"There's Not Many of Us Left Anymore," in *Southwest Review* (Dallas), Winter 1977.
"Bud's Love for the 851," in *Southwest Review* (Dallas), Spring 1978.

Verse

Harvest of Youth. Howe, Oklahoma, Scroll Press, 1930.
Man with a Bull-Tongue Plow. New York, Dutton, 1934; revised edition, 1959.
Album of Destiny. New York, Dutton, 1944.
Kentucky Is My Land. New York, Dutton, 1952.
Hold April: New Poems. New York, McGraw Hill, 1962.
Autumn Lovesong: A Celebration of Love's Fulfillment. Kansas City, Missouri, Hallmark Editions, 1971.
The World of Jesse Stuart: Selected Poems, edited by J.R. LeMaster. New York, McGraw Hill, 1975.
The Seasons of Jesse Stuart: An Autobiography in Poetry 1907-1976, edited by Wanda Hicks. Danbury, Connecticut, Archer Editions Press, 1976.

Other

Beyond Dark Hills: A Personal Story. New York, Dutton, and London, Hutchinson, 1938.
The Thread That Runs So True (autobiography). New York, Scribner, 1949.
The Beatinest Boy (juvenile). New York, Whittlesey House, 1953.
A Penny's Worth of Character (juvenile). New York, Whittlesey House, 1954.
Red Mule (juvenile). New York, Whittlesey House, 1955.
The Year of My Rebirth (autobiography). New York, McGraw Hill, 1956; London, Gollancz, 1958.
God's Oddling: The Story of Mick Stuart, My Father. New York, McGraw Hill, 1960.
The Rightful Owner (juvenile). New York, Whittlesey House, 1960.
Huey the Engineer (juvenile). St. Helena, California, Beard, 1960.
Andy Finds a Way (juvenile). New York, Whittlesey House, 1961.
A Jesse Stuart Reader: Stories and Poems. New York, McGraw Hill, 1963.
A Ride with Huey the Engineer (juvenile). New York, McGraw Hill, 1966.
Rebels with a Cause... (address). Murray, Kentucky, Murray State University, 1967.
To Teach, To Love. Cleveland, World, 1970.
Old Ben (juvenile). New York, McGraw Hill, 1970.
Come to My Tomorrowland (juvenile). Nashville, Aurora, 1971.
My World. Lexington, University Press of Kentucky, 1975.
Up the Hollow from Lynchburg, photographs by Joe and Junebug Clark. New York, McGraw Hill, 1975.
Dandelion on the Acropolis: A Journal of Greece. Danbury, Connecticut, Archer Editions Press, 1978.
Lost Sandstones and Lonely Skies and Other Essays. Danbury, Connecticut, Archer Editions Press, 1979.
The Kingdom Within: A Spiritual Autobiography. New York, McGraw Hill, 1979.
If I Were Seventeen Again and Other Essays. Danbury, Connecticut, Archer Editions Press, 1980.

Editor, with others, *Outlooks Through Literature*. Chicago, Scott Foresman, 1964.
Editor, with A.K. Ridout, *Short Stories for Discussion*. New York, Scribner, 1965.

*

Bibliography: *Jesse and Jane Stuart: A Bibliography* by Hensley C. Woodbridge, Murray, Kentucky, Murray State University, revised edition, 1969; *Jesse Stuart: A Reference Guide* by J.R. LeMaster, Boston, Hall, 1979.

Manuscript Collection: Murray State University, Murray, Kentucky.

Critical Studies: *Jesse Stuart: His Life and Works* by Everetta Love Blair, Columbia, University of South Carolina Press, 1967; *The*

Dark Hills of Jesse Stuart by Lee Pennington, Cincinnati, Harvest Press, 1967; *Jesse Stuart* by Ruel E. Foster, New York, Twayne, 1968; *Jesse Stuart: Essays on His Work* edited by J.R. LeMaster and Mary Washington Clarke, Lexington, University Press of Kentucky, 1977.

* * *

When the definitive history of modern American fiction is written, Jesse Stuart's name may well be near the top of the list. For Stuart, in the timeless vignettes of his fiction, has done what every great writer longs to do. He has created a *place* and wedged it everlastingly in the imagination of America. His fiction has given a voice to the far and lost lands of the Appalachians, a voice which calls us ever and delightedly into the outdoor world. The reader of any volume of Stuart's fiction opens the book and feels immediately the fine mist of nature blowing into his face. Stuart began as a short story writer and gradually worked into the novel. At the present time he is the author of over 400 short stories, published in a very wide variety of periodicals and books.

What is the "world" of his short stories? It is the mountain milieu he knew as a child, a milieu where family loyalty was as strong as religion and led to some spectacular feuds. It was a world where the people lived a hard life, laboring long over the meager soil for scanty returns. There were relaxations in the mountains, such as the burning pleasure of mountain moonshine, protracted religious meetings at Plum Grove church, basket dinners, public hangings, and the sporadic and joyous fights of the young bucks. Fox hunting gave a long nighttime delight to the males of all ages. Guns were a major source of pleasure to the men.

The essence of Stuart's method of fictional narration is its oral character. He uses the famous "talk style" that came into American fiction from the folk tale and the humorous tales of the old South West (J.J. Hooper and George Harris). He begins *in medias res* and tumbles the reader rapidly forward on a rising rush of events. His short stories are frequently told by a first person narrator, usually a mountain boy of eastern Kentucky. His early short stories are rich with mountain dialect. We read words like "casouse," "fittified," "fornenst," "slonchways." Stuart now seems to be our only living writer who can use this dialect unself-consciously. His short stories are marked also by their rich use of figurative language, their exuberant lyricism, tremendous gusto, abandon, and brimming joyous humor. Stuart is quite capable of the tall tale ("Sylvania Is Dead") and of a kind of surrealistic or Black Biles humor, in which we get the projection of the comic into the horrible as in the story "Word and the Flesh." There is also a deep tenderness in Stuart, a great pity and love for people. This tenderness appears in his poignant little story "Thanksgiving Hunter."

All of the above characteristics appear also in his novels. Like Thomas Wolfe, Stuart thinks of himself as a *writing man* and sees no great distinction between fiction and autobiography. He slides easily from one to another. The central fact about Stuart as a novelist is that he has created a spacious, complex imaginative world by projecting the actual one of W-Hollow onto an imaginative plane. His novels are in many ways prolongations of his short stories into a more spacious aesthetic scope. *Taps for Private Tussie* and *Hie to the Hunters* were both begun as short stories, became too long, and were recast and expanded to novel length. Stuart never outlines a novel except for a few notes which may be sketched out on an envelope. He has some image, some hunch, some node of interest in his own mind which is the real subject matter of the novel. His characters begin to come alive and dance their attitudes around this node of interest, shaping a fable which may mean something quite contrary to Stuart's original intent.

Stuart is, in a manner of speaking, the Grandma Moses of the novel. That is, he is a kind of "primitive" also. He uses strong, stark scenes, clearly and sharply delineated. He also has a certain affinity with Dickens. Like Dickens he characterizes obviously and bluntly, using name-typing, and some characterizing mannerism or gesture. Like Dickens his style is dramatic, kinetic, bustling with dialogue and action. Instead of *telling*, he *shows*; he loves the present tense. His style, though, is far simpler than that of Dickens. Stuart cannot be categorized as a realist or as a romantic. There is realism enough in his work, in the dialect, the customs of W-Hollow, in the living characters of his work, yet there is a romantic streak running through his novels, a kind of romantic primitivism in his treatment of nature and in his idealization of Grandpa Tussie in the latter stages of the novel *Taps for Private Tussie*. The romantic motif of the child as seer occurs frequently in his work as does his romantic idealization of the simple people of this world. If he has to be labelled, we can call him a regionalist, who mingles the modes of romanticism and realism in his work.

Consider his novels. His first novel, *Trees of Heaven*, relates the story of patriarch Anse Bushman, who loves the land and wants to own more of it. It is the story of Anse's son Tarvin falling in love with Subrinea Tussie, the beautiful daughter of Boliver Tussie, head of the family of poor white squatters. Anse actually dominates the book and bestrides the entire world of *Trees of Heaven*, as he comes tumultuously alive, striding in his nightshirt through a spring night or rain and lightning to feel the wakening life of the earth beneath his bare feet.

Next, in 1943, came Stuart's best-selling novel, *Taps for Private Tussie*, which has sold by now over two million copies. It is the story of a family of mountain poor whites who collect $10,000 life insurance on their soldier-son Private Tussie who has presumably been killed in World War II. The Tussies live joyously for a while in a wild, comic, free-loading spend-thrift spree in the best house in the nearby county seat. Once again the novel is dominated by a single character, Grandpa Tussie. There is a strong element of Huckleberry Finn in the narrator, Sid Tussie, the supposed grandson of Grandpa Tussie. Humor is endemic to the entire novel which carries various nuances of meaning. On one level it is a boisterous ballad of lolling reliefers and inherited indolence. On another level the novel is a sad-comic pastorale of a family caught in the turbulence of acute social change and not realizing the why of all the turbulence. Stuart, though, is an artist, not a polemicist. He does not inveigh against the welfare state. He laughs with Press Tussie who says, "I'm a-living just the way I like to live."

Stuart's next novel, *Foretaste of Glory*, is an episodic *Grand Hotel*-type of novel, which wheels about a central event, the sudden and apocalyptic appearance of the aurora borealis in a little mountain town. In a series of 36 chapters Stuart dramatizes the effect on the "*Lights!*" on the sensibilities of the simple mountain people. Fearing the Second Coming of Christ is at hand, they throng to the courthouse square and confess their most secret sins to their great discomfiture the following morning. The mode is comic, exuberant, joyous. Life throngs through the novel like a great painting by Brueghel the Elder.

In addition to these major novels, Stuart has published several minor ones, such as *Mongrel Mettle*, a novelette about a mongrel dog which has certain overtones relating to America as a melting pot. Then the novel *Hie to the Hunters*, a story in a Tom Sawyer vein of a city boy who goes to the mountain farm during the course of three months and learns through his pal, "Sparkie," the beauty and vigor and honesty of mountain life. Later Stuart published the novel *The Good Spirit of Laurel Ridge*, notable for the characterization of "Op" Akers, a kind of poor man's Henry David Thoreau. *Daughter of the Legend*, a tragic love story dealing with a mysterious people in this country known as Melungeons, is a romantic novel but does not have the power of *Taps* or *Trees of Heaven*. *Mr. Gallion's School*, an episodic novel recounting the efforts of a 49-year-old cardiac writer, an ex-teacher, to put a failing high school back on its feet, is very close to Stuart's autobiographical work *The Thread That Runs So True*, but does not have the lyric freshness that the young teacher displayed in his earlier work.

In his fiction, Stuart is an affirmer, a yea sayer. Like Thoreau he shows that life close to the bone is hard, but the taste is sweet. Equally important in the appeal of Stuart's work is the glimpse he gives us of the old days. He has refused to propagandize and slant his material. He is primarily a *maker*, a *poet*; he depicts things exactly and lets the universal shine through. In this sense he is a true artist. He digs into W-Hollow but says "yes" all along the way; "yes" in spite of sickness, injustice, and death. But he does not preach; he lets his world speak for itself. He has avoided literary cliques and coteries; he has fought alone. His real and lasting reputation is still ahead of him.

—Ruel E. Foster

STYRON, William. American. Born in Newport News, Virginia, 11 June 1925. Educated at Christchurch School, Virginia; Davidson College, North Carolina, 1942-43; Duke University, Durham, North Carolina, 1943-44, 1946-47, A.B. 1947. Served in the United States Marine Corps, 1944-45, 1951: 1st Lieutenant. Married Rose Burgunder in 1953; one son and three daughters. Associate Editor for McGraw Hill, publishers, New York, 1947. Since 1952, Advisory Editor, *Paris Review*, Paris and New York; since 1970, member of the Editorial Board of *The American Scholar*, Washington, D.C. Fellow of Silliman College, Yale University, New Haven, Connecticut, since 1964. Recipient: American Academy Prix de Rome, 1952; Pulitzer Prize, 1968; Howells Medal, 1970; American Book Award, 1980. D.H.: Wilberforce University, Ohio, 1967; Litt.D.: Duke University, 1968; New School for Social Research, New York; Tufts University, Medford, Massachusetts. Member, American Academy. Address: R.F.D., Roxbury, Connecticut 06783, U.S.A.

PUBLICATIONS

Novels

Lie Down in Darkness. Indianapolis, Bobbs Merrill, 1951; London, Hamish Hamilton, 1952.
The Long March. New York, Random House, 1956; London, Hamish Hamilton, 1962.
Set This House on Fire. New York, Random House, 1960; London, Hamish Hamilton, 1961.
The Confessions of Nat Turner. New York, Random House, 1967; London, Cape, 1968.
Sophie's Choice. New York, Random House, and London, Cape, 1979.

Uncollected Short Stories

"Autumn," and "Long Dark Road," in *One and Twenty*, edited by W.M. Blackburn. Durham, North Carolina, Duke University Press, 1945.
"Moments in Trieste," in *American Vanguard 1948*, edited by Charles I. Glicksburg. New York, Cambridge, 1948.
"The Enormous Window," in *American Vanguard 1950*, edited by Charles I. Glicksburg. New York, Cambridge, 1950.
"The McCabes," in *Paris Review 22*, Autumn-Winter 1959-60.
"Pie in the Sky," in *The Vintage Anthology of Science Fantasy*, edited by Christopher Cerf. New York, Random House, 1966.
"Shadrach," in *The Best American Short Stories 1979*, edited by Joyce Carol Oates and Shannon Ravenel. Boston, Houghton Mifflin, 1979.

Play

In the Clap Shack (produced New Haven, Connecticut, 1972). New York, Random House, 1973.

Other

The Four Seasons, illustrated by Harold Altman. University Park, Pennsylvania State University Press, 1965.
Admiral Robert Penn Warren and the Snows of Winter: A Tribute. Winston-Salem, North Carolina, Palaemon Press, 1978.
The Message of Auschwitz. Blacksburg, Virginia, Press de la Warr, 1979.

Editor, *Best Short Stories from the Paris Review.* New York, Dutton, 1959.

*

Bibliography: *William Styron: A Descriptive Bibliography* by James L. West, Boston, Hall, 1977; *William Styron: A Reference Guide* by Jackson Bryer and Mary B. Hatem, Boston, Hall, 1978; *William Styron: An Annotated Bibliography of Criticism* by Philip W. Leon, Westport, Connecticut, Greenwood, 1978.

Manuscript Collections: Library of Congress, Washington, D.C.; Duke University, Durham, North Carolina.

Critical Studies: *William Styron* by Robert H. Fossum, Grand Rapids, Michigan, Eerdmans, 1968; *William Styron* by Cooper R. Mackin, Austin, Texas, Steck Vaughn, 1969; *William Styron* by Richard Pearce, Minneapolis, University of Minnesota Press, 1971; *William Styron* by Marc L. Ratner, New York, Twayne, 1972; *William Styron* by Melvin J. Friedman, Bowling Green, Ohio, Popular Press, 1974; *The Achievement of William Styron* edited by Irving Malin and Robert K. Morris, Athens, University of Georgia Press, 1975.

* * *

Of the American novelists who have come onto the literary scene since the end of the Second World War, William Styron would seem to have worked most directly in the traditional ways of story-telling. As a writer from the American South, he was heir to a mode of fiction writing most notably developed by William Faulkner and practiced to striking effect by such fellow Southerners as Robert Penn Warren, Thomas Wolfe, Eudora Welty, and Katherine Anne Porter. It involved—as the mode of Hemingway did not involve—a reliance upon the resources of a sounding rhetoric rather than upon understatement, a dependence upon the old religious universals ("love and honor and pity and pride and compassion and sacrifice," as Faulkner once termed them) rather than a suspicion of all such external moral formulations, and a profound belief in the reality of the past as importantly affecting present behavior—an "historical sense," as contrasted with the dismissal of history as irrelevant and meaningless.

His first novel, *Lie Down in Darkness*, was strongly indebted to the example of Faulkner; Styron began it, he said after reading Faulkner night and day for several weeks. Yet though Styron portrayed a young Southern woman, Peyton Loftis, as she battled for love and sanity in a dreary family situation, doomed to defeat by her father's weak, self-pitying ineffectuality and her mother's hypocrisy and sadistic jealousy, and though the setting was a tidewater Virginia city among an effete upper-class society, what resulted was not finally Faulknerian. At bottom the causes of Styron's tragedy were familial, not dynastic; the deficiencies of Milton and Helen Loftis were not importantly those of decadent aristocracy whose concept of honor and pride has become empty posturing and self-indulgence, as they would have been for a writer such as Faulkner, but rather personal and psychological. When Peyton flees Virginia for New York City, there is little sense of her plight as representing isolation from the order and definition of a time and place that are no longer available. Instead, hers was a break for freedom, and the failure to make good the break is the result of the crippling conflict within her mind and heart imposed by the example of her parents, and which symbolizes the hatreds engendered by a society that does not know how to love. The suicide of Peyton Loftis represents a plunge into the moral abyss of a self-destructive modern world. Styron, in other words, wrote out of a tradition that taught him to measure his people and their society against the traditional values, and to see the absence of those values in their lives as tragic; but he did not depict that absence as a falling away from a more honorable, more ordered Southern historical past.

The success of *Lie Down in Darkness* was considerable, perhaps in part because a novel that could depict the modern situation as tragic, rather than merely pathetic, and could thus make use of the High Style of language to chronicle it, was all too rare. Styron followed in with *The Long March*, a novella set in a Marine Corps camp during the Korean War period (Styron himself was briefly recalled to active duty in 1951). Depicting the irrationality of war and the military mentality, it demonstrates the dignity, and also the absurdity, of an individual's effort to achieve nobility amid chaos.

Eight years elapsed before Styron's second full-length novel, *Set This House on Fire*. The story of a Southern-born artist, Cass Kinsolving, who is unable to paint, and is married and living in Europe, it involved a man in spiritual bondage, undergoing a terrifying stay in the lower depths before winning his way back to sanity and creativity. In Paris, Rome, and the Italian town of Sambucco, Cass Kinsolving lives in an alcoholic daze, tortured by his inability to create, wandering about, drinking, pitying himself, doing everything except confronting his talent. The struggle is on existential terms. Kinsolving has sought to find a form for his art outside of himself, looking to the society and the people surrounding him for what could only be located within himself: the remorseless requirement of discovering how to love and be loved, and so to create.

Set This House on Fire encountered a generally hostile critical reception, to some extent because it was sprawling and untidy, occasionally overwritten, and therefore so very different from his well-made first novel. It seemed, too, even further removed than *Lie Down in Darkness* from the customary Southern milieu: not only were there no decaying families, no faithful black retainers, no blood-guilt, and no oversexed Southern matrons, but we are told very little about the protagonist's past, either familial or personal, that might explain how he got the way he was. Yet there *was* a past; but Styron gives it to a friend of Kinsolving's, Peter Leverett, who tells the story. The fact is that Leverett's failure to find definition in his Southern origins is what really accounts for Kinsolving's present-day plight. Styron apparently could not avoid grounding his tragedy in history one way or the other. And after Kinsolving has fought his way back to personal responsibility and creativity, he leaves Europe and returns to the South. There is thus a kind of circular movement involved in the first two novels. Peyton Loftis finds the Southern community impossible to live within and love within, and she goes to New York. Cass Kinsolving, equally at loose ends, goes abroad and conducts his struggle for identity and definition there, and then comes home to the South. He has had in effect to ratify the individual and social worth of his attitudes and values away from the place and the institutions of their origins, and make them his own, not something merely bequeathed automatically to him.

If so, it was not surprising that Styron's next and most controversial novel, *The Confessions of Nat Turner*, once again was set in the South—in Southside Virginia, no more than an hour's automobile drive from Port Warwick where Peyton Loftis grew up and Newport News, Virginia, where Styron was born and raised—and that it concerned itself squarely with the Southern past, as exemplified in the presence and the role of the black man. For though *The Confessions of Nat Turner* is based upon a famous slave insurrection that took place in 1831, its implications involve race and racism, integration and separatism, and the use of violent means in order to achieve political and social ends. Styron's strategy, for what he termed his "meditation upon history," was to tell his story from the viewpoint of the slave leader Nat Turner, of whose actual life almost nothing is known. Rather than restrict his protagonist's language, however, to that which a plantation slave in the early 19th-century might be expected to have used, Styron decided that the range and complexity of such a man's mind could not be adequately represented in any such primitive fashion, and he cast Nat Turner's reflections in the rich, allusive, polysyllabic mode of the early Victorian novel. Styron was thus able to have his slave leader utilize the resources of a sounding rhetoric in order to look beyond his immediate circumstance into the moral and ethical implications of his actions.

The initial critical verdict on *The Confessions of Nat Turner* was highly favorable, with such critics as Alfred Kazin, Philip Rahv, C. Vann Woodward, and others declaring it an impressive contribution both to contemporary American fiction and to the knowledge of slavery. Almost immediately, however, the book became embroiled in a controversy, not so much literary as sociological, which made both novel and novelist into a *cause célèbre*. For in presuming, as a white man, to portray the consciousness of a black revolutionist of a century-and-a-half ago, Styron came into collision with the impetus of the black separatist movement. His novel appeared at a time when the black American was straining as never before to assert his identity and his independence of white paternalism, and the result was that numerous black critics, together with some white sympathizers, began heaping abuse on Styron for his alleged racism, his alleged unwarranted liberties with historical "fact," and his alleged projection of "white liberal neuroses" onto a revolutionary black leader's personality. A host of reviews and essays and even a book appeared in denunciation of Styron. Other critics rose to the rebuttal, and historians joined in to certify the controversy that may well interest future social historians almost as much as the Nat Turner insurrection itself.

In 1979 Styron entered the lists again with a lengthy novel on another controversial subject. *Sophie's Choice* involved the confrontation of a young and very autobiographically-clued Virginian with a Polish refugee who has undergone the horrors of concentration camp existence, and her lover, a young New York Jew who is a brilliant conversationalist but turns out to be quite mad. Written very much in the mode of Thomas Wolfe's fiction of encounter with the metropolis, Styron's novel records the growing helplessness of a youthful American in the face of a developing acquaintance with the enormity of human evil and irrationality. The novel drew much criticism for its excesses of rhetoric and the apparent irrelevance of much of its sexual material; in effect it would seem to imitate the author's own difficulties in coming to terms with the subject matter described. Yet is contains powerful sequences, and as always represents Styron's unwillingness to seek easy ways out or avoid central human problems.

—Louis D. Rubin, Jr.

SUKENICK, Ronald. American. Born in Brooklyn, New York, 14 July 1932. Educated at Cornell University, Ithaca, New York, B.A. 1955; Brandeis University, Waltham, Massachusetts, M.A. 1957, Ph.D. in English 1962. Married Lynn Luria in 1961. Lecturer, Brandeis University, 1956-57, and Hofstra University, Hempstead, New York, 1961-62; part-time teacher, 1963-66; Assistant Professor of English, City College, New York, 1966-67, and Sarah Lawrence College, Bronxville, New York, 1968-69; Writer-in-Residence, Cornell University, 1969-70, and University of California, Irvine, 1970-72. Since 1975, Professor of English, and director of the creative writing program, 1975-77, University of Colorado, Boulder. Founding Member, Fiction Collective; Chairman, Coordinating Council of Literary Magazines, 1975-77. Recipient: Fulbright Fellowship, 1958; Guggenheim Fellowship, 1976. Address: Department of English, University of Colorado, Boulder, Colorado 80309, U.S.A.

PUBLICATIONS

Novels

Up. New York, Dial Press, 1968.
Out. Chicago, Swallow Press, 1973.
98.6. New York, Fiction Collective, 1975.
Long Talking Bad Conditions Blues. New York, Fiction Collective, 1979.

Short Stories

The Death of the Novel and Other Stories. New York, Dial Press, 1969.

Uncollected Short Stories

"One Every Minute," in *Carolina Quarterly* (Chapel Hill, North Carolina), Spring 1961.
"A Long Way from Nowhere," in *Epoch* (Ithaca, New York), Fall 1964.
"The Endless Short Story: Verticals and Horizontals," in *Statements*, edited by Jonathan Baumbach. New York, Braziller, 1975.
"The Endless Short Story: Aziff," in *Tri-Quarterly* (Evanston, Illinois), Winter 1976.
"The Endless Short Story: Dong Wang," in *Statements 2*, edited by Jonathan Baumbach and Peter Spielberg. New York, Fiction Collective, 1977.
"The Endless Short Story: Five and Ten," in *Criss-Cross Art Communications 6*, March 1978.
"The Endless Short Story: What's Watts," in *New Letters* (Kansas City), Spring 1979.
"The Endless Short Story: Gorgonzola," in *Departures 2*, Fall 1979.
"The Endless Short Story: Bush Fever," in *Sub-Stance* (Madison, Wisconsin), Fall 1979.

Other

Wallace Stevens: Musing the Obscure. New York, New York University Press, 1967.

*

Critical Studies: "Getting Real: Making It (Up) with Ronald Sukenick," in *Chicago Review*, Winter 1972, and "A Persuasive Account: Working It Out with Ronald Sukenick," in *Seeing Castaneda*, edited by Daniel Noel, New York, Putnam, 1976, both by Jerome Klinkowitz; "Reading *Out*" by Melvin J. Friedman, in *Fiction International 1* (Canton, New York), Fall 1973; "Imagination and Perception" (interview), in *The New Fiction: Interviews with Innovative American Writers*, by Joe David Bellamy, Urbana, University of Illinois Press, 1974; "Tales of Fictive Power: Dreaming and Imagining in Ronald Sukenick's Postmodern Fiction" by Daniel Noel, in *Boundary 2* (Binghamton, New York), Fall 1976; "Obscuring the Muse: The Mock-Autobiographies of Ronald Sukenick" by Timothy Dow Adams, in *Critique* (Atlanta), xx, 1, 1978; "Way Out West: The Exploratory Fiction of Ronald Sukenick" by Alan Cheuse, in *Itinerary Criticism 7*, edited by Charles Crow, Bowling Green, Ohio, Bowling Green State University Press, 1978.

Ronald Sukenick comments:

My fiction is not "experimental."

* * *

The early prose of Ronald Sukenick was mostly playful fiction that "teased the form." The narratives relied heavily on verbal and visual tricks and games. The typography was unconventional. The plots were evasive. The characters were changeable and interchangeable. The theme seemed to be that experience is undependable, undefinable, but life is jolly. (Explicit sexual episodes were presented as being especially jolly.) The prose was often fiction as self-conscious process. Some critics compared Sukenick to Laurence Sterne. "One of the funniest books of the season, a hilarious outburst of wild comedy...," wrote one reviewer of an early Sukenick novel.

The first novel, *Up*, was the story of a writer named Ronnie Sukenick who is writing a novel. The tone is mischievous throughout. The writer and other characters blend in and out of the story with a kind of dissolve-and-appear film blur. Throughout the book the fiction is treated as play, as fantasy bearing no serious relationship to the world of "real" experience. The book is a clever example of the writing produced by contemporary anti-realists who begin with the principle that fiction is nothing but marks on paper; it is the kind of writing that greatly offends the earnest realist. Near the end of the novel, one character observes, "All novels are a load of crap anyway." And Ronnie, the narrator, ends the book by telling the reader, "I'm going to finish this today...I've had enough of this. I'm just playing with words anyway, what did you think I was doing?"

As Sukenick has gone on through novels like *98.6* and *Long Talking Bad Conditions Blues* he had continued to play the verbal and visual games. Line spacing on the pages is irregular; pages are left partially or totally blank, sometimes to suggest physical detail like snow, sometimes more abstract matters such as a breakdown in communication. The characters or the narrator continue to remind the reader that the fiction is merely fiction and the world presented there is fantasy. But much of the good humor that one expects in this sort of narrative has been left behind in the years. There is a grim numbness, sub-surface violence present in these later books. The narratives are twisted and confused. As in earlier books, the characters dissolve and reappear with new names and new identities, but now they have deep new terror and cold boredom. These characters are related to the post-counter-culture society of the 1970's, people still young (but not too young) after the social and cultural upheaval of the 1960's, the post flower-children group. Where now do they go?

These later novels picture a serious internal chaos, a lack of form to experience, life undefined. It is a fluid existence of fear and tedium. The confusion and sadness are everywhere present in the unpunctuated *Long Talking Bad Conditions Blues*, "individuals in a period of accelerated shatter." Such descriptions abound in the book, "...no aims no expectations no hopes and liked it that way....it was the condition of things the general disorientation and underlying disgust you might even say panic that uncertainty about the future and maybe worse about the past....sanity appeared futile so madness became chic." In all of this, the teasing of the form which was just a game in the early books has become an effective technique to dramatize the futility and terror which Sukenick sees just beneath the surface of modern life.

Sukenick has received considerable critical praise in the United States for his experiments in narrative form. He has been called a writer of the future who is concerned with significant relationships rather than static reality. Presumably this praise has something to do with his concentration on fiction as process. In one of his earlier books, a character wanted to write a "book like a cloud that changes as it goes." Sukenick has followed that desire into increasing incoherence and sadness. He gives a world of baseless change in which the knowing are totally bewildered.

—Leo J. Hertzel

SUMMERS, Hollis (Spurgeon, Jr.). American. Born in Eminence, Kentucky, 21 June 1916. Educated at Georgetown College,

Kentucky, A.B. 1937; Bread Loaf School of English, Middlebury College, Vermont, M.A. 1943; University of Iowa, Iowa City, Ph.D. 1949. Married Laura Vimont Clarke in 1943; two children. Taught at Holmes High School, Covington, Kentucky, 1937-44; Professor of English, Georgetown College, 1945-49, and the University of Kentucky, Lexington, 1949-59. Since 1959, Distinguished Professor of English, Ohio University, Athens. Adviser, Ford Foundation Conference on Writers in America, 1958; Lecturer, Arts Program, Association of American Colleges, 1958-63; Danforth Lecturer, 1963-66. Recipient: Fund for the Advancement of Education grant, 1951; *Saturday Review* Poetry Award, 1957; Colleges of Arts and Sciences Award, 1958; National Endowment for the Arts grant, 1974. LL.D.: Georgetown College, 1965. Address: 181 North Congress Street, Athens, Ohio 45701, U.S.A.

PUBLICATIONS

Novels

City Limit. Boston, Houghton Mifflin, 1948.
Brighten the Corner. New York, Doubleday, 1952.
Teach You a Lesson (as Jim Hollis, with James Rourke). New York, Harper, 1955; London, Foulsham, 1956.
The Weather of February. New York, Harper, 1957.
The Day after Sunday. New York, Harper, 1968.
The Garden. New York, Harper, 1972.

Short Stories

How They Chose the Dead. Baton Rouge, Louisiana State University Press, 1973.

Uncollected Short Story

"A Hundred Paths," in *Prize Stories 1977: The O. Henry Awards*, edited by William Abrahams. New York, Doubleday, 1977.

Play

A Note to Myself: A Thanksgiving Play. Chicago, Dramatic Publishing Company, 1946.

Verse

The Walks near Athens. New York, Harper, 1959.
Someone Else: Sixteen Poems about Other Children (juvenile). Philadelphia, Lippincott, 1962.
Seven Occasions. New Brunswick, New Jersey, Rutgers University Press, 1965.
The Peddler and Other Domestic Matters. New Brunswick, New Jersey, Rutgers University Press, 1967.
Sit Opposite Each Other. New Brunswick, New Jersey, Rutgers University Press, 1970.
Start from Home. New Brunswick, New Jersey, Rutgers University Press, 1972.
Occupant, Please Forward. New Brunswick, New Jersey, Rutgers University Press, 1976.
Dinosaurs. Athens, Ohio, Rosetta Press, 1978.

Other

Editor, *Kentucky Story: A Collection of Short Stories.* Lexington, University of Kentucky Press, 1954.
Editor, with Edgar Whan, *Literature: An Introduction.* New York, McGraw Hill, 1960.
Editor, *Discussions of the Short Story.* Boston, Heath, 1963.

*

Hollis Summers comments:

All we are trying to do, I suppose, is to tell it true.

A piece of writing, be it poem or novel, endeavors to draw a ring around experience. The experience and the drawing are of equal importance. The how and the what, the method and the matter are separable only for the luxury of discussion. The what of a piece of writing endures because of the how.

* * *

"We live enough on the edge of violence," sighs a Kentucky Baptist minister's wife in *Brighten the Corner.* She speaks for all Hollis Summers's characters. Summers knows this "edge" well. He has lived almost always in Kentucky and hilly southeastern Ohio, a long-time battleground of the guilt-ridden violence of the Fundamentalist rural South against the corporate-minded irresponsibility of the impersonal Northeast. Though possibly better known for his craftsmanlike poetry, Summers captures in his novels the obsessive bigotry barely masked by superficially whimsical manners and a charming concern with "breeding" of Kentucky's Bluegrass region, which is populated by a unique and distressing mixture of lovers of good bourbon and horse-racing and the self-appointed agents of the Lord in scourging such works of the devil. Summers's fictions arc over "the edge of violence," moving over 20 somewhat frustrating years in his native region towards a disciplined resignation to the inescapableness of violence but lately swinging toward a glimmering perception of new hope as he has increasingly escaped to other places—Mexico, Malta, New Zealand—where glimpses of unspoiled promise may still be caught.

The conclusion of his first novel, *City Limit*, is equivocal. A high school boy and girl, learning to love each other, but not yet ready for the commitment of marriage, are forced to marry anyway by hysterically repressed and repressive elders. Yet finally the girl can feel a hope that the reader is a little too apprehensive to share about the "little room" that awaits the couple beyond the "city limit" and the wreckage of their past.

Brighten the Corner presents us through the eyes of two growing sons with the life of a family of a Baptist minister at his first church in a Kentucky town. It could have been another superficial, episodic account of the minor tribulations of growing up in the United States were it not for the capturing of the tensions—often becoming explosive—generated by such highly charged figures as a retired minister who attempts to continue to dominate the church, a popular travelling evangelist who hates children, and the younger son, who unintentionally turns the spiritual life into a parody of itself. In *The Weather of February* a similarly dynamic woman who has come a long way from the similar parsonages where she grew up reflects on the husbands and lovers she has known and articulates the governing principle of a culture notorious for feuding. "You don't start all over in Lexington, Kentucky." Everything in this narrow, tense world that Summers exposes must be recalled, must be reckoned with as by the characters in short stories written over two decades and collected in *How They Chose the Dead.* These stories move—like the novels from *City Limit* to *The Day after Sunday*—from therapeutic accounts like that of the tranquilizing of an academic traveler on the verge of breakdown in "The Penitent" to the mercilessly skillful portrayals of the deadly games of empty people in tales like "The Terrible Death of Mister Vimont" to the almost unbearable uncapping of the forces of violence that ends in the complete social and artistic collapse of the neurasthenic characters in "The Woman Who Loved Everybody."

This movement culminates in *The Day after Sunday*, which begins with the hopelessly mixed-up only son of a couple that has ceased to be intimate visiting the bedroom of a love-starved spinster nearly his mother's age and making her pregnant. The story is built around three dreadful Mondays in the history of the family's decay; the central voice is that of the middle-aged father seeking to establish some human contact that may redeem him from alcoholism. He cannot find it through his wife, a Bluegrass Madame Bovary, who unmans three generations of "her men"—father, husband, son. The novel's power arises from Summers's making readers see that the heart-shattering irony of this situation is that these people could lead rewarding lives if they could only develop the courage to be honest and generous with each other. But since they cannot do this, they can only sink deeper into despair and drag a widening circle of others down with them.

With *The Garden*, set in Malta, Summers moves back from the tragic extremes that his vision has probed. Although a family that has fled that land where "folks never talked about love" finds violence and corruption even in a land that speaks another language, the wife is at the end the first of Summers's characters since the girl in *City Limit* to achieve a private vision that may make life bearable.

Perhaps all Summers's novels at heart inspire a similar vision. Like the younger son in *Brighten the Corner*, the novelist remains bright and artful in handling terrifying affairs. Perhaps he can awaken readers before they sleepwalk over "the edge of violence." His work partakes of the "revival" character that has been the glory and downfall of his native region; but he has achieved through art the reconciliation with life that eludes those obsessed with Judgment rather than understanding.

—Warren French

SWARTHOUT, Glendon (Fred). American. Born in Pinckney, Michigan, 8 April 1918. Educated at the University of Michigan, Ann Arbor, 1935-39, A.B. 1939, A.M. 1946; Michigan State University, East Lansing, 1952-55, Ph.D. 1955. Served in the United States Army Infantry, 1943-45: Sergeant. Married Kathryn Blair Vaughn in 1940; one child. Teaching Fellow, University of Michigan, 1946-48; Instructor, University of Maryland, College Park, 1948-51; Associate Professor of English, Michigan State University, 1951-59; Lecturer in English, Arizona State University, Tempe, 1959-62. Recipient: Theatre Guild Award, in playwriting, 1947; Hopwood Award, 1948; O. Henry Award, 1960; Western Writers of America Spur Award, 1976. Address: 5045 Tamanar Way, Scottsdale, Arizona 85253, U.S.A.

PUBLICATIONS

Novels

Willow Run. New York, Crowell, 1943.
They Came to Cordura. New York, Random House, and London, Heinemann, 1958.
Where the Boys Are. New York, Random House, and London, Heinemann, 1960.
Welcome to Thebes. New York, Random House, 1962; London, Heinemann, 1963.
The Cadillac Cowboys. New York, Random House, 1964.
The Eagle and the Iron Cross. New York, New American Library, 1966; London, Heinemann, 1967.
Loveland. New York, Doubleday, 1968.
Bless the Beasts and Children. New York, Doubleday, and London, Secker and Warburg, 1970.
The Tin Lizzie Troop. New York, Doubleday, and London, Secker and Warburg, 1972.
Luck and Pluck. New York, Doubleday, and London, Secker and Warburg, 1973.
The Shootist. New York, Doubleday, and London, Secker and Warburg, 1975.
The Melodeon. New York, Doubleday, and London, Secker and Warburg, 1977.
Skeletons. New York, Doubleday, and London, Secker and Warburg, 1979.

Uncollected Short Stories

"Pancho Villa's One-Man War," in *Cosmopolitan* (New York), February 1953.
"A Horse for Mrs. Custer," in *New World Writing 5*. New York, New American Library, 1954.
"What Every Man Knows," in *Collier's* (Springfield, Ohio), 17 February 1956.
"Ixion," in *New World Writing 13*. New York, New American Library, 1958.
"A Glass of Blessings," in *Esquire* (New York), January 1959.
"Attack on the Mountain," in *Saturday Evening Post* (Philadelphia), 4 July 1959.
"Going to See George," in *Esquire* (New York), August 1965.
"The Ball Really Carries in the Cactus League Because the Air Is Dry," in *Esquire* (New York), March 1978.

Other (juvenile)

The Ghost and the Magic Saber, with Kathryn Swarthout. New York, Random House, 1963.
Whichaway, with Kathryn Swarthout. New York, Random House, 1966; London, Heinemann, 1967.
The Button Boat, with Kathryn Swarthout. New York, Doubleday, 1969; London, Heinemann, 1971.
TV Thompson, with Kathryn Swarthout. New York, Doubleday, 1972.
Whales to See the, with Kathryn Swarthout. New York, Doubleday, 1975.

*

Manuscript Collection: Hayden Memorial Library, Arizona State University, Tempe.

* * *

Of the novels Glendon Swarthout has published since 1943, all are eminently readable; two—*They Came to Cordura* and *Bless the Beasts and Children*—are outstanding. Whether set in a World War II bomber plant in Michigan, or in a present-day boy's camp in Arizona, each reflects the author's intense involvement with the persons and places he writes of.

Willow Run, a novel about blue-collar workers in a World War II defense plant, is somewhat heavy on win-the-war speeches and lacks story and character development. And while the book is rhapsodic on the details of building airplanes and a bit obvious in the symbolism, it does give us a glimpse into the mind of the factory worker under stress.

Some 15 years later, Swarthout published his finest novel: *They Came to Cordura*. The tantalizing glance into a factory worker's psyche is explored with a probe—this time using the peace-time soldier as the object. Preparing for World War I, the country needed heroes. The time is 1916, and the place, the Mexican border, where the punitive forces of the U.S. Cavalry are trying to route the rebels of Villa. Five men are chosen to receive the Congressional Medal of Honor, and it is Major Thorn's duty to keep them alive to receive it. The story concerns their six-day journey to Cordura, during which the men are revealed to be pathetic, corrupt, hypocritical, cowardly, and degenerate. It is a remarkable book for its creation of tension and its probing into the motives which make men behave courageously and selflessly on the battlefield. A gripping novel in every respect, it demonstrates Swarthout's power as a writer of major dimensions.

Where the Boys Are, a commercial success, is the story of the annual student spring trek to Florida. Although there is some attempt to inject a serious note into the proceedings by pointing out the possible tragic consequences of sexual indiscretions, it is largely a novel about youth with an appeal to youth—somewhat dated in the light of the freedoms demanded by youth in the years since its publication.

After the huge commercial and critical success of *They Came to Cordura*, Swarthout and his family moved to southern Arizona. It is here that *The Cadillac Cowboys* is set. This work satirically depicts the pitfalls an Easterner faces in fitting into the not-so-wild West. Basically farcical, this novel nevertheless has elements of sentiment, poignancy, adventure, and nostalgia. Its main appeal, however, is its wild and often outrageous humor, bordering frequently on slapstick.

The same southern Arizona scene provides the background for *The Eagle and the Iron Cross*. The place is a prisoner-of-war camp; the time, 1945; the protagonists, two young German soldiers. They escape and ultimately find refuge with a bedraggled tribe of Indians. Despite the Indians' help, the soldiers meet violent death. Swarthout does not mask his bitterness in this novel: it is a tale of intolerable, misplaced faith, and wanton brutality. There are no winners and no heroes. The young Germans retain their dignity, even in death; the Indians retain theirs and endure life. Our villains are the American super patriots who, under the guise of retaliation, practice atrocities equal to those of the Nazis. It is not a pretty story.

Returning to his native Michigan, Swarthout in *Loveland* depicts the growing-up adventures of a young musician struggling with both adolescence and the depression of the 1930's. This story is told with warmth and humor, and captures the frantic era of a waning opulent society and a dying way of life. Heavily larded with the slang and idiom of the 1930's, the humor is occasionally strained; essentially though the lighter side of the era is handled tastefully and knowingly. Swarthout has been through this, we feel, and writes lovingly about those innocent days.

Bless the Beasts and Children brings the reader back to Arizona. Six sensitive boys from a summer camp witness a buffalo kill. Misfits and castoffs all their lives, their obsession leads them to free the remaining animals. Their nocturnal adventures and ultimate victory are interspersed with delicately handled flashbacks which probe to the core of each boy's personality problem. In the course of the adventure, there are humor, courage, suspense, and tragedy.

—Martin L. Kornbluth

SWINNERTON, Frank (Arthur). British. Born in Wood Green, Middlesex, 12 August 1884. Married Mary Dorothy Bennett in 1924; two daughters. Office boy, Hay Nisbet and Company, London, 1899-1900; Reception Clerk, and subsequently Confidential Clerk to Hugh Dent, J.M. Dent and Company, publishers, London, 1902-1907; proof reader, and subsequently Editor, Chatto and Windus, publishers, London, 1907-1926. Drama Critic, *Truth* and *The Nation*, London, 1919-21; Literary Critic, *The Evening News*, London, 1929-32; Novel Critic, *The Observer*, London, 1937-43; "John O'London" for *John O'London's Weekly*, London, 1949-54. President, Royal Literary Fund, 1962-66. Address: Old Tokefield, Cranleigh, Surrey GU6 8NR, England.

PUBLICATIONS

Novels

The Merry Heart: A Gentle Melodrama. London, Chatto and Windus, 1909; New York, Doubleday, 1929.

The Young Idea: A Comedy of Environment. London, Chatto and Windus, 1910; New York, Duffield, 1911.

The Casement: A Diversion. London, Chatto and Windus, and New York, Duffield, 1911.

The Happy Family. London, Methuen, and New York, Doran, 1912.

On the Staircase. London, Methuen, and New York, Doran, 1914.

The Chaste Wife. London, Secker, 1916; New York, Doran, 1917.

Nocturne. London, Secker, and New York, Doran, 1917.

Shops and Houses. London, Methuen, and New York, Doran, 1918.

September. London, Methuen, and New York, Doran, 1919.

Coquette. London, Methuen, and New York, Doran, 1921.

The Three Lovers. New York, Doran, 1922; London, Methuen, 1923.

Young Felix. London, Hutchinson, and New York, Doran, 1923.

The Elder Sister. London, Hutchinson, and New York, Doran, 1925.

Summer Storm. London, Hutchinson, and New York, Doran, 1926.

A Brood of Ducklings. London, Hutchinson, and New York, Doran, 1928.

Sketch of a Sinner. New York, Doubleday, 1929; London, Hutchinson, 1930.

The Georgian House: A Tale in Four Parts. New York, Doubleday, 1932; London, Hutchinson, 1933.

Elizabeth. London, Hutchinson, and New York, Doubleday, 1934.

Harvest Comedy. London, Hutchinson, 1937; New York, Doubleday, 1938.

The Two Wives. London, Hutchinson, and New York, Doubleday, 1940.

The Fortunate Lady. London, Hutchinson, and New York, Doubleday, 1941.

Thankless Child. London, Hutchinson, and New York, Doubleday, 1942.

A Woman in Sunshine. London, Hutchinson, 1944; New York, Doubleday, 1945.

English Maiden: Parable of a Happy Life. London, Hutchinson, 1946.

Faithful Company: A Winter's Tale. London, Hutchinson, and New York, Doubleday, 1948.

The Doctor's Wife Comes to Stay. London, Hutchinson, 1949; New York, Doubleday, 1950.

A Flower for Catherine. London, Hutchinson, 1950; New York, Doubleday, 1951.

Master Jim Probity. London, Hutchinson, 1952; as *An Affair of Love*, New York, Doubleday, 1953.

A Month in Gordon Square. London, Hutchinson, 1953; New York, Doubleday, 1954.

The Sumner Intrigue. London, Hutchinson, and New York, Doubleday, 1955.

The Woman from Sicily. London, Hutchinson, and New York, Doubleday, 1957.

A Tigress in Prothero. London, Hutchinson, 1959; as *A Tigress in the Village*, New York, Doubleday, 1959.

The Grace Divorce. London, Hutchinson, and New York, Doubleday, 1960.

Death of a Highbrow. London, Hutchinson, 1961; New York, Doubleday, 1962.

Quadrille. London, Hutchinson, and New York, Doubleday, 1965.

Sanctuary. London, Hutchinson, 1966; New York, Doubleday, 1967.

The Bright Lights. London, Hutchinson, and New York, Doubleday, 1968.

On the Shady Side. London, Hutchinson, 1970; New York, Doubleday, 1971.

Nor All Thy Tears. London, Hutchinson, and New York, Doubleday, 1972.

Rosalind Passes. London, Hutchinson, 1973; New York, Doubleday, 1974.

Some Achieve Greatness. London, Hamish Hamilton, and New York, Doubleday, 1976.

Uncollected Short Stories

"Marriage Arranged," in *Collier's* (Springfield, Ohio), May 1925.
"Lie," in *Woman's Home Companion* (Springfield, Ohio), March 1926.
"Celebrity," in *Saturday Evening Post* (Philadelphia), 4 April 1926.
"Stranger," in *Woman's Home Companion* (Springfield, Ohio), September 1926.
"Red-Headed Knight," in *Delineator* (New York), April 1927.
"The Shy Young Man," in *Woman's Home Companion* (Springfield, Ohio), July 1927.
"Gargoyle," in *Century* (New York), August 1927.
"Enchantress" and "Fugitive," in *Delineator* (New York), September 1927.
"The Chocolate Seller of Knightsbridge," in *Woman's Home Companion* (Springfield, Ohio), November 1927.
"Ivory Figurine," in *Delineator* (New York), February 1928.
"Better Than Fame," in *Collier's* (Springfield, Ohio), March 1929.
"Restaurant of the Silver Bells," in *Golden Book* (New York), September 1929.
"Miss Jedburys," in *Tales from Far and Near*, edited by Ernest Rhys and Catharine Scott. New York, Appleton, 1930.
"Percy and Pansy," in *Mr. Fothergill's Plot*, edited by John Fothergill. London, Oxford University Press, 1931.
"The Verdict," in *London Calling*, edited by Storm Jameson. New York, Harper, 1942.

Other

George Gissing: A Critical Study. London, Secker, and New York, Kennerley, 1912.
Robert Louis Stevenson: A Critical Study. London, Secker, and New York, Kennerley, 1914.
Women (published anonymously). London, Secker, 1918; New York, Knopf, 1919.
Tokefield Papers. London, Secker, and New York, Doran, 1927; augmented edition, as *Tokefield Papers, Old and New*, London, Hamish Hamilton, and New York, Doubleday, 1949.
A London Bookman. London, Secker, 1928.
Authors and the Book Trade. London, Howe, and New York, Knopf, 1932.
The Georgian Scene: A Literary Panorama. New York, Farrar and Rinehart, 1934; as *The Georgian Literary Scene 1910-1935*, London, Heinemann, 1935; revised edition, London, Hutchinson, 1938, 1950, 1969; New York, Farrar Straus, 1951.
Swinnerton: An Autobiography. New York, Doubleday, 1936; London, Hutchinson, 1937.
The Reviewing and Criticism of Books (lecture). London, Dent, 1939; New York, Oxford University Press, 1940.
The Cats and Rosemary (juvenile). New York, Knopf, 1948; London, Hamish Hamilton, 1950.
Arnold Bennett. London, Longman, 1950; revised edition, 1961.
The Bookman's London. London, Wingate, 1951; New York, Doubleday, 1952; revised edition, London, Baker, 1969.
Londoner's Post: Letters to Gog and Magog. London, Hutchinson, 1952.
Authors I Never Met. London, Frederick Books-Allen and Unwin, 1956; Los Angeles, Spencer, 1963.
The Adventures of a Manuscript, Being the Story of "The Ragged-Trousered Philanthropists." London, Richards Press, 1956.
Background with Chorus: A Footnote to Changes in English Literary Fashion Between 1901 and 1917. London, Hutchinson, 1956; New York, Farrar Straus, 1957.
Figures in the Foreground: Literary Reminiscences 1917-1940. London, Hutchinson, 1963; New York, Doubleday, 1964.
A Galaxy of Fathers. London, Hutchinson, and New York, Doubleday, 1966.
Reflections from a Village. London, Hutchinson, and New York, Doubleday, 1969.
Arnold Bennett: A Last Word. London, Hamish Hamilton, and New York, Doubleday, 1978.

Editor, *An Anthology of Modern Fiction.* London, Nelson, 1937.
Editor, *Literary Taste*, by Arnold Bennett. London, Cape, 1937.
Editor, *Conversations of James Northcote*, by William Hazlitt. London, Muller, 1949.
Editor, *The Journals of Arnold Bennett.* London, Penguin, 1954.

*

Manuscript Collection: University of Arkansas, Fayetteville.

Frank Swinnerton comments:

(1972) I have always written dramatic studies of character, at first set in the London suburbs as known to me, but increasingly in other environments. My aim has been to do in the novel what the Elizabethan playwrights did in their works. My two fundamental assumptions are that "character is Fate" and that "in life there are neither rewards nor punishments; there are consequences." Given the characters, I have built dramatic stories around them. My first model was Louisa May Alcott; my second Henry James; but of course I have chiefly been "inspired" by my own experience of life and my own observant temperament. I have never drawn people known to me; but have invented individuals (using experience solely as reference). This invention comes naturally; and the technique I use is to show the characters as it were stereoscopically, through the eyes of other persons. My grandfathers were both what are called "Master Craftsmen"; and while not claiming to be a master I do regard myself as, first of all, a craftsman. That is, I love my work, regardless of reward.

As critic, I write "by the light of Nature," being more interested in men and women than in their opinions or in aesthetic theory.

* * *

One hardly expects a novelist who is alive in the 1980's to be the contemporary of such giants as Conrad, James, Lawrence, or Forster. Yet the truth is that Frank Swinnerton's first novel, *The Merry Heart*, appeared in 1909, two years before Lawrence's *The White Peacock*, Conrad's *Under Western Eyes*, and James's *The Outcry*, and a year before Forster's *Howards End*. It is important to be aware of this, not for any matter of mere whimsicality, but because we need to recognise that Frank Swinnerton's "masters" could hardly be those tremendous innovators whose presence, sometimes shadowy, sometimes strong, we find behind such contemporary and senior novelists as Graham Greene, with his strong debt to Conrad, and Angus Wilson, who has always been ready to admit the influence of Forster on his writing.

If we are to begin to understand the nature and scope of Frank Swinnerton's fiction, then, we need to be alive to the fact that he began writing during the period of the sudden and vast upthrust of the modern novel, that many of the novelists who helped shape the course of 20th-century fiction were his acquaintances, and that he was able to write about them with easy familiarity in his critical guide *The Georgian Literary Scene*.

The Georgian Literary Scene is a useful work of reference, because of its author's encyclopaedic knowledge of the literature of the period about which he writes. It is a good deal more than useful in its shrewd summaries of the novelists of that era (Swinnerton is less sure on the poets). And, perhaps most important of all, it helps us to understand a good deal about Swinnerton as a novelist himself. For example, at the end of his generous and perceptive pages on Lawrence, Swinnerton remarks that in a hundred years Lawrence will in all probability still be on the literary map, "while I, and those like me, will have sunk without trace from every record of the Georgian era." Two things deserve our attention here. One, that Swinnerton's engaging modesty is in no sense false; he rightly thinks of himself as a minor novelist (though it needs to be said that there are good and bad minor novelists, and that Swinnerton is, so it seems to me, emphatically to be considered a good minor novelist). Two, Swinnerton identifies himself with the Georgian period, and this is very proper. For his fiction *is* essentially Georgian. But what is meant by calling Frank Swinnerton a Georgian novelist?

In the first place, we may note that Swinnerton, who was born in 1884, enjoys that sense of eager—one might almost say fervent—secularism that is so marked a feature of the novelists of the opening decades of the 20th century. Like Forster, Swinnerton believes in the holiness of carnal love, and in his autobiography, *Swinnerton*, he himself has said that he considers himself lucky to have escaped the sense of sin. Thus, when his novels deal with love, and they frequently do, they deal with it in what it seems fair to call a Georgian manner. That is to say, they express neither the sense of guilt or heavy conventionality of the Victorian novel, nor the metaphysical brooding of Lawrence. For Swinnerton, love is or ought to be simply enjoyable, and anything that impedes or prevents it from being so is for that very reason to be condemned. Putting it another way, we might remark that in dealing with intense personal relationships Swinnerton shows himself to be a true disciple of Meredith and a true contemporary of Forster.

Yet in another context Swinnerton is very unlike Forster. Indeed, although with his customary modesty and truthfulness Swinnerton calls Forster "the most intelligent of all the novelists of the 1880-1900 generation" what he has to say of Forster in *The Georgian Literary Scene* makes clear that Swinnerton finds a good deal to regret about Forster's fictional ways. In particular, he dislikes Forster's "fantasticality," which he sees as an evasion of realism and a refusal to let the life of the novel take over from his insistent moral themes. All of Forster's novels, Swinnerton says, have a quality of "radiant intelligence" but they also have two major faults. First, they are customarily deficient in emotion, in that Forster rarely shows any great involvement with his characters except in so far as they are figures in his moral theorems. Second, Forster is hampered because of his very limited knowledge of English life. Thus it is absurd, Swinnerton says, for Forster to pretend that Leonard Bast, the uneducated clerk of *Howards End*, would have responded as Forster claims he did to the courtesy of a Cambridge student. "My knowledge of clerks is very extensive," Swinnerton drily remarks, "and I have never met one who would be overwhelmed by decent behaviour on the part of an undergraduate, or one to whom such decent behaviour would seem less than his due."

Now this two-pronged criticism of Forster is instructive, not just because it directs us to faults which Forster certainly has, but because it makes clear that Swinnerton as a novelist himself is very much in the camp of realism. Perhaps we should not be surprised at this. For after all, the year of Swinnerton's *The Casement* (1911) was also the year in which Arnold Bennett published *Hilda Lessways*, the second of his *Clayhanger* trilogy. The following year, Swinnerton published *The Happy Family*, which seems to me one of his best pieces of sustained fiction in its unflurried and deliberately low-pitched observation of life and in its occasional sharp wit and the ready sympathy which the author displays with and for his characters. And in the same year he published *George Gissing: A Critical Study*. The fact is that Swinnerton has many points of similarity with both Gissing and Bennett, those champions of the realist novel (his *Shops and Houses*, 1918, is very akin to the kinds of study that one finds in so much of Bennett's writing, as for example, *Riceyman Steps*). And it is worth noting that Swinnerton writes with rare affection of Bennett in *The Georgian Literary Scene*.

Of all Swinnerton's many novels, *Harvest Comedy* is the one that perhaps most amply testifies to his gifts. It is extremely well-written, it is neatly but unobtrusively plotted, it has the realist's typical fascination with the contours of unremarkable yet unique lives (in this case the lives of three men), and its shows Swinnerton's unemphatic liberal moral position to its best advantage. That position is best summed up, perhaps, by the hero of *A Woman in Sunshine*, when he tells his wife that "You're infected by the pessimism of the children. You, and they, have gone away from simplicity. You're now trying to intellectualise the heart, which can't be done." The words are almost Forsterian, and very obviously they reflect "Georgian" concerns and attitudes. But in his best work Swinnerton finds his own ways of giving both concerns and attitudes a proper fictional life.

—John Lucas

SYMONS, Julian (Gustave). British. Born in London, 30 May 1912. Educated in various state schools. Married Kathleen Clark in 1941; one son and one daughter (deceased). Has worked as a shorthand typist, secretary for an engineering company, and advertising copywriter. Founding Editor, *Twentieth Century Verse*, London, 1937-39; Reviewer, Manchester *Evening News*, 1947-56; Editor, Penguin Mystery Series, 1974-77. Since 1958, Reviewer for the *Sunday Times*, London. Visiting Professor, Amherst College, Massachusetts, 1975-76. Co-Founder, 1953, and Chairman, 1958-59, Crime Writers Association; Chairman, Committee of Management, Society of Authors, 1969-71; Member of the Council, Westfield College, University of London, 1972-75. Since 1976, President, Detection Club. Recipient: Crime Writers Association Award, 1957, 1966; Mystery Writers of America Edgar Allan Poe Award, 1961, 1973; Swedish Academy of Detection Grand Master Diploma, 1977. Fellow, Royal Society of Literature, 1975. Address: Groton House, 330 Dover Road, Walmer, Deal, Kent, England.

PUBLICATIONS

Novels

The Immaterial Murder Case. London, Gollancz, 1945; New York, Macmillan, 1957.

A Man Called Jones. London, Gollancz, 1947.

Bland Beginning. London, Gollancz, and New York, Harper, 1949.

The Thirty-First of February. London, Gollancz, and New York, Harper, 1950.

The Broken Penny. London, Gollancz, and New York, Harper, 1953.

The Narrowing Circle. London, Gollancz, and New York, Harper, 1954.

The Paper Chase. London, Collins, 1956; as *Bogue's Fortune*, New York, Harper, 1957.

The Colour of Murder. London, Collins, and New York, Harper, 1957.

The Gigantic Shadow. London, Collins, 1958; as *The Pipe Dream*, New York, Harper, 1959.

The Progress of a Crime. London, Collins, and New York, Harper, 1960.

The Killing of Francie Lake. London, Collins, 1962; as *The Plain Man*, New York, Harper, 1962.

The End of Solomon Grundy. London, Collins, and New York, Harper, 1964.

The Belting Inheritance. London, Collins, and New York, Harper, 1965.

The Man Who Killed Himself. London, Collins, and New York, Harper, 1967.

The Man Whose Dreams Came True. London, Collins, 1968; New York, Harper, 1969.

The Man Who Lost His Wife. London, Collins, 1970; New York, Harper, 1971.

The Players and the Game. London, Collins, and New York, Harper, 1972.

The Plot Against Roger Rider. London, Collins, and New York, Harper, 1973.

A Three-Pipe Problem. London, Collins, and New York, Harper, 1975.
The Blackheath Poisonings. London, Collins, 1978; New York, Harper, 1979.
Sweet Adelaide. London, Collins, and New York, Harper, 1980.

Short Stories

Murder! Murder! London, Fontana, 1961.
Francis Quarles Investigates. London, Panther, 1965.
Ellery Queen Presents Julian Symons' How to Trap a Crook and Twelve Other Mysteries. New York, Davis, 1977.

Uncollected Short Stories

"The Post-Mortem," in *Ellery Queen's Mystery Magazine* (New York), May 1979.
"Flowers That Bloom in the Spring," in *Ellery Queen's Mystery Magazine* (New York), July 1979.
"Waiting for Mr. McGregor," in *Verdict of Thirteen*, edited by Julian Symons. London, Faber, and New York, Harper, 1979.
"Value for Money," in *Ellery Queen's Mystery Magazine* (New York), December 1980.

Plays

Radio Plays: *Affection Unlimited*, 1968; *Night Ride to Dover*, 1969.

Televison Plays: *I Can't Bear Violence*, 1963; *Miranda and a Salesman*, 1963; *The Witnesses*, 1964; *The Finishing Touch*, 1965; *Curtains for Sheila*, 1965; *Tigers of Subtopia*, 1968; *The Pretenders*, 1970; *Whatever's Peter Playing At*, 1974.

Verse

Confusions about X. London, Fortune Press, 1939.
The Second Man. London, Routledge, 1943.
A Reflection on Auden. London, Poem-of-the-Month Club, 1973.
The Object of an Affair and Other Poems. Edinburgh, Tragara Press, 1974.

Other

A.J.A. Symons: His Life and Speculations. London, Eyre and Spottiswoode, 1950.
Charles Dickens. London, Barker, and New York, Roy, 1951.
Thomas Carlyle: The Life and Ideas of a Prophet. London, Gollancz, and New York, Oxford University Press, 1952.
Horatio Bottomley. London, Cresset Press, 1955.
The General Strike: A Historical Portrait. London, Cresset Press, 1957; Chester Springs, Pennsylvania, Dufour, 1963.
The Thirties: A Dream Revolved. London, Cresset Press, 1960; Chester Springs, Pennsylvania, Dufour, 1963; revised edition, London, Faber, 1975.
A Reasonable Doubt: Some Criminal Cases Re-examined. London, Cresset Press, 1960.
The Detective Story in Britain. London, Longman, 1962.
Buller's Campaign. London, Cresset Press, 1963.
England's Pride: The Story of the Gordon Relief Expedition. London, Hamish Hamilton, 1965.
Crime and Detection: An Illustrated History from 1840. London, Studio Vista, 1966; as *A Pictorial History of Crime*, New York, Crown, 1966.
Critical Occasions. London, Hamish Hamilton, 1966.
Bloody Murder. London, Faber, 1972; as *Mortal Consequences*, New York, Harper, 1972.
Between the Wars: Britain in Photographs. London, Batsford, 1972.
Notes from Another Country. London, London Magazine Editions, 1972.
The Tell-Tale Heart: The Life and Works of Edgar Allan Poe. London, Faber, and New York, Harper, 1978.
Conan Doyle: Portrait of an Artist. London, G. Whizzard, 1979.
The Modern Crime Story. Edinburgh, Tragara Press, 1980.
Critical Observations. London, Faber, 1981.
The Great Detectives. New York, Abrams, 1981.

Editor, *An Anthology of War Poetry.* London, Penguin, 1942.
Editor, *Selected Writings of Samuel Johnson.* London, Grey Walls Press, 1949.
Editor, *Selected Works, Reminiscences and Letters*, by Thomas Carlyle. London, Hart Davis, 1956; Cambridge, Massachusetts, Harvard University Press, 1957.
Editor, *Essays and Biographies*, by A.J.A. Symons. London, Cassell, 1969.
Editor, *The Woman in White*, by Wilkie Collins. London, Penguin, 1974.
Editor, *The Angry 30's.* London, Eyre Methuen, 1976.
Editor, *Selected Tales*, by Poe. London, Oxford University Press, 1976.
Editor, *Verdict of Thirteen: A Detection Club Anthology.* London, Faber, and New York, Harper, 1979.
Editor, *The Complete Sherlock Holmes*, by Arthur Conan Doyle. London, Secker and Warburg, 1981.

*

Critical Study: in *Auden and After* by Francis Scarfe, London, Routledge, 1942.

Julian Symons comments:
I think the reason—well, one reason apart from money—for writing crime stories may be of interest. The quotation comes from the introduction to my Omnibus volume (Collins, 1967):

> Why put such ideas (as those in my books) into the form of crime stories, rather than "straight" novels? The thing that absorbs me most in our age is the violence behind respectable faces, the civil servant planning how to kill Jews most efficiently, the judge speaking with passion about the need for capital punishment, the quiet obedient boy who kills for fun. These are extreme cases, but if you want to show the violence that lives behind the bland faces most of us present to the world, what better vehicle can you have than the crime novel?

* * *

Julian Symons, a poet of the 1930's and later a distinguished literary critic (with books to his credit on Dickens and Carlyle) and social historian (author of *The Thirties* and *The General Strike*), took to writing crime novels as a sideline to his main literary interests, almost as a game, but during the years fiction has become one of the main currents of his life as a writer and a vehicle for his criticism of the world he lives in. He has become one of the few serious critics of the crime novel as well as one of its most prolific practitioners.

In his novels (such as *The Narrowing Circle*, *The Colour of Murder*, *The Progress of a Crime*, *The Immaterial Murder Case*, *The Broken Penny*) Symons has used the necessary structure of the thriller—the presence and explanation of a crime or an apparent crime—for many more purposes than those exploited by the writer of the ordinary neatly contrived detective story which depends on the solution of a complex puzzle. Symons's plots are often, by comparison, loose and even obvious, and his denouements are sometimes deliberately anti-climactic; there is a distinctly ironic element in his attitude towards such matters. What he injects into his deliberately disjointed version of the classic crime plot is the kind of content that comes from his own wider interests. He is concerned with the decay of a society, with cultural pretences, with politics as a corrupting element, with the manners of a world he has made his own: the Bohemian borderland where failed artists and hack writers, advertisement men and broadcasters, and their lesser hangers-on, come together to create a setting whose very alienation from moral stability tends to encourage the emergence of crime. It is a setting where the murderer and the victim seem to attract each other, a world of hollow men which suggests that as a novelist Symons has learnt lessons from Wyndham Lewis.

But it is not merely the landscape of a rotting society that is created. Within it there is likely to be enacted a pursuit in which the ambiguous guilts of unjustly accused men play their part. These novels, indeed, are often psychologically quite complex, and it is such inner drama that in the end is more important than the solution of the crime, or even the crime itself.

Indeed, in *The Thirty-First of February*, for example, there is no crime at all, and a man is grimly hunted to insanity, by a detective with a megalomaniac sense of being the agent of divine justice, for a death that was after all not a murder. This novel illustrates the ambiguity of Symons's attitude towards the policeman as a fictional type. Even when the police turn out in the end to be on the side of right, they are still menacing and unpredictable figures, and upon them Symons seems to focus the criticism of society that permeates his novels, and especially the dilemma of self-defeating authority and its semblances of justice which are hollow because they lack the core of justice.

—George Woodcock

SYMONS, (H.B.) Scott. Canadian. Born in Toronto, Ontario, 13 July 1933. Educated at Trinity College School, Port Hope, Ontario; Trinity College, University of Toronto, B.A. in modern history 1955; King's College, Cambridge, M.A. in English literature; the Sorbonne, Paris, Diplome d'Etudes Supérieures. Married; one child. Editorial Writer and Reporter, *Toronto Telegram*, *Quebec Chronicle Telegram*, *Montreal Presse*, and *Montreal Nouveau Journal*. Since 1962, has worked as Curator, Sigmund Samuel Canadiana Collection, and the Canadiana Gallery, Royal Ontario Museum, Toronto, Assistant Professor of Fine Art, University of Toronto, and Consultant, Smithsonian Institution, Washington, D.C. Taught a post-graduate course in Contemporary Art at the University of Pennsylvania, Philadelphia. Recipient: Beta Sigma Phi Award, 1968; Canada Council Senior Arts grant, 1973, 1977. Lives in Newfoundland. Address: c/o McClelland and Stewart Ltd., 25 Hollinger Road, Toronto, Ontario M4B 3G2, Canada.

PUBLICATIONS

Novels

Place D'Armes. Toronto, McClelland and Stewart, 1967.
Civic Square. Toronto, McClelland and Stewart, 1969.

Other

Heritage: A Romantic Look at Early Canadian Furniture. Toronto, McClelland and Stewart, and Greenwich, Connecticut, New York Graphic Society, 1971.

*

Manuscript Collection: Trinity College, University of Toronto.

Scott Symons comments:

> *Place D'Armes* is at once a first novel,
> a meticulously tangled diary,
> an insanely indiscreet autobiography,
> an existential Canadian allegory,
> a book of illicit imagination that is pure fact,
> an implacable manifesto.

* * *

As a "Para-Canadian, released from any allegiance to the Canadian State but obsessively devoted to the Canadian Nation," Scott Symons presents his novels as acts of faith in the inner logic of Canada. The country's Blandebeestes, Protestant architects of a new Canadian identity, have castrated Canadians by cutting them off from their land, love, heritage, and life; *Place D'Armes* is "an adventure in the senses" intended to reaffirm the sensibilities of the homosentient man, and to challenge the benignant Canadian Death "whose first trait is the social, sexual, moral security, passivity of smugness." "Decarnated," disembodied, detached from his roots as a Tory Radical, Hugh Anderson flees Ontario for Montreal, where he becomes a "demissionary" seeking to be touched by his French-Canadian friends, Roman Catholicism, antique furniture, even the buildings surrounding Old Montreal's Place D'Armes. His notes, Combat Journal (of the Holy War between reality and himself), and Novel gradually merge into an ontological discovery of the Real Presence of joy, of Body and Blood rather than the Bilingualism and Biculturalism of governmental Royal Commission. Anderson's numerous homosexual encounters are thus individual attempts at fusing the stability of English Canadians ("Cubed-Roots") and French Canadian carnality, just as in his growing madness, his heightened sensibility, he finds himself penetrated, "insited" by the Place itself.

Civic Square represents the other half of Symons's rhetorical diptych, an epistle to Ontario's Canadacult and the new orthodoxy of perverted Canadian nationalism which drove him to Montreal. His Civic Square is the "Torontoman," the prototype of the Canadian Cube ("An American-Square-in-Committee-of-the-Whole"), and the devil in Symons's seasonal liturgy. "Each season is a Man, a Landscape, a Religious Denomination, a form of Church Architecture, a Mode of Perception and of knowledge...and a Political Creed": the letters to "Dear Reader" comprising the novel are semi-autobiographical and scatalogical accounts of winter, the Great Canadian Heresy's urban-Liberal-Methodism/Presbyterianism, and of spring, rural-Conservative Anglicanadianism: a dialectical "Sensibility Sequence." Childhood memories, his private school, motor-racing and motor-cycling, heterosexual love, high tea with his parents in a fashionable Toronto suburb, metaphorical bird-watching at his small farm, all are data to dispute the reduction of Canadians to "mere Professional Canajuns first—dead on our feet."

Symons's fragmented prose, incorrigible punning and private mythology—accessible principally to readers familiar with Canadian literature and politics during the 1960's—reflect the tangled complexity of his central preoccupation: recapturing the delicately accretive emotional content linking him to his past and his environment. Both *Place D'Armes* and *Civic Square* are dedicated to demonstrating that "you cannot tamper with the inner logic of a people without destroying that people," even if the people themselves are only slowly coming to recognise that they are lamentably willing participants in their own destruction.

—Bruce Nesbitt

TAYLOR, Peter (Hillsman). American. Born in Trenton, Tennessee, 8 January 1917. Educated at Vanderbilt University, Nashville, 1936-37; Southwestern College, Memphis, Tennessee, 1937-38; Kenyon College, Gambier, Ohio, 1938-40, A.B. 1940. Served in the United States Army, 1941-45. Married Eleanor Lilly Ross in 1940; two children. Taught at the University of North Carolina, Chapel Hill, 1946-67. Since 1967, Professor of English, University of Virginia, Charlottesville. Visiting Lecturer, Indiana University, Bloomington, 1949; University of Chicago, 1951; Kenyon College, 1952-57; Seminar in American Studies, Oxford University, 1955; Ohio State University, Columbus, 1957-63; Harvard University, Cambridge, Massachusetts, 1964. Recipient: Guggenheim Fellowship, 1950; American Academy grant, 1952; Fulbright Fellowship, to France, 1955; O. Henry Award, 1959; Ford Fellowship, for drama, 1960. Member, American Academy, 1969. Address: 1841 Wayside Place, Charlottesville, Virginia 22903, U.S.A.

PUBLICATIONS

Novel

A Woman of Means. New York, Harcourt Brace, and London, Routledge, 1950.

Short Stories

A Long Fourth and Other Stories. New York, Harcourt Brace, 1948; London, Routledge, 1949.
The Widows of Thornton. New York, Harcourt Brace, 1954.
Happy Families Are All Alike: A Collection of Stories. New York, McDowell Obolensky, 1959; London, Macmillan, 1960.
Miss Leonora When Last Seen and 15 Other Stories. New York, Obolensky, 1963.
The Collected Stories of Peter Taylor. New York, Farrar Straus, 1969.
In the Miro District and Other Stories. New York, Knopf, and London, Chatto and Windus, 1977.

Uncollected Short Story

"The Old Forest," in *Prize Stories 1980: The O. Henry Awards*, edited by William Abrahams. New York, Doubleday, 1980.

Plays

Tennessee Day in St. Louis (produced Gambier, Ohio, 1956). New York, Random House, 1957.
A Stand in the Mountains (produced Abingdon, Virginia, 1971). Published in *Kenyon Review* (Gambier, Ohio), 1965.
Presences: Seven Dramatic Pieces. Boston, Houghton Mifflin, 1973.

Other

Editor, with Robert Penn Warren and Robert Lowell, *Randall Jarrell 1914-1965.* New York, Farrar Straus, 1967.

*

Critical Study: *Peter Taylor* by Albert J. Griffith, New York, Twayne, 1970.

* * *

Peter Taylor is part of the literary phenomena called the Southern Renaissance. In particular, his art springs from the same Middle Tennessee source that fed the New Criticism, Fugitive-Agrarianism of Ransom, Tate, Warren, Davidson, Lytle, and others. In common with his lustrous peers, Taylor delights in irony; he has superbly mastered his chosen art form; he has an acute consciousness of time, the presentness of the past, change, and the problem of identity; he is intensely aware of man's inevitable involvement in the subtleties and complexities of evil. Also like his peers, he has a keen sense of being deeply rooted to a place and its traditional values, but he is unique in being more intensely a Tennessean than any of his fellows and in choosing to express life's tensions entirely through the polite manners of Tennessee's gentle class. Tennessee becomes the very *modus operandi* of all his fiction, providing him with a set of manners from which to read and reveal character, with a literal setting and atmosphere for his actors, and with a staple symbol for ordering time, change, and chaos into meaning. Tennessee is the metaphor at the center of his universe.

Tennessee is time, and time is the central theme of all Taylor's works from "A Long Fourth" to "Tennessee Day in St. Louis," from "Venus, Cupid, Folly, and Time" to "Miss Leonora When Last Seen." Time is change measured from a fixed point in space, in character, or in social function. Time is also chance and chaos operating in a given place. Time is the erratic element against which man posits his will and control. Yet time is half man-made, a created part from which the whole is known, an artifical arrestment within movement, an artful ordering before new chaos. Whatever else time is, it is always betrayal.

Basic to Taylor's theme is the concept of role playing as the mark of man's personal as well as mankind's collective identity (civilization). *Theatrum mundi* concepts are as much in evidence in Taylor's novel as in his dramas and short stories where typically the tensions are drawn between acceptance or rejection of a role, between fidelity to or betrayal of a role, between knowledge or ignorance of the role and its relation to ultimate reality.

Roles are half the chancy doings and undoings of time; half the work of man. Within the circumference of chance are the roles one is offered, but the choice of role and the skill with which it is played are man's doing, outside but in time. A role can not be developed except through conventions, traditions, defined rules, arbitrary assigning of values, and the practice of manners. Man develops the role, ascribes to it values relative to some conception of the whole, learns its conventions, and plays it with whatever skill he may possess. Thus manners are the measure of man and their change is the measure of time. Taylor is mainly interested in the manners of those controlled, gentle, doomed people who play roles with the skill and conviction of artists who believe life imitates art.

For these people, identity is the role one plays. In a static society the roles are most clearly understood, the art of playing is most thoroughly appreciated, and the manners that express the role are the most subtly polished. Life in such societies can fully imitate art and maintain the illusion that art is reality. Life becomes ceremonies, rituals, traditions, manners, a clearly defined function relative to the whole. (The whole, for Taylor, is represented by the Southern family and all its extensive connections.) Like his great mentor Henry James, Taylor gives us brilliant portraits of such ladies and gentlemen who knowingly find and maintain their identity through conformation of self to the artful playing of a role. Literary descendents of James's Isabel Archer are Helen Ruth, "A Wife of Nashville," the other wives in "A Long Fourth," "Cookie," *Tennessee Day in St. Louis*, and "Death of a Kinsman," the uncle in "The Other Times," the bachelor brother in "Heads of Houses," the young boy searching for his role in "Promise of Rain," and the old couple in "Venus, Cupid, Folly, and Time," the only grotesques in all of Peter Taylor's work. But the maintenance of identity is no easy matter, because Tennessee is no longer a relatively static society and art is illusion and time the final reality. Reality is change and chance, forever making obsolete old roles and giving opportunity for new ones. The old role is betrayed for the new, or if one clings faithfully to the old role, it is betrayed by time making it irrelevant to the whole—functionless, useless, a curiosity from the past, unappreciated and misunderstood by the very society which originally created it. Thus, either way, time, for men, is betrayal, inevitable immersion in evil and knowledge, inescapable like original sin.

Such is man's doom in Taylor's world: betray or be betrayed. Only those flexible enough—one suspects that Taylor would say also those who are opportunists and disloyal enough—are the fittest for survival. But the civilized voice, the gentle voice, can not fail to mourn properly the nearly extinct American swan who sings most beautifully near death. Thus Taylor, as cold-eyed and realistic as he is, can not fail to mourn the art that time betrays and makes known most clearly its beauty just before its extinction. Taylor's most successful stories are concerned with gentle people who, having accepted and played a role with utmost skill, find their role is no longer wanted or understood and thus have no place to be themselves without self betrayal, yet they cling bravely and faithfully to the values of their identity and salvage what little they can from time's chaos. Such a one is Miss Leonora in "Miss Leonora When Last Seen" who is forced by "progress" into an orbit of no place and no time, assuming the outward, but for her meaningless, appearance modernism prescribes—rootless, chic, dyed, and painted—but held inevitably to a point in place and time to which she can never return. Another is Munsie in "What You Hear from 'Em?" Her role as one of the elect once unified public and private life. As black mother of a white family, as staunch preserver of the true wealth of human love and respect for the individual, as responsible citizen, she was a lady. She knew her role well and played it with utmost art that neglected no ceremony, no care, no ritual, no understood manner until time betrayed her private concrete life into a hopeless abstraction and her public life into a comic and degraded caricature of her race.

As artist, particularly as short story writer, Taylor too has accepted his role and played it with utmost skill. He apparently conceives of his role as that of awakener to the ironic beauty of illusion and the awful chaos of reality. He is also the recorder of change within the constancy of change, and, like his characters, practices such art that would freeze time for a moment so we may be more keenly aware of what is passing and about to pass. He would give order to change itself so we may see it in all its universality and individuality, its concreteness and abstraction, its manner and meaning, its surface and interior. Part of his role, too, is as elegist, most clearly seen in his skillful modulation of voices, always intelligent, always a little ironic, never so clever as those James employs, but infinitely more gentle and sad, speaking just at the point before full awareness of losses calls for utmost control. Full awareness and utmost control are left for Taylor and the reader.

—Robert L. Welker

TENNANT, Emma (Christina). British. Born in London, 20 October 1937. Educated at St. Paul's Girls' School, London. Has one son and two daughters. Travel correspondent, *Queen*, London, 1963; features editor, *Vogue*, London, 1966. Editor, *Bananas*, London, 1975-78. Agent: Gillon Aitken Ltd., 17 Belgrave Place, London, S.W.1. Address: 78 Elgin Crescent, London W.11, England.

PUBLICATIONS

Novels

The Colour of Rain (as Catherine Aydy). London, Weidenfeld and Nicolson, 1964.
The Time of the Crack. London, Cape, 1973; as *The Crack*, London, Penguin, 1978.
The Last of the Country House Murders. London, Cape, 1974; New York, Nelson, 1976.
Hotel de Dream. London, Gollancz, 1976.
The Bad Sister. London, Gollancz, and New York, Coward McCann, 1978.
Wild Nights. London, Cape, 1979; New York, Harcourt Brace, 1980.
Alice Fell. London, Cape, 1980.

Uncollected Short Stories

"Mrs. Ragley," in *Listener* (London), 1973.
"Mrs. Barratt's Ghost," in *New Statesman* (London), 28 December 1973.
"Philomela," in *Bananas*, edited by Tennant. London, Quartet-Blond and Briggs, 1977.
"The Bed That Mick Built," in *New Stories 2*, edited by Derwent May and Alexis Lykiard. London, Arts Council, 1977.
"Cupboard Love," in *New Stories 4*, edited by Elaine Feinstein and Fay Weldon. London, Hutchinson, 1979.
"Tortoise-Shell Endpapers," in *Time Out* (London), 21 December 1979.

Other

The Boggart (juvenile). London, Granada, 1980.

Editor, *Bananas*. London, Quartet-Blond and Briggs, 1977.
Editor, *Saturday Night Reader*. London, W.H. Allen, 1979.

* * *

With six novels published in rapid succession since 1973, Emma Tennant has established herself as one of the leading British exponents of "new fiction." This does not mean that she is an imitator of either the French *nouveaux romanciers* or the American post-modernists, although her work reveals an indebtedness to the methods and preoccupations of some of the latter. Like them, she employs parody and rewriting, is interested in the fictiveness of fiction, appropriates some science-fiction conventions, and exploits the possibilities of generic dislocation and mutation, especially the blending of realism and fantasy. Yet, although parallels can be cited and influences suggested, her work is strongly individual, the product of an intensely personal, even idiosyncratic, attempt to create an original type of highly imaginative fiction.

The first novel she published under her own name is *The Time of the Crack*. This futuristic fable about an ever-widening crack in the riverbed of the Thames, leading to the partial destruction of London and eventually to the breaking-off of the entire south of England and its Atlantis-like disappearance under the sea, is a fusion of black farce, wide-ranging satire, and apocalyptic vision. One reviewer described it as "Lewis Carroll technique applied to H.G. Wells material," but other names suggest themselves even more strongly, notably Orwell and Waugh. Like *Nineteen Eighty-Four, The Time of the Crack* is, in its bizarre way, a "condition of England" novel, projecting onto the immediate future current obsessions with decline and fall, and literalizing the metaphor of national disintegration. Stylistically, the book is characterized by a satirical panache recalling Waugh's early period, as Tennant mercilessly caricatures many aspects of contemporary society.

In 1973 *The Time of the Crack* seemed an original novel of great promise. Since then, with the changes in direction and emphasis of her work, critics have disagreed about whether these developments represent a fulfilment of that potential or a regrettable misuse of considerable talent. The comedy and satire of *The Time of the Crack*, together with its panoramic sweep and its visionary quality, have gradually given way to work narrower in focus, more intense, more introspective, more explicitly serious. There has been a gain in the sheer virtuosity of her writing, but there has also been a loss—especially of elements that made *The Time of the Crack* so immediately enjoyable and impressive.

Her next novel, *The Last of the Country House Murders*, is also set in the near future—Britain after the Revolution—and in its oblique way is another "condition of England" novel. Again like Orwell, Tennant extrapolates from the present a possible picture of the future, but what makes this novel so different from other dystopias is her ingenious fusion of the novel of pessimistic prophecy with an amusing parodistic reworking of the country-house brand of detective fiction. Indeed, the book increasingly focuses on the small group of peculiar, virtually caricature figures who arrive at Woodiscombe Manor to participate in the murder mystery planned by the government as a tourist attraction; the wider social and national issues become more marginal than in *The Time of the Crack*. The result is bizarre comedy, replete with the eccentricities, foibles, and oddities that recur throughout her *oeuvre*.

Eccentricity also pervades the small hotel that provides the setting for *Hotel de Dream*, in which the dreams and fantasies of the few residents, one of whom is a romantic novelist, play a much more important part than the framework of waking reality. Reality itself dissolves into fantasy and vice versa, and the various dreams and fictions merge with one another to create a super-reality of the collective unconscious, in which the dreamers acquire new identities and the romantic novelist's imaginary characters become as real as their creator. While the book is certainly not lacking in the weird humour of her two previous books, and actually abounds in the grotesque, there is a shift away from satirical comedy in favour of psychological fantasy, from a broad perspective to a closed world. Even so, Tennant still provides a tangentially symbolic comment on the "condition of England" issue through her characters and their dream-selves.

In both *The Last of the Country House Murders* and *Hotel de Dream*, Tennant plays self-consciously with novelistic conventions, but in *The Bad Sister*, another futuristic novel (it opens and ends in 1986), she attempts something much more daring and ambitious—some would say foolhardy. She models the entire book very closely on a literary masterpiece, Hogg's *Confessions of a Justified Sinner*. While setting her novel in the present and locating only part of it in Scotland, she adheres to Hogg's highly original structure, adopts some of the main features of his plot, and retains his embodiment of the Devil, Gil-Martin, though in a peripheral role. However, she does alter the sex of the main characters, the equivalent of the Justified Sinner being Jane Wild and her evil genius being Meg rather than Gil-Martin. This change allows Tennant to introduce the subject of feminism and the contemporary phenomenon of female urban guerrillas, but the main focus is not social or political but psychological—the split personality of Jane under the influence of the obsessional Meg. Like Hogg, Tennant is concerned with human duality, fanaticism, the subjectivity of reality, and the possibility of possession, but she interprets these in a contemporary context, developing the theme of the schizoid nature of modern woman.

If *The Bad Sister* is imaginatively claustrophobic, her two subsequent novels, *Wild Nights* and *Alice Fell*, are even more so, the dividing line between reality and fantasy being increasingly blurred and ambiguous. In *Wild Nights*, for example, the child-narrator presents a vision of the world controlled by the imagination rather than reason, in which magic and enchantment are an integral part of nature. Seasonal symbolism and archetypal images play a vital part, and the action seems timeless and placeless despite being located in postwar Scotland and England. For the most part, the relatively few characters in this closed world are strange, eccentric beings, more mythical than social. *Alice Fell* is strikingly similar to *Wild Nights* in a number of these respects, despite the differences that arise from it being a third-person narration. Tennant sustains the obsessive visionary quality of both novels by brilliant and evocative writing, but she does so at a price. In moving so far from *The Time of the Crack*, she has sacrificed some of her most attractive qualities as a novelist.

—Peter Lewis

TENNANT, Kylie. Australian. Born in Manly, New South Wales, 12 March 1912. Educated at Brighton College, Manly; University of Sydney, 1931. Married Lewis C. Rodd in 1932 (died, 1979); one daughter and one son (deceased). Full-time writer, 1935-59; worked as journalist, publisher's reader, literary adviser, and editor, 1959-69; resumed full-time writing career, 1969. Life Patron, Fellowship of Australian Writers; Member, Commonwealth Literary Fund Advisory Board, 1961-73. Recipient: S.H. Prior Memorial Prize, 1935, 1941; Australian Literary Society Gold Medal, 1941; Commonwealth Jubilee Stage Prize, 1951. Officer, Order of Australia, 1980. Address: Cliff View, via Shipley, Blackheath, New South Wales 2785, Australia.

PUBLICATIONS

Novels

Tiburon. Sydney, Bulletin Press, 1935.
Foveaux. London, Gollancz, 1939.
The Battlers. London, Gollancz, and New York, Macmillan, 1941.
Ride on Stranger. New York, Macmillan, and London, Gollancz, 1943.
Time Enough Later. New York, Macmillan, 1943; London, Macmillan, 1945.
Lost Haven. New York, Macmillan, 1946; London, Macmillan, 1947.
The Joyful Condemned. New York, St. Martin's Press, and London, Macmillan, 1953; complete version, as *Tell Morning This*, Sydney and London, Angus and Robertson, 1968.
The Honey Flow. London, Macmillan, and New York, St. Martin's Press, 1956.

Short Stories

Ma Jones and the Little White Cannibals. London, Macmillan, 1967.

Uncollected Short Stories

"A Bargain," in *Coast to Coast 1941*, edited by Cecil Mann. Sydney, Angus and Robertson, 1941.
"Foster Child," in *Tales by Australians*, edited by Edith M. Fry. London, British Authors' Press, n.d.
"The Face of Despair," in *Australia Writes*, edited by T. Inglis Moore. Melbourne, Cheshire, 1953.
"Eight-Hour Day," in *Australian Idiom*, edited by H.P. Heseltine. Melbourne, Chesire, 1963.
"The Antagonists," in *Summer's Tales 1*, edited by Kylie Tennant. London, Macmillan, 1964.
"The Cool Man," in *The Cool Man and Other Contemporary Stories by Australian Authors*. Sydney and London, Angus and Robertson, 1973.

Plays

John o' the Forest and Other Plays (juvenile). London, Macmillan, 1950.
Tether a Dragon. Sydney, Associated General Publications, 1952.
The Bells of the City and Other Plays (juvenile). London, Macmillan, 1955.
The Bushrangers' Christmas Eve and Other Plays (juvenile). Melbourne, Macmillan, 1959.

Other

Australia: Her Story: Notes on a Nation. London, Macmillan, and New York, St. Martin's Press, 1953; revised edition, London, Pan, 1964, 1971.

Long John Silver: The Story of the Film. Sydney, Associated General Publications, 1953; London, Robertson and Mullens, 1954.
The Development of the Australian Novel. Canberra, Commonwealth Literary Fund, 1958.
All the Proud Tribesmen (juvenile). London, Macmillan, 1959; New York, St. Martin's Press, 1960.
Speak You So Gently (travel). London, Gollancz, 1959.
Trail Blazers of the Air. Melbourne, Macmillan, 1965; London, Macmillan, and New York, St. Martin's Press, 1966.
The Australian Essay, with L.C. Rodd. Melbourne, Cheshire, 1968.
Evatt: Politics and Justice (biography). Sydney and London, Angus and Robertson, 1970.
The Man on the Headland (biography). Sydney, Angus and Robertson, 1971; London, Angus and Robertson, 1973.

Editor, *Great Stories of Australia 1-7.* London, Macmillan, and New York, St. Martin's Press, 1963-66.
Editor, *Summer's Tales 1* and *2.* London, Macmillan, and New York, St. Martin's Press, 1964-65.

*

Manuscript Collection: Australian National Library, Canberra.

Critical Studies: review by Frank Swinnerton, in *The Observer* (London), 5 January 1941; Richard Church, in *John O'London's*, 10 January 1941; M.C.R., in *Washington* (D.C.) *Star*, 10 August 1941; Ralph Thomson, in *New York Times*, 11 August 1941; Edwin Muir, in *The Listener* (London), 25 March 1943; *An Introduction to Australian Fiction* by Colin Roderick, Sydney, Angus and Robertson, 1950; "The Novels of Kylie Tennant" by Dorothy Auchterlonie, in *Meanjin 4* (Melbourne), 1953; "The Tragi-Comedies of Kylie Tennant," in *Southerly 1* (Sydney), 1957, and *Social Patterns in Australian Literature*, Sydney, Angus and Robertson, 1971, both by T. Inglis Moore; *The Novels of Kylie Tennant* by Margaret Dick, Adelaide, Rigby, 1966 (includes bibliography).

* * *

Kylie Tennant is an outstanding figure in the Australian literary scene. Versatile, original, with a strong creative flow, she has produced plays, history, biography, poetry, travel, and criticism, but primarily she is a novelist.

Her range is wide, her view of existence complex. High-spirited, humorous, with a pervading sense of the comic cross-purposes of the way life is lived, she combines a delighted appreciation of human idiosyncrasy with an open-eyed acceptance of man's innate destructiveness; affirms the value of life in the face of an ironic perception of the basic futility of the human predicament; uses the imagination of a poet to praise the prosaic and celebrate the commonplace.

When her first book, *Tiburon*, appeared she was hailed in some quarters as a social realist and it is true that there is an element of social challenge in all her work: politics, bureaucracy, education, law are derided with a good humour that did not in her early days as a writer save her from considerable backlash of indignation. Yet her sense of the intractability of human nature prevents her from supposing that a change in society would eradicate human perversity. Kylie Tennant, in fact, refuses to be pigeon-holed.

Certain themes recur—the instinctive against the civilised, the value of the outcast and the reject, the country against the city. The country has always been a refuge for her. Her spirits rise to the sights and sounds and smells of the bush, and her evocation of the Australian landscape in *The Battlers, Lost Haven*, and *The Honey Flow* are unsurpassed. Yet her feeling for the time she lives in insists that for good or ill our age is centred in cities. A line joining the one with the other is the axis on which her writing turns, preserving an almost perfect balance between the two.

Foveaux, Ride on Stranger, Tell Morning This together create a sense of Sydney that reflects the corruption of city life, the raffishness, crime, struggle, and despair that underlie the fine edifices of law and respectable custom. Only the gay comedy *Time Enough Later* adds a wholesome, softer note to the grim and grimy city symphony.

Each of Kylie Tennant's books is an exploration of an aspect of reality—a search for meaning and significance in life; yet her approach is pragmatic, her immediate attention directed outwards: her imagination needs firm roots in the actual. Before beginning a novel, she spends long periods immersed in the kind of life she means to represent—travelling for months with the unemployed along the long roads of Australia before writing *The Battlers*, living in a slum in Surry Hills before *Foveaux*, working on boat-building before *Lost Haven*, even contriving to be sent to gaol before *Tell Morning This.*

Her implication in many different ways of life gives her books a generously varied texture, but the effect is far from documentary. Each is a living world, seen in a tragi-comic perspective that is this writer's peculiar stamp: her mode is comedy, but her strength lies in the breadth of her vision and in her ability to handle a dynamic and complex system of relationships with vitality and freedom.

—Margaret Dick

THEROUX, Paul (Edward). American. Born in Medford, Massachusetts, 10 April 1941. Educated at Medford High School; University of Maine, Orono, 1959-60; University of Massachusetts, Amherst, B.A. in English 1963. Married Anne Castle in 1967; two sons. Lecturer, University of Urbino, 1963; Soche Hill College, Limbe, Malawi, 1963-65; Makerere University, Kampala, Uganda, 1965-68; University of Singapore, 1968-71; Writer-in-Residence, University of Virginia, Charlottesville, 1972. Recipient: *Playboy* award, 1971, 1977, 1979; American Academy award, 1977; Whitbread Award, 1978. D.Litt.: Tufts University, Medford, Massachusetts. Fellow, Royal Society of Literature, and Royal Geographical Society. Address: 35 Elsynge Road, London SW18 2HR, England.

PUBLICATIONS

Novels

Waldo. Boston, Houghton Mifflin, 1967; London, Bodley Head, 1968.
Fong and the Indians. Boston, Houghton Mifflin, 1968; London, Hamish Hamilton, 1976.
Girls at Play. Boston, Houghton Mifflin, and London, Bodley Head, 1969.
Murder in Mount Holly. London, Ross, 1969.
Jungle Lovers. Boston, Houghton Mifflin, and London, Bodley Head, 1971.
Saint Jack. London, Bodley Head, and Boston, Houghton Mifflin, 1973.
The Black House. London, Hamish Hamilton, and Boston, Houghton Mifflin, 1974.
The Family Arsenal. London, Hamish Hamilton, and Boston, Houghton Mifflin, 1976.
Picture Palace. London, Hamish Hamilton, and Boston, Houghton Mifflin, 1978.
The Mosquito Coast. London, Hamish Hamilton, 1981.

Short Stories

Sinning with Annie and Other Stories. Boston, Houghton Mifflin, 1972; London, Hamish Hamilton, 1975.

The Consul's File. London, Hamish Hamilton, and Boston, Houghton Mifflin, 1977.
World's End and Other Stories. London, Hamish Hamilton, and Boston, Houghton Mifflin, 1980.

Play

Screenplay: *Saint Jack*, with Peter Bogdanovich and Howard Sackler, 1979.

Other

V.S. Naipaul: An Introduction to His Work. London, Deutsch, and New York, Africana, 1972.
The Great Railway Bazaar: By Train Through Asia. London, Hamish Hamilton, and Boston, Houghton Mifflin, 1975.
A Christmas Card (juvenile). London, Hamish Hamilton, and Boston, Houghton Mifflin, 1978.
The Old Patagonian Express: By Train Through the Americas. London, Hamish Hamilton, and Boston, Houghton Mifflin, 1979.
London Snow (juvenile). London, Hamish Hamilton, and Boston, Houghton Mifflin, 1980.

*

Paul Theroux comments:

Both in my fiction and non-fiction I have tried to write about the times in which I have lived. Although I have been resident in various countries for the past 20 years, and these countries have been the settings for my books, I consider myself an American writer. I have a strong homing instinct.

* * *

Over the past decade, Paul Theroux has emerged as a major writer of novels, short fiction, and travel reportage. His fiction ranges over England, America, and many foreign settings, and it focuses on complex relationships between people and places. His travel books (*The Great Railway Bazaar*, *The Old Patagonia Express*) are vivid, minutely detailed, and ironically elegant. Theroux's fiction reflects the same qualities.

Some of the novels echo Joseph Conrad and V.S. Naipaul, centering on Westerners caught in remote and alien settings—*Girls at Play*, *Jungle Lovers*, *Saint Jack*, and the short stories in *The Consul's File*. An important theme is the stranger who can discover himself only in the strangeness of alien society. This appears also in *Fong and the Indians* but is most elaborately developed in *Saint Jack*. It recurs in the macabre *The Black House*, in which an Englishman must come home to discover a ghostly "foreigner." It appears in transmuted form in *The Family Arsenal*, in which IRA terrorists (led by an American) are the strangers, and London is the "foreign land." If Jack in *Saint Jack* is a Dostoevskian hoodlum-saint, a pander peddling material salvation, the bombers of *The Family Arsenal* are a parody of close community, offering not love and comfort but violence and death to the unsaved world of London.

Theroux has mastered the art of exact observation and cultivated his memory for sights, voices, and sensations. As Maude Coffin Pratt, the central character in *Picture Palace*, says of her photography: "art should require no instrument but memory, the pleasurable fear of hunching in a dark room and feeling the day's hot beauty lingering in the house." The drama in Theroux's fiction often arises in the complexity of his characters' sensibilities and in the sexual and spiritual desires they are driven to express.

Theroux's novels often revolve around physical violence—revolutions or civil wars in Africa or Asia, terrorism, casual assault—but also involve the violence of suppressed, warped, or mistaken desires. Frustrated desires lead to sadism, which leads inexorably to masochism. The colonialist who beats his servant keeps a closetful of chains and whips to be used on himself. Theroux opens these closets in England and America as well as in Malaysia. Maude Coffin Pratt of *Picture Palace* prepares for a 50-year retrospective photography show and reveals the single image that has warped her life—her thwarted incestuous desire for her brother, who preferred their sister. Alfred Munday of *The Black House* returns from haunted Africa to find a succubus in an English country house.

The characters Theroux depicts most sharply are complexly folded. His fiction shows us the disguises and distractions which shield them from the world. Hood, the sharply observant, ironic American terrorist of *The Family Arsenal*, sees his world turn alien:

> For every one who used the city as an occasion to perform, a thousand chose it as a place of concealment. In its depths bombs were stifled. His own was local, personal, a family matter; it had not been heard here.... He had thought the world was his to move in, an extension of his own world. But he had seen it grow unfamiliar, and smaller, and he was not moving at will.

Theroux's novels are urbane, paradoxical, and often comic. They also probe tragic fractures in the modern world and sensibility, in brightly evocative snapshots of foreign places—at home and abroad.

—William J. Schafer

THOMAS, Audrey (Grace). American; Canadian Landed Immigrant. Born in Binghamton, New York, 17 November 1935. Educated at Smith College, Northampton, Massachusetts, B.A. 1957; University of British Columbia, Vancouver, M.A. in English, 1963. Married Ian Thomas in 1958 (divorced); three daughters. Lived in Kumasi, Ghana, 1964-66. Recipient: *Atlantic* "Firsts" Award, 1965; Canada Council grant, 1969, 1971, 1972, 1974, Senior Arts grant, 1974, 1977, 1979. Address: R.R. 2, Galiano Island, British Columbia VON 1PO, Canada.

PUBLICATIONS

Novels

Mrs. Blood. Indianapolis, Bobbs Merrill, 1967.
Munchmeyer, and Prospero on the Island. Indianapolis, Bobbs Merrill, 1972.
Songs My Mother Taught Me. Indianapolis, Bobbs Merrill, 1973.
Blown Figures. Vancouver, Talonbooks, 1974; New York, Knopf, 1975.
Latakia. Vancouver, Talonbooks, 1979.

Short Stories

Ten Green Bottles. Indianapolis, Bobbs Merrill, 1967.
Ladies and Escorts. Ottawa, Oberon Press, 1977.

Plays

Radio Plays: *Once Your Submarine Cable Is Gone...*, 1973; *Mrs. Blood*, from her own novel, 1975.

*

Manuscript Collection: University of British Columbia Library, Vancouver.

Audrey Thomas comments:

I write primarily about women—modern women with their particular dreams, delights, despairs. Also how these women relate to men and the terrible things we do to one another in the name of love. I am also interested in what happens to a person set down in a strange city or country, without a familiar environment, friends, or job to define him, when he must ask serious questions. Madness, too, interests me, and the delicate balance between sanity and madness.

I like to tell a good tale, and at the same time I like to make the reader work. I assume my readers will want to run a bit for their money.

* * *

Audrey Thomas has demonstrated in her quasi-autobiographical fictions how small the territory of incident need be in order for the writer to create a continent of psychological complexity. Such categories as novel, novella, and short story are not easy to apply to Thomas's work. The short stories in *Ten Green Bottles* are closely inter-related. All of them are told by an unhappy female who, whether as a girl or a woman, appears to be the same person, so that in the end the book takes on in one's mind the character of a sequence of psychologically linked incidents. The two novellas in *Munchmeyer* and *Prospero on the Island* are not in fact separate works; they are linked by the fact that *Munchmeyer* (itself a kind of mirror work in which it is hard to tell what is meant as plot and what is the novelist-hero's fantasizing) is presented as the novel that has been written by Miranda, the narrator in *Prospero on the Island*, and being discussed by her with "Prospero," an elderly painter friend who lives in retreat on the same British Columbian island. And the two novels *Mrs. Blood* and *Songs My Mother Taught Me* are in turn constructed within loose frameworks, so that structurally there is not a great difference between the groups of inter-related stories and the highly episodic novels.

It soon becomes evident that the structural principle of Thomas's fictions is one in which the psychological patterns take precedence over the aesthetic or self-consciously formal. This fact is reinforced when one considers the content of the works. The experience in them is, in merely physical terms, limited and largely repetitious; it also runs fairly closely parallel to Thomas's own life. She was born and brought up in upper New York state, spent some time in England and in Ghana, and in recent years has been dividing her life between Vancouver and the nearby islands of the Gulf of Georgia. These are precisely the areas covered by her stories and novels, and it is impossible when reading them not to recognize that here one is on as tantalizing a frontier between the autobiographical and the invented as that in Proust's great work.

In fictional terms, however, it is more interesting to observe the fact that the central persona of the books appears to be the same, yet treated unchronologically, since the recently published work, *Songs My Mother Taught Me*, deals in the form of a rather shapelessly flowing narrative with the experiences of childhood, which recur as memories in the earlier works. *Mrs. Blood*, which harrowingly evokes a somewhat perilous pregnancy in West Africa, also incorporates the persona's sentimental adventures in England, while it is the novella *Prospero on the Island*, actually published between these two works, that brings one up to date with the persona-now-turned-novelist reflecting on the creative present to which these pasts contribute. As in the case of the novella *Munchmeyer* (the one wholly fictional item), it is hard to tell when the actuality of the author's life merges into the invented narration.

Constant throughout is the fact of suffering, and an acute awareness of suffering's psychological results—its power to distort our perceptions and our memories. A recurrent situation brings us to the appalling borderland—present up to now either as actual experience or as memory in every work of Thomas—between sanity and madness, always in the form of the madhouse where the adolescent heroine-narrator comes of emotional age; this is the mental deflowering that precedes the loss of physical virginity. Here, in its most concentrated form, appears the terror that haunts all Audrey Thomas's fiction; yet the essential quality of her work is not in the nightmare that shadows her psychologically complex characters and their inevitably imperfect grasp of experience, but rather in the precarious equilibrium between fear and the joy of existence which so intermittently they grasp.

—George Woodcock

TINDALL, Gillian (Elizabeth). British. Born in London, 4 May 1938. Educated at Lady Margaret Hall, Oxford, B.A. (honours) in English, M.A. Married Richard Lansdown in 1963; one son. Regular contributor to the *New Standard* and *New Society*, both London. Recipient: Mary Elgin Prize, 1970; Maugham Award, 1972. Agent: Curtis Brown Ltd., 1 Craven Hill, London W2 3EP, England.

PUBLICATIONS

Novels

No Name in the Street. London, Cassell, 1959; as *When We Had Other Names*, New York, Morrow, 1960.
The Water and the Sound. London, Cassell, 1961; New York, Morrow, 1962.
The Edge of the Paper. London, Cassell, 1963.
The Youngest. London, Secker and Warburg, 1967; New York, Walker, 1968.
Someone Else. London, Hodder and Stoughton, and New York, Walker, 1969.
Fly Away Home. London, Hodder and Stoughton, and New York, Walker, 1971.
The Traveller and His Child. London, Hodder and Stoughton, 1975.
The Intruder. London, Hodder and Stoughton, 1979.

Short Stories

Dances of Death: Short Stories on a Theme. London, Hodder and Stoughton, and New York, Walker, 1973.
The China Egg and Other Stories. London, Hodder and Stoughton, 1981.

Other

The Israeli Twins (juvenile). London, Cape, 1963.
A Handbook on Witches. London, Barker, 1965; New York, Atheneum, 1966.
The Born Exile: George Gissing. London, Temple Smith, and New York, Harcourt Brace, 1974.
The Fields Beneath: The History of One London Village (on Kentish Town). London, Temple Smith, 1977.

Translator, *Number One*, by René Masson. London, Hutchinson, 1964.

* * *

The women in Gillian Tindall's books have made a trade: in exchange for the insulation and pre-packaged lives that men present to them—and which they unthinkingly take—women give away the chance for a recognizable self. And they hardly notice this lack of independent personality, so smoothly and innocuously does daily life flow, until a violent event—a husband killed in a car crash

(*Someone Else*); a deformed baby murdered by the mother (*The Youngest*); the Six-Day Israeli War (*Fly Away Home*)—precipitates a search for the self deferred. "But this fragmentation would not have happened...if I had an inner personality...a self to fight against things and actions" (*Fly Away Home*). The nature of the quest involves an exploration of relationships, backward to mother, father and sister, and forward to husband and children.

Briefly, as an uncommitted young girl in Paris in the first two novels, the Tindall woman explores non-familial relationships with a personality that is almost a stereotype of youthful *sang-froid.* Her self-centeredness allows her to experience her first love affair, a painful miscarriage, the discovery of her French lover's homosexuality (*No Name in the Street*) and a presumed incestuous relationship (*The Water and the Sound*) with resiliency, courage and resourcefulness. But no sooner does she marry and beget children, as she does in the later books, than her spirit and enterprise dissipate.

By the first of the Grown-Woman novels, *The Edge of the Paper*, the wife, Meg, is completely powerless. She has married Roy King, a sadist, whose name symbolizes his place in the family matrix. At first he seems the perfect dream father-figure to Meg: rich, attractive, in command. But soon he is revealed as the ultimate destroyer, a man "who can only feel secure by beating someone else down." King is a psychotic, but he is only the extreme of a husband like Loic in *Someone Else* whose death reveals to his wife, Joanna, her own absorption into the strong personality of her husband. "Years ago she had transferred to Loic all the trust she had once placed in parent or deity." During her marriage her own responses atrophy and when Loic is killed she confronts the tragedy like a child, allowing other men to shield and protect her from bereavement.

This is the point to which the principal character always comes: a potentially dynamic, often creative woman finds herself living out a pattern others have set for her. Tindall structures the novels so that fairly early in the book one dramatic event tears the orderly pattern and out of necessity the woman begins her self-discovery. This movement results in a series of insights which the heroine interprets for herself and for the reader: "I began to realize again...how utterly real and inescapable the ties of blood and kin are, of race and class, in spite of the relative unimportance they may have in day-to-day life." The novels' undramatic style is often juxtaposed against strangely melodramatic plot devices such as abortion, incest, homosexuality, murder, car accidents, and infanticide.

But the author's strength is insight into people and their *milieu*. With the cold eye of her youthful protagonist, Tindall sees through the falsity of the Paris Bohemianism of the 1960's and the contrived artiness of London's TV-advertising-literary life. (Her dissection of fashionable child-raising in *Someone Else* is particularly sharp and fresh.) *Fly Away Home* catches the essential mores, pretensions, and fears of bourgeois French Jews. (She writes about Jews often, with a curious mixture of admiration and revulsion.) *The Youngest* highlights the demolition and renovation of London, which intimates a shifting class structure and the rapid change of the times. Amidst these unstable settings Tindall's woman tries to find a solid center within.

—Gloria Cohen

TINNISWOOD, Peter. British. Born in Liverpool, Lancashire, 21 December 1936. Educated at Sale County Grammar School, 1947-54; University of Manchester, 1954-57, B.A. 1957. Married Patricia Mallen in 1966; three children. Insurance clerk, Vienna, 1957; journalist for *The Star*, Sheffield, 1958-63, *Western Mail*, Cardiff, 1966-69, and *The Echo*, Liverpool, 1967. Recipient: Authors Club award, 1969; Winifred Holtby Prize, 1974; Welsh Arts Council bursary, 1974, and prize, 1975. Fellow, Royal Society of Literature, 1974. Agent: Anthony Sheil Associates Ltd., 1-3 Morwell Street, London WC1B 3AR, England.

PUBLICATIONS

Novels

A Touch of Daniel. London, Hodder and Stoughton, and New York, Doubleday, 1969.
Mog. London, Hodder and Stoughton, 1970.
I Didn't Know You Cared. London, Hodder and Stoughton, 1973.
Except You're a Bird. London, Hodder and Stoughton, 1974.
The Stirk of Stirk. London, Macmillan, 1974.
Shemerelda. London, Hodder and Stoughton, 1981.

Plays

The Investiture (produced Bristol, 1971).
Wilfred (produced London, 1979).
The Day the War Broke Out (produced London, 1981).

Radio Plays: *Hardluck Hall* series, with David Nobbs, 1964; *Sam's Wedding*, 1973; *The Bargeman's Comfort*, 1977; *A Touch of Daniel*, from his own novel, 1977; *The Umpire's Thoughts Regarding a Certain Murder*, 1979; *Jake and Myself*, 1979; *The Siege*, 1979; *A Gifted Child*, 1980; *Home Again* series, 1980; *An Occasional Day*, 1981.

Television Plays: scripts for *That Was the Week That Was* and *Not So Much a Programme* series, with David Nobbs; *Lance at Large* series, with David Nobbs, 1964; *The Signal Box of Grandpa Hudson*, with David Nobbs, 1966; *Never Say Die* series, 1970; *The Rule Book*, 1971; *The Diaries of Stoker Leishman*, 1972; *I Didn't Know You Cared*, 4 series, 1975-79; *Tales from a Long Room* series, 1980.

*

Critical Study: in *The New Review* (London), November 1974.

Peter Tinniswood comments:

I write very short sentences.

And very short paragraphs.

I try to make people laugh. I am a very serious writer, who has a gloomily optimistic outlook on life.

My books about the Brandon family contain all the above qualities.

* * *

Peter Tinniswood's reputation as the funniest novelist of his generation is founded on *A Touch of Daniel, I Didn't Know You Cared*, and *Except You're a Bird*, three interlinked but self-contained novels about the Brandon Family. The Brandons live in the North of England.

The characters in these novels exist, according to their lights, in noisy or muted desperation. Some want to be left alone, some want to chivvy away to get affairs moving. Whether terse or garrulous, their words rise from various mutations of what passes for the working-class heart to register comment on, or frustration at, life's endless capacity for being ordinary. Of course, whether the Brandons, Uncle Mort, Mrs. Partington *et alia* are prepared to accept things as they relentlessly persist, or whether they want them changed, the results are identical. When personalities are stubbed against the protruding end of life's sharp bedstead, when situations get so stultifyingly bad that people cannot see through their own blind and laughable prejudices, they are sometimes driven to dark outposts of expression and go to the kitchen to splash heavily under the cold tap. Sometimes they are driven even further and, in ultimate siberias of being badgered or misunderstood, can only rattle the knife-drawer. It is a crucial part of Tinniswood's invention that his central character, the Brandons' son Carter, caught as he is between his lusty zest for life and his bafflement, between love and the eager pernicketiness of Pat the loved one, gives out as comment on most circumstances an almost invariable "Mm." Tinniswood is a Lancastrian.

His characters don't realise it but what they want (given a fair ration of, say, fried tripe in batter and potato scallops, their bridge rolls and a pickled beetroot or two to go with their black-and-tan beer) is to be spirit. Mr. Brandon once ran away, but came back having got as far as Kensal Green. Mrs. Brandon wants a second honeymoon:

> "Do you fancy a second honeymoon, Les?"
> "No thank you," said Mr. Brandon.
> "Why not?" said Mrs. Brandon.
> "Well, I didn't reckon on much on the first one," said Mr. Brandon. "The breakfasts were a bloody disgrace."
> "There's no use skulking off, Les. I want a definite answer from you. Do you or do you not want a second honeymoon?"
> "No," said Mr. Brandon.
> "Don't prevaricate," said Mrs. Brandon.

Their daughter-in-law Pat gets badly injured in a car accident and Mr. Brandon assesses reality:

> Reality? It's all a bloody cod is reality. If there were such a thing as reality, you wouldn't have that poor lass fighting for her life with tubes sticking out of her.... If there was such a thing as reality, she'd be sitting in a garden with flowering peaches in full bloom and a fountain tinkling into a pond full of lilies and there'd be the buzz of bees and the song of nightingales and beer would only cost fivepence a pint.... If there were such a thing as reality, we'd turn into birds when unpleasantness cropped up and fly off to the sun until it all blew over.

Daniel is the baby begat by Uncle Mort and Auntie Lil when all Uncle Mort was doing was trying to keep warm. The infant is doomed to die, but not before it turns out that to touch him is to have some part of lost life restored. It is here that Tinniswood reaches a controlled audacity of imagination. For Daniel's spirit, moving through all the marvellous laughter, is the spirit of life itself. If that sounds too earnest it is not so in the texts. Carter Brandon carries on conversations with the dead Daniel who becomes his conscience and his goad:

> "What the hell's she on about, Daniel? What's this union she's talking about?"
> "The Amalgamated Society of Unborn Babies and Allied Trades. I'm the general secretary.... We held an emergency meeting in Pat's womb on account of a complaint received by one of our members—to wit, your baby. He said he had information to hand that led him to conclude that he was to be born with less than the agreed rate of grandfathers for the job—to wit, two."

Tinniswood has created for himself a form in which the precisely observed and the fantastic can live side by side and feed off each other. Because of his humour some have failed to see his poetic meaning. His invention is combined with a capacity delicately to amplify the ridiculous in ordinary speech. He has a savouring and loving eye for people's foibles. His knowledge of nature, especially ornithology, permits him to set his action against a changing cyclorama of vividly seen and stated details. Working at language with a fine chisel, he believes in telling a story; and it is obvious that he does not go along with those who think the novel is in crisis. Reading his work, one is on his side.

—John Ormond

TRACY, Honor (Lilbush Wingfield). British. Born in Bury St. Edmunds, Suffolk, 19 October 1913. Educated at the Grove School, Highgate, London, 1925-29. Specialist, Political Warfare (Japan), in London, 1942-45. Assistant Editor, *The Bell*, Dublin, 1946; Paris, Eastern Europe and Japan Correspondent, *The Observer*, London, 1947-48; Dublin Correspondent, *The Sunday Times*, London, 1950. Address: The Well House, St. George's Road, Bickley, Kent, England.

PUBLICATIONS

Novels

The Deserters. London, Methuen, 1954.
The Straight and Narrow Path. London, Methuen, and New York, Random House, 1956.
The Prospects Are Pleasing. London, Methuen, and New York, Random House, 1958.
A Number of Things. London, Methuen, and New York, Random House, 1960.
A Season of Mists. London, Methuen, and New York, Random House, 1961.
The First Day of Friday. London, Methuen, and New York, Random House, 1963.
Men at Work. London, Methuen, 1966; New York, Random House, 1967.
The Beauty of the World. London, Methuen, 1967; as *Settled in Chambers*, New York, Random House, 1968.
The Butterflies of the Province. London, Methuen, and New York, Random House, 1970.
The Quiet End of Evening. London, Eyre Methuen, and New York, Random House, 1972.
In a Year of Grace. London, Eyre Methuen, and New York, Random House, 1975.
The Man from Next Door. London, Hamish Hamilton, and New York, Random House, 1977.
The Ballad of Castle Reef. London, Hamish Hamilton, 1979; New York, Random House, 1980.

Uncollected Short Stories

"A Question of Minority," in *Horizon* (London), March 1944.
"Mr. Solomon Wastes a Rosebud," "Papa Is Dying," "The Ever Rolling Stream," "My Aunt and Ernest Hemingway," "I Am Peter," "A Strange Encounter," "The Connoisseur," in *Lilliput, Queen*, and *Punch* (all in London), and *Harper's Bazaar* (New York), 1944-56.
"The Behavior of Mr. Frumkin," in *Atlantic* (Boston), March 1953.
"Please Respect Our Grief," in *Mademoiselle* (New York), June 1961.
"Via Dolorosa," in *Winter's Tales 22*, edited by James Wright. London, Macmillan, 1976; New York, St. Martin's Press, 1977.

Plays

Radio Plays: *De l'Angleterre; or, Miss Austen Provides a Footnote; The Sorrows of Ireland*, 1967.

Other

Kakemono: A Sketch Book of Post-War Japan. London, Methuen, 1950; New York Coward McCann, 1951.
Mind You, I've Said Nothing: Forays in the Irish Republic. London, Methuen, 1953; Boston, Little Brown, 1955.
Silk Hats and No Breakfast: Notes on a Spanish Journey. London, Methuen, 1957; New York, Random House, 1958.
Spanish Leaves. London, Methuen, and New York, Random House, 1964.
Winter in Castille. London, Eyre Methuen, 1973; New York, Random House, 1974.

Translator, *The Conquest of Violence: An Essay on War and Revolution*, by Barthélemy de Light. London, Routledge, 1937; New York, Dutton, 1938.

*

Honor Tracy comments:

I haven't thought about my work in a general way. Roughly, if something interests, pleases, or amuses me I imagine it may do the same for other people and I try to pass it on. Also, I have an orderly mind, and writing is a sort of tidying up and clarifying of life.

* * *

Toward the end of *A Number of Things* appears a passage that casts light not only on this novel of Honor Tracy's. With necessary modifications it offers illumination that extends its light to most of the other novels of this writer—work intensely comic and, in its own way, intensely sensible. The hero of this novel, a young man named Henry Lamb, has had great success with his first novel; on the basis of this novel, he wins the appointment of roving correspondent for a new liberal publication entitled *Torch*. He is sent to a Caribbean island, to report on the flowering of new black political consciousness; his reports are expected to gratify the liberal prejudices of the magazine he serves. But Henry finds only nonsense rather than wisdom in the island he visits. After a series of farcical adventures, reports of which are deeply disturbing to his enlightened editor, he is deported under humiliating circumstances. He is finally allowed to pay a shore visit to the island of Madeira. He suddenly feels a sense of relief after the exotic nightmare of his Caribbean weeks. Henry's impression of deliverance takes this form: "I am in Europe! he thought. He had, suddenly, a quite vivid new sense of Europe, not as a place for holidays where the people behaved like foreigners, but of something wonderfully precious, that he had had to go all the way to the mindless tropics to discover, something as old as the hills and young as the flowers in the women's baskets." Something—Europe—that Henry had been too ready to discard is kindly restored to him, and Henry is beatifically grateful—grateful even for the prospect of once more having back a job for which he once had had contempt.

Henry Lamb's experience is one that is often retraced in the novels of Tracy. Her books are a celebration of the nonsense in which human beings allow themselves to be immersed and, by indirection at least, a celebration of the sense—dull, tedious, but as reliable as anything human can be—which exists as a criticism of nonsense. But if Tracy is a kind of moralist, she is one who tips her hand very delicately; the bulk of her fictional texture is indeed a reproduction of the follies that seduce persons from the relatively dull life of sense and rationality. Thus, the observer—if not the hero—of *The Straight and Narrow Path* is a dispassionate anthropologist who has come from labors in the Congo for a rest in an Irish village. To his English eyes—English rather than more generally "European" in this novel—the religious customs of the Irish village are no less strange than the primitivism he has been observing in Africa. The visitor observes and reports for the London press the behavior of nuns jumping over fires and assimilates the spectacle to ancient fertility rites practiced the world over. Unwittingly, he has affronted Catholic self-respect, becomes involved in a law-suit, and escapes the consequences of his imprudence only when a simple-minded Irish boy offers the distraction of an apparition of the Virgin. At the end of the novel, the visitor observes a pious procession that includes the only sensible Irishman he has met. Tracy's comment on her hero's discomfiture points up his confusion. "What he had just seen had bereft him of power to think.... Now he saw that the joke was far more complex and ramified than he had supposed, and that it was on him." The hero has been, throughout the novel, an apostle of prudent common sense in a world that is determined to lose itself in the superstition, puritanism, and deference to authority that are—as Tracy usually sees it—the mark of Irishry.

The common note of all Tracy's work, it should be plain, is to shoot folly where it flies. She is the tart enemy of all simplifying 20th-century expectations, and her powers of invention, as she pursues this task, are considerable. In addition to the themes already inspected—which come to the glorification of the wisdom of simple folk, whether in Ireland or the Caribbean—other modern expectations receive lethal arrows from Tracy. The cult of self-realization receives its just due in *A Season of Mists* and *The Butterflies of the Province*; satirical plotting and the justaposition of a raree-show of odd persons demonstrate that there are limits to the pursuit of pleasure and self-esteem. The delusions of the literary life receive their lashing in *Men at Work*; the book tells of the misfortunes of a successful novelist whose vanity and lack of personal scruple make him a sitting target for the sycophants that gather around him. *Settled in Chambers* brings to the English legal profession the same stringent regard that, in *Men at Work*, strips away the pleasing outer integuments of the literary career. There is, in all the novels, a kind of center—a kind of "Europe"—which amounts to a pervasive and yet unobtrusive judgment on the fretful ignorance of human limits that is the self-indulgence of the characters who move through the fiction.

In all the novels there is an electric vitality; the novels never run down. As in following novels, the unending inter-play of Irish fecklessness and English propriety produces rich and charmingly unexpected contrasts. Thus, in *The Prospects Are Pleasing*, the central plot concerns the efforts of a light-headed Irish youth to steal from the English a painting that "morally" should hang in an Irish gallery. Irish madness and English self-righteousness compose a ballet of opposed ideas and manners. This ballet surfaces again in *The Man from Next Door*: a dull English woman allows herself a brief dalliance with an Irish scoundrel who, without any sense of guilt, sees to it that the English woman lands in jail for handling counterfeit money. And *The Ballad of Castle Reef* pits the fox-hunting British resident in Ireland against vacillating Irish constabulary and mindless Irish terrorists. In such novels sense is on the side of neither the Irish nor the staid, habit-encrusted British. Sense, as always, is the possession of a small and select group: Tracy and her understanding readers. One might say that the novels are designed to be read with a glass of sherry in the hand, preferably in the company of persons as basically sensible as Honor Tracy herself.

—Harold H. Watts

TREVOR, William. Pseudonym for William Trevor Cox. Irish. Born in Mitchelstown, County Cork, 24 May 1928. Educated at St. Columba's College, Dublin, 1942-46; Trinity College, Dublin, B.A. 1950. Married Jane Ryan in 1952; two sons. History Teacher, Armagh, Northern Ireland, 1951-53; Art Teacher, Rugby, England, 1953-55; Sculptor, in Somerset, 1955-60; Advertising Copywriter, London, 1960-64. Recipient: *Transatlantic Review* prize, 1964; Hawthornden Prize, 1965; Society of Authors Travelling Fellowship, 1972; Allied Irish Banks Prize, 1976; Heinemann Award, 1976; Whitbread Prize, 1976; Irish Community Prize, 1979; Giles Cooper Award, for radio play, 1981. Member, Irish Academy of Letters. Honorary C.B.E. (Commander, Order of the British Empire), 1977. Address: Stentwood House, Dunkeswell, near Honiton, Devon, England.

PUBLICATIONS

Novels

A Standard of Behaviour. London, Hutchinson, 1958.
The Old Boys. London, Bodley Head, and New York, Viking Press, 1964.

The Boarding-House. London, Bodley Head, and New York, Viking Press, 1965.
The Love Department. London, Bodley Head, 1966; New York, Viking Press, 1967.
Mrs. Eckdorf in O'Neill's Hotel. London, Bodley Head, 1969; New York, Viking Press, 1970.
Miss Gomez and the Brethren. London, Bodley Head, 1971.
Elizabeth Alone. London, Bodley Head, 1973; New York, Viking Press, 1974.
The Children of Dynmouth. London, Bodley Head, 1976; New York, Viking Press, 1977.
Other People's Worlds. London, Bodley Head, 1980; New York, Viking Press, 1981.

Short Stories

The Day We Got Drunk on Cake and Other Stories. London, Bodley Head, 1967; New York, Viking Press, 1968.
Penguin Modern Stories 8, with others. London, Penguin, 1971.
The Ballroom of Romance and Other Stories. London, Bodley Head, and New York, Viking Press, 1972.
The Last Lunch of the Season. London, Covent Garden Press, 1973.
Angels at the Ritz and Other Stories. London, Bodley Head, 1975; New York, Viking Press, 1976.
Lovers of Their Time and Other Stories. London, Bodley Head, 1978; New York, Viking Press, 1979.
The Distant Past. Dublin, Poolbeg Press, 1979.

Uncollected Short Stories

"The Nicest Man in the World," in *Transatlantic Review* (London), Winter 1962.
"Memories of Youghal," in *Transatlantic Review* (London), Summer 1969.
"On Christmas Day," in *The Times* (London), 25 December 1969.
"The Only Story," "The Love of a Good Woman, " and "Alice and George and Isabel," in *The Seventh, Eighth,* and *Ninth Ghost Book,* edited by Rosemary Timperley. London, Barrie and Jenkins, 1971-73.
"Poppy and Alice," in *Encounter* (London), April 1974.
"Autumn Sunshine," in *Winter's Tales 26*, edited by A.D. Maclean. London, Macmillan, 1980; New York, St. Martin's Press, 1981.

Plays

The Elephant's Foot (produced Nottingham, 1965).
The Girl (televised, 1967; produced London, 1968). London, French, 1968.
A Night with Mrs. da Tanka (televised, 1968; produced London, 1972). London, French, 1972.
Going Home (broadcast, 1970; produced London, 1972). London, French, 1972.
The Old Boys, adaptation of his own novel (produced London, 1971). London, Davis Poynter, 1971.
A Perfect Relationship (broadcast, 1973; produced London, 1973). London, Burnham House, 1976.
The 57th Saturday (produced London, 1973).
Marriages (produced London, 1973). London, French, 1973.

Radio Plays: *The Penthouse Apartment*, 1968; *Going Home*, 1970; *The Boarding House*, from his own novel, 1971; *A Perfect Relationship*, 1973; *Scenes from an Album*, 1975; *Attracta*, 1977; *Beyond the Pale*, 1980.

Television Plays: *The Baby-Sitter*, 1965; *Walk's End*, 1966; *The Girl*, 1967; *A Night with Mrs. da Tanka*, 1968; *The Mark-2 Wife*, 1969; *The Italian Table*, 1970; *The Grass Widows*, 1971; *O Fat White Woman*, 1972; *The Schoolroom*, 1972; *Access to the Children*, 1973; *The General's Day*, 1973; *Miss Fanshawe's Story*, 1973; *An Imaginative Woman*, from story by Thomas Hardy, 1973; *Love Affair*, 1974; *Eleanor*, 1974; *Mrs. Acland's Ghosts*, 1975; *The Statue and the Rose*, 1975; *Two Gentle People*, from story by Graham Greene, 1975; *The Nicest Man in the World*, 1976; *Afternoon Dancing*, 1976; *Voices from the Past*, 1976; *Newcomers*, 1976; *The Love of a Good Woman*, from his own story, 1976; *The Girl Who Saw a Tiger*, 1976; *Last Wishes*, 1978; *Another Weekend*, 1978; *Memories*, 1978; *Matilda's England*, 1979; *The Old Curiosity Shop*, from the novel by Dickens, 1979; *Secret Orchards* from works by J.R. Ackerley and Diana Petre, 1980; *The Happy Autumn Fields*, from story by Elizabeth Bowen, 1980; *Elizabeth Alone*, from his own novel, 1981.

Other

Old School Ties (miscellany). London, Lemon Tree Press, 1976.

*

Critical Studies: in *Times Literary Supplement* (London), 5 March 1964, 15 October 1971, and 21 October 1973; by Malcolm Bradbury, in *New Statesman* (London), 3 October 1969; Auberon Waugh, in *Spectator* (London), 16 October 1971; Sean McMahon, in *Irish Press* (Dublin), 6 May 1972 and 13 January 1973; John Broderick, in *Hibernia* (Dublin), 12 May 1972.

* * *

Though he had written some fiction in the 1950's William Trevor's real career as a novelist seemed to spring full-blown, a decade later and in his own late thirties, from his years in an advertising agency. His expert phrasing, his skill with dialogue, his sense of the quirks of human nature may have been fostered there, adapted to the sweet uses of advertisement. But there was no visible foreshadowing of the rich inventiveness, the immensely effective observation of telling detail, the sardonic view of life, the already mature skill with comic character and ironic situation, that flowered in the first of his better-known novels. *The Old Boys* clearly marked an original new talent. The connecting link among his main characters, all ageing British males, was a class reunion—a device that Franz Werfel, among others, had used successfully before him; but he made it his own with his satiric insights into individuals and their pretensions and evasions. This justly, if surprisingly, won him the Hawthornden Prize.

Another novel in much the same vein, *The Boarding-House*, launched him on a full-time writing career. This time his characters were a mixed group of shabby-genteel boarders, mostly oldsters or eccentrics, in league against one another for succession to the management—and in league with each other against Death. His exposure of the fatuousness, futility, and low cunning of most of the types he wrote about in these two novels gives them an added dimension: the comedy, often close to travesty, has a Voltairean undertone.

The Love Department is less cynical, more pure fun: its exaggeratedly comic plot has many hilarious incidents, and it is about younger people. The "love department" of a women's magazine employs an innocent provinicial to track down a real Lothario, one Septimus Tuam, who has been playing havoc with the hearts of maids and matrons among its correspondents. The pursuit, on a borrowed bicycle through the highways and byways of Greater London, would be an adroit and playful farce, à la P.G. Wodehouse, were it not for Trevor's gift of serious irony.

Trevor's next two novels return to the group framework—odd characters living in rundown urban hostels. The locales are a bypassed street in old Dublin and a wasteland of London given over to the developers. The people, too, have noticeable likenesses. He does their aberrations and hangups superbly, as before, and with an increased compassion. But he attempts a deeper philosophical note by telling their stories around an outsider introduced as a touchstone or activator. In *Mrs. Eckdorf in O'Neill's Hotel* the activator is a visiting photographer who proves to be a madwoman. In *Miss Gomez and the Brethren* this role is given to a Jamaican girl, a former prostitute, with a religious obsession. Faith can work its wonders even when based on delusions. This device, in both cases, makes the novels seem more contrived and less credible, though carried off with verve and effective irony.

In *Elizabeth Alone*—a title that greatly understates his present range—Trevor deploys a full cast around four women patients in a London hospital. Except for a brief beginning and ending, we are no more nor less concerned with the 41-year-old Elizabeth, her ex-husband, her three daughters, and her feckless suitor than we are with the lives and multitudinous connections of the three other women.

This growth toward compassion reaches a peak in his two latest novels. The "villain" of *The Children of Dynmouth* is an obnoxious boy of 15 whose crazy dream, inspired by endless sessions on the telly, is to win a local talent show by re-enacting in person the murderer and the three victims of the famous "Brides in the Bath." For props to that end, he blackmails half the good townsfolk, causing heartbreak far beyond his insidious aims. In *Other People's Worlds* the characters are a cut above those of Dynmouth, but the themes are curiously related. This time his villain is a charmer of 33. He appears from the theatrical world to beguile the Gloucestershire gentry, including a gentle widow of 47. In marrying her and skipping out from their Italian honeymoon along with her jewels and cash, a lively and rather sordid past comes convincingly to light. But even here, as in Dynmouth, he offers Christian sympathy for villains as well as victims. The man and the boy both "live in fantasies and make-believe"; their wise neighbors call them "psychopaths." But the author lets us wonder how far off they are from the rest of us, and why. These last two novels, beautifully plotted and with hosts of sharply drawn minor characters, are neither farce nor pure social comedy, though they sometimes waver between them. They show the author at his best in his awareness of the human predicament—as he has also done increasingly in his many short stories.

—Marshall A. Best

TRICKETT, (Mabel) Rachel. British. Born in Lathom, Lancashire, 20 December 1923. Educated at the High School for Girls, Wigan, Lancashire; Lady Margaret Hall, Oxford, 1942-45, B.A. (honours) in English 1945, M.A. 1949. Assistant to the Curator, Manchester City Art Galleries, 1945-46; Lecturer in English, University College of Hull, Yorkshire, 1946-54; Fellow and Tutor, 1954-73, and since 1973, Principal, St. Hugh's College, Oxford. Visiting Lecturer, 1962-63, and Drew Professor, 1971, Smith College, Northampton, Massachusetts; Lecturer, Bread Loaf School of English, Middlebury, Vermont, 1967, 1969. Recipient: Commonwealth Fund Fellowship, 1949; Rhys Memorial Prize, 1953. Honorary Fellow, Lady Margaret Hall, 1978. Address: St. Hugh's College, Oxford OX1 3BD, England.

PUBLICATIONS

Novels

The Return Home. London, Constable, 1952.
The Course of Love. London, Constable, 1954.
Point of Honour. London, Constable, 1958.
A Changing Place. London, Constable, 1962.
The Elders. London, Constable, 1966.
A Visit to Timon. London, Constable, 1970.

Uncollected Short Story

"The Schoolmasters," in *Cornhill* (London), Summer 1965.

Plays

Antigone, music by John Joubert (broadcast, 1954). London, Novello, 1954.
Silas Marner, music by John Joubert (produced Cape Town and London, 1960). London, Novello, 1960.

Radio Play: *Antigone*, 1954.

Other

The Honest Muse: A Study in Augustan Verse. Oxford, Clarendon Press, 1967.
Browning's Lyricism (lecture). London, Oxford University Press, 1971.

*

Rachel Trickett comments:

I have always been particularly interested in my novels in the relationships between people, and between people and their environment. Place plays an important part in all my books. I have also grown increasingly interested in the essential solitude and uniqueness of my characters. This is not the same as the popular idea of alienation or isolation; it is rather the individual differentiating principle which identifies character and is most obviously exhibited in love where so often those who love each other are, consciously or not, learning to recognise their differences, their separateness. The passing of time has become an important element in my novels from *A Changing Place* to *A Visit to Timon*. My works are often retrospective in tone and mood as I am particularly interested in the way in which the imagination plays over the past and relates it to the present.

* * *

In one of Rachel Trickett's novels, *The Elders*, a character is asked, "And what is your contribution to the war effort?" to which she replies quite simply, "Literature." The ironic implications of this exchange are best understood in the context of the novel, but we see here one of the rare moments in this writer's work where the relation between the inner and outer worlds is given direct critical presentation. Her chosen territory appears to be the private world of personal relationships, often among highly cultivated people. Nevertheless her presentation of it is such that her work reflects very clearly the changing public world of her time. A tough searching out of the responses of individual sensibilities to private experience, given in language of unfailing clarity, inevitably leads to an accurate recording of how the inner world is affected by the outer. In *A Changing Place* a working-class hero's attachment to a girl from the upper middle class follows a course in which private emotions are seen as subtly bound up with the wider social circumstances of pre-war hardship, the war, and the disorientating effects of the war on people's private lives. A more recent novel, *A Visit to Timon*, shows a different reaction to experience on the part of a man whose retreat from public life is complicated by his relationship with a friend who works in television. Similarly, Trickett's ability to evoke a sense of place and of time passing is partly a matter of vividly realised landscape and a rare gift for the delineation of nostalgia, but also rests in a strong sense of the community, a recognition of the relations and tensions in a social structure. This may range in different novels from the non-conformist community of a small town in Yorkshire, to the life of industrial quarry workers in Lancashire, and again to the quite different structures of life in Oxford University.

A common theme is the confrontation between worlds, the invasion of one set of values by another. Often the clash is between spontaneity of feeling and the more sophisticated attitude to experience cultivated by certain artistic, literary, and academic circles. In *The Return Home* the simple and passionate young innocent, Christiana, becomes the victim of more sophisticated beings, but in

The Elders there is a comic reversal of this theme when the return from abroad of a spontaneous, romantic poet disturbs the existing pattern of relationships in an academic community and causes a reassessment of values by both old and young alike. These confrontations, too, are subject to the processes of time, and one of Rachel Trickett's gifts as a moralist is the careful account she takes of change and the complexity of the moral life in relation to it. Do civilised rituals of friendship really preserve love, or do they cause it to become atrophied, or do they perhaps simply come to disguise a lack of true commitment? In her work, this is a question that becomes increasingly important. It would be difficult to show by quotation the way in which she uses small acts, remarks, and gestures to build gradually a strong sense of the distinctive atmosphere peculiar to a relationship; but this extract from *A Changing Place*, in which she describes the refusal to envisage love, shows another important gift, the ability to describe emotional states with both elegance and accuracy:

> Love of the kind Sarah no longer envisaged is rare after all, because it is so seldom wanted. It seems dangerous in the dependence it creates, and some would rather have less than be threatened with the demand for this surrender. As they grow older the urge to protect themselves from it grows stronger and appears disguised as a sort of wisdom and settled maturity that can afford to smile at excesses of the heart and the imagination. But it is not emotion as such they fear; it is commitment, the loss of any part of themselves. The desire to conserve what remains of the self becomes so strong with age that it grows harder to believe that only he who loses his life shall save it. Superficially we become more generous with time and with new acquaintances and new responsibilities, all those things which have a touch of virtue in them and so often cover up for the lack of any real surrender of the self. It is like a religion that consists entirely of thinking and doing, of the theological arguments and pious duties and refuses to take into account feeling, because it is dangerous.

—Bridget O'Toole

TROCCHI, Alexander. British. Born in Glasgow, 30 July 1925. Educated at the University of Glasgow, 1942-43, 1946-50, M.A. 1950. Served in the Royal Navy, 1943-46. Married Lyn Hicks in 1956; one child. Painter and sculptor: Visiting Lecturer in Sculpture, St. Martin's School of Art, London. Editor, *Merlin* magazine, Paris, and *Paris Quarterly*, 1952-55; *The Moving Times*, London. Address: c/o John Calder Ltd., 18 Brewer Street, London W1R 4AS, England.

PUBLICATIONS

Novels

The Carnal Days of Helen Seferis (as Frances Lengel). Paris, Olympia Press, 1954; revised edition, as Alexander Trocchi, North Hollywood, Brandon House, 1967.

Helen and Desire (as Frances Lengel). Paris, Olympia Press, 1954; revised edition, as Alexander Trocchi, London, Olympia Press, and North Hollywood, Brandon House, 1967.

Young Adam (as Frances Lengel). Paris, Olympia Press, 1955; revised edition, as Alexander Trocchi, London, Heinemann, 1961; San Diego, Greenleaf, 1966.

School for Sin (as Frances Lengel). Paris, Olympia Press, 1955; revised edition, as *School for Wives*, as Alexander Trocchi, North Hollywood, Brandon House, 1967.

White Thighs (as Frances Lengel). Paris, Olympia Press, 1955; revised edition, as Alexander Trocchi, North Hollywood, Brandon House, 1967.

Thongs (as Carmencita de las Lunas). Paris, Olympia Press, 1956; as Alexander Trocchi, North Hollywood, Brandon House, 1967; London, Olympia Press, 1971.

The Fifth Volume of Frank Harris's My Life and Loves: An Irreverent Treatment. Paris, Olympia Press, 1958; London, New English Library, 1966.

Cain's Book. New York, Grove Press, 1960; London, Calder, 1963.

Sappho of Lesbos. New York, Castle, 1960; London, Tandem, 1971.

The Outsiders (includes *Young Adam* and short stories). New York, New American Library, 1961.

Short Stories

Four Stories, in *New Writers 3.* London, Calder and Boyars, 1965.

Verse

Man at Leisure. London, Calder and Boyars, 1972.

Other

Drugs of the Mind. London, Aldus, 1970.

Editor, with Richard Seaver and Terry Southern, *Writers in Revolt.* New York, Fell, 1963.

Translator, with R.E. Wyngaard, *I, Jan Cremer*, by Jan Cremer. London, Calder and Boyars, and New York, Shorewood, 1965.

Translator, *The Girl on the Motorcycle*, by André Pieyre de Mandiargues. London, Calder and Boyars, 1966.

Translator, *The Centenarian*, by René de Obaldia. London, Calder and Boyars, 1970.

Translator, *La Gana*, by Jean Douassot. London, Calder and Boyers, 1974.

* * *

Alexander Trocchi arrived in Paris in the early 1950's; there, from 1952 to 1955, he edited (with Richard Seaver and Austryn Wainhouse), the well-known expatriate avant-garde review *Merlin*. It published a number of pieces by Samuel Beckett, Christopher Logue, Patrick Bowles, Ronald Bottrall, and others of real distinction. During that same period. Trocchi became, according to Maurice Girodias, a "stalwart" of the Olympia Press. All Trocchi's works were banned by the French authorities, but most appear to be back in print by now in England or America. As the new editions are often described as "revised," and the English version of *Young Adam* has been somewhat rewritten for reasons both of style and decorum, the purist will naturally seek out the earlier editions.

In the late 1950's Trocchi is said to have collaborated with Asgar Jorn in the International Situationist movement, the journal of which dealt with visual arts ("pop" emphasis), environment and culture. After leaving Paris, Trocchi lived for some time on a scow on the Hudson River, where he wrote *Cain's Book*, his one book to have achieved, as yet, any literary prominence. In the mid-1960's he was to be found in London, active in the "sigma" project, his manifesto for which appeared in *New Saltire* and was reprinted in *City Lights Journal 2* (1964). It was a "Revolutionary Proposal" to bring art into life, leisure, and popular culture by means of "spontaneous universities" and cultural centers, and by making art available everywhere, from hoardings to matchboxes. In 1965 he was a co-organizer and master of ceremonies for the famous Albert Hall poetry reading, where Ferlinghetti, Ginsberg, and many others did indeed bring the New Poetry to an audience of thousands. Trocchi seems to have been in or near most "counter-culture" movements for 30 years; his collaborators, editors, and literary acquaintances would almost make up a directory to the underground.

Trocchi's pornography is lively, or, as Girodias puts it, "tingling with sex and fun." (See the *Olympia Reader* for some sketches of Trocchi and two samples of his work.) Girodias gives in his introduction a hilarious and circumstantial account of how Trocchi came to write, by Girodias's computation, four-fifths of *The Fifth Volume of Frank Harris*...in ten days, leaving "the odd twenty percent of real Harris...rejuvenated and revitalized." Indeed it is not easy to tell which is Trocchi and which Harris. (The Grove Press edition of the five volumes gives essentially the same text for Volume Five, with no attribution to Trocchi.) *Young Adam* (new edition) and *Cain's Book* are, in different ways, rather dreary. The former is an ordinary story of adultery and accidental murder (on a Scottish scow, this time), remarkable only for a very faint resemblance to Camus's *L'Etranger* (and anticipation of *La Chute*) in the detached, joyless, pleasure-seeking of its hero, his accidental and meaningless violence, and his narcotic semi-awareness of responsibility. *Cain's Book* is even less focussed and plotted than *Young Adam*; indeed it reads as if written in a drug haze. There is a simplistic adoption of the conventions of artifice: "the book I am writing is the book you are reading," and some solipsist, inconclusive brooding about awareness. But the book is essentially a blurred and unimaginative offshoot of the Henry Miller tradition of torrential pseudo-autobiography, and is really a rather dry little brook. There is some sex, but most of the characters' time and energy go into a lethargic search for the next "fix" and a morose description of the "fix" when found. Trocchi only summons up real energy to castigate the present drug laws or to give occasional flashback to his hero's Scottish youth. "Vol. 2" (excerpted in the *Evergreen Review*) augurs better; it has some sprightly, horrid satire in the Burroughs manner. The short stories have some good writing of a more conventional type, but, all in all, Trocchi remains more interesting as an important figure on a certain literary scene than for anything he seems yet to have written.

—Patricia Merivale

TUCCI, Niccolò. American. Born in Lugano, Switzerland, 1 May 1908; emigrated to the United States in 1938; naturalized, 1953. Educated in Florence, Italy, Dr. in law and political sciences, 1933. Married Laura Rusconi in 1936; two children. Writes in Italian and English. Correspondent, *Politics Magazine*, New York, 1943-46; Co-Founder, 1954, and Columnist ("The Press of Freedom"), *Village Voice*, New York; Columnist ("Offhand"), *Saturday Review*, New York, 1961-62. Writer-in-Residence, Columbia University, New York, 1965-66. Co-Founder, The Wide Embrace theatre company, New York, 1973. Recipient: Viareggio Prize, 1956; Ford grant, 1959; Bagutta Prize, 1969. Address: 25 East 67th Street, New York, New York 10021, U.S.A.

PUBLICATIONS

Novels

Il Segreto. Milan, Garzanti, 1956.
Those of the Lost Continent (in Italian: *Gli Atlantici*):
Before My Time. New York, Simon and Schuster, 1962; London, Cape, 1963.
Unfinished Funeral. New York, Simon and Schuster, 1964; London, Cape, 1965.
Gli Atlantici. Milan, Garzanti, 1968.
Confessioni Involontarie. Milan, Mondadori, 1975.
The Sun and the Moon. New York, Knopf, 1977; London, Allen Lane, 1979.

Uncollected Short Stories

"Where Anarchy Begins," in *Partisan Review* (New Brunswick, New Jersey), Spring 1944.
"Hey!," in *Twice a Year* (New York), Fall-Winter 1946-47.
"Excellency," in *Partisan Review* (New Brunswick, New Jersey), Winter 1946.
"The Siege," in *The Best American Short Stories 1947*, edited by Martha Foley. Boston, Houghton Mifflin, 1947.
"The Truce," in *New Yorker*, 5 July 1947.
"The Assignment," in *New Yorker*, 10 April 1948.
"Military Intelligence," in *New Yorker*, 29 May 1948.
"The Prisoner," in *New Yorker*, 23 October 1948.
"The Evolution of Knowledge," in *55 Stories from the New Yorker*. New York, Simon and Schuster, 1949.
"Tronco," in *Harper's* (New York), November 1949.
"History Comes C.O.D.," in *New Yorker*, 14 January 1950.
"Brother Lenin," in *New Yorker*, 1 April 1950.
"The Lonely Song," in *New Directions 13*, edited by James Laughlin. New York, New Directions, 1951.
"The Long Shadows," in *Botteghe Oscure* (Rome), 1951.
"The Underground Settlers," in *New Yorker*, 4 August 1951.
"Stolen Dream," in *New Yorker*, 19 January 1952.
"The Queen and I," in *New Yorker*, 3 May 1952.
"The Death of the Maid," in *Harper's* (New York), October 1952.
"Last Stand," in *New Yorker*, 17 April 1954.
"Those Long Shadows," in *Mademoiselle* (New York), September 1955.
"Morte di Scarandogi," in *Botteghe Oscure* (Rome), 1956.
"Special Ambassador," in *Mademoiselle* (New York), April 1956.
"Dollmaker," in *Atlantic* (Boston), September 1956.
"The Beautiful Blue Horse," in *New Yorker*, 13 April 1957.
"This Particular Rich Lady," in *Botteghe Oscure* (Rome), 1959.
"Terror and Grief," in *Stories from the New Yorker 1950-1960*. New York, Simon and Schuster, 1960.
"Death of the Professor," in *New Yorker*, 27 February 1960.
"The Trigger," in *New Yorker*, 10 June 1961.
"Fragments," in *Encounter* (London), August 1961.
"Four Dialogues," in *New Yorker*, 18 August 1962.
"The Announcement," in *New Yorker*, 29 December 1962.
"The Desert in the Oasis," in *The Best American Short Stories 1963*, edited by Martha Foley and David Burnett. Boston, Houghton Mifflin, 1963.
"The Worst," in *Esquire* (New York), August 1965.
"Strong Man," in *Insights*. New York, Aronson, 1973.

Play

Posterity for Sale (produced New York, 1967).

*

Niccolò Tucci comments:

(1972) Other Biographical Information: Slightly enlarged prostate but no enlarged horizons to match; liver, intestines, heart (touch wood) normal; bloodcount normal, pressure 80; defecation twice daily when I don't read the papers; no TV no radio; alcohol consumption only when good wines available, never more than one glass daily now that I am old; hiatus hernia; two sets of glasses: one to tell characters on page, one across the street; weight normal, no signs of weightlessness; no trace of taxable income; sex-count and telephone unlisted.

The reason I have never allowed anyone to translate me from one of my two present languages into the other is that I consider myself alive, and these two languages are the two parts of me into which my experiences were split, so that my daily effort is to weld them together again. Perhaps I am another Humpty-Dumpty who sees himself as a new Lazarus. I don't know but I see no great danger of self-delusion in this: Lazarus was not a great man and certainly not a writer, he was a poor guinea-pig, and we have never been told how he climbed back into life after his place was taken by his Absence. I only know that no one in the world is worth his absence, and *as a writer*, I feel this very intensely, for I associate with words more than with people. I still don't know how to write a good thank-you letter in English, French, or German, even in my native Italian, but the *word-population* of all languages is still at my orders for nonsense, fairy tales, plays, stories, polemical articles and even love letters, in spite of my venerable age. In fact I find it hard to limit myself to English and Italian, and none of the king's jet-planes and supermen, let alone his horses and men, could put me together again as well as I do every time I jump back into Italian or into English from that terrible wall. In the process of doing this almost daily repair-work I have learned a great deal about languages, and I know how to avoid the Temptations of the Writing Devil, namely hot-water and wind in the place of blood and soul to fill your characters with. It is an interesting life, but it dooms me to poverty as long as it lasts, because I can't let anyone bury me under *his* words while I am away from one of my two homes. But then this arrangement has its advantages too: the temptations of Success are far more sinister than those of habit, laziness or fatigue, in fact they are the *real* tools of the Devil.

* * *

The privileged deserve their literary investigators, as much as do the disadvantaged. Niccolò Tucci has devoted generous attention to an interesting minority group, the continental aristocracy and their heirs. Time and democracy have reduced their numbers and influence, but their fascination remains, less because of what they are than what they represent: the confluence of wealth, education, tradition, power, and social *élan* evidenced in a life style where eccentricity and self-will are not fatal flaws but the identifying stripes of their breed.

Like jet travel or new money, the clash of conflicting moral or social values is not Tucci's ostensible concern. Yet it is there, under the Tucci characters' public show of conservatism and propriety. A young Spanish woman in *Unfinished Funeral*, the author's second novel in English, is reminded that she is "a girl of 26" and that her honor may have to be avenged, not because she may or may not have been compromised by an elderly gentleman met on a train, but because all will assume she has been. "The defense of your honor is my business, not yours," her brother insists. To liberate woman is to deprive man of his protector image, and, always, appearances count. Yet paradoxically, the strongest characters in Tucci's English novels are women—not the equals of men, but their proven superiors in the art of tyranny.

Tucci's reputation as a short story writer was already established before his first English novel, *Before My Time*, appeared in 1962. The long novel, in part an autobiographical nod to the author's own Russian-Italian parentage, is not merely dominated, but overwhelmed, by the idiosyncratic widow, Mamachen. A rich Russian matriarch at the turn of the century, she plays czarina to the large, elegant, and slavish family entourage she pilots from Italy to Switzerland to France to Germany—and to despair at times. Yet there is no family revolution, least of all by the daughter, Mary, who verges on treason by falling in love with a humble Italian doctor, and then in turn makes him a family thrall. The possible rebels are really defectors, the daughter Ludmilla and the son Pierre, who find lives of their own elsewhere. Mamachen's eventual death, with tragicomic dividing of the spoils by her heirs, changes nothing, but merely hands on the matriarchal torch to Mary. Aristocracy persists, Tucci suggests, because its leaders are equal to those they succeed. And why not? They have been handpicked and rigorously trained.

Unfinished Funeral is another investigation of tyranny, this time very compressed in length and told in symbols (largely Freudian) so obvious that they themselves invite questions. Ermelinda, the widowed Duchess of Combon de Triton, is "the acrobat of pain" who has survived 36 major operations and innumerable heart attacks, having found that physical crises are the handles by which she can grasp and hold power. Her funeral cortege is always on call, yet she never dies—and so her son, Bernandrasse, and daughter, Eloise, never really live. The book states and restates a proposition rather than treating a question; hence those who seek ready answers are doomed to disappointment.

In all of Tucci's work the style is witty, clever, polished—appropriate to the worldly figures he illuminates but never dissects.

—Marian Pehowski

TUOHY, Frank (John Francis Tuohy). British. Born in Uckfield, Sussex, 2 May 1925. Educated at Stowe School; King's College, Cambridge, 1943-46, B.A. (honours) 1946. Lecturer, Turku University, Finland, 1947-48; Professor of English Language and Literature, University of Sao Paulo, Brazil, 1950-56; Contract Professor, Jagiellonian University, Krakow, Poland, 1958-60; Visiting Professor, Waseda University, Tokyo, 1964-67; Visiting Professor and Writer-in-Residence, Purdue University, Lafayette, Indiana, 1970-71, 1976, 1980. Recipient: Katherine Mansfield Prize, 1960; Society of Authors Travelling Fellowship, 1963; Black Memorial Prize, 1965; Faber Memorial Prize, 1965; E.M. Forster Award (USA), 1972; Heinemann Award, 1979. Fellow, Royal Society of Literature, 1965. Address: c/o Macmillan and Company, 4 Little Essex Street, London WC2R 3LF, England.

PUBLICATIONS

Novels

The Animal Game. London, Macmillan, and New York, Scribner, 1957.
The Warm Nights of January. London, Macmillan, 1960.
The Ice Saints. London, Macmillan, and New York, Scribner, 1964.

Short Stories

The Admiral and the Nuns with Other Stories. London, Macmillan, 1962; New York, Scribner, 1963.
Fingers in the Door. London, Macmillan, and New York, Scribner, 1970.
Live Bait and Other Stories. London, Macmillan, 1978; New York, Holt Rinehart, 1979.

Play

Television Play: *The Japanese Student*, 1973.

Other

Portugal. London, Thames and Hudson, and New York, Viking Press, 1970.
Yeats (biography). London, Macmillan, and New York, Macmillan, 1976.

*

Frank Tuohy comments:

Most of what I write seems to start off with the interaction between two cultures, modes of behaviour, ways of living, etc.

Sometimes this confrontation is between a foreigner and an alien environment, sometimes between groups in that environment itself. For me, the sense of displacement, loss, anxiety which happens to people derives from the world outside them, in their relationships with that world. If I thought of it as starting inside, as being a part of the Self, I probably would not write at all.

* * *

The novels and short stories of Frank Tuohy are marked by a strong sense of social reality. They are set in various places—England, Brazil, Poland—and give one a vivid sense of the physical place: the climate, landscape, local customs. Against the backdrop of special place, the drama of the characters' lives unfolds. In the short stories interest focuses usually on intense personal encounters in which the protagonist is made to face some unpleasant decision or harsh truth about himself or people close to him. These stories, sharply etched and intensely though quietly dramatic, have no apparent underlying theme. It is the revelation itself, the exquisitely rendered but "painful bite down on the rotten tooth of fact," to borrow a phrase from Tuohy, that one is meant to savor.

In his novels and longer stories there are the same sharp awareness of external reality and savoring of unpleasant fact, but there is also clearly a discernible moral structure. The writer's sympathies are with those who suffer and respond, who are capable of loyalty and self-abnegation. His dislike is for characters who, protected by money, indulge their appetites at the expense of those socially or culturally inferior or morally more sensitive.

The protagonist of Tuohy's first novel, *The Animal Game*, is Robin Morris, a young Englishman working in Sao Paulo, who encounters the beautiful corrupt daughter of a Brazilian aristocrat. Morris is attracted to this woman but is saved at the end of the novel from a relationship which, one sees, would have been sterile, self-indulgent, and ultimately destructive. Tuohy's moral sense is even more fully involved in his second novel about Brazil, *The Warm Nights of January*, which also deals with self-indulgence and sexual corruption. *The Ice Saints* takes place in Poland, some time after the Stalinist "thaw." Here the protagonist, an attractive, pleasant, but inexperienced and pampered young English woman visits her married sister and Polish brother-in-law with the idea of rescuing their son from what she regards as a grim and depressing existence, and taking him back to England to live. Although we are at first allowed to identify with the young woman's point of view (the horrors of Polish life are vividly presented), we are made to see, finally, the moral superiority of the Polish brother-in-law whose human qualitites outweigh his lack of polish and urbanity.

Tuohy's stories and novels are written in a style that is compressed and economical yet remarkably evocative. One has the immediate sense of a physical world vividly and objectively presented and yet one also feels, but unobtrusively, the authorial presence choosing and arranging for judgmental effect.

—W.J. Stuckey

TURNER, George (Reginald). Australian. Born in Melbourne, Victoria, 8 October 1916. Educated in Victoria state schools; at University High School, Melbourne. Served in the Australian Imperial Forces, 1939-45. Employment Officer, Commonwealth Employment Service, Melbourne, 1945-49, and Wangaratta, Victoria, 1949-50; Textile Technician, Bruck Mills, Wangaratta, 1951-64; Senior Employment Officer, Volkswagen Ltd., Melbourne, 1964-67; Beer Transferrer, Carlton and United Breweries, Melbourne, 1970-76. Since 1970, science-fiction reviewer, Melbourne *Age*. Recipient: Miles Franklin Award, 1962; Commonwealth Literary Fund award, 1968. Agent: Carl Routledge, 22 Knoll House, Carlton Hill, London N.W.8, England. Address: 87 Westbury Street, Balaclava, Victoria 3183, Australia.

PUBLICATIONS

Novels

Young Man of Talent. London, Cassell, 1959; as *Scobie*, New York, Simon and Schuster, 1959.
A Stranger and Afraid. London, Cassell, 1961.
The Cupboard under the Stairs. London, Cassell, 1962.
A Waste of Shame. Melbourne, and London, Cassell, 1965.
The Lame Dog Man. Melbourne, Cassell, 1967; London, Cassell, 1968.
Beloved Son. London, Faber, 1978; New York, Pocket Books, 1979.
Transit of Cassidy. Melbourne, Nelson, 1978; London, Hamish Hamilton, 1979.

Uncollected Short Story

"In a Petri Dish Upstairs," in *Rooms of Paradise*, edited by Lee Harding. Melbourne, Quartet, 1978; New York, St. Martin's Press, 1979.

Other

Editor, *View from the Edge.* Melbourne, Norstrilia Press, 1977.

*

George Turner comments:

I make few specific statements in my novels, and don't consider it my business to do so since the themes are usually such as bedevil the experts as much as they do the man in the street—insanity, alcoholism, the urge to meddle, the habit of making moral judgments and so on. I try to examine these themes under reasonably familiar circumstances, with no more of the exotic than is to be found in an average life, in the hope that some useful insight or recognition will emerge. The intention is that the reader will be able to identify with the problem as well as the characters.

To elimate personal point of view as much as possible, I do not plan a novel in detail in advance of writing it. I select my general theme on no better ground than that I find it interesting and challenging, conceive a few characters who could reasonably become involved in such a matter, and set them in motion. Since plot is very literally character in action, something useful usually emerges in 20 or 30 thousand words, and I know in which direction I am going.

Only at this point do I begin to shape the work as a whole (and it generally means scrapping everything so far written) but rarely have more than a generalised idea of what the climax and resolution will be. These must be decided by the interactions of the characters: authorial manipulation is restricted to the minimum necessary to give shape and balance to the work.

One personally useful by-product of this method is that I find that such concentration on a problem for many months often changes my original points of view about it, and the outcome is commonly rather far from what I had in mind during the shaping phase.

I am sufficiently old-fashioned to prefer a story with a beginning, a development, and a resolution (though not to the point of tying up every loose end in sight) but sufficiently of my time to avoid moral or ethical attitudes. Those of my characters who display them are apt to come to grief as the theme tests and retests them.

For this reason I have been termed "existentialist," which is probably true, and have also been said to have no moral or ethical views at all, which is not. I merely condemn rigidity of attitude and I suppose that in the final summation that is what my novels so far have been about.

George Turner's well-tailored stories of social pressure and private malaise read like nothing so much as Victorian narrative histories overlaid by 1930's "realism." On the surface the problems his characters face are bluntly modern: the hell of total war, political chicanery, alcoholism, mental instability, and broken homes. But underneath these, as the last volume of the Treelake saga (*The Lame Dog Man*) indicates most clearly, there murmurs an Arnoldian unease about the loss of order and the course of time: about Jimmy Carlyon (the social worker central to that book, *A Stranger and Afraid*, and *The Cupboard under the Stairs*), Turner writes: "Change ...had not so much touched Treelake as ridden roughshod through it.... His regret was personal. The severance from the past was inevitable, but the interregnum was violent and unsightly." Carlyon, of course, is in the public service, a cog in the System, attached to an order, but we soon learn that his job is his anodyne (for his troubled childhood) just as alcohol is Joe Bryen's, in the rather weaker novel *A Waste of Shame*. Half-consciously Jimmy knows this: "He made a virtue of...playing the observer who sees most of the game, but occasionally surprises a sense of incompletion in himself, of a shade of difference, of being an imitation smart enough to deceive the real." But for Turner that half-awareness is if anything more dangerous than ignorance, for it fosters dreams of power or self-possession that tempt individuals to overstep their limitations and sacrifice others for their own ends.

Turner's first and in many ways best—most self-contained—novel, examines just such a proposition. Set in New Guinea during World War II, it probes the motivations of three Australian soldiers: Scobie, who is thrust to position when his superior is killed and who discovers his taste for command; Payne, the rebel, who becomes Scobie's psychological slave too easily for Scobie's good; and Tolley, the new commander, who operates by rule instead of through human judgment. All three are inversions of each other and all inevitably come into a conflict that destroys them. What survives, to continue, is the army—not that Turner is praising military power particularly, but that in his novel it represents the community interdependence that he later explores in the town of Treelake. His world is one in which individuality is encouraged but in which every individual action has manifold ramifications in the intermarried, interlocked, intertwined town relationships. His approach to structuring a novel, therefore, is somewhat that of a chess player's: moves are plotted several plays ahead, and characters occupy a series of ratiocinative positions as they shift from ploy to ploy and struggle out of one innuendo into another.

Much of the movement of Turner's books depends on dialogue; much of its tone derives from the austere but sardonic balance of his sentences. On behaviour, for example, he writes: "You learned discipline and called it self-control, deprecation and called it modesty; you learned to take delight in the welfare of others—until the interest was not returned and the delight faded and the inturned motive was revealed." That assertion (tone and all) contains the basic Treelake theme. Carlyon ultimately knows that he will distribute compensation money to Johnson, a malingerer who does not deserve it; he also recognizes his mother's facade; but he accepts such deceit:

> Why, he thought, I really like the old fake. She plays a hard game, but she plays it with zest, and she plays it for the game's sake. Do that, and you can take your reverses for what they are worth, which is precious little. And life is the pleasure you take in the game.
>
> It seemed very profound and perceptive. It would do for a working basis, a working philosophy.

It seems perhaps more like an exchange of solipsisms. The humanity it reveals is brittle at best, always at the mercy of the social structure. Its range is narrow, and its deepest and most idealistic aspirations appear no more than the adaptations of personal ambition to the *status quo*.

—W.H. New

TUTUOLA, Amos. Nigerian. Born in Abeokuta, Western Nigeria, in June 1920. Educated at the Salvation Army School and the Anglican Central School, Abeokuta; Lagos High School. Served as a blacksmith in the Royal Air Force, Lagos, 1943-46. Married Victoria Alake in 1947; four sons and four daughters. Since 1956, Stores Officer, Nigerian (later, Federal) Broadcasting Corporation, Ibadan. Visiting Research Fellow, University of Ife, 1979. Founder, Mbari Club of Nigerian Writers. Address: Federal Broadcasting Corporation, Broadcasting House, New Court Road, Ibadan, Nigeria.

PUBLICATIONS

Novels

The Palm-Wine Drinkard and His Dead Palm-Wine Tapster in the Deads' Town. London, Faber, 1952; New York, Grove Press, 1953.

My Life in the Bush of Ghosts. London, Faber, and New York, Grove Press, 1954.

Simbi and the Satyr of the Dark Jungle. London, Faber, 1955; New York, Grove Press, 1962.

The Brave African Huntress. London, Faber, and New York, Grove Press, 1958.

Feather Woman of the Jungle. London, Faber, 1962.

Ajaiyvi and His Inherited Poverty. London, Faber, 1967.

Play

The Palm-Wine Drinkard, with Professor Collis, adaptation of the novel by Tutuola (produced Ibadan, 1962).

*

Critical Studies: *Amos Tutuola* by Harold R. Collins, New York, Twayne, 1969; *Critical Perspectives on Amos Tutuola* edited by Bernth Lindfors, Washington, D.C., Three Continents, 1975, London, Heinemann, 1980.

* * *

Amos Tutuola's six books follow the same basic narrative pattern. A hero (or heroine) with supernatural powers or access to supernatural assistance sets out on a journey in quest of something important and suffers incredible hardships before successfully accomplishing his mission. He ventures into unearthly realms, performs arduous tasks, fights with fearsome monsters, endures cruel tortures, and narrowly escapes death. Sometimes he is accompanied by a relative or by loyal companions; sometimes he wanders alone. But he always survives his ordeals, attains his objective, and usually emerges from his nightmarish experiences a wiser, wealthier man. The cycle of his adventures—involving a Departure, Initiation, and Return—resembles that found in myths and folktales the world over.

Tutuola's first and most famous book, *The Palm-Wine Drinkard and His Dead Palm-Wine Tapster in the Deads' Town*, which describes a hero's descent into an African underworld in search of a dead companion, was greatly influenced by oral tradition. Tutuola made use of common Yoruba tales and motifs, stringing them together like a fireside reconteur. As a consequence, the book's neat cyclical narrative pattern rests on a very loosely coordinated inner structure. The hero is involved in one adventure after another but these adventures are not well integrated. Like boxcars on a freight train, they are independent units joined with a minimum of apparatus and set in a seemingly random and interchangeable order. There is no foreshadowing of events, no dramatic irony, no evidence of any kind that the sequence of events was carefully thought out. Tutuola appears to be improvising as he goes along and employing the techniques and materials of oral narrative art in his improvisations. This is true of his other writings too.

Recent research has shown that none of Tutuola's works is entirely innocent of literary influence either. He clearly owes his greatest debt to D.O. Fagunwa, who began to publish folkloric "novels" in Yoruba in 1938. In his earliest fiction Tutuola tried to imitate Fagunwa's method of weaving a number of old stories into an elastic narrative pattern that could be stretched into a book. Both Fagunwa and Tutuola appear to have been stimulated by John Bunyan's *The Pilgrim's Progress* and *The Arabian Nights*, which were widely used in Nigerian elementary schools. Later Tutuola turned to other foreign sources of inspiration; Edith Hamilton's *Mythology* may have been responsible for the nymphs, satyrs, myrmidons, and phoenixes which started to inflitrate his African jungles. Goblins, imps, and gnomes also turned up regularly. Tutuola, like a great syncretic sponge, easily absorbed these alien creatures into his exotic imaginative universe.

This is not to say, of course, that all his writing is derivative or that it lacks originality or accomplishment. In descriptive ability and sheer visionary power Tutuola far surpasses most of his contemporaries. His fertile imagination, never fettered by reason or common sense, constantly begets the surprising, the unorthodox, the incongruous, the bizarre. Events are recounted with a hallucinatory energy that swiftly transports the reader into realms of fantasy. Characters are painted in the most vivid and memorable colors. Whatever Tutuola borrows from oral or literary tradition he immediately makes his own, enlarging it with details of his own invention. He is a master storyteller.

Tutuola's most conspicuous idiosyncrasy as a writer, and perhaps his most controversial, is his style, which Dylan Thomas once termed "naive English." Because he grew up speaking Yoruba and had only six years of formal schooling, Tutuola tends to make spectacular grammatical and spelling blunders on every page he writes. Some critics hold that this fractured idiom is one of his greatest assets for it adds extra tang to the primitive flavor of his works; his language is just as weird and unpredictable as the adventures he describes. Others argue that it is an unfortunate liability for it quickly tires the average reader who is not conditioned to jumping unfamiliar linguistic hurdles. It is unlikely that this critical debate will have any appreciable effect on Tutuola's writing, for he is not a conscious stylist experimenting with language. He is simply trying to do the best he can in a foreign tongue he has not adequately mastered.

The initial reaction to Tutuola's first books was mixed. Readers in Europe and America were enthusiastic for they had never seen anything quite like them before, and they were convinced that Tutuola was a marvellous "original," a diamond in the rough with rich and dazzling creative powers. Reviewers hailed him as an uncouth genius unspoiled by civilization, a mute, inglorious Milton who had suddenly found his voice, albeit a curiously cracked one. Many educated Nigerians, however, were extremely angry that such an unschooled author should receive so much praise and publicity abroad, for they recognized his borrowings, disapproved of his bad grammar, and suspected he was being lionized by condescending racists who had a clear political motive for choosing to continue to regard Africans as backward and childlike primitives. Since Nigeria was struggling to free itself from colonial rule at the time, Tutuola was more than merely an embarrassment; he was a disgrace, a setback, a national calamity. Later, after Nigeria had achieved its independence, Tutuola was no longer an explosive literary or political issue, and his works began to receive more intelligent critical attention. Today his reputation is secure both at home and abroad, for he has come to be accepted as a unique phenomenon in world literature, a writer who bridges two narrative traditions and two cultures by translating oral art into literary art.

—Bernth Lindfors

TYLER, Anne. American. Born in Minneapolis, Minnesota, 25 October 1941. Educated at Duke University, Durham, North Carolina, 1958-61, B.A. 1961; Columbia University, New York, 1961-62. Married Taghi Modarressi in 1963; two children. Recipient: American Academy award, 1977. Address: 222 Tunbridge Road, Baltimore, Maryland 21212, U.S.A.

PUBLICATIONS

Novels

If Morning Ever Comes. New York, Knopf, 1964; London, Chatto and Windus, 1965.
The Tin Can Tree. New York, Knopf, 1965; London, Macmillan, 1966.
A Slipping-Down Life. New York, Knopf, 1970.
The Clock Winder. New York, Knopf, 1972; London, Chatto and Windus, 1973.
Celestial Navigation. New York, Knopf, 1974; London, Chatto and Windus, 1975.
Searching for Caleb. New York, Knopf, and London, Chatto and Windus, 1976.
Earthly Possessions. New York, Knopf, and London, Chatto and Windus, 1977.
Morgan's Passing. New York, Knopf, and London, Chatto and Windus, 1980.

Uncollected Short Stories

"I Play Kings," in *Seventeen* (New York), August 1963.
"Street of Bugles," in *Saturday Evening Post* (Philadelphia), 30 November 1963.
"Nobody Answers the Door," in *Antioch Review* (Yellow Springs, Ohio), Fall 1964.
"I'm Not Going to Ask You Again," in *Harper's* (New York), September 1965.
"Everything But Roses," in *Reporter* (New York), 23 September 1965.
"As the Earth Gets Old," in *New Yorker*, 29 October 1966.
"Feather Behind the Rock," in *New Yorker*, 12 August 1967.
"Flaw in the Crust of the Earth," in *Reporter* (New York), 2 November 1967.
"Common Courtesies," in *McCall's* (New York), June 1968.
"With All Flags Flying," in *Redbook* (New York), June 1971.
"Bride in the Boatyard," in *McCall's* (New York), June 1972.
"Respect," in *Mademoiselle* (New York), June 1972.
"Misstep of the Mind," in *Seventeen* (New York), October 1972.
"Knack for Languages," in *New Yorker*, 13 January 1975.
"Geologist's Maid," in *New Yorker*, 28 July 1975.
"Some Sign That I Ever Made You Happy," in *McCall's* (New York), October 1975.
"Your Place Is Empty," in *New Yorker*, 22 November 1976.
"Average Waves in Unprotected Waters," in *New Yorker*, 28 February 1977.
"Foot-Footing On," in *Mademoiselle* (New York), November 1977.

* * *

Anne Tyler writes principally of life in Baltimore or in Southern small towns and is basically concerned with the theme of loneliness and human isolation and the difficulties people have both in understanding and in communicating with one another. When Ben Joe Hawkes, the protagonist of *If Morning Ever Comes*, returns for a visit to his home town of Sandhill, North Carolina, he ponders the gap which separates him from his family, although they are as friendly and as affectionate to him as their natures will allow. There is family unity at the same moment that there is family disunity. Ben Joe can reach his mother and sisters only half-heartedly, for within them and within himself mysterious factors in the human heart lure and yet resist complete harmony and understanding. Ben Joe comes to realize that his condition is life itself; he will never fully understand his wife or even his own children when they are eventually born. Parts of every human being and of life itself are forever closed to understanding. Such parts are sadly "unreachable."

This melancholy presentation of existence is related with a painfully sensitive awareness of the tragedy of things as they are. In *The Tin Can Tree* the parents of a six year old girl become exceedingly distraught over the child's accidental death. The mother, in particular, attempts to shut out any further life and light. But her only son suffers so intensely from her neglect that she finally comprehends that life even with its heartbreak and lack of fulfillment is all one has; and, as a consequence, the best should be made of it. Half-fulfilled relationships are better than no relationships at all. The ideal or even the semi-ideal cannot be reached in this life, and no matter how unhappy or disappointing life may be, it is life and not death. People are exalted most of all in Tyler's philosophy when they love other mortals although they consciously know that death awaits both themselves and the ones they love. And a further burden is added because the tin can tree is always rattling, never allowing anyone to forget the dead.

Individuals must arrive at deliberate choices on the relative scales of possibility and degree of bittersweetness. For example, one has a choice of imperfect love or no love at all. Tyler's protagonists generally prefer the former, or at least settle for what their consciousness informs them will be the most appropriate degree for them—although outsiders and even close friends continually insist that their selection is both incomprehensible and foolish. A "belonging to" someone else becomes necessary while life starts slipping away from everyone. Only the artist can really bear almost total loneliness; and despite intense dedication to his calling, even he is drawn by the needs of human love.

The search for belonging is just as pronounced in Tyler's most recent novels, *Earthly Possession* and *Morgan's Passing*. The characters sadly come to realize that they cannot "step inside" another's life. Nevertheless, individual barriers and inadequate relationships are juxtaposed with wry touches of humor and Tyler's delight in the contradictions and whimsies which accompany existence.

Tyler's principal themes are conveyed in crisp, delicate prose which often pleasantly startles because of the preciseness of word choice and the depth of insight. She writes simple descriptive passages and much fresh, graceful dialogue. Her closest literary progenitor is Carson McCullers, but Tyler's work is more wistful, probing, and tenderly perceptive. In her future work she will hopefully avoid occasional character improbability, a tendency to thematic repetitiveness, and a somewhat limited range of subject matter.

—Paul A. Doyle

UPDIKE, John (Hoyer). American. Born in Shillington, Pennsylvania, 18 March 1932. Educated in Shillington public schools; Harvard University, Cambridge, Massachusetts, A.B. (summa cum laude) 1954; Ruskin School of Drawing and Fine Arts, Oxford, 1954-55. Married 1) Mary Pennington in 1953 (marriage dissolved), two sons and two daughters; 2) Martha Bernhard in 1977. Staff Reporter, *New Yorker*, 1955-57. Recipient: Guggenheim Fellowship, 1959; Rosenthal Award, 1960; National Book Award, 1964; O. Henry Award, 1966. Member, American Academy, 1976. Address: 58 West Main Street, Georgetown, Massachusetts 01833, U.S.A.

PUBLICATIONS

Novels

The Poorhouse Fair. New York, Knopf, and London, Gollancz, 1959.
Rabbit, Run. New York, Knopf, 1960; London, Deutsch, 1961.
The Centaur. New York, Knopf, and London, Deutsch, 1963.
Of the Farm. New York, Knopf, 1965.
Couples. New York, Knopf, and London, Deutsch, 1968.
Rabbit Redux. New York, Knopf, 1971; London, Deutsch, 1972.
A Month of Sundays. New York, Knopf, and London, Deutsch, 1975.
Marry Me: A Romance. New York, Knopf, 1976; London, Deutsch, 1977.
The Coup. New York, Knopf, 1978; London, Deutsch, 1979.

Short Stories

The Same Door. New York, Knopf, 1959; London, Deutsch, 1962.
Pigeon Feathers and Other Stories. New York, Knopf, and London, Deutsch, 1962.
Olinger Stories: A Selection. New York, Knopf, 1964.
The Music School. New York, Knopf, 1966; London, Deutsch, 1967.
Penguin Modern Stories 2, with others. London, Penguin, 1969.
Bech: A Book. New York, Knopf, and London, Deutsch, 1970.
Museums and Women and Other Stories. New York, Knopf, 1972; London, Deutsch, 1973.
Warm Wine: An Idyll. New York, Albondocani Press, 1973.
Couples: A Short Story. Cambridge, Massachusetts, Halty Ferguson, 1976.
Too Far to Go: The Maples Stories. New York, Fawcett, 1979.
Problems and Other Stories. New York, Knopf, 1979; London, Deutsch, 1980.

Plays

Three Texts from Early Ipswich: A Pageant. Ipswich, Massachusetts, 17th Century Day Committee, 1968.
Buchanan Dying. New York, Knopf, and London, Deutsch, 1974.

Verse

The Carpentered Hen and Other Tame Creatures. New York, Harper, 1958; as *Hoping for a Hoopoe*, London, Gollancz, 1959.
Telephone Poles. New York, Knopf, and London, Deutsch, 1963.
Bath after Sailing. Monroe, Connecticut, Pendulum Press, 1968.
Midpoint and Other Poems. New York, Knopf, and London, Deutsch, 1969.
Seventy Poems. London, Penguin, 1972.
Six Poems. New York, Aloe, 1973.
Query. New York, Albondocani Press, 1974.
Cunts (Upon Receiving the Swingers Life Club Membership Solicitation). New York, Hallman, 1974.
Tossing and Turning. New York, Knopf, and London, Deutsch, 1977.
From the Journal of a Leper. Northridge, California, Lord John Press, 1978.
Sixteen Sonnets. Cambridge, Massachusetts, Halty Ferguson, 1979.

Other

The Magic Flute (juvenile), with Warren Chappell. New York, Knopf, 1962.
The Ring, with Warren Chappell. New York, Knopf, 1964.
Assorted Prose. New York, Knopf, and London, Deutsch, 1965.
A Child's Calendar. New York, Knopf, 1965.
On Meeting Authors. Newburyport, Massachusetts, Wickford Press, 1968.
Bottom's Dream: Adapted from William Shakespeare's "A Midsummer Night's Dream". New York, Knopf, 1969.
A Good Place. New York, Aloe, 1973.
Picked-Up Pieces. New York, Knopf, 1975; London, Deutsch, 1976.

Three Illuminations in the Life of an American Author. New York, Targ Editions, 1979.

Editor, *Pens and Needles*, by David Levine. Boston, Gambit, 1970.

*

Bibliography: *John Updike: A Comprehensive Bibliography* by B.A. Sokoloff and Mark E. Posner, Norwood, Pennsylvania, Norwood Editions, 1973.

Manuscript Collection: Harvard University, Cambridge, Massachusetts.

Critical Studies: interviews in *Life* (New York), 4 November 1966, and *Paris Review*, Winter 1968; *John Updike* by Charles Thomas Samuels, Minneapolis, University of Minnesota Press, 1969; *The Elements of John Updike* by Alice and Kenneth Hamilton, Grand Rapids, Michigan, Eerdmans, 1970; *Pastoral and Anti-Pastoral Elements in John Updike's Fiction* by Larry E. Taylor, Carbondale, Southern Illinois University Press, 1971; *John Updike: Yea Sayings* by Rachael C. Burchard, Carbondale, Southern Illinois University Press, 1971; *John Updike* by Robert Detweiler, New York, Twayne, 1972; *Rainstorms and Fire: Ritual in the Novels of John Updike* by Edward P. Vargo, Port Washington, New York, Kennikat Press, 1973; *Fighters and Lovers: Theme in the Novels of John Updike* by Joyce B. Markle, New York, New York University Press, 1973; *John Updike* by Suzanne H. Uphaus, New York, Ungar, 1980.

* * *

John Updike takes his place as a major figure in contemporary fiction not only by virtue of his steady production of praiseworthy novels and short stories since 1959, when both *The Poorhouse Fair* and *The Same Door* appeared, but also because he devotes a blessed gift for language to the process and dimensions of dissolution in religion, morality, and society that have characterized our culture in the post-Christian world. Updike is a traditional novelist whose literary mode is essentially although not always realistic and whose values derive from a mythic and Chrisitan past; the destruction of belief in that past and in those values is the theme in almost everything he has written.

Updike has said that good works of art direct us back outward to reality again; and that good writers focus on the excitements of normal, everyday life. He believes that contemporary fiction is thin in showing how the world operates and that it is an obligation for fiction to be factually right; he therefore tries to give convincing, accurate detail. If he succeeds, he believes that he can, as a writer, deliver the truth. The two assumptions that an apprehensible reality is available to the artist and that truth may be ascertained and grasped by the writer mark Updike as a legitimate swimmer in the traditional stream of fiction. These allegiances explain his admiration for Vermeer, a painter to whom he alludes frequently and whose verisimilitude he happily imitates. He has, like the masters of the Dutch school, the power to see precisely. When he looks at the world of nature, it is an act of discovery. When he shows us a girl biting into an apple, it is like Nabokov showing us Lolita at play on the tennis court—a self-contained thing of beauty. When he shows us the houses on the street where Rabbit and Janice live in *Rabbit, Run*, we can taste the grime and feel in our stomach the gray dreariness. He gives us the details of the linotype machine that Rabbit operates in *Rabbit Redux* or of architecture and construction as Piet practices these in *Couples*. Building on the capacity for sharp observation and the command of knowledgeable detail, Updike writes the kind of social comedy that reports on and analyzes the world around him. He is, among other things, a novelist of manners; his characters are often sophisticated metropolitan or suburban people, and his concerns are often marriage, divorce, and sex. *Marry Me* is a prime example of Updike's capacity for a carefully articulated anatomy of marriage, adultery, and divorce in suburbia. It is this talent for realism that makes Updike an indispensable observer of middle-class life in America.

He is, furthermore, an observer with a point of view. He has said that he does not wish to pronounce on great matters and that he disapproves of writers who have made a full commitment to ideas or social issues. Agreeing with John Cage, he has claimed that not judgments, but openness and curiosity are the artist's proper business. Yet he finds that he cannot altogether refrain from opinion, or even judgment. He does speak out, as he himself indicates when he describes his work as saying, "yes, but." Yes in *Rabbit, Run*, to urgent whispers, but the social fabric collapses; yes in *The Centaur* to self-sacrifice and duty, but what of private agony and dwindling? No in *The Poorhouse Fair* to homogenization and loss of faith, but listen to the voices speaking about the joy of persistent existence; no in *Couples* to a religious community founded on physical and psychical interpretations, but what else shall we do as God destroys our churches?

This dialectic, these fruitful tensions, arise in part from Updike's perception of the world in which he lives. Our century is celebrated for the breakdown of communication, he has said, resorting deliberately to the cliché; we live in an Age of Unconsummation in which we enjoy only solipsistic ecstasies. He had begun his career with a belief in the relevance of art; and he was concerned to forestall apocalypse, but some 20 years later he observes an interest on the part of some writers in bringing it on. When T.S. Eliot died in 1965, Updike has said, we were deprived of a cultural presence that extended the tradition of the presiding poet-critic into our time; as long as he was alive our literature seemed restrained from the apocalyptic formlessness and obscenity that it now seeks.

Updike's dilemma, which is both the subject and the generating force of his fiction, is to understand that his culture is in serious if not fatal disarray, moving inexorably toward the dissolutions of entropy. The stay against this drift into formlessness and anarchy is faith in some mythic or Christian structure of values. But the evidence is everywhere around us that the vitality has been sucked out of what were once life-giving myths. Recognizing that Christianity is an anachronism, Updike cannot commit himself to it. Yet he is unwilling to surrender altogether the attitudes and values that it represents to him and that he learned in his Lutheran boyhood. His fiction, therefore, cannot affirm anything, except a sense of loss. All is sullied o'er with hesitancy and skepticism and the nostalgic but forlorn hope that what we so confidently knew and had in the past might be in the present. He is the traditional novelist who celebrates the decay of tradition, recording its dissolution with meticulous accuracy.

In his first novel, the anti-Utopian *Poorhouse Fair*, Updike confronts the crisis of Christianity in the clash between a social scientist as a dehumanized humanitarian who would rationalize human behaviour and an old man who asserts that there is no goodness without a belief in God. On one side are progress and egalitarianism, on the other awe, ceremony, mystery, reverence for the past and for the spirit. But these latter qualities belong to the old and are fading into the past. In *Rabbit, Run* a half-articulated quest for Edenic nature fails, and a search for a sustaining religious faith fails, shattered in good part by a minister who himself has no faith. The consequences of failure in this novel are flight, escape, loss, as they are in other work. Updike's most pessimistic comment on the state of religion is in his portrayal of the Negro pusher in *Rabbit Redux* who, in a bitter parody, is made to see himself as the Christ of the Second Coming.

Updike's treatment of religion frequently involves a sexual dimension. Fornication in his fiction is accompanied by feelings of guilt and knowledge of sin, but the relationship between sex—love and passion—and Christianity goes well beyond these matters to speculation that sex may replace religion or that sexual vitality is an expression of the Christian life or that sexual passion destroys Christianity. In "Lifeguard" a divinity student recognizes the relation between concupiscence and piety. He sees the assault on heaven as a kind of lust. To desire a woman is to desire to save her. Every seduction is a conversion and every copulation is a rescue in Christ's name. In *A Month of Sundays* the bad priest whose belief in God has made his life a feast of inconvenience and unreason argues that sex is the exterior sign of interior grace. The fullest development of these ideas is in *Couples*, which asks the question, after Christianity, what? and tests the proposition that sexual vitality may defy death and lead to Christian fulfillment. The protagonist, who believes in the sovereignty of God, takes many women to bed as a way of serving his God and thinks that total sexual satiation, including fellatio and cunnilingus, is a celebration of the holiness of the flesh: to eat another is sacred, he decides. This man fails the test, but it is not altogether clear that Updike has rejected the notion that the unity of two in one during sex is like being one with God. Updike's ambiguity here avoids didacticism but does not rescue Christianity.

If Christianity cannot be made to work, then perhaps some other myth can. Updike has made two different extended explorations of myth. *The Centaur* is an effort to blend the lives of gods and men, using the Chiron variant of the Hercules myth, because it is one of the few classical examples of self-sacrifice, and it affords an opportunity to exploit the closeness of the name Chiron to that of Christ, as Updike has said. Unfortunately, it is precisely this intention that gives the key to the flaw in the novel: Updike does not fully commit himself to the classical myth, that is to the structure of belief in ancient Greece to which the myth belongs. Not only does he dilute the Greek world with the Christian, but also he fails to develop the Prometheus character, the son for whom the sacrifice is made. Ancient myth, in short, treated tentatively and incompletely, does not sustain Updike any more than Christian myth can. In *The Coup* Updike quite deliberately rejects myth. The dictator protagonist of a Third World country in this novel undertakes a perilous journey to the most fearsome corner of his country in order to destroy the spirit of the tyrannical king he has deposed and killed. In accomplishing his mission he will purify his own life, redeem the land, and bring fertility, i.e., rain, to it. But when he reaches the cave which contains the mystery—the deposed king's talking head—he finds that it has been wired for sound by his Russian allies; the cave, full of electronic equipment, has become a tourist attraction. Myth can exist only as parody in a world dominated by high technology and imperialism.

In Updike's fiction generally, it is contemporary culture that debases belief—in Christianity or myth—and values and renders them well-nigh impossible. His characters struggle to be moral, to take responsibility for others, but they find no acceptable authority, divine or human, to define for them a "good" life, and they cannot struggle successfully against a culture hostile to the genuine needs of human beings. Thus the vision of loss and disintegration pervades Updike's fiction. Everything decays: sexual and political morality, the family, patriotism, food (it is synthetic, plastic), sport, craftsmanship, language itself. In *Bech: A Book*, Updike comes, he says, to confess sterility, and he writes about how authors themselves betray literature and about the impotency of literature. A subtle writer and a master of paradox, Updike acts out in his own career an astonishing paradox: the survival of a writer who wishes, needs, to believe while demonstrating that belief is impossible.

—Chester E. Eisinger

UPWARD, Edward (Falaise). British. Born in Romford, Essex, 9 September 1903. Educated at Repton School, 1917-21; Corpus Christi College, Cambridge (Chancellor's Medal for Verse), 1922-24, M.A. 1925. Married to Hilda Maude Percival; one son and one daughter. Schoolmaster, 1928-62. Member of the Editorial Board, *The Ploughshare*, 1936-39. Address: c/o William Heinemann Ltd., 10 Upper Grosvenor Street, London W1X 9PA, England.

PUBLICATIONS

Novels

Journey to the Border. London, Hogarth Press, 1938.
The Spiral Ascent (includes *No Home But the Struggle*). London, Heinemann, 1977.
In the Thirties. London, Heinemann, 1962.
The Rotten Elements. London, Heinemann, 1969.

Short Stories

The Railway Accident and Other Stories. London, Heinemann, 1969.

Verse

Buddha. London, Cambridge University Press, 1924.

*

Manuscript Collection: British Library, London.

Critical Studies: Introduction by W.H. Sellers to *The Railway Accident and Other Stories*, 1969; by the author, in *London Magazine*, June 1969.

* * *

Edwrd Upward as a young writer in the 1930's achieved a great reputation, was indeed something of a legend, among a number of writers of his own age and younger. Christopher Isherwood has told in *Lions and Shadows* how he and Upward (called Chalmers in Isherwood's book) at Cambridge invented a fantasy world they called Mortmere which paralleled and parodied the world about them. Mortmere seems to have been at once sinister and comic, partly surrealist and partly Gothic. That it had affinities with Auden's early poetry, influenced as it was by Freud, seems clear, and something of it seems to emerge in the plays Isherwood wrote in collaboration with Auden, notably *The Dog Beneath the Skin*. Upward, however, overtly pursued the vein of fantasy in his fiction, but, even then politically committed, in the cause of Marxism. The central character of *Journey to the Border* is a middle-class young man employed as a tutor in the house of a rich man; he is constantly struggling against the implications and ignominies of his position but is unable to resolve them. He is persuaded against his will to accompany his employer to a race-meeting. On the way, and while there, he experiences a series of hallucinations that mount in intensity and are the counterparts of the debate going on in his mind. By the end of the novel he is forced to realise that the only solution to this problem, the only way to reality, is for him to identify himself with the working-class struggle.

When the novel was first published, reviewers read the influence of Kafka into it. This is not much apparent now, if it ever existed. Upward's novel is much less complex than Kafka's, and what begins as a work of symbolism peters out in simple allegory. Nevertheless, the voltage of imaginative excitement generated is high, and the dreamlike quality of the work is admirably sustained. It remains a brilliant experimental novel of a very unusual kind.

Upward published nothing for 25 years, and then in 1962 appeared *In the Thirties* (followed by *The Rotten Elements* and, as a complete trilogy incorporating *No Home But the Struggle*, *The Spiral Ascent*). These novels are based, it is impossible not to think, on the author's own life. *In the Thirties* describes the stages by which a young middle-class man comes to Communism. In a sense, the theme is that of *Journey to the Border*, but the treatment is entirely different. Fantasy has been replaced by literal realism, which is also the vein of the later volumes of the trilogy. In *The Rotten Elements* the hero of the earlier novel, a school teacher now married, finds himself compelled in the years immediately after the war to leave the Communist Party, not because he has lost his political faith but because for him and his wife the British Communist Party, under the influence of Moscow, has deviated from Marxism-Leninism. *No Home But the Struggle* shows them recommitted to the campaign for nuclear disarmament. The trilogy lacks the literary interest of *Journey to the Border*, but it has an anguish of its own and a documentary quality which suggests that, though it may not be read in the future for its artistic value, it will be essential reading for scholars concerned with the role of the Communist party in Britain.

—Walter Allen

URIS, Leon (Marcus). American. Born in Baltimore, Maryland, 3 August 1924. Educated in Baltimore city schools. Served in the United States Marine Corps, 1942-45. Married 1) Betty Beck in 1945 (divorced, 1965); 2) Margery Edwards, 1968 (died, 1969); 3) Jill Peabody, 1970; three children. Newspaper driver for the *San Francisco Call-Bulletin* in the late 1940's. Full-time writer since 1950. Recipient: Daroff Memorial Award, 1959; American Academy grant, 1959. Lives in Aspen, Colorado. Address: c/o Doubleday and Company Inc., 245 Park Avenue, New York, New York 10017, U.S.A.

PUBLICATIONS

Novels

Battle Cry. New York, Putnam, and London, Wingate, 1953.
The Angry Hills. New York, Random House, 1955; London, Wingate, 1956.
Exodus. New York, Doubleday, 1958; London, Wingate, 1959.
Mila 18. New York, Doubleday, and London, Heinemann, 1961.
Armageddon: A Novel of Berlin. New York, Doubleday, and London, Kimber, 1964.
Topaz. New York, McGraw Hill, 1967; London, Kimber, 1968.
Q.B. VII. New York, Doubleday, 1970; London, Kimber, 1971.
Trinity. New York, Doubleday, and London, Deutsch, 1976.

Plays

Ari, music by Walt Smith and William Fisher, adaptation of the novel *Exodus* by Uris (produced New York, 1971).

Screenplays: *Battle Cry*, 1955; *Gunfight at the OK Corral*, 1957; *Israel* (documentary), 1959.

Other

Exodus Revisited. New York, Doubleday, 1960; as *In the Steps of Exodus*, London, Heinemann, 1962.
The Third Temple, with *Strike Zion*, by William Stevenson. New York, Bantam, 1967.
Ireland, A Terrible Beauty: The Story of Ireland Today, with Jill Uris. New York, Doubleday, 1975; London, Deutsch, 1976.
Jerusalem: Song of Songs, with Jill Uris. New York, Doubleday, 1981.

* * *

Critics were willing to be charitable to Leon Uris's popular novel, *Battle Cry*, when it appeared in 1953. While it is a war novel not as psychologically complex as Wouk's *The Caine Mutiny*, nor as deeply probing into the nature of man and war as Mailer's *The Naked and the Dead* or Jones's *From Here to Eternity*, it is a good, straightforward, blood-and-guts adventure of the U.S. Marine Corps in which dialogue and action are matched well to characters. Though Uris's treatment by professional critics has generally been much harsher for the novels that have been published since, their disparagement of his work is, in an important sense, not entirely fair. There is no reason to suppose that the present is different from earlier periods in literary history when there has been a popular, ephemeral literature as distinct from a smaller body of serious and lasting literature with limited public appeal. Uris makes no pretense of contributing to an enduring *corpus* of American literature. He bulls his way forward on the sheer strength of his narrative ability, which was acknowledged at the beginning of his career, and though he may stumble over literary matters of characterisation, plot detail, dialogue, or theme, his handling of the story line unfailingly carries him through, and the book-buying public accaims him over the grumbling of critics.

Yet the faults are real and cannot be overlooked; they are in evidence in all of the novels. *The Angry Hills*, a romantic war adventure of Greek resistance to the Nazi occupation, contains obtrusively contrived circumstances. The invention of the love subplot of *Exodus*, between the Zionist hero Ari Ben Canaan and the gentile nurse Kitty Fremont, often seems gratuitous, and its execution pre-Cinemascope. *Armageddon*, like *Exodus* and Uris's other works, has its plot in large measure constructed by history, in this case Russian-American relations in Berlin after World War II, and especially the American airlift. And, like *Exodus*, it is plagued by a love affair that seems, at times, to be arbitrarily appended to the progression of historical events. It suffers, too, from a weakness of dialogue that is not unusual in Uris, and from the trite response of the main character, an American occupation officer, to the German and Russian nations in turn. *Mila 18* does an injustice to the Jews of the Warsaw ghetto, whose resolute defiance of the Nazis it chronicles, by transforming them into a series of stock characters. Here as elsewhere in his novels, Uris seems to be best when he is recounting the history he has researched and at his worst when he requires one of the obviously indispensable attributes of the novelist—the power to weave the plot line into a smooth integument of all the elements of fiction.

Yet there is the brute force of the narrative in all of the novels that compels the reader through to the finish despite all imperfections, even through the too-lengthy trial and concentration camp horrors of *Q.B. VII.* And, though it would be wrong to assume that Uris has begun to compose deathless prose at this late date, in pitting the American novelist Abraham Cady against the former camp inmate Adam Kelno, he demonstrates an ability now to create characters of interest and depth.

—Alan R. Shucard

URQUHART, Fred(erick Burrows). British. Born in Edinburgh, 12 July 1912. Educated at village schools in Scotland; Stranraer High School, Wigtownshire; Broughton Secondary School, Edinburgh. Worked in an Edinburgh bookshop, 1927-34; reader for a London literary agency, 1947-51, and for MGM, 1951-54; London scout for Walt Disney Productions, 1959-60; reader for Cassell and Company, London, 1951-74, and for J.M. Dent and Sons, London, 1967-71. Recipient: Tom-Gallon Trust Award, 1951; Arts Council grant, 1966, bursary, 1975. Address: Spring Garden Cottage, Fairwarp, Uckfield, Sussex, England.

PUBLICATIONS

Novels

Time Will Knit. London, Duckworth, 1938.
The Ferret Was Abraham's Daughter. London, Methuen, 1949.
Jezebel's Dust. London, Methuen, 1951.
Palace of Green Days. London, Quartet, 1979.

Short Stories

I Fell for a Sailor and Other Stories. London, Duckworth, 1940.
The Clouds Are Big with Mercy. Glasgow, Maclellan, 1946.
Selected Stories. Dublin, Fridberg, 1946.
The Last GI Bride Wore Tartan: A Novella and Some Short Stories. Edinburgh, Serif, 1948.
The Year of the Short Corn and Other Stories. London, Methuen, 1949.
The Last Sister and Other Stories. London, Methuen, 1950.
The Laundry Girl and the Pole: Selected Stories. London, Arco, 1955.
Collected Stories:
1. *The Dying Stallion and Other Stories*. London, Hart Davis, 1967.
2. *The Ploughing Match and Other Stories*. London, Hart Davis, 1968.

Proud Lady in a Cage: Six Historical Stories. Edinburgh, Harris, 1980.
A Diver in the China Seas. London, Quartet, 1980.

Uncollected Short Stories

"Hector's Hectic Hogmanay," in *Scottish Hogmanay Annual* (Edinburgh), 1950-51.
"Charlie Calling," in *Modern Reading* (London), Summer 1952.
"The Gay Gush Girls," in *Thy Neighbour's Wife*, edited by James Turner. London, Cassell, 1964.
"Water Water Wallflower," in *The Fourth Ghost Book*, edited by James Turner. London, Barrie and Rockliff, 1965.
"The Ghostess with the Mostest," in *Unlikely Ghosts*, edited by James Turner. London, Cassell, 1967.
"Two Lives: 1914," in *Texas Quarterly* (Austin), Autumn 1974.
"Witch's Kitchen," in *The Midnight Ghost Book*, edited by James Hale. London, Barrie and Jenkins, 1978.

Other

Scotland in Colour. London, Batsford, and New York, Viking Press, 1961.

Editor, with Maurice Lindsay, *No Scottish Twilight: New Scottish Stories*. Glasgow, Maclellan, 1947.
Editor, *W.S.C.: A Cartoon Biography* (on Winston Churchill). London, Cassell, 1955.
Editor, *Great True War Adventures*. London, Arco, 1956; New York, Arco, 1957.
Editor, *Scottish Short Stories*. London, Faber, 1957.
Editor, *Men at War: The Best War Stories of All Time*. London, Arco, 1957.
Editor, *Great True Escape Stories*. London, Arco, 1958.
Editor, *The Cassell Miscellany 1848-1958*. London, Cassell, 1958.
Editor, *Everyman's Dictionary of Fictional Characters*, by William Freeman, revised edition. London, Dent, and New York, Dutton, 1973.
Editor, with Giles Gordon, *Modern Scottish Short Stories*. London, Hamish Hamilton, 1978.

*

Manuscript Collections: National Library of Scotland, Edinburgh; University of Texas Library, Austin.

Critical Studies: review by Janet Adam Smith, in *New York Times Book Review*, 31 July 1938; Alexander Reid, in *Scotland's Magazine* (Edinburgh) February 1958; Iain Crichton Smith in *The Spectator* (London), 24 May 1968; *History of Scottish Literature* by Maurice Lindsay, London, Hale, 1977.

Fred Urquhart comments:

I never talk to people about my work. When I'm writing a story or novel I don't want anybody to see it or know anything about it until it is completely finished and it satisfies me. I can't understand the habit of some authors of reading their work aloud to their friends as the work progresses. It is only after I've written a story that I show it to friends, inviting criticism.

* * *

Fred Urquhart is a wonderful listener. He gets the exact lilt of Clydeside or the Mearns or Leith or Scots dialect modified by the army or navy. He seems to be fascinated by the corruption of language: how Glasgow speech adds an embroidering diminutive "ie"—flashie, steamie—but is itself a corrupted English from what was the Clyde ditch into which the fleeing Gaelic speakers piled themselves hoping for a puckle siller and a wee housie or roomie to live and love in. Those are his backgrounds. But his tongue or maybe his pen is as skilled as his deeply interested ear. He gets it all down often with a minimal plot but with such liveliness and such involvement of characters that the story line hardly matters. Indeed there are times when he has a good heart-throb ending but he usually gets away with it because of the way it is told.

These writings of his are too artful and delicate to be in fact the kind of stories which have been told into the unsympathetic ear of a tape recorder. Thus always another human but invisible listener may be asking the odd question that stirs the story up and this invisible other is infinitely aware of the fine points of dialogue and the hidden feelings of the characters, which only appear between the lines, making tensions which are never underlined. Oddly enough Urquhart is best with his women characters, his schoolmistresses and farmers' wives or daughters; his Glasgow lassies on the make or his dirty old wifies. He really gets into the skin of the "Last G.I. Bride." Why? Maybe he finds the toughness of the average male Scot a bit of a bore—as so many women also find it! But he is sensitive to other second class citizens, for instance the Italian prisoners working on a Lowland farm in one of his World War II stories.

He is not a quick writer. Perhaps that is why his novels are really longer short stories. On the whole he spends little time on the background unless it is farm detail, and here he is often away back to the days of splendid Clydesdale mares and comparatively unhygienic byres and dairies. Most comes through conversation or the fleeting thoughts which are near to speech. He is also very much interested in what other writers are doing, especially in Scotland. He must often have been sorely tempted to do a bit of quick slick writing for the "popular" family magazines; perhaps "The Year of the Short Corn" is partly autobiographical. But he believes that writers have a certain duty to tell the truth, even when it is displeasing to the audience they would most like—their own folk. This audience of course is what all writers want but few if any get, because of the corruption of the chosen hearers. It is hard luck to have to wait till you are dead before you are appreciated. One hopes this won't have to happen to Fred Urquhart.

—Naomi Mitchison

van der POST, Laurens (Jan). South African. Born in Philippolis, 13 December 1906. Educated at Grey College, Bloemfontein. Served in the British Army, in the Western Desert and the Far East, in World War II; Prisoner of War in Java, 1943-45; Military Attaché to the British Minister, Batavia, 1945-47: C.B.E. (Commander, Order of the British Empire), 1947. Married 1) Marjorie Wendt in 1929 (divorced, 1947), one son and one daughter; 2) the writer Ingaret Giffard in 1949. Reporter, *Natal Advertiser*, Durban, 1925-26; leader writer, *Cape Times*, Cape Town, 1930; editor, *Natal Daily News*, Durban, 1948; farmer in the Orange Free State, South Africa, 1948-65. Explorer: has made several missions to Africa for the Colonial Development Corporation and the British Government, including a mission to Kalahari, 1952. Recipient: Anisfield-Wolf Award, 1951; National Association of Independent Schools Award (USA), 1959; South African Central News Agency Prize, 1963, 1967. D.Litt.: University of Natal, Pietermaritzburg, 1964; University of Liverpool, 1976; Rhodes University, Grahamstown, 1978; St. Andrews University, Scotland, 1980; D. Univ.: University of Surrey, Guildford, 1971. Fellow, Royal Society of Literature, 1955. Knighted, 1981. Address: 27 Chelsea Towers, Chelsea Manor Gardens, London S.W.3; or, Turn-Stones, Aldeburgh, Suffolk, England.

PUBLICATIONS

Novels

In a Province. London, Hogarth Press, 1934; New York, Coward McCann, 1935.
The Face Beside the Fire. London, Hogarth Press, and New York, Morrow, 1953.
A Bar of Shadow. London, Hogarth Press, 1954; New York, Morrow, 1956.
Flamingo Feather. London, Hogarth Press, and New York, Morrow, 1955.
The Seed and the Sower (includes *A Bar of Shadow* and *The Sword and the Doll*). London, Hogarth Press, and New York, Morrow, 1963.
The Hunter and the Whale: A Tale of Africa. London, Hogarth Press, and New York, Morrow, 1967.
A Story like the Wind. London, Hogarth Press, and New York Morrow, 1972.
A Far-Off Place. London, Hogarth Press, and New York, Morrow, 1974.
A Mantis Carol. London, Hogarth Press, 1975; New York, Morrow, 1976.

Plays

Screenplays: *The Lost World of the Kalahari*, 1956; *A Region of Shadow*, 1971; *The Story of Carl Gustav Jung*, 1971; *All Africa Within Us*, 1975.

Other

Venture to the Interior. New York, Morrow, 1951; London, Hogarth Press, 1952.
The Dark Eye in Africa. London, Hogarth Press, and New York, Morrow, 1955.
Race Prejudice as Self-Rejection. New York, Workshop for Cultural Democracy, 1957.
The Lost World of the Kalahari. London, Hogarth Press, and New York, Morrow, 1958.
The Heart of the Hunter. London, Hogarth Press, and New York, Morrow, 1961.
Patterns of Renewal. Wallingford, Pennsylvania, Pendle Hill, 1962.
Intuition, Intellect, and the Racial Question. New York, Myrin Institute, 1964.
Journey into Russia. London, Hogarth Press, 1964; as *A View of All the Russias*, New York, Morrow, 1964.
A Portrait of All the Russias. London, Hogarth Press, and New York, Morrow, 1967.
A Portrait of Japan. London, Hogarth Press, and New York, Morrow, 1968.
The Night of the New Moon: August 6, 1945...Hiroshima. London, Hogarth Press, 1970; as *The Prisoner and the Bomb*, New York, Morrow, 1971.
African Cooking, with the editors of Time-Life. New York, Time, 1970.
Man and the Shadow. London, South Place Ethical Society, 1971.
Jung and the Story of Our Time: A Personal Experience. New York, Pantheon, 1975; London, Hogarth Press, 1976.
First Catch Your Eland: A Taste of Africa. London, Hogarth Press, 1977; New York, Morrow, 1978.

*

Critical Study: *Laurens van der Post* by Frederic I. Carpenter, New York, Twayne, 1969.

* * *

All the novels of Laurens van der Post have dealt, at least in part, with the life and problems of his native South Africa. All draw upon the author's actual life, which his most famous books of non-fiction (such as *Venture to the Interior*) have described autobiographically. All are distinguished by vivid descriptions of the natural scene, and by psychological depth. But each has been written from a different point of view, and has used a different technique.

In a Province is narrated in the first person by a young, white South African whose black friend runs afoul of the law. Both become involved with a communist agitator, and are finally killed by a posse of self-appointed commandos. The novel is realistic in technique, and is distinguished both by its wealth of incidents involving race relations, and by its balance between the theme of racial injustice on the one hand, and communist exploitation on the other. Although the author has opposed apartheid all his life, he has equally opposed communist subversion.

Nineteen years elapsed between the author's first and second novels—years including his move to England and his distinguished service in World War II, ending with his capture and imprisonment by the Japanese. *The Face Beside the Fire* deals with the problems of an expatriate South African artist in London. Narrated by a life-long friend of the hero, the novel covers a period of many years, and moves from Africa to England and back. Its many episodes find unity in the psychological theme of alienation. Its technique is that of the psychological novel pioneered by Thomas Mann.

Flamingo Feather is a fast-paced tale of mystery and adventure set in war-time South Africa. Narrated in the first person by a young anthropologist, the plot concerns a communist attempt to subvert a native tribe in the interior. The action includes a vividly narrated trek through tropical jungles. A mystery-melodrama, the novel is distinguished both by its fast action and its vivid description of the wild country of Africa.

The Seed and the Sower consists of three "novellas" describing warfare in Africa and Asia, but focusing on the life of the prisoner-of-war. The first novella, *A Bar of Shadow* (published separately in 1956), centers upon the narrator's attempt to understand his Japanese captors. The second (and longest) returns to South Africa to narrate the early experiences of another officer, and ends with his capture and execution by the Japanese. The third narrates a brief wartime romance. All focus upon the author's experiences as prisoner-or-war, which also shadow much of his autobiographical writing.

The Hunter and the Whale, subtitled *A Tale of Africa*, is narrated by a 17-year-old boy who serves as lookout on a whaling ship working out of Durban. The novel is richer and more complex than the others, and combines realistic with symbolic techniques. Its unusual subject matter and unusual techniques both suggest comparison with Melville's *Moby-Dick*, and help to explain both the fascination and the occasional difficulty of the novel.

A Story like the Wind narrates the adventures of a white boy whose ancestral farm in the interior of South Africa is attacked and captured by communist-led guerillas, and of his escape with the help of a Bushman friend of his own age. *A Far-Off Place* is a continuation of *A Story like the Wind*, though self-contained. The second novel tells of the long journey of these two across the southwest African desert to the coast, and their rescue. Both novels are fast-paced, and filled with adventure and the lore of the Africa which the author knows so well.

—Frederic I. Carpenter

VIDAL, Gore (Eugene Luther Vidal, Jr.). American. Born in West Point, New York, 3 October 1925. Educated at Los Alamos School, New Mexico, 1939-40; Phillips Exeter Academy, New Hampshire, 1940-43. Served in the United States Army, 1943-46. Editor, E.P. Dutton, publishers, New York, 1946. Member, Advisory Board, *Partisan Review*, New Brunswick, New Jersey, 1960-71; Democratic-Liberal candidate for Congress, New York, 1960; Member, President's Advisory Committee on the Arts, 1961-63; Co-Chairman, New Party, 1968-71. Address: 2562 Outpost Drive, Los Angeles, California 90068, U.S.A.

PUBLICATIONS

Novels

Williwaw. New York, Dutton, 1948; London, Panther, 1965.
In a Yellow Wood. New York, Dutton, 1947; London, New English Library, 1967.
The City and the Pillar. New York, Dutton, 1948; London, Lehmann, 1949; revised edition, Dutton, and London, Heinemann, 1965.
The Season of Comfort. New York, Dutton, 1949.
Dark Green, Bright Red. New York, Dutton, and London, Lehmann, 1950.
A Search for the King: A Twelfth Century Legend. New York, Dutton, 1950; London, New English Library, 1967.
The Judgment of Paris. New York, Dutton, 1952; London, Heinemann, 1953; revised edition, Boston, Little Brown, 1965; Heinemann, 1966.
Messiah. New York, Dutton, 1954; London, Heinemann, 1955; revised edition, Boston, Little Brown, 1965; Heinemann, 1968.
Three: Williwaw, A Thirsty Evil, Julian the Apostate. New York, New American Library, 1962.
Julian. Boston, Little Brown, and London, Heinemann, 1964.
Washington, D.C. Boston, Little Brown, and London, Heinemann, 1967.
Myra Breckinridge. Boston, Little Brown, and London, Blond, 1968.
Two Sisters: A Memoir in the Form of a Novel. Boston, Little Brown, and London, Heinemann, 1970.
Burr. New York, Random House, 1973; London, Heinemann, 1974.
Myron. New York, Random House, 1974; London, Heinemann, 1975.
1876. New York, Random House, and London, Heinemann, 1976.
Kalki. New York, Random House, and London, Heinemann, 1978.
Creation. New York, Random House, and London, Heinemann, 1981.

Novels as Edgar Box

Death in the Fifth Position. New York, Dutton, 1952; London, Heinemann, 1954.
Death Before Bedtime. New York, Dutton, 1953; London, Heinemann, 1954.
Death Likes It Hot. New York, Dutton, 1954; London, Heinemann, 1955.

Short Stories

A Thirsty Evil: Seven Short Stories. New York, Zero Press, 1956; London, Heinemann, 1958.

Plays

Visit to a Small Planet (televised, 1955). Included in *Visit to a Small Planet and Other Television Plays*, 1956; revised version (produced New York, 1957; London, 1960), Boston, Little Brown, 1957; in *Three Plays*, 1962.
Honor (televised, 1956). Published in *Television Plays for Writers: Eight Television Plays*, edited by A.S. Burack, Boston, The Writer, 1957; revised version, as *On the March to the Sea: A Southron Comedy* (produced Bonn, Germany, 1961), in *Three Plays*, 1962.
Visit to a Small Planet and Other Television Plays (includes *Barn Burning, Dark Possession, The Death of Billy the Kid, A Sense of Justice, Smoke, Summer Pavilion, The Turn of the Screw*). Boston, Little Brown, 1956.
The Best Man: A Play about Politics (produced New York, 1960). Boston, Little Brown; 1960; in *Three Plays*, 1962.
Three Plays (includes *Visit to a Small Planet, The Best Man, On the March to the Sea*). London, Heinemann, 1962.
Romulus: A New Comedy, adaptation of a play of Friedrich Dürrenmatt (produced New York, 1962). New York, Dramatists Play Service, 1962.
Weekend (produced New York, 1968). New York, Dramatists Play Service, 1968.
An Evening with Richard Nixon and... (produced New York, 1972). New York, Random House, 1972.

Screenplays: *The Catered Affair*, 1956; *I Accuse*, 1958; *The Scapegoat*, with Robert Hamer, 1959; *Suddenly Last Summer*, with Tennessee Williams, 1960; *The Best Man*, 1964; *Is Paris Burning?*, with Francis Ford Coppola, 1966; *Last of the Mobile Hot-Shots*, 1970.

Television Plays: *Barn Burning*, from the story by Faulkner, 1954; *Dark Possession*, 1954; *Smoke*, from the story by Faulkner, 1954; *Visit to a Small Planet*, 1955; *The Death of Billy the Kid*, 1955; *A Sense of Justice*, 1955; *Summer Pavilion*, 1955; *The Turn of the Screw*, from the story by Henry James, 1955; *Honor*, 1956; *The Indestructible Mr. Gore*, 1960.

Other

Rocking the Boat (essays). Boston, Little Brown, 1962; London, Heinemann, 1963.
Sex, Death, and Money (essays). New York, Bantam, 1968.
Reflections upon a Sinking Ship (essays). Boston, Little Brown, and London, Heinemann, 1969.
Homage to Daniel Shays: Collected Essays 1952-1972. New York, Random House, 1972; as *Collected Essays 1952-1972*, London, Heinemann, 1974.
Matters of Fact and of Fiction: Essays 1973-1976. New York, Random House, and London, Heinemann, 1977.
Great American Families, with others. New York, Norton, and London, Times Books, 1977.

Views from a Window: Conversations with Gore Vidal, with Robert J. Stanton. Secaucus, New Jersey, Stuart, 1980.

Editor, *Best Television Plays*. New York, Ballantine, 1956.

*

Bibliography: *Gore Vidal: A Primary and Secondary Bibliography* by Robert J. Stanton, Boston, Hall, 1978.

Manuscript Collection: University of Wisconsin, Madison.

Critical Studies: *Gore Vidal* by Ray Lewis White, New York, Twayne, 1968; *The Apostate Angel: A Critical Study of Gore Vidal* by Bernard F. Dick, New York, Random House, 1974.

* * *

At first glance the sheer number and range of Gore Vidal's books would seem to discourage any useful generalizations. Vidal is the author, as he puts it, of "what is probably in plain bulk the largest oeuvre of any contemporary American writer." The diversity of his fiction, from a massive "autobiography" of the Emperor Julian to reports on the American sexual underground, is more apparent, however, than real; for throughout the novels there is a persistent concern with naturalism—and its ethical and political consequences—as the only sensible guide to living. The early novels move toward this position; the later novels, as well as Vidal's vigorous critical essays, are essentially polemical defenses of naturalism against contending points of view.

For this position, which forms one of the dominant strains of western thinking from the pre-Socratics through Santayana, man is a finite, mortal, purely natural creature, living precariously and unsponsored in an accidental universe. Whatever meaning he finds and whatever values he cherishes can be derived only from a capacity to learn from his experiences in a world indifferent to his fate. But while it follows that reason will play a vital role in planning those adjustments necessary for living, the emotions and life of the body are no less real or natural. "Men are wise," reflects the hero of *The Judgment of Paris*, "when they love nature more than dogma"; the self is merely a "temporary arrangement of matter." The fullest statement of Vidal's naturalism, however, occurs in *Two Sisters*:

> listening to Dwight MacDonald talk on and on, entirely happy in his pursuit of thought, I said, "Don't you realize, Dwight, you have nothing to say, only to add?" He stopped short: said he found this a most impressive statement.... Yet what I said of him I really meant to say of myself, of us all. For what is there to *say* finally, except that pain is bad and pleasure good, death nothing? To these obvious texts, one can only add one's life which is so little, particularly if words are one's only means of telling what was, what is, and what ought to be.

The ethical corollary of Vidal's naturalism is a kind of urbane utilitarianism, or calculating hedonism, in which the diverse needs of natural man are satisfied to the fullest extent compatible with social order. The enemies of naturalism are the doctrines which repress these needs (hence Vidal's continuing fascination with Julian the Apostate as a figure who attempted to forestall the triumph of Christianity and its life-denying mandates), as well as the equally natural drive for power and domination over others, in sex or politics. "There is no virtue in any of us," complains the protagonist of *Washington, D.C.*, "we are savages"; we all play a game whose nature is, simply "war.... A conquers B who conquers C who conquers A. Each in his own way [struggles] for precedence and to deny this essential predatoriness [is] sentimental; to accommodate it wrong; to change it impossible." The narrator of *Two Sisters* concludes, "We come and we go and the time between is all we have. I am stoic, and I can be nothing else."

If this were all, however, Vidal's novels would be a good deal less lively than in fact they are, for despite his misgivings about the future of the race, he cannot help admiring human resourcefulness: as the central figure of *Messiah* puts it, our "conception of the inconsequence of human activity...is ever in conflict with a profound love of those essential powers that result in human action, a paradox certainly, a dual vision which restrains me from easy judgments." This "dual vision" is the source of Vidal's strength as a writer, even in those early novels which by any reasonable standards must seem fumbling and unpromising.

Williwaw is a "war novel" only in the sense that even this first novel defines men's lives as a battle against nature—and the vanity of their fellowmen. The three novels which follow deal in one way or another with the youthful search for freedom and satisfaction. Rather surprisingly the hero of *In a Yellow Wood* decides to "accept the pattern" of conventional behavior, after a thinly dramatized encounter with romantic love and unconventional sex (dismissed here as mere "self-indulgence" rather than genuine freedom). In *The Season of Comfort*—in which Vidal experiments uneasily with something beyond the "natural manner of the time...colorless, careful prose, deliberately confined to the surface of things"—the protagonist successfully breaks his ties to his mother and moves tentatively towards love and a career as an artist. *The City and the Pillar*, which caused something of a scandal by its earnest (and by current standards completely unsensational) revelations of homosexual life in America, has as its theme not sexual deviation so much as the more general problem of the "romantic fallacy," the fatal desire to recapture a past moment whose perfection was a naive illusion. (*The City and the Pillar* has far more in common with *The Great Gatsby* than with Genet.) Vidal has repudiated *In a Yellow Wood* and *The Season of Comfort*, as well as *A Search for the King* (a pale imitation of medieval romance), quite aware that he had not yet found his "own true voice and pitch."

Dark Green, Bright Red is a routine adventure story with a pleasantly ironic twist at the end, but in *The Judgment of Paris* Vidal's apprenticeship comes to an end. The theme is the familiar one—here a young man chooses love rather than political opportunity or "wisdom"—yet the writing is sharp and genuinely witty, revealing for the first time Vidal's great gifts as a comic caricaturist. *Messiah* is a philosophic fantasy, a parable in which the narrator struggles against the perverted naturalism of a powerful religious leader (the theme is repeated in the ambitious *Julian*, which despite its impressive moments finally sinks under the burden of its historical authenticity). *Washington, D.C.*, a panoramic account of power politics shrewdly contrived to have something for everyone, is, nevertheless, wholly engrossing. Vidal finds his "true voice," however, in *Myra Breckinridge*, a scabrous, brilliantly comic survey of American youth and sexuality and satiric dramatization of the familiar sex-as-domination motif. *Two Sisters* is a stylish exploration of vanity and, once again, the unrecapturability of the past, taking irresistible pot-shots along the way at everything and everyone Vidal dislikes, from Nabokov to the Bouvier sisters. Despite all the evidence that man is on a collision course with disaster, the final word for Vidal is an open-ended "Yet—": "Is there any word in English," he asks, "quite so useful, so hopeful, so truly pregnant as yet?" Given proper guidance it is still possible, he concludes, "that human freedom might be sustained, even increased."

—Elmer Borklund

VONNEGUT, Kurt, Jr. American. Born in Indianapolis, Indiana, 11 November 1922. Educated at Cornell University, Ithaca, New York, 1940-42; Carnegie Institute, Pittsburgh, 1943; University of Chicago, 1945-47. Served in the United States Army Infantry, 1942-45: Purple Heart. Married 1) Jane Marie Cox in 1945 (divorced, 1979), one son and two daughters; 2) Jill Krementz in 1979. Police Reporter, Chicago City News Bureau, 1946; worked in public relations for the General Electric Company, Schenectady, New York, 1947-50. Since 1950, free-lance writer. Since 1965, teacher, Hopefield School, Sandwich, Massachusetts. Visiting Lecturer, Writers Workshop, University of Iowa, Iowa City, 1965-67, and Harvard University, Cambridge, Massachusetts, 1970-71; Visiting Professor, City University of New York, 1973-74. Recipient: Guggenheim Fellowship, 1967; American Academy grant, 1970. M.A.: University of Chicago, 1971; Litt. D.: Hobart and William Smith Colleges, Geneva, New York, 1974. Member, American Academy, 1973. Agent: Donald C. Farber, 600 Madison Avenue, New York, New York, 10022. Address: Scudder's Lane, West Barnstable, Massachusetts 02668, U.S.A.

PUBLICATIONS

Novels

Player Piano. New York, Scribner, 1952; London, Macmillan, 1953; as *Utopia 14*, New York, Bantam, 1954.
The Sirens of Titan. New York, Dell, 1959; London, Gollancz, 1962.
Mother Night. New York, Fawcett, 1962; London, Cape, 1968.
Cat's Cradle. New York, Holt Rinehart, and London, Gollancz, 1963.
God Bless You, Mr. Rosewater; or, Pearls Before Swine. New York, Holt Rinehart, and London, Cape, 1965.
Slaughterhouse-Five; or, The Children's Crusade. New York, Delacorte Press, 1969; London, Cape, 1970.
Breakfast of Champions; or, Goodbye, Blue Monday. New York, Delacorte Press, and London, Cape, 1973.
Slapstick; or, Lonesome No More. New York, Delacorte Press, and London, Cape, 1973.
Jailbird. New York, Delacorte Press, and London, Cape, 1979.

Short Stories

Canary in a Cat House. New York, Fawcett, 1961.
Welcome to the Monkey House: A Collection of Short Works. New York, Delacorte Press, 1968; London, Cape, 1969.

Uncollected Short Stories

"Thanasphere," in *Collier's* (New York), 2 September 1950.
"Mnemonics," in *Collier's* (New York), 28 April 1951.
"Any Reasonable Offer," in *Collier's* (New York), 19 January 1952.
"The Package," in *Collier's* (New York), 26 July 1952.
"Poor Little Rich Town," in *Collier's* (New York), 25 October 1952.
"The No-Talent Kid," in *Saturday Evening Post* (Philadelphia), 25 October 1952.
"Souvenir," in *Argosy* (New York), December 1952.
"The Cruise of the Jolly Roger," in *Cape Cod Compass* (Provincetown, Massachusetts), April 1953.
"Custom-Made Bride," in *Saturday Evening Post* (Philadelphia), 27 March 1954.
"Ambitious Sophomore," in *Saturday Evening Post* (Philadelphia), 1 May 1954.
"Bagombo Snuff Box," in *Cosmopolitan* (New York), October 1954.
"The Powder Blue Dragon," in *Cosmopolitan* (New York), November 1954.
"A Present for Big Nick," in *Argosy* (New York), December 1954.
"Unpaid Consultant," in *Cosmopolitan* (New York), March 1955.
"The Boy Who Hated Girls," in *Saturday Evening Post* (Philadelphia), 31 March 1956.
"This Son of Mine...," in *Saturday Evening Post* (Philadelphia), 18 August 1956.
"A Night for Love," in *Saturday Evening Post* (Philadelphia), 23 November 1957.
"Find Me a Dream," in *Cosmopolitan* (New York), February 1961.
"Runaways," in *Saturday Evening Post* (Philadelphia), 15 April 1961.
"Hole Beautiful: Prospectus for a Magazine of Shelteredness," with Karla Kuskin, in *Monocle 5* (New York), 1962.
"2BR02B," in *Worlds of If* (New York), January 1962.
"Lovers Anonymous," in *Redbook* (New York), October 1963.
"The Big Space Fuck," in *Again, Dangerous Visions*, edited by Harlan Ellison. New York, Doubleday, 1972; London, Millington, 1976.

Plays

Happy Birthday, Wanda June (as *Penelope*, produced Cape Cod, Massachusetts, 1960; revised version, as *Happy Birthday, Wanda June*, produced New York, 1970; London, 1977). New York, Delacorte Press, 1970; London, Cape, 1973.
The Very First Christmas Morning, in *Better Homes and Gardens* (Des Moines, Iowa), December 1962.
Between Time and Timbuktu; or, Prometheus-5: A Space Fantasy (televised, 1972; produced New York, 1976). New York, Delacorte Press, 1972; London, Panther, 1975.
Fortitude, in *Wampeters, Foma, and Granfalloons*, 1974.
Timesteps (produced Edinburgh, 1979).
God Bless You, Mr. Rosewater, adaptation of his own novel (produced New York, 1979).

Television Play: *Between Time and Timbuktu*, 1972.

Other

Wampeters, Foma, and Granfalloons: Opinions. New York, Delacorte Press, 1974; London, Cape, 1975.
Sun Moon Star. New York, Harper, and London, Hutchinson, 1980.
Palm Sunday: An Autobiographical Collage. New York, Delacorte Press, and London, Cape, 1981.

*

Bibliography: *Kurt Vonnegut, Jr.: A Descriptive Bibliography and Annotated Secondary Checklist* by Asa B. Pieratt, Jr., and Jerome Klinkowitz, Hamden, Connecticut, Shoe String Press, 1974.

Critical Studies: *Kurt Vonnegut, Jr.*, by Peter J. Reed, New York, Warner, 1972; *Kurt Vonnegut: Fantasist of Fire and Ice* by David H. Goldsmith, Bowling Green, Ohio, Popular Press, 1972; *The Vonnegut Statement* edited by Jerome Klinkowitz and John Somer, New York, Delacorte Press, 1973, London, Panther, 1975; *Kurt Vonnegut, Jr.* by Stanley Schatt, Boston, Twayne, 1976; *Kurt Vonnegut* by James Lundquist, New York, Ungar, 1977; *Vonnegut: A Preface to His Novels* by Richard Giannone, Port Washington, New York, Kennikat Press, 1977; *Kurt Vonnegut: The Gospel from Outer Space* by Clark Mayo, San Bernardino, California, Borgo Press, 1977; *Vonnegut in America: An Introduction to the Life and Work of Kurt Vonnegut* edited by Jerome Klinkowitz and Donald L. Lawler, New York, Delacorte Press, 1977.

* * *

During the 1960's Kurt Vonnegut emerged as one of the most influential and provocative writers of fiction in America. His writing, indeed, constitutes an unintermittent protest against certain horrors of our century—the unending sequence of disastrous wars, the plunging decline in the livability of the environment, and the dehumanization of the individual in a society dominated by science and technology. Such protest is by no means new or unique in literature. The peculiar force of Vonnegut's voice among so many others may be traced to its complete contemporaneity. Fantasy (usually of the science variety), black humor, a keen sense of the absurd are the ingredients of his novels and stories.

Vonnegut has quite accurately described himself as "a total pessimist." And indeed his novels and most of his other writing offer little except wry laughter to counteract despair. This is certainly true of his first novel, *Player Piano*. The time of the novel is the not-too-distant future and the place is a one-industry city, Ilium, New York, which serves as the setting for much of Vonnegut's fiction and which resembles Schenectady, New York, where Vonnegut worked in public relations. In the novel not only the local industry but industries throughout the nation have been completely mechanized. Machines supplant human workers because machines make fewer errors. All national policy is determined by huge computers located in Mammoth Cave. A small elite of scientists are in charge of all production. The masses, who are provided with all material necessities and comforts, including an impressive array of gadgetry, serve in either military or work battalions. Acutely aware of their dehumanization and worthlessness except as mere consumers of the huge output of the machines, the common people revolt under the leadership of a preacher and several renegade scientists. Though the revolt in Ilium, at least, is successful and many of the objectionable machines are destroyed, Vonnegut denies his readers any sense of satisfaction. He records that the rebels destroyed not only obnoxious machinery but also the useful and necessary technological devices such as sewage disposal plants. What is more, they soon began to tinker with the unneeded machines with a view to making them operative again. In the face of such inveterate stupidity the leaders suicidally surrender to the government forces.

An obvious question arises: Why should Vonnegut or his readers concern themselves with the dehumanization of apparent morons? What, indeed, is there to be dehumanized? An answer is not readily forthcoming, but apparently Vonnegut considers that there is some value in attempting to save the human race from its own stupidity. In each novel there is at least one person who is aware of human folly, including his own, and thus is living proof that intellectual blindness is not universal. More frequently than not, moreover, these discerning individuals are reformers, as in *Player Piano*, who make self-sacrificing efforts to improve the lot of their fellow men. This is the case with *The Sirens of Titan*, which in plot is a rather conventional example of science fiction with an interplanetary setting. The reforming character in this book has been rendered immortal, omniscient, and virtually omnipotent by having been entrapped in a "chrono-synclastic-infundibulum." Thus endowed, he sets about uniting all nations of the world in the bonds of brotherhood by staging an abortive attack against the earth by Martians. The latter are earthlings abducted to Mars and converted to automatons by the insertion in their skulls of radio antennae through which orders are transmitted from a central directorate. These unfortunates are thus subjected to a ruthless dehumanization and exploitation, but to a worthwhile end. The scheme is successful; the earth becomes united after the defeat of the Martian attack and the unity is cemented by the establishment of a new religion, the Church of God the Utterly Indifferent. This happy outcome is somewhat clouded, however, by the revelation that the entire history of humanity has been determined by the trivial needs of the inhabitants of the planet Tralfamadore in one of the more remote galaxies.

Cat's Cradle and *God Bless You, Mr. Rosewater* also focus upon the efforts of altruistic individuals to allevate human misery. *Cat's Cradle* is notable for its presentation of an entirely new religion, Bokonism (named for its founder), much of the doctrine of which is written in Calypso verse. According to Bokonism, religion *should* be an opiate; its function is to deceive and, by deceiving, make people happy. It teaches that God directs human destinies and that mankind is sacred, and it promotes an ethic of love, which believers manifest by pressing the soles of their feet against those of fellow believers. Bokonism was founded and flourished on a Caribbean island oppressed by a Duvalier-type dictator. It flourished because it was outlawed, for, according to *Cat's Cradle*, at least, a religion functions most vigorously when opposed to the existing social order. There can be no doubt that Bokonism brings relief to the wretched islanders, the final horror of whose existence is that of being congealed, along with the rest of the world, by ice-nine, a discovery of an Ilium scientist. *God Bless You, Mr. Rosewater* recounts the efforts of an enormously wealthy philanthropist to alleviate human misery through the more or less random disbursement of the Rosewater Foundation's almost limitless funds. Like Bokonon, his purpose is to make existence more endurable for the masses. But he is less successful, for even with his millions he is able barely to scratch the surface of the world's wretchedness. He is taken advantage of by those whom he tries to help, and his friends and relatives consider him a lunatic. Yet he makes the effort and does achieve a degree of personal saintliness.

Two other novels, *Mother Night* and *Slaughterhouse-Five*, both of which focus upon World War II, contain no such reformers or philanthropists. In these the protagonists are never really in a position to be altruistic, even if they wish to be. In *Mother Night* Howard W. Campbell, Jr., serves schizophrenically as the Nazis' chief English-language radio propagandist at the same time that he is one of the allies' most effective spies. Years after the war he finds himself in an Israeli prison awaiting trial along with Adolph Eichmann. Here he commits suicide, even though a bizarre turn of events has ensured his acquittal. He has realized that one who has played his dual roles has betrayed beyond recovery his own humanity—a realization achieved by few Vonnegut characters in analogous situations.

Slaughterhouse-Five, perhaps Vonnegut's most powerful novel, presents two characters who can see beneath the surface to the tragic realities of human history but make no attempt to bring about change. These are the author himself, who is a frequent commentator, and the protagonist, Billy Pilgrim. The central event in the novel is the destruction of Dresden by bombs and fire storm—a catastrophe that Vonnegut himself witnessed as a prisoner of war. Billy Pilgrim's liberating insights are the outgrowth of his being freed from the prison of time and, as a result, seeing the past, present, and future as one and coexistent. One consequent realization is that death is an illusion. Though his periods of release from time occur on earth, their significance is explained to him by the inhabitants of the distant planet Tralfamadore, to which he is transported on a Tralfamadorian spaceship. Though Billy finds no way to improve the tragically absurd condition of man, he does arrive at an understanding of it and a resultant deepening of compassion.

Vonnegut's novels written durings the 1970's—*Breakfast of Champions*, *Slapstick*, *Jailbird*—continue to satirize human folly in its contemporary manifestations, and they still rely on fantasy, black humor, and the absurd as tools of satire. Yet their tone differs from that of the earlier fiction. The seriousness of theme and, above all, the compassion implicit in such books as *Cat's Cradle* and *Slaughterhouse-Five* are no longer noticeably present. *Slapstick*, indeed, would be appropriate as a title for any of the three. Fun and wit and laughs aplenty are not lacking, but thought is in short supply. The clown has shoved aside the thinker. But perhaps Vonnegut has concluded that is our only defense against the madness of our end-of-the century world.

—Perry D. Westbrook

WAGONER, David (Russell). American. Born in Massillon, Ohio, 5 June 1926. Educated at Pennsylvania State University, University Park, B.A. 1947; Indiana University, Bloomington, M.A. 1949. Served in the United States Navy, 1944-46. Married Patricia Parrott in 1961. Instructor, De Pauw University, Greencastle, Indiana, 1949-50, and Pennsylvania State University, 1950-54. Associate Professor, 1954-66, and since 1966, Professor of English,

University of Washington, Seattle. Elliston Lecturer, University of Cincinnati, 1968. Since 1966, Editor, *Poetry Northwest*, Seattle; since 1978, Editor, Princeton University Press Contemporary Poetry Series. Recipient: Guggenheim Fellowship, 1956; Ford Fellowship, for drama, 1964; American Academy grant, 1967; Morton Dauwen Zabel Prize (*Poetry*, Chicago), 1967; National Endowment for the Arts grant, 1969. Chancellor, Academy of American Poets, 1978. Address: 1075 Summit Avenue East, Seattle, Washington 98102, U.S.A.

PUBLICATIONS

Novels

The Man in the Middle. New York, Harcourt Brace, 1954; London, Gollancz, 1955.
Money, Money, Money. New York, Harcourt Brace, 1955.
Rock. New York, Viking Press, 1958.
The Escape Artist. New York, Farrar Straus, and London, Gollancz, 1965.
Baby, Come On Inside. New York, Farrar Straus, 1968.
Where Is My Wandering Boy Tonight? New York, Farrar Straus, 1970.
The Road to Many a Wonder. New York, Farrar Straus, 1974.
Tracker. Boston, Little Brown, 1975.
Whole Hog. Boston, Little Brown, 1976.
The Hanging Garden. Boston, Little Brown, 1980.

Uncollected Short Stories

"Afternoon on the Ground," in *Prairie Schooner* (Lincoln, Nebraska), Fall 1978.
"Wild Goose Chase," in *Georgia Review* (Athens), Fall 1978.
"Mr. Wallender's Romance," in *Hudson Review* (New York), Spring 1979.
"Cornet Solo, " in *Boston Globe Magazine*, 20 May 1979.
"The Water Strider," in *Boston Globe Magazine*, 14 October 1979.
"Fly Boy," in *Ohio Review 25* (Athens), 1980.
"The Bird Watcher," in *Georgia Review* (Athens), Spring 1980.
"Snake Hunt," in *Western Humanities Review* (Salt Lake City), Winter 1980.

Plays

An Eye for an Eye for an Eye (produced Seattle, 1973).

Screenplay: *The Escape Artist*, 1981.

Verse

Dry Sun, Dry Wind. Bloomington, Indiana University Press, 1953.
A Place to Stand. Bloomington, Indiana University Press, 1958.
Poems. Portland, Oregon, Portland Art Museum, 1959.
The Nesting Ground. Bloomington, Indiana University Press, 1963.
Five Poets of the Pacific Northwest, with others, edited by Robin Skelton. Seattle, University of Washington Press, 1964.
Staying Alive. Bloomington, Indiana University Press, 1966.
New and Selected Poems. Bloomington, Indiana University Press, 1969.
Working Against Time. London, Rapp and Whiting, 1970.
Riverbed. Bloomington, Indiana University Press, 1972.
Sleeping in the Woods. Bloomington, Indiana University Press, 1974.
A Guide to Dungeness Spit. Port Townsend, Washington, Graywolf Press, 1975.
Travelling Light. Port Townsend, Washington, Graywolf Press, 1976.
Collected Poems 1956-1976. Bloomington, Indiana University Press, 1976.
Who Shall Be the Sun? Poems Based on the Lore, Legends, and Myths of Northwest Coast and Plateau Indians. Bloomington, Indiana University Press, 1978.
In Broken Country. Boston, Little Brown, 1979.
Landfall. Boston, Little Brown, 1981.

Other

Editor, *Straw for the Fire: From the Notebooks of Theodore Roethke 1943-1963*. New York, Doubleday, 1972.

*

Manuscript Collections: Olin Library, Washington University, St. Louis; University of Washington, Seattle.

Critical Studies: "David Wagoner's Fiction: In the Mills of Satan" by William J. Schafer, in *Critique* (Minneapolis), ix, 1, 1965; "It Dawns on Us That We Must Come Apart," in *Alone with America* by Richard Howard, New York, Atheneum, 1969, London, Thames and Hudson, 1970, revised edition, Atheneum, 1980; "An Interview with David Wagoner," in *Crazy Horse 12* (Marshall, Minnesota), 1972; "A Conversation with David Wagoner," in *Yes* (Avoca, New York), iv, 1, 1973; "On David Wagoner," in *Salmagundi* (Saratoga Springs, New York), Spring-Summer 1973, and "Pelting Dark Windows," in *Parnassus* (New York), Spring-Summer 1977, both by Sanford Pinsker.

David Wagoner comments:

It is almost impossible for me to comment coherently on my own fiction, except to say that I began writing poetry first and received early encouragement as a writer of fiction from Edward J. Nichols at Penn State and Peter Taylor at Indiana University, and later from Malcolm Cowley at Viking Press and Catharine Carver who was then at Harcourt Brace. I seem to have a penchant for what might be called serious farce, but whether farce can stand the serious strains I put on it, I must leave to others to say. I also recognize my tendency to write what I believe critics call "initiation" novels. I tend to dramatize or write in scenes rather than to be discursive. One clear theme would seem to be the would-be innocent protagonist *vs.* the corrupt city, perhaps a result of my having grown up between Chicago and Gary, Indiana, where the most sophisticated and effective forms of pollution were first perfected.

* * *

In his novels, David Wagoner has pursued the themes of innocence and corruption, of the connections between past, present and future, of the individual trapped in a violent society. The novels depict individuals corrupted by modern urban life, protagonists essentially innocent and helpless damaged by the pressures of family life and further maimed by socity. Wagoner skilfully uses Dickensian comedy and drama to create a tragic myth of man stripped and abandoned by his parents and his fellows yet struggling to survive and to remain intact.

The Man in the Middle and *Money, Money, Money* describe helpless, childlike adults caught up in criminal machinations. *The Escape Artist* and *Where Is My Wandering Boy Tonight?* treat the same theme from the viewpoint of juvenile protagonists. Each novel involves criminals and corrupt politicans who pursue and persecute an innocent victim. There is a strong element of picaresque comedy in this drama of innocence adapting to a wicked world. The later novels also develop a complex sexual theme revolving around an Oedipal relationship—a child confronted and fascinated by a destructive mother figure. Each of the protagonists must overcome this infantile sexual bondage before he is free to live wholly, just as each must learn the depth of the world's wickedness before he can shed his infantile social innocence.

The Road to Many a Wonder continues Wagoner's comedy of

19th-century America (begun in *Where Is My Wandering Boy Tonight?*) and his parable of innocence and the Frontier. In it a gold-seeker, Isaac Bender, succeeds by the most improbable means, his questing innocence overcoming the money-corruption of the gold rush and the Hobbesian savagery of the raw West. The novel is marked by a comic sweetness and light that offsets the bleak portraiture of venal American character-types.

In *Rock* and *Baby, Come On Inside* Wagoner deals with the destructiveness of family life and the crippling effects of the past. Both stories concentrate on the conflict between leaving home and returning home: "You can't go home again" vs. "You *must* go home again." In each novel, the protagonist tries to recapture his past, to find a home place, but ends in confusion and further exile.

A recurrent pattern in Wagoner's novels is that of pursuit and flight, a nightmarish sense of implacable evil, and a recurrent scene is a metaphorical return to the womb, to primordial shelter. Charlie Bell in *The Man in the Middle* spends a night in a railway coin locker. Willy Grier is left in a garbage can in *Money, Money, Money*. Danny Masters in *The Escape Artist* hides out in a Goodwill Industries collection box and a US mailbox. The pattern of flight and hiding, a fragile individual pursued by a terrifying nemesis, occurs in a comic context—cynical wit and slapstick farce—for the dreamlike or mythic dimension of Wagoner's novels derives from their mixed tone. The stories encompass suspense, adventure, comedy, pathos, and a strong sense of the social and political life of midwestern cities.

Wagoner's tragicomedies of violence achieve effects somewhat like François Truffaut's *Shoot the Piano Player*. The mixture of naivety, tough-guy dialogue, violence, thriller action, and insight into complex states of mind creates a fantasy world as an accurate analogue for contemporary urban life. Danny Masters, in *The Escape Artist*, muses on violence and trickery and how to escape them:

> Danny felt his own life shut inside him, keeping as quiet as it could, shying away. Nobody should be able to break anybody open like a nut and clean out the insides, but some people did it, and he would never let them come close. That was why getting away was important, getting out, getting loose, because they had to make you sit still long enough so they could crack you open, otherwise it spoiled their aim. They were no good with moving targets, no good if you weren't where they thought you were. They knew a lot of tricks, and that was why you had to keep ahead of them, and then if you got a big enough lead, you could afford to let them know who you were, taunting them from a distance yet always ready to change shape to fool them.

Wagoner's novels reflect society's torments and traps and also explore the paths to freedom—self-understanding, imagination, and the uses of experience. While they detail corruption and destruction, they also reflect innocence and virtue. The possibilities in this world are tragic and comic, and the inevitable price of survival is loss of innocence.

—William J. Schafer

WAIN, John (Barrington). British. Born in Stoke-on-Trent, Staffordshire, 14 March 1925. Educated at the High School, Newcastle-under-Lyme, Staffordshire; St. John's College, Oxford, B.A. 1946, Fereday Fellow, 1946-49, M.A. 1950. Married 1) Marianne Urmston in 1947 (marriage dissolved, 1956); 2) Eirian James in 1960; three children. Lecturer in English, University of Reading, Berkshire, 1947-55; Professor of Poetry, Oxford University, 1973-78. Churchill Visiting Professor, University of Bristol, 1967; Visiting Professor, Centre Universitaire Expérimentale, Vincennes, France, 1969. First Holder, Fellowship in Creative Arts, 1971-72, and since 1973, Supernumerary Fellow, Brasenose College, Oxford. Recipient: Maugham Award, 1958; Heinemann Award, 1975, and Black Memorial Award, 1975, both for non-fiction. Fellow, Royal Society of Literature, 1960; resigned, 1961. Lives in Oxford. Address: c/o Macmillan and Company Ltd., 4 Little Essex Street, London WC2R 3LF, England.

PUBLICATIONS

Novels

Hurry on Down. London, Secker and Warburg, 1953; as *Born in Captivity*, New York, Knopf, 1954.
Living in the Present. London, Secker and Warburg, 1955; New York, Putnam, 1960.
The Contenders. London, Macmillan, and New York, St. Martin's Press, 1958.
A Travelling Woman. London, Macmillan, and New York, St. Martin's Press, 1959.
Strike the Father Dead. London, Macmillan, and New York, St. Martin's Press, 1962.
The Young Visitors. London, Macmillan, and New York, Viking Press, 1965.
The Smaller Sky. London, Macmillan, 1967.
A Winter in the Hills. London, Macmillan, and New York, Viking Press, 1970.
The Pardoner's Tale. London, Macmillan, 1978; New York, Viking Press, 1979.

Short Stories

Nuncle and Other Stories. London, Macmillan, 1960; New York, St. Martin's Press, 1961.
Death of the Hind Legs and Other Stories. London, Macmillan, and New York, Viking Press, 1966.
The Life Guard. London, Macmillan, 1971; New York, Viking Press, 1972.
King Caliban and Other Stories. London, Macmillan, 1978.

Plays

Harry in the Night: An Optimistic Comedy (produced Stoke-on-Trent, 1975).

Radio Plays: *You Wouldn't Remember*, 1978; *A Winter in the Hills*, from his own novel, 1981.

Verse

Mixed Feelings: Nineteen Poems. Reading, Berkshire, Reading University School of Art, 1951.
A Word Carved on a Sill. London, Routledge, and New York, St. Martin's Press, 1956.
A Song about Major Eatherly. Iowa City, Qara Press, 1961.
Weep Before God. London, Macmillan, and New York, St. Martin's Press, 1961.
Wildtrack: A Poem. London, Macmillan, and New York, Viking Press, 1965.
Letters to Five Artists. London, Macmillan, 1969; New York, Viking Press, 1970.
The Shape of Feng. London, Covent Garden Press, 1972.
Feng. London, Macmillan, and New York, Viking Press, 1975.
Poems for the Zodiac (12 booklets), illustrated by Brenda Stones. London, Pisces Press, 1980.
Poems 1949-1979. London, Macmillan, 1981.

Other

Preliminary Essays. London, Macmillan, and New York, St. Martin's Press, 1957.
Gerard Manley Hopkins: An Idiom of Desperation. London, Oxford University Press, and Folcroft, Pennsylvania, Folcroft Editions, 1959.
Sprightly Running: Part of an Autobiography. London, Macmillan, 1962; New York, St. Martin's Press, 1963.
Essays on Literature and Ideas. London, Macmillan, and New York, St. Martin's Press, 1963.
The Living World of Shakespeare: A Playgoer's Guide. London, Macmillan, and New York, St. Martin's Press, 1964; revised edition, 1979.
Arnold Bennett. New York, Columbia University Press, 1967.
A House for the Truth: Critical Essays. London, Macmillan, 1972; New York, Viking Press, 1973.
Samuel Johnson. London, Macmillan, 1974; New York, Viking Press, 1975; revised edition, Macmillan, 1980.
A John Wain Selection, edited by Geoffrey Halson. London, Longman, 1977.
Professing Poetry. London, Macmillan, 1977; New York, Viking Press, 1978.

Editor, *Contemporary Reviews of Romantic Poetry*. London, Harrap, and New York, Barnes and Noble, 1953.
Editor, *Interpretations: Essays on Twelve English Poems*. London, Routledge, 1955; New York, Hillary House, 1957.
Editor, *International Literary Annual*. London, Calder, and New York, Criterion, 2 vols., 1959-60.
Editor, *Fanny Burney's Diary*. London, Folio Society, 1960.
Editor, *Anthology of Modern Poetry*. London, Hutchinson, 1963.
Editor, *Pope*. New York, Dell, 1963.
Editor, *Selected Shorter Poems of Thomas Hardy*. London, Macmillan, and New York, St. Martin's Press, 1966; revised edition, 1975.
Editor, *The Dynasts*, by Thomas Hardy. London, Macmillan, and New York, St. Martin's Press, 1966.
Editor, *Selected Shorter Stories of Thomas Hardy*. London, Macmillan, and New York, St Martin's Press, 1966.
Editor, *Shakespeare: Macbeth: A Casebook*. London, Macmillan, 1968.
Editor, *Shakespeare: Othello: A Casebook*. London, Macmillan, 1971.
Editor, *Johnson as Critic*. London, Routledge, 1973.
Editor, *Lives of the English Poets: A Selection*, by Samuel Johnson. London, Dent, and New York, Dutton, 1975.
Editor, *Johnson on Johnson: A Selection of the Personal and Autobiographical Writings of Samuel Johnson*. London, Dent, and New York, Dutton, 1976.
Editor, *The Poetry of Thomas Hardy: A New Selection*. London, Macmillan, 1977.
Editor, *An Edmund Wilson Celebration*. Oxford, Phaidon Press, 1978.
Editor, *Personal Choice: A Poetry Anthology*. Newton Abbot, Devon, David and Charles, 1978.
Editor, *Anthology of Contemporary Poetry: Post-War to the Present*. London, Hutchinson, 1979.
Editor, *Everyman's Book of English Verse*. London, Dent, 1981.

*

Bibliography: *John Braine and John Wain: A Reference Guide* by Dale Salwak, Boston, Hall, 1980.

Manuscript Collection: Edinburgh University Library.

Critical Studies: "John Wain et le Magie de l'Individu" by Françoise Barrière, in *Le Monde* (Paris), 8 August 1970; "John Wain: Révolte et Neutralité" by Pierre Yvard, in *Etudes Anglaises* (Paris), October 1970; "The New Puritanism, The New Academism, The New..." by the author, in *A House for the Truth*, 1972.

*   *   *

In the middle 1950's John Wain first became widely known as a humorist and iconoclast. *Hurry on Down*, a mock-picaresque, became, in many journalistic accounts, a symbol for the irreverent rootlessness of the younger generation, making fun of any established social designation. And Wain's novels frequently followed switches in conventional expectation, as in the epigraph quoted from Trollope at the beginning of *The Contenders*: "Success is the necessary misfortune of human life, but it is only to the very unfortunate that it comes early." Yet, beneath the irreverence, beneath the prose that often reduced an emotion or a high-flown idea to the ordinary or the mechanical, images like "his heart lurched over and over in his breast like a cricket ball lobbed along a dry, bumpy pitch," Wain's perspective was that of the man of orthodox common-sense, the defender of a basic human dignity against the absurd pretenses of the modern world. Even the figure of despair, the central character of *Living in the Present*, about to commit suicide, decides that he cannot do so unless he also rids the world of the most loathsome and amoral creature he knows. Characteristically and appropriately, he chooses a snide, class-conscious neo-Fascist.

In his early work, Wain's central moral equation of plain English common-sense with a lack of pretense sometimes seemed slightly insular. In satirizing the follies of English class-consciousness (the stages of the journey in *Hurry on Down* are magnifications of various designations in the English class system), Wain often attached images of the Continent or of cosmopolitanism to the particular class-elaboration he was momentarily deriding. The central character of *The Contenders*, whose point of view Wain generally endorses, is the rumpled, unheroic, but basically sound and humane provincial who is contrasted to his boyhood friends who reach out for worldly success and lock themselves into inhumane and debilitating competition. The competitive artist, at one point, even requires a return to his provincial origins in order to regain himself and his talent. Although Wain is still interested in localism, still close to the fabric of specific social reference that chronicled the dingy night-life of London during the Second World War in *Strike the Father Dead* or the postwar world of Vespas and Scandinavian furniture in *The Contenders*, his attitudes have become far less provincial. The Welsh bard, for example, in *A Winter in the Hills*, a character true to himself and his past, is sympathetically connected with Bretons, Canadians, all who would preserve their local humanity in opposition to the contemporary corporate world. Wain has become less the defender of the specifically English as his career has progressed, become more seriously, deeply, and intelligently the critic of contemporary English society.

Much of Wain's early comedy was an exaggeration of the uncomfortable, the assaults of badly behaved children, the pains inflicted by sleeping on worn-out bedsprings, the gastronomic rumblings produced by bad food. Beneath this comedy is a sense of the difficulty of survival, of the effort and consciousness necessary to preserve oneself in an intrusive and demanding world. The worst of characters is always the bully, the worst of societies the totalitarian. The central character is often the victim of these intrusive forces, an element in Wain's fiction most patently visible in his sympathy for the gentle eccentric who seeks only to still the furies in his own brain by living in Paddington station and is, therefore, hounded to death by contemporary society. In much of his later fiction, however, Wain's central characters are less passive victims, become much more conscious of themselves and their relationships with others. The young man in *Strike the Father Dead* experiences consciously all the complicated and ambivalent stresses of revolt from his father, and a final reconciliation between the two, the young jazz musician and the rigid old scholar, so socially different and so personally alike, is made both moving and convincing. The central character in *A Winter in the Hills* works his past and his narrow fantasies into a more active engagement with contemporary life by helping both independent bus owner/drivers and poets to survive a little longer in a hostile world. In both these novels, probably Wain's best, the central characters are full of guilt that is both personal and social, guilt for having survived thus far through luck and narrow self-protection. In these novels the guilt is understood and surmounted, the central character connected with others and with contemporary experience. At times, Wain's thoughtful fiction is limited by simplicities in perspective, as in the overwhelming sexual guilts in *A Travelling Woman* or *The Pardoner's Tale* or, more superficially, in the exterior and political simplicities of *The Young Visitors*. At his best, however, Wain's sense of human dignity becomes much wider: women change from rewards or "instruments" to people with pasts, convictions, and experiences; children change from abrasive nuisances to people who need understanding and protection; morality grows beyond the mechanics of survival.

Wain's fiction also demonstrates a consistent interest in structure and the novel as metaphor. Often the novel seems designed as a set answer to a particular question: what would it be like to resolve rationally to commit suicide or live completely within Paddington station? what are the implications, for people and nations, of surviving the Second World War? how do people with guilts and pasts manage in a kind of Iris Murdoch world (in *A Travelling Woman*) of constantly shifting sexual attraction? how does a writer, as in *The Pardoner's Tale*, create fiction that both transposes and reveals himself? Sometimes the material in the novel, always observant and thoroughly detailed, seems to overwhelm the question, and the structure or the metaphor seems too ruthlessly to limit the novel. At other times, structure and content balance more effectively and depict comically the complexities of the moral and serious man in a difficult world that expands both historically and geographically. Wain's fiction always shows this struggle for shape, this use of conscious and intelligent effort by a man of letters (Wain is also a distinguished poet and literary critic) to give form to his searching perceptions and observations.

—James Gindin

WALKER, Margaret (Abigail). American. Born in Birmingham, Alabama, 7 July 1915. Educated at Northwestern University, Evanston, Illinois, B.A. 1935; University of Iowa, Iowa City, M.A. 1940, Ph.D. 1965; Yale University, New Haven, Connecticut (Ford Fellow), 1954. Married Firnist James Alexander in 1943; two sons and two daughters. Has worked as social worker, reporter, and magazine editor; taught at Livingstone College, Salisbury, North Carolina, 1941-42, 1945-46, and West Virginia State College, Institute, 1942-43. Since 1949, Professor of English, and since 1968, Director of the Institute for the Study of the History, Life and Culture of Black Peoples, Jackson State College, Mississippi. Recipient: Yale Series of Younger Poets Award, 1942; Rosenwald Fellowship, 1944; Houghton Mifflin Literary Fellowship, 1966; Fulbright Fellowship, 1971; National Endowment for the Arts grant, 1972. D.Litt: Northwestern University, 1974; Rust College, Holly Springs, Mississippi, 1974; D.F.A.: Denison University, Granville, Ohio, 1974; D.H.L.: Morgan State University, Baltimore, 1976. Address: 2205 Guynes Street, Jackson, Mississippi 39213, U.S.A.

PUBLICATIONS

Novels

Come Down from Yonder Mountain. Toronto, Longman, 1962.
Jubilee. Boston, Houghton Mifflin, 1966.

Verse

For My People. New Haven, Connecticut, Yale University Press, 1942.
Ballad of the Free. Detroit, Broadside Press, 1966.
Prophets for a New Day. Detroit, Broadside Press, 1970.
October Journey. Detroit, Broadside Press, 1973.

Recording: *The Poetry of Margaret Walker*, Folkways, 1975.

Other

How I Wrote "Jubilee." Chicago, Third World Press, 1972.
A Poetic Equation: Conversations Between Margaret Walker and Nikki Giovanni. Washington, D.C., Howard University Press, 1974.

* * *

Authenticating her facts by extensive research, Margaret Walker enlarged the experiences of her great-grandmother during and after slavery into the epic novel *Jubilee*. The heroine, Vyry, is two years old when she enters the story at the childbed death of her 29-year-old mother, who has borne 15 slave children in rural Georgia for her master, John Dutton. The 58 chapters are divided into three sections subtitled "The Ante-Bellum Years," "The Civil War Years," and "Reconstruction and Reaction."

The first section, beginning in 1837, introduces ten major characters, half of whom are removed by tragedy before the middle of the novel. The cook, Aunt Sally, irritably singing "mad-mood" songs, is sold. John Dutton, "yelling and cursing in the night," is dispatched by gangrene; and his "nigra"-hating wife, Big Missy Salina, dies ignominiously of a stroke. Young West Pointer Johnny Dutton and his pacifist brother-in-law, Kevin MacDougall, exit heroically but pitifully as war casualties. Old Brother Zeke, the slave preacher who secretly works for the Underground Railroad, succumbs later while a Union Army spy. Three other characters embody vigorous criticism of slavery and war: Lillian, Vyry's gentle white sister, who goes insane after the death of her Kevin and an assault by one of Sheridan's "bummers"; Ed Grimes, the brutal overseer, who lives to exploit his betters; and Randall Ware, proud blacksmith and freeman from birth, whose love for his wife Vyry "just got caught in the times" during his war service.

Of sections II and III, the former, replete with historical and military details, closely reflects the author's research. It introduces Innis Brown, who slowly convinces Vyry to end her seven-year wait for her husband. The title of the Reconstruction section, "Forty Years in the Wilderness," suits the ruinous adventures of Vyry, Innis, and the children building homes in Alabama. Flooded out, exploited in sharecropping, profoundly stricken when burned out by the Ku Klux Klan, Vyry becomes almost pathologically averse to building again. But by innate acts of humanity and racial dignity in Greenville, she inspires whites to help build the family's final home. An amicable understanding ensues between Innis and Randall Ware, who pays a visit with ideas like W.E.B. Du Bois's, and with money to educate the children.

The author's Dedication could have addressed her novel "to all the members of my race [not just 'family'] with all my love." The ancestry of almost every Black reader contains its own Vyry, thus revered in Chapter 57:

> She was only a living sign and mark of all the best that any human being could hope to become. In her obvious capacity for love, redemptive and forgiving love, she was alive and standing on the highest peaks of her time and human personality. Peasant and slave, unlettered and untutored, she was nevertheless the best true example of the motherhood of her race, an ever present assurance that nothing could destroy a people whose sons had come from her loins.

Vyry's actions, always credible, deserve that praise.

Jubilee is rich with history. Numerous details of slaves' medical and culinary arts, clothing, shelter, and marriages are given. Their legally enforced illiteracy, the planned destruction of their normal affections for one another, their physical oppressions (ranging from the Black Codes to savage plantation punishments and Confederate murders at Andersonville) are depicted. Over a dozen episodes and circumstances reveal the slaves' aggressive feelings: repressed hatreds, aid to abolitionists, revolts, and escapes after 1861 (including all 46 Dutton field slaves) to take up either guns or tools for the Union Army. Matters transcending their focus in the slavocracy come to the fore: political events, the birth of the Confederacy, the specie crisis, 1863 analyzed as a turning point in the war, the Freedmen's Bureau, and the maneuvered return of White Home Rule.

The author aims at a realistically balanced treatment. The "good whites" are represented by Lillian and Kevin, Doc, the Shackelfords, and nameless abolitionists—Lillian centralizing the tragedy of war and the psychopathy constantly threatening decent slaveholders. Vicious Grimes has no Black counterpart, and the slaveholders perform no noble deeds like Jim's bringing Johnny home to die. Regional balance is implicit in use of the New York draft riots and the indefensible destructiveness of Union soldiers after the end of the fighting.

Jubilee is history explicit in the prototypal experience of one slave woman, issuing contemporaneously in what Innis Brown saw as "a wisdom and a touching humility," and ultimately in what the author's speech in 1968 at the National Urban League Conference in New Orleans expresses as follows: "We are still a [Black] people of spirit and soul. We are still fighting in the midst of white American Racism for the overwhelming truth of the primacy of human personality and the spiritual destiny of all mankind."

—James A. Emanuel

WARNER, Rex (Ernest). British. Born in Birmingham, Warwickshire, 9 March 1905. Educated at St. George's School, Harpenden, Hertfordshire; Wadham College, Oxford (open classical scholar), B.A. (honours) in classics and English literature 1928. Served in the Home Guard, London, 1942-45. Married 1) Frances Chamier Grove in 1929, two sons and one daughter; 2) Barbara Lady Rothschild in 1949, one daughter; 3) remarried Frances Chamier Grove in 1966. Schoolmaster in Egypt and England, 1928-45; worked for the Control Commission in Berlin, 1945, 1947; Director, British Institute, Athens, 1945-47; Tallman Professor, Bowdoin College, Brunswick, Maine, 1962-63; Professor of English, University of Connecticut, Storrs, 1963-74. Recipient: Black Memorial Prize, 1961. D.Litt.: Rider College, Trenton, New Jersey, 1968. Honorary Fellow, Wadham College, 1973. Commander, Royal Order of the Phoenix, Greece, 1963. Address: Anchor House, St. Leonard's Lane, Wallingford, Oxfordshire, England.

PUBLICATIONS

Novels

The Wild Goose Chase. London, Boriswood, and New York, Knopf, 1937.
The Professor. London, Boriswood, 1938; New York Knopf, 1939.
The Aerodrome. London, Lane, 1941; Philadelphia, Lippincott, 1946.
Why Was I Killed? A Dramatic Dialogue. London, Lane, 1943; as *Return of the Traveller*, Philadelphia, Lippincott, 1944.
Men of Stones: A Melodrama. London, Lane, 1949; Philadelphia, Lippincott, 1950.
Escapade: A Tale of Average. London, Lane, 1953.
The Young Caesar. London, Collins, and Boston, Little Brown, 1958.
Imperial Caesar. London, Collins, and Boston, Little Brown, 1960.
Pericles the Athenian. London, Collins, and Boston, Little Brown, 1963.
The Converts. London, Bodley Head, and Boston, Little Brown, 1967.

Plays

Screenplays (documentaries): *World With End*, 1953; *The Immortal Land*, 1958.

Verse

Poems. London, Boriswood, 1937; New York, Knopf, 1938; revised edition, as *Poems and Contradictions*, London, Lane, 1945.

Other

The Kite (juvenile). Oxford, Blackwell, 1936; revised edition, London, Hamish Hamilton, 1963.
English Public Schools. London, Collins, 1945.
The Cult of Power: Essays. London, Lane, 1946; Philadelphia, Lippincott, 1947.
John Milton. London, Parrish, 1949; New York, Chanticleer Press, 1950.
Views of Attica and Its Surroundings. London, Lehmann, 1950.
E.M. Forster. London, Longman, 1950.
Men and Gods. London, MacGibbon and Kee, 1950; New York, Farrar Straus, 1951.
Ashes to Ashes: A Post-Mortem on the 1950-51 Tests, with Lyle Blair. London, MacGibbon and Kee, 1951.
Greeks and Trojans. London, MacGibbon and Kee, 1951.
Eternal Greece, photographs by Martin Hurlimann. London, Thames and Hudson, and New York, Viking Press, 1953.
The Vengeance of the Gods. London, MacGibbon and Kee, 1954.
Athens. London, Thames and Hudson, and New York, Studio, 1956.
The Greek Philosophers. New York, New American Library, 1958.
Look at Birds (juvenile). London, Hamish Hamilton, 1962.
The Stories of the Greeks. New York, Farrar Straus, 1967.
Athens at War: Retold from the History of the Peloponnesian War of Thucydides. London, Bodley Head, 1970; New York, Dutton, 1971.
Men of Athens: The Story of Fifth Century Athens. London, Bodley Head, and New York, Viking Press, 1972.

Editor, with Laurie Lee and Christopher Hassall, *New Poems 1954*. London, Joseph, 1954.
Editor, *Look Up at the Skies! Poems and Prose*, by Gerard Manley Hopkins. London, Bodley Head, 1972.

Translator, *The Medea of Euripides*. London, Lane, 1944; New York, Chanticleer Press, 1949.
Translator, *Prometheus Bound*, by Aeschylus. London, Lane, 1947; New York, Chanticleer Press, 1949.
Translator, *The Persian Expedition*, by Xenophon. London, Penguin, 1949.
Translator, *Hippolytus*, by Euripides. London, Lane, 1949; New York, Chanticleer Press, 1950.
Translator, *Helen*, by Euripides. London, Lane, 1951.
Translator, *The Peloponnesian War*, by Thucydides. London, Penguin, 1954.

Translator, *The Fall of the Roman Republic: Marius, Sulla, Crassus, Pompey, Caesar, Cicero: Six Lives*, by Plutarch. London, Penguin, 1958; revised edition, 1972.
Translator, *Poems of George Seferis*. London, Bodley Head, 1960; Boston, Godine, 1979.
Translator, *War Commentaries of Caesar*. New York, New American Library, 1960.
Translator, *Confessions of St. Augustine*. New York, New American Library, 1963.
Translator, with Th. D. Frangopoulos, *On the Greek Style: Selected Essays in Poetry and Hellenism*, by George Seferis. Boston, Little Brown, 1966.
Translator, *A History of My Times*, by Xenophon. London, Penguin, 1966.
Translator, *Moral Essays*, by Plutarch. London, Penguin, 1971.

*

Manuscript Collection: University of Connecticut, Storrs.

Critical Studies: *Rex Warner, Writer* by A.L. McLeod, Sydney, Wentworth Press, 1960, and *The Achievement of Rex Warner* (includes bibliography) edited by McLeod, Wentworth Press, 1965.

Rex Warner comments:

Most of my novels have been in some sense "political"; they have attempted to deal with contemporary problems of power, responsibility, and motivation. But they have not been "realistic." In the early novels, there is always an element of fantasy, but the later historical novels have still been dealing with the same general subjects.

* * *

By date of birth (1905), by education, and by accomplishment Rex Warner belongs to that unusual British generation which includes Auden, Isherwood, MacNeice, Aldous Huxley, Spender, Day Lewis, and Empson. That Warner has not been accorded the fame of many of those writers is an accident of publicity, not an indication of inferior merit. In a less cluttered time than ours, one has no question that Warner's stature would have been perceived from the outset and broadcast.

A classical scholar who has translated Aeschylus, Euripides, Thucydides, Xenophon, Caesar, and Plutarch, Warner began his career as a poet with *Poems*; it is our loss that he did not continue as poet. His first novel, *The Wild Goose Chase*, is unusual in English in that it displays the profound influence of the Czech writer, Franz Kafka. Although Auden and Isherwood in their early work indicated that they had read Kafka and some of the German expressionists, Warner's reaction to Kafka is without parallel in British writing unless one goes back to Carlyle's reaction to Goethe and Schiller. Warner's Kafkaesque work was not mere imitation, but an example of an original mind and temperament permeated and released by a profound influence.

Traditionally the English novelist has been concerned almost exclusively with social reality. In *The Wild Goose Chase* Warner writes expressionist allegory, a form quite foreign to the British mind and taste in prose fiction. Warner's unnamed country with its legendary frontier over which men pass at their peril comes directly from Kafka, while the three brothers and their quest for the wild goose, a symbol of man's political and spiritual hope, derive from myth and *Märchen*. Warner differs significantly from Kafka, however, in that Warner can write with humor as well as in Kafka's vein of the grotesque. At the same time Warner's themes are political and ethical, where Kafka's are suffocatingly psychological. *The Wild Goose Chase*, a near masterpiece, is flawed by the conclusion, in which the always tentative construction of reality dissolves into total expressionism, a theatrical resolution that does not in truth resolve the problems so scrupulously posed earlier on.

The Aerodrome, by contrast, written in 1941 during the war, is virtually unflawed. Kafka's influence is still discernible, but now it is totally assimilated and subordinated to a voice that is Warner's unchallenged own. The events of *The Aerodrome* simply relate the effects upon the villagers of the location of a flying field near their village. The villagers are exploited by a ruthlessness of the commanding Air Vice-Marshal, as in turn they are inevitable corrupted. Still writing in a nether region between the Kafkaesque and the realistic, Warner dramatizes the truism that war corrupts all whom it touches, while he does not fall into the expressionistic excesses of his first novel. Warner dominates any tendency to mannerism by intellectual control, and by his adaptation of a plot reminiscent of Greek myth and drama. Narrative economy and Greek directness allow him to write of subjects that in other hands often seem banal: love, hope, suffering, faith, endurance. The narrator's final words typify the qualities of the whole: " 'That the world may be clean,' I remembered my father's words. Clean indeed it was and most intricate, fiercer than tigers, wonderful and infinitely forgiving." *The Aerodrome* finally is a novel of ideas presented directly and dramatically. With his conviction of the pathos in the discrepancy between goodness and simplicity, and the necessary corruption of war, Warner achieves tragedy. No better novel appeared in English in the period between 1930 and 1970.

Warner's three novels *The Professor, Why Was I Killed?*, and *Men of Stones* form a second category in his work. They resemble *The Aerodrome* in theme in that they are political and ethical, but their range is narrower, and each novel is more fully determined by style and intellectual control than by imagination and inventiveness. They are lesser only in contrast to Warner's finest work however; in no sense are they negligible.

By the late 1950's, Warner launched into his third period as a novelist in those narratives based upon historical themes. In *The Young Caesar*, *Imperial Caesar*, or *Pericles the Athenian* one may see the classical scholar and translator as opposed to the young Warner who invented his own sources. Warner's historical novels, that is, are valuable for their insights into classical Athens and Rome, but as works of the imagination they are inferior to his early work. Either the historical novelist is bound by his materials, or if he distorts or ignores them, he offends as frivolous. Warner's historical scholarship is impeccable, but his tendency to the expository, present throughout his career, dominated in his third phase. The historical novels emphasize other qualities apparent from the outset in Warner's work: the fact that he possesses an historical view of reality, and that his first allegiance is to rationality. That alone may account for his relative lack of popularity, for as the 20th century grows older, it becomes anti-historical and anti-rational.

Given Warner's range and special kind of intelligence (and here his essays, *The Cult of Power*, must not be ignored), given his splendid style, the clear product of his work in classics in its elaborateness, its clarity, and its suppleness, one must believe that as long as men honor rationality even slightly, Warner will be read. Certainly *The Aerodrome* must survive, and if later generations sort out our contemporary clutter, Rex Warner will be assured his proper place.

—John McCormick

WARREN, Robert Penn. American. Born in Guthrie, Kentucky, 24 April 1905. Educated at Guthrie High School; Vanderbilt University, Nashville, Tennessee, B.A. (summa cum laude) 1925; University of California, Berkeley, M.A. 1927; Yale University, New Haven, Connecticut, 1927-28; Oxford University (Rhodes Scholar), B.Litt. 1930. Married 1)Emma Brescia in 1930 (divorced, 1950); 2) Eleanor Clark, *q.v.*, in 1952, one son and one daughter. Assistant Professor, Southwestern College, Memphis, Tennessee, 1930-31, and Vanderbilt University, 1931-34; Assistant and Associate Professor, Louisiana State University, Baton Rouge, 1934-42; Professor of English, University of Minnesota, Minneapolis, 1942-50. Professor of Playwriting, 1950-56, Professor of English, 1962-73, and since 1973, Professor Emeritus, Yale University. Member of the Fugitive Group of poets: Co-Founding Editor, *The Fugitive*, Nashville, 1922-25. Founding Editor, *Southern Review*, Baton Rouge, Louisiana, 1935-42. Consultant in Poetry, Library of Congress, Washington, D.C., 1944-45. Recipient: Caroline Sinkler Award, 1936, 1937, 1938; Levinson Prize, 1936, Union League Civic and Arts Foundation Prize, 1953, and Harriet Monroe Prize, 1976 (*Poetry*, Chicago); Houghton Mifflin Literary Fellowhip, 1939; Guggenheim Fellowship, 1939, 1947; Shelley Memorial Award, 1943; Pulitzer Prize, for fiction, 1947, for poetry, 1958, 1979; Robert Meltzer Award, Screen Writers Guild, 1949; Sidney Hillman Prize, 1957; Edna St. Vincent Millay Memorial Prize, 1958; National Book Award, for poetry, 1958; New York *Herald-Tribune* Van Doren Award, 1965; Bollingen Prize, for poetry, 1967; National Endowment for the Arts grant, 1968, and lectureship, 1974; Henry A. Bellaman Prize, 1970; Van Wyck Brooks Award, for poetry, 1970; National Medal for Literature, 1970; Emerson-Thoreau Medal, 1975; Copernicus Award, 1976; Presidential Medal of Freedom, 1980; Common Wealth Award, 1981. D. Litt.: University of Louisville, Kentucky, 1949; Kenyon College, Gambier, Ohio, 1952; University of Kentucky, Lexington, 1955; Colby College, Waterville, Maine, 1956; Swarthmore College, Pennsylvania, 1958; Yale University, 1959; Fairfield University, Connecticut, 1969; Wesleyan University, Middletown, Connecticut, 1970; Harvard University, Cambridge, Massachusetts, 1973; Southwestern College, 1974; University of the South, Sewanee, Tennessee, 1974; Monmouth College, Illinois, 1979; LL.D.: Bridgeport University, Connecticut, 1965; University of New Haven, Connecticut, 1974; Johns Hopkins University, Baltimore, 1977. Member, American Academy, and American Academy of Arts and Sciences. Address: 2495 Redding Road, Fairfield, Connecticut 06430, U.S.A.

PUBLICATIONS

Novels

Night Rider. Boston, Houghton Mifflin, 1939; London, Eyre and Spottiswoode, 1940.
At Heaven's Gate. New York, Harcourt Brace, and London, Eyre and Spottiswoode, 1943.
All the King's Men. New York, Harcourt Brace, 1946; London, Eyre and Spottiswoode, 1948.
World Enough and Time: A Romantic Novel. New York, Random House, 1950; London, Eyre and Spottiswoode, 1951.
Band of Angels. New York, Random House, 1955; London, Eyre and Spottiswoode, 1956.
The Cave. New York, Random House, and London, Eyre and Spottiswoode, 1959.
Wilderness: A Tale of the Civil War. New York, Random House, 1961; London, Eyre and Spottiswoode, 1962.
Flood: A Romance of Our Times. New York, Random House, and London, Collins, 1964.
Meet Me in the Green Glen. New York, Random House, 1971; London, Secker and Warburg, 1972.
A Place to Come To. New York, Random House, and London, Secker and Warburg, 1977.

Short Stories

Blackberry Winter. Cummington, Massachusetts, Cummington Press, 1946.
The Circus in the Attic and Other Stories. New York, Harcourt Brace, 1947; London, Eyre and Spottiswoode, 1952.

Uncollected Short Stories

"How Willie Proudfit Came Home," in *The Best Short Stories 1939*, edited by Edward J. O'Brien. Boston, Houghton Mifflin, 1939.
"Have You Seen Sukie?," in *The Best American Short Stories 1964*, edited by Martha Foley and David Burnett. Boston, Houghton Mifflin, 1964.
"It's a Long Way from Central Park to Fiddlersburg," in *Kenyon Review* (Gambier, Ohio), Winter 1964.
"Chicago," in *Georgia Review* (Athens), Winter 1976.

Plays

Proud Flesh (in verse, produced Minneapolis, 1947; revised [prose] version, produced New York, 1947).
All the King's Men, adaptation of his own novel (produced New York, 1959). New York, Random House, 1960.

Verse

Thirty-Six Poems. New York, Alcestis Press, 1935.
Eleven Poems on the Same Theme. New York, New Directions, 1942.
Selected Poems 1923-1943. New York, Harcourt Brace, 1944; London Fortune Press, 1951.
Brother to Dragons: A Tale in Verse and Voices. New York, Random House, 1953; London, Eyre and Spottiswoode, 1954; revised edition, Random House, 1979.
Promises: Poems 1954-1956. New York, Random House, 1957; London, Eyre and Spottiswoode, 1959.
You, Emperors and Others: Poems 1957-1960. New York, Random House, 1960.
Selected Poems: New and Old 1923-1966. New York, Random House, 1966.
Incarnations: Poems 1966-1968. New York, Random House, 1968; London, W.H. Allen, 1970.
Audubon: A Vision. New York, Random House, 1969.
Or Else: Poem/Poems 1968-1974. New York, Random House, 1974.
Selected Poems 1923-1975. New York, Random House, and London, Secker and Warburg, 1976.
Now and Then: Poems 1976-1978. New York, Random House, 1978.
Being Here: Poetry 1977-1980. New York, Random House, 1980.

Recording: *Robert Penn Warren Reads from His Own Works*, CMS, 1975.

Other

John Brown: The Making of a Martyr. New York, Payson and Clark, 1929.
I'll Take My Stand: The South and the Agrarian Tradition, with others. New York, Harper, 1930.
Understanding Poetry: An Anthology for College Students, with Cleanth Brooks. New York, Holt, 1938; revised edition, 1950, 1960.
Understanding Fiction, with Cleanth Brooks. New York, Crofts, 1943; revised editon, Appleton Century Crofts, 1959; abridged edition, as *The Scope of Fiction*, 1960.
A Poem of Pure Imagination: An Experiment in Reading, in *The Rime of the Ancient Mariner*, by Samuel Taylor Coleridge. New York, Reynal, 1946.
Modern Rhetoric: With Readings, with Cleanth Brooks. New York, Harcourt Brace, 1949; revised edition, 1958, 1972.
Fundamentals of Good Writing: A Handbook of Modern Rhetoric, with Cleanth Brooks. New York, Harcourt Brace, 1950; London, Dobson, 1952; revised edition, Dobson, 1956.
Segregation: The Inner Conflict in the South. New York, Random House, 1956; London, Eyre and Spottiswoode, 1957.
Remember the Alamo! New York, Random House, 1958.
Selected Essays. New York, Random House, 1958; London, Eyre and Spottiswoode, 1964.

The Gods of Mount Olympus (juvenile). New York, Random House, 1959; London, Muller, 1962.
How Texas Won Her Freedom. San Jacinto, Texas, San Jacinto Museum of History, 1959.
The Legacy of the Civil War: Meditations on the Centennial. New York, Random House, 1961.
Who Speaks for the Negro? New York, Random House, 1965.
A Plea in Mitigation: Modern Poetry and the End of an Era (lecture). Macon, Georgia, Wesleyan College, 1966.
Homage to Theodore Dreiser. New York, Random House, 1971.
John Greenleaf Whittier's Poetry: An Appraisal and a Selection. Minneapolis, University of Minnesota Press, 1971.
A Conversation with Robert Penn Warren, edited by Frank Gado. Schenectady, New York, The Idol, 1972.
Democracy and Poetry (lecture). Cambridge, Massachusetts, Harvard University Press, 1975.
Robert Penn Warren Talking: Interviews 1950-1978, edited by Floyd C. Watkins and John T. Hiers. New York, Random House, 1980.
Jefferson Davis Gets His Citizenship Back. Lexington, University Press of Kentucky, 1980.

Editor, with Cleanth Brooks and J.T. Purser, *An Approach to Literature: A Collection of Prose and Verse with Analyses and Discussions.* Baton Rouge, Louisiana State University Press, 1936; revised edition, New York, Crofts, 1939, Appleton Century Crofts, 1952.
Editor, *A Southern Harvest: Short Stories by Southern Writers.* Boston, Houghton Mifflin, 1937.
Editor, with Cleanth Brooks, *Anthology of Stories from the Southern Review.* Baton Rouge, Louisiana State University Press, 1953.
Editor, with Albert Erskine, *Short Story Masterpieces.* New York, Dell, 1954.
Editor, with Albert Erskine, *Six Centuries of Great Poetry.* New York, Dell, 1955.
Editor, with Albert Erskine, *A New Southern Harvest.* New York, Bantam, 1957.
Editor, with Allen Tate, *Selected Poems*, by Denis Devlin. New York, Holt Rinehart, 1963.
Editor, with Robert Lowell and Peter Taylor, *Randall Jarrell 1914-1965.* New York, Farrar Straus, 1967.
Editor, *Faulkner: A Collection of Critical Essays.* Englewood Cliffs, New Jersey, Prentice Hall, 1967.
Editor, *Selected Poems of Herman Melville.* New York, Random House, 1971.
Editor, *Selected Poems of John Greenleaf Whittier.* New York, Random House, 1971.
Editor, with Cleanth Brooks and R.W.B. Lewis, *American Literature: The Makers and the Making.* New York, St. Martin's Press, 2 vols., 1973.
Editor, *Katherine Anne Porter: A Collection of Critical Essays.* Englewood Cliffs, New Jersey, Prentice Hall, 1979.

*

Bibliography: *Robert Penn Warren* by Mary Nancy Huff, New York, Lewis, 1968; *Robert Penn Warren: A Reference Guide* by Neil Nakadate, Boston, Hall, 1977.

Manuscript Collection: Beinecke Library, Yale University, New Haven, Connecticut.

Critical Studies: *Robert Penn Warren* by Klaus Poenicke, Heidelberg, 1959; *Robert Penn Warren: The Dark and Bloody Ground* by Leonard Casper, Seattle, University of Washington Press, 1960; *The Faraway Country* by Louis D. Rubin, Jr., Seattle, University of Washington Press, 1963; *The Hidden God* by Cleanth Brooks, New Haven, Connecticut, Yale University Press, 1963; *Robert Penn Warren* by Charles H. Bohner, New York, Twayne, 1964; *Robert Penn Warren* by Paul West, Minneapolis, University of Minnesota Press, 1964; *The Burden of Time* by John L. Stewart, Princeton, New Jersey, Princeton University Press, 1965; *A Colder Fire* by Victor H. Strandberg, Lexington, University Press of Kentucky, 1965; *Robert Penn Warren: A Collection of Critical Essays* edited by John Lewis Longley, Jr., New York, New York University Press, 1965; *Web of Being: The Novels of Robert Penn Warren* by Barnett Guttenberg, Nashville, Vanderbilt University Press, 1975; *Robert Penn Warren: A Vision Earned* by Marshall Walker, New York, Barnes and Noble, 1979; *Robert Penn Warren: A Collection of Critical Essays* edited by Richard Gray, Englewood Cliffs, New Jersey, Prentice Hall, 1980.

* * *

Robert Penn Warren may well be America's most distinguished man of letters now at work. He has produced novels, short stories, poetry, and many essays on literary, sociological, and moral subjects, and he was one of the founding editors of *The Southern Review*, the leading literary journal of the 1930's in the United States. In each of these genres he has done distinguished work. Though younger than some of the others, he was one of the original New Critics and largely responsible for the dissemination of their ideas to generations of students and teachers. Since Faulkner's death Warren has certainly been the most influential novelist from the southern states. Although he studied at the University of California, at Yale, and as a Rhodes Scholar at Oxford, and has lived away from the South for many years, his work bears the marks of his origins. But his Southern credentials are not pure. He was born in Kentucky, a state which remained loyal to the Union, and received his early schooling in Tennessee, one of the last states to secede as well as one of the first to be reunited with the North. In a word, Warren is a border southerner, and his fiction reflects the division implicit in the term. His subject matter is strongly regional but his treatment of it objective and analytical.

A more particular influence, which did much to shape the pattern of Warren's system of values, was exerted by the Fugitives, a group of poets including Allen Tate, John Crowe Ransom, Andrew Lytle. "In a very important way," Warren has said, "that group was my education." It taught him that poetry was a vital activity, related to ideas and to life. Later, as he recalled, it taught him more specifically "how literature can be related to place and history." The famous Scopes Trial of 1925, testing a Tennessee law against the teaching of evolutionary theories in public schools, had polarized the cultural contrast between North and South. In a collection of essays entitled *I'll Take My Stand*, Warren and his friends defended the Southern point of view—Southern agrarianism against the encroachment of Northern industrialism, the contemplative life of the soul against materialism and its servants, science and rationalism. Some of their general principles continued to color Warren's thought and are reflected in his fiction. But he greatly revised his early view of the race problem. His contribution to *I'll Take My Stand* had been a defence of segregation. He had written the essay as a young man abroad, at the very time when he began writing fiction. And the way he later described that moment says a great deal about the impulse behind his fiction. He recalled the discomfort, the sense of evasion he experienced in writing the essay and, on the other hand, the free feeling, the "holiday sense" of writing his first novelette, "Prime Leaf." In the essay he had been "trying to prove something," in the narrative "to find out something, see something, feel something." When he had returned home he had soon realized that his views of segregation had changed: "it wasn't being outside the South that made me change my mind," he recalled later. "It was coming back home." And trying to write fiction—this, too, had made him change his mind, for in writing fiction "you can't allow yourself as much evasion as in trying to write essays." What Warren's backward glance projects with great clarity is the process of scrupulous exploration always behind his fiction and often dramatized by it—this and the light derived from going away and coming back, from contemplating native scenes with a mind schooled by distance. What it suggests is the rigorous discipline, conceptual and formal, which writing fiction is for him and which makes him the superb technician he is.

Warren has always been a reader of history, and his fiction reflects this interest. But he does not write historical novels. Although he has confessed to a romantic interest in the objects of American history, the focus of his novels is not on trappings but on issues. Much of his fiction starts from history. What he looks for in stories are actual events which have caught the public eye because, as he has said, they project "issues in purer form than they come to one ordinarily." Thus *Night Rider* deals with the Kentucky tobacco wars of 1909; *At Heaven's Gate* incorporates the case of a political murder which took place in Nashville in the 1920's; the Willie Stark of *All the King's Men* owes a great deal to the Louisiana politician Huey Long who was assassinated in 1935; *World Enough and Time* closely follows the so-called Kentucky Tragedy, a celebrated murder case of 1825, as well as certain political controversies of the period; *Band of Angels* and *Wilderness* reflect events of the Civil War; *The Cave* starts from a much publicized accident of the 1920's. In its historicity Warren's fiction has something in common with the fiction of Dos Passos; but whereas Dos Passos focussed primarily on the political issues of his own times, contemporaneity is less important to Warren and his focus is moral and philosophical. Indeed, as he wrote in his essay on Conrad's *Nostromo*, Warren fits his own definition of the philosophical novelist as

> one for whom the documentation of the world is constantly striving to rise to the level of generalization about values, ...for whom images always fall into a dialectical configuration, for whom the urgency of experience, no matter how vividly and strongly experience may enchant, is the urgency to know the meaning of experience. This is not to say that the philosophical novelist is schematic and deductive. It is to say quite the contrary, that he is willing to go naked into the pit, again and again, to make the same old struggle for his truth.

The transformation of fact into symbol is of course what distinguishes fiction or, in Aristotle's sense, poetry from history. And the general emphasis on moral values distinguishes Warren from Dos Passos, who remains closer to history and its accidents, as a comparison of *All the King's Men* with *Number One*, Dos Passos's version of the Huey Long story, would demonstrate. In Warren the truth struggled for is larger than in Dos Passos; it embraces a wider spectrum of human experience; and it produces characters more fully developed, more seen in the round.

The struggle for truth in Warren's fiction also produces form and style. His first book, a historical study entitled *John Brown: The Making of a Martyr*, already exemplifying the transformation of history into something else, gave him the type of his central figure—the idealist corrupted by his ideal. He is exemplified in novel after novel: by Percy Munn, the hollow man of *Night Rider*, by Slim Sarrett of *At Heaven's Gate*, by Willie Stark of *All the King's Men*, by Jeremiah Beaumont of *World Enough and Time*, by Adam Rosenzweig, the Bavarian Jew of *Wilderness*, who comes to America to fight for freedom on the Union side and stumbles into the "crime of monstrous inhumanity." But if the imaginative exploration of historical fact in *John Brown* rendered moral knowledge, in the novels that process is not only reproduced; it is made into a structural principle. It leads to Warren's characteristic experimentation with narrators and commentators, with the juxtaposition of past and present, and with the ironic parallels between main plots and illustrative parables (e.g., the story of Cass Mastern in *All the King's Men*). The very action of some of the novels consists in the exploration of the meaning of the events in which the narrators have participated. Frequently the narrator-protagonists are in quest of their own identities. Some are more perceptive than others; but whether we share their gradual illumination (as in *All the King's Men* and *Flood*) or learn by being made aware of their benightedness and confusion (as in *Night Rider* and *World Enough and Time*), the process always leads to the recognition of values, of moral wisdom. Warren always directs us to set our sights beyond historical fact on poetic truth.

One is tempted to say that the truth Warren aims at is none other than the eternal verities of the human heart Faulkner regarded as the novelist's great charge. The two writers have much in common. They are united in their awareness of history, in their devotion to the South, even if not to the same corner of it. They are united also in their experimentation with narrative structure, voice, and point of view. But unlike the protagonists of Faulkner's most successful novels, Warren's often serve as raisonneurs. As a result the skeleton of abstraction is in Warren more visible through the skin and flesh of fact. And yet the escape from naturalism into a kind of humanism is in Warren very much the same as in Faulkner. Indeed, what Warren said of his fellow Southerner applies to himself: although he, too, portrays his region and its history in vivid detail, he, too, claims our particular attention for "the world he creates out of the materials of the world he presents." He too uses "history" as parable and as raw material for the creation of another, less changeable realm.

—Christof Wegelin

WATEN, Judah (Leon). Australian. Born in Odessa, Russia, 29 July 1911. Educated at Christian Brothers College, Perth; University High School, Melbourne. Married Hyrell McKinnon Ross in 1945; one daughter. Former Public Servant: worked for the Australian Postal and Taxation departments. Since 1950, Member of the Committee, Fellowship of Australian Writers; since 1966, Reviewer for *The Age*, Melbourne, and since 1970 for the *Sydney Morning Herald*. President, P.E.N. Melbourne Centre, 1976-79. Recipient: *Sydney Morning Herald* Short Story Prize, 1947; Commonwealth Literary Fellowship, 1952, 1970; Melbourne Moomba Festival Award, 1965. Member, Order of Australia, 1979. Address: 1 Byron Street, Box Hill, Melbourne, Victoria 3128, Australia.

PUBLICATIONS

Novels

The Unbending. Melbourne, Australasian Book Society, 1954.
Shares in Murder. Sydney, Australasian Book Society, 1957.
Time of Conflict. Sydney, Australasian Book Society, 1961.
Distant Land. Melbourne, Cheshire, 1964; London, Angus and Robertson, 1965.
Season of Youth. Melbourne, Cheshire, 1966.
So Far No Further. Melbourne, Wren, 1971.

Short Stories

Alien Son. Sydney, Angus and Robertson, 1952; London, Angus and Robertson, and New York, Anglobooks, 1953.
Love and Rebellion. Melbourne, Macmillan, 1978.

Other

From Odessa to Odessa: The Journey of an Australian Writer. Melbourne, Cheshire, 1969.
The Depression Years 1929-1939. Melbourne, Cheshire, 1972.
Bottle-O! (juvenile). Melbourne, Cheshire, 1973; London, Cassell, 1975.

Editor, with Victor G. O'Connor, *Twenty Great Australian Stories*. Melbourne, Dolphin, 1946.
Editor, with Stephen Murray-Smith, *Classic Australian Short Stories*. Melbourne, Wren, 1974; North Pomfret, Vermont, David and Charles, 1975.

Translator, *Between Sky and Sea*, by Herz Bergner. Melbourne, Dolphin, 1946.

*

Manuscript Collection: Australian National Library, Canberra.

Critical Studies: "Three Realists in Search of Reality" by David Martin, in *On Native Grounds*, Sydney, Angus and Robertson, 1968; "The Sty of Circe: Judah Waten's *The Unbending*" by A.D. Hope, in *Native Companions*, Sydney, Angus and Robertson, 1974; *Red Letter Days* by Jack Beasley, Sydney, Australasian Book Society, 1979.

Judah Waten comments:

(1972) I think I am one of the first novelists and short story writers in Australia to write about foreign migrants, from the inside of a foreign community as well as being a member of the wider Australian community and having grown up in Australia.

My first published book, *Alien Son*, a collection of short stories about migrant life in a small town with the same main characters, was considered an original contribution to Australian literature and also, in the words of the critic of the *Sydney Morning Herald* in 1952, "a study of the problems of migrants, problems that may touch tens of thousands of New Australians today and also the Old Australians who meet them."

A considerable part of my work is about Jewish immigrants struggling to adapt themselves to Australia.

I should like to think that the *Times Literary Supplement* was right, on September 21, 1962, when it said that I was "a sensitive and humane novelist" and that I had made "an alien group part of Australian writing."

The *TLS* also suggested that behind my concepts of the novel and the short story "lies not the Anglo-American tradition followed by most Australian writers but the traditions of the French and Russian novelists, particularly that of Gogol, of Chekhov, and of Tolstoy." The *TLS* added that I had the sort of command of English that comes from learning it early in life and using it most of the time as my principal language.

(1981) My forthcoming novel, *They Thought the World Needed Changing*, deals with the fate of revolutionaries in a country without revolutionary perspective.

* * *

Judah Waten's fiction is usually related to two developments in Australian writing after the Second World War: the conscious effort of "social realist" writers to continue what they saw as the local traditon of proletarian "protest" literature, and the emergence of fiction concerned with the experience of European migrants in their new country. Waten's novels are too varied, however, to be fully covered by these labels.

He first established his reputation as a writer of short stories, especially with the *Alien Son* cycle organized around the theme of the conflicts experienced by European Jewish migrants and their children who are growing up in a strange new culture. In his novels, Waten's experience as a short story writer is apparent from the way he structures his narratives in a series of short scenes, a number of which could be extracted as self-contained episodes.

The first novel, *The Unbending*, retains the best qualities of the *Alien Son* stories—a gently humorous understanding of his migrants' problems and a delicacy in the presentation of the younger generation's cultural conflicts—and combines these with a compelling narrative pace. It opens with the dandified Russian Jew Solomon Kochansky arriving in Australia and settling, against his expectations, into a country town as a hawker. The dashing of Kochansky's high hopes, the education of his son Moses, the impact of the First World War and the conflicts between a conservative society and the International Workers of the World over conscription are the personal and political themes Waten integrates skilfully. The historic conflict over conscription is interesting in itself and it allows him to suggest a significance that goes beyond this small community.

Shares in Murder adapts the conventions of the detective thriller for its own purposes. Based on an actual murder case, it explores Melbourne's underworld with a convincing sense of careful documentation lying behind the relationship it discloses between organized crime and respectability. By turning the conventions he adopts on their heads, Waten implies that in a society as corrupt as contemporary Melbourne crime does pay.

Time of Conflict again presents historic events, but on a more extended scale and in a more overtly political way than in *The Unbending*. The early struggles of Nick Anderson to make his way in the world with the boxing skills he acquires in reform school, his travels, and his involvement with strikers during the depression are narrated compellingly. But the last third of the novel, concerned with Communist Party politics during the Second World War, strains both structure and characterization because it lacks the integration of dramatic life and significant theme found earlier in this novel, or in *The Unbending* as a whole.

Distant Land returns to the migrant theme with the story of another Russian Jewish couple who come to Australia at the beginning of the First World War and settle in a country town. The early scenes of Russian life and of the Kupelschmidts' struggles to prosper in their new land are absorbing and frequently humorous. Towards its end, however, the novel becomes something of a saga of the generations and, as with *Time of Conflict*, the sweep of events (personal rather than political in this case) tends to become external to the chief character.

Season of Youth has as its rogue hero a working class lad who wants to become a writer and moves against a varied social background as he pursues his ambition—and the ladies who help educate him.

Contemporary life and the conflicts felt by the children of immigrants are the subjects of *So Far No Further*. Waten overcomes the tendency of *Time of Conflict* and *Distant Land* to fall off towards the end by setting this novel in the present and working back in time to contrast the earlier experiences of the Italian and Polish Jewish parents with those of their children in the present. He uses his technique of working in short dramatic episodes very effectively here to present a broad social spectrum within the framework of the romance between two students; one, who has become involved in radical student politics, is the daughter of a Jewish businessman, the other is the more conservative son of an Italian fruiterer. Any political implication in this novel about contemporary politics seems untendentious—change and conflict are seen as an unavoidable part of life—and the novel remains optimistically open-ended.

—Brian Kiernan

WATERHOUSE, Keith (Spencer). British. Born in Leeds, Yorkshire, 6 February 1929. Educated at Osmondthorpe Council School, Leeds. Married Joan Foster in 1950 (divorced, 1968); one son and two daughters. Since 1950, free-lance journalist and writer in Leeds and London; currently, columnist, *Daily Mirror*, London. Governor, Leeds Theatre Trust. Recipient (for journalism): Granada Award, 1970; IPC Award, 1970, 1973; British Press Award, 1978. Agent: London Management, 235 Regent Street, London W1A 2JT. Address: 29 Kenway Road, London S.W. 5, England.

Publications

Novels

There Is a Happy Land. London, Joseph, 1957.

Billy Liar. London, Joseph, 1959; New York, Norton, 1960.
Jubb. London, Joseph, 1963; New York, Putnam, 1964.
The Bucket Shop. London, Joseph, 1968; as *Everything Must Go*, New York, Putnam, 1969.
Billy Liar on the Moon. London, Joseph, 1975; New York, Putnam, 1976.
Office Life. London, Joseph, 1978.
Maggie Muggins; or, Spring in Earl's Court. London, Joseph, 1981.

Plays

Billy Liar, with Willis Hall, adaptation of the novel by Waterhouse (produced London, 1960; Los Angeles and New York, 1963). London, Joseph, 1960; New York, Norton, 1961.
Celebration: The Wedding and The Funeral, with Willis Hall (produced Nottingham and London, 1961). London, Joseph, 1961.
England, Our England, with Willis Hall, music by Dudley Moore (produced London, 1962). London, Evans, 1964.
Squat Betty, with Willis Hall (produced London, 1962; New York, 1964). Included in *The Sponge Room and Squat Betty*, 1963.
The Sponge Room, with Willis Hall (produced Nottingham and London, 1962; New York, 1964). Included in *The Sponge Room and Squat Betty*, 1963; in *Modern Short Plays from Broadway and London*, edited by Stanley Richards, New York, Random House, 1969.
All Things Bright and Beautiful, with Willis Hall (produced Bristol and London, 1962). London, Joseph, 1963.
The Sponge Room and Squat Betty, with Willis Hall. London, Evans, 1963.
Come Laughing Home, with Willis Hall (as *They Called the Bastard Stephen*, produced Bristol, 1964; as *Come Laughing Home*, produced Wimbledon, 1965). London, Evans, 1965.
Say Who You Are, with Willis Hall (produced London, 1965). London, Evans, 1966; as *Help Stamp Out Marriage* (produced New York, 1966), New York, French, 1966.
Joey, Joey, with Willis Hall, music by Ron Moody (produced London, 1966).
Whoops-a-Daisy, with Willis Hall (produced Nottingham, 1968). London, French, 1978.
Children's Day, with Willis Hall (produced Edinburgh and London, 1969). London, French, 1975.
Who's Who, with Willis Hall (produced Coventry, 1971; London, 1973). London, French, 1974.
Saturday, Sunday, Monday, with Willis Hall, adaptation of a play by Eduardo de Filippo (produced London, 1973; New York, 1974). London, Heinemann, 1974.
The Card, with Willis Hall, music and lyrics by Tony Hatch and Jackie Trent, adaptation of the novel by Arnold Bennett (produced Bristol and London, 1973).
Filumena, with Willis Hall, adaptation of a play by Eduardo de Filippo (produced London, 1977; New York, 1980). London, Heinemann, 1980.

Screenplays, with Willis Hall: *Whistle Down the Wind*, 1961; *A Kind of Loving*, 1961; *The Valiant*, 1962; *Billy Liar*, 1963; *West Eleven*, 1963; *Man in the Middle*, 1964; *Pretty Polly* (*A Matter of Innocence*), 1968; *Lock Up Your Daughters*, 1969.

Radio Plays: *The Town That Wouldn't Vote*, 1951; *There Is a Happy Land*, 1962; *The Woolen Bank Forgeries*, 1964; *The Last Phone-In*, 1976; *The Big Broadcast of 1922*, 1979.

Television Plays: *The Warmonger*, 1970; *The Upchat Line*, 1977, second series, 1978; *Charlie Muffin*, from novels by Brian Freemantle, 1979; *West End Tales* series, 1981; with Willis Hall: *Happy Moorings*, 1963; *How Many Angels*, 1964; *Inside George Webley* series, 1968; *Queenie's Castle* series, 1970; *Budgie* series, 1971-72; *The Upper Crusts* series, 1973; *Three's Company* series, 1973; *By Endeavour Alone*, 1973; *Billy Liar* series, 1973-74; *Briefer Encounter*, 1977; *Worzel Gummidge* series, from stories by Barbara Euphan Todd, 1979; *Public Lives*, 1979.

Other

The Café Royal: Ninety Years of Bohemia, with Guy Deghy. London, Hutchinson, 1955.
How to Avoid Matrimony, with Guy Deghy (as Herald Froy). London, Muller, 1957.
Britain's Voice Abroad, with Paul Cave. London, Daily Mirror Newspapers, 1957.
The Future of Television. London, Daily Mirror Newspapers, 1958.
The Joneses: How to Keep Up with Them, with Guy Deghy (as Lee Gibb). London, Muller, 1959.
The Higher Jones, with Guy Deghy (as Lee Gibb). London, Muller, 1961.
The Passing of the Third-Floor Buck (*Punch* sketches). London, Joseph, 1974.
Mondays, Thursdays (*Daily Mirror* columns). London, Joseph, 1976.
Rhubarb, Rhubarb, and Other Noises (*Daily Mirror* columns). London, Joseph, 1979.
The Television Adventures [and *More Television Adventures*] *of Worzel Gummidge* (juvenile), with Willis Hall. London, Penguin, 2 vols., 1979.

Editor, with Willis Hall, *Writers' Theatre*. London, Heinemann, 1967.

* * *

Keith Waterhouse's fiction is distinguished by a sharp comic sense, a verbal facility that works on closely polished verbal, imagistic, and grammatical incongruities. For example, in the well-known *Billy Liar*, a character who is one of the two owners of the funeral establishment where Billy works, a man who keeps a copy of Evelyn Waugh's *The Loved One* on his desk in order to get new ideas and who looks forward to the day when all coffins will be made of fiberglass, is introduced: "He was, for a start, only about twenty-five years old, although grown old with quick experience, like forced rhubarb." In *Billy Liar on the Moon*, a sequel to *Billy Liar* that both takes place and was written about 15 years after the original, Billy invents a constant companion named Oscar: "Why Oscar spoke like an Australian actor playing an American bit-part in an English television play was because he didn't exist." In the same novel, which moves Billy from his Yorkshire locale of the late 1950's to a carefully designed community of shopping malls, motels, and perplexing one-way streets that lead only to motorways, a new housing estate is a "suburb of the moon" with "a Legoland of crescents and culs-de-sac with green Lego roofs and red Lego chimney stacks." In *The Bucket Shop* Waterhouse depicts the bumbling, self-deceptive owner of a tatty antique shop, unsuccessful alike in his business, his adulteries, and his efforts to make his wife and nine-year-old daughter, Melisande, fit his trendy definitions of "interesting" people. After a long passage developing Melisande's own fantasies about herself, Waterhouse adds, "She had William's gift for candid self-assessment." That kind of chilling comment, like the discordant contemporary images, the play with clichés, and the exploitation of grammatical incongruities, suggest comparisons with the comic prose of Evelyn Waugh.

Waterhouse builds his verbal texture on plots that often begin with a kind of adolescent humor. Billy, in *Billy Liar*, invents highly improbable stories, publicizing them fully and inconsistently, weaving a net of fantastic lies that is bound to be discovered by parents, bosses, and the three girl-friends to whom he is simultaneously engaged. He is full of elaborate compulsions: if he can suck a mint without breaking it or if he walks in certain complex patterns he feels he will escape the consequences of his stories. He is also a powerful leader in his fantasy land of Ambrosia. The point of view of the young boy in Waterhouse's first novel, *There Is a Happy*

Land, is made even more child-like. The boy plays at being blind or drunk or maimed, mimics all his elders (all Waterhouse's central characters are excellent mimics), and delights in calling out cheeky statements that annoy or embarrass adults. Neither child nor adolescent, the central character in *Jubb*, a rent-collector and youth-club leader in a planned "New Town," is also full of grandiose schemes that others always see through and mimics others' accepted pieties. All these characters, inventive, iconoclastic, and living almost wholly within their disordered imaginations, assault an adult world that pretends it's stable.

Underneath the texture of mimicry and iconoclasm, Waterhouse sometimes gradually shows a world far more sinister than the one suggested by the escapades of adolescent humor. As *There Is a Happy Land* develops, the tone shifts and the boy recognizes the sexuality, perversion, evil, and violence (including the murder of a young girl) in the abandoned quarries and behind the picture-windows of the lower-middle-class housing estate. The character of Jubb himself is gradually revealed as psychotic. Behind his fantasies and comic compulsions is the sexual impotence that has led him to become a peeping Tom, a pyromaniac, and a murderer. In *The Bucket Shop* William's incompetent management of money and women, as well as his incapacity to deal with the consequences of his fantasies, leads to the suicide of a dependent actress. Sometimes, as the humor fades from Waterhouse's novels, it leaves a melodramatic revelation of perverse and horrible humanity.

The two novels concerning Billy Liar are lighter and more sociological than Waterhouse's other fiction. Billy lies less to cover horror or perversion than "to relieve the monotony of living on the moon," where the moon is his arid contemporary civic and domestic life. And the comedy in these novels is more consistently sustained. Both also demonstrate a greater sense of focus in terms of sociological satire: in *Billy Liar* the target is, equally, romanticizing an old, rugged Yorkshire tradition and the "new" world of coffee bars, record shops, and the winner of the Miss Stradhoughton contest who delivers "whole sentences ready-packed in disposable tinfoil wrapper"; in *Billy Liar on the Moon* the target is civic pride, all the contemporary designs and shapes applied to experience and undermined both by their implicit fatuity and old-fashioned corruption. In both novels Billy, the comic, the spinner of fantasies, uses the vision of "London" as his potential escape from provincial dullness, ineptitude, and self-seeking. That any "real London" is no answer for Waterhouse is clear from the treatment of the same sort of amusingly inappropriate fantasy in the mind of William, the multiply incompetent central character in *The Bucket Shop*. Yet, the point in both books about Billy Liar is that he cannot, more than momentarily in the second book, manage the break to London, cannot do more than mimic, scoff, and invent within the limited world he is dependent on. Both as satire and as a potential means of revealing some deeply thought or deeply felt version of experience, Waterhouse's comedy is thin, a covering for a sense of the horror of experience in *There Is a Happy Land* and *Jubb*, a somewhat richer covering for a sense of the unchangeability of experience in the books centrally concerned with Billy Liar. The novels all seem staged (and Waterhouse, in conjunction with Willis Hall, has written a number of plays characterized by sharply witty dialogue and clever invention). As Billy himself says, in *Billy Liar on the Moon*, he is still only a "juvenile lead" in a "comedy," not the central character in a "tragedy" he imagines, not equipped for any part in a drama of "real life." At the end of the novel, he returns to Ambrosia. Yet, in spite of the thinness, the repetition, and the staged quality, Waterhouse, invariably an excellent mimic, often cogent and terse, has created a comic prose and a sense of the involuted logic of systematic fantasy that is strikingly effective and enjoyable.

—James Gindin

WATMOUGH, David. Canadian. Born in London, England, in 1926. Educated at the Coopers' Company School, London, 1937-43; King's College, University of London, 1945-49, degree in theology. Served in the Royal Navy, 1944-45. Reporter, *Cornish Guardian*, Bodmin, Cornwall, 1943-44; Editor, Holy Cross Press, New York, 1953-54; talks producer, BBC Third Programme, London, 1955; Editor, Ace Books, London, 1956; feature writer and critic, San Francisco *Examiner*, 1957-60; arts and theatre critic, Vancouver *Sun*, 1964-67; music and theatre critic, 1967-80, and host of a weekly television show ("Artslib"), 1979-80, Canadian Broadcasting Corporation, Vancouver. Recipient: Canada Council bursary, 1968, 1970, and Senior Arts Grant, 1976. Address: 3358 West First Avenue, Vancouver, British Columbia V6R 1C4, Canada.

PUBLICATIONS

Novel

No More into the Garden. New York, Doubleday, 1978.

Short Stories

Ashes for Easter and Other Monodramas. Vancouver, Talonbooks, 1972.
Love and the Waiting Game: Eleven Stories. Ottawa, Oberon Press, 1975.
From a Cornish Landscape. Padstow, Cornwall, Lodenek Press, 1975.

Uncollected Short Stories

"Terminus Victoria," in *Saturday Night* (Toronto), May 1976.
"Beyond the Mergansers, Above the Salal," in *Canadian Fiction* (Vancouver), Winter 1976.
"Nelly Moriarty and the Jewish Question," in *Matrix* (Lennoxville, Quebec), January 1981.
"Fury," in *Malahat Review* (Victoria, British Columbia), Spring 1981.
"All at Sea," in *Waves* (Toronto), Spring 1981.
"The Cross Country Run," in *Origins* (Hamilton, Ontario), Spring 1981.

Plays

Friedhof (produced Vancouver, 1966). Included in *Names for the Numbered Years*, 1967.
Do You Remember One September Afternoon? (produced Vancouver, 1966). Included in *Names for the Numbered Years*, 1967.
Names for the Numbered Years: Three Plays (includes *Do You Remember One September Afternoon?*, *Friedhof*, *My Mother's House Has Too Many Rooms*). Vancouver, Bau-Xi Gallery, 1967.

Other

A Church Renascent: A Study of Modern French Catholicism. London, SPCK, 1951.

*

Critical Studies: by Robert Fulford, in *Saturday Night* (Toronto), May 1976; "The Novel That Never Ends: David Watmough's Reminiscent Fictions" by George Woodcock, in *The World of Canadian Writing*, Seattle, University of Washington Press, 1980.

David Watmough comments:

In a very real sense I regard each successive volume of my fiction as part of an ongoing "novel" that will not be complete until I can no longer write. My work is an attempt to chronicle the private history of one man of Cornish ancestry living as a Canadian through the 20th century. My fictional protagonist, Davey Bryant, is depicted in childhood, adolescence, maturity, and, currently, middle age. If the work finally succeeds then it will be because I have been able to muster the kind of candour and honesty that such a confessional narrative demands. Another feature of the work is the depiction of private history—including the most intimate sexual and psychological detail—against the backdrop of public events.

* * *

David Watmough is a Canadian writer whose fiction has been set mostly in the land of his childhood, which is Cornwall. Up to now he has published a number of collections of short fiction and one open-ended novel, *No More into the Garden*.

One of the clues to the special nature of Watmough's work can be found in the fictions which he calls "monodramas." As distinct from his short stories, these are written in the area between fiction and drama, so that they can be read by one person—the writer—who in turn assumes all the roles within the story. It is dialogue fiction, resembling, as near as anything else one can think of, Peacock's novels if read by a versatile actor. Watmough has come to the monodrama and the kind of reminiscent short story he writes through long toil in more orthodox writing, such as radio and television plays and the early novels in a more conventional form which he rejected. But having discarded this earlier material, he has found the framework, reminiscent and ironic, into which all his fiction can be combined. It is an almost Proustian framework, and Watmough's assertion that he is really engaged in writing a single novel that will take a lifetime to complete should be taken with a certain seriousness.

In all the fictions Watmough has chosen to preserve—the stories and monodramas as well as the novel—the same central character, Davey Bryant, appears. In many ways he resembles Watmough, in the same way as some of his experiences resemble his creator's. Yet the character stands apart, observed with an irony and a candour that have sometimes made the monodramas as difficult for the audience to accept as for the writer to read. But the observation is from within as well as from without, and each story, each chapter of the novel, is a confession of ambivalent acts, ambivalent motives.

In a way the saga of Davey Bryant is in the classic tradition of modernist fiction—a portrait of the artist as a young man or dog. But real life—from which so much undoubtedly comes—is modified by memory and changed by art, and Watmough's fictions walk a variety of tightropes—between actuality and truth, between the oral and the written way of speaking.

These fictions are all essentially ironic, with the initial nostalgia of the vision always underlaid by the nagging memory, the jarring truth, that provokes the nostalgia. Among the monodramas some of the most telling are those which evoke moments of folly or unworthiness that stir the same shameful recollections in the audience or reader as the narrator experiences or, alternatively, make him uneasy because of the perilous closeness to the possibilities of his own life of the predicaments—frequently homosexual predicaments—that are delineated.

In *No More into the Garden* Davey Bryant is shown as the victim of ludicrous circumstances but equally often as the perpetrator of petty moral atrocities. The victim is impelled perpetually to seek a changed role as the victor, and all but one of Davey's homosexual relationships in *No More into the Garden* are marred by some element of cruelty that degrades one or other of the participants.

Apart from such unifying factors, which bind the chapters in a structure more organically cohesive than the sequences of an obviously conventional plot, there is a pervading elegiac consciousness that deepens as the novel proceeds. The longed-for garden that is never re-entered is in one sense the Cornwall of Celtic childhood happiness, but in another sense it is the state of collective innocence and safety to which all men, like Davey, seek a way back. Yet, as Davey remarks: "Things happen to you, without asking. They just steal up. And one day you wake up and realize you're cut off from everything you once thought would be there for ever." And so, in Blakeian terms, Davey's life moves on from innocence to experience, symbolized by the continent and the ocean that he puts between himself in his Canadian present and "that hurting Cornish terrain" of childhood. The garden finally becomes "a harvest of threats," and, by the novel's end, the fullness of life is revealed at the same time as the ever-presence of dying, for as the mind expands its borders, so in any life the physical possibilities narrow. Here, for Watmough, is the irony, and the elegy also; in his best work they are always coterminous.

—George Woodcock

WAUGH, Alec (Alexander Raban Waugh). British. Born in Hampstead, London, 8 July 1898; older brother of the novelist Evelyn Waugh. Educated at Ferndon Preparatory School; Sherborne School, Dorset; Royal Military Academy, Sandhurst, Berkshire. Served in the Dorset Regiment, 1917-19; prisoner of war, 1918; rejoined the Dorset Regiment, 1939, in France, 1940, the Middle East, 1941; with intelligence staff in Lebanon and Baghdad, 1942-45: Major. Married 1) Barbara Jacobs in 1919 (annulled, 1924); 2) Joan Chirnside in 1932 (died, 1969), two sons and one daughter; 3) the writer Virginia Sorensen in 1969. Member of the staff, 1919-24 and Literary Director, 1924-26, Chapman and Hall, publishers, London. Writer-in-Residence, Central State College, Edmond, Oklahoma, 1966-67. Fellow, Boston University Libraries, 1966. Lives in Tangier. Agent: A.D. Peters and Company Ltd., 10 Buckingham Street, London WC2N 6BU, England; or, Brandt and Brandt, 1501 Broadway, New York, New York 10036, U.S.A. *Died in September 1981.*

PUBLICATIONS

Novels

The Loom of Youth. London, Grant Richards, 1917; New York, Doran, 1920.
The Lonely Unicorn. London, Grant Richards, 1922.
Roland Whately. New York, Macmillan, 1922.
Card Castle. London, Grant Richards, 1924; New York, Boni, 1925.
Kept: A Story of Post-War London. London, Grant Richards, and New York, Boni, 1925.
Love in These Days: A Modern Story. London, Chapman and Hall, 1926; New York, Doran, 1927.
Nor Many Waters. London, Chapman and Hall, 1928; as *Portrait of a Celibate*, New York, Doubleday, 1929.
Three Score and Ten. London, Chapman and Hall, 1929; New York, Doubleday, 1930.
"Sir," She Said. London, Chapman and Hall, and New York, Farrar and Rinehart, 1930; as *Love in Conflict*, London, Severn House, 1977.
So Lovers Dream. London, Cassell, 1931; as *That American Woman*, New York, Farrar and Rinehart, 1932.
No Quarter. London, Cassell, 1932; as *Tropic Seed*, New York, Farrar and Rinehart, 1932.
Leap Before You Look. London, Benn, 1932; New York, Farrar and Rinehart, 1933.
Thirteen Such Years. London, Cassell, and New York, Farrar and Rinehart, 1932.
Wheels Within Wheels: A Story of the Crisis. London, Cassell, 1933; as *The Golden Ripple*, New York, Farrar and Rinehart, 1933.
Playing with Fire. London, Benn, 1933.

The Balliols. London, Cassell, and New York, Farrar and Rinehart, 1934.
Jill Somerset. London, Cassell, and New York, Farrar and Rinehart, 1936.
Going Their Own Ways: A Story of Modern Marriage. London, Cassell, 1938; New York, Farrar and Rinehart, 1939.
No Truce with Time. London, Cassell, and New York, Farrar and Rinehart, 1941.
His Second War. London, Cassell, 1944.
Unclouded Summer: A Love Story. London, Cassell, and New York, Farrar Straus, 1948.
Guy Renton: A London Story. New York, Farrar Straus, 1952; London, Cassell, 1953.
Island in the Sun. New York, Farrar Straus, 1955; London, Cassell, 1956.
Fuel for the Flame. London, Cassell, and New York, Farrar Straus, 1960.
The Mule on the Minaret. London, Cassell, and New York, Farrar Straus, 1965.
A Spy in the Family: An Erotic Comedy. London, W.H. Allen, and New York, Farrar Straus, 1970.
The Fatal Gift. London, W.H. Allen, and New York, Farrar Straus, 1973.
Brief Encounter (novelization of screenplay). London, W.H. Allen, 1975.
Married to a Spy. London, W.H. Allen, 1976.

Short Stories

Pleasure. London, Grant Richards, 1921.
The Last Chukka: Stories of East and West. London, Chapman and Hall, 1928.
Pages in a Woman's Life: A Group of Stories. London, Cassell, 1934.
Eight Short Stories. London, Cassell, 1937.
My Place in the Bazaar. London, Cassell, and New York, Farrar Straus, 1961.

Verse

Resentment. London, Grant Richards, 1918.

Other

The Prisoners of Mainz. London, Chapman and Hall, and New York, Doran, 1919.
Public School Life: Boys, Parents, Masters. London, Collins, 1922.
Myself When Young: Confessions. London, Grant Richards, 1923; New York, Brentano's, 1924.
On Doing What One Likes. London, Cayme Press, 1926.
The Coloured Countries (travel). London, Chapman and Hall, 1930; as *Hot Countries*, New York, Farrar and Rinehart, 1930.
"Most Women...." London, Cassell, and New York, Farrar and Rinehart, 1931.
The Sunlit Caribbean. London, Evans, 1948; revised edition, 1953; as *The Sugar Islands: A Caribbean Travelogue,* New York, Farrar Straus, 1949.
The Lipton Story: A Centennial Biography. New York, Doubleday, 1950; London, Cassell, 1951.
Where the Clocks Strike Twice. New York, Farrar Straus, 1951; as *Where the Clocks Chime Twice: A Travel Book*, London, Cassell, 1952.
Merchants of Wine: Being a Centenary Account of the Fortunes of the House of Gilbey. London, Cassell, 1957.
The Sugar Islands: A Collection of Pieces Written about the West Indies Between 1928 and 1953. London, Cassell, 1958; as *Love and the Caribbean: Tales, Characters, and Scenes of the West Indies*, New York, Farrar Straus, 1959.
In Praise of Wine. London, Cassell, 1959; as *In Praise of Wine and Certain Noble Spirits*, New York, Sloane, 1959.
The Early Years of Alec Waugh. London, Cassell, 1962; New York, Farrar Straus, 1963.
A Family of Islands: A History of the West Indies from 1492 to 1898, With an Epilogue Sketching Events from the Spanish-American War to the 1960's. New York, Doubleday, and London, Weidenfeld and Nicolson, 1964.
My Brother Evelyn and Other Profiles. London, Cassell, 1967; New York, Farrar Straus, 1968.
Wines and Spirits of the World, with the Editors of Time-Life Books. New York, Time, 2 vols., 1968.
Bangkok: The Story of a City. London, W.H. Allen, 1970; Boston, Little Brown, 1971.
A Year to Remember: A Reminiscence of 1931. London, W.H. Allen, 1975.
The Best Wine Last: An Autobiography Through the Years 1932-1969. London, W.H. Allen, 1978.

Editor, *These I Would Choose: A Personal Anthology.* London, Low, 1948.

*

Manuscript Collection: Mugar Memorial Library, Boston University.

* * *

At the conclusion of *The Fatal Gift* the first-person narrator of the novel—whom Alec Waugh acknowledges in the foreword to be himself—ruminates about Raymond Perrone, the protagonist: "The fatal gift of beauty....He had been too good looking, had had such grace and graciousness. He had showed such promise, seemed destined for the world's rewards. He had only to stretch out his hands to take them. The race had been won before the pistol went. He had been born to what others had to earn." At least to the extent that he may be referring to his early success and congenital verbal facility, Waugh, as narrator, is speaking of himself, too. A precocious as well as prolific novelist, Waugh published his first novel, *The Loom of Youth*, before he was 20. It is a strikingly mature first novel that reveals lucidly but not hysterically the intellectual flaccidness and moral emptiness of British public school life at the time of the First World War. Though Waugh has expanded the popularity that that first effort brought him, he has never perceptibly improved upon the literary techniques of *The Loom of Youth*, nor, perhaps, has he delved thematically deeper.

Waugh's strengths reside among his weaknesses. He is an accurate and supremely readable observer of modern mores, but he has a penchant for observing and glibly conveying the ordinary. That which would pluck a responsive chord deep in the imagination of a reader is missing; the extraordinary, the profound, misses Waugh's notice. In novel after novel—close to three dozen—he writes fluently, urbanely, but without depth, persuasion, or—one suspects—much conviction. He diverts, but he does not fascinate, much less enlighten. He often describes emotion rhetorically rather than shows it through action; he juggles plots, sometimes—as in *Wheels Within Wheels* and *No Truce with Time*—three to a volume, and has the characters serve them slavishly. He has a good sense of the autobiographical and historical past, and his family chronicle novels, such as *Three Score and Ten*, *No Quarter*, *The Balliols*, and *Jill Somerset*, are among his best works of fiction, but they tend to paint too many figures in a relatively small space so that they lack definition.

All this is to say that Alec Waugh writes novels that provide topical, entertaining—though occasionally a bit garish—light, but seldom much thematic heat. He writes the kind of popular in-flight entertainment that can translate easily, like *Island in the Sun*, into box-office cinema. He knows what his vast reading public wants, and he supplies it with consummate fluency and grace. His novels have, for example, clearly reflected the increasingly open sexuality of the 20th century, and he handles sex acts with a sensuous yet veiled delicacy that can simultaneously titillate a reader and keep a zealous censor quiescent. The initiation of the 13-year-old Raymond Perrone into sex by an aunt in *The Fatal Gift*, for instance, is a passage that relies on nothing more overt than birch whippings, hoisted shirts, open knees, and heavy breathing for its effect; it is remarkably erotic in a gentlemanly sort of way.

When Waugh has attempted to generate heat to explore significant themes—as well as light, as he did in *Nor Many Waters*, an examination of British divorce laws, the result has been an essay too thinly masquerading as a novel. It is to his credit that he has had the excellent instinct to create primarily light entertainments. "A siesta and a swim" is the suggestion that ends *The Fatal Gift*; for readers with no ready access to those diversions, there have been Alec Waugh's novels.

—Alan R. Shucard

WAUGH, Auberon (Alexander). British. Born in Dulverton, Somerset, 17 November 1939; son of the novelist Evelyn Waugh. Educated at Downside School, Somerset; Christ Church, Oxford (Exhibitioner in English, 1959-60). Served in the Royal Horse Guards (The Blues), 1957-58: Lieutenant; wounded in Cyprus, 1957; retired on pension, 1958. Married Teresa Onslow in 1961; two sons and two daughters. Reporter, *Daily Telegraph*, London, 1960-63; columnist, *Catholic Herald*, London, 1963-64; special writer, International Publishing, London, 1963-67; columnist, *News of the World* and *The Sun*, 1969-70, and *The Times*, London, 1970. Chief Political Correspondent, 1967-70, fiction reviewer, 1970-73, and since 1976, columnist, *The Spectator*, London. Reviewer and contributor, *Private Eye*, *New Standard*, *New Statesman*, and *Books and Bookmen*, all London, and *Esquire*, New York. Parliamentary candidate for Devon North, Dog Lovers' Party, 1979. Recipient (for journalism): British Press Association Award, 1976, 1978; Granada Award, 1980. Address: Combe Florey House, Taunton, Somerset, England; or, La Pesegado, 11320 Montmaur, France.

PUBLICATIONS

Novels

The Foxglove Saga. London, Chapman and Hall, 1960; New York, Simon and Schuster, 1961.
Path of Dalliance. London, Chapman and Hall, 1963; New York, Simon and Schuster, 1964.
Who Are the Violets Now? London, Chapman and Hall, 1965; New York, Simon and Schuster, 1966.
Consider the Lilies. London, Joseph, 1968; Boston, Little Brown, 1969.
A Bed of Flowers; or, As You Like It. London, Joseph, 1972.

Other

Biafra: Britain's Shame, with Suzanne Cronjé. London, Joseph, 1969.
Country Topics: Some Essays. London, Joseph, 1974.
Five Crowded Years: The Diaries of Auberon Waugh 1972-1976, edited by N.R. Galli. London, Private Eye-Deutsch, 1976.
In the Lion's Den: Fifty Essays. London, Joseph, 1978.
The Last Word: An Eye-Witness Account of the Thorpe Trial. London, Joseph, and Boston, Little Brown, 1980.

*

Critical Study: by John Davenport, in *Observer* (London), October 1960.

Auberon Waugh comments:

(1972) *The Foxglove Saga*, a first novel written when I was 19, dealt satirically with life in a monastic school and in the British army, using a complicated and baroque plot as a vehicle for this satire against Church and State which became a best seller in two continents.

Path of Dalliance satirized various political, artistic and philosophical excesses at Oxford University from the point of view of an innocent, sexually incompetent undergraduate.

Who Are the Violets Now? told the sad story of a hack writer for women's magazines, whose self respect was greater than his talent, but whose warm heart led him to work for various suspect organizations.

Consider the Lilies is a novel about the plight of Anglican clergymen today, with nothing whatever to do and time to kill, as fewer and fewer people attend their churches. It is not noticeably ecumenical in tone.

His recent novel, *A Bed of Flowers*, concerns itself with the political and moral implications of "dropping out," urging that politically and morally it is preferable to drop out of the modern world than to stay in and try to improve it.

(1976) As a novelist, I see it as my first duty to divert and stimulate the idle, educated reader; as a novel reviewer, I am appalled by the extent to which academic tastes and preoccupations have been allowed to influence the writing of novels. Where there is a decline in the vitality of the novel, it can almost always be traced to the novelist's angling for academic esteem—or even employment—instead of concentrating on his first duty. Academics have been able to establish a stranglehold in this way partly through the administration of literary prizes, but chiefly because editors are always tempted to cut costs by hiring them to review novels in place of reviewers. The result of novel reviews being unreadable is that fewer people take an interest in novels and more novelists are driven to seek academic jobs, twice as destructive of the creative impulse as any of Mr. Connolly's Enemies of Promise. A good example of the academic style of criticism in all its banal superciliousness and ponderous unreadibility may be seen below.

* * *

Packed away in Fowler's *Modern English Usage* is a useful, mock-Aristotelian outline for a poetics of the comic: the aim of humor, Fowler proposes, is discovery (of human inadequacies, presumably), the province is human nature and the method observation. More specifically, satire aims, by accentuation, at the amendment of manners and morals, while invective seeks to discredit misconduct by direct statement. The novels of Auberon Waugh suggest an unfortunate subcategory, close to invective but having as their aim something one can only call juvenile *Schadenfreude* of a particularly nasty sort. Waugh's first three novels, at any rate, are little more than sophomoric outbursts against some obvious disgraces of modern life, peppered with "daring" naughty little black jokes about cancer, old age and the church. What is distressing is not Waugh's choice of targets but the utter banality of his perceptions. In *The Foxglove Saga*, which Waugh describes as a "satire against Church and State," readers are informed that schoolboys are messy and foolish, the priesthood sometimes vain and mad, the upper classes cruelly selfish and hypocritical and the working class doltishly ignorant and vulgar. From *Path of Dalliance* we learn that Oxford undergraduates are faddish, foolish and cowardly (and dons eccentric) and that the middle class, while perhaps not so stupid as the workers, has its own appalling vulgarities. There are further startling revelations in *Who Are the Violets Now?*: slick women's magazines are mindlessly dishonest and the semi-educated young especially apt to be taken in by liberal action groups run by mendacious bigots. But the disclosures go no further; they barely touch an obvious surface, giving Waugh the penetration of, say, a moderately literate British Al Capp. Waugh is unable or unwilling to create characters and settles for crude caricatures; his plots are jerked forward by little bursts of simultaneous and paralleling actions, a technique obviously derived from Aldous Huxley's early comic-panoramic novels and perfected by the author's father, Evelyn Waugh. Unfortunately Auberon Waugh has none of Huxley's intellectual seriousness and nothing of his father's brilliant malice and moral indignation. "Compassion," asserts the narrator of *Consider the Lilies*, "is the base currency of second-rate minds, a substitute for thought." Possibly so; but for the would-be satirist simple minded contempt is equally ineffectual: there is nothing to discover in these novels but the obvious, no creative observation and no discernible motive other than self-indulgent peevishness.

Consider the Lilies is quite another matter. Here, for whatever motives, Waugh has an object for sustained contempt and something approaching genuine rage: he describes the novel as being "about the plight of the Anglican clergymen today, with nothing whatever to do and time to kill, as fewer and fewer people attend their churches." The central character and narrator, Trumpeter, is a genuine comic creation, a weary La Rochefoucauld the reader can detest with great pleasure; the plot, until the very end, is worked out with far more skill than Waugh had displayed in his first novels. *Consider the Lilies* is a special book, its range obviously limited, but within the terms it sets up it is a complex and almost wholly successful satire.

A Bed of Flowers is more difficult to place fairly—its range is broader, certainly, and if it fails it probably does so for honorable reasons. Waugh is obviously outraged by the horrors which benighted government policies can bring about, in Biafra or elsewhere. The problem here is that the political invective frames or is framed by an attack on another kind of mindlessness (innocents, potheads, and assorted misfits in a commune in Somerset). But bureaucratic wickedness and utopian irresponsibility would really seem to call for different kinds of assaults.

—Elmer Borklund

WEIDMAN, Jerome. American. Born in New York City, 4 April 1913. Educated at the City College of New York, 1930-33; Washington Square College, New York, 1933-34; New York University Law School, 1934-37. Served with the United States Office of War Information, 1942-45. Married Elizabeth Ann Payne in 1943; two sons. President, Authors League of America, 1969-74. Recipient (for drama): Pulitzer Prize, 1960; New York Drama Critics Circle Award, 1960; Tony Award, 1960. Agent: Brandt and Brandt, 1501 Broadway, New York, New York 10036. Address: 1966 Pacific Avenue, San Francisco, California 94109, U.S.A.

PUBLICATIONS

Novels

I Can Get It for You Wholesale. New York, Simon and Schuster, 1937; London, Heinemann, 1938.
What's in It for Me? New York, Simon and Schuster, 1938; London, Heinemann, 1939.
I'll Never Go There Any More. New York, Simon and Schuster, 1941; London, Heinemann, 1942.
The Lights Around the Shore. New York, Simon and Schuster, 1942; London, Hale, 1948.
Too Early to Tell. New York, Reynal, 1946.
The Price Is Right. New York, Harcourt Brace, 1949; London, Hammond, 1950.
The Hand of the Hunter. New York, Harcourt Brace, 1951; London, Cape, 1952.
Give Me Your Love. New York, Eton, 1952.
The Third Angel. New York, Doubleday, 1953; London, Cape, 1954.
Your Daughter Iris. New York, Doubleday, 1955; London, Cape, 1956.
The Enemy Camp. New York, Random House, 1958; London, Heinemann, 1959.
Before You Go. New York, Random House, 1960; London, Heinemann, 1961.
The Sound of Bow Bells. New York, Random House, 1962; London, Heinemann, 1963.
Word of Mouth. New York, Random House, 1964; London, Bodley Head, 1965.
Other People's Money. New York, Random House, and London, Bodley Head, 1967.
The Center of the Action. New York, Random House, 1969; London, Bodley Head, 1970.
Fourth Street East. New York, Random House, and London, Bodley Head, 1970.
Last Respects. New York, Random House, and London, Bodley Head, 1972.
Tiffany Street. New York, Random House, and London, Bodley Head, 1974.
The Temple. New York, Simon and Schuster, 1975; London, Bodley Head, 1976.
A Family Fortune. New York, Simon and Schuster, and London, Bodley Head, 1978.
Counselors-at-Law. New York, Doubleday, 1980; London, Bodley Head, 1981.

Short Stories

The Horse That Could Whistle "Dixie" and Other Stories. New-York, Simon and Schuster, 1939; London, Heinemann, 1941.
The Captain's Tiger. New York, Reynal, 1947.
A Dime a Throw. New York, Harcourt Brace, 1957.
Nine Stories. New York, Random House, 1960.
My Father Sits in the Dark and Other Selected Stories. New York, Random House, 1961; London, Heinemann, 1963.
Where the Sun Never Sets and Other Stories. London, Heinemann, 1964.
The Death of Dickie Draper and Nine Other Stories. New York, Random House, 1965.

Uncollected Short Stories

"The Absolute Darlings," in *McCall's* (New York), July 1965.
"The Friends of Mary Fowler," in *Redbook* (Dayton, Ohio), July 1965.
"Mrs. Gregory Is in Industrial Diamonds," in *Cavalier* (Greenwich, Connecticut), August 1965.
"The Wife of the Man Who Suddenly Loved Women," in *Ladies' Home Journal* (Des Moines, Iowa), June 1966.
"Second Breakfast," in *Playboy* (Chicago), February 1967.
"Good Man, Bad Man," in *Best Detective Stories of the Year 23*, edited by Anthony Boucher. New York, Dutton, and London, Boardman, 1968.

Plays

Fiorello!, with George Abbott, music and lyrics by Sheldon Harnick and Jerry Bock (produced New York, 1959; Bristol and London, 1962). New York, Random House, 1960.
Tenderloin, with George Abbott, music and lyrics by Sheldon Harnick and Jerry Bock, adaptation of the work by Samuel Hopkins Adams (produced New York, 1960). New York, Random House, 1961.
I Can Get It for You Wholesale, music by Harold Rome, adaptation of the novel by Weidman (produced New York, 1962). New York, Random House, 1963.
Cool Off!, Music by Howard Blackman (produced Philadelphia, 1964).
Pousse Café, music by Duke Ellington, lyrics by Marshall Barer and Frank Tobias (produced New York, 1966).

Ivory Tower, with James Yaffe (produced Ann Arbor, Michigan, 1968). New York, Dramatists Play Service, 1969.
The Mother Lover (produced New York, 1969).
Asterisk! A Comedy of Terrors (produced New York, 1969). New York, Dramatists Play Service, 1969.

Screenplays: *The Damned Don't Cry*, 1950; *The Eddie Cantor Story*, 1953; *House of Strangers*, 1955; *Slander*, 1957.

Television Plays: *The Reporter* series, 1964.

Other

Letter of Credit (travel). New York, Simon and Schuster, 1940.
Back Talk (essays). New York, Random House, 1963.

Editor, *The W. Somerset Maugham Sampler*. New York, Garden City Books, 1943; as *The Somerset Maugham Pocket Book*, New York, Pocket Books, 1944.
Editor, *Traveler's Cheque*. New York, Doubleday, 1954.
Editor, with others, *The First College Bowl Question Book*. New York, Random House, 1961.

*

Manuscript Collection: Humanities Research Center, University of Texas, Austin.

Critical Studies: Introductions to *The Horse That Could Whistle "Dixie" and Other Stories*, 1941, and *My Father Sits in the Dark and Other Selected Stories*, 1961.

* * *

In *Other People's Money* Jerome Weidman's protagonist muses as follows: "The trouble with a man who took a small piece of information and instead of conveying it in one lump broke it into bits...was that even a slow-witted listener was bound to put the pieces together more rapidly than the man who had broken them apart." This gives the key to Weidman's fictional method as it has developed over three decades of prolific writing. Indeed, it is difficult to see how he could have written these words without being conscious of their ironic application to himself as a story-teller.

Weidman seems to have admired the fat, rich products of such masters as Balzac and Dickens, and somewhat to have emulated such writers, but never to have had their panoramic vision of society as an organism. His postponed and prolonged revelations are of diminishing rather than increasing complexity and universality; the reader either guesses what is coming or feels let down when it comes.

Weidman's preoccupations from the beginning of his career in 1937 have been two: business and Jewishness. *I Can Get It for You Wholesale*, his first novel, is a fast-moving and highly-detailed examination of the ladies' garment industry in New York. It produced something of a sensation because of its realism and cheerful cynicism. In subsequent works of fiction he has explored other forms of industry, commerce, and finance. Concurrently he has explored the shape and substance of Jewish metropolitan life, at many different levels of poverty and wealth, ignorance and sophistication.

But however extensively Weidman as a writer has concerned himself with the workings of capitalism in the United States, and with the status of Jews in American life, it cannot be said that he has ever tried to draw up an indictment of capitalism, or a condemnation of racism. He is skilled at showing how large a part deception and meretriciousness play in the conduct of business, and he seems to take an artist's delight in depicting the gory details when dog eats dog. He is skilled in showing the many disguises and essential viciousness of anti-Semitism, and he can be really profound as he traces the inner contortions of Jews of various types as they "live with" pervading prejudice. But it is never his purpose to suggest that any kind of common action could make life hard for deceivers and cheaters, or increase man's stock of honesty and genuineness. Nor does he ever express any real pride in Jewishness as a tradition or a religion, or any firm hope that the strength to be drawn therefrom might be applied to defeat the Philistine and deliver God's people into freedom, milk, and honey.

A conversational exchange in *The Sound of Bow Bells* seems to sum up Weidman's whole moral, political and religious attitude:

> "When I first rented this office..., for fifteen cents they [the operators of a nearby small restaurant] gave you a sandwich you could hardly lift. Now...not only have the sandwiches gone up to fifty-five cents, but they're now about as big as a silver dollar, and...they're cutting the tuna fish by mixing it with diced white bread....Some world we live in, eh, Sam?"
> "Oh, it's not so bad," Sam said. "I imagine somebody was complaining about the size of the tuna fish sandwiches outside the tent of Henry V at Agincourt."

—Richard Greenleaf

WELDON, Fay (née Birkinshaw). British. Born in Alvechurch, Worcestershire, 22 September 1933. Educated at South Hampstead High School, London; St. Andrews University, Fife, M.A. in economics and psychology 1954. Has four sons. Recipient: Society of Authors travelling scholarship, 1981. Agent: Giles Gordon, Anthony Sheil Associates Ltd., 2-3 Morwell Street, London WC1B 3AR, England.

PUBLICATIONS

Novels

The Fat Woman's Joke. London, MacGibbon and Kee, 1967; as *...and the Wife Ran Away*, New York, McKay, 1968.
Down among the Women. London, Heinemann, 1971; New York, St. Martin's Press, 1972.
Female Friends. London, Heinemann, and New York, St. Martin's Press, 1975.
Remember Me. London, Hodder and Stoughton, and New York, Random House, 1976.
Words of Advice. New York, Random House, 1977; as *Little Sisters*, London, Hodder and Stoughton, 1978.
Praxis. London, Hodder and Stoughton, and New York, Summit, 1978.
Puffball. London, Hodder and Stoughton, and New York, Summit, 1980.

Short Stories

Watching Me, Watching You. London, Hodder and Stoughton, 1981.

Plays

Permanence, in *Mixed Blessings* (produced London, 1969). London, Methuen, 1970.
Time Hurries On, in *Scene Scripts*, edited by Michael Marland. London, Longman, 1972.
Words of Advice (produced London, 1974). London, French, 1974.
Moving House (produced Farnham, Surrey, 1976).
Friends (produced Guildford, 1978).
Mr. Director (produced Richmond, 1978).

Polaris (broadcast, 1978). Published in *Best Radio Plays of 1978: The Giles Cooper Award Winners*, London, Eyre Methuen, 1979.

Action Replay (produced Birmingham, 1978). London, French, 1980.

Radio Plays: *Spider*, 1972; *Mr. Fox and Mr. First*, 1974; *Housebreaker*, 1974; *The Doctor's Wife*, 1975; *Polaris*, 1978; *All the Bells of Paradise*, 1979; *Weekend*, 1979.

Television Plays: *Wife in a Blond Wig*, 1966; *The Fat Woman's Tale*, 1966; *What About Me*, 1967; *Dr. De Waldon's Therapy*, 1967; *Goodnight Mrs. Dill*, 1967; *The 45th Unmarried Mother*, 1967; *Fall of the Goat*, 1967; *Ruined Houses*, 1968; *Venus Rising*, 1968; *The Three Wives of Felix Hull*, 1968; *Hippy Hippy Who Cares*, 1968; *£13083*, 1968; *The Loophole*, 1969; *Smokescreen*, 1969; *Poor Mother*, 1970; *Office Party*, 1971; *On Trial* (*Upstairs, Downstairs* series), 1971; *Old Man's Hat*, 1972; *A Splinter of Ice*, 1972; *Hands*, 1972; *The Lament of an Unmarried Father*, 1972; *A Nice Rest*, 1972; *Comfortable Words*, 1973; *Desirous of Change*, 1973; *In Memoriam*, 1974; *Poor Baby*, 1975; *The Tale of Timothy Bagshott*, 1975; *Aunt Tatty*, from the story by Elizabeth Bowen, 1975; *Act of Rape*, 1977; *Married Love*, 1977; *Act of Hypocrisy* (*Jubilee* series), 1977; *Chickabiddy* (*Send in the Girls* series), 1978; *Pride and Prejudice*, from the novel by Jane Austen, 1980; *Honey Ann*, 1980; *Life for Christine*, 1980; *Watching Me, Watching You* (*Leap in the Dark* series), 1980.

Other

Editor, with Elaine Feinstein, *New Stories 4*. London, Hutchinson, 1979.

* * *

Fay Weldon's concern is personal relationships in contemporary society, focussing on women, especially as mothers, and thus widening to take in relationships between the generations: "By our children, you shall know us." She amusingly traces long chains of cause and effect, inexorable as Greek tragedy, stemming from both conscious and unconscious motivation, and from chance circumstances. She looks at society with devastating clearsightedness, showing how good may spring from selfishness, evil from altruism. Her liberating clarity, embracing as many points of view as possible, is compulsively readable.

Weldon's unique narrative style highlights the contradiction between the free will which her characters, like us, assume and the conditioning which we know we undergo. Her characters are continually referred to by their names, where English style would normally use a pronoun, and addressed directly in the second person by the author and commented on by her—"Lucky Lily" the author appraises a leading character in *Remember Me*, where she also "translates" passages of the characters' dialogue into what they *mean*, rather than say. Weldon's apparently *disingenuous* surface, with her own paragraphing lay-out, is underpinned by a whole battery of ironic devices, indicating the limitations on her characters'—and our—autonomy from cradle to grave. In *Puffball* this process is pushed back before the cradle, with the sections "Inside Liffey" about the growth of the foetus and its conditioning via the circumstances of the mother's life.

The Fat Woman's Joke, Weldon's first novel, tells what happens to a greedy couple on a diet. This novel originated as a television play, and Weldon hadn't fully developed her unique style. Her characteristic plangent note, that the worst can happen and does, is accompanied by a muted optimism, especially in her novels' endings: gradual progress occurs, at least for the majority if not for the unfortunate individual. *Down among the Women* concludes "We are the last of the women"—that is, the half of the population, defined earlier as living "at floor level, washing and wiping."

Weldon's feminism colours all her work, and is so powerful because she doesn't shrink from detailing the faults of individual women, or the way women exploit what advantages the system yields them. Men are the exploiting sex because the system favours them, and they take for granted the *status quo*. In *Female Friends*, focussing on three women friends and their mothers, Grace is shown as worthless, until perhaps the end, while Oliver and Patrick take what the system offers—and more.

The machinery of plot in *Remember Me* is ostensibly supernatural, as a dead divorced wife haunts her ex-husband's second *ménage*. Weldon's apparent reliance on the supernatural may seem unsatisfactory both here and in *Puffball*, where pregnant Liffey is "overlooked" by the local witch. But in both novels the psychology suggests something of Marjorie's realization about her "haunted" home in *Female Friends*: "it was me haunting myself, sending myself messages." Moreover, Weldon's version of "only connect," stressed in *Remember Me*, is that we should "pay attention to coincidence, and in general help the linkages along."

In *Little Sisters* Weldon turned to the very rich. This blackest of black comedies centres melodramatically on the wheelchair-bound Gemma, narrator of the story within a story. Weldon also uses this device in *The Fat Woman's Joke* and *Praxis*, and dialogue is used throughout her work for similar purposes. The story within a story device enables her to run different time-sequences simultaneously, perhaps to a point of convergence, emphasizing the interlocking of cause and effect between the generations, and also to highlight our imperfect understanding and information, dependent on each individual's partial perception.

Praxis charts the life of a woman who has served a prison sentence for killing "a poor little half-witted" baby, as we learn from one of the first-person chapters alternating at the start of the novel with the third-person chapters that subsequently take over. Weldon's female odyssey is entirely individual, though Praxis Duveen is inevitable sister to Dorothy Richardson's Miriam Henderson and May Sinclair's Mary Olivier.

Puffball, about Liffey's pregnancy in Somerset while her husband remains working in London, is as strongly feminist, by incorporating much information about female physiology and pregnancy. All Weldon's central characters are mothers, married or unmarried, apart from the disabled Gemma in *Little Sisters* who wants to be a mother. Ultimately, Weldon seems to be ambivalent about both the possibility of happiness for most people *without* a long-term relationship with someone, and the chances of such relationships succeeding. Thus Fay Weldon powerfully expresses a central dilemma of life today.

—Val Warner

WELTY, Eudora. American. Born in Jackson, Mississippi, 13 April 1909. Educated at Mississippi State College for Women, Columbus, 1926-27; University of Wisconsin, Madison, B.A. 1929; Columbia University School for Advertising, New York, 1930-31. Staff member, *The New York Times Book Review*, during World War II. Honorary Consultant in American Letters, Library of Congress, Washington, D.C., 1958. Recipient: O. Henry Award, 1942, 1943, 1968; Guggenheim Fellowship, 1942, 1948; American Academy grant, 1944, Howells Medal, 1955, and Gold Medal, 1972; Ford Fellowship, for drama; Brandeis University Creative Arts Award, 1965; Edward MacDowell Medal, 1970; Pulitzer Prize, 1973; National Medal for Literature, 1980; Presidential Medal of Freedom, 1980. D.Litt.: Denison University, Granville, Ohio, 1971; Smith College, Northampton, Massachusetts; University of Wisconsin, Madison; University of the South, Sewanee, Tennessee; Washington and Lee University, Lexington, Virginia. Member, American Academy, 1971. Address: 1119 Pinehurst Street, Jackson, Mississippi 39202, U.S.A.

PUBLICATIONS

Novels

The Robber Bridegroom. New York, Doubleday, 1942; London, Lane, 1944.
Delta Wedding. New York, Harcourt Brace, 1946; London, Lane, 1947.
The Ponder Heart. New York, Harcourt Brace, and London, Hamish Hamilton, 1954.
Losing Battles. New York, Random House, 1970.
The Optimist's Daughter. New York, Random House, 1972; London, Deutsch, 1973.

Short Stories

A Curtain of Green. New York, Doubleday, 1941; London, Lane, 1943.
The Wide Net and Other Stories. New York, Harcourt Brace, 1943; London, Lane, 1945.
Music from Spain. Greenville, Mississippi, Levee Press, 1948.
The Golden Apples. New York, Harcourt Brace, 1949; London, Lane, 1950.
Selected Stories. New York, Modern Library, 1954.
The Bride of Innisfallen and Other Stories. New York, Harcourt Brace, and London, Hamish Hamilton, 1955.
Thirteen Stories, edited by Ruth M. Vande Kieft. New York, Harcourt Brace, 1965.
The Collected Stories of Eudora Welty. New York, Harcourt Brace, 1980.
Moon Lake and Other Stories. Franklin Center, Pennsylvania, Franklin Library, 1980.

Verse

A Flock of Guinea Hens Seen from a Car. New York, Albondocani Press, 1970.

Other

Short Stories (essay). New York, Harcourt Brace, 1949.
Place in Fiction. New York, House of Books, 1957.
Three Papers on Fiction. Northampton, Massachusetts, Smith College, 1962.
The Shoe Bird (juvenile). New York, Harcourt Brace, 1964.
A Sweet Devouring (on children's literature). New York, Albondocani Press, 1969.
One Time, One Place: Mississippi in the Depression: A Snapshot Album. New York, Random House, 1971.
A Pageant of Birds. New York, Albondocani Press, 1975.
Fairy Tale of the Natchez Trace. Jackson, Mississippi Historical Society, 1975.
The Eye of the Storm: Selected Essays and Reviews. New York, Random House, 1975.
Ida M'Toy (memoir). Urbana, University of Illinois Press, 1979.

*

Bibliography: by Noel Polk, in *Mississippi Quarterly* (Mississippi State), Fall 1973; *Eudora Welty: A Reference Guide* by Victor H. Thompson, Boston, Hall, 1976.

Manuscript Collection: Mississippi Department of Archives and History, Jackson.

Critical Studies (selection): *Eudora Welty* by Ruth M. Vande Kieft, New York, Twayne, 1962; *A Season of Dreams: The Fiction of Eudora Welty* by Alfred Appel, Jr., Baton Rouge, Louisiana State University Press, 1965; *Eudora Welty* by Joseph A. Bryant, Jr., Minneapolis, University of Minnesota Press, 1968; *The Rhetoric of Eudora Welty's Short Stories* by Zelma Turner Howard, Jackson, University Press of Mississippi, 1973; *A Still Moment: Essays on the Art of Eudora Welty* edited by John F. Desmond, Metuchen, New Jersey, Scarecrow Press, 1978; *Eudora Welty: Critical Essays* edited by Peggy Prenshaw, Jackson, University Press of Mississippi, 1979; *Eudora Welty's Achievement of Order* by Michael Kreyling, Baton Rouge, Louisiana State University Press, 1980; *Eudora Welty* by Elizabeth Evans, New York, Ungar, 1981.

* * *

The most notable quality of Eudora Welty's fiction has been described very felicitously by Robert Penn Warren: "Eudora Welty's vision of—her feeling for—the world is multiple. She never, even when she nods, sinks into what Blake called 'the single vision and Newton's sleep.' " Each of Welty's five novels develops around the theme of multiplicity. A person is not the fixed quality that he at first may appear to be. The behavior of members of any sub-culture is not as predictable as members of adjoining sub-cultures delude themselves into believing.

Welty's first novel, set in frontier Mississippi in the first years of the 19th century, follows the outlines of a Grimm fairy tale; the robber bridegroom, contrary to expectations, is portrayed as a complex, multi-faceted character: bandit and rapist, respectable businessman, tender lover. Thus, Jamie Lockhart in one role is hired by the philosophical planter, Clement Musgrove, to apprehend the attacker of the planter's daughter, Jamie Lockhart in another role. It is not long, however, before Clement begins to penetrate the complexities of reality, and express the wish to meet the rapist of his daughter, for since the rape Rosamund's penchant for lying has disappeared. When Clement learns that Rosamund has become Jamie's wife, he declares that he would kill Jamie "if being a bandit were his breadth and scope." But through his own and his family's experiences, Clement has come to realize that "all things are double" and that "this should keep us from taking liberties...and acting too quickly to finish things off." And at the end of this brief novel, we have the omniscient narrator saying about Jamie, who with the greatest ease has been able to switch from bandit to merchant, that "he was a hero and had always been one, only with the power to look both ways and to see a thing from all sides."

While *Delta Wedding* is markedly different from *The Robber Bridegroom* in tone, in style, and in the richness of the narrative, the Mississippi aristocratic family that is focused on could be the descendants of Clement Musgrove one hundred years later. Twice the length of the first novel, *Delta Wedding* on the surface dwells in great detail on the activities of the Fairchilds during the week before the wedding of the family beauty Dabney to the plantation overseer Troy Flavin. But what Welty is really interested in are the sensibilities of the numerous members of the immediate and the extended family who come to the plantation for the wedding. One of the important criteria for judging the different characters is how they feel about receiving the overseer into the family. Again, Welty has used an omniscient narrator, and so events and people are seen from different points of view. Dabney's choice of the overseer seems to be a drastic mistake when it is thought about by her father, by an influential aunt, and by her elder sister, Shelley. However, when he is seen and listened to by her mother, Troy's basic goodness and fitness for Dabney become apparent. It becomes clear that objections to Troy are based on nothing more than the fact that his ancestry is undistinguished and that he was born poor. He is delighted with the quilt that his old mother, living alone in the hill country of the northeastern corner of the state, has sent him, and one is led to conclude that, in spite of everything else, a man of his humility and capacity for genuine affection will make a good husband for Dabney, a girl who while not especially perceptive is free of the snobbishness that afflicts other members of the family.

At the same time that the preparations for Dabney's marriage are going forward, the marriage of Dabney's uncle George endures a crisis. It is what some members of the family would have predicted, for in choosing Robbie Reid, who tended the counter in the general store in town, George married "beneath" him. While George's geniality and considerateness have made him a favorite with every member of the family, he is a man whom others find difficult to understand. He seems to love everyone equally, and thus to those, like his wife, who believe they are deserving of a larger portion of his love, he seems almost indifferent. When George risks his life to save the life of a retarded niece, Robbie is so piqued that she is driven to leave George. Robbie, however, in a display of humility that the Fairchild family can hardly believe, returns to George at the plantation two days before Dabney's wedding.

George is a type of man who fascinates Welty. He is goodness personified but seems to be deficient in feeling. The separation of George and Robbie causes Ellen Fairchild, who is married to George's older brother, Battle, to do a great deal of thinking about George. To Ellen, Dabney's mother, George "was the one person ...who did not have it in him to make of any act a facile thing or to make a travesty out of human beings....Only George left the world she knew as pure...as he found it; still real, still bad, still fleeting and hopelessly alluring to her." But Ellen is somewhat naive in her chastizing of Robbie: "George loves a great many people, just about everybody in the Delta....Don't you know that is the mark of a fine man...." As Ellen continues to think about him, she is forced to admit to herself that he is "far from kin to her, scarcely tolerant of her understanding, never dependent on hers or anyone's, or on compassion...." George is both infinitely complex and infinitely simple but at the same time very finite. Ellen is not moved to do anything that would upset the pattern of her life, but her thinking about George produces feelings of love, and she realizes that "she loved what was pure at its heart better than what was understood, or even misjudged, or afterwards forgiven. This was the dearest thing." Earlier, she had concluded that marrying into the Fairchild family had led her to realize "how deep were the complexities of the everyday, of the family, what caves were in the mountains, what blocked chambers, and what crystal rivers that had not yet seen light."

While it is clear that the values and temperament of Ellen Fairchild are the ones Welty most respects, one of the problems with *Delta Wedding* is that the cast is large and there are numerous voices and viewpoints, including those of nine-year-olds. In *The Ponder Heart* Welty has moved to the other extreme, and has her story told through only one voice. Edna Earle, proprietress of the Hotel Beulah in Clay, Mississippi, tells the story of her Uncle Daniel to a guest at the hotel who is not given the opportunity to speak a single word.

The mystery of Uncle Daniel Ponder is similar to that of George Fairchild. Uncle Daniel is constantly giving his money and possessions away to strangers. But he neglects to bestow any of his bounty upon his 17-year-old wife, Bonnie Dee Peacock, whom he became enamored of as she clerked in the local five and ten. Unlike George, Uncle Daniel is very distressed when his wife leaves him. When Edna Earle has heard Daniel's refrain "Where has Bonnie Dee gone?" innumerable times, she hits upon an idea for getting Bonnie Dee back. She places an advertisement in the form of a poem in the newspaper. The poem, a good imitation folk ballad beginning with the lines "O listen to me, Bonnie Dee Ponder,/Come back to Clay, or husband will wonder," includes this important bit of information: "Retroactive allowance will be given." Bonnie Dee returns, "and *things* began to pour into that house—you'd think there wouldn't be room." Welty then seems to pronounce judgment by having Bonnie Dee die during a lightning storm of heart failure.

The totally unexpected twist in plot is one of Welty's favorite narrative devices. The twist here is that the Peacock family press charges of murder against Daniel. Thematically, the purpose of the trial that then takes place is to expose the Peacocks, a farming clan mired in ignorance and poverty.

> We saw them come in....Old Lady Peacock wagged in first, big as a house, in new bedroom slippers this time, with pompoms on the toes. She had all of them behind her—girls going down stairsteps looking funnier in Bonnie Dee's parceled-out clothes, and boys all ages and sizes and the grown ones with wives and children, and Old Man Peacock bringing up the rear....He had a face as red as a Tom turkey and not one tooth to his name, but he had on some new pants. I noticed the tag still poking out the seam when he creaked in at the door.

The whole family settles on the courthouse steps for lunch, and afterwards the remains of the lunch are left there. Perhaps the worst quality of people like the Peacocks is their utter lack of imagination. "Poor Bonnie Dee: I never believed she had one whit of human curiosity. I never, in all the time she was married to Uncle Daniel, heard her say 'What next?' "

Ridicule of the Peacocks for their country ways is too easy. Even they are worthy of compassion. Thus on the final page of the novel, Welty has Edna Earle say of Bonnie Dee: "And you know, Bonnie Dee Peacock, ordinary as she was and trial as she was to put up with—she's the kind of person you do miss. I don't know why—deliver me from giving you the *reason*. You could look and find her like anywhere. Though I'm sure Bonnie Dee and Uncle Daniel were as happy together as most married people."

Almost 20 years later in *The Optimist's Daughter*, Welty again pits herself against a Bonnie Dee. This time her culturally and spiritually deprived nemesis is Fay Chisom, 30-year-old typist from Texas, who has become the second wife of 70-year-old Judge McKelva. The point of view is that of the Judge's 40-year-old self-sufficient daughter by his first wife. Laurel, home in Mississippi from her career in Chicago for her father's dying, struggles mightily to contain her contempt for Fay. But Fay is less amusing and meaner than Bonnie Dee. She is a person who is "without any powers of passion or imagination in herself and had no way to see it or reach it in the other person." To Welty, Fay seems to represent the growing number of Americans who are rootless and hence without traditions and a sense of appropriate behavior.

Losing Battles is Welty's most ambitious work. Into it she has attempted to cram a full lifetime's observations of and reactions to the people of her native region. She has a great deal to say, and, wisely, has wished to avoid the novelist's pitfall of direct statement. She uses the dramatic method. But, unfortunately, she has not avoided the pitfalls of that method. At least 95 per cent of the novel consists of dialogue, and that much dialogue, spoken in dialect by many different voices that frequently seem undifferentiated, is very wearing when it is the means of giving exposition, of pointing out local curiosities, of telling funny stories, of showing characters' penchants for trivia, and of making significant thematic statements, especially since at first the latter seem to be just as insignificant as the rest. Rejecting the single voice of *The Ponder Heart* and the omniscient narrator of *The Robber Bridegroom*, Welty has chosen a story-telling technique that is both tedious and confusing.

This long novel covers a period of only a day and a half. Again we have a large family gathered together; the occasion is the annual reunion and the celebration of the 90th birthday of Granny, who has recently become a great-great-grandmother. We have a family that could be the Peacocks or the Chisoms. But now we do not see them through the unsympathetic eyes of a town lady. We are with them in their home territory, for the most part at the farm home of Granny's youngest grandchild, Beulah Beecham Renfro, who is herself a grandmother. One of the several mysteries in this novel has to do with the circumstances under which Beulah's parents met their deaths together and left Beulah and six older children orphaned: "What errand was they both so beat on when they hitched and cut loose from the house so early and drove out of sight of Grandpa and Granny, children and all, that morning?" one voice asks. "Something between a man and wife is the only answer and it's what no other soul would have no way of knowing," another voice answered. From *The Robber Bridegroom* on, each marriage that Welty has dealt with has had its unique dynamics and tended to elude definition.

Granny, with her daughter and son-in-law dead, "just tied on her apron, dusted off her cradle, and started in all over again with another set of children." It was this heroic response that has brought Granny the unusual devotion of her grandchildren and that made their presence at the birthday reunion each summer so important to each of them.

For Jack Renfro, Beulah's 19-year-old son, this reunion at his own home is extremely difficult to get to. On the eve of the reunion he is across the state in the penitentiary, serving a two-year sentence for an act that any judge having first-hand familiarity with Jack's character would realize had to be more charitable than criminal. So that he may honor Granny by his presence, Jack makes a successful escape—one day before he would have been released on parole. This is typical of Jack's selflessness and devotion to others. It is also typical of the devil-may-care aspect of his character, and in terms of temperament makes him the descendant of George Fairchild and Uncle Daniel. All of his family recognize Jack's unique and prodigious virtue. But outsiders do not, including the school teacher who devoted her life to trying to bring knowledge and enlightenment to this family and to the other poverty-stricken, struggling families in these hills.

Throughout her novels, Eudora Welty is keenly aware of ambiguity and ambivalence, of irony, and how perspective affects judgment, of the imperfect knowledge of the knowledgeable. This awareness and concern place her in the mainstream of modern literature despite the sound and look of regionalism that her novels have.

—Paul Marx

WENDT, Albert. Samoan. Born in Apia, Western Samoa, 27 October 1939; member of the Aiga Sa-Tuala. Educated at New Plymouth Boys High School, New Zealand, graduated 1957; Ardmore Teacher's College, diploma in teaching, 1959; Victoria University, Wellington, 1960-64, M.A. (honours) in history 1964. Married Jennifer Elizabeth Whyte in 1964; two daughters and one son. Teacher, 1964-69, and Principal, 1969-73, Samoa College, Western Samoa. Senior Lecturer, 1974-75, and Assistant Director of Extension Services, 1976-77, University of the South Pacific, Suva, Fiji. Since 1978, Director, University of the South Pacific Centre, Apia, Western Samoa. Editor, *Bulletin*, now *Samoa Times*, Apia, 1966. Coordinator, Unesco Program on Oceanic Cultures, 1975-79. Recipient: *Landfall* Prize, 1963; Wattie Award, 1980. Agent: Tim Curnow, Curtis Brown (Australia) Pty. Ltd., P.O. Box 19, Paddington, New South Wales 2021, Australia. Address: University of the South Pacific Centre, Private Bag, Apia, Western Samoa.

PUBLICATIONS

Novels

Sons for the Return Home. Auckland, Longman Paul, 1973.
Pouliuli. Auckland, Longman Paul, 1977; Honolulu, University Press of Hawaii, 1980.
Leaves of the Banyan Tree. Auckland, Longman Paul, 1979; London, Allen Lane, 1980.

Short Stories

Flying-Fox in a Freedom Tree. Auckland, Longman Paul, 1974.

Uncollected Short Stories

"The Burden," in *Islands* (Auckland), September 1976.
"The Birth and Death of the Miracle Man," in *Hemisphere* (Woden, Australia), 1977.
"Exam Failure Praying," in *Education* (Wellington), 1977.

Plays

Comes the Revolution (produced Suva, Fiji, 1972).
The Contract (produced Apia, Western Samoa, 1972).

Verse

Inside Us the Dead: Poems 1961 to 1974. Auckland, Longman Paul, 1976.

Other

Editor, *Some Modern Poetry from Fiji* [*Western Samoa, the New Hebrides, the Solomon Islands*]. Suva, Fiji, Mana, 4 vols., 1974-75.
Editor, *Lali: A Pacific Anthology.* Auckland, Longman Paul, 1980.

* * *

As the Samoan novelist, short story writer, and poet, Albert Wendt, has said, he "belongs to two worlds in almost every way." For more than a decade after his early teens he experienced the difficulties of adapting himself to an alien culture in New Zealand, and his return to Samoa gave rise to a process of readjustment both to his ancestral past and to the post-independence present of his country. His writing stems in some measure from this bi-cultural predicament. It is a return to and a quest for the roots of his being. Significantly enough, "Inside Us the Dead" is the title of his volume of poems.

If his novels and short stories are the work of a self-acknowledged literary pioneer, they are much more than a welcome indication that a Polynesian literature is developing in the southwest Pacific. However difficult it may be to assess the ultimate value of productions for which in many important ways no firm basis for comparison exists, it is nonetheless clear that they achieve distinction as explorations of human relations and a way of life that have almost escaped the attention of romantic or racist outlanders.

Sons for the Return Home, Wendt's first novel, was published many years after his own return to Western Samoa. The simplicity of its plot and language is in marked contrast to the ambiguities and ironies of the pursuit of selfhood which, interwoven with a Samoan myth, provides the theme and gives substance and meaning to the narrative. Because it is mainly concerned with a Samoan family living in New Zealand, the fa'a Samoa or the Samoan way of life becomes an integral part of the novel's structure and not an intrusive element requiring unnecessary explanation. The doubts and difficulties implicit in the theme are developed in terms of incident and human relationship; and the disillusion experienced after "the return home" becomes the climax of the novel that offers no easy solution to the personal problems arising from cultural shock.

Wendt's later publications are centred on the extended families in the villages of Samoa, but they contain little to suggest that they are guide-books to an exotic and romantic island-world. In the short stories of *Flying-Fox in a Freedom Tree*, in *Pouliuli*, and in the three parts of *Leaves of the Banyan Tree* the quest for identity, the attempt to discover the true self caught between the claims of contending cultures, and the search for a precarious freedom from the dictates of competing orthodoxies are raised to a higher level. They are not merely the consequences of racial disharmony, but originate in the basic conditions of human existence. The flying-fox hangs upside-down in the freedom tree. The powerful head of an extended family rejects his past, repudiates his present, and in advanced old age seeks freedom in Pouliuli, in darkness. The rise and fall of another titled head of an aiga in *Leaves of the Banyan Tree*, his lust for power, his imitation of Papalagi (European) ways may be related to the social pollution of the islands, but have their source in a deeper corruption.

This long and powerful novel explores in myth and legend, in traditional social structure, in the changing post-independence present, not only what has happened to the fa'a Samoa, but what has happened to human beings. The comedy and the tragedy, the violence, the horror and the glory of human life, together with man's desperate search for the meaning of existence, are localised in a village setting populated by an extraordinary variety of characters. In its middle section an expanded version of *Flying-Fox in a Freedom Tree*, the novella that gives its title to the earlier volume of short stories, becomes an essential and thoroughly coordinated part of the whole book, linking the first section, "God, Money, and Success," to the third, "Funerals and Heirs," of this saga of a Samoan village.

As a Polynesian writer Wendt has not been satisfied to produce fiction that has entertainment value alone or to exploit the fa'a Samoa for the benefit of the foreign tourist. His aim has been far more ambitious, and he has taken greater risks. If at times he lays himself open to adverse critical comment and his intentions have not always been realised, his achievement is nonetheless impressive. He has set a standard that argues well for the future.

—H. Winston Rhodes

WESCOTT, Glenway. American. Born in Kewaskum, Wisconsin, 11 April 1901. Educated at the University of Chicago (President of the Poetry Society), 1917-19. Lived briefly in New Mexico, New York City and State, England, and Germany, 1919-25; lived in France and Germany, 1925-33; full-time writer from 1921. D.Litt.: Rutgers University, New Brunswick, New Jersey, 1963. President, National Institute of Arts and Letters, 1959-62. Address: Hay-Meadows, Rosemont, New Jersey 08556, U.S.A.

PUBLICATIONS

Novels

The Apple of the Eye. New York, Dial Press, 1924; London, Butterworth, 1926.
The Grandmothers: A Family Portrait. New York, Harper, 1927; as *A Family Portrait*, London, Butterworth, 1927.
The Pilgrim Hawk: A Love Story. New York, Harper, 1940; London, Hamish Hamilton, 1946.
Apartment in Athens. New York, Harper, 1945; as *Household in Athens*, London, Hamish Hamilton, 1945.

Short Stories

...Like a Lover. Macon, France, Monroe Wheeler, 1926.
Good-bye Wisconsin. New York, Harper, 1928; London, Cape, 1929.
The Babe's Bed. Paris, Harrison, New York, Minton Balch, and London, Simkin, 1930.

Verse

The Bitterns: A Book of Twelve Poems. Evanston, Illinois, Monroe Wheeler, 1920.
Native of Rock: XX Poems 1921-1922. New York, Francisco Bianco, 1925.

Other

Elizabeth Madox Roberts: A Personal Note. New York, Viking Press, 1930.
Fear and Trembling (essays). New York, Harper, 1932.
A Calendar of Saints for Unbelievers. Paris, Harrison, New York, Minton Balch, and London, Simkin, 1932.
12 Fables of Aesop, Newly Narrated. New York, Museum of Modern Art, 1954.
Images of Truth: Remembrances and Criticism. New York, Harper, 1962; London, Hamish Hamilton, 1963.

Editor, *The Maugham Reader.* New York, Doubleday, 1950.
Editor, *Short Novels of Colette.* New York, Dial Press, 1951.

*

Bibliography: "Glenway Wescott: A Bibliography" by Sy Myron Kahn, in *Bulletin of Bibliography 22* (Boston), 1956.

Critical Studies: *Glenway Wescott* by William H. Rueckert, New York, Twayne, 1965; *Glenway Wescott: The Paradox of Voice* by Ira Johnson, Port Washington, New York, Kennikat Press, 1971.

* * *

Glenway Wescott's literary reputation has been overshadowed by the reputation of his fellow upper midwestern writers, most of them like him expatriates during the 1920's: Ernest Hemingway and John Dos Passos from Illinois; Scott Fitzgerald and Sinclair Lewis from Minnesota (along with the presently neglected Kay Boyle); and Idaho's Ezra Pound. He has written comparatively little, but that little often comes close to an almost lapidary perfection of sentence, paragraph, and scene. Like other "minor" writers, Wescott tends to be forgotten by a public overwhelmed by publishers' announcements of yet more "major" novels and novelists; when the inflated press-releases are consigned to their place as part of the history of advertising rather than as part of literary judgment, however, Glenway Wescott will take his place as one of the finest literary artists in this period's prose for—if nothing else—his novel *The Pilgrim Hawk*, a work which like Joyce's "The Dead," Ford's *The Good Soldier*, and Porter's *Noon Wine*, comes as close to perfection as literary art is liable to allow. Wescott gained an early reputation for technical skill; but we mistake Wescott if we assume his sole virtue is technique.

In his first book, *The Apple of the Eye*, Wescott tells three stories; in one the stunted natural growth of the marsh-land setting frames and parallels the stunting of human feelings, emotions, ideals of a woman who must live in that setting; in the second the girl can find escape only through suicide in the marsh, whereas her seducer goes on about the pagan sensuousness of ancient Greeks; and in the third the conflict between stunted marshy landscape and the seduction of the past as made viable in language takes place within a boy. It is the best of the stories. The theme is, like most themes in fiction, a philosophical commonplace: the problem of moderation, a quality Wescott in his essays insists is a good thing in itself. It is decorum, moderation, the perilous balance of life which are the themes of Wescott's fiction. As in the contrast of hard-drinking German immigrants in the Midwest with Alwyn Tower's grandparents' teetotal puritanism, deviation to either side (decorum can be breeched as much by haughtiness as by rowdiness) brings distortion to human character; and it brings tragedy.

In *The Apple of the Eye* the boy is confronted with the conflict of family duty (as embodied in the disagreeable orthodoxy of his pioneering aunt) and a sort of pagan exuberance in natural beauty (as suggested by a friend's teaching). Such conflicts run through Wescott's fiction. Yet once the central character of most of the fiction, Alwyn Tower, has got free of the homeplace, he finds that his freedom is compromised by memory: he must find his proper relationship to the past if he is to live successfully in the present. So Alwyn Tower sits in his hotel room in the South of France, having told Wisconsin "goodbye," only to remember his past, a process which enabled Wescott to create one of the finest novels in modern American fiction, *The Grandmothers*.

In an essay in *Images of Truth*, Wescott tells of having been impressed by the passage in the *Odyssey* where the shades are called up so that Odysseus can obtain information he needs to find his way home. This is, of course, the "germ" of *The Grandmothers*; for near

Nice, Wescott heard and subsequently made Alwyn Tower hear, some drunken American sailors begin to sing "show me the way to go home," raising the question of where home is and how we truly arrive at the place—and know it, as Eliot says, for the first time. Alwyn Tower in a European hotel turns to a picture album; the visual images trigger his imaginative reconstruction of lives, his forebears from about 1840 down to his own parents: it is also a study of history and of what the past means, of the present and of how we come to know ourselves. Such a long look to the past is central to Wescott's works. In *The Pilgrim Hawk* Alwyn Tower in America looks back at a day in France; and in *Apartment in Athens* the very sight of the Acropolis from a window in the apartment's kitchen suggests the dimension of history in which a parable of freedom is played out in the 20th century.

The Pilgrim Hawk, subtitled "a love story," is a short novel in which a few people visit each other and a whole world of relationships is obliquely revealed. Wescott achieves in this novel a most difficult thing: a style which in its precision seems to be no style at all, and a technique so fused to theme and purpose that the story seems merely to tell itself. His is the art which conceals art. And he has used the first person narrator not just to tell a story, but in one sense to force upon the reader an examination of the very concept of perception—of how one perceives the world and then comes to knowledge, if at all. Wescott has made a tale of great complexity out of the simplest materials: one setting, a house and garden in France; a single afternoon in the 1920's, looked back on 20 years later; a plot consisting of triangular relationships of a small cast of characters—Alwyn Tower, the visiting American writer; his friend Alexandra Henry, owner of the house; two servants, Eva and Jean; and the Cullens, a wealthy roaming Irish couple who bring Ricketts, their chauffeur, and the pilgrim hawk. The action is quite limited. The Cullens arrive, displaying their rich eccentricity as well as their habit of preying on each other and the world; the hawk by contrast is for the most part hooded and quiet. Cullen gets drunk, tries to free the hawk which is recaptured; the narrator discovers the servants and chauffeur in a jealous quarrel in the kitchen; the Cullens leave. Shortly thereafter the Cullens return briefly, Mrs. Cullen with a revolver she carries for her protection, and took from her husband; the revolver is thrown in the lake; again the Cullens leave, and the narrator and his hostess chat briefly about the day's incidents.

Two triangles are at once apparent: the Cullens and the hawk, a triangle which reveals love in its possessive, jealous, even violent aspects, ranging from repressed to domineering, lyrical to savage; and the servants with the chauffeur, a triangle which parallels some of the perverse but vital attachments and needs which constitute involvements of the main triangles. The servant Eva flirts with the chauffeur Ricketts; yet she later explains that her husband, Jean needs to be made jealous so that he can express his love, a love otherwise the captive of his reticence. Freedom, then, is dependence, and captivity in love is liberty.

The third triangle is less dramatic, being entirely overlooked by some readers; yet it is central to the examination, in fictional terms, of the conflicts between appetite and control. In revealing Cullen's hatred, the narrator also reveals himself, his own self-interest and captivity. For as a writer he has missed life, as bound to his art as the hooded hawk on Mrs. Cullen's arm. One must finally wonder why the narrator elects to recall this one day when he was the guest of Alexandra Henry who later became his sister-in-law. The reader is not *told* about the conflict of love and art; instead he receives it, as a powerful undercurrent in the story of an Irish couple and a hawk, which is also a story about love and art, freedom and captivity.

Apartment in Athens undertakes to present the emotions and psychology of conqueror and conquered; yet it is also an extension of the theme of freedom and captivity, now presented in terms of ideology rather than of love. The fictional approach is direct, rather than oblique as in *The Pilgrim Hawk*, so that the war-time "message" is not obscured by subtle rendering; yet that very "message" has obscured for many readers the other themes of the novel.

A German officer is housed in an apartment in the Athens home of a Greek intellectual who tries to "adjust" to this intrusion of a victor; as the two men try to understand each other, we have a paradigm of part of human experience. When the Greek expresses sympathy for the German whose wife is dead, he is imprisoned and executed for "subversive" remarks—a dark and bitter end, if we read the book as something more than a war-time tract. The long letter smuggled out of jail is for the success of the novel unfortunate, for the blatant intrusion of propaganda unbalances the book, which is really about masks of submission, the reality of masks when deception becomes the reality; about the complex accommodations life requires.

In some of the early stories and in *The Pilgrim Hawk*, the narrator is an alien American in France; in *Apartment in Athens* the alien in Greece is a German enemy. This, together with other shifts in narrative style as well as the announced war-time propagandistic aim of the book, has tended to obscure the relationship of the novel to Wescott's other fictions and concerns: the nature of freedom, the types of captivity of which man is capable (whether by a marsh in *The Apple of the Eye* or an invader in *Apartment in Athens*), the ambiguous relationship of a man to his home place (Alwyn Tower says in *Good-bye, Wisconsin* that he has no land, only a family). One hopes that in the not too distant future, Wescott's prose fiction will again be in print so that it can take its place as one of the truly distinguished achievements in 20th-century literature in English.

—James Korges

WEST, Anthony (Panther). British. Born in Hunstanton, Norfolk, 4 August 1914; son of the writers H.G. Wells and Rebecca West, *q.v.* Educated at Stowe School. Married 1) Katharine Church in 1936, one son and one daughter; 2) Lily Dulany Emmet in 1952, one son and one daughter. Dairy Farmer, 1937-43; worked on the Far Eastern Desk, 1943-45, and in the Japanese Service, 1945-47, BBC, London. Since 1950, Staff Writer, *The New Yorker*. Recipient: Houghton Mifflin Literary Fellowship, 1950. Address: c/o The New Yorker, 25 West 43rd Street, New York, New York 10036, U.S.A.

PUBLICATIONS

Novels

On a Dark Night. London, Eyre and Spottiswoode, 1949; as *The Vintage*, Boston, Houghton Mifflin, 1950.
Another Kind. London, Eyre and Spottiswoode, 1951; Boston, Houghton Mifflin, 1952.
Heritage. New York, Random House, 1955.
The Trend Is Up. New York, Random House, 1960; London, Hamish Hamilton, 1961.
David Rees, Among Others. New York, Random House, and London, Hamish Hamilton, 1970.

Other

Gloucestershire. London, Faber, 1939.
D.H. Lawrence. London, Barker, 1951; revised edition, 1966; Folcroft, Pennsylvania, Folcroft Editions, 1973.
The Crusades. New York, Random House, 1954; as *All about the Crusades*, London, W.H. Allen, 1967.
Principles and Persuasions: Literary Essays. New York, Harcourt Brace, 1957; London, Eyre and Spottiswoode, 1958.
Elizabethan England. New York, Odyssey Press, and London, Hamlyn, 1965.

Mortal Wounds: The Lives of Three Tormented Women. New York, McGraw Hill, 1973; London, Robson, 1975.
John Piper. London, Secker and Warburg, 1979.

Editor, *The Galsworthy Reader.* New York, Scribner, 1968.

* * *

Anthony West is a journalist and critic as well as the author of several novels. *On a Dark Night*, *Another Kind*, and *The Trend Is Up* are concerned with the moral malaise of 20th-century man and its effect on his personal, political, and economic life. A different sort of novel is his third, *Heritage*; this and the collection of sequential stories *David Rees, Among Others* deal fictionally with problems similar to his own as a child and young man, the son of famous, brilliant parents who were not married. Both books treat the theme with courage and good humor; *Heritage*, as the young hero gets older and at last meets his father, becomes at times extremely funny. Irrepressible Max Town is an exuberant interpretation of H.G. Wells. The fictional mother—West uses the somewhat trite figure of a great actress—is less successful, and certainly bears little resemblance to Dame Rebecca West. It is Max Town's collisions with—and occasional surprising nostalgia for—conventionality that make the book live. In *David Rees, Among Others*, where the mother appears in the guise of a concert pianist, the study of her problems becomes more interesting. Both books afford subtle insights into the mind of a child and growing boy.

On a Dark Night, published just after the war crime trials, is a fantasia of the afterlife as John Wallis, who has just shot out his brains, quests for meaning in company with a German general whom he had helped hang. After reviewing many incidents in his past and rejecting an eternity of pleasure, he sees that there is "nothing vile in manhood" and that in avoiding moral responsibility he had chosen to "walk step by step away" from the goodness of life towards his eventual suicide. This theme of self-disgust is continued in his next novel, *Another Kind*, in which personal malaise, augmented by and contributing to economic sickness, brings contemporary England to a fascination with failure and a suicidal revolution. A defeated architect, Walter Jackson, attempts to put meaning in his life by an affair with a strong blonde courtesan, a former farm-girl, Anne. But his self-loathing taints everything he touches. West had just written a study of D.H. Lawrence, and in the first part of this novel the passages analyzing Walter's evasions and sudden repugnances betray Lawrentian models. Revolution comes and offers a heyday to black-marketeers (among them Walter), wastrels, and sadists. From this vineyard of wrath Anne effects a desperate escape and manages to get back to an old farm-mill to bear the child that Walter (now dead) had insisted that she abort.

The Trend Is Up, published after ten years of residence in the United States, ends on no note of hope: Gavin Hatfield, a quite decent New Englander who elected wealth and its power as his goal, is alone in his house in his Florida empire asking "Tell me, tell me what I did wrong!" This long book, lacking the sparkle of *Heritage* and the analysis of the first part of *Another Kind*, and needing concentration, is nevertheless a successful study of an economic boom and the dulling or distorting of the minds and emotions involved. It offers a wide screen of characters; though some tend to remain too allegorical, and Gavin's "northern" wife never comes to life, many are well grasped. Concerned with actualities, and building to a notable ironic climax, it is in some ways West's most powerful novel.

—Alice Bensen

WEST, Anthony C(athcart Muir). Irish. Born in County Down, Northern Ireland, 1 July 1910. Served in the Royal Air Force Pathfinder Force during World War II: Air Observer and Navigator Bomber. Married Olive Mary Burr in 1940; eleven children. Recipient: Atlantic Award, 1946. Address: c/o Midland Bank Ltd., Castle Street, Beaumaris, Anglesey, Gwynedd, North Wales.

PUBLICATIONS

Novels

The Native Moment. New York, McDowell Obolensky, 1959; London, MacGibbon and Kee, 1961.
Rebel to Judgment. New York, Obolensky, 1962.
The Ferret Fancier. London, MacGibbon and Kee, 1963; New York, Simon and Schuster, 1965.
As Towns with Fire. London, MacGibbon and Kee, 1968; New York, Knopf, 1970.

Short Stories

River's End and Other Stories. New York, McDowell Obolensky, 1958; London, MacGibbon and Kee, 1960.

Uncollected Short Stories

"Swineherd," in *Evergreen Review* (New York), Spring 1959.
"All the King's Horses," in *Transatlantic Review* (London), December 1960.
"The Fairy Midwife," in *Colorado Quarterly* (Boulder), Winter 1961.
"Myself and a Rabbit" (as Michael Mac Grian), in *Irish Stories and Tales.* New York, Washington Square Press, 1961.
"Looking for Bridie," in *Audience* (Cambridge, Massachusetts), Winter 1962.
"Song of the Barrow," in *In the Country*, edited by Eileen Buckle and Derek Lord. London, New English Library, 1979.

*

Critical Study: *Forces and Themes in Ulster Fiction* by John Wilson Foster, Dublin, Gill and Macmillan, 1974.

Anthony C. West comments:

I have a creative and an a-political interest in the human condition, wherever and however it may be found, with the incorrigible hope for social harmony and world tolerance.

* * *

The fiction of Anthony C. West is filled with poignant and great tenderness, yet it is not just lyric. The main characters of his novels are all very much attuned to nature, yet *in* the world if not entirely *of* it. He handles scenes of childhood well, yet his children grow up. *As Towns with Fire*, his latest novel, creates a focus, almost a culmination, for *The Native Moment* and *The Ferret Fancier*.

As Towns with Fire is the portrait of a man and a war. Beginning New Year's Eve, 1939, it traces the experiences of Christopher MacMannan, an Irishman who has settled in London to train himself as a writer, to the day of his discharge from the R.A.F. after the war has ended. During this time he has done odd jobs and worked with the A.R.P., married, had two children, gone to Belfast where he suffered employment, unemployment, and air raids, joined the Air Force, and flown many missions as observer in Mosquitoes.

There is almost too much in this book, but all of it is good. The war scenes are vivid and suspenseful. There is a charming lyric episode when MacMannan camps out in the hills of Northern Ireland. There is mystery in that, although a long flashback traces his childhood in detail, his history stops when he leaves school;

however, references throughout the story imply that between then and the beginning of the story proper, he had travelled widely and saved enough money for a free year in London, at the same time maturing without losing the sensitivity he had as a child. He refuses to submit his poetry for publication until it reaches some form of perfection known only to him. There is some sort of symbolism in his efforts to protect little ducks from the cruelty of thoughtless children.

A similar affinity with nature is in *The Native Moment*, an account of the day Simon Green goes to Dublin with a live eel in a pail; because London sales have dropped off, he is seeking an Irish market for the eels that abound in the northern lakes. He gets drunk, sleeps with a prostitute, is disappointed in a meeting with an old friend, and resolves to marry a girl made pregnant by her uncle. Yet so long as he can keep the eel alive, changing its water regularly he survives his crises. *The Ferret Fancier* is a pastoral in which the same kind of sensitive character is given a ferret as a pet when a child.

West has been compared with Joyce and Beckett, and if one does not seek word play or the broadly comic, it is possible to see the comparison. But in his feeling for nature, for the persons and places of the Irish countryside, he adds another ingredient. For all of their accomplishments this century, Irish writers have tended to be parochially Irish, or write mainly of urban settings or rural settings, but rarely both. West has broken through this barrier.

—William Bittner

WEST, (Mary) Jessamyn. American. Born in North Vernon, Indiana, 18 July 1902. Educated at Fullerton High School, California, graduated 1919; Whittier College, California, 1919, 1921-23, A.B. in English 1923; Fullerton Junior College, 1920-21; University of California, Berkeley, 1929-31. Married H.M. McPherson in 1923. Teacher and secretary, Hemet, California, 1924-29; has taught at Bread Loaf Writers Conference, Vermont; Indiana University, Bloomington; University of Notre Dame, Indiana; University of Utah, Salt Lake City; University of Washington, Seattle; Stanford University, California. Recipient: Thormod Monsen Award, 1958; Janet Kafka Prize, 1976. Honorary Degrees: Whittier College; Mills College, Oakland, California; Swarthmore College, Pennsylvania; Indiana University; Western College for Women. Lives in Napa, California. Address: c/o Harcourt Brace Jovanovich, 757 Third Avenue, New York, New York 10017, U.S.A.

PUBLICATIONS

Novels

The Witch Diggers. New York, Harcourt Brace, 1951; London, Heinemann, 1952.
Little Men, in *Star Short Novels*, edited by Frederik Pohl. New York, Ballantine, 1954; published separately, as *The Chilekings*, 1967.
South of the Angels. New York, Harcourt Brace, 1960; London, Hodder and Stoughton, 1961.
A Matter of Time. New York, Harcourt Brace, 1966; London, Macmillan, 1967.
Leafy Rivers. New York, Harcourt Brace, 1967; London, Macmillan, 1968.
The Massacre at Fall Creek. New York, Harcourt Brace, and London, Macmillan, 1975.
The Life I Really Lived. New York, Harcourt Brace, 1979.

Short Stories

The Friendly Persuasion. New York, Harcourt Brace, 1945; London, Hodder and Stoughton, 1946.
Cress Delahanty. New York, Harcourt Brace, 1953; London, Hodder and Stoughton, 1954.
Love, Death, and the Ladies' Drill Team. New York, Harcourt Brace, 1955; as *Learn to Say Goodbye*, London, Hodder and Stoughton, 1957.
Except for Me and Thee: A Companion to The Friendly Persuasion. New York, Harcourt Brace, and London, Macmillan, 1969.
Crimson Ramblers of the World, Farewell. New York, Harcourt Brace, 1970; London, Macmillan, 1971.

Plays

A Mirror for the Sky, music by Raoul Pène du Bois (produced Eugene, Oregon, 1958). New York, Harcourt Brace, 1948.

Screenplays: *Friendly Persuasion* (uncredited), with Michael Wilson, 1956; *The Big Country*, with others, 1958; *The Stolen Hours*, 1963.

Verse

The Secret Look. New York, Harcourt Brace, 1974.

Other

The Reading Public (address). New York, Harcourt Brace, 1952.
Friends and Violence. Philadelphia, Friends General Conference, n.d.
To See the Dream. New York, Harcourt Brace, 1957; London, Hodder and Stoughton, 1958.
Love Is Not What You Think. New York, Harcourt Brace, 1959; as *A Woman's Love*, London, Hodder and Stoughton, 1960.
Hide and Seek: A Continuing Journey. New York, Harcourt Brace, and London, Macmillan, 1973.
The Woman Said Yes: Encounters with Life and Death: Memoirs. New York, Harcourt Brace, 1976; as *Encounters with Death and Life*, London, Gollancz, 1977.
Double Discovery: A Journey. New York, Harcourt Brace, 1980.

Editor, *The Quaker Reader*. New York, Viking Press, 1962.

*

Critical Study: *Jessamyn West* by Alfred S. Shivers, New York, Twayne, 1972.

* * *

Jessamyn West's best-known book is *The Friendly Persuasion*, a collection of related short stories made into an immensely successful motion picture in 1956. Millions then saw the qualities which had impressed readers of her fiction since 1945. (In *To See the Dream* West described her work on William Wyler's film, a much closer collaboration than most novelists have enjoyed in Hollywood.) The film showed very faithfully that people like the Indiana Quakers Jess and Eliza Birdwell, who lead good and abundant lives, are still open to the full complexity of human experience. It also transferred some of her hard craftsmanship to the screen: the measure of surprise in her carefully constructed plots and the poetry which heightens her language.

She has written about two communities: her Quaker ancestors in the Ohio River Valley and her parents' generation of California settlers who developed the tracts which eventually became the suburbs of Los Angeles. One community cleared a wilderness and the other planted orange trees in a desert. Instead of the grim, nostalgic novels of pioneer life this heritage might have inspired, most of West's fiction is, far from such family sagas, a sketch book, an inquiry, a testament. A horse race, a broken vase, an adultery, and an imminent family death must all be gathered into lives significant enough to permit such a character as Jess Birdwell to observe to his wife that their frontier world has changed "except for me and thee."

West is one of those writers whose style was fully ripe by the time she published her first book, *The Friendly Persuasion*. She had talent enough to suggest the great wonder with which Jess Birdwell approached everything that happened to him, just as she was capable of showing the force that an artifact or a human being could have upon that wonder and how it could lead the men to wisdom. She knew how to write about such people without being patronizing, to show how, for example, Jess's love of music was irrepressible and yet, because he was a Quaker married to a Quaker preacher, how it could actually be repressed. Quite as convincingly as Carson McCullers developed a totally opposed theme, West has argued that the heart finds as well as hunts and that it is not impossible for two people ever to be completely together or to choose to be by themselves.

In *South of the Angels* she tried to be as perceptive about 40 peoples of all ages from childhood to dying old age who had descended on the Tract, one of the "God-given opportunities" promoted by Southern California property agents in the early 20th century. But the brief year in which they waited for water to be brought to their dry acres allowed the writer little more to develop than their transcience and frustration. This is enough, however, to establish this neglected book as a superior regional novel, the best so far about the orange groves and middle western towns that spread over the old ranchos. West and Raymond Chandler comprehend virtually all of Southern California regionalism from the turn of the century to World War II—she with her territory, he with "metropolitan L.A."

Cress Delahanty and *Leafy Rivers* are wise, humorous books about young women, one entering adolescence and the other giving birth to her first child. In the story collection *Love, Death, and the Ladies' Drill Team* one will find "The Mysteries of Life in an Orderly Manner," which is a better early statement about her writing than the essay "The Slave Cast Out," published in Granville Hicks's *The Living Novel* (1957). *The Massacre at Fall Creek* is based on an 1824 incident on the Indiana frontier in which five white men killed nine Indians, including two braves, three squaws, and four children. To their chagrin and bewilderment, the killers became the first American white men ever brought to trial for killing Indians, who were thereby recognized as murder victims for the first time in the young history of American justice. To prosecute the white men was to go against the frontier tradition of dealing with Indians as with wild animals, while to ignore the massacre was to defy Christian teaching and evade the implications of federal laws just reaching the settlements. West lets several variously shrewd and idealistic characters ponder these ambiguities through what is by all odds her most violent and melodramatic fiction.

Her best novels are probably *A Matter of Time* and *The Life I Really Lived*. At first reading, they seem her least characteristic works. *A Matter of Time* is the story of two sisters reunited by the younger one's terminal illness and committed to a plan in which suicide will thwart the illness. As they wait for the right moment, the older sister goes over scenes of their earlier lives, whose richness confirms them in their decision not to prolong existence beyond a day in which the patient could not live at least an hour free of either pain or narcotic dullness. (The impact of this novel is not diminished by the subsequent memoir, *The Woman Said Yes*, in which West defends a similar compact she had made with her sister, Carmen.) *The Life I Really Lived* is a novel about a novelist—not West—who has decided after 18 novels to deal with the joy and darkness of her own life. As Nancy Hale has written, "it is a novel about hidden things."

Jessamyn West chose a statement by Camus as an epigraph for *A Matter of Time*: "I shall tell of nothing but my love of life. But I shall tell it in my own way." It could serve as a comment on all her writing.

—David Sanders

WEST, Morris (Langlo). Australian. Born in Melbourne, Victoria, 26 April 1916. Educated at St. Mary's College, St. Hilda, Victoria; University of Melbourne, B.A. 1937. Served in the Australian Imperial Forces Corps of Signals, in the South Pacific, 1939-43: Lieutenant. Married Joyce Lawford in 1953; three sons and one daughter. For several years member of the Christian Brothers Order, and taught English, French, and European history in New South Wales and Tasmania, 1933 until he left the order before taking final vows, 1939. Secretary to William Morris Hughes, former Prime Minister of Australia, 1943. Publicity Manager, Radio Station 3 DB, Melbourne, 1944-45; Founder, later Managing Director, Australian Radio Productions Pty. Ltd., Melbourne, 1945-54. Since 1954, film and dramatic writer for the Shell Company and the Australian Broadcasting Network, and free-lance commentator and feature writer. Lived in England, 1956-58. Recipient: National Conference of Christians and Jews Brotherhood Award, 1960; Black Memorial Prize, 1960; Heinemann Award, 1960; Dag Hammarskjold Prize, 1978. D.Litt.: University of California, Santa Clara, 1969. Fellow, Royal Society of Literature, 1960. Fellow, World Academy of Arts and Sciences, 1964. Address: c/o Greenbaum Wolff and Ernst, 473 Madison Avenue, New York, New York 10022, U.S.A.

PUBLICATIONS

Novels

Moon in My Pocket (as Julian Morris). Sydney, Australasian Publishing Company, 1945.

Gallows on the Sand. Sydney, Angus and Robertson, 1956; London, Angus and Robertson, 1958.

Kundu. Sydney and London, Angus and Robertson, and New York, Dell, 1957.

The Big Story. London, Heinemann, 1957; as *The Crooked Road*, New York, Morrow, 1957.

The Second Victory. London, Heinemann, 1958; as *Backlash*, New York, Morrow, 1958.

McCreary Moves In (as Michael East). London, Heinemann, 1958; as *The Concubine*, as Morris West, London, New English Library, 1973; New York, New American Library, 1975.

The Devil's Advocate. London, Heinemann, and New York, Morrow, 1959.

The Naked Country (as Michael East). London, Heinemann, 1960; New York, Dell, 1961.

Daughter of Silence. London, Heinemann, and New York, Morrow, 1961.

The Shoes of the Fisherman. London, Heinemann, and New York, Morrow, 1963.

The Ambassador. London, Heinemann, and New York, Morrow, 1965.

The Tower of Babel. London, Heinemann, and New York, Morrow, 1968.

Summer of the Red Wolf. London, Heinemann, and New York, Morrow, 1971.

The Salamander. London, Heinemann, and New York, Morrow, 1973.

Harlequin. London, Collins, and New York, Morrow, 1974.

The Navigator. London, Collins, and New York, Morrow, 1976.

Proteus. London, Collins, and New York, Morrow, 1979.

The Clowns of God. London, Hodder and Stoughton, and New York, Morrow, 1981.

Plays

Daughter of Silence (produced New York, 1961). New York, Morrow, 1962.

The Heretic (produced London, 1970). New York, Morrow, 1969; London, Heinemann, 1970.

Screenplay: *The Devil's Advocate*, 1977.

Other

Children of the Sun. London, Heinemann, 1957; as *Children of the Shadows: The True Story of the Street Urchins of Naples*, New York, Doubleday, 1957.

Scandal in the Assembly: A Bill of Complaints and a Proposal for Reform on the Matrimonial Laws and Tribunals of the Roman Catholic Church, with Robert Francis. London, Heinemann, 1970.

* * *

The novels of Morris West bear the imprints of his varied background as religious novitiate, teacher, intelligence officer, political aide, publicist, and radio serializer. His autobiographical first novel (by "Julian Morris"), *Moon in My Pocket*, was about a disillusioned young religious, and West has never since abandoned this theme of the quest for moral identity and God's blessing. Two potboilers, *Gallows on the Sand* and *Kundu*, are significant only for providing the funds that allowed West to take up residence in Naples. There he wrote *Children of the Sun*, an outraged and compassionte study of southern Italy's street urchins which gained him attention and signalled his literary commitment to Christian responsibility. When he returned for financial reasons to publicity writing and to the novel of adventure, this deeper strain of moral concern had clearly, permanently been infused into his work.

The Big Story, though hastily written as a melodrama of murder and intrigue in Sorrento, suggests the "entertainments" of Graham Greene in its neat balance of swift, violent plot, and lonely, existential ponderings. Thus, the American journalist Richard Ashley risks his life to publish "the truth" about the corrupt Duke of Orgagna, only to find that "the truth" exposes everyone's sin and corruption, including his own. When Ashley has miraculously triumphed, his newspaper kills the big story because the publisher has just been appointed U.S. Ambassador to Italy. West in this novel raises another favorite theme, the difficulty of moral choice when individually righteous behavior threatens great social harm in a larger context (Ashley's published "truth" will adversely affect an upcoming election) or, conversely, when personally immoral behavior, such as betrayal or assassination, will result in significant social benefit.

There were three more potboilers between 1958 and 1960, *The Second Victory* and, under the pseudonym of Michael East, *McCreary Moves In* and *The Naked Country*. But it was *The Devil's Advocate*, West's seventh book in four years, that lofted him to the heights of bestsellerdom, Book-of-the-Month-Club selection, Reader's Digest condensation and high-priced sale of movie rights. This success, repeated with *Shoes of the Fisherman*, along with the common subject matter of theological and institutional practices inside the Catholic church, has contributed to the undervaluation of West's writings as "theological thrillers" and Biblical bestsellers. West's occasional tendencies to overwrite and to repeat purplish pet phrases ("he felt a chill as though a goose had walked over his grave") lend support to disdainful reviewers, but he is, nevertheless, a talented and well-informed novelist who deals with profound themes and significant events.

In *The Devil's Advocate* Monsignor Blaise Meredith, who expects to die of cancer within months, agrees to investigate the life and alleged miracle of Giacomo Nerone, an army deserter and father of an illegitimate son but nevertheless a candidate for sainthood. The dramatis personae struggle with their inner contradictions and ironies: Nerone's mistress, Nina, "the village whore," is an illiterate woman of intuitive wisdom and queenly bearing; the Countess de Sanctis is a nymphomaniac in sufficient despair either to commit suicide or to find God; Nicholas Black, artist-homosexual, on the verge of seducing Nerone's bastard son, finds redemption by hanging himself on the Judas tree; and, finally, the detached, scholarly Monsignor Meredith, who has misspent his priestly life because he has never loved anyone, develops a full heart under sentence of death and nearly qualifies for sainthood himself. Throughout the novel, the craggy landscape itself, the Calabrian towns of Gemello Minore and Gemello Maggiore, the cross, the office of "Devil's Advocate" and many characters and incidents take on a brooding symbolism and the rich suggestiveness of allegory. West's other best-known religious novel, *Shoes of the Fisherman*, though not as well-written, conveys the agony and loneliness of a contemporary non-Italian Pope, Kiril I, who tries to serve as keeper of the keys even as he would throw open the windows of the embattled fortress of the modern church. Matching Kiril's loneliness and courage is Father Telemond, a Jesuit scholar-scientist undoubtedly modeled on Teilhard de Chardin and more plausible and attractive as a character. West's Pope Kiril, as a combination of John XXIII and Haroun al Raschid, challenges credulity; his secret missions and personal diplomacy to avert World War III defy it. This novel, like *Daughter of Silence* before it and *The Ambassador* after it, is a *roman à clef* with a journalist-scholar's accurate and complete detailing of places and procedures.

In *The Ambassador* and *The Tower of Babel* West has ventured into the political novel with a degree of success. Although West gathered his data for *The Ambassador* in 1963, it offers a remarkably thorough, prescient description of the conditions and problems of American involvement in Vietnam. Told through the eyes of the newly arrived ambassador, the novel-documentary offers no heroes or villains but traces the inevitable failure, moral and political, personal and national, of the well-intentioned ambassador and the government he represents. *The Tower of Babel*, dealing with Middle East intrigue and crisis just prior to the Six Days War, diffuses its focus through the lives and point-of-view of five or six involved characters, but the author's basic approach and judgments are similar: in a complex violent world of conflicting needs and large blind forces, man needs compassion, love, and God; with these, personal catastrophe may come but it cannot destroy the dignity, meaning, or justice of life.

—Frank Campenni

WEST, Paul (Noden). British. Born in Eckington, Derbyshire, 23 February 1930. Educated at the University of Birmingham, B.A. (1st class honours) 1950; Oxford University, 1950-52; Columbia University, New York, M.A. 1953. Served in the Royal Air Force, 1954-57: Flight Lieutenant. Assistant Professor, then Associate Professor of English, Memorial University of Newfoundland, St. John's, 1957-62. Associate Professor, 1962-68, and since 1968, Professor of English and Comparative Literature, and Senior Fellow, Institute for the Arts and Humanistic Studies, Pennsylvania State University, University Park. Visiting Professor of Comparative Literature, University of Wisconsin, Madison, 1965-66; Pratt Lecturer, Memorial University of Newfoundland, 1970; Crawshaw Professor of Literature, Colgate University, Hamilton, New York, Fall 1972; Virginia Woolf Lecturer, University of Tulsa, Oklahoma, 1973; Melvin Hill Visiting Professor, Hobart and William Smith Colleges, Geneva, New York, Fall 1974. Contributor to *New Statesman*, London, 1954-62. Since 1962, regular contributor to *New York Times Book Review* and *Book World*, Washington, D.C. Recipient: Canada Council Senior Fellowship, 1960; Guggenheim Fellowship, 1962; Aga Khan Prize (*Paris Review*), 1974; National Endowment for the Arts Fellowship, 1975, 1980. Address: 117 Burrowes Building, Pennsylvania State University, University Park, Pennsylvania 16802, U.S.A.

PUBLICATIONS

Novels

A Quality of Mercy. London, Chatto and Windus, 1961.

Tenement of Clay. London, Hutchinson, 1965.
Alley Jaggers. London, Hutchinson, and New York, Harper, 1966.
I'm Expecting to Live Quite Soon. New York, Harper, 1970; London, Gollancz, 1971.
Caliban's Filibuster. New York, Doubleday, 1971.
Bela Lugosi's White Christmas. London, Gollancz, and New York, Harper, 1972.
Colonel Mint. New York, Dutton, 1972; London, Calder and Boyars, 1973.
Gala. New York, Harper, 1976.
The Very Rich Hours of Count von Stauffenberg. New York, Harper, 1980; London, Sidgwick and Jackson, 1981.

Uncollected Short Stories

"How to Marry a Hummingbird," in *Modern Occasions*. New York, Farrar Straus, 1966.
"The Season of the Single Women," in *New American Review 11*, edited by Theodore Solotaroff. New York, Simon and Schuster, 1971.
"The Man Who Ate the Zeitgeist," in *London Magazine*, April-May 1971.
"Invitation to a Vasectomy," in *Words* (Boston), Summer 1973.
"The Wet-God's Macho," in *Remington Review* (Elizabeth, New Jersey), Spring 1974.
"Tan Salaam," in *Paris Review*, Spring 1974.
"Brain Cell 99,999,999,999," in *New Directions 28*. New York, New Directions, 1974.
"The Universe and Other Fictions," in *New Directions 31*. New York, New Directions, 1975.
"The Sun in Heat," in *Remington Review* (Elizabeth, New Jersey), Spring 1975.
"The Monocycle," in *Carleton Miscellany* (Northfield, Minnesota), Spring 1975.
"Gustav Holst Composes Himself," in *New Directions 33*. New York, New Directions, 1976.
"Paganini Break," in *Tri-Quarterly* (Evanston, Illinois), Winter 1976.
"The Glass-Bottomed Boat," in *Mother Jones* (San Francisco), November 1976.
"Another Minotaur," in *New Directions 36*. New York, New Directions, 1978.
"The Basement of Kilimanjaro," in *Partisan Review* (New Brunswick, New Jersey), xlvi, 4, 1979.
"Field Day for a Boy Soldier," in *Iowa Review* (Iowa City), Spring 1979.
"Villa-Lobos in Winter," in *Review* (London), Winter 1979-80.

Verse

(Poems). Oxford, Fantasy Press, 1952.
The Spellbound Horses. Toronto, Ryerson Press, 1960.
The Snow Leopard. London, Hutchinson, 1964; New York, Harcourt Brace, 1965.

Other

The Fossils of Piety: Literary Humanism in Decline. New York, Vantage Press, 1959.
The Growth of the Novel. Toronto, Canadian Broadcasting Corporation, 1959.
Byron and the Spoiler's Art. London, Chatto and Windus, and New York, St. Martin's Press, 1960.
The Modern Novel. London, Hutchinson, 1963; New York, Hillary House, 1965.
I, Said the Sparrow (autobiography). London, Hutchinson, 1963.
Robert Penn Warren. Minneapolis, University of Minnesota Press, 1964.
The Wine of Absurdity: Essays in Literature and Consolation. University Park, Pennsylvania State University Press, 1966.
Words for a Deaf Daughter. London, Gollancz, 1969; New York, Harper, 1970.
Doubt and Dylan Thomas (lecture). St. John's, Newfoundland, Memorial University, 1970.

*

Manuscript Collections: Pattee Library, Pennsylvania State University, University Park; Mugar Memorial Library, Boston University.

Critical Studies: by John W. Aldridge, in *Kenyon Review* (Gambier, Ohio), September 1966; *New Literary History* (Charlottesville, Virginia), Spring 1970 and Spring 1976; "The Writer's Situation II" by the author, in *New American Review 10*, New York, New American Library, 1970; interview with George Plimpton, in *Caliban's Filibuster*, 1971; review by Frederick Busch, in *New York Times Book Review*, 20 June 1971; *Nation* (New York), 8 January 1977.

Paul West comments:

Looking back, I see myself as a late starter who, between thirty and forty, in a sustained and intensive spell of application, set down half a lifetime's pondering and moved from a restless contentment with criticism and fairly orthodox fiction to an almost Fellini-like point of view.

Imagination, as I see it, is an alembic in limbo; it invents, and what it invents has to be added to the sum of Creation—even though nothing imagination invents is wholly its own. In other words, I think the realistic novel has served its turn (for Western society as well as for me), should be put out to grass with an O.B.E. and a White House Medal. Fiction has to reclaim some of its ancient privileges, which writers like Lucian and Nashe and Rabelais and Grimmelshausen exploited to the full. I think that only the plasticity of a free-ranging imagination can do justice to late-20th-century man who, as incomplete as man ever was, keeps on arming himself with increasing amounts of data which, as ever, mean nothing at all.

My own fiction I have come to see as—I want it to be—a kind of linear mosaic, which is what my second novel, *Tenement of Clay*, was in a rudimentary form and which my two recent ones—*Caliban's Filibuster* and *Gala*—are in a much more advanced and demanding way. Actually, since both vocabulary and syntax are themselves fictive I don't regard my autobiographical writing as essentially different from my fiction: they're both part of the mosaic I invent.

* * *

For excellent reasons, Camden, the central character in Paul West's uneven, faintly gothic first novel, *A Quality of Mercy*, feels that "what was wrong was not that life was too much but that it was just too many. There was powder in the wind when there should have been crystals immune from every wind....Life was an unknown and unknowable quantity." Although now, more than 20 years later, West's fiction has grown so rich and apparently diverse that good readers will be suspicious of generalizations, it is still possible to see him as an artist working out unexpected variations on the theme Camden hints at indirectly, the problem of contingency. The final human tragedy, Santayana cooly observes, lies in our awareness that everything might just as well have been otherwise, in our consciousness that we are accidental creatures gratuitously existing in random places and forms. We might have been Caesar or we might have been a victim of the Holocaust; and in times when few can go on believing that angels were destined to be angels and stones stones, this can be a devastating insight. There are writers—Sartre, for example—who are in fact appalled by the idea; there are writers like Wallace Stevens and Iris Murdoch who are often exhilarated by the inexplicable variety of being; and there are also a few writers, like Nabokov and Paul West, who veer back and forth eloquently but uneasily between delight and disgust.

A good many of West's characters live condemned to this awareness of contingency, and to make matters worse, condemned to exist in exotic and unlovely forms. The archetypal figure is Caliban, an artist of sorts, howling for justice or at least freedom. In *A Quality of Mercy* there is Camden; in *Tenement of Clay* there are Lazarus, the defiant dwarf, and his mentor, Papa Nick, failed saint and keeper of a flophouse whose inmates he tries to reconcile to "the truth of life," and in helping them to swallow that truth to learn, himself, the proper "angle of drinking." In *Caliban's Filibuster*, there is Cal, the failed writer, and in West's most recent and finest novel Count von Stauffenberg, who must go on suffering beyond the grave for his failures. But clearest of all there is Alley Jaggers. At the start of that novel, Alley, longing for some dimly perceived beauty, is "enclosed and embattled but not closed up and defeated," but by the end he is both defeated and literally locked away. In *Bela Lugosi's White Christmas* Alley provides what is probably West's bitterest cry of rage:

> I never applied for admission to your so-called universe. I was kidnapped into it from a better place...where it is more *optional* than it is here and now, about the time old God Almighty was in a poxdoctoring dither, not sure which day was which, and wondering why the bejesus he got involved with the whole thing in the first place....My own feeling is this, in case you care, want it for your little black book: if only He'd kept at it all through the seventh day and maybe for all of the next week, we'd all of us be better off. It's just the same as saying the world—your so-called universe—is just a wee bit carelessly put together, fundamentally, firmamentally, fucked up, there being whole armies of folks with club foots, hare lips, folks with spines open to the fresh air and brains blown up as big as hunchback's humps, not to mention the deaf and the blind and the straightforward deformed, the slobberers and slaverers, the daft and St. Vitus dancers, the monkey-faced and the Siamese twins, folks whose hands grow out from their shoulders and folks with no especial sex at all. Don't tell me that twenty sets of quints can make up for all that. Why, it's like asking a pharmacist for an aspirin and getting gunpowder instead. Better to scrap it in the first place if he couldn't get it right or couldn't make up his mind.... Whatever blueprint there was, well, it was just a bit smudged. There ought to be laws against great minds bringing universes into being just for fun. There: that's AJ's first book of the bible; I could have done better myself once I'd gotten the sun to co-operate.

"Blow it all up then?" asks Alley's equally failed analyst, to which Alley replies, "*I* would, except I'd be loth to give your old universe a helping hand with a dead hand of my own."

It is natural enough to wonder where this view of things comes from, and tempting to conclude that it grew from West's experiences with his own deaf, brain-damaged daughter, Mandy. In such cases a parent's first response is often to ignore the handicap, to make it "go away"—or to make it go away by making the child go away. But there is another possible response: to see the handicap as a special kind of gift, and while trying to eliminate it still to "learn its nature by heart, as a caution." *Words for a Deaf Daughter* is the astonishing account of West's infinitely patient attempts to understand the world in which Mandy is enclosed but not, if he can help it, defeated; to grasp, by imaginative participation, the "supersensitivity" which such children often possess. The "caution," that is, the lesson, turns out to be an awareness of just how arbitrary our definitions of sense and madness can be. The world West and his readers learn to look at through Mandy's eyes is a world in which things are seen with cleansed perception.

Words for a Deaf Daughter is "fact"; *Gala* is "fiction," or, as West puts it, "the scenario of a wish-fulfillment," in which an adolescent Mandy comes to visit her father in America and finally speaks to him. The importance of this wish-fulfillment is central to West's fiction and makes it imperative to remember that something like Alley's cry of rage is not really West's own cry. For all of the pain which these characters must endure, West sees the act of expression, of imaginative creation, as an act of defiance and achievement, a substantial addition to the sum of existing things. In a 1971 interview he remarked:

> What a gratuitous universe it is, anyway; what a bloody surd...what with such defectives as waltzing mice, axolotls that should become salamanders but don't, children born without one of the human senses. Not that I'm harping on the universe's lapses rather than its norms; no, what impresses me finally is the scope for error within the constancy of the general set-up contrasted with the power to imagine things as otherwise—to rectify, to deform. What is man? He's the creature imaginative enough to ask that question. And although I know that the imagination had always to start with something not its own—hasn't *complete* underivedness—it can generate much pearl from little grit.

In *The Wine of Absurdity* he states even more emphatically that the imagination is "the only restorative each man has that is entirely his own....Imagination, trite and presumptuous as it may seem to express the fact, is the only source of meaning our lives can have." Thus imagining Mandy's visit and making her speak is a triumphant act; and having so imagined, West reports that "I can begin sentences with an *I* again, not so much glad or proud as astounded to be here on this planet as myself and not as a peppermint starfish, a thistle, an emu, a bit of quartz. Or a doorknob." It is the artist's imagination, then, which can turn Camden's irritating powder into crystals—if, of course, the artist has anything like Paul West's drive and dazzling verbal resources.

—Elmer Borklund

WEST, Rebecca. Pseudonym for Cicily Isabel Fairfield Andrews. British. Born in County Kerry, Ireland, 25 December 1892. Educated at George Watson's Ladies' College, Edinburgh. Had one son by H.G. Wells, Anthony West, *q.v.*; married Henry Maxwell Andrews in 1930 (died, 1968). Reviewer and political writer for *Freewoman*, London, 1911, and *Clarion*, London, 1912; Talks Supervisor, BBC, London, during World War II. Fellow of Saybrook College, Yale University, New Haven, Connecticut. D.Litt.: New York University. Member, Order of St. Sava, 1937; Chevalier, Legion of Honour, 1957. Fellow, 1947, Benson Medalist, 1966, and Companion of Literature, 1968, Royal Society of Literature. Member, American Academy of Arts and Sciences. C.B.E. (Commander, Order of the British Empire), 1949; D.B.E. (Dame Commander, Order of the British Empire), 1959. Address: c/o Macmillan Publishers Ltd., 4 Little Essex Street, London WC2R 3LF, England.

PUBLICATIONS

Novels

The Return of the Soldier. London, Nisbet, and New York, Century, 1918.
The Judge. London, Hutchinson, and New York, Doran, 1922.
Harriet Hume: A London Fantasy. London, Hutchinson, and New York, Doubleday, 1929.
War Nurse: The True Story of a Woman Who Lived, Loved, and Suffered on the Western Front (as Corinne Andrews). New York, Cosmopolitan, 1930.
The Thinking Reed. London, Hutchinson, and New York, Viking Press, 1936.

The Fountain Overflows. New York, Viking Press, 1956; London, Macmillan, 1957.
The Birds Fall Down. London, Macmillan, and New York, Viking Press, 1966.

Short Stories

The Harsh Voice: Four Short Novels. London, Cape, and New York, Doubleday, 1935.

Uncollected Short Stories

"Ruby," in *New Yorker*, 20 April 1940.
"The Man Who Came to Dinner," in *London Calling*, edited by Storm Jameson. New York, Harper, 1942.
"Thou Shalt Not Make Any Graven Image," in *Ten Commandments*, edited by Armin L. Robinson. New York, Simon and Schuster, 1943.
"Deliverance," in *Ladies' Home Journal* (Des Moines, Iowa), August 1952.
"Parthenope," in *Winter's Tale 21*, edited by A.D. Maclean. London, Macmillan, 1975; New York, St. Martin's Press, 1976.

Other

Henry James. London, Nisbet, and New York, Holt, 1916.
The Strange Necessity: Essays and Reviews. London, Cape, and New York, Doubleday, 1928.
Lions and Lambs (as Lynx), illustrated by Low. London, Cape, 1928; New York, Harcourt Brace, 1929.
D.H. Lawrence: An Elegy. London, Secker, 1930; as *Elegy*, New York, Phoenix Book Shop, 1930.
Arnold Bennett Himself. New York, Day, 1931.
Ending in Earnest: A Literary Log. New York, Doubleday, 1931.
St. Augustine. London, Davies, and New York, Appleton, 1933.
A Letter to a Grandfather. London, Hogarth Press, 1933.
The Modern "Rake's Progress," illustrated by Low. London, Hutchinson, 1934.
Black Lamb and Grey Falcon: A Journey Through Yugoslavia in 1937. New York, Viking Press, 2 vols., 1941; London, Macmillan, 2 vols., 1942.
Rebecca's Cookbook. Privately printed, 1942.
The Meaning of Treason. New York, Viking Press, 1947; London, Macmillan, 1949; revised edition, London, Penguin, 1965; as *The New Meaning of Treason*, Viking Press, 1964.
A Train of Powder (essays). London, Macmillan, and New York, Viking Press, 1955.
The Court and the Castle: Some Treatments of a Recurrent Theme. New Haven, Connecticut, Yale University Press, 1957; London, Macmillan, 1958.
The Vassall Affair. London, Sunday Telegraph, 1963.
McLuhan and the Future of Literature (address). London, Oxford University Press, 1969.
Rebecca West—A Celebration: A Selection of Her Writings. London, Macmillan, and New York, Viking Press, 1977.
The Young Rebecca: Selected Essays by Rebecca West 1911-1917, edited by Jane Marcus. London, Macmillan, 1981.
1900. London, Weidenfeld and Nicolson, 1981.

Editor, *Selected Poems of Carl Sandburg*. London, Cape, and New York, Harcourt Brace, 1926.

*

Manuscript Collection: Beinecke Library, Yale University, New Haven, Connecticut.

Critical Studies: *Rebecca West, Artist and Thinker* by Peter Wolfe, Carbondale, Southern Illinois University Press, 1971; *H.G. Wells and Rebecca West* by Gordon N. Ray, New Haven, Connecticut, Yale University Press, and London, Macmillan, 1974.

Rebecca West comments:

I have always written in order to discover the truth for my own use, on the one hand, and on the other hand to earn money for myself and my family, and in this department of my work I hope I have honoured the truth I had already discovered. I have like most women written only a quarter of what I might have written, owing to my family responsibilities. I dislike heartily the literary philosophy and practice of my time, which I think has lagged behind in the past and has little relevance to the present, and it distresses me that so much contemporary work is dominated by the ideas (particularly the political and religious ideas) of the late 18th or 19th century, and those misunderstood. I wish some novelist would arise who would write about the majority of people, who are as unhappy as the characters in modern fiction, but in ways never there referred to.

* * *

The "authentic" work of art, Rebecca West asserts in *The Court and the Castle*, is that which the artist creates by "analyzing an experience and synthesizing the results...into a form, which excites an appetite for further experience." For an understanding of all this, however, one has to turn to an earlier study, *The Strange Necessity*, in which West argues that the genuine work is essentially an analogue of cortical activity. Pavlov states that "the nervous system possesses on the one hand a definite analyzing mechanism, by means of which it selects out of the whole complexity of the environment those units which are of significance, and, on the other hand, a synthesizing mechanism by means of which individual units can be integrated into an excitatory complex." To this West responds, "but can it really be of the cortex he is speaking? For there never was a better statement of the duplex function that must be fulfilled by any work of art." In *The Strange Necessity* (the necessity being man's basic need to create and experience works of art) she develops a thoroughly behavioristic theory of the value of art in many respects similar to that of I.A. Richards. The artist's sensitive response to experience, his recognition of its component parts, and his synthesis, rendered in aesthetic (that is, organic) form allow the audience to become "much more completely the masters of reality." The artist is engaged in the same struggle to understand complex situations and states of feeling which all men face, and if we are capable of genuine response to his synthesis, our own capacity to cope with reality is strengthened. "Never, I perceive, am I a more healthy, sane, non-neurotic animal than when I let art dictate my reactions," West concludes; the authentic work permits a "new and satisfactory equilibrium for my will to live and my will to die."

The Court and the Castle extends the argument, insisting that artistic analysis and synthesis must have a bearing on "the question which concerns us more deeply of all: whether the universe is good or bad," but in this later work the simple psychologism of *The Strange Necessity* is subsumed by a frankly theological conception of the inherent corruption of the human will. Great works of fiction give

> impressive testimony against a heresy which [was] revived by the Renaissance and was steadily to gain adherents till it triumphed in the nineteenth century: against Pelagianism. It was an array of evidence against the theory that man is equally free to choose between good and evil, and that should he choose good, his own natural ability will enable him to reach moral perfection, and that our race could be changed and made innocent without search for a higher authority and submission to it.

Thus for West much of the "liberal" romantic tradition is heretical: "the truth that has to be embraced by the man who desires to be saved is cruel, unreasonable, and incomprehensible"—incomprehensible, that is, in purely human terms. West concludes with an eloquent endorsement of Kafka's aphorism, "The German word *Sein* has two meanings: it means to exist, and it means to belong to Him." The tendency of literature, when it "rises above a certain level, is to involve itself with statecraft and with religion: to exist and to belong to Him."

The ability to perceive complex experience accurately, to analyse it correctly, to synthesize a form suitable for its expression, and finally to reveal man's weaknesses and the possibility of grace—these are the qualities which West makes into critical requirements; and it is not surprising, perhaps, that judged by these ultimate standards her own work is never wholly successful. There can be no doubt about West's powerful capacity to observe the world around her or her passion to do so (with George Orwell she is one of the most distinguished political journalists of our time), nor about the sincerity of her convictions concerning the tragic consequences of human action ("Man is a political animal," observes one of the characters in *The Fountain Overflows*, "but seeing what the animal is, what may politics become?"). The difficulty is, rather, her inability to synthesize a truly satisfactory artistic form, that "perfect equilibrium" in which "there is no character which is not displayed in the right extent of space with the right degree of emphasis...there is no part which rebels against the whole, there is the peace of unity." And perhaps most important, West has thus far seemed unwilling to dramatize her essentially theological commitments.

The Return of a Soldier is an immature work, a sentimental romance distinguished only by some reliance on the Freudian conception of memory and repression which was soon to become a cliché of popular fiction and drama. *The Judge* is a much more ambitious novel, badly thrown off balance by a divided center of interest. In the first third of the book West is fitfully successful in rendering the perceptions of a naive young Scottish girl, a suffragette determined to wrest more from life than her poverty and sex permit. She marries a young man dominated by his mother, who then becomes the true protagonist of the work, a complex, suffering woman portrayed with a power and immediacy equal to Lawrence at his early best. The ending, however, degenerates into crude melodrama. *Harriet Hume* offers sad proof that West has little talent for fantasy or the comic. This heavy-handed parable about artistic sensitivity and political drive is spoiled by ponderousness, while the next novel, *The Thinking Reed*, is equally spoiled by untypical commercial slickness and some badly dated chic. Again there is an unsuccessful attempt to synthesize the basic elements of the story, in this case a young woman's marital ups and downs and West's rather superficial criticism of the sterility and waste of the world her heroine inhabits.

The Fountain Overflows, however, is an extraordinarily moving and real account of a dozen or so years in the life of an Edwardian family. The narrative tone is now completely consistent and assured; the portraits of the Aubreys' brilliant, erratic father and pathetic but finally heroic mother are achievements of the first order. Yet it is difficult not to regard this novel as something of an anachronism. In 1927 West admitted "I have got to live in a world where a large number of people are to varying degrees conditioned by a knowledge of *Ulysses*"; but the world of *The Fountain Overflows* is the world of Dickens, unconditioned by anything later than Bennett or Galsworthy. It is entertainment of remarkable innocence for these times, but wholly satisfying within the terms it sets up. In her latest novel, *The Birds Fall Down*, West once more seems unable to fuse her political acuity and technical control. Based on an actual incident in which a young girl unwittingly plays a part in frustrating a plot against her exiled Tsarist grandfather (in turn frustrating an attempt on the Tsar's life and thereby providing indirect aid for Lenin's rise to power), the novel remains a collection of splendid fragments. The information necessary for grasping the maddeningly tangled intrigue poses insuperable structural problems.

There is so much intelligence at work in West's fiction and in her unjustly neglected criticism that it may seem ungrateful to ask for more. But what one misses, finally, is a creative power equal to the high argument of *The Court and the Castle*.

—Elmer Borklund

WHITE, Jon (Ewbank) Manchip. British. Born in Cardiff, Glamorganshire, 22 June 1924. Educated at St. Catharine's College, Cambridge, 1942-43, 1946-50 (Open Exhibitioner in English Literature), M.A. (honours) in English, prehistoric archaeology, and oriental languages (Egyptology), and University Diploma in anthropology 1950. Served in the Royal Navy and the Welsh Guards, 1942-46. Married Valerie Leighton in 1946; two children. Story Editor, BBC, London, 1950-51; Senior Executive Officer, British Foreign Service, London, 1952-56; free-lance writer, 1956-67: Scenario Editor, Hammer Films, London, 1956-57; Screenwriter, Samuel Bronston Productions, Paris and Madrid, 1960-64; Professor of English, University of Texas, El Paso, 1967-77. Since 1977, Lindsay Young Professor of Humanities and Professor of English, University of Tennessee, Knoxville. Address: Department of English, University of Tennessee, Knoxville, Tennessee 37916, U.S.A.

PUBLICATIONS

Novels

Mask of Dust. London, Hodder and Stoughton, 1953; as *Last Race*, New York, Mill, 1953.
Build Us a Dam. London, Hodder and Stoughton, 1955.
The Girl from Indiana London, Hodder and Stoughton, 1956.
No Home But Heaven. London, Hodder and Stoughton, 1957.
The Mercenaries. London, Long, 1958.
Hour of the Rat. London, Hutchinson, 1962.
The Rose in the Brandy Glass. London, Eyre and Spottiswoode, 1965.
Nightclimber. London, Chatto and Windus, and New York, Morrow, 1968.
The Game of Troy. London, Chatto and Windus, and New York, McKay, 1971.
The Garden Game. London, Chatto and Windus, 1973; Indianapolis, Bobbs Merrill, 1974.
Send for Mr. Robinson. New York, Pinnacle, and London, Panther, 1974
The Moscow Papers. Canoga Park, California, Major, 1979.
Death by Dreaming. Cambridge, Massachusetts, Apple-Wood Press, 1981.

Plays

Screenplays: *Day of Grace*, with Francis Searle, 1957; *Man with a Dog*, 1958; *The Camp on Blood Island*, with Val Guest, 1958; *Mystery Submarine*, with Hugh Woodhouse and Bertram Ostrer, 1963; *Crack in the World*, with Julian Halevy, 1965.

Radio and Television Plays and Adaptations.

Verse

Dragon and Other Poems. London, Fortune Press, 1943.
Salamander. London, Fortune Press, 1946.
The Rout of San Romano. Aldington, Kent, Hand and Flower Press, 1952.
The Mountain Lion. London, Chatto and Windus, 1971.

Other

Ancient Egypt. London, Wingate, 1952; New York, Crowell, 1953; revised edition, London, Allen and Unwin, and New York, Dover, 1970.
Anthropology. London, English Universities Press, 1954; New York, Philosophical Library, 1955.
Marshal of France: The Life and Times of Maurice, Comte de Saxe. London, Hamish Hamilton, and Chicago, Rand McNally, 1962.

Everyday Life in Ancient Egypt. London, Batsford, 1963; New York, Putnam, 1964.
Diego Velazquez, Painter and Courtier. London, Hamish Hamilton, and Chicago, Rand McNally, 1969.
The Land God Made in Anger: Reflections on a Journey Through South West Africa. London, Allen and Unwin, and Chicago, Rand McNally, 1969.
Cortés and the Downfall of the Aztec Empire. London, Hamish Hamilton, and New York, St. Martin's Press, 1971.
A World Elsewhere: One Man's Fascination with the American Southwest. New York, Crowell, 1975; as *The Great American Desert*, London, Allen and Unwin, 1977.
Everyday Life of the North American Indian. London, Batsford, and New York, Holmes and Meier, 1979.

Editor, *Life in Ancient Egypt*, by Adolf Erman. New York, Dover, 1971.
Editor, *The Tomb of Tutankhamen*, by Howard Carter. New York, Dover, 1971.
Editor, *Manners and Customs of the Modern Egyptians*, by E.W. Lane. New York, Dover, 1972.
Editor, *Egypt and the Holy Land: 77 Historic Photographs by Francis Frith.* New York, Dover, and London, Constable, 1981.

Translator, *The Glory of Egypt*, by Samivel. London, Thames and Hudson, 1955.

*

Jon Manchip White comments:

My fiction seems to fall into two broad categories: the novel, as conventionally understood, and the romance, as defined by Northrop Frye in his *Anatomy of Criticism* and Edwin Muir in his *The Structure of the Novel.* From my Welsh birth and upbringing I derive my Celtic preoccupation with the fantastic, the bizarre, the unconscious, the intuitive; and from my education and training in England I derive my Saxon preoccupation with the directed, the conscious, the disciplined, the down-to-earth.

My romances comprise what I have come to describe as my Extravagant Tales: *Nightclimber*, *The Game of Troy*, *The Garden Game*, *Death by Dreaming*; while my novels comprise *Mask of Dust*, *Build Us a Dam*, *The Girl from Indiana*, *Hour of the Rat*, *The Rose in the Brandy Glass.* The two genres are not rigidly self-contained, and there is something of the romances in the novels and of the novels in the romances. Occasionally there is an obvious overlap, as in *No Home But Heaven* or *Send for Mr. Robinson.*

It might be worth noting that my fiction represents only half my literary output. My biographies, travel books, and books on archaeology and anthropology are in some ways even more significant vehicles of my general ideas, fleshing out as they do my personal attitudes and themes. In my own mind, my fiction and non-fiction constitute a single and indivisible tissue.

* * *

Jon Manchip White is first and foremost a novelist of adventure, a narrator of extraordinary events which take place in exotic settings and extend the human frame to the limit. He is a swift and adroit raconteur, not strong on characterisation, but capable of giving his plots an almost vertical take-off: thereafter the impetus is what matters, and the reader finds himself borne up on a steeply rising parabola of excitement. The typical pattern of his novels is that of a race, an escape, an inquisition, a test of endurance, skill or moral fibre. His heroes come through, but they are stretched up to and sometimes beyond the breaking-point: such is the toll of their exploits upon nerve and spirit. He has a weakness for those who are some way past their prime, and there is more of a touch of Hemingway in his fascination with physical ordeals and his mastery of the details of training and technique, of the weaponry and equipment of his soldiers and sportsmen.

Most of these elements are present in his first novel, *Mask of Dust*, which is still one of his best, a story of the world of the international motor Grand Prix. It is set in northern Italy, where the crowds hail this spectacular and lethal sport as the modern equivalent of charioteering. The central figure is a British champion, who in 1940 became a fighter pilot, and who after the war returns to racing, although arguably already "over the hill." Can he crown his career with one final international triumph, or has he stayed too long in the game—and what is the effect of this gamble on his young and beautiful wife? On this occasion White pursues an unashamedly romantic solution, and the novel reveals yet another characteristic which many of his heroes share: like Sherlock Holmes they indulge in unexpected intellectual or aesthetic relaxations. The British member of the driving team relieves his tensions by playing Debussy's *Arabesque*, "his fingers laid like strips of steel over the soft ivory"; the Italian plays chess; the Czech savours the odes of Horace in the original.

White's fiction has always been preoccupied with the rewards and penalties of individualism, and three later books are concerned with men on the run from society. The theme of *No Home But Heaven* is the natural and temperamental clash between the gipsy and the modern welfare state; *The Mercenaries* is an escape drama set in Argentina after the fall of Perón, where an ex-minister and his mistress struggle desperately to evade arrest by the revolutionaries and to find refuge in Paraguay; *Hour of the Rat* deals with the trial of a British civil servant, who kills a member of a Japanese delegation—his former persecutor at a prisoner of war camp—thus taking it upon himself, as he sees it, to avenge his war-time comrades. The one exception to these tales of action is *The Rose in the Brandy Glass*, yet here too the story involves an act of will as demanding as any mere demonstration of physical prowess: the plot hinges on the quixotic refusal of the hero, a retired cavalry colonel, against the wishes of all those nearest to him to put his name to an inaccurate statement in order to share out an inheritance. This is the author's most ambitious attempt to write a novel whose mainspring is social and pychological conflict rather than adventure, but the effort exposes his limitations in the field of characterisation.

White is an experienced writer of screenplays and more recently a strain of phantasmagoria has appeared in his writing, which suggests a cinematic influence on his technique: actuality and dream are juxtaposed, so that minute and sharply focussed details are contrasted with a background of delirium. Thus in *The Game of Troy* the plot is based on the legend of the Minotaur. The central character, a brilliant Daedalus-like architect, is commissioned by a Texas millionaire, with whose wife he has fallen in love, to design a modern labyrinth, complete with elaborate lighting and airconditioning systems. Awakening half-drugged underground, he finds himself being hunted by the murderous husband along the winding corridors and dead-ends of this nightmarish maze. But his most successful achievement in this genre is undoubtedly *Nightclimber*. The hero is an art-historian who is possessed by the craving, much in vogue in pre-war Cambridge, to climb high and dangerous buildings, and his obsession is diabolically exploited by a millionaire collector in search of a mysterious treasure in Greece. In the image of the nightclimber White has hit upon a symbol for the force which drives his heroes and inspires the type of adventure which he excels in chronicling. They are constantly impelled to push their luck, to take something more than a calculated risk, and much of the savour of the adventure lies in the possibility of being swept beyond the point of no return.

—Ian Scott-Kilvert

WHITE, Patrick (Victor Martindale). Australian. Born in London, England, 28 May 1912. Educated at schools in Australia, 1919-25; Cheltenham College, 1925-29; King's College, Cambridge, 1932-35, B.A. in modern languages 1935. Served in the Royal Air Force as an Intelligence Officer, in the Middle East, 1940-45. Travelled in Europe and the United States, and lived in London, before World War II; returned to Australia after the war. Recipient: Australian Literary Society Gold Medal, 1956; Miles Franklin Award, 1958, 1962; Smith Literary Award, 1959; National Conference of Christians and Jews Brotherhood Award, 1962; Nobel Prize for Literature, 1973. A.C. (Companion, Order of Australia), 1975. Address: 20 Martin Road, Centennial Park, Sydney, New South Wales 2021, Australia.

PUBLICATIONS

Novels

Happy Valley. London, Harrap, 1939; New York, Viking Press, 1940.
The Living and the Dead. London, Routledge, and New York, Viking Press, 1941.
The Aunt's Story. London, Routledge, and New York, Viking Press, 1948.
The Tree of Man. New York, Viking Press, 1955; London, Eyre and Spottiswoode, 1956.
Voss. New York, Viking Press, and London, Eyre and Spottiswoode, 1957.
Riders in the Chariot. New York, Viking Press, and London, Eyre and Spottiswoode, 1961.
The Solid Mandala. New York, Viking Press, and London, Eyre and Spottiswoode, 1966.
The Vivisector. New York, Viking Press, and London, Cape, 1970.
The Eye of the Storm. London, Cape, 1973; New York, Viking Press, 1974.
A Fringe of Leaves. London, Cape, 1976; New York, Viking Press, 1977.
The Twyborn Affair. London, Cape, 1979; New York, Viking Press, 1980.

Short Stories

The Burnt Ones. New York, Viking Press, and London, Eyre and Spottiswoode, 1964.
The Cockatoos: Shorter Novels and Stories. London, Cape, 1974; New York, Viking Press, 1975.

Plays

Return to Abyssinia (produced London, 1947).
The Ham Funeral (produced Adelaide, 1961; Crewe, Cheshire, 1969). Included in *Four Plays*, 1965.
The Season at Sarsaparilla (produced Adelaide, 1962). Included in *Four Plays*, 1965.
A Cheery Soul (produced Melbourne, 1963). Included in *Four Plays*, 1965.
Night on Bald Mountain (produced Adelaide, 1964). Included in *Four Plays*, 1965.
Four Plays (includes *The Ham Funeral, The Season at Sarsaparilla, A Cheery Soul, Night on Bald Mountain*). London, Eyre and Spottiswoode, 1965; New York, Viking Press, 1966.
Big Toys (produced Sydney, 1977). Sydney, Currency Press, 1978.
The Night the Prowler (screenplay). Melbourne, Penguin, 1977.

Screenplay: *The Night the Prowler*, 1979.

Verse

The Ploughman and Other Poems. Sydney, Beacon Press, 1935.

Other

Flaws in the Glass: A Self-Portrait. London, Cape, 1981.

*

Bibliography: *A Bibliography of Patrick White* by Janette Finch, Adelaide, Libraries Board of South Australia, 1966.

Critical Studies (selection): *Patrick White* by Geoffrey Dutton, Melbourne, Lansdowne Press, 1961, revised edition, Melbourne, London, and New York, Oxford University Press, 1971; *Patrick White* by Robert F. Brissenden, London, Longman, 1966; *Patrick White* by Barry Argyle, Edinburgh, Oliver and Boyd, 1967; *Ten Essays on Patrick White Selected from Southerly* edited by G.A. Wilkes, Sydney and London, Angus and Robertson, 1970; *The Mystery of Unity: Theme and Technique in the Novels of Patrick White* by Patricia Morley, Montreal, McGill-Queen's University Press, 1972; *Patrick White* by Alan Lawson, New York, Oxford University Press, 1974; *The Eye in the Mandala: Patrick White: A Vision of Man and God* by Peter Beatson, London, Elek, and New York, Barnes and Noble, 1976; *Patrick White: A General Introduction* by Ingmar Bjorksten, translated by Stanley Gerson, Brisbane, University of Queensland Press, and New York, Humanities Press, 1976; *Patrick White's Fiction* by William Walsh, London, Allen and Unwin, and Totowa, New Jersey, Rowman and Littlefield, 1977; *Patrick White: A Critical Symposium* edited by Ron E. Shepherd and Kirpal Singh, Bedford Park, South Australia, Flinders University Centre for Research, and Washington, D.C., Three Continents, 1978; *Patrick White* by Manly Johnson, New York, Ungar, 1980; *Patrick White* by Brian Kiernan, New York, St. Martin's Press, 1980.

* * *

As the only Australian to have received the Nobel Prize in literature, Patrick White represents a developed art both native and universal. Though an Australian from parentage and background, he was actually born in England while his parents, well-to-do sheep farmers, were visiting the British "homeland"; and he went back to England again for schooling in the British tradition, and served in the R.A.F. during World War II.

One or two early novels, which he no longer recognizes, were trial flights. But *Happy Valley*, the first to be noticed outside Britain and the Commonwealth (and very little known even there), may be called the first in what has become a series of 11 substantial novels. This is not a "series" in any literal sense—as were Galsworthy's, for example, or as were some of the novels of White's earlier compatriot, Henry Handel Richardson. Each novel is independent. Some are long, some shorter; some historical, some contemporary; most with Australia as the central scene, though the larger world impinges more and more often.

To follow them through may help to suggest the development of White's thought and art. It will appear that he has been continually reaching out for understanding, perhaps for his own identity—trying them in different forms, sometimes experimentally, sometimes more conventionally—and from time to time, after more specialized flights, he synthesizes in a major effort, usually taking longer than the others. It is dangerous to force such distinctions. Many consider *The Aunt's Story*—one of his earliest—to be also one of his best. Yet *The Tree of Man*, which followed it, was far more widely read and praised and was written on a much more generous scale.

In *Happy Valley* he identified himself with his Australian homeland in a true but quietly caustic idyll of farm life, uncomplicated and localized. It is more like Hardy than like Lawrence, though he later came closer in feeling to Lawrence. *The Living and the Dead* (which he is said to have written in America), was a throwback to his pre-War British years; it did not bespeak a new voice. Then, five years after the War, *The Aunt's Story* appeared—a total change. In tones both ironic and whimsical, with much free-wheeling imagination, he leads a maiden aunt from her Australian home to a pleasure garden in France with characters partly real and partly surrealist. Then, after personal dramas and a great fire, she dwindles into a new life in the real American desert.

The symbols as well as the actual manifestations of holocaust, with fire and storm, reappear often in his successive novels. The next turns away entirely from the Aunt's surrealism, but uses many of his new subtleties of speech and insights on individuals. In *The Tree of Man* he has come to the point of writing what could be thought a great Australian classic: an epic of the growth of the land in the life-story of one couple growing up in it. It, too, has the drama of a great fire, and it has an unforgettable flood; but these are worked into the lives of the couple, their children, and their neighbors in a pattern that keeps them in due perspective with the long range of their saga.

Another experiment followed. Turning to earlier history, White reached back to the Australian visit of an actual German explorer, Leichardt, for a fictional account, entitled *Voss*, in which Voss and a group of local men went deep into the unexplored Outback. Their personal relations as they encountered the hidden aborigines were dramatic subtle insights even more than their outward discoveries. Voss's telepathic communications with his sweetheart back in Sydney, which we still call para-normal, seem at odds with White's usual skepticism. Now both in Voss himself and in the kind of unexplained "magic" that his men encountered in the aborigines, he seemed to be seeking a non-material objective for his own beliefs.

This tendency, this longing for truths beyond material knowledge—"the search for some meaning and design," as he said in a *New York Times* interview—has continued to haunt him in his books, but not to predominate as in *Voss*. Only a year or so later, White finished a much longer and relatively more conventional novel. The focus of *Riders in the Chariot* is the imaginary town of Sarsaparilla (otherwise Sydney?), which White has begun to establish as his own bailiwick. It became the climax of this largest and most far-reaching of his novels. It tells itself in sections as the stories of four odd individuals brought together almost by chance: a native "Abo" who is a gifted artist; a local washerwoman of kind intent; a cultivated Jew who has escaped from the Nazi holocaust; and a genteel old lady who proves to be slightly cracked. To summarize their intertwining stories would be a desecration; but the Jew's self-told account of his escape, in the context of this far-off scene, is a novel in itself. And the role of the everyday folk of Sarsaparilla takes on a more sinister light. It explains why White increasingly dislikes the commonplace, the thoughtless, and the ignorant of his own or any other race—and perhaps why he was for so long ignored or underrated in his own country.

In *The Solid Mandala*, still absorbed with aspects of the problem of personal identity, he tried out his own version of the Cain and Abel legend in a story of two contemporary brothers. This book is often highly praised, and is one of his own favorites. George Steiner has called it "his best novel." To this reader it is a worthy "near miss"—stimulating but not convincing in its arbitrary re-shuffling of the brothers. But it has an added twist in the homely humor of the lesser local characters.

This was soon followed by a very different attempt, even more involved with identity. The principal in *The Vivisector*, an adopted child, strikes out for himself and becomes an artist. In brief, the intensity of his vision creates his own mystical drama, until he is lost in it. Again the inner vision, the non-material goad—but done with irony this time, not as in *Voss*.

Having tried these experiments, White enlarged them in a more traditional vein. *The Eye of the Storm* pursues a rich old lady in her terminal years in Sydney as she thinks back to her late husband, to her actor son and now-titled daughter in England, and as she follows the daily lives of the nurses and retainers round her today. The son and daughter plot for their own advantage, but even in dying she keeps the upper hand. Her retrospect of the great storm she endured as a girl of Brumby Island is White at his dramatic best. But this is only one episode out of many rich moments. The overtones of symbol, always present, are not forced here; and the members of the household as well as the children live out vivid individual lives. It is probable that this powerful book influenced the Stockholm judges who gave him the Nobel Prize after this appeared—though the award does not go to any particular book.

To switch to so different a book as *A Fringe of Leaves* is no surprise. He had already begun and put aside a different novel, to which he returned later. He had also been busy with plays and stories. More than that, he had now closely identified himself with local Sydney affairs—the Opera House and politics among them—and had arranged to donate his prize money as a foundation fund for less-known Australian authors. He was digging deep, also, into the country's history, preparing a large historical novel from the early period, as in *Voss*, but with elements of quite another sort. *A Fringe of Leaves* was his re-creation of an actual shipwreck in which the crew and the few passengers fell into the hands of untouched aborigines. Only one, a resourceful Englishwoman survived by accepting Abo life and finally made it back to civilization. Combining the two ways of life in one time and person was a tour de force that White managed with conviction, and with overtones that carried further his continuing pursuit of "meaning and design" in life. But he implied that the lucky survivor, having experienced the primitive past, would go back contentedly to her familiar present.

Then appeared the novel that appears to have come nearest to him in his private search. *The Twyborn Affair* is pure fiction, quite different from his own life in almost all outward particulars. Yet the story of Eddie Twyborn may be a parable from his inward autobiography, judging from the glimpses he has given us in public life and in his other writings. Eddie, after running away from a conventional marriage, first assumes the female role with a rich old Greek on the French Riviera. He then reverses himself, becomes a hero in the Great War, and returns to Australia as a sheep herder and self-sufficient male in the Outback. Fed up with his fellows—both men and women—he returns to Europe to become the sexless madame of the most prominent brothel in London.

Though richly imagined in its actions and filled with abundant humor, it is written with even more than White's usual subtleties, quizzical allusions, and wry attacks on human stupidity. He himself once said, while writing it, that "everybody is going to hate this." It obviously puzzled some critics. But Benjamin DeMott in the *New York Times*, for example, wisely saw at its core "the mystery of human identity." It's curious, in looking back, to see how often this mystery has echoed in the pages of White's novels—and in some of his short stories also. Not "everybody," but some at least, will feel that *The Twyborn Affair* is a rewarding climax.

To this reader, if a choice of menu were obligatory, the three great entrees would surely be *The Tree of Man, Riders in the Chariot*, and *A Fringe of Leaves*. But the appetizer should be *The Aunt's Story*, and the side dishes could cover almost all the others in sequence—with *The Twyborn Affair* as the dessert.

—Marshall A. Best

WIEBE, Rudy (Henry). Canadian. Born in Fairholme, Saskatchewan, 4 October 1934. Educated at the University of Alberta, Edmonton, 1953-56, 1958-60 (International Nickel Graduate Fellow, 1958-59; Queen Elizabeth Graduate Fellow, 1959-60), B.A. 1956, M.A. 1960; University of Tubingen, Germany (Rotary Fellow), 1957-58; University of Manitoba, Winnipeg, 1961; University of Iowa, Iowa City, 1964. Married Tena F. Isaak in 1958; three children. Research Officer, Glenbow Foundation, Calgary, 1956; Foreign Service Officer, Ottawa, 1960; high school teacher, Selkirk, Manitoba, 1961; Editor, The Mennonite Brethren *Herald*, Winnipeg, 1962-63; Assistant Professor of English, Goshen College, Indiana, 1963-67. Assistant Professor, 1967-70, and since 1970, Associate Professor of English, University of Alberta. Recipient: Canada Council Arts Scholarship, 1964, award, 1971, grant, 1977. Address: 5315 143rd Street, Edmonton, Alberta T6H 4E3, Canada.

PUBLICATIONS

Novels

Peace Shall Destroy Many. Toronto, McClelland and Stewart, 1962; Grand Rapids, Michigan, Eerdmans, 1964.
First and Vital Candle. Toronto, McClelland and Stewart, and Grand Rapids, Michigan, Eerdmans, 1966.
The Blue Mountains of China. Toronto, McClelland and Stewart, and Grand Rapids, Michigan, Eerdmans, 1970.
The Temptations of Big Bear. Toronto, McClelland and Stewart, 1973.
The Scorched-Wood People. Toronto, McClelland and Stewart, 1977.

Short Stories

Where Is the Wind Coming From? Toronto, McClelland and Stewart, 1974.
Alberta: A Celebration, edited by Tom Radford. Edmonton, Hurtig, 1979.

Play

Far as the Eye Can See, with Theatre Passe Muraille. Edmonton, NeWest Press, 1977.

Other

Editor, *The Story-Makers: A Selection of Modern Short Stories.* Toronto, Macmillan, 1970.
Editor, *Stories from Western Canada: A Selection.* Toronto, Macmillan, 1972.
Editor, with Andreas Schroeder, *Stories from Pacific and Arctic Canada: A Selection.* Toronto, Macmillan, 1974.
Editor, *Double Vision: An Anthology of Twentieth-Century Stories in English.* Toronto, Macmillan, 1976.
Editor, *Getting Here: Stories.* Edmonton, NeWest Press, 1977.
Editor, with Aritha van Herk, *More Stories from Western Canada.* Toronto, Macmillan, 1980.

*

Critical Studies: reviews in *Canadian Literature* (Vancouver), Winter 1963 and Fall 1966; *Fiddlehead* (Fredericton, New Brunswick), Winter 1971; *Saturday Night* (Toronto), April 1971; *The Banner* (Grand Rapids, Michigan), April 1971; *Christian Living* (Scottdale, Pennsylvania), July 1971.

Rudy Wiebe comments:

I believe that the worlds of fiction—story—should provide pleasure of as many kinds as possible to the reader; I believe fiction must be precisely, peculiarly rooted in a particular place, in particular people; I believe writing fiction is as serious, as responsible an activity as I can ever perform. Therefore in my fiction I try to explore the world that I know: the land and people of western Canada; from my particular world view: a radical Jesus-oriented Christianity.

* * *

Central to all of Rudy Wiebe's writings is the Mennonite faith in which he was reared, and central to that is the "extremely individualistic approach to religion" (as he puts it in the foreword to his first novel) which motivates the actions and attitudes of all his characters. His novels, fundamentally and forthrightly Christian (neither tub-thumping nor ritualistic), probe the nature of faith. Deliberately didactic, they investigate the lives of ordinary people with ordinary abilities but passionate minds, to show the virtue of individual action, the power of commitment, and the sterility of material competitiveness and moral apathy. Sometimes the Christian parables intrude awkwardly, artificially, "unfictionalized," into the narrative line and symbolic tapestry, as in *First and Vital Candle* or in the end of *The Blue Mountains of China*, but when the blend is right, Wiebe's indirect style closes in on the intricate balance between intellect and feeling.

The first novel is the simplest in form, taking its title from *Daniel*: "he shall magnify himself in his heart, and by peace shall destroy many: But he shall be broken without hand." The ironic contrast implicit in the book, between Hitler's militant arrogance and the prairie Mennonite Deacon Block's pacifist arrogance, serves to highlight their similarities. The Deacon, certain to himself, is aware only of rules and traditions; always when young members of the community enquire as to the *nature* of the traditions they are told to uphold, routine orders rather than illuminating answers await them. The Deacon destroys his own family by such narrowness. For the central character too, young Thom Wiens—striving to sharpen his mind, answer his conscience, weigh military service in an attractive cause against admirable but paradoxically "enforced" pacifism—the Deacon's negation is no answer either. But the prospect of abandoning his faith seems equally barren. Only the private relation with God and with man—lonely, terrifying, challenging, necessary—can arouse in him any promise of the true internal peace that governments cannot legislate nor other individuals rule.

The Blue Mountains of China, Wiebe's most ambitious book, explores in a flawed but compelling fashion exactly those traditions and histories that Thom sought to discover. Taking up again a theme from the earlier book's foreword, it traces the great Mennonite quest for paradise: "like ancient Israel, they were a religious nation without a country." In the minds of different generations recalling fragmentarily their own history and intuiting dimly their significance in the story of the community as a whole, the 100-year trek from Russia to China to Canada to Paraguay comes to life. But the novel is more than genealogy—more than *Exodus.* By positing the ambivalence of paradise, it tries to explore the impact of an ideal upon the communal mind of a people. From adolescent quarrels early in the book (over the innocence or sinfulness or sexuality), through dissatisfaction with Russian communes, Chinese deserts, Canadian commercialism, South American violence, and arid intellectual pretentiousness, routes to earthly paradises are one after the other quietly closed. Yet all the time *the people* is crossing borders, often in flight, undercover, at night, in the wilderness, or in another language (so that no-one can pinpoint the moment of crossing) and with each change there arises the possibility of metaphysical insight. The title mountains divide the Chinese winds, creating a "contrast between fertile Manchuria and arid Mongolia." As Wiebe metamorphoses them into the Canadian Rockies, they become an ambivalent marker of contemporary Canadian/Mennonite/individual choices, too, hinting that peace (in Vietnam or in the private spirit) is only possible when men surrender their will to control other men and turn to contemplating seriously their own moves and motives instead. Increasingly, for Wiebe's Canada, this means reflecting on the popular prejudices against the native Indians and acting to alter such attitudes. Above all it means acquiring faith in the basic humanity of men and pursuing one's way to the future that humane action can foster.

—W.H. New

WILLIAMS, John (Edward). American. Born in Clarksville, Texas, 29 August 1922. Educated at the University of Denver, B.A. 1949, M.A. 1950; University of Missouri, Columbia, Ph.D. 1954; Oxford University, 1963. Served in the United States Army Air Force, 1942-45. Married 1) Avalon Smith in 1949, two daughters and one son; 2) Nancy Gardner in 1970, four step-children. Instructor, University of Missouri, 1950-54. Assistant Professor, 1954-60, Director of the Workshop for Writers, 1954-59, and of the Creative Writing Program, 1954-74, Associate Professor, 1960-64, and since 1964, Professor of English, University of Denver. Writer-in-Residence, Wisconsin State University, Whitewater, summers 1964-66, 1968-69; Member of the Faculty, Bread Loaf Writers Conference, Vermont, 1966-72; Writer-in-Residence, Smith College, Northampton, Massachusetts, 1968; Hurst Professor of Creative Literature, Brandeis University, Waltham, Massachusetts, 1973. Editor, *Twentieth Century Literature*, Los Angeles, 1954-56, and *University of Denver Quarterly*, 1965-70. Recipient: Rockefeller grant, 1967; American Academy grant, 1969; National Book Award, 1973. Agent: Marie Rodell-Frances Collin Literary Agency, 156 East 52nd Street, New York, New York 10022. Address: Department of English, University of Denver, Denver, Colorado 80210, U.S.A.

PUBLICATIONS

Novels

Nothing But the Night. Denver, Swallow, 1948.
Butcher's Crossing. New York, Macmillan, and London, Gollancz, 1960.
Stoner. New York, Viking Press, 1965; London, Allen Lane, 1973.
Augustus. New York, Viking Press, 1972; London, Allen Lane, 1973.

Verse

The Broken Landscape. Denver, Swallow, 1949.
The Necessary Lie. Denver, Verb, 1965.

Other

Editor, *English Renaissance Poetry: A Collection of Shorter Poems from Skelton to Jonson.* New York, Doubleday, 1963.

*

Critical Studies: "The Western Theme: Exploiters and Explorers" by Robert B. Heilman, in *Partisan Review* (New Brunswick, New Jersey), March-April 1961; "Artist of Diversity" (interview), in *Dust* (Paradise, California), Winter 1966; "Accounts of Mutual Acquaintances to a Group of Friends: The Fiction of John Williams" by Robert J. Nelson, in *Denver Quarterly*, Winter 1973; "*Butcher's Crossing*: The Husks and Shells of Exploitation" by Jack Brenner, in *Western American Literature* (Fort Collins, Colorado), February 1973; "Good Men and Foes" by C.P. Snow, in *Financial Times* (London), 24 May 1973; "John Williams: An Introduction to the Major Novels" by Rex Stamper, in *Mississippi Review* (Hattiesburg), iii, 1, 1974.

John Williams comments:

Though I prefer to let my work speak for itself, I shall say three things about myself as a novelist. First, I consider myself a professional rather than an amateur; that is, I do things for the thing's sake rather than for my own. Second, I write rather slowly, being that kind of writer that Thomas Mann once described as one who finds writing more difficult than most people do. And third, I try not to repeat myself from novel to novel.

* * *

John Williams's fiction has revolved around the idea of history and the past's inexorable weight. In his four novels he had explored the symptoms of historical determinism from various perspectives. From *Butcher's Crossing*, set in mid-19th-century frontier America, to *Augustus*, set in Rome during Augustus Caesar's lifetime, Williams has concentrated on the individual in the context of his times.

Butcher's Crossing deals with man and nature on the violently expanding frontier of early America. Specifically it chronicles one of the last great buffalo kills at the height of the craze for buffalo robes, an example of the mindless waste of crude free enterprise. The story encompasses an expedition by Will Andrews, an innocent easterner determined to see the wilderness and taste adventure, and an obsessed buffalo-hunter, Miller, who knows a mountain valley that shelters the last great bison herd. The party reaches the valley, slaughters some 3,000 buffalo, stacks the hides, then is trapped by winter. Surviving the fierce Rocky Mountain winter, on the hazardous return they lose the buffalo hides. When they reach the town of Butcher's Crossing, from which they began, they discover that the demand for buffalo hides is gone—the market has totally collapsed. The ironies of the story multiply: Will Andrews has found more experience than he bargained for, and Miller, the super-annuated mountain man, goes violently mad when he realizes that his heroic feat has been meaningless. As in frontier ballads like "Buffalo Skinners," there is a strong sense here of the blind rapacity of the frontier and of the despair which generated such pointless blood-lust.

In contrast *Stoner* describes near-contemporary America, the life of a provincial university professor in the first half of our century. The story develops in sharp detail William Stoner's rise from rural poverty through a long career as a literature teacher. His life is a series of struggles and small triumphs that dissolve in losses: his wife is cold and neurotic, he fights petty battles with unscrupulous colleagues, has one brief and vivid affair with a student, and goes to his grave unrewarded for this intense devotion to learning. It is a small, minutely documented tragedy of a common man, set against the ideals of academe. Stoner is a talented but not brilliant teacher, an ethical man, but he is persistently defeated by people who do not hesitate to warp or betray ideals. In a small but distinct form, *Stoner* demonstrates the erosion of individual will in the face of apathy, malice, and neglect, a familiar theme of modern literature—and life.

At the other end of the historical spectrum is *Augustus*, which details the rise to ultimate power of a seemingly inept and uncalculating man. Constructed as a mock-documentary of letters, journals, military orders, and memoirs, the story recounts Augustus Caesar's political ascent from the viewpoints of both allies and enemies, and it shows how the complex strands of history are interpreted subjectively by all observers. The pastiche of documents gives a strong sense of a Hobbesian world of selfish motives and grasping egos. The man we see in this composite portrait is a complex individual skilfully manipulating the forces of his culture and shaping an ideology from the historical accidents around him. Yet *Augustus* demonstrates that the greatest power is ultimately as meaningless as the small man's impotence. *Augustus* concludes with Caesar's reflections on his career, a soliloquy summarizing his apparently matchless triumphs:

> The despair that I have voiced seems to me now unworthy of what I have done. Rome is not eternal; it does not matter. The barbarian will conquer; it does not matter. There was a moment of Rome, and it will not wholly die; the barbarian will become the Rome he conquers; the language will smooth his rough tongue; the vision of what he destroys will flow in his blood. And in time that is ceaseless as this salt sea upon which I am so frailly suspended, the cost is nothing, is less than nothing.

This small victory snatched from despair is very like Williams's Stoner's final meditation on his apparently futile career: "A kind of joy came upon him, as if borne in a summer breeze. He dimly recalled that he had been thinking of failure—as if it mattered. It seemed to him now that such thoughts were mean, unworthy of what his life had been." Like Gray's "Elegy," the two portraits bring together the mighty and the anonymous lives, demonstrating that the individual life is its own measure. A life examined from the inside is justified on its own terms, regardless of the defeats, confusions, and corrosive ironies of history.

—William J. Schafer

WILLIAMS, John A(lfred). American. Born in Jackson, Mississippi, 5 December 1925. Educated at Central High School, Syracuse, New York; Syracuse University, A.B. 1950. Served in the United States Navy, 1943-46. Married 1) Carolyn Clopton; 2) Lorrain Isaac; three children. Has worked for publishers, in an advertising agency, and for the American Committee on Africa, New York. Distinguished Professor of English, LaGuardia Community College, City University of New York, 1973-75; Visiting Professor, University of Hawaii, Honolulu, Summer 1974, and Boston University, 1978-79. Since 1979, Professor of English, Rutgers University, New Brunswick, New Jersey. Recipient: American Academy grant, 1962; Syracuse University Outstanding Achievement Award, 1970; National Endowment for the Arts grant, 1977. Litt.D.: Southeastern Massachusetts University, North Dartmouth, 1978. Address: 693 Forest Avenue, Teaneck, New Jersey 07666, U.S.A.

PUBLICATIONS

Novels

The Angry Ones. New York, Ace, 1960; as *One for New York*, Chatham, New Jersey, Chatham Bookseller, 1975.
Night Song. New York, Farrar Straus, 1961; London, Collins, 1962.
Sissie. New York, Farrar Straus, 1963; as *Journey Out of Anger*, London, Eyre and Spottiswoode, 1968.
The Man Who Cried I Am. Boston, Little Brown, 1967; London, Eyre and Spottiswoode, 1968.
Sons of Darkness, Sons of Light. Boston, Little Brown, 1969; London, Eyre and Spottiswoode, 1970.
Captain Blackman. New York, Doubleday, 1972.
Mothersill and the Foxes. New York, Doubleday, 1975.
The Junior Bachelor Society. New York, Doubleday, 1976.

Other

Africa: Her History, Lands, and People. New York, Cooper Square, 1962.
The Protectors (as J. Dennis Gregory, with Harry T. Anslinger) (on narcotics enforcement). New York, Farrar Straus, 1964.
This Is My Country, Too. New York, New American Library, 1965; London, New English Library, 1966.
The Most Native of Sons: A Biography of Richard Wright. New York, Doubleday, 1970.
The King God Didn't Save: Reflections on the Life and Death of Martin Luther King, Jr. New York, Coward McCann, 1970; London, Eyre and Spottiswoode, 1971.
Flashbacks: A Twenty-Year Diary of Article Writing. New York, Doubleday, 1973.
Romare Bearden. New York, Abrams, 1973.
Minorities in the City. New York, Harper, 1975.

Editor, *The Angry Black.* New York, Lancer, 1962.
Editor, *Beyond the Angry Black.* New York, Cooper Square, 1967.
Editor, *Amistad I* and *II.* New York, Knopf, 2 vols., 1970-71.

*

Manuscript Collection: Syracuse University, New York.

Critical Studies: *America as Seen by a Black Man* by Robert T. Haley, unpublished thesis, San Jose State College, California, 1971; "The Art of John A. Williams" by John O'Brien, in *American Scholar* (Washington, D.C.), Summer 1973; *The Evolution of a Black Writer: John A. Williams* by Earl Cash, New York, Third Press, 1974.

John A. Williams comments:

I think art has always been political and has served political ends more graciously than those of the muses. I consider myself to be a political novelist and writer to the extent that I am always aware of the social insufficiencies which are a result of political manipulation. The greatest art has always been social-political, and in that sense I could be considered striving along traditional paths.

* * *

James Baldwin was to remind us of the descent one must make to excavate history in *Just above My Head.* And it is similar to the theme the critic Addison Gayle deals with in *The Way of the New World*: "It is to history that one looks for the best example of modern black men; there that the falsity of the old images, stereotypes, and metaphors can be seen. History, then, rewritten and corrected, holds the key to success in the war against the imagists." Within the framework of this critical thinking John A. Williams wages war against the imagists, merging history into fiction to create new dimensions for the writings of Black novelists and fresh images for Black readers to digest.

Throwing off the image of the black protagonist struggling for confirmation of his self worth, Williams creates, in *The Man Who Cried I Am*, Max Reddick, a Black man who becomes a "success" in the white world who asks himself "was it worth what it cost?" Reddick's final confirmation of "self" comes not from the white world, but from himself, "All you ever want to do is remind me that I am black. But, goddamn it, I also am," he says.

The need for this new direction in Black writing has been documented; however, few writers have matched Williams in destroying illusions of the Black man as a victim subjugated by the pressures of racial injustice in the Western World. It is without uncertainty that Williams's protagonists know history, and understand its function. In *Sons of Darkness, Sons of Light* Eugene Browning mulls over the advantages of knowing his past: "Remember when we began to discover Negro history—twenty years old and blam there it was, and it was sort of like peeling an onion, one thing leading to another, translucent, slippery, thin...one morning I woke up and the enormity of what's been done to us was resting like a ball of badly digested lead in my stomach, but it got down, it went down, and I couldn't pretend anymore that it had meaning for me. Not only for me but for all the Negroes out there." But it is with reason and without anger, that Browning, after coming to the conclusion that civil rights and freedom marches would not bring justice to Blacks, employs Mafia tactics in the assassination of a policeman guilty of killing a 16-year-old black boy. "You could work...with all your heart and what was left of your soul, but you also had to know finally...that you had to obtain your goals by the same means as Chuck."

Williams's themes are the heightened level of group consciousness, self-resolve, and resourcefulness needed by blacks to eliminate racial injustices, through as Browning states, "Secrecy, apparent non-involvement, selected acts. That was the only answer." Williams leads us to the doorway of creating new values for the good of the group while unraveling Black people from a web of images, and stereotypes. "It is most imperative," Williams writes, "that the Negro be seen and seen as he is; the morality of the situation will then resolve itself, and truth, which is what we all presumably are after, will then be served." Williams does this well in leading us to the descent.

—Brenda R. Ferguson

WILLIAMS, Raymond (Henry). British. Born in Llanfihangel Crocorney, Wales, 31 August 1921. Educated at Abergavenny Grammar School, 1932-39; Trinity College, Cambridge, 1939-41, 1945-46, M.A. 1946, Litt.D. 1969. Served in the Anti-Tank Regiment, Guards Armoured Division, 1941-45: Captain. Married Joy Dalling in 1942; three children. Editor, *Politics and Letters*, 1946-47. Staff Tutor in Literature, Oxford University Delegacy for Extra-Mural Studies, 1946-61. Since 1961, Fellow of Jesus College, Cambridge; Reader, 1967-74, and since 1974 Professor of Drama, Cambridge University. Visiting Professor of Political Science, Stanford University, California, 1973. General Editor, New Thinkers Library, 1962-70. Reviewer for *The Guardian*, London. D. Univ.: Open University, Milton Keynes, Buckinghamshire, 1975; D.Litt.: University of Wales, Cardiff, 1980. Member of the Welsh Academy. Address: Jesus College, Cambridge CB5 8BL, England.

PUBLICATIONS

Novels

Border Country. London, Chatto and Windus, 1960; New York, Horizon Press, 1962.
Second Generation. London, Chatto and Windus, 1964; New York, Horizon Press, 1965.
The Volunteers. London, Eyre Methuen, 1978.
The Fight for Manod. London, Chatto and Windus, 1979.

Uncollected Short Stories

"Sack Labourer," in *English Story 1*, edited by Woodrow Wyatt. London, Collins, 1941.
"This Time," in *New Writing and Daylight*. London, Hogarth Press, 1943.
"A Fine Room to Be Ill In," in *English Story 7*, edited by Woodrow Wyatt. London, Collins, 1947.

Plays

Koba, in *Modern Tragedy*. London, Chatto and Windus, 1966.
A Letter from the Country (televised, 1966). Published in *Stand* (Newcastle upon Tyne), 1971.
Public Inquiry (televised, 1967). Published in *Stand* (Newcastle upon Tyne), ix, 1, 1967.

Television Plays: *A Letter from the Country*, 1966; *Public Inquiry*, 1967; *The Country and the City* (documentary; *Where We Live Now* series), 1979.

Other

Reading and Criticism. London, Muller, 1950.
Drama from Ibsen to Eliot. London, Chatto and Windus, 1952; New York, Oxford University Press, 1953; revised edition, London, Penguin, 1964; as *Drama from Ibsen to Brecht*, Chatto and Windus, 1968, Oxford University Press, 1969.
Drama in Performance. London, Muller, 1954; New York, Basic, 1969.
Preface to Film, with Michael Orrom. London, Film Drama, 1954.
Culture and Society, 1780-1950. London, Chatto and Windus, and New York, Columbia University Press, 1958.
The Long Revolution. London, Chatto and Windus, and New York, Columbia University Press, 1961.
Communications. London, Penguin, 1962; revised edition, London, Chatto and Windus, 1966; New York, Barnes and Noble, 1967.
The Existing Alternatives in Communications. London, Fabian Society, 1962.
Modern Tragedy. London, Chatto and Windus, and Stanford, California, Stanford University Press, 1966.
The English Novel from Dickens to Lawrence. London, Chatto and Windus, and New York, Oxford University Press, 1970.
Orwell. London, Fontana, and New York, Viking Press, 1971.
The Country and the City. London, Chatto and Windus, and New York, Oxford University Press, 1973.
Television: Technology and Cultural Form. London, Fontana, 1974; New York, Schocken, 1975.
Drama in a Dramatised Society (lecture). Cambridge, University Press, 1975.
Keywords: A Vocabulary of Culture and Society. London, Croom Helm, and New York, Oxford University Press, 1976.
Marxism and Literature. London and New York, Oxford University Press, 1977.
Politics and Letters: Interviews with "New Left Review." London, New Left, and New York, Schocken, 1979.
Problems in Materialism and Culture: Selected Essays. London, New Left, 1980; New York, Schocken, 1981.
Culture. London, Fontana, 1981.

Editor, *May Day Manifesto 1968*. London, Penguin, 1968.
Editor, *The Pelican Book of English Prose: From 1780 to the Present Day*. London, Penguin, 1970.
Editor, with Joy Williams, *D.H. Lawrence on Education*. London, Penguin, 1973.
Editor, *George Orwell: A Collection of Critical Essays*. Englewood Cliffs, New Jersey, Prentice Hall, 1974.
Editor, with Marie Axton, *English Drama: Forms and Development: Essays in Honour of Muriel Clara Bradbrook*. London, Cambridge University Press, 1977.

*

Critical Studies: by Dennis Potter, in *New Left Review* (London), 1961; Graham Martin, in *Views* (London), 1965; "The Novel, Truth and Community" by James R. Bennett, in *D.H. Lawrence Review* (Fayetteville, Arkansas), 1970-71; "Idea of a People" by Jeremy Hooker, in *Planet* (Llangeitho Tregaron, Dyfed), 1979.

Raymond Williams comments:

(1972) When I came out of the army in 1945 I began writing the novel which was eventually published as *Border Country*. It went through some seven rewritings. It has been described as autobiographical, but this is in many ways misleading. For example, the central character, Harry Price, is a railway signalman, as was my father, but I found I could not get the book right until I had invented another character, his friend and opposite Morgan Rosser, who is in many ways as close to my own father as the character usually taken as based on him. In its final version, the novel had moved far enough from anything that can ordinarily be called autobiography for it to have to be seen in quite other ways. The chapter on the General Strike in *Border Country* has nothing autobiographical in it, yet it is the chapter of my novel-writing that I am most satisfied with.

During that period of writing and rewriting I completed two other novels, *A Map of Treason* and *The Grasshoppers*, which are still in the desk drawer. During the early 1960's I wrote my second published novel, *Second Generation*, which seems to be preferred to *Border Country* only in Eastern Europe, though I think it is exactly what I wanted to write as the working-class experience—personal and social rather than political—of the 1960's. Since then I have been working on two novels, *The Brothers* and *The Volunteers*. The latter, set in Europe in the 1990's, will probably be the first published. The former, which is closer to *Border Country*, should be completed during the next two years.

I find novel-writing very important and rewarding, and I have given much more time to it than my list of publications might suggest. But I revise and rework a great deal, and shall be satisfied if by the time I have finished I have five or six novels which I can feel are really my own. The fact that I also write social criticism has led to a simple formula in which my novels are seen as by-products, but the two kinds of writing have always been equally important to me, and in fact the novel-writing came first and will, I think, go on longer. Some of the themes of the novels overlap with the social criticism, but I only write in novel form what I am sure could not be written in essays and analysis. As to method, although I found *Border Country* difficult to write, I think the form and language of memory and the past are more accessible to contemporary novelists than a form and language of the true present as attempted in *Second Generation*. *The Volunteers*, set in the future, has required much more extended technical experiment; this is the main reason why it has taken so long to write.

(1981) *The Brothers* is still in progress, but meanwhile I have completed the *Border Country* trilogy with *The Fight for Manod* which tackles one of its themes. I am also beginning work on an unusual kind of historical novel in which the continuity is not of people but of a place.

* * *

Raymond Williams has a well deserved reputation for his critical works such as *Culture and Society*, but has also ventured an unperformed play, included in the English edition of his *Modern Tragedy*, two good television plays (published in *Stand*) and several novels.

Border Country describes how a young university lecturer leaves his London home to return to the Welsh border village where he grew up, to visit his sick father. Back in his childhood environment, he finds himself on a border between his past and his present, between different classes, ambitions, and generations. Most of the novel consists of memories evoked by the visit, through which he tries to understand his father, the rural way of life, and the experiences that have made him what he is. Obviously this is intensely personal for Williams, a book he had to write. Personal recollections—the death of his grandfather, fears that he had lost a pound note—mingle with a wealth of detail about the village, like the Eisteddfod and the excitement of catching a swarm of bees.

Matthew explores his deep relationship with his father, who "lived direct, never by any other standard at all." Through his father and friends, the relationship between work and life is examined: the signalbox routine has provided a meaningful core, a necessary job, close to home. Because work matters, the outside world has a big impact with the 1926 General Strike and its moral problems, vividly conveyed. A lifelong friend has taken a different course and become a successful minor capitalist, while Matthew fears his job and life do not connect.

Further, Matthew feels the Border community has a strength missing in his own more mobile society, and looks at it reverently. As a local tells him, "Here it's got to be in the open, because in the end there's no hiding things, and none of us is going away....It isn't your kind of settlement, that any day might break up." The Eisteddfod adjudicator had come annually for years, remembering everyone, and Matthew "knew how much this ceremony of memory and identification meant to the silent and apparently unresponsive listeners." But lorries are turning the village into "a name you pass through, houses along a road." Ideas about old-time organic country life that we may have though sentimental gain a new reality from Williams's picture.

He represents truthfully the experience of child growing away from parent, leaving village for suburb, which can appeal directly to those who share it and explain much to those who do not. The novel is leisurely, dignified, always serious.

Second Generation is more ambitious and more uneven. Two brothers, who have come in the 1930's from Wales to work in a car factory in a university town, live side by side, Harold, an active unionist, and Gwyn, politically apathetic. Harold's wife, frustrated intellectually, has an affair with a lecturer she meets through the Labour Party. Their son is a graduate student studying "community" theoretically and doubting the value of his work, wondering also whether to marry a girl he has known a long time. Finally, declining an American offer, he decides to work in the factory to make "a new kind of enquiry, with ourselves involved in it."

Williams, explained Irving Howe in the *New Republic*, is showing "both the continuities and differences between the old England of 'classical' capitalism and the new England of the welfare state." So it has less personal feeling than *Border Country* and is more of a document—and sometimes very good on this level, especially in conveying what a strike and threat of redundancy are like. What Williams thinks is often prominent at the expense of what he knows. As fiction, too, *Second Generation* is weaker than the earlier book, with over-solemnity, clumsiness, and prolonged wordy dialogues more frequent and conspicuous.

—Malcolm Page

WILLIAMS, Tennessee (Thomas Lanier Williams). American. Born in Columbus, Mississippi, 26 March 1911. Educated at the University of Missouri, Columbia, 1930-32; Washington University, St. Louis, 1936-37; University of Iowa, Iowa City, 1938, A.B. 1938. Clerical Worker and Manual Laborer, International Shoe Company, St. Louis, 1934-36; held various jobs, including waiter and elevator operator, New Orleans, 1939; teletype operator, Jacksonville, Florida, 1940; worked at odd jobs, New York, 1942, and as a screenwriter for MGM, 1943. Since 1944, full-time writer. Recipient: Rockefeller Fellowship, 1940; American Academy grant, 1944, and Gold Medal, 1969; New York Drama Critics Circle Award, 1945, 1948, 1955, 1962; Pulitzer Prize, for drama, 1948, 1955; *Evening Standard* award, for drama, 1958; Brandeis University Creative Arts Award, 1964. Member, American Academy, 1976. Lives in Key West, Florida, and New York City. Agent: Mitch Douglas, International Creative Management, 40 West 57th Street, New York, New York 10019, U.S.A.

PUBLICATIONS

Novels

The Roman Spring of Mrs. Stone. New York, New Directions, and London, Lehmann, 1950.
Moise and the World of Reason. New York, Simon and Schuster, 1975; London, W.H. Allen, 1976.

Short Stories

One Arm and Other Stories. New York, New Directions, 1948.
Hard Candy: A Book of Stories. New York, New Directions, 1954.
Three Players of a Summer Game and Other Stories. London, Secker and Warburg, 1960.
Grand. New York, House of Books, 1964.
The Knightly Quest: A Novella and Four Short Stories. New York, New Directions, 1967; augmented edition, as *The Knightly Quest: A Novella and Twelve Short Stories*, London, Secker and Warburg, 1968.
Eight Mortal Ladies Possessed: A Book of Stories. New York, New Directions, 1974; London, Secker and Warburg, 1975.

Uncollected Short Story

"Tent Worms," in *Esquire* (New York), May 1980.

Plays

Cairo! Shanghai! Bombay! (produced Memphis, 1936).
The Magic Tower (produced St. Louis, 1936).
Headlines (produced St. Louis, 1936).
Candles in the Sun (produced St. Louis, 1936).
Fugitive Kind (produced St. Louis, 1937).

Spring Song (produced Iowa City, 1938).
The Long Goodbye (produced New York, 1940). Included in *27 Wagons Full of Cotton*, 1946.
Battle of Angels (produced Boston, 1940; New York, 1974). Murray, Utah, Pharos, 1945; revised version, as *Orpheus Descending* (produced New York, 1957; London, 1959), published as *Orpheus Descending, with Battle of Angels*, New York, New Directions, 1958; as *Orpheus Descending*, London, Secker and Warburg, 1958.
At Liberty (produced New York, 1968). Published in *American Scenes*, edited by William Kozlenko, New York, Day, 1941.
Stairs to the Roof (produced Pasadena, California, 1944).
You Touched Me, with Donald Windham, suggested by the story by D.H. Lawrence (produced Cleveland, 1943; New York, 1945). New York, French, 1947.
The Glass Menagerie (produced Cleveland, 1944; New York, 1945; London, 1948). New York, Random House, 1945; London, Lehmann, 1948.
27 Wagons Full of Cotton and Other One-Act Plays (includes *The Purification, The Lady of Larkspur Lotion, The Last of My Solid Gold Watches, Portrait of a Madonna, Auto-da-Fé, Lord Byron's Love Letter, The Strangest Kind of Romance, The Long Goodbye, Hello from Bertha*, and *This Property Is Condemned*). New York, New Directions, 1946; London, Grey Walls Press, 1947; augmented edition (includes *Talk to Me Like the Rain and Let Me Listen* and *Something Unspoken*), New Directions, 1953.
This Property Is Condemned (produced New York, 1946; London, 1953). Included in *27 Wagons Full of Cotton*, 1946.
Portrait of a Madonna (produced Los Angeles, 1946; New York, 1959). Included in *27 Wagons Full of Cotton*, 1946.
The Last of My Solid Gold Watches (produced Los Angeles, 1946). Included in *27 Wagons Full of Cotton*, 1946.
Lord Byron's Love Letter (produced New York, 1947). Included in *27 Wagons Full of Cotton*, 1946; revised version, music by Raffaello de Banfield (produced London, 1964); libretto published, Milan and New York, Riccordi, 1955.
Auto-da-Fé (produced New York, 1947; Bromley, Kent, 1961; London, 1979). Included in *27 Wagons Full of Cotton*, 1946.
The Lady of Larkspur Lotion (produced New York, 1947; London, 1968). Included in *27 Wagons Full of Cotton*, 1946.
The Purification (produced Dallas, 1954; Cambridge, England, 1955; New York, 1959). Included in *27 Wagons Full of Cotton*, 1946.
27 Wagons Full of Cotton (produced New Orleans and New York, 1955). Included in *27 Wagons Full of Cotton*, 1946.
Hello from Bertha (produced Bromley, Kent, 1961). Included in *27 Wagons Full of Cotton*, 1946.
The Strangest Kind of Romance (produced London, 1969). Included in *27 Wagons Full of Cotton*, 1946.
Mooney's Kid Don't Cry (produced Los Angeles, 1946; New York, 1947; London, 1971). Included in *American Blues*, 1948.
A Streetcar Named Desire (produced New York, 1947; London, 1949). New York, New Directions, 1947; London, Lehmann, 1949.
Summer and Smoke (produced Dallas, 1947; New York, 1948; London, 1951). New York, New Directions, 1948; London, Lehmann, 1952; revised version, as *The Eccentricities of a Nightingale* (produced Nyack, New York, 1964; Guildford, Surrey, 1967), published as *The Eccentricities of a Nightingale, and Summer and Smoke*, New York, New Directions, 1965; revised version (produced Buffalo, New York, and New York City, 1976).
American Blues: Five Short Plays (includes *Mooney's Kid Don't Cry, The Dark Room, The Case of the Crushed Petunias, The Long Stay Cut Short; or, The Unsatisfactory Supper*, and *Ten Blocks on the Camino Real*). New York, Dramatists Play Service, 1948.
Ten Blocks on the Camino Real, in *American Blues*, 1948; revised version, as *Camino Real* (produced New York, 1953; London, 1957), New York, New Directions, 1953; London, Secker and Warburg, 1958.
The Case of the Crushed Petunias (produced Cleveland, 1957; New York, 1958; Glasgow, 1968). Included in *American Blues*, 1948.
The Dark Room (produced London, 1966). Included in *American Blues*, 1948.
The Long Stay Cut Short; or, The Unsatisfactory Supper (produced London, 1971). Included in *American Blues*, 1948.
The Rose Tattoo (produced New York, 1951; London, 1959). New York, New Directions, 1951; London, Secker and Warburg, 1955.
I Rise in Flame, Cried the Phoenix: A Play about D.H. Lawrence (produced New York, 1953; London, 1971). New York, New Directions, 1951.
Talk to Me Like the Rain and Let Me Listen (produced Westport, Connecticut, 1958; New York, 1962; London, 1978). Included in *27 Wagons Full of Cotton*, 1953.
Something Unspoken (produced New York and London, 1958). Included in *27 Wagons Full of Cotton*, 1953.
Cat on a Hot Tin Roof (produced New York, 1955; London, 1958). New York, New Directions, 1955; London, Secker and Warburg, 1956; revised version (produced West Springfield, Massachusetts, 1973), New York, New Directions, 1975.
Three Players of a Summer Game (produced Westport, Connecticut, 1955).
Sweet Bird of Youth (produced Coral Gables, Florida, 1956; New York, 1959; Watford, Hertfordshire, 1968). New York, New Directions, 1959; London, Secker and Warburg, 1961.
Baby Doll: The Script for the Film, Incorporating the Two One-Act Plays Which Suggested It: 27 Wagons Full of Cotton and The Long Stay Cut Short; or, The Unsatisfactory Supper. New York, New Directions, 1956; as *Baby Doll: The Script for the Film*, London, Secker and Warburg, 1957.
Garden District: Something Unspoken, Suddenly Last Summer (produced New York and London, 1958). New York, New Directions, 1958; London, Secker and Warburg, 1959.
The Fugitive Kind: Original Play Title: Orpheus Descending (screenplay). New York, New American Library, 1958.
A Perfect Analysis Given by a Parrot (produced New York, 1976; London, 1978). New York, Dramatists Play Service, 1958.
The Enemy: Time, in *Theatre* (New York), March 1959.
The Night of the Iguana (produced Spoleto, Italy, 1959; revised version, produced New York, 1961; Croydon, Surrey, and London, 1965). New York, New Directions, 1962; London, Secker and Warburg, 1963.
Period of Adjustment: High Point over a Cavern: A Serious Comedy (produced Miami, 1959; New York, 1960; Bristol, 1961; London, 1962). New York, New Directions, 1960; London, Secker and Warburg, 1961.
To Heaven in a Golden Coach (produced Bromley, Kent, 1961).
The Milk Train Doesn't Stop Here Anymore (produced Spoleto, Italy, 1962; revised versions, produced New York, 1962; Abington, West Virginia, 1963; New York, 1964; London, 1968). New York, New Directions, and London, Secker and Warburg, 1964.
Slapstick Tragedy (*The Mutilated* and *The Gnädiges Fräulein*) (produced New York, 1966). New York, Dramatists Play Service, 2 vols., 1967; revised version of *The Gnädiges Fräulein*, as *The Latter Days of a Celebrated Soubrette* (produced New York, 1974).
Kingdom of Earth, in *Esquire* (New York), February 1967; revised version, as *Kingdom of Earth: The Seven Descents of Myrtle* (produced New York, 1968; Bristol, 1978). New York, New Directions, 1968.
The Two Character Play (produced London, 1967; revised version, produced London, 1969). New York, New Directions, 1969; revised version, as *Out Cry* (produced Chicago; 1971, New York, 1973), New Directions, 1973; revised version (produced New York, 1974).
In the Bar of a Tokyo Hotel (produced New York, 1969; London, 1971). New York, Dramatists Play Service, 1969.
I Can't Imagine Tomorrow (televised, 1970; produced London, 1976; New York, 1978). Included in *Dragon Country*, 1970.
Dragon Country: A Book of Plays (includes *In the Bar of a Tokyo*

Hotel; *I Rise in Flame, Cried the Phoenix*; *The Mutilated*; *I Can't Imagine Tomorrow*; *Confessional*; *The Frosted Glass Coffin*; *The Gnädiges Fräulein*; and *A Perfect Analysis Given by a Parrot*). New York, New Directions, 1970.

Tennessee Laughs: Three One Act Plays (*Some Problems for the Moose Lodge*; *A Perfect Analysis Given by a Parrot*; *The Frosted Glass Coffin*) (produced Chicago, 1980). *The Frosted Glass Coffin* and *A Perfect Analysis Given by a Parrot* included in *Dragon Country*, 1970.

Senso, with Paul Bowles, in *Two Screenplays*, by Luigi Visconti. New York, Orion Press, 1970.

A Streetcar Named Desire (screenplay), in *Film Scripts One*, edited by George P. Garrett, O.B. Harrison, Jr., and Jane Gelfann. New York, Appleton Century Crofts, 1971.

Small Craft Warnings (produced New York, 1972; London, 1973). New York, Dramatists Play Service, 1972; London, Secker and Warburg, 1973.

The Theatre of Tennessee Williams:

I. *Battle of Angels*, *A Streetcar Named Desire*, *The Glass Menagerie*. New York, New Directions, 1972.

II. *The Eccentricities of a Nightingale*, *Summer and Smoke*, *The Rose Tattoo*, *Camino Real*. New York, New Directions, 1972.

III. *Cat on a Hot Tin Roof*, *Orpheus Descending*, *Suddenly Last Summer*. New York, New Directions, 1972.

IV. *Sweet Bird of Youth*, *Period of Adjustment*, *Night of the Iguana*. New York, New Directions, 1972.

V. *The Milk Train Doesn't Stop Here Anymore*; *Kingdom of Earth*, revised version; *Small Craft Warnings*; *The Two Character Play*, revised version. New York, New Directions, 1976.

VI. *27 Wagons Full of Cotton and Other One Act Plays* (includes *The Unsatisfactory Supper*, *Steps Must Be Gentle*, *The Demolition Downtown: Count Ten in Arabic*). New York, New Directions, 1981.

VII. *Dragon Country*, *Lifeboat Drill*, *Now the Cats with Jewelled Claws*, *Now the Peaceable Kingdom*. New York, New Directions, 1981.

The Red Devil Battery Sign (produced Boston and New York, 1974; revised version, produced Vienna, 1976; London, 1977; Vancouver, 1980).

Demolition Downtown: Count Ten in Arabic—Then Run (produced London, 1976). Included in *The Theatre of Tennessee Williams VI*, 1981.

This Is an Entertainment (produced San Francisco, 1976).

Tiger Tail (produced Atlanta, 1978).

Vieux Carré (produced Nottingham and London, 1978; New York, 1979). New York, New Directions, 1979.

Lifeboat Drill (produced New York, 1979). Included in *The Theatre of Tennessee Williams VII*, 1981.

A Lovely Sunday for Creve Coeur (produced New York, 1979). New York, New Directions, 1980.

Kirche, Kütchen, und Kinder (produced New York, 1980).

Clothes for a Summer Hotel (produced Washington, D.C., and New York, 1980).

Will Mr. Merriwether Return from Memphis? (produced Key West, Florida, 1980).

A House Not Meant to Stand (produced New York, 1981).

Screenplays: *Senso* (*The Wanton Countess*; English dialogue, with Paul Bowles), 1949; *The Glass Menagerie*, with Peter Berneis, 1950; *A Streetcar Named Desire*, with Oscar Saul, 1951; *The Rose Tattoo*, with Hal Kanter, 1955; *Baby Doll*, 1956; *Suddenly Last Summer*, with Gore Vidal, 1960; *The Fugitive Kind*, with Meade Roberts, 1960; *Boom*, 1968.

Television Plays: *I Can't Imagine Tomorrow*, 1970; *Stopped Rocking*, 1975.

Verse

Five Young American Poets, with others. New York, New Directions, 1944.

In the Winter of Cities: Poems. New York, New Directions, 1956.

Androgyne, Mon Amour. New York, New Directions, 1977.

Other

Memoirs. New York, Doubleday, 1975; London, W.H. Allen, 1976.

Tennessee Williams' Letters to Donald Windham 1940-1965, edited by Windham. Privately printed, 1976; New York, Holt Rinehart, 1977.

Where I Live: Selected Essays, edited by Christine R. Day and Bob Woods. New York, New Directions, 1978.

*

Bibliography: *Tennessee Williams: A Bibliography* by Drewey W. Gunn, Metuchen, New Jersey, Scarecrow Press, 1980.

Critical Studies (selection): *Tennessee Williams* by Signi L. Falk, New York, Twayne, 1961, revised edition, 1979; *Tennessee Williams: The Man and His Work* by Benjamin Nelson, New York, Obolensky, and London, Owen, 1961; *Tennessee Williams, Rebellious Puritan* by Nancy Tischler, New York, Citadel Press, 1961; *The Broken World of Tennessee Williams* by Esther Jackson, Madison, University of Wisconsin Press, 1965; *Tennessee Williams* by Gerald Weales, Minneapolis, University of Minnesota Press, 1965; *Tennessee Williams: A Tribute* edited by Jac Tharpe, Jackson, University Press of Mississippi, 1977; *Tennessee Williams: A Collection of Critical Essays* edited by Stephen S. Stanton, Englewood Cliffs, New Jersey, Prentice Hall, 1977; *The World of Tennessee Williams* edited by Richard Freeman Leavitt, New York, Putnam, and London, W.H. Allen, 1978.

* * *

...when you attempt to set those details
down in a tale, some measure of obscurity
or indirection is called for to provide the same,
or even approximate, softening effect that
existence in time gives to those gross elements
in the life itself.

"Hard Candy"

Tennessee Williams's fiction is a series of euphemisms for situations actually less shocking than these disguises imply. Sometimes the language merely dresses up a physical fact: Mrs. Stone's domination by "the moon of pause." More often, the commonplace becomes mythic: "Desire and the Black Masseur" (*One Arm*), perhaps Williams's best-known story, turns a Turkish bath into an arena for religious passion and the masochistic Anthony Burns into an actual eucharist, while a Lenten crowd of disarrayed celebrants underlines the symbolism. The masturbation scene of "One Arm" transforms a mutilated hustler who "looked like a broken statue of Apollo" into a Christ holding a literal eternity in the palm of his hand: "Too late, the resurrection." His tardy recognition of the divinity of his sex echoes Lawrence's phallic Christ in "The Man Who Died" crying "I have risen." Despite the explicit language and sex of the recent stories in *Eight Mortal Ladies Possessed*, Williams continues coy euphemism in a title like "Miss Coynte of Greene" and uses a symbolic antique shop to suggest the decline of the South, and an annunciating angel to help the heroine live up to the promise of her name. Williams seems unable to resist weighting even a shaggy dog story with cosmic significance.

Thus, Williams's fiction, especially *One Arm* and *The Roman Spring of Mrs. Stone*, aims high and occasionally justifies its aspiratioins in an allegorical tale like "The Poet," which traces the last days of a pied piper for sexually awakening adolescents, a more cosmic version of Sebastian in the play *Suddenly Last Summer.* The arresting opening sentence—"The poet distilled his own liquor and had become so accomplished in this art that he could produce a fermented drink from almost any kind of organic matter"—works so well as a metaphor for the poet's craft that the more literal second sentence is momentarily shocking, though the story manages to sustain both levels: "He carried it in a flask...." Supported by only skeletal symbolic details, this work is the best of Williams's poet stories like "The Angel in the Alcove" and "The Important Thing" and dramatizes the dying artist's triumphant, if transient, power to incorporate death into his vision, an important theme in Williams.

Williams's later dramatization of some of his stories perhaps justifies their minimal dialogue and tendency toward summarized action, and suggests that they were either sketches for future plays or exercises in which the developing dramatist sought his real talent. Occasionally the stories have virtues that do not translate to drama: "Portrait of a Girl in Glass," when transformed to *The Glass Menagerie*, loses the wonderful detail of Laura's constant rereading of *Freckles*, the key index to her character. The stories also reveal the complex genesis of later plays: the name and some characteristics of Oliver Winemiller in "One Arm" apparently fuse with those of Alma Tutwiler in "The Yellow Bird" and undergo yet further changes in *The Eccentricities of a Nightingale* and *Summer and Smoke.*

Like his stories, Williams's novel *The Roman Spring of Mrs. Stone* also suffers from inadequate dramatization. The narrative's negative summary of the heroine's character and motivations does not mesh with what seems a normal post-menopausal awakening to sexuality and to the charms of a young Roman gigolo and does not validate the charge of an angry friend that Mrs. Stone is a female "Tiberius." Despite these flaws, however, the book is sufficiently engrossing to generate disturbing questions. How can Mrs. Stone be simultaneously a predatory monster constantly equated to a voracious bird of prey and an obvious victim of both her susceptibility and the centuries of Roman duplicity objectified in the Contessa who supplies young men to wealthy foreigners? (Even James's Daisy Miller faced nothing so formidable.) The book lacks the irony necessary to resolve these contradictory views of Mrs. Stone. Is the beautiful ubiquitous young man who reveals his intentions by urinating in public merely another stage in Mrs. Stone's "corruption" or an angel of death, as some hints suggest? (In the latter role, he seems to fuse with the wandering poet Jimmy Dobyne—"anybody" spelled backwards?—who successfully tries to comfort/dupe an even older American lady in "Man Bring This Up Road" and, ultimately, becomes a poet/Christ/death-angel in the various versions of the play *The Milk Train Doesn't Stop Here Anymore.*) Whether Mrs. Stone merits laughter or compassion, she commands enough attention to make these questions pertinent.

Less ambitious in conception than these earlier works are those collected as *Hard Candy.* The title story and "The Mysteries of the Joy Rio" employ the same gallery of a decaying movie theater as a setting for furtive homosexual encounters. Freed of the mythic parallels of "One Arm," these pieces proceed straightforwardly, despite apologetic comments on sex and a style occasionally as furtive as the characters. "Mysteries," in particular, creates a moving picture of the last act of an enduring homosexual union, reminiscent of McCullers's *The Heart Is a Lonely Hunter*, and develops a favorite Williams theme of love as the force mitigating the pain of death. "The Vine" and "Two on a Party" skillfully depict symbiotic relationships that salvage would-be losers, a married couple in "Vine" and a homosexual and an aging playgirl in "Party." Even in the "world's biggest necropolis," New York, the mutually lacerating lesbian relationship of "Happy August the Tenth" still satisfies enough to make the heroine, Elphinstone, choose life over death by following her lover's nagging advice to "begin her polio shots despite her childish dread of the prick of the needle." Elphinstone's mother, one of a group of tyrannical and messily dying older women who dominate many stories in *Eight Mortal Ladies Possessed*, sufficiently embodies the horror of solitary death to make plausible the ludicrous and grotesque sexual antics of the other characters.

This more relaxed mood carries over into *The Knightly Quest*, especially in "Grand," a deftly understated reminiscence of a grandmother's long life and painful death. "Mama's Old Stucco House" continues the symbiosis of "Vine" and "Party," in uniting a homosexual southern artist and his young Negro maid. While "The Kingdom of Earth," which became the play *The Seven Descents of Myrtle*, overdoes a broadly comic treatment of sex, the narrator, Chicken, is an amusing version of Williams's heterosexual boor, almost a parody of Stanley Kowalski, like Billy Spangle in the novella "The Knightly Quest." However, despite Billy's presence, "Quest," a paranoid vision of a conformist, incipiently fascistic America, remains unfocused, though there are some funny moments, and the improbable happy ending is almost a send-up of the entire piece. Ironically, it is the imperceptive husband in "Vine" who articulates this growing freedom from pretension and apology in Williams's later fiction: "No wonder people who lived those obscenely solitary lives did things while sober that *you* only did when drunk...."

The "*distinguished* failed writer" who narrates Williams's novel *Moise and the World of Reason* echoes this attitude with prissy irony: "Well, I'm a Southerner from a small town and it's traditional among those of such origin to be politely silent about whatever oddities they observe in the life styles and mannerisms of those who entertain them." A suicidal homosexual abandoned by his lover, the writer derives his only emotional strengh from a friendship with the unfashionable painter Moise, a woman totally committed to the world of "unreason" and art: "My linseed oil, gone, gone, and as for my brushes, well, I can paint with my fingers...." When the narrator rejects the comparative security of a liaison with the elderly dramatist, who seems a grim image of the future, to choose life with Moise, they enjoy a metaphysically weighted orgy with the two photographers interviewing Moise. Unfortunately, the novel wavers between presenting this conclusion as a serious triumph of the artistically pure or as parody. Further, *Moise* neither develops believable characters, nor gives coherence to its lengthy discussions of art and imagination. But these serious flaws fail to destroy the arresting mood of rage uniting the violence and sex. Though the obsessive grotesqueness of Williams's material creates a very limited world, this novel and some stories occasionally support, with the effect of frightening inevitably, the truth that the scatalogical is the only proof of the existence it degrades.

—Burton Kendle

WILLIAMS, Wirt (Alfred, Jr.). American. Born in Goodman, Mississippi, 21 August 1921. Educated at Delta College, Cleveland, Mississippi, 1937-40, B.A. in English and American literature 1940; Louisiana State University, Baton Rouge, 1940-41, M.A. in journalism 1941; University of Iowa, Iowa City, 1950-53, Ph.D. in English and American literature 1953. Served in the United States Navy, 1942-46: Gunnery Officer and Assistant Gunnery Officer, *U.S.S. Decatur*, 1942-44; Executive Officer and Navigator, 1944-45, and Commanding Officer, 1945-46, *U.S.S. LSM 437*; since 1954, Lieutenant-Commander, United States Naval Reserve. Married Ann Meredith in 1954; one child. Correspondent, Associated Press, Cleveland, Mississippi, 1938-40; News Editor, 1941-42, and capitol correspondent, 1946, *Shreveport Times*, Louisiana; reporter, special writer and City Editor, *New Orleans Item*, 1946-49. Assistant Professor, 1953-57, Associate Professor, 1957-60, and since 1960, Professor of English, California State University, Los Angeles. Guest Literary Editor, *Los Angeles Times*, 1960-61, 1968. Recipient: ABC Award, for reporting, 1949; Huntington Hartford Fellowship, 1958. Address: 2022 Avenue of the Trees, Carlsbad, California 92008, U.S.A.

PUBLICATIONS

Novels

The Enemy. Boston, Houghton Mifflin, 1951; London, Corgi, 1967.
Love in a Windy Space. New York, Reynal, 1957.
Ada Dallas. New York, McGraw Hill, 1959; London, Muller, 1960.
A Passage of Hawks. New York, McGraw Hill, 1963; London, Muller, 1964.
The Trojans. Boston, Little Brown, 1966; London, Barrie and Rockliff, 1967.
The Far Side. New York, Horizon Press, 1972; London, Bantam, 1976.

Uncollected Short Stories

Attack by Starlight," in *New Narratives 1944*, edited by Blanche Williams. New York, Appleton Century, 1944.
"The Unbeaten," in *Statement* (Los Angeles), Winter 1953.

Other

Translator, *The Blue Angel*, by Heinrich Mann. New York, New American Library, 1959.

*

Manuscript Collection: Boston University.

Critical Studies: by Robert Kirsch, in the *Los Angeles Times*, 8 October 1959 and 17 December 1966; *The Recent Political Novel in America* by Joseph Blotner, Austin, University of Texas Press, 1966; John Raymond, in *Punch* (London), 18 August 1967; "Tragic Themes in Three Novels by Wirt Williams" by Gay Chow, unpublished dissertation, State College, Mississippi State University, 1977.

Wirt Williams comments:

A novelist should really keep his mouth shut about his work. His explanation of what he is about limits the work fatally, and necessarily is so incomplete as to be downright false. Even the most self-conscious writer *knows* only a small part of what he has done. The great artificer is the subconscious, which creates those recurring patterns of structure and symbol that tell what the writer really means. His work is only as strong as the force of that subconscious—vision, if you will.

Still and all, the conscious is a partner, too, and up to a point, the more thoroughly the writer plans, the better are his chances of giving the subpsyche a full free run. So he has at least some idea of what he is up to, and perhaps at least once he ought to say. For better or for worse, I am an extremely self-conscious writer: I can never quite forget technical principles of the art of fiction that I learned, or at least had explained to me, in the classroom—broadly speaking, the principles of Flaubert and particularly of Hemingway. The central conception of the Imagist poets (which I took from Hemingway without at first knowing where he got it) has been unquestionably the biggest force operating on, and in, my fiction. This conception is (put much too simply) that the writer sends emotion and idea, and makes reality, through sharp, hard pictures—undiluted by reflection or rhetoric. Almost paradoxically, the other "official" moderns I have learned from have been, in language, working the other side of the street—Conrad, Faulkner, and more lately Jean-Paul Sartre.

I teach a seminar in tragedy and once read a great deal of formalistic (academic) criticism, and what I write has been marked by those exposures, also.

So what I *think* I am saying, most of the time, is that we define our lives by what we do in the face of the universal and inescapable catastrophe. Or that we must take our own meaning in an operationally hostile universe without apparent meaning. The theme is scarcely original: no theme is, but this one is as old as tragedy. At the same time, nuanced differently in each case, it seems to be the pervasive statement of 20th-century fiction.

My first novels were an attempt to beat personal experience into fictional form. *The Enemy* is about destroyers and aircraft hunting submarines they never see in the North Atlantic in World War II. Some saw it as a paraphrase of Camus's central metaphor—Sisyphus rolling the stone up the hill. Fair enough, but I had never read Camus at the time I wrote it, and I think my pattern was stronger for my ignorance. *Love in a Windy Space* was a love story set in Louisiana—a simple enough tragedy, with a couple of fables beneath about the state of the South and of the forlorn man. *Ada Dallas* was concerned with Louisiana politics (which I had covered as a political correspondent), was awarely tragic, and was invested with the familiar ethical fable.

No longer finding my own experience that interesting, now I make up or find designs on the outside, and hope that by analogy, the essence of my experience will somehow infuse that design. *A Passage of Hawks*, a deliberately Jacobean story of murder and wickedness, was suggested by T.S. Eliot's examination of Thomas Middleton's *The Changeling*—an examination, of course, far more interesting than the play. *The Trojans* was a multi-purposed attempt to say something about the relationship between the artist and the world, to put forward a species of existentialism, to explore all sorts of varieties of experience, and to come up with some interesting information about motion pictures. Its subject matter in the narrowest sense came from recent history of that industry.

The day of the publisher as patron has been over for some time, and if a novelist is to be heard (that is to say, published) he must offer one level of appeal—among all his levels of statement—to a large and completely non-literary audience. I have accepted the condition and find it just: there are many fine things a novelist can do, but the finest of all is to tell a wonderful story. The abiding, unanswerable question, of course, is: wonderful to whom?

* * *

Wirt Williams is a pure example of the American novelist who came to literary maturity shortly after World War II. He is well-grounded in criticism and theory; he teaches and is fluent in the history of the genre. His literary forebears are writers in the grand traditions of prose fiction: Flaubert, Conrad, James, Hemingway. Understandably his expectation for all prose fiction is lofty; everywhere in his own work the alignments of image, action, character, and meaning are exact. Seen together his works make a larger statement than the separate titles.

From a brilliant first novel (*The Enemy*) to a probable middle-ground of development (*The Trojans*), the overall pattern is clear: *The Enemy* concerns the author's line-experience in North Atlantic anti-submarine warfare; *The Trojans* concerns art and the movie industry and is narrated from a fully dramatic perspective by a cerebral writer/artist. The motif of a protagonist overwhelmed by tragic or near-tragic circumstances often occurs; the ancillary literary resources of the novels stem variously from fable, myth, Jacobean drama, and others. In summary, the literary resources of the novels are extraordinary.

Intentionally, characterization, plot-structure, and chronology are not notably experimental. Typically, a story unfolds from multiple points of view; the author's attitude towards his materials is seldom extreme although irony, especially in dialogue, reoccurs. Thus all the novels are "open," public; there is little obscurity of either language or motivation. Williams acknowledges the influence of his sometimes literary correspondent, Ernest Hemingway.

The prose is taut, informational, and well-calculated. The finest language occurs in brief, descriptive passages of the sea, the rural South, or the city at dawn or at night. From these passages emerges a pervasive atmosphere; so great is this strength that a delicately controlled atmosphere may become an important protagonist in the story. Williams deals best with large effects; his unit of comparison is the whole novel.

To place the novels in a mainstream of American literature calls for other, extrinsic considerations. For example, Williams was born and raised in Mississippi, in the Black Belt—a region of America which changed almost not at all until after World War II. His father was a Southern-trained classical historian; on occasion Williams taught his father's classes in Roman history. In addition to this classical background, and before he completed the Ph.D. in literary studies, Williams was a newspaperman in New Orleans. *Love in a Windy Place*, *A Passage of Hawks*, and *Ada Dallas* (also a film) are concerned with the provinciality, the passions, and enigmas of the South.

Not surprisingly, therefore, many of the protagonists are concerned with status, integrity of motive, and money; their often unconscious search for the lost "classical" values of valor, fidelity, friendship, and honor is a continuing criticism of modernity. These women and men come from a felt or remembered tradition and order; they are fated to live among the ruins of the 20th century. Typically these characters of above-average intelligence and education remain isolated or unresolved in the midst of apparent affluence. Too often the resolution they find is in personal oblivion, death, or patrician acceptance. Taken together, these concerns and attitudes suggest the novels are in the mainstream of the American novel of manners, the Romance of large-scale enterprise, the film industry and state-capitol politics included.

—James B. Hall

WILLINGHAM, Calder (Baynard, Jr.). American. Born in Atlanta, Georgia, 23 December 1922. Educated at The Citadel, Charleston, South Carolina, 1940-41; University of Virginia, Charlottesville, 1941-43. Married 1) Helene Rothenberg in 1945 (divorced, 1951), one son; 2) Jane Marie Bennett in 1953, three sons and two daughters. Recipient: Writers Guild of America West Award, for screenplay, 1968. Address: 7 West 51st Street, New York, New York 10019, U.S.A.

PUBLICATIONS

Novels

End as a Man. New York, Vanguard Press, 1947; London, Lehmann, 1952.
Geraldine Bradshaw. New York, Vanguard Press, 1950; revised edition, London, Barker, 1964.
Reach to the Stars. New York, Vanguard Press, 1951; London, Barker, 1965.
Natural Child. New York, Dial Press, 1952.
To Eat a Peach. New York, Dial Press, 1955; London, Mayflower, 1966.
Eternal Fire. New York, Vanguard Press, and London, Barker, 1963.
Providence Island. New York, Vanguard Press, and London, Hart Davis, 1969.
Rambling Rose. New York, Delacorte Press, 1972; London, Hart Davis MacGibbon, 1973.
The Big Nickel. New York, Dial Press, 1975; London, Hart Davis MacGibbon, 1976.
The Building of Venus Four. New York, Manor, 1977.

Short Stories

The Gates of Hell. New York, Vanguard Press, 1951; London, Mayflower, 1966.

Uncollected Short Stories

"What Star So Humble," in *New Yorker*, 16 January 1965.
"A Clowny Night in the Red-Eyed World," in *Playboy* (Chicago), March 1965.

Plays

End as a Man, adaptation of his own novel (produced New York, 1953).

Screenplays: *Paths of Glory*, with Stanley Kubrick and Jim Thompson, 1957; *The Strange One*, 1957; *The Vikings*, with Dale Wasserman, 1958; *One-Eyed Jacks*, with Guy Trosper, 1961; *The Graduate*, with Buck Henry, 1967; *Little Big Man*, 1970; *Thieves Like Us*, with Joan Tewkesbury, 1974.

*

Calder Willingham comments:

(1972) At the beginning of my career, I was contemptuous and skeptical of the typical "best-seller" that pandered to public fantasies, wish-fulfillment, class or regional or national prejudices, et cetera. As my career progressed, I became equally contemptuous and skeptical of the typical "literary" novel that pandered to the aesthetic dicta and passing fashions of an intellectual elite. Thus, I have contrived as a novelist to fall cleverly between two stools: my work in general has dissatisfied or distressed the mass best-seller audience and at the same time has infuriated or bemused the so-called literary audience. Lonely and awkward as it is down here between these stools, I like to think of my achievement as a considerable and perhaps even unique feat on the current writing scene.

Fortunately, this fall between stools has not been unqualified; certain of my novels have been highly praised by the critical and certain of them have reached a substantial audience. But to support my large family through the years it has been necessary for me to resort to the writing of screenplays. There has been too much disturbing reality and irony in my novels for them to be generally acceptable as escapist pap for a mass audience and I break far too many rules of literary fashion (practically all in fact) for my work to appear of any great significance to the intelligentsia. I would rather this be so than to have written wish-fulfillment trash or the tedious, inhuman, unreadable literary monstrosities now fashionable.

The critical fraternity, I am afraid, has not known what on earth to make of my writing. I have used ironic contradiction and seemingly cruel humor in ways that are singular—or were singular, let us say; much of so-called modern "black comedy" seems to have been inspired by some off-hand stories I wrote 20 or 25 years ago. But also (and here the puzzlement of my critics deepens) my principal novels have been optimistic, fond of their characters, affirmative, hopeful, joyous toward life. A bewildering thing indeed, this. How can a man perceive the terrors and horrors of life, and still remain an optimist able to love his fellow creatures? I would grant it takes more courage and heart than can be contained in the critical faculty, which in blind cowardice can only conclude that such a man must be a liar or a fraud or a maddening incomprehensible idiot. I certainly have never yet seen any truly intelligent detailed criticism of my writing and I do not expect it to appear in my lifetime and this pleases me. So long as I can keep the analytical brethren off-balance and bewildered, I know I myself am crossing the wire.

As for my movie work, I do not regard this as real writing of my own, because here my sensibility is at the tender mercies of those with whom I am associated. The only way I could make a motion picture truly my own would be to produce and direct it as well as write it. I am looking for an insane millionaire to give me the money to make a really great film. In the meanwhile I cannot take with genuine seriousness any of the films on which I have worked.

As for the theatre, to me the theatre is an amusement rather than a major form, no doubt because my background as a novelist causes the medium to seem to me too restrictive. Besides, poetry is not my forte but rather the inter-play of characters in time and space, i.e., classic narrative.

My real work has been as a novelist and that work readily falls into three periods. The first is that of my initial novel, *End as a Man*, an adolescent effort marked by youthful fury and a rather simplistic view of the human condition. The second is the *Geraldine Bradshaw* period ending with *To Eat a Peach*—it was I suppose during this period that I (according to *The New Yorker*) "inadvertently fathered black comedy." The third period is that of my maturity and it has seen thus far publication of two major efforts, *Eternal Fire* and *Providence Island*. Doubtful as I am of the literary world, it has nonetheless been a profound astonishment to me that these novels have not received far greater recognition. I expect they will someday; it is my belief I put more of whatever gifts I have into these books than all my other work combined. Thus, on this Christmas Eve in snowy New Hampshire in this the year of Our Lord 1970, I look back on my struggle as a novelist with both frustration and satisfaction even as I plan to return to the bitter fray and write another book or two, God willing.

*   *   *

The simplest and possibly truest way to characterize the fiction of Calder Willingham is to call it the work of a 20th-century Fielding, for Willingham is a comic chronicler of iniquity, a creator of mock-novels, an enemy of hypocrisy who turns its lies and pretenses back on themselves, and a moral seer who is able to espy the good always and only in the midst of a chaos of vice and folly. His first novel, *End as a Man*, revealed as much, but the novels (and stories) which have followed it have shown him to be a Fielding possessed of such a strong sense of the absurd, of the natural disorder of being, that he has discarded even conventional form in his search for an artistic expression of the real and living world. Traditional genres collapse in his hands like a shack in a hurricane and at the same time open out to reveal the free imaginative source of all form—literary and artistic forms and, in fact, the good, the true, and the beautiful.

His attack on the ponderous seriousness of the modern novel and short story has led him away from the path that seemed to open out from the success of his first novel. The very form of the serious novel failed him. He abandoned his plan to write a trilogy constructed from the lives of hotel bellmen after he had finished and published the first two volumes, *Geraldine Bradshaw* and *Reach to the Stars*. (He did revise the first volume for its English publication in 1964 so that it could stand alone, but, at the same time, he referred to the second as "a literary exercise.") The narrator of his next novel, *Natural Child*, decides at the end that neither he nor any other of the characters could have written such a book and that "Maybe the cat wrote it." *To Eat a Peach*, his fifth novel, professes to be the tale of "a happy little summer in the mountains down in the deep South where the dogwood and the sycamore grow, and the sun shines all day long, when it isn't raining." His novels turn into tall tales, his characters become caricatures, and the short stories in *The Gates of Hell* are more often than not "anti-stories." They collapse into playlets or take the form of brief and gloriously mindless essays. *Providence Island*, Willingham's longest novel, closes by calling itself "a seashell tale." *Rambling Rose* is a wonderfully comic and loving tale about a 19-year-old country girl who comes to work during the Great Depression for a family remarkably like Willingham's own. The novel hovers between fiction and memory, with Willingham admitting that the family is "based on real people who lived in this world," but adding "unequivocally and even humbly that the girls who worked for my family...were of excellent moral character and bore no resemblance whatsoever to the title character of this novel." The forms fail him, but he finds life in the absence of form, creates novels and stories that defy form.

Willingham's finest novel (and one of the most under-rated of modern American novels), *Eternal Fire*, is on the one hand a mock "Southern" novel full of sound and fury, and on the other a serious and meaningful novel expressing a moral sense which grows from an acceptance of the world with all its chaos and a forgiveness of it. One of its villans, Harry Diadem, is both as comical and as convincingly evil as any character in modern literature, but its simple hero manages to face up to the inescapable presence of evil even in the girl he loves, his "fallen angel," and to emerge "from eternal fire into manhood."

To be a man is all Willingham asks of any of us—a man who sees honestly what it is to be a man and nonetheless accepts and affirms his manhood. His fiction, which calls everything into question, even and perhaps especially itself, offers as answer only the need to live in the world that we see and to dare to see the world in which we live. And that, laughably, is enough.

—R.H.W. Dillard

WILSON, Angus (Frank Johnstone). British. Born in Bexhill, Sussex, 11 August 1913. Educated at Westminster School, London, 1927-31; Merton College, Oxford, B.A. (honours) in medieval and modern history 1936. Served in the Foreign Office, 1942-46. Staff Member, British Museum, London, 1937-55: Deputy Superintendent of the Reading Room, 1949-55. Lecturer, 1963-66, Professor of English Literature, 1966-78, and since 1978, Professor Emeritus, University of East Anglia, Norwich. Ewing Lecturer, University of California at Los Angeles, 1960; Bergen Lecturer, Yale University, New Haven, Connecticut, 1960; Moody Lecturer, University of Chicago, 1960; Northcliffe Lecturer, University College, London, 1961; Leslie Stephen Lecturer, Cambridge University, 1962-63; Beckman Professor, University of California, Berkeley, 1967; John Hinkley Visiting Professor, Johns Hopkins University, Baltimore, 1974; Visiting Professor, University of Delaware, Newark, 1977, 1980, University of Iowa, Iowa City, 1978, Georgia State University Atlanta, 1979, University of Michigan, Ann Arbor, 1979, and University of Minnesota, Minneapolis, 1980. Member of the Committee, Royal Literary Fund, 1966; Member of the Arts Council of Great Britain, 1966-69; Chairman, National Book League, London, 1971-74; President, Dickens Fellowship, London, 1974-75. Recipient: Black Memorial Prize, 1959; Prix de Meilleur Roman Etranger, 1960; *Yorkshire Post* Award, for non-fiction, 1971. D.Litt.: University of Leicester, 1978; University of East Anglia, 1979; University of Liverpool, 1979. Honorary Fellow, Cowell College, University of California, Santa Cruz, 1968. Fellow, 1958, and Companion of Literature, 1972, Royal Society of Literature; Honorary Fellow, American Academy, 1980. C.B.E. (Commander, Order of the British Empire), 1968. Knighted, 1980. Address: Felsham Woodside, Bradfield St. George, Bury St. Edmund's, Suffolk, England.

PUBLICATIONS

Novels

Hemlock and After. London, Secker and Warburg, and New York, Viking Press, 1952.
Anglo-Saxon Attitudes. London, Secker and Warburg, and New York, Viking Press, 1956.
The Middle Age of Mrs. Eliot. London, Secker and Warburg, 1958; New York, Viking Press, 1959.
The Old Men at the Zoo. London, Secker and Warburg, and New York, Viking Press, 1961.
Late Call. London, Secker and Warburg, 1964; New York, Viking Press, 1965.
No Laughing Matter. London, Secker and Warburg, and New York, Viking Press, 1967.
As If by Magic. London, Secker and Warburg, and New York, Viking Press, 1973.
Setting the World on Fire. London, Secker and Warburg, and New York, Viking Press, 1980.

Short Stories

The Wrong Set and Other Stories. London, Secker and Warburg, 1949; New York, Morrow, 1950.
Such Darling Dodos and Other Stories. London, Secker and Warburg, 1950; New York, Morrow, 1951.
A Bit off the Map and Other Stories. London, Secker and Warburg, and New York, Viking Press, 1957.
Death Dance: Twenty-Five Short Stories. New York, Viking Press, 1969.

Play

The Mulberry Bush (produced London, 1956). London, Secker and Warburg, 1956.

Other

Emile Zola: An Introductory Study of His Novels. London, Secker and Warburg and New York, Morrow, 1952; revised edition, Secker and Warburg, 1965.
For Whom the Cloche Tolls: A Scrapbook of the Twenties, illustrated by Philippe Jullian. London, Methuen, and New York, Curtis, 1953.
The Wild Garden; or, Speaking of Writing. Berkeley, University of California Press, and London, Secker and Warburg, 1963.
Tempo: The Impact of Television on the Arts. London, Studio Vista, 1964; Chester Springs, Pennsylvania, Dufour, 1966.
The World of Charles Dickens. London, Secker and Warburg, and New York, Viking Press, 1970.
Dickens Memorial Lecture 1970, with Kathleen Tillotson and Sylvère Monad. London, Dickens Fellowship, 1970.
The Naughty Nineties. London, Eyre Methuen, 1976.
The Strange Ride of Rudyard Kipling: His Life and Works. London, Secker and Warburg, 1977; New York, Viking Press, 1978.

Editor, *A Maugham Twelve*, by W. Somerset Maugham. London, Heinemann, 1966.
Editor, *Cakes and Ale, and Twelve Short Stories*, by W. Somerset Maugham. New York, Doubleday, 1967.
Editor, *Writers of East Anglia.* London, Secker and Warburg, 1977.

*

Manuscript Collection: University of Iowa, Iowa City.

Critical Studies: *The Free Spirit* by C.B. Cox, London, Oxford University Press, 1963; *Angus Wilson* by Jay Halio, Edinburgh, Oliver and Boyd, 1964; *Angus Wilson* by K.W. Gransden, London, Longman, 1969; "*The Middle Age of Mrs. Eliot* and *Late Call*" by Valerie Shaw, in *Critical Quarterly* (London), Spring 1970; *Harvest of a Quiet Eye: The Novel of Compassion* by James Gindin, Bloomington, University of Indiana Press, 1971; *Angus Wilson: Mimic and Moralist* by Peter Faulkner, New York, Viking Press, 1980.

Angus Wilson comments:

(1972) I shall confine this statement to noting certain received critical ideas about my work that seem to me misleading, or, at the very best, marginal. I have not seen the critical notice to appear with this statement nor do I know who is its author. If what I say disagrees with that notice, it is only necessary to point out that some people find authors' views of their own work illuminating, others misleading. The choice is with the reader.

1) My work is very frequently compared to that of E.M. Forster. In some ways I am, of course, flattered and gratified. It is also true that some of my early short stories, *Hemlock and After*, and above all my play, *The Mulberry Bush*, contain the sort of critique of liberal humanism that is to be found in Forster's novels, above all in *Howards End.* But there have always been wide divergences—above all in my deep distrust of money, property, and the sort of responsibility that goes with them; in my dislike of sentimentalism about the primitive, the unsophisticated, and the physically strong; in my acceptance, in general, of the city (London) as having values in many ways superior to, certainly equal with, the country; on the other hand in my placing great importance upon a close relation with animal and plant life (see my continuous concern with animal and flower imagery); in my acceptance of violence and uncontrolled passion as being in certain occasions a good; above all, in my open statement of the possibility of homosexual happiness within a conventional framework and my consequent, I believe, greater power of identifying truly sympathetically with my women characters. None of this is an attempt to suggest equality with Forster's work, only to underline differences, and to note a certain distaste that I feel for it—notably in the sentimentalization of Stephen Wonham, the treatment of Leonard and Jackie Bast (indeed what seems to me the whole coldhearted, withdrawn, judging quality of *Howards End*); nor do I share Forster's evolutionary optimism expressed by the end of *Howards End.* It seems to me that I am at once a more impulsive, a more bitchy, and a more compassionate author than E.M. Forster—that my humanism has less high hope for the future but more acceptance and liking for human beings as they are. I cannot share or hope to attain his curious mixture of cunning, love, withdrawal, and passivity. Of course, I except the wonderful *Passage to India* from all these criticisms, but then I have written nothing that can be seen in relation to it.

2) My early work was formally traditional. It was written out of my deep saturation in 19th-century novels and out of a certain feeling that, like many of my contemporaries, I had temporarily got all I could out of the "modernists'" experiments. I wrote one or two very ill-advised commitments to "traditionalism," which, together with a misunderstanding of my praise of Zola and Dickens, led me almost to be labelled as an anti-experimentalist, almost a social realist. Dickens and Zola for me, of course, have their value as poets, though also poets using all society to create their prose poems from. My early work was probably somewhat sharply "traditional" in form—in restoring 19th-century forms; but this was a protest against a conformity to post-Jamesian techniques. With a too great tyranny of neo-traditionalism in English novel writing, I have increasingly, from *The Old Men at the Zoo*, experimented, above all with pastiche. In the apparently conventional *Late Call* there are innumerable jokes, alienations, pastiches, and other non-traditional techniques that the critics failed to see. With *No Laughing Matter* experiment has greatly taken over. The chief influence in my last years has been Virginia Woolf, whom I had to attack fiercely before I felt free to recognize as the very great novelist she was. But my work continues and will, I think, continue to be social in its general material though probably increasingly experimental in form—I am interested in man's personality and soul, but I tend to see him first from the outside as a political and social creature.

3) This leads me to my last point. I am often spoken of as having a very narrow range of characters or as being the satirist of the middle classes. This has only a superficial truth, I think. Compared to most contemporary English novelists my social range seems wide, and my approach to the middle classes (the centre of my work) is as sympathetic as it is critical.

All this, of course, is a statement of intention (realized or unrealized I am not supposed, as an author, to be able to judge; though I suspect that authors can guess at their success with their intentions more than academic critics allow). Certainly it is not a judgement of quality—here the novelist must be his own most harsh critic and also his own most loving admirer—and about both he must say nothing.

* * *

Angus Wilson is a realistic novelist, with a very sharp ear and eye for the subtleties of English social behaviour. But there is another aspect of his work, not so obvious on a casual reading but never far below the surface, in which he is a writer deeply concerned with cruelty and horror and the intrusions of the nightmarish into civilized life. He began as a short-story writer and in some ways remains one, since his novels are usually episodic in organization, and are likely to be at their most impressive in their treatment of small units of narrative. His first two collections of stories, *The Wrong Set* and *Such Darling Dodos*, were sharply drawn sketches of English middle-class life during and just after the Second World War, with heavy emphasis on snobbery, self-deception, and genteel cruelty. Technically they were very adroit, though their despairing view of human motives was altogether too black and unrelieved for complete plausibility. In one of these stories, "Raspberry Jam," Wilson shows a characteristic awareness of the way in which an extremity of violence can shockingly erupt into a familiar domestic setting.

Wilson's first three novels, *Hemlock and After*, *Anglo-Saxon Attitudes*, and *The Middle Age of Mrs. Eliot*, are like much of modern English fiction, in their traditional, unselfconscious attitude to form, their precise registration of social nuance, and the nature of their moral preoccupations. At the same time, their peculiar mixture of detached observation and underlying obsession make them works that only Angus Wilson could have written. Despite a sense of what Henry James called "felt life" and, in the first two, an almost Dickensian range of characters, certain thematic preoccupations tend to be very obtrusive. The reader is invited to dwell on responsibility and guilt, and the tension between the public life of busy achievement and the private life of spiritual cultivation. In Wilson's world moral progress lies in the steady eradication of self-deception. Such preoccupations are, of course, part of a central tradition of the English novel, the line of Jane Austen and George Eliot and E.M. Forster. It must, however, be confessed that Angus Wilson's concern with these questions is at times a little fine-drawn and even parochial. It is not altogether easy to identify with the problems of the self-flagellating homosexual novelist, Bernard Sands, in *Hemlock and After*, or the spiritually sluggish historian, Gerald Middleton, in *Anglo-Saxon Attitudes.* In *Middle Age of Mrs. Eliot* Meg Eliot, an archetypal liberal heroine, is good-looking, sensitive, intelligent but not intellectual, and modestly complacent. Yet her husband is killed in an outbreak of casual political violence at the airport of an Asian country they are visiting; the rest of the novel shows her brave attempt to make something of her life in widowhood and poverty. Among other things, it suggests that Wilson is better at creating memorable female characters than male ones, and compared with its two predecessors it is a generally admirable and successful work.

In the first three novels Wilson's sense of nightmare appears in isolated incidents and recurring images, but in *The Old Men at the Zoo* it moves into the centre of the action. This work is unique in Wilson's *oeuvre* in being as much a fable as a work of realistic fiction. It is a prophetic fantasy of the near future, when England is at war with an alliance of European powers, and Wilson deals with larger moral dilemmas than he had projected in his earlier books. Politics impinges on private life in an un-English way. His hero, Simon Carter, secretary of the London Zoo, who is both an animal-lover and an efficient administrator, tries to carry on with his work as best he can after England has been defeated by the Europeans. In doing so he embodies the classical dilemma of the public servant in a period of defeat and oppression: should one try to keep society going and risk being labelled a collaborator, or should one keep up a possibly vain and even disastrous resistance? *The Old Men at the Zoo* is a bizarre and often violent narrative that seems to have enabled Wilson to face and, for a time at least, to subdue his own fantasies. His next novel, *Late Call*, is by contrast a work of relative serenity. In *Late Call* the sense of evil that had appeared in Wilson's earlier novels in elements of fantasy or marginal obsession is integrated with his principal strength as a novelist: his infallible sense of social fact. *Late Call* explores the spiritual desolation of life in a New Town in the English Midlands, where the gimmickry of affluence has become a way of life rather than an aid to living. Wilson employs the consciousness of Sylvia Calvert, a woman in her sixties, who has retired after a lifetime of managing small, unfashionable hotels. Accompanied by her sponging idler of a husband, who cares only for playing cards and reliving his days as a temporary officer in the First World War, she goes to live with her recently widowed son in the New Town of Carshall. Harold is a progressive headmaster and educational theorist: he welcomes his parents to his fine modern house with a great display of filial feelings. But why and how they cannot live with Harold and his three teenage daughters is the story that Wilson goes on to tell with considerable insight and sensitivity. Sylvia is one of his most successful fictional creations. She is not at all an educated woman, but she has much native shrewdness, and Wilson uses her honest but often baffled responses to make a remarkably sharp exposure of contemporary progressive attitudes. *Late Call* is better written and less diffuse than Wilson's previous novels, and despite, or perhaps because of, its deliberately limited theme, it is arguably his most uniformly successful novel.

Wilson has several times shown his interest in the pre-1914 world; it appears in several retrospective scenes in *Anglo-Saxon Attitudes* and in the prologue to *Late Call*, describing Sylvia's childhood in 1911. In *No Laughing Matter* he once more returns to it. He unfolds the fortunes of the Matthews family from 1912, when the book opens, up to 1967, when it closes. *No Laughing Matter* is a long, ambitious book with many local successes; it uses the several generations of the Matthews family to look at more than 50 years of English social history, and Wilson indulges to the full his love of the crowded fictional canvas. In comparison with his earlier fiction, his language is far more resourceful, and he uses it to convey a wider spectrum of feeling and to draw on a greater variety of technical devices. Yet the book, for all its richness, is uncomfortably episodic: one is frequently more conscious of Wilson as a brilliant short story writer than as a novelist who is really at home with an extended narrative. A similar criticism can be made of *As If by Magic*, another long and ambitious novel. It contains many characters and ranges in space rather than time, from contemporary England to India, Ceylon, Malaya, and Japan. In intention a penetrating anatomy of the modern world and its problems, this novel shows in practice a division between Wilson's large aims and his real, more restricted imaginative interests.

Angus Wilson is a writer of unusually fine intelligence, wide reading, and great sensitivity, who embodies certain traditional attitudes to life and the novel at a time when they are increasingly under attack. He is both a writer of broad middle-brow appeal and true literary seriousness, in itself a highly traditional combination, and one which makes him hard to subject to confident critical placing.

—Bernard Bergonzi

WILSON, Colin (Henry). British. Born in Leicester, 26 June 1931. Educated at Gateway Secondary Technical School, Leicester, 1942-47. Served in the Royal Air Force, 1949-50. Married 1) Dorothy Betty Troop in 1951 (marriage dissolved), one son; 2) Pamela Joy Stewart in 1960, two sons and one daughter. Laboratory Assistant, Gateway School, 1948-49; tax collector, Leicester and Rugby, 1949-50; labourer and hospital porter in London, 1951-53; salesman for the magazines *Paris Review* and *Merlin*, Paris, 1953. Since 1954, full-time writer. British Council Lecturer in Germany, 1957; Writer-in-Residence, Hollins College, Virginia, 1966-67; Visiting Professor, University of Washington, Seattle, 1968; Professor, Institute of the Mediterranean (Dowling College, New York), Majorca, 1969; Visiting Professor, Rutgers University, New Brunswick, New Jersey, 1974. Agent: David Bolt, Bolt and Watson Ltd., 8-12 Old Queen Street, Storey's Gate, London SW1H 9HP. Address: Tetherdown, Gorran Haven, Cornwall, England.

PUBLICATIONS

Novels

Ritual in the Dark. London, Gollancz, and Boston, Houghton Mifflin, 1960.
Adrift in Soho. London, Gollancz, and Boston, Houghton Mifflin, 1961.
The World of Violence. London, Gollancz, 1963; as *The Violent World of Hugh Greene*, Boston, Houghton Mifflin, 1963.
Man Without a Shadow: The Diary of an Existentialist. London, Barker, 1963; as *The Sex Diary of Gerard Sorme*, New York, Dial Press, 1963.
Necessary Doubt. London, Barker, and New York, Simon and Schuster, 1964.
The Glass Cage: An Unconventional Detective Story. London, Barker, 1966; New York, Random House, 1967.
The Mind Parasites. London, Barker, and Sauk City, Wisconsin, Arkham House, 1967.
The Philosopher's Stone. London, Barker, 1969; New York, Crown, 1971.
The Killer. London, New English Library, 1970; as *Lingard*, New York, Crown, 1970.
The God of the Labyrinth. London, Hart Davis, 1970; as *The Hedonists*, New York, New American Library, 1971.
The Black Room. London, Weidenfeld and Nicolson, 1971; New York, Pyramid, 1975.
The Schoolgirl Murder Case. London, Hart Davis MacGibbon, and New York, Crown, 1974.
The Space Vampires. London, Hart Davis MacGibbon, and New York, Random House, 1976.

Short Story

The Return of the Lloigor. London, Village Press, 1974.

Uncollected Short Story

"Timeslip," in *Aries 1*, edited by John Grant. Newton Abbot, Devon, David and Charles, 1979.

Plays

Viennese Interlude (produced Scarborough, Yorkshire, and London, 1960).
Strindberg (as *Pictures in a Bath of Acid*, produced Leeds, Yorkshire, 1971; as *Strindberg: A Fool's Decision*, produced London, 1975). London, Calder and Boyars, 1970; New York, Random House, 1971.
Mysteries (produced Cardiff, 1979).

Other

The Outsider. London, Gollancz, and Boston, Houghton Mifflin, 1956.
Religion and the Rebel. London, Gollancz, and Boston, Houghton Mifflin, 1957.
The Age of Defeat. London, Gollancz, 1959; as *The Stature of Man*, Boston, Houghton Mifflin, 1959.
Encyclopaedia of Murder, with Patricia Pitman. London, Barker, 1961; New York, Putnam, 1962.
The Strength to Dream: Literature and the Imagination. London, Gollancz, and Boston, Houghton Mifflin, 1962.
Origins of the Sexual Impulse. London, Barker, and New York, Putnam, 1963.
Rasputin and the Fall of the Romanovs. London, Barker, and New York, Farrar Straus, 1964.
Brandy of the Damned: Discoveries of a Musical Eclectic. London, Baker, 1964; as *Chords and Discords: Purely Personal Opinions on Music*, New York, Crown, 1966; augmented edition, as *Colin Wilson on Music*, London, Pan, 1967.
Beyond the Outsider: The Philosophy of the Future. London, Barker, and Boston, Houghton Mifflin, 1965.
Eagle and Earwig (essays). London, Barker, 1965.
Introduction to the New Existentialism. London, Hutchinson, 1966; Boston, Houghton Mifflin, 1967.
Sex and the Intelligent Teenager. London, Arrow, 1966; New York, Pyramid, 1968.
Voyage to a Beginning (autobiography). London, Cecil and Amelia Woolf, 1966; New York, Crown, 1969.
Bernard Shaw: A Reassessment. London, Hutchinson, and New York, Atheneum, 1969.
A Casebook of Murder. London, Frewin, 1969; New York, Cowles, 1970.
Poetry and Mysticism. San Francisco, City Lights, 1969; London, Hutchinson, 1970.
The Strange Genius of David Lindsay, with E.H. Visiak and J.B. Pick. London, Baker, 1970; as *The Haunted Man*, San Bernardino, California, Borgo Press, 1979.
The Occult. New York, Random House, and London, Hodder and Stoughton, 1971.
New Pathways in Psychology: Maslow and the Post-Freudian Revolution. New York, Taplinger, and London, Gollancz, 1972.
Order of Assassins: The Psychology of Murder. London, Hart Davis, 1972.
L'Amour: The Ways of Love, photographs by Piero Rimaldi. New York, Crown, 1972.
Strange Powers. London, Latimer New Dimensions, 1973; New York, Random House, 1975.
Tree by Tolkien. London, Covent Garden Press-Inca, 1973; Santa Barbara, California, Capra Press, 1974.
Hermann Hesse. London, Village Press, and Philadelphia, Leaves of Grass Press, 1974.
Wilhelm Reich. London, Village Press, and Philadelphia, Leaves of Grass Press, 1974.
Jorge Luis Borges. London, Village Press, and Philadelphia, Leaves of Grass Press, 1974.
A Book of Booze. London, Gollancz, 1974.
The Unexplained. Lake Oswego, Oregon, Lost Pleiade Press, 1975.
Mysterious Powers. London, Aldus, and Danbury, Connecticut, Danbury Press, 1975; as *They Had Strange Powers*, New York, Doubleday, 1975.
The Craft of the Novel. London, Gollancz, 1975.
Enigmas and Mysteries. London, Aldus, and New York, Doubleday, 1976.
The Geller Phenomenon. London, Aldus, 1976.
Mysteries: An Investigation into the Occult, The Paranormal, and the Supernatural. London, Hodder and Stoughton, and New York, Putnam, 1978.
Science Fiction as Existentialism. Hayes, Middlesex, Bran's Head, 1978.
The Search for the Real Arthur, with *King Arthur Country in Cornwall*, by Brenda Duxbury and Michael Williams. Bodmin, Cornwall, Bossiney, 1979.
Starseekers. London, Hodder and Stoughton, 1980; New York, Doubleday, 1981.
Anti-Sartre, with an Essay on Camus. San Bernardino, California, Borgo Press, 1980.
The War Against Sleep: The Philosophy of Gurdjieff. Wellingborough, Northamptonshire, Aquarian Press, 1980.
Frankenstein's Castle. London, Ashgrove Press, 1980.
The Quest for Wilhelm Reich. London, Granada, and New York, Doubleday, 1981.

Editor, *Colin Wilson's Men of Mystery.* London, W.H. Allen, 1977.
Editor, *Dark Dimensions: A Celebration of the Occult.* New York, Everest House, 1978.
Editor, with John Grant, *The Book of Time.* Newton Abbot, Devon, David and Charles, 1980.

Editor, with John Grant, *The Directory of Possibilities.* Exeter, Webb and Bower, and New York, Rutledge Press, 1981.

*

Manuscript Collection: University of Texas, Austin.

Critical Studies: *The Angry Decade* by Kenneth Allsop, London, Peter Owen, 1958; *The World of Colin Wilson* by Sidney Campion, London, Muller, 1963; "The Novels of Colin Wilson" by Richard Dillard, in *Hollins Critic* (Hollins College, Virginia), October 1967; *Colin Wilson* by John A. Weigel, New York, Twayne, 1975.

Colin Wilson comments:

I am unashamedly a writer of ideas, in the tradition of Shaw, Wells, or Sartre; I see myself as part of a European rather than English literary tradition. My novels are based firmly upon the "new existentialism" expressed in the six volumes of the "Outsider Cycle" (1956-1966) and *Introduction to the New Existentialism.* Although I count myself an existential phenomenologist, I am in fundamental disagreement with the pessimistic European tradition of Heidegger, Jaspers, Sartre, and Camus, and my philosophical work has been an attempt to show that their pessimism is the outcome of certain serious misunderstandings of Husserlian phenomenology, notably of the intentionality of consciousness. The foundation of my position could be expressed in the form of a contradiction of Sartre: Consciousness *does* have an "inside." Sartre's position is fundamentally Humeian: he believes the mind *adds* meaning to the chaotic and fragmented world as you might add milk to a bowl of cornflakes; I hold, with Whitehead, that meaning is an objective reality, and that the problem is the curious narrowness and inefficiency of human consciousness.

My novels are basically preoccupied with the problem of meaning, with what Peirce called the problem of "values in a universe of chance." In the first, *Ritual in the Dark*, this takes the form of an exploration of "the great mystery of human boredom." The hero has always wanted freedom and hated being tied down to an office job; yet when a small legacy gives him "a room of his own," he finds himself bewildered, bored, directionless. His meeting with a man who, he comes to suspect, is a mass-murderer of women produces a powerful sense of meaning and direction, but he feels that this is inauthentic—that he should have been capable of *doing it himself*—finding freedom *without help from outside.* This problem of freedom is at the core of all my novels. Man experiences his freedom both positively and negatively: positively in moments of intensity and ecstasy (sex, for example), negatively in the face of crisis or a threat to his existence. Both experiences reveal that the main trouble with everyday consciousness is its narrowness, its obsessive preoccupation with trivialities. There is something fundamentally wrong with human consciousness, a form of short-sightedness amounting almost to blindness. This is, in a sense, a "religious" vision—closely akin to that of T.E. Hulme, who preferred to call it "original sin."

The main influences on my fiction, in my late teens and early twenties, were Joyce and Faulkner, and I felt strongly that the novel had advanced as far as possible in the direction of experimentalism, attempting, so to speak, to approximate to the condition of music. The solution I chose was based upon the notion of Brecht's "alienation effect." In the theatre, Brecht invites his audience to acknowledge that they are watching actors in a play, not reality; it seemed to me that the novel could back out of the Joycean *cul de sac* by choosing to be, on one level, entertainment within a conventional framework; using the conventions of the *roman policier*, the *Bildungsroman*, science fiction, the spy novel, as a kind of symbolic form (in Cassirer's sense) which is freely acknowledged *not* to correspond to its content. This I saw as the only reasonable escape from the Joycean-Faulknerian dilemma of trying to distort the form to *correspond* to an increasingly complex content. Hence, in my fiction, I have used the form of the detective story, science fiction, spy story, etc. as the "persona" or mask of the book. This also offers one enormous advantage. The Joyce disciples, in their attempt to "render" their precise meaning once and for all, robbed themselves of the possibility of free expansion and development. By treating the form as a kind of carnival mask, I am able to re-explore the same meaning or inner-conflict from different angles, so to speak. For example, the same basic meanings are explored in *The Killer* (in the United States, *Lingard*) and *The God of the Labyrinth* (*The Hedonists*), although the first is a clinically precise study of a sexually motivated killer, and the second a literary "detective story" with more than a touch of Thorne Smith farce.

The central statement in my work occurs near the beginning of *Man Without a Shadow*: "Human beings are grandfather clocks driven by watch-springs." This is why consciousness *appears* to have no "inside." All human beings suffer, more or less, from the complaint of Sartre's café proprietor in *Nausea*: "When his café empties, his head empties too." Our sense of values, which ought to be absolute, appears to depend completely upon stimuli from the environment. This problem is explored most exhaustively in my "spy novel" *The Black Room*, in which I pose the question: How could a spy be trained to withstand total sensory deprivation in a black room? If such a method could be found, it would also be a method for creating supermen.

It is this Carlylean-Nietzschean preoccupation with the potentialities of man—and his present unsatifactoriness—that has led certain critics to accuse me of fascism, a curious accusation since, although my cast of mind is naturally conservative, I regard my work as wholly non-political.

* * *

Colin Wilson's many novels, which include psychological thrillers, mysteries, science-fiction fantasies, diary-confessions, and one of the first "beat" stories, are integral parts of an ambitious project which began in 1956 with the publication of *The Outsider*, that precocious "seminal book on the alienation of man." Although more like a collection of quotations and ideas from a youthful autodidact's notebooks than a coherently developed thesis, *The Outsider* impressed serious critics as well as journalists, who immediately exploited the colorful personality of the author and made the book a sensational best seller. Although Wilson still sees his first work as the most important book of its generation—and he may be right—the thoughtless enthusiasm for Wilson's erudition inevitably yielded to a more thoughtful skepticism. But the cruel change in mood toward his early success fortunately did not destroy the young man, who soon went to work again—less with a vengeance than a solemn determination to prove his significance.

Some 25 years and many books later, Wilson can no longer be dismissed as an amateur with only one lucky strike to his credit. Aware that he will eventually be judged as a philosopher, as the champion of a *new* existentialism which rejects the inevitability of despair, Wilson has neatly justified his fiction. "If I were to prescribe a rule," he wrote in 1958, "that all future philosophers would have to obey, it would be this: that no idea shall be expressed that cannot be expressed in terms of human beings in a novel—and perfectly ordinary human beings at that—not Peacockian brain-boxes. If an idea cannot be expressed in terms of people, it is a sure sign it is irrelevant to the real problems of life" (*Declaration*, p.58).

As a matter of fact none of Wilson's prose has that kind of finesse which awes literary critics not interested in ideas, yet it is adequate to its purpose. The fairest way to approach Wilson's novels is to cooperate with his objectives. His apparent preoccupation with violence, sexuality, and criminality is thematically related to his concern with the outsider syndrome. Furthermore, his methodology always participates in his urgency. In a hurry to clear away debris and passionately committed to his position, he is neither a Naturalist nor a Romantic weaving word-spells. He says that he has endorsed "the Brechtian alienation effect" in his fiction, and that he has *intended* that his novels announce their forms and make no claim to reality. In that sense they may be read as parodies of the genres they represent. Whether he has succeeded, however, is still debatable.

Since Wilson hopes to live almost forever, there is plenty of time to abide with his project. Recent experiments are currently validating his dreams of freeing humanity from the pessimism that correlates with determinism and traditional existentialism—at least as Wilson sees them. He is continuing his research into the sources of human energy, and there is certainly more to come from this indefatigable worker who says that even now he is just beginning. In 1966 in *Voyage to a Beginning* Wilson evaluated himself with characteristic candor. After modestly estimating that his first twenty years of work had not taken him far he added a firm *but*: "I know that I have come further than any of my contemporaries. I would be a fool if I didn't know it, and a coward if I was afraid to say so."

—John A. Weigel

WILSON, Sloan. American. Born in Norwalk, Connecticut, 8 May 1920. Educated at Harvard University, Cambridge, Massachusetts, B.A. 1942. Served in the United States Coast Guard, 1942-46. Married 1) Elise Pickhardt in 1942 (divorced); 2) Betty Stephens, 1963; three daughters and one son. Reporter, *Providence Journal*, Rhode Island, 1946-47; writer, Time Inc., New York, 1947-49; Assistant Director, National Citizens Commission for the Public Schools, New York, 1949-52; Director of Information Services, University of Buffalo, New York, 1952-55; Assistant Director, White House Conference on Education, Washington, D.C., 1956; Education Editor, *New York Herald Tribune*, 1956-58. Address: 207 Champlain Avenue, Ticonderoga, New York 12883, U.S.A.

PUBLICATIONS

Novels

Voyage to Somewhere. New York, Wyn, 1946.
The Man in the Gray Flannel Suit. New York, Simon and Schuster, 1955; London, Cassell, 1956.
A Summer Place. New York, Simon and Schuster, and London, Cassell, 1958.
A Sense of Values. New York, Harper, 1960; London, Cassell, 1961.
Georgie Winthrop. New York, Harper, and London, Cassell, 1963.
Janus Island. Boston, Little Brown, and London, Cassell, 1967.
All the Best People. New York, Putnam, 1970; London, Cassell, 1971.
Small Town. New York, Arbor House, 1978.
Ice Brothers. New York, Arbor House, 1979.
The Greatest Crime. New York, Arbor House, 1980.
Pacific Interlude. New York, Arbor House, 1981.

Uncollected Short Stories

"The Arrival of the Mail," in *New Yorker*, 18 August 1945.
"Party for the Veterans," in *New Yorker*, 20 April 1946.
"We've Got to Do Something," in *New Yorker*, 11 May 1946.
"The Best and Most Powerful Machines," in *Harper's* (New York), June 1946.
"Housewarming," in *New Yorker*, 3 May 1947.
"Drunk on the Train," in *New Yorker*, 3 January 1948.
"Reunion," in *New Yorker*, 6 March 1948.
"Bygones," in *New Yorker*, 18 June 1949.
"Hunt," in *Yale Review* (New Haven, Connecticut), March 1950.
"Alarm Clock," in *New Yorker*, 24 February 1951.
"Black Mollies," in *Harper's* (New York), December 1951.
"A Letter of Admonition," in *New Yorker*, 29 December 1951.
"Regatta," in *New Yorker*, 28 June 1952.
"School Days," in *The Best Short Stories of World War II*, edited by C.A. Fenton. New York, Viking Press, 1957.

Other

Away from It All. New York, Putnam, 1969; London, Cassell, 1970.
What Shall We Wear to This Party? The Man in the Gray Flannel Suit Twenty Years Before and After (autobiography). New York, Arbor House, 1976.

*

Manuscript Collection: Boston University.

Sloan Wilson comments:

My work consists of a running commentary on the world as I have seen it from 1944 to the present. Both my strength and my limitation derive from my determination to confine myself to first-hand experiences and observations. The Second World War is in my books because I fought through it. The worries and frustrations of business are on my pages because I suffered them for many years before I became a full-time writer. The joys, angers, desperation, and contentment which are part of many marriages are in my novels, because I have been married twice. Children appear in my books because I have four of them. The writing in my books is rather simple and straightforward because I have a story to tell and I want to get on with it. The English language, I believe, can be used for many purposes—to make the music of poetry, to give military orders, or to give the illusion of meaning without any meaning, as most politicians employ it. I use it to give my readers the thoughts and, most of all, the emotions which I have experienced. I want the readers to be deeply moved without becoming aware of the language which is transmitting the feelings of others to them. That's why I avoid "fancy writing"—it makes readers think about words instead of about human triumph or despair.

The men, women, and children in my books are concerned with bed-rock issues, such as how to stay alive in time of war without being a coward, how to make a good living in time of peace without selling one's soul cut-rate, and, most of all, how to understand and enjoy the mysteries of love without guilt and without hurting other people. Human beings in my books get tired, cross, and discouraged sometimes, but they doggedly pursue happiness and cling to a rather old-fashioned sense of honor to the best of their ability, which sometimes is not enough. Critics often believe my books are an over-simplification of life or a naive interpretation of it, but a few million readers tell me that for them my pages are mirrors.

* * *

The dust jacket of the American edition of Sloan Wilson's fifth novel, *Georgie Winthrop*, describes the book in these rather sensational terms: "The story of the man who lives next door to The Man in the Gray Flannel Suit—forty-five, intelligent, modest, decent, and catapulted by an extraordinary love into trying to grow up inside." Sloan Wilson has long been the victim of this kind of cliché-ridden, high-pressure advertising, of this nod toward a low-brow readership. If he enters literary history at all it will be as the creator of the man-in-the-gray-flannel-suit metaphor. Until now the critics have paid him scant attention. Despite his impressive output, even as comprehensive a reference work as the three-volume *Encyclopedia of World Literature in the 20th Century* (Ungar, 1967-71) does not devote an entry to him.

The typical Sloan Wilson protagonist is acutely aware of his Puritan ancestry, of his New England background, and tries desperately to "live in the present." Thus Ben Powers, in *Janus Island*, and George Winthrop, both 45-year-old family men, enter into relationships with younger women (in George's case a 17 year old) in vain attempts to ignore past commitments and future responsibilities. Tom Rath, before the present events of *The Man in the Gray*

Flannel Suit, had a wartime love affair with an Italian girl in another futile effort to freeze the present moment. Rath has a kind of Faulknerian obsession with time, which often expresses itself lyrically: "Time was given us like jewels to spend, and it's the ultimate sacrilege to wish it away."

Wilson called one of his novels *All the Best People*, a title which would serve handsomely for almost any of his books. Despite the intended irony of the phrase, there is always a certain respect in evidence in his fiction for the established eastern seaboard families, with their yachts, their islands, and their prep school and Harvard-Yale backgrounds. Dana, the main character in *All the Best People*, at one point defiantly remarks to his wife: "Of course! They call people like us WASPS, Caroline, white Anglo-Saxon Protestants." Later on, Caroline asserts formidably and characteristically: "my parents said I had to learn how to like Jews and Negroes, but they never said I had to like Middle Westerners."

Wilson has proved to be a skilled chronicler of social and historical events, from the Depression years through the aftermath of World War II. *All the Best People*, his most historical novel, shows the eroding effect of various upheavals in American life on a group of families who own property at Paradise Point, near Lake George, New York. *A Sense of Values* and *All the Best People* have long sequences devoted to the military experiences of the principal male characters. The Second World War, if somewhat obliquely, figures crucially also in *The Man in the Gray Flannel Suit* and *A Summer Place*. *Janus Island*, which describes more recent events than most of the other novels, is concerned, in passing, with the disruptive presence of Vietnam.

There is no mistaking the richness and vitality of Sloan Wilson's fiction. Still, as certain reviewers have remarked, there is a sense of *déjà vu* for anyone who reads through all of his work. Events, characters, and symbols have a way of being reused. Thus the war experiences of Nathan in *A Sense of Values* and those of Dana in *All the Best People* are more than passingly similar. There are crotchety caretakers, all cast from the same mold, in *The Man in the Gray Flannel Suit*, *A Summer Place*, and *Janus Island*. Magicians serve rather similar symbolical functions in *All the Best People* and *A Sense of Values*. Sylvia's "fake mink coat over her bathing suit" in *A Summer Place* reappears in the form of Caroline's "mink-dyed muskrat coat" in *All the Best People*. Both Nort in *Janus Island* and Nathan in *A Sense of Values* have the nervous habit of clenching and unclenching their hands. Dana, at the end of *All the Best People*, comes, uncannily, to resemble Hopkins in *The Man in the Gray Flannel Suit*, and Annabelle, in *A Sense of Values*, is a female—and somewhat more aggressive—Hopkins.

Critics have objected to the untidiness of Sloan Wilson's novels; their structures tend to be indecisively open-ended. Most of them are unduly episodic. They are as far removed as possible from the tautness of the best post-World War II fiction. Wilson obviously prefers a more leisurely, digressive pace. There is, however, a certain appropriateness about the rather old-fashioned open form of these novels; they deal, after all, with a world which holds on to the old pieties and stubbornly resists change. The underplayed, somewhat symbolic final remark of George Winthrop—which ends the only novel in the Wilson canon with a university setting—reveals how important traditional values are: "No, thank you very much, but I have to be getting home. I have a long drive ahead."

—Melvin J. Friedman

WINDHAM, Donald. American. Born in Atlanta, Georgia, 2 July 1920. Educated at Boys' High School, Atlanta. Editor, *Dance Index* magazine, New York, 1943-45. Recipient: Guggenheim Fellowship, 1960. Address: 230 Central Park South, New York, New York 10019, U.S.A.

Publications

Novels

The Dog Star. New York, Doubleday, 1950; London, Hart Davis, 1951.
The Hero Continues. New York, Crowell, and London, Hart Davis, 1960.
Two People. New York, Coward McCann, 1965; London, Joseph, 1966.
Tanaquil; or, The Hardest Thing of All. Privately printed, 1972; New York, Holt Rinehart, 1977.
Stone in the Hourglass. Privately printed, 1981.

Short Stories

The Hitchhiker. Privately printed, 1950.
Servants with Torches. Privately printed, 1955.
The Warm Country. London, Hart Davis, 1960; New York, Scribner, 1962.

Uncollected Short Story

"Rome," in *Paris Review 3*, Autumn 1953.

Plays

You Touched Me, with Tennessee Williams, suggested by the story by D.H. Lawrence (produced, Cleveland, 1943; New York, 1945). New York, French, 1947.
The Starless Air, adaptation of his own short story (produced Houston, 1953).

Other

The Kelly Boys. Privately printed, 1957.
Emblems of Conduct (autobiography). New York, Scribner, 1964.
L'Albero dei Palloni (juvenile), illustrated by the author. Milan, Emme Edizioni, 1974.

Editor, *E.M. Forster's Letters to Donald Windham.* Privately printed, 1975.
Editor, *Tennessee Williams' Letters to Donald Windham 1940-1965.* Privately printed, 1976; New York, Holt Rinehart, 1977.

*

Manuscript Collection: University of Georgia Libraries, Athens.

Critical Studies: Introduction by E.M. Forster to *The Warm Country*, 1960; Jeremy Larner, in *New York Times Book Review*, 1962; Ralph McGill, in *New York Times Book Review*, 12 April 1964; "Un amico straniero che ci vede come siamo" by Mario Soldati, in *Il Giorno* (Milan), 13 July 1965; Tim Dlugos, in *Little Caesar 12* (Los Angeles), 1981.

Donald Windham comments:

I try to write about reality. The belief that reality bears being portrayed seems to me the only optimism. I disagree with the idea "write about what you know." I write about what I *need* to know, in an effort to understand. I hope to sight and capture my theme without killing it. I disagree with the idea "never write a story unless you can put down the point of it on a postage stamp." I like a story to be concise. I have no impulse to spread out what I could set down in one square inch. I have written an autobiography (up to my nineteenth year), and can claim that of my writings only it is autobiographical; but I would rather claim that I have written about life only as I myself have found it and tried to understand it.

* * *

Donald Windham's novels, short stories, and autobiographical sketches demonstrate the significance of even the most trivial objects and events when made part of sharply delineated feelings. His writing abounds with the unexpected and precisely realized details of daily life: cats walking with "tails high in the air revealing their dry buttons," "the bright vacant cement of the Gulf filling station," workmen with "wet circles like dark suns beneath the pits of their arms." *Emblems of Conduct*, particularly, contains remembrances of the Georgia world of his boyhood lived amid fading prosperity and insular relatives—remembrances presented without the sentimentality or nostalgia of Thomas Wolfe or even Truman Capote.

The innocence and spontaneity of his childhood world contrast with Windham's principal concern, the tortured, self-deceptive, confused creatures of desire and disappointment we become as adults. Trapped in the patterns of their lives, the characters sometimes rebel and more often suffer in an agony of weakness, anger, and indecision, often torn between the desire for escape and the fear of losing their security. Windham himself escaped at 18 from family and Southern society on a bus to New York, unlike his less fortunate characters, for example, the widow with two children and little money in "Life of Georgia" trapped in a spiritless routine of dependence on her mother, in her mind the childhood memory "that tomorrow, somehow, something would happen more wonderful, or more terrible, than anything which ever had happened before."

The rebellious adolescent hero of Windham's first novel, *The Dog Star*, builds defenses against the world which are ultimately self-destructive. In a series of episodes burdened with obtrusive symbolism and indefinite existential motivation Windham examines the alienation that is both the result and cause of violence and insensitivity. Blackie Pride's contempt for human weakness and dependence following the suicide of his reform school friend, Whitey, grows into the contempt for life and the exaltation of personal freedom that are implicit in Blackie's suicide.

Elements of violence and alienation overshadow Dennis Freeman's rise to success as a playwright in *The Hero Continues*. Fame, money, and admirers only provoke his self-centered and paranoid responses to people and events, symptoms of his fears concerning his talent, his reputation, his friendships, and his virility, all ultimately concentrated in his fear of death. The terrible irony, however, is that his creativity arises out of his personal nightmare world of physical violence, self-deception, and alienation—his fictional life and his real life incompatible yet inseparable.

Homosexuality, a casual theme in *The Hero Continues*, is central to *Two People*, the story of a love affair between a married American in his thirties and an Italian boy. But for all Windham's sympathetic, delicate treatment of the man's absorbing passion, the love making, the boy's dual attraction to girlfriend and lover, Windham fails to realize the homosexual drive as more than an aberration conceived, satisfied, and abandoned in the interval of a Roman holiday. Here as elsewhere Windham falls short of a thorough exploration of the motives of his characters, but he also demonstrates his abiding virtues: emotional control, precision of detail, and compassionate treatment of subject.

—Dale K. Doepke

WISEMAN, Adele. Canadian. Born in Winnipeg, Manitoba, in 1928. Taught English at MacDonald College, McGill University, Montreal. Recipient: Beta Sigma Chi Award, 1957; Governor-General's Award, 1957; National Conference of Christians and Jews Brotherhood Award, 1957; Guggenheim Fellowship, 1957. Address: c/o Macmillan Company Ltd., St. Martin's House, 70 Bond Street, Toronto, Ontario M5B 1X3, Canada.

PUBLICATIONS

Novels

The Sacrifice. New York, Viking Press, and London, Gollancz, 1956.
Crackpot. Toronto, McClelland and Stewart, 1974.

Other

Old Markets, New Worlds. Toronto, Macmillan, 1964.
Testimonial Dinner. Erin, Ontario, Press Porcépic, 1976.
Old Woman at Play. Toronto, Clarke Irwin, 1978.

* * *

Adele Wiseman's second novel, *Crackpot*, gives animated voice to the central character, a fat prostitute named Hoda. Growing from a taunted childhood into middle age, Hoda manages a degree of optimism unusual in modern fiction. She comes to accept life with remarkable poise, even when her son (the relationship unknown to him) comes to her as a customer and she is called upon to initiate him and to engender in him a sense of worth.

If this novel can be seen as a singular study of an archetypal figure, Wiseman's first book, *The Sacrifice*, reads as a much more conventionally organized "novel of fathers and sons." It is a study of three generations of a Jewish family that emigrated from European pogroms to mid-Canadian urban stress. Living in either place has its problems, and the nature of life (of what it is to be a Jew, a Jew in Canada, or just to be) is the key question the book explores. The kosher butcher Abraham (with wife Sarah, son Isaac, and later grandson Moses) may seem too aptly named and employed to be fictionally credible, yet Wiseman deals with parallels and differences among individuals thoroughly enough (the subplots aid in such a structure) that the Old Testament references simply add mythical dimension to the problem she examines, and historical—genealogical—continuity to man's quest both for knowledge and for the ability to live with the knowledge he acquires.

The sacrifice of the title is thus many things at once, some admirable, others not—the Biblical story of Abraham's faith, the pagan ritual propitiation of angry gods, the immolation of self in the preservation of valued traditions, the ritual butchery, the education of one's sons to one's own ideas and standards, the accepted means for ceremonially renewing wonder, belief, and fear, and the fictional Abraham's murder of the prostitute Laiah in the belief that he is defeating Death and restoring vitality to his life and his community. For his act, Abraham is confined on Mad Mountain. Not content to be, he reflects later, he tried to be creator and destroyer, too, thus impinging on others' identity when the real struggle lay within himself. But understanding is its own punishment, he avers; it is the natural consequence of seeking beyond oneself—exemplified in the emigration as well as in the constant quest for knowledge—and the paradox of being human and alive.

Men occupy, however, various kinds of country—national political organizations, religious communities, families, economic and cultural groups, the world of life (at war with the world of death), the outlook of childhood, and the age of maturity. All blend in each man's separate identity, but all identities blend with each other in friendship and humane brotherhood. When Moses impulsively visits his "mad" grandfather, and sees his own hand taken in the older man's, he recognizes the continuity they represent—an affirmation of the cyclical progress of humanity and of the inevitability of men suffering understanding. Moses's friend Aaron departs at this point to help start the new (old, ancestral) country of Israel; Moses himself, who had been contemplating the same move, recognizes that he has a new country to explore already—not in Canada *per se*, but in the identity, the being, he has newly found, in his newly appreciated sense of heritage, and in the dimly lit recesses of his heart and mind. To shed light on some of those dark corners is the task Wiseman has attempted to dramatize; to arouse sympathy for the characters meeting their consciences in this way is the goal to which she has managed to win.

—W.H. New

WOIWODE, Larry (Alfred). American. Born in Carrington, North Dakota, 30 October 1941. Educated at the University of Illinois, Urbana, 1959-64, A.A. 1964. Married Carole Ann Peterson in 1965. Writer-in-Residence, University of Wisconsin, Madison, 1973-74. Member of the Executive Board, American P.E.N., 1972. Recipient: William Faulkner Foundation Award, 1969; Guggenheim Fellowship, 1971; American Academy Award, 1980. D.Litt.: North Dakota State University, Fargo, 1977. Agent: Candida Donadio and Associates, 51 East 42nd Street, New York, New York 10017. Address: c/o Farrar Straus and Giroux, 19 Union Square West, New York, New York 10003, U.S.A.

PUBLICATIONS

Novels

What I'm Going to Do, I Think. New York, Farrar Straus, 1969; London, Weidenfeld and Nicolson, 1970.
Beyond the Bedroom Wall: A Family Album. New York, Farrar Straus, 1975.

Uncollected Short Stories

"The Deathless Lovers," in *New Yorker*, 10 July 1965.
"Near the Straits of Mackinac," in *New Yorker*, 9 April 1966.
"The Brothers," in *New Yorker*, 21 May 1966.
"The Visitation," in *New Yorker*, 10 September 1966.
"On This Day," in *New Yorker*, 9 September 1967.
"The History Lesson," in *New Yorker*, 30 September 1967.
"Pheasants," in *New Yorker*, 18 November 1967.
"An Old Man," in *New Yorker*, 20 April 1968.
"The Long Trip," in *New Yorker*, 13 July 1968.
"The Boy," in *New Yorker*, 31 August 1968.
"The Horses," in *New Yorker*, 28 December 1968.
"Don't You Wish You Were Dead," in *New American Review 7*, edited by Theodore Solotaroff. New York, New American Library, 1969.
"What Can Blow the Wind Away?," in *Mademoiselle* (New York), February 1969.
"The Contest," in *New Yorker*, 1 November 1969.
"Owen's Father," in *Partisan Review* (New Brunswick, New Jersey), xxxvii, 3, 1970.
"The Beginning of Grief," in *New Yorker*, 17 October 1970.
"Burning the Couch," in *Atlantic* (Boston), November 1970.
"The Suitor," in *The Best American Short Stories 1971*, edited by Martha Foley and David Burnett. Boston, Houghton Mifflin, 1971.
"Pneumonia, 1945," in *New Yorker*, 13 February 1971.
"The Old Halvorson Place," in *New Yorker*, 8 May 1971.
"Marie," in *New Yorker*, 25 December 1971.
"Burial," in *New Yorker*, 19 November 1973.

Verse

Poetry North: Five North Dakota Poets, with others. Fargo, North Dakota Institute for Regional Studies, 1970.
Even Tide. New York, Farrar Straus, 1977.

*   *   *

Of Larry Woiwode's two novels, the first, *What I'm Going to Do, I Think*, may soon be forgotten, but the second, *Beyond the Bedroom Wall*, is sure to be ranked as one of the great achievements of American fiction of the 1970's. It is a midwestern novel, an American novel, a universal novel. It spans four generations, and could be set in almost any century. The book's significant events emerge out of the natural histories of human beings. It is about births and deaths, love and courtship, joy and grief, motherhood and fatherhood, childhood, adolescence, old age. It is about strength of character, spoiled character, redeemed character. It is about hardship and work, competence and incompetence, faith and distrust. It is about provincial bigotry and the lot of a Catholic family in a town of Methodists. It is about enduring.

Otto Neumiller emigrated from Germany in 1881. He went all the way to the Dakota plain, where he prospered and then lost most of what he had gained. In his old age, he is lonely and envied and unloved by his neighbors. His son Charles returns to the homestead to attend him at his death. In one of the book's finest chapters, Woiwode shows Charles at work making his father's coffin, lovingly washing and dressing his father's body, burying him in the unhallowed ground of the farm he loved. Like his father, Charles Neumiller has been a devout Catholic all his life; and so is Charles's son Martin. Most of the novel is the story of Martin, his wife Alpha, who dies at 34, and their six children. The older children, the fourth generation, are off on their own in the 1970's.

The great strength of this novel is in Woiwode's rendering of the commonplace. The Neumiller family may be a bit more intelligent and perhaps possess more fortitude than the average family, but they are not particularly special. In addition to the virtues, there certainly are waywardness, carelessness, and ill-considered impulsive behavior among them. Indeed, one of the beautiful ironies in the novel is that it is the ill-considered decision of Martin, usually so steady and prudent, to move his family from North Dakota to Illinois that brings disaster to the family, including ultimately his beloved wife's death. But the fabric of the novel is made of such scenes as the father telling stories to his children, the father's being overcome with frustration and kicking one of his sons viciously, the acting out of guilt feelings brought on by the nearly fatal illness of a child. An important motif running through the novel is the family's emotional involvement with each of the various houses in which they live.

The marriage of Martin and Alpha is old-fashioned ordinary. Except for what is done by acts of nature, it is a marriage that is not susceptible to disruption. This man and this woman become totally entangled with each other, and regardless of what befalls them they cannot imagine themselves married to anyone else. To Martin and Alpha, marriage is for better or for worse, forever.

Even in bulk *What I'm Going to Do, I Think* is not half the novel that *Beyond the Bedroom Wall* is. It has a small cast of characters, with the focus rarely leaving Chris or Ellen. It does not range over generations, but is concerned with only a few seasons in the lives of its young couple. It is lyrical and symbolic; unfortunately it is also murky. Its central situation is commonplace: the young woman is pregnant and the couple marry. They take an extended honeymoon at an isolated lodge up in northern Michigan. Only then does the nature of the commitment he has made become real to Chris. He is not single anymore; he must take account of another person. He is uncertain about which emotions to share and which to conceal. He experiences much anger, resentment, frustration, but he does not know what to do with such feelings in the new context. Their physical relationship is different under the blanket of marriage; expectation, disappointment, jealousy, fulfillment have a new texture. Neither Chris nor Ellen has had an appropriate model for the roles of husband and wife; Chris, especially, suffers as a result.

Both had unusual childhoods. Ellen's parents were killed in an accident, and she has been raised by dour grandparents. Chris's alienation from his parents is so severe that he hardly ever thinks of them; he does not invite them to his wedding, he does not attend his mother's funeral. It is the quality of Chris's earlier life that is suggested by the title of the novel. The words are part of a remark made by his father when Chris has hurt himself being clumsy at a chore. What his father thinks he is going to do is get himself a new kid.

The child Ellen is carrying is born dead. When Ellen calls her grandmother for consolation, she is told that what has happened is the wages of sin. Chris and Ellen do not have another child. The novel ends with the suggestion that Chris always will be a troubled man, and the marriage will not bring fulfillment or much joy to husband or wife. The lives of Chris and Ellen will never have the richness of the lives of Martin and Alpha. Standing by itself, the earlier novel does not have a meaning that clearly emerges from the interaction of character and plot. When it is put beside *Beyond the Bedroom Wall*, its theme is quite clear: without firm familial commitments, modern life will exact constant feelings of despair and loss.

At his best, Woiwode renders the commonplace with such emotional and psychological truth that all the reader's capacity for empathy and compassion is tapped. Woiwode often demonstrates marvelous descriptive power; at his best, his readers see and feel and learn with him making easy transfers of their fictional experience to their own lives.

—Paul Marx

WOLFE, Bernard. American. Born in New Haven, Connecticut, 28 September 1915. Educated at Yale University, New Haven, 1931-36, B.A. 1935 (Phi Beta Kappa). Married Dolores Michaels in 1964. Taught at Bryn Mawr College, Pennsylvania, 1936; Trotsky's secretary, Mexico, 1937; served in the United States Merchant Marine, 1937-39; Editor, *Mechanix Illustrated*, New York, 1944-45; ghostwriter for Billy Rose's syndicated column, "Pitching Horseshoes," 1947-50; taught creative writing, University of California, Los Angeles, 1966-68; Screenwriter, Universal-International Productions, and Tony Curtis Productions, Hollywood. Address: c/o Eliot Gordon Company, 8888 Olympic Boulevard, Beverly Hills, California, U.S.A.

PUBLICATIONS

Novels

Really the Blues, with Mezz Mezzrow. New York, Random House, 1946; London, Musicians Press, 1947.
Limbo. New York, Random House, 1952; abridged edition, as *Limbo '90*, London, Secker and Warburg, 1953.
The Late Risers: Their Masquerade. New York, Random House, 1954; London, Consul, 1962; as *Everything Happens at Night*, New York, New American Library, 1963.
In Deep. New York, Knopf, 1957; London, Secker and Warburg, 1958.
The Great Prince Died. New York, Scribner, and London, Cape, 1959; as *Trotsky Dead*, Los Angeles, Wollstonecraft, 1975.
The Magic of Their Singing. New York, Scribner, 1961.
Come On Out, Daddy. New York, Scribner, 1963.
Memoirs of a Not Altogether Shy Pornographer. New York, Doubleday, 1972.
Logan's Gone. Los Angeles, Nash, 1974.
Lies. Los Angeles, Wollstonecraft, 1975.

Short Stories

Move Up, Dress Up, Drink Up, Burn Up. New York, Doubleday, 1968.

Uncollected Short Stories

"Self Portrait," in *The Robot and the Man*, edited by Martin H. Greenberg. New York, Gnome Press, 1953.
"The Never Ending Penny," in *The Year's Best S-F 6*, edited by Judith Merril. New York, Simon and Schuster, 1961; London, Mayflower, 1963.
"The Dot and Dash Bird," in *The Playboy Book of Science Fiction and Fantasy*, edited by Ray Russell. Chicago, Playboy Press, 1966; London, Souvenir Press, 1967.
"The Biscuit Position" and "The Girl with the Rapid Eye Movements," in *Again, Dangerous Visions*, edited by Harlan Ellison. New York, Doubleday, 1972; London, Millington, 1976.

Plays

Television Plays: *Assassin!*, 1955; *The Ghost Writer*, 1955; *The Five Who Shook the Mighty*, 1956.

Other

How to Get a Job in the Aircraft Industry. Mount Vernon, New York, Wallach, 1943.
Full Disclosure, edited by Annette Welles. Los Angeles, Wollstonecraft, 1975.
Julie: The Life and Times of John Garfield. Los Angeles, Wollstonecraft, 1976.

Translator, with Alice Backer, *The Plot*, by Egon Hostovsky. London, Cassell, 1961.

*

Critical Study: *Bernard Wolfe* by Carolyn Geduld, New York, Twayne, 1972.

* * *

Bernard Wolfe began his writing career with a comical pseudobiography of a jazzman/conman; written in collaboration with Mezz Mezzrow, *Really the Blues* made clear Wolfe's inventive if somewhat erratic comic sense and his deep interest in music. His novels characteristically take a sidelong and usually satirical look at some distinct sub-group of American culture, and the very forms in which the stories are presented frequently take comic aim at specific literary conventions. Wolfe's first "solo" novel, *Limbo*, falls loosely within the genre of science fiction; set 18 years after a cataclysmic Third World War, it is an implicit criticism of the post-World War Two munitions race and, on a larger scale, of the almost irresistible destructive instinct of our times. William Peden recognized a dichotomy in this novel which manifests itself in almost all of Wolfe's fiction when he referred to it as "a mélange of Huxley fantasy and E. Phillips Oppenheim melodrama, together with serious dialectical overtones reminiscent of Dostoevsky and Thomas Mann." Aesthetic impulses and dialectical-political ones are often in conflict in Wolfe's writing, marring the structure of his work so that it can never be termed "well wrought" despite the frequent brilliance of conception and, indeed, of individual passages.

Wolfe's second novel, *The Late Risers*, cast the clichéd modern search for identity in a comic light, beginning with a Runyonesque cast of hipsters, whores, and has-beens whose nightmare adventures become increasingly grotesque but are always contained within the intellectual "joking" that gives the work its special tone. *In Deep*, perhaps the least successful of Wolfe's novels, appropriates the melodramatic spy chase as its vehicle; intrigue and insinuation proliferate, and Wolfe shows great narrative dexterity in manipulating the events of the novel, but it fails to sustain the weight of existential meaning with which he attempts to infuse it.

Wolfe's most overtly political novel is *The Great Prince Died*, a fictionalized account of the murder of the exiled Leon Trotsky. From his own brief experience as a member of Trotsky's staff in Mexico, Wolfe reconstructed in graphic and compelling detail the last days in the life of "Victor Rostov." For all the novel's force, it finally becomes ponderous and dull. As a study in human motivation it is at times provocative, but Wolfe seemed to lack the necessary emotional distance to transform his materials into a completely satisfactory novel.

His fascination with negativism, self-delusion, and the fragmented personality found its most imaginative expression in *The Magic of Their Singing*, Wolfe's satire on non-conformity and, in particular, on the Beat Generation. Similar themes were explored in *Come On Out, Daddy*, a sprawling, episodic novel about life in Hollywood. Like Nathanael West, Wolfe exploits with knowing humor the press-agentry, the bizarre nature and dietary fetishes, the macaronic architecture, and the "gyrating grotesques" of the dream capital of America.

Throughout his novels Wolfe has waged war on hypocrisy, mindless conformity, and mindless revolution; each of his works is a strong indictment of the life-denying impulses of our age, and he reinforces this vision with a sweeping comic sense and considerable technical adroitness.

—David Galloway

WOOLF, Douglas. American. Born in New York City, 23 March 1922. Educated at Harvard University, Cambridge, Massachusetts, 1939-42; University of New Mexico, Albuquerque, 1949-50, A.B. 1950. Served with the American Field Service, 1942-43; in the United States Air Force, 1943-45. Married 1) Yvonne Elyce Stone in 1949; two daughters; 2) Sandra Braman in 1976. Since 1950, free-lance writer and itinerant worker, in the western United States, Canada, and Mexico. Address: P.O. Box 10671, Eugene, Oregon 97440, U.S.A.

PUBLICATIONS

Novels

The Hypocritic Days. Majorca, Divers Press, 1955.
Fade Out. New York, Grove Press, 1959; London, Weidenfeld and Nicolson, 1968.
Wall to Wall. New York, Grove Press, 1962.
John-Juan. Kyoto, Origin, 1967.
Ya! and John-Juan. New York, Harper, 1971.
On Us. Santa Barbara, California, Black Sparrow Press, 1977.
HAD. Eugene, Oregon, Wolf Run, 1977.

Short Stories

Signs of a Migrant Worrier. Eugene, Oregon, Coyote's Journal, 1965.
Spring of the Lamb, with *Broken Field Runner: A Douglas Woolf Notebook*, by Paul Metcalf. Highlands, North Carolina, Jargon, 1972.
Future Preconditional. Toronto, Coach House Press, 1978.

*

Critical Studies: by Edward Dorn, in *Kulchur* (New York), 1963; J.H. Prynne, in *Prospect* (London), 1964; I.D. Mackillop in *Delta 45* (Cambridge), 1969.

Douglas Woolf comments:

For the writer these days there is a new urgency in the air, he is goaded to finish his present work before its reader disappears. Thus I feel privileged to have received lately three or four responses that seem to promise me some extra time. I'll nonetheless have my new novel ready soon.

* * *

The deserts, ghost towns and superhighways of Douglas Woolf's fiction are peopled by the maimed and exiled of the human race. Fleeing the desolation of modern existence, they find either that deliverance is not possible or that it is to be found in the bleak and desert places among others who are rejected and fleeing. Woolf paints a vivid surrealistic picture of a mechanistic society where the pressure for money and peer acceptance erases the last vestiges of humanity from hollow men. The wise run to preserve their souls and sometimes save another soul, too. Mr. Twombly of *Fade Out* induces his friend, Behemoth Brown, to forsake the beloved television set, and Al James of *Ya!* releases his teenage daughter, Joan, from the tightening bonds of materialism and superficiality.

Woolf's fine descriptive talent is especially notable given the unusual settings and characters he uses. *John-Juan*, for instance, captures dream-like experiences in a strong visual reality. Anyone who suffers in flight will find his painful symptoms faithfully recorded in "Off the Runway," one of the seven stories from *Signs of a Migrant Worrier*. In *Ya!* Woolf's depiction of Al James's Northwest odyssey combines vivid scenic descriptions with deft quick character sketches and concludes with a finely etched picture of James spending the night asleep in a hemlock tree high above the snowed-in-forest. John and Martha in "Bank Day" (*Migrant Worrier*) awake to a breakfast of cat food and eggs, an event which is clearly and economically described.

Although the themes are isolation and mankind's race toward destruction, the tone is usually humorous. In rare instances when the humor is too heavy-handed the work suffers—the short story "The Cat" is an example of this—but generally Woolf's comic writing is of a high order. In *Fade Out* there is a marvelous scene in which the old men visit a zoo where a science-fiction movie is being made with unresponsive tortoises cast as monsters.

With its fine balance of humor and human insight, *Fade Out* is a brilliant novel. Woolf details the cruelties visited on the aged by their families and society. Mr. Twombly has functioned in the middle-class mold for 50 years, but now retired he finds he is a nuisance to his family. His only friends are children and old people like himself, unwanted. Threatened with an ending in an old people's home, he takes his existence in hand and "fades out" to find a new life in an Arizona ghost town. His cross-country trip, accompanied by his ex-prize fighter friend, is wild and hilarious.

Woolf is a serious craftsman who writes from a perspective of detached sympathy. Seldom reviewed, he supports himself with itinerant work and takes off for solitary places to write when he has saved enough money. In 1963, he called his vocation "a desperate anachronism" and described his method as bringing his characters to a point where "some kind of balance is reached" so that the character and the reader can assess the character's position. Although he portrays a dismal society from which the wise can at best flee, he is obviously not quite willing to write "finis" for humanity.

—Barbara M. Perkins

WOUK, Herman. American. Born in New York City, 27 May 1915. Educated at Townsend Harris Hall, New York; Columbia University, New York 1930-34, A.B. 1934. Served in the United States Naval Reserve, 1942-46. Married Betty Sarah Brown in 1945; three sons (one deceased). Radio writer, 1935; scriptwriter for the comedian Fred Allen, 1936-41; Consultant, United States Treasury Department, 1941. Since 1946, full-time writer. Visiting Professor of English, Yeshiva University, New York, 1952-58. Trustee, College of the Virgin Islands, 1961-69. Recipient: Pulitzer Prize, 1952; Columbia University Medal of Excellence, 1952. L.H.D.: Yeshiva University, 1955; LL.D.: Clark University, Worcester, Massachusetts, 1960; D.Lit.: American International College, Springfield, Massachusetts, 1979. Lives in Washington, D.C. Agent: BSW Literary Agency, 3255 N Street, Washington, D.C. 20007, U.S.A.

PUBLICATIONS

Novels

Aurora Dawn. New York, Simon and Schuster, and London, Barrie, 1947.
The City Boy. New York, Simon and Schuster, 1948; London, Cape, 1956.
The Caine Mutiny. New York, Doubleday, and London, Cape, 1951.
Marjorie Morningstar. New York, Doubleday, and London, Cape, 1955.
Slattery's Hurricane. New York, Permabooks, 1956; London, New English Library, 1965.
Youngblood Hawke. New York, Doubleday, and London, Collins, 1962.
Don't Stop the Carnival. New York, Doubleday, and London, Collins, 1965.
The Lomokome Papers. New York, Pocket Books, 1968.
The Winds of War. Boston, Little Brown, and London, Collins, 1971.
War and Remembrance. Boston, Little Brown, and London, Collins, 1978.

Uncollected Short Stories

"Herbie Solves a Mystery," in *Feast of Leviathan*, edited by L.W. Schwarz. New York, Rinehart, 1956.
"Old Flame," in *Good Housekeeping* (New York), May 1956.
"Irresistible Force," in *Fireside Treasury of Modern Humor*, edited by Scott Meredith. New York, Simon and Schuster, 1963.

Plays

The Traitor (produced New York, 1949). New York, French, 1949.
Modern Primitive (produced Hartford, Connecticut, 1951).
The Caine Mutiny Court-Martial (produced Santa Barbara, California, 1953; New York, 1954; London, 1956). New York, Doubleday, 1954; London, Cape, 1956.
Nature's Way (produced New York, 1957). New York, Doubleday, 1958.

Screenplays: *Slattery's Hurricane*, with Richard Murphy, 1949; *Confidentially Connie*, with Max Shulman, 1953.

Other

The Man in the Trench Coat. New York, National Jewish Welfare Board, 1941.
This Is My God: The Jewish Way of Life. New York, Doubleday, 1959; London, Cape, 1960; revised edition, London, Collins, 1973.

*

Manuscript Collection: Columbia University Library Special Collections, New York.

Critical Study: "You, Me and the Novel" by the author, in *Saturday Review-World* (New York), 29 June 1974.

Herman Wouk comments:

No author should be trusted to discuss his own work in an encyclopedia or a compendium until he has been dead thirty or forty years. Then, if anyone still cares, and if he can be raised at a seance, his opinion might be sufficiently detached to be worth something.

* * *

Herman Wouk continues to enjoy wide readership and to suffer critical attack for essentially the same reasons. He has a strong commitment to established values, which he champions only after energetic and attractive presentation of the Devil's case. Often, he plays Devil's advocate so well that the book's concluding reversal to affirmation of the status quo suggests mere pandering to popular prejudice. When the book is done, the rebels emerge as villains and the evils rebelled against as blemishes on the face of a healthy world.

Thus *Aurora Dawn* is an attack on vulgarity and dishonesty in advertising, not on advertising itself, and the bullying boss is only a witless product of nepotism, not a true portrait of capitalism's face. Andrew Reale, who chases money at the price of his soul, finds salvation when his discarded fiancée inherits money and takes him back—after her millionaire husband gallantly releases her from a marriage made on the rebound. Thus, Andrew is saved from money-grubbing's debasements through a millionaire's generosity and an heiress' forgiveness.

In *The Caine Mutiny*, Wouk's Pulitzer-prize novel of World War II, a strong case is made out for mutiny aboard an American destroyer during a Pacific storm, when the paranoiac Captain Queeg breaks under pressure. When all is done, however, only the legal verdict goes to the rebels; morally, Lieutenant Keefer and his followers are guilty of deserting a military system which, despite its resident fascists, has protected American freedom against foreign fascism. *Marjorie Morningstar* chronicles the false emancipation of Marjorie Morgenstern from the values and authority of her hard-working Jewish parents to the glitter of the theatre and bohemian "freedom." Then, renouncing her renunciation, the beautiful, intelligent Marjorie readily accepts her suburban destiny as lawyer's wife, mother of two and community servant. Interestingly, in both novels the "intellectual" (Lt. Keefer and writer Noel Airman) is unmasked as an insubstantial fraud, while the philistine, even when vicious and insane like Queeg, is sincere and somewhat heroic. In both novels, the protagonists, Princetonian Willie Keith and Bronxite Marjorie, must learn that the old ways are the best ways: obedience, chastity before marriage, the faith of one's fathers, hard work and money, all sound dull but ring true. In form and style, Wouk is equally traditionalist, his early works ranging from parody of Fielding (*Aurora Dawn*) and Booth Tarkington (*City Boy*) to Victorian-sized melodramas (*Marjorie Morningstar*) bursting with incident and character.

His two next novels, *Youngblood Hawke* and *Don't Stop the Carnival*, also abound in plot and character but are below his best work. Wouk's gargantuan Arthur Youngblood was obviously modeled on Thomas Wolfe, then grafted onto a melodramatic plot of the artist turned businessman, with his talent destroyed by greed and scheming women. But Wouk does not succeed in portraying Wolfe-Hawke as a dedicated artist; instead, it is Wouk and Hawke who seem to blend in the intensity of "their" business interests and speculative shenanigans, so that the money parts of the book command more authority than the literary parts. In *Don't Stop the Carnival* Wouk returned to comedy with his middle-aged cardiac victim, Norman Paperman, who exchanges a Broadway press agent's life for ownership of a Caribbean hotel. Alas, on his island paradise, life proves even more frantic as foundation walls burst, typhoons rage, and mad employees decapitate others—but Norman copes. When all is under control, Paperman unaccountably sells out cheap (as Wouk seems to do) and returns to ulcer-ridden Broadway. But the novel does display the same comedic flair for oddball characters, clever dialogue, fast intercutting, and imaginative slapstick as had *Aurora Dawn*, *City Boy* (about a Jewish Penrod) and even *Marjorie Morningstar*.

Possibly, light comedy and fond satire are Wouk's forte, since his serious views seem uninspired and inhibited. But his recent two-volume series *The Winds of War* and *War and Remembrance* is surely his most ambitious work. The two books trace the lives of Navy Commander, later Admiral Victor Henry, and his family from 1939 through World War II, and the end of his marriage. The size and broad aims of the volumes suggests Tolstoy's *War and Peace*, but the quality of the writing is closer to Upton Sinclair's Lanny Budd series.

—Frank Campenni

WRIGHT, Charles (Stevenson). American. Born in New Franklin, Missouri, 4 June 1932. Educated in public schools in New Franklin and Sedalia, Missouri. Served in the United States Army, in Korea, 1952-54. Free-lance writer: Columnist ("Wright's World"), *Village Voice*, New York. Lives in New York City. Address: c/o Farrar, Straus and Giroux, 19 Union Square West, New York, New York 10003, U.S.A.

PUBLICATIONS

Novels

The Messenger. New York, Farrar Straus, 1963; London, Souvenir Press, 1964.

The Wig: A Mirror Image. New York, Farrar Straus, 1966; London, Souvenir Press, 1967.

Absolutely Nothing to Get Alarmed About. New York, Farrar Straus, 1973.

Uncollected Short Stories

"A New Day," in *The Best Short Stories by Negro Writers*, edited by Langston Hughes. Boston, Little Brown, 1967.

"Sonny and the Sailor," in *Negro Digest* (Chicago), August 1968.

*

Critical Studies: reviews in *New Yorker*, 2 November 1963, and *New York Times*, 23 February 1966.

Charles Wright comments:

(1972) Numbers. One number has always walked through the front door of my mind. But when I was writing my first book, *The Messenger*, I did not think of numbers. I was very bitter at the time. *The Messenger* was simply a money roof. I was amused at its success. Mini-popular first published thing. A pleasant dream with the frame of reality.

The Wig was my life. And as I write this on a night of the last week in April of 1971—I have no regrets. Let me explain: A year after the publication of *The Messenger* I was thinking of that folkloric, second novel, and began a rough draft of a novel about a group of Black men, very much like the Black Panthers. But, in 1963, America was not ready for *that* type of novel, nor were they ready for *The Wig*. Ah! That is the first horror hors d'oeuvre. My agent, Candida Donadio, said: "This is a novel. Write it." I will tell you quite simply...that I was afraid that I could not sustain the thing for say...fifty pages.

Now it was another year, another country (Morocco). Frightened, I returned to the states and rewrote *The Wig* in twenty-nine days...the best days of my life. The basic plot was the same but most of it was new. Thinking, working, like seven and, yes, sometimes fourteen hours a day. It took me less than three hours to make the final changes before the publishers accepted. I was *hot*...hot for *National Desire*...a short N. West-type of novel very much like *The Wig*, although *Race* would not have been the theme.

And.

And. Many things have happened to me and to my country since then. The country has always been like this, I suppose. I only know that something left me. As a result...I haven't written a novel in six years. I remember Langston Hughes saying: "Write another nice, little book like *The Messenger*. White folks don't like to know that Negroes can write books like that."

Ah, yes...dear, dead Friend. Then. Yes. Another *Messenger*. And, what follows? Something that I've always wanted to do, something different...say an action packed Hemingway novel and then say...a Sackville-West novel. All I've ever wanted was a home by the sea and to be a good writer.

* * *

The literary output of Charles Stevenson Wright has been slight in volume and promising, but not always effective, in practice. Wright's three small "novels" are each the size of Nathanael West novels, and they reflect the same mordant wit, yearning despair, and surrealistic lunacy of vintage West. Wright's world, however, is essentially a race-twisted society of black grotesques, of crippled lovers and dish-washer poets whose lives of wine, whores, and junkie-songs spell slow murder in white America.

The Messenger, *The Wig*, and *Absolutely Nothing to Get Alarmed About* portray an Inferno-world of sexual deviates: prostitutes (male and female), pimps, transvestites, poseurs, flower-children, sadistic cops. We meet not only lovers but pretenders, false black friends who set you up, genteel female perverts, white liberals whose children suddenly snarl "nigger," beloved black musicians who betray their heritage to gain white favor. Each novel centers around the efforts of a young protagonist ("Charles Stevenson" in the first and "Charles Wright" in the third novel) to cope with city life, where literally and metaphorically the protagonists prostitute themselves to survive. Each must dissemble, disguise, and sell himself; each finds the gimmicks and the humbling tricks to hustle an existence.

In *The Messenger*, which is heavily autobiographical, a young writer, Charles Stevenson, stumbles to find himself, moving from the South to the army to New York. As a writer, he knows he must feel and record; his literal job as messenger is unimportant compared to his literary obligation to spread the word about life. As a black, however, he is torn between his compassion for outcast blacks and his emotional shield compounded of numbness, indifference, and cynicism. Although the writing occasionally slips into clichés or strained metaphor, style is the novel's chief attraction and is marvelously wedded to content. The writing is terse, the narrator-hero's manner laconic and usually guarded. Most episodes are deliberately inconclusive and undeveloped, sketchy vignettes that affect the narrator more than he acknowledges. Deeply touching are the few pages in which the spiritually exhausted young veteran is united with his warm, righteous grandmother, while his athletic command performance in a Southern police station is outrageously comic and brilliantly symbolic of racial debasement.

If *The Messenger* seems like a patch-quilt of styles and moods, *The Wig* is more consistent in tone and mood, but regrettably so. For Wright's second novel goes all-out as black comedy, but despite its wildness it is more black, or malicious, than comic. There is a similar gallery of transvestites and other disguise-wearing freaks in quest of identity without guilt, failure, or self-hatred, but they are portrayed without hope or compassion. The hero, Lester Jefferson, is, like all the other blacks, on the make: he has conked and curled his Afro hair into a beautiful white "wig" that will open the doors to the Great (White) Society. Alas, he doesn't make it but we are not even sorry, for neither he nor the author reaches Ellison's solution that "visibility" begins with confronting and accepting one's truly created self. There are two or three successful comic achievements: Jimmy Wishbone, who once "kept 100 million colored people contented for years" as a Stepin Fetchit type in movies and who now wants to sue white society and redeem his lost fleet of cadillacs; and Lester himself, crawling the streets in a feathery chicken-suit as employee of the Southern Fried Chicken King.

The last exchange of dialogue in *The Messenger* goes: " 'Charles, what's wrong?' 'Nothing,' I said. 'Absolutely nothing.' " Wright's latest novelistic autobiography, *Absolutely Nothing to Get Alarmed About*, picks up from its predecessor's conclusion, although the locale has moved from mid-Manhattan to the Lower East Side. The mood is more uniformly despairing, with only a few attempts at the pathos and yearning of *The Messenger* or the caustic hilarity of *The Wig*. In place of the homosexual-junkie nightmare world of *The Messenger*, Wright's metaphor of our foundering American culture is here the yellow-black-white world of the Bowery. Appropriate to their original publication in New York's *Village Voice*, many chapters echo the vivid tone and the felt immediacy of "new journalism" prose.

—Frank Campenni

YAFFE, James. American. Born in Chicago, Illinois, 31 March 1927. Educated at Yale University, New Haven, Connecticut, 1944-48, B.A. (summa cum laude) 1948. Served in the United States Navy, 1945-46. Married Elaine Gordon in 1964; two daughters and one son. Since 1968, Adjunct Professor, Colorado College, Colorado Springs. Recipient: National Endowment for the Arts Award, for drama, 1968. Address: 1215 North Cascade Avenue, Colorado Springs, Colorado 80903, U.S.A.

PUBLICATIONS

Novels

The Good-for-Nothing. Boston, Little Brown, and London, Constable, 1953.
What's the Big Hurry? Boston, Little Brown, 1954; as *Angry Uncle Dan*, London, Constable, 1955.
Nothing But the Night. Boston, Little Brown, 1957; London, Cape, 1958.
Mister Margolies. New York, Random House, 1962.
Nobody Does You Any Favors. New York, Putnam, 1966.
The Voyage of the Franz Joseph. New York, Putnam, 1970.

Short Stories

Poor Cousin Evelyn. Boston, Little Brown, 1951; London, Constable, 1952.

Uncollected Short Stories

"Mom Knows Best," in *The Queen's Awards 7*, edited by Ellery Queen. Boston, Little Brown, and London, Gollancz, 1952.
"On the Brink," in *The Queen's Awards 8*, edited by Ellery Queen. Boston, Little Brown, and London, Gollancz, 1953.
"Mom Makes a Bet," in *Best Detective Stories of the Year 1953*, edited by David Coxe Cooke. New York, Dutton, 1953.
"Mom in the Spring," in *The Queen's Awards 9*, edited by Ellery Queen. Boston, Little Brown, and London, Gollancz, 1954.
"Mom Makes a Wish," in *The Queen's Awards 10*, edited by Ellery Queen. Boston, Little Brown, and London, Gollancz, 1955.
"Mom Sheds a Tear," in *Best Detective Stories of the Year 1955*, edited by David Coxe Cooke. New York, Dutton, 1955.
"One of the Family," in *The Queen's Awards 11*, edited by Ellery Queen. New York, Simon and Schuster, and London, Collins, 1956.
"Mom Sings an Aria,"in *All-Star Lineup*, edited by Ellery Queen. New York, New American Library, 1966; London, Gollancz, 1968.
"Mom and the Haunted Mink," in *Mystery Parade*, edited by Ellery Queen. New York, New American Library, 1969.

Plays

The Deadly Game, adaptation of a novel by Friedrich Dürrenmatt (produced New York, 1960; London, 1967). New York, Dramatists Play Service, 1960.
This Year's Genie (juvenile), in *Eight Plays 2*, edited by Malcolm Fellows. London, Cassell, 1965.
Ivory Tower, with Jerome Weidman (produced Ann Arbor, Michigan, 1968). New York, Dramatists Play Service, 1969.

Numerous plays for television, 1953-67.

Other

The American Jews. New York, Random House, 1968.
So Sue Me! The Story of a Community Court. New York, Saturday Review Press, 1972.

*

James Yaffe comments:

For me, to write novels has been to create characters and to combine and juxtapose those characters, involve them in confrontations, place them in situations which challenge them, strengthen them, destroy them, transform them, test their mettle—and out of a variety of such characters, to build a world. Where do I get the raw material for my characters? From my own experience, of course—mostly from my experience of the world I was born and brought up in, the world of middle-class, second- and third-generation Jews living in New York, Chicago, Los Angeles. I have chosen to write about this world because I know it instinctively and subliminally, because it was part of me before I was old enough to doubt my perceptions.

But I have always tried to treat this experience not analytically or sociologically or philosophically but novelistically—that is, by imagining, and trying to re-create, the world as seen through each character's eyes. The greatest novelists, it seems to me, are those who succeed in merging their personalities with the lives and feelings of their people. This is the special ability shared by writers as different as Tolstoy and Jane Austen, Trollope and Joyce (to mention a few of my favorites). The attempt to follow their example may be presumptuous and doomed to failure, but it is also inevitable for anybody who wants to write novels.

* * *

James Yaffe is considered a leading novelist of middle-class Jewish life in America. His early collection of short stories (*Poor Cousin Evelyn*) and his first novel (*The Good-for-Nothing*) are essentially drawing room comedies set in New York. As in the novels of Jane Austen, whom Yaffe admits a special fondness for, small conflicts are closely scrutinized within a closed society—in Yaffe's case, the Jewish family, with all its attendant social hierarchies, its patriarchs, its strongmen and its failures, its pressures of shame and guilt applied by loved ones to safeguard conformity and tradition. In these earlier works, characters are

simply drawn and situations directly presented, largely through dialogue.

A recurring Yaffe theme involves the "dreamer," an impractical or artistically oriented individual confronted with pressures to survive in a competitive business world of shady deals and opportunism. In *The Good-for-Nothing* this conflict is represented by two brothers, apparently very different from each other, yet mutally dependent. The one is college-educated and totally ineffectual in the business world, a charming sycophant. The other, a Certified Public Accountant, supports him, but in so doing restricts his own life. As they interact, it become unclear which is the "good for nothing," which the success or the failure: in different ways, both are unwilling to face responsibilities or the possibility of failure. Self-righteousness and self-indulgence, like sentimentality, are both forms of escape, excuses for not taking risks.

In a later novel, *Mister Margolies*, this pattern of self-deception is advanced to the point where the manipulation of reality becomes a life-style. Stanley Margolies, defeated in his early attempt to become a concert-pianist, yet unable to give up totally his dreams of a poetic life, withdraws into a world of fantasies. The reality of business and competition crashes in on this, and he withdraws deeper, erecting more elaborate defences. Yaffe's "dreamers" create worlds which are both sad and poetic, but they are not the demonic Rose-gardens of the totally mad. They are the tiny fantasies of little men, dreams reinforced by sympathetic and condescending friends with whom they still retain some form of contact.

Yaffe avoids several stereotypes popular in much contemporary Jewish literature: the dominant Jewish Mother, and the Jew-Gentile confrontation, particularly in matters sexual, as an expression of, or as a means of resolving feelings of inferiority. In general, he maintains a comic narrative tone—some of the scenes are funny—and though his characters are forever lecturing each other, their messages are frequently as confused as they are. The novels themselves preach little other than a deep compassion for the small man and his hopes.

The theme of the dreamer in search of his vision makes a terrifying appearance in *Nothing But the Night*, which is based on the Nathan Leopold-Richard Loeb murder case of 1924, and the celebrated defence by Clarence Darrow. The case history is seen through the eyes of one of the young men, not as an investigation of the criminal mind, but as a study of a lonely and creative child. As in Chekhov, Yaffe's characters take their emotions very seriously and ponder them deeply. They are often trapped by their own visions and the pressures to succeed imposed from outside. In their struggle to hold on to their dreams, they are destroyed, transformed, and occasionally liberated. An example of the latter is presented in *Nobody Does You Any Favors*, which despite its 1940's cinema-sounding title is perhaps his best novel. As opposed to the earlier New York novels which suggest short stories in their structural focus on a single event, *Nobody Does You Any Favors* with its time span of roughly 40 years allows for an extended development and growth in character. The confrontation between father and son is drawn with an understanding and passion valid beyond a scene of very special terror and insight. Certainly this novel is a significant contribution to American literature of the 20th century.

Yaffe's most recent novel, *The Voyage of the Franz Joseph*, represents an epic departure from his usual drawing room style. Like *Nothing But the Night*, it is based on an historical event, the sailing of the German liner *St. Louis* in 1939 with a thousand Jewish refugees searching for a homeland.

—Paul Seiko Chihara

YATES, Richard. American. Born in Yonkers, New York, 3 February 1926. Educated at the Avon School, Connecticut. Served in the United States Army Infantry, 1944-46. Married 1) Sheila Bryant in 1948 (divorced, 1959), two daughters; 2) Martha Speer in 1968. Financial reporter, United Press, New York, 1946-48; publicity writer, Remington Rand Inc., New York, 1948-50; free-lance public relations writer, 1953-60; Lecturer, New School for Social Research, New York, 1959-62, and Columbia University, New York, 1960-62; screenwriter, United Artists, Hollywood, 1962; speech writer for Attorney-General Robert Kennedy, Washington, D.C., 1963; screen-writer, Columbia Pictures, Hollywood, 1965-66. Lecturer, 1964-65, and since 1966, Assistant Professor of English, University of Iowa, Iowa City. Writer-in-Residence, Wichita State University, Kansas, 1971-72. Recipient: Guggenheim Fellowship, 1962; American Academy grant, 1963; Brandeis University Creative Arts Award, 1964; National Endowment for the Arts grant, 1966; Rockefeller grant, 1967; Rosenthal Foundation award, 1976. Address: 473 Beacon Street, Boston, Massachusetts 02115, U.S.A.

PUBLICATIONS

Novels

Revolutionary Road. Boston, Little Brown, 1961; London, Deutsch, 1962.
A Special Providence. New York, Knopf, 1969.
Disturbing the Peace. New York, Delacorte Press, 1975.
The Easter Parade. New York, Delacorte Press, 1976; London, Eyre Methuen, 1978.
A Good School. New York, Delacorte Press, 1978.

Short Stories

Eleven Kinds of Loneliness. Boston, Little Brown, 1962; London, Deutsch, 1964.

Uncollected Short Stories

"To Be a Hero," in *Saturday Evening Post* (Philadelphia), 25 September 1965.
"A Good and Gallant Woman," in *Prize Stories 1967: The O. Henry Awards*, edited by William Abrahams. New York, Doubleday, 1967.
"Bellevue," in *North American Review* (Cedar Falls, Iowa), Summer 1975.
"Oh, Joseph, I'm So Tired," in *Prize Stories 1980: The O. Henry Awards*, edited by William Abrahams. New York, Doubleday, 1980.
"Regards at Home," in *Atlantic* (Boston), August 1980.

Other

Editor, *Stories for the Sixties.* New York, Bantam, 1962.

*

Manuscript Collection: Boston University.

Critical Study: in *The Red-Hot Vacuum* by Theodore Solotaroff, New York, Atheneum, 1970.

Richard Yates comments:

(1972) Writing fiction is a very slow and difficult process for me. It is what I do best, but it has taken me nearly twenty years to produce three published books.

If my work has a theme, I suspect it is a simple one: that most human beings are inescapably alone, and therein lies their tragedy.

* * *

Richard Yates's fictional world is peopled with ordinary middle-class New Yorkers and suburbanites whose lives have gone awry. They come from broken homes; they naively believe that a mate, family, and material comfort make them happy. Their plans and dreams alike simply do not work out. Yates's men drink and seek solace in casual affairs; neither narcotic is sufficient to relieve the pain of their loneliness. His women have little promise: they glide easily through the moods of wifely reassurance, wife-as-mistress, and wife-as-cocktail companion. They always stop short of self-recognition and the admission that they cannot stand to be loved for the part they play, rather than for the person they are. In Yates's fictional world, there is "no settling of accounts, no resolution, no proof." People must make the best of a bad lot. Nurtured on songs about "the best of everything," his characters grow up to discover that the glow of good feeling lasts only moments and comes rarely. Their homes become prisons; their dreams, too fragile to withstand reality, become difficult to recall. They stumble through their lives.

The contours of Yates's stories are familiar—John Updike has written in the same vein—but it is his finely tuned powers of observation coupled with an ability to elect the right detail that make his scenes come alive and give his writing its distinction. His skill, too, as a technician enables him to create a language, colloquial and deftly ironic, to render his detail with unerring honesty. Like J.D. Salinger, Yates can capture scenes of awkward adolescence with all their excruciating humiliations. In *A Good School* he writes so vividly of a scene where a group of noisy adolescent boys strip their classmate, pin him down in his bed, and force his genitals to fufill their will that the reader winces, wanting to look away, but compelled by his or her own curiosity to see the scene to its humiliating end. Later Yates depicts the victim of this scene trying to befriend his two literary idols who he learns, to his mortification, have witnessed the hazing and judged him with contempt. At this kind of scene, Yates excels as a writer, capturing precisely the subtle, contradictory emotions such a scene evokes.

Yates's short stories and fiction both rely on some of Salinger's tricks of dialogue, situation, and character. But more important is his debt to Salinger for a way to handle point of view. Salinger's narrators in "For Esmé with Love and Squalor" and *Raise High the Roof Beams, Carpenters* seem to have inspired Yates's rendering of Bob Prentice, the protagonist of "Builders" from *Eleven Kinds of Loneliness* and *A Special Providence*. Prentice, like Salinger's narrators, recognizes that the writer is a "sensitive person," that the sensitivity ought to be disguised lest it be too unsettling for the reader, that the piece of fiction to be recounted must be "no-nonsense fiction," and that the wives of these sensitive writers are "dead logical" or "breathtakingly level-headed women." Yates also imitates Salinger's method of selecting a detail and presenting it with a nice misanthropic turn. Mrs. Fedder's attitude towards Seymour Glass's sickness is echoed in Mrs. Giving's treatment of John's mental disorders in *Revolutionary Road*. John's candor and outspokenness also resembles Seymour's outburst when a lady looks too markedly at his bare feet in "A Perfect Day for Bananafish." Yates's interest in children, their moods, sullenness, tantrums, and jealousies also shares with Salinger's. But if Yates imitates Salinger, this imitation is not slavish. He has his own voice, his own style—lucid, amusing, and artfully wrought—and his most recent book testifies to his independence from his mentor.

Revolutionary Road, *A Special Providence*, *Disturbing the Peace*, and *The Easter Parade* all touch on madness and suicide, and the profession which purports to treat their victims. April Wheeler in *Revolutionary Road* kills herself, helplessly confessing that she does not know who she is. In *The Easter Parade* the protagonist's plight is grimmer. She must go on living. At 50, Emily Grimes arrives at her nephew's door, turning to him to care for her, confessing she feels old and has never understood anything in her whole life. Her sister, an inveterate alcoholic and victim of her husband's beatings, dies after a fall. The novel leaves the reader and Emily with the sickening suspicion that Sarah's self-destruction was ultimately assisted by her husband's blow, that her death was not an accident but a murder. *Disturbing the Peace* is the story of John Wilder's crack-up, one from which he never mends. *A Special Providence* relates Bob Prentice's struggle for freedom from his neurotic mother. It is, finally, the humiliating and bitter experiences in a training camp that painfully teach Bob that he must stand alone if he is to survive, and that life has nothing to offer but survival.

Yates's collection of short stories and his first four novels all concern characters who fall in love with the postures of failure. Walter Henderson in "A Glutton for Punishment" is endlessly fascinated by the attitudes of collapse: as a child he loved to play at falling dead; as an adolescent, he was the best little loser, a real sport; and by the time he marries, failure has become a habit. In *Disturbing the Peace* Yates extends his study of failure to include a protagonist who leaves his wife and child to join his mistress and become the film producer he had always dreamt of being. The irony that the film he will make is one based on his own incarceration in Bellevue after an alcoholic binge is not one he feels until he is hopelessly enmeshed in his own actions. John Wilder, once a successful salesman, disintegrates, pursuing in life the role he has created for a film. His self-destruction is total. Believing that art offered a means to control his chaos, he flounders as we realize that his art is merely an extension of his chaos. *The Easter Parade* depicts the unhappy lives of Sarah and Emily Grimes, two girls from a broken home. Their dread of isolation pushes one into the arms of a handsome, brutish, uneducated man who looks like Olivier, and the other, first, into a bad marriage with a man who proves impotent and, then, into a series of affairs, one involving a writer who has lost his creativity. Three failed relationships leave Emily a confused, hurt woman whose independence, once a necessary defense, becomes intolerable.

A Good School, perhaps the most autobiographical of Yates's writings, offers a story in which the protagonist's creativity survives. The book recounts the schooldays of William Grove at Dorset Academy. Dorset "believes in individuality" and has a reputation for accepting boys which no schools, for a variety of good reasons, will accept. The story is set during World War II and the wartime economy ruins Dorset financially. William's schooldays bruise and build. Gawky, bookish, lacking in social background, William is subject to ridicule and neglect. Hanging on to what little dignity is left him after the vicious sexual attack from his virile and frustrated classmates, William befriends the editors of the *Dorset Chronicle* and ultimately becomes editor himself. The portrait of the school and William is convincing and moving. The war takes its toll on William's classmates and his school; William's awkward attempts to gain acceptance and his battles with his shyness and sexuality are told with humor and poignancy; and the novel ends with his coming of age while another age ends. In *A Good School* Yates's interest in writers is more affirmative than it has been before. He had aptly captured the syndrome of the failed writer in *The Easter Parade*; *A Good School* is the most forgiving story he has told. In it Yates is at once wry and ironic, light-hearted, and dumbly sad; never does he lapse into sentimentality. Many parts of this story have been hinted at in Yates's other writings. In some ways it is curious that Yates should attempt this genre five novels into his canon, and not earlier, but the maturity and the mellowing the book reflect argue for the delay. I trust the book will liberate Yates. He is a fine writer who has more than proved his competence. What he needs now is a different theme, tougher and more complex characters, and more significant action to stretch the talent that his writing has amply demonstrated.

—Carol Simpson Stern

YERBY, Frank (Garvin). American. Born in Augusta, Georgia, 5 September 1916. Educated at Paine College, Augusta, A.B. 1937; Fisk University, Nashville, Tennessee, M.A. 1938; University of Chicago, 1939. Married 1) Flora Helen Claire Williams in 1941 (divorced), two sons and two daughters; 2) Blanca Calle Pérez in 1956. Instructor, Florida Agricultural and Mechanical College, Tallahassee, 1938-39, and Southern University and A. and M. College, Baton Rouge, Louisiana, 1939-41; Laboratory Technician, Ford Motor Company, Dearborn, Michigan, 1941-44; Magnaflux Inspector, Ranger (Fairchild) Aircraft, Jamaica, New York, 1944-45; full-time writer from 1945; settled in Madrid, 1954. Recipient: O. Henry Award, 1944. Agent: Owen Laster, William Morris Agency, 1350 Avenue of the Americas, New York, New York 10019, U.S.A. Address: Edificio Torres Blancas, Apartamento 710, Avenida de America 37, Madrid 2, Spain.

PUBLICATIONS

Novels

The Foxes of Harrow. New York, Dial Press, 1946; London, Heinemann, 1947.
The Vixens. New York, Dial Press, 1947; London, Heinemann, 1948.
The Golden Hawk. New York, Dial Press, 1948; London, Heinemann, 1949.
Pride's Castle. New York, Dial Press, 1949; London, Heinemann, 1950.
Floodtide. New York, Dial Press, 1950; London, Heinemann, 1951.
A Woman Called Fancy. New York, Dial Press, 1951; London, Heinemann, 1952.
The Saracen Blade. New York, Dial Press, 1952; London, Heinemann, 1953.
The Devil's Laughter. New York, Dial Press, 1953; London, Heinemann, 1954.
Benton's Row. New York, Dial Press, 1954; London, Heinemann, 1955.
Bride of Liberty. New York, Dial Press, 1954; London, Heinemann, 1955.
The Treasure of Pleasant Valley. New York, Dial Press, 1955; London, Heinemann, 1956.
Captain Rebel. New York, Dial Press, 1956; London, Heinemann, 1957.
Fairoaks. New York, Dial Press, 1957; London, Heinemann, 1958.
The Serpent and the Staff. New York, Dial Press, 1958; London, Heinemann, 1959.
Jarrett's Jade. New York, Dial Press, 1959; London, Heinemann, 1960.
Gillian. New York, Dial Press, 1960; London, Heinemann, 1961.
The Garfield Honor. New York, Dial Press, 1961; London, Heinemann, 1962.
Griffin's Way. New York, Dial Press, 1962; London, Heinemann, 1963.
The Old Gods Laugh: A Modern Romance. New York, Dial Press, and London, Heinemann, 1964.
An Odor of Sanctity. New York, Dial Press, 1965; London, Heinemann, 1966.
Goat Song: A Novel of Ancient Greece. New York, Dial Press, 1967; London, Heinemann, 1968.
Judas, My Brother: The Story of the Thirteenth Disciple. New York, Dial Press, and London, Heinemann, 1969.
Speak Now. New York, Dial Press, 1969; London, Heinemann, 1970.
The Dahomean. New York, Dial Press, 1971; as *The Man from Dahomey*, London, Heinemann, 1971.
The Girl from Storyville: A Victorian Novel. New York, Dial Press, and London, Heinemann, 1972.
The Voyage Unplanned. New York, Dial Press, and London, Heinemann, 1974.
Tobias and the Angel. New York, Dial Press, and London, Heinemann, 1975.
A Rose for Ana María. New York, Dial Press, and London, Heinemann, 1976.
Hail the Conquering Hero. New York, Dial Press, 1977; London, Heinemann, 1978.
A Darkness at Ingraham's Crest. New York, Dial Press, 1979.

Uncollected Short Stories

"The Thunder of God," in *New Anvil* (Chicago), April-May 1939.
"Health Card," in *O. Henry Memorial Award Prize Stories 1944*, edited by Herschel Brickell and Miriam Fuller. New York, Doubleday, 1944.
"Roads Going Down," in *Common Ground* (New York), v, 4, 1945.
"The Homecoming," in *American Negro Short Stories*, edited by John Henrik Clarke. New York, Hill and Wang, 1966.
"My Brother Went to College," in *Black American Literature: Fiction*. Columbus, Ohio, Merrill, 1969.

*

Manuscript Collection: Mugar Memorial Library, Boston University.

Critical Studies: *Behind the Magnolia Mask: Frank Yerby as Critic of the South* by William Werdna Hill, Jr., unpublished thesis, Auburn University, Alabama, 1968; *The Unembarrassed Muse* by Russel B. Nye, New York, Dial Press, 1970; *Anti-Heroic Perspectives in the Life and Works of Frank Yerby* by James Lee Hill, unpublished thesis, University of Iowa, 1976.

Frank Yerby comments:

The work has consisted mostly of historical novels written both to instruct and to entertain. In them, I've tried to correct the reader's historical perspective, wildly distorted in my youth, on such themes as Negro slavery, the Civil War South, and Reconstruction.

To date, I have written only two modern novels, *The Old Gods Laugh*, largely an entertainment in the sense that Graham Greene uses the word, and *Speak Now*, a serious effort.

Of my historicals, I should rate *An Odor of Sanctity*, *Judas, My Brother*, *A Goat Song* and perhaps even *The Garfield Honor* as serious novels. The rest are entertainments, a fact of which I am *not* ashamed. Entertaining the reader is a legitimate function of a novelist.

I hope, in the future, however, to concentrate upon serious work. Present day taxation makes writing "entertainments" worth neither the boredom, nor the bother.

* * *

Few popular writers have been maligned for so many reasons as the historical novelist Frank Yerby. He has been indicted for superficial research, melodramatic plotting, purple prose and sub-freshman grammar, comic book characterization, and, above all, betrayal of his Negritude. All of these shortcomings are easily found in his many novels, but such documentation cannot explain away the enormous appeal of these novels or the determined energy that produced them.

Yerby's first published novel, *The Foxes of Harrow*, was quickly followed by five more, each selling more than a million copies, and several adopted by book clubs and sold to the movies. In America the genre of the historical novel enjoyed its highpoint from about the mid-1930's to the mid-1950's, and Frank Yerby was most in favor during the last decade of that trend. He has continued to write and to be read since *The Saracen Blade* and *The Devil's Laughter* but with intermittent and diminishing success, even though his later work is probably his best.

Following the popular acceptance of *Foxes of Harrow*, Yerby developed that novel into a loose trilogy; he then continued with a half dozen similar novels set in the South, especially New Orleans, during the middle and late 19th century. In this same period, Yerby also turned his hand to picaresque adventure and pirate heroes of the late 17th century (*Golden Hawk*), the crusades to the Holy Land

(*Saracen Blade*), and the French and American revolutions (*Devil's Laughter* and *Bride of Liberty*). That Yerby was writing by formula was evident, but it was not quite the typical romantic pattern of separated but undying love, of virtuous heroines and happy endings, of brave heroes and bold villains battling in a glamorized historical setting of reactionary politics and sharp class distinctions. Instead, Yerby's heroes are not faithful, the heroines not virtuous, the endings not happy; the characters' claims to aristocracy are spurious, the "colorful milieu" is sordid, the upper classes are mean-spirited, bigoted, and greedy.

In 1959 Yerby candidly described for *Harper's Magazine* his own formula for the "costume novel," rejecting the label "historical" since his editors cut out "ninety-nine and ninety-nine one-hundredths" of the historical material. Yerby discredits writing "about ill-treated factory workers, or people who suffered because of their religion or the color of their skins," since such material should deal with interesting "individuals." Yerby's own rules include writing "good, rousing tales" about picaresque "doers" (dominant males who are neither emotionally mature nor polygamous) and their involvements with beautiful, sexy heroines—though sex scenes should be minimal and understated. The plot should be dramatic and economically handled, focussing tightly on development and resolution of "a strong exteriorized conflict." There should be an "ennobling" unifying theme, such as the author's own favorite, "the eternal warfare between the sexes," but never must the writer propagandize and upset the "hypnotic suspension of his reader's sense of disbelief."

Actually, Yerby's initial recognition as a writer of fiction came through several short stories of social protest, such as "Health Card," "The Homecoming," and "My Brother Went to College," all dealing with racial injustice in contemporary America. After an unsuccessful attempt at a proletarian novel, he turned to historical melodrama, with which he has recently become disenchanted, despite his great skill in narration and suspense-building. His more recent novels move further back in time and show more evidence of research and an authentic sense of place and culture.

The Dahomean is Yerby's only book primarily about Negroes; ironically, its major flaws are a sluggish pace and excess anthropological detail. Yet this moving chronicle of the making of an African chief—tracing his life through adolescence, initiation, marriage, wars, kingship, and downfall—is written with such sympathy, seriousness, and control, all lacking in the earlier work, that *The Dahomean* emerges as his best work.

Although Yerby has shown limited development as a craftsman, his main technical faults almost disappear as his attitudes toward his material and his literary purpose grow less cynical. His earliest escapist view, stated flippantly, that most significant problems are unsolvable anyway, has been embodied and reformulated in recent fiction as a mature, tragic view of man. Thus, there are signs that Frank Yerby's best work may still be ahead of him.

—Frank Campenni

YGLESIAS, Jose. American. Born in Tampa, Florida, 29 November 1919. Educated at Black Mountain College, North Carolina, 1946-47. Served in the United States Navy, 1942-45: Presidential Citation. Married Helen Bassine in 1950; one son and two stepchildren. Dishwasher, bus boy, stock clerk; Film Critic, *Daily Worker*, New York, 1948-50; Assistant to the Vice-President, Merch Sharp and Dohme International, 1953-63; Regents Lecturer, University of California, Santa Barbara, 1973. Recipient: Guggenheim Fellowship, 1970, 1976; National Endowment for the Arts grant, 1974. Agent: Wallace and Sheil Agency, 177 East 70th Street, New York, New York 10021. Address: North Brooklin, Maine 04661, U.S.A.

PUBLICATIONS

Novels

A Wake in Ybor City. New York, Holt Rinehart, 1963.
An Orderly Life. New York, Pantheon, 1967; London, Hutchinson, 1968.
The Truth about Them. Cleveland, World, 1971.
Double, Double. New York, Viking Press, 1974.
The Kill Price. Indianapolis, Bobbs Merrill, 1976.

Uncollected Short Stories

"The Guns in the Closet," in *The Best American Short Stories 1972*, edited by Martha Foley. Boston, Houghton Mifflin, 1972.
"In the Bronx," in *American Review 19*, edited by Theodore Solotaroff. New York, Bantam, 1974.
"The American Sickness," in *The Best American Short Stories 1975*, edited by Martha Foley. Boston, Houghton Mifflin, 1975.

Other

The Goodbye Land. New York, Pantheon, 1967; London, Hutchinson, 1968.
In the Fist of the Revolution: Life in a Cuban Country Town. New York, Pantheon, 1968; as *In the Fist of the Revolution: Life in Castro's Cuba*, London, Allen Lane, 1968.
Down There (on Latin America). Cleveland, World, 1970.
The Franco Years: The Untold Human Story of Life under Spanish Fascism. Indianapolis, Bobbs Merrill, 1977.

Translator, *Island of Women*, by Juan Goytisolo. New York, Knopf, 1962; as *Sands of Torremolinos*, London, Cape, 1962.
Translator, *Villa Milo*, by Xavier Domingo. New York, Braziller, 1962.
Translator, *The Party's Over*, by Juan Goytisolo. New York, Grove Press, and London, Weidenfeld and Nicolson, 1966.

*

Manuscript Collection: Boston University.

Jose Yglesias comments:

I write to have my say. There are feelings and ideas that conversations and speeches and articles and reviews will not accomodate: these are the things that fiction, always so undiscriminating, finds room for. I thank God for the novel form.

* * *

A primary focus in all of Jose Yglesias's novels is the bearing of Hispanic heritage upon increasingly Americanized Cuban expatriates. Most especially it is the old extended family and Spanish "republican" predilections which he probes for contemporary life signs. His work always entails some marriage of these two concerns, which gives them a compelling blend of the personal and the sociopolitical. Moreover, he unfailingly discovers, happily or unhappily for his characters, analogical moral crises between the generations. This aspect of his work reaches its finest, albeit pessimistic, fruition in his fourth and least ethnic novel, *Double, Double*.

Yglesias is gifted at delineating the conflicting claims of private, even mercantile, aspirations as against social and altruistic ones. The former include not only a regard for capital and personal luxury (the narrator of his third novel remarks "a shame-faced admiration for gentility"), but particularly for the wonders of sexual gratification and familial warmth. The latter include a regard for the democratic struggle in Spain, the egalitarian yearnings of Tampa's cigar workers (often mere "cafe revolutionaries"), the fight for Cuban independence, and, increasingly after the first novel, the hopes of all minorities, including student radicals. None of this is rendered at the expense of psychological or existential curiosity or verisimilitude.

Set in Tampa's Cuban ghetto in 1958, *A Wake in Ybor City* involves action ironically heightened by the reader's knowledge of the then incipiently successful Castro revolution. The major conflict concerns an affluent Cuban woman and her penurious family. She attempts to abort the wake the others are planning for her nephew, contemptuously labeling it "barbaric." And in asserting that the affair would kill her mother she misses the obvious, for eschewing the ancient custom is precisely what would do that. The foils to this figure are a political activist, Estaban, and Robert Moran, a Cuban-American artist. Robert is reluctantly won over to Estaban's commitment and in helping to deliver weapons to Cuban freedom fighters he is the first of Yglesias's protagonists to experience the ramifications of ideology. But in this first novel, the family and the morality of its tenacious affections are the focal points.

The least overtly political of the novels, *An Orderly Life* is, still laced with socio-political motifs, which touch subtly upon the protagonist Rafe's curiously successful pursuit of a structured existence. Rafe's sense of order is not rigid, but "a kind of listening to music, a response to its swells, lulls and rhythms." To this end he strikes a balance between numerous but counterpointed forces. Free enterprise, sex as an end in itself, and marital love determine Rafe in half of his nature. In the other half he is directed by the influences of three very different friends. From Jerry comes his Marxist bent, sullied in Jerry's own life by his guilt-ridden capitulation with the Bitch Goddess; from Josh, a black radical gone homosexual, comes a gift for leavening too pure motives with pragmatic choices; from Mr. Sealy, a veritable "Southern Gentleman," comes aristocratic decorum, "the vision of order itself."

The pronoun in *The Truth about Them* is finely ambiguous. "They" are Spanish Americans; their truth is the integrity of their passional lives. "They" are also their myriad antagonists. The novel builds itself upon the narrator Pini's effort to elaborate and validate his familial past and to pass on to his son Ralph the "elegiac mood" it inspires in him. This mood is intensified by Pini's realization that his "*background*...[is] the agony of others." Yet he has also known, shamefully, ethnic embarrassment and, anxiously, the fear "that in another generation this ambience might at best only linger like a scent after a beautiful woman has left the room." Expelled from Columbia after the student strike, Ralph sees Ybor City too narrowly, as only "a pacified village in Vietnam." But the past and present are fused happily when his grandmother gently wins him with a lesson in the survival instincts of his ancestors.

Four well-realized aspects of *Double, Double* make it Yglesias's best work. The plot is the primary masterstroke. From this emanate an astute psychological rendering of Seth Evergood's character, a brilliant unfolding of how the limitations (if not the sins) of the father are visited upon the son, and a lucid vision of the deadly serious ramifications of political dissent in contemporary America. The old thematic interests remain but are assimilated by broader ones. The novel exposes, often comically and pathetically, the disturbing relationships of sub-cultures and right-wing police power, as it depicts the bumbling attempts of an intellectual to act out his social consciousness. One wants to compare this work with "The Short Happy Life of Francis Macomber," but Evergood is deprived of Macomber's relatively luxurious moment of self-realization because—from the rear as it were—he is exploded into oblivion. It only remains for the good-hearted but dim hippie to misevaluate totally what has transpired.

—David M. Heaton

YORK, Andrew. *See* **NICOLE, Christopher.**

YOUNG, Al. American. Born in Ocean Springs, Mississippi, 31 May 1939. Educated at the University of Michigan, Ann Arbor (Co-Editor, *Generation* magazine), 1957-61; Stanford University, California (Wallace E. Stegner Creative Writing Fellow), 1966-67; University of California, Berkeley, A.B. in Spanish 1969. Married Arline June Belch in 1963; one son. Free-lance Musician, 1958-64; Disc Jockey, KJAZ-FM, San Francisco, 1961-65; Instructor and Linguistic Consultant, San Francisco Neighborhood Youth Corps Writing Workshop, 1968-69; Writing Instructor, Teenage Workshop, San Francisco Museum of Art, 1968-69; Jones Lecturer in Creative Writing, Stanford University, 1969-74. Since 1966, Founding Editor, *Loveletter*, San Francisco; since 1972, Co-Editor, *Yardbird Reader*, Berkeley, California; Contributing Editor, since 1972, *Changes*, New York, and since 1973, *Umoja*, New Mexico. Recipient: National Endowment for the Arts grant, 1968, 1969, 1974; San Francisco Foundation Joseph Henry Jackson Award, 1969; Guggenheim Fellowship, 1974. Agent: Lynn Nesbitt, International Creative Management, 40 West 57th Street, New York, New York 10019. Address: 514 Bryant Street, Palo Alto, California 94301, U.S.A.

PUBLICATIONS

Novels

Snakes. New York, Holt Rinehart, 1970; London, Sidgwick and Jackson, 1971.
Who Is Angelina? New York, Holt Rinehart, 1975; London, Sidgwick and Jackson, 1978.
Sitting Pretty. New York, Holt Rinehart, 1976.
Ask Me Now. New York, McGraw Hill, and London, Sidgwick and Jackson, 1980.

Uncollected Short Stories

"My Old Buddy Shakes, Alas, and Grandmama Claude," in *Nexus* (San Francisco), May-June 1965.
"The Question Man and Why I Dropped Out," in *Nexus* (San Francisco), November-December 1965.
"Moon Watching by Lake Chapala," in *Aldebaran Review 3* (Berkeley, California), 1968.
"Chicken Hawk's Dream," in *Stanford Short Stories 1968*, edited by Wallace Stegner and Richard Scowcroft. Stanford, California, Stanford University Press, 1968.

Plays

Screenplays: *Nigger*, 1972; *Sparkle*, 1972.

Verse

Dancing. New York, Corinth, 1969.
The Song Turning Back into Itself. New York, Holt Rinehart, 1971.
Some Recent Fiction. San Francisco, San Francisco Book Company, 1974.
Geography of the Near Past. New York, Holt Rinehart, 1976.

Other

Editor, with Ishmael Reed, *Yardbird Lives!* New York, Grove Press, 1978.

*

Bibliography: in *New Black Voices*, edited by Abraham Chapman, New York, New American Library, 1972.

Critical Studies: "Reader's Report" by Martin Levin, in *New York Times Book Review*, 17 May 1970; "Growing Up Black" by L.E.

Sissman, in *The New Yorker*, 11 July 1970; "Jazzed Up," in the *Times Literary Supplement* (London), 30 July 1971; "Al Young's *Snakes*: Words to the Music" by Neil Schmitz, in *Paunch 35* (Buffalo), February 1972.

* * *

In his story "Chicken Hawk's Dream" Al Young tells of a young man who believes that as magically as in a dream he might become a jazz artist. Failing to bring even a sound out of a borrowed horn, Chicken Hawk retreats into dope and alcohol, but his delusion persists so that when the narrator meets him later on a Detroit street corner Chicken Hawk says that he is off to New York to cut a record—just as soon as he gets his instrument out of the pawnshop. The dream of Chicken Hawk with its refusal of discipline and lack of nerve represents a version of what Young terms "art as hustle." It is not titillation, he says in a "Statement on Aesthetics, Poetics, Kinetics" (in *New Black Voices*, 1972), but the touching of human beings so that both toucher and touched are changed that matters most in art as in life. Touch may be magical but before all else it is the sign of willingness to engage actual life.

Through the metaphor of touch and repudiation of attitudinizing Young explains most of his literary practice. His novels gain much of their force from his ability to limn the texture of experience. Precise detailing of speech demonstrates how individuals play roles uniquely significant to those with whom they have personal relationships, including readers; and ways of seeing, talking, becoming, in short, ways of expressing the feel of life's touch, engender the books' movement.

In his first novel, *Snakes*, Young infuses the traditional narrative of adolescent growth with a principle of fluidity affecting every aspect of structure, style, and theme. MC, whose journey to maturity is the story's subject, gets turned on to modern jazz, an art of process which illustrates that personality itself may derive from music. Stylistically the book is largely constructed out of raps, oral performances by MC's friends, and reminiscences of his grandmother. The first concur with the performance of improvisational music to convey the importance of expressive response; the latter carry process into biographical temporality where memory of past events maintains influence in the present. Style and structure together support Young's theme of the struggle to be free, outlined in MC's thoughts on a bus to New York where he, unlike Chicken Hawk, will cut a record: "For the first time in my life I don't feel trapped; I don't feel free either but I don't feel trapped and I'm going to try and make this feeling last for as long as I can."

Who is Angelina? picks up Young's theme in the story of a young woman who must regain the sense of not being trapped. In one answer to the question posed by the title, Angelina finds herself, in the words of a Pepsi-drinking fortune teller, poised between freedom to choose what she wishes and weaknesses which hold her back. A return to roots among family and neighborhood renews a sense of love for origins in Angelina but also demonstrates that she has no choice but to accept her distinct individuality; and to make the best of it, she must learn to move with awareness through her own becoming. Young allows Angelina to try transcendental meditation as a means of renewal, but her crucial realization of self occurs as it must, in the context of mundane experience. In a tussle with a purse snatcher she impulsively ventilates feelings of outrage that offend the liberal sentiments of friends and bystanders. Thereby she wipes out, for herself, the illusions one gains by living second-hand.

A year in the life of Sidney J. Prettymon, known as Sitting Pretty or sometimes plain Sit, provides the story line for Young's third novel. Sit's literary cousin is Langston Hughes's Jesse B. Semple, a.k.a. Simple. By the world's reckoning both Sit and Simple are ordinary men, but each has a philosophy and style that raises him above the average. In Sit's case the philosophy involves getting by without harming others and without succumbing to the values that will compromise integrity or happiness; thus, living is an improvisational performance. Rendered in the voice of Sit the novel *Sitting Pretty* works as the prose equivalent of an Afro-American musical composition alternatively echoing the situations of blues and celebratory riffs that are unique to the character's expressive style. Sit, jogging through the streets of Palo Alto, putting his two cents worth in on a radio talk show, caring deeply for his former wife in her time of trouble and his children when they don't even know they have problems, is a triumphant creation who deserves a place in the popular imagination right alongside Simple and probably, as Wallace Stegner suggested, Huckleberry Finn too.

Like Ishmael Reed, his colleague in *Yardbird* enterprises, Young is impatient with expectations that Black writers should show their ethnicity in some predictable or stereotypical way. O.O. Gabugah the militant poet was Young's satirical treatment of such message writing, and O.O. makes an appearance in *Sitting Pretty* also. Usually, though, Young makes his point, as in *Ask Me Now*, by unselfconscious narrative of the human trials of his characters. What makes the books Black is that the people, such as Woody Knight, the retired basketball player of his most recent novel, are granted a broad range of experience in which they talk and touch others in the style of Black culture. That style permits comedy right along with tribulation, the sort of love that yields happy endings and the losses that create frustration and anger. Reviewers loaded with prescriptions for the ethnic author and critics who want the message straight can be displeased, but Al Young's art will persist as a loving treatment of the versions of human process that are its source and subject.

—John M. Reilly

YOUNG, Marguerite (Vivian). American. Born in Indianapolis, Indiana, in 1909. Educated at Indiana University, Bloomington; Butler University, Indianapolis, B.A. 1930; University of Chicago, M.A. 1936; University of Iowa, Iowa City. Taught at Indiana University, 1942; University of Iowa, 1955-57; Columbia University, New York, 1958; New School for Social Research, New York, 1958-67; Fairleigh Dickinson University, Rutherford, New Jersey, 1960-62; Fordham University, Bronx, New York, 1966, 1967. Recipient: American Association of University Women grant, 1943; American Academy grant, 1945; Guggenheim Fellowship, 1948; Newberry Library Fellowship, 1951; Rockefeller Fellowship, 1954. Address: 375 Bleecker Street, New York, New York 10014, U.S.A.

PUBLICATIONS

Novel

Miss MacIntosh, My Darling. New York, Scribner, 1965; London, Owen, 1966.

Verse

Prismatic Ground. New York, Macmillan, 1937.
Moderate Fable. New York, Reynal, 1944.

Other

Where Is There Another? A Memorial to Paul Y. Anderson, with others. Norman, Oklahoma, Cooperative Books, 1939.
Angel in the Forest: A Fairy Tale of Two Utopias (on the New Harmony community). New York, Reynal, 1945; London, Owen, 1967.

* * *

Marguerite Young's titanic novel, *Miss MacIntosh, My Darling*

(1,198 pages), was in slow generation for more than 17 years. It is a mammoth epic, a massive fable, a picaresque journey, a Faustian quest, and a work of stunning magnitude and beauty. Her only published fiction to date, it is her masterwork. Its style is one of musicalizations, rhapsodies, symbolizations that repetitively roll and resound and double back upon themselves in an oceanic tumult. Its force is cumulative; its method is clarification through amassment, as in the great styles of Joyce or Hermann Broch or Faulkner. The major passages of the work are fluent and seminal and are grounded on four beings: Miss MacIntosh, once nursemaid to the voyager-narrator; Catherine Cartwheel, the narrator's "poor dreaming mother"; Mr. Spitzer, loyal companion to Catherine Cartwheel, composer of unheard, unwritten music and twin brother to a dead gambler with whose identity he is confounded; and Esther Longtree, a voluptuous waitress in a Wabash Valley cafe (the town of the novel is What Cheer, Iowa), who is cursed by an "everlasting, lonely pregnancy." These grand sections are procreative and fertile, spurting forth richly expressive and exhaustingly revealing passages of radiant prose. The minor sub-sections explore the submerged lives of several vivid and haunting personages. In these sections, the humor is folk, slapstick, Chaplinesque, melodramatic, and Satanic. *Miss MacIntosh, My Darling* is as often mischievously funny and devilishly humorous as it is incantatory and operatic. And, finally, the novel involves and depends on the basic and traditional American literary themes: smalltown, childhood memory, homesickness, nostalgia, quest.

—William Goyen

YURICK, Sol. American. Born in New York City, 18 January 1925. Educated at New York University, A.B. 1950; Brooklyn College, New York, M.A. 1961. Served in the United States Army, 1944-45. Married Adrienne Lash in 1958; one child. Librarian, New York University, 1945-53; Social Investigator, New York City Department of Welfare, 1954-59. Since 1959, full-time writer. Address: 220 Garfield Place, Brooklyn, New York 11215, U.S.A.

PUBLICATIONS

Novels

The Warriors. New York, Holt Rinehart, 1965; London, W.H. Allen, 1966.
Fertig. New York, Simon and Schuster, and London, W.H. Allen, 1966.
The Bag. New York, Simon and Schuster, 1968; London, Gollancz, 1970.
An Island Death. New York, Harper, 1975.
Richard A. New York, Arbor House, 1981.

Short Stories

Someone Just Like You. New York, Harper, 1972; London, Gollancz, 1973.

Other

Editor, *Voices of Brooklyn: An Anthology*. Chicago, American Library Association, 1973.

* * *

Taken singly, each of Sol Yurick's works constitutes a substantial contribution to the growing body of contemporary fiction that depicts the American megalopolis in perpetual crisis. Taken together, his novels make up the most compelling vision available to us (in fiction or in non-fiction) of the most nightmarish megalopolis of all: New York now. Yurick is (as surely befits someone who was involved for several years in attempting to construct a sound theoretical and practical base for action on the American left) not interested in formal experimentation in the novel for the novel's own sake. Yet neither is he a polemicist with little sense of artistic form. He is an extreme rarity: a social critic with broad theoretical and "street level" experience. Yet, he is at the same time an erudite novelist with a solid historical knowledge of the genre and great skill in handling the form. In a deliberate and obviously self-conscious way, he consistently attempts to close the gap between the Biblical and classical Greek world so often alluded to in his works and the world of welfare, of murder, and of political power plays, the three major elements in his portrait of New York today.

The Warriors is a novel about a decimated New York teenage gang whom we first met on hostile "turf" on their way back to their "homeland" after a gang conference which has just ended in attempted murder. The opening scene is prefaced by an epigraph drawn from Xenophon: "My friends, these people whom you see are the last obstacle which stops us from being where we have so long struggled to be. We ought, if we could, to eat them up alive." The anabasis of Hinton (the gang artist), Lunkface, Bimbo, The Junior, and Hector is filled with memories of Ismael, leader of the Delancey Thrones, organizer of the citywide gang conference, and victim of the violence with which the conference had come to an abrupt close. "Ismael," we are told, "had the impassive face of a Spanish grandee, the purple-black color of an uncontaminated African, and the dreams of an Alexander, a Cyrus, a Napoleon." He will return in *The Bag* as a saturnine figure (now with only one eye), a dope pusher, rent collector for a slum landlord (Faust), and stockpiler of rifles, waiting for that moment when the downtrodden of the city will rise up and use these arms to kill their ancient oppressors. Ismael is not alone in his reappearance. Though seemingly self-contained when read singly, the novels (much like those of Faulkner) shade from one into another. The gang artist, Hinton in *The Warriors*, reappears, for instance, as a major figure in *The Bag*. Hinton's mother, Minnie (permanently on welfare and having a new "lover"), and his brother the addict, Alonso, minor figures at the end of Hinton's anabasis, also return but now as full-fledged characters in *The Bag*.

In contrast to the lower depths of *The Warriors* and parts of *The Bag*, *Fertig* appears at first to be an exploration of a strictly middle-class New York Jewish milieu. But the death of Fertig's son as a result of indifference on the part of the staff of a New York hospital triggers such a paroxysm of grief that Fertig cold-bloodedly murders some seven people involved however tenuously in his son's death. As mass murderer, Fertig is then thrust into the company of the criminals, madmen, and junkies who populate Yurick's other two novels. We are also given our first view of the political elite of this mythical New York: Judge Mabel Crossland whose thighs have encompassed every prominent jurist in New York in her climb to the judgeship; Fertig's lawyer, Royboy, the small but handsome sexual athlete, with multiple obligations to his female admirers (including Mabel Crossland) on his way to becoming Senator Roy, a character whom we then meet in *The Bag*; and Irving Hockstaff, king-maker, the man who indirectly runs the whole political apparatus of the city. A pawn in the political games of the mighty, Fertig and Fertig's trial are painfully reminiscent of *An American Tragedy*.

The evocation in *Fertig* of another classic work of literature is an integral part of Yurick's aesthetic and political methodology. The book is shaped as a contemporary replay of a recurrent phenomenon: the destruction of "the little man" by the power elite. Fertig's name comments ironically on a phenomenon that never ends. Likewise Ismael and Faust in *The Bag* are conscious restatements on a theme as old as poverty. Minnie (referred to by Yurick as a black Cybele and as the Wyf of Bath) loves Alpha (Fertig or Omega's opposite?) who has left his wife, Helen. They share the world with Faust (a figure drawn not only from Goethe but from Kosinski's *Painted Bird*), with Faust's daughter, the lesbian Eve, and with Faust's ambitious urban renewal project: Rebirth. Finally, Rebirth and all the little men and women are crushed as the ghetto detonates despite the best efforts of the man from Agape (love, affection), the master of the government's counter-insurgency game plan. We know with Yurick at the end of *The Bag* (though it is never explicitly stated) that the future of this city that is all cities lies not with the Ismael's and others who seek social improvement but with the Royboys and the Hockstaffs. It is they who seem to believe: "It didn't matter how many people you killed so long as you contained it [the revolution] and cooled it and co-opted it and made it run smoothly." So it has always been says Yurick and so it will be: Alpha and Agape are Omega and Fertig. The end of Ismael in *The Bag* returns us not only to Ismael at the beginning of *The Warriors* but to the ancient admonition drawn from the *Anabasis*. The "homeland" lies permanently within sight but beyond reach. There is grave doubt that, all his aesthetic skill and political acumen notwithstanding, Sol Yurick will ever get us any closer, but his portrayal of anabasis itself is worthy of comparison with its ancient counterpart. That is his achievement.

—John Fuegi

APPENDIX

CLARK, Walter Van Tilburg. American. Born in East Orland, Maine, 3 August 1909. Educated at Reno High School, Nevada, graduated 1926; University of Nevada, Reno, 1926-31, B.A. 1931, M.A. 1932; University of Vermont, Burlington, M.A. 1934. Married Barbara Frances Morse in 1933 (died); one daughter and one son. English teacher and basketball coach, Cazenovia Central School, New York, 1933-45, and a school in Rye, New York, 1945-46; lecturer, 1950-53, and Writer-in-Residence, 1962-71, University of Nevada; Rockefeller Lecturer, 1953; Associate Professor of English, University of Montana, Missoula, 1953-56; Professor of English and Creative Writing, San Francisco State College, 1956-62; Fellow in Fiction, Center for Advanced Studies, Wesleyan University, Middletown, Connecticut, 1960-61. Recipient: O. Henry Award, 1945. Litt.D.: Colgate University, Hamilton, New York, 1958; University of Nevada, 1969. *Died 10 November 1971.*

PUBLICATIONS

Novels

The Ox-Bow Incident. New York, Random House, 1940; London, Gollancz, 1941.
The City of Trembling Leaves. New York, Random House, 1945; as *Tim Hazard*, London, Kimber, 1951.
The Track of the Cat. New York, Random House, 1949; London, Gollancz, 1950.

Short Stories

The Watchful Gods and Other Stories. New York, Random House, 1950.

Uncollected Short Stories

"Trial at Arms," in *Saturday Evening Post* (Philadelphia), 25 January 1941.
"Prestige," in *Saturday Evening Post* (Philadelphia), 19 April 1941.
"The Pretender," in *Atlantic* (Boston), April 1942.
"A Letter to the Living," in *The Nation* (New York), 13 June 1942.
"Personal Interview," in *New Yorker*, 12 December 1942.
"The Rise and the Passing of Bar," in *Virginia Quarterly Review* (Charlottesville), Winter 1943.
"The Ascent of Ariel Goodbody," in *Yale Review* (New Haven, Connecticut), Winter 1943.
"Chuangtse and the Prince of the Golden Age," in *Western Review* (Denver), Winter 1949.

Verse

Christmas Comes to Hjalsen, Reno. Reno, Nevada, Reno Publishing House, 1930.
Ten Women in Gale's House and Shorter Poems. Boston, Christopher, 1932.

Other

Editor, *The Journals of Alfred Doten, 1849-1903.* Reno, University of Nevada Press, 3 vols., 1973.

*

Bibliography: "Walter Van Tilburg Clark: A Bibliography" by Richard Etulain, in *South Dakota Review* (Vermillion), Autumn 1965.

Manuscript Collection: Library of Congress, Washington, D.C.

Critical Studies: *Walter Van Tilburg Clark* by Max Westbrook, New York, Twayne, 1969; *Walter Van Tilburg Clark* by L.L. Lee, Boise, Idaho, Boise State College, 1973.

In his three novels, Walter Van Tilburg Clark worked with the first-rank novelist's instinct for subject matter and sense of place: usually he sustained the concomitant interest in his characters and their development through the circumstances of plot. What barred him from the first rank, ultimately, was the lack of unerring sense of proportion in matching structure, plot, and characterization that makes great novels.

The publication of *The Ox-Bow Incident* in 1940 brought Clark deserved notoriety, for it is, for the most part, an incisive, exciting study of mob violence. Through the skilful manipulation of a variety of characters who debate what to do after the report of a murder reaches the cattle town of Bridger's Wells, Clark conveyed the insight that the tyranny of the mob can only triumph by default. Boredom and the will to do something are forces that cannot easily be stemmed if there is someone present strong enough to use them. The mob, soon a posse intent on finding and summarily hanging the culprits, seeks the most single-minded leadership available, and once such a ruthless, charismatic character as Major Tetley takes charge, even intelligent men are willing to be borne by the event they are making. In Bridger's Wells, there is simply no one, not even the over-articulate storekeeper, Davies, who is sufficiently committed or forceful to do whatever is necessary to stop the leader. It is not surprising that although the novel is set in the American West, in the days of gun law, many readers took *The Ox-Bow Incident* to be a parable of the rise of the European tyrants in the 1930's.

The Ox-Bow Incident suffers from a structural defect: while it is true that the street debate about whether the crowd should act or not does serve to delineate character and theme, it is so over-long that it interferes with the pacing of the novel. There is another, probably more serious, flaw: in an otherwise tautly written work, there are long, inappropriately sententious speeches by various characters, notably Davies, explaining states of mind and points of view. Yet there is no denying Clark's overall success in exploring his theme through a wide range of vivid characters.

Clark's second novel, *The City of Trembling Leaves*, is not a bad novel simply because its plot is implausible or its characters too contrived. It is poor precisely because the incidents in the rambling chronicle of Timothy Hazard, the sensitive musician who is the protagonist, are banal and the people in his life mostly stock characters. It is not a novel of maturation in the way that, say, *Huckleberry Finn* is, but of romantic adolescence that must surely appeal mainly to romantic adolescents. A tale of emotional development arrested at the stage of a schoolboy infatuation may arouse some sympathy, but little interest. Whatever strength the book has is derived primarily from Clark's use of the West, particularly of the mountains and desert of western Nevada, as a source of spiritual energy, much as Hemingway uses the mountains in *The Sun Also Rises*.

The artistic, as well as popular, success of *The Track of the Cat* demonstrated that *The City of Trembling Leaves* had been an aberrant second novel and that Clark was capable of fullfilling the promise of *The Ox-Bow Incident*. With a sense of gripping immediacy, the novel deals with the hunting of a marauding mountain lion in the premature Sierra winter by each of the three Bridges sons in turn, and simultaneously with the tense relationships among the members of the family who remain at the ranch. The killer cat is both a physical entity and the spiritual *bête noire* of its trackers, who have invested it with supernatural size. The cat becomes, in fact, a symbolic manifestation of the hunters' deficiencies: Arthur, the artist-dreamer, is struck down because he cannot cope with reality and forgets the menacing cat; Curt, the overbearing realist, is killed because he cannot manage the mystic quality the cat assumes, and is driven off a cliff by the fear of it.

Clark played an indoor drama in counterpoint to the hunt. The mother looms as large at the Bridges ranch as the panther does in the mountains, as she oversees Arthur's burial and attempts to break up the romance between Harold, the youngest son, and his visiting fiancée. Harold is able to move from ranch to mountain to destroy the panther at the end of the novel—and thereby fuse two subplots—because in his treatment of the mother he has shown that he has in him the necessary balance of dreamer and doer. As Joe Sam, the ancient, mystical Indian ranch hand, who is one of the important unifying elements of the novel, implies, Harold can slay the beast because it is not his own particular black cat.

The Track of the Cat, too, has its imperfections: the real and magical cat requires a greater adversary than Clark provided in the person of Curt, whose striving with the cat accounts for the bulk of the novel. The necessary intensity that is suggested in Curt early in the book proves to be mainly bluster; he is not long in the cold wilderness before he abandons the food he needs to survive. The father is a stereotypical drunk, a nuisance to people inside and outside of the book alike. Yet Walter Van Tilburg Clark's narrative power was strong enough, and the portrait of the mother memorable enough, to diminish the effect of the weaknesses and make the audience regret that he did not publish another novel in the more than two decades before his death. It was as if when he caused Harold to return to the Bridges ranch to take charge, Clark's own quest, expressed first through Art Croft, the cowboy narrator of *The Ox-Bow Incident*, then through Timothy Hazard, and finally through the hunters of the black cat, was snowbound in the cold of the Nevada winter.

—Alan R. Shucard

FARRELL, J(ames) G(ordon). British. Born in Liverpool, Lancashire, 23 January 1935. Educated at Rossall School; Brasenose College, Oxford, 1956-60, B.A. 1960. Recipient: Harkness Fellowship, for residence in the United States, 1966-68; Arts Council Award, 1970; Faber Memorial Prize, 1971; Booker Prize, 1973. *Died 12 August 1979.*

PUBLICATIONS

Novels

A Man from Elsewhere. London, Hutchinson, 1963.
The Lung. London, Hutchinson, 1965.
A Girl in the Head. London, Cape, 1967; New York, Harper, 1969.
Troubles. London, Cape, 1970; New York, Knopf, 1971.
The Siege of Krishnapur. London, Weidenfeld and Nicolson, 1973; New York, Harcourt Brace, 1974.
The Singapore Grip. London, Weidenfeld and Nicolson, 1978; New York, Knopf, 1979.
The Hill Station, edited by John Spurling. London, Weidenfeld and Nicolson, 1981.

*

Critical Study: "Ireland Agonistes" by Elizabeth Bowen, in *Europa 1* (London), 1971.

J.G. Farrell commented (1972):

About *Troubles*. It is a common misconception that when the historians have finished with a historical incident there remains nothing but a patch of feathers and a pair of feet; in fact, the most important things, for the very reason that they are trivial, are unsuitable for digestion by historians, who are only able to nourish themselves on the signing of treaties, battle strategies, the formation of Shadow Cabinets and so forth. These matters are quite alien to the life most people lead, which consists of catching colds, falling in love, or falling off bicycles. It is this *real* life which is the novelist's concern (though, needless to say, realism is not the only way to represent it). One of the things I have tried to do in *Troubles* is to show people "undergoing" history, to use an expression of Sartre's. The Irish troubles of 1919-1921 were chosen partly because they appeared to be safely lodged in the past; most of the book was written before the current Irish difficulties broke out, giving it an unintended topicality. What I wanted to do was to use this period of the past as a metaphor for today, because I believe that however much the superficial details and customs of life may change over the years, basically life itself does not change very much. Indeed, all literature that survives must depend on this assumption. Another reason why I preferred to use the past is that, as a rule, people have already made up their minds what they think about the present. About the past they are more susceptible to clarity of vision.

* * *

J.G. Farrell's rich and densely patterned comic style has familial links with other exiles such as Nabokov and Beckett. In contrast to them, however, it reveals a horrifying and revolting world of disease, death, and decay. That electrifying tension between the style and the vision is what powers all his work, which reached out in each new novel towards greater and greater artistic success.

When he died in 1979, Farrell had already established his reputation as perhaps the most talented novelist of his generation. Even his first novel, *A Man from Elsewhere*, which he later disowned, had its distinctive merits; and the story of how he became a novelist is typically Farrellian. He was a stalwart, rugger-playing hearty at Brasenose College, Oxford, when he caught polio, was put in an iron lung, and emerged thin and greying, his rugger days definitely behind him. From that experience of life-in-death emerged *The Lung*, with its semi-autobiographical, death-in-life world of the polio victim, Sands, surrounded by morbid fellow-patients, such as the ex-priest who covers up his sense of failure with a mordantly comic blasphemy. There is also old man Rivers who sits making baskets, "his mind a complete blank across which a naked woman passed from time to time." The only solaces left to men in Farrell's bizarre world are sex, humour, art and a compulsive, Sisyphean will to carry on.

His third novel, *A Girl in the Head* completed the first phase of his writing career. Its hero, Count Boris Slattery, is treated, as always, with a warmly pervasive irony which is more biting than the satire lavished lovingly on the blandly and horrifying normal people who surround the Count and from whom he becomes increasingly alienated. The desperate props with which people hide from the horror of reality (in this case a mindless middle-class cheerfulness) are more devastatingly demolished in his three major novels which followed.

With *Troubles*, Farrell found the distinctive setting for his gifts: the vast and decaying magnificence of the Majestic Hotel, with its burgeoning tropical plants and exploding population of cats who together are taking over the hotel. The Majestic is owned by an eccentric Anglo-Irish family with which a well-meaning English major becomes involved. Baffled and dismayed by the mutual hostility of Protestant and Catholic, he comes to acquire a sense of responsibility for the Majestic and its unwanted but undismissable old ladies who freeload or pay as and when possible. As in all of Farrell's novels, there is a subtle economy with which the terror prevailing in the countryside, and indeed the world, is brought insistently closer, and culminates in a horrifying denoument which the reader has come to half-expect.

Troubles and *The Siege of Krishnapur* belong to the same period of Farrell's development: Irish references throng *The Siege of Krishnapur* just as Indian references crowd *Troubles*; and they share an essentially similar method and humour, though *Siege* has perhaps a greater narrative drive. Will the garrison be rescued from the mutinying sepoys who beseige it? Which of the well-bred English ladies and gentlemen will find the resources to survive in this extreme situation? What cost will they have paid? Farrell acknowledges the courage and passionate sincerity of that absurd little British band of Empire-builders who argue about Progress, Religion, and Technology surrounded by a vastly hostile human and physical environment.

In *The Singapore Grip*, too, Farrell explores the conflict of values. Tactfully, he points up the irony that the capitalism which has created Singapore also prevents it, by its shortsightedness, exploitativeness, and divisiveness, from uniting against the Japanese. What emerges is a new kind of novel for Farrell, not as interested in comedy, but of greater narrative range, complexity, and power. It is not as great an achievement as either *Troubles* or *The Siege of Krishnapur* but it marked a new stage in Farrell's development and promised an even larger artistic success—a promise that was betrayed by Farrell's death.

His three great novels were meticulously and thoroughly researched; but facts turn in Farrell's hands into wonderfully tall stories, shot through with the exotic colours of fairytale and the uproarious absurdity of slapstick. Farrell believed that people had, generally, already made up their minds about the present; the only means by which they could be led to alter their views was through a consideration of the past. The grim attrition of human hopes by vast and impersonal historical forces which are not even comprehended by his protagonists and actors is meant to hammer home a single vision: "the bitter-sweet knowledge that nothing is invulnerable to growth, decay and death, not even one's most fiercely guarded memories." Farrell works by an Eastern and Irish exaggeration that scoffs at the manifestations of the Raj, whether in Ireland, India, or Singapore. And the Raj itself comes to symbolise all human pride and achievement. Nothing escapes the contemptuous probing of Farrell's scalpel—science and reason, statistics and religion, technology and sex, black men and white men: "the poor are just as stupid as the rich." But when the rot has been smilingly exposed, the reader realizes with a shock that Farrell still loves everything—the attractive exterior as much as the decaying interior—with a Buddhistic or Christian compassion. Farrell's artistic and life-sustaining affection as much as this demolition by artistic fiat of the 20th century's technological and civilized towers of Babel are, eventually, much more religious than Farrell realized or perhaps would have wished to recognize.

When Farrell's humour faltered, his art remained, though it was not enough to sustain his life. Readers will remain grateful to the life for the art; whether they are reduced to what he had left for solace depends on whether they seek, and whether they find, any substitute for the assumptions and methodology of the modern world and all its works, which Farrell rejected so thoroughly and persuasively.

—Prabhu S. Guptara

JACKSON, Shirley (Hardie). American. Born in San Francisco, California, 14 December 1919. Educated at Burlingame High School, California; Brighton High School, Rochester, New York; University of Rochester, 1934-36; Syracuse University, New York, 1937-40, B.A. 1940. Married the writer Stanley Edgar Hyman in 1940; two daughters and two sons. Recipient: Mystery Writers of America Edgar Allan Poe Award, 1961; Syracuse University Arents Medal, 1965. *Died 8 August 1965.*

PUBLICATIONS

Novels

The Road Through the Wall. New York, Farrar Straus, 1948; as *The Other Side of the Street*, New York, Pyramid, 1956.
Hangsaman. New York, Farrar Straus, and London, Gollancz, 1951.
The Bird's Nest. New York, Farrar Straus, 1954; London, Joseph, 1955; as *Lizzie*, New York, New American Library, 1957.
The Sundial. New York, Farrar Straus, and London, Joseph, 1958.
The Haunting of Hill House. New York, Viking Press, 1959; London, Joseph, 1960.
We Have Always Lived in the Castle. New York, Viking Press, 1962; London, Joseph, 1963.

Short Stories

The Lottery; or, The Adventures of James Harris. New York, Farrar Straus, 1949; London, Gollancz, 1950.

Plays

The Lottery, adaptation of her own short story, in *Best Television Plays 1950-1951*, edited by William I. Kauffman. New York, Merlin Press, 1952.
The Bad Children: A Play in One Act for Bad Children. Chicago, Dramatic Publishing Company, 1959.

Other

Life among the Savages. New York, Farrar Straus, 1953; London, Joseph, 1954.
The Witchcraft of Salem Village (juvenile). New York, Random House, 1956.
Raising Demons. New York, Farrar Straus, and London, Joseph, 1957.
Special Delivery: A Useful Book for Brand-New Mothers.... Boston, Little Brown, 1960; as *And Baby Makes Three...*, New York, Grosset and Dunlap, 1960.
9 Magic Wishes (juvenile). New York, Crowell Collier, 1963.
Famous Sally (juvenile). New York, Harlin Quist, 1966.
The Magic of Shirley Jackson, edited by Stanley Edgar Hyman. New York, Farrar Straus, 1966.
Come Along with Me: Part of a Novel, Sixteen Stories, and Three Lectures, edited by Stanley Edgar Hyman. New York, Viking Press, 1968.

*

Critical Study: *Shirley Jackson* by Lenemaja Friedman, Boston, Twayne, 1975.

* * *

Throughout her work Shirley Jackson focused on incongruities in an everyday setting, whether for comic or sinister effect. This is as true of her "disrespectful memoir" of her children, *Life among the Savages*, and its equally hilarious sequel, *Raising Demons*, as of the dark psychological explorations of her novels and short stories. In her later fiction, she wrote about extraordinary characters and situations, but these were always located in an everyday setting, whose juxtaposition provided her staple ingredient of incongruity.

Stories in *The Lottery* like "Dorothy and My Grandmother and the Sailors" delight in the incongruous for its own sake. However, most of the stories including the title story, whose publication in the *New Yorker* in 1948 caused a literary sensation, are informed by a sense of evil, reinforced by the epigraphs from Glanvill's *Sadducismus Triumphatus*. The collection is subtitled "The Adventures of James Harris," and this figure of the daemon lover appears in a number of short stories.

Like much of Jackson's work, *Hangsaman* is concerned with identity. It describes the young Natalie's growing up into the astounding realization, as she crosses a bridge, that "unless she actually jumped over the parapet into the river she was of small interest" to passers-by. This is a turning-point for a girl who before going to college pondered "a workable personality to take along," and once there, wondered if she possessed "*the* original mind." Natalie's earlier imaginary world of murders and detectives is explained in terms of her parents' unsatisfactory relationship, but perhaps intentionally the book's positive ending doesn't quite offset the vividness of these fantasies.

The Bird's Nest is also concerned with identity, but in a mentally disturbed girl. Under hypnosis, Elizabeth varies between "herself," Beth, Betsy, and Bess; around these four distinct voices Jackson triumphantly structures the book. Eventually Aunt Morgen and Dr. Victor Wright name the "heiress," whom they have helped to reconstitute, "Victoria Morgen." Like *Hangsaman* the book ends positively yet without removing all doubts as to the viability of the central character for the future.

In *The Sundial* Jackson focuses on an eccentric group of characters in the Halloran family house, where directed by a dead relative they await the end of the world in the belief that they alone will be saved. Almost allegorical relationships develop between Orianna Halloran, Gloria, and Essex. Their situation is a consciously *Crusoe* one, despite the baroque leitmotivs of the sundial itself and the maze. The narrative is both comic and macabre—sometimes simultaneously.

In *The Haunting of Hill House* (filmed as *The Haunting*) Jackson fused her psychological insight with a traditionally spine-chilling ghost story. A ghost-hunting team moves into the "clashing disharmony" of Hill House to record scientifically its phenomena. Jackson's brilliant heightening of suspense has given the book a wide appeal.

Like her two previous novels and many of her short stories, *We Have Always Lived in the Castle* centres on a house, and even more than in *The Sundial* the reader is induced to identify with its inhabitants—eccentric or criminal though they may be—against "them" in the world outside. Eighteen-year-old "Merricat" describes her life with her sister Constance after the latter's acquittal from a charge of poisoning the rest of their family, of which the local people believe her guilty. The destructive invasion of the world outside parallels the set-piece of the peaceable invasion of the locals invited to Orianna's final barbecue in *The Sundial*. The portrayal of the sisters' loving relationship, albeit in macabre circumstances, makes *We Have Always Lived in the Castle* the most remarkable of Shirley Jackson's books.

At her death, Shirley Jackson left the beginning of another novel, *Come Along with Me*, which returns to the theme of identity in an extreme case: the first-person narrator writes of herself, "And outside the dim nameless creature named herself Mrs. Angela Motorman and came steadily to the door." Most of Jackson's short stories centre round an isolated female. The early story "Pillar of Salt" is unusual in its protagonist, a happy mother whose disintegration is traced; here Jackson seems on the verge of drawing on the family life material of her two autobiographical books for her fiction. Generally her fiction is concerned with the daemon lover's inadequate victims, lost in the concrete jungle of the Kafkaesque city or making long-distance journey "to the end of the night." This theme is habitually announced by laughter, lines from songs and poems, or nursery rhymes, transmuted to sinister leitmotivs.

To portray the fragmented personality, Shirley Jackson resorted to a kind of zany verbal logic: dealing with an alcoholic friend, Natalie in *Hangsaman* wanted "to ask Elizabeth what she thought she had seen through the eyes which for Elizabeth registered what Elizabeth's brain recorded." Two stories in *The Lottery*, "Colloquy" and "My Life with R.H. Macy," depend on semantic irony, and *Life among the Savages* makes amusing use of a catalogue technique in tabulating "a conversation, or double-listening." Yet though there are passages in her work reminiscent of Borges, Shirley Jackson kept any experimental tendency in her writing subordinated to the demands of story-telling, her prime consideration as the lectures printed in *Come Along with Me* make clear.

—Val Warner

JONES, James. American. Born in Robinson, Illinois, 6 November 1921. Educated at the University of Hawaii, Honolulu, 1942; New York University, 1945. Served in the United States Army, 1939-44: Bronze Star; Purple Heart. Married Gloria Mosolino in 1957; one son and one daughter. Recipient: National Book Award, 1952. *Died 9 May 1977.*

Publications

Novels

From Here to Eternity. New York, Scribner, 1951; London, Collins, 1952.
Some Came Running. New York, Scribner, 1957; London, Collins, 1959.
The Pistol. New York, Scribner, and London, Collins, 1959.
The Thin Red Line. New York, Scribner, 1962; London, Collins, 1963.
Go to the Widow-Maker. New York, Delacorte Press, and London, Collins, 1967.
The Merry Month of May. New York, Delacorte Press, and London, Collins, 1971.
A Touch of Danger. New York, Doubleday, and London, Collins, 1973.
Whistle: A Work-in-Progress. Bloomfield Hill, Michigan, Bruccoli Clark, 1974; complete version, as *Whistle*, New York, Delacorte Press, and London, Collins, 1978.

Short Stories

The Ice-Cream Headache and Other Stories. New York, Delacorte Press, and London, Collins, 1968.

Uncollected Short Stories

"Million-Dollar Wound," in *Esquire* (New York), November 1977.

Play

Screenplay: *The Longest Day*, with others, 1962.

Other

Viet Journal. New York, Delacorte Press, 1974.
WWII, with Art Weithas. New York, Grosset and Dunlap, and London, Cooper, 1975.

*

Bibliography: *James Jones: A Checklist* by John R. Hopkins, Detroit, Gale, 1974.

Critical Study: *James Jones: A Friendship* by Willie Morris, New York, Doubleday, 1978.

* * *

When James Jones died in 1977, he had completed all but a few pages of *Whistle*, the last novel of the military trilogy that also includes *From Here to Eternity* and *The Thin Red Line*. It is now clear that his work was unevenly divided between these books and those in which he ventured uneasily into the swamps of civilian life. The army was home and family to Jones. He wrote about it as his contemporaries wrote about their childhoods and their marriages. The war was only the major episode in his trilogy; his abiding subject was the brotherhood of infantrymen. His nemesis was the disposal of his company by bullets and, more devastatingly, rehabilitation, reassignment, and discharge. The increasing eroticism in his fiction—a relentless summary of acts and gratifications—surely follows from his failure to find anywhere else the belief and loyalty that vanished when his company broke up.

Jones's greatest achievement was to portray infantrymen realistically and mythically, as he did best in *From Here to Eternity* and *The Thin Red Line*. Private Prewitt and Sergeant Warden are gentlemen rankers, enlisted *men*, on Oahu before Pearl Harbor. Their manhood is defined by their acceptance of discipline and military organization and by their reaction to any circumstance that threatens that acceptance. Duty, for Prewitt, does not include becoming one of the company jocks; it is, for Warden, the unsentimental command and care of a hundred and sixty men. The men of *The Thin Red Line*, a tough unit in a Pacific island campaign, are Warden's old company with curt new names—Welsh, Witt, Land—because Prewitt, indispensable as a character in the unfolding trilogy, had been killed off in Hawaii. The novel is "cheerfully dedicated to those greatest and most heroic of all human endeavors, WAR and WARFARE," and Jones, while intentionally ironic, obviously believed that they were second greatest and most heroic after the mere existence of the company itself. It is a more disciplined, less engaging novel than the first. The coherence of combat episodes deters Jones from his characteristic indulgence in catalogues of stray information. The plot consists of several men in the company being tested from moment to moment. It has the harrowing physical detail of Mailer's *The Naked and the Dead* with only those overtones that come out of the dedication.

Whistle came 15 years later, although, as Jones told his friend Willie Morris, it had been "turning on its spit in my head for nearly thirty years." The obsession has left its mark on a book in which Jones's view of the company is his despairing commentary on human existence at the same time that it is a case study of his writing defects. His fictional army company is finished with Winch (Welsh, Warden) in a padded cell, Prell (Witt, Prewitt) killed again, and Strange (Land, Stark) slipping over the side of a troop transport in mid-Atlantic incapable of moving on with a new company. He adds a significant new character in Landers, drafted out of college to become thoroughly absorbed in the company at the moment of its annihilation. Even comfortable middle-class adolescents, Jones suggests, will jump at the chance to leave all other ties for the shreds of a real unit. But in sealing the integrity of Jones's 30-year vision of the company, *Whistle* becomes like his later novels of civilian life. As in *Go to the Widow-Maker* and *The Merry Month of May*, the effort to understand what is going on in the world gives way to a monotonous record of sexual gratification. That oral copulation is the supreme experience in his later novels seems only the logical development of Jones's thesis that his people have nothing left to seek or prove. It was ironic that a man who was as consumed by his own work as Jones was—swept up by it not long after he left the army—could not himself write about occupations and trades outside the work details that came with military service.

When he published *Some Came Running* in 1957, Jones proclaimed himself, like Don Quixote, "at last free from the damnable books of romance." He was free, actually, to attempt the insuperable task of portraying a man like himself, loose at home in the United States during the interval between World War II and the Korean War. Nothing can help Dave Hirsch write his book, just as nothing can prevent Frank Hirsch from building his shopping center. One estranged brother drifts among fellow isolates in his Illinois town, while the other is the advance guard of franchised, astroturfed America. Numbingly long, the novel still towers over *Go to the Widow-Maker* and *The Merry Month of May*. The latter novel was set during the French student revolts of 1968. Everyone seems to be sympathizing with the students, but it is soon clear that Jones himself thinks they are as foolish as their old-fashioned liberal parents. Worse, they are incompetent. In the family struggle which accompanies the strikes, the son is no match for his father in assertiveness, and the final, exclusive pursuit of the perfect orgasm. Again, Jones dismisses civilian complexity to court the ecstasy that the narrator of *The Merry Month of May* calls "happy elation."

The best of James Jones came in *From Here to Eternity* and *The Thin Red Line* before his company broke ranks.

—David Sanders

KEROUAC, Jack. American. Born Jean Louis Lebris de Kerouac in Lowell, Massachusetts, 12 March 1922. Educated at Horace Mann School, New York; Columbia University, New York, 1940-41, 1942. Served in the United States Merchant Marine, and Navy, during World War II. Married in 1944 (annulled), and 1950 (divorced); married Stella Sampas in 1966; one daughter. Sports Reporter for the Lowell *Sun*, 1942; became a writer after the war, supporting himself by various odd jobs; worked as brakeman with the Southern Pacific Railroad, San Francisco, 1952-53; travelled throughout the United States and Mexico, 1953-56; fire lookout for the United States Agricultural Service in Washington state, 1956; full-time writer from 1957. *Died 21 October 1969.*

PUBLICATIONS

Novels

The Town and the City (as John Kerouac). New York, Harcourt Brace, 1950; London, Eyre and Spottiswoode, 1951.
On the Road. New York, Viking Press, 1957; London, Deutsch, 1958; edited by Scott Donaldson, Viking Press, 1978.
The Subterraneans. New York, Grove Press, 1958; London, Deutsch, 1960.
The Dharma Bums. New York, Viking Press, 1958; London, Deutsch, 1959.
Doctor Sax: Faust Part Three. New York, Grove Press, 1959; London, Evergreen, 1961.
Maggie Cassidy. New York, Avon, 1959; London, Panther, 1960.
Excerpts from "Visions of Cody." New York, New Directions, 1959.
Tristessa. New York, Avon, 1960.
Book of Dreams. San Francisco, City Lights, 1960.
Big Sur. New York, Farrar Straus, 1962; London, Deutsch, 1963.
Visions of Gerard. New York, Farrar Straus, 1963.
Visions of Gerard, and Tristessa. London, Deutsch, 1964.
Desolation Angels. New York, Coward McCann, 1965; London, Deutsch, 1966.
Satori in Paris. New York, Grove Press, 1966; London, Deutsch, 1967.
Vanity of Duluoz: An Adventurous Education 1935-46. New York, Coward McCann, 1968; London, Deutsch, 1969.
Pic. New York, Grove Press, 1971.
Visions of Cody. New York, McGraw Hill, and London, Deutsch, 1973.
Pic, and The Subterraneans. London, Deutsch, 1973.

Short Stories

Two Early Stories. New York, Aloe Editions, 1973.

Play

Pull My Daisy (screenplay). New York, Grove Press, 1961; London, Evergreen, 1961.

Screenplay: *Pull My Daisy*, 1959.

Verse

Mexico City Blues. New York, Grove Press, 1959.
Hymn—God Pray for Me. Privately printed, 1959.
Rimbaud. San Francisco, City Lights, 1960.
The Scripture of the Golden Eternity. New York, Totem-Corinth, 1960.
Poem. Privately printed, 1962.
A Pun for Al Gelpi. Privately printed, 1966.
Hugo Weber. New York, Portents, 1967.
Someday You'll Be Lying. Privately printed, 1968.
A Last Haiku. Privately printed, 1969.
Scattered Poems. San Francisco, City Lights, 1971.

Trip, Trap: Haiku along the Road from San Francisco to New York 1959, with Albert Saijo and Lew Welch. Bolinas, California, Grey Fox Press, 1973.

Heaven and Other Poems, edited by Donald Allen. Bolinas, California, Grey Fox Press, 1977.

Other

Lonesome Traveler, drawings by Larry Rivers. New York, McGraw Hill, 1960; London, Deutsch, 1962.

Sketching Language: Selected Experimental Writings, edited by Richard Kostelanetz. Layton, Utah, Peregrine Smith, 1979.

*

Bibliography: *A Bibliography of Works by Jack Kerouac (Jean Louis de Kerouac) 1939-1967* by Ann Charters, New York, Phoenix Bookshop, 1967; revised edition, 1975.

Critical Studies: *No Pie in the Sky: The Hobo as American Cultural Hero in the Works of Jack London, John Dos Passos, and Jack Kerouac* by Frederick Feied, New York, Citadel Press, 1964; *Kerouac: A Biography* by Ann Charters, San Francisco, Straight Arrow, 1973, London, Deutsch, 1974; *Kerouac's Town* by Barry Gifford, Santa Barbara, California, Capra Press, 1973, revised edition, Berkeley, California, Creative Arts, 1977, and *Jack's Book: An Oral Biography* by Gifford and Lawrence Lee, New York, St. Martin's Press, 1978, London, Hamish Hamilton, 1979; *Visions of Kerouac* by Charles E. Jarvis, Lowell, Massachusetts, Ithaca Press, 1974; *Heart Beat: My Life with Jack and Neal* by Carolyn Cassady, Berkeley, California, Creative Arts, 1976; *Jack Kerouac, Prophet of the New Romanticism: A Critical Study* by Robert A. Hipkiss, Lawrence, Regents Press of Kansas, 1976; *Desolate Angel: Jack Kerouac, The Beats, and America* by Dennis McNally, New York, Random House, 1979; *Kerouac's Crooked Road: The Development of a Fiction* by Tim Hunt, Hamden, Connecticut, Shoe String Press, 1981.

Theatrical Activities:

Actor: **Film**—*Pull My Daisy*, 1959.

* * *

Regarded in modern American fiction as the authentic voice of the "beat generation," Jack Kerouac thought of himself as a story teller in the innovative tradition of Proust and Joyce. He was an authentic original, writing with the same idealism as Emerson, Thoreau, Melville, and Whitman, reasserting the American dream of romantic individualism in each of his published books, which he regarded as one vast autobiographical statement.

Twelve of these books comprise "The Legend of Duluoz," or "The Legend of Kerouac," his fictional autobiography, one of the most ambitious projects conceived by any modern writer. Kerouac intended in his old age to gather these books together under uniform binding and insert the real names of his contemporaries into the narratives, so that his larger design might be more apparent. His first published novel, *The Town and the City*, was based on the model of Thomas Wolfe, and Kerouac later dismissed it as a fiction written before he found his own voice. The autobiographical "Legend of Duluoz" begins with the novel *Visions of Gerard*, which describes the first years of Kerouac's Catholic French-Canadian childhood in Lowell and the death of his brother Gerard in 1926, when Jack was four years old. *Doctor Sax* is a fantasy of memories and dreams about his boyhood (1930-36) in Lowell with an imaginary companion Doctor Sax, like the pulp magazine hero The Shadow, the champion of Good in a mythic battle against the forces of Evil. *Maggie Cassidy* is a more realistic novel about his adolescence in high school and his first love (1938-39). *Vanity of Duluoz* describes his years playing football at prep school and Columbia College, and his experience in the merchant marine and Navy during World War II. It was during these years (1939-46) that Kerouac met Allen Ginsberg and William Burroughs, Jr., named "Irwin Garden" and "Will Hubbard" in the novel. *On the Road*, Kerouac's most popular book, begins with his meeting the legendary Neal Cassady, called "Dean Moriarity" in the narrative, who took Kerouac ("Sal Paradise") on the road in 1947-50, hitch-hiking and riding buses and cars across the United States on a search for joyful adventure. In this book Ginsberg is "Carlo Marx," and Burroughs is "Old Bull Lee." *Visions of Cody* is what Kerouac called an "in-depth" description of this same period of his life with Cassady ("Cody Pomeray" here), a more richly humorous exercise in spontaneous prose extended narrative, considered too experimental to be published in its entirety during Kerouac's lifetime. *The Subterraneans* continues the autobiography as an intense account of an affair with a black girl in the summer of 1953; in this book Kerouac is "Leo Percepied," Ginsberg is "Adam Moorad," Burroughs is "Frank Carmody," and Gregory Corso is "Yuri Gligoric." In *Tristessa*, Kerouac describes a love affair in Mexico City during 1955-56, the same time period as *The Dharma Bums*. In *The Dharma Bums*, Kerouac ("Ray Smith") adventures in California with Ginsberg ("Alvah Goldbook"), Cassady ("Cody Pomeray"), Philip Whalen ("Warren Coughlin"), Michael McClure ("Ike O'Shay"), John Montgomery ("Henry Morely"), and Gary Snyder ("Japhy Ryder"), who taught Kerouac how to climb mountains and live as a Buddhist during the first year of the "Poetry Renaissance" in San Francisco. *Desolation Angels* picks up the narrative in 1956, where the previous book left off, and continues until Fall 1957, with the publication of *On the Road*, the novel that made Kerouac famous as the father of the "beats." *Big Sur* and *Satori in Paris* are the last books in the narrative of "The Legend of Duluoz," chronicling Kerouac's final years of alcoholism and anger at the media's distortion of his work and refusal to regard him as a serious writer.

The larger design in Kerouac's work, the integrity of his theme of individualism, his romantic optimism, and his reverence for life, as well as the humor of his novels and his remarkably abundant prose energy, were largely ignored by contemporary critics, intent upon ridiculing him as a hopelessly naive visionary or as an irresponsible "beatnik." Since his death in 1969, there has been more sympathy for his work, and greater awareness of the extent of the influence of his books on young readers. As Jess Ritter said in *The Vonnegut Statement*, "The great psychic migration of American youth since World War II can be charted by the novels they read and the novelists whose reputations they created.... Kerouac and the Beats represent the psychic revolt of the 1950's." What has become increasingly clear in the last 20 years is that the fabric of American culture has never been the same since this revolt, since it represented a resurgence of the dominant thread of individualism that has been present in varying hues in the country's history since its beginnings. Jack Kerouac was as much an American idealist as Thoreau. What he said he wanted was the same hut as Thoreau's but in his hometown of Lowell, Massachusetts, not at Walden Pond. Something of a martyr—like Thoreau—in his own time, Jack Kerouac was a necessary hero who chronicled in his "Legend" the rewards and hazards of American romantic optimism in mid-20th century.

—Ann Charters

MANNING, Olivia. British. Born in Portsmouth, Hampshire in 1915. Educated in private schools. Married Reginald Donald Smith in 1939. Press Officer, United States Embassy, Cairo, 1942; Press Assistant, Public Information Office, Jerusalem, 1943-44, and British Council, Jerusalem, 1944-45; novel reviewer for *Spectator*,

London, 1949-50, and *The Sunday Times*, London, 1965-66. Recipient: Tom-Gallon Trust Award, 1949; *Yorkshire Post* Award, 1977. C.B.E. (Commander, Order of the British Empire), 1976. *Died 23 July 1980.*

PUBLICATIONS

Novels

The Wind Changes. London, Cape, 1937; New York, Knopf, 1938.
Artist among the Missing. London, Heinemann, 1949.
School for Love. London, Heinemann, 1951.
A Different Face. London, Heinemann, 1953; New York, Abelard Schuman, 1957.
The Doves of Venus. London, Heinemann, 1955; New York, Abelard Schuman, 1956.
The Balkan Trilogy:
The Great Fortune. London, Heinemann, 1960; New York, Doubleday, 1961.
The Spoilt City. London, Heinemann, and New York, Doubleday, 1962.
Friends and Heroes. London, Heinemann, 1965; New York, Doubleday, 1966.
The Play Room. London, Heinemann, 1969; as *The Camperlea Girls*, New York, Coward McCann, 1969.
The Rain Forest. London, Heinemann, 1974.
The Levant Trilogy:
The Danger Tree. London, Weidenfeld and Nicolson, and New York, Atheneum, 1977.
The Battle Lost and Won. London, Weidenfeld and Nicolson, 1978; New York, Atheneum, 1979.
The Sum of Things. London, Weidenfeld and Nicolson, 1980; New York, Atheneum, 1981.

Short Stories

Growing Up: A Collection of Short Stories. London, Heinemann, and New York, Doubleday, 1948.
My Husband Cartwright. London, Heinemann, 1956.
A Romantic Hero and Other Stories. London, Heinemann, 1967.
Penguin Modern Stories 12, *with others*. London, Penguin, 1972.

Uncollected Short Stories

"Girls Together," in *Winter's Tales* 16, edited by A.D. Maclean. London, Macmillan, 1970; New York, St. Martin's Press, 1971.
"The Banana House," in *Winter's Tales* 17, edited by Caroline Hobhouse. London, Macmillan, 1971; New York, St. Martin's Press, 1972.

Plays

Screenplay: *The Play Room*, 1970.

Radio Plays: *The Little Ottleys*, from novels by Ada Leverson, 1964; *The Card*, from the novel by Arnold Bennett, 1964; *Futility*, 1973, and *The Polyglots*, 1977, from novels by William Gerhardie.

Other

The Remarkable Expedition: The Story of Stanley's Rescue of Emin Pasha from Equatorial Africa. London, Heinemann, 1947; as *The Reluctant Rescue*, New York, Doubleday, 1947.
The Dreaming Shore (travel). London, Evans, 1950.
Extraordinary Cats. London, Joseph, 1967.

*

Manuscript Collections: University of Texas, Austin; University of Tulsa, Oklahoma; British Library, London.

Critical Studies: *The Novel Today* by Anthony Burgess, London, Longman, 1963; *Tradition and Dream* by Walter Allen, London, Phoenix House, and New York, Dutton, 1964; "Olivia Manning" by James Parkhill Rathbone, in *Books and Bookmen* (London), August 1971; *Continuance and Change: The Contemporary British Novel Sequence* by Robert K. Morris, Carbondale, Southern Illinois University Press, 1972.

Olivia Manning commented (1972):

When I have completed a book, I feel I have said all I can say concerning it. My subject is simply life as I have experienced it and I am happiest when writing of things I have known.

* * *

Olivia Manning began as a painter, and, from her first novel, *The Wind Changes*, onwards, what seems a painter's eye for the visible world enabled her to render particularly well the sensuous surface of relatively exotic places and landscapes. This is particularly apparent in *School for Love*, a novel of Jerusalem in wartime as registered through the consciousness of a 16-year-old English boy stranded there by the chances of war. An aspect of her painter's eye is a pure and exact prose style: her sentences give pleasure in themselves. At the same time, her art has sometimes seemed an art of diminishing; her exactness has seemed almost too cruel. This is apparent in *A Different Face*, in which the hero returns to the seaside town of Coldmouth, on the south coast of England, to discover that the money he has invested in a private school there has been lost. Coldmouth is vividly—and chillingly—described, but in the end the place-name seems too appropriate. Manning's world, one began to feel, was essentially the world of the defeated, and somehow it seemed that her very excellence as a novelist went towards imparting this feeling. Her work was lucid, ironic, and cold. One admired and applauded the integrity but was daunted by the detachment, which seemed, perhaps, the product of too great a fastidiousness.

But lucidity, irony, detachment,and fastidiousness are also the hall-marks of her Balkan Trilogy, and its sequel, The Levant Trilogy, certainly one of the outstanding achievements in post-war fiction. The achievement is such as to suggest that in it, for the first time, Manning was tackling a subject commensurate with her talents, and part of her success in it certainly comes from the qualities that had formerly seemed somehow to diminish her characters.

These qualities do, in fact, define the central consciousness through which the events of the series are reflected, that of Harriet Pringle, the newly married wife of Guy Pringle, who is a member of the staff of a cultural organization uncommonly like the British Council. They travel to Bucharest together, and *The Great Fortune* deals with that city during the first year of the war. The second ends with its occupation by the Germans after the fall of France, and *Friends and Heroes*, dealing with the departure of the Pringles for Greece, ends with their escape from Greece after the fall of Crete to Alexandria. The Levant Trilogy continues their adventures in wartime Cairo and the surrounding desert, with well-researched battle scenes (including the Battle of El Alamein), accounts of hospital ships, and later wanderings in Palestine and Syria. This, then, is a series on recent history, a war novel written from the point of view of an English non-combatant in countries remote from the West. The action is inevitably complex and the canvas large, and everything depends precisely on the eye of the beholder, Harriet Pringle, lucid, ironical, detached, fastidious, and also newly married to a man she scarcely understands. Harriet herself is almost totally unpolitical; she ia a stranger in an exotic world. She is at once naive and shrewd, and it is this combination that gives her rendering of the fall of a nation its authority and authenticity. This, we feel, is exactly what it must have been like to be the helpless onlooker of the takeover of a country in time of war. As a recreation of history in fiction these novels are admirable; the novelist is doing her proper job, to show us the workings of historical events in living terms, to bring them to the human level. The place and the time, the sense of doom and the consequent corruption, seem caught perfectly. And the characters are drawn with delicacy and strength, etched with a fine clarity that often reduces them to absurdity but never lets us see them as anything but suffering human beings. Though the books do not indulge in sensationalism, the violence is never burked and comes over the more strongly because of Olivia Manning's almost Austenish precision. Nothing is exaggerated, and this, despite the horrors in the near background, the very real dangers which threaten Harriet and her husband and overwhelm some of their friends, makes the whole work a comedy of a very poignant kind. Everything is in the balance; we read the work with the advantage of hindsight. We might, otherwise, have been reading tragedy.

But this is not all. At the centre of the novel, the focal point that makes everything else real, is the relationship between Harriet and her husband Guy, the young man she scarcely knows, and sees in action in a world new to her. Harriet is constantly discovering new aspects of him. He is a committed man, secure, as he thinks, in his marriage. As Harriet notes: "Guy's attitude impressed her, though she had no intention of showing it. He had the advantage of an almost supernatural confidence in dealing with people. It seemed never to occur to him they might not do what he wanted. He had, she noted with surprise, authority.... Only someone capable of giving so much could demand and receive so much. She felt proud of him."

The quotation illustrates something of Harriet's—and her creator's—objectivity; and also her fairness, for Guy Pringle is not an easy man to be married to. He seems to take Harriet for granted when he is engaged on what may be called his errands of mercy. He is a relentless do-gooder. But the word is wrong. Guy Pringle is much more than that. He is a man of great physical presence, an intellectual from the working class, who appears at times something of a saint, something of a fool. And again it is Harriet's not wholly certain attitude towards him that convinces us of his reality. He convinces us as that most maddening of human beings, the good man, and the good man, as Dostoevsky discovered when writing *The Idiot*, was only convincing when made at least a little ridiculous. Guy Pringle is one of the most fascinating explorations of character in contemporary fiction.

So, in the background, great events: in the foreground a very subtle analysis of the relationship between a man and wife. The juxtaposition is everything. It assures us of the truth of both.

—Walter Allen

McCULLERS, (Lula) Carson (née Smith). American. Born in Columbus, Georgia, 19 February 1917. Educated at Columbia University, New York and New York University, 1935-36. Married Reeves McCullers in 1937 (divorced, 1940); remarried Reeves McCullers in 1945 (died, 1953). Recipient: Guggenheim Fellowship, 1943, 1946; American Academy grant, 1943; New York Drama Critics Award, 1950; Donaldson Award, for drama, 1950. Member, American Academy. *Died 29 September 1967.*

PUBLICATIONS

Novels

The Heart Is a Lonely Hunter. Boston, Houghton Mifflin, 1940; London, Cresset Press, 1943.

Reflections in a Golden Eye. Boston, Houghton Mifflin, 1941; London, Cresset Press, 1942.

The Member of the Wedding. Boston, Houghton Mifflin, and London, Cresset Press, 1946.

Clock Without Hands. Boston, Houghton Mifflin, and London, Cresset Press, 1961.

Short Stories

The Ballad of the Sad Café: The Novels and Stories of Carson McCullers. Boston, Houghton Mifflin, 1951; London, Cresset Press, 1952.

Seven. New York, Bantam, 1954.

Collected Short Stories. Boston, Houghton Mifflin, 1955.

The Shorter Novels and Stories of Carson McCullers. London, Barrie and Jenkins, 1972.

Plays

The Twisted Trinity, music by David Diamond. Privately printed, 1946.

The Member of the Wedding, adaptation of her own novel (produced New York, 1950; London, 1957). New York, New Directions, 1951.

The Square Root of Wonderful (produced New York, 1957; London, 1970). New York, Houghton Mifflin, 1958; London, Cresset Press, 1959.

Other

Sweet as a Pickle and Clean as a Pig (juvenile verse). Boston, Houghton Mifflin, 1964; London, Cape, 1965.

The Mortgaged Heart (uncollected writings), edited by Margarita G. Smith. Boston, Houghton Mifflin, 1971; London, Barrie and Jenkins, 1972.

*

Bibliography: *Katherine Anne Porter and Carson McCullers: A Reference Guide* by Robert F. Kiernan, Boston, Hall, 1976; *Carson McCullers: A Bibliography* by Adrian M. Shapiro, New York, Garland, 1980.

Critical Studies: *Carson McCullers: Her Life and Work* by Oliver Evans, London, Owen, 1965, as *The Ballad of Carson McCullers*, New York, Coward McCann, 1966; *Carson McCullers* by Lawrence Graver, Minneapolis, University of Minnesota Press, 1969; *The Lonely Hunter: A Biography of Carson McCullers* by Virginia Spencer Carr, New York, Doubleday, 1975, London, Owen, 1977; *Carson McCullers* by Richard M. Cook, New York, Ungar, 1975; *The Achievement of Carson McCullers* edited by Irving Malin, Deland, Florida, Everett Edwards, 1976; *Carson McCullers* by Margaret B. McDowell, Boston, Twayne, 1980.

* * *

One of that group of precocious, eccentric, Southern *enfants terribles* who flowered like rank hollyhocks in the 1940's, Carson McCullers was a unique sensibility. A celebrity at 22, she wrote her best fiction within 6 years. With Faulkner, Tennessee Williams, and Truman Capote, she cultivated a type of fiction that critics labeled Southern Gothic. Hostile reviewers called her work bizarre, morbid, extreme, decadent, "horror pornography"; others praised her for having achieved "a metaphysical fusion of horror and compassion"; McCullers herself noted the "fusion of anguish and farce" in Southern writing that caused reviewers to misread the seriously grotesque mode as Poe-like Gothic horror for its own sake. Like Sherwood Anderson and Faulkner, she deliberately makes grotesque characters expressionistic extensions of normal, universal human problems. Like Proust, she was obsessed with time and memory. Although her overt didacticism reveals her preference for

Tolstoy, McCullers is closer to Dostoevski, with his "radically tightened nervous tone" (her phrase). She once referred to *The Heart Is a Lonely Hunter* as her Russian (Dostoevskian) novel, *Reflections in a Golden Eye* as her short French (Flaubertian) novel, and *The Member of the Wedding* as her English (Woolfian) novel.

"The South is a very emotional experience for me, " McCullers once said. Physically, most of her fiction is set in small southern towns, modelled on Columbus, Georgia; psychologically, "the labyrinth of the heart"; metaphorically, a prison. Most of her fiction sets the mood *The Ballad of the Sad Cafe* does: "The town itself is dreary....lonesome, sad, and like a place that is far off and estranged from all other places in the world....You might as well walk down to the Forks Fall Road and listen to the chain gang." As most events occur in monotonous conditions of extreme heat and dryness that exacerbate states of boredom and melancholy, McCullers makes us feel the congruence of physical and psychological weathers.

In *A Member of the Wedding* Frankie, this century's most vivid symbol of the compulsion to belong, says to little John Henry, "Not to belong to a 'we' makes you too lonesome." All her characters are the "we" of Carson McCullers. Some of them are autobiographical, especially Frankie and Mick (of *The Heart Is a Lonely Hunter*). When McCullers said, "I become the characters I write about," she was referring to characters who have been called "strange, enigmatic, macabre, fantastic, fanatic, narcissistic, perverted, malicious, desperate, abnormal, diseased, pathological." Her response was to quote Terence: "Nothing human is alien to me." Among her Gothic grotesques are the physical cripples, giantess Amelia and the hunchback dwarf Cousin Lymnon; the mental cripple, Captain Penderton, a latent homosexual; the spiritual cripple, senile, egocentric Judge Clane. Each of her novels depicts, as one reviewer said, "a viper's nest of neurasthenic relationships." If the two girls Frankie and Mick are also grotesque, it is only in the sense that adolescence is a grotesque phase in every person's development. Richard Wright praised McCullers for handling "Negro characters with...ease." Berenice and Portia are almost as impressive as Faulkner's Dilsey. One might say more appropriately of McCullers than of most writers that all her work is autobiographical in the sense that whatever she read and whatever she imagined *really happened* to her.

An omniscient narrator, somewhat like George Eliot, McCullers roved among her characters. Much of the excellence of her work may be attributed to the effects of the omniscient point of view she almost always employed and to a simple style that conjures an air of wonder, awe, and mystery. At its worst, her style is wordy, precious, awkward, pseudo-literary, clumsy, too much in the passive voice, too epigrammatic, cliché-ridden. At its best, what it emits is radiance. Like Sherwood Anderson, McCullers makes deliberate, controlled use of the old-fashioned style, tone, and techniques of the tale, as the openings of her novels suggest: "The participants of this tragedy were two officers, a soldier, two women, and a horse." One reviewer remarked upon the "distant Olympian dispassionateness" of her style that makes us feel authorial distance, most severely in *The Ballad.* Tennessee Williams asks us to regard as deliberate McCullers' "absolute mastery of design," the austere "Grecian purity" of form in that *tour de force Reflections in a Golden Eye*; its aura of artificiality, stylization, and decadence is characteristic to some degree of all her fiction. It is the use of too many of the deceptive tricks and devices of the omniscient narrator that mars *Clock Without Hands*, her least successful novel, as when Judge Clane delivers a weakly motivated, double-barreled revelation concerning Jester's father and Sherman's mother. But in *Heart* the omniscient point of view controls an aesthetic concept that embodies theme and is structured by the hero-witness relationship that McCullers develops between the mute John Singer and four other characters. The novel is unified by a pattern of symbolic motifs and a well-wrought design in which alternate sections are devoted to the intimate viewpoints of the five major characters, with a different style for each. We encounter the blatant foreshadowing, the obvious, ironic symbolism (Singer as Christ the Savior), the static character descriptions, and the omniscient author's narrative summaries; but elements that are sometimes faults in the other works here sound a succession of almost perfect notes.

The growing social consciousness that made young McCullers attack capitalism, racism, and religion in *Heart* is rather muted in subsequent works until *Clock Without Hands*, which dramatizes the entanglement of personal with public radical dilemmas. Social problems are primarily objective correlatives for spiritual and emotional struggles. *Heart* is a realistic allegory of the paradoxical conflict between one's hunger for human understanding and one's simultaneous desire for inviolable privacy; in the context of society, both needs are frustrated. Isolated from society by its conditions and their own constitutions, each character is obsessed with one single idea, purpose, or personality disorder. If Singer is Christ, his obese feebleminded Greek beloved is his god, and the ironic cruelty of Antonapoulos's incomprehension suggests an allegorical statement about man and God and self-delusion.

That McCullers is a didactic writer is demonstrated in her compulsion to discuss theme and her vision of life directly with the reader. The lover and the beloved "come from different countries.... And the curt truth is that.... the state of being beloved is intolerable to many. The beloved fears and hates the lover, and with the best of reasons. For the lover is forever trying to strip bare his beloved. The lover craves any possible relation with the beloved, even if this experience can cause him only pain" (*The Ballad*). McCullers develops her novels within the tensions of paradoxical polarities: characters simultaneously crave life and death, privacy and ideal assimilation of self with other; hopeless, doomed, often nonsexual attractions become cruel, violent repulsions, expressing love and hate; mismatched characters in tangled relationships remain always spiritually isolated. Some of them break out of the prison of solitude in compulsive, sudden acts of violence. Some turn against themselves; when the Greek, the object of his worship, perishes, Singer, like Richard Cory, shoots himself. For McCullers's transfixed prisoners, talk frequently substitutes for action. Seldom do McCullers's characters make physical or sexual contact. They internalize society's prohibitions, mistaking them for forces of nature. In McCullers's vision, the world itself is unfinished, incomplete, and so therefore are its creatures, who, like the trio in the ugly kitchen in *A Member of the Wedding*, play the game of life with a deck in which cards are missing. For what is missing in reality, characters compensate in impossible dreams and self-generated illusions, and out of severe need demonstrate the transcendent power of human imagination.

Carson McCullers was a poetic symbolist with a touch of the logician. Despite a certain static quality in all her work, one feels an intensity of expression, a tension of structure, and over all a sense of the magical and the mysterious that moved Dame Edith Sitwell to call her "a transcendental writer." Her characters hunger for communication, which was for McCullers the only access to love. Her aesthetics and her themes are inseparable; she had a compulsion to transform experience into the charged images of art. For her, the generators of all good writing were "love, passion, compassion." At times she consorted with the Sentimental Muse, and yet *The Heart Is a Lonely Hunter* is one of the most pessimistic novels ever written; still, the reader, beholding the transcendent artistry of McCullers's intuitive-intellectual imagination, is exhilarated. A work of art is "like a flowering dream," and the writer is "a conscious dreamer," she said; between the writer's dream and the "logic of God," there is a "divine collusion."

—David Madden

O'CONNOR, (Mary) Flannery. American. Born in Savannah, Georgia, 25 March 1925. Educated at Peabody High School, Milledgeville, Georgia, graduated 1942; Georgia State College for Women, now Georgia College at Milledgeville, 1942-45, A.B. 1945; University of Iowa, Iowa City, 1945-47, M.F.A. 1947. Recipient: *Kenyon Review* Fellowship, 1953; American Academy grant, 1957; O. Henry Award, 1957, 1963, 1964; Ford Foundation grant, 1959; National Catholic Book Award, 1966; National Book Award, 1972. D.Litt.: St. Mary's College, Notre Dame, Indiana, 1962; Smith College, Northampton, Massachusetts, 1963. *Died 3 August 1964.*

PUBLICATIONS

Novels

Wise Blood. New York, Harcourt Brace, 1952; London, Spearman, 1955.

The Violent Bear It Away. New York, Farrar Straus, and London, Longman, 1960.

Short Stories

A Good Man Is Hard to Find and Other Stories. New York, Harcourt Brace, 1955; as *The Artificial Nigger and Other Tales.* London, Spearman, 1957.

Everything That Rises Must Converge. New York, Farrar Straus, 1965; London, Faber, 1966.

The Complete Stories. New York, Farrar Straus, 1971.

Other

Mystery and Manners: Occasional Prose, edited by Sally and Robert Fitzgerald. New York, Farrar Straus, 1969; London, Faber, 1972.

The Habit of Being: Letters of Flannery O'Connor, edited by Sally Fitzgerald. New York, Farrar Straus, and London, Faber, 1979.

Editor, *A Memoir of Mary Ann.* New York, Farrar Straus, 1961; as *Death of a Child*, London, Burns and Oates, 1961.

*

Bibliography: *Flannery O'Connor and Caroline Gordon: A Reference Guide* by Robert E. Golden and Mary C. Sullivan, Boston, Hall, 1977.

Manuscript Collection: Georgia College at Milledgeville.

Critical Studies (selection): *Flannery O'Connor: A Critical Essay* by Robert Drake, Grand Rapids, Michigan, Eerdmans, 1966; *Flannery O'Connor* by Stanley Edgar Hyman, Minneapolis, University of Minnesota Press, 1966; *The Added Dimension: The Art and Mind of Flannery O'Connor* edited by Melvin J. Friedman and Lewis A. Lawson, New York, Fordham University Pres, 1966; *The True Country: Themes in the Fiction of Flannery O'Connor* by Carter W. Martin, Nashville, Tennessee, Vanderbilt University Press, 1969; *The World of Flannery O'Connor* by Josephine Hendin, Bloomington, Indiana University Press, 1970; *Flannery O'Connor: Voice of the Peacock* by Kathleen Feeley, New Brunswick, New Jersey, Rutgers University Press, 1972; *Invisible Parade: The Fiction of Flannery O'Connor* by Miles Orvell, Philadelphia, Temple University Press, 1972; *Flannery O'Connor* by Dorothy Walters, New York, Twayne, 1973; *The Question of Flannery O'Connor* by Martha Stephens, Baton Rouge, Louisiana State University Press, 1973; *Flannery O'Connor* by Preston M. Browning, Jr., Carbondale, Southern Illinois University Press, 1974; *Flannery O'Connor* by Dorothy Tuck McFarland, New York, Ungar, 1976; *The Pruning Word: The Parables of Flannery O'Connor* by John R. May, Notre Dame, Indiana, University of Notre Dame Press, 1976; *Flannery O'Connor's Dark Comedies: The Limits of Inference* by Carol Shloss, Baton Rouge, Louisiana State University Press, 1980.

"Belief, in my own case anyway, is the engine that makes perception operate." As a religious writer, Flannery O'Connor had to confront the lack of a shared world-picture with the majority of her readers. Declaring that "my subject in fiction is the action of grace in territory held largely by the devil," she recognized that in the average reader the "sense of evil is diluted or lacking altogether, and so he has forgotten the price of restoration." The unique vision of Flannery O'Connor—violent, apocalyptic, grotesque—resulted from her endeavor to function as a believing writer in a non-believing world.

Brought up a Catholic in the "Christ-haunted" Bible Belt of the American South, O'Connor focused on the dominant Protestant Fundamentalism of the region, "those aspects of Southern life where the religious feeling is most intense and where its outward forms are farthest from the Catholic, and most revealing of a need that only the Church can fill." As she exaggerated violence in her evocation of Georgia she accentuated the individualism of her backwoods prophets, because the Christian novelist "may well be forced to take ever more violent means to get his vision across to this hostile audience."

The theme of both her novels is vocation. In a note to the second edition of *Wise Blood*, the author described "Haze" Motes as "a Christian *malgré lui.*" His preaching of "the Church Without Christ" involves him in killing a "false prophet" and is terminated by the destruction of his pulpit, his car; he blinds himself, and bears mute and solitary witness. Like all O'Connor's work, the book is tragi-comic since "the maximum amount of seriousness admits the maximum amount of comedy;" ironic use of profanity is a major source of humour.

Whereas *Wise Blood* is something of negative spiritual odyssey, as Hazel Motes encounters the fake blind preacher, Enoch Emery, and Onnie Jay Holy, *The Violent Bear It Away* has a tighter structure; it is rooted in the relationships of Francis Marion Tarwater with his great-uncle, a prophet, and with his uncle Rayber and his little idiot cousin Bishop. The rationalist Rayber believes that the old man "needed the assurance of a call, and so he called himself." On his great-uncle's death, Tarwater tries to reject his vocation as a prophet and his "first mission" to baptize Bishop. Inexorably, he drowns Bishop, baptizing him simultaneously. He ceases to struggle with "the bleeding stinking mad shadow of Jesus," but by then he seems as unbalanced as his great-uncle was considered to be.

The key to O'Connor's technique is her use of anagogical vision, which she defined as "the kind of vision that is able to see different levels of reality in one image or one situation." The same symbols recur in both novels; for instance, the stones in Hazel Motes's shoes with the other rock leitmotifs in *Wise Blood* gradually recall St. Peter, while in *The Violent Bear It Away* Bishop plays with a stone in a wastepaper basket. An elaborate infrastructure of interlocking symbolism maintains the characteristic "interior suspense" of O'Connor's work.

The violence of her content is conveyed in a raw, angular style, whose vigour frequently hardens into violent imagery. In her critical writing, brought together posthumously in *Mystery and Manners*, she emphasized the writer's eye: "everything has its testing point in the eye.... Judgment is something that begins in the act of vision." Imagery of the eye is outstanding in her novels and stories, with eyes likened to "two steel spikes" or "pitchfork prongs."

Adapted to the short-story form, these techniques produced stories wonderfully "long in depth," as O'Connor herself prescribed. Yet the collections of stories *A Good Man Is Hard to Find* and *Everything That Rises Must Converge* ought not to eclipse her supreme achievement, *The Violent Bear It Away.* The patterns of relationship in this novel recur in many of the stories, notably in "The Lame Shall Enter First"; another favourite relation is the mother-daughter one, where the mother runs a farm managing Negro and white trash labour. O'Connor's stress on "the mystery of personality" is delimited, at least for the humanist reader, by her invariable location of this in terms of pervasive religious symbolism. Against her usual "mythic background" of the South, "where belief can be made believable," her stories pivot on a character's acceptance or rejection of the moment of grace. In "The Artificial Nigger" the simultaneous delight of Nelson and Mr. Head at the sight of a plaster statue of a Negro reunites them after the grandfather's "denial" of Nelson to passers-by. The positive ending is unusual in *A Good Man*, while in *Everything That Rises* the element of violence is even stronger and most of the stories culminate in death.

This latter volume of stories was written while O'Connor was enduring the closing stages of chronic lupus, just before her early death. Her experience of suffering in her long illness may have reinforced her uncompromising vision. Though Flannery O'Connor was fond of quoting St. Thomas Aquinas's dictum that "a work of art is a good in itself," the generalized cathartic effect which her unique work has on most readers represents a dilution of its vision.

—Val Warner

SCOTT, Paul (Mark). British. Born in London, 25 March 1920. Educated at Winchmore Hill Collegiate School. Served in the British Army, 1940-43, and in the Indian Army, in India and Malaya, 1943-46. Married Nancy Edith Avery in 1941; two daughters. Company Secretary, Falcon Press and Grey Walls Press, London, 1946-50; Director, David Higham Associates, literary agents, London, 1950-60. British Council Lecturer, India, 1972; Visiting Lecturer, University of Tulsa, Oklahoma, 1976-77. Recipient: Eyre and Spottiswoode Literary Fellowship, 1952; Arts Council grant, 1969; Booker Prize, 1977. Fellow, Royal Society of Literature, 1963. *Died 1 March 1978.*

PUBLICATIONS

Novels

Johnnie Sahib. London, Eyre and Spottiswoode, 1952.
The Alien Sky. London, Eyre and Spottiswoode, 1953; as *Six Days in Marapore*, New York, Doubleday, 1953.
A Male Child. London, Eyre and Spottiswoode, 1956; New York, Dutton, 1957.
The Mark of the Warrior. London, Eyre and Spottiswoode, and New York, Morrow, 1958.
The Chinese Love Pavilion. London, Eyre and Spottiswoode, 1960; as *The Love Pavilion*, New York, Morrow, 1960.
The Birds of Paradise. London, Eyre and Spottiswoode, and New York, Morrow, 1962.
The Bender: Pictures from an Exhibition of Middle Class Portraits. London, Secker and Warburg, 1963; as *The Bender*, New York, Morrow, 1963.
The Corrida of San Feliu. London, Secker and Warburg, and New York, Morrow, 1964.
The Raj Quartet. London, Heinemann, and New York, Morrow, 1976.
  The Jewel in the Crown. London, Heinemann, and New York, Morrow, 1966.
  The Day of the Scorpion. London, Heinemann, and New York, Morrow, 1968.
  The Towers of Silence. London, Heinemann, 1971; New York, Morrow, 1972.
  A Division of the Spoils. London, Heinemann, and New York, Morrow, 1975.
Staying On. London, Heinemann, and New York, Morrow, 1977.

Short Story

After the Funeral. Andoversford, Gloucestershire, Whittington Press, 1979.

Plays

Pillars of Salt, in *Four Jewish Plays*, edited by H.F. Rubinstein. London, Gollancz, 1948.

Television Play: *The Mark of the Warrior*, from his own novel, 1959.

Verse

I, Gerontius. London, Favil Press, 1941.

*

Manuscript Collection: Humanities Research Center, University of Texas, Austin.

Critical Studies: by the author, in *Essays by Divers Hands*, London, Oxford University Press, 1970; *Paul Scott: Images of India* by Patrick Swinden, London, Macmillan, 1980.

* * *

Paul Scott's considerable achievement as a novelist is best represented by the four inter-connected novels that make up *The Raj Quartet*. This tetralogy, set in the years 1939 to 1947, the final years of the Raj, was extended by a short novel, *Staying On*, set in 1972 and dealing with an elderly couple who decide to remain in India after Independence.

Each novel in *The Raj Quartet* is complete in itself, yet taken together they provide for the reader a growing understanding of India and involve him more and more intimately in the decisions and events of the period. The volumes are not consecutive; *The Day of the Scorpion*, for instance, barely advances in time from *The Jewel in the Crown*, and is concerned with the same events, the attack on Miss Crane and the rape of Daphne Manners in the Bibighar Gardens, yet the emphasis is placed at a different angle, and characters who appear in the first novel are revealed as very different people in the second. This is especially relevant in portraying the character of Merrick, District Superintendent of Police, who is presented as a pillar of the community in *The Jewel in the Crown*, with just a few vague suspicions surfacing about his actions, yet is seen to be a ruthless and prejudiced sadist in the next volume.

The Towers of Silence covers almost the same period of time, but introduces new characters, mostly female, and continues to develop the mysterious Merrick, whose sinister side seems to be recognised more readily by the Indian than by the English. Set in the hill station of Pankot, *The Towers of Silence* provides yet another veil of comment on the central incidents of the attacks on Daphne Manners and Miss Crane; here, the Brigadier who ordered his troops to fire on unarmed crowds in Mayapore, and whose pompous memoirs are so deftly pilloried in *The Jewel in the Crown*, can be dismissed as "a bit of a duffer" by the Colonel's wives sitting out the War in the mountains. The tragic figure of retired missionary teacher Barbie Batchelor is developed here, and allows Scott to bring out one of the most important themes in the novels, that of the class conflicts within the British themselves in India. Scott has said of British society, "We have our Brahmins, our workers, our untouchables." Barbie Batchelor, a friend of Miss Crane, is relentlessly insulted and snubbed by the women of higher social status in Pankot, the same women who exploit Lucy Smalley, the chief character of *Staying On*.

A Division of the Spoils is an extensive volume in two parts, dealing with the ultimate retreat of the British and the Partition of India. Violence fills the novel, as the figure who seems to bring evil wherever he goes, Robert Merrick, is savagely murdered, and Hindu and Muslim begin systematically to butcher each other as the British depart, a betrayal that Scott felt deeply about. In an interview in 1975 Scott said, "How did we walk out with such a high sense of duty performed? The Indians almost contributed to the feeling that we had done our job and it was no fault of ours that

250,000 people were massacred in road convoys and on trains.... In the end it was a tragedy in the classical sense." Scott's sense of shame is symbolised by the use he makes of the old painting that Miss Crane uses to teach her class English, of Queen Victoria on her throne, supported by angels and receiving tribute from her loyal Indian subjects. This image of mutual love and care, of "man-bap," ironically appears for the last time as one of the effects packed with the murdered Merrick's trunk.

Technically, *The Raj Quartet* and *Staying On* share a sophisticated blend of narrative techniques: changing viewpoint, different narrative forms, time-shifts, and flashbacks. The unfolding of the story is constantly inventive; in the final volume the shadowy figure of the contemporary traveller depicts historical events by simply describing a series of cartoons in a Bombay newspaper. In *The Jewel in the Crown* the reader is drawn into a mosaic of fragmentary reportage: letters, memoirs, comments on the memoirs, a journal, a formal deposition; all invite the reader to take an evaluative stance on the events of the novel. At the end of *A Division of the Spoils* Merrick is buried with honour as "a gallant soldier"; his widow refers to him admiringly as someone who "never pretended," yet the reader has seen the strange pathways of Merrick's mind, his hidden homosexuality, his Pathan disguises and his ritual murder by the young Indian boys he exploits. But Susan is sincere in her view of her husband, and Scott convinces us of the value she places on him, thus making the reader feel the impossibility of ever really knowing the truth about another person, or of judging others impartially.

Staying On is a short, very poignant novel dealing mainly with two characters, Colonel Tusker Smalley and his wife Lucy, who never reached the top ranks of Anglo-Indian society and elected to remain in India after Partition rather than return to the pettiness and snobbery of England. Scott is particularly sensitive to the feelings of the elderly, and the novel precisely plots a relationship that functions not so much through words, but through the daily incidents that habit has made familiar.

Paul Scott's early novels contrast strongly to the lengthy, dense works of *The Raj Quartet*. Many are set in India and deal with experiences gained while he was on active service in India in World War II as an officer in an air supply unit. His first published novel, *Johnnie Sahib*, describes the activities of such a unit and vigorously explores the strands of power and conflict that are involved in leading a small group of men. Similar themes concerned with the idea of the soldier as leader are examined in *The Mark of the Warrior*, a much slighter novel with a distressing feeling of inevitability about its plot and characters. *The Alien Sky* concerns itself with British civilians who are about to leave India in 1947 and looks with unusual honesty at the situation of the English liberal who cannot understand why he is so hated by the Indians he longs to help.

The idea of the soldier and the dilemma of command are also central to *The Chinese Love Pavilion*, which shares with several of the early novels a charismatic, mysterious character who both repels and fascinates the central figure. This time it is a dangerously independent ex-planter Brian Saxby who teaches the newly arrived Brent how to love the India that Brent's family have served for generations. *The Birds of Paradise* reveals the beginnings of the slow-paced, richly embellished prose that was to form the basis of his last works. In this novel the image of the decaying, stuffed birds of paradise in the garden of an Indian palace allows the author to explore the techniques of flashback that he was to use so effectively in *The Raj Quartet*.

Only three of Scott's 13 novels are not set in India or the Far East: *A Male Child* is a drab novel set in London just after World War II, but already there are hints of the rich characterisation that was to emerge. *The Bender* is a mildly amusing tale about a feckless poor relation with an inadequate private income and provides some satiric barbs at the fashionable society of the time. Narrative intricacy is strained to the utmost in *The Corrida of San Feliu*, set in Spain, with flashbacks to the past intercut with portions of an unfinished novel being written by the chief character, Edward Thornhill.

Critical acclaim came late to Paul Scott and only in the last years of his life did a wide readership develop for his work. Although the slow pace of his novels with their gradual accumulation of detail may be very much against the modern trend to short, elliptical novels, the reader finds in the very complexities of his later works an invitation to share in the complexities of life itself, and to emerge with an extended vision as a result.

—Margaret Lewis

NOTES
ON
ADVISORS
AND
CONTRIBUTORS

ALLEN, Walter. See his own entry. **Essays**: Graham Greene; Olivia Manning (appendix); V.S. Pritchett; Edward Upward.

ANDERSEN, Richard. Free-lance writer. Author of four books—the most recent being a novel, *Muckaluck*—and of a forthcoming study of Robert Coover. **Essay**: William Goldman.

AUBERT, Alvin. Associate Professor of English, State University of New York, Fredonia; Editor of *Obsidian* magazine, and Advisory Editor of *Drama and Theatre*. Author of two books of verse, *Against the Blues*, 1972, and *Feeling Through*, 1975. **Essay**: Ernest J. Gaines.

BAKERMAN, Jane S. Associate Professor of English, Indiana State University, Terre Haute. Adviser and contributor to *American Women Writers*, 1979. Author of interviews with P.D. James in *Armchair Detective*, Ruth Rendell in *Mystery Nook*, and Daphne du Maurier in *Writer's Yearbook*. Contributor to those magazines and to *Mystery Fancier*, *Cloak and Dagger*, and *The Poisoned Pen*. **Essays**: Daphne du Maurier; May Sarton.

BARNES, John. Member of the Department of English, La Trobe University, Bundoora, Victoria. Author of essays on Peter Cowan, Hal Porter, and Patrick White. **Essay**: Peter Cowan.

BENNETT, Sally H. Cataloguer, Warner Memorial Library, Eastern College, Saint Davids, Pennsylvania. Reviewer for *Library Journal* and *Emergency Librarian*. **Essays**: Richard Condon; James A. Michener; Cynthia Ozick.

BENSEN, Alice. Professor of English, Eastern Michigan University, Ypsilanti. Author of *Rose Macaulay*, 1969. **Essays**: Margery Sharp; Anthony West.

BERGONZI, Bernard. Professor of English, University of Warwick, Coventry. Author of *Descartes and the Animals*, 1954; *The Early H.G. Wells*, 1961; *Heroes' Twilight*, 1965; *The Situation of the Novel*, 1970; *T.S. Eliot*, 1971; *Gerard Manley Hopkins*, 1977; *Reading the Thirties*, 1978; *Years: Sixteen Poems*, 1979; *The Roman Persuasion* (novel), 1981. Contributor to *The Observer*, *Times Literary Supplement*, and other periodicals. **Essays**: Anthony Burgess; Nigel Dennis; Margaret Drabble; David Lodge; Julian Mitchell; Andrew Sinclair; Angus Wilson.

BERMANT, Chaim. See his own entry. **Essay**: Bernice Rubens.

BEST, Marshall A. Editorial Consultant. Editor, 1925-34, General Manager, 1935-55, and Editorial Vice-President, 1956-68, Viking Press, New York. Poems, reviews, and translations published in *Atlantic Monthly*, *Saturday Review*, and other magazines. Translator of *Avarice House* by Julien Green, 1926. **Essays**: Rumer Godden; Thomas Keneally; Manohar Malgonkar; William Trevor; Patrick White.

BIRNEY, Earle. See his own entry.

BITTNER, William. Professor of English, Acadia University, Wolfville, Nova Scotia. Author of *Poe: A Biography*, *The Novels of Waldo Frank*, and of articles in *Atlantic Monthly*, *The Nation*, *Saturday Review*, *New York Post*, and other periodicals. **Essays**: William Bradford Huie; Hammond Innes; Anthony C. West.

BORDEN, William. Associate Professor of English, University of North Dakota, Grand Forks. Author of the novel *Superstoe*, 1968. Editor of *Black American Literature: An Anthology*, 1972. **Essay**: William Melvin Kelley.

BORKLUND, Elmer. Associate Professor of English, Pennsylvania State University, University Park. Former Associate Editor of *Chicago Review*. Author of *Contemporary Literary Critics*, 1977, and of articles in *Modern Philology*, *Commentary*, *New York Herald-Tribune Book Week*, *Journal of General Education*, and *World Book Encyclopedia*. **Essays**: John Barth; Brigid Brophy; Mavis Gallant; Christopher Isherwood; Mary McCarthy; Iris Murdoch; Susan Sontag; Gore Vidal; Auberon Waugh; Paul West; Rebecca West.

BOWERS, Frederick. Associate Professor of English, University of British Columbia, Vancouver. Author of articles on Arthur Hugh Clough, Gabriel Fielding, syntax, and semantics, in *Renascence*, *Studies in English Literature*, *Orbis*, *Journal of Linguistics*, and other journals. **Essays**: J.G. Ballard; Stan Barstow; Gabriel Fielding; Frederik Pohl; J.B. Priestley.

BOXILL, Anthony. Associate Professor of English, University of New Brunswick, Fredericton; Fiction Editor of *The Fiddlehead*; Associate Editor of *World Literature Written in English*. Author of articles in *The Fiddlehead*, *Présence Africaine*, *CLA Journal*. **Essays**: Roy A.K. Heath; Earl Lovelace; Christopher Nicole.

BRADBURY, Malcolm. See his own entry. **Essay**: William Cooper.

BRADFORD, M.E. Professor of English and American Studies, University of Dallas; Member of the Editorial Board of *Modern Age*. Author of *Rumors of Mortality: An Introduction to Allen Tate*, 1967, and *A Better Guide Than Reason*, 1980, and of articles in *Bear, Man, and God*, 1971, *Allen Tate and His Work*, 1971, and *Sewanee Review*, *National Review*, *Southern Review*, and other periodicals. **Essays**: Madison Jones; Andrew Lytle.

BRANDER, Laurence. Author of *George Orwell*, 1954; *Somerset Maugham*, 1963; *E.M. Forster*, 1968; *Aldous Huxley*, 1970. **Essay**: Ahmed Ali.

BROWN, Lloyd W. Member of the Department of Comparative Literature, University of Southern California, Los Angeles. Editor of *The Black Writer in Africa and the Americas*, 1973. **Essays**: Austin C. Clarke; Marion Jones; Ismith Khan.

BRUNAUER, Dalma H. Professor of Humanities, Clarkson College of Technology, Potsdam, New York. Author of *World Literature in Translation*, 1960, and of articles in *The New Catholic Encyclopedia*. Editor of *Literature and Religion: Albee and Beckett*, 1971. **Essays**: Carol Hill; Edward Newhouse.

BURGESS, Anthony. See his own entry.

BURKE, Herbert C. William Morley Tweedie Professor of English, Mount Allison University, Sackville, New Brunswick. Author of articles and reviews on modern fiction in journals; regular poetry reviewer for *Library Journal*; his own poems have been published in little magazines. **Essay**: Jack Ludwig.

CADOGAN, Mary. Secretary of an educational trust; governor of an international school. Author of three books on popular literature with Patricia Craig—*You're a Brick, Angela*, 1976, *Women and Children First*, 1978, and *The Lady Investigates*, 1981—and of *The Greyfriars' Characters*, 1975, *The Charles Hamilton Schoolgirls' Album*, 1979, and *The Morcove Companion*, 1981. **Essay**: Gillian Freeman.

CAMERON, Donald. Associate Professor of English, University of New Brunswick, Fredericton; Co-Editor of *The Mysterious East*. Author of *Faces of Leacock*, 1967, and of stories and articles in *Studies in Scottish Literature*, *Canadian Literature*, *Queen's Quarterly*, and other periodicals. **Essays**: Ernest Buckler; Thomas Head Raddall.

CAMPENNI, Frank. Associate Professor of English, University of Wisconsin, Milwaukee. Author of articles and reviews in periodicals. **Essays**: Barry Beckham; Howard Fast; Irvin Faust; Bruce Jay Friedman; Mark Mirsky; Leo Rosten; Michael Rumaker; Budd Schulberg; Terry Southern; Morris West; Herman Wouk; Charles Wright; Frank Yerby.

CARPENTER, Frederic I. Author of *Emerson and Asia*, 1930; *Emerson Handbook*, 1953; *American Literature and the Dream*, 1955; *Robinson Jeffers*, 1962; *Eugene O'Neill*, 1964; *Laurens van der Post*, 1969. Has taught at the University of Chicago, Harvard University, and the University of California, Berkeley. **Essay**: Laurens van der Post.

CARRUTH, Hayden. Professor of English, Syracuse University, New York; Member of the Editorial Board, *Hudson Review* and Poetry Editor, *Harper's*. Author of several books of verse—the most recent being *Brothers, I Loved You All*, 1978—*AppendixA* (novel), 1963, and a book on Camus. Editor of anthologies of poetry. **Essay**: J.F. Powers.

CHAMBERS, D.D.C. Associate Professor of English, Trinity College, Toronto. Author of the forthcoming book *The Lost Cities*. **Essays**: N. Scott Momaday; John Rechy.

CHARLES, Gerda. See her own entry. **Essays**: Chaim Bermant; Penelope Fitzgerald.

CHARTERS, Ann. Associate Professor of English, University of Connecticut, Storrs. Author of *A Bibliography of Jack Kerouac*, 1967 (revised, 1975); *Scenes Along the Road: Photographs of the Desolation Angels*, 1970; *Nobody: The Story of Bert Williams*, 1970; *Kerouac: A Biography*, 1973; *I Love: The Story of Vladimir Mayakovsky and Lili Brik*, with Samuel Charters, 1979. **Essay**: Jack Kerouac (appendix).

CHIHARA, Paul Seiko. Associate Professor of Music, University of California, Los Angeles. Composer of numerous works, including *Driftwood* (string quartet), 1969, *Forest Music for Orchestra*, 1970, and music for ballets and films. Author of "Revolution and Music," 1970, and other essays. **Essay**: James Yaffe.

CLANCY, Laurie. Lecturer in English, La Trobe University, Bundoora, Victoria. Author of the novel *The Collapsible Man*, 1975, and short stories and articles for Australian magazines. **Essays**: Xavier Herbert; C.J. Koch; Peter Mathers.

CLARK, Anderson. Associate Professor of English, Belmont College, Nashville. **Essays**: Shelby Foote; Jesse Hill Ford.

COHEN, Gloria. Member of the English Department, Roosevelt University, Chicago; Assistant Editor, *Chicago Scene Magazine*. Author of textbooks. **Essay**: Gillian Tindall.

COHN, Ruby. Professor of Comparative Drama, University of California, Davis; Editor of *Modern Drama* and Associate Editor of *Educational Theatre Journal*. Author of *Samuel Beckett: The Comic Gamut*, 1962; *Currents in Contemporary Drama*, 1969; *Edward Albee*, 1969; *Dialogue in American Drama*, 1971; *Back to Beckett*, 1974; *Modern Shakespeare Offshoots*, 1976; *Just Play: Beckett's Theatre*, 1980. **Essay**: Samuel Beckett.

COLMER, John. Professor of English, University of Adelaide, Australia; General Editor of *Studies in Australian Culture*. Author of *Coleridge: Critic of Society*, 1959; *Approaches to the Novel*, 1967; *E.M. Forster: "A Passage to India."* 1967; *Forster: The Personal Voice*, 1975; *Patrick White: "Riders in the Chariot,"* 1977; *Coleridge to "Catch-22": Images of Society*, 1978. Editor of works by Coleridge . **Essays**: Elizabeth Harrower; Shirley Hazzard.

CONROY, Mary. Senior Lecturer in English, Cambridgeshire College of Arts and Technology. **Essay**: Julian Gloag.

COOKE, Judy. Lecturer in the Extra-Mural Department, University of London. **Essays**: Martin Amis; A.L. Barker; Jennifer Dawson; Maureen Duffy; Stella Gibbons; Wolf Mankowitz; Penelope Mortimer.

COPLAND, R.A. Former Member of the Department of English, University of Canterbury, Christchurch, New Zealand. **Essay**: Maurice Gee.

COTTON, John. Headmaster of a comprehensive school in Hertfordshire; Editor of *The Private Library* and Publisher of Priapus Press. Author of several books of verse—the most recent being *Piers*, 1979—and of *British Poetry since 1965*, 1973. **Essays**: Brian Aldiss; John Masters.

DAHLIE, Hallvard. Professor and Head of the Department of English, University of Calgary, Alberta. Author of *Brian Moore*, 1969. Editor of the Canadian issue of *The Literary Half-Yearly*, 1972. **Essays**: Robert Kroetsch; Alice Munro.

DAVIES, Barrie. Professor of English, University of New Brunswick, Fredericton. Editor of *The Selected Prose of Archibald Lampman*. **Essays**: Matt Cohen; C.J. Newman.

DESY, Jeanne. Free-lance writer. **Essay**: Tom McHale.

DICK, Margaret. Author of the novels *Point of Return*, 1958, and *Rhyme or Reason*, 1959, and of *The Novels of Kylie Tennant*, 1966. Reviewer for Sydney *Morning Herald* and *The Australian*. **Essay**: Kylie Tennant.

DILLARD, R.H.W. Professor of English and Chairman of the Graduate Program in Contemporary Literature and Creative Writing, Hollins College, Virginia; Vice-President, *The Film Journal*. Author of three books of verse—the most recent being *After Borges*, 1972—*The Book of Changes*, 1974 (novel), a screenplay, and *Horror Films*, 1976. Editor of two collections of essays. **Essays**: George Garrett; Calder Willingham.

DOEPKE, Dale K. Free-lance writer; author of essays on 19th-century American literature. **Essays**: Eleanor Clark; Donald Windham.

DOYLE, Paul A. Professor of English, Nassau Community College, Garden City, New York; Editor, *Evelyn Waugh Newsletter* and *Nassau Review*; Contributing Editor, *Best Sellers*; Consultant, *Choice* and *English Literature in Transition*. Author of studies of Pearl S. Buck, Evelyn Waugh, Sean O'Faolain, Liam O'Flaherty, and Paul Vincent Carroll, and of bibliographies of O'Flaherty and Waugh, a concordance to Joyce's poems, and works on writing skills and bibliography. Editor of *Alexander Pope's Iliad: An Examination* and *Thoreau: Studies and Commentaries*. **Essays**: Thomas Flanagan; Liam O'Flaherty; Piers Paul Read; Anne Tyler.

DRABBLE, Margaret. See her own entry.

DUCKWORTH, Deborah. Free-lance writer. Former Instructor in English, Louisiana State University, Baton Rouge. **Essay**: Elaine Dundy.

EISINGER, Chester E. Professor of English, Purdue University, Lafayette, Indiana. Author of *Fiction of the Forties*, 1963, and of articles in *Proletarian Writers of the Thirties*, 1968, and *Saturday Review*. Editor of *The 1940's: Profile of a Nation in Crisis*, 1969. **Essays**: Louis Auchincloss; Saul Bellow; John Cheever; Robert Coover; Peter De Vries; William H. Gass; Shirley Ann Grau; John Updike.

ELLIOTT, Brian. Reader in Australian Literary Studies, University of Adelaide. Author of the novel *Leviathan's Inch*, 1946; *Singing to the Cattle and Other Australian Essays*, 1947; *Marcus*

Clarke, 1958; *The Landscape of Australian Poetry*, 1967. Editor of *Coast to Coast: Australian Stories 1948*, 1949, *Bards in the Wilderness: Australian Poetry to 1920* (with Adrian Mitchell), 1970, and *The Jindyworobaks*, 1980. **Essay**: Dal Stivens.

EMANUEL, James A. Professor of English, City College of New York; General Editor of the Critics Series, Broadside Press, Detroit. Author of four books of verse—the most recent being *Black Man Abroad*, 1978—and of *Langston Hughes*, 1967, and an article in *How I Write 2*, 1972. Editor, with Theodore L. Gross, of *Dark Symphony: Negro Literature in America*, 1968. **Essays:** James Baldwin; Amiri Baraka; Julian Mayfield; Ann Petry; Margaret Walker.

FEIN, Richard J. Professor of English, State University College at New Paltz, New York. Author of *Robert Lowell*, 1970, and essays on Edward Lewis Wallant, Thoreau, modern poetry, and the Jewish story. **Essay:** Henry Roth.

FERGUSON, Brenda R. Director of Public Relations, Morgan State University, Baltimore. Author of articles in *Substance Magazine*, *Towson News*, and *Morgan Magazine*. **Essay:** John A. Williams.

FIEDLER, Leslie. See his own entry.

FIELD, Paul F. Staff member, Save the Children Fund, London; free-lance writer. **Essay:** James McNeish.

FIGUEROA, John. Visiting Fellow in Multi-Cultural Studies, Bradford College, Yorkshire. Formerly, Dean and Professor of Education, University of the West Indies, Kingston. Author of three books of verse, *Blue Mountain Peak*, 1944, *Love Leaps Here*, 1962, and *Ignoring Hurts*, 1976, and of two studies of education in the West Indies. Editor of *Caribbean Voices: An Anthology of West Indian Poetry*, 2 vols., 1966-70. **Essay:** Vic Reid.

FOLEY, Barbara. Assistant Professor of English, Northwestern University, Evanston, Illinois. Author of articles on Dos Passos and other writers in *American Literature*, *Contemporary Literature*, *Genre*, *PMLA*, and *Modern Fiction Studies*. **Essay:** E.L. Doctorow.

FOOTE, Irving F. Associate Professor of English, Georgia Institute of Technology, Atlanta. **Essay:** David Karp.

FORSBERG, Roberta J. Professor of English, Whittier College, California. Author of *Madame de Staël and Freedom Today*, 1963; *Chief Mountain: The Story of Archdeacon S.H. Middleton and the Blackfoot Indians in Alberta, Canada*, 1964; *Madame de Staël and the English*, 1967; *The World of David Beaty*, 1971; *Antoine de Saint-Exupéry and David Beaty: Poets of a New Dimension*, 1974. **Essay:** David Beaty.

FOSTER, Ruel E. Benedum Professor of American Literature, West Virginia University, Morgantown. Author of *Work in Progress*, 1948, *William Faulkner: A Critical Appraisal*, 1951, and *Jesse Stuart*, 1968. **Essays:** John Knowles; Jesse Stuart.

FRENCH, Warren. Professor of English and Director of the Center for American Studies, Indiana University-Purdue University, Indianapolis; Member of the Editorial Board, *American Literature* and *Twentieth-Century Literature*; series editor for Twayne publishers. Author of *John Steinbeck*, 1961; *Frank Norris*, 1962; *J.D. Salinger*, 1963 (revised, 1976); *A Companion to "The Grapes of Wrath,"* 1963; *The Social Novel at the End of an Era*, 1966; and a series on American literature, *The Thirties*, 1967, *The Forties*, 1968, *The Fifties*, 1971, and *The Twenties*, 1975. **Essays:** Evan S. Connell, Jr.; R.K. Narayan; Guy Owen; Alan Paton; Tom Robbins; Khushwant Singh; Elizabeth Spencer; Hollis Summers.

FRIEDMAN, Alan Warren. Professor of English, University of Texas, Austin; Member of the Editorial Board, *Studies in Literature and Language*. Author of *Lawrence Durrell and the Alexandria Quartet*, 1970, and of essays in *Seven Contemporary Authors*, 1966, and journals. **Essay:** Lawrence Durrell.

FRIEDMAN, Melvin J. Professor of Comparative Literature, University of Wisconsin, Milwaukee; Advisory Editor of *Journal of Popular Culture*, *Studies in the Novel*, *Renascence*, *Journal of American Culture*, *Studies in American Fiction*, and *Fer de Lance*. Author of *Stream of Consciousness: A Study in Literary Method*, 1955. Editor of works about Beckett, Flannery O'Connor, Styron, Catholic novelists, and Ionesco. **Essays:** Raymond Federman; Robie Macauley; Wallace Markfield; Philip Roth; Sloan Wilson.

FROST, Lucy. Senior Lecturer in English, La Trobe University, Bundoora, Victoria; Editorial Consultant, *Meanjin*. Author of articles on Hawkes, Heller, W.S. Merwin, American fiction, and Australian women writers. **Essay:** Frank Moorhouse.

FUEGI, John. Professor of Comparative Literature, University of Wisconsin, Milwaukee; Managing Editor, *Brecht Yearbook*. Author of *The Wall* (documentary film), 1961, and *The Essential Brecht*, 1972. Editor of *Brecht Today*, 3 vols., 1972-74. **Essay:** Sol Yurick.

FULLER, Roy. See his own entry.

GALLOWAY, David. Professor of English, University of the Ruhr, Bochum, Germany. Author of *The Absurd Hero*, 1966 (revised, 1970), *Henry James: "The Portrait of a Lady,"* 1967, and of reviews in periodicals. Editor of *Edgar Allan Poe*, 1967, and *Ten Modern American Short Stories*, 1968. **Essays:** Paul Bowles; James Leo Herlihy; Evan Hunter; Robert Lowry; Bernard Wolfe.

GATES, Norman T. Professor of English, Rider College, Trenton, New Jersey. Author of *The Poetry of Richard Aldington*, 1974, and *A Checklist of the Letters of Richard Aldington*, 1977. **Essay:** James Stern.

GEERING, R.G. Associate Professor of English, University of New South Wales, Kensington, Australia; Member of the Editorial Committee, *Southerly*. Author of two books on Christina Stead, and the introduction to her *Seven Poor Men of Sydney*, 1965. **Essay:** Christina Stead.

GEHERIN, David J. Associate Professor of English, Eastern Michigan University, Ypsilanti. Author of *Sons of Sam Spade: The Private Eye Novel in the '70's*, 1980. **Essay:** Arthur Hailey.

GINDIN, James. Professor of English, University of Michigan, Ann Arbor. Author of *Postwar British Fiction*, 1962, *Harvest of a Quiet Eye: The Novel of Compassion*, 1971, and *The English Climate: An Excursion into a Biography of John Galsworthy*, 1979. Editor of *The Return of the Native*, by Hardy, 1969. **Essays:** Kingsley Amis; John Bowen; Malcolm Bradbury; John Fowles; Thomas Hinde; Elizabeth Jane Howard; Norman Mailer; Brian Moore; Irwin Shaw; Alan Sillitoe; David Storey; John Wain; Keith Waterhouse.

GORDON, Lois. Professor of English and Comparative Literature, Fairleigh Dickinson University, Teaneck, New Jersey. Author of *Stratagems to Uncover Nakedness: The Dramas of Harold Pinter*, 1969, *Donald Barthelme*, 1981, and articles on Eberhart, Jarrell, Faulkner, T.S. Eliot, and Philip Roth. **Essays:** Donald Barthelme; William Gaddis; John Gardner; Erica Jong.

GOYEN, William. See his own entry. **Essay:** Marguerite Young.

GREACEN, Robert. Author and Lecturer. Author of three books of verse—*One Recent Morning*, 1944, *The Undying Day*,

1948, and *A Garland for Captain Fox*, 1975—and of *The World of C.P. Snow*, 1962, and *Even Without Irene* (autobiography), 1969; reviewer for *Books and Bookmen*, *Tribune*, and other periodicals. **Essays:** Walter Allen; Storm Jameson; Bill Naughton.

GREENLEAF, Richard. General Columnist, *The Daily World*. Author of essays on British and American literary history in *Marxism and Christianity*, 1968, *For a New America*, 1970, and in the journals *Science and Society* and *Religion in Life*. Died, 1971. **Essays:** Josephine Johnson; Jerome Weidman.

GRELLA, George. Associate Professor of English, Rochester University, New York. Author of studies of Ian Fleming, Ross Macdonald, and John le Carré for *New Republic*, and articles on the detective novel and other subjects. **Essays:** Len Deighton; J.P. Donleavy; John Irving; Ross Macdonald.

GUERARD, Albert. See his own entry. **Essays:** John Hawkes; Janet Lewis.

GUPTARA, Prabhu S. Doctoral Research Student, University of Stirling, Scotland; Editorial Adviser, *Kunapipi*. Former lecturer at St. Stephen's College, Delhi University, and North-Eastern Hill University, Shillong, India. Author of *Beginnings* (verse), 1975, and of poems and articles in *Review of English Studies*, *Journal of Commonwealth Literature*, *Review of National Literature*, *Kunapipi*, and other periodicals. Editor of *Selected Poems of Leela Dharmaraj*, 1979, and an anthology of Indian religious poetry. **Essay:** J.G. Farrell (appendix).

HAHN, Emily. Member of the staff, *New Yorker* magazine. Has taught at Yale University, New Haven, Connecticut, University of Virginia, Charlottesville, and University of Missouri, Columbia. Author of many books, including *On the Side of the Apes*, 1971, and *For Love of Gold*, 1980. **Essay:** Hortense Calisher.

HALL, James B. See his own entry. **Essays:** R.V. Cassill; William Eastlake; Paul Horgan; Frederick Manfred; Mario Puzo; Wirt Williams.

HALL, John. Regular Feature Writer for the *Guardian*, London. **Essay:** Christine Brooke-Rose.

HANKIN, Cherry. Senior Lecturer in English, University of Canterbury, Christchurch, New Zealand. Author of the introduction to the critical edition of Maurice Shadbolt's *The New Zealanders*, 1974, and "Language and Theme in Janet Frame's Owls Do Cry," in *Landfall*, 1974; regular contributor to *The Listener*. Editor, *It Was So Late and Other Stories* by John Reece Cole, 1979. **Essay:** Maurice Shadbolt.

HARMON, Maurice. Lecturer in English, University College, Dublin; Editor of *Irish University Review*. Author of *Sean O'Faolain: A Critical Introduction*, 1966. Editor of *Synge Centenary Papers*, 1971. **Essay:** Sean O'Faolain.

HARREX, S.C. Senior Lecturer in English and Director of the Centre for Research in the New Literature in English, Flinders University of South Australia, Bedford Park. Author of *The Modern Indian Novel in English*, 1972, and of articles on Narayan, Markandaya, Rao, and other Indian novels. **Essays:** Ahmad Abbas; Bhabani Bhattacharya.

HARRISON-FORD, Carl. Free-lance writer; Editor of *New Poetry*, Sydney. **Essay:** David Foster.

HART, James A. Associate Professor of English, University of British Columbia, Vancouver; Member of the Editorial Board, *Canadian Review of American Studies*. Author of articles on Alan Seeger, American poetry of World War I, E.E. Cummings, Pope, and Chaucer. **Essays:** Allen Drury; Edward Hoagland.

HASSAN, Ihab. Vilas Research Professor of English and Comparative Literature, University of Wisconsin, Milwaukee. Author of several works of literary criticism, including *Radical Innocence*, 1961, *The Literature of Silence*, 1968, *The Dismemberment of Orpheus*, 1971, *Contemporary American Literature*, 1973, *Paracriticisms*, 1975, and *The Right Promethean Fire*, 1980. Editor of *Liberations: New Essays on the Humanities in Revolution*, 1971. **Essay:** Truman Capote.

HAWKES, John. See his own entry.

HEATON, David M. Associate Professor of Comparative Literature, and Chairman of the Comparative Literature Program, Ohio University, Athens. Verse, verse translations, and articles on Ted Hughes and Alan Sillitoe published in periodicals. **Essays:** Dannie Abse; Joan Didion; Toni Morrison; Hubert Selby, Jr.; Jose Yglesias.

HERTZEL, Leo J. Associate Professor of English, University of Wisconsin, Superior; Contributing Editor, *North American Review*. Author of many articles and reviews. **Essays:** Charles Israel; Ronald Sukenick.

HILL, James. Associate Professor of English, Michigan State University, East Lansing. Author of a forthcoming book on Tennyson. **Essay:** Ayn Rand.

HILL, Susan. See her own entry.

HOEFER, Jacqueline. Free-lance writer. Author of articles on Beckett and other modern writers. **Essay:** Kay Boyle.

HOKENSON, Jan. Member of the Department of Languages and Linguistics, Florida Atlantic University, Boca Raton. Author of articles on modern French and American writers. **Essays:** John Gardner; Bernard Malamud.

HUDZIAK, Craig. Teaching Assistant and graduate student, University of Wisconsin, Milwaukee. **Essay:** William Humphrey.

HULTS, Barbara. Free-lance writer. **Essay:** Susan Hill.

IKIN, Van. Senior Tutor in English, University of Western Australia, Nedlands; Editor of *Science Fiction: A Review of Speculative Literature*. **Essay:** David Ireland.

JACKSON, Blyden. Professor of English, University of North Carolina, Chapel Hill. Author of *The Waiting Years: Essays on American Negro Literature*, 1976. **Essay:** John Oliver Killens.

JAMES, Louis. Senior Lecturer in English and American Literature, Keynes College, University of Kent, Canterbury. Author of *The Islands in Between*, 1968, and *Fiction for the Working-Class Man 1830-1850*, 1974. **Essays:** O.R. Dathorne; John Hearne; C.L.R. James; V.S. Naipaul.

JEFFARES, A. Norman. Professor of English Studies, University of Stirling, Scotland; Editor of *Ariel: A Review of International English Literature*, and General Editor of the Writers and Critics series and the New Oxford English series. Past Editor of *A Review of English Studies*. Author of *Yeats: Man and Poet*, 1949, *Seven Centuries of Poetry*, 1956, and *A Commentary on the Collected Poems* (1958) and *Collected Plays* (1957) *of Yeats*. Editor of *Restoration Comedy*, 1974, and *Yeats: The Critical Heritage*. Chairman of the Literature Section of the Scottish Arts Council. **Essays:** Eric Ambler; Nicolas Freeling; William Haggard; Margaret Laurence; Mary Lavin; John le Carré.

JENKINS, Annibel. Associate Professor of English, Georgia Institute of Technology, Atlanta. **Essays:** Arthur Calder-Marshall; Emma Smith; Monica Stirling.

KEITH, Margaret. Free-lance writer and researcher; also an actress and director. Author of a forthcoming children's book, *Patrick and the Actors*, and of a study of Margaret Kennedy. **Essays:** Hugh Hood; Norman Levine.

KENDLE, Burton. Professor of English, Roosevelt University, Chicago. Author of articles on D.H. Lawrence, John Cheever, William March, Tennessee Williams, and others. **Essays:** Burt Blechman; Roald Dahl; Brendan Gill; Alan Lelchuk; Tennessee Williams.

KIERNAN, Brian. Senior Lecturer in English, University of Sydney. Author of *Images of Society and Nature* (on the Australian novel), 1971, *Considerations: New Essays on Slessor, White, Stewart*, and an article on Patrick White in *The Literature of Australia* edited by Geoffrey Dutton, 1976. **Essays:** Geoffrey Dutton; Barry Oakley; Judah Waten.

KLEIN, H.M. Lecturer in Comparative Literature, University of East Anglia, Norwich. Author of *Die Englische Komödie im 18, Jahrhundert* and a study of J.B. Priestley. Editor and translator of English dramatic texts. **Essays:** Ngaio Marsh; J.I.M. Stewart.

KLEIN, Marcus. Professor of English, State University of New York, Buffalo. Author of *After Alienation: American Novels at Mid-Century*, 1964. Editor of *The American Novel since World War II*, 1969, and, with Robert Pack, of *Literature for Composition on the Theme of Innocence and Experience*, 1966, and *Short Stories: Classic, Modern, Contemporary*, 1967. **Essays:** Jack Conroy; Wright Morris; Richard G. Stern.

KLINKOWITZ, Jerome. Professor of English, University of Northern Iowa, Cedar Falls. Author of *Kurt Vonnegut, Jr.: A Descriptive Bibliography* (with Asa B. Pieratt, Jr.), 1974; *Literary Disruptions*, 1975 (revised, 1980); *Donald Barthelme: A Comprehensive Bibliography* (with others), 1977; *The Practice of Fiction in America*, 1980; *The American 1960's*, 1980. Editor of *The Vonnegut Statement*, 1973, and *Writing under Fire: Stories of the Vietnam War*, 1978 (both with John Somer), and *The Diaries of Willard Motley*, 1979. **Essays:** Walter Abish; Jonathan Baumbach; Guy Davenport; Jerzy Kosinski; Clarence Major; Gilbert Sorrentino.

KORGES, James. Free-lance writer. Editor of *Critique: Studies in Modern Fiction*, 1962-70. Author of *Erskine Caldwell*, 1969. Died, 1975. **Essays:** Erskine Caldwell; William Goyen; Glenway Wescott.

KORNBLUTH, Martin L. Professor of English, Eastern Michigan University, Ypsilanti; Associate Editor, *Journal of Narrative Technique*, and Review Editor, *Choice*. Author of articles on Shaw, Goethe, the folk tale, and other subjects. **Essay:** Glendon Swarthout.

KOSTELANETZ, Richard. Poet, critic, and cultural historian; Co-Founder, Assembling Press and Proprietor, The Future Press; Co-Editor, *Precisely* and Contributing Editor, *The Humanist* and *Performing Arts Journal*. Author of several books of verse (most recently *Illuminations*, 1977), two novels, several collections of short stories (*Foreshortenings and Other Stories*, 1978), and critical works including *The Theatre of Mixed-Means*, 1968, *The End of Intelligent Writing*, 1974, and *Twenties in the Sixties*, 1978. Editor of many collections and anthologies, particularly of experimental writing. **Essay:** Leslie Fiedler.

KRAMER, Leonie. Professor of Australian Literature, University of Sydney; Editorial Adviser, *Poetry Australia*. Author of *Henry Handel Richardson and Some of Her Sources*, 1954, and two other books on Richardson, and *A Guide to Language and Literature*, with R.D. Eagleson, 1977. Editor of several works by Australian writers and collections of Australian writing. **Essay:** Hal Porter.

LAREDO, Ursula. Lecturer in English, Trinity and All Saints' College, Horsforth, Yorkshire. **Essays:** Jack Cope; C.J. Driver; Nadine Gordimer; Dan Jacobson; Uys Krige; David Lytton.

LAURENCE, Margaret. See her own entry. **Essay:** Dave Godfrey.

LEACH, Chet. Assistant Professor of English, University of Michigan, Ann Arbor. Author of two books of verse, *The Erotic Sense* and *Field Trip*. **Essay:** Michael Crichton.

LeCLAIR, Thomas. Professor of English, University of Cincinnati. Author of articles on and interviews with Burgess, Donleavy, Hawkes, Nabokov, Barth, Updike, and other contemporary writers in *Contemporary Literature*, *Critique*, *Twentieth Century Literature*, *Paris Review*, and *New Republic*, and reviews in *New York Times Book Review* and *Saturday Review*. **Essays:** Don DeLillo; Stanley Elkin; Joseph McElroy.

LEECH, Anastasia. Free-lance writer. **Essays:** Bruce Marshall; Nicholas Mosley.

LEHMANN, John. Founding Editor of *New Writing*, *Daylight*, *Penguin New Writing*, *The London Magazine*, and the BBC's *New Soundings*. His most recent book of verse is *The Reader at Night*, 1974; other recent books are *In My Own Time: Memoirs of a Literary Life*, *Thrown to the Woolfs: Leonard and Virginia Woolf and the Hogarth Press*, and *Rupert Brooke: His Life and His Legend*.

LEVIN, Harry. Irving Babbitt Professor of Comparative Literature, Harvard University, Cambridge, Massachusetts. Author of many critical books, the most recent being *The Myth of the Golden Age in the Renaissance*, *Grounds for Comparison*, *Shakespeare and the Revolution of the Times*, and *Memories of the Moderns*. Editor of works by Jonson, Rochester, Joyce, Shakespeare, and Hawthorne, and of anthologies.

LEWIS, Margaret. Part-time teacher at the University of Durham and the Open University. **Essays:** Ruth Prawer Jhabvala; Paul Scott (appendix).

LEWIS, Peter. Member of the Department of English, University of Durham. Author of *Radio Drama*, 1981, and of articles on contemporary writing. **Essays:** Paul Bailey; A.S. Byatt; Ian McEwan; Emma Tennant.

LINDBERG, Stanley W. Associate Professor of English, University of Georgia, Athens; Editor, *Georgia Review*. Editor of *The Annotated McGuffey*, 1976. **Essay:** Jack Matthews.

LINDFORS, Bernth. Professor of African and English Literature, University of Texas, Austin; Founding Editor, *Research in African Literatures*. Author of many articles on African literature, including essays on Richard Rive, La Guma, Achebe, Ekwensi, Tutuola, and D.O. Fagunwa. Editor of *Critical Perspectives on Nigerian Literatures* and *Critical Perspectives on Amos Tutuola*. **Essays:** Peter Abrahams; Ezekiel Mphahlele; Abioseh Nicol; Amos Tutuola.

LINDSAY, Jack. See his own entry. **Essay:** James Aldridge.

LUCAS, John. Professor and Head of the Department of English and Drama, Loughborough University, Leicestershire; Advisory Editor, *Victorian Studies*, *Literature and History*, and *Journal of European Studies*. Author of *Tradition and Tolerance in 19th-*

Century Fiction, 1966; *The Melancholy Man: A Study of Dickens*, 1970; *Arnold Bennett*, 1975; *Egilssaga: The Poems*, 1975; *The Literature of Change*, 1977; *The 1930's: Challenge to Orthodoxy*, 1978. Editor of *Literature and Politics in the 19th Century*, 1971, and of works by George Crabbe and Jane Austen. **Essays:** David Caute; Barry Cole; Martha Gellhorn; Simon Raven; Frank Swinnerton.

LYNCH, Robert E. Associate Professor of English, New Jersey Institute of Technology, Newark. Author of articles in *The Reader's Encyclopedia of Shakespeare*, 1966, and *The Reader's Encyclopedia of World Drama*, 1969. Editor of *The Example of Science: An Approach to College Composition*, 1981. **Essays:** Jerome Charyn; Frederick Forsyth; Leonard Michaels.

MADDEN, David. See his own entry. **Essay:** Carson McCullers (appendix).

MAES-JELINEK, Hena. Chargé de Cours, University of Liège, Belgium. Author of *Criticism of Society in the English Novel Between the Wars*, 1970, *The Naked Design*, 1976, and articles on Peter Abrahams, V.S. Naipaul, Patrick White, and Wilson Harris. Editor of *Commonwealth Literature and the Modern World*, 1975. **Essays:** Clive Barry; Wilson Harris.

MALIN, Irving. Professor of English, City College of the City University of New York. Author of *William Faulkner: An Interpretation*, 1957; *New American Gothic*, 1962; *Jews and Americans*, 1965; *Saul Bellow's Fiction*, 1969; *Nathanael West's Novels*, 1972; *Isaac Bashevis Singer*, 1972. Editor of casebooks and collections of essays on Bellow, Capote, Styron, Singer, and McCullers, and of *Psychoanalysis and American Fiction* and *Contemporary American-Jewish Literature*. **Essay:** James Purdy.

MARX, Paul. Professor of English, University of New Haven, Connecticut. Editor of *12 Short Story Writers*, 1970. **Essays:** Gail Godwin; Eudora Welty; Larry Woiwode.

MASSA, Ann. Lecturer in American Literature, University of Leeds. Author of *Vachel Lindsay: Fieldworker for the American Dream*, 1970, *The American Short Story since 1945*, 1975, and co-author of *American Literature: Nineteenth and Twentieth Centuries*, 1978. **Essay:** Shiva Naipaul.

MATHIAS, Roland. Poet and critic. Former Editor of *Anglo-Welsh Review*; Chairman of the Welsh Arts Council Literature Committee. Author of five books of verse, the most recent being *Absalom in the Tree*, a collection of short stories, and studies of Vernon Watkins and John Cowper Powys. Editor of works by Welsh authors and a collection of essays on David Jones. **Essay:** Emyr Humphreys.

MATTHEWS, Brian E. Lecturer in English, The Flinders University of South Australia, Bedford Park. Author of *The Receding Wave: A Study of Henry Lawson's Prose*, 1972. Editor of *Selected Stories of Henry Lawson*, 1972. **Essays:** Thea Astley; Jon Cleary.

McCONNELL, Frank D. Associate Professor of English, Northwestern University, Evanston, Illinois. Author of articles on William S. Burroughs, Byron, and Flaubert. **Essay:** Thomas Pynchon.

McCORMICK, John. Professor of Comparative Literature, Rutgers University, New Brunswick, New Jersey. Author of *Catastrophe and Imagination* (on the modern novel), 1957; *The Complete Aficionado*, 1967; *American Literature 1919-1932: A Comparative History*, 1971; *Fiction as Knowledge*, 1975. **Essays:** Nina Bawden; Rex Warner.

McDOWELL, Frederick P.W. Professor of English, University of Iowa, Iowa City. Author of *Ellen Glasgow and the Ironic Art of Fiction*, 1960; *Elizabeth Madox Roberts*, 1963; *Caroline Gordon*, 1966; *E.M. Forster*, 1968; *Forster: An Annotated Bibliography of Writings about Him*, 1976; and articles on Auden and Robert Penn Warren. **Essays:** Melvyn Bragg; John Braine; Gerda Charles; Frederic Raphael.

McDOWELL, Margaret B. Professor of Rhetoric and Women's Studies, University of Iowa, Iowa City. Author of *Edith Wharton*, 1975, and *Carson McCullers*, 1980. **Essays:** Angela Carter; Tillie Olsen.

McELROY, George. Lecturer at Indiana University Northwest, Gary. Author of textbooks and of regular reviews in *Opera News*. **Essay:** Maude Hutchins.

MEPHAM, John. Lecturer in Philosophy, Goldsmiths' College, University of London. Co-Author of *Issues in Marxist Philosophy*, 3 vols., 1979, and author of many articles on philosophy and literature. **Essay:** Gabriel Josipovici.

MERIVALE, Patricia. Professor of English, University of British Columbia, Vancouver. Author of articles in *Harvard Studies in Comparative Literature* and other periodicals. **Essays:** Jerzy Peterkiewicz; Alexander Trocchi.

MITCHISON, Naomi. See her own entry. **Essay:** Fred Urquhart.

MONTAGUE, John. Lecturer in Poetry, University College, Cork. Author of many books of verse including *The Rough Field* (collected edition, 1972) and, most recently, *The Great Cloak*, a play, and a collection of short stories. Editor of *The Dolmen Miscellany of Irish Writing* and *The Faber Book of Irish Verse*, and translator of a collection of Irish poetry and *November* by André Frénaud. **Essays:** Aidan Higgins; John McGahern.

MOORE, Gerald. Professor of English, University of Jos, Nigeria; Editor of the Modern African Writers series. Author of *The Chosen Tongue*, 1969, *Wole Soyinka*, 1971 (revised, 1978), and *Twelve African Writers*, 1980. **Essays:** Elechi Amadi; Michael Anthony; George Lamming; Garth St. Omer.

MOORE, Harry T. Research Professor of English Emeritus, Southern Illinois University, Carbondale; Editor of the Crosscurrents/Modern Critiques series. Author and editor of many books, including studies of Lawrence, Steinbeck, Forster, Rilke, Durrell, and James. Died, 1981. **Essays:** Anita Loos; David Madden; Francis Stuart.

MORPURGO, J.E. Professor of American Literature, University of Leeds. Author and editor of many books, including *The Pelican History of the United States*, 1955 (third edition, 1970), and volumes on Cooper, Lamb, Trelawny, Barnes Wallis, the publisher Allen Lane, and on Athens, Venice, and rugby football. **Essays:** Robertson Davies; Robert Graves; A.B. Guthrie, Jr.; Hugh MacLennan.

MORRIS, Robert K. Associate Professor of English, City College of the City University of New York. Author of *The Novels of Anthony Powell*, 1968, *The Consolations of Ambiguity: An Essay on the Novels of Anthony Burgess*, 1971, and *Continuance and Change: The Contemporary British Novel Sequence*, 1972. **Essay:** Anthony Powell.

MURRAY-SMITH, Stephen. Reader in Education, University of Melbourne; Founding Editor, *Overland* and Editor of *Melbourne Studies in Education*. Author of *Henry Lawson*, 1962. Editor of *The Tracks We Travel*, *An Overland Muster*, *His Natural Life* by Marcus Clarke, and, with Judah Waten, *Classic Australian Short Stories*.

MUSSELL, Kay J. Director of the American Studies Program,

American University, Washington, D.C. Author of "The Sexual Woman in Modern Gothic Fiction" in *Journal of Popular Culture*, 1975, an article on gothic novels in *Handbook of American Popular Culture*, 1978, and a forthcoming bibliographic study of American gothic and romantic writers. **Essays:** Patricia Highsmith; Laura Z. Hobson; Fletcher Knebel.

NARAYAN, Shyamala A. Free-lance writer. Author of *Sudhin N. Ghose*, a study of Raja Rao, and of articles and reviews in *The Hindu*, *New Quest*, *World Literature Today*, and other periodicals. Editor of the Indian section of *The Bibliography of Commonwealth Literature*. **Essays:** Sasthi Brata; Nayantara Sahgal.

NELSON, Tom. Adjunct Instructor of English, Ohio University, Athens. Author of "The Stepmother Tongue" in *West Virginia Association of College English Teachers Bulletin*, 1980, and "The Syntax of Sidney's Poetry" in *Style*, 1981. **Essay:** Penelope Gilliatt.

NESBITT, Bruce. Member of the Department of English, Simon Fraser University, Burnaby, British Columbia. Author of many articles and bibliographies. Editor of *Earle Birney*, 1974. **Essay:** Scott Symons.

NEW, W.H. Professor of English, University of British Columbia, Vancouver; Editor of *Canadian Literature* and Associate Editor of *World Literature Written in English*. Author of *Malcolm Lowry*, 1971, *Articulating West*, 1972, *Among Worlds*, 1975, *Malcolm Lowry: A Reference Guide*, 1978, and other books and articles. **Essays:** Janet Frame; Zulfikar Ghose; W.O. Mitchell; Orlando Patterson; Randolph Stow; George Turner; Rudy Wiebe; Adele Wiseman.

NORRIS, Leslie. Poet and lecturer. Author of several books of verse—the most recent being *Water Voices*, 1980—and of *Sliding and Other Stories*, 1976, and *Glyn Jones*, 1973. Editor of books about Vernon Watkins and Andrew Young. **Essay:** Glyn Jones.

NYE, Robert. See his own entry. **Essays:** Paul Ableman; Alan Burns; William S. Burroughs; Frederick Busch; Eva Figes; David Plante; Anthony Storey.

O'NEILL, John P. Associate Professor of English, Georgia Institute of Technology, Atlanta. Regular reviewer for the Atlanta *Journal and Constitution*. **Essay:** Sybille Bedford.

ORMOND, John. Documentary film-maker for the BBC, and poet. His films include *Under a Bright Heaven* (on Vernon Watkins), *A Bronze Mask* (on Dylan Thomas), *The Fragile Universe* (on Alun Lewis), and, most recently, *The Colliers' Crusade*, 1979. Author of several books of verse including *Definition of a Waterfall*, 1973. **Essay:** Peter Tinniswood.

O'TOOLE, Bridget. Lecturer in English, New University of Ulster, Coleraine. **Essay:** Rachel Trickett.

PACEY, Desmond. Vice-President (Academic), University of New Brunswick, Fredericton. Author of *Frederick Philip Grove*, 1945; *Creative Writing in Canada*, 1952 (revised, 1962); *The Picnic and Other Stories*, 1958; *Our Literary Heritage*, 1968; *Essays in Canadian Criticism*, 1969. Editor of *A Book of Canadian Stories*, 1947, and *Ten Canadian Poets*, 1958. Died, 1975. **Essay:** Sinclair Ross.

PAGE, Malcolm. Associate Professor of English, Simon Fraser University, Burnaby, British Columbia. Author of articles on John Arden, Arnold Wesker, English television drama and experimental drama, London's Unity Theatre, Canadian drama, and West Indian fiction, in *Modern Drama*, *Drama Survey*, *Theatre Quarterly*, *Novel*, *Twentieth-Century Literature*, and other periodicals. **Essays:** Michael Frayn; Simon Gray; Adrian Mitchell; Andrew Salkey; Raymond Williams.

PARISI, Joseph. Associate Editor of *Poetry* magazine, Chicago. Editor, with Daryl Hine, of *The "Poetry" Anthology 1912-1977*, 1978. **Essays:** Janet Burroway; Alison Lurie; Colin Spencer.

PEDEN, William. Professor of English, University of Missouri, Columbia. Author of *Night in Funland and Other Stories*, 1968, *Twilight in Monticello* (travel), 1973, and *The American Short Story: Continuity and Change 1940-1975*, 1975. **Essay:** Nancy Hale.

PEHOWSKI, Marian. Instructor in Comparative Literature, University of Wisconsin, Milwaukee. Author of articles and features in the Milwaukee *Journal* and other periodicals. **Essay:** Niccolò Tucci.

PERKINS, Barbara M. Director of Writing Improvement, Humanities Program, Eastern Michigan University, Ypsilanti. **Essays:** Richard E. Kim; Jerre Mangione; Douglas Woolf.

PERKINS, George. Professor of English, Eastern Michigan University, Ypsilanti. Author or editor of *Writing Clear Prose*, 1964; *Varieties of Prose*, 1966; *The Theory of the American Novel*, 1970; *Realistic American Short Fiction*, 1972; *American Poetic Theory*, 1972; *The American Tradition in Literature* (with others), fourth edition, 1974. **Essays:** Chandler Brossard; Robert Gover; John Clellon Holmes.

PHIPPS, Frank T. Chairman of the Department of English, University of Akron, Ohio. **Essay:** Joseph Mitchell.

PORTER, Hal. See his own entry.

POWELL, Anthony. See his own entry.

QUIGLY, Isabel. Free-lance writer and critic. Author of the novel *The Eye of Heaven*, 1955, a book on Charlie Chaplin, and of many articles and reviews in *The Times*, *The Guardian*, and other periodicals. Editor, with Susan Hill, of *New Stories 5*, 1980. Translator of works of European fiction and non-fiction. **Essays:** Bryher; W.H. Canaway; Lettice Cooper; Winston Graham; Pamela Hansford Johnson.

RAVENSCROFT, Arthur. Senior Lecturer in English Literature, University of Leeds; Founding Editor, *Journal of Commonwealth Literature*. Author of *Chinua Achebe*, 1969 (revised, 1977). Translator, with C.K. Johnman, of *Journal of Jan Van Riebeeck*, vol. 3, 1958. **Essays:** Chinua Achebe; T.M. Aluko; Cyprian Ekwensi; Bessie Head; Alex La Guma; John Munonye; Ngugi wa Thiong'o.

REID, Ian. Senior Lecturer in English, Adelaide University, Australia; Editorial Consultant, *Meanjin*. Author of *The Short Story*, 1977, and *Fiction and the Depression in Australia and New Zealand*, 1978. **Essay:** Leonard Mann.

REID, J.C. Professor of English, University of Auckland. Author of *The Mind and Art of Coventry Patmore*, 1957; *Francis Thompson, Man and Poet*, 1959; *Thomas Hood*, 1963; *Bucks and Bruisers: Pierce Egan and Regency England*, 1971. Died, 1972. **Essays:** Errol Brathwaite; M.K. Joseph.

REILLY, John M. Associate Professor of English, State University of New York, Albany. Author of many articles on Afro-American literature, popular crime writing, and social fiction, and bibliographical essays in *Black American Writers*, 1978, and *American Literary Scholarship*. Editor of *Richard Wright: The Critical eception*, 1978, and the reference book *Twentieth-Century Crime and Mystery Writers*, 1980. **Essays:** Cyrus Colter; Ralph Ellison;

Dick Francis; Granville Hicks; George V. Higgins; Chester Himes; Kristin Hunter; Paule Marshall; Peter Matthiessen; Larry McMurtry; Margaret Millar; Al Young.

REXROTH, Kenneth. Poet and Critic; Lecturer at the University of California, Santa Barbara. Author of many books of verse (most recently *The Morning Star*, 1979), plays (*Beyond the Mountains*, 1951), and non-fiction (most recently *The Elastic Retort*, 1973, and *Communalism*, 1975). Editor of several collections of poetry and translator of works by Asian, European, and classical authors. **Essays:** Djuna Barnes; Isaac Bashevis Singer.

RHODES, H. Winston. Professor of English (retired), University of Canterbury, Christchurch, New Zealand. Past Editor of *New Zealand Monthly Review*. Author of *New Zealand Fiction since 1945*, 1978, *Frank Sargeson*, 1969, and other books. Editor of six volumes of Rewi Alley's prose and verse and *I Saw in My Dream* by Sargeson, 1976. **Essays:** Dan Davin; Roderick Finlayson; Noel Hilliard; Witi Ihimaera; John A. Lee; O.E. Middleton; Bill Pearson; Frank Sargeson; Albert Wendt.

RIES, Lawrence. Staff member, Skidmore College, Saratoga Springs, New York. **Essay:** Aubrey Menen.

RODRIGUEZ, Judith. Senior Lecturer in English, La Trobe University, Bundoora, Victoria; Poetry Editor, *Meanjin*. Author of several books of verse, the most recent being *Angels* and *Arapede*, both 1979. **Essay:** David Malouf.

ROSS, Alan. Editor of *London Magazine* and Managing Director of London Magazine Editions. Author of several books of verse, the most recent being *Death Valley and Other Poems*, 1980, and of critical works, travel books, and books for children. Editor of works by John Gay and Lawrence Durrell and of several anthologies. Translator of four French works.

ROSSET, Barney. President of Grove Press, Inc. Editor of *Evergreen Review Reader 1* and *2*, 1979.

ROYLE, Trevor. Free-lance writer and broadcaster. Author of *We'll Support You Ever More: The Impertinent Saga of Scottish Fitba'*, with Ian Archer, 1976, *Jock Tamson's Bairns*, 1977, *Precipitous City: The Story of Literary Edinburgh*, 1980, and many articles in periodicals. **Essays:** George Mackay Brown; Brian Glanville; Giles Gordon; Benedict Kiely; Robert Nye.

RUBIN, Louis D., Jr. Professor of English, University of North Carolina, Chapel Hill; General Editor, Southern Literary Studies series; Co-Editor, *Southern Literary Journal*. Author and Editor of many books, including the novel *The Golden Weather*, 1961, and most recently, *William Elliott Shoots a Bear*, 1975, *The Wary Fugitives: Four Poets and the South*, 1978, and *The American South: Portrait of a Culture*, 1979. **Essays:** Howard Nemerov; William Styron.

SALZMAN, Jack. Associate Professor of English, Hofstra University, Hempstead, New York; Member of the Editorial Board, *Resources in American Literary Study* and *Dreiser Newsletter*. Editor of *Years of Protest*, 1967, *The Survival Years*, 1969, *Sister Carrie* by Dreiser, 1970, and, with David Ray, *The Jack Conroy Reader*, 1980. **Essays:** Robert Cantwell; Albert Maltz.

SANDELIN, Clarence. Member of the English Department, California State College, Los Angeles. **Essay:** Robert Nathan.

SANDERS, David. Professor of English, Harvey Mudd College, Claremont, California. Author of *John Hersey*, 1967, and of articles on Hemingway and Dos Passos. **Essays:** Vance Bourjaily; Joseph Heller; John Hersey; James Jones (appendix); Jessamyn West.

SANDERSON, Stewart F. Director of the Institute of Dialect and Folk Life Studies, University of Leeds. Author of *Hemingway*, 1961 (revised, 1970), and of many articles on British and comparative folklore and ethnology, and on modern literature. Editor of *The Secret Common-Wealth* by Robert Kirk, 1970, and *The Linguistic Atlas on England* (with others), 1978. **Essays:** Gerald Hanley; Geoffrey Household.

SCHAFER, William J. Professor of English, Berea College, Kentucky. Author of articles on David Wagoner and Ralph Ellison in *Critique* and *Satire Newsletter*. **Essays:** Elliott Baker; Stephen Becker; David Benedictus; Thomas Berger; Harry Crews; Nell Dunn; David Ely; Mark Harris; James A. McPherson; Reynolds Price; Ishmael Reed; Clancy Sigal; Paul Theroux; David Wagoner; John Williams.

SCHORER, Mark. Professor of English, University of California, Berkeley. Author of three novels, three collections of short stories, and several critical works, including studies of Blake, Lawrence, and Sinclair Lewis. Editor of anthologies of fiction and literary criticism and of works by Capote and Lawrence. Died, 1977.

SCOTT, Alexander. Reader in Scottish Literature, Glasgow University. Author of several books of verse, the most recent being *Poems in Scots*, 1978, plays, a biography of William Soutar, and *The MacDiarmid Makars 1923-1972*, 1972. Editor of works by William Jeffrey, Alexander Scott (1530-1584), and Soutar, and of anthologies of Scottish poetry. **Essays:** Clifford Hanley; Robin Jenkins; Naomi Mitchison.

SCOTT-KILVERT, Ian. Director of Publications and Recorded Sound Department, British Council; Editor of The Writers and Their Works series. Author of *John Webster* and *A.E. Housman*. Translator of two volumes of Plutarch's Lives. **Essays:** Mervyn Jones; Lynne Reid Banks; Jon Manchip White.

SECOR, Cynthia. Mid-Atlantic Director, Higher Education Resource Services, University of Pennsylvania, Philadelphia. **Essay:** Daphne Rooke.

SEIDEL, Kathryn L. Member of the Department of English, University of Maryland, College Park. **Essay:** Marge Piercy.

SHIPPEY, T.A. Professor of English, University of Leeds. Author of *Old English Verse*, 1972, *Poems of Wisdom and Learning in Old English*, 1976, and *Beowulf*, 1978, and of articles on medieval literature, Kipling, and science fiction. **Essay:** Samuel R. Delany.

SHUCARD, Alan R. Associate Professor of English, University of Wisconsin-Parkside, Kenosha. Author of two books of verse—*The Gorgon Bog*, 1970, and *The Louse on the Head of the Lord*, 1972. **Essays:** Walter Van Tilburg Clark (appendix); James B. Hall; Kathrin Perutz; Irving Stone; Leon Uris; Alec Waugh.

SIEGEL, Ben. Professor of English, California State Polytechnic University, Pomona. Author of *Isaac Bashevis Singer*, 1969, *The Controversial Sholem Asch*, 1976, and articles on Israel Joshua Singer, Bernard Malamud, and Philip Roth. **Essay:** Daniel Fuchs.

SILVA, Fred. Assistant Professor of English, State University of New York, Albany. Author of *Focus on "The Birth of a Nation,"* 1971. **Essay:** Wilfrid Sheed.

SMITH, Angela. Lecturer in Commonwealth Literature, University of Stirling, Scotland. Author of study guides to *Wuthering Heights* and *Persuasion*. **Essay:** Ayi Kwei Armah.

SMITH, Curtis C. Associate Professor of Humanities, University of Houston, Clear Lake City. Editor of the reference book

Twentieth-Century Science-Fiction Writers, 1981. **Essays:** Ray Bradbury; Arthur C. Clarke; Philip K. Dick; Ursula K. Le Guin.

SQUIRES, Radcliffe. Professor of English, University of Michigan, Ann Arbor; Editor of *Michigan Quarterly Review*. Author of several books of verse—the most recent being *Gardens of the World*, 1981—and of books on Robinson Jeffers, Robert Frost, Frederic Prokosch, and Allen Tate. Editor of a collection of essays on Tate. **Essay:** Frederic Prokosch.

STANFORD, Derek. Lecturer in Modern Literature, City Literary Institute, London. Author of two books of verse, and many books of literary criticism, including studies of John Betjeman, Muriel Spark, Stephen Spender, Louis MacNeice, and C. Day Lewis. Editor of several anthologies, including a collection of drama since 1945, and books on the 1890's. **Essays:** Alex Comfort; Arthur Koestler; Bernard Kops; Jay Neugeboren.

STANFORD, Donald E. Professor of English, Louisiana State University, Baton Rouge; Editor of *Southern Review*. Author of two books of verse and of articles on American literature in *Kenyon Review*, *Southern Review*, *New England Quarterly*, and other periodicals. Editor of *The Poems of Edward Taylor*, 1960, and selected poems by Robert Bridges and S. Foster Damon. **Essay:** Albert Guerard.

STEDMAN, Jane W. Professor of English, Roosevelt University, Chicago. Author of *W.S. Gilbert*, 1979, and of articles and reviews in *Opera News* and in journals of Victorian studies. Editor of *Gilbert Before Sullivan: Six Comic Plays*, 1967. **Essays:** Monica Dickens; Ira Levin.

STEPHENSON, George. Director of the Mid-Northumberland Arts Group, Northumberland County Technical College, Ashington. **Essay:** Sid Chaplin.

STERN, Carol Simpson. Associate Professor, Department of Interpretation, Northwestern University, Evanston, Illinois; Research Consultant and contributor, *English Literature in Transition*. Theatre and book reviewer for *Victorian Studies* and Chicago *Sun-Times*. **Essays:** A. Alvarez; Alfred Grossman; Elizabeth Hardwick; Doris Lessing; Charles Newman; Joyce Carol Oates; Richard Yates.

STEVENS, James R. Master, Federation College, Thunder Bay, Ontario. Author of *Legends of the Sandy Lake Cree*, 1971, and *The Stories of Chief Dan Kennedy*, 1972. **Essay:** Fred Bodsworth.

STEVENS, Joan. Professor of English, Victoria University, Wellington, New Zealand; now retired. Author of *The New Zealand Novel 1860-1965*, 1966, *New Zealand Short Stories: A Survey*, 1968, and articles on the Brontës, Thackeray, and Dickens. **Essays:** Sylvia Ashton-Warner; David Ballantyne; Ian Cross.

STOKES, Edward. Reader in English, University of Tasmania, Hobart; Co-Editor of *Australian Literary Studies*. Author of *The Novels of Henry Green*, 1959, and *The Novels of James Hanley*, 1964. **Essay:** James Hanley.

STUCKEY, W.J. Associate Professor of English, Purdue University, Lafayette, Indiana; Founding Editor of *Minnesota Review*, Fiction Editor of *Quartet*, and Reader for *Modern Literary Studies*. Author of *Pulitzer Prize Novels*, 1966 (revised, 1980), and *Caroline Gordon*, 1972. **Essays:** Walker Percy; Frank Tuohy.

TANNER, Tony. Director of English Studies, King's College, Cambridge. Author of books on Conrad and Bellow and of *The Reign of Wonder: Naviety and Reality in American Literature*, 1965, *City of Words: American Fiction 1950-1970*, and *Adultery in the Novel*, 1980. Editor of works by Jane Austen and Henry James, and of a collection of essays on James.

THOMAS, Roy. Lecturer in Education, University College of Swansea, Wales. Author of *How to Read a Poem*, 1961. **Essay:** Gwyn Jones.

THOMSON, Derick S. Professor of Celtic, University of Glasgow; Editor of *Gairm*, a Gaelic quarterly. Author of six books of verse in Gaelic and English, *An Introduction to Gaelic Poetry*, 1974, and studies of Macpherson's *Ossian* and Edward Lhuyd. Editor of works of medieval and Renaissance Gaelic literature, and, with Ian Grimble, of *The Future of the Highlands*, 1968. **Essay:** Iain Crichton Smith.

TOULSON, Shirley. Features Editor, *The Teacher*. Author of several books of verse—the most recent being *Four Ways with a Ruin*, 1976, and *Bones and Angels* (with John Loveday), 1978—and of *Education in Britain*, 1974, and guidebooks to Wales, East Anglia, and Derbyshire. **Essays:** John Berger; Jack Lindsay; Stanley Middleton.

TREVOR, William. See his own entry. **Essay:** Edna O'Brien.

TURNER, Roland. Head of the Reference Division, St. Martin's Press. Editor of the reference book *The Grants Register*. **Essay:** Emanuel Litvinoff.

VAN-SERTIMA, Ivan. Lecturer, Rutgers University, New Brunswick, New Jersey. Author of *The River and the Wall* (verse), 1958, and *Caribbean Writers*, 1968. **Essay:** Samuel Selvon.

VINSON, James. Editor of the Contemporary Writers, Great Writers, and Twentieth-Century Writers series of reference books. **Essay:** Daniel Stern.

VOGLER, Thomas A. Associate Professor of English, University of California, Santa Cruz. Author of *Preludes to Vision*, 1970. **Essays:** Richard Brautigan; Ken Kesey.

WALKER, Keith. Free-lance writer and editor. Author of the novels *Running on the Spot*, 1959, and *Horse Latitudes*, 1965. **Essay:** Peter Everett.

WALSH, William. Professor of Commonwealth Literature and Chairman of the School of English, University of Leeds. Author of *Use of Imagination*, 1958; *A Human Idiom*, 1964; *Coleridge*, 1967; *A Manifold Voice*, 1970; *R.K. Narayan*, 1971; *V.S. Naipaul*, 1973; *Patrick White's Fiction*, 1977; *Introduction to Keats*, 1981. **Essays:** Mulk Raj Anand; Morley Callaghan; Kamala Markandaya.

WARNER, Val. Member of the Department of English, University of Dundee, Scotland. Author of *Under the Penthouse* (verse), 1973, and of articles and reviews in periodicals. Editor of *Centenary Corbière*, 1974. **Essays:** Beryl Bainbridge; Caroline Blackwood; George Buchanan; Philip Callow; Isobel English; Elaine Feinstein; Shirley Jackson (appendix); Francis King; Ethel Mannin; Elizabeth Mavor; Flannery O'Connor (appendix); Julia O'Faolain; Grace Paley; Gilbert Phelps; Fay Weldon.

WATTS, Harold H. Professor of English, Purdue University, Lafayette, Indiana. Author of *The Modern Reader's Guide to the Bible*, 1949; *Ezra Pound and the Cantos*, 1951; *Hound and Quarry*, 1953; *The Modern Reader's Guide to Religions, 1964; Aldous Huxley*, 1969. **Essays:** Frederick Buechner; Herbert Gold; William Golding; Meyer Levin; William Maxwell; P.H. Newby; Harry Mark Petrakis; Mary Renault; J.D. Salinger; Wallace Stegner; Honor Tracy.

WEGELIN, Christof. Professor of English, University of Oregon, Eugene. Author of *The Image of Europe in Henry James*, 1958, and articles on Hemingway, the "international novel," and other subjects in *PMLA*, *Sewanee Review*, and other periodicals. **Essay:** Robert Penn Warren.

WEIGEL, John A. Professor of English, Miami University, Ohio. Author of *Lawrence Durrell*, 1965, *Colin Wilson*, 1975, and *B.F. Skinner*, 1977. **Essay:** Jo Sinclair; Colin Wilson.

WELCH, Dennis M. Associatee Professor of Humanities, Clarkson College of Technology, Potsdam, New York. **Essay:** Thomas McGuane.

WELKER, Robert L. Professor of English, University of Alabama, Huntsville. **Essays:** Harriette Arnow; Peter Taylor.

WESTBROOK, Perry D. Professor of English, State University of New York, Albany. Author of *Acres of Flint: Writers of Rural New England*, 1951; *Biography of an Island, 1958; The Greatness of Man: An Essay on Dostoevsky and Whitman*, 1961; *Mary Ellen Chase*, 1966; *Mary Wilkins Freeman*, 1967. **Essays:** Anita Desai; G.V. Desani; Raja Rao; Kurt Vonnegut, Jr.

WESTON, Peter R. Extra-Mural Lecturer, Birmingham University; Editor of *Speculation*, a science-fiction magazine. **Essays:** Isaac Asimov; Robert A. Heinlein; Fritz Leiber.

WILLY, Margaret. Free-lance writer and lecturer. Author of two books of verse—*The Invisible Sun*, 1946, and *Every Star a Tongue*, 1951—and of several critical works, including *Life Was Their Cry*, 1950; *Three Metaphysical Poets*, 1961; *Three Women Diarists: Celia Fiennes, Dorothy Wordsworth, Katherine Mansfield*, 1964; *A Critical Commentary on "Wuthering Heights,"*1966; *A Critical Commentary on Browning's "Men and Women."* 1968. Editor of two anthologies and of works by Goldsmith. **Essays:** Rosamond Lehmann; Muriel Spark.

WOODCOCK, George. Free-lance writer, lecturer, and editor. Author of verse (most recently *The Kestrel and Other Poems*, 1978), plays, travel books, biographies, and works on history and politics; critical works include *William Godwin*, 1946, *The Incomparable Aphra*, 1948, *The Paradox of Oscar Wilde*, 1949, *The Crystal Spirit* (on Orwell), 1966, *Hugh MacLennan*, 1969, *Odysseus Ever Returning: Canadian Writers and Writing*, 1970, *Mordecai Richler*, 1970, *Dawn and the Darkest Hour* (on Aldous Huxley), 1972, *Herbert Read*, 1972, and *Thomas Merton*, 1978. Editor of anthologies and of works by Charles Lamb, Malcolm Lowry, Wyndham Lewis, Hardy, Meredith, and others. **Essays:** Margaret Atwood; Earle Birney; Leonard Cohen; Marian Engel; Roy Fuller; Mordecai Richler; Julian Symons; Audrey Thomas; David Watmough.